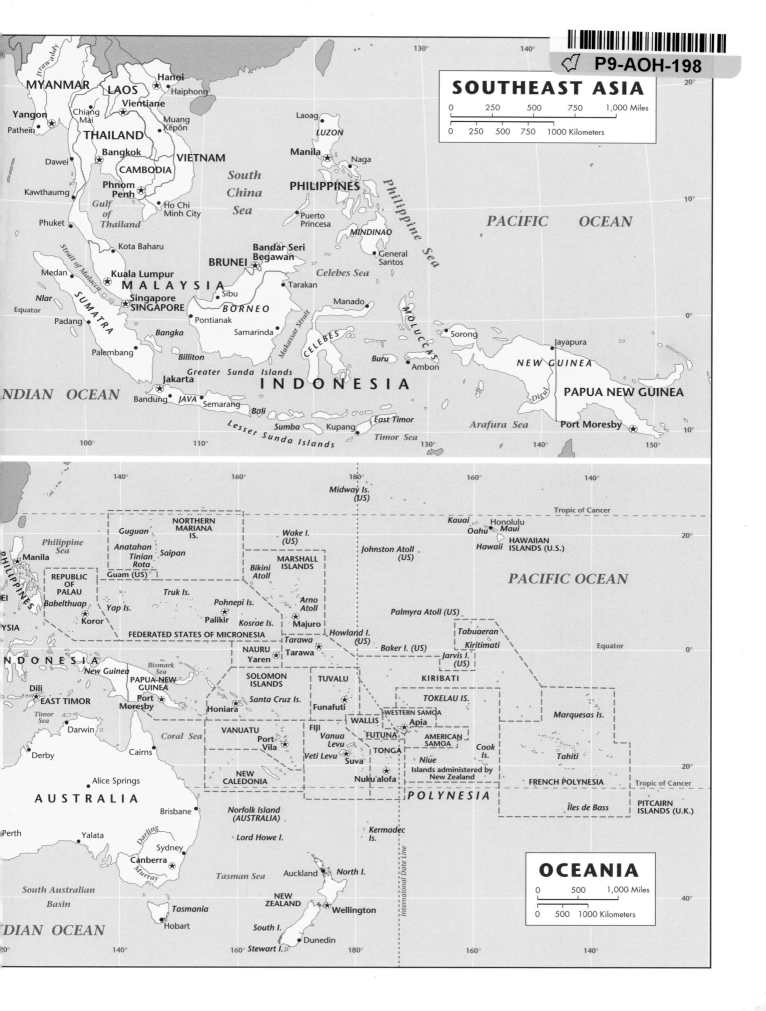

WORLDMARK
ENCYCLOPEDIA OF THE NATIONS

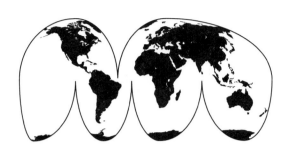

ASIA & OCEANIA

WORLDMARK
ENCYCLOPEDIA OF THE NATIONS, THIRTEENTH EDITION

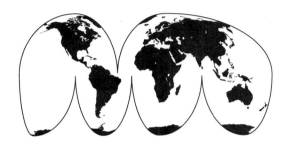

Volume 4
ASIA & OCEANIA

GALE
CENGAGE Learning·

Detroit • New York • San Francisco • New Haven, Conn • Waterville, Maine • Londoi

Worldmark Encyclopedia of the Nations, 13th Edition
Timothy L. Gall and Derek M. Gleason, Editors

Project Editors
Jason M. Everett and Kimberley A. McGrath

Contributing Editors
Kathleen J. Edgar and Elizabeth Manar

Managing Editor
Debra Kirby

Rights Acquisition and Management
Christine Myaskovsky

Imaging and Multimedia
John L. Watkins

Composition
Evi Abou-El-Seoud

Manufacturing
Rita Wimberley, Dorothy Maki

Product Manager
Douglas A. Dentino

Product Design
Kristine A. Julien

For product information and technology assistance, contact us at

Gale Customer Support, 1-800-877-4253.

For permission to use material from this text or product, submit all requests online at

www.cengage.com/permissions.

Further permissions questions can be emailed to

permissionrequest@cengage.com

While every effort has been made to ensure the reliability of the information presented in this publication, Gale, a part of Cengage Learning, does not guarantee the accuracy of the data contained herein. Gale accepts no payment for listing; and inclusion in the publication of any organization, agency, institution, publication, service, or individual does not imply endorsement of the editors or publisher. Errors brought to the attention of the publisher and verified to the satisfaction of the publisher will be corrected in future editions.

Library of Congress Cataloging-in-Publication Data

Worldmark encyclopedia of the nations / Timothy L. Gall and Derek M. Gleason, editors. -- 13th ed.
     p. cm.
  Includes bibliographical references and index.
  ISBN 978-1-4144-3390-5 (set) -- ISBN 978-1-4144-3391-2 (vol. 1) -- ISBN 978-1-4144-3392-9 (vol. 2) -- ISBN 978-1-4144-3393-6 (vol. 3) -- ISBN 978-1-4144-3394-3 (vol. 4) -- ISBN 978-1-4144-3395-0 (vol. 5) -- ISBN 978-1-4144-9090-8 (ebook)
  1. Geography--Encyclopedias. 2. History--Encyclopedias. 3. Economics--Encyclopedias. 4. Political science--Encyclopedias. 5. United Nations--Encyclopedias. I. Gall, Timothy L. II. Gleason, Derek M.
  G63.W67 2012
  910.3--dc23

                                2011049990

Gale
27500 Drake Rd.
Farmington Hills, MI 48331-3535

978-1-4144-3390-5 (set)   1-4144-3390-5 (set)
978-1-4144-3391-2 (vol. 1)   1-4144-3391-3 (vol. 1)
978-1-4144-3392-9 (vol. 2)   1-4144-3392-1 (vol. 2)
978-1-4144-3393-6 (vol. 3)   1-4144-3393-X (vol. 3)
978-1-4144-3394-3 (vol. 4)   1-4144-3394-8 (vol. 4)
978-1-4144-3395-0 (vol. 5)   1-4144-3395-6 (vol. 5)

This title is also available as an e-book
ISBN-13: 978-1-4144-9090-8   ISBN-10: 1-4144-9090-9
Contact your Gale, a part of Cengage Learning, sales representative for ordering information.

Printed in the United States
1 2 3 4 5 6 7 16 15 14 13 12

CONTENTS

For Conversion Tables, Abbreviations and Acronyms, Glossaries, World Tables, notes to previous editions, and other supplementary materials, see Volume 1.

READER'S GUIDE

GENERAL NOTE: The Thirteenth Edition of *Worldmark Encyclopedia of the Nations* (WEN) is comprised of five volumes. Volume 1 is dedicated to the United Nations and its related agencies. Volumes 2 through 5, "Africa," "Americas," "Asia and Oceania," and "Europe," contain entries on the countries of the world.

Reflecting the ever-changing status of the world geopolitical situation, the Thirteenth Edition includes entries for 196 countries and the Palestinian Territories, three more entries than the previous edition. This reflects the widely recognized independence of Kosovo and South Sudan that has occurred since the publication of the Twelfth Edition. It also recognizes the unique status of the Palestinian Territories, which, in the months leading up to the publication of this edition, were working to achieve membership in several peripheral United Nations agencies—a push toward formal recognition of statehood. Seven entries describe dependencies of the United Kingdom, United States, and the Netherlands. Previous editions have been cognizant of similar changes, including those in East Timor, Macau, and Hong Kong. Perhaps most dramatically, the Eighth Edition of this encyclopedia (1995) reported on the dissolution of the USSR, Czechoslovakia, and Yugoslavia; the unification of Germany; the unification of Yemen; and the independence of Eritrea. These changes resulted in 25 new country articles. Whereas the First Edition of the *Worldmark Encyclopedia of the Nations,* in one volume, contained 119 articles, the present Thirteenth Edition now contains 204.

Some notable foci for the Thirteenth Edition include coverage of the Arab Spring—the revolutionary fervor that carried across North Africa and the Middle East during 2011 and into 2012, deposing several longstanding dictators—and the global financial crisis, which, despite beginning in 2008, has led to economic recession or stagnation across much of the world that continued through 2011 and into 2012, especially among European countries and in other highly developed economies. Also for the Thirteenth Edition, each entry was submitted for review by subject-matter experts at universities across the United States and around the world, leading to greater continuity within each article and an authorial perspective conscious of region-wide context and historical relevance.

In compiling data for incorporation into the *Worldmark Encyclopedia of the Nations,* substantial efforts were made to utilize national government statistical resources, as well as all pertinent UN agencies, to compile the core information in each entry. Material received from official sources was reviewed and critically assessed by editors as part of the process of incorporation. In some cases, discrepancies between self-reported data and accepted international revisions, occasionally noted in figures such as unemployment and minority ethnic populations, highlight the political influences that weigh on national government statistic reporting. Materials and publications of the UN family and of intergovernmental and nongovernmental organizations throughout the world provided a major fund of geographic, demographic, economic, and social data.

In compiling historical, economic, and political data, primary materials generated by governments and international agencies were supplemented by data gathered from numerous other sources including newspapers (most notably *The European*, the *Financial Times*, the *New York Times*, and the *Wall Street Journal*); periodicals (most notably *Current History, Elections Today, The Economist*, the *Far Eastern Economic Review, Foreign Affairs*, and *World Press Review*); and thousands of World Wide Web sites hosted by government agencies and embassies. The base knowledge and access to a broad range of speciality academic publications enjoyed by subject-matter experts figures heavily in these sections as well.

The reader's attention is directed to the Glossary of Special Terms for explanations of key terms and concepts essential to a fuller understanding of the text.

COUNTRY NAMES: Country names are reported (as appropriate) in three forms: the short-form name (generally conformed to the US Central Intelligence Agency's *World Factbook 2011*), as commonly used in the text; the English version of the official name (generally conformed to the United Nations list of country names); and the official name in the national language(s). When necessary, textual usages of some short-form names have been rectified, usually through the substitution of an acronym for the official name, in order to strike a better balance between official usages and universal terminology. Thus the following short-form names have been adopted throughout (except in historical context to preserve accuracy): DROC (Democratic Republic of the Congo); ROC (Republic of the Congo); DPRK (Democratic People's Republic of Korea/North Korea); and ROK (Republic of Korea/South Korea).

MAPS: Spellings on the individual country maps reflect national usages and recognized transliteration practice. To clarify national boundaries and landforms, dark shading has been applied to waters, and lighter shading to lands not within that nation's jurisdiction. Cross-hatching has been used to designate certain disputed areas. Rivers that run dry during certain times of the year are indicated by dashed instead of solid lines.

FLAGS AND NATIONAL EMBLEMS: All depictions of flags, flag designations, and national emblems have been reviewed and, where necessary, corrected or changed to reflect their official usage as of 2012. In general, the term "national flag" denotes the civil flag of the nation.

CURRENCY: In most cases, currency conversion factors cited in the Thirteenth Edition are derived from figures available during the last quarter of 2011 or the first quarter of 2012. Differences between the official exchange rate and the actual exchange rate are noted as appropriate.

WEIGHTS AND MEASURES: The general world trend toward adoption of the metric system is acknowledged through the use of metric units and their nonmetric (customary or imperial) equivalents throughout the text. The two exceptions to this practice involve territorial sea limits, which are reported in nautical miles, and various production data, for which (unless otherwise stated) units of measure reflect the system in use by the country in question. All tons are metric tons (again, unless otherwise indicated), reflecting the practice of the UN in its statistical reporting.

HOLIDAYS: Except where noted, all holidays listed are official public holidays, on which government offices are closed that would normally be open. Transliterations of names of Muslim holidays have been standardized. For a fuller discussion on these points, and for a description of religious holidays and their origins and meanings, see the Glossary of Religious Holidays in this volume.

GEOGRAPHIC INFORMATION: To update the sections on Location, Size, and Extent; Topography, Climate, Flora and Fauna, and Environment, the World Bank's *World Development Indicators 2011* and CIA *World Factbook 2011* were two primary sources. Additional data was acquired from the Ramsar Convention on Wetlands (http://www.ramsar.org); UNESCO World Heritage Centre (http://www.whc.unesco.org); United Nations Environment Programme (http://www.unep.org); Weather Channel: Averages and Records (http://www.weather.com/common/home/climatology.html); and the International Union for Conservation of Nature (http://www.iucn.org).

POPULATION DATA: Data for the four rubrics describing population (Population, Migration, Ethnic Groups, Languages) were compiled from numerous publications of the US Department of State, the World Bank, the United Nations, and the Organization for Economic Co-Operation and Development (OECD), specifically its publication *Trends in International Migration*. Data on refugee populations generally comes from the United Nations. Population rankings are ordered based on data from the *World Factbook 2011* and include all full country entries in these volumes; this calculation excludes the Palestinian Territories and the seven dependency entries.

RELIGIONS: Data for this section were compiled in large part from the *2010 International Religious Freedom Report* released by the Bureau of Democracy, Human Rights, and Labor, US Department of State. This is an annual report to Congress compiled in compliance with Section 102(b) of the International Religious Freedom Act (IRFA) of 1998. The report includes the work of hundreds of State Department, Foreign Service, and other US government employees. The authors gathered information from a variety of sources, including government and religious officials, nongovernmental organizations, journalists, human rights monitors, religious groups, and academics.

TRANSPORTATION: Sources consulted for updated information on transportation include the *World Factbook 2011* and the World Bank's *World Development Indicators 2011*. Information on recent or ongoing transportation projects most often came from major news organizations such as the *BBC News International* and the *New York Times*.

HISTORY: In writing the History rubric, the entries relied heavily on the expertise of the academics reviewing and revising each country profile. Beyond the contributions of the subject-matter experts, the History rubrics have been maintained in previous editions and in between editions through the use of a variety of news and background information sources. Full country profiles—including information on the history, economy, political institutions, and foreign relations on most nations of the world—are provided by the US Library of Congress and by the US Department of State; similar formats are published by the *BBC News International*. In consulting news sources for up-to-date information on events, only reported facts (not editorials) were used. The *New York Times* and the *Washington Post* are more comprehensive than the *Wall Street Journal*, whose focus is placed on financial and business news. While the Web site of the United Nations was used extensively in compiling Volume 1 "United Nations," of the *Worldmark Encyclopedia of the Nations,* its coverage of such problems as politics in the Middle East and global terrorism pertained to and supported the updating of History rubrics of a number of countries. Other organizations that publish journals or studies on global current events, foreign policy, international relations, and human rights include Amnesty International; Human Rights Watch; *Foreign Affairs*, published by the Council on Foreign Relations; and *Great Decisions*, published by the Foreign Policy Association.

GOVERNMENT: The Government rubric is constructed by outlining the institutions of government as they were formed throughout a nation's modern history, up to those existing under the present constitution.

The US Library of Congress and the US Department of State chronicle constitutional changes and also provide information on the form of government. The online resource ElectionGuide (Electionguide.org) and the *World Factbook 2011* provide information on officeholders in place at the time of publication. The *BBC News International* "Country Profiles" cover current leaders and their political parties, and *The Economist* is comprehensive in its coverage of political structures and political forces in place and at work in the nations it profiles. The official government Web sites of individual nations were also consulted.

POLITICAL PARTIES: The *World Factbook 2011* was consulted for a list of political parties, and often, their leaders. *The Economist* also has sections in its country briefings labeled "political structure" and "political forces," which describe the political climate of each nation the magazine profiles. In addition, *The Economist* provides a brief history of the nation, which often includes the history of political parties. Editors also reviewed profiles of nations prepared by the US Department of State.

LOCAL GOVERNMENT: The *World Factbook 2011* lists the administrative subdivisions in each nation of the world. *The Economist* was consulted for a description of regional legislatures. ElectionGuide provides information on recent and upcoming subnational elections.

JUDICIAL SYSTEM: The US State Department *Background Notes* and the *World Factbook 2011* both provided basic information on each nation's judicial system. *The Economist* was consulted for a description of the legal systems of each nation it profiles. The US State Department's *Human Rights Reports* provide more in-depth details about the independence and fairness of the judiciary.

ARMED FORCES: Statistical data on armed forces was compiled from the *The Military Balance* (The International Institute for Strategic Studies), the *World Factbook 2011*, and other print and online sources including *Current World Nuclear Arsenals* maintained by the Center for Defense Information.

INTERNATIONAL COOPERATION: This section was updated using data provided by news agencies, the *World Factbook 2011*, and US State Department *Background Notes*.

ECONOMY: In addition to numerous official online sources, data on the economies of the world were compiled from the most recent editions of the following publications (and their publishers): *Country Commercial Guides* (US Department of State), *World Development Indicators 2011* (World Bank) and *Doing Business* reports (World Bank). *The Economist* was consulted for detailed information on economic structures and select indicators in its "Country Profiles" archive; it also included economic and political forecasts for the nations it profiled. *The Index of Economic Freedom* (Heritage Foundation) was also consulted for its measurement of independent variables into broad factors of economic freedom.

INCOME: Statistics on national income were obtained from sources published by the United Nations, the World Bank, and the US Central Intelligence Agency. CIA figures are for gross domestic product (GDP), defined as the value of all final goods and services produced within a nation in a given year. In most cases, CIA figures are given in purchasing power parity terms. Actual individual consumption, a statistic maintained by the World Bank, measures the percentage of a nation's GDP spent on various sectors of the consumer economy. Thus, public expenditures in sectors such as education, health, or military are not included in the calculation and account for the remaining percentage of GDP not included in actual individual consumption numbers.

LABOR: Labor statistics were compiled from the World Bank publication *World Development Indicators 2011* and the US State Department's *Human Rights Reports 2010*.

AGRICULTURE, FISHING, AND FORESTRY: In addition to government sources, statistical data for these sections was compiled from the following yearbooks published by the Food and Agriculture Organization of the United Nations: *Fishery Statistics; Production; Agriculture;* and *Forest Products*.

MINING: Data on mining and minerals production came from various online sources and from statistics compiled by the Minerals Information office of the US Geological Survey, US Department of the Interior, including the *Minerals Yearbook*. The *Minerals Yearbook* is published both electronically on the Internet and in various print formats available from the US Government Printing Office Superintendent of Documents. The *Yearbook* provides an annual review of mineral production and trade and of mineral-related government and industry developments in more than 175 countries.

ENERGY AND POWER: Key sources consulted include *Country Analysis Briefs* (US Energy Information Administration, US Department of Energy) and *World Development Indicators* (The World Bank). Special attention was given to renewable energy projects completed or underway in various countries; information for projects typically was found through major news agencies or on official government Web sites.

INDUSTRY: The primary source material for the Industry rubric was the *World Factbook 2011* and the US State Department's *Country Commercial Guides*, which provide a comprehensive look at countries' commercial environments, using economic, political, and market analysis. *Background Notes* were consulted for information on the industrial history and climate of each country profiled. *The Economist* and, to a lesser extent, *BBC News* were useful in providing background material for the Industry rubric.

SCIENCE AND TECHNOLOGY: Information in this section derived primarily from statistics of the UNESCO Institute for Statistics, the World Bank's *World Development Indicators,* and the World Intellectual Property Organization.

DOMESTIC TRADE: Source material for the Domestic Trade rubric came from the US State Department's *Country Commercial Guides* and *Background Notes.* Also used was *The Economist* and, to a lesser extent, the *BBC* for providing background material for the Domestic Trade rubric. The World Bank's *Doing Business* reports were consulted for information on conducting business in a nation, which included business hours and business regulations. Finally, most nations' government Web sites provided information on domestic trade.

FOREIGN TRADE: Sources consulted included the *Direction of Trade Statistics* (IMF Statistics Department, International Monetary Fund). The US State Department's *Country Commercial Guides* and *Background Notes* were also used. *The Economist* and the *World Factbook 2011* were consulted in listing import and export partners and key products traded. Various UN bodies—such as UNCTAD and UNESCO—provided up-to-date trade statistics. The principal trading partners table was constructed with information from the IMF's *Direction of Trade Statistics* publication.

BALANCE OF PAYMENTS: Balance of payments tables were computed from the International Monetary Fund's *Balance of Payments Statistics Yearbook.* In some cases, totals are provided even though not all components of those totals have been reported by the government of the country. Accordingly, in some instances numbers in the columns may not add to the total. Supplementing the IMF's *Balance of Payments Statistics Yearbook* were *The Economist*'s "Country Briefings," the *World Factbook 2011,* and information taken from the US State Department, in particular, the *Country Commercial Guides.*

BANKING AND SECURITIES: Statistical data on securities listings and market activity was compiled from *International Banking Statistics* (www.bis.org/statistics) and the *World Factbook 2011,* which provides both the discount rate and prime lending rate for most nations. Various Web sites specific to the individual countries of the world were also consulted, especially for the most current information on active publicly traded companies and market capitalization for domestic exchanges.

INSURANCE: Primary sources for information on insurance included the online resources of the Insurance Information Institute, Rowbotham and Co. LLP., PricewaterhouseCoopers, the Swiss Reinsurance Company, and J. Zakhour & Co., as well as numerous national Web sites dealing with insurance.

PUBLIC FINANCE: In addition to official government Web sites, analytical reports from the US Department of Commerce, the *World Factbook 2011,* and the *Government Finance Statistics Yearbook* (International Monetary Fund) were consulted.

TAXATION: Information on Taxation was compiled from country data sheets published by international accounting firms (Deloitte and Ernst & Young). Addition informational was obtained from the US Commerce Department, *Doing Business* reports from the World Bank, and government Web sites of the countries of the world.

CUSTOMS AND DUTIES: Information on Customs and Duties was compiled from country data sheets published by the accounting firms of Deloitte and Ernst & Young. Additional information was obtained from the US Commerce Department, the World Trade Organization, and the government Web sites of the countries of the world.

FOREIGN INVESTMENT: Source material for the Foreign Investment rubric included the US State Department's *Country Commercial Guides,* which provided a comprehensive analysis of the foreign direct investment environments of the countries of the world. The International Monetary Fund's publications *International Financial Statistics Yearbook* and *Balance of Payments Statistics Yearbook,* and the US State Department's *Background Notes* were consulted for the information on foreign direct investment. Also used was information contained in the *World Factbook 2011. The Economist* was consulted in providing basic FDI figures and other relevant data.

ECONOMIC DEVELOPMENT: Source material for the Economic Development rubric included the US State Department's *Country Commercial Guides* and *Background Notes. The Economist* was consulted for economic and political forecasts for selected nations. The *Index of Economic Freedom* was also consulted for its broad description of economic freedom and development. Information on foreign aid was taken from the print publications and Web sites of the International Monetary Fund, World Bank, and the United States Agency for International Development (USAID). Information on long-term development plans was found most often on individual government Web sites.

SOCIAL DEVELOPMENT: Publications consulted in the preparation of this rubric include the US State Department's 2010 *Human Rights Reports,* the US Social Security Administration reports for each nation, and the World Bank's *World Development Indicators 2011.* Additional information was obtained from country-specific Web sites and general news publications.

HEALTH: Statistical sources consulted included the World Health Organization health profiles for each country as well as statistical information maintained by UNESCO. Numerous Web sites of individual nations of the world were also utilized. The World Bank's *World Development Indicators 2011* served as an additional resource.

HOUSING: The latest government population and housing census information available was used for each country through access of official government Web sites. Also of use was the World Bank publication *World Development Indicators 2011*. Web sites consulted included Habitat for Humanity (http://www. habitat.org), United Nations Human Settlements Programme (http://unhabitat.org) and the US Agency for International Development (http://www.usaid.gov).

EDUCATION: Data on Education was obtained from various UNESCO publications and statistics from the World Bank. The *World Factbook 2011* and the US State Department's *Background Notes* were also consulted.

LIBRARIES AND MUSEUMS: Some information concerning libraries and museums was accessed through official government Web sites of various countries when links were available to tourism, education, and/or cultural ministries or departments. In addition, the following Web sites were consulted: American Library Association (http://www.ala.org); International Federation of Library Associations and Institutions (http://www.ifla.org); Museums of the World (http://www.museum.com); and UNESCO (http://www.unesco. org).

MEDIA: Primary sources for this section include the annual *Editor & Publisher* publication *International Year Book*—which lists circulation figures for periodicals—online data provided by UNESCO, and media sections of the "Country Profiles" featured on the Web site of *BBC News International*. In addition, government and other Web sites related to the countries of the world were consulted. Additional sources consulted included the *World Development Indicators 2011, World Factbook 2011,* and US State Department's *2010 Human Rights Reports* (particularly with regard to freedom of the press).

ORGANIZATIONS: Lists of member countries were obtained through the official Web sites of a variety of prominent international organizations and associations, such as the International Federation of Red Cross and Red Crescent Societies, Amnesty International, Kiwanis International, the World Alliance of YMCAs, the World Organization of the Scout Movement, etc.

TOURISM, TRAVEL, AND RECREATION: Statistical sources consulted included the *Tourism Factbook,* published by the UN World Tourism Organization in 2011. Tourism Web sites of individual countries were also consulted. US Department of State per diem travel allowances are published online.

FAMOUS PERSONS: Entries are based on information available through March 2012. Where a person noted in one country is known to have been born in another, the country (or, in some cases, city) of birth follows the personal name in parentheses.

DEPENDENCIES: Source material for the Dependencies rubric was taken primarily from statistical Web sites maintained by the sovereign nation overseeing each dependency. Information also came from *Background Notes* and from the Web site of the United Nations. *The Economist* and the Web site of *BBC News* were also consulted.

BIBLIOGRAPHY: Bibliographical listings at the end of country articles are provided as a guide to further reading on the country in question and are not intended as a comprehensive listing of references used in research for the article. Effort was made to provide a broad sampling of works on major subjects and topics as covered by the article; the bibliographies provide, wherever possible, introductory and general works for use by students and general readers, as well as classical studies, recent contributions, and other works regarded as seminal by area specialists. The country article bibliographies were supplemented with information obtained from a search conducted in November 2011. An extensive bibliography listing key references related to the facts in this encyclopedia follows. However, it is not a complete listing since many fact sheets, brochures, World Wide Web sites, and other informational materials were not included due to space limitations.

PRINT PUBLICATIONS CONSULTED

Almanac of Famous People. 10th ed. Farmington Hills, MI: Cengage Gale, 2011.

Balance of Payments Statistics Yearbook. Washington, D.C.: International Monetary Fund, 2011.

Asian Development Bank, ed. *Asian Development Outlook 2011: South-South Economic Links.* Manila, Philippines: Asian Development Bank, 2011.

Central Intelligence Agency. *World Factbook 2011.* Washington, D.C.: US Government Printing Office, 2011.

Commonwealth Yearbook 2011. London: Commonwealth Secretariat, 2011.

Compendium of Tourism Statistics (2005–2009). 2011 ed. Madrid: World Tourism Organization, 2011.

Crystal, David. *The Cambridge Encyclopedia of Language.* 2nd ed. New York: Cambridge University Press, 1997.

Direction of Trade Statistics. Washington, D.C.: International Monetary Fund, quarterly.

Doernberg, Richard L. *Doernberg's International Taxation in a Nutshell.* 9th ed. Eagan, MN: Thomson Reuters Westlaw, 2012.

Dowie, Mark. *Conservation Refugees: The Hundred-Year Conflict between Global Conservation and Native Peoples.* Cambridge, MA: MIT Press, 2011.

Editor and Publisher International Yearbook 2010. New York: The Editor and Publisher Company, 2011.

Ellicott, Karen. *Countries of the World and Their Leaders Yearbook 2012.* Farmington Hills: Cengage Gale, 2011.

Emerging Stock Markets Factbook 2000. Washington, D.C.: International Finance Corporation, 2002.

Entering the 21st Century: World Development Report 1999/2000. New York: Oxford University Press, 2000.

Evandale's Directory of World Underwriters 2010. London: Evandale Publishing, 2011.

Food and Agriculture Organization of the United Nations. *FAO Statistical Yearbook.* New York: United Nations, 2010.

———. *FAO Yearbook: Fishery Statistics.* New York: United Nations, 2009.

———. *FAO Yearbook: Forest Products.* New York: United Nations, 2009.

Future Demographic-Global Population Forecasts to 2030. London: Euromonitor, 2012.

Global Development Finance. Washington, D.C.: The World Bank, 2011.

Global Education Digest. Montreal: UNESCO Publishing, 2011.

Government Finance Statistics Yearbook. Washington, D.C.: International Monetary Fund, 2011.

Health in the Americas. 2007 ed. Washington, D.C.: World Health Organization, 2007.

Health Information for International Travel 2005–2006. Philadelphia, PA: Mosby, 2005.

Historical Statistics 1960-1993. Paris: Organization for Economic Co-Operation and Development, 1995.

Insurance in the Arab World: Facts and Figures. Beirut: J. Zakhour & Co., undated.

International Civil Aviation Organization. *ICAO Statistical Yearbook, Civil Aviation Statistics of the World.* Montreal: International Civil Aviation Organization, annual.

International Committee of the Red Cross. *ICRC Annual Report 2010.* Geneva: ICRC Publications, 2011.

International Finance Corporation. *Doing Business 2012: Doing Business in a More Transparent World.* Washington, D.C.: International Finance Corporation, 2011.

International Financial Statistics Yearbook. Washington, D.C.: International Monetary Fund, 2008.

The International Insurance Fact Book. New York: Insurance Information Institute, 2012.

International Marketing Data and Statistics 2012. London: Euromonitor, 2012.

International Institute for Strategic Studies. *The Military Balance 2011.* London: Routledge, 2011.

International Save the Children Alliance Annual Report 2010, London: Cambridge House, 2011.

International Trade Statistics Yearbook. New York: United Nations, 2011.

Insurance in the Arab World: Facts and Figures. Beirut: J. Zakhour & Co., undated.

The International Insurance Fact Book, New York: Insurance Information Institute, 2011.

Key World Energy Statistics. Paris: International Energy Agency, 2011.

Little Data Book. Washington, D.C.: The World Bank, 2011.

Making Decisions on Public Health: A Review of Eight Countries. Geneva: World Health Organization, 2004.

McCoy, John F., ed. *Geo-Data: The World Geographical Encyclopedia, 3rd ed.* Farmington Hills, MI: Gale Group, 2003.

National Accounts for OECD Countries, Main Aggregates, Volume I, 2003–2010. Paris: Organization for Economic Cooperation and Development, 2011.

National Accounts Statistics: Main Aggregates and Detailed Tables. New York: United Nations, 2011.

Nordic Statistical Yearbook 2010. Stockholm: Nordic Council of Ministers, 2011.

Nuclear Power Reactors in the World. Vienna: International Atomic Energy Agency, 2006.

Organisation for Economic Co-operation and Development (OECD). *OECD Factbook 2011–2012.* Paris: OECD, 2011.

———. *Agricultural Policies in OECD Countries at a Glance 2011.* Paris: OECD, 2011.

———. *Education at a Glance 2011.* Paris: OECD, 2011.

———. *Health at a Glance 2011.* Paris: OECD, 2011.

———. *Government at a Glance 2011.* Paris: OECD, 2011.

Organization for Economic Co-operation and Development (OECD). *Revenue Statistics of OECD Member Countries 1965–1992.* Paris: OECD, 1993.

Population and Vital Statistics Report, January 2011. New York: United Nations, 2011.

Science & Engineering Indicators 2010. Washington, D.C.: National Science Foundation, 2010.

Sivard, Ruth Leger. *World Military and Social Expenditures.* Washington, D.C.: World Priorities, Inc., 1996.

Sources and Methods: Labour Statistics. Geneva: International Labour Office, 1996.

The State of the World's Children 2011. New York: Oxford University Press, 2011.

The State of the World's Refugees: Human Displacement in the New Millenium. New York: Penguin Books, 2006.

The State of the World's Refugees: Fifty Years of Humanitarian Action. New York: Oxford University Press, 2000.

Stockholm International Peace Research Institute. *SIPRI Yearbook 2011: Armaments, Disarmament and International Security.* London: Oxford University Press, 2011.

Tourism Market Trends: Africa, Madrid: World Tourism Organization, 2008.

Tourism Market Trends: Americas, Madrid: World Tourism Organization, 2008.

Tourism Market Trends: East Asia & the Pacific, Madrid: World Tourism Organization, 2008.

Tourism Market Trends: Europe, Madrid: World Tourism Organization, 2008.

Tourism Market Trends: Middle East, Madrid: World Tourism Organization, 2008.

Tourism Market Trends: South Asia, Madrid: World Tourism Organization, 2008.

Trends in International Migration 2004. Paris: Organization for Economic Co-Operation and Development, 2005.

United Nations Department of Economic and Social Affairs. *World Population Policies 2009.* New York: United Nations, 2010.

United Nations Development Program. *Human Development Report 2011.* New York: United Nations, 2011.

US Agency for International Development, Bureau for Management, Office of Budget. *US Overseas Loans and Grants and Assistance from International Organizations (The Greenbook).* Washington, D.C.: US Government Printing Office, 2011.

US Arms Control and Disarmament Agency. *World Military Expenditures and Arms Transfers 2005.* Washington, DC: U.S. Arms Control and Disarmament Agency, 2009.

US Department of the Interior, US Geological Survey. *Mineral Industries of Africa and the Middle East.* Washington, D.C.: US Government Printing Office, 2009.

———. *Mineral Industries of Asia and the Pacific.* Washington, D.C.: US Government Printing Office, 2009.

———. *Mineral Industries of Europe and Central Eurasia.* Washington, D.C.: US Government Printing Office, 2008.

———. *Mineral Industries of Latin America and Canada.* Washington, D.C.: US Government Printing Office, 2009.

Working Time Laws: A Global Perspective. Geneva: International Labour Office, 2005.

World Data on Education. Paris: International Bureau of Education, 2000.

World Development Indicators 2011. Washington D.C.: The World Bank, 2011.

World Development Report 1990: Poverty. New York: Oxford University Press, 1990.

World Development Report 1995: Workers in an Integrating World. New York: Oxford University Press, 1995.

World Development Report 1996: From Plan to Market. New York: Oxford University Press, 1996.

World Development Report 2003: Sustainable Development in a Dynamic World. Washington, D.C.: World Bank, 2003.

World Development Report 2006: Equity and Development. Washington, D.C.: World Bank, 2005.

World Development Report 2011. Washington, D.C.: World Bank, 2011.

The World Health Report: Make Every Mother and Child Count. Geneva: World Health Organization, 2005.

The World Health Report: Working Together for Health. Geneva: World Health Organization, 2006.

The World Health Report: A Safer Future: Global Public Health Security in the 21st Century. Geneva: World Health Organization, 2007.

The World Health Report: Primary Health Care (Now More Than Ever). Geneva: World Health Organization, 2008.

World Health Statistics 2011. Geneva: World Health Organization, 2011.

World Migration Report. New York: United Nations, 2011.

World Population Projections to 2150. New York: United Nations, 1998.

World Population Prospects: 2011. New York: United Nations, 2011.

World Resources Institute; United Nations Environment Programme; United Nations Development Programme; World Bank. *World Resources Report 2010–11.* New York: Oxford University Press, 2011.

World Urbanization Prospects. New York: United Nations, 2011.

Worldwide Corporate Tax Guide. New York: Ernst & Young, 2011.

Yearbook of Labour Statistics 2005. Geneva: International Labour Office, 2011.

WEB SITES CONSULTED

In the course of preparing this edition, hundreds of Web sites were consulted including the official Web site of each country of the world and those of various nongovernmental organizations worldwide. Of special significance are the Web sites listed below. These sites were accessed in 2011 and 2012 for information relevant to the rubrics listed above.

African Development Indicators 2011. http://data.worldbank.org/sites/default/files/adi_2011-web.pdf

American Library Association. http://www.ala.org

Amnesty International. http://www.amnesty.org

Asia Society. http://asiasociety.org/policy

BBC News. *Country Profiles.* http://news.bbc.co.uk/2/hi/country_profiles/default.stm

Central Intelligence Agency. *The World Factbook, 2011.* http://www.cia.gov/cia/publications/factbook/index.html

Council on Foreign Relations. http://www.foreignaffairs.org/

Country Forecasts. http://www.countrywatch.com

Country Overviews. http://www.developmentgateway.org

The Economist. http://www.economist.com/countries/index.cfm

ElectionGuide. http://www.electionguide.org

Energy Information Administration. *Country Analysis Briefs, 2011.* http://www.eia.doe.gov/emeu/cabs/

Foreign Policy Association. http://www.fpa.org/

Growth Competitiveness Index Rankings. http://www.weforum.org

Habitat for Humanity. http://www.habitat.org

Human Rights Watch. http://www.hrw.org/

Index of Economic Freedom. http://www.heritage.org

Insurance Information Institute. http://www.internationalinsurance.org/

International Banking Statistics. http://www.bis.org/statistics/index.htm

International Federation of Library Associations and Institutions. http://www.ifla.org

International Labour Organization, Department of Statistics. http://www.ilo.org/stat/lang--en/index.htm

International Monetary Fund. http://www.imf.org/

International Union for Conservation of Nature. http://www.iucn.org

Jurist World Law. http://jurist.law.pitt.edu/world/

L'Outre-Mer. http://www.outre-mer.gouv.fr/

Latin Business Chronicle. http://www.latinbusinesschronicle.com

Minerals Information Office, US Geological Survey, US Department of the Interior. http://minerals.usgs.gov/minerals/pubs/country/

Museums of the World. http://www.museum.com

National Science Foundation. Science & Engineering Indicators 2012. http://www.nsf.gov/statistics/seind12/

New York Times. http://www.nytimes.com/pages/world/index.html

OPEC Annual Report 2010. http://www.opec.org/opec_web/static_files_project/media/downloads/publications/Annual_Report_2010.pdf

Organization of American States Annual Report of the Inter American Commission on Human Rights. http://www.oas.org/en/iachr/docs/annual/2011/TOC.asp

Patent Applications by Country. http://www.wipo.int/ipstats/en/statistics/patents/

Political Resources on the Net. http://www.politicalresources.net

Population and Vital Statistics Report, January 2011. Series A, Vol. LXIII. http://unstats.un.org/unsd/demographic/products/vitstats/default.htm

Ramsar Convention on Wetlands. http://www.ramsar.org

TradePort. http://www.tradeport.org

United Nations. http://www.un.org/

United Nations Conference on Trade and Development (UNCTAD). http://www.unctad.org

United Nations Educational, Scientific, and Cultural Organization (UNESCO). http://www.unesco.org

———. *Education for All Global Monitoring Report 2011.* http://unesdoc.unesco.org/images/0019/001907/190743e.pdf

———. Statistics on Research and Development. http://www.uis.unesco.org

———. World Heritage Centre. http://www.whc.unesco.org

United Nations Food and Agricultural Organization. http://www.fao.org/

———. Production Statistics. http: http://faostat.fao.org/site/339/default.aspx

———. Trade Statistics. http: http://faostat.fao.org/site/342/default.aspx

———. Resource Statistics. http: http://faostat.fao.org/site/348/default.aspx

———. Forestry Statistics. http: http://faostat.fao.org/site/630/default.aspx

———. Fisheries Statistics. http: http://faostat.fao.org/site/629/default.aspx

United Nations Schedule of Mission Subsistence Allowance (MSA). http://www.un.org/depts/OHRM/salaries_allowances/allowances/msa.htm

United Nations Human Settlements Programme (UN-HABITAT). http://unhabitat.org

United Nations Statistics Division. http://unstats.un.org/unsd/default.htm

US Agency for International Development. http://www.usaid.gov.

US Department of State. *Background Notes.* http://www.state.gov/r/pa/ei/bgn

———. *Country Commercial Guides.* http://www.state.gov/e/eb/rls/rpts/ccg/

———. *International Religious Freedom Report 2010.* http://www.state.gov/g/drl/rls/irf/2010/index.htm

———. *Human Rights Reports, 2010.* http//www.state.gov/j/drl/rls/hrrpt/

US Library of Congress. http://lcweb2.loc.gov/frd/cs/profiles.html

The Wall Street Journal. http://online.wsj.com/public/us

The Washington Post. http://www.washpost.com/index.shtml

The Weather Channel. "Averages and Records." http://www.weather.com

The World Bank. http://worldbank.org

———. *Doing Business* database. http://www.doingbusiness.org

World Development Indicators, Country Overviews. http://www.developmentgateway.org

World Health Organization. Countries. http://www.who.int/countries/en/

World Intellectual Property Organization. http://www.wipo.int/portal/index.html.en

GUIDE TO COUNTRY ARTICLES

All information contained within a country article is uniformly keyed by means of small superior numerals to the left of the subject headings. A heading such as "Population," for example, carries the same key numeral (6) in every article. Thus, to find information about the population of Albania, consult the table of contents for the page number where the Albania article begins and look for section 6 thereunder. Introductory matter for each nation includes coat of arms, capital, flag (descriptions given from hoist to fly or from top to bottom), anthem, monetary unit, weights and measures, holidays, and time zone.

SECTION HEADINGS IN NUMERICAL ORDER

1	Location, size, and extent	27	Energy and power
2	Topography	28	Industry
3	Climate	29	Science and technology
4	Flora and fauna	30	Domestic trade
5	Environment	31	Foreign trade
6	Population	32	Balance of payments
7	Migration	33	Banking and securities
8	Ethnic groups	34	Insurance
9	Languages	35	Public finance
10	Religions	36	Taxation
11	Transportation	37	Customs and duties
12	History	38	Foreign investment
13	Government	39	Economic development
14	Political parties	40	Social development
15	Local government	41	Health
16	Judicial system	42	Housing
17	Armed forces	43	Education
18	International cooperation	44	Libraries and museums
19	Economy	45	Media
20	Income	46	Organizations
21	Labor	47	Tourism, travel, and recreation
22	Agriculture	48	Famous persons
23	Animal husbandry	49	Dependencies
24	Fishing	50	Bibliography
25	Forestry		
26	Mining		

SECTION HEADINGS IN ALPHABETICAL ORDER

Agriculture	22	Income	20
Animal husbandry	23	Industry	28
Armed forces	17	Insurance	34
Balance of payments	32	International cooperation	18
Banking and securities	33	Judical system	16
Bibliography	50	Labor	21
Climate	3	Languages	9
Customs and duties	37	Libraries and museums	44
Dependencies	49	Local government	15
Domestic trade	30	Location, size, and extent	1
Economic development	39	Media	45
Economy	19	Migration	7
Education	43	Mining	26
Energy and power	27	Organizations	46
Environment	5	Political parties	14
Ethnic groups	8	Population	6
Famous persons	48	Public finance	35
Fishing	24	Religions	10
Flora and fauna	4	Science and technology	29
Foreign investment	38	Social development	40
Foreign trade	31	Taxation	36
Forestry	25	Topography	2
Government	13	Tourism, travel, and recreation	47
Health	41	Transportation	11
History	12		
Housing	42		

FREQUENTLY USED ABBREVIATIONS AND ACRONYMS

AD—Anno Domini
a.m.—before noon
b.—born
BC—Before Christ
C—Celsius
c.—circa (about)
cm—centimeter(s)
Co.—company
Corp.—corporation
cu ft—cubic foot, feet
cu m—cubic meter(s)
d.—died
E—east
e.g.—exempli gratia (for example)
ed.—edition, editor
est.—estimated
et al.—et alii (and others)
etc.—et cetera (and so on)
EU—European Union
F—Fahrenheit

fl.—flourished
FRG—Federal Republic of Germany
ft—foot, feet
ft³—cubic foot, feet
GATT—General Agreement on Tariffs and Trade
GDP—gross domestic products
gm—gram
GMT—Greenwich Mean Time
GNP—gross national product
GRT—gross registered tons
ha—hectares
i.e.—id est (that is)
in—inch(es)
kg—kilogram(s)
km—kilometer(s)
kw—kilowatt(s)
kWh—kilowatt-hour(s)
lb—pound(s)
m—meter(s); morning

m³—cubic meter(s)
mi—mile(s)
Mt.—mount
MW—megawatt(s)
N—north
n.d.—no date
NA—not available
oz—ounce(s)
p.m.—after noon
r.—reigned

rev. ed.—revised edition
S—south
sq—square
St.—saint
UK—United Kingdom
UN—United Nations
US—United States
USSR—Union of Soviet Socialist Republics
W—west

A fiscal split year is indicated by a stroke (e.g. 2011/12).
For acronyms of UN agencies and their intergovernmental organizations, as well as other abbreviations used in text, see the United Nations volume.
A dollar sign ($) stands for US$ unless otherwise indicated.
Note that 1 billion = 1,000 million.

AFGHANISTAN

Islamic State of Afghanistan
Dowlat-e Eslami-ye Afghanestan

CAPITAL: Kabul

FLAG: The national flag has three equal vertical bands of black, red, and green, with a gold emblem centered on the red band; the emblem features a mosque encircled by a wreath on the left and right and by a bold Islamic inscription above.

ANTHEM: *Milli Surood (National Anthem).*

MONETARY UNIT: The afghani (AFA) is a paper currency of 100 puls. There are coins of 1, 2, and 5 afghanis, and notes of 10, 20, 50, 100, 500, and 1,000 afghanis. AFA1 = US$0.02000 (or US$1 = AFA47.7) as of 2011.

WEIGHTS AND MEASURES: The metric system is the legal standard, although some local units of measurement are still in use.

HOLIDAYS: Now Rooz (New Year's Day), 21 March; May Day, 1 May; Independence Day, 18 August. Movable religious holidays include First Day of Ramadan, Eid al-Fitr, Eid al-Adha, Ashura, and Milad an-Nabi. The Afghan calendar year begins on 21 March (the Afghan year 1390 began on 21 March 2010).

TIME: 4:30 p.m. = noon GMT.

¹LOCATION, SIZE, AND EXTENT

Afghanistan is a landlocked country in South Asia with a long, narrow strip in the northeast (the Wakhan corridor). Afghanistan is slightly smaller than the state of Texas, with a total area of 647,500 sq km (250,001 sq mi), extending 1,240 km (770 mi) NE–SW and 560 km (350 mi) SE–NW. The country is bounded on the N by Turkmenistan, Uzbekistan, and Tajikistan; on the extreme NE by China; on the E and S by Pakistan; and on the W by Iran. Afghanistan has a total boundary length of 5,529 km (3,436 mi). Afghanistan's capital city, Kabul, is located in the east central part of the country.

²TOPOGRAPHY

Although the average altitude of Afghanistan is about 1,200 m (4,000 ft), the Hindu Kush mountain range rises to more than 6,100 m (20,000 ft) in the northern corner of the Wakhan panhandle in the northeast and continues in a southwesterly direction for about 970 km (600 mi), dividing the northern provinces from the rest of the country. Central Afghanistan, a plateau with an average elevation of 1,800 m (6,000 ft), contains many small fertile valleys and provides excellent grazing for sheep, goats, and camels. To the north of the Hindu Kush and the central mountain range, the altitude drops to about 460 m (1,500 ft), permitting the growth of cotton, fruits, grains, groundnuts, and other crops. Southwestern Afghanistan is a desert, hot in summer and cold in winter. The four major river systems are the Amu Darya (Oxus) in the north, flowing into the Aral Sea; the Harirūd and Morghāb in the west; the Helmand in the southwest; and the Kabul in the east, flowing into the Indus. There are few lakes.

Afghanistan is prone to earthquakes. There was an earthquake in the area of Samangan in the Hindu Kush region of northern Afghanistan with a magnitude 5.4 on 18 April 2010. On 29 October 2009 there was an earthquake with a magnitude of 6.2.

³CLIMATE

The ranges in altitude produce a climate with both temperate and semi-tropical characteristics, and the seasons are clearly marked throughout the country. Wide temperature variations are common from season to season and from day to night. Summer temperatures in Kabul may range from 16°C (61°F) at sunrise to 38°C (100°F) by noon. The mean January temperature in Kabul is 0°C (32°F); the maximum summer temperature in Jalālābād is about 46°C (115°F).

There is a substantial amount of sunshine, and the air is usually clear and dry. Rainfall averages about 25 to 30 cm (10 to 12 in); precipitation occurs in winter and spring, most of it in the form of snow. Wind velocity is high, especially in the west.

⁴FLORA AND FAUNA

The country is particularly rich in medicinal plants such as rue, wormwood, and asafetida; fruit and nut trees are found in many areas. Native fauna include the fox, lynx, wild dog, bear, mongoose, shrew, hedgehog, hyena, jerboa, hare, and wild varieties of cats, asses, mountain goats, and mountain sheep. Trout is the most common fish.

The World Resources Institute estimates that there are 4,000 plant species in Afghanistan. In addition, Afghanistan is home to 144 species of mammals, 434 species of birds, 109 species of reptiles, and 7 species of amphibians. The calculation reflects the total number of distinct species residing in the country, not the number of endemic species.

⁵ENVIRONMENT

The World Resources Institute reported that Afghanistan had designated 218,600 hectares (540,172 acres) of land for protection as of 2006. Water resources totaled 65 cu km (15.59 cu mi) while water usage was 23.26 cu km (5.58 cu mi) per year. Domestic water usage accounted for 2% of total usage and agricultural for 98%. Per capita water usage totaled 779 cu m (27,510 cu ft) per year.

The United Nations (UN) reported that in 2008 carbon dioxide emissions in Afghanistan totaled 715 kilotons.

Afghanistan's most significant ecological problems are deforestation, drought, soil degradation, and overgrazing. Neglect, scorched earth tactics, and the damage caused by extensive bombardments have destroyed previously productive agricultural areas, and more are threatened by tons of unexploded ordnance. Afghanistan has responded to the fuel needs of its growing population by cutting down many of its already sparse forests.

Another environmental threat is posed by refugees returning to Afghanistan, who have migrated to Kabul and other larger cities instead of returning to destroyed villages and fields. This migration has placed stress on the infrastructure of those cities, causing increased pollution and worsening sanitation conditions.

According to a 2011 report issued by the International Union for Conservation of Nature and Natural Resources (IUCN), 11 species of mammals, 14 species of birds, 1 species of reptile, and 3 plant species were threatened. Endangered species in Afghanistan included the snow leopard, long-billed curlew, Argali sheep, musk deer, tiger, white-headed duck, Afghani brook salamander, Kabul markhor, and the Siberian white crane. In 2002 there were thought to be fewer than 100 snow leopards, however, in 2011 it was reported that a healthy population had been found in the northeastern region.

⁶POPULATION

The US Central Intelligence Agency (CIA) estimated the population of Afghanistan in 2011 to be approximately 29,835,392, which placed it at number 40 in population among the 196 nations of the world. In 2011 approximately 2.4% of the population was over 65 years of age, with another 42.3% under 15 years of age. The median age in Afghanistan was 18.2 years. There were 1.05 males for every female in the country. The population's annual rate of change was 2.375%. The projected population for the year 2025 was 39,400,000. Population density in Afghanistan was calculated at 46 people per sq km (119 people per sq mi).

The UN estimated that 23% of the population lived in urban areas and that urban populations had an annual rate of change of 4.7%. The largest urban area was Kabul, with a population of 3.6 million.

These figures are unreliable, however, because many city dwellers have left their urban homes for refuge in rural areas. Approximately 20% of the population is nomadic.

Two decades of near-constant warfare make Afghanistan's population—never certain in any case—even more difficult to assess. As many as an estimated three million Afghans died, and an additional six million sought refuge in Pakistan, Iran, and elsewhere in the world.

⁷MIGRATION

Estimates of Afghanistan's net migration rate, carried out by the CIA in 2011, amounted to 3.31 migrants per 1,000 citizens. The total number of emigrants living abroad was 2.35 million, and the total number of immigrants living in Afghanistan was 90,900.

The Return of Qualified Afghans program, designed to bring back Afghan professionals living abroad, facilitated the return of 150 Afghans (14 female and 136 male) to take up work in Afghanistan consistent with their professional backgrounds by June 2005.

Of the world's total refugee population in 2004, Afghans constituted 23%, making it the largest country of origin of refugees under the care of the United Nations High Commission for Refugees (UNHCR). Tajikistan closed its border with Afghanistan in 2004.

All neighboring countries closed their borders with Afghanistan by September 2005. By mid-September 2005 the Pakistani government ordered the forcible expulsion of millions of Afghan refugees living in Pakistan's tribal areas. In the rush to meet the forced expulsion deadline, dozens of children died.

The continuing conflict between the Afghanistan government and the Taliban has caused a massive migration of citizens (particularly young Afghans) out of the country in search of security and jobs. Unfortunately, many of these citizens are using illegal smuggling channels to gain entry into other countries. Illegal migrants typically pay between $18,000 and $25,000 to smugglers who provide entry to destinations such as the United Kingdom, France, Greece, Italy, and Iran, where they then apply for asylum. Once there, however, many are detained in centers offering inadequate living conditions and thousands are deported back to Afghanistan after their applications are denied. In Iran, for instance, 700,000 Afghans were deported in 2008 when the government determined that they were not political refugees, but economic migrants. The International Organization for Migration has initiated campaigns against illegal migration, focusing on the dangers associated with illegal smuggling rings. The Afghani government, however, has done little to deter smuggling operations. As a result, many citizens who return to the country after one failed smuggling attempt simply find another smuggler and begin the process again.

⁸ETHNIC GROUPS

About the middle of the second millennium BC Indo-Aryans began to move into and through the present area of Afghanistan. Much later other ethnic groups came from Central Asia—Pactyes (from whom the present-day name Pashtuns derives), Sakas, Kushans, Hephthalites, and others, as well as a procession of Iranians and Greeks. In the 7th century AD Arabs arrived from the southwest, spreading the new faith of Islam. In the same century Turks moved in from the north, followed in the 13th century by Mongols, and, finally, in the 15th century by Turko-Mongols. This multiplicity of movements made Afghanistan a loose conglomeration of racial and linguistic groups. All citizens are called Afghans, but the Pashtuns (the name may also be written as Pashtoon, Pushtun, or Pukhtun, and in Pakistan as Pathan) are often referred to as the "true Afghans." Numbering about 42% of the population since 2005, they are known to have once been centered in the Sulaiman mountain range to the east; it is only in recent centuries that they moved into eastern and southern

AFGHANISTAN

LOCATION: 29°28′ to 38°30′ N; 60°30′ to 74°53′ E. BOUNDARY LENGTHS: China, 76 kilometers (47 miles); Iran, 936 kilometers (582 miles); Pakistan, 2,430 kilometers (1,511 miles); Tajikistan, 1,206 kilometers (750 miles); Turkmenistan, 744 kilometers (463 miles); Uzbekistan, 137 kilometers (85 miles).

Afghanistan, where they now predominate. They have long been divided into two major divisions, the Durranis and the Ghilzais, each with its own communities and sub-communities. The Tajiks, of Iranian stock, comprise nearly 27% of the population and are mainly concentrated in the north and northeast. The Hazaras (about 9%), who are said to have descended from the Mongols, are found in the central ranges. To the north of the Hindu Kush, Turkic and Turko-Mongol groups were in the majority until 1940. Each of these groups is related to groups north of the Amu Darya; among them are the Tajiks and Uzbeks (the Uzbeks number about 9% of the population). Other groups include the Aimaks (4%), Turkmen (3%), Baloch (2%), Farsiwans (Persians), and Brahiu. In the northeast are the Kafirs or infidels. After their conversion to

Islam at the end of the 19th century, they were given the name of Nuristanis or people of the light.

⁹LANGUAGES

Both Pashtu (or Pushtu) and Dari (Afghan Persian) are the official languages of the country. Pashtu is spoken by about 35% of the population while approximately 50% speak Dari. Although Pashtu has a literature of its own, over the centuries Dari, the language spoken in Kabul, has been the principal language of cultural expression, the government, and business. Both Pashtu and Dari are written primarily with the Arabic alphabet, however, there are some modifications. The Hazaras speak their own dialect of Dari. The Turkic languages, spoken by 11% of the population, include Uzbek and Turkmen. The Nuristanis speak some seven different dialects belonging to the Dardic linguistic group. There are about 30 minor languages, primarily Balochi and Pashai, spoken by some 4% of the population. Bilingualism is common.

¹⁰RELIGIONS

Almost all Afghans are Muslims. Approximately 80% of the population are Sunnis; 19% are Shias (including some Isma'ilis); and only about 1% practice other religions. The Pashtuns, most of the Tajiks, the Uzbeks, and the Turkmen are Sunnis, while the Hazaras are Shias. Most of the Sunnis adhere to Hanafi Sunnism, but a fairly sizable minority of Sunnis adheres to a more mystical version known as Sufism. The country's small Hindu and Sikh population is estimated at less than 3,000.

In 1994 the Islamic militants who called themselves the Taliban—literally "the Seekers," a term used to describe religious students—began to impose their strict form of Islam observance in the areas that they controlled. The Taliban, composed mostly of Pashtuns, were puritanical zealots. Women were ordered to dress in strict Islamic garb and were banned from working or from going out of their houses unless accompanied by a male relative. Some men were forced to pray five times a day and grow full beards as a condition of employment in the government. Under the Taliban repression of the Hazara ethnic group, who were predominantly Shias, was severe.

With the fall of the Taliban and the adoption of a new constitution in January 2004, Islam remains the state religion; however, the new constitution does allow for religious freedom. The constitution does not indicate a preference for Sunnism and there are no references made in the document to the use of Shari'ah law in the legal code. However, a 2009 law codified the implementation of Islamic family law for the Shia minority. The document does state that both the president and vice president must be Muslim. The Shia minority still faces some discrimination from the Sunni majority.

¹¹TRANSPORTATION

The CIA reports that Afghanistan has a total of 42,150 km (26,191 mi) of roads, of which 12,350 km (7,674 mi) are paved. There are 27 vehicles per 1,000 people in the country. Afghanistan has approximately 1,200 km (746 mi) of navigable waterways.

Many roads were built in the years prior to 1979 to connect the principal cities and to open up formerly isolated areas. Roads connect Kabul with most provincial capitals and with Peshāwar in Pakistan through the Khyber Pass. The road from Herāt to Mashhad in Iran was completed in 1971. The Salang Tunnel through the Hindu Kush, completed with Soviet assistance in 1964, considerably shortened the travel time between Kabul and northern Afghanistan. The tunnel was modernized in the mid-1980s. However, in May 1997 the Tajik leader, Ahmad Shah Masud, blew up the southern entrance of the tunnel in an effort to trap the invading Taliban forces. It was reopened in January 2002. The Qandahār-Torghundi highway in the south was completed in 1965.

The Khyber Pass in Pakistan is the best known of the passes providing land access to Afghanistan. Transit arrangements with Iran provide an alternative route for its commercial traffic. However, the great bulk of the country's trade moves through the former Soviet Union. At the same time, Afghanistan's highways are badly damaged from years of warfare and neglect. Land mines are buried on the sides of many roads.

The only railways in the country were a 9.6-km (6-mi) spur from Gushgy, Turkmenistan to Towrghondi; a 15-km (9.3-mi) line from Termez, Uzbekistan to the Kheyrabad transshipment point on the south bank of the Amu Darya; and a short spur into Spin Baldak in the southeast. In 2011 there were plans for the establishment of a National Rail Authority. Several projects that would connect Afghanistan to Iran and China were also underway. Ariana Afghan Airlines is the national carrier. Afghanistan has 53 airports, 19 with paved runways and 34 with unpaved runways. It also has 11 heliports.

¹²HISTORY

Afghanistan has existed as a distinct polity for less than three centuries. Previously, the area was made up of various principalities, usually hostile to each other and occasionally ruled by one or another conqueror from Persia and the area to the west or from central Asia to the north. The area was usually taken while these conquerors were on their way to India. These included the Persian Darius I in the 6th century BC and, 300 years later, Alexander the Great. As the power of his Seleucid successors waned, an independent Greek kingdom of Bactria arose with its capital at Balkh, west of Mazār-e Sharif, but after about a century it fell to invading ethnic groups (notably the Sakas, who gave their name to Sakastan, or Sistan). Toward the middle of the 3rd century BC, Buddhism spread to Afghanistan from India, and for centuries at least half the population of eastern Afghanistan was Buddhist.

Beginning in the 7th century AD Muslim invaders brought Islam to the region, and it eventually became the dominant cultural influence. For almost 200 years Ghaznī was the capital of a powerful Islamic kingdom, the greatest of the rulers during this time period, Mahmud of Ghaznī (r. 997–1030), conquered most of the area from the Caspian to the Ganges. The Ghaznavids were displaced by the Seljuk Turks, who conquered Persia and Anatolia (eastern Turkey) and by the Ghorids who, rising from Ghor (located southeast of Herāt), established an empire stretching from Herāt to Ajmir in India. They were displaced in turn by the Turko-Persian rulers of the Khiva oasis in Transoxiana who, by 1217, had created a state that included the whole of Afghanistan until it disintegrated under attacks by Genghis Khan in 1219. A distant descendant of Genghis Khan, Timur (also called "Timur the Lame" or Tamerlane), occupied all of what is now Afghanistan from 1365 to 1384, establishing a court of intellectual and artistic brilliance at Herāt. The Timurids came under challenge from the Uzbeks, who finally drove them out of Herāt in 1507. The great Babur, one of the Uzbek princes, occupied Kabul in 1504 and Delhi in 1526 establishing the Mughal Empire in which eastern Afghanistan was ruled from Delhi, Agra, Lahore, or Srinagar, while Herāt and Sistan were governed as provinces of Persia.

In the 18th century Persians under Nadir Shah conquered the area and, after his death in 1747, one of his military commanders, Ahmad Shah Abdali, was elected emir of Afghanistan. The formation of a unified Afghanistan under his emirate marked Afghanistan's beginning as a political entity. Among his descendants was Dost Muhammad who established himself in Kabul in 1826 and gained the emirate in 1835. Although the British defeated Dost in the first Afghan War (1838–42), they restored him to power. However, his attempts and those of his successors to play off Czarist Russian interests against the British concerns about the security of their Indian Empire led to more conflict. In the second Afghan War (1877–79) the forces of Sher Ali, Dost's son, were defeated by the British and his entire party was ousted. Abdur Rahman Khan, recognized as emir by the British in 1880, established a central administration and supported the British interest in a neutral Afghanistan as a buffer against the expansion of Russian influence.

Intermittent fighting between the British and Pashtun ethnic group from eastern Afghanistan continued even after the establishment, in 1893, of a boundary (the Durand line) between Afghanistan and British India. An Anglo-Russian agreement concluded in 1907 guaranteed the independence of Afghanistan (and Tibet) under British influence. Afghan forces under Amanullah Khan gained the upper hand in the third Afghan War; the Treaty of Rāwalpindi (1919) accorded the government of Afghanistan the freedom to conduct its own foreign affairs.

Internally, Amanullah's Westernization program, supported by the Soviet Union, was strongly opposed by the religious leaders and ethnic group chiefs. He was forced to abdicate in 1929. After a brief rule by Bachcha Saqaw ("water-carrier boy"), a community assembly chose Muhammad Nadir Shah as king. In his brief four years in power, he restored peace while continuing Amanullah's modernization efforts at a more moderate pace. After being assassinated in 1933 he was succeeded by his son, Muhammad Zahir Shah, who continued Amanullah's modernization efforts. Zahir Shah governed for 40 years, though he shared effective power with his uncles and a first cousin, who served as his prime ministers. It should be mentioned that from the time that it gained independence until the end of Zahir Shah's rule and decades thereafter, Afghanistan received Soviet aid in various forms.

In the 1960s there was considerable tension between Pakistan and Afghanistan as a result of Afghanistan's effort to assert influence among, and ultimately responsibility for, Pashtu-speaking Pashtun ethnic groups living on both sides of the Durand Line under a policy calling for the establishment of an entity to be called "Pashtunistan." The border was closed several times during the following years, and relations with Pakistan remained generally poor until 1977.

In 1964 a new constitution was introduced, converting Afghanistan into a constitutional monarchy. A year later the country's first general election was held. In July 1973 Muhammad Daoud Khan, the king's first cousin and brother-in-law, who had served as prime minister from 1953 until early 1963, seized power in a near-bloodless coup, establishing a republic and appointing himself president and prime minister of the Republic of Afghanistan. He exiled Zahir Shah and his immediate family, abolished the monarchy, dissolved the legislature, and suspended the constitution. Daoud ruled as a dictator until 1977, when a republican constitution calling for a one-party state was adopted by the newly convened Loya Jirga (Grand National Assembly), which then elected Daoud president for a six-year term.

Afghanistan Under Communist Rule

On 27 April 1978 Daoud was deposed and executed in a bloody coup (the "Saur Revolution" because it took place during the Afghan month of Saur), and the Democratic Republic of Afghanistan emerged. Heading the new Revolutionary Council was Nur Muhammad Taraki, secretary-general of the communist People's Democratic Party of Afghanistan (PDPA), assisted by Babrak Karmal and Hafizullah Amin, both named deputy prime ministers. The Soviet Union (which would break apart in 1991) strengthened its ties with the new regime and, in December 1978, the two nations renewed their treaty of friendship and cooperation. Soon after the coup, rural Muslim Afghan groups took up arms against the regime, which increasingly relied on Soviet arms for support against what came to be known as *mujahedeen*, or holy warriors.

Meanwhile, the Khalq (masses) and Parcham (flag) factions of the PDPA, which had united for the April takeover, became embroiled in a bitter power struggle within the party and the government. In September 1979 Taraki was ousted and executed by Amin, who had beat out Karmal to become prime minister the previous March and who now assumed Taraki's posts as president and party leader. Amin was himself replaced on 27 December by Karmal, the Parcham faction leader. This last change was announced not by Radio Kabul but by Radio Moscow and was preceded by the airlift of 4,000 to 5,000 Soviet troops into Kabul on 25–26 December, purportedly at the request of an Afghan government whose president, Hafizullah Amin, was killed during the takeover.

The Soviet presence increased to about 85,000 troops in late January 1980 and, by spring, the first clashes between Soviet troops and the *mujahedeen* had occurred. Throughout the early and mid-1980s the *mujahedeen* resistance continued to build, aided by Afghan army deserters and arms from the United States, Pakistan, and the nations of the Islamic Conference Organization (ICO). Much of the countryside remained under *mujahedeen* control as the insurgency waged on year by year while in Kabul, Soviet advisers assumed control of most Afghan government agencies.

By late 1987 more than a million Afghans had lost their lives in the struggle, while the UNHCR estimated that some five million others had sought refuge in Pakistan, Iran, and elsewhere. Soviet sources at the time acknowledged Soviet losses of 12,000–30,000 dead and 76,000 wounded. Soviet troop strength in Afghanistan at the end of 1987 was about 120,000, while according to Western sources, Afghan resistance forces numbered nearly 130,000.

In early 1987 Babrak Karmal fled to Moscow after being replaced as the head of the PDPA in May 1986 by Najibullah, former head of the Afghan secret police. Najibullah offered the *mujahedeen* a cease-fire and introduced a much-publicized national reconciliation policy; he also released some political prisoners, offered to deal with the resistance leaders, and promised new land reform. The *mujahedeen* rejected these overtures, declining to negotiate for anything short of Soviet withdrawal and Najibullah's removal.

International efforts to bring about a political solution to the war—including nearly unanimous UN General Assembly condemnations of the Soviet presence in Afghanistan—were pursued within the UN framework from 1982 onward. Among these efforts were "proximity talks" between Afghanistan and Pakistan conducted by Under Secretary-General Diego Cordovez, a special representative of the UN Secretary General. After a desultory beginning, these talks began to look promising in late 1987 and early 1988 when Soviet policymakers repeatedly stated, in a major policy shift, that the removal of Soviet troops from Afghanistan was not contingent on the creation of a transitional regime acceptable to the Soviet Union. On 14 April 1988 documents were signed and exchanged in which the Soviet Union agreed to pull its troops out of Afghanistan within nine months, the United States reserved the right to continue military aid to Afghan guerrillas as long as the Soviet Union continued to aid the government in Kabul, and Pakistan and Afghanistan pledged not to interfere in each other's internal affairs.

The Soviets completed the evacuation of their forces on schedule 15 February 1989, but in spite of continuing pressure by the well-armed *mujahedeen*, the Najibullah government remained in power until April 1992 when Najibullah sought refuge at the UN office in Kabul as *mujahedeen* forces closed in on the city.

Afghanistan after the Soviet Withdrawal

With the fall of the Najibullah government, the Seven-Party Alliance (SPA) of the Islamic groups based in Pakistan moved to consolidate its "victory" by announcing plans to set up the Afghan Interim Government (AIG) charged with preparing the way for elections. Meanwhile, they moved to assert their control of Afghanistan, but their efforts to establish the AIG in Kabul failed when, within ten days of Najibullah's departure from office, well-armed forces of the Hezb-e Islami and Jamiat-i-Islami—two of the seven SPA parties—clashed while fighting for control of the capital. In July Jamiat leader Burhanuddin Rabbani replaced Sibghatullah Mojaddedi as president of the AIG, as previously agreed by all the SPA parties but the Hezb-e Islami.

Continued fighting between Jamiat and Hezb-e Islami militias halted further progress. Rabbani's forces, under Commander Ahmad Shah Masoud, dug in to block those under the control of interim "Prime Minister" Gulbuddin Hekmatyar's Hezb-e Islami and his ally, General Rashid Dostum (a former PDPA militia leader turned warlord from northern Afghanistan), from taking control of Kabul. During a 24-hour rocket exchange in August 1992 in Kabul, an estimated 3,000 Afghans died; before the end of the year, upwards of 700,000 Afghans had fled the city. Deep differences among the SPA/AIG leadership, embittered by decades of bad blood, ethnic distrust, and personal enmity, prevented any further progress toward creating a genuine interim government capable of honoring the 1992 SPA pledge to write a constitution, organize elections, and create a new Afghan polity. Despite UN attempts to broker a peace and bring the warring groups into a coalition government, Afghanistan remained at war.

Rise of the Taliban

By the summer of 1994 Rabbani and his defense minister, Ahmed Shah Masoud, were in control of the government in Kabul, but internal turmoil caused by the warring factions had brought the economy to a standstill. It was reported that on the road north of Qandahār, Afghanistan's second largest city, a convoy owned by influential Pakistani businessmen was stopped by bandits demanding money. The businessmen appealed to the Pakistani government, which responded by encouraging Afghan students from the fundamentalist religious schools on the Pakistan-Afghan border to intervene. The students freed the convoy and went on to capture Qandahār. Pakistan's leaders supported the Taliban with ammunition, fuel, and food. The students, ultra-fundamentalist Sunni Muslims who called themselves the Taliban (the Arabic

word for religious students, literally "the Seekers") shared Pashtun ancestry with their Pakistani neighbors to the south. The Taliban also found widespread support among Afghan Pashtuns hostile to local warlords and tired of war and economic instability. By late 1996 the Taliban had captured Kabul, the capital, and were in control of 21 of Afghanistan's 32 provinces. When Rabbani fled the capital, Pakistan and Saudi Arabia officially recognized the Taliban government in Kabul. In areas under Taliban control, order was restored, roads opened, and trade resumed. However, the Taliban's reactionary social practices, justified as being Islamic, did not appeal to Afghanistan's non-Pashtun minorities in the north and west of the country, nor to the educated population generally. The opposition, dominated by the Uzbek, Tajik, Hazara, and Turkoman ethnic groups, retreated to the northeastern provinces.

In May 1997 the Taliban entered Mazār-e Sharif, Afghanistan's largest town north of the Hindu Kush and stronghold of Uzbek warlord Rashid Dostum. In the political intrigue that followed, Dostum was ousted by his second in command, Malik Pahlawan, who initially supported the Taliban. Dostum reportedly fled to Turkey. Once the Taliban were in the city, however, Pahlawan abruptly switched sides. In the subsequent fighting, the Taliban were forced to retreat with heavy casualties. The forces of Ahmad Shah Masoud, Tajik warlord and former defense minister in ousted President Rabbani's government, were also instrumental in the defeat of the Taliban in Mazār. Masoud controlled the high passes of the Panjshir Valley in the east of the country. The opposition alliance was supported by Iran, Russia, and the newly-formed Central Asian republics, which feared that the Taliban might destabilize the region.

By early 1998 the Taliban militia controlled about two-thirds of Afghanistan. Opposition forces under Ahmad Shah Masoud controlled the northeast of the country. Taliban forces mounted another offensive against their opponents in August–September 1998 and nearly sparked a war with neighboring Iran after a series of Shiite villages were pillaged and Iranian diplomats killed. Iran, which supplied Masoud's forces, countered by massing troops along its border with Afghanistan. Although the crisis subsided, tensions between the Taliban and Iran remained high. Masoud's opposition forces became known as the United Front or Northern Alliance in late 1999.

Despite attempts to broker a peace settlement, fighting between the Taliban and opposition factions continued through 1999 and into 2000 with the Taliban controlling 90% of the country. In March 1999 the warring factions agreed to enter a coalition government, but by July these UN-sponsored peace talks broke down and the Taliban renewed its offensive against opposition forces. By October the Taliban captured the key northern city of Taloqan and a series of northeastern towns, advancing to the border with Tajikistan. Fighting between the Taliban and Northern Alliance forces was fierce in early 2001.

In April 2001 Masoud stated that he did not rule out a peace dialogue with the Taliban, or even of setting up a provisional government jointly with the Taliban, but that Pakistan would have to stop interfering in the conflict first. He stated that elections would have to be held under the aegis of the UN and the "six plus two" countries including Iran, China, Pakistan, Tajikistan, Turkmenistan, Russia, and the United States. The Northern Alliance was receiving financial and military assistance from its old enemy Russia as well as from Iran. The Taliban was recognized as the legitimate government of Afghanistan by Pakistan, Saudi Arabia, and the United Arab Emirates. Masoud was assassinated on 9 September 2001 by two men claiming to be Moroccan journalists. His killers were thought to have been agents of the al-Qaeda terrorist group acting in concert with the plotters of the 11 September 2001 attacks on the United States.

Post-11 September 2001

The 11 September 2001 attacks carried out against the United States by members of al-Qaeda marked the beginning of a war on terrorism first directed against the Taliban for harboring Osama bin Laden and his forces. On 7 October 2001 US-led forces launched the bombing campaign Operation Enduring Freedom against the Taliban and al-Qaeda in Afghanistan. On 13 November the Taliban were removed from power in Kabul, and an interim government under the leadership of Hamid Karzai, a Pashtun leader from Qandahār, was installed on 22 December. In June 2002 a Loya Jirga—Grand Assembly of community leaders—was held, and Karzai was elected head of state of a transitional government that would be in place for 18 months until elections could be held. More than 60% of the cabinet posts in the government went to Ahmed Shah Masoud's Northern Alliance. Masoud was officially proclaimed the national hero of Afghanistan on 25 April 2002, and he was mentioned as a candidate for the Nobel Peace Prize. Between 2002 and 2004, Karzai survived two assassination plots.

In January 2004, a Loya Jirga adopted a new constitution providing for a strong presidency and defining Afghanistan as an Islamic republic where men and women enjoy equal status before the law. In October and November 2004, the first direct presidential election was held; Karzai was the winner with 55.4% of the vote. He was sworn in as president in December, amid tight security.

On 18 September 2005 Afghans went to the polls to elect a lower house of parliament and councils in each of the country's 34 provinces. The elections, which had been twice postponed, were part of the process of establishing a fully representative government. Several candidates and election workers were killed in Taliban attacks. In advance of the elections, the North Atlantic Treaty Organization (NATO) sent an extra 2,000 troops and a number of fighter jets to boost the 8,000-strong International Security Assistance Force (ISAF) protecting the country. Nearly 3,000 observers and media representatives registered to monitor the election.

The results of the 2005 elections showed that women, who were guaranteed 25% of seats in parliament, won 28%. Most of the candidates for parliament ran as independents, and a clear majority was predicted to support Karzai. However, many of the winners were former warlords, *mujahedeen* fighters, ex-Taliban figures, and opium dealers. Centrist and reformist figures did less well making the parliament, when it was seated on 19 December 2005, predominantly socially conservative and religious. The next election was scheduled for September 2009.

In 2005–06 several thousand troops from the US-led coalition in Afghanistan (most of them American) were engaged in battles with Taliban fighters in the eastern regions of the country bordering on Pakistani's tribal areas. The coalition forces also targeted members of the Hezb-e Islami group, whose leader, Gulbuddin Hekmatyar, has similar aims as the Taliban—to fight a *jihad* (holy war) to remove the Americans from Afghanistan and unseat Hamid Karzai's government. In October 2006 NATO assumed responsibility for the security of the entire country, heading the ISAF. Attacks by the Taliban continued, particularly in the southern part of the country.

In March 2007 NATO and Afghan forces began Operation Achilles, their largest offensive against the Taliban in the south. There was heavy fighting in the Helmand province. Also in March, Italy helped negotiate a prisoner exchange with the Taliban; in exchange for the release of kidnapped Italian reporter Daniele Mastrogiacomo, five Taliban rebels would be released by the Afghan government. Mastrogiacomo's driver and translator were beheaded. The deal was the first in which prisoners were openly exchanged for a hostage in either of the Afghan or Iraqi wars with the United States and its allies. The United States and other nations criticized the prisoner exchange; they said it would send the wrong signal to prospective hostage-takers and increase the risk of similar kidnappings of NATO and Afghan troops.

The war between the government and militant Islamists continued into 2009, particularly along the country's border with Pakistan where the Taliban has gained a great deal of popular support. Both the Taliban and al-Qaeda appeared to be growing in force. In 2009 several NATO countries pledged to increase their commitment to Afghanistan, both through troops and redevelopment financing.

The August 2009 elections were the first presidential polls organized by the Afghan government itself, with some international support. Throughout the weekend of the vote, at least 73 attacks were staged in and around polling stations by Taliban insurgents, though nearly 300,000 Afghan and NATO troops were on hand in many primary locations throughout the country. Voter turnout was considered to be low, with 40% to 50% of eligible voters participating. Immediately following the vote, hundreds of allegations of fraud, corruption, and ballot stuffing were reported to the United Nations-backed Electoral Complaints Commission (ECC). The results from about 600 polling stations were "quarantined" to allow for an official investigation. As a result, all of the ballots cast in 83 stations were invalidated because of fraud and the ECC announced a wider recount at about 2,500 polling stations across the country. Thousands of additional ballots were invalidated during the recount, leaving Karzai with less than 50% of the vote.

A run-off election was scheduled for 7 November between Karzai and his primary rival, Abdullah Abdullah. Abdullah demanded that several key poll officials be dismissed before the run-off took place. When this demand was immediately denied, he withdrew from the race leaving Karzai as the only candidate. Consequently, the run-off election was cancelled—as officials claimed the second round vote would only inspire a second round of violence from the Taliban—and Karzai was proclaimed the winner. International leaders were quick to congratulate Karzai on his reelection, despite previous allegations that he was involved in some way in the fraudulent activities of the August election. During his final term in office, the international community expected Karzai's administration to take a leading role in national security and to address the continuing issue of political corruption. The Taliban threatened to continue their fight against the government, calling Karzai a puppet of the West.

The United States increased its support of the war in Afghanistan in November 2009, as President Obama announced that an additional 30,000 troops would be sent to the nation. The troop increase came two months after the senior commander of US and NATO forces in Afghanistan, Gen. Stanley McChrystal, requested an additional 40,000 troops to subdue the Taliban. Obama's decision brought the total number of US forces in Afghanistan to 100,000. Shortly after Obama's announcement, several other NATO members collectively pledged an additional 7,000 troops. Together, the announcements placed troop levels in Afghanistan, after deployment, at about 145,000.

A new round of parliamentary elections, which was originally scheduled for May 2010, was rescheduled for September 2010 as the electoral commission cited a lack of funds and an increased concern for security at the polls. International observers hoped that the delay would allow time for the initiation of electoral reforms that could promote a smoother, safer election process than that of the 2009 presidential election, which was marred by fraud and violence. However, in February 2010 President Karzai issued a decree granting himself complete control over the Afghanistan Electoral Complaints Commission, the very group that questioned and investigated the outcome of the presidential elections in which Karzai ultimately prevailed. Karzai justified the decree by stating a need to limit Western "interference" in national elections. Western observers expressed great concern over the decree, believing that it would be a major hindrance to free and fair elections. The electoral commission needed approximately $50 million from the international community in order to host the elections. International discontent over the decree could jeopardize that funding and cause further delays.

At a major conference in Kabul in July 2010, Karzai set forth an ambitious goal to have Afghan forces entirely in control of security operations across the country by 2014. Although no formal agreements to that effect have been established, it seemed as if most of the 70 international representatives in attendance supported the idea. The British prime minister indicated that a withdrawal of British troops by 2014 seemed a very realistic goal, while the US secretary of state announced that the US hoped to turn over security to Afghan police and military by July 2011.

The 18 September poll featured more than 2,500 candidates running for 249 seats in the lower house (Wolesi Jirga or House of the People). The Independent Election Commission (IEC) announced that results for the election would not be released until the end of October. However, at mid October the IEC reported that 1.3 million of the 5.6 million votes had been cancelled due to fraud or other irregularities and 224 candidates were under investigation for suspicions of fraud. By November 2010, 24 winning candidates were disqualified due to fraud. The final results announced on 1 December gave 96 of the 249 seats to Pashtuns, 69 seats to Tajiks, and 41 seats to Hazaras. The final count displaced the previous Pashtu-speaking majority, leaving many officials concerned that the new ethnic balance in the government could lead to greater ethnic tensions throughout the nation. Despite the official tally, President Karzai continued to delay the inauguration of the new parliament. By mid-December a group of about 100 members of parliament organized under the name of the Administrative Board and passed a resolution in an attempt to force Karzai to act in convening the assembly. This move was partly motivated by rumors that the attorney general intended to annul the election results, even though he does not have the official power to do so. It was believed that Karzai supported the plan because of his own dissatisfaction with the results, which gave greater voice to the opposition.

Early in 2011 Taliban forces from both Afghanistan and Pakistan stepped up their campaign of violence within Afghanistan and along the border regions, presumably in an attempt to destabilize the region just as US forces were making plans to pull out (by July 2011). The surge in attacks also came in response to a surge in attacks by US Special Forces, which had begun to launch up to 20 attacks per day in an effort to capture hundreds of Taliban fighters. Hundreds of Taliban members were killed by ground attacks and drone missiles. This continued unrest brought several aid and development programs to a halt and hit the economy with dramatic increases in both fuel and food costs. From January 2011 through March of that year, more than 200 Afghan civilians were killed and hundreds more were wounded in Taliban attacks. Many of the most brutal attacks occurred in areas that NATO forces had previously deemed to be secure.

On 1 May 2011 US forces found and killed al-Qaeda leader Osama bin Laden in a house in Abbottabad, near Pakistan's capital city of Islamabad. Obama said that Pakistan helped develop intelligence that led to Bin Laden, although it was not notified before the US strike. Bin Laden, one of the most-wanted men in the world, had become a symbolic leader for the Taliban. His second in command, Ayman al-Zawahiri, remained at large.

On 16 June 2011 Ayman al-Zawahiri became the confirmed head of al-Qaeda.

13 GOVERNMENT

Between 1964 and 1973 Afghanistan was a constitutional monarchy for the first and only time in its history. The head of government was the prime minister, appointed by the king and responsible to the bicameral legislature. This system gave way to a more traditional authoritarian system on 17 July 1973, when Afghanistan became a republic headed by Muhammad Daoud Khan, who became both president and prime minister. A new constitution in 1977 created a one-party state with a strong executive and a weak bicameral legislature. The communist PDPA abrogated this constitution after they seized power in April 1978.

Between 1978 and 1980 a communist-style 167-member Revolutionary Council exercised legislative powers. The chief of state (president) headed the presidium of that council, to which the 20-member cabinet was formally responsible. A provisional constitution, introduced in April 1980 guaranteed respect for Islam and national traditions; condemned colonialism, imperialism, Zionism, and fascism; and proclaimed the PDPA as "the guiding and mobilizing force of society and state." Seven years later, a new constitution providing for a very strong presidency was introduced as part of the PDPA's propaganda campaign of "national reconciliation." Najibullah remained as president until April 1992 when he sought refuge at the UN office in Kabul as *mujahedeen* forces closed in on the city.

With the fall of the Najibullah government the SPA of the Islamic groups announced plans to set up the AIG charged with preparing the way for elections. However, Professor Burhanuddin Rabbani co-opted the process by forming a leadership council that elected him president. Subsequent fighting among warring factions plunged the country into anarchy and set the stage for the emergence of the ultra-conservative Islamic movement of the Taliban, which ousted the Rabbani government and controlled all but the northern most provinces of the country.

The Taliban, led by Mullah Mohammed Omar, formed a six-member ruling council in Kabul which ruled by edict. Ultimate authority for Taliban rule rested in the Taliban's inner Shura (Assembly) located in the southern city of Qandahār and in Mullah Omar.

With the fall of the Taliban in December 2001, an interim government was created under the leadership of Hamid Karzai by an agreement held in Bonn, Germany. In June 2002 Karzai was elected head of state of the Islamic Transitional Government of Afghanistan (ITGA) by the Loya Jirga convened that month. He named an executive cabinet, dividing key ministries between ethnic Tajiks and Pashtuns. He also appointed three deputy presidents and a chief justice to the country's highest court.

In January 2004 a Loya Jirga adopted a new constitution providing for a strong presidency and defining Afghanistan as an Islamic republic where men and women enjoy equal status before the law. Former King Zahir Shah held the honorific Father of the Country and presided symbolically over certain occasions, lacking any governing authority. The honorific is not hereditary. The president is both chief of state and head of government. The president's cabinet is made up of 27 ministers, appointed by the president and approved by the national assembly. The president and two vice presidents are elected by a direct vote for a five-year term; a president can only be elected for two terms.

The legislative branch is composed of a bicameral national assembly. The lower house is the 249-seat Wolesi Jirga, directly elected by each of Afghanistan's 34 provinces according to its population. Members serve a five-year term. The Kabul province has the most seats with 33. Women have 68 seats guaranteed in the Wolesi Jirga, and two on each provincial council. The 102-member House of Elders (Meshrano Jirga) is indirectly elected; one-third elected by the 34 provincial councils for a four-year term, one-third appointed by the president for a five-year term, and one-third elected by local district councils for a three-year term.

On rare occasions the government may convene the Loya Jirga on issues of independence, national sovereignty, and territorial integrity; it can also amend the provisions of the constitution and prosecute the president. The Loya Jirga is made up of members of the national assembly and chairpersons of the provincial and district councils.

In October and November 2004 the first direct presidential elections were held; Hamid Karzai was the winner with 55.4% of the vote. In September 2005 elections for the Wolesi Jirga and provincial councils were held; although a majority of the members of parliament who won would support Karzai, many warlords, former *mujahedeen* fighters, ex-Taliban figures, and opium dealers also won.

The last presidential elections were held on 20 August 2009. The next presidential elections were scheduled for 2014.

14 POLITICAL PARTIES

The 1964 constitution provided for the formation of political parties. However, since the framers of the constitution decided that political parties should be permitted only after the first elections and since the parliament never adopted a law governing the parties' operation, all candidates for the parliamentary elections of August and September 1965 stood as independents. Because a law on political parties was not on the books four years later, the 1969 elections were also contested on a nonparty basis. Through 1964–1973, however, the de facto existence of parties was widely recognized. Subsequently, the framers reversed their plan to allow political parties. Under the 1977 constitution only the National Revolutionary Party (NRP), the ruler's chosen instrument, was allowed.

The 1978 coup was engineered by the illegal PDPA, which had been founded in 1965. During its brief history, this Marxist party had been driven by a bloody struggle between its pro-Soviet Parcham faction and its larger Khalq faction. Babrak Karmal was the leader of the Parcham group, while the Khalq faction was headed by Nur Muhammad Taraki and Hafizullah Amin until 1979. The factional struggle continued after the 1978 coup, prompting the Soviet intervention of 1979. Factional bloodletting continued thereafter also, with repeated purges and assassinations of Khalq adherents as well as bitter infighting within Parcham, this last leading to Babrak Karmal's replacement as PDPA secretary-general in May 1986 by Najibullah.

The Islamic resistance forces opposing the PDPA government and its Soviet backers in Afghanistan represented conservative, ethnically based Islamic groups which themselves have had a long history of partisan infighting (and repression by successive Kabul governments). They came together in the early 1980s to fight the common enemy, the communist PDPA and the Soviet invaders and, in 1985, under pressure from Pakistan and the United States they were loosely united into the SPA, headquartered in Peshāwar, Pakistan. By 1987 commando groups affiliated with one or more of these seven parties controlled more than 80% of the land area of Afghanistan.

With arms flowing in from outside the country—a flow not halted until the end of 1991—the fighting continued, but with the final withdrawal of Soviet troops in February 1989, the SPA stepped up its military and political pressure on the communist PDPA government. However, President Najibullah proved to have more staying power than previously estimated. Using Soviet arms supplies, which continued to buttress his position until the end of 1991, Najibullah played upon divisions among the resistance, embraced nationalism and renounced communism, and even changed the name of the PDPA to the Wattan (Homeland) Party. It was only in April 1992 after the break-up of the Soviet Union, his army defecting from beneath him, and the *mujahedeen* closing on Kabul, that he sought refuge at the UN office in the capital, leaving the city in the hands of the rival ethnic and regional *mujahedeen* militias.

The leaders of the *mujahedeen* groups agreed to establish a leadership council. This council quickly came under the control of a professor, Burhanuddin Rabbani, who was subsequently elected president by the council. Fighting broke out in August 1992 in Kabul between forces loyal to President Rabbani and rival factions. A new war for the control of Afghanistan had begun.

On 26–27 September 1996 the Pashtun-dominated ultra-conservative Islamic Taliban movement captured the capital of Kabul and expanded its control to over 90% of the country by

2000. The Taliban was led by Mullah Mohammed Omar. Ousted President Rabbani, a Tajik, and his defense minister, Ahmad Shah Masoud, relocated to Takhar in the north. Rabbani claimed that he remained the head of the government. His delegation retained Afghanistan's UN seat after the General Assembly deferred a decision on Afghanistan's credentials. Meanwhile, the Taliban removed the ousted PDPA leader Najibullah from the UN office in Kabul, tortured and shot him, and hung his body prominently in the city. General Rashid Dostum, an ethnic Uzbek, controlled several north-central provinces until he was ousted on 25 May 1997 by his second in command Malik Pahlawan. Dostum fled to Turkey, but he returned that October. The Shia Hazara community, led by Abdul Karim Khalili, retained control of a small portion of the center of the country.

After the fall of the Taliban various warlords, leaders, and political factions emerged in Afghanistan. Dostum, as head of Junbish-e Melli Islami (National Islamic Movement), consolidated his power in Mazār-e Sharif. He was named interim deputy defense minister for the transitional government in 2002. Rabbani as nominal head of the Northern Alliance was also the leader of Jamiat-e-Islami, the largest political party in the alliance. Ismail Khan, a Shiite warlord of Tajik origin, earned a power base in the western city of Herāt by liberating it from Soviet control and for a time in the 1990s kept it from Taliban control. Khan was thought to be receiving backing from Iran. Abdul Karim Khalili was the leader of the Hezb-e-Wahdat (Unity Party) and the top figure in the Shia Hazara minority. Hezb-e-Wahdat was the main benefactor of Iranian support and the second most-powerful opposition military party. Gulbuddin Hekmatyar, the most notorious of the warlords who emerged from the fight against Soviet occupation, led the Hezb-e Islami party. Pir Syed Ahmed Gailani was a moderate Pashtun leader and wealthy businessman who was also the spiritual leader of a minority Sufi Muslim group. Gailani was supported by pro-royalist Pashtuns and Western-educated elites of the old regime. Former King Zahir Shah, a Pashtun, said he had no intention of returning to power, but volunteered to help build a power-sharing administration for the country. Zahir Shah died on 23 July 2007. Younis Qanooni, an ethnic Tajik who was named interior minister for the interim government, had also been the interior minister in the country's previous interim administration in 1996, before the Taliban came to power; he opposed the presence of UN peacekeepers in Afghanistan. Abdullah Abdullah, of the Northern Alliance, was a close friend of Ahmad Shah Masoud.

On 18 September 2005 Afghans went to the polls to elect a lower house of parliament and councils in each of the country's 34 provinces. The elections, which had been twice postponed, were part of the process of establishing a fully representative government. Some 12 million of an estimated 25–28 million Afghans were registered to vote. There were about 5,800 candidates standing for the 249-seat Wolesi Jirga and for seats in the provincial councils. There were more than 26,000 men-only or women-only polling stations in 5,000 locations. There were 69 different types of ballot papers, all including the names, pictures, and symbols of the candidates to enable voters who could not read to vote. Several candidates and election workers were killed in Taliban attacks. In advance of the elections, the NATO sent an extra 2,000 troops and a number of fighter jets to boost the 8,000-strong ISAF already protecting the country. Nearly 3,000 observers and media representatives registered to monitor the election. Final results for the elections were delayed due to accusations of fraud and were announced in November.

The results of the 2005 elections showed that women, who were guaranteed 25% of the seats in parliament, won 28%. Most of the candidates for parliament ran as independents, and a clear majority of them were predicted to support Karzai. However, many of the winners were former warlords, mujahedeen fighters, ex-Taliban figures, and opium dealers. Centrist, reformist figures did less well making the parliament, when it was seated on 19 December 2005, predominantly socially conservative and religious.

In the 2010 elections most of the newly elected officials were independents who maintained allegiance to their own ethnic groups, rather than to political organizations.

15 LOCAL GOVERNMENT

Afghanistan was traditionally divided into provinces governed by centrally appointed governors with considerable autonomy in local affairs. As of 2006 there were 34 provinces. During the Soviet occupation and the development of country-wide resistance, local areas came increasingly under the control of mujahedeen groups that were largely independent of any higher authority; local commanders, in some instances, asserted a measure of independence also from the mujahedeen leadership in Pakistan, establishing their own systems of local government, collecting revenues, running educational and other facilities, and even engaging in local negotiations. Mujahedeen groups retained links with the Peshāwar parties to ensure access to weapons that were doled out to the parties by the government of Pakistan for distribution to fighters inside Afghanistan.

The Taliban set up a shura (assembly), made up of senior Taliban members and important ethnic group figures from the area. Each shura made laws and collected taxes locally. The Taliban set up a provisional government for the whole of Afghanistan, but it did not exercise central control over the local shuras.

The process of setting up the transitional government in June 2002 by the Loya Jirga took many steps involving local government. First, at the district and municipal level, traditional shura councils met to pick electors—people who cast ballots for Loya Jirga delegates. Each district or municipality chose a predetermined number of electors, based on the size of its population. The electors then traveled to regional centers and cast ballots, choosing from among themselves a smaller number of Loya Jirga delegates, according to allotted numbers assigned to each district. The delegates then took part in the Loya Jirga.

The transitional government attempted to integrate local governing authorities with the central government, but it lacked the loyalty of warlords necessary to exert its governing authority. More traditional elements of political authority—such as Sufi networks, royal lineage, clan strength, age-based wisdom, and the like—still exist and play a role in Afghan society. Karzai relied on these traditional sources of authority in his challenge to the warlords and older Islamist leaders. The deep ethnic, linguistic, sectarian, racial, and regional divides present in the country create what is called Qawm identity, which emphasizes the local over higher-order formations. Qawm refers to the group to which the individual considers himself to belong, whether a sub-ethnic group, a village, a valley, or a neighborhood. Local governing authority relies upon these forms of identity and loyalty.

The constitution established in 2004 provided for directly elected provincial councils, which have 9–29 members depending on population. District and village councils are directly elected for a period of three years. Municipalities administer city affairs.

¹⁶JUDICIAL SYSTEM

Under the Taliban there was no rule of law or independent judiciary. Ad hoc rudimentary judicial systems were established based on Taliban interpretation of Islamic law. Murderers were subjected to public executions and thieves had a limb or two (one hand, one foot) severed. Adulterers were stoned to death in public. Taliban courts were said to have heard cases in sessions that lasted only a few minutes. Prison conditions were poor and prisoners were not given food as this was the responsibility of the prisoners' relatives who were allowed to visit to provide food once or twice a week. Those who had no relatives had to petition the local council or rely on other inmates.

In non-Taliban controlled areas, many municipal and provincial authorities relied on some form of Islamic law and traditional ethnic group codes of justice. The administration and implementation of justice varied from area to area and depended on the whims of local commanders or other authorities, who could summarily execute, torture, and mete out punishments without reference to any other authority.

After the fall of the Taliban, Afghanistan's judicial system was fragmented with conflicts between such core institutions as the Ministry of Justice, Supreme Court, and attorney general's office. In addition, the judicial system's infrastructure was destroyed; the absence of adequate court or ministry facilities, basic office furniture, and minimal supplies made substantive progress difficult. There were also tensions between secularly and religiously trained judges with regard to judicial appointments. Until Afghanistan's new constitution was adopted in 2004, the country's basic legal framework consisted of its 1964 constitution and existing laws and regulations to the extent that they were in accordance with the Bonn Agreement of 2001 and with international treaties to which Afghanistan was a party. The Ministry of Justice was charged with compiling Afghan laws and assessing their compatibility with international standards, but they did not have texts of Afghan laws, which were largely unavailable, even among attorneys, judges, law faculty, and government agencies. While in power, the Taliban burned law books. There was no adequate law library in the country as of 2002.

The 2004 constitution established an independent judiciary under the Islamic state. The judicial branch consists of a Supreme Court (Stera Mahkama), high courts, appeals courts, and local and district courts. The Supreme Court is composed of nine members who are appointed by the president for a period of ten years (non-renewable) with the approval of the Wolesi Jirga. The Supreme Court has the power of judicial review. Lower courts apply Shia law in cases dealing with personal matters for Shia followers.

¹⁷ARMED FORCES

In 2011 military branches in the Afghan armed forces included the Afghan National Army (ANA) and the Afghan Air Force (AAF), which was considered a part of the ANA. Relative to the rest of the world, Afghanistan's military manpower (citizens eligible for military service) ranked 78th.

The International Institute for Strategic Studies (IISS) reports that armed forces in Afghanistan totaled 136,106 members in 2011. The force is comprised of 131,906 from the army and 4,200 members of the air force. Armed forces represent 1.4% of the labor force in Afghanistan. Defense spending totaled $522.3 million and accounted for 1.9% of gross domestic product (GDP).

¹⁸INTERNATIONAL COOPERATION

Afghanistan has been a member of the UN since 19 November 1946. Within the UN, Afghanistan is part of several specialized agencies, such as the United Nations Educational, Scientific, and Cultural Organization (UNESCO); the UN Food and Agriculture Organization (FAO); and IAEA. The country also participates in the World Health Organization (WHO), IFAD, UNIDO, the International Monetary Fund (IMF), the World Bank and IFC, and the ILO. Afghanistan is an observer in the World Trade Organization (WTO). Afghanistan is part of the Asian Development Bank, the Colombo Plan, the Economic and Social Commission for Asia and the Pacific (ESCAP), G-77, the Islamic Development Bank (IDB), the Economic Cooperation Organization, the Council for Mutual Economic Assistance (CEMA), and the Organization of the Islamic Conference (OIC). Other groups include WFTU and Interpol. Afghanistan is also a part of the Nonaligned Movement, the Organization for the Prohibition of Chemical Weapons, and the Nuclear Test Ban. In cooperation on environmental issues, the country is part of the Convention on the International Trade in Endangered Species of Wild Flora and Fauna (CITES), the London Convention, and the UN Conventions on Desertification and Climate Change.

The Afghan, Coalition, and Pakistan militaries periodically discuss boundary issues. Afghan and Iranian commissioners have sought agreement on Afghanistan's damming of the Helmand River tributaries during periods of drought. Pakistani troops build fences in tribal areas areas along the Durand Line to prevent foreign terrorists and other illegal activities. Smuggling of poppy derivatives from Afghanistan through Central Asian countries is also a concern.

On 24 May 2009 the president of Afghanistan met with the presidents of Iran and Pakistan to sign the Tehran Statement, an agreement through which they have pledged to work together in efforts to fight Islamist extremism and drug smuggling across borders. The leaders discussed immediate security issues relating to the wars in both Afghanistan and Pakistan. The meeting was considered a major step toward establishing regional cooperation on security issues, without the control of Western governments.

¹⁹ECONOMY

Afghanistan's economy has been devastated by decades of war. Hampered by an economy that was not integrated until relatively late in the post–World War II period, only in the 1950s did the building of new roads begin to link the country's commercial centers with the wool-and fruit-producing areas. Largely agricultural and pastoral, the country is highly dependent on farming and livestock raising (sheep and goats). Approximately 80% of the workforce is engaged in agriculture, with the remainder equally divided between industry and the service sector. Agricultural crops include wheat, corn, barley, rice, cotton, fruit, nuts, karakul pelts, wool, and mutton. Industrial activity includes small-scale production of textiles, soap, furniture, shoes, fertilizer, cement, and hand-woven carpets. The country has valuable mineral resources, including large reserves of iron ore at Hajigak discovered before the 30-year-old war. Natural gas, coal, copper, and to some degree, salt, lapis lazuli, barite, and chrome, are also available to be exploited. The discovery of large quantities of natural gas in the north, for which a pipeline to the Soviet Union was completed in 1967, increased the country's export earnings at least until escalation of civil strife in the late 1970s and 1980s.

Since the outbreak of war in the late 1970s, economic data have been contradictory and of doubtful reliability. In September 1987 the Afghan foreign minister asserted that 350 bridges and 258 factories had been destroyed since the fighting began in 1979. By the early 1990s two-thirds of all paved roads were unusable, and the countryside appeared severely depopulated, with more than 25% of the population—twice the prewar level—residing in urban areas. What little is left of the country's infrastructure has been largely destroyed due first to the war and then to the US-led bombing campaign following the 11 September 2001 terrorist attacks.

Severe drought added to the nation's difficulties in 1998–2001. The majority of the population continued to suffer from insufficient food, clean water, electricity, clothing, housing, and medical care as of 2008; these problems were exacerbated by military operations and political uncertainties. The presence of an estimated 10 million land mines also hinders the ability of Afghans to engage in agriculture or other forms of economic activity. Inflation, at 13% in 2007, was down from 16% in 2005, but it remained a serious problem.

Opium poppy cultivation is the mainstay of the economy. Major political factions in the country profit from the drug trade. In 1999, encouraged by good weather and high prices, poppy producers increased the area under cultivation by 43% and harvested a bumper crop-a record 4,600 tons-compared with 2,100 tons the year before. A Taliban ban on poppy production cut cultivation in 2001 by 97% (to 1,695 hectares/4,188 acres) with a potential production of 74 tons of opium. However, production rebounded after the fall of the Taliban, despite efforts by the United States and its allies to limit production. The opium trade still accounts for $4 billion in illicit revenue annually. Afghanistan is also major source of hashish, and there are many heroin-processing laboratories throughout the country.

International efforts to rebuild Afghanistan have been addressed at three separate donor conferences, the first of which was the Tokyo Donors Conference for Afghan Reconstruction held in January 2002. At the conferences, more than 60 countries and international financial organizations pledged over $24 billion to rebuild the country over the period 2004–09. Priority areas for reconstruction included the construction of education, health, and sanitation facilities; enhancement of administrative capacity; the development of the agricultural sector; and the rebuilding of road, energy, and telecommunication links.

After decades of neglect, Afghanistan's economy is recovering. The fall of the Taliban (2001), infusion of international assistance, the recovery of the agricultural sector, and service sector growth are the main factors. Nevertheless, Afghanistan is extremely poor, landlocked, and highly dependent on foreign aid, agriculture, and trade with neighboring countries. Housing, clean water, electricity, medical care, and jobs are among the sectors of the economy that need particular attention. The inability of the government to enforce rule of law in all parts of the country is Afghanistan's greatest challenge for future economic growth. Afghanistan's living standards are among the lowest in the world. Over $67 billion given at four donors' conferences since 2002 has not been sufficient to rebuild Afghanistan's poor public infrastructure.

The Afghan economic base is so disjointed that it was almost futile for the government to undertake economic development. Nonetheless, the country's GDP grew from a meager $2.7 billion in 2000 to almost $6 billion in 2004 and to $8.8 billion in 2007. Consequently, the GDP growth rates appear spectacular: 28.6% in 2002, 15.7% in 2003, and 12.4% in 2007 (after a more modest 7.5% in 2004). GDP rate of change in Afghanistan, as of 2010, was 8.2%.

The unemployment rate was estimated at 35% as of 2008, which was the latest year for which there were figures as of 2011. Inflation dropped from 52.3% in 2002 to 10.2% in 2003, but rose again to 16% in 2004 and 2005. In 2010 inflation stood at 20.7%.

In September 2010 a major financial crisis began to take shape as it was discovered that Kabul Bank, the largest private bank in the country, had suffered major losses related to loans granted to relatives and allies of President Karzai and a series of risky real estate investments in Dubai made by top shareholders. The discovery was quickly followed by the dismissal of two top directors, along with allegations of corruption. The news led many large investors to withdraw funds, opening the door for potential collapse of the institution. The chairman of the Central Bank of Afghanistan announced that it would lend Kabul Bank as much as it needed to remain solvent and protect its citizen investors, if such assistance became necessary. However, such a bailout would most likely include reserve funds provided by the United States to prevent against a currency crisis. The possibility of using donated US funds for a private bank bailout in Afghanistan raised concerns for many officials and analysts. As of 7 September officials from Kabul Bank were optimistic that the bank could weather the storm on its own, claiming that accounts were still stable. As a precaution, the central bank froze the property and assets of several key shareholders of Kabul Bank.

20 INCOME

The CIA estimated that in 2010 the GDP of Afghanistan was $27.36 billion. The CIA defines GDP as the value of all final goods and services produced within a nation in a given year and computed on the basis of purchasing power parity (PPP) rather than value as measured on the basis of the rate of the exchange based on current dollars. The per capita GDP was estimated at $900. The annual growth rate of GDP was 8.2%. The average inflation rate was 20.7%. It was estimated that agriculture accounted for 31% of GDP, industry 26%, and services 43%.

According to the World Bank, remittances from citizens living abroad totaled $3.3 billion or about $111 per capita and accounted for approximately 12.1% of GDP.

It was estimated that in 2009 about 36% of the population subsisted on an income below the poverty line established by Afghanistan's government.

21 LABOR

The labor force in Afghanistan was estimated to be about 15 million in 2004. In country comparison to the world Afghanistan stands at 39. In 2009 78.6 % of the labor force was in agriculture, 5.7 % in industry, and 15.7% in services. The unemployment rate is 35% (2008 estimate).

The textile industry is the largest employer of industrial labor; weaving of cloth and carpets is the most important home industry.

As of 2005 Afghan law offered wide protection to workers, but little is known about the enforcement of labor statutes. Workers are unaware of their rights and there is no central authority to enforce those rights. There is no legal right to strike, nor does the country have a history of real labor-management bargaining. There are no courts or mechanisms for settling labor disputes. Wages are entirely subject to market forces, except for government employees, whose wages are set by the government. Although child and forced or compulsory labor are prohibited, little is known about enforcement. By law children under the age of 15 cannot work more than 30 hours per week, but there is no evidence this is enforced. According to the United Nations Children's Fund (UNICEF), it is estimated that there are one million children under the age of 14 in the workforce. Children as young as six years old are reportedly working to help sustain their families. The vast majority of Afghan workers are in the informal economy.

22 AGRICULTURE

Roughly 12% of the total land is farmed, and the country's major crops include opium, wheat, fruits, and nuts. Cereal production in 2009 amounted to 6.5 million tons, fruit production 754,709 tons, and vegetable production 964,016 tons.

In some regions, agricultural production had all but ceased due to destruction caused by the war and the migration of Afghans out of those areas. The average farm size is 1–2 hectares (2.5–5 acres). Absentee landlords are common and sharecropping is expanding in most provinces.

During periods when external forces are not influencing the ability of farmers to grow crops, Afghan farmers grow enough rice, potatoes, pulses, nuts, and seeds to meet the country's needs; Afghanistan depends on imports for some wheat, sugar, and edible fats and oils. Fruit, both fresh and preserved (with bread), is a staple food for many Afghans. Agricultural production is a fraction of its potential. Agricultural production is constrained by dependence on erratic winter snows and spring rains for water and irrigation is primitive. Relatively little use is made of machines, chemical fertilizer, or pesticides.

The variety of the country's crops corresponds to its topography. The areas around Qandahār, Herāt, and the broad Kabul plain yield fruit of many kinds. The northern regions from Takhar to Badghis and the Herāt and Helmand provinces produce cotton. Corn is grown extensively in the Paktia and Nangarhar provinces and rice mainly in the Kunduz, Baghlān, and Laghman provinces. Wheat is common to several regions and makes up 70% of all grain production. Nuts and fruit, including pistachios, almonds, grapes, melons, apricots, cherries, figs, mulberries, and pomegranates, are among Afghanistan's most important horticultural crops. By-products of orchard fruits, such as pomegranate rind and walnut husks, were traditionally used to dye carpets, as was the madder root, valued for the deep red hue it produces.

Afghanistan is the world's largest producer of opium. Although in 2008 poppy cultivation decreased 22% to 157,000 hectares, it still remains at a historically high level. If the entire opium crop were processed, 648 metric tons of pure heroin could potentially be produced. The Taliban and other anti-government groups participate in and profit from the opiate trade. In fact, this trade is a key source of revenue for the Taliban inside Afghanistan; counter-drug efforts are impeded by widespread corruption and instability. Most of the heroin consumed in Europe and Eurasia is derived from Afghan opium. The country is the regional source of hashish (2008) and a major center of drug money laundering through informal financial networks.

The Taliban are primarily responsible for the increase in opium production. Opium cultivation in Afghanistan grew by 17% in 2007 (as of August that year), reaching record levels for the second straight year. The number of hectares in Afghanistan cultivated with poppies grew to 193,000 in 2007 (476,913 acres), from 165,000 (407,724 acres) in 2006, or an increase of 17%. The amount of opium produced was estimated at 9,000 tons in 2007, from 6,700 tons in 2006, a 34% increase. Despite a $600 million American counternarcotics effort and an increase in the number of poppy-free provinces to 13 from 6, the amount of land in Afghanistan used for opium production is now larger than the amount of land used for coca cultivation in all of Latin America. Afghanistan in 2007 accounted for 93% of the world's opium. Opium production has dropped in the relatively stable north of the country but has grown in the south, where the Taliban control large areas and have encouraged farmers to grow opium. In the south, the number of labs processing opium into heroin grew to 50 from 30 in the Helmand province. The Helmand province had a 48% increase in opium production in 2007. The province produced 53% of Afghanistan's opium in 2007, an increase from 42% in 2006. The UN Office on Drugs and Crime stated that, in 2008, the growth in opium cultivation in the southwest appeared to be continuing. The United States has proposed aerial spraying of opium crops with herbicide but Afghan and British officials are opposed to this, saying it would increase support for the Taliban among farmers who fear the herbicide would poison them and their families. The UN Office on Drugs and Crime also noted in 2008 that Afghanistan had become the world's biggest supplier of cannabis, with cultivation estimated at 70,000 hectares. Cannabis is reportedly exported mostly through Pakistan, Iran, and neighboring countries to the south.

23 ANIMAL HUSBANDRY

The availability of land suitable for grazing has made animal husbandry an important part of the economy. There are two main types of animal husbandry: sedentary, practiced by farmers who raise both animals and crops; and nomadic, practiced by animal herders known as Kuchis. The northern regions around Mazār-e Sharif and Maymanah were the home range for about six million karakul sheep in the late 1990s. Most flocks move to pastures in the north in the highlands during the summer. Oxen are the primary draft power and farmers often share animals for plowing. Poultry are traditionally kept in most households.

The UN FAO reported that Afghanistan dedicated 30 million hectares (74.1 million acres) to permanent pasture or meadow in 2009. During that year the country tended 10.2 million chickens and 4.7 million head of cattle. Afghanistan also produced 15,000 tons of cattle hide and 14,700 tons of raw wool.

24 FISHING

Some fishing takes place in the lakes and rivers, but fish does not constitute a significant part of the Afghan diet. Using explosives for fishing, called dynamite fishing, became popular in the 1980s and is common practice. The annual capture totaled 1,000 tons according to the UN FAO.

25 FORESTRY

Approximately 2% of Afghanistan is covered by forest. Significant stands of trees have been destroyed by the ravages of the war. Exploitation has been hampered by lack of power and access roads. Moreover, the distribution of the forest is uneven, and most of the remaining woodland is presently found only in mountainous regions in the southeast and south. The natural forests in Afghanistan are mainly of two types: dense forests of oak, walnut, and other species of trees that grow in the southeast and on the northern and northeastern slopes of the Sulaiman ranges; and sparsely distributed short trees and shrubs on all other slopes of the Hindu Kush. The dense forests of the southeast cover only 2.7% of the country. The UN FAO estimated the 2009 roundwood production at 1.76 million cu m (62.2 million cu ft). The value of all forest products, including roundwood, totaled $6.24 million. The destruction of the forests to create agricultural land, logging, forest fires, plant diseases, and insect pests are all causes of the reduction in forest coverage. Illegal logging and clear-cutting by timber smugglers have exacerbated this destructive process.

26 MINING

Afghanistan has valuable deposits of barite, beryl, chrome, coal, copper, iron, lapis lazuli, lead, mica, natural gas, petroleum, salt, silver, sulfur, and zinc. Reserves of high-grade iron ore, discovered years ago at the Hajigak hills in the Bamiyan province, are estimated to total 2 billion tons. Additional reserves of iron, gold, cobalt, and lithium were discovered in 2010, worth an estimated $1 trillion.

It is estimated that the country has 73 million tons of coal reserves, most of which are located in the region between Herāt and Badakhshan in the northern part of the country. Production in 2010 amounted to 724,900 metric tons. In 2010 Afghanistan produced 186,100 metric tons of rock salt, 63,100 metric tons of gypsum, and 35,000 metric tons of cement. Deposits of lapis lazuli in Badakhshan are mined in small quantities. A copper mine in Aynak in the Logar province has an annual capacity of 180,000 metric tons. The $4.4 billion project was expected to begin production in 2014. Like other aspects of Afghanistan's economy, exploitation of natural resources has been disrupted by war. The remote and rugged terrain and an inadequate transportation network usually have made mining these resources difficult.

27 ENERGY AND POWER

The World Bank reported in 2008 that Afghanistan produced 832 million kWh of electricity and consumed 589.6 million kWh, or 20 kWh per capita. Two decades of warfare have left Afghanistan's power grid badly damaged. Three hydroelectric plants were opened between 1965 and 1970 at Jalālābād, Naghlu, and Mahipar, near Kabul; another, at Kajaki, in the upper Helmand River Valley, was opened in the mid-1970s. In addition to the Jalālābād , Naghlu, Mahipar, and Kajaki plants, other hydroelectric facilities that were operational included plants at Sarobi, west of Kabul; Pol-e Khomri; Darunta, in the Nangarhar province; Dahla, in the Qandahār province (restored to operation in 2001); and Mazār-e Sharif. In 1991 a new 72-collector solar installation was completed in Kabul at a cost of $364 million. The installation heated 40,000 liters (10,400 gallons) of water to an average temperature of 60°C (140°F) around the clock. Construction of two more power stations, with a combined capacity of 600 kW, was planned in Charikar City

Natural gas is Afghanistan's only economically significant export, going mainly to Uzbekistan via pipeline. Natural gas reserves were once estimated at 140 billion cu m (4.94 trillion cu ft). Production started in 1967 with 342 million cu m (12 billion cu ft) but had risen to 2.6 billion cu m (92 billion cu ft) by 1995. In 1991 a new gas field was discovered in Chekhcha in the Jowzjan province. Natural gas was also produced at Sheberghān and Sar-e Pol. As of 2002 other operational gas fields were located at Djarquduk, Khowaja Gogerdak, and Yatimtaq, all in the Jowzjan province. In 2010 natural gas production was 1 billion cu ft.

In August 1996 a multinational consortium agreed to construct a 1,430 km (890 mi) pipeline through Afghanistan to carry natural gas from Turkmenistan to Pakistan, at a cost of about $2 billion. However US air strikes led to cancellation of the project in 1998, and financing of such a project has remained an issue because of high political risk and security concerns.

Afghan energy sources are oil gas, electricity, and coal. A small quantity of crude oil is produced at Angot Oilfield in the Sar-i-Pol province. Primitive retorts are used at the field and near Sheberghan to refine produced oil. Natural gas is produced in the Sheberghan Area Gas Fields. The Djarquduk, Khowaja Gogerdak, and Yatimtaq natural gas fields are all located within 20 miles of Sheberghan. A pipeline also connects these natural gas fields to Mazar-i Sharif and to a 48 MW power plant near Mazar-i-Sharif and a 100,000 mt/y fertilizer plant. Electricity is produced at the Kajaki Dam located in the Helmand province near Kandahar. Small amounts of electricity are also produced at the Mahipar Dam (66 MW); the Naghlu Dam (100 MW); and the Mazar-i-Sharif Power Plant under 30 MW.

28 INDUSTRY

As with other sectors of the economy, Afghanistan's already beleaguered industries have been devastated by civil strife and war that began in the 1970s and left most of the country's factories and even much of the cottage industry sector inoperative. Still in an early stage of growth before the outbreak of war, industry's development has been stunted since; those few industries that have continued production remain limited to processing of local materials. The principal modern industry is cotton textile production, with factories at Pol-e Khomri, Golbahar, Begram, Balkh, and Jabal os Saraj, just north of Charikar. Important industries in 2000 included textiles, soap, furniture, shoes, fertilizer, cement, hand woven carpets, natural gas, coal, and copper.

Carpet-making is the most important handicraft industry, but it has suffered with the flight of rug makers during the civil war and since the 2001 US-led bombing campaign. Carpet-making is centered in the north and northwest regions of the country. Afghan carpets are made of pure wool and are hand-knotted, and women do much of the work. Production has fluctuated widely from year to year, increasing somewhat during the early 1990s with the establishment of selected "zones of tranquility" targeted for UN reconstruction assistance. Other handicrafts include felt making and the weaving of cotton, woolen, and silk cloth. Wood and stone carving have been concentrated in the northeastern provinces, while jewelry making has been done in the Kabul area. The making of leather goods has also been a handicraft industry.

29 SCIENCE AND TECHNOLOGY

The Afghanistan Academy of Sciences, founded in 1979, is the principal scientific institution. As of 2002 it had about 180 members. Prospective members of the academy must take a written exam, present samples of their work, and pass a proficiency exam in one of the official languages of the UN. Many Afghan scientists have migrated to Europe, the United States, and Pakistan since 1970. Under the Taliban, professors who did not teach Islamic studies were relieved of their duties.

The Department of Geology and Mineral Survey within the Ministry of Mines and Industries conducts geological and mineralogical research, mapping, prospecting and exploration.

The Institute of Public Health, founded in 1962, conducts public health training and research and study of indigenous diseases, has a government reference laboratory, and compiles statistical data.

Kabul University, founded in 1932, has faculties of science, pharmacy, veterinary medicine, and geo-sciences. Its faculty numbers close to 200. The University of Balkh has about 100 faculty members. Bayazid Roshan University of Nangarhar, founded in 1962, has faculties of medicine and engineering, and its faculty numbers close to 100. The Institute of Agriculture, founded in 1924, offers courses in veterinary medicine. Kabul Polytechnic College, founded in 1951, offers postgraduate engineering courses. Kabul Polytechnic was the site of the June 2002 Loya Jirga, and the international community spent over $7 million to refurbish part of the campus for the assembly. Buildings on campus had suffered heavy bomb damage. During the 1990s the campus was shelled and looted by *mujahedeen* groups, who fought amongst themselves for control of the capital. Boarding students studying under the rule of the Taliban lived in makeshift dormitories.

30 DOMESTIC TRADE

Kabul, Qandahār, Mazār-e-Sharif, and Herāt are the principal commercial cities of eastern, southern, northern, and western Afghanistan respectively. The first two are the main distribution centers for imports arriving from the direction of Pakistan, the latter two for materials arriving from Iran, Turkmenistan, Uzbekistan, and Tajikistan. Hours of business vary. The destruction of paved roads has severely constrained normal domestic trade in most rural parts of the country. Heavy fighting in Kabul completely destroyed the city's infrastructure. More than 25 reconstruction projects were undertaken in the transport, energy, and construction sectors. At least five projects were ongoing as of 2011.

Principal Trading Partners – Afghanistan (2010)

(In millions of US dollars)

Country	Total	Exports	Imports	Balance
World	4,600.0	400.0	4,200.0	-3,800.0
United States	2,446.8	79.2	2,367.6	-2,288.4
Pakistan	2,034.3	137.8	1,896.5	-1,758.7
Russia	610.6	17.7	592.9	-575.2
India	544.6	110.6	433.9	-323.3
Germany	367.7	26.5	341.2	-314.7
Turkey	290.4	4.6	285.8	-281.1
Turkmenistan	237.5	0.7	236.9	-236.2
Kazakhstan	211.8	0.5	211.2	-210.7
China	195.8	3.3	192.5	-189.2
Thailand	160.5	0.1	160.5	-160.4

(…) data not available or not significant.

(n.s.) not specified.

SOURCE: *2011 Direction of Trade Statistics Yearbook*, New York: United Nations, 2011.

31 FOREIGN TRADE

Afghanistan imported $5.3 billion worth of goods and services in 2008, including food, textiles, petroleum products, and most commodity items. Major import partners in 2009 were the United States, 24.9%; Pakistan, 22.3%; India, 7.7%; Germany, 5.1%; and Russia, 4.3% . Its major exports included opium, fruits and nuts, carpets, wool, cotton, hides and pelts, and gems, and totaled an estimated $547 million in 2009 (not including illegal exports). Afghanistan's primary export partners that year were the United States, 24.9%; India, 24.2%; Pakistan, 23.9%; and Tajikistan, 8.9%.

Although the Taliban had brought a repressive order to the 90% of the country under its rule, it was not able to gain international recognition nor did it attract foreign investment. Hyperinflation had increased the number of afghanis (the country's currency) needed to equal one US dollar from 50 in the early 1990s, to a virtually worthless 42,000 in 1999. On 7 October 2002 the first anniversary of the start of the US-led bombing campaign in Afghanistan, a new Afghan currency came into use. Also called the afghani, the new notes were worth 1000 of the old notes, which were phased out. The government planned to exchange the dostumi currency—used in northern Afghanistan and named for the region's warlord, Abdul Rashid Dostum—with the new afghani, at half the value of the old afghani. Around 1,800 tons of old afghanis were due to be burned or recycled.

32 BALANCE OF PAYMENTS

Between 1951 and 1973 Afghanistan's year-end international reserves were never lower than $38 million nor higher than $65 million. Increased trade in the late 1970s and 1980s resulted in a reduction of foreign exchange earnings, since trade surpluses are counted as a credit against future imports. Foreign exchange reserves declined from $411.1 million at the close of 1979 to $262 million as of 30 May 1987. The Afghan economy—and access to reliable statistical information about it—declined precipitously during the 1990s. Following the US-led invasion in 2001, billions of dollars in development projects flowed into the country. Foreign exchange reserves were estimated at $1.3 billion in 2004, up from $426 million in 2002 and $815 million in 2003. The public foreign debt in 2009 stood at $2.7 billion.

³³BANKING AND SECURITIES

Headquartered in Kabul, the nation's capital, the Bank of Afghanistan (founded in 1938) is headed by a governor, who also holds a position with the Asian Development Bank (ADB), as well as an alternate governor. Unlike other central banks around the world, the Bank of Afghanistan must completely rebuild the nation's banking system after more than 20 years of war, which had virtually wiped-out the country's financial system. The policy of the central bank has been to create a two-tiered banking system, consisting of a private commercial sector separate from the central bank. A new currency has also been introduced, although Pakistani rupees and United States dollars are still being used for some transactions.

Afghanistan's central bank is the largest bank in Afghanistan. The central bank issues all notes, executes government loans, and lends money to cities and to other banks. All private banks in Afghanistan were nationalized in 1975, mostly because a lack of clear terms for borrowers and lenders had made it difficult for people to use the country's credit resources. No stock market or other modern form of economic development exists in Afghanistan. Instead, archaic "money bazaars" provide loans and foreign exchange transactions.

In 1999 the UN Security Council passed a resolution placing the Bank of Afghanistan on a consolidated list of people and entities whose funds and financial resources should be frozen, due to the fact that the bank was controlled by the Taliban regime. The UN Security Council agreed to remove the bank from the list upon a request from the Interim Administration of Afghanistan in January 2002.

There is no organized domestic securities market. On 14 March 2004 the Kabul Bank was incorporated.

³⁴INSURANCE

The Insurance Corporation of Afghanistan was formed in 2007. Backed by international investors, the company was the first privately owned, multi-line insurance company in Afghanistan. It received full government licensing in 2008.

³⁵PUBLIC FINANCE

The fiscal year ends 20 March. Budget breakdowns have not been available since the 1979/80 fiscal year, when revenues totaled AFA15.788 billion and expenditures AFA16.782 billion. In 2002 the Interim and Transitional governing authorities were working with donor aid agencies to finance the rebuilding of Afghanistan's infrastructure and society. The Interim Administration was supported by the ADB, the Islamic Development Bank, UNDP, and the World Bank. An Implementation Group was established to operate an Operational Costs Trust Fund for Afghanistan, to be effective when the UNDP Start-up Fund ceased, to cover expenditures normally financed by domestic revenue. The Operational Costs Trust Fund was scheduled to cease to operate when the situation in Afghanistan reached fiscal normality, when the government would be able to finance most or all of its own costs.

In 2010 the budget of Afghanistan included $1 billion in public revenue and $3.3 billion public expenditures. The budget deficit

Public Finance – Afghanistan (2009)		
(In millions of afghanis, central government figures)		
Revenue and Grants	449,974	100.0%
Tax revenue	51,882	11.5%
Social contributions	974	0.2%
Grants	385,287	85.6%
Other revenue	11,830	2.6%
Expenditures	448,241	100.0%
General public services	29,333	6.5%
Defense	189,737	42.3%
Public order and safety	105,399	23.5%
Economic affairs	64,381	14.4%
Environmental protection	501	0.1%
Housing and community amenities	6,563	1.5%
Health	13,497	3.0%
Recreational, culture, and religion	2,261	0.5%
Education	29,212	6.5%
Social protection	7,356	1.6%

(…) data not available or not significant.

SOURCE: *Government Finance Statistics Yearbook 2010*, Washington, DC: International Monetary Fund, 2010.

amounted to 14.7% of GDP. In total $2.7 billion of the public debt is held by foreign entities.

³⁶TAXATION

In 2009 direct taxes accounted for about 6.4% of government revenues. The share provided by indirect taxes declined as revenues from natural gas and state enterprises played an increasing role in government finance. Tax collection, never an effective source of revenue in tribal areas, was essentially disabled by the disruption caused by fighting and mass flight. Under the Taliban, arbitrary taxes, including those on humanitarian goods, were imposed.

In 2005 the government introduced an income (or wage) tax. Employers with two or more employees were required to pay 10% on annual income over about $3,500 and 20% on income over about $27,000.

³⁷CUSTOMS AND DUTIES

Before the turmoil of the late 1970s customs duties, levied as a source of revenue rather than as a protective measure, constituted more than one-fourth of total government revenue. Both specific and ad valorem duties of 20–35% were levied on imports. Other costs included service and Red Crescent charges; monopoly and luxury taxes; authorization and privilege charges; and a commission-type duty.

After the fall of the Taliban, Afghanistan's warlords collected customs duties for themselves rather than transferring the funds to the Interim and Transitional authorities in Kabul. Only a small amount of the customs paid each month at Afghanistan's borders with Pakistan, Iran, and Uzbekistan reached the government treasury.

³⁸FOREIGN INVESTMENT

A 1967 law encouraged investment of private foreign capital in Afghanistan, but under the PDPA government, Western investment virtually ceased. Between 1979 and 1987 the Soviet Union provided technical and financial assistance on more than 200 projects, including various industrial plants, irrigation dams, agricultural stations, and a new terminal at the Kabul airport. After 1990 reconstruction investments from Russia, Japan, and the United States were channeled through the UN. The Taliban called for Western support to help reconstruct Afghanistan, but Western donors—already reluctant to support UN programs in the country—did not respond. After the fall of the Taliban, head-of-state Hamid Karzai invited foreign direct investment (FDI) in Afghanistan, first to reach the people in the provinces who required salaries and owed taxes, and then to invest in businesses that would lead to industrial and technological development.

One of the main policies of the government as of 2006 was to create a business-friendly environment and to attract foreign, as well as domestic, investments. Both national and international observers realized that the economy of Afghanistan could not be sustained long-term on the benefits of donor-led reconstruction and the trickle down effects of the opium economy. At the opening of the Hyatt Hotel in Kabul in April 2004, President Hamid Karzai declared that "Afghanistan is open for business."

FDI in Afghanistan was a net inflow of $185 million according to World Bank figures published in 2009. FDI represented 1.28% of GDP.

³⁹ECONOMIC DEVELOPMENT

The main growth engines of the Afghan economy are donor-led reconstruction, the opium business, agriculture, and carpeting. The first two cannot sustain the economy long-term, and Afghan policymakers faced a challenge to develop a strategy to grow other sectors of the economy. As of 2011 the country remained poor, landlocked, and dependent on farming, foreign aid, and trade with neighboring countries. Much of the population continued to live in abject conditions (without access to housing, clean water, energy, or medical care), and the labor market was far from dynamic. Its attractive 30 million person market was offset by the lack of good infrastructure and by security problems that still loom outside Kabul. Policymakers were hopeful, however, that political stability would enable the economy thrive and grow.

⁴⁰SOCIAL DEVELOPMENT

Social welfare in Afghanistan has traditionally relied on family and ethnic group organization. In the villages and small towns a tax to benefit the poor is levied on each man. Social welfare centers in the provincial capitals exist to care for disabled people, but these are able to assist only a small number of those in need. Most other welfare activities are still unorganized and in private hands. In the early 1990s a social insurance system provided old age, disability, and survivors' pensions; sickness and maternity benefits; and workers' compensation.

Traditionally, women have few rights in Afghanistan, with their role limited largely to the home and the fields. Advances in women's rights were made from 1920 onward, and by the 1970s women were attending school in large numbers, voting, held government jobs—including posts as cabinet ministers, and were active in the professions. The victory of the extremely conservative Taliban in 1996 reversed this trend. Strict limits on the freedoms of women were put in place. Under the constitution of 2004 the government provided for freedom of speech, the press, assembly, association, religion, and movement; however, serious problems remained in the area of human rights. Although the rule of law applied throughout the country, in practice its recognition was limited.

Violence, including rape and kidnapping, and societal discrimination against women and minorities persisted. Terrorist attacks and extreme violence continued. Extrajudicial and unlawful killings by the government or its agents and police continued to occur. Civilians were killed as rebel forces battled. Torture and excessive use of force were also reported. Detention conditions were inadequate.

With the end of the Taliban, women and girls were permitted to attend schools and universities, and the enforced wearing of the burka was ended. Men were allowed to shave, music and television were permitted, and a host of Taliban-imposed restrictions on society ended. Many women continued to wear the burka, or chadri, out of tradition, but also due to fear of harassment or violence. Reports claimed that trafficking in women and children for forced labor, prostitution, and sexual exploitation was increasing. The country was both a source and transit point for trafficking. Trafficking victims faced societal discrimination, especially with regard to sexual exploitation. There are no child labor laws or other legislation to protect child abuse victims. The law criminalizes homosexual activity.

Women in urban areas regained some measure of rights to public life, however lack of education under Taliban rule restrict employment possibilities. On the other hand, in 2004 regulations changed to allow married women to attend high school classes. Certain other restrictions on women were lifted in 1998. Women are allowed to work as doctors and nurses (as long as they treat only women) and are able to attend medical schools. Yet, women are denied adequate medical care due to the societal barriers discouraging them from seeking care from male health workers. Widows with no means of support are allowed to seek employment.

⁴¹HEALTH

According to the CIA, life expectancy in Afghanistan was 44 years in 2011. The country spent 7.4% of its GDP on healthcare, amounting to $51 per person. There were two physicians, five nurses and midwives, and four hospital beds per 10,000 inhabitants. The fertility rate was 6.5, while the infant mortality rate was 134 per 1,000 live births. In 2008 the maternal mortality rate, according to the World Bank, was 1,400 per 100,000 births. It was estimated that 76% of children were vaccinated against measles.

Starvation, disease, death, war, and migration had devastating effects on Afghanistan's health infrastructure in the 1990s. According to the WHO medication was scarce. Even before the war disrupted medical services, health conditions in Afghanistan were inadequate by Western standards. Most of the country's facilities are in Kabul, and those needing treatment must traverse the countryside to get there. Health care was being provided primarily by the international community.

⁴²HOUSING

Years of conflict have caused severe damage to the housing stock. Between 2001 and 2003, about 26% of all housing had been destroyed or seriously damaged. About 20–25% of the population did not have access to piped supplies of safe water and about 84% of the population had no sanitary toilets.

The UN UNHCR has been the leader in providing homes and shelter for returning Afghan refugees, internally displaced people, and the extremely poor. Over 100,000 rural homes were built through the collaboration of UNHCR and the Afghan Ministry of Refugees and Repatriation. Others funding housing development included the UN Development Program, the International Organization for Migration, and CARE International, while the agencies implementing the programs are the Ministry for Rural Rehabilitation and Development (MRRD) in Afghanistan, the United Nations Human Settlement Program (HABITAT), the International Rescue Committee (IRC), and an assortment of international and local nongovernmental organizations (NGOs).

Houses in farming communities are built largely of mud brick and frequently grouped within a fortified enclosure to provide protection from marauders. The roofs are flat with a coating of mixed straw and mud rolled hard above a ceiling of horizontal poles, although in areas where timber is scarce, separate mud brick domes crown each room. Cement and other modern building materials are widely used in cities and towns. Every town has at least one wide thoroughfare, but other streets are narrow lanes between houses of mud brick, taller than those in the villages and featuring decorative wooden balconies.

43 EDUCATION

In 2009 the World Bank estimated that 60% of age-eligible children in Afghanistan were enrolled in primary school. Secondary enrollment for age-eligible children stood at 27%. Tertiary enrollment was estimated at 4%. Overall, the CIA estimated that Afghanistan had a literacy rate of 28.1%.

Education is free at all levels. The primary education program covers six years. The secondary education (middle school and high school) includes another six year program. Theoretically, education is compulsory for six years. The new constitution proposed to change the standard to nine years of compulsory education.

Boys and girls are schooled separately. Children are taught in their mother tongue, Dari (Persian) or Pashtu (Pashto), during the first three grades; the second official language is introduced in the fourth grade. Children are also taught Arabic so that they may be able to read the Koran. The school year extends from early March to November in the cold areas and from September to June in the warmer regions.

In addition to the secular public education system, the traditional Islamic madrassa school system is functioning. At the madrassas, children study the Koran, the Hadith (sayings of the Prophet Muhammad), and popular religious texts.

In January 2011 the Taliban announced that they would no longer oppose the education of girls. The announcement came from Farroq Wardak, the Afghani education minister. Agreements were made across the country to allow girls and female teachers to return to schools. Despite the Taliban's statement, the education minister feared that the prejudice against female education was held not only in the Taliban's beliefs, but in the roots of Afghani society, making it harder to accept female education as a societal norm. Additionally, the Taliban said they were still against the use of education as a political or ideological tool to shape minds against them.

The University of Kabul, which is now coeducational, was founded in 1932. In 1962 a facility of medicine was established at Jalālābād in the Nangarhar province; this facility subsequently became the University of Nangarhar. There were at least eight universities and three other institutes of higher education.

44 LIBRARIES AND MUSEUMS

For centuries, manuscript collections were in the hands of the rulers, local feudal lords, and renowned religious families. Printing came fairly late to Afghanistan, but with the shift from the handwritten manuscript to the printed book, various collections were formed. Kabul Central Library is a public library (founded in 1920) with 60,000 volumes. The Khairkhona Library is the only other public library in Kabul. The library of the University of Kabul has about 250,000 volumes. There is a library at Kabul Polytechnic University with 6,000 volumes. A government library, at the ministry of education also in Kabul, houses 30,000 volumes.

Prior to the devastating civil war, the Kabul Museum (founded in 1922) possessed an unrivaled collection of stone heads, bas-reliefs, ivory plaques and statuettes, bronzes, mural paintings, and Buddhist material from excavations at Hadda, Bamiyan, Bagram, and other sites. It also contained an extensive collection of coins and a unique collection of Islamic bronzes, marble reliefs, Kusham art, and ceramics from Ghaznī. During several decades of warfare, however, the museum was plundered by various armed bands, with much of its collection sold on the black market or systematically destroyed. In March 2001 the Taliban dynamited the Bamiyan Buddhas and sold the debris and the remains of the original sculpture. Small statues of the Buddhas in Foladi and Kakrak were destroyed. Most of the statues and other non-Islamic art works in the collections of the Kabul Museum were destroyed, including those stored for security reasons in the ministry of information and culture.

UNESCO has undertaken a plan to conserve the archaeological remains and the minaret at Jam and to make it a World Heritage site. The minaret was built at the end of the 12th century and, at 65 m (215 ft), is the second-tallest in the world after the Qutub Minaret in New Delhi, India.

The National Archives of Afghanistan in Kabul was established in 1973. Holdings include government documents and ancient books, the most important being a 500 year-old Koran. Also in Kabul is the Kabul University Science Museum, with an extensive zoological collection and a museum of pathology. There are provincial museums in Bamiyan, Ghaznī, Herāt, Mazār-e Sharif, Maimana, and Qandahār. Major religious shrines have collections of valuable objects.

45 MEDIA

Limited telephone service to principal cities and some smaller towns and villages is provided by the government. In 2009 the CIA reported that there were 129,300 telephone landlines in Afghanistan. In addition to landlines, mobile phone subscriptions averaged 40 per 100 people. Internet users numbered 3 per 100 citizens. In 2009 there were 47 Internet hosts in the country.

The media in Afghanistan was severely restricted by the Taliban. Since the fall of that regime, freedom of expression has been provided for in the constitution. However, a 2002 press law contained an injunction against information that would be considered insulting to Islam and, while an independent media is beginning to grow, the state owned numerous publications and a majority of the electronic media.

The first television broadcast took place in 1978.

In January 2002 the independent newspaper *Kabul Weekly* began publishing again, after having disappeared during the period when the Taliban was in power. The first issue carried news in Dari, Pashtu, English, and French. News agencies include the state-operated Bakhtar News Agency and the privately owned Pajhwok Afghan News, Hindokosh, and Afghan Islamic Press.

46 ORGANIZATIONS

Afghanistan has over 2,300 registered NGOs and approximately 300 registered social organizations. Organizations to advance public aims and goals are of recent origin and most are sponsored and directed by the government.

The National Fatherland Front, consisting of ethnic and political groups that support the government, was founded in June 1981 to bolster the PDPA regime and to promote full and equal participation of Afghan nationals in state affairs. The Revolutionary Association of the Women of Afghanistan (RAWA), established in Kabul in 1977, is an independent political organization of Afghan women focusing on human rights and social justice.

With political changes in the country throughout the past decade, a number of new women's groups have developed since 1990. The Women's Welfare Society carries on educational enterprises, provides training in handicrafts, and dispenses charitable aid, while the Maristun, a social service center, looks after children, men, and women while teaching crafts and trades. Other women's groups include the Afghan Women Social and Cultural Organization (AWSCO, est. 1994), the Afghan Women's Educational Center (AWEC, est. 1991), the Afghan Women's Network (AWN, est. 1995), the Educational Training Center for Poor Women and Girls of Afghanistan (ECW, est. 1997), the New Afghanistan Women Association (est. 2002 as a merger of the Afghan Women Journalist Association and the Afghan Feminine Association), and the World Organization for Mutual Afghan Network (WOMAN, est. 2002).

The Union of Afghanistan Youth is an NGO representing the concerns of the nation's youth and young adults in the midst of transition and reconstruction. The organization serves as a multiparty offshoot of the Democratic Youth Organization of Afghanistan (DYOA), which has worked closely with the PDPA. Though the Scouting Movement of Afghanistan was disbanded in 1978, the World Organization of the Scout Movement (WOSM) conducts seminars to encourage and support the rebirth of scouting programs. There are a number of sports organizations throughout the country, including those for football (soccer), tennis, cricket, and track and field; many of these are linked to international organizations.

The Red Crescent, the equivalent of the Red Cross, is active in every province, with a national chapter of Red Crescent Youth also active. Afghanistan also hosts chapters of Habitat for Humanity and HOPE Worldwide.

An institute, the Pashto Tolanah, promotes knowledge of Pashtu literature, and the Historical Society (Anjuman-i-Tarikh) amasses information on Afghan history. The Afghan Carpet Exporters' Guild, founded in 1987, promotes foreign trade of Afghan carpets and works for the improvement of the carpet industry.

47 TOURISM, TRAVEL, AND RECREATION

The estimated daily cost to visit Kabul, the capital, was $28. The cost of visiting other cities averaged $15. The tourism industry, developed with government help in the early 1970s, has been negligible since 1979 due to internal political instability. A passport and visa are required for entrance into Afghanistan. Travel was highly restricted in the country due to the US-led campaign against the Taliban and al-Qaeda.

48 FAMOUS PERSONS

The most renowned ruler of medieval Afghanistan, Mahmud of Ghaznī (b. 971?– 1030), was the Turkish creator of an empire stretching from Ray and Isfahan in Iran to Lahore in India (now in Pakistan) and from the Amu Darya (Oxus) River to the Arabian Sea. Zahir ud-Din Babur (b. 1483–1530), a Timurid prince of Ferghana (now in the former Soviet Union), established his base at Kabul and from there waged campaigns leading to the expulsion of an Afghan ruling dynasty, the Lodis, from Delhi and the foundation of the Mughal Empire in India.

Many eminent figures of Arab and Persian intellectual history were born or spent their careers in what is now Afghanistan. Al-Biruni (b. 973–1048), the great encyclopedist from Khiva (now in Uzbekistan), settled in Ghaznī, where he died. Abdul Majid Majdud Sana'i (b. 1070–1140), the first major Persian poet to employ verse for mystical and philosophical expression, was a native of Ghaznī. Jalal ud-Din Rumi (b. 1207–1273), who stands at the summit of Persian poetry, was born in Balkh but migrated to Konya (Iconium) in Turkey. The last of the celebrated Persian classical poets, Abdur Rahman Jami (b. 1414–1492), was born in Khorasan but spent most of his life in Herāt. So did Behzad (b. 1450?– 1520), the greatest master of Persian painting.

The founder of the state of Afghanistan was Ahmad Shah Abdali (b. 1724–1773), who changed his dynastic name to Durrani. He conquered Kashmir and Delhi and, with his capital at Qandahār, ruled over an empire that also stretched from the Amu Darya to the Arabian Sea. Dost Muhammad (b. 1789–1863) was the founder of the Muhammadzai (Barakzai) dynasty and unified the country. His grandson, Abdur Rahman Khan (b. 1844–1901), established order after protracted civil strife. Amanullah Khan (b. 1892–1960), who reigned from 1919 to 1929, tried social reforms aimed at Westernizing the country but was forced to abdicate. Muhammad Nadir Shah (d. 1933), who was elected king by a community assembly in 1929, continued Amanullah's Westernization program. His son, Muhammad Zahir Shah (b. 1914–2007), was king until he was deposed by a coup in July 1973. Lieut. Gen. Sardar Muhammad Daoud Khan (b. 1909–1978), cousin and brother-in-law of King Zahir, was the leader of the coup and the founder and first president of the Republic of Afghanistan. Leaders in the violent years after the 1978 "Saur Revolution" were

Nur Muhammad Taraki (b. 1917–1979), founder of the PDPA; Hafizullah Amin (b. 1929–1979), Taraki's successor as president of the Revolutionary Council and secretary-general of the PDPA; Babrak Karmal (b. 1929–1996), leader of the pro-Soviet Parcham group of the PDPA and chief of state from December 1979 until May 1986; and Dr. Mohammad Najibullah (b. 1947–1996), former head of the Afghan secret police who was brutally executed by the Taliban militia after they seized control of Kabul. Ahmed Shah Massoud (b. 1953?–2001) played a leading role in driving the Soviet Union out of Afghanistan; after the rise of the Taliban, he became the military leader of the Northern Alliance. He allied himself with Burhanuddin Rabbani (1940–2011). Massoud was the victim of a suicide attack two days before the 11 September 2001 terrorist attacks on the United States; some speculate Osama bin Laden had a hand in his assassination, to ensure the protection and cooperation of the Taliban. Hamid Karzai (b. 1957) is the first democratically elected president of Afghanistan. Karzai worked to overthrow the Taliban. After the regime's demise in 2001, Karzai became the chairman of the transnational administration and interim president until his election in the first direct election in the country, held in 2004.

[49]DEPENDENCIES

Afghanistan has no territories or colonies.

[50]BIBLIOGRAPHY

Adamec, Ludwig W. Historical *Dictionary of Afghan Wars, Revolutions, and Insurgencies.* 2nd ed. Lanham, MD: Scarecrow Press, 2005.

Afghanistan Investment and Business Guide: Strategic and Practical Information. Washington, DC: International Business Publications USA, 2012.

Barry, Michael. *History of Modern Afghanistan.* New York: Cambridge University Press, 2006.

Chayes, Sarah. *Punishment of Virtue: Inside Afghanistan after the Taliban.* New York: Penguin Press, 2006.

Clements, Frank. *Conflict in Afghanistan: An Encyclopedia.* Oxford: ABC-Clio, 2003.

Emadi, Hafizullah. *Culture and Customs of Afghanistan.* Westport, CT: Greenwood Press, 2005.

Lansford, Tom. *9/11 and the Wars in Afghanistan and Iraq: A Chronology and Reference Guide.* Santa Barbara, CA: ABC-CLIO, 2012.

Misdaq, Nabi. *Afghanistan: Political Frailty and Foreign Interference.* New York: Routledge, 2005.

Rumer, Boris. *Central Asia at the End of the Transition.* Armonk, NY: M.E. Sharpe, 2005.

Runion, Meredith L. *The History of Afghanistan.* Westport, CT: Greenwood Press, 2007.

AUSTRALIA

Commonwealth of Australia

CAPITAL: Canberra

FLAG: The flag has three main features: the red, white, and blue Union Jack in the upper left quarter, indicating Australia's membership in the Commonwealth of Nations; the white five-star Southern Cross in the right half; and the white seven-pointed federal star below the Union Jack. The flag has a blue ground. Of the five stars of the Southern Cross, four have seven points and one has five points.

ANTHEM: *Advance Australia Fair.*

MONETARY UNIT: The Australian dollar (AUD) is a paper currency of 100 cents. There are coins of 5, 10, 20, and 50 cents and 1 and 2 dollars, and notes of 5, 10, 20, 50 and 100 dollars. AUD1 = US$1.02 (or US1 = AUD0.98) as of January 2012.

WEIGHTS AND MEASURES: Metric weights and measures are used. The Australian proof gallon equals 1.37 US proof gallons.

HOLIDAYS: New Year's Day, 1 January; Australia Day, 26 January; Labor Day (Western Australia), 5 March; Anzac Day, 25 April; Queen's Birthday, second Monday in June; Christmas, 25 December; and Boxing Day, 26 December. Movable religious holiday included Good Friday, Easter Sunday, and Easter Monday. In addition, several state holidays are observed in different parts of the country. Labour Day is celebrated on different dates in Western Australia, Victoria, Queensland, New South Wales, Australian Capital Territory, and South Australia; Eight-Hour Day is celebrated in Tasmania; Canberra Day is celebrated in Australian Capital Territory; May Day is celebrated in Northern Territory; Foundation Day is celebrated in Western Australia; and Melbourne Cup Day is celebrated in Melbourne.

TIME: There are three time zones in Australia. Australian Eastern Standard Time (noon GMT=10 p.m.) is used in New South Wales, Australian Capital Territory, Victoria, Tasmania, and Queensland; Australian Central Standard Time (noon GMT = 9:30 p.m.) is used in South Australia and Northern Territory; and Australian Western Standard Time (noon GMT = 8 p.m.) is used in Western Australia.

All states except for Northern Territory and Queensland observed daylight savings time from the first Sunday in October through the first Sunday in April.

¹LOCATION, SIZE, AND EXTENT

Lying southeast of Asia, between the Pacific and Indian oceans, Australia is almost completely surrounded by ocean expanses. Australia is slightly smaller than the 48 contiguous states of the United States, with a total land area of 7,682,300 sq km (2,966,164 sq mi). Australia is the only country to occupy an entire continent, and is the sixth largest country in the world.

The five mainland states are New South Wales, 801,600 sq km (309,500 sq mi); Queensland, 1,727,200 sq km (666,900 sq mi); South Australia, 984,000 sq km (379,900 sq mi); Victoria, 227,600 sq km (87,900 sq mi); and Western Australia, 2,525,500 sq km (975,100 sq mi). The island state of Tasmania has an area of 67,800 sq km (26,200 sq mi); the Northern Territory, 1,346,200 sq km (519,800 sq mi); and the Australian Capital Territory, 2,400 sq km (900 sq mi). The country, including Tasmania, extends about 4,000 km (2,500 mi) E–W and 3,180 km (1,980 mi) N–S.

Australia is bounded on the N by the Timor and Arafura seas, on the Ne by the Coral Sea, on the E by the Pacific Ocean, on the SE by the Tasman Sea, and on the S and W by the Indian Ocean, with a total coastline of 25,760 km (16,007 mi). As an island-nation, Australia has no land borders. The nearest neighboring countries are Papua New Guinea, East Timor, and Indonesia to the N and NW, and New Zealand to the SE.

Australia's capital city, Canberra, is located in the southeastern part of the country.

²TOPOGRAPHY

Australia is the lowest and flattest continental landmass on Earth.

The Western Plateau comprises the western half of the country, and consists of mountains near the west coast and lower elevations near the center. The region is generally flat and dry, although several mountain ranges including the Hamersley, MacDonnell, and Musgraves run through the area. To the west and north are several large rivers including the Murchison, Ashburton, and Victoria. The area is generally 300–600 m (1,000–2,000 ft) above sea level.

The Eastern Highlands separate the eastern coastal plain from the rest of Australia. This area is marked by temperate forests, abundant rainfall, and a wide variety of flora and fauna. Most of Australia's 18 million residents live in this area. Elevations range from 300 m to more than 2,100 m (1,000–7,000 ft). The area extends from Cape York Peninsula in northern Queensland southward to Tasmania.

The Central Lowlands lie between the Eastern Highlands and Western Plateau, and consist largely of a series of drainage basins running north to south. This Great Artesian Basin is 1,751,480 sq km (676,250 sq mi) in size and is the most extensive area of internal drainage in the world. There are also two large river systems in this area: the Murray-Darling Basin and Lake Eyre Basin.

Toward the southeastern corner is Tasmania, a large, mountainous island.

The Great Barrier Reef, the world's largest coral reef, is off the eastern coast and extends about 2,000 km (1,243 mi) off the east coast of Queensland.

The mainland has a total coastline length of 35,876 km (22,292 mi), and 23,859 km (14,825 mi) of island coastlines. In addition, there are 758 estuaries, mostly in tropical and subtropical zones. The coastline is smooth, with few bays or capes. The two largest sea inlets are the Gulf of Carpentaria in the north, between Arnhem Land and the Cape York Peninsula, and the Great Australian Bight in the south.

Erosion has lowered much of Australia's surface, and only about 6% of the continent is above 600 m (2,000 feet). The average elevation is less than 300 m (1,000 ft). The highest point is Mt. Kosciuszko, 2,229 m (7,350 ft), in the Australian Alps of the southeastern corner of New South Wales; the lowest point is Lake Eyre in South Australia, 15 m (49 ft) below sea level. In 1983, grains of rock from Western Australia were dated at 4.1–4.2 billion years old, making them the oldest ever found on earth.

Minor earthquakes occur frequently, and major earthquakes occur on average every five years.

The only river system with a permanent, year-round flow is formed by the Murray, Darling, and Murrumbidgee rivers in the southeast. The Murray River, Australia's largest, rises in the Australian Alps of New South Wales and flows some 2,600 km (1,600 mi) west and southwest to empty into the sea below Adelaide, South Australia. Several other rivers carry great amounts of water in the wet season and are dry for the rest of the year. The largest lakes have no outlet and are usually dry.

³CLIMATE

Australia, while considered one of the driest continents on earth, experiences a variety of climates.

The south has cool, wet winters and warm, dry summers. The climate is more tropical toward the north with a warm, dry season and a hot, wet season. Snow is common in the southeastern mountains during the winter when the Alpine snowfields are formed. The desert area is generally dry but floods during periodic torrential rains.

July mean temperatures average 9°C (48°F) in Melbourne in the southeast and 25°C (77°F) in Darwin in the north. January mean temperatures average 20°C (68°F) in Melbourne and 30°C (86°F) in Darwin. Summer readings often reach 38°C (100°F) or more in almost any area of the continent and may exceed 46°C (115°F) in interior regions. Winds are light to moderate, except along the coasts, where severe cyclones have occurred. One of the most consistent winds in the world, popularly known to Australians as the "Fremantle Doctor," blows across Perth and neighboring Fremantle on the southwest coast. The dry, hot climate of the interior often creates conditions favorable to periodic devastating bushfires.

The continent is subject to great variations in rainfall, but except for a few areas rainfall is insufficient, and the rate of evaporation is high. Mean annual rainfall is 465 mm (18.3 in). Only about 20% has more than 765 mm (30 in) of rain annually, but these areas suffer from a long dry season, while others have too much rain. Only Tasmania, Victoria, and parts of New South Wales have enough rainfall all year round. Drought conditions became very severe in the early 1980s, in 1994–95, and again in the early 2000s, leading to dust storms, fires, and multibillion-dollar crop losses.

The country's Bureau of Meteorology reported that 2010 was the third-wettest year since record-keeping began in 1900. The mean rainfall total was 690 mm (27 in), and the country with the exception of the southwestern region and Tasmania experienced above average rainfall. The second half of 2010 was the wettest on record. The rainfall helped end drought conditions that had persisted since 1996 in the southeast and across the Murray-Darling Basin, and replenished water storages in the basin from 26% in January 2010 to 80% by January 2011. The rains also resulted in significant flooding with the worst floods occurring between Christmas and the first two weeks of January 2011. The floods resulted in the deaths of at least nine people, destroyed properties in central and southern inland parts of Queenslands, ruined crops, and disrupted mining. More than 200,000 people and 70 towns were affected, and damage was estimated at $1.02 billion.

⁴FLORA AND FAUNA

The World Resources Institute estimates that there are 15,638 plant species in Australia. In addition, Australia is home to 376 species of mammals, 851 species of birds, 880 species of reptiles, and 229 species of amphibians. The calculation reflects the total number of distinct species residing in the country, not the number of endemic species. The coastal areas were home to 4,000 fish, 1,700 coral, and 50 marine mammal species.

The government's Department of Foreign Affairs and Trade stated the continent's geographic isolation had allowed a range of unique flora and fauna to thrive. Some notable vegetation included the Wollemi Pine which as a species dates back 65 million years; cycad palms, grass tree plants, and a variety of wildflowers including the waratah, Sturt's desert pea, banksia, and kangeroo paws. Hummock grasslands predominant in Western Australia, South Australia, and the Northern Territory, while tussock grasslands are found in Queensland.

There are some 500 species of Eucalyptus and at least 600 species of Acacia (called wattle by Australians). The golden wattle (*Acacia pycnantha*) is the floral emblem of Australia. Other trees are the baobab, blackwood (a type of acacia), red cedar, coachwood, jarrah (a type of Eucalyptus), river red gum (also a type of Eucalyptus), narrow-leaved tea tree, Queensland maple, silky oak, and walnut.

The country has the third most extensive mangrove area in the world, covering over one million ha. (Mangrove refers to the diverse habitat of tropical trees and shrubs growing near the seacoast, sometimes called mangrove forest or tidal forest.). As of January 2012, there were 19 natural UNESCO World Heritage Sites in Australia and 64 Ramsar wetland sites.

Nearly half of Australia's mammals are marsupials and included kangaroos, koalas, wallabies, and wombats. The Tasmanian Devil is a marsupial found only in Tasmania. Other mammals are the

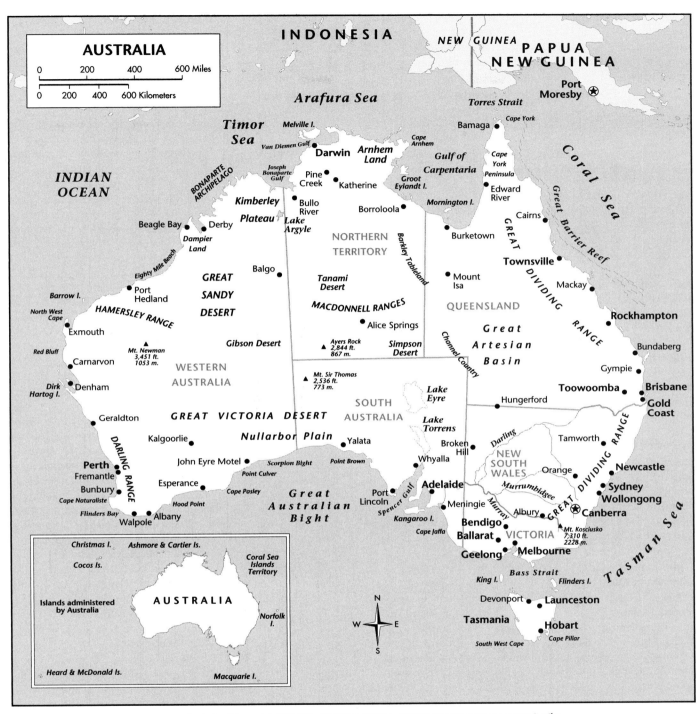

LOCATION:(including Tasmania): 113°09′ to 153°39′ E; 10°41′ to 43°39′S. TERRITORIAL SEA LIMIT: 3 miles.
note: Dotted outlines indicate lake beds that are dry except during rainy seasons.

dingo, a native wild dog; the river-dwelling platypus which has a duck-like bill, furred body, and webbed feet; and the echidna, an anteater.

About half of Australia's birds are found only on the continent. Some species are honeyeaters, emu, cassowaries, black swans, fairy penguins, kookaburras, lyrebirds, and currawongs. There are also 55 species of parrots.

Australia also has 21 species of venomous snakes. Marine life include the great white shark, the giant filter-feeding whale shark, Portuguese man-of-war, and box jellyfish.

Many species of trees, plants, and domestic animals have been imported, often thriving at the expense of indigenous types. Herds of wild buffalo, camels, donkeys, horses, and pigs, descendants of stock that strayed from herds imported by pioneers, roam the sparsely settled areas. The proliferation of rabbits resulted in a menace to sheep, and in the period 1901–07, a series of three fences stretching more than 2,000 miles were constructed to keep rabbits out of Western Australia and to control the incursion of emus, dingos, and other wild animals.

According to the 2011 International Union for Conservation of Nature and Natural Resources (IUCN) Red List Report, the number of threatened species include 55 types of mammals, 52 species of birds, 43 types of reptiles, 47 species of amphibian, 103 species of fish, 168 types of mollusks, 314 other invertebrates, and 67 species of plants. Endangered species include the banded anteater, greater rabbit-eared bandicoot, Leadbeater's possum, northern hairy-nosed wombat, woylie, bridled nail-tail wallaby, five species of turtle (western swamp, green sea, hawksbill, leatherback, and olive or Pacific ridley), Tasmanian freshwater limpet, granulated Tasmanian snail, African wild ass, western ground parrot, paradise parakeet, helmeted honeyeater, noisy scrub-bird, western rufous bristlebird, Lord Howe wood rail, Lord Howe currawong, small hemiphlebia damselfly, Otway stonefly, giant torrent midge, and Tasmanian torrent midge. Lord Howe stick insect, Gray's marble toadlet, the dusky flying fox, the Tasmanian wolf, and the banded hare wallaby are among the country's 42 extinct species. In March 2010, Australian scientists found a thriving community of yellow-spotted bell frogs, a species thought to be extinct for nearly forty years, in a remote Australian creek in New South Wales. To protect the community, the exact location was not announced. However, scientists in the country publicly discussed plans to launch a captive breeding program for the frogs.

5 ENVIRONMENT

The World Resources Institute reported that Australia had designated 73.41 million hectares (181.39 million acres) of land for protection as of 2006. Water resources totaled 398 cu km (95.49 cu mi) while water usage was 24.06 cu km (5.77 cu mi) per year. Domestic water usage accounted for 15% of total usage, industrial for 10%, and agricultural for 75%. Per capita water usage totaled 1,193 cu m (42,130 cu ft) per year.

The United Nations (UN) reported in 2008 that carbon dioxide emissions in Australia totaled 373,739 kilotons.

Australia faced many significant environmental issues in the second decade of the 21st century. Overgrazing, industrial development, urbanization and poor farming practices have resulted in significant soil erosion. Soil salinity was rising because of poor water quality, and desertification was an environmental threat. In addition, land-clearing that had been conducted for agricultural development was threatening the natural habitat of Australia's unique flora and fauna. Increased shipping and tourism activity was threatening the Great Barrier Reef. In addition, the country's natural freshwater resources were limited.

The government published its 2011 State of the Environment report on 12 December 2011. The report traced many of Australia's present-day environmental concerns to the impact of European contact, which began in the 18th century. Non-indigenous mammals such as cats, foxes, and rabbits have contributed to the decline of native species and degraded areas of farmland. In addition, introduced plants have damaged native vegetation and habitat. Camels, which were introduced in the mid-19th century, now

number more than 1 million and often trample vegetation and damage water pipes. Native species such as Australia's 140 marsupials also have competed with sheep and cattle for limited pasture and water resources. The carnivorous dingo also posed a threat to sheet and other livestock. According to the report, past practices of land clearing, wetlands draining, and overharvesting of fish stocks were continuing to exert pressure on the environment.

The 2011 State of the Environment report cited climate change as a significant issue, noting that average surface temperatures rose by nearly 1°C (1.8°F) between 1910 and 2009, with the first decade of the 21st century being the warmest on record.

The Australian government has taken steps to manage its environment. In 2001, the Natural Resource Management Ministerial Council (NRMMC) assumed jurisdiction over management of natural resources and the Environment Protection and Heritage Council (EPHC) took over management of environmental protection concerns. Other government ministries dealing with environmental matters are the Ministerial Council on Energy (MCE), and the National Environment Protection Council (NEPC). The Australian Antarctic Division, an agency of the Department of the Environment, Water, Heritage, and the Arts, works to ensure that the country's interests in Antarctica are protected. The Antarctic Division conducts research and administers the Australian Antarctic territories. The Department of the Environment, Water, Heritage, and the Arts was established on 3 December 2007 as the principal government institution responsible for environmental matters.

Several laws enacted since the 1970s are aimed at environmental stewardship. The Environment Protection (Impact of Proposals) Act of 1974 established procedures for ensuring that environmental impact is considered in governmental decision making. The Whale Protection Act of 1981 prohibited killing, capturing, injuring, or interfering with a whale, dolphin, or porpoise within Australia's 200 mi economic zone or, beyond the zone, by Australian vessels and aircraft and their crews. The Environment Protection (Nuclear Codes) Act of 1978 mandated the development of uniform safety standards for uranium mining and milling and for the transport of radioactive materials. The Protection of the Sea (Discharge of Oil from Ships) Act of 1981 and the Protection of the Sea (Prevention of Pollution from Ships) Act of 1983 prevented or limited pollution from oil or noxious substances. In 1999 the Environment Protection and Biodiversity Conservation Act (EPBC Act) was passed.

In 2004 Australia's Great Barrier Reef became the most protected reef on earth when Parliament passed a law banning commercial and recreational fishing and increasing protection of the reef system. By expanding the protected area of the existing Marine Park and World Heritage site by more than 109,000 sq km (42,000 sq mi), Parliament established the park as the world's largest marine protected area.

The government committed $2.25 billion in 2008 to develop its Caring For Our Country program. The initiative has supported the use of indigenous land and sea management practices to rescue the Great Barrier Reef, repair coastal ecosystems, save the endangered Tasmanian Devil, control feral animals and weeds, improve water quality, and to expand its indigenous protected area network.

Despite these measures, both natural and human-made disasters are ongoing environmental concerns. Australia's dry hot climate creates conditions favorable to periodic devastating bushfires. Deadly and damaging cyclones occasionally occur along the coastal regions. And in April 2010, a large Chinese vessel carrying 65,000 tons of coal ran aground in a restricted section of the Great Barrier Reef, rupturing its fuel tank and spilling tons of thick oil sludge into the reef. Three tons of engine oil escaped from the vessel, and ocean currents caused the ship to drag along a large section of the reef, scarring a corridor 3.1 kilometers (1.9 miles) long and 250 meters (820 feet) wide. Scientists estimated that it could take the reef twenty years to recover from the trauma.

As of 2011, Australia was party to the Antarctic-Environmental Protocol, Antarctic-Marine Living Resources, Antarctic Seals, and Antarctic Treaty. It also was party to international environmental agreements on biodiversity, climate change, desertification, endangered species, environmental modification, hazardous wastes, law of the sea, marine dumping, marine life conservation, ozone layer protection, ship pollution, tropical timber, wetlands, and whaling.

6 POPULATION

The Australian Bureau of Statistics estimated the population of Australia to be approximately 22,800,000 in January 2011, which placed it at number 55 in population among the 196 nations of the world. In 2011, approximately 14% of the population was over 65 years of age, with another 18.3% under 15 years of age. The median age in Australia was 37.7 years. There were 1.00 males for every female in the country. The population's annual rate of change was 1.148%. The projected population for the year 2025 was 26,900,000. Population density in Australia was calculated at 3 people per sq km (8 people per sq mi).

The UN estimated that 89% of the population lived in urban areas, and that urban populations had an annual rate of change of 1.2%. The largest urban areas, along with their respective populations, included Sydney, 4.4 million; Melbourne, 3.9 million; Brisbane, 2 million; Perth, 1.6 million; and Canberra, 384,000.

One-third of Australia is virtually uninhabited; another third is sparsely populated. The total population is quite small compared to the large land mass. Most of the cities are located in the east and southeast, with more than 80% of the population concentrated within 100 km (60 mi) of the coast.

7 MIGRATION

Estimates of Australia's net migration rate, carried out by the CIA in 2011, amounted to 9.42 migrants per 1,000 citizens. The total number of emigrants living abroad was 442,800, and the total number of immigrants living in Australia was 5.52 million.

After World War II, the government promoted immigration of the maximum number of persons Australia could absorb without economic disequilibrium. Most of the 4.2 million immigrants to Australia between 1945 and 1985 were from the United Kingdom, Italy, and Greece. The government encouraged immigrants of working age to settle in rural areas, but many immigrants preferred to work in the cities. The record high for new settlers was 185,099, in 1969–70.

In 1979, with the unemployment rate rising, the government tightened immigration requirements. As of January 2012, Australia was extending visas through its Migration Program for skilled migrants and family members, and for refugees, internally displaced persons, and asylum seekers through its Humanitarian Program.

The government granted 13,799 visas under its Humanitarian Program in 2010–11. Of that total, 4,828 visas were granted to individuals already in Australia while 8,971 visas were granted to a total of 54,396 applicants from Iraq, Myanmar, Afghanistan, Bhutan, the Democratic Republic of Congo, Ethiopia, Sri Lanka, Iran, Sudan, and Somalia.

The government estimated that it had granted 750,000 visas for humanitarian reasons from 1945–2011. Among the refugees, asylum seekers, and internally displaced persons, were individuals leaving the Indochinese Peninsula during the Vietnam War; ethnic Tamils from Sri Lanka seeking refuge from the 1983–2009 civil war; Iraqis, Iranians, and ethnic Kurds.

In 2001, the Migration Program allowed 80,610 entry visas, most granted under the family and skill based categories. By 2005–06, the number of entry visas the Migration Program planned to allow had increased to 140,000. The government granted 113,725 visas under its Migration Program in 2010–11.

More than 4 million immigrants have become citizens since Australian citizenship was introduced in 1949. In 2009–10 citizenship was granted to 119,791 people from 185 countries. The highest numbers of new citizens were from the United Kingdom (22,832 or 19.1%); India (17,781 or 14.8%); China (11,103 or 9.3%); South Africa (5,207 or 4.3%); the Philippines (4,503 or 3.8%). As of 2012, Australia did not recognize children born after 20 August 1986 as natural-born Australian citizens unless one of their parents was either a citizen or permanent resident at the time of their birth.

The majority of illegal immigrants are those who entered the country legally but remained beyond the expiration of their visas. The government was undertaking more stringent measures to identify and remove illegal aliens. Australia has also set up programs to assist the integration of migrants and refugees by providing services and education.

Christmas Island, a dependency of Australia in the Indian Ocean, has served as a controversial detention center for foreigners seeking to immigrate to Australia. Over the years, the number of asylum-seekers has swelled, leading to a serious problem in overcrowding. The center was designed to accommodate 800 people but, by December 2010, over 3,000 people were being held in the processing center. Other difficulties stem from disagreements over Australia's immigration policies, since some opposition leaders argue that granting asylum to immigrants seeking admission to Australia has the potential to upset Australia's social balance.

There also was a growing concern that Islamic radicals born or raised in Australia posed threats to national security. According to Prime Minister Kevin Rudd, these "home-grown terrorists" pose a serious threat to the nation, making terrorism a persistent and permanent feature of national security. In February 2010, following the release of a report on security issues compiled by intelligence agencies, the prime minister stated that the nation faces a permanent state of alert as the threat of militant attacks by Islamic radicals continues to increase. In response to that threat, Rudd announced the development of a new program that would tighten entry requirements for visitors from ten high-risk nations. The government expected to spend $62 million on biometric facilities to fingerprint and face-scan these visitors. The government has also announced plans to develop community-based programs designed to end radicalism by promoting the integration of various ethnic groups into mainstream society.

8 ETHNIC GROUPS

Most Australians are of British or Irish ancestry. According to some 2010 estimates, approximately 92% of the population was Caucasian, 7% was Asian, and 1% was Aboriginal or indigenous (Torres Strait Islander).

The Australian Bureau of Statistics reported in 2011 that the Aboriginal and Torres Strait Island population would reach 713,300–721,000 by 2021. The Aboriginal population declined from 300,000–1,000,000 prior to European contact in the late 18th century to about 60,000 by the 1920s. The population began to grow again, however, by the 1950s. The most recent national census, taken in 2006, showed the number of Aboriginal or Torres Strait Islander peoples at 517,200, 2.5% of the total population. New South Wales had the largest number of indigenous people with 148,200, followed by Queensland with 146,400, Western Australia with 77,900, and the Northern Territory with 66,600. The Australian government, however, reported that Queensland likely would have the largest number of Aboriginal and indigenous peoples by 2021, an estimated 212,908, followed by New South Wales at 208,341 and Western Australia at 92,587.

The Aboriginals' social organization is among the most complex known to anthropologists. They do not cultivate the soil but are nomadic hunters and food gatherers, without settled communities. Anthropologists believe the Aboriginals, also known as Australoids, are relatively homogeneous, although they display a wide range of physical types. Their serological, or blood-group, pattern is unique, except for a faint affinity with the Paniyan of southern India and the Veddas of Sri Lanka. The Aboriginals probably originated from a small isolated group subject to chance mutation but not to hybridization. There seems to be a sprinkling of Australoid groups in India, Sri Lanka, Sumatra, Timor, and New Guinea. In 1963, Aboriginals were given full citizenship rights, although as a group they continued to suffer from discrimination and a lower living standard than Australians of European descent generally.

Beginning in the 1960s, the government abandoned its previous policy of "assimilation" of the Aboriginals, recognizing the uniqueness of Aboriginal culture and the right of the Aboriginals to determine their own patterns of development. From the passage of the Aboriginal Land Rights (Northern Territory) Act in 1976 to mid-1990, Aboriginals in the Northern Territory were given ownership of about 34% of territorial lands (461,486 sq km or 178,180 sq mi). The South Australia state government and its Aboriginals also signed a land-rights agreement, and similar legislation was developed in other states during the 1980s. In all, Aboriginals held 647,772 sq km (250,104 sq mi) of land under freehold in mid-1989 and another 181,800 sq km (70,193 sq mi) under leasehold. A reservation in Western Australia consisted of 202,223 sq km (78,078 sq mi). By the mid-1990s, however, more than two-thirds of the Aboriginals had left rural lands to settle in urban areas.

The 2006 census reported that Australia's population included persons of US, Chinese, Croatian, Dutch, British, Filipino, French, German, Greek, Hungarian, Indian, Irish, Italian, Lebanese, Macedonian, Maltese, Maori, New Zealander, Polish, Russian, Scottish, Serbian, Sinhalese, South African, Spanish, Turkish, Vietnamese, Welsh and other origins. Figures from the 2011 census were to be released in June 2012.

9 LANGUAGES

The 2006 census reported that nearly 400 different languages were spoken in Australian homes. About 78.5% of the population used English primarily; 2.6% used Chinese; 1.6% used Italian, 1.3% Greek, 1.2% Arabic, and 1% Vietnamese. About 13.7% of the population used languages other than the above stated languages or did not specify a primary language.

The number of Cantonese-speakers grew by 21% over 1996; the number of Mandarin and Hindu speakers doubled during the same period. The number of European-language speakers declined during the decade: German-speakers declined by 24%, Italian-speakers declined by 15%, and Greek-speakers by 7% during the period 1996–2006. Many languages or dialects are spoken by the Aboriginal tribes, but phonetically they are markedly uniform. Historically there was no written Aboriginal language, but increased concern about the preservation of Aboriginal culture has led to the development of some written Aboriginal language. Aboriginal languages are in use in certain schools in the Northern Territories and, to a lesser extent, in schools of other states.

10 RELIGIONS

The 2006 census reported that 64% of Australia's citizens identified as Christian, 26% of whom were Roman Catholic, 19% Anglican, and 19% other Christian denominations. Buddhists made up 2.1% of the population, Muslims, 1.7%, Hindus 0.7%, Jews 0.4%, and other religious affiliations 0.5%. The census reported that among the indigenous community, 5,206 individuals (less than 0.03% of respondents) reported the practice of an indigenous traditional religion. About 20% of the population listed no religion.

Australia's constitution protects religious freedom, and the government generally respects that right.

From 1996–2006, the number of people affiliated with non-Christian faiths grew from 3.5% to 5.6% of the total population (from 600,000 to 1.1 million people).

Good Friday, Easter Monday, and Christmas are observed as national holidays.

Plans to build an Islamic school in a suburb of Sydney, New South Wales, in June 2009 prompted a lawsuit. The case was being appealed to the Australian Supreme Court as of late 2011.

Organizations promoting tolerance and mutual understanding between faiths include the Columbian Center for Christian-Muslim Relations, the National Council of Churches in Australia, the Aboriginal and Torres Strait Islander Ecumenical Commission, the Australian Council of Christians and Jews, and the Affinity Intercultural Foundation.

¹¹TRANSPORTATION

The CIA reported that Australia had a total of 818,356 km (508,503 mi) of roads in 2008. There were 687 vehicles per 1,000 people in the country. There were 465 airports, which transported 50.03 million passengers in 2009 according to the World Bank. Australia had approximately 2,000 km (1,243 mi) of navigable waterways.

Some railways are publically owned; private railways are primarily used by the iron ore industry in Western Australia.

Australia's railway systems do not interconnect well because the system is made up of three track gauges: standard (1.435-m); broad (1.600-m); and narrow (1.067-m). Of the three, the majority is standard gauge with 20,519 km (12,722 mi) of track as of 2006, followed by narrow gauge track at 14,074 km (8,726 mi), and by broad gauge at 3,727 km (2,311 mi). As a result, rail travel between principal cities can involve changing trains. Modern equipment is gradually replacing older stock. As of August 1991, all interstate freight movements by rail were brought under the control of the National Rail Corporation (NRC).

Most navigable waterways are on the Murray and Murray-Darling river systems and are used largely for recreational purposes. However, ocean shipping is important for domestic and overseas transport. Most overseas trade is carried in non-Australian ships, while most coastwise vessels are of Australian registry. Although the fine natural harbors of Sydney and Hobart can readily accommodate ships of 11 m (36 ft) draft, many other harbors have been artificially developed. Other international shipping ports include Adelaide, Brisbane, Cairns, Darwin, Devonport, Fremantle, Geelong, Launceston, Mackay, Melbourne, and Townsville. All main ports have ample wharfage, modern cargo-handling equipment, and storage facilities. There are some 70 commercially significant ports. The nation's merchant marine in 2008 included 50 vessels of 1,000 GRT or over, with a combined GRT of 1,531,461. Highways provide access to many districts not served by railroads.

Australia had 325 airports with paved runways in 2009. There was also one heliport. Principal airports include Adelaide, Brisbane, Cairns, Darwin, Melbourne International at Melbourne, Perth International at Perth, and Kingsford International at Sydney. In 1997, the government began privatizing many of the country's airports. The first round of such sales early in 1997 included the Melbourne, Brisbane, and Perth airports, which raised AUD$3.34 billion (US$2.5 billion). The main Sydney airport was explicitly excluded from the privatization plan. Domestic air services are operated primarily by the privately owned Ansett Airlines. The Australian overseas airline, Qantas, carries more than 3 million passengers per year to and from Australia, nearly 40% of the total carried by all airlines serving Australia. The Commonwealth government owned the airline until it was privatized in 1995.

¹²HISTORY

Stone objects that were found in 1978 but are still only tentatively dated suggest that human beings may have inhabited what is now Australia as long as 100,000 years ago. The Aboriginals migrated to Australia from Southeast Asia at least 40,000 years before the first Europeans arrived on the island continent. Living as hunters and gatherers, roaming in separate family groups or bands, the Aboriginals developed a rich, complex culture, with many languages. They numbered 300,000 by the 18th century; however, with the onset of European settlement, conflict and disease reduced their numbers.

Although maps of the 16th century indicate European awareness of the location of Australia, the first recorded explorations of the continent by Europeans took place early in the 17th century, when Dutch, Portuguese, and Spanish explorers sailed along the coast and discovered what is now Tasmania. None took formal possession of the land. In 1770, Capt. James Cook charted the east coast and claimed possession in the name of Great Britain. Up to the early 19th century, the area was known as New Holland, New South Wales, or Botany Bay.

The First Fleet under Capt. Arthur Phillip landed at Sydney on 26 January 1788. On 7 February 1788, the established of the Colony of New South Wales was proclaimed. The initial colony was a penal colony, and from 1788–1868 shipments of prisoners brought approximately 161,000 convicts to the area.

With the increase of free settlers, the country developed, the interior was penetrated, and additional colonies were created: Van Diemen's Land in 1825 (renamed Tasmania in 1856), Western Australia in 1829, South Australia in 1834, Victoria in 1851, and Queensland in 1859. These colonies along with New South Wales constitute the commonwealth of present-day Australia.

Sheep raising and wheat growing were introduced and soon became the backbone of the economy. The wool industry made rapid progress during the period of squatting migration, which began on a large scale about 1820. The grazers followed in the wake of explorers, reaching new pastures, or "runs," where they squatted and built their homes. Exports of wool increased from 111 kg (245 lb) in 1807 to 1.1 million kg (2.4 million lb) in 1831. With the increased flow of immigrants following the Ripon Land Regulations of 1831, the population grew from about 34,000 in 1820 to some 405,000 in 1850. The discovery of gold in Victoria (1851) attracted thousands, and in a few years the population had quadrupled. Under the stimulus of gold production, the first railway line-Melbourne to Port Melbourne-was completed in 1854. Representative government spread throughout the continent, and the colonies acquired their own parliaments.

Until the end of the 19th century, Australia's six self-governing colonies remained separate. However, the obvious advantages of common defense and irrigation led to the federation of the states into the Commonwealth of Australia in 1901, and the first federal Parliament was opened at Melbourne in May 1901 by the Duke of York (who later became King George V). The Northern Territory, which belonged to South Australia, became a separate part of the Commonwealth in 1911. In the same year, territory was acquired from New South Wales for a new capital at Canberra, and in 1927, the Australian Parliament began meeting there.

Liberal legislation provided for free and compulsory education, industrial conciliation and arbitration, the secret ballot, female suffrage, old age pensions, invalid pensions, and maternity allowances before World War I. On 9 October 1942, the Statute of Westminster Adoption Act was passed and officially established Australia's complete autonomy from the British Empire.

Child subsidies and unemployment and disability benefits were introduced during World War II.

Australian forces fought along with the British in Europe during World War I. In World War II, the Australian forces supported the UK in the Middle East between 1940 and 1942, and played a major role in the Pacific theater after the Japanese attack on Pearl Harbor.

After the war, a period of intense immigration began. The Labour government was voted out of office in 1949, beginning 23 years of continuous rule by a Liberal-Country Party (now known as the National Party) coalition. During this period, the government stepped up efforts to be more responsive to the rights of Australia's Aboriginal and indigenous peoples whose numbers had declined from 300,000 at the time of Capt. Cook's arrival in 1780 to about 60,000 by the 1920s. During that period, Australian foreign policy stressed collective security and support for the US presence in Asia, and Australian troops served in Vietnam between 1965 and 1971.

When Labour returned to power in December 1972, it began the process of disassociating Australia from US and UK policies and strengthening ties with non-communist Asian nations; in addition, it established diplomatic relations with the People's Republic of China. The Northern Territory was granted self-government in 1978. The Australia Act on 3 March 1986 eliminated most lingering vestiges of British legal authority. Self-government was granted to the Australian Capital Territory in 1988.

In 1975 a constitutional crisis resulted when Senate opposition successfully blocked the Labour Party's budgetary measures. The governor-general dismissed the Labour prime minister, Gough Whitlam, and called for new elections. The Liberal-National Party coalition swept back into power, where it remained until 1983. The Australian Labour Party (ALP) returned to power in 1983, following a campaign in which such economic issues as unemployment and inflation predominated.

In 1993, the Mabo Ruling on Native Title recognized the land rights of the indigenous people (Aborigines) inhabiting Australia prior to the arrival of the Europeans. The Mabo Ruling did not void existing leases, but did allow the Aborigines to reclaim land when the leases granted by the national or state governments expired. The Wik Judgment of 1996 extended the land rights of indigenous people to include their use of pastoral land for religious purposes.

In the March 1996 elections, the ALP was unseated by a coalition of the Liberal Party and the National Party, who chose Liberal MP John Howard to be prime minister. The newcomer Howard pledged to change the government, to make it more "rational." To that end, he cut ministries and cabinet posts, made budget cuts affecting higher education, Aborigine affairs, and jobs, and instituted an AUD\$15 billion (US\$15.44 billion) privatization program. Many government employees opposed these changes; violent demonstrations took place when the budget was made public. While the revised budget was less radical, social unrest continued and the October 1998 election found Howard's coalition party's majority greatly reduced, while the ALP gained in influence, winning 18 more seats than it did in the 1996 election.

In July 1998, the government passed amendments to the 1993 Native Title Act. The amendments removed the time limit for lodging native claims, but weakened the right of Aboriginal groups to negotiate with non-Aboriginal leaseholders concerning land use. In 1999 the government issued an official expression of regret for past mistreatment of Aborigines, but opposed issuing the formal national apology sought by Aborigine leaders, fearing that would encourage claims for compensation.

In September 1999, Australian troops led the UN-sanctioned peacekeeping forces into East Timor following that country's referendum decision to seek full independence from Indonesia. Australian civilian and military personnel formed part of the UN Mission of Support in East Timor (UNMISET), which was established to ensure the security and stability of East Timor after it became an independent nation-state on 20 May 2002. Over the next few years, unresolved maritime boundary disputes between Australia, Timor-Leste (East Timor), and Indonesia festered. Australia declared a 1,000-nautical mile-wide maritime identification zone, and asserted land and maritime claims to Antarctica in 2004. In January 2006, Australia and Timor-Leste signed an agreement to divide revenues from oil and gas deposits in the Timor Sea. The two countries agreed to defer discussions on the disputed maritime boundary for 50 years.

Parliamentary elections on 10 November 2001 resulted in Howard's coalition increasing its strength. Two events stood out in the election campaign that swung the vote to the Liberal Party-National Party coalition. The first was a controversy over refugees and asylum-seekers. In August 2001, a Norwegian freighter that had rescued a boatload of asylum-seekers was denied permission to land the human cargo in Australia. After that, the Howard government also tightened border protection laws, making it nearly impossible for any asylum-seeker landing in the remote island outposts of Australia to claim refugee status. Instead, the would-be refugees would be either turned back to Indonesian waters or transported to detention centers on Pacific nations such as Nauru or Papua New Guinea. The ALP criticized the government for this policy, which remained a major campaign issue.

In August 2002, Australia instituted a regional alliance with Malaysia to work together to fight suspected Islamic militants. On 12 October 2002, two popular nightclubs in Bali, Indonesia, were bombed, killing 202 people, 88 of them Australians, an act referred to as "Australia's September 11th." Australia added four more Islamic groups to its list of banned terrorist organizations. In November 2002, some 1,000 Australian protesters demonstrated against globalization and a possible war with Iraq. By January 2003, when Australia deployed troops to the Persian Gulf region ahead of a possible war, public protest was immediate. In the first-ever vote of no-confidence against a serving leader, the Senate passed the motion against Prime Minister John Howard over his handling of Iraq crisis.

Between July and October 2003, in "Operation Helpem Fren," an Australian-led peacekeeping force headed a mission to restore law and order in the Solomon Islands. In October 2003, US President George W. Bush was heckled at his appearance in Australia's Parliament. In November 2003, an Indonesian fishing boat, the *Minasa Bone*, with 14 Kurds aboard, sought asylum on Melville Island, but was forced to return to Indonesia.

Anti-Iraq war protests continued in 2004. In September 2004, a car bomb exploded outside the gates of the Australian Embassy in Jakarta, Indonesia, killing 8 people and wounding more than 160. Australia continued to bolster its security with a US cruise missile program that provided the "most lethal" air combat capacity in the region.

In October 2004, Prime Minister John Howard achieved a strong victory in Australia's federal election, winning a historic fourth term. In January 2005, Australia's free-trade agreement with the United States became effective. In February 2005, Howard continued the government's support of the war in Iraq, promising 450 extra troops to help reinforce Iraq's transition to democracy. By July 2005, 150 special forces troops were sent back into Afghanistan to resist rebel attacks. Australia further bolstered regional security with a NATO agreement to cooperate in the fight against international terrorism, weapons proliferation, and other global military threats, and with a security pact with Indonesia.

In December 2005, on Sydney's North Cronulla beach and in the surrounding neighborhood, young white Australians violently clashed with Lebanese-Australians, in attacks reflecting long-brewing racial and religious tensions. The violence led to intense debate and introspection nationwide about law and order and the widening cultural and religious divide between white Australians and Australian-Arab Muslims. Tensions were fueled by fears of terrorism and the government's efforts to tighten domestic security.

In August 2006, proposed legislation-under which future asylum-seekers who arrive by boat would be sent to offshore detention camps-was discarded after a revolt by ruling party lawmakers.

In December 2006, during the worst drought in a century, the government severely cut economic growth forecasts, reflecting a decline in farm output. In January 2007, Prime Minister Howard declared water security to be Australia's greatest challenge.

In June 2007, the government initiated a major controversial intervention in the Aboriginal communities of the Northern Territory by sending police, military troops, medical staff, and social workers into the communities. The Racial Discrimination Act was temporarily suspended in order to allow the intervention. The primary goal was to curb widespread child abuse and alcoholism. To that end, the measures imposed on the community included a ban on alcohol and pornography and tighter restrictions on how families could spend welfare payments. In August 2009, a UN human rights official reported that the intervention program was discriminatory and an infringement on the rights of self-determination, leading to greater stigmatization of the people. About 45,500 Aborigines from 500 communities were affected. The five-year intervention was to end in August 2012, though the government indicated it might extend the time period.

¹³GOVERNMENT

Australia's constitution, which took effect 1 January 1901, established the Commonwealth of Australia as an independent, self-governing nation within the Commonwealth of Nations. Queen Elizabeth II was the head of state as of January 2012 and officially Queen of Australia. The Queen was represented by a governor general at the federal level and by a governor in each state. Although the governor general conventionally has acted on the advice of the prime minister and other ministers, the governor general holds some reserve powers that allow for the dismissal of ministers.

The federal Parliament consists of a 76-member Senate and a 150-member House of Representatives. The Senate's membership consists of twelve senators from each of the six states and two from each of the two territories. Senators from the states are elected to six-year terms, and elections take place every three years. Senators from the territories are elected to three-year term. Seats in the House of Representatives are allocated on the basis of population, though each state is allowed at least five representatives. House members are elected to terms of three years, unless the House is dissolved and new elections are called for.

Members of Parliament must be Australian citizens of full age, possess electoral qualification, and have resided for three years in Australia. Parliament must meet at least once a year. Taxation and appropriation measures must be introduced in the lower house; the Senate has the power to propose amendments, except to money bills, and to defeat any measure it may choose.

The leader of the political party or coalition that wins a majority of seats in the House of Representatives serves as prime minister. The prime minister serves as the head of government, and nominates a Cabinet from members of parliament who are sworn in by the governor general.

As of January 2012, the governor-general was Quentin Bryce, who had held the position since 5 September 2008. Julia Ellen Gillard became prime minister following elections on 24 June 2010.

In the 1990s, the Labour Government, under the leadership of Prime Minister Paul Keating, proposed a referendum to change Australia to a republican form of government. The idea gained wide support. After the 1996 federal elections, the coalition majority decided to host a constitutional convention to decide the issue. The constitutional convention met in February 1998, and voted in favor of replacing the British monarch as the head of Australia's government (73 voted in favor, 57 against), and Australia becoming a republic by the year 2001 (89 voted in favor, 52 against). But in a November 1999 popular referendum, the proposal to convert Australia to a republic failed to carry even a single state.

Suffrage is universal for all persons 18 years of age and older, subject to citizenship and certain residence requirements. Voting is compulsory in national and state parliamentary elections.

The last House elections took place on 21 August 2010. Senate elections took place on 21 August 2010 and 1 July 2011. Elections were expected to take place before 30 November 2013.

¹⁴POLITICAL PARTIES

The main political parties as of 2012 were the Australian Greens, headed by Bob Brown; the Australian Labor Party, headed by Prime Minister Gillard; the Family First Party, headed by Steve Fielding; the Liberal Party, headed by Tony Abbott; and the Nationals, headed by Warren Truss.

The Australian Labor Party (ALP) is the country's oldest party, having been founded in 1890.

Except in 1929–31, when a Labor government was in office, governments between World War I and World War II were dominated by non-Labor groupings. When war seemed certain in 1939, the government was resolutely imperial, considering Australia to be at war automatically when the UK went to war. The Labor Party challenged this view. While they did not oppose a declaration of war on Germany, they wanted the step to be taken so as to show Australia's independence.

Labor was in office from 1941 to 1949. The Liberal and Country Parties were in office as a coalition from 1949 to 1972, and again beginning in December 1975 (by that time, the Country Party had become the National Country Party; it later became the National Party).

In the general elections of 13 December 1975, a caretaker government, formed the preceding month by the Liberal-National Country Party coalition after the dismissal of the Labour government of Prime Minister Gough Whitlam, obtained large majorities in both houses of the legislature. Although its majorities were eroded in the elections of December 1977 and October 1980, the coalition remained in power until March 1983, when Labour won 75 out of 147 seats in the House of Representatives. Robert Hawke, leader of the Labour Party, took office as prime minister; he was reelected in 1984, 1987, and 1990. Paul Keating replaced Hawke as Labour's leader, and as prime minister, in December 1991 after party members ousted Hawke. Keating led the ALP to an unprecedented fifth consecutive election victory in the 1993 general election, increasing both its percentage share of the vote and its number of seats in the legislature. In 1996, a Liberal-National Party coalition headed by John Howard ousted the ALP from the majority, with the Liberal-National coalition winning 94 seats compared to the ALP's 49 seats. John Howard was reelected prime minister in 1998, 2001, and 2004.

In elections held 24 November 2007, the Australian Labour Party, under the leadership of Kevin Rudd, unseated the incumbent coalition government led by John Howard.

In mid-2010, Prime Minister Rudd faced rising opposition from his own party as a result of a series of unpopular decision that include the shelving of an emissions trading scheme and support for a major tax on the mining industry. He left his post, and on 24 June 2010, Julia Gillard, was sworn in as his replacement.

The 21 August 2010 parliamentary elections resulted in the first minority government since World War II, as no single party or coalition gained enough seats to form a majority. For more than two weeks after the vote, officials worried over the prospect of political deadlock, while party members turned their sights on winning official support from the four independent seat holders. Prime Minister Gillard retained her position after two of these independents offered their backing to her Australian Labour Party (ALP).

A direct descendant of the governments of the 1920s and 1930s, the Liberal-National coalition is principally linked with business (Liberal) and farming (National) and is officially anti-socialist. In economic and foreign affairs, its outlook is still involved with the Commonwealth of Nations, but it supports the UN, as well as the alliance with the United States in the ANZUS pact. It is sympathetic toward the new Asian countries and values the link with these countries afforded by the Colombo Plan. The Labour Party is a trade-union party, officially socialist in policy and outlook. It initially maintained an isolationist posture, but since the early 1940s, its policy has been a mixture of nationalism and internationalism.

Smaller parties include the Democratic Labour Party, the Communist Party, the Australian Democrats Party, the Green Party, and the One Nation Party. Since its formation in 1997, the One Nation Party's platform has featured racial issues. In the 1998 Queensland state elections, it won 11 of 89 seats. In the federal elections of that same year, the One Nation Party called for an end to Asian immigration and a restriction to Aboriginal welfare programs, but failed to win any seats. The Green Party increased its strength by 2.3% in the 2001 elections, while the One Nation Party lost 4.1% of its strength.

15 LOCAL GOVERNMENT

Australia is divided into six states and two territories: the Australian Capital Territory and Northern Territory, and the states of New South Wales, Queensland, South Australia, Tasmania, Victoria, and Western Australia.

Each state is headed by a premier who is the leader of the party with a majority or working minority in the lower house of the state legislature, with the exception of Queensland which has a unicameral parliament. The two self-governing territories also have unicameral legislative bodies but operate similarly to the states. A chief minister heads each territory, and is the leader of the party with a majority or working minority in the territory's legislature.

In the states with bicameral legislatures, the lower houses are popularly elected while the upper houses are elected by franchise limited to property holders and to those with certain academic or professional qualifications. The state prime minister achieves office and selects his cabinet in the same fashion as does the Commonwealth prime minister.

More than 670 local councils oversee road maintenance, sewage treatment, recreational facilities, and other services.

Local communities (variously designated as boroughs, cities, district councils, municipalities, road districts, shires, and towns) have limited powers of government, but they are responsible for some health, sanitation, light, gas, and highway undertakings. Even the largest cities do not provide their own police protection, nor do they conduct or support education; these are state functions. Local aldermen or councilors ordinarily are elected on a property franchise, and mayors are elected annually or biennially by the aldermen from among their own number or by taxpayers. State departments of local government regulate the organization of local government. State governments directly control some large interior areas.

Each state also has an appointed governor who serves as the representative of the Queen.

16 JUDICIAL SYSTEM

The constitution vests federal jurisdiction in a High Court of Australia which consists of a chief justice and six associate justices appointed by the governor general, who acts on the advice of the government. The High Court has the authority to conduct constitutional review of state and federal legislation and is the supreme authority on constitutional interpretation. The High Court also has original jurisdiction over interstate and international matters.

Until 1985, in certain cases involving state law, appeals from courts below the High Court could be taken to the Privy Council in the United Kingdom, the final court of the Commonwealth of Nations. Special cases may be referred to a 25-member federal court that deals with commercial law, copyright law, taxation, and trade practices. There is also a family court.

States and territories have their own court systems. Cases in the first instance are tried in local or circuit courts of general and petty sessions, magistrates' courts, children's courts, or higher state courts. Capital crimes are tried before state supreme courts.

The state and federal courts are fully independent. The High Court has ruled that indigent defendants have a right to counsel at state expense. Criminal defendants are presumed innocent, and a plethora of due process rights include the right to confront witnesses and the right to appeal. In 2002 the High Court ruled on various Aboriginal cases. Aborigines were denied rights to oil or minerals found under tribal land now being used by mining companies. Two long running land claim cases were settled: in the northwest a remote area slightly larger than Greece was granted to an Aboriginal tribe; however, a claim in eastern Australia in the Murray River area, land now occupied by farmers, was denied.

The law provides for the right to a fair trial. In local courts, the magistrates sit alone. In the higher courts, trials are usually conducted by judge and jury. The law prohibits arbitrary interference with privacy, family, home, or correspondence.

[17] ARMED FORCES

The International Institute for Strategic Studies reported that armed forces in Australia totaled 56,552 members in 2011. The force is comprised of 28,246 from the army, 14,250 from the navy, and 14,056 members of the air force. Armed forces represent .5% of the labor force in Australia. Defense spending totaled $26.5 billion and accounted for 3% of gross domestic product (GDP).

As of 2011, Australia had the largest group of troops from a non-NATO country fighting in Afghanistan. According to the US State Department, Australia planned to increase its army to 30,617 in 2011–12 and to 31,076 by 2014–15. The government has planned to increase defense funding by 3% annually through 2018, and 2011–12 funds covered 59,000 full-time military personnel and 23,350 reserves.

In April 2011, the United States moved more troops into Australia in order to have better access to the Asian Pacific. The South China Sea has been a crucial point of interest for both the United States and Australia, who have been allies since World War I. China has built up its military and staked claims on sovereignty in the South China Sea, causing some international disputes.

Australia contributed to peacekeeping missions in East Timor, Ethiopia/Eritrea, Egypt, and the Middle East.

[18] INTERNATIONAL COOPERATION

Australia is a charter member of the UN, to which it gained admission on 1 November 1945. It belongs to ESCAP and all the nonregional UN specialized agencies, such as the FAO, IFC, ILO, UNESCO, WHO, and the World Bank.

Australia became a member of the World Trade Organization on 1 January 1995. The country participates in the Commonwealth of Nations and ANZUS (Australia, New Zealand, United States Treaty).Other regional memberships include the Asian Development Bank, the European Bank for Reconstruction and Development, APEC (which Australia founded), the ASEAN Regional Forum, Colombo Plan, OECD, South Pacific Commission, the Pacific Community, the South Pacific Regional Trade and Economic Cooperation Agreement, the Pacific Island Forum, and the Paris Club (G-10). Australia also has a position on the Permanent Court of Arbitration. It joined the International Criminal Court in 2002.

The country belongs to the Australia Group, the Nuclear Energy Agency (of the OECD), the Nuclear Suppliers Group (London Group), the Zangger Committee, and the Organization for the Prohibition of Chemical Weapons. Australia sent troops as part of the coalition forces in the Persian Gulf War (1991), in Afghanistan (2002), and in Iraq (2003). The country has also supported UN efforts in Ethiopia, Eritrea and East Timor (Timor-Leste).

The ANZUS Treaty, signed in 1951, is Australia's pre-eminent security treaty alliance. The country also participates in the Australia-New Zealand-UK Agreement and the Five-Power Defense Arrangements to protect Singapore and Malaysia, and in a Trilateral Security Dialogue with the US and Japan.

Australia held a non-permanent seat on the UN Security Council in 1985–86, and was seeking that status for 2013–14.

In 2005 East Timor and Australia agreed to defer for 50 years the resolution of a boundary dispute. During that period, the two countries will divide evenly any hydrocarbon revenues produced outside the Joint Petroleum Development Area covered by the 2002 Timor Sea Treaty.

[19] ECONOMY

The GDP rate of change in Australia, as of 2011, was 2.7%. Inflation stood at 2.9%, and unemployment was reported at 5.1%. Australia was ranked as the world's 13th largest economy with a GDP of $1.3 trillion.

The government has projected that the economy will grow by 2.7% a year to 2050. Services dominate Australia's economy. However, most of its exports are derived from its agricultural and mining sectors.

Much of the country's economic prosperity rests in its small population, large geographic mass, and an abundance of natural resources. It has rich reserves of coal, iron ore, copper, gold, natural gas, uranium, and renewable energy sources. Australia was the world's largest net exporter of coal, which accounted for 29% of all global coal exports.

The structure of Australia's economy has changed over the past century as agriculture has declined in importance. Manufacturing, which reached peak levels in the 1950s and 1960s, declined through the next several decades before stabilizing at about 8.6% of GDP at the start of the second decade of the 21st century. Services have been dominant since 1950, and continued in 2012 to constitute a significant share of GDP. The largest service industry is finance, property, and business services. Other major service industries include retail and wholesale trade, transportation and communications, and construction.

Since the 1980s, Australia has shifted its economy from being inward looking and highly protected to a more open, internationally competitive export-oriented economy. The government has been engaged in a program to transform the economy's orientation from import substitution industrialization (ISI) to export-driven, high-tech globalization. This helped introduce an economic expansion from 1991 that, as of 2011, had continued uninterrupted—the longest economic expansion in Australia since 1945. This economic growth was sustained despite slowdowns occasioned by the 1997 Asian financial crisis, the 2001–02 global economic downturn, one of Australia's worst-ever droughts in 2003, and the 2008–09 global financial crisis. Strong consumption growth provided the momentum for Australia to withstand the Asian financial crisis, as the buoyant domestic economy offset the deterioration in regional demand for Australian exports.

Australia's last economic recession was in 1990, from which it began to recover in mid-1991. However, the unemployment rate of about 11% that year was near a postwar record. From this high point, around which unemployment hovered throughout 1991–1993, unemployment has been on a general decline in Australia, with few exceptions. The growth has been aided by reforms, low inflation, a housing market boom, and growing ties with China. The country has a higher standard of living than any G7 country except the United States. The Australian-US Free-Trade Agreement (AUSFTA) was completed in 2005 and is the first free trade agreement the United States has signed with a developed economy since the North American Free Trade Agreement with Canada.

The government responded to the 2008 global economic crisis by introducing a fiscal stimulus package worth more than $60 billion, and the Reserve Bank of Australia cut interest rates to historic lows. These steps allowed the economy to grow by 1.2% in 2009, and to keep unemployment in check. Unemployment was expected to reach 8%-10% but peaked at 5.7% in late 2009. Growth continued in 2010 and 2011, although there were concerns of recession in 2012 amid the uncertainty surrounding a European debt crisis that had come to the economic forefront during 2011.

Economic activity is focused on the country's eastern seaboard, where most of the population lives. There is a clear divide in economic performance between the states: typically, growth in South Australia and Tasmania is considerably below the overall national rate, and Western Australia is heavily dependent upon mining.

[20] INCOME

The CIA estimated that in 2010 the GDP of Australia was $882.4 billion. The CIA defines GDP as the value of all final goods and services produced within a nation in a given year and computed on the basis of purchasing power parity (PPP) rather than value as measured on the basis of the rate of the exchange based on current dollars. The per capita GDP was estimated at $41,000. The annual growth rate of GDP was 2.7%. The average inflation rate was 2.9%. It was estimated that agriculture accounted for 4% of GDP, industry 24.8%, and services 71.2%.

According to the World Bank, remittances from citizens living abroad totaled $4.1 billion or about $188 per capita and accounted for approximately .5% of GDP. It was estimated that household consumption was growing at an average annual rate of 3.9%. Australia, with 0.33% of the world's population, accounted for 1.22% of the world's GDP. By comparison, the United States, with 4.85% of the world's population, accounted for 22.51% of world GDP.

As of 2011 the most recent study by the World Bank reported that actual individual consumption in Australia was 65.9% of GDP and accounted for 1.20% of world consumption. By comparison, the United States accounted for 25.44% of world individual consumption.

[21] LABOR

As of 2010, Australia had a total labor force of 11.87 million people. Within that labor force, CIA estimates in 2009 noted that 3.6% were employed in agriculture, 21.1% in industry, and 75% in the service sector.

Union membership in 2009 was estimated at 20% of the total workforce and 14% of the private sector workforce. The public sector was more unionized at 45%. Unionization was 4% in the agricultural sector, 13% in retail, 22% in mining, 25% in manufacturing, and 20% in construction. Most of the country's unions were affiliated with the Australian Council of Trade Unions.

The March 2009 Fair Work Act became effective in 2010, replacing a previous Workplace Relations Act as the basic labor law for private-sector workers. The law requires companies to negotiate with workers in good faith if they wish to form unions and allows union representatives greater access to workplaces.

The federal minimum wage was increased in 2010 to $570 a week from $544 previously. It also allowed casual and part-time workers, contractors, and self-employed workers to be eligible for payment of up to 18 weeks of the national minimum. The US State Department's Human Rights Report on Australia reported that most workers earned more than the federal minimum, and that the minimum wage provided for a reasonable standard of living for workers and family members. A taxpayer-funded paid parental leave benefit took effect in January 2011.

[22] AGRICULTURE

Roughly 6% of the total land is farmed, and the country's major crops include wheat, barley, sugarcane, and fruits. Cereal production in 2009 amounted to 34.9 million tons, fruit production 3.4 million tons, and vegetable production 1.9 million tons.

Agriculture declined from 20% of GDP in the 1950s to about 3% in 2010. Still, Australia remained an important producer and exporter of agricultural products as well as a major world supplier of cereals, sugar, and fruit.

According to the Australian government's Department of Agriculture, Fisheries and Forestry, wheat was the major winter crop grown in the country. Wheat was grown in Western Australia, New South Wales, South Australia, Victoria, and Queensland and exported primarily to Indonesia, Japan, South Korea, Malaysia, Vietnam and Sudan.

Raw and refined sugar was produced from sugarcane grown primarily in northern Queensland. More than 80% of the sugar was produced for export, and Australia was the second largest raw sugar exporter in the world. Key markets were South Korea, Indonesia, Japan, and Malaysia.

Cotton grown in the inland regions of northern New South Wales and southern Queensland was sold to spinning mills in China, Indonesia, Thailand, South Korea, Japan, Taiwan, Pakistan, and Italy. According to the government, Australia was one of the world's largest exporters of raw cotton and exported more than 90% of the cotton produced.

Rice also was grown for domestic use and export, primarily to Japan.

Australia's wide climate differences permit the cultivation of a range of fruits, from pineapples in the tropical zone to berry fruits in the cooler areas of temperate zones. Orchard fruit trees included orange, apple, pear, and mango. Production of fruit included oranges, bananas, pineapples, pears, peaches, tangerines, lemons and limes, apricots, grapefruit, mangoes, and plums. Australia has a significant wine industry.

Approximately 90% of the utilized land area is in its natural state or capable of only limited improvement and is used largely for rough grazing. Droughts, fires, and floods are common hazards.

Lack of water is the principal limiting factor, but unsuitable soil and topography are also important determinants.

Severe droughts in the first years of the 21st century followed by torrential flooding in 2010 caused significant strain to the country's agricultural sector. The 2006 census found that 10,636 families ceased farming between 2001 and 2006. In addition, the government has identified climate change as a key threat to Australia's agriculture. Its Climate Change Research Program was aimed at working with farmers to reduce greenhouse gas emissions and improve soil management practices to keep the agricultural sector resilient.

23 ANIMAL HUSBANDRY

The UN Food and Agriculture Organization (FAO) reported that Australia dedicated 372.9 million hectares (921.5 million acres) to permanent pasture or meadow in 2009. During that year, the country tended 95.4 million chickens, 27.9 million head of cattle, and 2.3 million pigs. The production from these animals amounted to 917,807 tons of beef and veal, 485,242 tons of pork, 829,440 tons of poultry, 130,952 tons of eggs, and 4.82 million tons of milk. Australia also produced 252,000 tons of cattle hide and 370,601 tons of raw wool.

Much of the livestock raised in Australia produced meat for both the domestic and export markets. Australia was one of the world's largest exporters of beef, mutton, and lamb. In addition, about half of the world's greasy wool was grown in Australia.

About 52% of Australia's land is used in stock raising. Animal husbandry is concentrated in the eastern highlands, but it spreads across the wide interior spaces and even to low-rainfall areas, in which up to 12 ha (30 acres) are required to support one sheep and from which cattle must be taken overland hundreds of miles to coastal meat-packing plants.

Sheep raising has been a mainstay of the economy since the 1820s, when mechanization of the British textile industry created a huge demand for wool. Wool demand grew through the 19th and much of the 20th century before stabilizing in the 1970s. As of the first decade of the 21st century, Australia accounted for 75% of the world's exports of wool apparel. However, droughts in the 1990s and early 21st century have caused the number of sheep in the country to diminish.

Sheep of the Merino breed, noted for its heavy wool yield, make up about three-quarters of Australian flocks.

Butter and honey also were produced in Australia.

24 FISHING

Australia had 1,100 decked commercial fishing boats in 2008. The annual capture totaled 178,576 tons according to the UN FAO. The export value of seafood totaled $939.1 million.

Australia's fishing zone is the third largest in the world, extending 200 nautical miles out to sea. The government reported that the waters were less productive than others in the region, and that Australia ranked 52nd in the world in terms of the volume of fish landed in 2008. According to the government, the commercial fishing and aquaculture industry was worth more than $2 billion annually. Fisheries production focused on lobsters, prawns, tuna, salmon, and abalone.

25 FORESTRY

Approximately 19% of Australia is covered by forest. The UN FAO estimated the 2009 roundwood production at 25.3 million cu m (893.6 million cu ft). The value of all forest products, including roundwood, totaled $1.48 billion.

Most timberland is neither exploited nor potentially exploitable. Native forests cover 50.2 million ha (124 million acres), 31% of the forested area, of which 23% is privately owned and 77% is state forest, crown land, and permanent national parks or reserves. National parks and wildlife preserves occupy about 3.8 million ha (9.4 million acres), or 9% of the total forestlands. About 60% of the state forest areas were available for sustainable logging. Native forests consist principally of hardwood and other fine cabinet and veneer timbers; eucalyptus dominates about 35 million ha (86.5 million acres).

Limited softwood resources had become seriously depleted, but new plantations were established in the 1980s at a rate of 33,000 ha (81,500 acres) annually. Softwood plantations supply more than half the timber harvested annually. Since 1990, plantings have shifted from primarily softwood to mostly hardwood. About 90% of the standing hardwood plantations were planted after 1990.

Australia's leading forest products are softwood logs and chips. Whereas all of the softwood log production is consumed at home, all commercial woodchip production is exported.

The government of Australia has established initiatives to encourage the growth of forestry plantations, and to support Aboriginal and indigenous people involvement in forestry enterprises.

26 MINING

Australia is one of the world's leading producers of minerals, ranking among the world's top nations in terms of economic demonstrated resources (EDR) for lead, mineral sands, nickel, silver, tantalum, uranium, and zinc. In addition, its EDR ranked the country among the top six for bauxite, black coal, brown coal, cobalt, copper, gem and near-gem diamonds, gold, iron ore, lithium, manganese ore, and rare-earth oxides, The country is virtually self-sufficient in mineral commodities, commercially producing more than 60 minerals and metals. In 2009, Australia was one of the world's leading exporters of alumina, bauxite, coal, diamond, ilmenite, iron ore (the country's fourth-largest minerals earner), refined lead, rutile, and zircon.

Gold production in 2009 was 222,000 kg, down from 296,410 kg in 2000. Western Australia was the largest gold producer. Australia has around 8% of the world's gold resources, and produces about 10% of the worlds mined gold output. This output ranks fourth in the world, behind China, South Africa and the United States, respectively.

Australia was the leading bauxite producer in 2009, with 64% coming from Western Australia. In 2009, Australia produced 19,948,000 tons of alumina and 65,231,000 tons of bauxite. Bauxite deposits in northern Queensland were among the world's largest; those in the Northern Territory were also in production.

Australia also ranked second in iron ore (with 17% of world production), mined cobalt, and mined zinc; and was fifth in mined copper. Australia produced 1,635 metric tons of mined silver in 2009.

In 2009, Australia produced 220,000 carats of gem diamond (15,136,000 carats in 2002), and 10,575,000 carats of industrial diamond (25,730,000 carats in 2005). Reserves were estimated at 105 million carats of gem and near-gem diamond, and 109 million of industrial diamond. Argyle's principal diamond ore body, the AK-1 lamproite pipe, near Kununurra, Western Australia, produced nearly twice the amount of diamond as any other in the world, able to supply 30 million carats a year, including some of the highest diamond grades-about 5% was of gem quality, including a small number of very rare pink diamonds; 40% was of near gem quality; and 55% was of industrial quality.

The value of opal produced in 2009 was AUD20 million. Lightning Ridge, in New South Wales, was the world's major source of black opal. Australia also produces 30% of the world's rough sapphire; commercial production came from alluvial deposits. Jade was discovered in the form of nephrite, at the world's largest identified resource, in the Eyre Peninsula. Australia produces most of the world's chrysoprase, known as Australian jade. Other gemstones produced in the country include agate, amethyst, chiastolite, emerald (aquamarine), garnet, rhodonite, topaz, tourmaline, turquoise, and zircon.

Iron ore production in 2009 was 394,000 tons, 97% percent of iron ore came from the Pilbara region. Reserves were estimated to be 28 billion tons.

The country produced 59,000 tons of contained copper in 2009, down from 930,000 in 2005. Reserves were estimated to be 80 million tons. WMC's Olympic Dam underground mine, in South Australia, was the country's largest copper mine, and a <empha-sis n="4">us</emphasis>$1.1 billion expansion program was expected to increase production from 200,000 tons per year to 235,000 tons. Queensland is the leading state for mined copper production, mostly from the Mount Isa region, accounting for 31% of Australia's output in 2009.

Zinc output in 2009 was 1,290,000 tons, 15% of world output, with reserves of 56 million tons. The McArthur River base-metal mine, in the Northern Territory, had record-setting tonnages of bulk concentrate.

In 2009, the country produced 4,451,000 tons of manganese ore (48% manganese content), with reserves of 181 million tons. Groote Eylandt Mining Co. mined about 10% of the world's manganese at its 3.1-million-ton capacity Eylandt open cut operations, in the Gulf of Carpentaria. Lead output, 56,600 tons (reserves of 29 million tons); nickel, 165,000 tons, all from Western Australia, with reserves of 24 million tons; and tin, 5,400 tons (2011), all by Australia's only producer, Renison Bell Mine, in Tasmania, with reserves of 176,000 tons.

Australia had a substantial portion of the world's mineral sand resources—about 29% for ilmenite, 31% for rutile, and 46% for zircon—and in 2009 produced 15% of the world's ilmenite (1,449,000 tons, with reserves of 200 million), 47% of the world's rutile (281,000 tons, with reserves of 23 million), and 474,000 metric tons of zirconium, with reserves of 40 million tons. The dominant producer of zircon was Iluka Resources, with a capacity of 300 tons per year. Australia was also one of the world's leading producers of titanium. In 2009, the Greenbushes Mine, south of Perth, was the world's largest and highest-grade resource for spodumene (a lithium ore), 197,482 tons of which was produced in the country.

Other industrial minerals produced in Australia in 2009 included clays, diatomite, gypsum (3.5 million tons), limestone (19 million tons), magnesite (125,000 metric tons, with reserves of 330 million tons), phosphate rock (2.8 billion tons), salt, sand and gravel, silica, and dimension stone (230,000 tons).

In June 2010, Prime Minister Gillard forged a compromise with mining companies to tax profits on coal and iron ore at 30%. However, under the new plan, Australia will forego roughly $1.3 billion in revenue over the first few years. Australia's federal government drafted a tax proposal to eliminate state royalty taxes on mining projects and replace them with a uniform national rent tax beginning in 2012 to shift the tax burden from low profitability projects to more profitable ones.

[27] ENERGY AND POWER

The World Bank reported in 2008 that Australia produced 257.1 billion kWh of electricity and consumed 240.4 billion kWh, or 11,044 kWh per capita. Roughly 95% of energy came from fossil fuels, while 1% came from alternative fuels. Per capita oil consumption was 6,071 kg.

Major electric power undertakings, originally privately owned and operated, were by 1952 under the control of state organizations. In the early 1990s however, many of the Australian state governments began privatizing sections of their energy utilities. Manufacturing has been developed most extensively in or near coal areas, and distribution of electricity to principal users is therefore relatively simple. All major cities except Perth use 240-volt, 50-cycle, three-phase alternating current; Perth has 250-volt, 40-cycle, single-phase alternating current.

The Snowy Mountains hydroelectric scheme in southeast New South Wales, Australia's most ambitious public works project, comprises 7 power stations, a pumping station, 16 large and many smaller dams, and 145 km (90 mi) of tunnels and 80 km (50 mi) of aqueducts. It provides electricity to the Australian Capital Territory, New South Wales, and Victoria. The project took 25 years to complete and has a generating capacity of 3,740 MW (about 10% of Australia's total generating capacity). The Snowy Mountains scheme and other large power projects in New South Wales, Victoria, and Tasmania have greatly increased the nation's aggregate installed capacity. The only state with water resources sufficient for continuous operation of large hydroelectric power stations is Tasmania, which possesses about 50% of Australia's hydroelectric energy potential. Production and use of such power is on the increase throughout the country, however.

Since 1986, Australia has been the world's largest exporter of coal and was expected to continue to dominate international coal trade; expansions and new terminals at the port of Newcastle could add more than 1.0 quadrillion Btu of additional coal export capacity in New South Wales. Queensland's Dalrymple Bay port was also expanding capacity. As of 2008, Australia was supplying 75% the demand in Asia for coking coal, which can be used as a fuel. The major market is Japan, which imports about 50% of Australia's coal exports. Around 80% of Australia's coal was bituminous and 20% was lignite. New South Wales and Queensland account for more than 95% of Australia's black coal production and virtually all its exports.

In early 1983, Alcoa Australia signed a contract with the Western Australian State Energy Commission, at an estimated cost of AUD11.2 billion, to supply natural gas from the Northwest Shelf (the North West Gas Shelf Project—NWGSP). In 1985 eight Japanese companies agreed to buy 5.84 million tons of liquefied natural gas (LNG) a year from 1989 to 2009. Capacity has continued to increase, due to completion of additional offshore platforms and onshore facilities. Proved reserves of natural gas were estimated at 3.115 trillion cu m in 2010.

In early 1992, petroleum exploration began in the Timor Sea; the area had been off limits for over a decade in order to establish a zone of cooperation with Indonesia. In 2001 Australia, Phillips Petroleum, and the newly independent state of East Timor renegotiated arrangements for development of the Bayu Undan oil field in the Timor Sea. Oil production, which began in 1964, totaled 549,200 barrels per day in 2010; proven reserves at the end of 2011 totaled 3.318 billion barrels.

28 INDUSTRY

The CIA estimated the industrial production rate of change at 4.5% in 2010. Key industries were mining, industrial and transportation equipment, food processing, chemicals, and steel.

Australia was one of the world's most highly industrialized countries as of 2012. It was the world's largest exporter of black coal, the second-largest exporter of gold, and the third-largest exporter of aluminum and bauxite. It also had exports of diamonds, iron ore, lead, rutile, zinc, and zirconium. About 50% of the mineral production was in Western Australia, where there were more than 1,200 operating mine sites and 170 processing plants. About 90% of the coal mined in Australia was in Queensland and New South Wales. Nearly 70% of the $500 million of mining equipment used in this industry was imported.

Another significant industry was oil and natural gas production, with $150 billion in projects underway in 2010, according to the US State Department's 2011 guide to Doing Business in Australia. Most oil and gas production occurred in areas offshore from Western Australia, where the Gorgon and Wheatstone projects were based. In Queensland, there was onshore drilling and production in areas where coal bed methane and oil shale were shored.

Australia in 2010 had emerged as a world leader in photovoltaic technology, as well as wind and hydro power. Projects worth nearly $1.5 billion were underway in 2010.

About 450 companies formed a strong biotechnology industry as of 2011. Working in Victoria, New South Wales, and Queensland, these companies were involved in human therapeutics (49%), agricultural biotechnology (16%), and diagnostics (13%).

Australia's aerospace and aviation industry included small and medium businesses that repaired and maintained aircraft, and manufactured airframe components, engines, and engine components.

The manufacturing sector underwent significant expansion in the early through mid 20th century but began to decline in the 1970s as a share of GDP as the services sector exploded.

According to the US State Department, it constituted about 8.5% of GDP in 2010 compared with 13% in 2000. Traditional textiles, processed foods, automobiles, chemicals, specialty steels, plastics, high speed ferries, telecommunications equipment, and motor vehicles were among the items produced.

Australia is self-sufficient in beverages, most foods, building materials, many common chemicals, some domestic electrical appliances, radios, plastics, textiles, and clothing; in addition, most of its needed communications equipment, farm machinery (except tractors), furniture, leather goods, and metal manufactures are domestically produced.

29 SCIENCE AND TECHNOLOGY

Patent applications in science and technology as of 2009, according to the World Bank, totaled 2,821 in Australia. Public financing of science was 2.06% of GDP.

Australia's research and development tradition has been long and consistent. The country's educational program emphasizes high-quality science education, and many of its 39 universities emphasize scientific, agricultural, and medical research. According to the US State Department about 2.5% of the world's published and patented research was produced in Australia.

The development of penicillin, Cochlear hearing implants, Resmed treatment of sleep apnea, Relenza flu drug, and the Gardasil cervical cancer vaccine all have been credited to Australian researchers.

According to the government, about 50,000 people in higher educational organizations were working in research and development in 2008, while 36,000 were employed in the business sector, and 19,000 in governmental agencies and laboratories. About 16,000 science students and 9,000 engineering students graduated annually from Australian universities.

The Commonwealth Scientific and Industrial Research Organization (CSIRO), founded in 1926, is an independent government agency that supports research in agribusiness, information technology, manufacturing, health, sustainable energy, mining and minerals, space exploration, environmental sustainability, and natural resources. As of 2008, its staff included 4,000 scientists and 2,500 others working in more than 50 laboratories and field stations.

The government has identified information and communications technology, biotechnology, manufacturing, mining, and the food industry as its research and development priorities.

30 DOMESTIC TRADE

There are many small specialty shops, but in the larger cities department stores sell all kinds of items. Supermarkets have been widely established and telephone shopping and delivery services are becoming popular.

The World Bank ranked Australia as the world's second easiest place to open a business in 2010. The US State Department's 2011 guide to Doing Business in Australia reported 1,025 business franchise systems operating in Australia along with 6,500 fuel retail outlets and 2,130 motor vehicle retail outlets. Most of these outlets were Australian owned.

The language, cultural environments, and customer expectations of Australians are similar to those of Americans. Business

Principal Trading Partners – Australia (2010)

(In millions of US dollars)

Country	Total	Exports	Imports	Balance
World	405,465.0	212,362.0	193,103.0	19,259.0
China	89,326.0	53,111.0	36,215.0	16,896.0
Japan	56,802.0	40,075.0	16,727.0	23,348.0
United States	29,921.0	8,464.0	21,457.0	-12,993.0
South Korea	25,407.0	18,840.0	6,567.0	12,273.0
India	16,844.0	15,029.0	1,815.0	13,214.0
Thailand	15,480.0	5,383.0	10,097.0	-4,714.0
Singapore	14,249.0	4,445.0	9,804.0	-5,359.0
New Zealand	14,000.0	7,365.0	6,635.0	730.0
United Kingdom	12,950.0	7,608.0	5,342.0	2,266.0
Malaysia	11,676.0	3,347.0	8,329.0	-4,982.0

(…) data not available or not significant.

(n.s.) not specified.

SOURCE: *2011 Direction of Trade Statistics Yearbook,* New York: United Nations, 2011.

hours generally are 9 a.m. to 5 p.m. Monday through Friday, with shops in major cities open on weekends and often on evenings. Banks are open from 9 a.m. to 4 p.m. Monday through Friday, and most have 24-hour automated teller machines.

Travelers checks and credit cards are widely accepted. A goods and services tax (GST) replaced wholesale and state sales taxes as of 1 July 2000. The GST, 10% as of 2010, applies to most goods and services with a few exceptions, including basic foods, education, and health care.

Most advertising is done through the press, radio, and television. Principal advertising agencies are in Sydney and Melbourne.

The business environment often slows in December and January when many Australians take annual vacations that coincide with the summer school vacation period.

Electronic commerce (e-commerce) is well established in Australia, and is growing at a rapid pace in both the business-to-consumer (B2C) and business-to-business (B2B) sectors.

31 FOREIGN TRADE

Australia imported an estimated $194.7 billion worth of goods and services in 2010, compared with $169 million in 2009. Major import partners in 2010 were China, 18.7%; the US, 11.1%; Japan, 8.7%; Thailand, 5.2%; Singapore, 5.1%; Germany, 5%; and Malaysia, 4.3%. Major import commodities were machinery and transportation equipment, computers and office machines, telecommunications equipment and parts, and crude oil and petroleum products.

Australia's exports for 2010 were estimated at $212.9 billion compared with $154.8 billion in 2009. Major export partners were China, 25.1%; Japan, 18.9%; South Korea, 8.9%; India, 7.1%; and the US, 4%. Major export commodities were coal, iron ore, gold, meat, wood, aluminum products, wheat, machinery and transportation equipment.

Australia has signed free trade agreements with New Zealand, the US, Chile, Singapore, and Thailand. As of 2011, it was negotiating or considering free trade agreements with China, Japan, Malaysia, South Korea, India, Indonesia, and the Gulf Cooperative Council.

The country participates actively in the World Trade Organization and the Asia Pacific Economic Cooperation (APEC), where it has promoted trade liberalization policies. About 70% of Australia's overall exports were going to APEC members as of 2011.

Australia has made its economy increasingly open to foreign trade since the 1980s. It has reduced high tariffs and other protective barriers to free trade, deregulated its financial services sector, and privatized many former government-owned monopolies. It also has simplified its taxation system with the introduction in 2000 of a broad-based Goods and Services Tax (GST), and cut income tax rates significantly.

US items constituted about one-third of Australia's construction machinery imports, from such manufacturers as Caterpillar, Case New Holland, John Deere, Ingersoll-Rank, Bobcat, Vermeer, Manitowoc, Terex, and Ditch Witch. Japan and Germany also were key machinery suppliers through Komatsu, Hitachi, Kobelco, Kawasaki, Kubota, Sumitomo, Liebherr, Demag, and Bomag. In addition, the US, Japan, and Germany supplied Australia with much of its mining equipment, and US software made up 38% of the country's software imports in 2009.

Mining exports accounted for 37.2% of total exports in the 12-month period ending October 2008, compared to 18.9% in the 12-month period ending October 1998. Manufacturing exports accounted for 35.3% of total exports in the 12-month period ending October 2008, down from 46.2% in the 12-month period ending October 1998. Agriculture exports accounted for 3.9% of total exports in the 12-month period ending October 2008, down from 8.7% in the 12-month period ending October 1998.

32 BALANCE OF PAYMENTS

The CIA estimated Australia's current account balance at -$30.4 billion in 2010 compared with -$43.89 billion in 2009. The current account deficit also was down from $52.5 billion in 2008. The

Balance of Payments – Australia (2010)

(In millions of US dollars)

Current Account		-31,990.0
Balance on goods		18,180.0
Imports	-194,670.0	
Exports	212,850.0	
Balance on services		-2,980.0
Balance on income		-45,803.0
Current transfers		-1,388.0
Capital Account		-213.0
Financial Account		32,940.0
Direct investment abroad		-24,526.0
Direct investment in Australia		30,576.0
Portfolio investment assets		-42,407.0
Portfolio investment liabilities		109,561.0
Financial derivatives		316.0
Other investment assets		-13,544.0
Other investment liabilities		-27,035.0
Net Errors and Omissions		-303.0
Reserves and Related Items		-434.0

(…) data not available or not significant.

SOURCE: *Balance of Payment Statistics Yearbook 2011,* Washington, DC: International Monetary Fund, 2011.

figure had been rising since 2003 when the current account deficit was $23.388 billion.

Australia's reserves of foreign exchange and gold were estimated at $42.27 billion as of 31 December 2010 compared with $41.74 billion on 31 December 2009.

33BANKING AND SECURITIES

The US State Department's 2011 guide to Doing Business in Australia described its banking system as one of the world's most resilient. Its four leading banks were among the world's top 12 in 2010 in terms of financial security and AA rankings. The total assets in Australia's largest banks were valued at $2.5 trillion in March 2010. About 1.1% of the country's bank loans were non-performing.

The Reserve Bank of Australia is responsible for setting monetary policy and regulating the payment system, while the Australian Prudential Regulation Authority is tasked with overseeing banks, credit unions, building societies, general insurance and reinsurance companies, life insurance, co-ops, and members of the superannuation industry. The institutions under the Authority's supervision held assets totaling $3.6 trillion.

The four largest retail banks are Westpac Banking Corp., Commonwealth Bank, Australian New Zealand Bank, and National Australia Bank. These banks controlled about 80% of the home mortgage market and managed 75% of deposits. There were a large number of smaller banks in the country as well as a number of foreign-owned banks.

The banking system has undergone progressive privatization and foreign investment since the deregulation of financial markets in the 1980s. Fifty banks operate in Australia, 35 of which are foreign-owned.

The Australian currency has floated freely since 1983. In the Statement on the Conduct of Monetary Policy issued in 2007, the Reserve Bank set a target for the annual inflation rate at 2–3%.

The Australian Stock Exchange (ASX) was established on 1 April 1987. In 2009, it was the 13th largest exchange in the world, with market capitalization of shares of domestic companies at $1.3 trillion. There were 2,050 listed companies in 2009.

34INSURANCE

The Australian government reported that the country's insurance sector was the 12th largest in the world as of 2010. The market generally includes life insurers, health insurers who products complement the government's Medicare health care scheme, and general insurers.

The Australian Prudential Regulation Authority oversees the insurance industry. According to a semi-annual reporting bulletin published on 21 December 2011, net premiums from 30 June 2010 through 30 June 2011 were AUD38.4 billion compared with AUD39.6 billion from the same period a year earlier. Net policy payments totaled AUD34.8 billion in the 30 June 2010 through 30 June 2011 period compared with AUD37.5 billion a year earlier.

Life insurance firms, through premiums on policies and interest earned on accumulated funds, account for substantial annual savings. The companies invest in government securities, in company securities (including shares and fixed-interest obligations), and in mortgage loans and loans against policies in force. Most loans (to individuals and building societies) are for housing.

Motor-vehicle third-party liability, workers' compensation, professional indemnity for certain professions, and Medicare coverage are compulsory.

35PUBLIC FINANCE

In 2010 the budget of Australia included $396.1 billion in public revenue and $426.5 billion in public expenditures. The budget deficit amounted to 3.4% of GDP. Public debt was 22.4% of GDP, with $1.268 trillion of the debt held by foreign entities.

The CIA reported in 2011 that the budget deficit would likely peak below 4.2% of GDP, and that budget surpluses could be restored by 2015.

The fiscal year begins 1 July and ends 30 June. After World War II, the government assumed greater responsibility for maintaining full employment and a balanced economy, as well as for providing a wide range of social services. Social security and welfare payments are the largest category of government expenditure. The central government has financed almost all its defense and capital works programs from revenue and has made available to the states money raised by public loans for public works programs.

In 2000, the government implemented a 10% goods and services tax (GST) on all items, while income tax and corporate tax rates were cut. In the budget year 2008–09, further tax cuts of over four years were announced.

The Australian government estimated that 2008/09 central government revenues amounted to AUD319.5 billion (25.5% of GDP) and had expenditures of AUD292.5 billion (23.8% of GDP). Revenues minus expenditures totaled approximately AUD27 billion.

36TAXATION

Australia's main federal taxes are a personal income tax, a corporate tax, and a goods and services tax. The income tax rate as of

---

Public Finance – Australia (2009)

(In millions of Australian dollars, central government figures)

Revenue and Grants	**309,678**	**100.0%**
Tax revenue	277,999	89.8%
Social contributions	674	0.2%
Grants	31,005	10.0%
Other revenue	...	...
Expenditures	**340,190**	**100.0%**
General public services	73,178	21.5%
Defense	21,932	6.4%
Public order and safety	3,558	1.0%
Economic affairs	24,513	7.2%
Environmental protection	1,768	0.5%
Housing and community amenities	3,985	1.2%
Health	49,153	14.4%
Recreational, culture, and religion	2,906	0.9%
Education	34,167	10.0%
Social protection	125,030	36.8%

(...) data not available or not significant.

SOURCE: *Government Finance Statistics Yearbook 2010,* Washington, DC: International Monetary Fund, 2010.

November 2010 was a progressive rate up to 45%; the corporate tax rate was 30% and the goods and services tax (GST) was 10%.

Individuals are also subject to capital gains taxes, fuel taxes, and excise taxes on alcohol, tobacco products, luxury cars, and oil. There is also a 1.5% levy on residents to fund the nation's healthcare program, plus a 1% surcharge for those in high income brackets.

At the state and municipal levels, property taxes, and stamp duties on land transfers are imposed. States also assess corporations a payroll tax based on wages paid out to employees.

The goods and services tax was introduced in July 2000 as part of a tax overhaul. The GST replaced most sales taxes. Basic foods, education, health, and some other sectors are exempted from the tax.

A First Home Owners Scheme (FHOS) that made grants available to first-time homebuyers was eliminated in 2010.

In 2011 the Australian Senate approved a carbon tax rate that was to take effect in July 2012. The tax charged the nation's top 500 polluters a fixed rate of A$23 (US$23.78) per ton of carbon emission through July 2015. After July 2015, companies would be able to participate in an emissions trading scheme.

[37] CUSTOMS AND DUTIES

According to the US State Department, custom duty rates are dependent on factors such as the type of goods entering Australia as well as the country of origin.

The Free Trade Agreement between the US and Australia, effective 1 January 2005, eliminated tariffs on 99% of US-made industrial and consumer goods and 100% of US agricultural products. Tariffs on non US products generally are 5% or less, except for such commodities as motor vehicles, clothing and footwear.

Before the 1980s, federal policy was to use the tariff to protect local industries (especially the automobile industry), but a three-decade long program of tariff reduction led to tariff rates of 5% or below in 2000. The GST of 10% applies for most imports and exports in addition to the duty. Tariffs on industrial machinery and capital equipment ordinarily are low where they do not compete with Australian enterprise and machinery and equipment required by new industries may be imported duty-free or at concessional rates under the Project-By-Law Scheme (PBS).

As a contracting party to GATT, Australia consented to a number of tariff reductions after 1947. Under the South Pacific Regional Trade and Economic Cooperation Agreement (SPARTECA), which went into effect on 1 January 1981, Australia and New Zealand offered the other South Pacific Forum members duty-free or concessional access to their markets. The Australia New Zealand Closer Economic Relations Trade Agreement (ANZCERTA, abbreviated to CER) opened bilateral trade between the two countries in 1983. Australia is also a member of the Asia Pacific Economic Cooperation (APEC) forum.

[38] FOREIGN INVESTMENT

Foreign direct investment (FDI) in Australia was a net inflow of $22.6 billion, according to World Bank figures published in 2009. FDI represented 2.44% of GDP.

Australia has welcomed foreign investment and its stable, well managed economy has attracted strong capital. The 2007 A.T.

Kearney FDI Confidence Index ranked Australia as the eleventh most attractive destination in the world for foreign direct investment. China ranked first followed by India, the United States, and the United Kingdom.

As of 2010, the US was the largest direct investor in Australia while Australia was the ninth largest source of FDI for the US. US investment in Australia totaled $514 billion in 2009, while Australian investment in the US totaled $404 billion. US FDI funds accounted for 23% of the total foreign investment in Australia and were largely in resources and energy, manufacturing, and non-bank financial services sectors. Other large sources of FDI in Australia were China ($26.6 billion), Japan ($22.1 billion), the UK ($20.3 billion), and France ($7.5 billion).

According to the US State Department, many multinational corporate players were engaged in projects in Australia. These companies included Apache, BP, Chevron, Conoco-Phillips, Exxon, Shell, BHP-Billiton, Santos, Woodside, Halliburton, Schlumberger, and Technip.

The 1975 Foreign Acquisitions and Takeovers Act regulates inward FDI. In 2008–09, 5,352 proposals received foreign investment approval compared with 7,841 in 2007–08.

Overall, the level of foreign investment had reached $1.9 trillion by 2009, while the level of Australian investment abroad had reached $1.13 trillion. Besides the US, Australian foreign investment was directed toward the UK, New Zealand, Canada, Japan, France, Hong Kong, and the Netherlands.

The worldwide commodities boom of 2006–07 boosted investment in Australia's mining industry, particularly in New South Wales which accounted for 22% of the national total. Overall, almost a quarter of foreign direct investment in Australia is invested in the mining industry. Manufacturing accounts for 19%, followed by wholesale and retail trade (17%), finance and insurance (15%), transport and communication (8.6%), and property and business services (6.5%).

[39] ECONOMIC DEVELOPMENT

Australia's economic health in the 20th century was rooted initially in its agricultural sector. As the nation industrialized, its rich mineral, oil, coal, and natural gas deposits became the primary economic driver. As Australia entered the second decade of the 21st century, the government defined knowledge-based systems and technologies as critical to its economy. According to the consulting firm A.T. Kearney, Australia was the third most technology-savvy country in the world by 2007.

The government sees aggressive promotion of Australia as an "information economy" as helping to reduce a competitive disadvantage caused by Australia's distant geographic location.

According to the US State Department's 2011 guide to Doing Business in Australia, numerous infrastructure projects were in place to increase the access and quality of Internet service throughout the country. The federal government planned to spend $30 billion on a high-speed fibre-to-the-home network across the country, and had implemented the project in parts of Tasmania by 2010. The Australian government reported that the country's information and communications technology market was worth approximately $89 billion in 2008, with 25,000 companies employing 236,000 information technology specialists.

Historically, the government has sought to keep the economy stable while working to ensure that basic needs of its people would be met. The pre-sovereign commonwealth and state governments devoted special attention to the production and marketing of main primary products, and after 1920, legislation provided subsidies or other marketing aids to certain commodities. Price controls were in effect during World War II and part of the postwar period.

Federal and state aid was given to industries established in approved fields of manufacture during the 1970s. The Export Market Development Grant Acts of 1974 provided government assistance in the development of export markets.

As an alternative to price controls, the Commonwealth government, in mid-1975, introduced a policy of wage indexing, allowing wages to rise as fast as, but no faster than, consumer prices. Major labor unions, however, opposed this restraint, which was ended in 1981, in the wake of the second oil shock and the onset of global recession. Monetary policy supported recovery from the recession of the early 1980s by holding to a low inflation rate. From the mid-1980s, Australia's government embarked on a basic re-orientation of the economy from inward-looking import substitution industrialization (ISI) to outward-looking export-led growth and liberalization. The transformation and opening of the economy helped produce consecutive economic growth from 1992 to 2011, exceeding in duration the expansions of the 1960s, 1970s, and 1980s.

This economic success has been strengthened by sound economic management. But it also has stretched the country's infrastructure to the limit, causing the government to create an organization in 2008 called "Infrastructure Australia" to address the problem. The US State Department reported in its 2011 guide to Doing Business in Australia that infrastructure improvements were planned in transportation, mining, electricity, telecommunications, sewers and water supply as well as freight and port facilities. These developments were expected to help Australia's construction industry grow 3.8% annually from 2013 to 18.

An increased demand for liquefied natural gas, oil, and petroleum products has been fueling exploration, development, and production in existing and new oil and gas fields across the country. Much of this demand is due to increased energy needs of Japan, Korea, and China. It also was due to a growing interest to use gas as a cleaner alternative to burning coal.

The government also has set a target of reducing greenhouse gas emissions by 60% from their 2000 levels by 2050, and has committed to supplying at least 20% of Australia's electricity supply from renewable energy sources by 2020. The government committed $2 billion to clean energy initiatives in its 2009–10 budget.

An important area of priority is care of the nation's indigenous peoples. On 19 October 2011, the government released an Indigenous Economic Development Strategy for 2011–18 that aimed to increase the well-being of its Aboriginal and indigenous population through five priorities: stronger economic development foundations in indigenous communities, educational investments, improved access to skills development and job opportunities, growth of indigenous business and entrepreneurship; and increasing the financial security and independence of indigenous individuals and communities through personal financial education.

40 SOCIAL DEVELOPMENT

Social Security measures have been in effect since 1908 and cover all residents. Old age pensions are payable to men 65 years of age and over, and to women 62.5 years of age and over, who have lived in Australia continuously for at least 10 years at some stage in their lives. The continuous-residence requirement may be waived for those who have been residents for numerous shorter periods. Disability pensions are payable to persons 16 years of age and older who have lived at least five years in Australia and have become totally incapacitated or permanently blind. The family allowance legislation provides for weekly payments to children under 16 years of age. Widows' pensions are also provided. Employed persons are covered by workers' compensation, and unemployment assistance is provided for those aged 21 to 65. Youths aged between 16 and 20 are eligible for the youth training allowance, administered by the Department of Employment, Education and Training. Work-related sickness and maternity benefits are provided, as well as medical benefits for all residents. There are numerous programs in place for families of limited means, including child care and rent assistance.

The Sex Discrimination Act bars discrimination on the basis of sex, marital status or pregnancy. The Office for Women was created to monitor the position of women in society. Sexual harassment is specifically prohibited by law, and is aggressively addressed by the government. Sex discrimination complaints were down in 2004 by seven percent. Domestic violence remains a problem, particularly in Aboriginal communities. The government has a strong commitment to the welfare of children.

In 2003–04 gay and lesbian issues were politicized. In May 2003, the resignation of Governor-General Peter Hollingworth followed his revelation that, as an Anglican archbishop in the 1990s, he permitted a known pedophile to remain a priest. In July of that same year, a congregation protested an Australian Christian church vote to allow homosexuals to become priests. In May 2004, the government introduced legislation to prohibit same-sex marriages. As of 2011, Same sex marriage was banned, although the Labour Party endorsed legalization, despite opposition from Prime Minister Gillard. The Labour Party agreed that any legalization legislation would be put to popular referendum. The government also announced that same-sex partners would be recognized for the first time by federal authorities as dependents.

Discrimination on the basis of race, color, descent or national or ethnic origin was prohibited in the Racial Discrimination Act of 1975. Despite these measures, Aboriginal Australians have poorer standards of living, are imprisoned more often, and die younger than white Australians.

41 HEALTH

According to the CIA, life expectancy in Australia was 82 years in 2011. The country spent 17.1% of its GDP on healthcare, amounting to $3,867 per person. There were 30 physicians, 96 nurses and midwives, and 38 hospital beds per 10,000 inhabitants. The fertility rate was 1.9, while the infant mortality rate was 4 per 1,000 live births. In 2008 the maternal mortality rate, according to the World

Bank, was 8 per 100,000 births. It was estimated that 94% of children were vaccinated against measles. The CIA calculated HIV/AIDS prevalence in Australia to be about 0.1% in 2009.

The federal and state governments fund approximately 69% of healthcare spending, through a government-funded program. The private sector funds the remaining percent.

42 HOUSING

According to 2006 national census figures, there were about 8.4 million private dwellings and 19,800 non-private dwellings (hotels, motels, nursing homes, hospitals, etc.) in the nation. The average number of persons per dwelling was 2.5. Despite this, the census data revealed that in the period 1986–2006, dwellings with four or more bedrooms increased from 15% to 28% of all private dwellings.

Home purchases slowed in 2010–11 due to an increase in interest rates as well as the end of the First Home Owner Grant that had been in effect since 2000.

Nationwide, about 74.4% of all dwellings are separate, single-family houses (about 5.3 million houses). About 9.3% are classified as semi-detached, row or terrace, or townhouse. Flats and apartments account for about 14.7% of all dwellings. Central heating, formerly available only in the most modern and expensive homes and apartments, is now generally available in the coldest areas of the country. Most apartments and houses are equipped with hot-water service, refrigeration, and indoor bath and toilet facilities.

43 EDUCATION

In 2008 the World Bank estimated that 97% of age-eligible children in Australia were enrolled in primary school. Secondary enrollment for age-eligible children stood at 88%. Tertiary enrollment was estimated at 77%. Of those enrolled in tertiary education, there were 100 male students for every 130 female students. Overall, the CIA estimated that Australia had a literacy rate of 99%. Public expenditure on education represented 4.5% of GDP.

Education is compulsory for children from the age of 6 to 15 (16 in Tasmania). Most children attend pre-school or kindergarten programs. Primary education generally begins at six years of age and lasts for six or seven years, depending on the state. Secondary schools have programs of four to six years. Free education is provided in municipal kindergartens and in state primary, secondary, and technical schools. There are also state-regulated private schools, which are attended by approximately one-third of Australian children. Correspondence courses and educational broadcasts are given for children living in remote areas and unable to attend school because of distance or physical handicap. One-teacher schools also satisfy these needs. Although most Aboriginal and Torres Strait Islander students use the regular school system, there are special programs to help them continue on to higher education.

Education is the joint responsibility of the federal government and each state government and territory. The federal government directly controls schools in the Northern Territory and in the Australian Capital Territory.

Australia has 39 universities in addition to more than 200 technical institutes. There is a state university in each capital city and each provincial area; a national postgraduate research institute in Canberra and a university of technology in Sydney with a branch at Newcastle. There are also a number of privately funded higher-education institutions including theological and teacher training colleges. Adult education includes both vocational and non-vocational courses. Most universities offer education programs for interested persons. In 2005, it was estimated that about 72% of the tertiary age population were enrolled in higher education programs; 64% of men and 80% of women.

44 LIBRARIES AND MUSEUMS

The National Library of Australia traces its origins back to 1902, but it was not until 1961 that it was legislatively separated from the Commonwealth Parliamentary Library and made a distinct entity. The National Library is now housed in modern facilities in Canberra and has over 4.7 million volumes.

Four other libraries in Australia of comparable size are the library of the University of Sydney (over three million volumes), founded in 1852; the State Library of New South Wales (over 1.9 million volumes), founded in 1826; the State Library of Victoria (over 1.5 million), founded in 1854, and the Library Information Service of Western Australia (2.7 million). The Australian Capital Territory (ACT) Library Service oversees nine public library branches and the ACT Government and Assembly Library. The state capital cities have large noncirculating reference libraries, as well as municipal public circulating libraries. The university libraries of Adelaide, Brisbane, Canberra, Melbourne, Monash, New South Wales, and Queensland all have sizable collections. Recent years have seen programs with increased cooperation between libraries, which has resulted in increased service. The Australian Institute of Aboriginal Studies in Acton has a specialized collection of 15,000 volumes, and dozens of museums and cultural centers house other specialized collections.

There are about 2,000 museums in Australia, of which over 200 are art museums. A national art collection has been assembled in the Australian National Gallery at Canberra, which was opened to the public in October 1982. The National Museum of Australia, founded 1980 in Canberra, exhibits Australian history and social history. In 2001 the museum opened new facilities in a stunning architectural structure on the shores of Lake Burley Griffin. There are eight other major museums, two each in Sydney and Melbourne and one in each of the other state capitals. Of note in Melbourne are a Performing Arts Museum (1978); the Ancient Times House (1954); and the Jewish Museum of Australia. The Melbourne Museum, completed in 2000, became the largest museum in the southern hemisphere. Sydney houses the Australian National Maritime Museum (1985), the Museum of Contemporary Art (1979) and the Nicholson Museum of Antiquities (1860). Some of the smaller cities also have museums. The National Gallery of Victoria in Melbourne has a fine collection of paintings and other artworks, and the South Australian Museum in Adelaide has excellent collections relating to Australian entomology, zoology, and ethnology. Botanical gardens are found in every capital city.

45 MEDIA

In 2009 the CIA reported that there were 9 million telephone landlines in Australia. In addition to landlines, mobile phone subscriptions averaged 111 per 100 people. There were 262 FM radio stations, 345 AM radio stations, and 1 shortwave radio station. Internet users numbered 72 per 100 citizens. Prominent newspapers in 2010, with circulation numbers listed parenthetically, included the *Herald Sun* (575,317), *Daily Telegraph* (500,000), and the *Sydney Morning Herald* (225,861), as well as 64 other major newspapers.

Responsibility for the nation's postal service is vested in the Australian Postal Commission and with the Australian Telecommunications Commission. Local and long-distance telephone services are rated highly, while mobile cellular phone use is expanding rapidly. In 2009 there were some 24.1 million mobile cellular phones in use. International service was provided by 19 satellite ground stations and submarine cables to New Zealand, Papua New Guinea, and Indonesia.

The government administers and supervises broadcasting through the Australian Broadcasting Commission, which operates a nationwide noncommercial radio and television service; the Australian Broadcasting Tribunal, which licenses and regulates commercial broadcasters; and the Special Broadcasting Service, which prepares and broadcasts multilingual radio and television programs. Federal government stations are financed from budget revenues, and the private commercial stations derive their income from business advertising. The primary news services are the Australian Associated Press and ABC News.

In 2010, the country had about 13.3 million Internet hosts. In 2009, there were about 15.8 million Internet users in the nation.

In general, news is presented straightforwardly, and political criticism is considered fair and responsible.

Though the Australian constitution does not have specific guarantees of freedom of expression, the High Court has, in two decisions, declared that freedom of political discourse is implied. The government is said to respect all such rights in practice.

46 ORGANIZATIONS

Chambers of commerce and chambers of manufacture are active throughout Australia, especially in the state capital cities; the Australian Chamber of Commerce and Industry, formed when the Australian Chamber of Commerce and the Confederation of Australian Industry merged in 1992. The Australian Consumers' Association is active. There are also trade unions and business associations in a wide variety of fields. Agricultural producers and industry workers are represented through the Australian Dairy Corporation, the Aus-Meat, the Australian Food and Grocery Council, and the Australian Chamber of Fruit and Vegetable Industries, to name a few.

There are professional associations or scholarly societies in the fields of architecture, art, international affairs, economics, political and social science, engineering, geography, history, law, literature, medicine, philosophy, and the natural sciences. Many, such as the Australian Academy of Science, publish scholarly journals.

The Australia Council (founded in 1943) encourages amateur activities in the arts and sponsors traveling exhibitions of ballet, music, and drama. Theatrical, musical, and dance organizations are present in the larger cities and towns. Other notable art and cultural groups are the Australia Council for the Arts,

the Australian Academy of the Humanities, the Australian Film Institute, and the National Trust of Australia.

Health and welfare organizations include the National Health and Medical Research Council, the Australian Council on Healthcare Standards, the Australian Dental Association, the Australian Medical Association, and the Australian Medical Council, among others. There are numerous associations for specialized fields of medicine and science.

Several sports organizations are present. Skiing and tobogganing clubs function in the mountainous areas. Sydney, Melbourne, Hobart, and several other cities have large yacht clubs. Every state capital city has swimming and surfing clubs.

There are numerous youth organizations. One of the most prominent is the National Union of Students (NUS), which was founded in 1987 by uniting the existing student unions in the Australian states. The President of NUS has a position on the Higher Education Council, which advises the Australian Minister for Education, Employment, and Workplace Relations. Other youth groups include the Australian Youth Hostel Association, Student Services of Australia, Tertiary Catholic Federation of Australia, the YMCA and YWCA, Young Liberal Movement, and the Young Nationals. Scouting organizations are also active throughout the country.

There are national chapters of the Red Cross Society, Caritas, Habitat for Humanity, the Christian Children's Fund, Doctors Without Borders, World Vision, Amnesty International, and UNICEF.

47 TOURISM, TRAVEL, AND RECREATION

The *Tourism Factbook*, published by the UN World Tourism Organization, reported 5.58 million incoming tourists to Australia in 2009; they spent a total of $27.9 billion. Of those incoming tourists, there were 3.2 million from East Asia and the Pacific, and 1.4 million from Europe. There were 692,327 hotel beds available in Australia, which had an occupancy rate of 63%. The estimated daily cost to visit Canberra, the capital, was $394. The cost of visiting other cities averaged $370.

Among Australia's natural tourist attractions are the Great Barrier Reef, a mecca for scuba divers; the varied and unusual flora and fauna; and the sparsely inhabited outback regions, which in some areas may be toured by camel. Other attractions include Ballarat and other historic gold-rush towns near Melbourne; wineries, particularly in the Barossa Valley, 55 km (34 mi) northeast of Adelaide; Old Sydney Town, a recreation of the Sydney Cove Settlement north of Sydney as it was in the early 19th century; and the arts festivals held in Perth every year and in Adelaide every two years, featuring foreign as well as Australian artists.

The sports that lure tourists are surfing, sailing, fishing, golf, tennis, cricket, and rugby. Melbourne is famous for its horse racing (Australia's most celebrated race is the Melbourne Cup) and for its 120,000-capacity cricket ground, reputedly the biggest in the world.

Except for nationals of New Zealand, visitors must have a valid visa. Immunizations are required only of tourists coming from an infected area.

The government actively promotes tourism and in 2010 launched a $20 million, four-year brand campaign to promote the nation as a prime destination for trade, tourism, and investment. The campaign carried the slogan, "So where the bloody hell are you?"

48 FAMOUS PERSONS

The most highly regarded contemporary Australian writer is Patrick White (1912–90), author of *The Eye of the Storm* and other works of fiction and winner of the 1973 Nobel Prize for literature. Other well-known novelists are Henry Handel Richardson (Henrietta Richardson Robertson, 1870–1946), Miles Franklin (1879–1954), Christina Stead (1902–83), and Thomas Michael Keneally (b. 1935). Henry Lawson (1867–1922) was a leading short-story writer and creator of popular ballads. Germaine Greer (b. 1939) is a writer on feminism. A prominent Australian-born publisher of newspapers and magazines in the United Kingdom, the United States, and Australia, is Keith Rupert Murdoch (b. 1931).

Three renowned scholars of Australian origin are Sir Gilbert Murray, O.M. (1866–1957), classicist and translator of ancient Greek plays; Samuel Alexander, O.M. (1859–1938), influential scientific philosopher; and Eric Partridge (1894–1979), authority on English slang. Mary Helen MacKillop (1842–1909) was an Australian Roman Catholic nun who dedicated herself to the care of needy children and the promotion of education; she was canonized by Pope Benedict XVI in 2010, becoming the first Australian saint.

Sir Howard Walter Florey (1898–1968) shared the 1945 Nobel Prize in physiology or medicine for the discovery of penicillin. An outstanding bacteriologist was Sir Frank Macfarlane Burnet, O.M. (1899–1985), director of the Melbourne Hospital and co-winner of the 1960 Nobel Prize for medicine. Elizabeth Kenny (1886–1952) made important contributions to the care and treatment of infantile paralysis victims. Sir John Carew Eccles (1903–1997) shared the 1963 Nobel Prize for medicine for his work on ionic mechanisms of the nerve cell membrane. John Warcup Cornforth (b. 1917) shared the 1975 Nobel Prize for chemistry for his work on organic molecules. Peter C. Doherty (b. 1940) shared the 1994 Nobel Prize in physiology or medicine for his work in immunology. Barry J. Marshall (b. 1951) and J. Robin Warren (b. 1937), both Australians, shared the 2005 Nobel Prize in physiology or medicine for their discovery of the *Helicobacter pylori* bacterium, which causes stomach ulcers and gastritis. The Tasmanian native Elizabeth Blackburn (b. 1948) was a co-recipient of the 2009 Nobel Prize in Medicine, along with her US colleagues, Carol Greider and Jack Szostak. Working in the United States, the team of three researchers discovered the process through which the ends of a chromosome (called telomeres) are copied with the help of the enzyme known as telomerase.

Among Australia's most prominent film directors are Fred Schepisi (b. 1939), Bruce Beresford (b. 1940), George Miller (b. 1943), Peter Weir (b. 1944), and Gillian Armstrong (b. 1950); film stars have included Australian-born Errol Flynn (1909–59), Paul Hogan (b. 1940), US-born Mel Gibson (b. 1956), Nicole Kidman (b. 1967), and Heath Ledger (1979–2008). Leading Australian-born figures of the theater include the actors Dame Judith Anderson (1898–1992) and Cyril Ritchard (1898–1977) and the ballet dancer, choreographer, and stage actor and director Sir Robert Murray Helpmann (1909–86). Musicians of Australian birth include the operatic singers Dame Nellie Melba (1861–1931), John Brownlee (1901–69), Marjorie Lawrence (1907–79), and Dame Joan Sutherland (b. 1926) and the composers Percy Grainger (1882–1961), Arthur Benjamin (1893–1960), Peggy Glanville-Hicks (1912–1990), and Peter Joshua Sculthorpe (b. 1929). Popular singers include Helen Reddy (b. 1941) and Olivia Newton-John (b. UK, 1948). Alfred Hill (1870–1960) is regarded as the founder of the art of musical composition in Australia. Albert Namatjira (1902–59), an Aranda Aboriginal, achieved renown as a painter, as did Sir Sidney Robert Nolan (1917–92) and Arthur Boyd (1920–99), who was a sculptor as well as a painter. The aviator Sir Charles Edward Kingsford-Smith (1897–1935) pioneered flights across the Pacific Ocean. A popular figure of folklore was the outlaw Ned (Edward) Kelly (1855?–80).

From about 1970 to 1990, the tennis world was dominated by such Australian players as Frank Sedgman (b. 1927), Lewis Hoad (1934–94), Kenneth Rosewall (b. 1934), Rod (George) Laver (b. 1938), John David Newcombe (b. 1944), and Evonne Goolagong Cawley (b. 1951). Sir Donald George Bradman (1908–2001) was one of the outstanding cricket players of modern times. Record-breaking long-distance runners include John Landy (b. 1930) and Herb Elliott (b. 1938). Jon Konrads (b. 1942) and his sister Ilsa (b. 1944) have held many world swimming records, as did Dawn Fraser (b. 1937), the first woman to swim 100 meters in less than a minute, and Murray Rose (b. 1939).

A notable modern Australian statesman is Sir Robert Gordon Menzies (1894–1978), who served as prime minister from 1939 to 1941 and again from 1949 to 1966. Subsequent prime ministers have included Edward Gough Whitlam, who held office from 1972 to 1975; John Malcolm Fraser, who succeeded Whitlam late in 1975; Robert James Lee Hawke, who served from 1983–91, Paul John Keating, who succeeded Bob Hawke in 1991; and John Winston Howard, who began his term as Australia's 25th prime minister in 1996; he was reelected four times before losing his seat in 2007, becoming the most electorally successful prime minister since Menzies.

49 DEPENDENCIES

Since 1936, Australia has claimed all territory in Antarctica (other than Adélie Land) situated south of 60°S and between 45° and 160°E, an area of some 6.1 million sq km (2.4 million sq mi), or about 42% of the continent. The Australian Antarctic Division, a division of the Department of the Environment, Water, Heritage and the Arts, is responsible for Australia's activities in the Antarctic. Three scientific and exploratory bases are now in operation: Mawson (established February 1954), Davis (established January 1957), and Casey (established February 1969). As of 2007, approximately 50 vessels were transporting an estimated 33,000 tourists to Antarctica annually.

Ashmore and Cartier Islands

The uninhabited, reef-surrounded Ashmore Islands, three in number, and Cartier Island, situated in the Indian Ocean about 480 km (300 mi) north of Broome, Western Australia, have been under Australian authority since May 1934. In July 1938, they were annexed as part of the Northern Territory. Cartier Island is now a marine reserve.

Christmas Island

Situated at 10°30'S and 105°40'E in the Indian Ocean, directly south of the western tip of Java, Christmas Island is 2,623 km (1,630 mi) northwest of Perth and has an area of about 135 sq km (52 sq mi). Until its annexation by the UK in 1888, following the discovery of phosphate rock, the island was uninhabited. The total estimated population in 2007 was 1,402, of whom 70% were Chinese and 10% were Malay. The only industry was phosphate extraction. The governments of Australia and New Zealand decided to close the mine in December 1987. Christmas Island was transferred from the UK to Australia on 1 October 1958. Abbott's booby is an endangered species on the island.

Cocos (Keeling) Islands

The Territory of Cocos (Keeling) Islands is a group of coral atolls consisting of 27 islands with a total land area of 14 sq km (5 sq mi) in the Indian Ocean, at 12°5'S and 96°53'E, about 2,770 km (1,720 mi) northwest of Perth. The estimated population of the two inhabited islands was 596 in 2007. A British possession since 1857, the islands were transferred to Australia in 1955 and are administered by the minister for territories. In 1978, the Australian government bought out the remaining interests (except for personal residences) of the Clunies-Ross heirs on the islands. The climate is pleasant, with moderate rainfall. Principal crops are copra, coconut oil, and coconuts.

Coral Sea Islands

The Coral Sea Islands were declared a territory of Australia in legislation enacted during 1969 and amended slightly in 1973. Spread over a wide ocean area between 10° and 23°30'S and 154° and 158°E, the tiny islands are administered by the minister for the Capital Territory and have no permanent inhabitants-although there is a manned meteorology station on Willis Island.

Territory of Heard and McDonald Islands

Heard Island, at 53°6'S and 72°31'E, about 480 km (300 mi) southeast of the Kerguelen Islands and about 4,000 km (2,500 mi) southwest of Perth, is about 910 sq km (350 sq mi) in size. Bleak and mountainous, it is dominated by a dormant volcano, Big Ben, about 2,740 m (8,990 ft) high. There was a station at Atlas Cove from 1947 to 1955, but the island is now uninhabited and is visited occasionally by scientists. Just north is Shag Island, and 42 km (26 mi) to the west are the small, rocky McDonald Islands. The largest island of the group was visited for the first time, it is believed, on 27 January 1971, by members of the Australian National Antarctic Expedition. The territory was transferred from the UK to Australia at the end of 1947.

Macquarie Island

Macquarie Island, at 54°30'S and 158°40'E, is about 1,600 km (1,000 mi) southeast of Hobart. The rocky, glacial island, 34 km (21 mi) long and about 3 to 5 km (2 to 3 mi) wide, is uninhabited except for a base maintained at the northern end since February 1948. Macquarie Island has been a dependency of Tasmania since the early 19th century. At the most southerly point, the island has what is believed to be the biggest penguin rookery in the world. Two small island groupings are off Macquarie Island: Bishop and Clerk, and Judge and Clerk.

Norfolk Island

Norfolk Island, with an area of 36 sq km (14 sq mi), is situated at 29°3'S and 167°57'E, 1,676 km (1,041 mi) east-northeast of Sydney. Discovered in 1774 by Capt. James Cook, it was the site of a British penal colony during 1788–1814 and 1825–55. In 1856, it was settled by descendants of the *Bounty* mutineers. As of 2008, the estimated permanent population was 2,128. The soil is fertile and the climate conducive to the growing of fruits and bean seed, as well as the famed Norfolk Island pine. Tourism is also important. As of 2003, endangered species on Norfolk Island included the gray-headed blackbird, Norfolk Island parakeet, the white-breasted silver-eye, the green parrot, the Morepork (Boobook owl), and the Bird of Providence (Providence Petrel). In 1996, Phillip Island was added to the Norfolk Island National Park.

50 BIBLIOGRAPHY

Australia Investment and Business Guide: Strategic and Practical Information. Washington, DC: International Business Publications USA, 2012.

Clancy, Laurie. *Culture and Customs of Australia.* Westport, CT: Greenwood Press, 2004.

Cotton, James. *East Timor, Australia and Regional Order: Intervention and Its Aftermath in Southeast Asia.* New York: RoutledgeCurzon, 2004.

Emerson, Arthur. *Historical Dictionary of Sydney.* Lanham, MD: Scarecrow Press, 2001.

Garden, Donald S. *Australia, New Zealand, and the Pacific: An Environmental History.* Santa Barbara, CA: ABC-CLIO, 2005.

International Smoking Statistics: A Collection of Historical Data from 30 Economically Developed Countries. New York: Oxford University Press, 2002.

Kabir, Nahid Afrose. *Muslims in Australia: Immigration, Race Relations and Cultural History.* London, Eng.: Kegan Paul, 2004.

Lilley, Ian, ed. *Archaeology of Oceania: Australia and the Pacific Islands.* Malden, MA: Blackwell, 2006.

McElrath, Karen, ed. *HIV and AIDS: A Global View.* Westport, CT: Greenwood Press, 2002.

Summers, Randal W., and Allan M. Hoffman, eds. *Domestic Violence: A Global View.* Westport, CT: Greenwood Press, 2002.

AZERBAIJAN

Azerbaijan Republic
Azarbaichan Respublikasy

CAPITAL: Baku

FLAG: Three equal horizontal bands of blue (top), red, and green; a crescent and eight-pointed star in white are centered in the red band.

ANTHEM: *Azerbaijan Marsi (March of Azerbaijan).*

MONETARY UNIT: The manat (AZN), consisting of 100 gopik, was introduced in 1992 and remains tied to the Russian ruble with widely fluctuating exchange rates. AZN1 = US$1.24456 (or US$1 = AZN0.8035) as of 2010.

WEIGHTS AND MEASURES: The metric system is in force.

HOLIDAYS: New Year's Day, 1 January; International Women's Day, 8 March; Novruz Bayrom (Holiday of Spring), 22 March; Day of the Republic, 28 May; Day of Armed Forces, 9 October; Day of State Sovereignty, 18 October; Day of National Revival, 17 November; Universal Azeri Solidarity Day, 31 December.

TIME: 4 p.m. = noon GMT.

¹LOCATION, SIZE, AND EXTENT

Azerbaijan is located in southeastern Europe/southwestern Asia between Armenia and the Caspian Sea. Comparatively, Azerbaijan is slightly smaller than the state of Maine with a total area of 86,600 sq km (33,436 sq mi). This area includes the Nakhichevan Autonomous Republic—an exclave separated from Azerbaijan by Armenia—and the Nagorno-Karabakh Autonomous Oblast—a region effectively under the control of Armenian-supported rebels. Azerbaijan shares boundaries with Russia on the N, the Caspian Sea on the E, Iran on the S, Armenia on the W, and Georgia on the NW. Azerbaijan's boundary length totals 2,013 km (1,251 mi). Azerbaijan's capital city, Baku, is located on the Apsheron Peninsula that juts into the Caspian Sea.

²TOPOGRAPHY

The topography of Azerbaijan features the large, flat Kura-Aras Lowland (much of it below sea level) surrounded on three sides by mountains. The Great Caucasus Mountains are to the north, the Lesser Caucasus Mountains are to the southwest, and the Talish Mountains are in the south along the border with Iran. The Karabakh Upland lies in the west. About 19% of Azerbaijan's land is arable with approximately 16% under irrigation.

The Nakhichevan exclave lies to the west, separated from the rest of Azerbaijan by Armenia. Nakhichevan also shares borders with Turkey and Iran.

³CLIMATE

The country's climate is subtropical in the eastern and central parts. In the mountainous regions the climate is alpine-like. The southeastern section of the country has a humid subtropical climate. The average temperature in the capital, Baku, in July is 25°C (77°F). In January the average temperature is 4°C (39°F). Rainfall varies according to climate zones. The average rainfall for most of the country is only about 15 to 25 cm (6 to 10 in). However, at the highest elevations of the Caucasus and in the Länkäran lowlands, annual rainfall can exceed 100 cm (39 in).

⁴FLORA AND FAUNA

The World Resources Institute estimates that there are 4,300 plant species in Azerbaijan. In addition, Azerbaijan is home to 82 species of mammals, 364 species of birds, 61 species of reptiles, and 10 species of amphibians. The calculation reflects the total number of distinct species residing in the country, not the number of endemic species.

⁵ENVIRONMENT

The World Resources Institute reported that Azerbaijan had designated 398,100 hectares (983,727 acres) of land for protection as of 2006. Water resources totaled 30.3 cu km (7.27 cu mi) while water usage was 17.25 cu km (4.14 cu mi) per year. Domestic water usage accounted for 5% of total usage, industrial for 28%, and agricultural for 67%. Per capita water usage totaled 2,051 cu m (72,430 cu ft) per year.

Azerbaijan's current environmental problems result in part from the effects of the economic priorities and practices of the former Soviet Union. General mismanagement of the country's resources has resulted in a serious threat to several areas of the environment. The combination of industrial, agricultural, and oil-drilling pollution has created an environmental crisis in the Caspian Sea. These sources of pollution have contaminated 100% of the coastal waters in some areas and 45.3% of Azerbaijan's rivers. The pollution of the land through the indiscriminate use of agricultural chemicals such as the pesticide DDT is also a serious problem.

Azerbaijan's war with Armenia has hampered the government's ability to improve the situation. Due to the severity of pollution on all levels, the country's wildlife and vegetation are also seriously affected. From the mid-1980s to mid-1990s, the amount of forest and woodland declined by 12.5%. The country had two Ramsar wetland sites: Agh-Ghol and Ghizil-Agaj.

According to a 2011 report issued by the International Union for Conservation of Nature and Natural Resources (IUCN), threatened species included 7 mammals, 14 birds, 9 reptiles, 10 fish, and 4 other invertebrates. Endangered species include the Barbel sturgeon, beluga, the Azov-Black Sea sturgeon, the Apollo butterfly, and the Armenian birch mouse.

The UN reported in 2008 that carbon dioxide emissions in Azerbaijan totaled 31,749 kilotons.

6 POPULATION

The US Central Intelligence Agency (CIA) estimates the population of Azerbaijan in 2011 to be approximately 8,372,373, which placed it at number 91 in population among the 196 nations of the world. In 2011, approximately 6.5% of the population was over 65 years of age, with another 23.2% under 15 years of age. The median age in Azerbaijan was 28.8 years. There were 0.97 males for every female in the country. The population's annual rate of change was 0.846%. The projected population for the year 2025 was 10,300,000. Population density in Azerbaijan was calculated at 97 people per sq km (251 people per sq mi).

The UN estimated that 52% of the population lived in urban areas, and that urban populations had an annual rate of change of 1.4%. The largest urban areas was Baku, with a population of 2 million.

7 MIGRATION

Estimates of Azerbaijan's net migration rate, carried out by the CIA in 2011, amounted to -1.14 migrants per 1,000 citizens. The total number of emigrants living abroad was 1.43 million, and the total number of immigrants living in Azerbaijan was 263,900. Azerbaijan also accepted 2,400 refugees. As a result of the war with Armenia, which ran from 1988 through 1994, more than one million people were forced to leave the region. The Law on Citizenship allows for the automatic acquisition of Azerbaijani citizenship by refugees from Armenia. Also, there are some 48,000 Meshketians, also known as Meskhis, who were forcibly resettled from Central Asia after bloody Soviet pogroms in 1989. The Meshketians, descendants of rural Muslim populations, were originally deported from Georgia to Central Asia under the Stalin era.

8 ETHNIC GROUPS

At the 1999 census, 90.6% of the population was Azeri; about 2.2% were Dagestani, 1.8% were Russian, another 1.5% were Armenian, and 3.9% were of other ethnic origins. Almost all of the Armenians live in the separatist Nagorno-Karabakh region. There have been many reports of discrimination against the ethnic Armenians in employment, schooling, and provisions of social services.

9 LANGUAGES

Azerbaijani (or Azeri) is a language related to Turkish and is also spoken in northwestern Iran. It is traditionally written in Arabic script. In 1999, an estimated 90.3% of the population spoke Azeri; 2.2% spoke Lezgi; 1.8% spoke Russian; 1.5% spoke Armenian; and 4.3% other or unspecified.

10 RELIGIONS

For most of the 20th century, from 1920–1991, the Azerbaijan Soviet Socialist Republic observed the restrictions in religious belief and practice common throughout the former Soviet Union. According to official figures available in 2010, the population was 96% Muslim (65% of whom were Shi'as, and 35% were Sunnis). However, the percentage of those who are active practitioners of the faith is believed to be much lower. Religious identity within the country tends to be primarily based on culture and ethnicity. Because of the Persian influence on Azerbaijan, most Azerbaijanis are Shi'as, even though all of the other Turkic groups of the former Soviet Union are Sunni Muslims. Islam (both Shi'a and Sunni), Russian Orthodox, and Judaism are considered to be traditional religions of the country. A majority of Christians (primarily Russian Orthodox) live in the Baku and Sumgait urban areas. There are two main groups of Jews: the Mountain Jews, who are believed to be descendents of those who first came to the northern part of the country over 2,000 years ago, and the Ashkenazi Jews, who are the descendant of European immigrants. The entire Jewish community has about 20,000 people. There are small communities of Evangelical Lutherans, Roman Catholics, Baptists, Molokans (an older branch of Russian Orthodox), Seventh-Day Adventists, Baha'is, Wahhabist Muslims, Jehovah's Witnesses, and Hare Krishnas. The constitution specifically provides that persons of all faiths may choose and practice their religion without restrictions. There are legal provisions which allow the government to regulate religious groups. All religious groups must be registered with the government through the State Committee for Work with Religious Associations, a department of the Ministry of Justice. Proselytizing by foreigners is against the law. Muslims who convert to non-Muslim faiths often face social discrimination, and even hostilities.

11 TRANSPORTATION

The CIA reports that Azerbaijan has a total of 59,141 km (36,749 mi) of roads, of which 29,210 km (18,150 mi) are paved. Railroads extend for 2,079 km (1,292 mi). There are 35 airports, which transported 839,514 passengers in 2009 according to the World Bank.

Baku is the rail hub and major port in Azerbaijan. In 2008, the merchant marine had 89 ships of at least 1,000 gross registered tons. Ships from the Caspian fleet have called at some 125 ports in over 30 countries. Azerbaijan has 27 airports with paved runways. There are flights from Baku's Bina Airport to more than 70 cities of the former Soviet Union.

12 HISTORY

The territory of present-day Azerbaijan has been continuously inhabited since the Paleolithic era. The first evidence of tribal alliances date to the first millennium BC, when such peoples as the Mannaians, the Medes, the Cadusiis, the Albanoi, and the Caspians appeared. In the 7th century BC, the state of Media appeared in what now is southern Azerbaijan, growing to cover large portions of the Near East. The Medians were displaced by the Persian dynasty of Achaemenids, who in turn were defeated by Alexander the Great. In the 4th century BC, another state arose, which Greek sources called Atropatena, or "Land of the Fire Keepers"; it is this name, reflecting the predominance of Zoroastrianism, which may have given the present state its name. Around the beginning of the common era, Atropatena was succeeded by a state called Albania, which the Romans attempted to conquer.

In the 3rd and 4th centuries AD, Azerbaijan existed with fluid boundaries between the Sassanid state in Persia and the Romans, whose battles inflicted great damage, leaving Azerbaijan open to raids by Turkic nomadic tribes from the north, including Khazars and Huns. Outside influence reappeared in the 7th and 8th centuries, when Arabs conquered much of Transcaucasia. As their influence receded, a number of small local states were established, the best known of which was the Shirvanshahs.

In the 11th century Azerbaijan was invaded by Oguz Turks, of the Seljuk dynasty. By the 13th century the gradual displacement of pre-Turkic local languages was complete, although many traces of non-Turkic predecessors remain in the Azerbaijani language. Persian, however, remained the language of art, science, and education.

In the 1230s Azerbaijan was conquered by Genghiz Khan, whose power remained in the Il-Khanid state, which at the end of the 14th century was displaced by the armies of Tamerlane. In the 16th century, the Safawid state emerged, coming to control most of the land between the Syr Darya and the Euphrates, and reestablishing agriculture and commerce destroyed under the Mongols. In the 17th century, the Safawids became Persianized, which made present-day Azerbaijan decline in importance.

In the 18th century Azerbaijan became the intersection of the Turkish, Persian, and Russian empires, as well as the focus of British and French attempts to block Russian expansion. The northern part of the territory was incorporated into Russia in the first third of the 19th century, but the area did not become important until the 1880s, when the area's abundant oil gained commercial importance. The southern portion of what was originally Azerbaijan has remained in Iran, except for the period 1941–46, when it was occupied by Soviet troops.

When the 1917 Russian revolution came, Ottoman Turkish troops moved into Azerbaijan, and later British forces controlled the capital, Baku. The Azerbaijani Musavat, or Equality Party, established a government, declared Azerbaijan's independence, and received diplomatic recognition from several states. Azerbaijan was invaded by the Russian Bolsheviks' Red Army in April 1920, and Azerbaijan was declared a Soviet state. In 1922 it was made part of the Transcaucasian Federated Socialist Republic, along with Georgia and Armenia. That was dissolved in 1936, when the three states were each made into separate Soviet Socialist Republics.

In 1988, calls by ethnic Armenians living in Azerbaijan's Nagorno-Karabakh (NK) region to be incorporated into the Armenian republic led to open conflict, which lasted until 1994. This predominantly Armenian area had been unsuccessfully claimed by the Armenians in the 1920s, at the time of the creation of Soviet Azerbaijan. Inability to solve the NK conflict was one of the problems that ultimately brought down Mikhail Gorbachev and broke apart the USSR. Ethnic and civil violence in January

LOCATION: 40°30′ N; 47°0′ E BOUNDARY LENGTHS: Armenia (W), 566 kilometers (352 miles); Armenia (S), 221 kilometers (137 miles); Georgia, 322 kilometers (200 miles); Iran (S), 432 kilometers (268 miles); Iran (SE), 179 kilometers (111 miles); Russia, 284 kilometers (177 miles); Turkey, 9 kilometers (6 miles).

1990 prompted the occupation of Baku by Soviet armed forces and Moscow's replacement of Abdulrakhman Vezirov with Ayaz Mutalibov as republic head. During this period of martial law, the legislature elected Mutalibov as president in May 1990.

Azerbaijan declared independence from the Soviet Union on 30 August 1991, and Mutalibov was reaffirmed as president in a popular, uncontested election in September 1991. In December 1991, NK's Armenians held a referendum (boycotted by local Azerbaijanis) that approved NK's independence and elected a Supreme Soviet, which on 6 January 1992, declared NK's independence and futilely appealed for world recognition. Following a late February 1992 massacre of Azerbaijani civilians in the town of Khojaly in NK, Mutalibov was accused of failing to protect Azeri citizens and forced by the nationalist oppositionist Azerbaijani Popular Front (APF) and others to resign as president. His replacement, legislative head Yakub Mamedov, was also forced to resign in May 1992, in the face of further Azerbaijani military defeats in NK. Mutalibov was then reinstated by loyalists in the Supreme Soviet, but he had to flee two days later, when the APF seized power. Former Soviet dissident and APF leader Abulfaz Elchibey, was elected president in a popular contest in June 1992.

The nationalist government took several moves to cut its ties to Russia, including demanding the withdrawal of Russian troops, refusing to participate as a member of the Commonwealth of Independent States, negotiating with Western firms to develop its oil resources, and improving relations with Turkey. Fighting with rebels in the NK region continued, leading to increasing military losses for Azerbaijan. In 1993, Heydar Aliyev, who had been the Communist Party leader of the republic from 1971–85 but then was ousted and disgraced by Soviet leader Mikhail Gorbachev, began to press for Elchibey's dismissal.

An abortive attempt by the Elchibey government in June 1993 to disarm paramilitary forces in the town of Ganja precipitated the fall of the government and provided the opportunity for Aliyev to regain power. These forces were led by Suret Huseynov, formerly in charge of troops in NK, who had been fired by Elchibey. Huseynov's forces, supplied with Russian equipment, defeated an Azerbaijani Army attack and began to march on Baku. His government in chaos, Elchibey invited Aliyev to come to Baku, and on 15 June, he endorsed Aliyev's election by the legislature as its new speaker. Elchibey fled to the Nakhchiveni Autonomous Republic (NAR) on 17 June. On 24 June 1993, a bare quorum of legislators met and formally stripped Elchibey of presidential powers, transferring them to Aliyev. Huseynov demanded and was given the post of prime minister.

On 3 October 1993, Aliyev was elected president with 98.8% of the vote. The referendum and election were viewed as not "free and fair" by many international observers because of suppression of APF and other opposition participation. In late September 1994, police and others in Baku launched a purported coup attempt. Aliyev darkly hinted at Russian involvement. After defeating the coup attempt, Aliyev also accused Prime Minister Huseynov of major involvement, and Huseynov fled the country. Other coup attempts were reported in 1995 and 1999. All of the alleged coup attempts triggered mass arrests of Aliyev's opponents.

The conflict with Armenian separatists over its Nagorno-Karabakh region continued to plague Azerbaijan. The Organization for Security and Cooperation in Europe (OSCE) began the "Minsk Group" peace talks in June 1992. A Russian-mediated cease-fire was agreed to in May 1994 and was formalized by an armistice signed by the ministers of defense of Armenia and Azerbaijan and the commander of the NK army on 27 July 1994 (and reaffirmed a month later). This was effectively a defeat for Azerbaijan, as the rebels retained control over most of the historic NK region and also substantial territory outside of NK. Moscow talks were held by the sides, with token representation by the OSCE, along with Minsk Group talks. With strong US backing, the OSCE at its Budapest meeting agreed in December 1994 to send OSCE peacekeepers to the region under UN aegis if a political settlement could be reached. Russia and the OSCE assented to merge their mediation efforts. France was nominated as a co-chair in 1996. This elicited criticism from Azerbaijan that the French had appeared pro-Armenian, leading to the seating of United States, French, and Russian co-chairs. (Many Azerbaijanis also have voiced reservations about Russia's objectivity as a mediator, citing its defense ties to Armenia.)

On 11 October 1998, incumbent President Aliyev defeated five other candidates and was elected to a second five-year term, receiving over 76% of 4.3 million votes cast. The major "constructive opposition" candidate running was Etibar Mamedov of the National Independence Party (NIP), who received 11.6% of the vote. Most international observers judged the vote not "free and fair," citing myriad irregularities, though also noting that the election marked some improvement in political pluralism.

In 2001, the United States lifted a ban on aid imposed during the NK conflict after Azerbaijan provided airspace and intelligence to the United States following the 11 September 2001 terrorist attacks. In September 2002, construction began on a multibillion-dollar pipeline to carry Caspian oil from Azerbaijan to Turkey via Georgia (the Baku-Tbilisi-Ceyhan pipeline, otherwise known as the BTC).

The government held a referendum on 24 August 2002 to approve 39 changes to the constitution. Some of the major articles at issue were the abolishment of the proportional system of election of deputies to the national parliament; making the prime minister, not the speaker of the parliament, a caretaker president in case the president is not able to carry out his duties; and giving lower level courts the right to ban political parties. Opposition leaders argued that abolishment of the proportional system would damage the multiparty system in the country and further strengthen the ruling elite. In addition to this, the opposition claimed that President Aliyev intended to appoint his son Ilham prime minister and then retire, thus paving the way for his son to become the next president. President Aliyev also approved adding a provision to the Law on State Secrets, which would make editors and journalists of local mass media accountable for disseminating state secrets. The government claimed that there was nearly 100% support for the constitutional changes with 88% voter turnout, while opposition groups stated turnout was closer to 15%, which would render the vote invalid. Demonstrators called for the resignation of President Aliyev and for holding free and fair elections. Supporters of more than 30 opposition parties, including the major parties Musavat, the Popular Front, the Azerbaijan Democratic Party, and the Azerbaijan National Independence Party, held marches on 14 September 2002 urging the authorities to cancel the results of the referendum. On 27 October and again on 24 November of that year, the opposition parties marched again under the banner of the United Opposition Movement, claiming that over 50,000 people participated in the marches.

In August 2003, Aliyev appointed his son Ilham prime minister. In October, Ilham Aliyev won a presidential vote by a landslide, in a poll that outside observers declared did not meeting international standards. This sparked opposition protests which were met by police violence; hundreds were arrested. In December, Heydar Aliyev died in a hospital in Cleveland, Ohio, in the United States; he had been suffering from heart and kidney problems.

In March 2005, outspoken opposition journalist Elmar Huseynov was shot and killed in Baku; thousands of Azerbaijanis mourned his death. After months of preelection tension and the suppression of riots, voters cast their ballots for parliament on 6 November 2005. The ruling Yeni Azerbaijan Party declared victory, while leaders of Azadliq ("Freedom"), a three-party opposition bloc, said the official results were a sham, and the races were tainted by fraud, falsification, and police action. During the campaign, beatings of demonstrators, arrests of opposition figures, and the continued use of government resources for its candidates took place. After the elections, thousands of opposition members protested the fraudulent elections, and the Azeri government was forced-in part by intense diplomatic pressure-to undo some of the most obviously falsified results, by firing two regional governors for interfering with vote counts, annulling the results for five parliamentary seats, and dismissing several election officials and opening criminal cases against them, in addition to carrying out investigations of complaints. The official results showed the Yeni Azerbaijan Party winning 58 parliamentary seats and the Azadliq bloc only 11. The rest of the seats were scattered among small parties and independents. Tens of thousands of citizens staged peaceful protests on 26 November 2005, calling on President Ilham Aliyev to resign, and chanting "freedom"; the protests were broken up by the police, who beat many of the participants.

In May 2005 the Baku-Tbilis-Ceyhan oil pipeline was completed, providing a major route for Caspian Sea fossil fuels to reach the Mediterranean and hence European and North American markets, while bypassing Russia. This pipeline brought significant income to the region but at the time exacerbated relations between the West and Russia as it was seen as meddling within Russia's historic sphere of interest.

In January 2007, the Azeri state oil company stopped pumping oil to Russia in a dispute over energy prices with Russia's state-backed oil giant, Gazprom. Russia in recent years has become more aggressive in using its energy resources for political purposes. In 2003–04, a large number of senior Russian officials and major energy companies visited Baku in the hopes of participating in energy projects in Azerbaijan. While maintaining diplomatic relations with Moscow, Azerbaijan is more hesitant when it comes to close cooperation with Russian energy companies. Azerbaijan fears that if Russia gains more assets in Azerbaijan, control of these assets will be used for political purposes. Such fears of Russia's actions in recent years have played out with other former Soviet republics as well. Political disagreements with Georgia, Ukraine, Armenia, and Belarus have resulted in Russia disrupting the supply of natural gas or significantly raising prices for it. For instance, in 2006, Azerbaijan played middleman in a dispute between Russia and Georgia. Russia's relationship with Georgia had worsened amid tension over Georgia's breakaway regions and its ties with NATO. Gazprom indicated that it would seek to more than double the price it charged Georgia for natural gas. Georgia said that it was close to obtaining an alternative supply from a British Petroleum (BP)-run platform in the Caspian Sea off of Azerbaijan. Georgia's President Mikhail Saakashvili secured the supply from the BP platform after talks with BP and Azerbaijan's President Ilham Aliyev. The gas will be sent through the Baku-Tbilisi-Ceyhan pipeline.

At the Group of 8 summit meeting in the German Baltic Sea town of Heiligendamm in June 2007, Russian President Vladimir Putin offered the United States the use of the Russian-leased Qabala radar station in Azerbaijan as an alternative to US plans to build a missile defense system in Europe. The George W. Bush administration wanted to build an X-band radar in the Czech Republic to guide antimissile interceptors, and to deploy the interceptors themselves in Poland. Russia earlier in 2007 indicated that if Poland and the Czech Republic agreed to host US missile defense systems in their countries, they could become targets of Russian missile attacks. President Putin warned of a growing "unipolar world," with the US the sole hegemonic power, and saw the plans for a US missile defense system as a direct threat to Russia's security. Thus the announcement by Putin at the Group of 8 summit of a possible sharing of missile defense data by the US and Russia came as something of a surprise. Russia uses the Qabala station under a lease agreement with Azerbaijan. Putin conferred with President Aliyev, who he said "stressed he will be only glad to contribute to the cause of global security and stability." US and NATO officials indicated that the Azerbaijan site was less useful than those selected for Poland and the Czech Republic because it is too close to Iran to intercept missiles fired from there. The potential threat posed by Iran is one of the main stated reasons behind the US plans for the missile defense system.

In 2006, residents of Nagorno-Karabakh again voted in favor of a declaration as a sovereign state, but this was not internationally recognized. In July 2007, Nagorno-Karabakh elected the former head of the security service Bako Sahakyan to replace Arkadiy Gukasyan as president.

In 2008 presidential elections, Ilham Aliyev was reelected, taking over 88% of the vote in an election that was boycotted by the major opposition parties. While the constitution originally limited the presidency to two terms, a referendum lifting the limits was passed in March 2009, clearing the way for a possible third term for Aliyev.

Into 2009, the conflict over Nagorno-Karabakh complicated Azerbaijan's relationship with Turkey too. Turkey is allied with Azerbaijan over the issue of Nagorno-Karabakh. As a result of this alliance, among other disputes, Turkey closed its border to Armenia in 1993. In April 2009, officials from Turkey and Armenia began a series of meetings to normalize relations. One month later, however, the government of Turkey stated that their border would not open to Armenia unless that country withdrew from Azerbaijan. Armenia likewise reiterated its continued support of Nagorno-Karabakh, thus leaving the talks at a stalemate. In September 2009, the New Azerbaijan Party issued a statement claiming that the opening of the Turkey-Armenia border and renewal of diplomatic ties between those nations would be unacceptable until the Nagorno-Karabakh conflict is resolved.

On 23 May 2010, residents of Nagorno-Karabakh took part in a legislative election that received swift condemnation from the European Union, Azerbaijan, and several other members of the international community. The European Union's foreign policy head, Catherine Ashton, called the election illegal, saying that it did nothing to settle the underlying conflict over the territory. Meanwhile, Bako Sahakian, the president of the disputed republic, hailed the election as a symbol of Nagorno-Karabakh's commitment to democracy. In the election, four parties vied for thirty-three, five-year seats in Nagorno-Karabakh's de facto legislature. The two dominant parties were the pro-government Free Fatherland party, which Armenian sources claimed won just under 46% of the vote, and the Democratic Party of Artsakh.

13 GOVERNMENT

Azerbaijan is a republic with a presidential form of government. Heydar Aliyev assumed presidential powers after the overthrow of his popularly elected predecessor and was elected president in 1993. Aliyev and his supporters from his home region of Nakichevan and elsewhere dominated the government and the legislature. Aliyev's son Ilham was elected president in 2003 and reelected in 2008. While the constitution originally limited the presidency to two terms, a referendum lifting the limits was passed in March 2009, clearing the way for a possible third term.

The Azerbaijani constitution was approved by 91.9% of voters in a referendum held in November 1995. It establishes a strong presidency, sets up a new 125-member legislature (the Milli Mejlis), declares Azerbaijani the state language, proclaims freedom of religion and a secular state, stipulates ownership over part of the Caspian Sea, and gives Nakhchiveni Autonomous Republic (NAR) quasi-federal rights. The president appoints and removes cabinet ministers (the Milli Mejlis consents to his choice of prime minister), submits budgetary and other legislation that cannot be amended but only approved or rejected within 56 days, and appoints local officials. It is extremely difficult for the Milli Mejlis to impeach the president. The transition to democracy has been impeded by government efforts to hinder the opposition. In NK, political turmoil and war damage have slowed development, and ethnic Azerbaijanis are prevented from returning to the region and surrounding areas by the lack of a peace settlement.

In June 2002, the Constitutional Court ruled that changes to the constitution proposed by President Heydar Aliyev did not conflict with the principles of Azerbaijan's basic law. One major change in the constitution concerned what happens if the president retires or becomes incapacitated. Prior to the 24 August 2002 referendum, under the constitution's Article 105, the speaker of parliament assumed the president's duties. Under the new rule, the prime minister, who is appointed by the president and is responsible to him, not the legislature, assumes presidential powers. An amendment to Article 101 changed the threshold for a candidate to be elected president in the first round of voting, from two-thirds to a simple majority. Members of the Milli Mejlis were previously elected on the basis of majority and proportional election systems under Article 83 of the constitution. Under the new provisions, proportional party lists were eliminated and deputies are elected only through winning majorities in districts. Changes to Article 3 forbid holding a referendum on issues that fall under the scope of executive institutions, such as taxes, the state budget, amnesties, elections and appointments to executive positions.

14 POLITICAL PARTIES

Some three dozen parties are registered, but some opposition parties have been arbitrarily refused registration. Some parties that are deemed explicitly ethnic or religiously based also have been refused registration. Under election legislation passed after Heydar Aliyev's accession, a party must have at least 1,000 members to be legally registered. Party membership is forbidden to government officials in agencies of the judiciary, law enforcement, security, border defense, customs, taxation, finance, and the state-run media. Six pro-Aliyev parties participated in the 1995 legislative party list vote, including Yeni Azerbaijan (YAP;

formed in November 1992; in English, the New Azerbaijan Party), Azerbaijan Democratic Independence (ADIP; broke off from NIP in late 1993), Motherland (formed in 1990), and the Democratic Entrepreneurs' Party (formed in 1994). Only the YAP gained enough votes to win seats in the party list vote (though these other parties won seats in constituency balloting). Two centrist or opposition parties participated and won seats in the party-list voting: the Azerbaijan Popular Front (APF-formed in 1988) and National Independence Party (NIP; broke off from APF in early 1992). Opposition parties excluded from the party list ballot included Musavat (formed in 1912). All parties are small; YAP is the largest. YAP, formed by Aliyev, encompasses many of his former Azerbaijani Communist Party (ACP) supporters. The APF was at the forefront of the nationalist and anticommunist movement and its chair, Abulfaz Elchibey, was elected president in 1992. With Heydar Aliyev's return to power, APF members and officials were arrested and harassed. NIP views itself as a moderate nationalist party in "constructive opposition" to Aliyev. Musavat has supported close ties with Turkey and has cooperated on some issues with the APF. The pro-Iranian Islamic Party was stripped of its registration in 1995. Preparing for the 1998 presidential race, in March 1998, 46 pro-government political parties and groups formed the Center for Democratic Elections (CDE). Five prominent opposition political leaders and others formed the Movement for Democratic Elections and Electoral Reform (MDEER) in May 1998: Elchibey (the AFP), Isa Gambar (Musavat), Lala Shovkat Hijyeva (Azerbaijan Liberal Party—ALP), former speaker Rasul Guliyev, and Ilyas Ismayilov (Democratic Party of Azerbaijan). The Democratic Party finally achieved registration in early 2000, but co-leader Guliyev remained in forced exile.

Other political parties include the Civil Solidarity Party (CSP), Civic Union Party, Compatriot Party, Justice Party, Liberal Party of Azerbaijan, and the Social Democratic Party of Azerbaijan (SDP). Opposition parties regularly factionalize and form new parties. The opposition bloc that fielded candidates in the November 2005 parliamentary election was called Azadliq ("Freedom").

Ilham Aliyev of the New Azerbaijan Party has held the presidency since 2003. He was appointed to the position by his father, Heydar Aliyev, a few months before the elder Aliyev died, then elected to the post. He was reelected in 2008, taking 89% of the vote in an election that was boycotted by the major opposition parties.

In the parliamentary elections of 7 November 2010, the ruling New Azerbaijan Party reportedly gained 90% of the vote, taking more than 70 of the 125 seats in parliament. The remaining seats were won by candidates considered to be loyalists of President Aliyev. While the Central Election Commission and election monitors from the Commonwealth of Independent States deemed the vote free and fair, Western observers claimed the election was marred by serious violations. Some election observers presented video evidence showing busloads of people being transported from one polling place to another, issuing multiple votes. Other observers reported that they were forced out of polling locations by police and/or detained during voting hours.

¹⁵LOCAL GOVERNMENT

Soviet-era Azerbaijan was subdivided administratively into one autonomous republic, Nakhichevan, an area separated from the rest of Azerbaijan by a thin strip of Armenian territory, which had its own parliament of 110 members; and an autonomous region, Nagorno-Karabakh (NK). Azerbaijan dissolved NK's status as an autonomous region in November 1991 in an attempt to reassert central control. NK has claimed an independent existence since December 1991, and a swath of territory around it has been occupied by NK Armenian forces. Azerbaijan has 59 districts (*rayons*) and 11 cities, whose executive heads or mayors are appointed and dismissed by the president. Although the constitution called for the local election of legislative assemblies (councils) by the end of 1997, these elections did not take place until December 1999 (with runoffs in some municipalities in March 2000). State contributions to municipal governments dwindled during the 2000s: state funds comprised 37% of municipal budgets in 2002 but only 10.7% in 2004. To offset the at best unpredictable and—most often—declining revenues, municipalities engaged in tax sharing to stabilize their budgets.

¹⁶JUDICIAL SYSTEM

The old Soviet court system has been essentially retained, consisting of district courts and municipal courts of first instance and a Supreme Court which usually performs the function of appellate review. However, the Supreme Court also performs the function of court of first instance for some serious cases. District courts consist of one judge and two lay assessors and hear criminal, civil, and juvenile cases. Criminal defendants have the right to an attorney and to appointed counsel, the right to be present at trial, to confront witnesses, and to a public trial.

The 1995 constitution provides for public trials in most cases, the presumption of innocence in criminal cases, and a defendant's right to legal counsel. Both defendants and prosecutors have the right of appeal. In practice, however, the courts are politically oriented, seeming to overlook the government's human rights violations. In July 1993, Heydar Aliyev ousted the Supreme Court chief justice because of alleged political loyalties to the opposition. The president directly appoints lower level judges. The president also appoints the Constitutional Court and Supreme Court judges with confirmation by the legislature.

Prosecutors (procurators) are appointed by the president with confirmation by the legislature. The minister of justice organizes prosecutors into offices at the district, municipal, and republic levels. The constitution provides equal status for prosecutors and defense attorneys before the courts, but in practice the arrest and investigatory powers of the prosecutors have dominant influence before the courts. Judges will often remand a case for further prosecutory investigation rather than render an innocent verdict. Investigations often rely on obtaining confessions rather than on gathering evidence.

The Azerbaijan government's human rights record is poor, although some public policy debate is allowed and human rights organizations operate. The government restricts freedom of assembly, religion, and association. Numerous cases of arbitrary arrest, beatings (some resulting in deaths), unwarranted searches and seizures, and other human rights abuses are reported.

Political oppositionists are harassed and arrested, and there are dozens of political prisoners in Azerbaijan. The conflict between NK Armenians and Azerbaijanis contributed to widespread human rights violations by both sides. Some opposition newspapers are allowed to exist. Ethnic Lezgins and Talysh have complained of human rights abuses such as restricted educational opportunities in their native languages.

¹⁷ARMED FORCES

The International Institute for Strategic Studies reports that armed forces in Azerbaijan totaled 66,940 members in 2011. The force is comprised of 56,840 from the army, 2,200 from the navy, and 7,900 members of the air force. Armed forces represent 2% of the labor force in Azerbaijan. Defense spending totaled $2.4 billion and accounted for 2.6% of GDP.

¹⁸INTERNATIONAL COOPERATION

Azerbaijan was admitted to the UN on 2 March 1992 and serves on several specialized agencies, such as the FAO, IAEA, IFC, ILO, IMF, UNESCO, and the World Bank. The country is also a member of the Black Sea Cooperation Group (BSEC), the Asian Development Bank, Council of Europe, OSCE (1992), EBRD, Economic Cooperation Organization (Turkey, Iran, Pakistan, Russia, the Central Asian states, and Afghanistan), the Islamic Development Bank, the Organization of the Islamic Conference, and the European-Atlantic Partnership Council. The country is also a member of the CIS and has observer status in the WTO. Azerbaijan is part of the group known as GUUAM (Georgia, Uzbekistan, Ukraine, Azerbaijan, Moldova). The group was formed in 2001; Uzbekistan withdrew in 2005.

The OSCE continues to mediate in the struggle between the Azerbaijani government and the ethnic Armenians of the Nagorno-Karabakh region. Under the terms of a 1994 cease-fire agreement, the region is legally a part of Azerbaijan but de facto controlled by the local ethnic Armenian government. In 2006, residents of Nagorno-Karabakh again voted in favor of a declaration as a sovereign state, but this was not internationally recognized. In 2008, leaders from Armenia and Azerbaijan signed an agreement to intensify efforts toward a peaceful resolution. Though the leaders met again in January 2009, no settlement was determined.

In environmental cooperation, Azerbaijan is part of the Basel Convention, the Convention on Biological Diversity, Ramsar, CITES, the London Convention, the Kyoto Protocol, and the Montréal Protocol.

¹⁹ECONOMY

The GDP rate of change in Azerbaijan, as of 2010, was 5%. Inflation stood at 5.1%, and unemployment was reported at 0.9%.

Azerbaijan is one of the oldest oil-producing regions of the world. Here in ancient times the Zoroastrians, for whom fire was a sacred symbol, built temples around the "eternal fires" of burning gas vents. At the beginning of the 20th century, as international competition increased in the first great era of economic globalization, Azerbaijan was supplying almost half of the world's oil. As a constituent republic of the USSR it was a leading supplier to the rest of the Union until the focus of Soviet oil development efforts shifted to the Ural mountains and western Siberia during the

1970s and 1980s. In addition, the country is endowed with ample deposits of iron, aluminum, zinc, copper, arsenic, molybdenum, marble, and fire clay.

Azerbaijan boasts a diversified industrial sector that grew rapidly in the late 1990s and early 2000s. Industrial activity account for less than 1/5 of GDP in 1998, increased to 1/3 by 2000, and by 2010 CIA estimates put it at 65.4% of GDP. In 2010 agriculture, which employed about 38% of the labor force and supporting 5% of GDP (including forestry), also rested on a relatively diversified base, producing cotton, tobacco, grapes, and a variety of foodstuffs. The transport sector is well developed, integrating the country's various regions and facilitating both domestic and external trade.

Despite its economic potential, Azerbaijan has been slow in making the transition from a command to a market economy. Large state companies continue to dominate the economy and below-market price controls still cover many key commodities. The war with Armenia has also slowed economic growth by disrupting trade ties and draining government revenues. In 1992, Azerbaijan implemented an economic blockade against both Armenia and the enclave of Nagorno-Karabakh, which is still in effect despite the cease-fire reached in 1994. In 1992 the United States passed Section 907 of the Freedom Support Act, restricting assistance to Azerbaijan until "demonstrable steps" were taken to lift the embargo and cease offensive actions. In January 2002, however, US president George W. Bush waived Section 907, purportedly due to Azerbaijan's support of the US-proclaimed War on Terror. In August 2002, CCC, a Greek-based construction and project management firm, won the tender for laying pipes for the Baku-Tbilisi-Ceyhan (BTC) oil pipeline officially approved September 2002 and scheduled to go into operation in 2005. Trade has traditionally been with Russia and the former Soviet republics, although their importance is decreasing, and the economy is still greatly affected by events in those countries.

In 1994, Russia, citing its own conflict in Chechnya, closed all rail and road borders with Azerbaijan. Cut off from its major source of production inputs and main outlet for manufactured projects, Azerbaijan's industrial production fell by more than 20% in 1995. Overall, it is estimated that from 1991 through 1995 the economy declined by about 60%. Since the late 1990s, Azerbaijan has shifted trade to Iran, Turkey, and Europe and away from Russia and Ukraine. The BTC pipeline is designed to avoid Russia. Foreign investment, the majority in hydrocarbons, began a period of steady growth in the late 1990s, and in 2001 the economy registered its fifth straight year of real GDP growth.

Azerbaijan's production of oil has increased every year since 1997, leading to strong economic growth in 2006 and 2007. Starting in 1997 the country partnered with foreign nations in production sharing arrangements (PSAs) for long-term oil-field development. The oil sector accounted for 52.8% of GDP in 2007 and more than 50% in 2008. In 2009 a high GDP growth rate of 9% was maintained in spite of the global economic downturn, reflecting the resiliency provided by oil exports as well as increasing diversification of the economy. Despite this diversification, which has included high growth in banking, construction, and real estate, the economy is still hindered by corruption. World oil prices and new pipeline projects will continue to determine the state of Azerbaijan's economy in the coming years.

20 INCOME

The CIA estimated that in 2010 the GDP of Azerbaijan was $90.79 billion. The CIA defines GDP as the value of all final goods and services produced within a nation in a given year and computed on the basis of purchasing power parity (PPP) rather than value as measured on the basis of the rate of the exchange based on current dollars. The per capita GDP was estimated at $10,900. The annual growth rate of GDP was 5%. The average inflation rate was 5.1%. It was estimated that agriculture accounted for 5.5% of GDP, industry 61.4%, and services 33.1%.

According to the World Bank, remittances from citizens living abroad totaled $1.3 billion or about $152 per capita, equal to approximately 1.4% of GDP.

The World Bank reports that in 2009, household consumption in Azerbaijan totaled $11.6 billion or about $1,389 per capita, measured in current US dollars rather than PPP. Household consumption includes expenditures of individuals, households, and nongovernmental organizations on goods and services, excluding the purchases of dwellings. It was estimated that household consumption was growing at an average annual rate of 12.5%.

As of 2011 the most recent study by the World Bank reported that actual individual consumption in Azerbaijan was 47.5% of GDP and accounted for 0.06% of world consumption. By comparison, the United States accounted for 25.44% of world individual consumption. The World Bank also estimated that 30.3% of Azerbaijan's GDP was spent on food and beverages, 5.5% on housing and household furnishings, 2.7% on clothes, 2.4% on health, 2.8% on transportation, 0.7% on communications, 1.1% on recreation, 1.0% on restaurants and hotels, and 2.3% on miscellaneous goods and services and purchases from abroad.

It was estimated that in 2009 about 11% of the population subsisted on an income below the poverty line established by Azerbaijan's government.

21 LABOR

As of 2010, Azerbaijan had a total labor force of 5.933 million people. Within that labor force, CIA estimates in 2008 noted that 38.3% were employed in agriculture, 12.1% in industry, and 49.6% in the service sector.

The constitution provides for the right to form labor unions, but as of 2010 US Department of State reports claimed the right was limited and unions were generally not independent from the government. The Azerbaijani Trade Union Confederation (ATUC) represented 37% of the formal workforce in 2010 and was only nominally free from government oversight. Collective bargaining is at a rudimentary level. Uniformed police, military, and customs personnel are prohibited from forming unions, and trade unions may not participate in political activity. The use of compulsory labor is limited to certain circumstances.

Government collaboration with multinational corporations in energy production, a major factor behind the mid 2000s rapid GDP growth, allowed labor laws to be circumvented. The PSA (production sharing agreements) did not provide for union membership although the ATUC acknowledged some improvement of the situation by 2009.

In 2010 the government raised the minimum wage to AZN84 ($104) per month. Domestic NGOs maintained that this was insufficient to provide a suitable standard of living for a family and that the rule was often not enforced. As a result, many rely upon outside income sources and the structure of extended families generally, to ensure a decent living. The legal workweek is 40 hours, although workers in dangerous occupations are limited to 36 hours per week. The maximum daily work shift is 12 hours, and lunch and rest periods are also required. There is a minimum working age of 15 with exceptions for children as young as 14 to work in family businesses.

Although health and safety standards have been set by law, these rules are mostly ignored and inspections by the government were ineffective and weak. Workers who leave their jobs due to health and safety hazards do so at the risk of losing their jobs.

22 AGRICULTURE

Roughly 23% of the total land is farmed, and the country's major crops include cotton, grain, rice, grapes, fruit, vegetables, tea, and tobacco. Cereal production in 2009 amounted to 2.9 million tons, fruit production 880,359 tons, and vegetable production 1.5 million tons. There are currently 59 agricultural regions in 10 geographic zones.

Wheat production in Azerbaijan suffers from a number of problems common in the former Soviet Union, including inadequate production credit and lack of inputs. Most wheat is still produced on state farms, as privatization is only beginning. Cotton production has been stagnant due to low producer prices, lack of incentives, and a shortage of both inputs and operating capital. Tobacco is also grown.

During the Soviet period, some 1,200 state and cooperative farms existed. Since independence, former state-owned farms have become more productive, and private fruit and vegetable farming is increasing. Azerbaijan has an expanding wine-producing industry whose wines have frequently won awards at international exhibitions.

23 ANIMAL HUSBANDRY

The UN Food and Agriculture Organization (FAO) reported that Azerbaijan dedicated 2.7 million hectares (6.6 million acres) to permanent pasture or meadow in 2009. During that year, the country tended 21.5 million chickens, 2.3 million head of cattle, and 10,299 pigs. The production from these animals amounted to 76,255 tons of beef and veal, 6,965 tons of pork, 58,852 tons of poultry, 46,890 tons of eggs, and 1.03 million tons of milk. Azerbaijan also produced 13,524 tons of cattle hide and 15,257 tons of raw wool.

24 FISHING

Azerbaijan had 12 decked commercial fishing boats in 2008. The annual capture totaled 1,517 tons according to the UN FAO. The export value of seafood totaled $7.28 million. The Caspian Sea is Azerbaijan's principal fishing resource. Commercial fishing traditionally centered on caviar and sturgeon.

25 FORESTRY

Approximately 11% of Azerbaijan is covered by forest. The UN FAO estimated the 2009 roundwood production at 3,300 cu m (116,538 cu ft). The value of all forest products, including roundwood, totaled $984,000. Soviet-era policies gave priority to high production and rapid growth at the expense of the environment. The State Committee for Ecology and Use of Natural Resources has introduced new regulations to protect forest resources.

26 MINING

Besides significant reserves of natural gas and petroleum, Azerbaijan has iron ore reserves near the disputed Nagorno-Karabakh region, and lead-zinc and copper-molybdenum deposits in the Nakhichevan area. Production of metallic and industrial minerals in 2009 included alumina (40,000 tons in 2009), bromine (3,500 metric tons), gypsum (45,030 metric tons), iodine (300,000 kg), limestone (4,342 metric tons), marble, sand and gravel, decorative building stone, and precious and semiprecious stones. In 2009, exports of aluminum amounted to 13,441 metric tons, down 76% from 2008, due to lack of global demand for aluminum products.

27 ENERGY AND POWER

The World Bank reported in 2008 that Azerbaijan produced 23.9 billion kWh of electricity and consumed 20.1 billion kWh, or 2,403 kWh per capita. Roughly 99% of energy came from fossil fuels, while 1% came from alternative fuels. Per capita oil consumption was 1,540 kg. Oil production totaled 1.03 million barrels of oil a day.

At the turn of the 20th century, Azerbaijan accounted for half of the world's oil production. Oil wells have been operating in Baku since the 1840s. As of the early 21st century, almost all production came from offshore in the Caspian Sea. Azerbaijan was one of only four former Soviet republics (along with Russian, Kazakhstan, and Turkmenistan) to be self-sufficient in petroleum. However, production declined following the 1991 breakup of the Soviet Union until foreign investment provided the capital for new development, turning this trend around in 1998. The State Oil Company of Azerbaijan (SOCAR) has planned for joint development of the offshore fields (which are now largely untapped) and has entered into several agreements to build oil pipelines.

Natural gas production has become more important in recent years, especially in Baku, where some of the oil wells have been exhausted. Proven reserves as of late 2010 totaled 30 trillion cu ft. Production of natural gas in 2010 totaled 589 billion cu ft. In January 2010 Azerbaijan and Iran struck an agreement that would allow 1.2 million cu m (425 million cu ft) of natural gas to flow daily from Azerbaijan to Iran. The deal expired in March 2010. Because its terrain impedes supply routes from the energy-rich south, Iran imports considerable amounts of natural gas to fuel its northern region. At the same time, highly lucrative Caspian gas is at the center of the geopolitical competition between Russia, Europe, and Iran. In securing large contracts with countries like Azerbaijan, Iran also strengthens its regional position.

Petroleum and natural gas resources are the basis for an extensive system of refineries, which produce gasoline, herbicides, fertilizers, kerosene, synthetic rubber, and plastics.

28 INDUSTRY

The oil and gas industry has traditionally been pivotal to the economy; in 1891, Azerbaijan produced more than half of the world's total oil production. Oil refining is concentrated in the Azerineftyag (Baku) refinery and the Azerneftyanajag (New Baku) refinery. Both refineries are in need of modernization, which the government estimates will cost $600 million to $700 million.

Failure to replace worn and outdated technology as well as falling demand in the rest of the former USSR resulted in a steady decline in the production of oil products since the early 1980s. The offshore Gunashli petroleum mining operation supplies half of the country's petroleum.

In line with the historic importance of the oil sector for the Azeri economy, the fabrication of equipment related to petroleum production had been one of the country's major industries. As a source of 70% of the former Soviet Union's oilfield equipment, it also held great importance for other oil-producing post-Soviet republics in the early years of the transition from Communism. Azerbaijan's petroleum equipment manufacturing industry comprised the second-largest concentration of such industries in the world (behind that of the United States). Like most other of the country's economic sectors, however, the industry was plagued by plant obsolescence.

Other important industrial sectors in the Azeri economy include electrical power production, chemicals, food processing, cars and other transport equipment, and tobacco goods, as well as various kinds of light manufacturing.

29 SCIENCE AND TECHNOLOGY

Patent applications in science and technology as of 2009, according to the World Bank, totaled 222 in Azerbaijan. Public financing of science was 0.17% of GDP. The Azerbaijan Academy of Sciences in Baku has departments of physical engineering and mathematical sciences, chemistry, earth sciences, and biology. The country has numerous other institutes conducting research in agriculture, medicine, and technology.

The Azerbaijan Technical University in Baku, founded in 1920, has faculties in automation and computing technology, electrical engineering, machine-building, automechanics, metallurgy, radio-engineering, robotics, and transport. Baku State University, founded in 1919, has faculties of mathematics, physics, chemistry, biology, geology, and geography. Azerbaijan also has five higher institutes offering courses in agriculture, medicine, petroleum engineering, engineering, and technology. The Azerbaijan Scientific and Technical Library is located in Baku.

30 DOMESTIC TRADE

Despite the government's claims that it is moving towards a free market economy, government ownership is still common among large industries. Since independence, there has been an informal privatization of the trading sector as many small shops have sprung up throughout Azerbaijan. Private traders now handle most retail sales. Private business people see trade as relatively low risk in an environment where private ownership rights do not exist. Business and retail hours can vary according to the owner's preference; however, most businesses are open from 9 a.m. to 6 p.m., Monday through Friday. Many businesses and offices also have Saturday hours. Private transactions are primarily in cash. Credit cards are not generally accepted, except in major hotels and restaurants. An 18% value added tax applies to all goods and services.

Principal Trading Partners – Azerbaijan (2010)

(In millions of US dollars)

Country	Total	Exports	Imports	Balance
World	27,924.1	21,324.8	6,599.3	14,725.5
Italy	7,162.5	7,044.2	118.4	6,925.8
France	1,993.0	1,856.5	136.4	1,720.1
Russia	1,918.6	773.6	1,145.0	-371.5
United States	1,912.9	1,706.6	206.3	1,500.2
Israel	1,804.2	1,744.8	59.4	1,685.5
Ukraine	1,354.2	888.6	465.6	423.1
Turkey	948.3	170.9	777.4	-606.6
China	926.5	338.9	587.6	-248.8
Croatia	789.1	787.2	1.9	785.3
Indonesia	788.5	782.2	6.4	775.8

(…) data not available or not significant.

(n.s.) not specified.

SOURCE: *2011 Direction of Trade Statistics Yearbook*, New York: United Nations, 2011.

31 FOREIGN TRADE

Azerbaijan imported $7.035 billion worth of goods and services in 2008, while exporting $28.07 billion worth of goods and services. Major import partners in 2009 were Russia, 17.5%; Turkey, 14.8%; Germany, 9%; Ukraine, 8.4%; China, 7.9%; UK, 4.5%; and the United States, 4.3%. Its major export partners were Italy, 25.8%; the United States, 11.9%; France, 9%; Israel, 8.4%; Russia, 5.1%; and Indonesia, 4.5%.

Like other post-Soviet economies, Azerbaijan is highly trade-dependent; however, it is endowed with a more diversified export structure than many other former Soviet countries, especially in neighboring Central Asia. While the centrally planned state ordering system is steadily losing its place as the basis for trade in the former Soviet Union, the Azeri Ministry of Foreign Economic Relations still controls the export of all products considered to be of strategic importance to the national economy.

32 BALANCE OF PAYMENTS

The war with Armenia in and around Nagorno-Karabakh had facilitated Azerbaijan's trade deterioration, which was further exacerbated by the collapse of the local currency. Reviving ruble-related trade links with Russia was a key reason for Azerbaijan's entry into the Commonwealth of Independent States in September 1992. In 2010 Azerbaijan had a foreign trade surplus of $13 billion, amounting to 0.4% of GDP. Azerbaijan's current account balance showed a surplus beginning in 2005—its first since independence from the Soviet Union—which continued through 2010 ($15.04 billion).

33 BANKING AND SECURITIES

The National Bank of Azerbaijan is the central bank of Azerbaijan. It is charged with regulating the money supply, circulating currency, and regulating the commercial banks of the country. However, the banking system in Azerbaijan is minimal and ineffective. An estimated $1 billion is held in cash or outside the banking sector, a considerable amount in comparison with the scope of the country's entire economy.

There are approximately 70 foreign and local banks in Azerbaijan. Of the four state-owned banks, only the International Bank of Azerbaijan (IBA) was solvent in 1999. The IBA was in the process of being privatized that year; completion of the privatization process was expected in mid-2012. Major commercial banks include the Promtekhbank, Azakbank, Azerdemiryolbank, Bacobank, Gunay International Bank, Halgbank, ILKBANK, and the Universal Bank. Most businesses use the IBA, or the British Bank of the Middle East, Baku.

In 2010, the discount rate, the interest rate at which the central bank lends to financial institutions in the short term, was 3%.

The Baku Stock Exchange, known as the BSE, opened in 2001 trading short-term treasury bonds and the common stock of recently privatized state-owned enterprises.

34 INSURANCE

At least eight insurance companies were operating in Azerbaijan in 2011. In 2010 per capita insurance premiums totaled AZN17.2 ($21.4). The sector showed strong growth in 2008–11.

35 PUBLIC FINANCE

Since 1996, the Azerbaijani government has emphasized privatization as a means towards consolidation of the public debt and revitalization of the economy. More than 20,600 companies were privatized during 1997 and 1998. The CIA estimated that in 2010 the budget of Azerbaijan included $14.19 billion in public revenue and $14.64 billion in public expenditures. The budget deficit amounted to .8% of GDP. Public debt was 4.6% of GDP, with $3.221 billion of the debt held by foreign entities.

36 TAXATION

On 1 January 2001, a new tax code went into effect. Personal income rates remained the same, at rates ranging from 12–35%, as

Public Finance – Azerbaijan (2008)		
(In billions of manat, central government figures)		
Revenue and Grants	10,371	100.0%
Tax revenue	6,363.3	61.4%
Social contributions	...	...
Grants	...	...
Other revenue	4,007.7	38.6%
Expenditures	10,233.4	100.0%
General public services	...	...
Defense	...	...
Public order and safety	...	...
Economic affairs	...	...
Environmental protection	...	...
Housing and community amenities	...	...
Health	...	...
Recreational, culture, and religion	...	...
Education	...	...
Social protection	...	...

(...) data not available or not significant.

SOURCE: *Government Finance Statistics Yearbook 2010*, Washington, DC: International Monetary Fund, 2010.

did the corporate tax rate, at 27%. However, by 2011, the corporate rate was set at 20%. The revised depreciation schedule for corporate assets favors investments in high-tech equipment and oil and gas exploration. Depreciation rates are 10% a year for buildings, 25% a year for equipment and computers, 25% for geological and exploratory costs, and 20% a year for all other assets. However, accelerated depreciation is allowed for capital spending allocated for production purposes at twice the standard rates. Included in this are expenditures on the building of those facilities that are to be used in the actual manufacture of goods. The value-added tax (VAT) was reduced from 20% to 18%, while the property tax was raised from .5% to 1% of assessed value. A 0.05% Road Fund Tax on turnover was abolished, but there is a highway tax imposed on foreign-registered vehicles collected by customs authorities. There are payroll taxes paid by the employer amounting to 32%, 30% going to the Social Protection Fund, and 2% going to the Employment Fund. There are excise taxes, but excise paid for goods used in production can be offset against excise charged for the finished product.

37 CUSTOMS AND DUTIES

Tariffs are set at 15%, 5%, 3%, or 0.5%. Most goods carry the 15% import customs duty. Capital goods and some primary goods are exempt. There is also a 20% value-added tax on certain imports. A dividend withholding tax of 15% is applicable to monies sent abroad.

In 1992, Azerbaijan signed trade agreements with all the republics of the former USSR except Armenia and Russia. Azerbaijan joined the Commonwealth of Independent States (CIS) in September 1993 and acceded to the CIS economic union treaty the same year. Azerbaijan is a member of the Economic Cooperation Organization. In 1999, Azerbaijan entered into a Partnership and Cooperation Agreement with the European Union and was seeking membership in the World Trade Organization, but as of 2012 was only an observer nation.

Balance of Payments – Azerbaijan (2010)		
(In millions of US dollars)		
Current Account		15,040.4
Balance on goods		19,730.0
Imports	-6,745.6	
Exports	26,476.0	
Balance on services		-1,732.1
Balance on income		-3,467.1
Current transfers		509.1
Capital Account		14.3
Financial Account		-12,695.0
Direct investment abroad		-232.0
Direct investment in Azerbaijan		563.1
Portfolio investment assets		-163.3
Portfolio investment liabilities		24.5
Financial derivatives		...
Other investment assets		-14,698.0
Other investment liabilities		1,810.6
Net Errors and Omissions		-989.7
Reserves and Related Items		-1,370.0

(...) data not available or not significant.

SOURCE: *Balance of Payment Statistics Yearbook 2011*, Washington, DC: International Monetary Fund, 2011.

³⁸FOREIGN INVESTMENT

Foreign direct investment (FDI) in Azerbaijan was a net inflow of $473.3 million according to World Bank figures published in 2009. FDI represented 1.1% of GDP.

Foreign investment plays a major role in financing the development of much of Azerbaijan's industrial sector, especially the oil and gas-related industries. The 1992 Law on Foreign Investment provided many basic guarantees to foreign investors, including nondiscriminatory treatment, the repatriation of profits, guarantees against expropriation, and dispute settlement. The Privatization Law passed in 1995 allowed foreign investors to acquire shares in state companies and purchase real estate jointly. Starting in 1997, foreign tax privileges were revoked. As of 1999, foreign investors were required to obtain a license and pay a fee in order to open business in Azerbaijan.

Although the US government had banned public aid to Azerbaijan in 1992, US investors played a large role in exploiting Azerbaijani oil reserves, increasingly so since January 2002 when the Bush administration waived the ban on public assistance (due to Azerbaijan's trade embargo against Armenia and Nagorno-Karabakh) because of Azerbaijan's support in the War on Terror.

Significant foreign investors in the energy sector included British Petroleum (BP)-the designated operator for both the ACG oil field and the Shah Deniz natural gas field-Unocal, ExxonMobil, Devon Energy (Pennzoil), Chevron, Conoco, Moncrief Oil, TPAO (Turkish Oil Company), Statoil (Norway), Lukoil (Russia), Itochu (Japan), Agip (Italy), and TotalfinaELF (France).

The Baku-Tbilisi-Ceyhan pipeline was completed in May 2005 and the first oil reached Ceyhan in May 2006. The pipeline provides an exit for Azeri hydrocarbons that avoids Russian territory and has brought significant income to the region.

³⁹ECONOMIC DEVELOPMENT

Rapid development of the Azeri economy in the former USSR was based on the expansion of both its industrial sector, led by oil-related industries, and its agricultural sector, led by grape, tobacco, and cotton production. With grape and wine production weakened by the effects of Gorbachev's anti-alcoholism campaign in the 1980s, and much of the country's industrial sector afflicted by technological obsolescence, overall economic growth in the republic had already begun to decline by 1989, when NMP dropped 6%. Real GDP contracted by almost 60% from 1990 to 1995. However, in the late 1990s, foreign investment in the country's oil and natural gas sectors opened a period of steady growth. Key strategies of the Azeri government to bring about economic revitalization have included both an economic restructuring program as well as efforts to expand its economic ties to countries beyond the former Soviet Union. To the latter end, Azerbaijan joined the Economic Cooperation Organization set up by Iran, Pakistan, and Turkey to promote trade among Muslim countries. It was also the first of the former Soviet republics to become a member of the Islamic Development Bank, which provides potential access to financing for programs related to agriculture, construction, training, and food aid. In 2002, economic prospects brightened considerably with progress made on its two major pipeline projects designed to connect the Caspian Sea to the Turkish Mediterranean to provide oil and gas for the European and North American markets, the

Baku-Tbilisi-Ceyhan Export Oil Pipeline (BTC) and the Baku-Tbilisi-Erzrum Gas Pipeline. The BTC particularly received an important impetus when the Azeri government came out as a strong ally of the United States in its War on Terror.

The restructuring program in Azerbaijan has been similar to those of other countries in the former USSR. Its main points include stabilization measures (price liberalization, introduction of national currency, and establishment of an exchange rate stabilization fund); introduction of new legislation regarding privatization, foreign investment, and employment; fiscal and monetary reform (including introduction of a VAT and controls on government expenditures); civil service reform; and development of the banking sector. Four committees on antitrust, support for enterprises, state property, and land reform have been established to oversee the implementation of reform legislation. Privatization of the state enterprise sector is moving at a slow pace. Particular attention is being directed at modernizing those strategic sectors of the economy with the greatest potential for export growth, particularly the oil industry and, to a lesser extent, textile production; the role of foreign investment is seen as pivotal in these areas.

Economic reforms in the early 2000s came under the conservative supervision of the IMF and the World Bank, which also took aim at the problem of pervasive corruption in the administration of taxes and custom duties. In 2002, Azerbaijan was under a three-year Poverty Reduction and Growth Facility (PRGF) program with the IMF, the objectives of which include establishing financial discipline in the energy sector, and increasing efficiency and transparency in the operations of the Ministry of Taxation and the State Customs Committee, and developing a comprehensive anti-corruption program.

In March 2002, Azerbaijan reached agreement with the World Bank for a second Structural Adjustment Credit (SAC-II) program, funded at $60 million. Azerbaijan's two previous privatization programs since its transition to a free market economy faltered on the lack security and market transparency. The first, from 1996 to 1998, focused on small and medium-sized enterprises was hindered by lack of resources to properly prepare assets for privatization and insufficient information about these enterprises. A presidential decree of August 2000 opened up case-by-case sales of some of the country's largest enterprises, and in March 2001 additional decrees were issued identifying about 450 enterprises to be privatized during the second privatization program. Progress continued to be slow, however. Attempts to privatize large state enterprises, such as the Azerboru pipe facility, failed for lack of qualified bidders, although by January 2002 the government had succeeded in placing the Baku electrical distribution network under the long-term private management of a Turkish firm, Barmek Holdings.

The diversification of the economy in the mid to late 2000s and the very strong GDP growth from 2006 to 2009 helped bolster the Azeri economy and provide new sources of revenue. Azerbaijan is strategically located between fast growing and high resource regions of Eastern Europe, Turkey, Iran, Russia, and the Central Asian states, and could be an important economic player regionally.

In 2012, approximately twenty years after the dissolution of the Soviet Union, the Azeri economy was still feeling the long term impact of its history. Corruption remained endemic, with NGO

Freedom House giving Azerbaijan a 6.5 out of 10 rating on corruption in 2010, and noting that corruption is the primary obstacle to economic development. Much of the soviet-era infrastructure has not been updated. Despite this, Azerbaijan's oil wealth has ensured consistent GDP growth since the late 1990s, although it has underachieved economically.

40 SOCIAL DEVELOPMENT

Old age, disability, and survivor benefits have been provided since 1956. Pensions are provided for men at age 62 with 25 years of employment, and at age 57 for women with 20 years of employment. Social insurance, instituted in 1997, covers all employed residents. Workers' compensation provides both short-term disability benefits and pensions. Unemployment benefits were introduced in 1991. To obtain benefits there must be at least 26 weeks of covered employment in the 12 months prior to unemployment. These benefits are suspended if the applicant refuses two acceptable job offers. Benefits amount to 70% of average gross monthly earnings but are not to exceed the national average monthly wage.

Women nominally enjoy the same legal status as men but are underrepresented in government and higher levels of the work force. Although women receive opportunities for education, work, and political activity, social traditions tend to keep them in subordinate positions. Violence against women is a serious problem especially in rural areas. The government is committed to protecting the rights of children, however economic hardship limits the ability to safeguard children.

Ethnic tensions and anti-Armenian sentiment are still strong. Many Armenians have either been expelled or emigrated. Other minorities, such as the Kurds and the Turks, also report problems of discrimination. The constitution provides for freedom of assembly, religion, and speech, but these rights are often restricted by the government. Azerbaijan's human rights record remains poor. Excessive force is used by police, and the judicial system continues to be inefficient and corrupt. Torture remains a problem, and harsh prison conditions continue.

41 HEALTH

According to the CIA, life expectancy in Azerbaijan was 70 years in 2011. The country spent 4.3% of its GDP on healthcare, amounting to $285 per person. There were 38 physicians, 84 nurses and midwives, and 79 hospital beds per 10,000 inhabitants. The fertility rate was 2.3, while the infant mortality rate was 30 per 1,000 live births. In 2008 the maternal mortality rate, according to the World Bank, was 38 per 100,000 births. It was estimated that 67% of children were vaccinated against measles. The CIA calculated HIV/AIDS prevalence in Azerbaijan to be about 0.1% in 2009.

42 HOUSING

About 67% of current dwellings were built within the period 1981–96. In the period 1991–95, construction of new housing fell by nearly 50% due to poor economic conditions and the government estimated that a total of about 107,000 homes had been lost due to the conflict over Nagorno-Karabakh.

About 94% of the population has access to piped water (cold), but only 19.2% have access to hot piped water. About 92% have access to appropriate sewage systems and 76% have central heating systems. Most private homes are located in rural areas. Housing construction was growing rapidly as of 2011, with 1.9 million sq m (20.5 million sq ft) of housing constructed that year, a 6.8% growth over 2010. Despite record constructions, the housing market declined by 6% during 2011.

43 EDUCATION

In 2009 the World Bank estimated that 85% of age-eligible children in Azerbaijan were enrolled in primary school. Secondary enrollment for age-eligible children stood at 93%. Tertiary enrollment was estimated at 19%. Of those enrolled in tertiary education, there were 100 male students for every 79 female students. Overall, the CIA estimated that Azerbaijan had a literacy rate of 98.8%.

Education is compulsory for students between the ages of 6 and 15. Primary school covers a program of four years, followed by a five-year basic program and a two-year secondary program. Secondary students might choose to attend a three-year technical program instead. The usual language of instruction is Azerbaijani, although Russian, Armenian, Georgian, and English are also offered by some schools. The academic year runs from September through May. The Ministry of Education and the Council of University Presidents are the primary national administrative bodies.

Azerbaijan's most important institutes of higher learning are the Azerbaijan Polytechnic Institute, located in Baku, with seven departments and an enrollment of 12,000 students; and the State University, also located at Baku and founded in 1919. It has an enrollment of over 15,000 students in 11 departments. Other institutions include the Medical University, Technological University, the Economic Institute, and the Oil and Chemistry Academy. Russian is more commonly used as the language of instruction at higher-level institutions, but this is slowly changing with a growing demand for the use of Azerbaijani.

Baku is sometimes referred to as an "oil academy" because of its ongoing research in the areas of turbine drilling, cementation of oil wells, and the development of synthetic rubber from natural gas.

44 LIBRARIES AND MUSEUMS

The Mirza Fatali Akhundov National Library of Azerbaijan is in Baku and contains about 4.4 million volumes. Other public libraries in Baku include City Central Library, the Kocharli Azerbaijan State Children's Library, and Jafar Jabbarly Republican Youth Library. The country has about 4,000 public libraries that are administered by the Ministry of Culture. Academic libraries include a library of Russian language and literature at the Azerbaijan Pedagogical University and a scientific library at Baku State University. The Azerbaijan Library Development Association was founded in 1999.

There are 115 recognized museums in the country, 27 of which are art museums, and there are 20 theaters. The country also has 6,571 monuments and historic sites. The Ichari Shahar, or Old Town, in Baku has the Shirvanshah Palace, an architectural monument from the 15th and 16th centuries which has been restored and is now a museum. Other museums are the Museum of History of Azerbaijan (1920), which exhibits archeological, ethnographic, and other relics; the Rustam Mustfayev Azerbaijan State Arts Museum, displaying works of Azerbaijani, Russian and

West European artists from the 15th–19th centuries along with the works of modern Azerbaijani artists; the State Museum of Azerbaijani Carpets and Folk and Applied Art; and the Nizami State Museum of Azerbaijani Literature, depicting the stages of literary development. The Gobustan Museum features prehistoric dwellings and cave paintings over 10,000 years old. Baku, the capital, remains an important cultural and intellectual center in Transcaucasia.

45 MEDIA

In 2009 the CIA reported that there were 1.4 million telephone landlines in Azerbaijan. In addition to landlines, mobile phone subscriptions averaged 88 per 100 people. There were 117 AM radio stations and 1 shortwave radio station. Internet users numbered 42 per 100 citizens. Prominent newspapers in 2010, with circulation numbers listed parenthetically, included *Azerbaijan*, *Azerbaijan Ganjlari* (161,000), and *Mukhalifat*.

Azerbaijan is connected to other former Soviet republics by land-line or microwave communications, and to other countries through Moscow. Overall, phone service is said to be of poor quality and inadequate. Most telephones are in Baku and other industrial centers. There are about 700 villages still without public telephone service.

A majority of radio and television broadcasting sources are controlled by the government, but some private stations have begun to flourish. Domestic and Russian television programs are received locally, while Iranian television is received from an Intelsat satellite through a receive-only earth station.

In 2010, the country had about 22,737 Internet hosts. As of 2009, there were some 2.4 million Internet users in Azerbaijan.

The constitution of Azerbaijan specifically outlaws press censorship; however, it is said that the government does not always respect freedom of the press in practice. Azerbaijan drew international attention and condemnation in November 2009 after an Azeri court sentenced two political bloggers, who often parody government officials, to over two years in prison. The bloggers were convicted of hooliganism for their involvement in a fight at a restaurant. The bloggers claimed that the Azeri government orchestrated the fight after they posted a mock press conference on YouTube depicting a government leader as a donkey. For their part, prosecutors in the case said the arrests had nothing to do with the video.

46 ORGANIZATIONS

The Azerbaijan Republic Chamber of Commerce and Industry is based in Baku. Azad Istehlakchilar Birliyi is an independent consumers' union. Important political associations in the Republic of Azerbaijan include the Helsinki Group, a human rights group, the National Democratic Movement, and Musavat (Equality). The Committee of Democracy and Human Rights in Azerbaijan, founded in 1993, is made up of both individuals and organizations focusing on promoting respect for human rights. The group publicizes human rights abuses and offers legal assistance to victims.

The Azerbaijan Medical Association promotes the rights of both physicians and patients and serves as a networking organization for a number of associations in specialized fields of medicine.

A number of groups promote and protect civil rights and humanitarian and development needs for women and children. These include: the Association for the Defense of Rights of Azerbaijan Women, the Azerbaijan Women's Association, Azerbaijan Women and Development Center, Azerbaijan Women's Intelligence Organization, Azerbaijani League for the Defense of the Rights of Children, and the Mothers Outcry Society.

There are over 20 youth organizations united and coordinated in part by the National Assembly of Youth Organizations of Azerbaijan (NAYORA), which was established in 1995. The Azerbaijan Union of the Democratic Youth (AUDY), established in 1994, is an independent group seeking to unite youth of all languages, religions, and nationalities into a single cause of patriotism for an independent and democratic Azerbaijan society. A scouting organization is also present. There are several athletic associations representing particular sports, including skating, weightlifting, handball, and track and field. There is a National Olympic Committee, a Paralympic Committee, and a chapter of the Special Olympics.

There are national chapters of the Red Crescent Society, UNICEF, World Vision, and Caritas.

47 TOURISM, TRAVEL, AND RECREATION

The *Tourism Factbook*, published by the UN World Tourism Organization, reported 1.83 million incoming tourists to Azerbaijan in 2009; they spent a total of $516 million. Of those incoming tourists, there were 1.5 million from Europe and 340,000 from South Asia. There were 30,571 hotel beds available in Azerbaijan, which had an occupancy rate of 55%. The estimated daily cost to visit Baku (Baki, Baky), the capital, was $194. The cost of visiting other cities averaged $163.

The capital city of Baku is one of the prime tourist destinations of the Caucasus region. Its Old Town, with the Shirvanshah Palace dating back to the 15–16th centuries, is especially popular with sightseers. Other attractions include the Museum of History and the State Arts Museum, as well as museums of folk art and literature. Elsewhere in Azerbaijan, the Gobustan Museum displays prehistoric dwellings and cave paintings, and the village of Surakhani attracts visitors to the Atashgah Fire-Worshipper's Temple. Visitors are also welcome at the carpet-weaving factory in the village of Nardaran, the Wine-making State Farm in the Shamakhi area, the Fruit and Vegetable State Farm around the town of Guba, and the Mashtagha Subtropical Fruit State Farm.

In November 2010, the traditional art of Azerbaijani carpet weaving was officially inscribed on the UNESCO Representative List of the Intangible Heritage of Humanity, an offshoot of the World Heritage program. The craft was deemed a living tradition by UNESCO, meaning that it is still passed from generation to generation and continues to create a sense of identity and community for those who participate. Such traditions have been approved by UNESCO for special consideration since 2001. For one that is inscribed, a special program is designed to protect and promote the practice and understanding of the tradition. In Azerbaijan, carpet weaving is a family tradition, with men tending and shearing sheep for wool and women dyeing, spinning, and weaving the fabric into intricately designed carpets. The techniques and patterns used in different regions of the country are taught from one generation to the next through oral tradition and practice.

48 FAMOUS PERSONS

Heydar Aliyev (1923?–2003) was president from 1993 until 2003, when he was succeeded by his son Ilham Aliyev (b. 1961). The poet Nizami Ganjavi (1141–1204) is celebrated for his *Khamsa*, a collection of five epic poems. Muhammed Fizuli (1438–1556) based his poems on traditional folktales, and his poetic versions provide the basis for many 20th century plays and operas. Satirical poet Sabir (1862–1911) was openly critical of the clergy at a time when their influence controlled much of society. Abul Hasan Bakhmanyar, an 11th century scientist, wrote respected books on mathematics and philosophy. Hasan Shirvani wrote a book on astronomy.

The composer Uzeyir Hajibeyov (1885–1948) wrote the first Azerbaijani opera, and also founded the Azerbaijani Symphonic Orchestra and composed Azerbaijan's National Anthem. Other famous composers from Azerbaijan include Gara Garayev (1918–82), Haji Khannmammadov (b. 1918), Fikrat Amirov (1922–84), and Vasif Adigozal (b. 1936). Vagif Mustafa Zadeh (1940–79) is considered the founder of the Azerbaijani music movement of the 1960s that mixed jazz with the traditional style known as *mugam*. His daughter, Aziza Mustafa Zadeh (b. 1969), is a noted jazz pianist.

Prominent modern Azerbaijani scientists include Lotfi Zadeh (b. 1921), pioneer of the "fuzzy logic" concept, and Ali Javan (b. Iran, 1928), inventor of the gas laser.

49 DEPENDENCIES

Azerbaijan has no territories or colonies.

50 BIBLIOGRAPHY

Azerbaijan Investment and Business Guide: Strategic and Practical Information. Washington, DC: International Business Publications USA, 2012.

Cornell, Svante E. *Azerbaijan Since Independence.* Armonk, NY: M.E. Sharpe, 2011.

De Waal, Thomas. *Black Garden: Armenia and Azerbaijan Through Peace and War.* New York: New York University Press, 2003.

———. *The Caucasus: An Introduction.* New York: Oxford University Press, 2010.

Elliot, Mark. *Azerbaijan with Georgia.* Cincinnati, OH: Seven Hills, 2001.

Leeuw, Charles van der. *Azerbaijan: A Quest for Identity.* New York: St. Martin's Press, 2000.

Liberman, Sherri. *A Historical Atlas of Azerbaijan.* New York: Rosen, 2004.

Streissguth, Thomas. *The Transcaucasus.* San Diego, CA: Lucent Books, 2001.

Terterov, Marat, ed. *Doing Business with Azerbaijan.* 2nd ed. London, Eng.: Kogan Page, 2005.

BAHRAIN

Kingdom of Bahrain
Mamlakat al Bahrayn

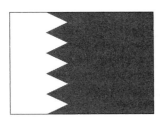

CAPITAL: Manama (Al-Manamah)

FLAG: The flag of Bahrain is red, the traditional color for flags of Persian Gulf states, with a vertical white serrated band (five white points) on the hoist side; the five points represent the five pillars of Islam.

ANTHEM: *Bahrainona (Our Bahrain).*

MONETARY UNIT: The Bahrain dinar (BHD) is divided into 1,000 fils. There are coins of 5, 10, 25, 50, and 100 fils, and notes of 500 fils and 1, 5, 10, and 20 dinars. BHD1 = US$2.65957 (or US$1 = BHD0.376) as of 2010.

WEIGHTS AND MEASURES: The metric system is the legal standard; local measures are also used.

HOLIDAYS: New Year's Day, 1 January; National Day, 16 December. Movable Muslim religious holidays include Hijra (Muslim New Year), Ashura, Milad an-Nabi, Eid al-Fitr, and Eid al-Adha.

TIME: 3 p.m. = noon GMT.

¹LOCATION, SIZE, AND EXTENT

Situated in the western Persian Gulf, 29 km (18 mi) NW of Qatar, the State of Bahrain consists of a group of 33 islands (6 inhabited) with a total area of 620 sq km (239 sq mi), extending 48 km (30 mi) N–S and 19 km (12 mi) E–W. Comparatively, Bahrain occupies slightly less than 3.5 times the area of Washington, DC. Bahrain, the main island, is linked by causeways and bridges to the Muharraq and Sitra islands and to Saudi Arabia; other islands include the Hawar group, Nabih Salih, Umm an Nasān, and Jiddah. The total coastline is 161 km (100 mi). Bahrain's capital city, Manama, is located on the northeastern coast.

²TOPOGRAPHY

A narrow strip of land along the north coast of Bahrain is irrigated by natural springs and artesian wells. South of the cultivable area, the land is barren. The landscape consists of low rolling hills with numerous rocky cliffs and wadis. From the shoreline the surface rises gradually toward the center, where it drops into a basin surrounded by steep cliffs. Toward the center of the basin is Jabal ad-Dukhan, a rocky, steep-sided hill that rises to 122 m (400 ft). Most of the lesser islands are flat and sandy, while Nabih Salih is covered with date groves.

³CLIMATE

Summers in Bahrain are hot and humid, and winters are relatively cool. Daily average temperatures in July range from a minimum of 29°C (84°F) to a maximum of 37°C (99°F); the average minimum temperature in January is 14°C (57°F), the average maximum 20°C (68°F). Rainfall averages less than 10 cm (4 in) annually and occurs mostly from December to March. Prevailing southeast winds occasionally raise dust storms.

⁴FLORA AND FAUNA

The World Resources Institute estimates that there are 195 plant species in Bahrain. In addition, Bahrain is home to 14 species of mammals, 196 types of birds, 18 species of reptiles, and 1 type of amphibian. The calculation reflects the total number of distinct species residing in the country, not the number of endemic species.

Outside the cultivated areas, numerous wild desert flowers appear, most noticeably after rain. Desert shrubs, grasses, and wild date palms are also found. Mammalian life is limited to the jerboa (desert rat), gazelle, mongoose, and hare. Larks, song thrushes, swallows, and terns are frequent visitors, and residents include the bulbul, hoopoe, parakeet, and warbler.

⁵ENVIRONMENT

The World Resources Institute reported that Bahrain had designated 800 hectares (1,977 acres) of land for protection as of 2006. Water resources totaled 0.1 cu km (0.024 cu mi) while water usage was 0.3 cu km (0.072 cu mi) per year. Domestic water usage accounted for 40% of total usage, industrial for 3%, and agricultural for 57%. Per capita water usage totaled 411 cu m (14,514 cu ft) per year.

The World Bank reported that carbon dioxide emissions in Bahrain totaled 22,478.7 kilotons in 2008.

Bahrain's principal environmental problems are scarcity of fresh water, desertification, coastal degradation, and pollution from oil production. Population growth and industrial development have reduced the amount of agricultural land and lowered the water table, leaving aquifers vulnerable to saline contamination. In recent years, the government has attempted to limit extraction of groundwater (in part by expansion of seawater desalinization facilities) and to protect vegetation from further erosion.

Bahrain has developed its oil resources at the expense of its agricultural lands. As a result, lands that might otherwise be productive are gradually claimed by the expansion of the desert. Pollution from oil production was accelerated by the Persian Gulf War and the resulting damage to oil-producing facilities in the Gulf area which threatened the purity of both coastal and ground water, damaging coastlines, coral reefs, and marine vegetation through oil spills and other discharges.

According to a 2011 report issued by the International Union for Conservation of Nature and Natural Resources (IUCN), threatened species included 3 types of mammals, 3 species of birds, 4 types of reptiles, and 8 species of fish. A wildlife sanctuary established in 1980 is home to threatened and at-risk Gulf species, including the Arabian oryx, gazelle, zebra, giraffe, Defassa waterbuck, addax, and lesser kudu. Bahrain has also established captive breeding centers for falcons and for the rare Houbara bustard. The goitered gazelle, the greater spotted eagle, and the green sea turtle are considered endangered species. There are two Ramsar international wetland sites in the country: the Hawar Islands and Tubli Bay.

⁶POPULATION

The US Central Intelligence Agency (CIA) estimated the population of Bahrain in 2011 to be approximately 1,214,705, which placed it at number 153 in population among the 196 nations of the world. In 2011 approximately 2.6% of the population was over 65 years of age, with another 20.5% under 15 years of age. The median age in Bahrain was 30.9 years. There were 1.24 males for every female in the country. The population's annual rate of change was 2.814%. The projected population for the year 2025 was 1,600,000. In 2010 population density in Bahrain was calculated at 1,660 people per sq km (4,299 people per sq mi).

The United Nations (UN) estimated that 89% of the population lived in urban areas, and that urban populations had an annual rate of change of 1.8%. The largest urban area was Manama, with a population of 163,000.

⁷MIGRATION

The total number of immigrants living in Bahrain was 315,403 as of 2010. Most are temporary workers from Iran, Pakistan, India, the Republic of Korea, and other Arab countries. Many skilled workers are Europeans.

A population of stateless inhabitants in Bahrain is the Bidun, a name derived from the Arabic expression meaning "without nationality." The Bidun have no proof of citizenship for their home country. In 2001 Bahrain granted the majority of 9,000–15,000 Bidun citizenship status, giving them the right to own land, start a business, or get government loans. Most Bahraini Bidun are of Iranian origin and are mostly Shiite, with some Christians.

⁸ETHNIC GROUPS

About 63% of the population consists of indigenous Bahrainis, the vast majority of whom are of northern Arab (Adnani) stock, infused with black racial traits. Asians account for 19% of the population; other Arab groups (principally Omanis) 10%; and Iranians 8%.

⁹LANGUAGES

Arabic is the official language of the country; the Gulf dialect is spoken. English is widely understood. Farsi and Urdu are spoken by small groups of people.

¹⁰RELIGIONS

In 2010 an estimated 98% of the country's citizens were Muslim, with about two-thirds practicing the Shia branch and the others Sunni. Foreigners make up 37% of the total population; roughly half are non-Muslim, including Christians, Jews, Hindus, Buddhists, Sikhs, and Baha'is. The primary Christian groups include Roman Catholics, Protestants, Syrian Orthodox, and Mar Thoma (originating in southwest India). All are free to practice their own religions, keep their own places of worship, and display the symbols for their religions. Islam, however, is the official religion and Islamic law is the basis for legislation and some of the legal system. Islamic holidays are observed as national holidays. Religious groups are required to obtain a license from the government through the Ministry of Islamic Affairs, but small unlicensed groups have operated without government interference. Sunni Muslims, though a minority, seem to enjoy a favored status, as Shias face discrimination and disadvantage in social and economic realms.

¹¹TRANSPORTATION

The CIA reports that Bahrain has a total of 3,851 km (2,393 mi) of roads, of which 3,121 km (1,939 mi) are paved. There are 509 vehicles per 1,000 people in the country. There are four airports, which transported 5.22 million passengers in 2009 according to the World Bank.

The outline of the present road network was traced in the early 1930s, soon after the discovery of oil. The four main islands and all the towns and villages are linked by excellent roads. A four-lane, 2.8-km (1.7-mi) causeway and bridge connects Manama with Al Muharraq, and another bridge joins Sitra to the main island. A four-lane highway atop a 24-km (15-mi) causeway links Bahrain with the Saudi Arabian mainland via Umm an Nasān and was completed in December 1986, financed by Saudi Arabia.

Bahrain's port of Mina' Salman can accommodate 16 ocean-going vessels drawing up to 11 m (36 ft). In 2008 Bahrain had a merchant fleet of nine ships of 1,000 gross registered tons (GRT) or over. There was one heliport. The international airport near Al Muharraq can handle large jet aircraft and serves more than two dozen international airlines. Gulf Air, headquartered in Bahrain and owned equally by the governments of Bahrain, Oman, Qatar, and the United Arab Emirates (UAE), flies to other Gulf countries, India, and Europe.

Construction on the world's longest marine causeway, the 40-km (24.85-mi) Friendship Bridge, is planned to connect the east coast of Bahrain with the west coast of Qatar with passenger and freight rail lines as well as a marine highway. Analysts estimated the cost of the project to fall between $3 and $4 billion, a significant sum to be shared equally by the governments of Qatar and Bahrain. Project officials expected the project to be completed by 2015.

12 HISTORY

The history of Bahrain has been traced back 5,000 years to Sumerian times. Known as Dilmun, Bahrain was a thriving trade center around 2000 BC; the islands were visited by the ships of Alexander the Great in the 3rd century BC. Bahrain accepted Islam in the 7th century AD, after which it was ruled alternately by its own princes and by the caliphs' governors. The Portuguese occupied Bahrain from 1522 to 1602. The present ruling family, the Khalifa, who are related to the Sabah family of Kuwait and the Saudi royal family, captured Bahrain in 1782. Following an initial contact in 1805, the ruler of Bahrain signed the first treaty with Britain in 1820. A binding treaty of protection, similar to those with other Persian Gulf principalities, was concluded in 1861 and revised in 1892 and 1951. After World War II, Britain maintained its headquarters for treaty affairs in the lower Gulf in Bahrain. Claims to Bahrain pressed by Iran were abandoned in 1971 after a UN mission ascertained that the Bahrainis wished to remain independent of that nation.

Between 1968 and 1971 Bahrain participated in discussions aimed at forming a federation of the nine sheikhdoms of the southern Gulf. On 14 August 1971 Sheikh 'Isa bin Salman al-Khalifa declared that, in view of the failure of the larger federation to materialize, Bahrain would declare its independence. Its treaties with the United Kingdom were replaced by a treaty of friendship and cooperation, and on 15 August the country became the sovereign State of Bahrain. Bahrain promulgated its first constitution in 1973, which occasioned the convening of an elective National Assembly; the legislature was dissolved in August 1975 amid charges of communist influence. The emir continued to set state policy and his brother, Crown Prince Hamad bin 'Isa al-Khalifa, directed government administration. In 1993 Bahrain established an appointive Consultative Assembly (Majlis al-Shura).

Owing to its small size, Bahrain generally takes its lead in foreign affairs from its Arab neighbors on the Gulf. A founding member of the Gulf Cooperation Council, it shares with the other five members a long-standing concern with pressures from Iran and Iraq. During the Iran-Iraq War, Bahrain joined most other Arab states in supporting Iraq. Subsequently, it has carefully tried to foster better relations with Iran through trade. When Iraq invaded Kuwait, Bahrain stood with the allies, contributing military support and facilities to the defeat of Iraq.

Bahrain has long assisted the US naval presence in the Persian Gulf. In 1977 a formal agreement for home-porting US naval ships was replaced by arrangements to continue ship visits and other security cooperation. Since the Gulf War, this cooperation has expanded with arms sales, plans for joint exercises, and US pre-positioning of military material for future contingencies. In 1991 the United States signed an agreement giving the US Department of Defense access to facilities on the island. The country is home to the US Navy's Fifth Fleet.

Since 1994 Bahrain, like several traditional emirates of the Gulf, experienced sometimes severe civil disturbances from a Shiite-led resistance opposed to the ruling family and supportive of establishing an Islamic democracy. In 1996 a band of 44 Bahraini Islamists were arrested for allegedly planning a coup to overthrow the ruling family. The emirate broke relations with Iran, which the former accused of fomenting its civil disturbances which between 1994 and 1996 had resulted in 25 deaths. In 1997 the United States

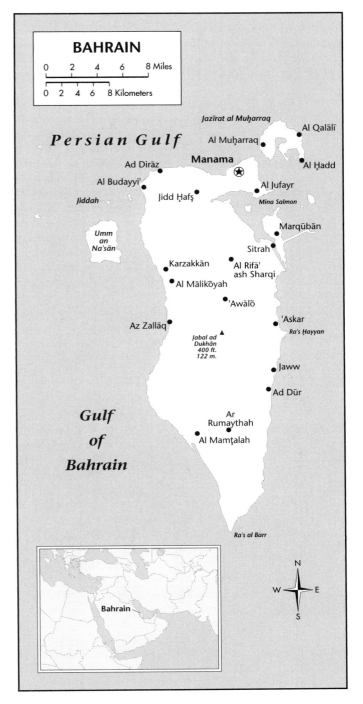

LOCATION: 25°47′10″ to 26°17′3″N; 50°22′45″ to 50°40′20′ E. TOTAL COASTLINE: 161 kilometers (100 miles). TERRITORIAL SEA LIMIT: 3 miles.

disclosed that it had uncovered a plot to attack its military forces stationed in the country.

On 6 March 1999 Sheikh 'Isa bin Salman al-Khalifa, who had ruled his country since its independence in 1971, died of a heart attack. He was succeeded on the throne by his son, Sheikh Hamad bin 'Isa al-Khalifa. Over the following year, there were signs that while the new ruler would continue his father's pro-Western foreign-policy orientation, domestically he would take a more liberal approach to government. In April Sheikh Hamad released a high-profile Shiite dissident, Sheik Abdul Amir al-Jamri, from jail along with hundreds of other political prisoners. Another broad pardon of dissidents took place in November. By February 2001 the emir had pardoned and released all political prisoners, detainees, and exiles.

On 16 March 2001 the International Court of Justice (ICJ) resolved a territorial dispute between Bahrain and Qatar over the potentially oil and gas rich Hawar Islands. The islands were controlled by Bahrain since the 1930s but were claimed by Qatar. Bahrain also claimed the town of Zubarah, which is on the mainland of Qatar. The dispute lasted for decades and almost brought the two nations to the brink of war in 1986. In its judgment, the ICJ drew a single maritime boundary in the Gulf of Bahrain, delineating Bahrain and Qatar's territorial waters and sovereignty over the disputed islands within. The ICJ awarded Bahrain the largest disputed islands, the Hawar Islands, and Qit'at Jaradah Island. Qatar was given sovereignty over Janan Island and the low-tide elevation of Fasht ad Dibal. The Court reaffirmed Qatari sovereignty over the Zubarah Strip.

On 14 February 2001 a referendum was held that endorsed a return to constitutional rule. Under the constitution amended 14 February 2002, the country is no longer an emirate, but a constitutional monarchy. Hamad assumed the new title of King of Bahrain. A two-house national assembly was established, along with an independent judiciary.

In August 2002 King Hamad made the first state visit to Iran since the Islamic revolution in 1979. The two countries voiced their support for solidarity with the Iraqi people. At that time, Iraq was under the threat of a military attack led by the United States for its alleged possession of weapons of mass destruction. Bahrain and Iran urged Iraq to implement all UN resolutions then pending, so that Iraq's territorial integrity and sovereignty could be honored. President Mohammed Khatami of Iran and King Hamad also noted the importance of preserving security and stability in the region and thus pledged to strengthen ties with one another. Several trade, taxation, and naval agreements were signed at the conclusion of the state visit. In addition, both countries agreed to "open a new page" in their bilateral relations, previously strained due to Iran's support for Bahraini opposition movements and Iran's criticism of the American military presence in Bahrain.

In January and March 2003 demonstrations took place in Bahrain in opposition to a potential US-led war with Iraq. By 13 January there were approximately 150,000 US troops in the Gulf region, many of which were stationed in Bahrain, in addition to Kuwait, Qatar, Saudi Arabia, and Oman. US naval operations were headquartered in Bahrain with 4,000 US troops stationed aboard Fifth Fleet ships. As anti-American sentiment in the Gulf increased, the government arrested five men for plotting attacks against Americans in February 2003. By July 2004 Americans were warned to leave. In May 2003 the king was petitioned by thousands of victims of alleged torture to cancel the law which prevented them from suing suspected torturers. Bahrain signed a free trade pact with the United States in September 2004. Under the terms of the agreement 100% of bilateral trade in consumer and industrial products became duty-free. In addition, Bahrain and the United States provided immediate duty-free access on virtually all products in their tariff schedules and planned to phase out tariffs on the remaining handful of products within 10 years. In Iraq, gunmen ambushed a senior Bahraini diplomat in July 2005. In the same month Bahrainis staged a demonstration about unemployment, estimated by economists to be at 20%.

Bahrain remains a Shia majority country controlled by a Sunni monarch, a situation that has been a source of tension in the country. Between March and June 2005 thousands attended protest marches led by Shiite opposition demanding a fully elected parliament. This sectarian issue became inflamed in March 2009, after an official in Iran, a Shia-controlled country, asserted that Bahrain was historically a province of Iran. The statement sent fiery ripples throughout the region. Morocco severed diplomatic relations with Iran. Qatar disinvited Iran to the Arab League Summit it planned to host in April. Saudi Arabia viewed the statement as one more indication that Iran harbored an expansionist ideology. The event led to a collective drubbing of Iran by Sunni governments throughout the region and inspired Iran to take an unusual stance and apologize.

In February 2011 activists organized demonstrations demanding a new constitution, release of hundreds of Shia prisoners, and an end to discriminations in all sectors of society. Some protestors, first camped in Pearl Roundabout, were imprisoned, wounded, or killed. Pearl Roundabout was destroyed in 2011 in response to protestors' encampments and escalating domestic tensions.

In March 2011, with the backing of the Gulf Cooperation Council (GCC), King Hamad declared a state of emergency, putting an end to the mass public gatherings and authorizing the military to take all measures to "protect the safety of the country and its citizens." Bahrain also invited Saudi and Emirati forces as part of a GCC deployment intended to quell demonstrations and maintain order. By April 2011, after Pearl Roundabout was demolished, security forces had largely relegated demonstrations to Shia neighborhoods and villages, and negotiations between the government and opposition groups reached a stalemate. The government subjected opposition groups and their supporters to mass firings, arrests, imprisonment, and sectarian incitement.

In March the GCC pledged $20 billion to Bahrain and over a 10-year period to support putting an end to protests. In June King Hamad lifted the state of emergency. The government held a by-election in September 2011 to fill 18 seats vacated earlier in the year when the political society al-Wifaq withdrew from the national assembly.

13 GOVERNMENT

Under its constitution, amended 14 February 2002, Bahrain is no longer an emirate but a constitutional hereditary monarchy. As a result of the change, the State of Bahrain became the Kingdom of Bahrain, and Sheikh Hamad bin 'Isa al-Khalifa became King Hamad by his own decree. A referendum held on 14 February 2001 endorsed a return to constitutional rule by 98.4%.

The legislature is called the National Assembly (Al-Majlis al-Watani). It consists of two houses, a king-appointed Consultative Council (Majlis al-Shura) and an elected Chamber of Deputies, or Council of Representatives (Majlis al-Nawab). The Chamber of Deputies consists of 40 members, each elected for a four-year term. The Chamber of Deputies elects a president and two vice presidents. The Consultative Council consists of 40 members appointed by the king for a four-year period. The king also appoints the Council speaker and the Shura Council elects two vice presidents. Both chambers must concur to pass legislation, which is then sent to the king for ratification. The king has the power to dissolve the Chamber of Deputies, but new elections are to be held within four months from the date of the dissolution; if they are not, the dissolved Chamber reassumes its constitutional powers and is reconvened. In April 2004 a woman was made health minister, the first woman to be appointed head of a government ministry.

The constitution specifies that Shari'ah (Islamic law) is a principal source of legislation but also pledges freedom of conscience. It guarantees equality of women with men "in political, social, cultural and economic spheres, without breaching the provisions of Shari'ah." The constitution states that every citizen is entitled to health care. It protects private property, but states that "all natural wealth and resources are state property." Discrimination is banned on the basis of sex, national origin, language, religion, or creed.

In the first parliamentary elections since 1973, 190 candidates ran for 40 seats in the Chamber of Deputies on 24 October 2002. In nearly half the races, runoff elections were held between the top two vote getters due to close election results. Under the new constitution, women have the right to vote and run for public office. Of the eight women seeking election in the October parliamentary elections, two forced runoff elections by being among the top two vote getters. As in municipal elections held in May 2002, women constituted over half of those voting. Leaders of Bahrain's Shia population and labor-oriented groups called for a boycott of the elections, claiming dissatisfaction with the structure of parliament. Voter turnout was 53.2%. Moderate Sunni Islamists and independents won 16 of 40 seats on 24 October. In a second round of elections held on 31 October, the independents won 12 seats and the Islamists 9. In total, secular representatives or independents secured a total of 21 of the 40 seats and Islamists 19.

After boycotting the first round of elections under the new constitution in 2002, Shia political societies participated in 2006 and 2010 in legislative and municipal elections. The largest Shia political society, al-Wifaq, won the largest bloc of seats in the lower house of legislature both times. The government held a by-election in September 2011 to fill 18 seats vacated when the political society al-Wifaq withdrew from the national assembly after the government quelled protests that began in February through mass arrest and detention, causing death and injury among demonstrators and supporters.

14 POLITICAL PARTIES

Political parties are illegal in Bahrain. Groups known as political societies, or blocs, remnants of the former Communist left and the Islamist right, hold some seats in parliament. Some of these groups are the al-Wifaq National Islamic Society, Islamic Action Society, National Democratic Action, Democratic Bloc, National Action Charter Society (al-Meethaq), Progressive Democratic Front, Nationalist Democratic Rally Society, National Justice Movement (al-Adala), and the Al-Asala Islamic Society. Several underground groups, including branches of Hezbollah and other pro-Iranian militant Islamic groups, have been active. Anti-regime dissidents have frequently been jailed or exiled. However, in 1999 Sheikh Hamad bin 'Isa al-Khalifa issued amnesty for most political prisoners, ended the house arrest of Shiite opposition leader Sheikh

Abdul Amir al-Jamri, and granted permission for the return of 108 people in exile. By February 2001 the emir had pardoned and released all political prisoners, detainees, and exiles. In addition, the reinstatement of dissidents fired from public sector jobs, the lifting of travel bans on political activists, and the abrogation of state security laws have all created a more open atmosphere for political expression.

Beginning with municipal elections in May 2002, candidates from a wide variety of political groups formed a more pluralistic political culture in Bahrain. These groups were not officially designated as political parties, but they had the attributes of democratic parties in the West as they fielded candidates in elections, organized activities, and campaigned freely. There are seven main political groups: the Arab-Islamic Wasat (Center) Society (AIWS); the Democratic Progressive Forum (DPF); the Islamic National Accord (INA); the National Action Charter Society (NACS); the National Democratic Action Society (NDAS); the National Democratic Gathering Society (NDGS); and the National Islamic Forum (NIF).

In addition, numerous other nongovernmental organizations (NGOs) were set up after the constitution was endorsed in February 2001, among them the Bahrain Human Rights Society, the Supreme Council for Bahraini Women, and the Organization Against Normalization with Israel. These organizations campaign on single-issue platforms, hold public discussions and meetings, consult with the government, and are members of Bahraini delegations to international forums.

The partially elected bicameral parliament that was approved in a referendum in 2001 held its first session in December 2002 after elections were held that October. In the 40-member directly elected House of Deputies, independents took 21 seats, Sunni Islamists won 9 seats, and other groups won 10 seats.

In the elections of 23 October 2010 the Shia opposition society, al-Wifaq, won 18 of the 40 seats in the lower house of parliament. An additional 13 seats were filled by Sunnis loyal to the ruling government. The remaining nine candidates (primarily pro-government) then competed in a run-off election on 30 October. In the second round, all of the remaining nine seats were won by pro-government Sunnis. The government held a by-election in September 2011 to fill 18 seats vacated earlier in the year when the political society al-Wifaq withdrew from the national assembly.

Khalifa bin Salman Al-Khalifa (an uncle of King Hamad) has served as prime minister since he was appointed by the monarch in 1971.

15 LOCAL GOVERNMENT

There are five municipal councils in Bahrain, each with 10 elected members and an appointed chairman. The first local elections since 1957 were held on 9 May 2002. Additional elections were held in 2006. The National Harmony Society won 20 of 50 municipal seats in the 2006 elections. Five women ran for office, but none were successful.

The democratic municipalities are responsible for the provision of local goods and services, including transportation, waste disposal, street cleaning and beautification, and enforcing health and safety standards.

¹⁶JUDICIAL SYSTEM

The law of Bahrain represents a mixture of Islamic religious law (Shari'ah), community law, and other civil codes and regulations. In 2001 the new constitution enshrined an independent judiciary. The Supreme Judicial Council supervises the courts. Courts have been granted the power of judicial review.

The new reforms establish a constitutional court, consisting of a president and six members appointed by the king for a specified period. Members are not liable to dismissal. The government, or either house of the national assembly, may challenge the constitutionality of any measure before the court. The king may refer to the court draft laws prior to their adoption, to determine their constitutionality.

Military courts are confined to military offenses only and cannot be extended to others without the declaration of martial laws.

Shari'ah governs the personal legal rights of women, although the constitution provides for women's political rights. Specific rights vary according to Shia or Sunni interpretations of Islamic law, as determined by the individual's faith, or by the courts in which various contracts, including marriage, have been made. While both Shia and Sunni women have the right to initiate a divorce, religious courts may refuse the request. Women of either branch of Islam may own and inherit property and may represent themselves in all public and legal matters. A Muslim woman may legally marry a non-Muslim man if the man converts to Islam. In such marriages, the children automatically are considered to be Muslim.

¹⁷ARMED FORCES

The International Institute for Strategic Studies (IISS) reported that armed forces in Bahrain totaled 8,200 members in 2011. The force was comprised of 6,000 members of the army, 700 members of the navy, and 1,500 members of the air force. Armed forces represented 5.2% of the labor force. Defense spending totaled $1.3 billion and accounted for 4.5% of gross domestic product (GDP).

In January 2010 Bahrain hosted its first international air show, which drew major aviation and defense manufactures from around the globe. During the show Bahrain finalized a deal with Sikorsky, a US aviation manufacturer, to deliver nine Blackhawk helicopters. The deal underscored the major military ties between the United States and Bahrain, which hosts the US Navy's Fifth Fleet.

¹⁸INTERNATIONAL COOPERATION

Bahrain joined the UN on 21 September 1971 and is a member of the Economic and Social Development Commission in Western Asia (ESCWA), all major regional organizations, and several non-regional specialized agencies. It also belongs to the Arab League, the Arab Monetary Fund, the Islamic Development Bank, OAPEC, the Organization of Islamic Conference (OIC), the Gulf Cooperation Council, and G-77. The country joined the World Trade Organization (WTO) on 1 January 1995. Bahrain was a founding member of the GCC, inaugurated in 1981. The country is also a part of the Nonaligned Movement and the Organization for the Prohibition of Chemical Weapons. In environmental cooperation, the country is part of the Basel Convention, the Convention on Biological Diversity, Ramsar, the Montréal Protocol, and the UN Conventions on the Law of the Sea, Climate Change, and Desertification.

¹⁹ECONOMY

The GDP rate of change in Bahrain, as of 2010, was 4.1%. Inflation stood at 3.3%, and unemployment was reported at 15%.

For centuries Bahrain depended almost exclusively on trade (or piracy), pearl diving, and agriculture. The discovery of oil on 1 June 1932 changed that. Although its economy has been based on oil for the last six decades, Bahrain's development has been tempered by relatively limited reserves. Proven reserves are 125 million barrels, all from one diminishing oil field, the Awali field. At current production levels, the field has a life of less than 10 years. Oil revenue accounts for 11% of GDP. However, it makes up 76% of government income. Aluminum is Bahrain's second major export after oil.

Significant progress has been made in enhancing Bahrain as an *entrepôt* (trade center) and as a service and commercial center for the Gulf region. Bahrain provides ample warehousing for goods in transit and dry dock facilities for marine engine and ship repairs. Bahrain also acts as a major banking, telecommunications, and air transportation center. Bahrain also began diversifying its economy to rely on services to a higher degree after the Lebanese civil war in the late 1970s and early 1980s essentially ended that country's status as a safe, regulation-free banking environment.

Although the Bahrain economy slowed considerably in the mid-1990s, foreign investment in the earlier part of that decade helped enable GDP to grow at an annualized rate of 4% between 1988 and 1998. Low world oil prices created a negative growth situation in 1998, but after that the International Monetary Fund (IMF) reported that real growth was shown every year until 2009, when it dropped amidst the global economic crisis. In 2006 Bahrain established the first Gulf state free trade agreement with the United States.

In 2010 the Canadian-based Fraser Institute ranked Bahrain as the most economically free Arab nation and the 18th freest economy in the world in the their Economic Freedom Reports. Bahrain has been listed as first in the Arab world since 2003. The Economic Freedom Reports compare five aspects of the economy, including the size of government (expenditures, taxes, and enterprises); commercial and economic law and security of property rights; access to sound money; freedom to trade internationally; and regulations for credit, labor, and business. Bahrain received an overall score of 8 out of 10 in the regional analysis and 7.58 in the worldwide analysis.

²⁰INCOME

The CIA estimated that in 2010 the GDP of Bahrain was $29.71 billion. The CIA defines GDP as the value of all final goods and services produced within a nation in a given year and computed on the basis of purchasing power parity (PPP) rather than value as measured on the basis of the rate of the exchange based on current dollars. The per capita GDP was estimated at $40,300. It was estimated that agriculture accounted for 0.5% of GDP, industry 56.6%, and services 42.9%.

As of 2011 the most recent study by the World Bank reported that actual individual consumption in Bahrain was 52.4% of GDP and accounted for 0.02% of world consumption. By comparison, the United States accounted for 25.44% of world individual consumption. The World Bank also estimated that 9.6% of Bahrain's GDP was spent on food and beverages, 13.6% on housing and household furnishings, 3.4% on clothes, 5.5% on health, 4.9% on transportation, 1.1% on communications, 1.7% on recreation, 1.1% on restaurants and hotels, and 6% on miscellaneous goods and services and purchases from abroad.

21 LABOR

As of 2010 Bahrain had a total labor force of 656,200 people. Within that labor force, CIA estimates in 1997 noted that 1% were employed in agriculture, 79% in industry, and 20% in the service sector.

Non-nationals in 2005 made up an estimated 44% of the country's population between the ages of 15 and 64.

Although the constitution permits workers to organize, the government bans trade unions. With this absence of legitimate trade unions, no collective bargaining entities or collective agreements exist. Workers may express grievances through joint labor-management committees (JLCs). JLCs are generally created at each major company and have an equal number of labor and management representatives. As of 2000 there were a total of 20 JLCs. There are no internationally affiliated trade unions, and foreign workers are underrepresented in the General Committee of Bahrain workers which coordinates the JLCs.

The government sets minimum wage scales for public sector employees and this generally provides a decent standard of living for workers and their families. For public-sector jobs, the minimum wage is specified on a contract basis.

As in several Gulf nations the economy of Bahrain depends heavily on foreign workers, most of whom will work for less money in menial jobs than would nationals, who may not have accepted the work anyway. However, the sponsorship system for foreign workers, known as *kafala*, has been widely criticized by international human rights organization. Under the system, workers are sponsored by their employers, meaning that the employer must accept full economic and legal responsibility for the employee. A number of abuses have emerged from the system. Workers are forced to accept the conditions imposed by their employer with no legal recourse. Employers also have the right to seize the passports of their contract employees, thus making it impossible for them to leave the country and creating a complete dependency on the employer. In 2009 the government announced its intention to reform the system by introducing a new arrangement through which foreigners will be sponsored by the official labor authority, rather than individual employers. A new system is expected to correct some of the unfair labor practices and introduce a more efficient process to monitor the number of immigrant workers within the country.

22 AGRICULTURE

Roughly 11% of the total land is farmed, and the country's major crops include fruit and vegetables. Fruit production amounted to 21,769 tons and vegetable production to 16,227 tons in 2009.

Ninety farms and small holdings produce fruit and vegetables, as well as alfalfa for fodder. The date palm industry has declined sharply in recent years due to heavy demands on the limited water supply, and dates have become a luxury item. The government's goal is for output to meet 16% of demand, compared with the current 6%.

23 ANIMAL HUSBANDRY

The UN Food and Agriculture Organization (FAO) reported that Bahrain dedicated 4,000 hectares (9,884 acres) to permanent pasture or meadow in 2009. During that year, the country tended 525,000 chickens and 10,000 head of cattle. Bahrain also produced 162 tons of cattle hide.

Most domestic meat consumption is supplied through imports of live cattle, goats, and sheep. About 40,000 sheep and 19,000 goats were kept for milk and meat production in 2010. A thriving poultry industry provided 6,260 metric tons of meat and 3,000 metric tons of eggs. A national dairy pasteurization plant has been established in order to centralize all milk processing and distribution. In 2009 milk production totaled 9,000 tons. An abattoir that opened in 1984 slaughters imported sheep and cattle.

24 FISHING

Bahrain had 159 decked commercial fishing boats in 2008. The annual capture totaled 14,177 tons according to the FAO. The export value of seafood totaled $10.79 million.

Although more than 300 species of fish found in Bahraini waters constitute an important food source for much of the population, local fishing and pearl diving have declined because of industrial pollution. The government operates a fleet of seven trawlers. By encouraging traditional angling, giving incentives to fishermen, improving fishing and freezing equipment, and establishing cooperatives, the government is attempting to increase the annual catch. There is a modern fishing harbor at Al Muharraq, which provides docking and landing facilities, storage areas, an ice plant, and a water supply.

25 FORESTRY

Approximately 1.3% of Bahrain is covered by forest. The value of all forest products, including roundwood, totals $5.71 million.

Bahrain's imports of forest products amounted to $53.2 million in 2010. That year, Bahrain re-exported about $5.7 million of forest products, including about 1,000 tons of industrial roundwood.

26 MINING

Bahrain's oil-based economy produced few minerals other than crude oil and natural gas. In 2010 crude oil and refined petroleum products accounted for around $11.5 billion of the nation's $18.4 billion in exports. Cement production in 2010 was reported at 700,000 metric tons, up from 438,000 metric tons in 2008. Sulfur production totaled 72,000 metric tons in 2010.

27 ENERGY AND POWER

The World Bank reported that in 2008 Bahrain produced 11.9 billion kWh of electricity and consumed 10.2 billion kWh, or 8,392 kWh per capita. All energy came from fossil fuels. The Directorate of Electricity operated plants at Manama, Sitra, and Rifaa. Power is principally derived from a municipal power station at Jufair, from the Sitra power and water station, from two gas turbines at Al Muharraq, and from the power station at East Rifaa, which was completed in 1985 and is the largest and most modern. The Bahrain National Oil Company (BANOCO) produces its own electricity from a 60 MW plant. Phase One of the Hidd power project, completed in 1999, created an additional 280 MW of gas-fired generating capacity. Completion of Phase Two would add another 630 MW.

The Arabian Peninsula's first oil well was drilled in Bahrain in 1932, and production began in 1934. From the 1930s to the mid-1970s oil development was a monopoly of the Bahrain Petroleum Company (BAPCO), which in 1936 came under the ownership of Caltex, a corporation registered in Canada and jointly owned by Texaco and Standard Oil of California. In 1975 the Bahrain government acquired a 60% holding in BAPCO, and it later formed BANOCO to take over full ownership. In 1980 BANOCO announced its acquisition of a 60% interest in Bahrain's main refinery, which had been wholly owned by Caltex.

Total daily crude petroleum production, after reaching a peak in 1970, has declined gradually. In 2009 per capita oil consumption was 11,896 kg (26,226 lbs). Oil production totaled 35,000 barrels of oil a day. From 1972 until 1996 Bahrain shared revenues from the Abu Safa oil field, which lies halfway within Saudi Arabian territorial waters, with Saudi Arabia. In 1996 the Saudi government ceded the remainder of its share of the field to Bahrain, increasing the government's revenue by about $200 million.

Bahrain gained the right to offer concessions in offshore oil fields in the Gulf of Bahrain after a territorial dispute with Qatar was settled by the International Court of Justice in March 2001 and Bahrain won control of the Hawar Islands. In November 2001 drilling rights were awarded to Petroliam Nasional Berhad (PETRONAS) and Chevron Texaco, and oil exploration began in late 2002.

28 INDUSTRY

Bahrain was the first Gulf state to discover oil and built the region's first refinery in 1935. Known as the Bahrain Oil Company, it has been 60% owned by BANOCO and 40% owned by the US company Caltex since 1980. BANOCO also maintains holdings in the BAPCO, which was formed in 2002 through a merger with a government-owned petroleum enterprise. Most of the crude oil processed in Bahrain's refinery comes from Saudi Arabia. Because Bahrain's own oil reserves are relatively limited, an agreement with Saudi Arabia allows the country to receive revenues from Saudi Arabia's Abu Safa offshore oilfield. Bahrain's oil production had stabilized at about 40,000 barrels per day in early 2006, and its reserves were expected to last 10 to 15 years.

Bahrain also has a gas liquefaction plant, operated by the Bahrain National Gas Company. Gas reserves are expected to last about 50 years.

Other petroleum enterprises include the Gulf Petrochemical Industries Company, a joint venture of the petrochemical industries of Kuwait, the Saudi Basic Industries Corporation, and the Government of Bahrain, which produces ammonia and methanol for export. Bahrain also has awarded exploration rights to two multinational companies—PETRONAS from Malaysia and Chevron Texaco from the United States.

A government-controlled aluminum industry, Aluminum Bahrain BSC (ALBA), was launched in 1971 with an original smelter capacity of 120,000 tons annually; the successful completion of a 1997 expansion project increased production to more than 500,000 metric tons in 1998 and to 851,000 metric tons in

2010. It is the world's second-largest aluminum smelter and is 77%- owned by the government. Other aluminum factories include the Aluminum Extrusion Company and the Gulf Aluminum Rolling Mill. Bahrain also has an iron ore palletizing plant and a shipbuilding and repair yard.

Overall industrial production accounts for 58% of GDP.

29 SCIENCE AND TECHNOLOGY

The World Bank reported in 2009 that there were no patent applications in science and technology in Bahrain. The economy depends heavily on advanced petrochemical technologies, and many Bahrainis have had or are receiving technical training. The University of Bahrain, at Isa Town, has a college of engineering and science. The Arabian Gulf University, founded in 1980 by the seven Gulf states, has colleges of medicine and applied sciences. The Bahrain Society of Engineers and the Bahrain Computer Society, in Manama, and the Bahrain Medical Society in Adliya, are leading professional groups. The College of Health Sciences, founded in 1976, had 528 students in 1996. The Bahrain Centre for Studies and Research, founded in 1981, conducts scientific study and research.

30 DOMESTIC TRADE

Bahraini shops have become increasingly modernized and specialized. American-style supermarkets are open in Manama and most supplies and services are available in shops throughout the country. Business hours for most shops are from 8:30 a.m. to 12:30 p.m. and from 4 p.m. to 8 p.m., Saturday through Wednesday, with a half day on Thursday. Government offices and banks are generally open Saturday through Thursday. Of all the Gulf states, Bahrain offers the most scope for consumer advertising through its publications, cinemas, direct mail facilities, and radio and television stations.

31 FOREIGN TRADE

Bahrain imported $11.19 billion worth of goods and services in 2010, while exporting $13.83 billion worth of goods and services.

Principal Trading Partners – Bahrain (2010)

(In millions of US dollars)

Country	Total	Exports	Imports	Balance
World	25,200.0	15,400.0	9,800.0	5,600.0
Sa'udi Arabia	3,633.6	857.5	2,776.1	-1,918.6
United States	1,780.0	405.6	1,374.5	-968.9
Japan	1,246.9	598.9	647.9	-49.0
India	1,242.8	561.2	681.6	-120.4
China	1,105.1	225.5	879.6	-654.1
United Arab Emirates	876.6	564.4	312.2	252.2
South Korea	837.2	535.7	301.6	234.1
Brazil	713.0	42.4	670.6	-628.2
France	687.8	126.8	561.0	-434.3
Germany	469.4	38.6	430.8	-392.3

(…) data not available or not significant.

(n.s.) not specified.

SOURCE: *2011 Direction of Trade Statistics Yearbook,* New York: United Nations, 2011.

Balance of Payments – Bahrain (2010)

(In millions of US dollars)

Current Account		770.1
Balance on goods		2,642.8
Imports	-11,190.4	
Exports	13,833.2	
Balance on services		2,142.0
Balance on income		-2,373.0
Current transfers		-1,641.8
Capital Account		50.0
Financial Account		352.4
Direct investment abroad		-334.0
Direct investment in Bahrain		155.8
Portfolio investment assets		2,051.6
Portfolio investment liabilities		2,704.2
Financial derivatives		...
Other investment assets		2,739.7
Other investment liabilities		-6,964.8
Net Errors and Omissions		107.1
Reserves and Related Items		-1,279.5

(…) data not available or not significant.

SOURCE: *Balance of Payment Statistics Yearbook 2011*, Washington, DC: International Monetary Fund, 2011.

Major import partners in 2010 were Saudi Arabia, 24.7%; the United States, 12.2%; China, 7.8%; Brazil, 6%; Japan, 5.8 %; and France, 5%. Its major export partners were Saudi Arabia, 2.9%; Japan, 2%; United Arab Emirates (UAE), 1.9%; and India, 1.9%.

Petroleum products drive Bahrain's economy and export market. Aluminum, which is manufactured in government-controlled enterprises, ranks as the country's second-largest export commodity. Other exports include apparel, iron, and chemicals.

32 BALANCE OF PAYMENTS

In 2010 Bahrain had a foreign trade surplus of $4.4 billion, amounting to 6.4% of GDP.

Traditionally, Bahrain relied on a substantial influx of funds from Saudi Arabia, Kuwait, Abu Dhabi, and Iran to finance capital outlays. In recent years, however, increased income from tourism and financial services has placed Bahrain in a favorable payments position.

The CIA reported that in 2010 the PPP of Bahrain's exports was $13.83 billion while imports totaled $11.19 billion. The country's current account balance was $239.5 million in 2010. Bahrain's foreign reserves totaled $4.789 billion in 2010. Since 1992 Bahrain has received $150 million annually from Saudi Arabia, the UAE, and Kuwait.

33 BANKING AND SECURITIES

Bahrain is considered the preeminent financial services center in the Middle East. The Bahrain Monetary Agency (BMA), Bahrain's equivalent of a central bank, issues and redeems bank notes, regulates the value of the Bahrain dinar, supervises interest rates, and licenses and monitors the activities of money changers. One factor contributing to Bahrain's growth as a Middle Eastern financial services center is that unlike some of its larger, richer neighbors, there is no serious religious opposition to western banking

practices—especially the accrual of interest—which some Islamic scholars consider to be contrary to Muslim teachings. There are, however, several large banks in Bahrain classified as Islamic; these banks don't pay or charge interest, don't finance or otherwise support "un-Islamic" enterprises, and make a conscious effort to invest in socially productive enterprises. Another important factor influencing the growth of the financial sector is the tax-free environment.

The value of assets and liabilities held by Bahrain's commercial banks rose by 43%, and offshore banking units (DBUs) rose by 20% between 1991 and 1995. The consolidated assets and liabilities of commercial and offshore banks in Bahrain reached over $82 million in 1997. In 2007 Bahrain was home to 28 commercial banks, 2 specialized banks, 61 offshore banks, 34 representative offices of international banks, 42 investment banks, 89 insurance companies, and 24 money changers and money brokers. Bahrain has 38 Islamic banks and financial institutions.

The Bahrain Stock Exchange (BSE) was planned in 1987 after the unofficial Kuwait Stock Exchange collapsed. The BSE has become an important Gulf center of share trading; volume or shares increased from its inception from 62 million in 1989 to almost 400 million in 1993. Beginning in 1995 the BSE listed foreign companies, bonds, and investment funds. Trading in foreign investment vehicles was made open to all Bahrainis and resident and nonresident foreigners in late 1996. As of 2004 there were 42 companies listed on the BSE. Market capitalization in 2010 stood at $20.429 billion.

The Islamic finance industry, through which Muslim scholars regulate financial transactions according to Shari'ah law, represents a large and growing sector in the Muslim world, with assets valued between $500 billion and $1 trillion. However, a lack of scholars competent in both finance and Islamic law may hinder growth in the sector. In 2006 Bahrain's central bank introduced the Waqf Fund for Research, Education, and Training to tackle this challenge. The Waqf Fund aims to train new scholars in the Islamic finance field to ensure that the sector can grow well into the 21st century. In April 2010 the fund held its inaugural training course, which was attended by about 30 scholars and Shari'ah auditors. Bahrain's central bank said that it planned to hold these courses regularly.

34 INSURANCE

The total value of direct premiums underwritten in 2010 in Bahrain was $558 million. Motor insurance constituted the largest class of business, generating premiums of $152 million, accounting for 27% of the market. In Bahrain, both conventional and Takaful insurance, which is grounded in Islamic banking, are available.

35 PUBLIC FINANCE

In 2010 the budget of Bahrain included $5.786 billion in public revenue and $7.009 billion in public expenditures. The budget deficit amounted to 5.4% of GDP. Public debt was equal to 60.1% of GDP, with $14.58 billion of the debt held by foreign entities.

The budget is presented biannually and regularly updated and represents a large section of economic activity. More than half of government revenues come from oil production and refining; the oil industry is completely controlled by the government. The

Public Finance – Bahrain (2009)

(In millions of dinars, central government figures)

Revenue and Grants	**1,708**	**100.0%**
Tax revenue	117.6	6.9%
Social contributions	...	...
Grants	28.4	1.7%
Other revenue	1,562	91.5%
Expenditures	**2,153.9**	**100.0%**
General public services	225.5	10.5%
Defense	358.8	16.7%
Public order and safety	279.8	13.0%
Economic affairs	398.9	18.5%
Environmental protection	28.9	1.3%
Housing and community amenities	138.4	6.4%
Health	203.2	9.4%
Recreational, culture, and religion	91.7	4.3%
Education	288.2	13.4%
Social protection	140.5	6.5%

(...) data not available or not significant.

SOURCE: *Government Finance Statistics Yearbook 2010,* Washington, DC: International Monetary Fund, 2010.

public deficit is covered by internal borrowing, loans from Arab funds, and the Islamic Development Bank (IDB), although privatization has become increasingly important to controlling the budget. The oil and aluminum industries are still controlled by the government, although utilities, banks, financial services, and telecommunications have started to fall into private hands.

In 2010 revenues were $5.786 billion and expenditures were $7.009 billion.

36 TAXATION

The only income tax in Bahrain is levied on oil, gas, and petroleum companies. In 2007 the government introduced a 1% "social insurance tax" to help fund unemployment benefits. A municipal tax of 10% is levied on property rentals. The rate is 7.5% on furnished rentals, office, and commercial rents. The only sales tax is on gasoline. As an offshore tax haven, Bahrain allows foreign firms to remit accumulated profits and capital without taxation.

37 CUSTOMS AND DUTIES

Import licenses for items sold in Bahrain are issued only to local companies that are at least 51% Bahraini-owned. Principal prohibited items are weapons, raw ivory, and cultured pearls. Customs duties are 20% on corn and palm oil; 5% on foodstuffs and non-luxuries; 7.5% on consumer goods; 20% on cars and boats; 70% on tobacco and cigarettes; and 125% on authorized imports of liquor. A free transit zone operates at the port of Mina Salman. Free trade is available with GCC countries if products have at least 40% local value-added content.

38 FOREIGN INVESTMENT

Foreign direct investment (FDI) in Bahrain was a net inflow of $155.7 million according to World Bank figures published in 2010.

Bahrain has well-established communication and transport facilities. The strength of its infrastructure, along with the generous

incentives it offers to foreign investors, have made the country home to many multinational companies doing business in the Persian Gulf. In recent years, the government has sought to control more of the country's key businesses. Bahrain, however, continues to court international investment; the country does not tax corporate or individual earnings. Only petroleum royalties are subject to taxation.

39 ECONOMIC DEVELOPMENT

Since the late 1960s the government has concentrated on policies and projects that will provide sufficient diversification in industrial, commercial, and financial activities to sustain growth in income, employment, and exports into the post-oil era. To this end, Bahrain in September 2004 became the first Gulf state to sign a free trade agreement with the United States. The pact was ratified by the Bahraini parliament in July 2005 and by the US Congress in December 2005. US president George W. Bush signed the agreement into law in January 2006; it entered into force that month.

Despite diversification efforts, the oil and gas sectors remain the cornerstone of the economy. The reliance on oil poses one of Bahrain's biggest long-term economic challenges. Unemployment and a shortage of long-range water resources also are issues. Much of Bahrain's labor force, estimated in 2009 at 591,876, consists of non-Bahrainis. In hopes of encouraging more employment among its citizenry, the country has adopted a policy of matching job seekers with potential employers. It also is promoting training programs that would give young adults marketable skills. The country also is considering a labor law that would stress the value of vocational training and require that benefits for public and private sector employees be equal. It also is considering introduction of a minimum wage law.

The strongest possibility for growth in Bahrain lies in its financial sector. Bahrain leads an effort to develop Islamic financial services and has 38 Islamic banks and financial institutions. More than 100 offshore banks also operate in Bahrain, which helped to boost financial services activity to 33% of GDP in 2008. In hopes of keeping the sector both vibrant and efficient, Bahrain has consolidated regulation of banks, insurance companies, and capital markets under one umbrella.

40 SOCIAL DEVELOPMENT

Impoverished families receive subsistence allowances from the Ministry of Labor and Social Affairs. Beginning in 2005 all establishments with one or more employees are covered by the social insurance system. A social security fund provides old age, disability, survivor, and accident insurance. Contributions amount to 5% of earnings by workers and 7% by employers. Work injury insurance exempts domestic servants, self-employed, and agricultural workers.

Islamic law, either Shia or Sunni, dictates the legal rights of Bahraini women. Women may initiate divorce proceedings, although religious courts often refuse the request. Men retain legal rights over children, even in case of divorce. Custody of young children is granted to women, but fathers automatically regain custody when the children reach the age of nine (for daughters) and seven (for sons). In 2009 women made up approximately 32% of the labor force. The majority of working women are young and single, and most women cease working outside the home after marriage. Bahrain's labor law does not recognize the concept of equal pay for equal work, and women are often paid less than men. Sexual harassment is a common problem. Spousal abuse is widespread, especially in economically deprived areas. It is estimated that 30% of married women are victims of domestic abuse, but few women seek assistance.

Bahrain's government regularly violates citizens' human rights. There was a continuation of torture, arbitrary arrest, denial of the right to a fair trial, and restrictions on freedom of speech, press, assembly, association, and workers' rights. The treatment of foreign workers, especially women employed as domestic help, is especially abusive.

41 HEALTH

According to the CIA, life expectancy in Bahrain was 76 years in 2011. The country spent 3.7% of its GDP on healthcare, amounting to $1,108 per person. There were 14 physicians, 37 nurses and midwives, and 19 hospital beds per 10,000 inhabitants. In 2009 the fertility rate was 2.6, while the infant mortality rate was 9 per 1,000 live births. In 2008 the maternal mortality rate, according to the World Bank, was 19 per 100,000 births. It was estimated that 99% of children were vaccinated against measles. The CIA calculated that fewer than 600 people in Bahrain were living with HIV/AIDS in 2007.

42 HOUSING

According to the 2010 government census, there were 151,580 housing units within the country. About 41% were private villas and 45% were flats. There were 24,021 apartment buildings. About 72% of all units were connected to the public water system. The greatest number of housing units (47,179) was available in Manama.

43 EDUCATION

In 2009 the World Bank estimated that 97% of age-eligible children in Bahrain were enrolled in primary school. Secondary enrollment for age-eligible children stood at 89%. About 47% of children three to five years of age attend preschool programs. It is estimated that 99% of all students complete their primary education. The literacy rate of Bahrain was estimated at 91%.

Education is compulsory for students between the ages of 6 and 15. Primary education lasts for six years followed by an intermediate program of three years. Students may then choose from three options for their secondary education: general (science or literary tracks), technical, or commercial. Each secondary program is a three-year course of study. The academic year runs from October to August. The primary languages of instruction are Arabic and English. The Ministry of Education is the primary administrative body. As of 2008 public expenditure on education was estimated at 2.9% of GDP.

Bahrain's principal university is the University of Bahrain, established in 1986 after a merger between the University College and Gulf Polytechnic. It is comprised of five colleges and an English language center; it has colleges of arts, sciences, engineering, education, and business administration. The Arabian Gulf University (founded in 1980) has departments of science, engineering and medicine, and is in fact a joint venture project among the six GCC members and Iraq. Each nation is allocated 10% of the seats (total

70%) and the remaining 30% are given to other countries. Also important is the Bahrain Training Institute, which currently has over 50% female students.

There are also 67 adult education centers in Bahrain, which have helped to reduce the illiteracy rate of the country. The adult literacy rate in 2009 was estimated about 91%.

44 LIBRARIES AND MUSEUMS

Manama Public Library was the first to open in the country in 1946; it contains the collection of UN-related publications. The Bahrain National Bank Public Library in Muharraq (opened in 1969 as the Muharraq Public Library) includes the Mohammed Hassan Al-Hassan Collection of over 400 books on national and international law (with volumes in Arabic and English), a library for the blind, a children's library, and a special section on travel and tourism. The Central Public Library in Isa Town has 124,000 volumes. There were at least nine public libraries nationwide under supervision of the Directorate of Public Libraries at the Ministry of Education. The University of Bahrain in Manama (1978) holds 140,000 volumes, while the Manama Central Library holds 155,000 volumes. In 2003 the first specialized law library opened at the University's Sakhir campus. The Educational Documentation Library in Manama holds the largest collection of educational research materials with about 22,000 books and nearly 200 periodicals; publications are available in Arabic and English. The Bahrain National Commission for Education, Science and Culture Library, also in Manama, was established in 1967, serving primarily as a research library; holdings include materials from four main international organizations: UN Educational, Scientific and Cultural Organization (UNESCO), Arab League Educational, Cultural and Scientific Organization (ALECSO), Arab Bureau of Education for the Gulf States (ABEGS), and Islamic Educational, Scientific and Cultural Organization (ISESCO).

The Bahrain National Museum in Manama holds art, archaeological, and historical exhibits, chronicling the rise of the Dilmun civilization. Muharraq Island hosts a few of traditional homes that are open to visitors. The Royal Tombs in A'ali are popular archeological sites.

45 MEDIA

In 2010 the CIA reported that there were 228,000 telephone landlines in Bahrain. In addition to landlines, mobile phone subscriptions averaged 199 per 100 people. There were two FM radio stations and three AM radio stations.

Modern telephone, cable, and telex systems are available. In 2010 there were 1.567 million mobile cellular phones in use. International service is provided by tropospheric scatter radio communications to Qatar and the UAE, microwave radio relay to Saudi Arabia, and by submarine cable to Qatar, the UAE, and Saudi Arabia. There was also one satellite ground station operating in Bahrain. Basic service is provided by the National Telephone Company (BATELCO).

Internet service is provided through the national phone company. In 2010 the country had about 53,944 Internet hosts. Government control restricts access to some Internet sites with content that is considered anti-Islamic or anti-government. Many districts of Manama have cyber cafés. Internet users numbered 82 per 100 citizens.

Bahrain's first daily newspaper in Arabic, *Akhbar al-Khalij*, began publication in 1976, and the first English daily, the *Gulf Daily News*, was established in 1991. *Al Ayam*, an Arabic daily, was founded in 1989.

Though the Bahraini constitution has provisions for freedom of expression, press criticism of the ruling family or government policy is strictly prohibited.

46 ORGANIZATIONS

In addition to the national Chamber of Commerce and Industry, Bahrain is a committee member of the International Chamber of Commerce. There are numerous Bahraini and multinational groups, including the Bahrain Red Crescent Society and the Children's and Mothers' Welfare Society. Health and welfare organizations include the Bahrain Family Planning Association and the Bahrain Diabetic Association. Youth organizations include those representing the Youth Hostel Federation, Red Crescent Youth, the Boy Scouts of Bahrain and the Girl Guides, and Arab Student Aid International (ASAI). The Bahrain Olympic Committee coordinates activities for about 12 national youth sports federations.

47 TOURISM, TRAVEL, AND RECREATION

The *Tourism Factbook*, published by the UN World Tourism Organization, reported 7.83 million incoming tourists to Bahrain in 2007, who spent a total of $1.87 billion. Of those incoming tourists, there were 5.5 million from the Middle East and 1.1 million from South Asia. The estimated daily cost to visit Manama, the capital, was $396.

Bahrain has been a fast growing destination in the Middle East since the early 1990s. Tourist attractions include archeological sites (notably Qal-at Al-Bahrain—The Portuguese Fort), the National Museum, and the Heritage Center. Recreational riding and horse racing are both popular in Bahrain. Pearl diving is also part of Bahrain's heritage.

48 FAMOUS PERSONS

Sheikh 'Isa bin Salman al-Khalifa (b. 1933–d. 1999) ruled from 1961 until his death in 1999. He was succeeded by his son, Sheikh Hamad bin 'Isa al-Khalifa (b. 1950).

49 DEPENDENCIES

Bahrain has no territories or colonies.

50 BIBLIOGRAPHY

Bahrain Investment and Business Guide: Strategic and Practical Information. Washington, DC: International Business Publications USA, 2012.

Gillespie, Carol Ann. *Bahrain*. Philadelphia: Chelsea House, 2002.

Holes, Clive. *Dialect, Culture, and Society in Eastern Arabia.* Boston: Brill, 2001.

Hourani, Albert Habib. *A History of the Arab Peoples*. Cambridge, Mass.: Belknap Press of Harvard University Press, 2002.

Nakhleh, Emile A. *Bahrain: Political Development in a Modernizing Society.* Lanham, MD: Lexington Books, 2011.

Seddon, David, ed. *A Political and Economic Dictionary of the Middle East.* Philadelphia: Routledge/Taylor and Francis, 2004.

Terterov, Marat, ed. *Doing Business with Bahrain: A Guide to Investment Opportunities and Business Practice.* 2nd ed. Sterling, VA: Kogan Page, 2005.

Tétreault, Mary Ann, Gwenn Okruhlik, et al. *Political Change in the Arab Gulf States.* Boulder, CO: Lynne Rienner Publishers, 2011.

Winkler, David F. *Amirs, Admirals & Desert Sailors: Bahrain, the U.S. Navy, and the Arabian Gulf.* Annapolis, MD: Naval Institute Press, 2007.

BANGLADESH

People's Republic of Bangladesh
Gana-Prajatantri Bangladesh

CAPITAL: Dhaka (formerly Dacca)

FLAG: The national flag is a red circle against a dark-green background.

ANTHEM: Amar Sonar Bangla (My Golden Bengal).

MONETARY UNIT: The taka (BDT) of 100 poisha is a paper currency. There are coins of 1, 2, 5, 10, 25, and 50 poisha, which are rarely used; there are coins of 1, 2, and 5 taka and notes of 10, 20, 50, 100, 500, and 1,000 taka. BDT1 = US$0.0132 (or US$1 = BDT75.815) as of October 2011.

WEIGHTS AND MEASURES: The metric system is used. Customary numerical units include the lakh (equal to 100,000) and the crore (equal to 10 million).

HOLIDAYS: New Year's Day, 1 January; National Mourning Day (Shaheel Day), 21 February; Independence Day, 26 March; May Day, 1 May; Victory Day, 16 December; Christmas, 25 December. Movable religious holidays include Jamat Wida, Shab-i-Bharat, Eid al-Fitr, Eid al-Adha, and Durga Puja.

TIME: 6 p.m. = noon GMT.

¹LOCATION, SIZE, AND EXTENT

Situated in South Asia, Bangladesh, before it became an independent state, was the eastern province of Pakistan, known as East Bengal and, later, as East Pakistan. Bangladesh is slightly smaller than the state of Iowa with a total area of 144,000 sq km (55,598 sq mi), extending 767 km (477 mi) SSE–NNW and 429 km (267 mi) ENE–WSW. Bangladesh is bordered in the W, N, and E by India, on the SE by Myanmar (Burma), and on the S by the Bay of Bengal, with a total boundary length of 4,246 km (2,638 mi). A border demarcation agreement was signed with Myanmar in May 1979. Demarcation of the marine boundary with India remained unresolved as of 2006. Bangladesh's capital city, Dhaka, is located near the center of the country.

²TOPOGRAPHY

Bangladesh is a tropical country, situated mainly on the deltas of large rivers flowing from the Himalayas. The Brahmaputra River, known locally as the Jamuna, unites with part of the Ganges to form the Padma, which, after its juncture with a third large river, the Meghna, flows into the Bay of Bengal. Offshoots of the Ganges-Padma, including the Burishwar, Garai, Kobadak, and Madhumati, also flow south to the Bay of Bengal. No part of the delta area is more than 150 m (500 ft) above sea level, and most of it is but a meter or two (a few feet) above sea level. Its soil consists mostly of fertile alluvium, which is intensively farmed; mineral deposits are negligible. During the rainy season, floodwater covers most of the land surface, often damaging crops and injuring the economy. The northwestern section of the country, drained by the Tista (Teesta) River, is somewhat higher and less flat, but the only really hilly regions are in the east, notably in the Chit-

tagong Hill Tracts to the southeast and the Sylhet District to the northeast. Near the Myanmar border in the extreme southeast is the Keokradong, which, at 1,230 m (4,034 ft), is the highest peak in Bangladesh.

³CLIMATE

Bangladesh has a tropical monsoon climate. Annual rainfall is high, averaging from about 119 cm (47 in) to 145 cm (57 in). There are three distinct seasons. The winter, which lasts from October through early March, is cool and dry, with temperature ranges from 5 to 22°C (41 to 72°F); total winter rainfall averages about 18 cm (7 in) in the east and less than 8 cm (3 in) in the northwest. Temperatures rise rapidly in March and during the summer season (March through May) average about 32°C (90°F). Rainfall also increases during this period. However, nearly 80% of the annual rainfall falls from May to September, the monsoon season, when moisture-laden winds blow from the south and southeast. Temperatures drop somewhat, seldom exceeding 31°C (88°F), but humidity remains high.

From April through June and from October through November, tropical cyclones, accompanied by high seas and heavy flooding, are common. There were cyclones in May 1963, May and December 1965, October 1966, and most notably during the night of 12–13 November 1970, when a storm and resultant flooding killed more than 200,000 people. A cyclonic storm on 24–25 May 1985 took more than 11,000 lives. A cyclone on 30 April 1991 left over 138,000 people dead and nine million homeless. The November 2007 Cyclone Sidr left a death toll of 3,500 people and rendered homeless at least one million people. In May 2009, Cyclone Aila swept through Bangladesh and parts of eastern India, killing over

120 people and displacing nearly 500,000 people. Massive mudslides are also common during the rainy season. Monsoon floods in 1974, 1980, and 1983 devastated the country and caused many deaths. The monsoon in August and September 1988 left three-fourths of the country flooded, 1,300 persons dead, and over three million people homeless, with damage to the country's infrastructure estimated at $1 billion. Following two days of torrential rains in June 2010, flooding and mudslides in the area around the beach resort of Cox's Bazar left 53 people dead.

Climate change due to global warming is a particular threat to Bangladesh, already being felt as storms become more severe and coastal wetlands are increasingly salinated. Rising sea levels are projected to inundate low-lying land, which could displace as many as 40 million Bangladeshis.

4 FLORA AND FAUNA

The World Resources Institute estimates that there are 5,000 plant species in Bangladesh. In addition, Bangladesh is home to 131 species of mammals, 604 species of birds, 113 species of reptiles, and 23 species of amphibians. These figures reflect the total number of distinct species residing in the country, not the number of endemic species.

Most of Bangladesh has the plant and animal life typical of tropical and riverine wetlands. The landscape, which for most of the year is lush green, is dominated by rice paddies and dotted with palms, bamboo, and fruit trees. The large mangrove forest area of the Sundarbans in the southwest is the home of the world's largest single population of the endangered Bengal tiger. Bangladesh also has leopards, crocodiles, elephants, sambar and chattel deer, monkeys and gibbons, boars, bears, and many varieties of birds and waterfowl.

5 ENVIRONMENT

Extreme population density has severely strained Bangladesh's limited natural resources. Nearly all arable land is already cultivated, and forestland has been greatly reduced by agricultural expansion and by timber and fuel wood cutting. Between 1983 and 1993, forest and woodland declined by 12.5% to 1.9 million hectares (4.7 million acres). By 2011, forest cover had diminished to less than 10% of the land, with 1.4 million hectares (3.4 million acres) and a deforestation rate of 3.3%, according to a United Nations Food and Agricultural Organization (UN FAO) satellite study.

Bangladesh's environmental problems have been complicated by natural disasters, such as cyclones and floods, straining an agricultural system supporting one of the world's most populous countries. Water supply is also a major problem because of population size, lack of purification procedures, and the spread of untreated contaminants by floodwaters. To ease these problems, the government has established drainage, irrigation, and flood protection systems. Water resources totaled 1,210.6 cu km (290.4 cu mi) while water usage was 11.96 cu km (2.87 cu mi) per year. Domestic water usage accounted for 3% of total usage, industrial for 1%, and agricultural for 96%. Per capita water usage totaled 560 cu m (19,776 cu ft) per year. Industrial waste, agricultural chemicals, and sewage have severely polluted the rivers of Bangladesh. The UN reported in 2008 that carbon dioxide emissions in Bangladesh totaled 43,715 kilotons.

The World Resources Institute reported that Bangladesh had designated 88,400 hectares (218,441 acres) of land for protection as of 2006. The Sundarbans is a natural UNESCO World Heritage Site and a Ramsar International Wetland Site. Despite passage of the Wildlife Preservation Act of 1973, wildlife continued to suffer from human encroachment. According to a 2011 report issued by the International Union for Conservation of Nature and Natural Resources (IUCN), threatened species included 34 types of mammals, 30 species of birds, 21 types of reptiles, 18 species of fish, and 16 species of plants. Threatened species included the Asian elephant, pygmy hog, Bengal tiger, gharial, and river terrapin. A critically endangered clouded leopard cub was captured in Bangladesh 2009.

6 POPULATION

The US Central Intelligence Agency (CIA) estimated the population of Bangladesh in 2011 to be approximately 158,570,535, which placed it at number 7 in population among the 196 nations of the world. In 2011, approximately 4.6% of the population was over 65 years of age, with another 34.3% under 15 years of age. The median age in Bangladesh was 23.3 years. There were 0.93 males for every female in the country. The population's annual rate of change was 1.566%, a result of comprehensive family planning programs. The projected population for the year 2025 was 195,000,000. In the 2011 Bangladesh census, population density was calculated at 964 people per sq km (2,497 people per square mi).

The UN estimated that 28% of the population lived in urban areas, and that urban populations had an annual rate of change of 3.1%. The largest urban areas, along with their respective populations, included Dhaka, 14.3 million; Chittagong, 4.8 million; Khulna, 1.6 million; and Rajshahi, 853,000. The city of Sylhet, in the northeast, experienced the highest growth rate as of the 2011 census.

7 MIGRATION

Estimates of Bangladesh's net migration rate, carried out by the CIA in 2011, amounted to -1.57 migrants per 1,000 citizens. The total number of emigrants living abroad was 5.38 million, and the total number of immigrants living in Bangladesh was 1.09 million. Bangladesh also was host to over 28,000 refugees. Since 1947, there has been a regular interchange of population between India and what is now Bangladesh, with Hindus migrating to India and Muslims emigrating from India. There was also substantial migration between Bangladesh (then East Pakistan) and West Pakistan until the 1971 war. Before and during the war, an estimated 8 million to 10 million Bengalis fled to India; most of these refugees returned after the independence of Bangladesh was firmly established.

In 1993, repatriation began of an estimated 56,000 Chakma refugees from the Indian state of Tripura to the Chittagong Hill Tracts of Bangladesh. In 1991–92, about 265,000 Rohingyas—Muslims from neighboring Myanmar—fled to Bangladesh to escape repression. As of October 2011 around 28,000 Rohingya refugees lived in southern Bangladesh in two official camps, while many others lived unofficially in Bangladesh.

Bangladeshi long-term migration to industrialized countries in the West began in the 1950s to the United Kingdom and in the

1960s to the United States. Labor migration to the Middle East and Southeast Asia began in the 1970s on short-term bases. Preferred Middle Eastern countries for labor migration have included Saudi Arabia, the United Arab Emirates, Kuwait, and Libya. Bangladeshis have sought political asylum in India and other countries.

8 ETHNIC GROUPS

Residents of Bangladesh are called Bangladeshis. About 98% of the people are of the ethnic group called Bengalis (or Banglas). The indigenous people of the Chittagong and Bandarban Hill Tracts, collectively totaling less than one million people, are ethnically distinct from the Bengalis, with their own languages. Some are related to peoples of neighboring Myanmar. The government's policy of resettling Bengalis in the region and extracting resources resulted in an indigenous peoples' insurgency, brutally repressed in the 1980s. About 250,000 of the national population consists of Biharis, non-Bengali Muslims who migrated from India to what was then East Pakistan after the partition of the subcontinent in 1947.

9 LANGUAGES

Bengali (Bangla), part of the Indo-European language family, is the official language of Bangladesh, and is spoken as a first language by about 98% of the population. The successful move to make Bengali coequal with Urdu as an official language was a hallmark of Bengali nationalism in the early 1950s. Although Bangla is the official language, English is also used for official and legal purposes and widely used in business. Among those speaking Bangla there are differences of dialect according to region. The people of Chittagong, Noakhali, and Sylhet are known for their distinctive dialects. Non-Bengali migrants from India still speak Urdu (and Hindi), and this language is widely understood in urban areas. A few indigenous groups speak distinct Tibeto-Burmese languages, akin to Burmese and Assamese.

10 RELIGIONS

Nearly 90% of the people are Sunni Muslims, making Bangladesh one of the world's largest Muslim countries. About 9% of the population is Hindu; the remainder are mainly Buddhists (Theravada) or Christians (mostly Roman Catholics). There are small numbers of Shi'a Muslims, Sikhs, Baha'is, Ahmadis, and animists. Islam was established as the state religion in 1988. Although freedom of worship is provided for in the constitution, in practice there have been reports of social, political, and economic discrimination, and sometimes violence, against non-Muslims. Major religious holidays of Muslims, Hindus, Buddhists, and Christians are observed as national holidays.

11 TRANSPORTATION

The large number of rivers and the annual flooding hazard make it difficult to build and maintain adequate transportation facilities in Bangladesh. Railways and waterways are the chief means of transportation. Railroads extend for 2,835 km (1,762 mi). The railways are managed by the government and reach most districts of the country. The quality of service has declined because of the expense of importing new equipment. Enlarging and improving

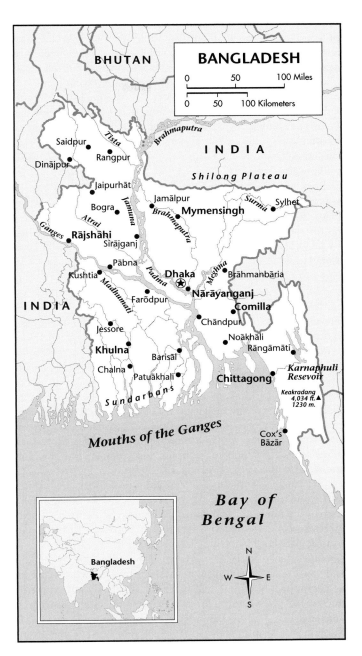

LOCATION: 20°34' to 26°38'N; 88°1' to 92°41' E. BOUNDARY LENGTHS: India, 4,053 kilometers (2,553 miles); Myanmar, 193 kilometers (122 miles); Bay of Bengal coastline, 580 kilometers (324 miles). TERRITORIAL SEA LIMIT: 12 miles.

the railway system is also costly, partly because of the number of bridges needed.

The country has two deep-water ports: Chittagong, serving the eastern sector, and Chalna, serving the west. Bangladesh has approximately 8,370 km (5,201 mi) of navigable waterways. There are five main river ports—Dhaka, Nārāyanganj, Chandpur, Barisal, and Khulna—and more than 1,500 smaller ports. The inland water system has 2,575 km (1,600 mi) of main cargo routes. The merchant marine fleet in 2010 consisted of 50 ships of 1,000 GRT or over.

The CIA reports that Bangladesh has 239,226 km (148,648 mi) of roads, of which 22,726 km (14,121 mi) are paved. A large part of the highway system becomes submerged in the rainy season; bridges, ferries, embankments, and dikes are therefore necessary to the inland transportation system. Because of the difficulties of land travel, the number of motor vehicles remains relatively small. There are 2 motor vehicles per 1,000 people in the country, a figure which excludes motorcycles, motor scooters, and scooter taxis, which are common in Bangladesh, as are bicycle rickshaws. Poor road conditions, untrained drivers, and lack of vehicle maintenance are blamed for the high number of vehicle accidents each year in Bangladesh. As many as 4,000 people die on Bangladesh roads every year.

There are 17 airports, which transported 1.41 million passengers in 2009 according to the World Bank. Zia International is the principal airport, located at Dhaka. There are also international airports at Chittagong and Sylhet. Bangladesh Biman is the national airline. It has a domestic network connecting major cities and operates international flights to cities in Asia, the Middle East, and Europe.

12 HISTORY

In ancient times, the area now known as Bangladesh was the eastern portion of a huge river delta region called Bang, where the Ganges and Brahmaputra River systems empty into the Bay of Bengal and Indian Ocean. The region became known as Bengal in more modern times, but recorded history of the region can be traced to the 4th century BC when it was home to an apparently flourishing riverine civilization. The oldest surviving remains of this civilization are the ruins of the city of Mahasthan, the ancient Pundranagar, which continued to flourish for more than 1,500 years, even though the region was conquered by the Hindu Maurya empire that reached its height under Emperor Asoka around 207 BC. From this time onward, the history of Bengal was part of the wider historical experience of the Indian subcontinent, and during most of India's classical Hindu period (AD 320 to AD 1000), Bengal was a loosely incorporated outpost of empires centered in the Gangetic plain.

Islam came to South Asia in the years following AD 800 but did not reach Bengal until Muslim invaders from the west secured a foothold there around AD 1200. In the 13th and 14th centuries, after successive waves of Turkish, Persian, and Afghan invaders, Islam began to take a firm hold in the area that is now Bangladesh. The region was annexed by the Mughal Empire in 1576 under Emperor Akbar and ruled by his successors into the 17th century. The fealty lesser Nawabs (or Nabobs) of the Bengal area paid to the Mughals ensured the political stability and economic prosperity of the region, which became known for its industries based on the weaving of silk and cotton cloth.

The arrival of the French and British East India companies in the early 18th century coincided with Mughal decline. By the middle of the 18th century, the British emerged supreme in what they created as the Bengal presidency, establishing themselves in Calcutta and expanding into all of what is now Bangladesh, as well as the Indian states of West Bengal, Bihar, Assam, and Orissa. From Calcutta, British traders and administrators successfully played off rivalries among the satraps of the late Mughal Empire to gain control of most of the subcontinent in the years between the Battle of Plassey in 1756 and the assumption of the company's domain by the British Crown in 1859. Calcutta remained the seat of British power in the subcontinent and the center of British control over the Indian Empire until 1931 when the capital was moved to the new city of New Delhi.

Well-to-do Hindus in Bengal generally prospered under the British, apparently taking more easily to British ways and British law than the numerically dominant Muslims. The Muslim aristocracy of eastern Bengal—feudal barons under the Mughals—resisted British rule. By the turn of the 20th century, both communities took offense at British efforts to impose western educational systems on local universities, reducing their independence. Hindus were further enraged by the British decision in 1905, in an effort to improve administration and to placate Muslims, to divide the overly large Bengal presidency in two, with the Muslim-dominant area of eastern Bengal and Assam to be a separate province. The 1905 partition was the first acknowledgment of a sense of separateness among Muslims by the British and foreshadowed events of 42 years later when Bengal was divided between Muslim-majority and Hindu-majority districts to create East Pakistan.

The 1905 action resulted in increasing acts of violence. This lasted until it was undone six years later in favor of reuniting Bengal and instead separating out what would become the provinces of Orissa and Bihar. But the agitation provoked by the 1905 partition and the Hindu-Muslim enmities it left behind continued to provoke terrorist actions against British rule until nonviolence emerged as a mode of political struggle, under the leadership of Mohandas (Mahatma) Gandhi of the Indian National Congress.

British reforms in 1909 and 1919 expanded local self-rule in their Indian domains, but the pace fell short of the pace of demands put forth by the rising tide of nationalism espoused by the Indian National Congress, which in 1929 committed itself to the goal of complete independence. As the struggle gained momentum, differences between Hindus and Muslims widened. While the majority Hindu community saw a single Indian polity committed to secularism and diversity as the goal of the independence movement, Muslims came to fear that their community would be a permanent electoral minority, an anxiety they saw borne out in the 1937 elections held under British auspices. To look after their unique cultural interests, they formed the All-India Muslim League, and under the Muslim League leadership, sentiment began to coalesce around the "two nation" theory propounded earlier by the poet Iqbal, a belief that South Asian Muslims and Hindus were and should be two separate nations, i.e. that Muslims required the creation of an independent nation of their own (Pakistan) in which they would predominate. In 1940, the Muslim League adopted this as its goal, under the leadership of Mohammad Ali Jinnah, who resisted all efforts at compromise through all the difficult days leading up to the grant of independence in 1947.

In language, culture, ethnic background, population density, political experience, and economic potential, East and West Pakistan were totally disparate. The primary bond was Islam. Pakistan's early years as a nation were dominated by unsuccessful attempts—punctuated by bouts of authoritarian rule—to create a national policy that would somehow bridge these differences. Larger in population and in economic importance than the west wing, the Bengali east wing chafed under national policies effectively dominated by the leadership residing in the west wing. When its influence was further reduced under repeated bouts of martial law and by the reconstruction of West Pakistan as a single province, demands for autonomy in the east began to mount. This demand proved more than the fragile sense of Islamic nationhood could sustain. The new state of Pakistan, made up of Muslim-majority districts in both eastern and western reaches of formerly British India, was at best an unwieldy creation. It cut across long-established lines of trade and communication, divided families, provoked a mass movement of millions of refugees caught on the "wrong" side of the partition markers, and forced the creation of a new but divided polity. Pakistan consisted of two distinct territories, Sindh, the Northwest Frontier, and (partially) Punjab (which, like Bengal, was also partitioned), separated by 1,600 km (1,000 mi) of secular but predominantly Hindu India. East Pakistan, its 42 million people including nearly 9 million Hindus, encompassed the eastern half of Bengal province as shaped in 1912, plus the Sylhet District of Assam.

Nationhood

After a round of martial law in Pakistan in 1969, national elections were scheduled for 1970. But when the popular verdict in those elections supported greater autonomy for East Pakistan than the West Pakistan-dominated national leadership was prepared to accord, the results were set aside. Subsequent civil unrest escalated quickly to civil war in East Pakistan. At least 300,000 people, mostly civilians, died in the war. Swamped with a million refugees from the fighting, India intervened militarily in December 1971, tipping the scales in favor of the rebels and facilitating the creation of Bangladesh in 1972. Sheikh Mujibur (Mujib) Rahman, leader of the Awami League and of the fight for autonomy, was released from prison in West Pakistan (which became the Islamic Republic of Pakistan) and became prime minister of the new nation of Bangladesh.

The 1971 civil war undid much of the limited progress East Pakistan had made in recovering from the 1947 partition. Flooding and official mismanagement of food distribution were causes of a 1974 famine in which over one million Bangladeshis perished. Mujib faced a task for which his administrative and political experience was lacking. He fought and won a massive victory at the polls in 1973, but two years later, he suspended the political process and took power into his own hands. Public opinion turned against Mujib, coalescing two main opposition groups that otherwise shared little in common besides their opposition to Mujib and to Indian influence: they were the ultra-conservative Islamic groups, led by the Jamaat-i-Islami, and the radical left, led by Maoists, who opposed both Indian and Soviet influence. On 15 August 1975, a group of young military officers seized power, killing Mujib and many of his family members and imposing martial law. A counter-coup three months later produced a new military government with Gen. Zia-ur Rahman at its head. In 1978, with limited political activity permitted, he was elected president and lifted martial law. In February 1979, he restored parliamentary government after elections gave his new party, the Bangladesh National Party (BNP) a two-thirds majority in parliament.

Zia was assassinated during an abortive military coup in May 1981. He was succeeded in power by his vice president, Abdus Sattar, who was deposed the following March by his army chief, Gen. Hussain Mohammad Ershad. Declaring martial law, Ershad became Chief Martial Law Administrator (CMLA), suspended the 1972 constitution, and banned political parties. Ershad gained support by cracking down on corruption and opening up the economy to foreign investment. In 1983, he assumed the presidency, and by January 1986, he had restored full political activity in which his own party, the Jatiya (People's) Party took a prominent part. He retired from the army and was elected president without opposition in October 1986, but in July 1987, mounting opposition to his often dictatorial rule among the united opposition parties led him again to declare a state of emergency, dissolve the assembly, and schedule new elections for March 1988. His Jatiya Party triumphed in those elections, due mainly to the refusal of the opposition parties to participate. At the end of 1990, in the face of widespread demonstrations and some Hindu-Muslim violence, his opposition had grown so strong that Ershad was forced to resign the presidency, turning the government over to Supreme Court Chief Justice Shahabuddin Ahmed, the unanimous choice of the opposition parties.

An interim government scheduled elections for February 1991, and the result was the election of an assembly in which the BNP, headed by Begum Khaleda Zia-ur Rahman, Zia's widow, held a plurality. However, the BNP lost popular support by March 1994, when opposition parties walked out of parliament and boycotted the government, claiming the BNP had rigged a regional election. The main opposition groups—the Awami League (AL), Jatiya Party, and the Jamaat-e-Islami—continued the protest for two years, boycotting February 1996 elections swept by the BNP. Amid further charges of vote-rigging, Khaleda Zia resigned, the BNP dissolved parliament, and a caretaker government conducted new elections in June 1996. The Awami League, led by Sheikh Hasina Wajed, daughter of Sheikh Mujid, gained control of parliament in the elections, contested by all parties and monitored by international observers.

Prime Minister Sheik Hasina had no easier time ruling Bangladesh than her predecessor. Her government faced continuing protests, strikes, and often-violent demonstrations organized by the BNP and other opposition parties. Targets for such actions included the government's historic agreement with India in December 1996 over sharing the waters of the Ganges River, higher taxes imposed by the government in July 1997, and problems of law and order in the country. Tensions were heightened by the conviction and death sentences passed on several people involved in the assassination of Sheikh Hasina's father, Sheikh Mujib. Among the AL government's achievements, however, were the Ganges water-sharing treaty, the December 1997 accord that ended the insurgency in the Chittagong Hill Tracts (CHT) in southeastern Bangladesh, and a restructuring of local government to increase grassroots involvement in politics. On the international stage, Bangladesh was elected to serve a two-year term on the Security Council of the United Nations, effective 1 January 2000.

One hundred fifty-five people were killed in violence leading up to the October 2001 parliamentary elections. In July, Prime Minister Hasina stepped down, handing power over to a caretaker authority that supervised the upcoming elections; she became the first prime minister in the country's history to complete a full five-year term. Former prime minister Khaleda Zia won a landslide victory on 1 October 2001, campaigning against lawlessness and corruption, in an election in which 75% of the registered voters went to the polls. The Awami League boycotted Parliament, protesting alleged rigging of elections and the persecution of religious minorities. In June 2002, the Awami League ended its boycott of parliament and attended for the first time since losing in the October 2001 elections. That October Prime Minister Zia engaged the army to contain terrorist attacks throughout the country in the absence of adequate logistic support from the police. The army was also directed to curb crime and corruption. As many as 44 people died in custody in the drive lasting from 16 October 2002 to 9 January 2003. Zia granted immunity to the armed forces for their actions during that period, a decision that was highly criticized by the opposition Awami League.

Like other Muslim-majority countries in Asia, Bangladesh saw an increase in Islamic militant activity following the attacks on the World Trade Center in the United States on 11 September 2001 and the US invasion of Afghanistan. Although the nation remains officially secular, calls to adopt Islamic law have grown since 2001. The threat of militant violence continued to grow through 2005. On 17 August of that year, about 100 small bombs exploded across the country, mainly at government offices, bus and train stations, and in public markets. Two people were killed and at least 125 others were wounded in the blasts. Leaflets from an Islamic group, Jamaat-ul-Mujahideen, were found at many of the bomb sites, calling for Islamic rule in Bangladesh.

In 2006 and 2007, Bangladeshi politics were still dominated by Khaleda Zia of the BNP and Sheikh Hasina Wajed of the Awami League. In October 2006, a caretaker authority was established under Iajuddin Ahmed to prepare for the elections after Khaleda Zia's five-year term as prime minister expired. However, the bitter feud between the two political leaders led to violent street protests, which brought about the suspension of the planned January 2007 elections and the declaration of a state of emergency. Dozens of people were killed and hundreds injured. Iajuddin Ahmed resigned from his role as interim government leader and was replaced by Fakhruddin Ahmed, a former head of the central bank, on 12 January 2007. The military-backed caretaker government widened a sweeping anti-corruption investigation in March 2007. Prominent public officials and business figures from the BNP and the Awami League were jailed on charges of corruption and related offenses. By April, Sheikh Hasina had been charged with murder and extortion, and Khaleda Zia was under virtual house arrest. In an effort to ease tensions, the government initially barred Sheikh Hasina from returning to the country (she was on a visit to the United States) and pressed Khaleda Zia to go into exile. However, by 26 April, those demands had been dropped. In August 2007, the government imposed a curfew on Dhaka and five other cities amid violent clashes between police and students who demanded an end to the state of emergency.

Parliamentary elections were held in December 2008, considered free and fair by international observers, with 230 seats won by the Awami League, representing the largest parliamentary majority since 1973. The BNP won only 30 seats in parliament. Khaleda Zia and her BNP initially rejected the results, claiming the vote was rigged. The caretaker government had hoped that both the AL and the BNP would drop the former prime ministers as party leaders to ensure political reform. But this approach, popularly known as the Minus Two formula, was not widely supported, as sentiments against the army-backed regime seemed to grow stronger than those against the party leaders. Sheikh Hasina Wa-

jed of the Awami League was appointed as prime minister in January 2009. Zillur Rahman was elected president in February 2009.

In 2010, Hasina's government initiated war crimes tribunals of Bangladeshis accused of collaborating with the West Pakistan Army in massacres during the independence war; defendants included prominent leaders of Jamaat-e-Islami.

¹³GOVERNMENT

Bangladesh inherited the provincial government under which first the dominion, then republic, of Pakistan was governed, a parliamentary system based on the Westminster model with a unicameral legislature. Following this model, the constitution of December 1972 (amended several times) established a unitary, democratic republic, with an indirectly elected president as nominal head of state and a prime minister as head of government and chief executive. The prime minister and his government are responsible to a unicameral legislature (*Jatiya Sangsad*) elected no less frequently than every five years and composed of 300 members. A constitutional amendment reserving 30 additional parliamentary seats for indirect election of women expired in 2001, and, in 2004, a constitutional amendment stipulated that a minimum of 15% of parliamentary seats must be for women.

The members of the parliament are elected by popular vote from single territorial constituencies. The prime minister is generally the leader of the majority party in parliament. The president is elected by parliament to serve a five-year term and is eligible for a second-term. An executive cabinet is chosen by the prime minister and appointed by the president.

The constitution incorporated four basic principles of state policy: nationalism, secularism, socialism, and democracy. Islam replaced secularism as a state principle by constitutional amendment in 1977.

¹⁴POLITICAL PARTIES

From 1947 through the end of 1971, East Pakistan (now Bangladesh) was governed as a single province, one of the two wings of Pakistan. There were more than 30 political parties operating in the east wing, most of them small, fractious, and with few elected members. The major parties at that time operated on the all-Pakistan level as well, and included the moderate Pakistan Muslim League (PML), a national movement that became the party of independence and the ruling party of Pakistan; the moderate socialist Awami (Freedom) League (AL), a spin-off from the Muslim League and the advocate of Bengali autonomy, with the bulk of its support in the east wing; the ultraconservative Islamic Jamaat-e-Islami (JI), grounded in Sunni Islamic orthodoxy and initially opposed to the 1947 partition; and the leftist peasants and workers party, the Krishak Sramik Party (KSP). The Communist Party of Pakistan (CPP) was banned in 1952 and remained illegal until its east wing component became the Bangladesh Communist Party (BCP) after 1971.

The PML governed East Pakistan from 1947, but in elections in 1954, the AL and the KSP, supported by the JI, ousted the Muslim League from office. After four years of political instability, however, the two parties were displaced by the central government under a "Governor's Rule" provision. When the East Pakistan government was restored in 1955, the KSP ruled in its own right until displaced by an AL government in 1956. Loss of Hindu support in

1958 cost the AL its majority in 1958, but "Governor's Rule" was again imposed. Martial law was imposed in Pakistan in 1965 and, in elections held thereafter under a limited political franchise, the Muslim League came to power briefly. Imposition of martial law in 1969 suspended political activity again until the scheduling of elections in 1970.

By 1970, the Pakistan People's Party (PPP) and the AL now advocating far-reaching autonomy for East Bengal, had become the dominant political forces, respectively, in West and East Pakistan. Elections confirmed this position, with the AL winning 167 of East Pakistan's 169 seats in parliament and absolute control in East Pakistan. The AL was the only constituent in the Bangla government-in-exile in 1971, with leftist parties in support and Islamic parties in opposition. After independence, the Islamic party leaders were jailed, their parties having been banned, and in 1973, Sheikh Mujibur (Mujib) Rahman's Awami League elected 293 members of the 300-elective seats in parliament.

In January 1975, with his power slipping, President Mujib amended the constitution to create a one-party state, renaming his party the Bangladesh Krishak Sramik Awami League (BKSAL). After the coup later in 1975, the BKSAL was disbanded and disappeared. When Zia-ur Rahman lifted the ban on political parties in 1978, his presidential bid was supported by a newly formed Nationalist Front, dominated by his Bangladesh National Party (BNP), which won 207 of the assembly's 300 elective seats. All political activity was banned anew in March 1982, when General Ershad seized power, but as he settled into power, Ershad supported the formation of the Jatiya (People's) Party, which became his vehicle for ending martial law and transforming his regime into a parliamentary government. In elections marked by violence and discredited by extensive fraud, Ershad's Jatiya Party won more than 200 of the 300 elective seats at stake. The Awami League, now under the leadership of Mujib's daughter, Sheikh Hasina Wajed, took 76 seats as the leading opposition party. Khaleda Zia's BNP, heading an alliance of seven parties, boycotted the elections and gained considerable respect by doing so. The BNP, the AL, and all other parties boycotted Ershad's 1988 election as well, discrediting the result that gave the Jatiya a two-thirds majority and fueling the fires of discontent that led to Ershad's resignation on 4 December 1990. Ershad was imprisoned on corruption charges.

A BNP plurality in the elections on 27 February 1991 enabled Khaleda Zia to form a government. The leader of the opposition was Sheikh Hasina Wajed of the Awami League (AL), which won 88 seats to claim the second-ranking position in the assembly. However, Khaleda Zia resigned, and parliament was dissolved in March 1996 amid vote-rigging charges and a two-year government boycott by opposition parties. June 1996 elections brought Sheikh Hasina and the AL to a majority role in the new parliament. The AL won 140 seats to the BNP's 116. The new prime minister, Hasina formed a cooperative government with the Jatiya Party, which won 32 seats. Although the Jatiya Party withdrew from the coalition in March 1997, the AL had by then acquired an absolute majority in the legislature and continued as the party in power.

From 1997 to 2001, the main opposition party, the BNP, hindered the work of the parliament by repeatedly boycotting its proceedings. The BNP supported public antigovernment demonstrations, and organized a three-day general strike in November 1998 to protest alleged government repression. October 2001 parliamentary elections ousted the AL, bringing Khaleda Zia's BNP back to power, in a coalition with three Islamic parties: Jamaat-e-Islami, Islami Oikya Jote, and the Naziur faction of the Jatiya Party. Khaleda Zia's term extended through 2007. A military-backed caretaker government declared emergency rule in January 2007 when violent clashes broke out over the coming elections. The caretaker government advised that the AL and BNP force Hasina and Zia to step down from leadership; neither did. The AL took 230 seats in the December 2008 elections, and the marginalized BNP won 30. Hasina again became prime minister in January 2009.

Zillur Rahman of the AL was elected president in 2009.

¹⁵LOCAL GOVERNMENT

The key administrative unit in Bangladesh is the district, of which there are 64 in all. Districts are grouped into (and report through) seven administrative divisions (Barisal, Chittagong, Dhaka, Khulna, Rajshahi, Rangpur, and Sylhet), under a Divisional Commissioner.

In 1997, Bangladesh reorganized its local government structure in rural areas. New legislation created a four-tier local government system: *gram* (village), *union* (collection of villages), *upazila* (subdistrict), and *zila* (district) councils. The purpose of this reorganization was to democratize government at the grassroots level. The 1997 law also reserved seats for women in local government. Other legislation made the *upazila* level the most important tier in local government, giving the *upazila* council power to collect revenue, prepare its own budget, and hire its own employees.

¹⁶JUDICIAL SYSTEM

The judicial system is modeled after the British system. Besides the 1972 constitution, the fundamental law of the land, there are codes of civil and criminal laws. The civil law incorporates certain Islamic and Hindu religious principles relating to marriage, inheritance, and other social matters.

The judicial system consists of a Supreme Court and subordinate courts. The Supreme Court, with a chief justice and judges appointed by the president, has two divisions: a high court and an appellate court. The lower judicial system consists of district and sessions courts, and magistrate courts. The upper-level courts have exercised independent judgment, ruling against the government on a number of occasions in criminal, civil, and even political trials. The trials are public. There is a right to counsel and right to appeal. There is also a system of bail. An overwhelming backlog of cases has been a major problem of the court system.

In March 2001, the World Bank announced the approval of a $30.6 million credit to assist Bangladesh in making its judicial system more efficient and accountable. Changes included the creation of legal aid committees to provide assistance to the poor, as well as the establishing of metropolitan courts of sessions in Dhaka and Chittagong. A permanent Law Commission was created to reform and update existing laws. The National Human Rights Commission was instituted in 2008 under the caretaker government and convened in June 2010. Bangladesh law provides for a national ombudsman to consider complaints of corruption and abuse of power, but, as of 2011, the appointment had never been made. Extrajudicial killings by security forces, as well as torture and death in police custody, were reported by Amnesty International and other human rights monitors in 2009–11.

17 ARMED FORCES

The International Institute for Strategic Studies reports that armed forces in Bangladesh totaled 157,053 members in 2011. The force is comprised of 126,153 from the army, 16,900 from the navy, and 14,000 members of the air force. Armed forces represent 0.3% of the labor force in Bangladesh. Defense spending totaled $3.4 billion and accounted for 1.3% of gross domestic product (GDP).

Since 2009, Bangladesh had been upgrading its navy to combat piracy and secure offshore petroleum fields. A military contingent from Bangladesh participated in the first Gulf War against Iraq in 1990 but did not join the US-led coalition in Iraq in 2003. According to the Armed Forces Division of the Bangladesh government, as of 2011, troops from Bangladesh have engaged in 45 UN peacekeeping missions in 32 countries. As of 2011, Bangladesh was the largest contributor of troops to UN peacekeeping.

18 INTERNATIONAL COOPERATION

Bangladesh joined the United Nations on 17 September 1974; it belongs to the Economic and Social Commission for Asia and the Pacific (ESCAP) and several non-regional specialized agencies. The country holds membership in the Asian Development Bank, the Colombo Plan, the Commonwealth of Nations, the Organization of the Islamic Conference (OIC), and G-77. The nation became a member of the WTO on 1 January 1995. In 1985, Bangladesh became one of seven constituent members of the South Asian Association for Regional Cooperation (SAARC), under which it is a signatory to the South Asia Preferential Trade Agreement.

Soon after independence, Bangladesh signed a friendship treaty with India, but relations between the two nations are often strained. In 1997, Bangladesh signed an agreement with India on sharing water from the Ganges River. Pakistan recognized Bangladesh in February 1974, and the two have developed good relations, their past differences notwithstanding. Friction with neighboring Myanmar has occurred over the flow of refugees into Bangladesh, border issues, and offshore petroleum rights.

Bangladesh has followed a nonaligned foreign policy, but by the late 1990s was seeking closer relations with other Islamic states, ASEAN, and China. Bangladesh maintains a friendly relationship with the United States, with which it has bilateral trade agreements. Bangladesh has contributed troops to UN efforts in Kosovo (1999), the Western Sahara (1991), Ethiopia and Eritrea (2000), Sierra Leone (1999), East Timor (2002), Georgia (1993), Côte d'Ivoire (2004), and Darfur (2007), among many other UN peacekeeping missions.

In environmental cooperation, Bangladesh is part of the Basel Convention, the Convention on Biological Diversity, Ramsar, CITES, the Kyoto Protocol, the Montréal Protocol, the Nuclear Test Ban Treaty, and the UN Conventions on the Law of the Sea, Climate Change, and Desertification.

19 ECONOMY

Bangladesh has experienced chronic poverty since its independence, but has also produced innovative methods for alleviating poverty, particularly microcredit loan programs. The prospect of return to elected government in 1990 helped produce an up-surge in growth in 1989/90, but in 1990/91 the combined effects of the Gulf War, domestic political disturbances, and a devastating cyclone resulted in a drop in the GDP growth rate. Pursuit of further stabilization and structural adjustment measures by the government in 1991 allowed Bangladesh to weather these crises, strengthen its revenue base, bring inflation to a record low of 1.4% in 1993, and maintain a good balance of payments position. However, political instability and a lack of continued economic reforms pushed inflation up in 1995. Sluggish development investments, limited growth in manufacturing, and bureaucratic inefficiency persisted. The election of the Awami League government helped calm the political situation, and the economy responded. GDP grew in 1996, while inflation eased.

In 1997, the government's delay in instituting reforms threatened to slow economic advances. Inflation rose, while GDP slowed. Although the Awami League promoted the exploration and production of oil and gas in Bangladesh in the late 1990s, exploration was delayed by political differences over how foreign companies would participate. The economy grew strongly during 1998, but growth slowed in 1999 and 2000. The global economic slowdown and the effects of the 11 September 2001 terrorist attacks on the United States, combined with continuing internal political turmoil, brought economic growth almost to a halt in Bangladesh in 2001–02. Severe flooding in 2004 damaged crops and infrastructure, illustrating once again the country's vulnerability to natural disasters.

Remittances from Bangladeshis working overseas decreased with the global economic crisis of 2008–09 but are recovering and have combined with exports to keep the economy healthy enough in 2010–2011 to allow some debt repayment. A related challenge to the economy has involved the return of thousands of newly unemployed workers back to Bangladesh. Many workers, particularly those in the construction industries of the Gulf states, lost their jobs and returned home, only to find an even bleaker job situation. Typically, these workers are heavily indebted to the brokers who secured the jobs originally, meaning that many faced losing their homes and land without a way to repay the debt.

The all-important agricultural sector has been periodically damaged by flooding, while manufacturing, including the vital export garment industry, has struggled with inadequate supplies of natural gas and electricity.

As of 2009, nearly 45% of all Bangladeshis were employed in the agricultural sector, with rice as the most important crop. But agriculture accounted for only 18.8% of GDP in 2010, with services making up 52.6% and industry 28.5%. The ready-made garment industry was responsible for about 80% of the nation's export earnings, but the industry is continually challenged by fluctuations in market demand and labor disputes.

According to the CIA, the GDP rate of change in Bangladesh, as of 2010, was 6%. Inflation stood at 8.1%, and unemployment was reported at 5.1%, a figure that does not include the country's chronic underemployment (estimated at 40%).

20 INCOME

The CIA estimated that, in 2010, the GDP of Bangladesh was $258.6 billion. The CIA defines GDP as the value of all final goods and services produced within a nation in a given year and computed on the basis of purchasing power parity (PPP) rather than value as measured on the basis of the rate of the exchange based on current dollars. The per capita GDP was estimated at $1,700. The annual growth rate of GDP was 6% as of 2011, and the average inflation rate was 8.1%. It was estimated that in 2010 agriculture accounted for 18.8% of GDP, industry 28.5%, and services 52.6%. According to the World Bank, remittances from citizens living abroad totaled $10.5 billion or about $66 per capita and accounted for approximately 4.1% of GDP.

The World Bank reports that, in 2009, household consumption in Bangladesh totaled $66.7 billion or about $421 per capita, measured in current US dollars rather than PPP. Household consumption includes expenditures of individuals, households, and nongovernmental organizations on goods and services, excluding the purchases of dwellings. It was estimated that household consumption was growing at an average annual rate of 5.9%.

As of 2011 the most recent study by the World Bank reported that actual individual consumption in Bangladesh was 77.7% of GDP and accounted for 0.37% of world consumption. By comparison, the United States accounted for 25.44% of world individual consumption. The World Bank also estimated that 40.6% of Bangladesh's GDP was spent on food and beverages, 16.4% on housing and household furnishings, 4.5% on clothes, 2.8% on health, 3.2% on transportation, 0.4% on communications, 0.6% on recreation, 1.7% on restaurants and hotels, and 3.1% on miscellaneous goods and services and purchases from abroad.

It was estimated that in 2010 about 40% of the population subsisted on an income below the poverty line established by Bangladesh's government.

21 LABOR

As of 2010, Bangladesh had a total labor force of 73.86 million people. Within that labor force, CIA estimates in 2008 noted that 45% were employed in agriculture, 30% in industry, and 25% in the service sector. Labor statistics may be unreliable because of a large, informal, unreported market. Bangladesh is an extensive exporter of labor to Saudi Arabia, Malaysia, Qatar, and Oman, among other countries.

In the formal sector of the economy, 1.8 million out of the 5 million workers were unionized. Strikes are a common form of workers' protest. There are industrial tribunals to settle labor disputes. The government can impose labor settlements through arbitration, as well as by declaring a strike illegal. Unions have become progressively more aggressive in asserting themselves, especially on the political scene. Civil service and security forces personnel are banned from joining unions. In addition, teachers in both the private and public sectors are prohibited from forming a trade union.

A series of wildcat strikes and street protests swept through the garment industry in June 2010, as tens of thousands of garment workers demanded an industry-wide increase in the minimum wage to a living wage level. In response, the Labor Ministry raised the rate from $24 a month (set in 2006) to $50 a month; the workers had called for $72 a month. As of November 2010, minimum wage rates for all sectors ranged from $43 to $132 per month.

By law, government employees, workers in nongovernmental organizations (NGOs) and banks, and other office workers are subject to a 40-hour workweek, with Fridays and Saturdays off. The legal workweek for factory workers is 48 hours, with up to 12 hours of overtime and one day off mandated. This law is rarely enforced, especially in the garment industry. Worker safety standards lack enforcement, and work-related accidents, factory fires, toxic materials, and road or boat accidents kill many workers each year. According to the Occupational Safety, Health and Environment Foundation of Bangladesh, 2,453 people died from work-related causes in 2009.

The prevalence of child labor in the nation has continued to be a serious problem according to international human rights groups. In response to criticism from major trade partners, the government passed a new labor law in 2006 that provided specific laws about child workers in the formal export-garment industry. However, the law does not apply to those working in home-based garment businesses or to other industries. The government discourages, but does not forbid, the employment of children under the age of 14. For many families, the small amount of money earned by each child is necessary to keep the family from starving. Some reports indicate that close to 8 million children are active in the workforce, with either part-time or full-time jobs. As children are sent to work rather than school, the nation must also deal with the challenge of employing and supporting a largely uneducated workforce. The International Labor Organization estimated in 2006 that 532,000 workers between ages 5 and 17 were employed in hazardous labor sectors, including construction, stone breaking, and dye works. Children are employed in agriculture, as domestic servants, street sellers and beggars, restaurant helpers, and in many other types of informal sector work.

22 AGRICULTURE

Roughly 58% of the total land is farmed, according to the World Bank (2008). The country's major crops include rice, jute, tea, wheat, sugarcane, potatoes, tobacco, pulses, oilseeds, spices, and fruit. According to the UN Food and Agriculture Organization (UN FAO), in 2009, cereal production amounted to 49.3 million tons, fruit production 3.6 million tons, and vegetable production 3.4 million tons.

Most farmers own no more than a few acres of land, and their holdings are badly fragmented. The land is fertile, but yields are low because of a lack of capital for input. While seasonal flooding is a vital element for agricultural production in Bangladesh, excessive rains and cyclonic storms have repeatedly devastated crops, as have periodic droughts.

Rice dominates production, with about 77% of all cropped land in Bangladesh and the country's food security depends completely on its supply. Of the varieties grown, aman rice, which can be raised in inundated land and saline soil, occupies nearly 60% of the total land under rice. Aus rice, which cannot be grown in flooded fields, is raised mostly in higher areas of Bangladesh. Boro rice is grown in the winter, mainly in the swamps and marshy areas, but government-supported irrigation projects have encouraged its extension to other areas. To meet the challenge of the food shortages, the government of Bangladesh and international aid programs introduced high-yield varieties. Hybrid and traditional varieties are grown.

Before 1992, the government artificially inflated rice prices by buying over one million tons per harvest. With subsidies gone, the subsequent fall in rice prices reflected an adjustment of the market after 20 years of prices propped up by government sales and purchases. According to the International Rice Research Institute, per capita rice consumption in Bangladesh is about 170 kg per year (378 lb), the highest in the world, and production was 48 million tons in 2009, making the country the world's sixth-largest rice producer. As of mid-2011, the Bangladesh government continued a ban on rice exports, in an effort to stabilize the price of the commodity; only high-quality rice in small amounts is normally exported. According to the government, 1.1 million tons of rice, along with 3.1 million tons of wheat, were imported in the first nine months of fiscal year 2010/11.

Jute is a leading cash crop of Bangladesh, which produces about one-quarter of the total jute supply of the world. Grown in most parts of the country, jute is harvested from July to September. Its strong fibers are used to produce carpets, burlap bags, mats, upholstery, and other products. Although Bangladesh is the world leader in exports of jute, its prominence in the economy has slipped since the 1970s, as world demand for jute has been replaced by synthetic fibers. Tea is the second most important agricultural export. Most tea plantations are in the Sylhet Region and the Chittagong Hill Tracts. Much of the tea is consumed domestically.

23 ANIMAL HUSBANDRY

The UN FAO reported that Bangladesh dedicated 600,000 hectares (1.48 million acres) to permanent pasture or meadow in 2009. During that year, the country tended 221.3 million chickens and 23 million head of cattle. The production from these animals amounted to 191,438 tons of beef and veal, 9 tons of pork, 172,136 tons of poultry, 208,600 tons of eggs, and 2.55 million tons of milk. Bangladesh also produced 31,900 tons of cattle hide and 2,171 tons of raw wool.

Livestock provide draft power, rural transportation, manure, and fuel, in addition to meat, milk, eggs, hides, and skins. Milk is an important item of consumption, especially in the form of clarified butterfat. There are over 20,000 small dairies. There were about 850,000 buffaloes, 34.5 million goats, and 1.26 million sheep in 2004.

Much of the cattle stock is smuggled from India because of the reduced local availability of cows and bulls, especially during the mid-year Muslim holiday of Id al-Adha, when cattle are sacrificed throughout the country. The cattle brought in from India may account for up to 30% of beef production. The scarcity of cattle in recent years is the result of lack of vaccines and fodder, natural disasters, and an absence of farmer incentives. An outbreak of anthrax on cattle farms began in 2010. H5N1 avian flu appeared in Bangladesh in 2003, necessitating destruction of poultry.

24 FISHING

Fish is a staple food of Bangladesh and the main source of protein. There are hundreds of varieties, including carp, hilsa, pomfret, shrimp, catfish, and many local varieties. In 2008, the annual capture totaled 1.56 million tons according to the UN FAO. While much of the fish is consumed domestically, Bangladesh exports a sizable quantity of freshwater fish to India and other neighboring countries, and shrimp and lobster are exported to a number of countries. In 2010, exports of frozen food, mainly shrimp and fish products, amounted to $437.4 million. Fishing cooperatives foster the use of modern fish-catching trawlers in the Bay of Bengal, and the government has established a fisheries corporation to stimu-

late production of freshwater fish for export. Fish farming has increased, with small-scale village ponds and river cages. Coastal shrimp farms are a threat to mangrove forest ecosystems.

25 FORESTRY

Only about 7% of Bangladesh is covered by forest. The UN FAO estimated the 2009 roundwood production at 282,000 cu m (9.96 million cu ft). The value of all forest products, including roundwood, totaled $2.03 million. The pressure of population has led to enormous deforestation due to conversion of forestland for agriculture, woodcutting for fuel, and illegal timber cutting (frequently by corrupt forestry officials). Most of the loss occurred before 1990, with a low deforestation rate of 1.2% since then. Over 98% of timber cut is used for firewood.

The main forest zone is the Sundarbans area in the southwest, consisting mostly of mangrove forests. Two principal species dominate the Sundarban forests: sundari trees, which grow about 15–18 m (50–60 ft) high and are of tough timber, and gewa trees, a softer wood. Sal and bamboo grow in the highly threatened remaining central and hill forests, and there are plantations of teak, pulpwood, and rubber.

26 MINING

Aside from its large identified natural gas reserves, Bangladesh has few mineral resources. The Bay of Bengal area was being explored for oil, and in some offshore areas, drilling was being conducted by international companies. Bangladesh had reserves of good-quality coal in the northern districts, but extraction has been difficult since many deposits were located at a depth of more than 900 m. Production estimates of mineral commodities in Bangladesh in 2009 included hydraulic cement, 5,000,000 metric tons; marine salt, 360,000 metric tons; and limestone (mined in the Sylhet and Chittagong regions), 70,000 metric tons.

27 ENERGY AND POWER

The World Bank reported in 2008 that Bangladesh produced 35 billion kWh of electricity and consumed 33.3 billion kWh, or 210 kWh per capita. Roughly 68% of energy came from fossil fuels (mainly natural gas), 33% from combustible biomass and fuel wood, and 1% came from alternative sources. Per capita oil consumption was 175 kg.

A potential source of industrial growth lies in Bangladesh's oil and natural gas reserves. According to the CIA, Bangladesh produces about 5,724 barrels of oil per day, and its proven reserves were estimated at 28 million barrels in 2011. An exploration/production contract was signed with US petroleum giant Conoco-Phillips in June 2011. In terms of natural gas, proven reserves were estimated between 195.4 billion cu m (6.9 trillion cu ft) in 2011. Consumption was estimated at 20.1 billion cu m (709 billion cu ft) in 2010. Production was estimated at 19.75 billion cu m (697 billion cu ft) in 2009.

As of 2011, solar energy was being promoted by the government, the Grameen Bank, and international donors as a way to mitigate chronic shortages of electrical power, with subsidized solar panels installed on new high-rise buildings and in rural areas not reached by the national grid. Energy-efficient kilns for brick making have been promoted as a measure to decrease fuel wood use.

28 INDUSTRY

Efforts to develop an industrial base faltered in the country's early years of independence when Bangladesh nationalized most of its industries. That led to much inefficiency and stagnation, and beginning in the mid-1970s, Bangladesh started to shift its strategy toward one of encouraging a move toward a market economy. Bangladesh developed policies to encourage private enterprise and investment through the mid-1980s. However, many stated objectives were not carried out, and Bangladesh has had difficulty achieving its major industrial goals. Privatization of industry occurred at a slow pace, partly because of worker unrest as well as a dysfunctional banking system.

The economic crisis that followed the 11 September 2001 terrorist attacks on the United States hit Bangladesh's garment industry particularly hard. Ready-made garments comprise Bangladesh's primary export. The growth of these exports, 18% annually before September 2001, slowed to 8%. The garment industry, however, remained the strongest export sector for Bangladesh. About 1.8 million jobs—mostly for women—have been created in the industry since the 1990s.

As of 2010 according to the CIA, industry accounted for 28.5% of GDP. A challenge is diversifying the export base. Garments accounted for about 80% of the country's exports in 2010, ranking fourth in the world with a 3% world market share in 2010, according to the WTO. Bangladesh also exports leather, frozen fish and shrimp, ceramics and its historic cash crop, jute. With a goal of expanding exports, the country has established export-processing zones. Bangladesh has seen growth in steel, sugar, tea, leather goods, newsprint, pharmaceuticals, and fertilizer production. The hazardous work of ship breaking, recycling decommissioned vessels by hand, continues in Bangladesh, providing an estimated 60% of the country's steel needs. Bangladesh's pharmaceutical industry supplies an estimated 97% of the domestic market.

29 SCIENCE AND TECHNOLOGY

Patent applications in science and technology as of 2009, according to the World Bank, totaled 29 in Bangladesh. In 2007, high technology exports totaled $96 million, just 1% of manufactured exports, according to the World Bank.

Research institutes focusing on agriculture include the Bangladesh Agricultural Research Institute, the Bangladesh Jute Research Institute, the Bangladesh Rice Research Institute, the Soil Resource Development Institute, and the Bangladesh Livestock Research Institute. Others include the Bangladesh Institute of Development Studies, the Bangladesh Medical Research Council, the Institute of Peace and Security Studies, the Bangla Academy (which sponsors translations of scientific and literary works into Bangla), the Asiatic Society, and the National Institute of Public Administration's Institute of Law and International Affairs. The Bangladesh Council for Scientific and Industrial Research, headquartered in Dhaka, operates seven research institutes, and the Bangladesh Atomic Energy commission, founded in 1973, operates two others.

The Geological Society of Bangladesh, founded in 1972 at Dhaka, is a government organization under the Ministry of Energy and Natural Resources. The Center for Environment and Geographic Services, founded in 2002, researches climate change effects. Professional groups include the Bangladesh Academy of Sciences, the Bangladesh Medical Association, the Jute Research Institute, and the Zoological Society of Bangladesh.

Principal Trading Partners – Bangladesh (2010)				
(In millions of US dollars)				
Country	Total	Exports	Imports	Balance
World	40,266.0	14,195.0	26,071.0	-11,876.0
China	4,872.0	191.0	4,681.0	-4,490.0
India	4,181.0	321.0	3,860.0	-3,539.0
United States	3,781.0	3,247.0	534.0	2,713.0
Germany	2,606.0	2,075.0	531.0	1,544.0
United Kingdom	1,599.0	1,244.0	355.0	889.0
Singapore	1,559.0	66.0	1,493.0	-1,427.0
Malaysia	1,370.0	54.0	1,316.0	-1,262.0
Japan	1,328.0	165.0	1,163.0	-998.0
France	1,097.0	998.0	99.0	899.0
Canada	1,059.0	553.0	506.0	47.0

(…) data not available or not significant.

(n.s.) not specified.

SOURCE: *2011 Direction of Trade Statistics Yearbook*, New York: United Nations, 2011.

30 DOMESTIC TRADE

Most commodities produced in Bangladesh are consumed inside the country. Since a majority of Bangladeshis earn their living from agriculture, many of the domestic commodities that are traded are farm products. Normally, farmers and fishing people sell to wholesalers, who, in turn, sell to distributors and retailers. Industrial commodities for domestic consumption are distributed through the same procedure. The middlemen in the distribution process have often benefited from excessive profits, creating hardships for farmers and consumers. To alleviate this situation, the government introduced ways for farmers to sell directly to cooperative agencies acting on behalf of buyers. The government has also set up fair-price shops for consumers. Foreign products are imported by large commercial concerns located in the capital city of Dhaka or in the ports, and are then distributed through wholesalers and retailers.

Much domestic trade in rural areas is conducted in open-air markets, where farmers sell directly to consumers. The large cities have numerous indoor shopping malls and supermarkets. Shops specializing in particular goods or repair work can be found in concentrated streets or districts of the cities and towns. Normal business hours are between 9 a.m. and 5 p.m., Sunday through Thursday, but most retail stores are open until 8 p.m. Many private businesses are open on Saturday as well. Advertising appears in newspapers, movie houses, outdoor displays, radio, television, and the Internet.

31 FOREIGN TRADE

Imports steadily ran more than double the value of exports between 1971 and 1991. With a surge in export growth since 1991, the trade deficit has improved; imports exceeded exports by about 56% in 1996, and by 62% in 1997. As a result of successful export promotion measures undertaken by the government during the 1980s, exports of ready-made garments became Bangladesh's leading earner of foreign exchange. Ready-made garments accounted for 80% of exports in 2010. Fish and crustaceans are frozen and exported. Jute and leather are other export commodities.

Bangladesh imported an estimated $21.34 billion worth of goods and services in 2010, while exporting $15.97 billion worth of goods and services. Major import partners in 2009 were China, 16.2%; India, 12.6%; Singapore, 7.6%; Japan, 4.6%; and Malaysia, 4.5%. The major export partners were the United States, 20.2%; Germany, 12.7%; the United Kingdom, 8.6%; France, 6.5%; and Netherlands, 5.9%. India's removal of tariffs of garment from Bangladesh in mid-2011 was expected to boost the nation's garment manufacturing sector with new export possibilities.

Bangladesh is a member of the WTO and the Bay of Bengal association known as BIMST-EC, with India, Myanmar, Sri Lanka, and Thailand. Bangladesh belongs to the South Asian Association for Regional Cooperation (SAARC). It joined the other SAARC members—Bhutan, India, Maldives, Nepal, Pakistan, and Sri Lanka—to create a South Asian Free Trade Area in 2006.

³²BALANCE OF PAYMENTS

In 2010, Bangladesh had a foreign trade deficit of $6.2 billion, amounting to 1.7% of GDP. According to the CIA, as of December 2010, Bangladesh had reserves of foreign exchange and gold amounting to $11.18 billion and external debt of $24.41 billion. Since independence, massive foreign aid and heavy short-term borrowing have been needed to handle Bangladesh's chronic balance-of-payments problem and fund development. Since 2008, however, the total income of exports and remittances has exceeded foreign aid. Foreign aid in fiscal year 2010/2011 was the lowest since independence, at $139.39 million, according to the government's Economic Relations Division, and the government was able to repay $911.32 million on outstanding debt. Disbursement remained problematic, as government agencies struggled to implement projects funded by foreign aid and loans within their designated timeframes.

³³BANKING AND SECURITIES

Central banking is conducted by the Bangladesh Bank, which has its head office in Dhaka. It is responsible for the circulation of money, supervision of commercial banks, and control of credit and foreign exchange. As of 2011, in Bangladesh there were 4 commercial government-owned banks, 5 development financial institutions, and 38 domestic private banks (including Islamic banks), as well as several foreign banks. The four major banks are state-owned: Sonali Bank, Janata Bank, Agrani Bank, and Rupali Bank. A Saudi Arabian prince's offer to purchase the state-owned Rupali Bank was cancelled by the government in 2008. In 2010, the central bank discount rate, the interest rate at which the financial institutions lend to one another in the short term, was 5%, according to the CIA.

Bangladesh is known for the innovation of microcredit loans. In 1976, economist Muhammed Yunus started the Grameen Bank on the theory that small, low-interest loans to individuals would be an effective, low-risk way to fight poverty and encourage grassroots development. The loans are usually made to rural women and finance investments in cottage industries, small-scale agriculture, and livestock raising to support their families. The Grameen Bank's microcredit programs have been widely adapted by other

Balance of Payments – Bangladesh (2010)		
(In millions of US dollars)		
Current Account		**2,502.4**
Balance on goods		-5,484.6
Imports	-24,723.4	
Exports	19,238.7	
Balance on services		-1,938.3
Balance on income		-1,406.4
Current transfers		11,331.8
Capital Account		**470.9**
Financial Account		**-1,626.4**
Direct investment abroad		-0.2
Direct investment in Bangladesh		967.6
Portfolio investment assets		-778.6
Portfolio investment liabilities		165.9
Financial derivatives		...
Other investment assets		-2,657.4
Other investment liabilities		676.3
Net Errors and Omissions		**-395.5**
Reserves and Related Items		**-951.5**

(…) data not available or not significant.

SOURCE: *Balance of Payment Statistics Yearbook 2011*, Washington, DC: International Monetary Fund, 2011.

developing countries and even in impoverished regions of developed nations. Yunus was awarded the Nobel Peace Prize in 2006. Studies have shown that microcredit loans have helped millions of Bangladeshis rise above the poverty level, but some analysts believe that microcredit loans, particularly from unscrupulous lenders, often end up trapping poor people in a cycle of multiple debts that they cannot repay. The Grameen Bank diversified, becoming the Grameen Family Foundation, a mixture of nonprofit and for-profit companies that includes telecommunications, solar energy, Internet, and manufacturing. Yunus has had disagreements with Prime Minister Sheikh Hasina, who attempted to set up an alternative political party in 2007. Her government, which is a 25% owner of Grameen Bank, forced Yunus to retire as the bank's managing director in May 2011.

Trade on the Dhaka Stock Exchange (DSE) was dormant until 1993. The fourth quarter of 1996 was marked by feverish activity on the DSE, and on the smaller Chittagong Stock Exchange (CSE); records were broken daily as share prices soared. Prices soon bore little relation to the current profitability or future prospects of the companies concerned. Up to 300,000 first-time buyers joined in the bonanza and market capitalization reached an unsustainable $6 billion, equivalent to some 20% of the country's GDP. The market crashed in 1996 despite the government's attempts at preventative measures. In 1997, 37 stockbrokers were charged with market manipulation in the DSE boom and crash.

In January 2011, the Dhaka Stock Exchange in Bangladesh fell by 660 points, or 9.25% in less than an hour. The crash was the most the market had fallen in one day in the previous 55 years, and affected more than three million people. As a result of the crash, there were protests and violent clashes in the streets near Dhaka's business district. The downturn following the January crash continued into March 2011, with an accumulated 40% loss in the market, or about $16 billion. At that time, the government

Public Finance – Bangladesh (2009)

(In millions of taka, central government figures)

Revenue and Grants	**697,384**	**100.0%**
Tax revenue	528,671	75.8%
Social contributions	…	…
Grants	17,478	2.5%
Other revenue	151,235	21.7%
Expenditures	**799,137**	**100.0%**
General public services	302,447	37.8%
Defense	62,100	7.8%
Public order and safety	52,650	6.6%
Economic affairs	132,988	16.6%
Environmental protection	543	0.1%
Housing and community amenities	52,485	6.6%
Health	50,643	6.3%
Recreational, culture, and religion	8,712	1.1%
Education	112,794	14.1%
Social protection	23,776	3.0%

(…) data not available or not significant.

SOURCE: *Government Finance Statistics Yearbook 2010*, Washington, DC: International Monetary Fund, 2010.

announced that it would set up a $700 million investment fund to stabilize the market. The fund was to be backed by state-run financial institutions. As of October 2011, there were 500 companies listed on the DSE.

34 INSURANCE

The insurance industry of Bangladesh dates back to the British colonial period. Insurance companies were nationalized in 1972 and privatized in the 1980s. The Insurance Development and Regulatory Authority was established in January 2011. Insurance companies in Bangladesh include Jiban Bima, Sunlife, Homeland Life, American Life, Delta Life, Prime Islami Life, Sadharan Bima, and Meghna Life. As of 2011, 17 private companies offered life insurance in Bangladesh. Forty-three private companies offered general insurance. Two insurance companies, Jiban Bima Corporation and Sadharan Bima, were state-owned. Islamic-law-compliant insurance was available from a few companies. Insurance coverage remains low in Bangladesh, with the vast majority of homes and small businesses uninsured, and less than $5 per capita spent on insurance yearly. Some nongovernmental organizations have devised programs of micro health insurance and crop insurance for the rural poor in Bangladesh.

35 PUBLIC FINANCE

In 2010, the budget of Bangladesh included $11.43 billion in public revenue and $15.9 billion in public expenditures. The budget deficit amounted to 4.2% of GDP. Public debt was 39.3% of GDP, with $24.41 billion of the debt held by foreign entities. The fiscal year runs from June to July. Government outlays by function for fiscal year 2010/11 included: education, 14.3%; interest, 11.2%; agriculture, 10.1%; local government/rural development, 8.1%; public services, 7.7%; defense, 7.2%; transport/communication, 6.7%; health, 5.9%; public order and safety, 5.8%; energy, 5.6%; recreation, culture, and religion, 1.2%; housing, 1%; industrial

and economic services, 0.7%. The $22 billion budget for fiscal year 2011/12, with spending up almost 28% over the previous fiscal year, placed emphasis on communications and energy infrastructure. It continued to subsidize the costs of fuel, electricity, fertilizer, and food to help those below the poverty line survive rising prices. The projected fiscal year 2011/12 budget would increase the deficit from 4.4% of GDP in the previous fiscal year to 5% of GDP, and would depend heavily on foreign and domestic loans.

36 TAXATION

According to the CIA, taxes and other revenues amounted to an estimated 10% of GDP in 2010. The principal direct taxes are progressive personal income taxes and corporate income taxes, and a value-added tax (VAT) of 15% levied on consumer goods. Exports and cottage industries are exempt from VAT. As of 2011, the basic corporate tax rate was 27.5% for publicly traded companies, with higher rates of 42.5% for banks, insurance and financial companies, and 35% to 45% for mobile telephone companies. Capital gains are taxed at 15%. The top income tax rate for individuals is 25%.

37 CUSTOMS AND DUTIES

Bangladesh gets a major portion of its current revenue from import duties and excise taxes. Customs duties vary by category, from 7% for basic raw material to 25% for finished products. Categories exempt from duties include relief goods, solar-power equipment, and raw materials for production of textiles. Imports of petroleum, metals, livestock, and agricultural products are prohibited. Bangladesh has eight export processing zones, offering duty-free manufacturing, located in Chittagong, Dhaka, Mongla, Ishwardi, Comilla, Uttara, Adamjee, and Karnaphuli. Bangladesh is a member of the South Asia Preferential Trade Agreement (SAPTA).

38 FOREIGN INVESTMENT

Bangladesh nationalized most industries in 1972 and set up nine corporations to oversee them. In the mid-1980s, the Bangladesh government privatized industry and began relaxing its policy toward foreign investment. Since then, government industrial policies have liberalized conditions for foreign investment much further—100% foreign equity is now allowed on investments anywhere in the country, and many regulations discriminating between foreign and domestic investors have been abolished. Foreign investment averaged about $7 million annually in 1990–96 before rising sharply in 1997–2000 to $196.8 million annually. The US State Department reported that total foreign direct investment in Bangladesh totaled $712 million in the period 1999–2003. Most of the increase was due to investments in Bangladesh's oil and natural gas reserves and other aspects of its energy sector.

Foreign investors in Bangladesh continue to face challenges of approval delays, inadequate power supply, and corruption. Foreign direct investment (FDI) in Bangladesh was a net inflow of $674.2 million, according to World Bank figures published in 2009. FDI represented 0.75% of GDP. According to the CIA, FDI was an estimated $5.939 billion as of December 2010, and Bangladesh invested an estimated $91 million overseas. According to the government's Board of Investment (BOI), foreign and joint venture investment in 2010 was mainly in the service sector, with a share of 89%. The largest investors for fiscal 2009/10, according to the BOI, were Saudi Arabia, South Korea, China, Hong Kong, India, and the Netherlands. Although Bangladesh has encouraged foreign oil companies to do business in the country, exploration has proven difficult, and disagreements over the licensing of foreign oil holdings have stalled growth in this sector. In June 2011, the government signed a contract for offshore exploration and production with petroleum multinational Conoco-Phillips from the US. The deal was criticized by activists and protesters opposed to a foreign company taking a large share of the profits from Bangladesh's natural resources and potentially using petroleum for export rather than local needs.

39 ECONOMIC DEVELOPMENT

The major objectives of planned development have been increased national income, rural development, self-sufficiency in food, and increased industrial production. However, political turmoil and natural disasters frequently derailed Bangladesh's economic goals. Bangladesh's first five-year plan (1973–78) aimed to increase economic growth by 5.5% annually, but actual growth averaged only 4% per year. A special two-year plan (1978–80), stressing rural development, also fell short of its projected growth target, as did the second five-year plan (1980–85), which targeted 7.2% annual growth. The third five-year plan (1985–90) had a 5.4% annual growth target though only 3.8% was actually achieved.

In 1991, a new economic program included financial sector reform and liberalization measures to encourage investment, in a structural adjustment program developed through the International Monetary Fund. Growth slowed during this period but was renewed in the late 1990s until the global economic crisis that followed the 11 September 2001 attacks on the United States all but halted new economic growth. A new government, led by Khaleda Zia, came into power in 2001 on a pledge of returning to the earlier economic liberalization policies. The IMF approved a $490 million plan in June 2003 to support economic reforms through the end of 2006.

The government has worked with foreign governments to open more jobs abroad for Bangladeshi workers, but low levels of education and a lack of desirable skill sets are a major concern. The government hopes to modernize and expand its international business and financial services sector with help from the European Union. In July 2009, the government signed a funding agreement with the European Union for $14.1 million, with funds designated for this purpose as part of the European Community's action program on the Accompanying Measures for Sugar Protocol Countries, established in 2008.

40 SOCIAL DEVELOPMENT

A system of pensions exists for public employees. There is a limited work injury compensation system and mandatory termination benefits. These programs are financed by employer contributions and cover only a small percentage of the population. Sickness and maternity benefits are offered on a very limited basis. In 2006, the government introduced a program of small allowance payments to senior citizens, widows, and the disabled poor. In practice, fees and demands for bribes often deny very poor people access to public social welfare programs.

Although the constitution prohibits discrimination against women, and women have gained increased employment and po-

sitions in political leadership, women still continue to experience social disadvantages. Violence against women, including attacks with corrosive acid, remained common. A bill criminalizing domestic violence was passed by the parliament in 2010, but there is a countrywide lack of support and shelter for victims. Women are sometimes punished with whippings or humiliations by local or religious courts in villages, although the Supreme Court ordered an end to such practices in 2010. Reports have continued of women being tortured and killed over dowry disputes. Rapes are underreported due to the social disgrace to the victims. Homosexual contact remained a criminal offense as of 2011, although enforcement of the law was rare.

According to a World Bank-sponsored survey, urban poverty levels in Bangladesh decreased from 28.4% in 2005 to 21.3% in 2010, and rural poverty decreased from 43.8% in 2005 to 35.2% in 2010. However, an estimated 48.6% of children suffer from malnutrition, according to UN agencies, as of 2011. Government incentives have increased school enrollment, but children continue to work in agriculture and other informal sector occupations, including hazardous jobs. Marriages below the legal age of 18 have continued, as has trafficking of women and children.

Security forces, particularly the anti-crime Rapid Action Battalions, have been involved in disappearances, extrajudicial executions, and torture in custody. Although the government is secular, discrimination against minority religions has at times led to conflict and violence. Refugees from neighboring Myanmar remain vulnerable to violent attacks.

41 HEALTH

According to the CIA, life expectancy in Bangladesh was 69 years in 2011. The country spent 3.4% of its GDP on healthcare, amounting to $18 per person. There were three physicians, three nurses and midwives, and four hospital beds per 10,000 inhabitants. The fertility rate was 2.6 children per woman, while the infant mortality rate was 50 deaths per 1,000 live births as of 2011. In 2008, the maternal mortality rate, according to the CIA, was 340 deaths per 100,000 births. The CIA calculated HIV/AIDS prevalence in Bangladesh to be less than 0.1% in 2009. Other infectious diseases include diarrhea, hepatitis A and E, typhoid fever, dengue fever, H5N1 avian flu, and H1N1 flu.

In the 1960s and 1970s, international agencies funded millions of tube wells in Bangladesh to provide safe drinking water. It was not until the 1980s that geological arsenic contamination of at least 40% of the tube wells was found to be putting more than 30 million Bangladeshis at risk of cancer. In 2010, researchers in Bangladesh announced a simple method for filtering out disease microorganisms in fresh water by filtering drinking water through folded cloth.

42 HOUSING

With extreme population density (964 people per sq km/2,497 people per square mi), adequate housing has been a challenge in Bangladesh. As of the 2011 census, the average household contained 4.4 persons. In the 21st century, Dhaka has become a mega-city, with urban sprawl, stressed infrastructure, and pollution. In Dhaka and Chittagong, urban development is conducted under the guidance of town planning authorities, which develop land and allocate it for private dwelling and commercial purposes.

Brick and concrete are used for apartment buildings and shop-houses in urban areas. Houses are built of wood, corrugated metal, bamboo, mud brick, and thatch in rural areas.

Since 1996, the government has launched a number of programs focusing on poverty and homelessness. The Asrayon (shelter) program provided group housing and agricultural plots on government land for about 50,000 families, according to a 2002 estimate. The Gahrey Phera (return home) program helped displaced rural families return to their villages. The Grihayan Tahabil (housing fund) was established through the Bangladesh Bank as a way to provide loans to non-government organizations that build shelters for the urban poor.

According to the CIA, as of 2008 only 53% of the population had access to improved sanitation; 85% of the urban population and 78% of the rural population had access to improved water sources.

43 EDUCATION

The principal administrative bodies for education are the Ministry of Education, the Ministry of Science and Technology, and the Association of Universities of Bangladesh. In 2009, the World Bank estimated that 86% of age-eligible children in Bangladesh were enrolled in primary school. Secondary enrollment for age-eligible children stood at 41%. Tertiary enrollment was estimated at 8%. Public expenditure on education represented 2.6% of GDP. According to the World Bank, as of 2009 Bangladesh's total literacy rate was 56%.

Education is compulsory for students between the ages of 6 and 10 (five years), and free for students for eight years. Secondary education for girls is subsidized, and there are government education stipends to encourage school enrollment for poor children. Primary education covers five years. Secondary education is divided into three cycles of junior (three years), upper (two years), and higher (two years) secondary programs. After their junior level, students may choose to attend a vocational training school for two years, followed by a higher technical course of two years, instead of following the general education track. There is also a Madrasah system (Islamic education), which is required to support national curricula, and a cadet college system of military schools. Most educational institutions are supported by the government, either fully or partially, but NGOs are active in running pre-schools and primary schools. The language of instruction is either Bangla (in public schools) or English.

There are 30 public universities and over 50 private universities in Bangladesh. They include University of Dhaka, Bangladesh Agricultural University in Mymensingh, University of Chittagong, National University, American University, Jahangirnagar University in Dhaka, Khulna University, University of Rajshahi, and Bangladesh University of Engineering and Technology. The university campuses have traditionally been very politically active and are sometimes affected by strikes, prolonged protests, or violent clashes. There are public and private medical colleges, agricultural colleges, and teacher-training colleges. Several polytechnical schools offer three-year courses in technical and engineering fields. Technical Training Centers offer certificate and diploma courses. The Bangladesh Open University offers degree and non-degree continuing education programs. Students from Bangladesh often seek undergraduate or postgraduate education overseas.

44 LIBRARIES AND MUSEUMS

The largest library in Bangladesh is Dhaka University Library (founded 1921, 5.5 million volumes). The National Library of Bangladesh, also in Dhaka, holds 200,000 books in Bengali, English, Persian, and Arabic and contains the National Archives collection. The Bangladesh Public Library System (founded in 1958) has over 1,550,000 volumes; besides the Central Library in Dhaka, there are 67 branches. The Bangla Academy maintains an excellent research collection, as does the Bangladesh Institute of Development studies in Dhaka.

The National Museum of Bangladesh began as the Dhaka Museum in 1913. It contains a variety of sculptures and paintings from the Buddhist, Hindu, and Muslim periods. Also in Dhaka is the Liberation War Museum. The Ahsan Manzil Museum is a 19th-century palace on the Buriganga River. There is a Folk Arts Museum in the historic village of Sonargaon. Comilla has 7th-century archaeological sites and museums, and the Varendra Museum in Rajshahi contains many artifacts from the ruins of an 8th-century Buddhist monastery excavated nearby, as well as significant relics from the Kushon, Gupta, Pala, and Sena periods of Bengali history. There are ethnological museums in Chittagong, Rangamati and Bandarban. Contemporary art is exhibited at the Dhaka Art Center, galleries in Dhaka and other cities, and other venues. The Central Public Library hosts film festivals and other cultural events. Artists from Bangladesh were represented at the Venice Biennale for the first time in 2011 with a group of installations commenting on social issues.

45 MEDIA

There is freedom of expression under the law in Bangladesh. The government has sometimes shut down opposition publications and imprisoned journalists. Reporters investigating corruption and other criminal activities have been killed.

As of 2010, 46% of households in Bangladesh owned televisions. Bangladesh Television is state-owned, and there are over 18 satellite and cable television stations, including Ekushey Television, ATN, Desh TV, NTV, and Diganta. Bangla movies, talk shows, and news are among the popular programs. The state-owned radio station is Bangladesh Betar, which broadcasts internationally on shortwave, and there are several private AM/FM radio stations and online radio stations.

Prominent newspapers in 2010, with circulation numbers listed parenthetically, included *Dainik Inqilab* (180,025), *Dainik Dinkal* (60,000), and *Dainik Purbanchal* (42,960), as well as 10 other major newspapers. English-language dailies include the *Bangladesh Observer* (43,000) and *Daily Star* (30,000). Bangladesh Sangbad Sangstha (BSS) and United News of Bangladesh (UNB) are the two main news agencies. Bdnews24.com is an online newspaper for Bangladesh.

The microcredit pioneer Grameen Bank entered the telecommunications market with Grameenphone in 1996 to fund its programs and to provide low-cost mobile phones to poor villages, resulting in telephone access for millions of new users in Bangladesh. In 2009, the CIA reported that there were 1.5 million telephone landlines and 50.4 million mobile cellular phones in use. As of 2009, mobile telephones were owned by an estimated 61% of households. An estimated 82% of urban households, and 51% of rural households owned at least one mobile telephone.

Use of telephones for text messaging is widespread in Bangladesh, and social media Internet use is growing quickly. In 2010, the country had about 68,224 Internet hosts. In mid-2011, the Internet Service Provider Association of Bangladesh predicted that by the year's end the number of Internet users would have grown to about 20 million. Internet connections were usually shared, in workplaces or Internet cafes, with an estimated 10 people using each connection. Internet services were offered by the state-owned Bangladesh Telecommunications Company and 60 private services. The Drik Picture Library, in Dhaka, is a media resource center with a gallery, photo agency, and online activism network.

46 ORGANIZATIONS

The Federation of Bangladesh Chambers of Commerce and Industry and the Foreign Investors' Chamber of Commerce and Industry are based in Dhaka. There are also many business and workers' associations, including the Bangladesh Teachers' Federation, Bangladesh Garment Manufacturers and Exporters Association, the Bangladesh Tea Board, and the Bangladesh Jute Mills Association. The Bangladesh Medical Studies and Research Institute and the Bangladesh Academy of Sciences promote research and education in a number of medical and scientific fields.

The people of Bangladesh have formed NGOs, large and small, to promote sustainable development, grassroots self-help programs, social justice and education for poor people, especially in rural areas. The Association for Social Advancement is a development organization assisting the poor. The Bangladesh Rural Advancement Committee (BRAC), founded in 1972, is the largest development NGO in the world. Maulik Chahida Karmashuchi promotes economic and social development for rural citizens. The Grameen Foundation provides social programs, including microcredit, in Bangladesh and other countries. Parbatya Bouddha Mission serves the indigenous people of the Chittagong Hill Tracts.

Poribesh.com is a website with information about Bangladesh's environment issues and links for organizations working on those issues. Bangladesh Poribesh Andolon is a network of environmental activists. There is also a Bangladesh Environmental Lawyers Association.

There are many other local NGOs and numerous international NGOs also at work on development and social justice issues in Bangladesh. The Red Crescent Society, Amnesty International, Habitat for Humanity, Caritas, UNICEF, and Society of Saint Vincent de Paul have chapters within the country.

Various associations for the Muslim, Hindu, Christian, and Buddhist communities have long been active in organizing religious festivals and social activities. Every town also has several cultural groups. Women's organizations include Banchte Shekha, Women to Women, and Bangladesh National Women Lawyers Association. Trade unions in the garment industry represent a mainly female workforce.

The National Federation of Youth Organizations in Bangladesh coordinates dozens of national youth organizations, and there are hundreds of local and regional youth groups. Bangladesh has several major student unions, which are often highly involved in politics. Youth groups include the Bangladesh Girl Guides, the Bangladesh Scouts, Junior Chamber Bangladesh, World Association of Muslim Youth, and the YMCA/YWCA. There are several sports associations, including groups for badminton, track and field, tae kwan do, tennis, and weightlifting.

47 TOURISM, TRAVEL, AND RECREATION

International tourism is not significant in Bangladesh, as the county's image has been damaged by natural disasters, political crises, and inadequate transport infrastructure. The *Tourism Factbook*, published by the UN World Tourism Organization, reported 267,000 incoming tourists to Bangladesh in 2009 with expenditures totaling $76 million. Of those incoming tourists, there were 102,000 from South Asia and 77,000 from Europe. There were 11,173 hotel beds available in Bangladesh, which had an occupancy rate of 52%. The estimated daily cost to visit Dhaka, the capital, was $266. The cost of visiting other cities averaged $135. A valid passport, onward ticket, and visa are required for visiting Bangladesh, with visa exceptions for some countries (mostly in the Caribbean and Africa).

Bangladesh's main tourist attractions include Dhaka's old Mughal capital and Ahsan Manzil place museum, the National Assembly Building (designed by Louis Khan) in Dhaka, and nearby Sonargaon with its ancient architecture and Folk Museum. The ancient Buddhist cultural center of Mainamati is near Comilla. The Sundarbans wetlands and the hill tracts appeal to adventurous travelers. Sylhet, in the northeast, is known for its tea plantations and cooler climate. Cox's Bazar, on the Bay of Bengal in the southeast, has one of the longest beaches in the world, with 120 km (74 mi) of sand; it is the top attraction for domestic tourism.

48 FAMOUS PERSONS

Many Bengalis distinguished themselves in political life before the creation of Bangladesh. A. K. Fazlul Huq (d. 1962), the former premier of Bengal Province, moved the Lahore Resolution of 1940, calling for an independent Pakistan, and dominated Bengali politics for half a century. H. S. Suhrawardy (1895–1964), another former premier of Bengal, served for a time as premier of Pakistan and was a mentor to the next generation of Bengali leaders. Sheikh Mujibur Rahman (1920–1975), a leader of the Awami League, led the successful fight for the independence of East Pakistan and was the first prime minister of Bangladesh. Maj. Gen. Zia-ur Rahman (1936–1981) was military ruler of the country from 1976 until his assassination. His widow, Khaleda Zia (b. 1945) leader of the Bangladesh National Party, served as prime minister from 1991–1996 and 2001–2006. Sheikh Hasina (b. 2009), daughter of Sheikh Mujibur Rahman and leader of the Awami League, was prime minister 1996–2001 and took office again in 2009. Muhammed Yunus (b. 1940), the 2006 Nobel Peace Prize laureate, developed microcredit loans for the poor with his Grameen Bank.

The Bengali (Bangla) poetry tradition has been of great importance in Bangladesh. Kazi Nazul Islam (1899–1976) is revered as "the rebel poet." Shamsur Rahman (1929–2006) was a prolific and influential poet. Taslima Nasrin (b. 1962) is a feminist novelist who since 1994 has lived in exile due to threats over her criticism of Islamic practices. Zaunul Abedin (1914–1976) was an important Bangladeshi painter whose works often had social and political themes. In the contemporary arts scene, Mahbubur Rahman (b. 1969) is a video and installation artist; Promotesh Das Pulak (b. 1980) works with photographs, video, and other media;

and Tayeba Begum Lipi (b. 1969) creates installations on feminist themes.

⁴⁹DEPENDENCIES

Bangladesh has no territories or colonies.

⁵⁰BIBLIOGRAPHY

Bangladesh Investment and Business Guide: Strategic and Practical Information. Washington, DC: International Business Publications USA, 2012.

Barter, James. *The Ganges.* San Diego, CA: Lucent Books, 2003.

Baxter, Craig, and Syedur Rahman. *Historical Dictionary of Bangladesh.* Lanham, MD: Scarecrow Press, 2003.

Dos, Santos A. N. *Military Intervention and Secession in South Asia: The Cases of Bangladesh, Sri Lanka, Kashmir, and Punjab.* Westport, CT: Praeger Security International, 2007.

Mitra, Subrata K., ed. *A Political and Economic Dictionary of South Asia.* Philadelphia: Routledge/Taylor and Francis, 2006.

Paratian, Rajendra. *Bangladesh.* Geneva: International Labour Office, 2001.

Saliba, Therese, Carolyn Allen, and Judith A. Howard, eds. *Gender, Politics, and Islam.* Chicago: University of Chicago Press, 2002.

Shah, Shekhar, and Pradeep Mitra. *Bangladesh: From Stabilization to Growth.* Washington, DC: World Bank, 1995.

Shrestha, Nanda R. *Nepal and Bangladesh: A Global Studies Handbook.* Santa Barbara, CA: ABC-CLIO, 2002.

Sisson, Richard. *War and Secession: Pakistan, India, and the Creation of Bangladesh.* Berkeley: University of California Press, 1990.

Stern, Robert W. *Democracy and Dictatorship in South Asia: Dominant Classes and Political Outcomes in India, Pakistan, and Bangladesh.* Westport, CT: Praeger, 2001.

Stiles, Kendall W. *Civil Society by Design: Donors, NGOs, and the Intermestic Development Circle in Bangladesh.* Westport, CT: Praeger, 2002

Wahid, Abu N., and Charles Weis. *The Economy of Bangladesh: Problems and Prospects.* Westport, CT: Praeger, 1996.

BHUTAN

Kingdom of Bhutan
Druk-Yul

CAPITAL: Thimphu

FLAG: The flag is divided diagonally into an orange-yellow field above and a crimson field below. In the center is a white thunder dragon.

ANTHEM: *Druk tsendhen (The Thunder Dragon Kingdom).*

MONETARY UNIT: The ngultrum (BTN) is a paper currency of 100 chetrum. There are coins of 25, and 50 chertrum and 1 ngultrum, and notes of 1, 5, 10, 20, 50, 100, and 500 ngultrum. The ngultrum is at pegged to par with the Indian rupee (INR), which also circulates freely. BTN1 = $0.02 (or $1 = BTN48.70) as of 2011.

WEIGHTS AND MEASURES: The metric system is the legal standard, but some traditional units are still in common use.

HOLIDAYS: Birthday of the Fifth King, 21–23 February; Birthday of the Third King, 2 May; Social Forestry Day, 2 June; Blessed Rainy Day, 23 September; Birthday of the Fourth King, 11 November; National Day, 17 December. Movable Buddhist holidays and festivals are observed. Bhutan's New Year, Losar, was 3–4 February 3 in 2011.

TIME: 5:30 p.m. = noon GMT.

¹LOCATION, SIZE, AND EXTENT

Bhutan, a landlocked country in the Himalayan mountain range, has an area of 47,000 sq km (18,147 sq mi), extending 306 km (190 mi) E–W and 145 km (90 mi) N–S. Comparatively, the area occupied by Bhutan is slightly more than half the size of the state that of Indiana. It is bordered on the east, south, and west by India and on the north and northwest by China, with a total boundary length of 1,075 km (668 mi). The capital city of Bhutan, Thimphu, is located in the west-central part of the country.

²TOPOGRAPHY

Bhutan is a mountainous country of extremely high altitudes and irregular, often precipitous terrain, which may vary in elevation by several thousand feet within a short distance. Elevation generally increases from south to north. The mountains are a series of parallel north-south ranges. The loftiest peaks, found in the Himalayan chain that stretches along the northern border, include Kula Kangri (7,554 m/24,783 ft) and Chomo Lhari (7,314 m/23,997 ft). Great spurs extend south from the main chain along the eastern and western borders. In the rest of the country are mainly ranges of steep hills separated by narrow valleys. Bhutan is drained by rivers flowing south between these ranges and for the most part ultimately emptying into the Brahmaputra River in India.

³CLIMATE

Because of the irregular terrain, the climate varies greatly from place to place. In the outer foothills adjoining the Indian plains, rainfall ranges from about 150–300 cm (60–120 in) a year; the forests are hot and steaming in the rainy season, while the higher hills are cold, wet, and misty. Violent Himalayan thunderstorms gave rise to Bhutan's Dzongkha name, Druk-Yul, which translates as "Land of the Thunder Dragon." Rainfall is moderate in the central belt of flat valleys (which have an elevation of 1,100–3,000 m/3,500–10,000 ft). The uplands and high valleys (above 3,700 m/12,000 ft) are relatively dry. There is less rainfall in eastern Bhutan. In general, the mountainous areas are cold most of the year. Temperatures there average 4°C (39°F) in January and 17°C (63°F) in July. The melting of Himalayan glaciers due to global warming has caused hundreds of lakes to form in Bhutan, dozens of which pose the threat of severe flooding in the valleys.

⁴FLORA AND FAUNA

The World Resources Institute estimates that there are 5,468 plant species in Bhutan. In addition, Bhutan is home to 92 mammal, 625 bird, 29 reptile, and 2 amphibian species. The calculation reflects the total number of distinct species residing in the country, not the number of endemic species.

Dense jungle growth is characteristic at altitudes below 1,500 m (5,000 ft). Above that height, the mountain slopes are covered with forest, including beech, ash, birch, maple, cypress, spruce, hemlock, and yew. At 2,400–2,700 m (8,000–9,000 ft) are forests of oak and rhododendron. Above this level, firs and pines grow to the timberline. Primulas, poppies (including the rare blue variety), magnolias, and orchids grow in Bhutan.

The relative abundance of wild animals has been attributed to Buddhist reluctance to take life and to the government's environmental policies, which have protected diverse habitats. Mammals include elephant, goral, musk deer, barking deer, sambar, takin, rhinoceros, bear, red panda, golden langur, tiger, and snow leopard. Birds include pheasants, ravens, hornbills, black-necked cranes, tragopans and cuckoos. The national animal is the takin, and the national bird is the raven. Bhutan is also known for its hundreds of butterfly species.

5 ENVIRONMENT

The government of Bhutan has prioritized conservation and sustainable development. Bhutan's constitution specifies that at least 60% of the land must be forest-covered. The most significant environmental problem in Bhutan has been soil erosion, occurring mainly because 50% of the land in Bhutan is situated on mountainous slopes that are subject to landslides during the monsoon season. The UN reported in 2008 that carbon dioxide emissions in Bhutan totaled a very low 579 kilotons. Bhutan's water resources totaled 95 cu km (22.79 cu mi) while water usage was 0.43 cu km (103 cu mi) per year. Domestic water usage accounted for 5% of total usage, industrial for 1%, and agricultural for 94%. Per capita water usage totaled 199 cu m (7,028 cu ft) per year. Increasing development of hydropower resources for export, as of 2011, have led to concerns about the environmental effects of larger dams, particularly as melting glaciers would make containment reservoirs necessary in a change from the prevalent run-of-the-river projects built in Bhutan.

The World Resources Institute reported that Bhutan had designated 1.24 million hectares (3.07 million acres) of land for protection as of 2006. Bhutan has an extensive system of national parks and wildlife sanctuaries, with connecting wildlife corridors. Protected areas include Jigme Dorji National Park, Royal Manas National Park, Black Mountains National Park, and Bomdeling Wildlife Sanctuary. Torsa Strict Nature Reserve is a wilderness area. Overgrazing and poaching have been problems in the protected areas, particularly along the Indian border. As of late 2011, environmentalists were trying to stop a highway being built through wildlife habitat in Thrumshingla National Park. According to a 2011 report issued by the International Union for Conservation of Nature and Natural Resources (IUCN), threatened species in Bhutan included 27 types of mammals, 18 species of birds, 1 species of amphibian, and 9 species of plants. Threatened species included the tiger, snow leopard, Asian elephant, and wild yak.

6 POPULATION

The US Central Intelligence Agency (CIA) estimates the population of Bhutan in 2011 to be approximately 708,427, which placed it at number 161 in population among the 196 nations of the world. In 2011, approximately 5.8% of the population was over 65 years of age, with another 28.9% under 15 years of age. The median age in Bhutan was 24.8 years. There were 0.94 males for every female in the country. The population's annual rate of change was 1.201%. The projected population for the year 2025 was 850,000. Population density in Bhutan was calculated at 18 people per sq km (47 people per sq mi).

As of 2010, according to the CIA, 35% of the population lived in urban areas, and urban populations had an annual rate of change of 3.7%. The largest urban area was Thimphu, population 89,000; Phuentsholing, on the India border, had a population of approximately 20,000. Few towns have more than 3,000 residents. Many place names incorporate the word *dzong*, which means "castle-monastery." A *dzong*, the official center of a region or district, often houses substantial numbers of Buddhist monks.

7 MIGRATION

Estimates of Bhutan's net migration rate, according to the CIA in 2011, amounted to zero. The total number of emigrants living abroad was 44,600, and the total number of immigrants living in Bhutan was 40,200. Bhutan opposes immigration and forbids the entry of new settlers from Nepal. Since 1959, when about 4,000 Tibetan refugees entered Bhutan, the border with Tibet has been closed to immigration. By 1980, most of the refugees had become citizens of Bhutan; the rest migrated to India. The border between Bhutan and India is open, and citizens of Bhutan are free to live and work in India.

Since the late 1980s, more than 110,000 refugees, ethnically related to the Nepalese, fled or were expelled from Bhutan to refugee camps in eastern Nepal. The ethnic Nepalese, who are primarily Hindu, claimed they faced systematic discrimination and "ethnic cleansing" in the primarily Buddhist nation. Beginning in 2007, many Western nations began programs to resettle the refugees in the West. As of early 2010, over 40,000 refugees from Bhutan had been resettled in Western nations, particularly the United States, Canada, and Australia. As of 2011, over 75,000 remained in Nepal, most of whom would be willing to accept resettlement.

8 ETHNIC GROUPS

The Ngalop (also called Bhote) are people of Tibetan origin who live in northern and western Bhutan and speak the Dzongkha language. They account for about 50% of the population. The Sharchop inhabit the eastern regions and also have ethnic affinities with the people of Tibet. Indigenous tribal peoples live in villages scattered throughout Bhutan and account for approximately 15% of the population. The remaining peoples are related to the Nepalese (about 35% of the population), living mostly in the south. They are known as the Lhotshampas, meaning "southerners" in the Dzongkha language.

9 LANGUAGES

Three main languages are spoken in Bhutan, but there are many other languages and dialects. The official language is Dzongkha, a Tibetan dialect spoken mainly by Ngalop people in the northern and western parts of the country. About 24% of the population speaks Dzongkha as a first language. Both Dzongkha and English are languages of instruction in all schools; Nepali was removed from school curricula in 1989. Nepali-related languages are spoken by about 22% of the population. Sharchopkha is spoken by about 28% of the population, most in eastern Bhutan. Bumthangkha, is spoken in central Bhutan.

10 RELIGIONS

About 75% of the Bhutanese practice Drukpa Kagyupa or Nyingmapa Buddhism. About 25% practice Indian- and Nepalese-influenced Hinduism. While the law provides for religious freedom, Drukpa Kagyup, a branch of Mahayana Buddhism, is the state religion, and the law prohibits religious conversions. The Drukpa (people of the dragon), introduced from Tibet in the 12th century, dominate the collective life of the Bhutanese through a large clerical body estimated at more than 6,000 lamas or monks, centered in 8 major monasteries (dzongs) and 200 smaller shrines (gompas) scattered throughout the land. This sect incorporates both the ideology of the classical Buddhist scriptures and the indigenous pre-Buddhist animistic beliefs called Bon. The Nyingmapa school of Mahayana Buddhism is also practiced, primarily in the eastern regions. The royal family practices a combination of Drukpa Kagyup and Nyingmapa Buddhism. Most Ngalops are of the Drukpa Kagyup school; they hold a majority of positions in the government. The Sharchops are primarily of the Nyingmapa school. Major Buddhist holidays are observed as national holidays. Among Hindus, the Shaivite, Vaishnavite, Shakta, Ghanapath, Paurinic, and Vedic schools are all represented. There are still a few Bon priests and followers in the country, and there are small numbers of Christians, with worship practices generally limited to the family home. The law provides for freedom of religion, but this right is limited in practice. Proselytizing is prohibited, and all religious organizations must have a license from the government in order to build a new place of worship. There have been reports of government discrimination against the Hindu Nepalese. A few Bhutanese Christians were jailed for proselytizing in 2006 and 2010.

¹¹TRANSPORTATION

Historically, Bhutan's communications were mostly with Tibet, through several strategic mountain passes. Prior to the 1961–66 development plan, there were no surfaced roads in Bhutan. Since then, a network of roads and suspension bridges was built by India. According to the World Bank, as of 2006, there were 2,100 km (m) of roads, and 33,000 motor vehicles in Bhutan. New roads were being constructed using environmentally friendly methods. Bus service links Paro Dzong and Thimphu with Indian border towns, and bus service goes from Thimphu to other areas of the country. There is express bus service from Phuentsholing to Kolkata, India. Many local travelers journey on foot or on ponies bred to withstand great altitudes and steep slopes. Goods are still transported by porters or on pack animals.

As of 2011, Bhutan had 2 airports, Paro Airport and the Yongphulla airstrip. According to the World Bank, 49,056 passengers arrived by air in Bhutan in 2009. The national air carrier, Druk Airlines, began operations in 1983 with regular flights between Calcutta and Paro. International flights arrived at Paro from India, Nepal, and Thailand, as of 2011. Besides Druk Air, the only other carrier flying to Paro was Nepal's private Buddha Air. A second airline for Bhutan, Tashi Air, was expected to commence business in 2012. Airports under construction at Bathpalathang and Gelephu had not opened as of October 2011 but were expected to commence domestic air travel in 2012.

¹²HISTORY

Little is known of the history of Bhutan before the 17th century. Buddhism was originally introduced from India in the 8th century, although the Buddhism of today's Bhutan is very much Tibetan in character. The forebears of the Bhotes (or Bhotias) came from Tibet, probably in the 9th century, when Tibetans invaded the area and met little resistance from the indigenous Tephu tribe. In the middle of the fifteenth century, Shabdrung Ngawang Namngyal, a Tibetan lama exercising temporal as well as spiritual power, united the country and built most of the fortified villages (*dzongs*). His successors in power established a dual system, sepa-

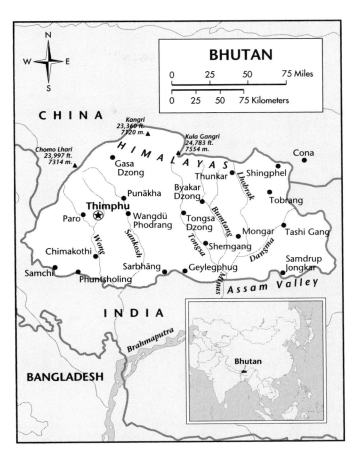

LOCATION: 26°42′ to 28°21′N; 88°45′ to 92°8′ E. BOUNDARY LENGTHS: India, 605 kilometers (378 miles); China, 470 kilometers (290 miles).

rating the temporal ruler (Desi or deb raja) and the spiritual ruler (Je Khenmpo or dharma raja).

The first recorded contact with the West occurred in 1772, when the British East India Company repelled a Bhutanese invasion of the princely state of Cooch Behar in India; they concluded a peace treaty two years later. During the 18th century and most of the 19th, British efforts to open trade with Bhutan proved futile, with the Bhutanese frequently attacking the relatively level areas of Assam and Bengal along their southern border. In 1865, the British finally defeated the Bhutanese, and Bhutan formally accepted a British yearly financial subsidy, which was dependent upon their keeping the peace.

With British approval, Gongsa Ugyen Dorji Wangchuck became the first hereditary king in 1907, replacing the temporal ruler; he was succeeded in 1926 by the second king, Jigme Wangchuck. In 1910, the Punakha Treaty was concluded between the British Indian Government and Bhutan, under which British India agreed explicitly not to interfere in Bhutanese internal affairs, while Bhutan accepted British "guidance" in handling external matters, a role independent India assumed after 1947. A formal Indo-Bhutanese accord, concluded in 1949, reaffirmed and amplified the earlier Punakha Treaty. It made India responsible for Bhutan's defense and strategic communications, committed India to avoid interfering in Bhutan's internal affairs, and affirmed Bhutan's agreement to be "guided by the advice of" India in foreign affairs. In 1952, the third king, Jigme Dorji Wangchuck, took the throne, and began reforms including establishment of a National Assembly, road construction, and strengthened ties with India.

In 1959, China published maps of the Himalayan frontier with South Asia that showed as Chinese part of the territory claimed by Bhutan as Chinese; Chinese representatives also asserted that Bhutan belonged to a greater Tibet. In response, Indian prime minister Jawaharlal Nehru warned that an attack on Bhutan would be deemed an act of war against India. Fighting between India and China in neighboring border regions in the fall of 1962 did not violate Bhutan's borders.

In April 1964, Bhutan's long-time prime minister, Jigme Dorji, was assassinated, revealing fissures among the ruling elite. The military plotters who were caught were executed, including the deputy commander of the army; others fled to Nepal. In the 1960s, Bhutan's advance toward modernization and the end of its insularity were accelerated by economic plans prepared and underwritten by India. Jigme Singye Wangchuck became the fourth king of Bhutan in 1974. His policies would emphasize what he termed "gross national happiness" (GNH) as an alternative of social and spiritual factors to the material "gross national product" (GNP). Bhutan's government policies were to be guided by GNH, with measures such as sustainable development, cultural preservation, and environmental conservation. The GNH concept became influential in international spheres far from the kingdom of Bhutan.

Relations with Nepal grew difficult in the late 1980s, due to a dispute with Nepal concerning Bhutanese refugees of Nepalese ethnicity. In contrast to Bhutan's Buddhist farmers, the Nepalese ethnic people were mostly Hindu, and many worked on roads and other building projects, having settled in the southern districts. The ethnic Nepalese, comprising approximately a third of Bhutan's population, had been granted citizenship in 1958. However, Bhutan changed its citizenship laws in the late 1980s, making many of the Nepalese Bhutanese illegal immigrants. A flawed census led to longtime residents, even government officials, being marked as illegal. The government's decision to promote a Ngalop ethnic identity for the whole country, with the clothing, language and codes of conduct of that ethnic group made mandatory for all citizens, was perceived by the Nepalese ethnic people as systematic discrimination, along with the decision that Nepali would no longer be used in Bhutan's schools. The government's actions appeared motivated by the fear that a growing Nepalese ethnic population might overthrow the monarchy and even cause annexation by a neighboring country, as had happened in neighboring Sikkim. In 1990, the Bhutanese government expelled 100,000 Nepalese ethnic Bhutanese to refugee camps in eastern Nepal.

Ethnic Nepalese activism, spearheaded by the Bhutan People's Party based in Nepal, continued through the early 1990s. It resulted in violence from both sides, and brought charges of violations of human rights against Bhutan's security forces. In 1996, "peace marches" of refugees from Nepal into Bhutan were met by force, and the marchers were deported by the Bhutanese police. The following year, the National Assembly adopted a resolution (later discarded) that prohibited family members of ethnic Nepalese refugees from holding jobs in the government or armed forces. The government also began resettling Buddhist Bhutanese from other regions of the country on land vacated by the refugees. In 1998, Foreign Minister Jigme Thinley took office with a mandate to settle the refugee issue. Although Bhutan and Nepal originally agreed in principal that the refugees would be divided into four categories (1) bonafide Bhutanese; (2) Bhutanese émigrés; (3) non-Bhutanese; and (4) Bhutanese who had committed crimes in Bhutan, the question of what to do with the more than 100,000 refugees living in the camps in Nepal remained unresolved. With repatriation elusive, Nepal agreed in 2007 to allow third-country resettlement of the refugees. More than 40,000 were resettled in Western countries by 2010, with third-country resettlement expected for most of the remaining 75,000.

In the 2000s, there was conflict on Bhutan's frontier with India's northeastern state of Assam. Two separatist groups from Assam—the United Liberation Front of Asom (ULFA) and the National Democratic Front of Bodoland (NDFB)—maintained bases in Bhutan. The separatist Kamatapur Liberation Organization (KLO) from West Bengal state was there as well. In late 2003, Bhutan launched a joint military operation with India to destroy the separatist bases.

Reforms introduced by King Jigme Singye Wangchuck in June 1998 marked a milestone in Bhutan's political and constitutional history. The king issued a royal edict relinquishing some of the monarch's traditional prerogatives and giving over a greater role in Bhutan's administration to elected government officials. On 3 December 2002, the king issued a first draft of a constitution for Bhutan, including the option of impeachment of the king by a two-thirds majority of the national assembly. The draft was discussed in the country's 20 districts before being presented for ratification, and the final document was released in March 2005. Plans were soon underway to initiate the nation's first parliamentary elections. King Jigme Singye Wangchuck abdicated the throne in December 2006, passing the monarchy to his son, Jigme Khesar, with the official coronation not to be held until after the parliamentary elections.

In December 2007, elections were held for the 25 members of the national council. In March 2008, Druk Phuensum Tshogpa (Bhutan Peace and Prosperity Party) gained 44 of the 47 seats in the nation's first national assembly. The People's Democratic Party earned the remaining 3. The parliament formally adopted the constitution on 18 July 2008. Jigme Khesar was officially crowned as king on 6 November 2008, becoming, at age 28, the world's youngest monarch. In the early years of his reign, the fifth king had a somewhat populist image, visiting remote villages, often traveling on foot, and on 13 October, 2011, he married Jetsun Pema, who was not a member of Bhutan's aristocracy. With neighboring Nepal having abolished its monarchy and elected a communist-led government, a small-scale underground Maoist party advocated similar actions in Bhutan and was suspected in bomb blasts in Nepal's southern towns in 2006, 2008, and 2011.

13 GOVERNMENT

Bhutan was an absolute monarchy until 2008, when the transition to a constitutional monarchy was completed. From 1972 to 2006, the king was Jigme Singye Wangchuck. In preparation for the transition in government, he abdicated to his son Jigme Khesar Namgyel Wangchuck, who was not officially crowned until 6 November 2008, after the new parliament was in place. The first parliament was established following elections in March 2008, and the first constitution was formally adopted on 18 July 2008.

The bicameral parliament consists of a non-partisan national council of 25 seats and the national assembly of 47 seats. Twenty members of the council are elected by majority vote in single-member electoral districts. They serve four-year terms. The remaining five members are appointed by the king. The members of the national assembly are elected by popular vote in multi-member districts to serve five-year terms. Under the new constitution, the king serves as chief of state, and the prime minister serves as head of government. The leader of the majority party of the national assembly is nominated as prime minister.

14 POLITICAL PARTIES

Under the absolute monarchy, political parties were discouraged, and none operated legally. That changed with the shift to a constitutional monarchy. In the first parliamentary elections, held in March 2008, Druk Phuensum Tshogpa (DPT—Bhutan Peace and Prosperity Party) won 44 of the 47 seats in the national assembly. The leader of DPT, Jigme Thinley, was appointed as the first prime minister. The People's Democratic Party (PDP), under the leadership of Tshering Tobgay, won the remaining 3 seats. At least 80% of the nation's registered voters cast a ballot in the first election. Suffrage is open to registered legal citizens age 18 and over. Underground political parties with members mostly from the Nepalese ethnic group have included the Bhutan People's Party and the Bhutan Communist Party (Marxist-Leninist-Maoist).

15 LOCAL GOVERNMENT

The country is divided into 20 districts (*dzongkhas*) under the supervision of elected district commissioners (*dzongdas*). Larger *dzongkhas* are subdivided into *dungkhags*. Villages are grouped into 201 *gewog*, which have elected leaders. Local government elections were held in June 2011, after long delays involving establishment of districts for representation, but voter turnout was a low 56%.

16 JUDICIAL SYSTEM

The legal system is based on English common law and Indian law. Bhutan does not have trial by jury. In 2010, Bhutan established a Supreme Court, overseeing constitutional issues. District court judges hear local cases, which can be appealed to a High Court and ultimately the Supreme Court. Judges are appointed by the National Judicial Commission and confirmed by the king. Defendants are presumed innocent, and capital punishment was abolished in 2004.

17 ARMED FORCES

The International Institute for Strategic Studies reports that armed forces in Bhutan totaled 8,000 members in 2011. The force is comprised of the army, the Royal Bodyguard, the national militia, the Royal Bhutan Police, and Forest Guards. Armed forces represent 2.6% of the labor force in Bhutan. Defense spending totaled $38.8 million and accounted for 1% of GDP.

18 INTERNATIONAL COOPERATION

Bhutan became a UN member on 21 September 1971; it participates in several specialized agencies of the UN, such as the FAO, ICAO, IDA, IFAD, IMF, ITU, UNESCO, the World Bank, UNIDO, and WHO. The country also belongs to the Colombo Plan, the Asian Development Bank, the SACEP, and G-77. In addition, Bhutan is a member of the Nonaligned Movement and was a founding member of the South Asian Association for Regional Cooperation (SAARC). Bhutan participates in the South Asian Free Trade Agreement (SAFTA). In 2004, Bhutan joined the Bangladesh, Indian, Myanmar, Singapore, and Thailand Economic Cooperation Forum (BIMSTEC).

In environmental cooperation, Bhutan is part of the Convention on Biological Diversity, the Kyoto Protocol, the Nuclear Test Ban Treaty, and the UN Convention on Climate Change. Japan, Switzerland, the Netherlands, Austria, Norway, Finland, Sweden, and Denmark formed the "Friends of Bhutan" donor group. Bhutan's closest diplomatic and economic ties are with India, and Bhutan does not have diplomatic relations with China or the US.

19 ECONOMY

The gross domestic product (GDP) rate of change in Bhutan, as of 2010, was 6.7%. Inflation stood at 4.3%. Bhutan's small-scale, agriculture-based economy has had the virtue of self-sufficiency in food production. Tourism, limited in numbers but marketed towards affluent travelers, provided foreign exchange and employment in the service sector. The major industry was production of hydropower for the country's own electricity needs and for export to India. Bhutan's traditional trade partner, India, continued to provide development aid.

The elected government of Bhutan vetted all programs and projects according to the "gross national happiness" policy of environmental, social, and cultural preservation. In the 2010s, modernization had begun to create demand for imported consumer goods in Thimphu and some other areas, as television and the Internet became popular, and creating gainful employment for the country's increasingly educated youth was a challenge. According to the CIA, as of 2009, unemployment was 4%.

20 INCOME

The CIA estimated that, in 2010, the GDP of Bhutan was $3.875 billion. The CIA defines GDP as the value of all final goods and services produced within a nation in a given year and computed on the basis of purchasing power parity (PPP) rather than value as measured on the basis of the rate of the exchange based on current dollars. The per capita GDP was estimated at $5,500. The annual growth rate of GDP was 6.7%. The average inflation rate was 4.3%. It was estimated that agriculture accounted for 17.6% of GDP, industry 45%, and services 37.4%.

As of 2011 the most recent study by the World Bank reported that actual individual consumption in Bhutan was 52.9% of GDP and accounted for less than 0.01% of world consumption. By comparison, the United States accounted for 25.44% of world individual consumption. The World Bank also estimated that 19.7% of Bhutan's GDP was spent on food and beverages, 11.7% on housing and household furnishings, 3.4% on clothes, 6.8% on health, 1.0% on transportation, 0.2% on communications, 1.8% on recreation, 0.0% on restaurants and hotels, and 5.1% on miscellaneous goods and services and purchases from abroad.

According to the CIA, It was estimated that as of 2008 about 23.2% of the population subsisted on an income below the poverty line established by Bhutan's government.

21 LABOR

As of 2008, Bhutan had a total labor force of 299,900 people. CIA estimates as of 2004 noted that 43.7% were employed in agriculture, 39.1% in industry, and 17.2% in the service sector. The salaried labor market is predominantly in government service and tourism. Other than hydropower production, most of the industrial sector consists of home-based handicrafts and privately owned small- or medium-scale factories producing consumer goods. Bhutan has employed guest workers from India in skilled and unskilled occupations. Bhutan's minimum working age of 18 was not well-enforced, and child labor has remained common in agriculture and the informal sector.

As of 2002, Bhutan had a government-set minimum wage of approximately BTN50 per day, which was doubled to BTN100 per day (approximately $2.00) in July 2011. At that time, wages were also increased for the National Work Force (NWF), people employed on government projects, ranging from BTN165 to BTN240 per day, with a bonus for high-altitude work. Workdays were legally 8 hours, with overtime payment. Compensation was made by the government in case of work-related injury. As of 2011, workers' associations were legal, although actual trade unions were not; collective bargaining and strikes were not allowed. In 2011, the government of Bhutan announced that it would join the International Labor Organization (ILO) in 2012.

22 AGRICULTURE

Roughly 15% of the total land was farmed, according to the FAO as of 2009. The country's major crops include rice, corn, and other grains, along with root vegetables, apples, and citrus. Cereal production in 2009 amounted to 143,410 tons, fruit production 58,740 tons, and vegetable production 24,998 tons.

With less than 8% of land suitable for cultivation, in Bhutan's mountainous terrain, fields are often terraced on hillsides. Stone aqueducts carry irrigation water. Almost all farm families own their own land. As of 2011, according to the Asian Development Bank, half of the country's farmers worked land of 1 hectare (2.47 acres) or less. Since the mid-1960s, the government has established demonstration farms, distributed fruit plants, and implemented irrigation schemes. High-yield varieties of rice, wheat, and corn seeds have been introduced. Lack of access to roads, on which farm products could be brought to market, has remained a severe problem for the agricultural sector.

The low-lying areas raise rice. Other cereals include wheat, maize, millet, buckwheat, and barley. Beer and distilled liquor are made from rice, barley, and millet. Paper is made from the daphne plant, and wild cannabis is used as livestock feed. Walnuts, citrus fruits, apples, and apricots are grown in orchards.

Bhutan's near self-sufficiency in food has permitted quantities of some crops, particularly fruit, to be exported to India, in exchange for cereals. Oranges are a primary cash crop for the country and one of the most important exports. In 2009, a deadly virus spread by the psyllid fly destroyed entire orchards in some areas of the country. In response, the government created a team to implement measures to prevent or stop the spread of the disease. Other cash and export crops include apples, cardamom, and potatoes. Specialty products for export include organic honey and high-quality red hill rice.

23 ANIMAL HUSBANDRY

The UN Food and Agriculture Organization (FAO) reported that Bhutan dedicated 407,000 hectares (1.01 million acres) to permanent pasture or meadow in 2009. During that year, the country tended 240,000 chickens, 326,017 head of cattle, and 36,000 pigs. Bhutan also produced 1,080 tons of cattle hide and 56 tons of raw wool. Meat and butter are important products from cattle and yaks raised by family farms and herding people. Yaks, cattle, and sheep graze in lowland pastures and, during the summer, in the uplands and high valleys. Draft and pack animals remain important, with horses, donkeys, and mules transporting goods in many areas not reached by roads.

24 FISHING

In 2008, the annual capture totaled 180 tons according to the UN FAO. The government established a hatchery and started a program of stocking Bhutan's rivers and lakes with brown trout. Freshwater fish, including carp, snow trout, mahseer, and loach, are found in most waterways.

25 FORESTRY

Approximately 85% of Bhutan is covered by forest, the highest percentage of any country in Asia. Bhutan's constitution mandates a minimum of 60% forest cover, and government policy has made sustainable yield mandatory to protect of forests and watersheds. With forest lands under strict protection, the country has experienced a shortage of construction timber. In October 2011, the government began to freely allow timber imports, to deal with the shortage. The UN FAO estimated the 2009 roundwood production at 257,000 cu m (9.08 million cu ft). The value of all forest products, including roundwood, totaled $7.51 million. There are a large number of small, privately owned sawmills and several small furniture factories throughout Bhutan, and several small furniture factories. Forest products other than timber include fuel wood, animal fodder and bedding, dyes, pitch, resins, wax, and medicinal plants.

26 MINING

The mineral industry of Bhutan was small, dominated by the production of cement, coal, dolomite, and limestone, and insignificant to its economy. Estimated production totals, in metric tons, for 2010 were: limestone, 715,956; dolomite, 1,192,374; cement, 295,000; gypsum, 344,134; quartzite, 104,580; ferrosilicon, 276,000; and talc, 26,302. Marble and slate were quarried for use as dimensional stones; production totals in 2010 were estimated at 716,700 metric tons. Dolomite has constituted an important export to India since 1960, and almost all the ferrosilicon output is exported to India. For centuries, silver and iron have been mined in Bhutan for handicrafts. Deposits of beryl, copper, graphite, lead, mica, pyrite, tin, tungsten, and zinc have also been found. A graphite-processing plant was established at Paro Dzong.

27 ENERGY AND POWER

The World Bank reported in 2008 that Bhutan produced 7.07 billion kWh of electricity. Hydroelectric power generated from Bhutan's rivers has supplied the country's energy needs and has become a vital export to India. Bhutan's first large power plant, the 336-MW Chukha hydroelectricity project (CHEP), came on line in early 1987, having been first agreed to as a turn-key operation with India in 1961, on what became a standard arrangement of 60% grant and 40% concessional loan. 70% of the power generated by the CHEP has been exported to India. Other large run-of-the-river projects, with funding from India, included Kurichu (operational in 2006), Punatsangchu-1, (2006), and Tala (2006). India's partner in the hydropower projects is a government-owned company called Druk Green.

As of 2011, the government planned to use hydropower export to become completely economically self-reliant. Bhutan's hydropower dams were run-of-the-river, but new projects with containment reservoirs were foreseen. Such mega-dam projects might compromise Bhutan's commitment to low-environmental-impact development. As of 2011, it was estimated that only about 5% of Bhutan's hydroelectric potential had been tapped. However, river flows were subject to seasonal changes, leading to power fluctuations and even power shortages during the dry winters.

Domestic consumption of petroleum (all of which was imported) and electricity has remained low in Bhutan, and many rural areas remain off the power grid. As of 2011, the government, in partnership with the Asian Development Bank, planned to promote renewable energy sources including solar, wind, biomass, and micro-hydro, particularly for rural electrification. A briquette fuel factory using sawdust and other wood byproducts was in operation in Romtokto.

28 INDUSTRY

Large development projects in Bhutan, such as road building and hydroelectricity projects, have relied on financing from Indian investors, as well as Indian guest workers. The building of new power projects led to growth in the transport and construction sectors, including a number of local cement operations. The country's first cement plant was completed in 1982 in Penden, a border town, by India, to which the bulk of its output is exported. A large Indian-subsidized dry-process cement plant began producing at Nganglam in 2011. Besides cement, there was a narrow range of other manufactures exported, including ferro-alloys, calcium carbide, processed foods, and particleboard. Bhutan Ferro Alloys, a joint venture between the government, the private Tashi Commercial Corporation, and Marubeni of Japan, produced ferro-silicon for export to India and Japan. Calcium carbide was produced at several private dolomite-mining operations, as well as private and joint public-private limestone mining operations. Copper wire and cable factories in Phuentsholing lost revenue as the price of copper (imported by Bhutan) rose in 2009 and demand fell in India, the export market. Industrial estates had been set up at Phuentsholing and Geylegphug, with others planned but not completed as of 2011.

Much of Bhutan's industrial production was craft-based, with homespun textiles—woven and embroidered cottons, wools, and silks—being the most important products. Other Bhutanese handicrafts included daphne paper, incense, leather objects, copper, iron, brass, bronze, and silver work, wood carvings, and split-cane basketry.

29 SCIENCE AND TECHNOLOGY

The World Bank reported in 2009 that there were no patent applications in science and technology in Bhutan. Royal Bhutan Polytechnic College, founded in 1974 in Deothang, offered courses in civil, mechanical and electrical engineering. The Royal Technical Institute in Phuentsholing offered courses in electronics and mechanics. Sherubtse Degree College, founded in 1983 in Trashigang, offered science courses as part of the Royal University of Bhutan. The Royal Institute of Health Sciences, also in the Royal University system, was founded in 1974. Bhutan also has an Institute of Traditional Health Services, which has a pharmaceutical research department. A new technical university, the Jigmeling Institute of Mechanical Engineering, was under construction as of 2011, as was the Thimphu Tech Park for information technology businesses.

30 DOMESTIC TRADE

Retail sales are carried out mainly in small, local bazaars. Bartering is used in remote areas, with grains, butter, and cloth being principal commodities of exchange, although both Indian and Bhutanese currencies are now used throughout the country. Access to markets remains very limited in rural areas due to lack of roads. Imports from India are distributed from Phuentsholing and other border towns. Several handicrafts shops cater to the tourist trade. Thimphu has stores selling imported appliances and electronic goods, and supplies for archery and other sports. A few small indoor shopping centers, department stores, and supermarkets have opened in Thimphu.

31 FOREIGN TRADE

Bhutan imported $621 million worth of goods and services in 2009, while exporting $509 million worth of goods and services, according to the CIA. Major import partners in 2009 were India, Hong Kong, Japan, Germany, Singapore, and Thailand. Bhutan's major export partners were India, Hong Kong, Japan, Germany, Singapore, and Thailand.

Bhutan's external sector has been almost exclusively oriented toward trade with India. With the completion in 2002 of the second hydroelectric power project financed by India—built largely with Indian labor and designed to deliver the majority of its power outputs to India—the dominance of India in terms of exports was about 85.6%. Some export industries, such as palm oil processing and copper wire manufacturing, were established on Bhutan's southern border because of tax advantages with India, but were virtually wiped out by increases in raw materials, changes in Indian duties, and the world economic crisis from 2008 on. In a multinational trade cycle, crude palm oil had been imported from Southeast Asia, refined in Bhutan, and exported to India in exchange for computer software, which was then exported from

Bhutan for tax advantages in Southeast Asia in exchange for crude palm oil.

Bhutan's import sources are increasingly diversified, although most imports still transit India. From 2010, Bhutan had increasing trade with Bangladesh, but the transit point remained India. Bhutan has had no diplomatic or trade relations with its other neighbor, China, since 1960.

Bhutan's principal exports include electric power (to India), cement, ferro-silicon, calcium carbide, copper wire and cable, manganese, particle board, and fruit products. The country's principal imports include fuel and lubricants, motor vehicles, machinery and parts, fabrics, electronic goods, and rice.

Bhutan signed the South Asian Free Trade Agreement (SAFTA) in 1994, joined the IFC in 2003, and became a member of the Bay of Bengal Initiative for Multi-Sectoral Technical and Economic Cooperation (BIMST-EC) in 2004. As of 2011, the government was not pursuing WTO membership, for reasons including not wanting to open trade with China, which would be necessary under WTO policy.

32 BALANCE OF PAYMENTS

The IMF reported in 2011 that Bhutan had a favorable growth outlook, driven by its hydropower exports to India. According to the IMF, foreign reserves covered about 11 months of import costs as of 2011. The IMF estimated that in the fiscal year 2010/2011, Bhutan's exports totaled $549 million, while imports totaled $896 million, resulting in a trade deficit of -$347 million, about 15% of GDP. Much of the imbalance reflected the import of equipment needed to construct and operate new hydropower plants. Foreign aid kept the balance of payments in surplus in spite of the trade imbalance, according to the IMF, but the hydropower projects in construction contributed to public debt amounting to an estimated 76% in the fiscal year 2010/2011.

33 BANKING AND SECURITIES

Bhutan's central bank is the Royal Monetary Authority, established in 1982 to manage currency and foreign exchange. The Bank of Bhutan was founded in 1968 as a joint venture with the State Bank of India; it was 80% government-owned, and an attempt to privatize the bank by reducing the government's share to 25% was stalled as of late 2011. A second commercial bank, the Bhutan National Bank (BNB), was established in 1997 as a public corporation, though the government retained 51%. The Bhutan Development Finance Corporation (BDFC) was set up in 1988 to finance small and medium enterprises. Druk Punjab National Bank, a joint venture, and T-Bank, owned by the Tashi commercial group, opened in 2010. As of 2010, according to the CIA, the discount rate, the interest rate at which the central bank lends to financial institutions in the short term, was 14.5%. Banking hours are mostly restricted to 9 a.m. to 4 p.m., Monday to Friday, and 9 a.m. to 12 a.m. on Saturday. ATMs were available in Thimphu and Phuentsholing. Mobile banking was available, and credit cards were accepted in hotels and other businesses catering to tourists. The small Royal Bhutan Stock Exchange (RBSE), established in

Balance of Payments – Bhutan (2010)		
(In millions of US dollars)		
Current Account		**-139.4**
Balance on goods	-298.8	
Imports	-843.3	
Exports	544.5	
Balance on services	-21.8	
Balance on income	-60.8	
Current transfers	241.9	
Capital Account		**79.7**
Financial Account		**104.8**
Direct investment abroad	...	
Direct investment in Bhutan	19.0	
Portfolio investment assets	...	
Portfolio investment liabilities	...	
Financial derivatives	...	
Other investment assets	-0.2	
Other investment liabilities	86.0	
Net Errors and Omissions		**61.4**
Reserves and Related Items		**-106.5**

(…) data not available or not significant.

SOURCE: *Balance of Payment Statistics Yearbook 2011*, Washington, DC: International Monetary Fund, 2011.

1993, traded 20 companies as of October 2011; there were four brokerage firms.

34 INSURANCE

The Royal Insurance Corporation of Bhutan (RICB) was founded by royal charter in January 1975, covering all classes of insurance. The RICB managed the government's rural house insurance scheme, a social welfare program which covered homes for fire, earthquake, flood, landslide, and storm damage. The government owned 39.25% of RICB, while private and public shareholders owned 60.25%. Bhutan Insurance, a private company, began offering general insurance policies in 2009. The two insurance companies were reinsured by financial institutions in India, Thailand, and Japan. In late 2011, the government announced that it was seeking the formation of local re-insurers, in order to keep revenues in the country, particularly on hydropower-related insurance.

35 PUBLIC FINANCE

In 2010, the budget of Bhutan included $302 million in public revenue and $588 million in public expenditures. The budget deficit amounted to 5.9% of GDP. In total, $836 million of the debt was held by foreign entities. Most of the annual budget deficit was covered by grants from India, the UN, and other international donors. According to the IMF, during the five year plan from 2008–2013, hydroelectric power sales to India were estimated to contribute 27% of revenue, while aid grants were estimated to amount to 37% (of which India would contribute 74%). The government announced that revenue collected for 2010 increased 11% over 2009. The fiscal year 2011/2012 budget allotted 24% of expenditures for health and education, and 10% for roads. Other government projects in the budget included water supply repair, urban housing, and new industrial estates. In 2011, the World Bank reported that

Public Finance – Bhutan (2009)

(In millions of ngultrum, central government figures)

Revenue and Grants	**20,624.1**	**100.0%**
Tax revenue	5,654.1	27.4%
Social contributions	71.3	0.3%
Grants	6,575.1	31.9%
Other revenue	8,323.7	40.4%
Expenditures	**20,317.7**	**100.0%**
General public services	6,500.9	32.0%
Defense	…	…
Public order and safety	1,133.9	5.6%
Economic affairs	5,482.2	27.0%
Environmental protection	891.7	4.4%
Housing and community amenities	1,930.5	9.5%
Health	…	…
Recreational, culture, and religion	773.1	3.8%
Education	3,605.5	17.7%
Social protection	…	…

(…) data not available or not significant.

SOURCE: *Government Finance Statistics Yearbook 2010,* Washington, DC: International Monetary Fund, 2010.

the parliament had little power to modify budgets proposed by the government's Ministry of Finance.

[36] TAXATION

As a low-income country, Bhutan has had a limited tax base. Personal income tax is charged progressively from 0% to 15%. The corporate tax on net profit was 30% as of 2011, with tax-free exceptions in the tourism industry and other sectors. Property transfers and interest were taxed at 5%. Sales tax varies by product but is generally low. In the fiscal year 2011/2012 budget, the government announced increases in excise taxes on alcohol (ranging from 35% to 75%) and beer (100% to 200%). Motor vehicles were taxed 40% to 50% in an effort to control the increasing traffic in the cities.

[37] CUSTOMS AND DUTIES

Under free trade agreements, trade flows between Indian and Bhutan without payment of customs duties. As a signatory of SAFTA, Bhutan was obliged to waive tariffs for member nations entirely by 2015. As of 2011, Bhutan had backed away from joining the WTO, due to not wanting to open up trade with China and not wanting to open up itself to unrestricted entry of foreign goods and companies. A dry-port project to expedite export and import formalities, which included Bhutan's first railway link, was announced in 2009 for the southern location of Toribari, but had not been completed as of late 2011.

Goods restricted for import include pharmaceuticals, plants, chemical, fertilizers, firearms, and precious metals. Duties of 100% are charged on alcohol and 50% on small juice packages, as of 2011. Import duties of 20% to 30% are charged on vehicles, but electric/hybrid vehicles are exempt. Increased import duties on automobiles were challenged in the court system in 2010, resulting in a ruling that the taxes had been imposed by the government without due process.

[38] FOREIGN INVESTMENT

Foreign investment has come primarily from India, carried out within the context of its and Bhutan's special relationship with India. Bhutan has relied on an increasingly diverse set of countries—Australia, Austria, Finland, Denmark, Sweden, Japan, the Netherlands, Norway, Canada, Switzerland, Germany, Italy, New Zealand, South Korea, the United Kingdom, and the United States—and multilateral institutions—the UN, the World Bank, and the Asian Development Bank (ADB)—to provide capital on a concessional basis, but India remains the dominant source.

The government's stance has been that foreign direct investment (FDI) has become increasingly necessary to meet the country's employment and self-sufficiency goals. However, it is limited due to sustainability restrictions and cultural concerns. FDI has been permitted in sectors including hydropower and tourism, with joint ventures with a consisting of a few luxury international hotel and resort chains. Foreign direct investment (FDI) in Bhutan was a net inflow of $36.4 million according to World Bank figures published in 2009. FDI represented 2.85% of GDP.

[39] ECONOMIC DEVELOPMENT

By the mid-1970s, tourism had surpassed the sale of postage stamps as the chief source of Bhutan's limited foreign exchange revenue. In turn, since the completion of the first large-scale hydroelectric project in 1988, power exports have become the leading source of a more comfortable hard currency position.

A series of five-year plans, initiated in 1961 and financed primarily by India, enhanced transportation, improved agriculture, and developed hydroelectric power. Realization of several hydroelectric and industrial projects during the 1980s helped increase industry's share of the GDP and helped overall GDP grow 7.3% annually during 1985–90. A slowdown in government project investment in the early 1990s caused GDP growth to stabilize at an average of 3%, although an upturn in economic activity brought the rate back up to 6% by 1995 and to 7.3% by 1998. In 1999, real GDP growth dropped to 5.5% but recovered to around the long-term average of 6% in 2000 and 2001. GDP was at 5.3% in 2003. In 2007, the real GDP growth ballooned to 22.4% as a result of hydropower exports to India.

One of Bhutan's greatest challenges will be creating jobs for its growing population of educated young people. Much of the educated workforce has been employed traditionally by the public sector; however, the IMF advised the government to encourage more private-sector development. With 47% of the population working in agriculture but only 8% of the land arable, improvements were needed in irrigation, erosion prevention, and access to markets. Bhutan has improved its infrastructure but still has many roadless areas. Domestic flights are being added, and the airline fleet has been expanded at considerable expense. Hydroelectric power is the crucial export, and India is the essential client. Seasonal power fluctuations still affect the export market and domestic industry. New trade outlets, including Bangladesh, are being actively sought, but access will still be through India, and opening up to trade with China is not under consideration, as of 2011.

Despite Bhutan's growth in the early 21st century, poverty in the country remains high in remote rural areas, and among the Nepalese ethnic group. Bhutan conducted its first Poverty Analysis Report in 2004 and found that 32% of its population was living below the poverty line. As of 2008, the population below the poverty line had decreased to 23%.

Bhutan embarked on its ninth five-year plan in 2002 with the goal of seeking "gross national happiness" rather than gross national income. This strategy is in keeping with the country's Buddhist traditions and helps maintain an intact environment, particularly in terms of forest cover. Bhutan's leaders remain cautious about future development, emphasizing maintenance of culture and protection of environment, and working to decrease poverty. In 2011, Prime Minister Jigme Thinley was predicting a future role for Bhutan as a regional center for education and medical services.

40 SOCIAL DEVELOPMENT

As of 2011, state pension plans covered government employees and the military. The government provided free healthcare for all citizens and home insurance in rural areas. Membership associations provide relief benefits in case of death or injury.

A pattern of discrimination against people of Nepalese ethnicity persists, and they are under-represented in government. Nepali was no longer taught in schools, as of 2011, and Ngalop national dress was required for official occasions. A generation gap exists between the culturally conservative elite and young people who are increasingly open to outside influences, and there is extreme disparity between the rural poor and the well-off urban population. Alcohol abuse is prevalent in rural and urban areas.

In Bhutan's traditional culture, dowry was not practiced, and land was divided equally between sons and daughters. Polygamy is legal, but only with the consent of the first wife. The law clarified the definition of sexual assault and imposed harsh penalties, but domestic violence is common, and often linked to alcohol abuse, particularly in rural areas. As of 2011, just 14% of seats in parliament were held by women. Bhutan has laws against same-sex relationships, but they are rarely enforced.

41 HEALTH

According to the CIA, life expectancy in Bhutan was 67 years in 2011. The country spent 5.5% of its GDP on healthcare, amounting to $98 per person. There was less than 1 physician, 3 nurses and midwives, and 17 hospital beds per 10,000 inhabitants. The fertility rate was 2.6, while the infant mortality rate was 52 per 1,000 live births. In 2008, the maternal mortality rate, according to the World Bank, was 200 per 100,000 births. It was estimated that 98% of children were vaccinated against measles. The CIA calculated HIV/AIDS prevalence in Bhutan to be about 0.2% in 2009. Other infectious diseases include diarrhea, hepatitis A, typhoid fever, malaria, and dengue fever.

Medical care is provided free of charge to all citizens in need, including a choice of western or traditional treatments, and transport out of the country if necessary. Doctors are trained in other countries, as Bhutan lacked a physicians' degree course as of 2011. Bhutan is known for its traditional medicine, in the Tibetan methodology, with an emphasis on botanical products. The government of Bhutan banned all tobacco sales for health reasons in 2005. A controversial crackdown on tobacco smuggling took place in 2011, leading to court cases and Facebook protests.

42 HOUSING

Houses are traditionally built of rammed earth in timber framing; some buildings are made of stacked stone. Roofs are gently inclined and often made of pine shingles kept in place by heavy stones. Walls are often whitewashed and decorated with paintings, and carved wood is used for doors and trim work. A 3-story house, with livestock quartered on the first floor, is typical in rural Bhutan. A serious shortage of housing in urban areas continued in 2011. Urban multi-unit buildings of cement and brick were being constructed to keep up with demand. The government building codes mandated use of traditional architectural elements in new buildings, and no building could be higher than 6 stories.

As of 2008, according to the CIA, 99% of urban and 88% of rural dwellers had access to improved water supplies, while 87% of urban and 54% of rural dwellers had access to improved sanitation.

43 EDUCATION

A modern educational system was introduced in Bhutan in the 1950s. Prior to that, education was provided only by monasteries. In the 20th century, Bhutan's aristocracy was educated at prestigious schools in India and the United Kingdom.

Free education is provided to citizens. Primary schooling covers a seven-year course of study followed by two years of junior high. This is followed by either a general secondary program (four years of high school) or a technical course of study. In 2009, the World Bank estimated that 87% of age-eligible children in Bhutan were enrolled in primary school. Secondary enrollment for age-eligible children stood at 47%. Tertiary enrollment was estimated at 7%. Of those enrolled in tertiary education, there were 100 male students for every 59 female students. Public expenditure on education represented 4.8% of GDP, as of 2008, according to the CIA.

As of 2007, according to the government's Bhutan Living Standard Survey, the adult literacy rate was 55.5%, with about 74% in urban areas, and 49% in rural areas. Women's literacy was estimated as 46%, while men's literacy was about 66%.

The Royal University of Bhutan (founded 2003) is comprised of 11 colleges, in Thimphu, Phuentsholing, Paro, Samtse and other locations; college specializations include business, science, traditional medicine, education, language, and natural resources. Thimphu is the site of the Center for Bhutan Studies (founded 1999), a research institute for culture and society. Royal Thimphu College (2009), located in Ngabiphu, is the country's first private college.

44 LIBRARIES AND MUSEUMS

The National Library at Thimphu (established in 1967) has an important collection of Mahayana Buddhist literature, and the entire 120,000-item collection has been digitized. The National Library includes the National Archives, and displays the world's largest book, *Bhutan: A Visual Odyssey Across the Last Himalayan Kingdom*. Jigme Dorji Wangchuck Public Library (1980) in Thimphu was the only public library in the country as of 2011, with over 18,000 volumes. Sherubutse College Library (1989) holds over 35,000 volumes. The Samtse Institute of Education library holds over 15,000 volumes, and the Royal Institute of Management library holds over 5,000 volumes. The library collection of the Institute of Traditional Medicine Services dates back to the 17th century.

The National Museum of Bhutan opened to the public in 1968 at Paro Dzong, in a seven-story 17th-century fortress, featuring religious art objects reflective of Bhutan's unique Buddhist culture, as well as historical objects. Some monasteries have valuable collections of Buddhist manuscripts and art objects. The National Textile Museum and the Folk Heritage Museum both were established in 2001, in Thimphu.

45 MEDIA

As of April 2011, according to the Ministry of Information and Communications, Bhutan had 26,292 landlines, in use by 3.78 out of 100 people. In contrast, mobile telephones were in use by over 56% of Bhutan's population. Bhutan Telecom Limited, a state-owned company, offers mobile service through its subsidiary B-Mobile, and a private company, Tashi Info Com, also offers mobile service. As of April 2011, there were 394,316 mobile telephone subscriptions.

The constitution guarantees the right of free expression in Bhutan, but the government continues to prohibit criticism of the king. Broadcast and cable television are government-controlled, and some foreign cable companies and programs were blocked as culturally offensive. Movies, including local films, are censored, and some websites are blocked.

Founded in 1986, Bhutan's first newspaper, *Kuensel*, was half government-owned, half public. It publishes twice a week in Dzongkha and English, with a total circulation of about 30,000 as of 2010. Private newspapers began only in 2006; they include Bhutan Today, Bhutan Observer, Druk Neytshuel, Journalist, and Business Bhutan. The newspapers are dependent on the government for advertising.

As of 2010, there were 10 FM radio stations and 1 short-wave station. Broadcasts are in Dzongkha, Nepali, English, and Sharchop. The government radio service is Bhutan Broadcasting Service (BBS); newer private stations include Radio Valley and Kuzoo. From 1989 to 1999, the government had imposed a ban on private television reception. Television broadcasting was reintroduced to the country in 1999 with the creation of the Bhutan Broadcasting Service (BBS). The same year, the government allowed for the licensing of cable companies. As of 2011, there was only one broadcast television station in operation, the state-owned BBS. Satellite television, although illegal because of its unrestricted foreign channels, has become popular in remote areas not reached by cable.

Druknet, the nation's first Internet service provider, was established in 1999 by the government owned Bhutan Telecom Limited. In 2010, the country had 9,147 Internet hosts. Internet users numbered 8 per 100 citizens. Facebook, blogs, and news sites such as Bhutantimes.com (defunct as of late 2011) have been used to express objections to government policies.

46 ORGANIZATIONS

Traditionally, regional monasteries provided community events and organizing in Bhutan. Villages put on festivals and religious ceremonies, and work on cooperative projects. Villages have committees for health and development, and there are farmers' associations. The Bhutan Chamber of Commerce and Industry is head-quartered in Thimphu, and there is an Association of Bhutanese Tour Operators.

The Bhutan Youth Development Association (BYDA), established in 1985, sponsors skills training for disadvantaged young people. Scouting programs for boys and girls are available through Bhutan Scout Tshogpa, formed in 1996. Sports associations represent several different pastimes, including the national sport of archery, tennis, tae kwan do, badminton, and track and field.

The National Women's Association of Bhutan was founded in 1981. Respect, Educate, Nurture, and Empower Women (RE-NEW, founded in 2004) works against domestic violence. The Voluntary Artists' Studio, Thimphu (VAST) encourages art activities for young people. The Royal Society for Protection of Nature was founded in 1987 and runs educational and conservation programs.

Several international non-governmental organizations operate in Bhutan, along with international government aid projects and multilateral aid agencies. Exiles of Nepalese ethnicity have formed the Human Rights Organization of Bhutan, the Bhutan Women and Children Organization, and other civil society groups.

47 TOURISM, TRAVEL, AND RECREATION

The *Tourism Factbook*, published by the UN World Tourism Organization, reported 23,500 incoming tourists to Bhutan in 2009 who spent a total of $51 million. Of those incoming tourists, there were 9,900 from Europe, 7,700 from East Asia and the Pacific, and 5,700 from the Americas. There were 3,531 hotel beds available in Bhutan, which had an occupancy rate of 12%. The estimated daily cost to visit Thimphu, the capital, was $392.

Bhutan has a heavily regulated tourism sector, with a "low volume, high value" policy, encouraging only upscale tourists to visit. All foreign visitors, except those from India, are required to enter on visa-providing package tours, paying a minimum of $250 per day, which includes accommodation, meals, transport, and guide. Some ultra-luxury hotels charged far more than the minimum. In 2010, the government announced plans to expand the tourist sector by opening new destinations for tourists, building and upgrading hotels, and upgrading credit card capabilities.

The beautiful Thimphu, Paro, and Punakha valleys, with their many monasteries, attract culture-oriented tourists. The "Tiger's Nest" cliff-side monastery at Taktsang is particularly famous. Eco-tourism and trekking through forests and high mountains have increased in popularity, as have kayaking and whitewater rafting adventures on the Pho Chhu and Mo Chhu rivers.

48 FAMOUS PERSONS

Jigme Dorji Wangchuck (1928–72) instituted numerous reforms during his reign as king of Bhutan. He was succeeded by his son Jigme Singye Wangchuck (b. 1955), who brought democracy to Bhutan and abdicated the throne in 2008 to his son, Jigme Khesar Namgyel Wangchuck (b. 1980). Ashi Dorji Wangmoa Wangchuck (b. 1955),

Bhutan's queen mother, is an author active in sustainable development work. Drungtsho Pema Dorji (1936–2009) was a doctor of traditional medicine who founded Bhutan's Institute of Indigenous Medicine. Khyentse Norbu (b. 1961), a Buddhist lama, directed *The Cup* and Bhutan's first feature film, *Travellers and Magicians*.

⁴⁹DEPENDENCIES

Bhutan has no territories or colonies.

⁵⁰BIBLIOGRAPHY

Aris, Michael. *The Raven Crown: The Origins of Buddhist Monarchy in Bhutan.* Singapore: Times Editions-Marshall Cavendish, 2005.

Berthold, John. *Bhutan: Land of the Thunder Dragon.* Boston: Wisdom Publications, 2005.

Bhutan Investment and Business Guide: Strategic and Practical Information. Washington, DC: International Business Publications USA, 2012.

Cooper, Robert. *Bhutan.* New York: Marshall Cavendish, 2001.

Fraser, Neil. *Geography of a Himalayan Kingdom: Bhutan.* New Delhi: Concept Publishing, 2001.

Hellum, A. K. *A Painter's Year in the Forests of Bhutan.* Edmonton: University of Alberta Press, 2001.

Rennie, Frank, and Robin Mason. *Bhutan: Ways of Knowing.* Charlotte, NC: Information Age Publishing, 2008.

BRUNEI DARUSSALAM

Nation of Brunei, Abode of Peace
Negara Brunei Darussalam

CAPITAL: Bandar Seri Begawan

FLAG: On a yellow field extend two diagonal stripes of white and black, with the state emblem centered in red.

ANTHEM: *Allah Peliharakan Sultan (God Bless His Majesty).*

MONETARY UNIT: The Brunei dollar (BND) of 100 cents is pegged to and is interchangeable with the Singapore dollar. There are coins of 1, 5, 10, 20, and 50 cents, and notes of 1, 5, 10, 50, 100, 500, 1,000, and 10,000 Brunei dollars. BND1 = US$0.8004 (or US$1 = BND$1.2855) as of 2011.

WEIGHTS AND MEASURES: Imperial weights and measures are in common use, as are certain local units, but a change to the metric system is slowly proceeding.

HOLIDAYS: New Year's Day, 1 January; National Day, 23 February; Anniversary of the Royal Brunei Armed Forces, 31 May; Sultan's Birthday, 15 July. Movable holidays include the Chinese New Year and various Muslim holy days.

TIME: 8 p.m. = noon GMT.

¹LOCATION, SIZE, AND EXTENT

Brunei occupies 5,770 sq km (2,228 sq mi) on the northwestern coast of the island of Borneo. Comparatively, Brunei is slightly smaller than the state of Delaware. It comprises two small enclaves separated by the Limbang River Valley, a salient of the Malaysian State of Sarawak, which surrounds Brunei on the E, S, and W. Brunei's total boundary length is 381 km (237 mi).

Brunei's capital city, Bandar Seri Begawan, is located in the northern part of the country.

²TOPOGRAPHY

Brunei's western enclave contains most of the country's population, as well as the capital; the thinly populated eastern zone is mainly dense forest. The land generally consists of primary and secondary tropical rainforest, with a narrow coastal strip on the western enclave. The eastern enclave is more hilly, rising to 1,850 m (6,070 ft) in the nation's highest peak of Mt. Pagon in the extreme south. The longest river in the country is the Belait River, which crosses through the western portion of the country and has a length of 209 km (130 mi).

³CLIMATE

The country has a tropical climate, with uniform temperatures ranging from 23–32°C (73–89°F). Humidity is high, about 80% all year-round, and annual rainfall varies from about 275 cm (110 in) along the coast to more than 500 cm (200 in) in the interior. Rainfall is heaviest during the northeast monsoon season (*landas*), especially in November and December.

⁴FLORA AND FAUNA

The country is largely covered by mangrove and peat swamp, heath, montane vegetation, and Dipterocarpaceae forest. The rainforest and swampland are inhabited by a plethora of small mammals, tropical birds, reptiles, and amphibians. Mammals include both wild and domesticated buffalo, honey bear, deer, and monkeys. Insects are abundant and sometimes harmful, in particular the malarial mosquito and biting midge.

The World Resources Institute estimates that there are 6,000 plant species in Brunei Darussalam. In addition, Brunei Darussalam is home to 112 mammal, 455 bird, 73 reptile, and 4 amphibian species. This calculation reflects the total number of distinct species residing in the country, not the number of endemic species.

⁵ENVIRONMENT

According to a 2011 report issued by the International Union for Conservation of Nature and Natural Resources (IUCN), threatened species included 34 types of mammals, 24 species of birds, 6 types of reptiles, 3 species of amphibian, 7 species of fish, and 100 species of plants. Endangered species included the black-faced spoonbill, Sumatran rhinoceros, the Siamese crocodile, and the painted batagur.

Brunei is a party to international agreements on ozone layer protection, endangered species, whaling, and ship pollution and in 1996 ratified the Law of the Sea.

The World Resources Institute reported that Brunei Darussalam had designated 324,000 hectares (800,621 acres) of land for protection as of 2006. Water resources totaled 8.5 cu km (2.04 cu mi) while water usage was 35 cu km (8.4 cu mi) per year. Per capita water usage totaled 243 cu m (8,581 cu ft) per year. The UN reported in 2008 that carbon dioxide emissions in Brunei Darussalam totaled 7,599 kilotons. The nation has an extensive oil industry with reserves that, in 2011, were estimated to last 25 years; national gas resources were expected to last 40 years.

6 POPULATION

The US Central Intelligence Agency (CIA) estimated the population of Brunei Darussalam in 2011 to be approximately 401,890, which placed it at number 175 in population among the 196 nations of the world. In 2011, approximately 3.6% of the population was over 65 years of age, with another 25.5% under 15 years of age. The median age in Brunei Darussalam was 28.4 years. There were 1.00 males for every female in the country. The population's annual rate of change was 1.712%. The projected population for the year 2025 was 480,000. Population density in Brunei Darussalam was calculated at 70 people per sq km (181 people per sq mi).

The UN estimated in 2010 that 76% of the population lived in urban areas, and that urban populations had an annual rate of change of 2.2%. The largest urban area was Bandar Seri Begawan, with a population of 22,000 (2009).

7 MIGRATION

Estimates of Brunei Darussalam's net migration rate, carried out by the CIA in 2011, amounted to 2.60 migrants per 1,000 citizens. There is little emigration except among the Chinese minority. Citizenship is based on parentage.

8 ETHNIC GROUPS

Malays make up about 66.3% of the population. Minorities include an estimated 11.2% Chinese, 3.4% indigenous, and 19.1% designated as other. There is a small Caucasian minority, chiefly of English, Dutch, American, and Australian stock.

9 LANGUAGES

Malay is the official language. English is also widely spoken, as is Chinese. The principal Chinese dialect is Hokkien, with Hakka, Cantonese, and Mandarin dialects also in use. Many native dialects are spoken as well.

10 RELIGIONS

The Shafeite sect of Sunni Islam, the official religion, dominates nearly every aspect of public and private life. According to CIA statistics, 67% of the population are Muslim; 13%, Buddhist; 10%, Christian; and 10% practice other faiths, including Hindu, Baha'i, Taoist, Sikh, and Nasrani. The Brunei government lists the Muslim population as being closer to 82%. Primary Christian denominations include Anglicans, Catholics, and Methodists.

Religious practice is controlled by the influential Ministry of Religious Affairs. The constitution allows for the peaceful practice of other faiths, but non-Muslims, as well as non-Shafeite traditions, are restricted in practice. Religious groups are required to register even to have the right of assembly. Some zoning laws prohibit the use of private homes as places of worship. Proselytizing of non-Muslim faiths is prohibited. All students are required to study Islam in school, including students at private Christian mission schools, where Christian instruction is prohibited. The *Melayu Islam Beraja* (Malay Islamic Monarchy) concept, a national philosophy, celebrates Brunei/Malay culture and adherence to strict Islamic principles. *Melayu Islam Beraja* discourages ecumenism and the general understanding of or openness to non-Muslim faiths. Chinese New Year, Christmas Day, Eid al-Fitr, Eid al-Adha, First Day of Ramadan, First Day of the Islamic Calendar, and the Prophet Muhammad's Birthday are all observed as national holidays.

11 TRANSPORTATION

Two seaports, at Muara and Kuala Belait, offer direct shipping services to Hong Kong, Singapore, and several other Asian ports; however, wharf facilities at the deepwater port of Muara, though expanded to about 550 m (1,800 ft) in the mid-1980s, remain inadequate. The Brunei River, which flows by the capital, is a major thoroughfare, but the country's approximately 209 km (130 mi) of navigable waterways are useable only by craft that draw under 1.2 m (3.9 ft).

The CIA reports that Brunei Darussalam has a total of 2,971 km (1,846 mi) of roads, of which 2,411 km (1,498 mi) are paved. Links between the capital and the other western towns are good. Taxi and limited bus services are available. River taxis and cars are for hire.

Brunei has two airports, only one of which has a paved runway. Brunei's airports transported 999,375 passengers in 2009, according to the World Bank. The national carrier, Royal Brunei Airlines, operates regular flights to Singapore, Hong Kong, Manila, Bangkok, Jakarta, Kuala Lumpur, and other cities. Some foreign airlines serve Brunei International Airport at Barakas, outside the capital.

A 13-km (8-mi) railway is operated by the Brunei Shell Petroleum Co.

12 HISTORY

From the 14th to the 16th century, Brunei was the center of a powerful native sultanate occupying what are now Sabah and Sarawak and extending northward through the Philippines almost to Manila. By the 19th century, much of this empire had been whittled away by war, piracy, and the colonial expansion of European nations. In 1847, the sultan concluded a treaty with Great Britain to suppress piracy and further commercial relations. In 1888, Brunei became a British protectorate; in 1906, a resident British commissioner was established. By a 1959 agreement (amended in 1971), Brunei was recognized as fully self-governing, with Britain retaining responsibility for defense and foreign affairs.

Brunei's first elections, held in 1962, resulted in a victory for the Brunei People's Party, militant nationalists who denounced Brunei's entry into a proposed federation with Malaysia, which had attained independence in 1957. Prevented from taking office, the nationalists, with Indonesian backing, revolted against Sultan Omar Ali Saifuddin in December 1962; the revolt was quickly put down with British assistance, but the sultan decided against federation in any case. From that time on, the sultanate has ruled by decree under a national state of emergency.

In 1967, Sultan Omar abdicated in favor of his son, Muda Hassanal Bolkiah. Sultan Omar, who, after his abdication, remained as defense minister and assumed the royal title of Seri Begawan, died in 1986.

During the 1970s, Brunei emerged as the richest state in Southeast Asia, profiting from its oil wealth and the steep increases in international oil prices. Much of this vast oil income was expended by the state on modernization and social services. Brunei renegotiated its treaty with the United Kingdom in mid-1978 and, on 7 January 1979, concluded a new treaty providing for independence within five years.

On 1 January 1984, the country attained full independence and was also proclaimed a member of the British Commonwealth. In 1984, Brunei joined both the Association of South-East Asian Nations (ASEAN) and the United Nations. Brunei is also a member of the Organization of Islamic Conference.

In the early 1990s, increasing emphasis on *Melayu Islam Beraja* (MIB) as a state ideology resulted in the affirmation of traditional values in light of increasing concern over an affluent and worldly younger generation. In 1991, the import of alcohol and the public celebration of Christmas were banned.

Brunei established diplomatic relations in 1993 with China, Vietnam, and Laos.

In 1998 Brunei's economy was hit simultaneously by falling oil prices, regional currency depreciation stemming from the region's economic crisis, and the collapse of the multibillion-dollar Amedeo conglomerate run by the sultan's brother, Prince Jefri Bolkiah, who was removed from his post as the country's finance minister. Tensions persisted between the sultan and his brother, who fled to London. Upon his return in early 2000, the government sued him and dozens of other persons for misuse of public funds.

As the new century began, Brunei's oil and gas reserves waned, and the nation was looking for ways to diversify its heavily petroleum-dependent economy. Brunei entered into an informal agreement with nine other members of the Association of Southeast Asian Nations (ASEAN) to create a free-trade zone by eliminating duties on most goods traded in the region by 2010.

In September 2004, Sultan Bolkiah took a tentative step toward giving some political power to the citizenry when he reopened Brunei's parliament with minimal powers, twenty years after it had been suspended. Seven months later, in May 2005, the cabinet was reshuffled in a major overhaul. New, younger members were ushered in, along with ministers with private-sector experience. In August 2005, the National Development Party registered as a political party.

The sultan dissolved the legislative council in March 2011, with no discussion of plans to reestablish it. Sultan Bolkiah celebrated 44 years on the throne in October 2011. As of 2001 the sultan was listed by *Forbes* magazine as one of the 15 wealthiest individuals in the world, with US$16 billion.

13 GOVERNMENT

Brunei is an independent Islamic sultanate. The 1959 constitution (parts of which were suspended in 1962) confers supreme executive authority to the sultan and provides for five constitutional councils: a privy council, council of cabinet ministers, legislative council, religious council, and council of succession to assist him. The members of these bodies are appointed by the sultan. The chief minister (*mentri besar*) is also appointed by the sultan and is responsible to him for the exercise of executive authority.

The legislative council was from time to time reconstituted until a cabinet-style government was introduced for the first time in 1984. At that time, an elected legislative council was considered as part of constitutional reform, but elections were considered unlikely for several years. In August 2000, the foreign minister confirmed that a review of the constitution had been submitted to the

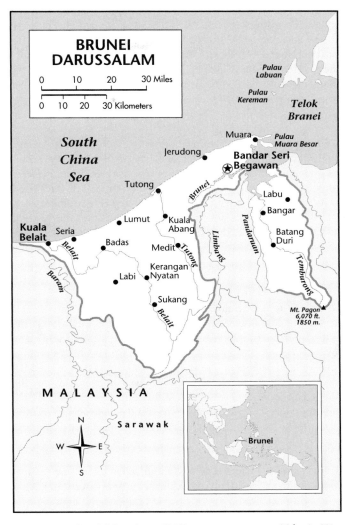

LOCATION: 4°2′ to 5°3′N; 114° to 115°22′E. BOUNDARY LENGTHS: Malaysia, 381 kilometers (237 miles); South China Sea and Brunei Bay coastlines, 161 kilometers (100 miles). TERRITORIAL SEA LIMIT: 12 miles.

sultan for approval, and that "an element of an election" was in this report. On 25 September 2004, Sultan Bolkiah reopened parliament 20 years after it had been disbanded. The new parliament had 21 members, all of them appointed. The sultan later signed a constitutional amendment, allowing for a 45-seat council with the direct election of 15 members of the next parliament. However, no future election dates were scheduled. In March 2011, the sultan dissolved the legislative council.

At his 1992 silver jubilee celebration, the sultan emphasized his commitment to preserving Brunei's political system based on the concept of *Melayu Islam Beraja* (MIB), or Malay Islam Monarchy, as the state ideology. MIB combines Islamic values and Malay culture within a monarchical political framework with the monarchy as defender of the faith.

14 POLITICAL PARTIES

Parties were organized shortly after self-government was achieved in 1959. However, when, in 1962, the Brunei People's Party won 98% of the legislative seats in the country's only election, the sultan barred its candidates from office and outlawed all political parties under a continuing state of emergency. Political parties reemerged in the 1980s but, in 1988, were banned and many of their leaders arrested. At that time, the political parties were the Brunei National Democratic Party (BNDP), founded in 1985, and the Brunei National United Party (BNUP), founded in 1986 by an offshoot of the BNDP. In contrast to the Malay-only BNDP, membership in the BNUP was open to other indigenous people, whether Muslim or not. The Chinese were left with the option of forming their own party.

In 1995, the Brunei National Solidarity Party (PPKB in Malay), one of the initial parties that had been banned in 1962, formally requested authorization to hold a convention and elected Abdul Latif Chuchu, the former secretary-general of the BNDP, as its president. In August 2005, the National Development Party (NDP) registered as a political party. The PPKB was deregistered in 2007. As of 2011, the NDP was the only officially registered party. The legislative council was dissolved by the sultan in March 2011.

15 LOCAL GOVERNMENT

There are four administrative districts: Brunei-Muara, Kuala Belait, and Tutong in the western enclave, and Temburong in the east. Government is centrally controlled, but allowance is made for local tribal customs. District officers responsible to the ministers of home affairs administer each district. As part of the MIB ideology, village consultative councils were introduced, making direct elections unnecessary. Instead, popularly elected headmen functioned as mediators between the people and the central government.

16 JUDICIAL SYSTEM

Brunei's judicial system is based on Indian penal code and English common law. Magistrates' courts hear ordinary cases involving minor disputes. Such cases may be appealed to the high court, a court of unlimited original jurisdiction in both civil and criminal matters. The high court is presided over by a chief justice and justices. Decisions of the high court can be taken to the court of appeal. The high court and court of appeal together comprise the Supreme Court. Judges from the United Kingdom are appointed as justices in the Supreme Court. A final appeal for civil cases can be brought before the Privy Council in London.

There are also Islamic courts that handle family matters such as marriage and divorce by applying Islamic law (Shari'ah).

17 ARMED FORCES

The International Institute for Strategic Studies reports that armed forces in Brunei Darussalam totaled 9,250 members in 2009. Armed forces represent 4.7% of the labor force in Brunei Darussalam. Defense spending totaled $918.3 million and accounted for 4.5% of gross domestic product (GDP) in 2006.

18 INTERNATIONAL COOPERATION

Brunei was admitted to UN membership on 21 September 1984, and is a member of ICAO, IMF, IMO, ITU, WHO, WIPO, the World Bank, and WMO. It is also a member of the Commonwealth of Nations, ASEAN, APEC, G-77, and the Organization of the Islamic Conference (OIC). Brunei became a member of the WTO 1 January 1995. The country is part of the Nonaligned Movement.

In environmental cooperation, Brunei is part of CITES, the Montréal Protocol, MARPOL, and the UN Conventions on the Law of the Sea and Climate Change.

19 ECONOMY

Brunei's wealth is deeply based in oil. Discovery of extensive petroleum and natural gas fields in the 1920s brought economic stability and modernization to the nation. Oil production peaked in 1980 at an estimated 270,000 barrels per day. Production was deliberately cut back since then to preserve the country's oil reserves, which were estimated to last through at least 2015. In 2011, it was estimated that Brunei would continue to have oil for the next 25 years and gas for the next 40 years. In 2011, the oil and gas sector accounted for about half of GDP, almost 90% of exports, and about 90% of government revenue.

While oil and gas exports account for the majority of Brunei's revenues, the country is attempting to diversify its economy. The government has increased efforts to promote Brunei as both a financial center and a destination for upscale tourism. The country's efforts to preserve the rainforest covering 70% of its land serve its goal of promoting ecotourism. Meanwhile, attempts to diversify the economy have moved slowly.

The GDP rate of change in Brunei Darussalam, as of 2010, was 4.1%. Inflation stood at 1.2%, and unemployment was reported at 3.7% (2008).

20 INCOME

The CIA estimated that, in 2010, the GDP of Brunei Darussalam was $20.38 billion. The CIA defines GDP as the value of all final goods and services produced within a nation in a given year and computed on the basis of purchasing power parity (PPP) rather than value as measured on the basis of the rate of the exchange based on current dollars. The per capita GDP was estimated at US$51,600. The annual growth rate of GDP was 4.1%. The average inflation rate was 2.7%. It was estimated that in 2010 agriculture accounted for 0.7% of GDP, industry 73.3%, and services 26%. It was estimated that household consumption was growing at an average annual rate of 2%.

In 2007 the World Bank estimated that Brunei Darussalam, with 0.01% of the world's population, accounted for 0.03% of the world's GDP. By comparison, the United States, with 4.85% of the world's population, accounted for 22.51% of world GDP.

As of 2011, the most recent study by the World Bank showed that actual individual consumption in Brunei Darussalam was 28.6% of GDP and accounted for 0.01% of world consumption. By comparison, the United States accounted for 25.44% of world individual consumption. The World Bank also estimated that 5.5% of Brunei Darussalam's GDP was spent on food and beverages, 4.8% on housing and household furnishings, 1.3% on clothes, 1.5% on health, 4.3% on transportation, 1.6% on communications, 2.2% on recreation, 1.5% on restaurants and hotels, and 1.6% on miscellaneous goods and services and purchases from abroad.

21 LABOR

As of 2008, Brunei Darussalam had a total labor force of 188,800 people. Within that labor force, CIA estimates in 2008 noted that

4.2% were employed in agriculture, 62.8% in industry, and 33% in the service sector. Unemployment was estimated at 3.7%.

Although all workers, including government employees, can join and form trade unions (excluding military personnel, police officers, and prison guards) the government neither facilitates nor encourages the establishment of unions. In addition, collective bargaining has no legal basis in the country, and strikes are illegal. The country's oil sector accounted for all three of Brunei's registered unions, with 5% of the industry's workforce unionized. However, in 2007, two of the unions were inactive, and the third had only very limited activity. Wages and benefits are set by market conditions.

Children under the age of 18 may only work with parental consent and the approval of the labor commission. The law prohibits employment of children under the age of 16. There are no reports of violations of these child labor laws. Although there is no minimum wage, most employees earn a generous living wage. The workweek is limited to 48 hours of work for five days, with two mandatory 24-hour rest days. The more than 100,000 foreign workers in Brunei who make up 30–40% of the total workforce do not receive the same conditions and wages as citizens.

22 AGRICULTURE

Roughly 2% of the total land is farmed. The country's major crops include rice, vegetables, and fruits. Cereal production amounted to 1,371 tons, fruit production 7,616 tons, and vegetable production 10,025 tons.

Rice production is low (only about 1,000 tons per year), and Brunei imports more than 80% of its requirements. Urban migration and more profitable jobs in the oil industry have led to a shortage of farm labor. An agricultural training center, sponsored by Brunei Shell and the Department of Agriculture, was established in 1978 to encourage young people to return to the land. Crops for home consumption include bananas, sweet potatoes, cassava, coconuts, pineapples, and vegetables.

23 ANIMAL HUSBANDRY

The UN Food and Agriculture Organization (FAO) reported that Brunei Darussalam dedicated 3,400 hectares (8,402 acres) to permanent pasture or meadow in 2009. During that year, the country tended 16 million chickens, 1,000 head of cattle, and 1,300 pigs. The production from these animals amounted to 2,133 tons of beef and veal, 2,245 tons of pork, 19,887 tons of poultry, 8,083 tons of eggs, and 49,708 tons of milk. Buffalo and goats are raised, as well. Brunei Darussalam also produced 100 tons of cattle hide.

Brunei has taken steps to become more self-reliant in regards to meat products. In 1978, the Mitsubishi Corporation and the government started McFarm, a cattle-breeding station in Brunei established in order to reduce meat imports and promote modern agricultural and livestock techniques. The government owns a cattle station in Australia that is larger in area than Brunei itself; this station supplies much of Brunei's beef.

24 FISHING

Traditional fishing declined during the late 1990s and into the mid-2000s, with only 60% of home consumption provided by local fishermen. The Fisheries Department supplied a small trawling fleet, and continuing efforts were being made to develop both freshwater and saltwater aquaculture. Fish hatcheries were in operation on a six-hectare (15-acre) site near Muara.

Brunei Darussalam had 1,970 decked commercial fishing boats in 2008 producing an annual capture totaling 2,358 tons, according to the UN FAO. The export value of seafood totaled $95.38 million.

25 FORESTRY

Approximately 72% of Brunei Darussalam is covered by forest. Forest reserves constitute about 41% of the forested area. In 2008, Brunei announced plans to increase the reserve to 55% in order to preserve the area's rich natural resources. Exports of timber are restricted. There is a small sawmill and logging industry for local needs. The UN FAO estimated the 2009 roundwood production at 112,100 cu m (3.96 million cu ft). The value of all forest products, including roundwood, totaled $2.47 million.

26 MINING

Brunei's mining industry was engaged primarily in the production and processing of crude oil and natural gas. Principle non-fuel mineral resources in 2009 were cement, carbonate rocks, coal, kaolin, sand, gravel, and other varieties of stone. As of 2011, the government was considering projects for the development of a silica-processing plant to produce silica plates from the country's reserves of high-quality silica sands. In 2009 cement production totaled 220,000 metric tons.

27 ENERGY AND POWER

The World Bank reported in 2008 that Brunei Darussalam produced 3.42 billion kWh of electricity and consumed 3.26 billion kWh, or 8,109 kWh per capita. All energy came from fossil fuels. Per capita oil consumption was 9,251 kg. Oil production totaled 136,162 barrels of oil a day. Commercial oil production, which began in 1929, dominates the economy. Exploratory drilling for new reserves has continued, and capital expenditure on petroleum development remains high. In 2011, proven reserves of oil were estimated at 1.1 billion barrels.

After peaking at 240,000 barrels per day in 1979, crude oil production was deliberately lowered in 1988, through a self-imposed conservation quota of 150,000 barrels of oil per day, to extend the life of Brunei's reserves. There are seven offshore fields belonging to Brunei, of which the largest is the Champion field, with about 40% of the country's total reserves. Brunei opened its first deep-water drilling areas in 2001 and accepted bids by two international consortia.

Brunei has been a major supplier of liquefied national gas to Japan under 20-year contracts, the last renewed in 1993 by the then-newly established Brunei Oil and Gas Authority. The LNG plant at Lumut is one of the largest in the world. In 2009, natural gas production was estimated 11.5 billion cu m and consumption was estimated at 2.69 billion cu m. Proved reserves of natural gas were estimated at 11.5 billion cu m in 2011.

28 INDUSTRY

Industry is almost entirely dependent on oil and natural gas production. Brunei is the fourth-largest oil producer in Southeast

Asia and the ninth-largest producer of liquefied natural gas in the world.

Brunei Shell Petroleum (BSP), a joint venture owned by the Brunei government and Royal Dutch/Shell, is the country's main oil and gas production company and is the largest employer after the government. It also operates Brunei's refinery, which has a distillation capacity of 10,000 barrels per day, and generally fulfills petroleum product needs within the country. Brunei reported in 2009 that Australia, Indonesia, India, and Korea together accounted for 70% of the nation's oil exports, with smaller quantities going to other countries including New Zealand and China.

Natural gas is mostly liquefied at a Shell Liquefied Natural Gas (LNG) plant, which opened in Brunei in 1972 and is one of the largest LNG plants in the world. Brunei sells about 90% of its liquefied natural gas to Japan under a long-term agreement. In addition, Mitsubishi, a Japanese company, is a joint-venture partner with Shell and the Brunei government in three companies: Brunei LNG, Brunei Coldgas, and Brunei Shell Tankers. Brunei also supplies liquefied natural gas to the Korea Gas Corporation.

Oil and gas exploration also are important industrial activities in Brunei, although deep-water exploration activities were put on hold in 2003 because of a dispute with Malaysia; the dispute was later resolved with a joint production resolution. The French oil company ELF Aquitaine, which began petroleum exploration activities in Brunei in the 1980s, operates in the country as Total E&P Borneo BV.

Brunei's small manufacturing sector includes production for the construction sector, sawmills, and brick and tile factories. Government support of small-scale projects in food and beverage processing, textiles, furniture making, and specialist optics has had limited results. Brunei's garment industry suffered after the United States eliminated import quotas in 2004. Even still, the United States remained Brunei's largest market for garments, with $66 million that year.

A $400 million methanol plant came online in 2010. Brunei also may establish a "cyber park" to encourage development of an information technology industry, and has announced plans to encourage the establishment of offshore financial institutions and Islamic banks. Other future development plans reported in 2011 included a proposed aluminum smelting plant in the Sungai Liang region and the addition of a giant container hub to the port at Muara.

29 SCIENCE AND TECHNOLOGY

Advanced science and technology have been imported in connection with development of the oil industry. Foreign technology expertise is employed in communications and other infrastructural programs. The Ministry of Industry and Primary Resources conducts agricultural research. The University of Brunei Darussalam, founded in 1985, has a faculty of science. The Technological Institute of Brunei, located in Bandar Seri Begawan, and the Jefri Bolkiah College of Engineering in Kuala Belair, offer engineering courses.

The World Bank reported in 2009 that there were no patent applications in science and technology in Brunei Darussalam.

30 DOMESTIC TRADE

Most food products and other consumer goods found in local markets come from Singapore, Japan, and Malaysia. Most of Brunei's beef is supplied by a government-owned cattle ranch in Australia, which is larger than Brunei itself. Food items, such as eggs and chickens, are produced and sold locally.

31 FOREIGN TRADE

Brunei's reliance on oil and gas production requires it to import a wide array of goods. Nevertheless, the dollar value of its exports is considerably greater than that of its imports, which has allowed the country to maintain strong foreign reserves. Exports totaled US$10.67 billion worth of goods and services in 2008. Major trading partners for exports were Japan, 46.8%; South Korea, 13.7%; Indonesia, 9%; Australia, 8.9%; India, 6.9%; and New Zealand, 4.6%.

Imports totaled US$2.61 billion in 2008. Key trading partners for imports in 2009 were Singapore, 37.1%; Malaysia, 19%; Japan, 7%; China, 6%; Thailand, 5%; the United States, 4.3%; and the United Kingdom, 4.1%. However, these figures include transshipments; most of Brunei's imports pass through Singapore en route to the country and thus fall under Singapore's total even if the products do not actually originate there. Japanese products dominate local markets for motor vehicles, construction equipment, electronic goods, and household appliances.

On 1 January 2010, a new free trade agreement was established between China and the six founding members of the Association of South East Asian Nations (ASEAN), including Brunei. A major point of the free trade agreement was the elimination of tariffs on nearly 90% of imported goods. The free trade area agreement was expected to allow for a major increase in exports and export earnings among the ASEAN countries. Cambodia, Laos, Vietnam, and Myanmar, the newest members of ASEAN, are expected to gradually become full members of the free trade area by 2015. In terms of population, this is the largest free trade area in the world. In terms of economic value, it is the third-largest, surpassed only by NAFTA and the European Union.

Principal Trading Partners – Brunei Darussalam (2010)

(In millions of US dollars)

Country	Total	Exports	Imports	Balance
World	11,250.9	8,253.4	2,997.5	5,255.9
Japan	3,897.2	3,732.5	164.7	3,567.7
South Korea	1,454.8	1,383.2	71.6	1,311.6
Singapore	1,158.7	118.5	1,040.2	-921.7
Australia	1,012.5	978.6	33.8	944.8
China	985.6	581.2	404.4	176.9
Indonesia	672.7	605.6	67.1	538.6
Malaysia	540.1	43.9	496.2	-452.3
New Zealand	418.0	415.2	2.8	412.3
Thailand	231.3	89.8	141.5	-51.7
United Kingdom	219.5	5.4	214.1	-208.7

(…) data not available or not significant.

(n.s.) not specified.

SOURCE: *2011 Direction of Trade Statistics Yearbook,* New York: United Nations, 2011.

Balance of Payments – Brunei Darussalam (2009)

(In millions of US dollars)

Current Account		**3,977.0**
Balance on goods		4,889.0
Imports	-2,282.0	
Exports	7,172.0	
Balance on services		-519.0
Balance on income		52.0
Current transfers		-445.0
Capital Account		**-11.0**
Financial Account		**1,607.0**
Direct investment abroad		...
Direct investment in Brunei Darussalam		326.0
Portfolio investment assets		139.0
Portfolio investment liabilities		...
Financial derivatives		...
Other investment assets		644.0
Other investment liabilities		498.0
Net Errors and Omissions		**-5,420.0**
Reserves and Related Items		**-154.0**

(…) data not available or not significant.

SOURCE: *Balance of Payment Statistics Yearbook 2011*, Washington, DC: International Monetary Fund, 2011.

Further boosting trade, the ASEAN Trade in Goods Agreement (ATIGA) was approved in 2009 and put into effect on 17 May 2010. The ATIGA represents the next step in realizing the free flow of goods within the region. It simplifies the processes and procedures necessary to create a single market and production base, to be known as the ASEAN Economic Community (AEC). The AEC was scheduled to be in place by 2015. Major points of ATIGA include tariff liberalization, a simplification of the rules of origin, and implementation of such rules. The comprehensive agreement also demands greater transparency in regional trade liberalization, aiding the work of businesses and investors. The ATIGA supersedes the Common Effective Preferential Tariff Scheme (CEPT) adopted in 1992.

[32] BALANCE OF PAYMENTS

In 2010 Brunei Darussalam had a foreign trade surplus of $4.4 billion. Brunei's account surplus was estimated by the International Monetary Fund (IMF) at $4.318 billion in 2009, approximately 40% of GDP.

[33] BANKING AND SECURITIES

Brunei has no central bank. The banking industry is controlled by the Ministry of Finance in liaison with the Brunei Association of Banks, which sets the prime lending rate. Brunei's Association of Banks is, in turn, a member of the ASEAN Bankers Association, of which ten nations are members. The ASEAN Bankers Association's objectives include cooperation and collaboration for the mutual benefit of all members. Three permanent committees exist, dealing with: banking education; cooperation in finance, investment, and trade; and inter-regional relations. In 2008, there were nine banks operating in Brunei, in addition to four finance companies. Some of the banks were locally incorporated and others foreign, among them Malayan Banking, Berhard, and Citibank. The

International Bank of Brunei, in which the sultan has a 51% stake, was in 1993 renamed the Islamic Bank of Brunei.

The Brunei Investment Agency (BIA) manages the nation's external assets and General Reserve Fund. Brunei has investments in several foreign countries, including Malaysia, France, Australia, and India.

[34] INSURANCE

In 2011 several commercial insurance companies operated in Brunei, providing general and life insurance. Some offered *takaful*, or Islamic insurance, which is based on profit sharing.

[35] PUBLIC FINANCE

In 2010, the budget of Brunei Darussalam included US$6.889 billion in public revenue and $4 billion in public expenditures. Revenues minus expenditures totaled approximately US$2.889 million, a budget surplus amounting to 38.9% of GDP. Foreign reserves totaled US$1.36 billion at the end of 2009.

[36] TAXATION

Citizens of Brunei pay no income taxes and are the beneficiaries of generous welfare subsidies. However, the Chinese, who make up an estimated 16% of the population, are excluded from citizenship and these benefits. Only corporations are subject to taxation. Taxation on petroleum income is subject to a 55% rate. In 2006 the standard corporate tax rate was 30% on earnings; however, tax cuts over the next five years reduced it to 22%, according to a report by the IMF.

In 2011 Brunei had double-taxation agreements with the United Kingdom, Indonesia, Singapore, and China. Similar agreements were under development with several other primarily Asian nations. Double-taxation agreements lessen the tax burden for companies doing business in two countries and encourage trade and investment between the two countries taking part in the agreement.

Exemption from taxes can be granted by the Sultan in Council to industries deemed essential to the country's development. By Income Tax Order 2001, companies granted a Pioneer Certificate, foreign or domestic, are exempted from corporate income tax for periods of 2 to 20 years, depending on the size of their capital investment. Pioneer industries are those that have not been previously carried out in Brunei on a scale adequate to meet the nation's needs. Examples of pioneer products include various medicines, some types of clothing, and airline meals. Pioneer and export industries are also exempt from customs duties on imports of raw materials and capital goods.

[37] CUSTOMS AND DUTIES

Brunei levies tariffs ranging from zero to 30% on selected items and has a single-column tariff structure. The country joined ASEAN in 1984 and has reduced trade barriers with member nations.

[38] FOREIGN INVESTMENT

The Brunei Investment Agency (BIA), which is part of the Ministry of Finance, manages the country's foreign reserves. Established in 1983, its mission is to increase the real value of the reserves through a diverse investment strategy. BIA offices in London and

Brussels manage French and other European investments. Brunei in 2011 had holdings in many countries, including the United States, India, Japan, Western Europe, and the Association of Southeast Asian Nations (ASEAN) countries. In 2008 foreign investments were reported to be more than US$30 billion.

The Brunei government encourages more foreign investment by offering tax incentives and through its already attractive climate of requiring not personal income or capital gains taxes. However, foreign investors are encouraged to maintain some level of local participation in whatever enterprises they set up. At least half of the directors of any company must be residents of Brunei.

The World Bank reported foreign direct investment (FDI) net inflow of US$325 million in 2009. The country's foreign reserves remain healthy. FDI stocks stood at $10.045 billion in 2007 and comprised 81.1% of GDP. About US$698 million in FDI funds left the country in 2007 for investments elsewhere.

39 ECONOMIC DEVELOPMENT

Two major themes shape Brunei's economic development plans: careful use of its oil and gas resources to prolong the capacity of the reserves and gradual diversification beyond the petroleum sector. While Brunei has successfully managed its reserves and invested much of its excess revenue abroad, efforts to diversify the economy have been sluggish, at best. In 2011, two projects under development were a 500-megawatt (MW) power plant to provide power for an aluminum smelting operation and a container hub at Brunei's Muara Port. Both projects depend on foreign direct investors.

Another challenge Brunei faces is balancing both its labor force and ownership of its businesses between its residents and foreigners. About 40% of the country's work force consists of foreigners, despite stringent immigration regulations set up to maintain the social cohesion of Brunei's society. One of the country's long-term goals is to encourage Brunei Malays to participate more in business leadership while at the same time maintaining its numerous relationships with multinational investors.

40 SOCIAL DEVELOPMENT

In September 2009, the government began briefing private sector companies on the requirements of the new Supplemental Contributory Pension (SCP) scheme, which amends the existing retirement plan known as the Employees' Trust Fund and supplements the old age pension plan. The SCP took effect 1 January 2010. The SCP is designed to ensure that every worker will be prepared to retire at the compulsory age of 60 with a minimum pension of US$400 per month. All citizens and permanent residents in the public, private, and informal sector are required to join the SCP and must contribute a minimum of 3.5% of their earnings each month. Mandatory contributions by employers vary. The SCP is expected to provide for workers for a minimum of 20 years after mandatory retirement.

The state provides free medical care, with remote regions served by mobile clinics and a flying doctor service. There is also a school health service, as well as an employer liability system for workers' compensation.

The social influence of Islamic traditions and customs has increased under the national philosophy of *Melayu Islam Beraja*.

There are no specific laws against domestic violence, and spousal rape is not regarded as a crime. However, protection against spousal abuse is provided under Islamic family law. The law does prohibit sexual harassment. Women are permitted to own property, though Islamic inheritance laws provide for men to receive twice the inheritance of women. Women have nearly equal access to employment and business opportunities.

41 HEALTH

According to the CIA, life expectancy in Brunei Darussalam was 78 years in 2011. In 2009, the country spent 2.3% of its GDP on healthcare, amounting to US$791 per person. There were 14 physicians, 49 nurses and midwives, and 27 hospital beds per 10,000 inhabitants. The fertility rate was 1.86, while the infant mortality rate was 11.5 per 1,000 live births. In 2008, the maternal mortality rate, according to the World Bank, was 21 per 100,000 births. It was estimated that 99% of children were vaccinated against measles. The CIA calculated HIV/AIDS prevalence in Brunei Darussalam to be about less than 0.1% in 2003.

Brunei's government has invested heavily in health care, with the result that the US State Department in 2011 described Brunei's health care system as one of the best in Asia, saying that malaria had been eradicated in Brunei, and cholera nearly so.

42 HOUSING

Since the mid-1970s, the government has supported an ongoing housing program through the National Development Plan to encourage and support homeownership for all citizens. In the ninth National Development Plan, covering the years 2007 through 2012, 16.4% of planned spending was allocated for national housing.

The National Housing Scheme provides 20- to 30-year subsidized rate loans for building new houses. However, there is sometimes a long waiting list for those wishing to receive such loans. Through the Landless Indigenous Citizens Housing Scheme (LICS), the government has constructed at least eight housing project sites to offer affordable, modern housing to low-income residents. In July 2011 the sultan presented keys to 650 new homeowners who had applied in previous years for the National Housing Scheme or LICS program.

In 2011 it was estimated that about half of all Bruneians owned their own homes, but the demand for new housing was also believed to be greater than the supply, as many young couples are choosing to buy homes of their own rather than live in multigenerational households. Homes and apartment buildings in Brunei are similar in construction to those found in Western countries.

43 EDUCATION

The state provides its citizens free education from kindergarten up, including university training abroad. Education is compulsory between the ages of 5 and 12. Six years of primary school are followed by seven years of secondary education, the latter being divided into three years of junior secondary, two years of senior secondary, and two years of university preparation studies. The official policy is to promote bilingual education, Malay and

English, in all government-supported schools. The academic year runs from August to May.

In 2009 the World Bank estimated that 93% of age-eligible children in Brunei Darussalam were enrolled in primary school. Secondary enrollment for age-eligible children stood at 89%. Tertiary enrollment was estimated at 17%. Of those enrolled in tertiary education, there were 100 male students for every 199 female students. The pupil-teacher ratio at the primary level was 13 to 1 in 2008; at the secondary level the ratio was 11 to 1. Foreigners often attend private schools, including mission schools. There are numerous religious academies.

There are two teacher-training colleges and five vocational technical schools, including an agricultural training center. Brunei also has a university, established in 1985, and institutes of education and technology. The University of Brunei Darussalam has faculties for education, arts and social sciences, science, and management and administration. Many students continue their education in foreign universities at government expense. The adult literacy rate in 2009 was estimated at 92.7%.

As of 2010, public expenditure on education was estimated at 4.4% of GDP, or 8.55% of total government expenditures.

44 LIBRARIES AND MUSEUMS

The University of Brunei at Gadon holds 29,000 volumes, while the Brunei Museum houses 60,000 volumes. The Dewan Bahasa dan Pustaka Library, established in 1963, is the primary public system. In 2009 it had over 385,000 volumes and subscriptions to more than 200 magazines and journals. It sponsors four district branch locations in the country and provides mobile library services with five library vans.

Notable museums include the Brunei Museum, which exhibits ethnology and the history of Borneo Island; the Malay Technology Museum; the Royal Regalia Gallery, a fine arts museum opened in 1992; and the Royal Brunei Armed Forces Museum, which features the world's fastest patrol boat.

45 MEDIA

As of 2009, there were 80,500 telephone mainlines and 425,000 mobile cellular phones in use throughout the country, averaging 107 mobile phone subscriptions per 100 people. Telephone service is generally considered to be of excellent quality. The government-operated Radio Television Brunei broadcasts radio programs in English, Malay, and Chinese, and television programs in Malay and English. In 2010, there was only one television station (government-owned). Three Malaysian television channels can also be accessed by some viewers. Two satellite television networks are also available, offering about 28 different channels, including the Cable News Network, the British Broadcasting Corporation World News, and several entertainment and sports channels. As of 2010, there were four government-owned radio channels and two operated by the British Forces Broadcast Service.

In 2010, the country had 50,997 Internet hosts. As of 2009, there were some 314,900 Internet users in Brunei, or 80 regular Internet users per 100 citizens.

The only commercial daily newspaper serving Brunei is the English *Borneo Bulletin,* with a circulation of 25,000 in 2010. The government publishes the Malay weekly *Peilta Brunei* (2002 circulation 45,000) and a monthly English newsletter, *Brunei Darussalam* (14,000). There is one other Malay-language press, the Media Permata, which circulates approximately 5,000 newspapers. The *Straits Times* of Singapore circulates widely in Brunei, as do Chinese papers from Sarawak.

In 2001, legislation took effect that places several restrictions on press freedoms. Editions of foreign newspapers or magazines with articles that were found to be objectionable, embarrassing, or critical of the Sultan, the royal family, or the government may be banned from the country. Journalists deemed to have published or written "false and malicious" reports may be subjected to fines or prison sentences. Magazine articles with a Christian theme have been censored. The government also retains the right to close down any newspaper without prior notice.

46 ORGANIZATIONS

There are four chambers of commerce in the country, including the International Chamber of Commerce and Industry in Bandar Seri Begawan. The Consumers' Association of Brunei (est. 2002) has worked to promote improvements in living conditions and legal rights of workers as well as serving as a consumer advocate group. There are some professional organizations, such as the Brunei Malay Teachers Association and the Women Business Council. There are also organizations promoting education and research in several fields, such as the Brunei Association for Science Education and the Medical Association in Brunei.

The powerful Religious Affairs Department permeates daily life; its activities include sponsoring Islamic pilgrimages and establishing village mosque committees. The Council of Women of Negara Brunei Darussalam, founded in 1985, strives to improve the economic, cultural, and social status of women. Nongovernmental youth movements in Brunei include the Brunei Youth Council, Boy Scouts, and Girl Guides. Sports facilities tend to be privately maintained, with some athletic groups sponsored through the Brunei Amateur Athletic Association. The Brunei National Olympic Committee coordinates activities for national youth sports federations.

There is a national chapter of the Red Crescent Society.

47 TOURISM, TRAVEL, AND RECREATION

Known for the abundance of flora and fauna in its rainforests and national parks, Brunei is growing as a unique tourism destination. Among Brunei's newest and most remarkable sights is the sultan's 1,788-room palace, built at a reported cost of $300 million and topped by two gold-leaf domes. Native longhouses and trips up the Brunei and Tutong rivers are also tourist attractions. Visas are not required for stays of up to 90 days, but a valid passport and onward/return ticket are necessary.

The *Tourism Factbook*, published by the UN World Tourism Organization, reported 157,000 incoming tourists to Brunei in 2009; they spent a total of $254 million. Of those incoming tourists, there were 122,000 from East Asia and the Pacific. There were 3,501 hotel beds available in Brunei Darussalam, which had an occupancy rate of 39%. The estimated daily cost to visit Bandar Seri Begawan, the capital, was $290. The cost of visiting other cities averaged $123.

[48] FAMOUS PERSONS

Omar Ali Saifuddin (1916–86) was sultan from 1950 to 1967 and minister of defense from 1984 to 1986. His son, Muda Hassanal Bolkiah (Bolkiah Mu'izuddin Waddaulah, b. 1946), one of the wealthiest men in the world, has been sultan since 1967.

[49] DEPENDENCIES

Brunei has no territories or colonies.

[50] BIBLIOGRAPHY

Brunei Investment and Business Guide: Strategic and Practical Information. Washington, DC: International Business Publications USA, 2012.

Brunei Women in Culture, Business, and Travel: A Profile of Bruneian Women in the Fabric of Society. Petaluma, CA: World Trade Press, 2010.

Gunn, Geoffrey C. *New World Hegemony in the Malay World.* Trenton, NJ: Red Sea Press, 2000.

Leibo, Steven A. *East and Southeast Asia 2011.* Lanham, MD: Stryker-Post Publications, 2011.

Lindsey, Tim, and Kerstin Steiner. *Islam, Law, and the State in Southeast Asia: Volume 3: Malaysia and Brunei.* London, Eng.: I.B. Tauris, 2012.

Sidhu, Jatswan. *Historical Dictionary of Brunei Darussalam.* 2nd ed. Lanham, MD: Scarecrow, 2009.

World Trade Organization. *Trade Policy Review: Brunei Darussalam.* Geneva, Switzerland: WTO; Lanham, MD: Co-published by Bernan Associates, 2001.

CAMBODIA

Kingdom of Cambodia
Preahreacheanachakr Kampuchea

CAPITAL: Phnom Penh

FLAG: The flag has a red center field with a white silhouette of the temple complex at Angkor Wat. The center field is bordered top and bottom by blue bands.

ANTHEM: Nokoreach (Royal Kingdom).

MONETARY UNIT: The riel (KHR) is a paper currency of 100 sen. KHR1 = US$0.024 (or US$1 = KHR4,059) as of 2011. US dollars are also widely used in Cambodia.

WEIGHTS AND MEASURES: Both the metric system and traditional weights and measures are in general use.

HOLIDAYS: National Day, 9 January; New Year, April; Labor Day, 1 May; Feast of the Ancestors, 22 September; Independence Day, 9 November.

TIME: 7 p.m. = noon GMT.

¹LOCATION, SIZE, AND EXTENT

Situated in the southwest corner of the Indochina Peninsula, Cambodia has an area of 181,040 sq km (69,900 sq mi), extending 730 km (454 mi) NE–SW and 512 km (318 mi) SE–NW. It is bounded on the NE by Laos, on the E and SE by Vietnam, on the SW by the Gulf of Thailand, and on the W, NW, and N by Thailand, with a total boundary length of 2,572 km (1,598 mi). Comparatively, Cambodia is slightly smaller than the state of Oklahoma.

In 1982, Cambodia signed an agreement with Vietnam on their mutual maritime frontier. A treaty delineating the land border was signed in December 1985.

Cambodia's capital city, Phnom Penh, is located in the south-central part of the country.

²TOPOGRAPHY

Cambodia is a country with forested mountains and well-watered plains. The central part of the country forms a gigantic basin for the Tonle Sap, or Great Lake, and the Mekong River, which flows down from Laos to the southern border with Vietnam. Between the Tonle Sap and the Gulf of Thailand lie the Cardamom Mountains and the Elephant Range, which rise abruptly from the sea and from the eastern plains. In the north, the Dangrek Mountains, 320 km (200 mi) long and 300–750 m (1,000–2,500 ft) high, mark the Thailand frontier. The short coastline has an important natural harbor, Kompong Som Bay (Chhâk Kâmpóng Saôm), where the port of Kompong Som (Kâmpóng Saôm, formerly Sihanoukville) is located.

The Mekong and the Tonle Sap dominate the life and economy of Cambodia. The Mekong overflows during the rainy season, depositing vast quantities of alluvial soil and causing the Tonle Sap to increase in size from about 2,590 sq km (1000 sq mi) to almost 24,605 sq km (9,500 sq mi).

³CLIMATE

The climate is tropical, with a wet season from May through November and a dry season from December to April. Temperatures range from 10 to 38°C (68 to 97°F), and humidity is consistently high. Rainfall averages 127–140 cm (50–55 in) in the central basin to about 508 cm (200 in) in the southwestern mountains.

⁴FLORA AND FAUNA

There are over 8,200 plant species in Cambodia. Palm, rubber, coconut, kapok, mango, banana, and orange trees are common, as well as bamboo and the high, sharp grass of the savannas. In addition, Cambodia is home to 127 species of mammals, 521 species of birds, 116 species of reptiles, and 11 species of amphibians. This calculation reflects the total number of distinct species residing in the country, not the number of endemic species. Cranes, pheasants, wild ducks, and mammals such as elephants, monkeys, gibbons, bats, deer, wild oxen, tigers, and bears exist in Cambodia. Fish, snakes, and insects are present in abundance. Irrawaddy dolphins are found along the Mekong River.

⁵ENVIRONMENT

Deforestation and the resulting soil erosion cause significant environmental problems in Cambodia. By 1985, logging activities, the clearing of the land for agricultural purposes, and war damage had resulted in the destruction of over 300 sq km (116 sq mi) of forestland. Between 1983 and 1993, the nation's forests and woodlands were reduced by an additional 11.3% to 11.7 million hectares (29 million acres). In 1995, there were only 9 million hectares (22 million acres). The World Resources Institute reported that Cambodia had designated 4.15 million hectares (10.27 million acres) of land for protection as of 2006.

According to a 2011 report issued by the International Union for Conservation of Nature and Natural Resources (IUCN), threatened species included 37 types of mammals, 24 species of birds,

15 types of reptiles, 3 species of amphibians, 42 species of fish, and 30 species of plants. Endangered species in Cambodia include three species of gibbon, several species of wild dog and wild cat, leopard, tiger, elephant, brow-antlered deer, kouprey, giant catfish, Indian python, Siamese crocodile, and estuarine crocodile.

Three-fourths of Cambodia's wildlife areas have been lost through the destruction of its forests, and strip mining for gems in the western part of the country poses an additional threat to the nation's biodiversity and wildlife habitats. Natural fisheries have been endangered by the destruction of Cambodia's mangrove swamps. There are three Ramsar Wetlands Sites. Cambodian NGOs work to preserve the ecosystems and endangered wildlife of the country, and villagers have staged protests to demand protection of forests and rivers. The dredging of sand from the Mekong River for export to Singapore has been condemned for its effect on the river ecosystem and fishing livelihoods.

Water resources totaled 476.1 cu km (114.2 cu mi), while water usage was 4.08 cu km (.979 cu mi) per year in 2008. Domestic water usage accounted for 2% of total usage and agricultural for 98%. Per capita water usage totaled 290 cu m (10,241 cu ft) per year. Most rural dwellers do not have access to pure water. The UN reported in 2008 that carbon dioxide emissions in Cambodia totaled 4,437 kilotons. Air pollution resulted from industry and traffic in urban areas and burning for agricultural purposes.

⁶POPULATION

The US Central Intelligence Agency (CIA) estimated the population of Cambodia to be 14,701,717 in 2011, which placed it at number 66 in population among the 196 nations of the world. In 2011, approximately 3.7% of the population was over 65 years of age, with another 32.2% under 15 years of age. The median age in Cambodia was 22.9 years. There were 0.96 males for every female in the country. The population's annual rate of change was 1.698%. The projected population for the year 2025 was 19,000,000. Population density in Cambodia was calculated at 81 people per sq km (210 people per sq mi).

Estimates of Cambodia's population varied with the assessment of the impact of the 1970–75 war and the millions killed in its tumultuous aftermath. At the war's end, in April 1975, the population of the capital, Phnom Penh, had swollen to nearly 3 million because of a mass influx of refugees. The new government immediately embarked on a forced evacuation of all urban areas, and by March 1976, only 100,000–200,000 were thought to remain in Phnom Penh. After the installation of the People's Republic of Kampuchea (PRK) in 1979, the population of Phnom Penh began to increase.

According to the CIA, 20% of the population lived in urban areas in 2010, and urban populations had an annual rate of change of 3.2%. The largest urban area was Phnom Penh, with a population of 1.5 million as of 2009.

⁷MIGRATION

Estimates of Cambodia's net migration rate, according to the CIA as of 2011, amounted to -0.34 migrants per 1,000 citizens. The total number of emigrants living abroad was 350,400, and the total number of immigrants living in Cambodia was 335,800. The first migrations in independent Cambodia took place during the 1950s and 1960s, when ethnic Chinese were permitted to settle in the mountainous and wasteland areas and cultivate land that otherwise would have remained unproductive. After 1970, about 200,000 Vietnamese living in Cambodia were repatriated to Vietnam, ostensibly as a security measure. With the insurgent victory in April 1975, most of the country's remaining Vietnamese were reported to have immigrated to Vietnam. In addition, thousands of refugees, including many former officials and military personnel, fled across the Thai border or were evacuated by US aircraft.

The new government launched a sweeping nationwide resettlement program under which some 2.5–3 million persons were moved from Phnom Penh and other cities into the countryside, where they were organized into work brigades. The food shortage in rural areas was only slightly less critical than in the cities, and widespread starvation led to the deaths of an estimated one million people during the transition. After the installation of the new government in January 1979, continued fighting and political instability resulted in a new exodus of refugees. About 630,000 Cambodians left the country between 1979 and 1981, of which about 208,000 were able to resettle in other countries, including 136,000 in the United States. Most of the rest remained in camps on the border with Thailand and were repatriated to Cambodia in May 1993.

Between 1979 and 1987, there was a new migration of ethnic Vietnamese into Cambodia. Official sources insisted that the total number was under 60,000 and consisted mostly of residents who had left in the early 1970s; opposition groups contended that the number totaled over 500,000 and was intended to consolidate Vietnamese control over the country.

In 1997, the conflicts between government forces and the National Army of Democratic Kampuchea (Khmer Rouge) drove rural populations from their homes. In 1997 and 1998, the United Nations High Commissioner for Refugees (UNHCR) assisted up to 60,000 Cambodian refugees who had fled the fighting in northwest Cambodia. Also in 1997, the UNHCR helped several thousand ethnic Vietnamese fisher families return to their Cambodian homes after having camped on the Vietnam border. Following the peace settlement between the government of Cambodia and resistance forces in December 1998, the repatriation of approximately 36,000 refugees remaining in camps in Thailand was rapidly implemented.

In December 2010, the government of Cambodia announced plans to close one of its Vietnamese refugee centers as of 1 January 2011. At the time of the announcement, the center housed 62 asylum-seekers known as Montagnards, members of an ethnic minority group that sided with the US forces during the Vietnam War. The Cambodian government refused to let these refugees settle in the country, and insisted that they either seek asylum in a third nation or return to Vietnam, where many feared persecution.

⁸ETHNIC GROUPS

Over 90% of the entire population are ethnic Khmers, descendants of the original population in the area. The largest minority groups are the Vietnamese, estimated at 5% of the population, and the Chinese, estimated at 1%. Groups designated as other comprise the remaining 4% of the population. National minorities include the Cham and a number of small indigenous groups.

⁹LANGUAGES

Khmer, the national language, is spoken by about 95% of all inhabitants. Unlike Thai or Vietnamese, Khmer is a non-tonal language; most words are monosyllabic. The Vietnamese and the Chinese use their own languages, as do other minorities. French and English are also spoken.

¹⁰RELIGIONS

Buddhism has been the state religion since 1989. About 93% of all inhabitants practice Theravada Buddhism. Many people also practice some forms of animism. The Chinese and most Vietnamese in Cambodia practice a traditional mixture of Mahayana Buddhism, Taoism, Confucianism, ancestor worship, and animism. In 2010, there were about 464,000 Muslims (between 3.5% and 5% of the population), representing the four branches: Shafi, Wahhabi, Iman-San, and Kadiani. The ethnic Chams are predominantly Muslim. About 2% of the population is Christian, with over 100 separate organizations or denominations represented.

In 1975, the Khmer Rouge government virtually abolished Buddhism, disrobing some 70,000 monks. Islamic spokesmen have claimed that 90% of Cambodia's Muslims were massacred after 1975. Of some 6,000 Roman Catholics left in Cambodia at the time of the revolution, only a few survived. The PRK regime that came to power in 1979 permitted the return of religious practice, and hundreds of Buddhist monasteries were reopened. Freedom of religion is guaranteed by the constitution and the government reportedly respects this right in practice. All religious groups register through the Ministry of Cults and Religions in order to build places of worship and freely conduct religious activities. In 2007, the ministry placed restrictions on door-to-door evangelism by non-Buddhist groups.

¹¹TRANSPORTATION

Land transport facilities suffered wholesale destruction during the 1970–75 war. Cambodia's first railway, a 385-km (239-mi) single-track from Phnom Penh to Paoy Pet, was badly damaged in the fighting; a 262-km (163-mi) line from Phnom Penh to Kampong Sam was also disabled. The line to Kampong Sam was restored in November 1979, and a Phnom Penh-Băttâmbâng railway was reopened in February 1980. Improvised railcars are used in some rural areas.

The CIA reports that Cambodia has a total of 38,093 km (23,670 mi) of roads, of which 2,977 km (1,850 mi) are paved. All major cities and towns are connected with Phnom Penh by highway, and from there roads connect to Vietnam, Laos, and Thailand. The US-built 214-km (133-mi) Khmer-America Friendship Highway links Phnom Penh with Kampong Sam. According to the Cambodian government, there were 139,634 motor vehicles in 2006.

Cambodia has approximately 2,400 km (1,491 mi) of navigable waterways. The Mekong is the most important inland waterway. The river port of Phnom Penh has been upgraded. Until 1975, Saigon was the major transshipment point for outgoing Cambodian and incoming foreign goods; the opening of the deep-water port of Kompong Som made Cambodia largely independent of Vietnam for oceangoing shipping. In 2010, the merchant marine fleet consisted of 620 vessels of 1,000 GRT or over. About 426 of these were foreign-owned.

There are 17 airports, which transported 183,503 passengers in 2009, according to the World Bank. As of 2009, Cambodia had six airports with paved runways. There was one heliport. The main airport is at Phnom Penh; there are regular flights between Phnom Penh and Hanoi, Bangkok, Beijing, and other Asian cities. The airport at Siem Reap, which also has direct international flights, is used by tourists visiting Angkor Wat.

¹²HISTORY

Most Cambodians are descendants of the Khmers, who in the 6th century established the Indian-influenced Angkor Empire and for the next 900 years ruled the area of present-day Cambodia. According to legend, the founder of the Khmer dynasty was Kampu Svayambhuva, from whose name "Kampuchea" derives. From the 10th to the 14th centuries, after years of military expansion, the Khmers reached their apogee. Their empire extended over most of Southeast Asia (from central Vietnam southwest into the Malay Peninsula, and from Thailand north to the border of Burma, now known as Myanmar). Angkor, the capital city, was a flourishing complex of great temples, palaces, and shrines. In the subsequent centuries, however, continuing attacks by the Thai (who captured Angkor in 1431) and the Vietnamese weakened the empire, and by the end of the 18th century much of Cambodia was dominated by the Thai and Vietnamese.

In 1863, the king of Cambodia placed the country under French protection. The French, joining Cambodia to Laos and Vietnam to form French Indochina, ruled the protectorate until the end of World War II. Cambodian nationalism received its greatest impetus during the World War II period, while Japan controlled Indochina. King Norodom Sihanouk, who had ascended the throne in 1941 and had been held a virtual prisoner under the Japanese occupation, proclaimed Cambodia independent in 1945 then yielded before a temporary resumption of the French protectorate, enforced by Allied troops, which occupied Phnom Penh. Cambodia became a constitutional monarchy on 6 May 1947 and was granted nominal independence within the French Union on 9 November 1949. King Sihanouk, meanwhile, assumed leadership of Cambodia's growing nationalist movement. On 17 October 1953, during the height of the French Indochina War (1946–54), he was granted full military control of his country by France. Sihanouk, a skilled politician, abdicated in March 1955 in favor of his father and mother, King Suramarit and Queen Kossamak, and then emerged as prime minister with the unanimous support of the national legislature. King Suramarit died on 31 April 1960, but Prince Sihanouk, although retaining the title of chief of state, did not return to the throne. During the French Indochina War, Communist-controlled Vietminh troops from Vietnam operated in Cambodia (1954) and gave support to a small Khmer Communist movement.

The Geneva agreements of July 1954, which ended the French Indochina War, secured the withdrawal of French and Vietminh troops from Cambodia and the surrender of most of the Khmer rebels. During the next 15 years, Sihanouk sought to keep Cambodia neutral in the deepening Vietnam conflict. This proved increasingly difficult, however, as the National Liberation Front (also known as the Vietcong) used Cambodian border areas as bases from which to launch attacks on the Republic of Vietnam (RVN or South Vietnam) and as the United States in 1969 launched an undeclared air war against the guerrilla sanctuaries. On 18 March 1970, Marshal Lon Nol, prime minister and army chief, overthrew the chief of state, Prince Sihanouk, while the prince was on a visit to the USSR; the right-wing coup ended 1,168 years of rule by Khmer monarchs. Sihanouk thereupon took up residence in Beijing, where, on 5 May, he announced formation of the Royal Government of National Union of Kampuchea (GRUNK) under the political auspices of the National United Front of Kampuchea. In the interim, on 30 April, US President Richard M. Nixon announced an "incursion" into Cambodia of 30,000 US and 40,000 Vietnamese troops with the object of destroying their opponents' strongholds along the Vietnam border. The operation was terminated on 30 June with its military objectives apparently unfulfilled, and bombing of the region continued to devastating effect on Cambodia's economy.

Formal diplomatic relations with the United States, severed by Sihanouk in 1965, were resumed on 2 July 1970, and Sihanouk was condemned to death (in absentia) three days later. On 9 October, the Lon Nol government in Phnom Penh abolished the monarchy and changed Cambodia's name to the Khmer Republic. In elections held during June 1972, Lon Nol was elected president of the republic. Pressures from GRUNK insurgents continued to mount, especially following the conclusion of a cease-fire in Vietnam in January 1973 and the withdrawal of the last US troops from that country in March. US aid to the Lon Nol government had been substantial, totaling $1.18 billion in military supplies and $503 million in economic assistance for the whole of the 1970–75 period with most of the aid concentrated in the early years of direct involvement. With the reversal of US policy in Vietnam, however, support for the Khmer Republic began to taper, and by the start of 1975, the Lon Nol government had plunged into a struggle for survival. In January, GRUNK military forces, generally referred to as the Khmer Rouge, launched a major offensive aimed at gaining control of the Mekong River and isolating Phnom Penh. Fierce and costly fighting ensued over the next three months, with the United States undertaking a massive airlift to Phnom Penh in February to fend off starvation and military collapse. On 1 April, the strategic Mekong ferry crossing at Neak Luong fell to the insurgents, clearing the way for a direct, final assault on the capital. On that day, Lon Nol fled the country, to be followed by much of the ruling hierarchy. On 17 April, the Khmer Republic government officially capitulated to GRUNK forces, which were commanded by Khieu Samphan.

The GRUNK government reported in March 1976 that the war had resulted in about 800,000 deaths. On 5 January 1976, the country was officially renamed Democratic Kampuchea (DK). On 20 March, the first general elections were held for a new 250-member People's Assembly. The assembly on 14 April named Khieu Samphan chairman of the state presidium, replacing Prince Sihanouk, who had returned to the country in September 1975, as head of state. Pol Pot was named prime minister. Even before these political reforms were undertaken, the GRUNK government had undertaken a massive reorganization of the country's economic and social life. As an initial step, the new government ordered the near-total evacuation of Phnom Penh, where food, shelter, and medical resources had been stretched to the limit by the press of some 2.5 million refugees. The country was plunged into almost complete isolation, even from its neighbors in Vietnam and Laos.

Currency was abolished, social relations completely overhauled, religion almost eradicated, education suspended, and families divided. From two million to three million people may have died from starvation, exhaustion, disease, or massacre under the Pol Pot (Cambodian Communist leader Saloth Sar) regime.

Meanwhile, tensions with Vietnam (a traditional enemy of Cambodia) were growing, and there were border clashes during 1977 and 1978. In December 1978, Vietnam invaded Cambodia with a force of more than 100,000 troops; by January 1979, they had installed a pro-Vietnamese government, the People's Republic of Kampuchea (PRK), headed by Heng Samrin, a former division commander in the GRUNK army. The PRK had to contend with resistance from the very beginning, and the Khmer Rouge rebels, who had fled to the jungles in the west and south, continued to harass the government despite Vietnamese counteroffensives. In order to improve its international standing, the Khmer Rouge began in 1981 to pursue a united front strategy; Pol Pot, branded with the 1975–79 atrocities, reportedly withdrew into the background, and Khieu Samphan, supposedly the most moderate of the Khmer Rouge leaders, emerged as chief spokesman. In 1982, the Khmer Rouge formed the Coalition Government of Democratic Kampuchea (CGDK), with two non-communist factions led by Prince Sihanouk and a former politician, Son Sann. The PRK had won recognition only from Vietnam, the former USSR, and their allies, with most nations joining the United States and China in giving qualified support to the CGDK.

Vietnam announced the repatriation of 50,000 troops from Cambodia in 1988 and the complete withdrawal of troops by late 1989 or early 1990. In 1989, Prince Sihanouk resumed leadership of the Democratic Kampuchean government-in-exile, later resigning from leadership of the National Front for an Independent, Neutral, Peaceful and Co-operative Cambodia (FUNCINPEC). As a further sign of its commitment to change, in April 1989, an extraordinary session of Cambodia's National Assembly ratified amendments to the constitution: the name of the country was changed to the State of Cambodia (SOC), and Buddhism was reinstated as the state religion. Hun Sen met in Bangkok with the Thai prime minister, who appealed for a cease-fire among the four Cambodian factions: the government of the Kampuchean People's Revolutionary Party (KPRP) installed by the Vietnamese (the Heng Samrin government), and an umbrella organization, The National Government of Cambodia (NGC), comprised of three antigovernment groups : FUNCINPEC, the Khmer Rouge, and the Khmer People's National Liberation Front (KPNLF). The Khmer Rouge rejected this suggestion, and throughout 1988 and 1989, continued to make military gains. In September 1989, Vietnam completed the timely withdrawal of its forces from Cambodia.

In June 1990, Prince Sihanouk and Hun Sen signed a conditional cease-fire in Bangkok. The UN Security Council in late August endorsed a plan for a comprehensive settlement in Cambodia: UN supervision of an interim government, military arrangements for the transitional period, free elections, and guarantees of the country's future neutrality. A special representative of the UN secretary-general would oversee the proposed United Nations Transitional Authority in Cambodia (UNTAC), and the UN would also assume control of government ministries. The four Cambodian factions accepted the UN proposals in September 1990. In addition, they agreed to the formation of the Supreme

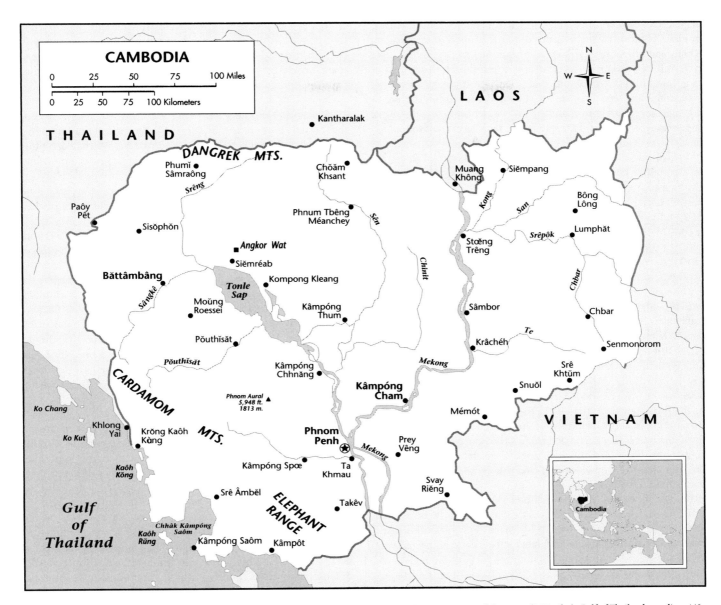

CAMBODIA

| 0 | 25 | 50 | 75 | 100 Miles |
| 0 | 25 | 50 | 75 | 100 Kilometers |

THAILAND

LAOS

DANGREK MTS.

Kantharalak

Phumĭ Sâmraông

Paôy Pêt

Srĕng

Chŏăm Khsant

Muang Không

Siĕmpang

Sĭsôphŏn

Phnum Tbêng Méanchey

Sĕn

Bông Lông

Kŏng

Băttâmbâng

Angkor Wat

Siĕmréab

Kompong Kleang

Tonle Sap

Stœ̆ng Trêng

Srêpôk

Lumphăt

Săn

Moŭng Roessei

Sângkê

Kâmpóng Thum

Chinit

Sâmbor

Chbar

Pŏuthĭsăt

Pŏuthĭsăt

Kâmpóng Chhnăng

Krăchéh

Te

Chbar

Senmonorom

Mekong

Phnom Aural 5,948 ft. 1813 m.

Kâmpóng Cham

Srê Khtŭm

Snuŏl

Ko Chang

Ko Kut

Khlong Yai

Krŏng Kaôh Kŭng

CARDAMOM MTS.

Phnom Penh

Mémót

VIETNAM

Mekong

Prey Vêng

Kaôh Kŏng

Kâmpóng Spœ

Ta Khmau

Svay Riĕng

Gulf of Thailand

Kaôh Rŭng

Chhâk Kâmpóng Saôm

Srê Âmbĕl

ELEPHANT RANGE

Takêv

Kâmpóng Saôm

Kâmpôt

Cambodia

LOCATION: 102°31′ to 108°E; 10° to 15° N. BOUNDARY LENGTHS: Laos, 541 kilometers (336 miles); Vietnam, 1,228 kilometers (763 miles); Gulf of Thailand coastline, 443 kilometers (275 miles); Thailand, 803 kilometers (499 miles). TERRITORIAL SEA LIMIT: 12 miles.

National Council (SNC), with six representatives each from the national government of Cambodia and Phnom Penh regime.

In 1991, Prince Sihanouk was elected to the chairmanship of the SNC and resigned as leader of the resistance coalition and as president of the national government of Cambodia. His replacement in both positions was Son Sann. From August through October, the SNC worked out the details of the armed forces reduction and election procedures. Elections would be held to establish a constituent assembly comprised of 120 seats, which would subsequently become a legislative assembly. The electoral system would be proportional representation based on the 21 provinces. The constituent assembly would adopt a new constitution. In October, the SOC released hundreds of political prisoners. The Kampuchean (or Khmer) People's Revolutionary Party (KPRP), the communist party aligned with the Vietnamese communist movement,

changed its name to the Cambodian People's Party (CPP), removed the hammer and sickle from the party emblem, and replaced Heng Samrin as chairman of the central committee with the conservative Chea Sim. Hun Sen was elected vice chairman of the CPP.

On 23 October 1991, what was hoped to be an end to 13 years of war in Cambodia was achieved with the signing of the Comprehensive Political Settlement for Cambodia by the 4 Cambodian factions and 19 participating countries. The agreement called for the creation of a United Nations Transitional Authority in Cambodia (UNTAC) to carry out the peacekeeping operations, which included the demobilization of 70% of each faction's army and enforcement of a cease-fire; the verification of the withdrawal of foreign forces; administering the country until an election in 1993; the assurance that human rights would be maintained; and the repatriation of 600,000 refugees and internally displaced people. In November 1991, a threat to the tenuous peace process occurred when a mob attacked Khmer Rouge leaders Khieu Samphan and Son Sen in a Phnom Penh villa. The SNC government's response was slow, and it was alleged that Hun Sen sanctioned this incident and that Vietnamese officials were involved in it. In December, violent student demonstrations protesting high-level corruption and in support of human rights were suppressed by the armed forces. Several high-level government officials were dismissed based on corruption charges.

Yasushi Akashi was appointed as the UN Special Representative to Cambodia in charge of UNTAC in 1992. The UN Security Council authorized mine-clearing operations and a 22,000-member peacekeeping force to establish UNTAC at an estimated cost of $2 billion. The Khmer Rouge denied free access to the zones it controlled and refused to comply with the disarmament phase. In May 1992, the Khmer People's National Liberation Front (KPNLF), the political and military party formed by Son Sann for the purpose of resisting the Vietnamese, was transformed into a political party called the Buddhist Liberal Democracy Party (BLDP). FUNCINPEC also became a party, headed by Prince Ranariddh. In August, the registration of parties for elections began. In September, the Khmer Rouge made two new demands: the resignation of Akashi and a redrawn border between Cambodia and Vietnam. In October 1992, UNTAC began voter registration. The Khmer Rouge boycotted voter registration and escalated destruction of bridges and roads, effectively cutting off its territory in the northeast from the rest of the country. The Khmer Rouge then announced the formation of the Cambodian National Unity Party to contest the elections. Ethnic and racial tensions were increasing as the Khmer Rouge incited and escalated actions against the Vietnamese based on deep-rooted Cambodian sentiments towards the Vietnamese.

In January 1993, Prince Sihanouk ceased cooperation with UNTAC and suggested that a presidential election be held prior to the legislative election, but, in February, he reversed his position. Voter registration was completed in February; registered voters numbered 4.5 million, and 20 political parties were registered. The election was set for 23–25 May 1993. The CPP intimidated its political rivals with attacks and stopped the gradual expansion of the Khmer Rouge into Phnom Penh government territory. In a dry-season offensive, the SOC attacked three of four of the Khmer Rouge's most important zones.

In early 1993, the Khmer Rouge refused to disarm and attacked UN offices, cars, helicopters, and personnel, as well as attacking ethnic-Vietnamese civilians. The UN goal was to have all refugees back in Cambodia by mid-April for elections. By 19 March, some 330,000 refugees were repatriated. The election took place 23–28 May 1993; four million Cambodians, or 85% of those registered, voted. FUNCINPEC won the election with 45% of the vote, or 58 of 120 seats in the constituent assembly; the CPP took 38% of the votes, or 51 seats in the assembly; the BLDP had over 3% of the votes, which gave them 10 seats; and, MOULINAKA (Movement for the Liberation of Kampuchea, a pro-Sihanouk group formed in 1979 by Kong Sileah, considered an offshoot of FUNCINPEC) took one seat. To the CPP, its political defeat was an unacceptable surprise, and it demanded a revote and threatened riots. The CPP's two leaders, hardliner Chea Sim and reformer Hun Sen, were engaged in an internal struggle. FUNCINPEC leader Prince

Norodom Ranariddh and CPP Prime Minister Hun Sen served as co-chairmen of the government, and control of the major ministries was divided. In August, for the first time the three government factions, royalist FUNCINPEC, former Phnom Penh ruling regime CPP, and the BLDP agreed to joint military operations.

Cambodia's new constitution was adopted on 21 September 1993. Prince Norodom Sihanouk was crowned king, resuming the title first bestowed on him in 1941. The minister of economics and finance, Sam Rainsy, set about to root out official corruption and centralize Cambodia's budget. The two co-prime ministers, First Premier Norodom Ranariddh and Second Premier Hun Sen, asked King Sihanouk for sanction to fire Rainsy, but instead received a statement praising Rainsy, who was becoming a popular hero.

The Khmer Rouge had expanded its territory, and its weaponry was intact. Cambodia had been critical of Thailand's support for the Khmer Rouge, which benefited Thailand with lucrative trade in gems and timber. The 1994 dry-season campaign by the Cambodian government against the Khmer Rouge was a failure. The need to remove the land mines infesting the fields of Cambodia was a high priority. For the first time since the 1970s, the United States provided military aid to Cambodia. The national assembly voted to outlaw the Khmer Rouge and seize its assets. The Khmer Rouge began to weaken in 1995, with mass defections of guerrilla fighters. Marginalization of the Khmer Rouge continued in 1996, as the group split between the leadership of ailing Pol Pot and a breakaway faction headed by Ieng Sary.

In February 1997, FUNCINPEC's Ranariddh began an alliance with Sam Rainsy in strong opposition to Hun Sen's CPP. A brief coup d'état set up Hun Sen as the sole power in charge. Ranariddh fled Cambodia and Hun Sen's forces killed many of Ranariddh's party leaders and supporters in the days immediately following the coup. Hun Sen moved to establish CPP legitimacy, with the party winning a flawed national election in July 1998 with 41.4% of the vote to FUNCINPEC's 31.7%. Ranariddh was able to return as an opposition leader, and he, along with Sam Rainsy, whose party gained 14.3% of the vote, condemned the election as rigged.

Throughout 1998, the Khmer Rouge continued to disintegrate, as Pol Pot, the architect of their genocidal regime, died on 15 April, and other leaders surrendered or were captured. With the entire top echelon of living Khmer Rouge leaders in custody, Cambodian government concerns from 1999 through 2001 centered on how to bring them to justice. Hun Sen's preference was for a series of trials conducted within Cambodia's own legal system, while the UN, fearing mere "show trials," called for an international tribunal. In August 2001, King Sihanouk signed legislation creating a special tribunal to prosecute the Khmer Rouge members responsible for the deaths of an estimated 1.7 million people through execution, torture, starvation, and hard labor. The trials were to be presided over by three Cambodian judges and two foreign judges. In 2004, an agreement between the UN and the Cambodian government on a tribunal system was formalized.

In October 2004, King Sihanouk abdicated after a 60-year reign. His son Norodom Sihamoni was chosen as the new monarch of Cambodia by a throne council and crowned on 29 October. The 51-year-old new monarch had grown up in Europe with a keen interest in Cambodian culture, particularly dance. He is unmarried, with no heirs, and has avoided the political involvement and commentary that marked his father's reign. In September 2008, he issued a royal pardon for his half-brother, Prince Ranariddh, who had been convicted of embezzling from the FUNCINPEC political party.

In February 2005, opposition leader Sam Rainsy left Cambodia after parliament stripped him of his immunity from prosecution, leaving him open to defamation charges brought by the ruling coalition. That December, Rainsy, in exile in France, was convicted by a Cambodian court of defaming Hun Sen. He was sentenced to nine months in prison. However, in February 2006, Rainsy received a royal pardon and returned to Cambodia after a year in exile. In May of that year, parliament voted to abolish prison terms for defamation. Rainsy again went into exile and was sentenced in absentia in September 2010 for false claims about Vietnam taking land from Cambodia.

After the UN had given the green light to Cambodia's international tribunal in 2005, the tribunal began questioning suspects about allegations of genocide in July 2007. That September, the most senior surviving member of the Khmer Rouge, Nuon Chea, was arrested and charged with crimes against humanity. In November 2007, the tribunal held its first public hearing, which was a request for bail from a former prison head, Kaing Guek Eav, better known as Comrade Duch. Also in November, Ieng Sary and Ieng Thirith, husband and wife who held senior positions in the Khmer Rouge government, were arrested and charged with crimes against humanity.

In July 2010, the infamous "Duch" was sentenced to 19 years in prison. It was the first conviction of a major Khmer Rouge leader, but many Cambodians considered it a lenient sentence for a man who oversaw the torture and killing of thousands. The four elderly surviving top Khmer Rouge leaders, Khieu Samphan, Nuon Chea, Ieng Sary, and Ieng Thirithm finally went on trial for genocide in June 2011, but court proceedings were delayed and not expected to resume until early 2012.

The 11th century Hindu temple Preah Vihear, a UNESCO World Heritage Site on Cambodia's western border, has repeatedly been a source of conflict between Cambodia and Thailand, each of which claim ownership. The International Court of Justice ruled in 2008 that Cambodia was the rightful owner. Military conflict between Cambodian and Thai forces erupted around the temple compound from February to April 2011, with deaths on both sides.

13 GOVERNMENT

Cambodia was a constitutional monarchy from 6 May 1947 until 9 October 1970, when Marshal Lon Nol formally established the Khmer Republic. On 30 April 1972, a new constitution was passed by a national referendum. It provided for a directly elected president and a bicameral legislature consisting of an elective 126-member national assembly and a 40-member senate. Upon the surrender of the Lon Nol government to insurgent forces on 17 April 1975, rule by the Royal Government of National Union of Kampuchea (Gouvernement Royal de l'Union Nationale de Kampuchea—GRUNK) was installed in Phnom Penh, with Prince Norodom Sihanouk as titular head of state. A new constitution, effective 5 January 1976, provided for a unicameral, 250-member people's assembly, elected for a five-year term by universal suffrage of citizens over age 18. The PRK government, installed in January

1979, enacted a new constitution in June 1981. Under this constitution, an elected national assembly was the supreme organ of state power; it was headed by a seven-member council of state, which the assembly elected from among its own members.

On 23 October 1991, the UN peace accord was signed by Cambodia's four factions. From 23–28 May 1993, a six-day election, the first multiparty election in more than 20 years, was held to determine the 120 members of the national assembly. This newly elected assembly was authorized to draft a constitution. The assembly ratified a new constitution on 21 September 1993. The monarchy was reestablished, and commitments to liberal democracy, the rule of law, and women's rights were included. Prince Norodom Sihanouk ratified the constitution and again became king of Cambodia.

In 1998, the number of seats in the assembly was increased to 122. As of 2011, the number of seats stood at 123.

In March 1999, amendments to Cambodia's 1993 constitution allowed the formation of an unelected 61-seat senate. Two senate seats are appointed by the king; two are elected by the national assembly; and 57 are elected by "functional constituencies." Members of the national assembly are elected by popular vote. Members of the assembly and the senate members serve five-year terms.

14 POLITICAL PARTIES

Under Sihanouk, the People's Social Community Party (Sang Kam) was the most important political group. In the 1955, 1958, 1962, and 1966 elections, with a platform of nonalignment, economic aid, and development, it captured all seats in the national assembly. Exiled in Beijing following his overthrow by Lon Nol in March 1970, Sihanouk allied himself with Cambodia's leftist insurgents under a group called the National United Front of Kampuchea (Front National Uni de Kampuchea—FNUK). Under the Khmer Republic government headed by Lon Nol, five political groups came to the fore. The Socio-Democratic Party (SDP), Lon Nol's own group, was quickly established as the most powerful political organization. Centrist opposition groups included the Republican Party and the Democratic Party. In the presidential elections held in June 1972, Lon Nol, the SDP's candidate, won by a relatively narrow margin of 55%.

With the victory of their forces in April 1975, leaders of the pro-communist FNUK became the dominant political power in Kampuchea. The leading element in FNUK was the Khmer Communist Party (KCP), founded in 1951 and dominated by radicals Pol Pot and Khieu Samphan. Khieu Samphan was named prime minister of the new regime, while Pol Pot remained party head. During the next few years, the Pol Pot faction systematically purged all suspected pro-Vietnamese members from the party organization. In late 1978, opposition elements, headed by Heng Samrin, formed the Kampuchean National United Front for National Salvation (KNUFNS) in an effort to overthrow the Pol Pot regime. Following a Vietnamese invasion in December, Heng Samrin became the head of the pro-Vietnamese PRK government installed in January 1979. In 1981, the KNUFNS was renamed the Kampuchean United Front for National Construction and Defense, the primary mass organization in the PRK. Popularly known as the Khmer Rouge, the movement allied during the

1980s with two non-Communist factions, the Sihanoukists and Son Sann's KPNLF.

Prince Sihanouk's main political organization, formed in 1981, was known as the National United Front for an Independent, Neutral, Peaceful, and Cooperative Cambodia, or its French acronym, FUNCINPEC; he resigned as its head in 1989. In 1992, FUNCINPEC was registered as a political party for the 1993 elections, and Prince Norodom Ranariddh was elected president. The Coalition Government of Democratic Kampuchea (CGDK), the tripartite, anti-Vietnamese resistance group formed in June 1982, changed its name to the National Government of Cambodia (NGC) in 1990.

In 1992, the Khmer People's National Liberation Front (KPNLF), headed by Son Sann, formed the Buddhist Liberal Democratic Party (BLDP). The military wing of the KPNLF was the KPNLAF, the Khmer People's National Liberation Army, formed under Son Sann in 1979. Although it boycotted the elections and attempted to undermine the peace process, the Khmer Rouge had also formed a party to contest the elections, the Cambodian National Unity Party, headed by Kieu Samphan and Son Sen.

The Kampuchean People's Revolutionary Party (KPRP), the Communist Party originally installed by Vietnam in 1979 as the People's Republic of Kampuchea (PRK), was also known as the Heng Samrin Government in the late 1980s. In 1991, the KPRP dropped the word "Revolutionary" from the party name, becoming the Khmer People's Party or Cambodian People's Party (CPP). Hun Sen remained chairman of the council of ministers, a position he had held since 1985. At an extraordinary party congress, 17–18 October 1991, Chea Sim was elected party president, replacing Heng Samrin, and Hun Sen was elected party vice president; these events signaled a shift from hard-line communist ideology to a reformist position prior to the UN-supervised elections. Chea Sim remained president of the national assembly.

In the coalition government following the 1993 election, Hun Sen was made second premier, and FUNCINPEC's Ranariddh became first premier. Hun Sen was able to push Ranariddh out of that position with a brutal coup d'état in 1997, and the CPP won enough seats in the 1998 election to establish Hun Sen as sole prime minister.

Perennial opposition leader and anti-corruption crusader Sam Rainsy transformed his unrecognized Khmer Nation Party into the eponymous Sam Rainsy Party, which won significant assembly seats in the 1998 election. Sam Rainsy has repeatedly stooped to race-baiting directed against Cambodia's Vietnamese population during his political career. At the same time, he has been an eloquent spokesman for increased democratization and openness in Cambodia and a persistent antiauthoritarian thorn in Hun Sen's side. He went into exile in 2005 and again in 2010.

In May 2002, Prince Ranariddh's half-brother formed a new party, the Norodom Chakrapong Khmer Soul party, to contest the national elections in July 2003, in which the CPP won the most votes and eventually formed a coalition government with FUNCINPEC. Hun Sen continued as prime minister. Violence again marred the election, with more than a dozen political killings during the campaign and voting.

FUNCINPEC and the CPP formed an alliance in September 2005 for mutual support in the 2008 general election, with CPP potentially backing Prince Ranariddh as prime minister. Prince Ranariddh was ousted from FUNCINPEC leadership in October 2006, and convicted in March 2007 on corruption charges related to the sale of party headquarters. The 27 July 2008 parliamentary elections were won by the CPP, with about 69% of the vote, for 90 seats. Opposition parties and international observers believed that the election was conducted unfairly, with voter bribery and media manipulation benefiting the CPP.

¹⁵LOCAL GOVERNMENT

Under the constitution adopted on 21 September 1993, People's Committees were established in all provinces, municipalities, districts, communes, and wards to be responsible for local administration, public security, and local order. Within this system, provincial officials and the governor effectively controlled the armed forces and security services, tax collection, civil service—and through them 80% of the Cambodian population. The country's provinces remained under the sway of the Cambodian People's Party (CPP) and responded to their old political loyalties rather than the central authority of the government. To alter this system, the assembly passed laws to secure central control of the economy. Effective 1 January 1994, a national budget and financial laws were enacted to try to ensure that all revenues came completely and directly to the national treasury. Provincial corruption remains a severe problem; communications and infrastructure are underdeveloped within Cambodia; and smuggling is rife.

In February 2002, Cambodia held its first local elections in 23 years. The CPP claimed victory in all but 23 of the 1,621 communes. FUNCINPEC won only seven of the village communes. At least 20 political activists, mostly from opposition parties, were killed in the run-up to the elections. The proportion of female candidates in the elections was 16%. Local elections were again held on 1 April 2007, with the CPP dominant, winning 1,592 of 1,621 communes. There were allegations of widespread vote-buying and fraud, allegations that were somewhat offset by less violence than in the 2002 local elections. As of 2011, local government is administered by 23 provinces (*khett*) and the city of Phnom Penh (*krong*).

¹⁶JUDICIAL SYSTEM

The 1993 constitution of the Kingdom of Cambodia provides due process protections such as presumption of innocence and also guarantees an independent judiciary. Efforts are still being made to train judicial personnel to implement these principles and to ensure basic human rights for Cambodians.

The legal system consists of lower courts, an appeals court, and a Supreme Court. There is also a military court system. The 1993 constitution provides for a constitutional council, and a supreme council of magistrates, which appoints and disciplines judges. With low revenues and high crime rates plaguing Cambodia, the justice system is burdened by substandard police procedures. Many serious crimes, notably political killings, go unsolved. Judicial corruption, police corruption, and abusive imprisonment conditions remain endemic. The long-delayed trials of Khmer Rouge officials for genocide and crimes against humanity are conducted as a joint tribunal by the United Nations and the Cambodian court system, with Cambodian and foreign judges, prosecutors and defense lawyers.

17 ARMED FORCES

The International Institute for Strategic Studies reports that armed forces in Cambodia totaled 124,300 members in 2011. The force is comprised of 75,000 from the army, 2,800 from the navy, 1,500 from the air force, and 45,000 members of provincial forces. Armed forces represent 2.4% of the labor force in Cambodia. Defense spending totaled $905.4 million and accounted for 3% of GDP.

18 INTERNATIONAL COOPERATION

Cambodia has been a member of the United Nations since 14 December 1955 and participates in the Economic and Social Commission for Asia and the Pacific (ESCAP) and several non-regional specialized agencies. Cambodia was admitted to the WTO 13 October 2004. Cambodia is also a member of the Asian Development Bank, the World Federation of Trade Unions, and G-77. Cambodia was accepted as the tenth member of the Association of Southeast Asian Nations (ASEAN) in 1999. The country is part of the Nonaligned Movement and a member of the Permanent Court of Arbitration. In environmental cooperation, Cambodia is part of the Basel Convention, the Convention on Biological Diversity, Ramsar, CITES, the Kyoto Protocol, the Montréal Protocol, MARPOL, and the UN Conventions on Climate Change and Desertification.

The Mekong River Commission (MRC) was founded by Cambodia, Thailand, Laos, and Vietnam in 1995 to coordinate regional development. Cambodia has strong trade, assistance, and diplomatic relations with China.

19 ECONOMY

Cambodia's economy has traditionally been based on agriculture. About 57.6% of the nation's workforce is employed in agriculture, most of which is small-scale, subsistence farming. About 85% of the cultivated area is devoted to the production of rice, while rubber trees account for a major part of the remainder. Prior to the war years, Cambodia's rice crop was usually ample enough to permit exports. The Tonle Sap is one of the major fishing reservoirs in Asia, and its products have played a key role in the Cambodian economy and diet. Cattle breeding is another important source of income.

Throughout the 1990s, Cambodia remained predominantly agricultural. In 1991–93, the transition period from a command to a market-driven system and the presence of 22,000 UN personnel aided the Cambodian economy, although the growth was mainly urban and barely affected rural areas. Consumer goods were readily available in Phnom Penh and other cities. On 4 January 1992, then-US-President George H.W. Bush announced the lifting of the US trade embargo against Cambodia.

The gross domestic product (GDP) averaged 6.4% from 2001 to 2004, due in large part to rises in tourism and the garment export industry. Inflation and unemployment remained at unthreatening levels. In 2005, a WTO agreement forced Cambodia to compete with other lower-priced producing countries. The country experienced 9% growth in 2007 and remained committed to supporting high labor standards.

The tourism industry continued to grow, and, in 2007, the government began a joint venture for two national airlines. In 2008, clothing accounted for more than 80% of all exports. The garment industry is the third-largest earning sector of the economy, after tourism and agriculture. GDP rate of change in Cambodia, as of 2010, was 6%. Inflation stood at 4.1%, and unemployment was reported at 3.5%.

20 INCOME

The CIA estimated that, in 2010, the GDP of Cambodia was $30.18 billion. The CIA defines GDP as the value of all final goods and services produced within a nation in a given year and computed on the basis of purchasing power parity (PPP) rather than value as measured on the basis of the rate of the exchange based on current dollars. The per capita GDP was estimated at $2,100. The annual growth rate of GDP was 6%. The average inflation rate was 4.1%. For 2009, it was estimated that agriculture accounted for 33.4% of GDP, industry 21.4%, and services 45.2%. According to the World Bank, remittances from citizens living abroad totaled $337.8 million or about $23 per capita and accounted for approximately 1.1% of GDP.

The World Bank reported that, in 2009, household consumption in Cambodia totaled $7.9 billion or about $538 per capita, measured in current US dollars rather than PPP. Household consumption includes expenditures of individuals, households, and nongovernmental organizations on goods and services, excluding the purchases of dwellings. It was estimated that household consumption was growing at an average annual rate of 1.6%. As of 2011, the most recent study by the World Bank reported that actual individual consumption in Cambodia was 86.0% of GDP and accounted for 0.04% of world consumption. By comparison, the United States accounted for 25.44% of world individual consumption. The World Bank also estimated that 43.9% of Cambodia's GDP was spent on food and beverages, 12.3% on housing and household furnishings, 1.6% on clothes, 6.6% on health, 6.2% on transportation, 0.2% on communications, 2.1% on recreation, 4.1% on restaurants and hotels, and 3.9% on miscellaneous goods and services and purchases from abroad.

It was estimated that, in 2007, about 31% of the population subsisted on an income below the poverty line established by Cambodia's government.

21 LABOR

As of 2010, Cambodia had a total labor force of 8.8 million people. Within that labor force, CIA estimates in 2009 noted that 57.6% were employed in agriculture, 15.9% in industry, and 26.5% in the service sector.

Although Cambodia's labor law provides the right for workers to form unions and bargain collectively, civil servants such as military personnel, judges, and teachers are excluded, along with household servants. In addition, aviation and maritime transport industry personnel are limited as to coverage, but can form unions. Forced or compulsory labor is also prohibited, but enforcement is inadequate and involuntary/unpaid overtime is widespread. Trade unions are concentrated in the footwear and garment industries. Relatively fair labor practices have been perceived as a competitive advantage for Cambodia over other lower wage exporting countries, because Cambodia could attract companies concerned about negative "sweatshop" images. This image advantage was marred by mass fainting and illnesses of exhausted workers at garment factories in 2011.

The global economic crisis of 2008–09, along with rising inflation, had a major impact on the garment workers themselves, as their $56 minimum monthly wage provided even less financial security than usual. Throughout 2010, a number of garment worker strikes took place, resulting in a $5-per-month increase in the minimum wage for workers in most unions.

A 48-hour work week and minimum safety and health standards are provided by law. However, these rules are not always enforced. Separate minimum wages are established for each sector of the economy, but average wages are so low that second jobs and subsistence agriculture are often necessary. In September 2010, over 200,000 garment workers went on a three-day strike to demand a living wage. The government proposed an increase of the garment workers' minimum wage from $50 per month to $61, but the unions called for $93. There were reprisals against leaders and workers involved in the strike, including arrests and hundreds of dismissals. In March 2011, an average of $10 per month was added to the $61 minimum wage for garment workers.

By law, the minimum legal working age is 15 years, with 18 as the minimum age for hazardous work. Minors between 12 and 15 can participate in light work that is not dangerous to their health and does not affect school attendance. However, enforcement remains inconsistent. Of all minors between the ages of 5 and 17, more than half (53%) are employed. About 71% are employed in the agricultural or forestry sectors, 21% in services or sales, and 7% in production.

22 AGRICULTURE

Agriculture remains the key sector in the economy. Roughly 21% of the total land is farmed. The country's major crops include rice, rubber, corn, vegetables, cashews, and tapioca. According to the UN Food and Agriculture Organization (UN FAO), in 2009, cereal production amounted to 8.5 million tons, fruit production 374,636 tons, and vegetable production 468,725 tons.

Rice provides the staple diet and prior to 1970 was Cambodia's major export, along with rubber. Production peaked at 3,200,000 tons in 1968; it began falling because of war. Upon coming to power in April 1975, the Pol Pot regime embarked on a major rice production program, but the highest output achieved was only 1,800,000 tons in 1976. During the 1980s, rice production gradually increased, from about 1,564,000 tons in 1980/81 to an estimated 1,680,000 tons in 1985/86. During the mid-1980s the Khmer Rouge government attempted to stimulate production by delaying its plans for collectivization of the countryside. In 1989, the new government returned agricultural land to the tiller, which significantly boosted food production; average annual production in 1989–91 was 2,524,000 tons. In the 2000s, five years of record yields, from expanded irrigation and double cropping, boosted rice production enormously. According to the US Department of Agriculture, in marketing year 2009/10, Cambodia's milled rice production reached 4.63 million tons, an increase of 2.4% over 2008/09. The government announced a goal of exporting 1 million tons of rice per year by 2015.

Rubber has traditionally been the second-most-important agricultural crop. However, rubber plantings, which covered 48,000 hectares (119,000 acres) in 1969, were almost completely destroyed by the end of 1971. By 2005–08, rubber production reached an estimated 20,000 tons per year, and increased to almost 50,000 tons in 2010. Cassava became another important plantation-grown crop, producing 3.5 million tons in 2009, according to the UN FAO.

23 ANIMAL HUSBANDRY

Livestock raised primarily by private households has traditionally supplied an important supplement to the Cambodian diet, and water buffalo are used to plow rice fields. The UN FAO reported that Cambodia dedicated 1.5 million hectares (3.71 million acres) to permanent pasture or meadow in 2009. During that year, the country tended 17 million chickens, 3.6 million head of cattle, and 2.2 million pigs. The production from these animals amounted to 71,667 tons of beef and veal, 133,038 tons of pork, 26,288 tons of poultry, 15,646 tons of eggs, and 80,115 tons of milk. Cambodia also produced 16,020 tons of cattle hide. In 2010, a revival of Cambodia's silk production was being attempted, with establishment of new silkworm farms.

24 FISHING

Production of freshwater fish, the main protein element in the Cambodia diet, traditionally ranks next to rice and rubber in the local economy. About half of Cambodia's freshwater catch comes from the Tonle Sap. Marine fishing developed significantly during the 1980s. In 2009, the annual harvest of fishery products totaled 515,000 tons, according to Cambodia's government. Fish and other seafood have remained primarily for domestic consumption rather than export.

25 FORESTRY

Approximately 57% of Cambodia is covered by forest, but very little of that is primary rainforest. According to the UN FAO, only 330,000 hectares (815,447 acres) of primary forest were left in 2005. Rampant illegal logging during the 1990s and continuing encroachment for fuel wood, agriculture, and rubber plantations have caused most of the loss of primary forest. The main products of the forest industry are timber, resins, wood oil, fuel, and charcoal. The UN FAO estimated the 2009 roundwood production at 118,000 cu m (4.17 million cu ft). The value of all forest products, including roundwood, totaled $20.1 million.

26 MINING

Cambodia's mineral resources, though limited, had not been extensively explored and developed in the 1980s and 1990s because of war, internal conflict, and the lack of appropriate legislation and policy to attract foreign investors. As part of the government's investment strategy, foreign investors are allowed full ownership of their mining investments in Cambodia. In 2009, the country produced aggregates, laterite blocks (estimated at 631,000 metric tons), phosphate rock, salt, sand (estimated at 14 million metric tons), gravel (estimated at 41,875 metric tons), and stones (estimated at 2.8 million metric tons). Other metallic minerals identified in the country were antimony, bauxite, chromium, copper, lead, manganese, molybdenum, silver, tin, tungsten, and zinc. In addition, Cambodia had resources of such industrial minerals as carbonate rocks, fluorite, quartz, silica sand, and sulfur. Iron deposits and traces of gold, coal, copper, and manganese have been reported in the Kampong Thum area. Substantial deposits of bauxite, discovered in the early 1960s north of Băttâmbâng and southeast of Phnom Penh, have yet to be worked. Potter's clay is common, and deposits of phosphates, used for fertilizer, existed in southern Kâmpât province and near Phnom Sampou. Precious gems were mined in the Pailin area and smuggled to Thailand. Highly valued gemstones, such as high-quality cornflower-blue sapphires and rubies, also have been found.

27 ENERGY AND POWER

The World Bank reported in 2008 that Cambodia produced 1.46 billion kWh of electricity and consumed 1.64 billion kWh, or 112 kWh per capita. Roughly 30% of energy came from fossil fuels. Per capita oil consumption was 358 kg. Firewood, often from defunct rubber plantations, is still used to produce steam for garment manufacturing. Attempts are being made to implement alternative fuels, such as biomass for factories and cheap solar panels for rural areas.

In 2005 oil and gas deposits were discovered offshore in Cambodian waters by the US multinational Chevron Corp., which as of late 2011 expected to produce oil in 2012, some of which would be for Cambodia's domestic use. Other petroleum deposits are located in a region of the Gulf of Thailand under competing claims by Cambodia and Thailand. With rapprochement between the two counties in late 2011, plans were made for joint development of that region.

28 INDUSTRY

Industrial activity had traditionally centered on the processing of agricultural and forestry products and on the small-scale manufacture of consumer goods. Rice milling has been the main food-processing industry.

Industrial expansion came to a virtual halt in 1970 with the outbreak of war. The Pol Pot government placed all industries under state control in 1975. In the course of the next four years, some 100 industries were abolished or destroyed. When the PRK took over in 1979, industrial plants began to reopen. By late 1985, there were a reported 60 factories in the state sector, producing household goods, textiles, soft drinks, pharmaceutical products, and other light consumer goods.

Efforts at recovery continued in the early 1990s, but were hampered by dilapidated equipment and shortages that continued to affect industrial production, principally textiles and rubber production. Construction in urban areas boomed with the signing of the Paris Peace Agreement in 1991. The garment export industry led the way for industrial development. In 1996, clothing industry exports more than doubled, with some 36 factories employing around 20,000 people. Industrial growth slumped in 1998 due to the effects of the Asian financial crisis, drought, and political disruptions. However, recovery was rapid in the industrial sector. From 1999–2001, the garment industry grew by 50%. According to the CIA, industry accounted for 21.4% of GDP in 2009. An industrial production growth rate of 5.7% was estimated for 2011.

29 SCIENCE AND TECHNOLOGY

The World Bank reported in 2009 that there were no patent applications in science and technology in Cambodia. The University of Health Sciences and the Institute of Technology are among the opportunities within Cambodia to pursue scientific training or research. The National Institute of Public Health conducts research independently and in collaboration with other institutes and universities. Other research centers include the Cambodian Research Center for Development (sustainable development), the Cambodian Agricultural Research and Development Institute, and the Cambodian Center for Study and Development in Agriculture (CEDAC). The government-affiliated Royal Academy of Cambodia serves as a comprehensive research and development center in social science, humanities, arts, science, and technology. Several research institutes and universities offer studies in science and technology focused on agriculture, forestry, and fisheries.

30 DOMESTIC TRADE

Phnom Penh has traditionally been Cambodia's principal commercial center. In 1986, the government began collecting license fees, rents, and utility fees from private businesses and substantially increased their taxes. Most retail shops are owned directly or subsidized by wholesalers. Sorya Shopping Center, opened in 2002, was the first indoor shopping mall, followed by the Sovanna Mall in 2008. Urban areas have supermarkets, wholesale outlets, and specialty stores. Villages rely on small shops and open food markets. E-commerce and online shopping has grown in popularity with Cambodians who have Internet access.

31 FOREIGN TRADE

Cambodia has traditionally been an exporter of primary products and an importer of finished goods. The country's normal trade patterns virtually disintegrated during the war as exports declined, and Cambodia was largely sustained by the US-subsidized imports. Under the Pol Pot regime, foreign trade ceased. The US trade embargo against Cambodia was lifted in January 1992 by President George H. W. Bush. With the installation of the PRK government, foreign trade began to rise in volume. Foreign trade is legally restricted to licensed private-sector firms and government agencies, although there is still considerable smuggling between Cambodia and Thailand.

Principal Trading Partners – Cambodia (2010)

(In millions of US dollars)

Country	Total	Exports	Imports	Balance
World	12,530.0	5,030.0	7,500.0	-2,470.0
United States	2,033.1	1,903.4	129.7	1,773.7
China	1,936.0	1,383.7	552.3	831.4
China	1,249.7	65.0	1,184.7	-1,119.7
Thailand	838.5	149.4	689.1	-539.8
Singapore	584.6	429.2	155.4	273.9
Vietnam	582.7	96.3	486.5	-390.2
Taiwan	487.1	10.9	476.2	-465.3
Canada	278.4	274.2	4.2	270.1
South Korea	272.3	24.5	247.8	-223.4
United Kingdom	241.6	235.2	6.5	228.7

(…) data not available or not significant.

(n.s.) not specified.

SOURCE: *2011 Direction of Trade Statistics Yearbook*, New York: United Nations, 2011.

Cambodia imported $6.005 billion worth of goods and services in 2008, while exporting $4.687 billion worth of goods and services. Major import partners in 2009 were China, 22.6%; Vietnam, 12.7%; Hong Kong, 12.4%; Thailand, 11.9%; South Korea, 5.4%; and Singapore, 5.4%. Cambodia's major export partners were Hong Kong, 33%; the United States, 31.2%; and Singapore, 9.7%. Cambodia's major exports include garments and footwear, rice, rubber, fish, and timber. Imports include petroleum, construction materials, cigarettes, gold, pharmaceuticals, machinery, and motor vehicles.

In an expected boost for trade, the ASEAN Trade in Goods Agreement (ATIGA), approved in 2009, entered into force on 17 May 2010. The ATIGA represented the next step in realizing the free flow of goods within the region by simplifying the processes and procedures necessary to create a single market and production base—known as the ASEAN Economic Community (AEC)—by 2015. Major points of ATIGA include tariff liberalization, a simplification of the rules of origin, and implementation of such rules. The comprehensive agreement also demands greater transparency in regional trade liberalization, aiding the work of businesses and investors. The ATIGA supersedes the Common Effective Preferential Tariff Scheme (CEPT) adopted in 1992.

Cambodia is expected to become a full member of the ASEAN-China free trade area by 2015. This trade agreement went into force 1 January 2010 between the founding members of ASEAN and China. A major point of the free trade agreement is the elimination of tariffs on nearly 90% of imported goods. In terms of population, this is the largest free trade area in the world.

The US-Cambodia bilateral Trade and Investment Framework Agreement (TIFA) was signed in 2006.

32 BALANCE OF PAYMENTS

Cambodia's balance-of-payments position showed a deficit every year during the period 1954–74. Transactions with other

Balance of Payments – Cambodia (2010)

(In millions of US dollars)

Current Account		-879.2
Balance on goods		-1,647.5
Imports	-6,790.7	
Exports	5,143.2	
Balance on services		655.9
Balance on income		-533.1
Current transfers		645.5
Capital Account		331.0
Financial Account		747.0
Direct investment abroad		-20.6
Direct investment in Cambodia		782.6
Portfolio investment assets		-36.7
Portfolio investment liabilities		...
Financial derivatives		...
Other investment assets		-643.2
Other investment liabilities		664.8
Net Errors and Omissions		-48.4
Reserves and Related Items		-150.3

(…) data not available or not significant.

SOURCE: *Balance of Payment Statistics Yearbook 2011*, Washington, DC: International Monetary Fund, 2011.

countries essentially ceased under the Pol Pot regime, when China conducted Kampuchea's external financial dealings. From 1979, Kampuchea continued to run a substantial trade deficit, much of which had been financed by grant aid and credits extended by the USSR and Vietnam.

Exports of goods and services reached $3.2 billion in 2004, up from $2.6 billion in 2003. Imports grew from $3.0 billion in 2003, to $3.7 billion in 2004. The resource balance was consequently negative in both years, reaching -$400 million in 2003, and -$500 million in 2004. The current account balance was also negative, deteriorating from -$105 million in 2003, to -$262 million in 2004.

By 2010, Cambodia had a foreign trade deficit of $972 million, amounting to 2.3% of GDP. According to the CIA, as of December 2010 Cambodia had foreign reserve and gold holdings of $3.802 billion.

33 BANKING AND SECURITIES

The National Bank of Cambodia (NBC) was initially established in December 1954, when Cambodia officially ceased to be a French colony. However, the bank and all other banking operations in the country ceased in April 1975, when the Pol Pot government seized power. In 1980, the bank was reborn as the People's Bank of Kampuchea when a money economy was reintroduced. In 1992, the national assembly restored the bank's original name. An independent organization, monetary policy is the bank's primary function, specifically price stability. It is also responsible for regulating the nation's banking and non-banking financial sectors. It has licensing approval and de-licensing powers and is the bank of issue for Cambodia. In 1991, the government created a state commercial bank to take over the commercial banking operations of the national bank. There were at least 50 commercial banks operating in 2001. Banks in Cambodia include the Cambodian Commercial Bank, Cambodian Farmers Bank, and the Cambodian Public Bank.

Cambodia's first stock exchange opened in July 2011, with transactions conducted in the local currency, the riel, although dollar transactions account for 90% of deposits and credits in Cambodia's banks. No companies were listed when the exchange opened, and the licensed securities traders were largely from other countries.

34 INSURANCE

The insurance industry is still in its early stages in Cambodia, with most insurance bought by foreign investors. Six insurance companies were operating in Cambodia as of 2011: Forte, Cambodia National, Asia Insurance, Campubank Lonpac, Infinity, and Cambodia-Vietnam Insurance. According to the General Insurance Association of Cambodia, in 2010 premiums increased 24% to $24.9 million, over $20.08 million in 2009. Fire insurance (25%) was the largest share of premium revenue, followed by motor insurance (20%).

35 PUBLIC FINANCE

All government budgets of the two decades preceding 1975 were marked by an excess of expenditures over domestic revenues; foreign aid and treasury reserves made up the difference. There probably was no domestic public finance system during 1975–78; any public funds in that period came from China. During the 1980s,

Public Finance – Cambodia (2009)

(In billions of riels, central government figures)

Revenue and Grants	6,610.8	100.0%
Tax revenue	4,163	63.0%
Social contributions	...	...
Grants	1,828.8	27.7%
Other revenue	619	9.4%
Expenditures	7,614.5	100.0%
General public services	...	...
Defense	...	...
Public order and safety	...	...
Economic affairs	...	...
Environmental protection	...	...
Housing and community amenities	...	...
Health	...	...
Recreational, culture, and religion	...	...
Education	...	...
Social protection	...	...

(...) data not available or not significant.

SOURCE: *Government Finance Statistics Yearbook 2010*, Washington, DC: International Monetary Fund, 2010.

public expenditures were financed by the former USSR, either directly or through Vietnam. From 1989–91, the public deficit nearly tripled as a result of falling revenue collection. As assistance from the Soviet bloc ceased after 1990, monetary expansion soared to cover the deficit. In 1992, with hyperinflation imminent, the government began a series of stabilization efforts to halt the fiscal deterioration. In the late 1990s and 2000s, foreign aid continued to enable public expenditures, but export and tourism revenues supported to the government budget as well.

In 2010, the budget of Cambodia included $1.413 billion in public revenue and $2.079 billion in public expenditures. The budget deficit amounted to 5.9% of GDP. In total, $4.428 billion of the debt was held by foreign entities.

36 TAXATION

Until 1975, indirect taxes were the most profitable source of domestic revenue, especially such monopoly excises as the sales tax on salt. Other indirect taxes included those on alcohol, tobacco, sugar, radios, and livestock. Taxes ceased to exist with the abolition of currency during the Pol Pot regime and were replaced by payments in-kind. In 1984, the PRK introduced an agricultural tax on profits earned by private farmers. The tax reportedly amounted to about 10% of total output. In 1986, taxes on private business were increased, which forced some shopkeepers out of business. As of 2010, Cambodia had a progressive salary tax of 0 to 20%, corporate tax of 20%, and value added tax (VAT) of 10%. The Finance Act in 2010 added a property tax of 0.1% on buildings and non-agricultural land.

37 CUSTOMS AND DUTIES

Cambodia has simplified its tariff system and eliminated most non-tariff barriers to trade. Customs duties are divided into four basic categories. The rate is 35% for finished products, alcohol, petroleum, vehicles, precious metal, and gems. The rate is 15% for capital goods, machinery, and locally available raw materials. The rate is 7% for primary products and raw materials. Goods including medical and educational materials are exempt from import tariffs but are still subject to the 10% VAT. Cambodia lowered customs duties to 0 to 5% for fellow ASEAN states, to comply with the ASEAN Free Trade Area (AFTA) deadline of 2010.

38 FOREIGN INVESTMENT

There was little private foreign capital in pre-1975 Cambodia. French capital in rubber plantations represented more than half of the total investment. Foreign investment was prohibited under the Pol Pot regime and was not resumed under its successor, the People's Republic of Kampuchea (PRK). As part of Cambodia's economic reforms, the July 1989 Foreign Investment Law and the regulations implementing the law contained in the May 1991 subdecree on foreign investment created a favorable foreign investment climate in Cambodia.

A foreign investment law was adopted by the national assembly on 4 August 1994. It guaranteed that investors shall be treated in a nondiscriminatory manner, except for land ownership; that the government shall not undertake a nationalization policy which adversely affects private properties of investors; that the government shall not impose price controls on the products or services of an investor who has received prior approval from the government; and that the government shall permit investors to purchase foreign currencies through the banking system and to remit abroad those currencies as payments for imports, repayments on loans, payments of royalties and management fees, profit remittances, and repatriation of capital. In October 1999, the government entered into a three-year program monitored by the International Monetary Fund that included as a priority goal making the country more attractive for foreign direct investment. In February 2000, this program was complemented by a World Bank program aimed at revising Cambodia's 1994 Law on Investment.

Companies from Thailand, Singapore, Taiwan, Hong Kong, South Korea, China, Vietnam, France, and the United States have invested in Cambodia, with projects including hotels, petroleum exploration, and cellular telephone systems. The primary hindrances to foreign investment have been the lack of infrastructure and endemic corruption. By 2002, over 100 US companies and companies representing US products and services were active in Cambodia. Foreign direct investment (FDI) in Cambodia was a net inflow of $530.2 million according to World Bank figures published in 2009. FDI represented 5.07% of GDP.

39 ECONOMIC DEVELOPMENT

Until 1975, Cambodian governments sought aid from public and private foreign sources and attempted to improve the climate for private foreign capital investment, although the volume of investment was small. Both Sihanouk and Lon Nol also increased local control of economic activities within the country. Aliens were prohibited from engaging in 18 professions or occupations, including those of rice merchant and shipping agent. The Sihanouk government promoted economic development through two five-year plans designed to improve the nation's light industrial sector and its educational and technological infrastructure. Progress was mixed. Strained economic conditions were a factor leading to the overthrow of Sihanouk in 1970. The outbreak of war following his fall brought almost all major production to a halt. The economic objectives of the 1975–79 Pol Pot regime were centered almost entirely on agriculture and the improvement of the irrigation network. Self-sufficiency was stressed, and foreign aid was almost nil, except for an estimated $1 billion from China.

When the PRK government took over, it inherited a shattered economy and a depleted population. The 1986–90 five-year plan stressed growth in the agricultural sector, the restoration of light industry (which faces shortages of raw materials and electrical supply), gradual socialist transformation of ownership, dependence upon the former USSR and its allies for foreign assistance, and an increase of economic cooperation with its Indochinese neighbors. The PRK signed a number of aid, trade, and cooperation agreements with the former USSR and other Eastern European countries and was receiving substantial technological aid from neighboring Vietnam. Development assistance from the CMEA bloc totaled an estimated $700 million between 1980 and 1984. The PRK moved slowly on its plan to transform the Cambodian economy to full socialist ownership. A small private manufacturing and commercial sector was recognized by the constitution in 1981, and farmers were introduced to collectivization through the formation of low-level "solidarity groups" which combined socialist and private ownership. PRK plans were to advance more rapidly toward socialist transformation during the 1990s. However, since the mid-1980s, the emphasis was placed on private sector economic activities. Newly introduced market-oriented reforms dismantled the old central planning regime.

In 1991, at the Tokyo Conference on the Rehabilitation and Reconstruction of Cambodia, $880 million in assistance was pledged to Cambodia by donor countries and multilateral institutions. An additional $80 million in aid was pledged by the Asian Development Bank, and the World Bank planned a $75-million assistance program. Under Sam Rainsy, then minister of finance and economy, the national assembly passed a budget and new Financial Structure Laws effective 1 January 1994. The government's aim was to establish central control of the economy and at the same time strike out at corrupt practices.

In October 1999, after the disruptions caused by civil unrest and the Asian financial crisis (1997–98), the government entered into a three-year arrangement with the IMF under its Poverty Reduction and Growth Facility (PRGF). The program focused on bank restructuring, reform of the Foreign Trade Bank, reform of forestry policy, and strengthening the public sector accounting and expenditure management. Concurrently, a Structural Adjustment Credit (SAC) loan program under the World Bank was approved in February 2000. The SAC program included conditionals related to a military demobilization program, public expenditure management, forestry policy, and revisions to the 1994 Law on Investment (LOI).

The economy grew at impressive rates in the late 1990s and early 2000s. This expansion was fueled by a strong manufacturing sector, especially the garment industry, but growth fluctuated with international economic crises affecting consumer demand. Tourism and increased rice production also helped strengthen the economy in the first decade of the 21st century. Cambodia continues to rely on foreign development aid, with $951 million received in 2009 and $1.1 billion pledged for 2010, according to the Cambodian government.

⁴⁰SOCIAL DEVELOPMENT

The Sihanouk and Lon Nol governments enacted limited social legislation regulating hours of work, wages, and workers' compensation. During the Pol Pot period, the social fabric of the country was ravaged. Although installation of the PRK government brought an end to the wide-ranging trauma of 1975–79, overall social conditions in Cambodia remained among the worst in Southeast Asia during the 1980s.

Cambodia's constitution provides equal rights for women in areas including work and marriage. Women have property rights equal to those of men and have equal access to education and certain jobs. Women are the majority of employees in the manufacturing sector. However, traditional views of the roles of women have continued to prevent women from reaching senior posts in government and business. Domestic violence against women has remained a widespread problem. Domestic abuse victims rarely issue formal complaints. Trafficking in women and children for prostitution has continued both domestically and across the nation's borders.

Cambodia's human rights record under the Hun Sen government has included a number of abuses, including extrajudicial killings, arbitrary arrests, and other uses of excessive force by security forces. Impunity for such abuses has remained a problem. Discrimination against the ethnic Vietnamese persists. Land disputes often have turned violent, particularly when farmers are forcibly evicted.

⁴¹HEALTH

According to the CIA, life expectancy in Cambodia was 62 years in 2011. The country spent 5.7% of its GDP on healthcare, amounting to $42 per person. There were 2 physicians, 8 nurses and midwives, and 1 hospital bed per 10,000 inhabitants. The fertility rate was 2.9 children born per woman, while the infant mortality rate was 55 deaths per 1,000 live births. In 2008, the maternal mortality rate, according to the World Bank, was 290 deaths per 100,000 births.

It was estimated that 92% of children were vaccinated against measles. The CIA calculated HIV/AIDS prevalence in Cambodia to be about 0.5% in 2009. Other infectious diseases include malaria, dengue, diarrhea, hepatitis, tuberculosis, and typhoid fever. While deaths from malaria have fallen due to better diagnosis and treatment, Cambodia has malaria strains that are resistant to multiple drugs.

Landmines left from the war years continue to pose a danger to Cambodians.

⁴²HOUSING

The traditional type of dwelling consists of one or more rooms raised on stilts some 3 m (10 ft) above the ground. Urban architecture now uses concrete and tile for shop-houses and apartment buildings. According to a 2004 survey, there were about 2.3 million dwellings in the country; 2.03 million of which were located in rural areas.

In 2008, according to Cambodian government statistics, 61% of the population had access to safe drinking water, 26% of households used electricity for their main light source, and 38% had indoor toilets.

⁴³EDUCATION

Under the Pol Pot regime, all children were sent to work in the fields; education was limited to political instruction. Most of the educated class had been killed by 1979. According to PRK sources, only 50 of 725 university instructors and 307 of 2,300 secondary-school teachers survived the Pol Pot era.

As of 2011, six years of primary education (ages 6–12) is compulsory. Following this, there are six years of secondary education, of which only the first three are compulsory. The academic year runs from October to July. The primary language of instruction is Khmer. According to the CIA, as of 2009 public expenditure on education represented 2.1% of GDP.

In 2009, the World Bank estimated that 95% of age-eligible children in Cambodia were enrolled in primary school. Secondary enrollment for age-eligible children stood at 34%. Tertiary enrollment was estimated at 10%. Of those enrolled in tertiary education, there were 100 male students for every 54 female students. The 2008 Cambodian census found adult literacy to be 85% for men and 71% for women.

Institutes of higher education include the University of Phnom Penh, the Institute of Technology of Cambodia, the Royal University of Agriculture, Royal University of Fine Arts, and the University of Health Sciences.

⁴⁴LIBRARIES AND MUSEUMS

The National Library is located in Phnom Penh and holds about 103,635 volumes in a variety of languages, including Khmer, French, English, Russian, Vietnamese, and Thai. The national document collection comprises 8,327 documents. Also in the capital is the Buddhist Institute (25,000 volumes), which contains collections on religion, philosophy, literature, linguistics, history, and art. The École Française de l'Extrême-Orient has a research library in Phnom Penh (engaged in manuscript conservation) as well as an archeological facility with a library in Siem Reap, near Angkor Wat. The Hun Sen Library of the Royal University of Phnom Penh (RUPP) opened in January 1997 and now houses a collection of at least 50,000 items in Khmer, English, and French. The Toshu Fukami Library of the University of Cambodia is open to the public, offering over 30,000 volumes.

Cambodia, in effect, is a museum of the cultural achievements of the Khmer Empire. Surviving stone monuments, steles, temples, and statuary attest to a formidable and unique artistic heritage. Particularly imposing are the world-famous temple of Angkor Wat and the Bayon of Angkor Thom. In the chaotic years of the 1980s and early 1990s, there were many press reports of pillaging of these historic sites. The National Museum of Phnom-Penh (1917), an excellent repository of national art, has an extensive collection of Khmer art from the 5th through 13th centuries, and there are provincial museums with important collections. Tuol Sleng, used as a prison and as a torture and extermination center by the Khmer Rouge from 1975 to 1979, has been made into a museum commemorating the victims of the genocide.

⁴⁵MEDIA

In 2009, the CIA reported that there were 54,200 telephone landlines in Cambodia and 5.5 million cellular mobile phones in use, with mobile phone subscriptions averaging 38 per 100 people. Text messaging is inexpensive and very popular, with functions including mobile banking, medical surveys, and political organizing.

TV-Kampuchea began color transmission in 1986. In 2010, there were nine local television stations. Satellite television is popular and many Cambodians watch programs from Thailand, South Korea and other Asian countries. In 2009, there were about 50 radio stations in Cambodia.

The official news agency is the Agence Kampuchea Presse (AKP). Prominent newspapers in 2010, with circulation numbers listed parenthetically, included *Cambodia Daily* (2,000) and *Reaksmei Kampuchea* (15,000). There are at least 100 newspapers in all, including weeklies, biweeklies, and monthlies, mostly in the Khmer language. Many receive significant funding from political parties or the government. There are several English language newspapers (the daily Phnom Penh Post, founded 1992, is the oldest) and magazines, as well as newspapers in Chinese and French.

In 2010, the country had 5,452 Internet hosts. In 2009, there were some 78,500 Internet users in Cambodia. The use of social media such as Facebook, Twitter, and the local Angkor One, grew in 2010–11 due to cheaper Internet and smartphone access. Cambodian bloggers, known as "cloggers," cover politics (often cautiously), tourism, and Khmer literature, among other subjects.

The constitution provides for freedom of speech and press, but the government has limited the press in practice. The violent intimidation of journalists which occurred in the 2000s has abated, but intimidation through lawsuits and self-censorship remained common in 2010–11. The Voice of America Khmer service faced contempt of court charges in 2011 for reporting on confidential documents from the Khmer Rouge tribunal. The government has continued to sporadically block some websites and blogs with political or human rights content and has temporarily shut down mobile phone text messaging during elections or political unrest.

⁴⁶ORGANIZATIONS

The Phnom Penh Chamber of Commerce was established in 1995. The Cambodian Federation of Employers' and Business Associations was established in 2000. Workers' organizations include the Free Trade Union of Workers of the Kingdom of Cambodia, Workers' Union for Economic Development, Cambodian Union Federation, Cambodian Federation of Independent Trade Unions, and the National Independent Federation Textile Union of Cambodia. There are professional organizations, including the Cambodia Medical Association.

Cambodia has national chapters of the Red Cross Society, Caritas, UNICEF, and Habitat for Humanity. Volunteer service organizations, such as the Lions Clubs International, are also present. The Khmer Youth Association, founded in 1992, has been very active in promoting education and job training, as well as the championing the rights of women and children. There is an organization of Girl Guides in the country, as well as independent national scouting groups that are partly affiliated with political parties. Several sports associations are present as well, representing such pastimes as tennis, badminton, weightlifting, and track and field.

The Cambodian Human Rights and Development Association, established in 1991, promotes respect for human rights and the rule of law by providing legal services and educational materials to the public. Environmental groups include local NGOs such as Save Cambodia's Wildlife, and international partnerships such as Flora and Fauna's Cambodian Elephant Conservation Group. Cambodia has many grassroots and alternative development groups, and women's self-help organizations, which include Cambodian Women Crisis Center and Cambodia Women's Development Association.

⁴⁷TOURISM, TRAVEL, AND RECREATION

Until the encroachments of war in the late 1960s, Angkor Wat and other remains of the ancient Khmer Empire were the major attractions for visitors to Cambodia. Under the Pol Pot regime, tourism was nonexistent, and it was not substantially revived under Vietnamese occupation. Since the 1992 UN peace plan, tourism rebounded. As well as Angkor Wat, tourists visit the Silver Pagoda and National Museum in Phnom Penh. The genocide commemoration sites at Tuol Sleng prison and the Choeung Ek "Killing Fields" are visited by numerous tourists who wish to learn about Cambodia's past. Forest eco-tours and the beaches of Sihanoukville became popular once security was restored. Sex tourism has been a problem in Cambodia, with arrests of foreigners for exploitation of children. The Angkor War temple ruins have begun to suffer the effects of too much tourism, through wearing away of stonework, pollution, and sprawling commercialized surroundings.

A valid passport and visa are required for visitors from all countries except Malaysia, Thailand, Vietnam, Laos, Singapore, and the Philippines. Visas are available upon arrival at the Phnom Penh and Siem Reap International Airports, or as e-visas online. Visas are valid for one month after arrival in Cambodia.

The *Tourism Factbook*, published by the UN World Tourism Organization, reported 2.16 million tourists visiting Cambodia in 2009 and spending a total of $1.31 billion. Of those incoming tourists, there were 1.4 million from East Asia and the Pacific and 470,000 from Europe. There were 63,787 hotel beds available in Cambodia, which had an occupancy rate of 64%. The estimated daily cost to visit Phnom Penh, the capital, was $227. The cost of visiting other cities averaged $85.

⁴⁸FAMOUS PERSONS

Foremost among ancient heroes were Fan Shihman, greatest ruler of the Funan Empire (150–550), and Jayavarman II and Jayavarman VII, monarchs of the Khmer Empire who ruled between the 10th and 13th centuries. Prince Norodom Sihanouk (b. 1922), who resigned the kingship and won Kampuchea's independence from France, is the best-known living Cambodian. In exile in China during 1970–75, he founded the GRUNK government, from which he resigned in April 1976. In July 1982, he became president of the CGDK. In 1993, he once again became king, until his abdication in 2004. Sihanouk was succeeded by his son Norodom Sihamoni (b. 1953). Khieu Samphan (b. 1931), a former Marxist publisher and leader of the insurgency in Kampuchea, was named chairman of the State Presidium in the GRUNK government in April 1976, replacing Sihanouk as chief of state. The de facto head of the GRUNK regime during 1975–79 was Pol Pot (1925–98), who presided over the drastic restructuring of society that left as many as 3 million dead in its wake. Heng Samrin (b. 1934) became president of the Council of State of the PRK in 1979; he lost his position in 1992. Photographer Dith Pran (b. 1943), whose ordeal with the Khmer Rouge was portrayed in the film *The*

Killing Fields, helped chronicle the atrocities of the Pol Pot regime. Sam Rainsy (b. 1949) is a controversial opposition leader. Hun Sen (b. 1952) has been Cambodia's prime minister for over two decades. Mu Sochua (b. 1954) is a politician and campaigner against human trafficking. Somaly Mam (b. 1970), a former child prostitute, started a foundation to help victims of the sex trade. Ek Sonn Chan (b. 1950) brought safe drinking water to urban Cambodia for the first time as head of the Phnom Penh Water Supply Authority. A Cambodian environmental scientist, Tuy Sereivathana (b. 1970) won the 2010 Goldman Environmental Prize for his work on human/elephant interactions. In March 2010 it was announced that a new species of gecko was named after Cambodian herpetologist and conservationist Neang Thy (b. 1970).

⁴⁹DEPENDENCIES

Cambodia has no territories or colonies.

⁵⁰BIBLIOGRAPHY

Altbach, Philip G. and Toru Umakoshi (eds.). *Asian Universities: Historical Perspectives and Contemporary Challenges*. Baltimore, MD: Johns Hopkins University Press, 2004.

Cambodia Investment and Business Guide: Strategic and Practical Information. Washington, DC: International Business Publications USA, 2012.

Coates, Karen J. *Cambodia Now: Life in the Wake of War*. Jefferson, NC: McFarland, 2005.

Cook, Susan E. (ed.). *Genocide in Cambodia and Rwanda: New Perspectives*. New Brunswick, NJ: Transaction, 2005.

Corfield, Justin J. *Historical Dictionary of Cambodia*. Lanham, MD: Scarecrow Press, 2003.

DK Eyewitness Travel Guide: Cambodia and Laos. London, Eng.: DK Publishing, 2011.

Higham, Charles. *The Civilization of Angkor*. Berkeley: University of California Press, 2002.

Hinton, Alexander Laban. *Why Did They Kill?: Cambodia in the Shadow of Genocide*. Berkeley: University of California Press, 2005.

Leibo, Steven A. *East and Southeast Asia 2011*. Lanham, MD: Stryker-Post Publications, 2011.

Marston, John and Elizabeth Guthrie (eds.). *History, Buddhism, and New Religious Movements in Cambodia*. Honolulu: University of Hawaii Press, 2004.

Roberts, David W. *Political Transition in Cambodia 1991–1999: Power, Elitism and Democracy*. Richmond, VA: Curzon, 2001.

Solomon, Richard H. *Exiting Indochina: U.S. Leadership of the Cambodia Settlement and Normalization of Relations with Vietnam*. Washington, DC: United States Institute of Peace Press, 2000.

U Sam Oeur, with Ken McCullough. *Crossing Three Wildernesses: A Memoir*. Minneapolis: Coffee House Press, 2005.

Wagner, Carol. *Soul Survivors: Stories of Women and Children in Cambodia*. Berkeley, CA: Creative Arts, 2002.

Wenk, Brian. *The Work of Giants: Rebuilding Cambodia*. Geneva: International Labor Organization, 2002.

CHINA

People's Republic of China
Zhonghua Renmin Gongheguo

CAPITAL: Beijing (Peking)

FLAG: The flag is red with five gold stars in the upper left quadrant; one large star is near the hoist and four smaller ones are arranged in an arc to the right.

ANTHEM: *Yiyongjun Jinxingqu (The March of the Volunteers).*

MONETARY UNIT: The renminbi, or "people's money," denominated in yuan (RMB), is equivalent to 10 jiao or 100 fen. There are coins of 1, 2, and 5 fen, 1, 2, and 5 jiao, and 1 yuan, and notes of 1, 2, and 5 fen, 1, 2, and 5 jiao, and 1, 2, 5, 10, 50, and 100 yuan. RMB1 = US$0.15492 (or US$1 = RMB6.455) as of 2011.

WEIGHTS AND MEASURES: The metric system is the legal standard, but some Chinese units remain in common use.

HOLIDAYS: New Year's Day, 1 January; Spring Festival (Chinese New Year), from the 1st to the 3rd day of the first moon of the lunar calendar, usually in February; International Women's Day, 8 March; May Day, 1 May; Army Day, 1 August; Teachers' Day, 9 September; and National Day, 1–2 October.

TIME: 8:00 p.m. = noon GMT

¹LOCATION, SIZE, AND EXTENT

The People's Republic of China (PRC), the fourth-largest country in the world and the largest nation in Asia, claims an area of 9,596,960 sq km (3,705,406 sq mi), including Taiwan, which the PRC claims as a province; the major administrative divisions, excluding Taiwan and the offshore islands, cover 9,444,292 sq km (3,646,448 sq mi). Comparatively, the area occupied by China is slightly larger than the United States. If the area of Taiwan is excluded, China is the fourth-largest country in the world, after Russia, Canada, and the United States. The mainland has an extension of 4,845 km (3,011 mi) ENE–WSW and 3,350 km (2,082 mi) SSE–NNW. The mainland's 5,774 km (3,588 mi) coastline, extending from the mouth of the Yalu River in the northeast to the Gulf of Tonkin in the south, forms a great arc, with the Liaodong and Shandong peninsulas in the north protruding into the Yellow Sea and the Leizhou Peninsula in the south protruding into the South China Sea. China's territory includes several large islands, the most important of which is Hainan, off the south coast. Other islands include the reefs and islands of the South China Sea, extending as far as 4°N. These reefs and islands include Dongsha (Pratas), to which Taiwan has also laid claim. China's claims to the Xisha (Paracel) and Nansha (Spratly) archipelagoes are also in dispute. In 1986, the United Kingdom agreed to transfer Hong Kong to the PRC in 1997; in March 1987, the PRC and Portugal reached an agreement for the return of Macau to the PRC on 20 December 1999.

China is bordered on the N by Mongolia (Mongolian People's Republic—MPR) and Russia; on the NE by the Democratic People's Republic of Korea (DPRK); on the E by the Yellow and the East China seas; along the southern border are Hong Kong, Macau, the South China Sea, the Gulf of Tonkin, Vietnam, and Laos; on the SW by Myanmar, India, Bhutan, and Nepal; on the W by India, Jammu and Kashmir (disputed areas), Pakistan (west of the Karakoram Pass), and Afghanistan; and on the NW by Tajikistan, Kyrgyzstan, and Kazakhstan. China's total boundary length, including the coastline (14,500 km/9,010 mi) is 36,647 km (22,771 mi). China's capital city, Beijing, is located in the northeastern part of the country.

²TOPOGRAPHY

China may be divided roughly into a lowland portion in the east, constituting about 20% of the total territory, and a larger section consisting of mountains and plateaus in the west. The principal lowlands are the Manchurian (Dongbei) Plain, drained by the Songhua (Sungari) River, a tributary of the Amur (Heilongjiang), and by the Liao River, which flows to the Yellow Sea; the North China Plain, traversed by the lower course of the Yellow (Huang He) River; the valley and delta of the Yangtze (Chang Jiang) River; and the delta of the Pearl (Zhu) River surrounding Guangzhou (Canton). West of these lowlands, the country's topography rises to plateaus of 1,200–1,500 m (about 4,000–5,000 ft): the Shanxi and Shaanxi loess plateaus, in central China, and the Mongolian Plateau, in the north.

Beyond lie the high plateaus of Tibet, with an average elevation of 4,600 m (15,000 ft), and the great mountain ranges. The highest mountains are the Kunluns and the Himalayas. North of Tibet are two plateau basins of Central Asia, the Tarim and the Junggar, which are separated from each other by the Tian Mountains. The Chinese portion of the Tian range, which also extends into several other countries, rises above 7,000 m (23,000 ft).

The great rivers of China flow eastward toward the Pacific. In the northeast, the Amur drains a great part of the Manchurian Basin as it winds along its 4,350 km (2,719 mi) course. Other northeastern rivers include the Liao, the Tumen, and the Yalu, the last two both rising in Mt. Paaktu, flowing respectively northeast and southwest, and forming the boundary between China and the

DPRK. The main river of north China, and the second-largest in the country, is the Yellow River (Huang He). From Gansu it winds about 4,671 km (2,903 mi) eastward to Shandong Province, where it empties into Bo Hai (Gulf of Zhili, or Chihli). The valley of the Yellow River covers an area of 1,554,000 sq km (600,000 mi).

Central China is drained mainly by the Yangtze and its tributaries. The largest river in China, the Yangtze travels 5,525 km (3,434 mi) and drains 1,808,500 sq km (698,300 sq mi) of land. As China's only long river with no natural outlet, the Huai River, flowing between the Yangtze and the Yellow (Huang He) and roughly parallel to them, is subject to frequent flooding. To the southwest are the upper courses of the Mekong (Lancang) and Brahmaputra (Yarlung Zangbo) rivers.

Northern China is in a major earthquake zone with some of the most destructive earthquakes on record. On 28 July 1976, a tremor measuring 7.5 on the Richter scale struck the city of Tangshan (145 km/90 mi east of Beijing), causing widespread devastation and the deaths of over 650,000 people. On 3 February 1996, a 6.6 magnitude quake occurred at Yunnan causing death for 322 people and injury to over 16,000. About 358,000 homes were completely destroyed and over 654,000 others were damaged. On 24 February 2003, a 6.4 magnitude quake in Southern Xinjiang killed at least 260 people and injured 4,000. It was recorded as the deadliest earthquake of the year worldwide. On 12 May 2009, a 7.9 magnitude earthquake killed about 70,000 people and left 18,000 missing. There were allegations against the government for corruption in the construction of schools that collapsed.

³CLIMATE

Although most of China lies within the temperate zone, climate varies greatly with topography. Minimum winter temperatures range from -27°C (-17°F) in northern Manchuria to -1°C (30°F) in the North China Plain and southern Manchuria, 4°C (39°F) along the middle and lower valleys of the Yangtze, and 16°C (61°F) farther south. Although summer temperatures are more nearly uniform in southern and central China, with a July mean of about 27°C (81°F), northern China has a shorter hot period and the nights are much cooler.

Rain falls mostly in summer. Precipitation is heaviest in the south and southeast, with Guangzhou receiving more than 200 cm (80 in), and diminishes to about 60 cm (25 in) in north and northeast China, and to less than 10 cm (4 in) in the northwest. The southern Pacific coastal regions are vulnerable to severe tropical storms and typhoons, particularly in the season from July through September. Floods during this same time of the year can also be severe. In August 2010, one of the worst flood seasons in decades led to a massive landslide in Zhouqu county, Gansu, in the central northwest portion of the country. More than 700 people were killed as mud slid down from the mountainous regions, covering buildings up to seven stories high. Many more people were listed as missing or presumed dead. Overall, the 2010 flood season resulted in death or displacement for more than 2,100 people throughout the country.

Approximately 31% of the total land area is classified as arid, 22% as semiarid, 15% as subhumid, and 32% as humid.

⁴FLORA AND FAUNA

Much of China's natural vegetation has been replaced or altered by thousands of years of human settlement, but isolated areas still support one of the world's richest and most varied collections of plants and animals. Nearly every major plant found in the tropical and temperate zones of the northern hemisphere can be found there. The World Resources Institute estimates that there are 32,200 plant species in China. In all, more than 7,000 species of woody plants have been recorded, of which there are 2,800 timber trees and over 300 species of gymnosperms. The rare gingko tree, cathaya tree, and metasequoia, long extinct elsewhere, can still be found growing in China. Among flowering plants, 650 of the 800 known varieties of azalea occur in China, while 390 of the 450 known varieties of primrose and about 230 of the 400 known varieties of gentian are also found there. The tree peony, which originated in Shandong Province, appears in 400 varieties.

The richest and most extensive needle-leaf forests occur in the Greater Hinggan Ling (Khingan) Mountains of the northeast, where stands of larch, Asian white birch, and Scotch pine flourish, and in the Lesser Hinggan Ling (Khingan) Mountains, with stands of Korean pine and Dahurian larch. In the Sichuan (Szechuan) Basin, vegetation changes with altitude to embrace a variety of conifers at high levels, deciduous trees and cypresses at middle elevations, and bamboo in lower elevations. Farther south, in subtropical Fujian and Zhejiang provinces, broadleaf evergreen forests predominate. Forests give way to natural grasslands and scrub in drier western and northwestern areas, especially in the semiarid regions of Shanxi and Shaanxi, in the steppes of Inner Mongolia, and along the desert margins of the Tarim and Junggar basins.

China is home to 502 mammal, 1,221 bird, 424 reptile, and 340 amphibian species. The calculation reflects the total number of distinct species residing in the country, not the number of endemic species. China's most celebrated wild animal is the giant panda, a rare mammal now found in the wild only in remote areas of Sichuan, Gansu, and Shanxi provinces. Other fauna unique to China include the golden-haired monkey, found in remote parts of Shaanxi, Gansu, Sichuan, Guizhou, and Yunnan; the northeast China tiger, found in the Lesser Hinggan Ling and Changbai mountains along the Korean border; the Chinese river dolphin (believed to be on the brink of extinction) and Chinese alligator, both found along the middle and lower Yangtze River; the rare David's deer and the white-lipped deer, the latter found mainly in Qinghai Province and Tibet; a rare kind of white bear found in Hubei Province; and the lancelet, an ancient species of fish representing a transitional stage between invertebrate and vertebrate development, now found only in Fujian Province. Among the rarer birds are the mandarin duck, the white-crowned long-tailed pheasant, golden pheasant, Derby's parakeet, yellow-backed sunbird, red-billed leiothrix, and red-crowned crane.

In October 2009, researchers announced the discovery of fossilized remains representing a new type of flying reptile (pterodactyls) now known as Darwinopterus, after Charles Darwin. The 20 fossil skeletons found in northeast China were dated at about 160 million years old and seem to bridge the gap between the two known groups of pterodactyls: primitive and advanced. The Darwinopterus has a head and neck of the advanced group (long jaw, pointed teeth), but a body and long tail similar to the primitives. Some scientists believe the Darwinopterus is evidence of modular

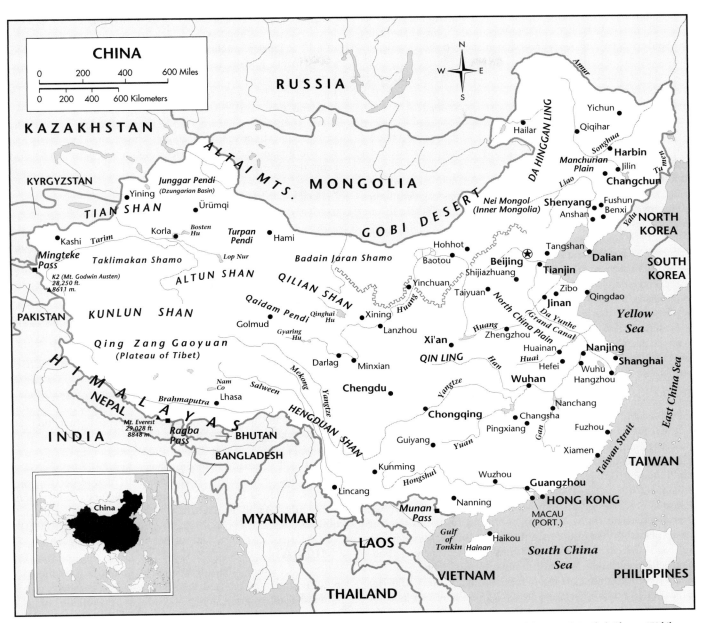

CHINA

LOCATION: (not including islands south of Hainan): 18°9′ to 53°34′ N; 78°38′ to 135°5′ E. BOUNDARY LENGTHS: Afghanistan, 76 kilometers (47 miles); Bhutan 470 kilometers (292 miles); Myanmar 2,185 kilometers (1,358 miles); Hong Kong, 30 kilometers (19 miles); India 3,380 kilometers (2,100 miles); Kazakhstan 1,533 kilometers (953 miles); North Korea 1,416 kilometers (880 miles); Kyrgyzstan 858 kilometers (533 miles); Laos, 423 kilometers (263 miles); Macau, 0.34 kilometers (0.21 miles); Mongolia 4,673 kilometers (2,904 miles); Nepal, 1,236 kilometers (768 miles); Pakistan, 523 kilometers (325 miles); Russia (NE) 3,605 kilometers (2,240 miles); Russia (NW) 40 kilometers (25 miles); Tajikistan 414 kilometers (257 miles); Vietnam, 1,281 kilometers (796 miles); total coastline, 14,500 kilometers (9,009 miles). TERRITORIAL SEA LIMIT: 12 miles.

evolution, a type of natural selection in which several traits change over a relatively short period of time, rather than one trait at a time over longer periods.

⁵ENVIRONMENT

It is estimated that China has lost one-fifth of its agricultural land since 1957 due to economic development and soil erosion. Since 1973, China has taken significant steps to rectify some of the environmental damage caused by rampant use of wood for fuel, uncontrolled industrial pollution, and extensive conversion of forests, pastures, and grasslands to grain production during the Cultural Revolution (1966–76). Reforestation, including construction of shelter belts, has emphasized restoration of the erosion-prone loesslands in the middle reaches of the Yellow River. In 1979, the Standing Committee of the Fifth National People's Congress adopted an Environmental Protection Law and a Forestry Law. In 1989, China began a nationwide program called the Great Green Wall of China which began to accelerate the rate of reforestation. The tree belt is supposed to stretch 4,480 km from western Xinjiang to eastern Heilongjiang to protect cities and cropland from floods and the desert. Scheduled for completion in 2050, the forested area—to cover over 400 million hectares or 42% of China's landmass—would be the largest man-made carbon sponge on the planet.

Water resources totaled 2,829.6 cu km (678.9 cu mi) while water usage was 549.7 cu km (131.88 cu mi) per year. Domestic water usage accounted for 7% of total usage, industrial for 26%, and agricultural for 67%. Per capita water usage totaled 415 cu m (14,656 cu ft) per year. Legislation provides for the protection of aquatic resources, including water quality standards for farmland irrigation and fisheries. In 2006, the Chinese Ministry of Water Resources reported that 70% of China's rivers and lakes are polluted. However, water supply and sanitation coverage continues to improve. Some 75% of China's population have access to safe drinking water.

The use of high-sulfur coal as a main energy source causes air pollution and contributes to acid rain. In 2007 China became the world's leading carbon emitter, surpassing the United States. However, greenhouse gas emissions per capita are still much lower compared to the United States. The United Nations (UN) reported in 2008 that carbon dioxide emissions in China totaled 6.53 million kilotons. Investment in pollution-reducing technology is required of all industrial enterprises. Penalties are imposed for noncompliance and incentives, in the form of tax reductions and higher allowable profits, are available for those enterprises that meet environmental standards. Beijing has implemented programs for controlling discharges of effluents, smoke and soot emissions, and noise pollution. Special success has been claimed for the recovery of oil from effluents of the Daqing oil field in Heilongjiang, refineries, and other oil-processing establishments; use of electrostatic precipitators and bag collectors by the cement and building industries; recovery of caustic soda and waste pulp from effluents of the pulp and paper industries; introduction of non-polluting processes into the tanning and depilating of hides; use of nonmercuric batteries; recovery of fine ash from coal-burning power plants for use in the manufacture of bricks, tiles, cement, and road-surfacing materials; and development of new methodologies for recycling coal wastes and marine oil discharges.

The World Resources Institute reported that China had designated 143.78 million hectares (355.28 million acres) of land for protection as of 2006. To protect the nation's botanical and zoological resources, a program was adopted in 1980 to establish 300 new reserves, with a total area of 9.6 million ha (23.7 million acres). That goal was achieved by the end of 1985, one year ahead of schedule. The largest reserve, covering 800,000 hectares (1,980,000 acres), is the Changbai Mountain Nature Reserve, in the northeast. Others include the Wolong reserve in Sichuan Province, covering 200,000 ha (494,000 acres) and famous for its research on the giant panda; the Dinghu Mountain reserve in Guangdong Province, where a subtropical evergreen broadleaf monsoon forest that has remained virtually untouched for four centuries provides opportunities for ecological studies; and the Nangun River area in Yunnan Province, where the principal focus of protection is the tropical rain forest. There are 37 Ramsar wetland sites and 12 natural and mixed properties designated as UNESCO World Heritage Sites.

According to a 2011 report issued by the International Union for Conservation of Nature and Natural Resources (IUCN), threatened species included 75 types of mammals, 86 species of birds, 32 types of reptiles, 87 species of amphibians, 113 species of fish, 14 types of mollusks, 27 other invertebrates, and 454 species of plants. Endangered species in China include Elliot's pheasant, Cabot's tragopan, yarkand deer, Shansi sika deer, South China sika, North China sika, the Chinese alligator, the Amur leopard, Thailand brow-antlered deer, the white-lipped deer, Bactrian camel, the giant panda, and the Siberian white crane. There are about nine extinct species, including the Yunnan box turtle and the wild horse. The Chinese river dolphin is believed to be near extinction or extinct.

⁶POPULATION

China, as the most populous country in the world, accounts for 21% of the estimated world population. Until 2001, it was also the only country to have attained the status of demographic billionaire, but in March that year, India also reached a one billion population. The government policy, launched in the 1990s calling for an extensive family planning program to limit population growth, has been successful.

The US Central Intelligence Agency (CIA) estimates the population of China in 2011 to be approximately 1,336,718,015. In 2011, approximately 8.8% of the population was over 65 years of age, with another 17.6% under 15 years of age. The median age in China was 35.5 years. There were 1.06 males for every female in the country. The population's annual rate of change was 0.493%. The projected population for the year 2025 is 1.48 billion. Population density in China was calculated at 139 people per sq km (360 people per sq mi).

The UN estimated that 47% of the population lived in urban areas, and that urban populations had an annual rate of change of 2.3%. The largest urban areas, along with their respective populations, included Shanghai, 16.6 million; Beijing, 12.2 million; Chongqing, 9.4 million; Shenzhen, 9 million; and Guangzhou, 8.9 million.

⁷MIGRATION

Estimates of China's net migration rate, carried out by the CIA in 2011, amounted to -0.33 migrants per 1,000 citizens. The total number of emigrants living abroad was 8.34 million, and the total number of immigrants living in China was 685,800. China also accepted 300,897 refugees from Vietnam and an estimated 40,000 from North Korea. The overseas migration of millions of Chinese reached its peak in the 1920s when thousands of farmers and fishermen from the southeastern coastal provinces settled in other countries of Southeast Asia. Chinese constitute a majority in Singapore, are an important ethnic group in Malaysia, and make up a significant minority in the Americas. In 1949, after the Communist victory, some two million civilians and 700,000 military personnel were evacuated to Taiwan.

Since in many places abroad the Chinese population has been growing at a rate faster than that of the local non-Chinese population, most countries have been trying to curtail the entrance of new Chinese immigrants. Emigration from China under the PRC government was once limited to refugees who reached Hong Kong, but is now denied only to a few political dissidents, if the state is reimbursed for postsecondary education costs. Immigration is for the most part limited to the return of overseas Chinese.

During the Cultural Revolution of the 1960s and 1970s, more than 60 million students, officials, peasant migrants, and unemployed were sent "down to the countryside" in a gigantic rustication movement. The goals of this program were to relocate industries and population away from vulnerable coastal areas, to provide human resources for agricultural production, to reclaim land in remote areas, to settle borderlands for economic and defense reasons, and, as has been the policy since the 1940s, to increase the proportion of Han Chinese in ethnic minority areas. Another purpose of this migration policy was to relieve urban shortages of food, housing, and services, and to reduce future urban population growth by removing large numbers of those 16–30 years of age. However, most relocated youths eventually returned to the cities.

Efforts to stimulate "decentralized urbanization" have characterized government policy since the late 1970s. Decentralized urbanization and the related relocation of industries away from established centers has also been promoted as a way for China to absorb the increasing surplus labor of rural areas. However, China's economic boom of the 2000s led to rapid growth of coastal provinces attracting inland rural males for construction and females to work in factories. This contrast extends to how children are perceived. Urban parents call their only child "little sun" (as in "center of the universe"), compared with rural parents, who call their child or children "left behind," (with their grandparents, as parents travel distances for work). For rural areas another split has developed: migrant work for the young and farming for the old.

Since Deng Xiaoping's Reform and Opening policy began in the late 1970s, China has witnessed the largest migration of people from the countryside to the city in human history. The profiles of the people on the move are changing. Those who left their rural villages in the 1980s and early 1990s were often driven by a family's need for cash and the desire to build a house back home. The new generation in the late 1990s to the present are younger and better educated than their predecessors; they are motivated less by the poverty of the countryside than by the opportunity of the city. In 2011, an estimated 153 million migrant workers were employed outside their home county, usually moving from the less economically developed central and western regions to the well off coastal regions. The six provinces of Henan, Anhui, Hunan, Jiangxi, Sichuan and Hubei contribute just under 60% of migrant workers nationally, while the six municipalities and provinces of Beijing, Shanghai, Zhejiang, Jiangsu, Guangdong and Fujian have absorbed almost 70% of cross-province migrant workers. In Beijing in 2011, about 40% of the total population were migrant workers, while in Shenzhen, nearly 12 million of the total 14 million population were migrants.

On 1 July 1997, the sovereignty of Hong Kong reverted back to China. Although in 1999 some 1,562 refugees and screened-out nonrefugees still remained in the Hong Kong Special Administrative Region (SAR), the population of refugees or asylum seekers was no more than 100 during 2008–10.

8 ETHNIC GROUPS

According to the 2000 census, the largest ethnic group, accounting for 91.5% of the total population, is the Han. The Han form a majority in most of the settled east and south but remain a minority, despite continuing immigration, in the west. The remaining 8.5% of the population is comprised of minority groups. Because of their predominance in strategically sensitive border areas, they hold a political and economic importance disproportionate to their numbers. The largest minority, at last estimate was the Zhuang, a Buddhist people, related to the Thai, who are primarily concentrated in Guangxi, Yunnan, and Guangdong. Other large minorities were the Manchu, concentrated in Heilongjiang, Jilin, and Liaoning; the Hui, a Chinese-speaking Muslim people concentrated in Ningxia, Gansu, Henan, and Hebei; the Uygur, a Muslim Turkic people of Xinjiang; the Yi, formerly called Lolo, a Buddhist people related to the Tibetans and concentrated in Yunnan, Sichuan, and Guizhou; the Miao, in Guizhou, Hunan, Yunnan, and Guangxi; and the Tibetans, concentrated in Xizang (Tibet), Qinghai, and Sichuan. Other minority nationalities, with estimated populations of more than one million, included the Mongolians; Tujia; Buyi; Koreans; Dong; Yao; Bai; Hani; Li; and the Kazaks, concentrated in Xinjiang, Gansu, and Qinghai.

9 LANGUAGES

Chinese, a branch of the Sino-Tibetan linguistic family, is a monosyllabic tone language written by means of characters representing complete words. The Chinese script is not phonetic and remains constant throughout China, but the spoken language has regional phonetic differences. Spoken Chinese falls into two major groups, separated roughly by a northeast-southwest line running from the mouth of the Yangtze River to the border of Vietnam. North and west of this line are the so-called Mandarin dialects, based on the Beijing dialect and known as *putonghua* ("common language"). The most important dialect south of the linguistic divide is that of Shanghai, the Wu dialect spoken in the Yangtze River Delta. Hakka and Hokkien are dialects of the southeastern coastal province. Cantonese, the Yue dialect spoken in southern China, is the language of the majority of Chinese emigrants. Others include the Minbei or Fuzhou dialect, the Xiang, and Gan dialects. Mandarin Chinese was adopted as the official language of China in 1955. To communicate in written Chinese, thousands of Chinese characters must be memorized. Since the establishment of the PRC in 1949, reform of the written language has been a major priority. A simplified system of writing, reducing the number of strokes per character, has been adopted, and the language restructured so that anyone familiar with the basic 2,000–3,000 characters is functionally literate (defined as being able to read a newspaper). A number of systems have been developed to transcribe Chinese characters into the Latin alphabet. The principal romanization scheme was the Wade-Giles system until 1979, when the PRC government adopted Pinyin, a system under development in China since the mid-1950s. Inside China, Pinyin is used in the schools to facilitate the learning of Chinese characters, in minority areas where other languages are spoken, and on commercial and street signs. Pinyin has replaced the Wade-Giles system in all of China's English-language publications and for the spelling of place names. In general, pronunciation of Pinyin follows standard American English, except that among initial sounds, the sound of *q* is like the sound of *ch* as in chart, the sound of *x* like the sound of *sh* as in ship, and the sound of *zh* like the sound of *j* as in judge, and among final sounds, the sound of *e* is like the sound of *oo* as in look, the sound of *eng* like the sound of *ung* as in lung, the sound of *ui* like the sound of *ay* as in way, and the sound of *uai* like the sound of *wi* as in wide. Of the 55 recognized minority peoples in China, only Hui and Manchus use Chinese as an everyday language. More than 20 minority nationalities have their own forms of writing for their own languages. Minority languages are used in all state institutions in minority areas and in all newspapers and books published there.

10 RELIGIONS

Three faiths—Confucianism, Buddhism, and Taoism—have long been established in China and the religious practice of the average Chinese traditionally has been an eclectic mixture of all three. Confucianism has no religious organization but consists of a code of ethics and philosophy; filial piety, benevolence, fidelity, and justice are among its principal virtues. Taoism, a native Chinese religion that evolved from a philosophy probably founded in the 6th century BC by Laotzu (Laozi), and Buddhism, imported from India during the Han dynasty, both have elaborate rituals. Tradition-minded Chinese base their philosophy of life on Confucianism, but such old habits of thought came under strong attack during the Cultural Revolution. Suppression of religion and the introduction of programs of antireligious indoctrination began in 1949 and intensified, with the closure of temples, shrines, mosques, and churches, from the mid-1960s through the mid-1970s. Overt anti-religious activity eased in 1976, and the government reactivated its Bureau of Religious Affairs. The constitution of 1982 provides for freedom of belief and worship; however, the government restricts religious practices and maintains a great deal of control over the growth of various religious organizations. The State Administration for Religious Activities and the United Front Work Department monitor religious organizations and supervise the implementation of government regulations for religious groups and activities. All groups are required to register with the government in order to legally participate in worship. Many groups refuse to register, however, either out of protest for government policies and control over religion or from fear of providing the names of religious leaders to government authorities. As of 2010, the country had five officially recognized religions, Buddhism, Taoism, Islam, Catholicism, and Protestantism. According to a 2007 survey, between 11% and 16% of citizens were Buddhists. Christians and Muslims each made up less than 5% of the population. Nearly all of the nation's Muslims are members of the ethnic minority nationalities; most belong to the Sunni branch, but the Tajiks are Shi'as. The tiny Jewish minority has virtually disappeared through emigration and assimilation. A majority of the population does not claim official religious affiliation.

11 TRANSPORTATION

Railways, roads, and inland waterways all play an important role in China's transportation system, which has undergone major growth since the 1940s. China's rail network forms the backbone of the transportation system. Chinese railways increased in length from 21,989 km (13,663 mi) in 1949 to 65,491 km (40,694 mi) in 2010. In the rush to expand rail facilities during the "Great Leap Forward," the Chinese laid rails totaling 3,500 km (2,175 mi) in 1958, with some 4,600 km (2,900 mi) added in 1959. Many major projects had been completed by the 1970s, including double-tracking of major lines in the east; the electrification of lines in the west, including the 671 km (417 mi) Baoji-Chengdu link; and

the addition of several new trunk lines and spurs, many providing service to the country's more remote areas. While the total rail network is more than twice what it was in 1949, the movement of freight is more than 25 times that of 1949. In 1991, China invested $8 billion for infrastructure improvements, including the upgrade of 309 km (192 mi) of double-track railway and the electrification of 849 km (528 mi) of track.

The construction of a major high-speed rail system linking several major cities is expected to provide a boom for the economy. One major line, from Beijing to Shanghai, opened on 1 July 2011. By that date, nearly half of the 10,000-mile network had been built and the project was on schedule for completion by 2020. However, a deadly rail crash on 23 July 2011 occurred near the city of Wenzhou when a signal failure brought one train to a standstill as a second train plowed right into it. Forty people were killed in the crash, which was met with public outrage as many believe the government has been disregarding safety concerns in its enthusiasm to complete its flagship project. In August 2011, the government ordered a temporary suspension of new high-speed projects, stating that each would be reevaluated for safety before final approval. The government also pledged to complete new safety inspections on existing lines and to implement new speed limits.

Road transportation has become increasingly important. Motor roads grew from about 400,000 km (249,000 mi) in 1958 to 550,000 km (342,000 mi) in 1964 and to 3,583,715 km (2,226,817 mi) by 2007. The CIA reports that in 2010 China had a total of 3.86 million km (2.40 million mi) of roads, of which 3.06 million km (1.90 million mi) are paved. Major roads completed in the 1970s included the 2,413 km (1,499 mi) Sichuan-Tibet Highway, the 2,100 km (1,305 mi) Qinghai-Tibet Highway, and the 1,455 km (904 mi) Xinjiang-Tibet Highway. Between 1981 and 1985, 50,000 km (31,000 mi) of highways and more than 15,000 bridges were built. In July 2011, China opened the world's longest bridge over open water, spanning 26.3 miles. The Jiaozhou Bay Bridge links the city of Qingdao to the island of Huangdao. The bridge was built to cut the driving time between the city and the island by about half an hour. The $2.3 billion dollar project beats out Louisiana's Lake Pontchartrain Causeway, which measures 24 miles. In 2010 there were 37 vehicles per 1,000 people in the country. Bicycles are the chief mode of transport in large cities. In Beijing, there are an estimated eight million bicycles, accounting for 83.5% of the city's road traffic.

In 2010 China had approximately 110,000 km (68,351 mi) of navigable waterways. About 25% of China's waterways are navigable by modern vessels, while wooden junks are used on the remainder. The principal inland waterway is the Yangtze River. Much work was done in the early 1980s to dredge and deepen the river, to improve navigational markers and channels, and to eliminate the treacherous rapids of the Three Gorges section east of Yibin. Steamboats can now travel inland throughout the year from Shanghai, at the river's mouth, upstream as far as Yibin, and 10,000-ton oceangoing vessels can travel inland as far as Wuhan in the high-water season and Nanjing in the low-water season. Major ports on the river include: Chongqing, the principal transportation hub for the southwest; Wuhan, its freight dominated by shipments of coal, iron, and steel; Wuhu, a rice-exporting center; Yuxikou, across the river from Wuhu and the chief outlet for the region's coal fields; Nanjing; and Shanghai. The Pearl River is navigable via a tributary as far as Nanning. The ancient Grand Canal, rendered impassable by deposits of silt for more than 100 years, has been dredged and rebuilt; it is navigable for about 1,100 km (680 mi) in season and 400 km (250 mi) year-round.

China's merchant fleet expanded from 402,000 gross registered tonnage (GRT) in 1960 to over 10,278,000 GRT in 1986, and to 18,724,653 GRT in 2005. In 2008, the merchant marine fleet consisted of 1,826 ships of 1,000 GRT or over. The principal ports are Tianjin, the port for Beijing, which consists of the three harbors of Neigang, Tanggu, and Xingang; Shanghai, with docks along the Huangpu River channel; Lüda, the chief outlet for the northeast and the Daqing oil field; and Huangpu, the port for Guangzhou, on the right bank of the Pearl River. Other important ports include Qinhuangdao; Qingdao; Ningbo, the port for Hangzhou; Fuzhou; Xiamen; and Zhanjiang.

The Civil Aviation Administration of China (CAAC) operates all domestic and international air services. Operations have grown significantly with the purchase, since the 1970s, of jet aircraft from the United States, United Kingdom, and other Western sources. In 2009 there were an estimated 425 airports with paved runways. There were also 45 heliports. According to the World Bank there were a total of 502 airports, which transported 229.06 million passengers in 2009. Principal airports include Capital at Beijing, Shuangliu at Chengdu, Hongqiao at Shanghai, Baiyun at Guangzhou, Wujiaba at Kunming, and Gaoqi at Xiamen. From Beijing there are scheduled daily flights to Shanghai, Guangzhou, Kunming, Chengdu, Shenyang, Changchun, Changsha, Wuhan, Zengzhou, and Harbin.

12 HISTORY

Fossils attest to hominid habitation in China more than 500,000 years ago, and Paleolithic cultures appeared in the southwest by 30,000 BC. Neolithic peoples appeared before 7000 BC; by 3000 BC there were millet-growing settlements along the Yellow River (Huang He). The original home of the Chinese (Han) people is probably the area of the Wei, Luo (Lo), and middle Yellow rivers. According to tradition, the Xia (Hsia) dynasty (c. 2200–c. 1766 BC) constituted the first Chinese state. Its successor, the Shang, or Yin, dynasty (c. 1766–c. 1122 BC), which ruled over the valley of the Yellow River, left written records cast in bronze or inscribed on tortoiseshell and bone. The Shang was probably conquered by the Western Zhou (Chou) dynasty (c. 1122–771 BC), which ruled a prosperous feudal agricultural society. Fleeing foreign attack in 771 BC, the Western Zhou abandoned its capital near the site of Xi'an and established a new capital farther east at Luoyang (Loyang). The new state, known as the Eastern Zhou dynasty (771–256 BC), produced the great Chinese philosophers Confucius (K'ung Fu-tzu or Kong Fuzi) and the semi-historical figure, Lao Tzu (Lao Zi). Between 475 and 221 BC, the Qin (Ch'in) dynasty (221–207 BC) gradually emerged from among warring, regional states to unify China. Shi Huangdi (Shih Huang Ti, r. 221–210 BC), the first Qin emperor (the outer edges of whose tomb, opened in the 1970s, were discovered to contain stunningly lifelike terra-cotta armies), ended the feudal states and organized China into a system of prefectures and counties under central control. For defense against nomadic proto-Mongolian tribes, Shi Huangdi connected walls of the feudal states to form what was later to become known as the Great Wall. By this time, the Yellow River had an irrigation system, and cultivation had begun in the Yangtze Valley. At the end of Shi Huangdi's reign, China probably had close to 40 million people. During the period of the Han dynasties (206 BC- AD 8, AD 25–220), China expanded westward, nomadic tribes from the Mongolian plateau were repelled, and contacts were made with Central Asia, the West, and even Rome. The Han saw the invention of paper. Under the later Han, Buddhism was introduced into China. After the Han period, the Three Kingdoms (Wei, Shu, and Wu) contended for power, and nomadic tribes from the north and west raided northern China. From the 4th century AD on, a series of northern dynasties was set up by the invaders, while several southern dynasties succeeded one another in the Yangtze Valley, with their capital at Nanjing (Nanking). Buddhism flourished during this period, and the arts and sciences were developed. The empire was reunited by the Sui (589–618) dynasty, which built the Grand Canal, linking the militarily strategic north with the economic wealth of the south and laying the basis for the Tang (T'ang, 618–907) dynasty.

Under the early Tang, especially under Emperor Taizong (T'aitsung, r. 627–49), China became powerful. The bureaucratic system, begun by the Han, was further developed, including the regular use of an examination system to recruit officials on the basis of merit. Handicrafts and commerce flourished, a system of roads radiated from the capital (at the site of Xi'an), successful wars were fought in Central Asia, and China became the cultural and economic center of Asia. Poetry and painting flourished, particularly under Emperor Xuan-Zong (Hsüan-tsung, r. 712–56). Civil wars and rebellion in the late Tang led to a period of partition under the Five Dynasties (r. 907–60) which was followed by the Northern and Southern Song (Sung) dynasties (960–1127, 1127–1279), distinguished for literature, philosophy, the invention of movable type (using clay and wood), the use of gunpowder in weapons, and the improvement of the magnetic compass. However, Mongol and Tatar tribes in the north forced the Song to abandon its capital at Kaifeng in 1126 and move it to Hangzhou (Hangchow). In 1279, Kublai Khan (r. 1279–94) led the Mongols to bring all of China under their control and became the first ruler of the Mongols' Yuan dynasty (1279–1368). The Mongols encouraged commerce and increased the use of paper money. The Grand Canal was reconstructed, and a system of relay stations ensured safe travel. Many European missionaries and merchants, notably Marco Polo, came to the Mongol court.

After a long period of peasant rebellion, Mongol rule was succeeded by the native Chinese Ming dynasty (1368–1644). The famous Ming admiral, Zheng He (Cheng Ho, 1371–1433) led seven naval expeditions into the South China Sea and the Indian Ocean between 1405 and 1433, reaching as far as the east coast of Africa. The Portuguese reached China in 1516, the Spanish in 1557, the Dutch in 1606, and the English in 1637. The Ming dynasty was overthrown by the Manchus, invaders from the northeast, who established the last imperial dynasty, the Qing (Ch'ing or Manchu, 1644–1911). The first century and a half of Manchu rule was a period of stability and expansion of power, with outstanding reigns by Kang xi (K'ang-hsi, 1662–1722) and Qian long (Ch'ien-lung, 1736–96). Although the Manchus ruled as conquerors, they adopted indigenous Chinese culture, administrative machinery, and laws. Under Manchu rule, Chinese territories included Manchuria, Mongolia, Tibet, Taiwan, and the Central Asian regions of

Turkestan. The population of over 300 million by 1750 grew to over 400 million a century later.

By the close of the 18th century, only one port, Guangzhou (Canton), was open to merchants from abroad, and trade was greatly restricted. Demands by the British for increased trade, coupled with Chinese prohibition of opium imports from British India, led to the Opium War (1839–42), which China lost. By the Treaty of Nanjing (1842), the ports of Guangzhou, Xiamen (Amoy), Fuzhou (Foochow), Ningbo, and Shanghai were opened, and Hong Kong Island was ceded to Britain. The T'aiping Rebellion (1850–64) nearly overthrew the Manchus and cost 30 million lives. A second war (1856–60) with Britain, joined by France, resulted in the opening of Tianjin (Tientsin) to foreign trade. The West's interest then turned from trade to territory. Russia acquired its Far Eastern territories from China in 1860. China's defeat in the Sino-French War (1884–85), in which it came to the defense of its tributary, Vietnam, resulted in the establishment of French Indo-China. In the First Sino-Japanese War (1894–95), Japan obtained Taiwan, the opening of additional ports, and the independence of Korea (which Japan subsequently annexed in 1910). This was a major turning point and led to the "scramble for concessions." In 1898, Britain leased Weihai in Shandong and the New Territories (for 99 years) of Hong Kong, Germany leased part of Shandong, Russia leased Port Arthur at the tip of Liaodong Peninsula, and France leased land around Guangzhou Bay in the south. The Boxer Uprising (1899–1901), led by a secret society seeking to expel all foreigners and supported by the Manchu court, was crushed by the intervention of British, French, German, American, Russian, and Japanese troops.

A revolution that finally overthrew Manchu rule began in 1911 in the context of a protest against a government scheme that would have handed Chinese-owned railways to foreign interests. The turning point was the Wuchang Uprising on 10 October 1911. The revolution ended with the abdication of the "Last Emperor" Puyi (P'u-yi) on 12 February 1912, which marked the end of over 2,000 years of Imperial China and the beginning of China's Republican era. The Chinese republic, ruled briefly by Sun Zhongshan (Sun Yat-sen), followed by Yuan Shikai (Yüan Shih-kai), entered upon a period of internal strife. Following Yuan's death in 1916, the Beijing regime passed into the hands of warlords. The Beijing regime joined World War I on the Allied side in 1917. In 1919, the Versailles Peace Conference gave Germany's possessions in Shandong to Japan, sparking the May Fourth Movement as student protests grew into nationwide demonstrations supported by merchants and workers. This marked a new politicization of many social groups, especially those intellectuals who had been emphasizing iconoclastic cultural change.

Meanwhile, civil war grew more intense. In the south, at Guangzhou, the Nationalists (Guomindang, Kuomintang) led by Sun Zhongshan in alliance with the Communists (whose party was founded in Shanghai in 1921) and supported by Russia, built a strong, disciplined party. After Sun Zhongshan's death in 1925, his successor, Chiang Kai-shek (Jiang Jieshi), unified the country under Nationalist rule in 1928 with the capital in Nanjing. In 1927, the Nationalists began a bloody purge of the Communists, who sought refuge in southern Jiangxi Province. Their ranks severely depleted by Nationalist attacks, the Communists embarked on their arduous and now historic Long March during 1934–35.

The Communists eventually reached Shaanxi Province in northwestern China, where, under the leadership of Mao Zedong (Tsetung), they set up headquarters at Yan'an (Yenan). Japan, taking advantage of Chinese dissension, occupied Manchuria (Dongbei) in 1931.

Increasing Japanese pressure against northern China led, in July 1937, to the second Sino-Japanese war, which continued into World War II and saw Japanese forces occupy most of China's major economic areas. Nationalist China, established in the southwestern hinterland with its capital at Chongqing, resisted with US and UK aid, while the Communists fought the Japanese in the northwest. Japan evacuated China in 1945 and both Communist and Nationalist forces moved into liberated areas. The rift between the two factions erupted into civil war. Although supported by the United States, whose mediation efforts had failed, the Nationalists steadily lost ground through 1948 and 1949, were expelled from the mainland by early 1950, and took refuge on Taiwan.

The People's Republic

The Communists, under the leadership of Mao, as chairman of the Chinese Communist Party (CCP), proclaimed the People's Republic of China (PRC) on 1 October 1949, with the capital at Beijing. A year later, China entered the Korean War (1950–53) on the side of the Democratic People's Republic of Korea (DPRK). In the fall of 1950, China entered Tibet, which had asserted its independence after the overthrow of the Manchu dynasty, despite formal claims to it by all subsequent Chinese governments. In 1959, the Dalai Lama fled to India during a Tibetan revolt against Chinese rule. Tibet became an autonomous region in 1965. The Nationalists held, in addition to Taiwan, islands in the Taiwan (Formosa) Strait: the Pescadores, Quemoy (near Xiamen), and the Matsu Islands (near Fuzhou).

In domestic affairs, a rapid program of industrialization and socialization up to 1957 was followed in 1958–59 by the Great Leap Forward, a crash program for drastic increases in output and the development of completely collectivized agricultural communes. The program ended in the "three bad years" of famine and economic crisis (1959–61), which produced 20 million deaths above the normal death rate, followed by a period of restoration and retrenchment in economics and politics. In the early 1960s, Chinese troops intermittently fought with Indian border patrols over conflicting territorial claims in Ladakh and the northeastern Indian state of Assam. Mediation attempts failed, but in 1963, the Chinese withdrew from the contested areas that they had occupied, and war prisoners were repatriated. Meanwhile, growing discord between China and the Union of Soviet Socialist Republics (USSR) had become more open, and in 1960, the USSR withdrew its scientific and technical advisers from China. Public polemics sharpened in intensity in the succeeding years, as the two powers competed for support in the world Communist movement.

After the Chinese economy recovered in 1965, Mao again steered the country onto the revolutionary path, and gradually built up momentum for the Great Proletarian Cultural Revolution, one of the most dramatic and convulsive periods in modern Chinese history. It continued until Mao's death in 1976, but the most tumultuous years were from 1966 to 1969, during which the cities witnessed a chaotic and violent pattern of factional fighting, accompanied by attacks on bureaucrats, intellectuals, scientists and technicians, and anyone known to have overseas connections.

Increasing confrontation between Mao and the party establishment, beginning in the fall of 1965, culminated in August 1966 with the CCP Central Committee's "16-Point Decision" endorsing Mao's Cultural Revolution policy of criticizing revisionism. In response to Mao's initiative, high levels of urban protest demonstrated widespread dissatisfaction with bureaucracies and privilege. In the latter half of 1966, the Red Guard movement of radical students attacked educational and state authorities and split into competing factions. Amid the rising conflict, the party institution collapsed in major cities. Liu Shaoqi, second to Mao in the political hierarchy and Chairperson of the People's Republic, was ousted from power as the chief target of the Cultural Revolution. In 1968, Liu was formally dismissed from all positions and expelled from the party. He died at the end of 1969. From January 1967 through mid-1968, the discredited political establishment was replaced by Revolutionary Committees, comprised of the new radical organizations, the officials who remained in power, and representatives of the army. Finally, the army was told to restore order. In 1968 and 1969, students were sent out of the cities into the countryside. Colleges did not reopen until 1970. At the Ninth Party Congress in April 1969, the military's role was confirmed when Lin Biao, the Minister of Defense, was named Mao's successor.

Estimates place the number of dead as a direct result of the Cultural Revolution from 1966 to 1969 at 400,000. Much of the countryside, however, was unaffected and the economy, despite a setback in 1968, suffered little. The remaining years of the Cultural Revolution decade, up to 1976, were marked by a legacy of struggles over policies and over political succession to the aging Mao (83 at his death in 1976). In September 1971, Lin Biao died in a plane crash, allegedly while fleeing to the USSR following an abortive coup. The decade from 1966 to 1976 left persistent factionalism in Chinese politics and a crisis of confidence, particularly among the young.

These years of domestic upheaval also brought profound changes in international alignments. In 1969, Chinese and Soviet forces clashed briefly along the Amur River frontier of eastern Heilongjiang Province. Throughout the late 1960s and early 1970s, China played a major role in supporting the Democratic Republic of Vietnam (North Vietnam) in the Vietnamese conflict. In November 1971, the PRC government replaced Taiwan's Nationalist government as China's representative at the UN and on the Security Council, following a General Assembly vote of 76–35, with 17 abstentions, on 25 October. Following two preliminary visits by US Secretary of State Henry Kissinger, President Richard M. Nixon journeyed to China on 21 February 1972 for an unprecedented state visit, and the two countries took major steps toward normalization of relations as the two nations sought common ground in their mutual distrust of Soviet intentions. In the period following the Nixon visit, US-China trade accelerated and cultural exchanges were arranged. In May 1973, the two countries established liaison offices in each other's capital and full diplomatic relations were established by 1979.

In 1975 at the Fourth National People's Congress, Zhou Enlai (Chou En-lai) announced a reordering of economic and social priorities to achieve the Four Modernizations (of agriculture, industry, national defense, and science and technology). Factional strife reminiscent of the late 1960s emerged between radical party elements led by Mao's wife, Jiang Qing (Chiang Ch'ing), and three associates (later collectively dubbed the Gang of Four), who opposed the modernization plans, and veteran party officials, such as Deng Xiaoping (previously associated with Liu Shaoqi and restored to power in 1973), who favored them. When Zhou died on 8 January 1976, the radicals moved to block the appointment of Deng (Zhou's heir apparent) as premier, with Mao resolving the impasse by appointing Hua Guofeng, a veteran party official and government administrator, as acting premier. Attacks on Deng continued until he was blamed for spontaneous disorders at a Beijing demonstration honoring Zhou on the Festival of the Dead, 5 April 1976, and, for the second time in his career, Deng was removed from all official positions.

After Mao

When Mao Zedong died on 9 September 1976, Hua Guofeng was quickly confirmed as party chairman and premier. A month later, the Gang of Four was arrested, and in early 1977, the banished Deng Xiaoping was again "reinstated." By 1978, Deng Xiaoping had consolidated his political dominance, and a new era of economic reforms began. The Third Party Plenum and the Fifth National People's Congress in 1978 adopted a new constitution and confirmed the goals of the Four Modernizations. Another new constitution in 1982 again confirmed policies of economic reform and emphasized legal procedure. The Cultural Revolution was officially condemned and Mao's historical role reevaluated. After a show trial from November 1980 to January 1981, the Gang of Four, together with Mao's former secretary and five others associated with Lin Biao, were convicted of crimes of the Cultural Revolution. Jiang Qing, whose death sentence was commuted to life imprisonment, committed suicide in 1991 after being diagnosed with cancer.

In 1980, Zhao Ziyang, a protégé of Deng Xiaoping, replaced Hua Guofeng as premier, and Hu Yaobang, another Deng protégé, became general secretary of the CCP while Hua resigned as party chairperson (a position which was abolished) in 1981. The 1980s saw a gradual process of economic reforms, beginning in the countryside with the introduction of the household responsibility system to replace collective farming. As the rural standard of living rose, reforms of the more complex urban economy began in the mid-1980s in an attempt to use the economic levers of the market instead of a command system of central planning to guide the economy. These included, with varying degrees of success, reforms of the rationing and price system, wage reforms, devolution of controls of state enterprises, legalization of private enterprises, creation of a labor market and stock markets, the writing of a code of civil law, and banking and tax reforms. At the same time, the Chinese pursued a policy of opening toward the outside world, establishing Special Economic Zones, and encouraging joint ventures and foreign investment.

In the 1980s and 1990s, China attempted to settle its relations with neighboring states. After a border clash with Vietnam in 1979, there were agreements with Great Britain in 1984 for the return of Hong Kong to China in 1997, and with Portugal in 1987, for the return of Macau—a Portuguese colony since the 16th century—in 1999. In May 1989, Soviet President Mikhail Gorbachev visited Beijing in the first Sino-Soviet summit since 1959. Top

Vietnamese leaders came to China in 1991, normalizing relations between the two countries after a gap of 11 years. In the early 1990s, China and South Korea established regular relations, with China also maintaining a relationship with North Korea.

Until 1989, economic reforms were accompanied by relatively greater openness in intellectual spheres. A series of social and political movements spanning the decade from 1979 to 1989 were critical of the reforms and reacted to their effects. In the Democracy Wall movement in Beijing in the winter of 1978–79, figures like Wei Jingsheng (imprisoned from 1979 to 1994 and subsequently reimprisoned) called for democracy as a necessary "fifth modernization." A student demonstration in Beijing in the fall of 1985 was followed in the winter of 1986–87 with a larger student movement with demonstrations of up to 50,000 in Shanghai, Beijing, and Nanjing, in support of greater democracy and freedom. In June 1987, blamed for allowing the demonstrations, Hu Yaobang was dismissed as party General Secretary, and several important intellectuals, including the astrophysicist Fang Lizhi and the journalist Liu Binyan, were expelled from the party. At the 15th Party congress of November 1987, many hard-line radicals failed to retain their positions, but Zhao Ziyang, who was confirmed as General Secretary to replace Hu, had to give up his position as Premier to Li Peng. By the end of 1988, economic problems, including inflation of up to 35% in major cities, led to major disagreements within the government, resulting in a slowdown of reforms. In December 1988, student disaffection and nationalism were expressed in a demonstration against African students in Nanjing.

On 15 April 1989, Hu Yaobang died of a heart attack. Students in Beijing, who had been planning to commemorate the 70th anniversary of the May Fourth Movement, responded with a demonstration, ostensibly in mourning for Hu, demanding a more democratic government and a freer press. Student marches continued and spread to other major cities. The urban population, unhappy with high inflation and the extent of corruption, largely supported the students and, by 17 May, Beijing demonstrations reached the size of one million people, including journalists, other salaried workers, private entrepreneurs and a tiny independent workers' organization, as well as students. On 19 May, martial law was imposed to no effect, and the government attempted to send troops to clear Beijing's Tiananmen Square, where demonstrators were camped, on 19–20 May and 3 June. Finally, in the early hours of 4 June 1989, armed troops, armored personnel carriers, and tanks, firing on demonstrators and bystanders, managed to reach the Square. Firing continued in the city for several days and estimates of the total number killed range from 200 to 3,000. The events of 4 June sparked protests across the country, and thousands were arrested as the movement was suppressed. On 24 June, Zhao Ziyang was dismissed as General Secretary and Jiang Zemin, the mayor of Shanghai, was named in his place.

Following 4 June 1989, economic reforms were curtailed and some private enterprises closed down as the leadership launched an anticorruption drive. Ideological expression, higher education, and the news media were more tightly controlled in the ensuing years. The move toward a market-oriented economy began again, with increased speed, after Deng Xiaoping made a publicized visit in the spring of 1992 to the most developed areas in southern China. China's economy became one of the most rapidly growing in the world but continued to be plagued by inflation, corruption,

and a growing disparity among the provinces. With a high rate of tax evasion, state revenues were shrinking and one-third went to subsidize state enterprises. Having been at the forefront of change in the early 1980s, peasants in the early 1990s were being left behind. In 1993 and 1994, there were peasant protests and riots over receiving IOUs for their produce and over local corruption. There were workers' disputes and strikes (250,000 between 1988 and 1993) in response to low pay and poor working conditions.

Labor unrest continued into 1997 as thousands of workers in several impoverished inland provinces rioted when promises of back pay went unfulfilled. A March 1997 labor protest involving 20,000 workers in Nanchong was the largest since the Communist revolution. China's uneven economic development also led to the growth of a migrant worker class. By 2005, it was estimated that some 100–150 million peasants left their homes in northern and western provinces in search of menial work along the coast. The unemployment rate in urban areas was 9.8% for 2004 with an overall unemployment rate of 20%; the unemployment rate does not include underemployment which also is a serious problem.

Parallel to but separate from the student and labor movements were ongoing demonstrations by ethnic minorities; there are 56 officially recognized minority groups in China. The most visible were those of the Tibetans (Buddhists), due to their international connections, but there have also been protests by other minorities, such as the Uyghurs (Muslims) in Xinjiang province. Violent Tibetan demonstrations in the fall of 1987 and spring of 1988 were forcibly suppressed, and from March 1989 to April 1990, martial law was imposed in Lhasa, Tibet. A Uyghur uprising in Xinjiang was met with force by the Chinese military in February 1997, leaving an estimated 100 ethnic Uyghur and 25 Chinese dead. But the situation in Tibet posed the most difficult for Beijing. China's efforts to control Tibet and dilute its culture led in 1995 to the indefinite detention of the six-year-old boy chosen by the exiled Dalai Lama as his reincarnation, or Panchen Lama. Beijing selected another six-year-old and forced Tibetan leaders to accept him. According to the CCP the Panchen Lama and his family are living in "protective custody," however, no international organization has been able to visit the family to verify their whereabouts since he was taken in 1995.

In September 1997, the CCP's 15th National Congress elected a Central Committee, which selected the 22-member Politburo. Jiang Zemin became the General Secretary of the party in addition to his title of president. Li Peng was appointed prime minister, and Zhu Rongji, deputy prime minister. During this Congress, political power was consolidated in the triumvirate, with Jiang Zemin officially taking the deceased Deng Xiaoping's position.

As the government prepared for the 50th anniversary of the proclamation of the People's Republic of China, it witnessed the return of Hong Kong (1 July 1997) and Macau (20 December 1999). Both former colonies were designated Special Administrative Regions (SAR) and Jiang stated that each SAR would continue to operate with a considerable degree of economic autonomy.

Also in 1999, Chinese nationalism increased with the US bombings of the Chinese Embassy in Belgrade, Yugoslavia in May as an outpouring of government-sanctioned anti-American demonstrations took place in Beijing. Despite rising nationalism, the political leadership felt threatened by a small but rapidly growing religious sect, the Falun Gong. On 22 July 1999, Chinese authorities banned the sect and arrested its leaders despite international human rights watch groups' criticism. The country celebrated its 50th anniversary on 1 October 1999 with a 500,000-person military parade showcasing its new technological achievements in armaments.

In February and March 1996, China test-fired missiles near Taiwan's two main ports, which caused the United States to send two aircraft carrier groups to the Taiwan Strait. It was the largest US naval movement in the Asia-Pacific region since the Vietnam War. The missile firings and accompanying military exercises were considered to be responses to Taiwan's presidential elections of March 1996, which President Lee Teng-hui, whom China accused of supporting Taiwanese independence, won.

In the run-up to Taiwanese presidential elections in March 2000, Chen Shui-bian of the Democratic Progressive Party, the eventual winner, issued pro-independence campaign speeches advocating "one country on each side," contradicting China's "one-country, two systems" policy. In March 2000, Zhu Rongji, the deputy prime minister, warned Taiwan and the United States that Taiwanese independence could lead to armed conflict. A Chinese newspaper also quoted a government white paper stating that war with the United States is inevitable in the future and that if the United States intervened on behalf of Taiwan, the Chinese may use nuclear weapons. Meanwhile, China began construction of military bases on the mainland across the Taiwan Strait. In 1996, China had fewer than 50 short-range missiles within striking distance of Taiwan. In April 2002, it was estimated that China's military forces had more than 350 missiles in the region and by 2005 the number had risen to 700.

On 1 April 2001, a US Navy EP-3 reconnaissance aircraft survived a mid-air collision with a Chinese F-8 fighter jet over the South China Sea. The Chinese fighter pilot was lost. The EP-3 conducted an emergency landing on Hainan Island, and the 24-member crew was detained there for 11 days in a standoff between the two countries. The United States and China blamed each other's aircraft for the crash. The EP-3 was later disassembled for transport back to the United States.

China expressed deep sympathy toward the United States following the 11 September 2001 terrorist attacks on the World Trade Center in New York and the Pentagon in Washington, DC. It has backed the American-led war on terrorism, and cited its own problems with what it considers to be terrorist activities led by ethnic Uyghurs fighting for an independent homeland in the northwest Xinjiang province. China has detained thousands of Uyghurs since 11 September 2001. China voted in favor of UN Security Council Resolution 1441 on 8 November 2002, which required Iraq to immediately disarm itself of weapons of mass destruction (chemical, biological, and nuclear weapons), to allow UN and International Atomic Energy Agency (IAEA) arms inspectors into the country, and to comply with previous UN resolutions regarding Iraq.

On 11 December 2001, China formally became a member of the World Trade Organization, representing international recognition of China's growing economic power. Several nongovernmental organizations and individuals worldwide protested China's accession to the body, due to its record on human rights violations. Another formidable problem for China, in regards to acceptance of WTO regulations, is the lack of adherence to intellectual property rights which involves industries as different as films to computer software. Most disconcerting is the availability of counterfeit medicine; thousands of Chinese are reported to have died from the ill effects of fake medicine. WTO regulations forbid counterfeiting although this has not yet affected China's membership in the organization.

In November 2002, China and the ten members of ASEAN signed an accord to resolve any conflicts over the Spratly Islands without armed force. The Spratlys are claimed by China, Taiwan, Brunei, Malaysia, the Philippines, and Vietnam, and are home to some of the world's busiest shipping lanes; they are also believed to be rich in oil and natural gas. Signatories to the accord agreed to cease further occupation of the islands, to help anyone in distress in the area, to exchange views with one another on defense issues, and to give advance warning of military exercises.

At the 16th Communist Party Congress held 8–14 November 2002, what is considered to be a "fourth generation" of Chinese leaders emerged, led by Hu Jintao, Jiang Zemin's replacement as Communist Party General Secretary. In addition to Hu, the other eight members of the 9-member Politburo Standing Committee were new appointees. In 2005 Hu advised the CCP not to focus solely on economic growth and instead integrate social and environmental factors into decision-making. Hu also took a number of high profile trips to the poorer areas of China. He also made the minutes of the Politburo Standing Committee meetings public.

In May 2006, work on the structure of the Three Gorges Dam, the world's largest hydropower project, was completed. It had begun in 1993. Scheduled to reach full capacity in May 2012, the dam had the potential to produce 85 billion kWh of electricity per year. The project is controversial, however. Critics say the human cost has been far too high: more than a million people have been moved to make way for the dam. At least 1,200 towns and villages will be submerged under the waters of the dam's reservoir. The government says those who have been relocated will be compensated, and be given new homes and jobs. The project also creates concern about its environmental impact: a region of superb natural beauty will be lost. Also, the reservoir behind the dam is already severely polluted and will likely get worse as much of the waste from big cities upstream flows into the Yangtze River.

In January 2007, China sent an interceptor missile into space to destroy a target satellite. It was the first successful demonstration of an antisatellite missile by any country in more than two decades. American Defense Department officials warned that the test had increased the threat to American satellites, and could spawn a new arms race. Space experts worried that it had created a cloud of orbiting debris. Interestingly, it was revealed in April 2007 that as the Chinese were preparing to launch the antisatellite weapon, American intelligence agencies had issued reports about the preparations being made. High-level Bush administration officials debated how to respond and began to draft a protest. Ultimately, however, the administration decided not to say anything to China until after the test.

China has reached out to African and other nations, looking for new sources of energy. In November 2006, African heads of state gathered for a China-Africa summit meeting in Beijing. The countries signed business agreements worth nearly $2 billion, and China promised billions of dollars in loans and credits. In February 2007, President Hu toured eight African countries to increase trade and investment. Western human rights groups criticized China for dealing with corrupt or abusive regimes, including Sudan, where the Darfur genocide was taking place. China has invested heavily in Sudan's oil industry.

China moved past the United States in 2007 as the world's largest emitter of carbon dioxide. (The United States continued to be the largest per capita emitter.) It is projected that China will add 331,000 megawatts of coal-fired generating capacity by 2015, for a total of 638,000 megawatts. China, still heavily dependent upon coal, is not only looking for new sources of petroleum, but is turning to clean nuclear energy as well.

China and Japan were attempting to reconcile differences over the interpretation of their shared history in 2007. In April of that year, Wen Jiabao became the first Chinese premier to address Japan's parliament. Former Japanese Prime Minister Junichiro Koizumi had often visited the Yasukuni shrine dedicated to Japan's war dead, provoking protests from China and other nations. The Yasukuni shrine also honors war criminals. In 2004, Japanese relations with Beijing deteriorated amid violent anti-Japanese protests in Chinese cities; the furor was a response to a Japanese textbook, which China said glossed over Japanese aggression in World War II, and Japan's treatment of the citizens of countries it occupied. In early 2007 another controversy arose, when Japanese Prime Minister Shinzo Abe denied that Japan's military had coerced women into sexual slavery during World War II. There are accounts of Japanese soldiers and sailors rounding up foreign women for use as sex slaves, euphemistically known as "comfort women."

In the summer and fall of 2007, international fears about the quality and safety of consumer products made in China began to grow. China's economic prowess has been fueled by cheap labor and smart cost-cutting measures; but in their desire to cut costs and secure contracts, some Chinese manufacturers have used inexpensive and illegal substances in making certain products. In the United States, Chinese toys contaminated with lead paint or toys with small, powerful magnets that could come loose and be swallowed by children were recalled, as were pet food, tires, toothpaste, and food items. One of the owners of a Chinese manufacturing company that made toys contaminated with lead paint committed suicide. In July 2007, the head of China's food and drug agency was executed for taking bribes.

In fall 2007, faced with a growing Chinese military buildup, Taiwan pursued plans to develop missiles that could strike mainland China. Taiwan successfully tested its first cruise missile with a range of 600 miles, which could reach targets as distant as Shanghai. Some of Taiwan's military brass have argued that Taiwan should develop offensive weapons, including missiles, as a deterrent to China, which has threatened to attack Taiwan if it were to declare formal independence. In March 2009, the Chinese government offered to begin peace talks with Taiwan. While the Taiwanese government has agreed to a number of economic deals with mainland China, Taiwanese officials have not committed to the idea of political reunification based on the "one-China" principle favored by the mainland.

In October 2010, the Chinese dissident Liu Xiaobo was named as the recipient of the 2010 Nobel Peace Prize. The announcement caused a great deal of controversy between China and the international community. Liu was a key leader in the 1989 Tiananmen Square protest and has often spoken out against the nation's track record for violations of human rights. In 2009, Liu was tried and convicted for inciting subversion after drafting a proposal called Charter 08, which called for greater respect for human rights from the Chinese government and for a change to a multiparty democracy. Liu was sentenced to 11 years in prison. The Chinese government immediately spoke out against the Norwegian Nobel committee, stating that it is an insult to the very principles of the peace prize to choose a man who is a duly convicted criminal in violation of Chinese law. The governments of several other nations called for Liu's release. A few days after the prize announcement, the Chinese government cancelled a diplomatic meeting with a Norwegian minister, indicating a potential diplomatic rift between China and Norway, despite the fact that the Norwegian government has no involvement in the actions of the independent Norwegian Nobel committee.

[13] GOVERNMENT

On 4 December 1982, China adopted its fourth constitution since 1949, succeeding those of 1954, 1975, and 1978. In theory, the highest organ of state power is the National People's Congress (NPC), in which legislative power is vested. The constitution stipulates, however, that the congress is to function under the direction of the Chinese Communist Party, headed by the general secretary. The NPC meets annually for about two weeks to review major new policy directions, to adopt new laws, and to approve the national budget submitted to it by the state council. Each congress consists of more than 3,000 deputies elected indirectly for a term of five years. The NPC elects a standing committee as its permanent working organ between sessions. The state council, the executive organ of the NPC, consists of a premier (the head of government), five vice-premiers, ministers, and heads of other major government agencies. The state council issues administrative regulations and both formulates and executes economic policy and the state budget. The 1982 constitution restored the largely ceremonial post of state chairman, or president, a position abolished by Mao Zedong in 1968. The eighth National People's Congress in March 1993 elected Jiang Zemin as president and reelected Li Peng, first elected in 1988, to a second five-year term as premier. At the ninth National People's Congress in March 1998, Li Peng was elected chairman of the NPC standing committee, and Zhu Rongji became premier. Since the 1980s, the NPC has slowly increased its function as a locus for discussion of issues instead of merely being a rubber stamp. The 1992 debate on the Yangtze River (Chang Jiang) dam project is an example of this.

The death of Communist Party patriarch Deng Xiaoping in February 1997 brought to a head the infighting between Jiang Zemin, Li Peng, and Zhu Rongji. At the 15th National People's Congress, Jiang was chosen to succeed Deng Xiaoping. The political leadership settled into one of shared leadership. At the 16th party congress held in November 2002, Jiang Zemin, Li Peng and Zhu Rongji resigned their posts in the Politburo standing committee, and the three gave up their positions as president and general secretary, chairman of the NPC standing committee, and premier, respectively, at the 10th NPC held in March 2003. Hu Jintao was named president (he had already been named general secretary of the Communist Party) and Wen Jiabao was named premier.

Democratic elections are held at the village level, but are forbidden above that level. The one lone opposition party, China Democratic Party, is acknowledged by the CCP, but it exists in theory only. Corruption, embezzlement, and bribery are all aspects of contemporary Chinese political life. The government owns all forms of media, including television, radio stations, and most newspapers. However, access to the Internet is widespread, especially in large cities and Western news outlets can be reached.

14 POLITICAL PARTIES

The Chinese Communist Party (CCP) has been the ruling political organization in China since 1949. Eight other minor parties have existed since 1949 as members of a United Front, but their existence has been purely nominal. The party, with 80 million members (2010 estimate), plays a decisive role in formulating broad and detailed government policies and supervising their implementation at all levels of administration. Party supervision is maintained not only through placement of CCP members in key government posts, but also through specialized organs of the central committee of the CCP, which focus their attention on given subjects (e.g., propaganda or rural work). The CCP also forms branches within individual government units, as well as in factories, communes, schools, shops, neighborhoods, and military units.

Theoretically, the highest organ of party power is the National Party Congress, which usually meets once every five years. At each party congress a central committee is elected to oversee party affairs between sessions. The central committee (356 members—198 full members and 158 alternate members) meets annually in a plenary session to elect a political bureau, or Politburo (with 24 members as of 2011), and its standing committee, the party's most powerful organ (9 members in 2011). Directing day-to-day party affairs at the highest level is the secretariat, headed by Hu Jintao as general secretary since November 2002. In 1982, the post of party chairman, formerly the most powerful in the nation, was abolished; the title had been held by Mao Zedong until his death in 1976, by Hua Guofeng from 1976 until his ouster in 1981, and by Hu Yaobang thereafter.

Deng Xiaoping, China's acknowledged political leader since 1977, retired from the central committee in 1987, retired as chairperson of the party's central military commission in 1989, and retired as chairperson of the state's central military commission, his last formal position, in 1990. A new CCP charter adopted at the 12th Communist Party congress in September 1982 forbids "all forms of personality cult" and, in an implicit criticism of Mao, decrees that "no leaders are allowed to practice arbitrary individual rule or place themselves above the party organization." A major purge of party members in the early 1980s sought to exclude elements opposed to Deng's modernization policies. The 13th party congress, convened in October 1987, affirmed Deng's reform policies and the drive for a younger leadership.

In the wake of the June Fourth massacre in 1989, Deng Xiaoping declared that Jiang Zemin, former mayor of Shanghai, should be the "core" of collective leadership after Deng's death. The Politburo announced prohibitions, largely ineffectual, against some forms of party privileges and nepotism, the corruption that had sparked the 1989 protests. The 14th party congress in October 1992 removed Yang Shangkun, state president (1988–93), from the Politburo, weakening the power of his clique in the military. In 1993, the National People's Congress reelected Jiang Zemin, already party general secretary, as chairperson of the central military commission and elected him as state president. This was the first time since the late 1970s that top, formal positions in the party, government, and military were concentrated in one leader's hands.

After the 15th Communist Party congress, a highly publicized anticorruption drive resulted in the execution of several prominent cases. In addition, Jiang began to remove the Communist Party from state-owned enterprises through an aggressive privatization strategy. In 2000, Jiang introduced a theory revamping the image of the Communist Party. Called the "three represents," it was written into the party constitution at the 16th party congress in November 2002. Seen as a re-orientation of the party away from its sole mission to serve the proletariat, the theory of the "three represents" emphasizes the importance of the middle class, stating that the party will represent not only workers and peasants, but the "advanced productive forces, advanced culture, and the broad masses of the people." Jiang resigned as chairman of the Central Military Commission in September 2004, his last official post.

Hu, who became state president at the National People's Congress in March 2003, was a protégé of Deng Xiaoping, chosen as the "core" of the younger generation. Seen as moderate and cautious, he was expected to proceed with Jiang's slow but steady policy of economic liberalization, and perhaps to introduce some administrative and political reform. Soon into his tenure, the SARS (severe acute respiratory syndrome) crisis broke out and Hu was criticized for not taking action quickly enough. Hu also chose to move China away from a policy of favoring rapid economic growth and toward a more balanced view of growth, most notably by establishing a "green" gross domestic product (GDP), taking into consideration the degradation of both natural resources and the environment.

15 LOCAL GOVERNMENT

The People's Republic of China (PRC) consists of 22 provinces (sheng—the PRC claims Taiwan as its 23rd province), five autonomous regions (zizhiqu), and four centrally administered municipalities (zhixiashi). Provinces and autonomous regions, in turn, are divided into "special districts," counties (xian), and cities (shi) under provincial jurisdiction, and into autonomous minor regions (zhou) and autonomous counties (zizhixian), where non-Han Chinese minority groups reside. Counties, autonomous counties, and autonomous zhou are divided into townships (xiang), autonomous townships (for small minority groups), towns, and rural communes. Hong Kong and Macau are designated as Special Administrative Regions (SAR).

From 1958 to 1982, local administrative authority formerly held by the xiang was transferred to the communes and their local people's councils. In 1988, Hainan Island, formerly part of Guangdong, was made China's newest province. The 1982 constitution returned local administrative control to the xiangs as the communes began to be disbanded. Local revolutionary committees, which replaced the local people's councils during the Cultural Revolution and under the 1975 constitution, were abolished in 1980. The restored local people's councils have the power to formulate local laws and regulations. The local people's governments are administrative organs of the state and report to the State Council.

In the 1980s an emphasis was placed on recruiting and promoting younger and better-educated officials in local party and government posts. Many provinces along the coastal regions have adopted more decentralized forms of administration while interior provinces remain highly beholden to the central party. Local elections involving multiple candidates have taken place, especially in the more urbanized coastal areas. Elections began on a trial basis in 1987, and in over 730,000 villages, peasants were scheduled to go to the polls every three years to elect local committees.

16 JUDICIAL SYSTEM

China's legal system, instituted after the establishment of the PRC in 1949, is largely based on that of the former USSR. However, after 1957, Mao Zedong's government consistently circumvented the system in its campaign to purge the country of rightist elements and "counter-revolutionaries." The Ministry of Justice was closed down in 1959, not to reopen until 1979, and the excesses of the Cultural Revolution wrought havoc on legal institutions and procedures. Efforts to reestablish a credible legal system resumed in 1977 (when there were no lawyers in China), as party moderates came to power. These efforts were accelerated in the early 1980s as China sought to provide the legal protection required by foreign investors.

The highest judicial organ is the Supreme People's Court, which, with the Supreme People's Procuratorates, supervises the administration of justice in the basic people's courts and people's tribunals (courts of first instance), intermediate people's courts, and higher people's courts. The judiciary is independent but subject to the Communist Party's policy guidance. The legal profession was still in an incipient stage of development in the mid-1980s. Over 25 law departments at universities and four special schools for training legal officials were in operation in 1987, when China had 26,000 lawyers. In 2011, China had 190,000 lawyers.

A major anticrime campaign during the autumn of 1983 resulted in public executions at the rate of at least 200 a month; capital punishment may be meted out for 65 offenses, including embezzlement and theft. Under the Chinese criminal codes, as revised in 1979, local committees may sentence "hoodlums" to terms in labor camps of up to four years, in proceedings that grant the suspect no apparent opportunity for defense or appeal. Government records for 1990 indicated that nearly 870,000 persons were assigned to such camps during the 1980s. In 2003, there were 250,000 people reported to be incarcerated in these camps. China does not permit international observation of prisons or labor camps. Since 1990, sentences to labor camps may be judicially challenged under the Administrative Procedures Law. In practice the review of such a sentence is rarely sought.

Due process rights are afforded in the 1982 constitution, but they have limited practical import. The Criminal Procedural Law requires public trials, with an exception for cases involving state secrets, juveniles, or personal privacy. Cases are rapidly processed and conviction rates are about 99%. The 1976 Criminal Code contained 26 crimes punishable by death. A 1995 law raised this number to 65, including financial crimes such as passing fake negotiable notes and letters of credit, and illegal "pooling" of funds. Appeal is possible but with little chance of success. However in 1996, the National Peoples' Congress passed new legislation to reform criminal procedure and the legal profession. The new legislation recognized for the first time that lawyers represent their clients, not the state. Under the new system lawyers may establish private law firms. Defendants may also ask near relatives or guardians to provide additional defense.

Amendments to the criminal procedure became effective in January 1997. The amendments state that suspects may retain a lawyer after being first interrogated by an investigative organ. Attorneys may conduct limited investigation, call defense witnesses, and argue their client's cases in open court. According to the amendments, defendants enjoy a presumption of innocence.

Beginning in 1998, the government began a comprehensive "internal shake-up" of the judiciary, resulting in the punishment or dismissal of over 4,200 judicial branch employees. In January 1999, the former head of the Anticorruption Bureau of the Supreme People's Procuratorate was dismissed for corruption.

China is party to many international organizations such as the UN, the ICC, ASEAN, and most recently the World Trade Organization. China's entry into the World Trade Organization (WTO) in December 2001 has caused China to undertake a full-scale revision of its laws and regulations in order to adhere to WTO rules. In opening its market up to sectors involving finance, insurance, telecommunications, commerce, transportation, construction, tourism, and other services, China will require its judicial system to perform in accordance with international standards.

Independent trade unions are illegal. Striking is also illegal although there have been increased use of strikes as a method of bargaining with mixed results. Sometimes leaders are arrested but other times not.

The oft misunderstood "one-child policy" has been clarified in recent years. The Population and Family Planning Law requires couples to employ birth control measures and technically limits the couple to only one child. This is well enforced in the cities, but less so in more rural areas. However, there are many avenues through which couples may have a second child. Two examples are as follows: ethnic minorities and farming families are able to have more than one child and couples in urban areas that are both the product of a one child family are entitled to produce a second child.

In March 2005, the State Council passed the Regulation on Religious Affairs, which human rights groups believe sharply curtailed both freedom of religious belief and freedom to express one's belief. However, Chinese officials claimed that the regulation safeguards "normal" religious activities, places of religious worship, and religious believers. At the same time religious believers are expected to abide by the government's laws. Religious activities that are banned if deemed "nonnormal" include publishing and distributing texts, selecting leaders, raising funds and managing finances, organizing training, inviting guests, independently scheduling meetings and choosing venues, and communicating freely with other organizations.

17 ARMED FORCES

The International Institute for Strategic Studies reports that armed forces in China totaled 2.29 million members in 2011. The force is comprised of 1.6 million from the army, 255,000 from the navy, 315,000 from the air force, and 100,000 members of strategic missile forces. Armed forces represent .4% of the labor force in China. Defense spending totaled $431 billion and accounted for 4.3% of

GDP. China has been modernizing its military at a rapid pace even as it reduces personnel.

Chinese military strength also includes a nuclear capability. It is suspected that China possesses 410 strategic and nonstrategic nuclear weapons.

The Chinese are involved in UN peacekeeping missions in 10 countries or regions around the world.

18 INTERNATIONAL COOPERATION

China has held a seat in the UN since 24 October 1945. After the Communist victory in 1949, UN representation was exercised by the Republic of China (ROC) government on Taiwan until November 1971, when the PRC replaced the ROC in the world organization and its member agencies. As of January 1988, the PRC belonged to ESCAP and several nonregional specialized agencies. The PRC displaced the ROC in the World Bank and IMF in 1980. China acceded to WTO membership on 11 December 2001. China also participates in APEC, the African Development Bank, the Asian Development Bank, and G-77. The country is an observer in the OAS and the Latin American Integration Association (LAIA), a nonregional member of the Caribbean Development Bank, and a dialogue partner in ASEAN.

The United States extended recognition to China on 15 December 1978 and resumed full diplomatic relations as of 1 January 1979. Continued US links with Taiwan in the 1980s, however, remained an irritant in US-PRC relations. The future of Hong Kong, for which part of the lease (the New Territories) expired in 1997, dominated UK-Chinese discussions, and in 1984, an agreement to give Hong Kong back to China in 1997 was formally signed. Relations with the USSR, severed during the Sino-Soviet split in the 1960s, improved somewhat in the 1980s but remained strained over China's support of anti-Soviet forces in Cambodia and Afghanistan. By the end of 1985, more than 130 nations had extended full diplomatic recognition to the PRC, with a parallel drop to about 10 in the number recognizing Taiwan's government. By the mid-1980s, the PRC had achieved normal relations with most of its Asian neighbors, including Japan, India, Pakistan, Malaysia, Thailand, and Singapore.

Relations with Vietnam, Cambodia, and Laos (all allies of the former USSR) were tense after the late 1970s, but improved in the 1990s. At the Eighth Summit of the Association of Southeast Asia Nations (ASEAN) held in November 2002, China forgave the debts of Vietnam, Laos, Myanmar, and Cambodia. Following the collapse of the Soviet Union in late 1991, China established diplomatic relations with the republics of the former Soviet Union. China normalized relations with the Republic of Korea in 1992. At an "ASEAN+3" (China, Japan, and the Republic of Korea) summit meeting held in November 2000, the three countries agreed to promote human and cultural exchanges between them. The ASEAN-China Free Trade Area (ACFTA) officially launched on 1 January 2010. The ACFTA comprises of China and ten Southeast Asian countries: Brunei, Cambodia, Indonesia, Laos, Malaysia, Myanmar, Philippines, Singapore, Thailand and Vietnam. ASEAN members and China have combined figures of 6 trillion GNP and 4.5 trillion trade volume. ACFTA is the world's third-largest free trade zone in volume after the European Economic Area and the North American Free Trade Area. It is the most populous free trade area, as well as the largest free trade zone among developing countries.

China is part of the Nuclear Suppliers Group (London Group), the Zangger Committee, and the Organization for the Prohibition of Chemical Weapons and participates as an observer in the Nonaligned Movement. In 2001, China joined with Russia, Kazakhstan, Kyrgyzstan, Tajikistan, and Uzbekistan to establish the Shanghai Cooperation Organization (SCO), a cooperative security partnership focused on combating terrorism, extremism, and separatism. China is also a member of the Permanent Court of Arbitration.

In environmental cooperation, China is part of the Antarctic Treaty, the Basel Convention, Conventions on Biological Diversity and Whaling, Ramsar, CITES, the London Convention, International Tropical Timber Agreements, the Kyoto Protocol, the Montréal Protocol, MARPOL, the Nuclear Test Ban Treaty, and the UN Conventions on the Law of the Sea, Climate Change, and Desertification.

19 ECONOMY

The GDP rate of change in China, as of 2010, was 10.3%. Inflation stood at 5%, and unemployment was reported at 4.3%.

Traditional China was predominantly agricultural. Adhering to farming patterns developed over a score of centuries, China could sustain a harsh level of self-sufficiency, as long as there were no natural calamities. For almost three decades prior to the proclamation of the People's Republic of China in 1949, the incessant ravages of civil disorder, foreign (principally Japanese) invasion, and gross economic neglect virtually decimated China's frail abilities to sustain itself. The first task of the new PRC government thus was to restore the flow of natural resources. By the early 1950s, the government had succeeded in halting massive starvation. Almost all means of production and distribution were brought under state control, and vast parcels of land were redistributed to the peasantry. During 1953–57, China's first five-year plan stressed heavy industry. Economic development was aided by imports of machinery and other industrial equipment from the USSR and Eastern European countries. In return, China exported agricultural produce to them. A major geological prospecting drive resulted in the discovery of mineral deposits that provided a major thrust toward industrialization.

The Great Leap Forward of 1958–59 initially produced sharp gains in industry and agriculture, but the zeal for increased quotas quickly resulted in undue strain on resources and quality. The Great Leap was followed by "three bitter years" of economic crisis brought on by bad harvests and the economic dislocation of the previous period. By 1961, the GNP had fallen to an estimated $81 billion, roughly the level reached in 1955. By 1965, however, a readjustment of expectations, coupled with a careful program of industrial investment, helped the economy to recover. China's trade patterns, meanwhile, had shifted radically away from the USSR and toward Japan and Western Europe.

During the late 1960s, in the Cultural Revolution period, long-range central economic planning was abandoned in favor of policies promoting local self-reliance. Self-sufficiency in grain production was particularly stressed. The negative impact of this emphasis on agricultural development, together with the turmoil of the Cultural Revolution, resulted in a drop in industrial production of 10–20%, while agricultural output, aided by good weather, improved only marginally.

Centralized planning resumed in 1970 with Zhou Enlai's announcement of key goals for the fourth five-year plan (1971–75), including an increase in grain output. The fifth five-year plan (1976–80), disrupted during the political upheaval that followed the deaths of Mao and Zhou in 1976, was restructured in 1978 to embody the Four Modernizations, with the use of Western technology as necessary. At the same time, a 10-year plan (1975–85) calling for the traditional expansion of agriculture and heavy industry was revamped to emphasize the growth of light industries and the accelerated development of industrial raw materials. Trade with the United States expanded after full diplomatic relations were restored in 1979, and four special economic zones were established as centers for foreign investment. The sixth five-year plan (1981–85), adopted in 1982, reflected this new pragmatic approach to economic development by emphasizing agriculture, light industry, energy, and improved transportation facilities.

Rural reforms launched in 1979, which linked remuneration to output and centered on household responsibility, had a profound and beneficial impact on the rural economy, and output and income rose to record levels for rural residents. The commune system was disbanded in 1983–84 and replaced by a system of townships, and the household or family became the main unit of rural production. In the wake of the success of these rural reforms, the CCP Central Committee published "A Decision on the Reform of the Economic Structure" in October 1984, with the goal of totally overhauling the national economy and bringing urban industrial organization in line with rural practice. The main points of the decision were that all urban enterprises would be responsible for their own profits and losses, managers would have greater decision-making authority, and national and local governments would relinquish direct control over enterprises and assume a regulatory and supervisory position. Remuneration would be based on productivity, subsidies would be abolished, wages and prices would find their own level, and private and collective enterprises would be encouraged.

The seventh five-year plan (1986–90) made reform its paramount concern. The reforms put forth in 1984 and firmly anchored in the 1988 Enterprise Law proved remarkably successful, leading to much higher rates of industrial and general economic growth than previously expected. Real GNP grew by an average of 9.6% annually between 1979–88, reaching 11% in 1988. By this time, however, indicators of a seriously overheated economy were also emerging; inflation accelerated to 20.7% and shortages in raw material and energy supply, as well as transportation capacity, rapidly worsened. Growth fell to only 4% in 1989 before austerity measures initiated by the government brought inflation to below 10% and eventually restored growth to double digit levels.

Infrastructure development was given special priority in China's eighth plan covering 1991–95. During this period economic growth accelerated, averaging more than 10% annually, giving China one of the fastest-growing economies in the world. With growth came rising inflation and infrastructural bottlenecks, which highlighted the need for further improvements in macroeconomic management. The 1996–2000 economic plan, which called for economic growth of 9–10% through 2000, reaffirmed the importance of the private sector and opening the economy to

the outside world. To attract and maintain foreign investors China needed to reform its legal and financial institutions. Despite the government's endorsement of market reforms, the plan continued to affirm the role of state-owned enterprises, which still accounted for more than one-third of total industrial output. In 1996, China committed two-thirds of fixed-asset investment to state-owned enterprises even though most were heavily in debt. By propping up the state sector China risked continuing budget deficits and the higher debt service that came with the borrowing necessary to pay for those expenditures. Investment in the state sector accounted for nearly all of the new investment in 1998, in the form of a special infrastructure-spending package forwarded by the government, supporting a GDP growth rate of 7% in 1999. Economic growth, which slowed during the late 1990s, recovered after China gained entrance to the World Trade Organization (WTO) in December 2001. After joining the WTO, China eliminated some trade barriers and opened up sectors of its economy to foreign investment.

In 2005 the government approved the 11th five-year plan, which focused on achieving more balanced wealth distribution and improving education, medical care, and social security. Some 40% of the country's industries were state-owned. The 11th five-year plan encouraged energy conservation and improvements in environmental protection.

The global financial crisis of 2008–09 affected the economy immediately as the demand for Chinese exports in the world market declined. From January through August 2009, trade with Japan declined by 20%, with an additional decline of 15.8% in trade with the United States and 19.4% with the European Union. A government economic stimulus package of $596 billion was implemented in mid-2009, allowing for a slight, but optimistic, recovery beginning in September 2009. Economic reports released in January 2010 showed that the Chinese economy had surged back to the rapid growth that had been its hallmark in the early 2000s. However, in March 2010 China posted its first month-to-month trade deficit in nearly six years, with the value of imports outpacing exports by $7.24 billion. Chinese authorities said they had repeatedly warned of a budget deficit in March, saying it was part of the broader campaign to keep the renminbi weak compared to the dollar.

In the twelfth five-year plan adopted in March 2011, the government vowed to continue reforming the economy and emphasize the need to increase domestic consumption in order to make the economy less dependent on exports for GDP growth in the future.

By mid-2011 economic growth showed a marked slowdown with a decline in the growth of both imports and exports. Imports had increased by 28.4% in May (compared to figures of the previous year), but grew by only 19.3% in June. Exports in May rose by 19.4%, while the June figure stood at only 17.9%. The slowdown of imports was attributed to a rise in consumer prices. In June 2011, prices rose by 6.4%, reaching the highest level of inflation in three years.

Economic growth in the second quarter of 2011 was marked at 9.5%, slightly down from the 9.7% of the second quarter 2010. However, the economy continued to exhibit signs of growth in 2011, when the trade surplus marked an increase of 41% compared to previous year figures.

20 INCOME

The CIA estimated that in 2010 the GDP of China was $10 trillion. The CIA defines GDP as the value of all final goods and services produced within a nation in a given year and computed on the basis of purchasing power parity (PPP) rather than value as measured on the basis of the rate of the exchange based on current dollars. The per capita GDP was estimated at $7,600. The annual growth rate of GDP was 10.3%. The average inflation rate was 5%. It was estimated that agriculture accounted for 9.6% of GDP, industry 46.8%, and services 43.6%.

According to the World Bank, remittances from citizens living abroad totaled $48.7 billion or about $36 per capita and accounted for approximately .5% of GDP.

The World Bank reports that in 2009, household consumption in China totaled $1.78 trillion or about $1,333 per capita, measured in current US dollars rather than PPP. Household consumption includes expenditures of individuals, households, and nongovernmental organizations on goods and services, excluding the purchases of dwellings. It was estimated that household consumption was growing at an average annual rate of 9.4%.

In 2007 the World Bank estimated that China, with 21.27% of the world's population, accounted for 9.70% of the world's GDP. By comparison, the United States, with 4.85% of the world's population, accounted for 22.51% of world GDP.

As of 2011 the most recent study by the World Bank reported that actual individual consumption in China was 43.0% of GDP and accounted for 6.12% of world consumption. By comparison, the United States accounted for 25.44% of world individual consumption. The World Bank also estimated that 11.3% of China's GDP was spent on food and beverages, 8% on housing and household furnishings, 2.7% on clothes, 2.7% on health, 1.7% on transportation, 1.8% on communications, 2.0% on recreation, 2.2% on restaurants and hotels, and 6.4% on miscellaneous goods and services and purchases from abroad.

21 LABOR

As of 2010, China had a total labor force of 815.3 million people. Within that labor force, CIA estimates in 2008 noted that 38.1% were employed in agriculture, 27.8% in industry, and 34.1% in the service sector.

Although workers in China are legally allowed the freedom of association, they cannot organize or join a union of their own choosing. Instead, workers are represented by the All-China Federation of Trade Unions (ACFTU), which is controlled by the Chinese Communist Party (CCP) and is headed by a top party official. The ACFTU controls all union activities and organizations, including those at the enterprise level. Independent unions are illegal. Union officials working outside the official confines of the ACFTU have reported being harassed and detained by authorities.

Unlike their urban counterparts, China's estimated 540 million rural labor force (including 300 million primary sector workers) were unorganized, with no similar organization to represent the nation's farmers. In addition, only a small number of the 130 million rural residents that work in village and township enterprises were unionized.

While collective bargaining for workers in all enterprise types is legal, in reality it falls way short of international standards.

Although forced and compulsory labor is prohibited by law, it was a serious problem in penal institutions. Those held in reeducation-through-labor facilities were frequently forced to work often with no or little remuneration. In some cases they were contracted to nonprison enterprises to the profit of the facilities and their respective managers.

There is a minimum working age of 16, but compliance with this is irregular, especially in the burgeoning and unregulated private economy. The huge surplus of adult labor reduces the incentive to employ children. Children are most often found working on farms in poorer, isolated areas. Those between the ages of 16 and 18 are considered "juvenile workers" and are prohibited from certain types of physical work, including laboring in mines. The minimum wage varies depending on the area of the country. There was no set national minimum wage rate as of 2011. Nonetheless, wages generally provides a decent standard of living for a family. The Labor Law provides that the standard workweek is 40 hours, with a mandatory 24-hour rest period weekly.

22 AGRICULTURE

With some 50% of the economically active population engaged in farming, agriculture forms the foundation of China's economy. The enormous pressures of feeding and clothing China's vast and growing population remain among the country's most compelling concerns. Agricultural output grew substantially between 1980 and 2010.

The PRC government expropriated large landholdings in a land reform carried out in 1951–52, redistributing the land among poor peasants. By the end of 1954, 11.5% of all peasant households had been collectivized; by 1955, 65%; and by 1965, 99%. The Chinese collective farms had virtually no mechanical equipment, but the peasants pooled their labor in various projects, such as water management, which were beyond the capacity of individual peasants. In 1958, the collective farms were merged into larger units as people's communes. The communes were concerned not only with agricultural output but also with subsidiary farm activities, such as light industry and handicrafts, usually produced for local consumption.

Far-reaching changes in the organization of communes took place during 1961–62. Formerly, the production brigade (the major division of a commune), of which there were about 719,438 in 1982, was regarded as the commune's "basic accounting unit." In 1962, however, the production team (the subdivision of a commune) became the commune's basic organizational element. The average production team consisted of 33 households and cultivated about eight hectares (20 acres). Production teams functioned almost autonomously, making basic decisions on production and distribution of income, while the commune mainly exercised the functions of a township government. Households, the final link in the system, were permitted the use of private plots, which made up about 5% of the arable land assigned to a team. In the early 1980s, these private holdings accounted for 19% of total agricultural output and the bulk of the country's production of vegetables, fruits, hogs, and poultry. Under the "responsibility system," which was introduced in 1978 and by 1983 was operating in 90% of rural China, all production in excess of assigned levels could be sold on the open market to yield a profit for individual production teams. In 1982, in addition to the rural communes, which provided most of China's agricultural output, there were 2,078 state farms working approximately 4.5% of all farmland. These farms, under the Ministry of State Farms and Reclamation, generally served as commodity production centers and as research units for the improvement of crop and livestock yields.

In 1983–84, a major reform of the agricultural system was launched. The 50,000 communes were disbanded and replaced by 92,000 townships, and the six million production brigades were broken up. Production decisions were now made by the household, which sets production targets in contracts with the government; households could sell their surpluses in the open market for cash. Crop diversification was encouraged. By the late 1980s, 60% of agricultural output was free of state controls, and most of China's peasants practiced the household responsibility system.

Roughly 16% of the total land was used in agriculture as of 2009. Grains are the chief crop, accounting for 70% of the total value of crop output and occupying 80% of all land under cultivation. Shandong, Jiangsu, and Henan together account for about 25% of the total crop value.

China's major crops include rice, wheat, potatoes, corn, peanuts, tea, millet, barley, apples, cotton, and oilseed. Cereal production in 2009 amounted to 483.3 million tons, fruit production 115.9 million tons, and vegetable production 522.7 million tons. China is the world's leading producer of rice. Over 90% of all rice is produced in southern China, with two (and in the far south, three) crops being grown each year where irrigation facilities permit. Early rice is planted in April and harvested in July; single-crop rice is planted in May and harvested in September; and late double-cropped rice is planted in June and harvested in October. Wheat is cultivated throughout the country, often as a dry-season crop in the rice-growing south, with specialized production centered in the Yangtze Valley and North China Plain.

Industrial crops occupy only 8–9% of the cultivated areas. Among the most important are cotton (the chief raw material for the important textile industry), various oil-bearing crops, sugar, tobacco, silk, tea, and rubber. Oilseed output derived from a diverse assortment of widely grown industrial crops, including sunflower seeds and rapeseed. Other oilseed products included castor beans, sesame seeds, and linseed. Most sugar is derived from sugarcane grown in the south; the remaining sugar comes from sugar beets grown in the north and northeast. Production of tea is an important traditional export, with most of the tea grown in hilly regions of the south and southeast. Most tobacco is produced as a sideline by commune householders working private plots. Most natural rubber is produced on specialized state farms.

China is the world's leader in irrigated land. The expansion of fertilizer production is viewed as a key to major growth in the agricultural sector.

23 ANIMAL HUSBANDRY

The UN Food and Agriculture Organization (FAO) reported that China dedicated 400 million hectares (988.4 million acres) to permanent pasture or meadow in 2009. During that year, the country tended 4.7 billion chickens, 84.1 million head of cattle, and 450.9 million pigs. The production from these animals amounted to 6.24 million tons of beef and veal, 44 million tons of pork, 15.8 million tons of poultry, 2.33 million tons of eggs, and 38.4 million tons of milk. China also produced 1.38 million tons of cattle hide and 364,002 tons of raw wool.

Except in outlying areas, nearly all of China's arable land is devoted to crops. Most agricultural units, however, also support the raising of large quantities of hogs and poultry. Natural grasslands for the grazing of sheep and cattle occupy 43% of China's total area; the four major pasture areas are Xinjiang, Gansu, Qinghai, and Inner Mongolia. In an effort to improve these pastures, 303 million hectares (749 million acres) were planted with improved forage seed strains from 1976 to 1980. Nonetheless, animal husbandry continues to be the weak link in the agricultural economy.

China leads the world in swine production. The provinces with the largest hog populations are Sichuan, Hunan, Henan, and Shandong. Pig raising, often pursued as a private sideline by peasants, is the fastest-growing sector of the livestock industry, and hogs and pork products are becoming valuable export earners.

The number of sheep expanded from 36.9 million in 1952 to 134 million in 2010. Most sheep are raised by pastoral herders, mostly the ethnic minorities, in the semiarid lands of Xinjiang, Inner Mongolia, Gansu, and Sichuan (Szechuan). Goats, also raised primarily in semiarid areas but increasingly promoted throughout China as a profitable household sideline for milk and dairy production, increased in number from 24.9 million in 1952 to 150 million in 2010. Provinces with the greatest numbers of sheep and goats include Shandong, Inner Mongolia, and Xinjiang. In 2010 there were also 6.8 million horses (792,000 in 1965) and 240,000 camels (448,000). Chickens and ducks are raised throughout China on private plots and constitute, together with fish and pork, China's chief sources of dietary protein. The provinces with the largest cattle populations are Shandong, Sichuan, and Guangxi. China is also a leading producer of honey and silk.

24 FISHING

With a coastline of some 6,500 km (4,000 mi) adjoining a broad continental shelf, China has excellent coastal fisheries. A vast number of inland lakes and ponds, covering a total area of about 300,000 sq km (116,000 sq mi), are also used for fish culture, and a 30 km (19 mi) section of the Yangtze below Gezhouba Dam at Yichang is a designated sturgeon preserve. The principal marine fisheries are located on the coast of southern and southeastern China, in the provinces of Guangdong, Fujian, and Zhejiang. China had 472,756 decked commercial fishing boats in 2008. The annual capture totaled 14.8 million tons according to the UN FAO. China's leading aquacultural products are carp, kelp, oysters, and scallops. Regulations for the protection of aquatic resources were enacted in 1979.

25 FORESTRY

Forest cover has grown from 8.6% of the land base in 1949 to 22% in 2009. Mature stands are decreasing, however, while the share of plantation and commercial forests continues to rise in response to government policies. Coniferous forest accounts for 47%; deciduous, 50%; and mixed, 3%. Most of the forests are in remote regions, however, and lack of transportation limits exploitation. China has three major forest areas: the northeast (Heilongjiang, Jilin, and Inner Mongolia); the southwest (Sichuan and Yunnan); and the southeast (Guangdong, Guangxi, Fujian, Jiangxi, and Hainan). Fujian, Zhejiang, Anhui, and Guangdong together account for about 30% of the total value of the forestry sector. Coniferous stands, which yield the most valuable commercial timber, are found mainly in the northeast and adjoining parts of Inner Mongolia. Deciduous trees are felled in Sichuan and Yunnan.

While China is a major producer of softwood logs and lumber, virtually all of its production is domestically consumed. Paper production, which has benefited from the substitution of rice-straw and other nonwood materials for wood pulp, nearly tripled during the 1980s. Special forestry products originating in southwestern China include tung oil, cassia oil, and aniseed oil. Wood imports can vary widely from year to year. The UN FAO estimated the 2009 roundwood production at 93.1 million cu m (3.29 billion cu ft). The export value of all forest products totaled $7.94 billion. About 60% of state quota timber production comes from plantations. Private mills dominate China's wood processing sector. There are more than 200,000 mills in China (located mostly in Hebei, Shandong, Jiangsu, Zhejiang, Guangdong, and Fujian), of which more than 90% are private.

Deforestation has been a persistent and serious problem in China, leading to massive erosion and desertification. The government has, from the start of its first five-year plan in 1953, given high priority to campaigns for afforestation. By 1980, 26 million hectares (64 million acres) of new forests had been planted, and during the 1980s, afforestation proceeded at the rate of 4.55 million hectares (11.24 million acres) per year. However, cutting of trees for fuel continued in rural areas, and many of the trees planted as part of afforestation efforts were lost because of neglect after planting. During 1990–2000, the forested area grew by an annual average of 1.2%. A massive afforestation program undertaken by the government in 1989, with a scheduled completion date of 2050, will cover over 400 million hectares or 42% of China's landmass.

[26]MINING

China produced more than 80% of the world's tungsten, was the largest producer and exporter of rare earths, the largest producer of cement, tin, and steel, and a world leader in the production of aluminum, antimony, barite, bismuth, copper, fluorspar, gold, graphite, indium, lead, lime, magnesium, manganese, molybdenum, phosphate rock, salt, silver, talc, and zinc. Intensive geologic exploration has yielded greatly expanded mineral reserves. The production of iron and steel was China's leading industry, coal production ranked second, and petroleum, cement, and chemical fertilizers were among the top eight.

Iron ore production in 2009 (gross weight) was 880 million metric tons, up from 824 million metric tons in 2008. The largest producers—Anshan Mining Co. (in Liaoning, Anshan) and Shoudu (Capital) Mining Co. (Beijing)—had annual capacities of 30 million tons and 20 million tons, respectively. As domestic iron deposits were of a low ore grade (less than 35% on the average) and required concentration, China imported more than 627 million tons of ore in 2009 (valued at $50.1 billion), and steel enterprises continued to look for joint-venture possibilities for iron mines in other countries.

Tungsten output in 2009, mainly from Jiangxi, was 51,000 metric tons (metal content), up from a revised figure of 50,000 metric tons in 2008. Copper output (metal content) was 970,000 metric tons in 2009, up from 940,000 tons in 2008. Other metallic ore

outputs in 2009 were: tin (chiefly in Yunnan), 115,000 metric tons, up from 110,000 metric tons in 2008; antimony (from Guangxi, Guizhou, and Hunan), 14,000 metric tons; bauxite (gross weight), 40 million metric tons, 35 million metric tons in 2008; lead (metal content), 1,600,000 metric tons, down from 1,550,000 metric tons in 2008; molybdenum, 93,500 metric tons; mercury, 1,400 metric tons; and zinc, 3.4 million metric tons, up from 3.3 million metric tons in 2008. China also mined alumina, bismuth, cobalt, gallium, germanium, gold, indium, manganese, nickel, platinum-group metals, silver, uranium, and vanadium. Henan geologists discovered a bauxite deposit in western Hunan Province that could contain reserves of 50 million tons and a significant amount of gallium. Another bauxite discovery, in Jingxi County, Guangxi Province, could contain reserves of 82 million tons (37 million tons of which could be economically developed), and a significant amount of gallium, niobium, scandium, and titanium.

The government since 2002 has eased restrictions on its gold market, allowing gold producers to sell their gold through the Shanghai Gold exchange, instead of to the Central Bank at a fixed price. However, imports and exports of gold ingot were still controlled by the government. The establishment of gold mining companies that were wholly owned by foreign investors was not permitted. Shandong province was the leading gold-producing province in China, followed by Henan, Fujain, Shaanxi, Liaoning, and Hebei provinces. In 2009, China produced 320,000 kg of gold, more than any other nation and equivalent to 13% of world production that year.

The output of rare-earth oxide content—60% from Nei Mongol, 18% from Sichuan, and 17% from Jiangxi—was 129,000 metric tons in 2009, up from 125,000 metric tons in 2008. Major portions were exported to France, Japan, and the United States. In Nei Mongol, rare-earth concentrate, known as Baotou rare-earth concentrate, was the by-product of producing iron concentrates, and contained oxides of the light rare-earth group—lanthanum, cerium, praseodymium, neodymium, samarium, europium, and gadolinium. In Mianning and Dechang (Sichuan), rare earths were mainly bastnasite, and, in Ganzhou (Jiangxi), the rare earths were of the ionic absorption type. A joint venture in Jiangsu province was to produce vanillin. The largest producers—Gansu Rare Earths Co. (in Jiangxi, Nanchang) and Baotou Iron and Steel and Rare Earths Corp. (in Nei Mongol, Baotou)—had capacities of 32,000 and 25,000 metric tons, respectively. China's rare-earth processing capacity expanded from 50,000 metric tons per year in 1995 to 95,000 metric tons per year in 2009. Rare earths remained a highly controlled sector, and a rare-earth quota was introduced in 1999 to control exports.

Hydraulic cement production in 2009 was 1,629 million metric tons, up from 1,400 million metric tons in 2008. Other industrial mineral production in 2009 included: fluorspar, 3.2 million metric tons; barite, 3.0 million metric tons (1.77 million metric tons of barium sulfate was exported, worth $122.1 million); magnesite, 15 million metric tons; gypsum, 4.5 million metric tons; graphite, 780,000 metric tons, down from 800,000 in 2008 (460,000 metric tons exported, for $134.1 million); talc and related materials, 2.3 million metric tons (400,000 metric tons exported, for $71.8 million); mine boron (boron oxide equivalent), 145,000 metric tons, up from 135,000 metric tons in 2008; asbestos, 380,000 metric tons; and bromine, 140,000 metric tons, up from 135,000 metric tons in 2008. China also produced diamond, diatomite, dolomite, kyanite and related materials, lithium minerals, nitrogen, phosphate rock and apatite, potash, salt, sodium compounds, and sulfur.

The government in 2000 approved the opening of a diamond exchange market in Shanghai. China became the world's eighth-largest consumer of precious stones (actual figures were difficult to ascertain because of smuggling and overseas purchases), and "Greater China," which included Hong Kong and Taiwan, was believed to be the world's third-largest diamond market, after the United States and Japan.

Also in 2000, the government issued several laws and regulations to improve the country's investment environment and foreign investors' confidence. The laws and regulations dealt with, among other things, mineral resource exploitation planning, land exploitation, mine ownership transfer, customs law, gold mining, Sino-foreign contractual joint ventures, foreign capital enterprises, and mineral-resource deposit size classification standards. The government continued its efforts to restructure the mining and metal sectors, abolishing nine bureaus, transferring responsibilities to industrial associations, dissolving three state-owned nonferrous enterprises, and, to help the industry become more efficient, ceding management to provincial and city governments. The government also offered incentives to companies—exemption from income tax, tariffs, and import value-added tax (VAT)—to invest in the poorer western provinces. It also began to phase out the preferential taxes for foreign enterprises, prepared to draft a "zero tariff rate" policy for exports, issued guidelines to allow foreign enterprises to conduct mineral exploration in China, and agreed to eliminate import quotas and dismantle export subsidies. China planned to increase production of cement, copper, fertilizer, iron, lead, nickel, salt, soda ash, and zinc, and expected to retain its dominance in the world market for antimony, barite, fluorspar, magnesite, rare earths, and tungsten.

27 ENERGY AND POWER

China's petroleum resources are a key to its industrial development. Crude oil production increased from 102,000 barrels per day in 1960 to 4.273 million barrels per day as of 2010. In 2008, per capita oil consumption was 1,598 kg. In 2010 China had proven reserves of 20.35 billion barrels. In November 2011 crude oil imports estimated at 5.55 million barrels per day, an 8.5% increase from November 2010. The major producing centers are the Daqing field in Heilongjiang, which came into production in 1965 and the Liaohe field, located in northeastern China. Although nearly 85% of China's oil production capacity is onshore, and in addition to numerous other mainland finds, China has potential offshore reserves in the Bo Hai area (thought to have reserves of over 1.5 billion barrels) and the South China Sea, especially in the vicinity of Hainan Island.

By the mid-1970s, China no longer had to rely on oil imports; petroleum exports had, in fact, emerged as a major source of foreign exchange earnings. More than 9,740 km (6,050 mi) of long-distance pipelines transport the oil from fields to refineries and other points of consumption and export. China, however, became a net importer of oil in 1996, because rapid increases in oil demand from high economic growth rates outpaced the slower increases in oil production.

After rising dramatically in the early 1980s, owing largely to the discovery and exploitation of vast deposits in Sichuan Province during the late 1950s and early 1960s, natural gas output stagnated somewhat in the late 1980s. As of 2003, natural gas supplied only an estimated 2.6% of the country's energy. The Chinese government wants natural gas to account for at least 10% of the country's energy consumption by 2020 and are building liquefied national gas (LNG) import terminals. China had proven reserves totaling an estimated 53.3 trillion cu ft as of 1 January 2005. In 2011, proven reserves were 107 trillion cu ft. In 2000, total national production reached 960 billion cu ft. By 2010, that figure had risen to an estimated 3.33 trillion cu ft. That same year, China consumed 3.77 trillion cu ft of natural gas, imported 577 billion cu ft and exported 144 billion cu ft. The West-East natural gas pipeline to transport natural gas from the Xinjiang province in the west to Shanghai in the east has the capacity of 17 billion cu m of natural gas. The 3,843 km pipeline's equipment was supplied by US-based GE Oil and Gas. It has been in operation since June 2011. Three additional west–east natural gas pipelines are being planned for construction.

Although China's rivers provide a vast hydroelectric potential (an estimated 378 million kW), only a small part has been developed. In the late 1990s, after economic growth slowed due to the Asian economic crisis, the government declared a two- to three-year moratorium on construction of new power plants due to an oversupply problem. The main hydroelectric projects include Ertan in Sichuan Province, Yantan in Guangxi Zhuang Autonomous Region, Manwan in Yunnan Province, Geheyan in Hubei Province, Wuqiangxi in Hunan Province, Yamzho Yumco in Tibet Autonomous Region, and Lijia Xia in Qinghai Province. In April 1992, the government approved the construction of the largest hydropower project in China—the Three Gorges Project on the middle reaches of the Yangtze River. Construction began in 1996 and was completed in 2009. The Three Gorges Project includes 26 hydropower generating units, at 700 MW each, producing a total of 18.2 GW of power. The Three Gorges Project required the relocation of 1.3 million people. Completed in 2010, the Yellow River Hydroelectric Development Corporation's scheme on the Yellow River became the world's second biggest hydro scheme with capacity of 15.8GW. It is centered on a 250-m (820-ft)high dam in Qinghai Province.

China's electrical generating capacity was estimated as of 1 January 2003 to stand at 338.3 GW, up from 115.5 million kW in 1988. Total output of electricity increased during the 1988–98 period from 545 billion to 1,098 billion kWh. Output in 2000 was 1,288 billion kWh, of which 81.8% was from fossil fuels, 16.8% from hydropower, and 1.2% from nuclear power. In 2003, electrical power output was estimated at 1,807 billion kWh, of which 1,484 billion kWh hours are from thermal sources, 279 billion kWh from hydroelectric sources, and 42 billion kWh from nuclear sources. Electricity consumption in 2000 was 1,206 trillion kWh. In 2002, consumption rose to 1,452.048 billion kWh. The World Bank reported in 2008 that China produced 3.45 trillion kWh of electricity and consumed 3.25 trillion kWh, or 2,433 kWh per capita. Roughly 87% of energy came from fossil fuels, while 4% came from alternative fuels. Electric power consumption is forecast to increase at an annual rate of 4.3% through 2025.

Traditionally, coal has been China's major energy source, with auxiliary biomass fuels provided by brushwood, rice husks, dung, and other noncommercial materials. The abundance of coal continues to provide cheap thermal power for electric plants. In 2010, China was both the world's largest coal producer, at 3.52 billion short tons, and the leading consumer of coal, at 3.7 billion short tons. China's coal production is projected to peak in 2027 with a peak production level of 5.1 billion short tons. Coal comes from over two dozen sites in the north, northeast, and southwest; Shanxi Province is the leading producer. Recoverable reserves as of 2008, were estimated at over 126.2 billion short tons. At the end of 2008, China accounted for 12.6% of the world's proven reserves of coal. Large thermal power plants are situated in the northeast and along the east coast of China, where industry is concentrated, as well as in new inland industrial centers, such as Chongqing, Taiyuan, Xi'an, and Lanzhou. As of July 2011, it was reported that coal accounted for 70% of primary energy consumption.

The development of nuclear power has become a major factor within China's electricity sector. The 279 MW Qinshan nuclear power plant near Shanghai began commercial operation in 1994. That same year, two 944 MW reactors at the Guangdong facility at Daya Bay also started commercial service. In 1995, Chinese authorities approved the construction of four more reactors. In May 2002, the 1 GW first unit of the Lingao nuclear power plant came online while a second 1 GW unit began operating in January 2003. An additional 600 MW generating unit also came online at Qinshan in February 2002. Net capacity for China's three nuclear reactors was estimated at 2,167,000 kW in 1996. At the start of 2002, installed capacity for nuclear power was placed at 2 GW. By mid-2005, that capacity had risen to 15 GW and further construction is being planned. A 6 GW complex is being planned for Guangdong province at Yangjiang (slated to begin commercial operation in August 2013), and a second facility is being planned for Daya Bay. By 2020, plans call for the completion of 27 GW of additional nuclear power generating capacity. Although China touts nuclear power as a way to cut its dependence upon fossil fuels and as a source of clean energy, by 2020 nuclear power will account for less than 5% of the nation's installed electric generating capacity.

In December 2009, the government celebrated the opening of a 1,800 km (1,100 mi) gas pipeline from Turkmenistan. The pipeline, which flows through Uzbekistan and Kazakhstan en route to Xinjiang in western China, is expected to deliver 40 billion cubic meters of gas per year by 2013. Turkmenistan produces about 70 billion cubic meters of gas per year. The Turkmen gas fields are being developed by the China National Petroleum Corporation.

28 INDUSTRY

China achieved a rapid increase in the gross value of industrial output (used before China switched to GNP accounting in 1986), which, according to official Chinese statistics, rose by 13.3% annually between 1950 and 1979. The greatest sustained surge in growth occurred during the first decade, with the rate averaging 22% annually during 1949–60. During 1961–74, the yearly growth rate fell to about 6%, partly as a result of the disruptions brought on by the collapse of the Great Leap Forward (which accompanied the withdrawal of Soviet technicians in mid-1960) and of work stoppages and transportation disruptions during the Cultural Revolution. Growth averaged 10% from 1970 to 1980 and 10.1%

from 1979 to 1985. Major policy reforms of 1984 further accelerated the pace of industrial growth, which reached 20.8% by 1988. After a brief retrenchment period in 1989–90 as government policies prioritized inflation control over other concerns, expansion of the country's industrial sector resumed apace, exceeding 20% in 1992 and 18% in 1994. Industrial output was officially up 13.4% in 1995, with state enterprises contributing the majority. The industrial production growth rate was 13% in 2011—the fourth-highest rate in the world.

While approximately 50% of total industrial output still derives from the state-owned factories, a notable feature of China's recent industrial history has been the dynamic growth of the collectively owned rural township and village enterprise as well as private and foreign joint-venture sectors. Also apparent has been the spatial unevenness of recent industrial development, with growth concentrated mainly in Shanghai, the traditional hub of China's industrial activity, and, increasingly, a number of new economic centers along the southern coast. The coastal provinces of Jiangsu, Guangdong, Shandong, Shanghai, and Zhejiang together account for close to 33% of the country's total industrial output and most of its merchandise exports. One key factor in this industrial geography has been the government's establishment of several Special Economic Zones in Guangdong, Fujian, and Hainan provinces, and its designation of over 14 "open coastal cities" where foreign investment in export-oriented industries was actively encouraged during the 1980s.

China's cotton textile industry is the largest in the world, producing yarn, cloth, woolen piece goods, knitting wool, silk, jute bags, and synthetic fibers. Labor-intensive light industries played a prominent role in the industrial boom of the late 1980s and early 1990s, accounting for 49% of total industrial output, but heavy industry and high technology took over in the late 1990s. In addition to garments and textiles, output from light industry includes footwear, toys, food processing, and consumer electronics. Heavy industries include iron and steel, coal, machine building, armaments, petroleum, cement, chemical fertilizers, and autos. High technology industries produce high-speed computers, 600 types of semiconductors, specialized electronic measuring instruments, and telecommunications equipment.

Since 1961, industry has been providing agriculture with farm machines, chemical fertilizers, insecticides, means of transportation, power, building materials, and other essential commodities. Handicraft cooperatives also have been busy making hand-operated or animal-drawn implements. Production of a variety of industrial goods has expanded, increasingly in order to supply the country's own expanding industrial base. In addition to fertilizers, the chemicals industry produces calcium carbide, ethylene, and plastics. Since 1963, great emphasis has been placed on the manufacture of transportation equipment, and China now produces varied lines of passenger cars, trucks, buses, and bicycles. In 1995, output included 1,452,697 motor vehicles (more than double the 1991 figure). Output for 1997 was over 1.6 million units. The industry underwent a major overhaul in the late 1990s in order to stimulate efficiency and production. In 2009 China became the world's leading producer of automobiles, with 13.79 million units. That year, Japan produced 7.93 million units, and the United States produced 5.7 million units.

High-tech manufacturing has gained ground, supplanting the low-technology, assembly-line production of the early 1990s. Though textiles still contribute largely to China's production output, industrial growth is increasingly in sectors producing advanced electronic goods such as cell phones and integrated circuits.

²⁹SCIENCE AND TECHNOLOGY

Modern China is the heir to a remarkably inventive civilization that pioneered in the development of the abacus (the first mechanical calculating device), paper (and paper money), printing by movable type, gunpowder, the magnetic compass, and the rocket. Contact with the West during the 19th century however, revealed how technologically backward China had become, and it is only in recent decades that the nation has begun to catch up.

China detonated its first fission device in 1964 and its first hydrogen bomb in 1967; the nation now possesses a variety of nuclear weapons mounted on missiles, bombers, submarines, and other delivery systems. Its first satellite was launched in 1970. By 1992, the PRC had launched an INTELSAT satellite on a Chinese launch vehicle. Other priorities have been the development of high-energy physics, laser research, powerful computer memory chips, color television broadcasting technology, and laser infrared devices, although the PRC still relies heavily on outside investment and technology transfer. Major advances have also been claimed in rice hybridization, insecticides, fertilizers, biogas digesters for rural electrification, and pollution control technology.

Two scientific exchange agreements between the United States and China were signed in January 1984 during Premier Zhao Ziyang's visit to Washington, D.C. China has proposed to several Western nations that it provide long-term storage facilities in remote provinces for radioactive waste—a proposal that Western observers believed would provide China not only with hard currency but also with nuclear materials for possible reprocessing.

China's principal technological handicap is lack of skilled personnel. Part of China's response to this shortage has been to send tens of thousands of students overseas for advanced study, especially in the United States. Scientific research is coordinated by the prestigious Chinese Academy of Sciences, founded in 1949 and headquartered in Beijing. Specialized learned societies in the fields of agriculture, medicine, science, and technology typically are affiliated members of the China Association for Science and Technology, which was founded in 1958. International science and technology cooperation is also increasing. However, concerns over human rights issues have had the effect of cooling US-PRC science and technology exchanges.

In 2009, public financing of science was 1.44% of GDP. Patent applications in science and technology as of 2009, according to the World Bank, totaled 229,096 in China.

³⁰DOMESTIC TRADE

Three types of retail trade outlets—the periodic market, the peddler, and the urban shop—constituted the basis of the traditional commercial structure. In the early 1950s, however, a number of state trading companies were established for dealing in commodities such as food grains, cotton, textiles, coal, building materials, metals, machinery, and medicines. These companies, under the control of the Ministry of Commerce, have established branch offices and retail stores throughout the country.

In the 1960s, the establishment of state-owned department stores and cooperative retail outlets virtually replaced private trade. There was a resurgence of periodic open markets and private traders when domestic trading regulations were relaxed in 1978. In addition, the government has progressively loosened or eliminated many of its former price controls; an estimated 90% of all retail sales are no longer controlled.

The Twelfth Five-Year Plan (2011–2015) formulated a development plan for China's domestic trade. The goal is to achieve continuous expansion of trade scale and new breakthrough in structural adjustments. It is expected that the volume of retail sales will double that of 2010, and the actual annual growth rate will reach 12% by the end of the Twelfth Five-Year Plan period. The domestic trade plan also puts an unprecedented emphasis on consumption expansion. According to Commerce Minister Chen Deming, this is the first time China has formulated a plan for domestic trade development in its history. Efforts will be made to further expand domestic consumption demand, vigorously promote consumption of residents in urban and rural areas, foster new consumption growth areas, accelerate circulation modernization, develop chain operations, and speed up the development of e-commerce.

The China Export Commodities Fair, also called the Canton Fair, is usually held each spring and fall in Guangzhou, since its inauguration in 1957. It was an important point of contact for Westerners doing business with China for more than twenty years. Though still important as an initial introduction to the full range of China's potential suppliers, the decentralization of trading activities in recent years has greatly reduced the fair's role in mediating sustained contact between producers and buyers.

Local foreign trade commissions in various industrial centers of the country have taken on a much more active role in organizing many of the services associated with the commodities fair, while any domestic enterprise with foreign trading rights may now participate directly in all events related to trade promotion. Guangzhou still hosts two annual trade fairs, though on a reduced scale. In the major cities, Friendship Stores and other restaurants, hotels, service bureaus, and taxis cater exclusively to foreign visitors; payment is made in foreign exchange certificates.

By the mid-1980s, international credit cards could be used to obtain cash advances in selected outlets and for direct purchases in Friendship Stores. The Friendship Store is a state-run store, which opened in the 1950s and initially sold exclusively to tourists, foreigners, diplomats, and government officials but since the 1990s it has no restrictions on customers such as ordinary Chinese citizens.

Although Internet commerce was initiated in China in the late 1990s, its full potential has yet to be realized. Impediments to an effective electronic commerce (e-commerce) sector include a preference by customers towards cash instead of credit cards, a lack of developed distribution channels that can provide effective delivery of items bought over the Internet, and Internet security. However, the number of Internet users in China is growing rapidly. In 2004, there were 90 million users in China. By December 2006, the number had increased to 132 million. In 2011, there were 551 million Internet users in China.

Government and business office hours in China run from 8 a.m. to 5 p.m., with an hour break around noon on weekdays. Banks are open Sundays through Saturdays from 9 a.m. to 6 p.m., while stores are open Sundays through Saturdays from 9 a.m. to 8 p.m.

31 FOREIGN TRADE

China's enormous trading potential, both realized and unrealized, has attracted great attention by both advanced and newly industrializing nations. Trade has performed important functions within the economy, providing needed capital goods and modern technology to abet development, as well as primary commodities (such as grains) to supplement local supply in slack years. Foreign trade is under the direction of a single Ministry of Foreign Economic Relations and Trade, created in 1982 through the merger of the former ministries of Foreign Trade and Foreign Economic Relations with the Export-Import and Foreign Investment commissions. A major issue since the early 1980s, however, has been the decentralization of trade management and greater reliance on currency devaluation (major devaluations were implemented in 1989 and 1991) and market incentives rather than direct export and import controls to promote desired trade patterns. After the Asian financial crisis of 1997, officials were tempted to devalue the currency once more; instead the Ministry of Foreign Trade and Economics (MOFTEC) spent massive sums of money on state industry, while dismantling trade barriers in anticipation of WTO membership in 2001.

Prior to 1949, some three-fourths of China's exports were agricultural products. This proportion ebbed to a low of 13% during the agricultural crisis of 1961. Foodstuffs and other primary products including crude nonfood raw materials, minerals and fuels averaged about 43–50% of exports through 1985, after which the proportion declined steadily to reach only 6% in 1998, as manufactured exports expanded rapidly. Textiles (excluding garments) accounted for 10% of all exports in 1994 and clothing for about 19.7% (up from 7.5% in 1985). However, China's efforts to emulate the success of Japan, British Hong Kong, Taiwan, and the ROK in basing economic expansion on textile and clothing exports en-

countered protectionist resistance from major potential markets in the United States and European Union.

The direction of China's trade has followed three major patterns since the 1930s. Prior to World War II, Japan, Hong Kong, the United States, and the United Kingdom together made up about three-fourths of the total trade volume. With the founding of the PRC in 1949, trade shifted in favor of the USSR and Eastern Europe. During 1952–55, more than 50% of China's trade was with the USSR; during 1956–60, the proportion averaged about 40%. As Sino-Soviet relations deteriorated during the 1960s, trade exchanges steadily declined, reaching a bare 1% of China's total volume in 1970 (3.6% in 1986). By the early 1980s, most of China's leading trade partners were industrialized non-Communist countries, and China's trade pattern overall reflected a high degree of multilateralism.

As China has rapidly enlarged its role on the international market, the importance of Hong Kong as an entrepôt and major source of revenue has increased. In 1992, Hong Kong accounted for close to 35% of China's total trade (up from about 21% in 1986). Hong Kong reverted to Chinese rule in 1997, but because of its enormous trade activity, Hong Kong's trade is often measured separate from China. During the 1990s, Japan ranked as the second-largest trading partner, importing oil and other raw material and claiming 15% of China's total trade. The most dramatic change in the mid-1980s was the emergence of the United States as China's third-largest trading partner; by 2000 the United States was China's second-largest trading partner, and the largest importer of Chinese goods.

China imported $1.307 trillion worth of goods and services in 2008, while exporting $1.506 trillion worth of goods and services. Major import partners in 2009 were Japan, 13%; South Korea, 10.2%; the United States, 7.7%; and Germany, 5.6%. Its major export partners were the United States, 18.4%; Hong Kong, 13.8%; Japan, 8.2%; South Korea, 4.5%; and Germany, 4.2%.

As of 1 January 2010, a new free trade area has been established between China and the six founding members of the Association of South East Asian Nations (ASEAN). A major point of the free trade agreement is the elimination of tariffs on nearly 90% of imported goods. The free trade area agreement is expected to allow for a major increase in exports and export earnings among the ASEAN countries. In terms of population, this is the largest free trade area in the world. Cambodia, Laos, Vietnam, and Myanmar, the newest members of ASEAN, are expected to gradually become full members of the free trade area by 2015.

32 BALANCE OF PAYMENTS

Both foreign trade and international financing in China are state monopolies, with policies and transactions administered by the People's Bank of China (PBC). Among its various functions, the PBC sets exchange rates for foreign currencies. The PBC releases foreign exchange to the Bank of China, which plays a major payments role through its branches in Hong Kong, Singapore, and other overseas financial centers. The government has, overall, maintained a record of financial stability, linked to a policy of stringent controls over its international transactions. Adhering generally to a principle of self-reliance, it has resorted to the use of commercial credit at certain junctures but until the 1970s avoided falling into long-term indebtedness as a means of financing major

Principal Trading Partners – China (2010)

(In millions of US dollars)

Country	Total	Exports	Imports	Balance
World	2,974,000.0	1,578,000.0	1,396,000.0	182,000.0
United States	385,638.0	283,679.0	101,959.0	181,720.0
Japan	296,566.0	120,262.0	176,304.0	-56,042.0
Hong Kong	227,706.0	218,205.0	9,501.0	208,704.0
South Korea	206,835.0	68,811.0	138,024.0	-69,213.0
Taiwan	145,287.0	29,642.0	115,645.0	-86,003.0
Germany	142,447.0	68,069.0	74,378.0	-6,309.0
Australia	86,926.0	27,228.0	59,698.0	-32,470.0
Malaysia	74,192.0	23,817.0	50,375.0	-26,558.0
Brazil	62,502.0	24,464.0	38,038.0	-13,574.0
India	61,736.0	40,880.0	20,856.0	20,024.0

(…) data not available or not significant.

(n.s.) not specified.

SOURCE: 2011 Direction of Trade Statistics Yearbook, New York: United Nations, 2011.

Balance of Payments – China (2010)

(In millions of US dollars)

Current Account		**305,374.0**
Balance on goods		254,180.0
Imports	-1,327,238.0	
Exports	1,581,417.0	
Balance on services		-22,118.0
Balance on income		30,380.0
Current transfers		42,933.0
Capital Account		**4,630.0**
Financial Account		**221,414.0**
Direct investment abroad		-60,151.0
Direct investment in China		185,081.0
Portfolio investment assets		-7,643.0
Portfolio investment liabilities		31,681.0
Financial derivatives		…
Other investment assets		-116,262.0
Other investment liabilities		188,708.0
Net Errors and Omissions		**-59,760.0**
Reserves and Related Items		**-471,659.0**

(…) data not available or not significant.

SOURCE: *Balance of Payment Statistics Yearbook 2011*, Washington, DC: International Monetary Fund, 2011.

development goals. In the period 1958–60, the Great Leap Forward and the succeeding years of economic crisis caused a sharp deterioration in China's international payments position. In 1960, large negative clearing account balances with Communist countries (-$625 million) were even more than the foreign exchange reserves of $415 million. By the end of 1964, however, the negative balance with Socialist nations had been reduced to $55 million, and China's net international financial resources stood at a surplus of $345 million, owing to monetary gold holdings of $215 million and foreign exchange balances from trade with non-Communist countries amounting to $185 million. By 1965, the Chinese had completely cleared their long-term debt to the USSR, and by 1968, China had redeemed all national bonds and was free of all long-term external and internal debts. Publication of official balance-of-payments statistics was discontinued during the Cultural Revolution and not resumed until September 1985.

According to Western analyses, the period 1978–81 saw a continuing surplus in current accounts, as rising levels of imports were generally matched or exceeded by increases in exports over the same period. In addition, transfers of an estimated $1.1 billion in 1978 and $1 billion in 1980, derived from increased earnings in tourism, shipping, and remittances from Hong Kong and other sources, resulted in overall current accounts surpluses of $900 million and $1.2 billion in 1978 and 1980, respectively. China's drive to industrialize under the Four Modernizations policy resulted in an unprecedented deficit on capital accounts of $1.1 billion in 1978. The subsequent unilateral decisions to cancel $2.6 billion in contracts with Japan (1979) and $2 billion with Japan and Western nations (1981) were interpreted by some observers as an indication of acute cash-flow problems and a reordering of investment priorities at the highest levels. The trade account was helped by the slow but steady devaluation that occurred after China went to a managed float exchange rate system in January 1991.

Tourism receipts and visitor figures also continued to grow, passing pre-Tiananmen levels.

Foreign investment boomed in the 1990s, with a total of nearly $45 billion committed in 1998 alone. Approximately half of China's loans came from the Asian Development Bank, the World Bank, and Japan; external debt reached $159 billion in 1998. A usually positive current account balance stockpiled China's reserves. In 1998, China had some $147 billion in official reserves, but state industries had accumulated a huge amount of what was called triangular debt with the state banks and other lending agencies. Government infrastructure and industrial projects received funding for goods that could not be sold domestically in 1999 due to lower demand, losing money for each party involved. In effect, external trade plays a secondary role in China's economy because of normally high, unsatisfied domestic demand.

During the 2000s, China's balance of trade remained positive due to the continued expansion of its share in world export markets. Frequently, however, China was criticized by the international community, in particular the United States, over allegations of currency manipulation that maintains a competitive advantage for Chinese exports. The current account balance was $305.4 billion in 2010 and $280.6 billion in 2011, nearly twice that of the nearest country (Saudi Arabia). Reserves of foreign exchange and gold were $2.895 trillion at year-end 2010 and $3.236 trillion at year-end 2011.

33 BANKING AND SECURITIES

As part of the Four Modernizations program adopted in 1978, the People's Bank of China (PBC) became China's central bank in 1982. It also turned over its commercial operations to the new Industrial and Commercial Bank. Headquartered in Beijing, the PBC is responsible for the formulation and implementation of the nation's monetary policy, and for the safety of the country's financial stability. Specifically, the PCB can issue and enforce regulations and orders, and is the sole issuer of currency. It can also administer the circulation of currency, and can regulate the inter-bank lending market and inter-bank bond market. It is also responsible for administering foreign exchange, and regulating the inter-bank foreign exchange market; regulation of the gold market; the holding and management of the nation's official exchange rate, and the nation's gold reserves; managing the national treasury; maintaining normal operation of the payment and settlement system; guiding and organizing the anti-money laundering work of the financial sector, and monitoring relevant fund flows; conducting financial statistics, surveys, analysis and forecasts; participating in international financial activities in the capacity of the central bank; and performing other functions specified by the State Council.

The PBC is managed by a Governor and a number of Deputy Governors. The Governor is appointed by the President of the People's Republic of China, and serves at the president's discretion. The Deputy Governors are nominated by the Premier of the State Council, and are approved by the National State Congress.

In 2010, the discount rate, the interest rate at which the central bank lends to financial institutions in the short term, was 3.25% for banks on mainland China. The commercial bank prime lending rate, the rate at which banks lend to customers was 6.6%.

The State Administration of Foreign Exchange (SAFE) helps set foreign exchange policy. Other specialized agencies include the People's Construction Bank, the Agricultural Bank of China, the Bank of China, the Bank of Communications, the China Development Bank, and the Export-Import Bank of China. The China Construction Bank (CCB) makes payments for capital construction according to state plans and budgets. The Agricultural Bank of China finances agricultural expansion, grants rural loans, supervises agricultural credit cooperatives, and assists in the modernization of agriculture. The Bank of China (BOC) handles foreign exchange and international settlements for the PBC. It has branches throughout China as well as in Singapore, Hong Kong, Paris, London, Luxembourg, New York, and Tokyo. The BOC is charged with financing China's foreign trade and also acquiring and channeling into appropriate areas the foreign capital needed for imports of industrial equipment and other items for modernization.

In 1987, stock exchanges opened in Shanghai and several other cities, and several stock and bond issues were floated domestically. Securities exchanges are controlled by the PBC, and trading in securities is very limited. In 1997, China accelerated stock-market listings of about 50 large and medium-sized state-owned enterprises (SOEs) and considered raising the number of enterprises piloting group holding structures from 57 to 100. In November 1996, the Shanghai Stock Exchange President, Yang Xianghai, predicted that China's two exchanges (Shanghai and Shenzhen) would number in excess of 1,000 companies by 2000. At the time he was speaking, there were 472 companies listed on the stock exchanges. By 2003, there were 746 listed companies and 871 listed securities being traded on the exchange. By 2011, the Shanghai and Shenzhen exchanges listed a combined total of more than 2,000 companies. Market capitalization of both exchanges in 2010 amounted to about $4 trillion. China's stock market is split into two sections, the "A" share market and the "B" share market. Foreigners may only participate in the B-share market, denominated in foreign currencies and consisting predominantly of foreign private companies. The A-share market is reserved for domestic investors (who are not allowed to participate in the B-share market) and dominated by state enterprises.

On 19 June 2010, China's central bank issued a statement saying that it would return to the currency policy used from 2005 to 2008, and set the value of the renminbi to a basket of other currencies, not just the US dollar. From 2005 to 2008, the renminbi rose 21 percent against the dollar, and investors and analysts alike interpreted the central bank's June 2010 statement as an affirmation of a controlled float policy, whereby the renminbi is again allowed to appreciate against the dollar. Chinese authorities sought to soothe domestic anxieties about the new policy, however, qualifying the announcement with guarantees that no abrupt or disruptive jumps in the currency value would be tolerated.

³⁴ INSURANCE

The People's Insurance Co. of China (PICC), formed in 1949, is authorized to handle all kinds of insurance, including the insurance of China's foreign trade and foreign insurance operations in China. In 2001, the People's Insurance Co. of China controlled 78% of China's property/casualty insurance industry, with 4,200 branches and a workforce of 110,000. Two additional state enterprises, the China Insurance Co. and the Tai Ping Insurance Co., are in operation, and several foreign insurance companies have established representative offices in Beijing. Demand for insurance projects is predicted to grow as economic reforms limit the social security benefits provided by state enterprises.

Motor-vehicle third-party liability for foreigners and for citizens in certain provinces, workers' compensation (in the Shenzhen Special Economic Zone), old age pension, unemployment insurance, and property (fire) in Shenzhen for commercial risks are compulsory.

³⁵ PUBLIC FINANCE

The annual state budget is prepared by the Ministry of Finance and approved by the National People's Congress. A major reform in public finance, introduced in 1980, was a new system of allocating revenues and expenditures between local and national levels of government. Previous revenue-sharing procedures allowed the central government to fix maximum spending levels for each province, autonomous region, and centrally administered municipality. The new system fixed for a five-year period the proportion of local income to be paid to the central government and (except for emergency appropriations for floods and other such disasters) the level of subsidies to be provided by the central government, as well as the proportion of local income to be retained by local governments. Autonomous regions receive proportionately greater state subsidies than the provinces and centrally administered municipalities, and they are entitled to keep all revenues from local industrial and commercial taxes. During the 1990s, the Chinese consolidated budget deficit grew at a rapidly increasing rate. According to the IMF, the 1998 budget deficit amounted to 4% of GDP, due to rising expenditures and tax evasion. Deficits are largely financed by domestic debt issuance rather than by money creation. In 1999, the central government performed an audit of embezzlement, finding that some $2.4 billion in state funds had

---

Public Finance – China (2008)

(In billions of yuan, budgetary central government figures)

Revenue and Grants	**3,701.9**	**100.0%**
Tax revenue	3,224.8	87.1%
Social contributions	...	...
Grants	165.8	4.5%
Other revenue	311.3	8.4%
Expenditures	**3,981.4**	**100.0%**
General public services	2,674	67.2%
Defense	411.9	10.3%
Public order and safety	64.9	1.6%
Economic affairs	635.1	16.0%
Environmental protection	6.6	0.2%
Housing and community amenities	31.4	0.8%
Health	5.4	0.1%
Recreational, culture, and religion	17.1	0.4%
Education	80.5	2.0%
Social protection	54.5	1.4%

(…) data not available or not significant.

SOURCE: *Government Finance Statistics Yearbook 2010*, Washington, DC: International Monetary Fund, 2010.

been diverted into private bank accounts, and that a total equaling one-fifth of the central government's tax revenues were misused. In all, the government's liabilities were equal to 100% of GDP in 2000, according to some sources. Taxes and other revenues equaled 23.6% of GDP as of 2011, one-fifth of which goes annually to paying interest on government debts.

For 2010, the CIA Factbook lists revenue at US$1.227 trillion and expenditures at US$1.323 trillion, creating a deficit equal to 1.6% of GDP. Public debt totaled 16.3% of GDP for the same year. In 2010 the budget of China included $1.149 trillion in public revenue and $1.27 trillion in public expenditures. The budget deficit amounted to 2.1% of GDP. Public debt was 17.5% of GDP, with $428.4 billion of the debt held by foreign entities. Total external debt was $529.2 billion by 31 December 2010.

36 TAXATION

According to the World Bank, China's corporate income tax rate was 20% with total tax rate 5.4% of profit in 2010. It was applicable to resident as well as those business operations that involved foreign investments, or so-called foreign investment enterprises (FIEs). In addition, local authorities were allowed to collect certain license and registration fees, as well as levy a surcharge. FIEs typically paid taxes at concessional rates, depending upon the type of business and location. Capital gains incurred by companies are generally considered income and are taxed as such.

On 1 January 1994, the PRC Individual Income Tax law came into effect in China. As of 2011, an individual's income is taxed progressively at 3%-45% for residents and foreigners, although foreigners listed as nonresidents (those living in China for less than one year) are taxed only on income sourced from China. People resident in China for five or more years are considered residents and are taxed on world-wide income. Capital gains claimed by individuals are taxed at 20%. However, the sale of a private dwelling is exempt from the capital gains tax, if the seller lived in it for at least five years. Nonresidents are subject to a 10% withholding tax. As of 2011, the sale or importation of goods and services are subject to a value-added tax (VAT) at a standard rate of 17% or at a lower rate of 13%. The lower rate applies to water, grain, edible oils, certain agricultural products such as fertilizers, and books. Small businesses with a turnover of less than the legally defined limit pay VAT at 3%. The VAT applies to a broad range of services including the sale of immovable property, construction, insurance and entertainment, the latter of which is subject to a 20% rate. Consumption/excise taxes also apply to goods, including cigarettes, motor vehicles, cosmetics, jewelry and alcoholic beverages.

37 CUSTOMS AND DUTIES

Although China is in the process of aligning its trade system with international standards, prohibitively high tariffs and quotas discourage many imports. It uses the Harmonized System for tariff classification. A minimum tariff rate is granted to countries that have special agreements with China, including the United States. Tariff rates range from 3–100% with the highest rates reserved for goods such as automobiles. Raw materials are exempt. In 1996, as a step toward WTO compliance, China reduced tariffs on more than 4,000 products by an average of 30%, and then reduced tariffs even further in 2001 in preparation for WTO accession. In 2000, the US-China Trade Relations Working Group successfully

opened trade relations with China, with such agreements as: reducing the automobile tariff from a maximum of 100% to a maximum of 25%; reducing auto parts tariffs from 23.4% to 10%; and eliminating quotas by 2005.

Official PRC policy is that direct trade with Taiwan is interregional, rather than international, since Taiwan is considered a province of China and, therefore, no customs duties are levied. There are free trade zones in Shanghai, Tianjin, Dalian, Haikou, the Hainan Island Special Economic Zone, and within the Shenzhen Special Economic Zone. Smuggling, reportedly well organized along the coasts of Guangdong, Fujian, and Zhejiang provinces and in the frontier regions of Tibet and Yunnan, is a major governmental concern.

38 FOREIGN INVESTMENT

China strongly emphasizes attracting foreign investment in projects that will enhance the nation's economic development. Beginning in the early 1970s, China contracted for the construction of a substantial number of complete plants, notably for iron and steel, automobile, fertilizer manufacture, and power generation, including nuclear power. Such agreements, often made with private firms from Japan, Germany, Italy, France, the United Kingdom, and Canada, as well as with agencies of the Communist states, all called for direct purchase of materials and services. Residual ownership by foreigners and remittance of profits from production were expressly disallowed. In 1979, China established the Foreign Investment Control Commission to attract and coordinate foreign investment, and the first four Special Economic Zones (SEZs) in southern China at Shenzhen, Xiamen, Shantou, and Zhuhai to attract foreign investment (the fifth SEZ was established on Hainan Island in 1988).

In the 1980s, foreign investment was restricted to export-oriented businesses, and foreign investors were required to enter into joint ventures (JVs) with Chinese counterparts in order to enter the market. Under the Joint Ventures Law, enacted in 1979 and revised in 1982, the development of joint ventures for the production of exports has been particularly stressed as a means of securing for China the foreign exchange needed to pay for purchases of advanced technology. Foreign investment in products for the domestic market, other than those needed for modernization, was discouraged. In 1984, further foreign investment opportunities were created with the designation of 14 open coastal cities— Shanghai, Guangzhou, Tianjin, Fuzhou, Dalian, Qinhuangdao, Yantai, Qingdao, Lianyungan, Nantong, Ningbo, Wenzhou, Zhanjiang, and Beihai—where preferential incentives could also be offered. Since then, 52 state-approved economic and technology zones have come into existence, and most provinces, regions, and major municipalities have their own international and trust investment corporations, of which the one in Shanghai is the largest. Special corporations for the attraction of investment by overseas Chinese have been established in Fujian and Zhejiang provinces.

In the early 1990s, the government began allowing foreign investors to manufacture and sell an increasingly wide variety of goods in the domestic market. From the mid-1990s, wholly foreign-owned enterprises (WFOEs) have been allowed to operate. In 2000 and 2001, China revised its laws on JVs and WFOEs to eliminate requirements for foreign exchange balancing, to eliminate domestic sales ratio requirements, to eliminate or adjust advanced technology and export performance requirements, and to modify provisions on domestic procurement of raw materials. With China's accession to the WTO in December 2001, foreign investment opportunities were further expanded with the removal of financial and distribution services from the restricted list. Only the production of arms and the mining and processing of certain minerals are currently off-limits to foreign investment.

China attracts capital in four ways: (1) by soliciting loans and credits from foreign governments and international financial institutions; (2) by floating bonds and debentures on international capital markets; (3) by promoting direct foreign investment through joint ventures and other cooperative enterprises; and (4) by accumulating trade surpluses from export sales.

From 1979 to 2000, according to Chinese government figures, FDI (foreign direct investment) totaled $350 billion. This figure includes investment from the Special Administrative Regions (SARs) of Hong Kong and Macao as well as from Taiwan. On an annual basis, this not-very-foreign proportion of FDI dropped from over two-thirds to an average of 45.5% for 1999 and 2000. (Analysts have also estimated that 10–30% of FDI from Hong Kong actually comes from Chinese mainland companies looking for a tax break.) From 1979 to 1990, double-digit annual growth rates in the early years (55% in 1984 and 38% in 1985) declined to a low of 2.7% in 1990, the year after the Tiananmen Square violence. However, in 1991, FDI increased 25% and then soared by triple digits in 1992 (152%) and 1993 (150%). By the end of 1995, over 258,000 foreign-invested enterprises had registered in China. In 1996 a World Bank study found that China attracted more than one-third of all investment in factories and other manufacturing plants in developing nations. Growth rates, of course, moderated after their early surge, but it was not until the Asian financial crisis of 1997–98, precipitated by China's reabsorption of Hong Kong in July 1997, that annual FDI levels stagnated, with a 0.45% growth rate in 1998, and then declined, with an 11.1% fall in 1999 from $45.46 billion to $40.4 billion annual FDI. In 1999 foreign invested firms numbered 300,000 and accounted for almost 50% of exports. In 2000, FDI only grew 0.9%, to $40.77 billion, but in 2001, a 14.6% increase sent annual FDI to a record $46.8 billion. FDI in China was a net inflow of $78.2 billion according to World Bank figures published in 2009. FDI represented 1.57% of GDP. The government's 2011 foreign investment catalogue, which came into effect on 1 January 2012 and replaced the 2007 catalogue, regulates investment by placing restrictions or incentives on various industries. In particular, the 2011 catalogue included regulations that encouraged greater foreign investment in advanced manufacturing—components for alternative energy vehicles and Internet system equipment, for example.

China continues to have no mergers and acquisitions law that would permit the involuntary take-over of a company. A company can be bought outright but the sale requires specific government approval, as do all investments in China. Indirect foreign (or portfolio) investment (FII) is limited to those willing to invest to the mainland companies listed on the Chinese stock exchange.

Until the early 1980s, the flow of Chinese funds abroad was confined to assistance to developing countries and to investment in Hong Kong real estate. In 1983, however, China began making direct investments overseas, in the United States, Canada, the Solomon Islands, and Sri Lanka. China has been a significant supplier of development aid to other countries. Recipients of Chinese military and economic assistance have included the DPRK, Vietnam, Egypt, Pakistan, and Tanzania.

[39]ECONOMIC DEVELOPMENT

A profound restructuring of China's economy began in 1949 following the founding of the PRC. Adhering to orthodox models borrowed wholesale from the former USSR, the PRC brought all major industrial, infrastructure, and financial enterprises directly under state ownership. Agriculture was collectivized. Management of the economy was closely controlled by central authorities, whose powers extended to the allocation of basic commodities and the basic division of resources into investment, consumption, and defense channels. Centralized planning for economic development was introduced in the form of five-year economic plans.

The first five-year plan (1953–57), belatedly announced in 1957, pursued rapid industrialization along Soviet lines, with a special emphasis on increases in steel and other heavy industries. The plan reportedly achieved its goals of a 5% gain in gross value of agricultural output and a 4% gain in grain production, and exceeded the 19% growth target in gross value of industrial output.

The second five-year plan (1958–62) was voided at its start by the social and economic upheavals of the Great Leap Forward. At the heart of the Great Leap was the establishment of the self-sufficient rural commune; decentralization of industry was stressed, and the rural unemployed put to work in "backyard steel furnaces" and other industrial enterprises of dubious efficiency. Incomes were determined by need, and coercion and revolutionary enthusiasm replaced profit as the motivation for work. Publication of economic data ceased at this time, but Western observers estimated a 1% decline in agriculture for the 1958–60 period, an increase in GNP of only 1%, and no more than a 6% increase in industrial output. After the bad harvests of 1960 and 1961, an "agriculture first" policy was adopted under which large areas of semiarid steppe and other marginal lands in the north and west were converted to agricultural use.

A third five-year plan (1966–70), formulated by governmental pragmatists and calling for rapid growth of all sectors, was aborted by the outbreak of the Cultural Revolution. In 1969, the government published a report calling for a more open approach to foreign assistance and trade. Domestically, it confirmed the use of the "mass line"—the system of calling upon workers and peasants to take responsibility and initiative, and to work without material incentives. It favored the simultaneous use of modern and traditional employment methods (the "walking on two legs" policy), and recommended expansion of industry through investment of profits derived from the sale of agricultural and light industrial products. At the heart of the 1969 policy was a reversion to the commune system of 1958—a program to make the countryside self-sufficient, with every commune not only growing its own food but also producing its own fertilizer and tools, generating its own electricity, and managing its own small handicrafts factories, health schemes, and primary schools. In contrast to the hastily organized communes of 1958–60, however, the new units frequently adhered to the traditional—and more manageable—structure of Chinese rural life.

Long-range economic planning resumed in 1970 with the announcement of a fourth five-year plan, for 1971–75. In late 1975,

Premier Zhou Enlai proclaimed the plan successful. Agricultural output was reported to have grown by 51% during the 1964–74 period, while gross industrial output was said to have increased by 190%. Specifically, the following growth rates (1964–74) for mining and industry were reported: petroleum, 660%; coal, 92%; steel, 120%; cotton yarn, 86%; tractors, 540%; chemical fertilizers, 350%; and electric power, 200%.

A fifth five-year plan (1976–80), announced in 1975, gave priority to modernization of the economy and, for the first time, emphasized the development of light rather than heavy industry. Implementation of this new departure was, however, delayed by the deaths of Mao and Zhou in 1976 and did not occur until 1978, by which time the economic pragmatists, led by Deng Xiaoping, had emerged victorious from the subsequent political and ideological struggles.

The sixth five-year plan (1981–85) reemphasized China's commitment to the pragmatic line and to the Four Modernizations. Approximately $115 billion was allocated for capital construction, and another $65 billion for renovation of existing infrastructure. GNP increased by an annual average of 10%, industrial output by 12%, and agricultural output by 8.1%.

The seventh five-year plan (1986–90), announced in March 1986 and called by Deng Xiaoping "The New Long March," featured the following major goals: increasing industrial output 7.5% annually (to $357 billion); increasing agricultural output 4% annually (to $95.4 billion); increasing national income 6.7% annually (to $252.7 billion); increasing foreign trade 40% (to $83 billion); spending $54 billion on 925 major development projects in energy, raw materials, transportation, and postal and telecommunications; and investing $74.6 billion in technological transformation of state enterprises. The goal for rural per capita income was $151 annually.

Concerns about the unevenness of China's economic development progress, both in geographic and sectoral terms, shaped the country's eighth five-year plan (1991–95). To ameliorate potentially crippling bottlenecks in the supply of raw materials, energy, transportation, and communications capacity, the government prioritized the financing of infrastructure investments. Streamlining of inefficient state industrial enterprises was targeted as well, with the setting up of an unemployment security fund planned in order to assist laid-off workers make the transition to employment in nonstate industry and the services sector. Direct foreign investment in industry, services, and infrastructure (especially energy and communications development) were promoted. The plan also emphasized better distribution of the country's development momentum. Inland cities, especially along the Russian, Mongolian, and North Korean borders were targeted for development as export-oriented special economic zones in addition to coastal areas. Particular emphasis was given to developing major infrastructure projects to link Hong Kong, Macao, and the Pearl River delta area of Guangdong province into an integrated economic area and major export base for the 21st century.

The ninth five-year plan (1996–2000) called for a shift from a centrally planned economy to a "socialist market economy." It also stressed resource allocation to achieve higher efficiency. The goals included continuing progress toward quadrupling the 1980 GNP by the year 2000 (a goal that had already been met by 1996) and doubling the 2000 GNP by the year 2010, a goal carried over into

tenth five-year plan (2001–05). By the end of 2002, the Chinese economy had come through two major external shocks (the Asian financial crisis of 1997–98 and the global economic slowdown of 2001–02) without seriously faltering, at least according to official government figures. Real GDP growth registered 8% in 2000 and dipped to 7.3% in 2001. Inflation held near zero or below, with a slight deflation in consumer prices (-0.8% in 1998, -1.4% in 1999, and -0.4% in 2002). In 2000 and 2001 inflation was below 1%, at 0.4% and 0.7%, respectively.

The tenth five-year plan (2001–05) called for a continuance of these trends: average GDP growth rates of 7% with a goal of reaching a GDP of $1.5 trillion by 2005 in the context of stable prices. The government estimated that the labor force would increase 40 million by 2005, and that there would also be 40 million surplus rural laborers to be transferred, as the proportion of the labor force in agriculture dropped from an estimated 50% in 2001 to a planned 44% by 2005. Under the tenth five-year plan the government sought to improve its "socialist market economy." Priorities include establishing a "modern enterprise system" in the state-owned enterprises (SOEs), improving social security, and increasing the depth and breadth of participation in the international economy. Registered urban unemployment, at 3.6% in 2001 and below 4% in 2002, was to be controlled at about 5% under the tenth plan. The CIA estimated that total urban unemployment was about 10% in 2001, and that there was substantial underemployment in rural areas; Chinese sources put unemployment overall at 20% in 2003. The tenth five-year plan foresaw agriculture's share in the GDP decreasing to 13% by 2005 from 17.7% in 2001, while industry's share was expected to increase from 49.3% to 51%, and the share of services, from 33% to 36%, across the planning period. Educational goals include attaining gross enrollments of 90% at the junior high school level, 60% in high school, and 15% in higher education. Environmental targets included attaining 18.2% forest coverage, 35% urban green rate, and an overall 10% reduction over 2000 levels in pollutants discharged.

In 2005 China's history of incrementalist economic restructuring for increased efficiency gains led to a GDP ten times higher than that recorded in the late 1970s. Such advances helped make China the second-largest economy in the world (in terms of purchasing power parity) after the United States. However, despite the country's economic advances as a whole, the low per capita income and millions of citizens living below the poverty line still placed China in a lower middle-income range. Economic development continued to be disproportionate, with more advances occurring in the eastern coastal provinces than in the rest of the country. Also, as state-owned enterprises (SOEs) have decreased, the government has been challenged to find work for the millions of former SOE employees who were unemployed as a result. Also challenging the government are charges to reduce corruption and economic crimes and to reduce environmental damage (air pollution, soil erosion, and the fall of the water table in the north) and social strife in the face of economic transformation. In July 2005, China revalued the yuan by 2.1%, and benefited from foreign investment and increased involvement in world trade and increasing employment in urban jobs, despite electricity shortages in the summer of 2005.

The 11th five-year plan included provisions to reduce energy consumption (per unit GDP) by 20% and increase GDP by 45% by

2010. It also included a resource conservation and environmental protection package supplementing the other policies and reforms. The twelfth five-year plan (2011–15) sought to address rising inequality and create an environment for more sustainable growth by prioritizing more equitable wealth distribution, increased domestic consumption, and improved infrastructure and social safety nets. The health and energy sectors were targeted as Strategic Emerging Industries and also fit into the government's concept of more inclusive economic growth. Minimum wage increases, while also working toward that end, were expected to raise labor costs for businesses, a hindrance the government intended to mitigate through the development of the labor force.

⁴⁰SOCIAL DEVELOPMENT

China does not yet have national social security legislation. Old age provisions in rural areas is tied to family support and community and state programs. According to the Labor Law, male workers and professional women are eligible to retire at age 60, female nonsalaried workers at 55, and other women at age 50. The amount of the pension is decided by the local or city government based on the standard of living in that area. The urban medical insurance program covers employees in urban enterprises. Local governments and employers adapt the guidelines and base rates according to local conditions. There are some local programs to provide for needy families.

Workers may receive six months' sick leave at 60–100% of salary. For work-related total disability, workers are entitled to lifetime compensation of 75–90% of the standard wage. Maternity leave at full pay is provided for up to 90 days. In addition, numerous health, day-care, and educational benefits are provided free of charge. In urban areas, housing rentals rarely exceed 5% of the monthly wage.

Despite constitutional provisions, women may face discrimination in the workplace. Women continue to report that unfair dismissal, sexual harassment, demotions, and wage disparity are significant problems. In addition, some enterprises are reluctant to hire women because of the additional costs of maternity leave. Sexual harassment is an ongoing problem and the first court cases were heard in 2003. Most women earn less than men, and are twice as likely to be illiterate. Violence against women remains a serious problem, and spousal abuse goes largely unreported. The suicide rate among women is three times the global average. Women are subject to pressure and sometimes physical coercion to submit to abortion or sterilization. The trafficking of women for the sex trade is a pervasive problem.

Since the 1970s, the government has emphasized family planning, imposing a "one child rule" on most families. As a result, population growth has been significantly reduced, but the one child rule has created a dramatic shift in the balance between the number of male and female births. Because some couples prefer to have male offspring, there has been an increase in the number of sex-selective abortions and adoptions of female infants. A study released in April 2009 reported that among the Chinese population age 20 and under there were 32 million more boys than girls. In 2011 the sex ratio at birth was 1.133 male(s)/female. The total population was 1.06 male(s)/female.

The general increase in the number of abortions has been a cause for concern in the nation. According to a report published in July 2009, there are an estimated 20 million births each year and about 13 million abortions, though the actual number of abortions may be even higher since there are a number of unregistered clinics in the country. This translates into an abortion rate of 24 per 1,000 woman of childbearing age. While many women choosing abortions are those who are married and already have one child, a large percentage are single young women between the ages of 20 and 29. Some authorities cite inadequate sex education programs and poor knowledge of birth control as primary factors in the heightened abortion rates.

Yet another result of the one-child policy is a rapidly aging society. In Shanghai, over 21% of the population is aged 60 or over and that percentage is expected to rise to over 33% by 2020. There are fewer younger workers to sustain the support system of the nation's retirees. Because of China's cultural expectations, children are required to take care and provide for both their elderly parents and their grandparents. With only one child per family, this now becomes more difficult as an only child must take on the responsibilities of two parents and four grandparents. In wealthier cities like Shanghai, nursing homes are constructed to accommodate the needs of citizens who do not have the capacity for the healthcare aid in their homes. In poorer towns, as elderly people live longer and develop diseases like dementia, many are sent to psychiatric wards because of the lack of treatment ability or diagnosis.

In 2009, officials in Shanghai began a special campaign to remind residents of an important exception to the one-child rule: couples who were both only children are permitted to have a second child. Family planning officials in the city began making home visits to urge eligible couples to have another child.

China's human rights record continued to draw international censure. Ongoing human rights abuses include arbitrary and lengthy detention, forced confessions, torture, and the mistreatment of prisoners. Repression of political dissent continues. Prison conditions are poor and China does not allow any independent monitoring of its prisons. Widespread human rights abuses have also been reported in Chinese-occupied Tibet. The government does not tolerate any political dissent or pro-independence movements in Tibet.

⁴¹HEALTH

The birth rate was 12.29 births per 1,000 in 2011. The fertility rate was 1.54, while the infant mortality rate was 16.06 per 1,000 live births. In 2008 the maternal mortality rate, according to the World Bank, was 38 per 100,000 births. It was estimated that 94% of children were vaccinated against measles. The CIA calculated HIV/AIDS prevalence in China to be about 0.1%. The country spent 4.3% of its GDP on healthcare, amounting to $177 per person.

A revamping of China's health system was underway in the late 1990s to manage serious diseases. These include strengthening epidemic prevention management systems and facilities. National health practices, including the provision of both Western and traditional Chinese health services are under the supervision of the Ministry of Health. The ministry has emphasized preventive medicine and general improvement of sanitary conditions.

Since the early 1950s, mass campaigns have been mounted to deal with major public health problems. These have included nationwide cleanup campaigns and mass educational programs in the sanitary preparation of food, the treatment of drinking water, personal hygiene, and waste disposal. The entire population was mobilized to eradicate the four pests—rats, sparrows, flies, and mosquitoes—with mixed results. Epidemic prevention centers were established to carry out massive immunizations, while parasitic diseases, affecting hundreds of millions in China, were also attacked. As a result, schistosomiasis, malaria, kala-azar, and hookworm are thought to have been largely brought under control.

There were 14 physicians, 14 nurses and midwives, and 41 hospital beds per 10,000 inhabitants.

During the Cultural Revolution, in an effort to even out the disparity between rural and urban health services, medical personnel from hospitals (as much as 30–50% of a hospital's medical staff) were sent to the countryside and the number of locally trained paramedical personnel, called barefoot doctors, expanded. These paramedical personnel—young peasants or middle-school graduates—were trained on the job by township doctors or in two-month courses at township health clinics. "Barefoot doctors" and brigade health stations are still major deliverers of healthcare in the countryside.

In the fight against disease, China received $539 million from the Global Fund to Fight AIDS, Tuberculosis and Malaria from 2003 to 2011. Since 2008, efforts toward greater cooperation have been handled in part through negotiations between the mainland-based Association for Relations Across the Strait and the Taiwan-based Straits Exchange Foundation. The groups met six times between 2008 and 2010. At the December 2010 meeting, negotiators signed a medical and health care cooperation agreement that will enhance cooperation in pharmaceutical research and safety management and strengthen prevention and emergency measures aimed at combating the spread of infectious diseases. The agreement also calls for the establishment of quality guarantees and enhanced research for traditional Chinese medicine. About 90 percent of the traditional medicines used in Taiwan come from the mainland.

42 HOUSING

China has an acute shortage of housing, attributable not only to the large annual increases in population (over 10 million a year), but also to the long-standing policy of directing investment funds into heavy industry rather than into housing and other social amenities. The government expected to build 486 million sq m (5,231.26 million sq ft) to 549 million sq m (5,909.39 million sq ft) of floor space each year between 2000 and 2020.

During the 1990s, the government began a program of transferring ownership of state-owned housing into private hands at fairly low costs and with subsidized mortgages. As a result, an estimated 73% of families owned their own residence by the end of the decade. In rural areas, homes tend to be smaller. Some newer rural homes are at about 50 sq m (538.2 sq ft) in size, with households of about three to six people. Though many rural homes are constructed with wood and earthen walls and tile or thatched roofs, some newer homes, such as those built by Habitat for Humanity, include red brick, stone, and compressed earth blocks.

43 EDUCATION

The Cultural Revolution affected education more than any other sector of society. Schools were shut down in mid-1966 to give the student Red Guards the opportunity to "make revolution" on and off campus. The Cultural Revolution touched off purges within the educational establishment. Upper- and middle-level bureaucrats throughout the system were removed from office, and virtually entire university faculties and staffs dispersed. Although many lower schools had begun to reopen during 1969, several universities remained closed through the early 1970s, as an estimated 10 million urban students were removed to the countryside to take part in labor campaigns. During this period and its aftermath, revolutionary ideology, and local conditions became the principal determinants of curriculum. A nine-year program of compulsory education (compressed from 12 years) was established for youths 7–15 years of age.

Education was reoriented in 1978 under the Four Modernizations policy, which restored the pre-1966 emphasis on competitive examinations and the development of special schools for the most promising students. The most striking changes were effected at the junior and senior high school levels, in which students were again streamed, according to ability, into an estimated 5,000 high-quality, well-equipped schools, or into lower-quality high schools, or into the technical and vocational schools, which were perceived as the least prestigious. In addition, 96 universities, 200 technical schools, and 7,000 primary schools were designated as "key" institutions. Universities were reopened, with a renewed emphasis given to science and technology. By 1998, there were 628,840 primary schools with 5,794,000 teachers and 139,954,000 students. At the secondary level, there were 4,437,000 teachers and 718,883,000 students.

In 2009 the World Bank estimated that 100% of age-eligible children in China were enrolled in primary school. There were 100 male students for every 104 female students. Overall, the CIA estimated that China had a literacy rate of 91.6%. The student-to-teacher ratio in primary school was 17:1.

There are over 1,000 colleges and universities in China. Among the largest and most prestigious institutions were Beijing University and Qinghua University, both in Beijing; Zhongshan University, in Guangzhou; Nanjing University and Nanjing Institute of Technology; Nankai University and Tianjin University, in Tianjin; and Fudan University, in Shanghai. In 2009, tertiary enrollment was estimated at 25%. Of those enrolled in tertiary education, there were 100 male students for every 104 female students. Overall, the World Bank estimated that the adult literacy rate for 2009 was 94%, with 97% for men and 91% for women.

Tuition has traditionally been free in vocational secondary schools, and in training schools for elementary teachers, as well as in colleges and universities; students in need of food, clothing, and textbooks receive state grants-in-aid. Primary and general secondary school students pay a nominal tuition fee. Part-time primary and secondary schools, evening universities, and correspondence schools exist for adult workers and peasants.

44 LIBRARIES AND MUSEUMS

The National Library in Beijing (founded in 1909) is the largest in China, with over 22 million volumes, including more than 291,000 rare ancient Chinese books and manuscripts. The Chinese Academy of Sciences Central Library, in Beijing, has a collection of 6.2 million volumes, with branches in Shanghai, Lanzhou, Wuhan, and Chengdu. The Capital Library in Beijing (2.6 million volumes) is the city's public library and operates lending, reference, and children's services. The Shoudu Library, also in Beijing, has 2.35 million volumes. Shanghai Central Library System, established in 2001 with support from the municipal government, includes about 36 branch libraries.

Small lending libraries and reading rooms can be found in factories, offices, and rural townships. The library of Beijing University, with over four million volumes, is the largest university library. Other important university collections are at Nanjing University in Nanjing (3.2 million volumes), Fudan University in Shanghai (3.6 million volumes), and Qinghua University in Beijing (2.5 million volumes). The Central Institute of Nationalities in Beijing—one of dozens of private institutions with libraries—has a collection of 800,000 volumes, including 160 foreign-language journals. The Library Association of China was founded in Beiping (modern-day Beijing), China, in 1925 and reorganized in T'aipei in 1953. The Hong Kong Library Association was founded in 1958.

China has a wealth of about 1,000 museums, most of them cultural in nature. The Imperial Palace Museum in Beijing houses collections of art, sculpture, silk fabric, and furniture. The Museum of the Chinese Revolution on Tiananmen Square has exhibits of the revolutionary movement in China from the Opium War to the founding of the PRC. In Shanghai is the Museum of Art and History, with some of the country's outstanding archaeological and art collections. Many museums are memorials to Chinese artists and writers, and house collections of their work. China also has 500 historical sites with exhibitions. With the return of Hong Kong to China, the country gained the Hong Kong Museum of Art, the University Museum and Art Gallery, the Hong Kong Museum of History, and the Hong Kong Space Museum.

45 MEDIA

Postal service and telecommunications facilities fall under the authority of the Ministry of Posts and Telecommunications. China continues to develop and improve its telecommunication infrastructure. Domestic and international services are increasingly being made available for private use, although domestic services are unevenly distributed, primarily serving major cities, industrial centers, and many towns. In 2009, there were some 313.7 million main phone lines and some 747 million mobile cellular phones in use. Mobile phone subscriptions average 56 per 100 people. In Hong Kong, there were some 3.85 million telephone main lines in 2006. There were 8.693 million mobile cellular phones in use in 2005.

Television broadcasting began in 1958, and color transmissions in 1973. As of 2009 China had 369 AM and 259 FM radio broadcasting stations. In 1997, China Central Television operated 209 government-owned television stations and 45 shortwave radio stations. There were also 31 provincial stations and almost 3,000 city stations. The most important station is Beijing's Central People's Broadcasting Station (CPBS); from there, programs are relayed by local stations. CPBS broadcasts daily on several channels using a variety of languages, including Mandarin (or standard Chinese), the Hokkien and Hakka dialects, Cantonese, Mongolian, Tibetan, Uigur, Kazakhi, and Korean. Many of the TV sets are installed in public meeting places and in government and economic enterprises, although increasingly a television set has

become a much-prized private acquisition. Since large segments of the rural population are as yet without radios and television sets, the government operates a massive wired broadcast network linked to over 100 million loudspeakers.

Despite controls, a rapidly growing number of Chinese have access to satellite television and the Internet. The government regulates access of the Internet through the Ministry of Information Industry and the Ministries of Public and State Security. In 2010, the country had 15.2 million Internet hosts. In 2011 there were some 551 million Internet users. Internet users numbered 29 per 100 citizens.

China's state-run news agency, Xinhua, announced in July 2010 that it would begin broadcasting a 24-hour global news channel in English. The station, which was originally piloted in Hong Kong, will expand into Europe, North America, and Africa in a bid to reach some 50 million viewers and put forward a Chinese perspective on international events. The Chinese government has long complained that Western media outlets portray China in an unflattering light, reporting mostly negative stories. Thus, the expansion of China's English-language television station offers the Chinese government a chance to counterbalance those perspectives with a better view of China. Chinese authorities stressed, however, that the station was structured as a news channel, not a propaganda station.

The press is closely controlled by the government, the CCP, or the various political and mass organizations associated with the CCP. Minority newspapers are published in Mongolian, Uygur, Tibetan, Korean, and other languages. The main news agencies are the official New China (Xinhua) News Agency; the China News Service, which supplies information to overseas Chinese newspapers and journals; and China Feature, which supplies articles to magazines and newspapers worldwide.

The Cultural Revolution caused substantial upheaval in the Chinese press establishment. Many publications closed down, and others underwent purges of editorial staffs. Publication of *Hongqi* (*Red Flag*), the most authoritative of the CCP publications, resumed in 1968.

Prominent newspapers in 2010, with circulation numbers listed parenthetically, included *Xin Min Wan Bao* (1,800,000), *Oriental Daily News* (650,000), and *Beijing Wanbao* (800,000), as well as 37 other major newspapers. The major newspapers, with their locations and circulations in 2002, are: *Gongren Ribao* (*Worker's Daily*), Beijing, 2,500,000; *Renmin Ribao* (*People's Daily*), Beijing, 2,150,000; *Xin Min Wanbao* (*Xin Min Evening News*), Shanghai, 1,800,000; *Wenhui Bao* (*Wenhui Daily*), Shanghai, 1,700,000; *Yangcheng Wanbao* (*Yangcheng Evening News*), Guangzhou, 1,300,000; *Jiefang Ribao* (*Liberation Daily*), Shanghai, 1,000,000; and *Jiefangjun Bao* (*Liberation Army Daily*), Beijing, 800,000.

Government-approved publishing houses are the only legal book publishers.

The increasing use of foreign languages in the media has become a concern for the government, which believes that such use has seriously damaged the purity of the language and has had an adverse cultural impact on the culture. In December 2010, the government banned newspapers, publishers, website managers, and radio and television broadcasters from using foreign words, abbreviations, and acronyms. If a word must be written in a foreign language, the author must also provide an explanation in Chinese.

Though China's constitution states that freedom of speech and of the press are fundamental rights, in practice the Communist Party and the government control all print and electronic media, which are compelled to propagate the current ideological line. All media are under explicit, public orders to guide public opinion as directed by the authorities.

46 ORGANIZATIONS

Prior to 1966, the leading mass organizations, all closely tied to the regime, were the Communist Youth League, the Women's Federation, the Federation of Literary and Art Circles, the Federation of Scientific Societies, and the Federation of Industry and Commerce. These bodies were to some extent eclipsed by the Cultural Revolution, which spawned a host of new groups. After the Cultural Revolution passed its peak, many of the new organizations lost ground, while local Communist Youth League organizations, including the Young Pioneers, gained prestige. By the mid-1980s, the pre-Cultural Revolution groups were once again ascendant.

There are professional and trade organizations representing a wide variety of professional fields. The All China Federation of Industry and Commerce promotes international trade. The All China Federation of Trade Unions serves as an advocate for worker's rights and benefits, particularly for women. The Asia Pacific Occupational Safety and Health Organization (APOSHO) is located in Hong Kong. Labor organizations in Hong Kong include the Employers' Federation of Hong Kong, the Hong Kong Confederation of Trade Unions, and the Hong Kong Federation of Trade Unions. The International Labour Organization has an office in Beijing.

Educational and cultural organizations include the China National Association of Literature and Fine Arts based in Taiwan. The Chinese Academy of Social Sciences promotes research in philosophy and the social sciences. The Hong Kong Arts Festival Society sponsors an international arts festival. The Royal Asiatic Society, dedicated to the history and culture of China, Hong Kong, and Asia, has a branch in Hong Kong. There are also several organizations dedicated to research and education in various fields of medicine and science. There are also many associations for hobbyists.

National women's organizations include the Association for the Advancement of Feminism (AAF), based in Hong Kong and the All China Women's Federation, based in Beijing. The largest youth association is the umbrella organization the All-China Youth Federation (ACYF), which is led by the Communist Party of China. Member organizations include the Rural Young Entrepreneurs Association, the Association for Young Journalists, the Communist Youth League (CYL) of China, the All-China Students Federation (ACSF), the YMCA and YWCA, and the Chinese Young Entrepreneurs Association (CYEA). Scouting groups exist in Hong Kong and Macau. A wide variety of sports organizations are active throughout the country, including the Chinese Table Tennis Association, which has gained international recognition.

The Asian Human Rights Commission (Hong Kong) is a multinational organization for human rights. There are national chapters of the Red Cross, Greenpeace, Habitat for Humanity, and Amnesty International.

47 TOURISM, TRAVEL, AND RECREATION

Chinese restrictions on tourism were eased to allow access by foreigners on group tours in 1976 and further relaxed in 1983, when the ban on individual travel was lifted. By 1985, there were 244 Chinese cities and scenic spots open to foreign tourists and a number of resorts specifically designed for foreigners were in operation. China was opened to tourists from Taiwan in 1987. All visitors to China must have a valid passport and visa; personal interviews may also be required upon entry.

The most famous tourist attraction in China is the Great Wall, the construction of which began in the 3rd century BC as a barrier against northern invaders. Other leading tourist attractions include the Forbidden City, or Imperial Palace, in Beijing; the nearby tombs of the Ming emperors; historic Hangzhou, with its famous West Lake and gardens; busy Shanghai, with its well-stocked stores and superb cuisine; Xi'an, the site of monumental Qin dynasty excavations; and Guangzhou, the center of Cantonese cooking, with an extensive Cultural Park.

Sports activities in China are coordinated by the State Physical Culture and Sports Commission and the All-China Sports Federation. Active sports, represented by national associations, include gymnastics, diving, basketball, football (soccer), tennis, cycling, swimming, volleyball, weight lifting, and mountain climbing. The 2008 Summer Olympics were held in Beijing, the first Olympic Games to be held in China.

Distinctively Chinese pastimes include wushu, a set of ancient exercises known abroad as gonfu (kung fu) or the "martial arts"; taijiquan, or shadow boxing, developed in the 17th century; and liangong shibafa, modern therapeutic exercises for easing neck, shoulder, back, and leg ailments. Qigong (literally "breathing exercises") is also widely practiced both as a sport and as physical therapy. A popular traditional spectator sport is Chinese wrestling. Traditional pastimes for the national minorities are horse racing, show jumping, and archery among the Mongolians; the sheep chase (in which the winner successfully locates and defends possession of a slaughtered sheep) among Uyghurs and Kazaks; and yak and horse racing among Tibetans.

In November 2010, the Peking opera was officially inscribed on the UNESCO Representative List of the Intangible Heritage of Humanity, an offshoot of the World Heritage program. The opera was deemed a living tradition by UNESCO, meaning that it is still passed from generation to generation and continues to create a sense of identity and community for those who participate. Such traditions have been approved by UNESCO for special consideration since 2001. For one that is inscribed, a special program is designed to protect and promote the practice and understanding of the tradition. Peking opera combines singing, acting, reciting, and martial arts to tell stories that are both informative and entertaining. Another addition to the list was traditional Chinese acupuncture and moxibustion, forms of Chinese medicine that treat disease through the precise placement of needles in the body and the burning of moxa (mugwort) cones or sticks that are placed on points of the body.

The *Tourism Factbook*, published by the UN World Tourism Organization, reported 126.5 million incoming tourists to China in 2009, who spent a total of $42.6 billion. Of those incoming tourists, there were 117.6 million from East Asia and the Pacific. There were 3.06 million hotel beds available in China.

In 2011, the estimated daily cost to visit Beijing, the capital, was $370. The cost of visiting other cities averaged $188.

48 FAMOUS PERSONS

Confucius (K'ung Fu-tzu or Kong Fuzi, 551–479 BC) is generally regarded as the most important historical figure and the greatest scholar of ancient China. His philosophy and social ideas include observance of filial piety, the sanctity of the family, and social responsibility. Other early philosophers were Laotzu (Laozi; Li Erh, 604?–531 BC), the traditional founder of Taoism; Mencius (Meng-tzu or Mengzi, 385–289 BC), who stressed the essential goodness of human nature and the right of subjects to revolt against unjust rulers; and Mo Ti (Di, 465?–390? BC), who stressed the theme of universal love. Among the principal early poets was Chu (Chü) Yuan, (340–278 BC), whose *Li Sao*, a melancholy rhapsody, is among the world's great poems. Sima Qian (Ssu-ma Ch'ien, 145–87 BC) produced the monumental *Shiji (Shih-chi; Historical Records)*, the first general history of China. Ban Gu (Pan Ku, AD 32–92) wrote *Qian Hanshu (Ch'ien-Han shu; History of the Former Han Dynasty)*, a continuation of Sima Qian's work. Zhang (Chang) Heng (78–139), an astronomer, is credited with having invented the first seismograph. Zhang Zhongjing (Chang Chung-ching, 152–219) was a celebrated physician, and Zu Zhongzhi (Tsu Chung-chih, 429–500) calculated the figure 3.14159265 as the value for pi. Three brilliant poets of the Tang dynasty were Li Bo (Po, 701–62), Du (Tu) Fu (712–70), and Bo Juyi (Po Chü-yi, 772–846). Li Shizhen (Shi-chen, 1518–93), an outstanding pharmacologist, wrote a monumental *Materia Medica*. Great authors of the Qing dynasty were Wu Jingzi (Ching-tzu, 1701–54), who wrote *Rulin Waishi (Ju-lin wai-shih; Unofficial History of the Scholars)*, a superb satire on the civil service system, and Cao Xueqin (Ts'ao Hsüeh-ch'in, 1715?–63), who produced a remarkable novel, *Honglou meng (Hung-lou meng; The Dream of the Red Chamber)*. Lu Xun or Lu Hsun (Zhou Shuren or Chou Shu-jen, 1881–1936) is generally regarded as China's greatest writer of the modern period. Mao Dun (Shen Yanbing, 1896–1981) and Ba Jin (Li Feigan, 1904–2005) are leading novelists. Lin Yutang (Yu-t'ang, 1895–1976) popularized Chinese culture in the West. Ha Jin (b. 1956) is a contemporary Chinese-American novelist born in Liaoning, China. His novel *Waiting* (1999) won the US National Book Award and PEN/Faulkner Award, and *War Trash* (2004) was a finalist for the Pulitzer Prize. Maxine Hong Kingston (b. 1940), born in California, is a Chinese-American writer whose *The Woman Warrior* (1976) won the National Book Critics Award for Nonfiction. In October 2009, Charles Kao (b. 1933), a native of Shanghai, China, was announced as a co-recipient of the 2009 Nobel Prize in Physics for his work in developing fiber optic cables. Ai Weiwei (b. 1957), an artist and human rights activist, was arrested by the Chinese government in April 2011 and held in secret for 81 days. He became a global cause célèbre.

Political Figures

Sun Yat-sen (Zhongshan or Chung-shan, 1866–1925) planned the revolution against the Manchus and became the first president (1911–12) of the republic. Mao Zedong (Tse-tung, 1893–1976), the foremost figure of postrevolutionary China, served as chairman of the Central Committee of the CCP from 1956 to 1976. Other prominent Chinese Communist leaders include Zhu De (Chu Teh, 1886–1976), who became commander in chief of the Red Army in 1931 and chairman of the Standing Committee of the NPC; Zhou Enlai (Chou En-lai, 1898–1976), first premier of China's State Council; Liu Shaoqi (Shao-ch'i, 1898–1969), who became China's head of state in 1959 and was purged during the Cultural Revolution but posthumously rehabilitated in 1985; and Lin Biao (Piao, 1908–71), who became deputy premier and minister of defense in 1959 and who, prior to his death and subsequent political vilification, had been certified as Mao's successor in the constitution drawn up in 1969. Women in the political hierarchy have included Song Qingling (Soong Ch'ing-ling, 1892–1981), Sun Zhongshan's wife, and Jiang Qing (Chiang Ch'ing, 1913–91), Mao's fourth wife, who emerged as a radical leader during the Cultural Revolution. Jiang, with other prominent radicals, was purged in the wake of the ascension of Hua Guofeng (b. 1921–2008) as CCP chairman in 1976. Deng Xiaoping (1904–97), twice disgraced (1966–73 and 1976) by radical administrations, reemerged in 1977 to become China's most powerful political figure, albeit without major office, and a major figure in its modernization drive; he officially retired in 1987. A protégé, Hu Yaobang (1915–89), was party secretary until his ouster in 1987. Another protégé was Zhao Ziyang (1919–2005), who became general secretary of the CCP in 1987; he was purged in 1989 for his support of student demonstrators in the Tiananmen Square protests of 1989, and spent the last 15 years of his life under house arrest. Li Peng (b. 1928) was chairman of the standing committee of the National People's Congress from 1998–2003. For his support of the violent suppression of the 1989 Tiananmen Square protests, he remains unpopular with a large part of the Chinese population. Jiang Zemin (b. 1926), is part of the "third generation" of Chinese leaders (after those surrounding Mao Zedong and Deng Xiaoping); he served as general secretary of the CCP from 1989–2002, as president from 1993–2003, and as chairman of the military from 1989–2004. Hu Jintao (b. 1942) is the fourth president of the People's Republic of China, general secretary of the CCP, and chairman of the central military commission, succeeding Jiang Zemin in those posts. He ushers in a "fourth generation" of leaders. In October 2010, the Chinese dissident Liu Xiaobo was named as the recipient of the 2010 Nobel Peace Prize. The announcement caused a great deal of controversy between China and the international community. Liu was a key leader in the 1989 Tiananmen Square protest and has often spoken out against the nation's track record for violations of human rights.

49 DEPENDENCIES

Hong Kong

Hong Kong consists of 237 small islands off the southeast coast of the mainland of China and a small peninsula adjoining Guangdong Province on the mainland between 22°29′ and 22°37′ N and 113°52′ and 114°30′ E. With a total area, including reclamation, of 1,068 sq km (412 sq mi), it comprises the island of Hong Kong and adjacent islands, 79 sq km (30 sq mi); the Kowloon Peninsula, 11 sq km (4 sq mi); and the New Territories (a leased section of the Chinese mainland) and the remaining islands, 978 sq km (377 sq mi). Most of Hong Kong territory is rocky, hilly, and deeply eroded. The climate is subtropical, with hot and humid summers. Rainfall is heavy and there are occasional typhoons.

Total population, which was under 600,000 in 1945, was approximately 7.1 million in 2011. Some 60% of Hong Kong's residents in 1996 were born there. The phenomenal increase since World War II (1939–45) resulted primarily from a large influx of mainland Chinese. During the late 1970s and early 1980s, hundreds of thousands of "boat people" arrived from Vietnam. Most have been resettled in other countries, and by mid-1987 only 8,500 remained in camps. In summer 1987, however, Hong Kong faced another influx of Vietnamese, most of them ethnic Chinese. These people—more than 6,000 of them—had fled to China after the Vietnam War but found it difficult to assimilate there.

About 95% of the inhabitants are Chinese and about 95% of the people live in metropolitan areas. Chinese (Cantonese dialect) is the principal spoken language; both Chinese and English are official languages. Taoists, Confucianists, and Buddhists constitute a majority of the population. The Christian population (10%) is split about evenly between Roman Catholics and Protestants. There are also Muslim and Hindu communities (1%). The capital is Victoria, commonly known as Hong Kong.

Hong Kong has regular shipping, air, cable, and wireless services to every part of the world. Government-maintained roads spanned 2,067 km (1,284 mi) in 2010. The mile-long Cross Harbour Road Tunnel connecting Hong Kong Island to Kowloon was opened in 1972, and the Lion Rock Tunnels link Kowloon with Sha Tin; the Aberdeen Tunnel beneath Hong Kong Island entered service in 1982. The government-owned Mass Transit Railway, a 38.6-km (24-mi) subway system, was begun in November 1975 and started operations in October 1979. The government also owns and operates a 56-km (35-mi) rail line, known as the Kowloon-Canton Railway. The railroad links up with the rail system of Guangdong Province and constitutes a major land-entry route to China; passenger service, suspended in 1949, was resumed in 1979. The Kowloon-Canton Railway operates a 34-km (21-mi) light rail system for the New Territories.

Hong Kong has one of the finest natural harbors. There are deepwater berths in Kowloon Peninsula and in Hong Kong; a container terminal at Kwaichung in Kowloon handles some 60% of Hong Kong's exports. An extensive ferry service connects Hong Kong's islands; hydrofoils provide service to Macau. The Hong Kong airport, Kai Tak, is the world's fourth-largest in terms of passenger traffic; it can handle upwards of 27 million passengers a year. A new airport, Chep Lap Kok, a US$20 billion project that included bridges, highways, tunnels, and a high-speed railway, opened in 1998. The first phase of the airport project, the West Kowloon expressway connecting the airport to Hong Kong Island, opened in February 1997. In April that year, another link—the Tsing Ma Bridge, the longest suspension bridge for road and rail travel in the world—opened with lavish ceremonies. Three days later, a tunnel with capacity for 180,000 cars a day opened to provide another link between Hong Kong Island and the West Kowloon expressway.

A bleak fisherman's island for most of its early history, Hong Kong was occupied in 1841 by the British. Formal cession by China was made in 1842 by the Treaty of Nanking. The Kowloon Peninsula and adjacent islands were added in 1860, and in 1898, the New Territories were leased from China for 99 years. Hong Kong

fell under Japanese occupation from 25 December 1941 to 30 August 1945. Negotiations between the United Kingdom and China culminated in an agreement on 26 September 1984 under which sovereignty over the entire colony would be transferred to China as of 1 July 1997. For a 50-year period, Hong Kong would be a Special Administrative Region and would retain its capitalist economy, its political rights, and its general way of life. A Basic Law, forming a constitution for this period, took effect in 1990.

In the interim, the colony was ruled by a UK-appointed governor, with an advisory Executive Council headed by the local commander of UK forces, and an appointed Legislative Council presided over by the governor. Chris Patten, appointed governor in 1992, held the post until the transfer of control to China 1 July 1997. The Urban Council of 30 members (15 elected and 15 appointed by the governor) dealt primarily with municipal affairs, and the government secretariat was responsible for the work of some 40 executive departments. The public sector's share of GDP decreased steadily after 1973. Under a 1981 defense agreement, about three-fourths of the cost of the maintenance of a garrison of 8,945 troops (including four Gurkha battalions) in Hong Kong was borne by the Hong Kong government. The currency unit is the Hong Kong dollar; exchange rates as of 2010 were HKD1 = US$0.129; US$1 = HKD7.76.

Located at a major crossroads of world trade, Hong Kong has become a center of commerce, shipping, industry, and banking. Rapid industrialization, accelerated by the influx of new labor, skills, and capital, changed the pattern of the economy after World War II. While heavy industries, such as shipbuilding and ship repairing, iron, and steel, remain important, light industries—especially watches, clocks, toys, and electronics—have developed more rapidly. The service sector has also experienced growth; as of 2011, approximately 93% of Hong Kong's GDP derived from services. In 2011, the GDP stood at US$353.7 billion, with annual growth that year of 6%.

Less than 10% of the total land area is used for farming, most of which is intensive vegetable cultivation. Agriculture does not represent a significant portion of Hong Kong's GDP and most of Hong Kong's agricultural produce is imported. Hong Kong is among the top export markets for US produce.

Electricity is supplied by two franchise companies. Water resources, for long a serious deficiency, have been increased by converting Plover Cove into a lake. About one-quarter of the water supply is purchased annually from China.

Imports in 2010 were estimated at US$437 billion, and exports at US$394 billion. As one of the world's largest banking centers, Hong Kong receives a continuous flow of outside capital. The Hong Kong Association of Banks was created in January 1981 to regulate charges and deposit interest rates and oversee banking standards. There is no central bank; currency is issued by two commercial banks. In addition to the licensed banks, many Chinese firms handle Chinese remittances from overseas.

Hong Kong is self-supportive except for external defense. Revenues in 2011 were estimated at US$47.55 billion, derived mainly from internal taxation and import duties. Government expenditures amounted to US$43.22 billion.

Tourism was an important industry prior to 1997, and remained so after the transfer of Hong Kong to China. About one-fourth of the total number of tourists travel to Hong Kong from the United States, Canada, and Western Europe, with another one-fourth from Japan.

Main line telephones numbered about 4.3 million in 2010; mobile cellular telephones numbered about 13.4 million that year. Broadcasting services are provided by a government station, Radio Television Hong Kong, and by commercial operators. Broadcasting services are in both Chinese and English. More than 90% of all households have one or more television sets. The Hong Kong press included 734 newspapers and periodicals. Almost all the newspapers are in Chinese; five are English-language dailies.

The infant mortality rate was 2.9 deaths per 1,000 live births in 2011, down from 5.73 deaths per 1,000 live births in 2002. The average life expectancy as of 2011 was 82.04 years (females, 84.97 years and males 79.32 years), up from 79.8 years in 2002.

The Hong Kong Housing Authority plans, builds, and manages public housing developments. About 40% of the population lived in public and aided housing as of the late 1990s.

In September 1980, education until the age of 15 was made compulsory; six years of primary and three years of secondary schooling are provided by the government free of charge. Schools are of three types: Chinese, English, and Anglo-Chinese. Prevocational training was offered in more than a dozen government-run institutions. Student enrollment in primary and secondary school is about a quarter of the population. Higher education is provided primarily by the University of Hong Kong and the Chinese University of Hong Kong. Hong Kong Polytechnic and the City Polytechnic of Hong Kong also provides postsecondary education for the colony's residents. As of 2010 approximately 97% of the population was literate.

On 1 January 2010, a group of 9,000 residents of Hong Kong protested outside of the Chinese government's liaison office in a call for full democracy to the semiautonomous region. While the constitution of Hong Kong provides for the eventual development of a more democratic system of government, the Chinese government maintains the power to veto any changes to the political system. In 2007, the Chinese government ruled that the territory cannot directly elect its own leader until 2017 and is not allowed to elect its own legislature until 2020. Opposition leaders and protesters believe the process toward democracy should move at a quicker pace.

MACAU

Macau (Macao) is situated on the south coast of China, at the mouth of the Pearl (Zhu) River, almost directly opposite Hong Kong, which is about 65 km (40 mi) away. Located at 22°6′ to 22°13′ N and 113°33′ to 113°37′ E, Macau consists of a peninsula, about 5 km (3 mi) long and 1.6 km (1 mi) wide, and two small islands, Taipa and Coloane. The total area is about 16 sq km (6 sq mi), and the total coastline is 41 km (25 mi). The climate is subtropical, with high humidity from April to October, when Macau receives most of its rainfall. Daily maximum temperatures average 29°C (84°F) during the summer; normal daily temperatures are less than 20°C (68°F) during the winter months.

Macau's population was estimated at 573,003 in 2011, up from 496,837 in mid-1996. The population density of over 29,000 people per sq km (79,000 per sq mi) was among the highest in the world. Chinese, many of them refugees from the People's Republic of China (PRC) before Macau reverted to the PRC in 1999, con-

stitute 94.3% of the total; the remaining 5.7% are Portuguese or of mixed Chinese-Portuguese ancestry. Large-scale movement of Chinese in and out of Macau has inevitably affected the economic and social life of the territory. The common language is Chinese, usually spoken in the Cantonese (85.7%), Hokkien (4%), or Mandarin (3.2%) dialect. As of 2010, Buddhism (17%) and Roman Catholicism (7%) were the dominant religions.

In 2009 there were about 413 km (257 mi) of highways. A causeway links Taipa and Coloane islands, and a 2.7-km (1.7-mi) bridge connects Macau and Taipa. Macau's main asset is its harbor; ferries, hydrofoils, and jetfoils offer shuttle service between Macau and Hong Kong. In 1994, a 240-km (149-mi) road connecting Macau and Hong Kong opened, running through Guangdong Province in the PRC.

Macau is the oldest European settlement in the Far East. The first Portuguese attempts to establish relations with China were made in the early 16th century. In 1557, the Chinese authorities agreed to Portuguese settlement of Macau, with leaseholder rights. The Portuguese, however, treated Macau as their possession and established a municipal government in the form of a senate of the local inhabitants. Disputes concerning jurisdiction and administration developed. In 1833, Macau, together with Timor, became an overseas province of Portugal under the control of the governor-general of Goa, and in 1849, Portugal succeeded in having Macau declared a free port. On 26 March 1887, China confirmed perpetual occupation and governance of Macau and its dependencies by Portugal, but the question of the delimitation of the boundaries was left unsettled.

As the only neutral port on the South China Sea during World War II (1939–45), Macau enjoyed a modicum of prosperity. In 1949, the government of the PRC renounced the "unequal treaty" granting Portuguese suzerainty over Macau. Civil disturbances in late 1966 between Macau police and Chinese leftist groups resulted in concessions to the territory's pro-China elements. The 1974 military coup in Portugal led to a constitutional change in Macau's status from a Portuguese province to a "special territory." In January 1976, Portugal's remaining few hundred troops were withdrawn from Macau. China and Portugal established diplomatic ties in 1980. In March 1987, the PRC and Portugal reached an agreement for the return of Macau to the PRC on 20 December 1999. The PRC has guaranteed not to interfere in Macau's capitalist economy and way of life for a period of 50 years.

Until December 1999, Macau was ruled by a governor appointed by Portugal, although it was empowered to make its own laws, appoint and control its own civil service, and contract directly for foreign loans.

Prior to and immediately following Macau's transfer to PRC control, the unit of currency was the Macau pataca (MOP) of 100 avos; Hong Kong dollars also circulated freely. There are coins of 10, 20, and 50 avos and 1 and 5 patacas, and notes of 5, 10, 50, 100, and 500 patacas. The pataca is linked to the Hong Kong dollar at the rate of HKD1= MOP1.03; as of 2010, the rate of exchange with US dollars was US$1 = MOP8.002 or MOP1 = US$0.1250. Corporate taxes and import duties are important sources of revenue; major expenditures are for finance, security, education, and health and welfare.

Macau's economy is consumer-oriented. There is little agriculture and the territory is heavily dependent on imports from

China for food, fresh water, and electricity. Important economic sectors are commerce, tourism, gambling, fishing, and light industry. There are small- and medium-scale enterprises concerned especially with the finishing of imported semimanufactured goods, in particular the manufacture of clothing, ceramics, electronic equipment, toys, and fireworks, and the printing and dyeing of cloth and yarn.

Macau's historic role has been that of a gateway for southern China. It has close trade relations with neighboring Hong Kong, another free port. Gold trading, formerly a major facet in Macau's economy, virtually came to a halt in 1974–75 following Hong Kong's decision to lift its own restrictions on gold trading. The principal exports were clothing, textiles, footwear, toys, electronics, and machinery and parts. Principal export partners in 2004 were the United States, 48.7%; China, 13.9%; Germany, 8.3%, Hong Kong, 7.6%, and the United Kingdom, 4.4%. The principal imports were raw materials and semi-manufactured goods, consumer goods (foodstuffs, beverages, and tobacco), capital goods, and mineral fuels and oil. Total imports in 2004 were valued at $3.478 billion, of which China provided 44.4%; Hong Kong, 10.6%; Japan, 9.6%; Taiwan, 4.9%; Singapore, 4.1%, and the United States, 4.1%.

Government schools are operated mainly for the children of civil servants and wealthier families, while poor Chinese students are educated in schools supported by China. Macau's University of East Asia opened in 1981. The Medical and Health Department, although critically understaffed, operates a 400-bed hospital. The 800-bed Kiang Vu Hospital has a largely China-trained staff.

There were 167,500 main telephone lines in 2011 and 1.122 million mobile cellular phone lines in use in 2010. Macau has three radio stations of which two are government-operated. Macau has access to satellite communications. There are newspapers published in Chinese and Portuguese. Macau receives television broadcasts from Hong Kong.

With its varied gambling facilities, gambling provides about 70% of government revenue. Travelers must have a valid passport and a visa, which is generally purchased at the point of disembar-kation. After the transfer of Macau to Chinese control in 1999, there was an increase in tourist arrivals from China.

50 BIBLIOGRAPHY

Aspalter, Christian. *Conservative Welfare State Systems in East Asia.* Westport, CT: Praeger, 2001.

Baranovitch, Nimrod. *China's New Voices: Popular Music, Ethnicity, Gender, and Politics, 1978–1997.* Berkeley: University of California Press, 2003.

Chang, Jung. *Mao: The Unknown Story.* New York: Knopf, 2005.

Chan, Ming K. and Shiu-hing Lo. *Historical Dictionary of the Hong Kong SAR and the Macao SAR.* Lanham, MD: Scarecrow, 2006.

Ebrey, Patricia B. *The Cambridge Illustrated History of China.* 2nd ed. New York: Cambridge University Press, 2010.

Hoare, Jim and Susan Pares. *A Political and Economic Dictionary of East Asia.* Philadelphia: Routledge/Taylor and Francis, 2005.

Kaye, Lincoln. *Cousin Felix Meets the Buddha.* New York: Farrar, Straus and Giroux, 2003.

LaFleur, Robert. *China.* San Diego, CA: ABC-CLIO, 2010.

McElrath, Karen, ed. *HIV and AIDS: A Global View.* Westport, CT: Greenwood Press, 2002.

Meyer, David R. *Hong Kong as a Global Metropolis.* New York: Cambridge University Press, 2000.

One China, Many Paths. London: Verso, 2003.

Reuvid, Jonathan and Li Yong, eds. *Doing Business with China.* 5th ed. Sterling, VA: Kogan Page, 2005.

Zhang, Yongjin. *China's Emerging Global Businesses: Political Economy and Institutional Investigations.* New York: Palgrave Macmillan, 2003.

Zurlo, Tony. *China.* San Diego, CA.: Greenhaven Press, 2003.

Zhang, Yongjin. *China's Emerging Global Businesses: Political Economy and Institutional Investigations.* New York: Palgrave Macmillan, 2003.

Zurlo, Tony. *China.* San Diego, Calif.: Greenhaven Press, 2003.

CYPRUS

Republic of Cyprus

Kypriaki Dimokratia

CAPITAL: Nicosia

FLAG: The national flag consists of the map of Cyprus in gold set above two green olive branches on a white field.

ANTHEM: *Ymnos eis tin Eleftherian (Hymn to Liberty).*

MONETARY UNIT: The euro (€) is the official currency of Cyprus; it replaced the Cypriot pound on 1 January 2008. There are seven paper denominations in the euro: 5, 10, 20, 50, 100, 200, and 500. There are eight euro coins: 1, 2, 5, 10, 20, and 50 cents; and €1 and €2 euros. €0.74 = US$1 (or US$1 = €1.35) as of November 2011. The Turkish lira (TRY) of 100 kuruş is the currency in the Turkish Cypriot zone.

WEIGHTS AND MEASURES: The metric system is the legal standard. Imperial and local measures also are used.

HOLIDAYS: New Year's Day, 1 January; Epiphany, 6 January; Late President Makarios' Day, 19 January; Greek Independence Day, 25 March; Cyprus National Day, 1 April; Labor Day, 1 May; Cyprus Independence Day, 1 October; Greek Resistance Day, 28 October; Christmas, 25 December; Boxing Day, 26 December. Holidays observed by the Turkish Cypriot community include Founding of the Turkish Federated State of Cyprus, 13 February; Turkish National Sovereignty and Children's Day, 23 April; Turkish Youth and Sports Day, 19 May; Turkish Victory Day, 30 August; Turkish Independence Day, 29 October. Movable Christian religious holidays include Green Monday, Good Friday, Holy Saturday, and Easter Monday. Movable Muslim religious holidays are observed in the Turkish Cypriot zone.

TIME: 2 p.m. = noon GMT.

[1] LOCATION, SIZE, AND EXTENT

Cyprus is the largest Mediterranean island after Sicily and Sardinia. Including small island outposts of Cape Andreas known as the Klidhes, its total area is 9,250 sq km (3,571 sq mi). Comparatively, the area occupied by Cyprus is about three-fifths the size of the state of Connecticut. Since 1974 the northern third of the island, or 3,367 sq km (1,300 sq mi), has been under the de facto control of the Turkish Cypriot Federated State (proclaimed in 1975), which on 15 November 1983 proclaimed its independence as the Turkish Republic of Northern Cyprus; the southern two-thirds (5,884 sq km/2,272 sq mi) are controlled by the government of the Republic of Cyprus. A narrow zone called the "green line," patrolled by UN forces, separates the two regions and divides Nicosia, the national capital.

Cyprus is situated in the extreme northeast corner of the Mediterranean; it is 71 km (44 mi) S of Turkey, 105 km (65 mi) W of Syria, and some 800 km (500 mi) E of the Greek mainland. Cyprus extends 227 km (141 mi) ENE–WSW from Cape Andreas to Cape Drepanon and 97 km (60 mi) SSE–NNW. The average width is 56–72 km (35–45 mi); the narrow peninsula known as the Karpas, which is nowhere more than 16 km (10 mi) wide, extends 74 km (46 mi) northeastward to Cape Andreas. Cyprus has a total coastline of 648 km (403 mi).

The capital city of Cyprus, Nicosia, is located in the north central part of the country.

[2] TOPOGRAPHY

Two dissimilar mountain systems, flanking a central plain, occupy the greater part of the island. The Troodos Massif in the southwest, attaining its highest point in Mt. Olympus (1,953 m/6,406 ft), sends out numerous spurs to the northwestern, northern, and southern coasts. In the north, a geologically older range, the Kyrenia Mountains, extends more than 160 km (100 mi) along the coast in a series of rocky peaks, capped often by medieval castles. Between these principal formations lies the Mesaoria, a low plain extending from Famagusta Bay on the east to Morphou Bay on the west. Once forested, this now treeless region, varying in width from 16–32 km (10–20 mi), contains the bulk of the island's cultivable and pastoral area. There are few lakes or rivers; rivers are little more than rocky channels that carry away torrents during the thaw of spring and early summer.

[3] CLIMATE

Cyprus is for the most part dry and sunny. The warm currents of the Mediterranean ensure mild winters but bring humidity to the coastal area in the summer, when the central plain is hot and dry. On the hills, daily sunshine is interrupted only occasionally by a wet period rarely lasting more than a week. The mean annual temperature is about 20°C (68°F). A cool, rainy season lasts from November to March. In winter, snow covers the higher peaks of the Troodos; elsewhere the temperature seldom falls below freezing, and conditions are mild and bracing. Rainfall is erratic and varies greatly in different parts of the island. The annual average precipitation ranges from below 30 cm (12 in) in the west-central lowlands to more than 114 cm (45 in) in the higher parts of the southern massif. The main agricultural areas receive rainfall of from 30 to 40 cm (12 to 16 in) annually. Earthquakes are not uncommon.

4 FLORA AND FAUNA

The World Resources Institute estimates that there are 1,682 plant species in Cyprus. In addition, Cyprus is home to 21 species of mammals, 349 species of birds, 30 species of reptiles, and 1 species of amphibian. This calculation reflects the total number of distinct species residing in the country, not the number of endemic species.

Except for some small lowland areas in which eucalyptus has been planted, the forests are natural growths of great antiquity, from which the Phoenician shipbuilders drew much of their timber. Forests consist principally of Aleppo pine; other important conifers, locally dominant, are the stone pine, cedar (which is becoming rare), Mediterranean cypress, and juniper, the last growing chiefly on the lower slopes of the Kyrenia Mountains. Oriental plane and alder are plentiful in the valleys, while on the hills, Olympus dwarf oak mingles with pines of various species. Wild flowers grow in profusion, and herbs are numerous.

Birdlife is varied and includes partridge, quail, snipe, plover, and woodcock. Eagles are commonly seen in the mountains.

5 ENVIRONMENT

The World Resources Institute reported that Cyprus had designated 89,500 hectares (221,159 acres) of land for protection as of 2006. Water resources totaled 0.4 cu km (0.096 cu mi) while water usage was 0.21 cu km (0.05 cu mi) per year. Domestic water usage accounted for 27% of total usage, industrial for 1%, and agricultural for 72%. Per capita water usage totaled 250 cu m (8,829 cu ft) per year.

The UN reported in 2008 that carbon dioxide emissions in Cyprus totaled 8,193 kilotons.

Under the Town and Country Planning Law of 1972, the government has the power to issue "reservation orders" in order to protect historic buildings, trees, or other specific points. Other conservation laws seek to preserve forests, restrict the hunting of wildlife, and maintain environmental health.

The most significant environmental problems in Cyprus are water pollution, erosion, and wildlife preservation. The purity of the water supply is threatened by industrial pollutants, pesticides used in agricultural areas, and the lack of adequate sewage treatment. Other water resource problems include uneven rainfall levels at different times of the year and the absence of natural reservoir catchments.

Another environmental concern is erosion, especially erosion of Cyprus's coastline. In accordance with the Foreshore Protection Law, several coastal areas have been zoned to prevent undesirable development. The Ministry of Agriculture and Natural Resources has primary responsibility for environmental matters. The expansion of urban centers threatens the habitat of Cyprus's wildlife.

According to a 2011 report issued by the International Union for Conservation of Nature and Natural Resources (IUCN),

threatened species included 5 mammals, 4 birds, 4 reptiles, 19 fish, and 18 plants. Threatened species included the Cyprus spiny mouse, the black vulture, the Mediterranean killfish, the imperial eagle, and the wild goat. About 20 species of flora are protected. The Cyprus mouflon or wild sheep is protected in the Paphos Forest game reserve.

6 POPULATION

The US Central Intelligence Agency (CIA) estimated the population of Cyprus in 2011 to be approximately 1,120,489, which placed it at number 155 in population among the 196 nations of the world. In 2011 approximately 10.4% of the population was over 65 years of age, with another 16.2% under 15 years of age. The median age in Cyprus was 34.8 years. There were 1.04 males for every female in the country. The population's annual rate of change was 1.617%. The projected population for the year 2025 was 1,100,000. Population density in Cyprus was calculated at 121 people per sq km (313 people per sq mi).

The UN estimated that 70% of the population lived in urban areas, and that urban populations had an annual rate of change of 1.3%. The largest urban area was Nicosia, with a population of 240,000.

7 MIGRATION

Estimates of Cyprus's net migration rate, carried out by the CIA in 2011, amounted to 11.21 migrants per 1,000 citizens. The total number of emigrants living abroad was 149,600, and the total number of immigrants living in Cyprus was 154,300. Cyprus suffered massive population shifts following the Turkish military occupation of the northern third of the island in July 1974. Some 120,000 Greek Cypriots fled from the occupied area to the south, and about 60,000 Turkish Cypriots fled in the opposite direction. In 2009 there were 200,000 internally displaced persons in Cyprus.

In the 1990s asylum seekers originated mainly from the Middle East and North Africa. Until 1998 a yearly average of 70 to 100 people applied for refugee status. Since then the number of asylum seekers has risen dramatically, driven in part by Cyprus's joining the EU in 2004. In the mid-2000s many of the asylum seekers were students from South Asia who entered the country legally as students, and later applied for asylum. As of January 2011 the United Nations High Commissioner for Refugees reported there were 5,396 persons in Cyprus with asylum applications pending.

Some asylum seekers are detained as illegal entrants or overstayers. While acknowledging the difficulties in dealing with the increased number of asylum seekers, the United Nations High Commissioner for Refugees (UNHCR) has encouraged the government to find alternatives to detention. Cyprus allows recognized refugees to remain with work permits while waiting for resettlement to a third country; however, resettlement is a lengthy process and many refugees never obtain employment. Local integration has been the preferred solution after adoption of the new refugee law. In 2002 an Amendment of the Citizenship Law allowed persons born after 16 August 1960 by a Cypriot mother and a foreign father to automatically acquire Cyprian citizenship. Previously, only children born of a Cypriot father were automatically permitted to attain citizenship.

8 ETHNIC GROUPS

Following the 16th-century Turkish conquest, Cyprus received a substantial permanent influx of Ottoman Turks. Many soldiers became owners of feudal estates, and there was immigration from Anatolia and Rumelia. There was virtually no intermarriage; each community preserved its own religion, language, dress, and other national characteristics, and major cities and towns had their Greek and Turkish quarters. The 1974 war had the effect of almost completely segregating the two communities. The most recent estimates available indicated that in 2001 about 77% of the population were Greek and about 18% were Turkish. The remainder of the population included Lebanese Maronites, Armenians, British, and others.

9 LANGUAGES

After independence in 1960, Greek and Turkish became the official languages. Since 1974 Greek has been the language of the south and Turkish the language of the north. English is also used extensively.

10 RELIGIONS

About 95% of the permanent residents in the government-controlled area of Cyprus are members of the Autocephalous Greek Orthodox Church of Cyprus. However, a 2006 poll indicated that only about 19% of Greek Cypriots attended church services once a week. Maronite Catholics, Armenian Orthodox, and Roman Catholics (referred to as Latins) are recognized as primary minority religious groups. There are about 2,000 members of the Jewish community in the Greek-controlled region. Nearly 98% of the Turkish Cypriots are Sunni Muslims, though only about 8% attend weekly religious services.

11 TRANSPORTATION

The CIA reports that Cyprus has a total of 14,671 km (9,116 mi) of roads. There are 659 vehicles per 1,000 people in the country. There are 15 airports, which transported 1.94 million passengers in 2009 according to the World Bank.

Internal transport is exclusively by road. In addition to numerous taxicabs, the chief towns are served by private buses, whose services are regulated by the Road Motor Transport Board.

Although off the main world shipping routes, Cyprus is served by passenger and cargo shipping lines. Famagusta on the east coast was the main port, but it and the ports of Kyrenia and Karavostasi were closed to national shipping after the Turkish invasion in 1974. The port of Famagusta was reopened by the Turkish Cypriots in 1978. The Limassol and Larnaca ports have been modernized and are now considered good deepwater harbors. Other ports include Moni, Vasiliko-Ziyyi, and Paphos. In 2010 there were 839 ships in the merchant fleet. About two-thirds of the trade passed through Limassol. There are no inland waterways.

In 2010 there were nine heliports. The civil airport at Nicosia was used by many international airlines until the 1974 war, after which nearly all flights were diverted to the new international airport built at Larnaca. In 1983 a new international airport opened in Paphos. Cyprus Airways has services to Middle Eastern countries, but there is no regular internal air service.

12 HISTORY

Numerous Stone Age settlements excavated in Cyprus indicate that as early as 4000 BC a distinctive civilization existed on the island. Living in circular huts, this Neolithic people produced decorated pottery of great individuality, and used vessels and tools ground from the close-grained rocks of the Troodos Mountains. Cyprus was famous in the ancient world for its copper, which, from about 2200 BC, was used throughout the Aegean in the making of bronze. The island is believed either to have derived its name from or to have given it to this mineral through the Greek word *kypros*—copper. Although celebrated also for its cult of Aphrodite (many temples devoted to the goddess were built in Paphos on the southwest coast), Cyprus was at first only a far outpost of the Hellenic world.

Greek colonizers came there in sizable numbers in 1400 BC, and were followed soon afterward by Phoenician settlers. About 560 BC Cyprus was conquered by Egypt. Coveted by each rising civilization, it was taken in turn by Persia, Alexander the Great, Egypt again, Rome, and the Byzantine Empire. Its Christian history began with the visits of Paul, accompanied first (as described in the Acts of the Apostles) by Barnabas, and later by the apostle Mark. For several centuries after AD 632, Cyprus underwent a series of Arab invasions. The island was wrested from its Byzantine ruler Isaac Comnenus in 1191 by Richard I (the Lion-Hearted) during the Third Crusade. Sold by the English king to the Knights Templar, it was transferred by that order to settle debts. Guy de Lusignan, the ruler of Jerusalem, received control of Cyprus. It was under his dynasty that the island experienced a brilliant period in its history, lasting some 300 years. In the period from 1468 until 1489, Cyprus was linked to Venice through a marriage. Cyprus fell to the Turks in 1571, and was thus part of the Ottoman Empire until 1878.

The administration of Cyprus by the United Kingdom began in 1878 at a convention with Turkey initiated by the British Prime Minister, Benjamin Disraeli, at the Congress of Berlin. He sought to establish Cyprus as a defensive base against further Russian aggression in the Middle East. When Turkey entered World War I, Cyprus was annexed to the British crown. It was declared a crown colony and placed under a governor in 1925.

For centuries under Ottoman and British rule, Greek Cypriots had regarded Greece as their mother country and had sought union (*enosis*) with it as Greek nationals. In 1931 enosis agitation, long held in check, broke into violence. The government house was burned amid widespread disturbances, and the British colonial administration applied severe repressive measures, including the deportation of clerical leaders. While British occupation was restrictive to many Cypriots, it also brought many benefits. The economy prospered, an efficient civil service was established, hospitals and roads were built, and investment in modernization was made.

Agitation for enosis was dormant until the close of World War II, when it recommenced, and demands that the United Kingdom cede the island to Greece were renewed. The National Organization of Cypriot Fighters (Ethniki Organosis Kyprion Agoniston–EOKA), led by retired Greek army officer Col. George Grivas, began a campaign of terrorism in 1955. The campaign was a series of carefully planned military attacks against British police, military, and other government institutions in Limassol, Larnaca,

Famagusta, and Nicosia. The results of these riots were the resignation of many Greek Cypriots from the police force and the replacement of the force by Turkish Cypriots. Upward of 2,000 casualties were recorded.

Problems were escalating rapidly in the island, and in 1957, because of tensions between the Greeks and the Turks, the Turkish Cypriots formed the TMT (Turk Mukavemet Teskilati) to fight the EOKA. The TMT was formed to protect Turkish Cypriots' interest and identity, should enosis occur. The TMT felt the only solution was to divide the island, with the Greek Cypriots living on one side and the Turkish Cypriots on the other.

The unity of the North Atlantic Treaty Organization (NATO) was endangered by the opposing positions taken on the Cyprus question by Greece and Turkey, and efforts by NATO members to mediate the dispute proved unsuccessful. Against this background, the prime ministers of Greece and Turkey met in Zürich, Switzerland, early in 1959 in a further attempt to reach a settlement. Unexpectedly, the Greek Cypriots set aside their demands for enosis and accepted instead proposals for an independent republic, with representation of both the Greek and Turkish Cypriot communities (including a Greek Cypriot president and a Turkish Cypriot vice president) guaranteed. A formula for the island's future, approved by the governments of the United Kingdom, Greece, and Turkey, also received the blessing of the Cyprus ethnarch, Archbishop Makarios III, who returned in triumph to the island after three years in exile, having been deported in 1956 by the British government on charges of complicity with terrorism.

Besides determining Cyprus's legislative institutions, the Zürich settlement provided for a number of instruments defining the island's future international status. Enclaves on Cyprus were set aside for the continuation of British military installations in an effort to restore constitutional order. The United Kingdom, Greece, and Turkey, the guarantor powers, had the right to act together or singly to prevent either enosis or partition. In addition, provision was made for Greek, Turkish, and Cypriot forces to be stationed together at a tripartite headquarters. By 1 July 1960 agreement was reached on all outstanding differences. Independence was officially declared and the constitution was made effective on 16 August 1960. The first general elections for the Republic of Cyprus House of Representatives were held 31 July of that same year. A month later the nation became a member of the United Nations (UN) and in the spring, a member of the Commonwealth of Nations. In December 1961 Cyprus became an official member of the International Monetary Fund and the World Bank.

No amount of independence, however, would ensure peace between the Turks and Greeks living in Cyprus. From the outset, the two Cypriot communities differed on how the Zürich settlement would be implemented, and how much autonomy the Turkish minority would enjoy. In December 1963 Turkish Cypriots, protesting a proposed constitutional change that would have strengthened the political power of the Greek Cypriot majority, clashed with Greek Cypriots and police. When fighting continued, the Cyprus government appealed to the UN Security Council. On 4 March 1964 the Security Council voted to send in troops. Turkey and Cyprus agreed on 10 August 1964 to accept a UN Security Council call for a cease-fire, but on 22 December, fighting again erupted in Nicosia and spread to other parts of the island. The UN General Assembly passed a resolution in December 1965 calling on all states to "respect the sovereignty, unity, independence, and territorial integrity of the Republic of Cyprus, and to refrain from any intervention directed against it." The General Assembly requested the Security Council to continue UN mediation.

Violent clashes between Greek and Turkish Cypriots nearly precipitated war between Greece and Turkey in 1967, but the situation was stabilized by mutual reduction of their armed contingents on Cyprus. By January 1970 the UN peacekeeping force numbered some 3,500 troops; both Greek Cypriot National Guard and Turkish Cypriot militia also maintained sizable national guards of their own. Although talks continued between the two communities, no agreement was reached on the two basic points of dispute. Politically, the Turks wanted full autonomy, while the Greeks demanded continued unitary majority rule. Territorially, the Turks wanted Cyprus divided into Greek- and Turkish-controlled zones, a position that was likewise at odds with the Greek Cypriot concept of a unitary state.

Meanwhile, tensions had developed between Makarios, who continued to oppose enosis, and the remnants of the military junta that had ruled Greece since 1967. On 2 July 1974 Makarios accused the Greek government of seeking his overthrow and called for the immediate withdrawal of 650 Greek officers in the Cypriot National Guard. Less than two weeks later, the guard toppled the Makarios government, forcing the archbishop into exile and installing Nikos Sampson as president. To counter the threat of Greek control over Cyprus, the Turks, supported by Turkish Cypriots, insisted on some form of geographical separation between the Greeks and the Turks living on the island. Turkish Cypriot leaders asked Turkey to intervene militarily. On 20 July 1974 Turkish troops landed on the island and the resulting conflict ended in the deaths of thousands of Greek and Turkish Cypriots. Within two days the UN forces had been augmented and a UN Security Council cease-fire resolution took effect. This action eventually led to the establishment of a corridor, known as the UN Buffer Zone or the "green line," separating the two groups. Sampson resigned as president on 23 July and Glafkos Clerides became acting president in accordance with the Cyprus constitution.

However, Turkey did not withdraw its forces, and while peace talks were conducted in Geneva, Switzerland, the Turkish military buildup continued. When talks broke down, a full-scale Turkish offensive began, and by mid-August, when a second cease-fire was accepted, Turkish forces controlled about 38% of the island. Makarios returned to Cyprus and resumed the presidency in December. On 13 February 1975, in an action considered illegal by the Cyprus government, the Turkish-held area proclaimed itself the Turkish Cypriot Federated State; Rauf Denktash, a former vice president of Cyprus, became president. A Security Council resolution on 12 March regretted the proclamation of the new state and called for the resumption of talks. The government of the Republic of Cyprus continued to be recognized as the legally constituted authority by the United Nations and by all countries except Turkey, although its effective power extended only to the area under Greek Cypriot control.

After the de facto partition, Greek and Turkish Cypriot leaders met several times under UN auspices to explore a possible solution to the Cyprus problem. President Makarios conferred with Denktash in Nicosia early in 1977. When Makarios died of a heart attack on 3 August, Spyros Kyprianou became president.

Kyprianou also held talks with Denktash in May 1979. Further negotiations between leaders of the two communities were held in August 1980, but again no agreement was reached.

On 15 November 1983 the Turkish sector proclaimed itself an independent state, the Turkish Republic of Northern Cyprus (TRNC). Denktash was named president, but only Turkey recognized the TRNC. The United Nations, which condemned the TRNC's declaration of independence, tried repeatedly to end the partition between north and south, but both parts rejected all proposals. The major stumbling block was the south's demand that the estimated 25,000 Turkish troops in the north be withdrawn before negotiations began and the north's refusal to remove the troops before a final solution was reached. In February 1988 George Vassiliou was elected president of Cyprus, and he stated that he would call for reunification talks with the Turkish Cypriots.

In 1991 the UN Security Council called on both sides to complete an overall framework agreement. Despite speculation in 1994 that UN peacekeeping forces might be withdrawn if some progress was not registered, the mandate was renewed. In 1993 voting, Glafcos Clerides, a conservative, replaced right-wing George Vassiliou as president. Clerides won reelection to a second five-year term in 1998.

August 1996 saw the most violent border clashes since the 1974 partition. In the space of one week, protestors broke through Greek Cypriot security lines and clashed with Turkish Cypriot and Turkish military forces in the buffer zone lying between the two divided parts of the island. Two Greek Cypriots were killed and over 50 were injured by the Turkish military. The killing of the protestors, who were unarmed, brought general expressions of condemnation from the West, but was supported by the Turkish government as acts of self-defense.

In November 2002 UN secretary general Kofi Annan presented a comprehensive peace plan for Cyprus, envisaging a Swiss-style confederation of two equal component states, presided over by a rotating presidency. To go into effect, the plan required a referendum on both sides of the island. In December 2002 the European Union (EU) issued a formal invitation to Cyprus to join, stipulating that the two communities agree to the UN peace plan for reunification. Without reunification, only the Greek Cypriot part of the island would gain membership.

In late 2002 and early 2003, thousands of Turkish Cypriots held rallies to call for the island's reunification and Denktash's resignation. Denktash was accused of blocking progress on the November 2002 UN peace plan. Denktash threatened to stand down as leader rather than sign the UN plan. Contributing to the failed peace negotiations was the election of hard-line nationalist Tassos Papadopoulos as president of Cyprus on 16 February 2003; he took office on 1 March 2003. In a surprise first-round win, Papadopoulos soundly defeated Clerides, with 51.5% of the vote to 38.8%.

Talks on Annan's reunification plan broke down on 11 March 2003, and Annan declared the island's two communities might not get a similar chance for peace for years. The Republic of Cyprus, remaining divided, signed the Accession Treaty for the European Union on 16 April 2003. In April 2004 referenda were held on each side of the island regarding the Annan plan; the Turkish north voted largely in favor, but the plan was soundly defeated in the south. Consequently, while the whole island was admitted to the

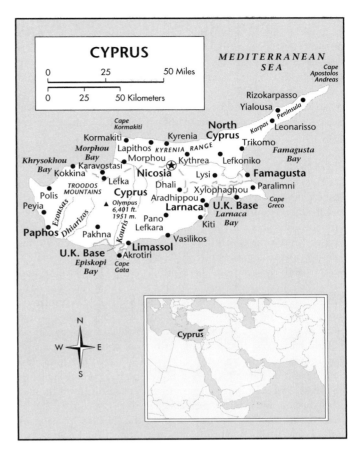

LOCATION: 34°33′ to 35°34′N; 32°16′ to 34°37′ E.
TERRITORIAL SEA LIMIT: 12 miles.

European Union on 1 May 2004, the rights and obligations of EU membership apply only to the southern Greek-controlled portion of the island; they are suspended in the Turkish-controlled north. In June 2005 the legislature ratified the proposed EU constitution, although France and the Netherlands had rejected it.

In April 2005 Rauf Denktash retired as president of the Turkish republic. Mehmet Ali Talat—who favored reunification—was elected in his place.

In May 2005 Greek Cypriot and UN officials began exploratory talks on prospects for a new peace effort. In May 2006 legislative elections were held and Greek Cypriots supported the ruling coalition. This meant voters gave the sign that they opposed reunification. That July, UN-sponsored negotiations between President Papadopolous and Turkish Cypriot leader Mehmet Ali Talat were held. The leaders agreed to a series of confidence-building measures and contacts between the two communities.

In 2008 Communist Party leader Demetris Christophas campaigned for president on a platform favoring ending the division of the island. When he was elected president by a wide margin in February 2008, one of the first actions Christophas undertook was to begin talks with Mehmet Ali Talat regarding ways to reunite the island.

In November 2009 the United Kingdom renewed an offer to relinquish control over half of its Sovereign Base Areas (SBAs) in Cyprus, if a comprehensive peace agreement were approved by both of the Cypriot governments and a majority of the population.

The two UK SBAs of Akrotiri and Dhekelia cover a total area of about 98 sq mi (254 sq km) on Cyprus and serve as military bases for the UK. If an agreement is reached, the UK government has pledged to hand over sovereign control of about 45 sq mi (116 sq km), with the understanding that both military bases would remain operational. This same offer was made during peace negotiations in 2004. The UK government hoped that the renewal of the offer would inspire greater efforts toward a comprehensive agreement.

13 GOVERNMENT

The 1960 constitution of the Republic of Cyprus respects the two existing ethnic communities, Greek and Turkish, by providing specifically for representation from each community in the government. The president must be Greek and the vice president Turkish. Under the constitution, these officers are elected for five years by universal suffrage by the Greek and Turkish communities, respectively; each has the right of veto over legislation and over certain decisions of the Council of Ministers. (The Council of Ministers is made up of seven Greek and three Turkish ministers, designated by the president and vice president jointly.) Legislative authority is vested in the 80-member Republic of Cyprus House of Representatives, elected by the two chief communities in the proportion of 56 Greek and 24 Turkish. In January 1964, following the outbreak of fighting, Turkish representatives withdrew from the house, and temporary constitutional provisions for administering the country were put into effect.

On 13 February 1975, subsequent to the Turkish invasion of Cyprus, the Turkish Cypriot Federated State (TCFS) was proclaimed in the northern part of the island. A draft constitution, approved by the state's constituent assembly on 25 April, was ratified by the Turkish Cypriot community in a referendum on 8 June. On 15 November 1983 the TCFS proclaimed itself the Turkish Republic of Northern Cyprus (TRNC), separate and independent from the Republic of Cyprus. In June 1985 TRNC voters approved a new constitution that embodied most of the old constitution's articles. The new constitution, however, increased the size of the legislative assembly to 50 seats.

14 POLITICAL PARTIES

The principal political parties of the Greek community in 2011 were the European Party (EURO.KO), Green Party of Cyprus, Movement for Social Democrats (EDEK), Progressive Party of the Working People (Communist Party-AKEL), the right-wing Democratic Rally (DISY), the center-right Democratic Party (DIKO), and the United Democrats (EDI). The Orthodox Church of Cyprus also exercises some political power within the island.

In the area administered by Turkish Cypriots, the principal parties were the National Unity Party (NUP), Republican Turkish Party (RTP), Democrat Party (DP), Communal Democracy Party (TDP), Freedom and Reform Party (ORP), and United Cyprus Party (BKP).

Party representation and percentages of the popular vote in the May 2011 election for the republic of Cyprus House of Representatives were as follows: DISY 20 seats (34.3%); AKEL (Communist) 19 seats (32.7%); DIKO 9 seats (15.8%); EDEK 5 seats (8.9%); EURO.KO 2 seats (3.9%); Other 1 seat (4.5%). (There are 80 seats in the House; 56 assigned to the Greek Cypriots and 24 to Turkish Cypriots, but only those assigned to Greek Cypriots are filled.)

The distribution of seats in the 50-seat Assembly of the Republic of the Turkish Republic of Northern Cyprus (TRNC) by party as of April 2009 were the National Unity Party (UBP), 25 seats; the Republican Turkish Party (CTP) 15 seats; the Democratic Party (DP) 5 seats; and other, 4 seats.

Communist party leader Demetris Christofias won the February 2008 Cypriot presidential election in the second round with a vote of 53.4%. Ioannis Kasoulides of the European People's Party and Democratic Rally came in second with 46.6% of the vote. In the April 2010 presidential election for the Turkish Republic of Northern Cyprus, Dervis Eroglu of the UBP was deemed the winner with 50.4% of the vote. The incumbent Mehmet Ali Talat of the CTP lost with 42.9% of the vote.

15 LOCAL GOVERNMENT

There are six administrative districts in the island: Kyrenia, Limassol, Nicosia, Paphos, and Famagusta. The Turkish areas include Kyrenia, and several small parts of Larnaca, Nicosia, and Famagusta. Elected municipal corporations manage chief towns and larger villages. The smaller villages are managed by commissions comprising a headman (*mukhtar*) and elders (*azas*).

The 1960 constitution provided for two communal chambers, these bodies having wide authority within the two main ethnic groups, including the power to draft laws, impose taxes, and determine all religious, educational, and cultural questions. The Greek Communal Chamber, however, was abolished in 1965, and its functions reverted to the Ministry of Education (later renamed the Ministry of Education and Culture). The Turkish Communal Chamber embraces municipalities that are exclusively Turkish. Originally the duties of the Turkish Communal Chamber were to supervise Turkish cooperatives, sports organizations, and charitable institutions. But since the late 1960s, the Turkish communities have maintained strict administrative control of their own areas and have insisted on civil autonomy.

16 JUDICIAL SYSTEM

In the Greek Cypriot area, the Supreme Court of Cyprus is the final appellate court and has final authority in constitutional and administrative cases. It deals with appeals from assize and district courts, as well as from decisions by its own judges, acting singly in certain matters. There are six district courts and six assize courts. The Supreme Council of Judicature appoints judges to the district and assize courts.

In the Turkish-held area, a Turkish Cypriot Supreme Court acts as final appellate court, with powers similar to those of the Supreme Court of Cyprus. In addition to district and assize courts, there are two Turkish communal courts as well as a communal appeals court.

The Cypriot legal system incorporates a number of elements of the British tradition including the presumption of innocence, due process protections, and the right to appeal. Both parts of Cyprus provide for fair public trials. Both in theory and in practice, the judiciary is independent of executive or military control.

¹⁷ARMED FORCES

The International Institute for Strategic Studies reports that armed forces in Cyprus totaled 10,000 members in 2011, all of which are members of the national guard. Armed forces represent 2.4% of the labor force in Cyprus. Defense spending totaled $882.4 million and accounted for 3.8% of gross domestic product (GDP).

As of 2011 Cyprus's armed forces were divided between the Greek and Turkish dominated areas.

¹⁸INTERNATIONAL COOPERATION

Cyprus was admitted to the United Nations on 20 September 1960 and is a member of ECE and several nonregional specialized agencies. Cyprus became a member of the European Union in 2004. The nation is also a member of the Commonwealth of Nations, the Council of Europe, the European Bank for Reconstruction and Development, the Central European Initiative, and the WTO. Cyprus belongs to the Alliance of Small Island States (AOSIS) and the OSCE and is an observer in the OAS.

Cyprus is part of the Nonaligned Movement, the Australia Group, and the Organization for the Prohibition of Chemical Weapons. It also belongs to the Nuclear Suppliers Group. In environmental cooperation, Cyprus is part of the Basel Convention, Conventions on Biological Diversity and Air Pollution, CITES, the London Convention, the Kyoto Protocol, the Montréal Protocol, MARPOL, the Nuclear Test Ban Treaty, and the UN Conventions on the Law of the Sea, Climate Change, and Desertification.

While tension between the Greek and Turkish Cypriots has sometimes resulted in violent clashes, a general peace has prevailed since 1996. The Green Line between the two areas is patrolled by United Nations (UN) troops. Talks between the governments have been mediated through the UN for several years, as both sides have expressed willingness for reunification. Unresolved issues include security matters, property disputes, and an equitable power-sharing agreement. The primarily Greek Republic of Cyprus considers the de facto Turkish Cypriot control of the north to be an illegal occupation. Since Cyprus joined the European Union (EU) in 2004, individual citizens of both nationalities are eligible for EU citizenship.

¹⁹ECONOMY

The gross domestic product (GDP) rate of change in Cyprus, as of 2010, was 1%. Inflation stood at 2.4%, and unemployment was reported at 5.6%.

Historically an agricultural country with few natural resources, Cyprus has been shifting from subsistence farming and light manufacturing to a service dominated economy. Farm mechanism has reached an advanced state. Large trade deficits have been partially offset by tourism and remittances from Cypriots working abroad. The Greek Cypriot economy has established itself as a business and service center for enterprises engaged in shipping, banking, and commerce. Cyprus is classified by the World Bank as a high-income country and its citizens have a per capita income near the EU average.

The 1974 coup and the Turkish armed intervention badly disrupted the economy. Physical destruction and the displacement of about a third of the population reduced the output of the manufacturing, agricultural, and service sectors. The lands occupied by Turkish forces accounted for about 70% of the country's prewar economic output. In general, the Greek Cypriot zone recovered much more quickly and successfully than the Turkish-held region, which was burdened with the weaknesses of Turkey's economy as well as its own. Scarcities of capital and skilled labor, the lack of trade and diplomatic ties to the outside world, and the consequent shortage of development aid have aggravated the problems of northern Cyprus. In the south, on the other hand, tourism has exceeded prewar levels, foreign assistance has been readily available, and the business community has benefited from the transfer to Cyprus of the Middle Eastern operations of multinational firms driven from Beirut by the Lebanese civil war.

The Republic of Cyprus saw strong economic growth throughout the 1990s. In 1992 the economy grew by over 8%. In 1995 and 1996 growth was more modest, but still robust. Growth slumped in 1997 to 3%, which was followed by three years of recovery. The global slowdown of 2001 impacted Cyprus's vulnerable economy. Although growth returned in 2002, it was at an anemic 2% level due mainly to the sharp decline in tourism following the 11 September 2001 terrorist attacks on the United States. Inflation and unemployment continued at low levels. From 1992 to 2001, the weighted annual rate of inflation was 2.48%, according to CIA estimates.

In the Turkish Republic of Northern Cyprus, however, the economy continued to grow more slowly, at less than 1% a year accompanied by persistently high inflation. In 2010, according to CIA estimates, the real growth rate was -0.6%. The inflation rate was 11.4% as of 2006 (the most recent figure available). Unemployment in the Turkish-held north was at an estimated 9.4% in 2005 (the latest year for which figures are available). North Cyprus is to a large extent dependent on transfers from the Turkish government. Its main domestic sources of revenue are the tourist industry and the education sector. According to the World Bank, gross domestic product per capita in the south was nearly double that of the north.

The aggressive and strict economic program preceding the transition from the Cyprus pound to the euro added to country's economic benefits. The high deficits of the mid-2000s were turned into a surplus in 2007. Water supplies are a perennial problem; desalination plants have been constructed to provide more regular access to fresh water. The government has also granted licensing for research in offshore drilling on the southern coast. About 12% of GDP comes directly from tourism. In January 2010 reports showed a 10.9% drop in tourist arrivals from 2008 to 2009. Over the same period, the economy contracted 0.5%.

The budget deficit in the first quarter of 2011 doubled to 2.1% of economic output, up from 0.9% the previous year. Additional reports said that while overall revenue fell, public spending rose.

Confidence in both the economy and government's ability to control it dwindled following an 11 July 2011 explosion at a navy base, which resulted in 12 deaths, more than 60 injuries, and severe damage to the nation's largest power station, as well as damage to more than 240 homes. The damage to the nearby power station resulted in rolling blackouts through the country that continued into August 2011, leaving many to fear that the already struggling economy would plunge into greater turmoil as a result of an energy crisis.

Within two weeks of the explosion, both Moody's and Standard and Poor's downgraded the nation's credit ratings. In addition to concerns that the explosion would hurt the economy, the downgrading was attributed to concerns over the country's exposure to Greece's debt. Amid continued public protests, the government cabinet resigned. President Christofias appointed new ministers on 5 August 2011, in hopes of restoring some level of domestic and international confidence in the government and the economy.

20 INCOME

The CIA estimated that in 2010 the GDP of Cyprus was $23.19 billion. The CIA defines GDP as the value of all final goods and services produced within a nation in a given year and computed on the basis of purchasing power parity (PPP) rather than value as measured on the basis of the rate of the exchange based on current dollars. The per capita GDP was estimated at $21,000. The annual growth rate of GDP was 1%. The average inflation rate was 2.4%. It was estimated that agriculture accounted for 2.1% of GDP, industry 18.6%, and services 79.3%.

According to the World Bank, remittances from citizens living abroad totaled $153.4 million or about $137 per capita and accounted for approximately 0.7% of GDP. It was estimated that household consumption was growing at an average annual rate of 7%.

In 2009 the World Bank estimated that Cyprus, with 0.01% of the world's population, accounted for 0.04% of the world's GDP. By comparison, the United States, with 4.85% of the world's population, accounted for 24.18% of world GDP.

As of 2011 the most recent study by the World Bank reported that actual individual consumption in Cyprus was 73.1% of GDP and accounted for 0.04% of world consumption. By comparison, the United States accounted for 25.44% of world individual consumption. The World Bank also estimated that 16.3% of Cyprus's GDP was spent on food and beverages, 15.2% on housing and household furnishings, 4.8% on clothes, 5.1% on health, 10.9% on transportation, 1.5% on communications, 6.6% on recreation, 9.5% on restaurants and hotels, and 2.9% on miscellaneous goods and services and purchases from abroad.

21 LABOR

As of 2010 Cyprus had a total labor force of 407,700 people. Within that labor force, CIA estimates in 2006 noted that 8.5% were employed in agriculture, 20.5% in industry, and 71% in the service sector. Unemployment was reported at 5.6%.

In both the Greek and Turkish parts of Cyprus, all workers have the right to join or form unions without prior authorization, excluding the military and police forces. In the Republic of Cyprus, about 70% of the Greek Cypriot workforce belonged to independent unions in 2010. In both Cyprus and the Turkish-administered region, collective bargaining is legal, but the bargaining agreements are not legally enforceable.

There is not a legislated minimum wage in the Greek Cypriot community, except for certain jobs which are considered vulnerable to exploitation. In 2010 the minimum wage was €835 ($1,121) per month for the first six months of employment for practical nurses, shop and nursery assistants, clerks, and hairdressers, rising to €887 ($1,191) per month after six months employment. In 2010 the Turkish Cypriot minimum wage was TRY1,300 ($710 per month). These wages are insufficient to support a wage earner and family, but most workers earn significantly more than this. The minimum working age in both communities was 15. In the Greek-controlled area, the legal workweek was 48 hours, including overtime. In the private sector, white-collar employees worked 39 hours, with 38 hours for blue-collar workers. Public sector employees worked fewer hours in the summer months. In the Turkish Cypriot community, the workweek was 39 hours year-round. Health and safety standards in the workplace continued to improve.

Women comprised about 44% of the workforce in 2010, an increase of some 11% over 1980 figures.

22 AGRICULTURE

Roughly 13% of the total land is farmed, and the country's major crops include citrus, vegetables, barley, grapes, olives, and vegetables. Cereal production amounted to 38,570 tons, fruit production 181,339 tons, and vegetable production 115,287 tons.

Agricultural methods are adapted to the island's hot and dry summers and generally limited water supply. Spring and early summer growth is dependent on moisture stored in the soil from the winter rains, but summer cultivation is dependent on irrigation.

Most farmers raise a variety of subsistence crops, ranging from grains and vegetables to fruits. Since 1960 there has been increased production of citrus fruits and potatoes. These two commodities, along with grapes, kiwi, and avocados are grown both for the domestic market and as exports to EU nations. Tomatoes, carrots, olives, and other fruits and vegetables are also grown. The areas that have been Turkish-held since 1974 include much of Cyprus's most fertile land; citrus fruits are a major export.

The Agricultural Research Institute, through experiments with solar-heated greenhouses, soil fertility, water usage optimization, and introduction of new varieties of grain, attempts to improve the efficiency of Cypriot agriculture.

23 ANIMAL HUSBANDRY

The UN Food and Agriculture Organization (FAO) reported that Cyprus dedicated 1,400 hectares (3,459 acres) to permanent pasture or meadow in 2009. During that year the country tended 2.9 million chickens, 55,589 head of cattle, and 464,932 pigs. The production from these animals amounted to 6,043 tons of beef and veal, 42,269 tons of pork, 28,255 tons of poultry, 8,601 tons of eggs, and 135,883 tons of milk. Cyprus also produced 693 tons of cattle hide and 160 tons of raw wool.

Output of pork, poultry, and eggs meets domestic demand, but beef and mutton are imported. Sheep and goats, which feed upon rough grazing land unsuitable for cultivation, provide most of the milk products.

Indigenous cattle, kept primarily as draft animals, are decreasing with the advance of farm mechanization. There is no indigenous breed of dairy cattle, but near main towns, dairy stock, mostly shorthorns, are kept under stall-fed conditions, and Friesian cattle have been imported from the Netherlands and the United Kingdom.

24 FISHING

Cyprus had 19 decked commercial fishing boats in 2008. The annual capture totaled 2,011 tons according to the UN FAO. The export value of seafood totaled $30.91 million.

Year-round fishing is carried on mostly in coastal waters not more than 3.2 km (2 mi) from shore. The fish in Cyprus waters are small from the lack of nutrient salts, and the catches are meager. There is no deep-sea fishing. Sponges of good quality are taken, mostly by licensed fishermen, from the Greek Dodecanese Islands.

25 FORESTRY

Approximately 19% of Cyprus is covered by forest. The UN FAO estimated the 2009 roundwood production at 6,160 cu m (217,538 cu ft). The value of all forest products, including roundwood, totaled $3.46 million.

About 173,000 hectares (427,000 acres) are forested; 137,800 hectares (340,500 acres) are reserves managed by the Forest Department, the remainder being natural growths of poor scrub used by village communities as fuel and as grazing grounds. Besides furnishing commercial timber, the forests provide protective cover for water catchment areas and prevent soil erosion. Their value is also scenic, numerous holiday resorts being situated in the forest reserves. Most numerous by far among forest trees is the Aleppo pine. The stone pine is found on the highest slopes of the Troodos Massif; the cedar, once a flourishing tree, has become a rarity. In the lowlands, eucalyptus and other exotic hardwoods have been introduced. Other important local species include cypress, plane, alder, and golden oak. The demand for timber during World War I resulted in some overcutting, and in 1956 large fires further reduced forests, particularly in Paphos, where 211,000 cu m (6 million cu ft) of standing timber were destroyed. To offset these losses, all felling of fresh trees for timber was stopped and systematic reforestation begun. The timber cut decreased from 152,415 cu m (5.4 million cu ft) in 1977 to 12,000 cu m (42.3 million cu ft) in 2003 (about 90% coniferous). Most of Cyprus's timber requirements must be met by imports.

26 MINING

In 2009 the mineral industry of Cyprus was dominated by the production of bentonite, cement, sand and gravel, and stone. Mineral production however, accounts for only a small portion of the country's GDP. In 2008 the value added by mining and quarrying amounted to $87.2 milion. In addition, production of Cyprus's historically important export minerals—asbestos, celestite, chromite, copper, and iron pyrite—has stopped. Cyprus was also a source of the mineral pigment umber. In 2004 preliminary umber production was put at 4,363 metric tons. Ownership and control of minerals and quarry materials were vested in the government, which may grant prospecting permits, mining leases, and quarrying licenses. Royalties on extracted mineral commodities ranged from 1 to 5%.

Preliminary production totals of the following products in 2009 were: hydraulic cement, 1,481,000 metric tons; 152,722 metric tons of bentonite; 15 million metric tons of sand and gravel; 317,000 metric tons of crude gypsum; 2.6 million tons of marl (for cement production), and 800,000 metric tons of crushed limestone (Havara). Other mine and quarry products for 2009 were common clays, hydrated lime, marble, building stone, and sulfur.

27 ENERGY AND POWER

The World Bank reported in 2008 that Cyprus produced 5.08 billion kWh of electricity and consumed 4.93 billion kWh, or 4,395 kWh per capita. Roughly 96% of energy came from fossil fuels, while 2% came from alternative fuels. Per capita oil consumption was 2,998 kg.

Cyprus's electricity is produced mainly by conventional thermal means, namely through the burning of fossil fuels. Its production, transmission and distribution are controlled by a semi-governmental corporation known as the Electricity Authority of Cyprus (EAC), which operates three generating stations: Dhekelia, Moni, and Vasilikos. The three facilities have a combined capacity of 1,118 MW.

Cyprus must also import virtually all the oil products it consumes. In 2010 consumption of all petroleum products totaled 61,000 barrels per day, with imports totaling 57,290 barrels per day (2009 estimates). There was no domestic oil production in 2010. Cyprus has no known coal reserves and therefore must import whatever coal it uses.

28 INDUSTRY

In 2010, according to the CIA, primary industries were tourism, food and beverage processing, cement and gypsum production, ship repair and refurbishment, textiles, and chemicals. In 2010 the industrial production growth rate, according to the CIA, was -0.3%.

Certain industrial sectors have increased considerably since 1990, namely mining and quarrying and the production of electricity, gas, and water treatment. Cyprus's leading products are textiles, cement and gypsum, light chemicals, metal products, wood, paper, and stone. In Greek Cyprus, industry accounts for about 18.6% of GDP and employs about 20.5% of the labor force. Manufactured goods account for nearly 60% of exports.

29 SCIENCE AND TECHNOLOGY

There were six patent applications in science and technology in Cyprus in 2009, according to the World Bank. Public financing of science was 0.47% of GDP in 2008. The Cyprus Research Center promotes research principally in the social sciences and in history, ethnography, and philology. In addition, Cyprus has three universities and several colleges offering degrees in basic and applied sciences. In 2008 there were 1,026 researchers in research and development per one million people in the country.

In August 2009 Cyprus signed an accession agreement with the European Space Agency, gaining observer status for the nation. Membership is viewed as an important step forward in the development of science and technology.

30 DOMESTIC TRADE

A flourishing cooperative movement provides facilities for marketing agricultural products. There are more than 500 Greek cooperative societies, with some 100,000 members. Many towns and villages have cooperative stores; the towns also have small independent shops, general stores, and bazaars. The nation is not self-sufficient and relies on imports for a number of food products and consumer goods. Since 1990 at least 12 US franchises have been established throughout the country; there are also many Greek franchises.

Government price controls have been virtually eliminated as the nation has realigned its economic policies to be acceptable to the European Union. The result has been a more open market with greater competition.

Business hours are from 8:30 a.m. to 5:30 p.m., Mondays through Fridays, with a half-hour break at noon. However, during the summer months, the break goes from 1 p.m. to 4 p.m. Government offices are open from 7:30 a.m. to 2:30 p.m. On Thursdays, government offices are open later, from 3 p.m. to 6 p.m. Shops on Mondays, Tuesdays, Thursdays, and Fridays are open from 8 a.m. to 7 p.m. But on Wednesdays and Saturdays shops are only open from 8 a.m. to 1 p.m. Normal banking hours are from 8:30 a.m. to 12:30 p.m. Tuesdays through Fridays, and from 8:30 a.m. to 3:15 or 4:45 p.m.on Mondays. Advertising is mainly through newspapers and television. Direct marketing/telemarketing has also been used.

As a result of the island's division in 1974, there is no trade between the two communities across the UN buffer zone.

31 FOREIGN TRADE

Cyprus imported $7.962 billion worth of goods and services in 2008, while exporting $2.232 billion worth of goods and services. Major import partners in 2009 were Greece, 20.1%; Italy, 10.8%; the United Kingdom, 8.9%; Germany, 8.7%; Israel, 6.9%; China, 5.5%; and the Netherlands, 4.8%. Major export partners were Greece, 24.4%; Germany, 9.1%; and the United Kingdom, 8.8%.

With limited natural resources, Cyprus is dependent on other countries for many of its needs. Other than some agricultural commodities, it has few surpluses, and the balance of trade has steadily grown more unfavorable.

In 2010 major imports were consumer goods, petroleum and lubricants, machinery, and transport equipment. Major exports were citrus, pharmaceuticals, potatoes, cement, and clothing.

Principal Trading Partners – Cyprus (2010)

(In millions of US dollars)

Country	Total	Exports	Imports	Balance
World	10,066.5	1,512.2	8,554.3	-7,042.1
Greece	1,940.9	324.9	1,616.0	-1,291.0
Germany	900.5	139.6	761.0	-621.4
Italy	840.3	34.4	805.9	-771.4
United Kingdom	823.6	113.7	710.0	-596.3
Israel	700.4	24.7	675.8	-651.1
China	467.6	20.7	446.9	-426.3
France	454.9	17.2	437.7	-420.5
Netherlands	413.6	24.3	389.3	-365.0
Spain	245.2	6.6	238.6	-232.0
Belgium	188.4	10.8	177.6	-166.8

(…) data not available or not significant.

(n.s.) not specified.

SOURCE: 2011 Direction of Trade Statistics Yearbook, New York: United Nations, 2011.

Balance of Payments – Cyprus (2010)

(In millions of US dollars)

Current Account		**-2,802.7**
Balance on goods		-6,514.1
Imports	-8,032.4	
Exports	1,518.4	
Balance on services		5,023.4
Balance on income		-1,267.1
Current transfers		2,312.8
Capital Account		**38.4**
Financial Account		**2,659.0**
Direct investment abroad		-1,003.9
Direct investment in Cyprus		1,885.9
Portfolio investment assets		-3,115.3
Portfolio investment liabilities		162.3
Financial derivatives		-176.7
Other investment assets		20,884.8
Other investment liabilities		-15,978.0
Net Errors and Omissions		**-152.4**
Reserves and Related Items		**257.7**

(…) data not available or not significant.

SOURCE: Balance of Payment Statistics Yearbook 2011, Washington, DC: International Monetary Fund, 2011.

Lack of international recognition for the Turkish Cypriots severely hampers their foreign trade. Because of the Greek Cypriot economic boycott, all goods originating in northern Cyprus must transit through Turkey, thereby adding to shipping costs. Moreover, a 1994 ruling by the European Court of Justice declared that phytosanitary certificates issued by the Turkish Republic of Northern Cyprus were invalid due to the illegality of the entity.

In 2007 North Cyprus's total exports reached $68.1 million free on board (FOB). Imports were $1.2 billion FOB. Main import commodities for North Cyprus were vehicles, fuel, cigarettes, food, minerals, chemicals, and machinery. Turkey remains the most important trade partner for North Cyprus.

32 BALANCE OF PAYMENTS

In 2010 Cyprus had a foreign trade deficit of $94 million, amounting to 5.9% of GDP.

Since Cyprus has persistently imported more than it exports, it consistently runs a trade imbalance, which has grown steadily over the past two decades. Cyprus's trade deficit has been somewhat offset by tourist dollars, spending by foreign military forces, and remittances from workers abroad.

The current account balance for Greek Cyprus was -$1.32 billion in 2010, down slightly from -$1.7 billion in 2009. External debt was estimated at $32.61 billion as of December 2008. The reserves of foreign exchange and gold were estimated at $1.14 billion in December 2010.

33 BANKING AND SECURITIES

The Central Bank of Cyprus acts as the central bank for the Greek portion of Cyprus, and is designated as the government's banking and currency clearing agent. The Banking law of 1997 provided for a properly-funded deposit insurance scheme, which was approved by the House of Representatives in late 1999. In general, banking services compare with the level experienced in European countries and the United States. The central bank is responsible for supervising the nation's private banks, which are required to meet standards set by the Bank for International Settlements. There are two dozen foreign bank branches operating in Cyprus.

In 2010 the central bank's discount rate, the interest rate at which the central bank lends to financial institutions in the short term, was 1.75%. The commercial bank lending rate was 6.815%.

The Cyprus Stock Exchange opened in March 1996. Foreign investors are not required to obtain the central bank's permission to invest in the CSE, although there are limits on foreign participation. Legislation passed in 1999 prohibited insider trading and a new screen-based automated trading system helped enhance investor confidence.

The banking sector of the northern Turkish portion of Cyprus is closely tied to the banking system of Turkey. There is a central bank that supervises the north's onshore banks. The bank is governed by a board of directors.

34 INSURANCE

Insurance companies, mostly British, make available life, fire, marine, accident, burglary, and other types of insurance. Third-party automobile liability and workers' compensation insurance are compulsory. All insurance companies in Cyprus must be members of the Insurance Association of Cyprus, and foreign ownership is subject to government approval. As of 2010 there were some 30 local insurance companies operating in Cyprus, and 20 international or foreign insurance companies.

35 PUBLIC FINANCE

In 2010 the budget of Cyprus included $9.308 billion in public revenue. The budget deficit amounted to 5.3% of GDP. Public debt was 61.1% of GDP.

The fiscal year follows the calendar year. Import duties and income tax are the principal sources of government revenue. The

Public Finance – Cyprus (2008)

(In millions of pounds, central government figures)

Revenue and Grants	**7,640.4**	**100.0%**
Tax revenue	5,300.5	69.4%
Social contributions	1,332.5	17.4%
Grants	...	...
Other revenue	...	...
Expenditures	**7,474.2**	**100.0%**
General public services	1,986	26.6%
Defense	295.7	4.0%
Public order and safety	363.7	4.9%
Economic affairs	725.3	9.7%
Environmental protection	6.5	0.1%
Housing and community amenities	369	4.9%
Health	516.8	6.9%
Recreational, culture, and religion	155.9	2.1%
Education	1,342.2	18.0%
Social protection	1,713.1	22.9%

(…) data not available or not significant.

SOURCE: *Government Finance Statistics Yearbook 2010,* Washington, DC: International Monetary Fund, 2010.

principal ordinary expenditures are education, defense, and police and fire services. Due to the introduction of a value-added tax and a more efficient tax collection system, Cyprus made steady progress in reducing its budget deficit in the early 1990s, which reached 1% of GDP in 1995.

For the Turkish-administered region, revenues amounted to $2.5 billion in 2006, and expenditures were $2.5 billion that same year.

36 TAXATION

Income taxes were first introduced in 1941, and a system of withholding in 1953. The first value-added tax (VAT) was enacted in 1992. With an eye to its hoped-for accession to the European Union in 2004, the Greek Cypriot government enacted a series of new tax laws in July 2002, effective as of 1 January 2003, designed to be fully compliant with OECD tax criteria and the EU tax Code of Conduct.

The new corporate income tax rate, applied to both local and international business companies (IBCs), is 10%. Dividends paid to Cypriot tax residents are subject to a 15% withholding tax. A major feature of the new tax code is the integration of corporation and withholding taxes, with income tax on distributed profits. The combination of the income tax and the withholding tax, assuming that 70% of the after-tax profits are distributed, produces a final tax rate of 19.45%, which is below the highest income tax rate of 25% before the reforms. Provisions for "special contributions to defense of the Republic" are changed under the new tax laws. The defense tax on interest income was raised from 3% to 10% except for recipients whose total income is less that €12,000 ($16,111), and except on interest from government bonds, pension funds, and deposits with the Housing Finance Corporation (HFC), which are taxed at 3%. With some exceptions, the defense levy on dividends received was increased from 3% to 15%. Interest income is subject to a final 10% withholding tax. All interest earned by individuals and 50% of the interest earned by corporations is exempt from income tax.

Income taxation of companies no longer depend on where they are registered but on where they are managed and controlled. Companies registered in Cyprus but managed and controlled from another country, are only be taxed in Cyprus on their Cyprus-source income. IBCs are not entitled to benefits under double taxation treaties, but they are also not be subject to the exchange of information requirements of such treaties.

Cyprus has a progressive individual income tax with a top rate of 30%, with the initial €19,500 ($26,182) tax-free. Cyprus residents are subject to a withholding tax on dividends and a withholding tax on interest. The capital gains tax, its rate of 20% unchanged under the new laws, is imposed only on the disposal of property situated in the Republic. Indirect taxes include a VAT that is assessed at four rates: 0%, 5%, 8%, or 15%.

Duty free facilities for expatriates were withdrawn in April 2003.

37 CUSTOMS AND DUTIES

By January 1998, tariffs on many goods imported from the European Union fell to zero as Cyprus adopted the EU's common customs tariff on most products from third-party countries. In addition, Cyprus is a member of the World Trade Organization. A

15% VAT is also levied, although most foodstuffs and agricultural products have a reduced rate of 5% or 8%.

³⁸FOREIGN INVESTMENT

Foreign direct investment (FDI) in Cyprus was a net inflow of $5.91 billion according to World Bank figures published in 2009. FDI represented 23.59% of GDP. In 2008, 36% of foreign investment came from EU nations and nearly 50% from non-EU countries in Europe. The largest investments were in financial intermediation (48%), real estate and business (30%), and trade and repairs (15%).

As part of its accession to the European Union, Cyprus endeavored to transform itself from an offshore tax haven, featuring a 4.25% corporate tax rate for ring-fence businesses (that is, those having no trade inside Cyprus) to what it calls a tax incentive country, free from the suspicion usually associated with tax havens. Under the new tax code, effective as of effect 1 January 2003, foreign companies already enjoying the tax haven of 4.25% (in 1996, for instance, there were some 1,168 offshore companies operating out of Cyprus) could continue to do so until the end of 2005, provided they have not traded inside Cyprus.

Since its accession to the European Union, foreign companies receive the same treatment as national companies for most sectors. The Cyprus Protection Investment Agency was created in 2007 by the government in order to attract and provide assistance to foreign investors.

In 2008 the UN Conference on Trade and Development, in its *World Investment Report*, ranked Cyprus as one of the world's top nations in terms of attracting foreign direct investment on a per capita basis.

There are no official statistics available for North Cyprus. Because it is recognized as a sovereign nation by Turkey only, it has attracted little foreign investment, despite an openness by the authorities to such investment. Most investment has come from Turkey and has been in the sectors of tourism and real estate.

³⁹ECONOMIC DEVELOPMENT

The first development plan (1962–66), designed to broaden the base of the economy and to raise the standard of living, resulted in an average annual real growth rate of 5.4%. The second development plan (1967–71) called for an annual growth rate of 7% in the GDP; actual growth during this period was nearly 8% annually. The third development plan (1972–76) envisaged an annual economic growth rate of 7.2%, but a drought in 1973 and the war in 1974 badly disrupted development programs. Physical destruction, a massive refugee problem, and a collapse of production, services, and exports made it impossible for Cyprus to reach the targets.

Since 1975, multi-year emergency economic action plans inaugurated by the Republic of Cyprus have provided for increased employment, incentives to reactivate the economy, more capital investment, and measures to maintain economic stability. The 1994–98 strategic development plan emphasized a free-market, private-sector economic approach with a target GDP growth of 4% annually. The plan called for a domestic savings rate of 22.3% of GDP; an increase of labor productivity of 2.8% between 1994–96; an inflation rate of approximately 3%, and unemployment no

greater than 2.8%. By 1996 Cyprus had largely met these goals with the exception of less than target levels of savings and productivity.

While Cyprus used to receive substantial amounts of development aid, due in part to its own improving economy and a recession in the European donor countries, it now receives little direct financial assistance from other nations.

Since its military intervention in 1974, Turkey has provided substantial financial aid to the Turkish Cypriot area. From 2003 to 2006, Turkey provided approximately $700 million in grants and loans to the Turkish region, which are usually forgiven.

Cyprus boasts an educated work force, close geographic proximity to three continents, good infrastructure, a sound legal system, and relatively low taxes. Tourism has historically been a strong driver of the economy, although it has been affected at times by economic conditions in the region and competition. In the 21st century, tourism, while still important, has been somewhat eclipsed by growth in the financial services and services sectors.

In North Cyprus, construction and education (numerous students from Turkey, and other parts of the world study at one of the area's five universities) have established themselves as the main engines of growth. However, as long as the dispute between the north and the south areas continues, development figures will not reach the island's potential.

⁴⁰SOCIAL DEVELOPMENT

A social insurance and social assistance system is in effect for all employed and self-employed persons. It provides unemployment and sickness benefits; old age, widow, and orphan pensions; maternity benefits; missing persons' allowances; and injury and disability benefits. Citizens become entitled to the old-age pension between the ages of 63 and 68, depending on earnings contributed to the system. There is a universal family allowance system, which allows for child and mother benefits; the cost is borne by the government.

Women generally have the same legal status as men. Laws require equal pay for equal work and this is enforced at the white-collar level. Sexual harassment is prohibited by law; however, incidents are usually not reported. Spousal abuse is a serious social problem and continued to receive attention.

Although human rights are generally respected, police brutality continued to be a problem. There are also reports of the mistreatment of domestic servants, usually of East or South Asian origin. Freedom of movement between the Greek and Turkish zones is restricted.

⁴¹HEALTH

According to the CIA, life expectancy in Cyprus was 80 years in 2011. The country spent 6% of its GDP on healthcare, amounting to $1,838 per person. There were 23 physicians, 40 nurses and midwives, and 37 hospital beds per 10,000 inhabitants. The fertility rate was 1.5 children per woman of childbearing years, while the infant mortality rate was 3 deaths per 1,000 live births. In 2008 the maternal mortality rate, according to the World Bank, was 10 deaths per 100,000 births. The CIA calculated HIV/AIDS prevalence rate in Cyprus to be about 0.1% in 2003.

The island has a low incidence of infectious diseases, but hydatid disease (echinococcosis) is endemic. Malaria has been eradicated and thalassaemia, which affected 15% of the population in 1960, has been eliminated. There are both public and private medical facilities, including rural health centers.

In 2007 an estimated 98% of children were vaccinated against measles and diphtheria, pertussis, and tetanus. The incidence of tuberculosis was 4 per 100,000 people in 2007. Approximately 95% of the population had access to health care services and 100% had access to safe water.

42 HOUSING

The 1974 war resulted in the displacement of more than 200,000 people and the destruction of 36% of the housing stock. The government provided temporary accommodations for about 25,000 displaced people and embarked on a long-term plan to replace the lost housing units. Between 1974 and 1990, 50,227 families were housed in a total of 13,589 low-cost dwellings.

According to a 2008 government report on construction and housing statistics, there were 374,000 dwelling units in the country, of which 63% were in urban areas. Nicosia had the largest number of new dwellings in 2008, with 4,788, followed by Paphos and Limassol. The average size of a new home in 2008 was 199 sq m (2,142 sq ft), and 118 sq m (1,270 sq ft) for new apartments.

Village homes in Cyprus are generally constructed of stone, sun dried mud bricks, and other locally available materials; in the more prosperous rural centers, there are houses of burnt brick or concrete.

Cyprus's housing market was one of the worst performing in Europe in 2010; housing prices dropped an average of 9% during the year.

Approximately 100,000 of the country's homes are owned by foreigners; more than half of these are owned by British nationals.

43 EDUCATION

In 2008 the World Bank estimated that 99% of age-eligible children in Cyprus were enrolled in primary school. Secondary enrollment for age-eligible children stood at 96%. Tertiary enrollment was estimated at 43%. Of those enrolled in tertiary education, there were 100 male students for every 96 female students. Overall, the CIA estimated that Cyprus had a literacy rate of 97.6% of GDP.

Since 1959 the Greek and Turkish communities have been responsible for their own school systems. In the Republic of Cyprus, education is compulsory for nine years, with children attending six years of primary school and six years of secondary. The secondary education is divided into two stages: gymnasium and lyceum. Each stage lasts three years. Students may choose vocational or technical schools for their secondary education as well. In 1995 a comprehensive lyceum program was established for secondary education, which combines both general and technical or vocational education. In the Turkish region, preschool education is provided for children between the ages of four and six. Primary and secondary education is free and compulsory; primary education lasts for five years and secondary education lasts for three years.

In the Republic of Cyprus in 2008, about 83% of children between the ages of three and five were enrolled in some type of preschool program. It is estimated that 100% of students complete their primary education. The student-to-teacher ratio for primary school was 14:1 in 2009; the ratio for secondary school was 10:1 in 2008.

The University of Cyprus (est. 1992) has six faculties: humanities, pure and applied sciences, social sciences and education, economics and management, letters, and engineering. There are a total of six universities in northern Cyprus and one teacher training college.

In 2007 the Republic of Cyprus's public expenditure on education was estimated at 4.1% of GDP.

44 LIBRARIES AND MUSEUMS

Cyprus has numerous school, private, and public libraries. The National Library in Nicosia holds 105,000 volumes and serves as the central library for the Republic of Cyprus. There are also municipal libraries in Famagusta, Limassol, Ktima, Larnaca, and Paphos, and bookmobile services in the Nicosia environs. Among the most important specialized libraries are those of the Cyprus Museum (15,000 volumes), the Phaneromeni Library of the Eastern Orthodox Church (33,000), and the Cyprus Turkish National Library (56,000), all in Nicosia. The University of Cyprus holds 150,000 volumes in Nicosia.

The Department of Antiquities is responsible for a wide, continuing program of research at Neolithic and classical sites. On behalf of ecclesiastical authorities, it conserves the cathedrals, mosques, monasteries, and other monuments, and over a period of many years has cooperated with numerous scientific expeditions. The entire range of archaeological discoveries from prehistoric to medieval times is displayed in the Cyprus Museum at Nicosia. In addition to the Cyprus Historical Museum and Archives and the Folk Art Museum in Nicosia, there are important collections in museums at Paphos, Larnaca, and Limassol. In all, there are about 20 museums in Cyprus, the majority being archaeological and historical. There are over 1,000 monuments and historic sites nationwide.

45 MEDIA

In 2009 the CIA reported that there were 500,788 telephone landlines in Cyprus. In addition to landlines, mobile phone subscriptions averaged 112 per 100 people. There were 7 FM radio stations, 60 AM radio stations, and one shortwave radio station.

The quality of the Cypriot telecommunications system in both the Greek and Turkish administrated areas is generally considered to be excellent. The domestic system consists of open-wire, fiber-optic cable, and microwave radio relay systems. International service is provided by tropospheric scatter communications, coaxial and fiber-optic submarine cables, and satellite ground stations. In the northern Turkish Republic, there were some 86,228 main phone lines and 147,522 cell phones in use as of 2002 (the latest year for which data was available).

The Cyprus Broadcasting Corp. (CBC) maintains regular service. Commercial spot announcements and a few sponsored programs are permitted on both radio and television. Radio programming in both AM and FM is transmitted by the CBC on two channels in Greek, Turkish, Arabic, and English. Private radio stations have been allowed since 1990. The main television transmitting station is located on Mt. Olympus. Since 1980, the television service has been linked via satellite with the Eurovision network for live transmission of major events in Europe.

Internet users numbered 50 per 100 citizens in 2009. In 2010 the country had 187,881 Internet hosts.

Nicosia has traditionally been the publishing center for the island and the editorial headquarters of nearly all the daily newspapers and weeklies. There is no censorship in the south and newspapers are outspoken on political matters. Prominent newspapers in 2010, with circulation numbers listed parenthetically, included *Phileleftheros* (26,000), *Alithia* (11,000), and *Cyprus Mail* (7,000), as well as two other major newspapers.

Freedom of speech and the press are mandated by law and are said to be in full support by the government. Private television and radio stations and university-run stations compete successfully with the government-controlled stations.

46 ORGANIZATIONS

The government encourages cooperative societies in many ways, including exemption from certain forms of taxation. The Cyprus Chamber of Commerce and Industry is the main commercial organization. There is also a Turkish Cypriot Chamber of Commerce in Nicosia. The Famagusta Chamber of Commerce and Industry is concerned primarily with international trade. The Employers and Industrialists Federation is based in Nicosia. The Pancyprian Federation of Labor serves as a general organization promoting the rights of employees. Professional and trade organizations cover a wide variety of careers, including those that also serve as forums for education and research, such as the Cyprus Medical Association. Some separate professional associations exist for Turkish Cypriot communities.

Some political parties have youth organizations. The Cyprus Scouts Association and Girl Guides are active in the country and there are branches of the YWCA. The Cyprus Sports Organization represents about 33 national sport federations and 500 athletic clubs throughout the country. There is an active organization of the Special Olympics and a Paralympic Committee.

Volunteer service organizations, such as the Lions Clubs International, are present in the country. There is an active national chapter of Caritas.

47 TOURISM, TRAVEL, AND RECREATION

The *Tourism Factbook*, published by the UN World Tourism Organization, reported 2.14 million incoming tourists to Cyprus in 2009, spending a total of $2.47 billion. Of those incoming tourists, there were two million from Europe. There were 84,327 hotel beds available in Cyprus, which had an occupancy rate of 56%. The estimated daily cost to visit Nicosia was $361. The cost of visiting other cities averaged $270.

The island's salubrious climate, proximity to continental Europe, scenic beauties, extensive roads, and rich antiquarian sites have attracted numerous visitors. Water parks and cultural centers are also popular attractions.

All visitors must have a valid passport and an onward/return ticket. Visas are not required for stays of up to 90 days.

48 FAMOUS PERSONS

The most widely known Cypriot in the pre-Christian world was the philosopher Zeno (335?–263? BC), who expounded his philosophy of Stoicism chiefly in the marketplace of Athens.

Makarios III (1913–77), archbishop and ethnarch from 1950 and a leader in the struggle for independence, was elected the first president of Cyprus in December 1959, and reelected in 1968 and 1973. His successor as president, Spyros Kyprianou (1932–2002), also was twice elected to the office, in 1978 and 1983. Tassos Nikolaou Papadopoulos (b. 1934) was elected president in 2003. Rauf Denktash (Denktaş b. 1924), the leader of the Turkish Cypriot community, was elected vice president of Cyprus in 1973, became president of the TCFS in 1975, and of the TRNC in 1983; he was reelected in 1985 and served until 2005. He was succeeded by Mehmet Ali Talat (b. 1952).

In 2010 the Nicosian native Christopher Pissarides (b. 1948) was awarded the 2010 Nobel Prize in economics, along with his American colleagues Peter Diamond and Dale Mortensen. The trio received the prize for their research and analysis of labor markets with search frictions. This research is applied to the understanding of labor markets at a time when unemployment remains high, even though the number of job vacancies appears to be large. Their research considers the factors of cost and time involved for both job seekers and employers as each group seeks to find the right match in filling a position.

49 DEPENDENCIES

Cyprus has no territories or colonies.

50 BIBLIOGRAPHY

Bolger, Diane and Nancy Serwint, eds. *Engendering Aphrodite: Women and Society in Ancient Cyprus*. Boston, MA: American Schools of Oriental Research, 2002.

Borowiec, Andrew. *Cyprus: A Troubled Island*. Westport, CT: Praeger, 2000.

Commission on Security and Cooperation in Europe. *The Situation in Cyprus: Briefing of the Commission on Security and Cooperation in Europe*. Washington, DC: The Commission, 2002.

Cyprus Investment and Business Guide: Strategic and Practical Information. Washington, DC: International Business Publications USA, 2012.

Ioannides, Christos P. *Realpolitik in the Eastern Mediterranean: From Kissinger and the Cyprus Crisis to Carter and the Lifting of the Turkish Arms Embargo*. New York: Pella, 2001.

Karageorghis, Vassos. *Early Cyprus: Crossroads of the Mediterranean*. Los Angeles, CA: J. Paul Getty Museum, 2002.

Seddon, David, ed. *A Political and Economic Dictionary of the Middle East*. Philadelphia: Routledge/Taylor and Francis, 2004.

EAST TIMOR

CAPITAL: Dili

FLAG: The national flag is rectangular. It features two isosceles triangles, the bases of which form the left edge and overlap each other. One triangle is black and its height is equal to one-third of the length of the flag. It overlaps the yellow triangle, whose height is equal to half the length of the flag. A white five-pointed star, signifying "the light that guides," is centered on the black triangle. The remaining part of the flag is red.

ANTHEM: *Pátria.*

MONETARY UNIT: East Timor has adopted the US dollar of 100 cents. There are coins of 1, 5, 10, 25, and 50 cents and 1 dollar, and notes of 1, 5, 10, 20, 50, and 100 dollars.

WEIGHTS AND MEASURES: The metric system is the legal standard.

HOLIDAYS: New Year's Day, 1 January; Labor Day, 1 May; Independence Day, 20 May; Assumption Day, 15 August; Consultation Day, 30 August; All Saints Day, 1 November; Santa Cruz Day, 12 November; Feast of the Immaculate Conception, 8 December; Christmas, 25 December. Movable holidays are Good Friday, Eid al-Fitr, and Eid al-Adha.

TIME: 9 p.m. = noon GMT.

¹LOCATION, SIZE, AND EXTENT

The main land area of East Timor lies on the eastern half of Timor, an island roughly the size of the Netherlands (32,000 sq km/12,355 sq mi) that forms an arc between Asia and Australia and is situated within the Nusatengarra Archipelago. The western half of Timor is Indonesian territory. East Timor is surrounded by the Indian Ocean at the south at the Pacific Ocean at the north. Its size rivals New Jersey or Israel, and its 15,007-km (9,325-mi) territory extends beyond its mainland to include the enclave of Ocussi-Ambeno in West Timor, and the islands of Atauro in the N and Jaco in the E. Dili, a small port city on the northern coast, is the capital.

²TOPOGRAPHY

The landscape offers a patchwork of rugged mountains, waterfalls, coastal lagoons, and diverse features that support variable vegetation, dry grasslands, savannah forests, gullies, and patches of dense rain forest. Gunung Tata Mai Lau, a mountain that forms the highest point on East Timor, reaches 2,963 m (9,721 ft) just south of the capital city of Dili, and the Laclo river in the north stretches some 80 km (50 mi), forming the longest river.

³CLIMATE

Temperatures in the dry season, from May to November, average 20–33°C (68–91°F). The weather during this season is pleasant and dry. Around October or November, oppressive humidity arrives and monsoon cloud activity builds up. The wet season, from December to April, sees average temperatures of 29–35°C (84–95°F), with heavy rains and flooding. In the mountains, daytime temperatures are warm to hot, but are cool to cold at night. Earthquakes, tsunamis, and tropical cyclones occur.

⁴FLORA AND FAUNA

The primary forest area of East Timor has been reduced to around 88,000 hectares (220,000 acres), or 1% of the territory. Dense forests are found only on the south coast or in mountainous areas. The vegetation consists mostly of secondary forests, savannah, and grasslands. Flora includes ironwood, eucalyptus, black eucalyptus, redwood, sandalwood, cendana, and lontarwood. Fauna include deer, monkeys, cockatoos, horses, cows, and beo kakoaks.

⁵ENVIRONMENT

East Timor's main environmental threats come from the widespread use of slash-and-burn agriculture, which has led to deforestation and soil erosion. According to a 2007 report issued by the International Union for Conservation of Nature and Natural Resources (IUCN), threatened species included five species of birds, one type of reptile, and four species of fish. Threatened species include the albacore tuna, Everett's tree frog, black kite, Timor sparrow, shirt-toed eagle, Japanese sparrow eagle, and red-cheeked parrot.

The World Resources Institute reported that East Timor had designated 93,800 hectares (231,785 acres) of land for protection as of 2006. The UN reported in 2008 that carbon dioxide emissions in East Timor totaled 183 kilotons.

⁶POPULATION

The US Central Intelligence Agency (CIA) estimated the population of East Timor in 2011 to be approximately 1,177,834, which placed it at number 158 in population among the 196 nations of the world. In 2011 approximately 3.6% of the population was over 65 years of age, with another 33.8% under 15 years of age. The median age in East Timor was 22.5 years. There were 1.03 males for every female in the country. The population's annual rate of change was 1.981%. The projected population for 2025 is 1,498,000. In 2011 the population density in East Timor was calculated at 79 people per sq km (205 people per sq mi).

The UN estimated in 2010 that 28% of the population lived in urban areas, and that urban populations had an annual rate of change of 5.0%. The largest urban area was Dili, with a population of 166,000.

7 MIGRATION

Estimates of East Timor's net migration rate, carried out by the CIA in 2011, amounted to zero. The total number of emigrants living abroad was 16,800, and the total number of immigrants living in East Timor was 13,800. "Timor" may be the Malay word for "Orient," but East Timor's people betray a long procession of migrations from the west, north, and east. The Portuguese arrived on the island in the early 16th century.

8 ETHNIC GROUPS

Historically the ethnic population was largely defined by the Atoni and the more dominant Belu, which was a blend of Malay, Melanesian, and Austronesian peoples who were fluent in the Tetum language. At independence in 2002, the approximate ethnic divisions in the population were as follows: 78% Timorese, 20% Indonesian, and 2% Chinese.

9 LANGUAGES

Tetum and Portuguese are the official languages. Indonesian and English are also prominent. In addition to Tetum, there are about 15 other indigenous languages spoken within East Timor. Tetum, Galoli, Mambai, and Tokodede are classified as Austronesian languages, while Bunak, Kemak, Makassai, Dagada, Idate, Kairui, Nidiki, and Baikenu are the non-Austronesian tongues.

10 RELIGIONS

According to a 2005 report, 98% of citizens were Roman Catholic, with 1% Protestant and less than 1% Muslim. The primary Protestant groups were Seventh-Day Adventists, Pentecostals, Jehovah's Witnesses, and the Christian Vision Church. It is believed that most citizens also practice some animistic beliefs in conjunction with Catholicism.

The 2002 constitution provides for the freedom of conscience, religion, and worship and this right is generally respected in practice. Though there is no state religion, the Catholic faith maintains a prominent influence in politics. Good Friday, Assumption Day, All Saints' Day, the Feast of the Immaculate Conception, Christmas, Eid al-Fitr, and Eid al-Adha are observed as national holidays.

11 TRANSPORTATION

Rebuilding the transportation infrastructure has been a key concern for the nation. The CIA reports that East Timor has a total of 6,040 km (3,753 mi) of roads, of which 2,600 km (1,616 mi) are paved. Driving accidents are frequent due to poor road conditions, lack of illumination, and the absence of required driving permits. Roads are widely shared by pedestrians and vendors, especially in city areas. Taxis, small buses, and minivans provide public transportation, but the system is generally overcrowded and not reliable.

In 2010 the merchant marine fleet consisted of one vessel of 1,000 gross registered tons or more. There are six airports, two of which had paved runways in 2010. There were also eight heliports.

12 HISTORY

Since the 1500s, the island of Timor and its lush offering of sandalwood lured both Portuguese and Dutch explorers, who contested for the territory until an official territorial division was determined through the Sentenca Arbitral in April 1913. Unlike the Dutch, Portugal's sphere of influence was concentrated in the local leadership of the East Timorese *liurai rei*, chieftains, and biracial families known as the "Black Portuguese" who were of mixed Timorese and Portuguese descent. While Portugal's colonial hold on East Timor failed to avail the local population of educational and general advancement opportunities, even leaving the island with barely 30 km (19 km) of paved asphalt road, its detachment enabled the East Timorese cultural identity to remain largely intact and unscathed by modernity.

Ironically, efforts to crush the East Timorese are not traced to the Portuguese, but to the Indonesian people and their brutal tactics for integration following Portugal's exodus from the island. When the Carnation Revolution of April 1974 in Portugal prompted the demise of nearly 50 years of dictatorship, the decolonization of East Timor, among Portugal's other colonies, seemed a favorable consequence. By the start of May 1974 three political parties surfaced within the island: the Timorese Democratic People's Union (Apodeast Timori), largely a device of the Indonesian government that advocated that East Timor be integrated into Indonesia; the Democratic Union of Timor (UDT), advocating a progressive process of autonomy under Portugal; and the Timorese Social Democratic Association (ASDT), which later became the left-wing independence movement FRETILIN (Revolutionary Front for an Independent East Timor), advocating the island's total independence.

The subsequent union and mounting popularity of UDT and FRETILIN by January 1975 proved threatening enough to the Indonesian government that then president Suharto, whose integrationist stance was already endorsed by the United States, Australia, Japan, and other nations, justified his military intervention in East Timor through the Operasi Komodo. Authored by the president's intelligence advisor Ali Moertopo (1924–84), Operasi Komodo essentially slandered FRETILIN, asserting that the party was secretly communist. This served to splinter its alliance with the UDT by May. Consequently, on 6 June 1975, Indonesia already occupied the Oecussi-Ambeno enclave under the guise of restoring order in East Timor.

Despite Indonesian presence and pressure within East Timor, FRETILIN still gained 55% of the popular vote in local elections on 29 July 1975. Thus again threatened, Indonesia manipulated the UDT to counter Portuguese authority and FRETILIN's influence through a coup staged 11 August–24 September 1975.

However, the coup against FRETILIN failed; in fact, FRETILIN instead gained control of the entire East Timorese territory and launched humanitarian advancements (in education, medical treatment, and local decision-making) that had been historically denied to the islanders. Still, monitoring by the US Central Intelligence Agency suggested continued Indonesian infiltration and fighting within East Timor and around its borders mid-September–October 1975. After capturing the violence on videotape, four foreign journalists were executed by Indonesian militia on 17 October 1975, and tension between pro- and anti-independence forces was heightened. On 28 November 1975, FRETILIN's formal assertion of an independent state of East Timor was answered the very next day by Moertopo's petition for the integration of East Timor into Indonesia through the Balibo Declaration, which UDT leaders were forced to sign.

On 7 December 1975, only one day after a visit to Jakarta by President Gerald Ford and Secretary of State Henry Kissinger of the United States, Indonesia deployed 10,000 troops—by sea, air, and land—into Dili, after an already devastating naval and aerial bombardment led by General Benny Murdani. Within days of an invasion marked by public torture, rape, and the random killing of mass civilians, Portuguese governor Mario Lemos Pire and his remaining administration made a covert and final exodus during the night to the island of Atauro, marking the end of over 460 years of colonization. On 17 July 1976, Indonesia claimed East Timor its 27th province, despite condemnation from the United Nations (UN). Indonesia kept up full-scale attacks through March 1979 through weaponry largely supplied by the United States under the administration of President Jimmy Carter. Within a year of the attack, an estimated 60,000 East Timorese had been killed, while tens of thousands sought refuge from the Armed Forces of the Republic of Indonesia (ABRI) in the rugged mountainous interior of East Timor, where FRETILIN guerrilla forces remained; others were forced into Indonesian resettlement camps, where disease, malnutrition, and death were rampant. The island was relegated to a "closed colony" status by the military from December 1975 through 1 January 1989.

It has been estimated that some 250,000 were killed between 1975 and 1999. Mass terror and killings were widespread, including 1,000 killed in Aitana in July 1981, 400 in Lacluta in September 1981, and, finally securing international attention, some 270 during the Santa Cruz massacre of 12 November 1991, in which peaceful mourners and demonstrators were killed when Indonesian troops' opened fire in a cemetery in Dili. While Indonesia experienced a shift in leadership with the forced resignation of President Suharto in 1997 and rise to power of his vice president, B. J. Habibie, East Timor endorsed FRETILIN leader José Alexandre "Xanana" Gusmão, then the president of the National Council of Timorese Resistance (CNRT). Their continued resistance against military occupation and terror, coupled with heightened international scrutiny of the atrocities within the island, may have prompted Habibie in January 1999 to extend the choice to East Timorese citizens: autonomy under Indonesian rule or outright independence.

An overwhelming 99% of eligible voters were present during the 30 August 1999 referendum; 78% voted for independence. Following the election, violent retribution on the part of

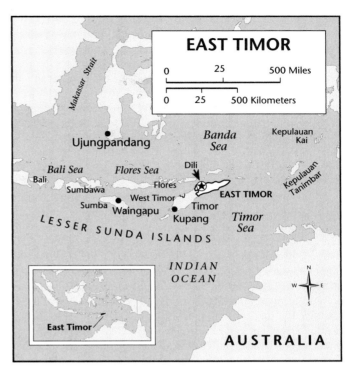

LOCATION: 8° 50′ S, 125° 55′ E. BOUNDARY LENGTHS: Indonesia, 228 kilometers (142 mi). coastline: 706 kilometers (439 mi).

Timorese militias supported by the Indonesian army led to the killing of more than 1,000 people and drove some 250,000 from East Timor. This was a dark reminder of East Timor's subjugation to the Indonesian military, which has long remained the source of ultimate government authority. Following a unanimous decision on 25 October 1999 by the UN Security Council, East Timor was governed by the UN Transitional Administration in East Timor (UNTAET) and the National Consultative Council (originally formed by 15 East Timorese whose representation was later increased to 33), with the mission to rebuild the island and establish a new government by the close of 2001. In September 2001, a constituent assembly was elected and given with the task of writing a constitution for East Timor. In April 2002, José Alexandre "Xanana" Gusmão defeated Xavier do Amaral for the presidency, and on 20 May 2002 East Timor became an independent nation. A successor mission to UNTAET, the United Nations Mission of Support in East Timor (UNMISET) was established to provide assistance to East Timor over a period 12 months, especially in matters of law enforcement and security. East Timor became the 191st UN member state on 27 September 2002.

Indonesia's attempts to bring to justice those responsible for the 1999 violence in East Timor were heavily criticized. Under intense international pressure, Indonesia set up a special human rights court to try those responsible for the violence. The court was criticized for its investigation of the involvement of Indonesia's most senior security officials and for its apparent willingness to acquit others in spite of alleged overwhelming evidence. The court indicted 18 suspects for atrocities in East Timor, but only one conviction stood. East Timor and Indonesia formed a Truth and Friendship Commission as a way to promote fact-finding about the 1999 human rights violations, and to achieve reconciliation, but the commission had no power of prosecution and was considered a diversion from the need for actual accountability.

In spring and summer 2006, violence spread across Dili once again, driving an estimated 150,000 residents to flee to villages in the countryside. The unrest, triggered when striking military were dismissed by the government in March 2006, undermined peace in the young nation. In June, Prime Minister Alkatiri resigned over his handling of the violence. On 10 July 2006, José Ramos-Horta was named prime minister. A non-military peacekeeping mission, the UN Integrated Mission in East Timor, or UNMIT, was established in August 2006.

In the presidential elections of 2007, then prime minister Ramos-Horta's victory raised hopes of greater stability in the nation. Ramos-Horta had taken an increasingly independent path, and was seen as being somewhat friendlier to the West and international investors than stalwarts in the FRETILIN Party. President Ramos-Horta was shot and severely wounded in a February 2008 attack led by rebel Alfredo Reinado. Reinado, an escaped prisoner accused of involvement in the violence of April and May 2006, was killed in the attack. Ramos-Horta was taken to Australia for medical treatment and returned in April 2008. The country was under an official state of siege until a group of rebels led by Gastao Salsinha surrendered in May of that year.

In December 2008, the UN Department of Peacekeeping Operations issued a confidential memo stating that the government of East Timor was at risk of political collapse. The report, which included a scathing indictment of the judicial and political conditions in the country, strongly advised against a withdrawal of UN and international peacekeeping forces. However, in May 2009, the government began the process of transferring control from UN security forces to the Timorese police. The UN was to remain in the nation to monitor the progress of the handover and to offer logistical support.

13 GOVERNMENT

East Timor's government was established in 2001 as a parliamentary republic with a president whose role is largely ceremonial and a prime minister who is the actual head of the government. The constitution that went into effect on 20 March 2002 was modeled largely on that of Portugal, although the German and US constitutions were consulted as well. Key components of the constitution include a ban on the death penalty, and the provision for fundamental political rights and civil liberties, including due process rights.

The unicameral parliament is composed of a minimum of 52 and a maximum of 65 members, serving five-year terms. Thirteen of the members are district representatives, corresponding to East Timor's 13 districts. For its first term of office, the parliament was comprised of 88 members on an exceptional basis.

A Council of State advises the president. It is composed of former presidents who were not removed from office, the prime minister, the speaker of parliament, five members elected from parliament, and five members appointed by the president. A Council of Ministers is comprised of the prime minister, any deputy prime ministers, and the ministers of state.

Corruption remains a serious issue in East Timor; many top government officials have been accused of the practice. In its 2009 rankings, the corruption monitoring group Transparency International ranked East Timor in the bottom 25% of its Corruption Perceptions Index. In February 2010, East Timor's parliament confirmed Aderito de Jesus, a university professor and human rights activist, as the country's first anti-corruption commissioner.

14 POLITICAL PARTIES

In 2011, East Timor's major political parties included FRETILIN, the National Congress for Timorese Reconstruction (CNRT), Democratic Party (PD), Social Democratic Party (PSD), Timorese Social Democratic Association (ASDT), National Unity Party (PUN), People's Party of Timor (PPT), Sons of the Mountain Warriors (KOTA), National Union of Timorese Resistance (UNDERTIM), and Frenti-Mudanca.

There were 16 registered parties for the constituent assembly elections held in August 2001. FRETILIN won 57.37% of the national votes and elected 12 of the 13 district representatives. The 11 other parties seating representatives in that election were: the Democratic Party (PD), 7 seats; the Social Democratic Party (PSD) and the Social Democratic Association of Timor (ASDT), 6 seats each; the Democratic Union of Timor (UDT), the Christian Democratic Party (PDC), the People's Party of Timor (PPT), the Nationalist Party of Timor (PNT), and the Timorese Monarchist Association also called Sons of the Mountain Warriors (KOTA), 2 seats each; the Liberal Party (PL), the Christian Democratic Party of Timor (UDC/PDC), the Socialist Party of Timor (PST), and an independent candidate, 1 seat each. Other parties include the Maubere Democratic Party (PDM) and the Timor Labor Party (PTT).

In the parliamentary elections of 2007, FRETILIN won 29% of the vote and 21 seats in parliament. The CNRT won 24.1% of the vote and 18 seats, followed by the alliance of the ASDT-PSD with 15.8% and 11 seats, the PD with 11.3% and 8 seats, the National Unity Party with 4.5% and 3 seats, the Democratic Alliance (KOTA and PPT) with 3.2% and 2 seats, and UNDERTIM with 3.2% and 2 seats. Kay Rala Xanana Gusmao of the CNRT was named as prime minister. The next parliamentary elections were scheduled for 2012.

The first presidential elections were held on 14 April 2002. José Alexandre "Xanana" Gusmão defeated Xavier do Amaral for the presidency, winning with 82.7% of the votes cast. Mari Alkatiri was chosen as East Timor's first prime minister. The next presidential elections were held in April and May 2007. José Ramos-Horta, a Nobel Peace Prize laureate and independent candidate, defeated FRETILIN president Francisco Guterres, 69.18% of the vote to 30.82%. The next presidential elections were scheduled for 2012.

15 LOCAL GOVERNMENT

East Timor is divided into 13 districts: Aileu, Ainaro, Baucau, Bobonaro, Covalima, Dili, Ermera, Lautem, Liquiçá, Manatuto, Manufahi, Oecussi, and Viqueque. The districts are further divided into 68 *postos* (sub-districts). A posto is further divided into *sucos*, or clusters of villages. There are approximately 500 sucos in the country. Sucos are divided into *aldeias* (villages); there are approximately 2,100 aldeias in East Timor. Local elections were held throughout East Timor in 2004 and 2005.

16 JUDICIAL SYSTEM

The Ministry of Justice was established in East Timor to guarantee an independent and impartial judiciary. A department of judicial affairs is responsible for the recruitment, appointment, and training of judges, prosecutors and public defenders.

In March 2000, the UN Transitional Administration in East Timor (UNTAET) created a civil law court system with 13 district courts and one national Court of Appeal. The law was later amended to include a court system of only four district courts and one national Court of Appeal. The four district courts are located in Dili, Baucau, Suai, and the Oecussi enclave. The district courts have jurisdiction over criminal and noncriminal offenses referred to as "ordinary crimes," whereas special panels within the Dili district court have exclusive jurisdiction over "serious criminal offenses." As of 2011, the Court of Appeals served as the supreme court, pending creation of an actual supreme court. Other courts include a high administrative, tax, and audit court; military courts; and maritime and arbitration courts.

The judicial system was considered the weakest government function in East Timor after independence. A backlog of cases raised human rights concerns, as cases pending trial and appeal were unable to be heard within a reasonable amount of time. From 2004, civil laws based on Portuguese codes began to supplant the UNTAET legal framework. A new penal code based on the Portuguese model passed in parliament and went into effect in 2009; new civil codes were to be in effect in 2011.

Portuguese and Tetum are the official languages of the court system.

17 ARMED FORCES

The International Institute for Strategic Studies reports that armed forces in East Timor totaled 1,332 members in 2011. The force is comprised of 1,250 from the army and 82 members of a naval element. Armed forces represent 0.3% of the labor force in East Timor.

In January 2001, East Timor's armed forces began training, with the goal of deploying 1,500 active military personnel and an additional 1,500 reservists into two infantry battalions. Basic training for the first group of recruits was aided by Portugal, with special training programs aided by Australia. In April 2002, UN peacekeeping forces totaled about 6,200 members from 20 countries. By 2005, the number of UN troops had fallen to 181 personnel from 9 countries. However, the 2006 strike of military personnel, and their subsequent dismissal, led to violent clashes within the nation. Faced with a crisis, East Timor government asked Australia, Malaysia, New Zealand, and Portugal to send security troops. In August 2006, the UN passed Resolution 1704, creating a mission to the beleaguered nation. The UN personnel were expected to stay until 2012, by which time policing efforts were expected to the turned over to East Timor's military and police.

East Timor's minimum military age is 18 years old. Both male and female recruits have been accepted.

18 INTERNATIONAL COOPERATION

East Timor joined the United Nations in September 2002; it has participated in the FAO, the World Bank, IFAD, the IFC, ILO, IMF, UNESCO, UNIDO, and WHO. The nation is also a member of the ACP Group, the Asian Development Bank, and G-77. It became a member of the ASEAN Regional Forum (ARF) in July 2005 and is applying for observer status in ASEAN. The United Nations Mission of Support in East Timor (UNMISET) was established in May 2002 to provide assistance in public security and law enforcement while the country establishes political stability following independence from Indonesia; 16 countries have offered support for the mission.

19 ECONOMY

As a result of the post-independence referendum violence in 1999 led by Indonesian troops and anti-independence militias, approximately 70% of the economic infrastructure was devastated and some 250,000 people moved into West Timor. Reconstruction efforts undertaken by the UN Transitional Administration in East Timor (UNTAET) improved both urban and rural areas.

East Timor's economic growth has been related to the foreign presence in country as part of the nation's rebuilding. During 2000–2001, both agriculture and the services sector expanded to meet the needs of the large international presence in East Timor. After mid-2002, growth was held back as a result of the winding-down of the international presence and of a drought in 2003. In 2004 GDP growth had recovered somewhat (1%). During the Indonesian occupation, tourism was not a large industry, but there is a great potential growth in this area. However, violent outbreaks in 2006 displaced 10% of the population and greatly hindered economic activity. The East Timorese economy stands to benefit in the long term from the development of the oil- and gas-rich seabed of the Timor Sea, but so far has been unable to effectively use these resources. For the amount of oil revenue that has been produced, the government passed a law in 2005 creating a petroleum fund to secure the value for the future; in September 2010 it was valued at $6.6 billion. The government announced plans in 2007 to increasing spending, reducing poverty, and improving the country's infrastructure. However, because the justice system remains cripplingly weak, difficulties continue in creating the economic reforms and institutions needed.

The rural areas lack infrastructure and the urban areas lack enough jobs. Unemployment and underemployment together are estimated in 2011 as being as high as 70%.

Agriculture is the main source of income in most of the country's villages, with only a small percentage of people selling a significant proportion of their rice or maize harvest.

The gross domestic product (GDP) rate of change in East Timor, as of 2011, was 6.1%, while inflation stood at 7.8%.

20 INCOME

The CIA estimated that in 2010 the GDP of East Timor was $3.051 billion. The CIA defines GDP as the value of all final goods and services produced within a nation in a given year and computed on the basis of purchasing power parity (PPP) rather than value as measured on the basis of the rate of the exchange based on current dollars. The per capita GDP was estimated at $2,600. The annual growth rate of GDP was 6.1%. The average inflation rate was 7.8%. It was estimated in 2010 that agriculture accounted for 27.9% of GDP, industry 18%, and services 54.1%.

It was estimated that in 2003 about 42% of the population subsisted on an income below the poverty line.

21LABOR

As of 2007, East Timor had a total labor force of 414,200 people. Subsistence agriculture accounted for 90% employment in 2006.

Official registration procedures for employer organizations and trade unions were established in 2004. As of 2005, workers were permitted to form and join labor organizations without getting prior approval; they were also allowed to engage in collective bargaining. However, inexperience, illiteracy, and a lack of organizational and negotiating skills have hampered attempts at organizing workers and at making them aware of their rights.

Children under the age of 18 are generally prohibited from working, but there are exceptions for minors between the ages of 15 and 18, and even for those under 15.

Although there is no legal minimum wage rate, a monthly wage rate of $85 was used by employers and employees as a minimum standard. The standard legal workweek was put at 40 hours per week, and included standard benefits such as days off, overtime, and health and safety standards.

22AGRICULTURE

Roughly 13% of East Timor's total land is farmed. With generally poor and shallow soil, steep terrain, and an unreliable climate, most farming is at a subsistence level, and based on slash-and-burn. In the north and a few fertile areas of the south, maize, cassava, cowpeas, and sweet potatoes are primary crops. Rice is cultivated in lowlands with the help of irrigation systems. The main harvest for maize occurs from February through April. The main harvest for rice occurs from May through September in the north and from August through November in the south. Other agricultural products include soybeans, cabbage, coffee, mangoes, bananas, vanilla, mung beans, taro (swamp and upland), onions, peanuts, sago, coconuts, and tobacco. Cereal production in 2009 amounted to 255,490 tons, fruit production 11,938 tons, and vegetable production 20,077 tons.

Coffee serves as an important cash crop, with over 60% of the country's organic coffee being produced in the Ermera district. The US Agency for International Development (USAID) supported East Timor's coffee industry in the early 2000s, especially through Cooperative Coffee Timor (CCT). Bobanaro, Oecussi, Viqueque, and Baucau are the most important food producing districts.

23ANIMAL HUSBANDRY

Most livestock production is based on household farms, with larger animals kept primarily for household use and consumption, while pigs and smaller animals are sold for cash. Although there are some large herds of cattle, buffalo, sheep, and goats, most farms keep smaller numbers of a variety of animals. In 2005, the livestock population included 80,000 goats, 25,000 sheep, 100,000 buffalo, and 48,000 horses.

The UN Food and Agriculture Organization (FAO) reported that East Timor dedicated 150,000 hectares (370,658 acres) to permanent pasture or meadow in 2009. During that year, the country tended 1 million chickens, 148,000 head of cattle, and 388,000 pigs. The production from these animals amounted to 1,660 tons of beef and veal, 9,712 tons of pork, 5,540 tons of poultry, 1,044 tons of eggs, and 3,122 tons of milk. East Timor also produced 198 tons of cattle hide.

24FISHING

East Timor's coastal communities have historically relied on fishing as a main source of food and income, with catches that include large tuna, flying fish, coral reef fish, and deepwater snapper. In 2008, the annual capture totaled 3,125 tons according to the UN FAO, but the industry is still recovering from the violence that followed independence. Nearly 90% of the boats and gear of these communities, as well as the onshore processing infrastructure, were damaged or destroyed. The industry has been moving toward recovery since that time through the work of the Department of Fisheries and the Marine Environment (DFME), and with the help of various international volunteers and agencies.

Besides working to recover maritime fishing activities, the DFME has explored options for inland hatcheries and freshwater fish production. One such project included breeding fish in rice fields.

25FORESTRY

Approximately 50% of East Timor is covered by forest. This is a critical resource for the country, with the value of all forest products, including roundwood, totaling $429,000 in 2009. Forest product imports totaled $565,000 that same year. The nation's forests are endangered by logging operations for teak, redwood, sandalwood, and mahogany for export, as well as by the use of wood as a primary fuel source.

In 2000, the UN Transitional Administration in East Timor (UNTAET) issued Regulation 2000–17 to prohibit any logging operations that would include the export of logs, lumber, and/or furniture from East Timor. Burning and destruction of remaining forests for any reason was also prohibited. The UN Development Program (UNDP) launched several programs to counter deforestation as well as begin reforestation. These included a nationwide seed propagation program to establish community nurseries and encourage replanting of forestlands, particularly on hillsides and in areas where erosion is a problem. There were also subsidy programs proposed to provide low-cost kerosene and cookers to rural residents in an effort to reduce dependency on wood as fuel. Other foreign governments and nongovernmental organizations have engaged in small-scale reforestation projects between 2000 and 2010.

26MINING

There are small deposits of gold, manganese, and copper throughout the nation, but not enough to be considered for major commercial industries. Marble is present in significant quantities, but it seems uncertain as to whether or not the exploitation of such deposits would have a significant impact on the country's economy in the near future.

27ENERGY AND POWER

East Timor's ability to develop its oil and gas reserves in the Timor Sea will greatly affect the economy. By 2003, the government planned to introduce a petroleum fund, designed to enhance transparency and accountability in the management of oil and gas revenues. A $1.8 billion gas recycling project in the Bayu Undan offshore gas field began in April 2004; a $1.2 billion liquid natural gas production operation began at Bayu Undan in February 2006. Revenues from that and other projects began to flow in 2006.

Disputes between Australia and Indonesia over parts of the oil- and gas-rich seabed of the Timor Sea led to the signing of the 1989 Timor Gap Treaty, which established a zone of cooperation and specified a 50–50 split of the royalties from the shared zone of undersea exploration between Australia and Indonesia. In May 2002, the treaty was renegotiated, and newly independent East Timor was granted 90% of the royalties, with Australia receiving 10%. However, the terms of the agreement were conditional on East Timor foregoing its territorial claim to almost the entire oil and gas field. Foreign officials estimated a potential revenue flow of several tens of millions of dollars per year to East Timor. In 2005 the Timor Gap fields were considered to be a source of tension, with East Timor's government accusing Australia of cutting humanitarian aid as a way to pressure East Timor into acceding to its contract terms.

In November 2009, East Timor threatened to abandon plans to develop the Greater Sunrise gas field located in the Timor Sea. In order for development to continue, East Timor has demanded that all gas exploits be piped 321 km (200 mi) to the country's mainland, where a processing plant would be constructed. Analysts have estimated the cost of the plant and pipeline to fall between $8 billion and 10 billion, while the estimated value of the gas fields is more than $50 billion. Looking at these numbers, Woodside, the Australia-based oil and gas giant that has been slated to develop the field, has claimed that East Timor's plan is cost prohibitive. Instead, Woodside promotes a plan to build a sea-based gas processing plant at the site of the fields, or construct an 804-km (500-mile) pipeline to an already existing plant near Darwin, a city in northern Australia. Bilateral treaties state that the Greater Sunrise gas fields belong in equal measure to Australia and East Timor. All plans to exploit the fields, therefore, require the approval of both countries. Government officials in East Timor said they would rather reserve the field for future generations than rush to exploit it under unfavorable conditions.

28 INDUSTRY

Industries include printing, soap manufacturing, handicrafts, and woven cloth. In 2010, industry accounted for 18% of GDP. The industrial production growth rate in 2006 was an estimated 8.5%.

29 SCIENCE AND TECHNOLOGY

The National Research Center of the National University of East Timor was established in 2001 to support the work of the five university faculties: agriculture, political science, economics, education and teacher training, and engineering.

The World Bank reported in 2009 that there were no patent applications in science and technology in East Timor.

30 DOMESTIC TRADE

Local businesses realized weak performance in the early 2000s, as they attempted to recover from violence that followed the referendum on independence. Traditional markets are filled by the local community, while foreign-owned businesses are largely

Balance of Payments – East Timor (2009)		
(In millions of US dollars)		
Current Account		**1,324.7**
Balance on goods	-361.1	
Imports	-370.3	
Exports	9.2	
Balance on services	-518.0	
Balance on income	1,844.4	
Current transfers	359.3	
Capital Account		**27.3**
Financial Account		**-1,272.6**
Direct investment abroad	…	
Direct investment in East Timor	49.9	
Portfolio investment assets	-1,325.1	
Portfolio investment liabilities	…	
Financial derivatives	…	
Other investment assets	8.4	
Other investment liabilities	-5.8	
Net Errors and Omissions		**-39.9**
Reserves and Related Items		**-39.5**

(…) data not available or not significant.

SOURCE: *Balance of Payment Statistics Yearbook 2011*, Washington, DC: International Monetary Fund, 2011.

patronized by the wealthy. In 2001, the World Bank launched a $4.85 million small enterprises project, offering loans of $500 to $50,000 to East Timorese with viable business plans. The project also financed the delivery of business skills training to small and medium-sized enterprises.

31 FOREIGN TRADE

Trade in East Timor is dominated by foodstuffs, construction materials, electronics, and clothing. Some 97% of manufactured goods are imported, with coffee being the sole significant export. East Timor in the mid-2000s was seeking trade partners to develop its oil and gas reserves, among them China and Malaysia. Coffee is exported to the United States, Australia, New Zealand, Italy, and the Netherlands, among other countries.

East Timor imported $202 million worth of merchandise in 2004, while exporting $10 million in merchandise in 2005 (excluding oil). Major import partners in 2009 were Australia, Europe, Indonesia, Japan, and the United States. Its major export partners were Australia, Europe, Japan, and the United States.

32 BALANCE OF PAYMENTS

The external current account was in large deficit by 2003 (-$230 million), resulting in large measure from imports associated with donor-assisted reconstruction activities. The deficit was more than financed by official transfers, however, and, inclusive of these transfers, the external current account was in surplus ($37 million). In 2005, the CIA estimated merchandise exports at $10 million, excluding oil, and imports at $202 million in 2004.

33 BANKING AND SECURITIES

The finance sector is small, with a limited central bank role played by the Banking and Payments Authority (formerly the Central Payments Office). In 2005 there were three operating branch offices of overseas banks (the ANZ Banking Group, Bank Mandiri, and the Banco Nacional Ultramarino). Informal lenders comprise the remainder of the finance sector.

34 INSURANCE

National Insurance Timor-Leste (NITL) opened in March 2010, becoming East Timor's first insurance company. It offers various types of personal and commercial insurance. While it is possible to obtain insurance for vehicles in East Timor, virtually no one does so. Most individuals involved in traffic accidents settle them informally. Third-party motor vehicle insurance is unavailable.

35 PUBLIC FINANCE

In 2010 the budget of East Timor included $1.481 billion in public revenue and $838 million in public expenditures. Revenues minus expenditures was $643 million.

East Timor receives foreign aid primarily from Australia, Japan, the European Union, the United States, Portugal, and China. Development assistance during the 1990s totaled $81 million, increasing from $1 million in 1989 to more than $12 million in 1999. As of 2002, East Timor was receiving $2.2 billion in economic aid. The United States alone provided $272 million in aid between 2000 and 2008, according to USAID, and Australia's official development assistance for 2010–11 was an estimated $103 million.

36 TAXATION

In 2000, the UN Transitional Administration in East Timor (UNTAET) issued a revenue system for East Timor, providing the basis for a tax regime. It largely adopted the Indonesian income tax law with some modifications. East Timor's tax system is designed to tax business profits and designated passive income. Business profits include capital gains. Passive income includes interest, royalties, and rental and dividend income. The standard income tax rates for resident companies and individuals are 10% on the first $3,368; 15% on the next $3,368; and 30% on income over $6,737.

Employment-related income initially was not subject to income tax; however, a wage income tax (WIT) was levied for wages received on or after 1 January 2001. WIT applies to employment-related remuneration only, as opposed to general personal income. WIT is due as follows: the rate is 0% on monthly salaries of $0 to $100; 10% on monthly salaries of $101 to $650; and 30% on monthly salaries of $651 or more.

37 CUSTOMS AND DUTIES

Excise taxes are imposed on the import or domestic production (but not both) of certain goods. Goods are exempt from excise taxes if they are exported from East Timor within 28 days of production and are exempt from import duty, or if they relate to the Timor Gap Treaty. Goods subject to excise taxes included (but are not restricted to) the following: confectionery, fruit juices, ice cream, soft drinks, tobacco, gasoline, diesel fuel, beer, wine, other alcohol, make-up, shampoos, toiletries, electrical goods, mobile phones, televisions, automobiles, motorcycles, and arms and ammunition.

As of 2011, all imported goods were subject to an import duty of 5% of the customs value (CIF value).

38 FOREIGN INVESTMENT

Most foreign investment is from Singapore and Australia, and is centered in the hotel and restaurant business, the importation of used cars, and construction. The government encourages foreign investment in light industries such as textile, garment, and shoe factories. Fishing and ecotourism also have potential for foreign investment (East Timor has some of the best scuba diving in Asia). Rudimentary infrastructure and a lack of skilled labor hamper investment. Investors have few guarantees regarding property rights, insurance, or bankruptcy. The labor law also serves to inhibit foreign investment because it is difficult for employers to fire East Timorese workers.

Foreign direct investment (FDI) in East Timor was unreported according to World Bank figures published in 2009.

39 ECONOMIC DEVELOPMENT

Since 2002, the nation's economic and social policies have been targeted toward the alleviation of poverty, development in the private sector, the strengthening of public institutions, and the achievement of public security. Into 2011, however, the nation continued to face significant challenges to economic stability and growth, including weak public governance and an inadequate physical infrastructure. The East Timor Strategic Development Plan 2011–2030 was designed to build on the initial 2002 development plan by presenting a general framework of short-term (1 to 5 years), medium-term (5 to 10 years), and long-term goals (10 to 20 years) that are closely aligned with the United Nations' Millennium Development Goals. An overall goal of the plan is to transition the nation from a low-income country to a middle-income country by 2030. To reach this goal, the government is expected to make major investments in infrastructure, health and education, security, good governance, and private sector development, particularly in agriculture, tourism, and the oil and gas sector. Development aid from Australia will most likely play an important part in reaching the nation's goals.

40 SOCIAL DEVELOPMENT

Some customary practices continue to discriminate against women, especially in remote villages. Despite a 2010 law prohibiting domestic abuse, domestic violence against women continues to be a problem exacerbated by the failure of officials to investigate or prosecute. As of 2010, East Timor was considered to be a destination country for human trafficking of women who are forced into prostitution. Most of the women come from Indonesia and China. It was believed that the nation might be a source country for women and girls sent to countries within Southeast Asia and as forced domestic labor. There have also been reports of men from Myanmar, Cambodia, and Thailand being brought in as forced labor on fishing boats around East Timor.

Child abuse, including sexual abuse, is considered to be a significant problem. There have been reports of children being forced into bonded labor by family members, generally to pay off debts.

East Timor's constitution includes important human rights protections, including the right to a fair trial, criminal due process, freedom of expression, freedom of association, and freedom of religion. The constitution forbids the death penalty and life imprisonment, and includes the right to be free from torture, servitude, and cruel or degrading treatment. However, problems relating to the criminal justice system, including lengthy pretrial detentions and abuse of authority, remained unresolved.

41 HEALTH

According to the CIA, life expectancy in East Timor was 62 years in 2011. In 2009, the country spent 12.3% of its GDP on healthcare. There were 22 nurses and midwives and 1 physician per 10,000 inhabitants. The fertility rate was 3.13 children born per woman, while the infant mortality rate was 48 deaths per 1,000 live births. In 2008 the maternal mortality rate, according to the World Bank, was 370 deaths per 100,000 births. It was estimated that 70% of children were vaccinated against measles.

42 HOUSING

Housing has been a serious problem since independence. Nearly 85,000 houses (about 70% of the nation's entire housing stock) were destroyed by the Indonesian military in September 1999. Though the UN Transitional Administration in East Timor (UNTAET) and a number of international aid organizations responded quickly with temporary shelter kits, rebuilding of permanent housing has been slow and property ownership disputes have not been fully addressed. It has been difficult to estimate housing demand.

Tens of thousands of residents fled the country during the violence and those who remained sought shelter in abandoned homes. As property owners returned to their homes, many found occupants claiming ownership and unwilling to leave. Some occupants have demanded large payments from the owners for "house-sitting" or "improvements" made to the homes in the owner's absence. Through a proposed Land and Property Commission, it has been generally recognized that the original owners or tenants of a property have the right to eventual restitution and reoccupancy, but administration and enforcement of such rights has been a low priority as the government struggled to rebuild an entire nation and care for the emergency needs of its people.

In urban areas such as Dili, Bacau, and Alieu, homes have been typically built from concrete. A majority of the population lives in rural areas with homes made from bamboo, wood, and thatch.

43 EDUCATION

Over 90% of all school buildings were severely damaged or destroyed by the Indonesian military. In the exodus of Indonesians out of East Timor, the nation lost 20% of its primary school teachers and 80% of secondary teachers, most of whom were not expected to return. UNICEF and other international aid organizations responded fairly quickly, however, reestablishing classes for 420 of the country's 800 primary schools by December 1999 plus an additional 273 schools by April 2000.

East Timor's educational system continued to recover. In 2009 the World Bank estimated that 82% of age-eligible children in East Timor were enrolled in primary school. Tertiary enrollment was estimated at 15%. Public expenditure on education represented 16.8% of GDP in 2009.

The education system includes six years of primary education and six years of secondary education. In 2000, the language of instruction was Indonesian, but this was phased out in favor of Portuguese, a troublesome decision since only 5% of the population speaks Portuguese, and few of the Portuguese speakers are children. Many are encouraging a switch to the national language of Tetum as a primary language with Portuguese and English as secondary languages, but this is complicated by the fact that Tetum, while widely understood in East Timor, is primarily an oral rather than written language.

The National University of East Timor (Universidade Nacional Timor Lorosae-UNTL) opened for classes on 27 November 2000 and had about 5,000 students in attendance in 2003. There are five faculties at the university: agriculture, political science, economics, education and teacher training, and engineering. All new students follow a course including human rights, ethics, philosophy of science, and Timorese history.

Overall, the CIA estimated that East Timor had a literacy rate of 58.6%. A full two thirds of all adult women were illiterate. Sixty percent of the population has never gone to school, but literacy continues to increase.

44 LIBRARIES AND MUSEUMS

As of 2002, it was proposed that a new National Library of East Timor would be established in the old Vila-Verde building, along with a national archive. A variety of Australian organizations have been raising funds to support the reconstruction of an East Timor public library system. In 2011 the new national library was still under development; an Australian librarian with East Timor experience was hired to serve as library specialist. She will help in developing physical infrastructure, educational policies, human resource requirements, and acquisition policies.

The National University of East Timor library, housed in a former gymnasium, opened for student access on 21 January 2002.

45 MEDIA

The World Bank in 2007 reported that East Timor has the highest telecommunications cost in the world. Australian companies have helped to restore the services cut off by the Indonesian government; by 2009, there were an estimated 2,400 main phone lines in use and an additional 116,000 mobile cellular phones (roughly 10 per 100 people). International communication authorities have approved an individual country code (670) for East Timor.

In 2010, the country had 206 Internet hosts. As of 2009, there were some 2,100 Internet users in East Timor. In January 2005, the country's domain name extension was officially changed from .tp to .tl.

As of 2011, there were three daily newspapers, two weeklies, and several bulletin-type newspapers with sporadic publication and circulation. These include the *Suara Timor Lorosae* (daily), *Timor Post* (daily), and *Jornal Nacional Semanario* (weekly). Timor Today and East Timor Centre for Investigative Journalism, were prominent news websites.

The government-operated Public Broadcast Service (PBS) has a radio station with nationwide reception and a television station that broadcasts only in Dili and Baucau. There were 16 community radio stations, with at least one in each district. The new constitution provides for the freedom of speech and press and the government generally respects these rights in practice.

46 ORGANIZATIONS

Student organizations in East Timor were influential in the nation's independence campaign and have continued to speak out for civil rights. The National Student Resistance of East Timor (Resistencia Nacional Dos Estudantes De Timor Leste) began in 1988 as an underground organization of Indonesian university students. The East Timor Students Solidarity Council originated in 1998 at the National University of East Timor. It has since set up regional groups throughout the country to represent the views of university and high school students and faculty. Student organizations were still active in 2010; an international student solidarity conference was held in Dili that year.

Other organizations in East Timor include Catholic youth groups, scouting groups, and a number of women's groups, covering political, health, and social issues, including Rede Feto Timor Lorosae, which serves as a network of about 15 individual groups.

The Cooperative Coffee Timor (CCT) is a federation of Timorese-owned organic coffee cooperatives that has received aid and developmental support from USAID. The Chamber of Commerce of East Timor and the National Association of East Timor Entrepreneurs are two major business associations in good standing.

There is a national chapter of the Red Cross Society.

47 TOURISM, TRAVEL, AND RECREATION

Tourism is limited due to a lack of infrastructure and tourist facilities. There are at least 25 hotels in Dili; one of Dili's two luxury hotels is an anchored cruise ship. Scuba diving and whale- and dolphin-watching are tourist attractions, in addition to the country's beaches. The northern coast features white sand beaches, while the southern coast is rocky with occasional black sand beaches. There are elaborate intact coral reefs, populated by over 1,000 aquatic species. East Timor's colonial towns and rugged mountains are also popular with visitors.

The *Tourism Factbook*, published by the UN World Tourism Organization, reported 44,000 incoming tourists to East Timor in 2009; they spent a total of $18 million. Of those incoming tourists, there were 26,300 from East Asia and the Pacific. There were 995 hotel beds available in East Timor. The estimated daily cost to visit Dili, the capital, was $210. The cost of visiting other cities averaged $89.

Passports are required. Visas may be obtained upon arrival for a fee, and are valid for 30 days. A certificate of vaccination against yellow fever is required if traveling from an infected area.

48 FAMOUS PERSONS

Martinho da Costa Lopes (1918–1991) was a Timorese priest with close ties to the Portuguese colonial government and an early advocate for the Timorese people. In 1996, exiled pro-independence leader José Ramos-Horta (b. 1949) and Bishop Carlos Filipe Ximenes Belo (b. 1948) shared the Nobel Peace Prize. Bishop Belo was the highest representative of the Roman Catholic Church in predominantly Catholic East Timor, and was a strong advocate of nonviolent resistance. Ramos-Horta served as the UN representative for the East Timorese cause from 1976–89. Ramos-Horta has since served as prime minister of East Timor (2006–2007) and subsequently as president (2007–). José Alexandre "Xanana" Gusmão (b. 1946) was a former Falintil (Armed Forces of National Liberation of East Timor) and FRETILIN guerrilla leader and East Timor's first president. He was imprisoned by the Indonesian army in 1992 and released in 1999. He was elected president in April 2002.

49 DEPENDENCIES

East Timor has no territories or colonies.

50 BIBLIOGRAPHY

Cardoso, Luís. *The Crossing: A Story of East Timor*. London, Eng.: Granta Books, 2000.

Chalk, Peter. *Australian Foreign and Defense Policy in the Wake of the 1999/2000 East Timor Intervention*. Santa Monica, CA: Rand, 2001.

Chomsky, Noam. *A New Generation Draws the Line: Kosovo, East Timor, and the Standards of the West*. New York: VERSO, 2000.

Cotton, James. *East Timor, Australia and Regional Order: Intervention and Its Aftermath in Southeast Asia*. New York: RoutledgeCurzon, 2004.

Cristalis, Irena. *Bitter Dawn: East Timor, a People's Story*. New York: Zed Books, 2002.

Durand, Frederic. *East Timor: A Country at the Crossroads of Asia and the Pacific*. Bangkok, Thailand: Silkworm Books, 2006.

East Timor (Timor-Leste). Washington, DC: Central Intelligence Agency, 2003.

Hainsworth, Paul and Stephen McCloskey, eds. *The East Timor Question: The Struggle for Independence from Indonesia*. New York: I.B. Tauris, 2000.

Kohen, Arnold. *From the Place of the Dead: A Biography of Bishop Carlos Ximenes Belo, Winner of the Nobel Prize for Peace, 1996*. New York: St. Martin's, 1997.

Leibo, Steven A. *East and Southeast Asia 2011*. Lanham, MD: Stryker-Post Publications, 2011.

Lennox, Rowena. *Fighting Spirit of East Timor: The Life of Martinho da Costa Lopes*. New York: Zed Books, 2000.

Marker, Jamsheed. *East Timor: A Memoir of the Negotiations for Independence*. Jefferson, NC: McFarland, 2003.

Nevins, Joseph. *A Not-So-Distant Horror: Mass Violence in East Timor*. Ithaca, NY: Cornell University Press, 2005.

Tanter, Richard, Mark Selden, and Stephen R. Shalom, eds. *Bitter Flowers, Sweet Flowers: East Timor, Indonesia, and the World Community*. Lanham, MD: Rowman and Littlefield, 2001.

Tiffen, Rodney. *Diplomatic Deceits: Government, Media, and East Timor*. Sydney, Aus.: UNSW Press, 2001.

FIJI

Republic of Fiji

CAPITAL: Suva

FLAG: The national flag of Fiji consists of the red, white, and blue Union Jack in the upper left corner of a light blue field, with the Fiji shield centered on the right side.

ANTHEM: *God Bless Fiji.*

MONETARY UNIT: The Fiji dollar (FJD) of 100 cents is the national currency. There are coins of one dollar, and 1, 2, 5, 10, 20, and 50 cents. Notes are available in denominations of 2, 5, 10, 20, and 50 Fiji dollars. FJD1 = US$0.54000 (or US$1 = FJD1.8482) as of 2011.

WEIGHTS AND MEASURES: The metric system is official, but some British weights and measures are still in use.

HOLIDAYS: New Year's Day, 1 January; Independence Day (Fiji Day), 10 October; Christmas Day, 25 December; Boxing Day, 26 December. Movable religious holidays include Good Friday, Easter Monday, Dewali, the Queen's Birthday, and Milad un-Nabi (Birthday of the Prophet Muhammed).

TIME: 12 midnight = noon GMT.

¹LOCATION, SIZE, AND EXTENT

Fiji, situated in the South Pacific about 4,450 km (2,765 mi) SW of Hawaii and 1,770 km (1,100 mi) N of New Zealand, comprises some 850 islands, of which only about 100 are inhabited. The island of Rotuma, added to Fiji in 1881, is geographically separate from the main archipelago and has an area of 44 sq km (17 sq mi). The total area (including Rotuma) is 18,270 sq km (7,054 sq mi). Comparatively, Fiji is slightly smaller than New Jersey. Fiji (not including Rotuma) extends 595 km (370 mi) SE–NW and 454 km (282 mi) NE–SW. The largest islands are Viti Levu, with an area of 10,386 sq km (4,010 sq mi), and Vanua Levu, with 5,535 sq km (2,137 sq mi). Fiji's total coastline is 1,129 km (702 mi).

Fiji's capital city, Suva, is located on the island of Viti Levu.

²TOPOGRAPHY

The larger Fiji islands are volcanic, with rugged peaks and flatland where rivers have built deltas. Coral reefs surround the islands. Viti Levu's highest point, Tomanivi, is 1,323 m (4,340 ft). About 28 other peaks are over 910 m (3,000 ft). The lowest point is at sea level (Pacific Ocean). The main river, the Rewa, is about 150 km (95 mi) long but is only navigable by small boats for 113 km (70 mi).

³CLIMATE

Temperatures at sea level range from 20 to 29°C (68 to 85°F); easterly trade winds blow during the greater part of the year. Annual rainfall is well-distributed and averages 305 cm (120 in) in Suva. At sea level on the leeward sides of the islands, there are well-de-fined wet and dry seasons, with a mean annual average of 178 cm (70 in) of rain.

The cyclone season, from November to April, brings storms that generally cause extensive property damage, loss of crops, and numerous deaths. In December 2009, Cyclone Mick passed over the main island of Viti Levu, killing three people and leaving thousands of people in need of temporary shelters. In March 2010, Cyclone Tomas hit the northern islands with winds up to 170 km (106 mi) per hour; 5,000 people were forced from their homes.

⁴FLORA AND FAUNA

The larger islands have forests on the windward side and grassland on the leeward slopes. Mangroves and coconut plantations fringe the coasts. Among indigenous fauna are bats, rats, snakes, frogs, lizards, and many species of birds. A red and white flowering plant called the tagimaucia is only found on the banks of the Tagimaucia River in the mountains of Taveuni island.

The World Resources Institute estimates that there are 1,518 plant species in Fiji. In addition, Fiji is home to 15 species of mammals, 112 species of birds, 34 species of reptiles, and 3 species of amphibians. This calculation reflects the total number of distinct species residing in the country, not the number of endemic species.

⁵ENVIRONMENT

The main challenges to the environment in Fiji are deforestation, soil erosion, and pollution. Approximately 30% of Fiji's forests have been eliminated by commercial interests. The rainfall pattern, the location of agricultural areas, and inadequate agricultural methods contribute to the loss of valuable soils. The land and water supply are polluted by pesticides and chemicals used in the sugar and fish processing industries. Fiji is also concerned about rising sea levels attributed to global warming caused by the burning of fossil fuels in the industrial world.

Fiji's natural environment is protected by a national trust, which under the 1981–85 development plan began to establish national parks to conserve the island's unspoiled landscape, reefs, and waters, as well as indigenous flora and fauna.

According to a 2011 report issued by the International Union for Conservation of Nature and Natural Resources (IUCN), threatened species included 6 types of mammals, 14 species of birds, 6 types of reptiles, 1 species of amphibian, 13 species of fish, 3 types of mollusks, and 65 species of plants. Threatened species included the Fiji banded iguana and crested iguana, the insular flying fox, and the Samoan flying fox. The bar-winged rail has become extinct.

The World Resources Institute reported that Fiji had designated 15,400 hectares (38,054 acres) of land for protection as of 2006. Water resources totaled 28.6 cu km (6.86 cu mi) while water usage was 0.07 cu km (.017 cu mi) per year. Domestic water usage accounted for 14% of total usage, industrial for 14%, and agricultural for 72%. Per capita water usage totaled 82 cu m (2,896 cu ft) per year.

The UN reported in 2008 that carbon dioxide emissions in Fiji totaled 1,458 kilotons.

6 POPULATION

The US Central Intelligence Agency (CIA) estimated the population of Fiji in 2011 to be approximately 883,125, which placed it at number 160 in population among the 196 nations of the world. In 2011, approximately 5.2% of the population was over 65 years of age, with another 28.9% under 15 years of age. The median age in Fiji was 26.9 years. There was one male for every female in the country. The population's annual rate of change was 0.798%. The projected population for the year 2025 was 920,000. Population density in Fiji was calculated at 48 people per sq km (124 people per sq mi).

The UN estimated that 52% of the population lived in urban areas, and that urban populations had an annual rate of change of 1.3%. The largest urban area was Suva, with a 2009 population of 174,000.

7 MIGRATION

Estimates of Fiji's net migration rate, carried out by the CIA in 2011, amounted to -7.24 migrants per 1,000 citizens. The total number of emigrants living abroad was 182,200, and the total number of immigrants living in Fiji was 18,500.

In the late 19th and early 20th centuries, about 50,000 Indian laborers arrived in the islands to work on sugar plantations. Recent immigrants have come from neighboring islands. There has been steady internal migration from rural to urban areas. There are no restrictions on emigration, and at least 40,000 have done so since 1987. Most of these emigrants were professionals or Indo-Fijians, with many of the Indo-Fijians leaving Fiji for Australia and New Zealand.

8 ETHNIC GROUPS

The indigenous Fijian population is predominantly Melanesian, with a Polynesian admixture. The population was estimated to be 57.3% indigenous Fijian and 37.6% Indian. About 1.2% of the population are Rotuman, the indigenous inhabitants of the island of Rotuma. European, other Pacific Islanders, and overseas Chinese are the minorities.

9 LANGUAGES

English and Fijian are official languages, but Hindi is also used in parliament. Fijian dialects belong to the Malayo-Polynesian language group; the Bau dialect is used throughout the archipelago except on Rotuma, where Rotuman is spoken. Hindustani (a local dialect of Hindi) is the lingua franca of the Indians of Fiji.

10 RELIGIONS

About 64.5% of Fijians are Christians, primarily Methodist (34.6%) and Roman Catholic (9.1%). About 27.9% of the people are Hindu, and 6.3% are Muslim (Sunni). Religion tends to run along ethnic lines. Most of the indigenous Fijians are Christian, while the Indians are Hindu or Muslim. Confucianism is practiced by a portion of the Chinese community.

The constitution provides for freedom of religion, and the government reportedly respects this right in practice. Though there is no state religion, the Methodist Church has been supported by a large number of the country's chiefs, leading to past accusations that the government was leaning toward the establishment of a Christian state. However, some church leaders and political party members associated with the Methodist Church were critical of the military government following a 2006 coup. As a result, church leaders reported some incidence of harassment, and the government prohibited the church from conducting its annual conference in 2010. At least 27 church members were later prosecuted for ignoring the ban and attempting to hold their annual meetings. Easter, Christmas, Diwali, and Milad un-Nabi are observed as national holidays.

11 TRANSPORTATION

The CIA reports that Fiji has a total of 3,440 km (2,138 mi) of roads, of which 1,692 km (1,051 mi) are paved. There are 175 vehicles per 1,000 people in the country. Fiji has approximately 203 km (126 mi) of navigable waterways. A private rail system of about 597 km (371 mi) serves most of the sugar-producing areas. Major ports are Suva, Lautoka, and Levuka.

In 2010, Fiji had ten merchant ships in service of 1,000 GRT or over. Inland waterways are navigable by motorized craft and 200-ton barges. There are 28 airports in Fiji, 4 with paved runways. An international airport at Nadi serves regularly scheduled flights to neighboring Pacific islands, Australia, and New Zealand, via Air Pacific. Fiji Air provides domestic and charter service. According to the World Bank, Fiji's airports transported 1.15 million passengers in 2009.

12 HISTORY

Voyagers from the east settled Fiji at least 2,500 years ago. Some of their descendants later moved on to settle the Polynesian islands to the west. The first known European contact came when the Dutch navigator Abel Tasman sighted the Fiji group in 1643.

English Captain James Cook visited it in 1774, and Charles Wilkes headed a US expedition there for three months in 1840.

European sandalwood traders, army deserters, and shipwreck survivors also landed on the islands during the first half of the 19th century, a period in which the chiefs of Bau rose to a dominant position. Protestant missionaries from Tonga arrived in 1835 and French Catholic priests in 1844. After a few chiefs had been converted, more and more Fijians embraced Christianity, usually in the form of Wesleyan Methodism.

In the course of a civil war in the 1850s, Cakobau, the most powerful chief in Fiji, combined forces with the king of Tonga to become paramount chief of western Fiji. The growing presence of Europeans contributed to political and economic instability. In 1871, some 3,000 Europeans supported Cakobau's claim to rule as king of all Fiji, but unrest continued. Cakobau's government appealed to Britain for assistance and, on 10 October 1874, Fijian chiefs signed a Deed of Cession making Fiji a British Crown colony.

From 1879 to 1916, more than 60,000 indentured laborers from India arrived to work on European-owned sugar plantations, and, by 1920, they had settled as free farmers. European settlers were granted elective representation in the legislative council in 1904, and Indians were admitted in 1929. Ethnic Fijian representation was based on traditional hierarchies until 1963, when the council was reconstituted; the franchise was extended to women, and direct election of Fijian members was provided. In 1966, the council was enlarged and again reconstituted, and Fiji attained virtual internal self-government.

On 10 October 1970, Fiji became a sovereign and independent state within the Commonwealth of Nations, with Kamisese K. T. Mara, head of the Alliance Party, as prime minister. He and his majority party won elections in 1972, 1977, and 1982 but lost the April 1987 elections to a coalition of the Indian-based National Federation Party and the Labour Party. The new government was short-lived, however; within a month, it was toppled by a military coup led by Lt. Col. Sitiveni Rabuka and aimed at restoring political leadership to ethnic Fijians. On 20 May, thousands of rioting Fijians attacked Indians. Under a compromise reached the next day, the governor-general temporarily was to head the government, assisted by an 18-member advisory council, including the coup leader and former prime minister Mara. Elections were to be held within six months, and the council was to propose constitutional revisions that would safeguard the political dominance of indigenous Fijians.

On 25 September 1987, however, Rabuka led a second coup. He subsequently suspended the constitution, dissolved the parliament, and declared Fiji a republic. The governor-general, Ratu Sir Penaia Ganilau, was appointed president of the republic, and Mara was reappointed prime minister. Full civilian rule returned in January 1990 when Rabuka gave up his position as minister of home affairs and returned to barracks as head of the armed forces.

The second coup in 1987 and the adoption of the 1990 constitution, which favored ethnic Fijian control of the government, led to heavy Indian emigration, especially among those Indians with sufficient capital to move. This emigration caused serious economic difficulties for Fiji, but it also ensured that the native Fijian population became the majority.

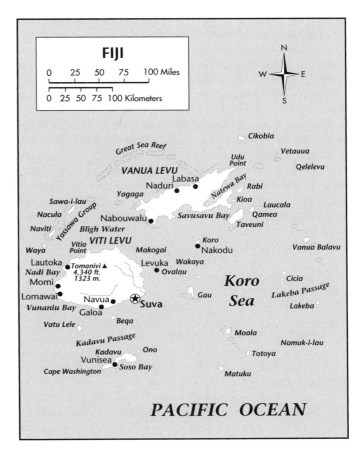

LOCATION: 15°43′ to 21°2′S; 176°54′E to 178°28′W (not including Rotuma, which is at 12°30′ S; 177°5′ E). TERRITORIAL SEA LIMIT: 12 miles.

In May of 1992, the Soqosoqo ni Vakavulewa ni Taukei (SVT) or the Fijian Political Party, led by now Major-General Rabuka, won 30 of the 37 seats reserved for ethnic Fijians. Rabuka formed a coalition government with the General Voters Party (GVP) and with the informal support of the Fijian Labour Party (FLP) became prime minister. After President Ganilau's death in December 1993, the Great Council of Chiefs elected Ratu Sir Kamisese Mara as the new president in January 1994. Rabuka's government fell in November 1993 when the legislature defeated the government's budget. New elections were held in February 1994. The SVT won 31 seats, and Rabuka was able to form a coalition government with the GVP. However, Rabuka's hold on power was tenuous as pressure mounted from within and outside the country for constitutional reform.

Beginning in 1995, a constitutional review commission spent almost two years to develop a system that would avoid purely ethnic politics and, at the same time, take account of the concerns of the native Fijian community. Its recommendations were unanimously adopted by parliament in July 1997. In 1999, parliamentary elections were held that resulted in a government led by Mahendra Chaudhry, leader of the Fiji Labour Party (FLP), who became the first Indian prime minister of Fiji.

On 19 May 2000, ethnic Fijian nationalist George Speight, a failed businessman and son of Sam Speight, an opposition member of parliament, took parliament by show of force and held Prime Minister Chaudhry and most of his multiracial cabinet hostage for 56 days. In exchange for the hostages' release, the military—which imposed martial law during the crisis—agreed to replace Chaudhry's government, grant an amnesty to the rebels taking part in the coup, and to abolish Fiji's multiracial constitution. One of Speight's demands was a new constitution that would permit only indigenous Fijians to hold the posts of prime minister and president. The coup resulted in widespread civil unrest and attacks against ethnic Indians, and caused a drop of 41% in tourism. Speight and 369 of his supporters were arrested in July 2000, and the military installed ethnic Fijian Laisenia Qarase as prime minister in a caretaker government. He was charged with organizing Fiji's next general election and drawing up a new constitution. Fiji's Great Council of Chiefs appointed Ratu Josefa Iloilo, a former father-in-law of Speight's brother, president.

Eighteen political parties fielded 351 candidates for office in parliamentary elections held in August and September 2001. Qarase was elected prime minister as the head of his newly created party, the nationalist Soqoso Duavata ni Lewenivuana Party (Fijian United Party or SDL), which took 32 out of 71 parliamentary seats. Qarase's campaign focused on indigenous Fijians' fears of political domination by ethnic Indians, who make up 44% of the population. Almost all ministers in Qarase's new government were indigenous Fijians. In February 2002, the Fijian Supreme Court ruled that Laisenia Qarase had to include ethnic-Indian members of the Fiji Labour Party in his cabinet.

In March 2006, the Great Council of Chiefs elected President Iloilo to a second five-year term. In May 2006, Qarase narrowly won parliamentary elections and was sworn in for a second term. However, in October and November 2006, tensions rose between Qarase and Frank Bainimarama, the head of the military, who threatened to oust the government after it tried but failed to replace him. Qarase went into hiding as the crisis escalated. A military coup took place in December, as Bainimarama took executive powers and dismissed Qarase. In January 2007, Bainimarama restored executive powers to President Iloilo and took on the role of interim prime minister. In April 2007, he dismissed the Great Council of Chiefs and suspended all future meetings, after the chiefs refused to endorse his government and his nomination for vice president.

In 2009, the Fijian court of appeal declared Bainimarama's interim regime illegal, inciting the president of Fiji, Ratu Josefa Iloilo, to remove the judiciary and postpone elections until 2014, instead of 2010. He also set aside the country's constitution. Although Bainimarama officially resigned his post as prime minister, it became clear that he had not relinquished any real power. Following the abrogation of the constitution, the government greatly curtailed the freedom of press, stationing soldiers in newsrooms across the country and detaining an array of local journalists. Bainimarama unveiled a roadmap that he claimed would help reestablish democracy in the country. The measures outlined included the introduction of a new constitution in 2013, elections in 2014, and a lowering of the voting age from 21 to 18. Bainimarama's plan was met with skepticism by many members of the international community. In September 2009, Fiji was suspended from the Commonwealth of Nations. It was also suspended from the Pacific Islands Forum, and suffered the loss of some aid programs from the European Union as well.

Upon completing a tour of the provinces in June 2010, Bainimarama stated that support for the existing government is overwhelmingly positive, so much so that most of the citizens he spoke to urged him to delay the 2014 elections in favor of extending his own rule. Bainimarama further claimed that citizens cited the government's support of agriculture, health, education, and infrastructure development plans as positive initiatives and seemed to be very happy with the government. However, opposition leaders from the Fiji Labour Party (FLP) claimed that their own feedback from citizens painted a very different picture, as many people were suffering economically, while the cost of living continued to rise. FLP officials suspected that Bainimarama's comments were simply a means of setting the groundwork for a deferment of the 2014 elections. They argued that Bainimarama should hold elections as scheduled and let the results prove or disprove the people's confidence in the existing government.

13 GOVERNMENT

The 1997 constitution specifies that the president, who is head of state, must always be a native Fijian. It also gives considerable recognition to the Great Council of Chiefs, which not only nominates and participates in electing the president, but also maintains its responsibility for matters relating to native Fijians. The bicameral parliament consists of two houses. The lower house, or House of Representatives, where all legislation must originate, has 71 members. Of these, 46 are communal: 23 for Fijians, 19 for Indians, 3 for general electors, and 1 for Rotumans. The remaining 25 are "open" seats contested on a common roll basis without any reference to ethnicity, either for the voters or for the candidates. The upper house, or Senate, consists of 32 appointed members: 14 nominated by the Great Council of Chiefs, 9 by the prime minister, 8 by the leader of the opposition, and 1 by the Council of Rotuma. Parliament serves for a maximum of four years after a general election, though the president on the advice of the prime minister can dissolve it.

The president appoints as prime minister the member of parliament who commands majority support in the lower house. The constitution also provides for mandatory power sharing in cabinet. Any party holding more than eight lower-house seats is invited to join the cabinet in proportion to the number of seats it holds.

A military coup in December 2006 resulted in Qarase's ouster; Frank Bainimarama, the head of the military, became acting prime minister. A new constitution was to be drafted in 2013; elections were to follow in 2014.

14 POLITICAL PARTIES

Fiji is host to a variety of political parties, some affiliated with ethnic groups, others not. After the May 2006 parliamentary elections, the National federation Party (NFP), for nearly 40 years the dominant Indian party, was entirely eliminated, as was the Fijian Political Party (SVT). The Fiji Labour Party (FLP), led by Mahendra Chaudhry, has a support base of trade unions, workers and farmers, providing it with an efficient, grassroots campaigning structure. The Soqoso Duavata ni Lewenivuana Party (Fijian United Party or SDL) was created by caretaker Prime Minister Laisenia Qarase in an attempt to consolidate his support and unite the Fijian vote. The SDL has been accused of not broadening its appeal to Indian voters, and some have accused it of racism. In the

2006 elections, the SDL won 36 seats, the FLP 31, the United People's Party (UPP) 2, and independents 2. The next parliamentary elections are tentatively scheduled for September 2014.

15 LOCAL GOVERNMENT

Local government is organized under provincial and urban councils. Fiji is divided into 4 administrative divisions, which are subdivided into 14 provinces, each with its own council. Some members are appointed, but each provincial council has an elected majority. The councils have powers to make bylaws and to draw up their own budgets, subject to central government approval. Within the provinces, districts and councils are organized around extended family networks, and have their own chiefs and councils. The cities of Suva and Lautoka have city councils and Nadi a town council, while certain other urban areas are administered by township boards. A few members of urban councils are appointed, but most members are elected from a common roll of taxpayers and residents.

16 JUDICIAL SYSTEM

Fiji's judicial system retains elements of the British system. The judiciary is independent of the other branches of government, and due process rights are similar to those in English common law. The courts include the magistrate courts, a high court, the courts of appeal, and the Supreme Court. There are no special courts, and the military courts try only members of the armed forces. Supreme Court judges are appointed by the president.

The magistrate courts are courts of first instance that try most cases. The high court hears more serious cases in first instance and hears appeals from decisions in the magistrate courts. The appellate courts, including the high court, may engage in constitutional review. The high court has jurisdiction to review violations of individual rights provided by the constitution.

Defendants have the right to a public trial and to counsel. A public legal adviser assists indigent persons in family law cases. Detainees must be brought before a court within 24 to 48 hours. Incommunicado and arbitrary detention are illegal. The criminal law permits corporal punishment as a penalty for certain criminal acts, but this provision is seldom invoked.

17 ARMED FORCES

The International Institute for Strategic Studies reports that armed forces in Fiji totaled 3,500 members in 2011. The force is comprised of 3,200 from the army and 300 members of the navy. Armed forces represent 1% of the labor force in Fiji. Defense spending totaled US$73.9 million and accounted for 1.9% of GDP in 2009.

The first two regular infantry battalions are generally stationed overseas and perform peacekeeping duties. Fiji's peacekeeping troops have been stationed in the Solomon Islands, Egypt, Sudan, Lebanon, Iraq, East Timor, and other locations.

18 INTERNATIONAL COOPERATION

Since joining the United Nations on 13 October 1970, Fiji has been a leading spokesman for Pacific island states and has contributed contingents to UN peacekeeping forces in Lebanon (1978) and the Sinai (1982). The country has also supported UN efforts in Kosovo (est. 1999) and East Timor (est. 2002). Fiji belongs to ES-CAP and all UN non-regional specialized agencies except IAEA. A member of the WTO, Fiji also is a member of the Asian Development Bank, the Colombo Plan, the ACP Group, G-77, the Alliance of Small Island States (AOSIS), Sparteca, and the Pacific Island Forum (formally called the South Pacific Forum). Its membership in the Commonwealth of Nations was suspended in September 2009, following the military coup.

On 10 December 1982, Fiji became the first nation to ratify the UN Convention on the Law of the Sea. Fiji's delegates had a prominent role in framing the document. Other efforts in environmental cooperation include participation in the Convention on Biological Diversity, CITES, International Tropical Timber Agreements, the Kyoto Protocol, the Montréal Protocol, the Nuclear Test Ban Treaty, and the UN Conventions on Climate Change and Desertification.

19 ECONOMY

Agriculture, mining, and fishing have dominated the economy in the past, but manufacturing and tourism are becoming progressively more important in Fiji. In the decades since Fiji gained its independence in 1970, the nation has endured recessions and enjoyed periods of rebounding growth.

Fiji has one of the most developed economies in the Pacific, but it continues to have a large subsistence sector. In 2009, the World Bank estimated that 31% lived below the poverty line. Tourism and sugar processing are the major sources of foreign exchange, but both industries suffered following the 2006 coup. Tourism was down 6% in 2007, with recovery uncertain. Flooding in 2009 also drove down tourism revenues. The sugar sector was impacted by the European Union suspending aid until elections would be held, resulting in related EU subsidy cuts, as European Union is Fiji's main sugar export market.

The gross domestic product (GDP) rate of change in Fiji, as of 2010, was 0.1%. Inflation stood at 5.1%, and unemployment was reported at 7.6%.

20 INCOME

The CIA estimated that in 2010 the GDP of Fiji was US$3.869 billion. The CIA defines GDP as the value of all final goods and services produced within a nation in a given year and computed on the basis of purchasing power parity (PPP) rather than value as measured on the basis of the rate of the exchange based on current dollars. The per capita GDP was estimated at US$4,400. The annual growth rate of GDP was 0.1%. The average inflation rate was 4.8%. It was estimated that agriculture accounted for 16.1% of Fiji's 2010 GDP, industry 24.4%, and services 59.5%.

According to the World Bank, remittances from citizens living abroad totaled US$128 million in 2010, or about US$160 per capita and accounted for approximately 3% of GDP.

In 2010, the CIA reported that Fiji, with 0.01% of the world's population, accounted for 0.004% of the world's GDP. By comparison, the United States, with 4.52% of the world's population, accounted for 19.89% of world GDP.

As of 2011, the most recent study by the World Bank reported that actual individual consumption in Fiji was 83.0% of GDP and accounted for 0.01% of world consumption. By comparison, the United States accounted for 25.44% of world individual consumption. The World Bank also estimated that 24.3% of Fiji's GDP was spent on food and beverages, 29.3% on housing and household furnishings, 1.9% on clothes, 4.6% on health, 6.3% on transportation, 0.3% on communications, 4.1% on recreation, 2.4% on restaurants and hotels, and 3.7% on miscellaneous goods and services and purchases from abroad.

It was estimated that, in 2009, about 31% of the population subsisted on an income below the poverty line established by Fiji's government.

21 LABOR

As of 2007, Fiji had a total labor force of 335,000 people. Within that labor force, CIA estimates in 2001 noted that 70% were employed in agriculture, 15% in industry, and 15% in the service sector.

Historically, the laws of Fiji protected the right of workers to unionize with some restrictions. All unions had to be registered, but they were not controlled by the government. Wages and conditions of employment were regulated by agreements between trade unions and employers. Workers had the right to collective bargain and strike, although a union could not strike in connection with a union recognition dispute. The only central labor organization was the Fiji Trade Union Congress (FTUC). About 31% of the paid workforce was unionized as of 2010.

The Essential National Industries (Employment) Decree of 2011 has negated these collective bargaining agreements. Under this decree, all unions are forced to re-register with the government. The government has the right to fire any union officials, and the right of the workers to strike is severely limited.

The normal workweek ranges from 40 to 48 hours, but there is no statutory regulated workweek for adult males. Adult females are prohibited from working in mines but are free to work elsewhere. There is no national minimum wage, and the enforcement of child labor regulations is ineffective. Minors under 12 years of age cannot be employed except in a family-owned business or agricultural enterprise. Children between 12 and 15 can be employed in non-industrial work that does not involve machinery, and under the provision that every night, they return home to their parents or guardian. Minors between the ages of 15 and 17 cannot be employed in occupations where heavy machinery is used, and they must also receive specified hours and rest breaks. Health and safety standards are not closely monitored.

22 AGRICULTURE

Agriculture is the smallest contributor to the GDP but the largest employer in the country, with a considerate number of people engaged in subsistence agriculture. Roughly 23% of Fiji's total land was farmed in 2011. The country's major crops include sugarcane, coconuts, cassava (tapioca), rice, sweet potatoes, and bananas. According to the UN FAO, in 2009 cereal production amounted to 12,194 tons, fruit production 19,561 tons, and vegetable production 22,245 tons.

More than three-quarters of all households engage in agriculture, livestock production, forestry, or fishing. Fijians retain legal ownership of the lands, but Indians farm it and produce about 90% of Fiji's sugar. Cane is processed into raw sugar and molasses by the Fiji Sugar Corporation, which is 68% owned by the government. The sugar industry is vital to the national economy; as such,

the government plays a leading role in all aspects of its production and sale.

23 ANIMAL HUSBANDRY

The UN Food and Agriculture Organization (FAO) reported that Fiji dedicated 175,000 hectares (432,434 acres) to permanent pasture or meadow in 2009. During that year, the country tended 3.5 million chickens, 312,000 head of cattle, and 145,000 pigs. The production from these animals amounted to 8,548 tons of beef and veal, 3,857 tons of pork, 15,632 tons of poultry, 3,002 tons of eggs, and 29,650 tons of milk. Fiji also produced 1,232 tons of cattle hide.

24 FISHING

Tuna, barracuda, snapper, grouper, mackerel, and mullet are the primary targets of Fiji's fishing industry. Other species, such as tilapia, have been grown in fish farms in the interior, first as animal feed, and later for human consumption. Concerns were raised that the accidental or intentional release of tilapia into lakes and streams has caused genetic weakening of the native, more desirable fish species. In September 2009, the government initiated a new milkfish farm project in the village of Vitawa. The US$20,800 project was expected to improve the food supply for residents along the northwestern coast of Viti Levu, the nation's largest island, where the fishing stock has been depleted by overfishing and the illegal use of dynamite in fishing. The project was administered by the Fisheries Department through August 2011.

Fiji had four decked commercial fishing boats in 2008. The annual capture totaled 48,453 tons according to the UN FAO. The export value of seafood totaled US$49.32 million.

25 FORESTRY

Approximately 56% of Fiji is covered by forest. The UN FAO estimated the 2009 roundwood production at 445,205 cu m (15.7 million cu ft). The value of all forest products, including roundwood, totaled US$23.6 million. Fiji exports wood chips, sawn lumber, plywood, and logs. The nation has long invested in reforestation, insuring that Fiji's forests will continue to be a source of valuable exports.

26 MINING

Fiji's mining sector in 2009 was centered on gold, produced solely at the Vatukoula Mine by Australian-based Emperor Mines Ltd., which is also the second-largest private employer, with more than 2,100 employees. Gold has been mined and exported continuously since 1933. The country also was endowed richly with deposits of copper, lead, and zinc. Gold production rose steadily in the mid-1990s, reaching 4,671 kg in 1997. It has since remained relatively static, with the 2009 total at 1,856 kg, down from 3,731 kg in 2002. Silver was also produced in 2009. Silver mine production that year totaled an estimated 500 kg. Hydraulic cement production was estimated at 100,000 metric tons in 2003. In addition to resources at existing sites, 930 million tons of copper (in Viti Levu) and gold reserves have been reported, and prospecting continued for oil and phosphates, and at base-metal sulfide deposits, disseminated porphyry copper deposits, epithermal precious-metal deposits, residual bauxite deposits, and manganese and heavy-mineral sand deposits that have previously been identified and evaluated. None has been shown to have sufficient tonnage to be economically viable. Ownership of minerals was vested in the state, which granted mining and prospecting rights.

27 ENERGY AND POWER

The World Bank reported in 2008 that Fiji produced 970 million kWh of electricity. The Fiji Electricity Authority, set up in 1966, is responsible for the generation and distribution of electricity. To lessen dependence on imported oil, the Monasavu hydroelectric project was completed in 1984, with a capacity of 80 MW. In 2009, oil imports were estimated at 18,850 barrels per day. In 2010, oil consumption was estimated at 15,000 barrels per day.

Exploration for oil and natural gas has taken place, and a 2008 report by the government's Mineral Resources Department demonstrated potential for oil mining in the Bligh Water Basin. Estimated production potential ranged from 5.4 to 20 billion barrels. In the 1990s, the government formed a state-owned petroleum company, Finapeco, to act as the exclusive petroleum importer to Fiji.

28 INDUSTRY

Most of the Fiji's revenues come from the services sector with industry taking the second spot and sugar processing accounting for a third of all industrial activity. Expensive power, lack of trained labor, and the limited local market have inhibited industrial production. Fiji's industry is based primarily on processing of agricultural products, mainly sugarcane and coconut, and on mining and processing of gold and silver. Other major product groups are processed foods and garments. The US State Department estimates that Fiji's exports for the first three quarters of 2010 totaled US$553.9 million.

The Fiji Sugar Corporation estimated that 2011 sugar production would be approximately 190,000 cubic tons, better than in the preceding two years, but significantly less than the previous norms of the late 1990s, which were close to 350,000 cubic tons. The government ascribes problems with sugar production to expiring land leases, poor mill performance, high incidence of cane burning, and cane transportation problems. Years of underinvestment in farms, sugar mills and power, water, and transportation infrastructure have resulted in declining quality as well as quantity.

The garment industry in Fiji began in 1988 and in 2002 produced a record value of about US$150 million; however, the industry declined by 47% in 2005 when the Agreement on Textiles and Clothing (ATC) quota system ended, and textiles were integrated into the World Trade Organization (WTO) General Agreement on Tariffs and Trade. In addition, garment industry exports declined as a result of disruptions in customer relations due to trade sanctions. In 2005, garments accounted for 9% of Fiji's exports.

29 SCIENCE AND TECHNOLOGY

The University of the South Pacific at Suva, founded in 1968, has schools of agriculture and pure and applied science and supports a research office. The Fiji School of Medicine in Suva also supports a research unit that works in collaboration with other regional centers and projects. The Sugar Research Institute of Fiji was established by the legislature in 2005 to promote advances in the sugar industry. In 2009, the Fiji Institute of Technology estab-

Principal Trading Partners – Fiji (2010)

(In millions of US dollars)

Country	Total	Exports	Imports	Balance
World	2,230.1	720.1	1,510.0	-789.9
Singapore	512.8	2.2	510.6	-508.4
Australia	488.9	175.5	313.4	-138.0
New Zealand	292.9	45.0	247.9	-202.9
United States	237.8	189.4	48.4	141.0
China	141.3	0.9	140.5	-139.6
Japan	104.7	72.9	31.8	41.1
Samoa	69.8	68.5	1.4	67.1
Thailand	66.3	9.5	56.8	-47.4
Tonga	61.7	60.2	1.5	58.7
Taiwan	52.3	6.3	46.1	-39.8

(…) data not available or not significant.

(n.s.) not specified.

SOURCE: *2011 Direction of Trade Statistics Yearbook*, New York: United Nations, 2011.

lished the Center for Applied Economic Research and the Center for Sustainable Technology and Development. The major learned societies are the Fiji Society, concerned with subjects of historic and scientific interest to Fiji and other Pacific islands, and the Fiji Medical Association, also in Suva.

The World Bank reported in 2009 that there were no patent applications in science and technology in Fiji.

30 DOMESTIC TRADE

Fiji has several large trading corporations and hundreds of small traders. The corporations own retail stores, inter-island ships, plantations, hotels, travel services, copra-crushing mills, and breweries. Small enterprises range from a single tailor or shopkeeper to larger family businesses, most of which are operated by Indians or Chinese.

Businesses are normally open from 8:30 a.m. to 5 p.m. on weekdays, and from 8:30 a.m. to 1 p.m. on Saturdays. Retail outlets are generally open from Monday through Friday, with half a day on Saturday. Most nonessential services and retail establishments are closed on Sundays. Though most major businesses and retail enterprises accept credit cards and travelers' checks, a number of smaller, local businesses and shops operate on cash only.

31 FOREIGN TRADE

Like most developing countries that export primarily basic commodities subject to wide market price fluctuations, and import high-valued manufactured products, Fiji has traditionally run a merchandise trade deficit. Fiji imported US$3.12 billion worth of goods and services in 2008, while exporting US$1.202 billion worth of goods and services. The CIA estimated that, in 2009, exports dropped to US$625.3 million and imports to US$1.3 billion.

In 2009, Fiji's major import partners were Singapore, 27.7%; Australia, 19.7%; NZ, 15.4%; China, 7.7%; and Thailand, 4.3%. Its major export partners were the United States, 15.1%; Australia, 12%; the United Kingdom, 11.1%; Samoa, 5.3%; Tonga, 4.7%; and Japan, 4.6%.

In 2008, sugar production was the largest contributor to Fiji's export revenues. Sugar accounted for 34% of the total revenue of

Balance of Payments – Fiji (2010)

(In millions of US dollars)

Current Account		-416.0
Balance on goods		-782.0
Imports	-1,601.4	
Exports	819.5	
Balance on services		351.7
Balance on income		-101.6
Current transfers		116.0
Capital Account		27.1
Financial Account		-13.0
Direct investment abroad		-5.8
Direct investment in Fiji		196.2
Portfolio investment assets		...
Portfolio investment liabilities		0.1
Financial derivatives		...
Other investment assets		38.7
Other investment liabilities		36.5
Net Errors and Omissions		257.1
Reserves and Related Items		-133.8

(…) data not available or not significant.

SOURCE: *Balance of Payment Statistics Yearbook 2011*, Washington, DC: International Monetary Fund, 2011.

Public Finance – Fiji (2009)

(In millions of dollars, budgetary central government figures)

Revenue and Grants	1,373.12	100.0%
Tax revenue	1,245.48	90.7%
Social contributions	...	...
Grants	6.4	0.5%
Other revenue	121.24	8.8%
Expenditures	1,529.72	100.0%
General public services	382.07	25.0%
Defense	82.62	5.4%
Public order and safety	143.52	9.4%
Economic affairs	217.6	14.2%
Environmental protection	3.35	0.2%
Housing and community amenities	143.96	9.4%
Health	142.99	9.3%
Recreational, culture, and religion	10.54	0.7%
Education	342.36	22.4%
Social protection	60.71	4.0%

(…) data not available or not significant.

SOURCE: *Government Finance Statistics Yearbook 2010*, Washington, DC: International Monetary Fund, 2010.

the five highest revenue export items, followed by fish (29%), mineral water (15%), apparel (15%), and tree products (7%, including timber, cork, and wood). In 2008, the five largest import items were mineral products, machinery/transportation equipment, vehicles/aircraft, medical/surgical supplies, and chemical products.

While water was a major export item in 2008, that changed in November 2010, when Fiji Water, one of the country's largest employers, stopped production after a 45-fold increase in taxes per liter, and deportation of the company's in-country head on accusations of interference in Fiji's domestic affairs.

32 BALANCE OF PAYMENTS

In 2009, Fiji had a foreign trade deficit of US$419 million, amounting to 2.9% of GDP. A decline in tourism from 2006 to 2008 grew the trade deficit, which reached US$676 million in 2006 and US$803 million in 2008. Increases in the price of imports such as mineral fuels, machinery, and appliances also contributed to the deficit.

33 BANKING AND SECURITIES

The Reserve Bank of Fiji is the central bank, (formerly the Central Monetary Authority), created in 1983 to replace the currency board. The bank is headed by a governor with a deputy governor and seven department managers. The Reserve Bank regulates the issue and supply of money, controls the availability of credit, and regulates international currency exchanges. The Fiji Development Bank is the main development finance agency.

In 2005, the money market rate, the rate at which financial institutions lend to one another in the short term, was 1.28%. In 2009, the discount rate, the interest rate at which the central bank lends to financial institutions in the short term, was 3.00%, down from 6.32% at the end of 2008. At the end of 2010, the nation's gold bullion deposits totaled 6,430.149 fine troy ounces. According to the CIA, at the end of 2009, Fiji had US$567.3 million in gold and foreign exchange.

Commercial banking facilities consist of the National Bank of Fiji (NBF) and branches of several foreign banks; in 2011, these included two Australian banks, a Papua New Guinea bank, and an Indian bank. The NBF enjoys the status of a commercial bank, but it does little business. The troubled NBF underwent a process of restructuring in 1996 following revelations of a high level of nonperforming loans. The government had to spend upwards of US$105 million to keep the bank operating. The government-owned Fiji Development Bank provides financing for development projects.

Growth in money supply has fluctuated widely in response to trends in foreign trade, affecting the level of reserves. The government tends to follow a cautious monetary policy, which has concentrated on maintaining price stability and on managing high levels of liquidity in the commercial banking system resulting from low levels of private investment.

The Suva Stock Exchange operates in Suva, Fiji.

34 INSURANCE

Third-party motor liability coverage is compulsory in Fiji. A number of insurance companies operate in Fiji, offering both life and non-life products. Companies listed as doing business in Fiji in 2011 included Dominion Insurance, Fiji Reinsurance Corp., Guardian Royal Exchange Assurance, National Insurance Co., the New India Assurance Co., Sun Insurance, Tower Insurance, and Queensland Insurance.

35 PUBLIC FINANCE

In 2010, the budget of Fiji included US$1.363 billion in public revenue and US$1.376 billion in public expenditures. The budget deficit amounted to 3.3% of GDP. In total, US$127 million of the debt was held by foreign entities.

³⁶TAXATION

Local councils levy taxes to meet their own expenses. In 2011, national taxes include a nonresident dividend withholding tax (15%), an interest withholding tax (10%), and a 15% tax on royalties. Dividends from a resident company paid to other resident companies are tax-exempt. The standard corporate tax rate in 2009 was 28% on resident companies. In 2011, income tax for residents ranged from 0% to 31%, and for non-residents from 20% to 30%. Other taxes include a land sales tax, an excise tax, and a value-added tax (VAT) of 12.5%. Gambling and financial services however, are exempt from the VAT.

³⁷CUSTOMS AND DUTIES

In 2006, approximately 17% of Fiji's revenues derived from customs duties, down from 20% in 2004. Tariffs range from 0–35% on most goods except motor vehicles, alcohol and tobacco, and chemical products, for which the tariffs imposed can be up to 60%, 60%, and 70%, respectively. Duties are levied on the cost, insurance, and freight (CIF) value of the goods.

There are several tax-free zones (TFZs) in Fiji; in 1996, there were as many as 133 tax-free factories (TFFs). TFZs offered a 13-year tax holiday, duty exemptions on capital goods and raw materials, and free repatriation of profits. By 2011, TFZs and TFFs were no longer available to new export companies, although the existing tax-free agreements continued to be in effect through their expiry dates. In place of the TFFs and TFZs, the government offered duty suppression schemes and tax deductions on export income.

³⁸FOREIGN INVESTMENT

The development of existing industries has been made possible largely by foreign investment. Fiji has continued to promote overseas capital investment through the Fiji Trade and Investment Board, which requires foreign goods and services to meet many of its needs, including domestic employment. Tax and tariff concessions are offered to newly approved industries, and special incentives apply to fuel-efficient or export-oriented enterprises. However, since the coup against the Chaudhry government in May 2000 and the subsequent coup in 2006, political tensions have seriously hampered Fiji's prospects for attracting foreign investment in two major ways: through concerns over nativist restrictions and labor problems and through concerns that trade sanctions could be imposed on the defiantly unconstitutional government. Most post-2006 foreign investments have been focused on resort hotel constructions and the tourism industry in general.

Foreign direct investment (FDI) in Fiji was a net inflow of US$56 million, according to World Bank figures published in 2009. FDI represented 1.98% of GDP.

³⁹ECONOMIC DEVELOPMENT

Political turmoil has been a major force hindering Fiji's economic development since 2005. Sugar and textile exports have suffered, with the sugar industry especially being plagued by reported qual-ity issues and technical obsolescence as well as the suspension of EU aid in the form of subsidies.

Following the 2006 coup, tourism was down 6% in 2007. It rebounded, only to be negatively impacted again in 2009 by severe flooding. Tourism was strong in 2011, with China announcing plans to build a new resort complex in Fiji, and tourism revenues in 2011 of approximately US$606 million.

Another source of hard currency are the remittances from Fijians working in Kuwait and Iraq.

⁴⁰SOCIAL DEVELOPMENT

Employed workers are eligible for retirement, disability, and survivor benefits, to which they contribute 8% of their wages, matched by their employers. In 2009, in an attempt to cut spending, the government decreed a mandatory retirement at 55 for all public servants. Employers also pay for workmen's compensation, covering both temporary and permanent disability benefits. Benefits include medical and hospital care, surgery, medicine, appliances, and transportation.

The constitution provides women with equal rights and includes affirmative action provisions for the disadvantaged. Fijian women primarily fulfill traditional roles, although some do attain leadership roles in the public and private sectors. Women are generally paid less than men for comparable work. Domestic abuse, incest, and rape remained pervasive problems. Women's rights groups continued to press for more effective prosecution and punishment for violence against women. Foreign governments provide funding for crisis centers.

The government overtly promotes the rights of ethnic Fijians over those of other ethnic groups. Ethnic Fijians predominate in senior government positions and in the ownership of land. Although Indo-Fijians may be found in senior positions in the private sector, few are in government. Indo-Fijians are sometimes subject to discrimination. Human rights abuses are occasionally reported.

⁴¹HEALTH

According to the CIA, life expectancy in Fiji was 69 years in 2011. The country spent 3.5% of its GDP on healthcare, amounting to US$130 per person. There were 5 physicians, 20 nurses and midwives, and 21 hospital beds per 10,000 inhabitants. In 2011, the fertility rate was 2.6 children per woman of childbearing age, while the infant mortality rate was 11 deaths per 1,000 live births. In 2008, the maternal mortality rate, according to the World Bank, was 26 deaths per 100,000 births. It was estimated that 94% of children were vaccinated against measles. The CIA calculated HIV/AIDS prevalence in Fiji to be about 0.1% in 2009.

⁴²HOUSING

According to government estimates, Fiji requires more than 4,200 new houses each year to maintain adequate housing standards. Natural disasters such as cyclones and tropical storms have caused problems in creating and maintaining adequate housing stock.

The Fiji Housing Authority provides accommodations for urban workers and extends credit for houses it builds and sells. At last estimate, housing stock exceeded 126,000 units, of which about 30% were made of corrugated iron or tin, 30% were concrete, and more than 25% were wood. At the last government census (2007), there were about 176,268 households. About 59.9% of all households had piped water, and 13.4% used well or river water. In 2008, 86% of all Fijians had electricity in their homes. About 43.6% had flush toilets. The average number of people per household was about 4.75 (2007).

43 EDUCATION

In 2008, the World Bank estimated that 89% of age-eligible children in Fiji were enrolled in primary school. Secondary enrollment for age-eligible children stood at 79%. The CIA estimated the adult literacy rate in 2004 as 93.7%, with 94.5% for men and 91.4% for women. Nearly all students complete their primary education. The student-to-teacher ratio for primary school was at about 25:1 in 2009; the ratio for secondary school was about 16:1.

There are government schools as well as private schools operated by individual groups or by missions under government supervision. Primary education lasts for eight years, which is followed by four years of junior secondary and two years of senior secondary school. Students may choose a final year of study known as seventh form, the completion of which is required for continuing in higher education. The academic year runs from February to November. The primary language of instruction is English.

The University of the South Pacific opened in Suva in 1968. Its students are drawn from several Pacific island states. Other institutions of higher education are the Fiji College of Agriculture at Nausori and the Fiji Institute of Technology and the Fiji School of Medicine, both in Suva. In 2003, there were about 115,400 students enrolled in higher education programs.

As of 2004, public expenditure on education was estimated at 6.2% of GDP.

44 LIBRARIES AND MUSEUMS

The Ministry of Education runs the Library Service of Fiji in Suva and provides public, special, and school services through 3 mobile libraries and 33 government libraries with a total collection of over 960,000 volumes. Suva maintains its own public library of 77,000 volumes, most of which is a children's collection. The library at the University of the South Pacific contains 750,000 volumes and serves as a depository library site for the United Nations. There are several libraries associated with theological institutions and colonial cultural centers. The Fiji Library Association was established in 1972. The Fiji Museum, established at Suva in 1906, has a collection of Fijian artifacts and documents Fijian oral traditions.

45 MEDIA

Suva and its surrounding area are served by an automatic telephone exchange. Fiji is a link in the world Commonwealth cable system and has radiotelephone circuits to other Pacific territories. In 2009, the CIA reported that there were 136,800 telephone landlines in Fiji. In addition to landlines, mobile phone subscriptions averaged 75 per 100 people.

The Fiji Broadcasting Commission offers programs in Fijian, English, and Hindustani over Radio Fiji on three channels. Fiji One TV, owned by private and government interests, was Fiji's first and only TV station until MAI TV began broadcasting in 2008. In 1999, Fiji had 541,476 radios and 88,100 television sets nationwide. In 2009, there were 13 FM radio stations and 40 AM radio stations.

In 2010, the country had 17,088 Internet hosts. In 2009, there were some 114,200 Internet users in Fiji, accounting for about 8.1% of the population.

The primary two daily newspapers are the private English-language *Fiji Times* (with an online version) and *Fiji Daily Post*, and the *Fiji Sun*. There are a few Hindi-language weeklies.

In April 2009, media came under official censorship. Radio relays of BBC and Radio Australia were suspended. The following year, the government announced a new law that mandated that all media organizations operating in Fiji must be 90% locally owned by September 2010. Among the affected media outlets was the *Fiji Times*, a Fijian newspaper that had been owned and run by the Australia-based publisher News Limited for 23 years. News Limited was forced to sell the paper to a Fijian company.

46 ORGANIZATIONS

The main chamber of commerce is located in Suva. Two organizations representing the interests of employers and business owners are the Fiji Commerce and Employers Union (previously called the Fiji Employers' Federation) and the Fiji National Training Council. The Fiji Trades Union Congress serves as a larger advocate for worker's rights. At last estimate there were more than 1,200 registered cooperatives. The International Labour Organization has an office in Suva.

Unions and professional associations exist for several occupations, including manufacturing industries, sugar cane growers, teachers, and optometrists. The Fiji Medical Association promotes research and education on health issues and works to establish common policies and standards in healthcare.

There are also several associations dedicated to research and education for specific fields of medicine and particular diseases and conditions. The Fiji Law Society promotes ethical standards and practices in the legal profession.

Youth organizations include the Fiji Youth and Student League, Junior Chamber, YMCA/YWCA, the Fiji Scout Association, and Fiji Girl Guides. There are several sports organizations promoting amateur competition in such pastimes as baseball, badminton, track and field, and tae kwon do.

There is also a Fiji Islands Blind Sport Association. Oceania National Olympic Committees encourages regional participation in the Olympic Games. National women's organizations include The National Council of Women, Women's Action for Change, and the Fiji Women's Rights Movement.

The Fiji Council of Social Services serves as an umbrella organization to promote the work of social and community welfare and development groups. There is a national chapter of the Red Cross Society.

47 TOURISM, TRAVEL, AND RECREATION

Fiji's beach resorts and traditional villages are popular tourist attractions. Spectator sports include football (soccer), cricket, rugby, and basketball; Fiji has excellent golf facilities. Visitors must have a valid passport, proof of sufficient funds, and an onward/

return ticket. A certificate of vaccinations against yellow fever is required if traveling from an infected area.

The *Tourism Factbook*, published by the UN World Tourism Organization, reported 605,000 incoming tourists to Fiji in 2009 who spent a total of US$606 million. Of those incoming tourists, there were 415,000 from East Asia and the Pacific.

There were 22,823 hotel beds available in Fiji. The estimated daily cost to visit Suva (on Viti Levu), the capital, was US$233. The cost of visiting other cities averaged US$171. Tourism, Fiji's major source of foreign currency, grew 16.3% in 2010, with reported gross earnings of over US$400 million.

48 FAMOUS PERSONS

The best-known Fijians are Ratu Sir Lala Sukuna (d. 1958), the first speaker of the Legislative Council in 1954; Ratu Sir George Cakobau (1911–89), the first Fijian to be governor-general; and Ratu Sir Kamisese K. T. Mara (1920–2004), considered the "founding father" of modern Fiji, who served as prime minister from 1970 to 1992 and as president from 1993 to 2000. Ratu Josefa Iloilovatu Uluivuda (b. 1920) has been president since 2000.

49 DEPENDENCIES

Fiji has no territories or colonies.

50 BIBLIOGRAPHY

Fiji Investment and Business Guide: Strategic and Practical Information. Washington, DC: International Business Publications USA, 2012.

Leibo, Steven A. *East and Southeast Asia, 2005.* 38th ed. Harpers Ferry, W.Va.: Stryker-Post Publications, 2005.

Lilley, Ian (ed.). *Archaeology of Oceania: Australia and the Pacific Islands.* Malden, Mass.: Blackwell, 2006.

Wilson, Stacey-Ann. *Politics of Identity in Small Plural Societies: Guyana, the Fiji Islands, and Trinidad and Tobago.* New York: Palgrave Macmillan, 2012.

Younger, Paul. *New Homelands: Hindu Communities in Mauritius, Guyana, Trinidad, South Africa, Fiji, and East Africa.* New York: Oxford University Press, 2010.

FRENCH PACIFIC DEPENDENCIES

FRENCH POLYNESIA

The overseas territory of French Polynesia (Polynésie Française) in the South Pacific Ocean includes five island groups. The Society Islands (Îles de la Société) were first visited by the British in 1767. They were named for the Royal Society and are the most important islands of French Polynesia. They include Tahiti (at 17°40′ S and about 149°20′ W), the largest French Polynesian island with an area of 1,042 sq km (402 sq mi); Moorea; and Raiatea. The French established a protectorate in 1844 and made the islands a colony in 1880.

The Marquesas Islands (Îles Marquises, between 8° and 11° S and 138° and 141° W) lie about 1,500 km (930 mi) northeast of Tahiti. The Marquesas were first visited by Spaniards in 1595 and annexed by France in 1842.

The Tuamotu Islands lie about 480 km (300 mi) SSW of the Marquesas. There are about 78 islands in the Tuamotus, scattered over an area of 800 sq km (310 sq mi). The Tuamotu Islands were first visited by Spaniards in 1606 and annexed by France in 1881.

The Gambier Islands, southeast of the Tuamotus, were first visited by the British in 1797 and annexed by France in 1881. Three of the islands—Mangareva, Taravai, and Akamaru—are inhabited.

The Tubuai or Austral Islands (Îles Australes), south of the Society Islands, were fist visited in 1777 by James Cook and annexed by France in 1880.

Clipperton Island (10°18′ N and 109°12′ W), an uninhabited atoll southwest of Mexico and about 2,900 km (1,800 mi) west of Panama, was claimed by France in 1858 and given up by Mexico, which also had claimed it, in 1932. In 1979, it was placed under direct control of the French government. Total area of the territory is between 3,600 and 4,200 sq km (1,400 and 1,600 sq mi).

The estimated July 2012 population of French Polynesia was 274,512, of whom about 78% are Polynesian, 12% Chinese, and 10% European. About 54% of the population is Protestant and 30% is Roman Catholic; there are also small animist and Buddhist minorities. The population was growing at an annual rate of 1.021% in 2012. The net migration rate was -0.94 per 1,000 population. Some 51% of the population lived in urban areas.

French and Polynesian are the official languages; English is also spoken. Marine life is abundant, both in the surrounding ocean and in rivers and streams; there are no indigenous mammals.

The territory is divided into five circonscriptions (administrative areas). A 57-member territorial assembly is elected every five years by universal suffrage. A council of ministers, headed by a president picked by the assembly, chooses a vice-president and other cabinet ministers. The president assists the French-appointed high commissioner, who is the administrator for the whole territory of French Polynesia. The Economic Social and Cultural Council, composed of representatives of industry and professional

groups, is a consultative body. Two deputies and a senator represent the territory in the French parliament.

Gross domestic product (GDP) in current US dollars was $4.718 billion in 2004 (most recent available information as of March 2012). Per capita GDP was $18,000. GDP growth was estimated at 2.7% (2005). In 2007 unemployment was estimated at 11.7%. The inflation rate was 1.1% that year. Historically, tourism has accounted for about one-fourth of GDP and served as a primary source of hard-currency earnings. However, tourism arrivals declined during the 2000s—only 160,447 tourists arrived in 2009, compared to 227,658 in 2000. While French arrivals have grown marginally during that period, US arrivals have decreased significantly. Obtaining official destination status from the Chinese government in 2008 offered French Polynesia the chance to expand its tourism industry in subsequent years. Pearl farming has become increasingly important industry, providing 60% of total export earnings in 2009.

Tropical fruit, vanilla, coffee, and coconuts are the principal agricultural products, although agriculture represented only 3.5% of GDP in 2005. Two-thirds of the agricultural area (about 12,000 hectares/29,653 acres) is dedicated to copra. Pineapple, citrus fruits, and watermelon accounted for 80% of total fruit production in 2008. Pigs are the primary livestock kept, with an estimated 30,000 head according to the 2000 census. Meat production totaled 24,731 tons in 2009, short of domestic demand. Fishing has intensified, especially for tuna and shark meat, although overfishing, combined with the effects of El Niño, negatively impacted the sector from 2003 to 2006. The industry's primary advantage is the breadth of French Polynesia's exclusive economic zone, which covers some 5 million sq km (1.93 million sq mi).

Phosphate deposits, mined on Makatea in the Tuamotu Islands, were exhausted by 1966. The Pacific Nuclear Test Center was constructed on the atoll of Mururoa in the 1960s. The Office for Overseas Scientific and Technical Research and the Oceanological Center of the Pacific (which experimented with shrimp and oyster breeding) operated in the region until its closure in 1996. Industry contributed 19% of GDP in 2006.

There are a number of hospitals and private clinics on the islands, and one large government hospital on Tahiti. As of 2007, public hospitals had more than 610 beds, and private hospitals had 260 beds. Life expectancy was 75 years in 2009. In 2012 the infant mortality rate was 4.88 deaths per 1,000 live births, and the fertility rate was 2.

The educational system is well developed. There were 236 nursery and primary schools as well as 99 secondary schools in 2007. Primary school students numbered 42,188 and secondary students 33,845. The Université de la Polynésie Française (UPF) was created in 1999, out of the former Université Française du Pacifique. During the 2009/10 school year, 2,922 degree students at-

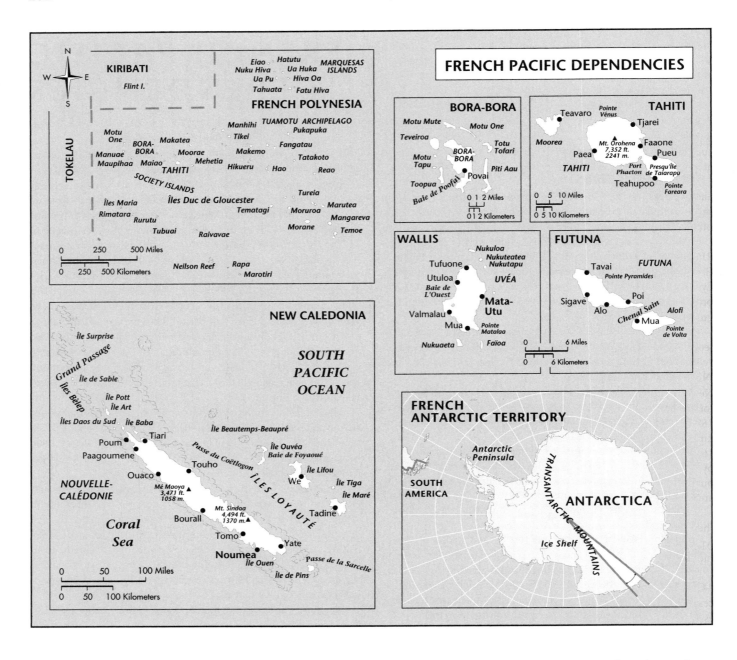

tended the university. Agricultural and technical schools also offer postsecondary education.

Fifty-four percent of the population had Internet access in 2009, with some 120,000 estimated daily users. Internet hosts numbered 37,360 as of 2011. There were 54,900 telephone landlines and 215,900 mobile cellular telephones in use as of 2010.

FRENCH SOUTHERN AND ANTARCTIC TERRITORIES

The French Southern and Antarctic Territories (Terres Australes et Antarctiques Françaises—TAAF) are an overseas territory of France. The territories are administered by an appointed administrator (Pascal Bolot since 29 February 2012) and consultative council from Paris. Most of the population in the territories are researchers. The Îles Eparses, which includes Europa Island, Bas-

sas da India, Juan de Nova, the Glorioso Islands, and Tromelin Island, became an integral part of the TAAF in 2007.

The Kerguélen Archipelago, situated at 48° to 50°S and 68° to 70° E, about 5,300 km (3,300 mi) SE of the Cape of Good Hope, consists of one large and about 300 small islands. The total area of the Kerguélen Archipelago is 7,215 sq km (2,786 sq mi). France maintains a captive register for French-owned merchant ships in the archipelago.

Crozet Archipelago, at 46° S and 50° to 52° E, consists of 5 main and 15 smaller uninhabited islands, with a total area of 505 sq km (195 sq mi).

St. Paul, at about 38° 25′ S and 77° 32′ E, is an uninhabited island with an area of about 7 sq km (2.7 sq mi). Some 80 km (50 mi) to the N, at about 37° 50′ S and with an area of about 54 sq km (21 sq mi), is Amsterdam Island.

Adélie Land (Terre Adélie), comprising some 432,000 sq km (167,000 sq mi) of Antarctica between 136° and 142° E, south of 67° S, was claimed for France by Dumont d'Urville in 1840.

Europa Island lies at 22°21′ S and 40°21′ E in the Mozambique Channel. It is about 340 km (210 mi) W of Madagascar. Europa is heavily wooded and has a meteorological station and airstrip.

Bassas da India also lies in the Mozambique Channel, at 21°27′ S and 39°45′ E. It is a low-lying volcanic rock 2.4 m (8 ft) high, surrounded by reefs. Bassas da India disappears under the waves at high tide.

Also in the Mozambique Channel, Juan de Nova (also known as Saint-Christophe, at 17°3′ S and 42°43′ E) lies about 145 km (90 mi) W of Madagascar. Juan de Nova is exploited for its guano and other fertilizers.

The Glorioso Islands (Îles Glorieuses) lie in the Indian Ocean 213 km (132 mi) NW of Madagascar, at about 11°34′ S and 47°17′ E. The Glorioso Islands consist of Grande Glorieuse, the Île du Lyse, and three tiny islets known as the Roches Vertes. Principal products of the Glorioso Islands are coconuts, corn, turtles, and guano.

Tromelin Island (15°53′ S and 54°31′ E) has an important meteorological station.

NEW CALEDONIA

New Caledonia (Nouvelle-Calédonie) is a French overseas territory NE of Australia in the South Pacific Ocean. It lies between 18° and 23° S and 162° and 169° E. The main island is about 400 km (250 mi) long and 50 km (30 mi) wide, with a surface area of 16,192 sq km (6,252 sq mi). Mountainous and partly surrounded by coral reefs, the island is mostly forested or covered with low bush. With its dependencies and protectorates, it has an overall area of 18,576 sq km (7,172 sq mi).

There are few native animals, but plant life is abundant. Among the plants unique to the territory is niaouli, a tree of the eucalyptus family whose leaves are processed for the pharmaceutical industry.

Total population in 2012 was estimated to be 260,166 of whom 44.1% were native Melanesians and 34.1% were Europeans (1996 census). French and various Melanesian and other local languages are spoken. Roman Catholicism is the majority religion, representing 60% of the population. Protestants account for 30%. The remaining 10% are unspecified.

New Caledonia was first visited in 1768 by Louis Antoine de Bougainville. It was named by James Cook, who landed there in 1774. Local chiefs recognized France's title in 1844, and New Caledonia became a French possession in 1853. In 1946, it became a French overseas territory, and in 1958, its assembly voted to maintain that status. Under 1976, 1984, and 1985 laws, New Caledonia is administered by an appointed high commissioner, an executive council, and a 54-seat territorial congress, consisting of the membership of the three provincial assemblies. New Caledonia has two representatives in the French national assembly and one in the senate. The territory is divided into three provinces (Îles Loyauté, Nord, and Sud); municipal communes play a role in primary education and social welfare. Although an independence referendum failed in 1998, an additional referendum was scheduled for sometime between 2014 and 2018.

GDP was $3.158 billion in 2003 (most recent available information as of March 2012), or about $15,000 per capita. As of 2011 agriculture accounted for 2% of GDP, industry 27.1%, and services 70.8%. Coffee, copra, potatoes, cassava, corn, wheat, and fruits are the main crops, but agricultural production does not meet domestic demand. New Caledonia is one of the largest sources of nickel in the world, with approximately 25% of the world's known nickel reserves. Trade is mainly with France, China, Australia, Singapore, South Korea, and Japan. In 2009 exports totaled $969.4 million; imports totaled $2.58 billion.

WALLIS AND FUTUNA

Wallis Island and the Futuna, or Hoorn, Islands in the southwest Pacific Ocean constitute a French overseas territory. The capital is Mata-Utu, on Wallis (also called Uvéa). Wallis lies about 400 km (250 mi) W of Pago Pago, American Samoa, at 13°22′ s and 176°12′ W. Wallis has an area of 154 sq km (59 sq mi) and is surrounded by a coral reef with a single channel. The Futuna Islands are about 190 km (120 mi) to the SW at 14°20′ S and about 177°30′ W. They comprise two volcanic islands, Futuna and Alofi, which, together with a group of small islands, have a total area of about 116 sq km (45 sq mi).

The Futuna group was first visited by Dutch sailors in 1616; Wallis (at first called Uvéa) was first visited by the English explorer Samuel Wallis in 1767. A French missionary established a Catholic mission on Wallis in 1837, and missions soon followed on the other islands. In 1842, the French established a protectorate, which was officially confirmed in 1887 for Wallis and in 1888 for Futuna.

As of mid-2012, Wallis and Futuna had an estimated 15,453 inhabitants. The population was growing at an annual rate of 0.356%. According to the 2003 census, about 89% of the population is Polynesian, 10.8% French, and 0.2% other. French and Uvean are the principal languages spoken; 99% of the population is Roman Catholic.

A high administrator, representing the French government, is assisted by a 20-seat territorial assembly. Principal commercial activities are the production of copra and fishing for trochus. The chief food crops are yams, taro, bananas, manioc, and arrowroot. GDP was estimated at $60 million in 2004 (most recent available information as of March 2012), or $3,800 per capita.

INDIA

Republic of India
Bharat Ganarajya

CAPITAL: New Delhi

FLAG: The national flag, adopted in 1947, is a tricolor of deep saffron, white, and green horizontal stripes. In the center of the white stripe is a blue wheel representing the wheel (chakra) that appears on the abacus of Asoka's lion capital (c. 250 BC) at Sarnath, Uttar Pradesh.

ANTHEM: *Jana gana mana (Thou Art the Ruler of the Minds of All People)*.

MONETARY UNIT: The rupee (INR) is a paper currency of 100 paise. There are coins of 5, 10, 20, 25, and 50 paise, and 1, 2, and 5 rupees, and notes of 2, 5, 10, 20, 50, 100, and 500 rupees. IRN1 = US$0.01958 (or US$1 = INR51.075) as of 2011.

WEIGHTS AND MEASURES: Metric weights and measures, introduced in 1958, replaced the British and local systems. Indian numerical units still in use include the lakh (equal to 100,000) and the crore (equal to 10 million).

HOLIDAYS: Republic Day, 26 January; Independence Day, 15 August; Gandhi Jayanti, 2 October. Annual events—some national, others purely local, and each associated with one or more religious communities—number in the hundreds. The more important include Shivarati in February; and Raksha Bandhan in August. Movable religious holidays include Holi, Ganesh Chaturthi, Durga Puja, Dussehra, Eid al-Fitr, and Dewali; also celebrated is Christmas, 25 December.

TIME: 5:30 p.m. = noon GMT.

¹LOCATION, SIZE, AND EXTENT

The Republic of India, Asia's second-largest country after China, fills the major part of the South Asian subcontinent (which it shares with Pakistan, Nepal, Bhutan, and Bangladesh) and includes the Andaman and Nicobar Islands in the Bay of Bengal and Lakshadweep (formerly the Laccadive, Minicoy, and Amindivi Islands) in the Arabian Sea. The total area is 3,287,590 sq km (1,269,345 sq mi), including 222,236 sq km (85,806 sq mi) belonging to Jammu and Kashmir; of this disputed region, 78,932 sq km (30,476 sq mi) are under the de facto control of Pakistan and 42,735 sq km (16,500 sq mi) are held by China. Comparatively, the total area occupied by India is slightly more than one-third the size of the United States. China claims part of Arunachal Pradesh. Continental India extends 3,214 km (1,997 mi) N–S and 2,933 km (1,822 mi) E–w.

India is bordered on the N by the disputed area of Jammu and Kashmir (west of the Karakoram Pass), China, Nepal, and Bhutan; on the E by Myanmar, Bangladesh, and the Bay of Bengal; on the S by the Indian Ocean; on the W by the Arabian Sea; and on the NW by Pakistan. The total boundary length is 21,103 km (13,113 mi), of which 7,000 km (4,340 mi) is coastline.

India's capital city, New Delhi, is located in the north-central part of the country.

²TOPOGRAPHY

Three major features fill the Indian landscape: the Himalayas and associated ranges, a geologically young mountain belt, folded, faulted, and uplifted, that marks the nation's northern boundary and effectively seals India climatically from other Asian countries; the Peninsula, a huge stable massif of ancient crystalline rock, severely weathered and eroded; and the Ganges-Brahmaputra Lowland, a structural trough between the two rivers, now an alluvial plain carrying some of India's major rivers from the Peninsula and the Himalayas to the sea. These three features, plus a narrow coastal plain along the Arabian Sea and a wider one along the Bay of Bengal, effectively establish five major physical-economic zones in India.

Some of the world's highest peaks are found in the northern mountains: Kanchenjunga (8,598 m/28,208 ft), the third-highest mountain in the world, is on the border between Sikkim and Nepal; Nanda Devi (7,817 m/25,645 ft), Badrinath (7,138 m/23,420 ft), and Dunagiri (7,065 m/23,179 ft) are wholly in India; and Kamet (7,756 m/25,447 ft) is on the border between India and Tibet.

The Peninsula consists of an abrupt 2,400-km (1,500-mi) escarpment, the Western Ghats, facing the Arabian Sea; interior low, rolling hills seldom rising above 610 m (2,000 ft); an interior plateau, the Deccan, a vast lava bed; and peripheral hills on the north, east, and south, which rise to 2,440 m (8,000 ft) in the Nilgiris and Cardamoms of Kerala and Tamil Nadu. The Peninsula holds the bulk of India's mineral wealth, and many of its great rivers—the Narmada, Tapti, Mahanadi, Godavari, Krishna, and Kaveri—flow through it to the sea. The great trench between the Peninsula and the Himalayas is the largest alluvial plain on earth, covering 1,088,000 sq km (420,000 sq mi) and extending without noticeable interruption 3,200 km (2,000 mi) from the Indus Delta (in Pakistan) to the Ganges-Brahmaputra Delta (shared by India and

Bangladesh), at an average width of about 320 km (200 mi). Along this plain flow the Ganges, Brahmaputra, Son, Jumna, Chambal, Gogra, and many other major rivers, which provide India with its richest agricultural land.

India is located in a seismically active region prone to destructive earthquakes. On 26 January 2001, a 7.7 magnitude earthquake hit northwest India with tremors felt through most of Pakistan as well. Over 20,000 people were killed and over 166,800 were injured. It was recorded as the deadliest earthquake of the year worldwide. The disastrous tsunami that struck Indonesia on 26 December 2004 also impacted India. The tsunami was caused by an underwater earthquake 324 km (180 mi) south of Indonesia's Sumatra island. More than 100,000 people were affected, and there were more than 10,000 casualties. On 8 October 2005, an earthquake measuring 7.6 on the Richter scale struck the Kashmir region. There were more than 140 aftershocks recorded; many measured at least 5.0 in magnitude. More than 1,300 were killed and at least 32,000 homes were destroyed. A magnitude 6.9 quake struck northeast India in September 2011, killing at least 30 people.

³CLIMATE

The lower east (Coromandel) and west (Malabar) coasts of the Peninsula and the Ganges Delta are humid tropical; most of the Peninsula and the Ganges-Brahmaputra Lowland are moist subtropical to temperate; and the semiarid steppe and dry desert of the far west are subtropical to temperate. The northern mountains display a zonal stratification from moist subtropical to dry arctic, depending on altitude.

Extremes of weather are even more pronounced than the wide variety of climatic types would indicate. Thus, villages in western Rajasthan, in the Thar (Great Indian) Desert, may experience less than 13 cm (5 in) of rainfall yearly, while 2,400 km (1,500 mi) eastward, in the Khasi Hills of Assam, Cherrapunji averages about 1,143 cm (450 in) yearly. Sections of the Malabar Coast and hill stations in the Himalayas regularly receive 250–760 cm (100–300 in) yearly; many areas of the heavily populated Ganges-Brahmaputra Lowland and the Peninsula receive under 100 cm (40 in).

Winter snowfall is normal for the northern mountains and Kashmir Valley, but for most of India, scorching spring dust storms and severe hailstorms are more common. The northern half of the country is subject to frost from November through February, but by May a temperature as high as 49°C (120°F) in the shade may be recorded. High relative humidity is general from April through September. Extratropical cyclones (similar to hurricanes) often strike the coastal areas between April and June and between September and December.

The monsoon is the predominant feature of India's climate and helps to divide the year into four seasons: rainy, the southwest monsoon, June–September; moist, the retreating monsoon, October–November; dry cool, the northeast monsoon, December–March; hot, April–May. The southwest monsoon brings from the Indian Ocean the moisture on which Indian agriculture relies. Unfortunately, neither the exact times of its annual arrival and departure nor its duration and intensity can be predicted, and variations are great. In 1987, the failure of the southwest monsoon resulted in one of India's worst droughts during the 20th century.

⁴FLORA AND FAUNA

The World Resources Institute estimates that there are 18,664 plant species in India. In addition, India is home to 422 mammal, 1,180 bird, 521 reptile, and 233 amphibian species. This calculation reflects the total number of distinct species residing in the country, not the number of endemic species.

Pine, oak, bamboo, juniper, deodar, and sal are important species of the Himalayas; sandalwood, teak, rosewood, mango, and Indian mahogany are found in the southern Peninsula. The neem tree, a native tropical evergreen tree, has been called the "village pharmacy" because many parts of the tree have been used for a variety of medicines and lotions.

Wild mammals, including deer, Indian bison, monkeys, and bears, live in the Himalayan foothills and the hilly section of Assam and the plateau. In the populated areas, many dogs, cows, and monkeys wander as wild or semiwild scavengers.

⁵ENVIRONMENT

Among India's most pressing environmental problems are land damage, water shortages, and air and water pollution. India lost 50% of its mangrove area between 1963 and 1977. The World Resources Institute reported that India had designated 15.17 million hectares (37.47 million acres) of land for protection as of 2006.

Despite decades of flood-control programs costing billions of dollars, floods have continued to claim thousands of lives, kill tens of thousands of cattle, and affect millions of people across 11.3 million hectares (28 million acres) of land. In October 2009, a cyclone in the Bay of Bengal resulted in a five-day storm of heavy rains in the southern states of Andhra Pradesh and Karnataka, causing the worst floods in that region in over 100 years. More than 350 villages were severely damaged or completely destroyed by the floods, with an estimated 10 million people left homeless. In some areas, authorities were forced to release water from dams and reservoirs in order to prevent them from breaking, thus causing even greater flooding. Large areas of farmland were completely submerged and thousands of livestock were killed.

Arable land had been damaged by the grazing of the nation's livestock, deforestation, misuse of agricultural chemicals, and salinization. Surface water has been polluted due to uncontrolled dumping of chemical and industrial waste, fertilizers, and pesticides.

Air pollution is most severe in urban centers, but even in rural areas, the burning of wood, charcoal, and dung for fuel, coupled with dust from wind erosion during the dry season, poses a significant problem. Industrial air pollution threatens some of India's architectural treasures, including the Taj Mahal in Agra, part of the exterior of which has been dulled and pitted by airborne acids. In what was probably the worst industrial disaster of all time, a noxious gas leak from a Union Carbide pesticide plant in Bhopal, the capital of Madhya Pradesh, killed more than 1,500 people and injured tens of thousands of others in December 1985. The United Nations (UN) reported in 2008 that carbon dioxide emissions in India totaled 1.61 million kilotons.

Water resources total 1,907.8 cu km (457.7 cu mi) while water usage is about 645.8 cu km (154.94 cu mi) per year. Domestic water usage accounts for 8% of total usage, industrial for 6%, and agricultural for 86%. Per capita water usage totals 585 cu m (20,659

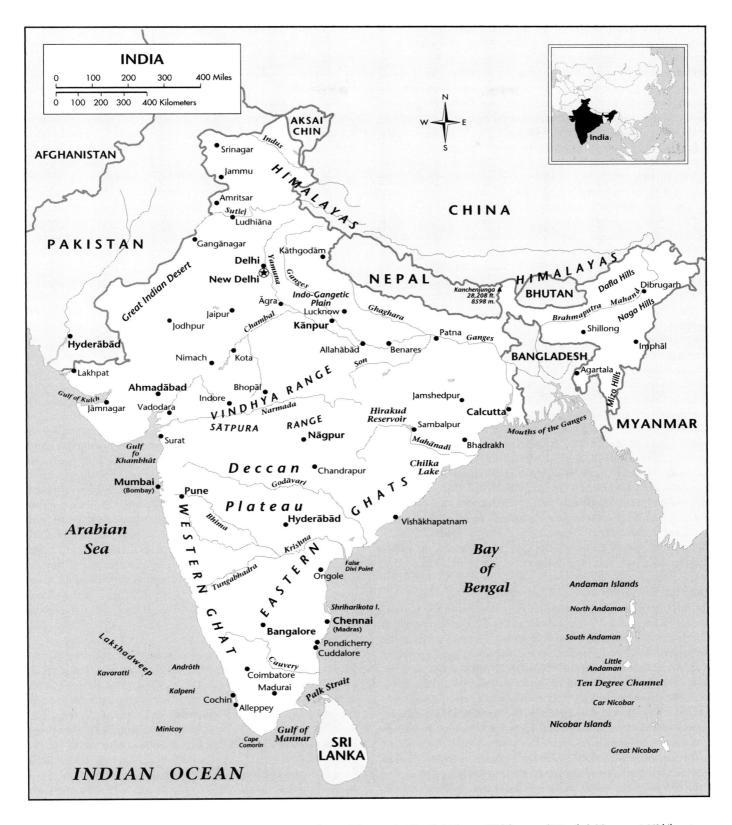

INDIA

| 0 | 100 | 200 | 300 | 400 Miles |
| 0 | 100 | 200 | 300 | 400 Kilometers |

AFGHANISTAN

PAKISTAN

CHINA

AKSAI CHIN

Srinagar

Jammu

Amritsar

Indus

HIMALAYAS

Sutlej

Ludhiāna

Gangānagar

Delhi

New Delhi

Great Indian Desert

Yamuna

Ganges

Āgra

Jaipur

Jodhpur

Indo-Gangetic Plain

Lucknow

Hyderābād

Lakhpat

Nimach

Kota

Kānpur

Chambal

Allahābād

Benares

Patna

Ghaghara

NEPAL

HIMALAYAS

Kanchenjunga
28,208 ft.
8598 m.

BHUTAN

Dafla Hills

Dibrugarh

Brahmaputra

Mahand

Naga Hills

Shillong

Imphāl

Ganges

BANGLADESH

Agartala

Mizo Hills

MYANMAR

Son

Ahmadābād

Indore

Bhopāl

VINDHYA RANGE

Narmada

Jamshedpur

Calcutta

Gulf of Kutch

Jāmnagar

Vadodara

SĀTPURA

RANGE

Nāgpur

Hirakud Reservoir

Sambalpur

Bhadrakh

Mahānadi

Mouths of the Ganges

Surat

Gulf fo Khambhât

Deccan

Mumbai
(Bombay)

Pune

Godāvari

Plateau

Bhima

Chandrapur

Chilka Lake

EASTERN GHATS

Hyderābād

Vishākhapatnam

Arabian Sea

Bay of Bengal

WESTERN GHATS

Krishna

Tungabhadra

Ongole

False Divi Point

Andaman Islands

North Andaman

South Andaman

Lakshadweep

Kavaratti

Andrôth

Bangalore

Shriharikota I.

Chennai
(Madras)

Pondicherry

Cuddalore

Little Andaman

Ten Degree Channel

Kalpeni

Cauvery

Coimbatore

Madurai

Palk Strait

Car Nicobar

Nicobar Islands

Minicoy

Cochin

Alleppey

Cape Comorin

Gulf of Mannar

SRI LANKA

Great Nicobar

INDIAN OCEAN

LOCATION: 8°4′ to 37°6′N; 68°7′ to 97°25′ E. BOUNDARY LENGTHS: Nepal, 1,690 kilometers (1,050 miles); Bhutan, 605 kilometers (373 miles); Myanmar, 1,463 kilometers (910 miles); Bangladesh, 4,053 kilometers (2,520 miles); total coastline, 7,000 kilometers (4,360 miles); Pakistan, 2,912 kilometers (1,800 miles). TERRITORIAL SEA LIMIT: 12 miles.

cu ft) per year. Water usage is a controversial subject in India, with some areas receiving much more drinkable water per capita than others.

India continues to build and expand large hydroelectric dams. Peasants living in areas flooded by dams are rarely given compensation for the loss of their land and livelihood. Opponents of large dam projects argue that there are other costs as well, such as water-logging, soil salinization, and silting.

In June 2011, India signed a loan agreement with the World Bank to support efforts to clean up the Ganges River, one of the world's dirtiest rivers. The World Bank issued a $1 billion dollar loan to manage untreated sewage and hydroelectric projects that have threatened the river's cleanliness for years.

The environmental effects of intensive urbanization are evident in all the major cities, although Calcutta—once a symbol of urban blight—has been freed of cholera, and most of the city now has water purification and sewer services. Analogous improvements have been made in other leading cities.

The Wildlife Act of 1972 prohibits killing of and commerce in threatened animals. There are about 20 national parks and more than 200 wildlife sanctuaries, including 5 natural UNESCO World Heritage Sites and 25 Ramsar wetland sites. According to a 2011 report issued by the International Union for Conservation of Nature and Natural Resources (IUCN), threatened species included 94 mammals, 78 birds, 30 reptiles, 71 amphibians, 212 fish, 6 mollusks, 116 other invertebrates, and 312 plants. Endangered species in India include the lion-tailed macaque, five species of langur, the Indus dolphin, wolf, Asiatic wild dog, Malabar large-spotted civet, clouded leopard, Asiatic lion, Indian tiger, leopard, snow leopard, cheetah, Asian elephant, dugong, wild Asian ass, great Indian rhinoceros, Sumatran rhinoceros, pygmy hog, swamp deer, Himalayan musk deer, Kashmir stag or hangul, Asiatic buffalo, gaur, wild yak, white-winged wood duck, four species of pheasant, the crimson tragopan, Siberian white crane, great Indian bustard, river terrapin, marsh and estuarine crocodiles, gavial, and Indian python. There are at least 10 extinct species. Although wardens are authorized to shoot poachers on game reserves, poaching continues.

6 POPULATION

The US Central Intelligence Agency (CIA) estimates the population of India in 2011 to be approximately 1,189,172,906, which placed it at number 2 in population among the 196 nations of the world. In 2011, approximately 5.4% of the population was over 65 years of age, with another 29.7% under 15 years of age. The median age in India was 26.2 years. There were 1.08 males for every female in the country. The population's annual rate of change was 1.344%. The projected population for the year 2025 is 1.44 billion. Population density in India was calculated at 362 people per sq km (938 people per sq mi).

The UN estimated that 30% of the population lived in urban areas, and that urban populations had an annual rate of change of 2.4%. The largest urban areas, along with their respective populations, included New Delhi, 21.7 million; Mumbai, 19.7 million; Kolkata, 15.3 million; Chennai, 7.4 million; and Bangalore, 7.1 million.

The US Census Bureau expected India's population to surpass China's by 2035. India's population grew rapidly from the 1920s until the 1970s, mostly due to a sharp decline in the death rate be-

cause of improvements in health care, nutrition, and sanitation. In 1921, when India's population stood at 251,321,213, the birth rate was 48.1, but the death rate was 47.2; by 1961, when the population reached 439,234,771, the birth rate was still high at 40.8, but the death rate had dropped by more than half to 22.8. The birth rate dropped from 41.1 in 1971 to 30.2 in 1990–91, presumably attributable to an aggressive program of family planning, contraception, and sterilization, but had little immediate impact on the compounded population growth rate, which averaged 2.1% in the 1980s and 1.9% in 1990–95. Despite the fact that the population growth rate has been steadily declining, the government continues to seek ways to slow population growth. The government considers the rapid population growth a serious problem, particularly in relation to reducing poverty. The goal of the Indian government is to reach zero population growth by 2050, with a population of 1.3 billion.

7 MIGRATION

Estimates of India's net migration rate, carried out by the CIA in 2011, amounted to -0.05 migrants per 1,000 citizens. The total number of emigrants living abroad was 11.4 million, and the total number of immigrants living in India was 5.44 million. India also accepted 77,200 refugees from Tibet, 69,609 from Sri Lanka, and 9,472 from Afghanistan. The partitioning of the South Asian subcontinent to create India and Pakistan in 1947 produced one of the great mass migrations in human history, involving some 20 million people. Historically, major migratory movements have been to and from Sri Lanka, Malaysia, Myanmar, and Bangladesh. Persons of Indian origin domiciled abroad (excluding Pakistan) reside mainly in Sri Lanka, Malaysia, Nepal, Myanmar, South Africa, Mauritius, Trinidad and Tobago, Guyana, Fiji, United States, and the United Kingdom. Indian minority groups in foreign countries generally do not become assimilated with the local population but live as separate groups, intermarry, and retain their own distinctive culture even after a residence of several generations.

There has been a steady migration within India from rural to urban areas. Linguistic differences limit the degree of interstate migration, as do efforts by some states to limit job opportunities for migrants and to give preference in public employment to long-time local residents.

8 ETHNIC GROUPS

India's ethnic history is extremely complex, and distinct racial divisions between peoples generally cannot be drawn clearly. However, estimates from 2000 stated that Indo-Aryans comprised 72% of the population, Dravidians 25%, and Mongoloids and others 3%. The Indo-Aryan are a taller, fairer-skinned strain dominant in the northwest. The dark-complexioned Dravidians of the south have a mixture of Mediterranean and Australoid features.

9 LANGUAGES

There are 211 recognized languages, of which Hindi is the most widely spoken (41% of the population). There are 16 official languages: Hindi, English, Bengali (8.1%), Telugu (7.2%), Marathi (7%), Tamil (5.9%), Urdu (5%), Gujarati (4.5%), Malayalam (3.2%), Kannada (3.7%), Oriya (3.2%), Punjabi (2.8%), Assamese (1.3%), Kashmiri, Sindhi, and Sanskrit. There are 24 languages that are each spoken by one million or more persons. The most important speech group, culturally and numerically, is the Indo-Aryan branch of the Indo-European family, consisting of languages derived from Sanskrit. Hindi, spoken as the mother tongue by about 41% of the total population, is the principal language in this family. Urdu differs from Hindi in being written in the Arabic-Farsi script and containing a large mixture of Arabic and Farsi words. Western Hindi, Eastern Hindi, Bihari, and Pahari are recognized separate Hindi dialects. Other Indo-Aryan languages include Assamese, Bengali, Gujarati, Kashmiri, Marathi, Oriya, Punjabi, Rajasthani, and Sindhi. Languages of Dravidian stock are dominant in southern India and include Telugu, Tamil, Kannada, and Malayalam. A few local languages of eastern India, such as Ho and Santali, fit into the aboriginal Munda family, which predates the Dravidian family on the subcontinent. Smaller groups in Assam and the Himalayas speak languages of Mon-Khmer and Tibeto-Chinese origin. English is widely employed in government, education, science, communications, and industry; it is often a second or third language of the educated classes.

According to government policy, Hindi is the national language; for that reason, Hindi instruction in non-Hindi areas is being rapidly increased, and large numbers of scientific and other modern words are being added to its vocabulary. However, there has been considerable resistance to the adoption of Hindi in the Dravidian-language areas of southern India, as well as in some of the Indo-Aryan-speaking areas, especially West Bengal. The importance of regional languages was well demonstrated in 1956, when the states were reorganized along linguistic boundaries. Thus, multilingual Hyderabad state was abolished by giving its Marathi-speaking sections to Mumbai (formerly Bombay, now in Maharashtra), its Telugu sections to Andhra Pradesh, and its Kannada sections to Mysore (now Karnataka). The Malayalam-speaking areas of Chennai (formerly Madras) were united with Travancore-Cochin to form a single Malayalam state, Kerala. Madhya Bharat, Bhopal, and Vindhya Pradesh, three small Hindi-speaking states, were given to Madhya Pradesh, a large Hindi state, which, at the same time, lost its southern Marathi areas to Mumbai state. Many other boundary changes occurred in this reorganization. Mumbai state originally was to have been divided into Gujarati and Marathi linguistic sections but remained as one state largely because of disagreement over which group was to receive the city of Mumbai. In 1960, however, it, too, was split into two states, Gujarat and Maharashtra, on the basis of linguistic boundaries. In 1966, the government of India accepted the demand of the Punjabi-speaking people, mainly Sikhs, to divide the bilingual state of Punjab into two unilingual areas, with the Hindi-speaking area to be known as Haryana and the Punjabi-speaking area to retain the name of Punjab. India has almost as many forms of script as it has languages. Thus, all of the Dravidian and some of the Indo-Aryan languages have their own distinctive alphabets, which differ greatly in form and appearance. Some languages, such as Hindi, may be written in either of two different scripts. Konkani, a dialect of the west coast, is written in three different scripts in different geographic areas.

10 RELIGIONS

India is the cradle of two of the world's great religions, Hinduism and Buddhism. The principal texts of Hinduism—the Rig Veda (Verses of Spiritual Knowledge), the Upanishads (Ways of Worship), and the Bhagavad-Gita (Song of the Lord)—were written between 1200 and 100 BC. The teachings of Buddha, who lived during the 6th–5th centuries BC, were first transmitted orally and then systematized for transmission throughout Asia. Jainism, a religion that developed contemporaneously with Buddhism, has largely been confined to India. The Sikh religion began in the 15th century AD as an attempt to reconcile Muslim and Hindu doctrine, but the Sikhs soon became a warrior sect bitterly opposed to Islam. An estimated 80.5% of the population are Hindus. Hindus have an absolute majority in all areas except Nagaland, Jammu, and Kashmir, and localized areas of Assam. Sikhs account for about 1.9% of the population and are concentrated in the state of Punjab. Other religious groups include Muslims (13.4% of the population, with about 85% Sunni and the remainder Shi'a) and Christians (2.3%). Large Muslim populations are located in Utar Pradesh, Bihar, Maharashtra, West Bengal, Andhra Pradesh, Kerala, Jammu, and Kashmir. The northeastern states of Nagaland, Mizoram, and Meghalaya have Christian majorities. Buddhists, Jains, Parsis (Zoroastrians), Jews, and Baha'is make up less than 2% of the total population. The caste system is a distinct feature of Hinduism, wherein every person either is born into one of four groups—Brahmans (priests and scholars), Kshatriyas (warriors and rulers), Vaisyas (shopkeepers, artisans, and farmers), and Sudras (farm laborers and menial workers)—or is casteless and thus untouchable. The untouchables are commonly known as Dalits or as Harijan (from the term used by Mahatma Gandhi). Although the constitution outlaws caste distinctions and discrimination, especially those applying to untouchability, progress in changing customs has been slow. Many Dalits have converted to other faiths in order to escape widespread discrimination in some areas; but several states have anticonversion laws in place for Dalits, and those who covert still have faced widespread social and economic discrimination from upper caste members. About 17% of the population are Dalits (also referred to by the government as the Scheduled Castes).

11 TRANSPORTATION

India's railway system is highly developed and constitutes the country's primary means of long-distance domestic transport with 63,273 km (39,319 mi) of track. Virtually all of India's railways are state-owned, and are the nation's largest public enterprise. It is also one of the largest railroad systems in the world. In addition to railways, India had a total of 3.32 million km (2.06 million mi) of roads according to the CIA in 2009.

India has approximately 14,500 km (9,010 mi) of navigable waterways. The most important inland waterways are the Ganges, Brahmaputra, Godavari, and Krishna rivers and the coastal plain canals of Kerala, Chennai, Andhra Pradesh, and Orissa.

In 2008, India's merchant fleet totaled 501 vessels of 1,000 gross registered tons (GRT) or more, sufficient to handle almost all of the country's coastal trade and much of its trade with adjacent countries. Eleven major ports handle the bulk of the import-export traffic; the leading ports are Mumbai and Mormugao. There are 140 smaller ports along the Indian coastline.

India has 352 airports, which transported 54.45 million passengers in 2009 according to the World Bank . International airports are at Mumbai, formerly Bombay (Santa Cruz); Calcutta (Dum Dum); Delhi (Indira Gandhi); Chennai; and Trivandrum. The government-owned Air-India operates long-distance services to foreign countries on five continents. Private airlines have grown in importance.

12 HISTORY

India is one of the oldest continuously inhabited regions in the world. In Harappa, an area in the Indus Valley (now in Pakistan), between 3000 and 2000 BC, scores of thriving municipalities developed a distinct urban culture. This civilization fell into decay around 1500–1200 BC, probably owing to the arrival of Aryan (Indo-European-speaking) invaders, who began entering the northern part of the subcontinent via Afghanistan. There followed over a thousand years of instability, of petty states and larger kingdoms, as one invading group after another contended for power. During this period, Indian village and family patterns, along with Brahmanism—one form of Hinduism—and its caste system, became established. Among the distinguished oral literature surviving from this period are two anonymous Sanskrit epics, the *Ramayana* (traditionally attributed to the legendary poet Valmiki) and the *Mahabharata* (the longest poem in the world, containing over 100,000 verses, including one of Hinduism's most sacred texts, the *Bhagavad-Gita*).

The South Asian subcontinent already had a population of about 30 million, of whom approximately 20 million lived in the Ganges Basin, when Alexander the Great invaded the Indus Valley in 326 BC. His successors were absorbed by the new Maurya dynasty (c. 321–c. 184 BC); under Chandragupta (r. c. 321–c. 297 BC), from his capital at Pataliputra (now Patna), the Mauryans subdued most of northern India and what is now Bangladesh. His successor, Ashoka (r. 273–232 BC), put all of India under unified control for the first time; an early convert to Buddhism, his regime was remembered for its sectarian tolerance, as well as for remarkable administrative, legal, and cultural achievements. Many Buddhist monuments and elaborately carved cave temples found at Sarnath, Ajanta, Bodhgaya, and other places in India date from the reigns of Ashoka and his Buddhist successors.

In the years following Ashoka, India divided again into a patchwork of kingdoms, as other invaders arrived from central and western Asia. In the process, Hinduism prevailed over Buddhism, which found wide acceptance elsewhere in Asia but remained widely practiced in India, its birthplace. Hindu kingdoms began to appear in what is present-day southern India after the 4th century AD. The era of the Gupta dynasty rule (AD 320–c. 535) was a golden age of art, literature, and science in India. Hindu princes of the Rajput sub-caste, ruling in the northwest, reached their peak of power from AD 700 to 1000, although their descendants retained much of their influence well into British days.

In the 8th century, the first of several Islamic invaders appeared in the northwest; between 1000 and 1030, Mahmud of Ghazni made 17 forays into the subcontinent. The first Muslim sultan of Delhi was Kutb-ud-din (r. c. 1195–1210), and Islam gradually spread eastward and southward, reaching its greatest territorial and cultural extent under the Mughal (or Mogul) dynasty. "Mughal" comes from the Farsi word for Mongol, and the earlier Mughals were descendants of the great 14th-century Mongol conqueror Timur (also known as "Timur the Lame" or Tamburlaine), a descendant in turn of Genghis Khan. Much of the population of the subcontinent began converting to Islam during the Mughal period, however, which helped weave Islam into the social fabric of India.

One of the Timurid princes, Babur (r. 1526–30), captured Kabul in 1504 and defeated the Sultan of Delhi in 1526, becoming the first of the Mughals to proclaim himself emperor of India. In 1560, Akbar (r. 1556–1605), Babur's grandson, extended the dynasty's authority over all of northern India. Akbar also attempted to establish a national state in and it was Akbar who was the first of the Muslim emperors to attempt the establishment alliance with Hindu rajahs (kings). Though illiterate, he was a great patron of art and literature. Among his successors were Shah Jahan and his son Aurangzeb, who left their imprint in massive palaces and mosques, superb fortresses (like the Lahore fort), dazzling mausoleums (like the Taj Mahal at Agra), elaborate formal gardens (like those in Srinagar), and the abandoned city of Fatehpur Sikri (37 km/23 mi W of Agra). Under Aurangzeb (r. 1658–1707), who seized his father's throne, the Mughal Empire reached its greatest extent and then began its decline, largely the result of his repressive policies. The Hindu Marathas fought the Mughals and established their own empire in western India.

Vasco da Gama reached India's southwest coast by sea in 1498, and for a century the Portuguese had a monopoly over the Indian sea. Although it continued to hold bits of Indian territory until 1961, Portugal lost its dominant position as early as 1612 when forces controlled by the British East India Company defeated the Portuguese and won concessions from the Mughals. The British East India Company, which had been established in 1600, had permanent trading settlements in Chennai (formerly Madras), Mumbai (formerly Bombay), and Calcutta by 1690.

Threatened by the French East India Company, which was founded in 1664, the two companies fought each other as part of their nations' struggle for supremacy in Europe and the western hemisphere in the 18th century. They both allied with rival Indian princes and recruited soldiers (*sepoys*) locally, but the French and their allies suffered disastrous defeats in 1756 and 1757, against the backdrop of the Seven Years' War (1756–63) raging in Europe.

By 1761, France was no longer a power in India. The architect of the British triumph, later known as the founder of British India, was Robert Clive, later Baron, who became governor of the Company's Bengal Presidency in 1764, to be followed by Warren Hastings and Lord Cornwallis in the years before 1800. The Company's rule spread up the Gangetic plain to Oudh and Delhi and, eventually, to western India, where the Maratha Confederacy, the alliance of independent Indian states that had succeeded the Mughal Empire there, was reduced to a group of relatively weak principalities owing fealty to the British in 1818.

The British government took direct control of the East India Company's Indian domain during the Sepoy Mutiny (1857–59), a widespread rebellion by Indian soldiers in the company's service, and in 1859, Queen Victoria was proclaimed Empress of India. The succeeding decades were characterized by significant economic and political change, but also by a growing cultural and political gap between Indians and the British. Indian troops were deployed elsewhere in the world by the Crown in defense of British interests but without any recourse of Indian views.

Nationalism and Independence

While the British moved gradually to expand local self-rule along federal lines, British power was increasingly challenged by the rise of indigenous movements challenging its authority. A modern Indian nationalism began to grow as a result of the influence of Western culture and education among the elite, and the formation of such groups as the Arya Samaj and Indian National Congress. Founded as an Anglophile debating society in 1885, the congress grew into a movement leading agitation for greater self-rule in the first 30 years of this century. Under the leadership of Mohandas Karamchand Gandhi (called the Mahatma, or Great Soul) and other nationalist leaders, such as Motilal and Jawaharlal Nehru, congress began to attract mass support in the 1930s with the success of noncooperation campaigns spearheaded by Gandhi and its advocacy of education, cottage industries, self-help, an end to the caste discrimination, and nonviolent struggle. Muslims had also been politicized, beginning with the abortive partition of Bengal during the period 1905–12. And despite the INC leadership's commitment to secularism, as the movement evolved under Gandhi, its leadership style appeared—to some Muslims—uniquely Hindu, leading some Muslims to look to the protection of their interests in the formation of their own organization, the All-India Muslim League.

National and provincial elections in the mid-1930s, coupled with growing unrest throughout India, persuaded many Muslims that the power the majority Hindu population could exercise at the ballot box could leave them as a permanent electoral minority in any single democratic polity that would follow British rule. Sentiment in the Muslim League began to coalesce around the "two nation" theory propounded by the poet Iqbal, who argued that Muslims and Hindus were separate nations and that Muslims required creation of an independent Islamic state for their protection and fulfillment. A prominent attorney, Muhammad Ali Jinnah, led the fight for a separate Muslim state to be known as Pakistan, a goal formally endorsed by the Muslim League in Lahore in 1940.

Mahatma Gandhi, meanwhile, had broadened his demand from self-rule to independence by 1929; in the 1930s, his campaigns of nonviolent noncooperation and civil disobedience electrified the countryside. In 1942, with British fortunes at a new low and the Japanese successful everywhere in Asia, Gandhi rejected a British appeal to postpone further talks on Indian self-rule until the end of World War II. Declining to support the British (and Allied) war effort and demanding immediate British withdrawal from India, he launched a "Quit India" campaign. In retaliation, Gandhi and most of India's nationalist leaders were jailed.

The end of World War II and the British Labor Party's victory at the polls in 1945 led to renewed negotiations on independence between Britain and the Hindu and Muslim leaders. Jawaharlal Nehru and the Congress leadership pressed anew for a single, secular nation in which the rights of all would be guarded by constitutional guarantees and democratic practice. But Jinnah and the Muslim League persevered in their campaign for Pakistan. In mid-August 1947, with Hindu-Muslim tensions rising, British India was divided into the two self-governing dominions of India and Pakistan, the latter created by combining contiguous, Muslim-majority districts in the western and eastern parts of British India, with the former, the new republic of India, consisting of the large remaining land mass in between. Partition resulted in one of the world's largest mass movements of people: Hindus, Muslims, and Sikhs who found themselves on the "wrong" side of new international boundaries sought to cross over. As many as 20 million people moved, and up to 3 million of these were killed as violence erupted along the borders. Gandhi, who opposed the partition and worked unceasingly for Hindu-Muslim amity, became himself a casualty of heightened communal feeling; he was assassinated by a Hindu extremist five months after Partition.

Kashmir Dispute

The Partition did not address the more than 500 princely states with which the British Crown had treaty ties. Most princely rulers chose one or the other dominion on grounds of geography, but the state of Jammu and Kashmir, bordering both new nations, had a real option. A Muslim-majority state with a Hindu maharaja, Kashmir opted first for neither but sought protection when invaded in 1948 by tribesmen from Pakistan. Quickly, Indian and Pakistani armed forces were engaged in fighting that cut to the heart of the "two-nation" theory and brought the dispute to the fledgling UN. A UN cease-fire in 1949 left the state divided, one-third with Pakistan and the rest, including the Vale of Kashmir, under Indian control. An agreement to hold an impartial plebiscite broke down when the antagonists could not agree on the terms under which it would be held. India and Pakistan went to war again in 1965, and relationships over Kashmir remained tense. A 1971 agreement formed an informal border, known as the Line of Control, which both nations agreed to honor. Both nations have stood by the agreement for the most part, although militant activity in Kashmir since the late 1980s has led to periodic clashes between Indian and Pakistani troops. Such clashes came close to war in 1999 when insurgents that India claimed were backed by Pakistan entered the Indian-held Kargil region in Kashmir. Heavy fighting between Indian and Pakistani troops ensued, until Pakistan withdrew from Kargil that year. On 24 December 1999, Kashmiri militants hijacked an Indian Airlines plane flying between Nepal and Delhi to Afghanistan, an incident India blamed on Pakistan. In July 2002, the United States announced that it did not support Pakistan's persistent demand for a plebiscite in Kashmir, a statement welcome to India. India and Pakistan declared a formal cease-fire in Kashmir in November 2003, and relations between the two countries were slowly improving. A bus link between the India- and Pakistan-controlled portions was established in April 2005, and both countries cooperated to some degree with the distribution of humanitarian aid following a deadly earthquake that struck the region on 8 October 2005. However, violence has continued intermittently, including bombings in Mumbai in 2008 by a Pakistan-based terrorist organization, Laskar-e-Taiba, in which 164 people were killed.

After Nehru's death on 27 May 1964, his successor, Lal Bahadur Shastri, led India in dealing with an unprecedented round of Hindu-Muslim violence occasioned by the theft of a holy Islamic relic in Kashmir. In August and September 1965, his government successfully resisted a new effort by Pakistan to resolve the Kashmir dispute by force of arms. India was victorious on the battlefield, and an agreement signed by both nations at Tashkent in January 1966 essentially restored the status quo ante. Shastri died of a heart attack at Tashkent, while at the height of his power, and his successor, Indira Gandhi (Nehru's daughter), pledged to honor the accords. India again went to war with Pakistan in December 1971, this time to support East Pakistan in its civil war with West Pakistan; Indian forces tipped the balance in favor of the separatists and led to the creation of Bangladesh from the former East Pakistan; in Kashmir, there were minor territorial adjustments. International tensions were heightened again in April 1974 when India conducted a successful test of an atomic bomb.

Weakening of Congress

Domestically, Indira Gandhi consolidated her power. The party lost its accustomed majority in parliament in the 1967 elections, but she continued to govern with the support of other parties and independents, winning again in 1972. In June 1975, after her conviction on minor election law violations in the 1972 polls, which required her to resign, she continued in power by proclaiming a state of emergency. By decree, she imposed press censorship, arrested opposition political leaders, and sponsored legislation that retroactively cleared her of the election law violations. These actions, although later upheld by the Supreme Court, resulted in widespread public disapproval.

Two years later, she held parliamentary elections in which she was defeated, forcing the Congress Party into the parliamentary opposition for the first time. The state of emergency was lifted, and Morarji Desai, formerly Nehru's deputy prime minister and the compromise choice of the winning five-party Janata coalition, became prime minister. But Janata did not last. Formed solely to oppose Indira Gandhi, the Janata coalition had no unity or agreed program, and soon collapsed. Indira Gandhi's newly reorganized Congress Party/I ("I" for Indira) courted Hindu votes to win a huge election victory in January 1980, and she regained office.

Rise of Communal Violence

Indira Gandhi's rule ended with her assassination by her Sikh bodyguards in October 1984. The assassination stemmed from her ordering of troops in 1983 to storm the Golden Temple in Amritsar, where Sikh militants agitating for an independent nation of Khalistan in the Sikh-dominant Punjab province were alleged to be storing arms. The Sikh factionalism occurred against a backdrop of communal violence that plagued India in 1983. Hindu mobs in the state of Assam attacked Muslims from Bangladesh and West Bengal, killing at least 3,000 persons. After widespread violence in Punjab, Indira Gandhi had imposed direct rule in the state.

Rajiv Gandhi immediately succeeded his mother as prime minister and, in parliamentary elections held in December 1984, led the CP/I to its largest victory. But during the next two years, Rajiv Gandhi's popularity declined precipitously as the public reacted to government-imposed price increases in basic commodities, his inability to stem escalating sectarian violence, and charges of military kickbacks and other scandals. In October 1987, Indian troops were sent to Sri Lanka to enforce an agreement he and the Sri Lankan president had signed in July, aimed at ending the conflict between the country's Sinhalese majority and Tamil minority.

In September 1989, Rajiv agreed with Sri Lanka's request to pull his 100,000 troops out of their bloody standoff with Tamil separatists by the end of the year. In elections later that fall, his Congress/I Party won only a plurality of seats in the Lok Sabha, and he resigned. Vishwanath Pratap Singh, formerly Rajiv's rival in the CP and leader of the second-largest party (Janata Dal) in the house, formed a government with the support of two other parliamentary groups. Despite an encouraging start, V.P. Singh's government lost first its momentum, then its ability to command a majority in the parliament. He resigned on losing a confidence vote 11 months later and was succeeded, with Congress/I support, by longtime Janata and Congress leader Chandra Shekhar, who resigned after four months.

During the election campaign that followed in the spring of 1991, Rajiv Gandhi was assassinated by a disgruntled Sri Lankan Tamil while in Tamil Nadu. Congress/I rallied around longtime party stalwart P. V. Narasimha Rao, a former minister under both Rajiv and Indira Gandhi, drawing on a sympathy vote, to finish close enough to a majority to form a minority government. As prime minister, Rao—who was also Congress Party president—faced one of the worst outbreaks of Hindu-Muslim violence since Partition. The violence was focused on a dispute over the Babri Masjid mosque in Ayodhya, Uttar Pradesh. Hindus had claimed that the mosque had been built on the site of a former temple, and a Hindu-nationalist political party, the Bharatiya Janata Party (BJP) exploited the long-simmering dispute into a carefully orchestrated grab for political power. Hindu militants succeeded in destroying the mosque on 6 December 1992, an act that led to widespread communal riots in Uttar Pradesh, Mumbai and much of the rest of the country. Communal riots have flared up throughout India ever since, and remained a persistent threat to the country's long-term stability. The worst outbreak of communal violence following the 1992 rioting occurred in February and March 2002, a group of Muslims in the town of Godhra in the state of Gujarat attacked and set fire to two train cars carrying Hindu activists returning from Ayodhya. Fifty-eight Hindus were killed in the 27 February attack. Starting the following day, Hindus attacked Muslims in Gujarat, leaving hundreds dead and tens of thousands displaced. In three months of violence, much of it sanctioned by India's Hindu nationalist-dominant federal and Gujarati state governments, approximately 2,000 individuals were killed, mostly Muslims.

In more positive developments, Rao initiated economic reforms that, beginning in the early 1990s, opened India to foreign investors and market economics. He lost his hold on power in 1996 and, in May of that year, President Shankan Dayal Sharma appointed Hindu nationalist Atal Bihari Vajpayee as prime minister, beginning a whirlwind of power struggles and political instability during which India changed governments four times in 11 months, with power shifting between the BJP and a United Front/Congress coalition. In an effort to retain its traditional grasp of power, Rajiv Gandhi's widow, Sonia Gandhi, was named president of the Congress Party. Her magnetism did little, however, to boost Congress' fortunes, and the power struggles culminated with Vajpayee's BJP-led party forming a government in 1998 after emerging as the largest single party in India's parliament. The BJP held power until general elections in 2004 dealt it a loss.

Nuclear Politics and World Terrorism

In May 1998, Vajpayee's government surprised the world by exploding several underground nuclear devices. Pakistan responded by holding its own nuclear tests later in the month. The tests brought economic sanctions against both India and Pakistan from the United States and other countries. Tensions eased somewhat in February 1999, however, when Vajpayee inaugurated the first ever bus service between India and Pakistan by traveling to Lahore to meet Pakistan's prime minister. This resulted in the Lahore Declaration (signed 21 February 1999), by which India and Pakistan pledged to resolve their differences peacefully and work for nuclear security. Nevertheless, both countries continued to test medium-range missiles capable of delivering nuclear warheads on targets throughout the region.

Following the September 2001 terrorist attacks on the United States, the United States lifted sanctions imposed on India following its 1998 nuclear tests, citing India's support in the US-led war on terrorism. India began to insist that Pakistan play a larger role in curtailing "cross-border terrorism" in Kashmir and India itself. On 13 December 2001, the Indian Parliament was attacked by five suicide fighters. Fourteen people died in the raid, including the five attackers. India blamed the attacks on two Pakistan-based organizations, Lashkar-e-Taiba and Jaish-e-Muhammad, which the United States also listed as terrorist groups. Following the attacks on parliament, diplomatic contacts were curtailed; rail, bus, and air links were severed; and close to one million troops amassed on India and Pakistan's shared border, the largest military build-up since the 1971 war. In January 2002, India successfully test-fired the Agni, a nuclear-capable ballistic missile, off its eastern coast. In May, Pakistan test-fired three medium-range surface-to-surface Ghauri missiles, capable of carrying nuclear warheads. In June, the United States and the United Kingdom undertook a diplomatic offensive to avert war, and urged their citizens to leave India and Pakistan. In October, India announced its troops had begun withdrawing from Pakistan's border.

On 19 March 2003, the US-led coalition launched war in Iraq. The war was seen as setting a precedent for authorizing preemptive strikes on hostile states. The notion that India and Pakistan might adopt such a policy toward one another caused international concern. In April 2003, spokesmen from both India and Pakistan asserted that the grounds on which the US-led coalition attacked Iraq also existed in each other's country. The situation became more uncomfortable in March 2006 when US President George W. Bush, in a visit to India, signed a deal that allowed India to import nuclear fuel and technology, a privilege not extended to Pakistan.

In September 2004, India, along with Brazil, Germany and Japan, launched an application for a permanent seat on the UN Security Council. The four countries are referred to as the G-4 nations. Their appeal was tabled at the September 2006 UN General Assembly meeting in New York. US president Barack Obama visited India in 2010, pledging support for India's bid to join the UN Security Council as a permanent member.

In December 2004, thousands of people were killed when tsunamis, caused by a powerful undersea earthquake off the Indonesian coast, devastated coastal communities in the south and in the Andaman and Nicobar Islands. In July 2005, more than 1,000 people were killed in floods and landslides caused by monsoon rains in Mumbai and the Maharashtra region.

India is still the scene of violence in many instances. On 29 October 2005, 62 people died in Delhi as a result of a series of bombs. A little-known Kashmiri group declared it was behind the attacks. On 7 March 2006, 14 people were killed by bomb blasts in the Hindu pilgrimage city of Varanasi. On 11 July 2006, more than 180 people were killed in bomb attacks on rush-hour trains in Mumbai. Investigators claimed Islamic militants based in Pakistan were responsible for the attacks. On 8 September 2006, explosions outside a mosque in the western town of Malegaon killed at least 31 people. On 18 February 2007, 68 passengers, most of them Pakistanis, were killed by bomb blasts and a fire on a train traveling from New Delhi to the Pakistani city of Lahore. In May 2007, at least nine people were killed in a bomb explosion at the main mosque in Hyderabad. Several other people died in subsequent rioting.

In February 2007, India and Pakistan signed an agreement aimed at reducing the risk of accidental nuclear war. In April 2007, India's first commercial space rocket was launched, carrying an Italian satellite.

Controversy erupted in India in December 2009 when the national government agreed to carve out a new state within Andhra Pradesh, a state in the southeast India. The decision to allow the new state, called Telangana, was made after large-scale demonstrations and a hunger strike by a leading, pro-independence politician captured the attention of national lawmakers. Within Andhra Pradesh, however, the decision caused political furor. Counter demonstrations were organized, major protests cropped up throughout the region, and hundreds of statewide lawmakers resigned, threatening government collapse in Andhra Pradesh. In addition to the local uproar, the national government's decision to carve out Telangana caused a host of other groups throughout India to make similar demands for statehood. Political boundaries in India have been redrawn several times since the country was originally carved into eighteen states in the 1950s. In 2011, there were twenty-eight states in India and seven federally administered areas, with the most recent additions (three new states) coming in 2000.

In August 2010, the parliament passed a law that opened the door to foreign companies wanting to build nuclear reactors to supply India's estimated $150-billion energy market. This followed the 2008 passage of the Indo-US civil nuclear agreement, which ended a three-decade-long period during which India was denied access to nuclear technology because it refused to sign the Nuclear Non-Proliferation Treaty (NPT) and developed nuclear weapons. In the August 2010 legislation, the government agreed to triple the amount (to $320 million) it would pay in the event of a nuclear accident, a point that addressed the requirements of foreign companies that their liabilities be limited in the event of an accident.

13 GOVERNMENT

India is a sovereign federal republic. Its constitution, which became effective 26 January 1950, provides for a parliamentary form of government, at the center and in the states. The constitution also contains an extensive set of directive principles akin to the US Bill of Rights. Legislative acts and amendments have weakened some of those guarantees, while a number of decisions by the Supreme Court have left some weakened and others—like the commitment to secularism and to representative government—strengthened. Suffrage is universal at age 18.

The parliament, or legislative branch, consists of the president, the Council of States (Rajya Sabha), and the House of the People (Lok Sabha). The Rajya Sabha has a membership of 245 members (2011), of whom 12 are appointed by the president and the remainder indirectly elected by the state legislatures and by the union territories for six-year terms, with one-third chosen every two years. The Lok Sabha has 543 directly elected members (530 from the states, 13 from the union territories) and two members appointed by the president to represent the Anglo-Indian community. The Lok Sabha has a maximum life of five years but can be dissolved earlier by the president.

The president and vice president are elected for five-year terms by an electoral college made up of the members of both parliamentary houses and the legislative assemblies of the states. Legally, all executive authority, including supreme command of the armed forces, is vested in the president, as head of state, who, in turn, appoints a council of ministers headed by a prime minister. The prime minister serves as the head of government. That individual is chosen by legislators of the political party, or coalition of parties, that commands the confidence of the parliament. The prime minister forms—and the president then appoints—the council of ministers, consisting of cabinet ministers, ministers of state, and deputy ministers to formulate and execute the government program.

By tradition, the presidency and vice presidency tradeoff between a northerner and a southerner, although a Muslim and a Sikh—nonregional identifications—have also held these positions.

14 POLITICAL PARTIES

India began its independent existence with the Indian National Congress supreme at the center and in all state legislatures. In its various manifestations, it controlled the government for most of the years since independence in 1947 before losing its dominant position with the rise of the Bharatiya Janata Party (BJP) in 1980. Founded in 1885, the Indian National Congress, known after 1947 as the Congress Party (CP), was the most powerful mass movement fighting for independence in British India. It became the ruling party of a free India by reason of its national popularity and because most leaders of the independence movement were among its members, including India's first prime minister, Jawaharlal Nehru. In its progression from independence movement to ruling party, the CP spawned many offshoots and continued to do so, as often for personal reasons as for matters of party policy. The first to do so was the socialist wing that split off shortly after independence to form a party in its own right, dividing again several times thereafter.

Other major parties at the time of independence included the Communist Party of India (CPI), with its origins in the peasants and workers parties of the past, representing, like them, the communist left. The CPI began the independence period under a cloud because of its Moscow-directed cooperation with the British during World War II. On the right were parties like the Hindu Mahasabha (HMS), doomed to ignominy when one of its kind killed Mahatma Gandhi in 1948. Within the political system, the HMS, nonetheless, reflected a vital Hindu nationalist strain that has seen several party iterations in the years since. It became a force to contend with as the BJP began to gain popularity after bringing together various strains of the Hindu nationalist movement into an "all-India" coalition party in 1980. By the early 1990s, the BJP has emerged as India's largest opposition party, and led a ruling coalition from 1998 to 2004.

Parties on the left, right, and center have continued to divide or split off over the years, and the number of single state linguistic, sectarian, and regional parties capable of governing only at the state level but available for coalition building at the center has grown significantly.

As of August of 2011, 36 political parties held seats in the People's Assembly (Lok Sabha). Leading parties in 2011 were the CP with 206 seats and the BJP with 116 seats. Manmohan Singh served as prime minister, and Pratibha Devisingh Patil served as president. The next elections were to take place by May of 2014.

15 LOCAL GOVERNMENT

The Republic of India is a union of states. The specific powers and spheres of influence of these states are set forth in the constitution, with all residual or nonspecified powers in the hands of the central government (the reverse of the US Constitution). The central government has the power to set state boundaries and to create and abolish states. The state governments are similar to the central government in form, with a chief minister and a cabinet responsible to the state legislature, which may be unicameral or bicameral. State governors, usually retired civil servants or politicians, are appointed by the president for a five-year term and act only on the advice of the state cabinet.

The constitution gives the president the power—on the advice of the prime minister—to dissolve a state legislature and dismiss a state government if no party commands the support of a majority or if the state's constitutional machinery is incapable of maintaining order. The Lok Sabha, which must approve each six-month extension of direct rule, acts as the state legislature during its imposition, governing through the governor. Termed as "President's Rule" in the constitution, this power derives from a provision for "Governor's Rule" in the Government of India Act of 1935 and survives in the Pakistan constitution of 1973 in that form. It was invoked for the first time in 1959 by Prime Minister Nehru, and on the advice of Indira Gandhi, who was then Congress Party president; in power herself, she invoked the power repeatedly, often for partisan political purposes and, especially in the early 1980s, in the wake of ethnic/communal violence in Punjab, Assam, and Jammu and Kashmir. Limitations on its partisan use were imposed in a Supreme Court decision in spring 1994.

Under the States Reorganization Act of 1956, there were 14 states and five union territories, organized, where appropriate, on linguistic grounds. Through a gradual process of reorganization and division, two former union territories have become states while new union territories have been created (there were seven as of 2011), and the number of states has grown to 28 (2011).

Administratively, the states and union territories are divided into districts, under the control of senior civil servants who are responsible for collecting revenues, maintaining law and order, and setting development priorities. Districts are further divided into subdivisions, and subdivisions into *taluks* or *tehsils*. State government and lower levels of representative councils vary in organization and function, but all are based on universal adult suffrage. Large towns are each governed by a corporation headed by a mayor; health, safety, education, and the maintenance of normal city facilities are under its jurisdiction. Smaller towns have municipal boards and committees similar to the corporations but with more limited powers. District boards in rural areas provide for road construction and maintenance, education, and public health. The constitution provides for the organization of village councils (*panchayats*), and nearly all the villages have been so organized. The panchayats are elected from among the villagers by all the adult population and have administrative functions and a judicial wing that enables them to handle minor offenses.

In the mid-1990s, there were several campaigns to form new states in India, carving new borders along factional lines in existing states. A promise by former Prime Minister Deve Gowda to create a new state in Uttar Pradesh in 1996 renewed separatist sentiments in several other states, most notably in Andhra Pradesh. Although Andhra Pradesh's elected officials supported the creation of a new state, Telangana, public resistance to the scheme put that plan on hold through 2011.

The Hindu nationalist party (BJP) proposed five new states in 1996, hoping to control their assemblies rather than fight political foes in larger entities. Both proposals ignore potentially chaotic consequences in favor of political gain; existing state boundaries were drawn on language differences, while there appeared to be no motive other than politics for the boundaries suggested by the new proposals. On its return to power in 1998, the BJP government succeeded in drafting bills that created three new states (Chhattisgarh, Uttaranchal, and Jharkhand), but put on hold its plans for making Delhi, presently a Union Territory, a state. Chhattisgarh, Uttaranchal, and Jharkhand became India's three newest states in November 2000.

16 JUDICIAL SYSTEM

The laws and judicial system of British India were continued after independence with only slight modifications. The Supreme Court consists of a chief justice and 25 associate judges, appointed by the president, who hold office until age 65. The court's duties include interpreting the constitution, handling all disputes between the central government and a state or between states themselves, and judging appeals from lower courts.

There are 18 high courts, subordinate to but not under the control of, the Supreme Court. Three have jurisdiction over more than one state. Each state's judicial system is headed by a high court whose judges are appointed by the president and over whom state legislatures have no control. High court judges can serve up to the age of 62. Each state is divided into districts; within each district, a hierarchy of civil courts is responsible to the principal civil courts, presided over by a district judge. The 1973 Code of Criminal Procedure, effective 1 April 1974, provides for the appointment of separate sets of magistrates for the performance of executive and judicial functions within the criminal court system. Executive magistrates are responsible to the state government; judicial magistrates are under the control of the high court in each state.

Different personal laws are administered through the single civil court system. Islamic law (Shari'ah) governs many noncriminal matters involving Muslims, including family law, inheritance, and divorce. There are strong constitutional safeguards assuring the independence of the judiciary. In 1993–94, the Supreme Court rendered important judgments imposing limits on the use of the constitutional device known as "President's Rule" by the central government and reaffirming India's secular commitment.

17 ARMED FORCES

The Indian Armed Forces have a proud tradition, having provided one million soldiers during World War I and two million during World War II for combat in Asia, Africa, the Middle East, and Europe. The armed forces are entirely volunteer and consist of a Strategic Forces Command, the regular army, navy, and air force, a territorial (reserve) army, and various full-time or reserve special purpose paramilitary units for border, transportation, and internal defense.

India's Strategic Forces Command is responsible for the country's strategic missile force. As of 2011, it was suspected that India possessed 80–100 nuclear weapons and had the capability for producing more.

In 2010 the government announced the establishment of two new army divisions. The divisions were to be deployed to the mountainous northeastern state of Arynachai Pradesh, which includes a large portion of land that the Chinese government claims as its own. The 56th and 71st divisions include a total of more than 36,000 men specifically trained for mountain warfare. The Indian army chief claimed that the increase in defenses against China was a necessary response to a similar Chinese build-up in Tibet, which began in 2007. India has also begun building paramilitary forces, known as the Arunachal Scouts and the Sikkim Scouts, to assist the army in protecting the Sino-Indian border in the states of Arunachal Pradesh and Sikkim.

The International Institute for Strategic Studies reported in 2011 that armed forces in India totaled 1.33 million members. The force is comprised of 1.13 million from the army, 58,350 from the navy, 127,200 from the air force, and 9,550 members of the coast guard. Armed forces represented 0.6% of the labor force in India. Defense spending totaled $101.7 billion and accounted for 2.5% of GDP.

18 INTERNATIONAL COOPERATION

India became a charter member of the UN on 13 October 1945 and belongs to ESCAP and several nonregional specialized agencies. India is also part of the Asian Development Bank, the African Development Bank, the Colombo Plan, SAARC, G-6, G-15, G-19, G-24, and G-77. India became a founding member of the World Trade Organization (WTO) on 1 January 1995. It is a dialogue partner with the ASEAN and an observer in the OAS. India is a member of the Commonwealth of Nations.

In June 2009, representatives from Brazil, Russia, India, and China—a group of countries with fast-developing economies, informally referred to as the BRIC group—convened their first-ever summit meeting in Moscow. A principal concern of the participating governments was the question of how to exert more control over the global financial system. At the time of the summit, the BRIC countries held a staggering 40% of global currency reserves and voiced concerns at the lack of diversity of these holdings, almost all of which were in US dollars.

India was a founder of the nonaligned movement during the Cold War and has pursued a formally neutralist foreign policy since independence. Relations with China, hostile during the early 1960s, have been normalized since 1976. India's primary ally among the superpowers had been the former USSR, with which a 20-year treaty of peace, friendship, and cooperation was signed in 1971.

Since independence, India has fought three wars with neighboring Pakistan, in 1947–48, 1965, and 1971. In 1998 both countries became nuclear powers, conducting a series of underground nuclear tests. Tension between the two nations was subject to periodic rises and falls, which continued through 2011.

In environmental cooperation, India is part of the Antarctic Treaty, the Basel Convention, Conventions on Biological Diversity and Whaling, Ramsar, CITES, International Tropical Timber Agreements, the Kyoto Protocol, the Montréal Protocol, MARPOL, the Nuclear Test Ban Treaty, and the UN Conventions on the Law of the Sea, Climate Change, and Desertification. The nation is also part of the South Asia Cooperative Environment Program (SACEP).

In 2010 India was elected for a two-year term on the UN Security Council. The term began on 1 January 2011.

¹⁹ECONOMY

India is rich in mineral, forest, and power resources. Its ample reserves of iron ore and coal provide a substantial base for heavy industry. Coal is the principal source for generating electric power although hydroelectric and nuclear installations supply a rising proportion of India's power needs. Anticipating a rapid growth in oil consumption in the near future, the government actively promotes oil exploration and development. Since 1997, under its New Exploration and Licensing Policy (NELP), foreign companies have been permitted to participate in upstream oil exploration, long restricted to Indian-owned firms.

The Indian economy is a mixture of public and private enterprises. Under a planned development regime following independence, the public sector provided the impetus for industrialization and for absorption of sophisticated technology. Nevertheless, a large proportion of the total manufacturing output continued to be contributed by small, unorganized industries. Since 1991, the government has placed greater emphasis on private enterprise to stimulate growth and modernization. During the 2000s, the Ministry of Disinvestment led a $2.5 billion in privatization effort. Sales included a strategic stake of Videsh Sanchar Nigam Ltd. (VSNL), India's premier international communications and internet service provider (ISP) company to the Tata Group, India's largest conglomerate; a strategic stake in IBP, the national petroleum marketing company, to Indian Oil; a strategic stake in Indian Petrochemical Company Ltd. (IPCL) to the Indian company, Reliance Industries; and a strategic share of Maruti Udyog Ltd. (MUL), India's top car maker, to Suzuki Maintenance Corporation (SMC) of Japan.

Following the proclamation of a state of emergency in June 1975, a 20-point economic reform program was announced. Price regulations were toughened, and a moratorium on rural debts was declared. A new campaign was mounted against tax evaders, currency speculators, smugglers, and hoarders. The reforms were buttressed by a 30-month arrangement under the IMF's Extended Fund Facility (EFF), from 9 November 1981 to 10 May 1984. After the collapse of world oil prices in 1986, India's average annual growth increased to 6.2% on the latter half of the decade. This expansion was accompanied, however, by numerous persistent weaknesses: slow growth in formal sector employment, inef-

ficiency and technological lags in the public sector, and increasing fiscal and balance of payments deficits, which by 1990 had produced double digit inflation. The oil shock accompanying the Persian Gulf War catalyzed an acute balance of payments crisis in early 1991.

Swift stabilization measures taken by the newly elected government, including two stand-by arrangements with the IMF, proved highly successful. Further reforms focused on trade liberalization, privatization, and deregulation helped push GDP growth to an average of 6.5% for the five years 1995 to 1999. Economic growth slowed significantly in 2000/01 reflecting both the global economic slowdown and also weak agricultural growth in India. In 2002/03 industrial and service growth recovered. By mid-2005, India's economy was booming. Industrial production had grown at its fastest rate in nine years, by 11.7% over the same period in 2004, including an increase in manufacturing of 12.5%. Exports were up by 19% on 2004, and imports by 30%. The stock market in mid-2005 had risen by more than 50% in one year, and foreign exchange reserves were building.

Despite its shining economy in 2006, India was suffering a stalling of economic reforms that had laid the basis for its successes. These reforms were begun in 1991 under Finance Minister Manmohan Singh, who by May 2004 had become prime minister. The government, led by the Congress Party, by 2005 had proved unable to pursue additional liberalizing economic reforms, as it relied upon support from a group of Communist parties that opposed many such reforms. In June 2005, those parties forced the government to formally abandon plans to sell stakes in 13 state-owned companies to strategic investors. However, by implementing a large public-works project, the government insisted it was implementing plans to reduce rural poverty, help fix rural infrastructure, and give power and rights to the very poor.

Although the global economic crisis of 2008–09 had a significant effect on the Indian economy, government stimulus packages helped pull the nation out of recession, leading to economic growth of 7.9% in the third quarter of 2009. Manufacturing was the primary growth sector.

The GDP rate of change in India, as of 2010, was 10.4%. In the second quarter of 2010 (July–September), GDP grew by 8.9% in comparison to the same period in 2009. Increases in farm production, vehicle sales, and bank lending were all noted as primary growth factors. During this period, farm production increased by 4.4%, manufacturing increased by 9.8%, and construction was up by 8.8%.

In 2011 the amount of exported goods, including industrial machinery, automobile parts, and refined petroleum products, grew by 37.5%, making up a $245.9 billion export industry. India has concentrated on products that require high-skill workers rather than garments and toys, which do not require technological skill and understanding. While India does export textiles, they make up less than 20 percent of India's exported goods.

India continues to take advantage of its well-educated, English-speaking workforce. India is investing in becoming a major exporter of software services and software workers. The United States remains India's largest trading partner. However, inflationary concerns have been fueled by strong growth combined with easy consumer credit and a real estate boom. India continues to receive funding from the United States as well as the World Bank.

²⁰INCOME

The CIA estimated that in 2010 the GDP of India was $4.1 trillion. The CIA defines GDP as the value of all final goods and services produced within a nation in a given year and computed on the basis of purchasing power parity (PPP) rather than value as measured on the basis of the rate of the exchange based on current dollars. The per capita GDP was estimated at $3,500. The annual growth rate of GDP was 10.4%. The average inflation rate was 11.7%. It was estimated that agriculture accounted for 16.1% of GDP, industry 28.6%, and services 55.3%.

Indians living in other countries are an important aspect of the Indian economy. According to the World Bank, remittances from citizens living abroad totaled $49.5 billion in 2009, about $42 per capita, and accounted for approximately 1.2% of GDP.

As of 2011 the most recent study by the World Bank reported that actual individual consumption in India was 63.4% of GDP and accounted for 4.29% of world consumption. By comparison, the United States accounted for 25.44% of world individual consumption. The World Bank also estimated that 22.8% of India's GDP was spent on food and beverages, 9.5% on housing and household furnishings, 3.3% on clothes, 4.6% on health, 9.7% on transportation, 1.0% on communications, 1.2% on recreation, 1.2% on restaurants and hotels, and 6.6% on miscellaneous goods and services and purchases from abroad.

The World Bank reports that in 2009, household consumption in India totaled $798.1 billion or about $671 per capita, measured in current US dollars rather than PPP. Household consumption includes expenditures of individuals, households, and nongovernmental organizations on goods and services, excluding the purchases of dwellings. It was estimated that household consumption was growing at an average annual rate of 7.4%. It was estimated that in 2007 about 25% of the population subsisted on an income below the poverty line established by India's government.

²¹LABOR

As of 2010, India had a total labor force of 478.3 million people. Within that labor force, CIA estimates in 2009 noted that 52% were employed in agriculture, 14% in industry, and 34% in the service sector.

Most trade unions are affiliated with political parties. The right to strike is often exercised, but public sector unions are required to give 14 days notice prior to an organized strike. Employers are prohibited from discriminating against union activity, and collective bargaining is practiced.

As of 2010, working hours are limited by law to 60 hours per week (48 normal and 12 overtime) for adults with eight-hour days. Minimum wages are set according to industry and by the various states. By law, earned income also includes a cost-of-living allowance and an annual bonus. However, these regulations were only applicable to factories and all other establishments covered by the Factories Act. Most workers covered under that law earned more than the minimum, and were subject to bonuses and other benefits. Agricultural workers were subject to separate state mandated minimum wage rates. In addition, some industries, such as apparel and footwear, had no official minimum wage rate. Although factory, mine, and other hazardous industry employment of children under 14 years of age was prohibited, India had no formal overall minimum age governing child labor. Estimates placed the number of child laborers as ranging from 12.7 to 60 million, as of 2010. Many of them work in the hand-knotted carpet industry. Bonded labor was abolished in 1976, but was still prevalent. Estimates of the number of bonded laborers range as high as 40 million. Health and safety standards are not regularly enforced.

²²AGRICULTURE

About 60% of the population is employed in the agricultural sector, and roughly 60% of the total land is farmed. India's major crops include rice, wheat, oilseed, cotton, jute, tea, sugarcane, lentils, onions, and potatoes. Rice leads all crops and, except in the northwest, is generally grown wherever the conditions are suitable. The combined acreage and production of other cereals, all to a large extent grown for human consumption, considerably exceed those of rice. These include jowar, a rich grain sorghum grown especially in the Deccan; wheat, grown in the northwest; and bajra, another grain sorghum grown in the drier areas of western India and the far south. In 2009, cereal production amounted to 246.7 million tons, while fruit production was 70.4 million tons, and vegetable production 92.8 million tons.

Nonfood crops are mainly linseed, cotton, jute, and tobacco. Cotton crops in the last decade were large enough to both supply the increasing demands of the domestic textile sector and provide export receipts. For centuries, India has been famous for its spices and today is one of the world's largest producers, consumers, and exporters of a wide range of spices. Of the 63 spices grown in the country, black pepper, cardamom, ginger, turmeric, and chilies are the most economically important. Since World War II (1939–45), India has been among the world's largest producers of black pepper. Pepper production is concentrated in the southern states of Kerlala, Karnataka, and Tamil Nadu.

India was the world's second-leading producer (after Brazil) of sugarcane in 2008. Production of raw sugar was enough to meet over 90% of domestic consumption. While sugar has been a major crop, both for domestic use and export, tight government controls on the industry have caused prices to fluctuate dramatically. The agricultural ministry sets minimum prices on the amount paid to sugar growers and places limits on how much sugar each mill may produce each month. In 2006, the government placed restrictions on sugar exports to drive domestic prices down, resulting in major surpluses as demand was easily supplied. Many farmers responded by cutting back on production, which in turn left many workers unemployed, and switching cultivation to other more profitable, and unregulated, crops. A sugar shortage occurred in 2009, leading to the need for imports to cover up to 30% of the nation's supply.

Tea, coffee, and rubber plantations contribute significantly to the economy, although they occupy less than 1% of the agricultural land (in hill areas generally unsuited to Indian indigenous agriculture), and are the largest agricultural enterprises in India. Tea, the most important plantation crop, is a large foreign exchange earner. It is grown mostly in Assam and northern Bengal, but also in southern India. Coffee is produced in southern India and rubber in Kerala.

Because of the ever-present danger of food shortages, the government tightly controls the grain trade, fixing minimum support and procurement prices and maintaining buffer stocks. The Food

Corp. of India, a government enterprise, distributes 12 million tons of food grains annually and is increasing its storage capacity.

23 ANIMAL HUSBANDRY

The UN Food and Agriculture Organization (FAO) reported that India dedicated 10.4 million hectares (25.7 million acres) to permanent pasture or meadow in 2009. During that year, the country tended 613 million chickens, 172.5 million head of cattle, and 13.8 million pigs. The production from these animals amounted to 1.8 million tons of beef and veal, 475,072 tons of pork, 662,358 tons of poultry, 2.41 million tons of eggs, and 80 million tons of milk. India also produced 386,000 tons of cattle hide and 40,000 tons of raw wool.

Animals as a whole play an important role in the agricultural economy even though they often receive inadequate nourishment. Slaughter of cattle in India is prohibited in all but a few states since Hindus believe that cows and other animals may contain reincarnated human souls. The slaughter of buffaloes is not as offensive to the religious beliefs of Hindus, and buffaloes are slaughtered for meat.

There are eight breeds of buffalo, 26 cattle breeds, and numerous crossbreeds. Bullocks (steers) and water buffalo are important draft animals. Dairy farming has made India self-sufficient in butter and powdered milk. Dairying in India is undertaken on millions of small farms, where one to three milk animals are raised on less than a hectare (2.5 acres), and yields consist of two to three liters of milk daily. Animal dung is also used for fuel and fertilizer.

24 FISHING

Fishing is an important secondary source of income to some farmers and a primary occupation in small fishing villages. The annual capture totaled 4.1 million tons according to the UN FAO in 2008. Almost three-fifths of the catch consists of sea fish. The bulk is marketed fresh; of the remainder, more than half is sundried. Deep-sea fishing is not done on a large scale. Inland fishing is most developed in the deltaic channels of Bengal, an area where fish is an important ingredient of the diet. The government has encouraged ocean fishing through the establishment of processing plants and the introduction of deep-sea craft. Fishing harbors have been built along the coasts of the Bay of Bengal and the Arabian Sea. Fish exports, still only a fraction of the potential, have shown a steady gain. In 2010, exports of fish products amounted to $2.84 billion.

25 FORESTRY

Approximately 23% of India is covered by forest. The major forestlands lie in the foothills of the Himalayas, the hills of Assam state, the northern highlands of the Deccan, the Western Ghats, and the Andaman Islands. Other forestlands are generally scrub and poor secondary growth of restricted commercial potential. India's forests are mostly broad-leaved; the most important commercial species are sal (10.9% of forest trees), mixed conifers (8.1%), teak (6.8%), fir (3.2%), chir-pine (2.4%), and upland hardwood (2.4%).

India's forests historically have suffered tremendous pressure from its large human and animal populations as a source of fuel wood, fodder, and timber. According to the government's national forest policy, 33% of the land area should be covered by forest. Most forests are owned by state governments and are reserved or protected for the maintenance of permanent timber and water supplies. The government has prohibited commercial harvesting of trees on public land, except for mature, fallen, or sick trees. In order to help meet the fuel needs of much of the population, harvesting dead and fallen branches is permitted in government forests, but this policy is widely violated.

The UN FAO estimated the 2009 roundwood production at 23.2 million cu m (819 million cu ft). The value of all forest products, including roundwood, totaled $390.1 million.

26 MINING

Well endowed with industrial minerals, India's leading industries in 2009 included steel, cement, mining, and petroleum. Gems and jewelry were leading export commodities to the United States. The minerals industry of India produced more than 80 mineral commodities in the form of ores, metals, industrial minerals, and mineral fuels, and is among the world's leading producers of iron ore, bituminous coal, zinc, and bauxite. The country exploits some 52 minerals—11 metallic, 38 nonmetallic, and 3 mineral fuels. In 2009, India also produced lead, monazite, selenium, silver, ilmenite, rutile, corundum, garnet, jasper, asbestos, barite (from the Cuddapah District mines, Andhra Pradesh), bromine, hydraulic cement, chalk, clays (including ball clay, diaspore, fireclay, and kaolin), feldspar, fluorspar, agate, zircon, graphite, kyanite, sillimanite, lime, magnesite, nitrogen, phosphate rock, apatite, ocher, mineral and natural pigments, pyrites, salt, soda ash, calcite, dolomite, limestone, quartz, quartzite, sand (including calcareous and silica), slate, talc, pyrophyllite, steatite (soapstone), vermiculite, and wollastonite. In 2009, India was among the top eight leading producers of aluminum, barite, bauxite, chromium, iron ore, kyanite, manganese ore, sheet mica, steel, talc, and zinc.

Output of iron ore and concentrate totaled 245 million tons in 2009, up from 220 million tons in 2007. Iron ore reserves, estimated at 4.9 billion tons of hematite ore containing at least 55% iron, were among the largest in the world. Principal iron ore output came from the rich fields along the Bihar-Orissa border, close to all major existing iron and steel works. Smaller amounts were mined in the Bababudan Hills of Karnataka and elsewhere.

India's output of bauxite by gross weight was 14 billion tons in 2009, down from 21.2 billion tons in 2008. Bauxite deposits were estimated at 539 million tons. The state-owned National Aluminum Co. Ltd. (Nalco), which doubled its mining capacity to 4.8 million tons per year, has been privatized by the government.

Production of zinc concentrates (zinc content) in 2009 was 365,000 metric tons, up from 337,000 metric tons in 2008.

Production of smelted gold in 2009 totaled 2,800 kg, while the output of mined and smelted silver totaled 53,600 kg in that same year. Gold and silver came largely from the Kolar fields of southeastern Karnataka, where the gold mines have reached a depth of more than 3.2 km (1.9 mi) and contained reserves of 55,000 kg of gold. The Geological Survey of India outlined three new gold resources—in the Dona block, Andhra Pradesh, 4.8 million tons averaging 1.9 grams per ton of gold; in the Banswar district, Rajasthan, 7.1 million tons averaging 2.96 grams per ton of gold; and in the Ghrhar Pahar block, Sidhi district of Madhya Pradesh, 3.3 million tons averaging 1.04 grams per ton of gold.

In 2009 diamond production (gem and industrial) totaled 52,000 carats. Industrial diamond output in 2009 totaled 38,000 carats, while gem diamond output totaled 14,000 carats. In 2009 Indian diamond processors sought $4 billion from the government amid a slump in jewelry exports that forced companies to lay off workers. About 50% of the diamond processing labor force was laid off due to the 2008–09 global financial crisis.

Content of manganese in mined ore produced was 980,000 tons in 2009. Manganese deposits were estimated at 77 million tons. Manganese was mined in Andhra Pradesh, Karnataka, the Nāgpur section of Maharashtra, northward in Madhya Pradesh, along the Bihar-Orissa border adjoining the iron ore deposits, along the Maharashtra-Madhya Pradesh-Rajasthan border, and in central coastal Andhra Pradesh.

Mineral production in 2009 included: 31,000 metric tons of mined copper ore; 3.8 million tons of gross weight chromite, compared to 3.9 in 2008; 2.6 million metric tons of gypsum; and 1,800 metric tons of crude mica, up from 1,800 metric tons in 2006. The best-quality mica came from Bihar.

There were extensive workable reserves of fluorite, chromite, ilmenite (for titanium), monazite (for thorium), beach sands, magnesite, beryllium, copper, and a variety of other industrial and agricultural minerals. However, India lacked substantial reserves of some nonferrous metals and special steel ingredients.

27 ENERGY AND POWER

India's proven petroleum reserves and crude refining capacity were estimated at 5.7 billion barrels (2011) and at 2.3 million barrels per day (2009), respectively. Oil production in 2008 was estimated at 751,300 barrels per day. Oil exploration and production are undertaken in joint ventures between government and private foreign companies. In 2010, oil accounted for roughly 30% of India's energy consumption. India's natural gas reserves were estimated at 1.074 trillion cubic meters, as of December 2011.

India's recoverable coal reserves were estimated in 2008 at total 66.8 billion short tons, leading to anxieties that India could run deplete its coal reserves almost entirely by 2040.

World Bank reported in 2008 that India produced 830.1 billion kWh of electricity and consumed 645.2 billion kWh, or 543 kWh per capita. Roughly 71% of energy came from fossil fuels, while 2% came from alternative fuels. Per capita oil consumption was 545 kg.

A 380 MW nuclear power station, India's first, was completed with US assistance in 1969 at Tarapur, near Mumbai. Another nuclear station in Rajasthan began partial operations in the early 1970s, and two more plants were added by the end of the decade. In 1996, India had 10 operating reactors with a combined capacity of 1,695 MW. By 2011, India had 20 nuclear reactors with a total capacity of 4780 MW.

28 INDUSTRY

Modern industry has advanced fairly rapidly since independence. Large modern steel mills and many fertilizer plants, heavy-machinery plants, oil refineries, locomotive and automotive works have been constructed; the metallurgical, chemical, cement, and oil-refining industries have also expanded. Moreover, India has established its role in the high-value-added sectors of the "new economy"—information technology (IT), computer hardware, computer software, media, and entertainment. Nine states (Maharashtra, West Bengal, Tamil Nadu, Gujarat, Uttar Pradesh, Bihar, Andhra Pradesh, Karnataka, and Madhya Pradesh) together account for most of Indian industry.

Industrial production expanded at an average annual rate of 5–6% between 1970 and 1990. Enforced austerity and demand management measures taken to stabilize rapidly worsening macroeconomic imbalances in 1991–92 slowed growth in the industry sector to 0% for that year. In 1995–96, the industrial growth rate jumped 11.7%, led by a 13% increase in manufacturing output, the highest in 25 years. A rebound evidenced in 6.6% growth in 1999–2000 was cut short by the global economic slowdown in 2001. The industrial production growth rate stood at 7.4% in 2004, and had climbed to 11.7% by June 2005. The industrial growth rate was 7.7% in 2010.

Under the planned development regime of past decades, government directives channeled much of the country's resources into public enterprises. Private investment was closely regulated for all industries, discouraging investors from formal entry into the sector. However, industrial policy has shifted towards privatization and deregulation. Since 1991 government licensing requirements have been abolished for all but a few "controlled areas": distillation and brewing of alcoholic drinks, cigars and cigarettes, defense equipment, industrial explosives, hazardous chemicals, and drugs and pharmaceuticals. Under the government disinvestment program announced at the end of 1999, only three sectors remain closed to private investment: defense, atomic energy, and railway transport. Credit and capital markets have also been greatly liberalized.

Textile production dominates the industrial field. On a broad level, the textile sector can be divided between the natural fiber segment (cotton, silk, wool, jute, etc.) and the man-made fiber segment (polyester filament yarn, blended yarns, etc.). In terms of operations, since the 1980s decentralized powerlooms have produced an increasingly large share of production as centralized mills have declined. In 1986, there were about 638,000 decentralized powerlooms in operation, and by 2008 these had increased 260% to about 1.9 million. Mumbai, Ahmadābad, and the provincial cities in southern India lead in cotton milling. Jute milling is localized at Calcutta, center of the jute agricultural area. In 2010 textile exports topped $20 billion despite a global recession.

India was the world's fifth-largest steel producer as of 2010, with a total output of 66.8 million tons. The industry consists of seven large integrated mills and about 180 mini steel plants. An Indian company, Mittal Steel, is among the largest steel-producing companies in the world. The metallurgical sector also produced 1.32 tons of aluminum products in 2010.

Automobile production, fed by both the steel and aluminum industries, has grown since liberalization in 1993, propelled by low interest rates, the expansion of consumer finance, and strong export demand. About 90% of vehicles produced are economy cars, and 10% are luxury cars and SUVs. In September 2009, US automakers General Motors (GM) and Ford each announced major investment projects in cooperation with the Indian auto industry.

In the field of computers and consumer electronics, production has been boosted by the liberalization of technology and component imports. The electronics market in India was worth $45 billion in 2010, and was projected to be the fastest-growing electronics market in several succeeding years.

In the petrochemical sector, India has a total refinery capacity of more than two million barrels per day. Almost half of India's refinery capacity has been built since 1998. The government's goal is to be self-sufficient in refined petroleum products. India's total refinery capacity should be able to meet domestic demand, but because of operational problems, it still has to import diesel fuel.

India's cement industry is the second-largest in the world, after China, with an installed capacity of some 209 million tons in 2009. That year India produced 178 million tons, only 3 million of which were for export. However, government financed infrastructure projects have also helped sparked a significant growth in construction.

India's fertilizer industry is one of the largest in the world and central to its efforts to increase agricultural productivity.

29 SCIENCE AND TECHNOLOGY

In 2010, India's total expenditures on research and development (R and D) amounted to 0.8% of GDP. Allocations are divided among government and industry, with government providing the major share. In 2009, the value of India's high technology exports totaled $10.14 billion. There has been a marked growth in the training of engineers and technicians. Patent applications as of 2008, according to the World Bank, totaled 36,812 in India.

Among the technological higher schools are the Indian Institute of Science at Bangalore and the Indian Institutes of Technology at Mumbai, Delhi, Kānpur, Kharagpur, and Chennai. One of the primary science and technology issues facing India is a "brain drain." Indian students often seek science and engineering degrees in the United States. Such an exodus reduced the quality of science and engineering education in India.

There are more than 2,500 national research and development institutions connected with science and technology in India. Principal government agencies engaged in scientific research and technical development are the Ministry of Science and Technology, the Council of Scientific and Industrial Research, the Ministry of Atomic Energy, and the Ministry of Electronics. The Council for Scientific and Industrial Research (founded in 1942) has dozens of national laboratories under its umbrella.

An importer of nuclear technology since the 1960s, India tested its own underground nuclear device for the first time in 1974 at Pokhran, in Rajasthan. In May 1996, India once again performed nuclear tests, dropping three bombs into 700-foot-deep shafts in the desert at Pokhran, with an impact of 80 kilotons. Pakistan responded later the same month with tests of its own. The first Indian-built nuclear power plant, with two 235-MW heavy-water reactors, began operating in July 1983.

The country's largest scientific establishment is the Bhabha Atomic Research Center at Trombay, near Mumbai, which has several nuclear research reactors and trains more than 100 nuclear scientists each year. In the area of space technology, India's first communications satellite, *Aryabhata,* was launched into orbit by the former USSR on 19 April 1975, and two additional satellites were orbited by Soviet rockets in 1979 and 1981. The Indian Space Research Organization constructed and launched India's first satellite-launching vehicle, the SLV-3, from its Vikram Sarabhai Space Center at Sriharikota on 18 July 1980. Indian-built telecommunications satellites have been launched into orbit from Cape Canaveral, Florida, by the US National Aeronautics and Space Administration, by the European Space Agency, and from French Guiana. India has established a satellite-tracking station at Kavalur, in Tamil Nadu. In 1984, the first Indo-Soviet manned mission was completed successfully; in 1985, two Indians were selected for an Indo-US joint shuttle flight.

Major learned societies in the country are the Indian Academy of Sciences (founded in 1934 in Bangalore), the Indian National Science Academy (founded in 1935 in New Delhi), and the National Academy of Sciences (founded in 1930 in Allahābād).

30 DOMESTIC TRADE

India is estimated to have more than 12 million retail outlets, most of which are small, family-owned or operated businesses. In the country's big cities some retailers will provide credit and home delivery. Retail outlets are often highly specialized in product and usually very small in quarters and total stock. Often the Indian retail shop is large enough to hold only the proprietor and a small selection of stock; shutters fronting the store are opened to allow customers to negotiate from the street or sidewalk. In most retail shops, fixed prices are rare and bargaining is the accepted means of purchase. Some department stores and supermarkets have begun to appear in shopping centers in major cities. These shopping centers usually offer entertainment and leisure activities as well. India's retail market size was estimated at $401 billion in 2010.

India's domestic trade is also characterized by a large, unorganized black market, and an informal gray market. The black market deals in a vast array of smuggled goods, such as food items, gold, computer parts, and cellular telephones. Merchants selling on the black market generally offer lower prices for the same commodities than would be found in the organized sector because they pay no taxes or tariffs, and sales are strictly on a cash basis. The gray market involves the sale of goods and services before they become legally available. This can include new shares of stock not yet available on the stock exchange.

Franchising is rapidly growing in India, the result of an equally rapid growth in the spending power of a large segment of the nation's population. However, franchising is not new to India, having operated in the country for several decades. Overall, India's franchising sector is evolving, and spans a diverse range of products and services such as education, food, health, apparel, entertainment, and fitness.

Direct marketing or selling is one of the fastest growing business sectors in India. According to the Indian Direct Selling Association, the country's direct selling industry reported a turnover of $915 million in fiscal year 2009/10. As of 2010, the direct selling industry in India employed over 3 million people.

Electronic commerce (e-commerce) is growing rapidly in India, fueled by an increasing number of Internet users and the declining cost of Internet access. According to the Internet and Mobile Association of India, the e-commerce market in 2009 was estimated at $300 million.

Government and business office hours are generally from 9:30 a.m. to 5:30 p.m., Monday through Friday, with a lunch break from 1 to 2 p.m. However, business offices may be open on Saturdays from 9:30 a.m. to 2 p.m. Shops are generally open from 9 a.m. to 7 p.m., Mondays through Saturdays. Normal banking hours are from 10 a.m. to 3 p.m. on weekdays and from 10 a.m. to 1 p.m. on Saturdays.

Principal Trading Partners – India (2010)

(In millions of US dollars)

Country	Total	Exports	Imports	Balance
World	552,048.0	222,883.0	329,165.0	-106,282.0
China	55,576.0	17,415.0	38,161.0	-20,746.0
United Arab Emirates	55,388.0	29,455.0	25,933.0	3,522.0
United States	40,481.0	23,696.0	16,785.0	6,911.0
Sa'udi Arabia	24,562.0	4,503.0	20,059.0	-15,556.0
Switzerland	19,628.0	622.0	19,006.0	-18,384.0
Germany	16,863.0	6,012.0	10,851.0	-4,839.0
Hong Kong	16,454.0	9,542.0	6,912.0	2,630.0
Singapore	15,938.0	9,107.0	6,831.0	2,276.0
Indonesia	13,789.0	4,579.0	9,210.0	-4,631.0
Iran	13,429.0	2,522.0	10,907.0	-8,385.0

(…) data not available or not significant.

(n.s.) not specified.

SOURCE: *2011 Direction of Trade Statistics Yearbook*, New York: United Nations, 2011.

31 FOREIGN TRADE

Initially, India's foreign trade followed a pattern common to all underdeveloped countries: exporting raw materials and food in exchange for manufactured goods. The only difference in India's case was that it also exported processed textiles, yarn, and jute goods. Until the late 1980s, the government's strongly import substitution-oriented industrial policy limited the significance of exports for the Indian economy. Stabilization and structural adjustment measures taken in 1991, including a 50% currency devaluation, improved the country's balance of trade position by depressing imports and making exports more competitive in the world market.

India imported $327 billion worth of goods and services in 2008, while exporting $201 billion worth of goods and services. Major import partners in 2009 were China, 11.2%; United States, 6.5%; United Arab Emirates, 6%; Saudi Arabia, 5.7%; Australia, 4.2%; Germany, 4.2%; and Iran, 4.1%. Its major export partners were United Arab Emirates, 12.5%; United States, 11.1%; China, 6.1%; Hong Kong, 4.2%; and Singapore, 4.1%.

In percentage terms, India's primary exports in 2010 were engineering goods; gems and jewelry; and textiles and garments. Major imports were petroleum and petroleum products, capital goods, and electronic goods.

In August 2009, India signed a trade deal with ASEAN to reduce and eventually eliminate tariffs on such goods as electronics, chemicals, machinery, and textiles—products that account for about 80% of the goods traded between India and ASEAN countries. Over 450 products are specifically excluded from the deal, including computer software. In January 2010, as a free trade agreement between India and South Korea took effect, the nations agreed to upgrade their relationship to a "strategic partnership." In the first four months of 2010, trade between the nations rose 70% compared to the same period in 2009.

32 BALANCE OF PAYMENTS

By November 1993, India's foreign exchange reserves had risen to $8.1 billion, the highest level since 1951. A substantial reduction in the trade deficit, increased inflows from foreign institutional investors, a stable exchange rate, and improved remittances all contributed in the growth of reserves. Although export growth remained strong, the current account deficit tripled from 1993–94 to 1995–96. The increase was attributed to a continuing surge in imports and higher debt service requirements. However, between 1995 and 1998 the current account deficit shrank to about 1% of GDP due to increased textile exports and a liberalizing trade regime. India's total external debt in 2001 was estimated at $100.6 billion, and at $117.2 billion in 2004. High international oil prices and strong domestic demand widened the merchandise trade deficit over the period 2006–08, but strong surpluses on services and transfers (remittances) lessened the deficit in the current-account. The global economic downturn of 2009 has negatively influenced India's current account, which grew to a $14.4 billion deficit in the second quarter of 2011. In 2010 India had a foreign trade deficit of $69 billion, amounting to 4.9% of GDP.

33 BANKING AND SECURITIES

A well-established banking system exists in India as a result of British colonialism. The Reserve Bank of India, founded in 1935 and nationalized in 1949, is the central banking and note-issuing authority. The Reserve Bank funds the Deposit Insurance and Credit Guarantee Corporation, which provides deposit insurance coverage to the banking sector. The Reserve Bank is also responsible for carrying out monetary policy, acts as a regulator and supervisor of the nation's financial system, manages the nation's foreign exchange reserves, grants licenses for branch operations, and acts as banker to the central and state governments. Most regional offices are in state capitals. In 2010, the discount rate, the interest rate at which the central bank lends to financial institutions in the short term, was 5.5%.

India's extensive banking system operates in both urban and rural areas. It is also a three-tiered system that consists of scheduled

Balance of Payments – India (2010)

(In millions of US dollars)

Current Account		**-51,781.0**
Balance on goods		-97,934.0
Imports	-323,435.0	
Exports	225,502.0	
Balance on services		6,920.0
Balance on income		-12,926.0
Current transfers		52,157.0
Capital Account		**-1.0**
Financial Account		**68,537.0**
Direct investment abroad		-13,151.0
Direct investment in India		24,159.0
Portfolio investment assets		-1,110.0
Portfolio investment liabilities		39,972.0
Financial derivatives		…
Other investment assets		-13,661.0
Other investment liabilities		32,328.0
Net Errors and Omissions		**-15,789.0**
Reserves and Related Items		**-966.0**

(…) data not available or not significant.

SOURCE: *Balance of Payment Statistics Yearbook 2011*, Washington, DC: International Monetary Fund, 2011.

commercial banks, regional rural banks, and cooperative and special purpose rural banks. Foreign banks are located in the nation's larger metropolitan areas. Over 100 branches of Indian commercial banks operate overseas as well, primarily in the United Kingdom, United States, Fiji, Mauritius, Hong Kong, and Singapore. As of 2011, there were over 40 foreign banks in India.

The main stock exchanges are located in Calcutta, Mumbai and Chennai, and there are secondary exchanges in Ahmadābad, Delhi, Kānpur, Nāgpur, and other cities. The Securities and Exchange Board of India supplies regulation of the stock market. Rules favor exchange members rather than public protection or benefit. Brokerage and jobbing are commonly combined. Of India's 21 stock exchanges, the Mumbai Stock Exchange (BSE) and National Stock Exchange (NSE) are the most important. There were 5,085 companies listed on the BSE as of 2011. Total market capitalization on the BSE's listed companies that year totaled $1.63 trillion. The NSE, however, is perceived as more transparent, has faster trading cycles, more timely settlements, and is in the process of setting up a share depository. Major efforts have been made to strengthen the stock market institutionally and make it less like a casino.

34 INSURANCE

The life insurance business was formally nationalized on 1 September 1956 by the establishment of the Life Insurance Corp. of India (LIC), which absorbed the life insurance business of 245 Indian and foreign companies. The general insurance business was nationalized as of 1 January 1973, and all nationalized general insurance companies were merged into the General Insurance Corp. (GIC) of India. In 1997, despite repeated promises to allow private insurers into the industry, an announcement on privatization in the financial services sector was postponed in the face of institutional resistance. The unions and left-wing parties led a struggle to stop an opening up of the insurance sector. They were alarmed by government plans to introduce legislation that would set up an independent Insurance Regulatory and Development Authority (IRA). Under the Insurance Regulatory and Development Authority Act of 1999, the IRA finally gained the power to issue licenses to private insurance companies in 2000 to Indians and foreigners. In India, third-party auto liability, public liability for hazardous material handling, workers' compensation, and third-party liability for inland water vessels are all compulsory.

35 PUBLIC FINANCE

The government's financial year extends from 1 April to 31 March, and the budget is presented to the parliament on the last day of February. The executive branch has considerable control over public finance. Thus, while parliament can oversee and investigate public expenditures and may reduce the budget, it cannot expand the budget, and checks exist that prevent it from delaying passage. Budgets in recent decades have reflected the needs of rapid economic development under rising expenditures of the five-year plans. Insufficient government receipts for financing this development have led to yearly deficits and a resulting increase of new tax measures and deficit financing.

Principal sources of government revenue are customs and excise duties and individual and corporate income taxes. Major items of expenditure are defense, grants to states and territories, interest payments on the national debt, and economic, social, and community services. In 2010 the budget of India included $170.7 billion in public revenue and $268 billion in public expenditures. The budget deficit amounted to 5.5% of GDP. Public debt was 55.9% of GDP, with $238 billion of the debt held by foreign entities.

Public Finance – India (2009)

(In billions of rupees, central government figures)

Revenue and Grants	**7,796.4**	**100.0%**
Tax revenue	6,410.8	82.2%
Social contributions	14.9	0.2%
Grants	21.4	0.3%
Other revenue	1,349.4	17.3%
Expenditures	**10,999.3**	**100.0%**
General public services	...	...
Defense	1,414.9	12.9%
Public order and safety	...	...
Economic affairs	2,131.6	19.4%
Environmental protection	...	...
Housing and community amenities	907.6	8.3%
Health	207.8	1.9%
Recreational, culture, and religion	...	...
Education	316.2	2.9%
Social protection	...	...

(…) data not available or not significant.

SOURCE: *Government Finance Statistics Yearbook 2010,* Washington, DC: International Monetary Fund, 2010.

36 TAXATION

Taxes are levied by the central government, the state governments, and the various municipal governments. The sources of central government tax revenue are union excise duties, the central value-added tax or CENVAT, corporate and personal income (nonagricultural) taxes, wealth taxes, and customs duties. The gift tax was abolished in January 1998. State government sources, in general order of importance, are land taxes, sales taxes, excise duties, and registration and stamp duties. The states also share in central government income tax revenues and union excise duties; and they receive all revenues from the wealth tax on agricultural property. Municipal governments levy land and other property taxes and license fees. Many also impose duties on goods entering the municipal limits. There is little uniformity in types or rates of state and municipal taxes.

Corporate income tax for domestic companies as of 2011 is 30%. The wealth tax is 1% of wealth exceeding INR3,000,000 ($58,000). Interest income is taxed at 10% to both foreign and resident companies; capital gains (short term only) are taxed at 15%. Dividends are taxed at 16.99%. The central government imposes a 12.5% value-added tax (VAT) called the CENVAT. However, lower rates of 4%, 1% and 0% are also levied on domestically manufactured goods.

37 CUSTOMS AND DUTIES

The majority of imports and some exports are subject to tariffs. There are both revenue and protective tariffs, although the former are more important and have long been a major source of central government income. The Indian government has been steadily reducing tariff rates in order to increase trade and investment. However, India's tariffs are still among the highest in the world. Additional, special duties can more than double the barriers to importing a product, including textiles and apparel. Gold is taxed at an added rate of 9% at the state level and at least an added 3% at the local level. Indians spend more money on gold than anything but oil. India's 28 states also impose duties on products coming in from other states.

38 FOREIGN INVESTMENT

Historically, foreign investment was closely regulated. Rules and incentives directed the flow of foreign capital mainly toward consumer industries and light engineering, with major capital-intensive projects reserved for the public sector. Under the Foreign Exchange Regulation Act of 1973, which went into effect on 1 January 1974, all branches of foreign companies in which non-resident interest exceeded 40% were required to reapply for permission to carry on business; most companies had reduced their holdings to no more than 40% by 1 January 1976. Certain key export-oriented or technology-intensive industries were permitted to maintain up to 100% nonresident ownership. Tea plantations were also exempted from the 40% requirement. Although the government officially welcomed private foreign investment, collaboration and royalty arrangements were tightly controlled. Government reform measures in mid-1991 changed this picture significantly. Under the New Industrial Policy, the amount of money invested in the country doubled annually from 1991 to 1995. In 1997 the New Exploration and Licensing Policy (NELP) was announced, permitting the participation of foreign oil companies in upstream exploration and development of oil and gas resources. Effective 1 April 2001, imports of crude oil and petroleum products were liberalized, with state-run enterprises losing their exclusive right to import certain petroleum products for domestic consumption. Also in 2001, India removed quantitative restrictions (QRs) from 715 items (147 agricultural products, 342 textile items, and 226 manufactured goods, including automobiles) in compliance with WTO standards. Under the New Industrial Policy as amended, most sectors have been opened for 100% foreign investment. Sectors such as banking, telecommunications, and print media are still restricted. In the early 2000s, the required approval by the Reserve Bank of India was removed from enterprises falling within categories allowing 100% foreign investment. Foreign direct investment (FDI) in India was a net inflow of $34.6 billion according to World Bank figures published in 2009. FDI represented 2.51% of GDP.

India has eight export processing zones (EPZs) designed to provide internationally competitive infrastructure and duty-free, low-cost facilities for exporters. Foreign investors in some industries can operate in EPZs, export oriented units (EOUs), special economic zones (SEZs) and Software Technology Parks of India (STPIs). SEZs are regarded as foreign territory for purposes of duties and taxes and sector caps that limit foreign direct investment (FDI) in different industries do not apply in the SEZs.

39 ECONOMIC DEVELOPMENT

The first five-year plan (1951–56) accorded top priority to agriculture, especially irrigation and power projects. The second plan (1956–61) was designed to implement the new industrial policy and to achieve a "socialist pattern of society." The plan stressed rapid industrialization, a 25% increase in national income (in fact, the achieved increase was only 20%), and reduction of inequalities in wealth and income. The focus of the third plan (1961–66) was industrialization, with 24.6% spent on transportation and communications and 20.1% on industry and minerals. Drought, inflation, and war with Pakistan made this plan a major disappointment; although considerable industrial diversification was achieved and national income rose, per capita income did not increase (because of population growth), and harvests were disastrously low. Because of the unsettled domestic situation, the fourth five-year plan did not take effect until 1969. The 1969–74 plan sought to control fluctuations in agricultural output and to promote equality and social justice. Agriculture and allied sectors received 16.9%, more than in any previous plan, while industry and minerals received 18.5%, transportation and communications 18.4%, and power development 17.8%, also more than in any previous plan.

The fifth plan (1974–79) aimed at the removal of poverty and the attainment of self-reliance. A total outlay of INR393.2 billion was allocated (26% less than originally envisaged), and actual expenditures totaled INR394.2 billion. Once again, the emphasis was on industry, with mining and manufacturing taking 22.5%, electric power 18.7%, transportation and communications 17.2%, and agriculture 12.1%. The fifth plan was cut short a year early, in 1978, and, with India enmeshed in recession and political turmoil, work began on the sixth development plan (1980–85). Its goal, like that of the fifth, was the removal of poverty, although the planners recognized that this gigantic task could not be accomplished within five years. The plan aimed to strengthen the agricultural and industrial infrastructure in order to accelerate the growth of investments and exports. Projected outlays totaled INR975 billion, of which electric power received 27.1%, industry and mining 15.4%, transportation and communications 12.7%, and agriculture 12.2%. The main target was a GDP growth rate of 5.2% annually. The seventh development plan (1985–90) projected 5% overall GDP growth (which was largely achieved and even exceeded) based on increases of 4% and 8% in agricultural and industrial output, respectively. Outlays were to total INR1.8 trillion.

The eighth development plan (for 1992–97), drafted in response to the country's looming debt crisis in 1990–91, laid the groundwork for long-term structural adjustment. The plan's overall thrust was to stimulate industrial growth by the private sector, and thereby free government resources for greater investment in basic infrastructure and human resources development. In addition to liberalized conditions for private and foreign investment, the foreign exchange system was reformed, the currency devalued, the maximum tariff reduced from 350% to 85%, import barriers generally loosened, and those for key intermediate goods removed altogether. Reform of the tax system, reduction of subsidies, and restructuring of public enterprises were also targeted. While the eighth plan generally supported expansion of private enterprise, unlike structural adjustment programs in other developing countries, it did not stipulate a large-scale privatization of the public sector. As the eighth plan came to an end in 1997, most analysts proclaimed it a success; economic growth averaged 6% a year, employment rose, poverty was reduced, exports increased, and inflation declined.

The ninth development plan (1997–2002) focused on the redistribution of wealth and alleviation of poverty, the further privatization of the economy and attraction of foreign investment, and the reduction of the deficit. Overall, there were improvements in the reform era including an increase in the GDP growth rate from an average of about 5.7% to about 6.1% in the eighth and ninth plan periods, a reduction of the percent in poverty from one-third of the population to one-fourth, increased literacy from 52% in 1991 to 65% in 2001, and India's emergence as a competitor in state-of-the-art technologies of the new information age economy. However, persistent inefficiencies—unemployment and underemployment, and welfare deficiencies.

In the tenth five-year plan, 2002–07, the government focused on accelerating economic growth. Agricultural development was viewed as the core element of the tenth plan with attention to sectors most likely to create employment opportunities. These included agriculture in its extended sense, construction, tourism, transport, small-scale industries (SSI), retailing, IT, and communications enabling services. Industrial policy included continued emphasis on privatization and deregulation.

The eleventh five year plan, 2007–12, set out the ambitious goal of doubling per capita income by 2016 while maintaining a growth rate of 8–10%. It had numerous other social goals as well, including an improvement in literacy rates and education, a reduction in infant mortality to 28, providing electricity to all villages 24 hours per day, providing broadband technology to all villages, the creation of 70 million new jobs, treating urban waste-water, increasing forest and tree cover by 5%, and the particularly ambitious goal of making clean drinking water available to all Indians.

40 SOCIAL DEVELOPMENT

An employees' provident fund was established in 1954. In 2004, a voluntary old age, disability, and survivor benefit scheme was implemented for some low-income employees and self-employed persons. Contributions are income related and at a flat rate. Provident fund old-age benefits are available at age 55, or at any age if the worker is leaving the country permanently. Workmen's compensation was first enacted in 1923. It provides coverage to lower income employees working for establishment with more than 10 employees. State governments arrange for the provisions of medical care for workers. Labor laws require employers to provide severance pay in certain situations.

The program for old age, disability, and death benefits are covered by a provident fund with deposit linked insurance for industrial workers in 177 categories. The system is partially funded by insured persons and employers, with a small pension scheme subsidized by the government. There is a social insurance system covering sickness and maternity as well as work injury. The law requires employers to pay a severance indemnity of 15 days pay for each year of employment.

Domestic violence is commonplace. Wife murder, usually referred to as "dowry death," is still evident. Although the law prohibits discrimination in the workplace, women are paid less than men in both rural and urban areas. Discrimination exists in access to employment, credit, and in family and property law. Laws aimed at preventing employment discrimination, female bondage and prostitution, and the *sati* (widow burning), are not always enforced. India is a significant source and destination for thousands of trafficked women. Not only does the male population exceed that of females, but India is also one of the few countries where men, on the average, live longer than women. To explain this anomaly, it has been suggested that daughters are more likely to be malnourished and to be provided with fewer healthcare services. Female infanticide and feticide is a problem in a society that values sons over daughters. It is estimated there are nearly 500,000 children living and working on the streets.

Human rights abuses, including incommunicado detention, are particularly acute in Kashmir, where separatist violence has flared. Although constitutional and statutory safeguards are in place, serious abuses still occur, including extrajudicial killings, abuse of detainees, and poor prison conditions. Despite efforts to eliminate discrimination based on the longstanding caste system, the practice remains unchanged. Prison conditions are harsh, and the judicial system is severely overloaded.

41 HEALTH

According to the CIA, life expectancy in India was 64 years in 2011. Great improvements have taken place in public health since independence. The country spent 4.2% of its GDP on healthcare, amounting to $45 per person. Yet the general health picture remained far from satisfactory. The government has paid increasing attention to integrated health, maternity, and child care in rural areas. An increasing number of community health workers and doctors are being sent to rural health centers. Primary healthcare is provided to the rural population through a network of over 150,000 primary health centers and sub-centers that are staffed by trained midwives and health guides.

In 2009 there were 6 physicians, 13 nurses and midwives, and 9 hospital beds per 10,000 inhabitants. There are also numerous herb compounders, along with thousands of registered practitioners following the Ayurvedic (ancient Hindu) and Unani systems.

India has modern medical colleges, dental colleges, colleges of nursing, and nursing schools. More than 100 colleges and schools teach the indigenous Ayurvedic and Unani systems of medicine and 74 teach homeopathy. New drugs and pharmaceutical plants, some assisted by the UN and some established by European and American firms, manufacture antibiotics, vaccines, germicides, and fungicides. However, patent medicines and other reputed curatives of dubious value are still widely marketed and used.

A short-term multi-drug therapy launched in India led to a dramatic fall in the leprosy prevalence. Smallpox was eradicated through a massive vaccination program. Many other diseases remain, especially deficiency diseases such as goiter, kwashiorkor, rickets, and beriberi. There is a national system to distribute vitamin A capsules to children because a lack of this vitamin contributes to blindness and malnutrition. Hypertension is a major health problem in India.

The HIV/AIDS adult prevalence rate was 0.3 percent in 2009.

42 HOUSING

Though progress has been made toward improving the generally primitive housing in which most Indians live, there are still some deficits in housing supply and access to basic utilities. A number of subsidized, low-cost housing schemes have been launched by the government, but the goal of providing a house for every homeless family cannot be met because of the prohibitive cost. The eleventh five-year plan established the ambitious goal of providing space for housing to all Indians by the end of 2012.

According to the 2011 national census, there were about 330,835,767 residential dwelling units nationwide. About 53% were considered to be in "good" condition and 41% were described as "livable." Many rural dwellings are constructed of mud brick or burnt brick walls with mud floors and a thatched or tiled roof. Urban dwellings are made from concrete or burnt brick. Only about 51.6% of all residential dwellings were considered to be permanent structures. About 44% of all households had drinking water within their premises. About 67% of dwellings had access to electricity. Only about 47% of all dwellings had bathroom facilities within the house.

43 EDUCATION

In 1986, the National Education Policy (NPE) was adopted in order to bring about major reforms in the system, primarily universalization of primary education. In 1988, a national literacy mission was launched, following which states, like Kerala and Pondicherry, achieved 100% literacy. The 2001 census estimated India's literacy rate at 61%. In 2008 the World Bank estimated that 91% of age-eligible children in India were enrolled in primary school. Tertiary enrollment was estimated at 13%. Public expenditure on education represented 6% of GDP. In August 2009, the Indian parliament passed a major education bill to provide free and compulsory education for all children between the ages of 6 and 14. Under the terms of the law, the government must establish numerous state-run neighborhood schools, including special schools for students with disabilities. Private schools were expected to reserve at least 25% of their enrollment for children from low-income families. Schools could no longer impose fees on parents in order to reserve a spot in the school, which had been a common practice. The law also ended some of the highly selective admission practices that had been common in many schools, thus ensuring admission for a larger number of students from a wider variety of backgrounds.

In the Indian school system, eight years of basic education are divided into three stages of lower primary school (five years), middle school (three years), and secondary school (two years). Following this, students may choose to attend a two-year senior secondary school or a three-year vocational school. The academic year runs from July to April.

India's system of higher education is still basically British in structure and approach. The university system is second in size only to that of the United States, with 150 universities and over 5,000 colleges and higher-level institutions. Educational standards are constantly improving and especially in the area of science and mathematics in which standards are as high as those found anywhere in the world. The older universities are in Calcutta, Mumbai, and Chennai, all established in 1857; Allahābād, 1877; Banares Hindu (in Varanasi) and Mysore (now Karnataka), both in 1916; Hyderābād (Osmania University), in 1918; and Aligarh and Lucknow, both in 1921. Most universities have attached and affiliated undergraduate colleges, some of which are in distant towns. In addition to universities, there are some 3,500 arts and sciences colleges (excluding research institutes) and commercial colleges, as well as 1,500 other training schools and colleges. The autonomous University Grants Commission promotes university education

and maintains standards in teaching and research. Many college students receive scholarships and stipends.

44 LIBRARIES AND MUSEUMS

The National Library in Calcutta, with over 22 million books and numerous other items, is by far the largest in the country. Some of the other leading libraries are the New Delhi Public Library (1.4 million volumes), the Central Secretariat Library in New Delhi (700,000 volumes), and the libraries of some of the larger universities. The Khuda Baksh Oriental Library in Patna, with a collection of rare manuscripts in Arabic, Urdu, and Farsi, is one of 10 libraries declared "institutions of national importance" by an act of parliament. The National Archives of India, in New Delhi, is the largest repository of documents in Asia, with 25 km (16 mi) of shelf space. There is an extensive public library system as well as cultural and religious institutions and libraries throughout the country.

Noted botanical gardens are located in Calcutta, Mumbai, Lucknow, Ootacamund, Bangalore, Chennai, and Darjeeling, and well-stocked zoological gardens are found in Calcutta, Mumbai, Chennai, Trivandrum, Hyderābād, Karnataka, and Jodhpur. Most of India's hundreds of museums specialize in one or several aspects of Indian or South Asian culture; these include 25 archaeological museums at ancient sites, such as Konarak, Amravati, and Sarnath. Some of the more important museums are the Indian Museum in Calcutta, the Prince of Wales Museum of Western India in Mumbai, and the National Museum and the National Gallery of Modern Art, both in New Delhi.

There are also municipal museums throughout the country and dozens of museums and galleries devoted to prominent South Asian artists. There are science museums in Bhopal, Calcutta, Mumbai, and New Delhi. Bhavongor houses the Gandhi Museum, one of several sites devoted to the history of the national hero. In 2001 the Broadcasting Museum was founded in Delhi. There also are thousands of architectural masterpieces of antiquity—the palaces, temples, mausoleums, fortresses, mosques, formal gardens, deserted cities, and rock-hewn monasteries—found in every section of the subcontinent.

45 MEDIA

India's telecommunications system has seen rapid growth take place, the result of deregulation and the liberalization of telecommunications laws and policies. While all regions of the country have access to local and long distance service, these services are largely concentrated in urban areas, although steady improvement is taking place. Nationally, telephone density remains low, with the lowest density found in rural areas. The fastest growth is in cellular service, with only modest growth in fixed lines. In 2010, there were some 35.7 million main phone lines and 670 million mobile cellular phones in use nationwide. Mobile phone subscriptions averaged 45 per 100 people in 2009.

All-India Radio (AIR), government owned, operates transmission through over 100 stations and broadcasts in all major languages and dialects for home consumption. AIR also operates external services in 24 foreign and 36 Indian languages. There are also privately licensed radio stations. In 2009, there were 153 FM radio stations, 91 AM radio stations, and 68 shortwave radio stations. In 1959, India's first television station was inaugurated in

Delhi, and color television broadcasting was inaugurated in 1982. Cable and satellite stations have fairly large audiences.

In 2010 the country had about 4.5 million Internet hosts. Internet users numbered 5 per 100 citizens.

While Hindi continues to be the official language in India, English has grown increasingly important and often overrides the national language. In 2011, it was reported that almost all Mumbai films had made the transition to English, including popular Hindi songs from their soundtracks. India has a thriving film industry, centered at Mumbai, Chennai, Calcutta, and Bangalore. Indians are avid film-goers.

The first newspaper in India, an English-language weekly issued in Calcutta in 1780, was followed by English-language papers in other cities. The first Indian-language newspaper (in Hindi) appeared in Varanasi (Benares) in 1845. There are hundreds of newspapers in circulation throughout the country, published in some 85 languages, primarily Hindi, English, Bengali, Urdu, and Marathi. The majority of Indian newspapers are under individual ownership and have small circulations. Prominent newspapers in 2010, with circulation numbers listed parenthetically, included the *Times of India* (4,100,000), *Gujarat Samachar* (1,542,115), and *Malayala Manorama* (1,761,000), as well as over 200 other major newspapers.

Freedom of the press has been nominally ensured by liberal court interpretations of the constitution, but the government has long held the right to impose "reasonable restrictions" in the interest of "public order, state security, decency, and morality." On a day-to-day basis, the press is essentially unfettered, and news magazines abound in addition to the newspapers.

46 ORGANIZATIONS

There are many political, commercial, industrial, and labor organizations, and rural cooperatives. Almost all commercial and industrial centers have chambers of commerce. The Center of Indian Trade Unions and All India Trade Union Congress are umbrella organizations representing the rights of worker's. There are unions for more specialized trades and fields as well, such as the Silk Association of India. There are a number of scholarly and professional societies and associations focused on education and research in various scientific and medical fields, including the national Indian Medical Association. There are also several associations dedicated to research and education for specific fields of medicine and particular diseases and conditions. The Indian Academy of Sciences was established in 1934 to promote research and education in a variety of branches of pure and applied sciences. The Indian National Science Academy similarly promotes public interest in science.

Cultural activities, especially traditional arts and crafts, are promoted throughout India by the National Academy of Fine Arts; the National Academy of Music, Dance, and Drama; the National Center for the Performing Arts; and the National Academy of Letters. Other state organizations for the furthering of cultural activities include the Ministry of Information and Broadcasting, the Indian Council for Cultural Relations, and the National Book Trust. There are a great many private cultural and institutional organizations based on religion and philosophy, language (including Sanskrit and Pali), drama, music and dancing, modern writing, the classics, and painting and sculpture.

Notable national youth organizations include the All India Students Federation, Girl Guides and Scouts of India, Indian National Youth Organization, National Council of YMCA's of India, Service Civil-Youth Volunteers of India, Student Christian Movement of India, Junior Chamber, Student Federation of India, the Bharat Scouts and Guides, Tibetan Youth Congress, UN Youth Organization of India, and Young Catholic Students of India. National women's organizations include All India Women's Conference, Women's Equal Rights Group, and Women's Protection League.

There are several national and local organizations and associations dedicated to providing assistance and services to the poor, disadvantaged, and marginalized, such as the Karnataka Welfare Society and Andhra Mahila Sabha. There are a wide variety of international organizations with chapters in India, including Christian Children's Fund, CARE, Caritas, Defence for Children International, Habitat for Humanity, the Red Cross, Amnesty International, Kiwanis, and Lion's Clubs. The International Health Organization has an office in New Delhi.

47 TOURISM, TRAVEL, AND RECREATION

The national Department of Tourism maintains tourist information offices at home and abroad. It has constructed many facilities for viewing wildlife in forest regions, by minibus, boat, or elephant; and operates tourist lodges in wildlife sanctuaries. The principal tourist attractions are India's distinctive music, dance, theater, festivals, and cuisines; the great cities of Calcutta, Mumbai, and Chennai; and such monuments as the Red Fort and Jama Masjid mosque in Delhi, the Taj Mahal at Agra, and the Amber Palace in Jaipur. Tourists and pilgrims also flock to the sacred Ganges River, the Ajanta temple caves, the temple at Bodhgaya where the Buddha is said to have achieved enlightenment, and many other ancient temples and tombs throughout the country.

The big-game hunting for which India was once famous is now banned, but excellent fishing is available. There are also many golf courses. Cricket, field hockey, polo, football (soccer), volleyball, and basketball are all popular, as are pony-trekking in the hill stations and skiing in northern India.

In 2010 three Indian performing art forms were officially inscribed on the UNESCO Representative List of the Intangible Heritage of Humanity, an offshoot of the World Heritage program. The Miudiyettu, a ritual dance drama performed every year after the summer harvest in Kerala, has been a tradition for more than 250 years. The Chhau, a tribal ritual dance in Orissa, Jharkhand, and West Bengal, also made the list. Both dance forms feature crafted masks and elaborate, prescribed movements. The folk songs and dances of the Kabelia community of snake charmers from Rajasthan were added to the list as well. To be added to the list, a tradition must be deemed a living tradition by UNESCO, meaning that it is still passed from generation to generation and continues to create a sense of identity and community for those who participate. Such traditions have been approved by UNESCO for special consideration since 2001. For one that is inscribed, a special program is designed to protect and promote the practice and understanding of the tradition.

All major cities have Western-style hotels that cater to tourists. The *Tourism Factbook*, published by the UN World Tourism Organization, reported 5.3 million incoming tourists to India in 2009; they spent a total of $11.5 billion. Of those incoming tourists, there were 1.9 million from Europe, 1.1 million from the Americas, and 1 million from South Asia. There were 242,184 hotel beds available in India. The estimated daily cost to visit New Delhi, the capital, was $400. The cost of visiting other cities averaged $291.

48 FAMOUS PERSONS

Siddhartha Gautama was (624–544 BC according to Sinhalese tradition; 563–483 BC according to most modern scholars) later known as the Buddha ("the enlightened one"). Born in what is now Nepal, he spent much of his life in eastern Uttar Pradesh and Bihar, propounding the philosophical doctrines that were later to become Buddhism. Contemporary with the Buddha was Vardhamana (599–527 BC), also known as Mahavira ("great hero"), a saintly thinker of Bihar from whose teachings evolved Jainism. Some of the noteworthy religious and political leaders were Chandragupta (r. 321–297 BC), founder of the Maurya Dynasty; Asoka (r. 273–32 BC), who made Buddhism the religion of his empire; Chandragupta II (r. AD 375–413), whose era marked a high point of Hindu art and literature; Shivaji (1627–80), a hero of much Hindu folklore; Nanak (1469–1539), whose teachings are the basis of Sikhism; and Govind Singh (1666–1708), the guru who gave Sikhism its definitive form. Akbar (1542–1605) greatly expanded the Mughal Empire, which reached its height under Shah Jahan (1592–1666), builder of the Taj Mahal, and his son, the fanatical emperor Aurangzeb (1618–1707).

Sanskrit grammarian Panini (5th–4th centuries BC), wrote the first book on scientific linguistics. The Bengali educator and reformer Rammohan Roy (1772–1833) has been called "the father of modern India." Swami Vivekananda (1863–1902), founder of the nonsectarian Ramakrishna Mission and a great traveler both in India and abroad, did much to explain the Hindu philosophy to the world and to India as well. Sarvepalli Radhakrishnan (1888–1975), a leading 20th-century Hindu scholar and philosopher, also served as president of India from 1962 to 1967. Another revered religious philosopher was Meher Baba (1894–1969). The rising position of India in science and industry is well exemplified by Jamshedji Nusserwanji Tata (1822–1904), founder of the nation's first modern iron and steel works and many other key industries; the physicist Jagadis Chandra Bose (1858–1937), noted for his research in plant life; Srinivasa Ramanujan (1887–1919), an amazingly original, largely self-taught, mathematician; Chandrasekhara Venkata Raman (1888–1970), who was awarded the 1930 Nobel Prize for research in physics; Chandrasekhara Subramanyan (1910–95), also a Nobel Prize laureate in physics, and Vikram A. Sarabhai (1919–71), the founder of the Indian space program. Mother Teresa (Agnes Gonxha Bojaxhiu, 1910–97, in what is now Serbia and Montenegro) won the Nobel Peace Prize in 1979 for her 30 years of work among Calcutta's poor.

In modern times no Indian so completely captured the Indian masses and had such a deep spiritual effect on so many throughout the world as Mohandas Karamchand Gandhi (1869–1948). Reverently referred to by millions of Indians as the Mahatma ("the great-souled one"), Gandhi is considered the greatest Indian since the Buddha. His unifying ability and his unusual methods of nonviolent resistance contributed materially to the liberation of India in 1947. A leading disciple of the Mahatma, Vinayak ("Vinoba") Narahari Bhave (1895–1982), was an agrarian reformer who persuaded wealthy landowners to give about 600,000 hectares (1,500,000 acres) of tillable land to India's poor. Venkatraman Ramakrishnan (b. 1952), a native of Tamil Nadu, was named as the co-recipient of the 2009 Nobel Prize in Chemistry for research on the structure and function of the ribosome, the part of the cell that produces protein.

Gandhi's political heir, Jawaharlal Nehru (1889–1964), had a hold on the Indian people almost equal to that of the Mahatma. Affectionately known as Chacha (Uncle) Nehru, he steered India through its first 17 years of independence and played a key role in the independence struggle. Indira Gandhi (1917–84), the daughter of Nehru and prime minister from 1966 to 1977 and again from 1980 to 1984, continued her father's work in modernizing India and played an important role among the leaders of nonaligned nations. Her son Rajiv (1944–91) succeeded her as prime minister and, in the 1985 election, achieved for himself and his party the largest parliamentary victory since India became independent. Subsequent prime ministers have been: P.V. Narasimha Rao (1921–2004, served 1991–96), Atal Behari Vajpayee (b. 1924, served 1996 and 1998–2004), and Dr. Manmohan Singh (b. 1932), who began his term in 2004.

A classical Sanskrit writer in Indian history was the poet and playwright Kalidasa (fl. 5th cent. AD), whose best-known work is *Shakuntala*. In modern times, Rabindranath Tagore (1861–1941), the great Bengali humanist, influenced Indian thought in his many songs and poems. Tagore received the Nobel Prize in literature in 1913 and through his lifetime wrote more than 50 dramas and approximately 150 books of verse, fiction, and philosophy. Another Bengali writer highly esteemed was the novelist Bankim Chandra Chatterjee (1838–94). Tagore and Chatterjee are the authors, respectively, of India's national anthem and national song. The novel in English is a thriving genre; notable modern practitioners include Rasipuram Krishnaswamy Narayan (1906–2001), Bhabani Bhattacharya (1906–88), Raja Rao (1908–2006) and Khushwant Singh (b. 1915). Other contemporary Indian-born novelists writing in English include: Anita Desai (b. 1937), Bharati Mukherjee (b. 1940), Salman Rushdie (b. 1947), and Arundhati Roy (b. 1961); Jhumpa Lahiri (b. 1967) is an American author of Indian descent. Influential poets of the last two centuries include the Bengalis Iswar Chandra Gupta (1812–59) and Sarojini Naidu (1879–1949), known as "the nightingale of India," a close associate of Gandhi and a political leader in her own right.

Modern interpreters of the rich Indian musical tradition include the composer and performer Ravi Shankar (b. 1920) and the performer and educator Ali Akbar Khan (1922–2009). Zubin Mehta (b. 1936) is an orchestral conductor of international renown. Uday Shankar (1900?–1977), a dancer and scholar, did much to stimulate Western interest in Indian dance. Tanjore Balasaraswati (1919?–84) won renown as a classical dancer and teacher. Preeminent in the Indian cinema is the director Satyajit Ray (1921–92).

49 DEPENDENCIES

Andaman and Nicobar Islands

The Andaman and Nicobar Islands are two groups of islands in the Indian Ocean, extending approximately 970 km (600 mi) N–S and lying about 640 km (400 mi) W of both the Tenasserim coast of Myanmar and peninsular Thailand. Their total area is 8,293 sq km (3,202 sq mi); their population was estimated at 379,994 according to the 2011 census. These islands together form a union territory with its capital at Port Blair. The legal system is under the jurisdiction of the high court of Calcutta.

The Andaman Islands extend more than 354 km (220 mi) between 10 and 14°N and 92°12′ and 94°17′ E. Of the 204 islands in the group, the three largest are North, Middle, and South Andaman; since these are separated only by narrow inlets, they are often referred to together as Great Andaman. Little Andaman lies to the south.

The Nicobars extend south from the Andamans between 10 and 6°N and 92°43′ and 93°57′ E. Of the 19 islands, Car Nicobar, 121 km (75 mi) S of Little Andaman, holds more than half the total population; the largest, Great Nicobar, 146 km (91 mi) NW of Sumatra, is sparsely populated.

The Andamans were occupied by the British in 1858, the Nicobars in 1869; sporadic settlements by British, Danish, and other groups were known previously. During World War II (1939–45), the islands were occupied by Japanese forces. They became a union territory in 1956. That same year, the Andaman and Nicobar Islands (Protection of Aboriginal Tribes) Act came into force; this act, designed to protect the primitive tribes that live in the islands, prohibited outsiders from carrying on trade or industry in the islands without a special license. Six different ethnic groups live in the Andaman and Nicobar Islands, the largest being the Nicobarese. There are lesser numbers of Andamanese, Onges, Jarawas, Sentinalese, and Shompens in the dependency. Access to tribal areas is prohibited.

Agriculture is the mainstay of the economy. The principal crops are rice and coconuts; some sugarcane, fruits, and vegetables are also grown. There is little industry other than a sawmill and plywood and match factories.

Lakshadweep

The union territory of Lakshadweep consists of the Laccadive, Minicoy, and Amindivi Islands, a scattered group of small coral atolls and reefs in the Arabian Sea between 10° and 13° N and 71°43′ and 73°43′ E and about 320 km (200 mi) W of Kerala state. Their total area is about 32 sq km (12 sq mi). Minicoy, southernmost of the islands, is the largest.

In 2011, the population of Lakshadweep was estimated at 64,429. The inhabitants of the Laccadives and Amindivis are Malayalam-speaking Muslims; those on Minicoy are also Muslim, but speak a language similar to Sinhalese. The islanders are skilled fishermen and trade their marine products and island-processed coir in the Malabar ports of Kerala. The main cottage industry is coir spinning. Politically, these islands were under the control of the state of Madras until 1956. The present territorial capital is at Kavaratti. Judicial affairs are under the jurisdiction of the high court of Kerala.

50 BIBLIOGRAPHY

Alexander, Yonah, ed. *Combating Terrorism: Strategies of Ten Countries*. Ann Arbor: University of Michigan Press, 2002.

Barter, James. *The Ganges*. San Diego, CA: Lucent Books, 2003.

Chakravarti, Ranabir, ed. *Trade in Early India*. New York: Oxford University Press, 2001.

Henderson, Carol E. *Culture and Customs of India*. Westport, CT: Greenwood Press, 2002.

India Investment and Business Guide: Strategic and Practical Information. Washington, DC: International Business Publications USA, 2012.

Mansingh, Surjit. *Historical Dictionary of India*. 2nd ed. Lanham, MD: Scarecrow Press, 2006.

Mitra, Subrata K. ed. *A Political and Economic Dictionary of South Asia*. Philadelphia: Routledge/Taylor and Francis, 2006.

Nilekani, Nandan. *Imagining India: The Idea of a Renewed Nation*. New York: Penguin Books, 2010.

Pavan, Aldo. *The Ganges: Along Sacred Waters*. London: Thames and Hudson, 2005.

Stern, Robert W. *Democracy and Dictatorship in South Asia: Dominant Classes and Political Outcomes in India, Pakistan, and Bangladesh*. Westport, CT: Praeger, 2001.

Vohra, Ranbir. *The Making of India: A Historical Survey*. 2nd ed. Armonk, NY: M. E. Sharp, 2001.

Wolpert, Stanley A. *A New History of India*. 8th ed. New York: Oxford University Press, 2009.Stern, Robert W. *Democracy and Dictatorship in South Asia: Dominant Classes and Political Outcomes in India, Pakistan, and Bangladesh*. Westport, Conn.: Praeger, 2001.

Tomlinson, B. R. *The Economy of Modern India, 1860–1970*. New York: Cambridge University Press, 1993.

Vohra, Ranbir. *The Making of India: A Historical Survey*. Armonk, N.Y.: M. E. Sharp, 1997.

Wolpert, Stanley A. *A New History of India*. 4th ed. New York: Oxford University Press, 1993.

INDONESIA

Republic of Indonesia
Republik Indonesia

CAPITAL: Jakarta

FLAG: The national flag, adopted in 1949, consists of a red horizontal stripe above a white stripe.

ANTHEM: *Indonesia Raya (Great Indonesia).*

MONETARY UNIT: The rupiah (IDR) consists of 100 sen. There are coins of 25, 50, 100, 500 and 1,000 rupiah, and notes of 1,000, 2,000, 5,000, 10,000, 20,000, 50,000, and 100,000 rupiah. IDR1 = US$0.0001 (or US$1 = IDR9,044.52) as of 2011.

WEIGHTS AND MEASURES: The metric system is standard.

HOLIDAYS: New Year's Day, 1 January; Independence Day, 17 August; Christmas, 25 December. Movable holidays include the Prophet's Birthday, Ascension of Muhammad, Eid al-Fitr, Eid al-Adha, Good Friday, Ascension of Jesus Christ, Buddha's birthday, Chinese New Year, and Balinese New Year.

TIME: Western, 7 p.m. = noon GMT; Central, 8 p.m. = noon GMT; Eastern, 9 p.m. = noon GMT.

¹LOCATION, SIZE, AND EXTENT

The Republic of Indonesia consists of five large islands and 13,677 smaller islands (about 6,000 of which are inhabited) forming an arc between Asia and Australia. With a total area of 1,919,569 sq km (741,149 sq mi), Indonesia is the fifth-largest Asian country, after China, India, Kazakhstan, and Saudi Arabia. Comparatively, the area occupied by Indonesia is slightly less than three times the size of the state of Texas. It extends 5,271 km (3,275 mi) E–W and 2,210 km (1,373 mi) N–S. The five principal islands are Sumatra; Java; Borneo, of which the 72% belonging to Indonesia is known as Kalimantan; Sulawesi, formerly called Celebes; and the western portion of the island of New Guinea. Indonesia has land boundaries with Malaysia (on Borneo), Papua New Guinea (on New Guinea), and East Timor (on Timor). It is bounded on the N by the South China Sea, on the N and E by the Pacific Ocean, and on the S and W by the Indian Ocean. Indonesia's total land boundary length is 2,830 km (1,758 mi). Its coastline is 54, 716 km (33,999 mi).

Indonesia's capital city, Jakarta, is located on the island of Java.

²TOPOGRAPHY

The Indonesian archipelago consists of three main regions. One of the regions consists of Sumatra, Java, Kalimantan, and the islands that lie between them, which stand on the Sunda shelf, where the ocean depths are never more than 210 m (700 ft). Another region consists of West Papua and the Aru Isles, which stand on the Sahul shelf, projecting northward from the north coast of Australia at similar depths. Between these two shelves are the Lesser Sunda Islands, the Maluku Islands (Moluccas), and Sulawesi, which are surrounded by seas with depths that reach 4,570 m (15,000 ft). The large islands have central mountain ranges rising from more or less extensive lowlands and coastal plains. Many inactive and scores of active volcanoes dot the islands, accounting for the rich volcanic soil that is carried down by the rivers to the plains and lowlands;

there are over 100 volcanoes. Peaks rise to 3,650 m (12,000 ft) in Java and Sumatra. Java, Bali, and Lombok have extensive lowland plains and gently sloping cultivable mountainsides. Extensive wetland forests and hill country are found in Kalimantan. Sumatra's eastern coastline is bordered by morasses, floodplains, and alluvial terraces suitable for cultivation farther inland. Mountainous areas predominate in Sulawesi.

Earthquakes and tsunamis have often devastated Indonesia. In 1992, an earthquake off the island of Flores caused more than 2,500 deaths. More than 200 people died in 1994 from an earthquake and tsunami in eastern Java. An earthquake in Sumatra with a magnitude of 7.9 on the Richter Scale killed more than 100 people in 2000. Java was struck by a 6.3 earthquake, causing over 5,700 deaths on 26 May 2006. A Sumatra earthquake (7.6) on 30 September 2009 caused over 1,000 deaths, and another Sumatra earthquake (7.7) on 10 October 2010 killed over 400 people.

A catastrophic tsunami struck Indonesia and other Indian Ocean countries on 26 December 2004. Stemming from an underwater earthquake about 324 km (180 mi) south off the coast of Sumatra, the city of Banda Aceh experienced a 10-minute earthquake, the longest duration ever recorded. The tsunami rolled waves onto the mainland at an estimated 800 km/h (500 mi/h), leaving about 131,000 confirmed dead and another 38,000 missing in Indonesia. The disaster obliterated entire villages on Sumatra.

The eruption of the Sidoarjo Lusi, a mud volcano in East Java, began in 2006 and continued into 2011. Some scientists predicted that the eruption could continue for another 26 years. Lusi is the world's largest mud volcano. As of 2011, the eruption had displaced 13,000 families. Scientists believed that the eruption was caused by a natural gas drilling blowout.

³CLIMATE

Straddling the equator, Indonesia has a tropical climate characterized by heavy rainfall, high humidity, high temperature, and low winds. The wet season is from November to March, the dry season from April to October. Rainfall in lowland areas averages 180–320 cm (70–125 in) annually, increasing with elevation to an average of 610 cm (240 in) in some mountain areas. In the lowlands of Sumatra and Kalimantan, the rainfall range is 305–370 cm (120–145 in); the amount diminishes southward, closer to the northwest Australian desert. Average humidity is 82%.

Altitude rather than season affects the temperature in Indonesia. At sea level, the mean annual temperature is about 25–27°C (77–81°F). There is slight daily variation in temperature, with the greatest variation at inland points and at higher levels. The mean annual temperature at Jakarta is 26°C (79°F); average annual rainfall is about 200 cm (79 in).

4 FLORA AND FAUNA

The World Resources Institute estimates that there are 29,375 plant species in Indonesia. In addition, Indonesia is home to 667 species of mammals, 1,604 species of birds, species of 749 reptiles, and 285 species of amphibians. The calculation reflects the total number of distinct species residing in the country, not the number of endemic species. The Wallace Line, drawn between Bali and Borneo in the north and Lombok and Sulawesi in the south, is a demarcation of species related to those of Asia in the north from species related to those of Australia in the south.

The plant life of the archipelago reflects a mingling of Asiatic and Australian forms with endemic ones. Vegetation ranges from that of the tropical rain forest of the northern lowlands and the seasonal forests of the southern lowlands, through vegetation of the less luxuriant hill forests and mountain forests, to subalpine shrub vegetation. Two of the world's largest flowers, the raffelsia and the titum arum, grow in Indonesia's rainforests.

The bridge between Asia and Australia formed by the archipelago is reflected in the varieties of animal life. The fauna of Sumatra, Kalimantan, and Java is similar to that of peninsular Malaysia, but each island has its peculiar types. The orangutan is found in Sumatra and Kalimantan, the siamang only in Sumatra, the proboscis monkey only in Kalimantan, the elephant and tapir only in Sumatra, and the wild ox in Java and Kalimantan. In Sulawesi, the Maluku Islands, and Timor, Australian types begin to occur-the bandicoot, a marsupial, is found in Timor. All the islands, especially the Malukus, abound in great varieties of bird life, reptiles, and amphibians. The extremely diverse marine life of Indonesia's extensive territorial waters includes a variety of corals.

5 ENVIRONMENT

The World Resources Institute reported that Indonesia had designated 20.31 million hectares (50.19 million acres) of land for protection as of 2006. As of 2011, Indonesia had 50 national parks, including 7 marine parks. Komodo National Park, Lorentz National Park, Ujung Kulon National Park, and the Sumatran rainforests are UNESCO World Heritage Sites, and there are five Ramsar wetland sites. Logging, wildlife poaching, and agricultural encroachment have been chronic problems in Indonesia's protected forests. Severe deforestation affected Indonesia as commercial logging and oil palm plantations decimated rainforests, particularly on Kalimantan and Sumatra, during the 1980s, 1990s, and early 21st century. According to the FAO, Indonesia had the world's highest deforestation rate from 2000 to 2009, losing 1.8 million hectares (4.4 million acres) of forest per year. Fires set deliberately to burn

away vegetation in logged areas and peatlands of Kalimantan and Sumatra were identified as the main cause of a smokey haze that caused air pollution in Indonesia and neighboring countries in 2006 and 2010. Although Indonesia has laws to protect the remaining forest, illegal logging continued to be pervasive, especially on Kalimantan, in the first decades of the 21st century. In September 2011, Indonesia's president Susilo Bambang Yudhoyono pledged that he would dedicate his last three years in office to protecting the country's forests and environment.

Water resources totaled 2,838 cu km (680.9 cu mi) while water usage was 82.78 cu km (19.86 cu mi) per year. Domestic water usage accounted for 8% of total usage, industrial for 1%, and agricultural for 91%. Per capita water usage totaled 372 cu m (13,137 cu ft) per year. Water pollution, air pollution, traffic congestion, and waste disposal inefficiency are among the environmental problems in Jakarta and other Indonesian cities. The United Nations (UN) reported in 2008 that carbon dioxide emissions in Indonesia totaled 396,819 kilotons. The burning of oil and coal, along with the misuse of fertilizers and pesticides, results in significant damage to the environment. In November 2011, the Asian Development bank loaned $100 million to Indonesia for programs aimed at reducing the country's greenhouse gas emissions by 2020. Indonesia was a major greenhouse gas producer as of 2011, due largely to the clearing of peatlands for expanding oil palm plantations.

A 2009 study completed by the Asian Development Bank (ADB) projected a general sea level rise of up to 70 cm (28 in) within 100 years due to global warming; such a change would damage or destroy coastal lands in Indonesia and the many homes and businesses located there. Agricultural lands are already susceptible to extreme weather conditions, ranging from droughts and forest fires to severe storms and floods. Climate change could also affect the delicate balance of marine life habitats. Indonesia was a founding member of the Coral Triangle Initiative, established in 2007 to promote cooperation among nations and international organizations in safeguarding marine and coastal resources under the threat of climate change.

According to a 2011 report issued by the International Union for Conservation of Nature and Natural Resources (IUCN), threatened species included 184 mammals, 119 birds, 32 reptiles, 32 amphibians, 140 fish, 5 mollusks, 242 other invertebrates, and 395 plants. Endangered species in Indonesia include the pig-tailed langur, Javan gibbon, orangutan, tiger, Asian elephant, Malayan tapir, Javan rhinoceros, Sumatran rhinoceros, Sumatran serow, Rothschild's starling, lowland anoa, mountain anoa, Siamese crocodile, false gavial, river terrapin, and four species of turtle (green sea, hawksbill, olive ridley, and leatherback). The Buhler's rat is extinct, the Javanese lapwing is considered critically endangered, and the Kalimantan mango tree is extinct in the wild.

6 POPULATION

The US Central Intelligence Agency (CIA) estimated the population of Indonesia in 2011 to be approximately 254,613,000, which placed it at number 4 in population among the 196 nations of the world. In 2011, an estimated 6.1% of the population was over 65 years of age, with 27.3% under 15 years of age. The median age in Indonesia was estimated at 28.2 years. The male to female ratio was equal, at 1 to 1. The population's annual rate of change was 1.069%, the result of decades of family planning promotion by the government and international agencies. The projected population for the year 2025 was 273,200,000. Population density in Indonesia was calculated at 134 people per sq km (347 people per sq mi).

The CIA estimated that 44% of the population lived in urban areas as of 2010, and that urban populations had an annual rate of change of 1.7%. The largest urban areas, along with their respective populations as of 2009, according to the CIA, included the "mega-city" of Jakarta, 9.1 million; Surabaya, 2.5 million; Bandung, 2.4 million; Medan, 2.1 million; and Semarang, 1.3 million. Java has a very high population density, containing nearly 60% of Indonesia's population on 6.6% of the land mass, according to the 2010 national census.

7 MIGRATION

Estimates of Indonesia's net migration rate, carried out by the CIA in 2011, amounted to -1.15 migrants per 1,000 citizens. The total number of emigrants living abroad was 2.5 million, and the total number of immigrants living in Indonesia was 122,900. Historically, there has been considerable migration from and to China. Following a decree banning foreigners from participating in retail trade in rural Indonesia, some 120,000 Chinese left Indonesia in 1960–61. After the attempted coup of 1965, deterioration in relations with China, and violence against local Chinese, many more Chinese left Indonesia; another outflow of Chinese Indonesians took place following severe violence targeting them in 1998. Migration between the Netherlands and Indonesia has been greatly reduced since independence. First asylum was granted to over 145,000 Indochinese refugees between 1975 and 1993. Of these refugees, 121,708 were from Vietnam, nearly all were resettled in western countries. According to the UN, as of 2010 there were from 6.5 to 9 million Indonesian migrant workers employed in Malaysia, the Middle East, and elsewhere.

Resettlement of people from crowded areas to the less populous outer islands has been official government policy, particularly during the 1980s. The 1979–84 National Economic Plan had as a target the "transmigration" of 500,000 families from Java, Bali, and Madura to Sumatra, Kalimantan, Sulawesi, Maluku Province, and Irian Jaya (now West Papua). Participation was voluntary, and the actual number of families that resettled was about 366,000, containing about 1.5 million people. Since the annual population increase of Java was more than two million, the costly transmigration scheme did little to relieve that island's human congestion, but it had a considerable impact in developing sparsely settled areas; it also provoked tensions with indigenous peoples. Transmigration was limited in scale after the end of the Suharto administration.

8 ETHNIC GROUPS

Ethnic groups of Indonesia include Achenese of north Sumatra; Bataks of northeastern Sumatra; Minangkabaus of west Sumatra; Sundanese of west Java; the Javanese in central and east Java; Madurese on the island of Madura; Balinese on Bali; Sasaks on the island of Lombok; Timorese on Timor; Dayaks in Kalimantan; and the Minahasa, Torajas, Makassarese, and Buginese on Sulawesi. The Javanese are the largest group in Indonesia, at 41.6% of the population, according to the 2010 census, followed by the Sundanese with 15.4%. The other ethnic groups each comprise less than 5%. Ethnic Chinese Indonesians live mainly in towns and cities, throughout the country. Many different ethnic groups are indigenous to West Papua; Polynesians including the Ambonese live on the Maluku Islands.

9 LANGUAGES

Bahasa Indonesia, a product of the nationalist movement, is the official language, serving as a common vehicle of communication for the various language groups. Based primarily on Malay and similar to the official language of Malaysia, it evolved as a trading language and contains many words from other Indonesian languages and dialects, as well as from Dutch, English, Arabic, Portuguese, Chinese, and Sanskrit. In 1973, Indonesia and Malaysia adopted similar systems of spelling. Malay/Indonesian is part of the far-ranging Austronesian language family, which ranges from Polynesia to Madagascar. During the Suharto administration, Bahasa Indonesia was emphasized in education and business for national unification. It is the official medium of instruction in public schools, through university level. Use of over 680 other languages continues, including Sundanese, Malay, and the most widely used, Javanese. English and Chinese are also used in industry and commerce.

10 RELIGIONS

Indonesia officially recognizes six religions: Islam, Protestantism, Catholicism, Hinduism, Buddhism, and Confucianism. Citizens are expected to have one of the six official religions listed on identity cards and marriage registrations, although other religions are allowed as cultural or social organizations. According to the 2010 census, about 87% of the inhabitants were adherents of Islam, almost 7% were Protestant, about 3% were Roman Catholic, and 1.6% were Hindu. Buddhists, Confucians, Sikhs, Jews, and adherents of indigenous religions together accounted for less than 1.3% of the population. Muslim, Christian, Buddhist, and Hindu holidays are observed as national holidays.

Muslim majorities are found in Java, Sumatra, Kalimantan, West Nusa Tenggara, Sulawesi, and North Maluku. The government supports Islamic religious schools and is in charge of annual pilgrimages to Mecca for Indonesians. The government of Aceh uses Shari'ah (Islamic law) for Muslim citizens, and some local governments apply aspects of Shari'ah for Muslims. Most Indonesian Muslims are Sunni, but the Shi'a, Amadhiyah, and Sufi branches are also represented. There are also smaller groups of al-Qiyadah al-Islamiya, Darul Arqam, Jamaah Salamulla (Salamulla Congregation), and members of the Indonesian Islamic Propagation Institute. The mainstream Muslim community is divided into modernists (who embrace modern learning but adhere to scriptural orthodox theology) and traditionalists (who are generally followers of charismatic religious scholars). Islamic sects considered "deviant", including Amadhiyah, have been subject to official pressure, including arrests, in Indonesia in the early decades of the 21st century, with three members of Amadhiyah killed by a mob on Java in February 2011. Islamic fundamentalist groups have been active on social issues, sometimes leading to mob violence and destruction of Christian churches. Religious-based violence occurred in Poso (central Sulawesi) and Ambon, Maluku, in 2011.

Hinduism was the religion of Java for several centuries, but after Islam swept over Indonesia in the 15th century, Hinduism became isolated to Bali. The Naurus on Seram Island practice a combination of Hindu and animist beliefs. In central Kalimantan and western New Guinea, as well as a few other areas, substantial numbers of Indonesians practice animism and other indigenous religion known collectively as Aliran Kepercayaan. Some animists on Kalimantan and elsewhere list themselves as "Hindu" to be included in the six official religions. Indonesian Chinese are usually Christian, or combined Buddhist-Confucian. Of the Indonesian Buddhists, about 60% ascribe to the Mahayana school and 30% adhere to the Theravada school. The chief Christian communities are found in the eastern part of the country, particularly West Papua and the Malaku islands. There are small Jewish communities on Sulawesi.

11 TRANSPORTATION

Indonesia is politically and economically dependent upon transportation among the islands. Piracy in Indonesia's busy sea lanes, particularly the Straits of Malacca between Sumatra and the Malay Peninsula, has been a chronic problem in the early 21st century. Indonesia's principal ports of international trade are Tanjungpriok (for Jakarta) and Tanjungperak (for Surabaya) in Java, and Belawan (near Medan) and Padang in Sumatra. Ports with less traffic but capable of handling sizable ships are Cirebon and Semarang in Java; Palembang in Sumatra; Banjarmasin, Balikpapan, and Pontianak in Kalimantan; Tanjungpinang in Bintan; and Ujung Padang in Sulawesi. As of 2010, Indonesia's merchant fleet included 1,244 vessels of 1,000 GRT or more. Smaller cargo boats and passenger ferries travel routes between the islands. Indonesia has approximately 21,579 km (13,409 mi) of navigable waterways. As of 2011 inland waterways formed the most important means of transportation in Kalimantan and in parts of Sumatra.

As of 2010, according to the CIA, Indonesia had 684 airports, of which 164 had paved runways. There were also 64 heliports. The center of international air traffic is Jakarta's Sukarno-Hatta International Airport. Other principal airports include Bali Ngurah Rai International Airport at Denpasar, Juanda International Airport near Surabaya, and Polonia International Airport at Medan. There are direct flights to the international airports from cities in Asia and Australia. Garuda Indonesia is the national airline, flying to 19 international and 31 domestic destinations, as of 2011. Indonesian low cost airlines include Lion Air, CitiLink, and Indonesia Air Asia. There are also Indonesian regional, cargo, and charter airlines. Safety concerns led to the EU banning all Indonesian airlines from flying to Europe in 2007–2009.

Indonesia's railway system is state owned, with narrow gauge tracks. According to the CIA, as of 2009, there were 5,042 km (3,132 mi) of tracks, 565 km (351 mi) of which had been electrified. The CIA reports that Indonesia has a total of 437,759 km (272,011 mi) of roads, of which 258,744 km (160,776 mi) were paved, as of 2008. There are 77 vehicles per 1,000 people in the country, according to the World Bank, as of 2008. Traffic congestion--including buses, cars, and motorcycles--and related air pollution are severe in Jakarta and other Indonesian cities.

12 HISTORY

Evidence for the ancient hominid habitation of Indonesia was discovered by in 1891; these fossil remains of so-called Java man (*Pithecanthropus erectus*) date from the Pleistocene period, when Indonesia was linked with the Asian mainland due to lower sea levels. In 2003, the partial skeleton of a small, apparently very ancient hominid was discovered on the island of Flores and given the scientific name *Homo floriensis,* although the discovery was met with controversy.

Most of Indonesia was probably populated by modern humans arriving from the Malay Peninsula. Indian influences permeated Java and Sumatra from the 1st to the 7th century. During this period and extending into the 15th century, local Buddhist and Hindu rulers established a number of powerful kingdoms. Among the most powerful of these was the Buddhist kingdom of Srivijaya, established on Sumatra in the 7th century; it prospered by gaining control of trade through the Strait of Malacca. To the east, in central Java, the Sailendra dynasty established its Buddhist kingdom in the 8th century. Relics of Sailendra rule include the great temple of Borobudur, Asia's largest Buddhist monument. Succeeding the Sailendra dynasty in 856 were followers of the Hindu god Shiva; they built the great temple at Prambanan, east of Yogyakarta. Other Hindu kingdoms subsequently extended Indian influence eastward into east Java and Bali. The last of these was the Hindu kingdom of Majapahit, which was at the height of its power during the 13th century, when Marco Polo visited Java and northern Sumatra. When Majapahit collapsed around 1520, many of its leaders, according to tradition, fled to Bali, the only island in Indonesia that retains Hinduism as the chief religion. Even before Majapahit disintegrated, Muslim missionaries, probably Persian merchants, had begun to convert much of the archipelago to Islam. About this time, also, the first Europeans arrived, and the first Chinese settlements were established. The Portuguese captured Malacca (Melaka), on the west coast of the Malay Peninsula, in 1511, and then gained control over the archipelago.

Dutch ships visited Java in 1596. The Dutch came in increasing numbers and soon drove the Portuguese out of the archipelago (except for the eastern half of the island of Timor), beginning nearly 350 years of colonial rule. The States-General of the Dutch Republic in 1602 incorporated the East Indian spice traders as the United East India Company and granted it a monopoly on shipping and trade and the power to make alliances and contracts with the rulers of Southeast Asia. By force and diplomacy, the company became the supreme ruler of what became known as the Dutch East Indies. Poor administration and corruption weakened the company after its early years of prosperity, and the Dutch government nullified its charter in 1799 and took over its affairs in 1800. The British East India Company ruled the Indies during the Napoleonic wars, from 1811 to 1816. When Dutch rule was restored, the Netherlands government instituted the "culture system" on Java, under which the Javanese, instead of paying a certain proportion of their crops as tax, were required to put at the disposal of the government a share of their land and labor and to grow crops for export under government direction. From a fiscal point of view the system was very successful for the Netherlands treasury, but this "net profit" or "favorable balance" policy fell under increasing moral attack in the Netherlands and was brought to an end about 1877.

The prosperity of the Netherlands at the expense of Indonesian living standards was increasingly resented. With the adoption of what colonial administrators called the "ethical policy" at the beginning of the 20th century, the first steps were taken to give Indonesians participation in government. A central representative body, the Volksraad, was instituted in 1918. At first it had only ad-

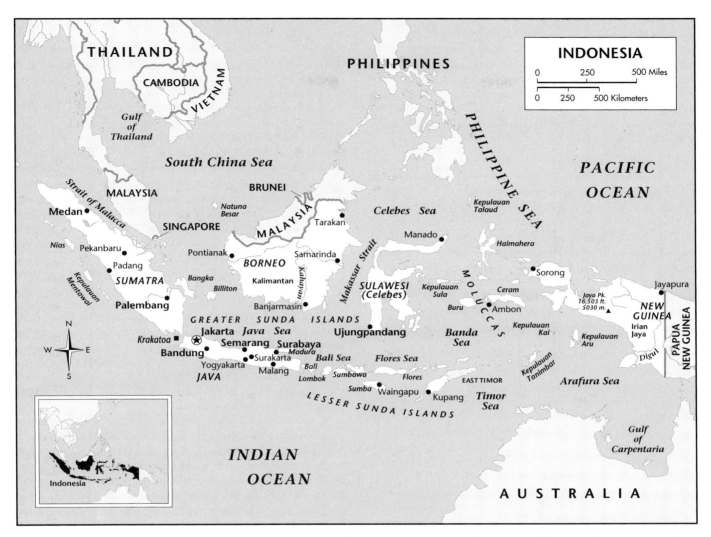

LOCATION: 95°1′ to 141°2′E; 6°5′N to 11°S. BOUNDARY LENGTHS: Malaysia, 1,782 kilometers (1,110 miles); Papua New Guinea, 820 kilometers (510 miles); total coastline, 54,716 kilometers (33,996 miles). TERRITORIAL SEA LIMIT: 12 miles.

visory powers, but in 1927 it was given co-legislative powers. An Indonesian nationalist movement began to develop during those years and steadily gained strength. The movement progressed during the World War II Japanese occupation (1942–45). A nationalist group under the leadership of Sukarno and Mohammad Hatta proclaimed an independent republic on 17 August 1945, adopted a provisional constitution providing for a strong presidential form of government, formed a revolutionary government, and resisted Dutch reoccupation. After four years of intermittent negotiations, frequent hostilities, and intervention by the UN, the Netherlands agreed to Indonesian demands.

On 27 December 1949, the Dutch recognized the independence of all the former Dutch East Indies except West New Guinea as the Republic of the United States of Indonesia. A few months later, on 17 August 1950, the federal system was rejected and a unitary state, the Republic of Indonesia, was established under a new constitution. West New Guinea remained under Dutch control until October 1962, when the Netherlands transferred the territory to the UN Temporary Executive Administration (UNTEA). On 1 May 1963, Indonesia took complete possession of the disputed

territory as the province of Irian Barat (West Irian); the province was renamed Irian Jaya in 1973. Indonesia, which aimed to acquire Sarawak and Sabah (which are on the island of Borneo with Kalimantan), opposed the formation of the Federation of Malaysia in September 1963 and announced a "crush Malaysia" policy. Indonesian guerrilla raids into Malaysian territory continued until August 1966, when a formal treaty was concluded between the two countries.

Sukarno became the first president of the new nation in 1949, and Hatta the vice president. Internal difficulties, fostered by a multiplicity of political parties inherited from Dutch colonial days, soon developed, and regional rivalries also threatened the unity of the new nation. Then as now, Java had some two-thirds of the country's population, but the great sources of wealth were found on the other, much less densely settled islands. Those living in the so-called Outer Islands believed too much governmental revenue was being spent in Java and too little elsewhere. After Vice President Hatta, a Sumatran, resigned in December 1956, many in the Outer Islands felt they had lost their chief and most effective spokesman in Jakarta. Territorial army commanders in Sumatra staged coups and defied the central government; other rebel movements developed in Sulawesi. The government took measures providing for greater fiscal and administrative decentralization, but discontent remained, and the rebellions were put down by force. Thereafter, Sukarno bypassed parliamentary procedures and pursued an increasingly authoritarian, anti-Western policy of "guided democracy." In 1959, he decreed a return to the 1945 constitution, providing for a centralized form of government, and consolidated his control.

Suharto Gains Control

Communist agitation within the country and secessionist uprisings in central and eastern Java came to a head in the 30th of September Movement under the direction of Lt. Col. Untung. Sukarno, whose foreign policy had turned increasingly toward the Communist Chinese, may have had advance knowledge of the Communist-led coup attempt on 30 September 1965, which was directed against Indonesia's top military men. The coup was crushed immediately by the army and in the ensuing anti-Communist purges more than 100,000 persons (mostly Indonesian Chinese) were killed and another 700,000 were arrested. By mid-October 1965, the army, under the command of Gen. Suharto, was in virtual control of the country.

On 12 March 1966, following nearly three weeks of student riots, President Sukarno transferred to Suharto the authority to take, in the president's name, "all measures required for the safekeeping and stability of the government administration." In March 1967, the People's Consultative Assembly (Majetis Permusyawaratan Rakyat—MPR) voted unanimously to withdraw all Sukarno's governmental power and appointed Gen. Suharto acting president. One year later, it conferred full presidential powers on Suharto, and he was sworn in as president for a five year term. The congress also agreed to postpone the general elections due in 1968 until 1971. Sukarno died in June 1970. On 3 July 1971, national and regional elections were held for the majority of seats in all legislative bodies. The Joint Secretariat of Functional Groups (Sekber Golongan Karya—Golkar), a mass political front backed by Suharto, gained 60% of the popular vote and emerged in control of both the House of Representatives (DPR) and the MPR.

In March 1973, the MPR elected Suharto to a second five-year term. Suharto, with key backing from the military, began a long period of dominance over Indonesian politics. Under Suharto's "New Order," Indonesia turned to the West and began following a conservative economic course stressing capital development and foreign investment. In foreign affairs, Suharto's government achieved vastly improved ties with the United States, Japan, and Western Europe, while also maintaining links with the USSR.

Following Portugal's withdrawal from East Timor, the Revolutionary Front for an Independent East Timor (Frente Revolucionário de Este Timor Independente—Fretilin) gained popularity and the Indonesian government sent troops into East Timor, taking full control of the territory. On 17 July 1976, the Suharto government incorporated the territory as an Indonesian province. This action was not recognized by the UN, which called on Indonesia to withdraw and allow the East Timorese the right to self-determination.

Suharto's Golkar Party gained an overwhelming majority in the elections of 1977. The government acknowledged holding 31,000 political prisoners; according to Amnesty International, the total was closer to 100,000. Student riots and criticism of government repression resulted in further government measures: political activity was suspended, and leading newspapers were temporarily closed. Suharto was elected by the MPR to a third five-year term in 1978; during late 1977 and 1978, some 16,000 political prisoners were released, and the remainder of those detained in 1965 were released by the end of 1979. Golkar made further gains in the 1982 elections, and Suharto was elected for a fourth five-year term in March 1983. Suharto called for greater loyalty by all political groups to the Pancasila ("five principles") framed by Sukarno in 1945. The credo included belief in one supreme being, humanitarianism, national unity, consensus democracy, and social justice. Muslim groups strongly objected to the new government program and organized demonstrations that took place in 1984 and 1985. Golkar made further gains in the 1987 elections, and Suharto was reelected for a fifth five-year term in March 1988.

The Indonesian Army (ABRI) continued to play a dual military and socioeconomic function, and this role was supported by legislation in 1988. The war against Fretilin in East Timor continued through the 1980s, with reports of massacres by government troops and severe economic hardship, including famine, among the Timorese. Negotiations with Portugal on decolonization began in July 1983. In Irian Jaya, the Organization for a Free Papua (Organisasi Papua Merdeka—OPM), which desired unification with Papua New Guinea and had been active since the early 1960s, increased its militant activities in 1986.

From 1969–92, the Transmigration Program, a policy aimed at redistributing population in Indonesia for political purposes and demographic reasons, resulted in almost 1,488,000 families moving from the Inner Islands to the Outer Islands. The Transmigration Program produced land disputes with indigenous people and environmental concerns over deforestation. In Irian Jaya, OPM attempted to sabotage the government's program, which was turning the indigenous majority into a minority. In 1989, tension from land disputes in Java and the Outer Islands produced social unrest that resulted in clashes between villagers and the armed forces. In 1990 an armed rebellion arose in Aceh, northern Sumatra, over Indonesian government exploitation of mineral resources and the transmigration program. The government fought the rebellion with a massive display of force.

In 1990 a group of prominent Indonesians publicly demanded that Suharto retire from the presidency at the end of his current term; in 1991 labor unrest increased with a rash of strikes, which the army was called in to quell. On 12 November 1991, during a funeral for a young Timorese killed in demonstrations against Indonesia's rule of East Timor, soldiers opened fire on the defenseless mourners, provoking worldwide condemnation. Western governments threatened to suspend aid, and demands were made linking aid to human rights issues. In early December 1992 government forces captured Xanana Gusmao, leader of Fretilin, and he was sentenced to life imprisonment. By 1993 US policy toward Indonesia shifted toward criticism of Indonesia's rule in East Timor and a threat to revoke trade privileges pursuant to Indonesia's treatment of the largest independent trade union, the Indonesian Prosperous Labor Union (SBSI). Adding further scrutiny to Indonesia's tarnished international image was a UN resolution on Indonesia's human rights violations placing the country on a human rights "watch list" in 1993. East Timor's Roman Catholic bishop, Carlos Filipe Ximenes Belo, and pro-independence advocate José Ramos-Horta, shared the Nobel Peace Prize in 1996. Hundreds of lives were lost in ethnic clashes in Kalimantan, which broke out in December 1996, between the indigenous Dayaks and Muslim settlers from the island of Madura.

Although its total share of votes declined, Golkar won the 1992 elections, securing 282 of the 400 elective seats. In March 1993, Suharto was elected to a sixth term as president. Try Sutrisno, the commander in chief of ABRI, was chosen as vice president. A major scandal occurred in March 1993 with the sale of $5 million in fake shares on the Jakarta Stock Exchange (JSE). Violent labor unrest broke out in Medan in April 1994 with the death of a union activist. Ethnic Chinese, who were only about 3% of the population of Indonesia, were the target of demonstrators; a Chinese factory manager was killed. In June 1994 the government closed *Tempo* and two other publications by revoking publishing licenses.

Violent outbreaks, clashes, land disputes, and riots increased in Indonesia from 1995–97. In 1997, the country experienced the dual effect of increased ethnic conflict and economic decline. The campaign for the 29 May 1997 elections was particularly violent. This followed the uproar resulting from the ouster of Megawati Sukarnoputri (daughter of Sukarno) as the Indonesian Democratic Party (PDI) chairperson in June 1996. Her political involvement was seen as a rallying point for democratic change. Golkar took 74% of the vote in elections that were seen as marked by fraud; over 200 people were killed during the campaign. The Muslim-oriented United Development Party (PPP) obtained 22% and the PDI, 3%. Violence continued after the elections and was worsened by the Asian economic crisis. After severe devaluation of the rupiah in August and October of 1997, Suharto accepted an International Monetary Fund (IMF) loan package but failed to carry out IMF-imposed conditions for economic reform. By December 1997, news of Suharto's declining health cast doubt on his ability to see Indonesia through a worsening economic and political situation. After Suharto won an unopposed presidential election in March 1998, student protests swept Jakarta. Chinese Indonesians were attacked in riots across Indonesia in May 1998, with over a thousand killed and many cases of rape. Army involvement in provoking and allowing the anti-Chinese riots was alleged. On 21 May 1998, Suharto resigned as president. B. J. Habibie, the former vice president, was sworn in as president.

Democracy Arrives

Upon assuming the presidency, Habibie adopted a conciliatory posture toward defusing the East Timor crisis by stating that East Timor could be given "special status" with increased autonomy within Indonesia. In August 1998, Portugal and Indonesia met to discuss the future of the province. After significant pressure from the UN, Australia, and Portugal, Habibie agreed on 27 January 1999 to hold a referendum for the province. Despite widespread violence instigated by pro-Indonesia armed militia, 98% of voters cast their ballots on 30 August, with 78.5% in favor of independence. This was followed by a rampage by pro-Indonesia forces that looted and burned the entire province creating a major humanitarian situation and refugee crisis. With the aid of Australian troops, the UN intervened to restore order and establish humanitarian programs. Meanwhile, in Irian Jaya and Aceh, the military

forces and the national police continued to commit extra-judicial killings in 2000. Thousands of people were killed when Muslims and Christians clashed in the Maluku islands in 1999–2002. Habibie's political fortunes waned in the aftermath of the UN-sponsored referendum in East Timor. Pressure on Habibie mounted and he subsequently resigned as a result of a no-confidence vote.

In 20 October elections in the People's Consultative Assembly, the first free elections in 44 years, Abdurrahman Wahid, the leader of the National Awakening Party and a near-blind Muslim cleric, ran against Megawati Sukarnoputri. Megawati's PDI-P (Indonesia Democracy Party-Struggle) party won the most votes, but rather than negotiate with other politicians to form a coalition, Megawati allowed the more experienced Wahid to become president. She became vice president. Wahid worked to curb the influence of the military and promised major reforms in the government. In July 2001, after months of opposition from legislators over the competence of his administration, Wahid declared a state of emergency and ordered parliament dissolved. On 23 July 2001, legislators in the People's Consultative Assembly voted 591–0 to remove Wahid from the presidency. He had been charged with corruption and incompetence, being accused of embezzling US$4.1 million in state funds and illegally accepting US$2 million from the Sultan of Brunei. He was cleared of all charges that May, but the parliament continued to insist upon impeachment proceedings based on dissatisfaction with his administration. Megawati was sworn in as president immediately after Wahid's removal.

Megawati, a Muslim who was identified with nationalist-secular policies, faced demonstrations upon assuming office from strict Islamic fundamentalists calling for the establishment of Shari'ah law. More than 1,000 people were killed in Aceh in 2001, adding to the thousands more that had been killed in the previous decade. Following the fall of Suharto, Indonesia had experienced a resurgence of Islamic militant activity. The main extremist Islamist organizations in Indonesia were Darul Islam, the Islamic Defender's Front, and Laskar Jihad. Megawati expressed support for the US-led war on terrorism following the 11 September 2001 terrorist attacks, and she visited the United States the following week. On 12 October 2002, Indonesia experienced its own major terrorist attack, when two nightclubs in the resort town of Kuta on Bali were bombed, killing 202 people. On 18 October, President Megawati issued an emergency decree to give the government expanded powers to fight terrorism. Megawati permitted the arrest of Abubakar Bashir, a Muslim cleric who was the spiritual leader of Jemaah Islamiyah, which was accused of staging the Bali bombings and had links to the al-Qaeda organization. Later bombing attacks took place in August 2003 outside the Marriott Hotel in Jakarta, killing 14 people; in September 2004 outside the Australian embassy in Jakarta, which killed 9; and in October 2005 on Bali, when three suicide bombings killed 22 people.

Following its independence referendum held in August 1999, East Timor was governed by the UN Transitional Administration in East Timor (UNTAET), and a National Consultative Council. A constituent assembly was elected in September 2001 with the task of writing a constitution for the country. In April 2002 José Alexandre "Xanana" Gusmão was elected president, and on 20 May 2002 East Timor became an independent nation. Irian Jaya was granted limited autonomy by parliament in October 2001, but many inhabitants rejected the measure and called for full independence. Irian Jaya was renamed Papua, and a separate peninsular province was created in 2003, to be called West Papua.

On 9 December 2002, the Indonesian government and the separatist Free Aceh Movement (GAM) signed a peace accord aimed at ending over three decades of violence. The accord provided for autonomy and free elections in Aceh; in return the GAM was to disarm. In May 2003, peace talks between the government and GAM broke down; the government mounted a military offensive against GAM separatists in Aceh and imposed martial law. In August 2005, the government and GAM separatists once again signed a peace agreement providing for the disarmament of rebels and the withdrawal of government soldiers from Aceh. In December 2006, the first direct elections were held in Aceh. Former separatist rebel leader Irwandi Yusuf was elected governor.

Demonstrators protested price increases on basic necessities such as fuel and electricity in January 2003. In April 2004, parliamentary and local elections were held: the Golkar party of former president Suharto took the greatest share of the vote, with Megawati's PDI-P coming in second. In July 2004, the country's first direct presidential election was held. Susilo Bambang Yudhoyono, a former army general who had served in Wahid's cabinet, representing the Democratic Party (PD), won 33%, the largest share of the votes, but was under the required 50% for election. In the run-off held on 20 September 2004, Megawati was defeated by Yudhoyono, who received 60.6% of the vote. The election was hailed as the first peaceful transition of power in Indonesia's history. Yudhoyono won with 61% of the vote in the 2009 presidential election, making him the first Indonesian president directly reelected. Yudhoyono was considered an anti-corruption reformist, as Indonesia's economy became a regional frontrunner in 2009–2011. He was constitutionally not allowed to seek a third term.

A series of natural major natural disasters struck Indonesia beginning in the mid 2000s. On 26 December 2004, a powerful undersea earthquake off the coast of Sumatra generated massive tidal waves. The tsunami devastated Indian Ocean communities as far away as Thailand, India, Sri Lanka, and Somalia. More than 169,000 people were dead or missing in Indonesia alone, with the worst destruction in Aceh. In March 2005, another earthquake off the coast of Sumatra killed at least 1,000 people, most of them on the island of Nias. In May 2006, a powerful earthquake killed approximately 5,800 people on Java. And in July 2006, yet another earthquake hit Java, in which more than 500 people were killed. On 30 September 2009, a 7.6 magnitude earthquake struck off the coast of Sumatra, causing the death of over 1,000 people, and on 10 October 2010, a 7.7 earthquake killed over 400 people.

13 GOVERNMENT

The provisional constitution of 17 August 1950 mandated a unitary republic. The president and vice president, "elected in accordance with rules to be laid down by law," were to be inviolable, but cabinet ministers were jointly and individually responsible. The House of Representatives was to be a unicameral parliament. Sukarno and Hatta, the first president and vice president, were elected by parliament; no term of office was stipulated by the constitution. In practice, the government was not truly parliamentary, since president Sukarno played a role far greater than is usual for the head of state in a parliamentary system. In 1957, Sukarno adopted a more authoritarian policy of "guided democracy." He fur-

ther strengthened his powers in 1959 by decreeing a return to the provisional 1945 constitution, which called for a strong president and stressed the philosophy of Pancasila as a national ideology. In 1960, Sukarno suspended parliament and began to rule by decree. He appointed a new 283-member parliament and later named another 326 legislators who, with the members of parliament, were to constitute the Provisional People's Congress. In 1963, the congress elected Sukarno president for life. Following the political upheavals of 1965–66, the army, led by Gen. Suharto, took over to establish a "New Order." In 1968, Suharto dismissed 123 members of the People's Consultative Assembly (Majelis Permusyawaratan Rakyat—MPR), an outgrowth of the Provisional People's Congress, and replaced them with his own nominees.

On 3 July 1971, general elections-the first since 1955-were held for portions of two reconstituted national bodies, a 460-seat House of Representatives (Dewan Perwakilan Raky—DPR) and a 920-seat People's Consultative Assembly or MPR. In 1987, the memberships were increased to 500 and 1,000, respectively. The number of seats in the MPR was later reduced to 700. The People's Consultative Assembly included the DPR plus 200 indirectly selected members; it met every five years to elect the president and vice president and to approve broad outlines of national policy and also had yearly meetings to consider constitutional and legislative changes. Legislative responsibility was vested in the DPR, which consisted of 462 elected members and 38 members appointed by the president from the military. In 1973, the MPR elected President Suharto to a second five-year term; he was reelected to a third term in 1978, a fourth in 1983, a fifth in 1988, a sixth in 1993, and a seventh in 1998. However, Suharto was forced to step down in May 1998 in favor of B. J. Habibie, his vice president. He too was forced to resign after the People's Consultative Assembly questioned his leadership, and the body chose Abdurrahman Wahid as president in October 1999. Wahid was eventually removed from office in July 2001, amid charges of corruption and political incompetence. The vice president, Megawati Sukarnoputri, the daughter of Sukarno, became president.

In August 2002, the People's Consultative Assembly (MPR) approved constitutional amendments to take effect in time for the presidential elections held in 2004. Seats in the DPR were no longer reserved for the armed forces; in return, members of the military were allowed to vote. Members of the DPR were to be elected for five-year terms. A second standing body, the Council of Regional Representatives (Dewan Perwakilan Daerah—DPD), now functions as a senate in Indonesia. As of 2011, the DPR had 560 members and the DPD had 132 members. Presidents are directly elected, and limited to two terms. In 2004, Megawati was defeated in the second round of the first direct presidential elections held in Indonesia. Susilo Bambang Yudhoyono ran with the newly formed Democratic Party (PD) and became president in a runoff election. He was reelected in 2009, winning a majority without needing a runoff election.

14 POLITICAL PARTIES

Until the autumn of 1955, when the first national elections were held, members of the House of Representatives were appointed by the president in consultation with party leaders. In the 1955 general election, six parties received more than one million votes each: the Indonesian Nationalist Party (Partai Nasional Indonesia—PNI), 22.3% of the total; the Council of Muslim Organizations (Masjumi), 20.9%; the Orthodox Muslim Scholars (Nahdlatul Ulama—NU), 18.4%; the Indonesian Communist Party (Partai Komunis Indonesia—PKI), 16.4%; the United Muslim Party, 2.9%; and the Christian Party, 2.6%. In all, 28 parties won representation in the 273-member parliament. Most of the political parties had socialist aims or tendencies.

In August 1960, Sukarno ordered the dissolution of the Masjumi and one other party on the grounds of disloyalty. A month later, political action by all parties was barred. Early in 1961, notice was given that all political parties were required to apply for permission to function. Parties certified to continue in existence included the PKI, PNI, and NU, as well as Islamic and Christian based parties. The PKI, which at the height of its power in 1965 had an estimated three million members and was especially strong on Java, was banned by Gen. Suharto in March 1966, by which time more than 100,000 PKI members were estimated to have been killed in riots, assassinations, and purges; many more PKI members were arrested.

Prior to the 1971 elections, Suharto's government formed a mass organization, known as Golkar, to be the political vanguard for its "New Order" program. In the 1971 elections, Golkar candidates received 63% of the vote, while winning 227 of the 351 contested seats in the House of Representatives. The Orthodox Muslim NU placed second in the balloting, with 58 seats; the moderate Indonesian Muslim Party (Parmusi), an offshoot of the banned Masjumi Party, won 24 seats; and the PNI, Sukarno's former base, won only 20 seats. An act of 1975 provided for the fusion of the major political organizations into two parties-the United Development Party (Partai Persuatan Pembangunan—PPP) and the Indonesian Democratic Party (Partai DemoKrasi Indonesia—PDI)-and Golkar. The PPP, then Golkar's chief opposition, was a fusion of the NU, Parmusi and other Muslim groups, while the PDI represented the merger of the PNI, the Christian Party, the Catholic Party, and smaller groups. In the third general election, held in 1977, Golkar won 232 seats in the House of Representatives, against 99 seats for the PPP and 29 seats for the PDI. Golkar made further gains in the elections of 1982, winning 246 of the 364 contested seats, against 94 for the PPP and 24 for the PDI. Both opposition parties charged that the government had falsified the vote totals. In the election of 1987, Golkar won 292 of the 400 elected seats (73.2%), against 64 for the PPP (16%) and 44 for the PDI (10.8%). In the 1992 election, Golkar won 68% of the popular vote, down by 5% from 1987. The PPP took 17% of the vote, and the PDI took 15%. These results in terms of DPR seats were: Golkar, 281; PPP, 63; and PDI, 56 seats.

The 29 May 1997 elections were marked by fraud and more than 200 people were killed during the campaigning. The ruling Golkar party took 74% of the vote, the PPP took 22% of the vote and the PDI, 3%. The 7 June 1999 elections resulted in a victory for Megawati Sukarnoputri's PDI-P (Indonesia Democracy Party-Struggle); however, she relinquished the presidency in favor of Abdurrahman Wahid. The PDI-P took 37.4% of the vote, Golkar took 20.9% of the vote, Wahid's National Awakening Party (PKB) took 17.4% of the vote, and the PPP took 10.7%. As vice president, Megawati became president on the removal of Wahid in July 2001.

The next parliamentary elections were held in April 2004, following constitutional amendments in 2002 and the formation of new political parties, some of which were vehicles for particular politicians and some of which promoted Islamist views. Golkar took 21.6% of the vote (128 seats), followed by the PDI-P, with 18.5% (109 seats). The PPP won 8.2% of the vote (58 seats). The National Awakening Party (PKB) won 10.6% of the vote (52 seats); the Democratic Party (PD) won 7.5% of the vote (55 seats); the National Mandate Party (PAN), 6.4% (53 seats); the Prosperous Justice Party (PKS), 7.3% (45 seats). Other parties won a collective 19.9% of the vote and held 50 seats. Due to election rules, the number of seats won does not always follow the number of votes received by the parties. When a direct presidential election was held in 2004, Susilo Bambang Yudhoyono of the PD won a runoff election against Megawati with 60.6% of the vote.

In the presidential election of 2009, Yudhoyono was reelected with 60.8% of the vote. In the parliamentary elections of 2009, his PD won 20.9% of the vote (148 seats), followed by Golkar with 14.5% (107 seats), PDI-P with 14% (94 seats), PKS with 7.9% (57 seats), PAN with 6% (46 seats), PPP with 5.3% (37 seats), PKB with 4.9% (28 seats), the Great Indonesia Movement Party (GERINDA) with 4.5% (26 seats), and the People's Conscience Party (HANURA) with 3.8% (17 seats). Twenty-nine other parties received less than 2.5% of the vote and did not obtain any seats. Officials of the PD were under scrutiny in corruption cases in 2011, which called into question PD leader Yudhoyono's reputation as an anti-corruption reformist.

15 LOCAL GOVERNMENT

Indonesia is divided into 30 provinces. In addition there are two special territories (Yogyakarta and Aceh), and the capital city of Jakarta is a special district. When Indonesia became a democracy following the Suharto administration, decentralization of power to regional governments was given particular priority. With the implementation of decentralization on 1 January 2001, in what is known as the "Big Bang," district (also called regency, kabupaten) and city governments became the key administrative units responsible for providing most government services. According to the World Bank, 16,000 public service entities were put under regional control.

Each province is administered by an elected governor. Aceh, Papua, and West Papua have special autonomous status, and in Yogyakarta, the sultan retains political powers. Provinces are divided into districts (kabupatens), and cities, with elected bupati administrators for districts and elected mayors for cities. There are subdistricts (kecamatan) headed by a camat, and villages, usually known as desa. The head of a desa is elected by the village community.

16 JUDICIAL SYSTEM

Government courts have jurisdiction in the first instance in civil and criminal cases. The high court hears appeals in civil cases and reviews criminal cases. The Supreme Court has as its primary function the review of decisions by lower courts; its judges are appointed by the president. On 16 August 2003, a separate Constitutional Court was invested by the president. In March 2004, the Supreme Court assumed administrative and financial responsibility for the lower court system from the Ministry of Justice and Human Rights.

By Indonesian law, defendants are guaranteed rights including innocence until proven guilty, the right to an attorney, and the right to call defense witnesses. Indonesia does not have jury trials; evidence is heard by a panel of judges. Corruption is a pervasive problem at all levels of the judicial system.

In villages, customary law (*adat*) procedures continue to be used for some civil arbitration. Islamic law (Shari'ah) governs many non-criminal matters involving Muslims, including family law, inheritance and divorce; however, the People's Consultative Assembly (MPR) rejected the imposition of Shari'ah for all Muslims of Indonesia in 2002. The exception is Aceh province, which is allowed to apply Shari'ah for its Muslim citizens.

Indonesia has several special courts for human rights violations. While official respect for human rights has improved enormously under Indonesia's democratic form of government, reports persisted of extrajudicial killings, torture, and other mistreatment in custody by police forces, and by members of the armed forces stationed in Papua, according to the US State Department as of 2010.

17 ARMED FORCES

The International Institute for Strategic Studies reports that armed forces in Indonesia totaled 302,000 members in 2011. The force is comprised of 233,000 from the army, 45,000 from the navy, and 24,000 members of the air force. Armed forces represent 0.5% of the labor force in Indonesia. Defense spending totaled $30.9 billion and accounted for 3% of gross domestic product (GDP). Indonesia's military purchases weapons and aircraft from a variety of sources, including Russia, the NATO countries, and China. As of 2011, Indonesia's army was engaged in counterinsurgency operations against pro-independence forces in Papua. In 2011, nearly 1,800 Indonesian peacekeeping troops were serving in Haiti, Congo, Darfur, and the Middle East, according to the UN.

18 INTERNATIONAL COOPERATION

Indonesia was admitted to the UN on 28 September 1950 and is a member of ESCAP and several non-regional specialized agencies. Following the seating of Malaysia in the Security Council, Indonesia withdrew from the UN on 7 January 1965; it resumed its seat on 28 September 1966. Indonesia is also a member of the WTO, the Asian Development Bank, Colombo Plan, G-15, G-77, APEC, the Organization of the Islamic Conference (OIC), and OPEC. Indonesia became one of the founding members of ASEAN in 1967. Indonesia was a founding member of the Nonaligned Movement.

In March 1970, a treaty of friendship was signed between Indonesia and Malaysia; the treaty also established the boundary between the two countries in the Strait of Malacca. Relations between Indonesia and much of the international community were strained following the 1999 East Timor referendum through which that nation voted for its independence from Indonesia. Indonesian military forces supported violent upheavals in East Timor immediately following the referendum, but these were calmed by the arrival of the Australian-led peacekeeping mission of the International Force for East Timor (INTERFET).

In environmental cooperation, Indonesia is part of the Basel Convention, the Convention on Biological Diversity, Ramsar, CITES, International Tropical Timber Agreements, the Kyoto Protocol, the Montréal Protocol, MARPOL, the Nuclear Test Ban Treaty, and the UN Conventions on the Law of the Sea, Climate Change, and Desertification.

19 ECONOMY

When President Susilo Bambang Yudhoyono took office in October 2004, his government launched an aggressive program of economic reforms aimed at improving the business and investment climate. The government began a "100 Day" program of legal reform and energy initiatives. In January 2005, transportation, water and sanitation, power, and other projects were announced. The government launched a vigorous anticorruption campaign, and Yudhoyono stressed the need for economic transparency and efficiency. Revisions of the tax, investment, and labor laws were underway in 2005. Yudhoyono's initiatives were also geared toward helping poverty-stricken Indonesians, first by directing government spending toward targeted development programs, especially in rural areas; and second by creating jobs, which would be accomplished through the reduction in corruption and increase in investment. Direct cash payments were also made to the poorest Indonesians, to help offset a reduction in fuel subsidies, while rice subsidies were expanded. Domestic consumption comprised the majority of GNP as of 2011, but Indonesia also exported lucrative petroleum and mineral commodities. The Yudhoyono administration has implemented financial reforms, including tax and customs reforms, the introduction of Treasury bills, and improved capital market supervision.

In the first quarter of 2011 the economy grew by 6.5%. The GDP rate of change in Indonesia, as of 2011, was 6.1%. Inflation stood at 5.1%, and unemployment was reported at 7.1%. While Indonesia still struggled with poverty, unemployment, natural disasters such as earthquakes, inadequate infrastructure, widespread corruption, a complex regulatory environment, and unequal resource distribution among regions, from 2006 through 2011 the nation had one of the best performing stock markets in Asia, debt ratio declined, and reserves were at an all time high. Foreign investment was strong from 2009 through 2011, with analysts touting Indonesia, Southeast Asia's largest economy, as the next step after China and India for major investment in Asia.

20 INCOME

The CIA estimated that in 2010 the GDP of Indonesia was $1 trillion. The CIA defines GDP as the value of all final goods and services produced within a nation in a given year and computed on the basis of purchasing power parity (PPP) rather than value as measured on the basis of the rate of the exchange based on current dollars. The per capita GDP was estimated at $4,200. The annual growth rate of GDP was 6.1%. The average inflation rate was 5.1%. It was estimated that agriculture accounted for 16.5% of GDP, industry 46.4%, and services 37.1%. According to the World Bank, remittances from citizens living abroad totaled $6.8 billion or about $27 per capita and accounted for approximately 0.7% of GDP.

The World Bank reported that in 2009, household consumption in Indonesia totaled $316.7 billion or about $1,244 per capita, measured in current US dollars rather than PPP. Household consumption includes expenditures of individuals, households, and nongovernmental organizations on goods and services, excluding the purchases of dwellings. It was estimated that household consumption was growing at an average annual rate of 4.9%.

As of 2011 the most recent study by the World Bank reported that actual individual consumption in Indonesia was 67.2% of GDP and accounted for 1.37% of world consumption. By comparison, the United States accounted for 25.44% of world individual consumption. The World Bank also estimated that 29.3% of Indonesia's GDP was spent on food and beverages, 15.4% on housing and household furnishings, 2.4% on clothes, 2.0% on health, 4.4% on transportation, 1.2% on communications, 1.2% on recreation, 4.1% on restaurants and hotels, and 3.6% on miscellaneous goods and services and purchases from abroad. It was estimated that in 2010 about 13.33% of the population subsisted on an income below the poverty line established by Indonesia's government.

21 LABOR

As of 2010, Indonesia had a total labor force of 116.5 million people. Within that labor force, CIA estimates in 2010 noted that 38.3% were employed in agriculture, 12.8% in industry, and 48.9% in the service sector. The law protects the right to form and join unions for all workers regardless of political affiliation. Ten or more workers can unionize, and thousands of unions have been registered. However, a union can be banned by the government if its foundation goes against the constitution. Sometimes there are clashes between different unions within one workplace. With the exception of civil servants, workers have the right to strike, after prior announcement and mandatory mediation. Illegal "wildcat" strikes are common. Collective bargaining is utilized, but most contracts do not provide workers with more than the government minimum standards. Labor issues included excessive mandatory overtime, and extreme disparity between the pay of local employees and foreign "expert" workers. According to the US State Department, as of 2010, 10% of workers in the formal sector were members of trade unions, while 65.6% of all workers were employed in the informal sector.

Although a 2005 law prohibited children under age 18 from working, the nation's laws recognized that some children must work to supplement family income. As a result, there is an exception for children as young as 13, who may work but are limited to working no more than three hours per day. In addition, they must have parental consent, cannot work during school hours, and must be paid legal wages. In addition, children under 18 are not legally permitted to work in hazardous occupations. The child labor laws are not effectively enforced. According to the US State Department, an estimated 6 to 8 million children were working more than the legal three hours per day, as of 2010.

There is no national minimum wage. Wages are set by area wage councils who estimate the amount a worker needs to earn to provide for his or her basic needs. In 2010, the minimum wage ranged from about $120 per month to about $60 per month. However, many employers do not pay this minimum wage, especially in the informal sector. The 40-hour work week and a 7- to 8-hour day are established by law throughout Indonesia, although these standards are not regularly enforced. Millions of Indonesians work overseas, where they are often vulnerable to human trafficking, abuse, and exploitation.

22 AGRICULTURE

Roughly 18% of the total land was farmed as of 2009, according to the FAO. The country's major crops include rice, cassava (tapioca), sugarcane, peanuts, rubber, cacao, coffee, oil palm, tobacco, vegetables, fruits, corn, soybeans, spices, and copra. Cereal production as of 2009 amounted to 82 million tons, fruit production 17.1 million tons, and vegetable production 9.1 million tons. The Indonesian government has sought to achieve food self-sufficiency through expansion of arable acreage, improved farm techniques (especially the use of fertilizers and improved seeds), extension of irrigation facilities, and expanded training for farmers. As of 2010, according to the CIA, agriculture accounted for 16.5% of GDP and employed 38.3% of the labor force.

Some 60% of the country's cultivated land is in Java. There are three main types of farming: smallholder farming (mostly rice), smallholder cash cropping, and over 1,800 large foreign-owned or privately owned estates, the latter two producing export crops as well as crops for domestic consumption. Although rice, vegetables, and fruit constitute the bulk of the small farmer's crops, about 20% of output is in cash crops. Of the estate-grown crops, rubber, tobacco, sugar, palm oil, fibers, coffee, tea, and cocoa are the most important. Indonesia was the world's second largest exporter of rubber, as of 2010, producing about 2,736,000 metric tons.

Rice is the staple food, and Indonesia is one of the world's top rice producers, but the country still must import rice, as well as corn (for poultry feed), and soybeans to fill gaps between domestic production and consumption. Climate change and excessive chemical pesticide use are cited by experts as damaging Indonesia's rice production. Sugarcane has been an important commercial crop, but production has been steadily declining, to 1.9 million tons of plantation white sugar in fiscal year 2009/2010, necessitating imports for domestic consumption.

Indonesia as of 2011 was the world's largest producer of palm oil, used for cooking, processed food, cosmetics, and biofuel. Crude palm oil production was estimated at 23.5 metric million tons in 2011, according to the Indonesian Palm Oil Association. The expanding palm oil industry, along with logging, was widely blamed for rampant deforestation and wildlife habitat loss in Kalimantan, Sumatra, and other regions, as well as the land-clearing fires in peatlands and rainforests which caused regional air pollution haze in 2006 and 2010. Palm oil production involving peatland clearing was reportedly the source of an estimated 80% of Indonesia's greenhouse gas emissions. Efforts to change to more sustainably produced palm oil, such as a moratorium on taking over forests and peatlands, and emphasis on planting on degraded lands instead, had been slow to make an impact as of 2011.

In 2011, Indonesia was the world's third-largest producer of coffee, producing 9.129 million bags in the 2010/2011 crop, according to the International Coffee Organization. Indonesia planned to boost production of high quality arabica coffee, as coffee beans from Sumatra, Sulawesi, and Papua have gained international prestige. In 2010, Indonesia was the second largest cacao (the raw material for chocolate) producer in the world, producing over 800 tons, but lagged behind in processing cacao, instead exporting 80% raw cacao beans. Plans were underway to produce artisanal organic chocolate for export in a new factory in Bali, as of 2011. The nation's tobacco industry was placed in jeopardy in 2010 when the World Health Organization (WHO) issued recommendations to ban the use of cloves and other flavor ingredients in tobacco products; 93% of the cigarettes produced in the country were clove cigarettes and the Indonesian tobacco market was the fifth largest in the world.

23 ANIMAL HUSBANDRY

The UN Food and Agriculture Organization (FAO) reported that Indonesia dedicated 11 million hectares (27.2 million acres) to permanent pasture or meadow in 2009. During that year, the country tended 1.3 billion chickens, 12.9 million head of cattle, and 6.9 million pigs. The production from these animals amounted to 433,479 tons of beef, 598,928 tons of pork, 1.35 million tons of poultry, 1.15 million tons of eggs, and 2.58 million tons of milk. Indonesia also produced 65,550 tons of cattle hide and 21,412 tons of raw wool.

The production of meat and cows' milk is secondary in Indonesia to the raising of draft animals for agricultural purposes. The government has established cattle-breeding stations and artificial-insemination centers to improve the stock and has been carrying on research to improve pastures. Beef demand has increased in the early 21st century, and as of 2009, Indonesia was importing more than 30% of the beef consumed, as well as importing 70% of milk. Pork was primarily consumed on Bali, and by Chinese Indonesians. H1N1 virus was detected in pigs in Indonesia during 2009. Technical and other assistance has been offered to rural smallholder farmers raising chickens and ducks. Indonesia also has large commercial poultry farms owned by international agribusiness companies. H5N1 avian influenza has been detected in Indonesia.

24 FISHING

Indonesia had 86,240 decked commercial fishing boats in 2008. The annual capture totaled 4.96 million tons according to the UN FAO. The export value of seafood totaled $1.8 billion. The Indonesia-Malaysia-Philippines region has the world's highest marine biodiversity. Important seafood products include tuna, mackerel, shark, shrimp, crab, cuttlefish, squid, and grouper. Methods used include pole and line, troll-line, longline, traps, and various types of nets. Fish farms, mainly on Java, produce carp, tilapia, catfish, milkfish, and shrimp. Coastal shrimp farms have caused major environmental damage, and in 2010 the government began requiring Indonesian shrimp farming operations to meet sustainability guidelines.

Indonesia's commercial commodity fishing is largely confined to a narrow band of inshore waters, especially off northern Java, but other fishing for domestic consumption takes place along the coast and in rivers, lakes, coastal swamps, artificial ponds, and flooded rice fields. The government has stocked the inland waters, encouraged cooperatives to provide credit facilities, introduced improved fishing methods, provided for the use of motorized fishing boats and improved tackle, and built or rehabilitated piers. Overfishing of Indonesia's seas, by local and foreign trawlers, has been an ongoing problem in the early 21st century.

25 FORESTRY

Approximately 52% of Indonesia is covered by forest. The UN FAO estimated the 2009 roundwood production at 36.6 million

cu m (1.28 billion cu ft). The value of all forest products, including roundwood, totaled $6.2 billion.

Indonesia has over 4,000 species of trees, including 120 types of hardwood considered suitable for commercial use. Timber estates produce fast growth species such as pine, eucalyptus, albizia, and acacia for the pulp and paper industry. Bamboo is cultivated as a sustainable product for pulp and building, and rattan is gathered for export and domestic use. Throughout Indonesia, deforestation has caused soil erosion, aggravated floods, and created water shortages. Most remaining primary forests are on Kalimantan, Sumatra, Papua, and West Papua. Those regions have been heavily logged from the 1980s through the early 21st century. Loss of forest from illegal logging and clearing of land for oil palm plantations has continued, as of 2011.

A hardwood log export ban was enacted in 1985 to try to protect rapidly diminishing forests. Prohibitive export taxes imposed in 1990 all but eliminated legal tropical hardwood exports, in order to conserve declining forest resources for production and export of higher value items such as plywood and furniture. The annual allowable cut of logs was set at 5.74 million cu m. However, up to 68 million cu m of logs are cut illegally, with some 10 million cu m of logs illegally shipped out of the country.

Controversially, Indonesia's Ministry of Forestry in 2011 began classifying oil palm plantations as forests. The replacement of forests with oil palm plantations had been widely cited as a major source of loss of primary rainforest and peatland forest. A moratorium on licenses for clearing primary and peatland forests was announced by Indonesia in a 2011 Norway-sponsored climate deal. Forest loss has been the main cause of Indonesia's high level of greenhouse gas emissions. At the September 2011 Forests Indonesia Conference, President Yudhoyono made a pledge to devote himself to protecting Indonesia's forests during his last three years in office.

26 MINING

Indonesia's principal mineral resources (excluding oil, natural gas, and coal) are copper, gold, nickel, and tin. It has large reserves of all of these metals and is a major world supplier of them. In addition, Indonesia is a leading regional producer of cement, bauxite, and nitrogen fertilizer. Indonesia also produces hydraulic cement, dolomite, feldspar, granite, gypsum, marble, nitrogen, salt, quartz sand, silica stone, sulfur, and zeolite.

Mined copper output (content in ore) in 2009 was 610,000 metric tons, down from 1,064,000 metric tons in 2005. Bauxite production in 2009 (wet basis, gross weight) was 1.2 million tons. Indonesia possesses large deposits of high-grade bauxite, from mines in Kijang (Bintan Island) and Sumatra. Most of the output was exported to Japan, the remainder to the United States.

Tin mine output in 2009 was 55,000 metric tons. The chief deposits of tin are in Bangka, Belitung, and Singkep, islands off the east coast of Sumatra. Indonesia is the world's second-largest producer of tin (after China). The industry in Indonesia is dominated by PT Koba Tin and PT Tambang Timah. However, the industry has, for several years, faced depleting resources, community conflicts in several mining sites, and illegal mining and smuggling, the latter resulting in increased compensation to company contractors to dissuade illegal actions. The government set a lower tin production target in 2010 and renewed its crackdown on illegal tin mining.

Gold mine output in 2009 was 65,000 kg, down from 130,620 kg in 2008. Illegal mining activity and associated mercury contamination was an ongoing problem for the Indonesian government and legal gold mining operators.

Nickel mine output in 2003 totaled 143,000 metric tons, up from 123,000 metric tons in 2002. Nickel is produced in Soroako (North Sulawesi), Pomalaa (South Sulawesi), and the Maluku and Gebe islands, with some of the largest reserves in the world.

Iron ore is found in sizable quantities, but was commercially exploited only in central Java. There are fair-to-good reserves of silver, iodine, diamond (industrial and gem quality), and phosphate rock, and considerable supplies of limestone, asphalt, bentonite, fireclay, and kaolin powder. In 1998 Herald Resources Ltd. of Australia announced the discovery of significant lead and zinc resources in the Dairi area, Bukit Barisan Highland; the exploration concentrated in the Anjing Hitam area; it was estimated that the deposit contained an indicated resource of 7.5 million tons of lead and zinc at 10.3% lead, 16.7% zinc, and 14 grams per ton of silver and an inferred resource of 2.5 million tons at 6.8% lead and 11.3% zinc. It was sold to a Chinese and Indonesian joint venture in 2008.

Indonesia's constitution places all natural resources in the soil and waters under the jurisdiction of the state. In 1999, the government increased taxes and royalties that created a less competitive investment environment. Restructuring and privatization of state-owned industries has been very slow, and new investment was still low. As the world's fourth-most-populous country, Indonesia could become one of the largest steel-consuming countries. However, its volatile political situation and uncertain economic climate hampered development. The state-owned general mining company, PT Aneka Tambang, was privatized during the 2000s, with its stock trading on the Jakarta Stock Exchange.

27 ENERGY AND POWER

The World Bank reported in 2008 that Indonesia produced 149.4 billion kWh of electricity and consumed 134.4 billion kWh, or 528 kWh per capita. Roughly 66% of energy came from fossil fuels, while 8% came from renewable fuels. Electricity was generated by coal or diesel burning plants. Fluctuations in energy supply are common throughout the country.

Per capita oil consumption was 874 kg. Oil production totaled 953,148 barrels of oil a day. Indonesia was a member of OPEC until 2008, when, its petroleum reserves in decline, the country began to import oil for its needs. Petroleum products such as kerosene (used for cooking and lighting), and gasoline, have been heavily subsidized by the Indonesian government. The Yudhoyono administration met with strong political resistance to proposed reductions in fuel subsidies. As of late 2011, Indonesia had achieved very little conversion to natural gas or renewable sources such as solar, wind, biomass, or geothermal, despite the enormous potential for alternative energy (particularly geothermal) in the archipelago.

28 INDUSTRY

The leading industries by value, according to the CIA, are petroleum products; textiles, apparel and footwear; mining; cement; chemical fertilizers; wood products; rubber; food; and tourism. Industrial expansion has been given a high priority in development plans. Labor-intensive industries have been stressed, together with industries producing consumer items for domestic consumption and export, and products accelerating agricultural development. Indonesia has a vast array of cottage industries, producing handicrafts including batik, jewelry, woodcarvings, and basketry, for local use and for export.

The government has encouraged industrial investors, particularly those who plan to export, to locate in bonded zones (BZ), free trade zones (FTZ) or export-processing zones (EPZ). From World War II until the 1990s, overall industrial growth was small, with agriculture the dominant sector of the Indonesian economy. However, in the 1990s, industry and services took over as the dominant sectors. In January 2005, the WTO abolished world textile quotas, and Indonesia's garment export industry suffered.

Industries that process Indonesia's natural and agricultural resources include those based on petroleum, wood, sugarcane, rubber, coffee, cacao, tea, coconuts, oil palm, sisal, kapok, rice, and cassava. Manufactured products include consumer goods such as tires, clothing, shoes, textiles, glass, paper, tractors, and trucks. Other industries include Krakatau Steel's six production facilities, plywood factories, cement works, spinning mills, knitting plants, iron works, and copper foundries. Petrochemicals and urea fertilizers are manufactured, and there are facilities for automobile assembly, shipbuilding, and aircraft manufacture. Indonesia's original "national car" was the Maleo, first produced in 1996 with over 80% locally made parts. In 2011, the government requested that Indonesia-based manufacturers begin to produce low cost, environmentally friendly "city cars" for the domestic market.

The petroleum refining industry declined in the early 21st century. Indonesia had eight refineries, operated by Pertamina, which was in transition from state owned to a public company as of late 2011. Urea fertilizers were produced from Indonesia's natural gas deposits, and Indonesia also produced nitrogen, phosphate, and potash fertilizers. The steel industry in Indonesia includes state owned Krakatau Steel-plus numerous small mills that use scrap steel as their raw material input. Wood products, including plywood, pulp and paper, are important industrial exports.

The Agency for Strategic Industries, a state-owned holding company including aircraft, telecommunications, and high-technology industries, has formed joint ventures to promote technology transfer to Indonesia. There has been a shortage of skilled technical personnel to support high-tech industries; most technology has been imported through joint ventures. In September 2011, the government announced plans to attract investment in high technology electronics manufacturing. Relatively low labor costs boosted manufacturing in consumer goods sectors like footwear during 2009–2011, although electricity shortages and other infrastructure deficiencies continued to hold back industrial development.

29 SCIENCE AND TECHNOLOGY

The World Bank reported in 2009 that there were no patent applications in science and technology in Indonesia. The Indonesian Institute of Sciences, a government agency established in 1967, has centers for research and development in biology, oceanology, geotechnology, applied physics and applied chemistry, metallurgy, limnology, biotechnology, electrical engineering, information and computer sciences, telecommunications, strategic electronics, component and material sciences, and metrology. It also oversees Indonesia's botanical gardens, including the world-renowned Bogor Botanical Garden. The Indonesian Center for Agricultural Library and Technology Dissemination, based in Bogor, is an information center with e-resources including the Rice Knowledge Bank. The country has over 40 other research institutes concerned with agriculture and veterinary science, medicine, the natural sciences, and technology. Courses in basic and applied sciences are offered at over 50 state and private universities. A Science and Technology Park, encouraging research and development, was planned for the city of Solo, on Java.

Indonesia's first locally designed and manufactured communications satellite was launched in 2007. In 2010, Indonesia and the United States embarked on their first joint deep sea exploratory mission, exploring one of the least understood and most diverse marine systems on earth, located just north of the Indonesian archipelago. Indonesian scientists have participated in expeditions in Papua's remote forests, finding previously undescribed species of plants and animals. In July 2011, the formation of a Partnership for Enhanced Engagement in Research, between Indonesia and the US, was announced, emphasizing cooperation on topics being addressed by Indonesian scientists, including alternative energy, climate change, infectious diseases, and marine science.

30 DOMESTIC TRADE

Jakarta, the capital and chief commercial city, is Indonesia's main distribution center. Most trade is conducted through small and medium-sized importers who specialize in specific product lines. Corruption among police and local officials has made transporting products long distances from a central warehouse within the country very expensive.

Retail outlets range from open air markets and small village shops, to urban supermarkets and mega-malls like Jakarta's Grand Indonesia and Mall Indonesia. Local and international franchise businesses operate in Indonesia, and the cities have stores representing imported luxury brands. Bali is known for its handicrafts shops and art galleries. Commercial business hours vary, but are usually 8 a.m. to 5 p.m., Monday through Friday, and from 8 a.m. to 1 p.m. on Saturday, although some Indonesians take Saturday off. Many shops are open from 9 a.m. to 10 p.m., Monday through Saturday. Muslims can take time off for prayers every Friday from 12 to 1 p.m. Local banks transact business from 9 a.m. to 3 p.m., Monday through Friday.

Newspapers, magazines, television, radio, posters, and billboards are the most popular advertising media. Electronic commerce (e-commerce) was slow to develop in Indonesia, due mainly to concerns about fraud, despite widespread use of mobile phones and the internet. As of mid-2011, Indonesia had only 7 million credit card users, and in December 2011, the central bank put caps on monthly allowed debt for card holders.

31 FOREIGN TRADE

Indonesia imported $36 billion worth of goods and services in 2010, according to the US State Department, while exporting $158 billion worth of goods and services. Indonesia's major import partners in 2010, according to the CIA, were China, 15.1%; Sin-

Principal Trading Partners – Indonesia (2010)

(In millions of US dollars)

Country	Total	Exports	Imports	Balance
World	289,922.0	157,823.0	132,099.0	25,724.0
Japan	42,748.0	25,782.0	16,966.0	8,816.0
China	36,117.0	15,693.0	20,424.0	-4,731.0
Singapore	33,964.0	13,723.0	20,241.0	-6,518.0
United States	23,718.0	14,302.0	9,416.0	4,886.0
South Korea	20,278.0	12,575.0	7,703.0	4,872.0
Malaysia	18,011.0	9,362.0	8,649.0	713.0
India	13,210.0	9,915.0	3,295.0	6,620.0
Thailand	12,038.0	4,567.0	7,471.0	-2,904.0
Canada	8,343.0	4,244.0	4,099.0	145.0
Taiwan	8,080.0	4,838.0	3,242.0	1,596.0

(…) data not available or not significant.

(n.s.) not specified.

SOURCE: *2011 Direction of Trade Statistics Yearbook*, New York: United Nations, 2011.

gapore, 14.9%; Japan, 12.5%; United States, 6.9%; Malaysia, 6.4%; South Korea, 5.7%; and Thailand, 5.5%. Major export partners in 2010 were Japan, 16.3%; China, 9.9%; United States, 9.1%; Singapore, 8.7%; South Korea, 8%; India, 6.3%; and Malaysia, 5.9%. In percentage terms, the major exports in 2010 were crude petroleum and petroleum products (17.8% of total exports); minerals (14.9%); textiles and footwear (8.9%); crude palm oil (8.5%); electrical appliances (8.2%); and rubber products (4.7%), according to the US State Department. Major imports include machinery and other industrial equipment, fuel and lubricants, food, and chemicals. According to the CIA, in 2009 Indonesia exported an estimated 404,100 barrels per day of petroleum, but imported 767,400 barrels per day; oil (crude and refined) is imported, while natural gas is exported.

Trade liberalization began in 1982 as an effort to increase non-oil exports. By 1987, non-oil exports matched revenue from oil and gas exports for the first time. Imports, which have been closely regulated in government efforts to restrain growth of consumer merchandise imports, have consisted mainly of machinery and raw materials. The late 1990s had shrinking exports of wood products, and slow growth in exports of garments and textiles. Emerging exports such as footwear and consumer electronics also showed weak growth. However, rising world prices for oil and rubber kept commodity exports high. In the early 21st century, Indonesia has had to import the main staple food, rice, as well as petroleum, to meet rising domestic demand. Palm oil has become a significant export commodity, sold to Asian countries such as China and India. Concerns about sustainability have slowed demand for Indonesian palm oil in Europe. Indonesian coffee has become a prestigious export in international markets.

Japan became Indonesia's dominant trade partner in the 1970s, and has remained important for both imports and exports. Other trade partners-including China, the United States, Singapore, and South Korea have become important to the economy as well, and Indonesia's diversified export markets keep it protected from risk in any one country. With the creation in 1992 of the ASEAN Free Trade Area (AFTA), trade within the region increased. As of 1 January 2010, a new free trade area has been established between

China and the six founding members of the Association of South East Asian Nations (ASEAN), including Indonesia. A major point of the free trade agreement is the elimination of tariffs on nearly 90% of imported goods. The ASEAN Trade in Goods Agreement (ATIGA), entered into force on 17 May 2010. The ATIGA represented the next step in realizing the free flow of goods within the region by simplifying the processes and procedures necessary to create a single market and production base-known as the ASEAN Economic Community (AEC)-by 2015. Major points of ATIGA include tariff liberalization, a simplification of the rules of origin, and implementation of such rules. The comprehensive agreement also demands greater transparency in regional trade liberalization.

32 BALANCE OF PAYMENTS

Indonesia had initial balance-of-payments difficulties from the time of independence, but Indonesia's payments position improved considerably in the late 1970s as a result of increases in oil prices. The current account deficit averaged -2% of GDP between 1992 and 1997, and then began a steady improvement, accruing a surplus of over 4% of GDP in 1998 due to currency devaluation and a one-third cut in imports. The current account balance averaged 3.9% of GDP over the 2001–05 period. After Indonesia posted balance of payments surpluses in 2006 ($14.5 billion) and 2007 ($12.5 billion), the global financial crisis weakened demand for Indonesia's exports in 2008, and a deficit of -$2.2 billion was posted. Indonesia headed back into surplus balance of payments with $4.0 billion in 2009, although rising costs of fuel imports kept the trade balance under pressure. In 2010 Indonesia had a current account balance of $6.294 billion, strengthened by the inflow of investment to capital and financial accounts, and had a foreign trade surplus of $21 billion, amounting to 1.7% of GDP. Reserves of foreign exchange and gold were estimated at $96.21 billion, as of December 2010, according to the CIA.

Balance of Payments – Indonesia (2010)

(In millions of US dollars)

Current Account		**5,643.0**
Balance on goods		30,628.0
Imports	-127,447.0	
Exports	158,074.0	
Balance on services		-9,324.0
Balance on income		-20,291.0
Current transfers		4,630.0
Capital Account		**50.0**
Financial Account		**26,151.0**
Direct investment abroad		-2,664.0
Direct investment in Indonesia		13,371.0
Portfolio investment assets		-2,511.0
Portfolio investment liabilities		15,713.0
Financial derivatives		...
Other investment assets		-1,725.0
Other investment liabilities		3,968.0
Net Errors and Omissions		**-1,559.0**
Reserves and Related Items		**-30,284.0**

(…) data not available or not significant.

SOURCE: *Balance of Payment Statistics Yearbook 2011*, Washington, DC: International Monetary Fund, 2011.

33 BANKING AND SECURITIES

The government's Bank Negara Indonesia (BNI) was established in 1953 as the successor to the colonial era Java Bank. In 1967, as part of the new government's policy of encouraging foreign investment, foreign banks were permitted to operate in Indonesia. The Indonesian banking system transformed after 1980, through a process of gradual but steady reform that culminated in the 1992 banking law. Joint ventures were allowed with Indonesian partners. The partial liberalization of the banking industry had a dramatic impact. A precipitous growth in bank credits threatened to undermine economic stability by stimulating a sharp increase in import demand and inflationary pressures. Responding to this threat, the government initiated an abrupt tightening of monetary policy during the 1990s. From 1992 until 1997, the rupiah was managed in relation to the dollar, but in 1997, the currency was allowed to float because of Asian currency depreciation. Political and social unrest resulted in a highly volatile currency. The 1998 economic failure brought about a major restructuring of the banking system. There were 128 private domestic commercial banks in 1998, 38 of which were liquidated in 1999, and 8 were taken over by the government. In 1999, four of the state banks were merged into the new Bank Mandiri.

Bank Indonesia (BI), the central bank, is responsible for the administration and regulation of the four state banks (Bank Mandri, Bank Negara Indonesia, Bank Rakyat Indonesia, and Bank Tabungan Negara). Bank Indonesia also oversees other banking operations, including measures to encourage foreign investment, and promotes the consolidation of smaller banks into larger financial entities. Among the state banks, Bank Rakjat Indonesia specializes in credits to agricultural cooperative societies but also provides fishing and rural credit in general. Bank Tabungan Negara promotes savings among the general public. Bank Negara Indonesia (BNI) provides funding for industry. According to the US State Department, as of March 2011, Indonesia had 122 commercial banks, 28 of which were joint ventures and 10 of which were foreign owned. Islamic, or Shari'ah, banking represented under 4% of Indonesia's banking sector, as of March 2011. Microfinance loans are provided to low income Indonesians by Bank Rakjat Indonesia, Bank Andara, Bank Tabungan Negara, and other institutions. ATMs and mobile phone banking are available in Indonesia.

The CIA reported that in December 2010, currency and demand deposits-an aggregate commonly known as M1-were equal to $67.34 billion. In 2010, M2-an aggregate equal to M1 plus savings deposits, small time deposits, and money market mutual funds-was $274.9 billion. As of December 2010, the commercial bank prime lending rate was 13.25%, according to the CIA. The discount rate, the interest rate at which the central bank lends to financial institutions in the short term, was 6.37%.

Indonesia's first stock exchange was established in December 1912 in Jakarta, although both this and two subsequent exchanges established in Surabaya and Semarang in 1925 were shut down during the Japanese occupation. An attempt to revive the capital markets in the early 1950s proved futile. It was not until August 1977 that the Jakarta Stock Exchange (JSE) was successfully relaunched amid a comprehensive set of institutional reforms that resulted in the establishment of the Capital Market Executive Agency (Badan Pelaksana Pasar Modal—BAPEPAM) to manage the market, as well as a state-owned securities firm, Danareksa, to facilitate the flotation of shares. In 2009–2001, the JSE was one of the best-performing stock markets in Asia, but shares fell in September 2011, as the financial crisis in Europe sparked panic selling along with a weak exchange rate for the rupiah. As of December 2011, there were 433 companies listed on the JSE.

34 INSURANCE

The insurance and reinsurance industry is governed by an insurance law issued in February 1992 that allows foreign ownership of insurance companies. A 1998 Financial Services Agreement with the WTO equalized capital requirements for both domestic and foreign insurance firms. The industry is regulated by the Ministry of Finance as well as the Insurance Council of Indonesia. The growth of the industry over the past decade is reflected in an impressive increase in many of the industry's financial variables, including assets, gross premiums, and investments. Third-party motor liability insurance, workers' compensation, and passenger accident insurance are compulsory. Workers' compensation must be insured with the government company, ASTEK, and employees have no right to sue. Marine cargo insurance is also a particularly important sector in Indonesia. Microinsurance, and Shari'ah-compliant insurance are available in Indonesia. Asuransi Jasa Indonesia was Indonesia's largest non-life insurer in the first half of 2009, while Asurani Jiwa Mega Life was the largest life insurer that same year. In 2009, the value of direct premiums written totaled $6.9 billion, with nonlife premiums accounting for the largest portion at $3 billion.

35 PUBLIC FINANCE

In 2010 the budget of Indonesia included $119.5 billion in public revenue and $132.9 billion in public expenditures. The budget deficit amounted to 1.9% of GDP. Public debt was 26.4% of GDP, with $196.1 billion of the debt held by foreign entities. President Yudhoyono vowed not to seek any IMF funding assistance in paying down debt. Foreign aid, in the form of loans, grants, and technical assistance, continued to be received by Indonesia, although some analysts questioned its necessity in a resource-rich G-20 "emerging economy" nation.

The 2010 budget expenditures included 20% for education, and 14.3% for subsidies. Rising costs of fuel subsidies increased government expenditures during 2011. Other government-subsidized commodities included electricity, fertilizer, seedlings, and food. Allocations in 2010 and 2011 also included health insurance programs, health clinics, family planning, social welfare, electric power generation, defense, public service improvements, and increased pay for government workers.

36 TAXATION

As of 2011, Indonesia's corporate tax was a 25% flat tax, with a 5% discount available for some public companies, and a 50% discount for small enterprises. Deemed profit margins were specified for shipping, airlines, petroleum drilling, and toys manufactured for export. Investment incentives included tax reductions and extensions. Gains from revaluations of fixed assets were taxed at 10%. Concessional rates are available for tax treaty countries, which are mainly in Asia and Europe.

Indonesia has a progressive individual income tax that ranges from 5% to a top rate of 30% on incomes over IDR500,000,000. Property taxes are 0.5%, and land/building sales tax is 5% of gross transfer value. Indirect taxes include a 10% value-added tax (VAT) that applies to a range of transactions, with many categories excepted. As of 2011, mining products, and basic food commodities were among the VAT-excepted items, as were medical, financial, and entertainment services, and transportation. Indonesia also imposes a 10% to 50% luxury tax on items including luxury homes, appliances, perfume, alcohol, and sports equipment. Luxury sales tax on vehicles ranges from 10% to 75%.

37 CUSTOMS AND DUTIES

Most tariffs are designed to stimulate exports and to protect domestic industries. However, corruption is pervasive, and evasion is widespread. Several types of goods, including food, garments, shoes, toys, and electronics, can be legally imported only through the seaports at Jakarta, Medan, Semarang, Surabaya, and Makasar, in a measure intended to control the smuggling and dumping of cheap foreign imports. There is a Free Trade Zone on Batam Island, near Singapore, that is exempt from all import and export taxes. Free Trade Zones have also been established near Tanjung Priok, the country's main port, and the Cakung manufacturing district in the vicinity of Jakarta. Indonesia has several Special Economic Zones (SEZ) for export processing, mainly near Jakarta and on the Riau Islands. In November 2011, the government announced plans for more SEZs in locations including Sumatra and Sulawesi.

Customs duties ranged from 0% to 170%, with restrictions or prohibitions on importing items including hazardous waste, explosives, and weapons. Exempt from import duties are machinery for starting industry, and goods used for science. In early 2011, the Indonesian government removed duties on 57 categories of imports, mainly staple foods and fertilizer, in an effort to control rising food prices.

Public Finance – Indonesia (2009)

(In billions of rupiah, budgetary central government figures)

Revenue and Grants	863,105	100.0%
Tax revenue	640,830	74.2%
Social contributions	...	...
Grants	1,150	0.1%
Other revenue	221,125	25.6%
Expenditures	956,824	100.0%
General public services	...	...
Defense	...	...
Public order and safety	...	...
Economic affairs	...	...
Environmental protection	...	...
Housing and community amenities	...	...
Health	...	...
Recreational, culture, and religion	...	...
Education	...	...
Social protection	...	...

(…) data not available or not significant.

SOURCE: *Government Finance Statistics Yearbook 2010*, Washington, DC: International Monetary Fund, 2010.

Indonesia participated in the ASEAN Free Trade Agreement and its Common Effective Preferential Tariff (CEPT), under which preferential duties and exemptions are granted for goods of ASEAN member countries' origin. A major point of the 2010 free trade agreement between China and the six founding members of ASEAN is the eventual elimination of tariffs on nearly 90% of imported goods. The ASEAN Trade in Goods Agreement (ATIGA), entered into force in May 2010; it included tariff liberalization.

Indonesia has imposed export taxes on palm oil and cacao, to encourage domestic processing of those commodities. In September 2011, the government announced a possible export tax for mineral ores, in preparation for a 2014 complete ban on exports of mining products in order to make sure they would be processed for added value before leaving Indonesia.

38 FOREIGN INVESTMENT

After independence, Indonesia's foreign investment law of 1958 attempted to provide guarantees to foreign investors and to establish safeguards for Indonesian interests. In the 1960s, the Sukarno government reversed this policy by nationalizing all foreign-owned commercial enterprises. This policy was again reversed after the ouster of Sukarno. The overall flow of private investments from overseas sources increased during the early 1970s, in response both to liberal terms offered under the Suharto government and to favorable world markets for Indonesian oil and other primary products. Since 1973, all foreign investment has been channeled through the Investment Coordinating Board (BKPM), and Indonesian partners were mandated for all foreign concerns established after 1974. Among the incentives for investment approved in 1986 were regulations allowing foreign investment in more industries (arms production is still prohibited) and granting foreign partners in joint ventures the right to distribute the products themselves. The Negative Investment List, amended in 2010, specifies the business fields that are closed to, or impose limitations on, foreign investors. Some conditions were placed on foreign investment in business fields including agriculture, livestock, forest products, fishing, energy, minerals, construction, and communications.

By the second decade of the 21st century, improved political and economic stability in Indonesia had encouraged investor confidence. Low labor costs, a thriving domestic market, and healthy financial institutions inspired some analysts to consider Indonesia Asia's best country for investment after China and India. However, as of 2011, issues including corruption, security risks, intellectual property violations, and labor instability, still challenged foreign investors. Foreign direct investment (FDI) in Indonesia was a net inflow of $86.15 billion in 2010, according to the CIA. FDI represented 0.9% of GDP. Indonesia's investment in other countries amounted to $32.85 billion in 2010, according to the CIA.

39 ECONOMIC DEVELOPMENT

The colonial economy of Indonesia depended upon the export of a relatively small range of primary commodities. In the 17th and 18th centuries, the basis of the export-oriented economy was spices. In the 19th century, it shifted to sugar and coffee; in the 20th century, production of petroleum, tin, timber, and rubber became fundamental. Public expenditures on the first five-year plan (1956–60) included 25% for mining and manufacturing, 25%

for transport and communications, 15% for power projects, and 35% for all other categories. Foreign aid played a major role in Indonesia's post-independence development. Before 1965, Indonesia, under Sukarno, received substantial aid from the USSR and other communist states. After 1966, Indonesia turned dramatically toward the West, as Suharto's government took steps to stabilize the economy. The government imposed strict controls on imports, encouraged foreign investment, and returned many nationalized assets to their previous owners. The fiscal crisis threatened by the accumulated debts of the Sukarno years was averted through debt rescheduling and improved economic management, but Indonesia continued to rely heavily on foreign aid through the mid-1980s.

Under the 1969–74 plan, the government successfully introduced fiscal and credit restraints, rescheduled internal debts, returned expropriated properties, liberalized foreign investment laws, and actively sought assistance from overseas. Economic growth was set back by the near-collapse in 1975 of Pertamina, the giant government-backed oil conglomerate; growth was restored as rising oil prices increased revenues in the late 1970s. The 1975–79 plan placed considerable focus on the rural economy, stressing labor-intensive industries along with improved provision of housing and education. Labor unions were encouraged to help improve the lot of plantation and industrial workers.

Efforts to restructure the economy in the 1980s resulted in an expansion of real GDP 6% annually on average. The 1979–84 development plan, called Repelita III, emphasized the "development trilogy" of economic growth, equity, and national stability. The 1984–89 five-year plan, called Repelita IV, emphasized industry, agriculture, transportation and communications, and construction. However, low oil prices caused the government to reduce its goals and to promote private and foreign investment. Rampant deforestation took place during that period, as vast quantities of logs from Indonesia's rainforests were exported. In Repelita V (1989–94) the development of mining and energy sectors were prioritized. In 1991, the share of manufacturing in GDP exceeded that of the agricultural sector for the first time.

The sixth five-year development plan (1994–99), Repelita VI, focused on the privatization of industry and further opening up of foreign investment. Indonesia's record of economic growth and diversification had been among the most successful in the developing world; but the onset of the Asian financial crisis in 1997 with Indonesia at the epicenter, followed by the 1998 political unrest and drought, contributed to a recession that hit the country hard, severely depressing the economy and halting economic growth. In November 1997 an international bail-out package was arranged that included a stand-by agreement with the IMF with an $11.5 billion line of credit, an $8 billion loan from the World Bank and the Asian Development Bank (ADB), $5 billion loan from its own reserves, and $3 billion in US loan guarantees. The extended impact of the crisis can be seen in the figures for 1998, when real GDP fell by over 13%, industrial production was down by 18.24%, and the net outflow of invested capital reached of about $13.8 billion. The political crisis of 1998 included violence attacks on businesses owned by Chinese-Indonesians. President Suharto resigned in 1998 and his designated successor was B. J. Habibie, the architect of Indonesia's ambitious shipping and aircraft manufacturing industry.

In 1999 real growth returned, although only at 0.2%, as there was a net outflow of investment funds of almost $10 billion-a net loss of $2.7 billion in FDI and a net loss of $7.2 billion in portfolio investment. In February 1999 the government estimated that 27% of the population was living in poverty, with inflation at 20%. In 2000, however, the economy showed signs of recovery with real GDP growth, a low budget deficit, and a low inflation rate. In February 2000, the government of Abdurrahman Wahid entered into an extended agreement with the IMF that included a $5 billion line of credit. In December 2000, Indonesia's agreement with the IMF was suspended, as Wahid was failing to implement the requirements of the IMF programs. The 2001–2004 National Development Plan had goals of democratization, good governance, economic recovery, and social welfare.

In 2002, with Megawati Sukarnoputri as president, the economy began to improve. The total debt-to-GDP ratio for the government fell from 90% for 2001 to 70% in 2002, and the annual budget deficit was estimated to have fallen to below 2% of GDP. Real GDP growth climbed in 2003 and 2004 at its fastest rate since the 1997 crisis. President Yudhoyono, elected in 2004, stated that he wanted the economy to grow by 7% or more, in part to generate enough jobs for Indonesia's large unemployed population. The National Development Plan for 2004–2009 emphasized fighting corruption, improving infrastructure, peace in petroleum-producing Aceh, poverty reduction, and increasing employment, exports, and investment. With declining petroleum production, Indonesia became a net oil importer in 2004, although still exporting natural gas. In March 2005, Yudhoyono reduced subsidies on various fuels, raising gas prices by some 30%. The government had been spending more on fuel subsidies than on health and education combined. Economists welcomed the move for Southeast Asia's largest economy, although the reduction in subsidies resulted in a decline in popularity for Yudhoyono. A recovery in investment demand enabled GDP growth to average an estimated 5.2% a year in 2006/07. Although export demand and investments were affected by the 2008–09 global financial crisis, Indonesia's GDP still grew at 6% in 2008, and 4.6% in 2009.

Yudhoyono restated his goal of 7% growth when he announced a "change, continuity, and unity" five-year development plan in 2009, emphasizing regional development, improved governance, and poverty reduction. His administration had also at various times announced goals including ending food insecurity, reducing carbon emissions, protecting forests, promoting high tech manufacturing, and ending mineral ore exports. Indonesia was often slow to implement such large-scale measures, but the Yudhoyono did show a willingness to address the big issues facing Indonesia, and to move towards new solutions. In 2010, Yudhoyono inaugurated a National Innovation Committee to advise on increasing national productivity and growth. The GDP growth rate for 2010 was 6.1%. Regional analysts predicted continued growth for Indonesia, driven by its domestic market and political/financial stability, as of 2011. Many challenges remained, including urban congestion, regional poverty, corruption, and dependence on imported fuel and food.

40 SOCIAL DEVELOPMENT

A state-administered social security program known as Jamsostek provides workers' compensation and health care through manda-

tory employer contributions; it also provides pensions through a combination of payroll deductions and employer contributions. The government has emphasized poverty alleviation and reduction with subsidies on food and fuel, development projects, and employment programs. As of 2010, 13.3% of the population was below the poverty line, according to the CIA.

Improvement of the status of women was specifically included in the guidelines for the 1979–84 national economic plan. A Ministry of Women's Affairs was created to promote the economic and social welfare of women. Gender equality has continued to be stressed in more recent development plans. Women's participation in politics has grown, with women comprising 18% of the parliament, and five out of 37 cabinet members, as of 2010. In spite of women's official equality, in practice they often find it hard to exercise their legal rights. Marriage laws define the husband as the head of the family, and divorce procedures are much more difficult for women. In the workplace, disparity in pay between men and women has steadily narrowed, with women's hourly wages at 83% of men's hourly wages, as of 2008, according to the ILO. Trafficking in women and children, for prostitution, domestic service, and other low wage labor, has remained a problem. Domestic workers are not covered by labor protection laws such as minimum wage, and were vulnerable to abuse whether working in Indonesia or overseas. As of 2010, according to the US State Department, rape was under-prosecuted in Indonesia. A Domestic Violence Act was passed in 2004 that criminalizes domestic violence. Shelters and special police desks are increasingly available for victims of domestic violence and human trafficking. In Aceh, conservative Islamic dress codes are enforced for Muslim women.

Gay and lesbian sex is banned under some local laws in Indonesia. Lesbian, gay, bisexual, and transgender organizations are allowed to operate, but were often harassed during 2010–2011, particularly by some militant Muslim organizations. In autonomous Aceh, a Shari'ah-based law passed by the local legislature in 2009 allowed penalties such as stoning to death for adultery and beating homosexuals, but as of late 2011, the governor of the province had refused to sign it. In December 2011, a punk rock concert was raided by police in Aceh, who detained concert-goers without charges for a week and shaved their heads. Young people identifying with punk rock, including street children employed in the informal sector, have been harassed in other parts of Indonesia as well.

As of 2011, the indigenous people of provinces including Kalimantan and Papua faced discrimination and the loss of their ancestral lands from mining, palm oil, and logging operations, as well as from migrant communities which had been settled in those regions. Indigenous Dayaks in central Kalimantan complained that their traditional land was taken out of their control for internationally-sponsored conservation schemes. Papuan independence activists were arrested, and several were killed during protests, as strikes and violent conflict continued during 2011.

41 HEALTH

According to the CIA, life expectancy in Indonesia was 71 years in 2011. The fertility rate was 2.1, while the infant mortality rate was 30 per 1,000 live births. In 2008 the maternal mortality rate, according to the World Bank, was 240 per 100,000 births. It was estimated that 82% of children were vaccinated against measles.

The country spent 2.3% of its GDP on healthcare, amounting to $55 per person. There were 3 physicians, 20 nurses and midwives, and 6 hospital beds per 10,000 inhabitants.

The national health system, administered locally, was underfunded, and there was little accountability for malpractice. The Jamkesmas low income healthcare insurance plan, begun in 2008, was not fully successful as of 2011, as cardholders are often denied medical service. Poor Indonesians often went without treatment, while the well-off went to Singapore for medical care. The CIA calculated HIV/AIDS prevalence in Indonesia to be about 0.2% in 2009. The government health system offered free antiretroviral drugs for HIV/AIDS, but additional medical fees often prevented patients from getting treatment. Other infectious diseases included diarrhea; hepatitis A, B and E; H5N1 avian influenza; tuberculosis; leptospirosis; typhoid fever; dengue fever; chikungunya fever; and malaria.

42 HOUSING

Since 1974, the government has sponsored a series of four major programs to build new housing and provide repair and maintenance for the large number of low-income housing units and slum areas. From 1974–93, the government adopted the Kampong Improvement Program, which was designed to upgrade slum settlements and thus provide more adequate housing for more than 36 million people; as of 2006, the program was part of the Urban Environment Upgrading Program, which relied on community initiatives. In 1990, an estimated 210,000 new housing units were completed. In 2003, the government announced the One Million Houses Development Program as a plan to inspire local governments, private businesses, and community initiatives to finance and build new housing. Floods, earthquakes (including the 2004 tsunami disaster), drought, fires, and violent conflicts have produced emergency shelter needs for displaced and homeless residents in Indonesia. Urban areas such as the mega-city of Jakarta are extremely crowded. According to Indonesia's Central Statistics Agency, Jakarta's population density was 14,476 people per sq km, as of August 2010.

Indonesia's urban housing includes concrete shophouses and high-rise apartment buildings, as well as the extremes of luxury townhouses and improvised shacks made from scavenged materials. Rural dwellings are often built of cement blocks, wood and bamboo, with metal roofing, and usually are on stilts above the ground. According to the CIA, as of 2008, 80% of the population had access to improved drinking water sources, and only 52% of the population had access to improved sanitation.

43 EDUCATION

In 2009 the World Bank estimated that 95% of age-eligible children in Indonesia were enrolled in primary school. Secondary enrollment for age-eligible children stood at 69%. Tertiary enrollment was estimated at 24%. Of those enrolled in tertiary education, there were 100 male students for every 92 female students. The student-to-teacher ratio for primary school was 17 as of 2009, according to the World Bank. Overall, the CIA estimated that Indonesia had a literacy rate of 90.4%. Public expenditure on education represented 2.8% of GDP.

Under the constitution, education must be nondiscriminatory, and nine years of basic education are free and compulsory (ages 7–15). In practice, however, the supply of schools and teachers is inadequate to meet the needs of the under-15 age group. Primary school covers six years of study, followed by three years of junior secondary school. Students may then choose to continue in three years of secondary studies in general studies (natural sciences, social sciences, and languages), Islamic studies, or vocational studies. Schools are coeducational, except for certain vocational and religious schools. Private (mostly Islamic religious) schools receive government subsidies if they maintain government standards. There are also public Islamic schools, administered by the Ministry of Religious Affairs.

Bahasa Indonesia is the language of instruction for public education through university level, although English is used for some university classes, particularly in scientific and technical subjects. Local languages may be used in primary education until the third level. As of 2011, English medium private schools were gaining in popularity with middle and upper class urban families. One famous product of Indonesian education is US president Barack Obama, who attended primary schools on Java; his administration pledged $90 million in aid for improving teacher training and other aspects of the Indonesian education system.

As of 2011, Indonesia had over 120 public, and over 50 private, universities, the largest of which are the University of Indonesia (in Jakarta, founded 1849) and the University of Gajah Mada (in Yogyakarta, founded 1949). Islamic University (in Yogyakarta, founded 1945) was the oldest private university, and Bandung Institute of Technology (1959) was the oldest technology and science university. There were also thousands of private colleges, polytechnic and vocational schools, and management institutes, offering diploma or certificate programs. The private institutions would have to undergo accreditation evaluation by 2012.

44 LIBRARIES AND MUSEUMS

Indonesia's largest library, Perbustakaan National Library (PNL) of Indonesia, was created in 1980 with the merger of four libraries, including the library of the National Museum, which was established in 1778. Located in Jakarta, PNL has a collection of over 1.9 million volumes, as well as a digital collection including historical maps, photographs, and manuscripts. The Indonesian Center for Agricultural Library and Technology Dissemination was founded in 1842 as a library associated with the botanical gardens in Bogor, on Java, it holds more than 400,000 volumes and also has e-resources on rice growing, appropriate technology, and other subjects. The Center for Scientific Documentation and Information of the Indonesian Institute of Sciences was founded in 1965 in Jakarta, and maintains digital collections of scientific papers and other research databases. University libraries tend to be autonomous faculty or departmental libraries lacking central coordination. The University of Indonesia in Jakarta has over 200,000 volumes and extensive electronic resources, with plans for a new "Crystal of Knowledge" library building as part of the "Green Campus" initiative. School libraries are generally underfunded; some international aid groups have donated books to increase their collections, particularly following the 2004 tsunami and other natural disasters. Since decentralization, public libraries have been administered by districts or cities. In addition, there are numerous private rental libraries, as well as small informal community libraries known as "reading gardens", many of which were originally formed to promote adult literacy.

Outstanding museums in Indonesia include the National Museum in Jakarta, which is a museum of Indonesian history and culture, founded in 1788, and the Zoological Museum in Bogor, on Java, founded in 1894. There is a Geological Museum in Bandung. Jakarta's Fatahillah Square includes the Jakarta Museum, the Fine Arts Gallery, the Ceramics Museum, and the Wayang Museum of puppetry. Jakarta also has a museum of crime, a large military museum, a museum chronicling the country's fight for independence, a maritime museum, a railway museum, and several other museums and historic buildings that are open to the public. The Sangiram museum near Solo, on Java, has prehistoric fossils on display. The Yogya Kemabli Monument, in Yogyakarta, Java, is a museum of the Indonesian revolution, in the shape of a pyramid. The OHD Museum in Magelang, on Java, shows modern Indonesian art, as does the Yuz Museum in Jakarta. Indonesia has many provincial museums of history and culture. Sumatra has the Bukittingi Museum and the Simalungun Museum, among others, and the Makkasar Museum is on Sulawesi. Kalimantan's museums include Museum Negari Pontianak, Balanga Museum, and Lambung Mangkurat Museum. Bali has several museums and numerous art galleries showing the work of local artists. The Bali Museum is in Denpasar. The Agung Rai Museum of Art in Bali holds a notable collection of works by Balinese, Javanese, and foreign artists.

45 MEDIA

Indonesia's constitution declares that everyone has the "right to freedom of opinion and expression." Indonesia's press, as of 2011, operated freely and independently, with the ability to criticize the government. However, individual journalists have been harassed and violently attacked, particularly when investigating corruption and other criminal activity.

Most newspapers are published in Bahasa Indonesia, with a small number appearing in local languages, English, and Chinese. Prominent newspapers in 2010, with circulation numbers listed parenthetically, included *Kompas* (523,453), *Pos Kota* (500,000), and *To O Nippo* (235,000), as well as 16 other major newspapers.

There were over 1,200 radio stations in Indonesia as of 2011, the vast majority privately owned. Programs originating in Jakarta are usually in Bahasa Indonesia; programs from regional stations are often in local languages. Radio Republik Indonesia, founded in 1945, is the national radio network. Its overseas service (Voice of Indonesia) broadcasts 11 hours daily in Arabic, Chinese, English, and other languages. Television service was inaugurated in 1962. Televisi Republik Indonesia (TVRI) is the state television network. There were more than additional 10 analog TV networks and 3 digital channels as of 2011, along with numerous regional stations. Terrestrial, cable, and satellite television are available in Indonesia. Popular programs include news shows, soap operas, music competitions, martial arts movies, and educational shows.

In 2009 the CIA reported that there were 34 million telephone landlines in Indonesia. In addition to landlines, mobile phone subscriptions averaged 69 per 100 people. Text messaging was in common use throughout the country, and of 2011, low-priced smartphones were rapidly gaining in popularity. In 2010 the country had 1.2 million Internet hosts. In 2010 there were some 34 million computer-based Internet users in Indonesia, a majority of whom used internet cafes, but millions more accessed the internet through mobile phones. Internet users numbered 23 per 100 citizens. As of 2011, social networks were hugely popular in Indonesia, with the world's second largest Facebook membership at over 40 million and nearly 5 million Twitter users. Indonesia had the largest number of users of the Singapore-based Mig33 social networking application for mobile phones. Over 70% of social media users accessed the sites by mobile phone. Indonesia also had over 4.5 million blogs. The government has made sporadic efforts to block internet pornography, and foreign films were monitored by a censorship institute, but rarely banned, as of 2011.

46 ORGANIZATIONS

Village unit cooperatives help meet the small farmer's need for credit and aid in marketing cash crops. Village unit cooperatives also exist for cottage industries such as textiles, which are important forms of employment in rural areas. Many trade and business promotional organizations are concerned with individual sectors of the business world. An Indonesian chamber of commerce and industries has connections with leading business organizations in the country. The Indonesian Consumers Association is active. The ASEAN Council on Petroleum, ASEAN Occupational Safety and Health Network, and ASEAN Regional Forum all have offices in Jakarta. The International Labour Organization also has an office in Jakarta. The myriad arts organizations include Yayasan Pecinta Budaya Bebali Foundation for textile arts; Kelola Foundation for performing arts; and the literary Lontar Foundation.

Among social welfare and women's organizations are the Indonesian Women's Congress, a federation founded in 1928; the National Council on Social Welfare; the Indonesian Planned Parenthood Association; and Alimat, an activist coalition of Muslim women's organizations. International organizations with chapters in Indonesia include Habitat for Humanity, World Wildlife Fund, Greenpeace, the Red Cross, Caritas, and the Kiwanis and Lion's clubs.

National youth organizations include the Indonesian Muslim Youth, IMKA/YMCA Indonesia, Junior Chamber, and Young Generation of Islam of Indonesia. There is also a national association for Boy Scouts and Girl Scouts (Indonesia Geraken Pramuka). There are many sports associations promoting both youth and adult participation in amateur competitions. 1001 Buku is an organization which supplies books to community "reading gardens."

There are a number of organizations promoting education and research into various arts and sciences, including the Indonesian Institute of Sciences and the Indonesian Medical Association. Indonesian environmental groups include The Indonesian Forum for Environment, Borneo Orangutan Survival Foundation, PILI-Green Network, Ecological Observation and Wetlands Conservation, Bali Environmental Education Center, and Gili Eco Trust. The Merah Putih Foundation, IDEP Foundation, Obor Tani Foundation, and Indigenous Peoples Alliance of the Archipelago, are among a great many Indonesian grassroots groups which work for sustainable development, support community projects, prepare disaster relief, and/or campaign for land rights.

47 TOURISM, TRAVEL, AND RECREATION

As a means of creating employment, tourism has been strongly promoted by Indonesia's government, which declared 2010 "Visit Indonesia Year". The tourist industry recovered quickly from setbacks due to the December 2004 tsunami, and terrorist bombings of nightclubs on Bali in 2002 and 2005. Among Indonesia's most popular tourist destinations are Bali, with its world-famous visual and performing arts, and beaches; the restored Borobudur Buddhist temple in Java; and historic Yogyakarta. Cultural attractions include traditional Balinese dancing, the percussive sounds of the Indonesian orchestra (*gamelan*), the shadow puppet (*wayang kulit*) theater, and Indonesian cuisines. Ecotourism and community-based cultural tours are promoted in some regions. Popular sports include badminton, football (soccer), the martial art of *silat*, and *sepak takraw*, a game where players volley a woven cane ball over a net. The tropical seas and reefs of the archipelago are destinations for world-class surfing and scuba diving.

The *Tourism Factbook*, published by the UN World Tourism Organization, reported 6.32 million incoming tourists to Indonesia in 2009, who spent a total of $6.77 billion. Of those incoming tourists, there were 4.8 million from East Asia and the Pacific. There were 519,205 hotel beds available in Indonesia. The estimated daily cost to visit Jakarta, the capital, was $233. The cost of visiting other cities averaged $146. Accommodations ranging from very inexpensive home-stay arrangements to ultra-luxurious resorts are available on Java, Bali, and other islands. Foreigners needed special permission to visit West Papua and Poso (central Sulawesi) as of 2011. A passport, valid for at least six months from the date of arrival is required of visitors, and citizens of most countries can purchase a visa on arrival, if they have an onward/return ticket. Visitors from 11 countries are eligible for a Visa-free 30 day visit permit on arrival.

48 FAMOUS PERSONS

Gajah Mada, prime minister under King Hayam Wuruk (r. 1350–89), brought many of the islands under one rule, the Majapahit Empire. Princess Raden Ajeng Kartini (1879–1904), founder of a school for girls, led the movement for the emancipation of women. Sukarno (1901–70), was the founder and leader of the nationalist movement, becoming president at independence. Mohammad Hatta (1902–80), one of the architects of Indonesian independence, served as Sukarno's vice president and concurrently as prime minister. Suharto (1921–2008) dominated Indonesia's political and economic life as president for three decades. Adam Malik (1917–84) established an international reputation as a negotiator while foreign minister and vice president. B. J. Habibie (b. 1936) became president in 1998, followed by Abdurrahman Wahid (1940–2009). Megawati Sukarnoputri (b. 1947) was the country's first female president. Susilo Bambang Yudhoyono (b. 1949) began his first of two presidential terms in 2004. Tri Mumpuni (b. 1964) has won international recognition, including the 2011 Magsaysay Award, for her work bringing alternative energy to villages on Java, and Prigi Arisandi (b. 1976) received the Goldman Environmental Prize in 2011 for his efforts to fight water pollution.

During the Sukarno and Suharto years, a number of writers risked punishment for political expression, including Pramudya Ananta Tur (1925–2006) an important novelist who was a political prisoner for many years, dramatist. W. S. Rendra (1935–2009), and Soe Hok Gie (1942–1969), an anti-dictatorship dissident writer. H. B. Jassin (1917–2000) was an influential literary critic and translator, Mochtar Lubis (1922–2004) was a novelist and free press advocate, and Goenawan Susatyo (b. 1941) is a poet and founder of the news magazine *Tempo*. Aya Utami (b. 1968) is a feminist author whose novel *"Saman"* symbolized an awakening after decades of dictatorship.

Affandi (1910–90) was a famous expressionist painter from Java. Gusti Nyoman Lempad (circa 1862–1978), an influential Balinese artist and architect, lived to an estimated 116 years. Nyoman Masriadi (b. 1973) is an avant-garde painter originally from Bali. Raden Irama (b. 1946) is a singer/actor known as "the king of *dangdut*", a popular music style. Anggun (b. 1974) is a pop music singer/songwriter from Jakarta who has had international hit albums.

49 DEPENDENCIES

Indonesia has no territories or colonies.

50 BIBLIOGRAPHY

Altbach, Philip G. and Toru Umakoshi, eds. *Asian Universities: Historical Perspectives and Contemporary Challenges.* Baltimore, MD: Johns Hopkins University Press, 2004.

Chandra, Satish and Baladas Ghoshal (eds.) *Indonesia: A New Beginning?* New Delhi: Sterling Publishers, 2002.

Cribb, Robert and Audrey Kahin. *Historical Dictionary of Indonesia.* Lanham, MD: Scarecrow Press, 2004.

Drakeley, Steven. *The History of Indonesia.* Westport, CT: Greenwood Press, 2005.

Forshee, Jill. *Culture and Customs of Indonesia.* Westport, CT: Greenwood Press, 2006.

Giannakos, S.A., ed. *Ethnic Conflict: Religion, Identity, and Politics.* Athens: Ohio University Press, 2002.

Gunn, Geoffrey C. *New World Hegemony in the Malay World.* Trenton, NJ: Red Sea Press, 2000.

Indonesia Investment and Business Guide: Strategic Information and Laws. Washington, DC: International Business Publications USA, 2012.

Martyn, Elizabeth. *Women's Movement in Postcolonial Indonesia: Gender and Nation in a New Democracy.* New York: Routledge-Curzon, 2004.

Mirpuri, Gouri. *Indonesia.* 3rd ed. New York: Marshall Cavendish Benchmark, 2012.

Suryadinata, Leo. *Indonesia's Foreign Policy Under Suharto: Aspiring to International Leadership.* Singapore: Marshall Cavendish Academic, 2005.

Tanter, Richard, Mark Selden, and Stephen R. Shalom, eds. *Bitter Flowers, Sweet Flowers: East Timor, Indonesia, and the World Community.* Lanham, MD: Rowman and Littlefield, 2001.

IRAN

Islamic Republic of Iran
Jomhuri-ye Eslami-ye Iran

CAPITAL: Tehrān

FLAG: The national flag consists of three equal horizontal bands of green (top), white (middle), and red (bottom). The national emblem (a stylized representation of the word Allah in the shape of a tulip—a symbol of martyrdom) drawn in red is centered in the white band. "Allah Akbar" ("God is Great") written in white Arabic script is repeated 11 times along the bottom edge of the green band and 11 times along the top edge of the red band. Green is the color of Islam and also represents growth, white symbolizes honesty and peace, and red stands for bravery and martyrdom.

ANTHEM: *Soroud-e Melli-e Jomhouri-e Eslami-e Iran (National Anthem of the Islamic Republic of Iran).*

MONETARY UNIT: The rial (IRR) is a paper currency of 100 dinars. There are coins of 1, 2, 5, 10, 20, 50, 100 rials, and banknotes of 100, 200, 500, 1,000, 2,000, 5,000, and 10,000 rials. IRR1 = US$0.000097 (or US$1 = IRR10,300.2) as of 2010.

WEIGHTS AND MEASURES: The metric system is the legal standard, but local units are widely used.

HOLIDAYS: National Day, 11 February; Oil Nationalization Day, 20 March; No Ruz (New Year), 21–24 March; Islamic Republic Day, 1 April; 13th Day of No Ruz (Revolution Day), 2 April. Religious holidays (according to the lunar calendar) include the Birthday of Imam Husayn; the Birthday of the Twelfth Imam; the Martyrdom of Imam Ali; the Death of Imam Ja'afar Sadiq; Eid al-Fitr; the Birthday of Imam Reza; Eid-i-Qurban; Eid-i-Qadir; Shab-i-Miraj; the Martyrdom of Imam Husayn; 40th Day after the Death of Imam Husayn; Birthday of the Prophet; the Birthday of Imam Ali.

TIME: 3:30 p.m. = noon GMT.

¹LOCATION, SIZE, AND EXTENT

Situated in southwestern Asia, Iran covers an area of 1,648,000 sq km (636,296 sq mi) and extends about 2,250 km (1,398 mi) SE–NW and 1,400 km (870 mi) NE–SW. Comparatively, the area occupied by Iran is slightly larger than the state of Alaska. Iran is bounded on the N by Armenia, Azerbaijan, Turkmenistan, and the Caspian Sea; on the E by Afghanistan and Pakistan; on the S by the Gulf of Oman and the Persian Gulf; on the W by Iraq; and on the NW by Turkey, giving Iran a total land boundary length of 5,440 km (3,380 mi). The coastline is 2,440 km (1,516 mi). The shoreline on the Caspian Sea is 740 km (460 mi). Iran's territory includes several islands in the Persian Gulf.

Iran's capital city, Tehrān, is located in the northwestern part of the country.

²TOPOGRAPHY

Most of the land area consists of a plateau some 1,200 m (4,000 ft) above sea level and strewn with mountains. The Zagros range runs north–south and the Elburz range runs east–west on the plateau. The apex is in the northwest, and within the lower area between the arms there are salt flats and barren deserts. Most of the drainage is from these two great ranges into the interior deserts, with limited drainage into the Caspian Sea and the Persian Gulf. The ranges run in parallel lines, creating long valleys that provide most of the agricultural land. Qolleh-ye Damāvand (Mt. Damavand), northeast of Tehrān, rises to 5,671 m (18,605 ft), while the Caspian littoral is below sea level and has a semitropical climate. Only the Kārūn River, emptying into the Persian Gulf, is navigable for any distance, but the rivers that rush down from high altitudes offer good sources of power. Harbors of limited depth are found along the Persian Gulf, and the Caspian Sea has similar facilities for coastal fishing and trade.

Iran is geologically unstable with some of the most severe and deadliest earthquakes on record. On 20 June 1990 a 7.4 magnitude quake caused the death of about 50,000 people, many of whom were caught in resulting landslides. On 22 February 2005 a 6.4 magnitude quake in the Kerman province in central Iran left at least 602 people dead and 991 injured. On March 31, 2006 there was a quake with a magnitude of 6.1 near Khorrambabad, and on 26 December 2011 there was a 4.6 magnitude quake northeast of Borujerd.

³CLIMATE

Iran has a continental type of climate with cold winters and hot summers prevalent across the plateau. The annual rainfall does not exceed 30 cm (12 in), with the deserts and the Persian Gulf littoral receiving less than 13 cm (5 in). Snow falls heavily on the mountain peaks and is the principal source of water for irrigation in spring and early summer. The Caspian littoral is warm and humid throughout the year, and the annual rainfall is about 100–150 cm (40–60 in). Clear days are the rule since the skies are cloudless more than half the days of each year. The seasons change abruptly. By the Persian New Year (the first day of spring) orchards are in bloom and wild flowers abound. In January the Tehrān temperature ranges from an average low of -3°C (27°F) to an average high of 7°C (45°F), and in July from an average minimum of 22°C (72°F) to an average maximum of 37°C (99°F).

⁴FLORA AND FAUNA

The World Resources Institute estimates that there are 8,000 plant species in Iran. In addition, Iran is home to 158 species of mammals, 498 types of birds, 220 species of reptiles, and 23 types of amphibians. The calculation reflects the total number of distinct species residing in the country, not the number of endemic species.

The most extensive plant growth is found on the mountain slopes rising from the Caspian Sea, with stands of oak, ash, elm, cypress, and other valuable varieties of trees. On the plateau proper areas of scrub oak appear on the best-watered mountain slopes, and villagers cultivate orchards and grow plane trees, poplar, willow, walnut, beech, maple, and mulberry. Wild plants and shrubs spring from the barren land in the spring and afford pasturage, but the summer sun burns them away. Bears, wild sheep and goats, gazelles, wild asses, wild pigs, panthers, and foxes abound. Domestic animals include sheep, goats, cattle, horses, water buffalo, donkeys, and camels. The pheasant, partridge, stork, and falcon are native to Iran.

⁵ENVIRONMENT

Iran's high grasslands have been eroded for centuries by the encroachment of nomads who overgrazed their livestock. Desertification resulting from erosion and deforestation of the high plateau pose additional dangers to Iran's environment. United Nations (UN) sources have estimated that 1–1.5 million hectares (2.5–3.7 million acres) of land per year turn into desert. The basic law controlling the use of forests dates from 1943. In 1962 the forests and pastures in Iran were nationalized in an effort to stop trespassing deforestation.

In early 1983 blown-out oil wells in the Persian Gulf war zone between Iran and Iraq caused a huge oil slick that threatened ocean and shore life along the southwestern Iranian coast. Air and water pollution continued to be significant problems in Iran in the aftermath of the 1991 Persian Gulf War. The water in the Persian Gulf is polluted with oil and black rain, and the burning of Kuwaiti oil wells caused significant air pollution as well.

The country has a large network of underground water canals called *qanats*. This network, once used as an irrigation source, covers an estimated 400,000 km (248,548 mi). Some analysts are encouraging a return to this source of irrigation water as an answer to regional water shortages.

Iran's Department of Environment was established under the Environment Protection and Enhancement Act of 1974; no information is available on how well the legislation has been implemented.

The World Resources Institute reported that Iran had designated 10.39 million hectares (25.67 million acres) of land for protection as of 2006. Water resources totaled 137.5 cu km (32.99 cu mi) while water usage was 72.88 cu km (17.48 cu mi) per year. Domestic water usage accounted for 7% of total usage, industrial for 2%, and agricultural for 91%. Per capita water usage totaled 1,048 cu m (37,010 cu ft) per year.

The UN reported in 2008 that carbon dioxide emissions in Iran totaled 495,582 kilotons.

According to a 2011 report issued by the International Union for Conservation of Nature and Natural Resources (IUCN), threatened species included 16 types of mammals, 20 species of birds, 12 types of reptiles, 4 species of amphibians, 29 species of fish, 19 species of invertebrates, and 1 type of plant. Endangered species in Iran include the Baluchistan bear, Asiatic cheetah, Persian fallow deer, Siberian white crane, hawksbill turtle, green turtle, Oxus cobra, Latifi's viper, dugong, and dolphins. The Syrian wild ass has been listed as extinct.

⁶POPULATION

The US Central Intelligence Agency (CIA) estimated the population of Iran in 2011 to be approximately 77,891,220, which placed it at number 18 in population among the 196 nations of the world. In 2011 approximately 5% of the population was over 65 years of age, with another 24.1% under 15 years of age. The median age in Iran was 26.8 years. There were 1.02 males for every female in the country. The population's annual rate of change was 1.248%. The projected population for the year 2025 was 87,100,000. Population density in Iran was calculated at 47 people per sq km (122 people per sq mi).

The UN estimated that 71% of the population live in urban areas and that urban populations have an annual rate of change of 1.9%. The largest urban areas, along with their respective populations, include Tehran, 7.2 million; Mashhad, 2.6 million; Esfahan, 1.7 million; Karaj, 1.5 million; and Tabriz, 1.5 million.

⁷MIGRATION

Estimates of Iran's net migration rate, carried out by the CIA in 2011, amounted to -0.13 migrants per 1,000 citizens. The total number of emigrants living abroad was 1.3 million, and the total number of immigrants living in Iran was 2.13 million. Iran also accepted 914,268 refugees from Afghanistan and 54,024 from Iraq. Until the late 20th century there was little immigration to Iran, with the exception of Shia Muslims coming from Iraq. There has been some emigration to Europe and the United States, particularly by Iranians who were studying overseas at the time of the revolution of 1979. About 100,000 Kurds were repatriated from Iran to Iraq during the mid-1970s after the suppression of a Kurdish rebellion in the latter country. Between 1980 and 1990, however, an increased number of Shia Muslims fled Iraq because of the Iran-Iraq and Gulf wars; at the end of 1992 there were some 1.2 million refugees in Iran. Perhaps 2.8 million Afghan refugees moved to Iran after the Soviet invasion of Afghanistan in December 1979. About 200,000 returned in 1992, and about 2.1 million remained in mid-1993. At least 50,000 refugees from Azerbaijan had fled to Iran by late 1993 to escape Armenian occupation. In the fall of 1996 some 65,000 Iraqi Kurds entered Iran due to ethnic fighting.

Iran has one of the largest refugee populations in the world, hosting some one million refugees, mainly from Afghanistan (80%) and Iraq (10%). Since 2006 Iranian officials have been working with the United Nations High Commission for Refugees (UNHCR) and Afghan officials for their repatriation. The total number of migrants in the country was 1,065,000 in 2010, down from 2,321,000 ten years earlier.

LOCATION: 25° to 40°N; 44° to 63°E. BOUNDARY LENGTHS: Afghanistan, 936 kilometers (582 miles); Armenia 35 kilometers (22 miles); Azerbaijan (N) 432 kilometers (268 miles); Azerbaijan (NW) 179 kilometers (111 miles); Caspian Sea coastline, 740 kilometers (460 miles); Gulf of Oman and Persian Gulf coastlines, 2,440 kilometers (1,516 miles); Iraq, 1,458 kilometers (906 miles); Pakistan, 909 kilometers (565 miles); Turkey, 499 kilometers (310 miles); Turkmenistan, 992 kilometers (616 miles). TERRITORIAL SEA LIMIT: 12 miles.

8 ETHNIC GROUPS

Present-day Iranians, or Persians, are considered to be direct descendants of the Aryans who moved into the plateau in the second millennium BC. They speak Persian, or Farsi, and number more than half the total population. In the Zagros range and its extensions there are Kurds, Lurs, Bakhtiari, Qashqa'i, and Qajars; the first three are said to be of stock similar to the Iranian ethnic group, and they speak languages that stem from ancient Indo-European languages. At various times after the 10th century AD, Turkish tribes settled in the region, and Turkish-speaking groups are still found in several parts of the country. One-eighth of the total population dwells in East and West Azerbaijan, and there are

sizable groups of Azerbaijanis in major cities elsewhere, including Tehrān. Arab groups arrived during and after the 7th century AD; their descendants live in the south and southwest and in scattered colonies elsewhere. In general, non-Iranian ethnic groups are found along the perimeter of the country. Of these, certain nomadic groups move back and forth across the frontiers. Tribal groups have been a conspicuous element in Iran for many centuries, migrating vertically in spring and fall between high mountain valleys and hot lowland plains. The important migratory groups include the Qashqa'i, Qajars, Bakhtiari, Balochi, and Turkmen. A large proportion of these people are now settled, however. The nomadic way of life is on the decline, and official policy seeks to resettle these groups on farmlands. According to the latest estimates, Persians account for 51% of the population, Azeri 24%, Gilaki and Mazandarani 8%, Kurds 7%, Arab 3%, Lur 2%, Balochi 2%, Turkmen 2%, and other 1%.

9 LANGUAGES

Farsi, commonly called Persian in the West, is the official language of Iran. An Indo-European language of the Indo-Iranian group Farsi derives from ancient Persian, with a mixture of many Arabic words. Arabic characters and script are used in writing modern Persian. Dialects of Turkish or Turki—especially Azeri, the language of the Azerbaijanis—are spoken throughout northwestern Iran, by the Qashqa'i tribe in the southwest, and in parts of the northeast by Turkmen tribes and others. The Lurs, Kurds, and Bakhtiari have languages and dialects of their own that descend from earlier Indo-European languages, and the Balochi language spoken in southeastern Iran also is of Indo-European origin. A small number of Brahui in the southeast speak a Dravidian language. The breakdown of languages spoken in the country as a whole is Persian 65%, Azeri 16%, Kurdish 10%, Luri 6%, Arabic 2%, Balochi 2%, Turkmen 1%, other 1%.

10 RELIGIONS

Iran is the only Islamic country where Ja'afari Shia Muslims hold the reins of power. Shia Islam is the official religion of the country and the president, prime minister, and cabinet ministers must all be Muslims. As of 2010 about 98% of the population were Muslim, with 89% of the people being Shia Muslims and 9% Sunni Muslims. Between 2 million and 5 million people practice Sufism. The largest non-Muslim group was the Baha'i faith, with between 300,000 and 350,000 members. Their faith, which sprang from the teachings of a 19th-century Muslim in Iran, has been denounced as heresy to Islam. People practicing the Baha'i faith have been severely persecuted by the Shia government since the 1979 revolution, and many of their religious leaders have been executed.

11 TRANSPORTATION

The CIA reports that Iran has a total of 172,927 km (107,452 mi) of roads, of which 125,908 km (78,236 mi) are paved. There are 128 vehicles per 1,000 people in the country. Railroads extend for 7,555 km (4,694 mi). There are 319 airports, which transported 13.05 million passengers in 2009 according to the World Bank. Iran has approximately 850 km (528 mi) of navigable waterways.

A1, a major paved highway, runs from Bazargan on the Turkish border to the border with Afghanistan. Another major highway, A2, runs from the Iraqi border to the Pakistani border. Much of the revolutionary government's road-building activity centered on improving roads in rural areas.

The main rail line runs south from Bandar Turkoman on the Caspian Sea, through Tehrān, to Bandar-e Khomeini on the Persian Gulf. There is also a rail line between Bafq and Sirjan.

Iran's main ports at Khorramshahr and Ābādān on the Persian Gulf were largely destroyed in fighting during the 1980–88 war with Iraq. Khorramshahr was restored to operation in November 1992. Other ports on the Gulf are Bandar-e Khomeini, Bandar-e 'Abbās, and Bandar-e Būshehr. Both Bandar-e Khomeini and Bandar-e Būshehr were damaged because of the war. The government is continuing the program to modernize the port at Bandar-e 'Abbās. On the Caspian Sea there are the ports of Bandar Anzeli (formerly Bandar Pahlavi) and Naushahr. In addition, there are the oil shipment ports of Kharg Island (a principal target in the war with Iraq) and Ābādān. The Shatt al Arab is usually navigable by maritime traffic for about 130 km (81 mi).

Iran has an estimated 133 airports with paved runways and 186 unpaved runways; there are 19 heliports. Principal airports include Bandar-e 'Abbās, Mehrabad International at Tehrān, and Shirāz International at Shirāz. The state-owned Iran Air maintains frequent service to 15 cities in Iran and is an international carrier. Lack of access to parts and the age of the fleet make travel on Iranian carriers hazardous.

12 HISTORY

As early as 6000 BC, communities on the Iranian plateau were engaged in agriculture, raising domestic animals, and producing pottery and polished stone implements. There are numerous sites that date to later than 3000 BC and these sites offer specimens of bronze instruments and painted pottery of the finest types. About 1500 BC masses of Indo-Europeans, or Aryans, began to cross the plateau of Iran. The Iranian group included Medes, Persians, Parthians, Bactrians, and others. The Medes settled in western Iran (Media) about 900 BC and established their capital at Ecbatana (modern Hamadān); the Persians settled to the south of them (Parsis) around 700 BC. The Median king Cyaxares (b. 625–d. 585 BC), along with the Chaldeans, destroyed the power of neighboring Assyria. In the area of Parsis, the Achaemenid clan became overlords, and in 550 BC their leader, Cyrus the Great, revolted against the Medes; forming a union of Medes and Persians, he then drove with armies both into Asia Minor and to the east of the Iranian plateau and established the Achaemenid Empire. Cambyses, Darius, Xerxes I, and Artaxerxes I were notable rulers of this line who penetrated Greece, Egypt, and beyond the Oxus. The Achaemenid power was centered at Susa and Persepolis; the ruined site of the latter is impressive even today. The religion of the rulers was Zoroastrianism. Some worshiped only Ahuramazda, some others worshiped Mithra and Anahita as well.

In his eastward sweep (334–330 BC), Alexander the Great defeated vast Achaemenid forces and went on to capture Susa and to burn Persepolis. In the 3rd century BC the Parthians moved into the area east of the Caspian and then into the Achaemenid Empire, establishing the new Parthian kingdom; later rulers moved west to come in contact with and then to fight the Roman Empire. The Parthians considered themselves spiritual heirs of the Achaemenids and adopted Zoroastrianism as the official religion. Weakened by long wars with Rome, the Parthians were followed by a local dynasty, the Sassanian, which arose in the area of Fars in southwestern Iran. Wars with Rome continued and were followed by a struggle with the Byzantine Empire. The Sassanian period (AD 226–641) was one of cultural consolidation and was marked by economic prosperity and by a series of enlightened rulers.

During the first half of the 7th century AD Arab warriors burst out of the Arabian Peninsula to overwhelm the Sassanian Empire and to spread the teachings of the prophet Muhammad, embodied in Islam. By the opening of the 9th century Islamic doctrine and precepts had spread over the plateau, and local dynasties faithful to the Muslim creed emerged. Early in the 11th century the Turkish Ghaznavid dynasty held power from western Iran to the Indus River. Their greatest ruler was Mahmud of Ghaznī, a renowned conqueror and a patron of the arts. The Ghaznavids were replaced by the Seljuks, who descended from Turkish nomad warriors enlisted in their service.

The Seljuk kingdom had its capitals at Ray, just south of Tehrān, and in Esfahān. It stretched from the Bosporus to Chinese Turkestan. Seljuk rulers like Tughril Beg, Alp Arslan, and Malik Shah did much to promote cultural pursuits and enhance the character of Persian civilization.

In 1219 Mongol hordes under Genghis Khan (Temujin) began to move into Iran; successive waves subdued and devastated the country. Hulagu, a grandson of Genghis, settled in Maragheh in Azerbaijan and as Il-khan, or chief of the tribe, gave this title to the Il-khanid dynasty. His successors, such as Ghazan Khan and Oljaitu, ruled from Tabriz and Sultaniya, and once again untutored invaders became converts to Islam and patrons of Persian science, learning, and arts. Rivalries within the military leadership brought about the breakdown of Il-khanid power in the second half of the 14th century.

In 1380 Timur ("Timur the Lame" or—in the West—Tamerlane) began to move into the Iranian plateau from the east. Within a decade, the entire area was in his power, bringing a renaissance of culture at Herāt (in modern Afghanistan) and other towns, but later rulers lacked the force and ability to hold the empire together. Early in the 16th century a number of smaller local dynasties emerged throughout Iran. The most powerful was the Safavid dynasty, whose leaders, descendants of a spiritual head of the Shia sect, imposed this form of Islam on their subjects. The fourth and greatest of this line, Shah Abbas (r. 1587–1628), moved the capital to Esfahān, where he had many splendid buildings constructed. The Safavid period proved to be a period of military power and general prosperity. However, decline set in, and in 1722 Esfahān fell to invading forces from Afghanistan. Nadir Shah, an Afshar tribesman from the north, drove off the Afghans and in 1736 established the Afshar dynasty. By the end of the 18th century Zand rulers, dominant in the south, were replaced by the Qajars, a Turkish tribe.

Qajar power began to fade at the turn of the 19th century. In the 1890s Shia clerics led a national boycott that made the shah rescind a decree awarding a tobacco monopoly to a foreign agent. In 1906 a coalition of bazaar merchants, clerics, intellectuals, and community leaders forced the shah to accept a constitution. This liberal initiative was frustrated, however, by the power of Brittan and the Soviet Union, who controlled spheres of influence in the south and north of Iran, respectively.

After a period of chaos, the British arranged for a Persian Cossack officer, Reza Khan, to come to power, first as minister of war in 1921, then as prime minister, and finally in 1925 as Reza Shah, the first sovereign of the Pahlavi dynasty. With ruthless authority, he sought to modernize Iran along the lines of Ataturk in Turkey. In 1941 the British, suspecting him of pro-German sympathies, forced Reza Shah to abdicate in favor of his 21 year-old son, Muhammad Reza. British and Soviet forces set up a supply line across Iran to the Soviet Union. In April 1946 the British left, but the Soviet Union refused to withdraw its forces. Under pressure from the UN, the United States, and promise of a concession regarding oil in the north of Iran, Soviet troops withdrew in December 1946.

Oil, the source of nearly all Iran's national wealth, quickly came to dominate politics after World War II. Muhammad Mossadeq, who, as leader of the National Front in the National Assembly (Majlis) led the fight in 1947 to deny the Soviet Union oil concessions in northern Iran, became chairman of the oil committee of the Majlis. On 15 March 1951 the Majlis voted to nationalize the oil industry, which was dominated by the Anglo-Iranian Oil Co. (AIOC), a prewar concession to the United Kingdom. When the government of Prime Minister Hosein Ala took no immediate action against the AIOC, the Majlis demanded his resignation and the appointment of Mossadeq, who became prime minister in April. The AIOC was nationalized, but its output rapidly declined when the United Kingdom imposed an embargo on Iranian oil, as well as other economic sanctions. As Iran's economic situation worsened, Mossadeq sought to rally the people through fervent nationalistic appeals. An attempt by the shah to replace him failed in the summer of 1952 but, by August 1953, Mossadeq had lost his parliamentary majority, although not his popular support. With the backing of a referendum, Mossadeq dissolved the Majlis and then refused to resign when the shah again tried to oust him. The shah fled Iran for four days, but returned on 22 August with backing from the military, the United States, and the United Kingdom. A new conservative government issued an appeal for aid; in September the United States granted Iran $45 million. Mossadeq was convicted of treason in December.

After 1953 the shah began to consolidate his power. New arrangements between the National Iranian Oil Co. and a consortium of US, UK, and Dutch oil companies were negotiated during April–September 1954 and ratified by the Majlis in October. The left-wing Communist Party, which had been banned in 1949 but had resurfaced as the Tudeh (Masses) Party during the Mossadeq regime, was suppressed after its organization in the armed forces was exposed. In 1957 two new pseudo-parties (both government-sponsored) arose; both contested parliamentary elections in 1960 and 1961. Meanwhile, Iran became affiliated with the Western alliance through the Baghdād Pact (later the Central Treaty Organization—CENTO) in 1955 (CENTO was dissolved after Iran pulled out in 1979). Frontier demarcation agreements were signed with the Soviet Union in April 1957.

US assistance and goodwill were essential for the shah. In 1961 President John F. Kennedy urged him to undertake a more liberal program. Under the "white revolution" of 1962–63 the shah initiated land reform, electoral changes (including, for the first time, the right of women to hold and vote for public office), and broad economic development. Opposition to the reform program, the dictatorial regime, and the growing American influence was suppressed. Political dissent was not tolerated.

The shah's autocratic methods, his repressive use of the secret police (known as SAVAK), his program of rapid Westernization (at the expense of Islamic tradition), his emphasis on lavish display and costly arms imports, and his perceived tolerance of corruption and of US domination fed opposition in the late 1970s. When, after 15 years, the economic boom came to an end, Islamic militants, radical students, and the middle class all joined in a revolt. In the end, virtually the entire population turned against the shah. Following nine months of demonstrations and violent army reactions, martial law was declared in Iran's major cities in September 1978, but antigovernment strikes and massive marches could not be stopped. On 16 January 1979 the shah left Iran, appointing an old-line nationalist, Shahpur Bakhtiar, as prime minister. However, the leader of the Islamic opposition, Ayatollah Ruhollah Khomeini (the term "ayatollah" is the highest rank of the Shia clergy), who had spent 15 years in exile first in Iraq and briefly in France, refused to deal with the Bakhtiar regime. Demonstrations continued, and on 1 February the ayatollah returned to a tumultuous welcome in Tehrān. He quickly asserted control and appointed a provisional government, which took power after a military rebellion and the final collapse of the shah's regime on 11 February.

After a referendum, on 1 April Khomeini declared Iran an Islamic republic. However, the provisional government, led by Medhi Bazargan and other liberal civilians, was unable to exercise control; revolutionary groups made indiscriminate arrests and summary executions of political opponents. Increasingly radical clerics sought to take power for themselves. The crisis atmosphere was intensified by the seizure, on 4 November 1979, of more than 60 US hostages (50 of them in the US embassy compound in Tehrān) by militant Iranian students who demanded the return of the shah from the United States (where he was receiving medical treatment) so he could stand trial in Iran. Despite vigorous protests by the US government, which froze Iranian assets in the United States, and by the UN over this violation of diplomatic immunity, 52 of the hostages were held for 444 days; in the intervening period, a US attempt to free the hostages by military force failed, and the shah died in Egypt on 27 July 1980. The crisis was finally resolved on 20 January 1981, in an agreement providing for release of the hostages and the unfreezing of Iranian assets. Relations between the United States and Iran remained poor. A new constitution providing for an Islamic theocracy was ratified by popular referendum in December 1979. In presidential elections in January 1980, Abolhassan Bani-Sadr, a moderate who supported the revolution, was elected president. Later elections to the Majlis resulted in victory for the hard-line clerical Islamic Republican Party (IRP).

In June 1981 President Bani-Sadr was ousted by Khomeini; later that month a bomb explosion at IRP headquarters in Tehrān killed Ayatollah Beheshti, who had been serving as chief justice, as well as four cabinet ministers, 20 paramilitary deputies, and dozens of others. Another bombing on 30 August killed the new president, Muhammad 'Ali Rajai, and his prime minister, Muhammad Javad Bahonar. The bombings were ascribed by the government to leftist guerrillas. By 1982 at least 4,500 people had been killed in political violence, and some estimates placed the total much higher. In September 1982 Sadegh Ghotbzadeh, who had been foreign minister during the hostage crisis, was executed on charges of plotting to kill Khomeini and establish a secular government.

Iraq, meanwhile, had taken advantage of Iran's political chaos and economic disorder to revive a border dispute that had been settled in 1975 when Iranian and Iraqi representatives reached agreement on the demarcation of their frontiers. Full-scale war erupted in September 1980, when Iraq demanded sovereignty over the entire Shatt al Arab waterway. Iraqi forces invaded Khuzestan in the southwest and captured the town of Khorramshahr and the oil refinery center of Ābādān. The Iranian army, decimated by the revolution, was slow to mobilize, but by June 1982 it had driven Iraqi soldiers out of Ābādān and Khorramshahr and from all undisputed Iranian territory. Iran then launched its own offensive, invading Iraq and thrusting toward Al Başrah (Basra), but

failed to make significant gains. At this point the land war became a stalemate, with Iranian and Iraqi troops both setting up an elaborate system of trenches. In 1983 Iraq broadened the war zone to include oil-tanker traffic in the northern Persian Gulf.

The Iraqis first attacked Iranian oil installations, disrupting, but not stopping, oil exports from the main oil terminal at Kharg Island. In mid-1983 Iraq took delivery of French jets bearing Exocet missiles. Iran said that it would close the Strait of Hormuz if Iraq used the missiles. The United States declared the strait a vital interest and said it would use military force to keep the strait open because of the large volume of oil that passed through it on the way to the West. During 1983 the Iraqis also began to attack civilian targets in Iran with long-range missiles. The attacks caused heavy casualties, and Iran responded by shelling Iraqi border cities. In 1984 Iran began to attack Arab shipping in the Persian Gulf.

Iranian forces staged a surprisingly effective attack on Iraqi forces in the Fao Peninsula in February 1986. After the attack the Iranians controlled Iraq's entire border on the Persian Gulf and were in reach of the major Iraqi city of Al Başrah. In April Khomeini renewed his demands for an end to the war: Iraqi president Saddam Hussein had to step down and Iraq had to admit responsibility and pay war reparations. Iran rejected all demands for a cease-fire and negotiations until these demands were met.

In November 1986 it was revealed that US National Security Advisor Robert McFarlane had secretly traveled to Iran to meet with government leaders. The United States supplied Iran with an estimated $30 million in spare parts and antiaircraft missiles in hopes that Iran would exert pressure on terrorist groups in Lebanon to release American hostages. This so-called Iran-Contra Affair caused a political scandal in the United States. In 1987 Iran attacked Kuwaiti oil tankers reregistered as American tankers and laid mines in the Persian Gulf to disrupt oil tanker shipping. The United States responded by stationing a naval task force in the region and attacking Iranian patrol boats and oil-loading platforms; in the process, the United States accidentally shot down a civilian passenger jet.

As the war continued to take a heavy toll in casualties and destruction and economic hardships persisted on the home front, the clerics maintained firm control through repression and Khomeini's charismatic hold over the people. In 1988 Iran finally yielded to terms for a cease-fire in the war. The borders were left effectively unchanged. Hundreds of thousands had died in both countries over the course of the war.

On 3 June 1989, a few months after calling for the death of novelist Salman Rushdie for blasphemy, Khomeini died of a heart attack. Over three million people attended his funeral. He was succeeded as the country's spiritual guide by Ali Khamenei. On 28 July 1989 Speaker of the Parliament Ali Akbar Rafsanjani, a moderate, was elected president with 95% of the vote. Iran remained neutral during the Gulf War, receiving (and retaining) Iraqi planes that were flown across the border for safekeeping. Iran also accepted thousands of Kurdish refugees from Iraq to add to its heavy burden of Afghan refugees from the civil strife in that country. Inflation, shortages, and unemployment—the products of revolution, war, and mismanagement—continued to generate widespread popular discontent, also fueled by dissatisfaction with the closed and repressive political system.

President Rafsanjani was reelected by a significantly smaller margin in 1993 but continued to press for free-market economic reforms. Rising prices in the wake of decreased government economic subsidies led to civil unrest in 1994 and 1995. Clerical conservatives led by Khamenei continued to battle the political moderates for dominance in the 1996 parliamentary elections, without a decisive victory for either side. Then, in the presidential election of May 1997, a moderate cleric, Mohammad Khatami, who favored economic reform, a more conciliatory foreign-policy stance, and less rigid clerical control of the government, won over two-thirds of the vote. In spite of continued opposition by Islamic conservatives, Khatami established a more tolerant climate in the country and expanded civil liberties. His policies received a decisive endorsement by the Iranian electorate when a political coalition led by the reformist president won 141 out of 290 parliamentary seats in the February 2000 elections and 189 seats in the May runoff elections, despite the shutdown of over a dozen liberal newspapers by conservative elements in the government in the weeks preceding the May polling. On 8 June 2001 Khatami won a landslide reelection victory, securing nearly 80% of the popular vote.

US president George W. Bush, in his 29 January 2002 State of the Union address, labeled Iran—along with Iraq and North Korea—an "axis of evil," responsible for seeking out weapons of mass destruction and supporting terrorists. Khatami, who long advocated a more pro-Western stance, urged anti-US demonstrators to turn out in large numbers to protest the speech, as the speech had come as a surprise to him. Although Iran did not support the US-led military campaign in Afghanistan to oust the Taliban regime in late 2001, it had expressed sympathy toward US citizens after the 11 September 2001 attacks on the United States and stated that it would aid any US service personnel in need on Iranian territory during the war in Afghanistan. Iran supported a greater role for the UN in Afghanistan and pledged resources to help train an Afghan army. Iran was concerned with securing its border with Afghanistan to prevent further destabilization of the region.

In January 2003 Iran urged Iraq to cooperate with UN resolutions requiring it to disarm itself of weapons of mass destruction, in an effort to avoid war. Iran took the position that the United States must not take unilateral military action in the dispute and said that it would not participate or allow its territory to be used in any military action against Iraq. Iran was again outraged by US President George W. Bush's 28 January 2003 State of the Union address, in which he alleged once again that Iran was developing weapons of mass destruction and supported terrorism.

Parliamentary elections, which marked the end of the campaign for political and social reform, were held on 20 February 2004. The conservative Guardian Council disqualified 43% of the 8,000 candidates who had entered the election, including most reformist incumbents who ran. There were calls for a boycott of the election. Reformists who chose to contest the election took only about 20% of the seats decided in the first round of voting. The conservative win was consolidated in the second round of voting in May. Another victory for conservatives came with the 2005 presidential election, when the ultraconservative former mayor of Tehrān, Mahmoud Ahmadinejad, beat former President Akbar Hashemi Rafsanjani with more than 61% of the vote in the second round. Ahmadinejad appealed to the poor in securing his win.

The United States and the European nations of France, Germany, and the United Kingdom have led efforts to persuade Iran to give up its nuclear research program. By 2005 Iran had resumed what it claimed was a civilian nuclear research program, but which Western nations fear could be used to develop nuclear arms. The International Atomic Energy Agency (IAEA) found Iran in violation of the Nuclear Non-Proliferation Treaty (NPT). In January 2006 Iran broke IAEA seals at its Natanz nuclear research facility, and in February the IAEA voted to report Iran to the UN Security Council over its nuclear activities. Iran then resumed uranium enrichment at Natanz. In December 2006 the UN Security Council voted to impose sanctions on Iran's trade in sensitive nuclear materials and technology. Iran condemned the resolution and said it would speed up its uranium enrichment work. In April 2007 President Ahmadinejad announced Iran was able to produce nuclear fuel on an industrial scale. The IAEA announced Iran had begun making nuclear fuel and said Iran had activated more than 1,300 centrifuge machines. That May the IAEA said Iran could potentially develop a nuclear weapon in three to eight years. In July 2007 Iran agreed to allow inspectors to visit the Arak nuclear plant following talks with the IAEA. In August 2007 the IAEA said Iran had 1,968 centrifuges enriching uranium at the Natanz plant, in addition to 328 in testing and 328 in assembly for a total of 2,624 centrifuges. In September President Mahmoud Ahmadinejad subsequently announced that Iran had reached its goal of developing 3,000 centrifuges. The goal of 3,000 centrifuges is significant as experts believe that if Iran could spin that many centrifuges continuously for a year, it could make enough highly enriched uranium for a single atom bomb.

Parliamentary elections held in March and April 2008 reinforced Ahmadinejad's strength, with a strong showing by candidates who support his hard-line conservative stance as well as more moderate conservatives. Conservative and Islamist candidates won 170 of the 290 seats in the Majlis to the reformers 46 seats. Many candidates who favored reform were barred from participating in the election.

In the presidential elections of June 2009, President Ahmadinejad was announced as the winner with 62% of the vote. However, a recount was quickly authorized following massive demonstrations by opposition groups claiming fraud. An early provincial review of results indicated majority wins for the incumbent in areas known to be heavily populated by opposition supporters, giving support to the claims of fraud. Hossein Mousavi, the primary opposition candidate, received only 33.8% of the total vote. Such a wide margin, with an 85% voter turnout, was unexpected. The recount, supervised by the Guardian Council, did show evidence of voting irregularities in at least 50 voting districts, including some localities in which the number of votes counted exceeded the number of eligible voters. However, the Guardian Council confirmed Ahmadinejad as the winner, ruling that the irregularities were not significant enough to affect the outcome of the election. Though a protest ban was initiated by the Ayatollah, violent demonstrations continued for over a week, leading to several deaths and the arrest or detainment of over 450 people. With hundreds of thousands of protestors involved on both sides of the issue, the demonstrations following the vote were the largest since the Iranian Revolution.

In September 2009 the Iranian parliament approved the appointment of the Islamic republic's first woman cabinet minister.

Fifty-year-old Marzieh Vahid Dastjerdi, the nation's health minister, trained as a gynecologist and was a leading conservative activist for women's health. In the past, Dastjerdi pushed for a plan of segregated health care in Iran through which female physicians would treat women and male physicians would treat men. The shortage of female physicians and specialists in the nation made the plan unviable. Two other women were nominated for ministerial positions, but were rejected. Ahmad Vahidi was approved as the nation's defense minister by an overwhelming majority of 227 votes out of 286 possible, despite international controversy. A warrant for Vahidi's arrest was issued by Argentina through Interpol for his involvement in a 1994 attack on the Israeli-Argentine Mutual Association, a Jewish community center; eighty-five people were killed in the attack.

Also in September 2009, just a few days before scheduled international talks in Geneva on nuclear disarmament and nonproliferation, the Iranian government revealed the existence of a nuclear enrichment facility near the city of Qum. While the disclosure increased international suspicions that Iran is actively working toward achieving nuclear weapons capacity, the government argued that the plant was producing enriched uranium consistent with a nuclear energy program, at levels of enrichment that are far less than those required for nuclear weapons. An official from Iran's Atomic Energy Organization announced that the government would consider a timetable for international inspectors to visit the new plant, but warned that the nuclear rights of the nation would not be accepted as a topic of conversation at the Geneva talks. While willing to discuss disarmament and nonproliferation of nuclear weapons, Iran has firmly asserted that it will not abandon its current nuclear activities. Expectations for a nuclear deal were diminished further in November 2009 when Iran's president announced that the country would build ten new uranium enrichment facilities.

In July 2010 the European Union (EU) announced a tough new package of sanctions against Iran, ramping up the pressure on Iran over its controversial nuclear program. The sanctions, which were described by officials as the toughest EU sanctions ever adopted against a single country, targeted the backbone of Iran's economy—foreign trade, financial services, transport, and the oil and gas sector. The sanctions prevent European companies from providing equipment or technical assistance to Iran in those key sectors, reducing Iran's ability to attract investors. The EU is Iran's largest trading partner and European companies will undoubtedly suffer from the sanctions too. However, EU officials described the sanctions as a necessary demonstration of seriousness that Iran's shadowy nuclear program would not be tolerated.

In December 2010 following two days of talks in Geneva with the permanent members of the UN Security Council, an Iranian negotiator announced that Iran would be willing to meet again in January 2011 in Istanbul for talks on issues of cooperation and shared concerns over nuclear issues. However, it was made clear that the government would not participate in any negotiations concerning Iran's nuclear rights or the nation's uranium enrichment program. In May 2011 Iran announced that the country would resume talks about its nuclear program with six major EU powers. Respecting the nation's rights and refraining from pressure were two of the country's stipulations if the talks commenced.

The United States and the EU continue to hold sanctions against the country.

13 GOVERNMENT

Before the 1979 revolution Iran was an absolute monarchy, with the constitution of 1906 modified in 1907 and amended in 1925, 1949, and 1957. The shah was the chief of state with sweeping powers. He commanded the armed forces, named the prime minister and all senior officials, and was empowered to dissolve either or both legislative houses. The legislative branch comprised the national assembly (Majlis) and the senate. Members of the Majlis were elected for four-year terms from 268 constituencies by adults 20 years of age and older. Half of the 60 senators were named by the shah, and half were elected. Members of the Majlis ostensibly represented all classes of the nation, while the somewhat more conservative Senate consisted of former cabinet ministers, former high officials, and retired generals.

The constitution of December 1979, which was approved in a public referendum and revised in 1989, established an Islamic republic in conformity with the principles of the Shia faith. Guidance of the republic is entrusted to the country's spiritual leader (*faqih*) or to a council of religious leaders. An appointed Council of Guardians consists of six religious leaders, who consider all legislation for conformity to Islamic principles, and six Muslim lawyers appointed by the supreme judicial council, who rule on limited questions of constitutionality. In accordance with the constitution, an 86-member Assembly of Experts chooses the country's spiritual leader and may nullify laws that do not conform to Islamic tenets. In 1998 seats on the council (which have eight-year terms) were opened for the first time to non-clerics.

The executive branch consists of a president and council of ministers. The president is elected by popular vote to a maximum of two consecutive four-year terms and supervises government administration. Candidates for the presidency and parliament must have the approval of Iran's spiritual leaders. The Majlis consists of 290 members elected directly to four-year terms. Iran has the lowest voting age in the world; suffrage is universal for those ages 15 and over.

There were more than 800 candidates for president in 2001, and the Council of Guardians narrowed them to 10. Mohammad Khatami was the sole moderate, with all of the other candidates having ties to conservative or hard-line parties. On 8 June 2001 Khatami secured 77% of the popular vote, with four-fifths of 43 million eligible voters turning out. In 2005 more than 1,000 candidates initially put forth their names for president, but the Council of Guardians disqualified all but seven. In the run-off election held on 24 June 2005, former president Akbar Hashemi Rafsanjani faced Tehrān Mayor Mahmoud Ahmadinejad. In a surprise victory, Ahmadinejad beat Rafsanjani with more than 61% of the vote. Almost 60% of all eligible voters turned out to cast their ballots. In the 2009 presidential election Ahmadinejad won 62% of the vote. This was challenged by reformists, who pointed to evidence of fraud, but the results stood after the Guardian Council confirmed Ahmadinejad's victory.

14 POLITICAL PARTIES

During the reign of Reza Shah (r. 1925–41), political parties were not permitted to function. After 1941 parties sprang up, but most of them were of an ephemeral nature. The Communist-oriented Tudeh Party was better organized than the others and benefited from the services of devoted followers and foreign funds. In 1949 an unsuccessful attempt to assassinate the shah was traced to the Tudeh and it was banned. It continued to work through front groups and its views were reflected in some periodicals, but the organization was extinguished in the shah's post-1953 crackdown.

In 1957 the government created facade political parties, the Nationalist (Mellioun) Party, headed by Manochehr Eqbal, then prime minister, and the People's (Mardom) Party, headed by former Prime Minister Asadullah Alam. Neither of these parties ever attracted any popular following. In 1975 the shah ordered the formation of a single political organization, the Iran Resurgence (Rastakhiz) Party, into which were merged all existing legal parties. Three cardinal principles were cited for membership in the party: faith in Iran's constitution, loyalty to the monarchical regime, and fidelity to the "white revolution." This party, like others before it, lacked a popular base.

After the overthrow of the shah's regime in February 1979, new political parties were formed, the most powerful being the IRP, which took control of the Majlis. However, power was wielded primarily by the military, the president, the clerical elite, and the heads of the *bonyads* (autonomous financial organizations that have considerable power and were formed from the confiscated wealth of the former royal family and its cronies).

As of 2006 Iran's parliament, or Majlis, was made up of various groups representing a spectrum of views ranging from hard-line radical Islam to moderates and liberals. Moderates generally hold less hostile views about the West while still believing in an Islamic republic. In 1997 a moderate politician, Mohammad Khatami, was elected president of Iran. The moderates scored a further triumph in the parliamentary elections of February and May 2000. A moderate reformist coalition headed by Khatami won 189 out of 290 seats in the Majlis, with radical Islamists winning 54, independents 42, and religious minority parties 5. The following organizations had success at the 2000 parliamentary elections: Assembly of the Followers of the Imam's Line, Freethinkers' Front, Islamic Iran Participation Front, Moderation and Development Party, Servants of Construction Party, and the Society of Self-sacrificing Devotees. Khatami was reelected president in 2001 after receiving just under 77% of the vote.

In 2004 the hard-line Guardian Council banned 3,605 reformist candidates out of a total 8,157 candidates running for parliament. About 80 of the candidates were sitting members of parliament. The first round of elections was held on 20 February 2004. Reformists who chose to contest the election took only about 20% of the seats decided in the first round. The conservative win was consolidated in the second round of voting in May. Conservatives held 190 seats, reformers took 50, independents, 43, religious minorities 5, and 2 seats were vacant as of 2005. Mahmud Ahmadinejad of the Alliance of Builders of Islamic Iran (a coalition of conservative groups) was elected president in 2005 and reelected in 2009.

The next legislative election was held in March and April 2008. Conservative and Islamist candidates won 170 of the 290 seats in the Majlis to the reformers' 46 seats. In fact, many candidates who favored reform were barred from participating in the election. Independents captured 71 seats and religious minorities 3 seats.

In September 2010 an Iranian court dissolved the nation's two leading reformist parties—the Islamic Iran Participation Front and the Islamic Revolution Mujahideen Organization. Both parties supported Hossein Mousavi in the 2009 presidential race. According to internal government reports, the parties were accused of undermining national security through their involvement in the 2009 election protests. The parties are now prohibited from any further activities.

15 LOCAL GOVERNMENT

Iran is divided into 28 *ostans* (provinces), each headed by a governor-general; the governor-general and district officials of each province are appointed by the central government. The *ostans* are subdivided into *sharestans* (counties), which are in turn divided into *bakhsh* (districts). Each *bakhsh* consists of two or more *dehistans*, which are composed of groups of villages or hamlets. Each of the municipalities (*shahrdarys*) is headed by a mayor. Some *sharestan* officials are elected, others are appointed by Tehrān.

16 JUDICIAL SYSTEM

The overthrow of the shah and the approval in 1980 of a constitution making Iran an Islamic state have radically changed Iran's judicial system. The 1980 constitution was revised in 1989.

In August 1982 the Supreme Court invalidated all previous laws that did not conform to the dictates of Islam, and all courts set up before the 1979 revolution were abolished in October 1982. An Islamic system of punishment, introduced in 1983, included flogging, stoning, and amputation for various crimes. There are two different court systems: civil courts and revolutionary courts. The Iranian court structure includes revolutionary courts, public courts, courts of peace, and Supreme Courts of Cassation. Public courts consist of civil, special civil, first class criminal, and second class criminal. Courts of peace—part of the civil court structure—are divided into ordinary courts, and independent courts of peace, and Supreme Courts of Cassation. There are 70 branches of the revolutionary courts.

The judicial system is under the authority of the religious leader (*faqih*). A supreme judicial council responsible to the faqih oversees the State Supreme Court, which has 33 branches. The chief justice of the Supreme Court is appointed by the *faqih* to a five-year term and must be a Muslim cleric and judicial expert. The Ministry of Justice oversees law courts in the provinces.

The revolutionary courts try cases involving national security, political offenses, narcotics trafficking, and "crimes against God." Although the constitution guarantees a fair trial, the revolutionary courts provide almost no procedural safeguards. The trials in revolutionary courts are rarely held in public and there is no guarantee of access to an attorney.

A special clerical court deals with crimes committed by members of the clergy, including what can be termed ideological offenses, such as issues like interpretations of religious dogma deemed not acceptable to the establishment clergy.

Elements of the prerevolutionary judicial system continue to be applied in common criminal and civil cases. In these cases the right to a public trial and the benefit of counsel are generally respected. In 1995 the government began implementing a law authorizing judges to act as prosecutor and judge in the same case.

The constitution states that "reputation, life, property, (and) dwelling(s)" are protected from trespass except as "provided by law." However, in practice, security forces do not respect these provisions.

17 ARMED FORCES

The International Institute for Strategic Studies (IISS) reported that armed forces in Iran totaled 523,000 members in 2011. The force is comprised of 350,000 from the army, 125,000 from the Revolutionary Guard Corps, 18,000 from the navy, and 30,000 members of the air force. Armed forces represent 1.9% of the labor force in Iran. Defense spending totaled $20.5 billion and accounted for 2.5% of gross domestic product (GDP).

There was also a reserve of the Popular Mobilization Army (Basij Resistance Force) which, upon mobilization, could reach up to one million combat capable personnel. It was widely believed that Iran was developing the capability to produce nuclear weapons.

18 INTERNATIONAL COOPERATION

Iran is a charter member of the UN, having joined on 24 October 1945 and belongs to ESCAP and several non-regional specialized agencies, such as the UN Food and Agriculture Organization (FAO); United Nations Educational, Scientific and Cultural Organization (UNESCO); UNIDO; the World Bank; and the World Health Organization (WHO). Iran is also a member of the Organization of the Islamic Conference (OIC), G-24, G-77 and the Colombo Plan. It is a founding member of the Organization of Petroleum Exporting Countries (OPEC) and a leading supporter of higher petroleum prices. Iran is one of ten members in the Economic Cooperation Organization (ECO).

During the 2011 Syrian uprising, Iran aided the Syrian government with technical and personnel support as well as riot control equipment, intelligence monitoring techniques, and oil. The outcome of the struggle of the Syrians against their government had consequences for the future of the Islamic Republic of Iran as well.

Iran's revolutionary government was aligned with the radical Arab states of Libya and Syria, which were the only Arab countries to support Iran in its war with Iraq (1980–88). Since before 1979 Iranian foreign policy has been to curtail superpower influence in the Persian Gulf area. It also encourages the Islamization of the governments throughout the Middle East, in such countries as Sudan, Algeria, Bahrain, and Saudi Arabia. This policy of Islamization includes strong anti-US and anti-Israeli sentiments. Despite past troubles with Iraq, Iran remained neutral during the 2003 US-led coalition invasion of Iraq, which resulted in the ousting of the Hussein government. Iran is considered to be a state sponsor of terrorism by the United States. Iran is part of the Nonaligned Movement.

In environmental cooperation, Iran is part of the Basel Convention, the Convention on Biological Diversity, Ramsar, CITES, the London Convention, the Montréal Protocol, the Nuclear Test Ban Treaty, and the UN Conventions on Climate Change and Desertification.

19 ECONOMY

A country with a substantial economic potential, Iran witnessed rapid economic growth during the reign of Shah Muhammad Reza Pahlavi, from 1941 to 1979. Development of its extensive agricultural, mineral, and power resources was financed through oil revenues. The traditional land tenure system, under which farmers were sharecroppers, was replaced through a land reform program inaugurated in 1962. Famous for its carpets, Iran also produced a variety of consumer goods and building materials. Oil, however, became the lifeblood of the economy. With the astonishing growth of its oil revenues, Iran became a major world economic power, whose investments helped several industrialized countries pay for their oil needs during the 1970s.

The economy changed drastically after 1979. The war with Iraq, which curtailed oil exports, coupled with the decrease in the price of oil, especially in 1986, sent oil revenues spiraling downward from $20.5 billion in 1979 to an estimated $5.3 billion in 1986. This forced annual GDP growth down from 15.2% in 1982 to 0.2% in 1984; GDP was estimated to have fallen by 8% in 1986. The war's drain on the state budget, the drop in oil prices, poor economic management, declining agricultural output, an estimated 1987 inflation rate of 30–50%, and large budget deficits combined to put enormous strains on the economy.

After Iran accepted a UN ceasefire resolution in 1988, it began reforming the economy with the implementation of the Islamic republic's first five-year social and economic development plan for 1989–94. The plan emphasized revitalizing market mechanisms, deregulating the economy, and rebuilding basic infrastructure. These reforms led to economic growth and lowered budget deficits. GDP grew an average 7% a year in real terms over 1989–92. The general government deficit was reduced from 9% of GDP in 1988 to an estimated 2% in 1992. The inflation rate decreased from 29% in 1988 to around 10% in 1990, but had redoubled to 20% in 1991–92.

Other impacts of the first plan included a growth in agricultural production of 5.6%; industrial production of 15%; water, gas, and electricity of 18.9%; and transport of 11.9%. In 1991 the government adopted a structural adjustment program similar in nature to the kind the International Monetary Fund (IMF) imposes on developing nations in exchange for aid. Iran, however, did not need aid, but rather imposed the adjustments on itself in an effort to liberalize its economy, making it more market-oriented while still retaining an authoritarian regime. The structural adjustments advocated by then-President Rafsanjani included privatizations of state-owned enterprises, deregulation, cutting government subsidies, and encouraging foreign investment. While marginally well-intentioned, the Rafsanjani reforms led to little economic improvement. Privatization was especially ineffective. Political corruption and rampant cronyism led to many enterprises ending up in the hands of a small clique of well-connected elites. By 1997, 86% of Iran's GDP came from state-owned businesses. Deregulation also hit considerable snags. In 1996 alone more than 250 regulations on imports and exports were issued by 24 ministries—many of them repetitive or contradictory.

In April 1995 the United States imposed trade and investment sanctions against Iran, in reprisal for what the United States believed was Iran's continued support of international terrorism. This move, which even the strongest allies of the United States did not match, had some economic impact—most notably a precipitous drop in the value of the rial, which the government was forced to prop up. Sanctions have generally grown stricter in the years since, and other nations have joined the United States in imposing them, with the expressed goal of pressuring Iran to stop its nuclear program.

The GDP growth rate stood at 5.28% in 2000, 5.82% in 2001, 7.64% in 2002, and 6.1% in 2003. For 2005 and 2006 real GDP growth averaged 5.6% and 4.8%, respectively. For 2007 the real GDP growth rate was estimated at 5.8%. Inflation, which had averaged 14.6% from 2001–05, stood at 17.5% in 2007. The Iranian government reported unemployment of 12% in 2007. The Iranian economy in the mid-2000s remained determined by its reliance upon oil and continued to pass through periods of boom and bust as oil prices rose and fell on the volatile international markets. The state remained the dominant economic factor, as it was the recipient of crude oil revenue. The oil sector's share of GDP has declined from highs of 30-40% during the 1970s. Nevertheless, oil revenue provided some 85% of government revenue as of 2007; therefore the hydrocarbons sector receives the vast majority of domestic and foreign investment flows. The services sector has grown, but bureaucracy, the uncertainty of long-term economic planning, and currency-exchange restrictions have made services a volatile sector. The agricultural sector has been aided by state investment, with the improvement of packaging and marketing helping to develop new export markets. Export-based agricultural products—such as dates, flowers, and pistachios—have seen substantial growth, aided by large-scale irrigation projects. In 2007 agriculture accounted for 10.7% of GDP, with industry contributing 42.9% and services 46.4%. As of 2007, 25% of the labor force was engaged in agriculture, with 31% in industry and 44% in services. The GDP rate of change in Iran, as of 2010, was 1%. Inflation stood at 11.8%, and unemployment was reported at 14.6%.

The 2008–09 global recession and continued international sanctions led to serious economic challenges. As a cost-cutting measure, in December 2010 the government initiated a series of cuts in energy and food subsidies, which generally amount to about $100 billion per year. The cuts resulted in a 400% increase in the price of gasoline. Prices for electricity, water, flour, and bread were also expected to increase significantly as a result of the cuts.

20 INCOME

The CIA estimated that in 2010 the GDP of Iran was $818.7 billion. The CIA defines GDP as the value of all final goods and services produced within a nation in a given year and computed on the basis of purchasing power parity (PPP) rather than value as measured on the basis of the rate of the exchange based on current dollars. The per capita GDP was estimated at $10,600. The annual growth rate of GDP was 1%. The average inflation rate was 11.8%. It was estimated that agriculture accounted for 11% of GDP, industry 45.9%, and services 43.1%.

According to the World Bank, remittances from citizens living abroad totaled $1 billion or about $13 per capita and accounted for approximately 0.1% of GDP. It was estimated that household consumption was growing at an average annual rate of 9.1%.

The World Bank estimates that Iran, with 1.12% of the world's population, accounted for 1.34% of the world's GDP. By comparison, the United States, with 4.85% of the world's population, accounted for 22.51% of world GDP.

As of 2011 the most recent study by the World Bank reported that actual individual consumption in Iran was 55.8% of GDP and accounted for 1.23% of world consumption. By comparison, the United States accounted for 25.44% of world individual consumption. The World Bank also estimated that 13.4% of Iran's GDP was spent on food and beverages, 16.8% on housing and household furnishings, 3.5% on clothes, 4.7% on health, 5.2% on transportation, 1.4% on communications, 2.0% on recreation, 0.9% on restaurants and hotels, and 3.7% on miscellaneous goods and services and purchases from abroad.

21 LABOR

The labor code grants workers the right to form and join their own organizations; however, the government-controlled Workers' House is the only authorized national labor organization. The Workers' House controls all workers according to government objectives. Strikes are not permitted. Islamic principles and dress are strictly observed at work with transgressions subjecting the worker to penalties. Workers cannot bargain collectively.

The Labor Law forbids employment of minors under 15 years of age, but these regulations are not enforced. Forced and bonded labor by children remains a serious problem. In 2009 the minimum wage was $263 per month. Many middle class citizens work several jobs to support their families. The Labor Code stipulates a 6-day, 48-hour workweek with one rest day.

As of 2010 Iran had a total labor force of 25.7 million people. Within that labor force, CIA estimates in 2007 noted that 25% were employed in agriculture, 31% in industry, and 45% in the service sector.

22 AGRICULTURE

Roughly 11% of the total land is farmed, and the country's major crops include wheat, rice, other grains, sugar beets, sugar cane, fruits, nuts, and cotton. Cereal production in 2009 amounted to 20.8 million tons, fruit production 1.3 million tons, and vegetable production 18.1 million tons.

Progress in Iranian agriculture was greatly stimulated by the land reform of 1962–63, under which 4,025,680 farmers and their family members had taken title to their land by 1975, after the old land tenure system was abolished. However, with a rapidly increasing population and a sharply rising standard of living, Iran is no longer self-sufficient in its agricultural production, and food imports have risen steadily.

In 2008 Iran was the largest producer of pistachios in the world and the third-largest producer of almonds (after the United States and Spain).

23 ANIMAL HUSBANDRY

The UN FAO reported that Iran dedicated 29.5 million hectares (73 million acres) to permanent pasture or meadow in 2009. During that year the country tended 513 million chickens and 8.1 million head of cattle. The production from these animals amounted to 451,557 tons of beef and veal, 1.42 million tons of poultry, 576,694 tons of eggs, and 4.79 million tons of milk. Iran also produced 49,734 tons of cattle hide and 74,655 tons of raw wool.

Not only is animal husbandry the major occupation of nomadic and semi-nomadic ethnic groups scattered over Iran, but each farming village also keeps flocks that graze on the less productive areas. Cattle are raised as draft animals and for milk and are not fattened for beef. Sheep produce many staple items: milk and butter, animal fat for cooking, meat, wool for carpet making, and skins and hides.

24 FISHING

The Caspian Sea provides a seemingly inexhaustible source of sturgeon, salmon, and other species of fish, some of which spawn in the chilly streams that flow into this sea from the high Elburz Mountains. Caviar of unrivaled quality is produced by the Iranian Fisheries Co., formerly a joint Russo-Iranian venture but now wholly owned by the government of Iran. About 200,000 kg (440,000 lbs) of caviar are sold per year, most of which is exported, providing a substantial share of the world's supply. The fishing grounds of the Persian Gulf were long neglected, but during the 1970s new fishing fleets and packing and conserving facilities were established. The Iran-Iraq war and consequent environmental damage retarded the development of fisheries in this region. In 2008 Iran had 2,900 decked commercial fishing boats. The annual capture totaled 407,842 tons according to the UN FAO. The export value of seafood totaled $48.95 million.

25 FORESTRY

Approximately 7% of Iran was covered by forest in 2010. The value of all forest products, including roundwood, totaled $8.28 million in 2009. The UN FAO estimated 819,000 cu m (28.9 million cu ft) of roundwood were produced in 2009; about 29% was used for fuel. Along the northern slopes of the Elburz Mountains from near sea level to an altitude of about 2,100 m (7,000 ft) are dense stands of oak, ash, elm, beech, ironwood, cypress, walnut, and a number of other tree varieties. The high plateau forests of Fars, Kurdistan, Luristan, and Khorasan comprise sparse stands of scrub oak, ash, maple, cedar, wild almond, and pistachio. Date palms, acacias, and tamarisks grow in the Persian Gulf area. The timber industry is controlled by the government.

A forest ranger school was started in 1957 as an extension of the government's forest service. In 1963 a forestry college was established at Karaj, west of Tehrān, to train forestry engineers.

26 MINING

Iran possesses extensive and varied mineral resources and is the world's third-largest producer of gypsum. As of 2009, most of Iran's 2,700 mines were privately owned and 2,000 were active, producing 42 minerals; some 65% of the mines produced building and construction materials and 20% were stone quarries. The mining sector accounted for 24% of Iran's industrial output of $15.4 billion, and mineral and metal exports amounted to $645 million. Mineral exports include chromite, refined sulfur, lead, zinc, copper, and decorative stone. Iron, steel, and chemicals are leading export commodities, while the petroleum and petrochemicals industries are Iran's top industries. In 2010 Iran was ranked 7th in the world in cement production by the US Geological Survey. The annual output in 2010 was 72 million tons.

Production of gypsum in 2008 (from the Semnan region, east of Tehrān) was an estimated 12 million tons, down from 13.82 million tons in 2002. Estimated production of iron ore and concentrate (by gross weight) in 2009 was 33 million tons up by 3.13% over 2008. Copper concentrate (29–35% Cu) output by gross weight in 2009 totaled 241,000 metric tons. Bauxite production (gross weight) totaled an estimated 500,000 metric tons in 2009,

while output of mined chromite concentrate (by gross weight) in 2008 was estimated at 188,000 metric tons. Lead concentrate production by gross weight in 2008 was estimated at 20,000 metric tons. Output of mined zinc concentrate by gross weight in 2009 was estimated at 100,000 metric tons, while manganese mine production by gross weight that same year was estimated at 110,000 metric tons. Mined molybdenum concentrate output by gross weight was estimated at 3,700 metric tons in 2009. Marble production (blocks, crushed, and slabs) was estimated at 7.7 million tons in 2003.

Iran also produces orpiment and realgar arsenic concentrates, gold, silver, asbestos, barite, borax, hydraulic cement, clays (bentonite, industrial, and kaolin), diatomite, feldspar, fluorspar, turquoise, industrial or glass sand (quartzite and silica), lime, magnesite, nitrogen (of ammonia and urea), perlite, natural ocher and iron oxide mineral pigments, pumice and related volcanic materials, salt, caustic soda, stone (including granite, marble, travertine, dolomite, and limestone), celestite strontium, natural sulfates (aluminum potassium sulfate and sodium sulfate), and talc. Iran may also produce ferromanganese, ferromolybdenum, nepheline syenite, phosphate rock, selenium, shell, vermiculite, and zeolite and has the capacity to mine onyx.

In 2000 the government merged the Ministry of Mines and Metals and the Ministry of Industry to form the Ministry of Industry and Mines. For its third five-year economic development plan (2000–05), the government proposed to privatize 40 mineral industry companies affiliated with the Ministry of Industry and Mines, having already divested itself of numerous smaller mineral enterprises. Since 1998 the government has allowed foreign investment in solid mineral exploration joint ventures and, in 1999, showcased 102 mining and mineral-processing projects at the First International Mines and Metals Investment Forum. The Iranian constitution prohibits foreign control over natural resources. To diversify and expand the economy in the wake of declining oil prices in the late 1990s, the government sought to increase metal production. In May 2011 the Ministry of Industry and Mines was merged into the Commerce Ministry to decrease the number of ministries.

27 ENERGY AND POWER

The World Bank reported in 2008 that Iran produced 214.5 billion kWh of electricity and consumed 174.3 billion kWh, or 2,238 kWh per capita. Roughly 99% of energy came from fossil fuels. Per capita oil consumption was 2,808 kg. Oil production totaled 4.08 million barrels of oil a day.

Iran's proven oil reserves as of 2011 were estimated by the Oil and Gas Journal at 138.4 billion barrels; these constituted 10% of the world's known reserves and were exceeded only by those of Saudi Arabia, Iraq, the United Arab Emirates, and Kuwait. However, in 2007 Iran's oil minister placed the country's proven oil reserves at 150 billion barrels after new discoveries in the Pars fields. In 2010 Iran produced around 4.25 million barrels of oil per day, and natural gas production was 138.5 billion cu m (4.9 trillion cu ft) per day. Domestic oil demand in 2010 was placed at an estimated 1.8 million barrels per day, with oil exports estimated for 2009 at 2.5 million barrels per day.

More than half of Iran's 40 producing fields contain over 1 billion barrels of oil. Most of the reserves are located in onshore fields in the Khuzestan region. The onshore Ahwaz, Marun, Gachsaran, Agha Jari, Bibi Hakimeh, and Pars fields alone account for half of annual oil production. In July 2011 the National Iranian Oil Company (NIOC) announced another large deposit of crude oil and natural gas in the South Pars field in the Persian Gulf. The Khayyam field is thought to have about 260 billion cu m (9.2 trillion cu ft) of gas reserves, as well as some crude reserves. OPEC said Iran's oil revenues will be about $100 billion in 2011.

Although the nation is a leading exporter of oil, it does not maintain a large domestic refining industry, resulting in a need to import refined petroleum products. In 2009 Iran signed a deal with Venezuela to import 20,000 barrels of gasoline a day. Under the terms of the deal, the money paid to Venezuela for the imports will be placed in a fund that Venezuela will then use to finance the purchase of machinery and technology from Iran. In 2010 Iran and Venezuela signed a $780 million deal to develop the South Pars gas field in Iran in exchange for investment by Iran in Venezuelan oil projects. In 2011 the Obama administration targeted sanctions on the Venezuelan State Oil Company.

In 2010 Iran's natural gas reserves were estimated at 29.61 trillion cu m, and are exceeded only by those in Russia. However, approximately 62% of Iran's natural gas reserves are situated in non-associated fields and have yet to be developed. More than one-quarter of Iran's natural gas reserves have been discovered since 1992. Domestic demand for natural gas was estimated for 2010 at 137.5 billion cu m (4.9 trillion cu ft), with exports and imports for that year estimated at 7.9 billion cu m (279 billion cu ft) and 6.9 billion cu m (244 billion cu ft), respectively. The national Iranian Gas Co. controls the exploitation of natural gas. Inside Iran, a network of pipelines connects Tehran, Qazvin, Esfahan, Abadan, Shiraz, and Mashhad to Ahvaz and the gas fields.

In January 2010 Azerbaijan and Iran struck an agreement that would allow 1.2 cu m (425 million cu ft) of natural gas to flow daily from Azerbaijan to Iran. Analysts said the deal could result in a total transfer of 100 million cu m (3.5 billion cu ft) by the time the contract expires in March 2010. Because its terrain impedes supply routes from the energy-rich south, Iran imports considerable amounts of natural gas to fuel its northern region. At the same time, highly lucrative Caspian gas is at the center of the geopolitical competition between Russia, Europe, and Iran. In securing large contracts with countries like Azerbaijan, Iran also strengthens its regional position.

Although Iran is one of the world's leading oil-producing countries, Iranian industry formerly depended on other energy sources, such as electricity, coal, and charcoal. Recently, however, oil and especially gas have been used increasingly in manufacturing. In 2009 Iran's electric power generating capacity was placed at 34.222 million kW, with 31.419 million kW dedicated to conventional thermal fuel plants. Hydropower accounts for 2.803 million kW of capacity for that year. Electric power output in 2009 came to 212.8 billion kWh, with consumption that year at 206.7 billion kWh. Iran plans to construct ten nuclear power plants by 2015 in order to provide about 20% of the country's power needs. As of 2000 there were five small nuclear reactors in operation.

28 INDUSTRY

Principal industries are oil refining, petrochemicals, steel, and copper. In 1987 there were six primary refineries—at Ābādān,

Bakhtaran, Tehrān, Shirāz, Esfahān, and Tabriz—with a potential capacity of 950,000 barrels per day. In late 1980 Iraqi bombing forced the closure of the Ābādān refinery, which had a total capacity of 600,000 barrels per day and was one of the world's largest refineries. Several other refineries suffered lesser damage during the war. The Kharg Island oil terminal also was severely damaged by bombing in 1985. Construction by a Japanese consortium of a $4 billion petrochemical complex at Bandar-e Khomeini, near the Iraqi border, was halted by the war; by mid-1983 the installation, which was 85% complete, had already been attacked six times. In September 1984 the Japanese withdrew their technicians from the site because of renewed Iraqi bombing. Iran took on much of the financial responsibility for the plant, and the ending of all payments of Japanese credits and loans in February 1986 meant that the plant would never be completed according to the original plans. After the cease-fire in 1988, Iran began to rebuild its damaged oil export facilities, concentrating mainly on the rehabilitation of Kharg Island. A 500,000-barrel reservoir terminal at Uhang Island was put into operation in March 1993. The oil complex on the southern island of Lavan was reopened after reconstruction at the end of April 1993. The Ābādān refinery became operational again at 200,000 barrels per day in May 1993. Esfahān's oil production unit became operational in 1992–93, while an additional refinery later opened at Bandar-e 'Abbās. Major refinery products are motor fuel, distillate fuel oil, and residual fuel oil. Oil refining manufacturers had a combined capacity of 1.86 million barrels per day in 2009.

In 2011 Iran had proven oil reserves of 137 billion barrels. Oil production in 2010 was 4.25 million barrels per day, of which 93% was crude oil. In 2009 Iran had estimated net exports of 2.523 million barrels of oil per day, the second-largest exporter in the Persian Gulf region. The Doroud 1 and 2, Salman, Abuzar, Foroozan, and Sirri fields comprise the bulk of Iran's offshore output, all of which is exported. Iran's major refineries in 2005 are at Ābādān, Esfahān, Bandar Abbās, Tehrān, Arāk, Tabriz, Shirāz, Kermānshāh, and Lavan Island.

The natural gas industry has boomed in Iran, with the second-largest proven reserves in the world (1,045 trillion cubic feet in 2010). In 2010 Iran produced 138.5 billion cubic feet of natural gas. In October 2004 Iran and China announced the signing of a deal for Chinese investment in Iran's oil fields and the long-term sale of Iranian natural gas to China, which could eventually be worth $100 billion. The gas agreement entailed the annual export of some 10 million tons of Iranian liquefied natural gas (LNG) for a 25-year period. The agreement could eventually reach 15–20 million tons a year, taking the total value to as much as $200 billion. Iran must first build the plants to liquefy the natural gas. This agreement was seen as a blow to US sanctions on Iran. In January 2009 Iran and China signed a $1.76 billion contract for the initial development of the North Azadegan oil field in western Iran. In March the two countries struck a three-year $3.39 billion deal to produce liquefied natural gas in Iran's mammoth South Pars natural gas field.

A plant in Ābādān for the production of plastics, detergents, and caustic soda was completed in the 1960s. Since then, the petrochemical industry has expanded considerably. By the mid-2000s Iran's attempt to diversify its economy resulted in its investing some of its oil revenue in the petrochemicals sector and other areas. The petrochemicals sector has been the main focus of the postwar industrialization program. The heavy metals industry began in 1972 with the start of steel production at the Esfahān National Steel Mill in Esfahān. Manufactured goods include diesel engines, motor vehicles, television sets, refrigerators, washing machines, and other consumer items.

The textile industry has prospered in recent years with increased production of cotton, woolen, and synthetic fabrics. The making of hand woven carpets is a traditional industry in Iran that flourishes despite acute competition from machine-made products. However, carpet exports declined throughout the war years. To promote self-sufficiency, Iran has encouraged development of the food-processing, shoemaking, paper and paper products, rubber, pharmaceutical, aircraft, and shipbuilding industries. Other industrial products include cement, nitrogenous fertilizer, phosphate fertilizers, and refined sugar.

Iran's industrialization program was set back by political turmoil and labor disruptions of the late 1970s and by the revolutionary government's nationalization of industries in the summer of 1979, causing a flight of capital and trained managers. Industrial production declined by -3.4% during the 1970s. However, the sector recovered somewhat by 1983–84, when the government reported a 23% gain in industrial production. The development plan of 1989–94 increased funding to develop heavy industry. A privatization decree in June 1991 led to the identification of 390 public manufacturing and trading firms for divestiture; of these, 185 were already divested. Industrial production grew at a rate of 5.3% during 1988–98,. The industrial production growth rate stood at 3% in 2005 (excluding oil); it was -1.1% in 2010. The majority of heavy industries including steel, petrochemicals, copper, automobiles, and machine tools remained in the public sector, with most light industry privately owned.

29 SCIENCE AND TECHNOLOGY

The "white revolution" of the 1960s, which emphasized industrialization, involved the importation of petroleum technology and the training of Iranian technicians abroad, but it did not improve Iran's indigenous technology. The principal scientific institution in Tehrān is the International Scientific Research Institute, founded in 1955. Specialized learning societies include the Iranian Mathematical Society and the Iranian Society of Microbiology, both headquartered in Tehrān. Also in the city are the Animal Husbandry Research Institute and the Institut Pasteur. Iran has 37 universities offering degrees in basic and applied sciences. Following the removal of the shah and the formation of an Islamic revolutionary government, Iran suffered a "brain drain" as foreign-trained scientists and engineers either fled the country or refused to return after their education. According to the World Bank, in 2006 the number of patent applications in science and technology totaled 5,970 in Iran. Public financing of science was 0.67% of GDP. As of 2006 there were 706 researchers per million people. High technology exports in 2006 were valued at $374 million, or 0.67% of GDP.

30 DOMESTIC TRADE

Outside the major cities, most goods are sold in small shops or open-air markets. Most large enterprises are controlled by the state. Privately owned shops for trade and services are typi-

cally small. Textile industries are located in Esfahān and Shirāz. Kermān is known for production and distribution of fine carpets. Hamadān is an important trade center for agricultural products from the surrounding areas.

Business hours are from 8 a.m. to 2 p.m. Saturdays–Wednesdays. Since Friday is the official Muslim holy day, many establishments close early on Thursday afternoons or are completely closed on Thursdays. Banking hours are 7:30 a.m. to 2 p.m. on weekdays and 7:30a.m. to 12 p.m. on Thursdays. Shops are open from 10 a.m. to 9 p.m. Saturdays–Thursdays, and department stores are open until 9:30 p.m.

31 FOREIGN TRADE

Iran imported $58.97 billion worth of goods and services in 2008, while exporting $78.69 billion worth of goods and services. Major import partners in 2009 were United Arab Emirates (UAE), 15%; China, 14.5%; Germany, 9.7%; South Korea, 7.3%; Italy, 5.2%; and Russia, 5.1%. Its major export partners were China, 16.3%; India, 13.1%; Japan, 11.5%; South Korea, 7.1%; and Turkey, 4.2%.

In 2010 major imports included industrial supplies, capital goods, food stuffs, other consumer goods, and technical services.

Iran's most valuable export is crude petroleum. Petroleum accounts for the majority of its commodity exports revenues (80%). Other exports included floor coverings and fruits and nuts. Iran accounts for 10% of the world's carpet exports.

32 BALANCE OF PAYMENTS

Throughout the 1960s and 1970s Iran had a favorable trade balance, but substantial imports of services resulted in an annual deficit on current accounts. Long-term capital inflows from private sources reached a peak in 1965; between 1968 and 1973 capital from foreign governments played a prime role in Iranian development. By 1974, with a net trade surplus of $17.7 billion and a current account surplus of $10.9 billion, Iran was one of the world's major exporters of capital. The current account balance remained in surplus annually until the massive economic and civic turbulence caused by the revolution of 1979 and the long, devastating war with Iraq (1980–88). By the time the war had ended, Iran's po-

Principal Trading Partners – Iran (2010)

(In millions of US dollars)

Country	Total	Exports	Imports	Balance
World	163,570.0	100,900.0	62,670.0	38,230.0
United Arab Emirates	23,317.0	871.0	22,446.0	-21,575.0
China	22,311.0	16,578.0	5,733.0	10,845.0
Japan	11,702.0	10,147.0	1,555.0	8,592.0
India	11,690.0	9,916.0	1,774.0	8,142.0
Turkey	10,756.0	6,950.0	3,806.0	3,144.0
South Korea	9,996.0	6,309.0	3,687.0	2,622.0
Italy	7,352.0	5,527.0	1,825.0	3,702.0
Germany	5,491.0	1,007.0	4,484.0	-3,477.0
Spain	4,624.0	4,089.0	535.0	3,554.0
Netherlands	3,725.0	2,564.0	1,161.0	1,403.0

(…) data not available or not significant.

(n.s.) not specified.

SOURCE: *2011 Direction of Trade Statistics Yearbook,* New York: United Nations, 2011.

sition as a net foreign creditor was badly eroded due to a substantial drop in the world price for oil and a sharp increase in dependence on imports—largely machinery and basic commodities to rebuild infrastructure. By 1993 Iran owed foreign creditors nearly $30 billion. In following years the government, still plagued by lessening oil revenues and a quota of production imposed on it by OPEC, was forced to reschedule the debt—with payments coming due in 1996, when foreign debt went down to approximately $22 billion. Foreign debt stood at approximately $8.2 billion in 2002. In 2011 Iran's foreign debt is $12.84 billion down from $14.34 billion in 2010.

High oil prices during 2000–04 allowed Iran to record substantial trade surpluses, even though import spending also rose quickly as strong foreign-exchange earnings and the easing of the country's debt-repayment schedule allowed the central bank to relax its import compression program. In 2010 Iran had exports of $84.92 billion and imports of $58.97 billion. The current account surplus was $15.42 billion or 6% of GDP. Foreign debt stood at $12.84 billion. Iran had $75.06 billion in foreign exchange reserves and gold.

³³BANKING AND SECURITIES

The Iranian fiscal year begins on 21 March and runs through 20 March of the following calendar year. Before the modern era in Iranian banking, which dates to the opening of a branch of a British bank in 1888, credit was available only at high rates from non-institutional lenders such as relatives, friends, wealthy landowners, and bazaar money lenders. As recently as 1988 these non-institutional sources of credit were still available, particularly in the more isolated rural communities. The Central Bank of Iran-Bank Markazi, established by the Monetary and Banking Law of 1960, issues notes, controls foreign exchange, and supervises the banking sector.

The revolutionary government nationalized all commercial banks shortly after taking office in 1979 and announced that banking practices would be brought in line with Islamic principles, which include a ban on interest payments. By 1993 there were five Islamic banks, which had incorporated the previous banks. Instead of paying interest, the new banks give "guaranteed returns" or commissions on loans. The commissions were introduced in 1984 and were known as "profit sharing." In Islamic terms, this meant that profit (interest) was acceptable only if a lender's money was "not at risk."

In 1991 measures were introduced to promote competition between banks and to loosen Bank Markazi's control in order to encourage savings within the official banking sector. In 1994 Bank Markazi introduced reforms allowing private banking operations to register officially and offer most services in competition with the public sector. However, the raft of new currency and export regulations that followed the collapse of the rial in April 1995 put the recently legalized private sector under huge pressure because, for many of the bazaar traders, currency dealings represented a significant share of their total business. There is a basic lack of confidence in the banking system. Many informal banking operations are run from the bazaars. In addition, Iranians who are able to do so operate bank accounts outside the country, importing funds as needed rather than using the domestic system.

Bank Melli, which has acted for the central bank, handles most Iranian banking operations outside the country. The requirements to abide by Islamic principles were never imposed on Bank Melli. According to the Central Bank of Iran (CBI), the country's liquidity amounted to some $174 billion by April 2008 and $197 billion by October 2009.

The Tehrān Stock Exchange, locally known as the Bourse, was created in 1968. Three years later, the National Bank of Iran and the Industrial and Mining Development Bank of Iran joined with the US firm of Merrill Lynch, Pierce, Fenner and Smith to begin international brokerage activities in Iran. The exchange has stayed open since the revolution but did not play a significant role in the nation's business until the 1990s. Since 1989 the stock exchange has expanded continuously. A total of 337 companies were being traded and the capitalization of the exchange was reported to be nearly $59 billion in 2006.

³⁴INSURANCE

Under a 1971 act of parliament, all companies operating in Iran were required to cede 25% of total acquired nonlife business and 50% of life business to Bimeh Markazi Iran, the central insurance company of Iran. The company writes all classes of insurance and reinsurance. On 25 June 1979 the revolutionary government announced the nationalization of all insurance companies. At the end of 2008 there were 20 insurance firms active in the market, only 4 of which were state-owned (with a 75% market share). Alternate statistics give the market share for private insurance companies since 2006 at 54% and 46% for governmental insurance companies. In 2008 the value of all direct premiums written totaled $4.3 billion, of which nonlife premiums accounted for 95% and 5% relate to life products. Approximately 60% of all insurance premiums are generated from car insurance. Payout ratios have shown consistent growth over the years. The industry average payout ratio was 86%. Iran has two re-insurers. Insurance premiums come to just below 1% of GDP.

³⁵PUBLIC FINANCE

Iran's fiscal year coincides with its calendar year, beginning on 21 March. The budget is prepared by the Finance Ministry and submitted to parliament. Trade reforms implemented since 1991 have boosted economic growth and reduced budget deficits. The general government deficit fell from 9% of GDP in 1988 to 2% in 1992, but was up to almost 7% again in 1998. By 2002, however, external debt was equivalent to less than 2% of GDP as a result of market reforms. By 2010, however, external debt was estimated to be $14.34 billion.

In 2010 the budget of Iran included $105.7 billion in public revenue and $98.83 billion in public expenditures. The budget surplus amounted to 5.9% of GDP. Public debt was 16.2% of GDP, with $14.34 billion of the debt held by foreign entities.

Government outlays by function averaged 50% on social policies, 17% on economic matters, 15% on national defense, and 13% on general affairs. On social and economic affairs payments have averaged 39% on education, health, and social security, 20% on other social affairs, 3% on agriculture, 16% on water, power and gas; 5% on manufacturing and mining, 12% on roads and transportation, and 5% on other economic affairs.

Public Finance – Iran (2009)

(In billions of rials, central government figures)

Revenue and Grants	1,042,321	100.0%
Tax revenue	302,247	29.0%
Social contributions	194,792	18.7%
Grants	...	...
Other revenue	545,282	52.3%
Expenditures	1,023,770	100.0%
General public services	93,808	9.2%
Defense	80,944	7.9%
Public order and safety	42,948	4.2%
Economic affairs	169,302	16.5%
Environmental protection	886	0.1%
Housing and community amenities	20,034	2.0%
Health	70,418	6.9%
Recreational, culture, and religion	25,560	2.5%
Education	145,018	14.2%
Social protection	374,852	36.6%

(…) data not available or not significant.

SOURCE: *Government Finance Statistics Yearbook 2010*, Washington, DC: International Monetary Fund, 2010.

36 TAXATION

Under tax laws written in May of 1992, individual income is taxed at rates varying from 12–54%. Capital gains and investment income are also taxable and employees pay a 7% social security contribution. As of 2011 corporate profits were taxed at 25%. Income derived from outbound international transport was taxed at 5%. Capital gains resulting from the transfer of real property were taxed at 5% of the value of the property according to regional value tables. Capital gains resulting from the sale of securities listed on the Tehrān Stock Exchange were taxed on 0.5% of the sales value. Also levied are real estate taxes, municipal taxes, and a levy on expatriate salaries. A value-added tax (VAT) or sales tax of 3% is applied to products considered final. Another tax is a public education cost levy to be paid by manufacturing and service companies.

Following the imposition of a series of new international sanctions on Iran during at after 2010, Ahmadinejad turned his attention to Iran's taxation system, claiming that paying tax was not "forced payment;" instead, it was the most important form of "participation in politics." Forty-one percent of Iranians were legally exempted from taxation, but a significant portion of regime officials—and not only the Revolutionary Guards (IRGC)—have a vested interest in keeping the current system unchanged so as to continue their illegal economic activities. Moreover, as anti-tax protests in Tehran's textile and gold markets during the 2000s illustrated, the government had a long way to go in persuading business owners to actually pay into the public purse. Ahmadinejad and his team sought a way to assure the public that their tax money would be spent on programs that directly improved their day-to-day quality of life. Traditionally, revenues generated from oil exports made the government reluctant to collect taxes, let alone reform the system. However, as more oil companies departed Iran—and more states refused to buy Iranian oil— Tehran was increasingly in need of new sources of income. The government seemed determined to implement painful tax reforms to increase revenue. This new enthusiasm was potentially a tactical move by the Ahmadinejad government to reduce the financial might of IGRC, whose smuggling activities deprived the state of $20 billion in annual tax revenues. Ahmadinejad listed the IGRC as an obstacle to tax reform, referring to them as "our smuggler brothers."

37 CUSTOMS AND DUTIES

Most goods entering Iran are subject to customs duties, the majority of which are on the CIF (cost, insurance, and freight) value. A number of government organizations and charitable institutions are permitted to import goods free of duty. The average tariff was 15% in 2008.

38 FOREIGN INVESTMENT

Until the early 1970s Iran rarely participated in foreign businesses. The NIOC invested in the construction of oil refineries in Madras, India, and other places and participated in several ventures with foreign oil firms that held concessions for Iranian oil. With the vast increase in oil revenues, Iran became one of the world's leading creditor nations; in 1974 alone bilateral agreements worth hundreds of billions of rials were signed with France, Germany, Italy, and the United Kingdom. In July 1974 Iran agreed to purchase a 25% interest in the German steel-making firm of Krupp Hüttenwerke, an investment believed to be the largest single stake purchased by any oil-producing nation in a major European firm up to that time. In 1975 Iran began negotiating investments through the UN Development Programme (UNDP) in developing nations.

Prior to World War II foreign companies had important investments in Iranian banks, insurance companies, transport, and the oil industry. In 1955 the legislature enacted a law providing for withdrawal of invested capital in the currency that was brought into Iran, for the export of annual profits, and for adequate compensation in the event of nationalization of the industry or business. In 1957 the United States and Iran exchanged notes recognizing that the United States would guarantee its private investments in Iran against loss through actions by Iran, and the following year the Majlis enacted a law protecting foreign capital investments. Foreign companies moved into Iran to exploit mineral resources, to establish banks in partnership with Iranian capital, to build factories, and to carry out segments of the shah's vast economic development program.

Since 1979 the instability of the revolutionary government and the catastrophic war with Iraq have had a chilling effect on Western investment in Iran. The country emerged from the war with Iraq in terrible economic shape. In 1995 desperate for Western assistance in rebuilding its oil sector, Iran contracted with the French oil company, Total, to develop its Sirri oil field. It was the first instance of foreign investment in the vital petroleum sector since the 1979 revolution. In 1995 Iran had negative direct foreign investment of about $50 million, reflecting repatriation of profits greater than inflows of new investment. In 1995 the United States imposed trade and investment sanctions on Iran for its support of international terrorism; the Iran-Libya Sanctions Act (ILSA) penalizes companies investing more than $20 million in Iran's oil and gas sector. The ILSA was renewed in 2001 for five more years, and US and other international sanctions have only grown more stiff in the years since.

Inward foreign investment outside the oil and gas sectors was comparatively minimal. Foreigners observe investment in Iran warily, although Iran hopes to attract billions of dollars worth of foreign investment by creating a favorable investment climate (by reducing restrictions and duties on imports and creating free trade zones). Additionally, disagreements between reformers and conservatives make foreign investors wary of doing business in Iran, as does the international standoff over the country's nuclear program. Foreign direct investment (FDI) in Iran was a net inflow of $3.02 billion according to World Bank figures published in 2009. FDI represented 0.91% of GDP.

39 ECONOMIC DEVELOPMENT

Iran's first development plan (1949–56) foundered because of the lack of oil revenues during the nationalization dispute and also because the International Bank for Reconstruction and Development (IBRD) refused to lend the hoped for one-third of the projected development expenditures. The second plan (1956–63) also ran into financial difficulties when the domestic budget consumed a larger proportion of the oil revenues than expected. An austerity program from 1960, however, facilitated economic recovery. The third plan (1963–68) was successful, and the period witnessed rapid economic growth. This plan placed emphasis not only on the building of an infrastructure but also on projects making use of local resources. The private sector exceeded the target planned for investment. Substantial foreign aid, varied in its sources, was also forthcoming, and foreign investment in Iran totaled more than $2.7 billion. The fourth plan (1968–73) was far more successful than the previous ones, with most of its objectives realized beyond expectation. The mean annual gross national product (GNP) growth was 11.2%, as compared with the projected figure of 9%. Similarly, per capita GNP rose to about $560 ($300 had been the goal).

In its revised form, the fifth plan (1973–78) provided for infrastructural development and other expenditures. However, a lag in oil revenues led to rescheduling of the plan for six years instead of five and the postponement or slowdown of individual projects. Because of political opposition and social unrest during the last year of the shah's reign, the plan was abandoned in 1978. The Islamic government that came to power in 1979 cut economic development funds because of a shortage of revenues, but in 1983 it proposed its own five-year development plan for 1983–88, with allocations totaling $166 billion and emphasis given to agriculture and service industries. However, the government's cutbacks on oil production (and, consequently, of the oil revenues that were to finance the plan), coupled with the diversion of resources to the war with Iraq, made it impossible to fulfill the plan's goals.

The next five-year plan (1989–94) authorized up to $27 billion in foreign borrowing. It aimed to increase productivity in key industrial and economic sectors and to promote the non-oil export sector. The 1994–99 plan aimed at investing money in transport, particularly in the railroad system and in the construction of a public underground for Tehrān. Other projects were aimed at revitalizing the petroleum sector and developing the natural gas sector. The five-year plan implemented from 2000–04 was to privatize at least six major state-owned enterprises (such as communications and tobacco) and at least 2,000 smaller state-owned firms. The conservative parliament that took office in May 2004 ruled against key reforms included in the 2005–09 economic plan. Nevertheless, Iran's five-year plans have envisaged a gradual move towards a market-oriented economy, but political and social concerns and external debt problems have hampered progress. Upon being elected president in June 2005, conservative populist Mahmoud Ahmadinejad pledged to fight poverty and corruption while creating new jobs in the public sector. He proposed sharing the nation's oil wealth more broadly and reducing the country's income gap between rich and poor. Ahmadinejad also favored the promotion, where possible, of local firms over foreign enterprises. Following his reelection in 2009, despite widespread objections, Ahmadinejad took the bold steps of reducing state subsidies in an attempt to simultaneously rationalize the economy and disenfranchise his middle-class critics and promising more targeted subsidies for the lower classes that support his government. The bill would phase out subsidies—which benefit Iran's upper and middle classes the most—over three to five years and replace them with cash payments to Iran's lower classes. However, the start of the program was delayed repeatedly throughout 2010 over fears of public reaction to higher prices. This is the most extensive economic reform since the government implemented gasoline rationing in 2007.

40 SOCIAL DEVELOPMENT

Traditionally, family and communities were supplemented by Islamic *waqf* (obligatory charity) institutions for the care of the infirm and the indigent. Social welfare programs include workers' compensation, disability benefits, maternity allowances, retirement benefits, death benefits, and family and marriage allowances. These programs cover all employed persons between the ages of 18 and 65 who reside in the country. There is a special pension system in force for public employees. Old age benefits are available at age 65 for men and age 60 for women. Seasonal workers are covered for medical services during the working season. Employed people in urban areas are covered by workers' compensation. Family allowances are available for working families with limited means.

Statistics on violence against women including spousal abuse are unavailable. Provisions in the Islamic Penal and Civil Code discriminate against women, especially in property rights. The testimony of a woman in court is worth half of a man's statement. Women receive more harsh punishments for criminal offenses. A woman can only divorce a man for limited reasons, but a man may divorce his wife without cause. Gender segregation is enforced in most public places. In August 2011, 20 universities announced they would be offering certain majors only to men or to women. Iranian police plan to heighten the enforcement of dress-code laws. This includes creation of local security centers to address dress-code violation by both men and women. Even distributors of clothes that are considered inappropriate will be pursued.

The Jewish, Christian, Zoroastrian, and Baha'i minorities face government discrimination in education, employment, and public accommodations. They also suffer harassment and abuse. Serious human rights abuses persist, including summary execution, disappearance, torture, rape, stoning, flogging, arbitrary arrest and detention, and harsh prison conditions. The Iranian government continues to restrict freedoms of speech, assembly, religion, association, and the press.

41 HEALTH

Beginning in the 1960s national campaigns against such major diseases as malaria and smallpox were undertaken. Other major health problems included high infant mortality, smallpox outbreaks, venereal disease, trachoma, typhoid fever, amoebic dysentery, malaria, tuberculosis, and the debilitating effects of smoking opium. The creation in 1964 of a health corps, consisting of physicians and high school graduates who agreed to spend the period of their military service serving in semi-mobile medical units in rural areas, helped to reduce the death rate. Roving health corps teams, comprising a doctor, a dentist, a pathologist, and (when possible) a nurse, served the villages, offering medical services to 10,000–15,000 rural inhabitants annually.

According to the CIA life expectancy in Iran was 70.06 years in 2011. The country spent 3.9% of its GDP on healthcare, amounting to $269 per person. There were 9 physicians, 16 nurses and midwives, and 14 hospital beds per 10,000 inhabitants. The fertility rate was 1.8, while the infant mortality rate was 42 per 1,000 live births. In 2008 the maternal mortality rate, according to the World Bank, was 30 per 100,000 births. It was estimated that 99% of children were vaccinated against measles. The CIA calculated HIV/AIDS prevalence in Iran to be about 0.2% in 2009.

The Islamic republic has continued to provide health care programs to rural areas. Many physicians left the country after the 1979 revolution and health conditions were reportedly deteriorating; however, by the mid-1980s many doctors who had been in exile during the shah's reign had returned. Approximately 85% of the rural population had access to healthcare services.

42 HOUSING

Historically, rapid urbanization and migration of refugees into the country have made housing one of the country's most acute social problems. During the fourth plan (1968–73), nearly 300,000 housing units were built. However, housing starts fell sharply after the 1979 revolution as construction declined precipitously because of lack of funding. In subsequent decades, development in urban and suburban areas has outpaced that of rural areas, although some rural areas that serve as domestic tourist destinations are on par with the largest urban areas. As of 2010, the government had dedicated $10.2 billion to the Mehr housing scheme, which constructed homes for Iran's poorest citizens. From March to October 2010, nearly 400,000 construction permits were issued, and 600,000 rural housing units were under construction, according to the government.

43 EDUCATION

Education is virtually free in Iran at all levels, from elementary school through university. At the university level, however, every student is required to commit to serve the government for a number of years equivalent to those spent at the university.

In 2007 the World Bank estimated that 99% of age-eligible children in Iran were enrolled in primary school. Secondary enrollment for age-eligible children stood at 75%. Tertiary enrollment was estimated at 36%. Of those enrolled in tertiary education, there were 100 male students for every 114 female students. Overall, the CIA estimated that Iran had a literacy rate of 77%. Public expenditure on education represented 4.7% of GDP.

During the early 1970s efforts were made to improve the educational system by updating school curricula, introducing modern textbooks, and training more efficient teachers. The 1979 revolution continued the country's emphasis on education, but Khomeini's regime put its own stamp on the process. The most important change was the Islamization of the education system. All students were segregated by sex. In 1980 the Cultural Revolution Committee was formed to oversee the institution of Islamic values in education. An arm of the committee, the Center for Textbooks (composed mainly of clerics), produced 3,000 new college-level textbooks reflecting Islamic views by 1983. Teaching materials based on Islam were introduced into the primary grades within six months of the revolution.

Education is compulsory for five years of primary school. A middle school program covers three years of study. After this stage, students may choose to continue in general academic studies or vocational studies for three years. Students interested in continuing on to university studies complete an additional year. The academic year runs from September to June.

The tradition of university education in Iran goes back to the early centuries of Islam. By the 20th century, however, the system had become antiquated and was remodeled along French lines. The country's 16 universities were closed after the 1979 revolution and were then reopened gradually between 1982 and 1983 under Islamic supervision. While the universities were closed, the Cultural Revolution Committee investigated professors and teachers and dismissed those who were believers in Marxism, liberalism, and other "imperialistic" ideologies. The universities reopened with Islamic curriculums.

The University of Tehrān (founded in 1934) has 10 departments, including a department of Islamic theology. Other major universities are at Tabriz, Mashhad, Ahvāz, Shirāz, Esfahān, Kermān, Babol Sar, Rasht, and Orūmiyeh. Iran currently has 54 state operated universities and 42 state medical schools.

In 2008 Iran had over 3.5 million students enrolled in universities. In 2011 Ahmadinejad indicated that many college courses taught by Iranian universities are too Westernized and do not comply with Muslim law. He stipulated that those courses should be changed to comply with Muslim law or be eliminated.

44 LIBRARIES AND MUSEUMS

The National Library at Tehrān has a good general collection of about 600,000 volumes. The Library of Parliament, with 170,000 volumes, has an extensive collection of manuscripts and an unrivaled collection of documentary material in Farsi, including files of all important newspapers since the inception of the press in Iran. The Central Library of the University of Tehrān holds some 650,000 volumes. There were over 1,000 public library branches throughout the country.

Tehrān has the Archaeological Museum, overflowing with fabulous treasures from the long cultural and artistic history of Iran, as well as the Ethnological Museum. Iran's crown treasures—manuscripts, jeweled thrones, and a vast variety of other objects—may be seen at the Golestan Palace. Museums at Esfahān, Mashhad, Qom, and Shirāz feature antique carpets, painted pottery, illuminated manuscripts, and fine craftsmanship in wood and metal; most of these objects date from the 12th to the 18th centuries.

⁴⁵MEDIA

Iran's telegraph, telephone, and radio broadcasting services are state-owned. The country's telecommunications system is generally seen as inadequate, although modernization and expansion efforts are underway. The goal is to improve efficiency and to expand not only call volume in the cities, but also to connect several thousand villages currently without telephone service. In 2009 there were some 25.8 million main phone lines in use and 52.5 million mobile cellular phones in use (an average of 72 per 100 people).

Both radio and television were nationalized in 1980. Principal stations are located in Tehrān, and other major stations broadcast from Ahvāz, Zahedan, Tabriz, Rasht, Kermānshāh, and Bandar-e Lengeh. As of 1999 there were 72 AM radio stations, 6 FM radio stations, 5 shortwave radio stations, and 28 television broadcast stations. Television of Iran, a privately owned station, began broadcasting in 1956 in Tehrān and Ābādān. The national radio organization and the government television network were merged in 1971 to form National Iranian Radio and Television (NIRT). After 1979 it became the Islamic Republic of Iran Broadcasting Company. Though there is an official ban on owning a satellite dishes, many still do, particularly wealthier citizens. In 2010 the country had 119,947 Internet hosts. Internet users numbered 38 per 100 citizens.

Prominent newspapers in 2010 included *Ettelaʿat*—Iran's oldest newspaper—*Kayhan News,* and *Tehran Times* (circulation 7,700). There are also several weeklies and special interest magazines. Most print media originate in Tehrān.

The constitution does not mention freedom of speech and limits freedom of the press; a press law requires publications to be licensed, and their editors are subject to imprisonment for printing reports the religious authorities deem insulting. There were many reports of continuing government infringement on freedom of the press.

⁴⁶ORGANIZATIONS

Long renowned for their individualism, Iranians now actively associate with modern public and private organizations. Under the shah the government greatly encouraged the growth of the cooperative movement; the first Workers' Consumers Society was established in 1948. Many villages have founded producers' cooperatives with official advice and support, and consumers' cooperatives exist among governmental employees and members of the larger industrial and service organizations. Rural cooperative societies are wide spread. The Chamber of Commerce, Industries, and Mines has its headquarters in Tehrān.

Private charitable organizations date from as early as 1923, when the Iranian Red Lion and Sun Society was established; this organization has since joined the corresponding international organization of the Red Crescent Society. Other charitable institutions include the Organization for Social Services and the Mother and Infant Protection Institute. The Islamic Women's institute is active. The Society to Combat the Use of Opium has waged a campaign against use of the drug. Human Rights Monitor is a multinational organization based in Tehrān.

For youth, the Boy Scout movement in Iran began before World War II. There are several sports associations active within the country, representing such pastimes as football, badminton, tennis, baseball, and track and field. There are active organizations of the Special Olympics.

⁴⁷TOURISM, TRAVEL, AND RECREATION

Political and civil unrest has kept many tourists from visiting Iran in recent years. Principal tourist attractions include historic and beautifully decorated mosques, mausoleums, and minarets. There are many sports and physical culture societies in Tehrān and the provinces, where the emphasis is on skiing and weight lifting. Other popular sports include football (soccer), wrestling, and volleyball. There were 164,083 hotel beds available in Iran. The estimated daily cost to visit Tehran, the capital, was $155.

In November 2010 the traditional craft of carpet weaving from Fars and Kashan was officially inscribed on the UNESCO Representative List of the Intangible Heritage of Humanity, an offshoot of the World Heritage program. The craft was deemed a living tradition by UNESCO, meaning that it is still passed from generation to generation and continues to create a sense of identity and community for those who participate. Such traditions have been approved by UNESCO for special consideration since 2001. For one that is inscribed, a special program is designed to protect and promote the practice and understanding of the tradition. The handwoven carpets from these regions have been treasured by buyers worldwide for many years. The skills and techniques of the craft and unique designs of each region are taught from one generation to the next. The weavers are usually women, but men are often involved in the family carpet making business through raising and shearing sheep for wool and building wooden looms. The music of the Bakhshis of the Khorasan Province, played on the traditional two-stringed, long-necked lute known as the *dotar*, was also inscribed on the list. The Pahlevani and Zoorkhanei rituals, dance-like displays of martial arts combining elements of Islam; Gnosticism; and ancient Persian beliefs were also added.

⁴⁸FAMOUS PERSONS

The long history of Iran has seen many conquerors, wise rulers and statesmen, artists, poets, historians, and philosophers. In religion there have been many diverse figures. Zoroaster (Zarathushtra), who probably lived around the 10th century BC, founded the religion known as Zoroastrianism, with Ahura-Mazda as the god of good. In the 3rd century AD, Mani attempted a fusion of the tenets of Zoroastrianism, Buddhism, and Christianity. The Bab (Sayyid ʿAli Muhammad of Shiraz, b. 1819–d. 1850) was the precursor of Baha'ism, founded by Baháʾuʾlláh (Mirza Husayn ʿAli Nuri—b. 1817–d. 1892).

Persian rulers of the pre-Christian era include Cyrus ("the Great," Kurush—r. 550–529 BC), Cambyses II (Kambuiya, r. 529–522 BC), Darius I ("the Great," Darayavaush—r. 521–486 BC), Xerxes I ("the Great," Khshayarsha—r. 486–465 BC), and Artaxerxes I (Artakhshathra, r. 464–424 BC). Before the Arab conquest, great Sassanid Kings including Ardashir I (r. 224–241 AD), Shapur I (r. 142–272 AD), and Khosrau I (r. 531–579 AD), prevented Rome and Byzantium from reestablishing Alexander the Great's rule over Iran. Shah ʿAbbas (r. 1587–1628) expanded Persian territory and took control of Baghdād from the Ottomans which allowed Shah ʿAbbas and Iranians access to the sacred Shia shrines of Kazimayn, Karbala and Najaf in Iraq. Prominent political figures of modern times are Reza Shah Pahlavi (b. 1877–d. 1944), who reigned from 1925 to his abdication in 1941 and his son, Muhammad Reza Pahlavi (b. 1919–d. 1980), who was shah from 1941 until his abdication in 1979. Iran was under the leadership of Ayatollah Ruhollah Khomeini (b. 1900–d. 1989) from 1979 until his death in 1989. Ayatollah Ali Khamenei (b. 1939) took over the position of Supreme Leader upon Khomeini's death.

The great epic poet Firdawsi (Abdul Qasim Hassan ibn-i-Ishaq ibn-i Sharafshah, b. 940–d. 1020), writing about AD 1000, produced the *Shahnama (Book of Kings)* dealing with Iran's mythical hero-saints, royal women, and larger than life champions. The book is full of romantic and heroic tales that retain their popularity today. Omar Khayyam (d. 1123?), astronomer and poet, is known in the Western world for his *Rubáiyât,* a collection of quatrains skillfully translated by Edward Fitzgerald. Important figures of the Seljuk period (11th and 12th centuries) include Muhammad bin Muhammad al-Ghazali (b. 1058–d. 1111), philosopher and mystic theologian, who exerted an enormous influence upon all later speculative thought in Islam; Farid ad-Din 'Attar (Muhammad bin Ibrahim, b. 1119–d. 1229?), one of the greatest of mystic poets; and Nizami (Nizam ad-Din Abu Muhammad, b. 1141–d. 1202), noted for four romantic epic poems that were copied and recopied by hand and illuminated with splendid miniatures. In the 13th century Jalal ad-Din Rumi (b. 1207–d. 1273) compiled his celebrated long mystic poem, the *Mathnavi,* in rhyming couplets and Sa'di (Muslih ud-Din, b. 1184?–d. 1291), possibly the most renowned Iranian poet within or outside of Iran, composed his *Gulistan (Rose Garden)* and *Bustan (Orchard).* About a hundred years later, in 1389, another poet of Shirāz, Hafiz (Shams ud-Din Muhammad), died; his collected works comprise nearly 700 poems, all of them ghazals or lyrical odes.

Poets of the modern period include Iraj Mirza (b. 1880–d. 1926), Mirzadeh Eshqi (d. 1924), Parveen Ettasami (d.1941), Nima Yushij, Forugh Farrukhzad, Nader Naderpur, Shamlu, and Akhavan Sales and the poet laureate Behar (Malik ash-Shuara Bahar, d. 1951). Preeminent among prose writers was Sadeq Hedayat (b. 1903–d. 1951), author of the novel *Buf i kur* (The Blind Owl) and numerous other works including films. Azar Nafisi (b. 1955) is an Iranian-born professor and writer residing in the United States whose book *Reading Lolita in Tehran* gained international acclaim and was translated into 32 languages.

Miniature painting came to full flower in the second half of the 15th century. The greatest figure in this field was Bihzad, whose limited surviving work is highly prized. The School of Herāt was composed of his followers. Abbas Kiarostami (b. 1940) is an influential and controversial post-revolutionary filmmaker who is highly respected in the international film community.

⁴⁹DEPENDENCIES

Iran has no territories or colonies.

⁵⁰BIBLIOGRAPHY

Cirincione, Joseph, Jon B. Wolfsthal, and Miriam Rajkumar. *Deadly Arsenals: Nuclear, Biological, and Chemical Threats.* 2nd ed. Washington, DC: Carnegie Endowment for International Peace, 2005.

Daniel, Elton L. *The History of Iran.* Santa Barbara, CA: Greenwood, 2012.

Daniel, Elton L, and Ali A. Mahdi. *Culture and Customs of Iran.* Westport, CT: Greenwood Press, 2006.

Hourani, Albert Habib. *A History of the Arab Peoples.* Cambridge, MA: Belknap Press of Harvard University Press, 2002.

Iran Investment and Business Guide: Strategic Information and Laws. Washington, DC: International Business Publications USA, 2012.

Lorentz, John H. *Historical Dictionary of Iran.* 2nd ed. Lanham, MD: Scarecrow Press, 2007.

Mackey, Sandra. *The Iranians: Persia, Islam and the Soul of a Nation.* New York: Dutton, 1996.

O'Sullivan, Meghan L. *Shrewd Sanctions: Statecraft and State Sponsors of Terrorism.* Washington, DC: Brookings Institution Press, 2003.

Paidar, Parvin. *Women and the Political Process in Twentieth-Century Iran.* Cambridge, England: Cambridge University Press, 2005.

Seddon, David, ed. *A Political and Economic Dictionary of the Middle East.* Philadelphia: Routledge/Taylor and Francis, 2004.

Shaffer, Brenda. *Borders and Brethren: Iran and the Challenge of Azerbaijani Identity.* Cambridge, MA: MIT Press, 2002.

IRAQ

Republic of Iraq

Al-Jumhuriyah al-'Iraqiyah

CAPITAL: Baghdād

FLAG: The national flag is a tricolor of red, white, and black horizontal stripes, with the Arabic expression *Allahu Akbar* ("God is Great") in green Arabic script centered in the white band.

ANTHEM: *Mawtini (My Homeland).*

MONETARY UNIT: The Iraqi dinar (IQD) is in circulation as 50, 250, 500, 1,000, 5,000, 10,000 and 25,000 bank notes. US$1 = IQD1,149.82 (IQD1 = US$0.00084) as of 2012.

WEIGHTS AND MEASURES: The metric system is the legal standard, but weights and measures in general use vary, especially in domestic transactions. The unit of land is the dunam, which is equivalent to approximately 0.25 hectare (0.62 acre).

HOLIDAYS: New Year's Day, 1 January; Army Day, 6 January; Republic Day, 14 July. Muslim religious holidays include Eid al-Fitr, Eid al-Adha, and Islamic New Year.

TIME: 3 p.m. = noon GMT.

¹LOCATION, SIZE, AND EXTENT

Present-day Iraq, comprising an area of 437,072 sq km (168,754 sq mi), corresponds roughly to the former Turkish provinces of Baghdād, Al Mawşil (Mosul), and Al Başrah (Basra). Comparatively, the area occupied by Iraq is slightly more than twice the size of the state of Idaho. It extends 984 km (611 mi) SSE–NNW and 730 km (454 mi) ENE–WSW. Iraq is bordered on the N by Turkey, on the E by Iran, on the SE by the Persian Gulf and Kuwait, on the S by Saudi Arabia, on the W by Jordan, and on the NW by Syria, with a total land boundary length of 3,650 km (2,268 mi) and a coastline of 58 km (36 mi).

Iraq's capital city, Baghdād, is located in the east-central part of the country.

²TOPOGRAPHY

Iraq is divided into three distinct zones: the desert in the west and southwest; the plains; and the highlands in the northeast, which rise to 3,000 m (10,000 ft) or more. The desert is an upland region with altitudes of 600 to 900 m (2,000–3,000 ft) between Damascus in Syria and Ar-Rutbah in Iraq, but declines gently toward the Euphrates (Al-Furāt) River. The water supply comes from wells and wadis that at times carry torrential floods and that retain the winter rains.

Dominated by the river systems of the Tigris (Dijlah) and Euphrates (Al-Furāt), the plains area is composed of two regions divided by a ridge, some 75 m (250 ft) above the flood plain, between Ar Ramādi and a point south of Baghdād that marks the prehistoric coastline of the Persian Gulf. The lower valley, built up by the silt carried by the two rivers, consists of marshland, crisscrossed by drainage channels. At Qarmat 'Ali, just above Al Başrah, the two rivers combine and form the Shatt al Arab, a broad waterway

separating Iraq and Iran. The sources of the Euphrates and Tigris are in the Armenian Plateau. The Euphrates receives its main tributaries before entering Iraq, while the Tigris receives several streams on the eastern bank within the country.

³CLIMATE

Under the influence of the monsoons, Iraq in summer has a constant northwesterly wind (shamal), while in winter a strong southeasterly air current (sharqi) develops. The intensely hot and dry summers last from May to October, and during the hottest time of the day—often reaching 49°C (120°F) in the shade—people take refuge in underground shelters. Winters, lasting from December to March, are damp and comparatively cold, with temperatures averaging about 10°C (50°F). Spring and autumn are brief transition periods. Normally, no rain falls from the end of May to the end of September. With annual rainfall of less than 38 cm (15 in), agriculture is dependent on irrigation.

⁴FLORA AND FAUNA

The World Resources Institute estimates that Iraq is home to 102 species of mammals, 396 species of birds, 99 species of reptiles, and 11 species of amphibians. The calculation reflects the total number of distinct species residing in the country, not the number of endemic species.

In the lower regions of the Tigris (Dijlah) and Euphrates (Al-Furāt) and in the alluvial plains, papyrus, lotus, and tall reeds form thick underbrush; willow, poplar, and alder trees abound. On the upper and middle Euphrates (Al-Furāt), the licorice bush yields a juice that is extracted for commercial purposes; another bush growing wild in the semiarid steppe or desert yields gum tragacanth for pharmaceutical use. In the higher Zagros Mountains grows the valonia oak, the bark of which is used for tanning leather. About 30 million date palms produce one of Iraq's important exports.

Wild animals include the hyena, jackal, fox, gazelle, antelope, jerboa, mole, porcupine, desert hare, and bat. Beaver, wild ass, and ostrich are rare. Wild ducks, geese, and partridge are the game birds. Vultures, owls, and ravens live near the Euphrates. Falcons are trained for hunting.

5 ENVIRONMENT

The World Resources Institute reported that water resources totaled 96.4 cu km (23.13 cu mi), while water usage was 42.7 cu km (10.24 cu mi) per year. Domestic water usage accounted for 3% of total usage, industrial for 5%, and agricultural for 92%. Per capita water usage totaled 1,482 cu m (52,336 cu ft) per year. Access to a sustainable water supply has long been a problem in the hot, dry climate. Salinization and soil erosion caused by river basin flooding has affected otherwise fertile agricultural lands.

Three major armed conflicts since 1980 have had a significant negative effect on the nation's environment. Chemical weapons deployed at various locations along the Iran-Iraq border during the 1980–88 war killed thousands of people. During the 1991 Gulf War, coalition forces initiated a massive air campaign that destroyed nuclear, biological, and chemical facilities, causing toxic agents to seep into the air, soil, and waterways. Electrical plants, oil facilities, and water and sewage treatment plants were heavily damaged in both the 1991 and 2003 conflicts, contributing increased levels of air, water, and soil pollution to an already distressed environment. Additionally, the Iraqi government's tactic of setting oil fires to ward off coalition forces set a broad range of toxic chemicals into the air and threatened many of the marshland ecosystems of the Tigris (Dijlah)-Euphrates (Al-Furāt) river basin.

According to a 2011 report issued by the International Union for Conservation of Nature and Natural Resources (IUCN), threatened species included 13 mammals, 16 birds, 2 reptiles, 1 amphibian, 11 fish, and 15 other invertebrates. Threatened species include the black vulture, the imperial eagle, the wild goat, the striped hyena, and the sand cat. The Saudi gazelle has become extinct.

The UN reported in 2008 that carbon dioxide emissions in Iraq totaled 100,046 kilotons.

6 POPULATION

The US Central Intelligence Agency (CIA) estimates the population of Iraq in 2011 to be approximately 30,399,572, which placed it at number 39 in population among the 196 nations of the world. In 2011 approximately 3.1% of the population was over 65 years of age, with another 38% under 15 years of age. The median age in Iraq was 20.9 years. There were 1.03 males for every female in the country. The population's annual rate of change was 2.399%. The projected population for the year 2025 was 44,700,000. Population density in Iraq was calculated at 69 people per sq km (179 people per sq mi).

The UN estimated that 66% of the population lived in urban areas, and that urban populations had an annual rate of change of 2.6%. The largest urban areas, along with their respective populations, included Baghdad, 5.8 million; Mosul, 1.4 million; Erbil, 1 million; Basra, 923,000; and As Sulaymaniyah, 836,000.

7 MIGRATION

Estimates of Iraq's net migration rate, carried out by the CIA in 2011, amounted to zero. The total number of emigrants living abroad was 1.55 million, and the total number of immigrants living in Iraq was 83,400. Iraq also accepted 12,500 refugees from Palestinian Territories, 11,773 from Iran, and 16,832 from Turkey.

Immigration into Iraq was limited until the beginning of the 1970s. However, the rise in oil prices and the increase of oil exports, as well as extensive public and private spending in the mid-1970s, created a market for foreign labor. The result was a stream of foreign (mainly Egyptian) workers, whose number may have risen as high as 1,600,000 before the first Gulf War. During the Iran-Iraq war, many Egyptians worked in the public sector, filling a gap left by civil servants, farmers, and other workers who were fighting at the front. A number of Iraqis, mainly from southern Iraq and influenced by family ties and higher wages, migrated to Saudi Arabia and Kuwait. To weaken local support in the north for Kurdish rebels, the government forced tens of thousands of Kurds to resettle in the south; in September 1987, a Western diplomat in Baghdād claimed that at least 500 Kurdish villages had been razed and 100,000 to 500,000 Kurds relocated.

In 1991 some 1.5 million Iraqis fled the country for Turkey or Iran to escape Saddam Hussein's increasingly repressive rule, but fewer than 100,000 remained abroad by 2005. Most of the refugees were Kurds who later resettled in areas in Iraq not controlled by the government. In September and October of 1996, around 65,000 Iraqi Kurds fled to Iran due to internal fighting among Iraqi Kurds.

As a result of the 2003 invasion and subsequent occupation by international forces and the ensuing conflict and instability, an estimated two million Iraqis fled Iraq. As of 2012 hundreds of thousands of them still resided in neighboring countries, namely Jordan and Syria. At the end of 2010 humanitarian agencies estimated that 1.3 to 1.6 million Iraqis had been internally displaced since 2006. This population of "newly" displaced added to an already-existing internally displaced population in the country

8 ETHNIC GROUPS

Arabs constitute about 75–80% of the total population. The Kurds, a Muslim, non-Arab people, are the largest and most important minority group, constituting about 15–20% of the population. A seminomadic pastoral people, the Kurds live in the northeastern Zagros Mountains, mostly in isolated villages in the mountain valleys near Turkey and Iran.

Other minorities (5%) include Turkomans, living in the northeast; Yazidis, mostly in the Sinjar Mountains; Assyrians, mainly in the cities and northeastern rural areas; Chaldeans, and Armenians. There are also a number of Black Iraqis, or citizens of African descent, with the largest community found in Basra. Kurdish opposition to Iraqi political dominance has occasioned violent clashes with government forces. While some Kurds throughout Iraq continue to report incidents of discrimination against them, there are many Kurds serving as representatives in federal and provincial governments and the strength of the Kurdish political parties continues to increase.

9 LANGUAGES

Arabic is the national language and is the mother tongue of an estimated 79% of the population. Kurdish—the official language in Kurdish regions—or a dialect of it, is spoken by the Kurds and Yazidis. Aramaic (also referred to as Neo-Aramaic or Assyrian), the ancient Syriac dialect, is retained by the Assyrians. The Turkomans speak a Turkic dialect. Armenian is also spoken.

10 RELIGIONS

Islam is the national religion of Iraq, adhered to by some 97% of the population. About 60–65% of Muslims belong to the Shi'a sect and 32–37% to the Sunni sect. Traditionally, the Shi'a majority has been governed and generally oppressed by members of the Sunni minority. There are also some syncretic Muslim groups, such as the Yazidis, who consider Satan a fallen angel who will one day be reconciled with God. They propitiate him in their rites and regard the Old and New Testaments, as well as the Koran, as sacred. About 3% of the population are adherents to Christianity and other religions. The Assyrians (who are not descended from the ancient Assyrians) are Nestorians. In the 19th century, under the influence of Roman Catholic missions, Christian Chaldeans joined the Uniate churches, which are in communion with Rome; their patriarch has his seat in Mosul. The Sabaean-Mandaeans are often called Christians of St. John, but their religious belief and their liturgy contain elements of many creeds, including some of pre-Christian Oriental origin. Other Christian groups include Roman Catholics, Armenian and Syrian Orthodox, Anglicans, and other Protestant groups. There are a small number of Jews. While the constitution provides for freedom of religion, it also claims Islam as the official religion and states that all laws must adhere to the tenets of Islam. While the government has publically endorsed religious freedom, religious minorities continue to face discrimination and persecution, and sectarian violence in the nation has restricted religious practices for all faiths. Islamist extremists have continued to pressure some Muslims to adhere to radical fundamentalist beliefs. Religious groups are required to register with the government but must have a minimum of 500 adherents within the country for approval. Islamic instruction is required in public schools. Though non-Muslim students are not required to attend these classes, most feel pressured to do so. Ashura, Arbai'n, Eid al-Fitr, Eid al-Adha, Milad an-Nabi (the Birth of the Prophet Muhammad), Nawruz, and Christmas are observed as national holidays.

11 TRANSPORTATION

The CIA reports that Iraq had a total of 44,900 km (27,900 mi) of roads as of 2002, of which 37,851 km (23,520 mi) were paved. Railroads extended for 2,272 km (1,412 mi) as of 2008. Major cities, towns, and villages are connected by a modern network of highways and roads, which have made old caravan routes extinct. The city of Baghdād has been reshaped by the development of expressways through the city and by bypasses built since the 1970s.

Railroads are owned and operated by the Iraqi State Railways Administration. A standard-gauge railroad connects Iraq with Jordan and Syria, and nearly all the old meter-gauge line connecting Arbil in the north with Al Baṣrah, by way of Kirkūk and Baghdād, has been replaced.

A long-closed rail link between Mosul, Iraq, and Gazientep, Turkey, reopened in February 2010. The link had been closed since the 1980s due to the conflicts within Iraq. The reopening serves as a show of good faith and renewed economic partnerships between the two countries. Trade between Turkey and the Kurdish regional government of Iraq amounted to about $10 billion per year. The Mosul-Gazientep link also completes the Berlin to Baghdad railway that began construction in Germany nearly one hundred years ago, as Germany hoped to open a trade route through Turkey to the Persian Gulf.

As of 2010 there were 104 airports, 75 of them with paved runways. There were also 21 heliports.

Baghdād, Al Baṣrah, and Al Mawṣil have international airports. Iraq Airways is the state-owned carrier. The main seaports and terminals are Al Basrah, Khawr az Zubayr, and Umm Qasr. Iraq has approximately 5,279 km (3,280 mi) of navigable waterways. The Euphrates River (Al Furāt-2,815 km/1,864 mi), the Tigris River (Dijlah-1,899 km/1,179 mi) and the Third River (565 km/351 mi) were the main waterways. In addition, the Shatt al Arab is usually navigable by maritime traffic for 130 km (81 mi). The Tigris and Euphrates have navigable sections for shallow-draft boats. Expansion of Iraq's merchant marine, which totaled 1.47 million gross registered tonnage (GRT) in 1980, was halted by decades of war. In 2010 there were only 2 ships in the merchant marine with 1,000 GRT or more.

12 HISTORY

Some of the earliest known human settlements have been found in present-day Iraq. Habitations, shrines, implements, and pottery found on various sites can be dated as early as the 5th millennium BC. Some sites bear names that are familiar from the Bible, which describes the region of the Tigris (Dijlah) and Euphrates (Al Furāt) rivers as the location of the Garden of Eden and the city of Ur as the birthplace of the patriarch Abraham. Scientific exploration and archaeological research have amplified the biblical accounts.

Recorded history in Mesopotamia (the ancient name of Iraq, particularly the area between the Tigris and Euphrates) begins with the Sumerians, who by the 4th millennium BC had established city-states. Records and accounts on clay tablets prove that they had a complex economic organization before 3200 BC. The reign of Sumer was challenged by King Sargon of Akkad (r. c. 2350 BC); a Sumero-Akkadian culture continued in Erech (Tall al-Warka') and Ur (Tall al-Muqayyar) until it was superseded by the Amorites or Babylonians (about 1900 BC), with their capital at Babylon. The cultural height of Babylonian history is represented by Hammurabi (r. c. 1792–c. 1750 BC), who compiled a celebrated code of laws. After Babylon was destroyed by the Hittites about 1550 BC, the Hurrians established the Mitanni kingdom in the north for about 200 years, and the Kassites ruled for about 400 years in the south.

From Assur, their stronghold in the north, the Assyrians overran Mesopotamia about 1350 BC and established their capital at Nineveh (Ninawa). Assyrian supremacy was interrupted during the 11th and 10th centuries BC by the Aramaeans, whose language, Aramaic, became a common language in the eastern Mediterranean area in later times. Assyrian power was finally crushed by the Chaldeans or Neo-Babylonians, who, in alliance with the

Medes in Persia, destroyed Nineveh in 612 BC. Nebuchadnez-zar II (r. c. 605–c. 560 BC) rebuilt the city-state of Babylon, but it fell to the Persians, under Cyrus of the Achaemenid dynasty, in 539 BC. Under his son Cambyses II, the Persian Empire extended from the Oxus (Amu Darya) River to the Mediterranean, with its center in Mesopotamia. Its might, in turn, was challenged by the Greeks. Led by the Macedonian conqueror Alexander the Great, they defeated the Persians by 327 BC and penetrated deep into Persian lands. The Seleucids, Alexander's successors in Syria, Mesopotamia, and Persia, built their capital, Seleucia, on the Tigris, just south of Baghdād. They had to yield power to the Parthians, who conquered Mesopotamia in 138 BC.

The Arabs conquered Iraq in AD 637. For a century, under the "Orthodox" and the Umayyad caliphs, Iraq remained a province of the Islamic Empire, but the 'Abbasids (750–1258) made it the focus of their power. In their new capital, Baghdād, their most illustrious member, Harun al-Rashid (ar-Rashid, r. 786–809), became, through the Arabian Nights, a legend for all time. Under Harun and his son Al-Ma'mun, Baghdād was the center of brilliant intellectual and cultural life. Two centuries later, the Seljuk vizier Nizam al-Mulk established the famous Nizamiyah University, one of whose professors was the philosopher Al-Ghazali (Ghazel, d. 1111). A Mongol invasion in the early 13th century ended Iraq's flourishing economy and culture. In 1258 Genghis Khan's grandson Hulagu sacked Baghdād and destroyed the canal system on which the productivity of the region had depended. Timur, also known as Timur Lenk ("Timur the Lame") or Tamerlane, conquered Baghdād and Iraq in 1393. Meanwhile, the Ottoman Turks had established themselves in Asia Minor and, by capturing Cairo (1517), their sultans claimed legitimate succession to the caliphate. In 1534 Süleyman the Magnificent conquered Baghdād and, except for a short period of Persian control in the 17th century, Iraq remained an Ottoman province until World War I.

Late in 1914 the Ottoman Empire sided with the Central Powers, and a British expeditionary force landed in Iraq and occupied Al Başrah. The long campaign that followed ended in 1918, when the whole of Iraq fell under British military occupation. The collapse of the Ottoman Empire stimulated Iraqi hopes for freedom and independence, but in 1920, Iraq was declared a League of Nations mandate under UK administration. Riots and revolts led to the establishment of an Iraqi provisional government in October 1920. On 23 August 1921 Faisal I (Faysal), the son of Sharif Hussein (Husayn ibn-'Ali) of Mecca, became king of Iraq. In successive stages, the last of which was a treaty of preferential alliance with the United Kingdom (June 1930), Iraq gained independence in 1932 and was admitted to membership in the League of Nations.

Faisal died in 1933, and his son and successor, Ghazi, was killed in an accident in 1939. Until the accession to the throne of Faisal II, on attaining his majority in 1953, his uncle 'Abdul Ilah, Ghazi's cousin, acted as regent. On 14 July 1958 the army rebelled under the leadership of Gen. 'Abd al-Karim al-Qasim (Kassim). Faisal II, Crown Prince 'Abdul Ilah, and Prime Minister Nuri al-Sa'id (as-Sa'id) were killed. The monarchy was abolished, and a republic established. Iraq left the anticommunist Baghdād Pact, which the monarchy had joined in 1955. An agrarian reform law broke up the great landholdings of feudal leaders, and a new economic development program emphasized industrialization. In spite of some opposition from original supporters and political oppo-

nents, tribal uprisings, and several attempts at assassination, Qasim managed to remain the head of Iraq for four and a half years. On 9 February 1963, however, a military junta, led by Col. 'Abd as-Salam Muhammad 'Arif, overthrew his regime and executed Qasim.

The new regime followed a policy based on neutralism and aimed to cooperate with Syria and Egypt and to improve relations with Turkey and Iran. These policies were continued after 'Arif was killed in an airplane crash in 1966 and was succeeded by his brother, 'Abd ar-Rahman 'Arif. This regime, however, was overthrown in July 1968, when Gen. (later Marshal) Ahmad Hasan al-Bakr, heading a section of the Ba'ath Party, staged a coup and established a new government with himself as president. In the 1970s the Ba'ath regime focused increasingly on economic problems, nationalizing the petroleum industry in 1972–73 and allocating large sums for capital development.

Since 1961 Iraq's Kurdish minority has frequently opposed—with violence—attempts by Baghdād to impose authority over its regions. In an attempt to cope with this opposition, the Bakr government passed a constitutional amendment in July 1970 granting limited political, economic, and cultural autonomy to the Kurdish regions. But in March 1974, Kurdish insurgents, known as the Pesh Merga, again mounted a revolt, with Iranian military support. The Iraqi army countered with a major offensive. On 6 March 1975 Iraq and Iran concluded an agreement by which Iran renounced support for the Kurds and Iraq agreed to share sovereignty over the Shatt al Arab estuary.

Bakr resigned in July 1979 and was followed as president by his chosen successor, Saddam Hussein (Husayn) al-Takriti. Tensions between Iraq and Iran rose after the Iranian revolution of 1979 and the accession to power of Saddam Hussein. In September 1980 Iraq sought to take advantage of the turmoil in Iran by suddenly canceling the 1975 agreement and mounting a full-scale invasion. Iraqi soldiers seized key points in the Khuzistan region of southwestern Iran, captured the major southern city of Khorramshahr, and besieged Abadan, destroying its large oil refinery. The Iraqi army then took up defensive positions, a tactic that gave the demoralized Iranian forces time to regroup and launch a slow but successful counterattack that retook Khuzistan by May 1982. Iraq then sought peace and in June withdrew from Iranian areas it had occupied. Iran's response was to launch major offensives aimed at the oil port of Al Başrah. Entrenched in well-prepared positions on their own territory, Iraqi soldiers repelled the attacks, inflicting heavy losses, and the war ground to a stalemate, with tens of thousands of casualties on each side.

Attempts by the UN and by other Arab states to mediate the conflict were unsuccessful; in the later stages of the war, Iraq accepted but Iran regularly rejected proposals for a compromise peace. Although most Arab states supported Iraq, and the Gulf oil states helped finance Iraqi military equipment, the war had a destabilizing effect both on the national economy and on the ruling Ba'ath Party. France also aided Iraq with credits to buy advanced weapons (notably, Super Étendard fighters and Exocet missiles), and it provided the technology for Iraq to construct the Osirak nuclear reactor near Baghdād. (In June 1981 this installation was destroyed in a bombing raid by Israel, which claimed that the facility would be used to produce nuclear weapons, a charge Iraq de-

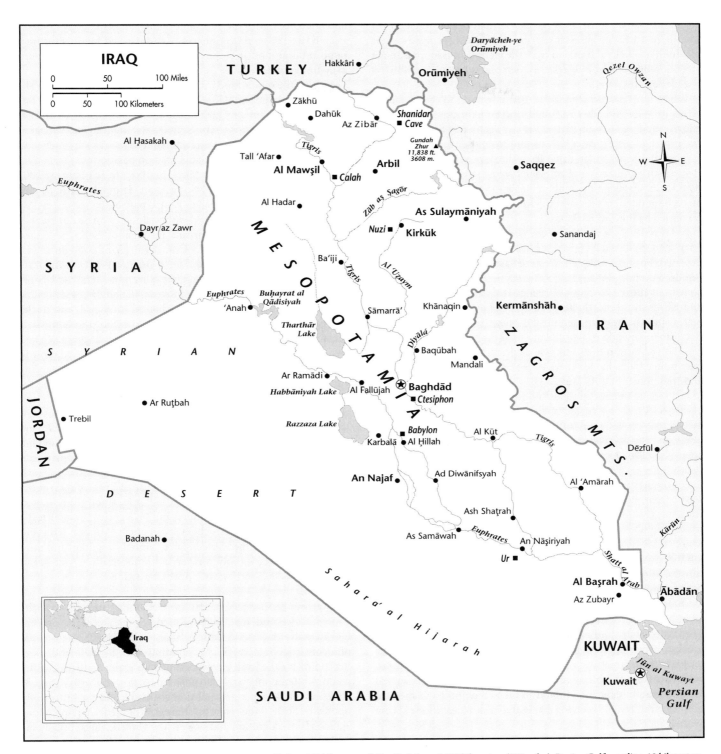

LOCATION: 29° to 37°30′N; 39° to 48°E. BOUNDARY LENGTHS: Turkey, 305 kilometers (190 miles); Iran, 1,458 kilometers (906 miles); Persian Gulf coastline, 19 kilometers (12 miles); Kuwait, 254 kilometers (158 miles); Saudi Arabia, 895 kilometers (556 miles); Jordan, 147 kilometers (91 miles); Syria, 603 kilometers (375 miles). TERRITORIAL SEA LIMIT: 12 miles.

nied.) Other Western countries provided supplies, financing, and intelligence to Iraq but denied the same to Iran.

In February 1986 the Iranians made their biggest gain in the war, crossing the Shatt al Arab and capturing Fao (Al-Faw) on the southernmost tip of land in Iraq. In early 1987 they seized several islands in the Shatt al Arab opposite Al Baṣrah. The war soon spread to Persian Gulf shipping, as both sides attacked oil tankers and ships transporting oil, goods, and arms to the belligerents or their supporters.

The war ended on 20 August 1988 after Iran accepted a UN cease-fire proposal on 18 July. Having suffered enormous casualties and physical damage plus a massive debt burden, Baghdād began the postwar process of reconstruction. Before and after the war, there were scores to settle, primarily against the Kurds, some of whom had helped Iran and were the victims of Iraqi poison gas attacks. Many border villages were demolished and their Kurdish populations relocated.

When Iraq's wartime allies seemed unwilling to ease financial terms or keep oil prices high and questioned Iraq's rearmament efforts, Saddam Hussein turned bitterly against them. Kuwait was the principal target. After threats and troop movements, Iraq reasserted its claim (which dated from the days of the monarchy) to that country and on 2 August 1990, invaded and occupied it. Saddam Hussein was unflinching in the face of various peace proposals, economic sanctions, and the threatening buildup of coalition forces led by the United States.

A devastating air war led by the United States began on 17 January 1991 followed by ground attack on 24 February. Iraq was defeated, but not occupied. Despite vast destruction and several hundred thousand casualties, Saddam's regime remained firmly in control. It moved to crush uprisings from the Shi'a in the south and Kurds in the north. To protect those minorities, the United States and its allies imposed no-fly zones that gave the Kurds virtually an independent state, but afforded much less defense for the rebellious Arabs in the south whose protecting marshes were being drained by Baghdād. There were several clashes between allied and Iraqi forces in both areas.

In 1996, in an effort to boost morale in Iraq and bolster its image abroad, Iraq conducted its first parliamentary elections since 1989. However, only candidates loyal to Saddam Hussein were allowed to run. A government screening committee reviewed and approved all 689 candidates, who either belonged to Hussein's Ba'ath Party or were independents that supported the 1968 coup that brought the party to power.

The Iraqi economy continued to decline throughout the 1990s, with the continuation of the UN sanctions, imposed in 1990, which prohibited Iraq from selling oil on the global market in major transactions and froze Iraqi assets overseas. The deteriorating living conditions imposed on the Iraqi population prompted consideration of emergency measures. In 1996 talks were held between Iraq and the UN on a proposed "oil for food" humanitarian program that would permit Iraq to sell a limited quantity of oil in order to purchase food and basic supplies for Iraqi citizens. The United States and Britain wanted money earmarked for Iraq's Kurdish provinces funneled through the existing UN assistance program there. They also raised the issue of equity with respect to Iraq's existing rationing system. In December 1996 the UN agreed to allow Iraq to export $2 billion in oil to buy food and medical supplies. Iraq began receiving 400,000 tons of wheat in the spring of 1997.

Since the end of the Gulf War, Iraq had demonstrated cooperation with UNSCOM, the special UN commission charged with monitoring weapons of mass destruction. However, Saddam Hussein refused to dismantle his country's biological weapons and had stopped cooperating with UNSCOM by August 1997, leading to increasing tension and a US military buildup in the region by early 1998. Personal intervention by UN Secretary General Kofi Annan helped diffuse the situation temporarily. However, renewed disagreements arose in the latter half of the year, ultimately leading to a December bombing campaign (Operation Desert Fox) by US

and UK forces, with the goal of crippling Iraq's weapons capabilities. In late 1998 the US Congress also approved funding for Iraqi opposition groups, in hopes of toppling Saddam Hussein politically from within.

In 1999 the oil for food program was expanded to allow for the sale of $5.25 billion in oil by Iraq over a six-month period to buy goods and medicine. By 2000 most observers agreed that the decade-long UN sanctions, while impoverishing Iraq and threatening its population with a major humanitarian crisis, had failed in their goal of weakening Saddam's hold on power.

The situation in Iraq intensified in 2002. In his January 2002 State of the Union Address, US President George W. Bush labeled Iraq, along with Iran and North Korea, part of an "axis of evil"—states that threatened the world with weapons of mass destruction (WMD) and sponsored terrorism. Throughout 2002, the United States, in partnership with the United Kingdom, brought the issue of the need to disarm the Iraqi regime of WMD to the forefront of international attention. On 8 November 2002 the UN Security Council unanimously approved Resolution 1441, calling upon Iraq to disarm itself of all biological, chemical, and nuclear weapons and weapons capabilities, to allow for the immediate return of UN and International Atomic Energy Agency (IAEA) weapons inspectors (they had been expelled from the country in 1998), and to comply with all previous UN resolutions regarding the country since the end of the Gulf War in 1991. UN and IAEA weapons inspectors returned to Iraq, but the United States and the United Kingdom were neither satisfied with their progress nor with Iraq's compliance with the inspectors. The United States and the United Kingdom began a military buildup in the Persian Gulf region (eventually 250,000 US and 45,000 British troops would be stationed there), and pressed the UN Security Council to issue another resolution authorizing the use of force to disarm the Iraqi regime. This move was met by stiff opposition from France, Germany, and Russia (all members of the Security Council at the time, with France and Russia being permanent members with veto power). Ultimately, the United States, United Kingdom, and their allies chose to act without further UN authorization. War began on 19 March 2003 and by early April, the Saddam Hussein regime had fallen.

After the regime fell, the troops remaining, mostly from the United States and the United Kingdom, attempted to prevent looting and violence, to disarm Iraqis, and to begin the process of reconstruction. Especially contentious was the issue of the formation of a new Iraqi government: Iraqi exiles returned to the country, attempting to take up positions of power; Kurds demanded representation in a new political structure; and the historically oppressed Shi'as (who make up some 60% of the Iraqi population) agitated for recognition and power. The United States initially installed retired US Army Lt. Gen. Jay Garner as head of the Office of Reconstruction and Humanitarian Assistance to oversee Iraq's civil administration while a new government was to be installed. Garner was replaced by former US State Department official L. Paul Bremer III in May 2003 in what some called an effort to put a civilian face on the reconstruction effort. The UN lifted economic sanctions as Bremer began to dismantle Saddam Hussein's power structure. Many Iraqi political figures in June labeled the allied campaign to remove the Saddam Hussein regime more like an "occupation" than a "liberation," and called for elections to a national assembly that would produce a new constitution for the country.

Iraq in the years after the coalition invasion was a dangerous and chaotic place. Various groups waged a guerilla warfare insurgency against the occupying forces and the new government, and hundreds of thousands of foreign troops remained in country to combat them and to try and rebuld Iraq's shattered infrastructure. There was also significant strife between various religious and ethnics groups within Iraq.

On 13 December 2003 Saddam Hussein was found alive, hiding in a hole 2.5-m (8-ft) deep, near his hometown of Tikrit. He was taken into custody and, beginning in October 2005, was put on trial in an Iraqi court for the killing of 148 Shi'as from Dujail, in retaliation for a failed assassination attempt in 1982. In November 2006 Saddam Hussein was found guilty of crimes against humanity for the Dujail killings and sentenced to death by hanging. Hussein was executed by hanging on 30 December 2006.

In March 2004 an interim constitution, called the Transitional Administrative Law, was passed. In June 2004 the United States disbanded the Coalition Provisional Authority led by Bremer and transferred sovereignty back to Iraq in the form of an interim government, headed by Prime Minister Iyad Allawi. On 30 January 2005 Iraqi voters elected a 275-member Transnational National Assembly. The Assembly was given the tasks of serving as Iraq's national legislature and forming a constitution. In April 2005 the National Assembly appointed Jalal Talabani, a prominent Kurdish leader, president. Ibrahim al-Jaafari, a Shi'a, whose United Iraq Alliance Party won the most votes in the January elections, was named prime minister. A constitution was written and presented to the people in a national referendum held on 15 October 2005: more than 63% of eligible voters turned out to vote. The constitution passed with a 78% majority, although three provinces voted against it, two of them by a two-thirds majority. Under election rules, had two-thirds of voters in each of the three provinces voted against the constitution, it would have failed. The vote was sharply divided along ethnic and sectarian lines: Shi'as and Kurds generally supported the document. As it was, the constitution was largely drafted by Shi'as and Kurds, who together make up some 80% of the population.

On 15 December 2005 the country turned out in new parliamentary elections to elect a permanent government. Turnout was high: 10.9 million out of 15.6 million registered voters cast ballots across the country. Official results were announced in January 2006, showing that the Shi'a and Kurdish coalitions once again dominated the voting. In all, four main coalitions won seats in the parliament, which was elected for a term lasting until 2009. The Kurdistan Alliance, an alliance of the primary Kurdish parties, won 53 seats. The Tawafuq Front (Iraqi Consensus Front), an alliance of predominantly Sunni parties, took 44 seats; the Iraqi National List, an alliance of the main secular parties, won 25 seats; and Fadilah won 15 seats.

Although the election held the fragile promise of a stable government, by the end of February 2006, sectarian violence had reached new levels. In January 2007 Bush announced a new Iraq strategy, known as "the surge," which involved deploying thousands more US troops to Baghdad. The move was controversial in the United States. Democrats in the US Congress began to call for the eventual pullout of forces from Iraq.

By August 2008 more than 4,000 US soldiers had been killed in Iraq. The number of Iraqi civilian deaths as of the end of September 2007 was calculated by the Iraq Body Count (IBC) at between 75,000 and 82,000 violent deaths, a figure which includes deaths caused by US-led coalition forces and paramilitary or criminal attacks by others. Those numbers reflect actual documented deaths, but the number of Iraqi civilian deaths could be much higher, as not all casualties are officially reported. While security remained tentative, with frequent acts of terrorism, the Iraqi government had slowly built up its own security forces, and the process of foreign troop withdrawals began: Australia ended its combat mission in Iraq in 2008, and Great Britain ended its combat mission in 2009. A formal handover of security duties took place on 30 June 2009 with the withdrawal of US troops from several cities. The day was declared a national holiday (Sovereignty Day) by the Iraqi government.

In November 2009 Transparency International released a report in which it listed Iraq as the fourth most corrupt country in the world. Although the report served as an indictment of a country that has received tremendous amounts of foreign aid, Iraq's levels of corruption have trended downward from 2008, when Transparency International listed the country as the third most corrupt in the world.

In the March 2010 parliamentary elections, the secular coalition led by former Iraqi Prime Minister Iyad Allawi narrowly beat out Prime Minister Nouri al-Maliki's State of Law bloc. Western analysts generally hailed the vote as fair; however, Maliki, whose personal polling predicted that he would win, angrily contested the result. Iraq's electoral commission launched a manual recount of the ballots in Baghdad to investigate the allegations of fraud. In May 2010 the commission announced that it had completed its recount of 11,298 ballot boxes in Baghdad and had found no violations or cases of fraud. Although the new parliament was seated and declared in session in June 2010, a coalition government was not immediately formed from among the four main parties, leaving vacant the offices of speaker and prime minister. Talks continued in an on and off cycle, suspended on occasion due to arguments among the members. An agreement was finally reached in December 2010, as Maliki was reappointed for a second term as prime minister and Allawi was appointed as chairman of the newly formed National Council for Strategic Policies, which was expected to oversee foreign policy and security issues. The two rivals expressed a commitment to the new unity government.

Under an agreement made between the United States and Iraq, all US troops were to leave the country by 31 December 2011; the last convoy of US troops departed the country on 18 December 2011.

13 GOVERNMENT

The coup d'état of 14 July 1958 established an autocratic regime headed by the military. Until his execution in February 1963, 'Abd al-Karim al-Qasim ruled Iraq, with a council of state and a cabinet. After its 1968 coup, the Ba'ath Party ruled Iraq by means of the Revolutionary Command Council, "the supreme governing body of the state," which selected the president and a cabinet composed of military and civilian leaders. The president (Saddam Hussein from 1979–2003) served as chairman of the Revolutionary Command Council, which exercised both executive and legislative powers by decree. He was also prime minister, commander-in-chief of the armed forces, and secretary-general of the Ba'ath Party. A national assembly of 250 members that was elected by universal suffrage in 1980, 1984, 1989, 1996, and 2000, had little real power. Most senior officials were relatives or close associates of Saddam Hussein; nevertheless, their job security was not assured.

The precarious nature of working in the regime of Saddam Hussein, even for relatives, was made evident in 1995 when two of his sons-in-law defected to Jordan along with President Hussein's daughters. The defection was widely reported in the international media and considered a great embarrassment to the regime as well as a strong indicator of how brutal and repressive its machinations were. After a promise of amnesty was delivered to the defectors by Iraq, the men returned and were executed shortly after crossing the border into Iraq.

In the aftermath of the Iraq war which began in March 2003, Iraq was effectively ruled by the US-installed Office of Reconstruction and Humanitarian Assistance, and then by a Coalition Provisional Authority. In June 2004 sovereignty was transferred back to Iraq and an interim Iraqi government was installed. On 30 January 2005 Iraqi voters elected a 275-member Transnational National Assembly. In April 2005 the National Assembly appointed a president and prime minister. A constitution was written and presented to the people in a national referendum held on 15 October 2005. More than 63% of eligible voters turned out to vote, and the constitution passed with a 78% majority.

Under the 2005 constitution, the government is broken down into four branches: legislative, executive, judicial, and independent associations. In the legislative branch, two councils were created: a Council of Representatives, the main law-making body, and the Council of Union, whose primary task is to examine bills related to regions and provinces. The executive branch is composed of a president, who is not directly elected and whose powers are primarily ceremonial; a deputy president; a prime minister, who as head of government is appointed by the president from the leader of the majority party in the Council of Representatives; and a cabinet chosen by the prime minister. The judiciary is independent and composed of the following: a Supreme Judiciary Council; a Supreme Federal Court; a Federal Cassation Court; a Prosecutor's Office; a Judiciary Inspection Dept.; and other federal courts organized by law. The "fourth branch" is that of independent associations whose actions are subject to legislation and supervision by the other branches. They include: a Supreme Commission for Human Rights; a Supreme Independent Commission for Elections; an Integrity Agency; an Iraqi Central Bank; a Financial Inspection Office; a Media and Communications Agency; Offices of (religious) Endowments; Institution of the Martyrs; and the Federal Public Service Council.

14 POLITICAL PARTIES

Until 1945 political parties existed but were ineffective as political factors. In 1946 five new parties were founded, including one that was Socialist (Al-Hizb al-Watani al-Dimuqrati, or the National Democratic Party), one avowedly close to communism (Ash-Sha'b, or the People's Party), and one purely reformist (Al-Ittihad al-Watani, or the National Union Party).

The response to these parties alarmed the conservative politicians. The Palestine War (1948) provided the pretext for suppres-

sion of the Sha'b and Ittihad parties. Only the National Democratic Party functioned uninterruptedly; in 1950, with the lifting of martial law, the others resumed work. In 1949 Nuri as-Sa'id founded the Constitutional Union Party (Al-Ittihad ad-Dusturi), with a pro-Western, liberal reform program to attract both the old and the young generations. In opposition, Salih Jabr, a former partisan of Nuri's turned rival, founded the Nation's Socialist Party (Al-Ummah al-Ishtiraki), which advocated a democratic and nationalistic, pro-Western and pan-Arab policy. In 1954, however, Sa'id dissolved all parties, including his own Constitutional Union Party, on the ground that they had resorted to violence during the elections of that year.

After the coup of 1958, parties "voluntarily" discontinued their activities. In January 1960 Premier Qasim issued a new law allowing political parties to operate again. Meanwhile, the Ba'athists, who first gained strength in Syria in the 1950s as a pan-Arab movement with strong nationalist and socialist leanings, had attracted a following among elements of the Syrian military. In February 1963 Qasim was overthrown and executed by officers affiliated with a conservative wing of Iraq's Ba'ath movement. In November, a second coup was attempted by Ba'athist extremists from the left, who acted with complicity of the ruling Syrian wing of the party. With the 1968 coup, rightist elements of the Ba'ath Party were installed in prominent positions by Gen. Bakr. These Ba'athists, organized as the Arab Ba'ath Socialist Party, were the ruling political group in Iraq for the next thirty-five years. In the national assembly elections of 1980, the Ba'athists won more than 75% of the seats at stake; in the 1984 elections they won 73% of the seats.

In 1991 the regime issued a decree theoretically allowing the formation of other political parties, but which in fact prohibited parties not supportive of the regime. Under the 1991 edict, all political parties had to be based in Baghdād and all were prohibited from having ethnic or religious affiliations.

Elections were held in March 1996, with only Ba'athists or independent supporters of Saddam Hussein allowed to run for seats in the Assembly. Altogether, 220 seats were contested by 689 candidates. Only Ba'ath Party members and supporters of the Saddam Hussein regime were allowed to run in the March 2000 elections as well.

Outside of Iraq, ethnic, religious and political opposition groups came together to organize a common front against Saddam Hussein, but they achieved very little until 2003. The Shi'a al Dawa Party was brutally suppressed by Saddam before the Iran-Iraq war. In the aftermath of the 2003 war, certain Shi'a clerics, including Grand Ayatollah Ali al-Sistani and Ayatollah Muhammad Bakr al-Hakim, emerged as political and religious leaders for the Shi'a community. In August 2003 al-Hakim was killed in a car bomb attack along with dozens of followers in the holy city of Najaf.

In March 2010 national parliamentary elections were held in Iraq. The Iraqi National Movement coalition led by former Prime Minister Ayad Allawi won the most seats (91), followed by Prime Minister Nuri al-Maliki's State of Law coalition (89 seats). The Kurdish bloc, headed by Kurdistan Democratic Party president Masud Barzani and Patriotic Union of Kurdistan president Jalal Talabani, won a total of 57 seats. The Iraqi National Alliance led by Muqtada al-Sadr ended up with 70 seats. Other smaller political and minority parties won 18 seats. In November 2010 the Council of Representatives convened to elect Jalal Talabani to another term as president of Iraq. Osama al-Nujayfi of the Iraqi National Movement coalition was elected as parliament speaker. In December 2010 the Council of Representatives approved President Talabani's nomination of Nuri al-Maliki for a second term as prime minister, as well as a majority of Prime Minister Maliki's Council of Ministers.

15 LOCAL GOVERNMENT

Until 2003 Iraq was divided into 18 provinces (three of which formed an autonomous Kurdish region), each headed by an appointed governor. Provinces were subdivided into districts, each under a deputy governor; a district consisted of counties, the smallest units, each under a director. Towns and cities were administered by municipal councils led by mayors. Baghdād's municipality, the "governorate of the capital," under its mayor, or "guardian of the capital," served as a model municipality. A settlement reached with the Kurds in 1970 provided for Kurdish autonomy on the local level. In 1974 the provisional constitution was further amended to provide the Kurdistan region with an elected 80-member legislative council; elections were held in 1980 and 1986, but, in fact, the Iraqi army controlled Kurdistan until the imposition of a UN-approved protected zone in the north at the end of the Gulf War. In May 1992 Kurds held elections for a new 100-member parliament for the quasi-independent region. This marked the only relatively free elections held in Iraq in several decades.

Local governing authority broke down following the fall of the Iraqi regime in April 2003. US and British troops were responsible for policing the country and for restoring electricity, running water, sanitation, and other essential services. Under the 2005 constitution, Iraq's federal system was made up of the capital of Baghdād, regions, decentralized provinces, and local administrations. The country's future regions were to be established from its 18 governorates (provinces). Any single province, or group of provinces, was entitled to request that it be recognized as a region, with such a request being made by either two-thirds of the members of the provincial councils in the provinces involved or by one-tenth of the registered voters in the province(s) in question. Provinces unwilling or unable to join a region still enjoy enough autonomy and resources to enable them to manage their own internal affairs according to the principle of administrative decentralization. With the two parties' approval, federal government responsibilities may be delegated to the provinces, or vice versa. These decentralized provinces are headed by provincial governors, elected by provincial councils. The administrative levels within a province are defined, in descending order, as districts, counties, and villages.

In January 2009 provincial council elections were held in all provinces except the three provinces of the Kurdistan Regional Government and Kirkuk province.

16 JUDICIAL SYSTEM

The court system until 2003 was made up of two distinct branches: a security component and a more conventional court system to handle other charges. There was no independence in the operation of the judiciary; the president could override any court decision.

The security courts had jurisdiction in all cases involving espionage, treason, political dissent, smuggling and currency exchange violations, and drug trafficking. The ordinary civil courts had jurisdiction over civil, commercial, and criminal cases except for those that fell under the jurisdiction of the religious courts. Courts of general jurisdiction were established at governorate headquarters and in the principal districts.

Magistrates' courts tried criminal cases in the first instance, but they could not try cases involving punishment of more than seven years in prison. Such cases were tried in courts of sessions that were also appellate instances for magistrates' courts. Each judicial district had courts of sessions presided over by a bench of three judges. There were no jury trials. Special courts to try national security cases were set up in 1965; verdicts of these courts could be appealed to the military supreme court. In other cases, the highest court of appeal was the court of cassation in Baghdād, with civil and criminal divisions. It was composed of at least 15 judges, including a president and two vice presidents.

For every court of first instance, there was a Shari'ah (Islamic) court that ruled on questions involving religious matters and personal status. Trials were public and defendants were entitled to free counsel in the case of indigents. The government protected certain groups from prosecution. A 1992 decree granted immunity from prosecution to members of the Ba'ath Party. A 1990 decree granted immunity to men who killed their mothers, daughters, and other female family members who had committed "immoral deeds" such as adultery and fornication.

Under the constitution ratified in 2005, the judiciary is independent and composed of the following: a supreme judiciary council; a Supreme Federal Court; a federal cassation court; a prosecutor's office; a judiciary inspection department; and other federal courts organized by law. The supreme judiciary council administers the judicial branch, nominates members of the courts and departments, and presents the judicial budget to the legislature. The Supreme Federal Court is the highest court in Iraq, oversees election results, and rules in the case of accusations against the president or prime minister. Private courts are banned.

17 ARMED FORCES

US military involvement in Iraq has long been a matter of controversy for both Iraqi and American politicians and citizens. The Ba'ath Party took control of Iraq in 1963, and Saddam Hussein first assumed the office of president in 1979. During the 1980s, the country fought a long war with its neighbor, Iran, which ended with a cease-fire proposed by the UN in 1988. In 1990 Iraq invaded Kuwait but was expelled by forces led by the United States. Following this war, the UN Security Council repeatedly called on Iraq to surrender its weapons of mass destruction and to submit to UN inspections of possible weapons manufacturing or storage sites. The Iraqi government, in turn, repeatedly refused to cooperate fully with the UN. As a result, in a 2003 invasion known as Operation Freedom, a coalition force led by the United States entered Iraq, ousted the Ba'ath regime, and installed a governing council. The coalition forces remained in the country to support the Iraqi Transitional National Assembly (TNA), which was elected in 2005 and drafted the country's new constitution. However, resistance groups have continued to fight against the new government. International troops remained steady for several years, maintaining a tentative security and providing training for Iraqi security forces in anticipation of troop withdrawals. Australia ended its combat mission in Iraq in 2008, and Great Britain ended theirs in 2009. US troops completed their withdrawal in December 2011.

The International Institute for Strategic Studies reports that armed forces in Iraq totaled 245,782 members in 2011. The force is comprised of 238,010 from the army, 2,605 from the navy, and 5,167 members of the air force. Armed forces represent 8.6% of the labor force in Iraq. Defense spending totaled $9.8 billion and accounted for 8.6% of GDP.

18 INTERNATIONAL COOPERATION

Iraq is a charter member of the UN, having joined on 21 December 1945, and participates in ESCWA and several nonregional specialized agencies. A founding member of the Arab League, Iraq also participates in the Arab Fund for Economic and Social Development, the Arab Bank for Economic Development in Africa, the Arab Monetary Fund, the Council of Arab Economic Unity, Organization of the Islamic Conference (OIC), G-19, G-77, OAPEC, and OPEC. Iraq holds observer status in the WTO.

Iraq has given both military and economic support to Arab parties in the conflict with Israel. The war with Iran preoccupied Iraq during the 1980s, and Iraq's relations with other countries in the Arab world have varied. During the 1980s Iraq maintained friendly relations with some Western countries, notably France, a major arms supplier to Iraq.

In November 1984 diplomatic relations between Iraq and the United States were renewed after a break of 17 years, but were broken off again when Iraq invaded Kuwait in August of 1990. The United States and its allies launched an air war against Iraq after diplomatic efforts and economic sanctions failed to convince Iraq to leave Kuwait. Iraq's international standing deteriorated badly and the nation was placed under an international trade embargo. Iraq was attacked by US and British forces beginning on 19 March 2003, and the regime led by Saddam Hussein was defeated by those forces that April.

In the postwar period, the country is undergoing reconstruction and the government is in transition. A Transitional National Assembly (TNA) was formed by direct democratic elections held on 30 January 2005. On 15 December 2005 a permanent 275-seat Council of Representatives was elected.

Iraq is a member of the Nonaligned Movement. In environmental cooperation, Iraq is part of the Nuclear Test Ban Treaty and the UN Convention on the Law of the Sea.

19 ECONOMY

In 1973 Iraqi oil revenue was $1.8 billion. By 1978 oil revenues peaked at $23.6 billion. GDP growth was in double digits from 1973 to 1980 with the exception of 1974, when it was 7.2%.

It was from these lofty heights that the regime of Saddam Hussein launched two wars, whose effects on the Iraqi economy, even aside from the tragic human costs, proved devastating. The Iraq-Iran War (1980–88) began with Iraq's attempt to seize control of the economically and strategically important Shatt al Arab from Iran, which the countries had agreed to divide in a treaty in 1975.

Saddam miscalculated that Iran could be easily dismembered during its revolutionary upheavals, and when the war ended eight bloody years later, the Shatt al Arab and all other border issues were unchanged, leaving Iraq with no material gain and a debt of over $100 billion, much of it owed to Kuwait. Annual oil revenues for Iraq and Kuwait were roughly even—averaging about $16 billion a year—but Kuwait, instead of spending on armaments, had invested sizeable amounts in the West, essentially doubling its returns.

Kuwait refused to see the debts owed it by Iraq as money spent for its own defense, and insisted on being repaid, providing the economic trigger for Iraq's second disastrous foray—the invasion of Kuwait on 2 August 1990. For the first time the UN Security Council agreed to support collective action against an aggressive power and Iraqi forces were driven out of Kuwait in the first Gulf War in February 1991. The UN imposed comprehensive economic, financial, and military sanctions, placing the Iraqi economy under siege. Acting on its own, the United States also froze all Iraqi assets in the United States and barred all economic transactions between US citizens and Iraq. Many other countries imposed similar sanctions on top of the UN-imposed embargo. UN Security Council resolutions authorized the export of Iraqi crude oil worth up to $1.6 billion over a limited time to finance humanitarian imports for the Iraqi people.

The effect of war in Kuwait and continuing economic sanctions reduced real GDP by at least 75% in 1991, on the basis of an 85% decline in oil production, and the destruction of the industrial and service sectors of the economy. Living standards deteriorated and the inflation rate reached 8,000% in 1992. Estimates for 1993 indicated that unemployment hovered around 50% and that inflation was as high as 1,000%. Because UN costs and reparations for Kuwait were taken out of permitted oil sales before being handed over to the Iraqi regime, the government's revenues were lower than total oil sales. The Organization of Arab Petroleum Exporting Countries (OAPEC) reported that Iraqi oil revenues at current prices were $365 million in 1994, $370 million in 1995, and $680 million in 1996. After the first Gulf War Iraq refused to provide economic data to the UN or any other international organization, and all estimates therefore were subject to wide variability and questions of reliability.

Uncertainty was increased by a flourishing black market that was responsible for an increasing share of domestic commerce. There were widespread expectations that the Hussein regime would soon fall from the weight of its disastrous political and economic miscalculations, but this did not happen, and by 1995 it had become apparent that the tight restrictions on oil sales were resulting in serious harm to the Iraqi people. The UN passed its first "oil-for-food" program (which the Iraqi regime refused to accept until 1996) allowing oil worth $5.26 billion to be sold every six months, with strict controls over how the money was spent. The "oil-for-food" program, finally implemented in December 1996, improved living conditions for the average Iraqi citizen. In December 1999 the UN Security Council lifted the limits on Iraq's oil production, which then rose from 550,000 billion barrels per day (bbl/d) in November 1996 to an average of about 2.6 million bbl/d during 2000.

By 2002 crude exports from Iraq had fallen below normal capacity (about two million bbl/d) to an average of 630,000 bbl/d.

According to UN assessments, this low export level created a $2.64 billion shortfall in the oil-for-food program. Low exports were blamed on illegal surcharges of 15–45 cents per barrel being levied by Iraq beginning in late 2000, and the tactic of "retroactive pricing" adopted by the United States and the United Kingdom in January 2001 to combat these surcharges. Both the surcharges and the retroactive pricing—whereby the price charged for Iraqi oil was revealed only after the sale, and then set at a level too high for a surcharge to be paid and still make a profit—raised the price and reduced demand for Iraqi oil. The concerns by the United States and the United Kingdom were that the surcharges were being used to fund a secret military build-up by Iraq.

UN estimates are that from 1996 to 2002 the "oil-for-food" program generated about $60 billion. The US government estimates that through smuggling and illegal surcharges the Iraqi government secured about $6.6 billion from 1997 to 2001. On 14 May 2002, after Iraq had resumed oil exports, the UN Security Council approved a change in the oil-for-food program to add an extensive list of "dual-use" goods (goods that could be used for military as well as nonmilitary purposes) that Iraq could not purchase with its oil revenues.

Sanctions against Iraq were lifted in May 2003 after coalition forces drove the Hussein regime from power. This allowed reconstruction efforts to begin, but serious security problems arising from an Iraqi insurgency hampered the rebuilding effort. In 2003 real GDP growth stood at -21.8% and the inflation rate was 29.3%. The "oil-for-food" program was phased out that May. A transitional government was elected in January 2005 and a referendum on a new constitution was held in October 2005, with the constitution being approved overwhelmingly. Elections for a permanent government were held in December 2005.

Estimates show that Iraq's unemployment rate in 2006 remained high (18–30%), but the overall Iraqi economy appeared to be improving somewhat. The continued sabotage of oil installations put a drag on the economy, however, but real GDP was forecast to grow at a rate of around 5% in 2007. In October 2003, a new Iraqi currency, the "new Iraqi dinar" was introduced, and by 2006 it had appreciated sharply. Iraq had requested formal membership in the World Trade Organization (WTO); the country was granted WTO observer status in February 2004 and began its WTO accession process in December 2004. On May 25, 2007 the Iraqi trade minister participated in a WTO meeting in Geneva, a first step in the WTO accession process. WTO membership is crucial to Iraq's integration into the international economy.

Iraq's oil export earnings were immune from legal proceedings, including debt collection, until the end of 2007. In 2004 the Paris Club of 19 creditor nations agreed to forgive up to 80% on $42 billion worth of loans, but the relief was contingent upon Iraq reaching an economic stabilization program with the IMF. Some $15.3 billion in foreign aid from sources other than the United States had been pledged during the period 2004–08.

The country's oil exports in 2005 were below 2004 levels. Oil production by 2008 was averaging 2.1 million barrels per day, up from levels below 2 million barrels per day in 2006. Persistent fuel shortages forced the government to raise the heavily subsidized price of gasoline in 2005. This sparked protests and rioting throughout Iraq. More than 75% of the country's GDP comes from oil. The high price of oil ($112 per barrel in August 2008, up from $63 per barrel in January 2006) mitigated the economic damage from lower production, and oil prices were forecast to remain high over the long term. By 2011 oil production had reached pre-2003 levels of some 2.5 million barrels per day. Iraq had signed contracts with oil companies that could enable the country to increase its oil revenue, however infrastructure will need to be improved in order to significantly expand processing and export capacity.

The GDP rate of change in Iraq, as of 2010, was 0.8%. Inflation stood at 4.2%, and unemployment was reported at 15.3%.

²⁰INCOME

The CIA estimated that in 2010 the GDP of Iraq was $113.4 billion. The CIA defines GDP as the value of all final goods and services produced within a nation in a given year and computed on the basis of purchasing power parity (PPP) rather than value as measured on the basis of the rate of the exchange based on current dollars. The per capita GDP was estimated at $3,800. The annual growth rate of GDP was 0.8%. The average inflation rate was 4.2%. It was estimated that agriculture accounted for 9.7% of GDP, industry 63%, and services 27.3%.

In 2007 the World Bank estimated that Iraq, with 0.46% of the world's population, accounted for 0.16% of the world's GDP. By comparison, the United States, with 4.85% of the world's population, accounted for 22.51% of world GDP. As of 2011 the most recent study by the World Bank reported that actual individual consumption in Iraq was 56.3% of GDP and accounted for 0.14% of world consumption. By comparison, the United States accounted for 25.44% of world individual consumption. The World Bank also estimated that 18.5% of Iraq's GDP was spent on food and beverages, 13.2% on housing and household furnishings, 2.9% on clothes, 8.6% on health, 5.2% on transportation, 0.7% on communications, 0.6% on recreation, 0.4% on restaurants and hotels, and 1.1% on miscellaneous goods and services and purchases from abroad.

In 2008 an estimated 25% of the population lived with incomes below the poverty level. According to the World Bank, remittances from citizens living abroad totaled $70.9 million or about $2 per capita and accounted for approximately 0.1% of GDP.

²¹LABOR

Although the constitution provides the right for citizens to form and join unions, some restrictions imposed by Saddam Hussein-era labor codes remained in place as of 2010. For instance, non-executive public sector workers were free to form and join unions, but most public workers were classified as executives. Unions for public employees and workers in state-owned enterprises are government run. Private-sector unions must have at least 50 employees in order to form a union, and workers are not permitted to strike.

Child labor is prohibited by law, but child labor remains a problem. Economic necessity and lack of government enforcement have increased the number of children of all ages that are employed.

The workday is eight hours, although regulations concerning length of the work day, rest periods, and overtime are generally not enforced. The minimum wage for a skilled worker in 2010 was less than $10 per day and less than $4.50 per day for an unskilled worker. Historically, working women have been accepted in Iraq, but the number of women in the workforce dramatically increased because of the prolonged war with Iran as well as the Persian Gulf War, as women replaced men in the labor market. Despite their presence in the workforce, women are subject to discrimination in terms of access to work and compensation. The security situation since 2003 has disproportionately impacted women's ability to work outside the home.

As a general rule, the quality of life has differed greatly between rural areas and the cities, especially that in Baghdād. This differential has resulted in massive rural to urban migration.

As of 2009 Iraq had a total labor force of 8.5 million people. Within that labor force, CIA estimates in 2008 noted that 21.6% were employed in agriculture, 18.7% in industry, and 59.8% in the service sector.

²²AGRICULTURE

The rich alluvial soil of the lowlands and an elaborate system of irrigation canals made Iraq a granary in ancient times and in the Middle Ages. After the irrigation works were destroyed in the Mongol invasion, agriculture decayed. Unlike the rain-fed north, southern Iraq depends entirely on irrigation, which is in turn heavily reliant on electricity and fuel supply to run the pumping networks. There are similar difficulties with the spring crop of vegetables in the south, also entirely dependent on irrigation. Over half the irrigated area in southern Iraq is affected by water-logging and salinity, diminishing crop production and farm incomes. Agriculture was once Iraq's largest employer and the second-largest sector in value. By 2010 it accounted for just under 10% of GDP. While it was no longer the country's largest employer, some 20% of the labor force was employed in the agricultural sector.

Under various agrarian reform laws—including a 1970 law that limited permissible landholdings to 4–202 hectares (10–500 acres), depending on location, fertility, and available irrigation facilities—about 400,000 previously landless peasants received land. Agrarian reform was accompanied by irrigation and drainage works, and by the establishment of cooperative societies for the provision of implements and machinery, irrigation facilities, and other services.

Agricultural production in Iraq declined progressively because of the war with Iran and the Persian Gulf War. During the 2003 conflict, most farmers in Iraq's three northern provinces were not displaced. The northern region produced some 30–35% of the grain crop.

Iraq currently imports almost $3 billion in food commodities annually. Aid programs are helping expand production of wheat to minimize food imports. Efforts on select Iraqi farms doubled wheat production in 2004. Since 2003, USAID's agriculture program has been working to restore veterinary clinics, introduce improved cereal grain varieties, repair agricultural equipment, and train farmers and Iraqi government staff. The US government has estimated that the Iraqi Ministry of Agriculture would require over $1 billion of agricultural inputs annually for Iraq's agricultural producers to boost production. Iraq will need to rely on imports to meet a large portion of its food and fiber needs, even with substantial gains in production.

Roughly 22% of the total land is farmed, and the country's major crops include wheat, barley, rice, vegetables, dates, and cot-

ton. Cereal production in 2009 amounted to 2.6 million tons, fruit production 1 million tons, and vegetable production 3.2 million tons.

²³ANIMAL HUSBANDRY

The UN Food and Agriculture Organization (FAO) reported that Iraq dedicated four million hectares (9.88 million acres) to permanent pasture or meadow in 2009. During that year, the country tended 27.5 million chickens and 1.6 million head of cattle. Iraq also produced 4,050 tons of cattle hide and 17,000 tons of raw wool.

Animal husbandry is widespread. Sheep raising is most important, with wool used domestically for weaving carpets and cloaks.

²⁴FISHING

Centuries of overfishing without restocking reduced the formerly plentiful supply of river fish, but the fishing industry has rebounded since the early 1970s. In 2008 the annual capture totaled 34,472 tons according to the UN FAO.

²⁵FORESTRY

Forests of oak and Aleppo pine in the north cover less than 2% of Iraq's entire area and have been depleted by excessive cutting for fuel or by fires and overgrazing. Since 1954 indiscriminate cutting has been prohibited, and charcoal production from wood has ceased. The forestry research center at Arbil has established tree nurseries and conducted reforestation programs. Approximately 2% of Iraq is covered by forest. The UN FAO estimated the 2009 roundwood production at 59,000 cu m (2.08 million cu ft). The value of all forest products, including roundwood, totaled $321,000.

²⁶MINING

Iraq's mineral resources (excluding hydrocarbons) are limited. Crude oil was Iraq's sole export commodity in 2009, and construction materials comprised another leading industry. In 2009, Iraq produced hydraulic cement, nitrogen, phosphate rock (from the Akashat open-pit mine), salt, and native Frasch sulfur from underground deposits at Mishraq, on the Tigris (Al Furāt) River, south of Al Mawṣil. Production figures for 2009, were (in metric tons): bauxite, 250; bentonite, 3,959; kaolin, 1,980; gypsum, 1,364; limestone, 316; iron stone, 3; and salt, 113,000. The output of Portland cement was 8,500,000 metric tons in 2009. In 2009, Iraq was still a leading regional importer of cement, importing an estimated 10 million metric tons to satisfy local demand, mainly from Iran and Turkey. Geological surveys have indicated usable deposits of iron ore, copper, gypsum, bitumen, dolomite, and marble; these resources have remained largely unexploited, because of inadequate transport facilities and lack of coal for processing the ores.

²⁷ENERGY AND POWER

Iraq's petroleum reserves are among the largest in the world. As of 1 January 2005, Iraq's proven oil reserves were estimated by the Oil and Gas Journal at 115 billion barrels, of which, about 75 billion barrels had yet to be developed. In 2011 the CIA gave the same estimate—115 billion barrels of proven oil reserves. However, the country's reserves may be significantly higher. Only about

10% of the country has been explored for oil and it is believed by some analysts that in Iraq's Western Desert region, deep oil-bearing formations may contain another 100 billion or more barrels of oil. Others are less optimistic, estimating that only another 45 billion barrels may lie undiscovered. In January 2011 a large block of oil was discovered in Kurdistan. The original estimate at the Shaikan well was 220 million barrels of oil. The new findings resulted in a 2.2 billion barrel estimate. Gulf Keystone Petroleum, the company that originally discovered the new surplus of oil, has a seventy-five percent stake in the block. As a result of the new findings, the company is contesting claims made from other oil companies stating they also hold interest in the new block.

Iraq's oil production has been deeply affected by the nation's wars, resulting in major drops in crude oil production. During Iraq's war with Iran, output dropped from 3,476,900 barrels per day in 1979 to 897,400 barrels daily in 1981. Oil production dropped from 2,897,000 barrels per day in 1989 to 305,000 barrels daily in 1991, following an embargo on Iraqi oil exports for Iraq's invasion of Kuwait in 1990. Iraq's oil production slowly increased to 600,000 barrels per day by 1996, and with the country's acceptance of UN Resolution 986, allowing limited oil exports for humanitarian reasons ("oil-for-food program"), production rose to about 2.58 million barrels per day in January 2003, just before the US-led invasion of Iraq in March of that year. Following the disruption in production caused by the war—production fell to 1,318,000 barrels per day in 2003—oil production has slowly recovered, growing each year during 2006–2010. In 2006 oil production was 2,009,411 barrels per day; by 2010 the number had risen to 2,408,465 barrels per day.

In June 2009 the Kurdistan Regional Government (KRG) began its first oil export project, transporting crude oil by pipeline from two oilfields to Turkey. The federal government supported the project, the revenues of which will be shared between the KRG, the federal government, and the oil company. In December 2009 the government announced an initial agreement with the Angolan state-owned oil company, Sonangol, to manage two major oilfields in the Nineveh province of Iraq. The two fields contain an estimated 1.7 billion barrels of oil, but Nineveh is one of the most dangerous areas of the country, suffering from frequent insurgencies by militant Sunnis and al-Qaeda. The preliminary contract offered Sonangol a payment of between $5 and $6 per barrel for their management of the fields, which is one of the highest fees ever awarded in an Iraqi oil deal.

Iraq's natural gas reserves were estimated, as of 1 January 2011, at 3.17 trillion cubic meters, the 11th largest natural gas reserve in the world.

Iraq's electric power sector has also been affected by the country's wars. During the 1990–91 Persian Gulf War, about 85–90% of the national power grid was destroyed or damaged. However, 75% of the national grid had been restarted by early 1992. Total electricity production in 2000 was 31,700 million kWh, of which 98% was from fossil fuels and 2% from hydropower. The country's generating capacity was about 9,500 MW in 2001. As of late May 2005, Iraq's available and operating generating capacity was placed at about 4,000 to 5,000 MW. Peak summer demand however, was forecast to be at 8,000 MW. The World Bank reported in 2008 that Iraq produced 36.8 billion kWh of electricity and consumed 35.7 billion kWh, or 1,176 kWh per capita. Roughly 99% of energy came from fossil fuels.

28 INDUSTRY

Main industries are petroleum, food processing, chemicals, textiles, leather goods, cement and other building materials, fertilizer, and metal processing. In 1964 the government took over all establishments producing asbestos, cement, cigarettes, textiles, paper, tanned leather, and flour. Iraq has eight major oil refineries, at Baiji, Al Başrah, Daura, Khānaqin, Haditha, Mufthiah, Qaiyarah, Al Mawşil, and Kirkūk. The Iraq-Iran War, Persian Gulf War, and Iraq War of 2003 seriously affected Iraqi refining. Iraq had a total refinery capacity of 598,000 barrels per day in 2009. The bulk of Iraq's refinery capacity is concentrated in the Baiji complex.

Industrial establishments before the 2003 war included a sulfur plant at Kirkūk, a fertilizer plant at Al Başrah, an antibiotics factory at Sāmarrā, an agricultural implements factory at Iskandariyah, and an electrical equipment factory near Baghdād. In the 1970s Iraq put strong emphasis on the development of heavy industry and diversification of its industry, a policy aimed at decreasing dependence on oil. During the 1980s the industrial sector showed a steady increase, reflecting the importance given to military industries during the Iran-Iraq war. By early 1992 it was officially claimed that industrial output had been restored to 60% of pre-Persian Gulf War capacity. Beginning in 1996, Iraq was permitted to export limited amounts of oil in exchange for food, medicine, and some infrastructure spare parts (the UN "oil-for-food" program). By 1999 the UN Security Council allowed Iraq to export as much oil as required to meet humanitarian needs. The program was phased out in May 2003 following the defeat of the Saddam Hussein regime.

In 2004 industry accounted for 66.6% of GDP. In 2010 it was 60.5% of GDP. Just under 19% of the labor force was employed in the industrial sector in 2008. The industrial production growth rate was 4.8% in 2010, ranking Iraq 85th in that category among the countries of the world.

29 SCIENCE AND TECHNOLOGY

Iraq has imported Western technology for its petrochemical industry. The Scientific Research Council was established in 1963 and includes nine scientific research centers. Multiple universities offer degrees in basic and applied sciences. In addition, the Ministry of Higher Education has 18 incorporated technical institutes. The Iraq Natural History Research Center and Museum (founded in 1946) and the Iraqi Medical Society (founded in 1920) are both headquartered in Baghdad. The World Bank reported in 2009 that there were no patent applications in science and technology in Iraq.

30 DOMESTIC TRADE

Modern shops and department stores have spread throughout the country, replacing traditional bazaars. Baghdād, Al Mawşil, and Al Başrah, as well as other large and medium-size cities, all have modern supermarkets. Baghdād leads in wholesale trade and in the number of retail shops.

International military interventions have caused great damage to the infrastructure and resulted in international sanctions that crippled the economy prior to the ousting of Saddam Hussein in

2003. That year the Trade Bank of Iraq (TBI) was established to facilitate transactions for humanitarian goods and reconstruction materials. The TBI—still operating as of 2011—is licensed by the Central Bank of Iraq. As of 2011, the retail and construction sectors were benefiting from increased security, although additional governmental reforms were needed.

31 FOREIGN TRADE

Iraq's most valuable export is oil, which has historically accounted for almost all of its total export value. Rising oil prices during the 1970s created increases in export revenues. However, the drop in world oil prices and Iraq's exporting problems due to international sanctions essentially put an end to Iraqi oil exports. The UN imposed trade restrictions on non-oil exports in August 1990. Non-oil exports (often illegal) were estimated at $2 billion for the 12 months following the March 1991 cease-fire. Iraq was traditionally the world's largest exporter of dates, with its better varieties going to Western Europe, Australia, and North America.

Until 1994, the UN committee charged with supervising what little international trade Iraq was permitted to engage in—food and medicine, essentially—kept records on the amount of goods it approved for import in exchange for oil. In the first half of 1994, the committee recorded $2 billion in food imports, $175 million in medicine, and an additional $2 billion in "essential civilian needs," a term that at that time referred to agricultural machinery, seeds, and goods for sanitation.

In 1995 the Iraqi government rationed its people only one-half of the minimum daily requirement in calories. In 1997 the UN permitted Iraq to expand its oil sales to increase its purchasing power of food and other sources of humanitarian relief. In the spring of that year the country received 400,000 tons of wheat to help feed its suffering population, who had been living under strict food rations for four years. Limited exports were organized by the UN, and the oil-for-food program brought in revenues during 1999 equaling $5.3 billion.

Iraq imported $43.92 billion worth of goods and services in 2010, while exporting $51.76 billion worth of goods and services.

Principal Trading Partners – Iraq (2010)

(In millions of US dollars)

Country	Total	Exports	Imports	Balance
World	95,550.0	53,050.0	42,500.0	10,550.0
United States	13,287.0	11,476.0	1,811.0	9,665.0
China	9,657.0	5,697.0	3,960.0	1,737.0
Turkey	7,871.0	1,231.0	6,640.0	-5,409.0
India	7,400.0	6,636.0	764.0	5,872.0
Syria	5,932.0	803.0	5,129.0	-4,326.0
South Korea	5,346.0	4,025.0	1,321.0	2,704.0
Italy	3,890.0	3,242.0	648.0	2,594.0
Japan	3,456.0	3,115.0	341.0	2,774.0
Canada	2,114.0	1,862.0	252.0	1,610.0
Netherlands	1,804.0	1,496.0	308.0	1,188.0

(…) data not available or not significant.

(n.s.) not specified.

SOURCE: *2011 Direction of Trade Statistics Yearbook,* New York: United Nations, 2011.

Balance of Payments – Iraq (2008)

(In millions of US dollars)

Current Account		**26,973.0**
Balance on goods	33,965.0	
Imports	-29,761.0	
Exports	63,726.0	
Balance on services	-6,000.0	
Balance on income	2,105.0	
Current transfers	-3,096.0	
Capital Account		**441.0**
Financial Account		**-3,146.0**
Direct investment abroad	-34.0	
Direct investment in Iraq	1,856.0	
Portfolio investment assets	-2,799.0	
Portfolio investment liabilities	…	
Financial derivatives	…	
Other investment assets	-850.0	
Other investment liabilities	-1,320.0	
Net Errors and Omissions		**-5,777.0**
Reserves and Related Items		**-18,491.0**

(…) data not available or not significant.

SOURCE: *Balance of Payment Statistics Yearbook 2011,* Washington, DC: International Monetary Fund, 2011.

Major import partners in 2010 were Turkey, 24.2%; Syria, 18.6%; China, 14.4%; and the United States, 6.6%. Its major export partners were the United States, 24.3%; India, 16.7%; China, 12.1%; South Korea, 8.2%; Italy, 6.9%; and Japan, 6.6%.

32 BALANCE OF PAYMENTS

The current account balance in 2010 was $3.105 billion. External debt was estimated at $52.58 billion.

33 BANKING AND SECURITIES

When Iraq was part of the Ottoman Empire, a number of European currencies circulated alongside the Turkish pound. With the establishment of the British mandate after World War I, Iraq was incorporated into the Indian monetary system, which was operated by the British, and the rupee became the principal currency in circulation. In 1931 the Iraq Currency Board was established in London for note issue and maintenance of reserves for the new Iraqi dinar. The currency board pursued a conservative monetary policy, maintaining very high reserves behind the dinar. The dinar was further strengthened by its link to the British pound. In 1947 the government-owned National Bank of Iraq was founded, and in 1949 the London-based currency board was abolished as the new bank assumed responsibility for the issuing of notes and the maintenance of reserves.

In the 1940s a series of government-owned banks was established: the Agricultural Bank and the Industrial Bank, the Real Estate Bank, the Mortgage Bank, and the Cooperative Bank. In 1956 the National Bank of Iraq became the Central Bank of Iraq. In 1964 banking was fully nationalized. The banking system comprised the Central Bank of Iraq, the Rafidain Bank (the main commercial bank), and three others: the Agricultural Cooperative Bank, the Industrial Bank, and the Real Estate Bank. In 1991 the government decided to end its monopoly on banking. After 1991 six new banks were established—the Socialist Bank, Iraqi Commercial Bank, Baghdād Bank, Dijla Bank, Al-Itimad Bank, and the

Private Bank—as a result of liberalizing legislation and the opportunity for large-scale profits from currency speculation.

Preference for investing savings in rural or urban real estate is common. Major private investments in industrial enterprises can be secured only by assurance of financial assistance from the government. The establishment of a stock exchange in Baghdād was delayed by practical considerations (such as a lack of computers), but it was eventually inaugurated in March 1992.

During the 2003 US-led war and subsequent occupation of Iraq, the financial sector essentially disappeared. The banking district of Baghdād was wrecked by the bombing campaign, and until the new government became stable it appeared that financial activity would remain at a standstill. Rejuvenation of Iraq's banking system was seen as a high priority. With the passage of the 2005 constitution, a central bank was established, which has the power to issue new currency and set interest rates in the hopes of managing the country's massive debts. USAID gave loans of up to $250,000 to small businesses and entrepreneurs in order to jumpstart the economy. Iraq's banking system had been one of the region's most advanced prior to the war, so the foundations were already in place for a sound financial sector.

In early 2010 the IMF approved $3.6 billion in support to Iraq, and the World Bank committed $250 million. The IMF's loan was intended to help Iraq implement its two-year economic plan, which included banking sector reforms.

34 INSURANCE

The Insurance Business Regulation Act of 2005 established the Iraqi Insurance Diwan, an independent body responsible for setting regulatory policies and procedures for the insurance industry. Domestic and foreign insurers are permitted to operate in Iraq, provided they abide by the established regulations.

35 PUBLIC FINANCE

In 2010 the budget of Iraq included $52.8 billion in public revenue and $72.4 billion in public expenditures, according to the CIA. The budget deficit amounted to 23.9% of GDP. The country's external debt was $52.58 billion.

36 TAXATION

Direct taxes are levied on income and on property. The rental value of dwellings, commercial buildings, and nonagricultural land is taxed, with a certain tax-free minimum. In 1939 graduated income tax rates were established on income from all sources except agriculture. Most agricultural income is not taxed.

Indirect taxation predominates. The land tax must be paid by all who farm government lands with or without a lease. Owners of freehold (lazimah) land pay no tax or rent. Much farm produce consumed on the farm or in the village is not taxed at all, but when marketed, farm products are taxed.

According to the World Bank, the corporate tax rate on a medium-size company was 28.4% as of 2010. In February 2010 a new law was passed establishing a tax rate of 35% for oil and gas companies.

37 CUSTOMS AND DUTIES

As of 1 March 2004 a 5% reconstruction levy based on the customs value of the product was imposed upon all imports. However, food, clothing, medicines, humanitarian goods, and books are exempt. The duty was expected to be increased in 2011, potentially to as high as 30%, but as of the end of 2011 the increase had been postponed.

38 FOREIGN INVESTMENT

UN sanctions effectively froze all of Iraq's foreign transactions in the 1990s. In October 1992 the UN Security Council permitted these frozen assets, including Iraqi oil in storage in Turkey and Saudi Arabia, to be sold without the permission of the Iraqi government. About $1 billion of frozen assets were to pay for compensation to Kuwaiti victims of the invasion and to cover UN operations inside Iraq.

In September 2003 the American-appointed Coalition Provisional Authority announced it was opening up all sectors of the economy to foreign investment in an attempt to deliver much-needed reconstruction in the war-torn country. The Iraqi Governing Council announced it would allow total foreign ownership without the need for prior approval. The program applied to all sectors of the economy, from industry to health and water, except for natural resources (including oil). The deal also included full, immediate remittance to the host country of profits, dividends, interest, and royalties. Income and business taxes for foreign investors were capped at 15% beginning in 2004. At a donors' conference in Madrid in 2003, more than $33 billion in foreign aid was pledged to Iraq for reconstruction efforts. Japan has been the largest contributor of soft loans. US assistance to Iraq since 2003 has totaled $58 billion, mostly for security and reconstruction (including technical assistance and capacity building).

Foreign direct investment (FDI) in Iraq was a net inflow of $1.07 billion according to World Bank figures published in 2009. FDI represented 1.63% of GDP. While investors showed increased interest in Iraq in 2010, they have been curtailed by regulatory impediments.

39 ECONOMIC DEVELOPMENT

Until the 2003 Iraq War, the government both controlled and participated in petroleum, agriculture, commerce, banking, and industry. In the late 1960s it made efforts to diversify Iraq's economic relations and to conserve foreign exchange. As an example, it was announced in 1970 that contracts for all planned projects would be awarded to companies willing to receive compensation in crude oil or petroleum products. The government also undertook to build an Iraqi tanker fleet to break the monopoly of foreign oil-transport companies.

The imposition of sanctions against Iraq in the 1990s destroyed all attempts to stabilize Iraq's payments on its foreign debt. Iraq also faced reparation claims. Iran separately pursued its claim for massive separation payments arising from the 1980–88 war. Iraq was also obligated by UN resolutions to pay for various UN agency activities.

Iraq had an estimated foreign debt in 2005 of $82.1 billion. However, a large portion of Iraq's debt had been forgiven by that time, and the IMF provided new funds as part of an effort to get Iraq back into capital markets, where it could secure the financing it needed to invest in the critical oil sector. The insurgency against coalition forces, in addition to underinvestment, prevented the oil industry from getting back on its feet. Work was being carried out to rebuild infrastructure, but by 2006, insurgents were destroying much of what was being built.

In 2011 the oil sector was the cornerstone of Iraq's economy, accounting for 90% of all foreign exchange earnings. Oil production was averaging 2.5 million barrels a day and two million barrels a day were being exported. The government had plans to increase significantly oil production over the next decade.

In order to significantly improve its economic outlook, the country will need to address a number of issues, including pervasive corruption, inadequate infrastructure, and current laws that inhibit investment.

40 SOCIAL DEVELOPMENT

A social security law passed in 1971 provided benefits or payments for disability, maternity, old age, unemployment, sickness, and funerals. The law applied to all establishments employing five or more people, but excluded agricultural employees, temporary employees, and domestic servants. The social insurance system was funded by employee contributions of 5% of their wages, and employer contributions of 12% of payroll. Oil companies were required to pay 25% of payroll. The retirement age was set at 60 for men and women at 55, after having worked for 20 years. Maternity benefits for employed women included 100% of salary for a period of 10 weeks. Work injury was covered and unemployment assistance was available.

Little is known about the extent of domestic violence in Iraq. Domestic abuse has historically been addressed within the family structure. As of 2011 there were both public and private shelters for women, although space was limited and service delivery was inadequate. Honor killings continue to be a serious problem in the country and are reported in every region. Legislation permits "honor" as a mitigating factor in sentencing. Women who do not wear traditional clothing are often subject to harassment.

Human rights are being addressed as the government undergoes significant transformation. The regime of Saddam Hussein was notorious for extensive human rights abuses.

41 HEALTH

After the 2003 overthrow of the Iraqi government, rebuilding the health care system has been a primary concern. Malnutrition and health problems related to lack of safe shelter and drinking water were immediate concerns. Before the war it was estimated that 93% of the population had access to health care services. Private hospitals are allowed to operate in Baghdād and other major cities. Considerable effort was made to expand medical facilities to small towns and more remote areas of the country, but these efforts have been hampered by a lack of transportation and a desire of medical personnel to live and work in Baghdād and the major cities. Before the war it was estimated that 85% of the population had access to safe drinking water and 79% had adequate sanitation. As of 2008 those numbers had declined to 79% and 73% respectively. There exists a marked disparity between urban and rural areas, with only 55% of people in rural areas having access to safe drinking water. Dentists and other specialists are almost unknown in rural districts. Child nutrition has been negatively affected by years of conflict.

According to the CIA, life expectancy in Iraq was 68 years in 2011. The country spent 3.3% of its GDP on healthcare, amount-ing to $98 per person. There were 7 physicians, 14 nurses and midwives, and 13 hospital beds per 10,000 inhabitants. The fertility rate was 3.9, while the infant mortality rate was 35 per 1,000 live births. In 2008 the maternal mortality rate, according to the World Bank, was 75 per 100,000 births. It was estimated that 69% of children were vaccinated against measles. The CIA calculated HIV/AIDS prevalence in Iraq to be less than 0.1% in 2001.

42 HOUSING

In the 20 years leading up to the 2003 Iraq War, living conditions for the vast majority of the population improved greatly. Electricity and running water were normal features of all Iraqi villages in rural areas. Mud huts in remote places were rapidly being replaced by brick dwellings. Major cities like Al Mawṣil, Al Baṣrah, and especially Baghdād had most of the amenities of modern living. Traditionally, Iraqis have lived in single family dwellings, but the government had built a number of high-rise apartments, especially in Baghdād. It had done so to control urban sprawl and to cut down on suburban service expenditures.

The 2003 invasion of Iraq by international coalition forces caused destruction and damage to a large portion of the housing sector, particularly in and around Baghdād. As a result of the civil conflict and instability that ensued with the fall of the regime, more than one million Iraqis were displaced within Iraq. According to UNHCR, hundreds of thousands of these displaced persons were living in dire conditions as of the end of 2011. Ongoing security and safety issues, destruction of their homes, and lack of access to services were the principal reasons why many of the displaced were unable to return home.

43 EDUCATION

In 2007 the World Bank estimated that 88% of age-eligible children in Iraq were enrolled in primary school. Secondary enrollment for age-eligible children stood at 43%.

Under the regime of Saddam Hussein, public education was forcibly secular and militarized, with most textbooks and other curriculum strongly based on promoting the causes of the government. The US-led invasion of Iraq beginning in 2003 and the overthrow of Hussein's regime continue to have damaging effects on the country's infrastructure. Many schools have been severely damaged or destroyed; but reconstruction efforts are being funded by a variety of international groups and governments. New developments in the post-Hussein system include the reprinting of textbooks and a greater freedom for teachers in designing and implementing curriculums. Some schools are beginning to adopt fundamental Islamic studies as a large part of their curriculum. This has caused some concern for new government officials and analysts, who fear that too much of a fundamentalist approach might lead to a new set of restrictions in academic freedom.

In general, six years of compulsory primary education has been in effect since 1978. Primary schools have provided the six-year course, at the end of which the student passes an examination to be admitted to secondary school. An intermediate secondary school program covers a three-year course of study. After this stage, students choose to attend a preparatory school or a vocational school, both of which offer three-year programs. In 2007 the student-to-teacher ratio for primary school was estimated at 24:1, while for secondary schools it was 14:1.

Education at all levels from primary to higher education has been free. Private schools are now permitted to operate. There are 20 state universities in Iraq and dozens of technical colleges and institutes. The University of Baghdād is the most important higher education institution in the country. Other universities include Al Mawşil, al-Mustansiriya, Al Başrah, and As Sulaymāniyah. In 2000 (the latest year for which data was available), the adult literacy rate was estimated at about 74.1%.

44 LIBRARIES AND MUSEUMS

Following the war in 2003, arsonists and looters ransacked the libraries and museums of Iraq, causing extensive destruction and damage and nearly eliminating some valuable historic and cultural collections of books, documents, and artwork. Various international groups have stepped forward to offer assistance in rebuilding and restocking the sites of what were Iraq's most prominent museums and libraries, but it is uncertain as to how many rare and valuable items can be recovered. The National Library and Archives in Baghdād was founded in 1961. Two noteworthy academic libraries are the Central Library of the University of Baghdād and the Central Library of the University of Al Mawşil. One of the country's outstanding libraries has been the Iraqi Museum Library (founded 1934), with modern research facilities. The Directorate of Antiquities in Baghdād houses a library as well. There are public library branches in many provincial capitals.

With the exception of the National History Research Center and Museum and the National Museum of Modern Art, museums have been under the control of the Department of the Directorate-General of Antiquities in Baghdād. One of the most outstanding collections was kept at the Iraqi Museum in Baghdād, which contained antiquities dating from the early Stone Age; however, this was one of the sites looted and damaged after the war. The Abbasid Palace Museum and the Museum of Arab Antiquities, both located in Baghdād, are housed in restored buildings from the 13th and 14th centuries, respectively.

45 MEDIA

Iraq's telecommunications system was severely disrupted by the invasion of the country in March 2003, and the continuing violence there. Although repair work has been carried out, sabotage remains a problem. Cellular service is widely available in the country's major urban areas. Mobile phone subscriptions averaged 63 per 100 people in 2009. The CIA reported that there were 1.1 million telephone landlines in Iraq. There were eight short-wave radio stations.

Internet users numbered 1 per 100 citizens in 2009. As of 2010 the country had only nine Internet hosts.

Satellite TV was watched by about 70% of television viewers in 2011. Iraqis had access to a host of foreign media, including British, French, and US. As television has become more popular, radio use has declined. *Al-Iraqiya* is the state-run public television station.

Prominent daily papers in 2011 included *Al-Sabah, Al-Mada, Al-Zaman, Al-Mashriq, Al-Dustur, and Al-Manarah. Iraq Today* is a popular English-language weekly.

The 2005 constitution guarantees freedom of speech, press, and assembly, although publicly insulting the Council of Representatives, the government, or public authorities is punishable (when authorized by the prime minister) by a fine or prison term.

46 ORGANIZATIONS

Chambers of commerce have been active in Baghdād, Al Başrah, and Al Mawşil. Cooperatives, first established in 1944, played an important social role, especially under the post-1968 Ba'ath government. There are many youth centers and sports clubs. Scouting programs are active. The General Federation of Iraqi Youth and the General Federation of Iraqi Women are government-sponsored mass organizations. The Women's Union of Kurdistan (WUK), established in 1989, works toward improving the lifestyle and social development of women by publishing educational magazines and presenting educational seminars on health, education, and legal issues. Red Crescent societies provide social services in many cities and towns.

47 TOURISM, TRAVEL, AND RECREATION

Tourism declined sharply in the 1980s during Iraq's occupation of Kuwait and the Gulf War, and has not recovered. The March 2003 attack on Iraq by US and UK forces and the subsequent fall of the government led to almost no tourist activity for many years. Prior to the political and military challenges of the 1980s, many visitors from other Arab states were pilgrims to Islamic shrines. The other principal tourist attraction is visiting the varied archeological sites. Popular forms of recreation include tennis, cricket, swimming, and squash.

The *Tourism Factbook*, published by the UN World Tourism Organization, reported 1.26 million incoming tourists to Iraq in 2009; they spent a total of $555 million. Of those incoming tourists, there were 1.2 million from South Asia.

48 FAMOUS PERSONS

The most famous kings in ancient times were Sargon (Sharrukin) of Akkad (fl. c. 2350 BC), Hammurabi of Babylon (r. 1792?–1750? BC), and Nebuchadnezzar II (Nabu-kadurri-utsur, r. 605?–560? BC) of Babylon.

Under the caliphs Harun al-Rashid (ar-Rashid ibn Muhammad al-Mahdi ibn al-Mansur al-'Abbasi, r. 786–809) and al-Mamun (abu al-'Abbas 'Abdullah al-Mamun, r. 813–33), Baghdād was the center of the Arab scholarship that translated and modified Greek philosophy. A leading figure in this movement was Hunain ibn Ishaq (d. 873), called Johannitius by Western scholastics. His contemporary was the great Arab philosopher Yaqub al-Kindi, whose catholicity assimilated both Greek philosophy and Indian mathematics. The founder of one of the four orthodox schools of Islamic law, which claims the largest number of adherents in the Muslim world, Abu Hanifa (d. 767) was also a native Iraqi. Another celebrated figure in theology, 'Abd al-Hasan al-Ash'ari (c. 913), who combated the rationalist Mu'tazila school, also lived in Baghdād; his influence still prevails in Islam. Al-Ghazali (Ghazel, d. 1111), though Persian by birth, taught at the Nizamiyah University in Baghdād; he is one of the best-known Islamic philosopher-theologians. Iraq also produced famous mystics like Hasan al-Basri (642–728) and 'Abd al-Qadir al-Jilani (1077–1166); the latter's followers are numerous among Asian Muslims, and his tomb in Baghdād draws many pilgrims.

Gen. Saddam Hussein (Husayn) al-Takriti (1937–2006), served as chairman of the Revolutionary Command Council and president of the country from 1979 until his ousting in 2003.

⁴⁹DEPENDENCIES

Iraq has no territories or colonies.

⁵⁰BIBLIOGRAPHY

Arnove, Anthony. *Iraq under Siege: The Deadly Impact of Sanctions and War*. Cambridge, MA: South End Press, 2000.

Block, Jeremy S. *Embracing the Occupiers: Conversations with the Future Leaders of Afghanistan and Iraq*. Westport, CT: Praeger Security International, 2009.

Cirincione, Joseph, Jon B. Wolfsthal, and Miriam Rajkumar. *Deadly Arsenals: Nuclear, Biological, and Chemical Threats*. 2nd ed. Washington, DC: Carnegie Endowment for International Peace, 2005.

Cordesman, Anthony H. *The War after the War: Strategic Lessons of Iraq and Afghanistan*. Washington, DC: CSIS Press, 2004.

Dalley, Stephanie. *The Legacy of Mesopotamia*. New York: Oxford University Press, 2005.

Fulanain. *The Tribes of the Marsh Arabs: The World of Haji Rikkan*. London, Eng.: Kegan Paul International, 2003.

Ghareeb, Edmund. *Historical Dictionary of Iraq*. Lanham, MD: Scarecrow, 2004.

Hiro, Dilip. *Iraq: In the Eye of the Storm*. New York: Thunder's Mouth Press/Nation Books, 2002.

Hourani, Albert Habib. *A History of the Arab Peoples*. Cambridge, MA: Belknap Press of Harvard University Press, 2002.

Hunt, Courtney. *The History of Iraq*. Westport, CT: Greenwood Press, 2005.

Iraq Investment and Business Guide: Strategic and Practical Information. Washington, DC: International Business Publications USA, 2012.

Lansford, Tom. 9/11 and the Wars in Afghanistan and Iraq: A Chronology and Reference Guide. Santa Barbara, CA: ABC-CLIO, 2012.

Natali, Denise. *The Kurds and the State: Evolving National Identity in Iraq, Turkey, and Iran*. Syracuse, NY: Syracuse University Press, 2005.

O'Sullivan, Meghan L. *Shrewd Sanctions: Statecraft and State Sponsors of Terrorism*. Washington, DC: Brookings Institution Press, 2003.

Seddon, David, ed. *A Political and Economic Dictionary of the Middle East*. Philadelphia: Routledge/Taylor and Francis, 2004.

ISRAEL

State of Israel
[Arabic] *Dawlat Israel*
[Hebrew] *Medinat Yisrael*

CAPITAL: Jerusalem (Yerushalayim, Al-Quds)

FLAG: The flag, which was adopted at the First Zionist Congress in 1897, consists of a blue six-pointed Shield of David (Magen David) centered between two blue horizontal stripes on a white field.

ANTHEM: *Hatikvah (The Hope).*

MONETARY UNIT: The new Israeli shekel (ILS), a paper currency of 100 new agorot, replaced the shekel at a rate of 1,000 to 1 in 1985; the shekel replaced the Israeli pound in 1980 at the rate of 10 pounds per shekel. There are coins of 5, 10, and 50 agora, 1 and 5 shekels and notes of 10, 50, 100, and 200 shekels. ILS1 = US$0.28 (or US$1 = ILS3.63) as of 2011. US dollars are commonly used as a unit of account and medium for long-term saving.

WEIGHTS AND MEASURES: The metric system is the legal standard, but some local units are used, notably the dunam (equivalent to 1,000 square meters, or about 0.25 acre).

HOLIDAYS: Israel officially uses both the Gregorian and the complex Jewish lunisolar calendars, but the latter determines the occurrence of national holidays: Rosh Hashanah (New Year), September or October; Yom Kippur (Day of Atonement), September or October; Sukkot (Tabernacles), September or October; Simchat Torah (Rejoicing in the Law), September or October; Pesach (Passover), March or April; Independence Day, April or May; and Shavuot (Pentecost), May or June. All Jewish holidays, as well as the Jewish Sabbath (Friday/Saturday), begin just before sundown and end at nightfall 24 hours later. Muslim, Christian, and Druze holidays are observed by the respective minorities.

TIME: 2 p.m. = noon GMT.

¹LOCATION, SIZE, AND EXTENT

Situated in southwestern Asia along the eastern end of the Mediterranean Sea, Israel claims an area of 21,643 sq km (8,357 sq mi), which makes it slightly smaller than New Jersey. Israel extends about 320 km (200 mi) N–S and 110 km (70 mi) E–W. At its narrowest point, just north of Tel Aviv-Yafo, it is 19 km (12 mi) across. Israel is bordered on the N by Lebanon, on the E by Syria and Jordan, on the S by the Gulf of Aqaba (Gulf of Eilat), on the SW by Egypt, and on the W by the Mediterranean Sea.

The total land boundary length is 1,017 km (632 mi), and the coastline is 273 km (170 mi). Israel's area includes the Golan Heights (1,176 sq km/454 sq mi), captured from Syria during the Six-Day War of 1967. The eastern section of Jerusalem, which was also captured in 1967, was annexed shortly thereafter. The official American position is that the status of Jerusalem must be settled in final negotiations. The Golan Heights were annexed on 14 December 1981; this annexation (technically described as the extension of Israeli "law, jurisdiction, and administration" to the region) was condemned by Syria and by unanimous resolution of the UN Security Council. The Labor Government in 1984 indicated that some (possibly all) of the Golan could be returned to Syria in a peace agreement. Other territories captured in 1967 and classified as administered territories were the West Bank (Judea and Samaria), 5,878 sq km (2,270 sq mi), and the Gaza Strip, 362 sq km (140 sq mi). The Sinai Peninsula, taken from Egypt, was restored to Egyptian sovereignty in 1983 in accordance with a 1979 peace treaty. In 1994, Israel returned small pockets of some of the land captured in the war to be administered in a less-than-totally-sovereign fashion by the Palestinian Authority (PA).Gaza City was transferred to the PA in 1993. Six more West Bank cities were included in Palestinian control in 1997. All seven West Bank cities were reoccupied by Israel in 2002, but Jericho was returned to the Palestinians in 2005. PA security forces police much of the West Bank at present.

Israeli troops and all 5,000 remaining Jewish settlers were unilaterally withdrawn from the Gaza Strip in 2003. The weak PA authority was defeated by Hamas in 2006, and the PA organization was forced out. Hamas, an Islamist movement, officially rejects the legitimacy of Israel and any possibility of a peaceful settlement with the "Zionists." For this reason, its authority is not recognized by the United States or the European Union. Egypt, which ruled Gaza from 1948 to 1967, blockaded Gaza until the overthrow of the Mubarak regime in 2011. Israel continues its naval blockade and selective land closings to date.

²TOPOGRAPHY

The country is divided into three major longitudinal strips: the coastal plain, which follows the Mediterranean shoreline in a southward widening band; the hill region, embracing the hills of Galilee in the north, Samaria and Judea in the center, and the Negev in the south; and the Jordan Valley. Except for the Bay of Acre, the sandy coastline is not indented for its entire length. The hill region, averaging 610 m (2,000 ft) in elevation, reaches its highest point at Mt. Meron (1,208 m/3,963 ft). South of the Judean hills, the Negev desert, marked by cliffs and craters and covering about half the total area of Israel proper, extends down to the Gulf of Aqaba on the Red Sea. The Jordan River, forming the border between Israel (including the West Bank) and Jordan, links the only bodies of water in the country, the Sea of Galilee (Yam Kinneret) and the heavily saline Dead Sea (Yam ha-Melah), which, at 408 m (1,339 ft) below sea level, is the lowest point on the earth's surface.

3 CLIMATE

Although climatic conditions are varied across the country, the climate is generally temperate. The coldest month is January; the hottest, August. In winter, snow occasionally falls in the hills, where January temperatures normally fluctuate between 4–10°C (40–50°F) and August temperatures between 18–29°C (65–85°F). On the coastal plain, sea breezes temper the weather all year round, with temperature variations ranging from 8–18°C (47–65°F) in January and 21–29°C (70–85°F) in August. In the south, at Eilat, January temperatures range between 10–21°C (50–70°F) and may reach 49°C (120°F) in August. The rainy season lasts from October until April, with rainfall averaging 118 cm (44 in) annually in the Upper Galilee and only 2 cm (0.8 in) at Eilat, although dewfall gives the south another several inches of water every year.

4 FLORA AND FAUNA

The Bible (Deuteronomy 8:8) describes the country as "a land of wheat and barley, of vines, and figs, pomegranates, a land of olive trees and honey." The original forests, evergreen and maquis, were largely destroyed under Turkish rule, but some 200 million new trees have been planted during this century in a major reforestation program sponsored by the Jewish National Fund. Vegetation cover is thin except in the coastal plain, where conditions are favorable to the cultivation of citrus fruit, and in the Jordan Valley with its plantations of tropical fruit. Among surviving animals, jackals and hyenas remain fairly numerous. There are wild boars in the Lake Hula region. With the growth of vegetation and water supplies, bird life and deer have increased.

The World Resources Institute estimates that there are 2,317 plant species in Israel. In addition, Israel is home to 115 mammal species, 534 bird species, 99 reptile species, and 8 amphibian species. These calculations reflect the total number of distinct species now found in the country.

According to a 2011 report issued by the International Union for Conservation of Nature and Natural Resources (IUCN), threatened species included 15 types of mammals, 13 species of birds, 9 types of reptiles, 36 species of fish, 7 types of mollusks, and 53 species of other invertebrates. Endangered species included the northern bald ibis, South Arabian leopard, Saudi Arabian dorcas gazelle, and three species of sea turtles. The Mediterranean monk seal, cheetah, Barbary sheep, and Persian fallow deer became extinct in the 1980s. The Israel painted frog and Syrian wild ass have also become extinct.

5 ENVIRONMENT

Water pollution and adequate water supply are major environmental issues in Israel. Industrial and agricultural chemicals threaten the nation's already depleted water supply. Afforestation efforts, especially since 1948, have helped to conserve the country's water resources and prevent soil erosion. Israel has reclaimed much of the Negev for agricultural purposes by means of large irrigation projects, thereby stopping the desertification process that had been depleting the land for nearly 2,000 years. Principal environmental responsibility is vested in the Environmental Protection Service of the Ministry of the Interior. The World Resources Institute reported that Israel had designated 337,100 hectares (832,992 acres) of land for protection as of 2006.

Water resources totaled 1.7 cu km (.408 cu mi) while water usage was 2.05 cu km (.492 cu mi) per year. Domestic water usage accounted for 36% of total usage, industrial for 6%, and agricultural for 58%, according to the Food and Agriculture Organization (FAO) in 2007. Per capita water usage totaled 305 cu m (10,771 cu ft) per year.

Air pollution from industrial sources, oil facilities, and vehicles is another significant environmental problem. The United Nations (UN) reported in 2008 that carbon dioxide emissions in Israel totaled 66,685 kilotons; these emissions have increased over the last two decades at the same rate as the gross domestic product (GDP).

6 POPULATION

The US Central Intelligence Agency (CIA) estimates the population of Israel in 2012 to be 7,590,758. This placed Israel at number 97 in population among the nations of the world. In 2010 Jewish population on the West Bank was estimated at somewhat over 311,000. Israel has about 200,000 Bedouin, a nomadic people now being settled in urban locations, mostly in the Negev region. There are also 40,000 Bedouin on the West Bank and many more in surrounding countries. In 2011, approximately 10.1% of the Israeli population was over 65 years of age, with another 27.6% under 15 years of age. The median age in Israel was 29.4 years. There were nearly 1.00 males for every female in the country. The population's annual rate of change was 1.54% in 2012. The projected population for the year 2025 was 9,400,000. Population density in Israel was calculated at 360 people per sq km (932 people per sq mi).

The UN estimated that 92% of Israel's population lived in urban areas and that urban populations had an annual rate of change of 1.5%. The largest urban areas are Tel Aviv-Yafo, 3.2 million; Haifa, 1 million; and Jerusalem, 768,000.

7 MIGRATION

Israel's declaration of independence publicly opened the state "to the immigration of Jews from all countries of their dispersion," and the 1950 Law of Return granted every returning Jew the right to automatic citizenship. The Nationality Law specifies other ways–including birth, residence, and naturalization–by which Israeli citizenship may be acquired. In 1948, 65% of Israel's Jewish population consisted of immigrants; many of these 463,000 immigrant Jews had fled from persecution in Russia and, especially during the Nazi period, from Central and Eastern Europe. In the years 1948–92, Israel took in 2,242,500 Jewish immigrants. During 1948–51, the flow was at its heaviest, averaging 171,685 per year, about evenly divided between Eastern European Jewish refugees and Oriental Jews from ancient centers of the Arab world. In the years 1952–56, most immigrants came from French North Africa; in 1957–58, there was a renewed inflow from Eastern Europe. After a lull in 1959–60, the flow of immigrants was renewed, reaching substantial proportions by 1963, when 64,364 Jews arrived. Immigration fell to an annual average of 20,561 people for 1965–68, then rose to an average of 43,258 per year for 1969–74, influenced by Israel's successful wars. Migration then declined to an average of 24,965 for 1975–79 and further to an average of 15,383 for 1980–89. Since 1990, with the collapse of the Soviet Union and its Warsaw Pact allies, immigration boomed. As of March 1995, around 525,000 immigrants had arrived in Israel, mostly from the former Soviet Union; this was the largest wave of immigration since Israel's independence.

In 1984–85, some 10,000 Ethiopian Jews, victims of famine, were airlifted to Israel via Sudan. In 1991, 14,000 more Ethiopian Jews immigrated thanks to the Operation Solomon airlift. In November 2010, the Israeli cabinet approved a plan to allow nearly 8,000 members of the Ethiopian Falash Mura community to emigrate to Israel. The Falash Mura are part of a Jewish community that once traced its roots to the biblical King Solomon. In the 19th century, most of the community was forced to convert to Christianity. As a result, in the 1980s and 1990s, as some Ethiopian Jews were welcomed into Israel under the Law of Return, members of the Falash Mura were deemed ineligible under the law because they were generally unable to prove they were Jewish. However, the Falash Mura have lived in extremely poor conditions in northern Ethiopia for many years. Recognizing that the interpretation of the law was perpetuating a humanitarian crisis, the Israeli cabinet agreed to a plan that would allow thousands of the community to go to Israel between 2010 and 2013.

The proportion of Jewish immigrants from Europe, the USSR, and North America varied during the 1960s, but it rose from 40.4% in 1968 to 97.3% in 1990. In 1992, the Jewish immigrant population was 39.4% of all Israeli Jews and 31.8% of all Israelis. By 2011, the total number of foreign-born immigrants living in Israel was 2.94 million. Estimates of Israel's net migration rate, carried out by the CIA in 2012, amounted to 1.94 migrants per 1,000 citizens.

A certain amount of emigration has always taken place, but the pace increased after 1975. In a typical year after 1980, about 10,000 Israelis were added to the number who had been away continuously for more than four years. The Central Bureau of Statistics has estimated that 260,000 more Israelis left the country than returned for a year or more. By 2011 the number of emigrants living abroad reached 1.02 million. From 1967 to 1992, Israel's government established 142 settlements in the occupied territories; about 130,000 Jews were living there by 1995, and, by 2011, the number had swelled to about 300,000, mostly close to Jerusalem.

Considerable Arab migration has also taken place since the late 19th century, including an apparent wave of Arab immigration into Palestine between World War I and World War II. During the 1948 war, there was a massive flight of an estimated 800,000 Palestinians. The UN Relief and Works Agency for Palestine Refugees in the Near East (UNRWA) was established in 1949 to provide assistance to the Palestinian Refugees of the ongoing Arab-Israeli conflicts. This mission, which was meant to be temporary,

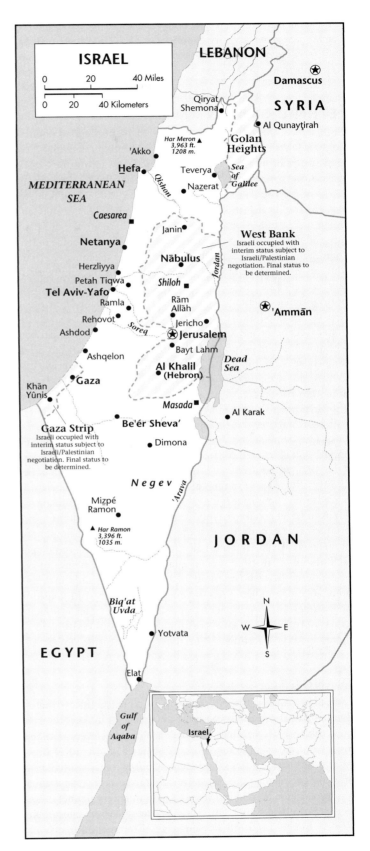

LOCATION: 29°29′ to 33°17′N; 34°16′ to 35°41′E. TERRITORIAL SEA LIMIT: 6 miles.

has been continually renewed; it continued during 2011. Ten nations serve on the advisory commission for UNRWA. As of 2011, there were registered 4.9 million Palestinian refugees and their descendants living in the areas around Israel under the mandate of UNRWA. Of these, about 40% reside in the West Bank and Gaza.

8 ETHNIC GROUPS

Estimates for 2004 indicate that about 76.4% of the total population was Jewish, with Israel-born Jews accounting for about 67.1% and European and American-born Jews accounting for 22.6%. African-born Jews made up 5.9% and Asian-born 4.2%. About 23.6% of the population was non-Jewish, mostly 1.37 million Arabs. The traditional ritual division of Jews into Ashkenazim (Central and East Europeans) and Sephardim (Iberian Jews and their descendants) is still given formal recognition in the choice of two chief rabbis, one for each community. A more meaningful ethnic division, however, would be that between Occidentals and Orientals (now also called Sephardim or Mizrachim). Including those born in Israel, Oriental Jews are in the majority. Many of them believe their group (known as 'adot ha-Mizrach) to have been educationally, economically, and socially disadvantaged by comparison with the Occidentals, particularly during the early years but up to the present. The minority non-Jewish population is overwhelmingly Arabic-speaking, but Israel's minorities include several small non-Arab national groups, such as Armenians and Circassians. The government of Israel has declared its intention to strive for both legal and practical equality between the Arab and Jewish sectors of the population. Israel's Arab citizens do not share fully in opportunities granted to, and levies imposed on, Jewish citizens. Arabs are not required to do military service, a condition for certain benefits. As an example of discrimination, Arab citizens are barred from some Jewish neighborhoods. The living standards of Arabs in Israel compare favorably with those of Arabs in non-oil-producing Arab countries, but they are considerably below those of the Jewish majority, especially the Occidentals. Arab municipal facilities are distinctly lower in quality. As a consequence of repeated wars between Israel and its Arab neighbors and the development of Palestinian Arab nationalism and terrorism, tensions between Jews and Arabs are a fact of daily life in Israel, especially in the West Bank and Gaza Strip. Many Israeli Arabs now identify themselves as "Palestinian." The rights of citizenship do not extend to Arabs in the administered territories.

9 LANGUAGES

The official languages are Hebrew and Arabic, the former being dominant. Hebrew is a west Semitic language of most of the Hebrew Bible (Old Testament). Modern Hebrew has been modified by absorption of elements from all historical forms of Hebrew and by development over the years, including a major admixture of west European languages, as well as some Arabic expressions. Modern Arabic is used by Arabs in parliamentary deliberations, in pleadings before the courts, and in dealings with governmental departments, and it is the language of instruction in schools for Arab children. English is taught in all secondary schools and, along with Hebrew, is commonly used in foreign business correspondence and in advertising and labeling. Coins, postage stamps,

and bank notes bear inscriptions in Hebrew, Arabic, and Latin characters.

10 RELIGIONS

The land that is now Israel (which the Romans called Judea and then Palestine) is the cradle of two of the world's great religions, Judaism and Christianity. Although the Declaration of Independence proclaims Israel as "the Jewish state," there is no official religion in Israel. Freedom of religion is guaranteed by the Basic Law on Human Dignity and Liberty, although occasional missionary efforts considered to violate public order are discouraged. While unrecognized groups were not hindered from practicing their religious beliefs, legally recognized groups enjoy some express benefits.

In the Hebrew Scriptures, Jewish history begins with Abraham's journey from Mesopotamia to Canaan, to which the descendants of Abraham would later return after their deliverance by Moses from bondage in Egypt. Jerusalem is the historical site of the First Temple, built by Solomon in the 10th century BC and destroyed by the Babylonians in 586 BC. The Second Temple was built about 70 years later and sacked by the Romans in AD 70.

Present-day Israel is the only country where Judaism is the majority religion, which is professed by 75.6% of the population (as of 2008). About 44% of the Jewish population describe themselves as secular or non-religious Jews. About 7% are Haredi (ultra-Orthodox) and about 10% are Orthodox, followers of the rabbinic interpretations of the Law (halacha). Supreme religious authority in the Jewish community is vested in the chief rabbinate, with Ashkenazim and Sephardim each having a chief rabbi and local clergy. There are also a number of adherents who claim affiliation with Conservative, Reform, and Reconstructionist branches of Judaism, but these are not officially recognized. There are about 10,000 Messianic Jews.

Belief in the life, teachings, crucifixion, and resurrection of Jesus of Nazareth (who, according to the Christian Scriptures, actually preached in the Second Temple) is the basis of the Christian religion. Spread by the immediate followers of Jesus and others, Christianity developed within three centuries from a messianic and apocalyptic Jewish sect to the established religion of the Roman Empire under the emperor Constantine. Israel's Christians are largely Greek Catholic or Greek (or Russian) Orthodox, but there are also Roman Catholics, Armenian Catholics, and Syrian Catholics and Syrian Orthodox, Chaldeans (Uniate Catholics), Maronites, and Protestants such as the Evangelical Episcopal Church. There is a small community of Jehovah's Witnesses. There are about 50,000 Christians in the West Bank and east Jerusalem and up to 3,000 Christians in the Gaza Strip.

Jerusalem is also holy to Islam; the Dome of the Rock mosque marks the site where, in Muslim tradition, Muhammad rose into heaven. Of the non-Jewish population, 16.5% are Muslims (primarily Sunni), 2.1% are Christians, and 1.7% are Druze. Most of the Muslims are Arabs. In the occupied territories under the jurisdiction of the Palestinian Authority, the Basic Law places Islam as the official religion and the principles of Shari'ah (Islamic law) as the basis for all legislation. About 98% of the Palestinian residents in the occupied territories are Sunni Muslims. The Druzes, who split away from Islam in the 11th century, have the status of a separate religious community. The Baha'i world faith is centered in Haifa.

The Ministry of Religious Affairs assists institutions of every affiliation and contributes to the preservation and repair of their holy shrines, which are protected by the government and made accessible to pilgrims. Nevertheless, relations between Muslims and Christians, Muslims and Jews, and secular and religious Jews have often been strained, as have those among different Christian sects, especially concerning the use of common shrines, such as the Church of the Holy Sepulchre in Jerusalem.

11 TRANSPORTATION

Railways built during pre-state times, buses, and shared taxis formerly constituted the principal means of passenger transportation up to the 1950s. Private car ownership began to increase with prosperity and nearly tripled during the 1970s. With the building in 1957 of a highway extension from Beersheva to Eilat, the Red Sea was linked to the Mediterranean.

By 2009, according to CIA reports, Israel had a total of 18,290 km (11,365 mi) of roads, all paved. There are now more than 1.9 million passenger cars (313 vehicles per 1,000 people) in the country. Israel's railroads extend for 1,005 km (624 mi).

There are also 48 airports, most of them small, which transported 4.61 million passengers in 2009, according to the World Bank. There also several heliports. The largest is the Ben Gurion International Airport, east of Tel Aviv, which recently opened Terminal One for domestic passengers and another for international visitors. From there and from Eilat's J. Hozman airport, 48,000 carrier departures were registered to worldwide destinations in 2009 with 4.6 million passengers. Air freight totaled 985 million tons. Of this traffic, shortly after Israel became a nation in 1948, Israel Airlines (El Al) alone accounted for 17 billion passenger-km and 606 million tons of cargo. Inland Airlines (Arkia) provides domestic service and is almost entirely owned by the government.

In 2008, Israel had 11 merchant vessels of 1,000 gross registered tonnage (GRT) or more. The long-established Haifa port can berth large passenger liners and has a 10,000-ton floating dock, though since the early 1980s Ashdod (south of Tel Aviv) has outstripped Haifa in cargo handled. Eilat is also a seaport with full-freight services. In 2009, Israeli ports handled 817,000 twenty-foot equivalents (TEU) of containers.

12 HISTORY

Archaeologists have found remains of human habitation in the land of Israel that are at least 100,000 years old. The world's earliest known city was Jericho, on the present-day West Bank, built about 7000 BC. The formative period of Israel began in approximately 1800 BC, when the "Hebrew" nomads entered Canaan, and resumed in approximately 1250 BC, during the reign of Ramses II (d. 1224 BC), when Israelite tribes returned to Egyptian-dominated Canaan after a period of residence in Egypt's heartland. At various times, the Israelites were led by patriarchs, judges, kings, prophets, and scribes. The first ancient kingdom of Israel was united by Saul and David in the early 10th century and became a strong Near Eastern power under Solomon (d. 922 BC), but much of the land was conquered by Assyrians in the eighth century, followed by Babylonians (or Chaldeans), Persians, and Saleucid (Syrian) Greeks. An independent Israelite kingdom existed after 168

BC, following the Maccabean revolt, but Rome took control during the next century. The ancient period neared its end in AD 70, when the Roman legions conquered Jerusalem after an unsuccessful Jewish zealot revolt and destroyed the Temple. Jewish authority ended in AD 135, when the Roman Empire exiled most Jews after another unsuccessful revolt, this time led by Simon Bar-Kokhba, and renamed the region Syria Palaestina. During the next five centuries, there were successive waves of Byzantine and Persian conquerors. According to historian Martin Gilbert, however, Jews still constituted the main settled population of Palestine from about 1000 BC until the Arab conquest in AD 636.

During the next 1,300 years, Arabs, Crusaders, Mongols, Turks, and Britons came to rule the area. Owing to forced emigration, most Jews remained in dispersion, where the pious nourished messianic hopes for an eventual return to Zion. However, Jews in varying numbers continued to live in Palestine throughout these years, mainly in the cities of Safed, Tiberias, Hebron, and Jerusalem—considered "the four holy cities of Judaism." There, important works of religious literature were composed and promulgated to world Jewry. From 1882 on (the "first Aliya"), more Jews began migration to Palestine to escape anti-Semitism in Europe, as well as in North Africa and the Middle East. During the second half of the 19th century, there were perhaps half a million total inhabitants of the land, much of which was barren, according to diplomatic sources and the writer Mark Twain, who visited northern Israel in 1867. It is estimated that by 1900, about 78,000 Jews were concentrated in certain parts of Turkish-ruled Palestine (less than 1% of the world Jewish population), compared with some 650,000 non-Jews, mostly Arabs.

Modern Zionism, the movement for the reestablishment of a Jewish state, dates from the late 19th century, with small-scale settlements by Russian and Romanian Jews on lands purchased by funds from Western European and US donors. The movement received impetus from the founding of the World Zionist Organization in Basel, Switzerland, in 1897 under the leadership of Theodor Herzl. Zionist hopes for a Jewish national homeland in Palestine were greatly bolstered when the British government pledged its support for this goal in the Balfour Declaration of 1917. This promise was subsequently incorporated in 1922 into the League of Nations mandate over Palestine (originally including Transjordan, now the Kingdom of Jordan, but cut off by Britain). Under the mandate, the Jewish community grew from 85,000 to 650,000, largely through immigration, on lands purchased from Arab owners. This growth was attended by rising hostility from the Arab community, which felt its majority status threatened by the Jewish influx. In 1939, shortly before the outbreak of World War II, the British mandatory authorities issued a White Paper that decreed severe restrictions on Jewish immigration and a virtual freezing of land purchase and settlement. Armed Jewish resistance to this policy, as well as growing international backing for the establishment of a Jewish state as a haven for the survivors of the Nazi Holocaust, finally persuaded the British government to relinquish the mandate after the war. As the post-war struggle for access to Jerusalem unfolded, many Arab villagers in Deir Yassin and elsewhere were killed by irregular Jewish militias in disputed circumstances.

On 29 November 1947, the UN General Assembly adopted a plan to partition Palestine into two economically united but politically sovereign states, one Jewish and the other Arab, with Jerusalem as an international city. The Arabs of Palestine, aided by brethren across the frontiers, at once rose up in arms to thwart partition. The Jews of Palestine accepted the plan; on 14 May 1948, the last day of the mandate, they proclaimed the formation of the State of Israel. The next day, the Arab League states—Egypt, Iraq, Jordan, Lebanon, Saudi Arabia, and Syria—launched a concerted armed attack. There followed a mass flight of hundreds of thousands of Palestinian Arabs abroad, partly at the urging of foreign Arab leaders and partly owing to actions of Israeli forces. The war left Israel in possession of a much larger territory than that awarded the Jews under the UN partition plan. The planned Arab state failed to materialize, as Jordan annexed the West Bank and east Jerusalem. Meanwhile, the Palestinian refugees were resettled in camps on both banks of the Jordan River, in the Gaza Strip (then under Egyptian administration), in southern Lebanon, and in Syria.

Armistice agreements concluded in 1949, which set a temporary "green line" border for Israel, failed to provide the contemplated transition to peace. Sporadic Arab incursions along the borders were answered by Israeli reprisals. Tensions were exacerbated by Arab economic boycotts and by Egypt's nationalization of the Suez Canal on 26 July 1956. On 29 October 1956, Israel (with British and French support) invaded Egypt and soon gained control of the Gaza Strip and the Sinai Peninsula. Fighting ended on 4 November, with Israel, under pressure from the United States's Eisenhower Administration, withdrawing from occupied areas by March 1957 to borders consistent with its military position at the end of the 1948 war. A UN Emergency Force (UNEF) patrolled the armistice line between Gaza and Sinai.

Violations by both sides of the armistice lines persisted, however, and in May 1967, Gamal Abdel Nasser's Egypt, fearing a rumored Israeli attack on its ally Syria, moved armaments and troops into the Sinai, ordered withdrawal of UNEF personnel from the armistice line, and closed the Strait of Tiran to Israeli shipping. On 5 June, Israel attacked Egypt, Syria, and Jordan (which had been drawn into the fighting). By 11 June, Israel had scored a decisive victory in the "Six-Day War" and took control of the entire Sinai peninsula, the Gaza Strip, the Golan Heights, the West Bank, and east Jerusalem, including the Jewish Quarter, with the famous "wailing wall" of the Temple Mount. The UN Security Council on 22 November unanimously adopted UK-sponsored Resolution 242, calling for establishment of a just and lasting peace in the Middle East, withdrawal of Israeli armed forces from territories occupied during the war, and acknowledgment of the "sovereignty, territorial integrity, and political independence of every State in the area and their right to live in peace within secure and recognized boundaries free from threats or acts of force." Israel indicated that return of captured territories would have to be part of a general settlement guaranteeing peace. Soon, however, the Israeli government began Jewish settlement in all these areas. Encouraged by later nationalist-liberal Likud governments, by 1997, there were some 160,000 settlers in the occupied territories.

Serious shooting incidents between Egypt and Israel resumed in June 1969, following Egypt's declaration of a war of attrition against Israel. In response to a US peace initiative, a cease-fire took effect in August 1970, but tensions continued, and Palestinian Arab militants mounted an international campaign of terror-

ism, highlighted in September 1972 by the kidnap and murder of Israeli athletes at the Olympic Games in Munich, Germany.

On 6 October 1973, during Yom Kippur, Egypt and Syria simultaneously attacked Israeli-held territory in the Sinai Peninsula and the Golan Heights. The Arabs won initial victories, but by 24 October, when a UN cease-fire took effect, the Israelis had crossed the Suez Canal westward and were 101 km (63 mi) from Cairo and about 27 km (17 mi) from Damascus. Under the impetus of the "shuttle diplomacy" exercised by US Secretary of State Henry Kissinger, formal first-stage disengagement agreements were signed with Egypt on 18 January 1974 and with Syria on 31 May 1974. On 4 September 1975, a second-stage disengagement pact was signed in Geneva, under which Israel relinquished some territory in the Sinai (including two oil fields) in return for Egyptian declarations of peaceful intent, free passage of nonmilitary cargoes to and from Israel through the Suez Canal, and the stationing of US civilians to monitor early warning systems.

On June 27, 1976, Palestinian and German terrorists attacked an Air France plane and forced it to land at the Entebbe Airport in Uganda. Of 100 hostages, 83 were Israelis. After six days, an elite team of the Israel Defense Force (IDF) freed them with the loss of three passengers and one soldier, Yonathan Netanyahu, older brother of Israel's future prime minister.

The 30-year cycle of Egyptian-Israeli hostilities was broken in November 1977, when Egyptian President Anwar al-Sadat (as-Sadat) paid a visit to Jerusalem on 19–21 November 1977 and addressed Israel's parliament. There, he affirmed Israel's right to exist as a nation, thereby laying the basis for a negotiated peace. In September 1978, at a summit conference mediated by US president Jimmy Carter at Camp David, Maryland, Israeli prime minister Menachem Begin and Sadat agreed on the general framework for a peace treaty eventually signed in Washington, DC, on 26 March 1979. The treaty provided for the withdrawal of Israeli forces from Sinai over a three-year period and for further negotiations concerning autonomy and future status of Arab residents of the West Bank and the Gaza Strip still under Israeli occupation. Israel withdrew from the Sinai oil fields within a year and from the remainder of Sinai by 25 April 1982. However, the two countries failed to reach agreement on Palestinian autonomy in the West Bank and Gaza, and Israel continued to establish Jewish settlements in the West Bank despite Egyptian protests. Sadat was assassinated by Muslim fundamentalists on 6 October 1981. Israel's relations remained tense with other Arab countries, however, which had ostracized Egypt for signing the peace accord.

Hostilities between Israel and the Palestine Liberation Organization (PLO) and Syria continued. In March 1978, Israel (which had long been supporting Lebanese Christian militias against the Palestine Liberation Organization and its Muslim backers) sent troops into southern Lebanon to destroy PLO bases in retaliation for a Palestinian terrorist attack. Israel withdrew under US pressure. In April 1981, Israeli and Syrian forces directly confronted each other in Lebanon; Israeli jets shot down two Syrian helicopters over Lebanese territory, and Syria responded by deploying Soviet-made antiaircraft missiles in the Bekaa (Biqa') Valley, which Syria had been occupying since 1976. On 7 June 1981, Israeli warplanes struck and disabled an Iraqi nuclear reactor under construction near Baghdād; the Israeli government asserted that the reactor could be employed to produce nuclear bombs for use against Israel. These uses of force reached a climax in early June 1982, when Israel launched a full-scale invasion of southern Lebanon, citing continued PLO shelling of the north and terrorist acts elsewhere. An estimated 90,000 troops rapidly destroyed PLO bases within a 40 km (25 mi) zone north of the Israeli border, captured the coastal towns of Tyre (Sur) and Sidon (Sayda), and then moved on to bomb and encircle Beirut by 14 June, trapping the main force of PLO fighters in the Lebanese capital and causing massive casualties and destruction. Meanwhile, Israeli warplanes destroyed Syria's Soviet-built missile batteries in the Bekaa Valley—the announced objective of the invasion—and dozens of Soviet-supplied jets. A negotiated cease-fire was arranged by US envoy Philip Habib on 25 June, allowing more than 14,000 Palestinian and Syrian fighters to evacuate Beirut in late August and relocate elsewhere. A multinational peacekeeping force of British, French, Italian, and US military personnel was stationed in the Beirut area. A UNIFIL mission, authorized in 1978 to supervise the withdrawal of Israeli troops and to aid the Lebanese government, remains in southern Lebanon. It now has the additional mission of helping Lebanese forces control the south of the country.

Within Israel, the lethal and indecisive Lebanese war was divisive, leading to protest rallies against the Begin government. After Israeli troops moved into West Beirut in the wake of the assassination of Lebanese President Bashir Gemayel, Christian militiamen were allowed to "mop up" remaining resistance in the Palestinian refugee camps of Sabra and Shatila. An Israeli investigating commission determined that some of Israel's civilian and military leaders were indirectly responsible for the massacres. This finding and further protests led to the resignation of Ariel Sharon as defense minister. Subsequent Israeli attempts to extricate its occupying forces from Lebanon by negotiating an agreement for the withdrawal of all foreign forces were rejected by Syria. In September, Israel pulled back its forces from the Shuf Mountains, east of Beirut, to south of the Litani River. In 1985, withdrawal from southern Lebanon took place in stages over six months, punctuated by terrorist acts of Shi'a Muslim militants against departing Israeli troops. Arrests and detention of hundreds of Lebanese resulted. Negotiations over a Trans World Airlines (TWA) jetliner hijacked en route from Athens to Rome by Shi'a militants in June 1985 led to gradual release by Israel of its Shi'a prisoners. In 1986, troubles continued despite the continued occupation of a swath of southern Lebanon, which Israel termed a "security zone," as Shi'a militants and Palestinian guerrillas had continued to infiltrate the border to launch attacks.

Continual war drained Israel's economy, already suffering from hyperinflation and huge foreign-exchange deficits. Prime Minister Menachem Begin resigned because of failing health in the autumn of 1983 and was replaced by the conservative nationalist Yitzhak Shamir. After inconclusive elections in 1984, Shamir was replaced on a rotational basis by Labor Party leader Shimon Peres. In 1986, a ground-breaking summit took place when Prime Minister Peres traveled to Morocco for two days of secret talks with King Hassan II. In that year, Israel also improved relations with Egypt when Prime Minister Peres conferred with Egypt's President Hosni Mubarak in the first meeting of the two nations since 1981. Shamir replaced Peres as prime minister in October 1986. In December 1987, Palestinians in Gaza began what became a long series of stone-throwing riots against Israeli troops in the occupied territories. In this uprising (or *intifada* in Arabic), well over 1,000 Palestinians were killed. Israeli use of lethal force, curfews, deportations, destruction of houses, and 10,000 detentions failed to stop the demonstrations while producing criticism abroad and anxiety at home. Elections were again held in November 1988, leading to a coalition government of the Labor and Likud parties. During the Gulf War of 1991, Israel was hit by Iraqi missile attacks, demonstrating for some the state's vulnerability and need to move toward peace with the Arabs. Prime Minister Shamir, who opposed the return of occupied territory, reluctantly accepted a United States and Russian invitation to direct peace talks in Madrid in October 1991.

These and subsequent negotiations produced few results until 1992, when Labor edged Likud in elections and was able to form a government supported by left wing and religious parties. Yitzhak Rabin, a former general, became prime minister with Shimon Peres as foreign minister. Both were publicly committed to reaching peace agreements with Israel's remaining Arab antagonists. Israeli and Palestinian representatives met secretly in Oslo to work out a peace agreement involving mutual recognition and transfer of authority in Gaza and Jericho to interim Palestinian rule with the final status of a Palestinian entity to be resolved in five years. Just prior to the signing, PLO leader Yasser Arafat sent Prime Minister Yitzhak Rabin a letter in which the Palestinian leader wrote that the PLO "recognizes the right of the State of Israel to exist in peace and security." The Oslo Accords were signed at the White House in Washington on 13 September 1993. Promises of international aid for the new Palestinian units poured in. The agreement was opposed by extremists on both sides. A massacre of 30 Muslims at prayer in the Hebron mosque on 25 February 1994 by a militant Israeli settler further inflamed the situation. After a delay of several months, however, a withdrawal of Israeli forces from certain sectors and establishment of Palestinian self-rule took place on 18 May 1994.

In November 1995, an extremist Israeli assassinated Prime Minister Yitzhak Rabin in retaliation for slowing Jewish settlement in the occupied territories and for his generally dovish policy toward the PLO. The nation then entered into a tumultuous period as Shimon Peres, Rabin's co-prime minister, took control of the government. Peres was not as popular as Rabin had been, and, in response to civil protest, he called for early elections, which were held in May 1996. For the first time, Israelis were given the opportunity to elect their prime minister directly. Peres, Likud, and Benjamin Netanyahu fought a bitter campaign, focusing mainly on the status of the occupied territories and the threat of terrorism from radical Palestinians. After a close race, Benjamin Netanyahu emerged as Israel's prime minister, with his Likud party winning a slight majority in coalition with a range of right-wing parties in the Knesset. Netanyahu immediately took a tough stance on the occupied territories, increasing the construction of Jewish settlements and enraging the Palestinians and the international community. Though six West Bank cities had been turned over to the Palestinian Authority, Israel balked at turning over control of Hebron even though it had previously agreed to do so. A 1997 Hebron Protocol split the city between Palestinian rule in one part of it and Israeli rule in the remaining 20% to guarantee the security of settlers living in Jewish enclaves. All seven of the major cities controlled by the Palestinian Authority were eventually reoccupied by Israel in 2002. As expected, progress in the Middle East peace process slowed under Netanyahu. Hostilities between Palestinians and Israeli soldiers in the fall of 1996, following the opening of a tunnel in the Old City of Jerusalem, were the worst to occur since the days of the *intifada*. In 1997 and 1998, peace talks stalled over the terms of Israeli withdrawal from the West Bank. A new agreement, the Wye Memorandum, was reached at an October 1998 meeting in the United States between Netanyahu, Yasser Arafat, and US President Bill Clinton. It set up a timetable for Israeli withdrawal from the West Bank. However, Netanyahu faced stiff opposition to the plan at home, and, by the end of 1998, his governing coalition had collapsed, and implementation of the Wye plan was suspended until a new government could be formed.

Labor candidate and former general Ehud Barak triumphed in the May 1999 elections and formed a coalition government in July. In September, Barak and Arafat signed an agreement reviving the Wye accord (the Sharm el-Sheikh Memorandum), and, in December, peace talks between Israel and Syria—broken off in 1996— were resumed. In May 2000, Israel unilaterally withdrew from the 14.5- (9-mi-) wide security zone in southern Lebanon.

Despite the earlier recognition letter, in 2009, Fatah (the moderates of the PLO) reaffirmed their charter, in which they mandate continuation of the armed struggle until the Palestinian Arabs have achieved "complete liberation of Palestine, and eradication of Zionist economic, political, military, and cultural existence." Later that year the official spokesman for Fatah celebrated "full conformity" between the programs of supposedly secular Fatah and the Islamist Hamas. Such statements to the Arab public, when noted within Israel, naturally excited suspicions about the ultimate intensions of the Palestinian movements. At the end of 1999 and into early 2000, nevertheless, three-way negotiations took place between Israel, the Palestinians, and the United States as mediator. In July 2000, President Clinton invited Barak and Arafat to Camp David, Maryland, for peace talks. The summit began on 11 July and ended on 25 July without an agreement being reached. Arafat refused Barak's offer of a return of some 95% of the West Bank. Arafat's failure to agree or even make a counteroffer was criticized by President Clinton and prominent Arab leaders.

On 28 September 2000, Likud leader Ariel Sharon and some other Knesset members visited the Temple Mount (Haram al-Sharif, the Noble Sanctuary, Arab name for the 35-acre complex that includes the remains of the Jewish temple) to assert their position that these holy places should remain under Israeli sovereignty. The day after Sharon's visit, on 29 September 2000, the second *intifada* erupted, bringing with it an abrupt reversal of the economic progress that had marked the first part of the year. Urgently renewed US-sponsored status negotiations in Taba, Egypt, in late January 2001 failed to produce an agreement and were allowed to lapse by the incoming George W. Bush administration.

By the end of 2000, Barak was presiding over an extremely violent situation. On 9 December 2000, Barak resigned, making necessary a special prime ministerial election in which he stated he would seek a new mandate to pursue peace with the Palestinians. On 6 February 2001, Sharon was elected prime minister in a landslide victory over Barak. The *intifada* intensified, with Israel assassinating Palestinian militants and conducting air strikes and incursions into Palestinian self-rule areas; Palestinian militants increased suicide bomb attacks in Israeli cities. In December 2001,

Israeli forces besieged Yasser Arafat's headquarters in Ramallah; he remained confined in his compound, and the next spring Israel launched its largest military offensive since the invasion of Lebanon. After being evacuated to Paris for an undisclosed illness, Arafat died on November 11, 2004.

In 2002, Israel began erecting a security barrier around the West Bank, intended to deter terrorist attacks. The barrier is part-fence and part-wall up to 30 ft (9 m) high in some areas and inconveniences Palestinian farmers nearby. When completed, it would stretch some 375 mi (603.5 km) through the West Bank to Jerusalem. In July 2004, the International Court of Justice (ICJ) ruled that the security barrier violates international law and must be torn down. Israel said it would ignore the ruling, but it later made changes in the barrier route according to a ruling of the Israeli Supreme Court.

In January 2003, Ariel Sharon's Likud Party won a strong victory in parliamentary elections, defeating the Labor Party and its chairman Amram Mitzna. The Shinui or "Change" Party, which campaigned on a platform of curtailing privileges and benefits the state offers to ultra-Orthodox Jews, also registered a clear win.

On 22 March 2004, Hamas founder and spiritual leader Sheikh Ahmed Yassin was assassinated in a targeted Israeli airstrike as he was leaving a Gaza City mosque. In another targeted killing in April, Abdel Aziz al-Rantissi, who took over the Hamas leadership after Yassin's death, was assassinated. These killings provoked widespread outrage among Palestinians. Palestinian attacks and kidnapping of Israeli soldiers near Gaza followed.

In January 2005 Prime Minister Sharon formed a unity government with Likud, Labor, and the United Torah Judaism parties to implement the planned withdrawal of Israeli settlements in the Gaza Strip. On 8 February 2005, a summit conference in Sharm el-Sheikh, Egypt, was held; attending were Sharon, Palestinian Authority President Mahmoud Abbas, Egyptian President Hosni Mubarak, and King Abdullah II of Jordan. Abbas and Sharon declared an end to violence. Israel announced it would release some 900 Palestinian prisoners and withdraw from Palestinian cities in the West Bank. Jordan and Egypt agreed to return ambassadors to Israel. The *intifada* that began in 2000 was declared over. However, after a Palestinian suicide bombing, Israel froze the return of Palestinian cities to Palestinian control. The evacuation of Israeli settlements from Gaza began on 15 August 2005 and continued until 24 August. Ultra-Orthodox Jews and ultra-nationalists sympathetic to the settlers' cause traveled to the settlements, held protests, and clashed with Israeli armed forces and police trying to remove them. The "disengagement plan" was marked by high emotions. That month, Netanyahu made a bid to challenge Sharon's leadership, threatening to split the Likud Party. He accused Sharon of betraying the core values of Likud in withdrawing from occupied territory and of moving to the left. On 21 November, Sharon resigned as head of Likud and dissolved parliament. Sharon formed a new center-right party, Kadima ("Forward"), to participate in elections on 28 March 2006. On 20 December 2005, Netanyahu was named Sharon's successor as head of Likud. On 4 January 2006, Sharon suffered a massive stroke and cerebral hemorrhaging. He underwent brain surgery. He was declared "temporarily incapable of discharging his powers," and Ehud Olmert, the deputy prime minister, was named acting prime minister of Israel.

Palestinian legislative elections were held on 25 January 2006. The radical Islamist party Hamas won an overwhelming victory, taking 76 out of 132 seats in parliament, deposing the former governing Fatah party, which won only 43 seats. A Hamas leader, Ismail Haniya, was named the new Palestinian prime minister in February 2006. This ended more than 40 years of domination by Fatah, the largest faction in the PA, which was criticized by many Palestinians as corrupt and ineffective. Hamas is regarded as a terrorist organization by Israel, the United States, and the European Union (EU). Israel declared it would not negotiate with a Palestinian administration led by Hamas, and refused to continue transferring about $50 million in monthly tax and customs receipts to the Palestinian Authority, collected on behalf of the Palestinians. These funds account for about two-thirds of PA annual revenue; of its total revenue 58% goes to wages in the public sector. The $100m debt owed the PA as of 2011 has contributed to the $1 billion the Palestinian authority owes private banks. The "Quartet"-composed of the United States, Russia, the EU, and the UN-has been seeking a way to continue financial support for the Palestinian Authority without providing direct assistance to a Hamas-led government. Hamas indicated it would turn to the Arab world to supplant the monthly tax and customs revenue being withheld by Israel. The PA had received approximately $1 billion of its $1.9 billion annual budget from outside donors.

On 12 July 2006, the Lebanese Hezbollah militia group seized two Israeli soldiers and killed three others in northern Israel. Israel responded with an air, sea, and land campaign against Hezbollah in Lebanon. The war continued until a UN cease-fire went into effect on 14 August 2006, although the war didn't end until 8 September, when Israel lifted its naval blockade of Lebanon. The last Israeli troops left Lebanon in December 2006. Some 1,200 people were killed in the war, about 900 of them Lebanese civilians; 117 Israeli soldiers and 41 Israeli citizens died in the fighting. Nearly one million Lebanese and some 300,000 Israelis were displaced from their homes. Much Lebanese infrastructure was severely damaged, including the Beirut Rafik Hariri International Airport. Despite Israel's overwhelming firepower, Hezbollah was not defeated, with the conflict ending as the result of a cease-fire. Therefore, Hezbollah claimed victory in the war, a claim with which Israel heartily disagreed.

Later in 2006 and early 2007, violence in the West Bank and Gaza broke out after the new ruling Hamas party accused the Fatah faction of trying to kill the Palestinian National Authority foreign minister, Mahmoud al-Zahar, after shots were fired at his convoy in Gaza City on December15, 2006. Mahmoud al-Zahar was not harmed in the attack but one of his bodyguards was killed and his son was wounded. After weeks of negotiations, a unity government was formed in March 2007, but tensions between Fatah and Hamas remained high. In mid-June, Hamas seized control of Gaza, defeating Fatah and Palestinian Authority forces there.

In late December, 2008, Israel attacked Gaza in Operation Cast Lead to free communities close to the border from missiles fired upon them by various groups from within the Strip. In an infantry attack on Hamas installations and Arab cities, some 1166 Palestinians were killed, more than half of them "terrorist operatives," according to the IDF. Considerable damage resulted. Thirteen Israeli soldiers died, and rockets hit Beersheva and Ashdod for the first time. A cease-fire was declared in late January. In a UN special mission headed by South African jurist Richard Goldstone, it was charged that Israel had deliberately targeted civilians, but Goldstone later reversed himself on this, though his colleagues did not. Hamas was also accused of war crimes in a report which attracted wide discussion and criticism for its methods.

While numerous attempts have been made to secure peace for the region, finding a compromise on the "final status" issues has stymied peace negotiators since 1979. These issues include the dismantling of certain Israeli settlements in the West Bank, the borders of a Palestinian state, the status of Jerusalem, security, and the fate of Palestinian refugees who left, or were forced to leave, their homes in Israel. Israel demands that the Palestinian Arabs recognize Israel as "the Jewish state." In April 2009, nonetheless, talks managed by Prime Minister Olmert came close to a deal with the PA, according to Mahmoud Abbas, but stalled over the issue of recognition of the Jewish state. While Palestinians have agreed to recognize the right of Israel to exist, they maintain that recognition of Israel as a Jewish state would deny the right of Palestinian refugees to return to their homeland, as Palestinian chief negotiator Saeb Erekat has explained in an Israeli newspaper. Palestinian leaders expect Israeli leadership to unequivocally affirm support of the two-state solution before peace talks can continue. Israeli and Palestinian leaders were persuaded to resume talks in September 2010, meeting in Egypt with mediation from the United States. A primary issue on the table was the imminent expiration of Israel's moratorium on Jewish settlements and proposed settlements for east Jerusalem, an area that the Palestinians hope to make their capital city. In October, Israel offered to extend the moratorium on new settlement construction, for a limited time, if the Palestinian leadership would unequivocally recognize Israel as the Jewish homeland. Negotiators for the Palestinians rejected the offer and accused the Israeli government of playing games instead of committing to serious negotiations, stating that the current issue involved the legality of the settlements, not the nature of the state of Israel. By the last week of October 2010, construction had already begun on more than 600 homes in the West Bank for Jewish settlers. The pace of building was four times faster than before the moratorium. In November, the government announced plans for an additional 1,300 new homes. From then and throughout 2011, despite American and European urging unconditional resumption of talks, no direct peace negotiations have occurred. The Netanyahu government continued to fund settlement activity on the West Bank and within Jerusalem, although it has sometimes removed tiny, unauthorized "outposts" set up by Jewish zealots.

Since 1967, Israel has settled nearly 500,000 Jews in more than 100 settlements in the West Bank. These settlements have been considered to be illegal under international law by most world governments. The Israeli government, however, contests that allegation, since Jordan's sovereignty over the occupied West Bank and Jerusalem was never recognized by the international community. Palestinian leaders are opposed to the rapid construction of Jewish settlements in areas that they believe should soon be designated as part of their own homeland. The settlement moratorium initiated by the Israeli government, set to expire on 26 September 2010, did not include Jerusalem, but officials temporarily halted major construction plans for east Jerusalem, partly in deference to international pressure for sensitivity on the issue. Meanwhile, Israel announced plans to accelerate 2000 new housing units in the

West Bank and to freeze transfer of tax and customs revenues that it collects on behalf of the PA. According to the World Bank, such a freeze would be ruinous for the PA, which already is suffering an "acute financial crisis." Frustrated for being punished for what they see as a non-violent path to statehood, the Ramallah government under Mahmoud Abbas may resign, leaving an uncertain and dangerous power vacuum.

In May 2010, Israel was invited to join the Organization for Economic Cooperation and Development (OECD). Israel's acceptance into the group affirmed the economic strides Israel had taken since its founding and stood testament to the effectiveness of Israeli diplomacy in the effort. Several Palestinian and human rights groups lobbied heavily to have Israel's invitation delayed.

In late May, 2010, Turkish peace activists aboard the ship *Mavi Marmara* attempted to run Israel's blockade of the Gaza coastline, along with six other vessels. The legal blockade was intended to prevent arms from reaching Hamas militants, with whom Israel remains in a state of war. Israeli naval commandos rappelled onto the ship, but outnumbered and encountering armed resistance, the Israelis opened fire. Nine of the Turks were killed, including one with US citizenship. International protests followed, particularly from Turkey, leading Israel to ease the blockade somewhat.

Later that year a very large natural gas deposit was discovered offshore. The "Leviathan" field is estimated to contain about 425 billion cubic meters. Along with nearby finds, the new reserves exceed the known reserves of the UK and could supply all of Israel's energy needs, as well as exports of LNG. Israel's use of natural gas in the mid-2000's was estimated at 200 million cubic meters a year.

In November 2010, the Israeli cabinet approved a plan for the withdrawal of troops from the northern half of the border village of Ghajar, which has been declared as part of Lebanon by the United Nations. Ghajar was once a part of Syria, but was captured and occupied by the Israelis during the Six Day War of 1967. Later, as the UN demarcated the border for Lebanon, the northern portion of the city was separated from Israeli control. The Israeli military occupation of southern Lebanon ended in 2000, but since the two nations were still technically at war, Israeli forces remained in the northern portion. The population of the entire village is about 2000, and many of the residents still consider themselves to be Syrian. A majority are opposed to falling under Lebanese control. Upon the withdrawal of Israeli troops, northern Ghajar will be placed under control of the UN Interim Force in Lebanon (UNIFIL) until further details can be worked out.

On October 18, 2011, Hamas freed Sgt. Gilad Shalit in exchange for 1027 Palestinian prisoners held in Israeli prisons. Shalit had been held for five years after he was taken wounded near the border fence at the southern end of the Gaza Strip.

During 2011 the PA applied to join the UN as a full member state, but the US threat to exercised its veto (if necessary) in the Security Council, together with Britain and France plans to abstain, deprived Palestinian bid of the needed nine votes in the Security Council. So the effort was dropped. Very possibly though, Palestine will be promoted to permanent observer status in the UN General Assembly. The Palestinian application to join UNESCO was approved, but the United States was obliged by law to freeze Palestinian funding upon its joining any UN body. That meant that UNESCO lost about a quarter of its funding. The fiscal crisis, caused by Israel's freeze of funds it owes the PA, may

force President Mahmud Abbas to reconcile with Hamas and relieve prime minister Salam Fayyad (a technocrat trusted in the West) of his post.

13 GOVERNMENT

Israel is a democratic republic, with no written constitution. Legislative power is vested in the unicameral Knesset (parliament), whose 120 members are elected for four-year terms by universal secret vote of all citizens 18 years of age and over under a system of proportional representation. New elections may be called ahead of schedule and must be held when the government loses the confidence of a majority of parliament. Predominantly Arab parties have long had several members (MKs) in the Knesset; there is one Bedou MK as well.

The head of state is the president, elected by the Knesset for a seven-year term. Shimon Peres was elected in 2007. The president performs largely ceremonial duties and traditionally chooses the prime minister from the ruling political party. In 1996, however, a new law went into effect whereby the prime minister would be directly elected by the people. In March 2001, the Knesset voted to change the system of direct elections and restore the one-vote parliamentary system of government that operated until 1996. The law went into effect with the January 2003 elections, won by Likud. The cabinet, headed by the prime minister, is collectively responsible to the Knesset.

14 POLITICAL PARTIES

Israel's multiparty system reflects the diverse origins of the people and their long practice of party politics in Zionist organizations. The first five Knessets were controlled by coalitions led by Mapai (Israel Workers Party), under Israel's first prime minister, David Ben-Gurion (1949–63), and then under Levi Eshkol (1963–69). Mapai formed the nucleus of the present Israel Labor Party, a democratic socialist party, which, in coalition with other groups, controlled Israel's governments under prime ministers Golda Meir (1969–74) and Yitzhak Rabin (1974–77 and 1992–95).

In September 1973, four right-wing nationalist parties combined to form the Likud, which thus became the major opposition bloc in the Knesset. Unlike the Israel Labor Party, whose core of support lies with secular Occidentals and older Israelis generally, the Likud has drawn much of its strength from Oriental Jewry, as well as from among the young and less-educated. Besides the State List and the Free Center, the Likud consists of the Herut (Freedom) Movement, founded in 1948 to support territorial integrity within Israel's biblical boundaries and a greater economic role for private enterprise, and the Liberal Party, formed in 1961 to support private enterprise, a liberal welfare state, and electoral reform. The Likud originally advocated retention of all territories captured in the 1967 war as a safeguard to national security. It won 39 seats in the 1973 elections and then became the largest party in the Knesset by winning 43 seats in the May 1977 elections to 32 seats for the Israel Labor Party-United Workers (MAPAM) alignment. Likud leader Menachem Begin became prime minister of a coalition government formed by Likud with the National Religious Party and the ultra-orthodox Agudat Israel. From that time on, Israel began to dismantle its socialist economic model in favor of a mixed capitalist one with considerable openness to the world economy.

In elections on 30 June 1981, Likud again won a plurality, taking 37.1% of the popular vote and 48 seats in the Knesset, compared to the Labor coalition's 36.6% and 47 seats. Begin succeeded in forming a new government with the support of smaller parties. The elections of July 1984 left both Labor (with 44 seats) and Likud (with 41) short of a Knesset majority; consequently, under a power-sharing agreement, each party held an equal number of cabinet positions in a national unity government, and each party leader served as premier for 25 months. Labor's Shimon Peres became prime minister in 1984, handing over the office to Likud's Yitzhak Shamir in late 1986. Elections in 1988 produced a similar power-sharing arrangement. In 1989, rotation was ended as Likud and Labor united in a coalition. After a vote of no confidence, Likud formed a coalition of religious and right-wing parties that held power for two years until 1992. Elections in June gave Labor 44 seats (32 for Likud) and enabled it to form a coalition with Meretz (a grouping of three left-wing parties) and Shas (a religious party) along with the support of two Arab parties.

In 1995, after Prime Minister Yitzhak Rabin was assassinated, Shimon Peres again became prime minister and called for early elections, which were held in May 1996. The main issue of the election was Israel's response to terrorist attacks and the disposition of the occupied territories. Labor favored continued negotiations with the PLO and the Palestinian Authority (PA), while Likud favored a tougher stance, increased settlement on occupied lands, a rethinking of the Oslo accords, and a slowing of the process of land-turnover. The elections were extremely close with the Likud-Geshe-Tsamet coalition winning a slim majority, 62 seats. In a separate poll, Benjamin Netanyahu was directly elected prime minister.

After Netanyahu's governing coalition collapsed at the end of 1998, new elections were called for May of 1999. In the prime ministerial election, Ehud Barak, heading a Labor-led center-left coalition (One Israel), defeated Netanyahu 56% to 44%. In the legislative elections, Barak's One Israel/Israeli Labor Party coalition won a 26-seat plurality. After Barak resigned in December 2000, Ariel Sharon won a special prime ministerial election in February 2001 with the largest vote margin ever in Israeli politics, 62.4% of the vote. In March 2001, the Knesset voted to replace the system of direct election for the prime minister established in 1996 with the parliamentary system.

Confronted with friction within his ruling coalition over the planned evacuation of Israeli settlements in the Gaza Strip, Ariel Sharon, in January 2005, formed a new unity government with Likud (40 seats in the Knesset), Labor (19 seats), and the United Torah Judaism (5 seats) parties. In November 2005, in response to dissent within his own Likud, Sharon dissolved parliament and formed a new party, Kadima ("Forward"). Benjamin Netanyahu took over the helm as leader of Likud. After Sharon suffered a massive hemorrhagic stroke in January 2006, Ehud Olmert took over as leader of Kadima.

In the parliamentary elections of February 2009, Kadima won 28 of 120 seats in the Knesset with 23.3% of the vote. Likud won 27 seats, followed by Yisrael Beiteinu (a mostly Russian party) with 15, Labor with 13, Shas (Misrachi religious) with 11, and United Torah Judaism (mostly Ashkenazi Orthodox) with 5. The United Arab List, the National Union, and the Democratic Front for Peace and Equality (HADASH) each won four seats. The Jewish Home, the New Movement-Meretz, and Balad parties each won three. Netanyahu was again named prime minister and governs with a right-of-center coalition of nationalist and religious parties.

15 LOCAL GOVERNMENT

Israel is divided into six administrative districts: Jerusalem, Tel Aviv, Haifa, Northern (Tiberias), Central (Ramla), and Southern (Beersheva). The Golan Heights is a subdistrict of the Northern District. Each district is governed by a commissioner appointed by the central government. At the local level, government is by elected regional and local councils, which govern according to by-laws approved by the Ministry of the Interior. Local officials are elected for four-year terms. Until 1994, Israel governed all of the occupied territories through the Civil Administration, which is responsible to the Ministry of Defense. More recently, Palestinian towns have Israeli-appointed mayors. Israeli settlers in the West Bank are subject to Israeli law. In 1994, a Palestinian National Authority (PA) was established; control over Gaza and some Palestinian towns on the West Bank were turned over to the PA.

16 JUDICIAL SYSTEM

Though Israel, like Britain, has no constitution, a series of "basic laws" provide fundamental rights. The law of Israel contains some features of Ottoman law, English common law, and other foreign law, but it is shaped by Knesset legislation. Judges are appointed by the president on recommendation of independent committees. There are 29 magistrates' courts, which deal with most cases in the first instance, petty property claims, and lesser criminal charges. Five district courts, serving mainly as courts of appeal, have jurisdiction over all other actions except marriage and divorce cases, which are adjudicated, along with other personal and religious matters, in the religious courts of the Jewish (rabbinical), Muslim (Shari'ah), Druze, and Christian communities. Besides its function as the court of last appeal, the Supreme Court also hears cases in the first instance brought by citizens against arbitrary government actions. The number of Supreme Court justices is determined by a resolution of the Knesset. Usually, twelve justices serve on the Supreme Court.

The judiciary is independent. Trials are fair and public. Legislation enacted in 1997 limits detention without charge to 24 hours. Defendants have the right to be presumed innocent and to writs of habeas corpus and other procedural safeguards. There is no jury system. Capital punishment applies only for crimes of wartime treason or for collaboration with the Nazis, and has been employed only once in Israel's modern history, in the case of Adolf Eichmann, who was executed in 1962. In the occupied territories, security cases are tried in military courts; verdicts may not be appealed, and the rules of habeas corpus do not apply. There are also labor relations and administrative courts.

The use of limited physical force during interrogations has been legal, but a high court ruling banned a variety of specific abuses, including sleep deprivation and violent shaking. Administrative detention without trial remains legal, but it is rarely used. Prison conditions for Palestinians have improved but still do not meet all international standards.

17 ARMED FORCES

The Israeli Defense Force began with the voluntary defense forces (principally the Haganah) created by the Jewish community in Palestine during the British mandate. Today, Jewish and Druze men between the ages of 18 and 26 are conscripted for 36 and 24 months, respectively. Ultra-Orthodox (*haredim*) men studying in religious institutions are commonly deferred; this traditional waiver now excuses about 50, 000 ultra-Orthodox students of military age from service. Bedouin sometimes serve voluntarily, as they also do in the diplomatic corps. Drafted Jewish women are trained for noncombat duties. Christians and Muslims may serve on a voluntary basis, but Muslims are rarely allowed to bear arms. All men and unmarried women serve in the reserves until the ages of 54 and 24, respectively. Men receive annual combat training until age 45.

The International Institute for Strategic Studies reports that armed forces in Israel totaled 176,500 active duty personnel in 2011. The force is comprised of 133,000 from the army, 9,500 from the navy, and 34,000 members of the air force. Reserves number about 565,000. The reserve forces can be effectively mobilized in 48–72 hours. Armed forces represent 6% of the labor force in Israel. Israel has three submarines and 57 patrol ships in its navy. IDF ground forces are well equipped with Dror and Uzi submachine guns, the Galil assault rifle, 1,680 Merkava tanks (and four other types), 1,550 Magach tanks made in the US, 1,500 M113 personnel carriers, and a variety of missiles and other weapons. Defense spending totaled $16 billion and accounted for 7.3% of GDP.

It is believed that Israel maintains a nuclear arsenal of up to 200 nuclear warheads.

18 INTERNATIONAL COOPERATION

Israel was admitted as the 59th UN member on May 11, 1949. The new nation subsequently joined several non-regional specialized agencies, such as the FAO, UNESCO, UNIDO, UNCHR, IAEA, IFC, the World Bank, and World Health Organization (WHO). It is also a member of the World Trade Organization (WTO) and the OECD. The country is a partner in the Organization for Security and Cooperation in Europe (OSCE). Israel holds observer status with the Council of Europe, the OAS, and the Black Sea Economic Cooperation Zone.

During the 1970s and early 1980s, Arab governments sought through the "oil weapon" to isolate Israel diplomatically and economically, but Israel's 1979 peace treaty with Egypt helped ease some of the pressure. A number of African countries reestablished diplomatic relations with Israel in the 1980s. After signing peace accords with the Palestinians in 1993 and 1994, Israel opened liaison and trade missions in certain Arab countries, including Qatar and Oman, plus 22 of the 43 sub-Saharan African countries. The accords brought to a formal end the Arab Boycott of Israel (BOI), in place since 1951, with the shutdown of the Central Boycott Office (CBO) in Damascus. The Gulf Cooperation countries effectively ended the boycott in 1994. Israel also signed a peace agreement with Jordan in 1994, and the two nations exchanged ambassadors in 1995. Altogether, Israel has diplomatic relations of some kind with 163 of the world's states. Foreign investment, once very hard to obtain, also grew substantially in years following the signing of the Oslo Accords. Tourism also benefited from

the Peace Accords. The Violence between Israel and the Palestinians resulting from the *intifada* that began in September 2000 increased tensions with the Arab world. In October 2000, however, following the eruption of the second *intifada* in September, the Arab League passed a resolution calling for the reinstatement of the BOI. In May 2002, in a meeting in Damascus, 19 Arab states drew up a list of firms to be blacklisted but did not publish it. In the month following the eruption of the renewed *intifada*, the number of tourists declined 43%, and an estimated 50,000 workers in the tourist industry were laid off. In 2002, the Israeli Ministry of Tourism estimated that revenues from tourism had fallen by over half.

To take part in environmental cooperation, Israel is a signatory of the Basel Convention, the Convention on Biological Diversity, Ramsar, CITES, the Kyoto Protocol, the Montréal Protocol, MARPOL, the Nuclear Test Ban Treaty, and the UN Conventions on Climate Change and Desertification.

The United States is Israel's major political, economic, and military ally, providing some $3 billion a year in mostly military assistance.

19 ECONOMY

Since independence, Israel's economy faced serious problems because of its significant defense burden and the need to absorb millions of refugees. Most of these immigrants were relatively well-educated, however, adding to Israel's already considerable base of technologically aware workforce and population. The government also makes large outlays for social welfare purposes. With limited natural resources, Israel must export on a large scale to maintain its relatively high standard of living; hence, it remains dependent on a continuing flow of investment capital and of private and public assistance from abroad. However, Israel's economy is technologically advanced, with machinery, cut diamonds, computer software, textiles, and agricultural products (fruits and vegetables) the leading products produced for export. Government infrastructure development since 1990 has played a large part in Israel's powerful economic performance in recent years. Major government projects include an expansion of the Ben-Gurion Airport, a subway for Tel-Aviv, a tunnel through Mt. Carmel, and a major new north-south highway.

The country is self-sufficient in producing its food supply, except for grain, which it imports. Agriculture accounts for 2% of GDP and employs 2% of the workforce. Industry, which includes aviation, communications, computer-aided design and manufacturing, medical electronics, and fiber optics, accounts for 32% of GDP and employs 16% of the workforce. Manufacturing value added as of 2005 included chemical products $3.4 million, instruments $2.3 million, electronics and telecommunications equipment $2.3 million. About 82% of the labor force is involved in the service sector, which accounts for an estimated 66% of GDP.

The United States is the destination for 35% of the country's exports; other export partners are Belgium and Hong Kong. Import partners include the United States, Belgium, Germany, and China. From 1992–95, Israeli exports to Asia grew by 86% and by 1999 accounted for 20% of Israel's total exports. Tourism grew to be Israel's second- or third-largest industry, a record 3 ½ million tourists in 2010.

Israel has achieved a fairly high rate of growth with lower inflation during the last 35 years. From 1975 to 1980, GNP grew at an annual rate of 3.1% (at constant prices). Between 1980 and 1985, real GNP growth was 10%. It was below this average in the period after 1989 during which the country had to absorb more than half a million new immigrants. From the inception of the Oslo process in the early 1990s, the Israeli economy has wavered between hopeful spurts of growth and recession, as openings and investor confidence increase or decrease, depending on the outlook for peace. In the period 1990–96, real GDP growth averaged 2.6%, but improved thereafter. Likud governments determined adherence to tight monetary and fiscal policies aimed at subduing Israel's chronically high inflation rate and tax burden. In the early 1980s, after the second oil shock, Israeli inflation had soared to triple digits, reaching a peak of 374 in 1985, the year before world oil prices collapsed. In 1986, in response to vigorous policies, inflation fell abruptly, and then, from 1987 to 1996, yearly inflation ranged from 10–20%. In 1997, Israel experienced its first single-digit level of inflation (9%) since 1970. Inflation rates continued to fall in 1998 and 1999. Strict monetary policies were not reversed by the return of a Labor-led government in 1999, as inflation fell to a record low in 2000. The moderate real GDP growth from 1997 to 1999, however, was not sufficient to prevent per capita income from declining somewhat during this period because of continued immigration from Russia and other Eastern European countries. In the recession that accompanied the emergence of the 2000 *intifada*, inflation remained low to moderate, at 1.1% for 2001 and accelerated for 2002. In 2005, rising consumer confidence, tourism, foreign investment in Israel, and a high demand for Israeli exports contributed to GDP growth. Due to improved fiscal management, the budget deficit was projected to decrease. 2007 saw growth at the fastest pace since 2000. Strong foreign investment, tax revenues, and private consumption, together with sensible fiscal policy and structural reforms put in place by all of Israel's governments since 2000, have resulted in impressive results. Average GDP growth for 2000–09 was 3.6% per year. In recent years, agriculture accounted for 2.4% of GDP, industry 32.6%, and services 65%. Inflation remained manageable. The GDP price deflator for 2000–08 was 2.6%, and consumer prices since 2000 rose between 2 and 3.5% a year. As of 2011, Israel's real gross domestic product was growing at a rate of 3.5%. Inflation of consumer prices stood at 2.9%, and unemployment was reported at 5.5%. According to the World Bank, in 2009 per capital income in Israel at purchasing power parity was $27,010, about the same as New Zealand or Greece. Israel's per capita income was more than twice that of its neighbor Lebanon and about five times those of Syria or Jordan.

Israel is an outstanding success in attracting venture capital. In 2007, $230 per capita was invested in Israel, and, in 2008, $270 per capita, more than twice that in the United States and four to five times rates in the United Kingdom, Ireland, Denmark, or the United Arab Emirates, according to Dow Jones and Thomson Reuters. Sixty-three Israeli companies were listed on the technology-rich NASDAQ exchange in 2009, as compared to 48 Canadian and only 6 Japanese companies.

The Oslo Accords explicitly acknowledged that peace could not be attained or sustained without the establishment of mutually beneficial economic relationships. Two annexes to the Oslo Accords laid out protocols for joint economic cooperation and regional development, listing specific projects to be pursued, including a Gaza seaport, a Gaza airport, a Mediterranean-Dead Sea Canal (MDSC) project (that would also provide water desalinization and farm irrigation), and a Red Sea-Dead Sea Canal (RSDSC) project (similarly aimed at providing desalinization and crop irrigation), as well general provisions for the establishment of border and local industrial estates to encourage economic cooperation and investment. International donors pledged more than $2.4 billion over the years 1994–99, much of which was to be used on the infrastructural projects identified in Oslo protocols. While the canal projects, which had been under consideration for many years, remained tied up in political and economic controversies, construction proceeded on the seaport and airport for Gaza and on the Kami Industrial Estate on the Gaza-Israeli border, funded primarily by aid from the United States and the European Union (EU). Following the second *intifada*, The economy under PA control all but collapsed. A World Bank report on Palestine in 2002 estimated that unemployment had risen from 10% in 2000 to 26% by December 2001, and that the average income had fallen 40%. Tourism is the leading industry in PA areas; it doubly suffered from the loss of security and the destruction of infrastructure in Israeli retaliatory incursions. Virtually all of the projects built under the protocols of the Oslo Accords, including the Gaza seaport, Gaza airport, and Kami Industrial Estate, were significantly damaged or destroyed in the fighting. Unemployment in the Gaza Strip and the West Bank stood at half the labor force, and more than 80% of the population lives below the poverty line. International aid in the amount of $2 billion to the West Bank and Gaza in 2004 prevented the complete collapse of the economy and allowed some reforms in the government's financial operations.

20 INCOME

The CIA estimated that, in 2010, the GDP of Israel was $219.4 billion. The CIA defines GDP as the value of all final goods and services produced within a nation in a given year and computed on the basis of purchasing power parity (PPP) rather than value as measured on the basis of the rate of the exchange based on current dollars. The per capita GDP was estimated at $29,800 at current exchange rates. Israel ranks 52nd in the world in per capita income; the United States ranks 16th. The World Bank categorizes Israel as a "high income" country.

According to the World Bank, remittances from citizens living abroad totaled $1.3 billion or about $170 per capita and accounted for approximately .6% of GNP. In 2009, household consumption in Israel totaled $111.4 billion or about $14,907 per capita, measured in current US dollars rather than PPP. Household consumption includes expenditures of individuals, households, and nongovernmental organizations on goods and services, excluding the purchases of dwellings. It was estimated that household consumption was growing at an average annual rate of 3.6%.

As of 2011, the most recent study by the World Bank reported that individual consumption in Israel was 68.0% of GDP and accounted for 0.28% of world consumption. By comparison, the United States accounted for 25.44% of world individual consumption. Of Israel's GDP, 10.2% was spent on food and beverages, 17.1% on housing and household furnishings, 1.9% on clothes, 6.6% on health, 6.6% on transportation, 2.2% on communications,

5.3% on recreation, 2.8% on restaurants and hotels, and 7.2% on miscellaneous goods and services and purchases from abroad.

It was estimated that, in 2007, about 23.6% of the population subsisted on an income below the poverty line established by Israel's government. As of the last survey (2001), the Gini coefficient, which measures inequality of income, was 39.2, with the top 10% of households enjoying a 28.8% share. The lowest 10% had a 2.1% share. Measured in these ways, Israel is somewhat more unequal than western European countries, but similar to the distribution in Portugal or New Zealand and more egalitarian than the US.

21 LABOR

As of 2010, Israel had a total labor force of 3.147 million people. Within that labor force, CIA estimates in 2008 noted that 2% were employed in agriculture, 16% in industry, and 82% in the service sector.

The majority of Israeli workers, including those in agriculture, are union members belonging to the General Federation of Labor (*Histadrut*, founded by Jewish farm workers in 1920), which has a membership of 650,000. Histadrut's collective bargaining agreements are also available to nonmembers. The right to strike is often exercised, but 15 days notice must be provided to the employer. Dismissal of employees is costly and sometimes difficult. Palestinians in the occupied territories are permitted to organize their own unions and have the right to strike.

Children under 15 are not permitted to work except for school holidays. Employment for those between the ages of 16 to 18 is restricted, and these laws are regularly enforced. The law provides for a maximum eight-hour day and 47-hour week, and establishes a compulsory weekly rest period of 36 hours. By collective agreement, the private sector has a maximum workweek of 45 hours, and the public sector went to a 42-hour week. Hours are fixed. The minimum wage is adjusted periodically for cost of living increases. The minimum wage, set as of July 2011, is ILS4100 per month (about $1130 at the current exchange rate) and is supplemented by family allowances.

The Tel-Aviv municipality estimates that there are 35,000 migrant workers in the city. Another 20,000 entered as guest workers but stayed illegally after their permits expired. The Ministry of Interior reports that 15,000 people entered Israel from Egypt in 2010, after some 25,000 the previous four years. During 2011, some 2,000 illegals entered the country, mostly from Africa via the Sinai peninsula. Israel normally employs labor from Thailand and Nepal. Thousands of Africans work in hotels and offices as janitors. Many of them do not qualify for refugee or asylum status. Controversial new laws are being considered that would allow three-year detention without trial for such illegals. Entrants from "enemy" states such as Sudan, with which Israel has no diplomatic relations, can be held indefinitely. Palestinian refugees can be prevented from "infiltrating" Israel under a 1954 law.

22 AGRICULTURE

Between 1948 and 2003, the cultivated area was expanded from 165,000 to 428,000 hectares (from 408,000 to 1,057,000 acres). Owing to the uniquely favorable soil and climatic conditions, Israel's citrus fruit has qualities of flavor and appearance commanding high prices when shipped promptly to the world market. Roughly 23% of the total land is currently farmed, and the country's major crops include citrus, vegetables, and cotton. Cereal production in 2009 amounted to 257,031 tons, fruit production (oranges, dates, grapefruit, apples, bananas, avocados, table grapes, peaches, olives, plums, pears, mangoes, etc.) 1.3 million tons, and vegetable (potatoes, tomatoes, etc.) production 1.6 million tons.

The main forms of agricultural settlement are the *kibbutz*, *moshav*, *moshav shitufi*, and *moshava* (pl. *moshavot*). In the *kibbutz*, all property is owned jointly by the settlement on land leased from the Jewish National Fund, and work assignments, services, and social activities are determined by elected officers. Although predominantly agricultural, many *kibbutzim* have taken on a variety of industries, including food processing and the production of building materials. Devoted entirely to agriculture, the *moshavim* (workers' smallholder cooperatives) market produce and own heavy equipment, but their land is divided into separate units and worked by the members individually. This form of settlement has had special appeal to new immigrants. The *moshavim shitufiyim* are 47 collective villages that are similar in economic organization to the *kibbutzim* but whose living arrangements are more like those of the *moshav*. The *moshavot* are rural colonies based on private enterprise. They were the principal form of 19th century settlement, and many have grown into urban communities.

New immigrants settling on the land are given wide-ranging assistance. The Jewish Agency, the executive arm of the World Zionist Organization, absorbs many of the initial costs; agricultural credits are extended on a preferential basis, and equipment, seeds, livestock, and work animals are supplied at low cost.

Israel has a high tariff on agricultural imports, subsidies on certain crops, and some price controls on essential items.

Israeli agriculture emphasizes maximum utilization of irrigation and the use of modern techniques to increase yields. A national irrigation system distributed water to 194,000 hectares (479,000 acres) in 2003, down from 219,000 hectares (541,100 acres) in 1986 but still far exceeding the 30,000 hectares (74,000 acres) served in 1948. Water is transported via pipeline from the Sea of Galilee to the northern Negev. More than 90% of Israel's subterranean water supply is being exploited, and annual freshwater withdrawals are 260% of internal sources. Of this water, some 58% is used in agriculture.

23 ANIMAL HUSBANDRY

The UN Food and Agriculture Organization (FAO) reported that Israel dedicated 125,000 hectares (308,882 acres) to permanent pasture or meadow in 2009. There is little natural pasturage in most areas, and livestock is fed mainly on imported feeds and farm-grown forage. During that year, the country tended 41.1 million chickens, 404,000 head of cattle, and 223,500 pigs. The production from these animals amounted to 187,689 tons of beef and veal, 18,108 tons of pork, 469,967 tons of poultry, 66,128 tons of eggs, and 1.24 million tons of milk. Israel also produced 9,300 tons of cattle hide and 790 tons of raw wool. Domestic beef production only satisfies between 33% and 40% of demand. Livestock farmers are aided by subsidies. There are 2,500 sheep and goat farms raising 455,000 head, 42% by the Bedu population, 36% by the Jewish sector, and 22% by the Arab and Druze populations. In 2005, there were 35,000,000 turkeys, 11,000 equines, and 5,300 camels. That year, honey production was estimated at 3,200 tons.

24 FISHING

Jewish settlers introduced the breeding of fish (mostly carp) into Palestine. In addition to carp, important freshwater fish include catfish, barbel, and trout. Israel had 181 decked commercial fishing boats in 2008. Their annual capture totaled 3,435 tons, according to the UN FAO. The marine catch consists mainly of gray and red mullet, rainbow trout, grouper, sardines, and bogue. Total fish production in 2007 was 26,236 metric tons, with aquaculture from 2,000 fish ponds accounting for 85%, mostly carp and tilapia. The export value of seafood totaled $12.83 million.

25 FORESTRY

Natural forests and woodlands cover about 132,000 hectares (326,000 acres), mostly in the north. About 180 million trees were planted between 1902 and 1986. Approximately 7% of Israel is now covered by forest. The UN FAO estimated the 2009 round-wood production at 24,957 cu m (881,348 cu ft). The value of all forest products, including roundwood, totaled $50.5 million. In 2004, forestry production included 181,000 cu m (6.4 million cu ft) of wood-based panels and 275,000 cu m (9.7 million cu ft) of paper and paperboard.

26 MINING

Israel accounted for 38% of world bromine production in 2009; 8% of magnesium, and 2% of phosphate rock. Israel also produces flint clay, kaolin, silica sand gypsum, magnesia and sulfur, as well as metals such as steel, lead, and magnesium. Diamond cutting (from imported rough diamonds) was also performed. In 2008, diamonds accounted for 18.8% of exports, mining and quarrying, 3.9%; and non-metallic minerals, 0.7%.

Mineral production in 2009 included beneficiated phosphate rock, 2.697 million metric tons, down from 3.088 million metric tons in 2008; potash, 2.1 million metric tons; elemental bromine, 128,000 metric tons; sulfuric acid, 16 million metric tons; and silica sand, 130,000 metric tons, down from 220,000 metric tons in 2007. Israel also produced in 2009, primarily for the construction sector, crude steel, refined secondary lead, magnesium metal, hydraulic cement, brick and Fuller's clays, gypsum, lime, magnesia, marble, phosphatic fertilizers, phosphoric acid, salt (mainly marine), sand, crushed stone, sulfur, sulfuric acid, and crude construction materials. Dead Sea Works in 2009 produced 2.1 million metric tons of potash. Although Israel did not mine diamonds in 2009, an estimated 382,000 carats of imported diamonds were cut, down from 526,000 carats in 2007.

The Negev Desert contained deposits of phosphate, copper (low grade), glass sand, ceramic clays, gypsum, and granite. Most of the phosphate deposits, located in the northeastern Negev, were, at best, medium grade, and were extracted by open-pit mining. The government was the principal owner of most mineral-related industries. Privately held industries included the diamond cutting and polishing industry and cement and potassium nitrate manufacturing.

27 ENERGY AND POWER

Israel's energy sector is largely nationalized and state-regulated, ostensibly for national security reasons. With extremely modest reserves of oil and natural gas and no coal reserves, Israel must rely almost entirely upon imports to meet its fossil fuel needs. In 2008, Israel imported 85% of its energy needs, according to the World Bank.

The World Bank reported in 2008 that Israel produced 56.4 billion kWh of electricity and consumed 51.6 billion kWh, or 6,899 kWh per capita. Roughly 97% of energy came from coal, lignite, natural gas, and some petroleum (100 barrels a day produced in the Negev), the rest from alternative fuels. Oil production totaled just 100 barrels per day, but new discoveries of natural gas deposits are expected to satisfy all domestic use and allow for exports. Per capita oil equivalent consumption was 3,011 kg. Israel has produced some oil in the Negev desert since 1955; exploration there continues. The country's own proven oil reserves were placed at two million barrels as of 1 January 2005. Oil fields in the Sinai were returned to Egypt in the peace agreements.

Nearly all electricity is supplied by the Israel Electric Corp. (IEC), a government-owned monopoly. Electricity is generated principally by thermal power stations. As of 31 December 2004, the IEC reported that installed electric power generating capacity totaled 10,083 MW, of which 79.1% of capacity was generated by coal, followed by fuel oil at 16.8%, and by gas oil at 4.1%. In 2008, total electric power was estimated at 52 billion kWh or 7.054kwH per capita, according to the World Bank. Transmission losses were only 2%.

28 INDUSTRY

More than half of the industrial establishments are in the Tel Aviv-Yafo area, but a great deal of heavy industry is concentrated around Haifa. Most plants are privately owned. State enterprises are mainly devoted to exploiting natural resources in the Negev, such as potassium nitrate and cement manufacturing. Some other enterprises are controlled by the Histadrut. Incentive schemes and productivity councils, representing workers and management, have been set up in an attempt to increase work output per hour. Whereas in the past Israel's industry concentrated on consumer goods to employ and provide for immigrant labor and their families, by the 1980s it was stressing the manufacture of capital goods.

In the early- and mid-2000s, manufacturing activity successfully branched out into such industries as electronics, albeit at the expense of traditional industries such as textiles and footwear. Textile and clothing firms have gone through structural changes and have outsourced labor-intensive activities to neighboring countries such as Jordan, Egypt, and Turkey, where wages are substantially lower than those in Israel. This allows Israeli manufacturers to concentrate on their comparative advantage in product design and trade agreements with the United States and EU as part of a free-trade zone. Despite the economic recession period that began in 2000, these and other medium- and low-technology export-oriented firms faired relatively well, largely due to greater levels of efficiency. The electronics, communications, and other high-tech industries have gone through high and low cycles in the early- and mid-2000s. The expansion of Israel's high-tech industries and start-up companies soared in 2000, reflecting strong global demand and intense financial market interest in this field. This sector became a focal point of foreign investment. Despite the dot-com bubble in the early part of the decade, efficiency measures, lower labor costs, and a depreciation of the shekel, many high-tech sub-sectors, particularly electronic component production and exports, recorded growth after 2002.

Today, Israel is research-and-development-oriented, as evidenced by the hundreds of foreign companies investing in Israel during the 1990s, the bulk in strategic high-technology projects in such fields as aviation, communications, computer-aided design and manufacturing (CAD/CAM), medical electronics, fine chemicals, pharmaceuticals, solar energy, and sophisticated irrigation. In the 1990s, major expansion took place in textiles, machinery and transport equipment, metallurgy, mineral processing, electrical products, precision instruments, and chemicals.

Industry remains handicapped by reliance on imported raw materials and relatively high wage costs but benefits from its reputation for innovation and product quality. High technology exports in 2009 brought in $10.3 billion; they constituted 23% of the country's total exports.

29 SCIENCE AND TECHNOLOGY

In 2000–08, Israel spent 4.86% of GDP on research and development (R and D) in science, engineering, agriculture, and medicine. This compares with 3.2% (2000–05) in Japan and 2.7% in the United States. In 2000 (the latest year for which the following data was available) business accounted for 69.9% of R and D spending, followed by the government at 24.7%, with foreign sources and higher education each accounting for 2.8%. National and local governments and industry shared equally in the funding.

A privatization program, begun by the government, has resulted in the creation of many science and technology parks and high technology towns, like Migdal He'Emek. Among scientific research institutes are seven institutes administered by the Agricultural Research Organization: the Rogoff-Wellcome Medical Research Institute; institutes for petroleum research, geological mapping, and oceanographic and limnological research directed by the Earth Sciences Research Administration; institutes of ceramic and silicate, fiber, metals, plastics, wine, and rubber research directed by the Office of the Chief Scientist, Ministry of Industry and Trade; the Institutes of Applied Research at the Ben-Gurion University of the Negev; the Israel Institute for Biological Research; the Israel Institute for Psychobiology; the National Research Laboratory; and the Soreg and Negev nuclear research centers attached to the Israel Atomic Energy Commission. The country has eight universities and colleges offering courses in basic and applied sciences; among them are the Weizmann Institute in Rehovot and the Technion-Israel Institute of Technology in Haifa. Science and engineering students accounted for nearly half of all college and university students.

In 2007 Israelis published 6,623 scientific and technical journal articles. Patent applications in science and technology as of 2009, according to the World Bank, totaled 1,387 in Israel. Immigrant scientists are an important resource in this scientific productivity.

30 DOMESTIC TRADE

In the Israeli wholesale trade sector, distribution companies generally serve the whole country. Various methods of distribution

Principal Trading Partners – Israel (2010)

(In millions of US dollars)

Country	Total	Exports	Imports	Balance
World	119,601.0	58,392.0	61,209.0	-2,817.0
United States	25,188.0	18,488.0	6,700.0	11,788.0
China	6,782.0	2,046.0	4,736.0	-2,690.0
Belgium	6,692.0	3,116.0	3,576.0	-460.0
Germany	5,379.0	1,701.0	3,678.0	-1,977.0
Hong Kong	5,313.0	3,915.0	1,398.0	2,517.0
India	4,735.0	2,890.0	1,845.0	1,045.0
United Kingdom	4,514.0	2,268.0	2,246.0	22.0
Switzerland	4,266.0	1,047.0	3,219.0	-2,172.0
Netherlands	3,920.0	1,818.0	2,102.0	-284.0
Italy	3,678.0	1,253.0	2,425.0	-1,172.0

(…) data not available or not significant.

(n.s.) not specified.

SOURCE: *2011 Direction of Trade Statistics Yearbook,* New York: United Nations, 2011.

are employed, based upon the type of product being sold. Non-stocking commissioned agents are used for commodities, industrial equipment, and raw materials, while high-volume items are handled by stocking agents. Consumer goods are usually sold through distributors and importers, although department stores and large retail chains are increasingly choosing to skip intermediaries and import directly into the country.

In the retail sector, shopping centers and malls are becoming more popular, with many US-based specialty shops, chain stores, and franchises doing business in those locations. There are over 200 malls nationwide and construction plans for many others. The institutional sector (the army, hospitals, hotels, restaurants, and places of employment) accounts for 30% of total turnover. In the non-institutional sector, more than 50% of the nation's food is sold through supermarkets and retail chains. The retail food market is dominated by three supermarket chains, which have hundreds of outlets nationwide. Small, open-air produce markets (such as Meah She'arim in the Orthodox section of Jerusalem) and groceries are still common and account for the rest. Foreign franchises have been well established since the mid-1980s, primarily in the fast-food and hardware industries.

Commercial sales and transactions are subject to a 16% value added tax (VAT). However, exports, hotel accommodations and tourist services, sales of unprocessed vegetables and fruit, and residential rents are not subject to the VAT.

Israel's electronic commerce (e-commerce) sector is composed of five players, four of which dominate the market, accounting for some 60% of online sales. Most of these sales are computer products and electrical appliances. Specialized niche sites comprise the remainder, focusing on books, flowers, entertainment tickets, food, and tourism.

Business hours vary widely, depending on the religion of the proprietor. Saturday closing is the custom for all Jewish shops, offices, banks, public institutions, and transport services. Generally, all businesses are closed on Saturdays, except for restaurants, coffee bars, cinemas, and shopping centers near large cities. Office hours are generally Sunday to Thursday, 8 a.m. to 7 p.m. Retail hours run from 9 a.m. to 7 p.m. Sunday through Thursday and 9 a.m. to 2p.m. on Fridays. Shops in malls usually stay open until 10 p.m. On days preceding holidays, shops shut down about 2 p.m., offices at 1 p.m. Banks are open 8:30 a.m. to 12:30 p.m. and 4 to 5:30 p.m.; they close at noon on Fridays and days before holidays and have no afternoon hours on Wednesdays. Many Islamic-owned establishments are closed all day Friday, while Christian-owned ones are closed on Sunday.

31 FOREIGN TRADE

Israel is a relatively small country with limited natural resources and a significant well-off citizenry. It is therefore dependent on international trade to supply its industry with natural resources and specialty machines and its populace with unusual and luxury items.

From 2000 to 2009 imports have risen about 1.8% a year in volume but 7.1% in value. Exports have grown at rates of 3.7% in volume and 8.7% in value. This means that Israel's net barter terms of trade have risen about 1.7% yearly, according to UNCTAD. The vast majority (66%) of Israeli exports are manufactured goods, and their primary destinations are the United States and the European Union, which together buy 65% of Israel's exports. Imports are primarily industrial resources (63%); other large sectors are capital goods (19%) and consumer products (11%). Cut diamonds top the list of Israel's export commodities in gross value though not in net value-added. In 2005, Israel's polished and rough diamond exports broke the $10 billion level for the first time, maintaining Israel's position as a major trading and manufacturing center for polished and rough diamonds. Net polished diamond exports were $6.7 billion, and rough diamond exports reached $3.5 billion. Net imports of rough diamonds totaled $5.3 billion, and Israel's imports of polished diamonds rose 9.3% in 2005 to reach $3.9 billion. The United States is the major export market for Israel's polished diamonds, although its export share dropped from 67% in 2004 to 61% in 2005, with exports to Europe and Asia increasing. Israel's imports of civilian goods (CIF) in 2008 were $65 billion, of which 20% was machinery and apparatus, 17% was petroleum, 14% uncut diamonds, 11% chemical products, and 8% transportation equipment. Exports were $61 billion, of which machinery and apparatus made up 22%; chemical products, 22%; polished diamonds, 11%, rough diamonds, 5%, petroleum and products, 5%, and scientific instruments, 2%. Imports came from or through the US, Belgium and Luxembourg (diamonds), China, Switzerland, and Germany. Exports went to or through the US, Belgium and Luxembourg, Hong Kong, India, and the Netherlands.

32 BALANCE OF PAYMENTS

Israel's foreign trade has consistently shown an adverse balance, owing mainly to the rapid rise in population and the expansion of the industrialized economy, requiring heavy imports of machinery and raw materials. The imbalance on current accounts has been offset to a large extent by the inflow of funds from abroad. Deficits are often offset by massive US aid, most of which is tied to American exports, and Jewish philanthropy. Even with these funds, however, Israel still runs significant trade deficits. Financing this deficit is easier on Israel than on many nations primarily because of its relationship with the United States.

For 2010–11, Israel's merchandise deficit will be an estimated -$14.7 billion, but the current account (which includes services

Balance of Payments – Israel (2010)

(In millions of US dollars)

Current Account		**6,396.0**
Balance on goods		-2,365.0
Imports	-58,039.0	
Exports	55,674.0	
Balance on services		6,648.0
Balance on income		-6,312.0
Current transfers		8,426.0
Capital Account		**983.0**
Financial Account		**1,248.0**
Direct investment abroad		-7,960.0
Direct investment in Israel		5,152.0
Portfolio investment assets		-8,901.0
Portfolio investment liabilities		8,602.0
Financial derivatives		30.0
Other investment assets		929.0
Other investment liabilities		-1,126.0
Net Errors and Omissions		**2,947.0**
Reserves and Related Items		**-11,573.0**

(…) data not available or not significant.

SOURCE: *Balance of Payment Statistics Yearbook 2011*, Washington, DC: International Monetary Fund, 2011.

and unilateral transfers) will be +$2.5 billion, which is 0.4% of the GDP.

33 BANKING AND SECURITIES

The structure of the banking industry is based on the central European model of "universal banking," whereby the banks operate as retail, wholesale, and investment banks and are active in all main areas of capital market activity, brokerage, underwriting, and mutual and provident fund management. However, the banks are barred from insurance operations and have only recently been allowed to enter the pension market.

The Bank of Israel (BOI), with headquarters in Jerusalem, began operations as the central state bank in December 1954. The BOI issues currency, accepts deposits from banking institutions in Israel, extends temporary advances to the government, acts as the government's sole banking and fiscal agent, and manages the public debt.

Among the largest commercial banks, ranked by assets as of 2005, are the Histadrut-controlled Bank Hapoalim (320 branches), the Bank Leumi le-Israel (232 branches), the Israel Discount Bank (195 branches), Mizrahi Tefahot (123), First International Bank (103). These banks had almost ILS800 billion in assets in that year or about 95% of the total banking assets in the country. There were about a dozen other licensed commercial banks and two mortgage banks listed by the Bank of Israel. Four international banks operate in Israel: Citibank, BNP Paribas, HSBCE, and the State Bank of India. There are also numerous credit cooperatives and other financial institutions. Among the subsidiaries of commercial banks are mortgage banks, some of which were also directly established by the government. The largest of these specialized institutions, the Tefahot Israel Mortgage Bank, provides many loans to homebuilders.

Industrial development banks specialize in financing new manufacturing enterprises. The Industrial Bank of Israel, formed in

1957 by major commercial banks, the government, the Manufacturers' Association, and foreign investors, has received aid from the International Bank for Reconstruction and Development (IBRD) and has played a major role in the industrial development of the Negev area. The government-owned Bank of Agriculture is the largest lending institution in that sector. The Post Office Bank, similar to France's La Poste, is concerned mainly with clearing operations, savings, sale of savings certificates, and postal orders.

The Bank of Israel's power to fix the liquidity ratio that banks must maintain against deposits has been an important instrument in governing both volume and types of loans. Legal interest rate ceilings formerly were 10% on loans to industry and agriculture and 11% for commercial loans, but, in the early 1980s, rampant inflation caused the large commercial banks to raise the interest rate to 13.6%. With the disinflation of the following years, by 2005, the discount rate had fallen to 4% and to 2.5% in 2008.

The International Monetary Fund reports that at the end of 2007, currency and demand deposits—an aggregate commonly known as M1—were equal to ILS77 billion. In that same year, money and quasi-money—an aggregate equal to M1 plus savings deposits, small-time deposits, and money market mutual funds—was ILS671 billion. Banking supervision and regulation conform to international standards, according to the *The Wall Street Journal*.

Banks have benefited from a very slow program of financial deregulation and the absence of foreign competition; until 2000, the only foreign bank licensed to operate in Israel was the Polish PKO Bank, more of a historical curiosity than a serious commercial consideration. By the mid-1990s, as Israel moved to liberalize its economy, the banking sector underwent significant reconstruction. In two sell-offs in 1997 and 1998, the government divested itself of a majority of Bank Hapoalim. It also sold sizeable shares of United Mizrahi Bank, Israeli Discount Bank, and Bank Leumi in the hopes of shedding all remnants of ownership in these banks. In addition to bank privatization, the Israeli government moved to reduce capital markets regulations. As deregulation progressed, foreign ownership of Israeli banks, in part or whole, was permitted. In 2000, Citibank set up a full branch in Israel, the first major international bank to do so; others soon followed.

Growing activity on the Israeli securities market made it necessary to convert the rather loosely organized Tel Aviv Securities Clearing House into the formally constituted Tel Aviv Stock Exchange (TASE) in 1953. A further expansion took place in 1955, when debentures linked either to the US dollar or to the cost-of-living index—with special tax privileges—made their first appearance on the market. The market is largely devoted to loans of public and semi-public bodies, with provident funds and banks acquiring most of the securities placed. There is only one quotation daily for each security. As of 2004, there was a combined total of 571 companies listed on the TASE and the S and P EMDB Israel indices, which in that year had a market capitalization of $95.505 billion. In 2011, the Tel Aviv-100 index stood at 1018, a rise of about 60% since 2004. The index recovered much of its decline in the 2008 world financial crisis by 2009, but fell more moderately from the end of 2010, -17% in local currency, along with other world markets.

As for the Arab sector, the Palestinian Authority began after 1994 to act within the constraints of the economic protocol to re-

vive the financial sector, supply liquidity, encourage savings and investments, and facilitate management of risk. In expectation of a boom in the financial sector, a number of Jordanian and Palestinian banks opened, or reopened, branches in the West Bank and Gaza. The banks have mainly limited themselves to establishing checking accounts and accepting deposits, specifically non-interest-bearing accounts. Despite their success in attracting deposits from Palestinians, the banks have maintained a limited role in lending. The reluctance to invest locally stems from doubts over the political environment. Instead, it is widely believed that banks are investing abroad, particularly in Central Bank of Jordan treasury bills. The Commercial Bank of Palestine, one of the first banks to open after the return of the Palestinian Authority, was capitalized at $14 million and raised its capital to $20 million by the end of 2003.

A key factor in the success of the banks will be the supervisory activities of the Palestinian Monetary Authority (PMA). The PMA has most of the functions of a central bank. It is empowered to act as the PA's adviser and sole financial agent: to hold its foreign currency reserves; to regulate foreign-exchange dealers; and to supervise the banking sector, as the self-rule areas come under PA jurisdiction. However, in the absence of a Palestinian currency, the PMA's ability to be a lender of last resort is questionable.

The Arab Palestine Investment Bank (APIB), organized in Amman, Jordan, in 1996, with four principal shareholders, Jordan's Arab Bank (55%), the International Finance Corporation (25%), the German Investment and Development Company (15%), and the Palestinian private-sector Enterprise Investment Company (5%). Total deposits of the Palestinian banking system expanded, but reportedly half the local deposits were invested abroad, despite PMA pressure to increase financial intermediation locally.

With the election of a Hamas government in January 2006, and Israel's subsequent decision to cease transferring some $50 million in monthly tax and customs receipts to the PA, Palestinians realized they would have to take significant steps to court new investment and development funds to support the economy, improve infrastructure, reduce poverty, and secure the living standards of the people. In January 2006, the Palestinian Minister for the National Economy pledged to provide a number of political and financial guarantees to those wishing to invest in Palestine; first on the list was a plan to establish a $250 million Investment Security Fund as insurance against further political action. The fund was to be established by various entities, including OPEC, the World Bank, the Islamic Investment Bank, German Investment Bank, European Investment Bank, and the Palestinian Investment Fund.

34 INSURANCE

There are 29 insurance companies offering life, property, and other types of policies, but the sector is dominated by a few large firms, of which Migdal and Clal Insurance (non-life) are the most prominent. However, the easy, cartel-like conditions that have characterized the sector for many years are beginning to crumble and new direct insurance companies are gaining market share. In 1997, the US-based AIG group entered the competition, via a direct insurance joint venture with an Israeli communications company, Aurec. This signaled the opening of the industry to much greater competition from both domestic and foreign entities.

The State Insurance Controller's Office may grant or withhold insurance licenses and determine the valuation of assets, the form of balance sheets, computations of reserves, and investment composition. According to the latest available reports from the State Controller, in 2003, the value of direct premiums written totaled $6.892 billion, of which non-life premiums accounted for $3.840 billion. Clal was Israel's top non-life insurer in 2002, with gross written non-life premiums of $479.3 million. Migdal, that same year was the country's leading life insurer, with gross written life premiums totaling $839.9 million.

Automobile liability insurance, workers' compensation, and aviation liability are compulsory. War-damage insurance is compulsory on buildings and also on some personal property.

35 PUBLIC FINANCE

In 2010, the budget of Israel included $60.59 billion in public revenue and $68.68 billion in public expenditures. Government spending was about 43% of GNP, but the government has been restricting the increase in its spending to 1.7% yearly since 2007. The budget deficit amounted to 3.8% of GDP. Public debt has been reduced and stood at 77.3% of GDP at the beginning of 2009, with $106 billion of the debt held by foreign entities.

As of 2007, budgetary revenue was collected 31% from income tax, 18% from the VAT, capital revenue (loans and grants) 29%, and other 22%. Expenditures were 32.5% on debt service, 18% on defense, 18% on social security and welfare, 11% on education, and 5.5% on health.

As of 2004, the PA in the West Bank and Gaza had revenues amounting to $964 million and expenditures amounting to $1.34 billion. The PA authority held no external debt at that time.

Public Finance – Israel (2009)

(In millions of new sheqalim, central government figures)

Revenue and Grants	**279,303**	**100.0%**
Tax revenue	176,994	63.4%
Social contributions	48,582	17.4%
Grants	13,213	4.7%
Other revenue	40,514	14.5%
Expenditures	**312,466**	**100.0%**
General public services	39,533	12.7%
Defense	51,532	16.5%
Public order and safety	12,262	3.9%
Economic affairs	19,062	6.1%
Environmental protection	811	0.3%
Housing and community amenities	2,631	0.8%
Health	40,795	13.1%
Recreational, culture, and religion	7,601	2.4%
Education	49,702	15.9%
Social protection	88,534	28.3%

(…) data not available or not significant.

SOURCE: Government Finance Statistics Yearbook 2010, Washington, DC: International Monetary Fund, 2010.

36 TAXATION

The personal income tax is progressive, from 10% up to a top rate of 45% on all earnings, including capital gains. In addition, there are personal income taxes on gross income from employment, trade, business, dividends, and other sources, with limited deductions. Rates on rentals and interest are lower. Special tax concessions, however, are granted to residents in border settlements, new settlements, and the Negev. Taxes of salaried persons are deducted at the source; self-employed persons make advance payments in 10 installments, subject to assessment. Also levied are a value-added tax (VAT) of 16% as of 2011, a purchase tax, high rates of excises on gasoline and tobacco, various land taxes, and a national health insurance premium tax on a rising scale up to 4.8%. Overall, Israel's government collects about 33.5% of GNP in taxes, a rate that is fairly high by world standards. By 2016, the government wishes to reduce the top personal rate to 39% and the top corporate rate to 18%.

The corporate income tax rate at present is 25%, although tax relief is available to "approved enterprises" and international trading companies. Municipalities and local and regional councils levy several taxes, too. There is an annual business tax on every enterprise, based on net worth, annual sales volume, number of employees, and other factors. General rates, a real estate tax (commonly based on the number of rooms and the location of the building), and water rates are paid by tenants or occupants rather than by owners.

37 CUSTOMS AND DUTIES

Israel has gradually reduced its import tariffs. As of 2008, the weighted average 1.1%, but there are non-tariff barriers in the form of some quotas and non-transparent government procurements.

Israel has a single-column import tariff based on the Brussels nomenclature classification. Ad valorem rates predominate, although specific and compound rates are also used. Most basic food commodities, raw materials, and machinery for agricultural or industrial purposes are exempt from customs duties. The highest rates are applied to nonessential foodstuffs, luxury items, and manufactured goods that correspond to a type produced in Israel.

A free-trade agreement between Israel and what is now the European Union took effect on 1 July 1975. Under this agreement, tariffs on Israel's industrial exports were immediately reduced by 60% and were subsequently eliminated in 1989. Preferential treatment has also been extended to Israel's agricultural exports. In return, Israel has granted concessions to the European Union on many categories of industrial and agricultural imports and agreed gradually to abolish its customs duties on imports from the European Union.

Israel belongs to the World Trade Organization (WTO) and operates its trade regime according to WTO guidelines. Most significantly, the WTO calls for the elimination of non-tariff barriers. Israel also signed a free trade agreement with the United States in 1985, which scheduled the elimination of all remaining duties on US-made products by 1 January 1995. However, Israel and the United States differ on the interpretation of the treaty, and it has yet to be fully implemented.

³⁸FOREIGN INVESTMENT

Israel is open to foreign investment, and the government encourages and supports the inflow of capital without screening. There are few restrictions on foreign investment, excepting parts of the defense industry, which are closed to outside investors on national security grounds. A 1951 law was designed to encourage foreign investment in those industries and services most urgently required to reduce Israel's dependence on imports and to increase its export potential. Applying mainly to investments in industry and agriculture, the law offers such inducements as relief from property taxes during the first five years, special allowances for depreciation, exemption from customs and purchase taxes on essential materials, and reductions in income tax rates. In a further effort to attract foreign investment, the government approved the "Nissim Plan" in 1990. This plan gives the investor the option of state loan guarantees for up to two-thirds of a project or the bundle of benefits offered under the "Encouragement of Capital Investments Law."

Most land is owned by the government or the Jewish National Fund, and sale is restricted. Commercial law is standardized and consistent, with no discrimination against foreigners. Arbitration of disputes is provided for.

Apart from reparations to victims of the Holocaust, capital imports mainly consist of long-term loans and grants designed for investment by the government or the Jewish Agency. Foreign direct investment (FDI) in Israel was a net inflow of $3.89 billion according to World Bank figures published in 2009. FDI represented 1.99% of GDP.

³⁹ECONOMIC DEVELOPMENT

The economy is a mixture of private, state, and cooperative ownership and holdings of the labor movement. In the first 35 years of Israel's existence, the number of industrial enterprises more than doubled; over 700 agricultural settlements were established; and there were notable advances in housing, transportation, and exploitation of natural resources.

Israel's privatization program, begun in 1986, was given a strong impetus after the election of the Likud-led government in 1996, highlighted by the 1997 divestment of Bank Hapoalim, the country's largest bank. Privatization continued in 1998 and 1999, and the election of a Labor-led coalition in 1999 did not result in a reversal of the privatization initiatives. Between 1986 and 2000, the total extent of privatization amounted to $7.7 billion, with 60% raised from 1998 to 2000. A total of 77 companies ceased to be state-owned during this period. Included among privatizations (whole or partial) by 2011 were Agridev in agriculture, Shikun Pituah le-Israel in construction, El Al (partial), Zim (the 13th largest shipping company in the world), Israel shipyards, Mizrahi Tefachot bank, Bank Hapoalim, Israel Discount Bank, Israel Chemicals, Paz Oil (filling stations), oil refineries, Bezek and Koor industries, Rafael defense electronics (partial), and several others. The energy sector is mostly state-owned and heavily regulated. There are plans to privatize Israel's postal service and Tadmor. Most of these have been sold to investment companies in private placement rather than offering shares on the stock market to the general public.

According to the 2011 Index of Economic Freedom, published by the Heritage Foundation and The Wall Street Journal, Israel ranks 43rd in the world, just ahead of Iceland. This survey attributes Israel's success as a "modern market economy" to a regulatory environment which permits considerable freedom to start, operate, or close a business, financial freedom, secure property rights, and flexible employment regulations. Property can be expropriated only on the ground of national security against terrorism. Since 2003, particularly, Israel has increased competition and entrepreneurship in its economy. Corruption is present, however, as Transparency International rates Israel only 32nd out of 180 countries rated in this regard. The Index notes that Israel's civil service is reported as more politicized than in the past. Israel signed the OECD Bribery Convention in 2009.

⁴⁰SOCIAL DEVELOPMENT

Israel has a universal social insurance system that covers all residents age 18 and over. Benefits are extensive and include old age pensions, disability, medical care, and family allowances. Employee-based programs include maternity benefits, worker's compensation for injuries, and unemployment benefits. These programs are funded by contributions by employees, employers, and the government. Beginning in 2004, the age for retirement is being increased until it reaches 67 for both men and women. All residents are covered for medical care.

The Equality of Women Law provides equal rights for women in the military, workplace, health, education, housing, and social welfare. It also entitles women protection from sexual harassment, exploitation, and violence. Nevertheless, there are still reports of spousal abuse and some harassment in the military. Although the law mandates equal pay for equal work, a wage gap remains. Jewish women are subject to military draft and can volunteer to serve in combat units. Jewish and Muslim women are subject to limitations in their respective faiths. Children's rights are protected, and education is free and compulsory. Gays and lesbians have equal rights and privileges. The government generally protects the human rights of its citizens.

⁴¹HEALTH

The Ministry of Health supervises all health matters and functions directly in the field of medical care. The Ministry also operates infant welfare clinics, nursing schools, and laboratories. The largest medical organization in the country, the Workers' Sick Fund (Kupat Holim, the health insurance association of Histadrut) administers hospitals, clinics, convalescent homes, and mother-and-child welfare stations. The Arab Department of the Ministry of Health recruits public health personnel from among the Arab population, and its mobile clinics extend medical aid to Bedouin tribes in the Negev.

According to World Bank statistics, the country spent 7.6% of its GDP on healthcare, amounting to $1,966 per person in 2009. Life expectancy at birth in Israel was 80 for males and 82 for females. The crude birth rate in 2008 was 22 per thousand, and the crude death rate was 8/1000. There were 36 physicians, 62 nurses and midwives, and 58 hospital beds per 10,000 inhabitants. The fertility rate in 2011 was 3.0 children for each woman during childbearing years. The maternal death rate (7 per 100,000 births) is the lowest in the Middle East and North Africa. Israel's Palestinian Arabs have a lower life expectancy as well as lesser educational achievement and employment opportunities than do Jews.

The infant (under 5) mortality rate was estimated at 4.12 per 1,000 live births in 2011. Immunization rates for children up to one year old were diphtheria, pertussis, and tetanus, 95%; polio, 93%; and measles, 95%. It was estimated that 96% of children were vaccinated against measles.

The CIA calculated HIV/AIDS prevalence in Israel to be about 0.2% in 2009. The incidence of tuberculosis was 9 per 100,000 people in 2007.

42 HOUSING

Israel suffered from a severe housing shortage at its creation. Despite an extensive national building program and the initial allocation of some abandoned Arab dwellings to newcomers, in early 1958, nearly 100,000 immigrants were still housed in transit camps. By the mid-1960s, however, the extreme housing shortage had been overcome, and newcomers were immediately moved into permanent residences. From 1960 to 1985, a total of 943,350 housing units were constructed. By 1986, 94% of all housing units had piped water, 58.2% had flush toilets, and 99% had electric lighting. During 1990–2001, a surge of immigration from the former Soviet Union and Ethiopia resulted in a dramatic increase in housing demand. The government responded with mortgage packages making it possible for new immigrants to afford housing.

As of the 1995 census, there were about 1,639,410 residential dwellings throughout the nation. By 2003, about 70% of all households lived in dwellings owned by a resident; all urban dwellings had improved sanitation facilities by 2008. Homelessness and overcrowding are serious problems in the West Bank and Gaza, however.

Israeli public opinion has been divided over the issue of new construction in Jewish settlements in east Jerusalem and the West Bank, which are heavily populated by Palestinians. In September 2009, 455 new housing units were authorized for construction in Jewish settlements in the West Bank by Israel's defense minister, Ehud Barak. Tensions mounted again in January 2010, when Israel approved the construction of four new apartment buildings in an Arab neighborhood of east Jerusalem. Palestinians claim Al-Quds as the future capital of their state. The international community, for the most part, does not accept the legitimacy of Israeli settlement construction in east Jerusalem and the West Bank, including apartment complexes that could not be considered "natural growth" for a preexisting Jewish settlement. However, Israel continued to approve a series of settlements, upsetting the peace negotiations that different US administrations wanted to push through. In total, approximately 180,000 Jews now live alongside 250,000 Palestinians in east Jerusalem, including the Jewish Quarter.

43 EDUCATION

In Israel, education is compulsory for 11 years and free for all children between 5 and 15 years of age. Primary education is for six years followed by three years of lower secondary and three more years of upper secondary education.

A state education law of 1953 put an end to the separate elementary school systems affiliated with labor and religious groupings, and established a unified state-administered system, with-

in which provision was made for state religious schools. Four types of schools exist: public religious (Jewish) and public secular schools (the largest group); schools of the orthodox Agudat Israel (which operate outside the public school system but are assisted with government funds); public schools for Arabs; and private schools, mainly operated by Catholic and Protestant organizations. The language of instruction in Jewish schools is Hebrew; in Arab schools it is Arabic. Arabic is taught as an optional language in Jewish schools, while Hebrew is taught in Arab schools from the fourth grade. The school year runs from October to June.

Most children between the ages of three and five are enrolled in some type of preschool program. In 2008, it was reported that 97% of age-eligible children in Israel were enrolled in primary school. Secondary enrollment for age-eligible children stood at 86%. Tertiary enrollment was estimated at 60%. Of those enrolled in tertiary education, there were 100 male students for every 131 female students. Overall, Israel had a literacy rate of 97.1%, nearly equal for men and women.

Public expenditure on education represented 5.9% of GDP in 2009, according to the World Bank. The student-to-teacher ratio for primary school was at about 13:1 in 2005 and 10:1 at the secondary level.

In June 2010, the Israeli supreme court ruled it illegal to segregate religious schools ethnically. The case concerned an Orthodox all girls' school in the West Bank settlement of Immanuel. Ashkenazi parents at that school did not want their daughters studying alongside Sephardi girls. The Ashkenazi parents cited the long history of separation between the groups. However, the supreme court dismissed that argument and ordered forty-three sets of parents from that school to jail. As a result, tens of thousands of Orthodox protesters took to the streets in protest.

Israel has eight main institutions of higher learning. The four largest are the Hebrew University in Jerusalem (founded in 1918), Tel-Aviv University (1956), and the Israel Institute of Technology (Technion, founded in 1912), and Haifa University. All receive government subsidies of about 50% of their total budgets; the remaining funds are largely collected abroad, as tuition is low. Other institutions include the Bar-Ilan University in Ramat-Gan, opened in 1955 under religious auspices; the Weizmann Institute of Science at Rehovot, notable for its research into specific technical, industrial, and scientific problems; and Ben-Gurion University of the Negev in Beersheva. An open university, promoting adult education largely through home study, was established and patterned on the British model. In 2005, about 58% of the tertiary age population was enrolled in some type of higher education program with 50% for men and 66% for women.

In the Palestinian school system, basic education covers 10 years of study followed by two years of secondary school or two years of vocational school. During the final two years of general secondary school, students are placed in either arts or science courses depending on their performance in their basic education. Primary school enrollment in 2005 was estimated at about 80% of age-eligible students. The same year, secondary school enrollment was about 95% of age-eligible students. Arab universities and community colleges on the West Bank offer higher education programs for adults. They include Bethlehem University, Islamic University, and Palestine Polytechnic Institute. In 2005, about 38%

of the tertiary age Palestinian population was enrolled in some type of higher education program.

⁴⁴LIBRARIES AND MUSEUMS

Israel's largest library, founded in 1924, is the privately endowed Jewish National and University Library at the Hebrew University in Jerusalem, with more than three million volumes. Important collections are housed in the Central Zionist Archives and the Central Archives for the History of the Jewish People, both also in Jerusalem. There are more than 950 other libraries. The Ministry of Education and Culture has provided basic libraries to hundreds of rural settlements. The Ben Gurion University of the Negev holds 720,000 volumes. Tel Aviv University holds two million volumes, including a Holocaust Studies collection.

The country's most important museum is the Israel Museum, opened in 1965 in Jerusalem. Found in the museum are the Bezalel Art Museum with its large collection of Jewish folk art; a Jewish antiquities exhibit; the Billy Rose Art Garden of modern sculpture; the Samuel Bronfman Biblical and Archaeological Museum; and the Shrine of the Book, containing the Dead Sea Scrolls and other valuable manuscripts. The Rockefeller Archaeological Museum (formerly the Palestine Museum), built in 1938, contains a rich collection of archaeological material illustrating the prehistory and early history of western Palestine and Transjordan. Also in Jerusalem is the Central Archives for the History of the Jewish People, containing documents from Jewish communities and organizations around the globe. The Tel Aviv Museum of Art, founded in 1926, has more than 30,000 paintings, drawings, and sculptures. Among Israel's newer cultural institutions are the Museum of the Diaspora in Tel Aviv-Yafo, founded in 1978 on the Tel Aviv University campus; the Bible Lands Museum in Jerusalem, founded in 1992; the Museum of Israeli Art in Ramat Gan, founded in 1987; and the Tower of David Museum of the History of Jerusalem at the Jaffa Gate in Jerusalem, founded in 1989.

⁴⁵MEDIA

Israel's telecommunications system, while not the largest in the Middle East, is certainly the most highly developed. The domestic system is fully digital and is based on microwave relay and coaxial cable technologies. International service is provided by submarine cables and satellite ground stations. The state owns and operates the major telephone communications services, although radio and television are increasingly privately owned. As of 2009, there were 3.3 million telephone landlines in Israel. Mobile phone subscriptions numbered about 121 per hundred people.

The state radio stations include the government's Israel Broadcasting Authority (*Shidurei Israel*), the army's Defense Forces Waves (*Galei Zahal*), and the Jewish Agency's Zion's Voice to the Diaspora (*Kol Zion la-Gola*), aimed mostly at Jewish communities in Europe and the United States. The Second Television and Radio Authority is a public organization that operates two privately owned television channels and 14 privately owned radio stations. There were 23 FM radio stations, 15 AM radio stations, and two shortwave radio stations. The state radio broadcasts in standard Hebrew, easy Hebrew for new immigrants, and English. There are three cable television companies and one satellite television company. In 2003, there were an estimated 526 radios, not counting automobile sets, and 330 television sets for every 1,000 people.

Of all households, 90% had television, except for ultra-Orthodox families, and nearly all had radios. Cable subscriptions are common. In 2010, the country had about 1.6 million Internet hosts. Internet users numbered 50 per 100 citizens.

All Israeli newspapers are privately owned and managed. Most newspapers have 4–16 pages, but there are weekly supplements on subjects such as politics, economics, and the arts. Prominent newspapers in 2010, with circulation numbers listed parenthetically, included *Yedioth Aharonoth* (300,000), *Ma'ariv Evening* (160,000), and *Al-Quds* (60,000), as well as nine other major newspapers. The English-language *Jerusalem Post* is published in the capital. An Arabic-language paper, *Al-Quds,* is published as well.

Although there is no political censorship within Israel, restrictions are placed on coverage of national security matters. Individuals, organizations, the press, and the electronic media freely and vigorously debate public issues and often criticize public policy and government officials.

⁴⁶ORGANIZATIONS

The World Zionist Organization (WZO) was founded by Theodor Herzl in 1897 for the purpose of creating "for the Jewish people a home in Palestine, secured by public law." The organization is composed of various international groupings represented in its supreme organ, the World Zionist Congress. The Jewish Agency, originally founded under the League of Nations mandate to promote Jewish interests in Palestine, functions as the executive arm of the WZO. Since 1948, it has been responsible for the organization, training, and transportation of all Jews who wish to settle in Israel. The United Israel Appeal (*Keren Hayesod*) is the financial instrument of the Jewish Agency; it recruits donations from world Jewry. The Jewish National Fund (*Keren Kayemet le'Israel*) is devoted to land acquisition, soil reclamation, and reforestation. Hadassah, the Women's Zionist Organization of America, is also active in Israel; it sponsors the Hadassah Medical Organization, which provides hospital and medical training facilities.

The main workers' organization is the General Federation of Labor (*Histadrut*), a complex whose interests include some of the largest factories in the country, an agricultural marketing society (*Tnuva*), a cooperative wholesale association (*Hamashbir Hamerkazi*), and a workers' bank. Trade and industry unions are fairly active, including such groups as the Manufacturers Association of Israel, Israel Association of Craft and Industry, and the Citrus Marketing Board of Israel. There are also professional associations representing a wide variety of fields. The Israel Medical Organization promotes research and education on health issues and works to establish common policies and standards in healthcare. There are several other associations dedicated to research and education for specific fields of medicine and particular diseases and conditions, such as the Israel Heart Society and the Israel Cancer Association.

Among numerous cultural and religious societies and organizations are the Israel Academy of Sciences and Humanities, which promotes public interest in science and cooperates with foreign academies in research and dissemination of information. The Hebrew Writers Association in Israel represents Hebrew writers worldwide.

Youth Aliyah, founded in 1934, has helped to rehabilitate and educate children from all countries of the world. Other national youth organizations include the Israeli Boy and Girl Scouts Federation, National Working Youth Movement of Israel, Orthodox Youth Movement of Israel (*Ezra*), Socialist Youth Movement of Israel, Sons of Akiva Youth Movement of Israel, Tel Aviv University Students' Association, Trumpeldor Covenant Youth Movement of Israel, United Kibbutz Youth Movement of Israel, Young Herut, Zionist Youth Movement, and chapters of the YMCA/YWCA. Sports associations, professional, semi-professional, and amateur, are also active for soccer, baseball, badminton, ice skating, cricket, and frisbee. A modern tennis center is located near Tel Aviv, and a golf course can be found near Caesarea. The Maccabi world organization conducts championships in athletics, swimming, and many other sports for world Jewish youth.

The Council of Women's Organizations in Israel is an umbrella organization promoting legal and social rights for women.

Disaster relief and aid services in Israel are organized by the Red Shield of David (*Magen David Adom*), which cooperates with the International Red Cross. Other international organizations include Defence for Children International and Amnesty International.

The Association for Arab Youth was founded in 2000 to promote pluralism and tolerance through educational and recreational youth activities. The Arab Association for Human Rights is in Nazareth, and the Association for Civil Rights in Israel is in Jerusalem. The Democracy and Workers Rights Center represents those working to create a civil society within the Palestinian-administered territories of the West Bank and the Gaza Strip.

47 TOURISM, TRAVEL, AND RECREATION

Principal Israeli tourist attractions are the many historic and holy sites sacred to three world religions. the Old City of Jerusalem contains the Western ("Wailing") Wall, the Dome of the Rock, and the Church of the Holy Sepulchre; nearby are the Mount of Olives and Garden of Gethsemane. Another holy place is Bethlehem, the traditional birthplace of both King David and Jesus of Nazareth. Also of great interest are the ruins of Jericho, the world's oldest city; the caves of Qumran, near the Dead Sea and the lowest spot on Earth; and the rock fortress of Masada, on the edge of the Judean Desert. Tourists are also drawn to Israel's rich variety of natural scenery, ranging from hills and greenery in the north to rugged deserts in the south. Popular tourist recreations include swimming, sailing, and fishing in the Mediterranean and the Sea of Galilee.

The UN World Tourism Organization reported 2.74 million incoming tourists to Israel in 2009; they spent a total of $4.33 billion. Of those incoming tourists, there were 1.4 million from Europe. There were 125,455 hotel beds available in Israel, which had an occupancy rate of 50%. The estimated daily cost to visit Jerusalem, the capital, was $466. The cost of visiting other cities averaged $359. Outbound Israeli tourists numbered about 4 million and spent $3.9 million while abroad.

A valid passport, sufficient funds, and onward/return ticket are required for tourists; a three-month visa may be issued upon arrival. The Tourist Industry Development Corporation fosters tourism by granting loans for hotel expansion and improvement. A total of 1,063,381 tourists visited Israel in 2003, a 23% increase from

2002. There were 46,368 hotel rooms with 114,041 beds and an occupancy rate of 45%. The average length of stay was two nights.

48 FAMOUS PERSONS

The State of Israel traces its ancestry to the settlement of the Hebrews in Canaan under Abraham (b. Babylonia, 18th century BC), the return of the Israelite tribes to Canaan under Moses (b. Egypt, 13th century BC) and Joshua (b. Egypt, 13th century BC), and the ancient kingdom of Israel, which was united by David (r. 1000?–960? BC) and became a major Near Eastern power under Solomon (r. 960?–922 BC). A prophetic tradition that includes such commanding figures as Isaiah (second half of the 8th century BC), Jeremiah (650?–585? BC), and Ezekiel (6th century BC) and spans the period of conquest by Assyria and Babylonia. The scribe Ezra (b. Babylonia, 5th century BC) and the governor Nehemiah (b. Babylonia, 5th century BC) spurred the reconstruction of the Judean state under Persian hegemony. Judas (Judah) Maccabaeus ("the Hammerer"; ca. 165–160 BC) was the most prominent member of a family who led a rebellion against Syrian Greek rule and established several decades of political and religious independence. During the period of Roman rule, important roles in Jewish life and learning were played by the sages Hillel (b. Babylonia, 30 BC–AD 9), Johannan ben Zakkai (1st century), Akiba ben Joseph (50?–135?), and Judah ha-Nasi (135?–220), the compiler of the Mishnah, a Jewish law code; by the military commander and historian Flavius Josephus (Joseph ben Mattathias, AD 37–100?); and Simon Bar-Kokhba (bar Kosiba, d. 135), leader of an unsuccessful revolt against Roman rule. Unquestionably, the most famous Jew born in Roman Judea was Jesus (Jeshua) of Nazareth (4? BC–AD 29?), the Christ, or Messiah ("anointed one"), of Christian belief. Peter (Simon, d. AD 67?) was the first leader of the Christian Church and, in Roman Catholic tradition, the first pope. Paul of Tarsus (Saul, b. Asia Minor, d. AD 67?) was principally responsible for spreading Christianity and making it a religion distinct from Judaism.

The emergence of Israel as a modern Jewish state is attributed in large part to Chaim Weizmann (b. Russia, 1874–1952), the leader of the Zionist movement for 25 years, as well as a distinguished chemist who discovered methods for synthesizing acetone and rubber. Theodor Herzl (b. Budapest, 1860–1904), the founder of political Zionism, is buried in Jerusalem. Achad Ha'am (Asher Hirsch Ginsberg; b. Russia, 1856–1927) was an influential Zionist and social critic. Vladimir Jabotinsky (1880–1940) was a dedicated advocate of Jewish self-defense, both in his native Russia and in Palestine. David Ben-Gurion (Gruen; b. Poland, 1886–1973), also a leading Zionist and an eloquent spokesman on labor and national affairs, served as Israel's first prime minister. Golda Meir (Meyerson; b. Russia, 1898–1978), like Ben-Gurion, a former secretary-general of Histadrut, became well known as Israel's prime minister from 1970 to 1974. Other prominent figures include Pinhas Sapir (b. Poland, 1907–75), labor leader and minister of finance; Abba Eban (Aubrey Eban; b. South Africa, 1915–2002), former foreign affairs minister and representative to the UN; and Moshe Dayan (1915–81), military leader and cabinet minister. Menachem Begin (b. Russia, 1913–92), the former leader of guerrilla operations against the British, was prime minister from 1977 to 1983 and received the Nobel Peace Prize in 1978. He was succeeded in 1983by Yitzhak Shamir (b. Poland, 1915–2011), who gave way to Shimon

Peres (b. Poland, 1923) in 1984. Shamir succeeded Peres in 1986. Yitzhak Rabin (1922–1995) was instrumental in the peace accords with the PLO signed in 1993 in Washington. Benjamin Netanyahu (b. 1949) succeeded Peres, who had succeeded the assassinated Rabin. Ehud Barak (b. 1942) followed Netanyahu as prime minister; Barak was succeeded by Ariel Sharon (b. 1928). Sharon suffered a hemorrhagic stroke in January 2006; because he was incapacitated, his deputy prime minister, Ehud Olmert (b. 1945), took over the duties of prime minister.

Israel's foremost philosopher was Martin Buber (b. Vienna, 1878–1965), author of *I and Thou*. Outstanding scholars include the literary historian Joseph Klausner (1874–1958); the Bible researcher Yehezkel (Ezekiel) Kaufmann (b. Ukraine, 1889–1963); the philologists Eliezer Ben-Yehuda (b. Lithuania, 1858–1922) and Naphtali Hertz Tur-Sinai (Torczyner; b. Poland, 1886–1973); the archaeologist Eliezer Sukenik (1889–1953); and the Kabbalah authority Gershom Gerhard Scholem (b. Germany, 1897–1982).

The foremost poets include Haim Nahman Bialik (b. Russia, 1873–1934), Saul Tchernichowsky (b. Russia, 1875–1943), Uri Zvi Greenberg (b. Galicia, 1896–1981), Avraham Shlonsky (b. Russia, 1900–1973), Nathan Alterman (b .Warsaw, 1910–70), Yehuda Amichai (b. Germany, 1924), and Natan Zach (b. Berlin, 1930); and the leading novelists are Shmuel Yosef Halevi Agnon (b. Galicia, 1888–1970), a Nobel Prize winner in 1966, and Hayim Hazaz (b. Russia, 1898–1973). Contemporary Israeli writers include Amos Oz (b. 1939), Aharon Appelfeld (b. 1932), and David Grossman (b. 1954). Painters of note include Reuven Rubin (b. Romania, 1893–1975) and Mane Katz (b. Russia, 1894–1962). Paul Ben-Haim (Frankenburger; b. Munich, 1897–1984) and Ödön Partos (b. Budapest, 1907–77) are well-known composers. Famous musicians include Daniel Barenboim (b. Argentina, 1942), Itzhak Perlman (b. 1945), and Pinchas Zukerman (b. 1948).

Significant contributions in other fields have been made by mathematician Abraham Halevi Fraenkel (b. Munich, 1891–1965); botanist Hugo Boyko (b. Vienna, 1892–1970); zoologist Shimon (Fritz) Bodenheimer (b. Cologne, 1897–1959); parasitologist Saul Aaron Adler (b. Russia, 1895–1966); physicist Giulio Raccah (b. Florence, 1909–65); rheologist Markus Reiner (b. Czernowitz, 1886–1976); gynecologist Bernard Zondek (b. Germany, 1891–1966); and psychoanalyst Heinrich Winnik (b. Austria-Hungary, 1902–82). In October 2009, Jerusalem native Ada Yonath (b. 1939) became the first Israeli woman to receive a Nobel Prize and only the fourth woman to receive the prize in chemistry. Aaron Ciechanover (2004), Avram Hersko (2004), and Daniel Shechtman (2011) all won the Nobel prize in chemistry. Daniel

Kahneman (2002) and Robert Aumann (2005) won the Nobel in Economic Sciences.

⁴⁹DEPENDENCIES

Israel has no formal dependencies, though it administers both the West Bank and the Gaza Strip.

⁵⁰BIBLIOGRAPHY

Alexander, Yonah, ed. *Combating Terrorism: Strategies of Ten Countries*. Ann Arbor, MI: University of Michigan Press, 2002.

Ben-Ami, Jeremy. *A New Voice for Israel: Fighting for the Survival of the Jewish Nation*. New York: Palgrave Macmillan, 2011.

Ben-Ami, Shlomo. *Scars of War, Wounds of Peace: the Israeli-Arab Tragedy*. New York: Oxford University Press, 2006.

Dershowitz, Alan. *The Case for Israel*. Hoboken, NJ: Wiley, 2003.

Eban, Abba. *My Country: The Story of Modern Israel*. New York: Random House, 1972.

Encyclopedia Judaica. 16 vols. Jerusalem: Keter, 1972.

Etzioni-Halevy, Eva. *The Divided People: Can Israel's Breakup Be Stopped?* Lanham, MD: Lexington Books, 2002.

Faure, Claude. *Dictionary of the Israeli-Palestinian Conflict: Culture, History and Politics*. Detroit: Macmillan Reference USA, 2005.

Frank, Mitch. *Understanding the Holy Land: Answering Questions about the Israeli-Palestinian Conflict*. New York: Viking, 2005.

Goodman, Hirsh. *The Anatomy of Israel's Survival*. New York: Public Affairs, 2011.

Ichilov, Orit. *Political Learning and Citizenship Education under Conflict: The Political Socialization of Israeli and Palestinian Youngsters*. New York: Routledge, 2004.

International Smoking Statistics: A Collection of Historical Data from 30 Economically Developed Countries. New York: Oxford University Press, 2002.

Pappae, Ilan. *The Forgotten Palestinians*. New Haven: Yale University Press, 2011.

Seddon, David (ed.). *A Political and Economic Dictionary of the Middle East*. Philadelphia: Routledge/Taylor and Francis, 2004.

Senor, Dan, and Singer, Saul. *Start-up Nation*. New York and Boston: Twelve, 2009.

Schindler, Colin. *Israel and the European Left*. New York: The Continuum International Publishing Group, 2012.

Tye, Larry. *Home Lands: Portrait of the New Jewish Diaspora*. New York: Henry Holt, 2001.

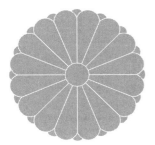

JAPAN

Nippon

CAPITAL: Tokyo

FLAG: The "circle of the sun" flag (*hi no maru*) consists of a red circle on a white background.

ANTHEM: *Kimigayo (The Emperor's Reign).*

MONETARY UNIT: The yen (JPY) of 100 sen is issued in coins of 1, 5, 10, 50, 100, and 500 yen, and notes of 1,000, 2,000, 5,000, and 10,000 yen. JPY1 = $0.013 (or $1 = JPY77) as of 2011.

WEIGHTS AND MEASURES: The metric system is the legal standard.

HOLIDAYS: New Year's Day, 1 January; Adults' Day, 15 January; Commemoration of the Founding of the Nation, 11 February; Vernal Equinox Day, 20 or 21 March; Greenery Day, 29 April; Constitution Day, 3 May; Children's Day, 5 May; Respect for the Aged Day, 15 September; Autumnal Equinox Day, 23 or 24 September; Health-Sports Day, 10 October; Culture Day, 3 November; Labor-Thanksgiving Day, 23 November; Emperor's Birthday, 23 December.

TIME: 9 p.m. = noon GMT.

¹LOCATION, SIZE, AND EXTENT

Situated off the eastern edge of the Asian continent, the Japanese archipelago is bounded on the N by the Sea of Okhotsk, on the E and S by the Pacific Ocean, on the SW by the East China Sea, and on the W by the Sea of Japan. The total area of Japan is 377,835 sq km (145,883 sq mi). Comparatively, the area occupied by Japan is slightly smaller than the state of California. It extends 3,008 km (1,869 mi) NE–SW and 1,645 km (1,022 mi) SE–NW and has a total coastline of 29,751 km (18,486 mi).

The five districts are Honshū, Hokkaidō, Kyūshū, Shikoku, and Okinawa. Each of the five districts consists of a main island of the same name and hundreds of surrounding islands.

Of the thousands of lesser islands, four are noteworthy: Tsushima, in the straits between Korea and Japan; Amami Oshima, of the northern Ryukyu Islands at the southern end of the Japanese archipelago; Sado Island in the Sea of Japan off central Honshū; and Awaji Island, lying between Shikoku and Honshū. Two groups of islands returned to Japan by the United States in 1968 are located some 1,300 km (800 mi) due east of the Ryukyus: the Ogasawara (Bonin) Islands, about 885 km (550 mi) south of Tokyo, and the Kazan (Volcano) Islands, directly south of the Ogasawara group.

Japan's principal island is Honshū, on which are located the capital city of Tokyo, many of Japan's principal cities and plains, and the major industrial areas. This island is divided into five regions: Tōhoku, from north of Kantō to Tsugaru Strait; Kantō, embracing seven prefectures in the Tokyo-Yokohama region; the Chūbu, or central, region, from west of Tokyo to the Nagoya area; Kinki, including the important cities of Kyoto, Osaka, Kobe, and Nara; and Chūgoku, a narrow peninsula thrusting westward from Kinki between the Sea of Japan and the Inland Sea, which lies between southern Honshū and the island of Shikoku.

Small islands at the fringes of Japan's archipelago remain contested between Japan and Russia and between Japan and South Korea. Of particular note are the southern islands in Russia's Kuril Island archipelago (*chishima rettō*), and Dokdo (*takeshima*), currently under South Korean administration.

Japan's capital city, Tokyo, is located on the east coast of the island of Honshū.

²TOPOGRAPHY

The Japanese islands make up the upper portions of vast mountains belonging to what is sometimes called the Circum-Pacific Ring of Fire, which stretches from Southeast Asia to the Aleutian Islands. Mountains cover more than 75% of the land's surface. Landforms are steep and rugged, indicating that, geologically, Japan is still a young area. Through the central part of Honshū, running in a north–south direction, are the two principal mountain ranges: the Hida (or Japan Alps) and the Akaishi mountains. There are 25 mountains with peaks of over 3,000 m (9,800 ft). The highest is the revered Mt. Fuji (*Fuji san*), at 3,776 m (12,388 ft). Japan has 265 volcanoes (including the dormant Mt. Fuji), of which about 20 remain active.

The plains of Japan are few and small and cover only about 29% of the total land area. Most plains are located along the seacoast and are composed of alluvial lowlands, diluvial uplands, and low hills. The largest is the Kantō Plain (Tokyo Bay region), about 6,500 sq km (2,500 sq mi). Others include the Kinai Plain (Osaka–Kyoto), Nobi (Nagoya), Echigo (north-central Honshū), and Sendai (northeastern Honshū). There are four small plains in Hokkaidō. The population is heavily concentrated in these limited flat areas.

Rivers tend to be short and swift. The longest is the Shinano (367 km/228 mi) in north-central Honshū, flowing into the Sea of Japan. The largest lake is Lake Biwa, near Kyoto, with an area of

672 sq km (259 sq mi). Lake Kussharo, in the Akan National Park of Hokkaidō, is considered the clearest lake in the world, having a transparency of 41 m (135 ft). Good harbors are limited because in most areas the land rises steeply out of the sea. Yokohama, Nagoya, and Kobe are Japan's most prominent harbors.

The Ryukyu Islands, among which Okinawa predominates, are the peaks of submerged mountain ranges. They are generally hilly or mountainous, with small alluvial plains.

Japan is considered to be one of the most seismically active areas in the world; about 20% of all magnitude of six or higher earthquakes in the world take place in this region. The country experiences an average of 1,500 minor shocks per year. One of the world's greatest recorded natural disasters was the Kantō earthquake of 1923, when the Tokyo-Yokohama area was devastated and upward of 99,000 people died. In 1995, a magnitude 7.2 quake shook Kobe and left over 6,400 people dead. On March 11, 2011, a magnitude 9.0 earthquake struck off the coast of Tōhoku, which was the most powerful earthquake ever known to have struck Japan. The earthquake and massive tsunami that it triggered were responsible for over 15,000 deaths, and the damage sustained by nuclear power plants along the coast left Japan in a state of social, economic, and political upheaval for months.

3 CLIMATE

Japan is located at the northeastern edge of the Asian monsoon climate belt, which brings much rain to the country. The weather is under the dual influence of the Siberian weather system and the patterns of the southern Pacific; it is affected by the Japan Current (*kuroshio*), a warm stream that flows from the southern Pacific along much of Japan's Pacific coast, producing a milder and more temperate climate than is found at comparable latitudes elsewhere. Northern Japan is affected by the Kuril Current (*oyashio*), a cold stream flowing along the eastern coasts of Hokkaidō and northern Honshū. The junction of the two currents is a bountiful fishing area. The Tsushima Current, an offshoot of the Japan Current, transports warm water northward into the Sea of Japan.

Throughout the year, there is fairly high humidity, with average rainfall ranging by area from 100 cm to over 250 cm (39–98 in). Autumn weather is usually clear and bright. Winters tend to be warmer than in similar latitudes except in the north and west, where snowfalls are frequent and heavy. Spring is usually pleasant, and summers are hot and humid. There is a rainy season that moves from south to north during June and July.

Average temperature ranges from 17°C (63° F) in the southern portions to 9°C (48° F) in the extreme north. Hokkaidō has long and severe winters with extensive snow, while the remainder of the country enjoys milder weather down to the southern regions, which are almost subtropical. The Ryukyus, although located in the temperate zone, are warmed by the Japan Current, giving them a subtropical climate.

The typhoon season runs from May through October, and each year several storms usually sweep through the islands, often accompanied by high winds and heavy rains. In September 2005, Typhoon Nabi hit southern Japan causing the deaths of at least 77 people and temporarily displacing more than 300,000.

4 FLORA AND FAUNA

The World Resources Institute estimates that there are 5,565 plant species in Japan. In addition, Japan is home to 171 species of mammals, 592 species of birds, 92 species of reptiles, and 64 species of amphibians. The calculation reflects the total number of distinct species residing in the country, not the number of endemic species.

Hokkaidō's flora is characterized by montane conifers (fir, spruce, and larch) at high elevations and mixed northern hardwoods (oak, maple, linden, birch, ash, elm, and walnut) at lower altitudes. The ground flora includes plants common to Eurasia and North America. Honshū supports a panoply of temperate flora. Common conifers are cypress, umbrella pine, hemlock, yew, and white pine. On the lowlands, there are live oak and camphor trees and a mixture of bamboo with the hardwoods. Black pine and red pine form the typical growth on the sandy lowlands and coastal areas. Shikoku and Kyūshū are noted for their evergreen vegetation. Sugarcane and citrus fruits are found throughout the limited lowland areas, with broadleaf trees in the lower elevations and a mixture of evergreen and deciduous trees higher up. Throughout these islands are luxuriant growths of bamboo.

The only indigenous primate is the Japanese macaque, a small monkey found in the north. There are 32 carnivores, including the brown bear, ermine, mink, raccoon dog, fox, wolf, walrus, and seal. Japan's waters abound with crabs and shrimp; great migrations of fish are brought in by the Japan and Kuril currents. There are large numbers and varieties of insects. The Japanese beetle is not very destructive in its homeland because of its many natural enemies.

5 ENVIRONMENT

The World Resources Institute reported that Japan had designated 3.45 million hectares (8.54 million acres) of land for protection as of 2006. Water resources totaled 430 cu km (103.2 cu mi), while water usage was 88.43 cu km (21.22 cu mi) per year. Domestic water usage accounted for 20% of total usage, industrial for 18%, and agricultural for 62%. Per capita water usage totaled 690 cu m (24,367 cu ft) per year.

The UN reported in 2008 that carbon dioxide emissions in Japan totaled 1.25 million kilotons.

Rapid industrialization has imposed severe pressures on the environment. Japan's Basic Law for Environmental Pollution Control was enacted in 1967, and the Environment Agency was established four years later.

Air pollution is a serious environmental problem in Japan, particularly in urban centers. Toxic pollutants from power plant emissions have led to the appearance of acid rain throughout the country. In the mid 1990s, Japan had the world's fourth-highest level of industrial carbon dioxide emissions, which totaled 1.09 billion metric tons per year, a per capita level of 8.79 metric tons per year. In 2000, the total of carbon dioxide emissions was 1.18 billion metric tons.

Generally seen as a leader in the pursuit of energy-efficient technologies, Japan was criticized by environmentalists when the government announced a new target plan to reduce greenhouse gas emissions by 15% by 2020 (using 2005 emission levels as a base). The June 2009 announcement was considered inadequate

LOCATION: 122°56′ to 153°59′E; 20°25′ to 45°33′ N. TOTAL COASTLINE: 29,751 kilometers (18,486 miles). TERRITORIAL SEA LIMIT: 12 miles.

by international environmental groups that look to Japan to be a leader in the cause of curbing global climate change. The new target translated into a cut of only about 8% from 1990 levels. The UN has recommended that developing nations cut emissions by at least 25% from 1990 levels by 2020. By comparison, the European Union has pledged to a reduction of 20%. The United States, which ranks first for the highest levels of greenhouse gas emissions, has pledged to a 17% reduction from 2005 levels. Japan,

ranking fifth, is already one of the leading nations in the development of alternative energy technologies. The government has also encouraged the use of alternative energies by offering subsidies to citizens for the use of solar power in homes and toward the purchase of "green" cars.

Water pollution is another area of concern in Japan. Increases in acid levels due to industrial pollutants have affected lakes, rivers, and the waters surrounding Japan. Other sources of pollution include DDT, BMC, and mercury. In the 1950s and 60s, mercury in the wastewater from an industrial chemical factory in the southwestern prefecture of Kumamoto led to widespread mercury poisoning of both animals and humans (a disease that came to be known as Minamata disease and has been linked to around 2,000 human deaths). This incident, among others, triggered the promulgation of the Water Pollution Control Law of 1971, but there remains widespread pollution of lakes and rivers from household sources, especially by untreated sewage and phosphate-rich detergents. Factory noise levels are regulated under a 1968 law. Airplanes may not take off or land after 10 p.m., and the Shinkansen trains must reduce speed while traveling through large cities and their suburbs.

Most of the nation's forests, which play a critical role in retarding runoff and soil erosion in the many mountainous areas, are protected under the Nature Conservation Law of 1972, and large areas have been reforested. Parks and wildlife are covered by the National Parks Law of 1967.

Japan has faced criticism from international environmental groups for several years over its whaling practices. The government officially ceased commercial whaling in 1986 in compliance with a global moratorium on the practice that was initiated by the International Whaling Commission (IWC). By 2011, Japanese whale hunts resumed as ventures in scientific research, which is permitted under the IWC, though there was considerable skepticism about the purpose of the whaling.

According to a 2011 report issued by the International Union for Conservation of Nature and Natural Resources (IUCN), threatened species included 28 types of mammals, 39 species of birds, 12 types of reptiles, 19 species of amphibians, 64 species of fish, 32 types of mollusks, 131 species of other invertebrates, and 15 species of plants. Endangered species in Japan included the Ryukyu sika, Ryukyu rabbit, Iriomote cat, Southern Ryukyu robin, Okinawa woodpecker, Oriental white stork, short-tailed albatross, green sea turtle, and tailless blue butterfly. The Ryukyu pigeon, Bonin thrush, Japanese sea lion, and Okinawa flying fox have become extinct.

⁶POPULATION

The US Central Intelligence Agency (CIA) estimated the population of Japan in 2011 to be approximately 126,475,664, which placed it at number 10 in population among the 196 nations of the world. In 2011, approximately 22.9% of the population was over 65 years of age, with another 13.1% under 15 years of age. The median age in Japan was 44.8 years. There were 0.95 males for every female in the country. The population's annual rate of change was -0.278%. The projected population for the year 2025 was 119,300,000. Population density in Japan was calculated at 335 people per sq km (868 people per sq mi).

The UN estimated that 67% of the population lived in urban areas, and that urban populations had an annual rate of change of 0.2%. The largest urban areas, along with their respective populations, included Tokyo, 36.5 million; Osaka-Kobe, 11.3 million; Nagoya, 3.3 million; Fukuoka-Kitakyūshū, 2.8 million; and Sapporo, 2.7 million.

⁷MIGRATION

Estimates of Japan's net migration rate, carried out by the CIA in 2011, amounted to zero. The total number of emigrants living abroad was 771,400, and the total number of immigrants living in Japan was 2.18 million. Japanese nationals living in other countries totaled more than 600,000 in the 1990s, including some 250,000 in the United States and over 100,000 in Brazil. More than one million Japanese have emigrated since 1880; about 70% of them arrived on the US mainland and in Hawaii during the decades prior to World War II. Emigration continued after the war, encouraged by government policy as a way to relieve population pressure. By the mid 1960s, emigration had considerably decreased, as economic opportunities and living standards in Japan improved. From the 1970s to 1990s, however, the number of emigrants rose, from 12,445 in 1975 to 34,492 in 1985 to 82,619 in 1992.

Immigration to Japan is generally small scale, although the illegal entry of workers from neighboring countries has come to be regarded as a problem. Since 1975, roughly 10,000 Indo-Chinese refugees have settled in Japan. In the mid 2000s, there were 1.9 million foreign residents in Japan, half ethnic Koreans and Chinese who were mostly born in Japan, followed by 350,000 ethnic Japanese from Latin America, often the descendents of Japanese who had emigrated.

Because citizenship is based on the nationality of parents rather than place of birth, registered aliens may have spent their entire lives in Japan. According to *Migration News*, Japan continued to struggle with Zainichi, a term that literally means "to stay in Japan," but is used as a shorthand for Koreans who came to Japan during Japan's colonial rule, and their descendants. Zainichi are often considered outsiders in both Japan and Korea. Their numbers have declined as more become naturalized Japanese.

Internal migration, providing a steady exodus of people from farm and mountain communities to the cities and suburbs, grew between 1952 and the late 1990s. Most such migrants flocked to the three major population centers—the Tokyo, Osaka, and Nagoya metropolitan areas. As pollution and congestion in these areas increased, the government instituted programs to decentralize industry by directing new growth to smaller cities of the north and west, and also began efforts to improve rural living conditions and employment opportunities.

⁸ETHNIC GROUPS

In 2008, 98.4% of the population was Japanese, while only 1.6% belonged to other ethnic groups (mostly Chinese, Korean, Brazilian, and Filipino). Although it is known that the Japanese are descended from many varied peoples of Asia, there is no agreement as to their origins or specific ethnic strains. In physical characteristics, the Japanese belong to the Mongoloid group, with faint admixtures of Malayan and Caucasoid strains. Waves of migration from the continental hinterland reached Japan during the end of the Paleolithic period, blending into a complicated and diverse ethnic, linguistic, and cultural system. It is believed that the Japanese have their roots in the Old Stone Age race of at least 30,000 BC. A major migration appears to have taken place in the 2nd and 3rd centuries AD, and, by the 4th century, this group, called the Yamato clan, had established a monarchy in the present Nara prefecture. Other ethnic strains may have come from Indonesia and

China in the south, Korea in the west, and Siberia and Alaska in the north. The one remaining distinct ethnic group in Japan is the Ainu. These people, living on the northern island of Hokkaidō, are physically distinct from the contemporary Japanese, having Nordic-like features, including more pervasive facial and body hair. There is no agreement as to their origins. There are also approximately 3 million Buraku, who are the descendants of the feudal-era outcasts and face lingering discrimination in Japanese society, although they are not ethnically distinguishable from other Japanese.

9LANGUAGES

Japanese is the official language. Most linguists agree that Japanese is in a language class by itself, although there is some inconclusive evidence that traces it to the Malayo-Polynesian language family. In vocabulary, Japanese is rich in words denoting abstract ideas, natural phenomena, human emotions, ethics, and aesthetics, but poor in words for technical and scientific expression. For these latter purposes, foreign words are directly imported and written in a phonetic system (katakana). A distinct characteristic is the use of honorifics to show proper respect to the listener and his social status. Written Japanese owes its origin almost entirely to Chinese forms. Having no indigenous script, the Japanese since the 5th century have used Chinese characters, giving them both an approximate Chinese pronunciation and a Japanese pronunciation. In addition, the Japanese invented phonetic symbols (kana) in the 9th century to represent grammatical devices unknown to the Chinese. Attempts have been made to reduce the complexity of the written language by limiting the number of Chinese characters used. The government has published a list of 1,850 characters for use in official communications. Newspapers adhere to this list.

10RELIGIONS

According to a 2007 report by the Agency for Cultural Affairs, about 82% of the population practice Shintōism, and 69% practice Buddhism. The percentages exceed 100% because religious identities are not mutually exclusive; many Japanese maintain affiliations with both a Buddhist temple and a Shintō shrine. Shintō, originally concerned with the worship of spirits of nature, grew under the influence of Chinese Confucianism to include worship of family and imperial ancestors and thus provided the foundation of Japanese social structure. Shintō became an instrument of nationalism after 1868, as the government officially sponsored and subsidized it, requiring that it be taught in the schools and that all Japanese belong to a state Shintō shrine. After World War II, Shintō was abolished as a state religion, and the emperor issued an imperial prescript denying divine origin. Shintō now exists as a private religious organization. Buddhism is considered by some the most important religion in Japan. Introduced through China and Korea around AD 552, Buddhism spread rapidly throughout Japan and has had considerable influence on the nation's arts and social institutions. There are 13 sects (shū) and 56 denominations, the principal shū being Tendai, Shingon, Jōdo, Zen, Sōtō, Ōbaku, and Nichiren. Japanese Buddhism was founded on the Mahayana school, which emphasizes the attainment of Buddhahood, whereas the Hinayana Buddhism of India emphasizes obedience to commandments and personal perfection. The great temples and gardens of Japan, the famous Japanese tea ceremony (chanoyu),

and Japanese flower-arranging arts (ikebana) owe their development to the influence of Buddhism.

Religions designated as "other" are practiced by about 6% of the population (including 0.5% practicing Christianity). Other faiths that were founded in Japan include Tenrikyō, Seichounoie, Sekai Kyusei Kyō, Perfect Liberty, and Risho Koseikai. Christianity, introduced to Japan by the Jesuit St. Francis Xavier in 1549, was first encouraged by feudal lords but then banned in 1613, often under penalty of death. After that time, a unique sect known as "hidden Christians" (kakure kirishitan) developed, with no tradition of churches or public displays of faith and a syncretic doctrine that incorporated local ideas and history. The prohibition against Christianity was enforced until 1873, following the reopening of Japan to international relations in 1854. Following World War II, when the emperor lost his claim to divinity, some Japanese gave up Shintō and converted to Christianity or Judaism. After World War II, a considerable number of new religious groups sprouted up. One of these, the Soka-Gakkai, a Buddhist offshoot, controlled a political party (Komeitō), the third-strongest political group in Japan, until politics and religion were officially separated in 1970. In addition to the established and new religions, Confucianism, an ethical system originating in China, has strongly influenced Japanese society since the earliest periods, providing one explanation for the underpinnings for some characteristically Japanese attitudes such as filial piety and patriarchy. There are between 100,000 and 110,000 Muslims. Freedom of religion is guaranteed by the constitution, and this right is generally respected in practice. Religious groups are not required to register for certification with the government, but those who do enjoy certain tax benefits.

11TRANSPORTATION

The CIA reports that Japan has a total of 1.20 million km (745,645 mi) of roads, of which 961,366 km (597,365 mi) are paved. There are 593 vehicles per 1,000 people in the country. Railroads extend for 20,036 km (12,450 mi). There are 176 airports, which transported 86.9 million passengers in 2009 according to the World Bank. Japan has approximately 1,770 km (1,100 mi) of navigable waterways.

Despite its rugged terrain, Japan has a highly developed transportation system. The government-owned Japan National Railways (JNR) was privatized in April 1987 and divided into six railway companies. Feeding into these six lines were 144 other private railroads. Like their counterparts elsewhere, Japan's rail lines face increasing competition from automotive, sea, and air transport, as well as rising operating costs. High-speed lines, however, have been successful in partially meeting these problems; the most famous of these is the bullet train, or Shinkansen, which began operation in October 1964 between Tokyo and Osaka and was extended in March 1975 to Fukuoka in northern Kyūshū. In 1984, the Shinkansen superexpress trains covered the 1,069 km (664 mi) between Tokyo and Fukuoka in less than seven hours, with maximum speeds of 210 km/hr (130 mph). In 1982, the first section of the northern Shinkansen line, between Tokyo and Omiya, began operations. This line was extended in 1983 to Niigata and to Morioka, in northern Honshū. By far the longest railway tunnel in the world, the 54.2 km (33.7 mi) Seikan tube linking Honshū with Hokkaidō, was opened in 1983 and completed in 1985. The tunnel, lying beneath the Tsugaru Strait, cost well over $2 billion.

A bridge links Honshū and Shikoku. Subway lines serve nine cities—Tokyo, Osaka, Nagoya, Kobe, Yokohama, Sapporo, Kyoto, Fukuoka, and Sendai. There are 410 km (255 mi) of track, with 196 km (122 mi) in Tokyo's 11 lines. Since 1964, downtown Tokyo has also been linked with that city's Haneda Airport by a monorail transport system, and several other monorails have been put into operation. In addition, a seven-km (4.3 mi) monorail serves the city of Yokohama.

Japan is one of the world's great maritime nations. The chief ports are Yokohama (for Tokyo), Nagoya, and Kobe. In 2008, Japan's merchant fleet included 683 ships of 1,000 GRT or more. After 1959, Japan emerged as the world's leading shipbuilder, but output declined in the late 1970s and 1980s in the face of a world-wide recession and increased competition from the Republic of Korea (ROK). It remains an important shipbuilding center but is no longer the world's leader. Inland waterways are not used by ocean-going vessels, which prefer to use the country's inland seas.

Japan had 144 airports with paved runways in 2009. There were also 32 heliports. Principal domestic airports include Haneda in Tokyo, Itami in Osaka, Itazuke in Fukuoka, and Chitose on Hokkaidō. Principal international facilities include Kansai International at Osaka and Narita at Tokyo. Japan Air Lines (JAL), the nation's major domestic and international airline, began operations in 1952 and inaugurated international flights in 1954. All Nippon Airways, established in 1957, began as a domestic system serving smaller areas of the country and acting as a feeder line to JAL but now serves overseas routes; it began to carry freight in 1987.

In March 2010, the Ibaraki airport became operational about 85 km (53 mi) north of Tokyo. In that month, the $220 million airport featured only one flight per day, to South Korea. A second daily flight to Kobe was set to begin in April. The project is considered by many to be the latest example of wasteful government expenditures. Proponents of the project believe the airport might someday serve as a major hub for budget carriers.

12 HISTORY

Archaeological discoveries revealed the existence of Paleolithic humans in Japan when the islands were connected to the Asian continental landmass. Little is known about the origins of the earliest Japanese beyond the fact that they migrated from the continent. The first distinctive Neolithic culture, the Jōmon, existed in Japan from 11,000 BC to 300 BC. The Jōmon was displaced by the Yayoi culture, which introduced new agricultural and metallurgical skills from the continent. Tradition places the beginning of the Japanese nation in 660 BC with the ascendance to the throne of the legendary Emperor Jimmu. It is generally agreed, however, that as the Yayoi developed, the Yamato clan attained hegemony over southern Japan during the first three or four centuries of the Christian era and established the imperial family line. Earlier contacts with Korea were expanded in the 5th century to mainland China, and the great period of cultural borrowing began: industrial arts were imported; Chinese script was introduced (thereby permitting the study of medical texts), the Chinese calendar and Buddhism also arrived from China. Japanese leaders adapted the Chinese governmental organization but based power on hereditary position rather than merit. The first imperial capital was established at Nara in 710. In 794, the imperial capital was moved to Heian (Kyoto), where it remained until 1868, when Tokyo became the nation's capital.

Chinese influence waned as native institutions took on peculiarly Japanese forms. Outside court circles, local clans gained strength, giving rise to military clan influence over a weakening imperial system. The Minamoto clan gained national hegemony as it defeated the rival Taira clan in 1185, and its leader, the newly appointed Yoritomo, established a military form of government at Kamakura in 1192, a feudal system that lasted for nearly 700 years. Under this shogunate system, all political power was in the hands of the dominant military clan, with the emperors ruling in name only. The Kamakura period was followed by the Ashikaga shogunate (1336–1600) which saw economic growth and the development of a more complex feudalism. Continuous civil war among rival feudal lords (*daimyo*) marked the last century of the Ashikaga shogunate. During this time, the first contact with the Western world took place with the arrival in 1543 of Portuguese traders. At the same time, the first guns were imported. Six years later, St. Francis Xavier arrived, introducing Christianity to Japan.

By 1590, the country was pacified and unified by Toyotomi Hideyoshi, a peasant who had risen to a top military position. Hideyoshi also invaded Korea unsuccessfully, in 1592–93 and in 1598, dying during the second invasion. Ieyasu Tokugawa consolidated Hideyoshi's program of centralization. Appointed shogun in 1603, Tokugawa established the Tokugawa shogunate (military dictatorship), which was to rule Japan until the imperial restoration in 1868. Tokugawa made Edo (modern Tokyo) the capital, closed Japan to foreigners except Chinese and Dutch traders (who were restricted to Nagasaki) and occasional Korean diplomats, and banned Christianity. For the next 250 years, Japan enjoyed stability and a flowering of indigenous culture, although from the end of the 18th century onward, Japan came under increasing pressure from Western nations to end its isolationist policy.

The arrival of Commodore Matthew C. Perry from the United States in 1853 with his famous "black ships" started a process that soon ended Japanese feudalism. The following year, Perry obtained a treaty of peace and friendship between the United States and Japan, and similar pacts were signed with Russia, Britain, and the Netherlands based on the principle of extraterritoriality. A decade of turmoil and confusion followed over the question of opening Japan to foreigners. A coalition of southern clans led by ambitious young samurai of the Satsuma and Chōshū clans forced the abdication of the Tokugawa shogun and restored the emperor as head of the nation. In 1868, Emperor Mutsuhito took over full sovereignty. This Meiji Restoration, as it is known, signaled the entry of Japan into the modern era.

Intensive modernization and industrialization commenced under the leadership of the restoration leaders. A modern navy and army with universal military conscription and a modern civil service based on merit formed the foundation of the new nation-state. The government undertook the establishment of industry by importing technological assistance. In 1889, a new constitution established a bicameral legislature (Diet) with a civil cabinet headed by a prime minister responsible to the emperor.

By the end of the 19th century, irreconcilable territorial ambitions brought Japan into open conflict with its much larger neighbors to the west. The Sino-Japanese War (1894–95) was fought over the question of control of Korea and the Russo-Japanese War

(1904–05) over the question of Russian expansion in Manchuria and influence in Korean affairs. Japan emerged victorious in both conflicts, its victory over the Russians marking the first triumph of an Asian country over a Western power in modern times. Japan received the territories of Taiwan and the southern half of Sakhalin Island, as well as certain railway rights and concessions in Manchuria and recognition of paramount influence in Korea. The latter became a Japanese protectorate in 1905 and was annexed by Japan in 1910.

During the Taishō era (1912–26), Japan participated in a limited way in World War I, in accordance with the Anglo-Japanese Alliance of 1902. Japan was one of the Big Five powers at the Versailles Peace Conference and in 1922 was recognized as the world's third-leading naval power at the Washington Naval Conference. The domestic economy developed rapidly, and Japan was transformed from an agricultural to an industrial nation. Economic power tended to be held by the industrial combines (*zaibatsu*), controlled by descendants of those families that had instituted the modernization of the country decades earlier. In 1925, universal male suffrage was enacted, and political leaders found it necessary to take into consideration the growing influence of parties.

In 1926, Emperor Hirohito ascended the throne, beginning the Shōwa era. By the 1930s, democratic institutions had atrophied, and the military-industrial complex had become dominant. With severe social distress caused by the Great Depression, an ultranationalist ideology emerged, particularly among young army officers. Acting independently of the central government, the military launched an invasion of Manchuria in 1931, eventually establishing the puppet state of Manchukuo. In 1932, a patriotic society assassinated the prime minister, bringing an end to cabinets formed by the majority party in the Diet. Japan withdrew from the League of Nations (which had protested the Manchurian takeover) in 1933, started a full-scale invasion of China (the Second Sino-Japanese War, 1937–45), and signed the Anti-Comintern pact with Germany in 1936, joining a triple alliance with Germany and Italy in 1940. The military leadership, viewing the former USSR and the United States as chief barriers to Japanese expansion, negotiated a nonaggression pact with the USSR in April 1941. This set the stage for the attack on Pearl Harbor and other Pacific targets on 7 December of that year, bringing Japan and the United States into World War II. With its capture of the Philippines on 2 January 1942, Japan gained control of most of East Asia, including major portions of China, Indochina, and the islands of the southwest Pacific. Japanese forces, however, could not resist the continued mobilization of the US military. A series of costly naval campaigns—including battles at Midway, Guadalcanal, and Leyte Gulf—brought an end to Japanese domination in the Pacific. By 1945, the Philippines had been recaptured, and the stage was set for a direct assault on Japan. After US troops captured Okinawa in a blood battle, US president Harry S. Truman argued that a full invasion of Japan would prove too costly and decided on aerial attacks to force Japan into surrendering. Four months of intense bombardment with conventional weapons ensued, destroying Japan's major cities (with the exception of Kyoto). The United States then dropped an atomic bomb on Hiroshima on 6 August 1945, and a second bomb on Nagasaki on 9 August. An estimated 340,000 people died from the two attacks and the subsequent effects of radiation.

On 14 August, Japan accepted the Potsdam Declaration for unconditional surrender with formal surrender documents signed aboard the USS *Missouri* on 2 September. Food and supply shortages continued for several years after the surrender. After the surrender, over 500 Japanese military officials committed suicide and hundreds more faced war crimes prosecution. A number of high-level officials, including former prime minister Tōjō Hideki were sentenced to death by hanging in the Tokyo War Crimes Tribunal. Emperor Hirohito was not declared a war criminal, and, although he lost all military and political power, he retained his royal title and became a symbol of the state until his death in 1989. The subsequent occupation (1945–52), under the direction of General Douglas MacArthur, Supreme Commander for the Allied Powers, began a series of ambitious reforms. Political reforms included the adoption of a parliamentary system of government based on democratic principles and universal suffrage, a symbolic role for the emperor as titular head of state, the establishment of an independent trade union, and the disarmament of the military. Economic reforms consisted of land reform, the dissolution of the zaibatsu, and economic and political rights for women. A new constitution was promulgated on 3 November 1946 and enforced on 3 May 1947.

The Postwar Period

Heavy economic aid from the United States and a procurement boom produced by the Korean War, coupled with a conservative fiscal and monetary policy, allowed the Japanese to rebuild their country relatively quickly. The standard of living quickly surpassed the prewar standard by a substantial margin. The state of war between the Western powers and Japan was formally ended by the San Francisco Peace Treaty, signed in September 1951 by 56 nations. The allied occupation ended officially when the treaty went into effect in April 1952. Japan renounced claims to many of its former overseas territories, including such major areas as Taiwan and Korea. The Amami island group, comprising the northern portion of the Ryukyu Islands, nearest to Kyūshū Island, was returned to direct Japanese control by the United States in December 1953; the remainder of the group, including Okinawa, was returned to full Japanese sovereignty in May 1972. The Ogasawara (Bonin) Islands and Kazan (Volcano) Islands were returned to Japanese sovereignty in June 1968. The USSR never signed the San Francisco Peace Treaty, and Japan and the USSR (and later, Russia) have continued to dispute sovereignty over the Kuril Islands, to the northeast of Hokkaidō, which the USSR occupied in 1945. In 1956, Japan and the USSR agreed to establish diplomatic relations.

Also in 1956, Japan was elected to UN membership. A revision of the 1952 defense treaty with the United States, under which a limited number of troops were to remain in Japan for defense purposes, was signed amid growing controversy in 1960. On 22 June 1965, Japan signed a treaty with South Korea normalizing relations between the two countries. The US-Japan Security Treaty was renewed in 1970 despite vigorous protest by the opposition parties and militant student organizations. In 1972, Japan moved to establish full diplomatic relations with the People's Republic of China. Formal diplomatic links with the Nationalist Chinese government on Taiwan were terminated by this move, but Japan's economic and cultural links with Taiwan nonetheless have survived virtually intact.

While Japan defined its new role in East Asian affairs, its remarkable economic expansion raised it to the level of a major trading power. Based on strong government support of export industries, political stability under the Liberal-Democratic Party (LDP), and public policy guidance from a powerful bureaucracy, Japan experienced a dramatic rise from the ruins of World War II. From 1955 to 1965, Japan experienced a nominal growth rate of 10–20% annually and real growth rates (adjusted for inflation) of 5–12%. In 1968, it surpassed the Federal Republic of Germany (FRG) to stand second after the United States among non-Communist nations in total value of GNP. The oil crisis of 1973—a combination of shortages and rising prices—revealed the crack in Japan's economic armor: the lack of domestic petroleum resources. A second oil crisis during the late 1970s was met by a reappraisal of Japan's dependence on foreign fuels and the institution of long-range programs for energy conservation and diversification. These oil crises led to a shift in the economy and to the creation of high-technology industries, most notably electronic appliances.

The yen declined in value in the early 1980s, causing Japanese exports to become cheaper in overseas markets and leading to huge trade surpluses with the United States and other leading trading partners, who began to demand that Japan voluntarily limit certain exports and remove the barriers to Japan's domestic market. During 1985–87, the yen appreciated in value against the dollar and, by 1994, the dollar had hit a post-World War II low, but Japan continued to register substantial trade surpluses.

Political stability, maintained since the 1950s by the majority LDP, began to unravel in the 1970s, following the retirement from politics of Prime Minister Eisaku Satō in 1972. Satō's successor, Kakuei Tanaka, was forced to resign in December 1974 amid charges of using his office for personal gain in the Lockheed Corporation bribery scandal. Takeo Miki succeeded Tanaka, and Takeo Fukuda became prime minister when Miki resigned in December 1976. Fukuda was defeated in intraparty elections by Masayoshi Ōhira in 1978. When Ōhira died in June 1980, he was succeeded by Zenkō Suzuki. Suzuki stepped down as prime minister in November 1982 and was replaced by controversial and outspoken Yasuhiro Nakasone. Noboru Takeshita became prime minister in November 1987.

Policy regarding military force has been a major political issue in the postwar years. According to Article Nine of the 1947 constitution, Japan renounced belligerency of the state. In the early 1950s as the Korean War was being fought and fear over the spread of Communism was growing, Japan re-developed its military as a "Self-Defense Force" (jieitai) with US support. In 1986, breaking a longstanding policy, the government increased military spending to over 1% of the GNP. The Diet (parliament) approved a bill allowing the deployment of troops abroad for international peacekeeping in 1992 with troops participating with the United Nations in Cambodia, Israel, Iraq, Sudan, Indonesia, and other states. The majority of work done by the Self-Defense Forces, however, is domestic, including major cleanup and aid missions after natural disasters, such as the March 2011 earthquake and tsunami.

Emperor Hirohito died of cancer of the small intestine on 7 January 1989, at the age of 87. He was succeeded by his eldest son, the Crown Prince Akihito, who was enthroned as the Heisei em-

peror in a formal ceremony in November 1990. The sense of entering a new era brought increased controversy over the assessment of Japan's role in the earlier part of the century, particularly during World War II. Some denied that Japan had committed atrocities during the war, and there were attempts to further soften the wording of school textbooks. In March 1989, Prime Minister Takeshita apologized to North Korea (DPRK) for the suffering Japan caused over the 36 years of occupation of Korea (1910–45), and Emperor Akihito expressed similar regrets to President Roh Tae Woo of South Korea (ROK) in May 1990. In the same month, the government removed the requirement for fingerprinting of people of Korean descent living in Japan. In 1992, Prime Minister Kiichi Miyazawa apologized for the forced prostitution of Korean, Chinese, and Japanese women in Japanese military brothels during World War II. However, many minorities in Japan, Chinese and Koreans included, claimed that they still experienced social and economic discrimination in Japan well after the war.

The 1980s ended with a major scandal involving illegal stock trading and influence peddling by the Recruit Cosmos Company. Between the summer of 1988 and the closing of the case in May 1989, the scandal led to the implication and resignations of prominent business people and politicians in top government positions, among them then-finance minister Kiichi Miyazawa, and the former prime minister, Yashuhiro Nakasone. Scandals continued into the 1990s, with stock rebates for politicians in 1991, and then, in 1992, contributions to politicians from a trucking company linked to organized crime became public knowledge.

The economy entered a period of major stagnation and distress in the early 1990s. In 1990, the stock market declined more than 25% from January to April. Then, during the spring of 1992, the stock index fell rapidly again, until in the summer, the index reached its lowest point in six years, 62% below the record high of 1989. By the end of 1993, Japan was in the midst of its worst economic downturn in at least 20 years. This also led to a debt crisis that resulted in many banks becoming unsustainable causing a massive consolidation. Although the long-term economic prospects for Japan were good, it was further retarded by the impact of the Asian financial crisis of 1997–98. In 1998, the Japanese economy witnessed a serious recession with a negative growth rate of 1.9%. In spite of this "bursting of the bubble" in the early 90s, Japan remained the world's second-largest economy until early 2011, when China took over this position.

Against the background of scandals and an economic recession, the political landscape began a major change. Taking responsibility for political problems caused by the Recruit scandal, Noboru Takeshita resigned as prime minister in April 1989 to be succeeded in May by Sōsuke Uno, who abruptly resigned when a sex scandal became public amidst the LDP loss of its majority in the upper House of the Diet. The next prime minister, Toshiki Kaifu, served his term from August 1989 to October 1991, but the LDP did not support him for a second term. Instead, Kiichi Miyazawa became prime minister in November 1991. When the lower House gave Miyazawa a vote of no confidence in June 1993 for abandoning electoral reform bills, Miyazawa dissolved the lower House and called for elections.

The dissolution of the House of Representatives and the ensuing election on 18 July 1993 marked a major turning point for Japanese politics, as the LDP lost its political dominance as new parties formed. One new party, the Japan New Party (JNP), was formed by Morihiro Hosokawa, a former LDP member, in May 1992. On 21 June 1993, 10 more members of the LDP, led by Masayoshi Takemura, left to form the Sakigake (Harbinger Party), and another 44 LDP members quit two days later to create the Shinseitō (Renewal Party), with Tsutomu Hata as its head. By 28 June, one fifth (57 members) of the LDP bloc of the dissolved lower House left the party. In the election for the 511 seats of the House of Representatives on 18 July 1993, the LDP, for the first time since its formation in 1955, failed to secure the 256 seats needed for a majority. Without a majority, the LDP was unable to form a government, and the new prime minister, Morihiro Hosokawa (JNP), was chosen on 29 July 1993, by a seven-party coalition of LDP defectors, socialists, and conservatives. Hosokawa's time in office, too, was tainted by questions regarding personal finances, and he stepped down as prime minister to be replaced by Tsutomu Hata (Shinseitō) in April 1994. Just as Hata took office, the Socialist Party left the governing coalition, leaving the prime minister as the head of a minority government for the first time in four decades. Hata soon resigned, and, in a surprise move, the LDP and the Socialist Party, traditionally opponents, allied to form a new coalition, which also included the Sakigake. The coalition selected as prime minister Tomiichi Murayama, the head of the Socialist Party and the first Socialist prime minister since 1948. Within the coalition, the LDP was the dominant factor, but the decades of LDP rule appeared to be over, and the nature of the LDP itself changed.

In June 1994, Tomiichi Murayama became prime minister in a coalition consisting of the LDP, the Social Democratic Party of Japan (SDPJ), and Sakigake. In an unprecedented move, Murayama recognized the legal right for the existence of the Japanese Self-Defense force, much to the disapproval of left-leaning party members. The tumultuous reign of Murayama included the Kobe earthquake, the sarin gas attacks on the Tokyo subway system, and political scandals which led to the resignation of the Justice Minister and the director of the Management and Coordination Agency. Elections in October 1996 resulted in a victory for the LDP, but the party still failed to obtain a majority of seats, capturing only 239 of 500. The Sakigake and Democratic Party of Japan agreed to support Prime Minister Ryūtarō Hashimoto. In July 1998, Hashimoto resigned after a poor performance of the LDP in the House of Councilors election and was replaced by Keizō Obuchi. During the Obuchi regime, the Japanese economy showed signs of recovering with major fiscal stimuli including a massive public works program.

In April 2000, Obuchi suffered a stroke, fell into a coma, and was replaced by Yoshirō Mori who called summarily for elections. On 25 June, parliamentary elections were held for the House of Representatives. Mori was reelected prime minister, with a ruling coalition of the LDP, the Buddhist-backed New Komeitō, and the New Conservative Party (NCP). In early 2001, the Nikkei stock average fell to its lowest level since 1985, and unemployment rates reached 4.9%, the highest since the end of World War II. Plagued by scandal and the depressed economy, Mori resigned in April 2001. Junichirō Koizumi won control of the LDP and became prime minister on 26 April, promising to reinvigorate Japanese politics and radically reform the economy. He appointed members of his cabinet without seeking nominations from major factions of the LDP, as had been the practice in the past.

Koizumi immediately raised controversy by making a visit to Tokyo's Yasukuni Shrine. Dedicated to Japan's war dead, it served as a symbol of nationalism during World War II and has been a lightning rod for anger among Asian nations that suffered under Japan's military aggression. He continued to visit the shrine annually. Japan was also the target of international criticism over its Education Ministry's approval of junior high-school textbooks that allegedly glossed over Japan's aggression in China, particularly the Nanjing Massacre and its annexation of the Korean Peninsula.

Koizumi's coalition dominated the July 2001 elections for the House of Councilors, with the LDP taking 65 of the 121 contested seats, its best performance in the House of Councilors since 1992. The victory was seen as a mandate for Koizumi. However, the economy remained in recession throughout 2002, which reduced his popularity.

In 2002, Japan began a diplomatic initiative to improve relations with North Korea. In September 2002, North Korean President Kim Jong Il apologized to Koizumi for North Korea's kidnapping of Japanese citizens during the 1970s and 1980s. Japan pledged a generous aid package to North Korea in return. In 2005, relations with South Korea and China soured over the continued use of Japanese junior high-school textbooks that downplayed the aggressive nature of Japan's role in WWII. In addition, South Korea objected to the reassertion of the Japanese claim to the Liancourt Rocks (dokdo/takeshima), which Korea occupies. China objected to the Japanese proposal for a permanent seat on the United Nations Security Council, while both countries objected to Japan's use of the East China Sea.

Elections in 2003 resulted in large gains for the opposition Democratic Party, but the LDP coalition retained a majority within the parliament. On 27 September 2004, Koizumi carried out a major cabinet reorganization in order to combat corruption and inefficiency, dubbing his new ministerial lineup the "Reform Implementation Cabinet." April 2005 public opinion polls showed Koizumi support ratings in the 40–50% range, which was very high by Japanese standards, and his tenure in office was one of the longest on record.

Koizumi called for early elections in September 2005 after he dissolved the lower House following the defeat in the upper House of his landmark proposals to reform the country's postal system. The upper House cannot be dissolved in Japan, and thus a two-thirds majority was needed in the lower House to be able to pass new legislation without the consent of the upper House. The result was the second-largest landslide in a general election in the LDP's history. In combination with allied parties, the LDP coalition held over two thirds of the seats, 296 out of 480. The results were a devastating setback for the Democratic Party, the main opposition, whose gains in 2001 and 2003 led some to believe that Japanese Democracy was evolving into a two-party system.

Koizumi retired in September 2006, and Shinzo Abe succeeded Koizumi as prime minister and head of the Liberal Democratic Party (LDP). Abe favored a more assertive role for Japan in world affairs, supported the revision of its pacifist constitution, and envisioned a closer relationship with the US.

China and Japan were once again attempting to reconcile differences over the interpretation of their shared history in 2007. In

April of that year, Wen Jiabao became the first Chinese premier to address Japan's parliament. It was an attempt to warm Japanese-Chinese relations that had grown tense over Japanese textbooks, which China says gloss over atrocities committed by the Japanese military during World War II; Japan's unwillingness to recognize its past war crimes; and former Prime Minister Koizumi's visits to the Yasukuni shrine dedicated to Japan's war dead, which also honors war criminals. In early 2007, another controversy arose when Prime Minister Shinzo Abe denied that Japan's military had coerced women into sexual slavery during World War II. There are accounts of Japanese soldiers and sailors rounding up foreign women for use as sex slaves, euphemistically known as "comfort women."

By mid 2007, Prime Minister Abe's popularity ratings were at an all-time low. On 29 July, the LDP lost control of the upper House of parliament for the first time in its history. On 9 September, Abe announced he had no intention of staying on as prime minister if members of parliament blocked a move to extend Japan's support of the US-led mission in Afghanistan. On 12 September 2007 Abe resigned. On 25 September 2007, the LDP chose Yasuo Fukuda, a mild-mannered moderate generally known for his ability to build consensus behind the scenes, to become Japan's next prime minister.

In the 30 August 2009 legislative elections for the lower House of parliament, the Democratic Party of Japan (DPJ) won a major victory over the Liberal Democratic Party (LDP), ending 50 years of nearly unbroken rule by the LDP. The DPJ gained 308 of the 480 seats in the lower House of parliament and formed a coalition with the New People's Party and the Social Democratic Party in order to hold a majority influence in the upper House. Yukio Hatoyama was sworn in as the new prime minister on 28 September 2009. He vowed to promote a "people-oriented society" while working toward economic revival and strengthening ties with the United States.

On 1 June 2010, facing the massive fallout over his decision to keep a US Marine base on Okinawa, Hatoyama resigned after serving for only nine months. Hatoyama's decision made him both the shortest-serving Japanese prime minister since 1994 and the fourth Japanese prime minister to resign in three years. As the Democratic Party of Japan grappled with the question of succession, Japanese leaders faced a host of pressing economic challenges, including the world's largest public debt. In early June, Naoto Kan, the former finance chief, was elected prime minister. Kan took power promising to address Japan's economic woes and to continue to make Japan's strong alliance with the United States a cornerstone of Japan's diplomacy. In assuming the premiership, Kan defeated Shinji Tarutoko, chairman of the lower House environmental committee, with members of his Democratic Party of Japan voting 291 to 129 in his favor.

On 11 March 2011, a 9.0 magnitude earthquake hit northern Japan. The earthquake was the most powerful to ever hit the country and set off a tsunami that prompted warnings for countries throughout the Pacific Ocean. Additionally, the nation experienced a number of explosions and radioactive leaks at its nuclear power facilities as a result of the earthquake and tsunami, adding another layer of disaster. The Fukushima Daiichi plant in northeastern Japan ruptured and was reported to have released high levels of radioactive steam, leading to the evacuation of a 20 km

(12 mi) zone around the plant. Over 15,000 Japanese died as a result of the earthquake and tsunami, and in April 2011 the World Bank estimated the total cost of the disaster could be a as high as $235 billion. Facing mounting public criticism over the government response to the 11 March earthquake, Prime Minister Kan resigned, and his finance minister, Yoshihiko Noda, became the new prime minister in late August 2011.

13 GOVERNMENT

Japan follows the parliamentary system in accordance with the constitution of 1947. The most significant change from the previous constitution of 1889 was the transfer of sovereign power from the emperor to the people. The emperor is now defined as "the symbol of the state and of the unity of the people." The constitution provides for the supremacy of the National Diet as the legislative branch of the government, upholds the separation of legislative, executive, and judicial powers, and guarantees civil liberties. It is officially termed a constitutional monarchy with a parliamentary government.

The executive branch is headed by a prime minister selected from the Diet by its membership. The cabinet consists of the prime minister and 17 state ministers (as of October 2011) elected by the prime minister, each heading a government ministry or agency. At least half the ministers must be selected from the Diet, to which the cabinet is collectively responsible. Upon a vote of no confidence by the House of Representatives, the cabinet must resign en masse.

The National Diet is bicameral. The House of Representatives (the lower House) has a membership of 480, with terms of office for four years, except that all terms end upon dissolution of the House. Of the 480 seats, 180 are elected from 11 multi-member constituencies by proportional representation, and 300 are elected from single-member constituencies. The House of Councilors (the upper House) has 242 members, 144 members in multi-seat constituencies and 98 by proportional representation. The term of office is six years, with one-half elected every three years. This means that, of the 121 members subject to election each time, 73 are elected from the 47 prefectural districts, and 48 are elected from a nationwide list by proportional representation. The lower House holds primary power. In case of disagreement between the two houses, or if the upper House fails to take action within 60 days of receipt of legislation from the lower House, a bill becomes law if passed again by a two-thirds majority of the lower House.

Suffrage is universal and the voting age 20 years, with a three-month residence requirement. The 1947 constitution granted suffrage to women. The 1996 elections resulted in the weakening of minor parties, in particular the SDPJ and Sakigake. Following Koizumi's decision to dissolve the lower House, elections for the House of Representatives took place in 2005, two years before the official end of the 2003 election term. The next elections for the House of Councillors took place in 2007; the Liberal Democratic Party lost control of this house for the first time in its history. Elections for the House of Representatives and the House of Councillors were held again in 2009 and 2010, respectively.

14 POLITICAL PARTIES

Most political parties in Japan are small local or regional parties, with the total number of parties exceeding 10,000. Japan's historically most popular party, the Liberal-Democratic Party (LDP) represents a wide spectrum of Japanese society but especially the conservative elements. Formed in 1955 by the merger of the two leading conservative parties, this party held the reins of government from its formation until July 1993. The LDP supports an alliance with the United States and the various security pacts enacted by the two countries.

The Japan Socialist Party (JSP) was Japan's principal opposition party, drawing its support mainly from the working class, but it suffers from ideological problems within its ranks. The JSP split into right and left wings over the ratification of the US-Japan Security Treaty of 1952. In October 1955, however, the two factions reunited, preceding the unification of the conservative parties and actually forcing the conservative groups into a unified front, thus creating a formal two-party system in Japan.

Beginning in the late 1960s, a shift took place toward a multiple-party system, with the gradual increase of opposition parties other than the JSP. The Democratic Socialist Party (DSP) represented moderate elements of the working class. The Komeitō (Clean Government Party), professing middle-of-the-road politics, was the political wing of the Sōka-Gakkai, a Buddhist sect. The Japanese Communist Party, founded as an underground group in 1922 and legalized after World War II, experienced major shifts in platform. The party had traditionally sided with China in the Sino-Soviet ideological dispute, although, in recent years, the Japanese Communists have focused instead on social conditions at home.

The LDP continued to hold its majority in both houses until 1993. Traditionally, the LDP has functioned as a coalition of several factions, each tightly organized and bound by personal loyalty to a factional leader. In the mid 1970s, policy differences among the factions and their leaders became acute, with the resignation under pressure of Prime Minister Tanaka in December 1974.

In the summer of 1993, after five years of scandals involving corruption, sex, organized crime, and in the midst of economic recession, the old political order disintegrated as dozens of younger LDP members defected to form new parties. Chief among these was the Japan New Party (JNP), formed in May 1992, and the Sakigake (Harbinger Party) and Shinseitō (Renewal Party), both formed in June 1993. A watershed election in July 1993 for the House of Representatives, the lower House of the parliament, resulted in a loss of its majority by the LDP for the first time since 1955. Of the 511 seats, the LDP won 223 seats (as compared with 275 in the 1990 election), the JSP won 70 seats (a loss of half of its previous seats), the Komeitō won 51 seats, the Shinseitō took 55 seats, the JNP won 35 seats, and the Sakigake won 13. A seven-party coalition, including new parties of LDP defectors, the JSP, and other conservative parties, formed the new cabinet, which governed for a year until the prime minister (Morihiro Hosokawa, JNP) resigned over a financial scandal. The coalition formed a new government, led by Tsutomu Hata of the Shinseitō, in April 1993. However, the JSP, finding itself maneuvered out of any voice in the coalition, broke away, and Hata, then with a minority in the House of Representatives, resigned after one month in office.

The next government was formed by a new, unorthodox coalition of the traditional opponents, the LDP and the JSP, as well as the Sakigake. Tomiichi Murayama, head of the JSP, was chosen prime minister in June 1994, the first Socialist to head a government since 1948, although the LDP appeared to be dominant in the coalition. This unusual partnership caused strains, leading to further defections within the LDP and within the JSP. The Shinseitō emerged as a serious focus of opposition, standing for an internationally more active Japan, including use of the military overseas, for a revision of the constitution, and for removing protective regulations to open the domestic economy to competition. The left wing of the JSP, unhappy with the alliance with the LDP, held that the Self-Defense Forces were unconstitutional, that the North Korean government (DPRK) was the legitimate government of all of Korea, and advocated the abolition of the security treaty with the United States.

Electoral reforms in 1994 changed the make-up of the House to a body of 500 members, 200 of which were elected on a proportional basis from multi-member districts, the rest on an individual basis in smaller districts. The number of proportionally-elected seats was reduced to 180 in 2000, leaving the total membership of the House at 480 members. After the dissolution of Shin Shintō, a highly factionalized party system emerged. Going into the 2000 election, the LDP had 266 seats, with the largest opponents the Democratic Party of Japan (DPJ) with 94 seats, the Komeitō with 52, the Liberal Party with 39, and the Communists with 23. The LDP worked closely with the Komei Party and the Liberal Party, effectively making the DPJ the only significant opposition.

The 2000 House of Representatives election produced the following distribution of seats: LDP, 233; DPJ, 127; Komeitō, 31; Liberal Party, 22; Japan Communist Party (JCP), 20; Social Democratic Party (SDP), 19; New Conservative Party (formed in 2000), 7; and 21 other seats. In the 2001 House of Councilors vote, the seats fell as follows: LDP, 110; DPJ, 59; Komeitō, 23; JCP, 20; SDP, 8; Liberal Party, 8; New Conservative Party, 5; and independents took 14 seats. A new party emerged in Japanese politics, the New Conservative Party, formed in March 2000 by members who split off from the Liberal Party.

In November 2003, an election for the House of Representatives was held, and Prime Minister Junichirō Koizumi, leading the LDP, emerged victorious, although with a reduced majority. The election was seen as a victory for the DPJ, which won 180 seats, its largest share ever. In 2005, the six largest parties represented in the national Diet were the Liberal Democratic Party (LDP), the Democratic Party of Japan (DPJ), the New Clean Party Government (Komeitō), the Japan Communist Party (JCP), the Socialist Democratic Party (SDP), and the Conservative New Party (CNP). The early election called by Koizumi in September of 2005, however, resulted in a firm majority for the LDP. Koizumi resigned as prime minister in 2006, and Shinzō Abe of the LDP took his place.

After the LDP lost power in elections for the House of Councilors in July 2007, Abe reshuffled his cabinet and then resigned in September 2007. The LDP chose Yasuo Fukuda to become Japan's next prime minister. In the 11 September 2007 election for the House of Representatives, the LDP won 47.8% of the votes and 296 seats. The DPJ won 36.4% and 113 seats.

In the 30 August 2009 legislative elections for the lower House of parliament, the Democratic Party of Japan won a major victory over the Liberal Democratic Party, ending 50 years of nearly unbroken rule by the LDP. The DPJ gained 308 of the 480 seats in the lower House of parliament and formed a coalition with the New People's Party and the Social Democratic Party in order to hold a majority influence in the upper House. Yukio Hatoyama was sworn in as the new prime minister on 28 September 2009. During his campaign, Hatoyama pledged to work toward the relocation of the US Marine base on Okinawa. However, in early 2010, he announced that the base would remain on Okinawa, through it would be moved to another location farther north. On 1 June 2010, facing the massive fallout over his decision to keep the Marine base, Hatoyama resigned after serving for only nine months. Naoto Kan of the Democratic Party of Japan was elected as his replacement. In September 2010, his post was challenged from within by Ichirō Ōzawa, a veteran member of parliament who was supported by a substantial number of DPJ members. However, Kan won the vote with 721 points to 491. Kan's time as prime minister would not last much longer, though, as he stepped down to be replaced by Yoshihiko Noda in September 2011.

15 LOCAL GOVERNMENT

Local government throughout Japan was strengthened by the Local Autonomy Law of 1947. Administratively, Japan is divided into 47 prefectures. Within these prefectures there are 670 cities and 2,562 towns and villages. The local chief executives, mayors, and village heads, together with prefectural assembly members, are directly elected. Governors and assembly members are elected by popular vote every four years. The 47 prefectures are divided as follows: 1 metropolitan district (Tokyo—*to*), 2 urban prefectures (Kyoto—*fu* and Osaka—*fu*), 43 rural prefectures (*ken*), and 1 district (Hokkaidō). Large cities are subdivided into wards (*ku*), and further split into towns, or precincts (*machi* or *chō*), or subdistricts (*shichō*) and counties (*gun*). The city of Tokyo has 23 wards.

Local public bodies have the right to administer their own affairs as well as to enact their own regulations within the law. The National Diet cannot enact legislation for a specific public entity without the consent of the voters of that district. Local governments control school affairs, levy taxes, and carry out administrative functions in the fields of land preservation and development, pollution control, disaster prevention, public health, and social welfare. However, the Ministry of Home Affairs has had enormous control designing the systems of local administration and over local finance and taxation. It also co-ordinates between the central government and local governments, although its purpose is to support and develop local and regional autonomy. The result of this power is a high level of organizational and policy standardization among the different local governments. Because Japan does not have a federal system, and its 47 prefectures are not sovereign entities in the sense that the United States are, most depend on the central government for subsidies. Mainly through the actions of the Ministry of Home Affairs, the Japanese government was seeking to funnel power through a process termed "controlled decentralization" away from Tokyo by allowing prefectures to exercise greater fiscal and budgetary autonomy.

16 JUDICIAL SYSTEM

The 1947 constitution provides for the complete independence of the judiciary. All judicial power is vested in the courts. There are five types of courts in Japan: the Supreme Court, High Courts (8 regional courts), District Courts (in each of the prefectures), Family Courts, and 438 Summary Courts. Family Courts, on the same level as the District Courts, adjudicate family conflicts and com-

plaints such as partitions of estates, marriage annulments, and juvenile protection cases.

The Summary Courts handle, in principle, civil cases involving claims which do not exceed 900,000 yen; and criminal cases relating to offenses punishable by fines or lighter penalties; and civil conciliations. They are situated in 438 locations nationwide. The cases are handled by a single summary court judge. The District Courts handle the first instance of most types of civil and criminal cases. They are situated in 50 locations nationwide (one in each of the 47 prefectures and one in the 3 cities of Hakodate, Asahikawa, and Kushiro) with branch offices in 203 locations. Most cases are disposed by a single judge, aside from those cases in which it has been decided that hearing and judgment shall be made by a collegiate court or cases in which the crimes are punishable by imprisonment with or without labor for a minimum period of not less than one year. The High Courts handle appeals filed against judgments rendered by the district courts, family courts, or summary courts. The cases are handled by a collegiate body consisting of three judges.

The Supreme Court is the highest and final court that handles appeals filed against judgments rendered by the High Courts. It is composed of the Chief Justice and 14 justices with a Grand Bench made up of all 15 justices. The Supreme Court is divided into three Petty Benches each made up of five justices to which cases are first assigned. Those cases that involve constitutional questions are transferred to the Grand Bench for its inquiry and adjudication. The chief justice is appointed by the emperor on designation by the cabinet; the other justices, by cabinet appointment. Judges of the lesser courts also are appointed by the cabinet from lists of persons nominated by the Supreme Court. Their term of office is limited to 10 years, with the privilege of reappointment.

The Supreme Court is the court of last resort for determining the constitutionality of any law, order, regulation, or official act that is challenged during the regular hearing of a lawsuit. Abstract questioning of a law is prohibited, and thus there is no judicial review. The constitution affords criminal defendants a right to a speedy and public trial by an impartial tribunal. There is no right to a trial by jury. The constitution requires a judicial warrant issued by a judge for each search or seizure. Japan accepts compulsory jurisdiction of the International Court of Justice with reservation.

Japan has the death penalty, and it can be enforced for the crimes of murder, arson, or crimes against humanity, although only two to three prisoners are executed a year. Japan has been widely criticized for giving lenient punishments for certain crimes, especially rape, which carries a typical sentence of two to five years in prison. On 18 May 2005, the Diet enacted a new law to improve the treatment of inmates and to help prevent recidivism. Executions in Japan are by hanging.

A form of jury trial was reintroduced in Japan in August 2009, its first such trial in over 60 years. In this new system, trials for some serious cases are conducted by three professional judges and six "lay judges," regular citizens chosen at random from a nationwide pool of eligible voters. Although juries were first introduced into the legal system in 1928, they were dropped in 1943 in favor of a simple panel of judges to preside over cases, issuing both verdicts and sentences. The reestablishment of jury trials is expected to ensure a more democratic, transparent, and speedy trial system.

A great deal of secrecy surrounded the judge-only trial system, which included private police interrogations that many believed led to false confessions and false convictions. At least one of the professional judges presiding over the trial must agree with the jury's decision in order for it to be upheld. While some legal experts have expressed concern that randomly selected jurors may not be qualified to decide the outcome of the most serious cases, others see the change as a step toward a more just system. The first trial under the new system, an August 2009 trial for murder, resulted in a conviction and a 15-year sentence.

17 ARMED FORCES

The International Institute for Strategic Studies reports that armed forces in Japan totaled 247,746 members in 2011. The force is comprised of 151,641 from a ground self-defense force, 45,518 of a maritime self-defense force, 47,123 from the air self-defense force, and 3,464 members of central staff. Armed forces represent 0.4% of the labor force in Japan. Defense spending totaled $34.7 billion and accounted for 0.8% of GDP.

The reestablishment of Japanese defense forces has been a subject of heated debate in the period since World War II. Article 9 of the constitution renounces war as a sovereign right and the maintenance of "land, sea, and air forces, as well as other war potential." During the Korean War, General MacArthur recommended the establishment of a national police reserve. Following the signing of the San Francisco Peace Treaty, the reserve force was reorganized into a National Safety Agency (1 August 1952). Laws establishing a Defense Agency and a Self-Defense Force became effective on 1 July 1954, both under firm civilian control.

Though the number has been gradually declining since the 1950s, the United States maintains around 35,000 troops in Japan. Japan participated in peacekeeping missions in the Middle East.

In April 2010, close to 100,000 people gathered on Okinawa to demand that the US military base on the island be closed. Under a 2006 agreement between the United States and Japan, the US Marine base was set to be relocated from central Okinawa to the coast of the island. However, then-prime minister Hatoyama pledged to relocate the base off the island while campaigning in 2009, and protesters rallied against the prime minister's failure to act on the promise.

18 INTERNATIONAL COOPERATION

Japan was admitted to the United Nations on 18 December 1956, and it holds membership in ESCAP and all the nonregional specialized agencies. It is a member of the WTO, participates in the Colombo Plan, and has permanent observer status with the OAS. In 1963, Japan became a member of IMF and the OECD. It is also a charter member of the Asian Development Bank, which came into operation in 1966; Japan furnished $200 million, a share equal to that of the United States. Japan is also a member of APEC, G-5, G-7, G-8, the Paris Club (G-10), the Inter-American Development Bank, and the Latin American Integration Association (LAIA). Japan is a dialogue partner in ASEAN, an observer to the Council of Europe, and a partner in the OSCE.

Japan has been actively developing peaceful uses for nuclear energy, and in 1970 it signed the Geneva Protocol, which prohibits the use of poisonous and bacteriological weapons. In June 1976, Japan—the only nation to have suffered a nuclear attack—became

the 96th signatory to the international Nuclear Nonproliferation Treaty. Japan also participates in the Australia Group, the Zangger Committee, the Nuclear Energy Agency, the Nuclear Suppliers Group (London Group), and the Organization for the Prohibition of Chemical Weapons and as an observer in the European Organization for Nuclear Research (CERN). The safety of having nuclear energy reactors in such an earthquake-prone country came under scrutiny after the 11 March 2011 earthquake, tsunami, and nuclear meltdown at the Fukushima Daiichi plant.

Japan has extended technical and financial aid to many countries, and, in 1974, it established the Japan International Cooperation Agency to provide technical assistance to developing nations. Japan also was instrumental in establishing the Asian Productivity Organization, the objective of which is to organize national productivity movements in various Asian countries into a more effective movement on a regional scale. Japan has entered into cultural agreements with many European and Asian nations and maintains an educational exchange program with the United States. Through the Japan Overseas Cooperation Volunteers, Japan sends youths to work in developing countries.

In environmental cooperation, Japan is part of the Antarctic Treaty, the Basel Convention, Conventions on Biological Diversity and Whaling, Ramsar, CITES, the London Convention, International Tropical Timber Agreements, the Kyoto Protocol, the Montréal Protocol, MARPOL, the Nuclear Test Ban Treaty, and the UN Conventions on the Law of the Sea, Climate Change, and Desertification.

An ongoing territorial dispute exists between Japan and Russia over four islands between the Sea of Okhotsk and the North Pacific. The islands, known as the Northern Territories by the Japanese and the Southern Kurils by the Russians, have been officially under Russian control since the end of World War II. The region surrounding the islands is a major fishing zone and offers a wealth of undersea gas and oil reserves. As a result of the dispute, the two nations have never signed a comprehensive post-war peace treaty. In May 2009, Vladimir Putin and Taro Aso, the prime ministers of Russia and Japan, respectively, met to establish their first nuclear energy cooperation agreement. Both leaders suggested that forging new economic ties could be a new step toward resolving the territorial conflicts. The nuclear energy agreement enables the transfer of Japanese technology to Russia and promises the sale of more nuclear fuel to Japan. Future mining and oil projects agreements were also discussed.

Japan served as the host country for the first international development conference on Afghanistan in January 2002. Since then, the Japanese government has offered nearly $1.78 billion in non-military aid to Afghanistan as that nation struggles in civil war with the Taliban. Most of the funds have gone toward reconstruction of the nation's damaged infrastructure, including an international airport terminal in Kabul and preservation efforts for the Buddhist ruins in Bamiam, which were damaged by the Taliban. In November 2009, the Japanese government pledged an additional $5 billion in aid to be distributed over a period of five years for projects that will include the construction of schools and highways, training programs for police officers, and rehabilitation programs for former Taliban militants.

19ECONOMY

The gross domestic product (GDP) rate of change in Japan, as of 2010, was 3.9%. Inflation stood at -0.7%, and unemployment was reported at 5.1%.

Japan has the third-largest overall economy in the world after the United States and China. The country tends to rank among the most technologically advanced economies, as well. In per capita GDP, Japan ranked 18th among nations of the world, with an estimated $43,137 per capita in 2010. Two unique features help the economy be so strong: first, a substantial portion of the labor force is guaranteed lifetime employment and second, suppliers, manufacturers, and distributors work in closely-knit groups. Japan was the first Asian country to develop a large urban middle-class industrial society. It was also the first Asian country where a sharp reduction in the birthrate set the stage for notable further increases in per capita income.

Since 1952, the number of farmers has fallen sharply, while expansion has been concentrated in industry and trade. Domestic raw materials are far too limited to provide for the nation's many needs, and imports must be relied on for such basics as raw cotton, raw wool, bauxite, and crude rubber, with fuels and foodstuffs heading the list of materials. The primary engine of Japan's modern growth has been the need to pay for these basic imports with manufactured exports. The exchange of high value-added finished products for low value-added commodities and raw materials has been the basis for both its high level of industrialization and its persistently high trade surpluses. Up until the mid 1980s, economic development depended on continued expansion in exports. With the steady appreciation of the yen in real terms after 1985, however, the country's economic structure underwent some adjustment. Business investment became the second major engine of growth. Facilitated by growing wage rates, favorable credit conditions, cuts in personal and corporate income tax rates and other stimulus measures by the government, domestic demand as well as direct foreign investment have played an increasingly important role as a source of growth in recent years.

After a period of recovery following World War II (from 1947 to 1960), Japan entered into about 15 years of rapid growth (1961–1975) that was arrested by the world oil crisis, signaled by the first oil shock in 1973. In 1974, for the first time since World War II, the GNP fell (by 1.8%). The recession was cushioned, however, by the nation's ability to improve its trade balance (by $11 billion) by increasing exports while reducing imports. The recovery of the mid 1970s was slowed by the second oil shock, in 1978–79, and although the Japanese economy continued to outperform those of most other industrial countries, growth in GNP slowed to an estimated 4.1% yearly in real terms for 1979–82, compared to 8.9% for 1969–72.

Meanwhile, the continued stimulation of exports, especially of automobiles and video equipment, combined with Japan's restrictive tariffs and other barriers against imports, led to increasingly strident criticism of the nation's trade practices in the United States and Western Europe. As early as 1971, Japan agreed to limit textile exports to the United States, and, in the 1980s it also imposed limits on exports of steel, automobiles, and television sets. Similar limits were adopted for exports to Canada, France (where criticism focused on videocassette recorders), and West Germany. Nevertheless, Japan's trade surpluses with the United States and other countries continued to swell through the mid 1980s, helped by a number of factors, most notably the misalignment of major currencies, particularly between the dollar and the yen.

During the late 1980s, a 70% appreciation of the yen's value against the US dollar helped narrow Japan's trade surplus by 19% for two consecutive years in 1988/89 and 1989/90. This was accompanied by low rates of unemployment as well as strong growth in consumer spending and private investment, in turn contributing to a healthy 5% annual growth rate in the GNP between 1987 and 1990.

The end of the period of high growth, 1975 to 1990, coincided with the collapse of the Cold War confrontation. The next twenty years were characterized by very low to stagnant growth, including several periods of recession. They are sometimes referred to as Japan's "lost decades." Japanese asset prices, such as urban real estate, had boomed to unsustainable levels in the late 1980s, and then crashed in the early 1990s. The Japanese stock market plummeted in value, by the summer of 1992 it had lost 62% of its peak 1989 value.

In 2006, despite a currency that rose more than 20% from 2002–05, Japan's economy was beginning to show signs of improvement. GDP was forecasted to grow by 2.1% in 2007. The central bank raised interest rates to 0.25% in 2006 and to 0.50% in February 2007. The unemployment rate held steady at 3.9% in 2006 and 2007. In 2008, Japan's generally growing economy was hit by the global recession--the nation's economy declined by 12.1% in the fourth quarter of 2008. Continuing into the new year, exports declined by 26% in the first quarter of 2009, leading to a 4% contraction of GDP. Still, Japan's May 2009 industrial production was down 30% from the previous year's figure, tempering enthusiasm. The price of imports in the third quarter 2009 fell by 2.6%, the largest drop since 1958.

Growth was remarkably slow into 2010, with a rise in GDP by only 0.1% from April through June 2010. Slow growth has led to some speculation concerning Japan's position in the world market. The World Bank noted that, from 2000 through 2008, Japan's economy expanded by only 5%, while the economy of China grew by 261%. In August 2010, the rising value of the yen against the US dollar and the euro became a concern, as analysts considered the effect this could have on the export market. In early 2011, China overtook Japan as the second-largest economy in the world.

In an effort to boost business, the central Bank of Japan announced plans to provide $33 billion in loans to commercial banks in order to allow them to issue more loans to private businesses. Businesses involved in the identified growth sectors of energy, the environment, and tourism will be targeted for loan approval under the plan. The Bank of Japan also announced that it would keep interest rates at a low 0.1%. The loan scheme began at the end of August 2010. Third quarter growth increased to 0.9%, but the boost was attributed primarily to domestic sales of items such as green cars, which were accompanied by government subsidies for consumers, and cigarettes, which were about to be subject to increased taxes.

In November 2010, parliament approved an additional $61 billion stimulus package with measures designed to assist small businesses and boost consumer spending.

On 11 March 2011, a 9.0 magnitude earthquake hit northern Japan and was immediately followed by a devastating tsunami that left thousands dead or missing and caused major destruction of buildings and infrastructure. In May 2011, Japan passed an emergency disaster relief budget of $49.31 billion in an effort to help rebuild the nation in the aftermath. The money will be used for removing debris, temporary housing, infrastructure repair, and financial support for businesses affected by the disaster.

20 INCOME

The CIA estimated that in 2010 the GDP of Japan was $4.3 trillion. The CIA defines GDP as the value of all final goods and services produced within a nation in a given year and computed on the basis of purchasing power parity (PPP) rather than value as measured on the basis of the rate of the exchange based on current dollars. The per capita GDP was estimated at $34,000. The annual growth rate of GDP was 3.9%. The average inflation rate was -0.7%. It was estimated that agriculture accounted for 1.1% of GDP, industry 23%, and services 75.9%.

According to the World Bank, remittances from citizens living abroad totaled $1.8 billion or about $14 per capita.

The World Bank reports that, in 2009, household consumption in Japan totaled $3.02 trillion or about $23,883 per capita, measured in current US dollars rather than PPP. Household consumption includes expenditures of individuals, households, and nongovernmental organizations on goods and services, excluding the purchases of dwellings. It was estimated that household consumption was growing at an average annual rate of 1%.

In 2011, the World Bank reported that actual individual consumption in Japan was 67.3% of GDP and accounted for 6.99% of world consumption. By comparison, the United States accounted for 25.44% of world individual consumption. The World Bank also estimated that 9.9% of Japan's GDP was spent on food and beverages, 16.8% on housing and household furnishings, 1.9% on clothes, 7.7% on health, 6.0% on transportation, 1.8% on communications, 5.2% on recreation, 4.3% on restaurants and hotels, and 9.6% on miscellaneous goods and services and purchases from abroad.

21 LABOR

As of 2010, Japan had a total labor force of 62.97 million people. CIA estimates in 2010 noted that, within that labor force, 3.9% were employed in agriculture, 26.2% in industry, and 69.8% in the service sector.

Employers tend toward traditional, paternalistic, often authoritarian, control over their workers, but in turn, most regular workers have traditionally enjoyed permanent status. Following the bursting of the economic bubble in the early 1990s, however, more and more young Japanese found themselves involved in part-time jobs or unemployed. The term "freeter" came to be used to describe those individuals who held part-time jobs but did not contribute to the pension system, and "neeto" (NEET) described those who were not in education, employment or training.

Union membership in 2005 was about 10.3 million or 19.2% of the workforce. Union strength is greatest in local government employees, automobile workers, and electrical machinery workers. Most members are organized in units called enterprise unions, which comprise the employees of a single firm. Virtually all organized workers are affiliated with national organizations, of which the largest is the Japanese Trade Union Confederation

(Shin-Rengō), established in 1987 following the dissolution of the Japanese Confederation of Labor (Dōmei), and incorporating the General Council of Trade Unions (Sōhyō) as of 1989. Collective bargaining is widely utilized, and the right to strike is available to most workers.

Strict enforcement of child labor laws as well as societal values protect children from exploitation in the workplace. Children under age 15 are not permitted to work, and those under 18 are restricted. As of 2011, the minimum wage ranged from $8.67 to $11.27 per hour, depending on region. Labor legislation mandated a standard workweek of 40 hours, with premium pay rates for overtime.

22 AGRICULTURE

Roughly 13% of the total land is farmed, and the country's major crops include rice, sugar beets, vegetables, and fruit. Cereal production in 2009 amounted to 11.5 million tons, fruit production 3.4 million tons, and vegetable production 10.5 million tons.

Crop production is vital to Japan despite limited arable land (13% of the total area) and the highest degree of industrialization in Asia. Steep land (more than 20°) has been terraced for rice and other crops, carrying cultivation in tiny patches far up mountainsides. With the aid of a temperate climate, adequate rainfall, soil fertility built up and maintained over centuries, and such a large farm population that the average farm has an area of only 1.2 hectares (3 acres), Japan has been able to develop intensive cultivation. Agriculture exists in every part of Japan but is especially important on the northern island of Hokkaidō, which accounts for 10% of national production. Since World War II (1939–45), modern methods, including commercial fertilizers, insecticides, hybrid seeds, and machinery, have been used so effectively that harvests increased substantially through the 1970s.

Almost all soybeans, feedstuffs, and most of the nation's wheat are imported. Overproduction of rice, as a result of overplanting and a shift to other foods by the Japanese people, led the government in 1987 to adopt a policy of decreasing rice planting and increasing the acreage of other farm products. For many years, the government restricted imports of cheaper foreign rice, but, in 1995, the rice market was opened to imports, as the government implemented the Uruguay Round agreement on agriculture.

As a result of the US-occupation land reform, which began in late 1946, nearly two thirds of all farmland was purchased by the Japanese government at low prewar prices and resold to cultivators on easy terms. By the 1980s, nearly all farms were owner-operated, as compared with 23% before reform. A more telling trend in recent years has been the sharp growth in part-time farm households. Farmers are aging, and 84% of farm income is derived from other sources, such as industrial jobs. Despite increasing urbanization, about half of all farms still cultivated less than one hectare (2.7 acres). As a result, Japanese agriculture intensively utilizes both labor and machinery for production.

23 ANIMAL HUSBANDRY

In 2009, the country tended 285.3 million chickens, 4.4 million head of cattle, and 9.9 million pigs. The production from these animals amounted to 1.09 million tons of beef and veal, 2.56 million tons of pork, 2.18 million tons of poultry, 2.5 million tons of eggs, and 9.74 million tons of milk. Japan also produced 31,500 tons of cattle hide. Livestock production has been the fastest-growing sector in Japanese agriculture. Japan is the single largest recipient of US agricultural exports; over a third of Japan's meat imports come from the United States.

24 FISHING

Japan had 339,470 decked commercial fishing boats in 2008. The annual capture totaled 4.25 million tons, according to the UN FAO. The export value of seafood totaled $1.25 billion. Japan is one of the world's foremost fishing nations, accounting on average for about 8% of the world's catch. The waters off Japan include cold and warm currents in which fish abound.

Japan has faced criticism from international environmental groups for several years over its whaling practices. The government officially ceased commercial whaling in 1986, in compliance with a global moratorium on the practice that was initiated by the International Whaling Commission (IWC).The Japanese whale hunts are now directed toward scientific research, which is permitted under the IWC. Whale meat that is not used in studies is sold to consumers, with proceeds reportedly going back toward more research. It is this practice that leads some environmental groups to believe that the hunts are primarily commercial in nature. While whale consumption is generally low in Japan, the meat can be found in many supermarkets and restaurants. The government places quotas (or targets) on the number of whales allowed in each season's catch. While the target is not always met, the quotas and the number of whales caught have increased each season. In 2009, the Fisheries Agency reported a catch of 679 minke whales and one fin whale, falling short of their target of 935 minke and 50 fin. The agency blames attacks by organizations such as the US-based Sea Shepherd Conservation Society for hindering their catch, since hunting ships have been damaged in intentional collisions by Sea Shepherd vessels.

Competition for overseas fishing privileges has at various times brought Japan into conflict with Canada over salmon, with Russia over fishing in the Sea of Okhotsk (between 1905 and 1945 Japan had special treaty privileges in these waters), with the ROK and China over their limitations on Japanese fishing operations, with Australia over pearl fishing in the Arafura Sea, with Indonesia over fishing in what Indonesia regards as inland waters, and with the United States, especially over fishing in north Pacific and Alaskan waters. Japan has been adversely affected by the adoption of the 200 mi fishing zone by the United States and more than 80 other world nations. Fishing in waters claimed by the United States (where about 70% of the Japanese catch originates) or by many other nations now requires payment of fees and special intergovernmental or private agreements.

Fish culture in freshwater pools, as well as in rice paddies, has long been practiced in Japan. Aquaculture provides an additional 1.2 million tons of fish annually. The leading species cultivated are laver (nori), yesso scallops, Pacific cupped oysters, and Japanese amberjack. Seaweed culture provides winter season activity for many fishermen. Pearl culture has for more than half a century been the foundation of a valuable export industry.

25 FORESTRY

Approximately 69% of Japan is covered by forest. The UN FAO estimated the 2009 roundwood production at 16.6 million cu m (586.9 million cu ft). The value of all forest products, including roundwood, totaled $2.42 billion.

Of 24 million hectares (59.5 million acres) of forest, the Japanese government owns 30%, which it maintains under strict regulations, limiting overcutting. On private forest lands, cutting is less controlled. About 6.6 million hectares (16.3 million acres) are reforested with trees less than 20 years old. Forest management and erosion control are urgent necessities in a land where gradients are very steep and flooding frequent. Japan is one of the world's leading producers of paper and paperboard.

About 45% of the forest area consists of plantations. The Japanese cedar (sugi), which grows in most of Japan, is the most exploited species, followed by Japanese cypress (hinoki), and Japanese red pine (akamatsu). These three species grow on 10 million hectares (24.7 million acres) of plantation forest and were first planted in the 1950s and 1960s. The production of roundwood has declined by more than 50% since the 1960s, and domestic roundwood comprises roughly half of Japan's total wood fiber demand.

During the 1980s and 1990s, Japan became more reliant on imported wood to satisfy domestic demand. Japan is the world's dominant importer of softwood and tropical hardwood logs and has become one of the largest importers of softwood lumber, which is mainly used for housing construction.

In the early 1960s, 42 public corporations were formed to help private landowners harvest and replant Japan's forests. Since timber prices have fallen 75% since the 1980s, many of these public corporations are now unable to pay back loans and are accruing large debts. The failure of these corporations left several prefectures with a great deal of unpaid loans.

26 MINING

The mining sector was the smallest of Japan's industrial-based economy, accounting for 0.1% of GDP. The mineral-processing industry, however, was among the world's largest and most technologically advanced, accounting for 6% of Japan's GDP, and it played a key role in supplying steel, nonferrous metals, and chemicals for the country's world-class manufacturing sector, as well as to those of the region. Japan is among the largest producers and consumers of cadmium and a leading producer of selenium metal, electrolytic manganese dioxide, titanium sponge metal iodine, pig iron, nickel metal, crude steel, copper metal, diatomite, zinc metal, and cement. Japan also produces and has considerable resources of limestone, carbonate rocks (construction aggregates and dolomite), clays (bentonite and fire clay), pyrophyllite, and silica. Since the beginning of the 20th century, most mineral production has undergone a steady decline, and Japan has become a net importer of minerals, relying heavily on imports for petroleum, iron ore, chromium, cobalt, copper concentrate copper metal, primary aluminum, ilmenite, rutile, natural gas, gallium, uranium, manganese (for all its requirements), indium, nickel and coal, although coal accounted for slightly more than half of all mineral production by value. With the exception of gold and zinc, Japan's ore reserves for other minerals, especially oil, gas, and metallic minerals, are very small.

In 2009, Japan imported about 1.2 million metric tons of copper, 99,000 metric tons of lead, and 470,000 metric tons of zinc, all in concentrates. Copper concentrate came mainly from Chile (30%), Indonesia (20%), and Peru (15%). Lead concentrate came from Australia (48%), the US (29%), and Bolivia (19%). Zinc concentrate was imported mostly from Australia (32%) and Peru (25%).

Among metal minerals, preliminary data for 2009 shows that Japan produced 7,708 kg of mine gold (metal content), and 1,500 kg of mine silver. In addition, Japan produced the metal minerals alumina, antimony oxide, high-purity arsenic, bismuth, mine copper, germanium oxide, iron ore, iron sand concentrate, mine lead, manganese oxide, rare-earth oxide (including oxide of cerium, europium, gadolinium, lanthanum, neodymium, praseodymium, samarium, terbium, and yttrium), elemental selenium, high-purity silicon, elemental tellurium, titanium dioxide, mine zinc, and zirconium oxide. Gold ore reserves totaled 159,000 kg (metal content); and zinc ore (metal content), 3.25 million tons.

Among industrial minerals, preliminary output totals for 2009 were hydraulic cement, 54.8 million tons; iodine, 9,600 metric tons; diatomite, 110,000 metric tons; limestone (crushed), 132.35 million tons; dolomite (crushed), 3.122 million tons; bentonite, 432,000 tons; crude fire clay, 440,000 metric tons; pyrophyllite (from Nagasaki, Okayama, and Hiroshima prefectures), 340,000 metric tons (estimated); silica sand, 2.856 million tons; and silica stone (quartzite), 9.189 million tons. In addition, Japan produced elemental bromine, kaolin clay, feldspar, aplite, gypsum, quicklime, nitrogen, perlite, salt, sodium compounds (soda ash and sulfate), sulfur, talc, and vermiculite. Reserves of iodine totaled 5 million tons; limestone, 40.4 billion tons; dolomite, 913 million tons; pyrophyllite, 59.7 million tons; silica sand, 73.6 million tons; and white silica stone, 462 million tons.

Japan's mineral industry consists of a small mining sector of coal and nonferrous metals, a large mining sector of industrial minerals, and a large minerals-processing sector of ferrous and nonferrous metals and industrial minerals. Mining and mineral-processing businesses are owned and operated by private companies. There were two major nonferrous metal mines and around 40 major industrial mineral mines in 2009. The mineral-processing industry produced, among other things, inorganic chemicals and compounds, ferrous metals, industrial minerals, nonferrous metals, petrochemicals, and refined petroleum products for domestic consumption and for export. Operating mines and employment in the mining industry have been in decline due to depleted ore reserves, high mining costs, and the availability of cheaper imports.

The government, through its Metal Mining Agency of Japan (MMAJ), collaborating with the Japan International Cooperation Agency, continued to promote overseas mineral exploration by providing loans and technical assistance and by carrying out basic exploration. In line with its mineral policy to secure and diversify its long-term supply of raw materials, Japan was expected to continue its active search for direct investment in joint exploration and development of minerals in developed and developing countries. The targeted minerals were antimony, chromium, coal, columbium (niobium), copper, gold, iron ore, lead, lithium, manganese, molybdenum, natural gas, nickel, crude petroleum, rare earths, silver, strontium, tantalum, titanium, tungsten, vanadium, and zinc.

27 ENERGY AND POWER

The World Bank reported in 2008 that Japan produced 1.08 trillion kWh of electricity and consumed 1.03 trillion kWh, or 8,149 kWh per capita. Roughly 83% of energy came from fossil fuels, while 16% came from alternative fuels. Per capita oil consumption was 3,883 kg. Oil production totaled 4,995 barrels of oil a day.

Japan's proven oil reserves are miniscule, and it must import a majority of the oil it consumes. Japan has been involved in exploration for petroleum and its production overseas. However, in 2000, Japan lost its drilling rights in Saudi Arabia. To make up for this loss, Japan began making investments in Iran and has sought equity stakes in the Caspian Sea region.

Japan ceased all coal production in January 2002, when it closed its last operating mine at Kushiro, on the island of Hokkaidō.

Electricity is provided by several private companies, with the public Electric Power Development Co. and the Japan Atomic Power Co. playing supplementary roles in distribution.

To reduce its reliance on oil and its carbon dioxide emissions, Japan has aggressively pursued the development of nuclear power since the 1980s. According to Japan's 10-year energy plan, which was approved in March 2002, nuclear generation was to be increased to 30% of total power production by 2011. It was anticipated that between 9 and 12 new nuclear plants would be needed. However, in light of the failures of the nuclear reactor at Fukushima Daiichi plant in northeastern Japan during the 2011 earthquake and tsunami, Prime Minister Naoto Kan announced that the plans made in 2010 to build 14 additional nuclear reactors by 2030 would be abandoned while the nation creates a new energy policy.

28 INDUSTRY

Manufacturing has been a key element in Japan's economic expansion during three periods of phenomenal growth. First, during the 50-year rise of Japan from a feudal society in 1868 to a major world power in 1918, output in manufacturing rose more rapidly than that of other sectors. Second, during the 1930s, when Japan recovered from the world depression earlier and faster than any other country and embarked on an aggressive course in Asia, manufacturing, especially heavy industries, again had the highest rate of growth. Third, in the remarkable recovery since World War II, manufacturing, which had suffered severely during the latter stages of the war, was again a leader, although commerce and finance expanded even more rapidly.

Japanese industry is characterized by a complex system of exclusive buyer-supplier networks and alliances, commonly maintained by companies belonging to the same business grouping, or *keiretsu*. Such a system utilizes a web of vertical, horizontal, and even diagonal integration within the framework of a few large conglomerations. Keiretsu firms inhibit the foreign acquisition of Japanese firms through nontransparent accounting and financial practices, cross-holding of shares among keiretsu member firms (even between competitors), and by keeping a low proportion of publicly traded stock relative to total capital.

Textiles and apparel, Japan's main exports during the years immediately following World War II, have steadily declined in importance. Output of cotton and woolen fabrics, yarns, rayon, and acetate reached peak levels in 1965. The Japanese textile industry has been diminished by competition from developing nations in East Asia.

During the 1970s and early 1980s, the rate of Japan's industrial growth surpassed that of any other non-Communist industrialized country. Of the 26 largest industrial companies in the world in the mid 1980s—those with sales of $20 billion or more—four were Japanese: Toyota Motor, Matsushita Electric, Hitachi, and Nissan Motor. Facing increasingly stiff competition from overseas trading partners in the 1980s, Japanese firms responded with several strategies, including product diversification, increased investment in overseas plants, and a greater focus on production for the domestic market. The electronics industry grew with extraordinary rapidity in the 1980s and continued to be a world leader in the 21st century. Despite declining profits with the economic downturn of the early 1990s, Japanese companies continued to make large investments in new plants and equipment

Restrictions imposed on Japanese automobile exports have promoted a marked increase in Japanese investment in automobile manufacturing facilities (engine manufacture, assembly as well as research and development) in the United States, Western Europe, and other overseas markets. Japanese manufactures have also sustained growth through greater focus on producing for the booming domestic motor vehicle market. Japan's superior technology in the design of bicycles, motorcycles, buses, and high-speed trains has been another major factor in the growth of the transport industry. In 2009, Japan produced 7,146,449 cars, trucks, and buses, of which about half were exported. Leading car makers included Daihatsu, Fuji, Hino, Mitsubishi, Nissan, Honda, Isuzu, Mazda, Suzuki, and Toyota. The 2011 earthquake and tsunami greatly disrupted supply chains for many car makers, resulting in production declines during that year. Two Toyota plants, producing 420,000 cars annually (13% of the company's domestic production), were directly hit.

The earthquake and tsunami also affected other industries, forcing the temporary suspension of operations of at least 20 electronics plants owned by major manufacturers such as Sony and Toshiba. By year end 2011, the Japanese electronics industry still managed to produce nearly $170 billion worth of electronic equipment. It produced nearly $200 billion in 2010. Beginning in the early 2000s, the Japanese consumer electronics industry has faced increasing competition from South Korea, which has forced some Japanese electronics companies to scale-back operations or merge with other domestic entities.

29 SCIENCE AND TECHNOLOGY

Patent applications in science and technology as of 2009, according to the World Bank, totaled 295,315 in Japan. Public financing of science was 3.44% of GDP. High technology exports represented 18% of all manufactured exports in 2010. The Japanese rank second only to the United States in spending on scientific research and technology development. Researchers in science and technology numbered 589 per 1,000,000 citizens in 2007.

In terms of the Japanese government's role in national science and technology, three ministries are important. The Ministry of Education, or Monbusho, provides most of the support and funding for scientific education and training at the university level in Japan. In the 1990s, Monbusho led a national effort to improve

science and technology education at universities, particularly in "basic" research (areas where research does not necessarily have to pay off in commercial products). Another organization, the Science and Technology Agency (STA) promotes science and technology policies, and acts as the prime minister's leading policy and budgetary agency. It performs this function through annual "white papers" which describe the current state and future goals of Japanese science and technology. The Ministry of International Trade and Industry (MITI), reorganized under the Ministry of Economy, Trade and Industry (METI) in 2001, is probably the ministry best-known by Americans. MITI was instrumental in providing close government-industry cooperation in many high technology fields—including computers, electronics, and biotechnology—which aided Japan's rapid ascent in the world market for high technology products.

Regional research institutions such as Tskuba Science City and Kansai Science Park also play a role in fostering Japanese research and development. Their growth since the 1970s has shifted some of the focus and power of the national government and industry in Tokyo to the regional prefectures. International cooperation with the United States in areas like global warming and space exploration offer opportunities for greater scientific research at local, regional, and national levels in Japan.

Japan has numerous universities and colleges that offer courses in basic and applied sciences. The country's National Science Museum, founded in 1877, is located in Tokyo. The University of Tokyo has botanical gardens that were established in 1684.

30 DOMESTIC TRADE

Traditionally, Japan's distribution system was characterized by a long term and carefully cultivated relationship that extended from the supplier and wholesaler, down to the retailer and the consumer. However, that relationship has begun to change. Japan's retail sector has been shifting away from small stores (those with five or fewer employees), toward larger outlets, such as self-service discount stores and so-called "superstores." Previously, at least half of all consumer goods were purchased through small, privately owned and operated shops, which rarely stocked imported goods. However, the economic stagnation and the accompanying deflation in prices that has afflicted the country's economy since the 1990s has taken a heavy toll on small stores. More importantly, Japanese consumers have begun to appreciate low prices. Another trend has been the growth of foreign retailers entering the Japanese market. Large retailers such as Toys 'R' Us, COSTCO and Walmart have either entered Japan's retail market or are in the process of doing so. In addition, there are an increasing number of specialty stores, many of which are also foreign-controlled. As of 2005, Japan's franchise industry was the second-largest in the world in total sales, with over 1,000 chains. The number of outlets in Japan exceeds 218,000.

As the number of large retail outlets has grown in Japan, legal revisions have loosened government regulation of these stores. In 2000, the Large-Scale Retail Store Location Law went into effect. This law limited local authorities' ability to regulate new large stores to only environmental issues. As a result, cities and towns in Japan have begun to implement laws governing such issues as parking and store operations.

At the wholesale level, the rise of larger, more efficient retailers has also reduced the number of layers in the Japanese distribution system. Direct importing is growing, bypassing traditional trading houses and other intermediaries, as the retail sector has become more cost-conscious and streamlined.

In retail, cash transactions have been traditional, but various forms of installment selling are increasingly being used, especially in the sale of durable goods. The use of charge accounts is growing rapidly. Promotion by displays, advertising, and other methods used in Western countries is increasing rapidly in Japan. Advertising appears in the daily press, in the numerous weekly and monthly magazines, and in special publications of many kinds. Radio and television also carry extensive advertising, excepting those channels run by the government's Japan Broadcasting Corporation.

Japan does not have a value added tax. Instead, a 5% consumption tax is imposed on most sales and services, and on imports.

Normal shop hours are 10 a.m. to 8 p.m., seven days a week, although department stores shut their doors at 6 p.m. and are closed two or three weekdays a month; government offices are open 10 a.m. to 5 p.m., Monday through Friday, and from 10 a.m. to noon on Saturdays. Banks are open from 9 a.m. to 3 p.m. Monday through Friday, and occasionally on Saturday mornings.

³¹FOREIGN TRADE

Japan imported $636.8 billion worth of goods and services in 2008, while exporting $765.2 billion worth of goods and services. Major import partners in 2009 were China, 22.2%; the United States, 11%; Australia, 6.3%; Saudi Arabia, 5.3%; and UAE, 4.1%. Its major export partners were China, 18.9%; the United States, 16.4%; South Korea, 8.1%; and Hong Kong, 5.5%.

Japan has historically had a low degree of openness to foreign trade, and therefore maintains a significant trade surplus. The closed nature of Japan's economy is also comparable to other countries in Asia, such as China. This phenomenon is due to official and unofficial restrictions on merchandise imports, which remain in place—despite pressure from the United States and other important trading partners—to protect the less-efficient sectors of Japanese industry, such as textiles, food, pulp, and paper. This lack of openness to foreign trade has been named one of the reasons for the poor productivity of companies in the nontradable sectors of the economy, for example, and for other structural economic problems.

Imports consist mostly of fuel, foodstuffs, industrial raw materials, and industrial machinery. Exports are varied, but manufactures now account for nearly all of the total. Cars represent a leading export product, with the United States, Canada, Australia, Germany, and the United Kingdom as the main markets. The export of office machinery, scientific and optical equipment is also important. South Korea, China, and Taiwan are among the main buyers of Japan's iron and steel, while plastic materials and fertilizers are shipped primarily to South Korea and the Southeast Asian countries, and woven fabrics are supplied to China, the United States, and Saudi Arabia. Only a small fraction of Japan's total exports consists of food items, mainly fish.

In light of growing overseas concern about Japan's continuing large trade surplus, the United States and Japanese governments collaborated on the Structural Impediments Initiative of 1989. Steps taken in the wake of the initial report included a variety of import and direct foreign investment promotion measures, including deregulation, accelerated government spending on public infrastructure, and support services for foreign businesses. The Initiative as a framework for US-Japan relations was ended in 1993.

Manufactured products make up most of Japan's commodity exports. Japan is the world's largest maker of machine tools and is one of the world's most important iron and steelmakers. The automobile is the country's most important industry, along with computers and electronic equipment.

Balance of Payments – Japan (2010)

(In billions of US dollars)

Current Account		**195.8**
Balance on goods	91.0	
Imports	-639.1	
Exports	730.1	
Balance on services	-16.1	
Balance on income	133.3	
Current transfers	-12.4	
Capital Account		**-5.0**
Financial Account		**-130.5**
Direct investment abroad	-57.2	
Direct investment in Japan	-1.4	
Portfolio investment assets	-262.6	
Portfolio investment liabilities	111.6	
Financial derivatives	11.9	
Other investment assets	-130.1	
Other investment liabilities	197.3	
Net Errors and Omissions		**-16.5**
Reserves and Related Items		**-43.9**

(…) data not available or not significant.

SOURCE: *Balance of Payment Statistics Yearbook 2011,* Washington, DC: International Monetary Fund, 2011.

Principal Trading Partners – Japan (2010)

(In millions of US dollars)

Country	Total	Exports	Imports	Balance
World	1,462,271.0	769,838.0	692,433.0	77,405.0
China	302,995.0	149,626.0	153,369.0	-3,743.0
United States	189,510.0	120,483.0	69,027.0	51,456.0
South Korea	90,919.0	62,270.0	28,649.0	33,621.0
Taiwan	75,478.0	52,395.0	23,083.0	29,312.0
Australia	61,057.0	15,869.0	45,188.0	-29,319.0
Thailand	55,255.0	34,222.0	21,033.0	13,189.0
Indonesia	44,173.0	15,918.0	28,255.0	-12,337.0
Hong Kong	43,822.0	42,303.0	1,519.0	40,784.0
Sa'udi Arabia	42,360.0	6,481.0	35,879.0	-29,398.0
Malaysia	40,352.0	17,637.0	22,715.0	-5,078.0

(…) data not available or not significant.

(n.s.) not specified.

SOURCE: *2011 Direction of Trade Statistics Yearbook,* New York: United Nations, 2011.

³²BALANCE OF PAYMENTS

In 2010, Japan had a foreign trade surplus of $23 billion.

Beginning in 1981, surpluses in Japan's current accounts increased rapidly, reaching $49 billion in 1985 and $86 billion in 1986, the latter being 18 times the level of 1981. These huge surpluses resulted largely from the high value of the dollar relative to the yen; price declines of primary goods, such as petroleum, also enhanced Japan's favorable trade position. Japan's mounting surpluses and the rising deficits of the United States forced the United States and other leading industrial nations to attempt to realign their currencies, especially the dollar and the yen, in September 1985. Within two years, the yen rose 70% against the dollar. The yen's appreciation increased the competitiveness of American products and contributed to the reduction of Japan's external imbalances through 1990, when the current account surplus fell by 37.4% due to higher expenses for imported oil and rising expenditures by Japanese traveling abroad. Whereas long-term capital outflows exceeded Japan's current account surplus from 1984 through 1990, by 1991 the outflow shifted predominantly to short-term capital, and overseas direct investment slowed.

Japan had the highest trade and current account surpluses in the world in the early 2000s; however, Japan is less open to trade than other highly developed economies. As a percentage of current-price GDP, the value of Japan's two-way foreign trade in 2003 was just 18%, compared with Germany's 54% and China's nearly 60%. This was due in part to restrictions on merchandise imports to protect the country's less-efficient industry sectors. Due to this lack of openness to trade, companies in the nontradable sectors were not productive, and this trend has continued to the present.

³³BANKING AND SECURITIES

Japan's highly sophisticated banking system continued to play a dominant role in financing the country's and the world's economic development, despite Japan's long period of economic stagnation. Banks provide not only short-term but also long-term credit, which often, in effect, becomes fixed capital in industry. In terms of sheer size, Japanese banks occupy some of the top spots in worldwide bank ratings.

The controlling national monetary institutions are the Bank of Japan (founded in 1882) and the Ministry of Finance. The Bank of Japan, as central bank, has power over note issue and audits financial institutions to provide guidance for improving banking and management practices. Ceilings for interest rates are set by the bank, while actual rates, commissions, and discounts are arranged by unofficial agreements among bankers and other financial institutions, including the National Bankers' Association.

As of 2009, six important city banks, with branches throughout the country, account for a majority of commercial bank assets, the rest accruing to 64 regional banks, 44 member banks of the Second Association of Regional Banks, 19 trust banks, 61 foreign banks, and 14 other banks. Foreign banks also have representative offices in Japan. Of special interest are the postal savings facilities, which are used by many Japanese families and have assumed many of the aspects of a huge state-owned banking business. In fact, the Japan Post Bank, established in 2006, was the world's biggest deposit holder as of 2008. As of 2011 it employed more than 12,000 people.

The Foreign Exchange Law was changed to totally liberalize cross-border transactions in 1998. Important foreign exchange banks include the city banks, long-term credit banks, trust banks, major local banks, major mutual loan and savings banks, and the Japanese branches of foreign banks. Governmental financial institutions also participate in foreign exchange markets.

In 2009, the discount rate, the interest rate at which the central bank lends to financial institutions in the short term, was 0.3%. In 2011, the nation's gold bullion reserves were valued at $49.11 billion (843.3 tons), the ninth-largest in the world.

Japan has securities exchanges in Tokyo, Fukuoka, Nagoya, Sapporo, and Osaka. Although prior to World War II, most stocks were held by large business firms (zaibatsu), stocks are now available for public subscription. The Tokyo Securities and Stock Exchange became the largest in the world in 1988, in terms of combined market value of outstanding shares and capitalization, while the Osaka Stock Exchange ranked third after Tokyo and New York. Both subsequently fell in value. As of November 2011, the Tokyo exchange remains the world's third largest in market capitalization, with 2,283 companies listed.

³⁴INSURANCE

After 56 years, the Japanese Insurance Business Law was revised in 1997. The purpose of the newly revised law is competition, to protect policy holders, and to promote greater management efficiency. The law allowed, for the first time, cross entries of life and non-life companies into each other's sector through the establishment of subsidiary companies.

Life insurance is by far the most extensive of all classes of insurance. Japan was the world's second largest holder of life insurance as of 2010. In the non-life field, automobile insurance, which is compulsory, is the largest sector. Personal accident insurance was next in importance, followed by fire, marine cargo, and marine hull insurance. Worker's compensation, nuclear liability, and health insurance are also compulsory. Tokio is the nation's leading non-life insurer.

The private insurance industry was insulated in large part from the losses incurred during the 2011 earthquake and tsunami. Many homeowners and businesses have property insurance through the government, as private firms are exceedingly expensive due to the high risk earthquakes. Additionally, insurance claims are capped at $60 billion, after which payouts are pro rated, limiting companies' exposure.

³⁵PUBLIC FINANCE

Plans for the national budget usually begin in August, when various agencies submit their budget requests to the Ministry of Finance. On the basis of such requests, the ministry, other government agencies, and the ruling party start negotiations. The government budget plan usually is approved by the Diet without difficulty, and the budget goes into effect in April. Deficits, financed by public bond sales, have steadily increased in size since the 1973 oil crisis. Since 1982, Japan has pursued tight fiscal policies and has attempted to constrain government debt. However, fiscal stimulus policies have contributed to an increasing budget deficit. Japan's government deficit was 4.3% of GDP in 1995. By 2002, the deficit had reached 7.8% of GDP. The budget deficit amounted to 7.7% of GDP in 2010. An aging population has

Public Finance – Japan (2009)

(In billions of yen, general government government figures)

Revenue and Grants	**155,594**	**100.0%**
Tax revenue	76,660	49.3%
Social contributions	55,506	35.7%
Grants	...	...
Other revenue	23,429	15.1%
Expenditures	**200,332**	**100.0%**
General public services	24,641	12.3%
Defense	4,662	2.3%
Public order and safety	7,204	3.6%
Economic affairs	22,617	11.3%
Environmental protection	7,126	3.6%
Housing and community amenities	3,578	1.8%
Health	39,859	19.9%
Recreational, culture, and religion	673	0.3%
Education	20,022	10.0%
Social protection	69,951	34.9%

(…) data not available or not significant.

SOURCE: *Government Finance Statistics Yearbook 2010*, Washington, DC: International Monetary Fund, 2010.

strained social service provisions—especially in healthcare—and diminished the labor force that contributes to government funding. In 2010, the budget of Japan included $1.638 trillion in public revenue and $2.16 trillion in public expenditures. Public debt was 208.2% of GDP in 2011, the second highest percentage in the world after Zimbabwe. Some $2.441 trillion of the debt was held by foreign entities.

36 TAXATION

After World War II, Japan adopted a tax system relying mainly on direct taxes, like those in the United States and the United Kingdom. The most important of these are the income tax and corporation tax.

Japan's standard corporate tax rate is 30%, but local enterprise and inhabitant taxes can push that rate to 41%. Corporations capitalized at JPY100 million or less are taxed at a 22% rate that is applied to the first JPY8 million of taxable income. Capital gains received by companies are taxed as income at normal tax rates. In the past, capital gains received from the sale of land had been subject to a special surplus tax. Dividends are generally subject to a withholding tax of 20%. However, dividends paid on listed shares from 1 April 2003 through 31 March 2008 are taxed at a lower 10% rate. Interest paid to residents and nonresidents is also subject to a 20% withholding rate, although interest received by nonresidents from debentures, bank deposits, and bonds is subject to a lower rate of 15%.

Japan has a progressive individual income tax that has a top rate of 37%. However, local taxes can push the effective rate to 50%. Local taxes can include municipal and prefectural inhabitant and per capita taxes. There is also a 5% consumption tax that is applied to most services and goods. However, a number of items are zero-rated. These include exports; foreign cargo handling, carriage, and storage; certain services to nonresidents; and patent, trademark and copyright loans or transfers to nonresidents. Exemptions include land transfers, medical services, residential rents, and financial services.

Additional national taxes include customs duties; a stamp tax; inheritance and gift taxes; a monopoly profits tax; a sugar excise tax; taxes on liquor, gasoline, and other commodities; and travel, admissions, and local road taxes.

In December 2009, Japanese prime minister Yukio Hatoyama raised the cigarette tax by one third in the hopes of addressing both the budgetary shortfall and rising health care costs that were plaguing the nation. As of 2009, Japan was the fourth-largest consumer of cigarettes in the world. The prime minister had campaigned with a promise to reduce the smoking rate in the country. The December 2010 tax hike was the fifth government-mandated boost on cigarette prices since 1985, and, with an increase of nearly four cents per cigarette (3.5 yen), it was the single largest tax increase in the period.

37 CUSTOMS AND DUTIES

The Japanese tariff system is administered by the Customs Bureau of the Ministry of Finance. As of 2011, Japan imposed tariffs ranging from 0 to 10% for many raw materials and home furnishings, and tariffs as high as 30% for specialty items such as certain types of footwear). However, import duties remained relatively high for certain agricultural and manufactured goods. In addition, quantity quotas and tariff quotas are still applied to some goods. There is also a 5% consumption tax on imports based on cost, insurance, and freight in addition to the duty. In August 2005, Japan imposed a 15% retaliatory duty on 15 products manufactured in the United States, including ball bearings, steel products, navigational instruments, machinery accessories, printing machines, forklift trucks, and industrial belts. There is a free trade zone at Naha, on Okinawa; no free trade zones function on the main islands.

38 FOREIGN INVESTMENT

Foreign investment in Japan has historically been less than in other G-7 countries. During the early- and mid-1990s, there was a significant imbalance in Japan's investment in other countries compared to other countries investing in Japan—the former was far greater than the latter. One reason for this is that, in the past, the Japanese government discouraged foreign investment. A second but perhaps more significant reason is the high cost of doing business in Japan, which, in turn, reduces profits. Some of the barriers became less significant with the signing of the US-Japan Investment Accord signed in 1995. Reforms in the financial, communications, and distribution sectors encouraged foreign investment in these sectors, and FDI stock in Japan more than tripled (on a yen basis) from 1998 to 2003. By 2005, Japan's government imposed few formal restrictions on FDI in Japan and had removed or liberalized most legal restrictions that applied to specific economic sectors. In 2005, President Koizumi promised to double the amount of FDI in Japan by 2010, and it accomplished this goal by 2008 (FDI would later decline, however). Foreign direct investment (FDI) in Japan was a net inflow of $11.8 billion according to World Bank figures published in 2009. FDI represented 0.23%

of GDP. In 2010, inward FDI was -$1.4 billion, and outward FDI amounted to $57.2 billion.

³⁹ECONOMIC DEVELOPMENT

Japan's phenomenal economic growth from the 1950s to 90s was based on an efficient blend of two economic tendencies. First was government activism in national planning and implementation, with guidance of the largely free economy via sophisticated and powerful monetary and fiscal policies. Second was the distinctively Japanese way of coupling largely private ownership of assets with conservative, public-spirited management. Especially significant was the role of the Ministry of International Trade and Industry (MITI), which coordinated national industrial policies consistent with economic and social growth. In a unique government-industry collaboration sometimes referred to overseas as "Japan, Inc.," MITI selected and nurtured industries targeted as important to Japan's future economic growth. Industries so targeted have included chemicals, iron and steel, shipbuilding, and transistor radios in the 1960s; automobiles and electronics in the 1970s; and computers, computer chips, and other high-technology industries for the 1980s. In addition to stimulating new industries, MITI also smoothed the way for plant closings and worker retraining in industries targeted for de-emphasis, such as textiles in the 1970s and the ailing coal-mining and shipbuilding industries in the 1980s. MITI, in collaboration with both domestic companies and foreign firms, also assumed an active role in lessening Japan's positive trade imbalances through a variety of import promotion measures. Close ties between government and industry are illustrated by the ministries' issuance of informal "administrative guidance" to Japanese companies, the frequent placement of retired bureaucrats in Japanese companies and trade associations, and the delegation of quasi-regulatory authority to trade associations (which are often allowed to devise and regulate their own insider rules). In 2001, MITI was reorganized as the Ministry of Economy, Trade, and Industry (METI).

The objectives of maintaining rapid GNP growth, controlling inflation, and developing Japan's social and industrial infrastructure have been the concern of the Economic Planning Agency, which produced the successful Ikeda plan (to double the national income between 1961 and 1970) and released projections of key indicators at frequent intervals (In 2001, the offices and functions of the Economic Planning Agency were reassigned to the newly-formed Cabinet Office, where they function as a secretariat to the Council on Economic and Fiscal Policy). The Ikeda plan consisted of a series of projections of growth in a free market economy, the basic assumption of which—the continued growth of Japan's overseas trade—was largely outside of government control. During the plan's 10-year span, an annual growth of 11% in GNP was realized, as against the forecasted rate of 7.2%. An economic and social development plan (1967–75) accomplished a GNP growth rate of 10.6%, against 8.2% projected.

A second economic and social plan (1970–75) projected a continued annual growth rate of 10.6%. The 1973 world oil crisis and its aftermath severely shook Japan's trade-dependent economy, however; in 1974, the GNP actually shrank by 1.8%, the first negative result in three decades. In 1975, the cabinet approved a new economic and social plan for 1979–85 calling for an average annual growth rate of 5.7%. However, the impact of the second oil cri-

sis in 1978 necessitated downward revisions of projected growth targets. Plans to stimulate the economy by increasing public-works spending and cutting taxes were approved in October 1983 and in May 1987. Also enacted in 1989 was a value-added tax to strengthen the government's revenue base while allowing reductions in personal and corporate income tax.

In 1988, a five-year plan was adopted to sustain real GNP growth at 3.8% per year, maintain low unemployment (2.5% per year), contain inflation, reduce the country's trade surplus, and improve the quality of life through a shorter workweek and stabilized property prices. Many of these objectives were achieved or surpassed in the closing years of the decade. After 1992, however, the economy's downturn was likened by some analysts to the 1974 recession in its severity and length. Economic indicators included steep declines and sluggish recovery in the stock market index after 1989, falling real estate prices, as well as a shrunken rate of GNP growth, despite surging exports. To prompt a recovery, the Ministry of Finance approved large stimulus packages for 1992 and 1993, totaling $85.6 billion and $119 billion in expenditures, respectively. Under the Structural Impediments Initiative, the government sought to sustain growth while also reducing the country's external trade imbalances. Among the main steps taken under the Initiative was a 10-year program targeting the expenditure of up to $8 trillion for the construction or renovation of airports, bridges, roads, ports, telecommunications systems, resorts, retirement communities, medical facilities, and other forms of public infrastructure development. Real growth during the 1990s hovered around 1% a year, however. The Asian Tigers, such as Singapore, Taiwan, and Hong Kong, saw their economies grow at a much higher rate than Japan's, and China's economic growth rate was 10% per year during the 1990s. In 1999, Japan began a tentative recovery from its longest and most severe recession since the end of World War II. By 2005, the economy was growing by a rate of approximately 2.3%.

Following the 2008 global financial crisis, the Japanese economy began to recover more quickly, and, in 2010, Japan's real GDP growth showed that it was the fastest-growing economy among the G-7 nations that year. The Japanese yen hit a 15-year high against the dollar in 2010, at around 84 yen to the dollar. It continued to grow in strength against the dollar, reaching a height of 75 yen to the dollar in October 2011. The strength of the yen is of concern to Japanese exporters and the economy as a whole, as it leads to losses for Japanese shares. Japan's economy took a major hit following the March 2011 earthquake and tsunami, with an estimated $235–310 billion worth of damages. The Bank of Japan pumped more than $300 billion into the economy in an effort to stabilize the financial market following the disaster.

Japan's financial assistance to developing countries and international agencies has grown significantly, making it one of the world's leading donor countries. The government has committed itself to large increases in official development assistance to developing countries and multilateral agencies since the late 1980s. Among the top recipients of bilateral ODA from Japan have been Indonesia, China, the Philippines, Thailand, Bangladesh, and Malaysia. Japan's increasing financial assistance to developing countries like China and Indonesia is an indication that the Japanese government is willing to sacrifice short-term gain for longer-term prosperity and stability. In essence, Japan is helping to create viable trading partners, and since Japan is a trading state, this strategy will enhance Japan's economic development over the long term. From 1992–2001, Japan was the largest donor of ODA in terms of raw dollars. That was until 2001, when the United States reclaimed that position, and Japan's amount of aid dropped by nearly $4 billion. A key factor accounting for this was the 12.7% depreciation of the yen.

⁴⁰ SOCIAL DEVELOPMENT

Living standards reflect Japan's rapid economic development since the mid 1960s. Greatly contributing to the social stability of the nation is the strong sense of family solidarity among the Japanese; virtually every home has its *butsudan*, or altar of the ancestors, and most elderly people are cared for in the homes of their grown children. A further source of social stability has been Japan's employment system, noted for its "lifetime employment" of workers from the time they enter the company after completing their education to the time they retire. Traditionally, layoffs and dismissals of employees were rare, even during times of recession.

The present social insurance system includes national health insurance, welfare annuity insurance, maternity coverage, unemployment insurance, workers' accident compensation insurance, seamen's insurance, a national government employees' mutual aid association, and day workers' health insurance. It also provides pension plans designed to maintain living standards for the elderly, based on years of employment, and for families of deceased workers. Per capita expenditure on social security programs remain low, however, in relation to expenditure in many other industrial nations. There is a family allowance for low-income residents with children under the age of nine.

Nearly the entire population receives benefits in one form or another from the health insurance system. Health insurance is compulsory for those employed at enterprises with five or more workers, and premiums are shared equally by the insured and their employers. Those not covered at work are insured through the National Health Insurance program. Other sickness and health insurance is in force among farmers, fishermen, and their dependents. Unemployment coverage is obligatory for all enterprises regardless of size; workers' compensation must also be provided by employers.

The Daily Life Security Law laid the groundwork for an ever-growing livelihood assistance program. Out of this have come laws pertaining to child welfare, physically handicapped people's welfare, social welfare service, welfare fund loans to mothers and children, aid to the war-wounded and ill, and aid to families of deceased soldiers. The system provides direct aid for livelihood, education, housing, medical, maternity, occupational disability, and funerals. More than a thousand welfare offices throughout the nation are staffed by full-time, salaried welfare secretaries and assisted by voluntary help. Institutions have been established to care for the aged, those on relief, and those needing rehabilitation. Numerous private organizations assist government agencies. There are special pension programs for public employees, private school teachers and employees, and employees of agricultural, forestry, and fishery cooperatives.

Women make up over 40% of the labor force. Although the law prohibits wage discrimination, there remains a significant gap between earnings for men and women. Women also retain the responsibility of child care and household chores. Domestic abuse and other violence against women are often unreported due to societal concerns about shame in the family. The government is taking some action in providing shelter facilities and passing laws to protect victims. There has been an ongoing problem with the molestation of women on crowded trains while commuting (called *chikan*), thus resulting in the establishment of women-only cars during specific hours. Sexual harassment in the workplace is prevalent.

Discrimination against ethnic Koreans and other non-Japanese minorities also continues. Human rights are generally respected by the government, but there have been some reports of abuse of detainees and prisoners.

⁴¹ HEALTH

According to the CIA, life expectancy in Japan was 83 years in 2011. The country spent 8.3% of its GDP on healthcare, amounting to $3,321 per person. There were 21 physicians, 41 nurses and midwives, and 138 hospital beds per 10,000 inhabitants. The fertility rate was 1.4, while the infant mortality rate was 2 per 1,000 live births. In 2008, the maternal mortality rate, according to the World Bank, was 6 per 100,000 births. It was estimated that 94% of children were vaccinated against measles. The CIA calculated HIV/AIDS prevalence in Japan to be about less than 0.1% in 2009.

The Ministry of Health, Labour and Welfare has become the central administrative agency responsible for maintaining and promoting public health, welfare, and sanitation. All hospitals and clinics are subject to government control with respect to their standards and spheres of responsibility. Every practitioner in the field of medicine or dentistry must receive a license from the Ministry of Health, Labour and Welfare. In addition, the ministry recognizes and authorizes certain quasi-medical practices, including massage, acupuncture, moxa-cautery, and judo-orthopedics, all based upon traditional Japanese health professions.

In 2009 the government introduced maximum waistline limits for men and women over 40 years of age—85 cm (33.5 in) for men and 90 cm (35.4 in) for women—in an effort to encourage citizens to live healthier lives and avoid health problems such as metabolic syndrome. The measure also sought to lower healthcare costs, which were projected to double by 2020. Citizens were required to undergo annual physicals at their places of work, and those who failed to meet the waistline obligations were required to undergo counseling. Employers that did not reduce the number of overweight employees potentially would pay more into the nation's healthcare system. Critics argued that the focus on waistline measurements was an incomplete measure of health.

Japan has held one of the world's highest suicides rates, with more than 30,000 suicides annually since 1998. In 2009, there were 32,000 suicides. Officials believe that depression related to the 2008–09 global financial crisis was a major factor in the increase. At the same time, the government also noted that depression and suicides came at a cost of $32 billion in lost incomes and the cost of treatment, marking the first time that such statistics were factored. The government hoped to increase awareness of the problem and promote the treatments available for those suffering from depression.

42 HOUSING

A severe housing shortage plagued Japan after World War II. It was estimated that, in 1947, two years after the war's end, the housing deficit amounted to more than four million units. A construction program resulted in 9.7 million new units by the end of 1965. The following year, the government undertook a five-year plan for the construction of 7.6 million houses by mid 1971; the plan was designed to fulfill the goal of "one house for each family."

Housing construction peaked at 1.9 million units in 1973; despite efforts to promote construction as a means of stimulating the domestic economy, construction lagged in later years, falling to between 1.1 million and 1.5 million units in the 1980s. The decline reflected not so much a saturation of demand—many Japanese regard their housing as inadequate—as a rapid rise in land and construction costs, especially in the Tokyo, Nagoya, and Osaka metropolitan areas, which put new housing out of the reach of potential buyers. In the mid 1990s, the average salaried worker in Tokyo could only afford a house 40 km outside the Tokyo metropolitan area. By the year 2000, about 58.5% of all households were living in detached houses. According to the government's 2008 housing survey, there were 27.5 million detached homes and 20.7 million apartments, out of a total housing stock of 49.6 million.

Following the March 2011 earthquake, tsunami, and nuclear meltdown, hundreds of thousands of Japanese found themselves without homes. Over a thousand temporary evacuation sites were set up in Iwate, Miyaki and Fukushima prefectures, and over a hundred thousand people sought refuge in them. In the three months following the disaster, over 30,000 temporary houses were built to house victims, though this number did not even accommodate a third of those still homeless in the summer of 2011. Emergency shelters closed in late August 2011 in Iwate, and late October 2011 in Miyagi prefecture. Evacuation shelters in Fukushima remained open until November 2011, with several hundred (mostly elderly) residents wishing to stay in them longer because they enjoyed the convenient location of the shelters and the food provisions they were given.

43 EDUCATION

In 2008 the World Bank estimated that 100% of age-eligible children in Japan were enrolled in primary school. Secondary enrollment for age-eligible children stood at 98%. Tertiary enrollment was estimated at 58%. Of those enrolled in tertiary education, there were 100 male students for every 88 female students. Overall, the CIA estimated that Japan had a literacy rate of 99%. Public expenditure on education represented 3.5% of GDP.

Japan's entire educational system was reorganized along US lines after World War II, adhering to a six-three-three-four plan (six years of primary school, three years of lower secondary school, three years of upper secondary school—full-time, part-time or correspondence—and four years of college). Education is compulsory and provided free of charge for the first nine years, from age 6 through 14. Entrance into high schools, the stage following the compulsory level, is by examination only, and most of these schools charge tuition. Coeducation has become an accepted principle.

In 2008, about 89% of age-eligible children were enrolled in some type of preschool program. Primary school enrollment that year was estimated at about 100% of age-eligible students, while secondary school enrollment was also estimated at about 100% of age-eligible students. The student-to-teacher ratio for primary school was at about 18:1 in 2009.

Prospective national and local public university students must pass entrance examinations in Japanese, English, mathematics, science, and social studies. There are three types of institutions for higher education—universities, junior colleges, and technical colleges—all of which receive prefectural and national support or annual subsidies. There are 95 national universities, with each prefectural capital having one school; the remainder are in the principal cities. The largest religious bodies, both Christian and Buddhist, maintain important universities and other educational institutions. There are many special schools for the handicapped.

Educational activities for adults and youths are organized both by government and private bodies. There is a board of education in each of the 47 prefectures and 3,000 municipalities, and these serve as the local education authority. The central education authority is the Ministry of Education, which provides guidance and financial assistance to the local bodies.

44 LIBRARIES AND MUSEUMS

In 1948, the National Diet Library Law established the National Diet Library to provide reference service to the Diet, other libraries, and the general public. In 1949, this library absorbed the Ueno Library (the former national library) as one of its branches. The National Diet Library acts as a legal depository for Japanese publications and is also a depository library for the United Nations. There are over 7.3 million volumes in the library's collection. The University of Tokyo (Tokyo Daigaku) has 7.6 million volumes, and Keio University, also in Tokyo, has libraries with holdings of over 1 million volumes.

Except in large cities, typical Japanese museums take the form of the treasure halls of shrines or temples, botanical gardens, and aquariums. Important museums include the National Science Museum, Museum of Contemporary Art, Calligraphy Museum, and the Tokyo Metropolitan Art Museum, all located in Tokyo. Also in Tokyo are the Baseball Hall of Fame and Museum, a criminal museum, and a clock museum. In 2002, the Hyogo Prefectural Museum of Art opened in Kobe. Osaka houses a museum of natural history and the National Museum of Ethnography, and Kyoto, the former capital, has many historical sites and monuments. Yokohama is home to an equine museum and Kanazawa Bunko, a general museum dating back to 1275 and featuring Zen Buddhist documents. There is a Peace Memorial and Museum in Hiroshima.

45 MEDIA

In 2009, the CIA reported that there were 44.4 million telephone landlines in Japan. In addition to landlines, mobile phone subscriptions averaged 90 per 100 people. There were 215 FM radio stations, 89 AM radio stations, and 21 shortwave radio stations. Internet users numbered 78 per 100 citizens. Prominent newspapers in 2010, with circulation numbers listed parenthetically, included *Asahi Shimbun-Osaka* (2,367,050), *Asahi Shimbun-Tokyo* (8,322,046), and *Mainichi Shimbun* (3,976,357), as well as over 150 other major newspapers.

Japan's telecommunications system is modern and highly developed. Service, domestically and internationally, is rated as excellent. In 2009, there were some 44.2 million main phone lines and 114.9 million mobile cellular phones in use.

A semigovernmental enterprise, the Japan Broadcasting Corp. (Nihon Hoso Kyokai—NHK), plays a large role in Japan's radio and television communications. Started in 1935, Radio Japan is also beamed by NHK throughout the world. There are five other national television networks. Some commercial stations are connected with large newspaper companies. Color television broadcasting began in 1960; multiplex broadcasting, for stereophonic or multiple-language programming, was made available in Tokyo and other metropolitan areas in 1978. In 2010, the country had about 54.8 million Internet hosts. As of 2009, there were some 99.1 million Internet users in Japan.

The Japanese press is among the world's largest in terms of newspaper circulation and is also a leader in ratio of copies to population. The leading Japanese dailies are: *Yomiuri Shimbun, Asahi Shimbun, Mainichi Shimbun, Nihon Keizai Shimbun, Sankei Shimbun, Tokyo Shimbun, Hōchi Shimbun, Osaka Nichi-Nichi Shimbun, Chūnichi Shimbun* (in Nagoya), *Nishi-Nippon Shimbun* (in Fukuoka), *Hokkaidō Shimbun* (in Sapporo), *Kyoto Shimbun* (in Kyoto), *Kobe Shimbun* (in Kobe), and *Chūgoku Shimbun* (in Hiroshima).

There are two domestic news agencies: the Kyōdō News Service, with 50 domestic bureaus and with foreign bureaus in every major overseas news center; and the Jiji Press, serving commercial and government circles.

The constitution of Japan provides for free speech and a free press, and the government is said to respect these rights in practice. The Japanese press operates under the constitutional provision of absolute prohibition of censorship.

46 ORGANIZATIONS

The Japan Chamber of Commerce includes several regional and local branches. Workers and employers are represented by a number of trade organizations, including the umbrella organizations of the General Council of Trade Unions, the Congress of Labor Unions, and Federation of Employers Associations. Specialized business and industry organizations include the Japan Silk Association, the Japan Whaling Association, and the Japan Pearl Exporters' Association.

The Japan Industrial Safety and Health Association serves an important role in regulating workplace safety standards. The Japan Medical Association promotes research and education on health issues and works to establish common policies and standards in healthcare. There are several other associations dedicated to research and education for specific fields of medicine and particular diseases and conditions. There are numerous professional associations representing a wide variety of careers.

There are several prominent youth organizations, including the Scout Association of Japan, Girl Guides, YMCA/YWCA, and the Japan Youth Association. Numerous sports associations and clubs promote amateur competition in such pastimes as tae kwon do, horse racing, squash, table tennis, track and field, and cricket.

The Institute of Art Research and the National Institute of Japanese Literature are important in the cultural field. The Society for International Cultural Relations, established in 1934, is active in the publishing field and in cultural exchange. The Motion Picture Association of Japan is a prominent entertainment organization. There are many associations and clubs available for hobbyists.

There are national chapters of the Red Cross Society, CARE, Greenpeace, Habitat for Humanity, and Amnesty International.

47 TOURISM, TRAVEL, AND RECREATION

The *Tourism Factbook*, published by the UN World Tourism Organization, reported 6.79 million incoming tourists to Japan in 2009 who spent a total of $12.5 billion. Of those incoming tourists, there were 4.9 million from East Asia and the Pacific. The estimated daily cost to visit Tokyo, the capital, was $496. The cost of visiting other cities averaged $334.

Tourism in Japan is regarded as a major industry, since many foreign visitors as well as the Japanese themselves tour the country extensively. Tourism expenditure receipts totaled $15.4 billion.

Japan's chief sightseeing attractions are in the ancient former capital of Kyoto: Nijō Castle, Heian Jingu Shrine, the 13th-century Sanjūsangendō temple, and the Kinkaku-ji (Temple of the Golden Pavilion); the Ryōan-ji (Temple of the Peaceful Dragon), famed for its garden of stones and raked sand; and numerous other ancient Buddhist temples and Shintō shrines. Nearby sights in the vicinity of Nara include the Great Buddha, a huge bronze statue originally cast in the eighth century; the Kōfuku-ji pagoda; and Hōryū-ji, the seventh century temple from which Buddhism spread throughout Japan. There are few historic sites in the capital—Tokyo was devastated by an earthquake in 1923 and virtually destroyed in World War II—but nearby attractions include Mt. Fuji and the hot springs of Fuji-Hakone-Izu National Park; Nikko National Park, site of the Toshogu Shrine, where the first Tokugawa shogun is entombed; and the summer and winter sports facilities in the mountains of central Japan—the so-called Japan Alps. The Hiroshima Peace Park and Peace Memorial Museum commemorate the destruction of the city by an atomic bomb in 1945.

Baseball is Japan's national pastime; there are two professional leagues, each with six teams. Sumō, a Japanese form of wrestling, is also popular, with tournaments held six times a year. Golf, an expensive sport because of the lack of open space, is used mainly as a means of entertaining business clients. Other pastimes include judō, karate, table tennis, fishing, and volleyball. Gardening is the most popular hobby among men and women alike. Japan has hosted the Olympic Games three times—the Summer Games in Tokyo in 1964, and the Winter Games in Sapporo in 1972 and Nagano in 1998.

In November 2010, Yuki-tsumugi, a technique for silk fabric production found in Yuki City and Oyama City, was officially inscribed on the UNESCO Representative List of the Intangible Heritage of Humanity, an offshoot of the World Heritage program. The craft was deemed a living tradition by UNESCO, meaning that it is still passed from generation to generation and continues to create a sense of identity and community for those who participate. Such traditions have been approved by UNESCO for special consideration since 2001. For one that is inscribed, a special program is designed to protect and promote the practice and understanding of the tradition. Yuki-tsumugi, which is entirely done by hand, is used to create the pongee silk traditionally made into kimonos. Another addition to the list was Kumiodori, a type of music theater tradition found on the Okinawa islands.

The costs of traveling in Japan, among the highest in the world, were reduced slightly when a 3% tourism tax, in effect since 1960, was abolished on 1 April 2000.

48 FAMOUS PERSONS

Murasaki Shikibu (late 10th–early 11th century) was the author of *The Tale of Genji,* probably the best-known Japanese literary classic in English since it was first translated in the 1920s. Zeami (Motokiyo, 1363–1443) was an actor who established Noh theater and wrote a number of plays that have been part of the Noh repertoire ever since. Monzaemon Chikamatsu (1653–1724) wrote plays for the Bunraku theater, many of which later became part of the repertoire of Kabuki. Bashō (Matsuo Munefusa, 1644–94) perfected the writing of the poetic form now known as haiku. In this genre, three other poets are also well-known: Buson Yosa (1716–83), Issa Kobayashi (1763–1827), and the modern reformer Shiki Masaoka (1867–1902). Ryūnosuke Akutagawa (1892–1927) is best known for his story "Rashomon." Prominent modern novelists include Jun'ichiro Tanizaki (1886–1965); Yasunari Kawabata (1899–1972), winner of the 1968 Nobel Prize for literature; Kōbō Abe (1924–93); Yukio Mishima (1925–70); Shūsaku Endō (1923–96); Haruki Murakami (b. 1949); and Kenzaburo Ōe (b. 1935) who won the 1994 Nobel Prize in literature. A leading modern writer and Zen Buddhist scholar was Daisetsu Teitarō Suzuki (1870–1966).

In art, Sesshū (1420–1506) was the most famous landscape artist of his day. Ogata Kōrin (1658–1716) was a master painter of plants, animals, and people. The leader of the naturalist school was Maruyama Ōkyo (1733–95). The best-known painters and wood-block artists of the "*ukiyo-e*" style were Kitagawa Utamaro (1754–1806), Katsushika Hokusai (1760–1849), Sharaku Tōshūsai (fl. 1794–95), and Hiroshige Utagawa (1797–1858). Four 20th-century Japanese architects whose work has had a marked influence on international style are Maekawa Kunio (1905–86), Hideo Kosaka (1912–2000), Kenzō Tange (1913–2005), and Yoshinobu Ashihara (1918–2003).

Noted Japanese film directors include Kenjii Mizoguchi (1898–1956), Yasujirō Ozu (1903–63), and Akira Kurosawa (1910–92). Toshirō Mifune (1920–97) was the best-known film star abroad. Important composers include Toshirō Mayuzumi (1929–97) and Tōru Takemitsu (1930–96). Seiji Ōzawa (b. 1935) is a conductor of world renown. The leading home-run hitter in baseball history is Sadaharu Oh (b. 1940), manager of the Yomiuri Giants, who retired as a player for the same team in 1980 after hitting 868 home runs.

Hideyo Noguchi (1876–1928), noted bacteriologist, is credited with the discovery of the cause of yellow fever and is famed for his studies on viruses, snake poisons, and toxins. Hideki Yukawa (1907–81), Japan's most noted physicist, received the 1949 Nobel Prize for research on the meson. In 1965, Shinichiro Tomonaga (1906–79), a professor at Tokyo University of Education, became one of the year's three recipients of the Nobel Prize for physics for work in the field of quantum electrodynamics. Leo Esaki (b. 1925, Reona Esaki) won the Nobel Prize for physics in 1973; Kenichi Fukui (1918–1998) shared the 1981 chemistry award; and Susumu Tonegawa (b. 1939) won the 1987 medicine award. Hideki Shirakawa (b. 1936) shared the 2000 Nobel Prize in chemistry; Ryōji Noyori (b. 1938) shared the chemistry prize in 2001; and Koichi Tanaka (b. 1959) shared the 2002 chemistry prize. Masatoshi Koshiba (b. 1926) shared the Nobel Prize in physics in 2002.

Hirohito (1901–89) became emperor of Japan in 1926. His eldest son, Akihito (b. 1933), succeeded him in 1990, and is to be succeeded by his eldest son, Crown Prince Naruhito. The leading statesman after World War II was Eisaku Satō (1901–75), prime minister from 1964 to 1972 and winner of the Nobel Peace Prize in 1974.

49 DEPENDENCIES

Japan has no territories or colonies.

50 BIBLIOGRAPHY

Alexander, Yonah, ed. *Combating Terrorism: Strategies of Ten Countries.* Ann Arbor: University of Michigan Press, 2002.

Altbach, Philip G. and Toru Umakoshi, eds. *Asian Universities: Historical Perspectives and Contemporary Challenges.* Baltimore, MD: Johns Hopkins University Press, 2004.

Aspalter, Christian. *Conservative Welfare State Systems in East Asia.* Westport, CT: Praeger, 2001.

Auslin, Michael R. *Negotiating with Imperialism: The Unequal Treaties and the Culture of Japanese Diplomacy.* Cambridge, MA: Harvard University Press, 2004.

Bellah, Robert Neelly. *Imagining Japan: The Japanese Tradition and Its Modern Interpretation.* Los Angeles: University of California Press, 2003.

Henshall, Kenneth G. *A History of Japan: From Stone Age to Superpower.* New York: St. Martin's Press, 2001.

Hoare, Jim and Susan Pares. *A Political and Economic Dictionary of East Asia.* Philadelphia: Routledge/Taylor and Francis, 2005.

Kage, Rieko. *Civic Engagement in Postwar Japan.* New York: Cambridge University Press, 2011.

Kingston, Jeff. *Contemporary Japan: History, Politics, and Social Change since the 1980s.* Malden, MA: Wiley-Blackwell, 2011.

Paprzycki, Ralph. *Foreign Direct Investment in Japan.* New York: Cambridge University Press, 2008.

Record, Jeffrey. *A War It Was Always Going to Lose: Why Japan Attacked America in 1941.* Washington, DC: Potomac Books, 2011.

Schirokauer, Conrad, ed. *A Brief History of Chinese and Japanese Civilizations.* 3rd ed. Australia: Thomson/Wadsworth, 2006.

Henshall, Kenneth G. *A History of Japan: From Stone Age to Superpower.* New York: St. Martin's Press, 2001.

Hoare, Jim and Susan Pares. *A Political and Economic Dictionary of East Asia.* Philadelphia: Routledge/Taylor and Francis, 2005.

International Smoking Statistics: A Collection of Historical Data from 30 Economically Developed Countries. New York: Oxford University Press, 2002.

Richardson, Bradley M. *Japanese Democracy: Power, Coordination, and Performance.* New Haven, Conn.: Yale University Press, 1997.

Schirokauer, Conrad (ed.). *A Brief History of Chinese and Japanese Civilizations.* 3rd ed. Australia: Thomson/Wadsworth, 2006.

Summers, Randal W., and Allan M. Hoffman (eds.). *Domestic Violence: A Global View.* Westport, Conn.: Greenwood Press, 2002.

Waswo, Ann. *Modern Japanese Society, 1868-1994.* Oxford: Oxford University Press, 1996.

Woronoff, Jon. *The "No Nonsense" Guide to Doing Business in Japan.* New York: Palgrave, 2001.

JORDAN

The Hashemite Kingdom of Jordan
Al-Mamlaka al-Urdunniyya al-Hashimiyya

CAPITAL: 'Ammān

FLAG: The national flag is a tricolor of black, white, and green horizontal stripes with a seven-pointed white star on a red triangle at the hoist.

ANTHEM: *As-Salam al-Maliki al-Urdoni (Long Live the King of Jordan).*

MONETARY UNIT: The Jordanian dinar (JOD) is a paper currency of 1,000 fils. There are coins of 5, 10, 25, 50, 100, and 250 fils, and ¼, ½, and 1 dinars, and notes of ½, 1, 5, 10, and 20 dinars. JOD1 = US$1.410944 (or US$1 = JOD0.709) as of 2011.

WEIGHTS AND MEASURES: The metric system is the legal standard, but some local and Syrian units are still widely used, especially in the villages.

HOLIDAYS: New Year's Day, 1 January; Labor Day, 1 May; Independence Day, 25 May; Accession of King Abdullah, 9 June. Muslim religious holidays include the 1st of Muharram (Islamic New Year), Eid al-Fitr, Eid al-Adha, Milad an-Nabi, and Eid al-Isra waal Mi'raj. Christmas and Easter are observed by sizable Christian minorities, and are public holidays as well.

TIME: 2 p.m. = noon GMT.

¹LOCATION, SIZE, AND EXTENT

Situated in southwest Asia, Jordan has an area of 89,342 sq km (55,514 sq mi). Jordan extends 562 km (349 mi) NE-SW and 349 km (217 mi) SE-NW. Comparatively, the area occupied by Jordan is slightly smaller than the state of Indiana. It is bounded on the N by Syria, on the NE by Iraq, on the E and S by Saudi Arabia, on the SW by the Gulf of Aqaba, and on the W by Israel. The nation has a total land boundary length of 1,635 km (1,016 mi) and a coastline of 26 km (16 mi).

Jordan's capital city, 'Ammān, is located in the northwestern part of the country.

²TOPOGRAPHY

The Jordan Valley has a maximum depression of 408 m (1,338 ft) below sea level at the Dead Sea; south of the Dead Sea the depression, called Wadi 'Araba, slowly rises to reach sea level about halfway to the Gulf of Aqaba. To the east of the Jordan River, the Transjordanian plateaus have an average altitude of 910 m (3,000 ft), with hills rising to more than 1,650 m (5,400 ft) in the south. Further eastward, the highlands slope down gently toward the desert, which constitutes 88% of the East Bank, and is constituted primarily by broad expanses of sand, dunes, and salt flats. The Jordan River enters the country from Israel to the north and flows into the Dead Sea; its main tributary is the Yarmuk, which near its juncture forms the border between Jordan and Syria. The Dead Sea is the lowest point on the earth's surface, at 408 m (1,339 ft) below the level of the Mediterranean. The Dead Sea has a mineral content of about 30%.

³CLIMATE

The Jordan Valley has little rainfall, intense summer heat, and mild, pleasant winters. The hill country of the East Bank—ancient Moab, Edom, and Gilead—has a modified Mediterranean climate, with less rainfall and hot, dry summers. The desert regions are subject to great extremes of temperature and receive rainfall of less than 12 cm (4.75 in) annually, while the rest of the country has an average rainfall of up to 58 cm (23 in) a year. Temperatures in 'Ammān range from about 4°C (39°F) in winter to more than 32°C (90°F) in summer.

⁴FLORA AND FAUNA

Plants and animals are those common to the eastern Mediterranean and the Syrian Desert. The World Resources Institute estimates that there are 2,100 plant species in Jordan. In addition, Jordan is home to 93 species of mammals, 397 species of birds, 80 reptile species, and 1 species of amphibian. The vegetation ranges from semitropical flora in the Jordan Valley and other regions, to shrubs and drought-resistant bushes in the desert. About 1% of the land is forested. The wild fauna includes the jackal, hyena, fox, wildcat, gazelle, ibex, antelope, and rabbit; the vulture, sand grouse, skylark, partridge, quail, woodcock, and goldfinch; and the viper, diced water snake, and Syrian black snake.

Jordan's wildlife was reduced drastically by livestock overgrazing and uncontrolled hunting between 1930 and 1960; larger wild animals, such as the Arabian oryx, onager, and Asiatic lion, have completely disappeared. Under a law of 1973, the government prohibited unlicensed hunting of birds or wild animals and unlicensed sport fishing, as well as the cutting of trees, shrubs, and plants.

According to a 2007 report issued by the International Union for Conservation of Nature and Natural Resources (IUCN), threatened species included 12 types of mammals, 8 species of birds, 5 types of reptiles, 14 species of fish, and 4 species of invertebrates. Endangered species in Jordan include the South Arabian leopard, the sand cat, the cheetah, and the goitered gazelle.

5 ENVIRONMENT

Jordan's principal environmental problems are insufficient fresh water resources, soil erosion caused by overgrazing of goats and sheep, deforestation, and desertification. Water pollution is an important issue in Jordan. It is expected that the rate of population growth will place more demands on an already inadequate water supply. Current sources of pollution are sewage, herbicides, and pesticides.

Total renewable water resources totaled 0.9 cu km (0.216 cu mi) while water usage was 1.01 cu km (0.242 cu mi) per year. Domestic water usage accounted for 21% of total usage, industrial for 4%, and agricultural for 75%. Per capita water usage totaled 177 cu m (6,251 cu ft) per year. The UN reported in 2008 that carbon dioxide emissions in Jordan totaled 21,434 kilotons.

The World Resources Institute reported that Jordan had designated 934,500 hectares (2.31 million acres) of land for protection as of 2006. Mujib, Jordan, which is part of the Dead Sea basin and the Jordan Rift Valley landscape, was listed as part of the United Nations Educational, Scientific, and Cultural Organization (UNESCO) Biosphere Reserve Program in July 2011. The spectacular landscape of the area includes the lowest terrestrial point on earth (420 m/1,339 ft below sea level). The area is home to more than 90 rare plant species at the national level, 1 fish species endemic to the Dead Sea Basin, and 24 species of mammals of national, regional, and global conservation importance.

6 POPULATION

The US Central Intelligence Agency (CIA) estimated the population of Jordan in 2011 to be approximately 6,508,271, which placed it at number 103 in population among the 196 nations of the world. In 2011 approximately 4.8% of the population was over 65 years of age, with another 35.3% under 15 years of age. The median age in Jordan was 22.1 years. There were 1.04 males for every female in the country. The population's annual rate of change was 0.984%. Population density in Jordan in 2008 was calculated at 69 people per sq km (179 people per sq mi).

The UN estimated that 79% of the population lived in urban areas in 2010, and that urban populations had an annual rate of change of 1.6%. The largest urban area was 'Ammān, with a population of 2.5 million.

7 MIGRATION

Estimates of Jordan's net migration rate, carried out by the CIA in 2011, amounted to -14.26 migrants per 1,000 citizens. The total number of emigrants living abroad was 733,600, and the total number of immigrants living in Jordan was 2.97 million. In 2010 there were almost 2.5 million people classified as refugees in Jordan, the vast majority of which were Palestinian. Jordan also accepted 500,000 refugees from Iraq, as well as 160,000 internally displaced people. There were 350,000 Jordanians in Kuwait before the 1990 Iraqi attack on Kuwait. Jordan sided with Iraq in the first Gulf War (1990–91), and as a result, most Jordanians were expelled from Kuwait.

The government granted nationality to approximately 700,000 people displaced from the West Bank after the 1967 war with Israel. There were three groups of Palestinians residing in the country, many of whom faced some discrimination. Those who migrated to the country and the Jordan-controlled West Bank after the 1948 Arab-Israeli war received full citizenship, as did those who migrated to the country after the 1967 war and held no residency entitlement in the West Bank. Those still residing in the West Bank after 1967 were no longer eligible to claim full citizenship but were allowed to obtain temporary travel documents without national identification numbers, provided they did not also carry a Palestinian Authority travel document. These individuals had access to some government services, but paid noncitizen rates at hospitals, educational institutions, and training centers. Refugees who fled Gaza after 1967 were not entitled to citizenship and were issued temporary travel documents without national numbers. These persons had no access to government services and were almost completely dependent on UNRWA services.

In February 2010 the US-based advocacy group Human Rights Watch (HRW) criticized the government of Jordan for revoking the citizenship of nearly 3,000 Jordanians of Palestinian origin between 2004 and 2007. The government maintained this policy was in line with efforts to implement disengagement from former claims to the West Bank.

8 ETHNIC GROUPS

Ethnically, the Jordanians represent a mixed stock. Most of the population is Arab (approximately 98%), but except for the Bedouin nomads and seminomads of the desert and steppe areas, this element is overlain by the numerous peoples that have been present in Jordan for millennia, including Greek, Egyptian, Persian, European, and African strains. The Palestinian Arabs now resident in Jordan tend to be sedentary and urban. Perhaps 1% of the population is Armenian and another 1% is Circassian. There are also small Kurd, Druze, and Chechen minorities.

9 LANGUAGES

Arabic is the official language of the country and is spoken even by ethnic minorities who maintain their own languages in their everyday lives. The spoken Arabic of the country is essentially a vernacular of literary Arabic; it is common to neighboring countries, but is quite different from the spoken language in Egypt. There also are differences between the languages of the towns and of the countryside. English is widely understood by the upper and middle classes.

10 RELIGIONS

Islam is the state religion. Most Jordanians (about 92%) are Sunni Muslims. Of the ethnic minorities, the Turkomans and Circassians are Sunni Muslims, but the Druze are a heterodox Muslim sect. Together the Shi'a Muslims, Baha'is, and Druze account for about 2% of the population. Christians make up approximately 6% of the population and live mainly in 'Ammān or the Jordan Valley; most are Greek Orthodox or Roman Catholic.

Other officially recognized denominations include Melkite (Greek) Catholics, Armenian Orthodox, Maronite Catholics,

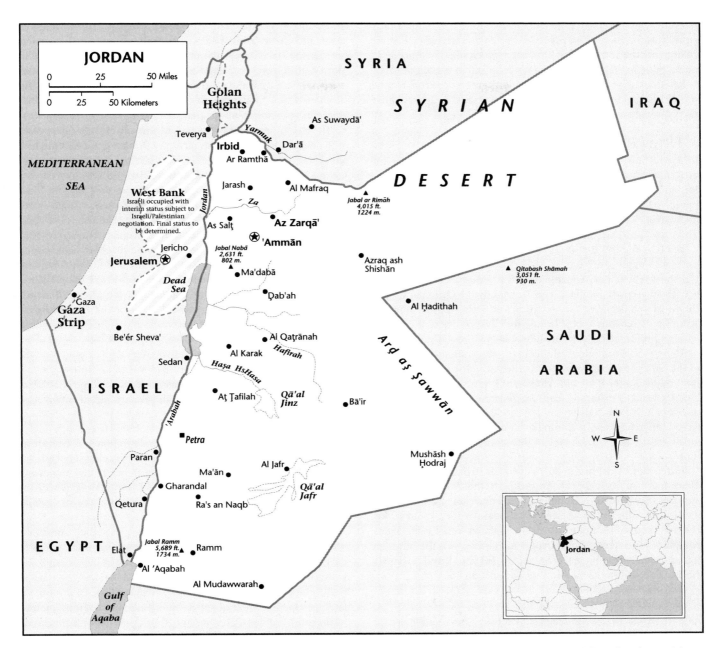

JORDAN

| 0 | 25 | 50 Miles |
| 0 | 25 | 50 Kilometers |

LOCATION: (1949): 29°17′ to 33°20′N; 34°53′ to 39°12′E. BOUNDARY LENGTHS: Syria, 375 kilometers (233 miles); Iraq, 181 kilometers (112 miles); Saudi Arabia, 728 kilometers (452 miles); Gulf of Aqaba, 26 kilometers (16 miles); Israel, 238 kilometers (148 miles); West Bank, 97 kilometers (60 miles). TERRITORIAL SEA LIMIT: 3 miles.

Assyrians, Coptics, Anglicans, Lutherans, Seventh-day Adventists, and Presbyterians. Some groups registered as religious societies by the government include Free Evangelicals, Nazarenes, the Christian Missionary Alliance, Assemblies of God, and The Church of Jesus Christ of Latter-day Saints (Mormons). The United Pentecostals and Jehovah's Witnesses are officially unrecognized groups. The Baha'i and Druze faiths are not recognized by the government, but their practice is not prohibited.

The members of the Coptic church are primarily Egyptian immigrants. The Baha'is are mainly of Persian stock. Chaldean and Syriac Christians are also represented among the Iraqi refugee population. A tiny community of Samaritans maintains the faith of its ancestors, which is a heterodox form of the ancient Jewish religion. There are numerous missionary groups within the country.

The constitution provides for religious freedom with the stipulation that all religious practices are within the semblance of "public order and morality." The constitution also places Islam as the state religions and stipulates that the king must be Muslim, of Muslim parents. Proselytizing is not expressly forbidden, but conversion from Islam to another faith is prohibited under Islamic law and converts face a great deal of legal and social discrimination and loss of civil rights. Shari'ah (Islamic law) applies to all Muslims in cases of family law and some other matters, and all matters of personal status—including religion, marriage, divorce, child custody, and inheritance—are under the jurisdiction of the relevant religious court; in personal law, converts are still considered Muslim. There is no provision for civil marriage or divorce. Islamic instruction is included as part of the public school curriculum, but Christian students are not required to participate.

Religious groups must apply for official recognition to own property and administer rites for legal marriage. Religious affiliation is noted on national identity cards.

11 TRANSPORTATION

Jordan's transportation facilities are underdeveloped, but improvements have been made in recent years. The CIA reports that Jordan has a total of 7,891 km (4,903 mi) of roads, of which 7,891 km (4,903 mi) are paved. The principal routes connect 'Ammān to al-'Aqabah, Irbid to al-'Aqabah, and 'Ammān to Jerash and Irbid. There are 146 vehicles per 1,000 people in the country.

The CIA reports that in 2010 Jordan had 507 km (315 mi) of railway, though rail travel is not a common form of passenger transport. The rail system contains a section of the old Hijaz railway (Damascus to Medina), constructed by the Ottoman Empire for Muslim pilgrims. It runs from the Syrian border through 'Ammān. A separate section runs from Ma'ān, where it connects with a spur line to the port of al-'Aqabah.

Al-'Aqabah, Jordan's only outlet to the sea, is situated at the head of the Gulf of Aqaba, an arm of the Red Sea. The port was initially developed after the 1948 Arab-Israeli war, which cut off Arab Palestine and Transjordan from Mediterranean ports; substantial development did not begin until the 1960s. The port has been enlarged for general use, including terminals for loading potash and fertilizers. In 2010 Jordan had 13 merchant ships of 1,000 GRT or more.

Jordan had 18 airports in 2010, of which 16 had paved runways. There was also one heliport. According to the World Bank, these airports transported 2.32 million passengers in 2009. The major airport is the Queen Alia International Airport, about 30 km (19 mi) south of 'Ammān, which was opened in the early 1980s. King Hussein International Airport in al-'Aqabah is the other international airport. The government-owned Alia-Royal Jordanian Airline operates domestic and international flights.

12 HISTORY

As part of the Fertile Crescent connecting Africa and Asia, the area now known as Jordan has long been a major transit zone and often an object of contention among rival powers. It has a relatively well-known prehistory and history. In the 16th century BC, the Egyptians first conquered Palestine, and in the 13th century BC, Semitic-speaking peoples established kingdoms on both banks of the Jordan. In the 10th century BC, the western part of the area of Jordan formed part of the domain of the Israelite kings David and Solomon, while subsequently what is now the West Bank became part of the kingdoms of Judah and Israel.

A succession of outside conquerors held sway in the area until, in the 4th century BC, Palestine and Syria were conquered by Alexander the Great, beginning about 1,000 years of intermittent European rule. After the death of Alexander, the whole area was disputed among the Seleucids of Syria, the Ptolemies of Egypt, and native dynasties, such as the Hasmoneans (Maccabees); in the 1st century BC, it came under the domination of Rome. In Hellenistic and Roman times, the Nabataean kingdom, a native Arab state

in alliance with Rome, developed a distinctive culture, blending Arab and Greco-Roman elements, and built its capital at Petra, a city whose structures hewn from red sandstone cliffs survive today. With the annexation of Nabataea by Trajan in the 2nd century AD, Palestine and areas east of the Jordan came under direct Roman rule. Christianity spread rapidly in Jordan and for 300 years was the dominant religion.

The Byzantine phase of Jordan's history, from the establishment of Constantinople as the capital of the Roman empire to the Arab conquest, was one of gradual decline. When the Muslim invaders appeared, little resistance was offered, and in 636 Arab rule was firmly established. Soon thereafter the area became thoroughly Arabized and Islamized, remaining so to this day, despite a century-long domination by the Crusaders (12th century). From the Arab conquest of Jordan until the Ottoman conquest in 1517, Jordan was ruled by a number of Islamic powers, including the Rashidun, Umayyad, and Abbasid empires, and the Ayubbids and Mamluks. Under the Ottoman Turks (1517–1917), the lands east of the Jordan were part of the Damascus *vilayet* (an administrative division of the empire), while the West Bank formed part of the *sanjak* (a further subdivision) of Jerusalem within the vilayet of Beirut.

During World War I, Sharif Hussein ibn-'Ali (Husayn bin 'Ali), the Hashemite (or Hashimite) ruler of Mecca and the Hijaz, aided and incited by the United Kingdom (which somewhat hazily promised him an independent Arab state), touched off an Arab revolt against the Ottomans. After the defeat of the Ottoman Empire in World War I, Palestine and Transjordan were placed under British mandate, with the semiautonomous Emirate of Transjordan established under the rule of Hussein's son Abdallah in 1922, while Palestine was administered by a British high commissioner. In 1946 Transjordan attained full independence, and on 25 May, Abdallah was proclaimed king of the Hashemite Kingdom of Transjordan.

After the Arab-Israeli War of 1948, King Abdallah annexed a butterfly shaped area of Palestine bordering the Jordan (thereafter called the West Bank), which was controlled by his army and which he contended was included in the area that had been promised to Sharif Hussein. On 24 April 1950, after general elections had been held in the East and West banks, an act of union joined Jordanian-occupied Palestine and the Kingdom of Transjordan to form the Hashemite Kingdom of Jordan. This action was condemned by some Arab states as evidence of inordinate Hashemite ambitions. Meanwhile, since the 1948 war Jordan had absorbed about 500,000 of some 1,000,000 Palestinian Arab refugees, mostly sheltered in UN-administered camps, and another 500,000 nonrefugee Palestinians. Despite what was now a Palestinian majority, power remained with the Jordanian elite loyal to the throne. On 20 July 1951 Abdallah was assassinated in Jerusalem by a Palestinian Arab, and his eldest son, Talal, was proclaimed king. Because of mental illness, however, King Talal was declared unfit to rule, and succession passed to his son Hussein I (Husayn ibn-Talal), who, after a brief period of regency until he reached 18 years of age, was formally enthroned on 2 May 1953. Jordan joined the United Nations in 1955.

Between the accession of King Hussein and the war with Israel in 1967, Jordan was beset not only with problems of economic development, internal security, and Arab-Israeli tensions, but also with difficulties stemming from its relations with the Western powers and the Arab world. Following the overthrow of Egypt's King Faruk in July 1952, the Arab countries were strongly influenced by "Arab socialism" and aspirations of Arab unity (both for its own sake and as a precondition for defeating Israel). Early in Hussein's reign, extreme nationalists stepped up their attempts to weaken the regime and its ties with the United Kingdom. Notwithstanding the opposition of most Arabs, including many Jordanians, Jordan maintained a close association with the United Kingdom in an effort to preserve the kingdom as a separate, sovereign entity. However, Israel's invasion of Egypt in October 1956, and the subsequent Anglo-French intervention at Suez, made it politically impossible to maintain cordial relations with the United Kingdom. Negotiations were begun to end the treaty with Britain in 1957, and thus the large military subsidies for which it provided; the end of the treaty also meant the end of British bases and of British troops in Jordan. The Jordanian army remained loyal, and the king's position was bolstered when the United States and Saudi Arabia indicated their intention to protect Jordan from any attempt by Syria to occupy the country. After the formation of the United Arab Republic by Egypt and Syria and the assassination of his cousin King Faisal II (Faysal) of Iraq in a July 1958 coup, Hussein turned again to the West for support, and British troops were flown to Jordan from Cyprus.

When the crisis was over, a period of relative calm ensued. Hussein, while retaining Jordan's Western ties, gradually steadied his relations with other Arab states (except Syria), established relations with the USSR, and initiated several important economic development measures. But even in years of comparative peace, relations with Israel remained the focus of Jordanian and Arab attention. Terrorist raids launched from within Jordan drew strong Israeli reprisals, and the activities of the Palestine Liberation Organization (PLO) often impinged on Jordanian sovereignty, leading Hussein in July 1966, and again in early 1967, to suspend support for the PLO, thus drawing Arab enmity upon himself. On 5 June 1967 a war broke out between Israel and the combined forces of Jordan, Syria, Egypt, and Iraq. These hostilities lasted only six days, during which Israel captured the Golan Heights in Syria, Egypt's Sinai Peninsula, and the Jordanian West Bank, including all of Jerusalem. Jordan suffered heavy casualties, and a large-scale exodus of Palestinians (over 300,000) across the Jordan River swelled Jordan's refugee population (700,000 in 1966), adding to the war's severe economic disruption.

After Hussein's acceptance of a cease-fire with Israel in August 1970, he tried to suppress various Palestinian guerrilla organizations whose operations had brought retaliation upon Jordan. The imposition of military rule in September led to a 10-day civil war between the army and the Palestinian forces (supported briefly by Syria, which was blocked by Israel), ended by the mediation of other Arab governments. Several thousand Palestinians were killed in this event. Subsequently, however, Hussein launched an offensive against Palestinian guerrillas in Jordan, driving them out in July 1971. In the following September, Premier Wasfi al-Tal was assassinated by Palestinian guerrilla commandos, and coup attempts, in which Libya was said to have been involved, were thwarted in November 1972 and February 1973.

Jordan did not open a third front against Israel in the Yom Kippur War (October 1973), but sent an armored brigade of about 2,500 men to assist Syria. After the war, relations between Jordan and Syria improved. Hussein reluctantly endorsed the resolution passed by Arab nations on 28 October 1974 in Rabat, Morocco, recognizing the Palestine Liberation Organization (PLO) as "sole legitimate representative of the Palestinian people on any liberated Palestinian territory," including, implicitly, the Israeli-held West Bank. After the Egyptian-Israeli Peace Treaty of 1979, Jordan joined other Arab states in trying to isolate Egypt diplomatically, and Hussein refused to join further Egyptian-Israeli talks on the future of the West Bank.

After the Israeli invasion of Lebanon in 1982 and the resulting expulsion of Palestinian guerrillas, Jordan began to coordinate peace initiatives with the PLO. These efforts culminated in a February 1985 accord between Jordan and the PLO, in which both parties agreed to work together toward "a peaceful and just settlement to the Palestinian question." In February 1986, however, Hussein announced that Jordan was unable to continue to coordinate politically with the PLO, which scrapped the agreement in April 1987. The following year, the king renounced Jordan's claim to the West Bank and subsequently patched up relations with the PLO, Syria, and Egypt.

Internally in the 1980s, Hussein followed policies of gradual political liberalization which were given new impetus by serious rioting over high prices in 1989. That year, for the first time since 1956, Jordan held relatively free parliamentary elections in which Islamists gained more than one-third of the 80 seats.

In 1990, owing largely to popular support for Saddam Hussein in Iraq, Jordan was critical of coalition efforts to use force to expel Iraqi forces from Kuwait. Relations with the United States and the Gulf states were impaired; Jordan lost its subsidies from the latter while having to support hundreds of thousands of refugees from the war and its aftermath. Jordan's willingness to participate in peace talks with Israel in late 1991 helped repair relations with Western countries. Martial law was ended in 1991 and new parliamentary elections were held in 1993. In June 1994, Jordan and Israel began meetings to work out practical steps on water, borders, and energy which would lead to normal relations. Later that year, Jordan and Israel signed a peace treaty, ending the state of war that had existed between the two neighbors for decades. Relations with the major players in the Gulf War also improved in the years after the war.

On 8 February 1999 King Hussein died, ending a 46-year reign. He was succeeded by his son Abdallah II, who pledged his support for the Middle East peace process, a more open government, and economic reforms. His first year in power reassured many observers, both at home and abroad. Domestically, he pushed through a series of trade bills that helped pave the way for the country's admission to the World Trade Organization (WTO), which came in April 2000, and declared his intention to implement wide-ranging administrative and educational reforms. On the international front, Abdallah played a role in the resumption of talks between Israel and Syria and also took a firm stance against the presence of Islamic extremists in his own country, driving the radical Hamas organization out of Jordan. Following the 11 September 2001 terrorist attacks on the United States, Jordan enacted a series of temporary laws imposing sharp restrictions on the right to public assembly and protest. One new law broadened the definition of "terrorism," and allowed for the freezing of suspects' bank accounts. The number of offenses carrying the death penalty was increased, and journalists who published articles which the government deemed harmful to national unity or to be incitement to protests were subject to three years' imprisonment.

In response to the January and February 2011 revolutionary protests, known as the Jasmine Revolution and the Arab Spring, that started in Tunisia and continued through Egypt, Yemen, Libya, and Syria, King Abdallah II bowed to public pressure and dismissed his own cabinet. Although he had changed his cabinet many times throughout his rule, this was the first time public protest came into play. Much of the country seemed relieved by the king's action, but the Islamic Action Front that served as the political arm of the Muslim Brotherhood saw the change as insufficient and called for further political freedom. In the change, Prime Minister Samir Rifai was replaced with Marouf al-Bakhit, a former general and former ambassador to Israel and Turkey. Unlike his predecessor, al-Bakhit did not have a history of corruption. Abdallah also instituted political reforms in the fields of representation, accountability, freedom of speech, and youth, resulting in the review of electoral law, the encouragement of the Anti-Corruption Commission, and the establishment of a national dialogue on sociopolitical issues, involving a broad swath of civil organizations, political parties, professional associations, economic entities, and women and youth forums.

13 GOVERNMENT

Jordan is a constitutional monarchy based on the constitution of 8 January 1952. The king has wide powers over all branches of government. The constitution vests legislative power in the bicameral national assembly composed of a 60-member senate and a 120-member lower house of representatives. Senators are appointed by the king for renewable four-year terms; representatives are elected through a single non-transferable vote system in a multi-member district for a four-year term, but the king may dissolve the house and order new elections. Twelve seats in the house are reserved for women. Nine seats are reserved for Christian candidates, nine for Bedouin candidates, and three for Jordanians of Chechen or Circassian descent. There is universal suffrage at age 18, women having received the right to vote in April 1973. General elections were held in 1989, 1993, 1997, 2003, and 2010.

The national assembly is convened and may be prorogued by the king, who has veto power over legislation, although his veto may be overridden by a two-thirds vote in both houses of the assembly. The executive power of the king is administered by a cabinet, or council of ministers. The king appoints the prime minister, who then selects the other ministers, subject to royal approval. The ministers need not be members of the assembly.

14 POLITICAL PARTIES

Political parties were abolished on 25 April 1957, following an alleged attempted coup by pan-Arab militants. In the elections of 1962, 1963, and 1967, candidates qualified in a screening procedure by the Interior Ministry ran for office, in effect, as independents. The Jordanian National Union, formed in September 1971 as the official political organization of Jordan and renamed the Arab National Union in March 1972, became inactive by the mid-1970s. In 1990 the election law was amended to ban bloc voting or by party lists, substituting instead a "one person, one vote" system.

Martial law was ended in 1991 and in 1992, political parties were again permitted; 22 were authorized to take part in elections. The principal opposition group has been the Islamic Action Front (IAF), the political arm of the Muslim Brotherhood. While Jordan has 30 political parties, the lack of organization and clear political platforms has hindered all but the IAF from playing a real role.

In the prolonged emergency created by the wars with Israel and by internal disorders, especially after 1968, King Hussein exercised nearly absolute power. The assembly, adjourned by the king in 1974, met briefly in 1976 to amend the constitution; legislative elections were postponed indefinitely because of the West Bank situation, and the assembly was then dissolved. In 1978 King Hussein established a national consultative council of 60 appointed members. The assembly was reconvened in 1984, as King Hussein sought to strengthen his hand in future maneuvering on the Palestinian problem. The freely elected houses of 1989 and 1993 played an increasingly active and independent role in governance, with open debate and criticism of government personalities and policies.

In the legislative elections of 8 November 1993, seats were widely dispersed among a range of largely centrist parties supportive of King Hussein's IMF-modeled reforms and his pro-Western stance. The largest bloc of seats, however, was won by the IAF. In 1997, nine pro-government parties, hoping to gain leverage against the large Islamist bloc in upcoming elections, banded together to form the National Constitutional Party. However, the grouping won only a total of three seats, and the Islamic opposition boycotted the elections altogether. Only six parties fielded candidates. Independent pro-government candidates representing local tribal interests won 62 out of the 80 contested seats; 10 seats were won by nationalist and leftist candidates; and 8 by independent Islamists.

New press restrictions were imposed in 1997, and a majority of opposition groups boycotted the elections that year. King Abdallah dissolved the assembly in June 2001 and postponed elections until June 2003. In the 2003 elections independents won 89.6% of the vote, or 92 seats; the IAF won 10.4% of the vote, or 18 seats. One of the six seats reserved for women was awarded to an IAF candidate.

In elections held in 2007, this opposition lost many seats to smaller political parties. The assembly was again dissolved in December 2009 as part of a wider effort aimed at strengthening governance and reform.

In the legislative elections of November 2010, a wide majority of the 120 seats in the lower house were filled with loyalists to King Abdallah II. Only 17 seats were won by candidates from opposition parties. Twenty seats were won by former cabinet ministers. The IAF boycotted the election in protest of a new law that reduced the number of representatives from urban areas and increased the number from tribal areas that were most supportive of King Abdallah.

15 LOCAL GOVERNMENT

Jordan is divided into 12 governorates-Ajloun, al-'Aqabah, 'Ammān, Irbid, al-Balqa, Jarash, al-Karak, Ma'ān, Ma'dabā, az-Zarqā', al-Mafraq, and at-Tafilah-each under a governor appointed by the king on the recommendation of the Interior Minister. The towns and larger villages are administered by municipal councils, which are elected by local residents. Half of the council of the

'Ammān municipality is elected, while the mayor and the other half are government appointees. Each village has a council that the governor appoints and can change as deemed necessary.

¹⁶JUDICIAL SYSTEM

Jordan's legal system is based on the Court Establishment Law of 1951, which established the judiciary as a separate and independent branch of government. Although the judiciary is independent, it is subject to political pressure and interference by the executive branch. The constitution prohibits arbitrary interference with privacy, family, and home, though this is not always respected in practice. Police must obtain a judicial warrant before conducting searches.

There are six jurisdictions in the judiciary: four levels of civil courts that adjudicate all civil and criminal cases; religious jurisdiction; and special military courts. Within the civil court system, magistrates' courts deal with minor crimes and misdemeanors and small claims civil actions. Courts of first instance have jurisdiction over civil and criminal matters that do not come under the jurisdiction of magistrates' courts; Major felonies courts have jurisdiction over serious criminal offenses that are not heard in military court. A court of appeal hear appeals from all lower courts. The Supreme Court, acting as a court of cassation, deals with appeals from lower courts. In some instances, as in actions against the government, it sits as a high court of justice.

Religious courts have jurisdiction in matters concerning personal status (marriage, divorce, wills and testaments, orphans, etc.), where the laws of the different religious sects vary. The Shari'ah courts govern the Muslim community, following the procedure laid down by the Ottoman Law of 1913, while councils within the main Christian sets handle similar cases involving their respective members. Though martial law in Jordan ended in 1991, crimes deemed relevant to national security are still tried in military courts. Their findings may be appealed before the Supreme Court.

¹⁷ARMED FORCES

The Jordanian military consists of three main branches: the army, air force, and navy. Following its peace treaty with Israel, Jordan ended mandatory conscription, though both men and women volunteer in the armed forces. The International Institute for Strategic Studies reported that armed forces in Jordan totaled 100,500 members in 2011. The force was comprised of 88,000 from the army, 500 from the navy, and 12,000 members of the air force. Armed forces represent 5.7% of the labor force in Jordan. Defense spending totaled $3 billion and accounted for 8.6% of gross domestic product (GDP).

In addition to military activities, the Jordanian armed forces are also involved in humanitarian efforts. Jordan had peacekeepers stationed in 11 regions or countries around the world. Further, they are active in research and development, particularly with wind energy, in infrastructure construction, and in afforestation programs.

¹⁸INTERNATIONAL COOPERATION

Jordan became a member of the United Nations on 14 December 1955 and belongs to the Economic and Social Commission for Western Asia (ESCWA) and several nonregional specialized agencies, such as the FAO, UNESCO, UNIDO, WHO, IFC, IMF, and the World Bank. Jordan became a member of the WTO in 2000. It is one of the founding members of the Arab League and also participates in the Arab Bank for Economic Development in Africa, the Arab Fund for Economic and Social Development, the Arab Monetary Fund, the Council of Arab Economic Unity, the Organization of the Islamic Conference (OIC), and G-77. It is a partner in the OSCE.

Jordan has greatly benefited from the work of UNICEF and of UNRWA, which helps the Palestinian refugees. Jordan and Israel signed a peace treaty in 1994 and exchanged ambassadors the following year. Jordan has sent medical and relief supplies to countries ranging from Bosnia and Herzegovina and Bangladesh to Iran and Japan. The late King Hussein was dedicated toward trying to bring about peace between Israelis and Palestinians, resulting in the Hebron Agreement of 1997. Jordan also played a role in temporarily moderating conflict in the Yemeni civil war and unsuccessfully attempted to mediate a resolution to the war in Chechnya.

In environmental cooperation, Jordan is part of the Basel Convention, the Convention on Biological Diversity, Ramsar, CITES, the London Convention, the Kyoto Protocol, the Montréal Protocol, the Nuclear Test Ban Treaty, and the UN Conventions on the Law of the Sea, Climate Change, and Desertification.

¹⁹ECONOMY

Jordan's economy has been profoundly affected by the Arab-Israeli conflict. The incorporation of the West Bank after the war of 1948 and the first exodus of Palestinians from the territory that became Israel tripled the population, causing grave economic and social problems. The loss of the West Bank in 1967 resulted not only in a second exodus of Palestinians, but also in the loss of most of Jordan's richest agricultural land and a decline in the growing tourist industry. The 1970–71 civil war and the Yom Kippur War in 1973 also brought setbacks to development plans.

The steadying influence has been foreign funds. An estimated 80% of annual national income in the early 1980s came from direct grants from and exports to oil-rich Arab countries and from remittances by Jordanians working there. Also important to the economy has been Western economic aid, notably from the United States, the United Kingdom, and Germany. The onset of the recession in Jordan in the mid-1980s, followed by the economic collapse of 1988–89 and the Gulf conflict in 1990, left the country with an unemployment rate of approximately 30–35%, high inflation, and about 25–30% of the population living below the poverty line.

On assuming the throne in 1999, King Abdallah II began implementing significant economic reforms, such as opening the trade regime, privatizing state-owned companies, and eliminating most fuel subsidies, which spurred economic growth by attracting foreign investment and creating some jobs. Tax reforms in the early 2000s included the lowering of top rates on personal and business income taxes, the elimination or reduction of a number of subsidies and exemptions, phased introduction of a value-added tax (VAT) regime, and, in connection with trade liberalization reforms, the reduction of many customs and tariffs.

The war in Iraq, beginning in 2003, significantly impacted the economy of Jordan; as in the first Gulf War, Iraq was an important trade partner and the main provider of oil. In 2008 the Jordanian government ended subsidies on petroleum and some consumer goods in an attempt to control the budget.

In the global financial crisis of 2008–09, Jordan's economy experienced some growth, but was hurt by lower-than-expected revenues and slow growth due to the global financial crisis. The global economic slowdown depressed Jordan's GDP growth, hitting export-oriented sectors, including manufacturing, mining, and re-exports, the hardest. The crisis most strongly affected the middle class, resulting in lower home ownerships and standards of living. The government approved two supplementary budgets in 2010, but planned sweeping tax cuts did not manifest because of the need for additional revenue to cover excess spending. Jordan's financial sector was relatively isolated from the international financial crisis because of its limited exposure to overseas capital markets.

The GDP rate of change in Jordan as of 2010 was 3.1%. Inflation stood at 4.4%. As of 2009 unemployment was officially 12.5%, while the unofficial rate was approximately 30%.

20 INCOME

The CIA estimated that in 2010 the GDP of Jordan was $34.53 billion. The CIA defines GDP as the value of all final goods and services produced within a nation in a given year and computed on the basis of purchasing power parity (PPP) rather than value as measured on the basis of the rate of the exchange based on current dollars. The per capita GDP was estimated at $5,400. The annual growth rate of GDP was 3.1%. The average inflation rate was 4.4%. It was estimated that agriculture accounted for 3.4% of GDP, industry 30.3%, and services 66.2%.

In 2007 the World Bank estimated that Jordan, with 0.09% of the world's population, accounted for 0.04% of the world's GDP. By comparison, the United States, with 4.85% of the world's population, accounted for 22.51% of world GDP.

According to the World Bank, remittances from citizens living abroad totaled $3.6 billion or about $553 per capita and accounted for approximately 10.4% of GDP in 2010. These were predominately from the 600,000 Palestinian-Jordanian expatriates who worked in Gulf countries.

The World Bank reported that in 2009, household consumption in Jordan totaled $20.9 billion or about $3,206 per capita. Household consumption includes expenditures of individuals, households, and non-governmental organizations on goods and services, excluding the purchases of dwellings. It was estimated that household consumption was growing at an average annual rate of 6.8%.

As of 2011 the most recent study by the World Bank reported that actual individual consumption in Jordan was 97.2% of GDP and accounted for 0.06% of world consumption. By comparison, the United States accounted for 25.44% of world individual consumption. The World Bank also estimated that 30.9% of Jordan's GDP was spent on food and beverages, 20.4% on housing and household furnishings, 5.2% on clothes, 7.5% on health, 8.6% on transportation, 3.5% on communications, 1.6% on recreation, 2.8% on restaurants and hotels, and 5.3% on miscellaneous goods and services and purchases from abroad.

It was estimated that in 2008 about 13.3% of the population subsisted on an income below the poverty line established by Jordan's government.

21 LABOR

As of 2010 Jordan had a total labor force of 1.719 million people, of which 313,000 were registered guest workers. Within that labor force, the US State Department estimated that services accounted for 34%, manufacturing 20%, public sector 19%, education 12%, health and social services 11%, and agriculture 3%. As of 2009 unemployment was officially 12.5%, while the unofficial rate was approximately 30%.

Workers in the private sector, some government-owned companies, and certain public sector professions have the right to form unions and must register to be legal. The General Federation of Jordanian Trade Unions, formed in 1954, was comprised of 17 trade unions and 200,000 members in 2002. Approximately 10% of the labor force is unionized. Unions are allowed to collectively bargain but they are not allowed to strike or demonstrate without a permit. Labor disputes are mediated by the Ministry of Labor. The government protects employees from antiunion discrimination. In August 2010 the Ministry of Labor issued a temporary law allowing foreign workers to join unions, though they could not create their own.

The national minimum wage was $213 per month in 2010 for all sectors except agriculture and domestic labor. This amount did not provide the average family with a living wage. The minimum working age is 16 and this is effectively enforced by the Ministry of Labor except for children working in family businesses or on family farms. The standard workweek is 48 hours, with up to 54 hours per week for hotel, restaurant, and cinema employees. An amendment to the labor law passed in July 2010 guaranteed 28 days of sick leave per year and the recalculation of annual leave to exclude weekends.

22 AGRICULTURE

Agriculture still plays a role in the economy, although 40% of the usable land consists of the West Bank, lost to Jordan since 1967. Rain-fed lands make up 75% of the arable land, while the remaining 25% is partially or entirely irrigated and lies mostly in the Jordan Valley and highlands. The dependence on rain for irrigation makes Jordan sensitive to climatic fluctuations; in 2009 agriculture in much of Jordan was threatened by drought.

Irrigation schemes and soil and water conservation programs have received emphasis in Jordan's economic development. The 77-km (48-mi) East Ghor Canal, substantially completed in 1966 and reconstructed in the early 1970s after heavy war damage, siphons water from the Yarmuk River and provides irrigation for about 13,000 hectares (32,000 acres). Water conservation in other areas had been undertaken with the rehabilitation of old water systems and the digging of wells. As of 2008 an estimated 82,000 hectares (292,626 acres) were irrigated.

Sixty percent of agricultural produce is grown in the Jordan Valley. While the system of small owner-operated farms, peculiar to Jordan among the Arab countries and originating in the Land Settlement Law of 1933, limits the number of large landowners and shared tenancy, the minuscule holdings have inhibited development. In 2010 agriculture accounted for roughly 3.4% of the

GDP, and employed 3% of labor force of the country, predominately in the form of cheap expatriate labor.

Roughly 5% of the total land was agricultural in 2008. The output of fruits and vegetables has been encouraging, in part because of increased use of fertilizers, herbicides, and plastic greenhouses by the nation's farmers in the Jordan Valley. The country's major crops include citrus, tomatoes, cucumbers, olives, strawberries, and stone fruits. Cereal production in 2009 amounted to 50,367 tons, fruit production 281,329 tons, and vegetable production 1.4 million tons.

The cooperative movement has made progress in the agricultural sector; the Central Cooperative Union, established in 1959, provides seasonal loans and advice to local cooperatives. The Agricultural Credit Corporation, founded in 1960, provides low-cost loans to finance agricultural investments.

23 ANIMAL HUSBANDRY

Raising livestock for both meat and dairy products is an important part of Jordanian agriculture. The UN Food and Agriculture Organization (FAO) reported that Jordan dedicated 743,000 hectares (1.84 million acres) to permanent pasture or meadow in 2009. Animal husbandry is usually on a small scale and is often of the nomadic or seminomadic type indigenous to the area, particularly in the semi-arid region of east Jordan. The large nomadic tribes take their camels into the desert every winter, returning nearer to the cultivated area in summer. The camels provide transportation, food (milk and meat), shelter, and clothing (hair); the sale of surplus camels is a source of cash. Sheep and goat nomads make similar use of their animals. Imported milk and meat are sold at subsidized prices.

Animal products account for about one-third of agricultural output. Sheep and goats account for 90% of the livestock and are raised for both meat and milk. In 2005 the number of sheep was estimated at 1,671,000 and goats at 444,000. Jordan produces about 30% of its needs in red meat and 50% of milk. During 2009 the country tended 25 million chickens and 64,520 head of cattle. The production from these animals amounted to 53,245 tons of beef and veal, 73 tons of pork, 159,310 tons of poultry, 24,424 tons of eggs, and 523,400 tons of milk. Jordan also produced 1,800 tons of cattle hide and 2,818 tons of raw wool.

24 FISHING

Fishing is unimportant as a source of food. The rivers are relatively poor in fish; there are no fish in the Dead Sea, and the short Gulf of Aqaba shoreline has only recently been developed for fishing. In 2008 the annual capture totaled 500 tons, according to the UN FAO.

25 FORESTRY

Jordan formerly supported fairly widespread forests of oak and Aleppo pine in the uplands of southern Jordan, but forestland now covers less than 1% of the total area. Scrub forests and maquis growths are the most common; the olive, characteristic of the Mediterranean basin, is widely cultivated. The important forests are around Ajlun in the north and near Ma'an.

By 1976, some 3,800 hectares (9,400 acres) had been newly planted as part of a government afforestation program. From 1976 to 1991, an additional 10,000 hectares (24,700 acres) were reforested, and as of 2011 the government had ongoing afforestation programs in place. Roughly half of Jordan's forests are naturally regenerated, while the other half are planted. Nonetheless, deforestation and the attendant soil erosion remain a concern. The UN FAO estimated the 2009 roundwood production at 4,000 cu m (141,259 cu ft). The value of all forest products, including roundwood, totaled $87.4 million.

26 MINING

In 2009 Jordan was among the world's leading producers of bromine, potash, and phosphate. Mining and quarrying contracted by 29% in 2009, affecting Jordan's GDP by -0.7% that year. Among Jordan's exports in 2009, potash accounted for $444 million, followed by: fertilizers (made from phosphate rock and potash) at $338 million, phosphate rock at $370 million, and phosphoric acid at $88 million. Jordan also produced common clay, feldspar, natural gas and petroleum (for domestic consumption), gravel, gypsum, kaolin, lime, limestone, marble, crushed rock, salt, silica sand, steel, dimension stone, sulfuric acid, and zeolite tuff. In 2009 Jordan mined no metals, although it had deposits of copper, gold, iron, sulfur, titanium, and, in the Dead Sea, bromine and manganese.

Phosphate mine output (gross weight) in 2009 was 5.282 million metric tons. Phosphate reserves totaled 1 billion tons. Production of potash crude salts-from Dead Sea potassium-was 1.2 million metric tons in 2009, down from 2.005 million metric tons in 2008. The World Bank has estimated that of the dissolved solids contained in the Dead Sea, 33 billion tons were sodium chloride and magnesium chloride and about 2 billion tons were potassium chloride.

Copper deposits between the Dead Sea and the Gulf of Aqaba remain undeveloped. Other potential for progress lay in the availability of bromine, dolomite, glass sands, iron, lead, oil shale, tin, travertine, and tripoli.

27 ENERGY AND POWER

In 2011 Jordan imported 96% of its energy needs from neighboring countries, particularly from Saudi Arabia and Egypt, accounting for almost 20% of the GDP. The major expense for imported energy has forced the government to search for alternative energy sources. As of 2011 Jordan was exploring nuclear power generation to forestall energy shortfalls, as well as indigenous and renewable energy sources, including wind and solar power and oil shale. In 2011 negotiations for the kingdom's first wind farm were in the final stages. The government aimed to generate 600MW by 2015, and had similar hopes for levels of solar energy by 2020.

Jordan's one oil refinery is in Az-Zarqa' and has a capacity of 90,400 barrels per day. Oil is supplied to it from Iraq by a fleet of 1,500 trucks traveling across 600 miles of desert highway. The oil trade was disrupted from 2003 until 2007, due to the US offensive in Iraq. Before the war, Iraq supplied all of Jordan's oil needs, delivering a portion for free, and the rest at one-third of market price. Saudi Arabia, the United Arab Emirates, and Kuwait supplied Jordan with oil at below-market value during the period Iraq was unable to. Following the resumption of trade, Iraq supplied Jordan with oil at $4 below market value. In July 2011, due to market demands, Iraq increased its shipment of oil from 10,000 to 15,000 barrels per day.

The World Bank reported in 2008 that Jordan produced 13.8 billion kWh of electricity and consumed 12.1 billion kWh, or 1,864 kWh per capita. Roughly 98% of energy came from fossil fuels, while 2% came from alternative fuels. Per capita oil consumption was 1,215 kg. Oil production totaled 20 barrels of oil a day.

28 INDUSTRY

With government encouragement, industry plays an increasingly important part in Jordan's economy. Industry in Jordan is divided into two main types: the mining sector and the manufacturing sector, which includes leather and footwear manufacturing, chemical, plastic, information technology, food, packaging, and chemical industries. Most industrial income comes from four industries: cement, oil refining, phosphates, and potash, though Jordan also produces clothing, fertilizers, pharmaceuticals, and inorganic chemicals. Pharmaceuticals accounted for $435 million in exports in 2007, while textiles accounted for $1.7 billion. Cement production has been rising since the 1980s. The industrial production growth rate was 2.5% in 2010. In 2010 industry as a whole accounted for 30.3% of GDP. This sector employed more than 173,000 workers.

In 1998 the government sold 33% of the Jordan Cement Factories Company (JCFC) to La Farge of France as part of its program of privatization begun in 1996. The 60-year old Jordan Phosphates Mine Company (JPMC) has a monopoly on phosphate mining in Jordan. In 2002 the government negotiated the sale of a 40% stake in JPMC to the Potash Company of Saskatchewan. The Arab Potash Company, a pan-Arab company, was granted a 100-year monopoly for potash mining in Jordan when it was founded in 1956.

29 SCIENCE AND TECHNOLOGY

Given the scarce supply of many necessary energy and agricultural resources, Jordan has spent considerable effort developing its science and technology sector. According to the World Bank, expenditures for research and development (R&D) totaled 2.07% of GDP in 2007. High technology exports in 2009 accounted for 20% of manufactured exports, totaling $48.77 million. There are 193 public and private scientific institutions, 82 of which have laboratory facilities totaling 379 laboratory units. The Islamic World Academy of Sciences, founded in 1986, is an international organization that promotes science, technology, and development in the Islamic and developing worlds. The Royal Scientific Society, founded in 1970, is an independent industrial research and development center. The Higher Council for Science and Technology, established in 1987, aims to increase awareness of scientific R&D and to fund and direct R&D activity toward developmental priorities. All three institutions are in 'Ammān. In 2007 there were 344 scientific and technical journal articles published in Jordan. In 2004, following a request by Abdallah II, an initiative was launched to advance the biotechnology sector. Patent applications in science and technology in of 2009 totaled 59 in Jordan, according to the World Bank.

30 DOMESTIC TRADE

Lack of proper storage facilities, inadequate transportation service, and a lack of quality controls and product grading have been chronic handicaps to Jordanian trade. However, these deficiencies have been alleviated, directly and indirectly, under progressive development plans. Traditional Arab forms of trade remain in evidence, particularly in villages, and farm products generally pass through a long chain of middlemen before reaching the consumer. In 'Ammān, however, Westernized modes of distribution have developed and there are supermarkets and department stores as well as small shops. Some local investors are beginning to take an interest in the potential for foreign franchises.

Business hours are from 8:30 a.m. to 1 p.m. and from 3:30 p.m. to 6:30 p.m., six days a week, though many offices and banks take half-days on Thursdays or Sundays. Shops close either on Friday for Muslims or on Sunday for Christians, and have more irregular hours, often from 9 a.m. until 8 or 9 p.m. Banks stay open from 8:30 a.m. to 12:30 p.m. and from 3:30 p.m. to 5:30 p.m., Sunday through Thursday.

31 FOREIGN TRADE

Jordan has traditionally run a trade deficit with imports at least doubling exports. During the 1990s fertilizers accounted for about a quarter of Jordan's commodity exports and amounted to almost a quarter of the world's total exports of crude fertilizers (23%). However, in 2000 Jordan's fertilizer exports plummeted, accounting for a mere 7.6% of exports. In 2011 the main exported items were apparel and accessories (14.7%), vegetables (14.3%), crude potash (11.3%) and crude phosphates (8.2%), pharmaceutical products (6.3%), and fertilizers (7.9), in addition to re-exported products and other commodities (37.3%).

In 2010 exports reached $7.333 billion, while imports grew to $12.97 billion. The bulk of exports went to the United States (15.6%), Iraq (15.4%), India (13.2%), Saudi Arabia (10.6%), the United Arab Emirates (4.3%), and Syria (4%). Imports included manufactured goods, machinery and transport equipment, crude oil and petroleum products, food and live animals, and mainly came from Saudi Arabia (19.8%), China (10.8%), Germany (6.1%), the United States (5.6%), Egypt (4.5%), and South Korea (4.2%).

In the period 1999–2002 the biggest single stimulus to the Jordanian economy came from the qualifying industrial zones

Principal Trading Partners – Jordan (2010)

(In millions of US dollars)

Country	Total	Exports	Imports	Balance
World	22,108.0	7,023.0	15,085.0	-8,062.0
Syrian Arab Republic	3,683.7	635.3	3,048.4	-2,413.1
Sa'udi Arabia	3,683.7	635.3	3,048.4	-2,413.1
United States	1,790.8	923.7	867.1	56.6
China	1,784.8	110.7	1,674.1	-1,563.4
India	1,163.7	776.0	387.7	388.3
Iraq	1,146.3	913.0	233.3	679.7
Germany	931.2	5.6	925.6	-920.0
Egypt	817.9	123.7	694.2	-570.5
South Korea	674.9	24.4	650.5	-626.1
United Arab Emirates	656.1	253.2	402.9	-149.7

(…) data not available or not significant.

(n.s.) not specified.

SOURCE: *2011 Direction of Trade Statistics Yearbook,* New York: United Nations, 2011.

(QIZs), a type of industrial estate authorized in a 1998 agreement among Jordan, Israel, and the United States, whereby manufactured exports from a QIZ could enter the US market duty free provided they contained at least 35% local content. QIZs particularly have nurtured a growing textile export industry. Jordan signed a free trade agreement (FTA) with the United States in 2001, an association accord with the European Union in 2004, and a FTA with Canada in 2010.

32 BALANCE OF PAYMENTS

Jordan's chronically adverse trade balance has long been offset by payments from foreign governments and agencies, especially from Jordan's oil-rich Arab allies, and by remittances from Jordanians working abroad, chiefly in Saudi Arabia and other Gulf states. The negative balance of payment is predominately due to Jordan's need to import energy. During the Gulf War (1990–91) expatriate remittances and aid from Arab countries dropped sharply, causing the improvement of the trade deficit to halt. This trend continued into the mid-1990s despite an increasing surplus in the services sector. In 2008 Jordan participated in a Paris Club debt buyback to retire more than $2 billion in debt using privatization proceeds that, at the time, reduced the percentage of external debt to GDP from 46% to 32%.

Exports reached $7.333 billion in 2010, up from $6.366 billion in 2009. Imports increased from $12.5 billion in 2009 to $12.97 billion in 2010. The resource balance was consequently negative in both years, slightly improving from -$6.134 billion in 2009, to -$5.637 billion in 2010. The current account balance was negative, though decreasing from -$1.27 billion in 2009 to -$974.5 million in 2010. Foreign exchange reserves (including gold) were to $13.4 billion on 31 December 2010. In 2010 Jordan had a foreign trade deficit of $5.4 billion, amounting to 8.5% of GDP.

Balance of Payments – Jordan (2010)

(In millions of US dollars)

Current Account		-1,311.5
Balance on goods	-6,650.4	
Imports	-13,678.7	
Exports	7,028.3	
Balance on services	890.5	
Balance on income	507.0	
Current transfers	3,941.4	
Capital Account		0.3
Financial Account		1,595.4
Direct investment abroad	-28.5	
Direct investment in Jordan	1,701.4	
Portfolio investment assets	41.0	
Portfolio investment liabilities	-20.4	
Financial derivatives	...	
Other investment assets	-1,228.7	
Other investment liabilities	1,130.6	
Net Errors and Omissions		425.7
Reserves and Related Items		-709.8

(…) data not available or not significant.

SOURCE: *Balance of Payment Statistics Yearbook 2011*, Washington, DC: International Monetary Fund, 2011.

33 BANKING AND SECURITIES

The Central Bank of Jordan, founded in 1964 with a capital of JOD2 million and reorganized in 1971, is in charge of note issue, foreign exchange control, and supervision of commercial banks, in cooperation with the Economic Security Council. In 1995 the Central Bank established the dinar as a fully convertible currency for noncapital remittances. In November of that year, the bank announced a fixed dollar-dinar rate for current payments. Because of Jordan's IMF-led structural adjustments and trade and investment liberalizations, it became the first Arab country to receive credit ratings from both Standard and Poor and Moody's.

In 2010 there were 25 banks operating in Jordan, including 13 commercial banks (5 of which are branches of foreign banks), 5 investment banks, 2 Islamic banks, and 1 industrial development bank, and other institutions. Commercial banks have a tradition of being both small, with a low capital base, and highly conservative. Jordan does not distinguish between investor banks and commercial banks. The Arab Bank, by far the largest "high street" bank, and the Housing Bank are the largest banks in Jordan. Jordanian banks have acted rapidly to fill the banking void in the occupied territories, since the agreement between the PLO and Israel transferred administrative authority to the Palestinians. State banks include the Arab Bank, The Bank of Jordan, Cairo 'Ammān Bank, Jordan-Kuwait Bank, and the Jordan National Bank. Commercial banks included those of Jordan, other Arab countries, the United Kingdom, and the United States. Foreign commercial banks in Jordan include the British Bank of the Middle East, Citibank (US), the Arab Land Bank, and the Arab Banking Corporation (Jordan). Jordan's strict regulations on lending, particularly mortgage lending, and limited integration with global financial markets, gave Jordanian banks resiliency in the global financial crisis. In 2008 the prime minister temporarily enacted a 100% government backing of bank deposits in response to the global crisis, which has since been repealed.

Loans are extended by the Jordan Industrial Bank, Agricultural Credit Corp., Jordan Co-operative Organization, and other banks and credit institutions. The Central Bank permits banks to extend loans and credit in foreign currency for export purposes only. Since 1992 moneychangers have been able to operate legally, having been closed down in February 1989, but their area of operation has been heavily circumscribed.

In December 2010 the money market rate, the rate at which financial institutions lend to one another in the short term, was 8.9%. In December 2009 the nation's discount rate, the interest rate at which the central bank lends to financial institutions in the short term, was 4.75%, down from 6.25% the previous year. At the end of 2010 the nation's gold bullion deposits totaled $13.4 billion.

Jordan's three key capital market institutions are the Jordanian Securities Commission (JSC), the 'Ammān Stock Exchange (ASE), and the Securities Depository Center (SDC). In 1999 the 'Ammān Stock Exchange was established as a privately managed institution, replacing the 'Ammān Financial Market (AFM), which had been in existence since the late 1970s. There were 149 listed public-shareholding companies at that time, with a market capitalization of approximately $6 billion. As of 2010 a total of 277 companies were listed on the ASE, which had a market capitalization of $30.9 billion that year. However, market capitalization was down nearly 46% from its 2008 record high of $57 billion, a result of the worldwide financial crisis. In 2010 the ASE General Index fell 6.3%. That year, the ASE launched an Internet Trading Service, in order to increase investors regardless of geographic location. Jordan issued its first bonds on the international market in November 2010, with $750 million in five-year bonds, carrying a fixed annual interest rate of 3.875%, payable every six months. These were purchase by 220 international investors.

34 INSURANCE

The Al-Ahlia Insurance Co. and the Jordan Insurance Co. offer commercial insurance. Several US and British insurance companies have branches or agents in Jordan. The Insurance Commission was created in 1999 to regulate and supervise the local insurance sector. In 2006 there were 286 insurance companies operating in Jordan, 1 specializing in life insurance, 7 in general insurance, and the rest in both categories. In 2006 the value of all direct premiums written totaled $365 million; life insurance accounted for 9.7% of premiums, while almost half of the premiums (46.8%) were for motor insurance. In that same year, the Arab Orient Insurance Company held 9.5% of the market for general insurance. The country's top life insurer that same year was American Life Insurance (Alico), with gross written life premiums of $17.7 million. In 2006 Jordan was last among Arab countries and 88th in the world for total insurance premiums; insurance premiums accounted for 2.4% of GDP in that year.

35 PUBLIC FINANCE

Jordan has had to rely on foreign assistance for support of its budget, which has increased rapidly since the 1967 war. During the late 1980s Jordan incurred large fiscal deficits, which led to a heavy burden of external debt. Efforts at cutting public expenditures reduced the budget deficit from 21% of GDP in 1989 to 18% in 1991. The Gulf War (1990–91), however, forced Jordan to delay the IMF deficit reduction program begun in 1989.

Public Finance – Jordan (2009)

(In millions of dinar, budgetary central government figures)

Revenue and Grants	4,521.2	100.0%
Tax revenue	2,879.9	63.7%
Social contributions	20.5	0.5%
Grants	333.4	7.4%
Other revenue	1,287.4	28.5%
Expenditures	**6,030.1**	**100.0%**
General public services	966.8	16.0%
Defense	996.7	16.5%
Public order and safety	694.3	11.5%
Economic affairs	552.5	9.2%
Environmental protection	4.8	0.1%
Housing and community amenities	291.7	4.8%
Health	697.7	11.6%
Recreational, culture, and religion	101.1	1.7%
Education	625.1	10.4%
Social protection	1,099.8	18.2%

(…) data not available or not significant.

SOURCE: *Government Finance Statistics Yearbook 2010*, Washington, DC: International Monetary Fund, 2010.

In 2010 Jordan's central government took in revenues of approximately $6.269 billion and had expenditures of $8.701 billion. Revenues minus expenditures totaled approximately -$2.5 billion. Public debt amounted to 64.1% of GDP. Total external debt was $6.391 billion in 2010. The International Monetary Fund (IMF) reported that in 2007, the most recent year for which it had data, government outlays by function were as follows: general public services, 16.15%; defense, 16.7%; public order and safety, 8.8%; economic affairs, 7.6%; environmental protection, 0.1%; housing and community amenities, 0.8%; health, 7.1%; recreation, culture, and religion, 0.87%; education, 13.9%; and social protection, 28%.

36 TAXATION

As of 2011 Jordan's corporate tax structure was divided into three tax rates, each targeted to the type of business operated. Hospitals, hotels, industrial, mining, construction, and transportation companies were subject to a 14% rate. Banks and financial institutions were subject to a 30% rate, while foreign exchange dealers, insurance, telecommunications, trade, and other companies were subject to a 24% rate. Jordan did not have capital gains tax. The value-added tax (VAT) rate in 2011 was 16%, with a higher rate for certain luxury items; basic foodstuffs, fertilizers, crops, fruits, seeds, and books and newspaper were exempt. Businesses with annual taxable turnover less than JOD30,000 ($42,254) per year were exempt from registering for the VAT. There were no capital gains or net worth taxes on individuals and social security taxes are paid jointly by employers and employees, with employers contributing 11% and employees 5.5% of salary. In 2011 personal income tax rates ranged from 7–14%, with the average taxpayer paying a marginal rate of 5%. In 2010 taxes accounted for 22.5% of GDP.

37 CUSTOMS AND DUTIES

Customs and excise duties used to provide a large portion of all tax revenues, but following accession to the World Trade Organization in 2000, they are no longer so high. All imports and exports are subject to licenses. Import duties are levied by cost, insurance, and freight (CIF) value, with a 0–30% rate, in addition to a 5% consumption tax. There is also a 16% VAT that is applied to both imported and domestically produced goods. Jordan grants preferential treatment to imports from Arab League countries, under bilateral trade agreements that exempt certain items from duty and under multilateral trade and transit agreements with Arab League countries. Jordan also signed a bilateral free trade agreement (FTA) with the United States in October 2000, which came into full force in January 2010, eliminating most duties and tariffs on commerce between Jordan and the United States.

38 FOREIGN INVESTMENT

In the past there was little foreign investment in Jordan apart from oil pipelines, but in the early 1970s the government began offering liberal tax inducements, including a six-year corporate tax holiday for firms established in ʿAmmān and a tax holiday of up to 10 years for those outside the capital. One hundred percent foreign ownership of local enterprises was permitted in some cases. In 1980 the government formed the Jordanian Industrial Estates Corp. near ʿAmmān to attract new industries to planned industrial complexes; investors were granted two-year income tax exemptions.

Jordan also established free trade zones, at Al-'Aqabah, Az-Zarqa', Karak, Karama, Sahab, and the Queen Alia International Airport. Profits in these free zones are tax-exempt for 12 years.

In 1999 with the succession of King Abdallah II to the throne, significant steps were taken towards encouraging further foreign investments in the country, including reforms in the banking, information technology, pharmaceuticals, tourism, and service sectors. Investment laws grant specific incentives to industry, agriculture, tourism, hospitals, transportation, and energy and water distribution. Foreign direct investment (FDI) in Jordan was a net inflow of $2.38 billion according to World Bank figures published in 2009. FDI represented 9.49% of GDP. According to the CIA, the stock of direct foreign investment was worth $20.67 billion in 2010, making Jordan 68th in the world.

³⁹ECONOMIC DEVELOPMENT

Before the upheavals caused by the war of 1967, the government had begun to design its first comprehensive development plans. The Jordan Development Board, established in 1952, adopted a five-year program for 1961–65 and a seven-year program for 1964–70, which was interrupted by war. In 1971 a newly created National Planning Council, with wide responsibility for national planning, prepared the 1973–75 plan for the East Bank. The main objectives were to reduce the trade deficit, increase the GNP, expand employment, and reduce dependence on foreign aid. At least 60% of the planned projects were completed, and a new five-year plan was instituted on 1 January 1976.

The 1976–80 plan achieved an annual GDP growth rate of 9.6%, below the goal of 11.9%. Notable development projects included port expansion at al-'Aqabah and construction of Queen Alia International Airport. The 1981–85 projected an economic growth rate of 10.4% annually (17% for industry and mining, 7% for agriculture). The plan envisioned completion of large potash and fertilizer installations, as well as the first stage of construction of the 150 m (492 ft) Maqarin Dam project on the Yarmuk River, which would store water for irrigation. This project also was to extend the East Ghor Canal 14 km (9 mi) from Karama to the Dead Sea. The Maqarin Dam project was shelved indefinitely, however.

The goals of the 1986–90 development plan were the following: realization of a 5.1% annual growth rate in the GDP; creation of 97,000 new employment opportunities; a decrease in imports and an increase in exports to achieve a more favorable balance of trade; expansion of investment opportunities to attract more Arab and foreign capital; development of technological expertise and qualified personnel; attainment of a balanced distribution of economic gains nationally through regional development; and expansion and upgrading of health, education, housing, and other social services.

In 1988 Jordan began working with the IMF on restructuring its economy. These plans were thrown into considerable disarray by political events in the Gulf, but new agreements were concluded in 1991, as Jordan began to institute democratic reforms. Foremost in the IMF plan were reductions in government spending, taming of inflation, increasing foreign exchange, and decreasing government ownership of economic enterprises.

In 1994 Jordan entered into another three-year structural adjustment program financed by IMF's Extended Fund Facility (EFF). The fiscal year 1994/95 saw real GDP growth of about 6%

and inflation of only about 3–3.5%. In order to build on these gains, and to incorporate the opportunities offered by the peace accord, a new three-year program was negotiated under the EFF, which ran officially from 6 February 1996 to 8 February 1999. In this case, the program fell well short of its targets, as real GDP growth slowed to an annual average of 1%, and budget deficits as a percent of GDP increased, instead of decreasing as envisioned. Further, this plan called for the removal of food subsidies, leading to riots over food prices.

Jordan instituted the National Economic and Social Development plan for 2004–2006, which aimed for sustained monetary and financial stability, partnership between public and private sectors, and targeting poverty and unemployment reduction. USAID also funded programs for economic development, giving priority to the use of American equipment. Free trade zones and trade agreements have made Jordan increasingly attractive to foreign investors.

As of 2011 the World Bank was partnered with Jordan in the Development Emergency Policy Loan program, which supported reforms in fiscal adjustment, financial sector policies, business environment, and social insurance and safety networks, helping Jordan to weather the negative fiscal effects of the global financial crisis. Further, on Jordan's request due to the financial crisis and the increase in energy and food prices, the World Bank continued to provide targeted technical assistance, supporting a new social security law and unemployment insurance program that provided coverage to all Social Security Corporation members from November 2010. In addition, the National Aid Fund's coverage for the targeted poor population increased from 20% in 2006 to 40% in 2010.

According to the US Commercial Service, in 2011 Jordan's main areas in need of economic development included alternative and renewable energy, IT, telecommunications, and electronic health and medical tourism.

⁴⁰SOCIAL DEVELOPMENT

Jordan's social insurance system provides old-age, disability, and survivor benefits, as well as workers' compensation. Public employees and workers over the age of 16 working in private companies with five or more employees are covered. Workers contribute 5.5% of their wages, employers pay 11% of payroll, and the government covers any deficit. The retirement age is 60 for men and 55 for women if coverage requirements are met. A funeral grant is also provided.

Women's rights are often dictated by Shari'ah law. Under Shari'ah law, men may obtain a divorce more easily than women, a female heir's inheritance is half that of a male, and in court, a woman's testimony has only half the value of a man's. Though women are not required by law to obtain their husband's permission to apply for a passport, some women have reported that authorities required the permission of a male custodian. Women do not have legal right to transmit citizenship to their children, affecting thousands of children whose fathers are of Palestinian origin.

In July 2009 the government established a special section within the criminal court to hear cases of "honor" crimes, involving men accused of murdering female relatives they believed to be immodest in order to "cleanse the honor" of their families. Sixteen of these honor killings were officially reported between 2007 and

2010. While this court generally hands out rulings of 10 years, the judge has discretionary ability to cut the sentence by half if the family of the victim does not press charges

Violence against women and spousal abuse are common. The rights of children are generally well respected in Jordan, and the government makes an effort to enforce child labor laws. In 2008 the Better Work Jordan program was launched by the Ministry of Labor, the International Labor Organization, and the International Finance Corporation to improve labor conditions and inspect forced labor allegations. Nonetheless, the US Department of Labor's Bureau of International Labor affairs has concluded that there are significant instances of forced labor in Jordan's garments sector.

Freedom of speech and of the press are restricted by the government. Human rights violations by the government included police brutality, arbitrary arrest and detention, and allegations of torture.

41HEALTH

According to the CIA, life expectancy in Jordan was 73 years in 2011. The country spent 9.4% of its GDP on healthcare, amounting to $336 per person. There were 25 physicians, 40 nurses and midwives, and 18 hospital beds per 10,000 inhabitants. The fertility rate was 3.4 children per woman, while the infant mortality rate was 16.42 deaths per 1,000 live births. In 2008 the maternal mortality rate, according to the World Bank, was 59 deaths per 100,000 births. It was estimated that 95% of children were vaccinated against measles. The CIA calculated HIV/AIDS prevalence in Jordan to be about less than 0.1% in 2007.

42HOUSING

According to 2004 national census, representing the latest official statistics available, there were 1,221,055 housing units nationwide, including 883,481 apartments, 301,071 *dar* (traditional, detached structures of one or more rooms), 1,188 barracks, and 4,530 tents. About two-thirds of all dwelling units were owner occupied. This census indicated a 44.7% increase in housing units from 1994. The average number of members per household was estimated at about 5.3.

In 2005 Jordan began several initiatives to provide housing for low-income groups, and in 2008 Jordan began a five-year plan to provide housing for an additional 100,000 Jordanians. However, the global financial crisis of 2008–09 impacted Jordan's middle class, resulting in lower rates of home ownership. Jordan's Housing and Urban Development Cooperation, established in 1992 and run by the Ministry of Public Works and Housing, had a 2010 budget of $165 million.

43EDUCATION

Education is compulsory between the ages of 6 and 15 and free until the age of 18. Ten years are devoted to primary education, followed by two years at the secondary stage. Vocational studies are offered as an option for secondary students. The United Nations Relief and Works Agency (UNRWA) operates schools in refugee camps. The academic year runs from September to June. The primary languages of instruction are Arabic and English.

According to World Bank estimates, primary school enrollment in 2008 was about 89% of age-eligible students, while secondary school enrollment was about 82% of age-eligible students.

According to UNICEF estimates, about 99% of all students completed their primary education in 2009. Tertiary enrolment was estimated at 41% in 2008. Of those enrolled in tertiary education, there were 100 male students for every 111 female students. Urban and rural rates of enrollment were roughly equal. The student-to-teacher ratio for primary school was at about 20:1 in 2005. Overall, the CIA estimated that Jordan has a literacy rate of 89.9%.

In 2007 Jordan had six public universities and 12 private universities, including the University of Jordan (founded in 1962), at 'Ammān; Yarmuk University at Irbid; Mut'ah University, in Karak governorate in southern Jordan; the University of Jordan for Science and Technology; the Hashemite University, the al-Bayt University, al-Balqaa University, and al-Hussein bin Talal University. In addition there were 51 community colleges. Women account for half of university students. In 2010, 11.8% of Jordanian women over the age of 15 had completed a bachelor's degree, while 10.3% were illiterate.

As of 2011 the World Bank was partnered with Jordan in the Education Reform for the Knowledge Economy program, which supported the development and implementation program of an outcomes-based curriculum, connecting schools to a high-speed learning network.

As of 2009 public expenditure on education was estimated at 4.5% of GDP, or 16% of total government expenditures.

44LIBRARIES AND MUSEUMS

The library at the University of Jordan had more than 1,008,000 volumes in 2011. In 1977, the Department of Libraries, Documentation, and Archives was founded to establish the national library, which has a number of holdings and manuscript collections. The Library of the Jordan University of Science and Technology holds 155,000 books and 45,000 back issues of periodicals. The Philadelphia University Library ('Ammān) holds about 108,811 volumes and 305 subscriptions to periodicals. Jordan's other universities all have extensive library collections.

More than half of Jordan's museums are archaeological and historical. 'Ammān has many major museums: the Jordan Archaeological Museum, the Folklore Museum, the Jordanian Museum of Popular Traditions, the National Gallery of Fine Arts, the Royal Automobile Museum, and the Children's Museum, and Mosaic Gallery. In addition, the University of Jordan houses both Archaeological and Anthropological Museums, while the Central Bank has a Numismatics Museum. The Department of Antiquities Museum opened in 2006 and is located in as-Salt. The Museum of Jordanian Heritage, one of the finest archeological museums in the country, is in Irbid, as is the Natural History Museum.

45MEDIA

Jordanian telecommunication services have improved through the use of digital switching equipment. Domestic service is provided through the use of microwave relay systems, and fiber-optic and coaxial cable systems. International service is provided through a mix of satellite ground stations, fiber-optic and submarine cables, and microwave relay systems. In 2009, there were some 501,200 main phone lines; mobile phone subscriptions averaged 101 per 100 people. The use of cellular phones in both rural and urban areas is reducing fixed-line services.

Radio and television broadcasts are dominated by the government-owned Jordan Radio and Television Corporation. Radio Jordan transmits AM and FM broadcasts in English, and the television stations broadcast programs in English, Arabic, French, and Hebrew on two channels. The first independent TV broadcaster aired in 2007; international satellite TV and Israeli and Syrian broadcasts are available, as are the transmission of multiple international radio broadcasters. As of 2009 there were 6 AM and 31 FM radio stations. In 2010 the country had 42,412 Internet hosts. As of 2009 there were some 1.642 million Internet users in Jordan. While an estimated 40% of homes had computers, only 18% were connected to the Internet. Jordan has a goal to achieve 50% Internet access by 2012.

Jordan's major daily newspapers (with 2010 estimated daily circulations) are *Al-Dustour* (*Constitution*, 100,000), *Al-Rai* (*Opinion*, 90,000), *Sawt Ash-Shaab* (*Voice of the People*, 30,000), and *Jordan Times* (15,000). All except the English-language *Jordan Times* are in Arabic; all are published in 'Ammān. *Al-Rai* is a government-controlled paper, founded after the 1970–71 civil war; *Al-Dustour* is 25% government owned. There are also weeklies and less frequent publications published in Arabic in 'Ammān. One weekly, *The Star*, is published in English. The press code, enacted in 1955, requires all newspapers to be licensed and prohibits the publishing of certain information, mainly relating to Jordan's national security, unless taken directly from material released by the government.

The constitution provides for freedom of speech and the press; however, in practice there are some significant restrictions on these rights. A 2009 Freedom House report on media freedom called Jordan "not free." Private citizens can be fined, prosecuted, and imprisoned for slandering the royal family, and the Press and Publication Law of 1993 restricts the media coverage of 10 subjects, including the military, the royal family, economic policy, and religious beliefs.

46 ORGANIZATIONS

Religious organizations still are of major importance, and membership in the *hamula*, the kinship group or lineage comprising several related families, also is of great significance as a framework for social organization. Literary and theatrical clubs have become popular, especially since World War II, but political organizations died out after the 1957 ban on political parties. Jordan serves as the home base for a number of multinational cultural and educational organizations, including the Islamic Academy of Sciences and the Arab Music Academy.

There are chambers of commerce in 'Ammān and other large towns. The Jordan Trade Association supports business owners with domestic and international holdings. Other labor and business organizations include the Jordan Exporters and Producers Association of Fruits and Vegetables and the Association of Banks in Jordan. There are several professional associations, particular those dedicated to research and education in medical and scientific fields. Jordan has a number of non-profit organizations, which cover issues ranging from rehabilitation of the physically challenged and breast cancer programs, to women and interfaith coexistence. The Noor Al-Hussein Foundation, founded in 1985, is a major national social welfare organization. The Red Crescent Society, Habitat for Humanity, and Caritas have national chapters.

National youth organizations include the Jordanian Association for Boy Scouts and Girl Guides (serving 15,521 scouts in 2011), YMCA/YWCA, Junior Chamber, National Union of Jordanian Students, and the Orthodox Youth Education Society. There are a variety of sports associations and clubs, representing such pastimes as tennis, track and field, and badminton. The Alliance for Arab Women and the Jordanian National Committee for Women are based in 'Ammān.

47 TOURISM, TRAVEL, AND RECREATION

Jordan's notable tourist attractions include the Greco-Roman remains at Jerash (ancient Garasi), which was one of the major cities of the Decapolis (the capital, 'Ammān, was another, under the name of Philadelphia) and is one of the best-preserved cities of its time in the Middle East. Petra (Batra), the ancient capital of Nabataea in southern Jordan, carved out of the red rock by the Nabataeans, is probably the most famous historical site. Natural attractions include the Jordan Valley and the Dead Sea, which at 392 m (1290 ft) below sea level is the lowest spot on Earth. Biblical sites include Bethany Beyond the Jordan, where Jesus was baptized by John the Baptist; and Mount Nebo, where Moses saw the Promised Land.

The beaches on the Gulf of Aqaba offer holiday relaxation for Jordanians, as well as tourists. Scuba divers can enjoy the Gulf of Aqaba's coral reefs. Sports facilities include swimming pools, tennis and squash courts, and bowling alleys. Eastern Jordan has modern hotel facilities in 'Ammān and al-'Aqabah, and there are government-built rest houses at some of the remote points of interest. A valid passport and visa are required for entry into Jordan. Visitors may obtain a visa, for a fee depending on nationality, at most international points of entry. Visitors must also pay a departure tax when leaving Jordan, which varies based on location of departure.

Medical tourism experts at the World Bank have ranked Jordan as a leader in the Arab world, and fifth in the world overall as a medical tourism hub. This sector annually generates over $1 billion in revenues, and the number of foreign patients in 2008 stood at over 200,100.

According to the *Tourism Factbook*, published by the UN World Tourism Organization, about 3.79 million tourists arrived in Jordan in 2009. Of these visitors, 1.9 million came from the Middle East. There were 42,842 hotel beds with an occupancy rate of 36%. Tourism expenditure receipts totaled $3.47 billion that year. The estimated daily cost to visit 'Ammān was $310. The cost of visiting other cities averaged $251.

48 FAMOUS PERSONS

The founder of Jordan's Hashemite dynasty—the term stems from the Hashemite (or Hashimite) branch of the tribe of the Prophet Muhammad—was Hussein ibn-'Ali (Husayn bin 'Ali, 1856–1931), sharif of Mecca and king of the Hijaz.

As a separate Arab country, Jordan has had a relatively short history, during which only several members of the royal family have become internationally known. The first of these was the founder of the kingdom, Abdallah ibn-Husayn (1882–1951). Although he was born in Hijaz and was a son of the sharif of Mecca, he made 'Ammān his headquarters. He was recognized as emir in 1921 and king in 1946. The second was his grandson, King

Hussein I (Husayn ibn-Talal, 1935–99), who ruled from 1953 until his death. In June 1978, 16 months after the death by helicopter crash of Queen Alia (1948–77), Hussein married his fourth wife, Queen Noor al-Hussein (Elizabeth Halaby, b. US, 1951), who has gained renown for her work against landmines and nuclear proliferation. King Abdallah II (b. 1962) has reigned since the death of his father in 1999. His wife, Queen Rania (b. 1970), has focused much attention on education in Jordan and abroad.

⁴⁹DEPENDENCIES

Jordan has no territories or colonies.

⁵⁰BIBLIOGRAPHY

Dew, Philip and Jonathan Wallace (eds.) *Doing Business with Jordan*. Sterling, VA: Kogan Page, 2004.

Elkhafif, Mahmoud A. T., Sahar Taghdisi-Rad, et al. *Economic and Trade Policies in the Arab World: Employment, Poverty Reduction, and Integration*. New York: Routledge, 2012.

Habeeb, William Mark, Rafael D. Frankel, et al. *The Middle East in Turmoil: Conflict, Revolution, and Change*. Santa Barbara, CA: Greenwood, 2012.

Knowles, Warwick M. *Jordan Since 1989: A Study in Political Economy*. New York: I.B. Tauris, 2005.

Lust-Okar, Ellen. *Structuring Conflict in the Arab World: Incumbents, Opponents, and Institutions*. New York: Cambridge University Press, 2005.

Milton-Edwards, Beverley, and Peter Hinchcliffe. *Jordan: A Hashemite Legacy*. London: Routledge, 2001.

Moore, Pete W. *Doing Business in the Middle East: Politics and Economic Crisis in Jordan und Kuwait*. New York: Cambridge University Press, 2004.

Ryan, Curtis R. *Jordan in Transition: From Hussein to Abdullah*. Boulder, CO: Lynne Rienner Publishers, 2002.

Seddon, David (ed.). *A Political and Economic Dictionary of the Middle East*. Philadelphia: Routledge/Taylor and Francis, 2004.

KAZAKHSTAN

Republic of Kazakhstan
Kazakstan Respublikasy

CAPITAL: Astana

FLAG: The flag features a golden sun with 32 rays positioned above a golden steppe eagle, both of which are centered on a sky blue background. The hoist side shows the "koshkar-muiz" (horns of the ram) national ornamental color in gold. The blue symbolizes cultural and ethnic unity as well as the endless sky and water. The sun represents life and energy as well as wealth. The rays of the sun take the shapes of grain, which represents abundance and prosperity. The eagle, which has been on the flags of Kazakh tribes for centuries, symbolizes freedom, power and future flight.

ANTHEM: *Menin Qazaqstanim (My Kazakhstan).*

MONETARY UNIT: The tenge (KZT), issued in 15 November 1993, is the national currency, replacing the ruble. There is a coin, the tyin. One hundred tyin equal one tenge. KZT1 = US$0.00675210 (or US$1 = KZT148.01 as of 2011).

WEIGHTS AND MEASURES: The metric system is in force.

HOLIDAYS: New Year, 1–2 January; International Women's Day, 8 March; Nauryz Meyramy (Kazak New Year), 22 March; Kazakhstan Nations Unity Holiday, 1 May; Victory Day, 9 May; Day of the Capital, 10 June; Constitution Day, 30 August; Republic Day, 25 October; and Independence Day, 16 December. The following religious holidays also were observed: Kurban Bayram, Ramadan, Easter, and Christmas. The celebration of Nauryz Meyramy was renewed after Kazakhstan gained independence from the Soviet Union, which had banned the holiday for 70 years on grounds that it was too religious.

TIME: 5 p.m. = noon GMT.

¹LOCATION, SIZE, AND EXTENT

Kazakhstan is located in central Asia between Russia and Uzbekistan, bordering on the Caspian Sea. It has a total land area of 2,724,900 sq km (1,052,090 sq mi), which makes it the ninth largest country in the world. Kazakhstan is approximately the same size as western Europe and nearly four times the size of the state of Texas. It also is larger than the other four former Soviet Republics in Central Asia combined.

Kazakhstan shares boundaries with Russia on the n and w, China on the e, Kyrgyzstan, Uzbekistan, and Turkmenistan on the s, and the Caspian Sea on the w. Kazakhstan's boundary length totals 12,185 km (7,501 mi). Its capital city, Astana, is located in the north-central part of the country.

About 6,000 sq km (2,317 sq mi) of Kazakhstan's territory enclosing the Baykonur Cosmodrome is being leased by Russia under a lease that in 2004 was extended to 2050.

²TOPOGRAPHY

The topography of Kazakhstan consists of vast flat steppe extended from the Volga River in the west to the Altai Mountains in the east and from the plains of western Siberia in the north to oases and deserts of Central Asia in the south. In the east and northeast, about 12% of the country consists of the Altay and Tian Shan mountain ranges.

However, more than three-quarters of the country is desert or semi-desert, with elevations below 500 m (1,640 ft). Much of the area along the Caspian Sea is below sea level.

Severe earthquakes are periodically experienced in the seismically active region along the Tian Shan.

The lowest point in the country is Vpadina Kaundy in the southwest region known as Karagiye Depression, which dips 132 m (433 ft) below sea level. The highest point is Khan Tangiri Shyngy, a mountain peak in the Tian Shan mountain range of the southeast at 6,995 m (22,949 ft).

Seven major rivers run through Kazakhstan and are more than 1,000 km (620 mi) in length: the Chu, Emba, Ili, Irtysh, Ishim, Syr Darva and Ural.

Two of the world's largest lakes are shared by Kazakhstan: The Caspian Sea (the world's largest lake) and the Aral Sea (the fourth-largest in the world). The largest inland lake completely within the borders of the country is Lake Balkhash, with an area of 18,200 sq km (7,300 sq mi).

³CLIMATE

Despite Kazakhstan's geographic diversity, its climate is primarily continental. Winters are cold, and summers are hot. Rainfall varies between 100 mm (3.94 in) and 200 mm (7.87 in) a year, and is generally heaviest in the south and in the eastern mountains.

The average temperature in Astana is -18°C (-4°F) in the winter, and 20°C (68°F) in the summer. The average temperature in Almany is -8°C(18°F) in the winter, and 22°C (72°F) in the summer.

⁴FLORA AND FAUNA

The World Resources Institute estimates that there are 6,000 plant species in Kazakhstan. In addition, Kazakhstan is home to 145 species of mammals, 497 species of birds, 51 species of reptiles, and 15 species of amphibians. The calculation reflects the total number of distinct species residing in the country, not the number of endemic species.

The varied terrain traditionally made Kazakhstan home to an array of species. However, rapid growth and environmental degradation have threatened many animals.

According to a 2011 report issued by the International Union for Conservation of Nature and Natural Resources (IUCN), threatened species included 16 mammals, 20 birds, 1 reptile, 1 amphibian, 14 fish, 4 other invertebrates, and 13 plants. Threatened species included the cheetah, the black vulture, the swan goose, the spotted eagle, the asp, the Siberian crane, and the great snipe.

The Ustyurt Plateau has been home to the critically endangered saiga antelope, which in the first decade of the 21st century was experiencing one of the fastest declines recorded for mammals in decades. Other mammals found in Kazakhstan are elk, wild boar, roe deer, the Siberian ibex, maral, wolves, foxes, badgers, lynx, bear, sable and polecats. There also were 140 hunting game birds.

⁵ENVIRONMENT

The World Resources Institute reported that Kazakhstan had designated 7.74 million hectares (19.13 million acres) of land for protection as of 2006. Water resources totaled 109.6 cu km (26.29 cu mi) while water usage was 35 cu km (8.4 cu mi) per year. Domestic water usage accounted for 2% of total usage, industrial for 17%, and agricultural for 81%. Per capita water usage totaled 2,360 cu m (83,343 cu ft) per year.

Kazakhstan faces several important environmental issues. As the site of the former Soviet Union's nuclear testing programs, areas of the nation have been exposed to high levels of nuclear radiation, and there is significant radioactive pollution. These sites posed significant health risks for both humans and animals. The nation also has 30 uranium mines, which add to the problem of uncontrolled release of radioactivity. Kazakhstan has sought international support to convince China to stop testing atomic bombs near its territory, because of the dangerous fallout.

Air pollution in Kazakhstan is another significant environmental problem. Acid rain damages the environment within the country and also affects neighboring countries. In 1992 Kazakhstan had the world's 14th highest level of industrial carbon dioxide emissions, which totaled 297.9 million metric tons (297,900 kilotons), a per capita level of 17.48 metric tons. By 2000, the total had dropped to 121.3 million metric tons (121,300 kilotons). However, by 2008, the United Nations (UN) reported that carbon dioxide emissions had climbed again to 227,208 kilotons.

Pollution from industrial and agricultural sources has also damaged the nation's water supply. The UN has reported that, in some cases, contamination of rivers by industrial metals was 160 to 800 times beyond acceptable levels.

Two of Kazakhstan's main rivers once flowed into the Aral Sea until being diverted for irrigation. The result of that diversion has been a drying up of the Aral Sea and a residue of chemical pesticides and natural salts. After being picked up by the wind, these substances have formed toxic dust storms. Most of what was once the Aral Sea is now dry land, with a few, much smaller, lakes remaining in the lowest areas.

There is also significant pollution in the Caspian Sea, and soil pollution from the overuse of agricultural chemicals. An expansion of oil operations along the Caspian coast has exacerbated the issue. The Kazakhstan government, however, has not made environmental protection of these areas a meaningful priority.

Kazakhstan as of 2011 was party to international environmental agreements on air pollution, biodiversity, climate change, desertification, endangered species, environmental modification, hazardous wastes, ozone layer protection, ship pollution, and wetlands.

⁶POPULATION

The US Central Intelligence Agency (CIA) estimates the population of Kazakhstan in 2011 to be approximately 15,522,373, which placed it at number 64 in population among the 196 nations of the world. In 2011, approximately 7.4% of the population was over 65 years of age, with another 21.6% under 15 years of age. The median age in Kazakhstan was 30.2 years. There were 0.93 males for every female in the country. The population's annual rate of change was 0.4%. The projected population for the year 2025 was 18,400,000. Population density in Kazakhstan was calculated at 6 people per sq km (16 people per sq mi).

The CIA estimated that 59% of the population lived in urban areas in 2010, and that urban populations had an annual rate of change of 1.3%. The largest urban areas, along with their respective populations, included Almaty, 1.4 million; and Astana, 650,000.

⁷MIGRATION

Estimates of Kazakhstan's net migration rate, carried out by the CIA in 2011, amounted to -3.27 migrants per 1,000 citizens. The total number of emigrants living abroad was 3.72 million, and the total number of immigrants living in Kazakhstan was 3.08 million. Kazakhstan also accepted 3,700 refugees from Russia and 508 from Afghanistan.

The imposition of Russian rule on present-day Kazakhstan in the late 19th and early 20th centuries led to a diaspora of ethnic Kazakhs to western China and other neighboring countries. Since the country became independent in 1991, the government has encouraged ethnic Kazakhs to return to the country by offering subsidies. In 1996, there was an organized return of 70,000 Kazakhs from Mongolia, Iran, and Turkey. During 1991–95, some 82,000 Ukrainians and 16,000 Belarussians repatriated. Between 1991–96, 614,000 Russians repatriated and 70,000 Kazakhs repatriated. During 1992–96, 480,000 ethnic Germans returned to Germany.

The World Bank reported in 2007 that Kazakhstan was the world's ninth-largest migrant receiving country in the world, and the seventh-largest migrant supplying country. Although many residents of the former Soviet republics in Central Asia were migrating to Kazakhstan for work opportunities in the first decade of the 21st century, many Kazakhstan residents were seeking work in Russia, the United Arab Emirates, Turkey, and elsewhere in Europe.

The International Organization of Migration reported in 2011 that internal migration was high in Kazakhstan, with thousands of rural residents moving to urban areas in search of employment. In

LOCATION: 48° N; 60°E. BOUNDARY LENGTHS: China, 1,533 kilometers (954 miles); Kyrgyzstan, 1,051 kilometers (653 miles); Russia, 6,846 kilometers (4,254 miles); Turkmenistan, 379 kilometers (236 miles); Uzbekistan, 2,203 kilometers (1,369 miles).

addition, environmental threats near the Aral Sea as well as near the nuclear testing site of Semey in northern Kazakhstan resulted in a high level of internal displacement in the 1990s.

Government statistics documented 7,585 stateless persons residing in Kazakhstan, as of 2010. However, the UN High Commission on Refugees estimated the figure to be between 60,000 and 100,000.

⁸ETHNIC GROUPS

As of the 2009 census, Kazakhs accounted for about 63.1% of the population, 23.7% were Russians, and 2.8% were Uzbeks, and 2.1% were Ukrainians. The remaining population consisted of Uighurs (1.4%), Tartars (1.3%), Germans (1.1%), and other groups.

⁹LANGUAGES

The constitution declares Kazakh to be the state language and requires the president to be a Kazakh speaker. Kazakh is a Turkic language written in Cyrillic script with many special letters (but in Roman script in China since 1960). Modern Kazakh utilizes many words of foreign origin from Russian, Arabic, Persian, Mongol, Chinese, Tatar, and Uzbek. Only about 64% of all Kazakhs can speak the language effectively. Almost everyone can speak Russian (95%), which has special status as the "language of interethnic communication" and is widely used in the realm of official business. English also is considered one of the country's official languages and appears on some signs.

¹⁰RELIGIONS

Approximately 47% of the population described itself as Muslim as of 2010. However, due in part to Kazakhstan's nomadic past and its years under Soviet rule, many residents were non-believers.

Ethnic Kazakhs, Uzbeks, Uighurs, and Tatars historically followed the Hanafi school of Sunni Islam. Other Muslims followed the Shafi'i Sunni (a school associated historically with Chechens),

Shi'a, Sufi, and Ahmadi schools. Most practicing Muslims as of 2010 resided in the south in the area bordering Uzbekistan. The country had 2,268 registered mosques in 2010, most of which were affiliated with the Spiritual Association of Muslims of Kazakhstan, a national organization with close ties to the government.

Russian Orthodox Christianity is common among ethnic Russians, Ukrainians, and Belarusians. Some ethnic Ukrainians and Germans are affiliated with a Roman Catholic archdiocese. Other ethnic Germans are Lutheran, while some ethnic Ukrainians are Greek Catholics. Other religions practiced in Kazakhstan are Buddhism; Hinduism, as affiliated with the International Society of Krishna Consciousness movement; Baha'i, Judaism, and various Christian-based denominational faiths.

11 TRANSPORTATION

The CIA reported that as of 2008 Kazakhstan had a total of 93,612 km (58,168 mi) of roads, of which 84,100 km (52,257 mi) were paved. There were 197 vehicles per 1,000 people in the country. Railroads extended for 14,205 km (8,827 mi). There were 97 airports, 65 with paved runways as of 2010. There were also 3 heliports. They transported 1.19 million passengers in 2009 according to the World Bank. Kazakhstan has approximately 4,000 km (2,485 mi) of navigable waterways.

The primary port is Guryev (Atyrau), on the Caspian Sea. Inland waterways are found predominantly on the Syr Darya and Irtysh rivers. Much of the infrastructure connects Kazakhstan with Russia rather than points within Kazakhstan. Although landlocked in the center of Eurasia and dependent on its transport connections through neighboring countries to deliver its goods to world markets, Kazakhstan as of 2008, had five merchant ships of 1,000 GRT or more.

The US State Department reported in 2010 that roads and transport systems in Kazakhstan were in need of modernization. The Asian Development Bank had provided the country an $800 million loan for road improvements.

12 HISTORY

Kazakhstan has been inhabited as far back as the Stone Age, more than 300,000 years ago, and many nomadic tribes passed through the area over the centuries. Achaemenid documents give the name Sacae to the first such group to be historically recorded. In the 3rd and 2nd centuries BC they were displaced by the Usun in the east, the Kangiui in the south central region, and the Alani in the west.

The area was ruled by a series of nomadic nations from the fourth century AD through the early 13th century. The first well-established state was that of the Turkic Kaganate, in the 6th century AD, replaced in the early 8th century by the Turgesh state. In 766, the Karluks established dominance in what now is eastern Kazakhstan. Some of the southern portions of the region fell under Arab influence in the 8th–9th centuries, and Islam was introduced. Western Kazakhstan was under Oghuz control in 9th to the 11th centuries; at roughly the same time the Kimak and Kipchak tribes, of Turkic origin, controlled the east. The large central desert of Kazakhstan is still called "Dashti-Kipchak," or the Kipchak Steppe.

The Karluk state was destroyed by invading Iagmas in the late 9th and early 10th centuries. They formed the Karakhanid state, which controlled extensive lands into what is now China. The Karakhanids were in a constant state of war with the Seljuks, to the south, and control of parts of what is now Kazakhstan passed back and forth between them. The Karakhanids collapsed in the 1130s when they were invaded by Khitans, who established the Karakitai state. In the mid-12th century, Khwarazm split off from the weakening Karakitais, but the bulk of the state survived until the invasion of Genghis Khan from 1219–1221.

The Mongol Empire established administrative districts in the area in the early 13th century and these districts eventually became territories in the Kazakh Khanate. During this period, the cities of Taraz and Turkestan were founded along the northern route of the Silk Road.

Kazakhstan was part of Batu's Golden Horde, which in the 14th century broke up into the White Horde and Mogulistan. By the early 15th century, the White Horde had split into several large khanates, including the Nogai Horde and the Uzbek Khanate.

Nomadic groups on the steppe and semi-desert lands that characterize Kazakhstan were constantly in search of new pasture to support their livestock-based economies. The ethnic Kazakhs emerged from a mixture of tribes living in the area around the 15th century, when clan leaders Janibek and Girei broke away from Abul Khair, who was the leader of the Uzbeks. They sought their own territory in Semirechie between the Chu and Talas rivers. Khan Kasym (1511–23) united the Kazakhs as a people and by the mid-16th century the group had developed a common language and culture.

The Nogai Horde and Siberian Khanates broke up in the mid-16th century, and tribes from both joined the Kazakhs. The clans separated into three Hordes: the Great Horde, which controlled Semirechie; the Middle Horde, which had central Kazakhstan, and the Lesser Horde, which had western Kazakhstan. The separation resulted in political disunity and competition among the hordes. These factors, along with the lack of an internal market, weakened the Kazakh Khanate.

Russian traders and soldiers began to appear on the northwestern edge of Kazakh territory in the 17th century, when Cossacks founded the forts which became the cities of Uralsk and Gurev. The Kazakh Khanate was badly pressed by Kalmyk invaders who had begun to move in from the east. Pushed west in what the Kazakhs call their "Great Retreat," the Kazakh position deteriorated until, in 1726, Khan Abul'khair of the Lesser Horde requested Russian assistance. From that point on the Lesser Horde was under Russian control. The Middle Horde was conquered by 1798. The Great Horde remained independent until the 1820s, when pressure from both the Kokand Khanate and Russia forced them to choose what they regarded as the lesser of evils, the Russians.

Khan Kenen (Kenisary Kasimov), of the Middle Horde and now regarded as a Kazakh national hero, led resistance against the Russians in 1836–47. Russian attempts to quell this resistance led to establishment of a number of forts and settlements in Kazakh territory, which made Kazakh nomadism impossible and destroyed the Kazakh economy. The Russian Empire seized territories that had belonged to the Great Horde in the 1860s and effectively ruled most of what is present-day Kazakhstan. Most of Kazakhstan was made part of the Steppe district of the Russian empire; the rest was in Turkestan.

Most Kazakhs resented Russian rule because it disrupted their traditional nomadic lifestyle and livestock-based economy, and forced many of the people to flee to western China and other neighboring countries. One product of that resentment was the emergence of a Kazakh national movement in the late 1800s that sought to preserve the Kazakh language and identity. Kazakhs periodically launched uprisings against the tsarist regime, and following the collapse of the Russian Empire in 1918 enjoyed a brief period of autonomy. At the time of the revolution a group of secular nationalists called the Alash Orda attempted to create a Kazakh government, but it lasted less than two years (1918–20) before surrendering to Russia's new communist government.

Kazakhstan became an autonomous republic within Russia in 1920 and a Soviet republic in 1936. In the period 1929–34, when Soviet dictator Josef Stalin was abolishing private agriculture and establishing huge collective farms, Kazakhstan suffered repeated famines which killed at least 1.5 million Kazakhs and destroyed 80% of the republic's livestock. As Soviet rule took hold, thousands of people who had been exiled from other parts of the Soviet Union were placed in Kazakhstan. Hundreds of thousands of people who were evacuated from World War II battlefields also settled in Kazakhstan, and the Kazakh Soviet Socialist Republic contributed five national divisions to the Soviet Union's military during World War II.

During World War II, much of the Russian industrial base was relocated to Kazakhstan. The republic's rich mineral resources also were exploited for the war effort. Despite this industrialization, Kazakhstan was still predominantly agricultural. Soviet planning after the war led to major developments of the Kazakh republic's agricultural sector. Soviet leader Nikita Khrushchev initiated the "Virgin Lands" program in 1953, which aimed to turn the traditional pasturelands into a grain-producing region for the nation. As wheat and cereal grains production intensified, thousands of Russians and other non-Kazakh peoples migrated to the area, leaving the ethnic Kazakhs as a minority.

On 16 December 1986, Mikhail Gorbachev replaced Kazakhstan's longtime leader Dinmukhamed Kunayev, a Kazakh, with a Russian from outside the republic. This action set off three days of rioting, and marked the first public nationalist protest in the Soviet Union. Soviet troops suppressed the riots and the government arrested dozens of protesters. However, the discontent continued to grow, and in June 1989, more civil disturbances hastened the appointment of Nursultan Nazarbayev as republic leader. A metallurgist and a Kazakh, Nazarbayev became prominent in the last Soviet years as a spokesman both for greater republic sovereignty and for the formation of a confederation of former Soviet republics.

Kazakhstan declared sovereignty as a republic within the Union of Soviet Socialist Republics in October 1990, and its parliament elected Nazarbayev president. Formal independence was declared in 16 December 1991, and Nazarbayev's election as president was reaffirmed in a public vote.

Kazakhstan's first two decades as an independent nation have been marked by healthy economic growth, market oriented reforms to the former Soviet command-based economy, and a political monopoly on power. A 1995 referendum extended Nazarbayev's presidential term to December 2000, and an early election in January 1999 returned him to office for a seven-year term. He was re-elected again in December 2005 for seven years, and was re-elected to a five-year term in April 2011.

As president, Nazarbayev has pursued close relations with Russia and other members of the Commonwealth of Independent States. He signed a Declaration of Eternal Friendship and Alliance Cooperation with former Russian president Boris Yeltsin in July 1998, and in early 1999 reaffirmed a CIS collective security agreement pledging the parties to provide military assistance in case of aggression against any one of them.

Following the 11 September 2001 terrorist attacks on the United States, Kazakhstan offered the use of its military bases, as well as air space for military and humanitarian purposes during the US-led military campaign in Afghanistan to oust the Taliban regime and al-Qaeda forces.

Nazarbayev has pledged to work to create a "democratic society with a market economy." While Kazakhstan has thrived economically since independence, Nazarbayev has wielded heavy control over the government and national policy priorities. He has stifled opposition parties and sidelined a bicameral parliament. Some members of Kazakhstan's elite have grown dissatisfied with the limited role they are allowed to play in the country's politics, and have made demands for more democratization of the society. Nevertheless, changes to Kazakhstan's constitution in 2007 removed all term limits on Nazarbayev, which could allow him to remain in office for life. None of the elections that have occurred since independence in Kazakhstan have been considered free and fair by international observers.

On 18 November 2001, a new political movement, the Democratic Choice of Kazakhstan (DCK) was established, however, Nazarbayev cracked down increasingly on the group. In what appeared to be politically motivated cases, two of the DCK's co-founders, Mukhtar Abliyazov and Galymzhan Zhakiyanov, were arrested, convicted of abuse of power and corruption during their tenure in government, and sentenced to prison. Abliyazov was freed from prison in 2003 after receiving an amnesty from Nazarbayev. Zhakiyanov was transferred from prison to a minimum security settlement colony in August 2004. In November 2005, opposition figure Zamanbek Nurkadilov, a strong critic of President Nazarbayev, was found shot dead at his home. In January 2006, Zhakiyanov was released on parole and returned to Almaty. In February 2006, opposition figure Altynbek Sarsenbaiuly, his bodyguard, and his driver, were found shot dead outside Almaty.

In January 2007, Prime Minister Daniyal Akhmetov resigned. He was replaced by former deputy prime minister Karim Masimov. Nazarbayev fired son-in-law Rakhat Aliyev and instigated criminal proceedings against him, and Nazarbayev's daughter Dariga Nazarbayeva divorced him. Aliyev subsequently left the country, and was sentenced in absentia on charges of abduction, racketeering, and coup plotting. Dariga Nazarbayeva has served as a member of parliament in the Nur Otan party, which is headed by her father.

Massive pro-democracy protests in the Middle East in 2011 prompted President Nazarbayeva to call for a snap parliamentary election in January 2012 that would allow for multiple parties to field candidates. The administration, however, appeared in July 2011 to have replaced leaders of an opposition party known as Ak Zhol (Bright Path) with supporters of the president in a bid to retain absolute control.

Riots erupted on 16 December 2011 in the town of Zhanaozen as Kazakhstan was celebrating its 20th anniversary of independence. Nazarbayev ordered a 20-day curfew and declared a state of emergency in the town. At least 14 people were killed and 100 others were injured in the clashes. Oil workers employed by Uzenmunaigaz, a subsidiary of the state-run Kazmunaigaz oil company in Zhanaozen had been striking since May. Opposition leaders, activists, and the international Human Rights Watch organization called for an independent investigation into the incident.

The January 2012 parliamentary elections were once again seen as unfree and unfair by outside observers. Nazarbayev's Nur Otan party won 81% of the vote. The Ak Zhol party and Communist People's Party were the only other organizations to win any spots in parliament.

13 GOVERNMENT

Kazakhstan is formally a constitutional republic with a strong presidency. The president serves as head of state and commander in chief of the armed forces. The president can veto legislation passed by the legislative branch, initiate constitutional amendments, appoint and dismiss the government, dissolve the legislative branch, and call referenda.

A prime minister serves at the pleasure of the president. The prime minister chairs the Cabinet of Ministers and serves as the head of government. The cabinet includes 17 ministers, and there are three deputy prime ministers.

The legislative branch consists of a bicameral parliament, with a lower house known as the Mazhilis and an upper house known as the Senate. The Mazhilis has 107 members, 98 of whom are elected by a party-list vote. The remaining nine members are elected by the Assembly of Peoples of Kazakhstan. The Senate consists of 47 members. Two senators are selected by each of the elected assemblies (Maslikhats) of the country's 16 administrative divisions, and the remainder are appointed by the president.

Presidential elections were held 3 April 2011 and were scheduled for 2016. Elections for the Mazhilis last took place on 15 January 2012. One-half of the Senate sat for elections on 4 October 2008, the other half in the January 2012 vote.

As of January 2012, Kazakhstan has had only one president: Nursultan Nazarbayev, who has ruled the country in an authoritarian fashion.

14 POLITICAL PARTIES

As of 2011, the main political parties were Nur Otan (Light-Fatherland), the Communist Party of Kazakhstan, Ak Zhol (Bright Path), the Republican People's Party of Kazakhstan, the Party of Patriots, the Communist People's Party of Kazakhstan, and OSDP Azat (the Freedom National Social Democratic Party) which was formed through a merger in October 2009 of the Azat and National Social Democratic Party.

Other parties included Auyl (Farm), Adilet & Justice, and Rukhaniyat (Spirituality).

Nur Otan won all of the seats in parliamentary elections that took place in 2007. A new decree calling for a multi-party parliament took effect in 2011, and was to allow for more than one party to participate in parliament following a 15 January 2012 vote. Ak Zhol and the Communist People's Party each won a small number of seats in that election but Nur Otan retained an overwhelming majority.

A 2002 law raised from 3,000 to 50,000 the number of members that a party must have to register, making it more difficult for political pressure groups to form actual opposition parties.

15 LOCAL GOVERNMENT

Kazakhstan is divided into 14 oblasts (provinces) and two municipal districts of Almaty and Astana. Each of these administrative units is headed by an akim (provincial governor). The president appoints akims for the oblasts, and the oblast akims appoint the akims for the municipal districts.

The akim appoints the staff members, who serve as local department heads. There is some discussion of shifting to local election of the regional akims.

In Uralsk (Western Kazakhstan) and Petropavlovsk (Northern Kazakhstan) there are Cossack obshchinas, or communities, agitating for autonomous status. Denied registry by Kazakhstan, many are active in Cossack obshchinas across the border in Russia, where Cossacks have the right to maintain military organizations and carry weapons.

16 JUDICIAL SYSTEM

Kazakhstan has a civil law system that is influenced both by Roman-Germanic law and by the theory and practice of law within the Russian Federation. The judiciary is under the administration of the president.

The US State Department reported in its 2010 Human Rights Report that the country's law did not provide for an independent judiciary, and that corruption marked every stage of the judicial process. Judges were among the most highly paid government employees, but lawyers and human rights advocates alleged that judges, prosecutors, and other judicial officials sought bribes in exchange for favorable rulings in most criminal cases. Prosecutors held a quasi-judicial role and had the power to suspend court decisions. Although a 2008 law transferred the power to sanction arrest from prosecutors to judges, most prosecutor arrests were sanctioned by judges.

A 2006 law allowed for jury trials in aggravated murder cases. However, the US State Department found that the juror selection process was inconsistent, and that judges would dominate juror deliberations.

Civil cases were handled by economic and administrative court judges under a structure that closely resembled the criminal court structure. Military courts also used the same criminal code as the civilian courts.

There are local and oblast (regional) level courts, and a national-level Supreme Court and Constitutional Council. A judgment by a local court may be appealed to the oblast level. The Supreme Court hears appeals from the oblast courts. The constitution establishes a seven member Constitutional Council to determine the constitutionality of laws adopted by the legislature. It also rules on challenges to elections and referendums and interprets the constitution. The president appoints three of its members, including the chair.

Under constitutional amendments of 1998, the president appoints a chairperson of a Supreme Judicial Council, which nominates judges for the Supreme Court. The Council consists of the chairperson of the Constitutional Council, the chairperson of the Supreme Court, the Prosecutor General, the Minister of Justice, senators, judges, and other persons appointed by the president. The president recommends and the senate (upper legislative chamber) approves these nominees for the Supreme Court. *Oblast* judges (nominated by the Supreme Judicial Council) are appointed by the president. Lower level judges are appointed by the president from a list presented by the Ministry of Justice. The Ministry receives the list from a Qualification Collegium of Justice, composed of deputies from the Mazhilis (lower legislative chamber), judges, prosecutors, and others appointed by the president). Under legislation approved in 1996, judges serve for life.

17 ARMED FORCES

The International Institute for Strategic Studies reports that armed forces in Kazakhstan totaled 49,000 members in 2011. The force is comprised of 30,000 from the army, 3,000 from the navy, 12,000 from the air force, and 4,000 members of the ministry of defense. Armed forces represent 0.9% of the labor force in Kazakhstan. Defense spending totaled $2.2 billion and accounted for 1.1% of gross domestic product (GDP).

Kazakhstan has participated in the US International Military Education and Training program as well as NATO's Partnership for Peace program. The US Central Command and the Ministry of Defense of Kazakhstan participated in a number of military cooperation events in 2005.

18 INTERNATIONAL COOPERATION

Kazakhstan was admitted to the UN on 2 March 1992. It also is a member of the UN Organization for Security and Cooperation in Europe, the North Atlantic Cooperation Council, the Commonwealth of Independent States, the Shanghai Cooperation Organizations, and the Eurasian Economic Committee. It served as chairman in office of the Organization for Security and Cooperation in Europe in 2010, and was a founding member of the Conference for Interaction and Confidence in Asia.

Kazakhstan has had observer status in the World Trade Organization, and has sought member status. International economic observers anticipated that the country would join the organization in 2012–13.

Kazakhstan also has played a strong international role in the disarmament of nuclear weapons. It renounced nuclear weapons in 1993, removed the last of its nuclear warheads in 1995, and completed the sealing of 181 nuclear test tunnels in 2000. It has signed the Comprehensive Test Ban Treaty.

President Nazarbayev has pursued close ties with Turkey, trade ties with Iran, and better relations with China, which many Kazakhs traditionally viewed with concern as a security threat. Kazakhstan has extensive trade ties with China's Xinjiang Province, where many ethnic Kazakhs and Uighurs reside.

19 ECONOMY

The GDP rate of change in Kazakhstan, as of 2010, was 7%. Inflation stood at 7.8%, and unemployment was reported at 5.5%. Based on 2010 estimates, services accounted for 51.8% of GDP, industry 42.8%, and agriculture 5.4%.

Kazakhstan is rich in fossil fuel reserves, minerals, and metals such as uranium, copper, and zinc. Oil and oil products accounted for 59% of its exports, while ferrous metals accounted for 19%. Its agricultural sector also is large and features livestock, cotton,

wheat and other grains. These endowments have made the Kazakhstan economy quite healthy since independence. The nation was on track to become one of the top 10 oil producing countries in the world by 2015.

Animal herding was the mainstay of the nomadic Kazakh population before the territory's incorporation into the Soviet Union. During the Soviet era, wool production remained an important agricultural product, along with grains and meat. Like other countries of the former USSR, Kazakhstan faced serious economic dislocation after 1991, resulting from the disruption of trade with other post-Soviet republics, an end to the flow of official revenues from the Soviet central government, the decline in state production orders, and the need for sudden currency adjustments. Positive if weak growth returned in 1996 and 1997, decline in 1998, and resumed again in 1999.

In 2000, Kazakhstan became the first former Soviet republic to repay all of its debt to the International Monetary Fund, and did so seven years ahead of schedule. The US Department of Commerce in March 2002 recognized the market economy reforms carried out by the government, and declared Kazakhstan to have market economy status under US trade laws. Kazakhstan also became the first country in the former Soviet Union to receive an investment grade credit rating in 2002. From 2000 through 2007, Kazakhstan's economy grew more than 9% a year.

Efforts have been made to privatize Kazakhstan's businesses as the country transitioned from the Soviet model of government control over the economy to a more capitalistic form of private ownership. Most small enterprises had been privatized by 2011, but many large companies remained government owned. The government has taken steps to consolidate the state holdings and as of 2010 there were five state-owned holding companies in Kazakhstan: Samruk-Kazyna, which managed state assets in the oil and gas, energy, transportation, telecommunication, and financial sectors; KazAgro, which managed agricultural holdings; Parasat, which oversaw the high-technology sector and managed several scientific institutions and funds; Zerde, which oversaw the communications sector; and National Medical Holding, which managed health services.

The U.S. State Department described Samruk-Kazyna as the largest buyer of goods and services in Kazakhstan, with procurement contracts in 2010 totaling $13.5 billion. As of February 2009, Samruk-Kazyna was granted the right to conclude large transactions between members of its holdings without public notification and was exempt from government procurement procedures. The prime minister served as chairman of its board of directors, and the board also included the ministers of Finance, Industry and Trade; Economic Development and Trade; and Oil and Gas as well as the assistant to the president of Kazakhstan.

Inflation has presented a challenge to Kazakhstan. After independence, inflation reached 2,000% in 1993. By 2002–04, inflation had come down to 6.6%-6.8% but climbed again as high as 18.8% in 2007 with rapid increases in global commodity prices.

The global financial crisis of 2008–2009 resulted in significant economic decline, primarily through the drop in oil prices and the effects of the worldwide credit crunch. The government took controlling stakes in the nation's two largest banks in early 2009 in an attempt to stabilize the banking industry. Small and medium business owners were particularly vulnerable during the crisis, with nearly 70% facing bankruptcy in early 2009. While the government earmarked $1 billion in funds for these struggling businesses, authorities indicated that a total of $10 billion would be required to save them all.

As a landlocked country, Kazakhstan must rely on neighboring countries to export its products. In addition, the country faces serious problems with its infrastructure. Its Caspian Sea ports and rail lines have been upgraded, but its aviation facilities were in need of improvements.

The economy has relied heavily on oil and extractive minerals and metal industries. In an effort to remedy the situation, the government has begun a diversification program aimed at developing its transport, pharmaceutical, telecommunications, petrochemicals, and food processing sectors.

20 INCOME

The CIA estimated that in 2010 the GDP of Kazakhstan was $196.4 billion. The CIA defines GDP as the value of all final goods and services produced within a nation in a given year and computed on the basis of purchasing power parity (PPP) rather than value as measured on the basis of the rate of the exchange based on current dollars. The per capita GDP was estimated at $12,700. The annual growth rate of GDP was 7%. The average inflation rate was 7.8%. It was estimated that agriculture accounted for 5.4% of GDP, industry 42.8%, and services 51.8%.

According to the World Bank, remittances from citizens living abroad totaled $123.7 million or about $8 per capita and accounted for approximately 0.1% of GDP.

The World Bank reports that in 2009, household consumption in Kazakhstan totaled $50.3 billion or about $3,240 per capita, measured in current US dollars rather than PPP. Household consumption included expenditures of individuals, households, and nongovernmental organizations on goods and services, excluding the purchases of dwellings. It was estimated that household consumption was growing at an average annual rate of 2.7%.

In 2007 the World Bank estimated that Kazakhstan, with 0.25% of the world's population, accounted for 0.24% of the world's GDP. By comparison, the United States, with 4.85% of the world's population, accounted for 22.51% of world GDP.

As of 2011 the most recent study by the World Bank reported that actual individual consumption in Kazakhstan was 55.3% of GDP and accounted for 0.22% of world consumption. By comparison, the United States accounted for 25.44% of world individual consumption. The World Bank also estimated that 12.1% of Kazakhstan's GDP was spent on food and beverages, 16% on housing and household furnishings, 4.9% on clothes, 5.4% on health, 4.7% on transportation, 1.1% on communications, 2.7% on recreation, 1.5% on restaurants and hotels, and 1.6% on miscellaneous goods and services and purchases from abroad.

It was estimated that in 2009 about 8.2% of the population subsisted on an income below the poverty line established by Kazakhstan's government.

21 LABOR

As of 2010, Kazakhstan had a total labor force of 8.611 million people. Within that labor force, CIA estimates in 2010 noted that 28.2% were employed in agriculture, 18.2% in industry, and 53.6% in the service sector.

A 2008 mining accident in Satpayev marked a significant change in labor policy, as the government began to encourage workers to sign memorandums of understanding in place of unionization. As of 1 March 2011 a pro-union collective bargaining campaign resulted in the signing of 47,362 collective agreements, and more than 8,000 large and medium-sized businesses had signed the memorandums of understanding to guarantee jobs and labor rights. Despite these proactive steps, the US State Department reported that the Kazakh government continued to favor state-affiliated unions over independent unions and often imposed restrictions on workers' rights to organize or join unions of their choice.

Approximately one-third of the workforce was organized as of 2011. The Federation of Trade Unions, which was a successor to the Soviet era labor organization, was still affiliated with the government, and remained the largest trade union association in the country.

The minimum age for employment was 16, but children between the ages of 14 and 16 were allowed to perform light work that would not interfere with their health or education. The maximum workweek was 40 hours, and 36 hours in sectors that required heavy manual labor or hazardous work. The monthly minimum wage of $102 was not enough to provide a decent standard of living for workers and their families, and multiple wage earners in families were common. Wages in urban areas generally were above the minimum level.

22 AGRICULTURE

Roughly 8% of the total land is farmed, and the country's major crops include grain (mostly spring wheat) and cotton. Cereal production in 2009 amounted to 20.8 million tons, fruit production 234,400 tons, and vegetable production 3.3 million tons. About 28.2% of Kazakhstan's labor force was employed in agricultural activities in 2010.

Most cropland is found in the northern steppes, where the failed Virgin and Idle Land Project of the 1950s occurred. Small-scale privatization resulted in the formation of 149,986 private farms, accounting for 94% of agricultural holdings by 2003. The average farm size in 2003 was about 110 hectares (270 acres). Despite the privatization, the state-run KazAgro holding company as of 2011 continued to oversee the wheat trade, leasing to farmers, livestock development, and other forms of financial assistance.

Agricultural output in Kazakhstan often suffers from summer droughts. Soft and durum wheat is grown in the north/northeast and parts of the west and central areas of the country while the eastern and southeastern agricultural areas produce oilseeds, sugar beets, corn, fruits, and vegetables. Fruits, vegetables, horticultural products, cotton and rice are also grown in the south.

The US State Department reported that agriculture accounted for about 6% of Kazakhstan's economic production. Major crops as of 2011 were wheat, barley, cotton, and rice. Wheat exports were a major source of hard currency.

23 ANIMAL HUSBANDRY

The UN Food and Agriculture Organization (FAO) reported that Kazakhstan dedicated 185.1 million hectares (457.4 million acres) to permanent pasture or meadow in 2009. During that year, the country tended 30 million chickens, 6 million head of cattle, and 1.3 million pigs. The production from these animals amounted to 407,714 tons of beef and veal, 234,231 tons of pork, 206,602 tons of poultry, 112,760 tons of eggs, and 4.05 million tons of milk. Kazakhstan also produced 49,628 tons of cattle hide and 36,400 tons of raw wool.

About 70% of Kazakhstan's total land area is permanent pastureland.

The government has been interested in increasing its livestock and poultry production, and beef and poultry breeding farms are eligible for reimbursements for money spent to obtain and maintain animals from foreign markets for the purposes of breeding. Subsidies for these endeavors were expected to increase by $275,000 in 2011.

24FISHING

Kazakhstan had 1,970 decked commercial fishing boats in 2008. The annual capture totaled 55,581 tons according to the UN FAO. The export value of seafood totaled $95.38 million.

A variety of sturgeons and pike-perch characterized the fishery sector. Most fishing was concentrated around the Caspian Sea, but water basins for fisheries were available for lease.

25FORESTRY

Approximately 1% of Kazakhstan is covered by forest. The UN FAO estimated the 2009 roundwood production at 197,900 cu m (6.99 million cu ft). The value of all forest products, including roundwood, totaled $6.55 million.

26MINING

The leading industries in Kazakhstan in 2008 were, in order, oil, coal, iron ore, manganese, chromite, lead, zinc, copper, titanium, bauxite, gold, silver, phosphates, and sulfur. In 2008, Kazakhstan accounted for 4% of world manganese production. The country was also a major producer of beryllium, bismuth, cadmium, chromium, ferroalloys, magnesium, rhenium, titanium, and uranium, and produced significant amounts of arsenic, barite (75% of the former Soviet Union's output), molybdenum, natural gas, phosphate rock, and tungsten. Among other minerals, Kazakhstan produced cobalt, magnesium, nickel, vanadium, and all grades of asbestos, as well as the industrial minerals boron, cement, and kaolin. Kazakhstan has commercial reserves of 3 ferrous metals, 29 nonferrous metals, 2 precious metals, 84 types of industrial minerals, and coal, natural gas, and petroleum. The eastern region of Kazakhstan is rich in alumina, arsenic, bauxite, beryllium, bismuth, cadmium, chrome, copper, gold, iron ore, lead-zinc, manganese, molybdenum, rhenium, silver, titanium, and tungsten. In 2007, mineral extraction accounted for 57% of the value of industrial production. Mining employed about 4.6% of the total labor force in 2008.

Output of metals in 2008 included: marketable iron ore (gross weight), 21.846 million metric tons, down from 23.834 million metric tons in 2007; manganese ore (gross weight), 2,485,000 metric tons; chromite, 3,269,000 metric tons; lead, 38,800; mined zinc, 387,400; mined copper, 421,700, up from 406,500 metric tons in 2007; bauxite, 5,160,600 metric tons; mined gold, 22,000 kg; silver, 700,000 kg, down from 800,000 kg in 2007; and alumina, 1.713 million tons.

Copper mining began to recover after foreign companies acquired management rights to the nation's copper producers, most notably the Zhezqazgan complex, which also included concentration, smelting, and refining facilities. Kazakhstan had supplied more than 95% of chromite production for the former USSR through the Donskoy mining and beneficiation complex at Khromtau. Iron ore found near Rudnyy supplied the iron and steel plants in the Russian Urals region as well as plants at Karaganda and Temirtau.

27ENERGY AND POWER

The CIA estimated that Kazakhstan in 2009 produced 75.61 billion kWh of electricity and consumed 77.9 billion kWh. Roughly 99% of energy came from fossil fuels, while 1% came from alternative fuels. Per capita oil consumption was 4,525 kg. Oil production totaled 1.61 million barrels of oil a day, based on a 2010 estimate by the CIA and natural gas production totaled 35.61 billion cu m, based on a 2009 estimate. Natural gas consumption was estimated at 8.572 cu m.

The country was estimated to have exported 2.483 billion kWh of electricity in 2008, and imported 1.94kWh, based on a 2009 estimate.

Kazakhstan has the Caspian Sea region's largest recoverable crude oil reserves. Proved oil reserves were estimated at 30 billion barrels as of 1 January 2011 and proved natural gas reserves were estimated at 2.407 trillion cu m.

Kazakhstan's oil and natural gas reserves have made the country a focal point in the battle for strategic energy pipelines. In 2009 Kazakhstan approved a Russian pipeline plan in which an additional 10 billion cubic meters of Kazakh gas will flow into Russia each year. As the European Union (EU) attempts to wean itself from Russian energy supplies, member nations worry that Kazakhstan's gas commitments to Russia will divert energy supplies away from Europe.

28INDUSTRY

Industry accounted for 42.8% of Kazakhstan's GDP in 2010, and employed 18.2% of its labor force. The industrial production growth rate was estimated at 10% for 2010, although the US State Department forecast more moderate growth of 3.6% for 2011. Key industries were oil, coal, iron ore, manganese, chromite, lead, zinc, copper, titanium, bauxite, gold, silver, phosphates, sulfur, uranium, iron and steel. In addition, Kazakhstan produced tractors and other agricultural machinery, electric motors, and construction materials.

Before its independence, Kazakhstan's designated manufactures included phosphate fertilizer, rolled metal, radio cables, aircraft wires, train bearings, tractors, and bulldozers. The country also had a well-developed network of factories that produced about 11% of the Soviet Union's military goods. Overwhelmingly dominated by state-owned enterprises under the centrally planned economy, independent Kazakhstan's economy has been substantially, if incompletely, privatized and reoriented to the market economy. According to the US State Department, the government was to invest $5.4 billion in 2011 for innovative industrial products, and a total of $15 billion from 2011 to 2013. The government also intended to continue privatizing its industry, with plans to sell off assets in its energy and banking sectors.

Oil production more than doubled in Kazakhstan between 2004 and 2011, and oil and oil products accounted for 59% of Kazakhstan's export income in 2010. The country's major producers were Tengiz, Karachaganak, CNPC-Aktobemunaigas, Uzenmunaigas, Mangistaumunaigas, and Kumkol. The three major oil fields were offshore Kashagan, onshore Karachaganak, and onshore Tengiz, and production from these fields was expected to grow as high as 3.5 million bbl/day by 2015.

Electric power generation accounted for about 10% of Kazakhstan's industrial output in 2011. Infrastructure in this sector, however, has been in need of modernization, and Kazakhstan has continued to import electricity. The government planned to build new power plants and reconstruct and modernize existing ones in hopes of boosting the total capacity to 124.5 billion kWh by 2015.

More than 230 enterprises formed Kazakhstan's mining sector as of 2010. These companies produced or processed coal, iron and steel, copper, lead, zinc, manganese, gold aluminum, titanium sponge, uranium, barites and other minerals. Mining account for 30% of export earnings, 16% of GDP, and 19% of the country's industrial employment. Kazakhstan was the world's ninth largest producer of coal in 2010, with a total of 103.5 million tons produced. It also holds the world's eighth largest iron ore reserves and second largest manganese ore reserves. The government was seeking to develop its gold and uranium mining in 2010.

The process of restructuring the industrial sector was initially painful. Industrial production declined by 13.8% in 1992, by 14.8% in 1993 and by 28.5% in 1994. Decline continued in 1995, but at the single digit rate of 8%. The first positive growth in industrial production after independence was a 0.3% improvement in 1996. Privatization moved ahead quickly in that year and into the summer of 1997, a year in which real GDP increased 4%. However, industrial production declined again in 1998-by 2%-due primarily to the combined effects of the Russian financial crisis and a fall in world oil prices. The president, citing the low fuel prices, decreed a halt to further privatization in the country's vital oil and gas sector, and slowed the negotiations on privatization of the remaining large state enterprises. Subsequently, industrial growth resumed at a moderate 3% in 1999, but then at robust double-digit rates of 16% in 2000 and 14% in 2001. For 2002, the estimated growth rate was 9.8%, slightly ahead of overall GDP performance. The share of industrial production fell from 25.9% of GDP in 1994 to 21.8% of GDP in 1995, but had risen to 30% by 2001. By 2005, industry accounted for 40.4% of GDP, and the industrial production growth rate stood at 10.7%.

Most of Kazakhstan's manufacturing, refining, and metallurgy plants are concentrated in the north and northeast, in Semey, Petropavl, and Aktobe. In south-central Kazakhstan, Shymkent is an important center for chemicals, light manufactures, metallurgy, and food processing; Almaty is important for light industry, machine building, and food processing.

²⁹SCIENCE AND TECHNOLOGY

Patent applications in science and technology as of 2009, according to the World Bank, totaled 11 in Kazakhstan. Public financing of science was 0.22% of GDP. The Kazakhstan Academy of Sciences, founded in 1946 in Almaty, has departments of physical and mathematical sciences, earth sciences, chemical-technological sciences, and biological sciences. Scientific training was available at a number of higher educational institutes.

The state-owned holding companies Parasat and Zerde were created to stimulate scientific and technological research and development. Parasat manages several scientific institutions and funds, and is chaired by the Minister of Education of Science. Zerde is charged with development of modern information and communication technologies, and stimulation of investment and innovation in commuications. Its managing board falls under oversight of the Ministry of Communication as well as the Prime Minister's office.

³⁰DOMESTIC TRADE

The wholesale and retail sector, previously dominated by state-controlled distribution channels, has seen the dynamic growth of independent small shops and traders. Price controls have been lifted for 90% of consumer and 80% of wholesale prices, although basic goods and services such as bread, flour, baby food, medicines, fodder, housing rents, utilities, and public transportation have been excluded from liberalization.

Business hours were normally 9 a.m. to 6 p.m.

Much of Kazakhstan's domestic business environment retains cultural ties to the country's history of clan and tribal relations. According to the U.S. State Department, business customs vary by ethnicity. Shaking hands and referring to people by their first name are customary at business meetings, and refreshments are usually served. Gifts are often given at the end of an initial meeting, and business cards are printed in Russian as well as English.

After business contacts are established, transactions often take place in more informal settings such as over meals, which feature rounds of toasts over a bottle of vodka or cognac. Weekend hunting and barbecues also provide informal means of building business relations.

The country sponsors a number of trade exhibitions through the year, including the Kazakhstan Oil and Gas Exhibition, held in Almaty every October, and a Consumer Expo in April.

³¹FOREIGN TRADE

Kazakhstan imported an estimated $31.96 billion worth of goods and services in 2010, compared with an estimated $28.96 billion in 2009. Major import items were machinery and equipment, metal products, and food stuffs. Major import partners were Russia (34.3%), China (27.7%), Germany (5.2%), and Ukraine (4%).

Exports were estimated at $60.84 billion in 2010 compared with $43.93 billion in 2009. Major export items were oil and oil products (59%), ferrous metals (19%), chemicals (5%), machinery (3%), and grain, wool, meat, and coal. Major export partners were China (20.2%), Germany (9.1%), Russia (8.5%), France (7.1%), Turkey (4.5%), Canada (4.5%), and Italy (4.1%).

In 1990, about 89% of Kazakhstan's exports and 88% of its imports represented trade with other former Soviet republics (at foreign trade prices). A serious disruption in the country's trading patterns occurred as the input procurement system within the Soviet centrally planned economy disintegrated and export demand from Eastern European countries shrank. To facilitate adjustment, the government decreed key trade liberalization measures in early 1992.

Principal Trading Partners – Kazakhstan (2010)

(In millions of US dollars)

Country	Total	Exports	Imports	Balance
World	81,268.0	57,244.0	24,024.0	33,220.0
China	20,238.0	10,031.0	10,207.0	-176.0
Russia	7,926.0	2,344.0	5,582.0	-3,238.0
Germany	6,430.0	4,498.0	1,932.0	2,566.0
France	3,903.0	3,545.0	358.0	3,187.0
Italy	3,464.0	2,041.0	1,423.0	618.0
Turkey	3,147.0	2,246.0	901.0	1,345.0
United States	2,570.0	1,759.0	811.0	948.0
Canada	2,372.0	2,223.0	149.0	2,074.0
Ukraine	2,128.0	697.0	1,431.0	-734.0
Netherlands	1,711.0	1,186.0	525.0	661.0

(…) data not available or not significant.

(n.s.) not specified.

SOURCE: 2011 Direction of Trade Statistics Yearbook, New York: United Nations, 2011.

Kazakhstan signed an investment incentive agreement with the U.S. in 1992, and since independence has ratified treaties on the avoidance of double taxation with 40 countries. It has also formed bilateral protection investment agreements with 45 countries including Great Britain, Germany, Italy, France, Russia, South Korea, Iran, China, Turkey, and Vietnam. It signed investment agreements with Romania, Austria, and Serbia in 2010.

As of 31 December 2010, Kazakhstan maintained a free trade regime with all members of the Eurasian Economic Community (Russia, Kyrgyzstan, Belarus, and Tajikistan). It also maintained free trade regimes with other members of the Commonwealth of Independent States, except for Turkmenistan. Russia, Kazakhstan, and Belarus formed a Customs Union which took effect on 1 July 2010, and had completed bilateral negotiations with all of the working party members of the World Trade Organization except for the U.S., European Union, and Saudi Arabia.

32 BALANCE OF PAYMENTS

In 2010 Kazakhstan had a foreign trade surplus of $9.4 billion, amounting to 2% of GDP.

The CIA estimated Kazakhstan to have a current account balance of $4.319 billion in 2010 compared with a negative balance of $4.221 billion in 2009. The current account balance was negative in 2009 due to the global economic crisis.

Reserves of foreign exchange and gold were estimated at $28.27 billion as of 31 December 2010 compared with $23.22 billion on 31 December 2009.

The CIA estimated the stock of direct foreign investment in Kazakhstan at $79.13 billion in 2010 compared with $69.11 billion in 2009. These figures represent investments made by foreigners, other than purchases of stock shares. The stock of direct foreign investment made by Khazakhstani residents in other countries was estimated at $13.76 billion in 2010 compared with $5.956 billion in 2009.

Kazakhstan's exports of oil and minerals allowed it to maintain a healthy balance of payments through the first decade of the 21st century, though changes in world oil prices and the global economic recession had a negative effect on the country. Kazakhstan also has benefited from large amounts of foreign direct investment.

33 BANKING AND SECURITIES

As of 2011, Kazakhstan maintained a two-tier banking system. The top tier was represented by the National Bank, which reported to the president and served as the country's central bank. The lower tier included 38 private commercial banks and one state-owned bank. The top ten banks in Kazakhstan controlled 90% of the country's banking assets. The largest commercial banks as of November 2010 were BTA bank, Kazkommertsbank, and Halyk Bank. Together they controlled 53.6% of Kazakhstan's total banking assets.

The National Bank is a successor of the Independent Kazakh, which had been known as the Almaty branch of Gosbank, the former Soviet State Bank. Although the central bank has the power under Kazakhstan's banking laws to regulate the commercial banking sector and to conduct monetary and credit policies, it is not independent of the governmental apparatus.

Banking sector assets grew rapidly from 2002–07, comprising 25.1% of GDP in 2002 and 87.8% by 1 January 2008. A freeze in global financial markets resulted in a loss of capital inflows to Kazakhstani banks; this resulted in a credit crunch and severe liquidity constraints. A sharp fall in oil and commodity prices in 2008 worsened the situation, and plunged Kazakhstan into recession. At the end of 2009, Kazakhstan's total external debt was $111.7 billion.

The government announced a $10 billion bailout package for banks in October 2008. It used its state-owned holding company Samruk-Kazyna to acquire majority stakes in four banks: 75.1% in BTA; 100% in Alliance Bank; 19.8% in Halyk Bank; and 21.24% in KazKommertsBank. By the end of 2009, BTA, Alliance Bank, Astana Finance and Temirbank all defaulted and underwent debt restructuring processes. After the restructuring, Samruk-Kazyna took over 81.48% of common shares of BTA and 67% of common shares of Alliance Bank.

Balance of Payments – Kazakhstan (2010)

(In millions of US dollars)

Current Account		4,319.0
Balance on goods	2,881.4	
Imports	-31,956.5	
Exports	60,837.9	
Balance on services	15,542.3	
Balance on income	-17,074.7	
Current transfers	-434.7	
Capital Account		7,888.2
Financial Account		-8,878.9
Direct investment abroad	7,805.9	
Direct investment in Kazakhstan	9,961.0	
Portfolio investment assets	-7,166.0	
Portfolio investment liabilities	15,878.0	
Financial derivatives	13.0	
Other investment assets	-6,351.8	
Other investment liabilities	-13,407.3	
Net Errors and Omissions		1,406.5
Reserves and Related Items		-4,734.7

(…) data not available or not significant.

SOURCE: Balance of Payment Statistics Yearbook 2011, Washington, DC: International Monetary Fund, 2011.

The restructuring stabilized the banking sector, with assets growing by 4.2% to $82 billion in 2010. The total bank equity capital was $9 billion as of 1 January 2011 compared with -$6.2 billion at the end of 2009. The US State Department noted, however, that the banking system faced numerous challenges in 2011.

Laws prohibit foreign banks from establishing branches in Kazakhstan but allow them to establish subsidiaries, joint ventures, and representative offices. As of December 2010, 29 foreign banks had representative offices, and 20 of the nation's banks had some foreign participation. From 2008 to 10, Sberbank and VTB of Russia, Bank Hapoalim of Israel, Kookmin Bank of South Korea, the Arab investment company Alnair Capital, and Islamic Al-Hilal bank of the United Arab Emirates all entered the Kazakhstan banking market. CenterCredit and ATF-UniCredit Bank are the two largest commercial banks with foreign participation. Citibank and HSBC of the United States have established subsidiaries, and several Dutch and Turkish banks have established joint ventures.

The Kazakhstani Stock Exchange has been in operation since 1993 but has not served as a significant source of investment. Trading was dominated by block trades primarily in foreign exchange operations. There were 354 listed companies on the exchange and total capitalization was $53 billion as of November 2010.

34 INSURANCE

Government figures indicated that 40 insurance companies were operating in Kazakhstan as of 1 January 2007. Five of the companies were life insurance companies. A 2007 Business Week article described the insurance market as in its infancy, with average per capita spending on premiums at $36. The gross premium average as of 1 May 2007 was $256 million, according to the article.

35 PUBLIC FINANCE

In 2010 the budget of Kazakhstan included $27.5 billion in public revenue and $31.6 billion in public expenditures. The budget deficit amounted to 2.6% of GDP. Public debt was 16.2% of GDP, with $97.57 billion of the debt held by foreign entities.

Although Kazakhstan's strong oil and mineral exports have made it one of the fastest growing economies in the world, the over-reliance on these exports for income have made the country vulnerable to global economic crises. This vulnerability plunged the country into recession in 1998 and again in 2008.

The government formed a sovreign wealth fund called the National Oil Fund in 2000 in an effort to lessen the country's budgetary dependence on oil prices and to accumulate savings for future generations. The Fund accumulates direct taxes and a percentage of revenues from the oil sector, revenues from the privatization of state property in mining and manufacturing, and revenues from sales of farmland. The Ministry of Finance owns the fund, and the National Bank serves as its trustee. Monies accumulated in the fund can be used to maintain macroeconomic stability and for savings. The fund is required by law to retain a minimum balance of no less than 20% of GDP.

As of 1 December 2010, assets in the National Fund totaled $30.24 billion.

36 TAXATION

Kazakhstan adopted a new Tax Code in January 2009 that lowered corporate income and value added taxes, replaced royalty payments with a mineral extraction tax, and introduced excess-profits and rent taxes on crude oil and natural gas exports.

The corporate income tax was set at 20%, compared with 30% previously. The value-added tax, which was 16% in 2006, was reduced to 12%. The code also set a flat 11% social tax on employee earnings and a personal income tax rate for residents of 10%.

37 CUSTOMS AND DUTIES

The 12% value added tax was required on top of all customs duties and excise taxes at the time of customs clearance. Kazakhstan also allows for a drawback of import duties and taxes when imported goods are processed in Kazakhstan and exported within two years of the importance. Manufacturing and assembly operations and repairs operations qualify for this drawback.

The country introduced a customs duty on crude-oil and gas-condensate exports in April 2008. The rate was set to zero in January 2009 but reintroduced at $20 a ton in August 2010. Companies who pay a rent tax were exempted from this duty.

The formation of the Customs Union with Russia and Belarus in 2010 required adoption of a common customs tariff, which raised the average level of customs fees from 6.2% to 10.6% on more than 5,000 types of goods. The Customs Union code also required Kazakhstan to implement tariff-rate quotes on poultry, beef, and pork imports. However, the code allowed for Kazakhstan to have no tariff on about 900 items that included modern aircraft, engines, and raw materials for the food processing industry. Agricultural combines and tractors also were exempted from customs duties if the import was financed through a government program. Pharmaceuticals, medical equipment, processed aluminum products, raw materials for the petrochemical industry, paper products and rail wagons also were subject to a transitional period of one and a half to five years.

Kazakhstan has established six special economic zones where businesses engaged in government-prescribed economic activities

---

Public Finance – Kazakhstan (2009)

(In billions of tenge, central government figures)

Revenue and Grants	**2,771.3**	**100.0%**
Tax revenue	1,370	49.4%
Social contributions	…	…
Grants	1,207.1	43.6%
Other revenue	194.2	7.0%
Expenditures	**3,107.6**	**100.0%**
General public services	789.8	25.4%
Defense	183	5.9%
Public order and safety	259.9	8.4%
Economic affairs	485.6	15.6%
Environmental protection	10.7	0.3%
Housing and community amenities	170.3	5.5%
Health	176.8	5.7%
Recreational, culture, and religion	104.4	3.4%
Education	231.2	7.4%
Social protection	695.9	22.4%

(…) data not available or not significant.

SOURCE: *Government Finance Statistics Yearbook 2010*, Washington, DC: International Monetary Fund, 2010.

enjoy certain tax preferences. The zones are the New Administrative Center in Astana, the Seaport of Aktau, the Alatau Information Technology Park near Almaty, the Ontustik Cotton Center in southern Kazakhstan, an international tourism zone Borabay, and the Atyrau National Industrial Petrochemical Techno park.

38 FOREIGN INVESTMENT

Foreign direct investment (FDI) in Kazakhstan was a net inflow of $13.6 billion according to World Bank figures published in 2009. FDI represented 11.81% of GDP.

The US State Department reported that as of 30 September 2010, Kazakhstan had received $139.3 billion in foreign direct investment. Between 1993 and 2009, investment in extractive industries accounted for 76% of total foreign investment in Kazakhstan.

U.S. companies have invested $6.5 billion in the oil sector. Key investors have included Chevron, ExxonMobil, and ConocoPhillips. Chevron has held a 50% stake in Tengizchevroil and ExxonMobil has held a 25% stake. The two companies invested $30.4 billion between 1993 and 2010. Other foreign investors in oil include the Chinese National Petroleum Corporation, Shell, British Gas, Total, Agip, Lukoil, Eni, and Inpex.

J Ray McDermott, S.A. has invested more than $400 million in manufacturing; JP Morgan Chase more than $300 million in business services; Marriott International $170 million in construction, and General Electric Transportation $78 million in a locomotive facility.

Kazakhstan restricts foreign ownership of media outlets to 20% and in the overall telecommunications sector to 49%.

Even before its formal independence, the government adopted the Foreign Investment Law of 1991 that allowed investment by foreign companies in any economic activity except the manufacture of military goods. The law contained provisions for duty-free imports as well as tax breaks for firms with foreign investment, especially those involved in producing consumer goods, agricultural goods, and electronic and medical equipment.

The regime was subsequently revised in a new Foreign Investment Law in 1994 (amended in 1997) to provide stronger guarantees against changes in Kazakhstan's legislation, greater clarity on investment requirements and on the credit facilities available to foreign investors, some additional customs exemptions, and a guarantee of the right to recourse to international arbitration to settle disputes.

From August to November 1996, the government pursued a vigorous privatization program. In 1997, a new law enabled investors to qualify for up to 100% tax relief for five years, and for up to 50% tax relief for the second five years. Priority areas were infrastructure, manufactures, housing, construction in Astana (designated the new capital as of December 1997), and agriculture. Following the recession in 1998, in 1999 the government began to change its stance on foreign investment from favorable treatment to national treatment. In January 2001, the government passed laws to control the transfer of capital out of the country. Foreign investors expressed concern over the increased authority given customs officials to regulate export and import transactions.

In 2001 the government moved to enact a new investment law to replace the 1994 and 1997 regulations. Because of strong opposition from foreign investors, the president did not sign the new law until January 2003. The new code, unlike the previous law, offers fewer protections to foreign investors and limits exemptions from customs fees to one year, with extensions limited to no more than five years. Particularly contentious was the removal of the right to international arbitration to settle disputes.

While Kazakhstan has sought foreign investment, a lack of economic reforms has stifled its success. New laws instituted by the national government often are not put into place properly at the local level, and the US State Department noted that this lack of transparency has led many companies to complain about the country's burdensome regulations.

39 ECONOMIC DEVELOPMENT

As a former Soviet Republic, Kazakhstan underwent rapid development of its agricultural and industrial sectors. Vast tracts of land were brought into cultivation with the expansion of irrigation under the USSR's "Virgin Lands" program, while within the industrial sector, development of its metallurgical, mining, and machinery industries were prioritized.

Since sovereignty was declared in December 1991, Kazakhstan has been embarked on a process of economic restructuring aimed at establishing a market economy. In 2002, President Nazarbayev reported that Kazakhstan was recognized by both the EU and the United States as a market economy, and that 75% of the country's GDP was derived from the private sector. This transformation, substantial if incomplete, involved reform on many fronts: privatization; lifting of price, capital, and profitability controls; the elimination of subsidies; debt restructuring; tax, customs, and banking reform; creation of a securities and exchange commission; and trade and investment liberalization.

In the first two decades of independence, 1991–2011, much of Kazakhstan's economic development focused on the oil and gas sectors, as well as the extraction of minerals. These developments allowed for strong economic expansion in the first decade of the 21st century, and made Kazakhstan one of the world's fastest growing economies. Kazakhstan also is becoming a key transit point between China and Europe, and was seeking new ways to use its wealth of natural resources and minerals to diversify its economy. The US State Department and other international observers identified the country's key challenges as being over-reliance on the oil, gas and mineral sectors; governmental and societal corruption; and political authoritarianism.

Key elements of the government's economic development plan for 2007–15 included upgrades of power facilities, the launch of a north-south power transmission line, and the building of hydropower plants to improve its electricity production. The government also identified the metallurgy sector as a targeted area for development in its Accelerated Industrial Innovation Development Program for 2010–14. The government planned to build two ore mining and processing enterprises in East Kazakhstan and Stepnogorsk. Plans also were in place to build a new nuclear power station, and to continue work on a 560-mile transmission line that would allow it to export electricity to Urumqi, China.

Numerous foreign aid agencies supported Kazakhstan's economic development. The World Bank provided 34 loans totaling $4.2 billion between July 1992 and December 2010, aimed at reforming the financial sector, privatizing businesses, and reforming the civil service. The World Bank had shifted its support in the early 21st century to investments in agricultural development, environmental protection, health, and general infrastructure. A $2.1 billion loan in April 2009 aimed to upgrade the South-West road between Aktobe and Shymkent. The European Bank for Reconstruction and Development had invested more than $2.6 billion as of 2010 in Kazakhstan's private enterprises, banking sector, and in infrastructure development. The Asian Development Bank also had 18 loan commitments in Kazakhstan as of 31 December 2009 in support of agricultural, natural resource, education, finance, transport, communications, water supply, sanitation, and irrigation programs. It approved a $700 million multi-tranche financing facility in 2009 to help finance the rebuilding of parts of an International Transit Corridor known as the Western Europe-Western PRC road project. The International Finance Corporation also had provided more than $1 billion to Kazakhstan between 1993 and December 2009.

Kazakhstan's economic prospects are promising because of its vast energy and mineral resources, low foreign debts, and well-trained work force. There is more Western private investment in Kazakhstan than elsewhere in Central Asia because of Kazakhstan's oil resources and efforts to attract investment.

40 SOCIAL DEVELOPMENT

Social security programs were first introduced in 1956, and were revised in 1991 and 1996 following independence. All employed persons, including noncitizens, qualify for old age, disability, and survivorship pensions. Employers contribute 30% of payroll, while employees contribute 1% of earnings. Residents of ecological disaster areas are entitled to early retirement. Workers' compensation is offered under a dual social insurance and universal system. The government funds a family assistance program for needy citizens, refugees, and stateless persons residing it the country.

Khazakhstani president Nazarbayev has stated that "the path from totalitarianism to democracy lies through enlightened authoritarianism." However, the authoritarian structure of Khazakhstan's government has led to rampant corruption, stiff restrictions on free expression, and several human rights violations.

The US State Department's 2010 Human Rights Report on Kazakhstan reported numerous human rights violations. According to the report, military hazing which led to deaths, suicides, and serious injuries occurred frequently, and police and prison officials would beat and abuse detainees to obtain confessions. Ministry of Internal Affairs hotlines maintained by the government received 13,617 complaints of police corruption and abuse in 2010. Prison conditions failed to meet international health standards, and nearly half of the inmate population suffered HIV/AIDS, tuberculosis, and other infectious diseases. Severe restrictions also were imposed on political participation, media coverage, and Internet usage.

Nazabayev signed a new law on domestic violence in December 2009 that outlined various types of violence, responsibilities of local and national authorities, and mechanisms for detention and sentencing. The US State Department reported little change in the domestic violence situation in Kazakhstan in 2010.

Ethnic tensions between Kazakhs and Russians continued to exist. Ethnic Kazakhs receive preferential treatment in housing, education, and employment.

41 HEALTH

According to the CIA, life expectancy in Kazakhstan was 68 years in 2011. The country spent 3.9% of its GDP on healthcare, amounting to $330 per person. There were 39 physicians, 78 nurses and midwives, and 77 hospital beds per 10,000 residents.

The fertility rate was 2.6, while the infant mortality rate was 26 per 1,000 live births. In 2008 the maternal mortality rate, according to the World Bank, was 45 per 100,000 births. It was estimated that 99% of children were vaccinated against measles. The CIA calculated HIV/AIDS prevalence in Kazakhstan to be about 0.1% in 2009.

The World Bank approved a $117.7 million loan in January 2008 for a Health Sector Technology Transfer and Institutional Reform Project that was to be implemented by 2013. The $296 million project was being co-financed by the government. In June 2008, the government established a state-owned joint stock company known as National Medical Holding that included the Kazakhstan Medical Academy, National Center for Maternal and Child Health, National Research Center for Emergency Care, Republican Center for Medical Rehabilitation, National Center for Neurosurgery, Republican Diagnostic Center and the National Research Center for Cardiac Surgery. The goal of this venture was to raise the quality and safety of health care and to ensure financial sustainability of health services.

The government allocated $2.75 billion of its 2010 budget to the health care sector in 2010, a 35% increase from the amount spent in 2009. Major improvements in medical personnel training, mother and child health services, preventative care, treatments of social diseases, and patient rehabilitation were planned.

42 HOUSING

Housing construction was a development priority for the government in the first decade of the early 21st century. A government report in 2008 noted that growing strength in Kazakhstan's market economy and rising populations in its urban areas had made housing construction an attractive area of development.

About half of the new homes being built were in Almaty and Astana. Housing prices, which had been on the rise in the early 2000s, began to decline in 2007. The government of Kazakhstan reported that as of 1 January 2008 defaults on construction debts were 1.39%, and mortgage defaults were 0.33%.

The CIA reported that as of 2008, 90% of the rural population and 99% of the urban population had access to improved drinking water, and that 98% of the rural population and 97% of the urban population had access to improved sanitation facilities.

The housing sector had been mostly privatized as of 2008.

43 EDUCATION

In 2009 the World Bank estimated that 89% of age-eligible children in Kazakhstan were enrolled in primary school. Secondary enrollment for age-eligible children stood at 89%. Tertiary enrollment was estimated at 41%. Of those enrolled in tertiary education, there were 100 male students for every 144 female students. Overall, the CIA estimated that Kazakhstan had a literacy rate of 99.5%. Public expenditure on education represented 2.8% of GDP.

Both at the primary and secondary level, education is free and state funded. Although Russian is the most commonly taught language, Kazakh, which is the official state language, is now gaining popularity and is being extended to all areas. A small percentage of students are also taught Uzbek, Uighur, and Tajik. Most children are enrolled in a kindergarten program at age six. This is followed by four years of primary school and five years of basic secondary studies. Students may then choose to continue in a two-year academic school, a two-year vocational school, or a four-year professional school. The academic year runs from September to June.

The US State Department reported that 107,543 students graduated from Khazakhstan high schools in 2010 and completed the United National Testing. Students who earn 50 out of 100 points on the testing are qualified to apply to local universities and other higher educational institutions. There were approximately 150 higher educational facilities in Kazakhstan in 2009, including 53 public institutions. Enrollment in these institutions was 620,442 in 2009.

In addition, Kazakhstan supported 494 private and state-funded vocational colleges, which had an estimated enrollment 490,997 students. The government also established in 1993 the Bolashak Scholarship that funded the education of Kazakhstan students in colleges and universities abroad, with a requirement that recipients return to Kazakhstan and work for five years after completing their education. Between 1994 and 2010, the government awarded 7,356 scholarships.

Major universities in Kazakhstan are: the University of Al-Farabi State Kazak University, which offeres history, philosophy, economics, sociology, journalism, mathematics, physics, chemistry, biology, and geography; Karaganda State University, which offers philosophy, economics, law, history, mathematics, physics, chemistry, and biology; and the Technical University at Karaganda Metallurgical Combine, which has faculties of metallurgy, mechanics and technology, and chemical technology.

44 LIBRARIES AND MUSEUMS

The National Library of the Republic of Kazakhstan in Almaty held 5.5 million volumes, and a new national library was being built as of 2009 in Astany. Other libraries are the Scientific and Technical Library of Kazakhstan also in Almaty (22.3 million volumes), and the Central Library of the Kazak Academy of Science (6.2 million volumes). The Al-Farabi Kazak State University Library in Almaty has 1.5 million volumes. Kazakhstan has an extensive public library system. The Pushkin Regional Public Library in East Kazakhstan is regarded as the oldest public library in the nation, with over 700,000 items, and a major cultural center for the region. The Karaganda Regional Public Library contains about 440,369 items.

Kazakhstan has dozens of museums. The Central State Museum of Kazakhstan in Almaty features 90,000 exhibits exploring the history and physical conditions of the region. The A. Kasteyer Kazak State Art Museum (formerly the Kazak T.G. Shevchenko State Art Gallery) in Almaty primarily contains works of Russian and Kazak artists from the 15th to 20th centuries. There are regional and general interest museums throughout the country. The Museum of Political Repression opened in June 2011 to document Soviet-era political repression of the 1930s, during which an estimated 4 million people from the Kazakh Soviet Socialist Republic were sent to prison camps in political purges led by Josef Stalin.

45 MEDIA

In 2009 the CIA reported that there were 3.8 million telephone landlines in Kazakhstan. In addition to landlines, mobile phone subscriptions averaged 94 per 100 people. There were 617 AM radio stations, and 9 shortwave radio stations. Internet users numbered 33 per 100 citizens.

In 2010 the country had 53,984 Internet hosts. As of 2009, there were some 5.2 million Internet users in Kazakhstan.

Although the constitution provides for freedom of speech and the press, the government has used laws, harassment practices, licensing regulations and other restrictions to control the media. State ownership of media is estimated at 20%. National laws prohibit insults to the president, president's family, and senior officials. A 2009 government tender put all radio frequencies in major cities and regions in the hands of one government-favored company. A similar government tender in 2008 was conducted for new television frequency licenses.

46 ORGANIZATIONS

The major economic organizations in Kazakhstan are the Union of the Chambers of Commerce and Industry of the Republic of Kazakhstan and the Union of Cooperative Entrepreneurs. The Zhardem International Charitable Fund promotes public interest in science and culture and operates cultural and educational centers for children and teenagers. There are many professional associations dedicated to research and education in the fields of medicine and other sciences. The Republican Council of Women's Organizations, established in 1985, promotes economic and social equality for women. National youth organizations include the Association of Young Leaders, Kazakhstan Youth Forum, and the Union of Youth of Kazakhstan. There are several sports associations and clubs for both youth and adult amateur athletes. There are national chapters of the Red Crescent Society and Caritas.

47 TOURISM, TRAVEL, AND RECREATION

The *Tourism Factbook*, published by the UN World Tourism Organization, reported 4.72 million incoming tourists to Kazakhstan in 2009, who spent a total of $1.18 billion. There were 49,849 hotel beds available in Kazakhstan, which had an occupancy rate of 20%. The estimated daily cost to visit Astana, the capital, was $365. The cost of visiting other cities averaged $236.

Almaty remains Kazakhstan's business and travel hub. Travelers arrive via Frankfurt, Amsterdam, London, Istanbul, Dubai, and Moscow, among other connecting cities. Direct service to the capital Astana is offered from Vienna, Moscow, Istanbul, and the United Arab Emirates. A high-speed overnight train runs between Almaty and Astana.

Kazakhstan offers a wide variety of natural landscapes to the hardier traveler, ranging from forests and mountain ranges to the vast steppes where Kazakh nomads live in tents called yurts and race thoroughbred horses and camels. The old capital, Almaty (Kazakh for "mountain of apples"), has no historic attractions but is an attractive city where tree-lined streets, parks, fountains, and canals give it a European flavor. In the winter, ice skating is popular on its waterways. Kazakhstan is open to both business travelers and tourists.

On 6 July 2010, Kazakhstan celebrated the grand opening of the world's tallest tent—a 150-m (490-ft) high structure that is designed to provide year-round recreational opportunities for residents. The tent, which was erected in Astana and opened on the 13th anniversary of the city's tenure as Kazakhstan's capital, was hailed as an engineering wonder that protects residents from Astana's notoriously harsh climate. The tent is Astana's tallest overall structure and contains a recreational park, an artificial beach, movie theatres, restaurants, and shops.

Kazakhstan requires visitors from the United States to register upon arrival through the 12 international airports, or the railway border point at Dostyk. Proof of registration is supplied through a migration card and is valid for three months.

Registration also was done at automobile border checkpoints in Khorgos, Dostyk Bakhty, Maikapchagai, Kordai, and Kolzhat, and at the seaports of Aktau and Bautino.

48 FAMOUS PERSONS

Nursultan A. Nazarbayev (b. 1940) was elected president of Kazakhstan in December 1991. Sergey Tereshchenko, Akezhan Kazhegeldin, Imangali Tasmagambetov, and Daniyal Akhmetov have each served as prime minister since independence in 1991. Abay Ibragin Kunanbayev (1845–1904) is internationally known as a 19th century humanist and poet, and is considered the founder of modern Kazakh literature. Writer Mukhtar Auezov (1897–1961) wrote *Abay,* a novel about steppe life that was translated into English. The novelist Kaltay Muhamedjanov is from Kazakhstan.

49 DEPENDENCIES

Kazakhstan has no territories or colonies.

50 BIBLIOGRAPHY

George, Alexandra. *Journey into Kazakhstan: The True Face of the Nazarbayev Regime.* Lanham, MD: University Press of America, 2001.

Kazakhstan Investment and Business Guide: Strategic and Practical Information. Washington, DC: International Business Publications USA, 2012.

Kort, Michael. *Central Asian Republics.* New York: Facts On File, 2004.

Markus, Ustina, Didar Kassymova, et al. *Historical Dictionary of Kazakhstan.* Lanham, MD: Scarecrow Press, 2012.

Nazpary, Joma. *Post-Soviet Chaos: Violence and Dispossession in Kazakhstan.* Sterling, Va.: Pluto Press, 2002.

Nysanbayev, Abdumalik. *Kazakhstan: Cultural Inheritance and Social Transformation.* Washington, DC: Council for Research in Values and Philosophy, 2004.

Olcott, Martha Brill. *Kazakhstan: Unfulfilled Promise.* Washington, DC: Carnegie Endowment for International Peace, 2002.

Peck, Anne E. *Economic Development in Kazakhstan: The Role of Large Enterprises and Foreign Investment.* New York: Routledge-Curzon, 2004.

KIRIBATI

Republic of Kiribati

CAPITAL: Tarawa

FLAG: Above a blue and white heraldic representation of Pacific waters, a golden sun rises against a red background, with a golden frigate bird at the top.

ANTHEM: *Troika kain Kiribati (Stand Kiribati).*

MONETARY UNIT: The Australian dollar (AUD) is the national currency. AUD1 = US$0.980603 (or US$1 = AUD1.01978) as of 2011.

WEIGHTS AND MEASURES: Kiribati is in transition from imperial to metric standards.

HOLIDAYS: New Year's Day, 1 January; Independence Day, 12 July; Youth Day, 4 August; Christmas Day, 25 December; Boxing Day, 26 December. Movable holidays include Good Friday, Easter, Easter Monday, Queen's Birthday (June), Bank Holiday (August), and Prince of Wales's Birthday (November).

TIME: Midnight = noon GMT.

¹LOCATION, SIZE, AND EXTENT

Kiribati (pronounced "Kiribass") consists of 33 islands in the central Pacific, situated around the point where the International Date Line intersects the equator. Scattered over more than 5 million sq km (2 million sq mi) of ocean are the 17 islands of the Gilbert group (including Banaba, formerly Ocean Island); the 8 Line Islands (including Christmas Island); and the 8 Phoenix Islands. The distance between Christmas Island in the E and Banaba in the W is more than 3,200 km (2,000 mi). Kiribati's total land area is 811 sq km (313 sq mi), and its total coastline is 1,143 km (710 mi). Comparatively, the land area occupied by Kiribati is about four times the size of Washington, DC.

Kiribati's capital city, Tarawa, is located on the island of Tarawa.

²TOPOGRAPHY

Kiribati is made up of three island groups. From west to east, they are: the Gilbert Islands (running NW-SE across the equator), the Phoenix Islands (clustered just south of the equator), and the Line Islands (running NNW-SSE across the equator). Most of the islands are coral atolls built on a submerged volcanic chain. Christmas Island is the largest atoll in the world, with an area of 606 sq km (234 sq mi). The highest point of the country is an unnamed point on the island of Banaba, which reaches a peak of 81 m (266 ft). The lowest point is at sea level (Pacific Ocean).

³CLIMATE

Tempered by prevailing easterly trade winds, the islands have a maritime equatorial climate, with high humidity during the November–April rainy season. Although the islands lie outside the tropical hurricane belt, there are occasional gales and even tornadoes. Rainfall varies from an average of 102 cm (40 in) near the equator to 305 cm (120 in) in the extreme north and south.

Severe droughts can also occur. On average, there is less than 1% variation between the cool and hot months, but daily temperatures range from 25 to 32°C (77 to 90°F), with an annual mean temperature of 27°C (81°F).

⁴FLORA AND FAUNA

The World Resources Institute estimates that there are 60 plant species in Kiribati. In addition, Kiribati is home to 1 mammal, 50 bird, and 6 reptile species. The calculation reflects the total number of distinct species residing in the country, not the number of endemic species.

Only babai (a kind of taro root), coconut palms, and pandanus trees grow easily on most islands. Pigs and poultry were probably introduced by Europeans. Sea life abounds.

⁵ENVIRONMENT

In 1992, the United Nations (UN) Report for Pacific Island Developing Countries identified the most significant environmental problems facing Kiribati, along with the other nations in this area of the world, as global warming and rising sea levels. Most of the nation rises only about 4 m (13 ft) above sea level, leaving the islands particularly vulnerable to rising sea levels associated with global climate change. Without the financial resources necessary to physically adapt to the change, the government has begun to promote education and job skills courses to prepare citizens for the possibility of international relocation. Local officials have called for the governments of Australia and New Zealand to offer financial assistance in the form of an adaptation fund that could be used for measures such as the construction of sea walls. Both nations would be the most likely destination of Kiribati immigrants should relocation be necessary.

Kiribati, along with the other nations in the area, is vulnerable to earthquakes and volcanic activity.

Top officials from Kiribati and thirteen other developing Pacific island nations and dependencies met in Vanuatu in 2010 to discuss the progress made in areas relating to sustainable development. At the summit, which was backed by the United Nations, participants attempted to streamline and concentrate efforts to address some of the issues unique to these low-lying, developing island states. These issues included climate change, sea-level rise, natural disasters, remoteness from major markets, and poverty. Another key objective of the meeting was to address the progress each nation had made in adopting the 2005 Mauritius Strategy, the only global blueprint that exists to combat the development challenges of small-island developing states.

There are several other environmental challenges facing Kiribati. The nation has inadequate facilities for handling solid waste, which has been a major environmental concern, particularly in the larger population centers. The lagoon of the southern Tarawa atoll has also been heavily polluted by solid waste disposal. Like other Pacific islands, Kiribati is sensitive to the dangers of pollution and radiation from weapons tests and nuclear waste disposal. The environment has also been adversely affected by metals and chemicals from mining activities, and agricultural chemicals have polluted coastal waters. The effects of phosphate mining have been especially devastating, rendering the island of Banaba almost uninhabitable. The Banabans, who were forced to move to the Fijian island of Rabi, sued the owners of the mines and won special compensation. Called the Phosphate Revenue Equalization Fund (PREF), in 1996 it amounted to AUD200 million.

Water pollution and occasional seasons of drought have led to water shortages in the past. Per capita water usage has been estimated at about 35 cu m (1,236 cu ft) per year.

The UN reported in 2008 that carbon dioxide emissions in Kiribati totaled 33 kilotons.

The World Resources Institute reported that Kiribati had designated 60,000 hectares (148,263 acres) of land for protection as of 2006. A region of 191,659 sq km (A 74,000 sq mi) comprising the Phoenix Islands and the surrounding coral reefs has been designated by the government as a marine reserve, making it the third largest of its kind in the world. Commercial fishing is banned in the reserve, which supports 120 species of coral and 520 species of fish. It is the first marine park to feature underwater mountains. The government receives funds from Conservation International and the New England Aquarium to cover some management expenses and to compensate for lost fishing revenues.

The UN report describes the wildlife in these areas as "among the most critically threatened in the world." According to a 2007 report issued by the International Union for Conservation of Nature and Natural Resources (IUCN), threatened species included 5 species of birds, 1 type of reptile, 6 species of fish, and 1 type of mollusk. Endangered species included the green sea turtle, the coconut crab, the giant grouper, the tiger shark, the pygmy killer whale, and the mukojima bonin honeyeater.

6 POPULATION

The US Central Intelligence Agency (CIA) estimated the population of Kiribati in 2011 to be approximately 100,743, which placed it at number 183 in population among the 196 nations of the world. In 2011, approximately 3.7% of the population was over 65 years of age, with another 33.9% under 15 years of age. The median age in Kiribati was 22.5 years. There were 0.97 males for every female in the country. The population's annual rate of change was 1.249%. The projected population for the year 2025 was 130,000. Population density in Kiribati was calculated at 124 people per sq km (321 people per sq mi).

The UN estimated that 44% of the population lived in urban areas and that urban populations had an annual rate of change of 1.9%. The largest urban area was Tarawa, with a population of 43,000.

Overcrowding is a problem in some areas of the nation, particularly in an around the capital of Tarawa. During 1988–93, some 4,700 people were resettled on the Teraira and Tabuaeran atolls of the Line Islands because of overcrowding on the main island group. During the 2000s, Kiribati planned to develop new urban centers on the outer islands in an effort to redistribute some of the population. The program had the backing of the Asian Development Bank and the United Nations Development Program and was aimed at reducing the flow of population to Tarawa.

7 MIGRATION

Estimates of Kiribati's net migration rate, carried out by the CIA in 2011, amounted to -2.85 migrants per 1,000 citizens. The total number of emigrants living abroad was 6,400, and the total number of immigrants living in Kiribati was 2,000. For the islanders, migration has been a perennial form of escape from drought and starvation. In the 19th century, recruiting ships forcibly took Gilbert Islanders for plantation work in Hawaii, Australia, Fiji, and Peru; some voluntarily reenlisted after the great drought of 1870. Although the majority eventually returned home, it is reckoned that between 1860 and 1890, some 10,000 islanders (of a total population of 30,000) were living overseas. In the 20th century, Fiji and the Solomon Islands continued to be popular places for Gilbert Islanders in search of work. Internal migration until 1979 was mainly to Banaba Island for work in the phosphate industry; since then, migration has been primarily to Nauru or to copra plantations in the Line Islands.

8 ETHNIC GROUPS

About 98.8% of the people are Gilbertese of Micronesian extraction. Polynesians, mainly from Tuvalu, make up 0.5% of the total; Europeans and people of mixed races make up 0.7%.

9 LANGUAGES

The principal languages spoken are Gilbertese, also called I-Kiribati or Kiribatese, and English. The official language is English, but it is seldom used on the outer islands. Gilbertese is an Austronesian language related to many other Pacific tongues.

10 RELIGIONS

Christian missionaries first arrived in 1857 when Dr. Hiram Bingham of the American Board of Foreign Missionaries began to spread Protestantism in the northern Gilberts with the help of Hawaiian pastors. In 1888, Catholicism was introduced to the islands by the Sacred Heart Mission. The American Board withdrew from the territory in 1917 and was succeeded by the London

Missionary Society which had placed Samoan pastors on the islands as early as 1870.

Virtually the entire population is Christian. According to the 2005 census, 55% of all residents are Roman Catholics and 36% belong to the Kiribati Protestant Church, formerly called the Congregational Church. Religious minorities include the Church of Jesus Christ of Latter-Day Saints (3%), the Seventh-Day Adventists (2%), and Baha'is (2%). Less than 1% of the population claimed no religious preference. The constitution provides for freedom of religion, and this right is generally respected in practice. Christmas, Easter, and National Gospel Day are celebrated as national holidays.

11 TRANSPORTATION

The remoteness of the scattered islands has severely hampered transport and communications. There are only about 670 km (416 mi) of roads, mostly on Tarawa. The Nippon Causeway, completed in 1987 with Japanese assistance, replaced ferry service between Betio and Bariki. A series of similar causeways links north and south Tarawa. In 2009, there were 70 vehicles per 1,000 people in the country.

There is no formal rail, river, or lake transport, although canoes travel freely on the lagoons. As of 2007, Kiribati had approximately 5 km (3.1 mi) of navigable waterways, primarily on the Line Islands. The main ports are located on Betio islet, near Tarawa, and on Tabuaeran and Christmas islands. Betio is equipped for handling containers, and Banaba has a cantilever for phosphate loading. In 2010, Kiribati had 71 ships of 1,000 GRT (gross registered tons) or over in the merchant marine fleet. A number of shipping lines call at the islands, and government boats provide interisland service. In 2010, there were 19 airports, of which 4 had paved runways. All the major islands have airstrips; the airports on Christmas Island and at Bonriki (Tarawa) are used for scheduled overseas flights. Air Tungaru, the national airline, operates regularly scheduled flights to Honolulu and Tuvalu.

12 HISTORY

The main wave of Micronesian settlement is thought to have come from Samoa in the 13th century, but Gilbertese tradition suggests that the Samoans were not the first settlers. European discovery dates from 1537, when Christmas Island was sighted by Spanish explorers. The English sea captain James Cook encountered the islands in 1777, and commercial activities in the region began early in the 19th century. The Gilbert Islands were a favorite whaling ground, and deserting crews began to settle on the islands in the 1830s. Trading ships were calling there regularly by the 1850s, and a flourishing copra and coconut trade was established by the 1860s, as well as an illicit human trafficking industry. The Office of British High Commissioner to the Western Pacific was created in 1877 to help suppress abuses by recruiting ships seeking labor for overseas service.

In 1888, Christmas, Fanning (now Tabuaeran), and Washington (now Teraina) islands were annexed by the British, and Phoenix Island was placed under their protection. A declaration of British protectorate over the Gilbert and Ellice groups followed in 1892. A handful of administrators established local native governments, and a period of stability ensued. Ocean Island was annexed by Britain in 1900 following Sir Albert Ellis's discovery of

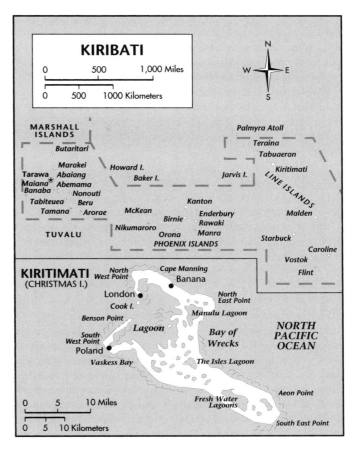

LOCATION: 4°N to 3°S; 168° to 176° E. TOTAL COASTLINE: 1,143 kilometers (710 miles). TERRITORIAL SEA LIMIT: 12 miles.

its valuable phosphate deposits. The Gilbert and Ellice groups (including Ocean, Fanning, and Washington islands) were declared a British colony in 1916. British control was extended to Christmas Island in 1919 and to the uninhabited Phoenix group in 1937, but after the United States laid claim to Canton and Enderbury, a joint British-American administration over these islands was established. During World War II, the Gilberts were occupied by Japanese forces until 1943, when the invaders were driven out by US forces after heavy casualties on both sides. Ocean Island was liberated by the Australians in 1945.

In a 1974 referendum, the Ellice Islands voted for separation, subsequently becoming the independent nation of Tuvalu. Internal self-government for the Gilberts was established as of 1 January 1977, and the islands became the independent Republic of Kiribati on 12 July 1979. In September 1979, the new nation signed a treaty of friendship with the United States (ratified by the US Senate in 1983), by which the United States relinquished its claim to the Line and Phoenix groups (including Canton, Enderbury, and Malden).

Ieremia Tabai, chief minister at the time of independence, became president of the new republic in 1979 and was reelected in 1982 and 1987. In 1991, Tabai stepped down and was replaced by Teatao Teannaki, head of the National Progressive Party. In 1994, the government of Kiribati underwent a crisis when President Teannaki was forced to resign following a no-confidence vote by the opposition in parliament, having been charged with misusing travel funds. Teburoro Tito was elected president in September 1994 and served until 2003. Within the first few months of his third term, Tito's government was toppled by a vote of no-confidence in the opposition-controlled parliament. In July 2003, Anote Tong was elected president.

Long-term elevation of the surrounding sea level due to global greenhouse emissions remains a serious concern for Kiribati, which reportedly has already lost two uninhabited islands and has been forced to move segments of its population inland, away from coastal regions.

13 GOVERNMENT

Under the independence constitution of 1979, Kiribati is a democratic republic within the Commonwealth of Nations. It has a 45-member unicameral assembly, the Maneaba ni Maungatabu. Forty-three members are elected for four-year terms, one appointed seat is reserved for a representative of the Banaban community, and the attorney general sits ex-officio as a nonelected member of parliament. The speaker is elected to office by members of parliament but is not a member of parliament. He has neither an original nor casting vote in parliamentary decisions.

After each legislative election, the newly seated parliament chooses three or four presidential candidates from its own membership. The president (*beretitenti*), who is both head of state and head of government, is then elected directly by popular vote for a term of up to four years. The president may serve a total of three terms. When the president no longer enjoys the confidence of the legislature, the parliament is dissolved and new parliamentary and presidential elections are held, with a Council of State (consisting of the head of the Civil Service Commission, the chief justice, and the speaker of the house) governing in the interim. The cabinet consists of the president, vice president, attorney general, and no more than 10 other ministers selected from parliament.

Anote Tong was elected president in 2003 and reelected in 2007 and 2012, with Teima Onorio serving as his vice president.

14 POLITICAL PARTIES

Kiribati has no formally organized political parties. But political organizations similar to parties have formed around common interests or in response to specific issues. In 1985, opponents of a controversial Soviet fishing agreement founded the Christian Democratic party, headed by Dr. Harry Tong. Other parties that formed after 1991 include the Boutokaan te Koaua Party (BTK); the Liberal Party; the New Movement Party; and the Health Peace and Honour Party.

As of 2011, the primary existing parties included the BTK, the Maneaban Te Mauri Party (MTM), the Maurin Kiribati Pati (MKP) and the National Progressive Party (NPP).

Anote Tong of the BTK won the 2003 presidential election. He was reelected for a second term in 2007 with 63.7% of the vote, and for a third term on 13 January 2012, with 42% of the vote.

15 LOCAL GOVERNMENT

There are fully elected local councils on all the islands in accordance with the local government ordinance of 1966. For administrative purposes the islands are divided into six districts: Tarawa (including the Phoenix group), Banaba, the Central Gilberts, the Line Islands, the Northern Gilberts, and the Southern Gilberts.

This structure has been further divided into 21 island councils, one for each of the inhabited islands. The geographic dispersion of the islands leaves considerable freedom for the districts; their councils have wide taxing powers, including the ability to tax land and draw up their own estimates of revenues and expenditures.

16 JUDICIAL SYSTEM

The 1979 constitution provides for a High Court with a chief justice and other judges, acting as the supreme court. There is also a court of appeal and magistrates' courts. Island courts were established in 1965 to deal with civil and criminal offenses. Native land courts have jurisdiction over property claims. The High Court and Court of Appeal judges are appointed by the president.

The judiciary is independent and free from government influence. Civil rights and civil liberties are guaranteed in the constitution and respected in practice. Procedural due process safeguards are based on British common law. Trials are fair and public. There is no trial by jury. The law prohibits arbitrary interference with privacy, family, home, and correspondence. The government authorities respect these provisions.

17 ARMED FORCES

Legislation providing for the establishment of a defense force of 170 men was repealed in 1978. Since then the nation has no standing military forces. Australia and New Zealand provide defense assistance. There is a small police force.

18 INTERNATIONAL COOPERATION

Kiribati was admitted to the United Nations (UN) on 14 September 1999 and is a member of several nonregional specialized agencies, including the FAO, ICAO, the World Bank, IMF, IFC, ILO, UNESCO, and WHO.

Kiribati participates in the Asian Development Bank, the ACP Group, the Pacific Island Forum, and the Alliance of Small Island States (AOSIS). The nation is also part of the Organization for the Prohibition of Chemical Weapons.

In environmental cooperation, Kiribati is part of the Basel Convention, the Convention on Biological Diversity, the London Convention, the Kyoto Protocol, the Montréal Protocol, and the UN Conventions on the Law of the Sea, Climate Change, and Desertification.

Kiribati opposes French nuclear testing in the Pacific and signed the 1985 Raratonga Agreement declaring the South Pacific a nuclear-free zone.

19 ECONOMY

Other than the sea, the nation has few natural resources. Its principal resource, phosphate, was already depleted by the time the nation became independent. However, the government still relies on funds drawn from the Revenue Equalization Reserve Fund, a trust fund established with phosphate earnings during peak production years. In 2009 the fund was worth approximately $500 million.

The government receives substantial revenues from licensing fees from the foreign fishing fleets of South Korea, Japan, Taiwan, China, and the United States. However, the nation also loses a significant amount each year from illegal, unlicensed, and unreported fishing operations in its difficult-to-patrol exclusive economic zone.

Only about 10% of the workforce participates in the formal wage and salary economy, and the majority of formal jobs are located in South Tarawa. A large portion of the nation's income is from foreign sources, such as remittances and development assistance from foreign governments.

The government has turned to tourism as a potential growth sector. However, economic development is constrained by the remote locale of the islands, a shortage of skilled workers, and a lack of infrastructure. As of 2009, the service sector accounted for 63.4% of the GDP and industry accounted for 9.15%. The gross domestic product (GDP) rate of change in Kiribati, as of 2010, was 1.8%. Inflation stood at 0.2%,

20 INCOME

The CIA estimated that in 2010 the GDP of Kiribati was $618 million. The CIA defines GDP as the value of all final goods and services produced within a nation in a given year and computed on the basis of purchasing power parity (PPP) rather than value as measured on the basis of the rate of the exchange based on current dollars. The per capita GDP was estimated at $6,200. The annual growth rate of GDP was 1.8%. The average inflation rate was 0.2% for 2009, and it was estimated that agriculture accounted for 27.4% of GDP, industry 9.15%, and services 63.4%.

According to the World Bank, remittances from citizens living abroad totaled $8.2 million or about $81 per capita and accounted for approximately 1.3% of GDP.

21 LABOR

Only about 10% of the population is employed earning salaries or regular wages and these people are primarily employed within the government sector. Official estimates place the unemployment rate at about 2%, but a much larger percentage of people are underemployed. Within the formal economy, the CIA estimates that 2.7% were employed in agriculture, 32% in industry, and 65.3% in the service sector. However, the percentage of those working in subsistence farming and fishing is considered to be much higher.

A small number of seasonal workers are officially sent to Australia each year, but the government has been negotiating with Australia to allow for a higher number of such workers. In 2011, only sixteen workers were expected to participate in Australia's seasonal worker scheme with Kiribati. The Kiribati government would like to increase the yearly number to 1,000.

In urban areas there is a small but strong trade union movement. Affiliates of the Kiribati Trades Union Congress (KTUC), founded in 1982 with Australian assistance, include the Fishermen's Union, the Cooperative Workers' Union, the Seamen's Union, the Teachers' Union, and the Public Employees' Association. Workers have the right to strike but rarely exercise this option. The government does not interfere with union activity. In 2005, about 10% of all wage earners were union members.

There is no statutory minimum wage; however, the government sets wage levels in the large public sector, which is the major employer in the cash economy. For others, the unofficial minimum wage is somewhere between $1.60 and $1.70 per hour. The unofficial standard workweek for those in the public sector was 36.25 hours, with overtime pay for any additional hours. Children may not work under the age of 14. This is effectively enforced by the government in the modern industrial sector of the economy, but many children do perform light labor in the traditional fishing economy.

22 AGRICULTURE

Out of 81,000 hectares (200,155 acres) of land in Kiribati, 2,000 hectares (4,942 acres) are arable. Roughly 42% of the total land is farmed. Official estimates place the number of people involved in formal agriculture at about 2.7%. These citizens are primarily engaged in work at coconut plantations. However, most residents are occupied in some level of substance farming. The primary commercial agricultural product is copra (dried coconut meat), which accounts for about two-thirds of total export revenues. Other crops include taro, breadfruit, sweet potatoes, and vegetables. In 2007, fruit production amounted to 8,591 tons and vegetable production to 6,233 tons. Overseas technical aid has allowed some islands to cultivate bananas and papaws for the Tarawa market.

In the wake of the 2008–09 global recession, food security became a problem for many residents of the country's outer islands, who account for about 60% of Kiribati's population. These islanders rely heavily on imported food due to their isolated location. With an increase in food prices, most residents were spending over half of their income on food. In June 2011, the World Bank agreed to send $2 million to the outlying Kiribati islands in relief.

23 ANIMAL HUSBANDRY

The islands do not have the resources necessary to sustain large-scale livestock production, but islanders do raise pigs, chickens, and goats for local consumption. The most recent estimates (2005) place the number of pigs maintained on the islands at more than 12,000. The Agricultural Division has introduced some improved breeds that are most suitable for the local environment.

24 FISHING

Sea fishing is excellent, particularly for skipjack tuna around the Phoenix Islands. Kiribati has one of the world's largest maritime zones, covering approximately three million sq km. Commercial fishing has expanded dramatically since 1979 as a result of projects funded by Japan, the United Kingdom, and the EU. Tuna is by far the most popular catch. Seaweed, pet fish, and shark fins are also exported. In 2008, the annual capture totaled 34,300 tons according to the FAO of the United Nations. Exports of fish products were valued at US$4.26 million in 2003.

Kiribati also receives revenue from the sale of licenses permitting foreign vessels to fish its offshore waters. Fishing fleets from South Korea, Japan, China, Taiwan, and the United States provide license revenues valued between $20 million and $35 million per year. However, it is believed that the nation loses millions of dollars each year from illegal, unlicensed fishing operations since the government does not have sufficient resources to properly police its territorial waters.

In March 2010, President Anote Tong met with fellow members of Parties of the Nauru Agreement (PNA) for their first presidential summit. The PNA was established in 1982 and is comprised of the nations of Palau, Micronesia, the Marshall Islands, Tuvalu, Kiribati, Papua New Guinea, Nauru, and the Solomon Islands. The purpose of the group is to work together for the conservation and management of tuna resources within their exclusive economic zones (EEZ). At the March meeting, which has been called the

Tuna Summit, members adopted the Koror Declaration, which aims, among other things, to establish cooperative management practices that will enhance commercial and economic opportunities for member states and to work toward the conservation and restoration of migratory tuna stocks. The waters of the PNA nations account for nearly 60% of all tuna catches in the western and central Pacific Ocean and 25% of the global tuna catches that supply canneries and processing facilities around the world.

25 FORESTRY

According to 2009 estimates, approximately 15% of Kiribati is covered by forest, but there is little useful timber on the islands.

26 MINING

There has been no mining in Kiribati since the closing of the Banaba phosphate industry in 1979. In its last year of operation, 445,700 tons of phosphates worth US$18 million were exported.

27 ENERGY AND POWER

Kiribati has no known reserves of oil, natural gas, or coal. Thus imports are relied upon to meet any fossil fuel needs.

In 2002, imports and consumption of refined petroleum products each averaged 210 barrels per day. There were no imports of coal or natural gas in 2002.

The government maintains electricity-generating plants on Tarawa and Christmas Island, and there are private generators on Banaba and several other islands. The World Bank reported in 2008 that Kiribati produced 22 million kWh of electricity. Estimates from the CIA place total consumption of electricity at 13.02 million kWh in 2007. Nearly all of the electric power was generated from fossil fuels. Solar power is used on some of the outer islands, but annual production of solar energy is less than 1% of the overall total.

28 INDUSTRY

According to 2009 estimates from the US Department of State, industry accounts for about 2.9% of the GDP. Most of the sector involves tuna processing and handicrafts. Some local industries have also included soft drink manufacturing, small boat-building shops, construction, furniture manufacturing, repair garages, bakeries, and laundries.

29 SCIENCE AND TECHNOLOGY

The World Bank reported in 2009 that there were no patent applications in science and technology in Kiribati. The Foundation for the Peoples of the South Pacific, founded in 1982 and located at Bairiki, Tarawa, provides technical assistance for agriculture and nutrition programs. Christmas Island is host to a Japanese Aerospace Exploration Agency tracking and monitoring station. The government of Australia has provided assistance in a variety of research and development programs for the nation, particularly those involving agriculture.

30 DOMESTIC TRADE

The domestic economy operates on a subsistence and barter basis. With very few local production or agricultural facilities, the nation relies heavily on imported goods of all types. Retail sales are handled by cooperative societies, which distribute the bulk of consumer goods and perform all merchandising functions not dealt with by the government. Although private trade is growing, cooperatives are preferred as a matter of public policy because they are closer to the local tradition than individual enterprises.

31 FOREIGN TRADE

The loss of the phosphate industry, copra price fluctuations, and the islands' remoteness have hindered overseas trade. Copra accounted for over 60% of total domestic exports in 2011. Coconut oil, fish, and seaweed were also exported. Kiribati's main export partners are Japan, Malaysia, Taiwan, the United States, Australia, Belgium, and Denmark. In 2009, Kiribati exported $33 million in goods and services. Kiribati relies heavily on imports to meet a wide array of consumer demands, including food and beverages, machinery, manufactured goods, fuel oil, and transport equipment. In 2009, the nation imported $74.5 million worth of goods and services. Major import partners in 2009 were Australia, Fiji, Japan, New Zealand, the United States, China, and Taiwan. Kiribati is a signatory to the South Pacific Agreement on Regional Trade (SPARTECA), which allows duty-free access to Australian and New Zealand Markets, and to the Pacific Islands Trade Agreement, which promotes the liberalization of trade in goods among member countries.

32 BALANCE OF PAYMENTS

In 2009, the total value of exports was estimated at US$33.36 million, and the total value of imports was estimated at US$74.54 million, resulting in a trade deficit of US$41.18 million. Continued deficits in the trade balance are often met by grants from the United Kingdom to the government's current and capital accounts. Foreign aid, in fact, accounts for between 25% and 50% of GDP.

33 BANKING AND SECURITIES

The Bank of Kiribati (ANZ Kiribati) in Tarawa is jointly owned by the Australia and New Zealand Banking group (75%) and the government of Kiribati (25%). It is the only commercial bank in the nation, sponsoring three branches on Tarawa and one on Christmas Island. The Development Bank of Kiribati opened in 1986 and lends to small businesses.

34 INSURANCE

The Kiribati Insurance Corporation provides a variety of insurance products including life, homeowners, fire, and motor vehicle insurance.

35 PUBLIC FINANCE

Local revenues are derived mainly from import duties, fishing fees, and investment income from the phosphate fund. The country has been running a capital account deficit since independence. Overall, budgetary deficits have appeared in recent years, growing substantially in the 1990s.

In 2005, the CIA estimated that the budget of Kiribati included $55.52 million in public revenue and $59.71 million in public expenditures, resulting in a budget deficit of $4.19 million. The budget deficit amounted to 2.8% of GDP. In total $10 million of the debt was held by foreign entities.

³⁶TAXATION

The main source of tax revenue, the phosphate industry, ended in 1979. Other taxes have brought meager returns, except for a copra export tax, with producers protected by a government stabilization fund. The Revenue Equalization Reserve Fund decreased from AUS\$658 million at the end of 2000 to AUS\$500 million at the end of 2009.

A progressive income tax is set at 25% of taxable income between AUS\$1,801 and AUS\$15,000; 30% for income between AUS15,000 and AUS50,000, and 35% on incomes over AUS50,000. Companies are taxed a flat rate of 30% of net profits for the first AUS\$26,001–60,000 and 35% on any net profits of AUS\$50,000 and above.

³⁷CUSTOMS AND DUTIES

Since a single-line tariff was introduced on 1 January 1975, trade preferences are no longer granted to imports from Commonwealth countries. Tariffs, applying mostly to private imports, are imposed as a service of revenue at rates up to 75%. Most duties are levied ad valorem, with specific duties on alcoholic beverages, tobacco, certain chemicals, petroleum, cinematographer's film, and some other goods.

³⁸FOREIGN INVESTMENT

The Foreign Investment Commission (FIC) grants licenses on a case-by-case basis. The commission may grant approval for investment plans with capital output estimated at less than AUS\$250,000; all others must also be approved by the cabinet. Performance criteria regarding employment, training, and production are often set. Certain local industries are closed to foreign investment, including pig farming, poultry farming, millionaire salad exportation, domestic interisland shipping, and wholesaling. Endangered species are protected. Fisheries and the agricultural sector are not closed, but are subject to restrictions. Foreign direct investment (FDI) in Kiribati was a net inflow of \$2.2 million according to World Bank figures published in 2009. FDI represented 1.72% of GDP. The main sources of investments have been the United States, Japan, the United Kingdom, Australia, and New Zealand.

³⁹ECONOMIC DEVELOPMENT

The government lays out National Development Plans at four-year intervals. The key policy areas identified under the Kiribati development Plan 2008–2011 included human resource development, economic growth and poverty reduction, health improvements, environmental sustainability, good governance, and improved infrastructure. Infrastructure development is likely to be a primary concern for the coming years as the government recognizes the need to provide improved and advanced services in order to attract foreign businesses and tourists. Under the category of economic growth, the government hopes to focus on private commercial investment in the production and marketing of marine products and the development of tourism resources.

⁴⁰SOCIAL DEVELOPMENT

The National Provident Fund provides old age, disability, and survivor benefits for all employees over 14 years old, with the exception of domestic workers. It is funded by employee contributions of 7.5%; employers pay an equal percentage of payroll. Retirement is allowed at ages 45–50 and benefits are paid as a lump sum. Workers' compensation is available for some employed persons and the cost is covered by the employer. A funeral grant is provided if there are no eligible survivors.

Women are accorded the same legal rights as men, but have traditionally been relegated to a subordinate role in society. However, women are gradually breaking out of their traditional role and entering both skilled and unskilled occupations. In 2005, about 56% of all professionals were women, primarily holding jobs as teachers and nurses. There have also been signs of affirmative action in government hiring and promotions. There is no law prohibiting sexual harassment, which is believed to be widespread. Domestic violence is a significant problem, and alcohol abuse is often in a factor in violence against women. Child abuse appears to be a growing problem, although the government is committed to the welfare of children. Child prostitution has been a problem as well, due largely to the lack of laws prohibiting prostitution. The legal age of consent is set at 15; however, the reasonable belief that a victim was 15 years or older at the time of sexual relations is a permissible defense for those arrested for statutory rape. Sodomy is illegal.

Overcrowding has become a problem in some towns as new residents come in search of jobs.

⁴¹HEALTH

According to the CIA, life expectancy in Kiribati was 64.39 years in 2011. The fertility rate was 2.78 children born for every woman of childbearing years, while the infant mortality rate was 38.89 deaths per 1,000 live births. The country spent 16.8% of its GDP on healthcare, amounting to \$159 per person. There were 3 physicians, 30 nurses and midwives, and 15 hospital beds per 10,000 inhabitants. It was estimated that 82% of children were vaccinated against measles.

According to the World Health Organization, approximately 90% of births are attended by skilled health personnel. According to data from the Population Reference Bureau, an estimated 36% percent of married women ages 15-49 used some form of contraception, and an estimated 31% used modern contraceptive methods.

⁴²HOUSING

Most Kiribatians live in small villages of 10 to 150 houses and construct their own dwellings from local materials. The use of more permanent building materials, such as concrete with corrugated aluminum roofing, is becoming common in urban areas. Loans to prospective homeowners are provided by the National Loans Board. Dwellings range from traditional houses with thatched roofs to nontraditional houses with metal roofs. At the 2005 census, there were 13,999 private households recorded, along with 43 non-private dwellings (including hospitals, hostels, prisons, dormitories, and meeting houses). The average household size was estimated at 6.3 people. More than 30% of the population lived in households with 10 or more persons; less than 1% lived alone. Open wells and rain water are primary sources of water for a majority of households. Very few households have flush toilets.

[43] EDUCATION

The government has gradually taken over control of primary education from the missions. Education has been made compulsory by the government for children between the ages of 6 and 15. They go through seven years of primary education and five years of secondary education. Secondary enrollment for age-eligible children stood at 69% in 2009. The World Bank estimated that 91% of age-eligible children in Kiribati were enrolled in primary school that same year. The student-to-teacher ratio for primary school stood at 25:1 and at 17:1 for secondary school in 2005. Secondary school pupils take the New Zealand school certificate. The estimated adult literacy rate is 92%.

Higher education courses are available at the Kiribati Extension Center of the University of the South Pacific (Fiji) in Tarawa. Other postsecondary education is provided by scholarships for study abroad. The Tarawa Technical Institute offers instruction in technical and vocational skills. The Japanese-funded Marine Training Center offers 18-month instruction in deck, engine room, and catering work on foreign shipping lines; there are approximately 200 students enrolled in these programs.

[44] LIBRARIES AND MUSEUMS

The National Library and Archives in Tarawa is the largest library in the country with a collection of 50,000 volumes, including those in small units throughout the islands. The University of the South Pacific has a campus in Tarawa with a small library of 5,700 volumes. The Kiribati Library and Information Network was formed in 2001 to promote libraries and the study and profession of library science in the nation. The Kiribati Cultural Centre in Bikenibeu houses the National Museum of Kiribati.

[45] MEDIA

In 2009, there were 4,000 main phone lines. In 2005, about 57% of all households had home phone service. In addition there were 1,000 mobile cell phones in use across the country, or about 1 per 100 people. In 2010, the country had 31 Internet hosts. As of 2009, there were some 7,800 Internet users in Kiribati, accounting for 2.1% of the population. Telecommunications services are provided by the government-owned Telecom Services Kiribati Limited.

Radio Kiribati, operated by the Broadcasting and Publications Authority (BPA), transmits daily in I-Kiribati and English and broadcasts a few imported Australian and New Zealand programs. There was 1 FM radio station, 2 AM radio stations, and 1 shortwave radio station. As of 2005, only 11% of all households owned a television, though more than 60% owned a radio.

There were no national television stations in operation. Kiribati is on the Peacesat network, which provides educational transmissions from Suva. A satellite link with Australia was established in 1985.

The BPA publishes a biweekly bilingual newspaper, *Te Uekera*. There is no commercial press; all publications are government- or church-sponsored. The Information Department at Tarawa publishes *Atoll Pioneer*, a weekly newspaper. *Te Itoi ni Kiribati*, a weekly newsletter, is published by the Roman Catholic Church. The constitution provides for legally guaranteed freedom of speech and press.

[46] ORGANIZATIONS

The most important organization is the *mronron* (meaning "sharing"), a cooperative society based on kinship or locality. There is a national Credit Union League and a teachers' union. The Foundation for the Peoples of the South Pacific—Kiribati works to design and implement programs promoting economic and environmental sustainability at the local level. National youth organizations include the Kiribati Students' Association, the Kiribati Scouts Association, and the Kiribati Girl Guides Associations. Sports clubs and associations represent amateur athletes in a variety of pastimes, including tennis, weightlifting, and track and field. The Kiribati Computer and Internet Society promotes the development of the nation's telecommunications network. There is a national chapter of the Red Cross Society.

[47] TOURISM, TRAVEL, AND RECREATION

Tourism, although important to the economy of Kiribati, is very limited.

In 2009, the islands welcomed about 5,000 visitors. Over 50% of these visitors came from East Asia. Through a new campaign initiated in 2010, the government hoped to boost that annual total to 8,000 or more by 2014, primarily through the promotion of such activities as fishing and surfing. There were 162 hotel rooms in 2002. The estimated daily cost to visit Tarawa, the capital, was $166 in 2010. A valid passport, visa, onward/return ticket, and proof of sufficient funds are required to travel in Kiribati. There is a visitors' bureau at Tarawa, and there are hotels in Betio and on Abemama and Christmas islands. The bureau makes available fishing, swimming, and boating facilities on Tarawa and arranges trips by sea or air to other islands. Ecotourism and World War II battle sites are also attractions.

Popular sports in Kiribati are football (soccer) and weightlifting. Kiribati first competed in the Olympic Games in Athens, Greece, in 2004. Traditional dancing and singing styles have survived.

[48] FAMOUS PERSONS

Ieremia Tabai (b. 1950) was president from independence until 1991. Teburoro Tito (b. 1953) was president and foreign minister from 1994 to 2003. Anote Tong (b. 1952) became president in 2003.

[49] DEPENDENCIES

Kiribati has no territories or colonies.

[50] BIBLIOGRAPHY

Leibo, Steven A. *East and Southeast Asia, 2005*. 38th ed. Harpers Ferry, WV: Stryker-Post Publications, 2005.

Piazza, Anne Di. *Sailing Routes of Old Polynesia: The Prehistoric Discovery, Settlement and Abandonment of the Phoenix Islands*. Honolulu: Bishop Museum Press, 2004.

Smith, George W. *Carlson's Raid: The Daring Marine Assault on Makin*. Novato, CA: Presidio Press, 2001.

Wright, Derrick. *Tarawa, 20–23 November 1943: A Hell of a Way to Die*. Marlborough, Eng.: Crowood Press, 2002.

Wukovits, John F. *One Square Mile of Hell*. New York: NAL Caliber, 2006.

KOREA, DEMOCRATIC PEOPLE'S REPUBLIC OF (DPRK)

Democratic People's Republic of Korea

Choson Minjujuui Inmin Konghwa-guk

CAPITAL: Pyongyang (Pyeongyang)

FLAG: A wide horizontal red stripe is bordered on top and bottom by narrow blue stripes, separated from the red by thin white stripes. The left half of the red stripe contains a red five-pointed star on a circular white field.

ANTHEM: *Aegukka (Patriotic Song).*

MONETARY UNIT: The won (KPW) of 100 ch'on (or jeon) is the national currency. There are coins of 1, 5, 10, and 50 ch'on, and 1 won, and notes of 1, 5, 10, 50, and 100 won. KPW1 = US$0.007407 (or US$1 = KPW135) as of 2011.

WEIGHTS AND MEASURES: The metric system and local Korean units of measurement are used.

HOLIDAYS: New Year's Day; Kim Jung Un's birthday, 8 January; Soellal (Lunar New Year), 23–25 January; Kim Jong Il's anniversary, 16 February; International Woman's Day, 8 March; Kim Il Sung's birthday (Day of the Sun), 15 April; Armed Forces Day, 25 April; May Day (Labor Day), 1 May; Surinal (Spring Festival), 24 June; Victory Day, 27 July; Liberation Day, 15 August; National Foundation Day, 9 September; Han'gawi (Harvest Moon Festival), 30 September; Hangawi holiday, 1–2 October; Founding of Korean Worker's Party, 10 October; Constitution Day, 27 December.

TIME: 9 p.m. = noon GMT.

¹LOCATION, SIZE, AND EXTENT

The Democratic People's Republic of Korea (North Korea—DPRK) occupies the northern 55% of the Korean Peninsula in East Asia. It has an area of 120,540 sq km (46,541 sq mi), extending 719 km (447 mi) NNE–SSW and 371 km (231 mi) ESE–WNW. Comparatively, the area occupied by the DPRK is slightly smaller than the state of Mississippi. It is bordered on the N by China; on the NE by Russia; on the E by the Sea of Japan (including East Korea Bay), known in Korea as the East Sea; on the S by the Republic of Korea (South Korea—ROK); and on the S and W by the Yellow Sea and Korea Bay, with a total land boundary length of 1,673 km (1,040 mi) and a coastline of 2,495 km (1,550 mi). A demilitarized zone (DMZ), 4,000 m (13,100 ft) wide, covering 1,262 sq km (487 sq mi)and located north and south of the 38th parallel, separates the DPRK from the ROK, which occupies the southern part of the Korean Peninsula. The DPRK's capital city, Pyongyang, is located in the southwestern part of the country.

²TOPOGRAPHY

The DPRK is mostly mountainous. Mt. Paektu (2,744 m/9,003 ft), an extinct volcano with a scenic crater lake, is the highest point; it is located on the border with China and forms part of the Mach'ol Range. Other peaks of note include Mt. Kwanmo (2,541 m/8,337 ft), in the Hamgyong Range; Mt. Myohyang (1,909 m/6,263 ft), in the Myohyang Range, north of Pyongyang; and Mt. Kumgang ("Diamond Mountain," 1,638 m/5,374 ft), in the Taebaek Range in

the southeast. Only about 20% of the country consists of lowlands and plains, but it is in these areas that the population is concentrated. The principal lowlands are the Unjon, Pyongyang, Chaeryong, Anju, and Yonbaek plains, extending from north to south along the west coast, and the Susong, Yongchon, Kilchu, Hamhung, and Yonghung plains, along the eastern shore.

The principal rivers are the Tumen and Yalu along the northern border of the peninsula, both of which rise in Mt. Paektu, and the Taedong, which flows past Pyongyang. The Imjin rises in the DPRK near the 38th parallel in the west and crosses into the ROK before entering the Yellow Sea. Yellow Sea tides on the west coast rise to over 9 m (30 ft) in some places; Sea of Japan tides on the east rise to only about 1 m (3 ft).

³CLIMATE

North Korea has a generally cool continental climate. The winter season, from December to March, is long and cold; mean temperatures in January range between about -7°C (20°F) in the south and -23°C (-10°F) in the northern interior. The summer, from June to September, is warm, with mean July temperatures nearing 21°C (about 70°F) in most places. Accordingly, the annual range of temperatures is large—about 30°C (54°F) at Pyongyang and about 43°C (77 °F) at Chunggang (Chunggangjin), where the lowest temperature in the Korean peninsula, -43.6°C (-46.5°F), has been recorded. Because of ocean currents and the mountain ranges bordering the narrow coastal lowlands, winter temperatures on

379

the east coast are some 3 to 4°C (5 to 7°F) higher than those of the west coast.

Most of the country receives about 101 cm (40 in) of precipitation annually. The northern inland plateau, however, receives only about 61 cm (24 in), and the lower reaches of the Taedong River valley, 81 cm (32 in); the upper Chŏngchŏn River area averages between about 122 and 132 cm (48 and 52 in) yearly. Some three-fifths of the annual precipitation falls in the four months from June to September; this heavy concentration of rainfall is related to the humid summer monsoon from the Pacific Ocean, which also produces occasional typhoons (tropical cyclones). Only a small portion of the total precipitation occurs in winter, generally as snow; snowfall can be locally heavy, such as in the T'aebaek Mountains. There are about 200 frost-free days along the coast but fewer than 120 in the northern Kaema Highlands.

⁴FLORA AND FAUNA

The World Resources Institute estimates that there are 2,898 plant species in the DPRK. Cold temperate vegetation, including firs, spruces, and other needled evergreens, predominate in mountainous areas of the DPRK, with alpine varieties flourishing at the higher altitudes. Animal species include 105 mammals, 369 birds, 20 reptiles, and 17 amphibians. The calculation reflects the total number of distinct species residing in the country, not the number of endemic species. The hilly terrain of Mt. Paektu is the home of bears, wild boar, deer, snow leopards, and lynx. Common at lower elevations are the roe deer, Amur goral, wolf, water shrew, and muskrat. Bird species include the black Manchurian ring-necked pheasant, black grouse, and three-toed woodpecker; the hawk owl, lesser-spotted woodpecker, and willow tit are indigenous to Mt. Paektu.

The DPRK's own estimates are higher than those from sources outside the country. For example, the official 1998 National Biodiversity and Action Plan notes that it is rich of fauna and flora species compared to the territorial size and even more than other neighboring countries in the rate per area. For plant life, the DPRK claims to have "higher plants" of 3,994 species and 420 bird species. Because of the nature of a relatively closed society, verification of data by external scientists is at times difficult to achieve. Prior to 1990, it was mainly scientists from communist bloc countries affiliated with the Soviet Union or China that had access and did studies in North Korea. The first list of North Korean insects was presented by D.R. Zhu in 1969, and it included 34 species of Tortricidae. In the 1970s and 1980s, the Hungarian Natural History Museum (HNHM; Budapest, Hungary) sent researchers to North Korea, and their studies contributed significantly to knowledge of the fauna of North Korea, as did researchers from the Polish Academy of Sciences.

Siberian Tigers, also popularly known as Amur Tigers, have not been found in Korea since 1922, when the last Siberian tiger was killed in North Gyeongsang. Today, Amur Tigers, now an endangered species, are mostly found in the far east region of Russia. Despite several field projects aimed at tracking a Siberian tiger within the peninsular DMZ region, none have yielded a result. In 2009, however, as part of a diplomatic move to improve bilateral ties with the Republic of Korea (ROK), Moscow pledged to give Seoul two male Siberian tigers and one female tiger. A symbol of the two nation's friendship, the three tigers were sent to the Seoul Zoo in June 2011.

⁵ENVIRONMENT

The World Resources Institute reported that the DPRK had designated 315,900 hectares (780,606 acres) of land for protection as of 2006. Water resources totaled 77.1 cu km (18.5 cu mi), while water usage was 9.02 cu km (2.16 cu mi) per year. Domestic water usage accounted for 20% of total usage, industrial for 25%, and agricultural for 55%. Per capita water usage totaled 401 cu m (14,161 cu ft) per year.

The UN reported in 2008 that carbon dioxide emissions in the DPRK totaled 70,653 kilotons. While greenhouse gas emissions have raised temperatures between one and two degrees worldwide, the effect of climate change is particularly evident on the peninsula in the rising occurrences of floods and droughts. As a water-deficient region, as classified by the UN, serious droughts and floods have compounded the peninsula's existing water scarcity and water security problems. With the projected global temperature increase due to increases in greenhouse gas emissions, scientists generally agree that the global hydrological cycle will intensify and suggest that extremes (such as droughts and floods) will become more common. Therefore, one major concern arising from climate change is its potential effects on water resources in terms of (increases in) droughts, and its impacts on different health, environmental, economic, and social sectors in both North and South Korea. Changes in the frequency and magnitude of droughts will have enormous impacts on water management, agriculture, and aquatic ecosystems. Various research efforts studying the impact of climate change on drought in Korea show that the risk of drought in Korea is growing.

The government has established 220 facilities to regulate environmental conditions, industrial areas, protected land, and water reserves. The government also created the Law of Environmental Protection. According to tothe International Union for Conservation of Nature and Natural Resources (IUCN) Red List of Threatened Species, threatened species in the DPRK as of 2011 included 9 mammals, 24 birds, 1 species of amphibian, 13 species of fish, 2 species of invertebrates, and 7 species of plants. Endangered species in the DPRK included the Amur leopard, Oriental white stork, Japanese crested ibis, and Tristram's woodpecker. The Japanese sea lion has become extinct.

Lack of information from external sources complicates the assessment of environmental damage caused by industrialization and urbanization. Electricity generation has largely been by hydroelectric dams and old coal burning technology transferred from the former Soviet Union and China when North Korea launched an ambitious program of industrialization modeled on the Soviet Union after the Korean War. By comparison, Poland, Czechoslovakia, and Romania, which pursued similar industrial policies, were found to have some of the world's worst pollution in the early 1990s when these countries opened up after the collapse of the Soviet Union. North Korea's use of coal is projected to increase five times from 2005 to 2020.

Productive land use was at a crisis level in 2011–2012. Major crop yields fell by almost two-thirds during the 1990s due to a host of reasons related to climate change, misguided policies, and natural disasters, including loss of forestland, droughts, floods and tidal waves, acidification due to overuse of chemicals, and shortages of fertilizer, farm machinery, and oil.

North Korea amended its environmental protection law in 2011, adding development of energy and environmental certification systems to the law.

⁶POPULATION

The US Central Intelligence Agency (CIA) estimated the population of the DPRK in 2011 to be approximately 24,457,492, which placed it at number 48 in population among the 196 nations of the world. Approximately 9% of the population was over 65 years of age, with another 22.4% under 15 years of age. The average lifespan of a man was 70 years and of women was 75 years. The median age in the DPRK was 32.9 years. There were 0.95 males for every female in the country. The population's annual rate of change was 0.538%. The projected population for the year 2025 was 23,600,000. Population density in the DPRK was calculated at 203 people per sq km (526 people per sq mi).

The UN estimated that 60% of the population lived in urban areas, with an annual rate of change of 0.6%. The largest urban areas included Pyongyang Hamhung, Chongjin, Wonsan, Nampo, Sinjuiju, and Kaesong.

⁷MIGRATION

Estimates of DPRK's net migration rate, carried out by the CIA in 2011, amounted to -0.04 migrants per 1,000 citizens. The total number of emigrants living abroad was 300,800, and the total number of immigrants living in DPRK was 37,100. During the generation of Japanese occupation (1910–45), some 3 million Koreans, mainly from the northern provinces, immigrated to Manchuria and parts of China; 700,000 to Siberia; some 3 million to Japan; and about 7,000 to the United States (mostly to Hawaii). From the end of World War II in 1945 through 1950, at least 1.2 million Koreans crossed the 38th parallel into the ROK, refugees either from Communism or the Korean War. Repatriation of overseas Koreans is actively encouraged in an attempt to ameliorate the nation's chronic labor shortages. Between 1945 and 1950, an estimated 300,000 Koreans were repatriated from Manchuria and Siberia; over 93,000 of about 600,000 Koreans living in Japan were repatriated to the DPRK between December 1959 and the end of 1974. The General Association of Korean Residents in Japan actively supports the DPRK, and the Pyongyang government subsidizes some Korean schools on Japanese soil.

Under the terms of a 1986 treaty with China that was still valid as of 2012, North Koreans apprehended as illegal immigrants in China are quickly returned to the DPRK, where they are severely punished and may be executed. Between 1992 and 1996, about 1,000 North Koreans fled to China, where refugees can avoid detection within large ethnic Korean communities. Both China and the ROK have constructed refugee camps in anticipation of a mass exodus of the population should the North Korean government collapse.

Fourteen official border crossings at twelve points connect China and North Korea. North Korea has reinforced border guards on its side with troops since 2004. Traffic on the bridges connecting China's Yanbian Autonomous Korean Prefecture with North Korea is moderate to light but has increased as China's trade with North Korea has increased.

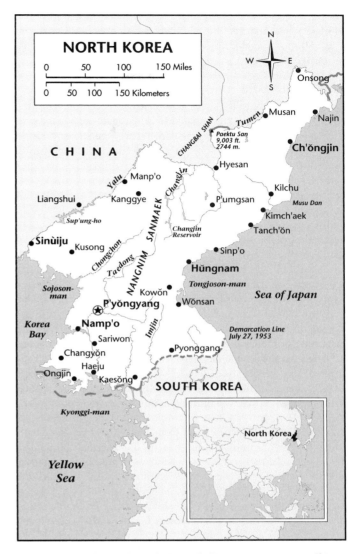

LOCATION: 37°38′ to 43°1′N; 124°13′ to 130°39′ E. BOUNDARY LENGTHS: China, 1,025 kilometers (637 miles); Russia, 16 kilometers (10 miles); ROK, 240 kilometers (149 miles); total coastline, 1,028 kilometers (639 miles). TERRITORIAL SEA LIMIT: 12 miles.

On the Chinese side of the border, press reports suggested that Chinese soldiers replaced many border guards in 2003, and in 2008 the Chinese moved 15,000 troops to the border area near North Korea. Troops were moved there as a contingency against a possible collapse of the North Korean government or economy to prevent North Korean refugees from flooding into northern China. Repatriations of North Koreans from China to North Korea have ranged from 150 to 300 per week from 2004 to 2010.

By 2001, 583 North Koreans had defected to the ROK. The following year, the figure nearly doubled to 1,138. By 2007, about 10,000 North Korean defectors had arrived in the South, and by December 2010, the number reached 20,360. This increase was expected to remain steady at about 2,500–3,000 per year, depending on North Korean policy and the degree of Chinese cooperation.

⁸ETHNIC GROUPS

The Koreans are believed to be descended primarily from Tungusic peoples of the Mongoloid race, who originated in the cold northern regions of Central Asia. There is scant evidence of non-Mongoloid admixture. There is a small Chinese community and a few ethnic Japanese; however, the DPRK has no sizable ethnic minority.

9 LANGUAGES

The Korean language is usually acknowledged as a member of the Altaic family and is clearly related to other agglutinative tongues such as Turkish, Mongolian, and Japanese. Linguistic unification of the Korean Peninsula apparently followed political unification in the 7th century AD, and today the dialect differences are comparatively slight, though residents of Seoul generally can identify a speaker as being from more rural areas, such as Cholla and South Cholla provinces by dialect and accent. Korean is written with a largely phonetic alphabet called Han'gul. Created in 1443 under the great King Sejong, the Korean alphabet originally consisted of 14 consonants and 10 vowels; since then, 5 consonants and 11 vowels have been added. Han'gul letters are combined into syllables by clustering. Before the invention of Han'gul, Koreans wrote in Chinese characters, or *Hanja*, which continued to be both the official written language and the written form of most Korean literature until the beginning of the 20th century. With the beginning of the Japanese colonial administration in 1910, Japanese became the official language, and the use of Korean was restricted. Since 1949, the DPRK has used only Han'gul (calling it *Choson Muntcha*) for writing. North Korean linguists have studied Han'gul extensively, publishing comprehensive dictionaries in 1963 and 1969. In 1964, Kim Il Sung called for the purification of Korean by replacing borrowings from English and Japanese with native Korean or familiar Chinese terms. During the colonial period, large numbers of Chinese character compounds coined in Japan to translate modern Western scientific, technical, social science, and philosophical concepts came into use in Korea. Following the armistice, however, the North Korean regime attempted to eliminate as many of these Japanese, Chinese, and Western loanwords as possible. All publications are printed exclusively in native Korean hangul, without the use of hancha (Chinese characters), and an attempt has also been made to create new words of exclusively Korean origin.

The traditional honorifics of polite language remain in use, though in simplified forms, and have been sanctioned by the government. Some Chinese (Mandarin dialect) and Russian are spoken in border areas.

There is considerable divergence in the Korean spoken north and south of the DMZ. Yet, despite arguments that the Korean language of the North is becoming archaic, both sides of the peninsula are linguistically similar—there are little to no grammatical rule and word formation rule differences between the two Koreas. Rather, expressions and differences in loanword origin represent the primary divergences between North and South Korean language.

10 RELIGIONS

According to current government estimates, the majority of the population professes no religion or is avowedly atheist. However, foreign observers indicate that religious activity within the country is much greater than the government suggests. Indigenous shamanism, notable for its emphasis on exorcising evil spirits, is practiced by a small percentage of the population, mostly in rural areas. The government reports that about 15,000 people are followers of the Ch'ondogyo Young Friends Party, a government-approved group based on the earlier religious movement that was forced underground in 1948. Ch'ondogyo offers an eclectic blend of both Christian and Buddhist elements. The government also estimates that 10,000 Buddhists remain active despite the conversion of many Buddhist temples to secular uses. Up to the mid-1940s, Pyongyang was an important center of Korean Christianity. Most of the nation's Christians, predominantly Protestants, fled to the ROK to escape persecution between 1945 and 1953. Christians make up less than 1% of the population, or about 12,800 people, according to the government. A number of Christian churches are overseen by lay leaders, since there are very few ordained priests and ministers. House churches may be more common among Christians; however, since these meetings are generally kept secret, there is no exact data concerning membership or participation. Those caught proselytizing may be arrested and are subject to harsh penalties. The constitution provides for freedom of religious beliefs, but in practice the government strongly discourages any religious activities that are not under official control. The state-controlled Chilgol Church (Protestant) in Pyongyang is dedicated in memory of Kang Pan-sok, the former leader Kim Il Sung's mother, who was a Presbyterian deaconess. There are three other state-controlled churches (all in Pyongyang): Bongsu Church (Protestant), Changchun Roman Catholic Church, and Holy Trinity Russian Orthodox Church.

11 TRANSPORTATION

The CIA reported that DPRK has a total of 25,554 km (15,879 mi) of roads, of which 724 km (450 mi) are paved. There are 79 airports, which transported 101,237 passengers in 2009 according to the World Bank. The DPRK has approximately 2,250 km (1,398 mi) of navigable waterways.

The rail network is the principal means of transportation, carrying nearly all of the nation's freight and most of its passenger traffic. Road transportation is of secondary importance. The exceptions are a superhighway connecting Pyongyang with Kaesŏng and two multilane highways, which link the national capital with the ports of Wonsan and Namp'o. Most of the nation's navigable waterways are suitable for small craft only. Rivers utilized for freight transportation are the Yalu, Taedong, and Chaeryong. The principal ports are Namp'o on the west coast, and Ch'ŏngjin and Hŭngnam (Hamhung) on the east coast.

Two airlines primarily run services in and out of North Korea. Air Koryo, the North Korean national airline, and Air China Ltd. Air Koryo conducts three flights a week between Beijing and Pyongyang, while Air China operates direct flights between the two cities twice a week. Air Koryo also operates regular international flights to Shenyang, China and occasional flights to domestic destinations. Diplomats, businesspeople, NGOs, and International Organizations primarily use these flight services. Since 2006, however, Air Koryo has been included on the EU airline blacklist on account of international safety standards, which in effect bar the airline from operating services to EU destinations. This ban was relaxed in 2010 when Air Koryo was permitted to resume operations for two of its aircrafts.

Currently, the government tightly controls all inbound travel to North Korea. The majority of outbound travel is done by the government and its ministers, who prefer to travel with Air Koryo. The largest travel operator in North Korea is the state-owned Korea International Travel Co (KITC), which is responsible for arranging inbound travel and tour guides to North Korea.

¹²HISTORY

The history of the Korean people begins with the migration into the Korean Peninsula of Tungusic tribes from northern China and Manchuria in about 3,000 BC. The archaeological evidence indicates that these tribes possessed a Neolithic culture. It was not until about the 8th century BC that the art of metalworking came to Korea from China. The recorded history of Korea begins around 194 BC, when the ancient kingdom of Choson ("Land of Morning Calm") in northwestern Korea was seized by Wiman, a military figure from China of either Chinese or Korean origin. He usurped the throne from a king who, according to legend, was a descendant of Kija, a historical Chinese nobleman who emigrated from China at the end of the Shang dynasty (c. 1122 BC). A popular Korean legend of much later origin asserts that Kija was preceded in his rule over the Korean Peninsula by a dynasty started in 2333 BC by the semidivine figure Tan-gun, an offspring of the son of the divine creator and a "bear woman" (possibly a woman from a bear-totem tribe). Both Tan-gun and Kija are still widely revered.

The primitive state controlled by Wiman's successors fell victim to expanding Chinese power in 108 BC, and more than four centuries of Chinese colonial rule followed. During this period, the advanced Chinese culture slowly spread into nearly every corner of Korea, giving impetus to the coalescence of the loosely knit Korean tribes into state-like formations. By AD 313, when the Chinese power was destroyed, three Korean kingdoms had emerged: Paekche, in the southwest; Silla, in the southeast; and Koguryo, in the northwest. The three kingdoms had advanced cultures for the time, each compiling a written history during the 4th–6th centuries. During the same period, Buddhism was introduced into Korea, from which it was later taken to Japan. Ultimately, the Silla kingdom crushed the other two and united all but the northernmost portion of the peninsula, ushering in the age of the Silla Unification (668–900). After rebellions broke out, Korea again suffered a threefold division until reunification was achieved in 936 under the leadership of Wang Kon, who proclaimed a new dynasty in the kingdom of Koryo (founded in 918), which derived its name from Koguryo; the name Korea is derived from Koryo.

Chinese influence on political and social institutions and on Korean thought went on at an accelerated pace during the Koryo period, and there were some notable cultural achievements, including the traditional invention of the use of movable metal type in printing in 1234. Beginning in 1231, however, the Mongols invaded Koryo, devastating the land and, from 1259 on, controlling the Korean kings. Following a revolt against the Mongol Empire in 1356 and a subsequent period of disorder, Gen. Yi Song-gye assumed the throne as King T'aejo in 1392, adopting the name Choson for Korea, moving the capital from Kaesŏng (the capital of Koryo since 918) to Seoul, and ushering in the long-lived Yi (or Li) Dynasty (1392–1910).

The first hundred years of Yi rule witnessed truly brilliant cultural achievements, especially during the reign of King Sejong (1418–50). The world's first authenticated casting of movable metal type was made in 1403. The Korean alphabet, Han'gul, was developed. A rain gauge was invented and put into use throughout the peninsula. A spate of basic texts—including histories, geographies, administrative codes, and works on music—were compiled and issued under state auspices. Scholars competed for government posts through the civil service examination system.

By about 1500, however, factionalism divided the kingdom, and the Yi rulers were ill prepared to meet foreign invasion. In 1592, in the course of an attempt to conquer China, the Japanese, under Hideyoshi Toyotomi, invaded Korea but were repulsed by an allied Chinese army and the Korean navy under Yi Sun-sin; in 1597, there was another invasion, which ended with Hideyoshi's death in 1598. After being invaded by the Manchus in 1636, Korea became a vassal state, eventually falling under the official but loose control of the Qing (Ch'ing), or Manchu, dynasty in China. During the 18th century, two energetic kings, Yongjo (r. 1724–76) and Chongjo (r. 1776–1800), were able to arrest the process of dynastic decline. However, the intellectual and cultural revival that they engendered, known as the Practical Learning Movement (Sirhak), was short lived.

The first six decades of the 19th century were marked by a succession of natural disasters, mounting peasant unrest and insurrection, and administrative relapse into corruption and inefficiency. Eventually, a Korean figure came forward to attempt to rescue the dynasty from impending collapse. This was Yi Ha-leng, known as the Taewon'gun (prince regent), who was the father of the king, Kojong, and held the actual power during the decade 1864–73. While his domestic reforms were generally enlightened and beneficial, he adopted an isolationist policy, including persecution of the growing Roman Catholic community in Korea. Soon after the Taewon'gun's downfall, the Kanghwa Treaty of 1876 with Japan opened Korea by force both to Japan and to the clamoring Western nations. During the last quarter of the 19th century, Korea was the prize in a complex rivalry for mastery of the peninsula among Japan, China, Western imperialist powers, and domestic political forces. Japan seized upon the pretext of peasant uprisings in Korea's southern provinces (the Tonghak Rebellion, led by followers of what later came to be called the Ch'ondogyo religion) during 1894–95 to destroy the waning Chinese power in Korea in the First Sino-Japanese War. A decade later, Japan turned back a Russian bid for supremacy in the Russo-Japanese War (1904–5). In 1910, with the tacit approval of the United States and the European powers, the Yi Dynasty came to an end with the formal annexation of Korea by Japan.

The Democratic People's Republic

For 35 years, Korea (renamed Choson) remained under the Japanese yoke, until it was liberated by US and Soviet troops at the end of World War II. Although Japanese colonial rule brought Korea considerable economic development along modern Western lines, the benefits went primarily to the Japanese, and the process was accompanied by ever harsher political and cultural oppression. The Korean people staged a nationwide passive resistance movement beginning on 1 March 1919 (the Samil or "March 1" Movement), only to have it swiftly and brutally crushed by their Japanese overlords. In the 1920s and 1930s, nationalist and Communist movements developed both within Korea and among Korean exiles in the former USSR, Manchuria (which was occupied by Japan in 1931), and the rest of China. After the onset of the Second Sino-Japanese War in 1937, the Japanese aimed to eradicate Korean national identity; even the use of the Korean language was banned.

After Japan accepted the Potsdam Declaration for unconditional surrender on 14 August 1945, the 38th parallel was chosen, as a result of US initiative, as a line of demarcation between Soviet occupation forces (who had entered the north on 8 August) and US occupation forces (who were introduced on 8 September). While the Americans set up a full military government allied with conservative Korean political forces, the Soviets allied their government with leftist and Communist Korean forces led by Kim Il Sung, who had been an anti-Japanese guerrilla leader in Manchuria. After a joint commission set up by the United States and the USSR failed to agree on plans for the reunification of Korea, the problem was placed on the UN agenda in September 1947. In accordance with a UN resolution, elections were held on 10 May 1948 in the ROK alone; North Korea did not recognize UN competency to sponsor the elections. The newly elected National Assembly formulated a democratic constitution and chose Syngman Rhee, who had been the leader of an independence movement in exile, to be the first president of the ROK, proclaimed on 15 August 1948. On 9 September, the DPRK was established in the north, with Kim Il Sung at the helm. Like its southern counterpart, the DPRK claimed to be the legitimate government of all Korea. In December, however, the ROK was acknowledged by the UN General Assembly as the only government in Korea to have been formed according to the original UN mandate. The next year and a half brought sporadic border clashes between the two Koreas, coupled with increasing guerrilla activity in the south.

On 25 June 1950, the People's Army of the DPRK struck across the 38th parallel at dawn in a move to unify the peninsula under Communist control. The DPRK forces advanced rapidly; Seoul, the ROK capital, fell within three days, and the destruction of the ROK seemed imminent. At US urging, the UN Security Council branded the DPRK an aggressor and called for the withdrawal of the attacking forces. President Harry S. Truman ordered US air and naval forces into battle on 27 June and ground forces three days later. A multinational UN Command was then created to join with and lead the South Koreans. An amphibious landing at Inch'on (15 September) in the ROK under General Douglas MacArthur brought about the complete disintegration of the DPRK's military position.

MacArthur then made a fateful decision to drive into the north. As the UN forces approached the Yalu River, China warned that it would not tolerate a unification of the peninsula under US/UN auspices. After several weeks of threats and feints, "volunteers" from the Chinese People's Liberation Army entered the fighting en masse, forcing MacArthur into a costly pell-mell retreat back down the peninsula. The battle line stabilized along the 38th parallel, where it remained for two years. On 27 July 1953, an armistice agreement was finally signed by the North Korean People's Army, the Chinese volunteers, and the UN Command at P'anmunjom in the DPRK, ending a conflict that had cost the lives of an estimated 415,000 South Koreans, 23,300 Americans (combat dead), and 3,100 UN allies; casualties among Communist forces were officially estimated by the DPRK at 50,000 but may have been as

high as two million. A military demarcation line, which neither side regarded as a permanent border, was established, surrounded by the DMZ. After the armistice agreement, all but a token force of UN Command troops withdrew, except those of the United States, which in 1954 guaranteed the security of the ROK under a mutual defense treaty. A postwar international conference held in 1954 to resolve the problem of Korea's political division was unable to find a satisfactory formula for reunification. Meanwhile, the DPRK, with the aid of China and the former USSR, began to restore its war-damaged economy. A series of purges consolidated political power in the hands of Kim Il Sung and his supporters. By the end of the 1950s, Kim had emerged as the unchallenged leader of the DPRK and the focus of a personality cult that developed around him and his family.

In 1972, the government replaced the original 1948 constitution with a new document (which would be further revised in 1992), and reunification talks, stalled since 1954, resumed under Red Cross auspices, though without lasting effect. Throughout the 1970s and 1980s, as part of its cold war with the ROK, the DPRK extended its diplomatic relations to over 100 countries. The ROK continued to charge the DPRK with attempts at sabotage and subversion, including infiltration by tunnels under the DMZ. In the 1980s, Korea's basic divisions remained unresolved. In 1980, President Kim proposed that both North and South Korea be reunited as a confederal state, with each part retaining regional autonomy and its own ideological and social system, but the ROK rejected the concept; the DPRK has likewise rejected the ROK's repeated proposals for the resumption of North-South talks on reunification unless the United States is a third party in the negotiations, but neither the ROK nor the United States has accepted that condition. Kim was unanimously reelected president in May 1990, but his son, Kim Jong Il (1942-), groomed since the 1960s as his designated successor, appeared to be running the nation's day-to-day affairs, though without the benefit of any formal administrative post. Indications of an improvement in relations between the North and South included material relief provided by the DPRK to the ROK after a flood in 1984, talks under Red Cross auspices that led to a brief reunion of separated families in 1985, economic discussions, and interparliamentary contacts. The DPRK did not participate in the 1988 summer Olympic Games, officially hosted by the ROK, since it was not named as co-host.

During the 1990s, the DPRK was less able to rely on its allies, the large communist states of the former Soviet Union and China. In 1990, the Soviet Union and the ROK opened formal diplomatic relations; however, by 1991, the collapse of the Soviet Union cut off an important source of economic and political support for the DPRK. The DPRK had reestablished ties with China in 1982, after a 12-year break since the DPRK sided with the former Soviet Union in the Sino-Soviet clash of 1969. In 1990, China and the ROK began to encourage mutual trade and in 1992 established formal diplomatic relations. Beginning in 1993, China demanded that all its exports to the DPRK be paid for with cash instead of through barter. The DPRK found itself increasingly isolated and in severe economic difficulty. Reunification talks and the DPRK's relations with the United States took on added urgency as the DPRK sought international recognition and economic aid.

In the first half of the 1990s, the DPRK's foreign relations revolved around issues of joint US-ROK military exercises and of nuclear capabilities. The DPRK repeatedly canceled negotiations with the ROK during the annual "Team Spirit" exercises of US and ROK militaries. In 1991, the United States withdrew its nuclear weapons from the ROK and the two Koreas signed a bilateral agreement to create a nuclear-free peninsula. Yet it was suspected that the DPRK was developing the capability to reprocess nuclear fuels and build nuclear weapons. (Both the ROK and Japan had stockpiles of plutonium.) Conflicts over the access of an International Atomic Energy Agency (IAEA) inspection team to a reprocessing plant, which the DPRK allowed into North Korea in May 1994, led to new tensions. These tensions were defused with an agreement for high-level talks between the United States and the DPRK, previously refused by the United States, to be held on 8 July 1994, followed on 25 July by a summit in Pyongyang between the presidents of the two Koreas, the first such summit since Korea was divided in 1945.

On 8 July 1994, just as the US-DPRK talks were beginning, President Kim Il Sung died, and the talks were suspended. Kim Jong Il replaced his father as leader of the country, without assuming Kim Il Sung's previous titles of state president and general secretary of the Korean Workers Party. The official mourning period for Kim Il Sung was extended to three years.

On 10 September 1995, Russia advised the DPRK that it would not extend the 1961 treaty on friendship, cooperation, and mutual assistance. The DPRK closed the Neutral Nations Supervisory Committee offices in the northern half of the joint security area at Panmunjom in an effort to dismantle the Military Armistice Agreement in May 1994, following the expulsion of the Czech and Polish representatives and the withdrawal of China, one of the three original signatories to the agreement. This post-Cold War framework was designed to pressure the United States into guaranteeing the DPRK's survival by means of a bilateral peace treaty. Marshall O Jin U, the armed forces supreme commander and second in the hierarchy behind Kim Il Sung, died 25 February 1995. He had been a prominent symbol of military acceptance of the younger Kim.

After he had served as North Korea's de facto leader for four years without formally being named as president, Kim Jong Il's position was made official. On 5 September 1998, the Supreme People's Assembly paid tribute to his father, Kim Il Sung, by permanently abolishing the post of president, which left Kim Jong Il, in his capacity as chairman of the National Defense Commission, the nation's top political official. At the same session, the assembly approved a number of other changes to the nation's constitution.

Later in 1998, tensions over North Korea's nuclear capabilities were revived when it reportedly fired a three-stage ballistic missile into the Pacific; claims that the vehicle was a satellite launcher were initially greeted with skepticism on the part of the United States and Japan, over which it had been fired.

Periodic, widespread flooding, due in part to North Korea's efforts to expand the land under collectivization by massive deforestation, has led to regular food shortages, including a national famine during the late 1990s. Relief efforts have not been able to raise nearly enough food to feed North Korea's starving population. The policies of North Korea's government have led to reticence on the part of those nations that normally would have contributed to the UN-sponsored World Food Program (WPF). Nevertheless, in 1998, the WPF mounted the largest aid effort on record in an attempt to save millions of North Koreans from starvation. That year, the DPRK accepted nearly $1 billion in food aid. Famine conditions continued during the 2000s, although it appeared the worst of the famine had receded. The UN estimated that between one and two million North Koreans died as a result of famine, economic mismanagement, and restrictions on the flow of information. Another factor contributing to the economy's poor performance, before and after the natural disasters of the 1990s, was the disproportionately large percentage of monies that were allocated to the military; some reports claim more than 25% of the GNP was spent for both offensive and defensive purposes. In 2005, North Korea had the fourth-largest army in the world. It had an estimated 1.2 million armed personnel, compared to about 650,000 in the South; 20% of men ages 17–54 are in the regular armed forces.

Due to economic reforms in 2002, a rudimentary free-market system in North Korea came into existence, mainly in the countryside, which allowed farmers to sell their products as their main source of income. However, the North Korean economy is centrally planned, and a large informal or black market exists for items such as food, clothes, appliances, and even cosmetics. The government assigns all jobs and prohibits private property. The government retains a high level of discrimination by giving all citizens security ratings of "core," "wavering," or "hostile." The lower the rating, the harder it is to find employment, educational opportunities, residence, and access to medical facilities. An increasing problem for North Korea is illegal migration of North Koreans into China to escape these harsh political and economic conditions.

As part of an effort to bring North Korea out of its self-imposed isolation, its government renewed diplomatic initiatives toward the South that had been interrupted by the death of Kim Il Sung in 1994. What became known as ROK president Kim Dae Jung's "sunshine policy" of rapprochement toward the North resulted in the signing of a joint agreement at a summit in Pyongyang between Kim Dae Jung and Kim Jong Il in June 2000. In 2003, incoming South Korean president Roh Moo Hyun pledged to continue the "sunshine policy," but by then relations with North Korea had deteriorated due to revelations in October 2002 that North Korea was undertaking a program to enrich uranium for use in nuclear weapons. This revelation came on the heels of US President George W. Bush's January 2002 State of the Union Address, in which he labeled North Korea (along with Iran and Iraq) a state that endangers the peace of the world by supporting terrorism and pursuing weapons of mass destruction (chemical, biological, and nuclear weapons). In late 2002, North Korea accused the United States of not adhering to the Agreed Framework between the two countries, established in 1994, in that the United States' construction of two light-water reactors in North Korea was far behind schedule. The North demanded the IAEA remove seals and surveillance equipment from its Yongbyon power plant, which the IAEA said was in danger of reprocessing spent fuel rods for plutonium.

In January 2003, North Korea announced it would withdraw from the Nuclear Nonproliferation Treaty and begin construction of nuclear missiles for self-defense. In February 2005, American officials claimed North Korea had admitted to having at least one nuclear weapon, although it had not been proven and was refuted by North Korea. However, the greatest fear was seen by many not to be that North Korea would create nuclear bombs for its own use, but that the country would sell plutonium or enriched uranium to rogue states or terrorists.

On 4 July 2006, North Korea test-fired at least six missiles, including a long-range Taepodong-2, despite repeated warnings from the international community. The next day it test-fired a seventh missile. The ROK suspended food aid to protest the missile tests. The UN Security Council unanimously voted to impose sanctions on North Korea. The resolution demanded UN members stop exports and imports of missile-related materials to North Korea and that North Korea put a halt to its ballistic missile program.

On 9 October 2006, North Korea carried out its first test of a nuclear weapon. Since then, North Korea has participated in talks with various nations and international groups on the issue of denuclearization without significant long-term resolutions. In April 2009, North Korea walked out of six-party talks after the UN Security Council criticized the government for launching a rocket. North Korea claimed that it had launched a communications satellite, but international observers widely presumed the launch to be a test of long-range missile technology. The next month, North Korea announced that it had resumed reprocessing of spent fuel rods and threatened to continue testing missiles unless the UN issued an apology for the Security Council's criticism of the April rocket launch.

While in the past the actual lines of power in the DPRK had been somewhat difficult to discern, an April 2009 revision to the constitution officially named Kim Jong Il as the supreme leader. Previously, his official post was as the chairman of the National Defense Commission, which was then the highest office in the state, while his deceased father, Kim Il Sung, retained the title of eternal president. The new constitution endorsed Kim Jong Il's "military first" policy as a guiding ideology and retained the dictate of a socialist system, but removed the term "communism" from the text. For the first time in history, the constitution explicitly stated that the country respected and protected the human rights of it citizens. Analysts believe the constitutional revision was designed to more clearly define Kim Jong Il's power as leader while attempting to persuade the international community that he was not entirely insensitive or inflexible in regards to the needs and demands of a changing world. Kim Jong Il designated his youngest son, Kim Jong Un, as his successor.

Following months of defiant rhetoric and action, North Korea began to pursue a conciliatory approach in September 2009, as it agreed to restore regular commercial crossings at its tense and heavily fortified border with the ROK. The decision to open the border came amidst a string of other gestures by the North designed to ease tension with the United States and the ROK. However, fresh on the minds of policy makers and political analysts in the United States was North Korea's nuclear test in May 2009, a move the United States, the ROK, and much of the international community viewed as unacceptable.

While North Korea attempted to patch a long-fractured relationship with the United States, crippling UN sanctions were affecting North Korea's commerce. A ban on North Korea's weapons transfers, which began after North Korea tested its nuclear device in May 2009, was being vigorously enforced by various nations in September 2009.

In November 2010, an exchange of artillery between the north and south in the maritime border region raised international concern. North Korea fired dozens of artillery shells at the border island of Yeonpyeong, making several hits on the South Korean military base. Two South Korean marines and two civilians were killed; another eighteen were injured. All of the 1,600 residents of the island were evacuated to shelters during the hour-long attack. North Korean officials accused the ROK of provoking the attack by firing shells into the maritime territory of the north. South Korean officials said that they had been conducting regular military drills off the coast of Yeonpyeong, but claimed that no artillery was ever fired into the northern region. In retaliation for the attack on Yeonpyeong, the ROK fired about 80 shells into the northern territory. There was no report of injuries from the north.

As the international community called for calm, the ROK announced plans to conduct another series of live-fire artillery exercises on and around Yeonpyeong. About two dozen Americans were expected to participate in the drills as observers. North Korea warned that any further drills would be considered a clear provocation, to which the government would retaliate in kind. Hoping to stop the escalating tensions, China called on fellow six-party nations to resume the talks that were stalled in April 2009. But the ROK and the United States reaffirmed their stand that talks would not resume until North Korea showed some commitment to halt its nuclear activity. The ROK went ahead with the artillery exercise on 20 December. To the surprise of many, the North did not retaliate, but later issued a statement saying that the action was not worth reaction, implying that the incident proved which side is interested in peace and which side showed the real provocation. The ROK scheduled two more military drills within the same week, including one that was set to take place 30 miles from the North-South demilitarized zone. In January 2011, North Korea invited the south to participate in discussions on economic ties. The ROK quickly declined.

In February 2011, the ROK agreed to participate in talks with North Korea for the first time since North Korea's November 2010 artillery attack. The talks ended abruptly on 9 February when the North Korean delegation walked out, refusing to take responsibility for the attack on Yeonpyeong Island. The talks had been planned to focus on the denuclearization of North Korea. For talks to continue, the ROK set the condition that North Korea accept responsibility for the November attack. No future sessions were scheduled.

In March 2011, relations between North and South Korea were further strained when South Korean activists started a massive anti–North Korea propaganda campaign. They sent helium-filled balloons over the border that carried leaflets, cassette tapes, and videos with anti–North Korean messages. The messages called for the people of North Korea to rise up against Kim Jong Il. The aim of the propaganda was to raise awareness of what was happening in the outside world, as North Koreans have almost no access to international news. As South Korean activists continued their balloon campaign against North Korea, in April the north responded by threatening a military attack on the border town of Imjingak, a small tourist town that had been the launching spot for the balloons, if the propaganda balloon launches did not stop. The South

Korean government, which initially intended to block the balloonists because their actions affected north-south relations, allowed the activists to continue the balloon launches.

On 17 December 2011, Kim Jong Il died from a heart attack. The government initiated a 12-day period of mourning and Kim Jong Il's youngest son, Kim Jong Un, who had been designated as next in line in 2009, was named his father's successor. Within hours after the announcement of Kim Jong Il's death, the ruling party issued a statement calling Kim Jong Un "the great successor to the revolution." However, there was some concern over whether the young Kim Jong Un (believed to be in his 20s) had enough experience and/or support from the military to serve as the new leader. Kim Jong Un was formally installed as the supreme leader on 29 December 2011. In the days and weeks following his installation, a number of rallies were held throughout the nation as citizens pledged support for their new leader. A military parade in Pyongyang on 9 January 2012 served as a public display of support by the armed forces for their new leader. In a move that some viewed as an additional measure to gain support, Kim Jong Un announced plans for a special pardon and release of an undisclosed number of political prisoners, effective 1 February 2012. The pardon served as part of national celebrations to honor the 70th anniversary of the birthday of Kim Jong Il (in February) and the 100th anniversary of the birth of Kim Il Sung (in April). The last special pardon was made in 2005 at the 16th anniversary of the Korean Workers' Party.

13 GOVERNMENT

North Korea has a centralized government under the rigid control of the communist Korean Workers' Party (KWP), to which all government officials belong. A few minor political parties are allowed to exist in name only. Kim Il Sung ruled North Korea from 1948 until his death in July 1994 as Secretary General of the KWP and President of North Korea. The latter post was abolished following Kim Il Sung's death, and he was given the title of the Eternal President of the Republic. Kim Jong Il served as North Korea's supreme ruler after his father's death and was at the time the only communist leader ever to have inherited power from his father. He died in 2011 and was succeeded by his son, Kim Jong Un.

The executive branch includes the president of the Presidium of the Supreme People's Assembly (chief of state) and the chairman of the National Defense Commission (head of government). The legislative branch is comprised of the Supreme People's Assembly (SPA), which has 687 seats. Little is known about the actual lines of power and authority in the North Korean Government apart from the formal structure set forth in its constitution. North Korea's 1972 constitution was amended in late 1992, September 1998, and April 2009.

The cabinet, formerly known as the State Administration Council (SAC), administers the ministries and has a significant role in implementing policy. The cabinet is headed by the premier and is the dominant administrative and executive agency. The National Defense Commission is responsible for external and internal security and has assumed a significant role in influencing policy. The Politburo of the Central People's Committee is the top policymaking body of the KWP, which also plays a role as the dominant social institution in North Korea.

The unicameral SPA selects members every four years. Usually only two meetings are held annually, each lasting a few days. A standing committee elected by the SPA performs legislative functions when the assembly is not in session. Further, though it is the nation's legislative body, the SPA generally delegates authority to the smaller Presidium chosen from among existing members. Thus, in reality, the SPA serves only to ratify decisions made by the ruling KWP, and is often considered a "rubber stamp," since elections are uncontested and policies are seldom debated. According to the Korean Constitution, any Korean citizen above the age of 17, irrespective of their party affiliation, political views, or religion, are eligible to be elected to the SPA. However, the elections are not democratic by international standards, as voters are presented with only one candidate for each post. The premier is assisted by three vice premiers and a cabinet of 27 ministers, all of whom are appointed by the SPA. A 28th minister, the minister of the People's Armed Forces, is not subordinate to the cabinet but answers directly to Kim Jong Un. However, some observers believe that the first vice chairman of the National Defense Commission is North Korea's most powerful military figure.

14 POLITICAL PARTIES

The KWP, the ruling party of the DPRK, was formed on 10 October 1945 through a merger of the Communist Party and the New Democratic Party. By the mid-1980s, party membership was estimated to have risen to over three million, or about 16% of the population, the largest percentage of any Communist country. The principal party organ is the National Party Congress. The congress adopts the party program and approves the political line set by its Central People's Committee.

In September 2010, the National Defense Commission held its first meeting in 30 years, during which Kim Jong Il was reelected as leader and Kim Jong Un was appointed as a four-star military general, despite the fact that he has had no military experience. Kim Jong Il's sister Kyong Hui was also elevated to the post of general, presumably to give her greater status as a political advisor. Following Kim Jong Il's death in December 2011, Kim Jong Un assumed leadership responsibilities.

15 LOCAL GOVERNMENT

There are three levels of local government. The first level includes provinces (*do*) and province-level municipalities (*chikalsi* or *jikhalsi*). The second level includes ordinary cities (*si* or *shi*), urban districts (*kuyk*), and counties (*gun* or *kun*). The third level is made up of traditional villages (*ri* or *ni*). North Korea is divided into nine provinces and two provincial-level municipalities—Pyongyang and Nasun (also known as Najin-Sonbong)—one special city, Nampo; and 24 cities. It also appears to be divided into nine military districts.

16 JUDICIAL SYSTEM

The judicial system consists of the Central Court, formerly called the Supreme Court; the courts of provinces, cities, and counties; and special courts (courts-martial and transport courts). Most cases are tried in the first instance by people's courts at the city or county level. Provincial courts try important cases and examine appeals from lower-court judgments. Members of the Central Court are named by the Standing Committee of the SPA; lower courts are appointed by the people's assemblies at the corresponding level. A prosecutor-general, who is also appointed by the SPA, is the country's chief law enforcement officer. He appoints prosecutors at the provincial, city, and county levels. The Central Court is the final court of appeal for criminal and civil cases and has initial jurisdiction over grievous crimes against the state. The Central Court supervises all lower courts and the training of judges. It is staffed by a chief judge or president, two associate chief judges or vice presidents, and an unknown number of regular judges.

[17] ARMED FORCES

The International Institute for Strategic Studies reported that armed forces in the DPRK totaled 1.19 million members in 2011. The force was comprised of 1.02 million from the army, 60,000 from the navy, and 110,000 members of the air force. Armed forces represented 11.2% of the labor force in the DPRK. The DPRK was actively pursuing a nuclear weapons program as of 2011.

[18] INTERNATIONAL COOPERATION

During the mid-1970s, the DPRK came out of its relative isolation to pursue a vigorous international diplomacy. By 1986, it had diplomatic relations with 103 countries, including 67 that also had relations with the ROK. The DPRK became a member of the UN on 17 September 1991 and belongs to several nonregional specialized UN agencies, including the Food and Agriculture Organization (FAO), International Civil Aviation Organization (ICAO), International Fund for Agricultural Development (IFAD), International Maritime Organization (IMO), International Telecommunication Union (ITU), United Nations Conference on Trade and Development (UNCTAD), United Nations Educational, Scientific and Cultural Organization (UNESCO), United Nations Industrial Development Organization (UNIDO), Universal Postal Union (UPU), World Health Organization (WHO), World Intellectual Property Organization (WIPO), and World Meteorological Organization (WMO). The county is also a part of the Association of Southeast Asian Nations (ASEAN) Regional Forum, G-77, and the Nonaligned Movement.

The DPRK retains treaties of friendship, cooperation, and mutual defense concluded with China and the republics of the former USSR in 1961. The DPRK was the only Asian Communist country to remain neutral in the Sino-Soviet dispute.

The demilitarized zone that separates North and South Korea has been in place since 1953, though both governments claim a desire for reunification. The DPRK withdrew from the Nuclear Nonproliferation Treaty in 2003, announcing that it would begin construction of nuclear weapons for self-defense. The first official nuclear missile test was in 2006. Since then, North Korea has participated in talks with various nations and international groups on the issue of denuclearization without significant long-term resolutions.

In environmental cooperation, the DPRK is part of the Antarctic Treaty, the Convention on Biological Diversity, the Montréal Protocol, MARPOL, and the UN Convention on Climate Change.

[19] ECONOMY

The Korean War devastated much of the DPRK economy, but growth after postwar reconstruction was rapid. The Communist regime used its rich mineral resources to promote industry, es-

pecially heavy industry. A generally accepted figure put annual industrial growth from 1956 to 1963 at about 25%. By 1965, industry accounted for 78% of the total output, and agriculture 22%, an exact reversal of their respective contributions in 1946. Until the oil crisis of the 1970s, the DPRK ranked as one of the most prosperous states in Asia, but the government's pursuit of self-reliance (juche) had, by the end of the 1960s, also transformed it into one the most isolated and strictly regulated economies in the world. After 1965, greater emphasis was placed on agriculture and light industry, the latter because of increased demand for consumer goods. The industrial growth rate slowed in the late 1960s to around 14% and averaged about 16% during the 1970s. In the meantime, the military government in the ROK began a series of five-year plans in 1962 that set it on the trajectory of export-led growth that vastly outpaced growth in the DPRK. Efforts in the DPRK to accelerate the growth rate during the mid-1970s, requiring substantial imports of heavy industrial equipment from Japan and Western Europe, led to a payments crisis, and the DPRK was repeatedly compelled to reschedule its foreign debt.

The seven-year plan for 1978–84 called for an annual increase in industrial output of 12%. Reliable data on the economy became increasingly difficult to obtain as Kim Il Sung's regime became more obsessed with passing power and his particular vision on to his son, Kim Jong Il. In the 1980s, the government also became seriously involved in the clandestine supply of missiles and nuclear technology to Pakistan and Middle East countries, particularly Iran. Estimates are that growth fell to no more than 2% or 3% in the early 1980s as about one-fourth of output went into the country's outsized military.

After a three-year "period of adjustment," the government announced its third seven-year plan for 1987 to 1993, which targeted an annual increase in industrial growth of 10%. The plan also called for increased allocations to agricultural production, fueling speculation that there were food shortages. In any case, the plan period spanned three watershed events that helped set the economy on its downward course. First was the ROK's successful hosting of the 1988 Olympics, which left the DPRK further isolated due to its decision to boycott the games. Second was the breakup of the Soviet Union in 1991, cutting off the DPRK's main source of trade and aid. Third was the admission of the ROK and the DPRK to the UN in 1991 as separate states, unblocked by a veto from either Russia or China.

In 1995 and 1996, the North Korean population became victims of widespread malnutrition and famine, worsened by the government's reluctance to admit the seriousness of the situation. The government called for the cultivation of marginal land with a target of doubling food production. However, the removal of tree cover from hillsides through the cultivation of marginal land made flooding worse in 1995 and 1996 when the country was hit by heavy rains and a typhoon. Drought conditions that followed worsened not only the food shortage but also the energy shortage by reducing the output from hydroelectric facilities. By 1997, most North Koreans had come to depend on government rations, which were reduced to 3.5–5.3 ounces of food per person per day. Estimates are that in real terms, the DPRK economy contracted 6.8% in 1997 and another 1.1% in 1998. In 1999, there were signs of positive growth, though small and from a low base, due mainly to government construction projects.

The Bank of Korea, the most reliable source of economic data on the DPRK, estimated that the economy expanded 1.3% in 2000 and 3.7% in 2001. Three new special economic zones (SEZs) were announced, making a total of four (the first one was established in 1991), designed to attract foreign investment, particularly from China and South Korea. Such reforms may have been meant to appease the US government, which had branded North Korea part of an "axis of evil" in 2002. In 2006, the gross domestic product (GDP) growth rate was estimated at1.1%, down from 2.2% in 2004. The country continued to suffer from high levels of technical unemployment. Food shortages were also a problem, with large-scale military spending eating up most of the resources. The government tried to respond by allowing private markets to sell a wider range of goods, and by permitting private farming on an experimental basis.

Severe summer flooding followed by dry weather conditions in the fall of 2006 caused poor crop yields, sending DPRK into its 13th year of food shortages. Flooding occurred again in the summer of 2007 but delivery of international food aid, mostly from China and the ROK, prevented full-scale famine.

In February 2010, the Financial Action Task Force (FATF), a powerful, membership-based intergovernmental organization that campaigns against money laundering and terrorist financing, placed tier-two, graduated sanctions on North Korea for failing to commit to an FATF-sponsored action plan to address concerns over illegal financial and terrorist activities within the nation. Listed along with North Korea in the tier-two bracket were Angola, Ethiopia, and Ecuador. The FATF is comprised of thirty-three of the most powerful nations and territories in the world, plus two regional organizations, including the Gulf Co-operation Council.

In August 2010, the United States expanded sanctions against North Korea with the hope of cutting key sources of income for the development of nuclear weapons. The sanctions involved a freeze on the assets of four North Koreans and five government agencies suspected of activities that supported the nuclear weapons industry, including the Munitions Industry Department and the Second Economic Committee. Three government-owned companies were also included in the sanctions—Korea Taesong Trading Co., Green Pine Associated Corp., and the Korea Heungjin Trading Co.

20 INCOME

The CIA estimated that in 2010 the GDP of the DPRK was $40 billion. The CIA defines GDP as the value of all final goods and services produced within a nation in a given year, computed on the basis of purchasing power parity (PPP) rather than value as measured on the basis of the rate of the exchange based on current dollars. The per capita GDP was estimated at $1,800. The annual growth rate of GDP was -0.9%. It was estimated that agriculture accounted for 20.9% of GDP, industry 46.9%, and services 32.1%.

21 LABOR

As of 2009, the DPRK had a total labor force of 12.2 million people. Within that labor force, CIA estimates in 2008 noted that 35% were employed in agriculture, 33% in industry, and 32% in the service sector. There are no free trade unions in North Korea; instead, there is one labor organization controlled by the government, the General Federation of Trade Unions of Korea, of which virtually all industrial and office workers are members. There is no minimum wage. Labor conditions are governed by a national labor law of 1978. The eight-hour workday is standard but most laborers work 12–16 hours daily during production campaigns. Although children under the age of 16 are prohibited by law from working, school children work in factories or on farms to meet production goals. Office and shop workers spend Fridays in public-works and urban-maintenance projects. In addition, some work time is spent on mandatory study of the writings of Kim Il Sung and Kim Jong Il.

22 AGRICULTURE

Roughly 25% of the total land is used in agriculture, and the country's major crops include rice, corn, potatoes, soybeans, and pulses. Cereal production in 2009 amounted to 4.5 million tons, fruit production 1.5 million tons, and vegetable production 4.6 million tons.

Most of the agricultural land is concentrated in the west coast provinces of North and South P'yongan and North and South Hwanghae. Irrigation, land reclamation, and flood-control projects have been carried out, especially in rice-growing areas; about one-half of the arable land is irrigated.

Rice is the principal crop. Improved rice yields have been achieved through the use of "miracle" rice strains, intensive application of fertilizer, and mechanization. Double-cropping of rice is not possible because of the climate, but double-cropping of other grains has been maximized through the use of cold-bed seeding and new seed varieties, so that an estimated half of all cultivated land yields two harvests. The leading grains after rice are corn, wheat, millet, and barley. Other important crops include soybeans, potatoes, sweet potatoes, pulses, oats, sorghum, rye, tobacco, and cotton. The DPRK long claimed to be self-sufficient in grain products, but this status has been affected by both widespread flooding and droughts.

The country's farms were collectivized after the Korean War. The movement began late in 1953, and the process was completed by August 1958, when all of the DPRK's 1,055,000 farm families became members of over 16,000 cooperatives. In order to establish larger and more efficient operating units, the cooperatives were merged in the autumn of 1958 into approximately 3,800 units with about 300 families each. Produce is delivered to the government, which controls distribution through state stores. Most farm workers retain small private plots (less than 100 sq m/1,100 sq ft) and can sell produce from them to the state or in peasant markets.

23 ANIMAL HUSBANDRY

The United Nations Food and Agriculture Organization (UN FAO) reported that the DPRK dedicated 50,000 hectares (123,553 acres) to permanent pasture or meadow in 2009. During that year, the country tended 13.9 million chickens, 576,000 head of cattle, and 2.2 million pigs. The production from these animals amounted to 21,751 tons of beef and veal, 176,579 tons of pork, 44,550 tons of poultry, 132,686 tons of eggs, and 114,358 tons of milk. The DPRK also produced 3,045 tons of cattle hide.

Since the 1950s, a major effort has been made to increase corn and fodder supplies, to improve breeding practices, and to raise sharply the numbers of livestock in all categories. Livestock raising is generally associated with the state farms.

²⁴FISHING

The DPRK had 82,803 decked commercial fishing boats in 2008. The annual capture totaled 205,000 tons according to the UN FAO. The export value of seafood totaled $1.04 billion.

The catch from the sea and from freshwater aquaculture includes mackerel, anchovy, tuna, mullet, rainbow trout, squid, kelp, sea urchin eggs, pollack eggs, and shrimp. Over 98% of fishing activity is marine, concentrated in the Sea of Japan. Much of the annual catch is now used for export.

The fishing industry is entirely socialized, with some 230 maritime cooperatives and more than 30 state-run fishery stations. The main fishing ports are on the east coast.

²⁵FORESTRY

Approximately 47% of the DPRK is covered by forest. The UN FAO estimated the 2009 roundwood production at 1.5 million cu m (53 million cu ft). The value of all forest products, including roundwood, totaled $14.4 million. There are rich stands of coniferous forests in the northern provinces. Predominant trees include oak, alder, larch, pine, spruce, and fir. Most of the timber cut was used for fuel. The Ministry of Forestry, created in 1980, promotes development of forest industries.

²⁶MINING

The DPRK (DPRK) has known deposits of coal, copper, fluorspar, gold, graphite, iron ore, lead, limestone, magnesite (magnesium carbonate), pyrite, salt, silver, tungsten, and zinc. Of these, the country has large reserves of coal, iron ore, limestone, and magnesite.

Gross weight of marketable iron ore and concentrate produced in 2009 was 5.3 million tons. High-grade iron ore deposits lay off the coast of Unryl County, South Hwanghae Province. Outputs of other minerals included: crude magnesite, 150,000 tons; graphite, 30,000 metric tons; mine copper (metal content), 12,000 metric tons; mined zinc, 70,000 metric tons; mined lead, 13,000 metric tons; mined gold, 2,000 kg; mined silver, 20 metric tons, unchanged since 2001; sulfur, 42,000 tons; phosphate rock, 300,000 metric tons, unchanged since 2002; and mined tungsten, 350 metric tons, down from 900 tons in 2006. North Korea also produced barite, hydraulic cement, fluorspar, nitrogen, salt, and pyrophyllite soapstone, and presumably produced varieties of stone, sand, and gravel. As North Korea began emerging from its isolation, mineral trade with the ROK increased, with the DPRK exporting coal, gold, steel, and zinc to the South. Since the collapse of the Soviet Union, North Korea has faced shortages of raw materials, in addition to shortages of fuel, food, and electricity. Molopo Australia NL had four gold projects in North Korea—Big Boy, Changjin, Danchon, and Hambung—and successfully processed 625 g of gold from a gravity separation plant in Changjin.

²⁷ENERGY AND POWER

The World Bank reported in 2008 that the DPRK produced 22.5 billion kWh of electricity and consumed 19.5 billion kWh, or 797 kWh per capita. Roughly 89% of energy came from fossil fuels, while 6% came from alternative fuels. Per capita oil consumption was 851 kg. North Korea has no known reserves of petroleum or natural gas but does have recoverable reserves of coal (661 million short tons as of 2008). The major coal-producing center is in South Pyongan Province, where the Anju, Sunchon, Tokchon, Pukchang, and Kaechon coal-producing complexes are located. Estimated coal production in 2010 was 34.79 million short tons. Domestic consumption that year came to 30.35 million short tons.

Although North Korea has a nuclear energy program, it is not directed toward the production of electric power, but to build nuclear weapons. In 1994 the United States and North Korea negotiated an Agreed Framework, by which North Korea agreed to give up its nuclear ambitions in exchange for the construction of two safer light water nuclear reactors and shipments of oil from the United States. In 2002, it was revealed that North Korea was engaged in pursuing a program of enriching uranium. (Enriched uranium is used for the production of nuclear weapons.) In January 2003, North Korea pulled out of the Nuclear Nonproliferation Treaty, and later admitted it was pursuing the reprocessing of plutonium, which also can be used in the building of nuclear weapons. In April 2003, North Korea stated it possessed nuclear weapons. In August 2003, six-nation talks between the United States, China, the ROK, Japan, Russia, and North Korea began to address the nuclear situation. As of early 2012, the issue of North Korea's nuclear program had yet to be resolved.

²⁸INDUSTRY

Under Japanese rule, northern Korea was regarded mainly as a supplier of war materials, while manufacturing and processing branches were neglected. The Communist regime, however, emphasized the development of manufacturing. By 1963, the metal-fabricating, textile, and food-processing industries accounted for 33%, 18.6%, and 13.7% of industrial output, respectively. By the late 1980s, heavy industry (including metal fabricating and textile production) accounted for 50% of total industrial production. Private enterprise in industry declined from 27.6% of total output in 1946 to only 2% in 1956, and the private sector was said to have disappeared by 1959. About 90% of all industry is state owned, and 10% is owned by cooperatives.

Under the second seven-year plan (1978–84), industrial output was scheduled to grow at an average annual rate of 12.2%; however, Western estimates put annual growth at 2% or 3% by the early 1980s. In the mid-1980s, the government became involved in clandestine missile production and supply. In 1985, the DPRK reached a bilateral accord with Iran, then in the midst of its war with Iraq, whereby North Korea would supply production technology and missiles in exchange for payments to finance engineering of the Scud-B missiles (a more accurate version of the original Scuds) and help in covert procurement of other necessary technologies. Ironically, because it became a matter of international security concern, the missile program is better documented than other aspects of the DPRK's secretive economy. In June 1987, North Korea delivered 90 to 100 Scud-B missiles, 12 launchers, and an undetermined number of HY-2 Silkworm missiles to Iran as part of the two countries' $500 million military assistance agreement.

In June 1990, the DPRK conducted the first successful test of the Scud-C, and in November concluded a second series of agreements with Iran believed to have covered the purchase of DPRK Scud-Cs and the conversion of an Iranian missile-maintenance facility into a production facility. In December 1990, during the run-up to the Persian Gulf War, the DPRK also agreed to sell Scud-B and Scud-C missiles to Iraq, but in February 1991, despite a personal visit from Iraq's deputy foreign minister, the DPRK backed out of the deal because of Iraq's inability to pay cash. Syria, having received $2 billion for participating on the side of the coalition, used some of it to purchase more than 150 North Korean Scud-C missiles for an estimated $500 million.

On 27 March 1992, the United States announced the imposition of sanctions on the DPRK and Iran for missile technology proliferation. In the mid-1990s, the DPRK recruited an estimated 160 Russian strategic weapons specialists to help with the DPRK's missile and nuclear programs. On 12 March 1993, North Korea announced its withdrawal from the Nuclear Nonproliferation Treaty (NPT) because of the International Atomic Energy Association's (IAEA's) efforts to conduct a special inspection of its nuclear facilities. During the spring of 1993, the successful launch of four missiles, one of which hit a target at 500 km (300 mi), raised international alarm to a new level. The DPRK representative to the UN denied that the government had ever supplied missiles to Iran. In a report issued in 1996, the South Korean Unification Ministry estimated that arms exports constituted about 30% of DPRK exports from 1980 to 1993, that annual Scud missile sales totaled about $500 million, and that the DPRK had a production capacity of about 100 Scud-B and Scud-C missiles a year.

The consequence of the DPRK's role as arms supplier to the Middle East was increasing isolation elsewhere. Japan banned the export of missile-related technology to the DPRK in 1988. In 1991, when the Soviet Union collapsed, North Korea lost its main source of fuel and fertilizer, as well as its main markets. As a result, the DPRK's nonmilitary industries atrophied while the government continued to build its military industry, developing nuclear ambitions.

In 2002, industry made up 34% of the economy. By 2010, the number had risen to 48%. Apart from military industries, other industries included mining, textiles, food processing, and tourism. However, the country's industrial stock continues to suffer from underinvestment and spare part shortages, and is considered to be beyond repair.

29 SCIENCE AND TECHNOLOGY

In 1970, the Fifth Party Congress called for the education of one million new technicians and specialists to aid economic modernization and development. By the mid-1990s, the government claimed that there were agricultural specialists on most rural cooperatives, although severe economic deprivation curtailed the DPRK agricultural output. Throughout this period, Russian and Chinese technicians helped train DPRK workers, and the DPRK actively sought to acquire advanced foreign technology through the importation of entire petrochemical and other manufacturing plants from Japan, France, Sweden, and other developed nations. Through 2012, the DPRK's nuclear energy program has gained international attention.

The principal scientific and technical institutions are the Academy of Sciences (founded in 1952), the Academy of Agricultural Science (founded in 1948), the Academy of Fisheries (founded in 1969), the Academy of Forestry (founded in 1948), the Academy of Medical Sciences, the Academy of Light Industry Science (founded in 1954), and the Academy of Railway Sciences. All of these academies are located in Pyongyang, and each has numerous attached research institutes.

By 1994, Kim Il Sung University in Pyongyang (founded in 1946) included faculties of computer science, chemistry, biology, atomic energy, geology, mathematics, and physics. Also in Pyongyang are the Kim Chaek University of Technology, the Pyongyang University of Agriculture, and the Pyongyang University of Medicine.

30 DOMESTIC TRADE

Wholesale and retail trade is almost entirely in state and cooperative hands. Wholesale distribution is administered by the state ministries and enterprises under the general jurisdiction of the Ministry of Material Supply. Most retail shops are run by the People's Service Committee, established in 1972. There are several state-run department stores in Pyongyang, and there is at least one in each provincial capital. All-purpose stores, cooperatives, factory outlets, and special stores for the military and for railroad workers also play an important part in retailing.

Improvements in industry and infrastructure have been slow, as the government continued to dedicate a large portion of funds to military, rather than social or domestic concerns. With the decay of the formal economy, black market activity has rapidly grown throughout the country, with the underground economy replacing formal domestic trade throughout much of the DPRK.

Normal business hours are from 9 a.m. to noon and 1 to 6 p.m., Monday through Friday. Saturday is a "study" day.

31 FOREIGN TRADE

In 2010 exports totaled $2.557 billion, while imports totaled $3.529 billion. Major import partners in 2009 were China, 61%; the ROK, 24%; Singapore, 2%; and India, 2%. Major export partners were the ROK, 47%; China, 40%; and Hong Kong, 2%. The DPRK's principal exports include rice, pig iron, rolled steel, cement, machinery of various types, chemicals, magnetite, textiles, armaments, and gold. Imports include petroleum, coking coal, wheat, cotton, and machinery.

Following the collapse of the Soviet Union, China took the lead as the DPRK's largest trading partner. Inter-Korean trade expanded particularly rapidly after 1988. As the DPRK economy has deteriorated, smuggling activity across the Chinese border has increased.

32 BALANCE OF PAYMENTS

During the late 1970s, the DPRK enjoyed consistent trade surpluses, due in part to increasing shipments of agricultural products, gold and silver, and armaments in exchange for hard currencies. Despite the improving trade picture, the DPRK had still not emerged from the shadow of foreign debt left over from the mid-1970s. Declining prices for precious metals in the early 1980s made it difficult for the nation to meet its debt obligations, even after repeated rescheduling. In 1987, a new rescheduling agreement was reached after Western banks threatened to freeze the DPRK's bank assets if it failed to service bank loans. In the early 2000s, the government focused on attracting foreign aid and earning hard currency without introducing market reforms. Desperately needed food and fuel aid from donor countries declined in 2002–03, due in part to the government's threats of nuclear weapons capabilities. The CIA reported that the trade deficit was $972 million in 2010.

³³ BANKING AND SECURITIES

The Central Bank, established in 1946, is the sole recipient of national revenues and the repository for all precious metals. It supplies basic operating funds to various sectors of the economy and is subordinate to the Ministry of Finance. The Central Bank is also an administrative organ that executes the fiscal policies of the State Planning Commission. It supervises the Foreign Trade Bank, established in 1959, and the Industrial Bank, established in 1964. The latter provides loans and credits to farm and fishing cooperatives and has an extensive system of branches that help to manage the financial operations of all cooperatives.

The Kumgang Bank is a specialized bank that handles transactions of foreign trade organizations dealing with exports and imports of machinery, metals, mineral products, and chemical products. The Daesong Bank handles transactions of the Daesong Trading Co. and other trading organizations. Another state bank is the Changgwang Credit Bank, founded in 1983.

There are savings facilities at all post offices, in industrial enterprises, and in the "trust" sections in the agricultural cooperatives. Through the latter, large farm and fishing cooperatives perform local banking functions, especially the raising and allocation of capital for local needs.

In 2009, North Korea revalued its currency in an effort to control prices and limit the impact of private markets allowed to develop during 2007–09. In a surprise move, on 30 November 2009, the DPRK recalled and reissued its currency, giving citizens just a week in which to exchange old money for new at the rate of 100 to 1, spurring inflation and panic in North Korean markets and rendering savings nearly worthless.

There are no securities exchanges in the DPRK.

³⁴ INSURANCE

The State Insurance Bureau and the Korea Foreign Insurance Co. carry fire and natural disaster insurance and, as appropriate, livestock, marine, and passenger insurance on a compulsory basis. Individuals may take out various types of property, life, and travel insurance, all provided by the government.

³⁵ PUBLIC FINANCE

In 2010, the budget of DPRK included $3.2 billion in public revenue and $3.3 billion in public expenditures. The budget deficit amounted to 0.4% of GDP. In total, $12.5 billion of the debt was held by foreign entities. The annual state budget is approved at regular sessions of the SPA. Foreign aid, important after the Korean War, has not appeared as budgetary income since 1961.

³⁶ TAXATION

All direct taxes were abolished in 1974; the DPRK thus became the first country in the world to abolish income taxes collected from its citizens. As a result, the population is dependent on the government for many services. The government collects a percentage (turnover tax) on all transactions between producers and state marketing agencies. Fees are charged to farmers for seeds, fertilizer, irrigation water, and equipment. Consumers pay a tax for the use of water and certain other household amenities. The tax

on collective farms is 15% of the harvest, paid in kind. Refugees from North Korea reported that a similar in-kind tax was being assessed on the private plots that proliferated during the 1990s, but there has been no official confirmation of this assessment.

All foreign-invested enterprises are subject to income, property, turnover, and local taxes. In the four special economic zones established by the government, one in 1991 and three in 2002, the tax on profits for most enterprises is set at 14%; for enterprises involving high technology, infrastructure construction, or light industry, the tax rate is 10%. Resident aliens in the DPRK must pay personal income taxes; the rate varies from 4% to a top rate of 20%.

³⁷ CUSTOMS AND DUTIES

No information is available.

³⁸ FOREIGN INVESTMENT

In 1984, the Joint Venture Act permitted foreign direct investment for the first time. Investment mainly came from Soviet-bloc countries, however, as both the United States and the ROK were closed to products from the DPRK. Companies found it difficult to do business in North Korea because of limits on equity ownership and a suffocating bureaucracy. In any case, the law was abruptly withdrawn in 1985, reinforcing perceptions of an unstable atmosphere for business.

In 1991, faced with the collapse of the Soviet bloc, the government announced plans to establish a multinational special economic zone (FETZ) in the Tuman River estuary region. On 11 December 1992, the Supreme People's Assembly passed three laws relating to foreign investment—the Foreign Investment Law, the Foreign Enterprise Law, and the Joint Venture Law. The laws allowed 10% foreign ownership and loosened government control over employee layoffs. Three types of enterprises were distinguished: contractual joint ventures, equity joint ventures, and "foreign enterprises." Citizens of the ROK were treated as foreigners under the investment laws. Foreigners were prohibited from establishing a "technologically backward" enterprise, or one that threatened DPRK national security. In practice, the most suspect categories are those involved in publishing, the press, broadcasting, and telecommunications. Also not permitted are businesses that do not conform to the "ideological emotions of the people."

Most trade with South Korean enterprises is conducted in the contractual joint-venture mode in which, typically, the DPRK partner takes responsibility for production and management while the ROK partner supplies both advanced technology and access to export markets. Most meetings between North and South Korean partners are held outside both countries. Applications for investment have remained limited; most have come from Japan-based Korean investors. Trade with the ROK dropped significantly following the sinking of a South Korean military vessel by the DPRK in 2010. As of 2011, joint operations continued only at the Kaesong Industrial Complex.

³⁹ ECONOMIC DEVELOPMENT

Until the 1990s, the economy operated on a planned basis, with priority given to the development of industry, particularly heavy industry. Planning began in 1947, when the economy operated first under two consecutive one-year plans (1947 and 1948), followed by a two-year plan (1949–50), which was interrupted by the Korean War in June 1950. After the war, economic reconstruction followed the terms of a three-year plan (1954–56) and a five-year plan (1957–61). The industrial goals of the five-year plan were fulfilled in just half the allotted time, so 1960 was set aside as a year of adjustment. An ambitious seven-year plan was then launched in 1961, with the general objectives of a 220% increase in industrial output and a 150% rise in grain production. This plan had to be extended until 1970, however, before its targets were fulfilled. In 1975, the DPRK announced completion of its six-year plan (1971–76) one year ahead of schedule, although certain outputs fell somewhat short of projected levels. Industrial growth slowed in 1976. A second seven-year plan (1978–84) called for a 12% annual industrial growth rate. Although the government claimed that its goals had been met or exceeded, neither the actual results nor a new plan was announced during the following three years. During this period the DPRK experienced the double trauma of ballooning international debt (to more than $5 billion, nearly $2 billion owed to Communist creditors) and watching the ROK's per capita income soar past its own.

There was a three-year hiatus before the government set forth the third seven-year plan (1987–93). (The death of President Kim Il Sung on 8 July 1994 marked the end of multiyear planning.) Annual growth of 10% was targeted under the third seven-year plan, part of which would be derived from missile production and export. Its stated targets were a 90% increase in industrial output, 40% in agricultural production, and 70% in national income. The DPRK government publishes no official economic data, but estimates by the ROK Bank of Korea, the most reliable source of information on the North Korean economy, suggest that actual performance fell far short of these targets, in some areas by as much as 50%, and that overall industrial output decreased. The plan period spanned the breakup and economic liberalization of the Soviet bloc in 1991. President Kim Il Sung made a gesture at keeping up with the trends, decreeing the establishment of the Rajin-Sonborg Free Economic and Trade Zone (FETZ). However, the lack of infrastructure and low investor confidence in the regime made the FETZ ineffective in attracting investments.

In late 1993, statements released by the Korean Workers' Party Central Committee for the first time admitted to the overall failure in achieving the goals of the economic plan. Another three-year period of adjustment was announced during which, again, agricultural production, light industry, and infrastructure projects were to be prioritized.

The so-called Agreed Framework of October 1994 embodied the offer to replace the DPRK's heavy-water nuclear facilities (suitable for producing weapons-grade fuel) with light-water reactors (LWRs, not as suitable), with construction and financing arranged by the United States. An annual supply of 500,000 metric tons of heavy oil would be donated by a consortium of 17 countries. In exchange, the DPRK committed to freeze and eventually dismantle its heavy-water facilities. The Korea Peninsula Energy Development Corporation (KEDO) was created to administer the agreement. Besides maintaining the freeze, the DPRK was also dissuaded in 1999 from test-firing its most advanced missile, the Taepodong-II, which has a range of over 6,000 km (3,728 mi).

The Agreed Framework began to unravel in early 2002, after US president George W. Bush, in his State of the Union address,

branded North Korea as part of an "axis of evil." In July 2002, the DPRK introduced a number of market-based economic reforms. Three special economic zones were officially established in 2002, including a special autonomous region (SAR) in Sinuiji to attract Chinese investment, and zones at Mt. Kumgang and near Kaesŏng to attract South Korean investment. The government also announced it would be presenting a formal economic plan in 2003. These gestures were overwhelmed by increased tensions following the October 2002 announcement from the US State Department that the DPRK regime had admitted it was pursuing a secret nuclear weapons program. Oil shipments through KEDO were stopped after November 2002, and by the end of December, North Korea had expelled all IAEA inspectors and removed their monitoring devices. In February, the IAEA referred North Korea's nuclear program to the UN Security Council. In April 2003, Kim Jong Il asked for a nonaggression pact with the United States, arguing that the United States was planning to overthrow his regime. No economic plan had been issued.

The way North Korea guards the access to indicators that might highlight its level of economic health prevents any solid analysis of economic growth perspectives. It is believed, however, that the country still suffers from food shortages and lacks a coherent future development strategy. The DPRK moved again against free-market tendencies in December 2009 by issuing a new, revalued currency in an effort to combat rising inflation. The program limited the amount of old money people could exchange for new bills. This move angered individuals and merchants who had large stores of the old currency. In North Korea's state-run economy, food and goods are rationed through state-run stores, which sell the products at low, fixed prices determined by the state. Because North Korea suffers from supply shortages, citizens are often willing to pay more for these products than the state charges, and therefore turn to the black market where food and goods are resold at higher prices. North Korea's rough currency revaluation was designed to do three things: reduce inflation, damage the vibrancy of the black market, and redistribute wealth by limiting the amount of old money citizens could exchange for new. But in a country where supply shortages are constant, analysts noted that this cycle would recur, just under a new currency. The pessimistic predictions about the program proved accurate. Within the first months of the revaluation, the program failed to meaningfully address the underlying economic stagnation of North Korea, and social unrest was mounting. Facing pressure to act, North Korean authorities were reported to have arrested and executed the country's top financial chief in March 2010, Pak Nam-gi. Pak Nam-gi faced charges of intentionally harming North Korea's economy.

The sinking of a South Korean military vessel—presumably by a DPRK torpedo—worsened economic relations between the two countries. During 2011 and continuing into 2012, the DPRK sought greater Chinese investment in North Korean special economic zones, as well as the potential construction of a natural gas pipeline from Russia to the ROK that would pass through the DPRK.

40 SOCIAL DEVELOPMENT

All men and women of working age are required to work, and all economic activity is run by the state. The government provides any medical, pension, or other welfare program to the workers. The country relies heavily on international aid for basic subsistence.

Although the constitution grants equal rights for women, few women have reached high levels in the government. The state provides nurseries and day-care centers, and large families are encouraged. Like men, women are obligated by law to work, although few occupy high official positions. Women with large families are entitled to shorter work hours. Female workers are legally guaranteed five weeks of maternity leave.

The government rejects international human rights standards, and human rights organizations are not permitted to operate. Dissent is not tolerated, and capital punishment is meted out for a wide variety of offenses, including attempted defection.

The government classifies all citizens into three groups: core, wavering, and hostile. These security ratings reflect the perceived degree of loyalty exhibited by citizens. These ratings may be taken into account in the allocation of housing, employment, medical care, and other benefits. All citizens are subjected to extensive indoctrination. Listening to foreign broadcasts or possession of banned reading materials is punishable by death. Travel within the country is also strictly controlled. Travel passes must be requested for intervillage travel.

41 HEALTH

According to the CIA, life expectancy in the DPRK was 67 years in 2011. There were 33 physicians, 41 nurses and midwives, and 132 hospital beds per 10,000 inhabitants. The fertility rate was 1.9, while the infant mortality rate was 26 per 1,000 live births. In 2008 the maternal mortality rate, according to the World Bank, was 25 per 10,000 births. It was estimated that 98% of children were vaccinated against measles. The HIV/AIDS adult prevalence rate was estimated at less than 0.10 per 100 adults in 2007.

The Ministry of Public Health is responsible for all national health services, including disease prevention and sanitation. All of the population has access to health care. Polio has been nearly eradicated. Western medicine is used alongside traditional Eastern medicine (*tonguihak*). Cancer is the leading cause of death, followed by heart disease and hypertension.

42 HOUSING

A serious housing shortage resulted from the government's early stress on industrial rather than residential construction. The housing deficit was aggravated by the Korean War, which demolished about one-third of the country's housing. Since then, residential housing has received serious attention. The construction of hundreds of thousands of homes was often included in multiyear development plans. Natural disasters such as floods have rendered thousands homeless.

43 EDUCATION

Overall, the CIA estimated that the DPRK has a literacy rate of 99%. Both primary and secondary education are free and compulsory for 10 years, beginning at age five. Children ages one through five are cared for in nursery schools, followed by one year of kindergarten, four years of primary school, and six years of secondary school. Subjects such as the Korean language, mathematics, and physical education account for most of the instructional time

in the classroom; however, an estimated 10% of instructional time is spent on the "Great Kim Il Sung" and "Communist Morality."

Kim Il Sung University was founded in 1946 in Pyongyang. Admission to the university is gained by intensely competitive examination. Song Kyun University of Koryo was founded in 1992, along with three medical schools. Other institutions of higher learning include the Kimch'aek Polytechnic Institute, Pyongyang Agricultural College, and Pyongyang Medical School. A system of adult schools, correspondence courses, and workplace schools makes higher education widely available. There are over 100 schools offering specialized workers' training.

44 LIBRARIES AND MUSEUMS

The DPRK has more than 200 public libraries, the largest being the Grand People's Study House in Pyongyang (also serving as the national library), with 20 million volumes. Also in Pyongyang, there is a fairly new German library holding 4,000 scientific books in natural and social sciences, plus leading German newspapers and magazines. This is the first public institution to allow citizens to freely read foreign books. In addition, there are research libraries at the academies of sciences and social sciences and at Kim Il Sung University.

Museums include the Korean Central Historical Museum, the Memorial Museum of the War of Liberation, the Korean Art Gallery, the Ethnographic Museum, and the Korean Revolutionary Museum, all in Pyongyang. There is a large museum at Mangyongdae, Kim Il Sung's birthplace, near the capital.

45 MEDIA

In 2009, the CIA reported that there were 1.2 million telephone landlines in DPRK. There were 17 FM radio stations, 14 AM radio stations, and 14 shortwave radio stations. Postal, telephone, and telegraph services are operated by the government. Telephones are believed to be used primarily for government business. Private lines are for local calling only; international phone lines are available only under very restricted circumstances.

The Korean Central Broadcasting Station in Pyongyang has a 1,500-kW transmitter. Broadcasts reach to every corner of the country through a system of more than one million loudspeakers, as well as through private radios. In addition, news is broadcast to other countries in English, Russian, French, and Spanish. There are two radio networks (Korean Central Radio and Radio Pyongyang) and two television networks (Korean Central TV and Mansudae TV). Internet access is permitted only to foreign visitors and high-ranking government officials. In 2010, there were only three Internet hosts.

In 2010, North Korea joined Twitter. Operating under the name *uriminzok* ("our nation" in Korean), North Korea began sending daily tweets condemning the United States and the "puppet" regime of South Korea. The move to join Twitter corresponded with a decision to also begin broadcasting propaganda videos on YouTube. North Korea's Twitter and YouTube accounts are operated by a user based in Pyongyang named "uriminzokkiri." The website www.uriminzokkiri.com is run by the Committee for the Peaceful Reunification of Korea, a main North Korean propaganda agency.

All newspapers and periodicals in the DPRK are published by government, party, or front organizations; each edition is subjected to prepublication review and censorship. The leading national newspapers and their publishers are *Rodong Sinmun* (Central Committee of the Korean Workers' Party), *Minju Choson* (Presidium of the Supreme People's Assembly and the cabinet), *Joson Immingun* (Korean People's Army Daily), and *Rodong Chongnyon* (Kim Il Sung Socialist Youth League). Each province has a newspaper, and other mass organizations have their own publications. A state news service, the Korean Central News Agency, is the sole organ for the gathering and dissemination of news.

Though there are articles of the constitution that provide for freedom of speech and the press, in practice the government prohibits the exercise of these rights, controlling all information. The receipt of foreign broadcasts is illegal, as is any criticism of the government in any media.

⁴⁶ORGANIZATIONS

Mass organizations established for specialized political, economic, or cultural purposes include the powerful Democratic Front for the Reunification of the Fatherland, commonly known as the Fatherland Front. Among its constituent members are the Kim Il Sung Socialist Youth League (formerly known as the Socialist Working Youth League), under the direct guidance of the Central Committee of the Korean Workers' Party; the Young Pioneer Corps, open to children ages 9–15; and the Korean Democratic Women's League. Also important is the Korean Agricultural Workers' Union. There are a number of sports associations and clubs throughout the country. There is a national chapter of the Red Cross Society.

⁴⁷TOURISM, TRAVEL, AND RECREATION

The estimated daily cost to visit Pyongyang, the capital, was $271. Most sightseeing takes place in the capital city of Pyongyang. Travel outside Pyongyang is closed to individual tourists but available to groups. Nampe, the port city for Pyongyang, has a beach resort area. The two most outstanding tourist sites outside the capital are the Kumgang (Diamond) Mountains in the southwest and Packdu Mountain on the Chinese border. Wrestling, tug-of-war, chess (with pieces different from the European form), and kite fighting are traditional sports. Also of note are the Arirang Mass Games, held from August through October, and the Grand Mass Gymnastics and Artistic Performance, held in the capital's Rungrado May Day Stadium. All visitors need valid passports and visas secured in advance. Tourists from the United States and South Korea may need an invitation to travel to the DPRK.

⁴⁸FAMOUS PERSONS

Among the many historical figures of united Korea are Ulchi Mundok, a Koguryo general of the early 7th century AD; Kim Yo-sin (595–673), a warrior and folk hero in Silla's struggle to unify the peninsula; Wang Kon (877–943), the founder and first ruler of the Koryo Dynasty; Yun Kwan (d. 1111), a Koryo general who repulsed Chinese invaders; Kim Pu-sik (1075–1151), a scholar-official who wrote the great *History of the Three Kingdoms;* Yi Song-gye (1335–1408), a general and founder of the Yi (or Li) Dynasty; King Sejong (1397–1450), who called for the invention of Han'gul and was Korea's greatest monarch; Yi Hwang (1501–70) and Yi I (1536–84), Neo-Confucianist philosophers and officials; Yi Sun-sin (1545–98), an admiral who invented the "turtleboat," the first ironclad ship, and defeated the Japanese in every naval engagement of the Hideyoshi invasions, dying in the climactic battle; Chong Yag-yong (1762–1836), a pragmatic scholar-official and prolific writer; and Yi Ha-ung (1820–98), known as the Taewon'gun (Prince Regent), the regent for his son, Kojong, and the central political figure of the late 19th century.

The preeminent political figure of the DPRK is Kim Il Sung (1912–94), the leader of the nation from 1948 until his death. Other influential figures have included Kim Il (1910–84), a prominent officeholder since 1954; Kim Jong Il (1941–2011), the son and successor of Kim Il Sung; Nam Il (1914–76), a chief of staff who became well known as an armistice negotiator at P'anmunjom (1951–53); and Marshal O Jin U (1918–95), head of the army from 1976 until 1993. Kim Jong Un (b. 1983?), the son of Kim Jong Il, succeeded his father in December 2011.

⁴⁹DEPENDENCIES

The DPRK has no territories or colonies.

⁵⁰BIBLIOGRAPHY

Cirincione, Joseph, Jon B. Wolfsthal, and Miriam Rajkumar. *Deadly Arsenals: Nuclear, Biological, and Chemical Threats.* 2nd ed. Washington, DC: Carnegie Endowment for International Peace, 2005.

Connor, Mary E. *The Koreas.* Santa Barbara, CA: ABC CLIO, 2009.

Dudley, William, ed. *North and South Korea: Opposing Viewpoints.* Farmington Hills, MI: Greenhaven Press, 2003.

Edwards, Paul M. *The Korean War: A Historical Dictionary.* Lanham, MD: Scarecrow Press, 2003.

Foley, James A., ed. *Korea's Divided Families: Fifty Years of Separation.* New York: RoutledgeCurzon, 2003.

Gause, Ken E. *North Korea under Kim Chong-Il: Power, Politics, and Prospects for Change.* Santa Barbara, CA: Praeger, 2011.

Hoare, J. E. *A Political and Economic Dictionary of East Asia.* Philadelphia: Routledge/Taylor and Francis, 2005.

———, and Susan Pares. *A Political and Economic Dictionary of East Asia.* Philadelphia: Routledge/Taylor and Francis, 2005.

Kim, Ilpyong J. *Historical Dictionary of North Korea.* Lanham, MD: Scarecrow Press, 2003.

Lan'kov, A. N. *From Stalin to Kim Il Sung: The Formation of North Korea, 1945–1960.* New Brunswick, NJ: Rutgers University Press, 2002.

Lee, Hy-Sang. *North Korea: A Strange Socialist Fortress.* Westport, CT: Praeger, 2001.

McNamara, Dennis L. *The Colonial Origins of Korean Enterprise, 1910–1945.* New York: Cambridge University Press, 2006.

North Korea's Engagement: Perspectives, Outlook, and Implications. Washington, DC: National Intelligence Council, 2001.

Park, Han S. *North Korea: The Politics of Unconventional Wisdom.* Boulder, CO: Lynne Rienner, 2002.

Seth, Michael J. *A History of Korea from Antiquity to the Present.* Lanham, MD: Rowman and Littlefield, 2011.

KOREA, REPUBLIC OF (ROK)

Republic of Korea
Taehan Min-guk

CAPITAL: Seoul

FLAG: The flag, called the T'aegukki, shows, on a white field, a central circle divided into two parts, red on top and deep blue below, in the shape of Chinese yin and yang symbols. Broken and unbroken black bars in each of the four corners are variously arranged in sets of three, representing divination diagrams.

ANTHEM: *Aegukka (The Song of Patriotism).*

MONETARY UNIT: The won (KRW) is the national currency. There are notes of 500, 1,000, 5,000, and 10,000 won. KRW1 = US$0.00087 (or US$1 = KRW1,152) as of 2012.

WEIGHTS AND MEASURES: Both the metric system and ancient Korean units of measurement are used.

HOLIDAYS: New Year's Days, 1–3 January; Independence Movement Day, 1 March; Labor Day, 10 March; Arbor Day, 5 April; Children's Day, 5 May; Buddha's Birthday (8th Day of the fourth Lunar Month); Memorial Day, 6 June; Constitution Day, 17 July; Liberation Day, 15 August; Armed Forces Day, 1 October; National Foundation Day, 3 October; Han'gul (Korean Alphabet) Day, 9 October; Christmas, 25 December.

TIME: 9 p.m. = noon GMT.

1LOCATION, SIZE, AND EXTENT

Occupying the southern 45% of the Korean Peninsula in East Asia, the Republic of Korea (South Korea—ROK) has an area of 98,480 sq km (38,023 sq mi), extending 642 km (399 mi) NNE–SSW and 436 km (271 mi) ESE–WNW. Comparatively, the area occupied by South Korea is slightly larger than the state of Indiana. Bounded on the N by the Democratic People's Republic of Korea (North Korea—DPRK), on the E by the Sea of Japan (known in Korea as the East Sea), on the S by the Korea Strait, and on the W by the Yellow Sea, the ROK has a total land boundary length of 238 km (148 mi) and a coastline of 2,413 km (1,508 mi). A demilitarized zone (DMZ), 4,000 m (13,100 ft) wide, covering 1,262 sq km (487 sq mi) and located north and south of the 38th parallel, separates the ROK from the DPRK, which comprises the northern part of the Korean Peninsula.

Over 3,000 islands, most of them off the southern and western coasts and belonging to the ROK, add another 8,600 km (5,350 mi) of coastline.

The ROK's capital city, Seoul, is located in the northwestern part of the country.

2TOPOGRAPHY

Elevations in the southern part of the Korean Peninsula are generally lower than those in the north. Only about 30% of the Republic of Korea (ROK) consists of lowlands and plains. The principal lowlands, all bordering the Yellow Sea along the west coast, include the Han River Plain, near Seoul; the Pyongtaek and Honam plains, south of the capital; and the Yongsan Plain in the southwest. Mt. Halla (1,950 m/6,398 ft), on volcanic Cheju Island, is the

nation's highest point, while Mt. Chiri, or Chii (1,915 m/6,283 ft), is the highest point on the mainland.

Principal rivers of South Korea include the Han (514 km/319 mi), with Seoul near its mouth; the Kum (401 km/249 mi) and Yongsan (116 km/72 mi), which water the fertile plains of the southwest; and the Somjin (212 km/132 mi), in the south. The longest river in the ROK is the Naktong (521 km/324 mi), which waters the southeast. Yellow Sea tides on the west coast rise to over 9 m (30 ft) in some places, while Japan Sea tides on the east coast rise only about 1 m (3 ft).

3CLIMATE

The average January temperature ranges from -5°C (23°F) at Seoul to -2°C (28°F) at Pusan and 4°C (39°F) on Cheju Island. During the hotter summer months, however, the regional variation in temperature is not nearly so marked, with average temperatures ranging from 25°C to 27°C (77°F to 81°F) in most lowland areas. Average rainfall is 100 to 150 cm (40 to 50 in). Nearly all the rainfall occurs in the April-September period, especially during the rainy season, late June to early August. From one to three mild typhoons normally strike the south in the early fall, with a severe one occurring every two or three years. Southern regions can experience up to 240 days free of frost during a given year. Yet during the colder months, climates can reach frigid temperatures that are often unexpected of the peninsula.

4FLORA AND FAUNA

The World Resources Institute estimates that there are 2,898 plant species in the Republic of Korea. In addition, Korea is home to 89 mammal, 423 bird, 24 reptile, and 14 amphibian species. The calculation reflects the total number of distinct species residing in the country, not the number of endemic species.

The Korean Peninsula is rich in varieties of plant life typical of temperate regions. Warm temperate vegetation, including camellias and other broad-leaved evergreens, predominate in the south and on Cheju Island. Zoologists have identified more than 130 freshwater fishes. Bear, wild boar, deer, and lynx still are found in the highlands, but the shrinking of the forested area has reduced the animal population in recent years. Migratory water fowl, cranes, herons, and other birds are visible on the plains. Noxious insects and household pests infest the warmer regions, and aquatic life is generally infected with parasites.

The largest and oldest fruit-bearing tree is located in South Korea—the ginkgo tree. Allegedly, it was planted in the 10th century by a Shilla prince on the temple grounds of Yongmunsa Temple. Its trunk circumference is 54 feet, and its height is 175 feet. Koreans have found that most plants and flowers have medicinal or edible value and there is a widespread commercial and home-based homeopathic medicine culture and industry.

5 ENVIRONMENT

The World Resources Institute reported that the Republic of Korea had designated 350,200 hectares (865,363 acres) of land for protection as of 2006. Water resources totaled 69.7 cu km (16.72 cu mi), while water usage was 18.59 cu km (4.46 cu mi) per year. Domestic water usage accounted for 36% of total usage, industrial for 16%, and agricultural for 48%. Per capita water usage totaled 389 cu m (13,737 cu ft) per year.

Efforts to control the detrimental effects of rapid industrialization, urbanization, and population growth focus on the Office of Environment, established in 1980 to control air, water, and land pollution and manage solid wastes. The Environmental Preservation Law, revised in 1979, covers air, water, and noise pollution; soil preservation; and disposal of solid wastes.

The purity of the nation's water is threatened by agricultural chemicals. Air pollution, associated mainly with the use of coal briquettes for home heating and the increase in automobile traffic, is also severe, with smog a common problem in Seoul. In the mid-1990s, South Korea had among the world's highest level of industrial carbon dioxide emissions, which totaled 289.8 million metric tons per year, a per capita level of 6.56 metric tons per year. In 1996, the total rose to 408 million metric tons. In 2000, the total of carbon dioxide emissions was at 427 million metric tons. The South Korea government reported in 2009 that carbon dioxide emissions increased 2.9 percent—totaling 620 million tons—in 2007.

There are 16 Ramsar Wetland Sites in the country. Although 28 species of birds and 8 species of mammals—chipmunk, wild boar, squirrel, raccoon dog, badger, hare, river deer, and roe deer—are still classified as game species, hunting was banned by the government from August 1972 through December 1981, except in such game preserves as that of Cheju Island. According to a the International Union for Conservation of Nature and Natural Resources (IUCN) Red List of Threatened Species, threatened species as of 2011 included 9 mammals, 29 birds, 1 reptile, 2 amphibians, 19 fish, and 3 species of invertebrates. Endangered species in the Republic of Korea (ROK) included the Amur leopard, Oriental white

stork, Japanese crested ibis, and Tristram's woodpecker. The Japanese sea lion has become extinct.

6 POPULATION

The US Central Intelligence Agency (CIA) estimated the population of the Republic of Korea in 2011 to be approximately 48,754,657, placing it as the 26th most populous state in the world. Population density was about 504 people per sq km (1,305 people per sq mi). Approximately 11.4% of the population was over 65 years of age, with another 15.7% under 15 years of age. The median age in the ROK was 38.4 years. There were 1.07 males for every female in the country. The population's annual rate of change was 0.23%. The projected population for the year 2025 was estimated to reach about 49,100,000.

The UN estimated that 83% of the South Korean population resided in urban areas, with an annual rate of change of 0.6%. The largest urban areas, along with their respective populations, included Seoul, 9.8 million; Busan (Pusan), 3.4 million; Incheon (Inch'on), 2.6 million; Daegu (Taegu), 2.5 million; and Daejon (Taejon), 1.5 million. Gyeonggi Province, which encompasses Seoul, Incheon (South Korea's third-largest city), and Suwon, comprises 48% of the entire country's population.

Korea is the most rapidly aging society in the world. After becoming an "aging" society in 2000 (with 7% percentage of the population 65 years and older), Korea was projected to reach an "aged" society in 2019 (14% over 65) and a "super-aged society" by 2026 (20% over 65). Korea's elderly population is expected to rise to 24.3 percent of the total in 2030 and to 38.2 percent in 2050, far higher than the rate projected for other economically advanced nations.

7 MIGRATION

Estimates of the Republic of Korea's net migration rate, carried out by the CIA in 2011, amounted to zero. The total number of emigrants living abroad was 2.08 million, and the total number of immigrants living in the Republic of Korea was 534,800. During the Japanese occupation (1910–45), some three million Koreans immigrated to Manchuria and other parts of China, 700,000 to Siberia, approximately three million to Japan, and about 7,000 to the United States (mostly to Hawaii). The great majority of those who went to Japan were from the populous southern provinces, and large numbers (1.5–2 million) of them returned home following the end of hostilities in 1945. In addition, from 1945 through 1949, at least 1.2 million North Koreans crossed the 38th parallel into the Republic of Korea (ROK), refugees from Communism or from the Korean War. Under the Emigration Law of 1962, the ROK government encouraged immigration to South America (especially Brazil), Germany, the Middle East, and elsewhere. Most of the emigrants are workers who remit earnings back home. A total of 409,922 Koreans emigrated during the 1962–80 period; emigration peaked at 48,270 in 1976 but declined to 27,163 by 1990. Koreans have immigrated permanently to the United States in large numbers since 1971; the population in the United States of Korean origin was 798,849 in 1990 (72.7% foreign born) but by 2007 had risen to 2,102,283. China has 2,336,771 Koreans living within its borders and Japan, 912,770. Together these three countries are home to 78.44% of the entire Korean diaspora. Migration within South Korea, mainly from the rural areas to the cities, remains substantial despite government efforts to improve village living conditions.

In 1993, South Korea developed two programs allowing employers to hire migrant workers: the industrial trainee system and the work permit program. The training program was undercut by the fact that as unauthorized workers, trainees could earn a higher wage, even with expenses. Employers face fines of up to 20 million won ($19,080) and up to three years in prison for hiring illegal foreigners. Since August 2004, foreigners can enter Korea as workers under the Employment Permit System. This system benefits the employers as the workers are not quitting their jobs.

8 ETHNIC GROUPS

Koreans are believed to be descended primarily from Tungusic peoples of the Mongoloid race, who originated in the cold northern regions of Central Asia. There is scant evidence of non-Mongoloid admixture. There are about 20,000 Chinese living in South Korea; however, the ROK has no sizable ethnic minority.

9 LANGUAGES

The Korean language is usually held to be a member of the Altaic family; there are only slight differences among the various dialects. Korean is written in a largely phonetic alphabet called Han'gul, created in 1443. The Korean alphabet originally consisted of 14 consonants and 10 vowels; since then, 5 consonants and 11 vowels have been added. Han'gul letters are combined into syllables by clustering, in imitation of Chinese characters. Republic of Korea (ROK) governments have launched several "language beautification" drives designed to purge Korean of borrowings from Japanese and other languages, but more than half of the vocabulary consists of words derived from Chinese. English is widely taught in junior high and high school.

10 RELIGIONS

Most South Koreans are quite eclectic in their religious beliefs, the majority subscribing to varying mixtures of Taoism, Confucianism, Buddhism, Christianity, Ch'ondogyo (Religion of the Heavenly Way, an indigenous sect originating in 1860), and local animism. There is a humorous adage that in Korea "you are born Buddhist, live Confucian and die Christian," reflecting the generally ecumenical spiritual nature of Koreans. Shamanism, especially its aspect of exorcism of evil spirits, survives in some rural areas of the Republic of Korea (ROK) and has taken on new cultural expressions even in modern, urban areas. Geomancy is also used in matters such as the selection of auspicious building and tomb sites. At the 2005 census, Buddhists accounted for about 22.8% of the population, followed by Protestants at 18.3% and Roman Catholics at 10.9%. Protestant denominations included Methodist, Lutheran, Baptist, Presbyterian, and Anglican, and the Korean Gospel Church Assembly. Ten of the eleven largest Christian congregations in the world are in Seoul.

Other religions with significant popular followings include Taejongyo, based on the worship of a trinity of ancient deities, and Soka Gakkai, a Buddhist sect of Japanese origin. There are also practicing Muslims, members of the Unification Church, Mormons, and Jehovah's Witnesses. The constitution provides for freedom of religion, and this right is generally respected in practice. The Religious Affairs Bureau of the Ministry of Culture and Tour-

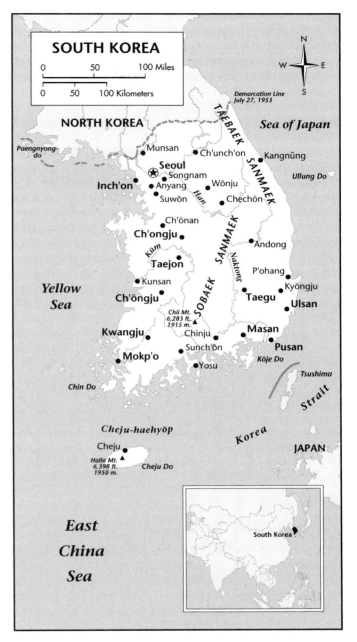

LOCATION: 33°7′ to 38°38′N; 124°36′ to 130°56′ E. BOUNDARY LENGTHS: DPRK, 240 kilometers (149 miles); total coastline, 1,318 kilometers (819 miles). TERRITORIAL SEA LIMIT: 12 miles.

ism sponsors such groups as the Korea Religious Council and the Council for Peaceful Religions in an effort to promote interfaith understanding. Buddha's Birthday and Christmas are observed as national holidays.

11 TRANSPORTATION

The CIA reported that the Republic of Korea had a total of 103,029 km (64,019 mi) of roads in 2006, of which 80,642 km (50,109 mi) were paved. There are 346 vehicles per 1,000 people in the country. The ROK road system carries 90% of the country's transportation. Bus transportation networks of varying quality serve most of the rural towns.

Railroads extend for 3,378 km (2,099 mi). The ROK railway system is mostly government controlled. The Seoul Metropolitan Subway, first opened in 1974, is one of the most heavily used rapid transit systems in the world, with well over 8 million trips daily on the system's thirteen lines. It has a daily ridership of 5.6 million. Construction of Pusan's first subway line was completed in 1985.

The ROK has approximately 1,608 km (999 mi) of navigable waterways. Maritime shipping expanded rapidly during the 1970s. Pusan is the country's chief port. Other major ports include Inch'on (the port for Seoul), Kunsan, and Mokp'o. Hyundai Heavy, Samsung Heavy, and Daewoo Shipbuilding, South Korea's three largest shipbuilders, helped make South Korea the largest shipbuilder in the world in the 2000s. China has since challenged this dominance.

There are 116 airports, which transported 34.17 million passengers in 2009 according to the World Bank. Major airports include Cheju International at Cheju, Kimhae International at Pusan, and Kimpo International at Seoul. Korean Air Lines (KAL), privately owned since 1969, grew rapidly during the 1970s and now ranks as a major world carrier. On the morning of one September 1983, a KAL jetliner en route from New York to Seoul via Anchorage, Alaska, strayed over airspace of the former USSR and was shot down by Soviet interceptors, reportedly because they thought it was a military aircraft engaged in espionage; all 269 persons on board were killed, and worldwide protest followed. In November 1983, 115 people were killed when a bomb was detonated aboard a KAL jet en route to Seoul.

12 HISTORY

[For Korean history before 1948, see Korea, Democratic People's Republic of.]

The Republic of Korea (ROK), headed by President Syngman Rhee (Rhee Syngman), was proclaimed on 15 August 1948 in the southern portion of the Korean Peninsula, which had been under US military administration since 8 September 1945. Like the Democratic People's Republic of Korea (DPRK), established in the north on 9 September 1948 with Soviet backing, the ROK claimed to be the legitimate government of all Korea. The ROK was recognized as the legitimate government by the UN General Assembly.

At dawn on 25 June 1950, following a year and a half of sporadic fighting, a well-equipped People's Army of the DPRK struck across the 38th parallel. Proclaiming that the war was for national liberation and unification of the peninsula, the DPRK forces advanced rapidly; Seoul fell within three days, and the destruction of the ROK seemed imminent. At US urging, the UN Security Council (with the Soviet delegate absent) branded the DPRK an aggressor and called for the withdrawal of the attacking forces. On 27 June, US president Harry S. Truman ordered US air and naval units into combat, and three days later, US ground forces were sent into battle. The United Kingdom took similar action, and a multinational UN Command was created to join with and lead the ROK in its struggle against the invasion. Meanwhile, DPRK troops had pushed into the southeast corner of the peninsula. At that juncture, however, UN lines held firm, and an amphibious landing at Inch'on (15 September 1950) in the ROK under General

Douglas MacArthur brought about the complete disintegration of the DPRK army.

MacArthur, commanding the UN forces, pushed North Korean forces back over the 38th Parallel. As the UN forces approached the Yalu River, the border with China, China warned that it would not tolerate a unification of the peninsula under US/UN auspices. After several weeks of threats and feints, "volunteers" from the Chinese People's Liberation Army entered the fighting en masse, forcing MacArthur into a costly retreat down the peninsula. Seoul was lost again (4 January 1951) and then regained before the battle line became stabilized very nearly along the 38th parallel. There it remained for two weary years, with bitter fighting but little change, while a cease-fire agreement was negotiated.

On 27 July 1953, an armistice agreement finally was signed at P'anmunjom in the DPRK. The Korean War was ended, but it had brought incalculable destruction and human suffering to all of Korea, with some 1,300,000 military casualties, including 415,000 combat deaths, for the ROK alone, and estimates of between 3.5 and 4.0 million civilian casualties. The war left the peninsula still more implacably divided. A military demarcation line, which neither side regarded as a permanent border, was established, surrounded by the DMZ. The international conference envisioned in the armistice agreement was not held until mid-1954. This conference and subsequent efforts failed to reach an agreement on unification of the North and South, and the armistice agreement, supervised by a token UN Command in Seoul and by the Military Armistice Commission and the Neutral Nations Supervisory Commission, both in P'anmunjom, remains in effect.

In 1954, the United States and ROK signed a mutual defense treaty, under which US troops remained in the country. Financial assistance throughout the 1950s was provided by the United States, averaging $270 million annually between 1953 and 1958, and by other nations under UN auspices. Syngman Rhee ran the government until 1960, when his authoritarian rule provoked the "April Revolution," the culmination of a series of increasingly violent student demonstrations that finally brought about his ouster. The Second Korean Republic, which followed Rhee, adopted a parliamentary system to replace the previous presidential system. The new government, however, was short-lived. Premier Chang Myon and his supporters were ousted after only 10 months by a military coup in May 1961 headed by Maj. Gen. Park Chunghee. The military junta dissolved the National Assembly, placed the nation under martial law, established the Korean Central Intelligence Agency (KCIA) as a means of detecting and suppressing potential enemies, and ruled by decree until late 1963 through the Supreme Council for National Reconstruction. General Park created a well-organized political party—the Democratic-Republican Party (DRP)—designed to serve as a vehicle for the transition from military to civilian rule, and in October 1963, under a new constitution, he easily won election as president of the Third Republic.

During the summer of 1965, riots erupted all over the ROK in protest against the ROK-Japan Normalization Treaty, which established diplomatic relations and replaced Korean war-reparation claims with Japanese promises to extend economic aid. The riots were met with harsh countermeasures, including another period of martial law and widespread arrests of demonstrators. Further demonstrations erupted in 1966, when the ROK's decision to send 45,000 combat troops to Vietnam became known. Park was elected to a second term in May 1967, defeating his chief opponent, Yun Po-sun, and the DRP won a large majority in the National Assembly. In 1969, Park pushed through the National Assembly a constitutional amendment permitting him to run for a third term. He defeated Kim Dae Jung, leader of the opposition New Democratic Party (NDP), in the elections of April 1971, but Kim's NDP made significant gains in the National Assembly elections that May.

Student demonstrations against the government in the fall of 1971 prompted Park to declare a state of national emergency on 6 December. Three weeks later, in a predawn session held without the knowledge of the opposition, the National Assembly granted Park extraordinary governmental powers. These failed to quell mounting opposition and unrest, and in October 1972 martial law was declared. A new constitution, promulgated at the end of the month and ratified by national referendum in November 1972, vastly increased the powers of the presidency in economic as well as political affairs. Under this new document, which inaugurated the Fourth Republic, Park was elected for a six-year term that December, with a decisive legislative majority for his DRP. Soon the economy began to expand at a rapid rate, but Park's regime became increasingly repressive. The abduction by KCIA agents of Kim Dae Jung from a Japanese hotel room back to Seoul provoked considerable friction between Japanese and Korean officials. On 15 August 1974, a Korean gunman carrying a Japanese passport and sympathetic to the DPRK attempted to assassinate the president but killed Park's wife instead. Park responded by drafting a series of emergency measures; the harshest of these, Emergency Measure No. 9, issued in May 1975, provided for the arrest of anyone criticizing the constitution and banned all political activities by students.

Park was reelected for another six-year term in July 1978, but the NDP, now led by Kim Young Sam, made major gains in the National Assembly. In October 1979, Kim was expelled from the legislature after calling for governmental reform. Riots protesting Kim's ouster were reported in several major cities. On 26 October 1979, in what may have been an attempted coup, Park was assassinated by KCIA director Kim Jae-gyu, who was later executed. Martial law was again imposed, and a period of relative calm followed as some of the more restrictive emergency decrees were lifted by Park's constitutional successor, Prime Minister Choi Kyu-hah, who promised a new constitution and presidential elections.

In December 1979, Maj. Gen. Chun Doo Hwan led a coup in which he and his military colleagues removed the army chief of staff and took effective control of the government. Demonstrations led by university students spread during the spring of 1980, and by mid-May, the government had once more declared martial law (in effect until January 1981), banned demonstrations, and arrested political leaders. In the city of Kwangju, more than 200 civilians were killed in what became known as the Kwangju massacre (these numbers may be conservative). Choi Kyu-hah was pressured to resign and Chun Doo Hwan, now retired from the military, was named president in September 1980. Chun Doo Hwan came to power under a new constitution inaugurating the Fifth Republic. A total of 567 political leaders, including Kim Dae Jung and Kim Young Sam, were banned from political activity. Kim Dae Jung, arrested several times after his 1973 kidnapping,

was originally sentenced to death but allowed to go to the United States in 1982. All existing political parties were dissolved and all political activity banned until three months before the 1981 elections.

Twelve new parties (later reduced to eight) were formed to enter the 1981 elections, in which Chun Doo Hwan was elected to a seven-year presidential term by a new electoral college and his Democratic Justice Party (DJP) secured a majority in the reconstituted National Assembly. Despite harsh controls, opposition to Chun continued. In 1982, 1,200 political prisoners were released, and in early 1983, the ban on political activity was lifted for 250 of the banned politicians. On 9 October 1983, Chun escaped an apparent assassination attempt in Yangon (Rangoon), Burma, when an explosion took the lives of 17 in his entourage, including 4 ROK cabinet ministers. Chun subsequently blamed the DPRK for the bombing. In 1984, under increasing pressure for political reforms prior to the 1985 parliamentary elections, the government lifted its ban on all but 15 of the 567 politicians banned in 1980; in 1985, the ban was lifted on 14 of the remaining 15. Kim Dae Jung was allowed to return from exile in the United States in 1984 but was rearrested. He remained banned from all political activity because of his conviction for sedition in 1980.

Opposition groups quickly formed the New Korea Democratic Party (NKDP) to challenge the DJP in the 1985 election; the new party became a strong minority voice in the National Assembly. The issue of constitutional reforms, particularly changes in the way in which presidents are elected and the way in which "bonus" seats in the legislature are distributed, became prominent, especially after Chun reaffirmed a commitment to step down in February 1988 and, in April 1986, dropped his long-standing opposition to any constitutional changes prior to that date. Demonstrations against Chun continued and became violent at Inch'on in May 1986 and at Konkuk University that fall. Opposition groups began collecting signatures on a petition demanding direct (instead of indirect) election of the president. In April 1987, as demonstrations became increasingly violent, Chun banned all further discussion of constitutional reform until after the 1988 Olympic Games in Seoul. The ban, which could have guaranteed the election of a hand-picked DJP successor, set off violent antigovernment demonstrations throughout the nation. In June 1987, the DJP nominated its chairman, Roh Tae Woo, a former general and a close friend of Chun, as its candidate for his successor. When Roh accepted opposition demands for political reforms, Chun announced in July that the upcoming election would be held by direct popular vote. On 8 July, 100,000 people demonstrated in Seoul in the largest protest since 1960 and, on the same day, the government restored political rights to 2,000 people, including the longtime opposition leader, Kim Dae Jung.

In the elections, held on 16 December 1987, Roh Tae Woo, as the DJP candidate, won a plurality of 37%, defeating the two major opposition candidates, Kim Young Sam and Kim Dae Jung, who had been unable to agree on a single opposition candidacy and split 55% of the total vote. Two minor candidates divided the remainder. A reported 89% of all eligible voters participated. The two leading opposition candidates charged massive fraud, and a series of demonstrations was held to protest the results. However, no evidence of extensive fraud was produced, and the demonstrations did not attract wide support. Roh Tae Woo was inaugurated as president in February 1988 when Chun Doo Hwan's term expired.

In the elections for the National Assembly, held on 26 April 1988, President Roh Tae Woo's party, the DJP, won only 34% of the vote. This gave the DJP 125 seats in the assembly, while Kim Dae Jung's Peace and Democracy Party (PDP) gained 70 seats; other parties included Kim Young Sam's Reunification Democratic Party (RDP), 59 seats; the new Democratic Republican Party (NDRP), 35 seats; and independent candidates, 10 seats. Thus, for the first time in 36 years, the government did not have a controlling vote in the National Assembly, which quickly challenged President Roh's choice for head of the Supreme Court and by year's end forced the president to work with the assembly to pass the budget.

In the fall of 1988, the National Assembly audited the government and held public hearings on former President Chun's abuses of power. In November, Chun apologized to the nation in a televised address, gave his personal wealth to the nation, and retired into a Buddhist temple. Following the revision of the constitution in 1987, South Koreans enjoyed greater freedoms of expression and assembly and freedom of the press, and in 1988, several hundred political dissidents were released from prison.

Unrest among students, workers, and farmers continued, however, and beginning in April 1989, the government repressed opposition. In October 1989, the government acknowledged making 1,315 political arrests so far that year. The National Assembly became less of a check on President Roh after two opposition parties (RDP, NDRP), including that of Kim Young Sam, merged with Roh's DJP, forming a new majority party, the Democratic Liberal Party (DLP) in January 1990. Kim Dae Jung was then left as the leader of the main opposition party (PDP).

There were continuing demonstrations into 1990 and 1991, calling for the resignation of President Roh and the withdrawal of US troops. In May 1990, 50,000 demonstrators in Kwangju commemorated the 10th anniversary of the massacre, resulting in clashes with police that lasted several days. The United States agreed to withdraw its nuclear weapons from the ROK in November 1991. On the last day of the year, the ROK and the DPRK signed an agreement to ban nuclear weapons from the entire peninsula.

In the presidential election on 19 December 1992, Kim Young Sam, now leader of the majority DLP, won with 41.9% of the vote, while Kim Dae Jung (DP) took 33.8%. Inaugurated in February 1993, Kim Young Sam began a new era as the first president in 30 years who was a civilian, without a power base in the military. President Kim granted amnesty to 41,000 prisoners and instituted a series of purges of high-ranking military officials, including four generals who had roles in the 1979 coup. Among political and economic reforms was a broad anticorruption campaign, resulting in arrests, dismissals, or reprimands for several thousands of government officials and business people. In March 1994, a former official of the National Security Planning Agency made public President Roh Tae Woo's authorization of a covert program to develop nuclear weapons at the Daeduk Science Town through 1991.

South and North Korea continued to have a rocky relationship. On three successive days in April 1996, North Korean troops violated the 1954 armistice that had ended the Korean War by entering P'anmunjom. The soldiers, who were apparently conducting training exercises, withdrew after a few hours on all three occasions. In September of the same year, a small North Korean sub-

marine was grounded off the eastern coast of South Korea and 26 crew members fled into the interior of South Korea. The ship appeared to be carrying a team of North Korean spies who intended to infiltrate South Korea to carry out what remain unknown missions against South Korean targets. Twenty-four of the crewmen were killed, one escaped, and one remains at large. In a surprise move, the North Korean government apologized in February of 1997 for the incursion.

Meanwhile, domestic events inside South Korea were equally tumultuous. In August of 1996, former President Chun Doo Hwan and his successor, Roh Tae Woo, were tried and found guilty of treason and mutiny for the 1980 coup that brought them to power and the subsequent Kwangju massacre, in which troops killed more than 200 prodemocracy demonstrators (those numbers may be conservative). The court gave Chun a death sentence (extremely rare in South Korea) and sentenced Roh to 22.5 years in prison. An appellate court later reduced Chun's sentence to life imprisonment and Roh's sentence to 17 years. When Kim Dae Jung was inaugurated as president in 1998, both leaders were released from prison under Kim's grant of amnesty.

On 11 April 1996, legislative elections took place amid allegations of corruption that reached the inner circle of President Kim Young Sam and his New Korea Party (NKP). During the preelection campaign, Kim promised to launch an anticorruption effort if his party gained power; in a major upset, the NKP captured 139 of the 299 seats, while the main opposition party (National Congress for New Politics-NCNP) of Kim Dae Jung won only 79 seats. Kim Dae Jung lost his own seat in the legislature. Several important New Korea Party officials and even Kim Young Sam's son were implicated on charges of taking or giving millions of dollars in bribes to arrange loans to Hanbo Steel Industry Co., which eventually went bankrupt under $6 billion of debt. Some of those officials were indicted in February of 1997, but Mr. Kim's son, Kim Hyun Chul, was cleared. However, in May of the same year, Kim Hyun Chul was arrested on bribery and tax-evasion charges unrelated to the Hanbo scandal.

By 1997, many of the large *chaebol* (business conglomerates) were reporting serious problems with debt in what became known as the 1997–1999 Asian Economic Crisis, hitting nearly all countries of the region. The crisis was triggered by contagion and currency speculation, starting in Thailand and rapidly spreading to other Asian countries, including Korea. Market overreaction produced a negative impact on exchange rates, raising the costs of trade and settlement of contracts (mostly denominated in dollars) followed by a drop in asset prices. Deeper problems in Korea related to structural fundamentals: large current account deficits, foreign debt (dollar denominated), foreign exchange reserves (below the standard of sufficient currency to cover 3 months worth of imports), excessive leveraging by corporations to fund operations, and a lack of focus on profitability.

In Korea, the Asian Economic Crisis was really a corporate crisis. The Korean economy was more concentrated on industry-centered businesses than its Organization for Economic Cooperation and Development (OECD) counterparts. 42% of Korean GDP at the time came from the industrial sector. Chaebol dominated the structure of Korean economy. At the highest level, the "Top 5" (Hyundai, Daewoo, SK, Samsung and LG) were quantitatively distinct from the 6- to 64th-ranked chaebol. They were characterized as having huge asset bases, were highly diversified into dozens of businesses, had tremendous political clout, and represented the country's strategic industries: shipbuilding, steel, autos, semiconductors, and petrochemicals. The problem exposed during the economic crisis was that the chaebol had expanded through excessive leveraging (often short-term loan for long-term and fixed investments), and that the government of Korea's "policy loans" to the chaebol contributed to and exacerbated the problem. Aggressive leveraging worked as long as economy expanded.

As the economic crisis unfolded, five major groups among the chaebol quickly failed, affecting 107,000 employees and Won 26.7 Trillion (about $25 Billion) in assets—including Kia (autos), Halla (construction, steel), and Jinro (brewing/distillery). By October 1998, more than 50% of the 30 largest corporations were in trouble and were being restructured, covering 255,000 employees and Won 104 Trillion of debt. Eventually, the cost of restructuring the chaebol and recapitalizing the banks came to 164 Trillion Won.

The ensuing financial panic coincided with presidential elections on 18 December 1997, the month that negotiations with the International Monetary Fund (IMF) began. In the 1997 presidential elections, South Koreans elected former political exile Kim Dae Jung, who became the country's first opposition candidate to win a presidential election. In the election, Kim Dae Jung narrowly defeated the ruling party's candidate, Lee Hoe Chang, by 40.3% to 38.7%. Kim Dae Jung pledged to adhere to IMF conditionality and reform government-business relations in South Korea by increasing transparency. In 1998 and 1999, the government reduced the role of government intervention in the domestic economy despite numerous strikes by workers protesting layoffs. By January 1999, the economy showed a slight return to growth, and by April of that year the Korean government moved to begin closing World Bank loans it had taken to deal with the crisis.

By mid-2000, Kim Dae Jung had managed to steer Korea's economy out of the worst of the crisis. The economy had started to grow in 1999 and topped 10% growth rate in 2000, although economic growth stabilized at 4.4% by 2004. South Korea faced a steady unemployment rate of 3.6% between 2000 and 2005, which seems modest except in the Korean context of historical unemployment rates of about 2%. In April 2000, the legislative elections improved the position of Kim's party, renamed the New Millennium Party (NMP), to 115 seats. However, the Grand National Party (GNP), successor to the NKP, obtained 133 seats and the United Liberal Democrats, allied with the GNP, won 17. Thus, Kim's objective to continue economic reform was imperiled.

In June 2000, Kim Dae Jung traveled to P'yŏngyang, the capital of the Democratic People's Republic of Korea (North Korea), for a historic meeting with his counterpart, Kim Jong Il. The two agreed to pursue further cooperation in the future. This summit marked the high point of what became known as Kim Dae Jung's "sunshine policy" of rapprochement toward the North. He was awarded the Nobel Peace Prize in 2000 for his commitment to democracy and human rights in Asia.

Roh Moo Hyun was elected president in the December 2002 election, taking 49% of the vote; he was inaugurated in February 2003. While campaigning, Roh stated he would continue Kim Dae Jung's "sunshine policy" toward the North, but prior to his election, it was revealed that North Korea was secretly developing a program to enrich uranium for use in nuclear weapons. In June 2003, the United States announced it would redeploy some of its 37,000 troops in South Korea to positions south of the DMZ, in an effort to create more agile and mobile forces. South Korea is also an integral part of the six-state team that meets periodically to assess North Korean nuclear ambitions. Roh's attempts to engage North Korea came under increasing attack, since North Korea admitted to having a uranium-enrichment program as well as nuclear reactors.

Of major importance to contemporary South Korea is the stance of Japan regarding its military activities during World War II. South Korea often criticizes the Japanese educational system for overlooking Japan's military aggression in Asia during World War II, and is in continual negotiations with Japan over this topic. Of great concern is South Korean animosity concerning South Korean women taken as sex slaves by the Japanese Imperial Army during World War II. Although the Japanese government admitted deception, coercion, and official involvement in the recruitment and kidnapping of South Korean women in 1995, there has been no official apology and there is much tension in South Korean-Japanese relations. Former Japanese Prime Minister Junichiro Koizumi further inflamed this animosity by making a yearly visit to the Yasukuni Shrine, which is dedicated to Japanese war dead. Japan regards all World War II compensation claims as settled through treaties signed in 1964. In early 2007, Japanese Prime Minister Shinzo Abe denied that Japan's military had coerced women into sexual slavery during World War II, initiating an international row over the issue. South Korea also contests Japanese claims to Liancourt Rocks (Tok-do/Take-shima), occupied by South Korea since 1954.

In April 2009, a formal talk between the leaders of South and North Korea lasted for only 22 minutes, with no official report on the discussion. Days earlier, the North Korea government walked out of six-party talks after the UN criticized their launch of a rocket. North Korea claimed the launch was a communications satellite, but international observers widely presumed it to be a test of long-range missile technology. South Korean officials refuse to consider further economic cooperation with North Korea until its nuclear weapons are surrendered.

In November 2010, an exchange of artillery between the north and south in the maritime border region raised international concern. North Korea fired dozens of artillery shells at the border island of Yeonpyeong, making several hits on the South Korean military base. Two South Korean marines and two civilians were killed; another eighteen were injured. All of the 1,600 residents of the island were evacuated to shelters during the hour-long attack. North Korean officials accused South Korea of provoking the attack by firing shells into the maritime territory of the north. South Korean officials said that they had been conducting regular military drills off the coast of Yeonpyeong, but claimed that no artillery was ever fired into the northern region. In retaliation for the attack on Yeonpyeong, South Korea fired about 80 shells into the northern territory. There was no report of injuries from the north.

As the international community called for calm, South Korea announced plans to conduct another series of live-fire artillery exercises on and around Yeonpyeong Island. About two dozen Americans were expected to participate in the drills as observers. North Korea warned that any further drills would be considered a clear provocation, to which the government would retaliate in kind. Hoping to stop the escalating tensions, China called on fellow six-party nations to resume the talks that were stalled in April 2009. But South Korea and the United States reaffirmed their stand that talks would not resume until North Korea showed some commitment to halt its nuclear activity. South Korea went ahead with the artillery exercise on 20 December. To the surprise of many, the North did not retaliate, but later issued a statement saying that the action was not worth reaction, implying that the incident proved which side is interested in peace and which side showed the real provocation. South Korea scheduled two more military drills within the same week, including one that was set to take place 30 miles from the North-South demilitarized zone. In January 2011, North Korea invited the ROK to participate in discussions on economic ties. South Korea quickly declined.

In February 2011, South Korea agreed to participate in talks with North Korea for the first time since North Korea's November 2010 artillery attack. The talks ended abruptly on 9 February when the North Korean delegation walked out, refusing to take responsibility for the attack on Yeonpyeong Island. The talks had been planned to focus on the denuclearization of North Korea. For talks to continue, South Korea set the condition that North Korea accept responsibility for the November attack. As of early 2012, no future sessions were scheduled.

In March 2011, relations between North and South Korea were further strained when South Korean activists started a massive anti-North Korea propaganda campaign. They sent helium-filled balloons over the border that carried leaflets, cassette tapes, and videos with anti-North Korean messages. The messages called for the people of North Korea to rise up against Kim Jong Il. The aim of the propaganda was to raise awareness of what was happening in the outside world, as North Koreans have almost no access to international news. As South Korean activists continued their balloon campaign, in April the north responded by threatening a military attack on the border town of Imjingak, a small tourist town that served as the launching spot for the balloons, if the propaganda balloon launches did not stop. The South Korean government, which initially intended to block the balloonists because their actions affected North-South relations, allowed the activists to continue the balloon launches.

¹³ GOVERNMENT

The Republic of Korea's (ROK) first constitution was adopted on 17 July 1948. Through repeated revisions, power remained concentrated in the hands of the president until the most recent revision, adopted by 93.1% of the vote in a popular referendum on 28 October 1987. Under the new constitution, which took effect in February 1988, the president is elected by direct popular vote, rather than indirectly as before, for a single term of five years. There are also a prime minister and two deputy prime ministers, who head the State Council (the cabinet).

The ROK legislature is the unicameral National Assembly (Kuk Hoe). It has 299 seats: 245 in single-seat constituencies and 54 by proportional representation. During the first four decades of the ROK, the National Assembly had little authority. The 1987 constitution strengthened the National Assembly, giving it power to audit government activities and removing the president's power to dissolve the Assembly. Suffrage is universal at age 20.

¹⁴ POLITICAL PARTIES

From 1948 to 1988, politics in the Republic of Korea were dominated by the executive arm of the government with military backing. Despite this, there were active opposition parties and, with the implementation of the revised 1987 constitution, political parties have had a greater governmental role. In the presidential election of December 1987, the governing Democratic Justice Party (DJP), with Roh Tae Woo as its candidate, won 37% of the vote; the Reunification Democratic Party (RDP), with Kim Young Sam, won 28%; the Peace and Democracy Party (PDP), with Kim Dae Jung, won 27%; and the New Democratic-Republic Party (NDRP), with Kim Jong Pil, won 10%. In a crucial election for the National Assembly in April 1988, the DJP gained only 34% of the popular vote, allowing the opposition parties to control the assembly. This was the first time since 1952 that the government party did not have a majority in, and hence control of, the National Assembly.

In a surprise move in January 1990, the DJP merged with two of the opposition parties, the RDP and the NDRP, to form a new majority party, the Democratic Liberal Party (DLP). In July of that year, two opposition parties, the PDP and the Democratic Party (DP) merged, retaining the latter's name. In September 1991, the DP agreed to merge with another opposition party, the New Democratic Party (NDP), then led by the veteran oppositionist, Kim Dae Jung, forming a new DP.

The National Assembly election on 24 March 1992 saw 38.5% of the vote go to the DLP; 29.2% to the DP; 17.3% to the Unification National Party, which later changed its name to the United People's Party (UPP); and 15% to other parties. The actual distribution of seats in the National Assembly shifts as members frequently switch among parties. In the presidential election on 18 December 1992, 41.5% of the vote went to Kim Young Sam of the DLP, 33.8% to Kim Dae Jung of the DP, 16.3% to Chung Ju Yung of the UPP, and 8% to candidates of various smaller parties.

Following the 1992 elections, Korea's largest political parties began a period of reorganization. The DLP transformed into the New Korea Party (NKP), while Kim Dae Jung formed a new opposition party, the National Congress for New Politics (NCNP). In the National Assembly election on 11 April 1996, the NKP won 139 seats; the NCNP, 79 seats; the ULD, 50 seats; and the DP, 15 seats. The remaining 16 seats were won by independents. The surprise of the election was the success of the ULD, a conservative party led by former premier Kim Jong Pil.

In the presidential election of 18 December 1997, Kim Dae Jung won 40.3% and Yi Hoe Chang of the Grand National Party (GNP) won 38.7%. In January 2000, Kim reorganized his cabinet; his party, the National Congress for New Politics, assumed a new name, the Millennium Democratic Party (MDP). The 13 April 2000 election involved Kim Dae Jung's MDP, which captured 115 seats; the former governing GNP obtained 133 seats; and a minor party, the United Democratic Liberal Party, captured 17 seats. Two seats were held by the Democratic People's Party, one seat was held by the New Korea Party of Hope, and five seats went to independents. In the December 2002 presidential election, Roh Moo-hyun of the MDP won the post with 48.9% of the vote.

The 15 April 2004 election showed a surprise outcome of the Uri Dang party, a liberal party, overtaking the Grand National Party with 152 seats; the Grand National Party retained 121 seats and the MDP came in fourth place with only 9 seats.

Lee Myung-bak of the GNP was elected president in December 2007 and began his term in February 2008. In the 9 April 2008 legislative elections, the Grand National Party won 153 seats, followed by the United Democratic Party with 81 seats.

In August 2010, President Lee Myung-bak reshuffled his cabinet, appointing South Korea's youngest prime minister in 39 years. The prime minister–designate, Kim Tae-ho, was just 47 at the time of his appointment—a significant detail, as Korean society places tremendous value on seniority. A few weeks later, however, Kim Tae-ho resigned amid allegations of unethical behavior during parliamentary confirmation hearings. Kim was accused of lying about his personal connections to a businessman accused of bribery. The candidates nominated for cultural minister (Shin Jae-min) and minister of knowledge economy (Lee Jae-hoon) also resigned as allegations of unethical behavior surfaced against them during confirmation hearings. Kim Hwang-sik was appointed as prime minister in October 2010.

The next presidential and legislative elections were scheduled for 2012.

15 LOCAL GOVERNMENT

The Republic of Korea (ROK) is divided into is divided into one special city (*teukbyeolsi*), six metropolitan cities (*gwangyeoksi*), and nine provinces (*do*). These are further subdivided into a variety of smaller entities, including cities (*si*), counties (*gun*), wards (*gu*), towns (*eup*), districts (*myeon*), neighborhoods (*dong*), and villages (*ri*). Between 1961 and March 1990, there were no local elections.

16 JUDICIAL SYSTEM

The highest judicial court is the Supreme Court, under which there are five intermediate appellate courts. Lower tribunals include district courts, of which there are 15, and a family and administrative court. There are 103 municipal courts in South Korea. Since 1988, constitutional challenges go to the Constitutional Court.

The president, with the consent of the National Assembly, appoints the chief justice, the other 13 justices of the Supreme Court, and the Constitutional Court. The chief justice, in consultation with the other justices of the court, appoints lower court justices.

The constitution provides for a presumption of innocence, protection from self-incrimination, the right to a speedy trial, protection from double jeopardy, and other procedural due process safeguards. The constitution provides for an independent judiciary. There are no jury trials. The legal system combines some elements of European civil law systems, Anglo-American law, and classical Chinese philosophies.

17 ARMED FORCES

The International Institute for Strategic Studies reported that armed forces in the Republic of Korea totaled 655,000 members in 2011. The force was comprised of 522,000 from the army, 68,000 from the navy, and 65,000 members of the air force. Armed forces represented 2.7% of the labor force in Korea. Defense spending totaled $39.5 billion and accounted for 2.7% of GDP.

Historically, since the Korean War and through the 1980s and 1990s, the US stationed between 37,000 and 40,000 troops in South Korea. With the decade of war in Iraq and Afghanistan following the 11 September 2001 attacks on the United States, US troops were drawn down in Korea to support the war effort. The United States maintained a military presence of over 27,000–28,500 military personnel in the ROK during 2011. In 2012, the United States was scheduled to relinquish wartime command of US troops in Korea to the South Korean military.

18 INTERNATIONAL COOPERATION

The ROK became a member of the UN on 17 September 1991 and participates in the Economic and Social Commission for Asia and the Pacific (ESCAP) and several nonregional specialized agencies, such as the Food and Agriculture Organization (FAO), United Nations Educational, Scientific and Cultural Organization (UNESCO), International Finance Corporation (IFC), International Monetary Fund (IMF), World Bank, International Labour Organization (ILO), UN Industrial Development Organization (UNIDO), and World Health Organization (WHO). The ROK participates in the African Development Bank, Asian Development Bank, Asia-Pacific Economic Cooperation (APEC), Association of Southeast Asian Nations (ASEAN) Regional Forum, Colombo Plan, European Bank for Reconstruction and Development, Latin American Integration Association (LAIA), and OECD. The country is a dialogue partner in ASEAN, a partner in the Organization for Security and Cooperation in Europe (OSCE), and an observer in the Organization of American States (OAS).

South Korea has hosted major international events such as the 1988 Summer Olympics, the 2002 World Cup Soccer Tournament (co-hosted with Japan), and the 2002 Second Ministerial Conference of the Community of Democracies. In 2010, the country hosted the ROK-Japan-China Trilateral Summit as well as the G-20 Seoul Summit. South Korea won the bid for hosting the 2018 Winter Olympics.

Korean foreign policy places economic considerations and trade at the center of its policy. It seeks to build on its development as an economic and trading powerhouse to increase its regional and global status and assume more leadership roles in international organizations. It is a founding member of the APEC forum and chaired the organization during the 2005 summit in Busan. Ban-Ki Moon's election as the eighth Secretary-General by the UN in 2007 is celebrated as a milestone in South Korea in advancing its role and status internationally. The Republic of Korea maintains diplomatic relations with over 170 countries. It remains in a security alliance with the United States under the 1953 Mutual Defense Treaty.

As Korea's status as a developing country changed with its emergence as one of the Asian economic "tigers" in the 1980s and 1990s, the country moved from net recipient of aid to net donor status. The Korea International Cooperation Agency (KOIKA) was founded as a government agency on 1 April 1991 in order to maximize the effectiveness of Korea's grant aid programs for developing countries by implementing the government's grant aid and technical cooperation programs. With its ascension to the OECD, an acknowledgment of Korea's emergence as a modern industrialized country, the nation began to play a larger role in overseas development assistance.

The UN Commission on the Unification and Rehabilitation of Korea was dissolved in 1973, but the UN Command originating from the Korean War continues to supervise implementation of the 1953 armistice agreement. The ROK pursues a vigorous international diplomacy, and in recent years has modified both its militant anticommunist stance and its close alliance with the United States. By 1986, the ROK was recognized by 122 nations, 67 of which also had diplomatic relations with the Democratic People's Republic of Korea (DPRK). The demilitarized zone that separates North and South Korea has been in place since 1953, though both governments claim a desire for reunification. The nation is a guest in the Nonaligned Movement.

The ROK is part of the Australia Group, the Zangger Committee, the Nuclear Energy Agency, the Nuclear Suppliers Group (London Group), and the Organization for the Prohibition of Chemical Weapons. In environmental cooperation, the nation is part of the Antarctic Treaty, the Basel Convention, Conventions on Biological Diversity and Whaling, Ramsar, the Convention on International Trade in Endangered Species of Wild Fauna and Flora (CITES), the London Convention, International Tropical Timber Agreements, the Kyoto Protocol, the Montréal Protocol, MARPOL, the Nuclear Test Ban Treaty, and the UN Conventions on the Law of the Sea, Climate Change, and Desertification.

[19]ECONOMY

Under a centralized planning system initiated in 1962, the Republic of Korea (ROK) became one of the fastest-growing developing countries, shifting from an agrarian to an industrial economy and then to a high-tech "new economy" in the course of only a few decades. In 1996, the ROK was officially admitted to the 30-member Organization for Economic Cooperation and Development (OECD) of advanced industrialized countries. In 2007, industry contributed 39.4% of GDP compared to 16.2% in 1965, while agriculture, forestry, and fishing accounted for 3%, down from 46.5%. Much of this industrialization was fueled by the government's stimulation of heavy industry, notably steel, construction, shipbuilding, and automobile manufacture, as well as its support of technological advances in communications and information technology (CIT). To finance industrial expansion, the ROK borrowed heavily. By the end of 2007, its foreign debt equaled about 33.4% of gross national product (GNP), down from 52% in 1986 when it was one of the world's four most deeply indebted developing economies. Financial and corporate structural reforms helped bring this ratio down.

The average annual rate of GDP growth declined from an average of 9.5–9.7% in the period 1965–90 to 6.57% in the next decade (1991–2000) as export growth slowed, labor costs rose, and the won steadily appreciated against the US dollar. The economy grew by 9.1% in 1995 and 1996. However, after June 1997, when Hong Kong reverted to Chinese rule, South Korea became engulfed in the Asian financial crisis. GDP growth averaged only 5% in 1997, and then turned negative (-6.6%) in 1998 in the country's first economic contraction since the Korean War.

South Korea's economy made a strong recovery in 1999 and 2000, with GDP growth rates of 10.9% and 9.3%, respectively, while inflation, which had reached 4% in 1998, was held to 1.9% in 1999 and 2.8% in 2000. The recovery was sharply interrupted, however, by the collapse of the dot.com boom in early 2001, the decline in international investment in the aftermath of the 11 September 2001 terrorist attacks on the United States, and the slowdown in the global economy.

Real GDP growth dropped to 3.23% in 2001, stood at 6.27% in 2002, and fell again to 2.7% in 2003. In 2007, the real GDP growth rate was estimated at 5%, reflecting a strengthening of domestic demand. However, rises in global oil prices in could slow economic recovery. The GDP rate of change in the ROK as of 2010 was 6.1%. Inflation stood at 3%, and unemployment was reported at 3.3%.

One problem South Korea faces is that it has not yet developed a strong and diverse local economy, despite its skilled workforce and large middle class. It has relied upon increasing exports, which benefit a few huge conglomerates (chaebol), in ways that stifle domestic demand. This dependency on exports led the nation into recession during the 2008–09 global financial crisis, as worldwide demand for major export products declined. In December 2009, however, overseas shipments showed an increase of 33.7% from that of December 2008. Products such as petrochemicals, semiconductors, and display panels were particularly in demand. China is the nation's largest export partner.

[20]INCOME

The CIA estimated that in 2010 the GDP of Korea was $1.5 trillion. The CIA defines GDP as the value of all final goods and services produced within a nation in a given year, computed on the basis of purchasing power parity (PPP) rather than value as measured on the basis of the rate of the exchange based on current dollars. The per capita GDP was estimated at $30,000. The annual growth rate of GDP was 6.1%. The average inflation rate was 3%. It was estimated that agriculture accounted for 3% of GDP, industry 39.4%, and services 57.6%.

According to the World Bank, remittances from citizens living abroad totaled $2.5 billion, or about $52 per capita, and accounted for approximately 0.2% of GDP.

The World Bank reported that in 2009, household consumption in Korea totaled $439.9 billion or about $9,022 per capita, measured in current US dollars rather than PPP. Household consumption includes expenditures of individuals, households, and nongovernmental organizations on goods and services, excluding the purchases of dwellings. It was estimated that household consumption was growing at an average annual rate of 0.2%.

The World Bank estimated that the ROK, with 0.79% of the world's population, accounted for 1.87% of the world's GDP. By comparison, the United States, with 4.85% of the world's population, accounted for 22.51% of world GDP.

As of 2011, the most recent study by the World Bank reported that actual individual consumption in the ROK was 58.6% of GDP and accounted for 1.57% of world consumption. By comparison, the United States accounted for 25.44% of world individual consumption. The World Bank also estimated that 9.1% of South Korea's GDP was spent on food and beverages, 10.8% on housing and household furnishings, 2.2% on clothes, 4.8% on health, 5.6% on transportation, 2.8% on communications, 3.8% on recreation, 3.9% on restaurants and hotels, and 9.5% on miscellaneous goods and services and purchases from abroad.

[21]LABOR

As of 2010, Korea had a total labor force of 24.75 million people. Within that labor force, CIA estimates in 2010 noted that 7.3%

were employed in agriculture, 24.3% in industry, and 68.4% in the service sector.

Before 1987, the labor movement was heavily controlled by the government, but since 1991, democratic reform has brought some changes. With the exception of public-sector employees, workers enjoy the right to join unions, even with as few as two members. All unions must register with the Labor Ministry, although unions not formally recognized by the ministry have generally not been interfered with by the government. Unions often exercise the right to strike, and collective bargaining is prevalent.

Children under the age of 15 are generally prohibited from working, and those under 18 must obtain written approval from their parents. In July 2004, the five-day, 40-hour workweek was adopted, applicable to certain types of companies with 1,000 or more employees. In other areas, employees can work up to 44 hours in one week, so long as the average over two weeks is 40 hours per week. Overtime pay is mandatory for extended hours. The new minimum wage rate covers all businesses and workplaces except seamen, family business hiring only family members, and housework employees. In 2010, the minimum wage was 4,320 won ($3.75) per hour.

22 AGRICULTURE

The country's major crops include rice, root crops, barley, vegetables, and fruit. Cereal production in 2009 amounted to 7.4 million tons, fruit production to 2.9 million tons, and vegetable production to 12 million tons. About 70% of the land is sown with grain, the majority of which is rice. In 1965, agriculture (including forestry and fishing) contributed nearly 50% to gross national product (GNP). Double-cropping is common in the southern provinces. Despite increased yields due to mechanization, the use of hybrid seeds, and increased employment of fertilizers, the ROK runs a net deficit in food grains every year. Virtual self-sufficiency has been attained in rice production, but at a cost of nearly $2 billion per year in direct producer subsidies.

Hemp, hops, and tobacco are the leading industrial crops. The orchards in the Taegu area are renowned for their apples, the prime fruit crop. Pears, peaches, persimmons, and melons also are grown in abundance. About two-thirds of vegetable production is made up of the *mu* (a large white radish) and Chinese cabbage, the main ingredients of the year-round staple kimchi, or Korean pickle.

Until the Korean War, tenant farming was widespread in the ROK. The Land Reform Act of June 1949, interrupted by the war, was implemented in 1953; it limited arable land ownership to three hectares (7.4 acres) per household, with all lands in excess of this limit to be purchased by the government for distribution among farmers who had little or no land. By the late 1980s, farms averaged 0.5–1 hectare (1.2–2.5 acres). The New Village (Saemaul) Movement, initiated in 1972, plays a major role in raising productivity and modernizing villages and farming practices.

The ROK has one of the most protected agricultural economies of the world, with high production costs supported by government purchases, and high tariffs protecting domestic producers from import competition. In 2004, a free trade agreement with Chile became effective, whereby trade duties were lifted on many of Chile's agricultural goods. The agreement was strongly opposed by the ROK's agricultural sector. The government agreed to a farm support program worth $100 billion during 2004–11, whereby farmers received compensation for the losses caused by Chilean imports.

23 ANIMAL HUSBANDRY

The UN Food and Agriculture Organization (FAO) reported that Korea dedicated 58,000 hectares (143,321 acres) to permanent pasture or meadow in 2009. During that year, the country tended 138.8 million chickens, 3.1 million head of cattle, and 9.6 million pigs. The production from these animals amounted to 538,482 tons of beef and veal, 1.49 million tons of pork, 630,272 tons of poultry, 495,953 tons of eggs, and 1.29 million tons of milk. Korea also produced 46,710 tons of cattle hide.

The raising of livestock, traditionally a supplementary occupation among ROK farmers, expanded rapidly during the 1970s and 1980s. The silkworm industry has declined radically since the mid-1970s. Although the dairy industry has been protected by import restrictions, an incremental lifting of such trade constraints was underway in 2011, which will eventually include livestock imports. In 2011, the Agriculture Ministry acknowledged the incidence of foot-and-mouth disease (FMD) at a cattle farm in Pohang city. Some 9.7 million cattle, pigs, and poultry were culled in 2011 due to disease outbreaks such as FMD and bird flu. As a result of disease outbreaks, inflation increased and meat imports rose.

South Korea's self-sufficiency in pork production dropped to its lowest point since statistics have been kept in 2010–11 due to the massive culling of pigs in the wake of FMD outbreaks. The self-sufficiency ratio of meat declined 20.6% between 2010 and 2011, according to data provided by the Ministry for Food, Agriculture, Forestry and Fisheries.

In 2011, South Korea became the first Asian country to implement the antibiotic ban in animal feed. Fishery exports reached a new high in 2011, largely led by increased imports by China and Japan.

South Korea has been in a big push to negotiate and complete free trade agreements with countries all over the world. The KO-RUS FTA (Korea-US Free Trade Agreement) was ratified in 2011, which finally opened South Korea to US beef imports that had been mostly banned since 2005. With the FTAs, South Korea expanded its support for the fishery and agricultural sectors to ease prospective losses to the local industry from a massive influx of outside products under free trade agreements. According to the ministry, the government planned to spend KRW24.1 trillion ($20.8 billion) to provide fiscal support for domestic fishing and agricultural households until 2017.

24 FISHING

Korea had 82,803 decked commercial fishing boats in 2008. The annual capture totaled 1.94 million tons according to the UN FAO. The export value of seafood totaled $1.04 billion. Korean waters are some of the best fishing grounds in the world. The Sea of Japan off the east coast provides deep-sea fishing, with an average water depth of 1,700 m (5,600 ft). Warm and cold water alternate each season; the area is known for its Alaskan pollack, cod, squid, king crab, hairy crab, turban shell, and abalone. Off the west coast, the Yellow Sea has an average depth of 44 m (144 ft); major species include corker, hairtail, mackerel, surf clam, large clam abalone, lobster, Japanese paste shrimp, and blue crab. Off the south coast, the warm Pacific Ocean currents move toward the northeast, bringing diverse species such as anchovy, mackerel, oyster, mussels, shellfish, octopus, beka squid, laver, and sea mustard. This has at times caused serious conflict with Korea's neighbors, Japan and China, who both have large fishing industries.

25 FORESTRY

Approximately 64% of the Republic of Korea is covered by forest. The UN FAO estimated the 2009 roundwood production at 3.18 million cu m (112.2 million cu ft). The value of all forest products, including roundwood, totaled $1.9 billion. Wood supplies are grossly inadequate to meet the needs of the fast-growing plywood and paper industries. Most of the original forests were destroyed during the Korean War and have been transformed into pine forests under a massive government reforestation program. Conifers account for 45% of the forest; broad-leaved species (such as oak), 28%; and mixed forests, 27%. About 21% of all forested land is nationally owned and is the focus of extensive reforestation efforts. The government supported local efforts to invest in forest development projects abroad. Because of low quality, domestic roundwood is mainly used for chopsticks, crates, match wood, and wood chips. Whereas plywood and wood pulp were once traditional export items, the role of forestry products in generating export earnings is shrinking. The ROK imports about 95% of its forest products. Imports have been boosted by a growing demand for single and multifamily wood frame houses.

26 MINING

The Republic of Korea (ROK) does not have significant natural resources, and its limited supplies of iron ore, coal, copper, lead, and zinc have to be supplemented by imports. In 2009, 455,000 metric tons of iron ore and concentrate (gross weight) were produced, up from 366,000 metric tons in 2008. Output of mined lead in 2009 was 2,064 metric tons. There was no recorded mined zinc output in 2009. Mined copper production in 2009 was 14 metric tons. The ROK also produced the metals bismuth, cadmium, gold, nickel, and silver. Among industrial minerals, the ROK produced barite, hydraulic cement, diatomaceous earth, feldspar, graphite, kaolin, limestone, mica, nitrogen, quartzite, salt, sand (including glass sand), soda ash (manufactured), sulfur, and talc and pyrophyllite. In 2009, mining and quarrying production decreased by 9%; output or industrial minerals accounted for 70% of ROK's mineral production value that year.

After four years of prospecting, Ivanhoe Mines Ltd. of Canada announced the discovery of two epithermal gold-silver veins near Haenam, Cholla Province, with potentially high-grade gold-silver mineralization. The government continued to support state-owned or privately owned enterprises that invested in such mineral-rich countries as Australia, Brazil, Canada, and Chile. The Korea Development Bank sold off the government's equity in Pohang Iron and Steel Co. Ltd. (POSCO), which had diversified interests and holdings, including a high-grade iron ore deposit in the Pibara region of Western Australia with proven reserves of 200 million tons. Two-way trade with North Korea continued to grow.

27 ENERGY AND POWER

The World Bank reported in 2008 that Korea produced 443.9 billion kWh of electricity and consumed 430.3 billion kWh, or 8,826 kWh per capita. Roughly 81% of energy came from fossil fuels, while 18% came from alternative fuels. Per capita oil consumption was 4,669 kg. South Korea has no known reserves of oil or natural gas, and must rely on imports to meet all its oil and natural gas needs. As the ninth-largest consumer of oil in the world, South Korea consumed over 2.2 million barrels of oil per day in 2010. South Korea has 3 of the 10 largest crude oil refineries in the world and produced almost 2.5 million barrels per day of refined products in 2009. The country also consumed 1.5 trillion cu ft of natural gas in 2010, an increase of 25% from 2009. South Korea is the second-largest importer of liquefied natural gas in the world behind Japan.

The country does have recoverable coal deposits, which are the country's primary source of domestic fossil fuel output, but the deposits are small and South Korea must import the bulk of the coal it consumes. Most of the domestic coal is low-quality anthracite and is used mainly for home cooking and heating; imports of higher-grade coal are required for industry.

Nuclear power accounts for more than one-third of South Korea's electricity generation.

28 INDUSTRY

Until the 1960s, manufacturing was chiefly confined to production for domestic consumption, and a substantial proportion of the output was produced by handicraft methods in homes and small factories. While textiles, apparel, and footwear were the first modern industries to be developed, heavy industry grew rapidly over the next four decades, promoted by a series of development plans. In the 1980s, the manufacture of metals, machinery, and electronic and other equipment overtook textile production as the country's leading industries in terms of value, employment, and export earnings. In the 1990s, high-tech electronics became the leading sector as South Korea became the world's leading semiconductor manufacturer as well as the leading shipbuilder. Prosperity brought higher labor costs, and in the past decade, South Korea began outsourcing production—particularly textiles and footwear but also consumer electronics—to overseas locations in Southeast Asia, Eastern Europe, China, Mexico, and Turkey. The Republic of Korea (ROK) ranks as a major Asian producer of electronics, automobiles, chemicals, ships, steel, textiles, clothing, shoes, and processed food.

Manufacturing in the ROK has been dominated by a few dozen vertically integrated industrial conglomerates (chaebol), which have privileged access to financing and set the standards for contracting and procurement throughout the country. Many of the country's chaebol have racked up huge debts in order to finance industrial expansion, some more than five times their annual intake. In 2005, the government instituted a program of corporate restructuring designed to make the business activities of Korean companies, including the chaebol, more transparent and more accountable to shareholders, but this was still a work in progress. Despite efforts since the Asian Economic crisis to diversify the economy and stimulate more small and medium enterprise development, the chaebol continued to dominate the economy in 2011.

Joint-venture production with major US and Japanese car companies, growing domestic demand, and successful penetration of overseas markets by Korean-owned corporations have fueled steady growth in automobile output. ROK is also one of the world's leading producers of large ships.

Production of electronics has shifted from assembly of imported parts to the manufacture of competitive high-technology products, such as office automation systems, for both the international and domestic markets. Daewoo Electronics (the second-largest chaebol, with substantial debts), LG, and Samsung Electronics dominate the production of consumer electronics in the ROK; the televisions, cell phones, stereos, refrigerators, washing machines, and microwave ovens produced by these companies are sold across the world. Daewoo Electronics also operates 36 facilities overseas. South Korea is a major producer of radio communications, including cell phones; the electronics sector accounts for 25% of domestic output.

P'ohang Iron and Steel Co. (POSCO) produces about half the nation's total steel output. There are about 200 steel companies in South Korea. According to the World Steel Association, in 2010 POSCO produced 34.5 million tons of steel and remained the fifth-largest steel company in the world.

²⁹SCIENCE AND TECHNOLOGY

Patent applications in science and technology totaled 127,316 in Korea as of 2009, according to the World Bank. Public financing of science was 3.21% of GDP. The ROK has often been compared to its powerful neighbor, Japan, but is said to be about 10 years behind that nation in scientific and technological innovation. However, in areas such as semiconductor memory chips, cars, and steel, Korean industries provide innovation equal to that of the United States and Japan.

Two organizations provide most of the main support for Korean science and technology. The Korean Institute of Science and Technology (KIST) was started in 1965 with the help of the United States. The Korean Advanced Institute of Science and Technology (KAIST), the leading university in scientific research, attracts researchers from all over the world and is considered one of the top universities for electrical and molecular engineering and computer science.

South Korea launched its first satellite into orbit from its own territory on 25 August 2009. The South Korean–built satellite was deployed to monitor atmospheric and oceanic conditions. While being hailed for its scientific merits in South Korea, the launch carried heavy implications for geopolitics in the region. South Korea's satellite launch took place four months after North Korea launched a satellite of its own. South Korea successfully courted Russia for technological expertise in completing this project. With the launch, South Korea became the fourth nation in the region—behind Japan, China, and North Korea—to have a domestic space program.

³⁰DOMESTIC TRADE

Traditionally, the retail sector in Korea has been characterized by the small family store. However, this has begun to change as large-sized discount stores have started to enter the nation's retail market. The nation's large stores tend to be located in the country's major cities where most consumer products are sold. Large re-

tailers such as Costco, Walmart, Carrefour (France), and E-mart (Korea) have become highly popular in Korea, and plans were being made to expand the number of these stores throughout the country. In rural areas, itinerant peddlers, mobile sidewalk stands, and periodic market fairs can still be found. However, the increasing presence of large discounters may mean that the days of such small retailers in the countryside are numbered.

Although Seoul is the nation's wholesaling center, the cities of Pusan, Incheon, Daegu, and Gwangyang are also important distribution centers.

Franchising has been growing rapidly in Korea, led initially by fast food restaurants but spreading to cleaning and mailing services, clothing, family restaurants, and discount stores. Direct marketing, in particular door-to-door sales, is still fairly popular.

Most private offices are open from 9 a.m. to 6 p.m. weekdays. Some businesses are open from 9 a.m. to 1 p.m. on Saturdays, but Korean companies are moving toward the five-day workweek. Korean government offices keep similar hours. Banking hours are 9 a.m. to 5 p.m., Monday through Friday. Department stores are open from 10:30 a.m. to 8 p.m. seven days a week, although typically one day a month (usually a Monday) department stores are closed (closings vary according to each store).

³¹FOREIGN TRADE

Major ROK import partners in 2009 were China, 16.8%; Japan, 15.3%; the United States, 9%; Saudi Arabia, 6.1%; and Australia, 4.6%. Its major export partners were China, 23.9%; the United States, 10.4%; Japan, 6%; and Hong Kong, 5.4%. Potential new markets in Eastern Europe and the rest of Asia were being explored. Saudi Arabia and Indonesia have been major providers of oil and liquefied natural gas. Australia is one of South Korea's leading suppliers of iron ore, coal, and grains.

In 2010, South Korea exported $341 billion and imported $310 billion worth of goods and services. Electric and electronic products, automobiles, various types of machinery, and chemicals were

Principal Trading Partners – Korea, Republic of (ROK) (2010)

(In millions of US dollars)

Country	Total	Exports	Imports	Balance
World	891,596.0	466,384.0	425,212.0	41,172.0
China	188,412.0	116,838.0	71,574.0	45,264.0
Japan	92,472.0	28,176.0	64,296.0	-36,120.0
United States	90,581.0	49,992.0	40,589.0	9,403.0
Sa'udi Arabia	31,377.0	4,557.0	26,820.0	-22,263.0
Taiwan	28,477.0	14,830.0	13,647.0	1,183.0
Hong Kong	27,240.0	25,294.0	1,946.0	23,348.0
Australia	27,098.0	6,642.0	20,456.0	-13,814.0
Germany	25,007.0	10,702.0	14,305.0	-3,603.0
Singapore	23,094.0	15,244.0	7,850.0	7,394.0
Indonesia	22,883.0	8,897.0	13,986.0	-5,089.0

(…) data not available or not significant.

(n.s.) not specified.

SOURCE: *2011 Direction of Trade Statistics Yearbook,* New York: United Nations, 2011.

Balance of Payments – Korea, Republic of (ROK) (2010)

(In millions of US dollars)

Current Account		**28,214.0**
Balance on goods	41,876.0	
Imports	-422,425.0	
Exports	464,301.0	
Balance on services		-11,201.0
Balance on income		768.0
Current transfers		-3,230.0
Capital Account		**-174.0**
Financial Account		**1,937.0**
Direct investment abroad		-19,230.0
Direct investment in Korea, Republic of (ROK)		-150.0
Portfolio investment assets		-3,542.0
Portfolio investment liabilities		42,094.0
Financial derivatives		-7.0
Other investment assets		-12,258.0
Other investment liabilities		-4,971.0
Net Errors and Omissions		**-2,805.0**
Reserves and Related Items		**-27,172.0**

(…) data not available or not significant.

SOURCE: *Balance of Payment Statistics Yearbook 2011*, Washington, DC: International Monetary Fund, 2011.

the most important commodity exports. The ROK's other major exports included woven fabrics and ships.

Oil and related products, machinery, semiconductors, electronic machinery, and raw materials were major imports, as most raw inputs for the country's industrial sector are imported. A lack of small companies and technological research compels the ROK to import components and production machines for the cars, consumer electronics, computer chips, and ships that it manufactures.

³²BALANCE OF PAYMENTS

Robust export performance turned the overall balance-of-payments deficit into a $1.7 billion surplus in 1986, which grew to $12.1 billion in 1988. The balance-of-payments surplus later declined; in 1990, the balance of payments had a deficit of $274 million because of declining exports, rising imports, and a current account deficit. The deficit grew to over 4% of GDP in 1996 before subsiding in 1997 due to a shrinking currency base. At the end of 1998, South Korea had $20.2 billion in net outstanding loans, but by the end of 1999, it had become a net creditor. By the end of April 2001, $33.3 billion in outstanding loans were owed the country. In 2010, the Republic of Korea had a foreign trade surplus of $39 billion. The current account balance was $28.21 billion that year.

³³BANKING AND SECURITIES

The Bank of Korea serves as the central bank, the bank of issue, and the depository for government funds. It was established on 12 June 1950. The banking system is regulated by the Financial Supervisory Service. Other banking services are provided by the state-run Korea Development Bank, the Export-Import Bank of Korea, and nine state-run specialized banks.

In 1986, as part of the government's economic stabilization program initiated in 1980, all of the five commercial banks previously

under government control were denationalized. In 1993, the Korean government began a five-year financial-sector reform program, including the deregulation of interest rates and liberalization of foreign exchange. During the financial crisis of late 1997 and 1998, nonperforming loan levels skyrocketed. The credit hunger of South Korean corporations can be explained in part by the failure of the stock exchange to generate the equity capital they needed. On 25 June 1998, the Korean government ordered the takeover of five failing banks, and seven other banks were put on a warning list. Of the seven, five merged, and two continued operations. Banks directly affected by these measures included Shinhan Bank, the Housing and Commercial Bank, Kookmin Bank, KorAm Bank, Hana Bank, and Hanvit Bank, among others. In 1998, efforts continued to stabilize the banking sector by increasing the capital adequacy ratio to 8%, and the government encouraged lending to small and medium-sized companies as opposed to the large conglomerate *chaebol*.

In 2009 the nation's discount rate, the interest rate at which the central bank lends to financial institutions in the short term, was 1.25%. The commercial bank prime lending rate, the rate at which banks lend to customers, was 5.508% in 2010.

The Korean Stock Exchange (KSE), a share-issuing private corporation, functioned as the country's only stock exchange through 1998, when the Korea Securities Dealers Automated Quotations (KOSDAQ) began holding stock transactions for small and medium-sized firms. Direct access to the stock market by foreigners has been allowed since 1992, with Seoul implementing unrestricted foreign access in 1998 and establishing international links in 2000.

³⁴INSURANCE

The insurance industry in the Republic of Korea is overseen by the Financial Supervisory Service. Leading life insurance companies include Samsung Life, Korea Life, Kyobo Life, and Allianz. Leading nonlife insurance companies include Samsung, Hyundai, Dongbu, LG, and Oriental. Workers' compensation, medical insurance, third-party automobile liability, nuclear and aviation liability, and unemployment insurance are all compulsory.

³⁵PUBLIC FINANCE

In 2010, the budget of Republic of Korea included $248.3 billion in public revenue and $267.3 billion in public expenditures. The budget surplus amounted to 1.2% of GDP. Public debt was 23.7% of GDP, with $380.6 billion of the debt held by foreign entities.

³⁶TAXATION

The principal sources of tax revenue as of 2011 were customs duties, corporate taxes, a defense tax surcharge imposed on corporations, a value-added tax (VAT) of 10%, personal income taxes, and excise taxes ranging from 5% to 20%. The rates for corporate taxation ranged from 10% for income up to KRW200 million ($174,000) to 22% beyond that amount, with an additional 10% surcharge. A local income tax of 0.5% and property taxes of 0.3% (buildings), 0.24–4.8% (land), and 0.14% (city planning) were also applied. Employers pay into national pension, health,

Public Finance – Korea, Republic of (ROK) (2009)

(In billions of won, central government figures)

Revenue and Grants	245,477	100.0%
Tax revenue	164,542	67.0%
Social contributions	40,220	16.4%
Grants	...	...
Other revenue	40,715	16.6%
Expenditures	247,789	100.0%
General public services	51,729	20.9%
Defense	27,745	11.2%
Public order and safety	12,030	4.9%
Economic affairs	49,724	20.1%
Environmental protection	...	...
Housing and community amenities	11,133	4.5%
Health	2,792	1.1%
Recreational, culture, and religion	2,525	1.0%
Education	36,717	14.8%
Social protection	53,393	21.5%

(…) data not available or not significant.

SOURCE: *Government Finance Statistics Yearbook 2010*, Washington, DC: International Monetary Fund, 2010.

and accident insurance plans. Personal income tax ranged from 6% to 35%.

37 CUSTOMS AND DUTIES

As of 2011, South Korea had an average tariff of 7.9%. Other import taxes included a value-added tax of 10% and excise taxes ranging from 15% to 100%. The special excise tax on consumer electronic goods and automobiles was cut by 30% in 1998. The Information Technology Agreement (ITA) dropped most IT tariffs by 2000, with the remainder phased out by 2004.

38 FOREIGN INVESTMENT

Foreign direct investment (FDI) in the Republic of Korea was a net inflow of $1.51 billion according to World Bank figures published in 2009. FDI represented 0.18% of GDP.

The Foreign Investment Promotion Act (FIPA) and related regulations have governed foreign investment in the Republic of Korea since May 1998, when a five-year liberalization plan was announced covering a total of 11 sectors, including real estate, financial services, and petroleum. The policy emphasis shifted from "control and regulate" to "promote and support." Tax benefits and incentives were provided for foreign investors in high-tech and services sectors.

To facilitate further technology transfer, the government offers particular incentives to foreign companies in more than 500 categories of high-technology industries. Four free export zones geared toward highly technical business activities have been established at Masan (near Pusan), Iri (near Kunsan), Daebul, and Iksan, to provide additional incentives for investment in favored industries. Six industrial parks exist, which are for the exclusive use of Korean firms with heavy foreign investment.

39 ECONOMIC DEVELOPMENT

The Republic of Korea (ROK) has a market economy in which both private enterprise and foreign investors play an important role. From 1962 to 1997, overall economic development was guided by the Economic Planning Board and a series of five-year plans. The Korean economy was devastated by the Korean War, even requiring foreign food aid. As late as 1965, per capita income was only $88 a year. Since 1965, South Korea has been transformed from an underdeveloped agricultural economy to a leading newly industrialized country (NIC) to a leader in the new information technology (IT) economy. Nominal GDP was $3 billion in 1965; in 2003, it was projected at $514 billion, 171 times higher. In 2004, South Korea joined the trillion-dollar club of world economies.

The seventh five-year economic and social development plan for 1992–96 aimed at establishing the ROK as an advanced industrialized economy by the year 2000. More specific goals included improving social and economic equity, continuing liberalization, and improving industrial and export competitiveness, as well as strengthening the role of the private sector while reducing government intervention in economic management, especially in the financial sector. The plan targeted an annual GDP growth rate of 7% and a decline of consumer price inflation to 3%. The plan was derailed by the Asian financial crisis. South Korea was assisted in weathering the crisis by a $58 billion international support program mobilized through the IMF, the World Bank, and the Asia Development Bank (ADB). In May 1998, the government introduced its five-year liberalization program. The ROK's recovery from the Asian financial crisis was remarkably strong, aided by a show of international confidence and its government's embrace of trade and investment liberalization reforms. However, the collapse of the dot.com boom and the global economic slowdown that began in 2001, combined with the aftermath of the 11 September 2001 terrorist attacks on the United States, dealt serious blows to the economy's forward momentum. Progress in reducing the share of nonperforming loans (NPLs) in the financial sector and reducing dependency on foreign borrowing were brought to a halt.

Major foreign acquisitions in the financial sector by 2006 prompted a backlash against further market opening, although this remained desirable, especially in the service sector. In order for the economy to grow at a faster rate in the long-term, South Korea, despite its skilled workforce and large middle class, must develop a strong and diverse local economy instead of relying on exports for growth, which tends to benefit the chaebol and stifle domestic demand. In addition to concerns about dependence on exports, South Korea's government also faced the challenge of an aging population in 2011.

40 SOCIAL DEVELOPMENT

The devastation of the Korean War left 348,000 war widows, most of them with dependent children, and 100,000 war orphans. Some 595,260 homes were destroyed, 5,000 villages wiped out, and many large cities badly damaged. Military relief payments consist mainly of financial support to veterans and their families.

A social insurance system provides old-age, disability, and survivors' benefits to all residents ages 18–59. There is a separate system for public employees, school teachers, self-employed individuals, and military personnel. Workers and employers contribute 4.5% of earnings and payroll. Retirement is set at age 65 but is gradually increasing. Unemployment insurance covers all employees younger than 65 years of age.

Conservative Confucian tradition encourages married women to remain at home. Women continue to suffer legal and societal discrimination. Despite equal opportunity laws, very few women achieve high levels of professional success. The wage of the average female worker is roughly half that earned by a male counterpart. Violence against women, domestic abuse, and child abuse are prevalent. Prostitution is illegal but widespread. Divorce remains socially unacceptable in most sectors of Korean society, and this leads many women to remain in abusive marriages.

In May 2009, the Supreme Court upheld a landmark ruling concerning a patient's right to die. The family of a 76-year-old woman petitioned for the right to remove life support for the woman, who had been comatose for one year and declared brain-dead. Doctors refused to withhold life-sustaining treatment. The opinion from the court claimed that sustained treatment of such a terminally ill patient was a violation of personal dignity. This was the first right-to-die case of its kind in the nation.

Korean citizenship is determined exclusively by genealogy, and as a result, many Chinese born and raised in Korea are deprived of citizenship rights. Human rights are generally respected by the government. Some abuses have been reported involving detainees, but these are declining.

In 2009 South Korea had one of the highest suicide rates in the world, officially registering 31 suicides per 100,000 people according to the WHO. The rate has risen dramatically compared to previous decades. The suicide rate was 13.6% in 2000 and 7.4% in 1990. Suicide rates also vary by age groups. In 2009, 2,504 elderly (ages 65 and older) committed suicide in Korea. Elderly suicides comprised 25.2% of the total number of suicides. Some 56.1%, or 5,575 cases, were by citizens between 35 and 64 years of age. Among the young, 1,260 suicides were by those between 25 and 34 years of age, making up 12.1% of the total, while Koreans under 25 accounted for 588 suicides, or 6% of total cases.

The problem of suicide, which experts attribute to a hypercompetitive social atmosphere and the decline of traditional social networks, is so great that the government has launched programs to combat the epidemic. Religious leaders from across the country and across faiths joined together in March 2010 to promote the prevention of suicide. That month, the Korean Council of Religious Leaders, which includes Catholic, Protestant, and Buddhist leaders, convened to plan public education programs to combat what remains the leading cause of death among South Koreans in their 20s and 30s.

Most media and public attention falls on the educational stress and competitive pressures to gain admission to the best colleges that may lead many of Korea's youth to commit suicide, but suicide is also prevalent among Korea's elderly population.

In 2008, nearly 13 elderly citizens committed suicide every day, and the elderly committed nearly 1 in 3 of the total suicides that year. Even within the statistical group of over 61 years, suicide rates in Korea generally increase with age for the elderly, with 48 per 100,000 among the 60–64 age group and 89 for the 75–79 age group. The rate of attempted suicide for the elderly population is lower than that of young people, but the success rate is much higher (1 out of 200 attempted suicides for young adults vs. 1 in 4 for the elderly). Potential causes of suicide include depression, loneliness, and poverty.

41 HEALTH

According to the CIA, life expectancy in the Republic of Korea was 80 years in 2011. The country spent 6.5% of its GDP on health care, amounting to $1,108 per person. There were 20 physicians, 53 nurses and midwives, and 123 hospital beds per 10,000 inhabitants. The fertility rate was 1.3, while the infant mortality rate was 5 per 1,000 live births. In 2008 the maternal mortality rate, according to the World Bank, was 18 per 100,000 births. It was estimated that 93% of children were vaccinated against measles. The CIA calculated HIV/AIDS prevalence in Korea to be about less than 0.1% in 2009.

The substantial improvement in health care is directly related to improvement of diet, a rise in living standards, and the development of health and medical programs. Since the late 1970s, medical security, in the form of medical insurance and medical aid, has been expanded to cover a substantial portion of the population. The national medical insurance system was expanded in 1989, covering 94% of the population.

Leading causes of death are illnesses related to cardiovascular disease and deaths caused by traffic motor vehicle accidents.

42 HOUSING

After liberation in 1945, Allied-occupied Korea south of the 38th Parallel faced a housing shortage greatly compounded by high population growth rates. In the late 1980s, the government planners promoted a policy called the "Two Million Home Construction Plan," designed to address the persistent shortages in housing and soaring housing prices. Five new towns (Bundang, Ilsan, Pyeongchon, Sanbon, and Joongdong) have since been built around the city of Seoul. By 2002, there were an estimated 11,892,000 housing units nationwide, still short of demand from 12,099,000 households. The ongoing push to meet housing demand saw about 543,000 new housing units built that year. Due to population density and limited land for development, most new housing in Korea is in the form of large 12–15 story apartment buildings. By the mid-1990s, the New Town phenomena spread throughout every major metropolitan area in the nation.

Though real estate is a fully private capitalist exchange system, land ownership is regulated by the state, which has had a major impact on real estate transactions involving extensive land expropriation and land-use planning. The Korean state used different strategies to manage trends and land development projects from the 1950s to the 1970s, and Public Management Development projects were the main mechanism of urban development in the 1980s. The urban development system was feasible because of the state's extensive control over access to financing for housing, which would go to the development firms and construction companies rather than individuals.

In the mid-1990s there was a shift towards greater private sector involvement in urban development. However, the distributional effects of the urban development process have been highly inequitable. Subsidized home ownership for middle-income families has been favored over provision of public rental housing for low-income families, and the basis of selecting beneficiaries of public subsidies has been very arbitrary. Thus, the system has promoted significant land concentration and land speculation particularly by private companies, including the large chaebol. Once a chaebol construction firm knew of a targeted area for development they could buy up land, raising prices and values.

After the Asian financial crisis in 1997, banks turned their attention away from company loans toward private credit, targeting families as new customers. Since then, household debt in South Korea has grown by an average of 13% a year, almost twice as fast as the country's GDP.

While the constant price hike across the housing market reinforced the system, stagnation resulting from the 2008–09 global financial crisis has made household debt a government concern. In contrast to soaring property values elsewhere in Asia, residential real estate prices declined 10% in the greater Seoul area and 20% or more in other regions of the country. Consumers face steep interest payments as well, especially as over 90% of Korea's loans have a variable interest rate. Meanwhile, total debt for Korea Land & Housing, the state-run funder of home and government construction, stood at $101 billion in 2011.

43 EDUCATION

In 2008 the World Bank estimated that 99% of age-eligible children in Korea were enrolled in primary school. Secondary enrollment for age-eligible children stood at 95%. Tertiary enrollment was estimated at 98%. The CIA estimated that the Republic of Korea had an overall literacy rate of 98%. Because of the nearly perfect literacy rate in the past decade, the Korean government has stopped reporting on it.

The Education Law of 1949 provided for a centralized system under the control of the Ministry of Education and made six-year elementary schools free and compulsory for children between 6 and 12 years of age. Children then attend middle school for three years, and subsequently attend either general academic high school or vocational high school for the remaining three years. The Korean Ministry of Education, Science and Technology has promoted the adoption of technology in schools, and the average number of students per computer overall in primary and secondary education is 5.5.

The government supports a university system in which the universities' primary source of financial support is the national government. Seoul National University (SNU) is the highest ranked and most renowned university in Korea, though the Korean Advanced Institute for Science and Technology (KAIST) is ranked higher in international rankings. There are 10 regionally based "flagship" national universities, including Chonnam National and Busan National, and 16 specialized national universities that include the military academies, science and technology institutes, a maritime university and a railroad university. Thirteen other national universities are scattered across the country. The principal private institutions, all of them in Seoul, are Korea, Sung Kyun Kwan, Yonsei, Kyung Hee, Hanyang, Chungang, and Ewha universities; Ewha is one of the largest women's universities in the world. Tuition fees for national institutions are set by the Ministry of Education and have begun to rise due to increased costs and budget tightening in the national government. These tend to be lower than the fees set by private institutions, which are free to set their own fees.

Of those enrolled in post-secondary higher education, there were 100 male students for every 70 female students in 2009. It has been estimated that nearly all men attend some type of higher education program, while only about 69% of women enroll in a program. According to the World Bank, public expenditures on education as of 2008 were estimated at 4.8% of GDP.

In Korea, a culture of cram schools known as *hagwons* has developed. Hagwon is the Korean term for a private tutoring academy or institute. According to the Korean Ministry of Education, Science, and Technology, in 2007, there were 67,649 private tutoring institutes in Korea, spanning a variety of fields but concentrated in assisting students pass entrance exams, certification exams, or supplementary courses to their programs (such as a language). Spending on hagwons exceeded $16 billion in 2008. It was estimated that 74% of all students engaged in private instruction in 2010. Hagwons are a way of life for most Korean children and youth. However, hagwons have been controversial. Their cost has been a major point of contention because it widens the education gap between social classes and has caused financial hardship for many families trying to advance their children's education. The cost of hagwons has even impacted Korean demography by reducing the birth rate as a mechanism to cope with the economic burden of educating children. They also significantly impact students' abilities to get into both high school and the upper echelons of universities, which have traditionally determined future socioeconomic status. The government has begun limiting both the fees and the opening hours of hagwons, and the number of youth educated abroad has started to change the working culture.

44 LIBRARIES AND MUSEUMS

The Central National Library, founded in 1923, has approximately 4 million volumes. Most other sizable libraries in the ROK are found at universities. The largest academic collection is at the Seoul National University Library (2.2 million volumes).

The National Museum, with centers in Seoul, Kyongju, Kwangju, Puyo, Chinju, Chunju, Chongju, and Kongju, contains art objects reflecting more than 5,000 years of cultural history, including statuary pieces, ceramics, and painting. A major private museum is the Ho-Am Art Museum in Seoul. The National Museum of Modern Art in Seoul presents many special exhibits as well a permanent collection. The National Science Museum of Korea in Daejon was completed in 1990. The ROK also possesses collections of early printing, dynastic histories, and art in its palaces and Buddhist temples and in university, college, and public libraries.

45 MEDIA

In 2009, the CIA reported that there were 19.3 million telephone landlines in Republic of Korea. In addition to landlines, mobile phone subscriptions averaged 98 per 100 people. There were 61 FM radio stations, 150 AM radio stations, and 2 shortwave radio stations. Internet users numbered 81 per 100 citizens. Prominent newspapers in 2010, with circulation numbers listed parenthetically, included *Pusan Ilbo* (427,000), *Chosun Ilbo* (1,960,000), *JoongAng Ilbo* (2,200,000) and *Dong-A Ilbo* (2,150,000), as well as 39 other major newspapers.

The South Korean media has a long history of censorship and attempts at state control. The country's first president Syngman Rhee, for example, used the US military government's Ordinance 88 to outlaw leftist publications. The advent of the military dictatorship under Chung-hee Park brought even more stringent suppression, as measures legal and extralegal were employed to stifle criticism and coverage of the opposition. This era saw a high degree of media consolidation as numerous independent outlets were subsumed under the state control, while others were closed or otherwise severely restricted. News agencies were limited not only in what stories they were allowed to cover but also in their geographic scope; many newspapers were banned from having offices in provincial cities and were confined to Seoul. In total, the Park regime closed 834 newspapers and other news agencies within a month of the 16 May 1961 coup d'état, permitting only 82 newspapers throughout the entire country to continue circulation. The number of news agencies in Seoul alone was reduced from 241 to a mere 11. State censorship ultimately culminated in the Basic Press Act of 1980, which set nationwide qualifications for journalists as well as daily "reporting guidelines" issued by the Office of Public Information Policy. Following the liberalization of the late 1980s, South Korean media outlets witnessed a renaissance as independent news agencies resumed operations and new agencies were formed. AM and FM radio stations combined grew from 75 to 125 between 1985 and 1989. Newspapers witnessed similar growth. There was an explosive growth in print media in the 1990s, and as of 2011 there were some 6,500 periodicals—2,000 weeklies, 3,300 monthlies, and 1,200 quarterlies—in publication.

The mobile service market is dominated by Korean Telecom (KT), LG U Plus (LGU+), and SK Telecom (SKT). Mobile devices are supplied predominantly by Samsung and LG Electronics, with estimated market shares of 51.5% and 17.55%, respectively, in July 2011. Samsung and LG not only dominate domestic markets but also stand at number 2 and 3 in world rankings, respectively. As of mid-2011, 80% of all mobile subscriptions were estimated to be 3G. U+ and SK introduced 4G LTE subscriptions in July 2011, and KT launched their own LTE services in January 2012.

Cisco Systems Inc. rated South Korea as the world leader in broadband quality for both 2009 and 2010, with an estimated 100% broadband penetration. Accordingly, South Korea has developed a vibrant Internet culture, complete with its own social networking sites, search engines, blogs, and online news portals. Internet-based social mobilization is widely credited with the 2002 election of President Myoo-Hyun Roh—who garnered support among young voters via the websites *Rohsamo* and alternative Internet-based news publications *Hankyoreh* and *Ohmynews*—and the December 2011 election of NGO leader and activist Won-Soon Park as Mayor of Seoul . Online media have likewise been credited with a series of protests against a US-Korean free-trade agreement in 2008, which led to the resignation of several senior officials, as well as the suicides of a handful of Korean celebrities following Internet-based smear campaigns.

46 ORGANIZATIONS

Clan and county associations are a conspicuous aspect of Korean social life. The National Agricultural Cooperative Federation comprises millions of farmers who work in cooperatives. The Korea Chamber of Commerce and Industry is based in Seoul. Other groups include the Agricultural and Fishery Marketing Corporation and the Federation of All Korean Trade Unions. The Consumers' Union of Korea is active. The Federation of Korean Industries is the key lobbying and business association of the chaebol,

which has in recent years expanded its mission to encompass a number of economic, political, and environmental issues.

South Korean nongovernmental organizations (NGOs) underwent a period of significant growth following the end of the military dictatorship in the late 1980s. The labor struggles of July, August, and September 1987, for example, gave birth to the organization that was to become the Korean Confederation of Trade Unions (KCTU). In July 1989, the Citizens' Coalition for Economic Justice (CCEJ) was formed to combat real estate speculation. In addition to the establishment of these new, progressive organizations, a number of previously state-controlled organizations, such as the Federation of Korean Trade Unions (FKTU) and the National Agricultural Cooperative Federation, took on a more independent and populist character.

While the late 1980s may be characterized as a time of ideological diversification among Korean NGOs, the 1990s saw a proliferation of public-interest organizations and a process of "competitive differentiation." Smaller, more focused interest groups emerged from the progressive monopolies of the late 1980s and competed both with their predecessors and one another. The 1990s were also a time of geographic expansion for the NGO movement, as the centralization imposed by the government weakened and allowed regionally based organizations to flourish. According to data from the 2000 *Directory of Korean NGOs*, 21% of the country's NGOs were founded during the 1980s and 56.5% during the 1990s, as compared with a mere 9% in the 1970s, for instance.

This explosive growth in Korean NGOs has had a major impact on Korean politics and society. The "NGO Movement," which by the mid-1990s included upwards of 40,000 organizations (including some as small as one or two people registering the organization to support some cause), put the political Left and political Right increasingly at odds with each other. The People's Solidarity for Participatory Democracy (PSPD) formed in 1994, for example, played a leading role in the election of its founder, Won-Soon Park, as mayor of Seoul in 2011.

Cultural and arts organizations include the Academy of Korean Studies, the Korea Foundation, and the National Academy of the Arts. Organizations for advancement and research in science include the Korean Medical Association and National Academy of Sciences of the Republic of Korea. National youth organizations include the Boy Scouts and Girls Scouts of Korea, Free Asian Youth Alliance, Korea Young Buddhists Federation, Korean 4-H, Junior Chamber, Korean Student Christian Federation, Korean World University Service, YMCA/YWCA, Seoul Association for Youth Service, and the Young Christian Workers of Korea. There are several sports associations throughout the country. Among the most notable are the base offices of the International Judo Federation and the World Tae Kwon Do Federation. National organizations for women include the Korean Association of University Women, Korean Institute for Women and Politics, and the Korean Women's Institute.

The Korea Welfare Foundation works with children and youth, the disabled, and the elderly. International organizations with active chapters within the country include Amnesty International, Habitat for Humanity, Caritas, and the Red Cross.

⁴⁷TOURISM, TRAVEL, AND RECREATION

The *Tourism Factbook*, published by the UN World Tourism Organization, reported 7.82 million incoming tourists to Korea in 2009. They spent a total of $12.9 billion. Of those incoming tourists, there were 6.0 million from East Asia and the Pacific. There were hotel beds available in Korea. The estimated daily cost to visit Seoul, the capital, was $350. The cost of visiting other cities averaged $135.

Major tourist attractions include Seoul, the former royal capital of the Yi (or Li) Dynasty, and Kyongju, with its treasures from the ancient kingdom of Silla. Along the eastern coastline, from Hwajinpo to Busan, are popular resorts with skiing in the winter and swimming and water sports in the summer. Football (soccer) and baseball are the most popular modern sports. Traditional sports for men are wrestling, archery, kite fighting, and tae kwon do (a martial art). Popular games include *paduk*, the Korean name for the Japanese board game *go*,;*changgi*, a type of Korean chess; and *yut*, or Korean dice, played with four wooden sticks. Seoul hosted the Summer Olympic Games in 1988.

In 2009, the Royal Tombs of the Joeson Dynasty, a collection of 40 tombs scattered over 18 locations throughout the country, were inscribed as a cultural UNESCO World Heritage Site. Built from 1408 through 1966, the tombs feature the burial sites, shrines, and associated guardhouses of the royal family that reigned from 1392 to 1910. South Korea is home to eight additional UNESCO World Heritage Sites.

In 2010, the traditional South Korean song cycle known as *gagok* was officially inscribed on the UNESCO Representative List of the Intangible Heritage of Humanity, an offshoot of the World Heritage program. This vocal song form was deemed a living tradition by UNESCO, meaning that it is still passed from generation to generation and continues to create a sense of identity and community for those who participate. Such traditions have been approved by UNESCO for special consideration since 2001. For one that is inscribed, a special program is designed to protect and promote the practice and understanding of the tradition. The gagok song cycle includes 26 songs for men (*namchang*) and 15 songs for women (*yeochang*). The songs are accompanied by a small orchestra of traditional instruments. The traditional wooden architecture known as *daemokjang* was also inscribed on the Intangible Heritage list. The traditional wooden structures are designed and built by craftsmen who learn the trade through apprenticeship.

Korea has also become increasingly popular as a destination for medical tourism. It has rigorous training and licensing protocols, resulting in a highly qualified medical community. It is relatively inexpensive compared to similar countries. Medical tourism has centered on cosmetic procedures, though other types of procedures for more debilitating medical conditions are on the rise. Traditional medicine is also increasing in popularity for both regional tourists and larger international tourists.

Cheju (more commonly known as Jeju) Island is often referred to locally as the "Hawaii of Korea." Though it is not tropical, it shares with Hawaii the characteristic of being volcanic and a honeymoon destination with many beaches and resort hotels. It is mountainous and the biggest island in South Korea, with the warmest climate of the whole country. It has a large tourism industry with over 4 million visitors each year and is famous among Japanese tourists for the high quality of its many sushi and sashimi restaurants. Its most notable mountain is Hallasan (also known as Mt. Yeongjusan). Mt. Hallasan is famous for its vertical ecosystem of plants that results from the varying temperatures along the mountainside. Over 1,800 kinds of plants and 4,000 species of animals (3,300 species of insects) have been identified including unique flora and fauna, some endangered species and others endemic to the island. Hallasan National Park is a UNESCO World Heritage Site.

⁴⁸FAMOUS PERSONS

The dominant political figures of the contemporary period in the Republic of Korea (ROK) have been Syngman Rhee (1875–1965), president from 1948 to 1960, and Park Chung-hee (1917–79), president from 1963 until his assassination in 1979. Chun Doo Hwan (Chon Du-hwan, b. 1931) became president in 1981. Other well-known modern figures include Kim Chong-p'il (b. 1926), prime minister, 1971–75; Bishop Daniel Chi (Chi Hak-sun, b. 1921); and Kim Dae Jung (Kim Tae-jung, 1925–2009) and Kim Young Sam (Kim Yong-sam, b. 1927), prominent opposition leaders during the 1970s and 1980s who both went on to become president. Kim Dae Jung won the 2000 Nobel Peace Prize for his policy of engagement with North Korea. Roh Moo Hyun (b. 1946) became president in 2003. The Rev. Sun Myung Moon (Mun Son-myong, b. 1920), a controversial evangelist and founder of the Tong-il (Unification) Church, and Kyung Wha Chung (Chung Kyung-wha, b. 1943), a violinist, are both well known internationally.

⁴⁹DEPENDENCIES

The Republic of Korea has no territories or colonies.

⁵⁰BIBLIOGRAPHY

Altbach, Philip G. and Toru Umakoshi, eds. *Asian Universities: Historical Perspectives and Contemporary Challenges.* Baltimore, MD: Johns Hopkins University Press, 2004.

Armstrong, Charles K., ed. *Korean Society: Civil Society, Democracy, and the State.* 2nd ed. New York: Routledge, 2007.

Buzo, Adrian. *The Making of Modern Korea.* 2nd ed. New York: Routledge, 2007.

Connor, Mary E. *The Koreas.* Santa Barbara, CA: ABC CLIO, 2009.

Dudley, William, ed. *North and South Korea: Opposing Viewpoints.* Farmington Hills, MI: Greenhaven Press, 2003.

Edwards, Paul M. *The Korean War: A Historical Dictionary.* Lanham, MD: Scarecrow Press, 2003.

Foley, James A., ed. *Korea's Divided Families: Fifty Years of Separation.* New York: RoutledgeCurzon, 2003.

Hoare, Jim, and Susan Pares. *A Political and Economic Dictionary of East Asia.* Philadelphia: Routledge/Taylor and Francis, 2005.

Korea, South Investment and Business Guide: Strategic and Practical Information. Washington, DC: International Business Publications USA, 2012.

Nahm, Andrew C., and James E. Hoare. *Historical Dictionary of the Republic of Korea.* 2nd ed. Lanham, MD: Scarecrow Press, 2004.

Seth, Michael J. *A History of Korea from Antiquity to the Present.* Lanham, MD: Rowman and Littlefield, 2011.

KUWAIT

State of Kuwait

Dawlat al-Kuwayt

CAPITAL: Kuwait (Al-Kuwayt)

FLAG: The flag, adopted in 1961, is a rectangle divided equally into green, white, and red horizontal stripes, with a black trapezoid whose longer base is against the staff and equal to the breadth of the flag, and whose shorter base is equal to the breadth of the white stripe.

ANTHEM: *Al-Nasheed Al-Watani (National Anthem).*

MONETARY UNIT: The Kuwaiti dinar (KD) has 1,000 fils. There are coins of 1, 5, 10, 20, 50, and 100 fils, and notes of 250 and 500 fils and of 1, 5, 10, and 20 Kuwaiti dinars. KD1 = US$3.60 (or US$1 = KD0.276) as of 2011. The Kuwaiti dinar is the world's highest-valued currency unit.

WEIGHTS AND MEASURES: The metric system is the legal standard, but imperial weights and measures also are in use, and some US measures are recognized.

HOLIDAYS: New Year's Day, 1 January; Emir's Accession Day, 25 February. Movable religious holidays include Muslim New Year (1st of Muharram); Laylat al-Miraj; Milad an-Nabi; Eid al-Fitr; and Eid al-Adha.

TIME: 3 p.m. = noon GMT.

¹LOCATION, SIZE, AND EXTENT

Kuwait is situated at the western head of the Persian (or Arabian) Gulf. Its area is estimated at 17,820 sq km (6,880 sq mi). Comparatively, Kuwait is slightly smaller than the state of New Jersey. Kuwait extends 205 km (127 mi) SE–NW and 176 km (109 mi) NE–SW. Islands that form part of Kuwait include Faylakah (an archaeological site that is the only inhabited island), Bubiyan, Maskan, 'Auha, Al-Warbah, Al-Kubr, Umm al-Maradim, Umm al-Nami, and Qaruh. Bounded on the E by the Persian Gulf, on the S and W by Saudi Arabia, and on the NW and N by Iraq, Kuwait has a total land boundary length of 462 km (287 mi) and a coastline of 499 km (310 mi).

Kuwait's boundary with Iraq historically has been unsettled. Following Kuwait's declaration of independence in June 1961, the emir requested assistance from the United Kingdom to ward off an Iraqi invasion; the British forces were later replaced by troops from Arab League states. The UN upheld Kuwait's sovereignty, and in October 1963, Iraq formally recognized Kuwait's independence. In March 1973, there were armed clashes on the Iraq-Kuwait border, but a settlement was announced in June 1975; negotiations to demarcate the border have continued intermittently. Again in August 1990, Iraq invaded Kuwait, asserting their right to reclaim it as their territory. US-led international forces responded with a massive air attack in January 1991, and Iraq was defeated. Some Iraqi officials continued to assert their claim to Kuwait, and relations between the two countries remained tense. On 27 May 1993, the UN Security Council reaffirmed the established border between the two nations. In 1994, Iraq formally accepted the UN-demarcated border, and the UN mandate in the area was completed in 2003. A 500-m buffer zone was established in 2010.

Kuwait's capital, Kuwait City, is located on the Persian Gulf coast.

²TOPOGRAPHY

Kuwait consists almost entirely of flat rolling desert and mud flats. There is a 360-m (1188-ft) ridge at Mina' al-Ahmadi and a 290-m (951-ft) prominence in the southwest corner. There are no permanent rivers or lakes, but there are some desert wadis that collect water during the rains.

³CLIMATE

During the summer, which lasts roughly from May to October, the air generally is dry, but southeasterly winds often raise daytime humidity to 90% for a few weeks in August or September. Summer temperatures range from 29°C (84°F) in the morning to more than 49°C (120°F) in the shade at noon. Between November and April, the climate is pleasant, with cool nights and warm sunny days. In December and January, night temperatures occasionally touch the freezing point. Frost, almost unknown on the coast, is common in the interior. Annual rainfall, which averages less than 25 cm (10 in), comes in the form of showers or storms between October and April. Cloudbursts have amounted to as much as 6.4 cm (2.5 in) of rain in one day, and can heavily damage roads and houses. The prevailing northwest wind (shamal) is a cooling breeze in summer.

⁴FLORA AND FAUNA

The World Resources Institute estimates that there are 234 plant species in Kuwait. In addition, Kuwait is home to 23 species of mammals, 358 species of birds, and 23 species of reptiles. The calculation reflects the total number of distinct species residing in the country, not the number of endemic species.

Plants and animals are those common to the arid parts of Arabia. There is little vegetation except camel thorn in the desert and some shrubs along the coastal strip. Between October and March, however, when sufficient rain falls at intervals, the desert is transformed: Grass and foliage are plentiful, flowers and plants appear in great variety, and in the spring truffles and mushrooms can be found.

The fox and jackal have decreased in numbers; other mammals found in Kuwait include gerbils, jerboas, and desert hares. Reptile species include various lizards, geckos, and snakes. Fish are plentiful in offshore waters. Among the species of migratory birds are swallows, wagtails, chiffchaff, skylarks, wrens, eagles, cormorants, hoopoes, and terns.

5 ENVIRONMENT

The World Resources Institute reported that Kuwait had designated 300 hectares (741 acres) of land for protection as of 2006. Water resources totaled 0.02 cu km (0.005 cu mi) while water usage was 0.44 cu km (0.106 cu mi) per year. Domestic water usage accounted for 45% of total usage, industrial for 2%, and agricultural for 53%. Per capita water usage totaled 164 cu m (5,792 cu ft) per year.

According to a 2011 report issued by the International Union for Conservation of Nature and Natural Resources (IUCN), threatened species include 6 types of mammals, 8 species of birds, 2 types of reptile, and 11 species of fish. The slender-billed curlew and hawksbill turtle are on the endangered list. The Saudi gazelle has become extinct in the wild.

The Persian Gulf War of 1991 and its aftermath caused severe environmental problems for Kuwait, releasing large quantities of oil into the environment and threatening the water supply. Kuwait has no renewable water resources and must rely on wells and desalination of sea water. The nation has some of the largest and most advanced desalination plants in the world, which provide much of its water.

The UN reported in 2008 that carbon dioxide emissions in Kuwait totaled 86,075 kilotons.

6 POPULATION

The US Central Intelligence Agency (CIA) estimates the population of Kuwait in 2011 to be approximately 2,595,628, which placed it at number 138 in population among the 196 nations of the world. In 2011, approximately 2% of the population was over 65 years of age, with another 25.8% under 15 years of age. The median age in Kuwait was 28.5 years. There were 1.54 males for every female in the country. The population's annual rate of change was 1.986%. The projected population for the year 2025 was 4,100,000. Population density in Kuwait was calculated at 146 people per sq km (378 people per sq mi).

The UN estimated that 98% of the population lived in urban areas, and that urban populations had an annual rate of change of 2.1%. The largest urban area was Kuwait City, with a population of 2.2 million.

7 MIGRATION

Estimates of Kuwait's net migration rate, carried out by the CIA in 2011, amounted to 0.65 migrants per 1,000 citizens. The to-

tal number of emigrants living abroad was 259,400, and the total number of immigrants living in Kuwait was 2.1 million. With the discovery of oil and the consequent rise in living standards, Kuwait acquired a large immigrant population, attracted by jobs, free education for their children, and free medical care. The number of foreign residents more than doubled during the 1970s, and in 1994 they accounted for an estimated 56.4% of the population. Through the early 2000s the number of foreign residents continued to increase. After the Persian Gulf war, Kuwait deported tens of thousands of foreign workers from countries whose leaders had backed Iraq in the conflict. Of the estimated 400,000 Palestinians living in Kuwait before the 1990–91 Gulf War, reportedly only about one-sixth were allowed to remain. Only about 120,000 of the 220,000 prewar Bedouins (mostly nomads from Syria, Jordan, and Iraq) were allowed to stay. These stateless Arabs had remained in Kuwait under Iraqi occupation and were suspected of collaboration. Most other foreign workers were able to return to their home countries. By 1996, however, Egyptians, Pakistanis, Filipinos, and others had filled the void that the previous foreign workers had left behind. Kuwait carried out amnesty plans for illegal foreigners in 1988, 1996, and 2002.

8 ETHNIC GROUPS

Ethnic Kuwaitis are mostly descendants of the tribes of Najd (central Arabia) but some descend from Iraqi Arabs. Still others are of Iranian origin. The number of non-Kuwaitis are divided roughly in half between Arabs and non-Arabs such as Iranians, Indians, Pakistanis, and Filipinos. According to the latest estimates, about 45% of the population are Kuwaiti, 35% are other Arab, 9% South Asian, 4% Iranian, and 7% other. It has also been estimated that over 100,000 people are considered to be bidoon residents, that is, Arabs who have long-standing residency in the nation but no documented proof of nationality.

9 LANGUAGES

Arabic is the official language. The Arabic spoken in Kuwait is closer to classical Arabic than to the colloquial Arabic spoken in many other parts of the Middle East. English is generally used by business people, employees of oil companies, foreign residents, and students, and it is the second language taught in the schools.

10 RELIGIONS

Islam is the state religion. According to a 2010 report, about 70% of all citizens were Sunni Muslims and most of the remaining 30% were Shi'a Muslims. Of the total population (including foreigners) about 85% are Muslims. The total Christian population has been estimated at more than 450,000 people, including Roman Catholics (300,000), Coptic Orthodox (70,000), the National Evangelical (Protestant) Church (40,000), Armenian Orthodox (4,000), Greek Orthodox (3,500), Greek Catholics (Melkite 1,000–2,000), and Anglicans (200). There were also Latin, Maronite, Coptic Catholic, Armenian Catholic, Malabar, and Malankara congregations. There is a small congregation of The Church of Jesus Christ of Latter-Day Saints (Mormons) as well as some small communities of the Indian Orthodox Syrian Church, Mar Thoma, and the

Seventh-Day Adventists. The number of Hindus is estimated at 300,000. Buddhists at 100,000, Sikhs at 10,000, and Baha'is at 400.

The constitution provides for freedom of religion, but this right is limited in some cases by the government, in that religious practices are not permitted to conflict with public policy or morals. Blasphemy, apostasy (of Muslims), and proselytizing are illegal, with the exception of the Islam Presentation Committee, which encourages the conversion on non-Muslims to Islam. Family law is administered through the Islamic court system. Religious affairs are overseen by the Ministry of Awqaf and Islamic Affairs. Only seven non-Muslim groups have some form of legal recognition from the government: the Roman Catholics, Coptic Orthodox Church, Armenian Orthodox, Greek Orthodox, Greek Catholics, Anglicans, and the National Evangelical Church. These groups are offered a certain amount of freedom operating churches and welcoming religious workers into the country. Religious groups not sanctioned by the Koran (Koran), including Buddhists, Baha'is, Hindus, and Sikhs, are not permitted to build religious facilities or public places of worship. All unofficial groups are generally allowed to worship freely in private homes. Islamic New Year, Birth of the Prophet Muhammad, Ascension of the Prophet, Eid al-Fitr, and Eid al-Adha are observed as national holidays.

11 TRANSPORTATION

The CIA reports that in 2009 Kuwait had a total of 5,749 km (3,572 mi) of roads, of which 4,887 km (3,037 mi) were paved. There were seven airports, which transported 2.6 million passengers the same year according to the World Bank. In 2009 there were an estimated four airports with paved runways. There were also four heliports. The principal airport, Kuwait International Airport, is located south of the city of Kuwait. Air transportation is highly advanced, with Kuwait Airways providing service to and from the major Middle Eastern and European cities.

Kuwait has a modern network of roads, with all-weather highways running north to Iraq and south to Saudi Arabia. Kuwait has five ports, including a cargo port at Ash-Shuwaykh, on Kuwait Bay, and an oil port at Mina' al-Ahmadi that is equipped with a huge pier at which eight large tankers can be loaded simultaneously. In 2008, Kuwait had 38 merchant ships in service of 1,000 gross registered tons or more. Kuwait has regular calls from ocean shipping, and local sailing craft carry goods between Kuwait and the neighboring sheikhdoms, Iraq, and Saudi Arabia. Sea transport accounts for most of Kuwait's foreign trade.

12 HISTORY

The historical records of the Arab coast of the Persian Gulf are meager. Archaeological discoveries on Faylakah Island reveal an ancient civilization about 2800 BC that had trade links with the Sumerians. By the 6th century BC, this part of the Gulf was a principal supply route for trade with India. There is evidence of early migrations to the East African coast by the seafaring inhabitants. The historical turning point for the entire Arabian Peninsula was the conversion of the people to Islam in the 7th century AD, during the lifetime of Muhammad.

Kuwait's recent history starts in 1716, when several clans of the tribe of Aniza migrated from the interior of the Arabian Desert to a tiny Gulf coastal locality, later to be called Kuwait (a diminutive of the word *kut*, meaning "fort"). In 1756, the settled tribesmen

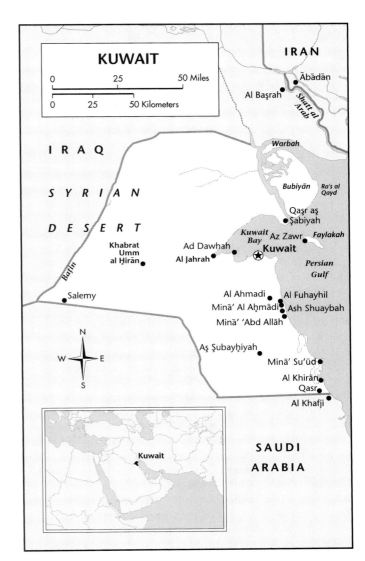

LOCATION: 28°32′ to 30°6′N; 46°33′ to 48°27′E. BOUNDARY LENGTHS: Persian Gulf shoreline, 499 kilometers (312 miles); Saudi Arabia, 222 kilometers (139 miles); Iraq, 242 kilometers (151 miles). TERRITORIAL SEA LIMIT: 12 miles.

rallied around the As-Sabah family and chose as their ruler Sheikh Sabah 'Abd ar-Rahim, founder of the present ruling dynasty. During the latter part of the century, raids by land and by sea resulted in the decline of Kuwait, but after the British suppression of piracy in the region, trading and shipbuilding prospered.

During the period in which Sheikh 'Abdallah as-Sabah ruled Kuwait (1866–92), a dynastic battle raged in Arabia between the rival houses of Ar-Rashid and As-Sa'ud. The Ottoman Turks, supporting Ibn Rashid, sought to extend their control over the coastal area to the south of Kuwait. Fearing that his territory would be lost to the Turks who considered it part of their province of Basra, Sheikh Mubarak as-Sabah (r. 1896–1915) asked to be taken under British protection. The British were concerned not only because of the Turkish claims but also because the Russians were seeking to set up a coaling station in Kuwait, and both the Germans and the Turks had planned to make it a terminus of the Berlin-Baghdād railroad. In 1899, Sheikh Mubarak agreed not to alienate any of his territory or to receive representatives of any foreign power without British consent. In return, the British offered their services as well as an annual subsidy to support the sheikh and his heirs.

On 19 June 1961, the protective treaty relations with the United Kingdom were terminated by mutual consent, and Kuwait declared itself fully sovereign and independent. By this time, the sheikhdom had already become a major oil producer and had acquired a controlling interest in the petroleum industry. Iraq refused to recognize Kuwait's independence, asserting it had inherited the Ottoman claim to the territory. Baghdād's threat of an invasion was foiled by the dispatch of British troops and later the support of the Arab League for Kuwait. Iraq then appeared to acquiesce in Kuwait's sovereignty, although border issues were never definitely resolved. During the next two decades, Kuwait succeeded in establishing an open and prosperous economy, based in large part on foreign, especially Palestinian and Egyptian, labor.

During the Iran-Iraq War, Kuwait, albeit technically neutral, rendered important assistance to Baghdād, including the transshipment of goods and the provision of over $6 billion in loans. As a response, members of Kuwait's large Shi'a minority and other radical dissidents waged a war of terrorism against the government. Throughout the 1980s, there were bombings, assassination attempts, hijackings, and sabotage against oil facilities.

In 1987 Iranian attacks on Persian Gulf shipping led Kuwait to request US protection for its supertankers. Washington agreed, and when a "reflagged" Kuwaiti vessel was attacked, American forces retaliated against an Iranian offshore oil rig.

With the end of the war, Iraq-Kuwait relations were stable until 1990, when Saddam Hussein accused his neighbor of waging economic warfare against Iraq by illegally drilling oil from the shared Rumailia field, overproducing oil to drive down prices and unfairly demanding repayment of wartime loans. Tensions could not be defused by negotiations or mediation and on 2 August 1990, Iraqi forces invaded Kuwait, asserting that they were rightfully reclaiming their territory. Kuwaiti defense forces offered little resistance and most senior officials fled the country.

The United States led an international coalition of Arab and other nations to demand the withdrawal of Iraqi forces. After a lengthy buildup of forces, Iraq was assaulted by massive air and land forces; after six weeks, its defenses collapsed and Kuwait was liberated in February 1991. Kuwait's leaders returned to find a disgruntled population that resented their abandonment and demanded greater political participation. Enormous physical damage had been inflicted on the country, including over 700 oil well fires that did serious ecological damage before being extinguished after almost nine months' effort.

The regime, and many Kuwaitis, turned harshly against those suspected of collaboration with Iraq. As a consequence, much of the large Palestinian community was ejected from the country. Relations with Iraq naturally remained tense, with some Baghdād officials continuing to assert their claim to Kuwait. On 27 May 1993, the UN Security Council reaffirmed the decision of a Boundary Demarcation Commission establishing the border between the two nations. Kuwait's vulnerability to possible attack from Iraq or Iran drew the nation closer to the United States, which has been willing to offer enhanced security collaboration.

In October 1994, Iraq began moving 60,000 troops to within 32 km (20 mi) of the Kuwaiti border. The UN Security Council voted unanimously to condemn Iraq's actions, and the United States, the United Kingdom, and other countries came to Kuwait's assistance. Kuwait agreed to allow the United States to station a squadron of 24 warplanes there as part of a broad effort to curb Iraqi military power. The plan kept reserves of American warplanes and a division's worth of tanks and armor stationed in the region. On 10 November 1994, Iraq agreed to recognize the independence and current borders of Kuwait, a major step apparently aimed at allowing at least some UN sanctions against Iraq to be lifted. However, in August 1995, Iraqi troop movements along the Kuwaiti border caused alarm again, and the United States began sending ships carrying equipment and supplies to the Persian Gulf. In April 1996, an international military exercise (involving forces of the United States, the United Kingdom, Russia, China, Italy, and other Arab nations) was held in Kuwait. The UN also renewed its multinational force of border observers in April 1996 to oversee the 14-km (9-mi) demilitarized zone that separates Kuwait from Iraq.

Although some of its neighbors in the Persian Gulf began to pursue a rapprochement with Iraq over the following years, Kuwait maintained its vigilance against the regime of Saddam Hussein. Early in 1998, it granted expanded staging areas to the United States in anticipation of possible military action in response to Iraq's failure to cooperate with UN weapons inspections. At the end of 1998, it supported NATO air strikes against Iraq over the same issue. In January 1999, Kuwait placed its military on full alert in response to renewed threats from Iraq. As of 2000, a special UN commission had awarded $15.7 billion in reparations for damages suffered in Iraq's 1990 invasion of Kuwait. In January 2003, Iraqi and Kuwaiti officials resumed talks on the fate of people who had gone missing during the Iraqi occupation of Kuwait in 1990–91. Kuwait claims Iraq must account for more than 600 Kuwaitis who disappeared during the occupation. Iraq insists it holds no such detainees, and accuses Kuwait of failing to account for more than 1,000 Iraqis.

On 8 November 2002, the UN Security Council passed Resolution 1441, calling on Iraq to disarm itself immediately of weapons of mass destruction (chemical, biological, and nuclear weapons), to abide by all former UN resolutions regarding the country since the end of the 1991 Gulf War, and to allow for the reintroduction of UN and IAEA weapons inspectors (they were expelled from the country in 1998). The United States adopted a firm position toward Iraq's disarmament, which it disputed, and by March 2003, was preparing for war. Since Kuwait's liberation from Iraq in 1991, it has become the world's largest per capita defense spender. As of 2003, Kuwait had purchased Patriot antimissile batteries, F/A-18 warplanes, and Apache attack helicopters for a military force estimated at 15,500, with 23,700 in reserves. However, Kuwait was not expected to take part in the expected US-led invasion of Iraq; instead, its forces were to defend the country from retaliation or other forms of attack by Iraq. By early March 2003, nearly 140,000 US and British military personnel had arrived in Kuwait.

On 21 January 2003, a civilian contractor for the US military was killed and another wounded when their car was fired upon outside Kuwait City. A Kuwaiti man was arrested and claimed responsibility for the shooting, expressing support for Osama bin-Laden's al-Qaeda organization. Kuwait is concerned about a rise in Islamic fundamentalism and anti-American sentiment.

On 19 March 2003, the United States launched air strikes on Baghdād, and the war in Iraq began. Iraq fired a number of missiles at Kuwait, and one struck a mall in Kuwait City but resulted in no deaths. Most of the missiles were destroyed by defensive Patriot missiles. The regime of Saddam Hussein was toppled on 9 April, but the U.S.-led coalition soon became embroiled in an effort to restore order and put down a violent insurgency. Kuwait remained an important supply hub and staging area for forces in Iraq.

In May 1999, the emir of Kuwait dissolved the National Assembly in the wake of a long-standing political deadlock between government and opposition forces. However, the opposition gained even more ground in national elections held in July, with both Islamists and liberals gaining additional seats. Among the matters awaiting parliamentary consideration was a controversial decree by the emir that would allow women to vote and run for office by the next election, scheduled for 2003. Parliament on 23 November 1999 voted against the emir's decree to grant full political rights to women.

Traditionally, the emir has appointed the crown prince as prime minister. In July 2003, he appointed Sheikh Sabah al-Ahmad al-Sabah prime minister, separating the post from the role of heir to the throne for first time since independence. In the legislative elections on 5 July 2003, 148 candidates ran for 50 places. Voter turnout was 81%, electing new candidates to half of the Assembly seats: procabinet, 20 seats; Islamist, 16 seats; independents, 12 seats; and liberals, 2 seats. In May 2005, parliament approved constitutional amendments to give women full political rights. In June, the first woman cabinet minister was appointed.

Sheikh Jabir al-Ahmad died in January 2006. Though the crown prince, Sheikh Saad al-Abdullah, would have taken his place, there were too many concerns over his health for the new appointment to be approved by the parliament. Sheikh Sabah al-Sabah, the former prime minister, became emir instead.

May 2009 marked a historic election for the nation as four women were voted into parliament. The special election came as a result of the dissolution of parliament announced in March 2009, when the emir accepted the resignation of the prime minister, Sheik Nasser Mohammad al-Ahmad al-Sabah.

During the 2010–11 uprisings across the Arab world, bidoons (residents with no documented proof of nationality) staged minor protests seeking citizenship, jobs, and other benefits provided to Kuwaiti nationals. In March 2011, young activist groups and students staged protests to put an end to government corruption. With the support of opposition legislators and the prime minister's rivals, the protesters rallied for the eviction of the prime minister and his cabinet. Similar protests were staged in September of 2011.

On November 28, 2011 Sheikh Nasser and his cabinet resigned amidst accusations of political corruption. The resignation was accepted by the emir, but the government was asked to remain in place until a new one is formed.

13 GOVERNMENT

According to the constitution of 16 November 1962, Kuwait is an independent sovereign Arab state under a constitutional monarch. Executive power is vested in the emir, who exercises it through a Council of Ministers. Succession is restricted to descendants of Mubarak al-Sabah; an heir apparent must be appointed within one year of the accession of a new ruler. The emir appoints a prime minister after traditional consultations and appoints ministers on the prime minister's recommendation. Emir Sabah al-Salim al-Sabah died in December 1977 after a reign of 12 years and was succeeded by Emir Jabir al-Ahmad al-Jabir as-Sabah. When Emir Jabir died in 2006, the crown prince, Sheikh Saad al-Abdullah, was considered too ill to take over. Sheikh Sabah al-Sabah was set as emir instead. The al-Sabah family, advised by wealthy merchants and other community leaders, dominates the government.

The national assembly (Majlis) consists of 50 elected representatives. Elections are held every four years among adult literate males who resided in Kuwait before 1920 and their descendants; candidates must be Kuwaiti and at least 21 years of age. Women were allowed the right to vote in 2005. In 1996, naturalized citizens who did not meet the pre-1920 qualification but had been naturalized for 30 years became eligible to vote. The assembly may be dissolved at any time by the emir. This power has been used somewhat frequently, leading to at least seven assembly elections since 1991. The usual cause is conflict between parliament and the cabinet. In March 2009, members of parliament wanted to question the prime minister, Sheik Nasser, concerning allegations of corruption and mishandling of economic policy. Nasser, who is the nephew of the emir, chose to resign rather than face such questioning. The emir accepted the resignation and dissolved parliament. Again in late November of 2011, amidst accusations of political corruption, Sheik Nasser resigned and dissolved parliament. While a new election brings a few new faces into parliament, it is common for the emir to reappoint the same cabinet members and even the same prime minister. Cabinet members are typically members of the ruling family, and tradition opposes any questioning of their actions by other public officials. The frequent reshuffling of parliament and cabinets has led to a call for constitutional changes that would revamp the parliamentary system. In particular, opponents of the current system are calling for a "popular government," meaning a cabinet that does not have members of the ruling family.

14 POLITICAL PARTIES

Political parties are prohibited, but opposition groups are active in the nation's political life. Several political groups act as de facto parties: Bedouins, merchants, Sunni and Shi'a activists, and secular leftists and nationalists. Political opinions are freely expressed in informal gatherings in the homes of government officials and leading citizens.

The Islamists are divided between the Ikhwan, which traces its political antecedents to Egypt's Muslim Brotherhood, and two Salafi groups that draw inspiration from Saudi Arabia. Current political groupings include the Islamic Constitutional Movement (ICM) and the Islamic Popular Group (of the Salafi tendency), two Sunni organizations; the Islamic National Alliance, the main faction for Shi'a Muslims; the Kuwait Democratic Forum (KDF), a loose association of groups with Nassarist and pan-Arabist foundations; and the National Democratic Group, composed of generally secular progressives with liberal tendencies. The rest are independents or are tribal confederations.

The 2009 elections gave 25 of the 50 assembly seats to tribal Sunni Muslims, primarily of the Al-Mutairi, Al-Azmi, Al-Ajmi, and Al-Rasheedi tribes. Shi'a Muslims took nine seats, while secular liberals earned seven seats, and independents earned six. Three seats went to Salafi (Sunni) Islamists.

15 LOCAL GOVERNMENT

There are five governorates (Ahmadi, Al-Jahrah, Al-Kuwayt, Hawalli, and Al-Farwaniyah), but political authority is highly centralized in the capital. A tradition of *diwaniyya*, or family or tribal gatherings, serves as a forum for debate in society, largely oriented around the proceedings of parliament.

16 JUDICIAL SYSTEM

The system of Muslim law (Shari'ah) was augmented by 1959 legislation that established courts of law, regulated the judicial system, and adopted modern legal codes. In each administrative district of Kuwait, there is a summary court composed of one or more divisions, each presided over by one judge. The summary courts deal with civil and commercial cases and leases. A tribunal of first instance has jurisdiction over matters involving personal status, civil and commercial cases, and criminal cases, except those of a religious nature and cases in which the amount involved exceeds KD1,000. The High Court of Appeals is divided into two chambers, one with jurisdiction over appeals involving personal status and civil cases, the other over appeals involving commercial and criminal cases. State security court decisions may be appealed to the Court of Cassation. Ordinary criminal cases may be appealed to the High Court of Appeals. The five-member Superior Constitutional Court is the highest level of the Kuwaiti judiciary. The Superior Constitutional Court interprets the constitution and deals with disputes related to the constitutionality of laws, statutes, and by-laws. A military court handles offenses committed by members of the security forces. Religious courts, Sunni and Shi'a, decide family law matters, but there is also a separate domestic court for non-Muslims. There is no Shi'a appellate court. Shi'a cases are adjudicated by Sunni courts of appeals.

While the 1962 constitution guarantees an independent judiciary, the executive branch retains control over its administration and budget. The emir, after recommendation of the Justice Ministry, appoints judges in the regular courts. Kuwaiti nationals receive lifetime appointments; non-Kuwaiti judges receive renewable terms of one to three years.

The constitution gives the authority to pardon and commute sentences to the emir. The Special State Security Court was abolished in 1995.

17 ARMED FORCES

The International Institute for Strategic Studies reports that armed forces in Kuwait totaled 15,500 members in 2011. The force is comprised of 11,000 from the army, 2,000 from the navy, and 2,500 members of the air force. Armed forces represent 1.5% of the labor force in Kuwait. Defense spending totaled $7.2 billion and accounted for 5.3% of GDP. The UN provided troops and observers in Kuwait during the Persian Gulf War. In addition, the United States as of 2011 maintained a military presence with 25,250 troops stationed in the country in eight major bases

18 INTERNATIONAL COOPERATION

Kuwait was admitted to the UN on 14 May 1963 and is a member of ESCWA and several nonregional specialized agencies, such as

UNESCO, UNIDO, IAEA, FAO, IFC, IMF, the World Bank, ILO, and WHO. It belongs to the Arab League, the Arab Bank for Economic Development in Africa, the African Development Bank, the Arab Monetary Union, the Council of Arab Economic Unity, the Central African States Development Bank (BDEAC), the Organization of the Islamic Conference (OIC), G-77, OPEC, WTO, and OAPEC; in 1981, it was a leader in forming the Gulf Cooperation Council with Saudi Arabia and four other Gulf states.

Kuwait played a key role in Operation Iraqi Freedom (2002–03) by offering land use and finances for the US-led coalition forces. The nation has also continued to support reconstruction efforts in Iraq. Kuwait is part of the Nonaligned Movement. In environmental cooperation, Kuwait is part of the Basel Convention, the Montréal Protocol, the Nuclear Test Ban Treaty, and the UN Conventions on the Law of the Sea, Climate Change and Desertification.

In December 2009, the Kuwaiti parliament unanimously approved a plan to join in regional efforts to create a Persian Gulf monetary union. However, parliament stopped short of fully supporting a unified currency and adopted a resolution to require another vote before a single Gulf-state currency could be adopted. Kuwait is one of six members of the Gulf Cooperation Council (GCC). At the time of the announcement, Saudi Arabia had already approved the plan and the parliaments in Bahrain and Qatar were expected to ratify the deal. With a lack of consensus among the member-states who were receptive to the idea of the monetary union, it is unclear how the countries will join together to determine the value of a single currency. Of the GCC states, Kuwait is the only country not to have its currency pegged to the dollar.

19 ECONOMY

The discovery of oil in 1934 transformed the economy. As of 2010, Kuwait's enormous oil reserves of 104 billion barrels represented 8% of the world's total. In addition huge quantities of natural gas have provided the base for an economic presence of worldwide significance. The Kuwaiti standard of living was among the highest in the Middle East and in the world by the early 1980s. Oil wealth has stimulated trade, fishery development, and service industries. The government has used its oil revenues to build ports, roads, an international airport, a seawater distillation plant, and modern government and office buildings. The public has also been served by the large-scale construction of public works, free public services, and highly subsidized public utilities, transforming Kuwait into a fully developed welfare state. Prudent management of budgetary allocations and development priorities, as well as substantial interest from overseas investment, helped cushion the adverse impact of the collapse in world oil prices during the mid-1980s and the 1980–88 Iran-Iraq War. In addition, acquisition of 5,000 retail outlets in Western Europe (marketed under the name "Q-8") and expansion into the manufacture and sale of refined oil products have bolstered the Kuwaiti economy.

Oil extraction and processing accounted for about 50% of GDP, 95% of export earnings, and 80% of government revenues as of 2007. Kuwait's economy suffered enormously from the effects of the Gulf War and the Iraqi occupation, which ended in February 1991 with the destruction of much of Kuwait's oil production capacity and other economic infrastructure. The damage inflicted on the economy was estimated at $20 billion. Economic improvement from 1994 to 1997 came largely from growth in the industrial and financial sectors. The Difficult Debts Law, which aided investors with losses incurred during the Iraqi invasion and an informal stock crash in the early 1980s, significantly improved investor confidence. The recovery of oil prices beginning in the second half of 1999 resulted in a growth in GDP of 17.22% in 1999 followed by an extraordinary 26.88% in 2000. From 1999 to 2007, per capita GDP rose from $13,082 to $39,300. Kuwait's portfolio of investments have generally served to double the income it receives from its basic oil industry.

While the GDP growth rate slumped in the negatives in 2001 and 2002 (-1.0% and -0.4% respectively), it quickly recovered, jumping to 9.9% in 2003, and 7.2% in 2004; in 2007, the economy expanded by 4.6%. The 2008 global financial crisis sent the Kuwaiti Stock Exchange into a tumble, as the exchange showed a loss of nearly 40% of its market capitalization throughout the year. However, high oil prices kept the national budget in check until 2009, when weaker oil prices caused Kuwait's economy to contract by between 1.5% and 2% in 2009. In March 2010, the governor of Kuwait's central bank announced that the country's economy was expected to increase by 4% to 5% in 2010, a reflection of stabilizing global oil prices. The governor's predictions were consistent with those released by the International Monetary Fund, which predicted Kuwait's economic growth to hit 3.3% in 2010. The true figure was 2.2%.

In 2010 the Canadian-based Fraser Institute ranked Kuwait as the second most economically free Arab nation in the world (after Bahrain) in the latest edition of their Economic Freedom of the Arab World report. The Economic Freedom reports compare five aspects of an economy, including the size of government (expenditures, taxes, and enterprises), legal structure and security of property rights, access to sound money, freedom to trade internationally, and regulation of credit, labor, and business. Kuwait received an overall score of 7.8 out of 10 in the regional analysis.

In February 2010, the Kuwaiti parliament approved a massive, $100 billion economic development plan that authorized the government to spend heavily on mega-projects designed to reorient the country's economy towards the post-oil world. Among the projects planned was a $77 billion business hub that will be known as Silk City.

The GDP rate of change in Kuwait, as of 2011, was 5.7%. Inflation stood at 3.8%, and unemployment was reported at 2.2%.

20 INCOME

The CIA estimated that in 2010 the GDP of Kuwait was $136.5 billion. The CIA defines GDP as the value of all final goods and services produced within a nation in a given year and computed on the basis of purchasing power parity (PPP) rather than value as measured on the basis of the rate of the exchange based on current dollars. The per capita GDP was estimated at $48,900. It was estimated that agriculture accounted for 0.3% of GDP, industry 48.1%, and services 51.6%.

The World Bank estimates that Kuwait, with 0.04% of the world's population, accounted for 0.20% of the world's GDP. By comparison, the United States, with 4.85% of the world's population, accounted for 22.51% of world GDP.

As of 2011 the most recent study by the World Bank reported that actual individual consumption in Kuwait was 38.1% of GDP and accounted for 0.09% of world consumption. By compari-

son, the United States accounted for 25.44% of world individual consumption. The World Bank also estimated that 5.7% of Kuwait's GDP was spent on food and beverages, 12.1% on housing and household furnishings, 3.1% on clothes, 2.1% on health, 4.7% on transportation, 1.0% on communications, 1.6% on recreation, 0.9% on restaurants and hotels, and 2.1% on miscellaneous goods and services and purchases from abroad.

21 LABOR

As of 2010, Kuwait had a total labor force of 2.112 million people. The government-owned oil industry dominates the economy. In 2009, 45% of Kuwait's economic activity was comprised of the oil and gas sectors. Kuwaiti nationals play by far the most important role in upper echelon decision making, accounting for 93% of employees in the public/government sector.

Although workers are legally permitted to join unions, less than 5% of the labor force are union members. Virtually all are affiliated with the Kuwait Trade Union Federation, the only trade federation allowed by law. The government performs a pervasive supervisory role of all unions, both subsidizing union expenses and carefully monitoring union activities. The right to strike is severely limited, and strikes rarely occur. About 10% of union members are foreign workers, but foreign workers must be in Kuwait for five years before they can join a union and then may not vote in elections or hold official positions.

In general, all workers are entitled to a 48-hour workweek, compensation for overtime, sick leave, termination pay, and access to arbitration for settlement of disputes. However, many laborers from developing countries are willing to tolerate poor or unhealthy working conditions in order to earn a wage that is significantly higher than in their own countries. The minimum working age is 18, although children who are at least 16 may work limited hours in nonhazardous occupations. Foreign workers must be at least 18 to work in Kuwait. Starting in 2002, the public-sector minimum wage was about $742 per month for citizens and $296 per month for noncitizens. In 2010 Kuwait introduced its first private sector minimum wage of $208 dollars per month. Health and safety standards remain lax in regard to foreign workers.

22 AGRICULTURE

Despite the absence of rivers and streams and the paucity of rain, the development of agriculture has been actively pursued. The government apportions arable land at nominal prices on a long-term basis among farmers to stimulate production of vegetables and other crops. It also provides farmers with long-term loans and low-cost irrigation. The state has supplied extension services and demonstration centers for new farming techniques in an attempt to increase agricultural production.

Roughly 1% of the total land is farmed. Cereal production in 2009 amounted to 3,550 tons, fruit production 17,242 tons, and vegetable production 243,573 tons. Dates are a major fruit tree crop.

23 ANIMAL HUSBANDRY

The UN Food and Agriculture Organization (FAO) reported that Kuwait dedicated 136,000 hectares (336,063 acres) to permanent pasture or meadow in 2009. During that year, the country tended 33.5 million chickens and 31,500 head of cattle. The production from these animals amounted to 5,895 tons of beef and veal and 304,101 tons of milk. Kuwait also produced 402 tons of cattle hide and 451 tons of raw wool.

When the desert is green (from the middle of March to the end of April), about one-fourth of Kuwait's meat supply is provided locally. Kuwait's poultry production has recovered from damages inflicted during the 1990 invasion. A small number of Bedouins raise camels, goats, and sheep for meat and milk.

24 FISHING

Kuwait had 890 decked commercial fishing boats in 2008. The annual capture totaled 4,373 tons according to the UN FAO. The export value of seafood totaled $789,000.

Locally, small boats catch enough fish to satisfy demand. Species caught include sardines, mackerel, tuna, shark (for the fins exported to China), barracuda, and mullet. Crabs, crayfish, and oysters are plentiful, and undik and zubaidi (butterfish) are both tasty and very popular. Shrimp are produced for a growing export market.

25 FORESTRY

Kuwait has no natural forests. The value of all forest products, including roundwood, totaled $18.3 million in 2009. The government's afforestation projects cover an area of about 5,000 hectares (12,300 acres). Since 1966 government programs have used sewage and other wastewater from Kuwait city to support planted forests representing a mix of native *Acacia spp.*, *Prosopis spp.*, and introduced *Eucalyptus* and *Acacia spp.*

26 MINING

In addition to petroleum and natural gas, the country's main commodities, Kuwait produces caustic soda, chlorine, cement, clays, clay products, fertilizer, lime, salt, and sand and gravel. The cement and fertilizer production plants were damaged by retreating Iraqi troops during the 1991 Gulf War. Cement production in 2010 was estimated at 2 million metric tons, unchanged from 2009. Ammonia production (nitrogen content) in 2009 was 485,000 metric tons, and output of urea (nitrogen content) was 430,000 tons metric tons.

27 ENERGY AND POWER

The Persian Gulf is geologically unique. Sedimentary deposits are combined with large, relatively unbroken folding that results in underground oil reservoirs 16 to 240 km (9 to 150 mi) long, containing billions of barrels of oil. Kuwait's known petroleum deposits are among the world's largest. As of 2010, Kuwait's proven oil reserves came to an estimated 104 billion barrels, approximately 8% of the world's total. This includes 2.5 billion barrels that are held in the Saudi Arabia-Kuwait neutral zone. The neutral zone covers an area of 6,200 sq mi and holds an estimated 5 billion barrels of oil and 1 trillion cu ft of natural gas.

As a member of the Organization of Petroleum Exporting Countries (OPEC) Kuwait's crude oil output is limited by a production quota. Kuwait's cost of production is perhaps the lowest in the world because its vast pools of oil lie fairly close to the surface and conveniently near tidewater. The oil rises to the surface under its own pressure and, owing to a natural gradient, flows downhill to dockside without pumping. Kuwait exports more than 60 per-

cent of its oil to Asian countries, although exports are also sent to Europe and the United States.

A vast amount of natural gas is found and produced along with oil. Kuwait is looking to expand its production and consumption of natural gas so as to free up more oil for export. The country is also hoping to cut the flaring or burning-off of natural gas.

All electric power is produced thermally from oil or natural gas. Generating capacity has grown dramatically during the past two decades. Electric power production increased from 30.6 billion kWh in 2000, to an estimated 32.4 billion kWh in 2002. In 2008, Kuwait produced 51.8 billion kWh of electricity and consumed 45.7 billion kWh, or 17,602 kWh per capita.

Most of the country is provided with electrical service; electric refrigeration and air conditioning are widely available. An extensive diesel power generating system serves outlying villages.

In September 2009, the Kuwaiti government signed a deal with US General Electric and Hyundai Heavy Industries of South Korea for the construction of a $2.7 billion power plant in the northern town of Subbiya. The new 2,000-megawatt plant will be completed in 2012 but is expected to be semi-operational by 2011. The plant is expected to be one of several new ventures in meeting the government's plans to boost power capacity. The demand for electricity is projected to grow by eight percent per year for several years to come.

28 INDUSTRY

Although oil extraction continues to be the economic mainstay, Kuwait has diversified its industry. Small-scale manufacturing plants produce ammonia, fertilizer, paper products, processed foods, and other consumer goods. The food processing industry includes vegetable oils, beverage bases, breakfast cereals, poultry parts, cheese, frozen vegetables, and snack foods. Major petroleum refinery products are fuel oil, gas oil, naphtha, kerosene, and diesel fuel. Industrial products include desalinated water, chemical detergents, chlorine, caustic soda, urea, concrete pipes, soap, flour, cleansers, asbestos, and bricks. The construction industry is highly developed.

29 SCIENCE AND TECHNOLOGY

The World Bank reported in 2009 that there were no patent applications in science and technology in Kuwait. Public financing of science was 0.09% of GDP. High technology in Kuwait has been largely confined to the oil industry and has been imported, along with the scientists and technicians needed to install and operate oil refineries and related facilities.

The Kuwait Institute for Scientific Research, founded in 1967 at Safat, promotes and conducts scientific research in the fields of food resources, water resources, oil-sector support, and environmental studies. The Agriculture Affairs and Fish Resources Authority has an experimental research station in Safat.

Kuwait University, founded in 1962 at Safat, has colleges of science, engineering and petroleum, medicine, and allied health sciences and nursing. The College of Technological Studies, in Shuwaikh, was founded in 1976. The Telecommunications and Navigation Institute, at Safat, was founded in 1966.

³⁰DOMESTIC TRADE

Until the early 1960s, the traditional small shop or market stall dominated retail trade. In recent decades, however, modern business centers with hundreds of new shops and offices have opened, and some smaller villages have developed retail stores with impressive stocks of foreign goods. Franchising is also becoming well established, though most of the franchise market is currently held by American fast-food and restaurant firms. The city of Kuwait is the distribution center for the emirate and serves the transit trade of nearby states.

Usual business hours in summer (May to October) are from 6 a.m. to 12 noon and from 4 p.m. to 6 p.m.; and during the rest of the year, from 7 a.m. to 12 noon and from 3 p.m. to 6 p.m. Stores are closed Fridays.

³¹FOREIGN TRADE

For many years, Kuwait maintained a boycott of imports from Israel. However, after liberation from Iraqi occupation in 1991, Kuwait relaxed its trade policies so that Israeli companies previously subject to boycott were permitted to do business in Kuwait. Kuwait also reduced economic ties with countries it regarded as having supported Iraq during the occupation—Jordan, Yemen, Tunisia, Sudan, Algeria, and Mauritania.

The export of fuels sustains Kuwait, accounting for the vast majority of commodity exports. Major trading partners have diversified and changed since the 1990s. Kuwait imported $20.36 billion worth of goods and services in 2008, while exporting $65.03 billion worth of goods and services.

Major import partners in 2009 were the United States, 11.2%; China, 9%; Germany, 7.8%; Japan, 7.2%; Saudi Arabia, 6.3%; Italy, 5%; France, 4.8%; South Korea, 4.3%; and India, 4.2%; UK, 4% . Its major export partners were Japan, 17.2%; South Korea, 15.3%; India, 14.4%; the United States, 7.6%; China, 6.7%; and Singapore, 5.3%.

Balance of Payments – Kuwait (2010)

(In millions of US dollars)

Current Account		**36,822.0**
Balance on goods	47,908.0	
Imports	-19,065.0	
Exports	66,973.0	
Balance on services	-5,901.0	
Balance on income	7,818.0	
Current transfers	-13,003.0	
Capital Account		**2,158.0**
Financial Account		**-34,686.0**
Direct investment abroad	-2,068.0	
Direct investment in Kuwait	81.0	
Portfolio investment assets	-6,921.0	
Portfolio investment liabilities	-815.0	
Financial derivatives	-3.0	
Other investment assets	-14,498.0	
Other investment liabilities	-10,461.0	
Net Errors and Omissions		**-3,683.0**
Reserves and Related Items		**-611.0**

(…) data not available or not significant.

SOURCE: *Balance of Payment Statistics Yearbook 2011,* Washington, DC: International Monetary Fund, 2011.

³²BALANCE OF PAYMENTS

Kuwait enjoys a highly favorable payments position because of its huge trade surpluses. The Kuwaiti dinar is completely covered by the country's reserve fund, 50% of which must be in gold.

The CIA reported that in 2001, the purchasing power parity of Kuwait's exports was $16.2 billion, while imports totaled $7.4 billion, resulting in a trade surplus of $8.8 billion. A decade later this favorable trade surplus had increased greatly to $31 billion in 2010, representing 20% of GDP.

³³BANKING AND SECURITIES

The Central Bank of Kuwait, established in 1969, formulates and implements the nation's monetary policy, regulates the currency, and controls the banking system. Foreign banks are not permitted to operate within Kuwait or to own shares in Kuwaiti banks. Kuwaiti bank shares are typically closely held, either by the government and its agencies or by the merchant families who founded them. The preeminent bank is the National Bank of Kuwait.

The Central Bank of Kuwait only took on a serious regulatory role in 1984, after a debt crisis engulfed commercial banks, all of which had exposure to the collapsed informal stock market. In 2010 the commercial bank prime lending rate was 2.9%. The discount rate, the interest rate at which the central bank lends to financial institutions in the short term, was 6%. At the end of 2010 the nation's total reserves of foreign exchange and gold equaled $21.36 billion.

There are three specialized banks, one of which, Kuwait Finance House, operates as a commercial bank restricted to Islamic financial transactions. The other two, Industrial Bank of Kuwait and Kuwait Real Estate Bank, were created to provide long-term credit at a time when the supply of fresh capital from the public sector was not constrained. In the more austere environment since the war, they function like a US investment bank. The idea of establishing more Islamic banks has been welcomed.

Principal Trading Partners – Kuwait (2010)

(In millions of US dollars)

Country	Total	Exports	Imports	Balance
World	87,950.0	65,950.0	22,000.0	43,950.0
South Korea	11,017.0	9,864.0	1,153.0	8,711.0
Japan	10,911.0	9,352.0	1,559.0	7,793.0
India	9,592.0	7,765.0	1,827.0	5,938.0
United States	8,134.0	5,079.0	3,055.0	2,024.0
China	8,113.0	6,080.0	2,033.0	4,047.0
Taiwan	5,724.0	5,568.0	156.0	5,412.0
Singapore	2,604.0	2,405.0	199.0	2,206.0
Netherlands	2,522.0	2,084.0	438.0	1,646.0
Pakistan	2,246.0	2,142.0	104.0	2,038.0
Sa'udi Arabia	1,902.0	334.0	1,568.0	-1,234.0

(…) data not available or not significant.

(n.s.) not specified.

SOURCE: *2011 Direction of Trade Statistics Yearbook,* New York: United Nations, 2011.

Kuwait's official securities exchange, the Kuwait Stock Exchange (KSE), first introduced in 1962, was founded in 1977 and handles only government bonds and securities of Kuwaiti companies. An unofficial and unregulated securities exchange, the Souk al-Manakh, listing the stocks of 45 Gulf companies outside Kuwait and considered highly speculative, collapsed suddenly in August 1982. At the time of the crash, some 6,000 investors and $94 billion in postdated checks drawn in anticipation of future stock price increases were said to be involved. In order to limit the effect of the collapse on the Kuwaiti economy, the government created a special rescue fund to pay compensation to small investors for validated claims. All trading operations of the KSE were suspended on the Iraqi invasion of Kuwait on 2 August 1990. The KSE recommenced trading on 28 September 1992. By the end of 2001, 88 companies were listed with a total capitalization of KD26.7 billion ($86.9 billion) and a trading value of KD11.7 billion ($38 billion). By the end of 2010 there were 214 companies listed. May 2010 saw a privatization bill that allowed the government to sell assets to private investors.

34 INSURANCE

The insurance sector is closed to foreign institutions. As of 2010, the insurance sector was dominated by three companies: Ahlia Insurance, Gulf Insurance, and Kuwait Insurance Co., and Warba Insurance Co. Marine, fire, accident, and life insurance policies constitute the bulk of all policies issued. Third-party liability insurance for motor vehicles is compulsory.

35 PUBLIC FINANCE

Improvement in public finances has been the result of higher oil prices and production rather than government reforms. Subsidies, such as those for utilities and healthcare, are one of the most contentious and politicized measures. The US Central Intelligence Agency (CIA) estimated that in 2005 Kuwait's central government took in revenues of approximately $47.2 billion and had expenditures of $20.7 billion. In 2010 the budget of the Kuwait government included $64.81 billion in public revenue and $38.12 billion in public expenditures. The budget surplus amounted to 22.7% of GDP. Public debt was 12.6% of GDP, with $54.54 billion of the debt held by foreign entities. Revenues minus expenditures totaled approximately $26.4 billion.

36 TAXATION

In 2012 the World Bank reported a total tax rate of 15.5% on corporate profits. Companies that are registered in Kuwait or in countries that are members of the Gulf Cooperation Council (GCC) and are wholly owned by Kuwaiti and/or citizens of GCC countries are not subject to income tax. However, foreign companies carrying on trade or business in Kuwait are subject to varying corporate tax rates based on defined income levels and where the operations are located. As of 2012 Kuwait had a 4% profit tax. Operations on the Kuwaiti mainland are subject to tax rates contained in the Amiri Decree No. 3 of 1955, which range from 0–55%, covering 11 income levels. Operations located on the islands of Kubr, Qaru, and Umm Al Maradim are subject to the tax rates contained in Law No. 23 of 1961, which has two income levels and rates of 20% and 57%. Foreign companies doing business in the portion of the offshore area of the partitioned neutral zone that is under

Public Finance – Kuwait (2010)

(In millions of dinars, budgetary central government figures)

Revenue and Grants	**17,473**	**100.0%**
Tax revenue	296	1.7%
Social contributions	...	...
Grants	...	...
Other revenue	17,177	98.3%
Expenditures	**11,591**	**100.0%**
General public services	1,352	11.7%
Defense	1,249	10.8%
Public order and safety	890	7.7%
Economic affairs	2,354	20.3%
Environmental protection	...	...
Housing and community amenities	627	5.4%
Health	851	7.3%
Recreational, culture, and religion	289	2.5%
Education	1,093	9.4%
Social protection	1,564	13.5%

(...) data not available or not significant.

SOURCE: *Government Finance Statistics Yearbook 2010,* Washington, DC: International Monetary Fund, 2010.

Saudi Arabian administration are subject to a tax of 50% of what they would pay under Amiri Decree No. 3 of 1955. Capital gains derived from the sale of assets and shares are treated as normal business profits subject to the appropriate tax rate. Other taxes include social security levies of 11% on employers; a 1% levy on a shareholding company's profit, payable to the Kuwait Foundation for Scientific Research; and a 2.5% employment tax on net annual distributable profits.

37 CUSTOMS AND DUTIES

Customs duties are generally 5% ad valorem, but many goods are admitted duty free. Imports of liquor are prohibited by law. Protective tariffs may be levied at up to 25%.

38 FOREIGN INVESTMENT

Through tax concessions, Kuwait welcomes foreign investment in heavy and light industries but continues to resist foreign investment in the oil sector. In May 2000, the government passed the Indirect Foreign Investment Law, allowing the purchase of up to 100% of the stock of companies listed on the Kuwait Stock Exchange, except for banks. In March 2001 the government passed a liberalized Foreign Investment Law that, together with a five-year privatization plan announced July 2001, expected to substantially increase foreign investment in Kuwait. Previously, foreign investment was not permitted in certain sectors, such as banking or insurance, and was restricted to less than 49% of ownership shares in permitted areas. Foreign investors are no longer required to have a Kuwaiti sponsor but are subject to a 55% corporate tax that Kuwaiti companies do not pay. Foreign direct investment (FDI) has historically been low and not encouraged by a government concerned with the "Kuwaitization" of the economy.

Low inward investment contrasts with remarkably high outward investment, though the government does not publish any statistics for these activities. Kuwaiti outward investment consists of portfolio investments held by the Kuwait Investment Authority (KIA), other direct investments by other government entities, and outward investments by private citizens. Entities like the Kuwait Petroleum Corp. have sizeable investments in production, refining and marketing activities abroad, but only the roughest estimates as to their value can be made. Investments by private citizens are thought to at least equal the government's holdings.

Foreign direct investment (FDI) in Kuwait was a net inflow of $144.9 million according to World Bank figures published in 2009.

39 ECONOMIC DEVELOPMENT

Since the mid-1970s, Kuwait has restrained its spending on economic development and fostered a policy of controlled growth. From 1977 to 1982, allocations for development projects remained steady at $1.7–2.5 billion annually, of which 76% was spent on public works, electric power plants, and desalination and irrigation projects. Development plans for the 1980s, stressing industrial diversification, included the expansion of local oil refineries and major projects in petrochemicals, electricity, water supply, highway construction, and telecommunications. Overseas, refining and marketing operations were stepped up.

Postwar economic planning was hampered by the expulsion of the mainly Palestinian middle-ranking civil servants in various government departments. The Industrial Bank of Kuwait played a major role in the industrial redevelopment of the emirate following the war. Diversification and privatization continue to be the strategic goals of the government to increase employment and counter the abrupt swings in the economy due to the heavy dependence on the oil sector. Increased foreign investment has come to be seen as essential to these goals. In May 2000, the government passed the Foreign Investment Law, allowing foreign investors to buy up to 100% of companies listed on the Kuwait Stock Exchange (KSE), except for banks. The government, however, controls which companies are publicly traded. In March 2001, the Foreign Direct Investment Law was passed, allowing up to 100% ownership of a company operating in Kuwait, although with the disincentive that the profits of the foreign company would be subject to a 55% tax. In July 2001, the government announced a five-year privatization program.

Despite suffering a recession in 2009, the economy as a whole has continued to grow at strong rates—3.4% in 2010 and 5.7% in 2011.

The Kuwaiti government passed a privatization bill in 2010 to allow the government to sell assets to private investors, and in 2011 the government passed an economic development plan that pledged to spend up to $130 billion in five years to diversify the economy away from oil, attract more investment, and boost private sector participation in the economy.

40 SOCIAL DEVELOPMENT

Kuwait has a widespread system of social welfare that is operated on a paternalistic basis and financed by government oil revenues. Social insurance legislation provides for old-age, disability, and survivor pensions, for which the worker pays 5% of earnings, the employer pays 11% of payroll, and the government provides a subsidy. Retirement benefits range from 65–95% of earnings, de-

pending upon the length of employment. The government pays for medical care in case of work injury.

Women are denied equal rights and legal protection under Kuwaiti law. Women (including foreign women) who wear Western clothing are often subject to harassment. Domestic abuse is common and often goes unreported, as men bribe police officials to ignore the claim. Rape and abuse of foreign domestic workers is widespread. Spousal rape is not considered a crime.

Bedouin minorities face considerable legal discrimination. They are not entitled to citizenship, but beginning in 2004, they were able to enroll their children in school, and health care became available in 2005.

In March of 2011, amidst the protests now known as the Arab Spring, bidoons staged protests demanding citizenship, jobs, and other privileges held by Kuwaiti nationals.

41 HEALTH

Kuwait has a highly advanced public health service that is extended to all Kuwaiti residents, regardless of citizenship. The entire population has access to health care services. In 2009, the country spent 2.0% of its GDP on healthcare, amounting to $1,416 per person. The urban population has access to safe water and adequate sanitation. As of 2011, there were 18 physicians, 46 nurses and midwives, and 18 hospital beds per 10,000 inhabitants. The incidence of typhoid fever and most infectious diseases is comparatively low; however, influenza is common and measles has resulted in a high fatality rate among children up to age five. It was estimated that 97% of children were vaccinated against measles in 2008. Life expectancy in 2011 was 78 years. The fertility rate was 2.2, while the infant mortality rate was 8 per 1,000 live births. In 2008 the maternal mortality rate, according to the World Bank, was 9 per 100,000 births.

42 HOUSING

For centuries, housing in Kuwait consisted primarily of small cottages, mud huts, and a few larger dwellings built of coral and plastered with cement and limestone. However, improved housing for the general population has been a main government objective since 1970, and many of the traditional Arab houses have been replaced with new government model housing.

The National Housing Authority built about 50,000 dwelling units in 1977–85. Between 1989 and 1994, 25,213 applications were presented for the housing distribution program. According to the 1995 census, there were 255,477 households in Kuwait. The total number of dwellings that year was 251,682, of which 234,153 were private and 17,529 were collective dwellings. Including vacant dwellings and those under construction, the total number was 287,574 in 1995. About 50% of all housing units were apartments, 19% were villas, 15% were traditional dwellings, 10% were annexes, and 4% were shacks and other marginal dwellings.

43 EDUCATION

In 2008 the World Bank estimated that 88% of age-eligible children in Kuwait were enrolled in primary school. Secondary enrollment for age-eligible children stood at 80%. Overall, the CIA estimated that Kuwait had a literacy rate of 93.9%. Public expenditure on education represented 3.8% of GDP. The student-to-teacher ratio for primary school was at about 8:1 in 2010.

Kuwait offers its citizens free education, including free food, clothing, books, stationery, and transportation from kindergarten through the fourth year of college. Schools below university level are segregated by sex. Four years of primary school are compulsory. Students may then move on to four years of intermediate school and four years of secondary school. For the last two years of schooling, students may choose a specialized curriculum in science, arts, or religious studies. The Ministry of Education oversees all aspects of secondary education, both public and private, for general and Islamic schools. The school year runs from September to June.

Kuwait University opened in 1966. Additional universities such as the American University of Kuwait, the Kuwait Maastricht Business School, and the Australian College of Kuwait, have opened in subsequent years. There are several colleges offering programs, as well as a Cadet Academy sponsored by the military. Kuwaiti students who complete their secondary school science courses in the upper 80% of their class and arts courses in the upper 70% are eligible to study abroad at government expense.

44 LIBRARIES AND MUSEUMS

The National Library of Kuwait has over 150,000 volumes, 90% of them in Arabic; it has established 22 branches throughout the country. The Kuwait University Library system has over 294,000 volumes. The Arab Planning Institute in Safat has a library of about 48,000 volumes. Other schools and oil companies maintain special libraries.

The Kuwait National Museum in Kuwait City displays ancient Kuwaiti artifacts (recovered from excavations on Faylakah Island), as well as exhibits concerning Islamic art, and local plant, bird, and animal life. The Kuwait Museum of Islamic Art in Kuwait City was founded in 1983. The Educational Science in Safat Museum was established in 1972 and features sections on natural history, space, oil, health, and meteorology.

45 MEDIA

The government administers telephone, television, radio, postal, and telegraph services. Kuwait's telecommunications system is modern and highly developed. Domestic service is handled by a mix of microwave radio relay, coaxial and fiber-optic cables, and open wire systems. Mobile cellular service operates country-wide. International services are provided by microwave radio relay, coaxial cable, and satellite ground station systems. In 2010, there were some 566,300 main phone lines, and 4.4 million mobile cellular phones in use.

Government-controlled Kuwait Television operates four networks and a satellite channel. Radio Kuwait broadcasts on a number of channels, with programs in English, Urdu, Persian, and Arabic. In 2009 there were 6 FM radio stations, 11 AM radio stations, and 1 shortwave radio station. In 2009, Internet users numbered 39 per 100 citizens. In 2010 the country had 2,485 Internet hosts.

Prominent newspapers in 2010, with circulation numbers listed parenthetically, included *Al-Watan* (110,000), *Al-Qabas* (79,700), and *Al-Seyassah* (49,000) as well as 2 other major newspapers. English-language dailies include the *Arab Times* (41,920), and *Kuwait Times* (28,000). The popular monthly magazine *Al-'Arabi*

(350,000 in 1995), similar to *Reader's Digest*, is widely read in Kuwait.

The constitution provides for freedom of speech and the press, and with a few exceptions, citizens are said to freely criticize the government in all media. However, a Press Law, revised in 2003, prohibits the publication of any materials that criticize the emir or are deemed an insult to God or Islam.

46 ORGANIZATIONS

There is a chamber of commerce and industry in the capital. Workers are represented through a number of associations, including the Kuwait Trade Union Federation. The Ministry of Social Affairs and Labor encourages and supports cultural and recreational organizations and sponsors theatrical activities for youth. The Kuwait National Commission for Education, Science, and Culture is the primary organization for the advancement of science, art, and culture. Organizations such as the Kuwait Medical Association promote research and education in specialized fields. The multinational Islamic Organization for Medical Sciences and the Arab Center for Medical Literature are in Kuwait. National youth organizations include the National Union of Kuwaiti Students and the Boy Scouts and Girl Scouts Associations. There is a national chapter of the Red Crescent Society.

47 TOURISM, TRAVEL, AND RECREATION

By 1992, the second anniversary of the Iraqi invasion, many of the physical scars of war and occupation had already been erased. The government has restored many of the country's extensive prewar accommodations and amenities. Kuwait City offers gardens and parks, along with landmarks such as the Kuwait Towers; Seif Palace was built in 1896 and boasts original Islamic mosaic tilework. A valid passport and visa are required of all visitors.

The *Tourism Factbook*, published by the UN World Tourism Organization, reported 5.09 million incoming tourists to Kuwait in 2009, who spent a total of $553 million. Of those incoming tourists, there were 3 million from the Middle East and 1.3 million from South Asia. There were 13,612 hotel beds available in Kuwait. The estimated daily cost to visit Kuwait City, the capital, was $466.

48 FAMOUS PERSONS

During the reign of Emir Sir 'Abdallah al-Salim al-Sabah (1870–1965), Kuwait attained a prominent position among the great oil-producing nations of the world, and the state adopted a social welfare program founded on a unique patriarchal system; the emir was revered as a man of simplicity, devotion, and deep concern for his people. He was succeeded as emir by Sabah al-Salim al-Sabah (1913–77), from 1965 to 1977; Jabir al-Ahmad al-Sabah (1926–2006), from 1977 to 2006; and Sabah IV al-Ahmad al-Jaber al-Sabah (b. 1929), who became emir in 2006.

49 DEPENDENCIES

Kuwait has no territories or colonies.

50 BIBLIOGRAPHY

Casey, Michael S, Frank W. Thackeray, and John E. Findling. *The History of Kuwait*. Westport, CT: Greenwood Press, 2007.

Fernea, Elizabeth Warnock, ed. *Remembering Childhood in the Middle East: Memoirs from a Century of Change*. Austin, TX: University of Texas Press, 2002.

Hourani, Albert Habib. *A History of the Arab Peoples*. Cambridge, MA: Belknap Press of Harvard University Press, 2002.

Kennedy, Paul D. *Doing Business with Kuwait*. 2nd ed. Sterling, VA: Kogan Page, 2004.

Khadduri, Majid. *War in the Gulf, 1990–91: The Iraq-Kuwait Conflict and its Implications*. New York: Oxford University Press, 2001.

Kuwait Investment and Business Guide: Strategic and Practical Information. Washington, DC: International Business Publications USA, 2012.

The Middle East. Washington, DC: CQ Press, 2005.

Moore, Pete W. *Doing Business in the Middle East: Politics and Economic Crisis in Jordan and Kuwait*. New York: Cambridge University Press, 2009.

Seddon, David, ed. *A Political and Economic Dictionary of the Middle East*. Philadelphia: Routledge/Taylor and Francis, 2004.

Tétreault, Mary Ann. *Stories of Democracy: Politics and Society in Contemporary Kuwait*. New York: Columbia University Press, 2000.

KYRGYZSTAN

Kyrgyz Republic
Kyrgyz Respublikasy

CAPITAL: Bishkek

FLAG: The national flag consists of a red field with a yellow sun in the center. The sun features 40 rays representing the 40 Kyrgyz tribes. A red ring crossed by two sets of three lines in the center of the sun represents the "tunduk", which is the crown of a Kyrgyz yurt. The color red represents bravery and valor while the symbol of the sun represents peace and wealth.

ANTHEM: *Kyrgyz Respublikasynyn Mamlekettik Gimni (National Anthem of the Kyrgyz Republic).*

MONETARY UNIT: The primary currency, introduced in May 1993, is the Som (KGS). KGS1 = US$0.0214431 (or US$1 = KGS46.6350) as of 2011.

WEIGHTS AND MEASURES: The metric system is in force.

HOLIDAYS: New Year's Day (1 January), Russian Orthodox Christmas (7 January), International Women's Day (8 March), Nooruz (Krygyz New Year, 21 March), Labour Day (1 May), Constitution Day (5 May), Victory Day (9 May), Independence Day (1 August), Orozo Ait (End of Ramadan), and Kurban Ait (Feast of the Sacrifice). Dates vary for religious holidays.

TIME: 5 p.m. = noon GMT.

¹LOCATION, SIZE, AND EXTENT

Kyrgyzstan is located in Central Asia, between China and Kazakhstan. Comparatively, it is slightly smaller than the state of South Dakota, with a total area of 199,951 sq km (77,202 sq mi). Kyrgyzstan shares boundaries with Kazakhstan on the N, China on the E, Tajikistan on the S, and Uzbekistan on the W. The country's boundary length totals 3,051 km (1,896 mi), and its capital city, Bishkek, is located in the north central part of the country.

²TOPOGRAPHY

The topography of Kyrgyzstan features the peaks of Tian Shan, which rise to over 7,000 m (23,000 ft), and associated valleys and basins which encompass the entire nation. About 90% of Kyrgyzstan has an elevation exceeding 1,500 m (4,900 ft). About 10,196 sq km (3,937 sq mi) is under irrigation.

Seismic activity occurs along the Tian Shan as these mountains continue to be uplifted. As a result, frequent and sometimes devastating earthquakes occur within the region. These also trigger massive mudslides and avalanches that have been known to destroy villages. In August 1992, a 7.3 magnitude earthquake occurred near Jala-Abad, killing 75 people and leaving several thousand homeless. A 6.6 magnitude earthquake in 2008 left 75 dead.

³CLIMATE

The climate of Kyrgyzstan ranges from continental to marine, largely because of its mountainous landscape and the large lake Issyk-Kul. Near the lake temperatures are milder, ranging between -4°C (25°F) and -9°C (16°F) in the winter and 20°C (68°F) to 27°C (81°F) in the summer. In more mountainous areas, winter temperatures can drop as low as -50°C (-58°F) in the winter and climb as high as 43°C (109°F) in the summer. The intrusion of cold air into the Issyk-Kul hollow often produces storm winds, and thunderstorms are a frequent phenomenon, particularly in June and July. Rainfall and other precipitation averages 230–500 mm (8–20 in) a year but can reach 1500 mm (59 in) in the mountains.

⁴FLORA AND FAUNA

Kyrgyzstan had the world's largest natural growth walnut forest, according to the CIA. The World Resource Institute estimated that there are 4,500 plant species in Kyrgyzstan. In addition, Kyrgyzstan was home to 58 species of mammals, 207 species of birds, 30 species of reptiles, and 7 species of amphibians. The calculation reflects the total number of distinct species residing in the country, not the number of endemic species.

Meadows, bushes, and forests cover much of the country's northern slopes' steppes while the southern slopes are characterized more by desert-like vegetation. Many wild plants of economic importance such as tinning joinweed, saltwort, barberries, rhubarb, thyme varieties and other herbs are found in the country. In addition, the country has apple, pear, cherry, barberry, almond, pistachio, and hawthorn trees.

Wildlife includes brown bears, wild rams, marmots, hares, mountain goats, snow leopards, and wolves. Birds found in the mountains include red belly redstarts, mountain finches, mountain gees, pigeons, partridges, and bullfinches.

⁵ENVIRONMENT

The World Resource Institute reported that Kyrgyzstan had designated 621,000 hectares (1.53 million acres) of land for protection as of 2006. Kyrgyzstan has established 83 specially protected natural territories, comprising nearly 4% of its total land, for the protection of its pristine natural resources. Water resources totaled 46.5 cu km (11.16 cu mi) while water usage was 10.08 cu km (2.42 cu mi) per year. Domestic water usage accounted for 3% of total usage, industrial for 3%, and agricultural for 94%. Per capita water usage totaled 1,916 cu m (67,663 cu ft) per year.

The UN reported in 2008 that carbon dioxide emissions in Kyrgyzstan totaled 6,075 kilotons.

Water pollution is Kyrgyzstan's greatest environmental threat. Many people use water from contaminated streams and wells, and water-borne diseases are prevalent. In addition, faulty irrigation practices have led to increases in soil salinity.

Kyrgyzstan is party to international environmental agreements on air pollution, biodiversity, climate change, desertification, hazardous wastes, ozone layer protection, and wetlands.

According to a 2011 report issued by the International Union for Conservation of Nature and Natural Resources (IUCN), threatened species included 6 mammals, 12 birds, 2 reptiles, 3 other invertebrates, and 14 plants. Threatened animal species include the great bustard, European bison, snow leopard, field adder, and tiger.

⁶POPULATION

The US Central Intelligence Agency (CIA) estimates the population of Kyrgyzstan in 2011 to be 5,587,443, which placed it at number 110 in population among the 196 nations of the world. In 2011 approximately 5.3% of the population was over 65 years of age, with another 29.3% under 15 years of age. The median age in Kyrgyzstan was 25 years. There were 1.053 males for every female in the country. The population's annual rate of change was 1.427%. The life expectancy for males in 2011 was about 66 years for males and 74 years for females. About 35% of the population lived in urban areas. The largest city was Bishkek with a population in 2009 of 854,000.

⁷MIGRATION

Estimates of Kyrgyzstan's net migration rate, carried out by the CIA in 2011, amounted to -2.60 migrants per 1,000 citizens. The total number of emigrants living abroad was 620,700, and the total number of immigrants living in Kyrgyzstan was 222,700.

The UN High Commission on Refugees reported that violence in June 2010 displaced 300,000 people internally and resulted in 75,000 residents fleeing temporarily to Uzbekistan. The State Committee for Migration and Employment reported 205 refugees and 130 asylum seekers as of 31 December 2010. Refugees had come from Afghanistan, Syria, Iran, and North Korea. Officially registered asylum seekers included 41 Afghans, 116 Uzbeks, 15 Russians, and 15 individuals from other countries.

A 2008 report sponsored by the UN High Commission on Refugees found nearly 13,000 individuals living in three oblasts in the south with no official documentation of citizenship. Some of these individuals continued to hold outdated passports for the former USSR while others had renounced Kyrgyz citizenship in hopes of becoming Russian citizens. The total number of stateless persons in the country was estimated at 20,000. From late 2009 to the end of 2010, the UNHCR worked with the government to improve the process of applying for citizenship, which resulted in 10,000 persons gaining citizenship in 2010.

⁸ETHNIC GROUPS

The US State Department reported in 2010 that 68.9% of the people are ethnically Kyrgyz. Russians made up 9.1% of the population and Uzbeks made up 14.4%. Dungans (ethnic Chinese Muslims) and Uighurs each made up 1% of the population; Tajiks 0.9%; Kazakhs 0.8%; Tatars 0.7%; Koreans 0.4%; and Germans 0.3%.

⁹LANGUAGES

Kyrgyz and Russians are the official languages. Based on a 1999 census, the CIA reported in 2011 that 64.7% of the population spoke Kyrgyz; 12.5% Russian; 13.6% Uzbek, and 1% Dungan. About 8.2% used other languages.

¹⁰RELIGIONS

According to a 2009 report, Muslims (mostly Sunni) accounted for an estimated 75% of the population. An estimated 20% were Russian Orthodox. The next largest group was the Protestant Church of Jesus Christ, with an estimated 11,000 members. Other Protestant groups included Baptists, Lutherans, Pentecostals, Presbyterians, and Seventh-Day Adventists. There were three Roman Catholic congregations and a small number of Jehovah's Witnesses. There was one Jewish synagogue, one Buddhist temple, and 12 houses of worship for the Baha'i faith.

The constitution provides for freedom of religion in a secular state, but there have been a number of laws and policies that limit this freedom. In practice, some minority Muslim groups as well as non-Muslim groups have reported discrimination by the government and social groups. Eid al-Adha, Eid al-Fitr, and Orthodox Christmas are observed as national holidays.

¹¹TRANSPORTATION

The CIA reports that as of 2007 Kyrgyzstan had a total of 34,000 km (21,127 mi) of roads. In 2010, railroads extended for 417 km (259 mi). There were 28 airports, which transported 309,488 passengers in 2009 according to the World Bank. Kyrgyzstan had approximately 600 km (373 mi) of navigable waterways. In 2009 there were 18 airports with paved runways. The principal airport is Manas, located at Bishkek.

As of 2008 the largest portion of Kyrgyzstan's rail system was a single east-west rail line of 370 km (230 mi) that went from Issykkul' across the Chuskaya region into Kazakhstan. Public transportation service often was irregular.

¹²HISTORY

The Kyrgyz people are believed to have been of Turkic descent and were organized loosely into nomadic tribes. However, their lives during the ancient and medieval periods of history included encounters with numerous conquerors, making the present-day Kyrgyz an amalgamation of various peoples as the tribes incorporated themselves into fresh waves of conquerors.

Kyrgyz and Chinese historians date Kyrgyz history to 201 BC, when the earliest descendents of the Kyrgyz people lived in the northeastern section of present-day Mongolia. Archeologists suggest that two types of economies developed in the territory—farming and pastoral nomadism. By the 7th century BC, nomadism had become predominant, and the area was controlled by various

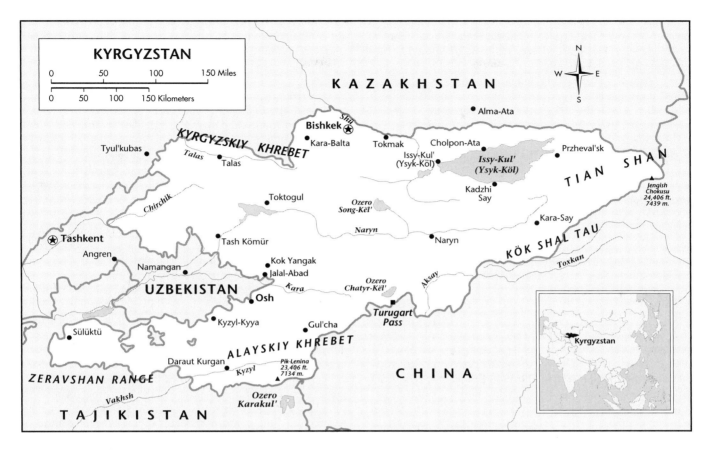

LOCATION: 41°30′ N; 75°0′ E. BOUNDARY LENGTHS: China, 858 kilometers (533.2 miles); Tajikistan, 870 kilometers (541 miles); Uzbekistan, 1,099 kilometers (683 miles); Kazakhstan, 1,051 kilometers (653 miles).

tribal alliances. In the north the Saki (7th–3rd century BC) were succeeded by the Usuni (2nd century BC–5th century AD); in the south, the Parkan state (2nd–1st century BC) was replaced by the Kushani kingdom (1st–4th century AD).

Some of the Kyrgyz tribes migrated to what is present-day southern Siberia in the sixth century ad, and settled along the Yenisey River. These tribes lived in that area until the eighth century, and then began migrating across what is now the Tuva region of the Russian Federation. This area was part of the Karakhanid state from 950 to 1150, during which the urban population was involved with trade and manufacturing along the Silk Road. Conversion to Islam occurred during this period, and Islam became the predominant religion in the region in the 12th century.

Genghis Khan's Mongols conquered the area in the 13th century, destroying most of the Karakhanid culture and introducing large numbers of new peoples into the area, of Turkic, Mongol, and Tibetan stock. The resulting mix of tribes was almost certainly the basis for the present-day Kyrgyz people, who retain much of the memory of those origins in the orally preserved genealogies of their 40 clans and tribes. However, with the rise of the Mongol Empire in the 13th century, the Kyrgyz began moving to the south.

The Kyrgyz began settling the territory that comprises the present-day Kyrgyz Republic in the 15th and 16th centuries. The southern part of that territory came under control of the Khanate of Kokand. The Russian Empire's expansion into what it called

the Steppe included this region, and much of northern Kyrgyzstan was incorporated into the Russian Empire by 1863. The south was incorporated in 1876 when Russia destroyed the Kokand Khanate. The empire split what is present-day Kyrgyzstan into four *guberniias*, and beginning in the 1890s, Russian and other European farmers began moving into the fertile river valleys. The Russian tsarist incorporation led to numerous revolts. These revolts along with the settlement by Europeans forced many of the traditionally nomadic Kyrgyz into the Pamir mountains and Afghanistan.

By 1916, Russian policies of livestock requisition and land use had left the Kyrgyz badly impoverished. When Russia attempted to issue a draft call-up for Central Asian males, including the Kyrgyz, widespread fighting broke out all across the territory. The uprisings were suppressed, with great loss of life; population in the northern part dropped as much as 40%, and many of the surviving Kyrgyz migrated to China. Since independence in 1991, the state has commemorated the 1916 uprising as genocide.

Hostility to tsarist authority prompted some Kyrgyz to support the 1917 Bolshevik revolution. That support diminished when it became clear that Lenin would not allow for the development of independent national states within what was emerging as the Union of Soviet Socialist Republics (USSR). The Kyrgyz continued sporadic resistance to the Russians through the mid-1920s in what Russian historians have described as the "Basmachi Rebellion."

Soviet authority established Kyrgyzstan as an autonomous political unit known as the Kara-Kyrgyz Autonomous Oblast within the Russian Federal Socialist Republic in 1924 and as the Kyrgyz Autonomous Soviet Socialist Republic within the Russian republic in 1926. Ten years later, on 5 December 1936 the Kyrgyz republic became the Kyrgyz Autonomous Soviet Socialist Republic and was established as a full union republic of the former USSR.

The Kyrgyz Republic saw much cultural, educational, and social development in the 1920s. As literacy increased, a standard literary language was introduced, codifying the Kyrgyz language. An Arabic-based Kyrgyz alphabet was introduced in 1924, and replaced by a Latin script in 1928. A Cyrillic script subsequently replaced the Latin script in 1941. This era of development helped create a distinct Kyrgyz national culture and identity despite the repressive policies of Soviet dictator Joseph Stalin who controlled the USSR through the late 1920s to 1953.

Despite the advances made through the 1920s, the Kyrgyz republic was regarded as one of the least developed of the Soviet states, politically and economically. Nevertheless, a new publication, Literaturny Kirghizstan, was established in the 1980s. And while Soviet policies prohibited the formation of political groups, several groups emerged in 1989 to deal with an acute housing crisis.

Ethnic tensions between Uzbeks and Kyrgyz in part of the Osh Oblast, where Uzbeks formed a numerical majority, flared into violence in June 1990. The Soviet Union declared a state of emergency and introduced a curfew. During this time, the Kyrgyzstan Democratic Movement began to develop into a significant political force, and in October 1990 the Kyrgyz became the first of the Soviet republics to elect their own president, Askar Akayev, president of the Kyrgyz Academy of Sciences. Akayev appointed a new government, introduced a new political structure, and helped bring many younger, reform-oriented politicians to power. Despite these moves toward independence, the economic impoverishment of the area made many residents hesitant to secede from the Soviet Union. A March 1991 referendum on the preservation of the USSR led 88.7% of the Kyrgyz residents to support retention of the USSR as a renewed federation.

On 19 August 1991, the State Committee for the State of Emergency assumed power in Moscow. On the same day, a coup attempted to depose Akayev. The coup collapsed and Akayev and vice president German Kuznetsov resigned from the Communist Party of the Soviet Union. The Supreme Soviet declared independence from the USSR on 31 August 1991, Kyrgyz became the new nation's official language in the following month, and voters elected Akayev president in a direct election on 12 October 1991.

Political corruption, poor interethnic relations, and terrorism marked the first two decades of Kyrgyzstan's existence as an independent nation, and these issues continued to challenge the nation at the end of 2011.

A constitution was adopted on 5 May 1993. An economic and political crisis led to the resignation of the first government in December 1993, but Akayev's presidency was reaffirmed by a popular referendum of support on 30 January 1994. Over 95% of registered voters participated in the referendum; 97% of those who voted supported Akayev. Akayev won re-election to five-year terms in 1995 and 2000.

Islamic extremism threatened Kyrgyzstan in July–August 1999. Guerrillas from Tajikistan entered the nation, seized hostages and took control of several villages. After Kyrgyzstan called out military reservists and acknowledged that its military was unprepared for combat, it received air support from neighboring Uzbekistan and Kazakhstan.

National protests erupted in March 2002 when police in the southern district of Aksy shot dead six people protesting the arbitrary arrest of an opposition politician. Akayev initiated a constitutional reform process, which led to a February 2003 referendum, which was marred by voting irregularities. The referendum led to constitutional amendments that weakened the powers of the parliament and constitutional court and allowed the president additional control. A previously bicameral parliament became a 75-seat unicameral legislature under these amendments.

Widespread fraud in parliamentary runoff elections in March 2005 led to calls for the government to resign. Police and pro-government thugs attacked pro-opposition demonstrators, who had gathered in the capital city of Bishkek. The protestors seized the presidential administration building, and President Akayev fled the country, going first to Kazakhstan and then Russia. Looting in Bishkek on 24 March 2005 caused an estimated $100 million in damaged. The opposition formed a broadly inclusive "Committee of National Unity" and named opposition leader Kurmanbek Bakiyev acting president and prime minister. Bakiyev formed an alliance with rival Feliks Kulov in which Kulov agreed to drop out of the presidential race if Bakiyev appointed him prime minister.

Bakiyev won the 2005 presidential election, but opposition grew against him as citizens protested the slow progress of constitutional reform. New constitutional amendments were introduced to strengthen the power of parliament, but later were invalidated. Bakiyev won re-election to the presidency in a 23 June 2009 election, but protests against his rule continued. In April 2010, they turned violent in Talas and Bishkek, with dozens of reported deaths. Bakiyev fled to Belarus, a provisional government headed by President Roza Otunbayeva took office, and organized a referendum on a new constitution. That referendum took place on 27 June 2010. Voters approved a new constitution and confirmed Otunbeyeva as president until 31 December 2011.

Ethnic clashes between Kyrgyz and Uzbek residents erupted on 15 June 2010 when Uzbeks in Osh took control of a local government-owned oil depot and threatened to blow it up if the interim government tried to take it by force. The riots forced 75,000 to 80,000 Uzbeks to flee into Uzbekistan, but that government had closed the border on 14 June. The United Nations began a series of airlifts to provide relief to refugees.

In a 1 November 2011 election, former prime minister Almazbek Atambayev received more than 63% percent of the vote and was confirmed as president. Atambayev declared after the vote an intention to close a U.S. airbase established in Kyrgyzstan in 2001 when the lease for the base expired in 2014. The New York Times reported in December 2011 that violence from ethnic clashes in 2010 had worsened tensions between Kyrgyz and Uzbeks. Uzbeks often faced arbitrary arrests and ongoing abuse from the predominantly Kyrgyz leadership. Ongoing poverty and instability characterized Kyrgyzstan at the end of 2011.

13 GOVERNMENT

A new constitution was adopted in 2010, following the ousting of Kurmanbek Bakiyev as president. The goal of the constitution, which was supported by Bakiyev's interim successor Roza Otunbayeva, was to lessen the powers of the president. The constitution defines Kyrgyzstan as a sovereign, democratic, secular, unitary, and social state, and states that the prime minister is the head of the executive branch. The constitution gives the president certain powers as head of state. It also defines the judicial branch as being comprised of a Supreme Court and local courts, and defines the legislative branch as being comprised of a 120-member unicameral parliament.

The constitution marked an attempt to move away from excessive presidential power and toward a more balanced system not just in Kyrgyzstan but in central Asia more broadly. Parliamentary elections will be held every five years and the president will be limited to a single six-year term. The referendum to approve the constitution passed with a vote of 91.8% in favor.

When Kyrgyzstan was still a Soviet republic, the legislature elected Askar Akayev president. Under his leadership, Kyrgyzstan declared independence and drafted a new constitution, ratified 5 May 1993. This constitution established a democratic presidential system with separation of powers and expansive human rights guarantees. In early September 1994, Akayev's supporters in the legislature boycotted the last session of the legislature, which led to dissolution of the legislature. Akayev took over legislative powers, and decreed that legislative elections would be held by the end of the year. He also decreed that a referendum would be held in October 1995 to approve amendments to the constitution, including provisions revamping the legislative system to weaken it relative to the presidency. He argued that legislative and other provisions of the May 1993 constitution were too "idealistic" because the "people are not prepared for democracy," and a "transitional period" was needed. The referendum questions were approved by over 80% of the voters.

Under 1996 amendments, the president received expanded powers to veto legislation, dissolve the legislature, and appoint all ministers (except the prime minister) without legislative confirmation, while making legislative impeachment more difficult. Akayev further introduced a referendum on 10 February 1996 to further alter the constitution. These amendments defined Kyrgyzstan as a secular, unitary state with three branches of government: executive, legislative, and judicial. The Jogorku Kenesh (parliament or supreme council) held legislative responsibilities. The Jogorku Kenesh was made up of two houses-the 35-member legislative assembly and the 70-member assembly of people's representatives. The legislative assembly was responsible for day-to-day operations of the legislature, such as interpreting laws and ratifying international treaties. The executive branch is comprised of the cabinet of ministers, or ministries, appointed by the president and approved by the parliament. The head of the cabinet is the prime minister, also appointed by the president and confirmed by the parliament.

Despite restrictions on its powers, in 1997–98, the legislature showed increasing signs of independence from executive power. Moving to further weaken it, Akayev spearheaded another referendum on 17 October 1998 to amend the constitution. Approved by 91.14% of voters, the amendments sharply restricted the legislature's influence over bills involving the budget or other expenditures, limited a legislator's immunity from removal and prosecution, increased the size of the legislative assembly to 60, and decreased the size of the assembly of people's representatives to

45. It also provided for private land ownership and upheld freedom of the press.

The erosion of democratic reforms grew apparent in 2000 legislative elections when numerous legally registered political parties were disqualified from fielding candidates. On 29 October 2000, Akayev was reelected president with 74% of the vote in an election marred by serious irregularities. Police used force and arrests to disperse and discourage democratic expression.

On 13 January 2003, Akayev announced a referendum would be held on 2 February for amendments to the constitution, including the abolition of the two-chamber parliament in favor of a single chamber, the abolition of party-list voting for parliament, and immunity from prosecution of former presidents and their families. Voters could not vote on the changes individually, but were to approve or reject them wholesale. They also had to indicate whether or not they wanted Akayev to remain in office until his term expired in December 2005. 76.6% of Kyrgyz citizens supported the amendments in the referendum, and 78.7% of voters determined Akayev should remain in office. Turnout was over 86%. The opposition, which called for a boycott of the vote said turnout had been less than 40%, failing to reach the 50% threshold for the referendum to be valid.

Elections for a new unicameral body (Jorgorku Kenesh) were held 27 February 2005, but the vast majority of positions remained undecided and protests over electoral irregularities culminated in the March Revolution which ousted Akayev from office. Kurmanbek Bakiyev was elected president in July 2005 with 88.6% of the vote.

The Kyrgyz parliament on 8 November 2006 approved a new constitution that significantly reduced the president's powers in favor of the legislature. The constitution was thought to make Kyrgyzstan the first Central Asian nation to have strong parliamentary checks and balances on the powers of the president. On 15 January 2007, however, Bakiyev signed into law a new version of the constitution, which empowered the president to nominate the prime minister subject to parliamentary confirmation and to appoint and dismiss regional governors and security chiefs without legislative approval. Bakiyev was removed from power in April 2010.

14 POLITICAL PARTIES

Approximately 26 parties and political leaders were active in Kyrgyzstan politics as of 2011. Many of the parties were small, and most legislators claimed no party affiliation.

The nation's first parliamentary elections under the constitution that was approved in a 2010 referendum were held in October 2010. The constitution stipulates that a party must receive a minimum of 5% of the vote in order to gain seats in parliament. Five of the twenty-nine parties participating in the 2010 election met this requirement, with the highest percentage of votes going to the nationalist Ata Zhurt Party, which won 8.8% of the vote and 28 of the 120 seats. The Social Democratic Party gained 8% of the vote and 26 seats, followed by Ar-Namys with 7.7% and 25 seats, Respublika with 7.2% and 23, and Ata-Meken with 5.6% and 18 seats. Because no single party had a majority presence, a coalition government needed to be negotiated. A little more than a month after the election, the Social Democrats, Respublika, and Ata-Meken agreed to a coalition that placed the Social Democrat leader Almazbek Atambayev as prime minister, Respublika leader Omurbek Babanov as deputy prime minister, and Ata-Meken leader Omurbek Tekebayev as speaker of parliament.

The US State Department listed the following parties and leaders as active in Kyrgyzstan at the end of 2011: Ata Jurt, (Fatherland) Kamchybek Tashiyev; Social Democratic Party of Kyrgyzstan, Almazbek Atambayev; Party of Communists of Kyrgyzstan, Iskhak Masaliev; Ar Namys (Dignity) Party, Feliks Kulov; Ata-Meken (Fatherland) Party, Omurbek Tekebaev; Respublika, Omurbek Babanov; Jany Kyrgyzstan Party, Usen Sydykov; Erkindik (Freedom) Party, Shamshibek Utebaev; Zamandash (Contemporary) Party, Muktarbek Omurakunov; Ak Shumkar (White Falcon) Party, Temir Sariyev; Asaba (Flag), Azimbek Beknazarov; Green Party, Erkin Bulekbayev.

15 LOCAL GOVERNMENT

The republic is divided into seven administrative regions, known as oblasts, plus the capital city of Bishkek. In addition, there are rayons, or districts. The oblasts, as of 2011, were Batken, Chuy, Jalal-Abad, Naryn, Osho, Talas, and Ysyk-Kol. Bishkek was known as the administrative unit *shaar*. Continuing into 2012, some officials continued to press the national government to divest more powers to local authorities.

16 JUDICIAL SYSTEM

Kyrgyz laws provide for an independent judiciary. However, a 2011 U.S. State Department Human Rights report found that the executive branch often interfered in judicial matters, and that both lawyers and citizens believed judges to be open to bribery.

Cases generally originate in local courts, and can be appealed to courts at municipal or regional levels and ultimately a Supreme Court. The judiciary system includes separate military courts and a separate arbitration court system for economic disputes. Elders' courts, which are under the supervision of the Prosecutor's Office, handle property, family law, and low-level crime.

As of 31 December 2010, a 2007 law allowing for jury trials in Bishkek and Osh had not been implemented.

A 27 June 2010 referendum dissolved the Constitutional Court, which previously dealt with matters of a constitutional nature.

17 ARMED FORCES

The International Institute for Strategic Studies reported that armed forces in Kyrgyzstan totaled 10,900 members in 2011. The force was comprised of 8,500 from the army and 2,400 members of the air force. Armed forces represented 0.8% of the labor force in Kyrgyzstan. Defense spending totaled $61.2 million and accounted for .5% of GDP.

Kyrgyzstan provided the UN with a total of 14 observers in four African countries. The United States, Denmark and Russia each have small contingents in Kyrgyzstan.

18 INTERNATIONAL COOPERATION

Kyrgyzstan joined the United Nations on 2 March 1992 and, with US sponsorship , became part of the World Trade Organization (WTO) in December 1998.

The country has maintained close relations with other former Soviet republics, particularly Kazakhstan and Russia. Kyrgyzstan withdrew from the ruble zone and introduced its own currency in May 1993. This move initially caused Kazakhstan and Uzbekistan to suspend relations, but the tensions were short-lived and the three countries formed an economic union in January 1994. The Eurasian Economic Community was formally established in 2000 with Kyrgyzstan, Kazakhstan, Russia, Belarus, and Tajikistan as members. Kyrgyzstan also has participated in joint military exercises with Uzbekistan and Kazakhstan troops.

The cultural and ethnic links between Kyrgyz and Turks have led to warm bilateral relations between Turkey and Kyrgyzstan. The country also belongs to the OSCE, the CIS and the Shanghai Cooperation Organization. It also has hosted Manas Transit Center, a logistical hub for the coalition effort in Afghanistan , since December 2001. Kyrgyzstan also has received humanitarian support, nonlethal military aid, and assistance in support of economic and political reforms from the United States.

19 ECONOMY

The gross domestic product (GDP) rate of change in Kyrgyzstan, as of 2010, was -1.4%. Inflation stood at 4.8%, and unemployment was reported at 18%.

Kyrgyzstan is among the poorest of the post-Soviet countries. Coal, gold, mercury, and uranium deposits are considerable, but the country boasts few of the oil and gas reserves found in neighboring Central Asian republics.Kyrgyzstan's economy is primarily agricultural, with cotton, tobacco, wool, and meat being the primary agricultural products, although only cotton and tobacco are exported in any significant quantities. In 2009, 29.8% of GDP was in the agricultural sector; industry accounted for 19.7% and services for 50.6%. About 48% of the labor force was engaged in agriculture. The economy depends heavily on gold exports, primarily from the Kumtor gold mine.

The break-up of the Soviet Union in December 1991 had severe effects on Kyrgyzstan's economy, but production began to recover and exports began to increase in mid-1995. The CIA noted that Kyrgyzstan improved its regulatory system, and instituted land reforms following its establishment as a sovereign nation. It was the first country from the Commonwealth of Independent States to be accepted into the World Trade Organization, and much of the former governmentally held enterprises have been privatized.

A medium-term poverty reduction and economic growth strategy was initiated in 2005, and Kyrgyzstan became eligible for the Heavily Indebted Poor Countries Initiative the following year.

The government has worked to control a substantial fiscal deficit, and GDP grew about 8% annually in 2007–08 before slowing to 2.3% in 2009. The overthrow of former President Bakiev in April 2010 and ethnic clashes that followed caused serious damages to the country's infrastructure and have hurt trade and agricultural production.

The 2008–09 global financial crisis of also hurt the economy as the demand for goods dropped among its main export partners of Russia, China, Kazakhstan, Switzerland, and Afghanistan. Industrial production fell by 19% in the first half of 2009. A drop in the amount of remittances from citizens working abroad also had an adverse effect on the economy. The government received substantial aid from Russia to alleviate some of the effects of the crisis.

In July 2010, the World Bank and other international donors pledged $1.1 billion to Kyrgyzstan for reconstruction and recovery efforts in the country. Officials said the money would be spent over a thirty-month period to jumpstart growth. Donors earmarked the funds for various projects, including reconstructing destroyed homes in Osh and Jalal-Abad and developing the nation's infrastructure.

20INCOME

The CIA estimated that in 2010 the GDP of Kyrgyzstan was $12.02 billion. The CIA defines GDP as the value of all final goods and services produced within a nation in a given year and computed on the basis of purchasing power parity (PPP) rather than value as measured on the basis of the rate of the exchange based on current dollars. The per capita GDP was estimated at $2,200. The annual growth rate of GDP was -1.4%. The average inflation rate was 4.8%. It was estimated that agriculture accounted for 24.6% of GDP, industry 25%, and services 50.4%.

According to the World Bank, remittances from citizens living abroad totaled $991.8 million or about $178 per capita and accounted for approximately 8.3% of GDP.

The World Bank reported that in 2009, household consumption in Kyrgyzstan totaled $4.3 billion or about $774 per capita, measured in current US dollars rather than PPP. Household consumption included expenditures of individuals, households, and nongovernmental organizations on goods and services, excluding the purchases of dwellings. It was estimated that household consumption was growing at an average annual rate of 4.4%.

The World Bank estimates that Kyrgyzstan, with 0.08% of the world's population, accounted for 0.02% of the world's GDP. By comparison, the United States, with 4.85% of the world's population, accounted for 22.51% of world GDP.

As of 2011 the most recent study by the World Bank reported that actual individual consumption in Kyrgyzstan was 93.3% of GDP and accounted for 0.03% of world consumption. By comparison, the United States accounted for 25.44% of world individual consumption. The World Bank also estimated that 46.2% of Kyrgyzstan's GDP was spent on food and beverages, 9.4% on housing and household furnishings, 7.5% on clothes, 3.9% on health, 8.6% on transportation, 2.5% on communications, 2.3% on recreation, 2.5% on restaurants and hotels, and 4.6% on miscellaneous goods and services and purchases from abroad.

21LABOR

As of 2007, Kyrgyzstan had a total labor force of 2.344 million people. Within that labor force, CIA estimates in 2005 noted that 48% were employed in agriculture, 12.5% in industry, and 39.5% in the service sector.

The Federation of Trade Unions was the only umbrella trade union in the country. It claimed a membership of 200,000 workers. The Union of Entrepreneurs and Small Business Workers, which was not affiliated with the federation, claimed a membership of 60,000.

The US State Department reported that average wages for women were significantly smaller than those for men, and that instances of forced labor were reported among foreign workers in the agricultural sector and among children in coal mining industries.

There was no minimum wage as of 2011, and the US State Department found that the government's nominal minimum monthly wage of $7.20 (used solely for purposes such as calculating court fines) was not adequate to provide workers and their families with a decent standard of living. The standard work week was 40 hours, and government owned industries were required to allow a 24-hour rest period in the work week. Overtime was limited to four hours a week, or 20 hours a week.

Safety and health conditions in factories were found to be poor, with the government failing to enforced legal occupational health and safety standards.

22AGRICULTURE

Roughly 7% of the total land is farmed, and the country's major crops included wheat, sugar beets, tobacco, cotton, potatoes, vegetables, grapes, fruits and berries. Cereal production in 2009 amounted to 1.9 million tons, fruit production 212,761 tons, and vegetable production 984,854 tons.

Since independence, most state farms have been privatized. The US State Department reported that the private agricultural sector provided one-third to one-half of the annual harvests by the early 1990s. As of 2010, agriculture accounted for 55% of GDP and 32% of the Kyrgyz labor force. Agricultural processing also formed a key sector of the industrial economy and provided an attractive sector for foreign investment.

Cultivation occurs primarily in the Shu, Talas, and Fergana valleys.

23ANIMAL HUSBANDRY

The UN Food and Agriculture Organization (FAO) reported that Kyrgyzstan dedicated 9.4 million hectares (23.2 million acres) to permanent pasture or meadow in 2009. During that year, the country tended 4 million chickens, 1.2 million head of cattle, and 63,328 pigs. The production from these animals amounted to 75,625 tons of beef and veal, 28,491 tons of pork, 20,342 tons of poultry, 21,352 tons of eggs, and 958,440 tons of milk. Kyrgyzstan also produced 10,298 tons of cattle hide and 11,006 tons of raw wool.

The mountain terrain of Kyrgyzstan has made it especially good for livestock raising. About 48% of the total land area is considered permanent pastureland.

24FISHING

In 2008, the annual capture totaled 8 tons according to the UN FAO. The Naryn River is the primary site of fishing activity, but fishing is of little commercial significance. The Lake Issyk-Kul is slightly saline and not conducive to the development of fresh water species fishing.

25FORESTRY

Approximately 5% of Kyrgyzstan is covered by forest. The UN FAO estimated the 2009 roundwood production at 9,300 cu m (328,426 cu ft). The value of all forest products, including roundwood, totaled $2.81 million.

With 85% of the country covered by high-altitude mountain ranges, and coupled with an underdeveloped transportation system, the forestry sector is not commercially significant

26MINING

Kyrgyzstan's southwestern region contains most of the nation's mineral wealth, including, most importantly, antimony (often found with lead-zinc), mercury (often found with fluorspar), and gold. Principal deposits of these minerals are found in the Kadamzhayskiy Rayon and Khaydarkan regions, in the Alay foothills. The Khaydarkan mercury mining and metallurgical complex, in the Osh region, was the major producer of metallic mercury in the former Soviet Union. Kyrgyzstan's leading mineral sector now is gold mining, with development of the Kumtor gold deposit by Cameco Corp. of Canada.

In 2009 Kyrgyzstan produced 320 metric tons of metallic mercury. Antimony metal and compounds production in 2009 totaled 918 metric tons. The mountains also contained deposits of gold, mercury, tungsten, molybdenum, rare earth metals, indium, sulfur, tin, and arsenic. Gold production in 2009 was estimated at 76,950 kg. Output figures in 2009 included fluorspar concentrate, estimated at 4,000 metric tons; and cement, 1,100,000 metric tons.

27 ENERGY AND POWER

The World Bank reported in 2008 that Kyrgyzstan produced 11.9 billion kWh of electricity and consumed 7.65 billion kWh, or 1,369 kWh per capita. Roughly 69% of energy came from fossil fuels, while 32% came from alternative fuels. Per capita oil consumption was 542 kg. Oil production totaled 1,000 barrels of oil a day.

The CIA estimated that Kyrgyzstan had proved oil reserves of approximately 40 million barrels as of 1 January 2011. While Kyrgyzstan produced 946 barrels per day as of 2010, the country was importing significantly more oil than it produced. Oil imports totaled 15,940 barrels in 2010.

Natural gas proved reserves were 5.664 billion cubic meters. Natural gas production was 15.4 million cubic meters in 2009, and was produced completely for domestic use.

28 INDUSTRY

Industry accounted for 28% of GDP in 2010 and employed 12.5% of the workforce. The industrial production growth rate was estimated at 9.8% in 2010. Key industries include the mining of gold and rare earth metals, small machinery and electric motors plants, textile factories, food processing facilities, cement-making, sawn log production, and the manufacture of shoes, refrigerators, and furniture.

The economy has been heavily dependent on gold exports, mainly from the Kumtor gold mine. Other industrial exports were mercury, uranium, natural gas, and electricity.

During the Soviet era, Kyrgyzstan relied on the other republics for raw materials and other resources for its industrial base. Between 1985 and 1989, industrial output increased at a rate of over 5% annually. With the disruption of traditional supply and export arrangements within the former USSR, however, industrial output declined sharply in the early 1990s. By mid-1995, production began to recover and began to grow substantially, due largely to the mining and export of gold.

In the early- and mid-2000s, the mining sector accounted for the majority of foreign investment. The high world price for gold also contributed to a rise in GDP and attracted foreign investment in the mid-2000s.

The government passed the Privatization and Denationalization Act in December 1991, authorizing the transfer of all small, medium, and large-scale industrial enterprises to the private sector. As of 2011, much of the government's stock in business enterprises had been sold. One important conversion involved the participation of a South Korean firm in establishing electronics manufacture at a plant previously geared toward military-related production.

Violence resulting from the 2010 overthrow of President Bakiev and ethnic clashes later that year has damaged much of the country's infrastructure. Repairing the infrastructure and continuing to reform domestic industry were key priorities for Kyrgyzstan at the end of 2011.

29 SCIENCE AND TECHNOLOGY

Patent applications in science and technology as of 2009, according to the World Bank, totaled 135 in Kyrgyzstan. Public financing of science was 0.23% of GDP.

The primary research body for Kyrgyzstan is the National Academy of Sciences of the Kyrgyz Republic, which was formally established as the supreme public scientific institution in 1993. The academy initially was established in the early 20th century, and was named the Academy of Sciences of the Kyrgyz Soviet Socialist Republic in 1943. Its primary activity in the first decade of the early 21st century was to promote scientific and technological development as well as to support research in culture, education, literature and the arts.

30 DOMESTIC TRADE

Kyrgyzstan has been making a slow transition from the planned economy model of the former Soviet Union to a more market oriented capitalistic economy. The World Bank reported in 2011, however, that governmental reforms in 2009–11 had made the country's domestic environment more business friendly. The government established a one-stop shop for starting businesses in 2009 and eliminated minimum capital requirements and various post-registration fees in 2010.

A 2011 article through the Central Asia Online News Service reported that 82,000 people were operating small- and medium-sized businesses in Kyrgyzstan at the end of 2010, and that these small enterprises accounted for nearly 40% of GDP. Businesses included retail establishments, real estate enterprises, services, and farms.

Most businesses open around 9 a.m. and close at about 6 p.m., with lunch taken sometime between noon and 2 p.m. Some offices are open from 9 a.m. to 1 p.m. on Saturdays. Retail shops are usually open from 7 a.m. to 8 p.m., with an afternoon lunch period. Department stores, bookstores, and other shops usually open according to state institution hours. Bazaars are open from 6 a.m. until 7 or 8 p.m.

31 FOREIGN TRADE

Kyrgyzstan imported $3.075 billion worth of goods and services in 2008, while exporting $1.682 billion worth of goods and services. Major import partners in 2009 were China, 70.8%; Russia, 12.3%; and Kazakhstan, 4.1%. Its major export partners were Russia, 34.5%; Uzbekistan, 21.2%; Kazakhstan, 16.8%; UAE, 5%; China, 4.6%; and Afghanistan, 4.2%.

The country's primary exports were nonferrous metals (mostly gold) and minerals, woolen goods, agricultural products, electric energy, and engineering goods. Its main imports were oil and natural gas, ferrous metals, chemicals, machinery, wood and pa-

Principal Trading Partners – Kyrgyzstan (2010)

(In millions of US dollars)

Country	Total	Exports	Imports	Balance
World	4,982.9	1,759.8	3,223.1	-1,463.3
China	4,572.7	63.2	4,509.5	-4,446.2
Russia	1,424.7	351.8	1,072.9	-721.1
Kazakhstan	623.0	204.5	418.4	-213.9
Uzbekistan	435.8	257.9	177.9	80.0
Turkey	170.2	28.1	142.1	-114.0
South Korea	117.5	2.5	115.0	-112.5
Belarus	101.5	7.5	94.0	-86.5
United States	90.0	3.7	86.2	-82.5
Ukraine	88.2	5.6	82.5	-76.9
United Arab Emirates	65.6	54.6	10.9	43.7

(…) data not available or not significant.

(n.s.) not specified.

SOURCE: *2011 Direction of Trade Statistics Yearbook,* New York: United Nations, 2011.

per products, foods and construction materials. Antimony, mercury, rare-earth metals, and chemical products were Kyrgyzstan's primary exports to the United States as of 2011. Its primary imports from the United States were grains, medicines and medical equipment, vegetable oil, paper products, rice, machinery, agricultural equipment, and meat. Exports to the United States totaled $90.3 million in 2010 while imports from the United States totaled $188.2 million that year.

32 BALANCE OF PAYMENTS

In 2010 Kyrgyzstan had a foreign trade deficit of $1.1 billion, amounting to 1.4% of GDP. With the exception of 2004, Kyrgyzstan has had a negative account balance each year between 1992 and 2010. The CIA reported that Kyrgyzstan had a negative current account balance of an estimated $397.4 million in 2010 compared with an estimated negative current account balance of $300.2 million in 2009. Foreign exchange reserves (including gold) were estimated at $1.72 billion as of 31 December 2010 compared with $1.585 billion as of 31 December 2009.

The Economic Intelligence Unit report that while tax collections rose in January–August 2011 by 29.4% over the same period a year earlier, the country's deficit would likely widen. The Kyrgyz parliament in September approved a government agreement with the World Bank which would bring $30 million in budget support for 2012. Approximately half of that amount was to come in the form of direct aid and the remainder as loan.

33 BANKING AND SECURITIES

The National Bank of the Kyrgyz Republic regulates the banking sector. As of 1 December 2011, there were 22 domestically operated commercial banks, including a Bishkek branch of the National Bank of Pakistan. Total assets of the Kyrgyz banks decreased 13.8% in 2010 from 2009. Non-interest income increased 5.3% and expenses associated with non-interest income rose 13.5%. Interest income decreased 18.2% and expenses associated with interest income rose 34.7%.

There were two specialized finance and credit institutions, 217 credit unions, and 397 microfinance organizations under the National Bank's purview. Total assets in these non-bank institutions rose 22% in 2010.

Microfinance, particularly micro-lending, has been an active part of Kyrgyzstan's banking sector, and the size of the loan portfolio among non-finance credit institutions increased in 2010 by 24.7%. The number of borrowers increased by 20.5% and totaled 391,000 people.

As of 2010, there were three stock exchanges in Kyrgyzstan: the Closed Joint Stock Company, the Kyrgyz Stock Exchange, and the Central Asian Stock Exchange. The Kyrgyz Stock Exchange was established in 1994 as a non-profit member organization and was reorganized as a joint stock exchange in 2000. Twelve companies were listed in 2011, and the exchange had 17 shareholders.

34 INSURANCE

There were 19 insurance companies operating in Kyrgyzstan as of 31 December 2009. Two of these firms were reinsurance companies. AUB Insurance was the largest company. The insurance sector's assets as a share of GDP was 0.38% in 2009, nearly triple that of 2006.

35 PUBLIC FINANCE

In 2010 the budget of Kyrgyzstan included $980 million in public revenue and $1.46 billion in public expenditures. The budget deficit amounted to 6.1% of GDP. In total $3.738 billion of the debt held by foreign entities.

36 TAXATION

The State Committee on Taxes and Duties of the Kyrgyz Republic supervises the collection of taxes. As of 2007, there were approximately 17 taxes in the country. National taxes included a profit tax, income tax, value added tax, excise tax, and automobile road tax.

Balance of Payments – Kyrgyzstan (2010)

(In millions of US dollars)

Current Account		**-467.0**
Balance on goods	-1,202.2	
Imports	-2,980.9	
Exports	1,778.7	
Balance on services	-231.1	
Balance on income	-343.2	
Current transfers	1,309.5	
Capital Account		**-62.1**
Financial Account		**646.0**
Direct investment abroad	…	
Direct investment in Kyrgyzstan	437.6	
Portfolio investment assets	182.5	
Portfolio investment liabilities	-18.2	
Financial derivatives	…	
Other investment assets	106.8	
Other investment liabilities	-62.7	
Net Errors and Omissions		**-95.5**
Reserves and Related Items		**-21.4**

(…) data not available or not significant.

SOURCE: *Balance of Payment Statistics Yearbook 2011,* Washington, DC: International Monetary Fund, 2011.

Public Finance – Kyrgyzstan (2009)

(In millions of soms, budgetary central government figures)

Revenue and Grants	48,006.3	100.0%
Tax revenue	30,256.1	63.0%
Social contributions	...	...
Grants	10,201.1	21.2%
Other revenue	7,549.1	15.7%
Expenditures	50,660.3	100.0%
General public services	...	...
Defense	...	...
Public order and safety	...	...
Economic affairs	...	...
Environmental protection	...	...
Housing and community amenities	...	...
Health	...	...
Recreational, culture, and religion	...	...
Education	...	...
Social protection	...	...

(…) data not available or not significant.

SOURCE: *Government Finance Statistics Yearbook 2010*, Washington, DC: International Monetary Fund, 2010.

Local taxes on land, automobiles, health resorts, advertising, parking, garbage collection, hotels, and retail sales also were levied.

Businesses paid the profit tax at a 10%. Personal income tax also was 10%.

37 CUSTOMS AND DUTIES

Kyrgyzstan is a member of the World Trade Organization, which limits the tariff levels of member nations. Eight regional customs centers have been established in the country, and there are city customs centers in Bishkek, Kara-Balta, and Tokmak. In addition, there is a railway customs center and a center at the Manas Airport.

In 2011 Kyrgyzstan joined the Russian-sponsored Customs Union, which is aimed primarily at protecting domestic Russian production from cheaper foreign imports. That same year, the average tariff in Kyrgyzstan was 5.1%, while the average tariff in the Customs Union was 10.6%.

38 FOREIGN INVESTMENT

Foreign direct investment (FDI) in Kyrgyzstan was a net inflow of $189.4 million according to World Bank figures published in 2009. FDI represented 4.14% of GDP.

Kyrgyzstan has sought foreign investment to help build its economy, and has relied on US support in this area. The areas of mining, electronics, and agricultural processing offered particularly strong opportunities.

Political unrest in 2010 deterred many investors. On 26 October 2011, the USAID Local Development Program initiated a series of seminars on foreign investment for representatives of the country's local governments, oblast administrations, and branches of the national government. The goal of the eight-month program, running through May 2012, was to help educate local leaders on investment and marketing opportunities for attracting foreign direct investment.

39 ECONOMIC DEVELOPMENT

Kyrgyzstan's County Development Strategy for 2009–11 identified economic growth that enhanced the quality of life of its people and lessened the corruption of its public administration as its primary economic goal. The country, which remained one of the poorest of the former Soviet Republics in 2011, has been working with foreign aid organizations to make a slow, often painful transition from the centrally planned economy to which it was subject under Soviet leadership to a market based economy under its current democratic regime.

Under the Soviet system, economic planning efforts in Kyrgyzstan focused on increasing agricultural production (particularly in the meat and dairy subsectors during the 1980s) and specialized development of industrial sectors in line with the wider Soviet economy. Transfer payments from the central government as well as capital inflows into state enterprises covered the republic's modest balance of trade deficit with its Soviet trading partners and countries beyond. With this support, GDP growth was sustained at moderately high levels in the late 1980s, averaging 5.1% in 1985–89.

Kyrgyzstan declared its independence in 1991. Since then, the Kyrgyzstan government faced the task of sustaining a viable national economy despite the sudden cessation of transfers from the central government, the country's critical dependence on oil and gas imports, and its landlocked geographic position that has hampered development of trading ties outside the economically troubled former Soviet Union.

Kyrgyzstan experienced declines in gross domestic product (GDP) from 1991–94. Both per capita income and overall output fell to well below the 1990 level. Agricultural output fell by an estimated 20%, and industrial output, by 42%. By 1996, however, Kyrgyzstan had begun to show progress, especially when compared to the other former Soviet republics, in the areas of privatizing state enterprises, ending the state ordering system, lifting price controls, and converting military enterprises to civilian uses.

Because of its commitment to democracy, Kyrgyzstan has received favorable treatment from international economic aid agencies including the Asian Development Bank, the World Bank, and the International Monetary Fund. Kyrgyzstan also has received substantial support from the United States.

In 2001, the government published its Comprehensive Development Framework (CDF) for 2001–10. The CDF contains the following goals for strengthening the economic stability of the country: modernization of the telecommunications, transportation, and tourism infrastructures; reduction and rationalization of the government's regulatory role in the economy; implementation of more sound fiscal, monetary, and taxation policies; reform of the judicial system to protect property rights; poverty reduction and employment creation, especially among Kyrgyz youth; and strengthening and reforming the banking sector. In addition to these goals, by 2006 other ingredients of future growth included progress fighting corruption, further restructuring of domestic industry, and success in attracting foreign investment.

In 2010, an estimated 40% of the population lived below the poverty level. The 2009–11 plan called for improvements in the standard of living that would bring at least 50% of the population to a middle-class standard. The plan also sought to maintain the country's annual GDP growth at 7.5–8% through a promotion of foreign trade, the development of domestic jobs, and tax reforms. Economic development suffered in 2010 with the political violence that erupted in April and the ethnic clashes between Kyrgyz and Uzbek peoples in July. The global financial crisis of 2008–09 also continued to take its toll on Kyrgyzstan, leading the National Bank of the Kyrgyz Republic to support the liquidity of the banking system with stabilizing loans.

The US State Department has identified the agricultural sector as attractive to potential foreign investment and growth. As of 2011, however, Kyrgyzstan had not shown significant success in attracting investment outside of its gold production industry.

A December 2011 analysis of the Kyrgyz economy in the magazine Global Finance suggested that the 1 November 2011 election of President Atambayev to office may restore the country's stability. Observers suggested that Kyrgyzstan may turn more to Russia as well as its neighboring countries for foreign investment, a move that might change the country's relationship with the US and other Western democracies. Ataybeyev began his presidency with an announcement of his intention to close the US military base at Manas in 2014 when the current contract expires, pledged to join a customs union with Russia, Kazakhstan, and Belarus, and to seek subsidized loans and lower fuel tariffs from Russia.

40 SOCIAL DEVELOPMENT

Old age, disability, and survivorship pensions are provided to all employed persons and members of cooperatives and collective farms. Contributions of 8% of earnings from employees, and 25% of payroll by employers finance the program. A universal medical care system exists for all residents. Maternity benefits for employed women include 100% of pay for 126 days of leave. Workers' compensation, unemployment benefits, and family allowances are also provided.

Women were not restricted from participating in politics, and the successor to President Bakiev was Roza Otunbeyeva, a woman. Despite her presence in politics, the US State Department has reported that women have been hindered from holding office or participating actively in politics. There were 28 women representing five political parties in parliament in 2011 as a result of an election code that mandated that male and female candidates could not be more than three spaces apart on party lists, and that a maximum 70% of candidates on a party list could be of the same gender.

National minorities make up 35% of the population and generally were underrepresented in government positions, despite laws that require at least 15% of party lists to be made up of minorities. Fourteen of the 120 parliament members were minorities. Ethnic Uzbeks particularly face discrimination. Many Uzbeks who were arrested for carrying out violence against the Kyrgyz in June 2010 were subject to unfair trials, torture, lack of access to attorneys, and threats of violence. Discrimination in hiring practices also was reported.

41 HEALTH

According to the CIA, life expectancy in Kyrgyzstan was 67 years in 2011. The country spent 5.7% of its GDP on healthcare, amounting to $57 per person. There were 23 physicians, 57 nurses and midwives, and 51 hospital beds per 10,000 inhabitants. The fertility rate was 2.8, while the infant mortality rate was 32 per

1,000 live births. In 2008 the maternal mortality rate, according to the World Bank, was 81 per 100,000 births. It was estimated that 99% of children were vaccinated against measles. The CIA calculated HIV/AIDS prevalence in Kyrgyzstan to be about 0.3% in 2009.

42 HOUSING

Kyrgyzstan faced a severe lack of urban housing during the Soviet era, with nearly 18.6% of its population on waiting lists to receive housing. Overcrowding continued to be a problem as of 2011.

A 1999 census showed 1,109,716 households in the country, and the average number of members per household to be 4.3. Ten years later, the results of a 2009 census showed that the number of households had increased slightly to 1,145,800 while the average number of members per household had risen to 4.6. In some oblasts the average household size was unusually large: 5.9 members per household in Osh and 5.4 in Jalal-Abad. Residential areas included houses, shared homes, apartments, dormitories, dachas, hotels, huts, trains, yurts, tents, garages, kiosks, and farm structures.

43 EDUCATION

In 2009 the World Bank estimated that 84% of age-eligible children in Kyrgyzstan were enrolled in primary school. Secondary enrollment for age-eligible children stood at 79%. Tertiary enrollment was estimated at 51%. Of those enrolled in tertiary education, there were 100 male students for every 136 female students. Overall, the CIA estimated that Kyrgyzstan had a literacy rate of 98.7%. Public expenditure on education represented 5.9% of GDP.

The law provided for compulsory and free education for the first nine years of schooling, or until age 14; secondary education was free and universal until age 17. However, financial constraints prevented the government from providing free basic education for all students, and the system of residence registration restricted access to social services, including education, for certain children, such as refugees, migrants, and noncitizens. Legally, all textbooks should be free of charge, but the government was unable to provide them to all students.

There were 28 colleges, universities, and other institutes of higher learning in Kyrgyzstan in 2011. Some of the main institutions were the Kyrgyz Russian Slavic University, founded in 1992, Kyrgyz National University, founded in 1924, and the International University of Kyrgyzstan, founded in 1993.

44 LIBRARIES AND MUSEUMS

The main library is the National Library of Kyrgyzstan and the American University of Central Asia also maintains a library.

There are numerous museums in Bishkek, with the major institutes being The Historical Museum, the Museum of Fine Arts, and the Frunze Museum, which documents the life of Bolshevik fighter Mikhail Frunze.

45 MEDIA

In 2009 the CIA reported that there were 498,300 telephone landlines in Kyrgyzstan. In addition to landlines, mobile phone subscriptions averaged 84 per 100 people, with a total of 4.4 million in use. There were three FM radio stations, 23 shortwave radio stations. Internet users numbered 41 per 100 citizens. Prominent newspapers in 2010, with circulation numbers listed parenthetically, included *Vechernii Bishkek* (51,500).

Telephone links to other former Soviet republics are via land line or microwave, and to other countries through Moscow. In 2010, the country had 97,976 Internet hosts. As of 2009, there were some 2.1 million Internet users in Kyrgyzstan.

⁴⁶ORGANIZATIONS

A handful of organizations have formed in Kyrgyzstan to preserve the country's traditional handicrafts including the Central Asia Craft Support Association, Altyn Kol: Women's Handicraft Cooperative, and the Kyrgyz Heritage Women's NGO. The Forum of Women's Non-Governmental Organizations of Kyrgyzstan has been working in support of the women's movement in the country. The Chamber of Commerce and Industry has a number of branches throughout the country. In addition, many political underground organizations are believed to exist, and terrorism groups, though banned, have maintained cells in the country.

⁴⁷TOURISM, TRAVEL, AND RECREATION

The *Tourism Factbook*, published by the UN World Tourism Organization, reported 2.15 million incoming tourists to Kyrgyzstan in 2009, who spent a total of $506 million. There were 4,990 hotel beds available in Kyrgyzstan. The estimated daily cost to visit Bishkek, the capital, was $302. The cost of visiting other cities averaged $111.

The Sulamain-Too Sacred Mountain, located in the Fergana Valley near the city of Osh, became the nation's first UNESCO World Heritage Site in 2009. Around the five peaks and slopes of the mountain there are numerous ancient worship sites, seventeen of which are still in use. Many worshippers, practicing a blend of pre-Islamic and Islamic rituals, believe that there are healing powers associated with these ancient altars. Two reconstructed 16th century mosques are also located on the mountain. The slopes are full of caves, with over one hundred known examples of ancient petroglyphs.

Bishkek is surrounded by some of the highest mountain ranges in the world, and is known for its large public parks and gardens, shady avenues, and botanical gardens.

Kyrgyzstan has set aside 761,300 hectares of land, nearly 4% of its total land area, into 83 specially protected natural territories. The best known of these areas was Ala Archa. The National Parks has created these territories with a goal of organizing tourism that is not harmful to the country's pristine natural environment.

⁴⁸FAMOUS PERSONS

Askar A. Akayev was elected president of the republic of Kyrgyzstan, in October 1990, prior to the republic declaring its independence. He remained president until 2005, when he was deposed in the popular uprising known as the "Tulip Revolution." Kurmanbek Bakiyev (b. 1949) became acting president in 2005 before being ousted in 2009. Chinghiz Aitmatov (b. 1928), winner of two Lenin Prizes for literature, is a native Kyrgyzstani. The wrestler Kojumkul (1889–1995) has had a village named in his honor, and a statue showing him lifting a horse was erected in 2004 outside the Sports Palace in Bishkek.

⁴⁹DEPENDENCIES

Kyrgyzstan has no territories or colonies.

⁵⁰BIBLIOGRAPHY

Abazov, Rafis. *Historical Dictionary of Kyrgyzstan.* Lanham, MD: Scarecrow, 2003.

Commission on Security and Cooperation in Europe. Human Rights and Democracy in Kyrgyzstan: Hearing Before the Commission on Security and Cooperation in Europe, One Hundred Seventh Congress, First Session, December 12, 2001. Washington, D.C.: U.S. Government Printing Office, 2002.

Handrahan, Lori. *Gendering Ethnicity: Implications for Democracy Assistance.* New York: Routledge, 2002.

Hiro, Dilip. *Inside Central Asia: A Political and Cultural History of Uzbekistan, Turkmenistan, Kazakhstan, Kyrgyzstan, Tajikistan, Turkey, and Iran.* New York: Overlook Duckworth, 2009.

King, David C. *Kyrgyzstan.* New York: Marshall Cavendish Benchmark, 2006.

Kort, Michael. *Central Asian Republics.* New York: Facts On File, 2004.

Kyrgyzstan Investment and Business Guide: Strategic and Practical Information. Washington, DC: International Business Publications USA, 2012.

Landau, Jacob M, and Barbara Kellner-Heinkele. *Politics of Language in the Ex-Soviet Muslim States.* Ann Arbor: The University of Michigan Press, 2004.

Mitchell, Laurence. *Kyrgyzstan.* Guilford, CT: Globe Pequot Press, 2008.

Seddon, David, ed. *A Political and Economic Dictionary of the Middle East.* Philadelphia: Routledge/Taylor and Francis, 2004.

LAOS

Lao People's Democratic Republic
Sathalanalat Paxathipatai Paxaxon Lao

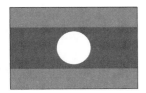

CAPITAL: Vientiane (Viangchan)

FLAG: The national flag, officially adopted in 1975, is the former flag of the Pathet Lao, consisting of three horizontal stripes of red, dark blue, and red, with a white disk representing the full moon, at the center.

ANTHEM: *Pheng Xat Lao (Hymn of the Lao People).*

MONETARY UNIT: The kip (LAK) is a paper currency of 100 at (cents). There are notes of 10, 20, 50, 200, 500, 1,000, 2,000, 5,000, 10,000, 20,000, 50,000 and 100,000 kip. No coins are in circulation. US dollars and Thai baht are also commonly used in Laos. LAK1 = US$0.000125078 (US$1 = LAK7,995) as of November 2011.

WEIGHTS AND MEASURES: The metric system is the legal standard, but older local units also are used.

HOLIDAYS: Anniversary of the Founding of the Lao People's Democratic Republic, 2 December. To maintain production, the government generally reschedules on weekends such traditional festivals as the Lao New Year (April); Boun Bang-fai (Rocket Festival), the celebration of the birth, enlightenment, and death of the Buddha (May); Boun Khao Watsa, the beginning of a period of fasting and meditation lasting through the rainy season (July); Boun Ok Watsa (Water Holiday), a celebration of the end of the period of fasting and meditation (October); and That Luang, a pagoda pilgrimage holiday (November).

TIME: 7 p.m. = noon GMT.

¹LOCATION, SIZE, AND EXTENT

Laos is a landlocked country on the Indochina Peninsula near the eastern extremity of mainland Southeast Asia. Laos occupies an area of 236,800 sq km (91,429 sq mi), extending 1,162 km (722 mi) SSE–NNW and 478 km (297 mi) ENE–WSW. Comparatively, the area occupied by Laos is slightly larger than the state of Utah. It is bordered on the N by China, on the E and SE by Vietnam, on the S by Cambodia, on the W by Thailand, and on the NW by Myanmar, with a total boundary length of 5,083 km (3,158 mi).

The capital of Laos, Vientiane, is located along the country's southwestern boundary.

²TOPOGRAPHY

The terrain is rugged and mountainous, especially in the north and in the Annam Range, along the border with Vietnam. The mountains reach heights of more than 2,700 m (8,860 ft), with Pou Bia, the highest point in Laos, rising to 2,817 m (9,242 ft) in the north central part of the country. Only three passes cross the mountains to link Laos with Vietnam. The Tran Ninh Plateau, in the northeast, rises to between 1,020–1,370 m (3,350-4,500 ft), and the fertile Bolovens Plateau, in the south, reaches a height of about 1,070 m (3,500 ft). Broad alluvial plains, where much of the rice crop is grown, are found only in the south and west along the Mekong River and its tributaries. Of these, the Vientiane plain is the most extensive.

Except for a relatively small area east of the main divide, Laos is drained by the Mekong and its tributaries. The Mekong flows in a broad valley along the border with Thailand and through Laos for 1,805 km (1,122 mi). In its low-water phase, it is almost dry, but it rises more than 6 m (20 ft) during the monsoon period. The

river is wide, and except for a navigable stretch between Vientiane and Savannakhét, rapids are numerous. Below Savannakhét and at the extreme south there are large rapids and waterfalls. Floods are common in the rainy season.

³CLIMATE

Laos has a tropical monsoon climate with three main seasons. The rainy season is from May through October, when rainfall averages 127–229 cm (50–90 in). November through February is a cool, dry season. March through April is a hot, dry season, during which temperatures can be as high as 40°C (104°F). Humidity is high throughout the year, even during the season of drought. Average daily temperatures in Vientiane range from 14–28°C (57–82°F) in January, the coolest month, and from 23–34°C (73–93°F) in April, the hottest.

⁴FLORA AND FAUNA

The forests of southernmost Laos are an extension of the Cambodian type of vegetation, while the highland forests of the north, consisting of prairies interspersed with thickets, resemble central Vietnam. Bamboo, lianas, rattan, and palms are found throughout Laos.

The World Resource Institute estimates that there are 8,286 plant species in Laos. In addition, Laos is home to 215 species of mammals, 704 species of birds, 147 species of reptiles, and 59 species of amphibians. This calculation reflects the total number of distinct species residing in the country, not the number of endemic species. The elephant, until 1975 depicted on the national flag as the traditional symbol of Lao royalty, has been used throughout history as a beast of burden; fewer than one thousand remain in the wild in Laos. From 500 to 600 tigers survive in Laos. A local breed of water buffalo is used as a draft animal. Reptiles include cobras, geckos, kraits, and crocodiles. Irrawaddy dolphins dwell in the Mekong River near the southern border.

5 ENVIRONMENT

Soil erosion, deforestation (from legal and illegal logging and agricultural encroachment), and flood control have been the principal environmental concerns in Laos. Reforestation projects have been promoted by the government as a means of increasing timber exports and of restoring valuable hardwoods to logged-out forest areas. Each person was required to plant five trees in the course of the 1981–85 economic plan. In 1986 the government prohibited the cutting of 15 different varieties of trees. At that time forests were reportedly being consumed at a rate of 300,000 hectares (741,000 acres) per year. Between 1983 and 1993 Laos suffered a further decline of 11.3% in its forest and woodland area. From 1990 through 2000 the rate of deforestation was about 0.4% per year. According to the United Nations Food and Agriculture Organization (UN FAO), the annual deforestation rate for 2005–10 averaged 0.6%. The World Resource Institute reported that the Lao People's Democratic Republic had designated 3.75 million hectares (9.28 million acres) of land for protection as of 2006.

The nation's water supply has begun to decrease due to a combination of factors, among them the loss of forestland, uncontrolled agricultural practices, and drought. Pollution from fires, dust, and motor vehicles is also becoming a problem. The UN reported in 2008 that carbon dioxide emissions in Laos totaled 1,535 kilotons. Water resources totaled 333.6 cu km (80.03 cu mi) while water usage was 3 cu km (0.72 cu mi) per year. Domestic water usage accounted for 4% of total usage, industrial for 6%, and agricultural for 90%. Per capita water usage totaled 507 cu m (17,905 cu ft) per year.

According to a 2007 report issued by the International Union for Conservation of Nature and Natural Resources (IUCN), threatened species included 34 types of mammals, 22 species of birds, 11 types of reptiles, 4 species of amphibians, 6 species of fish, and 21 species of plants. Endangered species in Laos include the douc langur, three species of gibbon, tiger, Asian elephant, Thailand brow-antlered deer, kouprey, Heude's pig, Siamese crocodile, and the extremely rare double horned saola. Laos has been a center for trafficking in endangered wildlife.

6 POPULATION

The US Central Intelligence Agency (CIA) estimated the population of Lao People's Democratic Republic in 2011 to be approximately 6,477,211, which placed it at number 103 in population among the 196 nations of the world. In 2011 approximately 3.7% of the population was over 65 years of age, with another 36.7% under 15 years of age. The median age in Laos was 21 years. There were 0.98 males for every female in the country. The population's annual rate of change was 1.684%. The projected population for the year 2025 was 8,300,000. Population density in Laos was calculated at 27 people per sq km (70 people per sq mi).

The UN estimated that 33% of the population lived in urban areas in 2010, and that urban populations had an annual rate of change of 4.9%. The largest urban area was Vientiane, with a population of 799,000.

7 MIGRATION

Estimates of the Lao People's Democratic Republic's net migration rate, carried out by the CIA in 2011, amounted to -1.16 migrants per 1,000 citizens. The total number of emigrants living abroad was 366,600, and the total number of immigrants living in Lao People's Democratic Republic was 18,900. There has been only limited population movement into Laos in modern times. During the late 1960s and early 1970s, under pressure of combat operations, Black Tai ethnic people moved southward into the Mekong River valley. Between 1975 and 1990 hundreds of thousands of Hmong, having backed the United States in the Vietnam War (sometimes referred to as the Second Indochina War), fled the Communist takeover and were eventually resettled in the United States, Australia, and other countries. In 2009 Thailand forcibly returned several thousand Hmong asylum-seekers to Laos. In the mid-1990s, as Laos opened up to international investment and development, Vietnamese workers began migrating to Laos—although in relatively small numbers—primarily to work in the construction industry.

8 ETHNIC GROUPS

The Lao-Loum, or lowland Lao, related to the people of Thailand, account for between 40% and 50% of the population; thought to have migrated to Laos from southwestern China in the 8th century, the Lao-Loum are concentrated in the lowlands along the Mekong. On the hillsides live the Lao-Theung, or slope dwellers, a diverse group dominated by the Lao-Tai (with various subgroups, including the Black Tai), who are ethnically related to the Lao-Loum. At higher altitudes are the Lao-Soung, or mountain dwellers. Important among the Lao-Soung are the Hmong (Meo), a people of Tibeto-Burman origin who supported the American presence during the Vietnam War until 1975 and, because of their continuing insurgency, became the targets of harassment by government and Vietnamese troops. The Hmong account for about 8% of the population. Other important upland tribes, all with customs and religions considerably different from those of the lowland Lao, are the Ho, Kha, Kho, and Yao (Mien). Ethnic Vietnamese and Chinese account for 1% of the population. There are 49 official ethnic groups in the country, but some reports indicate there are more than 100 ethnic groups.

9 LANGUAGES

Lao, the official language and the language of the ethnic Lao, is closely related to the language of Thailand. It is monosyllabic and tonal and contains words borrowed from Sanskrit, Pali, and Farsi. Pali, a Sanskritic language, is used by the Buddhist clergy. Other groups speak Tibeto-Burman, Mon-Khmer, or Miao-Yao languages. French, formerly the principal language of government and higher education, has been largely replaced by Lao. English, French, Thai, and various ethnic languages are also spoken.

10 RELIGIONS

Theravada Buddhism is practiced by most of the Lao-Loum (accounting for between 40% and 50% of the population). The Lao-Theung and the Lao-Soung, including the upland tribes, are almost exclusively animists, although influenced by Buddhism to some extent. About 2% of the population are Christians, with about 100,000 Protestants and 45,000 Roman Catholics. Most Protestants are members of the Lao Evangelical Church or Seventh-Day Adventists, which are the only two officially recognized Protestant groups. Christian groups not recognized by the government include Methodists, Jehovah's Witnesses, members of the Church of Christ and Assemblies of God, Lutherans, Mormons (The Church of Jesus Christ of Latter-Day Saints), and Baptists. Other minority religions include the Baha'i faith, Islam, Mahayana Buddhism, Taoism, and Confucianism.

Buddhist monasteries, found in every village, town, and city, serve as intellectual as well as religious centers. Vientiane and Luang Prabang have been called the cities of thousands of temples. More than 70 pagodas were built in Vientiane alone in the 16th century, including the famous Wat Phra Keo and That Luang. In addition to the major role that Buddhism, its temples, and its monks have played in Laotian life, the average lowland Lao regulates a large part of daily activities in accordance with animistic concepts. Certain spirits (*phi*) are believed to have great power over human destiny and to be present throughout the material world, as well as within nonmaterial realms. Thus, each of the four universal elements (earth, sky, fire, and water) has its special phi; every road, stream, village, house, and person has a particular phi; and forests and jungles are inhabited by phi. Evil phi can cause disease and must be propitiated by sacrifices.

Freedom of religion has been legally guaranteed since the constitution of 1991. However, the government reserves the right to serve as the final arbiter of permissible religious activities, which the government loosely defines as those practices that serve to promote national interests. Although there is no official state religion, Theravada Buddhism enjoys an elevated status due to its historic and cultural significance. Religious affairs are overseen by the Lao Front for National Construction (LFNC), an organization of the Lao People's Revolutionary Party. The government recognizes four religions—Buddhism, Christianity, Islam, and the Baha'i faith—but not all groups or denominations within these faiths are recognized. Lao citizens are allowed to proselytize, but foreigners are not. The That Luang Festival and the Lao (Buddhist) New Year are observed as national holidays.

11 TRANSPORTATION

Most of the roads in Laos were damaged by US bombing in the Vietnam War, but the main links with Vietnam (notably Highway 9, from Savannakhét to the Vietnamese port of Da Nang, and Highways 7 and 13, from Vientiane and Savannakhét to the Vietnamese port of Vinh and Ho Chi Minh City, respectively) were rebuilt with Vietnamese aid. Under the 1981–85 economic plan, 844 km (524 mi) of roads were built or improved. The CIA reported that as of 2009 Lao People's Democratic Republic had a total of 39,568 km (24,586 mi) of roads, the majority of which are unpaved.

Laos has approximately 4,600 km (2,858 mi) of navigable waterways. Landlocked, Laos's only water transport link with the outside world is via the Mekong, which forms a large part of the border with Thailand and flows through Cambodia and Vietnam into the South China Sea. The Mekong is navigable for small transport craft and, with its tributaries in Laos, forms an inland waterway system, although rapids make necessary the transshipment of cargo. However, another 2,897 km (1,802 mi) are navigable by small

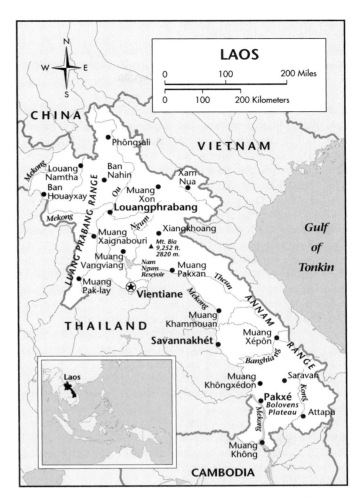

LOCATION: 100° to 107°E; 13°40′ to 22°40′N. BOUNDARY LENGTHS: China, 425 kilometers (264 miles); Vietnam, 1,555 kilometers (966 miles); Cambodia, 541 kilometers (336 miles); Thailand, 1,754 kilometers (1,090 miles); Myanmar, 238 kilometers (148 miles).

craft that draw under 0.5 m (1.6 ft). Upstream dams on China's section of the Mekong have been blamed for flooding and damage to fisheries in Laos, and China's dredging of the river and blasting away rapids for cargo navigation has been opposed by Laotian farmers and fishing people.

In March 2009 the nation's first international rail link was opened, a short track over the Thai-Lao Friendship Bridge to the new Thanaleng terminal, funded primarily by the Thai government as a segment of the Trans-Asian Railway. Proposed rail links to China and Vietnam were not yet under construction as of late 2011.

There were 41 airports (only 9 with paved runways), which in total transported 302,596 passengers in 2009 according to the World Bank. The national airline is Lao Airline and the international airport is Vientiane's Wattay International, with flights to Vietnam, Cambodia, Thailand, China, and Malaysia.

12 HISTORY

Although archaeological evidence indicates that settlers along the Mekong had learned agriculture, metallurgy, and pottery making by 3000 BC, little is known about the early history of the land that today bears the name of Laos. The lowland Lao are believed to be the descendants of Thai tribes that were pushed southward in the 8th century. According to tradition, the kingdom called Lan Xang ("a million elephants") was established in 756 by King Thao Khoun Lo. In 1353 it was reunified by Fa-Ngoum, who had been raised at the court of Angkor in Cambodia and returned with a force of Khmer troops. He is also credited with the introduction of Buddhism into Laos. Lan Xang waged intermittent wars with the Khmers, Burmese, Vietnamese, and Thai, and developed an effective administrative system, an elaborate military organization, and an active commerce with neighboring countries. In 1707 internal dissensions brought about a split of Lan Xang into two kingdoms, Luang Phrabang in the north (present-day upper Laos) and Vientiane in the south (lower Laos). Strong neighboring states took advantage of this split to invade the region. Vientiane was overrun and annexed by Siam (Thailand) in 1828, while Luang Phrabang became a vassal of both the Chinese and the Vietnamese. In 1893 France, which had already established a protectorate over what is now central and northern Vietnam, extended its control to both Vientiane and Luang Phrabang, and Laos was ruled by France as part of Indochina.

During World War II (1939–45) Laos was occupied by Japan. After the Japanese proclaimed on 10 March 1945 that the colonial status of Indochina had ended, the king of Luang Phrabang, Sisavang Vong, was compelled to issue a declaration of independence. The nationalist Free Lao (Lao Issarak) movement deposed the monarch soon after, but French forces reoccupied Laos, and on 27 August 1946 France concluded an agreement establishing him as king of Laos and reimposing French domination over the country. In May 1947 the king established a constitution providing for a democratic government. On 19 July 1949 Laos nominally became an independent sovereign state within the French Union. Additional conventions transferring full sovereignty to Laos were signed on 6 February 1950 and on 22 October 1953. All special economic ties with France and the other Indochinese states were abolished by the Paris pacts of 29 December 1954. In the meantime, Vietnamese Communist (Vietminh) forces had invaded Laos in the spring of 1953. A Laotian Communist movement, the Pathet Lao (Lao State), created on 13 August 1950 and led by Prince Souphanouvong, collaborated with the Vietminh during its Laotian offensive. Under the Geneva cease-fire of 21 July 1954 all Vietminh and most French troops were to withdraw, and the Pathet Lao was to pull back to two northern provinces, pending reunification talks with the national government under the leadership of Souvanna Phouma (Souphanouvong's half-brother). The negotiations were completed on 2 November 1957, and the Pathet Lao transformed itself into a legal political party called the National Political Front (Neo Lao Hak Xat). However, a political swing to the right that led to the ouster of Souvanna Phouma as prime minister, coupled with the refusal of the Pathet Lao forces to integrate into the Royal Lao Army, led to a renewal of fighting in May 1959.

A bloodless right-wing coup in January 1960 was answered in August by a coup led by paratroops under the command of Capt. Kong Le; in the ensuing turmoil, Souvanna Phouma returned to power. After a three-day artillery battle that destroyed much of Vientiane, right-wing military elements under Gen. Phoumi Nosavan and Prince Boun Oum occupied the capital on

11 December. A new right-wing government under Prince Boun Oum was established, but further military reverses, despite a heavy influx of US aid and advisers, caused the government to ask for a cease-fire in May 1961. An international conference assembled in Geneva to guarantee the cease-fire. All three Laotian political factions agreed on 11 June 1962 to accept a coalition government, with Souvanna Phouma as prime minister. On 23 July the powers assembled at Geneva signed an agreement on the independence and neutrality of Laos, which provided for the evacuation of all foreign forces by 7 October. The United States announced full compliance, under supervision of the International Control Commission (ICC) set up in 1954. Communist forces were not withdrawn. Fighting resumed in the spring of 1963, and Laos was steadily drawn into the role of a main theater in the escalating Vietnam War.

The Laotian segment of the so-called Ho Chi Minh Trail emerged as a vital route for troops and supplies moving south from the Democratic Republic of Vietnam (DRV), also known as North Vietnam, and was the target for heavy and persistent US bombing raids. While the Vientiane government was heavily bolstered by US military and economic support, the Pathet Lao received key support from the DRV, which was reported to have 20,000 troops stationed in Laos by 1974. Efforts to negotiate a settlement in Laos resumed with US backing in 1971, but a settlement was not concluded until February 1973, a month after a Vietnam peace agreement was signed in Paris. On 5 April 1974 a new coalition government was set up with equal representation for Pathet Lao and non-Communist elements. Souvanna Phouma, 73 years old and in failing health, stayed on as prime minister, while Prince Souphanouvong was brought closer to the center of political authority as head of the newly created Joint National Political Council.

The Pathet Lao had by this time asserted its control over three-fourths of the national territory. Following the fall of the US-backed regimes in Vietnam and Cambodia in April 1975, the Laotian Communists embarked on a campaign to achieve complete military and political supremacy in Laos. On 23 August Vientiane was declared liberated by the Pathet Lao, whose effective control of Laos was thereby secured. On 2 December 1975 the Lao People's Democratic Republic (LPDR) was established, with Prince Souphanouvong as president and Kaysone Phomvihan as prime minister. King Savang Vatthana abdicated his throne, ending the monarchy that had survived in Laos for 622 years. Elections for a new national assembly were called for April 1976; however, voting was put off indefinitely, amid reports of civil unrest and sabotage. A Supreme People's Assembly was convened, meanwhile, with Prince Souphanouvong as chairman, and was charged with the task of drafting a new constitution.

During the late 1970s the Communists moved to consolidate their control and socialize the economy. Private trade was banned, factories were nationalized, and forcible collectivization of agriculture was initiated. Reeducation camps for an estimated 40,000 former royalists and military leaders were established in remote areas. A 25-year friendship treaty with Vietnam, signed in July 1977, led to closer relations with that country (already signaled by the continued presence in Laos of Vietnamese troops) and with the former USSR, and also to the subsequent dismissal from Laos of all Chinese technicians and advisers. China, for its part, began to give support and training to several small antigovernment guerrilla groups. With the economy in 1979 near collapse, in part because of severe drought in 1977 and flooding in 1978, the Laotian government slowed the process of socialization and announced a return to private enterprise and a readiness to accept aid from the non-Communist world. Throughout the 1980s armed opposition to the government persisted, particularly from the Hmong hill tribe rebels. At the fourth party congress of the Lao People's Revolutionary Party (LPRP), in December 1986, a New Economic Mechanism (NEM) was set up, aiming at granting increased autonomy in the management of formerly state-run enterprises to the private sector.

In 1988 the Lao national assembly, the Supreme People's Assembly (SPA), adopted new election laws, and the first elections since the formation of the LPDR in 1975 were held. Local and provincial elections were held in 1988, and on 27 March 1989 national elections took place for an enlarged SPA. In March 1991 the fifth party congress of the LPRP changed Kaysone Phomvihan's title from prime minister to president, elected a new 11-member politburo, pledged to continue economic reforms in line with free-market principles while denying the need for political pluralism, and changed the national motto by substituting the words "democracy and prosperity" for "socialism." The newly elected SPA drafted a constitution adopted on 14 August 1991. The constitution provided for a national assembly functioning on principles of "democratic centralism," established the LPRP as the political system's leading organ, created a presidency with executive powers, and mandated a market-oriented economy with rights of private ownership.

President Kaysone Phomvihan died on 21 November 1992. A special session of the assembly on 24 November 1992 elected hard-line Communist Nouhak Phoumsavan as the next president. Gen. Khamtai Suphandon, who had been prime minister since 15 August 1991, remained in that post. Assembly elections were held in December 1992. One day before these elections, three former officials who called for a multiparty democracy and had been detained in 1990 were sentenced to 14 years imprisonment. The assembly convened in February 1993 and approved government reorganization designed to improve public administration. On 9 January 1995 longtime leader Prince Souphanouvong died, unofficially marking an end to Laos's long dalliance with hard-line Marxism. Although the NEM had initiated an opening up to international investment and improved relations with the rest of the world, there remained elements of the old guard in positions of power. With the death of Souphanouvong, the only old-time hard-line Marxist still in power as of 1996 was the country's president, Nouhak Phoumsavan. Khamtai Siphandon, prime minister and party chief, was more powerful than Nouhak and is largely credited with exerting a moderating influence on the hard-liner. Throughout the 1990s, a strongly conservative mindset among the politburo members pulled the government back from economic flexibility or any hint of political liberalization.

On 26 February 1998 Khamtai Siphandon was elected president. He was reelected in March 2001. A glimpse of popular discontent emerged with reports of an October 1999 demonstration in Vientiane, led by students and professors calling for democracy and human rights. The protest was quickly suppressed, and Khamtai's government disavowed all knowledge of its occurrence.

Beginning in 2000 Vientiane was hit by a series of bomb blasts, attributed to antigovernment groups based abroad. Bombings targeted crowded markets and buses in the city during 2003. Triggered by Thailand's closing of refugee camps on its side of the Laos-Thai border, tens of thousands of exiles were forced to return home. Most were expected to be jailed or executed for their antigovernment activities, but instead, the government encouraged their settlement among the lowland population. Certain right-wing guerrilla factions among the Hmong, long fighting the Pathet Lao, subsequently reacted violently to the government's pacification efforts to integrate moderate Hmong villagers. On 6 February 2003, near Vang Vieng, a bus and two Western bicyclers were attacked by gunmen, who killed 12 people. Militant Hmong were blamed for the attack. The government launched a major military crackdown on Hmong insurgents during 2004. In 2005 former Hmong guerrilla General Vang Pao was accused in US court, along with other Hmong and American supporters, of conspiring to overthrow the government of Laos. The charges were dropped in September 2009, and Vang Pao died in January 2011 in California.

Laos held celebrations of the 30th year of Communist rule on 23 August 2005. In 2009 several people who had been involved in the 1999 student protest were arrested, apparently to prevent a ten-years-later demonstration from being staged in Vientiane.

13 GOVERNMENT

With the establishment of the Lao People's Democratic Republic in December 1975, governmental authority passed to a national congress made up of 264 delegates elected by newly appointed local authorities. The congress in turn appointed a 45-member Supreme People's Assembly (SPA). The SPA adopted new election laws in 1988, and the first national elections under the new government took place in March 1989 (local elections were held in 1988). The newly elected SPA set out to draft a constitution, which was finished in mid-1990, and adopted on 14 August 1991. The SPA was then renamed as the Lao National Assembly.

Pursuant to the 1991 constitution (amended in 2003), the executive branch consists of the president, prime minister and two deputy prime ministers, and a council of ministers (cabinet) appointed by the president with the approval of the assembly. As of 2011 the legislative branch consists of the 132-member assembly, which is elected by popular vote through universal suffrage for a period of five years. All candidates for the assembly are selected by the Lao People's Revolutionary Party.

The constitution calls for a strong legislature, but most political power continues to rest with the party-dominated council of ministers, which is much aligned with the military. From 2006 to 2011 the assembly seemingly began to assert more power, acting in oversight of the executive branch, taking a stance on government land acquisition and participating in forcing the resignation of Prime Minister Bouasone. Analysts believe that there is some tension between pro-China and pro-Vietnam factions within the government.

14 POLITICAL PARTIES

The formation of the Lao People's Democratic Republic in December 1975 effectively established the Communist Lao People's Revolutionary Party (LPRP), the 1955 political incarnation of the

Pathet Lao movement, as the sole political force in Laos. Kaysone Phomvihan, general secretary of the LPRP, was named head of government, and Prince Souphanouvong head of state. The LPRP plays the leading role in the Lao Front for National Reconstruction, which seeks to promote socialism and national solidarity.

The first two party congresses were held in 1955 (to establish the organization as the Lao's People's Party) and in 1972 (when the name was changed to the Lao People's Revolutionary Party). The third party congress of the LPRP, and the first since the party assumed control, was held in Vientiane in April 1982. The congress, whose 228 delegates represented a party membership of 35,000, elected an enlarged central committee with 49 full and 6 alternate members. The central committee reelected Kaysone as general secretary. The fourth party congress, held in Vientiane in December 1986, established the New Economic Mechanism.

In 1988 the Supreme People's Assembly (SPA) adopted new elections laws and elections were held the next year–the first since 1975. The name of the assembly was changed to the Lao National Assembly. In 1991 the fifth party congress changed Prime Minister Phomvihan's title to president, a post he held until his death one year later. Elevated to the post of prime minister was Khamtai Suphandon, a generally pro-free market, antidemocratic pragmatist. Suphandon had for a time studied Marxism in Hanoi, but in his position as prime minister was considered essentially a transitional figure between the old guard and a new generation of leaders. After Phomvihan's death in 1992, a special session of the assembly elected an old-guard communist, Nouhak Phoumsavan, to the presidency.

Elections for the assembly were again held in 1992, but they were marred by the sentencing of three pro-democracy activists to 14 years in prison on the day before balloting. By 1996 Laos's leadership was made up primarily of party functionaries, regardless of the makeup of the assembly. A 1998 election retrenched the hard-liners, as "technocrats" vanished from the pre-approved slate, replaced with old style LPRP functionaries. This was viewed as a reaction to the social tensions (such as crime and corruption) arising with economic openness, as well as an attempt to reestablish centralized control over provincial matters.

The seventh party congress, which took place in March 2001, reelected all eight surviving members of the nine-member politburo. The decision was a clear sign that the party had opted for continuity rather than change. The eighth party congress, March 2006, kept seven of the same aging members in charge and added the first female, Pany Yathotou. In June 2006 the politburo named Choummaly Sayasone president and Bouasone Bouphavanh prime minister.

Choummaly was kept as president by the ninth party congress in March 2011. Bouasone stepped down for "family reasons," apparently forced out by the assembly. He was replaced as prime minister by Thonsging Thammavong, the former assembly leader. Thonsging had instituted a public access hotline, which reportedly inspired the assembly to raise policy issues in response to citizens' complaints.

While not all members of the assembly are members of the LPRP, only candidates approved by the LPRP are permitted to run in legislative elections. In the 2002 all but one of the 166 candidates were from the LPRP. The LPRP won 108 of the 109 seats in that year's assembly. Elections were again held in 2006, with only two independent candidates for 115 seats. For the April 2011 elections, the assembly was expanded to 132 seats. Only four independent candidates won seats.

Several governments-in-exile have been set up by former ministers of pre-1975 regimes, and overseas Hmongs and other dissidents have formed opposition organizations. A young pretender to the throne, Prince Soulivong Savang, has rallied some support in exile. Hmong groups and others continued a very low-level insurgency in rural Laos.

15 LOCAL GOVERNMENT

As of 2011 the administrative divisions of Laos consisted of 16 provinces (*khoueng*) and the municipality of Vientiane. The provinces are subdivided into districts (*muong*), townships (*tasseng*), and villages (*ban*). Since 1975 local administration has been restructured, with elected people's committees in the villages functioning as basic units. Both suffrage and candidacy are open to citizens 18 and over. The president appoints provincial governors and mayors of municipalities. The prime minister appoints deputy provincial governors and deputy mayors and district chiefs.

16 JUDICIAL SYSTEM

The People's Supreme Court is the highest in the judicial system. The president of this court is elected by the assembly and judges are appointed by a standing committee of the assembly. All judges are members of the LPRP. There are provincial and municipal courts, district courts, and military courts. The law allows for open trials and defendants are said to be presumed innocent. However, some reports indicate that in practice some judges will decide the guilt or innocence of a defendant in advance, based on police reports. Litigants may acquire legal representation from members of the nominally independent Lao Bar Association, but many choose not to have such representation, in part due to the fact that attorneys cannot affect the decisions of the court.

17 ARMED FORCES

The International Institute for Strategic Studies reports that armed forces in Lao People's Democratic Republic totaled 29,100 members in 2011. The force is comprised of 25,600 from the army and 3,500 members of the air force. Although Laos did not have a formal navy, the army did have an estimated 600-man marine section that operated 4 amphibious landing craft and 52 patrol/coastal boats. Laotian paramilitary forces consisted of a village home guard known as the Militia Self-Defense Forces, which numbered more than 100,000 members. Armed forces represent 4.2% of the labor force in Laos. Defense spending totaled $79.4 million and accounted for 0.5% of the gross domestic product (GDP).

18 INTERNATIONAL COOPERATION

Laos has actively improved its already "special relations" with Vietnam and Cambodia, while seeking to improve relations with Thailand, the People's Republic of China (PRC), and the United States. Laos and the PRC restored full diplomatic relations in 1989 and are now full-fledged trading partners. The government of Laos has attempted to balance the diplomatic and economic influence of China with that of Vietnam, and apparently has internal pro-China and pro-Vietnam factions. There is reportedly some feeling among the citizens that China's influence over Laos has gone too far.

Since 1961 Laos has been a member of the Nonaligned Movement. Laos's main diplomatic, economic, and military allies have been Vietnam and the former USSR. In 1977 Laos signed a 20-year treaty of cooperation with Vietnam. Territorial clashes between Laos and Thailand in 1987–88 caused hundreds of casualties. Mutual suspicions, characterizing the relationship between Laos and Thailand, improved with agreements to withdraw troops and resolve border disputes, and agreements between the UN High Commissioner for Refugees (UNHCR) to repatriate or resettle nearly 60,000 Lao refugees in Thailand. In 2003 Laos and Thailand signed a cooperation agreement that addresses issues of labor and counternarcotics. Laos has cooperated with the United States in recovering the remains of US soldiers missing in action in Laos since the Vietnam War and in efforts to suppress drug trafficking.

Laos, a UN member since 14 December 1955, belongs to (the Economic and Social Commission for Asia and the Pacific (ESCAP) and several non-regional specialized agencies, such as FAO, UNESCO, UNIDO, ILO, WHO, IMF, and the World Bank. The nation participates in the Asian Development Bank, the Colombo Plan, and G-77. It has observer status with the WTO and is expected to become a member in 2012. The Mekong River Commission (MRC) was founded in 1995 by Thailand, Cambodia, Laos, and Vietnam to coordinate development in the region. In 1997 Laos joined the Association of South East Asian Nations (ASEAN).

In environmental cooperation, Laos is part of the Convention on Biological Diversity, the Kyoto Protocol, the Montréal Protocol, the Nuclear Test Ban Treaty, and the UN Conventions on the Law of the Sea, Climate Change, and Desertification. Laos is also a member of the Mekong River Commission with Cambodia, Thailand, and Vietnam.

¹⁹ECONOMY

Poorly developed infrastructure and government corruption are serious obstacles to economic development. Mostly subsistence agriculture accounts for about 29.2% of the economy. Primary crops include rice, sweet potatoes, coffee, sugarcane, tobacco, and cotton. Industry focuses on mining, with copper, gold, tin, and gypsum the primary products. The country relies heavily on foreign aid and foreign investment, which has been generally directed toward development in mining, hydropower, and construction. Because industrialization is minimal, Laos imports nearly all the manufactured products it requires.

The hostilities of the 1960s and 1970s badly disrupted the economy, forcing the country to depend on imports from Thailand to supplement its daily rice requirements. During 1978–80, the government gave priority to postwar reconstruction, collectivization of agriculture, and improvements in rice production. In 1994 a liberalized Foreign Investment Law was passed as the government sought greater economic integration regionally and internationally.

By 1997 Laos had made modest improvements. In international investment, it had opened up its economy considerably. In April 1997 the government signed a trade and cooperation agreement with the European Community, and in July of that year Laos became a full member of ASEAN and AFTA. However, the Asian financial crisis of 1997–98 dealt the economy a series of blows. Laos's economy was particularly dependent on Thailand, the source of 42% of its foreign investment, 45% of imports, and 37% of export purchases, all of which was severely affected by the crisis. Growth increased in 1999, propelled by both industry and agriculture, and continued at moderate rates in 2000 and 2001. However, high inflation and declining foreign investments persisted. In the mid-2000s the growth rate increased, but inflation still posed a problem, along with corruption, lack of transparency, inconsistent regulation, and official impunity.

In late 2004 Laos gained Normal Trade Relations status with the United States, which allowed local producers to export at lower tariffs. Since then the nation has taken steps toward reforms that would align economic policy with the necessary standards to achieve membership in the World Trade Organization (WTO) in 2012.

The GDP rate of change in Lao People's Democratic Republic, as of 2010, was 7.7%. Inflation stood at 6%, and unemployment was reported at 2.5%.

²⁰INCOME

According to the CIA, in 2010 the GDP of Laos was $15.69 billion. The CIA defines GDP as the value of all final goods and services produced within a nation in a given year and computed on the basis of purchasing power parity (PPP) rather than value as measured on the basis of the rate of the exchange based on current dollars. The per capita GDP was estimated at $2,500. The annual growth rate of GDP was 7.7%. The average inflation rate was 6%. It was estimated that agriculture accounted for 29.2% of GDP, industry 32.4%, and services 30.3%.

The World Bank estimated that in 2010 Laos, with 0.09% of the world's population, accounted for 0.02% of the world's GDP. By comparison, the United States, with 4.85% of the world's population, accounted for 22.51% of world GDP.

According to the World Bank, remittances from citizens living abroad totaled $37.6 million or about $6 per capita and accounted for approximately 0.2% of GDP. It was estimated that household consumption was growing at an average annual rate of 3.3%. As of 2011 the World Bank reported that actual individual consumption in Laos was 62.9% of GDP and accounted for 0.02% of world consumption. By comparison, the United States accounted for 25.44% of world individual consumption. The World Bank estimated that 33.3% of Laos's GDP was spent on food and beverages, 9.6% on housing and household furnishings, 1.1% on clothes, 1.9% on health, 6.6% on transportation, 0.3% on communications, 1.9% on recreation, 1.9% on restaurants and hotels, and 2% on miscellaneous goods and services and purchases from abroad.

In 2010 the CIA estimated that 26% of the population subsisted on an income below the poverty line established by the government of Laos.

²¹LABOR

As of 2010 Laos had a total labor force of 3.69 million people. Within that labor force, the CIA estimated in 2010 that 75.1% were employed in agriculture.

Labor is organized into a single Federation of Lao Trade Unions (FLTU), which is controlled by the Lao People's Revolutionary

Party. Most of the 155,000 members of the FLTU (as of 2010) were in the public sector. There is no right to organize, strike, or bargain collectively. Labor disputes have been infrequent and the workers have little bargaining power.

Children under the age of 15 are forbidden by law from working, but many children work for their families in farms or in shops due to economic hardship. As of 2009 the daily minimum wage for private sector workers was about $1.60. Employers were also required to pay a $1 per day meal allowance. The minimum wage for civil servants and state enterprise employees was set at about $47.80 per month in 2008. Civil servants receive additional benefits as well. The labor code limits the workweek to 48 hours with at least one day of rest per week.

22 AGRICULTURE

According to the World Bank, as of 2008 about 9.6% of the total land was being farmed. According to the UN FAO, in 2009 cereal production amounted to 4 million tons, fruit production 259,008 tons, and vegetable production 1 million tons.

The main crop is rice, particularly the glutinous variety. Except in northern Laos, where farmers grow dry rice in forest clearings or on hillsides, most Laotians are wet-rice farmers. Yields, which are relatively low, could be raised substantially through wider use of irrigation and fertilizers. Production, which averaged 609,000 tons annually during 1961–65, rose to 2,529,000 tons in 2004. Typhoon Ketsana in 2009 and a drought/flood cycle in 2010 led to severe rice crop losses. According to the UN FAO, rice production for the harvest season of 2010/2011, at about 3 million tons, was about 6% lower than the previous year, necessitating 38,000 metric tons of imported rice.

Less important crops include corn, favored by some upland people and stressed by the government as a means of increasing livestock production. The main commercial crops, emphasized by the government as part of its export drive, are coffee, cotton, and tobacco. Also grown are cardamom, tea, ramie, hemp, sugar, bananas, and pineapples. In the 21st century, companies from China began establishing large-scale rubber plantations in northern Laos.

The mountain peoples traditionally have grown large quantities of poppies for opium, sold to dealers from the plains and often refined into heroin. Alternative income programs had decreased opium cultivation to its lowest recorded level in 2007, but opium cultivation came back strongly, reaching 3,000 hectares (7,413 acres) in 2010, 58% more than the previous year, according to the UN Office on Drugs and Crime.

23 ANIMAL HUSBANDRY

The UN FAO reported that Laos dedicated 878,000 hectares (2.17 million acres) to permanent pasture or meadow in 2009. During that year, the country tended 22.5 million chickens, 1.4 million head of cattle, and 2.9 million pigs. The production from these animals amounted to 42,231 tons of beef and veal, 46,000 tons of pork, 20,307 tons of poultry, 11,467 tons of eggs, and 28,223 tons of milk. Laos also produced 2,316 tons of cattle hide. Cattle raising is important, especially in the southern plains and in the valleys of the Noy, Banghiang, and Don rivers. Water buffalo are used for rice field plowing.

24 FISHING

Freshwater fish, found in the Mekong and other rivers, constitute the main source of protein in the Laotian diet. The prize catch is the Mekong giant catfish, weighing 205 kg (450 lb) or more. Proposed dams on the Mekong threaten spawning grounds for this and three more of the world's largest freshwater fish species. Fish are also farmed in ponds. In 2008 the annual capture totaled 26,925 tons, according to the UN FAO.

25 FORESTRY

Approximately 68% of Lao People's Democratic Republic is covered by forest. The UN FAO estimated the 2009 roundwood production at 217,749 cu m (7.69 million cu ft). The value of all forest products, including roundwood, totaled $96.6 million.

Laos traditionally relied on forests for timber including teak, ironwood, rosewood, and mahogany, with elephants used for moving logs. Aside from timber, firewood, and charcoal, forestry products include bamboo, copra, kapok, rattan, and resins. Agricultural encroachment and excessive logging have decreased forest cover not only in accessible central and southern areas, but in northern hill country as well. In 1999, in an attempt to halt massive deforestation, the government banned export of raw logs. In July 2011 the Environmental Investigation Agency (London) reported that enormous amounts of timber from Laos were being illegally cut and trafficked to Vietnam by bribery of Lao officials.

26 MINING

Laos's mining sector is dominated by tin, gypsum, gold, and limestone. However, mining is the country's smallest, sector, contributing less than 1% to GDP. Although much of the country remained unprospected, the nature of the terrain has led to ardent speculation about the nation's mineral resources. Other mineral resources thought to possibly exist in Laos were magnesium, antimony, bismuth, copper, lead, manganese, potash, iron ore, silica sand, and tungsten. Also produced in 2009 were barite, cement, gemstones, rock salt, silver, bituminous coal, and zinc. Copper, gemstones, gold, iron ore, lead, potash, tin, and zinc were earmarked for further exploration. Undiscovered resources of iron ore, potash, and rock salt were believed to be substantial.

Tin mine output in 2009 was estimated at 350 metric tons, down from 690 metric tons in 2008. Gypsum production, by the State Gypsum Mining Operation from the Dong Hene Mine, in Savannakhét Province, was estimated at 775,000 metric tons for 2009, unchanged since 2006. The mine's proven ore reserves were estimated to be 18 million tons. Three other gypsum mines operate in Savannakhét and Khammouane provinces. Although gold production ceased in 1998–2002, it was resumed in 2003, with 5,033 kg produced in 2009. Important iron deposits, with reserves of 68% ore estimated at 11 billion tons, have been discovered on the Plain of Jars near Xiangkhoang. A substantial deposit of low-grade anthracite coal has been found at Saravan. Output of gemstones in 2009 was estimated at 1,200,000 carats, unchanged since 2006. Tungsten and copper deposits and gold-bearing alluvials produced a limited income for the local population but have not been exploited by modern industrial methods. Increases in the production of potash are expected in the next few years as new mines and plants completed construction in 2010 and 2011.

27 ENERGY AND POWER

As of 2010, according to the CIA, Laos produced 1.55 billion kWh of electricity and consumed 2.23 billion kWh. Exports of electricity were estimates at 341 million kWh. Laos produces no petroleum. In 2010 oil imports were estimated at about 1,918 barrels per day and oil consumption was estimated at 3,000 barrels per day.

Many rural areas still do not have electricity. The government of Laos has planned 70 hydropower dam projects for domestic and export energy. These have been very controversial for their potential environmental effects, with the Xayaburi dam on the Mekong indefinitely postponed because of concerns about its threats to fishing stocks and Vietnam's agricultural Mekong delta. Multinational lenders and neighboring countries have continued to finance the giant dam projects, including the World Bank funded Nam Theun 2 dam, which could generate power for Thailand and is projected to earn Laos $2 billion over a quarter of a century.

28 INDUSTRY

Industrial development has been slow to reach Laos. Industry includes mining operations, charcoal ovens, cement and brick manufacture, tobacco processing, breweries, coffee and tea processing, rice mills, sawmills, furniture factories, and garment manufacturing. Newer resource developments include hydroelectric projects and the Vientiane sylvite field.

As of 2010 as many as 100 garment factories were operating in Laos, comprising the second biggest export sector after electric power. Garment manufacturers from Laos compete for orders on the basis of low wages, but are affected by labor shortages and chronic inflation. Handicrafts account for an important part of the income of many Laotians. Some villages or areas specialize in certain types of products, such as silk weaving, baskets, lacquerware, or jewelry. Bricks, pottery, iron products, and distilled beverages are made in individual villages.

From 1998 to 2001 industry grew at an average annual rate of 8.7%. The growth was in large part attributable to government-sponsored construction projects, particularly hydroelectric power projects. By 2002 hydroelectric power had taken the place of garments as the country's leading industrial export, and its leading source of foreign exchange. In 2005 industry accounted for 25.9% of economic output and services had a 25.5% share, while agriculture was the main economic sector, with a 48.6% share in the GDP. The industrial production growth rate was 13% in 2005, almost double the GDP growth rate-an indicator that industry had become one of the country's main economic engines. According to the CIA, in 2010 industry accounted for 32.4% of GDP. The 2010 industrial growth rate was an extremely high 17.7%, the sixth-highest in the world, as Laos experienced its own industrial revolution, moving from a rice subsistence economy towards an economy based on export of electric power, minerals and garments, along with important construction and tourism sectors.

29 SCIENCE AND TECHNOLOGY

The World Bank reported in 2009 that there were no patent applications in science and technology in Laos. Laos continues to depend on external expertise in science and technology. Research centers include the National Agriculture and Forestry Institute, the Research Institute of Science, and the Institute of Research for Development. A National Science Council was founded in 2002 to promote research. The National University of Laos, founded in 1996, has departments of sciences, forestry, medicine, agriculture, engineering, and environmental studies.

30 DOMESTIC TRADE

In the countryside of Laos, barter has often been the principal method of exchange. Items historically used as media of exchange have included tea, opium, tobacco, salt, silver, and gold. Markets are held at regular intervals, generally one day a week, at central villages or smaller towns.

Before the Pathet Lao came to power, there was a growing market in Laos for capital and consumer goods. Vientiane was the wholesale distributing point for much of the country. In late 1975 private trade was banned and many small traders and businesspeople—including Chinese, Japanese, Pakistani, Thai, and Vietnamese—fled the country. The new government subsequently made it clear that the trend toward consumerism would be reversed in favor of a production-oriented society. The Pathet Lao entered directly into the distribution and sale of essential commodities, such as rice and sugar, and prices were brought under control. In 1979, however, the ban on private trade was lifted.

The New Economic Mechanism (NEM), a set of economic reforms, was instituted in 1986 across all sectors of the economy. The government freed the market price of rice and other food staples in 1986. Later reforms—floating the national currency, the kip, and freeing interest rates—stimulated a market-based economy. Major land reforms in 1988 included the freedom to sell products at market-determined prices. Inflation has been a chronic problem for consumers in Laos, with a rate of 5.7% in 2010, according to the CIA. Manufactured consumer goods are largely imported from Thailand and China, and are usually paid for in Thai baht or US dollars.

The usual hours of business are from 8 a.m. to 4 p.m., Monday through Friday. Some factories and private companies extend the workday to 5 p.m. and factories are permitted to maintain a six-day workweek. Banking hours are 8:30 a.m. to 3:30 p.m., Monday through Friday.

31 FOREIGN TRADE

In 1991 Laos's largest export earner, logging, was banned pending steps to prevent further destruction of the forests. The ban on log exports was later modified to allow the export of already cut logs and logs from stipulated cutting areas, and large scale illegal timber smuggling to Vietnam and other neighbors has continued. The export of electricity and minerals (including tin, copper, gold), and the sale of garments, wood products and coffee have been sources of foreign earnings.

In 2010 imports totaled an estimated $1.75 billion and exports totaled $1.95 billion. Major import partners in 2010, according to the CIA, were Thailand, 65.6%; China, 14.6%; and Vietnam, 6.6%. Major export partners were Thailand, 31.1%; China, 23%; Vietnam, 12.9%. Exports were estimated at $1.95 billion and imports at $1.753 billion.

Laos became a member of ASEAN in 1997. In a boost for trade, the ASEAN Trade in Goods Agreement (ATIGA) entered into force on 17 May 2010. The ATIGA represented the next step in

Principal Trading Partners – Laos (2010)

(In millions of US dollars)

Country	Total	Exports	Imports	Balance
World	3,806.8	1,746.4	2,060.4	-314.0
Thailand	3,038.1	689.7	2,348.4	-1,658.7
China	1,035.0	510.9	524.1	-13.2
Vietnam	483.5	265.2	218.3	46.9
South Korea	141.7	18.2	123.5	-105.3
Japan	102.4	34.2	68.3	-34.1
United Kingdom	75.4	69.9	5.6	64.3
Germany	74.7	53.4	21.4	32.0
United States	69.6	56.3	13.3	43.0
Belgium	37.5	17.1	20.4	-3.4
Hong Kong	33.2	3.1	30.0	-26.9

(…) data not available or not significant.

(n.s.) not specified.

SOURCE: *2011 Direction of Trade Statistics Yearbook*, New York: United Nations, 2011.

realizing the free flow of goods within the region by simplifying the processes and procedures necessary to create a single market and production base—known as the ASEAN Economic Community (AEC)—by 2015. Major points of ATIGA include tariff liberalization, a simplification of the rules of origin, and implementation of such rules. The comprehensive agreement also demands greater transparency in regional trade liberalization, aiding the work of businesses and investors. The ATIGA supersedes the Common Effective Preferential Tariff Scheme (CEPT) adopted in 1992. Laos is also expected to become a full member of the ASEAN-China free trade area by 2015. This new trade agreement went into force 1 January 2010 between the founding members of ASEAN and China. A major point of the free trade agreement is the elimination of tariffs on nearly 90% of imported goods. In 2004 Laos achieved Normal Trade Relations status with the United States.

Laos expected to join the WTO in 2012.

32 BALANCE OF PAYMENTS

Laos has experienced severe trade deficits since independence. In June 1975 the flight of gold and hard currencies from the country forced the government to ban exports of gold and silver bullion. In the 1980s financing came mainly from the former USSR, with smaller amounts from multilateral agencies, but with the collapse of communism in Europe, Laos lost this means of support. Even with its attraction of international investment in mining, hydropower, construction and garment manufacturing, Laos still relies heavily on foreign aid. Sources include multinational lenders such as the IMF, and other countries, including the United States and Japan. According to the CIA, in fiscal year 2009/2010 the government of Laos received $586 million in foreign aid. In 2010, according to the CIA, Laos had a foreign trade deficit of $195 million, with exports of $1.95 billion and imports of $1.75 billion; reserves of foreign exchange and gold were an estimated $806.1 million as of December 2010.

33 BANKING AND SECURITIES

The large-scale flight of foreign currency that accompanied the Pathet Lao's ascendancy to power led the new government to shut

down Vientiane's banks in September 1975. Officials subsequently announced the expropriation of most private accounts, claiming they were the property of former rightists and "traitors." Until 1988 the wholly state-controlled system serviced the needs of the command economy, offering uncompetitive rates of interest to savers or producers in need of regular credit. Laotians continued to save by investing in gold and jewelry. Banking reforms of the 1988–89 period opened Laos to foreign banks. The system suffered severe liquidity problems in 1990–91 when the "privatization" of former state-owned enterprises was at its peak: old debts were not repaid and new capital arriving as a result of the opening of the economy to foreign investors was coming in too slowly. Laos was badly hit in 1997 by the Asian financial crisis, leading to further liquidity problems in 1998.

All banks now provide basic business services and offer a range of deposit and credit facilities. Interest rates are increasingly responsive to market conditions but tend to remain close to rates set by the central bank. Public confidence in the banking system as measured by the level of domestic capital mobilization is still low. Corruption has apparently been pervasive in loans made by government-owned commercial banks. Micro-credit loans for farmers and small businesses have recently been introduced. A few banks have ATMs. Credit card use in Laos is very low.

The central bank, the National Bank of Laos, is tightly controlled by the government. It is in charge of the floating rate of the currency. It regulates an expanding sector of national and foreign-owned banks under the terms of the Commercial Bank and Financial Institutions Act of January 1992. Most of the wholly foreign-owned banks are Thai (such as the Thai Military Bank and Siam Commercial), and many of the joint-venture banks are backed by Thai financiers (such as the Joint Development Bank). Banks in Laos include: Banque Pour le Commerce Exterieur Lao, Bank for Agricultural Development, Lao Development Bank, Joint Development Bank, ANZ Laos, and Phongsavan Bank.

Balance of Payments – Laos (2010)

(In millions of US dollars)

Current Account		**29.3**
Balance on goods		-314.0
Imports	-2,060.4	
Exports	1,746.4	
Balance on services		247.9
Balance on income		-83.2
Current transfers		178.6
Capital Account		…
Financial Account		**476.5**
Direct investment abroad	…	
Direct investment in Laos		278.8
Portfolio investment assets	…	
Portfolio investment liabilities	53.8	
Financial derivatives	…	
Other investment assets	-173.9	
Other investment liabilities	317.8	
Net Errors and Omissions		**-403.2**
Reserves and Related Items		**-102.6**

(…) data not available or not significant.

SOURCE: *Balance of Payment Statistics Yearbook 2011*, Washington, DC: International Monetary Fund, 2011.

Public Finance – Laos (2009)

(In billions of kip, budgetary central government figures)

Revenue and Grants	8,173.6	100.0%
Tax revenue	6,336.9	77.5%
Social contributions	...	...
Grants	1,143.2	14.0%
Other revenue	693.5	8.5%
Expenditures	...	...
General public services	...	...
Defense	...	...
Public order and safety	...	...
Economic affairs	...	...
Environmental protection	...	...
Housing and community amenities	...	...
Health	...	...
Recreational, culture, and religion	...	...
Education	...	...
Social protection	...	...

(...) data not available or not significant.

SOURCE: *Government Finance Statistics Yearbook 2010*, Washington, DC: International Monetary Fund, 2010.

The Lao Securities Exchange opened in January 2011, offering shares in two state-owned companies: EDL Generation Public PDL and Banque Pour Le Commerce Exterieur Lao. As of October 2011 they were still the only companies listed.

34 INSURANCE

As of 2010 six insurance companies operated in Laos, including Champa, Tokojaya Lao, Lao-Viet, MSIG, and Assurances Generales du Laos. Although car insurance was compulsory by law, in actuality less than 20% of the population was reported to have insurance of any kind.

35 PUBLIC FINANCE

In 2010, according to the CIA, the budget of Laos included $1.136 billion in public revenue and $1.338 billion in public expenditures. The budget deficit amounted to 3.2% of GDP. In total $4.63 billion of the debt was held by foreign entities.

The civil war rendered normal budgetary procedures impossible, the budget being covered largely by US aid and monetary inflation. Deficit financing continued in the 1970s and 1980s, covered mostly by foreign aid from communist nations. With the collapse of this support, however, Laos has increasingly looked to foreign investment capital and Western lending agencies for financial support. Beginning in 1994 the IMF initiated an annual program of loans to assist the country with a structural adjustment program.

36 TAXATION

In 1977 the government introduced a progressive agricultural tax on production. The tax revenues were to be used to develop forestry and mining without the need for outside aid, but the tax had the unwanted side effect of discouraging production by some of the largest landowners and slowing the achievement of self-sufficiency in food. The 1992–93 budget included a new profits tax and a law requiring foreign firms engaged in construction projects to pay taxes. The agricultural tax was replaced by a land tax, and consumption taxes were raised on fuel oil, liquor, beer, and tobacco.

Pursuant to a 2005 tax law, personal income tax rates were levied in six tiers, ranging from 0% for those earning LAK300,000 ($37.52) or below to a top rate of 25% for those earning LAK15 million ($1,876) or above. The top corporate tax rate is 35%. A value-added tax (VAT) of 5% to 10% was instituted in 2010. The top corporate tax rate is 35%. A VAT of 5% to 10% was instituted in 2010.

37 CUSTOMS AND DUTIES

Import duties are determined on an ad valorem basis and range from 5–40%. The 40% duty applies to items such as alcohol, cigarettes, motorbikes, and motor vehicles. A turnover tax of 3%, 5%, or 10% applies to many goods. Excise taxes are also imposed on items such as alcohol, soft drinks, perfume and cosmetics, and vehicles, to name a few.

The ASEAN Trade in Goods Agreement (ATIGA) entered into force on 17 May 2010. Major points of ATIGA include tariff liberalization, a simplification of the rules of origin, and implementation of such rules. The ATIGA supersedes the Common Effective Preferential Tariff Scheme (CEPT) adopted in 1992. Laos is also expected to become a full member of the ASEAN-China free trade area by 2015.

Laos bans import of weapons, toxic chemicals, hazardous materials, illegal drugs, pornography, and some agricultural products. The export of timber and lumber is restricted by quotas set by the government; Laos bans exports of weapons, antiquities images of Buddha, wildlife, and raw or processed rattan.

38 FOREIGN INVESTMENT

Before 1975 Laotian foreign economic relations were conducted under the FEOF and the US Commodity Import Program, under which dollar exchange was provided; Laos in turn allocated dollars to local importers, who then made kip payments to the government for the purchase of foreign goods. There was little direct foreign investment (FDI), however. From 1975 until the mid-1980s all foreign capital was in the form of development assistance. Reforms, as part of the New Economic Mechanism (NEM) initiated in 1986, included the introduction of the Laos Foreign Investment Code and Decree in 1989, which established the Foreign Investment Management Cabinet (FIMC). The FIMC oversees the Committee for Investment and Foreign Cooperation (CIFC) with power to authorize and approve investment. All investment proposals, no matter how small, must be submitted to the CIFC of the FIMC, which passes it for screening by the relevant line ministries. The Code and Decree focus on three types of transactions: contractual business, joint ventures, and wholly foreign-owned enterprises. Investment was allowed in the areas of agriculture, forestry, industry, communications, transport, services, and tourism, for projects using the indigenous raw materials and natural resources of Laos. The decree detailed the permitted sectors of foreign investment and outlines restrictions and prohibitions.

In 1994 a new foreign investment law streamlined regulations and tax structures. The contractual business mode of foreign investment was eliminated. Although the law stipulated that the pre-approval process for new investment was to take only 60 days, delays in fact have been a year or more.

In 2010 the foreign investment rules were amended with incentives such as discounted taxes, streamlined permission, and land ownership, in an effort to attract more investment outside of the resource extraction sector. The Ministry of Industry and Primary Resources, the Economic Planning Unit, which monitors existing and new businesses, and the Economic Development Board (EDB), which assists in the establishment of new industries, facilitate foreign investment in most sectors of the economy.

Foreign investment in Laos has largely been in hydropower (the dominant sector since 2000), mining, garment manufacturing, agriculture, tourism, and services. FDI in Lao People's Democratic Republic was a net inflow of $318.6 million in 2009, according to World Bank figures. FDI represented 5.36% of GDP.

According to the government of Laos, Vietnam has become the largest foreign investor as of mid-2011, with hydropower and mining projects as well as consumer goods and golf courses. China, particularly Yunnan Province, which borders Laos, ranked second, with major mining operations, although China's economic influence was thought to be controversial within the ruling party of Laos. Thailand has been a major infrastructure investor in Laos. The opening of the Mittaphap (Friendship) Bridge over the Mekong between Laos and Thailand (1994) improved opportunities for trade and tourism. Thai companies have invested in hydropower, cement, and agriculture. South Korea, France, Japan, India, and Australia are also important investors in Laos.

39 ECONOMIC DEVELOPMENT

The National Plan and Foreign Aid Council was established in June 1956 to prepare a general plan for the development of Laos and to set up a series of five-year plans. In view of its limited capital resources, the government sought increased private foreign investment, continued US governmental economic assistance, and help from international monetary bodies and the Colombo Plan organization. An economic plan drafted by the Laotian government in 1962 was never fully implemented, however, owing to internal instability. US aid to Laos began in 1955 and continued until the US pullout in 1975. During this period, the Laotian economy became almost totally dependent on US aid, which amounted to over $900 million in nonmilitary loans and grants and $1.6 billion in military assistance. Following the Pathet Lao takeover in 1975, efforts were made to restructure the Laotian economy along socialist lines. The source of most foreign assistance shifted to China between 1975 and 1979. By 1979, however, with the economy reduced to a virtual standstill because of poor harvests, rapid inflation, and the absence of private incentives, the government abandoned central planning for a mixed model of state-run enterprises, cooperatives, and private ventures.

Laos's first five-year plan (1981–85) after the removal of the Pathet Lao government envisioned increases of 65–68% in the gross social product, 23–24% in agricultural production, and 100–120% in industrial production, as well as completion of repairs on major highways and waterways. During this period the source of aid again shifted, this time to the USSR, Vietnam, and their allies. In 1985 the US ban on aid was lifted, largely because of Laotian cooperation in accounting for US military personnel missing in action in Laos during the Vietnam War.

The targets for the first five-year plan were largely not met, a failure ascribed to an overly rigid central planning approach. In August 1986, as a major part of the second five-year plan (1986–90), the New Economic Mechanism (NEM) was introduced. The New Economic Mechanism (NEM) approved in 1986 introduced free enterprise initiatives including decentralized decision making, deregulation of pricing and financial systems, and promotion of domestic and international trade and foreign investment. In 1988 land use reforms and market determined prices were introduced. In 1989 the tax system was modified, the Foreign Investment Code and Decree was implemented, the banking system was restructured, and the privatization of state economic enterprises commenced. Creation of a national taxation system and a customs administration were aimed at increasing government revenue. Incentives offered to encourage the development of industrial and commercial enterprises include allowing 100% foreign ownership, emphasized export of food products, strengthening of economic management, rehabilitation of routes to seaports and rural feeder roads, reform of general education and training, and development of small- and medium-scale projects.

The third five-year plan (1991–95) continued previous policies of infrastructure improvement, export growth, and import substitution. Four sectors were considered priority areas for future income for Laos: mining and energy; agriculture and forestry; tourism; and service, as a way-station and service center between China, Vietnam, and Cambodia. Major hydroelectric projects were built, in order to export electrical power. At the sixth party congress, held in March 1996, Laotian officials debated the country's slow pace of opening up to the international investment community. By that year, the country had allowed more than 500 foreign investors, in a variety of sectors, to either establish or buy (in whole or in part) Laotian businesses. The majority of $5 billion (75%) was invested in hydroelectric power.

In February 1997 Laos joined ASEAN, though some raised questions about its ability to afford even to attend all the organization's 200 or so annual meetings. Balance of payments problems had emerged almost as soon as the economy opened up to foreign trade and investments, with imports regularly running about 40% above exports. By 1997 Laos had entered into two stand-by arrangements with the IMF, a one-year arrangement under the Structural Adjustment Facility (SAF), and a three year arrangement under the Extended Structural Adjustment Facility (ESAP). The credit line for the ESAP arrangement amounted to about $49 million and ran until 7 May 1997. The Asian financial crisis of 1997–98 had devastating effects on Laos's economic development ambitions. From June 1997 to June 2002 the kip depreciated from 1,171 to more than 10,000 to one US dollar. FDI dropped from $179 million in 1997 to $23.9 million in 2001.

Normal trade relations (NTR) status was passed by the United States in 2004, reducing US tariffs on Laotian imports from an average of over 40% to about 3%, and allowing bilateral trade and investment agreements with the United States. In turn, this would open the way for the World Bank to issue guarantees for foreign investment projects in Laos. Healthy growth rates continued from 2004 through 2007. Following the global financial crisis of 2008–09, the growth engine for Laos continued to be the industrial sector, mining, and construction in particular. Agriculture has remained vulnerable to weather conditions, particularly disastrous flooding in 2008, 2009, and 2011. Tourism is a sector with strong potential, although held back by still weak infrastructure.

⁴⁰SOCIAL DEVELOPMENT

Poverty persists, with 26% of the population living below the poverty line as of 2010, according to the CIA. The World Bank and Asian Development Bank fund anti-poverty programs. The only government social security program is for Pathet Lao war veterans.

In general, the lowland Lao have the highest living standards, with lower standards prevailing among the upland tribes. Minority highland indigenous people and other rural people lack social, political, and economic power. They are increasingly vulnerable to land rights violations as agribusiness and plantation forestry concessions take over vast tracts of land.

Although the constitution establishes equal rights for women, social disparities continue, with women less educated and earning less than men. The Family Code provides women with equal inheritance and marriage rights. Trafficking in women and girls for the sex trade has persisted.

Political dissent is not tolerated, trials are not conducted fairly and detention without due process is not uncommon. Prison conditions are harsh, and the government suppresses the freedoms of speech, assembly, and association. Religious freedom is also problematic, with imprisonment of Christian house church worship leaders reported in 2009–11.

⁴¹HEALTH

According to the CIA, life expectancy in Lao People's Democratic Republic was 65 years in 2011. The country spent 4.0% of its GDP on healthcare, amounting to $36 per person. There were 3 physicians, 10 nurses and midwives, and 12 hospital beds per 10,000 inhabitants. The fertility rate was 3.4 children born per woman, while the infant mortality rate was 46 deaths per 1,000 live births. In 2008 the maternal mortality rate, according to the World Bank, was 580 deaths per 100,000 births. It was estimated that 59% of children were vaccinated against measles. The CIA calculated HIV/AIDS prevalence in Laos to be about 0.2% in 2009. Other infectious diseases include malaria, tuberculosis, H5N1 avian flu, diarrhea, hepatitis A, and typhoid fever.

⁴²HOUSING

Rural houses are typically built of wooden planks and bamboo, with a thatched roof, and raised off the ground on wooden pilings. In towns and cities, housing is built of concrete, brick, and tile. According to the CIA, as of 2008 about 57% of the population had access to improved water sources and 53% had access to improved sanitation.

⁴³EDUCATION

Education in Laos is compulsory for five years of primary education. This is followed by three years of lower secondary and three years of upper secondary studies. At this stage, students may choose to continue to a three-year technical school or higher technical college. The academic year runs from September to July.

In 2010 the World Bank estimated that 93% of age-eligible children in Laos were enrolled in primary school. Secondary enrollment for age-eligible children stood at 36%. Tertiary enrollment was estimated at 13%. Of those enrolled in tertiary education, there were 100 male students for every 78 female students. According to the CIA, education expenditures accounted for about 2.3% of GDP in 2008. Schools are badly supplied and understaffed, and teachers' pay is low.

There are five universities in the country: National University of Laos (Vientiane, founded in 1996), University of Health Sciences (Vientiane, founded in 1969), Souphanouvong University (in Luang Prabang, 2003), Champassak University (in Champassak Province, 2003), and Savannakhet University (Savannakhet, 2009). The newer provincial universities have struggled with limited funding. There are also regional technical colleges and several teacher training colleges. The adult literacy rate according to the 2005 census was 73%.

⁴⁴LIBRARIES AND MUSEUMS

The National Library (Vientiane), with volumes in French, Lao, and English, is the nation's largest library and has a program for the preservation of traditional manuscripts in Buddhist temples around the country. Vientiane has a city library and there are several provincial public libraries, as well as 18 academic libraries.

The Lao Revolutionary Museum, founded in 1985, was expanded to become the Lao National Museum in 2000. The Luang Prabang National Museum, in the former royal palace, opened in 1976. There are other provincial museums, a dinosaur museum, a Buddhist sculpture garden and private textile museums. Luang Prabang is a UNESCO World Heritage Site, as is the Khmer temple complex Wat Phu Champassak. The Plain of Jars is an important prehistoric archeological site.

⁴⁵MEDIA

Beginning in 1992 telephone owners were able to direct dial internationally, and private fax machines were permitted. In 2009 the CIA reported that there were 132,200 telephone landlines in Laos and 3.2 million mobile phones, with mobile phone subscriptions averaging 51 per 100 people. Mobile phone companies included Lao Telecom, ETL, Beeline, and Unitel. Planet Online Laos offered 4G mobile coverage in Vientiane in 2011.

Regular radio broadcasts were begun from Vientiane in 1968. There are 7 FM radio stations, 14 AM radio stations, and 2 shortwave radio stations. Most broadcasts are in Lao, but government news broadcasts are also in English, French, and other languages. Domestic television service from Lao National TV began in 1983; in addition, it is possible to pick up Thai television broadcasts. Cable television and satellite television are legally available for access to foreign broadcasts.

Although there are constitutional provisions for freedom of speech and the press, the government exerts broad control over the exercise of these rights. All domestically produced newspapers, radio, and television are controlled by the Ministry of Information, which suppresses any expressions of political dissent. The country's news agency is Laos News Agency. Prominent newspapers in 2010, with circulation numbers listed parenthetically, included *Pasason* (28,000), *Vientiane Mai* (2,500), and *Vientiane Times* (3,000).

According to the CIA, in 2010 the country had 1,468 Internet hosts. In 2009 there were some 300,000 Internet users in Laos. Lao Telecom and other providers had begun to offer wireless access by mid-2011. The government of Laos, although censoring all domestic, traditional media, had apparently not taken steps to limit or censor Internet access as of late 2011.

46 ORGANIZATIONS

The National Chamber of Commerce and Industry is located in Vientiane. The Lao People's Revolutionary Party and its numerous allied social and political groups in the Lao Front for National Reconstruction have dominated Laotian life. Virtually all domestic organizations in Laos remain under Party control, although many international nongovernmental organizations (INGOs) operate in Laos. There is a Lao Bar Association, a Lao Writers' Association and the Lao Medical Association, which promotes research and education on health issues and works to establish common policies and standards in healthcare. There are several sports associations promoting amateur competition in such pastimes as tennis, badminton, tae kwon do, and track and field. The Red Cross is active.

47 TOURISM, TRAVEL, AND RECREATION

The *Tourism Factbook*, published by the UN World Tourism Organization, reported 2.01 million incoming tourists to Laos in 2009, spending a total of $271 million. Of those incoming tourists, there were 1.8 million from East Asia and the Pacific. There were 37,492 hotel beds available in Laos, which had an occupancy rate of 54%. The estimated daily cost to visit Vientiane (Viangchan), the capital, was $194. The cost of visiting other cities averaged $114.

The main tourist destinations are the capital, Vientiane, and Luang Prabang. Facilities are limited in other parts of the country, although intrepid backpackers journey to the Plain of Jars and travel the Mekong River by local speedboat. Vientiane is popular for its Buddhist pagodas, French colonial architecture, and landmarks like the Patuxai arch. The old city of Luang Prabang is located at the junction of the Nam Khan and Mekong Rivers in the North. Since becoming a World Heritage Site in 1995, it has been overwhelmed by tourists, and there is some international donor discussion of limiting visitors to preserve the quiet Buddhist way of life for which the city was originally known.

Visas are required for entry into Laos, except for Japanese citizens. For most foreign visitors, visas can be obtained upon arrival. If purchased upon arrival, the visa is valid for up to 30 days.

48 FAMOUS PERSONS

One of the most cherished figures in Laotian history is Fa-Ngoum, who unified Lan Xang in the 14th century. Another dynastic personage still revered is the monarch Sethathirat, in whose reign (1534–71) the famous That Luang shrine was built. Chao Anou (r. 1805–28) is remembered for having fought a war to recover Laotian independence from the Siamese (Thais) and for having restored Vientiane to a glory it had not known since the 16th century. Important 20th-century figures include Souvanna Phouma (1901–84), former prime minister; Prince Souphanouvong (1902–95), a half-brother of Souvanna Phouma, leader of the Pathet Lao and president of Laos from 1975 to 1986; and Kaysone Phomvihan (1920–1992), former chairman of the Council of Ministers. Vang Pao (1929–2011) was a US-backed leader of Hmong troops against the communists. In the arts, Thongkham Onemanisone (b. 1949) is a poet and essayist, Khamsouk Keomingmuang (b. 1942) is a landscape painter, and Vong Phaophanit (b. 1961) is an installation artist.

49 DEPENDENCIES

Laos has no territories or colonies.

50 BIBLIOGRAPHY

Adams, Kathleen M., and Kathleen Gillogly. *Everyday Life in Southeast Asia*. Bloomington: Indiana University Press, 2011.

Chua, Liana, et al. *Southeast Asian Perspectives on Power*. New York: Routledge, 2011.

Kremmer, Christopher. *Bamboo Palace: Discovering the Lost Dynasty of Laos*. New York: HarperCollins, 2003.

Laos Investment and Business Guide: Strategic and Practical Information. Washington, DC: International Business Publications USA, 2012.

Leibo, Steven A. *East and Southeast Asia 2011*. Lanham, MD: Stryker-Post Publications, 2011.

Mansfield, Stephen. *Lao Hill Tribes: Traditions and Patterns of Existence*. New York: Oxford University Press, 2000.

Pyle, Richard. *Lost over Laos: A True Story of Tragedy, Mystery, and Friendship*. Cambridge, MA: Da Capo Press, 2003.

Stuart-Fox, Martin. *Historical Dictionary of Laos*. 3rd ed. Lanham, MD: Scarecrow Press, 2008.

------. *The A to Z of Laos*. Lanham, MD: Scarecrow Press, 2010.

LEBANON

Republic of Lebanon
Al-Jumhuriyah al-Lubnaniyah

CAPITAL: Beirut (Bayrut)

FLAG: The national flag, introduced in 1943, consists of two horizontal red stripes separated by a white stripe which is twice as wide; at the center, in green, is a cedar tree.

ANTHEM: *Kulluna lil watan lil'ula lil'alam (All of Us for the Country, Glory, Flag).*

MONETARY UNIT: The Lebanese pound, or livre libanaise (LBP), is a paper currency of 100 piasters. There are coins of 1, 2½, 5, 10, 25, and 50 piasters and 1 Lebanese pound, and notes of 1, 5, 10, 25, 50, 100, 250, 1,000 and 10,000 Lebanese pounds. LBP1 = US$0.00066 (or US$1 = LBP1,500) as of 2011.

WEIGHTS AND MEASURES: The metric system is the legal standard, but traditional weights and measures are still used.

HOLIDAYS: New Year's Day, 1 January; Arab League Day, 22 March; Independence Day, 22 November; Evacuation Day, 31 December. Christian religious holidays include Feast of St. Maron, 9 February; Good Friday; Easter Monday; Ascension; Assumption, 15 August; All Saints' Day, 1 November; and Christmas, 25 December. Muslim religious holidays include Eid al-Fitr, Eid al-Adha, and Milad un-Nabi.

TIME: 2 p.m. = noon GMT.

¹LOCATION, SIZE, AND EXTENT

Situated on the eastern coast of the Mediterranean Sea, Lebanon has an area of 10,400 sq km (4,015 sq mi), extending 217 km (135 mi) NE–SW and 56 km (35 mi) SE–NW. It is bordered on the N and E by Syria, on the S by Israel, and on the W by the Mediterranean Sea, with a total boundary length of 679 km (422 mi), of which 225 km (140 mi) is coastline. Comparatively, the area occupied by Lebanon is about three-fourths the size of the state of Connecticut.

The Lebanon of today is the Greater Lebanon (Grand Liban) created by France in September 1920, which includes the traditional area of Mount Lebanon—the hinterland of the coastal strip from Şaydā (Sidon) to Tarābulus (Tripoli)—some coastal cities and districts such as Beirut and Tarābulus (Tripoli), and the Bekaa (Biqā') Valley in the east. After January 1988 more than two-thirds of the territory was under foreign military occupation. In May 2000 Israeli troops withdrew from a 1,000 sq km (400 sq mi) strip along the Israeli border. Syrian forces, which had held northern Lebanon and the Bekaa Valley since 1976 and West Beirut and the Beirut-Şaydā coastal strip since February 1987, withdrew in April 2005.

Lebanon's capital city, Beirut, is located on the Mediterranean coast.

²TOPOGRAPHY

The name of the country comes from the name Djebel Libnan, which is the Arabic name for the Mount Lebanon range stretching from northeast to southwest through the center of the country. This area is rugged; there is a rise from sea level to a parallel mountain range of about 2,000–3,000 m (6,600–9,800 ft) in less than 40 km (25 mi), and heavy downpour of winter rains has formed many deep clefts and valleys in the soft rock. The terrain

has profoundly affected the country's history, in that virtually the whole landscape is a series of superb natural fortresses from which guerrilla activities can render the maintenance of control by a centralized government an intermittent and costly affair.

East of the Mount Lebanon Range is the Bekaa Valley, an extremely fertile flatland about 16 km (10 mi) wide and 129 km (80 mi) long from north to south. At the eastern flank of the Bekaa rise the Anti-Lebanon Range and the Hermon extension, in which stands Mount Hermon straddling the border with Syria. Lebanon contains few rivers, and its harbors are mostly shallow and small. Abundant springs, found to a height of 1,500 m (4,900 ft) on the western slopes of the Lebanon Mountains, provide water for cultivation up to this height.

³CLIMATE

Lebanon's extraordinarily varied climate is due mainly to the wide range of elevation and the westerly winds that make the Mediterranean coast much wetter than the eastern hills, mountainsides, and valleys. Within a 16-km (10-mi) radius of many villages, apples, olives, and bananas are grown; within 45 minutes' drive in winter, spring, and fall, both skiing and swimming are possible. Rainfall is abundant by Middle Eastern standards, with about 89 cm (35 in) yearly along the coast, about 127 cm (50 in) on the western slopes of the mountains, and less than 38 cm (15 in) in the Bekaa. About 80% of the rain falls from November to March, mostly in December, January, and February. Summer is a dry season, but it is humid along the coast. The average annual temperature in Beirut is 21°C (70°F), with a range from 13°C (55°F) in winter to 28°C (82°F) in summer.

⁴FLORA AND FAUNA

The World Resources Institute estimates that there are 3,000 plant species in Lebanon. In addition, Lebanon is home to 70 mammal species, 377 bird species, 44 reptile species, and 3 amphibian species. This calculation reflects the total number of distinct species residing in the country, not the number of endemic species.

Olive and fig trees and grapevines are abundant on lower ground, while cedar, maple, juniper, fir, cypress, valonia oak, and Aleppo pine trees occupy higher altitudes. Vegetation types range from subtropical and desert to alpine. Although hunting has killed off most wild mammals, jackals are still found in the wilder rural regions, and gazelles and rabbits are numerous in the south. Many varieties of rodents, including mice, squirrels, and gerbils, and many types of reptiles, including lizards and snakes (some of them poisonous), may be found. Thrushes, nightingales, and other songbirds are native to Lebanon; there are also partridges, pigeons, vultures, and eagles.

5 ENVIRONMENT

The World Resources Institute reported that Lebanon had designated 4,600 hectares (11,367 acres) of land for protection as of 2006. Water resources totaled 4.8 cu km (1.15 cu mi) while water usage was 1.38 cu km (0.331 cu mi) per year. Domestic water usage accounted for 33% of total usage, industrial for 1%, and agricultural for 66%. Per capita water usage totaled 385 cu m (13,596 cu ft) per year.

Lebanon's forests and water supplies suffered significant damage in the 1975–1990 civil war. Rapid urbanization has also left its mark on the environment. Coastal waters show the effects of untreated sewage disposal, particularly near Beirut, and of tanker oil discharges and oil spills. The water pollution problem in Lebanon is in part due to the lack of an internal system to consistently regulate water purification.

Air pollution is a serious problem in Beirut because of vehicular exhaust and the burning of industrial wastes. The UN reported in 2008 that carbon dioxide emissions in Lebanon totaled 13,344 kilotons. Control efforts have been nonexistent or ineffective because of political fragmentation and recurrent warfare since 1975.

The effects of war and the growth of the nation's cities have combined to threaten animal and plant life in Lebanon. In 1986 the National Preservation Park of Bte'nayel was created in the region of Byblos to preserve wooded areas and wildlife. Lebanon has four Ramsar wetland sites. According to a 2011 report issued by the International Union for Conservation of Nature and Natural Resources (IUCN), threatened species included 10 types of mammals, 8 species of birds, 6 types of reptiles, 5 species of invertebrate, and 22 species of fish. The Mediterranean monk seal, African softshell turtle, and dogfish shark are on the endangered list. The Arabian gazelle and Anatolian leopard are extinct.

6 POPULATION

The US Central Intelligence Agency (CIA) estimates the population of Lebanon in 2011 to be approximately 4,143,101, which placed it at number 127 in population among the 196 nations of the world. In 2011 approximately 9% of the population was over 65 years of age, with another 23% under 15 years of age. The median age in Lebanon was 29.8 years. There were 0.96 males for every female in the country. The population's annual rate of change was 0.244%. The projected population for the year 2025 was 4,700,000.

Population density in Lebanon was calculated at 398 people per sq km (1,032 people per sq mi).

The UN estimated that 87% of the population lived in urban areas, and that urban populations had an annual rate of change of 0.9%. The largest urban area was Beirut, with a population of 1.9 million.

7 MIGRATION

Estimates of Lebanon's net migration rate, carried out by the CIA in 2011, amounted to -6.04 migrants per 1,000 citizens. The total number of emigrants living abroad was 664,100, and the total number of immigrants living in Lebanon was 758,200. Lebanon also has some 400,000 Palestinian refugees and 55,000 refugees from Iraq. The economic roots of emigration may be traced to the increase of crop specialization during the 19th century and to the subsequent setbacks of the silk market toward the end of the century. Political incentives also existed, and many Lebanese left their country for Egypt (then under British rule) or the Americas at the turn of the century. After the mid-1960s, skilled Lebanese were attracted by economic opportunities in the Persian Gulf countries. Large numbers fled abroad, many of them to France, Syria, Jordan, Egypt, and the Gulf countries, during the civil war that began in 1975. In 1986 the Lebanese World Cultural Union estimated that some 13,300,000 persons of Lebanese extraction were living abroad, the largest numbers in Brazil, the United States, and Argentina.

Since the outbreak of war in 1975, internal migration has largely followed the pattern of hostilities, peaking in 1975/76 and again after the Israeli invasion of 1982. In 1993 the number of internally displaced people in various parts of the country was estimated at over 600,000.

The status of Palestinian refugees living in Lebanon represents a deeply complex and controversial issue. Because a majority of the Palestinian refugees are Muslim, many Christian political parties, such as the Phalange party and Lebanese Forces, oppose any measures that lean towards naturalization. Hundreds of thousands of Palestinian refugees live in camps scattered across Lebanon. Those refugees have been denied access to government social services and are barred from working and traveling overseas. In August 2010, however, Lebanon announced that it would grant Palestinian refugees living in the country the same right to work status as people of other nationalities living in Lebanon. Human rights groups praised the decision but noted that serious challenges remain for Palestinian refugees. Under Lebanese law, certain professions are reserved for Lebanese citizens. Many other professions, including law, medicine, and engineering, require employees to be members of the relevant professional association. Foreign membership in these trade associations is often contingent on reciprocity being granted in the member's home country. Palestinian refugees in Lebanon, who do not have an official state, are thus kept out of certain prestigious professions, such as medicine. The new law lifted the restrictions that kept Palestinian refugees entirely out of the labor market, but kept them subject to the same restrictions as other foreign workers.

8 ETHNIC GROUPS

Ethnic mixtures dating back to various periods of immigration and invasion are represented, as are peoples of almost all Middle Eastern countries. A confusing factor is the religious basis of ethnic differentiation. Thus, while most Lebanese are Arabs, they are divided into Muslims and Christians, each in turn subdivided into a number of faiths or sects, most of them formed by historical development into separate ethnic groups. The Muslims are divided into Sunnis and Shi'as. The Druzes, whose religion derives from Islam, are a significant minority. The Christians are divided mainly among Maronites, Greek Orthodox, and Greek Catholics. All the major groups have their own political organizations, paramilitary units, and territorial strongholds. Other ethnic groups include Armenians (most of them Armenian Orthodox, with some Armenian Catholics) and small numbers of Jews, Syrians, Kurds, and others. The number of Palestinian refugees is estimated at 390,000. As of 2010 population estimates stood at 95% Arab, 4% Armenian, and 1% other. Many Christians do not consider themselves to be Arabs, but rather descendants of the Phoenicians.

⁹LANGUAGES

Arabic is the official language and is spoken throughout the country. Much of the population is bilingual, with French as the main second language. There are also significant numbers of English, Armenian, and Turkish speakers. The distinctive Lebanese Arabic dialect contains various relics of pre-Arabic languages and also shows considerable European influence in vocabulary.

¹⁰RELIGIONS

Religious communities in the Ottoman Empire were largely autonomous in matters of personal status law and were at times treated as corporations for tax and public security matters. Membership in a millet, as these religious communities were called in Ottoman law, gave the individual citizenship, and this position, although somewhat modified, has given Lebanese politics its confessional nature. Religion is closely connected with civic affairs, and the size and competing influence of the various religious groups are matters of overriding political importance. The imbalance of power between Christians and Muslims, aggravated by the presence of large numbers of Palestinians, was a major factor contributing to the bitter civil war that began in 1975. According to a 2010 report, Sunni Muslims account for about 27% of the population, with Shi'a Muslims accounting for another 27%. There were three other legally recognized Muslim groups—Alawite or Nusayri, Druze, and Isma'ilite. Maronite Christians made up 21% of the population, followed by Greek Orthodox at 8%, Druze at 5%, and Greek Catholics at 5%. About 7% belong to other smaller Christian denominations, including Armenian Orthodox (Gregorians), Armenian Catholics, Syriac Orthodox (Jacobites), Syriac Catholics, Assyrians (Nestorians), Chaldeans, Copts, evangelicals (including Protestant groups such as Baptists), and Latins (Roman Catholic). There were also small numbers practicing Judaism, Buddhism, Hinduism, or Baha'ism. The Church of Jesus Christ of Latter-Day Saints has a small community as well.

The constitution provides for freedom of religion. However, there are some restrictions in religious practice. For instance, proselytizing is not prohibited, but is generally discouraged, and public blasphemy is prohibited under the law. Under an unwritten agreement made at the time of the National Covenant of 1943, the president of Lebanon must be a Maronite Christian, the prime minister a Sunni Muslim, and the speaker of parliament a Shi'a

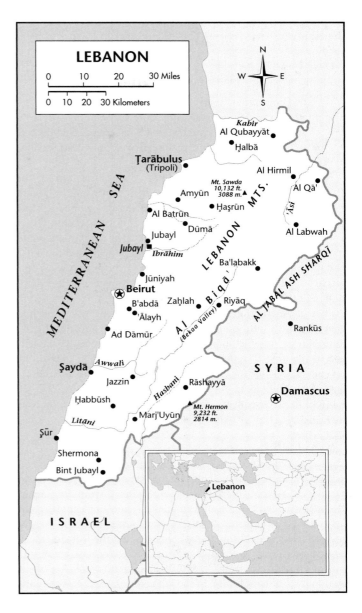

LOCATION: 35°6' to 36°36'E; 33°4' to 34°41' N. BOUNDARY LENGTHS: Syria, 359 kilometers (223 miles); Israel, 102 kilometers (63 miles); Mediterranean coastline, 195 kilometers (121 miles). TERRITORIAL SEA LIMIT: 12 miles.

Muslim. The agreement was reaffirmed by the Ta'if Agreement in 1989, though this arrangement has subsequently ceased to reflect the strength of competing religious groups in the population and is widely criticized. Religious groups must be officially recognized by the government in order for the group or its members to participate in certain activities. For instance, members of unrecognized faiths cannot run for parliament. As of 2010 there were 18 officially recognized religious groups, including 4 Muslim, 12 Christian, the Druze, and Judaism. Armenian Christmas, Eid al-Adha, Saint Maroun Day, Islamic New Year, Ashura, Good Friday, Easter (both Western and Eastern rites), the birth of the Prophet Muhammad, All Saints' Day, Feast of the Assumption, Annunciation, Eid al-Fitr, and Christmas are observed as national holidays.

11 TRANSPORTATION

The CIA reports that Lebanon has a total of 6,970 km (4,331 mi) of roads. There are seven airports, (five of which have paved runways), which transported 1.31 million passengers in 2009 according to the World Bank.

Construction of new roads frequently has been delayed by recurrent hostilities. Many roads were badly in need of repair; since 1982, fully one-third of the country's roads have been rehabilitated.

Due to damage suffered during the civil war, only short sections of railway are operable.

Beirut, a major Mediterranean port, was closed during the 1975–76 war and intermittently thereafter, reopening by March 1991. When the Beirut port was closed, Ṣaydā (Sidon) became the principal port for Muslims and Jūniyah for Christians. Other ports include Tarābulus (Tripoli) and Tyre. The rehabilitation and modernization of Beirut port was initiated in 2005, and the rehabilitation and development of Tarābulus (Tripoli) port was completed in 2001. As of 2011 Lebanon had a merchant fleet of 29 ships of 1,000 GRT or more.

Beirut International, Lebanon's principal airport, remained generally open until bombing during the Israeli invasion forced its closure in June-October 1982. It had handled 1,660,000 passengers in 1980; by 1985, the number was down to 599,000. Lebanon's two airlines, Middle East Airlines (MEA) and Trans-Mediterranean Airways (TMA), suffered heavy losses during the 1975–76 war and the Israeli invasion. As of 2011 MEA was Lebanon's national carrier; TMA was an all-cargo airline.

12 HISTORY

The geographical features of Lebanon have had a major effect on its history. Its mountains enabled the minority communities to survive the despotisms that submerged the surrounding areas. The sea provided trade routes in ancient times for exports from Lebanese cedar and spruce forests, and for commerce in copper and iron during the time of the Ptolemies and the Romans. Both Lebanon and Syria were historically associated from early times as part of Phoenicia (c. 1600–c. 800 BC), and both were later swept up into the Roman Empire. In the 7th century AD the Arabs conquered part of Lebanon. Maronite Christians had long been established there; Islam gradually spread by conversion and migration, although the country remained predominantly Christian. In the 11th century the Druzes established themselves in the south of the Mount Lebanon area as well as in Syria. Parts of Lebanon fell temporarily to the Crusaders; invasions by Mongols and others followed, and trade declined until the reunification of the Middle East under the Ottoman Empire.

For the most part, Ottoman officials of the surrounding areas left the Mount Lebanon districts to their own emirs and sheikhs. Fakhr ad-Din (1586–1635) of the Ma'an family set out to create an autonomous Lebanon, opened the country to Western Europe through commercial and military pacts, and encouraged Christian missionary activity. In 1697 the Shihab family acquired dominance, and from 1788 to 1840, except for a few intervals, Mount Lebanon was ruled by Bashir II of the Shihab family, who extended his power and was partly successful in building a strong state. The Egyptian occupation of Syria (1832–40) opened the Levant to large-scale European penetration and tied Lebanese affairs to

international politics. It also heightened the antipathy between Christians and Druzes, with the occupiers from time to time using armed groups of one against the other. The British invasion of 1840–41 served to deliver Lebanon from Egyptian rule and forced Bashir II into exile, but it also involved France and the United Kingdom in the problem of finding a modus vivendi for the religious factions. A partition of government did not work. Economic discontent was inflamed by religious antagonisms, and the Druzes, feeling their power dwindling, organized a major onslaught against the Christians in 1860. When the latter, fearing annihilation, requested European intervention, major powers sent fleets into Syrian waters and the French sent an army into Mount Lebanon. Under European pressure, the Ottoman government agreed to the establishment of an international commission to set up a new, pro-Christian government; an autonomous province of Mount Lebanon was created in 1864, with a Christian governor who, though the servant of the Ottoman state, relied upon European backing in disputes with his sovereign.

The entry of the Ottoman Empire into World War I led to an Allied blockade, widespread hunger, and the destruction of Lebanese prosperity. An Anglo-French force took the country in 1918, and in 1920, an Allied conference gave France a mandate over Syria, in which Mount Lebanon was included. The French separated from Syria the area they called Greater Lebanon (Grand Liban), which was four times as large as the traditional Mount Lebanon and included a Muslim population almost as large as the Christian. The mandate years were a time of material growth and little political development.

Lebanon came under Vichy control in 1940, but in 1941, Lebanon and Syria were taken by a combined Anglo-Free French force. The Free French proclaimed Lebanese independence in November 1941, but when a strongly nationalistic government was created in 1943, the French intervened and arrested the new president, Bishara al-Khuri. An insurrection followed, prompting UK intervention and the restoration of the government. In 1945 agreement was achieved for the withdrawal of both UK and French forces, and in 1946 Lebanon assumed complete independence.

The 1950s and 1960s were generally characterized by economic and political stability. Beginning in 1952, Lebanon received increased US aid and also benefited from an influx of Western commercial personnel and from growing oil royalties. It also seemed the calmest center of the Middle East, taking little part in the Arab-Israeli war of 1948 and no action in the wars of 1967 and 1973. In 1958, however, a reported attempt by President Camille Chamoun (Sha'mun) to seek a second term precipitated a civil war, and in July the United States sent forces to help quell the insurrection; this move was in keeping with the Eisenhower Doctrine, which pledged US military and economic aid to any country requesting it in order to counter a Communist threat. The crisis was settled when Gen. Fu'ad Shihab (Chehab), who was supported by both government and opposition groups, was elected president in July. By October US forces were withdrawn, and public security was reestablished.

In the late 1960s and early 1970s Lebanon's economy was disrupted by conflict in the Middle East, vividly brought home by the presence, near the border with Israel, of thousands of well-armed Palestinian guerrillas, many of whom had come from Jordan following the "Black September" fighting there in 1970–71.

Serious clashes between them and the Lebanese army occurred in 1969. Fearing civil war, the government that year signed the so-called Cairo Accord with the Palestinian Liberation Organization (PLO), which virtually made it a state within the state. The PLO gained the right to establish military bases and launch cross-border raids into Israel. This inevitably led to Israeli reprisals, and PLO interference in Lebanese affairs accelerated a slide toward anarchy. In April and May 1974 a series of Palestinian attacks on Lebanese villages killed scores of persons and injured hundreds. Government efforts to deal with the problem were denounced as insufficient by Christian rightists, while Muslim leftists defended the Palestinians, and both factions formed private militias.

During the early months of 1975, sporadic violence between the two factions gradually erupted into a full-scale civil war that pitted Maronite Christians against Muslims and against other Christian sects, and rightist militants against Palestinian guerrillas and other leftist Arab forces. At least 100,000 people on all sides were killed and some 600,000 persons displaced during the 18 months of fighting. In April 1976 Syrian forces entered Lebanon in an apparent effort to prevent an all-out victory by left-wing Muslims and Palestinians; by the fall, some 20,000 Syrian troops controlled the Bekaa Valley. A cease-fire arranged through the mediation of Saudi Arabia and other Arab countries enabled a peacekeeping force (including Syrian troops) to separate the combatants and end the war in October. The conflict not only devastated Lebanon economically, but so weakened the central government that effective power lay with the Syrians, the Palestinians, and some 30 sectarian militias. In general, the Christian Phalangists held sway over east-central Lebanon; fighters loyal to Maj. Sa'ad Haddad, a right-wing Lebanese army officer, controlled the southern border area, in a security zone set up by Israel; and the PLO, other Muslim leftists, and Syrian forces occupied northern and eastern Lebanon.

Intermittent fighting between the armed factions continued, and raids by Palestinian guerrillas based in southern Lebanon drew Israel into the conflict. In March 1978 the Israeli army invaded southern Lebanon, destroyed PLO bases, and then withdrew when the UN Interim Force in Lebanon (UNIFIL) was established to keep the peace. Continuing PLO rocket attacks on northern Israel and Syria's installation of antiaircraft missiles in the Bekaa Valley prompted Israel to launch a full-scale invasion of Lebanon in June 1982. Israeli forces quickly destroyed PLO bases in the south and in Tyre and Şaydā (Sidon), penetrated to the outskirts of Beirut, and disabled the Syrian missile bases. Several cease-fires arranged by US envoy Philip Habib broke down, but following a two-month Israeli siege of West Beirut, where the Palestinians were encamped, a truce was agreed to by Israel, the PLO, and Syria; by 1 September, more than 14,000 Palestinian and Syrian fighters had been evacuated. The Lebanese estimated their war casualties at more than 19,000 dead and 30,000 wounded (figures disputed by Israel). A multinational peacekeeping force, comprising British, French, and Italian soldiers and US marines, was stationed in the Beirut area in early September.

Despite the truce, the violence continued. On 14 September Bashir Gemayel, a Phalangist leader who in August had been elected president by the Lebanese parliament, was assassinated. Almost immediately, Israeli troops moved into West Beirut to wipe out pockets of Palestinian resistance causing tens of thousands of casualties. Phalangist forces were allowed into the Sabra

and Shatila refugee camps, and at least 600 Palestinians (some estimates put the number much higher, in the thousands), many of them unarmed civilians, were massacred; a subsequent Israeli government inquiry was critical of senior officials for indirect responsibility for the killings. In 1983 Israeli and Syrian troops still occupied large portions of Lebanon, and they became targets of attack by Muslim and Druze forces. In May 1983 Lebanon, Israel, and the United States signed an agreement by which Lebanon and Israel agreed to end their state of war. Israel agreed to withdraw all its forces, and both countries agreed to establish a security zone in southern Lebanon patrolled by Lebanese forces and joint Israeli-Lebanese teams. However, Syria opposed it and the agreement, never implemented, was repudiated by Lebanon in 1984.

The American embassy in Beirut was bombed in April 1983, and US marines were harassed by sniper fire. On 23 October, 241 American servicemen, including 220 marines, were killed by a truck-bomb explosion in their barracks at Beirut airport; on the same day, a similar bombing caused at least 58 deaths at a French paratroop barracks. Shortly before, Lebanon and Syria had agreed to a cease-fire pending a reconciliation conference, which began in Switzerland in November, with all major Lebanese political factions participating. Meanwhile, fighting broke out between a radical Syrian-supported PLO faction and guerrillas loyal to Yasser Arafat, chairman of the PLO; defeated at Tarābulus (Tripoli), Arafat withdrew from Lebanon in December.

As 1984 began, the position of the government headed by Amin Gemayel, who had been elected president to succeed his brother, was deteriorating. In February the United States, the United Kingdom, and Italy pulled their ground troops and nonessential personnel out of the Beirut area. In March the Lebanese reconciliation conference dissolved without reaching substantial agreement. The following month a "national unity" government was formed, bringing together the leaders of all the major warring factions. But it almost never met and could not pacify the country; intermittent clashes between factions continued. Israel's withdrawal of its troops from Lebanon (except the south) in early 1985 left in its wake renewed fighting for the evacuated territory. In December a Syrian-sponsored cease-fire agreement that included constitutional reforms was signed by the Druze, Amal (Shi'a), and Christian factions, but its terms were never implemented. The general lawlessness encouraged terrorist groups of all kinds to promote their own ends by assassinations, kidnappings, and bombings. Among the most feared was the Hezbollah, or Party of God, which was aligned with fundamentalist Iranian Revolutionary Guards.

In 1985–86 there was sporadic fierce fighting between Palestinian and Shi'a Amal militia. Syria pushed for political reform and, when opposed by Gemayel and militant Christians, influenced Muslim ministers not to deal with the president, thus paralyzing the government. With the economy in serious decline, Prime Minister Rashid Karami was assassinated, to be succeeded by Salim al-Huss. The badly divided factions could not agree on a successor to Gemayel when his term expired in September 1988. Christian Army Commander Michel Aoun asserted himself as prime minister, giving Lebanon two governments—a Muslim one in West Beirut and a Christian one in East Beirut. Aoun was opposed by the Syrians and Muslims and by rival Christian factions. In January 1989 the Arab League appointed a committee on Lebanon which, in September, arranged for a seven-point cease-fire and convened a meeting of Lebanese parliamentarians in Taif, Saudi Arabia. The Taif Accord that resulted in November led to the election of Elias Hrawi, a Maronite Christian, as president. He named al-Huss prime minister. When forces of General Aoun (who was technically deposed by Hrawi) attacked Christian and Syrian positions, they retaliated in strength and finally obliged him to take exile in France in 1991.

In 1991–92 the government gradually began to reassert its authority. Militias, except notably Hezbollah and the Israeli-backed army of South Lebanon, were dissolved in May 1991. Palestinian militants were repressed in Ṣaydā (Sidon) in July. In May 1992 the last Western hostages were released after years of confinement. Lebanon joined the Israeli-Arab peace talks in Madrid in October 1991. Internally, the poor economy aggravated political instability, but parliamentary elections, the first in 20 years, were scheduled for 1992. Poor preparations, widespread irregularities, and Christian abstention produced results that did not prepare Lebanon for an assured future. Yet, the appointment of Prime Minister Rafiq al-Hariri in November 1992 promised a serious effort at reconstruction.

Al-Hariri, a self-made billionaire who made his fortune in Saudi Arabia, was perceived by many to be a savior of sorts for the war-torn country. He had a long history of philanthropic giving, donating large sums to rebuild Beirut, for instance. As prime minister he was frequently accused of corruption and of making sure government rebuilding efforts were directed toward companies under his control. Still most Lebanese approved of his efforts to stabilize the country and unite its many long-warring factions. In 1996 al-Hariri was reelected prime minister in a unanimous vote of parliament.

In 1996 Lebanon was still subject to political violence, especially in the Israeli-occupied south, where that year 255 people were killed (27 Israeli soldiers) in violence. Some 54 of the dead were members of Hezbollah, and 19 were militiamen in the Israeli-controlled South Lebanon Army (SLA). The violence continued into 1997.

President Ilyas Hrawi had been elected to the six-year post in 1989. In 1995 when his term was set to expire in accordance with the constitution, parliament extended his term for an additional three years. Hrawi proved to be a weak leader and his standing with the Maronites was low. Émile Lahoud, of a prominent Maronite family, had been promoted to major-general in 1985 and general and army commander in 1989. In 1998 his name surfaced as a potential successor to Hrawi. In October 1998 the assembly introduced an amendment to the constitutional clause requiring senior public officials to leave office before running for president. Within two days Lahoud was elected president of the National Assembly. Lahoud was sworn in on 24 November 1998 as Lebanon's 11th president. On 4 December 1998 Salim al-Huss began his fifth term as prime minister after Hariri's sudden resignation.

In early 1999 fighting in southern Lebanon escalated as Hezbollah staged attacks on Israeli forces and the Israeli-backed SLA. Israel retaliated on Hezbollah strongholds, and by February, expanded air strikes beyond the "security zone" to southern and northern Lebanon. The al-Huss government's fiscal austerity aimed at reducing the deficit, which had grown to 15% of gross domestic product, met with resistance from the trade unions. On 24 June 1999 Israel destroyed bridges and power stations with its heaviest air raids in three years. In July 1999 the UN Security Council renewed for six months the mandate for UNIFIL, and restated its support of the territorial integrity and sovereignty of Lebanon.

At the end of 1999 in anticipation of elections in August 2000, the government passed a law creating 14 constituencies of suspiciously varying sizes, based on rewarding or punishing political foes or friends. A bill to curb the media—limiting all elections news, advertisements, and coverage to the state-run Tele-Liban and Radio Liban—and to limit campaign spending was also drafted. On 24 May 2000 Israel made a quick withdrawal from southern Lebanon. With the Israeli withdrawal the SLA disintegrated. The exact border between Lebanon and Israel remained unsettled as they disputed ownership of the Shabaa Farms. The Lebanese government sent police and intelligence officers to the newly liberated area, but refused to deploy troops until there was evidence of stability or a comprehensive peace treaty with Israel.

In March 2001 Lebanon began to divert waters from the Wazzani River to supply villages in southern Lebanon. The Wazzani feeds into the Hatzbani, which in turn flows into the Jordan River watershed and Lake Kinneret (Lake Tiberias or the Sea of Galilee), a major source of Israel's water supply. In September 2002 Israel's prime minister Ariel Sharon identified measures to divert water from Israel as a cause for war.

Syrian troops withdrew from Beirut in June 2001 to redeploy in other parts of Lebanon, in response to greater Lebanese criticism of Syria's presence there. In February 2003 the Syrian army completed its redeployment out of north Lebanon. The majority of the Syrian army remaining in Lebanon was assembled in a stretch of the Bekaa Valley on the Syrian border.

Parliamentary elections held 27 August and 3 September 2000 had resulted in the appointment on 23 October of Rafiq al-Hariri as prime minister once again. In October 2004 Hariri stood down as prime minister in protest over the continued presence of Syrian troops in Lebanon. On 14 February 2005 Hariri and 19 others were killed in a massive bomb blast in central Beirut. The UN Security Council unanimously authorized an international investigation into the assassination. In the wake of Hariri's murder, numerous public demonstrations took place, both for and against the presence of Syrian troops and security agents in Lebanon. The cabinet of then-prime minister Omar Karami resigned two weeks after the first wave of anti-Syrian rallies. After Karami resigned, a moderate pro-Syrian member of parliament, Najib Mikati, was named prime minister. Syria pulled all of its military forces (15,000 troops) out of Lebanon by the end of April 2005, in what was dubbed the "Cedar Revolution."

Parliamentary elections were held in May and June 2005 (they had been postponed for one year). An anti-Syrian alliance led by Saad Hariri, son of the late Rafiq Hariri, won control of parliament, and parliament chose an ally of Rafiq Hariri, Fouad Siniora, to become prime minister. The anti-Syrian alliance won 72 of 128 seats in parliament. Also in June, George Hawi, anti-Syrian former leader of the Lebanese Communist Party, was killed when his car blew up. In September 2005, four pro-Syrian generals were charged in connection with Rafiq Hariri's assassination.

On 12 July 2006 Hezbollah seized two Israeli soldiers and killed three others in northern Israel. Israel responded with an air, sea, and land campaign against Hezbollah. The war continued until a United Nations cease-fire went into effect on 14 August 2006, although the war didn't end until 8 September, when Israel lifted its naval blockade of Lebanon. The last Israeli troops left Lebanon in December 2006. Some 1,200 people were killed in the war, about 900 of them Lebanese civilians; 117 Israeli soldiers and 41 Israeli citizens died in the fighting. Nearly one million Lebanese and some 300,000 Israelis were displaced from their homes. Much Lebanese infrastructure was severely damaged, including the Beirut Rafiq Hariri International Airport. Despite Israel's overwhelming firepower, Hezbollah was not defeated. Since the conflict ended as the result of a cease-fire, Hezbollah claimed victory in the war, a claim with which Israel heartily disagreed.

In November 2006 leading Christian politician and government minister Pierre Gemayel was assassinated. In December hundreds of thousands of opposition supporters led by Hezbollah demonstrated in Beirut to demand the resignation of the government. In January 2007 the opposition further pressed its demands for the government to resign by calling a general strike.

From May to September 2007, a siege of the Palestinian refugee camp Nahr al-Bared, home to 30,000 people, followed clashes between the militant group Fatah al Islam and the Lebanese army. More than 300 people died and 40,000 residents fled before the army gained control of the camp. Fatah al Islam is a group made up of radical Sunni Muslims inspired by the al Qaeda terrorist organization.

On 25 September 2007, when parliament met to elect a new president, it had to disband without taking action because there weren't enough members present. To achieve a quorum, two-thirds of its members must be present and the session fell short of that number. Parliament postponed the election, first until 23 October and then indefinitely. On 21 November the United States, with Lebanon's primary anti-Syrian Christian leader Samir Geagea, accused Syria of blocking an agreement on a new Lebanese president, just two days before the pro-Syrian president, Émile Lahoud, was due to leave office. Lahoud left office on 23 November, and asked the military to take charge of the nation's security, as the speaker of parliament once again postponed for a week a vote to choose a new president. However, a caretaker government led by Prime Minister Fouad Siniora and his cabinet assumed the powers of the presidency.

In May 2008 parliament finally elected a president, General Michel Suleiman, who was unopposed. He was the leader of Lebanon's armed forces and was regarded as having the respect of both the government and the Hezbollah-backed opposition in Lebanon. He is a Maronite Christian, a requirement for the president according to Lebanon's system.

13 GOVERNMENT

As defined by the constitution of 1926 and subsequent amendments, Lebanon is an independent republic. Executive power is vested in a president (elected by the legislature for six years) and a prime minister and cabinet, chosen by the president but responsible to the legislature. Under an agreement dating back to the French mandate, the president must be a Maronite Christian, the prime minister a Sunni Muslim, and the president of the National Assembly a Shi'a Muslim. Decisions by the president must be countersigned by the prime minister and concerned minister(s) after approval by the National Assembly.

Legislative power is exercised by a 128-member National Assembly (formerly the Chamber of Deputies), elected for a four-year term by universal adult suffrage (compulsory for males age 21 or over, permitted for women age 21 or over with elementary education). The electoral reform law of 1960 determined the denominational composition of the legislature as follows: 30 Maronites; 20 Sunni, 19 Shi'a; 11 Greek Orthodox; 6 Greek Catholics; 6 Druzes; 4 Armenian Orthodox; 1 Armenian Catholic; 1 Protestant; and 1 other. Deputies were elected to the legislature in 1972, but elections scheduled for 1976 were postponed because of the war, and the legislature extended its term every two years until 1992. The Taif Accord of 1989 set the Christian-Muslim balance in parliament at 50–50, but the failure of Christians to participate in the elections of 1992 and 1996 gave Muslim groups the largest number of seats in the legislature. There has been no official census in the country since 1932, but most observers believe Muslims now form the majority with the Shi'a as the largest single group. The denominational composition of the legislature following the 1989 Taif Accord is: 34 Maronites, 27 Sunni, 27 Shi'a, 14 Greek Orthodox, 8 Greek Catholics, 8 Druzes, 5 Armenian Orthodox, 2 Alaouites, 1 Armenian Catholic, 1 Protestant, and 1 Christian Minorities.

14 POLITICAL PARTIES

Political life in Lebanon is affected by the diversity of religious sects and the religious basis of social organization. The mainly Christian groups, especially the Maronites, favor an independent course for Lebanon, stressing its ties to Europe and opposing the appeals of Islam and pan-Arabism. The Muslim groups favor closer ties with Arab states and are opposed to confessionalism (political division along religious lines). As of 2012, the two major political groups were coalitions: the 8 March Coalition and the 14 March Coalition. The Democratic Gathering Bloc and the Metn Bloc were two major parties operating outside these coalitions, but neither held seats in parliament.

In parliamentary elections held in May and June 2005 (previously postponed for one year), An anti-Syrian alliance led by Saad Hariri, son of the late Rafiq Hariri (assassinated earlier that year), won control of parliament, and parliament chose an ally of Rafiq Hariri, Fouad Siniora, to become prime minister. Saad Hariri's bloc took 72 of the 128 seats in the National Assembly. Syrian military forces pulled out of Lebanon in April 2005, following massive street demonstrations.

In the June 2009 parliamentary elections, the moderate 14 March Alliance maintained its control in parliament, winning 71 of 128 seats. Saad Hariri was named he new prime minister. The election served as a referendum against more extremist elements in Lebanese politics, like Hezbollah. Many observers had projected Hezbollah to win a majority in the elections.

Hariri's unity government won a vote of confidence by an overwhelming majority of parliamentary members in December 2009. Of the 128-seat assembly, 122 members approved the coalition. The most controversial aspect of Hariri's government concerned a clause that declared the right of "Lebanon, its government, its people, its army and its resistance" to liberate all Lebanese territory. That clause was viewed by analysts as an affirmation of Hezbollah's right to armed resistance—a troubling prospect for Christian members of parliament. Still, the need for the government to address several urgent social and economic issues, such as Lebanon's mounting debt and failing infrastructure, seemed to trump concerns over the clause.

On 12 January 2011, Hezbollah ministers and their allies resigned from the unity government, forcing its collapse. The resignation was in protest over a UN tribunal that is investigating the assassination of former prime minister Rafiq Hariri in 2005. Hezbollah then chose Najib Miqati, who had served as prime minister from April to July 2005, to head the new government. Anti-Hezbollah protestors marched in the streets after the news of Miqati's nomination was announced.

Palestinian refugees have no right to vote, despite numbering approximately 350,000.

15 LOCAL GOVERNMENT

Lebanon is divided into the six provinces (*muhafazat*) of Beirut, North Lebanon, South Lebanon, Bekaa, Mount Lebanon, and Nabatiye. As of 2011 two new provinces, Aakar and Baalbek-Hermel, had been legislated but not yet instituted. The muhafazat are subdivided into districts (*aqdiya*), municipalities, and villages. Provincial governors and district chiefs are appointed by presidential decree. In most villages, councils of village elders or heads of families or clans still play a considerable role.

Since May 1998 municipal elections have been held every six years. In 2010, 963 municipal councils were elected and 2,753 *mukhtars* or mayors. Elections were held in four rounds according to province. Voter turnout was approximately 74%, although that figure varied greatly between municipalities. In 2001 municipal elections took place in the newly liberated areas of South Lebanon after the Israeli withdrawal of May 2000.

16 JUDICIAL SYSTEM

Ultimate supervisory power rests with the minister of justice, who appoints the magistrates. Courts of first instance are presided over by a single judge and deal with both civil and criminal cases. Appeals may be taken to the courts of appeal, each made up of three judges. Of the four courts of cassation, three hear civil cases and one hears criminal cases. A six-person Council of State handles administrative cases. A Constitutional Council, called for in the Taif Accord, rules on the constitutionality of laws upon the request of 10 members of parliament. Religious courts—Islamic, Christian, and Jewish—deal with marriages, deaths, inheritances, and other matters of personal status in their respective faiths. There is also a separate military court system dealing with cases involving military personnel and military related issues.

The law provides for the right to a fair public trial and an independent and impartial judiciary. In practice, politically influential elements succeed in intervening to obtain desired results.

Matters of state security are dealt with by a five-member Judicial Council. The Judicial Council is a permanent tribunal, and the cabinet, on the recommendation of the Ministry of Justice, decides whether to bring a case before the Judicial Council.

In the refugee camps, the Palestinian elements implement an autonomous system of justice in which rival factions try opponents without any semblance of due process. Hezbollah applies Islamic law in the area under its control.

17 ARMED FORCES

The International Institute for Strategic Studies reports that armed forces in Lebanon totaled 59,100 members in 2011. The force is comprised of 57,000 from the army, 1,100 from the navy, and 1,000 members of the air force. Armed forces represent 5.4% of the labor force in Lebanon. Defense spending totaled $1.8 billion and accounted for 3.1% of GDP.

The conflict of 1975–90 split the regular Lebanese army along Christian-Muslim lines. The force was later reformed, first by the United States, then by Syria.

Much of the opposition militia has disbanded, and the Muslim Hezbollah (3,000 active) is the only significant communal army remaining. Also stationed in Lebanon were a number of UN peacekeeping troops; as of 2011 they numbered slightly more than 12,000. Some 16,000 Syrian troops, in the country as part of the UN peacekeeping force, were removed in April 2005.

18 INTERNATIONAL COOPERATION

Lebanon is a charter member of the United Nations, having joined 24 October 1945, and belongs to ESCWA and several nonregional specialized agencies, such as the FAO, IAEA, the World Bank, the ICAO, ILO, UNESCO, UNHCR, and WHO. Lebanon was one of the founding members of the Arab League. It also serves as a member of the Arab Bank for Economic Development in Africa, the Arab Fund for Economic and Social Development, the Arab Monetary Fund, G-24, G-77, and the Organization of the Islamic Conference (OIC). The country has observer status in the OAS and the WTO.

Lebanon is part of the Nonaligned Movement. Lebanon and Israel have a longstanding unresolved dispute concerning boundaries in the Golan Heights region. In 2000 the United Nations mapped out a Lebanese-Israeli line of separation known as the Blue Line, pending negotiations to determine a final international border. Israeli forces withdrew from their occupation across the Blue Line; however, the UN monitors have reported violations of the agreement from both countries. The United Nations Interim Force in Lebanon (UNFIL), which was originally established in 1978, continues to monitor the area and to assist in reestablishing Lebanese authority in the region.

In environmental cooperation, Lebanon is part of the Basel Convention, the Convention on Biological Diversity, Ramsar, the Montréal Protocol, MARPOL, the Nuclear Test Ban Treaty, and the UN Conventions on the Law of the Sea, Climate Change, and Desertification.

In November 2010 the Israeli cabinet approved a plan for the withdrawal of troops from the northern half of the border village of Ghajar, which has been declared as part of Lebanon by the United Nations. Ghajar was once a part of Syria, but was captured and occupied by the Israelis during the Six Day War of 1967. Later, as the UN demarcated the border for Lebanon, the northern portion of the city was separated from Israeli control. The Israeli military occupation of southern Lebanon ended in 2000, but since the two nations are still technically at war, Israeli forces remained in the northern portion. The population of the entire village is about 2,000, and many of the residents still consider themselves to be Syrian. A majority are opposed to falling under Lebanese control. Upon the withdrawal of Israeli troops, northern Ghajar will be placed under control of the UN Interim Force in Lebanon (UN-FIL) until further details can be worked out.

19 ECONOMY

The gross domestic product (GDP) rate of change in Lebanon, as of 2010, was 7.5%. Inflation stood at 3.7%, and unemployment was reported at 8.98%.

Lebanon is traditionally a trading country, with a relatively large agricultural sector and small but well-developed industry. Until the civil war, it had always figured prominently as a center of tourist trade. The 1975–76 war caused an estimated $5 billion in property damage and reduced economic activities to about 50% of the prewar level. The cost of reconstruction after the Israeli-Palestinian-Syrian war of 1982 was estimated at $12–15 billion. Lebanon has been able to survive economically because of remittances from abroad by Lebanese workers and companies, external aid by the United States, France, Germany, and Arab countries, and foreign subsidies to various political groups. A residual effect of the 1982 war was political uncertainty, which poisoned the economic climate in the following years. In 1984 and after, there was a pronounced deterioration in the economy. In 1987 inflation peaked at 487%. After the 1989 Taif Accord for National Reconciliation ended hostilities, the economy began to recover. Economic activity surged in 1991, and in 1993 the Hariri government was able to stabilize the economy, and launch a program to reconstruct the economy's infrastructure. Real GDP grew 4.2% in 1992, after growing by about 40% in 1991.

After 1988 the economy posted growth rates averaging 7.5%, although a rising budget deficit threatens to hamper economic reforms. Israel's Operation Grapes of Wrath in April 1996 cut economic development short, but in the same year, the stock market had reopened, and investment had made significant returns. In 1997 unemployment remained high, although inflation had been reduced by 1998. Gross domestic product grew in 1998, but was flat by 2000. Inflation was zero in 2000. High unemployment remained a persistent problem, at 20–25% in 1999 and 2000. According to the World Bank, total unemployment among youth was 22% in 2007.

In 2002 the government met with international donors to seek bilateral assistance in restructuring its massive domestic debt at lower rates of interest. Receipts from donor nations helped to stabilize government finances in 2003, but did little to reduce the debt, which stood at approximately 200% of GDP in 2005. In 2004 the Hariri government issued Eurobonds to try to manage maturing debt. Hariri stepped down as prime minister later in 2004, and was assassinated in February 2005, which led to a downturn in the economy. Prime Minister Fuad Siniora pledged to push forward with economic reforms, including privatization and more efficient government.

The Israeli-Hezbollah conflict in July-August 2006 caused over $3 billion in infrastructure damage. Donors aided the country and in 2007 pledged over $7.5 billion to Lebanon for development projects and budget support. However Lebanon had to promise to pursue economic and social reform. Lebanon continued to be economically hindered by political tensions.

In 2010 the Canadian-based Fraser Institute ranked Lebanon as the third most economically free Arab nation (after Bahrain and Kuwait) in the latest edition of their Economic Freedom of the Arab World report. The Economic Freedom reports compare five aspects of an economy, including the size of government (expenditures, taxes, and enterprises), legal structure and security of property rights, access to sound money, freedom to trade internationally, and regulation of credit, labor, and business. Lebanon received an overall score of 7.6 out of 10 in the regional analysis.

20 INCOME

The CIA estimated that in 2010 the GDP of Lebanon was $59.37 billion. The CIA defines GDP as the value of all final goods and services produced within a nation in a given year and computed on the basis of purchasing power parity (PPP) rather than value as measured on the basis of the rate of the exchange based on current dollars. The per capita GDP was estimated at $14,400. The annual growth rate of GDP was 7.5%. The average inflation rate was 3.7%. It was estimated that agriculture accounted for 5.1% of GDP, industry 15.9%, and services 79%.

According to the World Bank, remittances from citizens living abroad totaled $7.6 billion or about $1,824 per capita and accounted for approximately 12.7% of GDP.

The World Bank estimates that in 2010 Lebanon, with 0.06% of the world's population, accounted for 0.06% of the world's GDP. By comparison, the United States, with 4.5% of the world's population, accounted for 23% of world GDP.

As of 2011 the most recent study by the World Bank reported that actual individual consumption in Lebanon was 90.6% of GDP and accounted for 0.08% of world consumption. By comparison, the United States accounted for 25.44% of world individual consumption. The World Bank also estimated that 28% of Lebanon's GDP was spent on food and beverages, 15.3% on housing and household furnishings, 5.7% on clothes, 7.5% on health, 6.8% on transportation, 1.3% on communications, 2.7% on recreation, 4.9% on restaurants and hotels, and 2.2% on miscellaneous goods and services and purchases from abroad.

In the most recent figures available, it was estimated in 1999 that about 28% of the population subsisted on an income below the poverty line established by Lebanon's government.

21 LABOR

As of 2007 Lebanon had a total labor force of 1.481 million people.

As of 2010 there were some 160 labor unions in Lebanon. The General Confederation of Workers is the largest labor group, composed of 22 unions with about 200,000 members. Organized labor has grown slowly, partly because of the small number of industrial workers, but also because of the availability of a large pool of unemployed. Agricultural and most trade workers are not organized. Palestinians in Lebanon are free to organize their own unions. While Lebanese workers have the right to strike, there are limitations on public demonstrations which somewhat undermine this right. Lebanese workers have the right to organize and bargain collectively and this is the standard practice in employment situations.

A monthly minimum wage of US$333 had been in effect since 2008. In October 2011 the government voted to increase the minimum wage to US$467, averting a planned strike by labor unions. The standard workweek is set at 48 hours, with a 24-hour rest period. In practice, most laborers average around 35 hours of work per week. The law does not protect foreign domestic workers. Workers as young as 14 may legally work with restrictions as to working hours and conditions. However, age limitations are not effectively enforced.

22 AGRICULTURE

Roughly 30% of the total land is farmed, and the country's major crops include citrus, grapes, tomatoes, apples, vegetables, potatoes, olives, and tobacco. Cereal production in 2009 amounted to 192,436 tons, fruit production 961,297 tons, and vegetable production 851,138 tons.

The expansion of cultivated areas is limited by the arid and rugged nature of the land. Agricultural production was severely disrupted by the 1975–76 war, and production of citrus fruits, the main crop, was reduced to low levels in the fertile Bekaa Valley by Israeli-Syrian fighting during 1982. Two profitable, albeit illegal, crops produced are opium poppy (for heroin) and cannabis (for hashish). A joint Lebanese-Syrian eradication effort has practically wiped out the opium crop and significantly reduced the cannabis crop.

23 ANIMAL HUSBANDRY

The UN Food and Agriculture Organization (FAO) reported that Lebanon dedicated 400,000 hectares (988,422 acres) to permanent pasture or meadow in 2009. During that year, the country tended 37.5 million chickens, 77,000 head of cattle, and 9,500 pigs. The production from these animals amounted to 80,801 tons of beef and veal, 9,586 tons of pork, 110,107 tons of poultry, 19,952 tons of eggs, and 441,246 tons of milk. Lebanon also produced 4,050 tons of cattle hide and 2,139 tons of raw wool.

Much of Lebanon's livestock was lost during the protracted hostilities that began in 1975. In 2005 there were an estimated 430,000 goats and 346,000 sheep. As Lebanon's own meat and milk production is below consumption needs, animal and milk products are imported.

24 FISHING

Lebanon had 16 decked commercial fishing boats in 2008. The annual capture totaled 3,811 tons according to the UN FAO.

The fishing industry has not progressed significantly, despite a government-sponsored effort to reduce fish imports and provide employment in the canned-fish industry.

25 FORESTRY

Approximately 13% of Lebanon is covered by forest. The UN FAO estimated the 2009 roundwood production at 7,150 cu m (252,500 cu ft). The value of all forest products, including roundwood, totaled $28.7 million.

Most of the forests are in the central part of the country, with pine and oak predominant. Few of the ancient cedars have survived; small cedar forests have been planted at high altitudes. Fires in 2006 and 2007 were estimated to have destroyed more than 1,500 hectares (3,707 acres) of forest.

26 MINING

Lebanon's mineral industry makes only a small contribution to the economy. Mining activity is limited to the production of salt and the quarrying of raw materials for the construction industry, particularly limestone and silica for cement manufacture. In 2009 hydraulic cement production was estimated at 4.9 million metric tons, up from an estimated 3.9 million metric tons in 2007. Gypsum production in 2009 was estimated at 30,000 metric tons, while lime production in that same year was estimated at 14,000 metric tons; and salt output estimated at 3,500 metric tons. In 2009 Lebanon also produced phosphatic fertilizers, phosphoric acid, and sulfuric acid. Modest deposits of asphalt, coal, and iron ore existed, and the country had no petroleum or gas reserves. The success of Lebanon's minerals industry depended on the long-term restoration of peace and stability in the country. In 2009 exports of pearls and precious stones totaled $1.1 billion, or 32% of total exports.

27 ENERGY AND POWER

The World Bank reported in 2008 that Lebanon produced 10.6 billion kWh of electricity and consumed 9.51 billion kWh, or 2,295 kWh per capita. Roughly 95% of energy came from fossil fuels, while 1% came from alternative fuels. Per capita oil consumption was 1,250 kg.

Lebanon, as of 1 January 2011, has no known proven reserves of oil or natural gas. As a result, the country must import all the oil and natural gas it consumes. Although Lebanon had two coastal refineries, Tarābulus (Tripoli) in the north and Zahrani in the south, neither is operational, with the refinery in Tarābulus (Tripoli) closed since 1982.

In 2010 oil consumption averaged 106,000 barrels per day. Oil imports in 2009 were 78,760 barrels per day. There were no recorded imports or consumption of natural gas in 2010.

Lebanon's electric power generating sector is controlled by a state-owned public utility, Electricite du Liban (EdL). EdL is in charge of power generation, distribution and transmission.. In 2009 production was estimated at 10.41 billion kWh. Lebanon's power plants—hydroelectric, thermal, gas turbine, and combined cycle power—are known to be operating below capacity and the country must import power. In 2009 Lebanon imported 1.114 billion kWh. Daily and weekly electricity blackouts are common, although not all parts of the country are affected equally.

28 INDUSTRY

The 16-year civil war that ended in 1991 caused tremendous damage to the industrial sector, with losses totaling $1.5 billion. Since then, industrial recover has been gradual, with the industrial production growth rate pegged at 2.1% in 2010. Major industries included banking, tourism, food processing, wine, jewelry, cement, textiles, mineral and chemical products, wood and furniture products, oil refining, and metal fabricating.

29 SCIENCE AND TECHNOLOGY

The World Bank reported in 2009 that there were no patent applications in science and technology in Lebanon. Lebanon's advanced technology is limited to oil refining, the facilities for which were installed by international oil companies. The National Council for Scientific Research, established in Beirut in 1962, draws up national science policies and fosters research in fundamental and applied research. The council operates a marine research center at

Al-Batrun. Seven colleges and universities in Beirut offer degrees in basic and applied sciences.

³⁰DOMESTIC TRADE

Trade is by far the most important sector of the Lebanese economy. Before the 1975–90 civil war, Beirut was an important commercial center of the Middle East. During the first year of civil violence alone, 3,600 commercial establishments were destroyed, burned, or looted. Reconstruction and returning confidence have improved commercial activities since 1995.

The main trading activity is related to the importation of goods and their distribution in the local market. Distribution is generally handled by traders who acquire sole right of import and sale of specific trademarks, and although competition is keen, the markup tends to be high. Distribution of local products is more widely spread among traders. Franchising has become popular, with major firms representing the restaurant, hotel, and clothing industries.

Prices are generally controlled by the Consumer Protection Department of the Ministry of Economy and Trade. Retail credit is common, and advertising has developed rapidly in motion picture theaters, television, radio, and the press.

Government offices are generally open from 8 a.m. to 2 p.m. Monday through Thursday, from 8 to 11 a.m. on Friday, and from 8 a.m. to 1 p.m. on Saturday. Most banks are open with similar hours, occasionally with a half-day on Saturday as well. Private businesses and shops have varying hours, sometimes exceeding a 40-hour workweek.

³¹FOREIGN TRADE

Lebanon imported $17.97 billion worth of goods and services in 2008, while exporting $5.187 billion worth of goods and services. Major import partners in 2009 were France, 10.6%; the United States, 9.2%; Syria, 9.2%; Italy, 6.8%; China, 6.8%; Germany, 5.4%; Ukraine, 4.4%; and Turkey, 4.4% . Its major export partners were

Principal Trading Partners – Lebanon (2010)

(In millions of US dollars)

Country	Total	Exports	Imports	Balance
World	23,481.0	5,021.0	18,460.0	-13,439.0
Syrian Arab Republic	3,076.6	1,068.3	2,008.3	-940.1
United States	2,103.4	79.8	2,023.6	-1,943.7
Italy	1,524.8	33.5	1,491.3	-1,457.9
China	1,482.9	24.8	1,458.1	-1,433.4
France	1,382.9	38.4	1,344.5	-1,306.0
Ukraine	1,140.4	3.8	1,136.6	-1,132.8
Germany	1,072.3	30.1	1,042.2	-1,012.1
Sa'udi Arabia	1,006.5	255.3	751.2	-495.9
Turkey	887.9	207.8	680.2	-472.4
United Arab Emirates	754.8	537.2	217.6	319.6

(…) data not available or not significant.

(n.s.) not specified.

SOURCE: *2011 Direction of Trade Statistics Yearbook,* New York: United Nations, 2011.

Balance of Payments – Lebanon (2010)

(In millions of US dollars)

Current Account		**-9,415.0**
Balance on goods		-12,263.0
Imports	-17,728.0	
Exports	5,466.0	
Balance on services		2,259.0
Balance on income		45.0
Current transfers		544.0
Capital Account		**345.0**
Financial Account		**5,719.0**
Direct investment abroad		-574.0
Direct investment in Lebanon		4,955.0
Portfolio investment assets		-1,016.0
Portfolio investment liabilities		-108.0
Financial derivatives		…
Other investment assets		2,074.0
Other investment liabilities		388.0
Net Errors and Omissions		**6,411.0**
Reserves and Related Items		**-3,059.0**

(…) data not available or not significant.

SOURCE: *Balance of Payment Statistics Yearbook 2011,* Washington, DC: International Monetary Fund, 2011.

Syria, 25.8%; UAE, 14.3%; Saudi Arabia, 6.8%; Switzerland, 5.6%; and Qatar, 4.4%.

Foreign trade has been important in the economic life of Lebanon as a source of both income and employment. Some 40% of total exports are actually reexports, principally machinery, metal products, foods, wood products, textiles, and chemicals.

The most expensive products that Lebanon exports are gold, silverware, jewelry, and precious stones. Other exports include fruits, nuts and vegetables, chemicals, textile fibers, and construction minerals. Major imports include petroleum products, cars, meat and live animals, machinery and transport equipment, consumer goods, and chemicals.

³²BALANCE OF PAYMENTS

In 2010 Lebanon had a foreign trade deficit of $8.6 billion, amounting to 8.3% of GDP.

Lebanon traditionally maintained a favorable balance of payments, with rising trade deficits more than offset by net earnings from services, transfers of foreign capital, and remittances from Lebanese workers abroad. Although the trade deficit increased substantially between 1977 and 1984, a balance of payments deficit was recorded only for the last two years of the period. By 1985 a surplus of $249 million was again achieved, with a modest trade recovery following in 1986–87. Hostilities in the industrial and prosperous areas of Lebanon in 1989–90 triggered a substantial outflow of capital and a deficit in the balance of payments. Order was restored in 1991 and a resumption of capital inflows averted larger deficits in the following years. In 1995 net capital inflows offset a large trade deficit to produce a $256 million surplus in the balance of payments. A large portion of the trade imbalance consists of imports of machinery that should ultimately increase productivity. In 2000 the balance of payments registered a deficit of $289 million.

In 2003 exports of goods and services totaled $2.9 billion, and imports totaled $7.6 billion. The trade deficit widened in 2005 that year, Lebanon's exports totaled $1.782 billion, and imports were valued at $8.855 billion. The current-account balance in 2010 was estimated at -$8.8 billion.

³³BANKING AND SECURITIES

The Bank of Lebanon, established on 1 April 1964, is now the sole bank of issue. Its powers to regulate and control commercial banks and other institutions and to implement monetary policy were expanded by amendments to the Code of Money and Credit promulgated in October 1973. To encourage the movement and deposit of foreign capital in Lebanon, a bank secrecy law of 1956 forbids banks to disclose details of a client's business even to judicial authorities. There are no restrictions on currency conversions and transfers, and no foreign exchange controls effect trading.

In the late 1990s, the banking sector was undergoing a period of expansion and consolidation with a number of banks listed on the Beirut Stock Exchange. In 1998, over 70 banks were operating in Lebanon with total assets of around $31 billion.

In 2010 the discount rate, the interest rate at which the central bank lends to financial institutions in the short term, was 3.5%. The commercial bank prime lending rate, the rate at which banks lend to customers, was 8.337%.

The Beirut Stock Exchange was established by a decree from the French Commissioner in 1920. In its early years, trading was restricted to gold and currency. Trading was opened to companies in the 1930s, and by the 1950s it included 50 listed bonds from industrial, banking, and service companies. Trading activity waned during political unrest beginning in 1975; it was formally suspended from 1983 to 1996. In 2001 the stock market remained sluggish, with only 12 companies listed. Market capitalization was around $1.2 billion. In 2011 the Beirut Stock Exchange listed 24 companies; as of October that year, it had a total market capitalization of $10.5 billion, as compared to $2.3 billion in 2004.

Public Finance – Lebanon (2009)

(In billions of pounds, budgetary central government figures)

Revenue and Grants	**11,877**	**100.0%**
Tax revenue	8,995	75.7%
Social contributions	95	0.8%
Grants	166	1.4%
Other revenue	2,620	22.1%
Expenditures	**16,213**	**100.0%**
General public services	8,469	52.2%
Defense	1,696	10.5%
Public order and safety	810	5.0%
Economic affairs	3,377	20.8%
Environmental protection	3	<0.1%
Housing and community amenities	30	0.2%
Health	481	3.0%
Recreational, culture, and religion	78	0.5%
Education	1,096	6.8%
Social protection	172	1.1%

(…) data not available or not significant.

SOURCE: *Government Finance Statistics Yearbook 2010,* Washington, DC: International Monetary Fund, 2010.

³⁴INSURANCE

Activities of insurance companies are regulated by the National Insurance Council. All insurance companies must deposit a specific amount of money or real investments in an approved bank and must retain in Lebanon reserves commensurate with their volume of business. There are at least 85 insurance companies operating in Lebanon, most of them national insurance companies. According to a 2007 report by Lebanon's Central Administration of Statistics, nearly 48% of employed persons were not covered by health insurance and 79% of unemployed persons age 15 and above did not have health insurance.

³⁵PUBLIC FINANCE

In 2010 the budget of Lebanon included $9.001 billion in public revenue and $10.95 billion in public expenditures. The budget deficit amounted to 7.4% of GDP. Public debt was 150.7% of GDP, with $31.28 billion of the debt held by foreign entities.

The annual budget of the central government must be approved by the National Assembly. The Lebanese government annually faces the formidable problem of financing a massive deficit resulting from heavy financial obligations and huge shortfalls in revenues. To reduce the deficit, the government has tried to increase revenues by raising taxes and tightening the budget. The government relies heavily on grants and loans from multilateral agencies, Arab governments, and the French to cover the deficit.

The International Monetary Fund (IMF) reported that in 2009, budgetary central government revenues were LBP12.7 billion and expenditures were LBP17 billion.

³⁶TAXATION

A graduated tax is imposed on individual salaries, real profits, and real estate income. Corporations and joint stock companies generally are taxed on net real profits derived in Lebanon at a flat rate of 15%. Dividends, interest and royalties are generally subject to a 10% withholding tax. Bank interest is subject to a 5% rate. Also levied are inheritance and gift taxes, social security payroll taxes, flat and graduated property taxes, and a stamp duty.

³⁷CUSTOMS AND DUTIES

Customs duties, based on the Harmonized System of tariffs, depend on the type of product and range from 0% from 70%, averaging 15%. Lebanon acceded to Arab League's Arab Free Trade Area agreement in 1997 and also has bilateral free trade agreements with Egypt, Kuwait, Syria, and the United Arab Emirates. It also adheres to the Arab League boycott of Israel. Lebanon has applied for World Trade Organization membership and is in negotiations for accession.

³⁸FOREIGN INVESTMENT

Foreign direct investment (FDI) in Lebanon was a net inflow of $4.8 billion according to World Bank figures published in 2009. FDI represented 13.91% of GDP. Other forms of capital inflow—remittances, repatriated capital and placements in treasury bills—far outweigh inward FDI.

Lebanon's liberal investment policies are designed to attract foreign direct investment to foster economic recovery and rebuild its war damaged infrastructure. Some analysts estimated that the rebuilding costs would exceed $18 billion with construction accounting for a large part of foreign investment. By 2006, French, Italian, German, British, Korean, and Finnish companies were the predominant investors in Lebanon. Their presence is most strongly felt in the fields of electricity, water, and telecommunications. US-based investment was only $7 million in 1996, though this had climbed to $65 million by 1999. The movement of funds in and out of Lebanon is free from taxes, fees, or restrictions. The top corporate tax rate is 15%. Lebanon also has bilateral trade investment agreements with China and a number of European and Arab countries.

To conserve cash, the government uses "build, operate, transfer" (BOT) agreements in which major construction projects are funded by fees charged to the government by companies, rather than companies charging tariffs to consumers.

39 ECONOMIC DEVELOPMENT

Since World War II, Lebanon has followed free-enterprise and free-trade policies. The country's favorable geographical position as a transit point and the traditional importance of the trading and banking sectors of the economy helped make Lebanon prosperous by the early 1970s. Lebanon became a center of trade, finance, and tourism by means of a stable currency backed largely with gold, by a conservative fiscal policy, by various incentives for foreign investors, and by minimization of banking regulations.

Lebanon's development went awry in the mid-1970s, as factional conflict, always present in Lebanese society, erupted into open warfare. The loss to the economy was enormous, particularly in Beirut. In November 1979 Saudi Arabia and six other oil-producing Arab countries promised to contribute $2 billion for Lebanon's reconstruction effort over a five-year period, but only $381 million had been provided by October 1987. (After Israel invaded Lebanon in June 1982, the Arab countries decided to withhold future funds until Israeli forces had withdrawn completely.)

Under the leadership of Prime Minister Rafiq al-Hariri, Lebanon embarked on the Horizon 2000 program in 1993. Areas of major activity targeted by the plan were the rehabilitation of telecommunications, electricity grids, highways, sewage, waste management, water networks, Beirut International Airport, harbors, the education system, and housing. The plan also called for investment in commercial facilities to reestablish Beirut as an international business center in competition with Hong Kong and Singapore. The government established a private company, Solidere, to carry out the reconstruction and development of downtown Beirut. Under the Horizon 2000 guidelines, no single investor would be permitted to hold more than a 10% share in the company. The parliament also established a public company, Elyssar, for developing southwest Beirut. Under the government's five-year program (2001–05) the "three pillars" of reform were affirmed by the Hariri government to be 1) economic revival and sustained growth with the private sector as the engine of growth; 2) fiscal consolidation and administrative reform; and 3) monetary, financial, and price stability.

In 2002, in response to growing indebtedness, donors pledged $4.4 billion to Lebanon at the Paris II donors' conference. By 2006 the country had failed to make progress against its debt although the Lebanese government was continuing its plans for economic reforms. These included an improvement in the management of the national debt (in 2005, it stood at over 200% of GDP); an expansion of state revenues by widening the tax base, improving the collection of revenues, and rationalizing expenditure; and strengthening financial management. In 2007, at Paris III, $7.6 billion was pledged by international donors, to be contingent on Lebanon meeting agreed benchmarks.

40 SOCIAL DEVELOPMENT

A government social security plan is intended to provide sickness and maternity insurance, accident and disability insurance, family allowances, and end-of-service indemnity payments. The employer contributes 8.5% of payroll, while the employee and government make no contribution. The system provides lump sum payments only for retirement, disability, and survivor benefits. Foreigners employed in Lebanon are entitled to benefits if similar rights are available for Lebanese in their home countries. Family allowances are provided for workers' families with children and nonworking wives. Voluntary social work societies also conduct relief and welfare activities.

Careers in government, the professions, and, less commonly, business, are open to women. However, in some segments of society, social pressure prevents them from taking full advantage of employment opportunities. Cultural norms for women are not absolutely uniform and are informed by religion, socio-economic status, and region. Lebanese citizenship is passed on only by fathers to their children. The children of Lebanese women married to foreigners are unable to secure citizenship. Many of the religious laws governing family and personal status discriminate against women. Despite these circumstances, there are a growing number of women in business and in government. Domestic abuse and violence affects a significant percentage of women. The absence of economic independence and the fear of losing custody of children prevent women from leaving abusive spouses. Foreign domestic servants are frequently abused.

Human rights abuses include arbitrary arrest and detention and the use of excessive force and torture. Prison conditions are substandard and include severe overcrowding. Human rights organizations are allowed to operate freely.

41 HEALTH

According to the CIA, life expectancy in Lebanon was 72 years in 2011. The country spent 8.5% of its GDP on healthcare, amounting to $663 per person. There were 35 physicians, 22 nurses and midwives, and 35 hospital beds per 10,000 inhabitants. The fertility rate was 1.8, while the infant mortality rate was 11 per 1,000 live births. In 2008 the maternal mortality rate, according to the World Bank, was 26 per 100,000 births. It was estimated that 53% of children were vaccinated against measles. The CIA calculated HIV/AIDS prevalence in Lebanon to be about 0.1% in 2009.

The Lebanese Ministry of Health's review of hospital use identified major health problems to be hypertension, diabetes, and asthma, in addition to eye and ear diseases, cardiac conditions, and dermatological problems. According to the World Bank, approximately 100% of the population had access to an improved water source, although the accuracy of this statistic is disputed: access to water varies by location, and many people purchase water to meet their needs. According to a 2009 World Bank report, only 53% of households connected to the public water network use the water for drinking; safety was the most frequently cited concern.

About 61% of married women used contraception in 2007. Life expectancy in 2011 was 75.01 years and the infant mortality rate was 15.85 per 1,000 live births. Immunization rates for children up to one year old included diphtheria, pertussis, and tetanus, 92%, and measles, 96%. Vitamin deficiencies are a problem; an estimated 25% of all school-age children have goiter.

42 HOUSING

Despite substantial construction activity since World War II and a boom in construction during the 1960s, which increased the number of housing units to 484,000 in 1970, there was a housing shortage, especially of low-cost residential units, in the early 1970s. The situation was aggravated by the civil war (ending in 1990) and subsequent factional strife in which half of the country's real estate was severely damaged or destroyed. About 750,000 people were displaced. Under the CDR 1983–91 plan, nearly 30% of total expenditures were allocated to build new dwellings and to restore war-damaged houses. According to Lebanon's Central Administration of Statistics, there were a total of 888,814 housing units in 2007.

43 EDUCATION

In 2009 the World Bank estimated that 90% of age-eligible children in Lebanon were enrolled in primary school. Secondary enrollment for age-eligible children stood at 75%. Tertiary enrollment was estimated at 53%. Of those enrolled in tertiary education, there were 100 male students for every 124 female students. Overall, the CIA estimated that Lebanon had a literacy rate of 87.4%, with 93.1% for men and 82.2% (as of 2003) for women. Public expenditure on education represented 1.8% of GDP.

Free primary education was introduced in 1960, but about two-thirds of all students attend private schools. Public schools typically suffer from a lack of material resources, and poor infrastructure is not uncommon. Primary school covers six years of study, followed by three years of complementary (intermediate) courses. It is estimated that about 90% of all students complete their primary education. The student-to-teacher ratio for primary school was 14:1 in 2005. Based on their performance at the basic levels of education, students are assigned to general secondary school (studying economics, life sciences, humanities, and science) or a technical secondary school (with about 55 different field options). The academic year runs from October to June.

In 2005 about 74% of age-eligible children were enrolled in some type of preschool program.

Leading universities include the American University in Beirut; St. Joseph University; the Lebanese (State) University; the University of the Holy Spirit; and the Arab University of Beirut.

44 LIBRARIES AND MUSEUMS

Lebanon has about a dozen sizable libraries with specialized collections of books, manuscripts, and documents. Most libraries are in Beirut, but there are also collections at Şaydā (Sidon) and Harissa. The National Library of Lebanon, founded in 1921, had more than 100,000 volumes when it was destroyed at the beginning of the war in 1975. By 2002 it had restored that collection to 150,000 volumes. The Arab University Library has 200,000 volumes, but the largest library is that of the American University in Beirut, with 546,000 volumes. St. Joseph University has several specialized libraries, including the Bibliothèque Orientale, with 400,000 volumes. The library of the St. John Monastery in Khonchara, founded in 1696, contains the first known printing press in the Middle East. The Université Saint-Esprit de Kaslik in Jounieh has the largest provincial collection with 200,000 volumes. The Municipal Public Library of Beirut has two branches; the Bachoura branch, opened in 2004, maintains a collection that includes 20,000 books in Arabic, French, English, Armenian, Spanish, and German, plus audio books, CD-ROMs, videos, and DVDs. There are at least 25 other public and municipal libraries throughout the country that are organized through the Assabil library network, a nongovernmental organization established in 1997; these branches include National Library of Baakline, Cultural Center for Francophone Activities, Public Library of the Cultural League in Tarābulus (Tripoli), and the Library for the Blind (in Beirut).

The National Museum of Lebanon (1920) in Beirut has a collection of historical documents and many notable antiquities, including the sarcophagus of King Ahiram (13th century BC), with the first known alphabetical inscriptions. The American University Museum also has an extensive collection of ancient artifacts. Beirut also houses the Museum of Fine Arts and the Museum of Lebanese Prehistory of St. Joseph University. The Gibran Museum in Bsharri, celebrating the life and work of the prophet Khalil Gibran, is a popular site. The Planet Discovery Children's Science Museum is located in Beirut.

45 MEDIA

In 2009 the CIA reported that there were 750,000 telephone landlines in Lebanon. In addition to landlines, mobile phone subscriptions averaged 36 per 100 people; there were an estimated 1.5 million cellular phones in use. There were 222 AM radio stations and four shortwave radio stations. Internet users numbered 24 per 100 citizens. In 2011 it was reported that Lebanon had one of the slowest internet connections in the world.

Government-controlled Radio Lebanon broadcasts in Arabic, and Tele-Liban broadcasts on three channels in Arabic, French, and English. All other radio and television stations are privately owned. In 2007 there were more than 30 radio stations and seven television stations. In 2003 there were an estimated 182 radios and 357 television sets for every 1,000 people. About 29.9 of every 1,000 people were cable subscribers. In 2010 the country had 51,451 Internet hosts.

Historically, Lebanon has had the freest press in the Arab world. Even during the civil war some 25 newspapers and magazines were published without restriction. Newspapers freely criticize the government but refrain from criticizing political groups that have the power to retaliate forcibly. There have been high-profile precedents of journalists being assassinated. In 2005 Samir Qasir, a journalist with the daily *An Nahar*, was killed by a car bomb. Prominent newspapers in 2010, with circulation numbers listed parenthetically, included *An-Nahar* (77,595), *As-Safir* (50,000), and *Al Hayat* (31,034), as well as 4 other major newspapers.

Though the constitution provides for freedom of the press, the government uses several means short of censorship to control freedom of expression. The Surete Generale is authorized to approve all foreign materials, including magazines, plays, books, and films. The law prohibits attacks on the dignity of the head of state or foreign leaders, prosecuting through a special Publications Court.

46 ORGANIZATIONS

There are chambers of commerce and industry in Beirut, Tarābulus (Tripoli), Şaydā (Sidon), and Zahlah. The Chamber of Commerce, Industry, and Agriculture of Beirut and Mount Lebanon promotes tourism as well as international trade. The International Labour Organization Regional Office for the Arab States is in Beirut. Lebanon has a French Chamber of Commerce, and an Association of Lebanese Industries.

The Amel Association is a major social welfare organization providing emergency relief and social, medical, and educational services. The National Council for Scientific Research offers major support for promoting scientific study and research. A smaller organization, the Nadim Andraos Foundation, also provides financial support for medical and scientific studies.

National youth organizations include the Lebanese Scout Federation, Lebanese Youth and Student Movement for the United Nations, the Progressive Youth Organization, the Democratic Youth Union, and YMCA/YWCA. There are several sports associations representing a variety of pastimes, such as squash, aikido, badminton, yachting, tennis, and track and field. There are active branches of the Paralympic Committee and the Special Olympics.

There are Rotary and Lion's Clubs in Beirut. There are national chapters of the Red Cross Society, Defence for Children, and Habitat for Humanity.

47 TOURISM, TRAVEL, AND RECREATION

The *Tourism Factbook*, published by the UN World Tourism Organization, reported 1.84 million incoming tourists to Lebanon in 2009 that spent a total of $6.77 billion. Of those incoming tourists, there were 762,000 from the Middle East and 455,000 from Europe. There were 32,217 hotel beds available in Lebanon. The estimated daily cost to visit Beirut, the capital, was $197.

Before 1975, Lebanon's antiquities—notably at Şaydā (Sidon), Tyre, Byblos, and Baalbek—combined with a pleasant climate and scenery to attract many tourists (more than two million in 1974), especially from other Arab countries. During the civil war that began that year, however, fighting and bombing destroyed or heavily damaged major hotels in Beirut and reduced the number of tourists to practically zero. With the rebuilding of the country, the tourism industry has steadily grown. The luxury hotels have attracted tourists along with the famous Pigeon Rocks in Raouche. Many attractions are historical sites in Tyre and Tarābulus (Tripoli). The temple complex in Baalbek, which includes the remains of the temples of Jupiter, Bacchus, and Venus, is one of the largest in the world and has been designated a World Heritage site by UNESCO. Horse racing is also popular in Lebanon, with races held every Sunday.

Visas are required to enter Lebanon, along with passports valid for six months when applying for the visa. Tourism was badly affected by the 2006 war between Israel and Hezbollah but eventually rebounded. Lebanon's social freedoms and Western mores, particularly evident in Beirut, make the country a popular destination for Arabs from more conservative countries.

48 FAMOUS PERSONS

Khalil Gibran (Jibran, 1883–1931), a native of Lebanon, achieved international renown through his paintings and literary works. He is best known for *The Prophet*, a book of philosophical essays. Charles Habib Malik (1906–87), for many years Lebanon's leading diplomat, was president of the 13th UN General Assembly in 1958/59. Rafiq Hariri (1944–2005), twice prime minister of Lebanon, was assassinated in February 2005; massive demonstrations held after his death led to the eventual withdrawal of Syrian troops from Lebanon in April 2005.

49 DEPENDENCIES

Lebanon has no territories or colonies.

50 BIBLIOGRAPHY

El-Khazen, Farid. *The Breakdown of the State in Lebanon, 1967–1976.* Cambridge, MA: Harvard University Press, 2000.

Habeeb, William Mark, Rafael D. Frankel, et al. *The Middle East in Turmoil: Conflict, Revolution and Change.* Santa Barbara, CA: Greenwood, 2012.

Hamzeh, Ahmad Nizar. *In the Path of Hizbullah.* Syracuse, NY: Syracuse University Press, 2004.

Harris, William W. *Lebanon: A History, 600–2011.* New York: Oxford University Press, 2012.

Jabbour, Samer, Rouham Yamout, et al. *Public Health in the Arab World.* Cambridge, Eng.: Cambridge University Press, 2012.

Khalaf, Samir. *Civil and Uncivil Violence in Lebanon: A History of the Internationalization of Communal Contact.* New York: Columbia University Press, 2002.

Khater, Akram Fouad. *Inventing Home: Emigration, Gender, and the Middle Class in Lebanon, 1870–1920.* Berkeley: University of California Press, 2001.

Lattouf, Mirna. *Women, Education, and Socialization in Modern Lebanon: 19th and 20th Centuries Social History.* Lanham, Md.: University Press of America, 2004.

Lebanon Investment and Business Guide: Strategic and Practical Information. Washington, DC: International Business Publications USA, 2012.

Makdisi, Samir A. *The Lessons of Lebanon: The Economics of War and Development.* New York: I.B. Tauris, 2004.

Najem, Tom. *Lebanon: The Politics of a Penetrated Society.* London: Routledge, 2002.

Seddon, David (ed.). *A Political and Economic Dictionary of the Middle East.* Philadelphia: Routledge/Taylor and Francis, 2004.

MALAYSIA

CAPITAL: Kuala Lumpur

FLAG: The national flag consists of 14 alternating horizontal stripes, of which 7 are red and 7 white; a gold 14-pointed star and crescent appear on a blue field in the upper left corner.

ANTHEM: *Negara Ku (My Country).*

MONETARY UNIT: The Malaysian ringgit (MYR), or dollar, is divided into 100 sen, or cents. There are coins of 1, 5, 10, 20, and 50 sens and 1 ringgit, and notes of 1, 5, 10, 20, 100, 500, and 1,000 ringgits. MYR1 = US$0.31918 (or US$1 = MYR3.13) as of 2011.

WEIGHTS AND MEASURES: The metric system became the legal standard in 1982, but some British weights and measures and local units also are in use.

HOLIDAYS: National Day, 31 August; Christmas, 25 December. Movable holidays include Wesak Day (Buddha Day), Birthday of His Majesty the Yang di-Pertuan Agong, Hari Raya Puasa (the end of Ramadan), Hari Raya Haji, the 1st of Muharram (Muslim New Year), Milad an-Nabi, Dewali, Thaipusam, and the Chinese New Year. Individual states celebrate the birthdays of their rulers and other holidays observed by native ethnic groups.

TIME: 7 p.m. = noon GMT.

¹LOCATION, SIZE, AND EXTENT

Situated in Southeast Asia, Malaysia, with an area of 329,750 sq km (127,317 sq mi), consists of two noncontiguous areas: peninsular Malaysia (formerly West Malaysia), on the Asian mainland, and the states of Sarawak and Sabah, known together as East Malaysia, on the island of Borneo. Comparatively, the area occupied by Malaysia is slightly larger than the state of New Mexico. Peninsular Malaysia, protruding southward from the mainland of Asia, comprises an area of 131,587 sq km (50,806 sq mi), extending 748 km (465 mi) SSE–NNW and 322 km (200 mi) ENE–WSW. It is bordered on the N by Thailand, on the E by the South China Sea, on the S by the Strait of Johore, and on the W by the Strait of Malacca and the Andaman Sea, with a total boundary length of 2,068 km (1,285 mi).

Sarawak, covering an area of 124,449 sq km (48,050 sq mi), on the northwest coast of Borneo, extends 679 km (422 mi) NNE–SSW and 254 km (158 mi) ESE–WNW. It is bounded by Brunei on the N, Sabah on the NE, Indonesia on the E and S, and the South China Sea on the W. Sarawak's total boundary length is 2,621 km (1,629 mi). Situated at the northern end of Borneo, Sabah has an area of 74,398 sq km (28,725 sq mi), with a length of 412 km (256 mi) E–W and a width of 328 km (204 mi) N–S. To the N is the Balabac Strait, to the NE the Sulu Sea, to the SE the Celebes Sea, to the S Indonesia, to the SW Sarawak, and to the W the South China Sea, with a total boundary length of 2,008 km (1,248 mi). The total boundary length of Malaysia is 7,344 km (4,563 mi), of which 4,675 km (2,905 mi) is coastline.

Malaysia claims several atolls of the Spratly Island group in the South China Sea. The claim, in a region where oil is suspected, is disputed by China, the Philippines, Taiwan, and Vietnam. Malaysia's capital city, Kuala Lumpur, is located in the western part of peninsular Malaysia.

²TOPOGRAPHY

Four-fifths of peninsular Malaysia is covered by rain forest and swamp. The northern regions are divided by a series of mountain ranges that rise abruptly from the wide, flat coastal plains. The highest peaks, Gunong Tahan (Mt. Tahan-2,187 m/7,174 ft) and Gunong Korbu (2,183 m/7,162 ft), are in the north central region. The main watershed follows a mountain range about 80 km (50 mi) inland, roughly parallel to the west coast. The rivers flowing to the east, south, and west of this range are swift and have cut some deep gorges, but on reaching the coastal plains they become sluggish. The western coastal plain contains most of the country's population and the main seaports, George Town (on the offshore Pulau Pinang) and Kelang (formerly Port Swettenham). The eastern coastal plain is mostly jungle and lightly settled. It is subject to heavy storms from the South China Sea and lacks natural harbors.

Sarawak consists of an alluvial and swampy coastal plain, an area of rolling country interspersed with mountain ranges, and a mountainous interior. Rain forests cover the greater part of Sarawak. Many of the rivers are navigable. Sabah is split in two by the Crocker Mountains, which extend north and south some 48 km (30 mi) inland from the west coast, rising to over 4,101 m (13,455 ft) at Mt. Kinabalu, the highest point in Malaysia. Most of the interior is covered with tropical forest, while the western coastal area consists of alluvial flats making up the main rubber and rice land.

³CLIMATE

The climate of peninsular Malaysia is equatorial, characterized by fairly high but uniform temperatures (23–31°C/73–88°F) throughout the year, high humidity, and copious rainfall averaging about 250 cm/100 in annually. There are seasonal variations in rainfall, with the heaviest rains from October to December or January; except for a few mountain areas, the most abundant rainfall is in the eastern coastal region, where it averages over 300 cm (120 in) per year. Elsewhere the annual average is 200–300 cm (80–120 in), the northwestern and southwestern regions having the least rainfall. The nights are usually cool because of the nearby seas. The climate of East Malaysia is relatively cool for an area so near the equator.

⁴FLORA AND FAUNA

The World Resources Institute estimates that there are 15,500 plant species in Malaysia. In addition, Malaysia is home to 337 species of mammals, 746 species of birds, 388 species of reptiles, and 200 species of amphibians. The calculation reflects the total number of distinct species residing in the country, not the number of endemic species.

In peninsular Malaysia, camphor, ebony, sandalwood, teak, and many varieties of palm trees abound. Rain forest fauna includes seladang (Malayan bison), deer, wild pigs, tree shrews, honey bears, forest cats, civets, monkeys, crocodiles, lizards, and snakes. The seladang weighs about a ton and is the largest wild ox in the world. An immense variety of insects, particularly butterflies, are found.

On Sabah and Sarawak, lowland forests contain some 400 species of tall dipterocarps (hardwoods) and semi-hardwoods; fig trees abound, attracting small mammals and birds; and groves are formed by the extensive aerial roots of warangen (a tree sacred to indigenous peoples). As altitude increases, herbaceous plants-buttercups, violets, and valerian-become more numerous, until moss-covered evergreen forests are reached at elevations of 1,520–1,830 m (5,000–6,000 ft). Brilliantly colored birds of paradise and a great wealth of other bird species inhabit the two states.

⁵ENVIRONMENT

The environment of Malaysia faces a variety of threats. Discharge of untreated sewage has contaminated the nation's water; the most heavily polluted areas are along the west coast. Malaysia's water pollution problem also extends to its rivers, of which 40% are polluted. The Environmental Quality Act of 1974 and other environmental laws are administered by the Division of Environment of the Ministry of Science, Technology, and Environment. Discharge of oil by vessels in Malaysian waters is prohibited. The World Resources Institute reports that Malaysia had designated 5.97 million hectares (14.76 million acres) of land for protection as of 2006. Water resources totaled 580 cu km (139.2 cu mi) while water usage was 9.02 cu km (2.16 cu mi) per year. Domestic water usage accounted for 17% of total usage, industrial for 21%, and agricultural for 62%. Per capita water usage totaled 356 cu m (12,572 cu ft) per year.

Malaysia's cities have produced an average of 1.5 million tons of solid waste per year. Clean-air legislation limiting industrial and automobile emissions was adopted in 1978; however, air pollution from both of these sources is still a problem. In the mid-1990s, Malaysia ranked among 50 nations with the world's highest industrial carbon dioxide emissions, which totaled 70.5 million metric tons per year. By 2000, total carbon dioxide emissions had doubled to 144 million metric tons. By 2008, according to a United Nations (UN) report, carbon dioxide emissions in Malaysia totaled 194,317 kilotons.

According to a 2011 report issued by the International Union for Conservation of Nature and Natural Resources (IUCN), threatened species included 70 mammals, 45 birds, 24 reptiles, 47 amphibians, 64 fish, 32 mollusks, 211 other invertebrates, and 694 plants. Threatened species in Malaysia include the orangutan, tiger, Asian elephant, Malayan tapir, Sumatran rhinoceros, Singapore roundleaf horseshoe bat, four species of turtle (green sea, hawksbill, olive ridley, and leatherback), and two species of crocodile (false gavial and Siamese). At least three species have become extinct, including the double-banded argus.

Malaysia has the world's fifth-most-extensive mangrove area, which total over a half a million hectares (over 1.2 million acres), but the country's forests are threatened by commercial interests. Protected areas included two natural UNESCO World Heritage Sites and six Ramsar wetland sites.

⁶POPULATION

The US Central Intelligence Agency (CIA) estimates the population of Malaysia in 2011 to be approximately 28,728,607, which placed it at number 43 in population among the 196 nations of the world. In 2011, approximately 5% of the population was over 65 years of age, with another 29.6% under 15 years of age. The median age in Malaysia was 26.8 years. There were 1.01 males for every female in the country. The population's annual rate of change was 1.576%. The projected population for the year 2025 was 34,900,000. Population density in Malaysia was calculated at 87 people per sq km (225 people per sq mi).

The UN estimated that 72% of the population lived in urban areas, and that urban populations had an annual rate of change of 2.4%. The largest urban areas, along with their respective populations, included Kuala Lumpur, 1.5 million; Klang, 1.1 million; and Johor Bahru, 958,000.

⁷MIGRATION

Malaysia is a relatively well-off nation surrounded by poorer nations. Many refugees and immigrants arrive without official documentation. As such, it is hard to accurately estimate the number of refugees and immigrants in the country. In 2011, Malaysia's prime minister gave the number of refugees as 178,000. Others place the figure at closer to 100,000. Refugees International states there are 80,000 officially registered refugees. In 2011 there were believed to be millions of "economic migrants" from Indonesia, as well as 340,000 Burmese, including 87,000 refugees registered with the UN High Commission for Refugees (UNHCR) and an unknown number of Cambodians.

Estimates of Malaysia's net migration rate, carried out by the CIA in 2011, amounted to -0.39 migrants per 1,000 citizens. The total number of emigrants living abroad was 1.48 million. Many of those were of Chinese or Indian ethnicity; approximately one third were well educated. The total number of immigrants living in Malaysia was 2.36 million. Malaysia also accepted 15,174 refugees from Indonesia and 21,544 from Burma.

Not until British economic enterprise first attracted foreign labor after 1800 did large-scale Chinese, Indian, and Malaysian migration (nonnative Indonesians and Borneans) take place. The

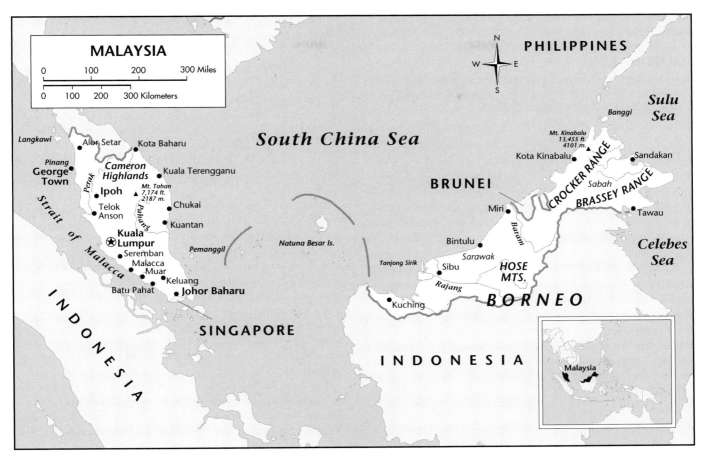

LOCATION: Peninsular Malaysia: 1°17′ to 6°43′ N; 99°38′ to 104°39′E. Sarawak: 0°52′ to 4°59′ N; 109°38′ to 155°43′E. Sabah: 4°6′ to 7°22′ N; 115°7′ to 119°17′E.
BOUNDARY LENGTHS: Peninsular Malaysia: Thailand, 506 kilometers (316 miles); coastline, 2,068 kilometers (1,292 miles). East Malaysia: Brunei, 381 kilometers (238 miles); Indonesia, 1,728 kilometers (1,080 miles); coastline, 2,607 kilometers (1,629 miles).
TERRITORIAL SEA LIMIT: 12 miles.

early migrants were transients; however, migration data for subsequent years show a general tendency toward permanent settlement by these non-indigenous portions of the population. By 1953, the Malays were a minority in their own territory. The government enacted legislation restricting further immigration, and by 1968 the Malays formed slightly more than 50% of the population. Regulations that took effect in 1968 concerning passports and border crossings between Malaysia and Indonesia and between Malaysia and the Philippines were also intended to restrict immigration.

Between October 2004 and February 2005, 380,000 unauthorized foreigners left or were expelled. Employers then claimed a shortage of workers on plantations and in construction. The government resumed the practice of permitting entrants on tourist visas to work if they found a job. In July 2005 the government declared that the 60,000 refugees in the country would be allowed to work.

In October 2011 Malaysia announced plans to deport 1,000 Burmese refugees being detailed in Malaysia in return for Malaysian immigrants being held in Burma. Human rights groups in Malaysia raised concerns that the exchange breached the UN Refugee Convention principle of not returning refugees to situations of danger; subsequently the deal fell through. A "Malaysian Solution" developed by Australia and Malaysia, in which Aus-

tralia would take some 4,000 certified refugees from Malaysia in exchange for Malaysia taking 800 asylum seekers from Australia was judged unlawful by the Australian High Court in part because Malaysia, not being a UNHCR signatory, could not guarantee the fair treatment of refugees.

8 ETHNIC GROUPS

The population of Malaysia consists of three main ethnic groups-Malays, Chinese, and peoples of the South Asian subcontinent. Collectively, indigenous groups are known as Bumiputras ("sons of the soil"). Estimates for 2004 reported the following distribution: Malays, 50.4%; Chinese, 23.7%; Bumiputras, 11%; Indians, 7.1%; and other groups, 7.8%. Malays predominate in the rural areas, while the Chinese are concentrated in urban and mining areas, where they control much of the nation's wealth; enmity between ethnic Malays and Chinese has occasionally erupted into violence. The non-Malay indigenous groups on the peninsula, collectively called the Orang Asli (aborigines), number about 150,000; as a large marginalized group, they represent the poorest in the country. Non-Malay indigenous tribes constitute about half of Sarawak's residents; the largest indigenous group consists of the Sea Dayaks, or Ibans, followed by the Land Dayaks, or Bidayuh. The majority of Sabah's population consists of indigenous peoples, principally Kadazans, Bajaus, and Muruts. The balance is dominated by Chinese.

9 LANGUAGES

Bahasa Malaysia, or Malay, is the national language and the lingua franca of all Malaysia. The traditional Bahasa Malaysia script is Jawi, which derives from Arabic script, but Rumi, based on the Roman alphabet, is officially used in government, education, and business. English is widely employed in government and commerce and is a compulsory subject in all schools. Chinese (notably the Mandarin, Cantonese, Hokkien, Hakka, Hainan, and Foochow dialects), Tamil, Telugu, Malalalam, Punjabi, and Thai are also spoken. In addition, in East Malaysia several indigenous languages are spoken, the largest of which are Iban and Kadazan. Most Malaysians are bilingual or multilingual.

10 RELIGIONS

While Islam is the official religion of Malaysia, a wide range of religions co-exist in the nation, with the blessing of the government which officially endorses freedom of religion. According to a 2000 government census, about 60% of the population were Muslim, 19% Buddhist, 9% Christian, and 6% Hindu. About 3% practiced Confucianism, Taoism, or other traditional Chinese religions. Other faiths include animism, Sikhism, and Baha'ism. Religious lines generally follow ethnic lines. Almost all Malays are Muslims; most Indians are Hindus, with a substantial minority of Muslims, Sikhs, and Parsees; and most Chinese are Confucian Buddhists, with a minority Muslim representation. Christianity has won some adherents among the Chinese and Indians. The indigenous peoples of Sabah and Sarawak are still largely animist, although many have become Christian. Shamanism is also practiced on East Malaysia.

Malaysia's head of state, the yang di-pertuan agong, is also the national leader of the Islamic faith. While the constitution guarantees freedom to profess, practice, and propagate other religions, in practice the religious practices of Islamic groups other than Sunni Muslims are restricted. The government lists 56 sects of Islam as deviant and has the authority to detain Muslims adhering to the tenets of these sects for "rehabilitation" toward accepted Sunni principles. Proselytizing of Muslims to non-Muslim religions is prohibited. Despite the strict rules regarding Islamic religious practices, followers of non-Islamic religions are able to practice their religions freely. The national holidays include Muslim (Hari Raya Puasa, Hari Raya Qurban, the Birth of the Prophet Muhammad, Awal Muharram), Hindu (Dewali and Thaipusam), Buddhist (Wesak Day), and Christian (Christmas) holidays.

The nation has a dual court system, which includes Shari'ah (Islamic law) courts as well as civil courts. While the Shari'ah courts are generally meant to handle cases of religious and family law pertaining only to Muslims, some non-Muslims have expressed concerns that civil courts sometimes cede jurisdictional control to Shari'ah courts in some matters involving both Muslims and non-Muslims. Under Shari'ah law, there are often severe punishments enacted for violations of the Islamic code on matters such as dress (especially for women) or alcohol consumption.

11 TRANSPORTATION

The major highways on peninsular Malaysia run north–south along the east and west coasts. East–west links connect George Town and Kota Baharu in the north and Kuala Lumpur and Kuantan farther south. The East–West Highway (Federal Route 2) crosses peninsular Malaysia, while the Klang Valley Expressway connects Kuala Lumpur to Port Klang. The 924-km (574-mi) North–South Highway along the west coast of peninsular Malaysia connects Thailand and Singapore. The CIA reports that Malaysia has a total of 98,721 km (61,342 mi) of roads, of which 80,280 km (49,884 mi) are paved. There are 334 vehicles per 1,000 people in the country.

Malaysia's railway system extends for 1,665 km (1035 mi) and consists of standard and narrow gauge railroads. Rail lines on peninsular Malaysia are operated by the country's Malayan Railway Administration. These lines provide links to Thailand, Singapore, and the eastern parts of the peninsula. On the island of Borneo, the Sabah State Railways provides diesel service along the west coast and in the interior for 136 km (85 mi). There are no railroads in Sarawak, but in 2011 feasibility studies were underway for development of a railway system to provide transportation to 57% of the state's area, and support the Sarawak Corridor of Renewable Energy (SCORE) project launched by the prime minister in February 2008.

The three leading ports, all located on the busy Strait of Malacca, are Kelang (the port for Kuala Lumpur), Johor Baharu, and George Town. Kuching is the main port for Sarawak, and Kota Kinabalu the main port for Sabah. The Malaysian merchant fleet in 2010 consisted of 321 ships of 1,000 GRT or more. In addition, Malaysia has approximately 7,200 km (4,474 mi) of navigable waterways.

Malaysia's airports transported 23.77 million passengers in 2009, according to the World Bank. There are two heliports and 118 airports, 38 of which have paved runways. Most international flights enter or leave Malaysia through Kuala Lumpur International Airport. Other principal airports include Kota Kinabalu, Kuching, and Penang. The Malaysian Airline System (MAS) provides domestic service to most major cities of the peninsula and to Sarawak and Sabah.

12 HISTORY

The ancestors of the Malays came down from South China and settled in the Malay Peninsula about 2000 BC. Sri Vijaya, a strong Indo-Malay empire with headquarters at Palembang in southern Sumatra, rose about AD 600 and came to dominate both sides of the Strait of Malacca, until the 14th century, when Sri Vijaya fell, and Malaysia became part of the Majapahit Empire. About 1400, a fugitive ruler from Temasik (now Singapore) founded a principality at Malacca and embraced Islam. It was at Malacca that the West obtained its first foothold on the peninsula, when in 1511 the Malacca principality fell to Portugal. The Portuguese were driven out by the Dutch in 1641. The British East India Company laid the groundwork for British control of Malaya in 1786 by leasing the island of Pinang from the sultan of Kedah. Fourteen years later, it obtained from him a small area on the mainland opposite Pinang. In 1819, Sir Thomas Stamford Raffles obtained permission to establish a settlement at Singapore; in 1824, the island was ceded to the British East India Company. In the following year, the Dutch settlement at Malacca was ceded to Great Britain. Pinang, Singapore, and Malacca were combined under British rule in 1829 to form the Straits Settlements. The states of Perak and Selangor in 1874 secured treaties of protection from the British. Similar treaties were subsequently made with the sultans of Negri Sembilan (1874–89) and Pahang (1888). In 1895, these four states became a federation (the Federated Malay States), with a British resident-general and a centralized government. In 1909, under the Bangkok Treaty, Siam (now Thailand) ceded to British control the four northern states of Kelantan, Trengganu, Perlis, and Kedah. These four, together with Johor, which in 1914 was made a British protectorate, became known as the Unfederated Malay States. Separate British control was extended to Sabah, then known as North Borneo, in 1882. Six years later, North Borneo and Sarawak each became separate British protectorates. Tin mining and rubber cultivation grew rapidly under British rule, and large numbers of Chinese and Indian laborers were imported for these industries.

Japanese forces invaded Malaya and the Borneo territories in December 1941 and occupied them throughout World War II. Within a year after the Japanese surrender in September 1945, the British formed the Malayan Union, consisting of the nine peninsular states, together with Pinang and Malacca; also in 1946, Singapore and the two Borneo protectorates became separate British crown colonies. The Malayan Union was succeeded by the Federation of Malaya on 1 February 1948. Over the next decade, the British weathered a Communist insurgency as Malaya progressed toward self-government. On 31 August 1957, the Federation of Malaya became an independent member of the Commonwealth of Nations. On 1 August 1962, Great Britain and Malaya agreed on the formation of the new state of Malaysia-a political merger of Singapore and the British Borneo territories (Sarawak, Brunei, and North Borneo) with the Federation. On 1 September 1962 Singapore voted for incorporation in the proposed Malaysia, but Brunei elected not to join. On 16 September 1963, the Federation of Malaya, the State of Singapore, and the newly independent British colonies of Sarawak and Sabah merged to form the Federation of Malaysia ("Federation" was subsequently dropped from the official name). On 7 August 1965, Singapore seceded from the Federation. From the outset, Indonesia's President Sukarno attempted to take over the young nation and incorporate it into Indonesia; cordial relations between the two countries were not established until after Sukarno's ouster in 1966. Internal disorders stemming from hostilities between Chinese and Malay communities in Kuala Lumpur disrupted the 1969 national elections and prompted the declaration of a state of emergency lasting from mid-1969 to February 1971. Successive governments managed to sustain political stability until 1987, when racial tensions between Chinese and Malay increased over a government plan to assign non-Mandarin-speaking administrators to Chinese-language schools.

Between 1978 and 1989 Malaysia provided asylum to about 230,000 Vietnamese refugees awaiting resettlement in the West. In March 1989 Malaysia responded to the continuing influx of refugees and the Western nations' slow efforts to place them with a plan to screen refugees in order to separate economic migrants from political refugees. This policy was confirmed by the UN.

In October 1987 the Malaysian government, under provisions of the Internal Security Act (ISA), which allows detention without trial on grounds of national security, arrested 79 political and civil leaders and closed four newspapers in an effort to stifle dissent. The government called its actions necessary to prevent racial violence, but many prominent Malaysians, including Tunku Abdul Rahman, the country's first prime minister, condemned the actions. At the same time the government clamped down on all news sources disseminating what the government considered false news, and new legislation denied licensing to news sources not conforming to Malaysian values.

In 1981 Dato' Hussein bin Onn was succeeded as prime minister by Sato' Sei Dr. Mahathir Mohamad, whose leadership came under criticism from within the United Malays National Organization (UMNO) and other political parties as racial tensions increased. A legal suit claimed that some of the delegates to the UMNO elections of 1987 had not been legally registered, and therefore the election should be declared null and void. The High Court ruled that, due to the irregularities, UMNO was an unlawful society and that in effect the election was invalid. Mahathir held that the ruling did not affect the legal status of the government; he was supported by the ruling head of state, Tunku Mahmood Iskandar. In 1988 Mahathir formed a new UMNO, Umno Baru, and declared that party members would have to reregister to join. (Umno Baru was thereafter referred to as UMNO.)

Under provisions of the ISA four people linked to the Parti Bersatu Sabah (PBS) were detained over alleged involvement in a secessionist plot in Sabah in June 1990. In July 1990 elections, the PBS won 36 of 48 seats in the Sabah State Legislative Assembly. Prior to the general election of 1990 the PBS aligned itself with the opposition, which had formed an informal electoral alliance, People's Might (Gagasan Rakyat). The National Front (BN) won 127 of the 180 seats, maintaining control of the House of Representatives with the two-thirds majority necessary to amend the constitution. The opposition increased its seats from 37 to 53. In 1992 the People's Might registered as a political organization.

In 1990 the restructuring of the portfolio of the Ministry of Trade and Industry was rationalized into two new ministries— the Ministry of International Trade and Industry (MITI) and the Ministry of Domestic Trade and Consumer Affairs (MDTCA). In an action that was widely regarded as politically motivated, Datuk Seri Joseph Pairin Kitingan, chief minister of Sabah and president of the PBS, was arrested in January 1991 and charged with corruption, then released on bail. After subsequent meetings with Mahathir it was announced that the PBS state government had proposed power sharing with United Sabah National Organization (USNO). The head of USNO, Tun Mustapha Harun, resigned from USNO and joined UMNO. This switch necessitated a by-election and in May 1991 UMNO took its first seat in Sabah. The rise of Dayak nationalism in Sarawak was considered as less of a threat after the 1991 state elections. The Sarawak Native People's Party (Parti Bansa Dayak Sarawak—PBDS) retained only 7 of the 15 seats it had won in the 1987 election. A High Court ruling in 1991 upheld a ruling by the Ministry of Home Affairs banning the public sale of party newspapers. Speculation was that by targeting limited media outlets the government was muzzling the opposition press.

In 1991 UMNO raised the issue of the alleged abuse of privilege by Malaysia's nine hereditary rulers. A resolution tabled in 1990 had demanded the rulers be restrained from interfering in politics. In January 1993 constitutional amendments were passed removing the rulers' immunity from prosecution. Immediately after passage of the bill, royal privileges other than those sanctioned and allocations not expressly provided in the constitution were withdrawn. The nine hereditary rulers first rejected the constitutional changes; however, they eventually agreed to a compromise formula on the bill that effectively removed the blanket legal immunity granted to them. The compromise upheld the constitutional stipulation of royal assent for laws affecting the monarchy. Criticism arose over Mahathir's handling of this situation, as it emphasized the antipathy between his authoritarian style and the "Malay way." These constitutional changes also highlighted Mahathir's moves to strengthen executive power at cost of the judiciary, to consolidate UMNO's control of the legislature, and to control the press. On 17 January 1994 Sabah's chief minister, Datuk Joseph Pairin Kitingan, was found guilty of corruption. The fine imposed on him fell short of the minimum required to disqualify him from office. Although the PBS won the Sabah polls in February 1994, Pairin resigned as the PBS's leading members joined the National Front, and the Sabah wing of UMNO (with 18 of 48 seats) was about to be installed. In August 1994 the government moved to ban the radical Islamic sect, Al-Arqam.

In the general election held 25 April 1995, the ruling National Front captured 162 parliamentary seats out of a possible 192, its biggest victory ever. The coalition won 64% of the popular vote and easily retained its two-thirds parliamentary majority.

The Asian economic crisis of 1997 affected both the economy and the political landscape in Malaysia. By early 1998, the Malaysian economy had undergone its first downturn in 13 years, and tensions over the handling of the crisis erupted between Prime Minister Mahathir, an economic isolationist, and his deputy, Anwar Ibrahim, who favored open-market policies. In September 1998, Mahathir removed Anwar from his cabinet and party posts and imposed currency controls. When Anwar publicly protested these moves and attempted to rally opposition to his former mentor's policies, he was arrested and later tried for corruption and sexual misconduct (sodomy). In 1999 Anwar was sentenced to six years in prison, and his wife launched a new political party, Keadilan (Justice), to contest the upcoming national elections.

The economy began to recover by the end of 1998 and in August 1999 the government officially announced that the recession was over. Responding to an April 2000 deadline for national elections, Mahathir called a snap election in November 1999. Although the arrest of Anwar and his treatment while in custody ignited widespread criticism of Mahathir and his government, the UMNO-led coalition maintained its two-thirds majority in parliament and Mahathir remained in power. However, electoral gains by the Islamic Party of Malaysia (Parti Se-Islam Malaysia—PAS) suggested a significant challenge to the popularity of the government and made PAS the country's largest opposition party.

On 9 March 2001, a wave of violence between Malays and ethnic Indians began on the outskirts of Kuala Lumpur, the worst in more than 30 years. Six people, including five of Indian origin, were killed and over 50 were injured. Most of the wounded were ethnic Indians. When opposition leaders claimed the casualty figures were higher, the government threatened to charge them with sedition, although charges were never brought.

In early April 2001, days before public protests were scheduled for the second anniversary of the sentencing of Anwar, 10 opposition leaders were detained under Malaysia's Internal Security Act (ISA).Most of the detainees were members of the opposition party Keadilan founded by Anwar's wife, Wan Aziziah. The government used a variety of laws to restrict freedom of expression, and peaceful rallies were broken up by the police. An Anti-ISA Movement (AIM) was formed to work for the repeal of the ISA, which as of 2010 was still in effect.

In September 2001, Malaysia and Singapore came to a series of agreements over issues that had strained relations between them for years. Largely prodded by concern over the growing influence of Islam in Malaysian politics, Singapore agreed to a Malaysian proposal that the causeway linking the two countries be demolished and replaced by a bridge and undersea tunnel after 2007. Malaysia agreed to supply water to Singapore after two water agreements expire in 2011 and 2061. Also discussed were disputes over the use of Malaysian-owned railway land in Singapore, and requests by Singapore to use Malaysian air space. In April 2006, plans for the construction of the bridge to Singapore were shelved when Singapore cited concerns over the environmental impact and costs of the project, and Malaysia was not willing to grant Singapore access to its air space.

With the rise in popularity of the Islamic PAS party, Malaysia's image as a moderate Islamic state began to be questioned. In the aftermath of the 11 September 2001 terrorist attacks on the United States, countries in Southeast Asia were asked by the United States to increase their security plans and efforts to combat terrorism. However, many nations were cautious of a broad sweeping link between Islam and terrorist activities. In May 2002, members of Association of Southeast Asian Neighbors (ASEAN) met in Kuala Lumpur to form a united anti-terror front (including strengthening laws to govern the arrest, investigation, prosecution, and extradition of suspects), and pledged to set up a strong regional security framework. Alleged militants with suspected ties to Osama bin Laden's al-Qaeda organization were arrested in Malaysia. ISA detention was used as an antiterrorism measure, as were tightened laws against money laundering and harsher criminal penalties passed in 2003. The government continued to keep "extremist" Muslim organizations under surveillance.

In June 2002, Mahathir shocked the country with the news that he would resign in October 2003. It was to be the first transfer of the prime ministerial office in over 20 years. His successor was Abdullah Ahmad Badawi, one of three UMNO vice presidents. Badawi pledged to continue Mahathir's policies, but has a far more low-key political style. After just four months as an appointed prime minister, Badawi won an overwhelming mandate in the March 2004 national election, in which his UMNO took 90% of the parliamentary seats, soundly defeating a challenge from the PAS opposition. During the election campaign, Badawi pledged more transparency in government. He also promoted a policy of Islam Hadhari (Civilized Islam) as a moderate, open, and tolerant alternative to fundamentalist or militant Islam.

Malaysia's Federal Court overturned the sodomy conviction of Anwar Ibrahim in September 2004, and he was freed after nearly six years of imprisonment. This was seen as the real end of the Mahathir era's authoritarianism. However, with Badawi's UMNO landslide victory in the 2004 elections, the status of the opposition as represented by Anwar had diminished.

A devastating tsunami in December 2004 caused far less damage in Malaysia than in neighboring Thailand and Indonesia; there were fewer than 100 deaths in Malaysia and the Malaysian government did not seek international tsunami relief. A health emergency was declared in August 2005 when smoke from Indonesian forest fires enveloped Kuala Lumpur. Indonesia announced plans to indict 10 companies for burning forest land for plantations; 8 of the companies were Malaysian.

The Badawi government's policies seemed inconsistent in regard to illegal immigrants from strife-prone areas of Indonesia and Myanmar, when an amnesty was followed by a crackdown in March 2005. Immigrant workers were detained, imprisoned, and deported. With a need for workers, particularly in the construction sector, Malaysia continued to attract immigrants in 2005, and government policy appeared unclear regarding the political refugees and asylum seekers among those foreign workers.

In 2006, Badawi's government unveiled a multibillion-dollar Ninth Malaysia Plan geared to take on the problem of rural poverty and promote economic growth. The plan is intended to help Malaysia achieve developed nation status by 2020 and achieve balanced growth through the creation of five regional development corridors.

Major flooding in the south throughout December 2006 and January 2007 displaced more than 130,000 people. In February 2007, Malaysia, Indonesia, and Brunei Darussalam signed an agreement to protect 77,220 square miles (200,000 sq km) of rainforest on the island of Borneo.

In May 2007, Anwar Ibrahim tried to make a political comeback but lost in a by-election. The following year he was again charged with sodomy. The long-running trial was expected to conclude late in 2011.

Also in May 2007, Malaysian, Indonesian, and Saudi Arabian partners were on track to build a 193 mile (310 km) pipeline to bypass the Malacca Strait, so that oil tankers could load crude oil away from the busy and often dangerous waterway. Two refineries would also be built, one on the western coast of Malaysia, and one on the eastern coast. This $14.5 billion project was to be a joint project of the National Iranian Oil Company and a local Malaysian company, but as of 2011 the pipeline was still not built. Some analysts expressed concern that a pipeline lacked the flexibility sea shipping provides, in that in times of strife, a ship can take an alternate route. In contrast, a pipeline is fixed in place; whoever controls the land the pipeline passes through has some control over the oil flowing through the pipe.

In February 2008 the yang di-pertuan agong dissolved Parliament a year early at the prime minister's request. A 13-day campaign period was followed by elections which gave the ruling coalition its worst results in decades. It won by simple majority but no longer had its two thirds majority and lost control of five states as Indian and Chinese voters deserted the party. Analysts pointed at inflation, crime, and ethnic tensions as the causes of the coalition's loss of popularity.

Thousands crowded the streets of the capitol city in July 2011, in a rally organized by the Coalition for Clean and Fair Elections, also known as Bersih, which means "clean." Police responded with tear gas and water cannons, arresting 1,700. The changes the protestors were demanding included using indelible ink on voters' fingers to ensure voters could only vote once, giving all political parties equal access to the media, and introducing a minimum of a 21-day campaign period prior to elections. In August the government promised to set up a commission to review the country's electoral process.

13 GOVERNMENT

Malaysia is a constitutional monarchy consisting of 13 states, 9 of which were formerly sultanates under British protection and 4 of which (Melaka, Pulau Pinang, Sarawak, and Sabah) were former British settlements ruled by appointed governors.

The constitution, promulgated on 31 August 1957 and subsequently amended, derives from the former Federation of Malaya, with provisions for the special interests of Sabah and Sarawak. It provides for the election of a head of state, the yang di-pertuan agong (paramount ruler), for a single term of five years by the Conference of Rulers. The constitution also provides for a deputy head of state, chosen in the same manner and for the same term.

The Conference of Rulers consists of the nine hereditary sultans. Its consent must be obtained for any law that alters state boundaries; affects the rulers' privileges, honors, or dignities; or extends any religious acts, observances, or ceremonies to the country as a whole. The conference must also be consulted on proposed changes of administrative policy affecting the special position of the Malays or the vital interests of other communities.

The yang di-pertuan agong, who must be one of the hereditary sultans, is commander in chief of the armed forces and has the power to designate judges for the federal court and the high courts on the advice of the prime minister, whom he appoints. Until January 1984, the paramount ruler had the right to veto legislation by withholding his assent; this right was lost in a constitutional compromise that gave the paramount ruler the right to delay new laws for up to 60 days but also stipulated that, if passed by a two-thirds majority, a bill may become law after six months without his signature.

The yang di-pertuan agong from 1979 to 1984 was Ahmad Shah al-Musta'in Billah Ibni al-Marhum, the sultan of Pahang. The leading candidate to succeed him was Idris al-Mutawakil Allahi Shah Ibni al-Marhum, the sultan of Perak, but when Idris died of a heart attack on 31 January 1984, the Conference of Rulers selected Mahmud Iskandar Ibni al-Marhum Sultan Ismail. As crown prince of Johor he was convicted of homicide in a shooting incident in 1977 but was pardoned by his father and became sultan in 1981. In 1989 the sultan of Perak, Azlan Muhibuddin Shah, became the yang di-pertuan agong. He was succeeded in 1994 by Tuanku Ja'afar ibni Al-Marhum Tuanku Abdul Rahman, who was in turn succeeded in 1999 by Salehuddin Abdul Aziz Shah ibni Al-Marhum Hismuddin Alam Shah. Salehuddin died in office on 21 November 2001 and was succeeded in 2002 by Tuanku Syed Sirajuddin ibni Almarhum Tuanku Syed Putra Jamalullail, the sultan of Perlis. In December 2006, Sultan Mizan Zainal Abidin became yang di-pertuan agong.

Executive power rests with the cabinet, chosen by the prime minister, who is the leader of the majority party or coalition of the house of representatives (Dewan Rakyat), the lower house of parliament. In April 2009, Dato' Sri Mohd Najib bin Tun Abdul Razak was appointed Malaysia's 6th prime minister. The 193 members of the house of representatives must be at least 21 years old; they are elected by universal adult suffrage (at age 21). Their term is five years unless the house is dissolved earlier. The 69-member senate (Dewan Negara) consists of 26 elected members (2 from each state); 2 members appointed by the paramount ruler to represent the federal territory of Kuala Lumpur, and 1 to represent the island of Labaun; and 40 members appointed by the paramount ruler on the basis of distinguished public service or their eligibility to represent the ethnic minorities. Senators must be at least 30 years old; they hold office for six-year terms.

Sabah and Sarawak retain certain constitutional rights, including the right to maintain their own immigration controls.

14 POLITICAL PARTIES

Before World War II, there was limited political activity in Malaya, but the Japanese occupation and its aftermath brought a new political awareness. Postwar political parties sought independence, and although the Malays feared domination by the populous minorities, particularly the economically stronger Chinese, the United Malays National Organization (UMNO), the leading Malay party, and the Malaysian Chinese Association (MCA) formed the Alliance Party in 1952. This party was later joined by the Malaysian Indian Congress (MIC) and became the nation's dominant political party. The Malayan Communist Party, a powerful and well-organized group after the war, penetrated and dominated the trade unions. In 1948, after the Communists had resorted to arms, they were outlawed.

In the elections of April 1964, the Alliance Party won a majority of 89 of the 154 House seats. The third general election since independence was held in peninsular Malaysia on 10 May 1969; in the balloting, the Alliance Party suffered a setback, winning only 66 seats. The election was followed by communal rioting, mainly between Malays and Chinese, resulting in much loss of life and damage to property. The government suspended parliament and declared a state of emergency; elections in Sarawak and Sabah were postponed until July 1970. By the time parliament was reconvened on 22 February 1971, the Alliance had achieved a two-thirds majority (required for the passage of constitutional amendments) with the addition of 10 unopposed seats from Sabah and through a coalition with the Sarawak United People's Party, which controlled 12 seats.

The elections for state assemblies resulted in a setback for the Alliance Party, which before the elections had controlled 10 of the 13 state assemblies, but after the elections only 7. In September 1970, Tunku Abdul Rahman retired as prime minister and was replaced by the deputy prime minister, Tun Abdul Razak. In 1973, the Alliance Party formed a broader coalition consisting of the UMNO, MCA, MIC, and eight minority parties. Known as the National Front or Barisan Nasional, and led by the UMNO, the coalition has won control of parliament in every election since 1974, typically by wide margins. Legislative apportionment in Malaysia favors ethnically Malay voters, which impacts the ability of non-Malay opposition parties to win seats in parliament. Sato' Sei Dr. Mahathir Mohamad of UNMO became prime minister in 1981, and went on to hold that position for the next 22 years. In April 1987, Mahathir narrowly overcame a challenge to his leadership of the UMNO.

As of 2003 there were more than 20 registered parties. The governing coalition is the Barisan Nasional (National Front), led by the United Malays National Organization (UMNO) and comprising 13 other parties, most ethnically based. Major opposition groups are the Muslim Unity Movement (APU), dominated by the Parti sa Islam Malaysia (PAS); the Democratic Action Party (DAP), which is predominantly Chinese and socialist; the Parti Bersatu Sabah (PBS); and Keadilan, formed by Wan Aziziah Wan Ismail, the wife of government official Anwar Ibrahim, who was jailed from 1999 to 2004.

In the March 2004 general election, the UMNO-dominated Barisan Nasional (BN) coalition took 198 of 219 seats in parliament's lower house, and won control of 11 of 12 state governments contested. The opposition Parti Islam sa Malaysia (PAS) won only six seats, losing even in conservative Muslim states. The Democratic Action Party (DAP) won 12 seats, making DAP's Lim Kit Siang the opposition leader in the Malaysian parliament. The PAS and the DAP were at odds over religious policy issues and the opposition was in a particularly weakened position. The next national election, scheduled to take place by 2009, occurred a year early when the yang-di-pertuan agong dissolved parliament in February 2008. The ruling coalition won the ensuing national election with a simple majority (140 seats), its smallest margin in decades. Opposition parties won 82 seats.

The next national election is scheduled to take place by 2013.

15 LOCAL GOVERNMENT

Of the 11 peninsular Malaysian states, 9 are headed by sultans, who act as titular rulers and as leaders of the Islamic faith in their respective states. The other two peninsular states, Pinang and Melaka, are headed by federally appointed governors. State governments are parliamentary in form and share legislative powers with the federal parliament. Effective executive authority in each state is vested in a chief minister, selected by the majority party in the state legislature. The legislative assembly, composed of elected members, legislates in conformity with Malaysian and state constitutions, subject to the sultan's assent. In peninsular Malaysia the states are divided into districts, each of which consists of 5 to 10 subdistricts, called mukims (derah in Kelantan). Each mukim is responsible for varying numbers of kampongs (villages or compounds). The mukim may include villages or consist of large, sparsely populated tracts of land. Each one is headed by a penghulu (penggawa in Kelantan), a part-time official locally elected for five years, who serves as the principal liaison between the district and the village. The village elects a ketua (chief).

Upon incorporation into the Federation of Malaysia in 1963, Sabah and Sarawak adopted separate constitutions for their local self-government; each is headed by a chief minister, appointed by the majority party of the elective legislature. In Sarawak, divisions and districts are the main subdivisions; in Sabah their counterparts are residencies and districts. The district officer is the most important link between the governing and the governed. His responsibilities are administrative, fiscal, and judicial. Kuala Lumpur, the national capital and former capital of Selangor State, was constituted as a separate federal territory, under the national government, on 1 February 1974. The mayor is appointed by the paramount ruler on the advice of the prime minister.

¹⁶JUDICIAL SYSTEM

Malaysia has a unified judicial system; all courts take cognizance of both federal and state laws. The legal system is founded on British common law. Most cases come before magistrates and sessions courts. Religious courts decide questions of Islamic law and custom, basing decisions on Shari'ah law. In 1988, Malaysia's constitution was amended such that civil courts cannot hear cases that fall under the jurisdiction of Shari'ah courts. This has led to a situation in which non-Muslims are required to take such cases to Shari'ah courts, but non-Muslim lawyers can't present cases there. The use of religious law by states, and selective, inconsistent enforcement by religious officers, has become controversial. The use of the Internal Security Act (ISA) against dissidents and restrictions of the press and freedom of expression remain concerns of civil libertarians and international human rights organizations.

The Federal Court, the highest court in Malaysia, reviews decisions referred from the High Court of Peninsular Malaysia, the High Court of Sabah and Sarawak, and subordinate courts. The Federal Court, of which the yang di-pertuan agong is lord president, has original jurisdiction in disputes among states or between a state and the federal government. The Federal Court consists of the chief justice, the two chief judges from the High Courts, and seven other judges. Administrative detention is permitted in security cases, in which certain other guarantees of due process are reportedly suspended.

The judiciary has traditionally functioned with a high degree of independence. Most civil and criminal cases are fair and open. The accused must be brought before a judge within 24 hours of arrest. Defendants have the right to counsel and to bail. Strict rules of evidence apply in court and appeal is available to higher courts. Criminal defendants may also appeal for clemency to the paramount ruler or to the local state ruler. Severe penalties, including the death penalty, are imposed for drug-related offenses.

High courts have jurisdiction over all serious criminal cases and most civil cases. The sessions courts hear the cases involving landlord-tenant disputes and car accidents. Magistrates' courts hear criminal cases in which the maximum sentence does not exceed 12 months. The Court of Appeals has jurisdiction over high court and sessions court decisions.

¹⁷ARMED FORCES

The International Institute for Strategic Studies reports that armed forces in Malaysia totaled 109,000 members in 2011. The force is comprised of 80,000 from the army, 14,000 from the navy, and 15,000 members of the air force. Armed forces represent 1.1% of the labor force in Malaysia. Defense spending totaled $8.4 billion and accounted for 2% of GDP.

Malaysia has provided support to 10 UN peacekeeping missions. Australia provides a small training mission.

¹⁸INTERNATIONAL COOPERATION

Malaysia became a member of the UN on 17 September 1957, and participates in ESCAP and several non-regional specialized agencies, such as the FAO, UNESCO, UNIDO, IFC, IAEA, the World Bank, and the WHO. It also belongs to the WTO, the Asian Development Bank, the Commonwealth of Nations, APEC, the Arab Bank for Economic Development in Africa, the Colombo Plan, the Organization of the Islamic Conference (OIC), and G-77. Malaysia was a founding member of ASEAN, the Association of Southeast Asian Nations.

Before the 1970s, Malaysia pursued a pro-Western policy, but it later promoted the neutralization of Southeast Asia while establishing ties with China, the Democratic People's Republic of Korea, and Cuba, and strengthening relations with the USSR and other East European states. Links with its traditional allies, including the United States, remained strong in the course of this transition. Relations with the United Kingdom were strained in the early 1980s, after the British imposed surcharges on foreign students attending universities in the United Kingdom and issued new regulations reducing opportunities for foreign takeovers of British-owned companies. Malaysia agreed to drop its "buy British last" campaign in 1983 after the United Kingdom expanded scholarship opportunities for Malaysian students.

In 1986 there was some friction with Singapore because of its improved relations with Israel. Malaysia shares the anti-Zionist ideology of the Arab League countries. The nation has offered support to UN missions and operations in Kosovo (est. 1999), Western Sahara (est. 1991), Ethiopia and Eritrea (est. 2000), Liberia (est. 2003), Sierra Leone (est. 1999), East Timor (est. 2002), and Burundi (est. 2004), among others. The country is part of the Nonaligned Movement.

In the 1990s and early 2000s Malaysia worked to build better relations with its neighbors. Malaysia has cooperated with the ASEAN Regional Forum (ARF), a 23-member Asian security network, helping to reduce tensions over the disputed Spratley Islands in the South China Sea. Malaysia also seeks increased economic integration in Southeast Asia. In 1990, Prime Minister Mahathir proposed the creation of an East Asian Economic Caucus, an idea that was initially regarded with skepticism, but was subsequently taken up by the ASEAN+3 group (the ten ASEAN members plus China, Japan, and South Korea) as a way of strengthening financial and trade ties between those states.

Malaysia's relationship with Indonesia has been strained by contention over the status of Indonesian workers in Malaysia, and by disputes over maritime boundaries.

In environmental cooperation, Malaysia is part of the Basel Convention, the Convention on Biological Diversity, Ramsar, CITES, International Tropical Timber Agreements, the Kyoto Protocol, the Montréal Protocol, MARPOL, the Nuclear Test Ban Treaty, and the UN Conventions on the Law of the Sea, Climate Change, and Desertification.

¹⁹ECONOMY

The GDP rate of change in Malaysia, as of 2010, was 7.2%. Inflation stood at 1.7%, and unemployment was reported at 3.5%.

Malaysia is one of the most prosperous nations in Southeast Asia, albeit with the mood swings inherent in an export-oriented economy. Until the 1970s, Malaysia's economy was based chiefly on its plantation and mining activities, with rubber and tin the principal exports. Since then, however, Malaysia has added palm oil, tropical hardwoods, petroleum, natural gas, and manufactured items, especially electronics and semiconductors, to its export list. This diversification greatly reduced the nation's dependence on overseas commodity markets. By 1980, rubber accounted for about 7.5% of the value of all exports, down from 30%

in the 1970s, and tin for about 4.3%, down from about 20% in the 1970s. Sarawak's basic economy is subsistence agriculture, supplemented by petroleum production and refining, the collection of forest produce, fishing, and the cultivation of cash crops, primarily rubber, timber and pepper. Sabah's economy rests primarily on logging and petroleum production.

In 1990, Malaysia was the world's largest producer of natural rubber, accounting for one-quarter of world production. By 1993, however, production was overtaken by both Thailand and Indonesia. During the late 1990s, production of synthetic rubbers undercut the natural rubber industry. In 1990 Malaysia was the world's largest exporter of tropical hardwood, the world's fourth-largest producer of cocoa, and the source of 60% of the world's palm oil. By 2001, Malaysia exported over half of the world's fixed vegetable oils, accounting for approximately 6.7% of Malaysia's exports. In 2002, electronics accounted for two-thirds of total exports.

The worldwide recession in 1981–82 hurt the Malaysian economy. Prices of Malaysia's traditional commodity exports were depressed, growth slowed, and investment fell. Government efforts to stimulate the economy through spending on heavy industry and infrastructure projects financed by borrowing pushed foreign debt from $4 billion in 1980 to $15 billion in 1984. In 1985, the GDP in current prices was estimated at $31 billion, up from $25 billion in 1981. In 1985–86 Malaysia's period of high growth was halted abruptly as both oil and palm oil prices were halved. Recovery began in late 1986 and 1987, spurred by foreign demand for exports. Growth rates reached an average 8–9% from 1987–92, and for most of the 1990s, the economy grew annually by just under 9%.

The Asian financial crisis put an end to 13 years of uninterrupted growth with a decline in GDP of -7.4% in 1998. The government's response was to embark on a massive economic recovery program, aimed at stabilizing the currency, restoring market confidence, maintaining market stability, strengthening economic fundamentals, furthering socioeconomic goals, and reviving badly affected sectors. The program featured two fiscal stimulus packages amounting to 2.25% of GDP and the establishment of three special purpose agencies: the Danaharta-also known as the National Asset Management Co.-to acquire and dispose of nonperforming loans (NPLs); the Danamodal, charged with implementing government policy on recapitalizing financial institutions; and the Corporate Debt Restructuring Committee (CDRC), to facilitate voluntary debt restructuring between creditors and viable corporate debtors. More controversially, the government proceeded in 2000 with merger plans to consolidate Malaysia's banks into 10 "anchor" banks and to consolidate Malaysian domestic brokerage houses into 15 "universal brokers." The rationale behind the consolidations was that larger entities would be better able to compete with international counterparts. GDP growth recovered in 1999 and 2000, but was reduced in 2001 as the global economic slowdown and the aftermath of the 11 September 2001 terrorist attacks on the United States helped produce a 10.6% reduction in exports.

Government or government-owned entities dominate a number of sectors (plantations, telecommunications, and banking). Since 1986 the government has moved toward the eventual privatization of telecommunications, ports, highways, and electricity production and distribution. In the 1990s, the government embarked on a privatization program aimed at creating a Malaysian

business elite as part of its *bumiputera* (literally, "sons of the soil") policy. However, virtually all the major privatized companies failed in the Asian financial crisis of 1997–98 (including the carmaker Proton, Malaysian Airlines, the engineering group Renong, and the media group, Malaysian Resources) and were renationalized in the aftermath.

On 1 September 1998, the government pegged the ringgit at MYR3.8 = US$1. The government maintained this fixed exchange rate until 21 July 2005, when the peg was replaced by a managed floating exchange rate based on a basket of trade-weighted currencies. Current account surpluses continued from 2007 to 2010, peaking in 2008 at $38.9 billion.

In 2002, the economy continued to recover, reaching an annual growth rate of about 3.5%. The official unemployment rate hovered around 3.6% in 2001–05. The inflation rate from 2001–2005 stayed between 1.5 and 3%. Malaysia, like most countries in Southeast Asia, is dependent upon exports for its growth. In 2004, a double-digit surge in exports lifted the region's growth to 6.3%. But in remaining export-driven, the region is vulnerable to the vagaries of the world economy. Boosting domestic consumption is seen as a key to the region's successful economic future. Malaysia has made it its goal to be a fully developed country by 2020.

Since late 2001, Malaysia has taken a leading role, with Bahrain, in seeking to institutionalize Islamic banking. In November 2001 Malaysia signed an agreement with Bahrain, Indonesia, Sudan and the Saudi-based Islamic Development Bank (IDB) to establish the International Islamic Financial Market (IIFM). This is an extension of its domestic efforts to foster Islamic banking going back to the Islamic Banking Act of 1983, under which it was the first Islamic economy to issue bonds on an Islamic basis. In June 2002 Malaysia took the lead in offering the world's first Islamic global bond issue.

The Islamic bond required special handling because Islam forbids paying or receiving interest. The 144a offering (not subject to SEC disclosure regulations) in the name of the Malaysia Global Sukuk (MGS) involved MGS buying from the Malaysian government the Ministry of Finance building, two hospitals, and a civil service accommodation, and leasing them back to the government for a period of five years, during which time the government issued trust certificates to the investors with payments exactly equal to lease rental payments being made by the government to MGS. At the end of five years, in 2007, the government bought back the properties at the face value of the bond. These arrangements were judged compliant with Islamic law. The Trust Certificates had their primary listing on the Luxembourg Stock Exchange in August 2002, and their secondary listing on Malaysia's Labuan International Financial Exchange (LFX) in September 2002. The LFX is part of Malaysia's Labuan International Offshore Financial Centre (IOFC), established in October 1990 by the government to provide a full array of financial services for multinational corporations and investors. The MSG certificates are part of an effort to provide Shari'ah-compliant instruments for a growing Islamic financial market, estimated in 2002 at $200 billion. The Labuan Offshore Financial Services Authority (OFSA) took credit for initiating the idea for the establishment of the IIFM in November 2001. A Malaysian heads the IIFM and the Islamic Financial Service Organization (IFSO) is headquartered in Malaysia. As host country for the IFSO, Malaysia took the lead in formulating and developing standards for the regulation of Islamic financial institutions.

On 30 June 2009, Malaysia announced a series of economic liberalization measures designed to attract more foreign investment and ease domestic political pressures from minority groups. The most sweeping change involved rolling back a policy that gave advantage to the ethnic Malay majority. In the former policy, the Malay majority was required to hold a 30% combined stake in companies listed on the Malaysian stock exchange. The economic liberalization measures reduced that figure to 12.5% for newly-listed companies and provided room for further cuts if companies issue more shares. The new policy affords foreign investors the opportunity to hold majority shares (up to 70%) in Malaysian stock brokerages, although they are still limited to minority stakes in so-called strategic industries, like telecommunications and energy.

Despite a recession in 2009, strong economic growth between 4.8 and 7.2% was registered between 2007 and 2010. In 2011 analysts expected the Malaysian economy to continue to be strong through 2012, due to the strong banking system and efficient capital markets. In May 2011, the government announced that it would begin to cut fuel subsidies to try to bring the budget deficit under control. In 2011, fuel subsidies were budgeted at $2.9 billion. With a gradual cuts to subsidies, the government hopes to reduce the budget deficit from 5.6 percent to 5.4 percent, with a goal of 2.8 percent by 2015.

20 INCOME

The CIA estimated that in 2010 the GDP of Malaysia was $414.4 billion. The CIA defines GDP as the value of all final goods and services produced within a nation in a given year and computed on the basis of purchasing power parity (PPP) rather than value as measured on the basis of the rate of the exchange based on current dollars. The per capita GDP was estimated at $14,700. The annual growth rate of GDP was 7.2%. The average inflation rate was 1.7%. It was estimated that agriculture accounted for 9.1% of GDP, industry 41.6%, and services 49.3%.

According to the World Bank, remittances from citizens living abroad totaled $1.1 billion or about $39 per capita and accounted for approximately .3% of GDP.

The World Bank reports that in 2009, household consumption in Malaysia totaled $96.3 billion or about $3,351 per capita, measured in current US dollars rather than PPP. Household consumption includes expenditures of individuals, households, and non-governmental organizations on goods and services, excluding the purchases of dwellings. It was estimated that household consumption was growing at an average annual rate of 0.7%.

The World Bank estimates that Malaysia, with 0.43% of the world's population, accounted for 0.54% of the world's GDP. By comparison, the United States, with 4.85% of the world's population, accounted for 22.51% of world GDP.

As of 2011 the most recent study by the World Bank reported that actual individual consumption in Malaysia was 51.2% of GDP and accounted for 0.39% of world consumption. By comparison, the United States accounted for 25.44% of world individual consumption. The World Bank also estimated that 9.6% of Malaysia's GDP was spent on food and beverages, 11.3% on housing and household furnishings, 1.1% on clothes, 2.5% on health, 6.5% on transportation, 2.7% on communications, 2.1% on recreation,

3.9% on restaurants and hotels, and 6.9% on miscellaneous goods and services and purchases from abroad.

It was estimated that in 2007 about 3.6% of the population subsisted on an income below the poverty line established by Malaysia's government.

21 LABOR

As of 2010, Malaysia had a total labor force of 11.63 million people. Within that labor force, CIA estimates in 2005 noted that 13% were employed in agriculture, 36% in industry, and 51% in the service sector.

Workers have the right to engage in union activity, but only about 9% of the workforce were unionized in 2005 and were covered by 617 trade unions. Negotiations between unions and employers are voluntary and strikes are permitted but limited due to many restrictions. In addition, unions must be registered with the director general of trade unions, the latter of which can refuse or revoke a union's registration, thus making the union an unlawful association. If a labor dispute has been referred to an industrial court for settlement, the employees are prohibited from engaging in a strike.

As of 2005, the employment of children under the age of 14 is prohibited by law, although some exceptions-which include public entertainment, family businesses, as an approved apprentice, and work in school or a training facility for the government-are permitted. However, child labor persists in some areas of the country and protective labor legislation in Malaysia is more extensive than in most Asian countries. The workweek is set at a maximum of 48 hours, 5–6 days per week, 8 hours per day. Actual weekly hours tend to be closer to 44 hours. There is a legal requirement of one rest day per week.

In October 2011, the National Wage Consultative Council held its first meeting to discuss setting a minimum wage for workers. There had been no national minimum wage up to that point, the government preferring to leave wage rates to market forces. Opponents warned that setting a minimum wage could discourage foreign investment and cause inflation to spiral and businesses to fail. Prevailing market wages provide a decent standard of living for a worker and family, although this was not the case with all migrant workers. Occupational safety and health provisions are set by law but are erratically enforced. The provisions are more rigorously enforced in the formal economic sector and are least enforced on plantations and construction sites where immigrant workers are employed. These foreign workers have no legal protections and are prohibited from forming unions.

22 AGRICULTURE

While much of Sabah and Sarawak is covered with dense jungle and unfarmed, peninsular Malaysia is predominantly an agricultural region. Cultivation is carried out on the coastal plains, river valleys, and foothills. Roughly 24% of the total land is farmed. The country's major crops include palm oil, cocoa, rice, subsistence crops, coconuts, and rice. Cereal production in 2009 amounted to 2.5 million tons, fruit production 1.5 million tons, and vegetable production 759,115 tons.

Domestic rice cultivation furnishes peninsular Malaysia with about 80% of its requirements; however, most of the rice supply for Sabah and Sarawak must be imported. About 70% of milled rice comes from peninsular Malaysia. The government has promoted diversification through the development of newer crops, such as oil palm, cocoa, and pineapples. Although Malaysia typically accounts for over one-third of the world's rubber exports, rubber is no longer the country's primary source of export income. Competition from Thailand and Indonesia has diminished the Malaysian market share for rubber. The Rubber Research Institute of Malaysia has concentrated on improving rubber production, but many former rubber estates have switched to production of the more profitable oil palm.

Malaysia produced more palm oil and palm kernel oil than any other country in the world. More than 90% of all rubber and palm oil is produced in peninsular Malaysia. Black and white peppers are grown on Sarawak.

23 ANIMAL HUSBANDRY

Peninsular Malaysia is free of most of the infectious and contagious diseases that plague livestock in the tropical zone, but the livestock industry is of minor importance. The swamp buffalo and indigenous breeds of cattle are used mainly as draft animals. Malaysia is self-sufficient in pork and poultry production and also exports to other countries in the region, particularly Singapore and Japan. Sarawak's poultry sector was growing by 7% annually in response to increased demand from neighboring Kalimantan, Indonesia, where during certain festival months there is a poultry shortage. Malaysia experienced outbreaks of bird flu between 2004 and 2009, but no human cases were reported. The avian outbreaks were believed to have been caused by poultry smuggled along the Malaysia-Thailand border. The government prohibits the importation of chicken and chicken parts in order to protect domestic producers. Hog-raising and export are handled mainly by non-Muslim Chinese.

The UN Food and Agriculture Organization (FAO) reported that Malaysia dedicated 285,000 hectares (704,250 acres) to permanent pasture or meadow in 2009. During that year, the country tended 205 million chickens, 800,000 head of cattle, and 2.1 million pigs. The production from these animals amounted to 158,284 tons of beef and veal, 204,489 tons of pork, 918,398 tons of poultry, 324,972 tons of eggs, and 979,595 tons of milk. Malaysia also produced 3,690 tons of cattle hide and 144 tons of raw wool.

24 FISHING

Malaysia had 17,272 decked commercial fishing boats in 2008. The annual capture totaled 1.4 million tons according to the UN FAO. The export value of seafood totaled $615.9 million. The Fisheries Department expressed concerns in 2011 that destructive fishing techniques, such as using dragnets in the breeding grounds, would deplete the nation's marine resources before 2050.

The government promotes fishing as both a means of reducing unemployment and as a primary source of protein in the country's diet. A government training program in navigation and engine care is accelerating the use of powerboats. Freshwater fishing, which accounts for 2% of the total catch, occurs in paddy fields or irrigation ditches and is integrated with rice farming and hog production.

25 FORESTRY

Approximately 62% of Malaysia is covered by forest. About 33% of the forest area is located in peninsular Malaysia, 22% in Sabah, and 45% in Sarawak. Of the total natural forest area, 14.2 million hectares (35 million acres) of forested land is designated as Permanent Forest Estate, of which 78% is available for sustainable production. The UN FAO estimated the 2009 roundwood production at 20.1 million cu m (710.7 million cu ft). The value of all forest products, including roundwood, totaled $3.48 billion.

In response to the global economic crisis, in 2009 timber exports were down 14.48% from the previous year. Demand picked up in 2010 as the global economy improved. Exports of timber products in 2009 were estimated to be worth $6.21 billion, or 2% of total exports. Of this total production, wooden furniture accounted for 30.4%; logs, 10%; sawn lumber, 12.4%; plywood, 25.8%; fiberboard and particleboard, 7.5%; veneer, 1.5%, and mouldings, 3.7%. (Smaller contributors to the total 100% have not been listed.) Exports of tropical hardwoods in 2009 included (in thousands of cubic meters) logs, 18,372; lumber, 57.53; veneer, 753.52; and plywood, 3,655.21. In keeping with the National Forestry Policy of 1978, exports of sawn logs are being progressively reduced (in fact, many states ban the export of logs) in favor of domestic development of veneer, plywood, furniture, and other wood-using industries. Only Sarawak exports tropical hardwood logs, but its state government has placed further restrictions on exporting logs in order to encourage expansion of value-added activities. As of 2011, nine states have received government certification for forest management, and 171 timber companies have been certified for chain of custody through the government's timber certification program, which is intended to provide assurance of sustainable and legal sources of forest products to buyers of Malaysian timber.

26 MINING

Malaysia is a producer of bauxite, coal, ilmenite, iron ore, kaolin, monazite, sand and gravel, struverite, tin, zircon, and natural gas and oil. The country's mining sector in 2010 accounted for roughly 15% of GDP, with gas and oil accounting for 95% of that sector. Malaysia's tin mining sector has been declining because of depleted high-grade reserves and lower tin resources. In 2009, Malaysia mined 2,380 metric tons of tin, less than one half of the 6,307 metric tons produced in 2000. To revitalize the tin-mining industry, the Malaysian Chamber of Mines recommended that the government of Perak, one of the two main tin-mining states (Selangor being the other), change the royalty rate to a flat rate. In 2010, Malaysia's total exports were valued at $204.10 billion, of which mining products accounted for 15%, with the bulk being from crude oil/petroleum products and liquefied natural gas ($18.05 billion and $12.37 billion, respectively), and the balance from major minerals.

Subsoil resources are public property of the states, which grants prospecting licenses and mining leases. Royalties on coal and gold accrue to the states. Export duties are levied on other minerals by the government, which returns a portion to the states.

Iron ore production (by gross weight) in 2009 totaled 950 thousand metric tons, down from 982 thousand metric tons in 2008. Bauxite production had fallen off in the years 2003 – 2005, but recovered beginning in 2006, with production in 2009 of 280 thousand metric tons. Malaysia ceased copper production in 1999. As a result, silver production, most of which was a by-product of copper mining, dropped from 9,647 kg in 1997 to 367 kg in 2009. Other metal minerals extracted include gold, columbite, and titanium dioxide (from Terangganu). Malaysia is a net importer of coal, despite reports of untapped coal resources in Sabah and Sarawak said to be worth $47.5 billion. Malaysia also imports ilmenite, rare earths, and zircon concentrate, and most of its smelted tin. Industrial minerals produced in 2009 include hydraulic cement, clays and earth metals, feldspar, mica, nitrogen, silica sand, and stone. Silica sand comes mainly from natural sand deposits in Sarawak (56.6 million tons of estimated reserves) and Johor and from tin-mine-tailings sand in Perak and Selangor; 85% was exported and 63% of exports went to Singapore.

27 ENERGY AND POWER

The World Bank reported in 2008 that Malaysia produced 97.4 billion kWh of electricity and consumed 94.3 billion kWh, or 3,282 kWh per capita. Roughly 95% of energy came from fossil fuels, while 1% came from alternative fuels. Per capita oil consumption was 2,693 kg. Oil production totaled 553,960 barrels of oil a day. Malaysia's large reserves of natural gas and its exports of oil make the country a key player in the world's energy markets. Natural gas reserves were estimated at 83 trillion cu ft in 2011. Oil reserves were estimated at 4 billion barrels. Oil is produced offshore, primarily in the peninsular region. However, of new and increasing importance are large offshore natural gas deposits. Production of oil and natural gas is controlled by the National Petroleum Co. (PETRONAS).

28 INDUSTRY

Early industrialization efforts centered on the establishment of import-substitution industries (ISI) and resulted in construction of sugar refineries and motor vehicle assembly plants. Industrialization accelerated after the mid-1960s under the provisions of the Investment Incentives Act and the formation of the Malaysian Industrial Development Authority (MIDA). Special incentives were offered for industries that were labor-intensive, export-oriented, or that utilized domestic rubber, wood, and other raw materials. In the mid-1980s the Malaysian economy changed from a commodity-based to a manufacturing-based economy. In 1986, the leading manufacturing industries included rubber processing, the manufacture of tires and other rubber products, palm oil processing, tin smelting, and the manufacture of chemicals, plywood, furniture, and steel. Other industries were textiles, food processing, and the manufacture of electronic and electrical components. Most early industries were controlled by ethnic Chinese and foreigners, but government policies in the 1990s and early 2000s called for greater participation by ethnic Malays. In 1998, as part of its policy to encourage manufacturing industries, the government relaxed restrictions on foreign ownership of new manufacturing projects. Any new manufacturing project for which the Malaysian Industrial Authority (MIDA) approves a license may have up to 100% foreign ownership, regardless of its involvement in exporting.

In 2010 industry accounted for 41.4% of GDP. Of total exports of manufactured goods in 2010, electronics and electrical products accounted for 54.2%; chemicals and chemical products, 8.8%; machinery, appliances, and parts, 4.7%; manufactures of metal, 4%; optical and scientific equipment, 4%; rubber products, 3.5%; wood products, 3.2%; processed food, 2.6%; transportation equipment, 2%; plastic manufactured goods, 2%; with 10.9% categorized as "other." In peninsular Malaysia, the leading industries by value of annual output are rubber and palm oil processing and manufacturing, light manufacturing, electronics, tin mining and smelting, and logging and processing timber. In Sabah, the leading industries are logging and petroleum production, while in Sarawak, they are agricultural processing, petroleum production and refining, and logging.

Malaysia has five oil refineries, with a total capacity in 2011 of 551,700 barrels per day (BPD). In 2010, crude oil production amounted to 664,800 barrels per day. Proven reserves have dropped from 4.3 billion in 1996 to an estimated 4 billion in 2011. Malaysia's national oil and gas company, PETRONAS, has invested in oil exploration projects in more than 30 foreign countries, including Syria, Turkmenistan, Iran, Pakistan, China, Vietnam, Burma, Algeria, Libya, Tunisia, the Sudan, and Angola. Overseas operations made up 30% of PETRONAS's operations in 2007. Japan, Thailand, South Korea, and Singapore continue to be the major customers for Malaysian crude oil. Malaysia's domestic oil fields are split between the South China Sea off Borneo and those off peninsular Malaysia. All exploration is conducted under production-sharing contracts (PSCs) between PETRONAS, the national oil company, and foreign companies. In 2011, foreign oil companies involved in the production of oil and gas in Malaysia included Exxon Mobil Corp., Royal Dutch Shell Plc, and Sonoco. Gas reserves were being developed to fuel power stations and to supply industries in peninsular Malaysia and Singapore. In 2009, Malaysia's LNG exports were second in volume only to those of Qatar. In 2010, Malaysia had proven LNG reserves of 83 trillion cubic feet.

At the end of the 20th century, Malaysia had as a top industrial priority the development of the "multimedia super corridor" (MSC), an ambitious project aimed at transforming a 15-by-40 km (9.3-by-25 mi) area south of Kuala Lumpur into Asia's version of California's Silicon Valley. It was composed of a number of projects: the tallest twin towers in the world, the 450-m (1,483-ft) Petronas Twin Towers (opened in 1999) ; two of the world's first Smart Cities—Putrajaya, the $8-billion new seat of government and administrative capital of Malaysia (the government seat as of 1999), where the concept of electronic government will be implemented, and Cyberjaya (opened in 1997), an intelligent city with multimedia industries, research and development centers, a multimedia university, and operational headquarters for MSC; the construction of a $3.6 billion international airport (built in 1998); and the installation of a fiber-optic telecommunications system linking them all.

In 2011 PETRONAS announced plans to build a $20 billion refinery complex, with a capacity of 300,000 bpd in the southern state of Johor, near the border with Singapore. The complex, scheduled to be completed in 2016, will produce gasoline, jet fuel, and diesel for both local use and export. It will also contain a naphtha cracker capable of producing 3 million tons of ethylene, propylene and olefins per year. A LNG import and re-gasification terminal is also under consideration as part of the complex. The refinery hub is anticipated to attract foreign investors.

29 SCIENCE AND TECHNOLOGY

According to the World Bank, Malaysia's patent applications in science and technology totaled 818 as of 2009. Public financing of science was 0.64% of GDP. Training in science, technology, and related subjects was promoted at all levels during the 1970s and 1980s. Enrollment at technical and vocational secondary schools rose from 4,510 in 1970 to 20,720 in 1985. The National University of Malaysia at Selangor, the University of Malaya at Kuala Lumpur, the University of Agriculture at Selangor Darul Ehsan, the University of Science at Penang, the Technological University at Johor Bahru, Kolej, Damansaura Utama College at Selangor, Politeknik Kuching at Surawak, and Tunku Abdul Rahman College at Kuala Lumpur offer degrees in basic and applied sciences. In 1987–97, science and engineering students accounted for 54% of college and university enrollments. National science policy is administered by the Ministry of Science, Technology, and Environment. The Ministry of Agriculture undertakes all aspects of research for improvement of crops. The Institute of Medical Research is a branch of the Ministry of Health.

The Forest Research Institute Malaysia (FIRM), the Freshwater Fish Research Center, the Malaysian Agricultural Research and Development Institute (MARDI), the Malaysian Institute of Microelectronic Systems (MIMOS), and the Rubber Research Institute of Malaysia are all located in Kuala Lumpur.

In 2009 high-tech exports were valued at $51.56 billion and accounted for 47% of manufactured exports.

30 DOMESTIC TRADE

Imported goods are channeled into the Malaysian market through local branches of large European mercantile firms; by local importers with buying agents abroad; through branch offices and representatives of foreign manufacturers; by local Chinese, Indian, and Arab merchants who import directly; and by commission agents. Chinese merchants occupy an important place in the marketing structure and control a large share of the direct import trade. For warehousing of imported goods, the facilities of the port of Singapore are used, while rubber for export is warehoused mainly on plantations.

Malaysia's government has been described as one of the most franchise-friendly in the world. It has a government agency that invests in foreign franchise expansion into Malaysia by providing loans and equity assistance to Malaysians wanting to buy a franchise. Franchising by foreign companies is well established in Malaysia. As of 2010, there were 447 franchises (144 of them international companies) and 4000 franchisees. Franchises were said to contribute 6% to the total retail sector in 2009. Many of the franchise sales were accounted for by US-based firms (followed by those from the UK, Taiwan, Singapore, and Australia), which dominate the fast food and restaurant industry. US franchisers in Malaysia include KFC, McDonald's, Starbucks, Pizza Hut, Hard Rock Café, Dairy Queen, TGIF, and Outback Steak House.

Starting in the commercial bank sector, e-commerce has slowly begun to filter down to other sectors of the economy. Malaysia Airlines, the national carrier, and Air Asia, its low cost competitor, each have on-line reservation systems. However, among Malaysian consumers, the idea of using the Internet to conduct business is only slowly being accepted, the issue of transactional security

a major concern of consumers there. A government agency, the Multimedia Development Corporation, was created in 1996 to encourage e-commerce in Malaysia by boosting confidence in online trading, preparing a regulatory framework, building a mass of internet users, and introducing an electronic payment system.

The usual business hours are from 9:00 a.m. to 5:00 p.m., Monday-Friday including an hour-long lunch break, with most businesses operating for a half-day on Saturday. All public service departments and some banks close on the first and third Saturday of the month. In Kelantan, Terengganu, Johor, Perlis, and Kedah states, businesses close for a half-day on Thursday (in keeping with Islamic practice) and Friday is the day of rest. Shop hours run from 10 a.m. to 10 p.m. English is widely used in commerce and industry.

Newspaper and motion picture advertising is directed toward the higher-income consumer, while radio advertising, outdoor displays, and screen slides are used for the lower-income consumer who is less likely to be literate. A code of practice and ethics governing advertising is in force, with restrictions on advertising of some products, such as alcohol and tobacco. Trade fairs are supervised by the Ministry of Trade and Industry.

31 FOREIGN TRADE

Malaysia imported $174.3 billion worth of goods and services in 2008, while exporting $210.3 billion worth of goods and services. Major import partners in 2009 were China, 12.6%; Japan, 12.6%; Singapore, 11.4%; the United States, 10.7%; Thailand, 6.2%; and Indonesia, 5.6%. Its major export partners were Singapore, 13.4%; China, 12.6%; Japan, 10.4%; the United States, 9.5%; Thailand, 5.3%; and Hong Kong, 5.1%.

While Malaysia exported mostly primary products such as wood and rubber in the 1970s, by 2010 it was one of the world's largest exporters of electrical good, solar panels, semiconductors, and communication technology products.

The primary exports in 2010 were: electronics and electrical machinery (39.1% of all exports); crude petroleum (4.9%); refined petroleum (4.5%); liquefied natural gas (6.0%); chemicals and chemical products (6.4%); palm oil (7.6%); and machinery, ap-

Principal Trading Partners – Malaysia (2010)

(In millions of US dollars)

Country	Total	Exports	Imports	Balance
World	363,533.0	198,800.0	164,733.0	34,067.0
China	45,751.0	25,068.0	20,683.0	4,385.0
Singapore	45,402.0	26,597.0	18,805.0	7,792.0
Japan	41,369.0	20,640.0	20,729.0	-89.0
United States	36,529.0	18,989.0	17,540.0	1,449.0
Thailand	20,867.0	10,603.0	10,264.0	339.0
South Korea	16,449.0	7,515.0	8,934.0	-1,419.0
Indonesia	14,774.0	5,621.0	9,153.0	-3,532.0
Hong Kong	14,074.0	10,128.0	3,946.0	6,182.0
Taiwan	13,712.0	6,290.0	7,422.0	-1,132.0
Germany	12,056.0	5,405.0	6,651.0	-1,246.0

(…) data not available or not significant.

(n.s.) not specified.

SOURCE: *2011 Direction of Trade Statistics Yearbook,* New York: United Nations, 2011.

pliances, and parts (3.4%). The primary imports were: electronics and electrical machinery (35.7%); chemicals and chemical products (8.6%); machinery, appliances, and parts (8.3%); manufactures of metal (5.5%); transportation equipment (5.4%); refined petroleum products (5.1%); iron and steel products (4.0%); crude petroleum (3.5%); and optical and scientific equipment (3.3%).

On 1 January 2010, a new free trade area was established between China and the six founding members of the Association of South East Asian Nations (ASEAN), including Malaysia. A major point of the free trade agreement was the elimination of tariffs on nearly 90% of imported goods. The free trade area agreement was expected to allow for a major increase in exports and export earnings among the ASEAN countries. In 2010, Malaysia's total exports to ASEAN states increased by 14.1%; however, this was less than the overall 15.6% increase in Malaysia's total exports. In terms of population, ASEAN is the largest free trade area in the world. Cambodia, Laos, Vietnam, and Myanmar, newer members of ASEAN, are expected to gradually become full members of the free trade area by 2015.

In another expected boost for trade, the ASEAN Trade in Goods Agreement (ATIGA), approved in 2009, entered into force on 17 May 2010. It represented the next step in realizing the free flow of goods within the region by simplifying the processes and procedures necessary to create a single market and production base known as the ASEAN Economic Community (AEC) by 2015. Major points of ATIGA include tariff liberalization, a simplification of the rules of origin, and implementation of such rules. The comprehensive agreement also demands greater transparency in regional trade liberalization, aiding the work of businesses and investors. The ATIGA supersedes the Common Effective Preferential Tariff Scheme (CEPT) adopted in 1992.

32 BALANCE OF PAYMENTS

In 2010 Malaysia had a foreign trade surplus of $42 billion, amounting to 6.4% of GDP.

Malaysia sustained a favorable trade balance throughout the 1960s and 1970s, recording its first trade deficits in 1981 and 1982, as world prices for tin, crude oil, rubber, and palm oil, the major exports, weakened simultaneously. Malaysia's balance of payments, like that of many other producers of primary products, was adversely affected in 1981–82 by the prolonged recession in the world's industrial nations. From 1983 to 1986, however, Malaysia registered trade surpluses. In the 1990s, a significant growth in exports and a decrease in imports led to trade surpluses, along with a fairly large services deficit. In the early 2000s, exports declined, but so did imports of intermediate components used in the manufacture of the country's electronics exports; this contributed to continuing strong trade surpluses.

The current-account recorded a surplus of $34.14 billion in 2010, lifted by a large merchandise trade surplus. The services and income balances remained in deficit. In 2009, the current-account surplus amounted to $34.08 billion. Exports totaled an estimated $197 billion in 2010, and imports were estimated at $152.6 billion.

33 BANKING AND SECURITIES

In 1958, the Bank Negara Tanah Melayu (renamed the Bank Negara Malaysia in 1963) was created as the central banking institution. Bank Negara requires banks to maintain a minimum

Balance of Payments – Malaysia (2010)

(In millions of US dollars)

Current Account		27,290.0
Balance on goods	41,672.0	
Imports	-157,283.0	
Exports	198,954.0	
Balance on services	544.0	
Balance on income	-8,142.0	
Current transfers	-6,783.0	
Capital Account		-51.0
Financial Account		-5,919.0
Direct investment abroad	-13,513.0	
Direct investment in Malaysia	9,167.0	
Portfolio investment assets	...	
Portfolio investment liabilities	...	
Financial derivatives	-212.0	
Other investment assets	...	
Other investment liabilities	...	
Net Errors and Omissions		-21,358.0
Reserves and Related Items		37.0

(…) data not available or not significant.

SOURCE: *Balance of Payment Statistics Yearbook 2011*, Washington, DC: International Monetary Fund, 2011.

risk-weighted capital ration (RWCR) of 8%. At the end of 2011, Malaysia had 24 licensed commercial banks, 17 Islamic banks, 4 international Islamic banks, 15 investment houses, and 6 money brokers. A total of 16 foreign banks have offices in Malaysia, but their banking privileges are restricted. Six of the Islamic banks and all of the international Islamic banks are foreign. Specialized credit institutions include the Federal Land Development Authority (FELDA), the Agricultural Bank of Malaysia (Bank Pertanian Malaysia), and Bank Rakyat, serving rural credit cooperative societies. International trade is financed mainly by the commercial banks. Total banking system assets were $469.6 billion in 2010. There were 50 offshore banks operating on the island of Lauban in 2011.

Malaysia offers Islamic banking, which is based on the concept of profit sharing as opposed to the use of interest in the conventional banking system. One such Islamic bank is Bank Islam Malaysia Berhad. The central bank has embarked on a plan to develop Malaysia as a regional Islamic financial center. Toward this end, the central bank formed a consultative committee on Islamic banking in January 1996 to serve as a think-tank group to develop strategies and proposals to map out the future direction of Islamic banking. Although Islamic operations were only a small proportion of total business, Malaysia has achieved more than most other Islamic countries in this respect and its developments are regarded as models.

The International Monetary Fund reported that in 2010, currency and demand deposits, an aggregate commonly known as M1, were equal to $71.05 billion. In that same year, M2, an aggregate equal to M1 plus savings deposits, small time deposits, and money market mutual funds, was $335.66 billion.

In 2010, the central bank discount rate was 2.83%. The commercial bank prime lending rate was 5.05%. At the end of 2010, the nation's gold bullion deposits totaled 1.17 million fine troy ounces.

The principal market for securities is the Bursa Malaysia, also known as the Kuala Lumpur Stock Exchange (KLSE). A second, smaller exchange has operated since 1970 to serve indigenous Malay interests. Originally part of the joint Stock Exchange of Malaysia and Singapore, in October 1991 the KLSE completely severed its links with the Singapore Stock Exchange. Foreign investors are permitted to buy and sell on the stock market, subject only to compliance with regulatory requirements. In June 1995, a wide range of measures liberalizing the Malaysian capital market were introduced. These included the lowering of commission rates on the KLSE, the easing of controls on loans secured against shares, and less stringent conditions for overseas fund managers. Overseas funds can now set up 100% subsidiaries for conducting non-Malaysian business and rules on work permits for expatriate staff have been relaxed. The KLCI index of the KLSE stood at 1465.39 in December 2011, with a 52 week low of 1310.53 and a 52 week high of 1597.08. As of 2011, roughly 1000 companies were listed on the KLSE and had a market capitalization of $404.21 billion.

34 INSURANCE

In Malaysia, third-party automobile liability, workers' compensation, and social security are compulsory insurances. The law requires insurance firms to maintain a minimum of 80% of their assets in authorized Malaysian holdings, including (by an amendment passed in 1978) 24% in government securities. Foreign insurance companies may operate by obtaining a license. The government's insurance branch, the MNRB Holding Berhad (previously known as the Malaysian National Reinsurance Berhad), generated MYR1.463 billion ($467 million) in revenue during fiscal year 2011.

In 2011 the Foreign Worker Hospitalization and Surgical Insurance Scheme was passed, requiring that all foreign workers have health insurance. Employers are required to provide the insurance, as a means of reducing the number of unpaid medical bills attributed to uninsured foreign workers. In addition, under the "Foreign Worker Compensation Scheme," employers are required to provide foreign employees with compensation insurance.

35 PUBLIC FINANCE

Malaysia's economy, heavily industrial and heavily dependent on export revenues, is impacted by the economic downturns of its trading partners. Thus during the 1997–1998 Asian economic crisis, Malaysia's economy suffered, and when the US economy began to slow down at the end of 2000, so did Malaysia's exports to the United States, as well as Malaysia's economy. During the 2008–2009 global financial crisis, the nation's economy fared better than in previous crises by implementing fiscal strategies learned during previous economic downturns, namely avoiding overexposure to sub-prime investments.

In 2010 the budget of Malaysia included $46.78 billion in public revenue and $46.34 billion in public expenditures. The budget deficit amounted to 5.6% of GDP. Public debt was 53.1% of GDP, with $72.6 billion of the debt held by foreign entities.

36 TAXATION

Income tax is levied on all individual and corporate income accrued in Malaysia during the previous year. As of 2010, income of resident individuals was progressively taxed, with a top rate of

Public Finance – Malaysia (2009)

(In millions of ringgit, budgetary central government figures)

Revenue and Grants	158,639	100.0%
Tax revenue	106,504	67.1%
Social contributions	...	...
Grants	...	...
Other revenue	52,135	32.9%
Expenditures	202,361	100.0%
General public services	68,395	33.8%
Defense	13,974	6.9%
Public order and safety	9,566	4.7%
Economic affairs	34,808	17.2%
Environmental protection	...	...
Housing and community amenities	10,693	5.3%
Health	14,768	7.3%
Recreational, culture, and religion	...	...
Education	50,158	24.8%
Social protection	...	...

(…) data not available or not significant.

SOURCE: *Government Finance Statistics Yearbook 2010,* Washington, DC: International Monetary Fund, 2010.

26%. Nonresidents are taxed at a flat rate of 26%. Resident and nonresident companies are charged a flat rate of 25%. A 38% income tax is levied on petroleum corporations. Royalties and technical fees are subject to a 10% withholding tax, while the withholding rate for interest is 15%. Dividends are treated as income and are not subject to a withholding tax, if the appropriate amount of tax has already been paid on the company's income.

Incentives are available for pioneer industries and for certain capital investments. Capital gains taxes are levied on the sale of real estate. Indirect taxes include a general 10% sales tax (5% for essential items, 20% for liquor, and 25% for cigarettes) and a 5% services tax.

37 CUSTOMS AND DUTIES

Import tariffs on textiles and other items already produced in Malaysia are applied in order to protect domestic industries. In 2009, most imports were charged with a tariff on an ad valorem basis, with a simple average tariff of 7.4%; however, on roughly 80 products, mostly agricultural, tariff charges are much higher, with an average duty of 392%. Imports are also subject to a 10% sales tax and excise taxes. Imported luxury goods have the highest rates. Items imported for industrial development, including machinery and raw materials imported for processing and re-export, are usually duty-free. Exports are generally free of control, except that licenses and export duties apply to exports of petroleum (25%), rubber, tin, palm oil, timber, and pepper.

As a member of the ASEAN free trade area, Malaysia is a part of the Common Effective Preferential Tariff Scheme (CEPT), which aims to liberalize trade in the region. As of 2003, all tariffs on manufactured goods were reduced to 0–5% between member countries. Malaysia has bilateral trade agreements with 59 countries as well. There are several free zones and a free port at Port Klang.

38 FOREIGN INVESTMENT

Foreign direct investment (FDI) in Malaysia was a net inflow of $1.39 billion according to World Bank figures published in 2009. FDI represented 0.72% of GDP.

Assets attracting foreign investors to Malaysia are location, cultural ties with Singapore and Taiwan, economic and political stability, an increasingly competent labor force, and good infrastructure. The main barriers have been restrictions put on foreign investment and ownership as a part of the government's *bumiputera* policy, which sought particularly to insure Malay dominance of domestic markets. Despite this policy, in 2011, the World Bank ranked Malaysia as 23rd of 183 world economies in terms of ease of doing business, and anticipated it would rise to 18th in 2012. The government encourages foreign investors with a tax holiday of up to 10 years for investments in new industries and assurance of convertibility and repatriation of capital and profits.

The Malaysian government has long been concerned with affirmative action for its ethnic Malay majority. In 1975, the Industrial Coordination Act established new equity participation guidelines that required a substantial majority of Malaysian ownership of new import-substitution industries catering to the domestic market and using local technology. Some of these restrictions regarding foreign ownership and investment were eased under the fifth Malaysia plan (1986–90), with the Promotion of Investment Act of 1986 which allowed 100% foreign ownership if a company exported at least 50% of its product and did not compete with local industry, or if it exported at least 80% of its product regardless of competition.

In 1998, 100% foreign ownership was granted to projects exporting at least 80% of output, 79% foreign ownership for exports of at least 51% of output, up to 50% foreign ownership for exporting at least 20% of output, and a maximum foreign ownership of 30% for projects exporting less than 20%, regardless of the origin of raw materials. Also, for new manufacturing projects, 100% foreign ownership was permitted in any project approved by the Malaysian Industrial Development Authority (MIDA). The MIDA screened all proposals for manufacturing projects to determine if they were compatible with the Second Industrial Master Plan (1996–2005), and government strategic and social policies.

In 2009, restrictions were further loosened. 30% ownership by ethnic Malays was no longer required for most industries, although the restriction remained for certain strategic industries, including telecommunications, energy concerns, ports, and water. The Foreign Investment Committee was stripped of many of its powers, including the approval of all purchases of property by foreigners. In addition, the government announced plans to establish an equity plan to buy private companies and hand them over to Malay managers.

The Federal Territory of Labuan, established in 1990, serves as an International Offshore Financial Center (IOFC) providing offshore banking and insurance, trust fund management, offshore investment holding and licensing companies, and other financial services for multinational companies.

In the period following the 11 September 2001 terrorist attacks on the United States, Malaysia took the lead in seeking to institutionalize Islamic banking and attract Islamic investment, serving as a founding member of the International Islamic Financial Market (IIFM), along with Bahrain, Indonesia, Sudan, and the Islamic Development Bank (IDB) based in Saudi Arabia. In June 2002 the Malaysian government put together the world's first global Islamic bond issue. The Labuan Offshore Financial Services Authority (OFSA) takes credit for initiating the idea of the establishment of the IIFM. The Islamic Financial Service Organization (IFSO), which has developed standards for the regulation of Islamic financial institutions, is headquartered in Malaysia.

By 2006, 14 free-trade zones (FTZs) had been established in Malaysia. (FTZs are specially designated geographic areas with regulations, including minimum customs controls and formalities when importing raw materials, parts, machinery, and equipment, specifically designed to serve export-oriented industries.) There are specially designated FTZs for businesses engaged in commercial activities including trading, breaking bulk, grading, repacking, relabeling, and transit. Within an FTZ, goods are allowed to be imported without being subject to customs procedures, provided the goods are ultimately exported after processing.

39 ECONOMIC DEVELOPMENT

Malaysia's economy has been transformed from a protected low-income supplier of raw materials to a middle-income emerging multi-sector market economy driven by manufactured exports, particularly electronics and semiconductors. Since 1970 and the institution of the New Economic Policy (NEP) following deadly riots in 1969 against economically dominant ethnic Chinese, the government's commitment to the free market has been hedged by its *bumiputera* (literally, "sons of the soil") policies aimed at providing "constructive protection" for Islamic Malays against economic competition from other ethnic groups and foreign investors, particularly in the domestic market. In the Asian financial crisis of 1997, most of the major companies that the government had privatized and reserved for bumiputera leadership (including Proton, the national car company, Malaysian Airlines, the Renong engineering group, and the Malaysian Resources media group) had to be renationalized to prevent their collapse. A vigorous recovery program mounted by the government that was showing positive results in 1999 and 2000 ran abruptly into the wall of the 2001 global economic slowdown. Worldwide, foreign direct investment dropped almost 50%, and in Malaysia the decline was an even more precipitous 85%. GDP growth dropped to 0.7% for 2001, from its usual 7- 9%.

Business in Malaysia remains dominated by non-Malays. In 1970, a government holding company, Perbadanan Nasional (PERNAS), was created to encourage Malay-controlled businesses; in 1975, the government attempted, through PERNAS, to strengthen Malaysian interests in the tin-mining sector. Also in 1974, the government established the National Oil Co. (PETRONAS), with the overall aim of acquiring majority control of the country's petroleum operations. The Industrial Coordination Act of 1975 attempted to accelerate indigenous Malay participation in the economy by setting limits on foreign participation in the processing, domestic distribution, and export of local raw materials. In 1971, the New Economic Policy (NEP) was adopted, with the aim of channeling a greater share of future economic growth into Malay hands. It specifically called for raising the level of corporate ownership by Malays to 30% by 1990, reducing corporate ownership by other Malaysians (i.e., Chinese and Indians) to 40%, and restricting foreigners to ownership of no more than 30%. Short-term investment strategies are set forth in a series of economic plans. The fourth Malaysia plan (1981–85) proposed a level of development spending of MYR42.8 billion and called for acceleration of the NEP goals for bumiputera economic participation. Major industrial and infrastructural development projects included a MYR900 million bridge between Pulau Pinang and the mainland and a MYR600 million automobile-manufacturing plant, both of which opened in 1985. Economic planning stressed a "look East" policy, with Malaysia attempting to emulate the economic successes of Japan and the Republic of Korea by importing technology from those countries. In response to deteriorating prices for oil and other exports, the fifth Malaysia plan (1986–90) moved away from the goals of the NEP, aiming instead at promoting foreign investment, particularly in export industries.

The year 1990 marked the culmination of several economic development plans: the fifth Malaysia plan (FMP), 1986–90; the conclusion of the first outline perspective plan (OPP1) 1971–1990; and the completion of the new economic policy (NEP) 1971–1990. The FMP emphasized industrialization. Specific targets were formulated to ensure that the distribution of ownership and participation in the commercial and industrial sector would be characterized by ethnic group participation, 30% bumiputera (Malays and other indigenous peoples), 40% other Malaysians (Chinese and Indian descent), and 30% foreign. The government provided funds to purchase foreign-owned shareholding on behalf of the bumiputera population, increasing their equity to 20% by 1990. These policies are part of the new national development policy, although specific targets and timetables have been dropped.

A post-1990 NEP defined Malaysian economic strategy for full development by 2020. Three ten-year outline perspective plans, which included a new development plan and six five-year plans, made up the NEP. A second outline perspective plan (OPP2) 1991–2000 aimed to sustain growth momentum and to achieve a more balanced development of the economy. The sixth Malaysia plan called for an average annual growth rate of 7.5%, and expenditures on infrastructure were included to ensure prospects for further development. Development trends were toward privatization, encouraging the spread of industry throughout the country, increasing manufacturing in the free trade zones, and providing financing for industry through the establishment of specialized financing institutions.

A five-year development plan announced in 1996 forecasted average growth of 8% per year for 1996–2000. In 1997–98, low productivity, a skills shortage, and a gaping current-account deficit along with a global financial crisis based in Asia, combined to cause an economic downturn. Massive capital and infrastructure projects have attracted foreign investment and international respect.

The Ninth Malaysia Plan was announced in 2006 to focus on improving supply-side issues, such as the promotion of new sources of value-added economic growth, the liberalization of the financial sector, and further measures to strengthen small- and medium-sized firms. Reducing the deficit was a policy priority, as fiscal stimulus had increased the budget deficit in the early 2000s. The government, as with those in other Southeast Asian countries, was committed to finding ways to revive domestic consumption instead of relying primarily upon exports for economic growth,

which would help insulate Malaysia from the vagaries of the global economy.

In March 2010, the government unveiled a New Economic Model, which aimed to transform Malaysia into a high-income country. The prime minister's plan promoted private-sector investment and altered a long-standing affirmative action policy that analysts criticized for stunting economic dynamism. The change to the affirmative action policy shifted the focus away from lifting just ethnic Malays, the majority group in Malaysia, from poverty, to aiding all disadvantaged people, irrespective of ethnic background. The New Economic Model, which was widely praised by economic analysts, pushed for the development of a higher-skilled workforce and encouraged Malay citizens working abroad to return home. The prime minister's stated goal was to lift per capita annual income from $7,000 to $20,000 by 2020.

40 SOCIAL DEVELOPMENT

A provident fund provides lump-sum benefits for old age, disability, and death. Pensions are funded by 11% contributions of earnings by workers, and 12% of payroll by employers. Domestic servants, foreign workers, and the self-employed are not covered by the system. The retirement age is 55. Work injury insurance and disability pensions to low-income workers are available, with a special system for public employees.

The government has taken active measures to improve the rights and standing of women. The Islamic Family Law was revised to strengthen the inheritance rights of Muslim women and to increase their access to divorce. The government passed a domestic violence bill that allows the courts to protect victims of spousal abuse. However, this law falls short of making domestic violence a criminal act, and women's groups called for amendments in 2004. Most Muslim women play subordinate roles in public and private life in spite of their growing legal rights. Although women make up more than half of university students, they represent only 15% of key posts in public sector jobs. Custom favors men in matters of inheritance.

Human rights abuses occurring in Malaysia include arbitrary arrest and detention, torture, and other types of prisoner abuse. Caning is still used for some crimes. The government restricts the freedom of press, religion, association, and assembly.

41 HEALTH

According to the CIA, life expectancy in Malaysia was 75 years in 2011. The country spent 4.3% of its GDP on healthcare, amounting to $336 per person. There were 9 physicians, 27 nurses and midwives, and 18 hospital beds per 10,000 inhabitants. The fertility rate was 2.7, while the infant mortality rate was 15 per 1,000 live births. In 2008 the maternal mortality rate, according to the World Bank, was 31 per 100,000 births. It was estimated that 95% of children were vaccinated against measles. The CIA calculated HIV/AIDS prevalence in Malaysia to be about 0.5% in 2009.

Malaysia enjoys a comparatively high standard of health, the result of long-established health and medical services. As of 2011, Malaysia had achieved significant population coverage for clean water supply, as well as child immunizations and nutrition. Contemporary threats include the spread of HIV/AIDS and upgrading information and management systems for major disease outbreaks.

42HOUSING

With about 72% of the population living in urban areas, the need for urban housing is acute. It has been estimated that over 20% of Kuala Lumpur's population consists of squatters living in overcrowded shantytowns with few urban amenities. The government is working toward the vision of being a developed country by 2020, and sees as part of that goal the ability to ensure that all residents, regardless of income level, can own a home or place of shelter. Squatters have proven in some cases to be unwilling to leave their squatting residence to make room for the development of those areas, but there has still been a marked decrease in the number of squatting households in the two states that adopted a zero squatters policy, with the aim of having no squatters by 2005. The goal was not attained, but government efforts did result in a marked decrease in squatters.

In 2004–2008, the government built 100,000 low cost units. It has also built rental units in urban areas to assist low-income residents unable to purchase their own homes.

43EDUCATION

In 2008 the World Bank estimated that 94% of age-eligible children in Malaysia were enrolled in primary school. Secondary enrollment for age-eligible children stood at 68%. Tertiary enrollment was estimated at 36%. Of those enrolled in tertiary education, there were 100 male students for every 130 female students. Overall, the CIA estimated that Malaysia had a literacy rate of 88.7%. Public expenditure on education represented 4.1% of GDP. The student-to-teacher ratio for primary school was at about 16:1 in 2007; the ratio for secondary school was about 17:1.

Six years of free primary education are followed by three years of general lower secondary education. Two further years of education at the upper secondary level, in either a vocational or an academic program, are offered. Technical schools also offer secondary program, but students must have a strong math and science background in order to attend. A selective one-year pre-university course prepares students for admission to the universities. Malay is the medium of instruction in primary and secondary schools, with English as a compulsory second language. Muslim religious instruction is compulsory for all Muslim children while private Christian schools offer religious training to their students. The academic year runs from July to March.

Malaysia moved in July 2009 to reverse its six-year-old policy of teaching math and science classes in English, in favor of the country's national language, Bahasa Malaysia. The decision to abandon English as the language of math and science remains deeply controversial in Malaysia. Many analysts argue that the switch was motivated by political, not educational concerns. Some teachers have also expressed concern over the decision, citing the fact that most of the scientific developments of the past 300 years have been expressed in English. Because Bahasa Malaysia has not developed the ability to express these new and complex ideas, they argue, Malaysian children will be at a competitive disadvantage to other students who have studied in English.

The primary institutions of higher education include the Universiti Kebangsaan Malaysia (the National University of Malaysia), the University of Malaya, and the Technological University of Malaysia, all in or near Kuala Lumpur, and the University of Science Malaysia (formerly the University of Pinang). The MARA Institute of Technology is the largest postsecondary institute in the country.

44LIBRARIES AND MUSEUMS

The National Library of Malaysia, with more than 1.3 million volumes, was established in 1971 and has been charged with wide responsibilities under the National Library Act. Both the National Library and the National Archives are in Kuala Lumpur. The National University of Malaysia (Universiti Kebangsaan Malaysia) in Bargi has 945,000 volumes. Other important libraries are those at the universities; the Sabah (380,000) and Sarawak (500,000) state libraries; Tun Abdul Razak Library at the MARA University of Technology (569,000); and the library of the Malaysian Rubber Board (120,000). The largest public libraries are in Denang, Malacca, and Selangor.

The National Museum of Malaysia in Kuala Lumpur, constructed on the site of the former Selangor Museum (destroyed in World War II), houses extensive collections of Malayan archaeology, ethnography, and zoology. The Perak Museum in Taiping, founded in 1883, has a varied collection exhibiting antiquities, ethnographic, and zoological materials. Also in Kuala Lumpur are the Museum of Asian Art (1974), the Postal Museum, the Air Force Museum, and the National Art Gallery (1958). Sabah and Sarawak maintain anthropological and archaeological collections pertinent to East Malaysia. There is an Aboriginal Affairs Museum in Gombak.

45MEDIA

Malaysia's government-owned telecommunications system is modern, well developed, and able to provide excellent to good international and domestic services. Domestic service is provided by a microwave radio relay system and a domestic satellite communications system. International service is provided by satellite ground stations and submarine cables to India, Singapore, and Hong Kong. In 2009, there were some 4.3 million main phone lines and 30.3 million mobile cellular phones in use.

Radio-Television Malaysia (RTM) operates radio and television stations in Kuala Lumpur, Sabah, and Kuching, and there is a commercial station, Sistem TV-3 Berhad, in Kuala Lumpur as well. Broadcasts are in English, Malay, five Chinese dialects, Tamil, and numerous local languages and dialects. As of 2009 Malaysia had 35 AM and 391 FM radio stations. In 2006, there were 88 television stations. In 2000, there were 420 radios and 168 televisions sets for every 1,000 people. In 2010, the country had 344,452 Internet hosts. Internet users numbered 58 per 100 citizens.

There are about 80 English, Malay, Chinese, and Tamil daily and weekly newspapers. The Malay-language press is the largest segment, followed by English, Chinese, Tamil, Punjabi, and Kadazan. In Kuala Lumpur, there are three major dailies published in Chinese: China Press, with a 2010 circulation of 220,000; Nanyang Siang Pau, with a 2007 circulation of 120,000; and See Hua Daily News, with a circulation in 2010 of 80,000. There are also two major dailies published in Malay, Berita Harian (circulation 350,000 in 2010) and Utusan Malaysia (240,000). The New Straits Times is an English-language paper. Malaysian Nanban is a Tamil-language daily.

In Petaling Jaya leading newspapers include two Chinese publications, New Life Post (every other week, circulation 231,000 in

2002) and *Sin Chew Jit Poh* (daily, 360,000 in 2007). *The Star* is published in English and had a 2002 circulation of 220,490 daily.

Though the constitution provides for freedom of speech and a free press, in practice the government is said to restrict the flow of information deemed "sensitive," including issues regarding citizenship of non-Malays and the special position of Malays in society. Under the Printing Presses and Publications Act, every publisher must obtain a license, to be renewed annually by the government. The government has the right to restrict or ban such publications if their content is considered to contain malicious or distorted views of the government. As such, the media generally practices self-censorship, providing laudatory, noncritical coverage of government activities.

46 ORGANIZATIONS

The Malaysian government promotes thrift, credit, processing, marketing, farming, consumer, and housing cooperatives. The cooperative movement was introduced in Malaya in 1922. The Chinese are organized along clan, common dialect, or occupational lines into rural credit associations. These local associations set up and maintain schools, build temples, and provide burial, relief, and employment services. In the larger cities, chambers of commerce, organized along ethnic lines, promote the economic welfare of the group represented. Specialized trade and industry associations include the Pepper Marketing Board, Malaysian Pineapple Industry Board, and the Malaysia Cocoa Board. The National Chamber of Commerce and Industry of Malaysia is in Kuala Lumpur. Professional associations are available for a wide variety of occupations.

Cultural organizations include the multinational Royal Asiatic Society and the International Institute of Islamic Thought and Civilization. Educational and research organizations include the Malaysian Medical Association and the Malaysian Scientific Association. There are several other associations dedicated to research and education for specific fields of medicine and particular diseases and conditions, such as the National Heart Association of Malaysia.

Youth organizations include the Federation of Malay Student Unions, Girl Guides Association of Malaysia, Malaysia Council of Churches Youth Division, Muslim Youth Movement of Malaysia, Junior Chamber, National Union of Malaysian Muslim Students, and the United Malaysian Youth Movement. YMCA/YWCA chapters are also active. There are several sports associations in the nation, including the regional ASEAN Football Federation. There are active branches of the Special Olympics.

Kiwanis and Lion's clubs have programs in the country. There are national chapters of the Red Crescent Society, Habitat for Humanity, UNICEF, and Amnesty International.

47 TOURISM, TRAVEL, AND RECREATION

The *Tourism Factbook*, published by the UN World Tourism Organization, reported 23.6 million incoming tourists to Malaysia in 2009, who spent a total of $17.2 billion. Of those incoming tourists, there were 20.8 million from East Asia and the Pacific. The estimated daily cost to visit Kuala Lumpur, the capital, was $195. The cost of visiting other cities averaged $154.

Most large hotels are in the major cities of Kuala Lumpur and George Town. The best-known hill resort areas are Cameron Highlands, Raub, and Pinang Hill. Island resorts off the coast of the peninsula are Langkawi and Pangkor. Horse racing, football (soccer), rugby, cricket, and sepak raga (a form of badminton) are popular spectator sports. Kite fighting and top spinning are traditional pastimes for children and adults, and silat (a Malay martial art) is popular in rural areas.

Passports are required of all entrants. Citizens of most countries, including the United States, Australia, and China, are required to have visas. Precautions against yellow fever, typhoid, and malaria are recommended before travel to Malaysia.

48 FAMOUS PERSONS

Among the foremost Malaysian leaders of the past was Sultan Mahmud, 16th-century ruler of Malacca. A great figure in Malay culture was 'Abdallah bin 'Abd al-Kabir (surnamed Munshi, 1796–1854), sometimes called the greatest innovator in Malay letters. The best-known figure in the political life of modern Malaysia is Tunku Abdul Rahman Putra bin Abdul Hamid Halimshah (1903–1990), first prime minister of the Federation of Malaysia. Other political leaders are Tun Abdul Razak (1922–76), the nation's second prime minister (1970–76); Datuk Seri Mahathir bin Mohamed (b. 1925), prime minister 1981–2003, succeeding Dato Onn bin Ja'afar (1895–1962), a founder of the United Malays National Organization; and Sir Cheng-lock Tan (1883–1960), leader of the Malaysian Chinese Association. Abdullah bin Haji Ahmad Badawi (b. 1939) succeeded Mahathir bin Mohamed as prime minister in 2003.

49 DEPENDENCIES

Malaysia has no territories or colonies.

50 BIBLIOGRAPHY

Altbach, Philip G., and Toru Umakoshi, eds. *Asian Universities: Historical Perspectives and Contemporary Challenges*. Baltimore, MD: Johns Hopkins University Press, 2004.

Bunnell, Tim. *Malaysia, Modernity and the Multimedia Supercorridor: A Critical Geography of Intelligent Landscapes*. New York: RoutledgeCurzon, 2004.

Chio, Vanessa C. M. *Malaysia and the Development Process: Globalization, Knowledge Transfers and Post-Colonial Dilemmas*. New York: Routledge, 2005.

Gunn, Geoffrey C. *New World Hegemony in the Malay World*. Trenton, NJ: Red Sea Press, 2000.

Hooker, Virginia Matheson. *A Short History of Malaysia: Linking East and West*. Crows Nest, N.S.W., Aus.: Allen and Unwin, 2003.

Jaaffar, Johan. *History of Modern Malay Literature*. Kuala Lumpur, Malaysia: Desan Bahasa dan Pustaka, Ministry of Education Malaysia, 1992.

Kaur, Amarjit. *Historical Dictionary of Malaysia*. Lanham, Md.: Scarecrow Press, 2001.

Koh, Jaime, and Lee-Ling Ho. *Culture and Customs of Singapore and Malaysia*. Santa Barbara, Calif: Greenwood Press, 2009.

Leibo, Steven A. *East and Southeast Asia, 2011*. Harpers Ferry, WV: Stryker-Post Publications, 2011.

Lindsey, Tim, and Kerstin Steiner. *Islam, Law, and the State in Southeast Asia: Malaysia and Brunei*. London: I.B. Tauris, 2012.

Lye, Tuck-Po. *Changing Pathways: Forest Degradation and the Batek of Pahang, Malaysia.* Lanham, MD: Lexington Books, 2004.

McNair, Sylvia. *Malaysia.* New York: Children's Press, 2002.

Malaysia Investment and Business Guide: Strategic and Practical Information. Washington, DC: International Business Publications USA, 2012.

Malaysian Eclipse: Economic Crisis and Recovery. New York: Zed, 2001.

Munro-Kua, Anne. *Authoritarian Populism in Malaysia.* Basingstoke: Palgrave, 2002.

Stewart, Ian. *The Mahathir Legacy: A Nation Divided, A Region at Risk.* London, Eng.: Orion, 2003.

Westhuizen W. J. van der. *Adapting to Globalization: Malaysia, South Africa, and the Challenges of Ethnic Redistribution with Growth.* Westport, CT: Praeger, 2002.

MALDIVES

Republic of Maldives

Dhivehi Raajjeyge Jumhooriyyaa

CAPITAL: Malé

FLAG: The national flag consists of a white crescent at the center of a green field which, in turn, is at the center of a red field.

ANTHEM: *Gaumee Salaam (National Salute).*

MONETARY UNIT: The Maldivian rupee, or rufiyaa (MVR), is a currency of 100 laari. There are notes of 5, 10, 20, 50, 100, and 500 rufiyaa. Coins are 1, 2, 5, 10, 25, and 50 laari, and 1 and 2 rufiyaa. The dollar circulates freely and is the only currency accepted at some resorts. MVR1 = US$0.06382 (or US$1 = MVR15.6) as of 2011.

WEIGHTS AND MEASURES: The metric system is used, but some local units also remain in use.

HOLIDAYS: National Day, January or February, date varies; Independence Day, 26 July; Republic Day, 11 November. Eid al-Fitr, Eid al-Adha, and Milad an-Nabi are some of the Muslim religious holidays observed.

TIME: 5 p.m. = noon GMT.

¹LOCATION, SIZE, AND EXTENT

The smallest country in Asia, the Republic of Maldives consists of an archipelago of nearly 1,200 coral islands and sandbanks in the Indian Ocean, fewer than 200 of which are inhabited. The chain of islands sits astride the equator, S of India and W of Sri Lanka, extending 823 km (511 mi) but occupying an area of just 300 sq km (116 sq mi). The area occupied by Maldives is slightly more than 1.5 times the size of Washington, DC. Grouped in 26 atolls, with a total coastline of 644 km (400 mi), the northernmost atoll lies some 110 km (70 mi) S of India's Minicoy Atoll, about 480 km (300 mi) SE of India's Cape Comorin, and 649 km (400 mi) W of Sri Lanka.

Maldives' capital, Malé, is situated on a 5.7 sq km (2.2 sq mi) island, the largest in the entire chain, in the Malé Atoll.

²TOPOGRAPHY

The islands vary from tiny banks to real islets. Some of the islands are in process of formation and are constantly increasing in size; others are gradually washing away. The islands are level and extremely low-lying, with elevations rarely exceeding 1.8 m (6 ft) above sea level. Many contain freshwater lagoons.

In 1997 the nation initiated a massive land reclamation project which involved the construction of an island, Hulhumale, a short distance away from Malé. In 2011, the new island was about the same size as Malé; developers hoped that by about 2040 Hulhumale would be twice the size of Malé and provide housing for 153,000 people.

The disastrous tsunami that struck Indonesia on 26 December 2004 also impacted Maldives. The tsunami was caused by an underwater earthquake 324 km (180 mi) south of Indonesia's Sumatra island. Waves reaching 6 m (20 ft) were absorbed by Maldives' coral reefs before they could severely damage the atolls. The

northernmost and southernmost islands suffered the brunt of the damage. More than 20,000 residents were left without homes in Maldives, and at least 55 were found dead.

³CLIMATE

The Maldives' equatorial climate is generally hot and humid, with a mean temperature of about 27°C (81°F). The weather during the northeast monsoon (November–March) is mild and pleasant; the southwest monsoon (June–August) is violent and very rainy. The northern atolls are subject to more violent storms than those in the south. Annual rainfall in the south averages about 380 cm (150 in); in the north, 250 cm (100 in).

⁴FLORA AND FAUNA

The World Resources Institute estimates that there are 583 plant species in Maldives. In addition, Maldives is home to 15 species of mammals, 166 species of birds, and 8 species of reptiles. The calculation reflects the total number of distinct species residing in the country, not the number of endemic species.

Most of the islands are covered with a dense scrub of palms and screw pine. The northern and southern islands are more fertile than those in the central group, and the eastern islands generally are more fertile than the western. Coconut, breadfruit, plantain, papaya, mango, and banyan trees flourish. Shrubs and flowers are widespread. Rats, rabbits, and flying foxes are the only indigenous mammals. Birds include ducks, bitterns, herons, crows, curlews, snipes, and various sea birds including frigate birds and terns. Small scorpions, spiders, beetles, and land crabs are common. Inland lagoons and coastal reefs contain tropical ocean fish, crustaceans, and turtles; the surrounding waters hold tuna, sharks, manta rays, eels, swordfish, and porpoises. The Maldives has more than 2,000 fish species, of which 300 are reef fish, according to the World Wildlife Fund.

5 ENVIRONMENT

The World Resources Institute reported that Maldives had designated 583,000 hectares (1.44 million acres) of land for protection as of 2006. Maldivian environmental organization Bluepeace has campaigned for uninhabited islands to be made into nature reserves, instead of converting them into new tourist resorts. According to a 2011 report issued by the International Union for Conservation of Nature and Natural Resources (IUCN), threatened species included 2 mammals, 3 birds, and 18 fish. The hawksbill turtle, green turtle, and blue whale are on the endangered list.

In 2010 Maldives declared that its 90,000-sq-km (35,000-sq-mi) exclusive economic zone would become a shark sanctuary. Analysts noted that Maldives's decision to protect the sharks in its waters served the nation's economic self-interest. Scuba diving represents a huge draw for tourists on Maldives, and the designation of a shark sanctuary may draw even more tourists. The reefs of Baa Atoll, Maldives, became part of the UNESCO Biosphere Reserve Program in 2011. The site had great potential with for demonstrating sustainable development throughout the Maldives and improving an integrated management system.

Water resources totaled 0.03 cu km (0.007 cu mi) while water usage was 0.003 cu km (0.001 cu mi) per year. Domestic water usage accounted for 98% of total usage and industrial usage for 2%. Per capita water usage totaled 9 cu m (318 cu ft) per year. Pollution of groundwater and surrounding seawater was a problem in the densely populated capital city, Malé. Destruction of the nation's coral reefs, sand dredging and erosion from new harbors, and solid waste pollution are other major environmental concerns for the nation. Refuse from Malé and resort islands was brought to a reclaimed "garbage island" which, as of December 2011, was over its capacity, with rubbish being dumped in the island's lagoon.

Vehicles cause air pollution on Malé's 5.7 sq km (2.2 sq mi) island. The United Nations (UN) reported in 2008 that carbon dioxide emissions in Maldives totaled 898 kilotons. In 2009, President Mohamed Nasheed announced his plan for Maldives to work towards carbon neutrality by 2010, through use of alternative energy technologies, in order to show the way for other nations to fight global warming. Urgent concerns about climate change were also voiced by the previous president, Maumoon Abdul Gayoom. At the UN World Summit on Sustainable Development held in August and September 2002 in South Africa, President Gayoom warned that his country could be submerged if a rise in sea levels due to the melting of polar ice caps continued. "A mere one-meter rise would mean the death of a nation," he stated. As world temperatures rise, the effects on the Maldives would include coastal erosion, increasing salinity of fresh water sources, altered tidal ranges and patterns, and the gradual destruction of the coral reefs that form the islands and their breakwaters.

As president, Nasheed wasa vocal international advocate for measures against global warming. He held the world's first underwater cabinet meeting in October 2009, to demonstrate Maldives' extreme vulnerability to rising sea levels from climate change. The possible need to relocate the entire population of the nation in the future, due to global warming, has been discussed. Climate change has already affected Maldives as rising sea temperatures damage coral reefs and drive fish deeper in the ocean to feed on plankton.

6 POPULATION

The US Central Intelligence Agency (CIA) estimated the population of Maldives in 2011 to be approximately 394,999, which placed it at number 170 in population among the 196 nations of the world. In 2011, approximately 4.1% of the population was over 65 years of age, with another 21.5% under 15 years of age. The median age in Maldives was 26.2 years. There were 1.40 males for every female in the country. The population's annual rate of change was -0.151%. The projected population for the year 2025 was 400,000. Population density in Maldives was calculated at 1,326 people per sq km (3,434 people per sq mi). The UN estimated that 40% of the population lived in urban areas, and that urban populations had an annual rate of change of 4.2%. The largest urban area was Male, with a population of 120,000 as of 2009.

7 MIGRATION

Estimates of Maldives's net migration rate, according to the CIA in 2011, amounted to -12.62 migrants per 1,000 citizens. According to the government's Statistical Yearbook of Maldives 2010, there were 70,259 expatriate workers in Maldives as of 2009. Human trafficking of migrant workers from Bangladesh and other South Asian countries to Maldives was a concern as of 2011. The total number of emigrants living abroad was 2,000. Inter-island migration has mostly been limited to settlement in Malé; between 1967 and 2000, population in the capital rose from one-tenth to nearly one-quarter of the national total.

8 ETHNIC GROUPS

The original inhabitants of the Maldives are thought to have been of south Indian and Arab origin. The people of the northern atolls have, to some extent, intermarried with peoples from western India, Arabia, and North Africa. Inhabitants of the southern islands may be more related to the Sinhalese of Sri Lanka. Black African slaves imported from Zanzibar and Arabia also intermarried with the Maldivians, and there are also some Caucasian and Malayan ancestors.

9 LANGUAGES

The Maldivian language, called Divehi, is similar to the old Sinhala (Elu) of Ceylon. It has contributed the word "atoll" to international terminology. In recent years, the language has been influenced by Arabic and Urdu. Thaana, developed during the 17th century, is the corresponding script, written from right to left. While Divehi is the official language, English is spoken by most government officials.

10 RELIGIONS

Though there is evidence that the early Maldivians were Buddhists, their conversion to Islam dates from 1153. The 2008 constitution places Sunni Islam as the official religion and a variety of laws prohibit citizens from practicing any other religion or renouncing Islam. Both land ownership and citizenship are limited to adherents of Islam. The president must be a Sunni Muslim. The nation's civil law is based on Shari'ah (Islamic law). Islamic holy days are national holidays. Non-Muslim foreigners working in or visiting the country are only permitted to practice their own religion privately; there are no non-Muslim places of worship. Proselytizing for non-Muslim faiths is prohibited and foreigners are not permitted to import items that are considered contrary to Islam, such as religious statues or icons, or pork products. In 2010, the Ministry of Islamic Affairs initiated a set of regulations pursuant to the Protection of the Religious Unity Among Maldivians Act, which provided for even tighter regulation and oversight of Islamic practice and the deterrence of non-Muslim practices.

Islamic fundamentalist pressure groups became more high-profile in Maldives after 2008, and in 2011 Islamic groups protested "idolatrous" monuments left there by countries including Pakistan and Sri Lanka, which participated in the November 2011 South Asian Association for Regional Cooperation (SAARC) summit. Small public gatherings promoting religious freedom were held in Malé in 2010 and 2011.

¹¹TRANSPORTATION

Malé, the capital, and some other islands have fairly good streets. Most people travel on land by motorbike, bicycle or on foot. Only a few of the islands are big enough to support automobiles. The CIA reports that Maldives has a total of 88 km (54.7 mi) of roads. There are 23 vehicles per 1,000 people in the country.

Inter-island transport is mainly by means of *dhonis* (small boats) powered by sails or engines. As of 2010, the Maldives had a merchant fleet of 24 vessels with 1,000 GRT or more. Resorts have private boat taxis for their guests and air taxis are available for tourists.

The Maldives has five airports, which transported 85,448 passengers in 2009 according to the World Bank. Malé International Airport, at Hulhulé, 2 km (1.24 mi) away over water from the capital, was completed in 1966. It consists of two islands that were joined together to create a runway. Direct flights are available from Europe, India, Singapore, China, Hong Kong and Sri Lanka. Maldivian is the national carrier, and Mega Maldives is a charter airline; both have international flights.

¹²HISTORY

The first inhabitants of the Maldives were probably Dravidian speakers from south India, followed by Indo-European speaking Sinhalese from Ceylon in the 4th and 5th centuries BC. The island chain first became known in the West through the writings of Ptolemy, during the 2nd century AD. The island chain may have been ruled in ancient times by the Chinese; later, its rulers paid an annual tribute to principalities of western India. Maldivians were converted to Sunni Islam from Buddhism by Arab traders from east Africa and the Middle East in the middle of the 12th century, and from 1153, an unbroken line of 92 sultans served as local rulers for 800 years until 1953. In 1343, Ibn Battutah, the Arab traveler and historian, visited the islands and served for a time as a qadi (Islamic judge.)

After their discovery by the Portuguese traveler Dom Lourenço de Alameida in 1507, the Maldives were occupied by the Portuguese and forced to pay a tribute to Goa, the center of Portugal's South Asian holdings. The Portuguese were driven out in 1573 by Muhammad Thakurufaani al-Azam, who, after becoming sultan, introduced a monetary system, a new script, and a standing militia. In the 17th century, the Dutch, who controlled neighboring Ceylon (now Sri Lanka), made a treaty with the sultanate, which

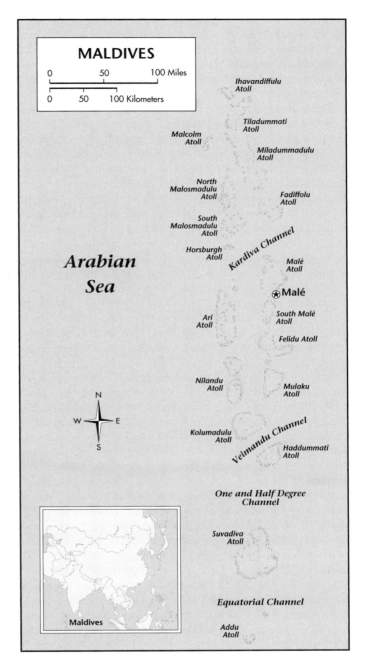

LOCATION: 7°7′ N to 0°43′ S; 72°31′ to 73°46′E. TERRITORIAL SEA LIMIT: 12 miles.

thereafter paid tribute to the rulers of Ceylon and claimed their protection.

The British completed their occupation of Ceylon in 1815 and British responsibility for the protection of the Maldives was formally recorded in 1887. By terms of the compact, the sultan recognized the suzerainty of the British sovereign and disclaimed all rights or intention to enter into any treaty or negotiations with any foreign state except through the (British) ruler of Ceylon. When Ceylon became independent in 1948, a new agreement was signed with the British government, providing for the Maldives to remain under the protection of the British crown, for external affairs to be conducted by or in accordance with the advice of the British government, for Britain to refrain from interfering in the internal affairs of the islands, and for the sultan to afford such facilities for British forces as were necessary for the defense of the islands or the Commonwealth. No tribute was to be paid by Maldives. New agreements reaffirming these provisions were signed in 1953, 1956, and 1960.

The sultanate, dominated by the Didi family since 1759, was abolished in 1953, and the Maldives was declared a republic. The first president, Amin Didi, ordered the emancipation of women and other reforms that were resented by more conservative elements, and nine months later he was overthrown. His cousins Muhammad Farid Didi and Ibrahim Ali Didi became co-presidents in September 1953, and a month later the National Assembly voted to restore the sultanate. The new sultan, Muhammad Didi, was installed at Malé on 7 March 1954, and Ibrahim Ali Didi, the prime minister, formed a new government.

The government's agreement in 1956 to permit Britain to maintain an air base on Gan Island in the southern Maldives produced a public reaction so strong that Prime Minister Ibrahim was forced to resign in December 1957. Ibrahim Nasir, who succeeded him, asserted that the British base would violate Maldivian neutrality, but when his government sent a representative to Gan to tell the islanders to stop working for the British, the islanders attacked him.

Early in 1959, the people of Addu Atoll, in which Gan Island is located, declared their independence. At the same time, a rebellion broke out in the three southernmost atolls (including Addu). The rebel headmen declared the formation of the United Suvadiva Republic (with a population of 20,000) and demanded recognition from London. The British refused to comply, but the Nasir government made public its suspicions that the coup had been engineered by the British. In the event, government forces crushed the rebels in two of the atolls but made no attempt to interfere on Gan or any of the other seven main islands in the Addu group. By March 1960, the Suvadiva Republic was declared dissolved, and a committee ruling under the sovereign control of the sultan was set up, including among its members Abdallah Afif, leader of the rebellion.

In February 1960, the Maldivian government made a free gift to the British government of the use of Gan Island and other facilities in Addu Atoll for 30 years, and a fresh agreement was drawn up between the governments. In return, the British agreed to assist in bringing about a reconciliation between the Maldivian government and the disaffected inhabitants of the southern islands. But by 1962, resentment had grown against the British owing to their lack of progress in implementing the agreement; in late 1962 a Royal Navy frigate was sent to the capital island of Malé to protect British citizens. Abdallah Afif was evacuated by the British to the Seychelles.

The Sultanate of the Maldive Islands achieved complete independence on 26 July 1965, with the British continuing to retain use of the facilities on Gan in return for the payment of $2,380,000, most to be spent over a period of years for economic development. In March 1968, a referendum resulted in an 81% vote to abolish the sultanate and to reestablish a republic. A new republican constitution came into force on 11 November 1968, establishing the Republic of Maldives, and Nasir-then prime minister-became president. With the British secure in their control of facilities they shared with the United States outside the Maldives in Diego Garcia, 650 km (400 mi) east of Gan, Britain vacated the Gan air base on 31 December 1975, and the UK-Maldivian accord was formally terminated the following year.

Nasir declined re-nomination and was succeeded as president on 11 November 1978 by Maumoon Abdul Gayoom, who was chosen by the Citizens' Majlis (parliament) in June and was confirmed in a popular referendum by a majority of 90% on 28 July. Reelected president by the Majlis in August 1983, Gayoom won confirmation in a national referendum on 30 September with a majority of 95.6%. Gayoom was reelected to a third term in August 1988. He successfully resisted a brief attempt to overthrow him by Sri Lankan Tamil mercenaries in November 1988, with the help of an Indian military contingent flown to the Maldives at his request.

Gayoom was reelected for a fourth term as president in August 1993 and confirmed by popular referendum in September. He was reelected to a fifth term, unopposed, in 1998, and was reelected to a sixth term, again unopposed, in 2003. Gayoom's only principal rival for the presidency came in the 1993 election when his brother-in-law Ilyas Ibrahim ran against him. Ibrahim subsequently was tried in absentia for violation of the constitution, found guilty of treason, and sentenced to more than 15 years banishment from the islands. In 2003, the human rights organization Amnesty International accused the Maldives government of political repression and torture. It said arbitrary detentions, unfair trials, and long-term imprisonment of government critics were commonplace. That September, unprecedented antigovernment riots broke out in Malé; Amnesty International blamed the unrest on political repression and human rights abuses. In August 2004, a state of emergency was imposed after a pro-democracy demonstration became violent. Nearly 100 people were jailed.

On 26 December 2004, the Maldives suffered severe damage as a result of a massive tsunami triggered by a powerful underwater earthquake off the coast of Indonesia. At least 55 people were killed, and the government said the disaster set back development work by 20 years.

In June 2004, President Gayoom promised constitutional changes to limit the presidential term of office and to allow political parties to form. In June 2005, parliament voted to allow multiparty politics. In elections held in October 2008, former political prisoner Mohamed Nasheed of the Maldivian Democratic Party defeated Gayoom to win the presidency with 54.2% of the vote. Gayoom had been one of Asia's longest-serving leaders, a fact that had become a major issue for many Maldivian voters, who were eager for change.

The Nasheed administration had trouble introducing the political and economic reforms that were promised during his campaign, as many motions were blocked by parliament. On 29 June 2010, Maldives's thirteen-member cabinet resigned in protest, with members saying they could no longer work with an opposition that, blocking everything, was making the country "ungovernable." The mass resignation came after the opposition threatened to bring a vote of no confidence against every member of the cabinet. Of the seventy-seven-member parliament, the opposition Maldivian People's Party maintained more than forty seats. Meanwhile, Nasheed's party, the Maldivian Democratic Party, had the support of thirty-two lawmakers. The numbers put the country in a political deadlock. Nasheed had no power to dissolve the parliament, and the opposition lacked the two-thirds majority to impeach Nasheed. The entire cabinet was reappointed by Nasheed a week later, but the reappointments of 7 cabinet members were rejected by the parliament. Replacements acceptable to the parliament were not completed until March 2011.

While Nasheed maintained a positive image in international circles due to his tireless activism on global warming's threats to the very existence of Maldives, at home the acrimony between his administration and the Maldivian People's Party continued through 2011, along with allegations of pervasive corruption, rising national debt, rising crime, and increasing religious intolerance. In January 2012, President Nasheed ordered the army to arrest the chief justice of the criminal court, a supporter of former president Gayoom. This was seen by many in the Maldives as overstepping his authority and led to protests that were eventually joined by members of the police. On 7 February 2012 Nasheed announced his resignation. He was replaced by Vice President Waheed Hassan. Shortly thereafter, however, Nasheed said that he had really been deposed by a coup, and that his resignation had been made under duress and was invalid. Violence and political turmoil continued in the ensuing weeks.

13 GOVERNMENT

The constitution of the Republic of Maldives that came into force in 1968 (and was amended in 1970, 1972, and 1975) was repealed and replaced by a new constitution enacted in January 1998. Under this law, the Citizens' Majlis (parliament) nominated a single candidate for the presidency, who was confirmed in office thereafter by popular referendum. Another new constitution was ratified 7 August 2008, under which the president is elected by direct vote to serve a five-year term, with eligibility for a second term. The president heads the executive branch and appoints the cabinet. The president serves a five-year term of office.

The unicameral Majlis is a body of 77 members, directly elected by universal suffrage of citizens over 21, with two from each administrative atoll and the city of Malé. Eight members are appointed by the president. Elections for the Majlis are scheduled for 2014. The Majlis drafts legislation that becomes law after ratification by the president.

14 POLITICAL PARTIES

The primary political parties of the Maldives have included the Adhaalath Party (AP), Maldivian People's Party (Dhivehi Rayyithunge Party—DRP), Islamic Democratic Party (IDP), Maldivian Democratic Party (MDP), Social Liberal Party (SLP), Dhivevi Quamee Party (DQP), People's Alliance (PA), and the Republican Party (Jumhooree Party—JP).

In the October 2008 presidential elections, Mohamed Nasheed of the MDP was elected with 54.3% of the vote. His leading opponent was former president Maumoon Abdul Gayoom of the DRP, who won 45.7% of the vote. On 7 February 2012 Nasheed resigned from office, but later claimed he had been forced out in a coup. Waheed Hassan assumed the presidency.The next presidential election is set for 2013.

In the legislative elections of May 2009, the DRP won 28 of the 77 seats in the assembly with 36.4% of the vote. The MDP won 26 seats (with 33.8% of the vote), followed by the Pa with 7 seats

(9.1%), the DQP with 2 seats (2.6%), and the Republican Party with 1 seat (1.2%). Thirteen seats were won by independent candidates. The next legislative elections are set for 2014.

15 LOCAL GOVERNMENT

Under the Decentralization Act of 2010, Maldives was divided administratively into 20 atolls. Malé and Hulhulé (the island of the international airport) are geographically in Kaafu Atoll, but are treated as a separate administrative entity. Malé and Addu City (Seenu atoll) have city councils. The atolls have elected atoll councils, and island councils form the local administration for the 189 inhabited islands within the atolls.

16 JUDICIAL SYSTEM

Maldives has an independent judicial system overseen by a Judicial Services Commission, under the 2008 constitution. Traditional Islamic law (Shari'ah) remains influential in the legal system. The continued use of flogging in Maldives for punishment of adultery and other offenses has been criticized by the UN and international human rights organizations. According to the US State Department, Maldives did not have political prisoners as of 2010.

The seven member Supreme Court, mandated in 2008 and appointed by the president, was sworn in at Malé in August 2010. The High Court was appointed in March 2011. The inhabited islands have magistrate's courts. In criminal cases there is no jury trial. The accused may call witnesses and may be assisted by a lawyer. Laws presuming innocence until proven guilty and against arbitrary detention are upheld. Maldives does not have the death penalty.

17 ARMED FORCES

Defense spending accounted for 5.5% of gross domestic product (GDP) in 2007. The Maldives National Defense Force is all-volunteer and consists of a Coast Guard, Marine Corps with Rapid Reaction Groups, Special Forces, and support units including engineering, medical, transport, and an Air Wing.

18 INTERNATIONAL COOPERATION

The Maldives, which joined the UN on 21 September 1965, is a member of ESCAP and several non-regional specialized agencies, such as the FAO, ICAO, IFC, IMF, the World Bank, UNESCO, UNIDO, and WHO. Maldives is also a member of the Asian Development Bank, the Commonwealth of Nations, the Colombo Plan, G-77, the Organization of the Islamic Conference (OIC), the South Asia Cooperative Environment Program (SACEP), the Alliance of Small Island States (AOSIS), and the 7-member South Asian Association for Regional Cooperation (SAARC).

An active member of the Nonaligned Movement, Maldives has led efforts to declare an Indian Ocean Peace Zone, free of nuclear arms. Sri Lanka traditionally served as the Maldives' focus in its external affairs. However, this has been broadened in the last few decades as the Maldives entered into diplomatic relations with more countries, and communication and transportation have opened up the outside world. As a member of the UN Human Rights Council, Maldives was prominent in calls for an end to repression in Syria during 2011.

In environmental cooperation, the Maldives is part of the Basel Convention, the Convention on Biological Diversity, the Kyoto

Protocol, the Montréal Protocol, and the UN Conventions on the Law of the Sea and Climate Change. Maldives has taken on an important role in multinational meetings on global warming.

¹⁹ECONOMY

The GDP rate of change in Maldives, as of 2010, was 8%, according to the CIA. Since the 1990s, tourism has been the mainstay of the economy, accounting for about 30% of GDP as of 2011. Besides tourism, Maldives' GDP is composed of distribution, construction, fisheries, agriculture, transportation and communication, government administration, manufacturing, and electricity. Sectors such as construction, transportation and agriculture are directly related to tourism. Although the 2004 tsunami and 2008–2009 international economic crisis negatively impacted Maldives' tourism industry, increases in tourism from other Asian nations drove economic recovery in 2010–2011. Inflation was 6% in 2011 due mainly to the cost of food, most of which (other than fish) was imported, and unemployment was high at 14.5%.

²⁰INCOME

The CIA estimated that in 2010 the GDP of Maldives was $2.734 billion. The CIA defines GDP as the value of all final goods and services produced within a nation in a given year and computed on the basis of purchasing power parity (PPP) rather than value as measured on the basis of the rate of the exchange based on current dollars. The per capita GDP was estimated at $6,900. The annual growth rate of GDP was 8%. The average inflation rate was 6%. It was estimated by the CIA that services accounted for 77.5% of GDP, industry 16.9%, and agriculture 5.6%, as of 2009. According to the World Bank, remittances from citizens living abroad totaled $3.7 million or about $9 per capita and accounted for approximately .1% of GDP.

It was estimated that in 2008 about 16% of the population subsisted on an income below the poverty line, according to the CIA. There is income disparity between residents of urban areas and those of smaller outlying islands. As of 2011 the most recent study by the World Bank reported that actual individual consumption in Maldives was 53.8% of GDP and accounted for less than 0.01% of world consumption. By comparison, the United States accounted for 25.44% of world individual consumption. The World Bank also estimated that 13.4% of Maldives's GDP was spent on food and beverages, 17.9% on housing and household furnishings, 1.9% on clothes, 5.1% on health, 1.8% on transportation, 1.7% on communications, 1.9% on recreation, 0.6% on restaurants and hotels, and 2% on miscellaneous goods and services and purchases from abroad.

²¹LABOR

As of 2010, Maldives had a total labor force of 110,000 people, according to the CIA. Within the labor force, CIA estimates in 2006 noted that 11% were employed in agriculture, 23% in industry, and 65% in the service sector. Tourist resorts and other sectors employed thousands of migrant workers, mainly from other Asian countries, and human trafficking was a problem as of 2010, according to the US State Department. The fishing industry was a major source of employment for Maldivians. Unemployment was severe, particularly for women and urban youth.

Maldives joined the ILO in 2009. Although the rights to form trade unions and to strike were guaranteed in the 2008 constitution, resort workers who have gone on strike to protest low wages or lack of wages have been threatened and detained, according to the International Trade Union Confederation's 2011 Annual Survey, and members of the Tourism Employees Association of the Maldives have been harassed and fired from their jobs.

Minimum wage for government workers was approximately $241 per month, as of 2010. The work week was set at 48 hours with the 2008 Employment Law. The minimum working age is 16, although younger children continue to work in family agricultural and fishing enterprises, and as domestic servants in Malé.

²²AGRICULTURE

Roughly 43% of the total land is farmed. Cereal production amounted to 147 tons, fruit production 17,758 tons, and vegetable production 28,152 tons as of 2009, according to the UN Food and Agriculture Organization (FAO). Coconuts, corn, sweet potatoes, breadfruit, mangoes, papayas, limes, bananas, pumpkins, watermelon, taro, and chili peppers, are gown, largely in home gardens or for use by tourist resorts. Rice, edible oil, and most other staple foods are imported.

²³ANIMAL HUSBANDRY

The FAO reported that Maldives dedicated 1,000 hectares (2,471 acres) to permanent pasture or meadow in 2009. Livestock production amounted to 1,507 tons of beef, 5,136 tons of poultry, 3,442 tons of eggs, and 23,799 tons of milk. Goats and chickens are raised by individual households.

²⁴FISHING

In 2008, the annual capture totaled 133,086 tons according to the UN FAO. Despite constituting only 3.2% of GDP, fishing is crucial to the local diet, is the only significant export commodity, and provides more than half of the jobs for Maldivians. It has declined in GDP value as fish stocks have become seriously depleted. While the Maldives fishing fleet uses sustainable pole and line methods in small locally-built boats, foreign fleets use large nets and fish attraction devices in nearby waters, contributing to depletion. The main commercial varieties have been skipjack and yellowfin tuna. About half the annual harvest is frozen, canned, or dried for export, with 49% going to Thailand for processing and re-export. The Maldives government has banned fishing for reef sharks, hunting sea turtles, and gathering coral.

²⁵FORESTRY

Approximately 3% of Maldives is covered by forest, which is largely along shorelines with mangroves, screw pine, and palm. The value of all forest products, including roundwood, totaled $14,000 in 2009. Wood from coconut palm groves is used for building boats and houses. Imports of forest products amounted to $4.2

million in 2004 and most wood for boats and construction is imported from elsewhere in Asia as of 2011.

26 MINING

There are no known mineral resources in the Maldives.

27 ENERGY AND POWER

The World Bank reported in 2008 that Maldives produced 260 million kWh of electricity, generated from imported diesel fuel. Imported petroleum was used for air, land and water transportation. Renewable energy sources gained importance as the government attempted to reach the goal of zero carbon emissions for the nation by 2020, set by Maldives president Nasheed as an example to the world of how to fight global warming. Household solar panels, wind turbine arrays, electric-powered boats and vehicles, and the use of coconut husks to power the electrical plant were planned as replacements for the country's costly imports of petroleum. Maldives was also looking into obtaining energy from wave, tidal, and ocean geothermal sources.

28 INDUSTRY

The manufacturing sector is small in Maldives. The boat building industry uses local and imported materials to produce small fishing boats. Fish-processing facilities include tuna canneries. There are small factories for consumer products, beverages, and processed foods, although most of those goods are imported. Tourism has created needs for resort construction, inter-atoll transport, bottled water, and handicrafts. Several apparel factories were in operation between 2000 and 2005, until US garment quotas expired.

29 SCIENCE AND TECHNOLOGY

The World Bank reported in 2009 that there were no patent applications in science and technology in Maldives. International and local scientists in Maldives study the effects of climate change on the islands, and patterns of weather and currents in the Indian Ocean. Maldives Science Society is a local NGO. Derived from the

Balance of Payments – Maldives (2010)

(In millions of US dollars)

Current Account		**-462.7**
Balance on goods	-798.0	
Imports	-978.0	
Exports	180.0	
Balance on services	462.2	
Balance on income	-60.3	
Current transfers	-66.7	
Capital Account		...
Financial Account		350.1
Direct investment abroad	...	
Direct investment in Maldives	163.8	
Portfolio investment assets	...	
Portfolio investment liabilities	...	
Financial derivatives	...	
Other investment assets	-1.8	
Other investment liabilities	188.1	
Net Errors and Omissions		158.6
Reserves and Related Items		-46.0

(…) data not available or not significant.

SOURCE: *Balance of Payment Statistics Yearbook 2011*, Washington, DC: International Monetary Fund, 2011.

Maldives Science Center, Maldives National University (founded 2011) offers degrees in health sciences and engineering.

30 DOMESTIC TRADE

Malé is the chief commercial center, where importers, exporters, and wholesalers do business. Small shops serve the residents and tourists of the other inhabited islands, and a convention center has been built at Gan, on Addu atoll. Most shops are open from 8 a.m. to 1:30 p.m. and from 2:30 to 5 p.m., Sunday through Thursday. Banks and government offices are open from 9 a.m. to 1 p.m. on the same days. Most establishments are closed on Fridays.

31 FOREIGN TRADE

In 1989, the government initiated an economic reform program that lifted import quotas and opened exports of some commodities to the private sector (until then, exports had been entirely controlled by a state trading organization). Exports were estimated at $163 million for 2009, according to the CIA. In 2010, Maldives main export partners were, according to the CIA, Thailand, 17.9%; Sri Lanka, 16.9%; France, 14.2%; UK, 12.1%; Italy 9.2%; and Tanzania 4.9%. Fish, particularly frozen or canned tuna, accounted for virtually all export business.

Maldives has remained heavily dependent on imports of petroleum, food, construction materials, and manufactured goods. In 2009, imports amounted to an estimated $967 million, according to the CIA. The major import partners in 2010 were Singapore, 24.7%; UAE, 17.2%; India, 8.6%; Malaysia, 8.1%; Sri Lanka, 5.7%; Thailand, 5.7%; and China, 5.6%, according to the CIA.

32 BALANCE OF PAYMENTS

Because Maldives' economy is dependent on a constant influx of foreign exchange from tourism and fish exports, it is extremely vulnerable to downturns in those sectors. This led to a balance of

Principal Trading Partners – Maldives (2010)

(In millions of US dollars)

Country	Total	Exports	Imports	Balance
World	1,169.1	74.0	1,095.1	-1,021.1
Singapore	308.5	2.3	306.3	-304.0
United Arab Emirates	213.1	0.0	213.1	-213.1
India	138.8	28.4	110.5	-82.1
Thailand	89.6	19.0	70.6	-51.7
Sri Lanka	88.8	17.8	71.0	-53.2
Malaysia	88.3	3.4	84.8	-81.4
China	69.9	0.1	69.8	-69.8
United States	32.9	1.6	31.2	-29.6
Bahrain	29.2	...	29.2	-29.2
Germany	28.5	15.1	13.5	1.6

(…) data not available or not significant.

(n.s.) not specified.

SOURCE: *2011 Direction of Trade Statistics Yearbook*, New York: United Nations, 2011.

payments crisis in 2009, necessitating a $79.3 million IMF loan, which was not completely disbursed due to the Maldives government's failure to comply with IMF-prescribed austerity measures such as pay cuts for civil servants. A rebound in the tourism sector did not offset rising import costs in 2010 and Maldives had a foreign trade deficit of $307 million, amounting to 26.5% of GDP.

33 BANKING AND SECURITIES

The Maldives Monetary Authority, established 1 July 1981, issues currency, advises the government on banking and monetary matters, supervises commercial banks, and manages exchange rates and exchange assets. Other banking services are provided by the Bank of Maldives (created in 1982) which has branches in Malé and the other atolls, with ATMs, debit cards and internet banking services. The Maldives Islamic Bank opened in 2011. There are also commercial banks with headquarters in India, Pakistan, Mauritius, UK, and Sri Lanka.

The CIA reported that in 2010, currency and demand deposits-an aggregate commonly known as M1-were equal to $588 million. In that same year, M2-an aggregate equal to M1 plus savings deposits, small time deposits, and money market mutual funds-was $1.239 billion. The Commercial bank prime lending rate was 10.38% in December 2010, according to the CIA.

The Maldives Stock Exchange began operations in 2008. As of December 2011, it had 6 companies listed.

34 INSURANCE

Allied Insurance was founded in 1985 as a joint venture with a UK company. Sri Lanka Insurance, Ceylinco Insurance, and Amana Takaful (Islamic law compliant), are all companies from Sri Lanka which operate in Maldives.

35 PUBLIC FINANCE

As of 2011, tax revenue provided the majority of public revenue, and other sources included tourist resort leases, and state owned

Public Finance – Maldives (2009)

(In millions of rufiyaa, central government figures)

Revenue and Grants	**5,947.2**	**100.0%**
Tax revenue	2,653.9	44.6%
Social contributions	...	...
Grants	602.4	10.1%
Other revenue	2,690.9	45.2%
Expenditures	**10,950.3**	**100.0%**
General public services	2,619.1	23.9%
Defense	635.5	5.8%
Public order and safety	1,114.4	10.2%
Economic affairs	1,600.2	14.6%
Environmental protection	115.3	1.1%
Housing and community amenities	810.7	7.4%
Health	845.2	7.7%
Recreational, culture, and religion	370.5	3.4%
Education	2,066.5	18.9%
Social protection	772.9	7.1%

(...) data not available or not significant.

SOURCE: *Government Finance Statistics Yearbook 2010*, Washington, DC: International Monetary Fund, 2010.

companies including Maldives Shipping Management. Government revenues were estimated at $476 million, and expenditures at $758 million, with a budget defect of -15.1% of GDP, and in total $943 million of the debt was held by foreign entities, according to the CIA. Public services, including salaries for government workers, education and health were major areas of expenditure in 2010–2011, with conversion to alternative energy expected to become an important budget item due to the government's goal of carbon neutrality by 2020.

36 TAXATION

Maldives had no income tax or property tax as of late 2011. Banks are charged a profit tax. In 2011, the government introduced two new taxes, a Goods and Services Tax on Tourism (GST) and a 15% Business Profit Tax. The GST of 3.5%, applied to accommodation, recreation, transportation, and food, was in addition to a hotel tax of $8 per bed per night. The GST was to increase to 6% as of January 2012. President Nasheed linked the GST to raising revenue for Maldives' carbon neutrality goal. License fees are charged for boats and motor vehicles. The government leases island land for resorts or farming.

37 CUSTOMS AND DUTIES

Customs duties are a significant source of government revenues and vary from 5% to 200%, depending upon the type of import. New customs regulations were implemented in October 2011. Following the introduction of the Goods and Services Tax on Tourism (GST), import duties were abolished for products including staple foods, construction materials and tourism-related goods. Reduced duty rates are available on imports that enter at Addu or Kulhudufushi ports. Maldives does not charge export duty. Maldives does not allow visitors to bring in alcohol, pork products, or dogs.

38 FOREIGN INVESTMENT

Foreign direct investment (FDI) in Maldives was a net inflow of $112.3 million according to World Bank figures published in 2009. FDI represented 7.63% of GDP. Invest Maldives is the government agency for foreign investors, encouraging investment projects that are capital intensive, enhance technology transfer, introduce new skills and offer training to local employees, and are environmentally friendly.

Resort management is the main area of investment, with several large international hotel chains invested in Maldives' island resorts. Other FDI sectors include financial services, telecommunications, air transport, and manufacturing. Incentives for foreign investors include lack of income or property tax, right to 100% foreign ownership, long term land leases, emphasis on carbon neutrality, and ease of repatriating profits. Drawbacks include pervasive corruption and lack of private land ownership.

Maldives received $33.26 million in ODA (Official Development Assistance) during 2009, according to the World Bank. Except for the period immediately following the 2004 tsunami, ODA has not been a significant source of revenue for Maldives in the 21st century. In 2009, a balance of payments crisis led Maldives to seek a $79.3 million loan from the IMF; the loan was not completely disbursed. ODA grants and loans have usually not been necessary for Maldives because of foreign exchange revenues from tourism.

³⁹ECONOMIC DEVELOPMENT

Maldives began the long, gradual transition from a fishing economy to a tourism economy when the first tour group arrived in 1972. Maldives' shipping and transportation infrastructure was improved in the 1980s. In 1986, Malé's new commercial harbor was opened, considerably speeding up cargo handling. Also in the late 1980s, Malé's international airport was upgraded, a critical factor in the growth of the country's tourism sector. In 1989 the government lifted import quotas and liberalized some sectors of trade. GDP growth rates averaged about 10% in the 1980s and about 7% in the 1990s. In 1997, the Companies Act governed the formation, registration, and management of companies doing business in Maldives.

The economy had been on an upward surge when, in December 2004, the Indian Ocean tsunami devastated much of the country, killing 55, leaving 12,000 displaced, and causing damages of over $300 million. The economy made a remarkable recovery, due to tourism. Continued expansion of tourism has been particularly targeted in government development plans, along with facilitating a spread of economic activity to outlying island groups, new urban areas, and ports. Maldives has been able to successfully promote itself as an upscale, "clean and green" destination, appealing to tourists from the European and Asian markets. However, the tourism industry relies on imported construction materials, food, fuel, and workers.

Public sector corruption, inflation and unemployment affected Maldives' economy as of 2011. Long term concerns for Maldives include finding employment other than tourism for the local population, which has a double digit unemployment rate while foreign migrant workers are employed in increasing numbers; and devising alternatives to fishing for employment and food security as fish catches have been increasingly depleted. Maldives under the Nasheed administration has seen climate change brought on by global warming both as an impending crisis (effects on fisheries, need to relocate population from islands or build new ones) and an opportunity to show the way to environmental improvement (the goal of Maldives' carbon neutrality by 2020). As of 2011, the government believed that the initial investment costs of alternative energy sources would be paid for quickly when the nation is no longer dependent on expensive imported petroleum.

⁴⁰SOCIAL DEVELOPMENT

The government has focused its spending on social services and health services. Assistance is traditionally provided through the extended family. Employees are entitled to medical and maternity leave. In 2009, a Pension Project was introduced, covering local and foreign workers, in which private and public sector employers would contribute at least 7% of pay to a pension fund.

In spite of traditional Islamic restrictions on the role of women, they have increased their participation in public life. Under the terms of the constitution, men and women are considered equal before the law. According to the US State Department, approximately 40% of government employees were women, as of 2009. The tourism industry employs mainly men, who are able to work away from their home islands at resorts for long periods of time. A

Gender Equality Council was created to assist the government in strengthening the role of women in society. However, the Islamic-based legal system discriminates against women in matters of divorce and inheritance. Gender-based violence against women and domestic abuse were frequent occurrences, according to Maldives' media and NGOs, but were not effectively dealt with by the criminal justice system. Abuse of migrant workers has reportedly included forced labor and the trafficking for prostitution of women and children. Bangladesh does not grant work permits for women to go to Maldives, because of such allegations.

According to the US State Department, gay or lesbian conduct is prohibited by law in Maldives, punishable by imprisonment, flogging, banishment to an outer island or house arrest. Gay bloggers in Maldives report social pressure for gays and lesbians to remain "in the closet". Non-Muslim citizen bloggers in Maldives report that they must remain anonymous under threat of legal prosecution for apostasy.

Although children's rights are explicit in law and provisions are in place to protect children from abuse, education is only compulsory for seven years. Female children are much more likely to be withdrawn from school than boys. Youth unemployment, violent crime, drug abuse, and street gangs have been reported in densely populated Malé and other islands.

⁴¹HEALTH

According to the CIA, life expectancy in Maldives was 72 years in 2011. The country spent 13.7% of its GDP on healthcare, amounting to $331 per person. There were 16 physicians, 45 nurses and midwives, and 26 hospital beds per 10,000 inhabitants. The fertility rate was 1.81, while the infant mortality rate was 27.45 per 1,000 live births as of 2011, according to the CIA. In 2008 the maternal mortality rate, according to the World Bank, was 37 per 100,000 births. It was estimated that 98% of children were vaccinated against measles. The CIA calculated HIV/AIDS prevalence in Maldives to be about 0.1% in 2009. Infectious diseases were rare in Maldives as of 2011, and malaria had been absent since 1984. As of December 2011, the government was planning a universal health insurance scheme for Maldives.

⁴²HOUSING

Malé is a high density urban area with multistory apartment buildings, shop-houses, and very little green space; it is protected by a concrete tetrapod seawall. Concrete buildings comprise new urban areas at Gan and the reclaimed-land island of Hulhumale. "Social housing" apartment buildings for lower income people have been constructed in Malé and Hulhumale. Most residential units in the rest of the country have brick walls, some of which are also plastered, and roofs of galvanized metal sheets. Some migrant workers live in shacks built from scavenged materials.

As of 2008, 91% of the population had access to improved drinking water, and 98% of the population had access to improved sanitation facilities, according to the CIA. Firewood, charcoal, and imported petroleum were the primary cooking fuels, as of 2011, but the government planned to replace those with alternative energy sources as part of its carbon neutrality plan.

43 EDUCATION

In 2008 the World Bank estimated that 96% of age-eligible children in Maldives were enrolled in primary school. Secondary school enrollment for age-eligible children stood at 69%. Overall, the CIA estimated that Maldives had a literacy rate of 93.8%. Public expenditure on education represented 11.2% of GDP as of 2009.

Primary level education is for seven years and secondary education is for five years. Education is freely available and compulsory for seven years. Most schools are English medium; there are also traditional religious schools (*makhtabs*), which teach the Koran, basic arithmetic, and the ability to read and write Divehi and Arabic. Primary and secondary schooling is based on the British educational system. Students from outlying islands often board in Malé for secondary education. Distance educational courses are also provided.

Science Education Center, founded in 1979 in Malé provided pre-university courses for students planning on continuing their education overseas. It merged with business, teacher training, and management schools to become the degree-granting Maldives College of Higher Education in 1999. In February 2011, Maldives College of Higher Education became The Maldives National University, which offers courses in maritime studies, tourism, health, education, engineering, and Islamic law, among other subjects. Mandhu College, Cyryx College, and Villa College, all privately run, provide courses in information technology and other subjects.

44 LIBRARIES AND MUSEUMS

The National Library, founded in 1945, contains over 38,000 volumes in English, and over 10,000 in Dhivehi, as well as publications in Arabic and Urdu. The Maldives National University has a library system with over 60,000 items. The National Center for Linguistic and Historical Research (founded 1982), and the National Archives are in Malé. Most primary and secondary schools have small libraries, and many atolls have privately-run libraries. The Center for the Holy Koran Library has a collection of more than 7,000 items, most in Arabic.

National Museum Maldives, in an old palace in Malé, was founded in 1952 to conserve and display historical items. The National Art Gallery, with an emphasis on contemporary art, opened in 2005 in Malé. The Addu Cultural Center opened in 2011, as an historical re-enactment village with traditional Maldivian atoll architecture.

45 MEDIA

In 2009 the CIA reported that there were 49,913 telephone landlines in Maldives. Mobile phone subscriptions averaged 167 per 100 people, the 18th highest teledensity rate in the world, as of 2011, according to the Telecommunications Authority of Maldives. Companies offering mobile phone coverage included Micromax, Wataniya and Dhiraagu. Mobile phones were used for text messages and internet access.

The 2008 constitution strongly guarantees freedom of expression with the exception of anything "contrary to any tenet of Islam." Newspapers include *Haveeru Daily* (4,500 circulation as of 2010) and *Miadhu Daily News* (3,000). Online news sites include Minivan News and Sandhaanu. The state-owned Voice of Maldives broadcasts in Divehi and English, on AM and FM. Television Maldives and the associated TVM Plus entertainment channel are the two public television channels. As of 2009, according to UNESCO, Maldives also had six private radio stations and two private television stations.

Internet users numbered 28 per 100 citizens as of 2009. In 2010 the country had 2,164 Internet hosts. From 2009 to 2011, the government blocked websites and blogs considered pornographic or offensive to Islam. Bloggers dealing with controversial issues in Maldives often maintained anonymity.

46 ORGANIZATIONS

The Maldives National Chamber of Commerce and Industry is located in Malé, along with the Maldives Traders' Association, and Maldives Association of Tourism Industry. Workers' groups include Tourism Employees Association of the Maldives and Teachers Association of the Maldives. The Maldives National Youth Council was formed in 1984 to assist in organizing national programs for youth. Scouting programs are available through the Scout Association of Maldives and the Girl Guides. The Society for Health Education and the Care Society work on issues of health and social welfare. Bluepeace is an environmental organization of Maldives, in operation since the 1980s. Transparency Maldives is a nongovernmental organization against corruption. Thirees Nuvaeh ("39") was founded in 2010 to promote traditional Maldivian culture.

47 TOURISM, TRAVEL, AND RECREATION

The *Tourism Factbook*, published by the UN World Tourism Organization, reported 656,000 incoming tourists to Maldives in 2009, who spent a total of $608 million. Of those incoming tourists, there were 462,000 from Europe. There were 24,650 hotel beds available in Maldives, which had an occupancy rate of 70%. The estimated daily cost to visit Maldives was $367.

The principal source of employment and leading foreign exchange earner for Maldives, tourism has been developing since the first beach resort opened in 1974. Maldives has been promoted as a luxurious, quiet, "getaway" destination with pristine beaches and excellent scuba diving. Natural attractions of the atolls are crystal-clear lagoons and white sand beaches that are ideal for swimming, fishing, snorkeling, and scuba diving. Modern, one- and two-story tourist facilities have been built on various otherwise uninhabited islands, mainly in the Malé atoll but also in neighboring atolls. Developed with foreign assistance and investment, such resorts are located away from Malé and other settlements of local people, allowing the country to profit from the presence of foreign tourists while shielding its citizens from the consumption of alcoholic beverages and other un-Islamic holiday activities of tourists. Maldivian resort workers maintain their homes and families on other islands, and foreigners from Bangladesh, Sri Lanka, and elsewhere, often work in tourism and related construction.

Although there was damage to various hotels and tourism facilities in the 2004 tsunami, much of the tourism infrastructure remained intact, and arrivals continued to increase through 2011. In the second decade of the 21st century, increasing numbers of arrivals were from China and other Asian countries. Budget travel became more of an option with the opening of less expensive guest houses priced for surfers and other independent visitors. Passports and return tickets are required of all visitors, and 30 day visas are issued on arrival.

48 FAMOUS PERSONS

Ibn Battutah (Muhammad bin 'Abdallah bin Battutah, b. Tangier, 1304–77), the Arab traveler and geographer, lived in the Maldives for several years, served as a quadi (Islamic judge) and married the daughter of a Maldivian vizier. Sultan Iskandar Ibrahim I, who reigned for nearly 40 years during the 17th century, had the Hukuru Miskit (the principal mosque on Malé Island) built in 1674. Modern-day leaders include Amir Ibrahim Nasir (1926–2008) and Maumoon Abdul Gayoom (b. 1937). Mohamed Nasheed (b. 1967) was elected president in 2008 and is an international activist about global warming. Fathimath Dhiyana Saaed (b. 1974) was at-torney general of Maldives and became the first female secretary-general of SAARC in 2011.

49 DEPENDENCIES

Maldives has no territories or colonies.

50 BIBLIOGRAPHY

Forbes, Andrew. *Maldives: Kingdom of a Thousand Isles*. Leicester, Eng.: Cordee, 2002.

Maldives Investment and Business Guide: Strategic and Practical Information. Washington, DC: International Business Publications USA, 2012.

NgCheong-Lum, Roseline. *Maldives*. 2nd ed. New York: Marshall Cavendish Benchmark, 2011.

Reynolds, C. H. B. *Maldives*. Santa Barbara, CA: Clio Press, 1993.

MARSHALL ISLANDS

Republic of the Marshall Islands

CAPITAL: Majuro, Majuro Atoll

FLAG: The flag, adopted in 1979, is blue, with two diagonal strips of orange over white; in the canton is a white star with 4 large rays and 20 shorter ones.

ANTHEM: *Forever Marshall Islands.*

MONETARY UNIT: The US dollar is the official medium of exchange.

WEIGHTS AND MEASURES: British units are used, as modified by US usage.

HOLIDAYS: New Year's Day (January 10), Nuclear Survivor's Day (March 1), Constitution Day (May 1), Fisherman's Day (first Friday in July), Rijerbal Day (Worker's Day, first Friday in September), Manit Day (Customs Day, last Friday in September), President's Day (November 17), Kamolol Day (Thanksgiving Day, third Thursday in November), Gospel Day (first Friday in December), Christmas Day (December 25).

TIME: 11 p.m. = noon GMT.

¹LOCATION, SIZE, AND EXTENT

The Republic of the Marshall Islands (RMI) is located in the central Pacific Ocean, just north of the equator. Isolated from major population centers, Majuro, the capital, lies 3,438 km (2,136 mi) W of Honolulu, 3,701 km (2,300 mi) SE of Tokyo, and 3,241 km (2,014 mi) SE of Saipan, the former trust territory capital. The country consists of 29 atolls, containing more than 1,000 small islets, and 5 major islands, extending over a sea area exceeding 1,942,500 sq km (750,000 sq mi). The main land area is only about 181 sq km (70 sq mi). Comparatively, the area occupied by the Marshall Islands is slightly larger than Washington, DC. The atolls and islands form two almost parallel chainlike formations: the Ratak (Sunrise), or Eastern, group and the Ralik (Sunset), or Western, group. The largest atolls in the Ratak group are Mili, Majuro, Maloelap, Wotje, Likiep, and Bikini; in the Ralik group, Jaluit, Kwajalein, Wotho, and Enewetak. The Marshall Islands have a coastline of 370.4 km (230 mi). The capital city of the Marshall Islands, Majuro, is located on the island of Majuro.

²TOPOGRAPHY

The majority of islands are in typical atoll formations, consisting of low-lying narrow strips of land enclosing a lagoon. Soils are porous, sandy, and of low fertility. Kwajalein Atoll in the Ralik, or Western, atoll is the largest coral atoll in the world.

³CLIMATE

The maritime tropical climate is hot and humid, with little seasonal temperature change. Diurnal variations generally range between 21–34°C (70–93°F). Trade winds from the northeast cool the high temperatures from December through March.

Rainfall averages about 30–38 cm (12–15 in) per month, with October and November the wettest and December to April the driest. Average rainfall increases from the north to the south; the northern atolls average 178 cm (70 in) annually, compared with 432 cm (170 in) in the southern atolls.

⁴FLORA AND FAUNA

The World Resources Institute estimates that there are 100 plant species in the Marshall Islands. In addition, the Marshall Islands is home to 4 mammal, 57 bird, and 9 reptile species. The calculation reflects the total number of distinct species residing in the country, not the number of endemic species. The flora consists of species resilient to porous soils, salt spray, and relatively strong wind force. The dominant tree species include coconut palms, pandanus, breadfruit, and citrus trees. The reef systems of the islands support about 160 coral species. Fauna include rodents and indigenous strains of pig.

⁵ENVIRONMENT

Among the Marshall Islands' more significant environmental problems are water pollution due to lack of adequate sanitation facilities, inadequate supplies of drinking water, and the rise of sea levels. The threat of rising sea levels, blamed on global warming, is one that the nation takes seriously. With a 20-inch rise in sea level, the Marshall Islands would lose 80% of its land area. In one effort to address the most immediate threats, in 2010 the government announced plans to construct a 5-kilometer (3-mile) seawall on the leeward coast of Majuro Atoll to protect the shoreline and serve as a containment wall for the landfill of some small bay areas. The landfill project will increase the landmass of the island and provide an even greater coastal buffer from rising sea levels and frequent storms and floods. Nearly half of the nation's population lives in Majuro and most of their homes are within 10 meters (32.8 feet) or less of the shore. The full cost of the project has not been announced, but officials launched an appeal for $20 million in international donations in order to begin the design and engineering phase of the project. The UN ambassador called on member countries to provide funds as part of a larger program involving the distribution of climate change aid for vulnerable countries.

In 2010 the Marshallese government gained the support of scholars from the Center for Climate Change Law at Columbia University to investigate the legal issues of sovereignty and nationality in light of the impending climate change crisis. For example, as sea levels rise and the islands become increasingly uninhabitable, more residents could be forced to relocate to other countries. However, whereas there are international laws in place concerning the welfare of refugees fleeing persecution, there are no laws regarding the status of those displaced by climate change. Under the Marshallese Compact of Free Association with the United States, residents may freely enter the United States for work or study, but do not have an automatic right to permanent residency. The Marshallese government also worries about the status of the nation in the event that major portions of land are submerged by the sea. In particular, the government is concerned about its rights over the current exclusive economic zone, which covers an area about the size of Mexico and provides a significant income to the nation through the sale of tuna fishing licenses to foreign fleets.

The Marshall Islands Environmental Protection Agency, established in 1984, is concerned with programs for water quality standards, solid waste disposal, earthworks, and use of pesticides. The UN reported in 2008 that carbon dioxide emissions in the Marshall Islands totaled 99 kilotons.

The environments of the Bikini, Enewetak, Rongelap, and Utirik atolls were contaminated by nuclear testing carried out in the region from 1946 to 1958. The people of Bikini and Enewetak, along with those exposed to radioactive fallout in the 1954 Bravo Blast, fought for compensation from the United States, which in February 1990 agreed to pay $45 million to the victims of the nuclear testing program. In October 1999, the United States, through the Majuro-based Nuclear Claims Tribunal, paid nearly $2.3 million toward the $45 million originally promised in 1990, bringing the amount paid toward the total to $39.4 million. Fifty years after testing began, Bikini Island began to attract a few tourists; scientific surveys have declared the island habitable again, although there is still a danger in eating too many of the local coconuts. Despite the scientific assurances, the US government has yet to issue a statement saying that the island is safe to inhabit.

The World Resources Institute reported that the Marshall Islands had designated 100,000 hectares (247,105 acres) of land for protection as of 2006. According to a 2011 report issued by the International Union for Conservation of Nature and Natural Resources (IUCN), threatened species included 2 mammals, 4 birds, 2 reptiles, 11 fish, and 1 mollusk. The hawksbill turtle and green turtle are on the endangered species list.

6 POPULATION

According to the US Central Intelligence Agency (CIA) the population of the Marshall Islands in 2011 was estimated at approximately 67,182, which placed it at number 188 in population among the 196 nations of the world. In 2011, approximately 3% of the population was over 65 years of age, with another 38.2% under 15 years of age. The median age in the Marshall Islands was 21.8 years. There were 1.04 males for every female in the country. The population's annual rate of change was 1.954%. The projected population for the year 2025 was 60,000. Population density in the Marshall Islands was calculated at 371 people per sq km (961 people per sq mi). The UN estimated that 72% of the population lived in urban areas, and that urban populations had an annual rate of change of 2.3%. The largest urban area was Majuro, with a population of 30,000.

7 MIGRATION

In 2011 the CIA estimated a net migration rate of -5.19 migrants per 1,000 citizens. The total number of emigrants living abroad was 10,500, and the total number of immigrants living in Marshall Islands was 1,700. Population has been steadily migrating from the outer atolls to the urban concentrations on Majuro and Ebeye. As a result, outer atolls have been left with unbalanced population structures of children, females, and the aged. Provisions under the Compact of Free Association with the United States permit unrestricted entry into the United States and allow high-school graduates to join the US armed forces.

8 ETHNIC GROUPS

The Marshallese people are Micronesians, who are physically similar to the Polynesian peoples. The largest non-Marshallese ethnic group is from Kosrae in the Federated States of Micronesia. As of 2006, about 92.1% of the population identified as Marshallese, while 5.9% identified as mixed Marshallese. There are also small numbers of Americans and Filipinos.

9 LANGUAGES

Both Marshallese and English are official languages. Marshallese is a Malayo-Polynesian language and the common source of each of the atolls' dialects. About 98.2% of the population speaks Marshallese, with two major Marshallese dialects. English is widely spoken as a second language and used along with Marshallese in official communications and in commerce. Japanese is also spoken.

10 RELIGIONS

The people are almost entirely Christian, primarily Protestant, as a result of the arrival of American and Hawaiian Protestant missionaries in the 1860s. The United Church of Christ is the principal denomination, representing some 51.5% of the population. The United Church of Christ is the successor of the Congregationalists from New England and Hawaii who converted the islanders in the latter half of the 19th century. Other religious denominations represented include Assemblies of God (24.2%), Roman Catholics (8.4%), the Church of Jesus Christ of Latter-Day Saints (Mormon, 8.3%), Bukot Nan Jesus (also called Assembly of God Part Two, 2.2%),and Baptists (1%). Seventh Day Adventists and members of the Full Gospel church each account for less than 1% of the population. Baha'is also account for less than 1% of the population. Jehovah's Witnesses are also represented. There are fewer than 20 Jews and only a few Ahmadiyya Muslims. Freedom of religion is guaranteed by the constitution and that right is generally respected in practice. While there is no state religion, Christianity serves as the dominant cultural influence. Religious groups are not required to register with the government. Good Friday, Gospel Day, and Christmas are observed as national holidays.

11TRANSPORTATION

According to the CIA, the Marshall Islands had a total of 2,028 km (1,260 mi) of roadways in 2007. On the outer islands, roads consist primarily of cleared paths and roads surfaced with stone, coral, or laterite. There are few motor vehicles. The many scattered atolls separated by long distances make sea and air transportation essential. Domestic sea transportation is provided by inter-island ships, which service each of the outer islands about once every three months. The nation has 13 deepwater docks capable of handling ocean-going vessels. The primary commercial ports are found at Majuro and Ebeye. A third port is located at Jaluit. In 2010, the merchant fleet consisted of 1,381 ships with a capacity of 1,000 GRT or more.

There were 15 airports in 2010, four of which had paved runways. A total of 27,692 passengers were accommodated by these airlines in 2009. Majuro International Airport, completed in 1974, accommodates aircraft up to Boeing 707 size. In May 2010, the Amata Kabua International Airport on Majuro opened its new US-financed Aircraft Rescue and Fire Fighting Facility, marking a major milestone for improved safety at the airport. Although the airport routinely handles only one international carrier (Continental Micronesia), it is a popular and important refueling site for flights between Asia and the United States. The opening of the new facility came at the end of a three-year project of airport improvements, which also included a newly paved runway and the development of a training program for safety and security personnel. In all, the US Federal Aviation Administration invested more than $50 million in the project. The government-owned Airline of the Marshall Islands (AMI), established in 1980, provides service to all outer islands with airstrips. International airline connections are provided to Tarawa in Kiribati, Funafuti in Tuvalu, and Nadi in Fiji. Air Micronesia/Continental Airlines links Majuro with major foreign destinations, including Hawaii, Guam, Manila, and Tokyo.

12HISTORY

Sighting of the islands was first recorded by the Spanish navigator Alvaro de Saavedra in 1529. The British captain John Marshall, after whom the islands are named, explored them in 1788. Throughout the late 1800s and early 1900s, foreign powers ruled the islands for such advantages as trade, religious propagation, exploitation of resources, strategic considerations, and maintenance of sea routes. Spain claimed the islands in 1874, but sold them to Germany in 1899. At the outbreak of World War I, Japanese naval squadrons took possession of the Marshalls and began formal administration under a League of Nations mandate in 1920.

In World War II, after bitter fighting between US and Japanese forces that included battles for Kwajalein and Eniwetok (now Enewetak), the islands came under US control. In 1947, the Marshalls became a district of a UN trusteeship, called the Trust Territory of the Pacific Islands, which was administered by the United States. The United States used Bikini and Enewetak atolls as nuclear testing sites from 1946 to 1958, exploding 66 atomic and nuclear tests during this period. Radiation contamination from the nuclear testing program resulted in the displacement of the indigenous people of Bikini and Enewetak. The Marshallese people adopted a constitution in 1978, under which the Marshalls were designated the Republic of the Marshall Islands. In 1979,

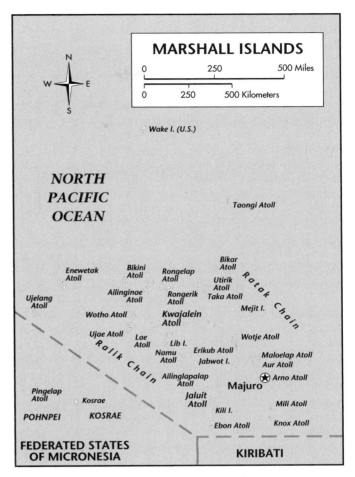

LOCATION: 4° to 14° N; 160° to 173° E.

the constitution went into effect and the republic became a self-governing territory, with Amata Kabua elected the Republic's first president.

In 1983, a Compact of Free Association with the United States, providing for full self-government except for defense, was approved by plebiscite. Section 177 of the compact stated that the United States would provide a $150 million settlement for damages resulting from the nuclear testing. The money formed the basis of a trust fund which was to generate enough money to provide annual proceeds of $18 million through 2001, to be distributed to benefit the people on the affected atolls. In January 1986, the compact was ratified by the United States, and on 21 October 1986 it went into effect. The UN Security Council voted in December 1990 to terminate the Marshall Islands' status as a UN Trust Territory. The Republic became an independent state and joined the UN in September 1991. The Compact of Free Association with the United States expired in 2001, but the provisions of the compact were subsequently extended though September 2003. A new agreement was negotiated and US president George W. Bush signed the Amended Compact of Free Association in December 2003. The new 20-year compact provides for annual payments of at least $57 million per year, including contributions to a trust fund of more than $800 million to replace the compact in 2024, and grants the United States exclusive military access to the Marshall Islands, in return for which the United States would provide protection against any third parties. Marshallese concerns were raised when the trust funds lost value following the September 2001 terrorist attacks in the United States.

Global warming and the possibility of rising sea levels have raised concern over the long-term prospects for the islands in the middle of the Pacific Ocean. The Marshall Islands, along with Kiribati and Tuvalu, rise only a few feet above sea level. The Intergovernmental Panel on Climate Change has suggested that the sea could rise 45.7 cm (18 in) by 2100, but that figure could be much lower or higher.

Litokwa Tomeing was elected as the fourth president of the Marshall Islands on 7 January 2008, replacing Kessai Note, who had served two four-year terms from 2000 to 2008. Tomeing was removed from office through a vote of no confidence in 2009 and replaced by Jurelang Zedkaia.

¹³GOVERNMENT

The Marshall Islands is an independent republic. The constitution effective on 1 May 1979 incorporates a blend of the British and American constitutional concepts. It provides for three main branches of government: the legislature, the executive, and the judiciary. Legislative power is vested in the parliament, known as the Nitijela, which consists of 33 members elected from 24 electoral districts, each corresponding roughly to an atoll. Representatives are elected by popular vote to serve four-year terms. The Council of Iroij (chiefs) has 12 members, whose main functions are to request reconsideration by the Nitijela of any bill affecting customary law, traditional practice, or land tenure, and to express an opinion to the cabinet on any matter of national concern. The president, serving as chief of state and head of government, is elected by Nitijela from among its members to serve a four-year term. The constitution requires the president to nominate not more than 10 or fewer than 6 members of the Nitijela as cabinet members. All citizens who have attained the age of 18 are eligible to vote.

¹⁴POLITICAL PARTIES

There is no tradition of organized political parties in the Marshall Islands; what has existed more closely resembles factions or interest groups because they do not have party platforms, headquarters, or party structures. However, two major groupings have competed in legislative balloting. The Kabua Party of former President Amata Kabua was in ascendance from 1979 to 1999; during that time, Kabua was elected to five 4-year terms as president. Following the death of Kabua in December 1996, the newly formed United Democratic Party (UDP), led by Litokwa Tomeing, became more powerful, winning a majority in parliament in November 1999, and again in the November 2003 elections. In legislative elections on 19 November 2007, the Kabua Party and its coalition members gained primary control of the Nitijela. Only four seats were won by independent candidates.

In January 2012, three candidates who lost in the November 2011 legislative elections jointly challenged the results of the election in the high court, calling for the rejection of improperly notarized ballots mailed in from Marshallese voters in the United States and a recount of the remaining legal ballots. The final results of the November election were delayed as the electoral board continued to receive and count numerous ballots arriving from the United States.

Kessai Note was elected president in legislative sessions in 2000, becoming the first commoner to become president (in place of a traditional chief); in January 2004, he was reelected to a second 4-year term by a vote of 20 to 9. Litokwa Tomeing replaced Note through a vote of 18 to 15 in the 7 January 2008 elections. However, in 2009 he was removed from office after a vote of no confidence by the Nitijela, and replaced by Jurelang Zedkaia. In January 2012 Christopher Loeak was elected by parliament to serve as the sixth president of the nation. The traditional chief and former senator was elected by a vote of 21 to 11.

¹⁵LOCAL GOVERNMENT

There are 24 local governments for the inhabited atolls and islands. Typically, each is headed by a mayor, and consists of an elected council, appointed local officials, and a local police force. Local elections are held every four years, usually at the same time as legislative elections.

¹⁶JUDICIAL SYSTEM

The judiciary consists of the Supreme Court, the high court, the district and community courts, and the traditional rights courts. The Supreme Court has final appellate jurisdiction. The high court has trial jurisdiction over almost all cases and appellate jurisdiction over all types of cases tried in subordinate courts. The district courts have limited civil and criminal jurisdiction nationwide. Community courts in local government areas adjudicate civil and criminal cases within their communities. The traditional rights court was established to determine questions relating to titles or land rights and other legal interests involving customary law and traditional practice. The constitution provides for an independent judiciary. The constitution also provides for the right to a fair trial. Defendants may choose between a bench trial or a jury trial with a four-member jury.

¹⁷ARMED FORCES

There are no armed forces in the Marshall Islands. Under the Compact of Free Association, the United States is responsible for security and defense.

¹⁸INTERNATIONAL COOPERATION

The Marshall Islands was admitted to the United Nations (UN) on 17 September 1991, and participates in several specialized agencies including the FAO, IAEA, the World Bank, UNCTAD, UNESCO, and the WHO. In 1992, it became a member of ESCAP. The country is also a member of the ACP Group, the Asian Development Bank, G-77, SPARTECA, and the Pacific Island Forum. In 1996 the Marshall Islands joined with 38 other nations to form the Alliance of Small Island States (AOSIS). The alliance, concerned with global warming and rising sea levels, wants the industrialized nations to reduce greenhouse gas emissions. In other environmental cooperation, the Marshall Islands is part of the Convention on Biological Diversity, the Kyoto Protocol, the Montreal Protocol, MARPOL, and the UN Conventions on the Law of the Sea, Climate Change, and Desertification. The Marshall Islands operates under the Compact of Free Association signed with the United States on 25 June 1983. Amendments to the CFA went into effect on 1 May 2004, extending the compact for another 20 years.

19 ECONOMY

The Marshall Islands' small island economy is largely supported by US government assistance, which accounted for 61.3% of the nation's budget for fiscal year 2010. The primary portion of that assistance comes from the Amended Compact of Free Association that was signed in 2003. Under the terms of the compact, the United States is expected to provide $57 million per year to the Marshall Islands until the end of 2023. A trust fund made up of US and RMI contributions was also established to continue annual payments after the compact expires. However, the United States has continued to provide additional assistance as well, and has been calling on the Marshall Islands to lessen their dependency on such aid.

According to most recent estimates, agriculture makes up about 31% of the nation's gross domestic product (GDP) and employs about 21% of its workforce. An urban small-business sector is made up in part by restaurants, banks, construction, and professional services. The government is the largest employer, with 46% of the workforce on its payroll. The nascent tourist industry employs less than 10% of the labor force, but is considered to be a primary growth sector. The islands have few natural resources and imports exceed exports. The gross domestic product (GDP) rate of change in Marshall Islands, as of 2008, was -0.3%.

20 INCOME

The CIA estimated that in 2008 the GDP of the Marshall Islands was $133.5 million. The CIA defines GDP as the value of all final goods and services produced within a nation in a given year and computed on the basis of purchasing power parity (PPP) rather than value as measured on the basis of the rate of the exchange based on current dollars. The per capita GDP was estimated at $2,500. The annual growth rate of GDP was -0.3%. The average inflation rate was 12.9%. For 2004, it was estimated that agriculture accounted for 31.7% of GDP, industry 14.9%, and services 53.4%.

21 LABOR

As of 2010, the Marshall Islands had a total labor force of about 18,500 people. An estimated 21.4% were employed in agriculture (primarily subsistence), 20.9% in industry, and 57.7% in the service sector. In 2006, an estimated 61% of the all those of working age were unemployed or inactive in the work force. Although the constitution provides for the freedom of association, there have been very few efforts to unionize, due primarily to the fact that there are few major employers with a substantial number of workers. The nation's public school teachers formed the first union in 2009, with about 10% of all teachers participating. There is no statutory provision permitting strikes by workers nor is there a right to collectively bargain or organize. Generally wages are set in accordance with the minimum wage regulation and determined in part by market influence. A minimum wage of $2 per hour was put in place by the government in 2010. There are no laws concerning maximum work hours or health and safety in the workplace. There is no prohibition against child labor but the law requires compulsory education until the age of 14. In practice this requirement is not effectively enforced, and many children work, especially on family farms and in the fishing industry.

22 AGRICULTURE

Out of 18,000 hectares (44,478 acres) of land in Marshall Islands, 2,000 hectares (4,942 acres) are arable and roughly 56% of the total land is farmed. About 31.7% of the population is involved in agriculture, primarily on a subsistence level. The traditional interplanting of root crops and other vegetables with coconuts, which maintained self-sufficiency in food and provided the Marshallese with dietetic variety before modern times, is still widely practiced as a subsistence activity. Dried coconut meat, known as copra, is produced on almost all islands and atolls and has provided the most significant export crop; however, with a declining economy, the government has had to provide subsidies to keep coconut plantations operational. Other major crops include bananas, pandanus, taro, breadfruit, and a variety of vegetables grown for local consumption. The nation is not self-sufficient in food and, therefore, must rely on imports to meet local demands.

23 ANIMAL HUSBANDRY

The UN Food and Agriculture Organization (FAO) reported that the Marshall Islands dedicated 3,000 hectares (7,413 acres) to permanent pasture or meadow in 2009. Livestock on the islands consists primarily of pigs and poultry. Most families raise pigs for subsistence and for family and community feasts. In 1981, pigs were imported from New Zealand to improve the strains of the local breed.

24 FISHING

While subsistence fishing for inshore species is carried out from all atolls, there is little domestic commercial fishing in the nation. However, the Marshall Islands has an exclusive economic zone of over 2,000,000 sq km (770,000 sq mi) of ocean that supports significant stocks of tuna. Since 1990 the nation has offered ship registration under the Marshall Islands flag and receives $4 million annually from the endeavor. As of 2011, the Marshall Islands registered about 2,300 vessels, making it the 3rd largest fleet in the world. Tuna processing is a primary, though relatively small, industry.

The Marshall Islands had 11 decked commercial fishing boats in 2008. The annual domestic capture totaled 35,436 tons according to the UN FAO. The export value of seafood totaled $30.12 million. Other principal marine resources include prawns, shrimp, seaweed, sponges, black pearls, giant clams, trochus, and green mussels. Colorful baby giant clams for ornamental aquariums are grown for export to the United States. The Marshall Islands Marine Resource Authority was established in 1997 to organize all marine resource activities, including protection, management, and development, under one agency.

In March 2010, the Marshall Islands and seven other Pacific nations met in Palau for the First Presidential Summit of the Parties of the Nauru Agreement (PNA). The PNA was established in 1982 and is comprised of the nations of Palau, Micronesia, the Marshall Islands, Tuvalu, Kiribati, Papua New Guinea, Nauru, and the Solomon Islands. The purpose of the group is to work together for the conservation and management of tuna resources within their exclusive economic zones (EEZ). At the March meeting, which has been called the Tuna Summit, members adopted the Koror Declaration, which aims, among other things, to establish cooperative management practices that will enhance commercial and economic opportunities for member states and to work toward the conservation and restoration of migratory tuna stocks. The waters of the PNA nations account for nearly 60% of all tuna catches in the western and central Pacific Ocean and 25% of the global tuna catches that supply canneries and processing facilities around the world. The official PNA Office was opened in Majuro in April 2010.

25 FORESTRY

Approximately 72% of the Marshall Islands is covered by forest. Coconut palms account for a large number of the trees found on the islands. Pine species are under experimentation in a windbreak tree project on Ebeye. In 1984 a sawmill was purchased for processing coconut trunks and other tree species as lumber. In 2004, forest product imports totaled $1.9 million.

26 MINING

There was no mining of mineral resources. However, preliminary surveys have revealed the presence of phosphate and manganese nodules in the seabed within the territorial waters. Lagoon dredging of sand and coral for construction purposes was undertaken in Majuro and Ebeye.

27 ENERGY AND POWER

The Marshall Islands is nearly 100% dependent on imported fossil fuels for electric power generation. The urban centers of Majuro and Ebeye have major generating facilities. The Majuro power plant, commissioned in 1982, has an installed power capacity of 14,000 kW. A 5,200 kW power plant was commissioned in Ebeye in 1987. The low power requirements in the outer islands are met by solar-powered systems. However, as of 2003, there were still outer island residents without adequate access to electricity because they were not supplied with solar power. Electricity production was 57 million kWh in 1994 (the last date that statistics were available through the CIA).

28 INDUSTRY

The economy's small manufacturing sector, localized largely in Majuro, accounts for less than 4% of the gross revenues generated in the private sector. The largest industrial operation is a copra-processing mill under a government and private-sector joint enterprise. (Copra is dried coconut meat.) The rest of the manufacturing sector consists of small-scale and domestic operations, such as coir making (coconut fibers), handicrafts (particularly from seashells and pearls), and small boat making. A major tuna processing plant is operating in Majuro.

Manufacturing output increased rapidly in the early 1990s climbing from $853 million in 1991 to a peak of $2.7 billion in 1995, a 215% increase. The growth was not sustained, and by 1998, manufacturing output had fallen almost 45% to $1.48 billion. By 2000 manufacturing output had climbed to $1.72 billion. In the period from 1988 and 1999, the percent of the work force engaged in industry more than doubled, from 10% to 21%. For 2004 the industrial sector accounted for about 14.9% of GDP.

29 SCIENCE AND TECHNOLOGY

The World Bank reported in 2009 that there were no patent applications in science and technology in the Marshall Islands. While there are no institutions involved in scientific research or training, the College of Micronesia nursing facility and science center, located in the Majuro Hospital, provides instruction in nursing technology and science.

30 DOMESTIC TRADE

Domestic trade accounts for the majority of the total gross trade revenue from urban private enterprises. The modern commercial/retail sectors are located in Majuro and Ebeye and consist mainly of service establishments and imported goods, although increasing amounts of locally produced vegetables and fish were being marketed. Most imports are purchased and consumed at these two main locations. Domestic trade in outer island areas is primarily for basic necessities.

31 FOREIGN TRADE

Heavy and increasing trade deficits result from limited exports and dependency on imports for consumer and capital goods. Over 90% of the value of exports is accounted for by fish, coconut oil, and copra cake (made of dried coconut meat). The major imports are foodstuffs, machinery and equipment, fuels, beverages, and tobacco. Major trading partners in 2009 were the United States, Japan, Australia, China, Hong Kong, New Zealand, and Taiwan.

32 BALANCE OF PAYMENTS

The economy suffers from a long-standing imbalance of trade, with imports far exceeding exports. A comprehensive record of international transactions in the form of standardized balance-of-payments accounts was not maintained during the trusteeship period (prior to 1986). The chronic trade deficit is offset by official unrequited transfers, predominantly from the United States. Exports of goods and services totaled $19.4 million in 2008, while imports grew to $79.4 million, leaving a deficit of $60 million.

33 BANKING AND SECURITIES

Financial services are provided by two commercial banks: the Bank of Guam, with branches in Majuro, Kwajalein, and Ebeye, and the Bank of the Marshall Islands, with branches in Majuro, Jabor, Jaluit, and Arno, as well as two mobile ship branches. The Development Bank of the Marshall Islands in Majuro was established as an independent government corporation in 1988. The Marshall Islands has no stock issues or securities trading.

34 INSURANCE

Two foreign insurance companies, located in Majuro, provide coverage. A US insurance company provides loan protection policies to credit unions.

35 PUBLIC FINANCE

Government revenues are derived from domestic sources and US grants. Domestic revenues are from taxes and nontax sources (fishing rights, philatelic sales, and user charges). The leading areas of expenditure include health services, education, public works, and transportation and communication. In 2008 the CIA reported government revenues at $123.3 million, while expenditures were noted at $1.213 billion. The budget deficit amounted to 674.1% of GDP. In total $87 million of the public debt was held by foreign entities.

36 TAXATION

Businesses must pay a gross revenue tax of $80 per year on the first $10,000 of gross revenue and 3% of the gross revenue in excess of $10,000 per year. The income tax rates start at 8% per year on the first $10,400 of taxable income earned by an employee, and 12% on higher earnings. Employees whose gross annual wages are $5,200 or less are allowed an exemption of $1,040 per year (or $20 per week). Sales taxes are imposed by local governments. Both the employer and the employee are required to make quarterly contributions for social security and health insurance.

37 CUSTOMS AND DUTIES

Import taxes are generally ad valorem; duties range from 5 to 75%. The average rate is 10%. Specific duties apply to cigarettes, soft drinks, beer, spirits, wine, gasoline, and other gases and fuels, with some proceeds designated as supplemental funding for the College of the Marshall Islands.

38 FOREIGN INVESTMENT

The government favors joint ventures with foreign private investors but efforts to attract foreign investment and develop new export products have been largely unsuccessful. There are some restrictions for foreign companies that also hinder investment. For instance, foreigners may lease but not own land, but there are provisions for land to be leased in perpetuity. Foreign investors are not permitted to operate in certain reserved activities, which include smaller scale operations that include agriculture and for local markets, bakeries, small retail shops, and motor garages. Some tax incentives are available for investors who invest at least $1 million or provide employment and wages in excess of $150,000 per year for citizen workers in the fields of offshore or deep-sea fishing, manufacturing, and hotel and resort facilities. Tourism and marine and fisheries resources are regarded as key growth sectors. Foreign direct investment (FDI) in the Marshall Islands was unreported according to World Bank figures published in 2009.

39 ECONOMIC DEVELOPMENT

The first five-year national development plan (1986/87–1990/91), constituted the first phase of a 15-year development program. The plan focused on economic development, with emphasis on private-sector expansion, personnel development and employment creation, regional development, population planning and social development, and cultural and environmental preservation. Total funding across the 15-year span of the agreement was envisioned at about $1 billion or about $65 million dollars per year in financial aid from the United States. Aid was gradually decreased across the 15-year period, and a down-step in 1996 caused a budget deficit that the government filled with debt financing. Paying off the bond obligations kept government expenditures and investment strapped until they were paid off in 2001. By that time, the size of the government had been significantly reduced. Compared to 1994/95, 2002 expenditures were 25% less in current dollar terms. Also, US aid had dropped to an estimated $39 million. Under Title 11 of the Compact of Free Association, funding was scheduled to expire in 2001, with provision of a two-year extension equal to the average level of assistance over the last 15 years. This increased US grant aid to almost $60 million for 2001, above the average of $45.33 million for 1997 to 2001.

In 2001, the government announced Vision 2018, which included the nation's next 15-year development plan. After the adoption of Vision 2018, various government agencies developed master plans and action plans for growth in the areas of human resources development, outer islands development, culture and traditions, environment, resources and development, information technology, private sector development, infrastructure, and tourism. All of the plans are designed to lead the nation towards greater self-sufficiency and economic sustainability.

In 2001 the government paid off all commercial debt but usable fiscal resources remained short because of a need to set aside about $30 million in 2001 and 2002 for the initial capitalization of the Marshall Islands Intergenerational Trust Fund (MIITF). The MIITF is the government's long-term solution to the island's public finance needs, but is not projected to provide substantial yearly dividends until at least 2024. In the meantime, the government renegotiated the terms of Title II of the Compact. In an agreement that went into effect in 2004, US aid was extended for 20 years, to 2023, with a base grant of $57 million per year. Each year, an increasing portion of this grant money is earmarked for deposit into the MIITF. The agreement also established the RMI-US Joint Economic Management and Financial Accountability Committee (JEMFAC) to monitor and oversee the spending of the grant money.

The United States has continued to provide additional assistance as well, and has been calling on the Marshall Islands to lessen their dependency on such aid. The Marshallese government was expected to produce an appropriate plan of action by the end of 2010, but that deadline was extended as no such plan was made by mid 2010. The priority targets set for spending are education, health, and infrastructure. Another agreement reached in April 2003 was a 50-year extension of the US lease of land on the Kwajalein atoll as a defense site, with an option to extend an additional 20 years. As the current lease was set to expire in 2016, this meant an extension to 2066. In calculating its assistance to the Marshall Islands, the United States includes not only the $13 million a year paid for the Kwajalein lease under the Military Use and Operating Rights Agreement (MUORA) but also an estimated $21 million in tax dollars that are infused through salaries, tax payments and telecom services, plus an estimated $10 million worth of federal programs, like the postal service. The RMI government expressed concerns that the assistance is insufficient to prevent economic stagnation, and social and infrastructure deterioration, and/or prevent recourse to debt financing to fill revenue shortfalls.

40 SOCIAL DEVELOPMENT

Among government agencies, the Ministry of Social Services is involved in five major areas: housing, women's and youth development, feeding programs, aging, and other community development welfare programs. Funding of these services is provided almost entirely by the United States. A social security system provides old age, disability, and survivor benefits, paid for by employers and employees. The program is funded by 7% contributions from both employers and employees. Retirement is set at age 55.

The Marshallese society retains a traditional matrilineal structure. Each person belongs to the bwij, or clan, of his or her mother, and has the right to use the land and other property of the bwij. The head of the bwij is called an alap. The alap is the spokesperson between the clan members and the members of the iroij, or royal clan. Inheritance of traditional rank and of property is matrilineal, and women occupy important positions within the traditional social system. However, within the economic system, many hold low-paid dead-end jobs. Spousal abuse is common, usually in conjunction with alcohol use.

In 2011 the US Department of State ranked the Marshall Islands as a top destination country for women subjected to sex trafficking. This designation was based on reports of foreign women being forced into prostitution after being given the promise of legitimate work. The government is committed to protecting and promoting the rights of children. The government fully respects the human rights of its citizens.

41 HEALTH

There is a private clinic and a public hospital in Majuro, and a second public hospital in Ebeye. According to the CIA, life expectancy in the Marshall Islands was 72 years in 2011. The country spent 14.6% of its GDP on healthcare, amounting to $422 per person. There were 6 physicians, 25 nurses and midwives, and hospital beds per 10,000 inhabitants. The fertility rate was 3.44 children per woman of childbearing age, while the infant mortality rate was 23.7 deaths per 1,000 live births. It was estimated that 94% of children were vaccinated against measles.

Rudimentary health care on the outer atolls is provided through dispensaries staffed by health assistants. Emergency cases are sent to the Majuro or Ebeye hospital and, when necessary, to hospitals in Honolulu. Dental services to the outer atolls are provided by periodic visits by dental teams from Majuro and Ebeye.

42 HOUSING

In 1999 (the date of the last full census), there were about 6,478 households with an average of 7.8 people per household. About 70% of households relied on rain water as a primary water source, 38% of households had access to flush toilets (either inside their own residence or outside), and 63% had access to electricity for lighting and/or cooking. Houses in the urban centers are usually simple wooden or cement-block structures, with corrugated iron roofs; because of the limited land availability, houses are heavily crowded. In the outer atolls houses are constructed of local materials, with thatched sloping roofs and sides of plaited palm fronds. The Ministry of Social Services provides housing grants, principally to low-income families, through a low-cost housing

program and a grant-in-aid program. Government housing is administered by the Public Service Commission.

43 EDUCATION

Education is compulsory for eight years. Primary school covers six years of study, followed by six years of secondary school. A high school entrance examination is given to all eighth graders in order to determine who will be admitted into the two public high schools each year. For students who are admitted to high school, a comprehensive four-year program of secondary education provides instruction in general studies, college preparatory courses, and vocational training.

In 2009 the World Bank estimated that 80% of age-eligible children in the Marshall Islands were enrolled in primary school. Secondary enrollment for age-eligible children stood at 52%. The student-to-teacher ratio for primary school was at about 17:1 in 2005; the ratio for secondary school was also about 17:1. In 2005, private schools accounted for about 24% of primary school enrollment and 34% of secondary enrollment. Higher education is provided through formal programs of teacher training and the provision of grants for university training abroad. The Majuro campus of the College of Micronesia opened its School of Nursing and Science Center in 1986. In 1991, the Marshall Islands campus separated from the College of Micronesia system and became accredited by the Accrediting Commission for Community and Junior Colleges of the Western Association for Schools and Colleges (WASC). On 1 April 1993, the College of the Marshall Islands was established as an independent institution with its own Board of Regents. In 2002, about 17% of the tertiary age population was enrolled in some type of higher education program.

Overall, the CIA estimated that Marshall Islands had a literacy rate of 93.7%. As of 2004, public expenditure on education was estimated at 12% of GDP.

44 LIBRARIES AND MUSEUMS

The College of Marshall Islands Library has about 10,000 volumes, while the High Court Library holds 50,000. In Majuro, the Alele Museum, which also houses a library, was completed in 1973. Alele Museum showcases both the traditional and colonial history of the Marshalls. The library houses historical documents and photographs from the trust territory archives. More than 2,000 glass-plate negatives taken between 1890 and 1930 are on loan to the museum. One of Alele's latest attractions was the elaborate shell collection from Mili Atoll.

45 MEDIA

The inter-island communications network consists of shortwave outer-island radio stations, which link all major islands and atolls. In 2009, there were 4,400 main phone lines. There were about 1,000 mobile cell phones in use nationwide, or about 2 per 100 people. The island of Ebeye is linked to Majuro by radio and also by satellite. As of 2009, there were four radio stations and one US military satellite radio station. The US military also provides a satellite television station. The government radio station, which has advertising, relays world news from Voice of America and Radio Australia. AFN Kwajalein operates the country's only AM radio station for the US military. In 2010, the country had three Internet hosts. In 2009 Internet users numbered 4 per 100 citizens.

There are no daily newspapers. A weekly newspaper, *The Marshall Islands Journal* (2010 circulation 3,700), is published in Majuro in English and Marshallese. *The Marshall Island Gazette*, established in 1982, is a free, four-page government newsletter, printed in English. The constitution provides for free expression and the government is said to respect these provisions in practice.

46 ORGANIZATIONS

A number of consumers' cooperatives are in operation. The Chamber of Commerce is located on Majuro. Marshallese society is matrilineal and organized on the basis of the clan (*bwij*). The head of the clan (*alap*) serves as spokesman between clan members and members of the royal clan. At the community level there are youth organizations, including Boy Scouts and Girl Scouts, women's organizations, and various religiously affiliated social organizations. Sports associations exist for such activities as tennis, weightlifting, baseball, and track and field. A national women's organization began in 1986. The Red Cross is also active.

47 TOURISM, TRAVEL, AND RECREATION

According to the UN World Tourism Organization, in 2009 there were 5,400 incoming tourists to the Marshall Islands who spent a total of $2.7 million. Of those incoming tourists, there were 3,300 from East Asia and the Pacific. The estimated daily cost to visit Majuro, the capital, was $204. The cost of visiting other cities averaged $83.

Tourist attractions include the sandy beaches on the atolls, protected lagoons, underwater coral reefs, and abundant marine life, including large game fish. Diving and fishing tours are also popular. The outer atolls of Mili, Maloelap, Wotje, and Jaluit offer many Japanese and American relics from World War II. Tourist facilities are available in Majuro, the capital, however, tourism remains limited in the outer atolls and there are few accommodations for visitors.

Visas are not required for citizens from the United States, United Kingdom, Federated States of Micronesia, Palau, Pacific Islands Forum countries (including Australia and New Zealand citizens), and members of the European Union,. Citizens of all other countries will need to obtain an entry visa before traveling to the Marshall Islands. A vaccination certificate may be required if traveling from an infected area. An AIDS test may be necessary if staying for over 30 days.

48 FAMOUS PERSONS

Amata Kabua (1928–96), president from 1979 until his death, was founder and leader of the Political Movement for the Marshall Islands Separation from Micronesia in 1972. He previously served as a member of the Congress of Micronesia and guided his country to self-governing status under the US-administered UN trusteeship. He was a graduate of Maunaolu College in Hawaii and taught secondary school before starting his political career. Kunio Lemari (1942–2008) was in office for a month in 1996–97; Imata Kabua (b. 1943) was president from 1997 to 2000. Kessai Hesa Note (b. 1950) was elected president in 2000 and reelected in 2004.

49 DEPENDENCIES

The Marshall Islands have no territories or colonies.

50 BIBLIOGRAPHY

Compacts of Free Association with the Marshall Islands, Federated States of Micronesia, and Palau. Washington, DC: U.S. Government Printing Office, Congressional Sales Office, 1998.

Dibblin, Jane. *Day of Two Suns: US Nuclear Testing and the Pacific Islanders.* New York: New Amsterdam, 1990.

The Final Victories. New York: Marshall Cavendish, 2011.

Harris, Michael. *The Atomic Times: My H-Bomb Year at the Pacific Proving Ground: A Memoir.* New York: Presidio Press/Ballantine Books, 2005.

Leibo, Steven A. *East and Southeast Asia, 2005.* 38th ed. Harpers Ferry, WV: Stryker-Post Publications, 2005.

Republic of the Marshall Islands Supplemental Nuclear Compensation Act. Washington, DC: U.S. Government Printing Office, Congressional Sales Office, 2010.

Rudiak-Gould, Peter. *Surviving Paradise: One Year on a Disappearing Island.* New York: Union Square Press, 2009.

Weisgall, Jonathan M. *Operation Crossroads: The Atomic Tests at Bikini Atoll.* Annapolis, MD: Naval Institute Press, 1994.

MICRONESIA, FEDERATED STATES OF

Federated States of Micronesia

CAPITAL: Palikir, Pohnpei Island

FLAG: Adopted in 1978, the flag is light blue, bearing four five-pointed stars arranged in a diamond in the center.

ANTHEM: *Patriots of Micronesia.*

MONETARY UNIT: The US dollar is the official medium of exchange.

WEIGHTS AND MEASURES: British units are used, as modified by US usage.

HOLIDAYS: New Year's Day, 1 January; Federated States of Micronesia Day, 10 May; Independence Day, 3 November; Christmas Day, 25 December.

TIME: In Pohnpei and Kosrae, 10 p.m. = noon GMT; in Yap and Chuuk, 9 p.m. = noon GMT.

¹LOCATION, SIZE, AND EXTENT

The Federated States of Micronesia (FSM) is located in the western Pacific Ocean within the Carolinian archipelago. The four states consist of 607 islands with a total area of 7,866 sq km (3,037 sq mi), comprising 702 sq km (271 sq mi) of land, and 7,164 sq km (2,766 sq mi) of lagoons. Comparatively, the area occupied by the FSM is slightly less than four times the size of Washington, DC. Kosrae, the smallest and easternmost state, consists of five closely situated islands. Pohnpei consists of the single large island of Pohnpei and 25 smaller islands within a barrier reef, in addition to 137 outer islands, of which the major atolls are Mokil, Pingelap, Kapingamarangi, Nukjuoro, and Ngatik. Chuuk includes the large Chuuk lagoon, enclosing 98 islands, and major outer island groups, including the Mortlocks, Halls, Western, and Namwunweito islands. Yap, the westernmost state, consists of four large islands and seven smaller islands surrounded by barrier reefs, in addition to 134 outer islands, of which the largest groups are Ulithi and Woleai. The cumulative coastline distance is 6,112 km (3,798 mi).

The capital city of the Federated States of Micronesia, Palikir, is located on the island of Pohnpei.

²TOPOGRAPHY

The 607 islands constituting the four states include large, mountainous islands of volcanic origin and coral atolls. Kosrae is largely mountainous, with two peaks, Fenkol (634 m/2,080 ft) and Matanti (583 m/1,913 ft). Pohnpei contains a large volcanic island, with the highest elevation that of Mt. Totolom (791 m/2,595 ft). Chuuk (Truk) contains 14 islands that are mountainous and of volcanic origin. Yap contains four large high islands, with the peak elevation that of Mt. Tabiwol (178 m/584 ft). The outer islands of all states are mostly coral atolls. Though the country is not generally known to have major earthquakes, a 6.6 magnitude quake occurred on Yap on 16 January 2005.

³CLIMATE

The climate is maritime tropical, with little seasonal or diurnal variation in temperature, which averages 27°C (80°F). The islands are subject to typhoons. The short and torrential nature of the rainfall, which decreases from east to west, results in an annual average of 508 cm (200 in) in Pohnpei and 305 cm (120 in) in Yap.

⁴FLORA AND FAUNA

The World Resources Institute estimates that there are 1,194 plant species in the Federated States of Micronesia. In addition, Micronesia is home to 8 species of mammals, 97 species of birds, and 13 species of reptiles. These figures reflect the total number of distinct species residing in the country, not the number of endemic species.

There is moderately heavy tropical vegetation, with tree species including tropical hardwoods on the slopes of the higher volcanic islands and coconut palms on the coral atolls. The only native land mammal is the tropical bat. A rich marine fauna inhabits the open sea, reefs, lagoons, and shore areas.

⁵ENVIRONMENT

Solid waste disposal in urban areas is a continuing problem, and toxic pollutants form mining operations threaten the land. Micronesia's water supply is also threatened by industrial and agricultural pollutants. Untreated sewage and contaminants from industrialized countries in the region add to the problem of water pollution. The United Nations (UN) reported in 2008 that carbon dioxide emissions in Micronesia totaled 62 kilotons.

UN research shows that global warming and the rise of sea levels are a threat to Micronesia's forests, agricultural areas, and water supply. Pollution from industrial and agricultural sources also threatens the nation's mangrove areas. The fish population is endangered by waterborne toxins and explosives used in commercial fishing. The country also has a problem with the degeneration of its reefs due to tourism. In 1984 the government established an Environmental Protection Board.

In 2010 top officials from Micronesia and thirteen other developing Pacific island nations and dependencies met in Vanuatu to address some of the issues unique to these low-lying, developing island states. These included climate change, sea-level rise, natural disasters, remoteness from major markets, and poverty. Another key objective of the meeting was to address the progress each nation had made in adopting the 2005 Mauritius Strategy, the only global blueprint that exists to combat the development challenges of small-island developing states.

The World Resources Institute reported that the Federated States of Micronesia had designated 5,100 hectares (12,602 acres) of land for protection as of 2006. According to a 2011 report issued by the International Union for Conservation of Nature and Natural Resources (IUCN), threatened species included 7 mammals, 10 birds, 4 reptiles, 16 fish, 4 mollusks, and 5 plants. Threatened species include the Chuuk flying fox, the Chuuk monarch, and the Mortlock Islands flying-fox. The Kosrae crake and the Kosrae mountain starling have become extinct.

6 POPULATION

For 2011 the US Central Intelligence Agency (CIA) estimated the population of the Federated States of Micronesia to be approximately 106,836, which placed it at number 180 in population among the 196 nations of the world. In 2011 approximately 3% of the population was over 65 years of age, with another 33.6% under 15 years of age. The median age in Micronesia was 22.7 years. There were 1.05 males for every female in the country. The population's annual rate of change was -0.313%. The projected population for the year 2025 was 120,000. Population density in Micronesia was calculated at 159 people per sq km (412 people per sq mi). The UN estimated that 23% of the population lived in urban areas, and that urban populations had an annual rate of change of 1.3%. The largest urban area was Palikir, with a population of 7,000.

7 MIGRATION

In 2011 the CIA estimated Micronesia's net migration rate at -20.99 migrants per 1,000 citizens. The total number of emigrants living abroad was 21,900, and the total number of immigrants living in Micronesia was 2,700. No significant permanent emigration has occurred; most emigration has been undertaken temporarily for higher education.

8 ETHNIC GROUPS

The islanders are classified as Micronesians of Malayo-Mongoloid origins. The people of the Nukuoro and Kapingamarangi atolls in southwestern Pohnpei are of Polynesian descent. In total, there are nine ethnic Micronesian and Polynesian groups. Since each of the four states has a different language and culture, these state groups are sometimes referred to as ethnic groupings. At the 2000 census, 48.8% of the population were Chuukese, 24.2% Pohnpeian, 6.2%

Kosraean, and 5.2% Yapese. Asians accounted for about 1.8% of the population and Polynesians accounted for 1.5%. Noncitizens are prohibited from owning land and holding certain occupations. Non-Micronesians are generally not granted citizenship.

9 LANGUAGES

English is the official language and is taught in the schools. The indigenous languages are of the Malayo-Polynesian family. Yapese, Ulithian, Woleaian, Trukese, Pohnpeian, and Kosraean are classed as Malaysian. Kapingamarangi and Nukuoro, spoken on two isolated atolls of the same names in Pohnpei, are Polynesian languages. Chuukese is a Trukic language of the Malayo-Polynesian family.

10 RELIGIONS

Roman Catholicism and Protestantism have been widely accepted throughout the country following their introduction by missionaries in the 1880s. Protestantism is predominant in Kosrae. The largest Protestant denomination is the United Church of Christ. Other Christian groups include Baptists, Seventh-Day Adventists, Mormons, members of the Salvation Army, Jehovah's Witnesses, and members of the Assemblies of God. Roman Catholics are dominant on Chuuk and Yap. There is a small Buddhist community of Pohnpei. There is also a small number of Baha'is in the country.

11 TRANSPORTATION

The CIA reports that Micronesia has a total of 240 km (149 mi) of roads, of which 42 km (26.1 mi) are paved. Over 90% of all vehicles are located on the main islands of Pohnpei, Moen (in Chuuk), Kosrae, and Yap. The state of Yap provides public bus transportation, primarily used by students. International shipping services are provided by eight companies, some of them Japanese. There are commercial harbor facilities at Colonia, Lele, and Pohnpei. The Federated States of Micronesia's merchant fleet, as of 2010, consisted of three vessels (one cargo and two passenger/cargo of 1,000 GRT or over). Interisland shipping service is provided by six government-owned vessels. In 2010 all six airports had paved runways. International and interstate airline services are provided by Continental Micronesia.

12 HISTORY

The Carolinian archipelago was sighted by European navigators in the 16th century. In 1686 the Spanish captain Francisco Lezcano named Yap Island "La Carolina" after King Charles II of Spain; the name was later generalized to the islands as a whole. Until the end of the 19th century, the islands were under Spanish colonial administration. In 1899 following the Spanish-American War, Spain sold the islands to Germany. Japanese administration commenced at the end of World War I, and in 1947, following World War II, the four states of the FSM came under US administration as part of the UN Trust Territory of the Pacific Islands. Beginning in the 1960s, the people of Micronesia began making clear their desire for political independence. The United States, ever interested in maintaining good relations with the strategically significant Pacific islands, gave in to such demands and helped Micronesia to form a consultative body, called the Congress of Micronesia, in

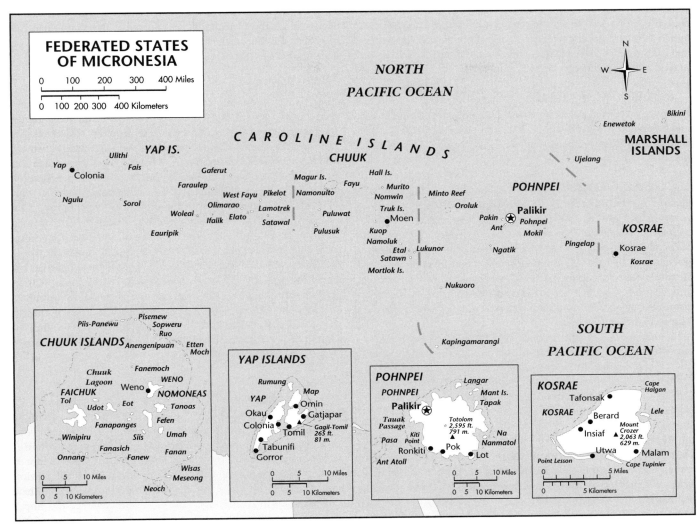

FEDERATED STATES OF MICRONESIA

0   100   200   300   400 Miles

0   100   200   300   400 Kilometers

NORTH
PACIFIC OCEAN

N
W   E
S

CAROLINE ISLANDS

Bikini

Enewetok

MARSHALL ISLANDS

Ujelang

YAP IS.

CHUUK

Yap
Colonia
Ulithi
Fais
Gaferut
Magur Is.
Fayu
Hall Is.
Murito
Nomwin
Minto Reef

POHNPEI

Ngulu
Faraulep
West Fayu
Pikelot
Namonuito
Truk Is.
Oroluk
Palikir

KOSRAE

Sorol
Olimarao
Lamotrek
Puluwat
Moen
Pakin
Pohnpei
Ant
Mokil
Woleai
Ifalik
Elato
Satawal
Pulusuk
Kuop
Namoluk
Etal
Lukunor
Ngatik
Pingelap
Kosrae
Eauripik
Satawn
Mortlok Is.
Kosrae

Nukuoro

Kapingamarangi

SOUTH
PACIFIC OCEAN

CHUUK ISLANDS
Piis-Panewu
Pisemew
Sopweru
Ruo
Anengenipuan
Etten
Moch

Chuuk
Lagoon
Fanemoch
FAICHUK
Weno
WENO
Tol
NOMONEAS
Udot
Eot
Tanoas
Fanapanges
Fefen
Winipiru
Siis
Umah
Fanasich
Fanan
Onnang
Fanew
Wisas
Meseong
Neoch

0   5   10 Miles
0   5   10 Kilometers

YAP ISLANDS
Rumung
YAP
Map
Okau
Omin
Colonia
Gatjapar
Tomil
Gagil-Tomil
265 ft.
81 m.
Tabunifi
Gorror

0   5   10 Miles
0   5   10 Kilometers

POHNPEI
Langar
POHNPEI
Mant Is.
Palikir
Tapak
Tauak
Passage
Totolom
2,595 ft.
791 m.
Na
Kiti
Point
Nanmatol
Pasa
Pok
Ronkiti
Lot
Ant Atoll

0   5   10 Miles
0   5   10 Kilometers

KOSRAE
Cape
Halgan
KOSRAE
Tafonsak
KOSRAE
Berard
Lele
Mount
Crozer
Insiaf
2,063 ft.
629 m.
Point Lesson
Utwa
Malam
Cape Tupinier

0   5 Miles
0   5 Kilometers

LOCATION: 0° to 14° N; 135° to 166° E.

1967. The congress declared the area sovereign in 1970. The history of the FSM as a political entity began on 12 July 1978, when a constitution drafted by a popularly elected constitutional convention was adopted; it went into effect on 10 May 1979. The government of the FSM and the government of the United States executed a Compact of Free Association in October 1982; in November 1986, that compact went into effect. Under the Compact of Free Association, the United States is responsible for defense and security issues. The UN Security Council voted in December 1990 to terminate the FSM's status as a UN Trust Territory. A new capital was built about 10 km (6 mi) southwest of Kolonia in the Palikir Valley; it has served the FSM since 1990. The FSM became an independent state and joined the UN in September 1991.

The first Compact of Free Association between the FSM and the United States expired in 2001. In 2003, after four years of discussion, negotiators agreed upon an amended document providing 20 years of ongoing assistance in the amount of approximately $100 million per year until 2023; the compact took effect in 2004.

Continuing into the new millennium, global warming and the possibility of rising sea levels have raised concerns over the long-term prospects for the islands in the middle of the Pacific Ocean. The Intergovernmental Panel on Climate Change has suggested that the sea could rise by about .5 m (18 in) by 2100, but that figure could be much lower or higher. The existence of low-lying nations such as FSM would be threatened by any rise in sea level. The country also faced the challenge of lessening its dependence on foreign aid. Tourism was considered as a possible solution.

13 GOVERNMENT

The government of the FSM can be characterized as a confederation, with strong state governments and a weaker central government. The national executive branch includes the president, who is both chief of state and head of government, and a vice president. Both are elected by the congress from among the four senators at large to serve a four-year term. Following a presidential election, a special election is held to fill the senate seats vacated by the new executives. The cabinet consists of the vice president and the heads of eight executive departments who are appointed by the president, with the advice and consent of congress.

The legislature consists of a unicameral congress of 14 senators elected by popular vote. Of the senators, four are elected at large, one from each state, and ten on the basis of population apportionment. The four at-large senators serve four-year terms, and the remaining senators serve two-year terms.

14 POLITICAL PARTIES

There are no formal political parties. Emanuel Mori from Chuuk was first elected as president in 2007 and reelected in 2011. Alik L. Alik from Kosrae was chosen as Mori's vice president in both elections.

15 LOCAL GOVERNMENT

Each of the four states has its own constitution, providing for governments headed by governors and lieutenant-governors, popularly elected for four-year terms. State legislatures consist of members popularly elected on the basis of proportional representation. The state governments hold a considerable amount of power, particularly in the development and implementation of budgetary policies. Municipalities are districts composed of a number of small communities (sections), some of which may be located in different islands.

Municipal government is considered by many to be the most important level of government in Micronesia. The leaders of local bodies are generally traditional chiefs, who are considered by a sizable body of Micronesians to be more important figures than nationally elected politicians. The local council of chiefs can veto any legislation it considers detrimental to traditional ways.

16 JUDICIAL SYSTEM

The national judiciary consists of a Supreme Court with both trial and appellate divisions. Justices, including the presiding chief justice, are appointed by the president, with the advice and consent of congress, and serve for life.

A traditional mediation system also exists to deal with local offenders. A large number of cases are resolved through such mediation rather than more formal legal trials.

The constitution provides for an independent judiciary and the government respects this provision in practice.

17 ARMED FORCES

The Federated States of Micronesia maintains no armed forces. Under the terms of the Compact of Free Association, external security is the responsibility of the United States. There are small, civilian-controlled national, state, and local police forces.

18 INTERNATIONAL COOPERATION

The FSM became a member of the United Nations on 17 September 1991; it is a part of ESCAP and serves on nonregional specialized agencies such as the FAO, the World Bank, the IFC, IMF, UNESCO, and the WHO. The FSM participates in the ACP Group, the Asian Development Bank, G-77, the Pacific Island Forum, the South Pacific Regional Trade and Economic Cooperation Agreement (Sparteca), and the Alliance of Small Island States (AOSIS).

The FSM and the United States signed the Compact of Free Association on 3 November 1986. Amendments to the compact went into effect on 1 May 2004.

In environmental cooperation, the FSM is part of the Basel Convention, the Convention on Biological Diversity, the Kyoto Protocol, the Montréal Protocol, and the UN Conventions on the Law of the Sea, Climate Change, and Desertification.

19 ECONOMY

The primary economic activities in Micronesia are agriculture, fishing, and tourism. Agriculture is primarily a subsistence activity, though exports of products such as bananas and black peppers contributed a small percentage to the GDP. Marine exports and licensing fees from commercial fishing fleets provide an even more significant contribution to the economy. Tourism, while still a relatively small industry, shows some potential for growth. Government services have become a major contributor to the economy as well, accounting for more the 40% of the gross domestic product (GDP) in 2011. The GDP rate of change in Micronesia, as of 2005, was estimated at -1.5%. Inflation stood at 2.2%.

Like most Pacific island nations, there is a high demand for imports and a relatively low level of exports, resulting in continual trade deficits for the nation. Micronesia is therefore highly dependent on financial assistance from the United States. Under the terms of the amended Compact of Free Association (2004), the United States will provide $100 million in direct assistance each year through 2023.

20 INCOME

The CIA estimated that in 2008 the GDP of Micronesia was $238.1 million. The CIA defines GDP as the value of all final goods and services produced within a nation in a given year and computed on the basis of purchasing power parity (PPP) rather than value as measured on the basis of the rate of the exchange based on current dollars. The per capita GDP was estimated at $2,200. The annual growth rate of GDP was -1.5% in 2011. The average inflation rate was 2.2% in 2005. In 2004 the CIA estimated that agriculture accounted for 28.9% of GDP, industry 15.2%, and services 55.9%.

It was estimated that in 2000 about 26.7% of the population subsisted on an income below the poverty line established by Micronesia's government.

21 LABOR

In 2008 Micronesia's national labor force was estimated at about 16,360. As of 2011 it was estimated that more than half of those in the formal workforce were employed in government services, either at the national or local levels. Most of the remaining population is employed in subsistence agriculture or fishing. Unemployment has been estimated as high as 22%.

The law provides the right to form or join associations. However, no such associations have been formed as of 2011. This lack of unions has been attributed to the fact that most private sector employment is very small, with businesses owned and operated primarily by families employing extended family members and friends.

The minimum wage for national government workers was reported at $2.65 per hour in 2011. Each state government imposes its own minimum wage for local government workers. As of 2011, the minimum hourly wages were reported as $2 in Pohnpei, $1.25 in Chuuk, $1.42 in Kosrae, and $1.60 in Yap. Only Pohnpei had a minimum wage for private sector workers. In 2011 it stood at $1.35 an hour. There is no minimum working age for children and many children assist their families in subsistence farming activities, though few are involved in the formal wage economy. While there were no laws concerning work hours, a 40-hour week has been standard practice.

22 AGRICULTURE

Out of 70,000 hectares (172,978 acres) of land in Micronesia, 2,000 hectares (4,942 acres) are arable. Agricultural production has traditionally been for subsistence and was based on a system of shifting cultivation in the high islands. Staple crops include taros, sweet potatoes, bananas, cassavas, and breadfruit. Yams are grown on Pohnpei, Kosrae, Yap, and Fais islands. Other vegetables, such as cucumbers, eggplant, head cabbage, Chinese cabbage, bell peppers, green onions, and tomatoes, are also produced. Other fruits include mangoes, papayas, pandanus, pineapples, lemons, and limes, with oranges and tangerines also produced on Kosrae. The ubiquitous coconut palm is used for a wide range of subsistence purposes, and copra is the main cash crop and the nation's leading export. Black and white peppers were introduced to Micronesia in 1938, but pepper growing only began in Pohnpei (the FSM's most important pepper-producing island) in 1960. Rich volcanic soil and heavy rainfall make gourmet Pohnpei peppers highly regarded.

In 2009 cereal production amounted to an estimated 248 tons, fruit production 3,333 tons, and vegetable production 3,318 tons.

23 ANIMAL HUSBANDRY

The UN Food and Agriculture Organization (FAO) reported that Micronesia dedicated 3,000 hectares (7,413 acres) to permanent pasture or meadow in 2009. Livestock in 2005 included some 13,900 head of cattle, 32,000 pigs, and 4,000 goats. Pigs, traditionally kept by many households for ceremonial purposes, are being upgraded through the introduction of improved strains. Two pig farms operate on Pohnpei. The largest cattle herd is on Pohnpei Island. Eggs are produced commercially and limited success has been achieved by commercial poultry chicken projects in the states of Pohnpei and Chuuk. Chickens are kept by many households. Goat projects are also operating in Kosrae and Chuuk. A few head of water buffalo are privately raised on Pohnpei and on Pata in Chuuk. In the mid-1990s, the government started encouraging domestic feed production in order to decrease the reliance on imported feed meal.

24 FISHING

Inshore marine resources of the reefs and lagoons are harvested mainly for subsistence. The FSM's exclusive economic zone covers some 2.9 million sq km (1.1 million sq mi) of ocean, which contains the world's most productive tuna fishing grounds. In 2008 the annual national fish capture totaled 21,699 tons according to the UN FAO. There is some aquaculture along the reefs and lagoons, involving specialty products such as giant clams, eucheuma seaweed, sponges, pearls, and green snails. Foreign fleets pay more than $16.9 million annually for the right to fish in FSM waters. Revenues from these licensing fees account for about 28% of national government revenues each year. In 2011 it was estimated

that marine exports account for about 85% of export revenues each year.

The Micronesian Maritime Authority and the National Fisheries Corporation assist in the development and promotion of commercial fisheries. As a signatory of the Parties of the Nauru Agreement (PNA), Micronesia works for the conservation and management of tuna resources. The waters of the PNA nations account for nearly 60% of all tuna catches in the western and central Pacific Ocean and 25% of the global tuna catches that supply canneries and processing facilities around the world. In 2010 the PNA held its First Presidential Summit. Called the Tuna Summit, members adopted the Koror Declaration, which aims, among other things, to establish cooperative management practices that will enhance commercial and economic opportunities for member states and to work toward the conservation and restoration of migratory tuna stocks.

25 FORESTRY

Approximately 91% of the Federated States of Micronesia is covered by forest. Exploitation of the nation's forestry resources is limited, and virtually all lumber used in construction is imported ($2.1 million in 2004). Mangrove timber is used for handicrafts and furniture making.

26 MINING

There are deposits of phosphates on Fais Island in Yap and bauxite in Pohnpei, Truk, and Yap, but there has been no commercial exploitation. Clays, coral, sand, rock aggregate, and quarry stone works supplied construction materials.

27 ENERGY AND POWER

The nation is dependent on imported petroleum for its energy needs. In 2002, the latest date that data was available, Micronesia produced 192 million kWh and consumed 178.6 million kWh. Diesel-powered generators at government power stations located in each state center supply most of the electricity. About half the electricity produced was used by the government. Small quantities of electricity are produced in outer island communities.

28 INDUSTRY

Manufacturing activity is nearly nonexistent and accounts for only a fraction of a percent of GDP. Cottage industries involving handicrafts and small-scale processing are carried out in all states and constitute an important source of income for those not integrated into the monetary economy. More formal manufacturing operations involve garment making, coconut processing, boat building, breadfruit flour processing, brick-manufacturing, and wood processing. In late 1999, a tuna processing plant opened in Majuro.

29 SCIENCE AND TECHNOLOGY

The World Bank reported in 2009 that there were no patent applications in science and technology in Micronesia. There are no educational institutions for advanced instruction or research and development in science and technology. A medical school was established in Pohnpei in 1987. The Western and Central Pacific Fisheries Commission, established in 2004 with headquarters in Pohnpei, has established a scientific committee to promote and contribute to research applicable to sustaining fish stocks in the Pacific islands.

30 DOMESTIC TRADE

There are numerous small retail shops and some wholesale establishments dealing primarily with imported products. Most trade is highly localized in the four state centers of Kolonia, Tofol, Moen, and Colonia. There are some major US retailers located in Pohnpei.

31 FOREIGN TRADE

With a high dependency on imports, the FSM typically sustains a severe trade deficit. Food, fuel, manufactured goods, textiles, machines, transport and equipment, and electrical appliances are among the primary imports. Exports include agricultural products (coconuts, bananas, betel nuts, cassava, and sweet potatoes), pigs, chickens, and re-exports of fish. Major import partners in 2009 were United States (50%); Japan (11%); and others (39%). Its major export partners were Japan, 21%; United States, 25%; and others, 53%.

32 BALANCE OF PAYMENTS

Micronesia imported $132.7 million worth of goods and services in 2008, while exporting $14 million worth of goods and services, resulting in a trade deficit of $118.7 million. Much of the annual deficit is covered by direct aid from the United States under the Compact of Free Association.

33 BANKING AND SECURITIES

Commercial banking services are provided by the Bank of the Federated States of Micronesia, which has one branch in each state. This bank is jointly owned by federal and state governments (80%) and local investors (20%). The publicly owned Bank of Guam has branches in Pohnpei and Chuuk. The FSM Development Bank commenced operations in 1982. It provides loans for projects that meet criteria based on the government's development priorities and is authorized to provide loan guarantees to other financial institutions in the FSM. However, it can only make loans of up to $200,000 because of capital limitations. The FSM Employees Credit Union was chartered in 1986. Additional credit unions have been established in some island communities. The government of Pohnpei state supports the Small Business Guarantee and Finance Corporation (est. 2000) to support small- and medium-sized enterprises within the state. Tradable securities are not issued by the FSM government, state governments, or enterprises residing in the FSM.

34 INSURANCE

The Public Service System administers life insurance and workers' compensation programs. In 1984 a government employee group health insurance program was instituted, and in 1987 a retirement pension program—for both state and national government employees—was initiated.

35 PUBLIC FINANCE

In 2007 the budget of Micronesia included $166 million in public revenue and $152.7 million in public expenditures. The budget surplus amounted to 5.6% of GDP. In total $60.8 million of public debt was held by foreign entities.

36 TAXATION

The national government imposes a business revenue tax and a personal income tax. The income tax rate is set at 6% of the first $11,000 and 10% on all income exceeding this amount. Those earning less than $5,000 per year are entitled to a deduction of $1,000 before taxes are computed. The gross revenue tax for businesses is set at $80 for the first $10,000 of gross revenues and 3% on all exceeding amounts.

The states are constitutionally limited in the types of taxes they may impose; they may levy sales taxes on alcoholic beverages, soft drinks, and cigarettes. The municipal governments usually levy head taxes and boat license and business license fees.

An important tax revenue service is from the sale of tuna fishing rights, which rose from $12.7 million in 1990 to about $16.9 million in 2010.

37 CUSTOMS AND DUTIES

An import tax is imposed on nearly all products brought in for resale. Rates range from as high as 100% ad valorem for laundry bar soap to 3% ad valorem on food for human consumption. A rate of 25% ad valorem applies to items such as perfumes, cosmetics, toiletries, soft drinks, coffee, tea, and other nonalcoholic beverages. Most other products have a rate of 4% ad valorem. A rate of 25% ad valorem applies for cigarettes, other tobacco products, beer, malt beverages, and wine regardless of whether they are imported for personal use or resale, with some duty free exemptions allowed for personal use only.

All imports are subject to physical inspection, and all import taxes must be paid before the products are released from customs.

38 FOREIGN INVESTMENT

While the government actively encourages foreign investment, there have been few investors in the 2000s. Foreign direct investment (FDI) in the Federated States of Micronesia was unreported according to World Bank figures published in 2009. Applicable regulations are outlined by the Foreign Investment Act of 1997, with amendments in 2005, and the Foreign Investment Regulations of 1998. Areas promoted for investment include agriculture, aquaculture, apparel manufacturing, fishing, and tourism.

39 ECONOMIC DEVELOPMENT

Despite past efforts to achieve greater economic self-sufficiency, the nation's economy has continued to rely heavily on US assistance. Under the terms of the Compact of Free Association, the United States provided about $1.3 billion from 1986–2001 in grant aid, along with additional assistance. A multi-million dollar US-implemented capital improvement plan to improve infrastructure was completed in the early 2000s. It included new airports, docks, water and sewage systems, paved roads, and hospitals.

The first Compact of Free Association between the FSM and the United States expired in 2001. In 2003 after four years of discussion, negotiators agreed upon an amended document providing 20 years of ongoing aid in the amount of approximately $100 million per year in direct assistance until 2023. The payment schedule included a systematic reallocation of a portion of the direct aid, so that each year a larger portion is placed in a jointly managed Trust Fund that will accumulate over the 20-year period and provide income once the compact expires.

A large portion of funding from the first compact was channeled into the national and state governments, with a successful result of establishing a stable democratic government system. However, this inflated the public sector at the expense of the private sector. In the *FSM Strategic Development Plan (2004–2023)*, development of the private sector is noted as a major priority. This will require continued reforms in the regulatory environment as well as the design and implementation of strategies to attract private investment. The comprehensive development plan also includes goals and strategies for improvements in agriculture, fisheries, tourism, health, education, gender equality, and the environment.

40 SOCIAL DEVELOPMENT

The extended family and clan system, headed by traditional leaders or chiefs, is retained in varying degrees, especially in the outer islands. A social insurance system includes old age, disability, and survivor benefits. Employees contribute 6% of their earnings; employers make a 6% payroll contribution.

In spite of constitutional safeguards, social discrimination against women continues to be a problem, primarily under the guise of tradition. Though women are becoming more active in the formal workforce, women's roles within the family remain largely traditional. Sexual abuse and domestic violence have persisted. There are no laws prohibiting domestic abuse, and in many cases the victims are reluctant to press charges against family members, partly from fear of reprisal, but also from a belief that such matters are private and should be handled within the extended family. In 2010 the government held a National Women's Conference to address issues that included improvements in women's health, promotion of women in education and business, and self-employment among women. The conference also addressed the need for national and state laws to protect women from abuse. Women do not face discrimination in education and women are well represented in middle and lower levels of government, usually receiving equal pay for equal work. Child abuse is illegal.

Minorities do not face widespread discrimination or prejudice. Noncitizens, however, are prohibited from owning land. Human rights are generally respected.

41 HEALTH

There are hospitals in each state center and a medical school in Pohnpei. In the outer islands, primary medical services are provided through dispensaries staffed by health assistants. A dispensary was created in the Lower Mortlock Islands to serve people scattered on seven atolls. Tertiary medical treatment is provided through patient referral to hospitals in Guam and Hawaii. All of Micronesia has access to safe water and sanitation. In 2011 there were an estimated 6 physicians, 23 nurses and midwives, and 33 hospital beds per 10,000 inhabitants.

The infant mortality rate in 2011 was 24.34 per 1,000 live births, and the life expectancy was 71.52 years. The total fertility rate in 2011 was estimated at 2.74. The maternal mortality rate was 121 per 100,000 live births in 2007. Immunization rates for Micronesian children under one year of age were as follows: measles, 96%; polio, 85%; and diphtheria, tetanus, and pertussis, 94%. Although polio has been eradicated, there have been cases of tuberculosis, and measles. Anemia has presented in some children under the age of five.

As of 2011 Micronesia spent an estimated 18.9% of GDP on healthcare, amounting to $337 per person. The government relies on grants from the United States and international organizations such as UNICEF and the World Health Organization for additional funding.

42 HOUSING

At the 2000 census, there were 15,273 occupied households, with about 44.4% on Chuuk, 35.8% on Pohnpei, 12.9% on Yap, and 6.9% on Kosrae. The average number of members per household was 6.8. About 26.8% of households had nine or more members. An estimated 30% of the housing stock was built in 1993 or later, with another 8.8% of all housing built in 1969 or earlier. Materials for housing construction are generally imported. Metal sheeting and concrete are the most common materials for walls and roofs. About 53.6% of all households had electricity and 50% had access to piped water. Only 25% of all households have access to improved sanitation systems.

43 EDUCATION

The state governments are responsible for the provision of education. Elementary education is compulsory and free up to the eighth grade or until age 15. Free secondary education is offered for those who pass a qualifying examination. Secondary education was provided through five public high schools (one in each state center and one in Falalop on the Ulithi atoll, serving Yap's outer islands) and five private secondary schools (two in Chuuk and three in Pohnpei).

The only postsecondary institution is the College of Micronesia (COM), which has five campus locations and offers two-year programs in business, teaching, accounting, marine science, and hospitality and tourism. FSM students are eligible for postsecondary education grants from the US government and attend institutions mainly in Guam, Hawaii, and the US mainland. Vocational education is provided by the Pohnpei Agriculture and Trade School and the Micronesian Occupational College in Palau.

A 2000 census report indicated that of all citizens aged 25 years or older, 12.3% had no formal schooling, 36% had completed only an elementary school education, 32.3% had completed their high school education, and about 18.4% had completed some college education. Overall, the CIA estimated that Micronesia had a literacy rate of 89%.

⁴⁴LIBRARIES AND MUSEUMS

Library materials are contained in the primary and secondary schools and at the College of Micronesia, which holds about 33,000 volumes and serves as the depository for documents from the trust territory government's archives in Saipan. The Pohnpei Public Library has about 30,000 books. The library of the Congress of the Federated States of Micronesia holds 15,000 volumes. There is a small museum in Kolonia, Pohnpei. The Nan Madol archaeological site was designated a historical landmark in 1986.

⁴⁵MEDIA

The FSM Telecommunications Corp. provides interstate telecommunications via its satellite ground station in each state center and international connections through the Pohnpei and Chuuk stations. An interstate and international telex service has been available through the Pohnpei station since 1984. Telecommunications services to all inhabited outer islands are provided by radio links with the Pohnpei, Chuuk, and Yap stations. In 2009 there were 8,700 main phone lines and 38,000 mobile cell phones in use nationwide, with an average of 34 mobile phone subscribers per 100 people. Internet users numbered 15 per 100 citizens.

As of 2011 there were five FM radio stations and one AM radio station, plus three television broadcast stations. Cable television is also available. In 1997 there were 127 radios and 10 television sets per 1,000 people. In 2010 the country had 3,097 Internet hosts. In 2009 there were 15 Internet users per 100 people.

Most of the papers and newsletters are sponsored by the state governments. The *National Union* is published fortnightly by the federal government. The *Kaselehile Press* of Pohnpei State is published fortnightly and available online. The constitution provides for free speech and a free press, and the government is said to respect these rights in practice.

⁴⁶ORGANIZATIONS

There are Community Action Agencies in Yap, Chuuk, and Pohnpei, which organize youth clubs and community self-help projects. Private institutions, most of them church-affiliated, play an active role in youth and community development. There are sports associations representing such pastimes as weightlifting, lawn tennis, tae kwon do, and track and field. Many municipalities sponsor local women's organizations and community centers. There is a national chapter of the Red Cross Society.

⁴⁷TOURISM, TRAVEL, AND RECREATION

Limited tourist facilities have been developed in each state. Tourist attractions include the spectacular beauty of the high islands; the rich marine environment; World War II artifacts, including sunken Japanese ships in the Chuuk lagoon; and remains of an ancient culture on Yap Island, including stone platforms and large circular stones used as money. All visitors must have an onward/return ticket and a present proof of citizenship or passport valid for 120 days after leaving Micronesia. A valid entry permit is also necessary if staying for more than 30 days. There are no vaccination requirements unless traveling from an infected area.

The nation hosted about 22,000 visitors in 2008. The estimated daily cost to visit Palikir was $177. The cost of visiting other cities averaged $190 per day.

⁴⁸FAMOUS PERSONS

John Haglelgam (b. 1949), a former senator in the congress, was president of the FSM from 1987 to 1991. Jacob Nena (b. 1941) served as the fourth president from 1996 to 1999. Leo Falcam (b. 1935) served as the fifth president from 1999 to 2003. He was succeeded by Joseph John Urusemal (b. 1952). In 2000 FSM's first five-story building (and first building with an elevator) opened; it was named for Raymond Setik (d. 1997), a successful businessman and one of the first members of the legislature in 1979.

⁴⁹DEPENDENCIES

The FSM has no territories or colonies.

⁵⁰BIBLIOGRAPHY

Gillespie, Rosemary G., and David A. Clague, eds. *Encyclopedia of Islands.* Berkeley: University of California Press, 2009.

Hezel, Francis X. *The New Shape of Old Island Cultures: A Half Century of Social Change in Micronesia.* Honolulu: University of Hawaii Press, 2001.

Kirch, Patrick Vinton, and Jean-Louis Rallu. *The Growth and Collapse of Pacific Island Societies.* Honolulu: University of Hawaii Press, 2007.

Levesque, Rodrigue, ed. *History of Micronesia.* 20 vols. Honolulu: University of Hawaii Press, 2008.

Micronesia Investment and Business Guide: Strategic and Practical Information. Washington, DC: International Business Publications USA, 2012.

Poyer, Lin. *The Typhoon of War: Micronesian Experiences of the Pacific War.* Honolulu: University of Hawaii Press, 2001.

Rainbird, Paul. *The Archaeology of Micronesia.* New York: Cambridge University Press, 2004.

Zabus, Chantal J., and Silvia Nagy. *Colonization or Globalization: Postcolonial Explorations of Imperial Expansion.* Lanham, MD: Lexington Books, 2010.

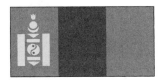

MONGOLIA

Mongol Uls

CAPITAL: Ulaanbaatar

FLAG: The national flag, adopted in 1946, contains a blue vertical stripe between two red stripes; in gold, on the stripe nearest the hoist, is the *soyombo*, Mongolia's national emblem. The *soyombo* is a columnar arrangement of abstract and geometric representations for fire, sun, moon, earth, water and the yin-yang symbol. The blue represents the sky while the red represents progress and prosperity.

ANTHEM: *Mongol Ulsyn Toriin Duulal (National Anthem of Mongolia).*

MONETARY UNIT: The Tugrug/Tugrik (MNT) is the official currency. Notes come in denominations of 10000; 5000; 1000; 500; 100; 50; 20; 10; 5; and 3. Coins come in 200; 100; 50 and 20. MNT1 = US$0.00072595 (or US$1 = MNT1,377.50) as of 2011.

WEIGHTS AND MEASURES: The metric system is the legal standard.

HOLIDAYS: New Year's Day, 1 January; International Women's Day, 8 March; Mother's and Children's Day, 1 June; Nadaam (National Day), 11–13 July; and Independence Day, 26 November. In addition, the government declared 29 December 2011 a public holiday in celebration of the 100th anniversary of the National Liberation Revolution; and Tsaagan (Mongol New Year) is celebrated in February or March.

TIME: 8 p.m. = noon GMT, in central and eastern Mongolia, and 7 p.m. = noon GMT in western Mongolia.

¹LOCATION, SIZE, AND EXTENT

Mongolia is located in northern Asian between China and Russia. It has an area of 1,565,000 sq km (604,250 sq mi), extending 2,368 km (1,471 mi) E–W and 1,260 km (783 mi) N–S. It is the seventh largest country in Asia and the 19th largest in the world. Its surface area is slightly smaller than the state of Alaska, and about the same as France, Germany, Holland, Belgium, Spain, and Portugal combined.

The largest landlocked country in the world, Mongolia is bordered on the N by Russia and on the E, S, and W by China, with a total boundary length of 8,220 km (5,108 mi).

²TOPOGRAPHY

The topography of Mongolia features vast semidesert and desert plains, with an average elevation of 914 m to 1,524 m (3,000 to 5,000 ft), as well as a grassy steppe area, mountains in the west and southwest, and the Gobi Desert in the south central part of the country. Its lowest point is Hoh Nuur at 560 m (1,837 ft) and the highest point is Nayramadlin Orgil (Huyten Orgil) at 4,374 m (14,350 ft).

The Altai mountains in the west extend in an arc that reaches the Gobi Desert. The Khangai mountains run through the central part of the country and are the source of the Selenge River, which is Mongolia's largest river. The river flows into Lake Baikal, a gigantic inland sea that extends across the northern border into Russia's Siberia. The Khentii mountains stretch to the east of the capital and feature abundant forests.

Numerous lakes, rivers, streams and springs are located in the north. The Khovsgol lake in northwest Mongolia is an immense blue lake 135 km (84 mi) long and 35 km (21.75 mi) wide.

The north and west parts of the country include good pasture areas, meadows, steppes, and forests. The south, by contrast, is primarily sagging plates and desert. The east includes vast steppes and plains.

³CLIMATE

Mongolia is known as "the land of blue sky" and averages about 250 sunny days a year. It enjoys warm summers and long, dry, and cold winters. Temperatures in most of the country are below freezing from November to March, and just above freezing in October and April. Winter night temperatures of -40°C (-40°F) are common. Summer temperatures can reach 40°C (104°F) in the Gobi Desert and 33°C (91°F) in Ulaanbaatar.

Winters often are dry and snowless. Most rainfall occurs in the summer months as remnants of the southeasterly monsoon pass through the country. Annual precipitation ranges from 25 to 38 cm (10 to 15 in) in mountain areas to less than 10 cm (4 in) in the Gobi.

⁴FLORA AND FAUNA

The World Resources Institute estimates that there are 2,823 plant species in Mongolia. In addition, Mongolia is home to 140 species of mammals, 387 species of birds, 23 species of reptiles, and 8 species of amphibians. The calculation reflects the total number of distinct species residing in the country, not the number of endemic species.

Urbanization, illegal hunting, mineral extraction, and livestock herding all have posed threats to Mongolia's wildlife since the early 1990s. About 30% of the territory has protected area status, but many species have experienced dramatic declines. Among the threatened species are the Bactrian camel and long-eared jerboa, which inhabit the Gobi Desert; and the Saiga antelope, which inhabits the western mountains. Several birds, rodents, reptiles, and amphibians also are threatened.

Protected areas included 11 Ramsar wetland sites. According to a 2011 report issued by the International Union for Conservation of Nature and Natural Resources (IUCN), threatened species included 11 types of mammals, 20 species of birds, 1 species of fish, and 3 species of invertebrates. Przewalski's horse (also called takh) is considered to be the last existing ancestor of the modern domesticated horse. The species was extinct in the wild of Mongolia by 1970, but a special government project of breeding the remaining animals in captivity has resulted in more than 1,500 horses reintroduced to a nature reserve at Hustain Nuruu.

⁵ENVIRONMENT

The World Resources Institute reported that Mongolia had designated 21.79 million hectares (53.85 million acres) of land for protection as of 2006. Water resources totaled 34.8 cu km (8.35 cu mi) while water usage was 0.44 cu km (0.106 cu mi) per year. Domestic water usage accounted for 21% of total usage, industrial for 27%, and agricultural for 52%. Per capita water usage totaled 166 cu m (5,862 cu ft) per year.

The United Nations (UN) reported in 2008 that carbon dioxide emissions in Mongolia totaled 10,574 kilotons.

The World Bank reported in 2011 that hundreds of rivers and lakes had disappeared in Mongolia, and that the diversity of plant species had plummeted by a third since 1997. Other experts have noted that climate change has resulted in longer and colder winters as well as drier summers.

The government of Mongolia has expressed a public commitment to restoring and protecting its natural resources. However, the US State Department reports that rapid urbanization and industrial growth policies have caused the environment to deteriorate. Burning of soft coal by homeowners, power plants, and factories in Ulaanbaatar has severely polluted the air. Overgrazing, increased crop production and mining development have cause soil erosion and water pollution. The government has established a restoration fund that is financed by polluter fees. It also has initiated several sustainable energy projects to reduce its reliance on its aging power plants.

Mongolia is party to international environmental agreements on biodiversity, climate change, desertification, endangered species, environmental modification, hazardous wastes, law of the sea, ozone layer protection, ship pollution, wetlands, and whaling.

⁶POPULATION

The US Central Intelligence Agency (CIA) estimates the population of Mongolia in 2011 to be approximately 3,133,318, which placed it at number 133 in population among the 196 nations of the world. In 2011, approximately 4% of the population was over 65 years of age, with another 27.3% under 15 years of age. The median age in Mongolia was 26.2 years. There were 1.00 males for every female in the country. The population's annual rate of change was 1.489%. The projected population for the year 2025 was 3,300,000. Population density in Mongolia was calculated at 2 people per sq km (5 people per sq mi).

The UN estimated that 62% of the population lived in urban areas, and that urban populations had an annual rate of change of 1.9%. The largest urban area was Ulaanbaatar, with a population of 949,000.

⁷MIGRATION

Estimates of Mongolia's net migration rate, carried out by the CIA in 2011, amounted to zero. The total number of emigrants living abroad was 32,100, and the total number of immigrants living in Mongolia was 10,000.

Between 1955 and 1962, some 20,000 Chinese laborers entered Mongolia to work on construction projects, but in 1964 Mongolia expelled about 2,000 Chinese nationals who had refused to take part in an agricultural resettlement program. In addition, Mongolia expelled 7,000 ethnic Chinese between 1983 and 1993. The independence of Kazakhstan in 1991 prompted thousands of ethnic Kazakh Mongolians to emigrate to Kazakhstan, but according to the UN High Commission on Refugees many of these individuals returned to Mongolia and were designated as stateless after being unable to gain Kazakhstani citizenship.

Mongolia's people traditionally were nomadic. A paper presented at the 25–29 May 2007 8th International Conference of Asia Pacific Migration Research Network in Fuzhou, Fujain province, China, reported that the nomadic tradition became more tied to work opportunities in the 20th century as Mongolia was governed by various Communist regimes. Rapid industrialization, the collectivization of agriculture, and urbanization brought many people from rural to urban areas during these years. Following the collapse of communism, the trend reversed as people began returning to rural areas. In the first decade of the 21st century, the trend shifted again with more migration to cities.

According to the paper, Mongolians in the early 21st century have migrated, often illegally, to South Korea, China, Japan, and the United States.

⁸ETHNIC GROUPS

According to the US State Department, ethnic Mongols made up 95% of Mongolia's population. The bulk of that population was Khalkha. Other groups were present and distinctions could be made among the various ethnic Mongols on the basis of linguistic dialect. The non-Khalkha population included Dorvod, Tuvan, and Buriat Mongols in the north and Dariganga Mongols in the east.

Turkic groups including Kazakhs, Turvins, and Khotans made up 5% of Mongolia's population, along with Tungusic speakers.

⁹LANGUAGES

Khalkha Mongol is used by 90% of the population. Russian and Turkic are also used. Mongol derives from the Altaic Mountain of Central Asia, and is a language family comprised of Turkic, Tungusic, and Mongolic subfamilies with some relation to Turkic, Korean, and possibly Japanese.

Early in the 13th century, the Mongols adopted an alphabet written in vertical columns from the Turkic Uighurs. The literary language differed increasingly from the living spoken language

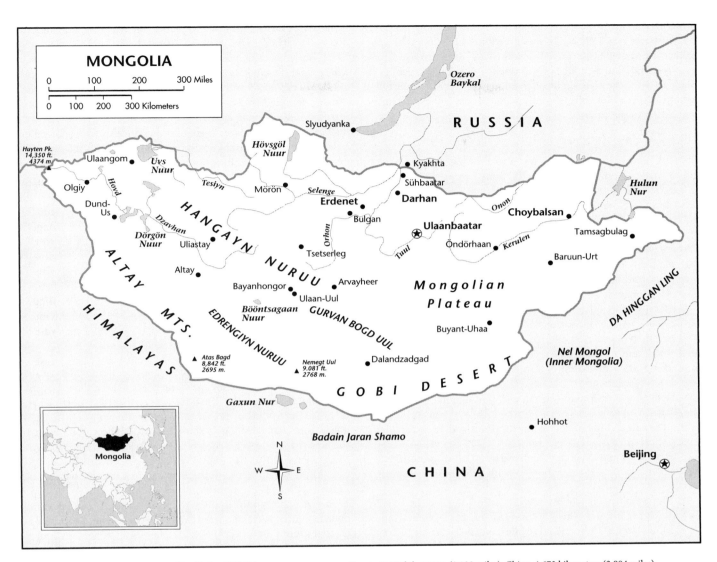

LOCATION: 87°47′ to 119°54′E 41°31′ to 52°16′N. BOUNDARY LENGTHS: Russia, 3,441 kilometers (2,138 miles); China, 4,673 kilometers (2,904 miles).

and, in 1941, the Mongolian government decided to introduce a new phonetic alphabet that would accurately reflect modern spoken Mongolian. The new alphabet consisted of the Cyrillic letters used in Russian, except for two special characters needed to render the Mongolian vowels represented as ö and ü in Western European languages. After a period of preparation (1941–45), the new alphabet was introduced in 1946 in all publications and in 1950 in all business transactions, but, following independence, some began to call for a return to the traditional Mongolian script. The differences between the Khalkha language spoken in Mongolia, the Buryat language spoken in the Buryat Republic of the Russian Federation, the Chahar and Ordos languages of China's Inner Mongolian Autonomous Region, and other Mongolian dialects are comparatively small and chiefly phonetic. A characteristic phonetic feature of Mongolian is the law of vowel harmony, which requires that a word contain either the so-called back vowels, represented as a, o, and u in Western European languages, or the so-called front vowels, represented as e (ä), ö, and ü, but not an association of the two types of vowels.

10 RELIGIONS

The US State Department's 2010 International Religious Freedom Report on Mongolia stated that more than 90% of Mongolia's citizens follow some form of Buddhism, although religious practices varied widely. The Lamaist Buddhist of the Tibetan tradition was practiced most dominantly.

Ethnic Kazakhs generally practiced Islam, and the Mongolian Muslim Association estimated that 120,000 Kazakh Muslims and 30,000 Khoton Muslims resided in the country. Christians accounted for about 4% of the population. Some practices of shamanism were followed.

There were 253 Buddhist temples, 223 Christian churches, and 41 Muslim mosques registered with the government.

Before the government's campaign against religion in the 1930s, there were 700 Buddhist monasteries with about 100,000 lamas in Mongolia. During 1936–39, the Communist regime closed virtually all monasteries, confiscated their livestock and landholdings, tried the higher lamas for counterrevolutionary activities, and induced thousands of lower lamas to adopt a secular mode of life. In the mid-1980s, only about 100 lamas remained. When the constitution of 1992 established freedom of religion, Mahayana Buddhism made a surprising resurgence. Former monasteries were restored, and a seminary was opened at Gandantegchinlen Hiyd. In 1992, Roman Catholic missionaries were also encouraged to come to Mongolia to continue the presence they had initiated earlier in the century.

11 TRANSPORTATION

The CIA reports that Mongolia has a total of 49,249 km (30,602 mi) of roads, of which 3,015 km (1,873 mi) are paved. There are 72 vehicles per 1,000 people in the country. Railroads extend for 1,814 km (1,127 mi). There are 46 airports, which transported 257,233 passengers in 2009 according to the World Bank. Mongolia has approximately 580 km (360 mi) of navigable waterways.

There were 14 airports with paved runways in 2009. There was also one heliport. Mongolia's first air service began operating between Ulaanbaatar and Verkhneudinsk in eastern Siberia in 1926. Miat-Air Mongol is the principal airline.

The Trans-Mongolian Railway connects Mongolia with both China and Russia. Ulaanbaatar has been connected to the Trans-Siberian Railway via Bayantümen since 1939 and via Sühbaatar since 1950, and to the Chinese Railways via Dzamïn üüd since the end of 1955. Choybalsan is also connected to the Trans-Siberian system via Ereenstav. Ulaanbaatar Railways has been linked to Nalayh since 1938 and to Darhan and Tamsagbulag since 1964. The Sharïn Gol Open-Pit Coal Mining Industry was connected to the Darhan industrial center during the third five-year plan (1961–65) by a 60-km (37-mi) rail line. A 200-km (124-mi) rail line connects Erdenet, a copper-molybdenum mining and industrial center near the Russian border, with the Trans-Mongolian Railway.

Of Mongolia's navigable waterways, only Lake Hovsgol (135 km) was in regular use. The 270 km (168 mi) Selenge River and the 175 km (109 mi) Orhon River, while navigable, carry little traffic. In addition, the country's lakes and rivers are only open from May through September due to freezing in winter. Although landlocked, Mongolia, as of 2008, had a merchant fleet of 77 vessels of 1,000 gross registered tons or more.

12 HISTORY

Archaeological investigations show that the land now known as Mongolia has been inhabited since the Lower Paleolithic period, more than 130,000 years ago. By about 1000 BC, animal husbandry of the nomadic type had developed, and by the 3rd century BC, a clan style of organization based on horsemanship had emerged. The Huns, a Turkic-speaking people, driven westward during the Han dynasty in China (206 BC–AD 220), created a nomadic empire in central Asia that extended into Europe, beginning about ad 370. It reached almost to Rome under the leadership of Attila (r. 433?–453) and declined after his death.

A single Mongolian state was formed based on nomadic tribal groupings under Genghis ("Chinggis") Khan in 1206. He and his immediate successors conquered nearly all of Asia and European Russia, and sent armies into central Europe and Southeast Asia. The Mongols set up their capital at Karakorum.

After the death of Genghis Khan in 1227, his empire was divided among his sons into Mongol states, or khanates: the Great Khanate of East Asia, which included the Yüan dynasty of China, and reached its peak under Kublai Khan (r. 1260–94), who established his capital at Cambaluc (now Beijing); the Khanate of Chaghadai (Djakhatai) in Turkestan; the Hulagid Khanate, founded by Hulagu Khan in Persia; and the Golden Horde in southern Russia, founded by Batu Khan, who invaded Poland and Hungary in 1240. Having crossed the Danube River, Batu withdrew in 1241. The Mongols' century of dominance in Asia allowed for great trade and cultural interchange but also led to the spread of the bubonic plague to Europe.

The Mongol states disintegrated in the 14th century. The Yüan dynasty in China collapsed in 1368, to be replaced by the Ming dynasty; the western part of the Turkestan Khanate was incorporated into the empire of Timur in 1390; Hulagu's Persian empire disintegrated after 1335; and the Golden Horde was attacked and shaken by the forces of Prince Dmitry Donskoy in Russia in 1380 but ruled South Russia into the 15th century. In 1369, at the age of 33, Timur, also called Timur Lenk ("Timur the Lame") or Tamerlane, proclaimed himself ruler of all the land lying between the Tien Shan and the Hindu Kush mountain ranges. Babur, a descendant of Timur, founded the Mughal (or Mogul) Empire (from the Farsi word for "Mongol") in India in 1526; it lasted until the 18th century.

With the downfall of the Mongol states, the ethnic Mongols returned to their original steppe homelands, where they split into three major groups: the Khalkha Mongols settled north of the Gobi Desert into an area that came to be known as Outer Mongolia; The Chahar Mongols settled south of the Gobi Desert in the area that came to be known as Inner Mongolia; and the Oirat Mongols moved to the west. Buddhism, which had been introduced by Tibetan monks in the 15th century, became widespread in the 16th and 17th centuries.

The Manchus conquered China in 1644 and formed the Qing dynasty. After a cleavage developed between the Khalkha and Chahar groups, nobles of the Khalkha groups swore an oath of allegiance to the Manchu emperor. The Manchus gained control of the northern and southern Mongolian areas, but under the oath of allegiance, the Khalkha tribe enjoyed considerable autonomy in Outer Mongolia, which was a Chinese province from 1691 through the end of the Qing dynasty in 1911.

Russia and China signed the Treaty of Khiakta in 1727, which delimited the border between China and Mongolia, and assigned the western Buryat region to Russia. The Manchus finally destroyed the western Mongols in 1758.

As Manchu power waned, Russia and Japan confronted each other. Russia provided military and diplomatic support to Mongol nationalists in Outer Mongolia. A Chinese revolt overthrew the Manchus in 1911 and the Mongols of Outer Mongolia proclaimed independence from Chinese rule.

Outer Mongolia signed a treaty with Russia's tsarist government to continue acceptance of Russian assistance for the autonomous state. This made Outer Mongolia an autonomous state under Russian protection from 1912–19. After the Bolshevik Revolution, the Chinese exploited Russia's weakness, and reoccupied Outer Mongolia in 1919.

Soviet military victories over White Russian forces in the early 1920s brought the Soviets into the then-Mongolian capital of Urgoo in July 21. Mongol revolutionary leaders Sukhe Baatar and

Khorloin Choybalsan received assistance from the Soviet Red Army to establish a constitutional monarchy, which with the death of a religious figure known as the Living Buddha, became on 25 November 1924 the Mongolian People's Republic.

The Mongolian People's Revolutionary Party consolidated its power as a communist regime between 1925 and 1928. Mongolia during the time period was a nomadic society with widespread illiteracy and none of the industrial proletariat that was said to be characteristic of communist states. Wealth was shared by an aristocratic and religious elite, and the new governing leaders had little experience. The revolutionary leaders confiscated large feudal landholdings, and carried out religious purges between 1932 and 1945 that resulted in the desecration of hundreds of Buddhist institutions and the imprisonment of more than 10,000 people. These actions produced a series of anti-communist uprisings.

The Soviet Union and Mongolian People's Republic formed a 10-year mutual assistance treaty in 1936, which was renewed for an additional 10 years in 1945. Mongolians used Soviet support to defeat Japanese forces along the Mongolian-Manchurian border in the eastern part of the country.

After a virtually unanimous plebiscite by the Mongolians in favor of independence, the Nationalist government of the Republic of China formally recognized the Mongolian People's Republic in 1945 (it withdrew its recognition in 1953 and nationalists in Taiwan still claim Mongolia as part of China). On 14 February 1950, the People's Republic of China and the former USSR signed a treaty that guaranteed Mongolia's independence. In October 1961, Mongolia became a member of the UN.

The Mongolian government, with strong Soviet backing, began the post-World War II era with a focus on civilian enterprise. It established relationships with North Korea and the new communist governments of Eastern Europe. As tensions developed between the Soviet Union and People's Republic of China, Mongolia initially tried to maintain a neutral position. China and Mongolia settled boundary disputes on 26 December 1962, and the Soviet Union and Mongolia signed a 20-year treaty of friendship, cooperation, and mutual assistance on 30 June 1964. However, in 1966, it signed an agreement with the Soviet Union that brought Soviet ground forces into the country as part of a Soviet buildup along the Sino-Soviet frontier. Mongolian society during this time period also underwent a significant transformation, shifting from being 78% rural in 1956 to being 52% urban by 1980. Much of its development was due to labor from ethnic Chinese, 7,000 of whom had been sent to Mongolia to assist with construction projects. Mongolia's relationships with China began to deteriorate in the 1960s, however, and in 1983, Mongolia began expelling ethnic Chinese.

Mongolia established diplomatic relations with the US on 27 January 1987. As the Soviet polices of *glasnot* (openness) and *perestroika* (restructuring) took hold, democratic activism in Mongolia took root with popular reform demonstrations occurring in December 1989. The Mongolian Democratic Association was formed and large-scale demonstrations took place through 1990. The government introduced economic reforms and on 2 March 1990, announced with the Soviet Union that all Soviet troops would be withdrawn from Mongolia by 1992. The constitution, which had been ratified in 1960, was amended to allow for multi-party elections to be held on 29 July 1990.

The governing party, the Mongolian People's Revolutionary Party (MPRP), won a majority (85% of the seats) in the legislature, the People's Great Hural (PGH), which took office in September. The PGH elected as president a member of the MPRP, Punsalmaagiyn Ochirbat, but invited the opposition parties to join in forming the new government.

During 1991, the new government discussed Mongolia's economic and political transformation. It issued vouchers to all citizens for the purchase of state property as a step toward privatization. Economic reform was made more difficult by the collapse of the Soviet Union. In 1991, Russia insisted on trade based on cash rather than barter and dramatically cut aid. In 1991, the PGH also discussed the writing of a new constitution, which took effect in February of the next year. Based on that constitution, elections in June 1992 created a new legislature (with a MPRP majority), and the State Great Hural (SGH). By September 1992, all troops from the former Soviet Union had withdrawn from the country. In June 1993, President Ochirbat was reelected (but with the support of a coalition of new parties, not the MPRP) in the first direct presidential elections.

Mongolia's transition from a one-party authoritarian government to a more democratic multi-party system presented challenges to the society in the 1990s as established elites attempted to retain power while younger, democratically oriented political novices agitated for reforms to continue at a faster pace.

In the 1996 parliamentary elections, discontent, especially among the young, led to the defeat of the MPRP. The leaders of the winning Democratic Union Coalition (DUC), mostly political novices, promised to intensify market reforms. The election results marked the first smooth transfer of power in Mongolia's modern history and one of the most peaceful among all the former communist nations. In the following years, however, the stability and effectiveness of Mongolia's democratic government were hobbled by disunity within the majority DUC and by the political stalemate between the DUC and the ex-communists of the opposition MPRP. In late 1996 and early 1997, the MPRP prevailed in local elections, and its candidate, Natsagiyn Bagabandi, was elected president. After the resignation of two prime ministers, the nation was left with an interim government in the second half of 1998, as Bagabandi rejected multiple DUC nominees for the post. By August 1999, yet another DUC government had fallen, and Rinchinnyamiin Amarjargal, the 38-year-old former foreign minister, became Mongolia's third prime minister in 15 months.

On 2 July 2000, parliamentary elections were held that resulted in an overwhelming victory for the MPRP. The MPRP took 72 of 76 seats in the State Great Hural, with only 4 seats going to opposition members. Nambaryn Enkhbayar was named prime minister. On 20 May 2001, Bagabandi was reelected president with 58% of the vote, giving the MPRP control of both the presidency and parliament. The elections were characterized by international observers as free and fair. MPRP candidate Nambariin Enkhbayar was elected president in May 2005.

In 2006 the MPRP ministers resigned from the coalition government, blaming government leaders for slow economic growth. A new coalition government was formed, led by the MPRP with the participation of four smaller parties, and Miyeegombo Enkhbold was named prime minister. Enkhbold resigned on October 2007 and was replaced by Sanjaa Bayar. In parliamentary elections in June 2008, the MPRP retained control. However, the Democratic Party claimed that the polls had been rigged and protesters took to the streets. The ensuing violence led to five deaths and hundreds of injuries. President Enkhbayar called a four-day state of emergency to end the riots. The Democratic Party prevailed in the 2009 presidential elections when party leader Tsakhiagiin Elbegdorj gained a narrow victory over the incumbent Nambaryn Enkhbayer. Elbegdorj campaigned with an anti-corruption platform.

On 29 October 2009, the Mongolian parliament approved Sukhbaatar Batbold as prime minister. Batbold, the country's former foreign minister and one of the richest men in Mongolia, replaced Sanjaagiin Bayar, who voluntarily stepped down due to liver problems. The new prime minister pledged to support a pro-business platform that capitalizes on Mongolia's rich resources and the increasingly fierce global demand for them. The ruling party's support of Batbold was so great that only one of its 180-member leadership did not back his bid for the premiership.

In April 2010, more than 5,000 protesters swarmed the streets of Ulaanbaatar demanding the dissolution of the country's parliament. The majority of the protesters came from rural and poor areas around the capital, where they acutely felt the country's poverty and strained social services. Protest organizers and activists expressed frustration that the government has failed to alleviate poverty and fulfill promises made during the 2008 campaign. During the run-up to the 2008 election, both dominant political parties promised to distribute the country's significant mining revenue through grants or a fund similar to the Alaska Permanent Fund, which pays Alaska residents for the oil revenue that the state earns.

As of 2011, Mongolia was the world's least densely populated country. The country was largely agrarian with more than 800,000 herders. A severe winter in 2010 resulted in the death of about 17% of its livestock, and while the country possesses great mineral and mining riches, 22% of its people lived on $1.25 a day or less, and 29% were undernourished. According to The New York Times, Mongolia's leaders believed democracy would ultimately allow the country to prosper.

Parliamentary elections were to take place in 2012.

13 GOVERNMENT

Mongolia's government is a mixed parliamentary/presidential system. A constitution that took effect 12 February 1992 replaced a constitution that had been in effect since 1960. The executive branch consists of a president and prime minister, and the legislative branch consists of a 76-member unicameral body known as the State Great Hural. The president is elected by popular election, and the prime minister is nominated by the president and confirmed by the State Great Hural.

The State Great Hural enacts and amends laws, sets domestic and foreign policy, ratifies international agreements, and has the power to declare a state of emergency. It meets semi-annually for 3–4 month sessions. Its members are popularly elected by district to four year terms. Its members elect a chairman and vice chairman, both of whom serve for four years. The parliamentary body cannot be dissolved.

The president serves as head of state, commander in chief of the armed forces, and as head of the National Security Council. The president is elected for four years and is limited to two terms. The president can call for the government's dissolution in consultation with the State Great Hural chairman, initiate legislation, veto legislation, and issue decrees which become effective after the prime minister signs them.

The prime minister heads the government, serves a four-year term, and is empowered to choose a cabinet.

The government can be dissolved with the prime minister's resignation, simultaneous resignation of half the cabinet, or after the State Great Hural votes for dissolution.

Elections for the State Great Hural were scheduled to take place in June 2012 and for the president in May 2013.

14 POLITICAL PARTIES

There were 17 political parties in Mongolia as of December 2011.

They included the Mongolian People's Party (which changed its name from the Mongolian People's Revolutionary Party in 2010 and has served as the ruling party for much of independent Mongolia's history); a new Mongolian People's Revolutionary Party; the Democratic Party; the Motherland-Mongolian Democratic New Socialist Party; the New National Party; the Civil Will Party; the Mongolian Green Party; the Mongolian Traditional United Party; the Mongol Liberal Democratic Party; the Republican Party; the Mongolian Women's National Party; the Mongolian Liberal Party; the Mongolian Social Democratic Party; the Freedom Implementing Party; the Civil Movement Party; the Development Program Party; and the Motherland Party.

The Mongolian People's Party (formerly the MPRP) was the single ruling party under the former communist regime from 1924–92. It legalized opposition parties in 1990. The largest opposition parties were the Democratic Party (DP), established in 2000 through the merger of Mongolian National Democratic Party (MNDP) and the Mongolian Social Democratic Party (MSDP).

In the first election for the State Great Hural (SGH) 28 June 1992, the MPRP won 56.9% of the vote and 71 of 76 seats in the SGH. In the first direct presidential election, 6 June 1993, President Punsalmaagiyn Ochirbat (first elected president 3 September 1990) was reelected with 58% of the vote. A former member of the MPRP, Ochirbat defeated that party's candidate, running as head of a coalition of the MSDP and MNDP.

In the elections of 30 June 1996, the Democratic Union Coalition (which included the MNDP, the MSDP, and two smaller parties) defeated the MPRP, winning 50 of 76 seats (an increase of 44 seats). The MPRP won 25 seats, and the remaining seat went to the MCP.

In the July 2000 parliamentary elections, MRPR candidates won 72 or the 76 seats, with the remaining 4 seats won (one each) by MNDP, the Civil Courage Party or Civil Will Party (CWP) in alliance with the Mongolian Green, the Motherland Alliance (the Mongol Democratic New Socialist Party and the Mongolian Labor Party), and an independent nonpartisan candidate.

General elections held in 2004 resulted in an impasse, as neither the MPRP nor the main opposition, the Motherland Democratic Party (MDP), held the 39 seats required to form a government. The MPRP was dealt a devastating blow with a reduction in parliamentary seats from 72 to 36. Electoral fraud was suspected on the part of the MDC and a recount was ordered. Parliament was not able to meet for the first half of 2004 as neither side wished to pursue legislation while the electoral investigation was ongoing. In August, the MPRP formed a coalition with the MDC and Tsakhilganiin Elbegdorj retained his post of prime minister for a second term.

In the 29 June 2008 parliamentary elections, the Mongolian People's Party won a majority with 46 seats in the SGH, with the Democratic Party winning 27 seats. The Civil Will party won one seat. Sukhbaatar Batbold of the Mongolian People's Party was named prime minister. Former prime minister Tsakhilganiin Elbegdorj of the Democratic Party was elected president in 2009 with 51.2% of the vote.

15 LOCAL GOVERNMENT

Mongolia administratively consists of 21 provinces (*aymag*), divided into 334 counties (*soums*) and lesser administrative units called *baghs*, as well as one autonomous city, Ulaanbaatar, which is divided into districts and *horoos*. Each level of local administration has its own legislative body, or *hural*. These *hurals* nominate the provincial governors, who are then appointed by the prime minister.

16 JUDICIAL SYSTEM

Prior to the 1992 constitution, justice was administered through a Supreme Court elected by the People's Great Hural; province and city courts, elected by the corresponding assemblies of people's deputies; and lower courts. The 17-member Supreme Court remains the highest judicial body with a Constitutional Court vested with sole authority for constitutional review. The local courts (people's courts) handle most routine civil and criminal cases. Provincial courts hear more serious cases and review local court decisions. The Supreme Court hears appeals from the local and provincial courts. The old specialized military justice and railway courts have been abolished. All courts are now organized under a single unified national system.

The General Council of Courts nominates and the president appoints the lower and the Supreme Court judges. The new constitution provides for a completely independent judiciary. It also promises procedural due process rights to a fair trial, legal assistance, right to appeal, and access to requests for pardons.

17 ARMED FORCES

The International Institute for Strategic Studies reports that armed forces in Mongolia totaled 10,000 members in 2011. The force is comprised of 8,900 from the army, 800 from the air force, and 300 construction troops. Armed forces represent 1.2% of the labor force in Mongolia. Defense spending totaled $154.9 million and accounted for 1.4% of gross domestic product (GDP).

18 INTERNATIONAL COOPERATION

Mongolia joined the UN on 27 October 1961. It is a member of the World Trade Organization, Asian Development Bank, Colombo Plan, European Bank for Reconstruction and Development, the ASEAN Regional Forum, the Pacific Economic Cooperation Council, and was seeking to join the Asian Pacific Economic

Council in 2011. It also has observer status in the Shanghai Cooperation Organization but does not intend to seek membership, and began a two-year chairmanship of the Community of Democracies in July 2011. Mongolia also serves on the UN's Economic and Social Council.

Mongolia's principal ally from 1961–1990 was the Union of Soviet Socialist Republics, which provided substantial economic and military assistance, although it developed relationships with other nations including North Korea and most of the former eastern European Communist bloc nations. Following the disintegration of the Soviet Union, Mongolia began to pursue a more independent and nonaligned foreign policy. Since 1991, it has formed strong ties with Russia, Japan, South Korea, the United States and the European Union. The US government recognized Mongolia in January 1987, and established an embassy in Ulaanbaatar in June 1988.

Mongolia began to normalize relations with China in 1986, by establishing a five-year trade agreement between the two countries, restoring air service and improving rail service between them, and exchanging consular delegations for the first time. China was the largest foreign investor in Mongolia, as of 2011.

Mongolia hosted a closed meeting between two Six-Party members, North Korea, and Japan in 2007, and hosted the planning meeting of the Asia-Pacific Democracy Partnership in Ulaanbaatar on 1 July 2008. It also has been host to a regional workshop of the Comprehensive Nuclear Test Ban Treaty Organization in March 2010 and to the Asia Pacific Parliamentary Forum in January 2011. Mongolia became chair of the Board of Governors of the International Atomic Energy Agency in September 2010.

Russia and Mongolia have renewed military ties through education, joint exercises focused on repairing Mongolia's Soviet-built equipment , and in December 2010 an expansion of training exchange programs.

19 ECONOMY

The GDP rate of change in Mongolia, as of 2010, was 6.1%. Inflation stood at 13%, and unemployment was reported at 11.5%.

With the growth of cities around the mining industry, Mongolian society shifted from being 78% rural in 1956 to being 52% urban in 1980, to 57% urban in 2005, and 62% urban in 2010. The CIA estimated the rate of urbanization to be 1.9% for 2010–15.

Economic activity in Mongolia traditionally was based on herding and agriculture, and agriculture was estimated to have accounted for 19.7% of GDP and to have employed 34% of the labor force in 2010. However, the country also holds extensive copper, gold, coal, molybdenum, fluorspar, uranium, tin, and tungsten deposits. This wealth of minerals began to attract foreign investment in the first decade of the 21st century. Mining and related industrial activity accounted for an estimated 35% of GDP in 2010 and employed 5% of the labor force. Services accounted for 45.2% of GDP, based on 2010 estimates, and employed about 61% of the labor force.

Mongolia was a centrally planned economy for the first 70 years of its independence, from 1941 to 1991. Under the centrally planned regime, Mongolia's industrial sector grew rapidly, while its agricultural sector declined. However, animal husbandry remained dominant in the nation's economy. Live animals and animal products accounted for a major share of exports, and livestock accounted for much of the raw material processed in industries.

The breakup of the Soviet Union in 1991 resulted in a sudden cessation of economic aid and disrupted trade with communist bloc partners. These factors, along with a severe winter in 1990–91, caused steep declines in economic activity, drops in GDP growth rate, and severe energy shortages. The government embarked on an economic transformation program and privatized most previously state-owned enterprises. These changes helped restore economic growth, and helped inflation drop from 325% in 1992 to about 4% by 1995.

In the early 2000s, the country began to exploit its copper and gold resources. Growth averaged nearly 9% per year from 2004–08 because of high copper prices and new gold production. At the same time, however, inflation soared in 2008 to nearly 30%. By late 2008, falling commodity prices due to the global financial crisis helped lower inflation but also resulted in governmental spending cuts due to a loss of revenue. Nevertheless, coal production and exports continued to increase, reaching 10.95 million tons in the first three quarters of 2010. At the same time, the drop in prices resulted in a 2011 budget deficit of about 9.9% of GDP.

The CIA reports that a $236 million stand-by arrangement formed in early 2009 between Mongolia and the International Monetary Fund helped stabilize the economy. In addition, the government passed legislation in October 2009 to develop the Oyu Tolgoi mine, which holds one of the largest untapped copper deposits in the world. The *New York Times* reported that the government had formed agreements with Canada-based Ivanhoe Mines and the Rio Tinto Group in 2009, and was in negotiations with US-based Peabody Energy to mine a Tavan Tolgoi coal deposit. The government has estimated that development of Oyu Tolgoi will produce $30 billion in revenue, and Tavan Tolgoi will produce $2 billion in revenue.

The economy grew 6.1% in 2010, largely because of exports to nearby countries, and international reserves reached $1.6 billion in September 2011. The economy continues to be strongly influenced by neighboring countries, with 95% of oil products and substantial electrical power purchased from Russia and heavy reliance on China as a receiver of Mongolia's exports.

Slightly more than one-third of the country's people, 36.1%, were living below the poverty line, as of 2004. The US State Department noted in its 2011 Background Notes on Mongolia that the country's success in sustaining long-term economic growth depends on how quickly it can mobilize international investment in its natural resources and advantageous locale between Russia and China.

20 INCOME

The CIA estimated that in 2010 the GDP of Mongolia was $11.02 billion. The CIA defines GDP as the value of all final goods and services produced within a nation in a given year and computed on the basis of purchasing power parity (PPP) rather than value as measured on the basis of the rate of the exchange based on current dollars. The per capita GDP was estimated at $3,600. The annual growth rate of GDP was 6.1%. The average inflation rate was

13%. It was estimated that agriculture accounted for 15% of GDP, industry 31%, and services 54%.

According to the World Bank, remittances from citizens living abroad totaled $199.6 million or about $64 per capita and accounted for approximately 1.8% of GDP. The US State Department and CIA reported that remittances fell sharply in 2008–09 as a result of the global economic crisis.

The World Bank reported that in 2009, household consumption in Mongolia totaled $2.1 billion or about $670 per capita, measured in current US dollars rather than PPP.

In 2007 the World Bank estimated that Mongolia, with 0.04% of the world's population, accounted for 0.01% of the world's GDP. By comparison, the United States, with 4.85% of the world's population, accounted for 22.51% of world GDP.

As of 2011 the most recent study by the World Bank reported that actual individual consumption in Mongolia was 62.3% of GDP and accounted for 0.01% of world consumption. By comparison, the United States accounted for 25.44% of world individual consumption. The World Bank also estimated that 23.7% of Mongolia's GDP was spent on food and beverages, 12.8% on housing and household furnishings, 6.7% on clothes, 3.3% on health, 3.9% on transportation, 1.2% on communications, 2.0% on recreation, 0.3% on restaurants and hotels, and 1.8% on miscellaneous goods and services and purchases from abroad.

21 LABOR

As of 2008, Mongolia had a total labor force of 1.068 million people. Within that labor force, CIA estimates in 2008 noted that 34% were employed in agriculture, 5% in industry, and 61% in the service sector.

A shortage of skilled labor has required the procurement of a large supplementary workforce from the former USSR, North Korea, and Eastern Europe.

The right to organize trade unions and professional organizations is granted by the 1990 constitution. In that year, the Association of Free Trade Unions, (AFTU) which includes about 70 unions, was chartered. In 2002, there were 400,000 unionized workers, amounting to less than 50% of the workforce. Nonessential workers have a right to strike.

The legal minimum wage of $87 a month was not considered high enough to provide a decent standard of living for a worker and family members. The US State Department found that employees of smaller companies in rural areas often received less than the minimum wage.

According to the labor code, the working week is fixed at 40 hours. Children aged 14 and 15 could work up to 30 hours a week, while those who were 16 and 17, could work a maximum of 36 hours. and for those under 18, 36 hours. In reality, regulations regarding child labor are not effectively enforced.

Trade unions are legal, although with the continued sale of many state factories, membership in trade unions has declined to approximately one-half the population in 2005. Strikes and collective bargaining are legal except in what the government considers "essential sectors," which are transportation, law enforcement and utilities.

²²AGRICULTURE

Roughly 0.76% of the total land was being farmed, and the country's major non livestock crops included wheat, barley, vegetables, and forage crops. Cereal production in 2009 amounted to 391,659 tons, fruit production 147 tons, and vegetable production 77,995 tons.

Mongolia's short summers and long, cold winters have made development of a non-livestock agricultural sector difficult. Climatic stress, according to a UN report often results in harvest losses of 10% to 30%. The report found that since the move toward a free-market economy that began in 1990, privatization of crop production had failed.

²³ANIMAL HUSBANDRY

The UN Food and Agriculture Organization (FAO) reported that Mongolia dedicated 115.1 million hectares (284.4 million acres) to permanent pasture or meadow in 2009. During that year, the country tended 399,000 chickens, 2.6 million head of cattle, and 25,808 pigs. The production from these animals amounted to 42,465 tons of beef and veal, 403 tons of pork, 1,417 tons of poultry, 2,742 tons of eggs, and 379,413 tons of milk. Mongolia also produced 14,448 tons of cattle hide and 21,000 tons of raw wool.

Animal husbandry is the backbone of Mongolia's economy, employing some 160,000 persons. After Mongolia became the world's second communist country in 1924, many nomads settled down to raise livestock on state-owned collectives. The end of communist rule in 1990 brought the resurgence of traditional animal herding methods. Pastures constitute about 75% of the national territory. Because of the harsh climate, Mongolians consume much fat and meat during winter, and dairy products in the summer.

Extreme temperature fluctuations and harsh winters often have left those engaged in animal husbandry practices vulnerable to hardship. UN relief officials reported in 2011 that nearly 8 million cows, yaks, camels, horses, goats, and sheep died during a severe winter in 2010, representing about 17% of the country's livestock and impacting 800,000 herders. The harsh winter was reminiscent of three consecutive harsh winters between 1999 and 2002 when thousands of herders were forced to abandon their nomadic life and flee to the city in search of work.

Another challenge facing the animal husbandry sector is a growth in livestock, which quadrupled to 40 million heads of cattle between 1990 and 2010. Environmental and governmental officials fear that the surge in livestock may lead to overgrazing. At the root of the challenge is a boom in exports of cashmere, which resulted in the breeding of significantly more goats than sheep. The grazing practices and sharp hooves of the goals have threatened the ecology of Mongolia's steppe, damaging fragile pasture areas, promoting soil erosion, and encouraging desertification.

²⁴FISHING

In 2008 the annual capture totaled 88 tons according to the UN FAO.

Although the government has made some effort to develop a fishing industry, fishing was not a significant part of Mongolia's economy as of 2011. Few ethnic Mongolians consume fish, and any fish that were caught were primarily eaten by foreigners residing in the country.

²⁵FORESTRY

Approximately 7% of Mongolia is covered by forest. The UN FAO estimated the 2009 roundwood production at 40,000 cu m (1.41 million cu ft). The value of all forest products, including roundwood, totaled $392,000.

Forests cover about 6.8% of the total territory of Mongolia, mainly in the area around Hövsgöl Lake. It is estimated that the country's total timber resources represent at least 1.25 billion cu m (44 billion cu ft). Birch, cedar, larch, and fir trees predominate.

²⁶MINING

Mongolia was the world's third-largest producer of fluorspar (after China and Mexico) and among the top three producers in Asia and the Pacific of copper and molybdenum. In 2009, Mongolia exported nearly all of its copper and molybdenum concentrates, while fluorspar was sent to Japan and Russia. Construction, mining (of coal, copper, molybdenum fluorspar, and gold), and oil were Mongolia's top three industries. Geological surveys have uncovered deposits of some 80 minerals, which were largely untapped. Also produced in 2009 were cement, hydrated lime, quicklime, varieties of stone, and silica. Most mining operations were in the eastern and north-central regions, including the Erdenet copper mining center.

Output in 2009 included (in metric tons): mine copper (metal content), 129,800; fluorspar (including acid grade and sub-metallurgical), 459,000; mine molybdenum, 2,140; and mine tungsten, 39,000. Gold output for 2009 was 9,803 kg, down from 15,184 kg in 2008. Gold mining increased significantly in the 1990s, and the number of companies engaged in gold mining grew to more than 100; total reserves were estimated to be 2,000 tons gold in 17 regions, the most important being Naran, Tolgoi, and Zamar. No tin has been mined in recent years. Uranium production ceased after 1997. The Erdenet copper-molybdenum mine, completed in 1981, was developed by the state in cooperation with the former USSR, and was 51% owned by the Mongolian government and 49%, by the Russian government. Clay, gold, gypsum, limestone, molybdenum, salt, sand and gravel, silver, precious stones, and tungsten were also mined by small operations.

Mongolia's minerals sector accounted for around 28% of GDP and 65% of exports in 2009. The government encouraged foreign investment and adopted a number of long-term programs to explore for and develop metallic and nonmetallic minerals. Ivanhoe Mines Ltd. estimated that the Oyu Tolgoy had as much as 750 million tons of copper and gold resources. Oyu Tolgoy is scheduled to open in 2013 as the largest copper and gold mine in the world, employing 18,000 workers. The Tsagaan Suvraga porphyry copper deposit, in southwestern Sayanshand City, in the northern part of the Ulaan-Uul structural-formational zone of the south Gobi mineral belt, contained 240 million tons of sulfide ore at a grade of 0.53% copper and 0.018% molybdenum. The government was looking for investors to develop a 500-million-ton iron ore deposit north of Darkhan City.

Parliament-approved guidelines for 2001–04 would privatize 27 state-owned enterprises and restructure 25 state-owned enterprises and organizations. Copper mining remained state owned. In 1997, the government modified mining laws to increase the land open to exploration to 40%, change policies regarding exploration

Principal Trading Partners – Mongolia (2010)

(In millions of US dollars)

Country	Total	Exports	Imports	Balance
World	6,177.1	2,899.2	3,277.9	-378.7
China	3,882.5	2,288.3	1,594.2	694.2
Russia	1,102.1	71.9	1,030.2	-958.3
Canada	254.3	225.4	28.9	196.5
South Korea	246.1	35.3	210.8	-175.5
Japan	198.6	21.5	177.1	-155.5
United States	138.0	11.6	126.4	-114.8
Germany	130.0	9.3	120.7	-111.4
Singapore	82.3	0.6	81.8	-81.2
United Kingdom	63.1	46.8	16.3	30.5
Italy	58.9	38.3	20.7	17.6

(…) data not available or not significant.

(n.s.) not specified.

SOURCE: *2011 Direction of Trade Statistics Yearbook*, New York: United Nations, 2011.

licenses, and grant tax incentives to promote mining. The government is trying to protect itself from potential losses that could be incurred by creating investment policies that could bring rapid foreign investment, while it evaluates how to develop a sustainable mining industry.

27 ENERGY AND POWER

The World Bank reported in 2008 that Mongolia produced 4.15 billion kWh of electricity and consumed 3.89 billion kWh, or 1,242 kWh per capita. Roughly 96% of energy came from fossil fuels. Per capita oil consumption was 1,193 kg.

The CIA estimated that Mongolia imported 214.1 million kWh in 2010, mostly from Russia. Electricity exports were estimated at 20.7 million kWh in 2010.

Mongolia has no proved reserves of oil or natural gas. The country was estimated to have imported 15,730 bbl of oil per day in 2010, and 11,790 cu m of natural gas.

28 INDUSTRY

The CIA estimated Mongolia's industrial production growth rate at 3%, as of 2006. Key industries were construction and construction materials, mining of coal, copper, molybdenum, fluorspar, tin, tungsten, and gold; oil processing; food and beverage products; processing of animal products; and the manufacture of cashmere and other natural fibers. These products accounted for most of Mongolia's exports in 2010.

The US State Department estimated that mining made up 21.8% percent of GDP in 2009, manufacturing 6.4%, and utilities for electricity, gas, and water production 2.4%

Small-scale processing of livestock and agricultural products has historically been a mainstay of Mongolia's industrial sector. With the establishment of the Erdenet copper plant in the late 1970s, metal processing also became an important part of the economy.

Mongolia's industrial development was severely affected by dwindling imports of fuel, spare parts, and equipment formerly obtained from the former USSR and allied trading partners. As a result, total output from the industrial sector generally declined

in the early 1990s but began to recover by 1997. About 72% of the economy had been privatized by 2000.

29 SCIENCE AND TECHNOLOGY

Patent applications in science and technology as of 2009, according to the World Bank, totaled 103 in Mongolia. Public financing of science was 0.23% of GDP.

A Science and Technology Master Plan for 2007–20, developed by 24 Mongolian scholars through support from UNESCO reported that in 2006, there were 2,642 people working in 51 research institutes, research and development corporations, and universities in the country. The report described the level of innovative technological development in Mongolia as weak and noted that the economy was highly dependent on foreign technology. It cited a need to strengthen links between research scientists and industry and to decentralize R&D outside of the capital city.

The government-run Mongolian Academy of Sciences includes 17 research institutes and centers, and nine scientific production corporations.

The Mongolian University of Science & Technology (MUST), founded in 1969, had nearly 40 research centers. As of 2009, 150 research works had been completed under the guidance of 96 chaired professorships. About two-thirds of university-educated Mongolians complete degrees through MUST.

30 DOMESTIC TRADE

Prior to economic reforms of the early 1990s, consumer goods produced at Ulaanbaatar or imported from abroad were distributed by state marketing agencies to retail outlets in local administrative centers. Prices for all items except consumer services and some luxury goods were set by the government. With steady price liberalization undertaken since 1990, prices are now closely regulated for only a few staples, such as fuel, rice, and flour.

A 2010 Economic Growth Assessment by the US Agency for International Development reports that 70% of Mongolia's economy had been privatized by 2008. Citing National Statistical Office figures, the report said there were 32,105 registered businesses in Mongolia as of 2007, and that 70% were small enterprises employing 20 or fewer people. The businesses included 57.4% engaged in manufacture and services; 35.7% in trade; and 7% in the social sector. Most of the businesses were in the capital region of Ulaanbaatar. These businesses contributed 57.4% to overall GDP.

Among the small enterprises were 172 dairy farms, 48 cattle farms, 57 meat and wool sheep farms, 172 swine farms, 225 chicken farms, 56 bee farms, 10 rabbit farms, 28 meat processing plants, 32 slaughterhouses, and 90 dairy processing facilities.

USAID predicted that the number of small businesses would double in Mongolia by 2020.

31 FOREIGN TRADE

Mongolia imported $3.3 billion worth of goods and services in 2008, while exporting $2.899 billion worth of goods and services. Major import partners in 2009 were Russia, 33.2%; China, 30.5%; Japan, 6%; and South Korea, 5.5%. Its major export partners were China, 84.8%; Canada, 3.6%; and Russia, 2.7%.

The main export items were copper, apparel, livestock, animal products, cashmere, wool, hides, fluorspar, coal, and nonferrous metals. The main import items were machinery and equipment,

Balance of Payments – Mongolia (2010)

(In millions of US dollars)

Current Account		**-886.5**
Balance on goods		-180.4
Imports	-3,088.9	
Exports	2,908.5	
Balance on services		-294.4
Balance on income		-598.9
Current transfers		187.0
Capital Account		**152.2**
Financial Account		**1,369.9**
Direct investment abroad		-46.6
Direct investment in Mongolia		1,454.7
Portfolio investment assets		143.3
Portfolio investment liabilities		751.0
Financial derivatives		...
Other investment assets		-1,040.2
Other investment liabilities		107.8
Net Errors and Omissions		**239.3**
Reserves and Related Items		**-874.8**

(…) data not available or not significant.

SOURCE: *Balance of Payment Statistics Yearbook 2011*, Washington, DC: International Monetary Fund, 2011.

Public Finance – Mongolia (2009)

(In billions of togrogs, central government figures)

Revenue and Grants	**1,901.4**	**100.0%**
Tax revenue	1,090.1	57.3%
Social contributions	315.8	16.6%
Grants	133	7.0%
Other revenue	362.4	19.1%
Expenditures	**2,171.1**	**100.0%**
General public services	...	...
Defense	...	...
Public order and safety	...	...
Economic affairs	...	...
Environmental protection	...	...
Housing and community amenities	...	...
Health	...	...
Recreational, culture, and religion	...	...
Education	...	...
Social protection	...	...

(…) data not available or not significant.

SOURCE: *Government Finance Statistics Yearbook 2010*, Washington, DC: International Monetary Fund, 2010.

fuel, cars, food products, industrial consumer goods, chemicals, building materials, sugar, and tea.

The US Agency for International Development's 2010 Economic Growth Assessment for Mongolia stated that Mongolia overall engaged in trade with 118 countries in 2009.

Greater economic independence in the foreign trade sector presented a challenge as Mongolia entered the second decade of the 21st century. Most of its imports came from Russia, and most of its exports went to China, creating little diversity in the country's overall foreign trade portfolio.

The Ministry of Foreign Affairs and Trade has been working to establish free trade agreements with China, Japan, Korea, and the European Union, which in 2008 was Mongolia's third biggest trading partner.

32 BALANCE OF PAYMENTS

In 2010 Mongolia had a foreign trade deficit of $332 million, amounting to 4.5% of GDP.

Mongolia consistently imports more than it exports. The CIA estimated Mongolia to have a current account balance of -$378.8 million in 2010 compared with a balance of -$341.8 million in 2009.

Reserves of foreign exchange and gold were estimated at $2.288 billion as of 31 December 2010 compared with $1.327 billion on 31 December 2009.

33 BANKING AND SECURITIES

The Bank of Mongolia (also known as Mongolbank) serves as the central bank of Mongolia. It initially was established in June 1924, and replaced a widespread informal and chaotic system of bartering and private lending by monasteries, foreign banks, and money-lenders.

Economic reforms since 1990 have allowed for the formation of a commercial banking sector. The banking system as of 2011 oper-

ated on a two-tier system, where control of the money supply was given to the central bank. Bank of Mongolia set lending rules and reserve requirements for the commercial banks.

As of 2010, there were 15 banks. Total assets were $3 billion as of July 2010 compared with $263 million on 31 December 2000. Four banks—Khan, Golomt, TDB, and Xac—controlled 66% of total loans. Total bank loans grew from $61 million in 2000 to $2.2 billion by July 2010.

The USAID Economic Growth Assessment for Mongolia reported in 2010 that the banking sector in Mongolia was in its early stages. Mobile banking services were available and large banks were offering mortgages. Ten banks had formed a Mongolian Mortgage Corporation to help individuals acquire housing loans. At the same time, loans were often expensive to obtain and heavily dependent on collateral, putting them out of reach for many lower-income Mongolians.

The Mongolian Securities Exchange opened in August 1995 but as of 2010 it remained the world's smallest stock exchange in terms of market capitalization. US Aid's Economic Growth Assessment described the exchange's equities market as "essentially defunct" with total market capitalization of $610 million as of July 2010. There were 339 companies listed on the exchange, although it was estimated that as many as 200 of those firms were no longer in business.

34 INSURANCE

Insurance as of 2010 was not mandatory to purchase in Mongolia. However, several private companies offered life, health/illness/disability, auto, travel, agricultural, property, and commercial insurance packages.

In the 1980s, insurance was offered by the State Directorate for Insurance, or Mongoldaatgal, which was under the control of the Ministry of Finance. The government was planning to introduce health insurance in 1993 as a cooperative effort between individuals, government agencies, and the private sector.

35 PUBLIC FINANCE

In 2010 the budget of Mongolia included $2.26 billion in public revenue and $2.26 billion in public expenditures. The budget surplus amounted to .6% of GDP. In total $1.86 billion of the debt held by foreign entities.

36 TAXATION

A 1991 Corporate Income and Personal Income Tax Law and 1993 General Law of Taxation provide the basis for Mongolia's taxation system. General taxes include a corporate income tax, customs duty, value added tax, excise tax, gasoline and diesel fuel tax, royalty, personal income tax, and windfall profit tax.

The World Bank reported that in December 2010 employer-paid contributions on wages and salaries were 11%. The corporate income tax was 10%, and the value-added tax was 10%. In addition, businesses were charged a 2% tax on property transfers and a 0.6% property tax. Personal income taxes were 10%, but often were higher for non-residents working in the country.

37 CUSTOMS AND DUTIES

Mongolia collects a general import tariff of 5% and a VAT of 13% on most imported items. The import duty was not imposed on hospital equipment and tools. Imported items that were used to produce goods for export were subjected on paper to both the general import tariff and VAT; however, the taxes were deducted when the finished products left the country.

However, gold is subject to a 10% VAT, while imports of technological equipment and machinery imported under the country's Law of Foreign Investment are exempt. Customs duties have been insignificant, yielding less than 1% of total state revenues. An additional excise tax was added to alcoholic beverages, tobacco and tobacco products, petroleum and petroleum products, and automobiles.

38 FOREIGN INVESTMENT

Foreign direct investment (FDI) in Mongolia was a net inflow of $623.6 million according to World Bank figures published in 2009. FDI represented 14.84% of GDP.

Before 1990, Mongolia derived much of its investment capital from government loans and grants. Most of these funds came from the Soviet Union and other members of the communist bloc, and private investment was virtually non-existent. Since 1990, the situation has changed greatly. Mongolia registered 9,940 foreign investors from more than 95 countries between 1990 and 2009. The portfolio from these investments totaled $3.8 billion. Leading investors came from China, Canada, South Korea, Japan, Russia, the US, Netherlands, and Singapore. Of the total investment, 61.3% was in geology, mining, and oil; 19.7% in trade and catering; 3.1% in banking and finance; 2.8% in light industry; 1.9% in construction; and 1.4% in animal processing. As of 2011, China was the largest source of foreign investment in Mongolia.

The Foreign Investment Law of 1993 provides the legal basis and incentive for foreign investments. Total income tax exemptions are granted to businesses engaged in infrastructural projects. Mining operations, metallurgy operations, chemicals production, and machinery and electronics manufacturing receive a 10-year tax holiday, and a 50% tax exemption for the following five years.

Companies that export more than 50% of production receive a three-year tax holiday, and 50% tax exemption for another three years.

Independent Mongolia's long-standing relationship with the Soviet Union has evolved into the development of strong ties with Russia and other former Soviet republics. Mongolia and Russia signed trade agreements and treaties of friendship in 1990, 1993, 1999, and 2000. Mongolia declared it had settled a debt it owed to Russia in 2003 with a negotiated payment of $250 million. The Russian government stated, however, that much of the debt was unpaid as of 2009 but declared the debt settled in December 2010. Russia and Mongolia also announced the establishment of a joint venture in Dornod Province in December 2010 to mine uranium. Mongolia and Russia also maintain joint ownership of Mongolia's railroad and its Erdenet copper mine.

The United States began to emerge as an important source of foreign investment after 1990. In 1994, Mongolia concluded a Bilateral Trade and Investment Agreement (BTIA) with the United States, in 1997 joined the WTO, and in 1999 was granted normal trade relations (NTR) status by the United States. A July 2004 Trade and Investment Framework Agreement between the US and Mongolia has aimed to promote economic reform and more foreign investment, and the US Agency for International Development (USAID) provided $214 million in grant assistance between 1991 and 2011 to promote economic growth, good governance, and management of its mining sector. The US government also approved $13 million in supplemental funds in August 2009 to ease effects of the global financial crisis, and signed a $10 million cash transfer to the government of Mongolia to help it meet deficit reduction targets. The US and Mongolia also established a Millennium Challenge Account initiative that called for $285 million to be spent on four projects between September 2008 and 2013. The projects were initially focused on rail modernization, property rights, vocational education, and health.

In the private sector, Peabody, a US mining firm, was among the companies who secured mining deals in 2011. Peabody was one of the stakeholders in a consortium with Russian and Chinese partners to develop the Tavan Tolgoi coal deposit.

39 ECONOMIC DEVELOPMENT

Mongolia unveiled an ambitious 16-year economic growth strategy in its Millennium Development Goals-based Comprehensive National Development Strategy in 2009. The first phase, which was to run until 2015, calls for average annual economic growth of 14%; increases in per capita GDP to at least $5,000; development of a knowledge-based economy; and the establishment of a foundation for intensive economic development that would allow the country to leave the level of the world's middle income nations. The strategy outlined increases in labor productivity, more investment efficiency, economic diversification, more export trade, and better technology as the vehicles by which the goals would be met.

In the past, Mongolia operated on the basis of a planned economy, with five-year plans implemented from 1947 until 1990, with assistance from the former USSR and China. In 1990, with the establishment of a new consensus government, there followed a three-year plan that aimed for achieving greater efficiency in the allocation of resources and a diversified economic base by undertaking a sustained transition to a free market economy. The change was a fundamental shift, as the government relinquished its role as the primary factor in the economy and began limiting itself to policies supporting a market-oriented economy. Main components of the government's program include privatization of state enterprises, price liberalization, changes in national law, and an action plan for environmental protection.

In 1996, the initial phase of privatization of state property was completed. By 2000, the private sector accounted for 72% of GDP. In September 2001, the administration entered into a three-year arrangement with the IMF under its Poverty Reduction and Growth Facility (PRGF) supported by stand-by funds of about $40 million.

In July 2002, a pledge meeting of the Consultative Group (CG) for Mongolia, consisting of donors from 20 countries and 18 international organizations in addition to representatives of various civil and private organizations, agreed on the importance of the government's addressing governance issues: ensuring accountability, promoting transparency, controlling corruption, reforming the judiciary and strengthening the rule of law. Priority areas of action stressed were energy and information and communications technology (ICT), as well as preparation of a long-term strategy for rural development. The donors pledged $333 million in support of Mongolia's development efforts in 2003.

Mongolia's economic development plans focus heavily on growth in the mining sector. However, the government and economic policy makers have shown a desire to diversify the economy, and to work particularly on improving the high-technology research sectors.

The country's biggest challenge is its reliance on external revenue from a few key nations, which leaves it vulnerable to economic downturns in those countries. Mongolia buys most of its energy from Russia, which makes it vulnerable to price increases. Similarly, China receives more than 75% of Mongolia's exports. In addition, remittances from overseas Mongolians—while sizeable—have dropped because of the global economic framework. Despite these challenges, many economic observers in 2011 praised Mongolia's effort to move from a centrally planned economy to a free market system within a democratic political framework. That effort, coupled with its rich deposits of coal, minerals, and metals, made Mongolia's prospects for raising the living standard of its citizens appear promising at the beginning of 2012.

40 SOCIAL DEVELOPMENT

The social insurance program provides for free medical services, benefits for temporary disability, and pensions for permanent disability and old age.

Women have equal rights and freedoms under Mongolian law, with the exception of a law barring them from hazardous work. Women account for approximately half of the work force, generally receive equal pay for equal work, and many hold mid-level government and professional jobs. Domestic abuse and violence remain serious problems. New laws went into effect in 2005 to combat domestic violence.

Although the government generally respects the human rights of its citizens, there are reports of mistreatment of detainees and prisoners. Human rights organizations operate openly in Mongolia.

The constitution bars arbitrary arrest, although this continued to occur. Prisoners also report beatings and torture while in detention. Deaths in prison are reported, although this is most likely due to disease exacerbated by poor conditions like lack of food, heat and medical services. Mongolia vowed to concentrate resources on prison reform by 2010.

In January 2010, Mongolian president Tsakhia Elbegdorj issued a moratorium on the death penalty and called for the abolishment of the practice. Elbegdorj has said that capital punishment hurts the dignity of Mongolia. Since coming to office in 2009, Elbegdorj commuted at least three sentences; in addition, several people were awaiting capital sentences when Elbegdorj issued the moratorium. The abolishment of the punishment would put Mongolia in a club of 95 other nations that have banned the practice.

The US State Department's 2010 Human Rights Report on Mongolia noted that widespread alcoholism and parental abandonment had forced many children to support themselves with work in petty trade, small-scale mining, herding, and dumpsite scavenging. The National Center for Children estimated that the number of children in the work force was as high as 77,000.

41 HEALTH

According to the CIA, life expectancy in Mongolia was 67 years in 2011. The country spent 3.8% of its GDP on healthcare, amounting to $74 per person. There were 28 physicians, 35 nurses and midwives, and 59 hospital beds per 10,000 inhabitants. The fertility rate was 2.0, while the infant mortality rate was 24 per 1,000 live births. In 2008 the maternal mortality rate, according to the World Bank, was 65 per 100,000 births. It was estimated that 94% of children were vaccinated against measles. The CIA calculated HIV/AIDS prevalence in Mongolia to be about less than 0.1% in 2009.

Health care is administered under state auspices and all medical and hospital services are free. The government gives special priority to increasing the number of physicians and other health personnel and expanding facilities in rural areas. Each province has at least two hospitals and each agricultural cooperative and state farm has a medical station.

42 HOUSING

The availability of safe, clean, and modern housing was one of Mongolia's biggest challenges at the end of 2011.

Although there are many stone and wood buildings in Ulaanbaatar and some of the larger provincial centers, the traditional housing structure is the *ger*, a tent-like wooden frame structure covered in woolen felt. Economic decline in the countryside and harsh weather conditions resulted in an increase in rural-urban migration in the first decade of the 21st century. Many rural residents simply packed up their *ger*, moved toward cities such as Ulaanbataar, Darkhan, and Erdenet, and set up their ger on the outskirts. Over time, ger districts formed, creating an acute crisis on urban infrastructure, services, and environmental quality.

An estimated 60% of Ulaanbataar's people lived in such districts in 2009. *Ger* life lacked water, improved sanitation, and adequate heating. Although residents eventually might replace a *ger* with a small house of wood, concrete, or brick, these structures also often lacked basic services.

The government considered housing for the poor as a key part of its economic development plan. With support from the World

Bank, clean water was being piped to water stations, more efficient stoves for heating and cooking have been provided, and a clean air project was under way. Several aid agencies were offering support, and the International Finance Corporation was planning to offer micro-housing finance options so that residents could improve their homes. XacBank, a client bank of the International Finance Corporation, was financing construction of low-cost apartments and making available loans that would allow people to make their homes more energy efficient. In addition, the Mongolian Mortgage Company was creating a secondary mortgage market aimed at addressing the problem. Residents also were working together in several neighborhoods on tree planting and other improvement projects designed to increase the overall standard of living.

⁴³EDUCATION

In 2009 the World Bank estimated that 90% of age-eligible children in Mongolia were enrolled in primary school. Secondary enrollment for age-eligible children stood at 82%. Tertiary enrollment was estimated at 53%. Of those enrolled in tertiary education, there were 100 male students for every 157 female students. Overall, the CIA estimated that Mongolia had a literacy rate of 97.8%. Public expenditure on education represented 5.6% of GDP.

Eight years of schooling is compulsory starting at age eight, and free of charge. Primary school covers four years of study, followed by four years of junior secondary school and two years of upper secondary school. There are technical and vocational schools, which admit students after their primary education is complete. Many children in rural areas are withdrawn from school in order to work at home. An absence of heat in many rural schools is also a problem that may contribute to poor enrollment levels. More than 70% of students from rural areas reside in dormitories adjoining the schools. The academic year runs from September to July.

Women were more likely than men to graduate from high school, and more than two-thirds of all university students were women.

While higher and professional education is not free, tuition fees for poor students are subsidized by the government. There were 16 colleges and universities in Mongolia in 2011. Top institutions included the National University of Mongolia, the Mongolian University of Science & Technology, and the Institute of Commerce and Business.

⁴⁴LIBRARIES AND MUSEUMS

The National Library of Mongolia, which until 2009 was known as the State Central Library, was the largest library in Mongolia with more than 3 million books and publications. The library also held a collection of 1 million rare books and manuscripts.

The National Library also is part of a Mongolian Library Consortium that was formed in the first decade of the 21st century to improve technology and access to resources within the country's libraries. Other libraries within the consortium were the Ulaanbaatar Public Library, the Children's Book Palace, the National University of Mongolia, the Mongolian University of Science and Technology, the Institute of Finance and Economics, and the Open Society Forum.

Most of Mongolia's major museums were in Ulaanbaatar. They included the National Museum of Mongolian History, the Natural History Museum, the Zanabazar Museum of Fine Arts, and The Gandhian Monastery.

⁴⁵MEDIA

In 2009 the CIA reported that there were 188,900 telephone landlines in Mongolia. In addition to landlines, mobile phone subscriptions averaged 84 per 100 people. There were 7 FM radio stations, 115 AM radio stations, and 4 shortwave radio stations. Internet users numbered 13 per 100 citizens. Prominent newspapers in 2010, with circulation numbers listed parenthetically, included *Ardyn Erh* (77,500) and *Unen*.

In 2009, there were 2.2 million mobile cell phones in use nationwide. In 2010, the country had 7,942 Internet hosts. As of 2009, there were some 330,000 Internet users in Mongolia.

A 1999 media law banned censorship of public information, and many independent newspapers and media outlets exist. However, to the extreme poverty in the country, the main source of news is the state-owned Radio Mongolia. Internet access and Western news media are available in all major cities and not hampered by government censorship. Parliamentary meetings are also broadcast to the public.

⁴⁶ORGANIZATIONS

The Mongolian National Chamber of Commerce and Industry, founded in 1960, is in Ulaanbaatar.

Oyuny Chadvar was established in 2006 as a youth-run organization aimed at fighting unemployment and helping young people gain leadership skills.

The Mongolian Amateur Radio Society was named in 2008 as a successor organization to the Mongolian Radio Sport Federation.

There were several international organizations with branches in Mongolia. As of December 2011, these organizations included the Adventist Development and Relief Agency, the Asia Foundation, the Hans Zeidel Foundation, the Japan International Cooperation Center, the Korea International Cooperation Agency, the Mongolia-Japan Center for Human Resource Development, the Mongolian Foundation for Open Society (which was affiliated with the Soros Society), the Swiss Agency for Development and Cooperation, and the International Federation of Red Cross and Red Crescent societies.

⁴⁷TOURISM, TRAVEL, AND RECREATION

The *Tourism Factbook*, published by the UN World Tourism Organization, reported 468,000 incoming tourists to Mongolia in 2009, who spent a total of $253 million. Of those incoming tourists, there were 241,000 from East Asia and the Pacific and 154,000 from Europe. The estimated daily cost to visit Ulaanbaatar, the capital, was $166. The cost of visiting other cities averaged $102.

USAID's 2010 Economic Growth Assessment for Mongolia reported that the government has hopes of developing a resort area at Kharhorin.

Points of interest include the largest monastery in Mongolia, Gandan Lamasery in Ulaanbaatar, and the ruined city of Karakorum, once the capital of the Mongol Empire. Mongolia offers abundant and varied scenery, including forests, steppes, lakes, and deserts, and a wide variety of wildlife. The national sports of Mongolia are wrestling, archery, and horse racing. Mongols also participate in boxing and sumo wrestling.

In November 2010, the traditional national festival of Naadam was officially inscribed on the UNESCO Representative List of the Intangible Cultural Heritage of Humanity, an offshoot of the World Heritage program. The festival was deemed a living tradition by UNESCO, meaning that it is still passed from generation to generation and continues to create a sense of identity and community for those who participate. Such traditions have been approved by UNESCO for special consideration since 2001. For one that is inscribed, a special program is designed to protect and promote the practice and understanding of the tradition. Naadam is a nationwide cultural festival celebrated each year from 11 to 13 July. The traditional games of horseracing, wrestling, and archery are important activities in the festival, as are a number of performing arts. The traditional art of Khöömei, a form of singing that originated in the Altai Mountains of western Mongolia, was also inscribed on the list. This form features a technique of singing through which a single performer can emit two distinct vocal sounds simultaneously. The songs generally imitate sounds of nature.

A valid passport is required for entry into Mongolia, an onward/return ticket, and a visa if staying for more than 90 days.

48 FAMOUS PERSONS

A long line of Mongol khans have left their mark on history ever since Temujin, or Genghis Khan (1162–1227), set up the first Mongol empire in 1206. Outstanding among them were Kublai Khan (1216–94), a grandson of Genghis, who conquered most of China; Hulagu Khan (1217–60), a brother of Kublai, who conquered Persia and Syria; Batu Khan (d. 1255), Kublai's cousin, who overran Russia, Poland, and Hungary; Timur, also known as Timur Lenk ("Timur the Lame") or Tamerlane (1336?–1405), a descendant of Genghis, who extended his military power for short periods into southern Russia, India, and the Levant; and Babur (Zahir ad-Din Muhammad, 1483–1530), a descendant of Timur, who established an empire in India.

In recent times, two national leaders were Sukhe Baatar (1894–1923) and Khorloin Choybalsan (1895–1952). Yumjaagiin Tsedenbal (1916–91), intermittently general secretary of the Central Committee of the MPRP since 1940, became chairman of the Council of Ministers in 1952, was elected chairman of the Presidium of the People's Great Hural in 1974, and was named the MPRP general secretary in 1981. Jambyn Batmunkh (1926–97) became chairman of the Council of Ministers in 1974 and was elected chairman of the Presidium and general secretary of the MPRP in 1984. Natsagiyn Bagabandi (b. 1950) was the president of Mongolia from 1997 to 2005; he was succeeded by Nambaryn Enkhbayar (b. 1958), who was prime minister from 2000–04.

The founder of modern Mongolian literature is D. Natsagdorj (1906–37). Tsendyn Damdinsuren (1908–86) is one of the most important writers. Leading playwrights are Ch. Oydov (1917–63) and E. Oyuun (1918–2001). Other prominent writers are B. Rindhen (1905–78), D. Namdag (1911–82), U. Ulambayar (b. 1911), and Ch. Lodoydamba (1917–70). B. Damdinsuren (1919–92) and L. Murdorzh are noted composers. Jugderdemidiyn Gurragcha (b. 1947) became the first Mongolian in space in 1981, when he was carried into orbit aboard the former USSR's Soyuz 39.

49 DEPENDENCIES

The MPR has no territories or colonies.

50 BIBLIOGRAPHY

Hanson, Jennifer. *Mongolia*. New York: Facts On File, 2004.

Hoare, Jim and Susan Pares. *A Political and Economic Dictionary of East Asia*. Philadelphia: Routledge/Taylor and Francis, 2005.

May, Timothy M. *Culture and Customs of Mongolia*. Westport, CT: Greenwood Press, 2009.

Mongolia Investment and Business Guide: Strategic and Practical Information. Washington, DC: International Business Publications USA, 2012.

Sanders, Alan J. K. *Historical Dictionary of Mongolia*. 3rd ed. Lanham, MD: Scarecrow, 2010.

Soucek, Svatopluk. *A History of Inner Asia*. New York: Cambridge University Press, 2009.

MYANMAR

Union of Myanmar
Pyidaungzu Myanma Naingngandaw

CAPITAL: Naypyidaw

FLAG: The national flag has three horizontal stripes, yellow, green, and red, from top to bottom; with a five-pointed white star at the center.

ANTHEM: *Kaba Ma Kyei (Until the End of the World).*

MONETARY UNIT: The kyat (MMK) is a paper currency of 100 pya. There are coins of 1, 5, 10, 50, and 100 kyat, and notes of 10, 20, 50, 100, 200, 500, 1000, and 5,000 kyat. MMK1 = US$0.15 (or US$1 = MMK6.51) at the official rate as of December 2011, with an unofficial, more prevalent rate of (US$1 = MMK770) as of October 2011.

WEIGHTS AND MEASURES: Metric weights and measures are in general use, but British and local units also are employed.

HOLIDAYS: Independence Day, 4 January; Union Day, 12 February; Peasants Day, 2 March; Armed Forces Day, 27 March; Labor Day, 1 May; Martyrs Day, 19 July; National Day, November 20; Christmas, 25 December. Movable religious holidays include Full Moon of Tabaung, February or March; Thingyan (Water Festival), April; Full Moon of Kason, April or May; Waso (Beginning of Buddhist Lent), June or July; Thadingyut (End of Buddhist Lent), October; and Tazaungdaing, November.

TIME: 6:30 p.m. = noon GMT.

¹LOCATION, SIZE, AND EXTENT

Situated in Southeast Asia, Myanmar has an area of 678,500 sq km (261,970 sq mi), extending 1,931 km (1,200 mi) N–S and 925 km (575 mi) E–W. Comparatively, the area occupied by Myanmar is slightly smaller than the state of Texas. It is bounded on the N and E by China, on the E by Laos, on the SE by Thailand, on the S by the Andaman Sea, and on the W by the Bay of Bengal, Bangladesh, and India; with a total boundary length of 7,806 km (4,850 mi), of which 1,930 km (1,197 mi) is coastline.

Myanmar's capital, Naypyidaw, is located in the central part of the country.

²TOPOGRAPHY

Myanmar is divided into four topographic regions: a mountainous area in the north and west, ranging from about 1,830–6,100 m (6,000–20,000 ft) in altitude, and including the Arakan coastal strip between the Arakan Yoma mountain range and the Bay of Bengal; the Shan Highlands in the east, a deeply dissected plateau averaging 910 m (2,990 ft) in height and extending southward into the Tenasserim Yoma, a narrow strip of land that projects some 800 km (500 mi) along the Malay Peninsula, in the southeast; central Myanmar, a principal area of cultivation, bounded by the Salween River in the east and the Irrawaddy River and its tributary, the Chindwin, in the west; and the delta and lower valley regions of the Irrawaddy and Sittang rivers in the south, covering an area of about 25,900 sq km (10,000 sq mi). Good harbors are located along the coastline.

Myanmar is located in a seismically active region of the Eurasian tectonic plate. As such, the nation experiences frequent earthquakes and tremors. Although these are usually minor, be-

low 5.0 magnitude on the Richter scale, a 6.6 magnitude earthquake occurred on 21 September 2003, and a 6.6 magnitude earthquake affected the north on 24 March 2011.

³CLIMATE

Myanmar has a largely tropical climate with three seasons: the monsoon or rainy season, from May to October; the cool season, from November to February; and the hot season, generally from March to April. Rainfall during the monsoon season totals more than 500 cm (200 in) in upper (northern) Myanmar and over 250 cm (100 in) in lower (southern) Myanmar and Yangon (formerly Rangoon). Central Myanmar, called the dry zone, and Mandalay, the chief city in the area, receive about 76 cm (30 in). The mean annual temperature is 27° c (81° f); average daily temperatures in Yangon (Rangoon) range from 18–32° c (64–90° f) in January, during the cool season, and from 24–36° c (75–97° f) in April, during the hot season. The climate in upper Myanmar, particularly at altitudes ranging from about 300–1,220 m (1,000–4,000 ft), is the most temperate throughout the year, while lower Myanmar, especially in the delta and coastal regions, is the most humid. The low-lying delta area is periodically affected by cyclones. Cyclone Nargis, which struck the delta on 5 May, 2008, was one of the most devastating cyclones ever recorded, causing an estimated 138,000 deaths.

⁴FLORA AND FAUNA

The World Resources Institute estimates that there are 7,000 plant species in Myanmar. In addition, Myanmar is home to 288 mammal, 1,047 bird, 285 reptile, and 89 amphibian species. The calculation reflects the total number of distinct species residing in the country, not the number of endemic species. The remaining tropical and temperate forests of Burma are considered biodiversity hotspots. Teak forests, occurring mainly in hill regions, are largely depleted. Bamboo grows throughout Myanmar. Mangroves and palms are found in the wetlands along the coast; mixed temperate secondary forests and rolling grasslands in the Shan Highlands; and scrub vegetation in the dry central area. There are more than 15 primate species, including monkeys, gibbons, and slow lorises; as well as small surviving populations of tigers, leopards, wild elephants, gaurs, and tapirs. Fish and shellfish habitats are along the coastline, in the tidal waters of the Irrawaddy delta, and in the rivers and streams. The numerous bird species include hornbills, pheasants, sunbirds, pittas, bulbuls, barbets, and storks.

5 ENVIRONMENT

The World Resources Institute reported that Myanmar had designated 3.55 million hectares (8.78 million acres) of land for protection as of 2006. Areas designated as parks are often encroached on by agribusiness plantations, logging, and other commercial operations. Wildlife poaching and trafficking in wild animal products are threats to Myanmar's rare and endangered species. According to a 2011 report issued by the International Union for Conservation of Nature and Natural Resources (IUCN), threatened species included 45 mammals, 43 birds, 24 reptiles, 39 fish, 2 mollusks, 63 other invertebrates, and 44 plants. Endangered and vulnerable species include the banteng, gaur, Asian elephant, hillock gibbon, red panda, Malayan tapir, clouded leopard, freshwater sawfish, Siamese crocodile, hawksbill turtle, and dugong. The Sumatran rhinoceros was considered critically endangered.

Deforestation for farming or economic gain has decimated Myanmar's tropical and temperate forests since 1990, when loggers from neighboring countries were granted concessions. By 1994, two-thirds of Myanmar's tropical forests had been eliminated. Myanmar enacted laws to protect the remaining forests, but illegal logging, often with Myanmar military cooperation, persisted in the early 21st century, particularly along the border with China.

The United Nations (UN) reported in 2008 that carbon dioxide emissions in Myanmar totaled 8,876 kilotons. While emissions from vehicles remained low in Myanmar as of 2011, deforestation was considered a contributor to climate change. Scientists believe that global warming is increasing the violence of the cyclones affecting Myanmar from the Bay of Bengal.

Water resources total 1,045.6 cu km (250.9 cu mi) while water usage is 33.2 cu km (7.97 cu mi) per year. Domestic water usage accounts for 1% of total usage, industrial for 1%, and agricultural for 98%. Per capita water usage totals 658 cu m (23,237 cu ft) per year. Evidence of industrial and agricultural pollutants has been found in the air, water, soil, and food. Inadequate sanitation and water treatment are leading contributors to disease. Mining and agriculture have caused pollution, soil erosion, and deforestation. In the 21st century, several mega-dam projects raised environmental issues. The government suspended the Chinese-backed Myitsone dam project at the confluence of the Irrawaddy River, in October 2011, after concerns about its watershed effects were raised by citizens. Until that time, there had been little sign of government response to environmental problems, and most campaigns on environmental issues were run by exiles from outside of the country.

6 POPULATION

The US Central Intelligence Agency (CIA) estimated the population of Myanmar in 2011 to be 53,999,804, which placed it at number 24 in population among the 196 nations of the world. In 2011, approximately 5% of the population was over 65 years of age, with another 27.5% under 15 years of age. The median age in Myanmar was 26.9 years. The male to female ration was virtually at parity. The population's annual rate of change was 1.084%. The projected population for the year 2025 was 61,800,000. Population density in Myanmar was calculated at 80 people per sq km (207 people per sq mi).

The UN estimated that 34% of the population lived in urban areas, and that urban populations had an annual rate of change of 2.9%. The largest urban areas, along with their respective populations, as of 2009, included Yangon (formerly Rangoon), 4.3 million; and Mandalay, 1 million.

7 MIGRATION

Estimates of Myanmar's net migration rate, calculated by the CIA in 2011, amounted to -0.31 migrants per 1,000 citizens. The total number of emigrants living abroad was over 514,200, and the total number of immigrants living in Myanmar was 88,700. Citizens of China (PRC) have increasingly resided in Myanmar for business purposes, during the early 21st century. Immigrants from the Indian subcontinent arrived in large numbers until World War II, when hundreds of thousands fled the Japanese invasion; after independence in 1948 the government instituted rigid restrictions on Indian immigration. Under military rule, the government sought to curtail both immigration and emigration, although hundreds of thousands of people have managed to flee the country since 1962.

About 187,000 Muslim Rohingyas, who fled to Bangladesh from Myanmar's Rakhine state in 1978, were repatriated with the help of UN agencies by the end of 1981; they lost their citizenship in 1982. In 1992, some 250,000 Rohingya refugees began arriving in Bangladesh, fleeing human rights abuses in Myanmar. Most were repatriated with assistance from the UN High Commissioner for Refugees (UNHCR). As of 2011, nearly 30,000 Rohingya refugees were still living in Bangladesh. The population of refugees from Myanmar in Thailand was estimated at over 120,000, and there were large populations of refugees and other migrant workers from Myanmar in Malaysia and India as well, mostly in urban areas. Refugees from Myanmar were resettled from Thailand and Malaysia to the United States, Australia, and European counties, particularly after 2008. As many as 30,000 Chinese-ethnic people fled conflict in northeast Myanmar, returning to China in 2009. In 2011, conflict in northern Myanmar's Kachin and Shan states caused an estimated 30,000 civilians to leave their homes, becoming internally displaced persons (IDPs) along the border of China.

About 500,000 poor urban residents were forcibly relocated by the military government to new settlements between 1989 and 1992. Rural peoples have also been subject to large-scale forced resettlement in connection with military operations and infrastructure projects.

8ETHNIC GROUPS

The Burman, speaking a language in the Tibeto-Burman group, constitute an unverified estimated 68% of Myanmar's total population. In ancient times, the Burman, migrants from the hills east of Tibet, descended the Irrawaddy Valley, where the Mon and Pyu peoples had previously settled. Many other peoples entered from the northeast and northwest to settle in what is now Myanmar: the Shan, Rakhine, Karen, Kachin, Kayah (Karenni), and Chin are among the more numerous. Urban areas have significant Chinese and Indian ethnic populations. According to unverified estimates, the Shan make up about 9% of the population, the Karen 7%, Rakhine 4%, Chinese 3%, Mon 2%, Indian 2%, and others 5%. While their percentage of the population is smaller than that of the Burman, the areas where the other ethnic peoples such as the Shan, Karen, Chin, and Kachin, predominate comprises a larger land area and holds many of Myanmar's most important natural resources.

Most of the non-Burman ethnic groups retain distinct identities, and many have sought to preserve cultural and political autonomy, or have even sought to secede. Dating back to independence from England, the military rulers of Burma-later Myanmar-have been in conflict with non-Burman ethnic peoples, using tactics that have amounted to a persistent pattern of severe human rights violations, which some international observers believe may fit legal definitions of genocide. The ethnic Karen have fought for greater autonomy from the central government since 1948, mainly with the Karen National Union (KNU). Over 100,000 Karen refugees fled the country during the course of the conflict. There have also been armed groups formed by the Shan, Wa, Mon, Kayah, Pa-O, Palaung, Kachin, Chin, Rakhine, Rohingya, and other ethnic peoples, particularly in the decades after the military takeover of Burma in 1962. As of 2011, the ethnic armies controlled little territory, and some were in ceasefire agreements with the government. The Muslim Rohingyas of Rakhine state are not recognized as an ethnic group by the Burmese government and have been denied citizenship.

9LANGUAGES

Burmese, the official language, is called *Myanmar* by the government, and spoken by at least 80% of the population, including use as a second language. Although Burmese is monosyllabic and tonal like other Tibeto-Chinese languages, its alphabet of 10 vowels and 32 consonants is derived from the Pahlavi script of South India; loan words from other languages, especially English are common. Other languages of Myanmar are in the Tibeto-Burman, Sino-Tai, Mon-Khmer, and Indo-European language families.

10RELIGIONS

After independence in 1948, Buddhism was made the state religion by the civilian government of U Nu. Since 1962 the government has been controlled by authoritarian military regimes which have generally placed restrictions on religious freedom, with religious publications and sermons subject to official approval and censorship. Although the military rulers have exhibited a strong preference for Theravada Buddhism, sponsoring monasteries and building pagodas, violent crackdowns have taken place against political activity by Buddhist monks. In August-September 2007,

LOCATION: 92°10′ to 101°11′E; 9°35′ to 28°28′ N. BOUNDARY LENGTHS: China, 2,185 kilometers (1,358 miles); Laos, 238 kilometers (148 miles); Thailand, 1,799 kilometers (1,118 miles); total coastline, 2,276 kilometers (1,414 miles); Bangladesh, 233 kilometers (145 miles); India, 1,403 kilometers (872 miles). TERRITORIAL SEA LIMIT: 12 miles.

tens of thousands of Buddhist monks, nuns, and lay supporters marched in the streets of cities and towns throughout Myanmar, chanting prayers of compassion and calling attention to popular discontent with the economy and lack of democracy. Armed soldiers were brought in to suppress the protests, and dozens or more of the monks were reportedly killed in the streets and in raids on monasteries. Leaders of the dissident monks were imprisoned or went into exile.

According to government statistics, Theravada Buddhism is practiced by about 90% of the population. Many Buddhists also follow traditional practices such as astrology, numerology, fortune-telling, and the veneration of supernatural beings called *nats*. The Chinese in Myanmar practice a traditional mixture of Mahayana Buddhism, Taoism, Confucianism, and ancestor worship; and the Indians there are mainly Hindus. Although Christian missionaries have had success with peoples of the hill areas—the Karen, Kayah, Kachin, and Chin—conversion among the Burman, Rakhine and Shan ethnic groups has been negligible. An estimated 4% of the population are Christian, with Baptists, Catholics, and Anglicans being the primary denominations. The government claims that about 4% of the population are Muslim, mostly Sunni, although the percentage may actually be much higher. There is a very small community of Jews in Yangon.

11 TRANSPORTATION

Because of Myanmar's near encirclement by mountain ranges, Myanmar has historically been dependent on sea and river transport externally and internally. Myanmar has approximately 12,800 km (7,954 mi) of navigable waterways. Inland waterways have been key to internal transportation, partly compensating for limited railroad and highway development. Hundreds of thousands of small river craft ply the Irrawaddy (navigable for about 640 km/400 mi), the Salween, the Sittang, and numerous tributaries. The Irrawaddy Delta, the focus of most water transportation, has some 2,700 km (1,679 mi) of rivers and streams, providing a seaboard for all types of craft. The state merchant fleet totaled 26 ships in 2010. Yangon, on the Yangon (Rangoon) River about 34 km (21 mi) inland from the Andaman Sea, is the chief port for ocean shipping, handling the majority of the country's seaborne trade; it is also the principal terminus for the highways, railroad, inland waterways, and airlines. Other ports include Sittwe (Akyab), serving western Myanmar; Pathein (Bassein), serving the delta area; and Mawlamyine (Moulmein), Dawei (Tavoy), and Mergui, in the southeast. As of 2011, a major new port construction project was planned for Dawei for development by Thailand, and an extensive river transport project was planned from Sittwe to the India border. A port project was also under development at Kyaukphyu, south of Sittwe, to serve petroleum pipelines to China.

The government operates all railroads, which are entirely 1.00 narrow gauge. The main lines are from Yangon (Rangoon) to Prome (259 km/161 mi) and from Yangon to Mandalay (621 km/386 mi) and then to Myitkyina (1,164 km/723 mi from the capital).

The Burma Road, connecting Lashio with Kunming in southern China, and the Ledo Road between Myitkyina and Assam, northeastern India, were built during World War II, but are now in disrepair. The CIA reports that as of 2006, Myanmar had a total of 27,000 km (16,777 mi) of roads, of which only 3,200 km (1,988 mi) were paved.

As of 2010 there were 76 airports, of which 37 had paved runways, according to the CIA. Yangon International Airport is the principal airport. The international airports are Yangon and Mandalay, with flights from Thailand, China, Indian, Malaysia, Vietnam, Cambodia, and Singapore. On 19 December 2011, a third international airport was inaugurated at Naypyidaw. Myanmar Airways is the national carrier; other airlines include Air Mandalay, Yangon Airways, Air KBZ, Asian Wings Airways, and Air Bagan.

12 HISTORY

The Pyu people settled what later became known as Burma in the 2nd century BC, founding city-states along the river valleys. Mon civilization rose across Southeast Asia, including southern Burma in the 9th century AD. The Burman kingdom of Pagan, founded in 1044 by Anawrahta, survived until 1287, when it was destroyed by the Mongol army of Kublai Khan. Centers of civilization also arose in lands controlled by Arakanese and Shan aristocracies. Independent indigenous peoples lived in mountain villages. In 1754, Alaungpaya defeated the Shan kingdom in northern Myanmar and the Mon kingdom in southern Myanmar and founded a Burman dynasty, which was in power until the British arrived in the early 19th century.

The British conquest spanned 62 years: the first Anglo-Burmese War took place during 1824–26, when the British East India Company, acting for the crown, took possession of the Arakan and Tenasserim coastal regions. In 1852, at the end of the second war, the British acquired the remainder of lower (southern) Burma; and on 1 January 1886, following Burma's defeat in the third war, total annexation was proclaimed. Incorporated into the British Indian Empire, Burma was administered as a province of India until 1937, when it became a separate colony. From 1886 to 1948, there was popular agitation for independence. The nationalists who finally gained independence for Burma were a group of socialist-minded intellectuals, called the Thakins, from the University of Rangoon. They included Aung San, who would be one of the founders of modern Burma; U Nu, independent Burma's first premier; Ne Win, the military dictator; and Than Tun, a Communist leader. At the start of World War II, these anti-British nationalists collaborated with the Japanese, and with the aid of the Burma Independence Army, led by Aung San, the capital, Rangoon, fell to Japan on 8 March 1943. They were soon disappointed with the Japanese occupation, however, and the Burma Independence Army was converted into an anti-Japanese guerrilla force called the Anti-Fascist People's Freedom League, which later assisted the British retaking of Burma. Many of the ethnic nationalities of the frontier regions, such as the Karen and Kachin, remained loyal to the British, as valued fighters for the Allies. After the war, Aung San negotiated with frontier ethnic leaders, signing the Panglong Agreement on 12 February 1947 with them, as a pledge of autonomy and other rights.

Having assumed leadership of the nationalist movement following the 19 July 1947 assassination of Aung San and six of his associates, U Nu signed an agreement with British Prime Minister Clement Attlee, and on 4 January 1948, the sovereign Union of Burma came into being. After severe setbacks in 1948–49, the U Nu government was able to control a Communist insurgency and consolidate its own power, and in 1951 the nation held its first parliamentary elections. The 1950s also brought the implementation of an ambitious land reform program and an attempt to forge a neutralist foreign policy, in the face of sporadic Communist resistance. U Nu appointed General Ne Win to head an interim "care-taker government" during a period of instability from 1958 to the 1960 national election, which U Nu's Anti-Fascist People's Freedom League (AFPFL) won.

Ne Win returned to power with a coup d'etat on 2 March 1962. The U Nu government was overthrown, and a military regime led by Ne Win assumed control. Student protests following the 1962 coup, and again in 1974, were crushed by the army with many civilian casualties. Most major political figures in the democratic governments of the years 1948–62, including U Nu, were arrested but were released in 1966–68. Ne Win rejected a return to a multiparty parliamentary system and proclaimed the Socialist Republic of Burma on 3 January 1974. Under a new constitution, Ne Win became president, and the government continued to be dominated by the military. Ne Win retired as president in November 1981, with Gen. San Yu succeeding him in office; but Ne Win retained his dominance, as chairman of the country's only legal political organization, the Burma Socialist Program Party (BSPP). Insurgency by the underground Communist Party of Burma (CPB) and numerous ethnic armies had begun just after World War II and continued throughout Ne Win's time in power. The general sought to unify the country by imposing a Burman-ethnic majority-identity, and to defeat insurgency with the "four cuts policy" of taking civilian support away from the rebels. Instead, the tactics of his armed forces in ethnic regions drove more and more inhabitants into rebellion.

In the 1980s, Ne Win continued to make all major and many minor government policy decisions. One such decision, to withdraw large currency notes from circulation in September 1987, made 80% of the country's currency valueless, touching off student-led demonstrations. Admitting his personal responsibility for dire economic conditions, Ne Win resigned as BSPP party chairman in July 1988. A protégé of Ne Win, Sein Lwin, was made president, and his appointment triggered nationwide revolts. A broad spectrum of the population joined in, marching in the streets and holding general strikes throughout Burma. The army opened fire on unarmed protesters, killing thousands, particularly during the first week of August. Sein Lwin resigned on 12 August and Maung Maung, a civilian, was appointed his successor on 19 August. Although Maung Maung proposed multiparty elections, his refusal to step down provoked further protests. On 18 September 1988 the army abolished the BSPP, took over the government and formed a junta called the State Law and Order Restoration Council (SLORC), headed by the army Chief of Staff, General Saw Maung, who named himself prime minister. Several days of violence occurred countrywide with thousands of civilians, including children, students, and monks, killed by the armed forces. In announcing the takeover, Saw Maung stated that the military rule would be temporary and that multiparty elections would be held once law and order were reestablished. In June 1989 the SLORC renamed Burma "Myanmar Naing Ngan," a formal historical Burmese name for the country; democracy advocates and the US government continue to use the name "Burma." Place names including cities and rivers were given new official spelling, as well, so that, for instance, Rangoon became Yangon.

Political parties formed for the 1990 elections. First to organize was U Nu's League for Democracy and Peace, later known as the League for Democracy. The BSPP was reformed as the pre-regime National Union Party (NUP). In 1988 Aung San Suu Kyi, daughter of assassinated legendary hero General Aung San, had come to popular prominence by delivering speeches opposing the military regime. On 24 September 1988, Aung San Suu Kyi, with senior civilian political figures, formed the National League for Democracy (NLD). Aung San Suu Kyi was placed under house arrest in Yangon (Rangoon) on 20 July 1989. The NUP was the party favored by the SLORC; other parties had immense difficulty in campaigning and obtaining publicity. Despite Aung San Suu Kyi's incommunicado house arrest, the NLD won the 27 May 1990 general elections by a landslide (87.7% of the votes, 392 candidates elected). The NUP took only 2.4% of the votes for 10 seats. In June 1989 Saw Maung indicated that the transfer of power to the winners of the election would not occur until a new constitution, meeting SLORC's approval, was drafted.

1990–2011

In September 1990 SLORC revealed its intention to remain in power for a further 5 to 10 years. Saw Maung resigned due to ill health in April 1992 and was replaced as Chairman of SLORC by General Than Shwe who was also named Chief of State and Head of the Government. The First Secretary was Lt.-General Khin Nyunt. In early 1993, a National Convention of 700 members met to draft a new constitution, but the convention was adjourned until June 1993, then again adjourned until January 1994, when it approved measures which would perpetuate the power of the military.

In March 1991, the UN Human Rights Commission passed a resolution to condemn and monitor the human rights abuses of SLORC, and in subsequent years Special Rapporteurs have been appointed to investigate Myanmar's human rights situation. Aung San Suu Kyi was awarded the 1991 Nobel Peace Prize, while she was under house arrest. The use of forced labor in Myanmar drew international attention; it was used on a vast scale throughout Myanmar, on many building projects including roads and railroads, as well as for carrying supplies and munitions for the SLORC troops in insurgent areas. According to the testimony of escapees, the labor was accompanied by beatings, rape, execution of the ill or slow, and use of civilians as human shields and human mine-detectors. Asia Watch also reported in 1994 that the government turned a "blind eye to traffic in women and girls from Myanmar to Thailand for forced-prostitution." It was estimated that there were about 20,000 women from Myanmar in Thai brothels, where they were at severe risk of HIV/AIDS infection.

The Communist Party of Burma (CPB) collapsed with the withdrawal of Chinese support and the mutiny of its Wa troops in 1989. The CPB split into four different ethnic armies. Khin Nyunt guided the SLORC to negotiate separate ceasefire agreements with individual armed ethnic groups. In 1989 the former CPB Wa were promised development assistance and were allowed to retain their arms, maintain control of their areas, and engage in any kind of business. In exchange they promised not to attack government forces. In 1990–1991 several other groups signed agreements to stop fighting the Tatmadaw, the SLORC's armed force, which had increased its troop strength from approximately 190,000 to well over 300,000 since the suppression of 1988's pro-democracy uprising. The Kachin had been the largest military group in a coalition of anti-SLORC ethnic forces. In February 1994 the Kachin

Independence Organization (KIO) signed a ceasefire agreement with SLORC. Armed conflict between the SLORC and Shan, Karen, and other groups continued. As many as 250,000 Muslim residents of Arakan, called the Rohingyas, fled to Bangladesh in the early 1990s.

Myanmar has been one of the world's largest producers of opium and heroin. Since 1990, illicit methamphetamine has also been produced, particularly in the Wa region. The HIV/AIDS virus spread through Myanmar in the 1990s, through the use of contaminated needles by drug addicts, unsafe medical practices, and sexual transmission, often involving prostitution. Myanmar's government has been slow to allow or promote any education and prevention measures against the epidemic.

In the 1990s, the countries of the region for the most part entered into "constructive engagement" with SLORC, gaining trade and investment opportunities. Up to and following Myanmar's acceptance into the Association of Southeast Asian Nations (ASEAN) in July 1997, ASEAN countries and Japan argued that "engaging" Myanmar was more productive than "isolating" it. This approach gained them controversial timber concessions, petroleum concessions, and some tourism and manufacturing opportunities. The United States and European Union (EU) imposed economic sanctions, but allowed their petroleum corporations to remain in Myanmar as major investors. Aung San Suu Kyi's NLD supported economic sanctions, including a tourism boycott. The Mon armed group in southern Myanmar signed a cease-fire agreement, but numerous Tatmadaw battalions were brought in to protect a gas pipeline project in their region. The multinational petroleum companies involved in the pipeline, Total of France and Unocal from the United States, were accused by human rights and environmental groups of complicity in human rights violations committed by the SLORC's security forces. Victims of such abuses sued Unocal, achieving a multi-million dollar settlement, in a groundbreaking US court case. The pipeline began bringing natural gas from Myanmar's Andaman Sea to an electrical generating plant on the Thai side of the border in 1999.

SLORC released Aung San Suu Kyi from house arrest on 10 July 1995. Her freedom was short-lived, however. After large crowds of people began gathering in front of her house for weekly speeches, she was forbidden to address such gatherings. In November 1995, the NLD withdrew from the National Convention which was to formulate a SLORC-approved constitution, in protest of undemocratic policies. SLORC renamed itself the State Peace and Development Council (SPDC) in November 1997. In 1999, Aung San Suu Kyi's terminally ill British husband was denied a visa to see her one last time before he died. Long jail sentences were handed down for even mild forms of public protest, and human rights groups reported that torture of student dissidents was routine in Myanmar's prisons. Min Ko Naing, an important leader of the 1988 demonstrations, was imprisoned, often in solitary confinement. Leo Nichols, an honorary consul for European nations, died in a Myanmar prison, where he was held for unauthorized possession of a fax machine.

Aung San Suu Kyi was again placed under house arrest in September 2000. She was released in May 2002, and toured the country, speaking in support of democratization. The most violent attack on the NLD occurred 30 May 2003 at Depayin in northern Burma. A convoy carrying Aung San Suu Kyi, and her supporters was attacked by a mob of young men, reportedly under the instigation of the military. Dozens of NLD supporters were killed in the assault, and many more were arrested. Aung San Suu Kyi was injured and placed under house arrest in Yangon. SPDC freed about 40 political prisoners in November 2004. The highest-profile dissident released at that time was Min Ko Naing.

In August 2003, Khin Nyunt became prime minister. He negotiated ceasefire agreements with several ethnic armies and planned to hold a convention in 2004 on drafting a new constitution as part of a "road map to democracy". In May 2004, the constitutional convention started, despite a boycott by the NLD. The convention adjourned in July. That October Khin Nyunt was replaced as prime minister and arrested. The ousting of Khin Nyunt left the SPDC firmly under the control of General Than Shwe. In February 2005, the constitutional convention resumed, without the participation of the main opposition and ethnic groups, and stopped again in January 2006.

As Myanmar's turn to take the chairmanship of the Association of Southeast Asian Nations (ASEAN) for 2006 approached, the international community called for Myanmar to be deprived of that honor because of the SPDC's human rights violations, and in July 2005, Myanmar relinquished the position. In November 2005, Myanmar suddenly announced that its seat of government would move to a new site near the small central town of Pyinmana. In March 2006, the elaborate new capital, called Naypyidaw ("abode of kings"), hosted its first official event, an Armed Forces Day parade.

The government raised the price of fuel for consumers in Burma on 15 August, 2007. Reacting to the hardship this caused for working people, and ongoing repression in Myanmar, a few survivors of the 1988 demonstrations held small public protests in Yangon, beginning on 19 August 2007. This was followed in September by a series of street processions by Buddhist monks and nuns, which grew into enormous marches, eventually joined by other people, in the largest protests since 1988, with up to 100,000 people participating. The monks chanted prayers of compassion, and their leaders, including U Gambira, called for nonviolent change in Myanmar. News of the demonstrations was sent to the outside world through digital videos by the underground journalists of Democratic Voice of Burma (DVB) and other exile-based media; the marches captured world attention and became known as the Saffron Revolution. In late September, troops were sent in to quell the protests in Yangon. On 26–30 September, monks, other marchers, and a Japanese photojournalist were killed by the security forces; monasteries were raided and monks were beaten and imprisoned as the protest movement was suppressed.

Cyclone Nargis smashed the Irrawaddy delta on 5 May, 2008, causing more than 134,000 deaths and destroying or seriously damaging over 800,000 homes. More than 2.4 million people were impacted by the storm. It was estimated that about 75% of the hospitals and clinics in the region were also damaged, and the delta's fertile rice-growing land was flooded with salt water. The military government was widely criticized for denying entry to foreign aid agencies until nearly a month after the disaster.

Myanmar's new constitution was put up for a public approval referendum on 10 May 2008, with the voting delayed in some areas affected by Cyclone Nargis. After approval by what the government claimed was a majority of over 90%, parliamentary elections were scheduled for November 2010. In May 2009, Aung San Suu Kyi was put on trial for allowing an uninvited American, who apparently swam to her house, to stay there overnight. Her house arrest was extended for several months. In May 2010, the main opposition party, Aung San Suu Kyi's NLD, was officially disbanded by the government for failure to register for the upcoming elections. In the 7 November 2010 legislative elections, candidates from the Union Solidarity and Development Party (USDP), the primary military-backed party, won about 80% of the vote. Opposition groups raised allegations of fraud and called the vote a sham. Of the nearly 3,000 candidates in the race, about two thirds were from parties associated with the military junta. Under existing rules, at least 25% of the seats in parliament have been reserved for the military. Following the November election, Aung San Suu Kyi was released from her latest term of house arrest on 13 November 2010. She called for peaceful change through negotiation, and the freeing of hundreds of other political prisoners.

On 30 March 2011, Myanmar's new government was sworn in, with a former general, Thein Sein, as president. During 2011, Aung San Suu Kyi was able to travel within Myanmar, and she held talks with government officials, including a meeting with Thein Sein on 19 August 2011. In the second half of 2011, the new parliament became increasingly willing to raise controversial issues, censorship of Myanmar's local media was drastically reduced, labor laws were strengthened, and some political prisoners were released, although hundred remained behind bars. Thein Sein was increasingly seen as a reformer, and Aung San Suu Kyi emphasized her willingness to work with his government for improvements. On 18 November 2011 the NLD announced that it would participate in parliamentary by-elections in April 2012; Aung San Suu Kyi and her party won 40 of the 45 contested seats in that election. Following a November 2011 ASEAN meeting in which Myanmar was approved as the 2014 chair of the organization, US secretary of state Hillary Clinton visited Myanmar, meeting separately with Thein Sein and Aung San Suu Kyi on 1 and 2 December.

Demands by the government for ethnic armies in ceasefire to become part of a Border Guard Force (BGF) led to conflict in 2009, when a Chinese-related Kokang ethnic militia refused and was ousted; tens of thousands of refugees fled to China. The Kachin Independence Organization (KIO) also refused the BGF demand, and began preparing for a return to war in 2011. Conflict between the KIO and government troops erupted on 9 June 2011 near a Chinese-backed hydroelectric dam site. Another Chinese project, the Myitsone dam, in construction on the confluence of the Irrawaddy River, was opposed by the KIO. In September 2011, controversy over the Myitsone dam's potentially disastrous effects on the entire watershed of Myanmar's most important river began to receive press coverage within Myanmar, and objections to the dam were raised in the Naypyidaw parliament. On 30 September, Thein Sein announced that the dam project was suspended, which was an unprecedented rejection of an infrastructure project backed by Myanmar's most powerful ally, China. Fighting continued between the Tatmadaw and the KIO through the end of 2011, with an estimated 30,000 civilians displaced by the conflict along the China border. The government held talks with a number of ethnic armed groups, including the KNU and KIO, as the year ended, and newly emboldened civil society groups and individuals within Myanmar began to call for peace and organize aid donations for war victims.

Numerous governmental reforms—including the release of many prominent political prisoners—led to a US announcement in January 2012 that the two countries would exchange ambassadors. The announcement was seen as a reward to Myanmar's government for its liberalization efforts.

13 GOVERNMENT

The Socialist Republic of the Union of Burma was announced on 3 January 1974, after a new basic law had been approved by plebiscite. Under the 1974 constitution there was a unicameral People's Assembly (Pyithu Hluttaw). The head of state was the chairman of the Council of State and the prime minister headed the Council of Ministers. Nationwide legislative elections were held in 1974, 1978, 1981, and 1985; in each election there was only a single slate presented by the ruling Burma Socialist Program Party (BSPP). General Ne Win, head of the BSPP was actually the supreme power, setting all policy. Suffrage was universal at age 18, although voting was often restricted in practice. In September 1988 a junta called the State Law and Order Restoration Council (SLORC) took over the government, under martial law. The earliest formation of the State Law and Order Restoration Council (SLORC) was made up of 17 active military commanders of the Defense Services. In June 1989, the official title of the country was changed to Myanmar Naing Ngan.

In the multiparty election held 27 May 1990, Aung San Suu Kyi's National League for Democracy (NLD) received 87.7% of the total vote and took 392 of its 447 contested seats, and the National Unity Party (NUP), the former BSPP re-registered as a new party, took only 10 seats with 2.4% of the votes. SLORC refused to hand over power to the NLD, instead voiding the election and insisting that a new constitution need be drafted and approved by referendum, and by SLORC, prior to the transfer of power. General Saw Maung resigned as chairman of SLORC on 23 April 1992, and was replaced by General Than Shwe. SLORC renamed itself the State Peace and Development Council (SPDC) in November 1997.

Government ministries were suddenly compelled to leave Yangon (Rangoon) on 6 November 2005 for a new capital still under construction at Pyinmana in the mountains 400 km north of Yangon. The motives for the large-scale relocation to a place with little infrastructure completed were not disclosed, but speculation ranged from fear of military attack, to an attempt at more centralized control of the country, to a form of "preventive magic." Civil servants were compelled to move to the new government complex at Pyinmana, named Naypyidaw, "Abode of Kings."

After years of sporadic constitutional convention meetings, without the participation of the NLD, a new constitution was revealed on 9 April 2008 and put up for an approval referendum on 10 May 2008. The government claimed approval rates of over 90%. The constitution designated 25% of seats in the Union Assembly (Pyidaungsu Hluttaw) parliament for active military personnel. This resulted in 56 out of 224 seats in the National Assembly upper house, and 110 seats out of 440 in the People's Assembly lower house, being held by military officers in uniform. Most of the civilian representatives were former military officers. The president is the head of state. Elections for the new parliament took place on 7 November 2010, with the NLD not able to participate. The election was considered unfair by international analysts, and the military-backed Union Solidarity and Development Party (USDP) gained around 80% of the vote. Myanmar's new National Assembly and People's Assembly were inaugurated on 30 March, 2011, and former general Thein Sein became president . Elections for unfilled parliamentary seats were to be held in 2012, with the NLD allowed to participate.

14 POLITICAL PARTIES

Between 1948 and 1962, Burma's parties were mostly socialist. The Anti-Fascist People's Freedom League (AFPFL), gained independence for the country and included the distinct Burma Socialist Program Party. The AFPFL governed the country from 1948. In 1958, tensions within the government, and insurgency in the countryside, prompted Prime Minister U Nu to temporarily hand over power to a "caretaker" government headed by General Ne Win. When U Nu's new Union Party won a landslide victory in 1960 elections, Ne Win relinquished power to him. Then on 2 March 1962, Ne Win staged a coup d'etat and began his long rule with the one-party (Burma Socialist Program Party, BSPP) state. Communist parties, and all other parties except the ruling military-dominant BSPP, were banned in 1974. The well-armed Communist Party of Burma (CPB) insurgents based themselves primarily in northeast Burma, along the China border. In 1989 the CPB was overthrown by its troops, many of whom regrouped as the United Wa State Army, which soon signed a cease-fire deal with the State Law and Order Restoration Council (SLORC).

Burmese independence leader General Aung San had negotiated the Panglong Agreement with representatives of frontier ethnic groups in 1947, but issues of autonomy and federalism have never been resolved. Numerous ethnic parties with armed wings were formed in the mid- to late-20th century, including the Karen National Union, Kachin Independence Organization, New Mon State Party, Karenni National Progressive Party, Shan State Progress Party, Arakan Liberation Party, and Chin National Front. In the 1990s, many ethnic organizations signed ceasefire agreements with the SLORC. Several of those groups participated in a coalition called the Ethnic Nationalities Council, as of 2011. Most of the ethnic leaders favor a federal union of Burma based on ethnic regions.

The democracy uprising of 1988 ended with the 18 September takeover by the junta called the State Law and Order Restoration Council (SLORC, renamed State Peace and Development Council, SPDC, in 1997). The Burma Socialist Program Party was formally abolished, and all governing authority was concentrated in SLORC. A general election was scheduled for 27 May 1990. Only the military-associated National Unity Party (NUP) was completely free to campaign. Aung San Suu Kyi and several senior civilian political figures formed the National League for Democracy (NLD), and her campaign speeches around the country were wildly popular, despite the junta's attempts to restrict her travel. A total of 93 parties fielded 2,209 candidates who, along with 87 independent candidates, contested 485 seats out of a total of 492 constituencies designated for holding elections. In voting considered by analysts to have been largely free and fair, the NLD won a resounding 87.7% of the vote and gained 392 seats; the NUP trailed with 2.4%, for 10 seats. The remaining seats mostly went to ethnic-based parties including Shan Nationalities League for Democracy (1.7%, 23 seats), and Rakhine Democratic League (1.2%, 11 seats.)

The 1990 election results were not honored by SLORC, which instead announced that a new constitution would be drafted. From 1990 on, opposition politicians and parties were harassed by SLORC/SPDC, with NLD leader Aung San Suu Kyi placed under house arrest from 20 July 1989 to 10 July 1995, from 2 September 2000 to 6 May 2002, and from 30 May 2003 to 13 November 2010. NLD members were imprisoned and pressured to renounce their membership at public rallies of the junta-sponsored Union Solidarity Defense Association (USDA) a mass organization formed in September 1993 to support the ruling military.

When the 2008 constitution was in place, elections were called by SPDC for 7 November, 2010, but with Aung San Suu Kyi still under arrest, the NLD refused to participate and was forced to disband. In September 2010, SPDC's election commission announced that 37 political parties had been officially qualified to present candidates for the election. A total of 47 parties had applied for qualification. Five established political parties were officially disbanded. The NUP and the new Union Solidarity and Development Party (USDP) were the main SPDC-backed parties, with candidates largely recently-retired military officers. The USDP won the 7 November 2001 vote in a landslide; analysts considered the election unfair due to lack of NLD participation and other flaws. The USDP gained 74.8% of the vote and 129 seats in the National Assembly, and 79.6% of the vote and 259 seats in the People's Assembly. Other parties with seats in parliament included Rakhine Nationalities Development Party, NUP, National Democratic Force, and Chin Progressive Party. Aung San Suu Kyi was released from house arrest following the election, and the NLD resumed functioning as a political party. On 18 November 2011, the NLD announced that, with previous restrictions on it lifted, it would run candidates for all or most of the 45 seats up for a vote in a parliamentary by-election to be held in April 2012. In that election, Aung San Suu Kyi and the NLD party took 40 of the 45 seats.

15 LOCAL GOVERNMENT

Myanmar is a unitary nation, comprised of seven states and seven divisions. The main distinction between the two kinds of units, which are functionally the same, is that the states represent an area where a non-Burman ethnic group is the local majority. The states are Rakhine (Arakan), Chin, Kachin, Kayin (Karen), Kayah (Karenni), Mon, and Shan. The divisions are Ayeyarwadt (Irrawaddy), Magway (Magwe), Mandalay, Bago (Pegu), Sagaing, Yangon (Rangoon), and Tanintharyi (Tenasserim). As of late 2011, there were also official self-administered zones of ethnic ceasefire groups including the Wa, Pa-O, and Palaung, and some remaining frontier areas where armed ethnic groups in opposition to the government provided their own administration and social services.

States and divisions are segmented into 317 townships. Village tracts consist of villages, and towns are divided into wards. Villages usually have a headperson, either appointed from outside or locally chosen.

Representatives were elected to 14 regional assemblies in the 2010 general election, with 25% of seats reserved for active members of the military. Most of the other regional assemblies' seats went to USDP candidates, although there was some local ethnic representation, particularly in Shan state and Rakhine states. Regional commanders of the Tatmadaw continued to be very powerful in setting local government policy throughout Myanmar as of late 2011.

16 JUDICIAL SYSTEM

The British-style judicial system with which Burma began its independence, including a supreme court, were disbanded by Ne Win's Revolutionary Council. The 1974 constitution, suspended in 1988, provided for a Council of People's Justices, state and divisional judges' committees, and township, ward, and village tract judges' committees. Military tribunals which enforced orders issued by the State Law and Order Restoration Council (SLORC) were abolished in 1992. Civilian courts then handled such cases, with heavy military influence. There are courts at the township, district, state, and national levels.

The military government used laws such as the Emergency Provisions Act and the Unlawful Associations Act to crack down on dissent; as of late 2011, they were still in effect. UN agencies and international human rights organizations have strongly criticized the military government for unfair trials and arbitrary imprisonment, as well as the use of torture, forced labor by captives, and summary execution. Myanmar's prisons and labor camps were described as "harsh and life-threatening" by the US State Department as of 2010.

Myanmar's 2011 constitution mandated a Supreme Court and a Constitutional Tribunal; it granted immunity from prosecution for acts committed by present or past government members as part of their official duties. The judiciary is not independent, there is no jury trial, and defendants are not presumed innocent. It was very difficult for persons not connected with the military to succeed in civil litigation, such as land rights cases, as of 2011. Aung San Suu Kyi stated in late 2011 that Myanmar's highest priority should be establishment of "the rule of law" for its citizens. In October 2011, about 200 political prisoners were released as part of a mass amnesty, but hundreds more remained imprisoned at the year's end.

17 ARMED FORCES

The International Institute for Strategic Studies estimated that armed forces in Myanmar totaled 492,000 members as of 2010. According to the Myanmar government's budget figures for 2011, about $2.04 billion, amounting to around 23% of expenditures would go to the military, over 4% of gross domestic product (GDP), with purchase of Russian fighter jets prioritized. Analysts believe that military spending was actually higher, due to military-run businesses and hidden funding sources.

Myanmar's 2010 constitution mandates that men and women over 18, with some exceptions, should be trained for military service. International human rights organizations estimated that Myanmar had as many as 70,000 child soldiers in the Tatmadaw, during the early 21st century, and reported that forced conscription and mistreatment of lower ranking troops were common.

Myanmar has purchased weapons, equipment, and aircraft from China, Russia, India, and Singapore, among other countries. In 2010, exiled dissidents released reports, vetted by international experts, alleging that Myanmar's military government was working on developing a nuclear weapons program in underground bunkers, under advice from North Korea.

18 INTERNATIONAL COOPERATION

Myanmar was admitted to the UN on 19 April 1948; it is a member of ESCAP and several non-regional specialized agencies, such as FAO, IAEA, UNSECO, UNIDO, and WHO, and WTO. As of 2011, Myanmar had membership in the Asian Development Bank (ADB); G-77; the Colombo Plan; and Bangladesh, India, Myanmar, Sri Lanka, and Thailand Economic Cooperation (BIMSTEC). Myanmar is a member of the Nonaligned Movement. In environmental cooperation, Myanmar is part of the Convention on Biological Diversity, CITES, the Kyoto Protocol, the Montréal Protocol, MARPOL, the Nuclear Test Ban Treaty, and the UN Conventions on the Law of the Sea, Climate Change, and Desertification. A member of ASEAN since 1997, Myanmar was approved in November 2011 to become chair of the organization for the first time in 2014.

In the early 21st century, China was Myanmar's closest ally and trade partner. Relations with the governments of neighboring Thailand and India were also friendly and business-based, but ties with Bangladesh were strained over boundary disputes including offshore petroleum rights. The US and European Community were often critical of Myanmar's human rights violations and lack of democracy, and had imposed economic sanctions which were still in effect as of December 2011.

19 ECONOMY

Although Myanmar is rich in resources and has much land suitable for agriculture, inefficient economic policies and constant mismanagement have resulted in a severely underdeveloped economy. The GDP rate of change in Myanmar, as of 2010, was 5.3%, according to the CIA. Inflation stood at 9.6%, and unemployment was reported at 5.7%, as of 2011. Myanmar government statistics are often unavailable or unreliable. There is an enormous informal sector, and a huge illicit economy including timber smuggling and the production of narcotics.

An estimated 43.2% of the GDP was from the agricultural sector, as of 2010, according to the CIA. A major rice exporter in colonial times, Myanmar's production initially declined under military rule, and production in the Irrawaddy delta region was badly set back by Cyclone Nargis in 2008. However, exports were expected to double to 1.5 million metric tons in 2012, and the government was encouraging additional rice planting.

Substandard infrastructure remains a major impediment to economic growth. Water treatment and distribution, sewage disposal, and irrigation systems, as well as power transmission and distribution, require upgrading. Industry faces chronic shortages of electricity. Roads are poor and many are not passable during parts of the year. Communications facilities have remained insufficient, with landline, mobile phone, and internet use lagging far behind most other Asian countries. Government priorities have centered on military expenditures and, since 2005, on the construction of an extravagant new capital at Naypyidaw.

Because of Myanmar's poor human rights record, the United States, Australia, Canada, and the European Union (EU) imposed economic sanctions on the country, with imports banned by the US. Myanmar's economy is driven by resource extraction, including timber (largely depleted as of 2011), metals, gems, natural gas, and hydroelectric power. Large infrastructure projects were planned and implemented as joint ventures between government entities and foreign investors, mostly from China and a few other Asian countries. These projects were often controversial for their environmental effects and displacement of local populations. The China backed Myitsone dam project was suspended by president Thein Sein in October 2011, following objections to its potential effects on the Irrawaddy River watershed, in an unprecedented show of Myanmar government responsiveness to popular concerns.

In October 2010, Transparency International listed Myanmar as the second most corrupt nation in the world (after Somalia). Following the economy change from a socialist to a free market system in 1989, successful businesses have largely been run by relatives or cronies of the military elite, or in some cases by narcotics warlords. The military elite has reportedly siphoned off earnings from joint-venture projects to private offshore bank accounts.

Myanmar's financial sector suffers from excessive bureaucratic red tape and an extremely unrealistic official exchange rate. The government drafted new laws on banking as steps toward improvement in the financial sector, and the new government took steps to increase transparency in 2011. President Thein Sein's reforms during 2011, and his willingness to talk with the opposition, as exemplified by Aung San Suu Kyi, led to a more optimistic foreign investment climate and an expectation that international sanctions would eventually be discarded. Tourism began to rebound in 2011, as the NLD no longer called for a tourism boycott.

20 INCOME

The CIA estimated that in 2010 the GDP of Myanmar was $76.47 billion. The CIA defines GDP as the value of all final goods and services produced within a nation in a given year and computed on the basis of purchasing power parity (PPP) rather than value as measured on the basis of the rate of the exchange based on current dollars. The per capita GDP was estimated at $1,400. The annual growth rate of GDP was 5.3%. It was estimated that agriculture accounted for 43.2% of GDP, industry 20%, and services 36.8%.

According to the CIA, as of 2007 about 32.7% of the population subsisted on an income below the poverty line established by Myanmar's government. As of 2011, Myanmar, on the UN's list of Least Developed Countries despite abundant resources, had low wages in all sectors, chronic underemployment and a massive gap between a wealthy, military-connected elite and a subsistence-level majority. Lack of opportunity in Myanmar has led to a brain drain of professionals and workers from all sectors seeking employment in other Asian countries like Thailand and Malaysia; according to the World Bank, remittances from citizens living abroad totaled $137 million or about $3 per capita and accounted for approximately 0.2% of GDP.

21 LABOR

In 1988 SLORC banned the workers' and peasants' organizations of the previous government, thereby eliminating any right to bargain collectively. Under the military government, labor rights activists, particularly members of the outlawed Free Trade Union of Burma, were harassed and imprisoned. Myanmar's 2008 constitution guaranteed the right of workers to organize, and by late 2011, a new Labor Organizations Law allowed unions to be registered, although collective bargaining was not included. During 2011, strikes and other wage protests were increasingly tolerated when they took place at private factories.

As of 2010, Myanmar had a total labor force of 31.68 million people, according to the CIA. At least 70% were employed in agriculture. Wage levels continued to be low and had been eroded by inflation, as of 2011. As of 2010, salaried government workers had a 35 hour work week, and a minimum wage of less than $4 per day, an amount that did not provide a living wage. Even such low minimum wages did not apply to most other sectors, and workplace health and safety standards were not regulated.

Forced labor by conscripted civilians has been used extensively by the military for building projects, carrying supplies for troops, and other purposes; it is often in conjunction with other human rights violations such as torture, rape, and summary execution. Prison labor is also commonly used, with prisoners taken on military operations to carry supplies for the Tatmadaw.

While the official minimum working age was 13 as of 2011, the use of child labor was widespread in Myanmar. In cities, children worked in small or family-owned businesses or the informal sector, sometimes in dangerous conditions, while in rural areas children were employed in agriculture and at mineral extraction sites. Children have been used for forced labor on the military's construction projects.

22 AGRICULTURE

As of 2010, according to the CIA, agriculture accounted for about 43% of Myanmar's GDP. According to the World Bank, about 18% of the total land was farmed, as of 2008. The country's major crops include rice, pulses, beans, vegetables, fruits, tea, cotton, tobacco, jatropha, oil palm, rubber, sesame, jute, peanuts, tapioca, corn, and sugarcane. According to the FAO, as of 2009, cereal production amounted to 34.3 million tons, fruit production 2.1 million tons, and vegetable production 4.9 million tons.

Rice is by far the most important agricultural product and the staple food throughout Myanmar. The vast majority of rice is grown in wet paddy fields, with some hill rice grown in mountainous areas. The most productive land lies in the fertile Irrawaddy delta region, the lower valleys of the Sittang and Salween rivers, and along the Arakan and Tenasserim coasts. However, the war caused extensive damage to the economy, and Myanmar did not achieve prewar levels of rice acreage and output until 1964. Low and unstable prices, lack of irrigation and fertilizer, lack of fuel for farm machinery, and difficulties in market transportation were among factors leading to rice production declines during Myanmar's decades of military rule. Irrawaddy delta rice production was badly set back by salt water inundation and infrastructure damage from Cyclone Nargis in 2008. Prior to World War II (1939–45), Myanmar was the world's leading exporter of rice. Although farming in the Irrawaddy delta began to recover in the years after Cyclone Nargis, rice crops were badly affected by drought in 2009. A 50 year cycle of bamboo flowering led to a rat population explosion in 2008, destroying rice harvests in upland areas of western Myanmar. Rice milling operations were held back by a lack of electrical power. According to US Department of Agriculture estimates, Myanmar's rice production was 10.6 million tons in 2009, with 1 million tons exported on the official market.

Crops grown for the production of edible oils, including sesame, peanuts, oil palm, mustard, and nigella are important in Myanmar. In the early 21st century, agribusiness plantations with foreign financing began growing oil palms, rubber, tapioca, and other crops; some of these operations were accused of taking land away from local villagers and adding to deforestation. In 2005–2007, the military government pressured citizens throughout Myanmar to grow jatropha, as a fuel oil crop, an effort that largely failed and took land away from food crops. Land confiscation by the military, forced relocations, and forced labor have had negative effects on agriculture in many rural areas of Myanmar. Opium poppies, providing the raw material for heroin, have traditionally been an important crop for upland areas with little market access for other farm products.

23 ANIMAL HUSBANDRY

The UN Food and Agriculture Organization (FAO) reported that Myanmar dedicated 305,000 hectares (753,671 acres) to permanent pasture or meadow in 2009. During that year, the country tended 125 million chickens, 13 million head of cattle, and 7.8 million pigs. The production from these animals amounted to 159,587 tons of beef, 410,826 tons of pork, 803,249 tons of poultry, 198,557 tons of eggs, and 1.25 million tons of milk. Myanmar also produced 24,510 tons of cattle hide and 403 tons of raw wool.

Zebu cattle and water buffalo are mainly raised as draft animals. Beef cattle are also raised, but dairy farming is not widespread. The Chin people of western Myanmar raise mithuns, a type of ox related to the wild gaur, for ceremonial purposes. Working elephants are still in use in some parts of Myanmar, for hauling logs and other transportation. Pigs and poultry are raised by individual households throughout Myanmar. H5N1 avian influenza first appeared in Myanmar in 2006 and H5N1 was detected at poultry farms in western Myanmar during 2011, leading to the destruction of over 100,000 chickens.

24 FISHING

Myanmar had an estimated 1,917 decked commercial fishing boats in 2008. The annual capture totaled 2.49 million tons according to the UN FAO. The export value of seafood totaled $460.1 million. Fish, which supply the main protein for most people of Myanmar, often are dried and salted for marketing. They are also consumed fresh or as fish paste. Roho and various carp are among the main species caught. Traditionally, freshwater fish has been preferred for local consumption. In 1990, the military government granted fishing concessions in the Bay of Bengal and Andaman Sea to foreign trawler fleets, leading to rampant overfishing of shrimp and other seafood. Many migrant workers from Myanmar are employed on Thailand's fishing boats, often in unsafe and exploitive conditions. Direct exports of seafood from Myanmar have been affected by international sanctions and allegations of chemical additives. Bay of Bengal cyclones, including the 2008 Cyclone Nargis, have killed fishing people and destroyed boats and fish farms. Shrimp/prawn farms have been established on Myanmar's coasts, reportedly leading to mangrove deforestation and pollution. Stocks of freshwater fish, in locations including Shan State's Inle Lake, have decreased due to pollution from agricultural chemicals and other sources.

25 FORESTRY

Approximately 49% of Myanmar was covered by forest as of 2010, but this figured included secondary forest and scrub woodlands; less than 10% of the 49% was primary forest. The FAO estimated Myanmar's 2009 roundwood production at 4.26 million cu m (150.5 million cu ft), and an estimated value of all forest products, including roundwood, totaled $385.7 million.

During British colonial times, Burma was the world's leader in production of valuable teakwood, harvested sustainably under the Burma Selection System. Forests were largely intact before the SLORC takeover in 1988; the country had the largest tropical rainforest area in mainland Southeast Asia, and logging was done selectively, on a small scale, often using elephants for log hauling. As SLORC opened up Myanmar's economy, in 1989–1990, logging concessions were granted to firms from neighboring Thailand, resulting in rapid clear-cutting of the world's last major teak forests and other tropical hardwoods for export. Myanmar lost an estimated 17.8% of its forest between 1990 and 2005, according to FAO statistics.

Forest protection guidelines were included in the Ministry of Forestry's Forest Law of 1992, and the 1995 Forest Policy, including limitations on log exports. However, massive illegal timber exporting continued in the early 21st century, particularly on the northern border with China, with cooperation of elements of the military and ethnic armies under ceasefire agreements. Areas designated as protected forests have been encroached on by mining operations, agribusiness plantations, wildlife poachers, and infrastructure projects.

Import sanctions imposed by the US and EU prohibited direct import of forest products from Myanmar, as of 2011, but furniture and other products made from Myanmar-origin wood still reached those markets via China and other Asian countries. There was little value-added industry for wood products in Myanmar, other than furniture and building materials for local use. Fuelwood and charcoal are widely used for cooking. Other forest products include bamboo, which is extremely important for construction and many other uses, rattan, lac, resins, medicines, and orchids.

26 MINING

Myanmar has a large variety of mineral resources. The government has controlled all official mineral exploration, extraction, regulation, and planning through the Ministry of Mines. However, tungsten, tin, antimony, gold, and jadeite were mined in, and exported from, areas controlled by armed ethnic opposition groups, including the Karen National Union and Kachin Independence Organization. Under military rule, development of the mining sector was slow, and was often accompanied by environmental damage. Gold and copper mining have caused water pollution and soil erosion in northern Myanmar, and in December 2011, President Thein Sein announced a moratorium on large-scale gold mining, which was mainly done by companies from China. Other foreign investors in mining have included Canada and Australia.

Mines in northern Myanmar have produced an estimated 90% of the world's supply of rubies. Myanmar's Kachin State has the world's primary deposits of jadeite (precious jade). Rubies and jadeite have been a significant export commodity for Myanmar's state-owned mining companies. A government gem emporium for international buyers is held at least once a year. The global financial crisis of 2007–08 led to a drop in demand from Asian buyers, including Thailand, China, and India. US sanctions against Myanmar include a ban on imports, including gems.

Exports of base metals and ores were valued at $40.9 million in 2009, 0.6% of total exports. Copper, tin, tungsten, iron, construction materials, and fertilizer were among the country's leading industrial products in 2009. Estimated outputs for 2009 were: copper (metal content), 8,000 metric tons, down from 35,000 metric tons in 2005; tin (metal content, from tin and tin-tungsten concentrate), 672 metric tons; tungsten (metal content, from tin and tin-tungsten concentrate), 87 metric tons; jadeite, 25.4 million kg, up from 19.4 million kg in 2005; and spinel rubies and sapphires, 1.1 million carats, down from 2.4 million carats in 2005. Metallic ores of chromite, gold, lead, manganese, nickel, silver, and zinc were mined. There are also deposits of limestone, iron, and antimony. Industrial mineral production included construction aggregates, barite, hydraulic cement, fire clay, feldspar, gypsum, limestone, salt, sand and gravel, and silica sand. Lead, zinc, silver, copper, nickel, and cobalt were produced at the Bawdwin mine, in Namtu, Shan State. In 2009, a Chinese mining group announced an $800-million project for the development of the Tagaung Taung ferro-nickel mine in Mandalay Division.

27 ENERGY AND POWER

The World Bank reported in 2008 that Myanmar produced 6.43 billion kWh of electricity and consumed kWh, or 89 kWh per capita. Oil production totaled 20,239 barrels of oil a day. The petroleum and petrochemical sector in Myanmar is entirely state-owned. After SLORC began offering petroleum exploration concessions to multinational corporations in 1990, the development of offshore natural gas reserves for export became a hard currency lifeline for the military government. In 1997/98 the energy sector grew by 37.7% (from virtual nonexistence) due to investment in the Yadana natural gas pipeline to Thailand, which came online in 1999. The $1.2 billion pipeline was a joint venture between multinationals Total, Unocal, Petroleum Authority of Thailand (PTT), and the Myanmar military government. Unocal paid damages in a US court case based on claims of abuse of villagers by pipeline security forces. Myanmar exported an estimated 8.29 billion cu m of natural gas exports in 2009, according to the CIA. As of 2011, two Myanmar-China petroleum pipelines were under construction, one for natural gas from Myanmar's offshore fields, and one to carry oil to China from tankers shipping it from the Middle East.

Although Myanmar has become a petroleum (natural gas) exporter, most homes and industries lacked a reliable supply of electricity as of 2011, with brownouts and blackouts common even in the cities. Large hydroelectric dam projects, financed by China and India, were intended for the export of electricity rather than local use. One such project, the Myitsone dam, was cancelled by the government following public concern about its danger to the Irrawaddy River watershed, but other dam projects remained controversial for their potential environmental effects and population displacement. As of 2011, a Thailand-backed port development plan on the southern coast at Dawei (Tavoy) included a coal-burn-

ing power plant. Alternative energy sources such as solar power were rarely in use in Myanmar, and reliance on diesel generators, kerosene lamps, and charcoal stoves was normal in most of the country. In December 2011, the government announced a 50% increase in electrical power fees.

28 INDUSTRY

According to the CIA, industry accounted for 20% of GNP, and the industrial production growth rate was 4.3% as of 2010. Industry is largely connected to the processing of agricultural and mineral products. Principal industrial products include cement, steel, bricks and tiles, fertilizer, metals, and processed foods. Consumer goods manufactured domestically include sugar, paper, glass products, bicycles, pharmaceuticals, beverages, and cigarettes. Vehicles including trucks and farm machinery were assembled in factories in Myanmar, with plans to increase passenger car production through foreign joint venture plants, as of 2011. In the late 1990s, private companies opened factories in Myanmar to produce garments for export. The garment industry declined severely after 1997, due to decreases in demand, competition from other Asian countries, and economic sanctions imposed by the US and EU. Myanmar had more than 600 government-owned factories, and 18 privately-owned special industrial areas, mainly around Yangon and Bago, as of 2011. Traditional cottage industries produce items such as woven silk, toys, lacquerware, and cheroots.

29 SCIENCE AND TECHNOLOGY

The World Bank reported in 2009 that there were no patent applications in science and technology in Myanmar. The Universities of Mandalay and Yangon offer degrees in the sciences, with graduate programs including medical schools. Each state and division has at least one "computer university" and at least one "technological university". University of Computer Studies, Yangon became an independent institution in 1998. Yatanarpon Cyber City was built near Naypyidaw, starting in 2007, to promote high tech businesses; it includes a technological university, opened in 2010. Many students from Myanmar seek undergraduate and graduate education in science at institutions in other countries; there has been a severe brain drain of professionals since the military takeover in 1962. Foreign assistance programs have funded training in technology, agricultural science, and fisheries science.

30 DOMESTIC TRADE

In 1964, Ne Win's military government nationalized all wholesale businesses, and large private and cooperative shops; small retail shops, hotels, restaurants, and village cooperatives were exempted. The People's Stores Corp. was initially responsible for imports, exports, and domestic sales. In 1970, the "people's stores," most of which had been unsuccessful, were replaced by consumer cooperatives. Beginning in 1966, the government set all commodity prices and controlled distribution systems; in September 1987, the Burmese people were told that they could buy, sell, and store rice and other grains free of government restrictions. After the SLORC takeover in 1988, domestic wholesale and retail trade was opened up to private business. Numerous new retail outlets, including a few shopping centers, appeared in cities and towns. Rural areas have outdoor markets and small household shops, while cities have large marketplaces with individual stalls for food, clothing, and other goods. Foreign franchise retail businesses had not entered Myanmar, as of 2011. Private trading companies, most run by businesspersons with military links, trade in commodities like timber and gems, and serve as local distributors for electronics and other imported goods. Although significant commerce is done at Bago (Pegu), Mandalay, Mawlamyine (Moulmein), Pathein (Bassein), Henzada, Akyab (Sittwe), and Dawei (Tavoy), Yangon (Rangoon) is Myanmar's most important business center. Citizens of China residing in Mandalay have invested heavily in retail and wholesale businesses.

Normal business hours are 9:30 a.m. to 4:30 p.m., Monday through Friday; small private shops keep longer hours than government offices and enterprises. Banks are usually open 10 a.m. to 2 p.m., Monday through Friday. Credit cards are not widely accepted. Advertising media includes outdoor display, television, and print publications.

31 FOREIGN TRADE

According to the CIA, Myanmar imported an estimated $4.224 billion worth of goods and services in 2010, while exporting $8.586 billion worth of goods and services; the CIA noted that official export figures are underestimated due to large volumes of goods (including narcotics, gems, timber, and rice) which are smuggled to other countries in the region; likewise official import figures were low because of the value of goods smuggled from regional countries. Major import partners in 2010 were China, 38.9%; Thailand, 23.2%; Singapore, 12.9%; and South Korea, 5.8%, according to the CIA, while major export partners were Thailand, 38.3%; India, 20.8%; China, 12.9%; and Japan, 5.2%.

Despite political repression and a difficult business environment, Myanmar has been considered a significant trading partner by some fellow members of ASEAN, including Thailand, Malaysia, and Singapore. The ASEAN Trade in Goods Agreement (ATIGA), approved in 2009, entered into force on 17 May 2010, as a step towards creating a single market and production base-known as the ASEAN Economic Community (AEC)-by 2015. Major points of ATIGA include tariff liberalization, a simplification of the rules of origin, and implementation of such rules. The comprehensive

---

Balance of Payments – Myanmar (Burma) (2010)

(In millions of US dollars)

Current Account		1,526.9
Balance on goods	3,455.8	
Imports	-4,375.5	
Exports	7,831.3	
Balance on services	-430.5	
Balance on income	-1,739.6	
Current transfers	241.0	
Capital Account		...
Financial Account		1,128.7
Direct investment abroad	...	
Direct investment in Myanmar (Burma)	910.3	
Portfolio investment assets	...	
Portfolio investment liabilities	...	
Financial derivatives	...	
Other investment assets	...	
Other investment liabilities	218.4	
Net Errors and Omissions		-2,089.9
Reserves and Related Items		-565.7

(…) data not available or not significant.

SOURCE: *Balance of Payment Statistics Yearbook 2011*, Washington, DC: International Monetary Fund, 2011.

---

agreement also demands greater transparency in regional trade liberalization, aiding the work of businesses and investors.

US sanctions banned the import of all commodities from Myanmar as of 2011, although the US petroleum company Chevron remained in a joint venture producing natural gas for sale to Thailand. The export of natural gas to Thailand by pipeline was Myanmar's predominant foreign trade sector as of 2011. Agricultural products, particularly beans and pulses, were also major export commodities. In 2010–2011, Myanmar was a low volume rice exporter; rice exports were temporarily halted in mid-2011 to stabilize domestic prices. Yearly government emporiums for gems have attracted buyers from China and elsewhere in Asia, as Myanmar produced significant quantities of precious jade, rubies and other gemstones. Metals, including tin, gold, copper, and tungsten, were exported. Timber was exported to China, mostly illegally, as of 2011, although in diminishing amounts as Myanmar's hardwood forests dwindled.

Some of Myanmar's border towns, such as Myawaddy and Tachilek, have become important for the legal and illegal importing of consumer goods. Myanmar's major imports include fuel, fertilizer, machinery, motor vehicles, aircraft, cement, palm oil, electronics, and fabric.

32 BALANCE OF PAYMENTS

As of 2010, according to the CIA, the value of Myanmar's exports was $8.586 billion, and that of imports was $4.224 billion. Myanmar's official figures are severely underestimated due to the value of smuggled imports and exports, as well as hidden wealth diverted to foreign bank accounts by the military elite, and other aspects of a very low-transparency economic system. According to the CIA, in 2010, the current-account balance was estimated at $1.549 million. That year, total external debt was estimated at $7.993 billion. Foreign assistance to Myanmar has been hampered

---

Principal Trading Partners – Myanmar (2010)

(In millions of US dollars)

Country	Total	Exports	Imports	Balance
World	13,556.2	8,748.7	4,807.5	3,941.2
Thailand	4,870.4	2,590.3	2,280.2	310.1
China	4,702.4	873.6	3,828.8	-2,955.2
Singapore	1,346.7	74.8	1,271.9	-1,197.1
India	1,311.5	1,010.6	300.9	709.8
South Korea	672.1	145.4	526.7	-381.3
Japan	643.9	353.4	290.5	62.9
Malaysia	613.2	208.4	404.7	-196.3
Indonesia	341.5	29.0	312.6	-283.6
Taiwan	175.8	57.8	118.0	-60.3
Australia	98.0	14.5	83.5	-69.0

(…) data not available or not significant.

(n.s.) not specified.

SOURCE: *2011 Direction of Trade Statistics Yearbook,* New York: United Nations, 2011.

by resistance to oversight and other interference on the part of the military government, although substantial aid and debt forgiveness have been provided by China and Japan. US sanctions have prevented World Bank and IMF involvement in Myanmar since the late 1980s; the ADB also stopped finance for Myanmar at that time. As of late 2011, following a visit by US secretary of state Hillary Clinton, it appeared that the multilateral lenders would soon re-engage with Myanmar.

33BANKING AND SECURITIES

In 1963, all of Burma's commercial banks were nationalized and combined into 4 state banks. After subsequent reorganizations of the banking system, these became Central Bank of Myanmar, Myanma Investment and Commercial Bank, Myanma Economic Bank, and Myanma Foreign Trade Bank. Agricultural credit was provided by a separate Myanmar Agricultural and Rural Development Bank. As SLORC opened up Myanmar's economy in 1990–94, licenses to open representative offices were issued to 19 banks from overseas. Eventually, 54 foreign banks had offices in Myanmar, but in 2000–02, 21 of them left the country. US sanctions imposed in 1997 prohibited new investment in Myanmar by US companies, and US sanctions imposed in 2003 blocked funds belonging to Myanmar senior government officials in US-owned banks.

As of 2009, there were 15 private local banks and 13 foreign banks in operation, according to the Myanmar Ministry of Finance. Some banks from Europe and Asia had representative offices, rather than actual branches, in Myanmar. As a sign of reform, the government announced that 11 private local banks would be allowed to trade in foreign currency as of November 2011. The first ATMs appeared in Myanmar that month, although they were not connected to international systems. Credit cards were not in use as of late 2011.

The CIA reported that in 2010, currency and demand deposits—an aggregate commonly known as M1—were equal to $6.53 billion, with the note that this figure represented the "vastly over-valued official exchange rate"; while M2—an aggregate equal to M1 plus savings deposits, small time deposits, and money market mutual funds—was $10.89 billion. According to the CIA, as of December 2010, the discount rate, the interest rate at which the central bank lends to financial institutions in the short term, was 10%. In late 2011, the IMF began talks aimed at advising the government of Myanmar on reforming the exchange rates to reach a more realistic medium in line with ASEAN trading policies.

As of late 2011, the Myanmar Securities Exchange Center (MSEC), a joint venture with Daiwa Securities from Japan, established in 1996, had only two companies listed: Forest Products Joint Venture and Myanmar Citizens Bank.

34INSURANCE

All 78 foreign insurance companies registered in Myanmar were nationalized in 1963. Since then, all forms of insurance, including life, fire, marine, automobile, workers' compensation, personal accident, and burglary, have been handled by the state-owned Myanma Insurance Corp. As of late 2011, Myanma Insurance continued to be the country's sole insurance company, although a variety of foreign companies provided reinsurance and insured joint venture projects in Myanmar. In November 2011, it was an-

nounced that Myanma Insurance Corp. would begin to insure small amounts of bank deposits.

35PUBLIC FINANCE

In 2010 the budget of Myanmar included $1.411 billion in public revenue and $3.042 billion in public expenditures, according to the CIA. The budget deficit amounted to 3.8% of GDP. In total $7.998 billion of the debt was held by foreign entities, as of December 2010, according to the CIA. As of mid- to late 2011, the government appeared to be trying to reduce its deficit by curbing spending, with a moratorium on new construction at Naypyidaw and an announced 50% increase in fees for electricity.

The government presents its budget in March for the 1 April-31 March fiscal year. The fiscal year 2011–12 budget was not debated in Myanmar's new parliament, as it had been set and approved by SPDC chairman Than Shwe before the January 2011 transition in government. Military spending has remained the highest priority for the government in the early 21st century. According to the Myanmar government, about 23% of the fiscal year 2011–12 budget was allocated to the military; energy, 3%; education, 4.13%; and health, 1.3%

Myanmar's revenue sources have included profits from state owned companies, taxes, import/export duties, foreign aid, and goods confiscated by the military. Analysts believe that with an exceptionally un-transparent economic system, enormous amounts of wealth have been siphoned from the public accounts by the military elite, using manipulation of exchange rates and other methods, with much of it transferred to offshore banks in Singapore and elsewhere.

36TAXATION

Residents pay a progressive individual income tax ranging from 2% to 35%. In December 2011, the government announced that citizens working overseas would no longer be required to pay income tax. The corporate tax rate is 30%, and there is a 10% capital gains tax (40% for nonresidents). Indirect taxes include a commercial tax on goods and some services (trading, transport, hotels, restaurants, and entertainment), ranging from 5–30%, and a 30–200% tax on luxury items. Property taxes include 20% of annual value as a general tax, plus 5% for lighting, 12% for water, and 15% for conservancy. There are also social security taxes, customs duties, royalties on natural resources, and a stamp tax. Myanmar's military has engaged in the informal, coerced taxation of civilians, on a massive scale, since the 1960s, in the form of forced labor, land confiscation, and confiscation of property.

37CUSTOMS AND DUTIES

Import licenses are required for shipment of goods into Myanmar, but smuggling is ubiquitous on all land borders and by sea. The huge disparity between the official exchange rate and the unofficial rate can amount to an informal duty on imported goods, including relief aid. When Myanmar joined ASEAN in 1997, a new official tariff schedule went into effect ranging from zero to 15% for most industrial inputs to a maximum of 40% for cars and luxury items. In 1998 a charge of 8% was enacted on all border-trade exports. In August 2011, Myanmar's government announced that a number of products would be exempt from export taxes until February 2012. Exempt goods included rice, beans and pulses, sesame, corn, rubber, seafood, and animal products. In September 2011, export taxes were reduced for value-added forest products until February 2012.

38 FOREIGN INVESTMENT

In the postwar period, and particularly after independence, government policies of economic nationalism strongly discouraged private foreign investment. After the nationalization of industry in 1963–64, private foreign investment was eliminated entirely. Foreign investment in Myanmar has been permitted only since the SLORC takeover in 1988. The Foreign Investment Commission (FIC) screens proposals for export generation potential, technology transfer, and the size of the investment. Various investment incentives are provided, such as exemption from income tax, and exemption from customs duties. Bureaucratic procedures and antiquated, inadequate infrastructure discourage foreign and local investments alike. Foreign entities cannot own land in Myanmar. Foreign investors may fear being criticized, boycotted, or sanctioned for investing in a country with a long record of human rights violations. Lawsuits were brought against Total and Unocal in US and European courts, for human rights abuses connected with the Yadana natural gas pipeline. New US investment in Myanmar was banned in 1997. Numerous foreign companies, including Pepsi, Heineken, Shell, ARCO, Texaco, Yukong, Motorola, and Philips, withdrew after initially investing in the 1990s; other refused to invest because of the human rights situation or other factors. Myanmar's fledgling garment industry went into decline in the late 1990s, as US companies stopped sourcing there, and the Asian financial crisis affected demand. In 2003, the US government banned the importing of goods from Myanmar to the US, and banned the export from the United States to Myanmar of financial services. The US also blocked financial assets of Myanmar government officials.

In the early 21st century, as ASEAN recovered from the Asian financial crisis, investments in Myanmar from countries such as Thailand, Malaysia, Indonesia, and Singapore increased. Extractive industries, including mining, timber, petroleum, and hydropower, accounted for the vast majority of foreign investment, with China taking the lead by initiating dam, port, and pipeline projects. In fiscal year 2008/09, foreign investments reached $985 million, according to Myanmar government statistics. Foreign investments decreased by a steep 68% in fiscal year 2009/10, affected by the world economic crisis and a delay in Chinese payments. According to Myanmar government statistics, foreign investment totaled $315 million for fiscal year 2009/10, with significant input from Malaysia, the UAE, Thailand, China, and Hong Kong, in sectors including petroleum, mining, and tourism. A sharp recovery was in evidence in fiscal year 2010/11, as record-breaking investments worth more than $20 billion poured into Myanmar. According to Myanmar government statistics, China invested $7.75 billion (part of which was for the Myitsone dam project, suspended in October 2011); Hong Kong, $5.79 billion; South Korea, $2.67 billion; Thailand, $2.14 billion; United Kingdom, $799 million; and Singapore, $226 million. Petroleum ($10.17 billion), hydroelectric power ($8.21 billion), and mining ($1.39 billion), were the leading foreign investment sectors.

39 ECONOMIC DEVELOPMENT

The economy of Burma was extensively disrupted by World War II. After 1962, under Ne Win's "Burmese Way to Socialism", all foreign companies, all banks, the entire transport system, all foreign and much domestic trade, and all the main branches of industry were nationalized; this put the economy in the hands of the ruling military elite, except for an extensive informal/illegal market and the areas of the country held by opposition armies.

Economic development proceeded slowly under the four-year plan for 1974–78. The 1978–82 development program was allocated 60% more funding than its predecessor and achieved an annual growth rate exceeding 6%. The four-year plan for 1982–86, costing an estimated $5 billion, set an average annual growth target of 6.2%. The plan stressed infrastructural development, with particular emphasis on agriculture, construction, and energy production. After the SLORC junta took over, announcing a free market economy, the four-year plan for 1986–90 encouraged foreign investment, but the military elite remained in direct or indirect control of joint ventures, financial institutions, and most other aspects of the economy.

An influx of foreign investment in extractive industries, particularly logging and petroleum exploration, took place in the early 1990s. Large reserves of natural gas were discovered, and a pipeline was built for the sale of gas to Thailand. Garment factories opened to take advantage of Myanmar's very low wages. However, outside economic pressure built up during the mid to late 1990s, in the form of consumer boycotts of companies doing business in Myanmar, and limited US economic sanctions which included an import ban but allowed Unocal to remain heavily invested in Myanmar's natural gas extractive industry. The Myanmar government reported that the economy grew by 6% in 1995 and 6.8% in 1996. Growth was estimated by the US State Department at 1.1% for 1998. Two trends were apparent in the government's economic policies throughout the 1990s: the capture of revenues from short term, quick turnover sources such as hardwoods, prospecting rights, and natural gas export rights; and spending patterns that emphasized acquisition of armaments. In June 1999, the International Labor Organization of the UN essentially expelled Myanmar from its ranks, following a detailed investigation of forced labor under the SPDC. In early 2000, the World Bank issued a report highly critical of Myanmar's economic and political climate. The IMF, the World Bank, and the ADB extended no credit to Myanmar from 1988 through 2011.

In 2001, the government introduced its third five year short-term plan, with a targeted average growth rate of 6%. Burma's trade with China, Thailand, and India increased in the early 21st century, and China invested in large scale infrastructure projects including dams, ports, and petroleum transport. Income from foreign investment did not always reach the national budget, apparently being siphoned off to private offshore bank accounts of the military elite; the exchange rate disparity was apparently one mechanism used by the military for skimming profits from foreign investments. Growth was held back by unproductive state-owned enterprises, lack of private sector credit, and the extremely unrealistic official exchange rate, among other factors. In February 2003, a major banking crisis affected the country's 20 private banks, closing them and disrupting the economy.

Myanmar's five year plan for fiscal year 2006–11 ambitiously targeted 12% growth. In actuality, according to the ADB, growth rates were estimated at 5.5% in 2007, 3.6% in 2008, and 5.1% in 2009. Despite a massive inflow of foreign investment from China, the GDP growth rate held steady at 5.3% in 2010, according to the CIA. Government programs pressuring citizens to grow jatropha as a biofuel failed in 2005/2007 and were considered by analysts of Myanmar's economy to be a sign of irrational centralized planning. Cyclone Nargis in 2008 devastated one of Myanmar's most important rice growing regions, as the country struggled to become a rice exporter. In 2009, a privatization campaign by the government divested state owned companies in many sectors. Critics noted that the companies were mostly bought up by people closely associated with the military. Agribusiness plantations, growing crops such as tapioca for export, were set up by foreign companies in rural areas, amid accusations of land confiscation and the displacement of local people. The Chinese-financed Myitsone dam, in Kachin state at the Irrawaddy River confluence, designed to provide hydroelectric power to China, caused conflict and controversy within Myanmar. In October 2011, the project was suspended by Thein Sein, president of Myanmar's new, nominally civilian, government. This was not only a rare sign of responsiveness to public opinion, it also showed a willingness to go against the intentions of China, Myanmar's most powerful neighbor, closest ally, and largest investor.

In 2011, reforms in banking, labor laws, and export regulations were underway; an increasingly uncensored press gave an impression of improved transparency and the possible beginning of government accountability. Investor confidence was rising at the end of 2011, with a real estate boom in Yangon, and various peace initiatives in frontier areas holding the possibility of opening up those regions to new business. With a history of projects such as pipelines and dams causing environmental harm and disruption of local populations in the resource-rich but impoverished country, it remained to be seen if projects like the Myanmar/China petroleum pipelines, Kaladan Multi-modal Transport system, Dawei Port, and hydroelectric dams, would be able to go forward without reconsideration or increased oversight. As Aung San Suu Kyi's NLD prepared to participate in the 2012 parliamentary by-elections, some of Myanmar's business people began holding meetings with her, as did US secretary of state Hillary Clinton and Thailand's prime minister Yingluck Shinawatra, which indicated that the NLD had developed into a viable political and economic force in a changing Myanmar.

40 SOCIAL DEVELOPMENT

Although Burma was one of the richest countries in Asia prior to World War II, poverty has persisted and increased in the decades since, with an estimated 32.7% of citizens below the poverty line as of 2007, according to the CIA. Although a 1.5% social security payroll tax was levied on employees of companies with five or more workers, actual benefits such as pension plans were largely restricted to government and military employees in Myanmar, as of 2011. Buddhist monasteries and other religious institutions traditionally provide many social services, such as caring for orphans, the disabled, and the elderly, in lieu of government programs. The Free Funeral Services Society began in 2001 as a way to see that people who died indigent were properly cremated

or buried; it expanded into other social welfare activities but has come under government pressure, as have other civil society charity groups. A number of private groups and individuals from academic, business, and other sectors organized much of the relief effort immediately after Cyclone Nargis in 2008, but were often harassed by the military government. Some UN agencies and international nongovernmental organizations provide assistance in healthcare, education, rural development, water purification, food relief, and alternative technology.

Myanmar's military has systematically engaged in human rights violations since coming to power in 1962. Arrests have often been made arbitrarily and many detainees are held incommunicado. Mistreatment of prisoners has been the norm. Thousands of nonviolent urban demonstrators were killed by the government's armed forces in 1988, and in 2007 Buddhist monks and other protesters were summarily executed. Human rights abuse has been most prevalent in areas of ethnic armed conflict, where torture, rape, massacres, forced labor, extortion, forced relocation, and other violations by the government's military were documented and reported every year, including 2011 (after the nominally civilian government took over), by entities including the US State Department, UN rapporteurs, and international human rights organizations. People of non-Burman ethnic groups have often faced discrimination, including restriction of travel, lack of access to higher education, and denial of citizenship.

Women have had equal status in Myanmar's civil society and economic life, including equal property and inheritance rights with men. However, traditional cultural views of women often prevent them from entering male dominated occupations, and they do not always receive equal pay for equal work. During the decades of military government, women were not participants in the upper levels of the BSPP or SLORC/SPDC. In the new 664 member parliament, as of March 2011, there were just 20 women. As of late 2011, a decades-long pattern of deliberate severe violence against women by the military, especially in ethnic conflict areas, continued. Numerous cases of rape of women and girls by the government's soldiers have been reported each year, according to human rights organizations. Domestic violence, and trafficking of women to neighboring countries for prostitution, were also common in Myanmar, as of 2011. Gay, lesbian, bisexual, and transgender people were usually treated with tolerance within Myanmar's civil society, but "abnormal" sexual behavior was illegal.

41 HEALTH

According to the CIA, life expectancy in Myanmar was 62 years in 2011. The country spent 2% of GDP on healthcare. There were 5 physicians, 8 nurses and midwives, and 6 hospital beds per 10,000 inhabitants. The fertility rate was 2.26, while the infant mortality rate was 50 per 1,000 live births. It was estimated that 87% of children were vaccinated against measles. With the exception of some private clinics in urban areas, and special facilities for the military and high-ranking government workers, medical care was extremely substandard throughout Myanmar, as of 2011. Fees for hospital care and medicines were out of reach for much of the population. Expired or fake pharmaceuticals were commonly for sale. Natural disasters, displaced populations, lack of properly trained medical personnel, low quality sanitation and drinking water supplies, and extreme income disparity were all contributing factors to the spread of infectious diseases and other health problems. The CIA calculated HIV/AIDS prevalence in Myanmar to be about 0.6% in 2009. Education about prevention and access to treatment for HIV/AIDS patients have improved, but funding for clinics remained difficult, as of 2011. Other infectious diseases included hepatitis, typhoid, malaria (with drug-resistant strains in some areas), dengue fever, H5N1 avian influenza, and leptospirosis.

⁴²HOUSING

As of 2008, according to the CIA, about 75% of the population had access to improved water sources and 86% of the population had access to improved sanitation. Urban apartment buildings are overcrowded and often unsafe, with improvised and irregular electricity supplies. A few enclaves of luxury housing have been built in Yangon and Mandalay. Naypyidaw is an entirely new capital, built since 2005, with housing for government employees and high ranking military officers. Cyclone Nargis destroyed an estimated 450,000 homes, and damaged 350,000 more, in the Irrawaddy Delta region in 2008. Rural housing is usually built of wood and woven bamboo, often on stilts, with metal or thatched roofs.

⁴³EDUCATION

In 2009 the World Bank estimated that 83% of age-eligible children in Myanmar were enrolled in primary school. Secondary enrollment for age-eligible children stood at 50%. Tertiary enrollment was estimated at 3%. The CIA reported the Myanmar had a literacy rate of about 90% as of 2006. According to the Myanmar government, about 4.13% of the fiscal year 2011–12 budget was allocated for education.

Public education is said to be free, but school-related fees were increasingly imposed starting in the late 1990s. Primary education is compulsory, covering a five-year course of study, although school fees and the need to work prevent many children from attending. Primary school may be followed by four years of middle school, and two years of high school or technical school. Burmese is the language of instruction, and English is taught in the secondary schools. English became the medium of instruction in the universities in 1982. Few school materials are available in languages spoken by non-Burman ethnic groups. Buddhist monasteries, informal community schools, and elite private schools provide alternatives to government-run primary and secondary education. English-medium private secondary schools prepare students for overseas tertiary education.

Under military rule, the entire educational system went into decline. Universities were closed for years at a time, following the student-led democracy protests of 1988. "Distance learning," with diplomas awarded based on three year courses with little actual class attendance, was promoted by the government. Military academies train future Tatmadaw officers. Corruption and political favoritism are alleged in faculty hiring, examination results and grades; a course of study is not chosen by the student and is often an arbitrary assignment. Academic freedom of expression has been extremely curtailed, although that may change if more freedom of expression becomes the norm in Myanmar. Many students seek to go overseas for higher education.

As of 2011, most of Myanmar's colleges and universities were government-owned. Each state and district has a technical university and a computer university. Yangon University (founded in 1878 as Rangoon College) and Mandalay University (founded in 1925) are the leading institutions of higher learning. There are also several teacher-training colleges, performing arts schools, and agricultural institutes. Chin State and Kachin State have Christian theological colleges, and International Theravada Buddhist Missionary University is located in Yangon.

⁴⁴LIBRARIES AND MUSEUMS

The Myanmar National Library in Yangon, is a research library established in 1952 and derived from the Bernard Library, established in 1883. It contains over 220,000 items, including over 16,000 palm leaf manuscripts and more than 340 literary manuscripts. The National Library moved to a new building in Yangon in 2008; in mid-2011 it was announced that construction was suspended on a new National Library building at Naypyidaw. The Yangon University library system has over 350,000 volumes. The Ministry of Religious Affairs library collection includes 45,200 books and more than 12,200 palm leaf manuscripts, and International Theravada Buddhist Missionary University has a library with over 25,600 items. There are also several other academic libraries, as well as state libraries at Pathein (Bassein), Kyaukpyu, Mandalay, and Mawlamyine (Moulmein). Myanmar has hundreds of community libraries and school libraries. Cities and towns have book rental shops and stalls. During decades of military repression in Myanmar, underground book discussion groups and book sharing clubs were formed. Reading rooms at the US, British, and other embassies in Yangon offered access to uncensored publications and safe discussion groups.

The National Museum of Art and Archaeology in Yangon was founded in 1952 and includes among its collections traditional arts, natural history, and historical artifacts; it moved to a new location in 1996. Yangon also has a Martyrs Museum, a Gems Museum, and a Defense Museum. The precolonial royal city of Mandalay has museums including the Mandalay Palace Cultural Museum and the Mandalay Traditional Folk Arts Museum. There are archeological museums at Bagan (Pagan) and Mrauk-U. In mid-2011, the government suspended construction of a new National Museum and a new Tatmadaw Museum at Naypyidaw.

⁴⁵MEDIA

According to the CIA, as of 2010 there were 604,700 telephone landlines in Myanmar, and 594,000 mobile telephone subscriptions. Myanmar Posts and Telecommunications, a state owned company, was the only telephone network provider, as of 2011. Fixed line and mobile phone market penetration remained extremely low, with both at about 1%.

Under military rule, domestic and foreign films and print publications were scrutinized by a Censorship Board. Content considered politically, socially, or culturally objectionable was physically cut out or obscured and entire publications were often banned. Censorship was also applied to works of art, literature, music, comedy, and performance. State owned print and broadcast media expressed the party line of the BSPP and policies of SLORC/SPDC. Myanmar was considered one of the most repressive countries for journalists, with many imprisoned.

Prominent newspapers in 2010, with circulation numbers listed parenthetically, included *Botahtaung* (96,000), *Loktha Pyithu Nayzin* (160,000), *Myanmar Alin* (400,000), and *New Light of Myanmar* (14,000). Private magazines and weekly newspapers cover sports, business, health, entertainment, and other topics. During 2011, censorship was lifted entirely for non-news magazines, and eased for news publications. In 2011, as censorship eased, magazines and weekly newspapers began to venture into coverage of political topics, even covering controversial issues such as the Myitsone dam. In late 2011, pictures of Aung San Suu Kyi and positive coverage of the NLD began to appear in local magazines.

As of 2011, radio and television remained government controlled. Radio stations included the government's shortwave Voice of Myanmar and seven state-private owned FM radio stations. There were five government/military owed television stations; satellite dish television was prohibitively expensive, due to high fees. Burmese language shortwave radio broadcasts by the BBC, VOA, Radio Free Asia, and others were a major source of news during military rule. Numerous media outlets were formed overseas by exiles from Myanmar, including the Democratic Voice of Burma (radio, Internet, and television), and The Irrawaddy (print and Internet), as well as ethnic news agencies and news websites.

Myanmar had just 172 Internet hosts as of 2010, and 110,000 Internet users as of 2009, according to the CIA. Internet usage was often at cyber cafes, and the military government made efforts to restrict, block, and censor access to websites it found objectionable, as well as keeping track of cyber cafe patrons and websites visited. However, proxy servers were in wide use, allowing free access to foreign websites. Despite restrictions, bloggers operate from inside and outside of Myanmar; some have been imprisoned under the Electronics Transactions Law, including the dissident comedian Zarganar, who was released in 2011. In September 2011 the government stopped blocking a number of websites, including foreign news outlets, YouTube, and exile-run news websites.

46 ORGANIZATIONS

Business organizations include the Union of Myanmar Federation of Chambers of Commerce and Industry, and Myanmar Egress. Myanmar Medical Association promotes research and education on health issues; there is also a Myanmar Red Cross Society, and a Myanmar Maternal and Child Welfare Association. Myanmar has numerous Buddhist, Muslim, and Christian organizations. The YMCA and YWCA have members throughout Myanmar. Several sports associations are active throughout the country. Social welfare groups include The Free Funeral Services Society, Myanmar Youths in Action, ICE Youth, Metta Foundation, and Information Center for Every Youth. There are clubs and venues for sports including boxing, badminton, football (soccer), and *chinlone,* in which a woven rattan ball is passed without using the hands.

47 TOURISM, TRAVEL, AND RECREATION

The *Tourism Factbook*, published by the UN World Tourism Organization, reported 263,514 incoming tourists to Myanmar in 2009. Of those incoming tourists, there were 149,631 from Asia. The estimated daily cost to visit Yangon (Rangoon), the largest city, was $159. When the military government declared 1996 "Visit Myanmar Year", a tourism boycott grew, in order to deprive the regime of foreign exchange earnings; the boycott was endorsed by Aung San Suu Kyi's NLD. Severe repression of protests by Buddhist monks in 2007 led to a downturn in tourism. As of 2011, with signs of reform in Myanmar, the boycott appeared to have gone out of effect, and tourist arrivals were rising.

Principal attractions include the massive golden Shwe Dagon Pagoda in Yangon, and Mandalay's Buddhist temples, monasteries, and royal palace. Bagan (Pagan) was declared a UNESCO World Heritage Site for its vast plain of ancient pagodas, but efforts by the government to increase appeal for tourists by restoring the ruins have been criticized by experts for damaging the structures. The tourist attraction of Inle Lake is under threat from chemical pollution. Mt. Popa and Kyaiktiyo Pagoda are Buddhist pilgrimage sites. There are hill districts including Kalaw and Pyin Oo Lwin (Maymyo), and beach resorts at Ngapoli. As of late 2011, Naypyidaw, the capital, was not open to tourists, although hotels and a zoo had been built there. Some regions of Myanmar, including Chin State, required special permission for foreigners to visit. Most border crossings were officially closed to foreigners, but tourists were allowed to visit Tachilek by bridge from the Thai town of Mae Sai, on limited passes. Visitors from China could enter several border towns, particularly in Wa controlled ceasefire areas. Gambling casinos were established on the Myanmar side of the China border in the early 21st century, but had been closed down as of 2011. Visitors to Myanmar require a visa; if arriving at Yangon or Mandalay airports, a 28 day visa can be granted on arrival. Travelers were encouraged to carry cash as credit cards were not accepted, as of 2011.

48 FAMOUS PERSONS

Anawrahta founded the early Burman kingdom of Pagan in 1044 and established Hinayana Buddhism as the official religion. Other important historical figures were the Toungoo warrior-king Bayinnaung (r. 1551–81) and Alaungpaya (r. 1752–60). Natshinnaung (1578–1613) was a poet-warrior of the Toungoo dynasty. Aung San (1916–47), led Burma to independence from Britain. U Nu (1907–95) was independent Burma's first premier (1948–62). U Thant (1909–74) served as UN secretary-general from 1961 through 1971. Ne Win (1911–2002) was Burma's dictator from 1962 to 1988. Than Shwe (b. 1933) was the military ruler from 2004 to 2011. Thein Sein, an ex-general, (b. 1945) became president under the new constitution in 2011. Min Ko Naing (b. 1962) was a student leader of the 1988 pro-democracy protests. Aung San Suu Kyi (b. 1945) founded the National League for Democracy, was awarded the 1991 Nobel Peace Prize, and was elected to parliament in 2012. Cynthia Maung is a Karen doctor who established health clinics for refugees along the border with Thailand.

The painter U Ba Nyan (1897–1945) introduced Western-style art techniques to Burma. Ludu Hla (1910–1982) was a social activist writer; his wife Ludu Daw Amar (1915–2008) was also a politically active author. Sai Htee Saing (1950–2008) was a popular Shan singer-songwriter. Zargana (b. 1961) is a dentist, comedian, political dissident, and charity worker. Htein Lin (b. 1966) is an internationally known painter and performance artist. Zayar Thaw (b. 1981) started Myanmar's first hip hop band, and was imprisoned for his political views.

⁴⁹DEPENDENCIES

Myanmar has no territories or colonies.

⁵⁰BIBLIOGRAPHY

Aung San Suu Kyi, *Freedom from Fear*. New York: Penguin Press, 1991.

Burma: Political Economy under Military Rule. New York: Palgrave, 2001.

Charney, Michael. *A History of Modern Burma*. New York: Cambridge University Press, 2009.

Dorai, Francis. *Burma Myanmar*. Updated 8th ed. Singapore: APA Publications, 2000.

Fink, Christina. *Living Silence*. London, Eng.: Zed Books, 2001.

Larkin, Emma. *Everything is Broken*. New York: Penguin Press, 2010.

Leibo, Steven A. *East and Southeast Asia 2011*. Lanham, MD: Stryker-Post Publications, 2011.

Lintner, Bertil. *Aung San Suu Kyi and Burma's Struggle for Democracy*. Chiang Mai, Thailand: Silkworm Book, 2011.

McClelland, Mac. *For Us, Surrender is Out of the Question*. Berkeley, CA: Soft Skull Press, 2010.

Seekins, Donald M. *Historical Dictionary of Burma (Myanmar)*. Lanham, MD: Scarecrow, 2006.

Skidmore, Monique, ed. *Burma at the Turn of the Twenty-first Century*. Honolulu: University of Hawaii Press, 2005.

Smith, Martin. Burma: Ethnicity and the Politics of Insurgency. London, Eng.: Zed Books, 1999.

Steinberg, David I. *Burma/Myanmar: What Everyone Needs to Know*. New York: Oxford University Press, 2010.

NAURU

Republic of Nauru
Naoero

CAPITAL: There is no formal capital. The seat of government is in the district of Yaren.

FLAG: The flag has a blue background divided horizontally by a narrow gold band, symbolizing the equator. Below the band on the left side is a white 12-pointed star, representing the island's 12 traditional tribes.

ANTHEM: *Nauru Ubwema (Nauru, Our Homeland).*

MONETARY UNIT: The Australian dollar (AUD) of 100 cents is the legal currency. AUD1 = US$1.02191 (or US$1 = AUD0.97) as of 2011.

WEIGHTS AND MEASURES: Imperial weights and measures are used.

HOLIDAYS: New Year's Day, 1 January; Independence Day, 31 January; Constitution Day, 17 May; National Youth Day, 25 September; Angam Day, 26 October (a celebration of the day on which the population of Nauru reached the pre-World War II level); Christmas Day, 25 December; and Boxing Day, 26 December.

TIME: 11:30 p.m. = noon GMT.

¹LOCATION, SIZE, AND EXTENT

Situated in the western Pacific, Nauru is one of the world's smallest independent nations, with an area of 21 sq km (8.1 sq mi), extending 5.6 km (3.5 mi) NNE–SSW and 4 km (2.5 mi) ESE–WNW. Comparatively, the area occupied by Nauru is about one-tenth the size of Washington, DC. It lies between two island groups, the Solomons and the Gilberts, 53 km (33 mi) S of the equator and 3,930 km (2,442 mi) NNE of Sydney; its nearest neighbor is Banaba (formerly Ocean Island, now part of Kiribati), situated 305 km (190 mi) to the E. Nauru has a coastline of 30 km (18.6 mi). The Yaren district, which holds the seat of the government, is located on the southern coast of the Nauru.

²TOPOGRAPHY

Nauru, one of the largest phosphate-rock islands in the Pacific, is oval-shaped and fringed by a wide coral reef. It has no natural harbor or anchorage. A relatively fertile belt varying in width from 150–300 m (490–980 ft) encircles the island. From this belt a coral cliff rises to a central plateau about 60 m (200 ft) above sea level. Buada Lagoon, a permanent, often brackish lake, covers some 300 acres (1.2 km/0.47 sq mi) in the southeastern end of the plateau. Apart from some brackish ponds and an underground lake, the nation's water supply is provided by rainfall.

³CLIMATE

Nauru has a dry season, marked by easterly trade winds, and a wet season with westerly monsoons extending from November to February. The average annual rainfall is about 200 cm (79 in), but the amount varies greatly from year to year, and long droughts have been a recurrent problem. Temperatures remain steady,

between 24–33°C (75–91°F) the year round, and relative humidity is also constant at about 80%.

⁴FLORA AND FAUNA

The plateau area contains large phosphate deposits that almost completely inhibit any natural growth useful for subsistence or commerce. Large areas of scrub and creeper, with occasional coconut and tamanu trees, grow in this region. On the coastal belt, coconut palms and pandanus (a type of screw pine) thrive. Some hibiscus, frangipani, and other tropical flowers grow, but they do not abound here as on other Pacific islands. Bird life is not plentiful, although noddies, terns, and frigate birds frequent the island. There are no indigenous land animals; however, hogs and poultry were introduced many years ago. Fish life is abundant in the seas encircling Nauru and good catches of tuna and bonito are taken.

⁵ENVIRONMENT

Nauru's phosphate mining industry has done significant damage to the land. In 1987, the Nauruan government began to investigate the nation's mining operations with the goal of developing a plan to regenerate the land and replace lost vegetation.

Nauru filed a claim with the International Court of Justice in 1989 for compensation from Australia for the loss of nearly all its topsoil from phosphate mining during the League of Nations mandate and the UN trusteeship. Australia agreed to pay a lump sum of AUD107 million plus AUD2.5 million per year for 20 years to settle the case. Nauru's government announced plans to rehabilitate the island at the 1994 Small Island States Conference on Sustainable Development.

Vegetation in the coastal areas, such as pandanus and coconut palms, is plentiful. Nauru has limited freshwater resources.

Its residents collect rainwater in rooftop storage tanks. Periodic droughts pose an additional hazard to the environment. Nauru's areas of lower elevation are at risk from tidal surges and flooding.

According to a 2011 report issued by the International Union for Conservation of Nature and Natural Resources (IUCN), threatened species included 1 mammal, 2 birds, 9 fish, and 62 other invertebrates.

In 2010 top officials from Nauru and thirteen other developing Pacific island nations and dependencies met in Vanuatu to discuss the progress made in addressing some of the issues unique to these low-lying, developing island states. These issues include climate change, sea-level rise, natural disasters, remoteness from major markets, and poverty. Another key objective of the meeting was to address the progress each nation had made in adopting the 2005 Mauritius Strategy, the only global blueprint that exists to combat the challenges of small-island developing states. The UN reported in 2008 that carbon dioxide emissions in Nauru totaled 143 kilotons.

⁶POPULATION

The US Central Intelligence Agency (CIA) estimates the population of Nauru in 2011 to be approximately 9,322, which placed it at number 195 in population among the 196 nations of the world. In 2011, approximately 1.7% of the population was over 65 years of age, with another 33.0% under 15 years of age. The median age in Nauru was 24.2 years. There were 0.99 males for every female in the country. The population's annual rate of change was 0.611%. Population density in Nauru was calculated at 444 people per sq km (1,150 people per sq mi).

The UN estimated that 100% of the population lived in urban areas, and that urban populations had an annual rate of change of 0.6%.

Most Nauruans live around the coastal fringes, in their traditional districts. About half the population consists of immigrant contract laborers, technicians, and teachers. Most Chinese, as well as immigrants from Kiribati and Tuvalu, are settled in communities near the phosphate works.

⁷MIGRATION

Estimates of Nauru's net migration rate, carried out by the CIA in 2011, amounted to -15.55 migrants per 1,000 citizens. Immigration to Nauru is strictly controlled by the government. Nauruans are free to travel abroad. The nation once served as host to two Australian refugee processing camps that were established as part of the Australian Pacific Solution, a program designed to manage the thousands of asylum seekers that enter Australia each year. In exchange for its cooperation, the Nauruan government received millions of dollars in aid from Australia. However, the controversial program ended in 2008 and the Nauruan centers were closed.

⁸ETHNIC GROUPS

The Nauruan people are the only indigenous ethnic group on the island. They are of mixed Micronesian, Melanesian, and Polynesian origin and resemble the last strain most closely. Nauruans are traditionally divided into 12 clans or tribes, in which descent is matrilineal, although kinship and inheritance rules have some patrilineal features. The 12 clans are Eamwit,

Eamwidumwit, Deboe, Eoaru, Emea, Eano, Emangum, Ranibok, Eamwidara, Iruwa, Irutsi (extinct), and Iwi (extinct). Admixtures of Caucasian and Negroid lineage in the 19th century and frequent intermarriage with other Pacific islanders have changed the present-day features of Nauruans from those of their forebears. The Caucasians on the island are almost all Australians and New Zealanders employed in administrative or teaching posts or in the phosphate industry. The Chinese and immigrants from Kiribati and Tuvalu originally came to the island as laborers in the phosphate industry, some being accompanied by their families. Filipino contract workers are also present but are not permitted to bring their families. According to the latest estimates, about 58% of the population are Nauruan, 26% are other Pacific Islander, 8% Chinese, and 8% European.

⁹LANGUAGES

Nauruan, which is distinct from all other Pacific tongues, is the official language. However, English is still commonly used in the schools, in government, and in business transactions. Most Nauruans are bilingual but use Nauruan in everyday life.

¹⁰RELIGIONS

The Nauruans have accepted Christianity as a primary religion since the end of the 19th century. A 2004 report indicated that about two-thirds of the population was Protestant and one-third was Roman Catholic. Missionary groups include Anglicans, Methodists, Mormons, and Jehovah's Witnesses. Buddhism and Taoism are also represented, particularly among the Chinese community. The constitution provides for religious freedom and this right is generally respected in practice. However, the government claims the right to restrict any organizations which it feels poses a threat to public safety, public order, or public morality. Under this assumption, the government has restricted Mormons and Jehovah's Witnesses from proselytizing of native-born citizens, claiming that such actions are likely to break up families. Only three denominations are registered to operate in an official capacity, meaning they may holds public services, build churches, and proselytize. These denominations are the Roman Catholic Church, the Nauru Congregational Church, and the Kiribati Protestant Church. Easter and Christmas are observed as national holidays.

¹¹TRANSPORTATION

The CIA reports that Nauru has a total of 24 km (14.9 mi) of roads, of which 24 km (14.9 mi) are paved. There is one airport, which does have a paved runway. Transport to and from Nauru has traditionally been by ships calling at the island to unload freight and pick up phosphates for delivery to Australia, New Zealand, and other countries. There is no merchant marine, but the public Nauru Pacific Line has a fleet of six ships. The government-owned Air Nauru flies regular air services to the Pacific islands, Taiwan, the Philippines, Hong Kong, Japan, Australia, and New Zealand.

Apart from a 5 km (3.1 mi) railway (used to carry phosphates), a school bus service, and fewer than 2,000 registered motor vehicles, there is no local transport.

¹²HISTORY

The original settlers are thought to have been castaways who drifted to Nauru from another Pacific island. The first recorded discovery of Nauru by a Westerner was made by Captain John Fearn of the whaling ship Hunter in November 1798. He named the island Pleasant Island. From the 1830s to the 1880s, the Nauruans had a succession of visitors—runaway convicts, deserters from whaling ships, and other men who can be classed as beachcombers. The beachcombers provided the Nauruans with their first real contact with Western civilization and introduced them to firearms and alcohol. They acted as a buffer between two cultures but were often a bad influence on the Nauruans. Several times beachcombers and Nauruans attempted to cut off and capture visiting ships, so that eventually Nauru came to be avoided as a watering place by ships whaling in the area. The advent of firearms also disturbed the balance of power between the tribes on the island; sporadic tribal warfare culminated in a 10-year civil war from 1878 to 1888 that reduced the native population to less than 1,000.

The British and German imperial governments agreed to the partition of the Western Pacific in 1886. Their purely arbitrary line of demarcation left Nauru in the German sphere of influence quite accidentally. It was not until 1888, on the petition of the beachcombers-turned-traders, that the German government annexed Nauru as a protectorate and disarmed the people. Christian missionaries arrived in 1899 and had a greater impact on the Nauruan culture than did the German administration.

In 1901, Sir Albert Ellis, a New Zealand geologist, discovered that there were large deposits of phosphate on both Nauru and Banaba (then called Ocean Island). Phosphate mining on Nauru began in 1907, after the German government had granted a concession to the British-owned Pacific Phosphate Co. Laborers from the German Caroline Islands were hired because the Nauruans had no interest in working in the mines.

Nauru was occupied by the Australian Expeditionary Force in 1914, and phosphate continued to be shipped all through World War I. In 1919, Nauru was made a League of Nations mandate of the British Empire, and the governments of Australia, New Zealand, and the United Kingdom agreed to administer the island jointly through an administrator to be appointed by Australia. At the same time the three governments obtained the mandate, they jointly purchased the Pacific Phosphate Co.'s rights to Nauruan phosphate for £3.5 million and began to work the deposits through a three-man board called the British Phosphate Commissioners (BPC).

The phosphate industry expanded greatly in the years between the wars. Australian and New Zealand farmers enjoyed substantial savings, for Nauru phosphate was sold at a much lower price than phosphate from other countries. As for the Nauruans, with their small royalty of eightpence a ton in 1939, they opted out of the industry completely and turned to their own culture for sustenance.

War came to Nauru in December 1940, when the island was shelled by a roving German raider, and four phosphate ships were sunk. Nauru was flattened by Japanese bombings beginning in December 1941, and all its industrial plant and housing facilities were destroyed. The Japanese occupied the island from August 1942 until the end of the war three years later. They deported 1,200 Nauruans to build an airstrip on Truk, a small atoll about 1,600 km (1,000 mi) northwest of Nauru, and many died there. Australian forces reoccupied Nauru in September 1945, and the surviving Truk Nauruans, who had been reduced in number to

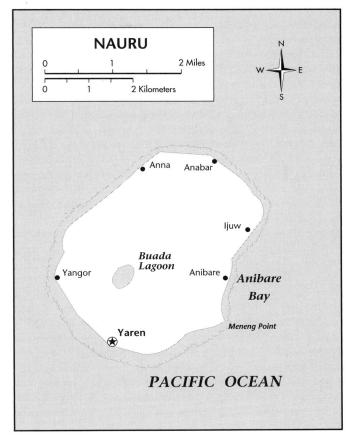

LOCATION: 0°32′ S and 166°56′ E. TERRITORIAL SEA LIMIT: 12 miles.

only 737, were repatriated in January 1946. Nauru's population thus fell from 1,848 in 1940 to 1,369 in 1946.

The three mandatory governments placed the mandate of Nauru before the UN. On 1 November 1947, the UN approved an agreement by which the island became a trust territory administered jointly by Australia, New Zealand, and the United Kingdom, who were to share the task of developing self-government on the island. The Nauruans had a Council of Chiefs to represent them since 1927, but this body had advisory powers only. Dissatisfied Nauruans made a number of complaints to the administering authority and to the UN Trusteeship Council, with the result that a Nauruan local government council was established by the election of nine council members in December 1951. Since control of the council was exercised by the administrator, however, the Nauruans continued to press for further political power. They asked for positions of importance in the administration and an increase in royalty payments, and expressed concern about the future of the island because the increased rate of phosphate exportation would, it was feared, exhaust the deposits by the end of the century. By constant negotiations, the Nauruans forced the BPC to pay royalties on a rights rather than needs basis, and with the establishment of a world price in 1964, phosphate royalties were raised. The Nauruans achieved control of the industry in 1967 by purchasing the plant and machinery owned by the BPC, and in 1970 they took over the industry completely.

Meanwhile, in 1964, Australia had attempted to resettle the Nauruans on Curtis Island, off the coast of Queensland. The

Nauruans, although in principle not averse to resettlement, refused it because of political considerations. They wanted to own their island and to maintain their identity by political independence. Australia would not agree to this, and the plan collapsed. This failure reinforced the Nauruans' desire for political independence. With the support of the Trusteeship Council, they established an elected Legislative Council in 1966. Although Australia wished to maintain control of defense and external affairs, the Nauruans insisted on complete self-determination. Thus, on 31 January 1968, the 22nd anniversary of the return of the Nauruan survivors from Truk, Nauru became the smallest independent republic in the world. Since that time, Nauru has pursued a policy of isolation and nonalignment, although it does have a role in Commonwealth affairs. In October 1982, Queen Elizabeth II visited the island, the first British monarch to do so. Nauru established diplomatic ties with the former Soviet Union in 1988. Nauru became a member of the Commonwealth of Nations in May 1999 and joined the United Nations in September of the same year.

Since winning its independence in 1968, Nauru experienced many changes in leadership with frequent votes of no confidence ousting presidents who were often returned to office only a short time later. Marcus Stephens, who was elected as president in 2007, faced a major challenge in 2008 as the country slipped deeper and deeper into debt and parliament became deadlocked over budget issues, with nine members supporting the president and nine opposed. To end the deadlock, Stephen dissolved the assembly and declared a state of emergency. In snap elections held in April 2008, every member of the parliament was replaced, with a final count of 12 members supporting Stephen and 6 opposed.

In March 2010, a second crisis arose, again over the budget, and the loyalties of parliament members shifted once again, resulting in another nine-nine split of support for the president. As opposition members lodged a motion for a vote of no confidence, Stephen again dissolved parliament, calling new elections for April. Those elections proved fruitless, however, as every incumbent member of parliament was reelected, leaving the budget stalemate intact and creating yet another impasse, as the members of parliament found they could not agree on a nomination for speaker. According to the constitution, parliament must elect a speaker before transacting any other business, including the election of a new president and the consideration of new bills.

The stalemate continued until 11 June 2010, when Stephen, acting as the caretaker president, issued a state of emergency and dissolved parliament. The political wrangling did not resolve until 1 November 2010 as former president Ludwig Scotty accepted the nomination as speaker or parliament. His unopposed election swayed the parliament in favor of the established government. As a result, Stephen was officially reelected as president by a secret ballot vote of 11 to 6. Stephen's first order of business was to end the state of emergency. Into 2011, the government continued to struggle with the issue of a declining economy and enormous government debt.

13 GOVERNMENT

The constitution of the Republic of Nauru, adopted at the time of independence and subsequently amended, provides that the republic shall have a parliamentary type of government. It contains provisions for the protection of fundamental rights and freedoms—a subject of particular importance because many of the inhabitants are short-term migrants ineligible for citizenship (defined in the constitution as being restricted to those of Nauruan or of Nauruan and Pacific islander parentage). Legislative power is vested in the parliament, composed of 18 members elected for a three-year term by Nauruan citizens who have attained the age of 20 years. Seven of the eight constituencies (representing 10 out of 14 districts) return two members each, and the constituency of Ubenide (representing 4 districts) returns four members. The first woman was elected in 1986.

Executive power is exercised by the president, who also fulfills the residual duties of head of state; he is elected by parliament and is assisted by a cabinet, which he appoints.

In 2005, the parliament undertook a review of the Nauru's constitution. One goal of the review was to initiate reforms that would reduce the frequencies of votes of no confidence and the resulting political instability. However, the constitutional referendum that took place in February 2010 failed to pass.

14 POLITICAL PARTIES

There have been ad hoc political parties since independence in Nauru, but politics is generally based on personal loyalties and occasionally on issue-based coalitions. After DeRoburt's reelection in 1987, Kennan Adeang formed the Democratic Party of Nauru, which aimed to curb the power of the presidency. Other parties as of 2011 included the Nauru First Party and an informal Nauru Party.

In the legislative elections of June 2010, all 18 seats in parliament were won by independent candidates. Marcus Stephen was reelected as president in November 2010 by a parliamentary vote of 11 to 6. The next elections are set for 2013.

15 LOCAL GOVERNMENT

There is no local government for the island. The Nauru Island Council, which once served as a representative assembly focused on local needs, was dissolved in 1999; all assets and liabilities became vested in the Government of Nauru. For general administrative purposes, the nation is divided into 14 districts.

16 JUDICIAL SYSTEM

The constitution provides for a Supreme Court, with a chief justice presiding. Cases are also heard in the district court or family court. There are two other quasi-courts: the Public Service Appeal Board and the Police Appeal Board. The chief justice presides over both as chairman of the panel, with two members for each board.

The Supreme Court, which has original and appellate jurisdiction, is the supreme authority on the interpretation of the constitution. Appeals against decisions of the Supreme Court on certain matters go to the Appellate Court of Nauru, which is comprised of two judges. Cases also may be appealed to the High Court of Australia. Parliament cannot overturn court decisions.

The judiciary is independent of the executive. The constitution guarantees protection of fundamental human rights which in practice are generally respected.

Many cases never reach the formal legal system. Most of the conflicts are resolved by the traditional reconciliation process.

¹⁷ARMED FORCES

Nauru has no armed forces. Although there is no formal agreement, Australia ensures its defense. There is a small police force under civilian control.

¹⁸INTERNATIONAL COOPERATION

Nauru was admitted to the United Nations on 14 September 1999 and participates in ESCAP and several other nonregional specialized agencies, such as the FAO, ICAO, ITU, UNESCO, and the WHO. The nation belongs to the Pacific Island Forum, the South Pacific Commission, the ACP Group, the South Pacific Regional Trade and Economic Cooperation Agreement (Sparteca), the Asian Development Bank, the Alliance of Small Island States (AOSIS), and the South Pacific Applied Geoscience Commission. The country is a special member of the Commonwealth of Nations, taking part in some Commonwealth functions but not represented at heads-of-government conferences.

In environmental cooperation, Nauru is part of the South Pacific Regional Environmental Program, the Basel Convention, the Convention on Biological Diversity, the London Convention, the Kyoto Protocol, the Montréal Protocol, and the UN Conventions on the Law of the Sea, Climate Change, and Desertification.

Nauru established diplomatic relations with the Republic of Abkhazia—the breakaway region of Georgia—in December 2009, becoming just the fourth country in the world to recognize the enclave as an independent state. The move culminated an intensive, fifteen-month lobbying effort by Russia that reportedly involved pledges of tens of millions of dollars in aid to Nauru.

¹⁹ECONOMY

Nauru's per capita gross domestic product (GDP) was once one of the world's highest, thanks to its phosphate reserves; these reserves are now almost depleted. When it became apparent that the phosphate reserves were nearly gone, trust funds were set up to help provide for the nation's economic future. However, heavy spending by the government has depleted the funds. Though the phosphate industry was revived in 2006, it makes very little profit. There are no other major natural resources.

A further blow to the economy was the closing of an Australian refugee processing center in 2008, which had generated millions of dollars of funds. As a result, the government is struggling against bankruptcy. Australia is the nation's last major supporter; it sends aid in the form of necessities to the island. The government subsidizes imports so that food and other necessities are available at nominal cost.

Fishing licenses for foreign fleets operating in the nation's exclusive economic zone are a primary source of income. Offshore financial operations bring in some revenue.

²⁰INCOME

The CIA estimated that in 2005 the GDP of Nauru was US$60 million. The CIA defines GDP as the value of all final goods and services produced within a nation in a given year and computed on the basis of purchasing power parity (PPP) rather than value as measured on the basis of the rate of the exchange based on current dollars. The per capita GDP was estimated at US$5,000. The average inflation rate was 2.2%.

²¹LABOR

The workforce is primarily engaged in the state-owned phosphate industry, with public administration, education, and transportation providing employment as well. In a 2006 government survey (the last available statistics as of 2011), the total resident workforce of citizens 15 years or over was estimated at about 3,156 people were wage or salary earners. Only about 1% of employment is in the private sector. As of 1992, there were some 3,000 guest workers in Nauru, mostly from Vanuatu or Kiribati. There are no formal trade unions, but there are a few trade associations that provide varying levels of assistance to workers. These include the Nauru Fisherman's Associations and the Buada Lagoon Owners' Association. The right to strike is neither protected nor prohibited. Collective bargaining does not take place.

There is no official minimum wage for the private sector. There is a graduated salary system for government workers, but those at the lower salary levels do not earn enough to provide a decent standard of living. The workweek for office employees is set at 35 hours, and for manual laborers the standard is 40 hours. The minimum age for employment is 17 years, although some younger children work in the few family-owned small operations. The government enforces health and safety standards in the workplace.

²²AGRICULTURE

The only fertile soils lie along the narrow coastal belt and the inland Buada Lagoon. Coconut palms are the primary agricultural product, but bananas and pineapples are also grown. In 2009, fruit production amounted to 356 tons and vegetable production to 463 tons.

²³ANIMAL HUSBANDRY

Pigs and chickens roam uncontrolled on the island; hence, there is no organized production. In 2005, there were an estimated 2,800 pigs.

²⁴FISHING

While there are substantial fishing resources in the nation's exclusive economic zone, the government has yet to develop its own commercial fishing resources. The total catch in 2003 was 43 tons. The government does earn revenues from the sale of fishing licenses to foreign fleets.

In March 2010, the president of Nauru met with fellow members of the Parties of the Nauru Agreement (PNA) for their First Presidential Summit. The PNA was established in 1982 and is comprised of the nations of Palau, Micronesia, Marshall Islands, Tuvalu, Kiribati, Papua New Guinea, Nauru, and the Solomon Islands. The purpose of the group is to work together for the conservation and management of tuna resources within their exclusive economic zones. At the March meeting, which was called the Tuna Summit, members adopted the Koror Declaration, which aims, among other things, to establish cooperative management practices that will enhance commercial and economic opportunities for member states and to work toward the conservation and restoration of migratory tuna stocks. The waters of the PNA nations account for nearly 60% of all tuna catches in the western and central Pacific Ocean and 25% of the global tuna catches that supply canneries and processing facilities around the world.

[25] FORESTRY

There are no forests on Nauru. All building timber has to be imported.

[26] MINING

High-grade phosphate rock extracted from the surface mine on the central plateau in the island's interior was once Nauru's most valuable natural resource. However, the depletion of reserves led to a sharp decline of production in the 1990s, with 613,000 tons in 1994 dropping to 487,000 tons in 1998. All phosphate rock was exported to New Zealand, Australia, the Philippines, and South Korea and the associated coral was used domestically for road aggregate. Operations were briefly suspended in 2005, but revived on a much smaller scale in 2006 under the state-owned Republic of Nauru Phosphate Company, or RONPhos. Most of the citizens involved in the formal wage sectors are employed by RONPhos. Foreign workers are also contracted by the company, due to the lack of skilled labor locally. Nauru also produces some common clays, sand and gravel, and stone.

[27] ENERGY AND POWER

Nauru has no proven reserves of oil, natural gas, coal, or refining capacity. All fossil fuel needs are met by imports. In 2007, oil imports averaged 1,026 barrels per day. For 2009, consumption averaged 1,000 barrels per day. Per capita oil consumption was 3,506 kg. A diesel oil generator to which nearly all buildings are connected produces electric power. The World Bank reported in 2007 that Nauru produced 31 million kWh of electricity and consumed 28.83 million kWh, or 3,089 kWh per capita.

[28] INDUSTRY

The phosphate industry is the primary manufacturing industry on the island. As of 2006, it is under the control of state-owned Republic of Nauru Phosphate Company, or RONPhos. The industry is not expected to grow, however, as reserves are nearly depleted. The government has made some efforts to promote investment in small-scale manufacturing to meets the domestic needs.

[29] SCIENCE AND TECHNOLOGY

The World Bank reported in 2009 that there were no patent applications in science and technology in Nauru. Nauru has little advanced technology, and Nauruans must travel abroad, usually to Australia, for scientific training.

[30] DOMESTIC TRADE

The island is completely dependent on imported goods; foodstuffs come mainly from Australia. There are several small retail shops providing imported food and goods for local consumers. Handicrafts are sold in owner-operated stores or roadside stalls.

[31] FOREIGN TRADE

Nauru's primary export is phosphate rock, the value of which fluctuates as world phosphate prices rise or decline. Nearly all consumer goods must be imported, including machinery and construction materials, food, fresh water (from Australia), fuel, and other necessities. Virtually all manufactured goods must be imported. Major import partners in were Russia, Australia, South Korea, United States, Germany, and Japan. Its major export partners were South Korea, India, New Zealand, Australia, Indonesia, and United States.

[32] BALANCE OF PAYMENTS

In 2009 exports were valued at US$100.2 million while imports were valued at US$145.1 million, resulting in a trade deficit of US$44.9 million.

[33] BANKING AND SECURITIES

The government-owned Bank of Nauru, founded in 1976, began to collapse in the early 2000s as a result of the nation's debt crisis, and was closed for active business in 2006. In 2011, the government appointed a liquidator from Deloitte to comb through years worth of poorly kept records to determine what, if any, remaining assets the bank could still claim. At that time, it was estimated that nearly 3,500 deposit holders were still owed money. Officials also speculated that some of the assets were located in Australia, Asia, and other parts of the Pacific. Since the closure of the bank, the nation has essentially operated as a cash economy. There is no stock exchange.

During the 1990s and early 2000s, the nation's offshore banking industry gained a reputation as a major tax haven and money-laundering center, thereby earning a spot on the Financial Action Task Force blacklist. Facing international pressure, the government revoked nearly all its offshore licenses in 2004 and reformed its banking laws before reissuing new licenses. It was removed from the blacklist in 2005.

[34] INSURANCE

The Nauru Insurance Corp., founded in 1974, went into bankruptcy in the early 2000s. As of 2011, the company had not been reestablished. It is the primary licensed insurer and reinsurer on the island. It underwrites all classes of insurance, including aviation and marine. Other insurance policies were available only from foreign firms that offered global coverage.

[35] PUBLIC FINANCE

A large portion of government revenues comes in the form of foreign aid. The parliament frequently struggles to agree upon a balanced budget. For 2006–07, total government revenues were reported at AUD22.28 million while government expenditures were listed at AUD22.2 million. However, for 2009–10 the government reported total debt at AUD869 million, or about 20 times the annual GDP. About one-third of this debt is external.

[36] TAXATION

There is no income tax in Nauru, although parliament has power to impose such tax. A 7% tax on all goods was implemented in 2004. There is also an airport departure tax of about AUD50.

[37] CUSTOMS AND DUTIES

There are duty-free allowances for a number of imported items, including tobacco and alcohol. Additional information on customs and duties was unavailable in 2011.

38 FOREIGN INVESTMENT

Foreign direct investment (FDI) in Nauru was unreported according to World Bank figures published in 2009.

Apart from the investment in the phosphate industry, now owned by the government of Nauru, there has been little investment on the island. There is some potential for investment in commercial fishing operations.

39 ECONOMIC DEVELOPMENT

Political and economic instability left the nation virtually bankrupt by 2005. The National Sustainable Development Strategy 2005–2025 includes a number of goals and strategies designed to rebuild the economy from square one. Short-term priorities include the reestablishment of a central bank; projects to improve physical infrastructure, utilities, and access to telecommunications; development of the private sector; and promotion of commercial fisheries. In this 20-year plan, the government has also placed the development of the agricultural sector as a priority, hoping to promote initiatives that will enhance local production primarily for local consumption. It is hoped that the rehabilitation of mining lands will result in additional land resources for such agricultural endeavors. The plan recognizes the need to create a more stable legislative environment in order to attract foreign investment. The plan also includes a number of social priorities, including improvements in the education and health care systems to develop a stronger, more highly skilled workforce.

40 SOCIAL DEVELOPMENT

General health care, education (until age 16), old age and disability pensions, and other social welfare benefits (until age 16) are provided by the government. The constitution guarantees women equal rights with men, although traditional social values, and persistent poverty, still discourage many from pursuing advanced education and professional careers. Domestic abuse is not prevalent, and the government treats reports of violent incidents in a serious manner. Human rights are generally well respected.

41 HEALTH

There are two modern hospitals. One hospital serves phosphate industry employees; the other provides free medical treatment for the rest of the population. Patients who need specialized care are flown to Australia.

Tuberculosis, leprosy, diabetes, and vitamin deficiencies have been the main health problems. A national foot care education program was launched in 1992 to decrease the number of diabetic amputations. With modern facilities and treatments, many of these diseases have been brought under control. Cardiovascular disease has also been a major cause of illness and death.

Life expectancy as of 2011 was estimated at 65.35 years. The infant mortality rate was an estimated 8.66 per 1,000 live births in that year. The total fertility rate in 2011 was estimated at 3.08 children born per woman. Total healthcare expenditure was estimated at 14% of GDP, amounting to US$233 per person. There were 7 physicians, 49 nurses and midwives, and hospital beds per 10,000 inhabitants. A 2007 government health survey indicated that at least 85.5% of all children under two years of age had been fully immunized for measles, diphtheria, tetanus, and pertussis, polio, and tuberculosis were usually above 75%. The same survey indicated that 35% of women used contraceptives. There were no reported cases of polio or AIDS.

42 HOUSING

At the 2002 census (the latest full census as of 2011), there were 1,677 dwellings listed, of which 828 (49%) were permanent single-family dwellings and 578 (34.5%) were apartment units. A 2006 government survey indicated that the average household was comprised of 6.1 residents. About 20.6% of all households consisted on nine or more members. About 71% of all households had access to improved sanitation facilities and about 90% of all households had access to an improved water source. Nearly all households had access to electricity.

43 EDUCATION

Attendance at school is compulsory and free for Nauruan children from 6 to 16 years old. Both public and private schools (primarily parochial) are available. The Education system is based on a 3-6-4 model, with three years of preschool (beginning at age four), six years of primary school, and four years of secondary school. According to a 2006 government survey, primary school attendance was listed at 88% of students of eligible age, while secondary school attendance was noted at 60%. The Nauru Vocational Training Center provides training in technical skills. Higher education overseas, mainly in Australia, is assisted by the government in the form of competitive scholarships. There is also a university extension center affiliated with the University of the South Pacific.

As of 2003, public expenditure on education was estimated 6.9% of total government expenditures. In 2011, the literacy rate was estimated at 97.1%.

44 LIBRARIES AND MUSEUMS

The Nauru Bureau of Statistics maintains a small library which serves as a depository site for the Asian Development Bank. Nauru has one small lending library. The Nauru Military Museum contains WWII artifacts and displays donated by Stan Gajda.

45 MEDIA

Communication with the outside world is maintained by a ground satellite station established in 1975, providing 24-hour telephone, telegraph, and telex services worldwide. In 2009, there were 1,900 main phone lines. In 2002, there were 1,500 mobile phones in use throughout the country, or about 16 mobile phone subscriptions for every 100 people.

The government-owned Nauru Broadcasting Service provides radio broadcasts in English and Nauruan. Though there is no local news reporting, the station rebroadcasts news services from Radio Australia and the BBC. As of 2008, there was one television station in operation, broadcasting programs from New Zealand. According to a 2006 government survey, about 39.6% of all households had a radio, while 75.3% of all households had a television and 21% had a computer. In 2010, the country had 4,158 Internet hosts. As of December 2002 (the latest year for which data was available), there were some 300 Internet users in Nauru, accounting for 2.6% of the population. In 2006, there were 52 Internet hosts.

Most newspapers are imported. There are three regular publications: the fortnightly the *Central Star News* and *The Nauru Chronicle*, and the weekly government publication, *The Nauru Bulletin*.

The constitution provides for free expression, and the government is said to support this in practice.

46 ORGANIZATIONS

The Boy Scouts, Girl Guides, and similar organizations function on the island. The Nauru National Youth Council was established in 1990 to encourage the development of various youth organizations. Sports associations are popular on the island. The Women's Information and News Agency monitors issues relating to women and government.

47 TOURISM, TRAVEL, AND RECREATION

Nauru has great potential for the development of tourism, and the government is working on expanding the very limited industry. Its sandy beach, snorkeling, deep sea fishing, and scuba diving on the coral reef helps visitors enjoy the tropical climate and sea breezes. Island tours of the mines and the National Museum are also attractions. Popular sports are weightlifting, basketball, and badminton. A valid passport, visa, onward/return ticket, and proof of lodging are required to visit Nauru. Vaccinations are not mandatory, although recommended for typhoid.

48 FAMOUS PERSONS

The best-known Nauruan is its first president, Hammer DeRoburt (1923–92), who led the Nauruan people to political independence; he was president from 1968 to 1976 and again from 1978 until his death in 1992 (except for a brief period in 1986).

49 DEPENDENCIES

Nauru has no territories or colonies.

50 BIBLIOGRAPHY

Craig, Robert D. *Historical Dictionary of Polynesia*. Lanham, MD: Scarecrow, 2002.

Leibo, Steven A. *East and Southeast Asia, 2005*. 38th ed. Harpers Ferry, WV: Stryker-Post Publications, 2005.

McDaniel, Carl N. *Paradise for Sale: A Parable of Nature*. Berkeley, CA: University of California Press, 2000.

Pilkey, Orrin H. *The Rising Sea*. Washington, DC: Island Press Shearwater Books, 2009.

Ward, Peter Douglas. *The Flooded Earth: Our Future in a World without Ice Caps*. New York: Basic Books, 2010.

NEPAL

Federal Democratic Republic of Nepal
Sanghiya Loktantrik Ganatantra Nepal

CAPITAL: Kāthmāndu

FLAG: The national flag consists of two red adjoining triangles, outlined in blue and merging at the center; the points are at the fly. On the upper triangle, in white, is a symbolic representation of the moon; on the lower triangle, of the sun.

ANTHEM: *Sayaun Thunga Phool Ka (Hundreds of Flowers).*

MONETARY UNIT: The Nepalese rupee (NPR) is a paper currency of 100 paisa. There are coins of 1, 5, 10, 25, and 50 paisa and 1, 2, 5, 10 rupees, and notes of 1, 2, 5, 10, 20, 25, 50, 100, 500, and 1,000 Nepalese rupees. NPR1 = US$0.01265 (or US$1 = NPR79; as of 2011).

WEIGHTS AND MEASURES: The metric system is in use, but some traditional Indian standards also are employed.

HOLIDAYS: Martyrs' Day, 30 January; Rashtriya Prajatantra Divas—National Democracy Day, 18 February; Nepalese Women's Day, 8 March; Navabarsha—Nepalese New Year's Day, mid-April; Constitution Day, 9 November. Hindu and Buddhist religious holidays including Basanta Panchami, Chaite Dashain, Holi, Buddha Jayanti, Krishna Janmashtami, and Laxhmi Puja are celebrated as national holidays. Saturday is the general day of rest.

TIME: 5:45 p.m. = noon GMT.

1 LOCATION, SIZE, AND EXTENT

Between India and China, landlocked Nepal has an area of about 140,800 sq km (54,363 sq mi), extending 885 km (550 mi) SE–NW and 201 km (125 mi) NE–SW. Comparatively, Nepal is slightly larger than Arkansas. In its length lie some 800 km (500 mi) of the Himalayan mountain chain. Nepal is bounded on the N by China (Tibet) and on the E, S, and W by India, with a total boundary length of 2,926 km (1,818 mi). Nepal's capital city, Kāthmāndu, is located in the central part of the country.

2 TOPOGRAPHY

Nepal is made up of three strikingly contrasted areas. Southern Nepal has much of the character of the great plains of India, from which it extends. Known as the Terai, this region comprises both cultivable land and forest preserves. The Terai contains about one-third of Nepal's population and makes up about one-fourth of the total area.

The second and by far the largest part of Nepal is formed by the Mahabharat, Churia, and Himalayan mountain ranges, extending from east to west. Their altitude increases toward the north, culminating on the Tibetan border in Mt. Everest (Sagarmatha in Nepali). Eight of the world's highest mountains are situated in the Himalayan range on the Tibetan border. Triangulated in 1850, Mt. Everest was officially given the status of the world's highest peak in 1859. The summit (8,850 m/29,035 ft) was reached for the first time on 29 May 1953 by Tenzing Norgay, a Nepalese Sherpa, and Edmund Hillary, a New Zealander. Three principal rivers originate from glaciers and snow-fed lakes, break southward through deep Himalayan gorges, and enter, respectively, the Karnali, Gandak, and Kosi basins. Flowing toward India, they become tributaries (as are all Nepal's rivers) of the Ganges system.

The third area is a high central region, some 890 km (344 sq mi) in extent between the main Himalayan and Mahabharat ranges; this region is known as the Kāthmāndu Valley, or the Valley of Nepal. Overlooked by mountains, the valley, with its fertile soil and temperate climate, supports thriving agriculture. Here, Kāthmāndu, the capital, is situated, with the foothill towns of Bhaktapur and Patan nearby. This is the only region of Nepal that has any considerable population density.

3 CLIMATE

Below the Kāthmāndu Valley and throughout the Terai, the climate is subtropical and, in the wetlands and forests, extremely humid. The valley itself enjoys the temperate conditions generally found between altitudes of 1,200–3,400 m (4,000–11,000 ft). At 1,300 m (4,300 ft) above sea level, the elevation of Kāthmāndu, the rainy season lasts from June to October; 80% of annual precipitation falls during this monsoon season. Colder weather follows, lasting until the middle of March, when the warm season begins. The warm season increases in intensity until broken by the rains, which account for precipitation of about 150 cm (60 in) annually. Temperatures in Kāthmāndu in January range from an average minimum of 2°C (36°F) to an average maximum of 18°C (64°F); the July range is 20–29°C (68–84°F). Northward of the Kāthmāndu Valley, a subalpine zone continues to altitudes of about 4,300 m (14,000 ft); above that elevation, the country is

569

covered with snow during the long winter, and extreme cold is experienced in the upper Himalayas.

⁴FLORA AND FAUNA

The World Resources Institute estimates that there are 6,973 plant species in Nepal. In addition, Nepal is home to 203 species of mammals, 864 species of birds, 123 species of reptiles, and 50 species of amphibians. The calculation reflects the total number of distinct species residing in the country, not the number of endemic species.

The wide range of climate accounts for correspondingly marked contrasts in flora and fauna between different regions of the country. In the south, the sal, sisu, and other subtropical trees grow; in the extreme north, junipers are seen even at the altitude of the glacial moraines. Many kinds of conifers also exist in the alpine zone, along with the yew, hollies, birch, dwarf rhododendrons, and other alpine flora.

Dominant in the Langtang Valley are the chir pine, willow, alder, and evergreen oak. Blue pine and silver fir are frequent in the subalpine zone, which also supports tree rhododendrons—magnificent plants often reaching a growth of 12 m (40 ft). Ground orchids, lilies, yellow and blue poppies, and crimson anemones are prevalent in central Nepal. The profusion of wild flowers extends to very high altitudes; at 5,200 m (17,000 ft), several varieties of primula, pink and white cotoneaster, and white erica have been gathered, along with many kinds of alpine mosses and ferns.

The tiger, hyena, and jackal still exist in southern Nepal, although in decreasing numbers. Rhesus monkeys and a variety of other small mammals and rodents are common. At middle altitudes are found the black bear, several species of cats, squirrel, hare, deer, and antelope. Higher in the mountains, wild sheep and goats, marmots, and a species of tailless mouse-hare are numerous. Snow leopards live in the mountains of the north. Wild yaks can still be found in the mountains of Nepal. The wild yak, an endangered species that holds the distinction of being the mammal that lives at the highest altitudes, can live at altitudes up to 6,096 m (20,000 ft). Small black spiders were found at 6,900 m (22,500 ft) on rocky ledges traversed by the Mt. Everest expedition of 1953.

Birds of Nepal include the green finch, dove, woodpecker, nuthatch, warbler, flycatcher, bulbul, and many others. At about 2,700 m (9,000 ft) are found the hill partridge, pheasant, yellow-backed sunbird, minivet, and many of the flowerpeckers; the redstart, pipit, wagtail, snow pigeon, snowcock, and golden eagle live in both the alpine and subalpine zones.

⁵ENVIRONMENT

Nepal's environment has suffered the effects of agricultural encroachment, deforestation and consequent soil erosion, and contamination of the water supply. Between the mid-1960s and the late 1970s, forestland declined from 30% to 22% of the total area, mainly because of the felling of timber for firewood. All of Nepal's forests were nationalized in 1957, but reforestation efforts have been ineffective. A forest conservation program, begun in 1980, included the establishment of village tree nurseries, free distribution of seedlings, and provision of wood-burning stoves of increased efficiency. By 1985, however, deforestation averaged 839 sq km (324 sq mi) per year, while reforestation was only 4,000

hectares (9,900 acres) per year. An additional 4.4% of forest and woodland was lost between 1983 and 1993.

In the 1990s, community forestry was promoted as a way to encourage the local people to protect and maintain forests. Gains from these programs were compromised by corruption in oversight agencies and at the local level. As of 2000, the annual rate of deforestation was about 1.8%. According to the FAO, forest cover was 22% as of 2010. The Nepal parliament's Committee on Natural Resources and Means issued a report in 2010 concluding that deforestation was at its worst since 1979, due to government corruption allowing rampant timber-cutting in regions such as the Terai. Firewood continued to provide 70% of energy in Nepal as of 2010. Deforestation has caused landslides and flooding.

The World Resources Institute reported that Nepal had designated 2.28 million hectares (5.64 million acres) of land for protection as of 2006. Nepal has two natural UNESCO World Heritage Sites: Sagarmatha National Park and Chitwan National Park (habitat of rhinoceros and tiger). There are nine Ramsar Wetland Sites. According to a 2011 report issued by the International Union for Conservation of Nature and Natural Resources (IUCN), threatened species included 31 types of mammals, 31 species of birds, 8 types of reptiles, 3 species of amphibians, and 9 species of plants. Species classified as endangered in Nepal included the snow leopard, tiger, Asian elephant, pygmy hog, Indian rhinoceros, Assam rabbit, swamp deer, wild yak, and gavial. Poaching, wildlife trafficking and habitat encroachment have increased the threats to species including tigers, rhinoceros, and snow leopards.

Air and water pollution are significant environmental problems in Nepal. The UN reported in 2008 that carbon dioxide emissions in Nepal totaled 3,422 kilotons. Water resources totaled 210.2 cu km (50.43 cu mi) while water usage was 10.18 cu km (2.44 cu mi) per year. Domestic water usage accounted for 3% of total usage, industrial for 1%, and agricultural for 96%. Per capita water usage totaled 375 cu m (13,243 cu ft) per year. The use of contaminated drinking water creates a health hazard. Untreated sewage is a major pollution factor: the nation's cities have produced an average of 0.4 million tons of solid waste per year. Garbage left by climbing expeditions has marred the Everest base camp area and the mountain itself. Climate change due to global warming is causing Himalayan glaciers to melt, forming lakes that pose a threat of catastrophic floods.

⁶POPULATION

The US Central Intelligence Agency (CIA) estimated the population of Nepal in 2011 to be approximately 29,391,883, which placed it at number 41 in population among the 196 nations of the world. In 2011, approximately 4.3% of the population was over 65 years of age, with another 34.6% under 15 years of age. The median age in Nepal was 21.6 years. There were 0.96 males for every female in the country. The population's annual rate of change was 1.596%. The projected population for the year 2025 was 35,700,000. Population density in Nepal was calculated at 200 people per sq km (518 people per sq mi).

The UN estimated that 19% of the population lived in urban areas, and that urban populations had an annual rate of change of 4.7%. The largest urban area was Kāthmāndu, with a population of 990,000.

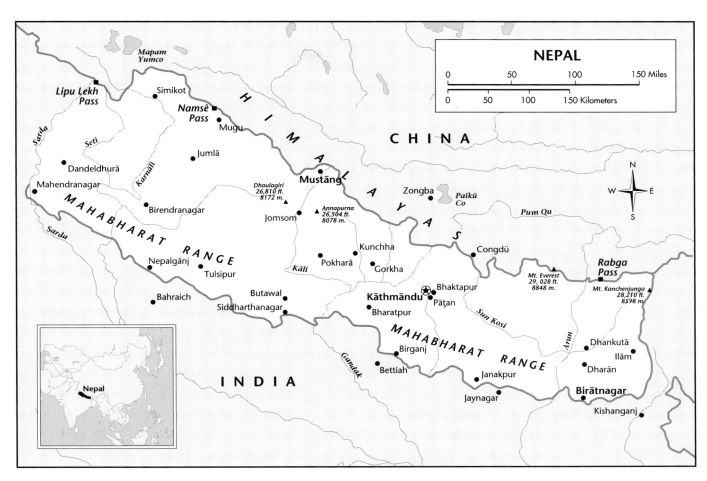

LOCATION: 26°20' to 30°16'N; 80°15' to 88°15' E. BOUNDARY LENGTHS: China, 1,236 kilometers (772 miles); India, 1,690 kilometers (1,046 miles).

⁷MIGRATION

Estimates of Nepal's net migration rate, carried out by the CIA in 2011, amounted to 0.61 migrants per 1,000 citizens; this statistic did not reflect the high rate of migrant workers. According to a 2009 World Bank survey, 2.1 million Nepalese workers were overseas, with 41% in India, 38% in Gulf states, and 12% in Malaysia. According to the government's Nepal Living Standard Survey, as of 2010, an estimated 55% of households in Nepal received remittances from workers in other countries. Over 350,000 workers left Nepal in the 2010/2011 fiscal year.

Hundreds of thousands of Indians reportedly live and work in Nepal, most undocumented and in the informal sector. According to the United Nations High Commissioner for Refugees (UNHCR), as of 2011, Nepal had 75,000 refugees from Bhutan and 20,000 from Tibet. An influx of Bhutanese refugees into Nepal began in late 1991 and peaked in 1992; the flow of new arrivals slowed after 1997. The refugees from Bhutan were being resettled in third countries at a rate of over 15,000 per year. Nearly 20,000 Tibetans arrived in Nepal between the Chinese annexation of Tibet in 1959 and 1989. About 1,000 Tibetan refugees travel through Nepal on their way to India each year, according to the UNHCR. Tibetan refugees have faced arrest, deportation, and other harassment, as Nepal maintains close relations with China.

⁸ETHNIC GROUPS

Nepal consists of ethnic peoples who originally migrated to Nepal by way of Tibet, Sikkim, Assam, and northern Bengal; and ethnic peoples who originally came from the Indian plains and from the sub-Himalayan hill areas to the west of Nepal. These can be broken down into more than 75 ethnic groups. There are also small remnants of Dravidian tribes. Bhotes, of Tibetan origin, are the principal occupants of northern Nepal. In the central valley, Newars, considered one of the earliest groups of inhabitants, and Murmis predominate, the former being responsible for most of the agriculture and trade. Less numerous groups include Gurungs and Magars in west-central Nepal and Kirantis and Rai in the east. Sherpas, a Himalayan people, have become well-known as guides for mountain climbing expeditions. The indigenous Tharus live in the southern Terai region. The Brahman and Chetri caste groups are believed to be descendants of Indian settlers. The Dalit people have faced discrimination due to the caste system.

⁹LANGUAGES

Nepali is the official language, although some 50 different languages are spoken. Nepali is spoken by about 47.8% of the population and is the language for most inter-ethnic communication; it is used in government publications and has been the language of most of the written literature since the Gurkha unification of

Nepal. About 12.1% of the people speak Maithili as their first language, 7.4% Bhojpuri, 5.8% Tharu, 5.1% Tamang, 3.6% Newar, 3.3% Magar, and 2.4% Awadhi. Except in primary schools, where children are taught in their own languages, Nepali or English is the medium of instruction. English is taught as a second language in secondary schools and colleges and is widely understood in business and government circles.

10 RELIGIONS

The 2001 census indicated that about 81% of the population identified as Hindu, while 11% were Buddhist. Muslims constituted about 4.2% of the population, and Kirants (followers of an indigenous animist religion) were 3.6%. Minorities include Christians, Baha'is and Jains. Nepal is a secular state as established by the constitution. Certain Hindu holidays are recognized as national holidays, as is the birthday of the Buddha. Religious freedom is respected, and proselytizing is banned.

Hinduism and Buddhism exist side by side in Nepal and to some extent are intermingled. The importance of both in the national life is manifested everywhere; more than 2,700 temples and shrines have been counted in the Kāthmāndu Valley alone, while innumerable others are scattered along trails and roads extending to the most distant mountain passes. Bodhnath and Shambunath are famous Buddhist temples, and Gautama Buddha's birthplace is at Lumbini. The ancient temple of Chandrahigiri is dedicated to both religions. The Baghmati River, flowing through central Nepal, is considered sacred and is visited by pilgrims, as are certain mountains and lakes.

11 TRANSPORTATION

The CIA reports that Nepal has a total of 17,282 km (10,739 mi) of roads, of which 10,142 km (6,302 mi) are paved. Porters with pack animals are still an important means of transport in mountainous areas without roads. The main highways are the 190 km (118 mi) road that penetrates the Kāthmāndu Valley, connecting it with the Indian border; the 87 km (54 mi) road between Kāthmāndu and Kodari on the Tibetan (Chinese) border; the 862 km (536 mi) east-west Mahendra Highway; and the 200 km (124 mi) Kāthmāndu-Pokhara highway.

All of Nepal's railways are narrow-gauge and close to the Indian border. Opened in 1927, the line runs from Jayanagar, in India, to Janakpur, a distance of 52 km (32 mi), of which 10 km (6 mi), running from Raxaul, India, to the frontier town of Birganj, is government-owned. Electrically driven ropeways for cargo have ceased to function. There are no waterways in Nepal. The only practical seaport for goods bound for Kāthmāndu is Kolkata in India.

Much of Nepal is easily accessible only by air. There are 47 airports. The leading air terminal is Tribhuvan Airport at Kāthmāndu. According to Tribhuvan Airport, there were 1,554,701 domestic passengers in 2010. Nepal Airlines (formerly Royal Nepal Airlines) is the flag carrier, with domestic flights as well as flights to Europe, the Middle East, India and other Asian countries. Numerous private airlines, including Buddha Air, Cosmic Air, Shangril-La Air, Gorkha Airlines and Yeti Air, offer domestic and some regional flights.

12 HISTORY

Nepal's historical literature traces the origins of the country to the distant past when Nepal was allegedly founded by Ne-Muni and derived its name from this source. A reliable chronology can be established only after the conquest of Nepal by Harisinha-deva, rajah of Simraun in about 1324. Under the Malla dynasty, Nepal was administered in four separate states: Banepa, Bhadgaon (now Bhaktapur), Kantipur (modern Kāthmāndu), and Lalitpur (now Pātan).

Prithwi Narayan Shah, the ruler of Gorkha, a small principality west of Kāthmāndu, established the modern kingdom of Nepal in 1768 by incorporating the Kāthmāndu Valley into his domain and unifying with it many small independent principalities and states. Under his descendants, most of the present boundaries of Nepal were established, and Hinduism was introduced from India as the official religion.

Nepal came in contact with the influence of larger powers outside South Asia in the late 18th century as a consequence of the British East India Company's conquest of India to its south and a trade dispute with Tibet that led to a Nepalese confrontation with China. Peace was imposed by China in 1792, after Chinese forces had invaded, then withdrawn from Nepal. In the same year, a commercial treaty was ratified between Britain and Nepal. Relations with the British in India remained peaceful until 1814 when a border dispute led to inconclusive hostilities between Nepal and the British East India Company. When the fighting ended two years later, Nepal's independence was preserved in an agreement in which Nepal yielded a large piece of territory to the Company on its southern border and agreed to the establishment of a permanent British resident at Kāthmāndu.

The 1816 agreement (reaffirmed by a formal treaty of friendship in 1923) also laid the groundwork for more than a century and a half of amicable relations between Britain and Nepal. Included under the agreement was Nepalese approval for British recruitment of Nepalese Gurkha mercenaries for the British-officered Indian army. During the Indian Mutiny of 1857, Nepal's Rana prime minister sent some 12,000 additional Nepalese troops in support of British garrisons; he also offered troops to US president Abraham Lincoln in 1866 during the US Civil War. Over the years, the Gurkha regiments serving overseas in the British Indian army (and after 1947 under both Indian and British flags) won renown for their bravery, skill, and endurance.

In 1846, Shumshere Jung Bahadur (Rana) became Nepal's de facto ruler, banishing the king and ruling as regent for the king's minor heir. The prime ministership became a hereditary office in his Rana family, which ruled successively until 1951. Following the end of World War II, the termination of British rule on the South Asian subcontinent in 1947 caused deep stirrings of change in Nepal. Resentment grew against the autocratic despotism of the Ranas, who—as regents—had kept successive monarchs virtual prisoners. A political reform movement, begun in 1946 with the founding of the Nepali Congress Party on the model of the Indian Congress Party, won the support of King Tribhuvana Bir Bikram Shah, but in a power struggle in 1950, the king was forced to flee from the Ranas to India. With Indian support, insurgents began operations against the Rana government until, with the mediation of Indian Prime Minister Nehru, a political compromise was reached that returned the king to Kāthmāndu and ended a century of hereditary Rana family rule. By late 1951, a new government had taken office, headed by Matrika Prasad Koirala, with his brother, a co-founder of the Nepali Congress Party (NC).

Political life in Nepal in the years since the restoration of the monarchy in 1951 was dominated by the struggle between the monarchy and the country's political elements to define the terms under which they might co-exist and bring the country into the modern world. Six different cabinets, each lacking popular support and riddled with dissension, held office in rapid succession between 1951 and 1957, and in 1957–58, King Mahendra Bir Bikram Shah, who had succeeded to the throne upon the death of his father in 1955, ruled directly for a period of months. In April 1959, he promulgated a democratic constitution, providing for a constitutional monarchy, two houses of parliament, and a cabinet and prime minister responsible to the lower house, in the Westminster model. Bisweswar Prasad Koirala of the NC assumed office on 24 July 1959 as first prime minister under this constitution.

Less than 18 months later, on 15 December 1960, the king suspended the constitution, dissolved parliament, dismissed the cabinet, and again established his own government, this time with an appointed council of ministers. He ruled directly until April 1962 when he promulgated a new constitution establishing an indirect, nonparty system of rule through a tiered system of panchayats (council) culminating in a National Panchayat. Five years later, after growing agitation and hit-and-run attacks by NC elements based in India, the king—again under Indian pressure—promulgated a series of amendments introducing gradual liberalization.

In January 1972, Mahendra was succeeded by his 27-year-old son, Birendra Bir Bikram Shah Dev. The young monarch, who had attended Harvard University, was committed to maintaining the authority of the monarchy while keeping Nepal on the course of gradual political and social reform set by his father. Student demonstrations in early 1979 led him to call for a national referendum on whether to continue the panchayat system or create a more conventional multiparty system. With the king promising further liberalization, the existing panchayat system was endorsed by 55% of the voters in May 1980, and later that year, the king's subsequent constitutional amendments established direct elections and permitted the Panchayat, not the king, to choose the prime minister. The king's failure to lift the ban on political parties led party members to ineffectively boycott the elections of 1981, in which Surya Bahadur Thapa, who had become prime minister in 1979, was reaffirmed and continued in office until 1983 when he was replaced by Lokendra Bahadur Chand following the government's loss of its majority on an opposition "no confidence" motion.

In nonparty elections to the National Panchayat in May 1986, again in the face of a major party boycott, a majority of the incumbents were defeated, and Marich Man Singh Shrestha became prime minister. Most new members were opponents of the panchayat system, foreshadowing a new struggle between the king and his legislators. By early 1990, the NC and the United Leftist Front (ULF), a Communist alliance of seven parties, again went to the streets, organizing agitations that forced the king to make further constitutional changes in April; included were an end to the ban on political parties and their activities. The king dissolved the National Panchayat and appointed NC president Krishna Prasad Bhattarai interim prime minister, who was assisted by a cabinet made up of members of the NC, the ULF, independents, and royal appointees. A Constitutional Reforms Commission produced a new constitution in November 1990 that ended the panchayat era and restored multiparty democracy in a constitutional monarchy. In May 1991, the first openly partisan elections in 32 years were held, resulting in an NC majority in the new House of Representatives that then chose Girija Prasad Koirala as prime minister.

In 1996, a "people's war" was launched by several Maoist organizations in the central-western hill districts of Nepal. The Maoists' aims were the removal of the constitutional monarchy and the eradication of rural poverty, as well as women's rights. The insurgents called themselves the Communist Party of Nepal (Maoist), modeled after Peru's Maoist Shining Path guerrillas. They were led by Chhabi Lal Dahal, or "Prachanda," who was seen by his followers as charismatic and by his enemies as fanatical.

On 1 June 2001, crown prince Dipendra Bir Bikram killed most of the royal family with an assault rifle as they sat around a dinner table. Although many theories circulated as to the motive for the killings, it is generally accepted that he turned against his family because his mother did not approve of a young woman as his choice of bride. Dipendra murdered his father, King Birendra, his mother, Queen Aishwarya, his sister, Princess Sruti, his brother, Prince Nirajan, and five others. He then shot himself in the head. Dipendra was anointed king while in a coma; two days later he died, and his uncle, Gyanendra Bir Bikram Shah Dev, was named king.

Not long after, in July 2001, the Maoists came into direct combat with the Nepalese army for the first time and stepped up their campaign of violence. Koirala, who was prime minister at the time, resigned after losing support from his ruling coalition and alluded to the violence as a reason that the country needed to work for national consensus. Sher Bahadur Deuba became prime minister. In November 2001, after more than 100 people were killed in four days of violence, the king called a State of Emergency. The emergency measures restricted freedom of the press, as well as freedom of assembly, expression, and movement. Suspects could be detained for three weeks without charges.

In February 2002, international donor agencies and individual nations pledged US$2.5 billion to Nepal, and the government increased military activity against the insurgents. In April, more than 300 people were killed in two of the most serious attacks of the rebellion, and the Maoists ordered a five-day national strike. Parliament was dissolved on 22 May, and national elections were scheduled for 13 November. In October, Prime Minister Deuba asked the king to put off the national elections for a year due to the mounting Maoist violence. King Gyanendra dismissed him and indefinitely put off the elections. King Gyanendra appointed Lokendra Bahadur Chand interim prime minister. Chand served seven months before resigning, The king then appointed Surya Bahadur Thapa as his replacement in 2003. However, Deuba was reinstated as prime minister in 2004. Finally in February 2005, King Gyanendra dismissed Prime Minister Deuba (again), dissolved the cabinet, and assumed direct rule of the country himself, with a stated goal of reestablishing democratic rule within three years.

In 2004, the latest cease-fire between the Maoist rebels and the government had collapsed. The killings increased on both sides with the Maoist rebels assassinating government officials, usually at the local level, and bombing and attacking Indian-owned establishments. The government officially invited the Maoists to negotiate again in 2004, but the rebels refused. In November 2005, the Maoist rebels and main political parties opposed to the king's direct rule agreed on a program intended to restore democracy. By December 2005 , the Maoists controlled 45% of Nepal and had brought the economy and political system to a virtual standstill. More than 12,000 people had been killed in the fighting.

In April 2006, King Gyanendra agreed to reinstate parliament, following weeks of violent strikes and protests against direct royal rule. Koirala was once again appointed prime minister. The Maoist rebels called for a three-month cease-fire. That May, parliament voted unanimously to scale back the king's political powers. The government and the Maoist rebels began peace talks, the first in nearly three years. On 16 June 2006, Prachanda and Koirala held talks, the first such high-level meeting between the two sides, and agreed that the Maoists should be brought into an interim government. That November, the two sides signed a peace agreement, declaring a formal end to the insurgency. The rebels agreed to join a transitional government and place their weapons under UN supervision.

An interim parliament was formed in January 2007, and an interim constitution was unanimously endorsed. Nepal became a federal republic on 28 May 2008, and the monarchy was officially terminated in June 2008. Elections for a constituent assembly were held in April 2008, with members to serve as parliament with a primary mandate to draft a new constitution. The Maoist party (officially known as the Unified Communist Party of Nepal–Maoist) emerged as the largest party. In August 2008, the leader of the Maoist insurgency, Prachanda, was elected prime minister; however, his term was a short one. In May 2009, Prachanda resigned after his bid to oust conservative army chief General Rookmangud Katawal was unsuccessful. Prachanda and the Maoist party accused the general of undermining the civilian government. With Prachanda's resignation, an alliance of 22 opposition parties quickly formed, with plans to form a new Communist government under the leadership of Madhav Kumar Nepal, the chairman of the Communist Party of Nepal (Unified Marxist-Leninist—CPN/UML). In protest, the Maoists refused to announce a candidate and boycotted the election. As a result, Madhav Nepal was declared the unopposed winner for the seat of prime minister. Prachanda led members of the Maoist party in several demonstrations, calling for the resignation of both General Katawal and the president and for a government based on "civilian supremacy."

On 30 June 2010, Madhav Kumar Nepal resigned amidst pressure from the CPN/M so that a new power-sharing deal could be reached. For seven months, parliament held successive elections, each time failing to choose a prime minister. In February 2011, Jhalanath Khanal of the CPN/UML finally won a majority of votes, but he stepped down in August 2011, unable to finalize demobilization of Maoist troops or produce a new constitution. Baburam Bhattarai (CPN/M) was elected prime minister in his place on 28 August 2011, becoming the fourth prime minister since 2008. The deadline for the constitution was extended for the third time, to November 2011.

13 GOVERNMENT

A peace agreement between the Maoists and the Seven Party Alliance (SPA) was signed on 21 November 2006. As part of that agreement, an interim Nepalese parliament was formed in January 2007 and an interim constitution was unanimously endorsed on 15 January 2007. The monarchy was ended, and Nepal became a federal republic. Elections for a constituent assembly were held in April 2008, with parliament members given a primary mandate to draft a new constitution. The unicameral constituent assembly consists of 601 seats. Through the fourth amendment to the interim constitution, the constituent assembly established, for the first time, a largely ceremonial president as the constitutional head of state, as well as a vice president. The prime minister continues to be the head of the government, with the president as ceremonial head of state. Deadlines for finalizing the new constitution have been repeatedly extended. As of January 2012 work was still underway, with a deadline of May 2012.

14 POLITICAL PARTIES

The 1962 constitution originally prohibited the formation of political parties and associations, even though political groups continued to exist and operate underground, at times on a quasi-legal basis. Parties were legalized in 1990. The main party through Nepal's modern history—providing nearly all of the country's prime ministers even when the ban on parties prohibited party activity—was the Nepali Congress Party (NC). Inspired by the socialist wing of the Indian National Congress and founded in 1946 by the Koirala brothers, M.P. and B.P., the party led Nepal's first democratic government in 1959. Most of its leaders were imprisoned during the 1960s, but with Indian help, the party operated from India, mounting hit-and-run attacks and maintaining an underground presence in Nepal.

The NC leadership led the opposition to King Mahendra's tiered panchayat system of indirect government. Although NC leaders called for a boycott of the May 1986 elections to the National Panchayat, 1,547 candidates ran for office, and only 40 of the previously elected members retained their seats. After these elections, a Democratic Panchayat Forum (DPF) was formed by NC members to mobilize voters on a nonparty basis to counter the influence in local elections of the Communist Party of Nepal (CPN), whose members had won 16 seats in the National Panchayat.

The communist movement in Nepal has been severely fragmented for years by personal and ideological schisms, some of them occasioned by splits and the loss of orthodoxy in the communist movement worldwide in the 1960s and 1980s. Operating for electoral and agitational purposes in the 1980s as the United Leftist Front (ULF), the Communist Party (CPN) and its several communist allies have since split, fragmenting the movement into a number of splinter parties. As of 2011, the two leading communist parties were the Unified Communist Party of Nepal–Maoist (CPN/M), which was the political party of the powerful Maoist insurgents, and the rival CPN/UML.

In the April 2008 parliamentary elections, the CPN/M won 229 seats in the constituent assembly (with 38% of the vote). The Nepali Congress came in next with 115 seats (19%), followed by the CPN/UML with 108 seats (18%), the Madhesi People's Right Forum with 54 seats (9%), and the Terai Madhes Democratic Party with 21 seats. The remaining seats were filled by candidates from smaller parties. Madhav Kumar Nepal of the CPN/UML was chosen as prime minister in 2009; he resigned in 2010. After several parliamentary attempts to choose a new prime minister, Jhalanath Khanal of the CPN/UML took office in February 2011 and was soon replaced by Baburam Bhattarai of the CPN/M.

15 LOCAL GOVERNMENT

For centuries, the heads of small principalities within Nepal exercised local judicial, police, and other powers. Under the panchayat reforms introduced in 1962, the country was divided into 14 zones, which in turn were divided into 75 districts. The zones were directly administered by commissioners appointed by the central government, and the zonal panchayats were executive bodies elected from the 11-member panchayats at the district level, the members of which were in turn selected from village and town panchayats. Each of the 3,600 villages with populations of more than 2,000 and each of the 33 towns with populations over 10,000 also had an 11-member panchayat, as well as its own local assembly.

In April 1990, the partyless panchayat system was abolished as a result of a people's movement organized by the Nepali Congress Party and several leftist parties. However, the country remains divided into 14 zones (headed by appointed commissioners) and 75 districts (under the charge of district officers responsible for law and order, collecting revenues, and setting development priorities). The districts are further divided into smaller units—into municipalities and village development committees (VDC). A VDC consists of 9 wards, and the municipalities consist from 9 to 35 wards. Municipalities and VDCs are directly elected. In 1999, the Local Self Governance Act stipulated that women should comprise 40% of candidates for municipal councils.

16 JUDICIAL SYSTEM

Each district has a court of first instance, civil and criminal, as well as a court of appeals and 14 zonal courts. There are five regional courts—at Kāthmāndu, Dhankutā, Pokharā, Surkhet, and Dipayal—to which further appeals may be taken. Corruption of judges has been a severe problem at the local level, although the interim constitution of 2006 included reforms of the judicial appointments process. Court backlogs and forced confessions are other persistent flaws in the criminal justice system.

The Supreme Court in Kāthmāndu is empowered to issue writs of habeas corpus and decide on the constitutionality of laws. The court is composed of a chief justice, assisted usually by six other judges, with seven additional judges in reserve. The Supreme Court is the court of last resort. In April 2001, the Supreme Court appointed its first female judge.

The 1990 constitution set a number of procedural safeguards for criminal defendants, including the right to counsel and protection from double jeopardy and from retroactive application of laws; it also declared the independence of the judiciary. The Supreme Court has exercised considerable independence in practice, declaring unconstitutional provisions of the Citizenship Act of 1991 and parts of the Labor Act of 1992. In 1995, the constitutional court also ruled that the dissolution of the parliament at the request of a former primer minister was unconstitutional. The 2007 interim constitution prohibited torture and detention without cause, and mandated the right to counsel for the accused and presumption of innocence.

There is no jury system. The first independent public defender service was opened in 2008. International human rights organizations have reported police violence against demonstrators and people in custody. Efforts to establish a Truth and Reconciliation Committee, in order to investigate human rights violations by both sides during the Maoist insurgency, had not been successful as of October 2011.

17 ARMED FORCES

The International Institute for Strategic Studies reports that armed forces in Nepal totaled 95,753 members in 2011, all of which were members of the army. Armed forces represented 1.2% of the labor force in Nepal. Defense spending totaled $575.1 million and accounted for 1.6% of gross domestic product (GDP). In October 2011, Nepal's government announced that 6,500 former Maoist soldiers would be accepted into the national army, while the remaining 125,000 would be given payments to help them re-enter civilian life.

As of 2011 the United Kingdom maintained a small military presence in Nepal involved in the recruitment and training of Gurkha troops. Under separate treaty arrangements going back to 1816, Gurkhas (especially Magars, Gurungs, Rais, and Limpus) are recruited in Nepal by the United Kingdom and, since 1947, by India. Under British and Indian flags and with arms, training, and officers provided by their foreign recruiters, Gurkhas are among the world's most renowned fighters with extensive international service in both World Wars, UN actions, and the Iraq and Afghanistan Wars. Remittance of pay by Gurkha soldiers has long been an important part of Nepal's economy, and Gurkha veterans have demanded pension equality and the right to reside in the United Kingdom. Women have been recruited as Gurkha soldiers since 2007. Nepalese troops have served on 28 missions as UN peacekeepers.

18 INTERNATIONAL COOPERATION

Nepal was admitted to the United Nations on 14 December 1955 and is a member of ESCAP and several non-regional specialized agencies, including the FAO, the World Bank, ILO, IMF, UNESCO, UNIDO, and the WHO. It also belongs to the WTO, the Asian Development Bank, the Colombo Plan, and G-77. In 1985, Nepal joined with six other Asian nations to form the South Asian Association for Regional Cooperation (SAARC); the secretariat is in Kāthmāndu. In 2006, Nepal signed the agreement for the South Asian Free Trade Area (SAFTA). Nepal is a member of the Nonaligned Movement.

Due to Nepal's location between India and China (Tibetan Autonomous Region), the country's foreign policy attempts to balance relations with two powerful rivals. Nepal's communist parties have shown some affinity for China, and Nepal has endorsed the "One China" policy. Repression and deportation of Tibetan refugees has apparently been the result of Chinese pressure, but in mid-2011, the Nepalese government rejected a multi-billion dollar Chinese plan to develop Lumbini, the Buddha's birthplace, into a special economic zone. India, while a long-term trade partner, is seen by some politicians as economically exploitive of Nepal and dominant over the Himalayan region.

In environmental cooperation, Nepal is part of the South Asia Cooperative Environment Program (SACEP), the Basel Convention, the Convention on Biological Diversity, Ramsar, CITES, International Tropical Timber Agreements, the Montréal Protocol, the Nuclear Test Ban Treaty, and the UN Conventions on the Law of the Sea, Climate Change and Desertification.

19 ECONOMY

Despite social and economic reforms begun in the 1950s, Nepal's per capita income was just $1,100 in 1998, and had only increased to $1,200 by 2007. General living standards have remained very low. Eight development plans, extending from 1955 to 1992, slowly improved the nation's infrastructure, but the industrial sector is still small. Structural adjustment measures initiated in 1989 reduced the regulation of industry and imports and were supported by similar liberalization in India, to which Nepal's economy is closely tied. Aggregate economic growth remained sluggish during the early 1990s, then accelerated in the later part of that decade.

The GDP growth rate was negative in 2002 (-0.3%), but the economy recovered in 2003 and 2004, expanding by 2.8% and 3.4%, respectively, in spite of political turmoil and insurgency. In 2007, the GDP growth rate was 2.5%. The inflation rate has fluctuated, with a high level of 6.4% in 2007, a very high level of 10.4% in 2010, and decreasing to a still-high 8.6% in 2011. The GDP rate of change in Nepal, as of 2010, was 4.6%. Nepal remained one of the poorest countries in the world, land-locked, with weak infrastructure and meager connections to outside markets. In spite of income from remittances and tourism, Nepal had a substantial trade deficit and continued to rely heavily on foreign development aid. The economy has been based on subsistence agriculture, which engaged about 76% of the labor force as of 2010 but was limited by a shortage of arable land and irrigation in relation to population. As of 2011, with communist parties dominant in government, economic policy appeared to be moving towards increased state control and extensive subsidy programs.

20 INCOME

The CIA estimated that in 2010 the GDP of Nepal was $35.81 billion. The CIA defines GDP as the value of all final goods and services produced within a nation in a given year and computed on the basis of purchasing power parity (PPP) rather than value as measured on the basis of the rate of the exchange based on current dollars. The per capita GDP was estimated at $1,200. The annual growth rate of GDP was 4.6%. The average inflation rate was 8.6 %. It was estimated that agriculture accounted for 33% of GDP, industry 15%, and services 52%. The World Bank estimated that Nepal, with 0.41% of the world's population, accounted for 0.05% of the world's GDP, as of 2010. By comparison, the United States, with 4.85% of the world's population, accounted for 22.51% of world GDP.

According to the CIA, it was estimated that in 2008 about 25% of the population subsisted on an income below the poverty line established by Nepal's government. The World Bank reported that, in 2009, household consumption in Nepal totaled $9.9 billion or about $338 per capita, measured in current US dollars rather than PPP. As of 2011, the World Bank reported that actual individual consumption in Nepal was 84.7% of GDP and accounted for

0.06% of world consumption. By comparison, the United States accounted for 25.44% of world individual consumption. The World Bank also estimated that 44% of Nepal's GDP was spent on food and beverages, 13.6% on housing and household furnishings, 5.3% on clothes, 7.5% on health, 3.3% on transportation, 0.2% on communications, 0.9% on recreation, 2.0% on restaurants and hotels, and 4% on miscellaneous goods and services and purchases from abroad.

21 LABOR

As of 2009, Nepal had a total labor force of 18 million people. Within that labor force, CIA estimates in 2010 noted that 75% were employed in agriculture, 7% in industry, and 18% in the service sector. Unemployment was reported at 46% as of 2008 according to the CIA, a statistic that does not reflect pervasive underemployment. In some sectors, a labor shortage was actually being felt in 2010–2011, as workers sought more lucrative employment in other countries. There has also been an ongoing shortage of skilled labor. Most agriculturists are subsistence farmers, and there are many seasonal wage laborers.

Unions are allowed to organize and strike. The three largest trade unions are associated with political parties and often reflect the rivalries between those parties. About 20% of the workforce is covered by collective bargaining agreements. Trade unions have lobbied for the right to organize, the right to strike, and collective bargaining to be included in the new constitution (not finalized by October 2011).

Nepal's mandatory minimum wage, adjusted in 2008, ranged from 4,600 nr ($59) per month for unskilled workers to 4,950 nr ($63) per month for highly skilled workers as of 2011 in the organized industrial sector. Trade unions did not consider the 2008 minimum wage to be a living wage because of high inflation. The minimum wage for agricultural workers was revised in October 2011 to reach 221 nr ($2.84) per day. Wages can actually be as low as 50% of the minimum in the informal economy and the agricultural sector. Few employers pay any type of benefits, such as health insurance. The law established a minimum employment age of 16 years in industry and 14 years in agriculture. Child labor remains very common, in agriculture, rug manufacture, and other occupations; the US State Department reported that more than 20,000 children were bonded (indentured) workers in Nepal as of 2010.

22 AGRICULTURE

Roughly 17% of the total land is currently farmed, and the country's major crops include pulses, rice, corn, wheat, sugarcane, jute, and root crops. According to the UN FAO, in 2009, cereal production amounted to 8.1 million tons, fruit production 1.2 million tons, and vegetable production 2.8 million tons. In 2010, according to the CIA, agriculture provided about 33% of GDP and employed about 75% of the population.

Regional imbalance, lack of market integration, transportation difficulties, and inadequate storage facilities are factors leading to food insecurity in Nepal. Agriculture has been held back by the lack of irrigated land, the small size of farms, and inefficient farming methods. Nepal has officially abolished tax-free estates (*birta*), eliminated the feudal form of land tenure (*jagira*), set a limit on landholdings, and redistributed land to farm tenants. Economic plans have promoted the use of fertilizers, insecticides, improved seeds, and better implements; the extension of irrigation; and the construction of transportation and storage facilities.

Rice, Nepal's most important cereal, is grown on more than half the cultivated land, mainly in the Terai but also on every available piece of ground in the Kāthmāndu Valley during the monsoon season. Sugarcane, jute, and tobacco are major raw materials for Nepal's own industries. Potatoes are grown in Ilam and fruit mainly in Dharan, Dhankuta, and Pokhara. Tea is also grown in Ilam and elsewhere. Raising orchard fruits such as apples, peaches, pears, lychees, mangos, and guavas for juice production has become increasingly important in Nepal's agriculture sector and export market.

Aid for agriculture was offered in August 2009, as the European Union (EU) allocated over $12.9 million in grant funds to benefit small farmers in Nepal, supporting projects of crop diversification and collective farming to improve the efficiency of small farms and boost local production. In association with the UN World Food Program, additional projects provided food in exchange for work on irrigation and flood prevention projects. All of these projects were designed to address the challenge of food security in the nation and to boost the local economy. The lack of adequate irrigation can pose a serious problem, especially during periods of drought like that in late 2010. In early 2011, the government was working to start new programs to boost irrigation management.

23 ANIMAL HUSBANDRY

The UN Food and Agriculture Organization (FAO) reported that Nepal dedicated 1.7 million hectares (4.29 million acres) to permanent pasture or meadow in 2009. During that year, the country tended 24.5 million chickens, 7.2 million head of cattle, and 1 million pigs. The production from these animals amounted to 196,326 tons of beef and veal, 16,128 tons of pork, 16,420 tons of poultry, 28,481 tons of eggs, and 1.16 million tons of milk. Nepal also produced 4,688 tons of cattle hide and 584 tons of raw wool.

Livestock, adapted to many uses, forms an essential part of the economy. Livestock accounts for about 30% of gross agricultural output. Bullocks plow fields, cows produce butter and yogurt, and yaks or horses are used as pack animals in the mountains. Sheep and goats are raised for food and wool, including fine pashmina fiber.

24 FISHING

In 2008, the annual capture totaled 21,500 tons according to the UN FAO. In the Terai there are many small fishponds and several government fish farms. Common fish species are carp, catfish, gar, and mural; there are also mahseer and snow trout.

25 FORESTRY

According to the FAO, approximately 22% of Nepal was covered by forest, as of 2010. The FAO estimated the 2009 roundwood production at 1.26 million cu m (44.5 million cu ft). The value of all forest products, including roundwood, totaled $5.3 million. Community forest-stewardship programs have failed to halt deforestation. Most wood is cut for use as fuel, but timber is still illegally cut in remaining southern forests, reportedly by bribery of officials.

26 MINING

Although mining in Nepal was an ancient occupation, the country's mineral resources have been little exploited. Mining and quarrying was dominated by the production of cement, red clay, coal, limestone, magnesite, and marble. In 2010, cement production totaled 295,000 metric tons, while red clay output came to 9,000 metric tons. Coal output that same year (bituminous and lignite) totaled 16,000 metric tons, while limestone production totaled 715,916 metric tons. In 2009, the country also produced quartz, quartzite, salt, talc, and tourmaline. A lead and zinc deposit near Lari had reserves of two million tons, and there were known deposits of iron, copper, graphite, cobalt, mica, and slate. Development plans included the encouragement of small-scale mining, and provided for continuing mineral surveys.

27 ENERGY AND POWER

The World Bank reported in 2008 that Nepal produced 3.08 billion kWh of electricity and consumed 2.57 billion kWh, or 87 kWh per capita. Per-capita oil consumption was 340 kg. Roughly 11% of energy came from fossil fuels, while 3% came from alternative fuels. Nepal has remained a low consumer of petroleum, which is not produced in the country, but consumption of scarce wood for fuel is an ongoing problem. International and local organizations have promoted alternative energy such as solar panels and sustainable technology including efficient ovens.

Many regions of Nepal are still not reached by the energy grid, and chronic power shortages have led to load-shedding power outages. Hydroelectric power, supplying an estimated 73% of the country's electricity, comes from medium-scale projects, which do not entirely dam rivers, including the Kulekhani, Marsyangdi, Kali Gandaki, Khimti Khola, and Bhote Koshi. There are also many small-scale hydroelectric projects and hundreds of village micro-hydro generators. Large-scale dams have been proposed for exporting electricity to India or China, but as of late 2011, no large-scale hydroelectric projects had been approved or funded, and they remained environmentally, socially, and politically controversial. Building dams on Nepal's rivers has been considered a possible way to stop flooding in India's Ganges Basin, but a World Bank report released in August 2011 found that not to be the case.

28 INDUSTRY

Starting in the 1930s, a number of public enterprises (PEs) were established by the government with an aim of building an industrial and manufacturing base. PEs in the industrial sector included cement factories, brick factories, sugar mills, textile mills, jute products factories, tool factories, foundries, and industrial chemical and fertilizer factories. The oldest PE was the Biratnagar Jute Mills (BJM), set up in 1936. The jute industry has been in decline since 1966, as synthetics replaced the natural fiber. From 2002, BJM was operated by a private conglomerate, and the mill shut down in 2006, leaving thousands of workers unemployed. From the early 1990s, there have been planned campaigns to reform and privatize the PEs. By the beginning of the Ninth Five-Year Plan (1997–2002), 16 PEs, over half industrial, had been transferred to private owners, and four had been shut down. A list of 30 PEs, 13 in the industrial sector, were scheduled for privatization during the Ninth FYP, but, in fact, only one, the Nepal Tea Development

Corporation, was privatized. The slowdown of the reform was attributable to both the outbreak of the Maoist insurgency in 1996 and a growing resistance to the privatization program from many sides, but particularly from workers' unions who perceived jobs as threatened.

Manufacturing as a percent of total GDP rose from 4.2% in 1980 to 6.1% in 1990 to an estimated 22% in 2000. Manufacturing was hit particularly hard by the Maoist insurgency and the intensification of violence after 2001. The industrial production growth rate for 1999/2000 was 8.7%, but it had dropped to less than 1% for 2001/02 according to IMF estimates. In February 2002, the government set up a special financing facility at 3% interest to encourage commercial banks to provide concessional loans to ailing industries, particularly those in the garment and hotel industries, which through exports and tourism were major earners of foreign exchange. Nepal's garment industry was decimated by the phasing out of garment export quotas in 2005. In 2008, the industrial production growth rate was still only 1.8%, rising to 3.3% in 2010 but expected to slow to 1% in 2011, affected by power shortages and energy costs. Labor unrest and shortages of skilled workers have been chronic in the industrial sector. Transport difficulties, resource shortages, political instability, and lack of financial transparency have also negatively affected industrial development. As of 2010, according to the CIA, industry was 14.4% of GDP.

Major industries in Nepal include small-scale mills for rice, jute, sugar, and oilseed, as well as factories producing cement, clay products, and bricks. Tourism is a very important industry in Nepal, along with carpets and textiles. Cottage handicraft industries produce items such as woodcarvings, handmade paper, and jewelry for local use and for the tourist market. Heavy industry includes a steel-rolling mill, established in 1965, which uses imported materials to produce stainless steel.

29 SCIENCE AND TECHNOLOGY

The World Bank reported in 2009 that there were no patent applications in science and technology in Nepal. In 1982, the Royal Nepal Academy of Science and Technology was established at Kāthmāndu to aid in socioeconomic development. The National Council for Science and Technology formulates science and technology policy, promotes scientific and technological research, and coordinates research among ministries and Mehendra Sanskrit University. Tribhuvan University has faculties of science and technology, medicine, agriculture and animal science, engineering, and forestry.

Although a brain drain of skilled professionals and students going overseas keeps Nepal lacking in research and development personnel, many NGOs and INGOs operate programs for sustainable technology, often innovative and in remote areas. A local NGO, Rural Integrated Development Service-Nepal, operates a high altitude research station at 3,000 m (9,842 ft) above sea level for evaluation of new technology.

Medicinal plants are found in the forests and at high altitudes. In 1961, the government established a department of medicinal plants to encourage Nepal's commercially important herb exports. There are regional herbal research farms at Kāthmāndu and Nepalganj, and there is also a research laboratory for botanical drug analysis. Nepal has several notable wildlife scientists,

and Nepal's Center for Molecular Dynamics has a tiger genome project.

30 DOMESTIC TRADE

For the six and one-half years of the Maoist insurgency in Nepal, domestic trade was severely blocked in rural areas. For many Nepalese, local trade is a part-time activity, limited to products such as cigarettes, salt, kerosene, and cloth. Marketing centers are along main roads and trails and are supplemented by small local markets. Distribution channels generally move from manufacturer to distributor to retailer. Poor transport infrastructure has made extensive domestic trade impractical. However, one major impediment, the local tax on trade called octroi, was eliminated in 1997. Also, in the early 1990s, domestic airline routes were privatized, quadrupling domestic air traffic.

Kāthmāndu and other tourist areas have extensive shopping bazaars for handicrafts, including fair trade emporiums connected to development projects, bookshops, and suppliers of mountaineering gear. Kāthmāndu also has a few supermarkets and shopping malls, featuring imported goods. Most shops are open from 10 a.m. to 8 p.m. Businesses and government offices generally operate from 9 a.m. to 5 p.m. Most stores and businesses are closed on Saturdays.

31 FOREIGN TRADE

Historically, Nepal's foreign trade was limited to Tibet and India. After 1956, Nepalese trading agencies in Tibet were restricted by the Chinese authorities. In 1980, however, Nepal and China agreed to open 21 new trade routes across the Tibetan frontier. Treaty arrangements with China strictly regulate the passage of traders in either direction across the border.

Until 1989, treaty agreements between India and Nepal allowed for unrestricted commerce across 21 customs posts along the border and duty-free transit of Nepalese goods intended for third-party countries through India. In 1989, a breakdown in the treaty renewal negotiations resulted in retaliatory actions by both sides. Despite the severe shock sustained by the Nepali economy,

Principal Trading Partners – Nepal (2010)

(In millions of US dollars)

Country	Total	Exports	Imports	Balance
World	6,450.0	950.0	5,500.0	-4,550.0
India	2,466.0	420.4	2,045.6	-1,625.2
China	815.9	10.4	805.5	-795.2
Singapore	93.7	2.9	90.8	-87.9
United States	91.3	60.2	31.1	29.1
Thailand	77.2	0.3	76.9	-76.6
Sa'udi Arabia	71.3	1.0	70.3	-69.3
Germany	61.5	32.3	29.2	3.0
Bangladesh	59.2	48.4	10.8	37.6
United Arab Emirates	58.2	5.5	52.7	-47.2
Japan	56.4	8.9	47.5	-38.7

(…) data not available or not significant.

(n.s.) not specified.

SOURCE: *2011 Direction of Trade Statistics Yearbook*, New York: United Nations, 2011.

the signing of a new interim agreement (renewed every 5 years) in 1990 prevented a prolonged crisis. Under the renewal of the bilateral trade treaty with India in 1997, Nepali goods entered India essentially duty-free and quota-free. As a result, exports to India grew for four years, from 1997 to 2001, at an average rate of 42% a year. The 2002 India-Nepal Treaty of Trade continued to allow Nepal's manufactures to enter the Indian market on a non-reciprocal, preferential, or duty-free basis, with rules of origin less restrictive than the international norm. However, it placed quotas on four sensitive imports: vegetable fats, acrylic yarn, copper products, and zinc oxide, all at volumes lower than Nepali exports to India. The treaty was renewed again on 6 March 2007. Nepal also has a treaty that allows it to trade through the Indian seaport at Kolkata. Nepal signed the 2006 South Asian Free Trade Area (SAFTA) agreement, to eventually eliminate tariffs for the members, Bangladesh, Bhutan, India, Maldives, Pakistan, and Sri Lanka.

The end of the 1990s saw robust growth in Nepal's exports, which increased nearly 12% in 1997/98, nearly 18% in 1998/99 and 37.4% in 1999/2000. The export growth rate fell, however, to 4.6% in 2000/01, according to the IMF. The decline in the growth rate of Nepal's exports in the early 21st century was attributed to the intensification of the country's Maoist insurgency in 2001, removal of quotas for the garment industry, and declines in demand from Nepal's export partners in the post-9/11 atmosphere and again in the world economic crisis of 2009. According to the CIA, as of 2009, Nepal's exports totaled an estimated $849 million and imports $5.26 billion. However, the figure for exports does not include unrecorded border trade with India, including substantial gold smuggling. Major import partners in 2009 were India, 52.5% and China, 15.1%. Imported goods included petroleum, machinery, pharmaceuticals, and electrical equipment. Nepal's major export partners were India, 58.2%; the United States, 8.2%; Bangladesh, 6.3%; and Germany, 5.1%. Items exported included garments, textiles, carpets, jute, and fruit juices.

32 BALANCE OF PAYMENTS

Despite large recorded trade deficits, in the 1990s Nepal maintained a surplus in its current accounts because of surpluses in services (including tourism), official aid transfers, and increasingly large remittances from Nepalese living abroad. However, in 2001/02, Nepal began to show a negative balance of payments, due primarily to lessening foreign aid. Exports declined, and tourism was affected by political turmoil through the first decade of the 21st century.

In 2010, Nepal had a foreign trade deficit of $3.6 billion. According to the US State Department, Nepal had a balance of payments deficit in 2009/2010 of -$36 million. The current account balance as of 2010, according to the CIA, was -$449 million. External debt was $4.5 billion as of 2009, according to the CIA. Foreign aid was 4.7% of GDP in 2009 as reported by the World Bank. According to the US State department, Nepal was the recipient of foreign aid from multilateral lenders and agencies, including the UN, World Bank, IMF, and ADB, as well as countries including India, the US, UK, Japan and the EU. Foreign aid disbursement by government agencies was slow, and severe corruption at the local government level continued to impede

Balance of Payments – Nepal (2010)

(In millions of US dollars)

Current Account		**-438.0**
Balance on goods		-4,114.5
Imports	-5,016.4	
Exports	901.9	
Balance on services		-199.1
Balance on income		93.5
Current transfers		3,782.0
Capital Account		**185.5**
Financial Account		**167.5**
Direct investment abroad		...
Direct investment in Nepal		87.8
Portfolio investment assets		...
Portfolio investment liabilities		...
Financial derivatives		...
Other investment assets		-355.2
Other investment liabilities		434.8
Net Errors and Omissions		**-186.3**
Reserves and Related Items		**271.3**

(…) data not available or not significant.

SOURCE: *Balance of Payment Statistics Yearbook 2011*, Washington, DC: International Monetary Fund, 2011.

implementation of development aid projects. According to the World Bank, as of 2011, remittances accounted for 23% of GDP.

33 BANKING AND SECURITIES

Nepal Bank Limited (NBL) was the country's first commercial bank, founded in 1937, and the central bank of Nepal is the Nepal Rastra Bank (NRB), established in 1956. The state-owned Rastriya Banijya Bank (RBB), founded in 1966, is Nepal's largest commercial bank. Foreign joint-venture banks arrived in Nepal in the 1980s. The number of banking and financial institutions grew rapidly during the 1990s and 2000s. As of 2011, Nepal had over 30 commercial banks, over 75 development banks, and 18 microcredit banks. Growth and competition in the banking sector culminated in a liquidity crisis in 2009/2010 and 2010/2011, as loans outweighed deposits, and real estate loans went unpaid. Corruption, inefficiency and lack of transparency continued to characterize the banking sector, and, in October 2011, the chairman of Nepal Share Market and Finance Bank was arrested on charges of embezzling $34 million.

The CIA reported that, in 2010, currency and demand deposits—an aggregate commonly known as M1—were equal to $2.844 billion. In that same year, M2—an aggregate equal to M1 plus savings deposits, small-time deposits, and money market mutual funds—was $10.34 billion. As of 2010, the discount rate, the interest rate at which the central bank lends to financial institutions in the short term, was 6.5%.

Nepal's currency has been pegged only to the Indian rupee since 1997. Banks and private businesses are licensed to exchange foreign currency, and unofficial "black market" exchange of foreign currency is also common. Credit cards are rarely used in Nepal, except in tourism-related businesses; ATM machines are available in Kāthmāndu and some larger towns.

The Security Exchange Center (SEC), set up in 1981, was converted into the Nepal Stock Exchange (NEPSE) in 1984. As of late

2011, there were 204 companies listed and 14 licensed securities businesses.

³⁴INSURANCE

As of 2005, Nepal had 21 insurance companies, of which 14 were private, 6 were foreign or joint-venture, and 1 was government owned. Nepal Insurance Company, the country's first insurer, was founded in 1947. The first private insurance company, National Life and General Insurance Company, started in 1987. In 1992, the Insurance Act established the National Insurance Board as an oversight agency. Insurance coverage has remained rare in Nepal as of 2011. Insurance for motor vehicles was not mandatory. In 2007, foreign employment insurance for workers going overseas was made mandatory by Nepal's government, and nine companies were offering the policies, at fixed rates, as of October 2011.

³⁵PUBLIC FINANCE

Most deficits on capital account have been financed by foreign grants, while domestic revenues have been sufficient to cover expenditures. The Maoist insurgency until 2006 had severe impacts on Nepal's public finances, interfering with tax collections and disrupting production while at the same time requiring increased public spending on security and to repair damaged infrastructure. Following the peace agreement, public finances were affected by inefficiency, as the government lagged in producing budgets and disbursing aid and was plagued by pervasive corruption.

In 2010, according to the CIA, the budget of Nepal included $3 billion in public revenue and $4.6 billion in public expenditures. Taxes and other revenues amounted to 18.9% for 2009/2010, and the budget deficit amounted to 10.1% of GDP. Nepal's fiscal year ends on July 15. In the budget for 2010/2011, government workers' salaries were raised, while poverty reduction programs and improvement of roads and other infrastructure were emphasized.

Public Finance – Nepal (2010)

(In millions of rupees, central government figures)

Revenue and Grants	**214,717**	**100.0%**
Tax revenue	156,291	72.8%
Social contributions	...	...
Grants	37,117	17.3%
Other revenue	21,309	9.9%
Expenditures	**237,266**	**100.0%**
General public services	39,145	16.5%
Defense	17,522	7.4%
Public order and safety	19,472	8.2%
Economic affairs	60,118	25.3%
Environmental protection	...	...
Housing and community amenities	20,612	8.7%
Health	16,657	7.0%
Recreational, culture, and religion	...	...
Education	46,295	19.5%
Social protection	17,446	7.4%

(...) data not available or not significant.

SOURCE: *Government Finance Statistics Yearbook 2010*, Washington, DC: International Monetary Fund, 2010.

³⁶TAXATION

In 2002, the government put into effect a new Income Tax Act, which replaced the previous act of 1958 and was developed in close cooperation with the IMF. The principle sources of domestic revenue are customs tariffs, value-added taxes (VAT), excise duties, and income taxes on personal and corporate incomes. There are also local development taxes, as well as license and registration fees for houses, land, and vehicles.

As of 2010, the standard corporate income tax rate was 20–30%. Special reduced rates were available for technology and electricity firms and for companies operating in remote and undeveloped regions. In the fiscal year 2011/2012 budget, the government announced tax breaks for technology companies, jute companies, and hydropower projects; excise taxes were raised on alcohol and tobacco. Excise taxes are applied mainly to goods deemed hazardous to health, such as alcoholic beverages, cigarettes, and soft drinks. Capital gains were taxed at a 20% rate, as of 2010, according to the World Bank. Nepal's income taxes are progressive in a range from 1% to 25%.

The VAT was introduced in November 1997 as a reform designed to replace sales taxes and most excises. The "octori," a traditional local tax on trade, was also eliminated at this time. As of 2010, the VAT rate was 13%, collected at every stage of selling goods and services. Goods exempted for the VAT included primary foodstuffs, agricultural products, and industrial machinery. There was no VAT on goods for export, on raw materials imported by an export promotion industry, or the products of such an industry.

³⁷CUSTOMS AND DUTIES

Customs and duties are a principle source of domestic revenue. Import tariffs are generally assessed on an ad valorem basis, with duties ranging from 0–140%. Most primary products, including live animals and fish, enter duty-free, as do educational materials. Machinery and goods related to basic needs are charged 5%. Duties on food imports were fixed at 10%. Cigarettes and automobiles are charged at 130%. Preferential rates apply to India and other SAARC/SAFTA nations, as well as to China. There are restrictions on export of antiquities (objects over 100 years old.)

An unchecked smuggling trade in both directions between India and Nepal has continued, with commodities including gold, timber, medicinal herbs, wildlife, construction equipment, tobacco, sugar, currency, weapons, and fertilizer. Wildlife products and rare wood species have been smuggled from India to China by going through Nepal.

³⁸FOREIGN INVESTMENT

In 1991, Nepal undertook economic reforms that were aimed at making Nepal attractive to foreign investors, beginning with the Foreign Investment and One Window Policy Act of 1992 and the establishment of an Investment Promotion Board. Steps were taken to privatize some government-owned public enterprises (PEs) and to open up for private investment previous government monopolies in telecommunications, hydroelectric power, and air transportation. Licensing requirements were streamlined, and 100% foreign ownership was permitted. In 1999, minimum investment requirements were also lifted. But foreign direct investment in Nepal, always low, saw annual decreases across the five years of the Ninth economic plan (1997 to 2002) and did not recover from 2002 to 2011, as garment manufacturing was sidelined by the end of quotas in 2005.

Foreign direct investment (FDI) has been discouraged by bureaucratic delays, inefficiency, and inconsistent or contradictory policies, as well as political instability, labor unrest and violence. Problems doing business in Nepal have included lack of direct access to airports, poor land transportation, lack of skilled labor and technological expertise, unclear rules on labor relations, inadequate electrical power, inadequate water supply, few local raw materials, nontransparent tax administration, and inadequate and obscure commercial legislation. FDI in Nepal was a net inflow of $38.2 million according to World Bank figures published in 2009. FDI represented just 0.3% of GDP, one of the lowest rates in the world.

In Nepal, most FDI has been in light manufacturing and the tourism industry. Investors in Nepal have included India, the United States, China, the British Virgin Islands, Norway, Japan, and South Korea. India has dominated in FDI in Nepal, not only because of its proximity, but also due to incentives for Indian investors to take advantage of the preferential trade regime, which India extends to Nepal's manufactures through their bi-lateral trade agreements. Some political parties are wary of India's economic power and seek increased investment from China. Large projects proposed by both neighbors have been cancelled by Nepal due to concerns about environmental and social effects.

39 ECONOMIC DEVELOPMENT

Planned economic development in Nepal began in 1953 with construction of roads and airfields and irrigation projects to bring more acreage under cultivation. In 1956, these projects were integrated into the first five-year plan (1956–61) to assist existing industries, revive and expand cottage industries, encourage private investment, and foster technological training. With the second plan (1962–65), the government introduced land reform with programs to set ceilings on land holdings and to redistribute land to the landless. However, large landholders were able parcel out land to relatives, and the poor were often forced to sell their redistributed land to pay debts. The third economic plan (1965–70), was the first to be administered under the panchayat system, the system overthrown in the economic reforms of the early 1990s. The fourth (1970–75) and fifth (1975–80) five-year plans emphasized infrastructure development. The sixth development plan (1980–85) allocated nearly one-third of its total expenditure to agriculture and irrigation. However, money targeted for development projects was used for other purposes. The objectives of the seventh plan (1986–90) were to increase production, create opportunities for employment, and fulfill basic needs; it was heavily dependent on foreign aid.

With the establishment of multiparty government in 1991, a comprehensive set of reforms affecting all sectors of the economy was initiated under the eighth five-year plan (1992–97). Nepal's public enterprises were slated for privatization; government monopolies in hydroelectric power, telecommunications, and transportation were opened to private investment; and the country was declared open to foreign investment. The ninth plan (1997–2002) emphasized investments in agriculture and hydroelectric power;

liberalization and privatization of the economy; and reform of the tax system and banking practices. Under the tenth plan (2002–2008), priorities shifted to security and poverty reduction, as the Maoist insurgency took hold in regions across Nepal. The percentage of the population below the poverty line had decreased significantly, from 42% of the population in 1997, to 38% in 2003, to 25% in 2008. The economy from 2008 through 2011 depended heavily on remittances from Nepal's workers overseas, as well as on infusions of foreign aid.

Nepal has development potential in hydroelectric power resources, which are estimated at 83,000 MW, of which less that 1% has been brought on line. However, environmental, social, and political concerns have put off large-scale hydroelectric power development, particularly for export. Shortages of electrify within Nepal have been a major deterrent to foreign investors and the manufacturing sector. As of 2011, other promising growth sectors included air transportation and telecommunications, both open to private investment, and tourism. Diversified agriculture, with exports of fruit products, also had potential if transportation could be improved. With two three-year interim economic plans (2007–2010) and (2010–2013), the communist-led government emphasized poverty reduction and infrastructure improvement. The communist-led government sought to strengthen ties with China as a balance to India's economic dominance. Challenges to Nepal's economic development have remained formidable. These include limited natural resources, difficult topography, landlocked location, poor infrastructure, outflow of skilled labor, high inflation, pervasive corruption, and political instability.

40 SOCIAL DEVELOPMENT

Rural poverty, economic inequality, and gender discrimination were causes of widespread support for the Maoist insurgency. Poverty reduction with support for labor rights has been a major goal of the government led by the CPN/M and the CPN/UML after 2006. The government maintains a countrywide network of Village Development Committees for food, clothing, shelter, health services, and education. The Employee Provident Fund administers a program of old age, disability, and death benefits for government, military, and corporate employees. Retirement is at age 55 but in some cases can be deferred to 60. There is a social assistance program that provides benefits to Nepalese citizens aged 70 or older, and citizens over 75 receive free treatment in government hospitals. Employees of establishments with 10 or more workers are covered by work injury insurance, which is funded by the employer through a private carrier. Severance pay is also mandated in some circumstances. Paid maternity benefits and sick leave were mandated by the Labor Act of 1992.

Freedom of expression and assembly were strongly respected in Nepal as of 2011. Security forces continued to use excessive force against some protestors and against suspects in custody, however. The right to a fair trial was compromised by pervasive corruption in the legal system. Tibetan refugees in Nepal were harassed and restricted in their political activities in 2010–2011.

Women were 33% of the Constituent Assembly, the Vice Chairman was a woman, and there was a Women's Caucus as of 2011. However, there were only 5 female ministers in the 43-member cabinet, and women were under-represented in leadership of the main political parties. Although women were legally entitled to equal pay for equal work, they continued to be subject to gender discrimination, especially in culturally traditional rural areas. Women's inheritance and marriage rights were strengthened in the Gender Equality Act of 2006, but women still suffered discrimination in both areas. Women's land ownership was encouraged by a 2008 tax exemption. Domestic abuse, rape, and other violence against women continued to be serious societal problems in Nepal. Early marriage and the tradition of dowry remained strong, and the killing of brides for default has continued. Trafficking of women and girls to India to work as prostitutes remained a serious problem. Increasing numbers of women from Nepal were working overseas, often as domestic servants, and they were often vulnerable to abuse by agencies and employers. As of 2011, the government had shown commitment to legal reforms in favor of equality for Lesbian, Gay, Bisexual and Transgender (LGBT) people, and Nepal was being promoted as a LGBT tourism destination. Caste discrimination has persisted against the Dalit group; the government has special programs for their economic benefit.

41 HEALTH

According to the CIA, life expectancy in Nepal was 67 years in 2011. Total healthcare expenditure was 6.0% of GDP, amounting to $25 per person. There were 2 physicians, 5 nurses and midwives, and 50 hospital beds per 10,000 inhabitants. As of 2011, the fertility rate was 2.4, while the infant mortality rate was 44 per 1,000 live births. In 2008, the maternal mortality rate, according to the World Bank, was 380 per 100,000 births. Increased health care access had substantially improved the maternal and infant survival rates since 2001. The CIA calculated HIV/AIDS prevalence in Nepal to be about 0.4% in 2009. Other infectious diseases included diarrhea, hepatitis A, typhoid fever, malaria, dengue fever, and Japanese encephalitis.

42 HOUSING

Most of the population lived in rural villages where houses were made of stone or mud bricks, with thatched roofs. Bamboo and reed dwellings were built in some rural areas, while wood, straw, cardboard, and plastic sheeting were used for improvised urban shelters. Most houses had two stories, but some contained only two rooms, a sleeping room and a room for cooking. In the Kāthmāndu Valley, residential buildings included shop-houses, apartments, and single-family homes; they were constructed of concrete or brick, traditionally with carved wooden trim.

According to the government's Nepal Living Standard Survey, as of 2010, about 90% of households were owned by the residents, and about 70% had access to electrical power. About 18% of households used liquefied petroleum gas (LPG) for cooking. Wood remained the most commonly used fuel for cooking. According to the CIA, as of 2008, a total of 31% of the population had access to improved sanitation (27% rural, 51% urban.) 88% of the population had improved drinking water sources (87% rural, 93% urban.)

43 EDUCATION

Nepal's adult literacy rate was a low 56% as of 2011, according to the government's Nepal Living Standards Survey, with a gender gap of 71% literacy for men and 44% for women. In 2009, the World Bank estimated that 71% of age-eligible children in Nepal were enrolled in primary school. Public expenditure on education represented 4.6% of GDP as of 2009, according to the CIA. In the fiscal year 2011/2012 government budget, Dalit caste students and all female students were to be eligible for free education in community schools through secondary school.

Traditional schools (pathshalas) in Nepal provided a classical education emphasizing languages. Gompas along the Tibetan border trained boys and men to become Buddhist religious leaders. The children of Nepal's elite were educated at prestigious private schools in India. English-medium schools in Nepal were modeled after those in India. Under a 1954 plan, a national school system with a single curriculum replaced the traditional schools. Free primary education was introduced in 1975. Schooling is compulsory for five years, which is the duration of primary school studies. Students then move on to either technical school (8 to 10 years) or general secondary school (about 7 years). Primary school enrollment in 2008 was estimated at about 91% of age-eligible students, with equal numbers of boys and girls, according to Nepal's Ministry of Education. Secondary school enrollment in 2011 was about 43% of eligible students, 46% for boys and 41% for girls, according to UNICEF, and it was estimated that about 75% of students completed their primary education.

Tribhuvan University, founded in 1959, includes 5 institutes (medicine, engineering, science and technology, agriculture and animal science, and forestry), 4 research centers, and 4 faculties (humanities and social science, management, law, and education) at 61 constituent and over 200 affiliated campuses, with 389,460 students enrolled in the system as of academic year 2011–2012. Other institutions of higher learning, all public, include the Mahendra Sanskrit University, Kāthmāndu University, Purbanchal University, Pokhara University, Siddhartha University, and B. P. Koirala Institute of Health Science. There are also hundreds of private colleges, some specializing in business or medical training. Tri-Chandra College was Nepal's first institute of higher learning, founded in 1916; it later became part of Tribhuvan University. Students from Nepal often look to India or other countries for undergraduate and graduate studies.

44 LIBRARIES AND MUSEUMS

The National Library in Kāthmāndu, founded in 1957, has about 86,000 volumes in Nepali, English, Sanskrit, Hindi, and other Indian languages. The Bir Library collection, originating in the 19th century, became the National Archives, containing over 35,000 manuscripts. Other important collections are maintained by the library of Tribhuvan University (over 300,000 volumes) and the Nepal-Bharat (62,000) in Kāthmāndu. The Kaiser Library, also in Kāthmāndu, contains the private collection of Kaiser Shumsher Jung Bahadur Rana; with about 50,000 volumes, it also serves as a reference library open for public use. The Asha Archives contains Nepalese manuscripts. The Kāthmāndu Valley Public Library was founded in 2003, with over 45,000 volumes. There are about 600 public libraries within the country, most of which have small collections and are severely underfunded. International voluntary organizations have sponsored hundreds of new community and school libraries.

The National Museum (founded 1928), with archeological and historical collections, and the Natural History Museum (1975) are both in the Kāthmāndu Valley. The former Narayanhity Royal Palace, where much of the royal family was massacred in 2001, was turned into a museum after the monarchy was abolished in 2008. The National Art Gallery is housed in an old palace in Bhaktapur. The Patan Museum, on the town's historic square, contains valuable works in stone, wood and metal. There is an Ethnographic Museum, and there are also regional museums at Lumbini, Pokhara, and Chitwan.

45 MEDIA

As of 2011, freedom of the press was respected by Nepal's government, and media outlets were not restricted in their news coverage or expression of opinions. However, journalists were at risk, as they were often threatened or assaulted while investigating corruption or other criminal activity, and, in some cases, political groups used intimidation against members of the press. Prominent newspapers in 2010, with circulation numbers listed parenthetically, included the government-owned *Gorkhapatra* (75,000, also published as the English-language *Rising Nepal*); the *Kāthmāndu Post* (40,000); and the *Nepali Hindi Daily* (40,000). Hundreds of other newspapers and magazines were published daily or weekly.

According to the government's Ministry of Information, 319 radio stations were operating as of 2011. Radio Nepal, a state-owned network, broadcasted in Nepali, English and other languages, on both short and medium wavelengths. In 1997, Radio Sagarmatha was established as Nepal's first independent community radio station; over 180 independent nonprofit community radio stations have been licensed since then. Radio is particularly popular in rural areas and can be listened to on mobile telephones.

Television was introduced into the Kāthmāndu Valley in 1984. Nepal Television, operated by the government, was the only television channel from 1984 to 2002, when private channels were allowed. According to the government's Telecommunications Authority, as of mid-2011, Nepal had 15 television stations, most of which were privately owned. Kantipur TV had the most market share, followed by Nepal Television and Avenues Television. Cable television is available in urban areas, and the use of satellite dishes is popular throughout the country.

In 2009 the CIA reported that there were 820,500 telephone landlines in Nepal. According to Nepal's Telecommunications Authority, as of mid-2011, 10 million mobile telephone lines were in use, with 1 for every 3 people. Text messaging on mobile telephones was used for political organizing and social causes.

In 2010, the country had 43,928 Internet hosts, according to the CIA. In 2011 there were 3.1 million Internet users in Nepal, penetration of nearly 11%, according to the Nepal Telecommunications Authority. Internet use was largely in urban areas as of 2011, but development organizations were starting to bring wireless access to some very remote regions of Nepal. Social media such as Facebook, with one million users, was becoming popular, and Nepal had thousands of bloggers. The government requested that Internet Service Providers (ISPs) block some websites and blogs in 2010; the ISPs refused to comply and protested with a temporary shutdown of service.

46 ORGANIZATIONS

The leading commercial organization is the Federation of Nepalese Chambers of Commerce and Industry. Professional organizations include the Nepal Medical Association, The Garment Association of Nepal, and the Nepal Journalists Association. Organizations involved in educational pursuits include the Environment, Culture, Agriculture, and Research Development Society in Nepal and the Nepal Academy of Science and Technology. Student groups are often affiliated with political parties and include the All Nepal National Free Students Union and Democratic National Youth Federation. Youth groups include the Nepal Scouts, YMCA/YWCA, and Youth for Human Rights Nepal. Women's organizations include the Nepal Association of University Women, Rural Women's Network Nepal, and All-Nepal Women's Association (Revolutionary). Maiti Nepal works to stop human trafficking, and Pourakhi assists workers exploited and abused in overseas employment. The Blue Diamond Society promotes equal rights for Lesbian, Gay, Bisexual and Transgender people.

International Organizations with national chapters include Amnesty International, CARE, Habitat for Humanity, and the Red Cross. Many international non-governmental organizations (INGOs) have social, environmental and development projects in Nepal. Local non-governmental organizations (NGOs) in those fields include Rural Integrated Development Service-Nepal, Informal Sector Service Center, Nepal Social Educational Environmental Development Services, Pro Public, and Eco Himal.

47 TOURISM, TRAVEL, AND RECREATION

In 1951, the government of Nepal reversed its longstanding policy and began to encourage visitors; before then, mountaineering expeditions had been permitted into the country only under severe official scrutiny and regulations. Since then, Nepal's tourism has continued to grow, from the days of the "hippie trail" in the 1960s and 70s to a time of organized adventure travel. Foreign travelers continued to arrive even during the Maoist insurgency, although parts of the country were officially off-limits. Tourism supports cottage industries, with handicrafts emporiums, and encourages cultural exchange and volunteer programs.

Accommodations from budget guesthouses to luxury hotels are available. For mountain trekkers, travel agencies in Kāthmāndu provide transportation, guides, and porters. There are charges for trekking permits. Villages along popular trekking routes offer teahouses, restaurants, and accommodation. Whitewater rafting and kayaking trips on Nepal's rivers are also popular, along with viewing of tigers and other wildlife in the Terai. Even remote frontier areas such as Mustang have been opened to foreign tourism. Expeditions to climb Everest and other Himalayan peaks are a steady source of revenue in fees, and employment for local guides, porters and outfitters. A number of Sherpa men and women, known for their guiding skills, have themselves become prominent mountaineers, setting high-altitude climbing records.

Nepal has two cultural UNESCO World Heritage Sites: the Kāthmāndu Valley with its distinctive town squares and carving-decorated architecture, and Lumbini, the Buddha's birthplace. There are also two natural UNESCO World Heritage Sites: Chitwan National Park, in the Terai, known for tigers and rhinoceros; and Sagarmatha National Park in the high Himalayas. The newest national park is Banke, established in May 2010 in midwestern Nepal. Many visitors from India and other South Asian countries are attracted by spiritual pilgrimage sites. Nepal also has several gambling casinos.

The *Tourism Factbook*, published by the UN World Tourism Organization, reported 510,000 incoming tourists to Nepal in 2009, who spent a total of $397 million in 2010. This was expected to increase substantially, with a goal of one million arrivals, during 2011, which was declared "Nepal Tourism Year" to promote the destination. Of the incoming tourists in 2010, there were 151,000 from South Asia, 144,000 from Europe, and 135,000 from East Asia and the Pacific. There were 28,485 hotel beds available in Nepal. The estimated daily cost to visit Kāthmāndu, the capital, was $213. The cost of visiting other cities averaged $102. A visa is required to enter Nepal, except for citizens of India. Visitors from most countries may obtain a tourist visa on arrival at specified ports of entry.

48 FAMOUS PERSONS

Buddhism, one of the world's great religions, is based on the teachings of Siddhartha Gautama, who became known as the Buddha ("Enlightened One"). He was born (traditionally about 624 BC but according to most modern scholars about 563 BC) in Lumbini, in the Terai, and died at Kushinagara (traditionally about 544 BC but according to the modern view about 483 BC). Amar Singh Thapa, Nepalese military leader of the 19th century and rival of Gen. David Ochterlony in the war between British India and Nepal, is a national hero. The two best-known Rana prime ministers were Jung Bahadur Rana (1817–77) and Chandra Shamsher Jang Rana (1863–1929). The most highly regarded writers are Bhanubhakta, a great poet of the 19th century, and the dramatist Bala Krishna Sama (Shamsher, 1902–81).

Mahendra Bir Bikram-Shah (1920–72), the king who introduced the partyless political system based on the Nepalese tradition of the village panchayat (council), was succeeded on the throne by his son, Birendra Bir Bikram Shah Dev (1945–2001), who democratized the panchayat system. Gyanendra Bir Bikram Shah Dev (b. 1947) ascended to the throne in 2001 and was deposed in 2008. Well-known political leaders include the brothers Matrika Prasad Koirala (1912–1997), head of the Nepali Congress Party and the first post-Rana prime minister of Nepal and Bisweswar Prasad Koirala (1915–82), head of the Nepali Congress Party and the first elected prime minister of Nepal. Chhabi Lal Dahal, known as "Prachanda" (b. 1954) was the leader of the Maoist insurgency and served as prime minister in 2008–2009.

World renown was gained for Nepal by Sherpa porter and mountaineer Tenzing Norgay (1914–86), who, with Edmund Hillary, a New Zealander, ascended to the summit of Mt. Everest in 1953. Dipprasad Pun (b. 1980), a Gurkha soldier, was award the British Conspicuous Gallantry Cross in 2011, for heroism in Afghanistan. Charimaya Tamang (b. 1980) and Anuradha Koirala (b. 1949) have won international awards for their efforts against human trafficking. Jhamak Ghimire (b. 1980) is a prominent poet who has also written about overcoming being born with cerebral palsy. Sunil Babu Pant (b. 1972) is a gay rights activist who was elected to the Constituent Assembly. Prabal Gurung (b. 1974) is a well-known fashion designer based in New York.

49 DEPENDENCIES

Nepal has no territories or colonies.

50 BIBLIOGRAPHY

Financial Accountability in Nepal: A Country Assessment. Washington, DC.: World Bank, 2003.

Hutt, Michael, ed. *Himalayan People's War: Nepal's Maoist Rebellion.* Bloomington: Indiana University Press, 2004.

Kincaid, Jamaica. *Among Flowers: A Walk in the Himalaya.* Washington, DC.: National Geographic, 2005.

Lawoti, Mahendra. *Towards a Democratic Nepal: Inclusive Political Institutions for a Multicultural Society.* Thousand Oaks, CA: Sage Publications, 2005.

Nepal Investment and Business Guide: Strategic and Practical Information. Washington, DC: International Business Publications USA, 2012.

Shrestha, Nanda R. *Nepal and Bangladesh: A Global Studies Handbook.* Santa Barbara, CA: ABC-CLIO, 2002.

Shrestha, Nanda R. and Keshav Bhattarai. *Historical Dictionary of Nepal.* Lanham, Md.: Scarecrow, 2003.

Whelpton, John. *A History of Nepal.* New York: Cambridge University Press, 2005.

NEW ZEALAND

CAPITAL: Wellington

FLAG: The flag has two main features: the red, white, and blue Union Jack (the national flag of the United Kingdom) in the upper left quarter and the four-star Southern Cross constellation in the right half. On the blue state flag the stars are red outlined in white. On the red national flag, used by individuals or commercial institutions at sea, the stars are white.

ANTHEM: *God Defend New Zealand.*

MONETARY UNIT: The New Zealand dollar (NZD) is a paper currency of 100 cents; it replaced the New Zealand pound on 10 July 1967. There are coins of 5, 10, 20, and 50 cents and 1 and 2 dollars, and notes of 5, 10, 20, 50, and 100 dollars. NZD1 = US$0.819 (or US$1 = NZD1.22) as of 2012.

WEIGHTS AND MEASURES: Metric weights and measures are used.

HOLIDAYS: New Year's Day, 1 January; Waitangi Day, 6 February; Anzac Day, 25 April; Queen's Birthday, 1st Monday in June; Labor Day, 4th Monday in October; Christmas Day, 25 December; Boxing Day, 26 December. Movable holidays are Good Friday and Easter Monday. Each province has a holiday on its own anniversary day.

TIME: 12 midnight = noon GMT.

¹LOCATION, SIZE, AND EXTENT

Situated in the southwest Pacific Ocean, New Zealand proper, with a total area of 267,710 sq km (103,363 sq mi), consists of the North Island, covering 114,669 sq km (44,274 sq mi) including small islands nearby; the South Island, 149,883 sq km (57,870 sq mi); Stewart Island, 1,746 sq km (674 sq mi); and various minor, outlying islands. Comparatively, the area occupied by New Zealand is about the size of the state of Colorado. The Chatham Islands, lying 850 km (528 mi) e of Lyttelton, on South Island, have a land area of 963 sq km (372 sq mi). Other outlying islands have a combined area of 778 sq km (300 sq mi). New Zealand extends 1,600 km (994 mi) nne–ssw and 450 km (280 mi) ese–wnw. It has a total coastline of 15,134 km (9,404 mi).

New Zealand's capital city, Wellington, is located on the southern tip of North Island.

²TOPOGRAPHY

Less than one-fourth of the land surface of New Zealand lies below the 200-m (656-ft) contour. The mountain ranges in the North Island do not exceed 1,800 m (6,000 ft) in height, with the exception of the volcanic peaks of Egmont, or Taranaki (2,518 m/8,261 ft), Ruapehu (2,797 m/9,176 ft), Ngauruhoe (2,290 m/7,513 ft), and Tongariro (1,968 m/6,457 ft), the last three of which are still active. This volcanic system gives rise to many hot springs and geysers.

The South Island is significantly more mountainous than the North Island, but is without recent volcanic activity. The Southern Alps, running almost the entire length of the South Island from north to south, contain 19 peaks of 3,000 m (9,800 ft) or above,

of which the highest is Mt. Cook or Aoraki, 3,764 m (12,349 ft). There are also several glaciers in the Southern Alps, the largest being the Tasman Glacier, 29 km (18 mi) long and 1 km (0.6 mi) wide. The rivers are mostly swift-flowing and shallow, few of them navigable. There are many lakes, those in the South Island being particularly noted for their magnificent mountain scenery.

Seismic activity in New Zealand results in thousands of earthquakes each year. Though most of them are too small to be felt, with a magnitude of 5.0 or lower on the Richter scale, periodically earthquakes of higher magnitudes strike. On 4 May 2003, a 6.7 magnitude earthquake occurred at the Kermadec Islands; the same year, a 7.2 magnitude quake occurred at South Island on 21 August, causing structural damage but no reported injuries. A 7.1 magnitude earthquake occurred on 22 November 2004 with a center off the coast of South Island. In 2007, two quakes measuring 6.7 and 6.8 caused US$1.5 million and US$30 million in residential damages respectively. In September 2010 a 7.1 magnitude quake struck Darfield, but resulted in no deaths. The following year, in February 2011, Christchurch was devastated by a 6.2 quake resulting in more than 180 dead and more than 100,000 buildings damaged or destroyed. Most of the damage in the Christchurch event was the result of liquidification, in which soil is shaken to the point that it acts like a liquid, undermining buildings and other structures.

Studies have revealed that New Zealand is a prime location for "slow-slip" earthquakes. Slow-slip earthquakes take place over months, instead of seconds, but can cause underground movement on the same scale as medium and large earthquakes. Over time, these movements may have triggered major earthquakes in the country. Additional studies are being made to determine whether slow-slip earthquakes, in fact, release pent-up energy and lessen seismic activity.

³CLIMATE

New Zealand has a temperate, moist ocean climate without marked seasonal variations in temperature or rainfall. The prevailing winds are westerly, with a concentration of strong winds in the Cook Strait area. The generally mountainous nature of the country, however, causes considerable variation in rainfall (e.g. between the eastern and western sides of the Southern Alps), and, by preventing stratification of air into layers of different density, results in an absence of extensive cloud sheets and a consequent high percentage of sunshine. Mean annual temperatures at sea level range from about 15°c (59°f) in the northern part of the North Island to 12°c (54°f) in the southern part of the South Island. Mean annual rainfall ranges from around 30 cm (12 in) near Dunedin to more than 800 cm (315 in) in the Southern Alps.

⁴FLORA AND FAUNA

Like other regions separated from the rest of the world for a long period, New Zealand has developed a distinct flora, including some of the world's oldest plant forms. The World Resources Institute estimates that there are a total of 2,382 plant species in New Zealand. Although roughly 80% of the native flora is unique, the flowering plants, conifers, ferns, and other species that constitute much of the land vegetation show affinities with plants of the Malayan region, supporting the theory of an ancient land bridge between the two regions. More than 250 species are common to both Australia and New Zealand.

The Antarctic element, comprising more than 70 species related to forms in the flora of South America and the Southern Ocean islands, is of great interest to botanists. The kauri pine, now found only in parts of the North Island, for more than a century has been world famous for its timber. The rimu and the totara are also timber trees. Other handsome trees include the evergreen pohutukawa and the rata, both of which bear red flowers, while the kowhai bears yellow flowers. Harakeke (or New Zealand flax) is actually a type of lily; it was formerly of great importance in the Maori economy.

Undergrowth in the damp forests consists largely of ferns, of which there are 145 species; they clothe most of the tree trunks and branches, and tree ferns form part of the foliage. Tussock grass occurs on all mountains above the scrub line and over large areas in the South Island.

Apart from seals and two species of bats, none of New Zealand's 73 mammal species are indigenous. Some of the land mammals introduced to New Zealand, such as the rabbit, the deer, the pig (now wild), and the Australian possum, have become pests. Sea mammals include whales and dolphins.

There is a great diversity among New Zealand's 351 species of birds, which include both breeding and migratory species. Among the most interesting birds is the kiwi, a flightless bird that is New Zealand's national symbol and the only known bird with nostrils at the tip of the bill instead of at the base. Other characteristic birds are the kea, a mountain parrot, and the tui, a beautiful songbird. All but one of the genera of penguins is represented in New Zealand.

Several species of birds, the most famous being the bar-tailed godwit, migrate from breeding grounds in the Arctic Circle to spend spring and summer in New Zealand. In 2007, a tagged godwit's migration was recorded by Massey University scientists, who reported that the godwit flew 10,200 km (6,340 miles) from New Zealand to Yalu Jiang in China before continuing to fly an additional 5,000 km (3,000 miles) to the godwit breeding grounds in Alaska. In September, the bird's tag recorded a journey of 11,500 km (7,150 miles), when her return flight from Alaska to New Zealand was accomplished in just eight days.

There are many flightless insects, 54 reptile species, 6 amphibian species, and a diversity of small life forms. In all cases of species numeration within this section, the calculation reflects the total number of distinct species residing in the country, not the number of endemic species.

⁵ENVIRONMENT

Because of its relatively small population, New Zealand's natural resources have so far suffered less from the pressures of development than have those of many other industrialized nations. Air pollution from cars and other vehicles is an environmental concern in New Zealand. The use of fossil fuels contributes to the problem. New Zealand's concern about the effects of air pollution on the atmosphere is, in part, due to the fact that the nation is among the world leaders in incidence of skin cancer. In 1996, New Zealand produced 29.7 million metric tons of carbon dioxide emissions from industrial sources. In 2000, the total of carbon dioxide emissions within the country was at 32.1 million metric tons; by 2008, according to UN reports, it had increased to 32.635 million metric tons.

Water pollution is a problem due to industrial pollutants and sewage. Water resources total 397 cu km (95.25 cu mi) while water usage is 2.11 cu km (0.506 cu mi) per year. Domestic water usage accounts for 48% of total usage, industrial for 10%, and agricultural for 42%. Per capita water usage totals 524 cu m (18,505 cu ft) per year.

Another environmental issue in New Zealand is the development of its resources—forests, gas and coal fields, farmlands—which in the past has come at serious cost to natural beauty and ecological balance. Two thirds of the nation's forests have been eliminated. The Ministry for the Environment (established in 1986) is the government's principal advisory agency on environmental sustainability. The Department of Conservation is charged with conservation of both natural and historic areas. The World Resource Institute reported that New Zealand had designated 6.47 million hectares (15.99 million acres) of land for protection as of 2006.

In September 2010, a 7.1 earthquake rocked the city of Christchurch, followed by more than 80 aftershocks over the next few days, with at least one measuring a magnitude of 5.1. Nearly 100,000 of the city's 160,000 homes were damaged by the quakes, with many of them considered to be beyond repair. A number of historic buildings were also destroyed or severely damaged. An initial estimate of the cost to repair the visible damage was placed at US$1.4 billion. In February 2011, another 6.3 earthquake hit Christchurch, killing 181 people. The earthquake proved to be New Zealand's deadliest natural disaster in 80 years.

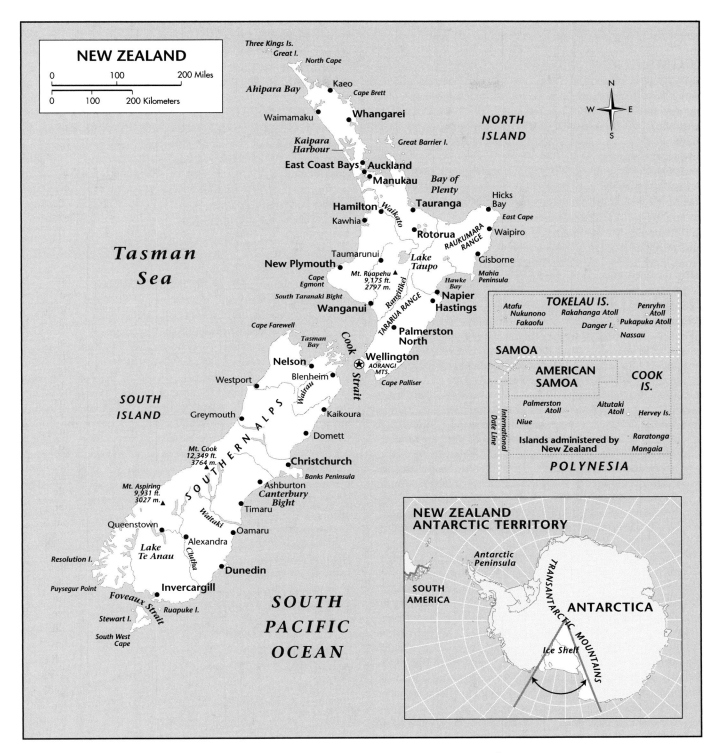

LOCATION: 33° to 53°S; 162°E to 173°W. TERRITORIAL SEA LIMIT: 12 miles.

There are two natural UNESCO World Heritage Sites in the country and six Ramsar wetland sites. According to a 2011 report issued by the International Union for Conservation of Nature and Natural Resources (IUCN), threatened species included 9 mammals, 70 birds, 13 reptiles, 4 amphibians, 23 fish, 5 mollusks, 10 other invertebrates, and 21 plants. Endangered animal species in New Zealand include the takahe, two species of petrel (black and New Zealand Cook's), the black stilt, orange-fronted parakeet, kakapo, and Codfish Island fernbird. Extinct are the bush wren, laughing owl, Delcourt's sticky-toed gecko, South Island kokako, New Zealand quail, and New Zealand grayling. Endangered species on the Chatham Islands were the Chatham Island petrel, magenta petrel, Chatham Island oystercatcher, New Zealand plover, Chatham Island pigeon, Forbes's parakeet, and Chatham Island black robin. The Chatham Island swan and Chatham Island rail are extinct.

6 POPULATION

The US Central Intelligence Agency (CIA) estimated the population of New Zealand in 2011 to be approximately 4,290,347, placing it at number 126 in population among the 196 nations of the world. In 2011, approximately 13.3% of the population was over 65 years of age, with another 20.4% under 15 years of age. The median age in New Zealand was 37 years. There were 0.99 males for every female in the country. The population's annual rate of change was 0.882%. The projected population for the year 2025 was 5,000,000. Population density in New Zealand was calculated at 16 people per sq km (41 people per sq mi).

The UN estimated that 86% of the population lived in urban areas, and that urban populations had an annual rate of change of 0.9%. The largest urban areas, along with their respective populations, included Auckland, 1.36 million; and Wellington, 391,000.

7 MIGRATION

Estimates of New Zealand's net migration rate, carried out by the CIA in 2011, amounted to 4.25 migrants per 1,000 citizens. The total number of emigrants living abroad was 624,900, and the total number of immigrants living in New Zealand was 962,100. Between 1946 and 1975, New Zealand experienced a net gain from migration of 312,588; from 1975 to 1990, however, there was a net outflow of 110,877. Under the 1974 immigration policy guidelines, immigrants were selected according to specific criteria, such as job skills, health, character, age, and family size. The same restrictions applied to British subjects as to others who wished to take up permanent residence. Citizens of Fiji, Tonga, and Samoa could be admitted under special work permits for up to 11 months. About 7,000 Indochinese refugees settled in New Zealand between 1975 and 1990. In 1998 immigration policy initiatives were passed aimed at making New Zealand a more appealing choice for entrepreneurs, investors, and students.

In 2004 New Zealand's Skilled Migration scheme was overhauled. A "Skilled Migrant" category was created, replacing the "General Skills" category, with the intent of attracting migrants to areas of growth experiencing skilled labor shortages. Applying for residency now involved two steps: an Expression of Interest and an Invitation to Apply for Residency. Applicants were scored on a points system, with points awarded according to the applicant's age, health, character, skills, and so forth. In order to lodge an Expression of Interest, the applicant was required to score at least 100 points. A score of at least 140 or an existing job offer guaranteed an applicant selection for Application for Residency.

New Zealand is one of only 10 countries in the world with an established resettlement program for people designated as quota refugees by the UN High Commission for Refugees (UNHCR). UNHCR quota refugees include, among other groups, protection cases, women at risk, and medical/disabled cases. New Zealand takes approximately 750 quota refugees per year; in 2009, the greatest number came from Iraq, Somalia, Ethiopia, Afghanistan, and Burma/Myanmar. In addition, New Zealand accepts other asylum seekers recognized as refugees by the local authorities. These are referred to as convention refugees. Approximately 300 convention refugees per year are family members sponsored by refugees already residing in New Zealand, through the Refugee Family Support Category. The largest numbers of convention refugees come from Iran, Iraq, Sri Lanka, Afghanistan, and Somalia.

Australia is the preferred destination for New Zealanders departing permanently or long term.

8 ETHNIC GROUPS

About 56.8% of the population was classified as European by the 2006 census, down from 80% in the 2001 census. According to a 2010 report, Pacific Islanders make up about 7% of the population, while Asians make up about 10%. The most significant minority group, the indigenous Maori people, numbered 565,329 in 2006, up from 526,281 in 2001. About 15% of the population claims some level of Maori ancestry.

The Maori are a Polynesian group with a distinctive culture and a well-ordered social system. Although the Treaty of Waitangi (1840) guaranteed to the Maori people all the rights and privileges of British subjects and full and undisturbed possession of their lands, these guarantees were often overlooked. As a result of war and disease, the Maori population declined to fewer than 42,000 by 1896. At the turn of the century, however, a group calling itself the Young Maori Party began to devote itself to the betterment of Maori welfare and status. Although Maori acquisition and development of land have been promoted, there is not enough land to afford a livelihood to more than about 25% of the Maori population. Thus, many Maori leave their tribal villages to seek job opportunities in the towns and cities. Though the law prohibits discrimination against the indigenous population, the Maori continue to report occasions of social discrimination. As a group, the Maori show higher levels of unemployment than other ethnic groups within the country. In 2006, 87% of all Maori lived on the North Island; 24.3% of those lived in the Auckland region. In 1956, more than 60% of all Maori lived in rural areas, but by 2010, 86% lived in urban areas.

Increasing numbers of migrants from New Zealand's former colonies and from other Pacific islands have come to New Zealand. Many of these, especially the Cook Islanders, are Polynesians having ethnic and linguistic ties with the Maori. There have been some reports of discrimination against Pacific Islanders and Asians.

9 LANGUAGES

English, New Zealand Sign Language, and Maori, a language of the Polynesian group, are the official languages. According to the 2006 census, Maori was spoken by 3.9% of the population. Maori joined English as an official language in 1987, with the right of use in courts of law and before a number of tribunals. There are Maori-language preschools, immersion primary schools, and many radio stations. Approximately 30,000 non-Maori speak the Maori language. A total of 24,090 people reported that they were able to use New Zealand Sign Language, which became an official language in 2006. Between 2001 and 2006, the number of people able to speak Hindi almost doubled, from 22,749 to 44,589; the number able to speak Mandarin increased from 26,514 to 41,391; the number able to speak Korean increased from 15,873 to 26,967; and the number able to speak Afrikaans increased from

12,783 to 21,123. French and Samoan are also spoken by minority populations.

10 RELIGIONS

According to the 2006 census, about 56% of the population identified themselves as Christian. Anglicans represented the largest Christian denomination with about 13.8% of the population. About 12.6% were Roman Catholic, 10% Presbyterians, and 3% Methodists. Other Christian groups include Baptists, Mormons (The Church of Jesus Christ of Latter-day Saints), and two syncretic Maori Christian groups, Ringatu and Ratana, which are indigenous to New Zealand. Buddhists account for 1.3% of the population, Hindus account for about 1.6%, and Muslims account for 1%. About 34.7% of the population stated no religious affiliation. The law provides for freedom of religion and calls for equal treatment of all religious groups. Religious groups are not required to register with the government, but those wishing to gain certain tax benefits must register as a charitable trust with the Inland Revenue Department. Good Friday, Easter Sunday, and Christmas are observed as national holidays.

11 TRANSPORTATION

The mountainous nature of New Zealand has made the development of rail and road communications difficult and expensive, particularly on the South Island. In 2010, there were 4,128 km (2,565 mi) of railways in operation, all of it narrow gauge. New Zealand has electrified some 506 km (314 mi) of its rail lines in order to reduce dependence on imported fuel.

Capital investment in roads exceeds that for all other forms of transport service. The CIA reports that New Zealand has a total of 93,911 km (58,354 mi) of roads, of which 61,879 km (38,450 mi) are paved. There are 733 vehicles per 1,000 people in the country.

New Zealand's merchant marine in 2008 consisted of 13 ships of 1,000 GRT or over. New Zealand is largely dependent on the shipping of other nations for its overseas trade. Auckland and Wellington, the two main ports, have good natural harbors with deepwater facilities and modern port equipment. Other ports capable of efficiently handling overseas shipping are Whangarei, Tauranga, Lyttelton (serving Christchurch), Bluff, Napier, Nelson, Dunedin, and Timaru.

There are 122 airports, which transported 12.1 million passengers in 2009 according to the World Bank. Of these airports, 41 had paved runways. Thirteen are major air facilities, of which those at Auckland, Christchurch, and Wellington are international airports. The government-owned Air New Zealand Ltd. operates air services throughout the Pacific region to Australia, Singapore, Hong Kong, Tokyo, Honolulu, and Los Angeles, among other destinations.

Inland waterways are of little importance in satisfying total transportation requirements.

12 HISTORY

New Zealand's first people were the Maori. Owing to the absence of written records, it is impossible to give any accurate date for their arrival, but according to Maori oral traditions, they migrated from other Pacific islands to New Zealand several centuries before any Europeans came, with the chief Maori migration taking place about 1350. It seems likely, however, that the Maori arrived from Southeast Asia as early as the end of the 10th century.

The first European to discover New Zealand was Abel Tasman, a navigator of the Dutch East India Company, who sighted the west coast of the South Island in 1642. He did not land, because of the hostility of the Maori inhabitants. No other Europeans are known to have visited New Zealand after Tasman until Captain James Cook of the British Royal Navy made his four voyages in 1769, 1773, 1774, and 1777. In this period, he circumnavigated both islands and mapped the coastline.

In the 1790s, small European whaling settlements sprang up around the coast. The first mission station was set up in the Bay of Islands in 1814 by Samuel Marsden, chaplain to the governor of New South Wales. In 1840, the Maori chieftains entered into a compact, the Treaty of Waitangi, whereby they ceded sovereignty to Queen Victoria while retaining territorial rights. In the same year, the New Zealand Company made the first organized British attempt at colonization. The first group of British migrants arrived at Port Nicholson and founded the city of Wellington. The New Zealand Company made further settlements in the South Island: in Nelson in 1842, in Dunedin in 1848 (with the cooperation of the Presbyterian Church of Scotland), and in Canterbury in 1850 (with the cooperation of the Church of England).

The New Zealand Wars (sometimes called the New Zealand Land Wars, and formerly known as the Maori Wars) were fought between the European settlers and the indigenous Maori during the period 1843–72. The conflict (or series of conflicts) was triggered by colonial New Zealand's official land policy as the colony rapidly increased in wealth and population. The violence eventually subsided as Europeans gradually gained control of various regions. Discovery of gold in 1861 resulted in a large influx of settlers. The introduction of refrigerated shipping in 1882 enabled New Zealand to become one of the world's greatest exporters of dairy produce and meat. The depression of the early 1930s revealed to New Zealand the extent of its dependence on this export trade and led to the establishment of more local light industry.

The British Parliament granted representative institutions to the colony in 1852. In 1907, New Zealand was made a dominion, and in 1947 the New Zealand government formally claimed the complete autonomy that was available to self-governing members of the British Commonwealth under the Statute of Westminster, enacted by the British Parliament in 1931.

New Zealand entered World Wars I (1914–18) and II (1939–45) on the side of the United Kingdom; New Zealand troops served in Europe in both wars and in the Pacific in World War II. After World War II, New Zealand and US foreign policies were increasingly intertwined. New Zealand signed the ANZUS Pact in 1951 and was a founding member of the Southeast Asia Treaty Organization (SEATO) in 1954. New Zealand troops fought with UN forces in the Korean conflict and with US forces in South Vietnam. The involvement in Vietnam touched off a national debate on foreign policy, however, and all New Zealand troops were withdrawn from Vietnam by the end of 1971. New Zealand's military participation in SEATO was later terminated.

In 1984, a Labour government led by Prime Minister David Lange took office under a pledge to ban nuclear-armed vessels from New Zealand harbors; a US request for a port visit by one of its warships was denied because of uncertainty as to whether the ship carried nuclear weapons. The continuing ban put a strain on New Zealand's relations within ANZUS, and in 1986 the United States suspended its military obligations to New Zealand under that defense agreement, also banning high-level contacts with the New Zealand government. The United States ended its ban on high-level contacts in March 1990; however, New Zealand's official stance against nuclear presence in its territory remained strong.

In the late 1990s, New Zealand's environmental concerns extended beyond nuclear issues. In 1999, when pirates decimated the population of Patagonian toothfish in the Southern Ocean off Antarctica, threatening not only fish, but also the sea birds that fed upon them, New Zealand responded to the threat to the fragile ecosystem by sending a patrol frigate to the area.

Extensive Maori land claims (to all the country's coastline, 70% of the land, and half of the fishing rights) led, in December 1989, to the formation of a new cabinet committee designed to develop a government policy towards these claims. The committee, including former Prime Minister Lange, aimed to work with the 17-member Waitangi Tribunal, established in 1975 to consider complaints from the Maori.

The 1993 general election resulted in the governing National Party (NP) winning a bare majority of 50 seats to the Labour Party's 45. In 1996 the NP formed a coalition government with the New Zealand First Party. The coalition was led by James Bolger, who in 1994 lobbied to convert New Zealand into a republic, a move that was met by NP resistance and public apathy.

The 1994 election was the first under New Zealand's 1993 referendum on proportional representation. It resulted in Bolger's third term as prime minister. Winston Peters, a fierce critic of Bolger, became the country's deputy prime minister and treasurer, a new post responsible for New Zealand's budget. Peters brought the First Party into the coalition over the Labour Party, which won 37 of the 120 seats in the 1996 election. In 1996 the government settled a NZD170 million agreement with the Waikato Tainui tribe in the North Island for its wrongful confiscation of lands during the 1860s. England's Queen signed the legislation, which also contained an apology.

The National Party-First Party coalition government remained in power until 1999, when the Labour Party won 49 seats and again became the majority government. The Labour Party formed a government in coalition with the progressive Alliance Party, with Helen Clark as prime minister. In 1999 tension arose between the Maori and white New Zealanders, centering on the growing Maori claims to the natural resources of the country. The Clark administration expressed its commitment to goals aimed at benefiting all New Zealanders and closing the economic gap between the Maori and the rest of the population. The Labour-Alliance coalition also built international alliances with other nonnuclear states and worked to strengthen the Nuclear Free Zone in the South Pacific.

The general elections of 27 July 2002 resulted in a Labour Party victory that returned Helen Clark as prime minister. The Labour Party entered into coalition with Jim Anderton's Progressive Party and received support from the United Future Party. The National Party recorded its worst showing in 70 years. General elections held in September 2005 resulted in a Labour Party victory again. Labour lost its majority in the elections of November 2008, when

the National Party captured 58 of the 122 seats in Parliament and John Key became prime minister.

In May 2006, New Zealand sent troops to join an intervention force (including Australia, Portugal, and Malaysia) in Timor-Leste (East Timor), in order to put an end to violence there. A conflict had broken out between members of Timor-Leste's military over discrimination within the military; and general violence escalated from there. By August, some troops had withdrawn from the country.

Also in August 2006, the Maori queen, Te Arikinui Dame Te Atairangikaahu, died at age 75 after a reign of 40 years. Her death prompted a week of mourning.

In October 2007, New Zealand's police arrested 17 people in anti-terror raids. Prosecutors accused Maori activists of planning a violent campaign against the nation's white majority.

In November 2011, election campaigning was underway. The ruling National Party announced new tough law and order policies, stating that if they won a second term, high risk violent offenders would be retained in civil custody after completion of their sentences, rather than being totally released into the civilian population. Labour's campaign promises included a major investment in child health and well-being. Elections were held in November 2011; Prime Minister John Key of the National Party won reelection.

13 GOVERNMENT

New Zealand is an independent member of the Commonwealth of Nations. Like the United Kingdom, it is a constitutional monarchy, the head of state being the representative of the crown, the governor-general, who is appointed for a five-year term.

The government is democratic and modeled on that of the United Kingdom. The single-chamber legislature, the House of Representatives, has 122 members (two seats were added in the 2008 election), elected by universal adult suffrage for a term of three years. Adult male suffrage dates from 1879; adult women received the right to vote in 1893. The voting age was lowered to 18 in November 1974. Since 1867, the House has included representatives of the Maori, and in 1985, the Most Reverend Paul Reeves, Anglican archbishop of New Zealand, became the first person of Maori descent to be appointed governor-general.

As of 2009, seven seats in the 122-member parliament were reserved for representatives of the native Maori minority population. Persons of at least half-Maori ancestry may register in either a Maori electoral district or a European district. Elections have resulted in coalition governments; a two-party system usually operates. The party with a majority of members elected to the House of Representatives forms the government; the other party becomes the opposition.

On his appointment, the prime minister, leader of the governing party, chooses 20 other ministers to form the cabinet. Each minister usually controls several government departments, for which he is responsible to the House of Representatives. Although the cabinet is the de facto governing body, it has no legal status. Members of the cabinet and the governor-general form the Executive Council, the highest executive body.

An act of 1962 established the post of ombudsman, whose principal function is to inquire into complaints from the public relating to administrative decisions of government departments and related organizations. In 1975, provision was made for the appointment of additional ombudsmen under the chief ombudsman.

In a September 1992 referendum, nearly 85% of voters rejected the established electoral system of simple plurality in favor of a system based upon a mixed member proportional system, as used in Germany. Final approval came in a second referendum held as part of the 1993 general election, and the proportional voting system was introduced during the 1996 elections. Under New Zealand's proportional representation system, each voter casts two votes, one for a candidate and one for a political party. Each party is awarded seats according to its share of the overall vote, with a minimum set at 5%.

Throughout the 2000s, Transparency International has consistently listed New Zealand as one of the least corrupt nations in the world. It was listed as the least corrupt nation during 2009–2011.

14 POLITICAL PARTIES

Although the New Zealand legislature began to function in 1854 under an act of 1852, it was not until near the end of the century that political parties with a national outlook began to form. This development was hastened by abolition of the provincial parliaments in 1876.

From 1890 to 1912, the Liberal Party was in power. It drew its strength from small farmers and from the rapidly increasing working class in the towns. It enacted advanced legislation on minimum wages, working conditions, and old age pensions, and established the world's first compulsory system of state arbitration. A Reform Party government replaced the Liberal government in 1912; the main items in the Reform platform were the "freehold" for certain types of farmers (i.e., the right to purchase on favorable terms the land they leased from the crown) and the eradication of patronage in the public service. During part of World War I, there was a coalition of Reform and Liberal parties. The Labour Party was formed in 1916 when several rival Labour groups finally came together. This party derived partly from old Liberal tradition, but its platform on socialization and social welfare was more radical.

The Reform Party continued in office until 1928 and was then succeeded by the United Party, a revival of the old Liberal Party. In 1931, these two parties came together, governing as a coalition until 1935. In that year, after a severe economic depression, a Labour government came to power. Labour remained the government until 1949, although for periods during World War II a coalition war cabinet and later a war administration were created in addition to the Labour cabinet. During its term of office, Labour inaugurated an extensive system of social security and a limited degree of nationalization.

After their defeat in 1935, the old coalition parties joined to form the National Party. Coming to power in 1949, this party held office until 1957, when it was replaced by Labour. The National Party returned to power in the 1960 election, and maintained its majority in the elections of 1963, 1966, and 1969. A Labour government was elected in 1972, but in 1975 the National Party reversed the tide, winning 55 seats and 47.4% of the total vote; a National Party cabinet was formed, with Robert Muldoon as prime minister. Led by Muldoon, the National Party was returned again in the 1978 and 1981 elections, but by much lower margins.

On 14 July 1984, the National Party was defeated at the polls, winning only 37 seats (36% of the vote) to 56 seats (43%) for Labour. The Social Credit Political League won 2 seats (8%), and the New Zealand Party, a conservative group formed in 1983, won most of the remaining popular vote, but no seats. David Lange formed a Labour government and was reelected in August 1987, when Labour won 56 seats and 47.6% of the vote, and the National Party won 41 seats and 45% of the vote. No other parties won seats.

David Lange resigned as prime minister on 7 August 1989 after Roger Douglas, a political foe in the Labour Party, was reelected to the cabinet. Labour's MPs selected Geoffrey Palmer as prime minister and party leader. Palmer resigned as prime minister in September 1990 and was replaced by Michael Moore, also of the Labour Party.

In October 1990 the National Party, led by Jim Bolger, won a general election victory. Bolger's government instituted major cuts in New Zealand's welfare programs. The National Party won reelection in the November 1993 general election, capturing 50 of 99 seats. The Labour Party won 45, and both the New Zealand First Party, led by Winston Peters, and the Progressive Alliance Party, led by Jim Anderton, won 2 seats. In December 1993 Helen Clark replaced Michael Moore as leader of the Labour Party, becoming the first woman to lead a major party in New Zealand.

The 1996 elections were the first under proportional representation. James Bolger was elected as prime minister for a third term to lead a coalition government formed by the National Party and the First Party. The National Party won 44 seats; Labour, 37; New Zealand First Party, 17; Progressive Alliance Party, 8; and the United Party, 1.

In the November 1999 elections, the balance of power once again shifted, with the New Zealand National Party losing 5 seats and capturing only 30.5% of the total vote, while the New Zealand Labour Party gained 12 seats and took 38.7% of the vote, thus becoming the majority party. Under Prime Minister Helen Clark, a coalition government was formed between the Labour Party and the Progressive Alliance Party, which consisted of five small parties: the New Labor Party, the Democratic Party, the New Zealand Liberal Party, the Green Party, and Mana Motihake.

In the July 2002 elections (held early), the Labour Party captured 41.3% of the vote and 52 seats to the National Party's 20.9% and 27 seats. The New Zealand First Party took 10.4% of the vote and 13 seats. It was the worst showing for the National Party in 70 years. Prime Minister Helen Clark formed an alliance with the United Future Party, after forming a coalition with Jim Anderton's Progressive Party. United Future claimed it would not form a coalition with the Labour Party, but would support the government.

While the Liberal and Reform Parties, and in more recent times the Labour and National Parties, have played the major roles in New Zealand's government, many other political groups have existed over the years, with varying agendas and membership. In 2002, those with enough support to win parliamentary seats included ACT New Zealand (libertarian), the New Zealand First Party (nationalistic), the Green Party of Aotearoa (ecologist), the United Future Party (liberal), and the Progressive Party (progressive). There were 21 registered political parties as of June 2002.

The results of the 2008 legislative elections were as follows: the National Party 44.9%, 58 seats; Labour Party 34%, 43 seats; Green Party 6.7%, 9 seats; New Zealand First Party 4; ACT New Zealand

3.7%, 5 seats; Maori 2.4%, 5 seats; Progressive Coalition 0.9%, 1 seat; and United Future 0.9%, 1 seat.

The November 2011 elections resulted in 48% of the vote and 60 seats for the National Party, 27.1% and 34 seats for the Labour Party, 10.6% and 13 seats for the Green Party, 6.8% and 8 seats for the New Zealand First Party, 1.4% and 3 seats for the Maori Party, and about 1% of the vote and 1 seat for several smaller parties. After forming a coalition with two, one-seat parties, Key and the National Party secured an additional term in power. The next elections were to be held by November 2014.

15 LOCAL GOVERNMENT

The Local Government Act (1974), with subsequent modifications, substantially changed the structure of local government in New Zealand. The previous system was based on territorial local authorities: boroughs, which served concentrated populations of at least 1,500; counties, which were predominantly rural; and town districts, an intermediate form. In addition, there were special-purpose authorities to administer harbors, hospitals, electricity and water distribution, and other public services. The 1974 legislation added two tiers to this structure. Regional bodies—including united councils, which are appointed by the constituent territorial authorities in a region, and regional councils, which are directly elected—are charged with two mandatory functions: regional planning and self-defense. They may also undertake other regional functions. Moreover, within territorial local authorities, communities may be established. Each community may have either a district community council (if the population is 1,500 or more), which exercises nearly all the powers of its parent territorial authority, or a community council, to which the parent authority may delegate powers. The purpose of these community bodies is to increase residents' participation in local government. The Local Government Act also introduced a new form of territorial local authority, the district council, established to serve areas of mixed rural and urban character.

In 2010, there were 78 local authorities representing all areas of New Zealand: 11 regional councils, 12 city councils, 54 district councils, and one Auckland council. The city, district, and Auckland councils are considered territorial authorities. In 2010, New Zealand had 108 regional councilors, 718 territorial authority councilors, 149 Auckland local board members, and 67 mayors. Most units of local government are elected at three-year intervals. In boroughs the mayor is elected directly by the voters, while the council itself elects the chairman of a county council.

In 2007, the Local Government Commission conducted a survey to determine the level of New Zealanders' knowledge of local government. The survey results revealed that 54% of all New Zealanders aged 18 and older had "some" knowledge of the regional and local councils, while 45% reported that they knew "very little." Some 22% of respondents were not aware there was a difference between local council and regional council, and 30% were not aware of the existence of community boards. The Local Government Commission sought to improve citizen involvement and participation in the election and operation of regional and local councils.

16 JUDICIAL SYSTEM

New Zealand's judicial system is based on the British judicial system and derived from two main sources: common law, which is the body of law developed from legal decisions made in New Zealand and in the UK; and statute law, which consists of the laws made by Parliament. The judiciary is independent and impartial, providing citizens with a fair and efficient judicial process.

The highest court is the Supreme Court, which was established in 2004, replacing the Judicial Committee of the Privy Council located in London for final appeals. Below the Supreme Court, in descending order, are the Court of Appeal, the High Courts, and the District Courts. Most civil and criminal cases are heard first in District Courts, but cases involving an amount greater than US$200,000 are addressed in the High Court, as are cases dealing with specified serious crimes such as murder. The Court of Appeal is an intermediate appellate court.

There are also several special courts, such as the Family courts established in 1980, to hear cases involving domestic issues. Other special courts include the Employment Court, the Environmental Court, the Coroner's Court, the Courts Martial Appeal Authority, and the Maori Land Court (Te Kooti Whenua Maori), which hears matters relating to Maori land. Less than 5% of New Zealand's land is designated as Maori freehold land. The Maori Land Court conducts business, observing traditional Maori customs. Many court hearing are conducted in the Maori language, and begin and end with a prayer.

The law prohibits arbitrary interference with privacy, family, home, or correspondence, and the authorities respect these provisions in practice.

17 ARMED FORCES

The International Institute for Strategic Studies reports that armed forces in New Zealand totaled 9,673 members in 2011. The force is comprised of 4,905 from the army, 2,161 from the navy, and 2,607 members of the air force. Armed forces represent 0.4% of the labor force in New Zealand. Defense spending totaled US$1.2 billion and accounted for 1% of GDP.

New Zealand forces have a history of participation in NATO, UN, European Union, or other missions in a supporting or peacekeeping role. In 2011, New Zealand defense forces joined those of Australia and Papua New Guinea to clear old WWII ordinance from Rabaul Harbor in Papua New Guinea, in a mission called "Operation RENDER SAFE." In November 2011, New Zealand had army troops operationally deployed in Afghanistan, East Timor, the Solomon Islands, Egypt, the Middle East, Sudan, Iraq, South Korea, and Antarctica. Previous deployments include Bosnia-Herzegovina, Kosovo, Lebanon, and Tonga.

18 INTERNATIONAL COOPERATION

New Zealand is a charter member of the United Nations (UN), having joined on 24 October 1945; it participates in ESCAP and several non-regional specialized agencies, such as the FAO, IAEA, ILO, the World Bank, UNESCO, UNHCR, UNIDO, and the WHO. In addition, New Zealand belongs to the WTO, the Asian Development Bank, APEC, the Commonwealth of Nations, the European Bank for Reconstruction and Development, the Colombo Plan, OECD, the South Pacific Commission, the Pacific Island

Forum, and the South Pacific Regional Trade and Cooperation Agreement (SPARTECA). It is a dialogue partner in ASEAN.

New Zealand also forms part of the ANZUS alliance with Australia and the United States; in 1986, however, following New Zealand's decision to ban US nuclear-armed or nuclear-powered ships from its ports, the United States renounced its ANZUS treaty commitments to New Zealand.

New Zealand is part of the Australia Group and the Nuclear Suppliers Group (London Group). In environmental cooperation, New Zealand is part of the Antarctic Treaty, the Basel Convention, Conventions on Biological Diversity and Whaling, Ramsar, CITES, the London Convention, International Tropical Timber Agreements, the Montréal Protocol, MARPOL, the Nuclear Test Ban Treaty, and the UN Conventions on the Law of the Sea, Climate Change and Desertification.

New Zealand has a strong interest in Antarctica. It was one of the 12 original signatories to the Antarctic Treaty, which was signed in December 1959 and went into effect in 1961. Avoiding international tensions in Antarctica depends on the Antarctic Treaty, which provides a mechanism for settling disputes about sovereignty. Peaceful relations over Antarctica form the basis for New Zealand's relations with several other countries. New Zealand, the United States, and Italy share resources in support of their respective Antarctic programs. New Zealand scientists cooperate on Antarctic research with scientists from many countries. In 2002 the New Zealand government issued the Revised New Zealand Statement of Strategic Interest, which confirmed the country's commitment to conservation of Antarctica and the Southern Ocean.

¹⁹ECONOMY

While New Zealand's economy was traditionally based on pastoral farming, in 1968 it lost the protected market for its agricultural goods when the United Kingdom joined the European Community (now the European Union). New Zealand responded with a government-led program to transform the economy into an independent, more industrialized competitor in the world market. When inflation and stagnation struck in the early 1980s, New Zealand responded with a neoliberal transformation of the economy, combining a strict monetary regime to eliminate inflation, liberalization of the country's trade and investment regimes, and deregulation and privatization of the domestic economy. The liberalization and stabilization program transformed New Zealand from a heavily protected and regulated economy to one of the most market-oriented and open in the world.

During the 1990s there was great expansion in light industries such as plastics, textiles, and footwear, mostly to supply the home market. Heavy industry also grew, with a trend toward the development of resource-based industries and expansion in the forest industry, with pulp, log, and paper products becoming a major earner of overseas exchange.

For financing imports both of raw materials and of a high proportion of manufactured goods, New Zealand has traditionally relied on the receipts from the export of its restricted range of primary products (mainly wool, meat, and dairy products). This dependence on the income from so few commodities makes the economy vulnerable to fluctuations in their world prices, and

sharp drops in these prices, as have occurred periodically, inevitably result in the restriction of imports or a substantial trade deficit.

Despite increased fuel costs that sent inflation to 4% in 2000, real GDP growth improved to 4.6%. The global slowdown in 2001–02 had a relatively mild impact on New Zealand's economy, reducing real GDP growth to 2.3%. Gross public debt fell from 36% of GDP in 1999 to 20.7% of GDP in 2007. Real GDP growth averaged 3.5% over the 2001–05 period, when inflation averaged 2.5%. Real GDP growth slowed slightly to 3.0% in 2007, as domestic demand weakened. Inflation was 2.4% in 2007. The public debt in 2007 was estimated at 20.7% of GDP. The unemployment rate in 2008 was estimated at 4%.

Late 2008 marked the nation's first recession since 1998. Reports indicated that the GDP fell in each quarter of 2008 and, in the wake of a global financial crisis, the economy was expected to decline another 2% through 2009. In a report released in March 2010, the International Monetary Fund (IMF) forecast the country's economy to grow at 3% in 2010 and 2011. It additionally warned that the New Zealand's currency was overvalued by 10% to 25%. The country's currency overvaluation risked widening the country's deficit, which was already growing, as New Zealand's exports became less attractive to the global market.

In 2010, agricultural production amounted to approximately 4.7% of GDP, industry 24.3%, and services 71%. Important industries included the manufacture of machinery and transportation equipment, banking and insurance, and eco-tourism.

After the February 2011 earthquake that hit Christchurch, the New Zealand economy suffered as the government cut interest rates in an attempt to improve businesses and consumer confidence in March 2011. The cut in rates from the central bank took the country back to the same place it stood during the global economic crisis, from which it had barely begun to recover.

The gross domestic product (GDP) rate of change in New Zealand, as of 2010, was 1.5%. Inflation stood at 2.6%, and unemployment was reported at 6.5%.

²⁰INCOME

The CIA estimated that in 2011 the GDP of New Zealand was US$123.3 billion. The CIA defines GDP as the value of all final goods and services produced within a nation in a given year and computed on the basis of purchasing power parity (PPP) rather than value as measured on the basis of the rate of the exchange based on current dollars. The per capita GDP was estimated at US$27,900. The annual growth rate of GDP was 2%. The average inflation rate was 4.5%. It was estimated that agriculture accounted for 4.7% of GDP, industry 24%, and services 71%.

According to the World Bank, remittances from citizens living abroad totaled US$627.7 million or about US$146 per capita and accounted for approximately 0.5% of GDP.

The World Bank reports that in 2009, household consumption in New Zealand totaled US$74.5 billion or about US$17,359 per capita, measured in current US dollars rather than PPP. Household consumption includes expenditures of individuals, households, and nongovernmental organizations on goods and services, excluding the purchases of dwellings. It was estimated that household consumption was growing at an average annual rate of 0.5%.

The World Bank estimates that New Zealand, with 0.07% of the world's population, accounted for 0.18% of the world's GDP. By comparison, the United States, with 4.85% of the world's population, accounted for 22.51% of world GDP.

As of 2011 the most recent study by the World Bank reported that actual individual consumption in New Zealand was 70.5% of GDP and accounted for 0.20% of world consumption. By comparison, the United States accounted for 25.44% of world individual consumption. The World Bank also estimated that 11.4% of New Zealand's GDP was spent on food and beverages, 17.2% on housing and household furnishings, 2.7% on clothes, 7.4% on health, 8.3% on transportation, 1.8% on communications, 8.4% on recreation, 4.6% on restaurants and hotels, and 3.5% on miscellaneous goods and services and purchases from abroad.

21 LABOR

As of 2010, New Zealand had a total labor force of 2.328 million people. Within that labor force, CIA estimates in 2006 noted that 7% were employed in agriculture, 19% in industry, and 74% in the service sector.

As of 2008, workers in New Zealand had the right to organize and join a union, to engage in collective bargaining and exercise the right to strike. However, members of the armed forces are prohibited from organizing a union and collective bargaining. Also, uniformed and plainclothes police (excluding support and clerical staff) were banned from striking or any other form of industrial action, but can organize and bargain collectively. All unions are required to register with the government, have at least 15 members, and be governed by democratic rules. Unions cannot engage in collective bargaining over political or social issues. About 17% of New Zealand's workforce in 2009 was unionized.

Official minimum wage rates are reviewed each year. On 1 April 2011, the minimum wage was increased to NZD13.00 per hour. For those 16 and 17 years old, the minimum wage rate was increased to NZD10.40 per hour, which is 80% of the adult minimum wage.

By law, employees in most occupations have a 40-hour workweek, eight hours a day, five days a week. Excess hours are generally paid at overtime rates. Legislation or industrial contracts secure sick leave, paid holidays, and accident compensation for all workers. Children under 15 years of age cannot work in mining, forestry or manufacturing, and cannot work between 10 pm and 6 am. Children attending school cannot be employed, even after school hours, if the employment interferes with their education. The safety, health and welfare benefits, holiday provisions, hours of work, and overtime of all workers are closely regulated.

22 AGRICULTURE

Roughly 12% of New Zealand's land is farmed. The country's major crops include dairy products, lamb and mutton; wheat, barley, potatoes, pulses, fruits, and vegetables. Cereal production in 2009 amounted to 1.1 million tons, fruit production 1.1 million tons, and vegetable production 950,147 tons. Capital investment in land improvement and mechanization has contributed greatly to the steady growth in agricultural production without an increase in the farm labor force. Agriculture contributed about 4.7% to GDP in 2010. Cereal cultivation, more than 90% of which takes place on the South Island plains and downlands, fluctuates in terms of both acreage and size of crop.

New Zealand is largely self-sufficient in horticultural products, many of which it exports. Its climate supports a wide variety of fruit crops. Some, such as kiwi, apples, and avocados, are grown primarily for export; about 70% of apple exports are derived from the Braeburn, Gala, and Royal Gala varieties developed in New Zealand. In 2011 fruit exports were quoted as bringing in roughly US$1.5 billion per year. Kiwi sales alone were worth over US$1 billion in 2010, although New Zealand's market share in kiwi production has declined as other countries expand their own domestic kiwi production. Wine exports are of approximately the same value as kiwi sales. Other fruit crops such as berries and citrus fruits are grown primarily for the domestic market. The export of processed fruit products such as juices and jams amounted to sales of US$100 million per year in 2011.

The Department of Agriculture and the Department of Scientific and Industrial Research provide farmers and horticulturalists with advice and encouragement on new farming methods, elimination of plant diseases, and improvement of unproductive land. Government subsidies to farmers were phased out in 1984.

23 ANIMAL HUSBANDRY

Relatively warm temperatures combined with ample rainfall make New Zealand one of the world's richest pastoral areas. Even in the south, where winters may be quite severe, animals need not be housed. Dairying and beef production are concentrated in the North Island, while sheep farming is more evenly distributed between the North and South islands. Products of animal origin account for more than half the total value of New Zealand's exports, with meat industry products in 2009 accounting for about 12% of exports, and dairy about 22%. New Zealand is the world's largest exporter of mutton and lamb, second-largest exporter of wool, and a leading exporter of cheese. New Zealand accounts for over 50% of the world's mutton exports.

The UN Food and Agriculture Organization (FAO) reported that New Zealand dedicated 10.9 million hectares (26.8 million acres) to permanent pasture or meadow in 2009. During that year, the country tended 13.1 million chickens, 10 million head of cattle, and 322,788 pigs. The production from these animals amounted to 134,742 tons of beef and veal, 96,071 tons of pork, 145,499 tons of poultry, 39,169 tons of eggs, and 435,175 tons of milk. New Zealand also produced 58,000 tons of cattle hide and 179,242 tons of raw wool.

The natural tussock land in the mountainous areas of the South Island and the surface-sown grassland in the less steep parts of the North Island are used to raise sheep for wool. The extensive use of aircraft for the spread of top dressing has greatly improved hill pasture, most of which is not readily accessible to normal top dressing with fertilizers. Although fine-woolen Merino sheep have grazed in New Zealand since the 1830s, most of the clip nowadays comes from Romney sheep, whose coarser, thicker wool is ideal for carpet-making and knitting yarns.

Some 24,000 farms stock mainly sheep, with an average flock of 1,800 head. In 2009, there were 34.2 million sheep, less than half as many as in the mid-1980s. The decrease in sheep farming was blamed on changes in government subsidies, dry weather, and difficult economic times. Some farmers replaced sheep with dairy cows, or in some cases, grapes, or even urban development. In 2009, 350 sheep farms were converted to dairy operations. Clean wool exports fell 8.3% in 2009, reflecting the reduced number of sheep in the country as well as the reduced wool prices.

With many more cows than people to milk them, New Zealand pioneered and relies on mechanical milking machines which pump whole milk through coolers to vats where it is transferred to tanker trucks. Milkfat production averages about 336,000 tons annually, of which 13% is consumed as milk or fed to stock. The balance is used for dairy products.

Although wild goats and deer were once regarded as vermin, over the last decade, the profitability of venison and mohair exports led to the domestication of both animals. About 1.7 million deer and 155,000 goats are being farmed. Alpacas, llamas, and water buffalo have been imported to improve the breeding potential as well as wool and meat production.

24 FISHING

Although many kinds of edible fish are readily obtainable in New Zealand waters, the fishing and fish-processing industry has remained relatively small. Since the 1960s, however, the government has taken a number of measures to expand the industry and increase fishery exports. In 1978, the government began implementing a 322-km (200-mi) exclusive economic zone. During the next four years, it approved nearly 40 joint ventures with foreign companies in order to exploit the zone, which, with an area of about 1.3 million sq mi (nautical), is one of the world's largest. These waters support over 1,000 species of fish, about 100 of which have commercial significance.

In 2008 the annual capture totaled 451,052 tons, according to the UN FAO. New Zealand's domestic vessels, which included 2,037 decked commercial fishing boats, accounted for about 60% of the catch. About 90% of the catch is exported, mostly to the United States, Japan, and Australia. The principal finfish species caught included blue grenadier, mackerel, whiting, snoek, and orange roughy. The most valuable part of the catch is made of orange roughy, hoki, squid, and rock lobster. Oyster and mussel aquaculture are well established; scallop, salmon, and abalone farming are developing.

25 FORESTRY

At the time Europeans began coming to New Zealand, about 70% of the land was forest, with beech, kauri, rimu, taraire, and tawa as the major indigenous tree species. By 2009, this proportion was reduced by settlement, farming, and exploitation to about 31%. Much of the remaining natural forest is reserved in national parks, or as protected forest on mountain land. About 7% of New Zealand is covered by planted forests, which provides a large and sustainable volume of wood. The Ministry of Agriculture and Forestry (MAF) estimated the planted forest area at 1.8 million hectares (4.4 million acres) in 2011, with 70% on North Island and 30% on South Island.

For wood production, New Zealand relies heavily on its planted forests of quick-growing exotic species, mainly radiata pine, which can be harvested every 25–30 years. These provide over 90% of the wood for production of sawn timber, wood panel products, pulp, paper, and paperboard. Due to these replanting efforts and privatization of forest lands, exports of softwood logs have skyrocketed since the early 1980s. Timber production is expected to pick up again around 2010 from the large number of trees planted in the 1980s and early 1990s. Exports of forestry products in 2009 amounted to US$1.98 billion; about 35% is exported as logs. Most of New Zealand's softwood logs and lumber go to Australia, the Republic of Korea, and Japan. Forestry accounted for about 3% of GDP in 2011. Imports of forest products consist mostly of specialty papers.

Roundwood production in 2009 was estimated at 20.2 million cu m (713.7 million cu ft). Softwood logs for export and lumber production that year were estimated at 7.1 million and 1.6 million cu m (250.6 million and 56.5 million cu ft), respectively. Plywood production for 2004 was estimated at 296,000 cu m (10.5 million cu ft).

The Forestry Corporation (FC) was established as a state-owned enterprise in April 1991. The FC manages 188,000 hectares (465,000 acres) of forest in the Bay of Plenty on North Island. The FC consists of three principal forests: Rotoehu Forest, Whakarewarewa Forest, and the Kaingaroa Forest in the Rotorua district that covers 149,735 hectares (370,001 acres) and is claimed to be the largest planted forest in the world. In 1996, the government sold FC for NZD2 billion to a joint venture consortium, which planned to invest NZD260 million over the next several years. New Zealand's forestry sector has become more fragmented as the large companies that previously dominated the industry have divested much of their business. Prior to this change, harvests were becoming of poorer quality, as younger trees were being harvested to satisfy a strong export market. The ownership change to long-term investment now focuses on wood processing.

26 MINING

Because of its diverse geology and dynamic tectonic history, New Zealand had a wide variety of potentially profitable mineral deposits, although few have been extensively exploited. Mining was a leading industry in 2009, with gold and silver dominating the metal mining sector. In 2009, mining exports were valued at NZD1.1 billion. Major mineral exports included ironsand, halloysite clay (for the manufacture of high-quality ceramics), cement, salt (by solar evaporation of seawater), and silver. Most output of industrial minerals was for domestic use, because the distances to overseas markets limited most exports to the high-value commodities or products with unique applications or specifications.

Gold was discovered in New Zealand in the early 19th century when European sealers and whalers were first exploring the country. The mining industry began in 1852, upon the discovery of hard-rock gold on the Coromandel region, North Island, by European settlers. Gold deposits were discovered on the South Island in 1861. By 1870, copper, iron, lead, and silver deposits had been discovered and worked, and deposits of antimony, arsenic, chromium, zinc, and other minerals had been located. After World War II, industrial minerals, aggregate, and stone production grew steadily, coal mining fluctuated, and gold output declined. Extensive exploration in the 1950s and 1960s found natural gas and gas condensate, ironsand, and geothermal energy.

Gold production for 2009 was 13,442 kg. Production came from two large hard-rock mines: the Martha Hill, at the base of the Coromandel Peninsula, at Waihi, southeast of Auckland; and the Macraes open cut mine, north of Dunedin; as well as the Reefton gold mine on the west coast of South Island. Reefton has four open pits and a processing plant with an annual capacity of 1 million metric tons, and accounted for about 50% the country's production in 2009.

In 2009, 1,585,000 tons of ironsand (titaniferous magnetite) was extracted. Iron ore in the form of titanomagnetite-rich sand derived from the coastal erosion of the Mount Taranaki volcanics was mined from beach and dune sands, concentrated at two sites along the western coast of North Island. Although the existence of large quantities of iron-bearing sands has been known for more than a century, the steel industry was not able to exploit them until the late 1960s.

Silver mine output in 2009 was 14,264 kg. Output of building materials in 2009 included an estimated 7,198,000 tons of sand and gravel for building aggregate, and 15,471,000 tons of limestone and marl for roads. New Zealand also produced bentonite, clays for brick and tile, diatomaceous earth (which included zeolite), dolomite, kaolinite (pottery), lime, marble, nitrogen, perlite (which included zeolite), quartzite, rock for harbor work, salt, sand and gravel (including silica [glass] sand and amorphous silica), serpentinite, and dimension stone. Considerable potential for platinum and platinum-group metals from hard-rock deposits and alluvial concentrations existed, the most promising area being the Longwood Range, in western Southland. Uranium-bearing minerals have been located on the South Island.

State-owned "Crown minerals," based on the British legal system, were owned and regulated by the New Zealand Crown Minerals Act 1991 and the Crown Minerals Amendment Act (No. 2), passed in 1997. Crown-owned minerals included all naturally occurring gold, silver, and uranium; substantial amounts of coal; other metallic and nonmetallic minerals and aggregates; and all petroleum. Minerals not designated as Crown owned were privately owned. New Zealand has not enacted native title legislation to gain access to Maori lands, claims for which were handled through the Treaty of Waitangi Tribunal.

27 ENERGY AND POWER

The World Bank reported in 2008 that New Zealand produced 43.8 billion kWh of electricity and consumed 40.5 billion kWh, or 9,445 kWh per capita. Roughly 67% of energy came from fossil fuels, while 27% came from alternative fuels. Per capita oil consumption was 3,967 kg. Oil production totaled 53,038 barrels of oil a day.

New Zealand has modest reserves of oil, natural gas, and coal. Most of its electricity comes from hydroelectric sources. As of 2008, New Zealand had proven reserves of petroleum and natural gas of 55 million barrels and 29.67 billion cu m, respectively.

28 INDUSTRY

Industrial production has increased rapidly since the end of World War II, stimulated by intermittent import controls that often enabled domestic industry to increase output without competition. A most significant feature of New Zealand industry in recent decades has been the establishment of heavy industry with Commonwealth and US capital. Plants include metal and petroleum processing, motor vehicle assembly, textiles and footwear, and a wide range of consumer appliances. The New Zealand Steel company manufactures billet slabs and ingots using domestically pro-

duced iron sands; Pacific Steel, which processes scrap metal, uses billets from New Zealand Steel. The Tiwai Point aluminum smelter, operated by an Australian-Japanese consortium, has an annual capacity of some 250,000 tons. The small but growing electronics industry produces consumer goods as well as commercial products, such as digital gasoline pumps. Wool-based industries have traditionally been an important part of the economy, notably wool milling, the oldest sector of the textile industry. Other significant industrial areas include a diverse food-processing sector, tanneries, sheet glass, rubber, and plastics.

Progressive withdrawal of government support beginning in 1985 led manufacturing to decline due to a more competitive environment; however, after cutting overcapacity, many firms increased productivity and were ultimately in a stronger financial position, leading industrial output to recover. The manufacturing sector, which until the mid-1980s focused on production for the small domestic market, has increasingly been geared toward export markets. By 2007, industry accounted for some 26% of GDP.

29 SCIENCE AND TECHNOLOGY

Scientific research in New Zealand is funded by the government, principally by the Foundation for Research, Science, and Technology, which invests nearly NZD500 million a year in science and technology research on behalf of the New Zealand government. In 2009, public financing of science was 1.21% of GDP. The Ministry of Research, Science, & Technology manages investment, advises on policy, and encourages innovation and commercialization of new ideas. Additional funding for research comes from the Ministry of Agriculture and Forestry. A research and development tax credit was introduced on 1 April 2008; it was expected to encourage private-sector investment in research and development. Patent applications in science and technology as of 2009, according to the World Bank, totaled 1,555 in New Zealand.

The Cawthron Institute at Nelson, established in 1919, conducts research in chemistry, biology, and environmental and marine studies. New Zealand has 20 other institutes conducting research in agriculture, veterinary science, medicine, and general sciences and 17 universities and technical institutes offering degrees in basic and applied sciences.

In 2007, of all bachelor's degrees awarded, 17.6% were in the sciences (natural, mathematics and computers, engineering). Among New Zealand's 42 scientific and technical learned societies, the most prominent is the Royal Society of New Zealand, founded in 1867.

In 2010, research and development (R and D) expenditures totaled US$2.5 billion, up 13% from 2008. This amounted to 1.3% of GDP. 70% of this was for applied R and D, with a trend toward more commercially focused projects. Of that amount, the largest portion, 46%, came from government sources, followed by the business sector at 38%. Higher education and foreign sources accounted for 8% and 5%, respectively. In 2008, there were approximately 4,400 researchers engaged in R and D per million people. In 2009, New Zealand's high technology exports totaled US$616 million, or 9.53% of the country's manufactured exports.

30 DOMESTIC TRADE

New Zealand has developed an open market economy since the mid 1980s, as the government has given up control of many areas

Principal Trading Partners – New Zealand (2010)

(In millions of US dollars)

Country	Total	Exports	Imports	Balance
World	64,105.0	32,287.0	31,818.0	469.0
Australia	12,814.0	7,243.0	5,571.0	1,672.0
China	8,400.0	3,499.0	4,901.0	-1,402.0
United States	5,921.0	2,705.0	3,216.0	-511.0
Japan	4,699.0	2,437.0	2,262.0	175.0
South Korea	2,076.0	1,018.0	1,058.0	-40.0
United Kingdom	1,791.0	1,099.0	692.0	407.0
Singapore	1,781.0	596.0	1,185.0	-589.0
Germany	1,734.0	473.0	1,261.0	-788.0
Malaysia	1,632.0	559.0	1,073.0	-514.0
Thailand	1,484.0	493.0	991.0	-498.0

(…) data not available or not significant.

(n.s.) not specified.

SOURCE: *2011 Direction of Trade Statistics Yearbook,* New York: United Nations, 2011.

of domestic economic regulation, including the elimination of agriculture subsidies and controls on prices and wages. The trend in retail establishments has increasingly moved from small shops to supermarkets and shopping centers. Several retail establishments have converted to self-service operations. There is very little retail mail-order trade. Automobiles and large appliances are increasingly being sold on the installment (hire-purchase) plan. General and trade papers, regional publications, and television and radio are used extensively as advertising media.

New Zealand has the highest number of franchises per capita in the world, with 450 franchise systems and 23,600 franchise holders in 2011. Local New Zealand businesses make up 70% of the franchises, the balance coming from overseas companies. New Zealand's policy of deregulation means there are no regulations specific to franchises. They are governed by normal commercial law.

Electronic commerce (e-commerce) is well developed in New Zealand. Although e-commerce usage is small in comparison to that of the United States, the degree of penetration is extremely high.

A goods and services tax (GST) is applied to most products and services. In October 2010, the GST was increased from 12.5% to 15%. Business hours vary, especially since the introduction of staggered work hours, known as glide time. Offices open as early as 7:30 a.m. and remain open until about 6 p.m. Stores may be open at any time between 7 a.m. and 9 p.m., Monday through Saturday. Weekend trading is becoming more prevalent at popular beach resorts near the larger urban areas; in the cities, many shops and malls are open seven days a week. Most offices and all banks are closed on Saturdays, Sundays, and statutory holidays. Banking hours are 9:30 a.m. to 4:30 p.m., Monday to Friday.

³¹FOREIGN TRADE

New Zealand's trade per capita and as a percentage of GNP is among the highest in the world. New Zealand produces a large amount of food, including meat, dairy products, fruits and nuts, and fish. Other exports include live animals, metals, chemicals, and mechanical and electrical machinery and equipment.

New Zealand imported US$30.24 billion worth of goods and services in 2008, while exporting US$33.24 billion worth of goods and services. Major import partners in 2009 were Australia, 18.4%; China, 15.1%; the United States, 10.5%; Japan, 7.2%; Germany, 4.2%; and Singapore, 4.1%. Its major export partners were Australia, 23.4%; the United States, 9.6%; China, 9.2%; Japan, 7.1%; and the United Kingdom, 4.2%.

While in the mid 1970s more than 70% of export receipts derived from meat, dairy products, and wool, in the decades that followed this figure declined, and manufactured goods and forest products represented an increasing share of the total.

³²BALANCE OF PAYMENTS

In 2010 New Zealand had a foreign trade surplus of US$1.3 billion, amounting to 3.1% of GDP.

³³BANKING AND SECURITIES

The Reserve Bank of New Zealand, established in 1933, exercises control over monetary circulation and credit. It is the bank of issue, handles all central government banking transactions, manages the public debt, and administers exchange control regulations. The Reserve Bank of New Zealand Amendment Act (1973) empowers the Bank to regulate credit from all sources and requires it to make loans (as the minister of finance may determine) in order to ensure continued full employment.

New Zealand's financial services sector is dominated by the commercial banks, leaving only a minor role for nonbank finance companies and savings institutions. In part this reflects the impact of deregulation since the mid-1980s. Before 1984, the financial sector was highly segmented with tight government controls on what different institutions could offer. (For example, only trading banks could offer checking accounts to clients.) The easing of regulations means that there are now only two formal categories of

Balance of Payments – New Zealand (2010)

(In millions of US dollars)

Current Account		**-4,994.0**
Balance on goods		2,344.0
Imports	-29,539.0	
Exports	31,883.0	
Balance on services		-310.0
Balance on income		-7,000.0
Current transfers		-29.0
Capital Account		**2,162.0**
Financial Account		**2,824.0**
Direct investment abroad		-573.0
Direct investment in New Zealand		701.0
Portfolio investment assets		-2,331.0
Portfolio investment liabilities		4,685.0
Financial derivatives		…
Other investment assets		-990.0
Other investment liabilities		1,332.0
Net Errors and Omissions		**855.0**
Reserves and Related Items		**-848.0**

(…) data not available or not significant.

SOURCE: *Balance of Payment Statistics Yearbook 2011,* Washington, DC: International Monetary Fund, 2011.

financial institution: registered banks and other financial institutions. However, both can offer a wide range of financial and banking services. To be defined as a bank, a financial institution must register with the central Reserve Bank and meet a range of eligibility criteria, such as minimum capital adequacy, experience in the financial intermediation industry, and a commitment to stability of the financial system. The number of registered banks peaked at 24 in 1994; in 2010 there were 19.

A number of bank mergers have increased the concentration of total banking assets in foreign ownership. In 2010 over 90% of total banking assets were foreign-owned, compared with 65% in 1990. The New Zealand banking industry is increasingly influenced by developments in Australia, since Australian banking groups control over two-thirds of banking assets in New Zealand.

In 2008, the money market rate, the rate at which financial institutions lend to one another in the short term, was 8.15%. The discount rate, the interest rate at which the central bank lends to financial institutions in the short term, was 8.25%.

The Stock Exchange Association of New Zealand, the forerunner to the New Zealand Stock Exchange (NZSE), was founded in 1915. In May 2003, the NZSE became the New Zealand Exchange Limited (NZX). The stock exchanges in Auckland, Wellington, Christchurch, Dunedin, and Invercargill are members of the NZX, with headquarters in Wellington. The main functions of the New Zealand Exchange Limited (NZX) are to provide an orderly market for the trading and transfer of securities, to protect investors' interests, and to ensure that the market is fully informed.

Official listing is granted to companies that comply with the Exchange's requirements. These do not impose qualifications as to share capital but do provide that the company must be of sufficient magnitude and its shareholding sufficiently well distributed to ensure a free market for its shares. Subject to the recommendation and approval of the stock exchange nearest to the registered offices, companies may secure unofficial listing for their shares. All transactions in shares quoted in the unofficial list are subject to special brokerage rates. As of 2009, there were 233 companies listing 213 securities worth US$49.024 billion on the NZX. In November 2011, the NZSX 50 Index stood at NZD3,322. Its 52 week range was NZD3,055.09–3,584.46. New Zealand is advantageously placed, since its trading day opens before the US market closes and before the Asian and Australian markets open.

The IMF reports that in 2008, currency and demand deposits—an aggregate commonly known as M1—were equal to US$18.379 billion. In that same year, M2—an aggregate equal to M1 plus savings deposits, small time deposits, and money market mutual funds—was US$54.008 billion.

³⁴INSURANCE

New Zealand has one of the world's highest ratios of value of life insurance policies to national income. Life insurance offices mobilize long-term household savings in conjunction with the provision of life insurance coverage and are also closely associated with the management of pension and superannuation funds. The long-term contractual nature of household-sector savings through life insurance offices gives them the capacity to acquire long-term government and corporate debt instruments and to take equity positions in commercial property and company shares. In addition, they may provide mortgage financing to policy holders. Gen-

eral insurance companies have substantial funds available for investment to cover claims outstanding and unexpired risks. These funds are available on a short-term basis and are invested mainly in marketable securities and liquid assets. New Zealand has a no-fault compensation scheme for personal injury, established in 1992 under the Accident Rehabilitation and Compensation Insurance Act of 1992. All people, including visitors, are eligible for the benefits. Under the same act, however, the right to sue for compensation was abolished. Additional personal injury can be purchased from insurers.

Like its Australian counterpart, the New Zealand insurance market is one of the most competitive in the world, with some 50 general insurers and the same number of life insurers. In 2010, the value of all direct insurance premiums written totaled US$3.995 billion, of which nonlife premiums accounted for US$2.673 billion. New Zealand's top nonlife insurer that same year was IAG New Zealand, which had gross written nonlife premiums of US$969 million.

³⁵PUBLIC FINANCE

In 2010 the budget of New Zealand included US$56.24 billion in public revenue and US$62.18 billion in public expenditures. The budget deficit amounted to 5.3% of GDP. Public debt was 25.5% of GDP, with US$81.1 billion of the debt held by foreign entities.

The government budget for fiscal year 2009/2010 showed outlays by function as follows: economic development, 16.3%; education, 17.7%; government administration, 2%; health, 40.5%; infrastructure, 11.7%; law and order, 12.3%; research, science, and technology, 1.7%; and social services, 7.7%. The preceding figures total more than 100% because they do not take into account various adjustments and line by line review savings.

³⁶TAXATION

Effective with the 2012 taxation year, the income tax rate for corporations, including subsidiaries of overseas corporations, was

Public Finance – New Zealand (2007)

(In millions of New Zealand dollars, central government figures)

Revenue and Grants	**65,859**	**100.0%**
Tax revenue	56,207	85.3%
Social contributions	101	0.2%
Grants	…	…
Other revenue	9,551	14.5%
Expenditures	**60,247**	**100.0%**
General public services	6,484	10.8%
Defense	1,948	3.2%
Public order and safety	3,021	5.0%
Economic affairs	5,064	8.4%
Environmental protection	…	…
Housing and community amenities	1,246	2.1%
Health	10,003	16.6%
Recreational, culture, and religion	1,977	3.3%
Education	10,058	16.7%
Social protection	20,446	33.9%

(…) data not available or not significant.

SOURCE: *Government Finance Statistics Yearbook 2010*, Washington, DC: International Monetary Fund, 2010.

28%, applied to aggregate income. There were also tax incentives for exporters. Generally, capital gains were not taxed, although gains from the sale of personal property that was related to a person's business or where the property was acquired for resale could be taxed as business income. Dividends were subject to a withholding tax of 30%, with interest and royalty income, and payments made to contractors subject to a withholding rate of 15%. Earnings were taxed in one combined general income and social security tax, which for wage and salary earners was deducted by the employer on a pay-as-you-earn basis (called PAYE), with annual adjustments The fringe benefits tax (FBT) was payable quarterly by employers on the value of fringe benefits provided to employees and shareholders. Employers could choose to pay a flat rate of 49.25% or fully or partially attribute the value of the fringe benefits to the individual's income and pay at the appropriate rate. Capital gains were charged as the same rate as other income.

Effective with the 2012 tax year, New Zealand had a progressive personal income tax with a top rate of 33%. In addition there was a system of low-income rebates that included, in addition to standard deductions for the taxpayer and dependents, rebates for housekeeping or child-care expenses, and tuition. There were also rebates for certain dividend and interest income, life insurance premiums, and contributions to retirement funds.

The main indirect tax is a value-added tax (VAT), called the goods and services tax (GST), set at 15% in 2010. Exported goods, goods held overseas, services in connection with temporary imports and exported goods were zero-rated for the GST. Excise taxes were imposed on motor vehicles, gasoline, tobacco products, and alcoholic beverages. The government ratified the Kyoto Protocol on climate change in December 2002, and planned to introduce an appropriate carbon tax, but as of November 2011 had not yet passed the legislation.

Local authorities are largely dependent on property taxes. There are three main systems of rating: (1) capital (land improvements) value; (2) annual value; (3) unimproved value. The actual amount of the rate is fixed by each local authority.

37 CUSTOMS AND DUTIES

Customs taxation is based principally on an ad valorem scale, but specific duties are applied to some goods. Rates of duty payable depend on the country of origin. With the exception of some automotive products, preferential rate scales for the United Kingdom were phased out by 1 July 1977, as a result of that nation's entry into the European Community. In 1978, preferential rates for Commonwealth countries were also discontinued. New Zealand has a long-standing revised generalized system of preferences (GSP) favoring the developing countries. Tariffs range from 0–30%. There is also a goods and services tax (GST) of 15% that applies to Free on Board (FOB; cost of the product, plus all transportation costs from the manufacturer to the port of departure, plus costs of loading the vessel) value.

38 FOREIGN INVESTMENT

Foreign direct investment (FDI) in New Zealand was a net outflow of US$1.26 billion according to World Bank figures published in 2009. FDI represented -0.99% of GDP.

Investment in New Zealand's economy by overseas companies grew substantially after the large-scale privatizations of the late 1980s and 1990s. By March 2010, the total stock of direct investment was NZD371.3 billion, a clear sign of international investor confidence. In contrast, New Zealand's direct investment abroad was NZD125 billion. Australia, with NZD128.65 billion in investments in March 2010, was the largest investor in New Zealand; its investments make up 34.6% of the total investments. Australia, the United Kingdom, and the United States together make up 68.4% of the total investments. Other major investors include the Netherlands, Germany, Singapore, and Japan.

The legal framework for FDI in New Zealand is laid out in the Overseas Investment Act of 2005, administered by the Overseas Investment Office (OIO). The act was designed to protect sites of special historic, cultural, or environmental significance while at the same time encouraging investment important to the economy. Under the regulations an overseas person must obtain consent to acquire or establish 25% or more ownership in any New Zealand business; property worth more than US$100 million; "sensitive land," for instance, land that is or includes foreshore or seabed; or certain fishing quotas.

39 ECONOMIC DEVELOPMENT

Economic policy is implemented through taxation, Reserve Bank interest rates, price and monopoly controls, and import and export licensing. From 1958 to the mid 1970s, import controls were employed to correct deficits in the balance of payments. The government began an industrial restructuring program focused on certain industries, such as textiles, footwear, automobiles, and electronics, whose domestic prices were much higher than those of foreign substitutes, with the aim of reducing the protection granted such products. The government gradually liberalized import controls, and by 1981 about 79% of private imports to New Zealand were exempt from licensing.

In June 1982, in an effort to control mounting inflation, the government announced a freeze on wages, prices, rents, and dividends. The freeze was lifted in March 1984, temporarily reimposed by a new Labour government, and then terminated late in 1984. In March 1985, the New Zealand dollar was floated as part of a broad-based deregulation of the economy. The Reserve Bank has not intervened since. The termination of the freeze, combined with a devaluation of the dollar, led to a resumption of high inflation, which lasted until the crash of financial markets in October 1987. From this point the government began implementing a strict monetary policy designed to achieve a stable price level. The immediate cost was a sharp rise in unemployment (from 7% to 10.4%), but by 1991 inflation had been brought down to the low levels that have prevailed since. The target set by the government is a range between 1% and 3% per year, though it was at 4% in 2000. It dropped after that year, but was estimated to have risen to 4.5% in 2011.

Also from the mid-1980s, the New Zealand government has embarked on a major restructuring program to transform the economy from an agrarian economy dependent on preferences in the British market to a competitive and more industrialized free market economy with per capita incomes on par with the leading industrialized nations. Consequently, New Zealand has been changed from being one of the most regulated in the OECD to one of the most deregulated.

The Labour-Alliance government elected in November 1999 set as its goals the transformation of New Zealand into a competitive, knowledge-based economy with emphasis on the development of high skills, high employment, and high value-added production. Monetary policy remains guided by the Reserve Act of 1989, which aimed at maintaining price stability. Fiscal policy is guided by the framework set out in the Fiscal Responsibility Act of 1994. Specific goals include keeping gross governmental debt below 30% of GDP, holding government expenditures to around 35% of GDP, and running an operating surplus in order to build up a fund (the New Zealand Superannuation Fund or NZS Fund) to meet the future costs of publicly provided retirement income. The major foci of the government's economic policy have been building conditions for enhancing New Zealand's sustainable economic growth rate and making it back into the top half of the OECD in terms of per capita income.

In 2006, economic transformation became one of the government's main objectives for the next decade. The main priorities of the program were improving broadband services, developing innovative responses to environmental issues, increasing workplace skills, and making companies globally competitive. Of concern is the population's historically low savings rate. The program also seeks to position Auckland as a world-class city through the development of globally competitive firms.

In furtherance of these goals, the 2008 budget devoted money to facilitate high speed broadband in urban areas and to extend the reach of broadband into underserved regions. It also allocated almost NZD2 billion in operating expenditure and NZD1.7 billion in capital expenditure to economic transformation. Also in 2008, the government signed a Free Trade Agreement with China and reached an agreement with Toll Holdings Ltd for the purchase of Toll New Zealand's rail and ferry business.

New Zealand's processed food industry developed rapidly in the first decade of the 21st century. Infant formula exports, for example, grew from US$27 million in 2000 to US$476 million in 2010, demonstrating a compound annual growth rate of 34%. In 2010 the government set a goal of tripling its food and beverage exports by 2025. New Zealand was seen to be in the process of transitioning from feeding the west to feeding an Asian-Pacific market, trending toward products meeting that market's demand.

A free trade agreement with India was being negotiated in 2011, with implementation expected for 2012. The agreement aims to treble commerce between New Zealand and India by 2015.

40 SOCIAL DEVELOPMENT

A dual system of universal and social assistance is provided to all residents. Old age pensions have been in place since 1898. The New Zealand Superannuation (NZS) is the flat-rate public pension to be available to all New Zealand residents aged 65 or older who have met residency requirements. The New Zealand Superannuation Fund was created to reduce the tax burden associated with NZS. Investment in the fund began in 2003. In July 2007, the government made a new program, known as KiwiSaver, available to citizens for retirement savings. KiwiSaver is a subsidized contribution retirement savings plan offered by private-sector providers; it was modified in 2011 to reduce government subsidies and increase private contributions. As of 2009, NZS represented approximately 4% of GDP and was the government's largest single budget item. As the population ages, the cost of NZS was projected to rise to 6.9% of GDP by 2050.

In addition to retirement benefits, the government pays benefits for unemployment, sickness, and emergencies; and to widows, orphans, families, invalids, and minors. Medical benefits include medical, hospital, and pharmaceutical payments.

Work injury compensation legislation provides for dual universal and compulsory insurance systems. The plan is financed by insurance premiums paid by employers and the self-employed and by a contribution from general revenue. Maternity benefits are provided for women for six months. There are extensive benefits for families including a child disability allowance, low income family support, and child, parental, and family tax credits.

Although prohibited by law, discrimination in the workplace still exists. Women continue to earn less than men, and sexual harassment is a serious problem. The Ministry of Women's Affairs aggressively addresses these issues. Domestic violence and abuse is a growing concern, although the law penalizes spousal rape. The law broadened the definition of domestic violence to include various kinds of psychological abuse. The government provides support to victims of domestic violence.

The government respects the human rights of its citizens. It also protects the rights of citizens living in the territories of Tokelau, Niue, and the Cook Islands.

41 HEALTH

According to the CIA, life expectancy in New Zealand was almost 81 years in 2012. The country spent 9.7% of its GDP on healthcare, amounting to US$2,634 per person. There were 24 physicians, 109 nurses and midwives, and 62 hospital beds per 10,000 inhabitants. The fertility rate was 2.1, while the infant mortality rate was 4.72 per 1,000 live births. In 2008 the maternal mortality rate, according to the World Bank, was 14 per 100,000 births. It was estimated that 89% of children were vaccinated against measles. The CIA calculated HIV/AIDS prevalence in New Zealand to be about 0.1% in 2009.

The New Zealand Public Health and Disability Act 2000 allowed for the creation of District Health Boards (DHS). As of 2008, there were 21 DHBs functioning in the country. The DHBs provide and/or fund health and disability services in their district. The DHBs are supervised by the Ministry of Health and are charged with implementing the New Zealand Health Strategy and the New Zealand Disability Strategy. The goals of the strategies include reduction of smoking, obesity, violence in relationships, and suicide attempts; minimization of harm caused by alcohol and illicit drugs; reduction of the impact of cancer, cardiovascular disease, and diabetes; improvement of nutrition and oral health; and encouragement of increased physical activity.

Public hospitals are managed under the supervision of the Ministry of Health by local hospital boards, whose members are elected; all costs are borne by the state. Private hospital costs are partly paid for by the state; additional fees may be claimed from patients. Voluntary welfare organizations make valuable contributions to public health and are assisted by grants from public funds. Most physicians practice under the National Health Service, established by the Social Security Act of 1938, but private practice outside the scheme is permitted.

The health of the Maori people, although greatly improved over recent decades, is still not on a par with that of the general population.

⁴²HOUSING

In 2006 it was stated that approximately 20,000 new homes were built each year, with about 80% separate, single family houses. Since that time there have been busy periods of new construction and rebuilding activity due to the heavy earthquake damage of 2010. About 66.9% of all dwellings are owner occupied. The average household has 2.7 people. The average private dwelling has three bedrooms, a living room, dining room, kitchen, laundry, bathroom, toilet, and garage. Most units are built of wood and have sheet-iron or tiled roofs. The estimated number of dwellings nationwide at the end of 2011 was 1,643,200; this figure does not take into account the Canterbury earthquakes, which resulted in a decrease in permanent structures and an increase in temporary structures.

In July 2008, housing prices remained 1.4% below their level in July 2007. The central bank governor Alan Bollard predicted that housing prices would decline by 7.7% during 2008. In 2011, modest recovery in housing prices was expected.

⁴³EDUCATION

Education in New Zealand is compulsory for 10 years for children between ages 6 and 16, although most children attend school from the age of 5. Many children also attend some type of pre-school program. Public primary and secondary schools are administered by district education boards (or boards of governors) and school committees (the latter elected by householders), under the authority of the Ministry of Education. Kindergartens are run either by private persons or by voluntary organizations with partial state subsidies. Primary education lasts for eight years and is given at primary and intermediate schools (the latter giving the last two years of primary education). Secondary education covers five years of study and is offered through general secondary schools, technical high schools, or consolidated schools for pupils who live in rural areas. Evening classes are given by technical and secondary schools, and adult education classes are offered by the universities. Most state schools are coeducational, but some private schools are not. New Zealand has about 2,300 state primary schools and 60 privately owned schools. At the secondary level, there are 315 state-run schools and 15 private schools. The academic year runs from February to November. The student-to-teacher ratio for primary school was at about 14.5 in 2010; the ratio for secondary school was about 12.8.

In 2008 the World Bank estimated that 99% of age-eligible children in New Zealand were enrolled in primary school. Secondary enrollment for age-eligible children stood at 91%. Tertiary enrollment was estimated at 78%. Of those enrolled in tertiary education, there were 100 male students for every 148 female students. Overall, the CIA estimated that New Zealand had a literacy rate of 99%.

Attendance at vocational schools has grown tremendously. For children in isolated areas, there is a public Correspondence School of New Zealand that provides distance learning. In some regions there are special state primary and secondary schools for Maori children, but most Maori children attend public schools. Private primary and secondary schools are operated by individuals and religious bodies. Since 1975, under new legislation, many private schools have been voluntarily integrated into the public system.

There are seven universities, all operating under the aegis of the New Zealand Qualifications Authority: the University of Auckland, University of Waikato (at Hamilton), Massey University (at Palmerston North), Victoria University of Wellington, University of Canterbury (at Christchurch), and University of Otago (at Dunedin). All universities offer courses in the arts, social sciences, commerce, and science. Lincoln University in Christchurch offers degrees in such subjects as agriculture, commerce, environmental management, landscape architecture, and recreation management. Law is offered at Auckland, Waikato, Victoria, Canterbury, and Otago, and medicine at Auckland and Otago. There are 24 polytechnic institutions. There are evening classes for adults interested in continuing their education at secondary schools, institutes and community centers. University tuition fees are low, and financial assistance is given to applicants who have passed special qualifying examinations.

As of 2007, public expenditure on education was estimated at 6.1% of GDP. In 2009 public spending on education accounted for 17.7% of total government expenditures.

⁴⁴LIBRARIES AND MUSEUMS

The Alexander Turnbull National Library of New Zealand was founded in 1966 by the amalgamation of three state libraries and service divisions. It contains a general lending collection of over 530,000 volumes, plus a large number of materials in special collections. Its Extension Division provides services to public and school libraries throughout the country, and the Library School offers courses for the training and certification of librarians. The two largest university libraries are at the University of Auckland (1.6 million volumes) and the University of Canterbury at Christchurch (571,000). The largest public library systems are in Auckland, Christchurch, Dunedin, and Wellington.

Outstanding art galleries and museums are the Auckland Art Gallery (European and New Zealand paintings); the Canterbury Museum, Christchurch (ornithology, anthropology, and history); the Dunedin Public Art Gallery (paintings, period furniture, and china); the Otago Museum, Dunedin (ethnography, classical antiquities, ceramics); and the Museum of New Zealand in Wellington (botany, ethnology, history). The nation's largest collection of Maori and Polynesian artifacts is found in the Auckland War Memorial Museum, which was founded in 1852. There is also a Melanesian Mission House highlighting the Christian conversion of the indigenous peoples. There are hundreds of other historical and anthropological museums and sites throughout the country.

⁴⁵MEDIA

New Zealand's domestic and international telecommunications systems are considered to be excellent. In 2010 the CIA reported that there were 1.87 million telephone landlines in New Zealand, and that mobile phone subscriptions averaged 109 per 100 people. International service is by submarine cable to Fiji and Australia, and by satellite ground stations. There were 124 FM radio stations, 290 AM radio stations, and 4 shortwave radio stations. Internet users numbered 83 per 100 citizens. Prominent newspapers in 2010, with circulation numbers listed parenthetically, included the

New Zealand Herald (210,910), the *Dominion Post* (175,000), and the *Press* (91,111), as well as 26 other major newspapers. Weeklies based in Auckland included the *Sunday Star Times, Sunday News,* and *The New Zealand Listener;* Dunedin was served by the *Dunedin Star Weekender.*

The national broadcasting system is united under one central board, the New Zealand Broadcasting Corporation. Under its authority are the Radio New Zealand, which broadcasts over three networks, and TVNZ, which operates four national television networks as well as an on-demand computer based system.

The law provides for freedom of expression including free speech and a free press. Aside from the usual British legal limit for libel, the press enjoys complete editorial freedom.

⁴⁶ORGANIZATIONS

Almost all aspects of New Zealand life have their appropriate organizations. A few of the more important ones are the Federated Farmers of New Zealand, the Horticulture New Zealand, the Business New Zealand/Export NZ Alliance, the Returned Servicemen's Association, the Plunket Society (which deals with child welfare), the Royal Society of New Zealand, the New Zealand Medical Association, the New Zealand Press Association, the Institute of Public Administration New Zealand, and the New Zealand Public Service Association.

Important cultural organizations are the New Zealand Symphony Orchestra, the NBR New Zealand Opera, Creative New Zealand Arts Council of New Zealand, the Royal NZ Ballet, the Queen Elizabeth II Arts Council of New Zealand, the New Zealand Academy of Fine Arts, and the Musical Theatre Federation of New Zealand. There are also several associations available for hobbyists.

National youth organizations include the Girl Guides Association of New Zealand, New Zealand Scouting Association, National Council of the YMCA/YWCAs of New Zealand, branches of the Junior Chamber, New Zealand Federation of Young Farmer Clubs, UN Youth Association of New Zealand, and New Zealand Union of Students' Associations. There are numerous sports associations for all ages, including a National Rifle Association.

Social action groups include the National Advisory Council on the Employment of Women, the National Council of Women of New Zealand, and New Zealand Men for Equal Rights Association. Volunteer service organizations, such as the Lions Clubs and Kiwanis International, are also present. International organizations with national chapters include Amnesty International, Greenpeace, Habitat for Humanity, Salvation Army, Caritas, Save the Children Fund, and the Red Cross.

⁴⁷TOURISM, TRAVEL, AND RECREATION

New Zealand draws many thousands of tourists to its shores because of the beauty, diversity, and compactness of its natural attractions and its varied sporting facilities. There are 14 national parks; of these, Fiordland is the largest, with some portions still unexplored. Te Urewera, noted for its forests and bird life, is the park in which early Maori culture is most strongly preserved; Tongariro includes two active volcanoes and is an important ski resort; and Mount Cook National Park includes Tasman Glacier, the largest glacier outside the polar regions. New Zealand has numerous thermal spas, particularly in the Rotorua area, which also offers

Maori villages where traditional arts and crafts may be observed. The Waitomo Cave, on the North Island, is lit by millions of glow-worms and may be toured all year. Lake Taupo and its streams form one of the world's richest trout fishing areas; Christchurch is home to one of the world's finest botanical gardens. Skiing is available on both the North and South Islands, and good deep-sea fishing is enjoyed along the North Island coast. New Zealand has first-class golf courses. Spectator sports include horse racing, football (soccer), cricket, and rugby.

The *Tourism Factbook*, published by the UN World Tourism Organization, reported 2.45 million incoming tourists to New Zealand in 2009; they spent a total of US$4.4 billion. Of those incoming tourists, there were 1.6 million from East Asia and the Pacific. The estimated daily cost to visit Wellington, the capital, was US$355. The cost of visiting other cities averaged US$230.

All overseas visitors need passports valid for at least three months beyond their intended stay in New Zealand. Visas are not required for Australian citizens with Australian passports or nationals of the 50 countries who hold visa waivers. There are no vaccination requirements.

⁴⁸FAMOUS PERSONS

Among New Zealand's best-known statesmen are Sir George Grey (1812–98), governor and later prime minister; Richard John Seddon (1845–1906), prime minister responsible for much social legislation; William Ferguson Massey (1856–1925); and Peter Fraser (1884–1950), World War II prime minister. Robert David Muldoon (1921–92) was prime minister from 1975 to 1984, when David Lange (1942–2005) became the youngest man to hold that office in the 20th century. Sir John Salmond (1862–1924) was an eminent jurist. William Pember Reeves (1857–1932), outstanding journalist, politician, and political economist, was the director of the London School of Economics. Frances Hodgkins (1869–1947) was a highly regarded painter. Katherine Mansfield (Kathleen Beauchamp Murry, 1888–1923), author of many evocative stories, was a master of the short-story form. Other well-known authors include Sylvia Ashton-Warner (1908–84) and Maurice Shadbolt (1932–2004). Two outstanding leaders of the Maori people were Sir Apirana Ngata (1874–1950) and Sir Peter Buck (1880–1951). Sir Truby King (1858–1938) pioneered in the field of child care.

Lord Ernest Rutherford (1871–1937), pioneer in atomic research and 1908 Nobel Prize winner for chemistry, was born in New Zealand. Other scientists include Sir Harold Gillies (1882–1960) and Sir Archibald McIndoe (1900–62), whose plastic surgery methods did much to rehabilitate war victims; Sir Brian G. Barratt-Boyes (1924–2006), a researcher in cardiac-thoracic surgery; and Albert W. Liley (1929–83), a researcher in perinatal psychology. Prominent in the arts have been ballet dancers Alexander Grant (1925–2011) and Rowena Jackson (b. 1926); the singer and actor Inia Watene Te Wiata (1915–71); and the soprano Kiri Te Kanawa (b. 1944). Film actor Russell Crowe (b. 1964) was born in New Zealand. Filmmakers Jane Campion (b. 1954) and Peter Jackson (b. 1961) have both won Academy Awards. In 1993, Campion won the Oscar for best screenplay for her film, *The Piano.* In 2003, Jackson's film, *The Return of the King,* the third film in *The Lord of the Rings* trilogy, won 11 Oscars, 3 for Jackson himself (best picture, best director, and best screenplay). Sir Edmund Percival Hillary (1919–2008) was the conqueror of Mt. Everest. The celebrated political cartoonist David Low (1891–1963) was born in New Zealand.

49 DEPENDENCIES

Cook Islands

The Cook Islands, 15 islands lying between 8° and 23°S and 156° and 167°W, more than 3,220 km (2,000 mi) northeast of New Zealand, were discovered by James Cook in 1773. They became a British protectorate in 1888 and were annexed to New Zealand in 1901. They consist of the Southern Group-8 islands, the largest of which are Rarotonga (6,666 ha/16,472 acres) and Mangaia (5,191 ha/12,827 acres); and the Northern Group-7 islands, varying in size from Penrhyn (984 ha/2,432 acres) to Nassau (121 ha/299 acres). The total area is 241 sq km (93 sq mi). The northern islands are low-lying coral atolls, while the southern islands, including Rarotonga, the administrative seat, are elevated and fertile, and have the greater population. Except for Rarotonga, the islands suffer from lack of streams and wells, and water must be conserved. The islands lie within the hurricane area and sometimes experience destructive storms.

The population (estimated in 2011 at 11,124, down from 20,811 in 2002) is Polynesian and close in language and tradition to the New Zealand Maori. They are converts to Christianity. The islands are visited by government and freight vessels, and interisland shipping services are provided by commercially owned boats. An international airport opened for full services in 1973. There were 6,900 telephone lines and 7,000 cellular phones in use in 2009, and six radio stations, one of which could reach all the islands. In 2009 there was one privately owned television station. There were 2,521 internet hosts and 6,000 Internet users.

Part of New Zealand since 1900, the Cook Islands became internally self-governing on 4 August 1965. The Cook Islands Constitution Act of 1964 established the island group as wholly self-ruling but possessed of common citizenship with New Zealand. New Zealand exercises certain responsibilities for the defense and external affairs of the islands, in consultation with the Cook Islands government.

A parliamentary type of government, like New Zealand's, characterizes the new political relationship, with a cabinet composed of a prime minister and six other ministers. The 24-member Legislative Assembly—to which the prime minister and other cabinet members are responsible—is elected by the adult population of the islands every four years and can void the applicability of New Zealand laws to the territory under its jurisdiction. The constitution of the autonomous islands also allows a declaration of independence, if ever this should be the wish of the political leadership. The New Zealand high commissioner is appointed by the New Zealand government. Cook Islands products continue to enter New Zealand freely, and the level of subsidies to the islands from the New Zealand government has persisted.

As of 2010, the New Zealand foreign ministry began consideration of a new plan that could lead to greater efficiency and less bureaucracy in the disbursement of funds to the Cook Islands by redirecting development aid as direct budget support. This would require the Cook Islands to employ an experienced financial secretary who would be given responsibilities to monitor projects that are currently handled by several different officials. The

change would centralize many project financing functions. For instance, instead of a having a dozen different tourism development projects that are monitored and managed individually, the Cook Islands would maintain a single overall tourism program that would provide budgetary support under the oversight of the financial secretary. The change could lead to less bureaucracy, fewer delays in project completion and operations, greater efficiency in monitoring progress on development projects, and greater efficiency in financial transactions. The New Zealand foreign minister was quick to note that this type of budgetary support would still be granted with very specific expectations, so that the Cook Islands government would be able to use funds only as approved by New Zealand.

The economy is based on tourism, pearls, fish, and agriculture. The main agricultural exports are copra and fresh and canned citrus fruit. Total exports were valued at US$4.9 million in 2010, down from US$5.222 million in 2005 and US$9.1 million in 2000. The main imports are foodstuffs, textiles, fuels, timber, and capital goods. In 2009, imports amounted to US$290 million.

Revenue for public finances is derived mainly from import duties and income tax. The 2008–09 budget envisioned revenues of US$72.91 million and expenditures of US$77.71 million. The New Zealand government provided grants and subsidies for capital development in health, education, other social services, economic development, and other purposes, covering one third of the budget.

Free compulsory education is provided by the government at primary and secondary levels for all children between the ages of 6 and 15, and an estimated 95% of the population is literate. All Cook Islanders receive free medical and surgical treatment, and schoolchildren receive free dental care.

Niue

An isolated coral island, Niue is 966 km (600 mi) northwest of the southern Cook Islands, and located at 19°02′ S and 169°52′ W. Niue became a British protectorate in 1900 and was annexed to New Zealand in 1901. Although Niue forms part of the Cook Islands, because of its remoteness and cultural and linguistic differences it has been separately administered. Niue has an area of 258 sq km (100 sq mi). Its population (of Polynesian stock) was 1,311 in 2011, down from 2,134 in 2002, and less than one third the number, 5,194, at the peak in 1966. The population decline was principally due to emigration to New Zealand, where Niueans outnumber those remaining on the island by three to one. Citizens enjoy a relatively high standard of living. Life expectancy for both men and women is 69.5 years, infant mortality is 17.5 per 1000 live births, and 98% of the population is literate.

Niue became self-governing on 19 October 1974, in free association with New Zealand. Under the constitution, the former leader of government became the premier. An assembly of 20 members is elected by universal suffrage; 14 members represent village constituencies, and 6 are elected at large. The constitution provides for New Zealand to exercise various responsibilities for the external affairs and defense of Niue and to furnish economic and administrative assistance.

Niue's soil, although fertile, is not plentiful; arable land is confined to small pockets of soil among the coral rocks, making agriculture difficult, although the economy is based mainly on agriculture. Since there are no running streams, the island is dependent on rainwater. Exports include canned coconut cream, copra, honey, vanilla, passion fruit products, pawpaws, root crops, limes, footballs, postage stamps, and handicrafts; in 2006 income from exports was US$264,000. As of 2008, there were 120 km (72 mi) of road, all of which were paved. A telephone system, with nearly 1,100 main lines as of the 2009, connects the villages, and an airport became fully operational in 1971. In 2004 there were about 600 mobile phones lines in use on the island.

In January 2004 the island suffered extensive damage from a cyclone, requiring several years of rebuilding. Budget deficits are met by the New Zealand government, which also makes grants for capital development. Health services and education are free. Education is compulsory for children 5 to 14 years of age.

The New Zealand government has become increasingly concerned over the amount of money being spent on the territory of Niue, which shows very little potential for an independent sustainable economy. Niue stands as a self-governing state in free association with New Zealand, a status ratified by its 1974 Constitution Act. This means, in effect, that while its defense and external affairs remain the official responsibility of New Zealand, Niue writes its own laws, maintains full executive powers, and, in recent years, has even conducted its own foreign policy. However, New Zealand must provide substantial economic and development assistance for the territory. As a result, Niue receives US$21.5 million in aid each year to support a population of only 1,200. In December 2010, a parliamentary committee of New Zealand introduced the idea of establishing the island as a major retirement village. Committee members noted that retirees could provide a steady flow of cash for local businesses, which could in turn expand to meet the needs of the population and provide greater employment opportunities.

Tokelau Islands

The Tokelau Islands, situated between 8° and 10°S and 171° and 173°W, about 483 km (300 mi) north of Samoa, consist of three atolls, Fakaofo, Nukunonu, and Atafu. Total area is about 12.2 sq km (4.9 sq mi). Each atoll has a lagoon encircled by a number of reef-bound islets varying in length from about 90 m to 6.4 km (100 yards to 4 mi), in width from a few meters to 200 m (3–220 yards), and extending more than 3 m (10 ft) above sea level. Nukunonu is 4.7 sq km (1.9 sq mi), Fakaofo is 4 sq km (1.6 sq mi), and Atafu is 3.5 sq km (1.4 sq mi). All villages are on the leeward side, close to passages through the reefs. Lying in the hurricane belt, the islands have a mean annual rainfall of 305 cm (120 in).

Total population in 2011 was estimated at 1,411, down from 1,760 in 1992. The inhabitants, of Polynesian origin, are British subjects and New Zealand citizens. Formerly part of the Gilbert and Ellice Islands group, the Tokelaus were transferred to New Zealand at the beginning of 1949. The Tokelau Islands Amendment Act 1967 gave Tokelauans the power to deal with distribution of land, but restricted the passage of property to non-indigenous people; land generally passes from generation to generation within families. New Zealand maintains a reserve fund of US$60,000 for seawall projects.

Executive functions are carried out on each atoll by appointed Tokelau mayors, magistrates, clerks, and other officials. An administrative officer based in Samoa coordinates administrative

services for the islands. Samoan is the official language. The question of self-government was first put to a referendum in February 2006, when 60% of voters, short of the two-thirds majority, supported the option of self-government in free association with New Zealand. A second referendum was held in October 2007, with technical assistance from the New Zealand Chief Electoral Office. The outcome, 64.4% voting in favor of self-government in free association with New Zealand, was just short of the two-thirds majority required to change Tokelau's status. Thus, Tokelau remained a non-self-governing territory, as categorized by the UN.

Subsistence farming and the production of copra for export are the main occupations. The total fish catch was estimated to be in the range of 350–375 tons in 2009. Visits are made regularly by New Zealand Air Force planes, and a chartered vessel makes regular trading visits. Sources of revenue are an export duty on coconuts, copra, customs dues, postage stamps, and trading profits.

Government expenditure is devoted mainly to agriculture, the provision of social services, and administrative costs. Annual deficits are met by New Zealand government subsidies. New Zealand's budgetary aid was US$43 million for the three year period 2008–2010. Nutrition and health are reasonably good.

Ross Dependency

The Ross Dependency is defined as all the islands and territories between 160°E and 150°W and south of 60°S. The Ross Dependency includes the Ross Ice Shelf, the Balleny Islands, Scott Island, and other adjacent land and islands. This area of the Antarctic continent was claimed by the United Kingdom in 1923. The UK issued an Order-in-Council that year, assigning the administration of the Ross Dependency to New Zealand. New Zealand collected fees for whaling licenses for the waters around Antarctica until 1928. Three decades later during the International Geophysical Year, the New Zealand government established Scott Base; Sir Edmund Hillary became the leader there. Scott base was located near where the United States had also established a base. (The US base later became McMurdo Station.) The cooperative research undertaken there eventually led to the formation of the Antarctic Treaty.

The area of the Ross Dependency is estimated at 414,400 sq km (160,000 sq mi). It is almost entirely covered by ice and is largely uninhabited. New Zealand activities in the dependency are coordinated and supervised by Officers of the Government of the Ross Dependency, who are appointed annually.

New Zealand criminal law extends to criminal acts committed in the Ross Dependency under the Antarctica Act 1960. Anyone born in the Ross Dependency is a citizen of New Zealand under the New Zealand Citizenship Act 1977. The Territorial Sea, Contiguous Zone and Exclusive Economic Zone Act 1977 was enacted by the New Zealand legislation to establish an economic zone beyond the outer limit of the territorial sea of the Ross Dependency.

50 BIBLIOGRAPHY

Belich, James. *Making Peoples: A History of the New Zealanders, From Polynesian Settlement to the End of the Nineteenth Century.* Honolulu: University of Hawaii Press, 1996.

Bohan, Edmund. *Climates of War, New Zealand in Conflict 1859–69.* Christchurch, New Zealand: Hazard Press, 2005.

Brooking, Tom. *The History of New Zealand.* Westport, CT: Greenwood Press, 2004.

Chatham Islands: Heritage and Conservation. Christchurch, New Zealand: Canterbury University Press, 2008.

Craig, Robert D. *Historical Dictionary of Polynesia.* Lanham, MD: Scarecrow, 2002.

Garden, Donald S. *Australia, New Zealand, and the Pacific: An Environmental History.* Santa Barbara, CA: ABC-CLIO, 2005.

Jackson, Keith, and Alan McRobie. *Historical Dictionary of New Zealand.* Lanham, MD: Scarecrow Press, 2005.

New Zealand Investment and Business Guide: Strategic and Practical Information. Washington, DC: International Business Publications USA, 2012.

Sinclair, Keith. *The Oxford Illustrated History of New Zealand.* 2nd ed. Auckland, New Zealand: Oxford University Press, 2008.

OMAN

Sultanate of Oman
Saltanat 'Uman

CAPITAL: Muscat (Masqat)

FLAG: The flag is red with a broad stripe of white at the upper fly and green at the lower fly. In the upper left corner, white crossed swords overlay a ceremonial dagger.

ANTHEM: *Nashid as-Salaam as-Sutani (Sultan's National Anthem).*

MONETARY UNIT: The Omani riyal (OMR), established in November 1972, is a paper currency of 1,000 baizas. There are coins of 2, 5, 10, 25, 50, 100, 250, and 500 baizas, and notes of 100, 250, and 500 baizas (the last two being replaced by coins) and 1, 5, 10, 20, and 50 riyals. OMR1 = US$2.56410 (or US$1 = OMR0.39) as of 2011.

WEIGHTS AND MEASURES: The metric system was adopted on 15 November 1974. The imperial and local systems are also used.

HOLIDAYS: Accession of the Sultan, 23 July; National Day, 18 November; Sultan's Birthday, 19 November. Eid al-Adha, Islamic New Year (Hijra), Milad an-Nabi, the Prophet's Ascension, and Eid al-Fitr are observed as national holidays

TIME: 4 p.m. = noon GMT. Solar time also is observed.

¹LOCATION, SIZE, AND EXTENT

The Sultanate of Oman is the second-largest country (after Saudi Arabia) on the Arabian Peninsula, with an area of about 309,500 sq km (119,500 sq mi). Comparatively, the area occupied by Oman is approximately the size of New Mexico. Oman's territory includes an exclave on the tip of the Ra's Musandam, which juts into the Strait of Hormuz, and is a vital transit point for crude oil shipments. This is separated from the rest of Oman country by the territory of the United Arab Emirates. Oman is bordered on the N by the Strait of Hormuz, on the NE by the Gulf of Oman, on the E and S by the Arabian Sea, on the SW by Yemen, on the W by Saudi Arabia, and on the NW by Saudi Arabia and the United Arab Emirates. Oman's land boundaries total 1,374 km (854 mi), and its coastline stretches 2,092 km (1,300 mi).

²TOPOGRAPHY

Physically, Oman, except for the Dhofar (Zufar) region, consists of three divisions: a coastal plain, a mountain range, and a plateau. The coastal plain varies in width from 16 km (10 mi) to practically nothing near Muscat, where the hills descend abruptly to the sea. The highest point, Jabal Shams, is at 2,980 meters (9,777 ft) in the Al Jabal range of the north. The plateau has an average height of about 300 m (1,000 ft) and is mostly stony and waterless, extending to the sands of the Ar-Rub' al-Khali. The coastline southward to Dhofar is barren and forbidding. From Salalah, a semicircular fertile plain extends to the foot of a steep line of hills, some 1,500 m (4,920 ft) high, and forms the edge of a stony plateau.

³CLIMATE

Oman has a sub-tropical dry, hot desert climate. It experiences low rainfall and very hot temperatures in the summer months. Daily maximum temperatures often exceed 40°C (104°) between June and September. The climate in the spring and autumn is mostly dry and pleasant with maximum temperatures reaching between 25°C (77°F) and 35°C (95°F) in the daytime and 15°C (59F) and 22°C (72°F) at night.

The Shamal, a hot, dust-laden wind, blows through Oman between March and August. These winds often result in sandstorms. Rainfall tends to occur in short, sudden cloudbursts and thunderstorms. Oman also has experienced cyclones in recent years. In 2007 Cyclone Gonu killed 54 people in Oman and Iran. In 2010 Cyclone Phet killed 16 people.

⁴FLORA AND FAUNA

The World Resources Institute estimated that there were 1,204 plant species in Oman. Oman has a variety of trees, shrubs, and herbs. The date palm grows widely, and the frankincense tree in the Dhofar region grows only in Oman, Yemen, and Somalia.

Oman is home to 74 species of mammals, 483 species of birds, 69 species of reptiles, and 3 species of amphibians. This calculation reflects the total number of distinct species residing in the country, not the number of endemic species. The Arabian leopard, though rare, is indigenous to Oman, and reserves have been set up to protect the Arabian oryx and tahr. Camels, donkeys, and goats roam near roads and towns, and desert life includes the sand cat, fox, desert hare, gerbils, snakes, and geckos. Migratory birds such as the white stork, nightjar, golden oriole, little green bee eaters,

Indian roller, and hoopoe—as well as some eagles—often pause in Oman in the spring and autumn months. Marine life includes tropical fish, jellyfish, sea snakes, corals, sharks, whales, and turtles. A turtle reserve has been established at Ras al-Had.

5ENVIRONMENT

The World Resources Institute reported that Oman had designated 22,000 hectares (54,363 acres) of land for protection as of 2006. Water resources totaled 1 cu km (0.24 cu mi) while water usage was 1.36 cu km (0.326 cu mi) per year. Domestic water usage accounted for 7% of total usage, industrial for 3%, and agricultural for 90%. Per capita water usage totaled 529 cu m (18,681 cu ft) per year. Sandstorms and limited rainfall have made Oman vulnerable to periodic droughts.

In 2011 Oman's greatest environmental issues included rising soil salinity; beach pollution resulting from oil spills; and limited fresh water from natural resources. Oman is party to international treaties on biodiversity, climate change, desertification, hazardous wastes, marine dumping, ozone layer protection, ship pollution, and whaling. The United Nations (UN) reported in 2008 that carbon dioxide emissions totaled 37,289 kilotons.

According to a 2011 report issued by the International Union for Conservation of Nature and Natural Resources (IUCN), threatened species included 9 mammals, 11 birds, 4 reptiles, 26 fish, 26 other invertebrates, and 6 plants. Decrees have been passed to protect endangered species, which include the South Arabian leopard, mountain gazelle, goitered gazelle, Arabian tahr, green sea turtle, hawksbill turtle, and olive turtle. The Arabian Oryx Sanctuary is a UNESCO World Heritage Site.

6POPULATION

The US Central Intelligence Agency (CIA) estimated the population of Oman in 2011 to be approximately 3,027,959, which placed it at number 134 in population among the 196 nations of the world. In 2011 approximately 3.1% of the population was over 65 years of age, with another 31.2% under 15 years of age. The median age in Oman was 24.1 years. There were 1.05 males for every female in the country. The population's annual rate of change was 2.023%. Oman's total population in 2011 included 577,293 non-nationals.

The CIA estimated that 73% of the population lived in urban areas, and that urban populations had an annual rate of change of 2.3%. The largest urban area was Muscat, with a population of 634,000.

7MIGRATION

Estimates of Oman's net migration rate, carried out by the CIA in 2011, amounted to -0.48 migrants per 1,000 citizens. According to the US State Department, about 580,000 non-nationals lived in Oman and comprised the majority of Oman's work force. Most non-nationals were guest workers from India, Pakistan, Bangladesh, Nepal, Sri Lanka, Egypt, Jordan, and the Philippines.

The ongoing Omanization effort to reduce the country's reliance on non-national workers continued through 2011. More than 86% of the public sector labor force was comprised of Omanis in 2009.

8ETHNIC GROUPS

Oman's population consists largely of Arabs and Baluchis. Guest workers are primarily Indian, Pakistani, Bangladeshi, and Sri Lankan.

9LANGUAGES

The official language is Arabic. Urdu, Baluchi, Swahili, Hindi, and several Indian dialects are also spoken, especially in the cities of Muscat and Matrah. English is taught as a second language.

10RELIGIONS

Most Omani citizens (75%) are Muslim and follow either the Sunni or Ibadhi sects, and the sultan is himself a member of the Ibadhi community. About 5% of the Muslim community is Shi'a Muslim; this community is based primarily in the capital area and along the northern coast. About 25% of the population is Hindu or Christian. Members of these latter religious communities are generally naturalized ethnic Indians. There are also small numbers of Buddhists, Sikhs, and Baha'is in Oman.

More than 50 Christian groups are active in the Muscat area. The capital city also hosts three officially recognized Hindu temples and two Sikh temples. Other temples are located at workplaces where there are large followers of the Hindu and Sikh faiths.

The country's basic law declares Islam to be the state religion but protects the right of non-Muslims to practice on the condition that religious rites do not disrupt public order.

Religious groups must register with the Ministry of Endowments and Religious Affairs and gain ministerial approval to practice. Non-Muslims are required to worship publicly only in governmental-approved areas, and these areas generally are located on land donated by the sultan. Muslim children must take part in Islamic studies in schools, but non-Muslims are exempt from this requirement.

11TRANSPORTATION

The CIA reports that Oman has a total of 53,430 km (33,200 mi) of roads, of which 23,223 km (14,430 mi) are paved. The road system is generally well-developed throughout the country and includes a $400 million highway that links the northern and southern regions. Plans were underway to construct four new airports, and passenger and cargo capacity has been increased at the two main international airports at Seeb and Salalah.

There are 130 airports, which transported 2.36 million passengers in 2009 according to the World Bank. Eleven of the airports contained paved runways, and there were three heliports in Oman as of 2011. Seeb International Airport, 30 km (19 mi) northwest of Muscat, is served by numerous international carriers, including Gulf Air, in which Oman holds a 20% interest. A second modern airport, at Salalah in the south, serves domestic flights.

Oman had three major commercial ports as of 2011, and a fourth port was being built and expected to come online in 2012. Port Sultan Qaboos in Muscat serves as the country's main import/export hub. The Port of Salalah in southern Oman is a leading center for container trans-shipments in the Indian Ocean, and the shipping line Maersk serves as its principal customer. This port also is the only port between Europe and Singapore that can accommodate S-Class container vessels. Plans were under way in 2011 to add a new general cargo terminal and liquid jetty to Salalah's facilities. The port also is located adjacent to a free-trade zone. The Port of Sohar, located just outside the Strait of Hormuz, was being expanded as well in 2011. It handles primarily aggregates, minerals, and dry bulk commodities and is located next to a heavy industrial area. The new commercial Port of Duqm was to include a dry dock, shipping repair yard, and fish processing services.

12 HISTORY

Oman's history can be traced to very early times. In Genesis 10:26–30, the descendants of Joktan are said to have migrated as far as Sephar (now Dhofar). The area was already a commercial and seafaring center in Sumerian times, and Phoenicians probably visited the coastal region. Other groups that likely came to the area in ancient times include the Baida and Ariba, Semitic tribes from northern Arabia, now extinct; the first Himyar dynasty from Yemen, which fell to the Persians in the time of Cyrus, about 550 BC; ancient Greek navigators; and the Parthians (174–136 BC).

The entire population was converted to Islam during the 7th century, during the lifetime of Muhammad (570–632), but Oman soon became—and remains today—the center of the Ibadhi sect, which maintained that any pious Muslim could become caliph or imam, and that the imam should be elected. Omani tribes have elected their imams since the second half of the 8th century.

Portuguese warships captured parts of Oman's coastal region beginning in 1508, establishing the first contact with Europe. The Portuguese were expelled in 1650. The Sultan of Oman began resisting Persian attempts to take over the country, and in doing so, conquered Zanzibar, parts of the eastern African coast, and parts of the southern Arabian Peninsula. Ibadhi imams who were elected religious leaders previously had held political control of the country. This control shifted to hereditary sultans who established trading posts on the Persian and Makran coasts (present-day Pakistan). The sultans established a capital in Muscat, and by the early 19th century, Oman was the most powerful state in the Arab world.

French and British powers rivaled for control of Oman through the 18th century, and Oman and the United Kingdom signed several treaties of friendship through the 19th century. The death of Sultan Sa'id bin Sultan al-Busaid in 1856 resulted in a quarrel among his sons over the succession. The British government moved to mediate the power struggle and divided the Omani empire into two principalities in 1861: Zanzibar, and Muscat and Oman. A second dispute erupted in the late 19th century when members of the Ibadhi sect residing in Oman's interior wanted to be ruled by their religious leader, the Imam of Oman, and not the Sultan of Muscat. The Treaty of Seeb in 1920 resolved the conflict by granting the imam autonomous rule of the interior. The conflict, however, resurfaced in 1954 when oil was discovered in the interior. The Sultan of Muscat tried to extend the government's control into the interior, and succeeded in defeating rebels led by the interior's imam in 1959 with British help. After regaining control of the interior, the sultan terminated the Treaty of Seeb and eliminated the imam's authority. The imam went into exile in Saudi Arabia. Meanwhile, the Sultanate of Muscat was proclaimed

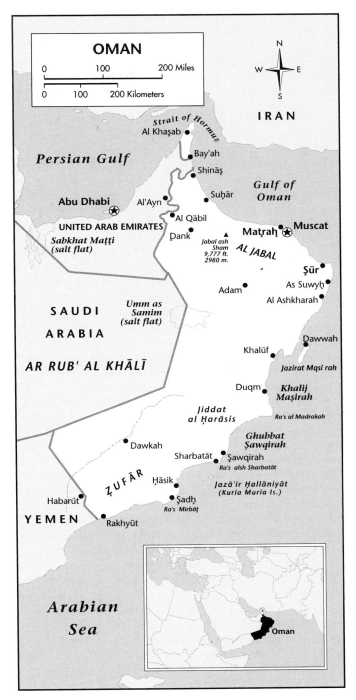

LOCATION: 51°50′ to 59°40′E; 16°40′ to 26°20′ N. BOUNDARY LENGTHS: Total coastline, 2,092 kilometers (1,301 miles); Yemen, 288 kilometers (179 miles); Saudi Arabia, 676 kilometers (420 miles); UAE, 410 kilometers (255 miles).
TERRITORIAL SEA LIMIT: 12 miles.

an independent and sovereign state on 10 March 1962, and was known as Muscat and Oman.

A Marxist inspired revolt erupted in 1964 in Dhofar Province when individuals who sought separation of the Dhofar region from Oman formed the Dhofar Liberation Front. The organization later merged with the Marxist oriented Popular Front for the Liberation of Oman and the Arab Gulf, whose goal was to overthrow all of the traditional regimes in the Persian Gulf region. The organization changed its name to the Popular Front for the Liberation of Oman in 1974, and continued to wage guerrilla war in Dhofar. In the meantime, Qaboos bin Sa'id organized a palace coup against his father, Sultan Sa'id bin Taymur, and seized power on 23 July 1970. Sultan Qaboos, who continued to rule Oman through 2011, renamed Muscat and Oman the Sultanate of Oman, abolished many of the harsh restrictions that his father had established, encouraged Omanis to return to the country, and began modernizing Oman's governmental, educational, and health facilities. He also brought Oman into the UN in 1971 and expanded the armed forces in an effort to end the Dhofar insurgency. That war ended in 1975, and Sultan Qaboos began to take steps to regain the allegiance of the Dhofar people. The sultan also initiated diplomatic relations in 1983 with South Yemen, whose leftist leaders had supported the insurgency, which eased tensions further.

Sultan Qaboos has actively promoted Middle East peace efforts throughout his tenure. Oman became a founding member of the Gulf Cooperation Council in 1971 and signed an agreement with the United Arab Emirates in 1999 to end a long-running border dispute. While maintaining diplomatic relations with Iraq during the 1990–91 Persian Gulf War, Oman also sent troops to join the US-led coalition forces. Oman also has supported the US-led efforts against terrorism following the 11 September 2001 attacks on the United States. Oman also deepened its relationship with the United States through a free trade deal signed in 2006.

Sultan Qaboos generally has maintained strong support among Omanis. In 2005 nearly 100 suspected Islamists were arrested, and 31 individuals were convicted of trying to overthrow the government. The convicted individuals received pardons from the sultan several months later.

In February and March 2011, hundreds of Omani citizens took to the streets in protest against the government, calling for immediate and sweeping political and economic reforms. The demonstrations were inspired by similar protests occurring in Egypt and Libya. While the Omani protests began peacefully, there were a number of clashes with police and several reported deaths, the latter of which were not confirmed by the government. Sultan Qaboos bin Said reshuffled his cabinet, promised to create up to 50,000 new jobs, and promised to grant legislative and regulatory powers to the Council of Oman. The demonstrations continued, however, as protesters called for the trial of all ministers and the abolition of all taxes. The Omani demonstrations called only for government reform, not regime change.

13 GOVERNMENT

Oman is a sultanate with an absolute monarch as leader. Sultan Qaboos al-Said has ruled since 1970 and has the sole authority to amend laws through royal decree. Government-run ministries draft laws, and citizens are able to offer input through the Majlis al-Shura, an 84-member consultative council. Elections took place on 15 October 2011, with more than 1,000 candidates competing for the 84 seats. Seventy candidates were women.

The Majlis al-Shura, created in 1981, had been allowed only an advisory role. However, following riots in early 2011, the sultan promised to expand the power of the council, and a proposed law would grant it full legislative authority. The law would establish a bicameral legislative system, with the Majlis al-Shura serving as

a lower house and the Majlis al-Dawla, whose members were appointed by the sultan, acting as upper chamber.

All Omani citizens over age 21 were eligible to vote in 2011, except for members of the military and security services.

14 POLITICAL PARTIES

There were no legal political parties in Oman, as of 2011. However, some women's organizations and environmental associations have organized and have provided input to the Majlis al-Shura.

15 LOCAL GOVERNMENT

In 2011 the nation was divided into eight administrative regions: Muscat Governorate, Dhofar Governorate, Musandam Governorate, Al-Buraimi Governorate, Al Batinah, Al Dhahirah, Al Dakhliya, Al Shariqiya, and Al Wusta. Within those regions were 61 wilayats (local districts), governed by walis.

Most wilayats are small in area, but can vary greatly in population. The walis is appointed by and responsible to the Minister of Interior. The walis is responsible for resolving local disputes, collecting taxes, and maintaining peace. The governors of Muscat, Musandam, Dhofar, and al-Buraymi are appointed directly by the Sultan and hold Minister of State rank.

16 JUDICIAL SYSTEM

Shari'ah traditionally has provided the foundation for Oman's judicial system. Oman enacted a criminal code in 1974, and its courts are under the jurisdiction of the Ministry of Justice and the Ministry of Endowments and Religious Affairs. A 1996 Basic Statute, Oman's equivalent of a national constitution, ensures judicial independence. However, the sultan's decree placed the court system in 1999 under the financial supervision of the Ministry of Justice.

As of 2010, Oman had established an independent Office of the Public Prosecutor and a Supreme Court, and was considering the use of regional court complexes to house courts of first instance and Shari'ah cases involving family law and inheritance. Many Shari'ah and small criminal court cases are heard at the wilayat level.

Reforms initiated in the wake of 2011 citizen protests led to the abolition on 22 September 2011 of the state security court. This court had reviewed cases involving national security or sensitive criminal matters. Such cases were moved to civilian and military criminal courts.

17 ARMED FORCES

The International Institute for Strategic Studies reported that armed forces in Oman totaled 42,600 members in 2011. The force was comprised of 25,000 from the army, 4,200 from the navy, 5,000 from the air force, 2,000 foreign forces, and 6,400 members of the Royal Household. Armed forces represented 4.3% of the labor force in Oman. Defense spending totaled $8.6 billion and accounted for 11.4% of gross domestic product (GDP).

In a sign of growing Omani-Indian military cooperation, a group of Indian warships traveled to Oman in 2009 to participate in war exercises with the Omani Royal Navy. The five-day training games represented the seventh joint Indian-Omani military exercise and stood as a testament to the increasingly complex and deep military ties between the nations. The Indian Ocean region is considered by military experts to be a growing battleground for naval influence. The United States, India, and, increasingly, China all vie for power in the third-largest body of water in the world. Analysts have noted that in reaching out to smaller regional powers like Oman, India seeks to solidify its influence in the area.

18 INTERNATIONAL COOPERATION

On 7 October 1971, Oman gained membership in the UN; it belongs to ESCWA and several nonregional specialized agencies, such as the FAO, ILO, UNESCO, UNIDO, the World Bank, and the WHO. Oman also participates in the WTO, the Arab Bank for Economic Development in Africa, the Arab Fund for Economic and Social Development, the Arab Monetary Fund, the Organization of the Islamic Conference (OIC), G-77, the Gulf Cooperation Council, and the Arab League.

Oman and the United States signed a free trade agreement on 19 January 2006 that took effect on 1 January 2009. Oman also has increased trade with China since 2007 and has been making diplomatic overtures to Central Asian republics. In 2011 Oman was involved in a joint oil pipeline project with Kazakhstan.

Oman has been a party to a number of international environmental initiatives on biodiversity, climate change, desertification, hazardous wastes, marine laws, ozone layer protection, ship pollution and whaling.

19 ECONOMY

The GDP rate of change in Oman, as of 2010, was 4.2%. Inflation stood at 3.256%. Unemployment, last reported in 2004, was 15%. Oman was regarded in 2011 as a middle-income economy heavily dependent on oil and natural gas resources. Since the discovery of oil in Oman in 1964, the oil industry has been the most important sector of the economy. Oman's oil exports in 2010 totaled $23.925 billion, and oil and gas revenues were expected to account for 81 percent of the government's 2011 revenue.

Oman's oil and gas resources are dwindling, which has prompted the government to seek foreign investment in other sectors including industry, data technology, tourism, transportation, and higher education. The country is developing its natural gas resources, metal industrial manufacturing, petrochemical development, and international transshipment ports. The government hoped to reduce the oil sector's contribution to GDP from about 40% to 9% by 2020. Enhanced oil recovery techniques also have helped Oman increase its oil production. Increased global oil prices through 2010 and 2011 provided the country with additional economic security. As of 2011, Oman's proven oil reserves were estimated at 5.5 billion barrels. Proven reserves of natural gas were 30 trillion cu ft.

The government has used its surplus of oil revenues both to diversify the economy and reduce its dependence on expatriate labor. The Omanization campaign, promoted since 2000, has sought to increase educational and employment opportunities for Omanis, in an effort to replace expatriate workers. The Ministry of Manpower reported that 985,715 foreign workers were employed in March 2011 in Oman's private sector, and that these workers and their families made up about one-third of the country's population. Demonstrations in early 2011 increased the call to employ Omanis, and companies were encouraged to invest in training programs.

20 INCOME

The CIA estimated that in 2010 the GDP of Oman was $75.84 billion. The CIA defines GDP as the value of all final goods and services produced within a nation in a given year and computed on the basis of purchasing power parity (PPP) rather than value as measured on the basis of the rate of the exchange based on current dollars. The per capita GDP was estimated at $25,438. It was estimated that agriculture accounted for 1.6% of GDP, industry 51%, and services 47.5%. The International Monetary Fund estimated Oman's share of the world's total GDP to be 0.11% in 2010.

According to the World Bank, remittances from Omani citizens living abroad totaled $39 million or about $13 per capita and accounted for approximately 0.1% of GDP.

21 LABOR

As of 2007 Oman had a total labor force of 968,800 people, about 60% of which was comprised of non-nationals.

The government has extended the right to form unions to workers in the private sector, but this right does not extend to members of the armed forces, public security institutions, governmental workers, or domestic employees. Nearly 100 unions were in existence in late 2010. Unions were required to notify the government of meetings at least one month in advance, and to notify employers of an intention to strike three weeks in advance. Despite laws prohibiting forced or compulsory labor, the US State Department reported incidents of such practices, particularly among domestic services and low-skilled workers in the construction, agricultural, and service sectors.

Child labor laws prohibit individuals under age 15 from working. Employment hours are limited to 6 a.m. to 6 p.m., with six-hour shifts for those between 15 and 18 years of age.

The minimum wage of OMR140 ($360) per month does not provide an adequate income for workers and their families. The minimum wage does not apply to all occupations, and human rights agencies report cases of migrant laborers being forced to work more than 12 hours a day for as little as OMR30 ($78) a month. The private sector workweek is 40 to 45 hours, with Thursday afternoon through Friday as a rest period. Government workers generally follow a 35-hour work week.

22 AGRICULTURE

Although agriculture accounted for only 1.6% of GDP in 2010, Oman had a strong agricultural society prior to the discovery of oil in 1964. Approximately 35% of the population remained engaged in subsistence agriculture as of 2011. Roughly 6% of the total land was being farmed, and the country's major crops included dates, limes, bananas, alfalfa, and vegetables. In 2009 cereal production amounted to 16,264 tons, fruit production 326,840 tons, and vegetable production 219,249 tons.

The main agricultural region of Oman is the coastal Batinah plain, which extends north–west from Muscat to the United Arab Emirates border. Dates, limes, mangoes, bananas and other fruits are grown in this area for export, while vegetables such as tomatoes, onions, and eggplants are grown for local consumption. Dates, fruits, and vegetables are also grown in the interior, and coconut palms flourish on the southern coastal plain near Salalah.

Oman's Ministry of Agriculture and Fisheries promotes the development of agriculture in the country and has embarked on projects to identify and cultivate the most suitable strains of agricultural products grown in Oman.

23 ANIMAL HUSBANDRY

The UN Food and Agriculture Organization (FAO) reported that Oman dedicated 1.7 million hectares (4.2 million acres) to permanent pasture or meadow in 2009. During that year, the country tended 4.2 million chickens and 325,500 head of cattle. Oman also produced 450 tons of cattle hide.

The Ministry of Agriculture and Fisheries describes Oman as the leading livestock producer in the Persian Gulf region. Much of the livestock production is aimed at domestic consumption, and the government is working to increase goat production in order to reduce reliance on imports. Cows, goats, sheep, and camels are raised in Oman.

24 FISHING

Oman had 56 decked commercial fishing boats in 2008. The annual capture totaled 145,631 tons according to the UN FAO. The export value of seafood totaled $102.6 million. Fishing was a traditional way of life in Oman before the discovery of oil, and the government is encouraging investment in fish production as part of its campaign to diversify the economy. The waters of the Gulf of Oman are rich in sardines, mackerel, shrimp, lobster, crayfish, tuna, barracuda, grouper, and sharks. Fisheries have been established for the cultivation of kingfish, tuna, shrimp, lobster, and abalone, among other fish and shellfish.

25 FORESTRY

The use of wood for fuel and overgrazing by goats had depleted the forests of Oman as of 2011. According to the UN FAO, Oman produced 5,594 tons of wood charcoal and about 84,000 tons of paper and recovered paper products in 2010. Imports of forest products totaled $155 million.

26 MINING

Petroleum and natural gas dominate Oman's economy. Large deposits of copper have been discovered northwest of Muscat, with other deposits also discovered at Hajl al-Safi and at Rakah, in Ibri; mined copper production totaled just 1,500 metric tons in 2009. An estimated 16,000 metric tons of smelted copper was produced from copper ore imports. In 2009, 28 kg of gold was produced, down from 49 kg in 2008 and 125 kg in 2007. Silver production in 2009 was 15 kg. At the end of 2009, Oman had about 500 active industrial minerals operations, including 150 for landfill material, 183 for crushed stone, 71 for chromium, 57 for marble, 4 each for clay, gypsum, and laterite, 3 for sandstone, 2 for limestone, and 1 for salt. Output of chromium (gross weight) in 2009 was 636,482 metric tons, down from 859,748 metric tons in 2008. Sand and gravel production in 2009 was estimated at 77.1 million metric tons, while marble output in 2009 totaled 587,892 metric tons. Oman also produced gypsum, salt, sulfur and hydraulic cement.

27 ENERGY AND POWER

The CIA reported that Oman produced 17.63 billion kWh of electricity in 2009 and consumed 13.25 billion kWh, or 4,502 kWh per capita. All energy came from fossil fuels. Per capita oil consumption was 5,903 kg. Oil production totaled 867,900 barrels of oil a day in 2010, and consumption was 142,000 barrels a day. Natural gas production totaled 24.76 billion cu m per day, and consumption was 14.72 billion cu m.

Oman's reserves of oil and natural gas are modest in size when compared to other countries in the Middle East. However, the country's importance to the world's oil markets lies in its geographic location overlooking the Strait of Hormuz. Oman is not a member of the Organization of the Petroleum Exporting Countries (OPEC) but is a leader in IPEC, the main independent petroleum exporter's organization.

Oman's proven oil reserves totaled 5.5 billion barrels (2011), most of which were located in its central and northern regions. Oman's primary customers are China, Japan, South Korea, Thailand, and the United Arab Emirates.

In 2010 Oman announced a plan to increase daily oil production to 900,000 barrels per day within two years. The plan was announced as new technologies became available to allow oil companies to more efficiently squeeze resources from aging and diminished oil fields. The 900,000-barrel-per-day target represented a long-term, plateau objective for Oman.

28 INDUSTRY

Industry accounts for 51% of Oman's GDP. The main industry sectors are crude oil production and refining, natural and liquefied natural gas production, construction, cement, copper, steel, chemicals, and optic fiber. The industrial production growth rate was 4.6% in 2010.

The Omani government continued to diversify its industrial base through 2011 and has provided financial support to sectors based on renewable resources. This diversification effort aimed to reduce the sultanate's reliance on oil and natural gas, both of which are non-renewable resources. New areas of focus were agriculture and fishing, tourism, and light industry.

29 SCIENCE AND TECHNOLOGY

The World Bank reported in 2009 that there were no patent applications in science and technology in Oman. Sultan Qaboos University, founded in 1985, encourages research in environmental and geological studies, water, oil and gas, and biotechnology. High technology exports totaled $18 million in 2008, according to The World Bank and made up 0.7% of the country's manufactured exports.

30 DOMESTIC TRADE

A free trade agreement between Oman and the United States went into effect in 2009. Since then, domestic and international trade organizations have noted Oman's efforts to make its business environment more hospitable. A number of multi-national restaurant chains and retailers operate in the country, and the government actively encourages foreign investment.

Businesses generally operate from 8 a.m. to 5 p.m., Saturday through Wednesday, and close for lunch between 1 p.m. and 2:30 p.m. Government offices are open 8 a.m. to 2 p.m. Banks generally are open 8 a.m. to 12:30 p.m., Sunday through Thursday. Automated teller machines are available 24 hours and accept most international bank cards.

³¹FOREIGN TRADE

Oman imported $19.3 billion worth of goods and services in 2008, while exporting $36.12 billion worth of goods and services. Major import partners in 2009 were the United Arab Emirates, 23.8%; Japan, 15%; the United States, 6.5%; India, 5.9%; China, 4.8%; and Germany, 4.3%. Major export partners were China, 20.1%; South Korea, 15.5%; Japan, 12.5%; UAE, 11.6%; India, 9.6%; and Thailand, 7.9%.

Oman traditionally has had a considerable trade surplus because of its oil exports. The surplus fell 32% in 2009—due to mounting inflation—but continued to rise in 2010 and 2011. The surplus was reported at $1.6 billion in April 2011, largely the result of higher exports of hydrocarbons. Major exports included oil, gas, petrochemical products, fish, metals, and textiles.

³²BALANCE OF PAYMENTS

In 2010 Oman had a foreign trade surplus of $7.8 billion.

Oman's balance of payments account is dominated by crude oil export earnings, consumer and capital goods and services, imports payments, and by large outgoing remittances by foreign workers.

The current account balance was estimated at $2.007 billion for 2010, compared with a negative balance of $603 million in 2009. Foreign exchange reserves were estimated at $13.03 billion (including gold) as of 31 December 2010, compared with an estimate of $12.2 billion at the end of 2009.

³³BANKING AND SECURITIES

The Central Bank of Oman, established in 1974, regulates Oman's financial services industry. The Central Bank has powers to regulate credit and is authorized to make temporary advances to the government.

As of 2010, there were 17 commercial banks in Oman: seven were locally incorporated, and the remainder were branches of

Principal Trading Partners – Oman (2010)

(In millions of US dollars)

Country	Total	Exports	Imports	Balance
World	56,376.0	36,601.0	19,775.0	16,826.0
China	9,908.0	8,870.0	1,038.0	7,832.0
United Arab Emirates	9,224.0	3,663.0	5,561.0	-1,898.0
Japan	7,522.0	4,098.0	3,424.0	674.0
South Korea	4,455.0	3,724.0	731.0	2,993.0
India	4,281.0	3,286.0	995.0	2,291.0
Thailand	2,824.0	2,213.0	611.0	1,602.0
United States	1,947.0	736.0	1,211.0	-475.0
Taiwan	1,668.0	1,563.0	105.0	1,458.0
Sa'udi Arabia	1,261.0	436.0	825.0	-389.0
Singapore	888.0	742.0	146.0	596.0

(…) data not available or not significant.

(n.s.) not specified.

SOURCE: *2011 Direction of Trade Statistics Yearbook*, New York: United Nations, 2011.

foreign banks. The local banks were Bank Muscat, National Bank of Oman, Oman International Bank, Oman Arab Bank, Bank Dhofar, Bank Sohar, and Al Ahli Bank. No US banks were operating in Oman, but five local banks had correspondents with US-based banking institutions. Local banks held about 88% of the total banking system assets, and the three largest banks accounted for 60% of the total assets, 63% of total credit, and 57% of total deposits.

Two government-owned banks—the Oman Housing Bank and Oman Development Bank—also offer financing to Omanis to buy or build residential properties, and to investors for small projects.

The CIA estimated Oman's stock of narrow money (the amount of total currency in circulation) at $53.08 billion in 2010, compared with an estimate of $45.8 billion in 2009. Total assets held in Omani banks were estimated at $71.42 billion in 2010, and the stock of domestic credit was estimated at $21.8 billion. The market value of publicly traded shares was $20.27 billion.

An Omani stock market, the Muscat Securities Market (MSM), was officially established in 1988, but trading did not begin until the following year. In 2011 there were 124 companies listed on the exchange with a market capitalization of approximately $20.24 billion. The MSM has established links with stock exchanges in several other Persian Gulf countries—including Bahrain, Qatar, and the United Arab Emirates—that allow for shares to be cross-listed. In 2010 the MSM 30 Index closed out the year at 6,743.92.

³⁴INSURANCE

Major insurance companies operating in Oman in 2011 included the Muscat-based Oman United Insurance Co., the United Arab Emirates-based Oman Insurance Company, the Oman-Qatar Insurance Company, and Al Alia. IRSA Oman acquired Oman's oldest insurance company, Al-Ahlia, in 2010.

³⁵PUBLIC FINANCE

In 2010 the budget of Oman included $20.5 billion in public revenue and $20.1 billion in public expenditures. The budget deficit amounted to 0.2% of GDP. Public debt was 4.4% of GDP, with $8.211 billion of the debt held by foreign entities.

Balance of Payments – Oman (2010)

(In millions of US dollars)

Current Account		5,096.0
Balance on goods	18,726.0	
Imports	-17,874.0	
Exports	36,601.0	
Balance on services		-4,764.0
Balance on income		-3,162.0
Current transfers		-5,704.0
Capital Account		-65.0
Financial Account		-2,372.0
Direct investment abroad		-390.0
Direct investment in Oman		2,333.0
Portfolio investment assets		250.0
Portfolio investment liabilities		703.0
Financial derivatives		…
Other investment assets		-3,765.0
Other investment liabilities		-1,502.0
Net Errors and Omissions		-1,161.0
Reserves and Related Items		-1,499.0

(…) data not available or not significant.

SOURCE: *Balance of Payment Statistics Yearbook 2011*, Washington, DC: International Monetary Fund, 2011.

Oil revenues accounted for about 63% of the government's total revenue in 2009 and were estimated to account for about 67.5% of expenditures. These figures reflected modest improvements in Oman's efforts to diversify its economy away from its reliance on oil and natural. The government owns 60% of Petroleum Development (Oman) Ltd., the main oil company.

Government outlays in 2010 were 56% for civil ministries; 36% for defense and security; 7% for oil and gas production; and 2% for interest payments on loans. The civil ministries expenses were for basic governmental services, expansions in education and health services, operational expenses of the ministries, and new projects.

36 TAXATION

Oman had no personal income tax as of 2011. Corporate profits were taxed at a flat rate of 12% above $78,000. Companies also paid municipal, tourism, and labor related taxes, though exemptions were available to businesses in manufacturing, mining, agricultural, fisheries, tourism, education and health sectors.

37 CUSTOMS AND DUTIES

General import duties were modest as of 2010 and rarely exceeded 10%. The US-Oman Free Trade Agreement removed most duties for US-made products as of 2009. Remaining duties were to be phased out by 2016.

38 FOREIGN INVESTMENT

Foreign direct investment (FDI) in Oman was a net inflow of $2.21 billion according to World Bank figures published in 2009. FDI represented 4.79% of GDP.

According to the US State Department, foreign ownership of shares in the Muscat Securities Market was 23% in December 2009, and foreign capital made up 24% of the shares held in finance, 21% in manufacturing, and 23% in insurance and services. The largest foreign investor was Royal Dutch Shell Oil, which held 34% ownership in the state-owned Petroleum Development (Oman) Ltd. and 30% ownership in Oman Liquid Natural Gas. Other large investors in the oil and gas sectors were included Occidental Petroleum, BP Amoco, Novus Petroleum, Hunt, British Gas, and Nimr.

US-based water pump manufacturer Gorman Rupp and wellhead equipment maker FMC were participating in joint ventures with Omani firms. Other major foreign investors were AES of the United States, Suez-Tractabel of France, Alcan of Canada, LG of South Korea, Veolia of France, SinoHydro of China, and National Power of the UK.

Oman has tried to diversify its economic base by actively seeking private foreign investors in information technology, tourism, and higher educational fields.

39 ECONOMIC DEVELOPMENT

Oman's economic policy operates under five-year development plans. Oman's second five-year plan (1981–85) suffered to some extent from the impact of declining oil prices in the early 1980s. The objectives of the third development plan (1986–90) were to encourage the private sector to play a larger role in the economy and to expand such areas as agriculture, fishing, manufacturing, and mining. The fourth five-year development plan (1991–95), aimed to achieve average annual GDP growth rates of just over 6%

and the diversification of the sources of national income in order to reduce dependence on the oil sector. The declared aim of the fifth five-year plan (1996–2000) was to achieve a balanced budget. The fall in oil prices to near-record lows in 1998 subverted the goal of a zero budget deficit in 2000, but rising oil prices in 2000 allowed the government to cut the deficit to only 1.5% of GDP ($301 million). Oman's sixth five-year development plan (2001–05) aimed to decrease dependence on government spending and employment, and to increase the role of the private sector. The seventh five-year plan (2006–11) focused on spending in industrial and tourism projects as well as further job creation for Omanis. The government also has invested substantially in schools, hospitals, and clinics since 1970.

The government's long-run development strategy is the Sultan's "Oman Vision 2020," which is designed to see the economy through the depletion of oil reserves. Emphases are on processes of Omanization of the workforce, industrialization, and privatization.

40 SOCIAL DEVELOPMENT

According to the US State Department in 2010, the Omani government generally respects human rights, in accordance with the country's 1996 Basic Law. The judicial system and a quasi-independent human rights commission provide a means for individual abuses to be addressed. Major human rights issues centered on a lack of consistent inspection of prisons and restrictions on freedoms of speech, press, assembly, and religion.

Women continued to face societal discrimination, and cases of domestic violence were found. Employers often put expatriate laborers in abusive environments.

Laws regarding women's welfare were weak. While rape was a criminal offense in 2010, spousal rape was not. In addition, no laws were in place regarding sexual harassment despite a 2009 study in which 11% of women reported being sexually harassed. Despite prohibitions on performing female genital mutilation in hospitals, the practice continued, particularly in rural areas. However, some steps toward improving the welfare of women were taken. On 6 May 2010, women gained the right to marry without parental consent, and on 17 October 2010 Oman instituted a National Oman Women's Day.

Oman maintains a social security system that provides old-age pensions, disability, and survivorship benefits to employed citizens ages 15–59 that are under a permanent work contract. This program is funded by 5% contributions from employees, 2% by the government, and 8% by employers. Retirement is set at age 60 for men and age 55 for women. Work injury legislation provides disability and medical benefits for injured workers. Hospitalization and medical care are provided to workers.

41 HEALTH

According to the CIA, life expectancy in Oman was 74 years in 2011. Healthcare expenditures totaled 3% of GDP, amounting to $497 per person. There were 19 physicians, 41 nurses and midwives, and 19 hospital beds per 10,000 inhabitants. The fertility rate was 2.87, while the infant mortality rate was 15 per 1,000 live births. In 2008 the maternal mortality rate, according to the World Bank, was 20 per 100,000 births. The CIA calculated HIV/AIDS prevalence in Oman to be about 0.1% in 2009. Approximately

1,100 people were estimated to be living with HIV/AIDS, and fewer than 100 AIDS related deaths were reported. About 88% of the total population had access to improved drinking water facilities, and about 87% to improved sanitation facilities.

42 HOUSING

Oman has invested heavily in housing under the leadership of Sultan Qaboos in an effort to provide affordable housing to its citizens. In May 1973, Sultan Qaboos approved the Law of People's Housing to make housing loans to needy Omanis. As of 2011 the Oman Housing Bank distributed these loans along with the Alliance Housing Bank, which was incorporated in 1997. Most of the loans granted through the Oman Housing Bank were subsidized by the government.

Women have the right to own property, but few landowners are women. In April 2009, the government began allocating more land to women to address concerns about inequalities in land ownership.

Omani housing includes a range of apartments and villas. Many homes were built to accommodate extended families and often included communal swimming pools, restaurants, tennis courts, and traditional Arab gathering halls known as *majlis*.

Land ownership is limited to Omani citizens. However, foreigners living in Oman are able to obtain mortgages in Integrated Tourism Complexes.

43 EDUCATION

In 2009 the World Bank estimated that 77% of age-eligible children in Oman were enrolled in primary school. Secondary enrollment for age-eligible children stood at 82%. Tertiary enrollment was estimated at 26%. Overall, the CIA estimated that Oman had a literacy rate of 81.4%. Public expenditure on education represented 3.9% of GDP.

Elementary school (primary) covers a six-year course of study, which is followed by three years of preparatory school and three years of general secondary school. Academic results of the preparatory exams determine the type of secondary education the student will receive—either arts or sciences. Islamic schools offer the same courses as preparatory schools, as well as religious and Arabic studies. At the secondary level, boys may choose to attend a technical school. The academic year runs from September to June.

Oman's government considers educating its citizens a high priority and part of the effort to reduce reliance on immigrant workers. Oman opened its first university, Sultan Qaboos, in 1986 and has recently added a law college to the campus. While Sultan Qaboos is the only public university in the country, Oman has about 20 technical colleges, teaching training colleges, and health institutes. The government also has awarded more than 300 full and partial scholarships each year to citizens who wish to study abroad. Omani colleges include three private universities, a banking college, a fire and safety college, a dentistry college, and several business and management colleges. In 2011 about 40% of Omani high school graduates were pursuing two- or four-year post-secondary degrees.

44 LIBRARIES AND MUSEUMS

The Ministry of Information recognized at least nine museums in Oman as of 2012. These include centers for natural history, architecture and traditional weaponry, inscriptions, currency, and postal items. A museum known as the Land of Frankincense opened in 2007 and features two halls showcasing Oman's history and maritime tradition.

Oman has few public libraries. The library at Sultan Qaboos University has 145,000 volumes, and the Muscat Technical and Industrial College has 10,000 volumes. A British Council Library of almost 8,000 volumes was founded in 1973 in Matrah. The Library of Manuscripts and Documents (1976) contains the Sultanate's most extensive collection of rare manuscripts.

45 MEDIA

In 2009 the CIA reported that there were 300,100 telephone landlines in Oman. In addition to landlines, mobile phone subscriptions averaged 140 per 100 people. There were three FM radio stations, nine AM radio stations, and two shortwave radio stations. Internet users numbered 44 per 100 citizens. In addition, the government owed two television stations and had licensed one privately owned satellite-based television station, as of 2011.

Eight privately owned newspapers, four in Arabic and four in English, were in circulation in 2011. In addition, the government owned two newspapers and operated the Oman News Agency. Prominent newspapers in 2010, with circulation numbers listed parenthetically, included *Oman Daily Observer* (22,000) and the *Times of Oman* (15,000).

Although Omani law provides for limited freedom of speech and the press, governmental policies and courts have interpreted this law to prohibit criticism of the sultan or any other public official. Some criticism of the government is tolerated, but generally journalists and writers have exercised self-censorship.

As of 2011, Oman's government continued to prohibit public and media appearances of poet and human rights activist Abdullah al-Riyami, journalist Mohamed al-Yahyai, and poet Mohamed al-Harthy for voicing opinions that the government found objectionable. Al-Riyami and a-Yahyai were convicted in 2005 of attempting to overthrow the government. They eventually were pardoned, but their freedom of expression remained restricted.

46 ORGANIZATIONS

There is a Chamber of Commerce and Industry in Muscat. Al Noor Association for the Blind, National Association for Cancer Awareness, Dar Al Atta Charity, Environment Society of Oman, and charities supporting children with special needs, the disabled, and those with hereditary blood disorder are among some of the non-governmental social service organizations. There are also a number of women's organizations, professional organizations, an Anglo-Omani Society, and an Omani historic association.

47 TOURISM, TRAVEL, AND RECREATION

The *Tourism Factbook*, published by the UN World Tourism Organization, reported 1.59 million incoming tourists to Oman in 2009, who spent a total of $1.11 billion. Of those incoming tourists, 917,000 were from Europe. There were 16,681 hotel beds available in Oman. The estimated daily cost to visit Muscat, the capital, was $372. The cost of visiting other cities averaged $303. Most large hotels have clubs that offer various recreational activities, and many tourists enjoy water.

In November 2010, the traditional Bedouin chant and dance known as Al-Bar'ah was officially inscribed on the UNESCO Representative List of the Intangible Heritage of Humanity, an offshoot of the World Heritage program. The dance was deemed a living tradition by UNESCO, meaning that it is still passed from generation to generation and continues to create a sense of identity and community for those who participate. Al-Bar'ah is a musical tradition from the Dhofar Mountains of southern Oman. The warlike dance is performed to an accompaniment of drums and the chanting of poetry. Each tribe has its own form of Al-Bar'ah, with varying dance steps, drum rhythms, and chant texts.

48 FAMOUS PERSONS

Oman's great Islamic religious leader, whose followers are called Ibadhis, was 'Abdallah bin Ibad (fl. 8th century); many of his teachings are still followed in Oman. Ahmad ibn Sa'id (r. 1741–83), founder of the present dynasty, freed Muscat from Persian rule. Sultan Qaboos bin Sa'id (b. 1940) has ruled Oman since his removal of Sa'id bin Taymur (1910–72), his father, in 1970.

49 DEPENDENCIES

Oman has no territories or colonies.

50 BIBLIOGRAPHY

King, David C. *Oman.* New York: Marshall Cavendish Benchmark, 2009.

Oman and the United Arab Emirates. London: Lonely Planet, 2000.

Oman Investment and Business Guide: Strategic and Practical Information. Washington, DC: International Business Publications USA, 2012.

Rabi, Uzi. *The Emergence of States in a Tribal Society: Oman under Sa'id bin Taymur, 1932–1970.* Portland, OR: Sussex Academic Press, 2006.

Seddon, David, ed. *A Political and Economic Dictionary of the Middle East.* Philadelphia: Routledge/Taylor and Francis, 2004.

PAKISTAN

Islamic Republic of Pakistan
Islami Jamhooria Pakistan

CAPITAL: Islāmābād

FLAG: The national flag is dark green, with a white vertical stripe at the hoist and a white crescent and five-pointed star in the center.

ANTHEM: *Qaumi Tarana (National Anthem).*

MONETARY UNIT: The rupee (PKR) is a paper currency of 100 paisa. Paisa coins ceased issue in 1994, but I and 2 rupee coins continue to be issued. There are notes of 2, 5, 10, 50, 100, 500, 1000 and 5000 rupees. PKR1 = US$0.01152 (or US$1 = PKR86.77) as of 2011.

WEIGHTS AND MEASURES: The metric system was introduced in 1966 and made mandatory as of 1 January 1979.

HOLIDAYS: Kashmir Day (5 February); Pakistan Day (23 March); Labor Day (1 May); Independence Day (14 August); Defense Day (6 September); Birthday of Muhammad Iqbal (9 November); Birthday of Muhammad Ali Jinnah (25 December). Muslim holidays by the Islamic calendar: Eid al-Fitr, Eid al-Adha, Ashura and Milad an-Nabi.

TIME: 5 p.m. = Noon GMT.

¹LOCATION, SIZE, AND EXTENT

Situated in South Asia, Pakistan covers an area of 803,940 sq km (310,403 sq mi) – almost twice the size of California, or the UK and France combined. At its greatest extent, Pakistan stretches 1,875 km (1,165 mi) NE–SW, and 1,006 km (625 mi) SE–NW. Pakistan is bordered on the N by China, on the NE by the disputed territory of Kashmir, on the E and SE by India, on the S by the Arabian Sea, on the SW by Iran, and on the W and NW by Afghanistan. The total land boundary length is 6,774 km (4,209 mi), sharing 2,912 km (1,809 mi) with India, 2,430 km (1,510 mi) with Afghanistan, 909 km (565 mi) with Iran and 523 km (325 mi) with China. The coastline on the Arabian Sea is 1,046 km (650 mi).

²TOPOGRAPHY

Geographers divide Pakistan into three major geographical areas: 1) The Northern Highlands; 2) The Indus Plain; and, 3) The Baluchistan Plateau. The Northern Highlands include parts of the Hindu Kush, the Karakoram Range, and the Himalayas. More than half the peaks are over 4,500 m (13,500 ft), and more than fifty peaks reach above 6,500 meters (19,500 ft). K2 (Mount Godwin Austin) at 8,619 m (28, 251 ft) is the second highest mountain in the world. High alpine valleys support some agriculture.

The Indus Plain is named for the Indus River. Originating in the Tibetan Plateau and entering Pakistan through the Northern Highlands, this 3,180 km (1980 mi) river flows in a generally southerly direction through the entire length of the country, fanning into a delta before entering the Arabian Sea. The Indus is also fed by four major tributaries from the east (Jhelum, Chenab, Ravi and Sutlej) and two from the west (Kabul and Zhob). The High

Plain (or Potwar Plateau) borders the Northern Highlands, in the foothills of Himalayas (e.g. Margalla Hills). The Upper Indus Basin lays to the south of that, defined by the areas crossed by the four eastern tributaries, followed by the Lower Indus Basin, which extends through the delta to the coast. The Indus Plain is Pakistan's prime agricultural region, but it occupies less than one-fifth of the country's total land-area. The region is also bordered on the east by three deserts (Thal, Thar, and Cholistan).

The western edge of the Indus Plain is marked by three mountain ranges. The most northerly Safed Koh Range is an extension of the Hindu Kush, and is crossed by the Kabul River and Khyber Pass. Its highest peak reaches to 4,761 m (15,620 ft), while lower elevations support agriculture in the valleys. The far more arid Sulaiman Range rises to the south, as high as 3,487 m (11,440 ft), and is bordered to its south-east by the more diminutive Kirthar Range, whose highest points do not exceed 2,500 m (7,500 ft). South and west of the Sulaiman and Kirthar Range extends the Baluchistan Plateau. Covering almost half of Pakistan's total land-area, this high, arid region does not support intensive agriculture.

³CLIMATE

Pakistan's climate varies with its topography. The Northern Highlands and the Baluchistan Plateau experience the greatest extremes, with expectedly heavy snows and sub-zero winters at high elevations and, particularly in the case of the Baluchistan Plateau, hot summers. The Indus Plain is also hot in summer, with a mean temperature of 37°C (100°F), but winters do not usually drop below 4°C (39°F). Sea breezes moderate the coastal belt. The Northern Highlands and Upper Indus Plains receive precipitation from the Western Disturbance, and from June to September the South West Monsoon brings widespread rains.

4 FLORA AND FAUNA

Diverse topography and climate are complemented by a wide array of plants and animals in Pakistan. According to the World Resources Institute, there are 4,950 plant species and 195 mammal, 625 bird, 190 reptile, and 17 amphibian species. Of these, 7.5% of flora and 3.5% of fauna are endemic.

The Northern Highlands support forests of coniferous alpine and subalpine trees such as deodar cedar (Pakistan's national tree), spruce, pine, birch, juniper and dwarf willow. Mammals found include markhor (Pakistan's national animal) and ibex goats, marco polo sheep, urial sheep, black and brown Himalayan bears, and the rare snow leopard.

Although the Indus Plains have largely been cleared for agriculture, they continue to support tropical and subtropical dry and moist broadleaf forestry as well as tropical and xeric shrubs. The trees include mulberry (shisham), acacia, eucalyptus, date and coconut palms. Northern foothills also support phulai, kao, chinar, walnut, olive, chestnut, oak and ash. Mangrove forests skirt much of the coastal areas.

The fauna of the Indus Plains includes jackals, mongoose, jungle cat, civet cat, desert cat, scaly anteaters, wild hare, boars, deer, porcupines and a variety of rodents and reptiles. Arid and desert regions are home to a jackals, hyenas, wild cats, panthers, and leopards. The rare Asiatic cheetah has also been sighted. The Indus River itself is home to a variety of fish species, crocodiles and the blind Indus River dolphin.

The Baluchistan Plateau and associated mountain ranges support many of the same plants species as the Northern Highlands at higher elevations, as well as tamarisk and a variety of grasses and scrub plants. In the xeric regions, date palms and ephedra are common floral varieties.

The most common bird species in Pakistan are crows, sparrows, myna, hawks, falcons, and eagles. Black and grey partridges, species of sand grouse, the Indian courser and peafowl are also found in the Indus Plains and associated desert regions. Many migratory species also winter in Pakistan, making their way from Europe, Central Asia and India.

5 ENVIRONMENT

Primary responsibility for environmental matters in Pakistan belongs to the Environmental and Urban Affairs Division of the Ministry for Housing and Works. Laws to manage forests were first drafted in 1927, and consideration of legislation to set air and water quality standards and regulate coastal zones to prevent pollution began in the 1980s. The Pakistan Environmental Protection Agency was created and charged with overseeing the Pakistan Environmental Protection Act of 1997. Some 6.53 million hectares (16.15 million acres) of land (approximately 4% of total land area) has been officially protected as of 2006.

Despite such regulatory bodies and legislation, the state of the environment in Pakistan is deteriorating on all fronts. As of 2010, 1,687,000 hectares, about 2.2% of total land area, was forested; down from 4.1% in 1993. The rate of decline has actually been increasing. Deforestation has also contributed to increased soil erosion, declining soil fertility, and severe flooding. Similarly, fauna

has been affected. According to a 2011 report issued by the International Union for Conservation of Nature and Natural Resources (IUCN), threatened species included 23 types of mammals, 27 species of birds, 10 types of reptiles, 34 species of fish, and 4 species of plants. Endangered species included the Indus dolphin, Baluchistan bear, tiger, Pakistan sand cat, snow leopard, Indian wild ass, green sea turtle, olive ridley turtle, gavial, Central Asian cobra, Kabul markhor, chi pheasant, western tragopan, great Indian bustard, and Siberian white crane.

Air quality has also suffered. By the mid-1990s, Pakistan was among the 50 nations with the world's highest levels of industrial carbon dioxide emissions, which totaled 71.9 million metric tons per year, a per capita level of 0.59 metric tons per year. In 2000, the total of carbon dioxide emissions was at 104.8 million metric tons. The UN reported in 2008 that carbon dioxide emissions have risen further to 156.2 million metric tons.

Water resources total 233.8 cu km (56.09 cu mi), with water usage at 169.3 cu km (40.62 cu mi) per year. Domestic water usage accounts for 2% of total usage, industrial for 2%, and agricultural for 96%. This supply is at risk due to untreated sewage along with agricultural and industrial pollutants. It is estimated that about 80% of the nation's diseases are related to impure water.

Agriculture, industry, population growth and lack of government oversight are the prime reasons for environmental degradation.

6 POPULATION

The US Central Intelligence Agency (CIA) estimated the population of Pakistan in 2011 to be 187,342,721, which placed it at number 6 in population among the 196 states of the world. In 2011, approximately 4.2% of the population was over 65 years of age, with another 35.4% under 15 years of age. The median age in Pakistan was 21.6 years. There were 1.07 males for every female in the country. The population's annual rate of change was 1.573%. Life expectancy at birth was 67 and infant mortality 71/1000.

The UN estimates that 36% of the population lives in urban areas, and that urban populations have an annual rate of change of 3.1%. The largest urban areas, along with their approximate populations, include: Karachi, 13.2 million; Lahore, 7.1 million; Faisalabad, 2.8 million; Rawalpindi, 2 million; Multan, 1.6 million; Hyderabad, 1.5 million; Gujranwala, 1.5 million; Peshawar, 1.4 million; Quetta, 900,000; and Islamabad, 832,000. Population density in Pakistan was calculated in 2011 at 235 people per sq km (609 people per sq mi).

In addition, Pakistani-administered portions of Kashmir comprise two administrative units: Azad Jammu and Kashmir (total area: 13,297 sq km/5,134 sq mi) with a population of 4,567,982 (2008); and Gilgit-Baltistan (total area: 72,496 sq km/27,991 sq mi) with a population of 1,800,000 (2008).

7 MIGRATION

Estimates of Pakistan's net migration rate, calculated by the CIA in 2011, amounted to -2.17 migrants per 1,000 citizens. The total number of emigrants living abroad was 4.68 million, and the total number of immigrants living in Pakistan was 4.23 million. The

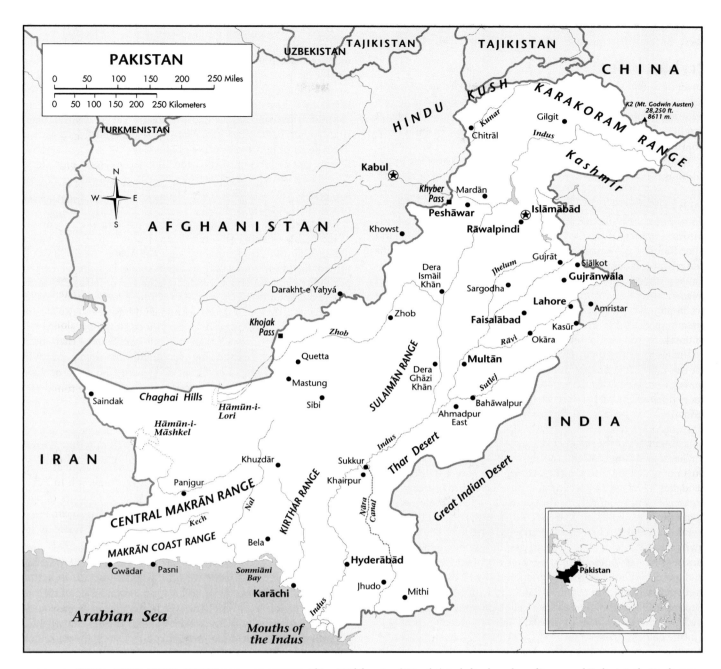

LOCATION: 23°41′ to 37°5′N; 60°52′ to 77°49′ E. BOUNDARY LENGTHS: China, 523 kilometers (325 miles), including boundary of Jammu and Kashmir to the Karakoram Pass; India, 2,912 kilometers (1,812 miles); Arabian Sea coastline, 1,046 kilometers (655 miles); Iran, 909 kilometers (568 miles); Afghanistan, 2,430 kilometers (1,510 miles). TERRITORIAL SEA LIMIT: 12 miles.

five largest immigrant communities are Afghanis, Bangladeshis, Tajiks, Uzbeks, Iranians, Indians and Britons of Pakistani origin.

According to the National Alien Registration Authority, there were also an approximated 3.35 million illegal immigrants from more than 76 countries in Pakistan as of 2004, 1.8 million of them in Karachi alone. Some are students, others work as menial laborers or as prostitutes, but most intend to use Pakistan as a transit point on the road to Europe or North America.

Refugees are also present in large numbers. As of 2009, approximately 1.78 million registered refugees, and more than three mil-

lion unregistered, as well as three thousand asylum seekers, resided in Pakistan. For more than three decades, Pakistan has hosted the largest refugee population in the world, mostly from Afghanistan, but also from Indian-administered Kashmir, Iraq, Somalia and other states in the region.

8 ETHNIC GROUPS

Pakistan is a multi-ethnic state. The major ethnic groups by population percentage are: Punjabi (44%); Pathan (Pashtun, 15%);

Sindhi (14%); Siraiki (8%), Muhajir (immigrants from India and their descendants, 8%); Balochi (4%); Kashmiri (1%); other (6%).

9 LANGUAGES

Urdu and English are the official languages of Pakistan. Urdu is the lingua franca of most of the population, but English plays an additional role among the elite and in government. The major mother- tongues of Pakistanis are: Punjabi (44%); Pashtu (15%); Sindhi (14%); Siraiki (10%); Urdu (8%); Balochi (4%); Hindko (2%); Brahui (1%); Kashmiri (1%); Other (1%). Most of the population is at least bilingual.

10 RELIGIONS

As of 2011, an estimated 95% of the population of Pakistan was Muslim, making it the 2nd largest Islamic country in the world after Indonesia. Approximately 80% of these Muslims are Sunnis (largely belonging to the Hanafi school of law) and 20% Shi'as (including Ithna Asharis and Ismailis). Sufism, the mystical branch of Islam, overlaps Sunni and Shi'a affiliations and is very prominent in the popular practices of Pakistanis, with thousands of tombs/ shrines dedicated to prominent mystics scattered throughout the country. In addition, Ahmadis, numbering 2-4 million by most estimates, consider themselves Muslims, but are not officially recognized as such since 1973. An estimated 5% of the population professes other faiths: Christians (1.5%): Hindus (1.5%); others, including Baha'is, Sikhs, Zoroastrians/Parsis, Buddhists, Jains and Jews (2%).

11 TRANSPORTATION

Pakistan has a total of 260,760 km (162,029 mi) of roads as of 2010, of which 180,910 km (112,412 mi) are paved. Railroads extend for 7,791 km (4,841 mi) and have been a major carrier of passenger and freight traffic, but since 2011, 115 routes and all freight haulage has been suspended due to shortages of locomotives and fuel. Even before these extreme measures, the road network carried 85% of all goods and passengers moving within the country. Major additions to these networks include the 800 km (500 mi) Karakoram Highway, built jointly by Pakistan and China and opened in 1979 to connect Islāmābād with western China. In November, 1997, the Lahore-Islāmābād Motorway was opened for traffic. In 2004, the Makran Coastal Highway added 653 km (425 mi) of road along the Arabian Sea, linking Karachi with Gwadar. Road traffic drives on the left.

The harbor of Karāchi, which provides Pakistan with its major port, covers an area of 6.5 sq km (2.5 sq mi) and handles over 10.5 million tons annually. Port Qasim, 22 km (14 mi) south of Karāchi, was developed during the 1970s to help handle the increased shipping traffic. Gwadar Port, developed with Chinese assistance on the coast of Baluchistan, was added in 2008. As of 2010, Pakistan's merchant marine operated 10 oceangoing vessels of 1,000 gross registered tons or more.

Pakistan had 101 airports with paved runways in 2010. There were also 19 heliports. Karāchi Airport is the main international terminus. As of 2011, along with the government-run Pakistan International Airlines (PIA), two private carriers, Airblue and Shaheen Air International (SAI), were operating on domestic as well as flights to Europe, the United States, and the Far East. Thirteen charter airlines are also in operation.

12 HISTORY

Pakistan joined the comity of nation-states on 14 August 1947. Its independence represents the convergence various factors. Most significant are the peoples habiting the Indus River Valley and its surrounding mountains and deserts; the advent of Islam; and, the impact of British colonial rule across South Asia.

Modern humans first settled the area today constituting Pakistan about 50,000 years ago. They subsisted with hunter-gather lifestyles until the Neolithic era (12000–3000 BC), when agriculture began to develop world-wide. The earliest Neolithic site in South Asia is Mehrgarh (7500–3500 BC), in Baluchistan. Farming, artisanship and local trade sustained this community of approximately 7000 individuals.

Mehrgarh and other such communities were the precursors of the highly urbanized Bronze Age cultures of the Indus Valley (3500–1250 BC), contemporary with the major river valley cultures of Egypt and Mesopotamia. For example, Harappa in the Upper Indus Plains and Mohenjodaro in the Lower Indus Plains are two of oldest and largest cities of the Bronze Age (approx. 50,000 inhabitants). They maintained sea and land-based trade links with Mesopotamia and Central Asia, besides engaging in brisk internal trade between no less than 1,052 culturally associated cities and towns spread over the largest contiguously urbanized area in the period. Although succumbing to climatic and environmental changes by 1250 BC, this Indus Valley Civilization influenced various aspects of Pakistani and broader South Asian societies that arose in their wake.

The same climatic and environmental factors that eventually extinguished the Indus Valley Civilization, also contributed to driving the Indo-European migrations, a branch of which began entering the Indus Valley by 1750 BC, continuing on to the Ganges Basin by 1250 BC. The interaction between these Indo-European speaking nomadic people and the indigenous agrarian cultures of the Indus Valley and Ganges Basin gave rise to Vedic Culture; named for the Vedas written in Sanskrit between 1500 and 500 BC. Much of the theology and many of the institutes of later Hinduism were laid down during this period. This culture's political products were 16 Mahajanapadas (kingdoms), spread across the Indus and Ganges regions of South Asia. The most significant in the Indus region was Gandhara, which was flourishing as a center of agriculture, commerce and learning by the 6th century BC.

From the 6th to the late 4th century BC, Gandhara and much of the Indus Valley were governed as satraps of the Achaemenid Empire of Iran. Zoroastrianism and other Persian institutes were introduced during that period. The fall of the Achaemenids to the forces of Alexander of Macedon, brought Greek/Hellenic influence in the 4th century BC. Soon after, the region was annexed to the Ganges-based Mauryan Empire, which ruled until 180 BC, firmly planting the then up-and-coming tradition of Buddhism in the region. Bactrian Greeks established themselves in Gandhara following Mauryan decline, but were themselves converted to and patrons of Buddhism. Under the Scythians and Kushans, Central Asian nomads who began seizing the region during the 1st century BC, Buddhism further expanded its influence. It not only became the official creed of the Kushans, who ruled a vast Central Asian empire from Gandhara's ancient capital, Taxila, but the region became the crucible of the Mahayana Buddhist tradition and its transmitter via the Silk Road to China, Tibet and beyond.

The Kushan Empire was gradually reduced by the rise of the Zoroastrian Sassanids of Iran to the west and the Hindu Guptas of the Ganges Basin to the east in the 4th century AD. Gupta rule was short lived, however, as the Turko-Persian Hephthalites (White Huns) extinguished Kushan remnants and pushed the Guptas eastward to establish themselves in the Upper Indus Plains. This period began the decline of Buddhism as a major influence in the region, the Hephthalites destroying many Buddhist monasteries and stupas in Gandhara. Hinduism, on the other hand, rose in stature to the point that the Hephthalites, ruling from Sialkot in contemporary Pakistan, adopted it as their creed in the early 6th century. The rival Buddhist Shahis displaced Hephthalite rulers in the mid-7th century, but established themselves as rulers of the Upper Indus Plains as the Hindu Shahis by the 9th century. On the Lower Indus Plains, the Hindu Rai dynasty, followed by the Chachar, ruled between the 5th and 8th centuries.

The vibrant collage of historical influences that defined the Indus Plains and immediate environs, quite distinct from other parts of South Asia, yet intimately connected, was added the colors of Islam in the 7th century. Arab traders, themselves only recently introduced to the faith, had long relations with trading communities of South Asia. During the era of the Rashidun Caliphate (632–661), however, the areas today constituting Baluchistan, then provinces of the Iranian Sassanids, became the first parts of the region brought under Muslim rule by 654. The advent of the Umayyad Caliphate (661–750) added the Lower Indus Plain as far north as Multan in 714, known to them as Sindh, then under the rule of the Hindu Chachar dynasty. Both Baluchistan and Sindh passed to the Abbasid Caliphate in 750, and remained as their eastern most provinces until the end of the 10th century.

While the Hindu Shahis retained sovereignty over the Upper Indus Plains until the 11th century, the period of Caliphal rule had begun transforming the Lower Indus Plains. The influx of Arab soldiers, bureaucrats, jurists, scholars and Sufi mystics complemented merchants as conduits not only for the transmission of Islamic culture into the region, but also the arts and sciences of South Asia westward. The majority of the population remained Hindu, Buddhist or Jain, evincing a generally honored policy of religious tolerance. Political, merchant and outcaste/tribal classes were among the first to begin adopting Islam as their faith during this period. When Abbasid authority ended in 998, local Sindhi Muslim dynasties (Soomros and Sammas) replaced them in the Lower Indus Plains, retaining authority intermittently to the 16th century.

The Upper Indus Plains and environs were brought under Muslim rule by the Turkic Ghaznavid Sultanate (975–1187), reducing the Hindu Shahis to vassals in the reign of Sultan Mahmud (r. 997–1030). Mahmud then launched the earliest Muslim incursions into the Ganges Basin, looting many important Buddhist and Hindu centers. The Ghaznavids were displaced by the Persian Ghurid Sultanate, Multan falling in 1175 and Lahore in 1186. The Ghurids went on to conquer most of the Ganges Basin, but were themselves limited in authority, then extinguished, when the Delhi Sultanate established by the their leading Turkic generals seceded in 1206. Successive dynasties of Delhi Sultans, only briefly interrupted by the incursions of Amir Timur (Tamerlane), ruled the Upper Indus Plains until they were displaced by the Turkic Mughal Sultanate in 1526. The Mughals, with their capitals in La-

hore, Delhi and Agra, more firmly extended central authority over the Lower Indus Plains and Baluchistan as well. Whereas the Caliphates had brought Arab influences to the region, along with Islam, the Ghaznavids, Ghurids, Delhi Sultans and Mughals introduced and embedded Turko-Iranian influences. It was during this period that Islam (Sunni and Shi'a) began significantly displacing Hinduism and Buddhism as the prime religious affiliation of the region's population. As well, syncretic faiths like Sikhism and the infusion of Arabic and Persian into the Baluchi, Sindhi, Punjabi and Pashtu languages began finding expression in rich vernacular cultures still present.

Mughal authority crumbled in the early 18th century, opening the door to the predations of the Iranian Nadir Shah, followed by the brief annexation of the Upper Indus Plains and Baluchistan by the Afghani Durrani Shahs. By the late 18th century, the Sikh kingdom of Ranajit Singh began establishing its authority over the Upper Indus Plains, continuing until 1849. The collapse of Mughal authority in Lower Indus Plains first led the Mughal's governors of Sind, the Sindhi Kalhoras, followed by the Baluchi Talpurs, rule of the area as its independent Amirs until 1843.

The Sikh kings of the Upper and Muslim Amirs of the Lower Indus Plains were conquered by the British East India Company, soon after which the 1857 Uprising (Mutiny) led to the assumption of direct rule over South Asian possessions by the British government in 1858. Further conquests to the west settled the Baluchistan boundary with Iran in 1872, and the border (Durand Line) with Afghanistan in 1893. Each line respectively split Baluchi and Pashtun populations between two states. These lines draw Pakistan's present western borders, as they have since 1947.

The drawing of the eastern border was still more intimately connected with the effects of British rule. With colonialism came political, judicial, fiscal and, educational reforms along British Victorian lines. Local thought and institutions were pushed aside, particularly for upper classes with access to education in English and employment in colonial institutions. As part of the process, the ideology of nationalism and the rhetoric of parliamentary government were internalized by such classes, leading to the creation of such political parties as the Indian National Congress (1885). Many Muslim intellectuals of the day, such as the educator and reformer Sayyid Ahmad Khan, worried that nationalism and parliamentary government would disenfranchise Muslims, who had been identified by British censuses as a minority everywhere except in the environs of the Indus Valley and eastern Bengal. Arguing that nationalism depended on homogeneous populations, they submitted evidence that at least two nations (Hindu and Muslim) co-habited British India. This 'Two Nation Theory' led to the founding of the All-India Muslim League in 1906, and the proposal for 'Separate Electorates' for each of British India's major religious and caste-based communities. The Government of India Act of 1909, which introduced limited franchise at local levels, adopted the proposal, as did the following Acts of 1919 and 1935.

The Lucknow Pact between the Congress and League in 1916 endorsed Separate Electorates as a formula for the future constitution of an independent, united India, allowing joint anti-colonial action to ensue. Congress and League members participated together in M.K. Gandhi's non-cooperation movement of 1919–22. This unity fell apart by the time Congress leadership issued the Nehru Report in 1927, repudiating Separate Electorates in any future independent constitution. The President of the League, Muhammad Iqbal, responded in 1930 with a call for the creation of sovereign Muslim states in the Muslim majority provinces of British India. Chaudhry Rehmat Ali, a student in England at the time, coined the term 'Pakistan' for the western provinces; an acronym for Punjab, Afghania (Khyber-Pukhtunkhwa), Kashmir, Sindh and Baluchistan, meaning 'Land of the Pure.' The call for sovereignty was taken up by Muhammad Ali Jinnah (Quaid-i Azam/ Great Leader) and adopted by the League as its official platform in the Lahore Declaration of 1940.

Rather than multiple states in the Muslim majority provinces of British India, as called for in the Lahore Declaration, one state comprising two 'wings' emerged on 14 August 1947. They were also not created on the basis of Muslim majority provinces, but rather by combining contiguous Muslim majority districts. The British Indian provinces of Punjab and Bengal were therefore partitioned. An estimated twenty million Muslims, Hindus and Sikhs caught on the 'wrong' side of the borders were pushed to migrate by growing violence that claimed an estimated three million lives, mostly in Punjab and Bengal. As well, the status of the Princely States of Kashmir and Junagadh was left undecided; the former being a Muslim majority state ruled by a Hindu prince, the latter being a Hindu majority state ruled by a Muslim prince.

Pakistan: 1947–1971

The Pakistani state that emerged in 1947 was beset with problems. Millions of refugees from India had to be accommodated. The areas comprising Pakistan also excluded the major industrial hubs of Punjab and Bengal, which were awarded to India. The agreed division of assets between India and Pakistan was also suspended by India. And finally, the Hindu prince of Kashmir signed a declaration joining India, despite its majority Muslim population, leading to the first Indo-Pak War (1947–49), which divided Kashmir into a Pakistani-held third and an Indian-held two-thirds of Kashmiri territory (much as it stood in 2011). Junagadh, where the prince joined Pakistan despite a Hindu majority population, was invaded and annexed to India in November 1947. Both matters were taken to the United Nations by Pakistan, which declared Kashmir a disputed territory and called for a plebiscite to decide its status. As of 2011, no plebiscite had been conducted.

The question of a constitution also proved difficult, mostly due to the question of representation for both 'wings' and the role of Islam. The death of Muhammad Ali Jinnah in 1948 and the assassination of the first Prime Minister, Liaqat Ali Khan, in 1951, contributed further to factionalism. Nevertheless, the leaders of the new state labored mightily to overcome the economic dislocations of Partition, which had cut former economic linkages. As well, they managed to promulgate the Constitution of 1956, declaring the state the 'Islamic Republic of Pakistan,' and enjoining parity between the east and west 'wings' in a parliamentary system, with Urdu and Bengali as national languages. However, the constitution was abrogated by a military coup d'état in 1958, led by Field Marshal Ayub Khan.

As Chief Marshal Law Administrator and President, Ayub Khan drafted a new constitution, which was promulgated in 1962, replacing the parliamentary system with a presidential system. The provinces of the west were amalgamated into a single province, West Pakistan, enjoying parity with the Bengali-speaking province of East Pakistan. The state was renamed the 'Republic of Pakistan.' In 1965, Ayub Khan confirmed his place as President through bitterly contested and allegedly rigged elections, defeating his main opponent, Fatima Jinnah, the sister of Muhammad Ali Jinnah. Political agitation in West and East Pakistan continued, coming to a head in 1968–69, forcing Ayub Khan to resign. Rather than devolving power to the speaker of the National Assembly as required by his own Constitution of 1962, Ayub Khan handed government to the Army Chief, General Yahya Khan, who imposed Martial Law on 25 March 1969.

Ayub Khan's presidency played a pivotal role in determining Pakistan's future. In foreign affairs, Ayub Khan sought security from India by aligning Pakistan with the United States and NATO, entering the Baghdad Pact (later the Central Treaty Organization; CENTO) and the South East Asian Treaty Organization (SEATO). A number of development projects were initiated and socio-economic reforms introduced leading to impressive agricultural and industrial growth. However, Ayub Khan's tenure was weakened by the Indo-Pak War of 1965, ostensibly driven by the unresolved dispute over Kashmir. Relations with the United States soured when the latter refused to come to Pakistan's defense against India. They were worsened by Pakistan's turn to China for security and economic needs. The Tashkent Agreement of 1966, which brought an end to war, was also widely viewed at home as a capitulation, and for East Pakistan in particular, the outcome of the war revealed the inability of West Pakistan to defend the East, adding to grievances about unequal development spending and access to state institutions. All such factors contributed to the popular agitation that led to Ayub Khan's resignation.

General Yahya Khan attempted to restore popular government by means of general elections in 1970. The result was an overwhelming win for the separatist Awami League in East Pakistan, under Mujibur Rehman, and the Pakistan People's Party (PPP) in West Pakistan, recently formed by Zulfikar Ali Bhutto. Although Rehman's party had won sufficient seats to form a government, Bhutto refused, leading to widespread dissent in East Pakistan. Yahya Khan responded with a military crackdown including the disarming of Bengali police and army personnel. Rehman was taken into custody in a wave of mass arrests and the Awami League was banned. Soon after, a rebellious general in the Pakistan Army, Ziaur Rehman, declared East Pakistani independence on 26 March 1971, and various regiments joined with the Mukhti Bahini (a guerrilla outfit) to fight the Pakistan Army. Millions of refugees fled the fighting into the Indian state of West Bengal, providing India the pretext to formally join the conflict on the side of East Pakistan on 3 December 1971. The brutal Indo-Pak War of 1971 ended with the surrender of Pakistani forces on 16 December 1971. East Pakistan was formally severed from Pakistan to become the People's Republic of Bangladesh.

1971–2011

The loss of East Pakistan led to Yahya Khan's resignation and brought Zulfikar Ali Bhutto to the presidency. His populist PPP had won a majority of seats in West Pakistan in the 1970 general election. A longtime minister under Ayub Khan, Bhutto quickly charted a new course for what remained of Pakistan. Bhutto implemented limited land reform, nationalized banks and industries, and obtained support among all parties to promulgate the Constitution of 1973, restoring a strong prime ministership, which position he then stepped down to fill. The state was renamed the 'Islamic Republic of Pakistan.' He distanced foreign policy from the United States, seeking security from India with a more nonaligned and Pan-Islamic ideology. Bhutto also concluded the Shimla Accord with India in 1972, but launched a long mooted nuclear weapons program in the wake of India's successful nuclear weapons tests of 1974. In the years following, Bhutto grew more powerful, more capricious, and autocratic. His regime became increasingly dependent on harassment and imprisonment of foes and his popular support seriously eroded by the time he called for elections in March 1977.

At the polls, the PPP was opposed by the Pakistan National Alliance (PNA), a nine-party coalition of all other major parties, including leftists, centrists, conservatives and Islamists. Although the results gave the PPP a two-thirds majority in parliament, allegations of widespread fraud and rigging undercut its credibility. PNA leaders demanded new elections, and Bhutto's exercise of emergency powers to arrest them led to widespread civil strife. On 5 July 1977, the army intervened and ousted Bhutto. Army Chief General Muhammad Zia ul-Haq suspended the Constitution of 1973, imposed martial law, and assumed the post of Chief Martial Law Administrator. He promised elections for October 1977, but for the first of many times to come, reversed himself before the event. In the meantime, he created a cabinet-like Council of Advisers comprising military officers and senior civil servants, chief among whom was Bhutto's Defense Secretary, Ghulam Ishaq Khan. Bhutto was brought to trial for conspiracy to murder a political rival. His conviction was upheld by the Supreme Court in March 1979, and he was hanged on 4 April.

Meanwhile, neighboring Afghanistan experienced a communist-led coup d'état in 1978 and Soviet invasion in 1979. Also prompted by the Iranian Revolution in 1979, the United States turned to Pakistan as a bulwark against both Soviets and Iranians. Zia ul-Haq obliged, drawing additional support from the Arab World, Europe and the UN. In the 1980s, the United States and Pakistan signed economic and security assistance agreements worth $3.2 and $4.02 billion. The so-called 'Islamization' of Pakistan reached new peaks during the same period, when sweeping restrictions were placed on religious minorities and women. The policy was designed and succeeded in bolstering Zia ul-Haq's authority and churning out mujahidin to fight the Soviets in Afghanistan. Relations with India, however, were further strained in 1984, when Indian forces occupied the Siachen Glacier of Kashmir, widely acknowledged as lying on Pakistan's side of the 1972 Line of Control (1949 ceasefire line).

General elections, on a nonparty basis, were eventually announced for February 1985. The PPP-led Movement for the Restoration of Democracy boycotted, but the Jamaat-i Islami and part of the Pakistan Muslim League (PML) supported the regime. The elections gave Zia ul-Haq a majority in the reconstituted National Assembly and left the opposition in further disarray. On 30 December 1985, Martial Law was repealed and the Constitution of 1973 restored, but not before amending it to grant the President the right to dissolve Parliament. As the Eighth Amendment to the constitution, these changes were approved by the National Assembly in October 1985. Day-to-day administration was handed to the PML's Mohammad Khan Junejo, appointed as Prime Minister

in March, but by May 1988, the President dismissed Junejo, alleging corruption and a lack of support for his Islamization and Afghanistan policies. New elections were scheduled for November 1988. However, Zia ul-Haq was among 18 officials (including the US Ambassador) killed in the crash of a Pakistan Air Force plane. Two months later, Chairman of the Senate, Ghulam Ishaq Khan, confirmed elections for November. Benazir Bhutto, Zulfikar Ali Bhutto's daughter, won a thin majority, and with her support, Pakistan's electoral college chose Ghulam Ishaq Khan as President of Pakistan on 12 December 1988.

Citing corruption, Ghulam Ishaq Khan used his powers as President to remove Benazir Bhutto from the prime ministership on 20 August 1990, declaring yet another a state of emergency, dissolving the National Assembly and calling for new elections on 24 October. On that date, the voters gave a near-majority to the Islamic Jamhoori Ittehad (IJI), a multiparty coalition resting mainly on a partnership of the PML and the JI. Mian Muhammad Nawaz Sharif, PML leader and former Chief Minister of Punjab, became Prime Minister on 6 November, ending the state of emergency. However, when Sharif challenged the President's choice of a new Army Chief, Ghulam Ishaq Khan again used his Eighth Amendment powers to dismiss the government and dissolve the assembly on 18 April 1993, again alleging mismanagement and corruption. But public reaction to the President's actions was strong, and on 26 May, a Supreme Court ruling restored Sharif to power, creating a period of constitutional gridlock until 18 July when the Army Chief brokered a deal in which both Ghulam Ishaq Khan and Sharif resigned.

General elections were held on 19 October 1993, and the PPP, leading a coalition called the People's Democratic Alliance (PDA), was returned to power, with Benazir Bhutto again Prime Minister. On 13 November, with her support, longtime PPP stalwart Farooq Leghari was elected President. Three years later in 1996, Leghari dismissed Benazir Bhutto and dissolved the National Assembly. She challenged the President's actions in the Supreme Court, but in a 6–1 ruling, the court upheld the President's actions and concurred with corruption charges.

Sharif won the general election held in February 1997 with one of the largest mandates in Pakistan's history. He immediately set about consolidating his hold on power by repealing major elements of the Eighth Amendment. This transferred sweeping executive powers from the President to the Prime Minister. Within the next few months Sharif dismissed the Chief of Naval Staff, arrested and imprisoned Benazir Bhutto's husband, Asif Ali Zardari, for ordering the killing of a political opponent, and froze the Bhutto family's assets. In March 1998, a warrant was issued for the arrest of Benazir Bhutto on charges of misuse of power during her prime ministership.

During this period, Sharif also ordered the successful tests of six nuclear devices on 28 May and 30 May 1998. This was in response to India's nuclear tests earlier in the month. Tensions eased when Sharif and India's Prime Minister, Atal Behari Vajpayee, signed the Lahore Declaration on 21 February 1999, committing their countries to a peaceful solution of their problems. In May 1999, however, several hundred Pakistani troops and Islamic militants infiltrated the Indian-held Kargil region of Kashmir, seeking to cut Indian supply lines to the Siachen Glacier. Two months of intense fighting brought Pakistan and India to the brink of all-out war. Under intense diplomatic pressure from the United States, but against the wishes of Pakistan's military, Sharif ordered a withdrawal from Kargil in July 1999. This decision contributed to the Prime Minister's eventual downfall in October 1999.

General Pervez Musharraf was then army chief and is generally believed to have authorized the Kargil operation. Sharif dismissed Musharraf on 12 October 1999, but troops loyal to the general arrested Sharif. Another state of emergency was declared, the constitution was suspended and Musharraf assumed power. In January 2000, Musharraf required all judges to take an oath of loyalty to his regime, seriously compromising judicial autonomy. By 23 March 2000, he announced local, not general, elections to be held between December 2000-July 2001. Sharif was tried and found guilty of hijacking and terrorism and sentenced to life in prison on 16 April 2000. In December, he was pardoned and went into exile in Saudi Arabia. With political opposition at bay, Musharraf named himself president on 20 June 2001, while retaining the post of army chief.

The nuclear tests in 1998, the Kargil War and Musharraf's coup d'état in 1999, had seriously strained relations with a United States then forging closer economic and strategic ties with India. The attacks on the US on 11 September 2001, however, once again turned Pakistan into a frontline state in a US-led war. Musharraf supported the US-NATO invasion of Afghanistan with the lease of Pakistani military bases and transit rights for the majority of US-NATO supplies, though by his own account under threat of US bombardment. Musharraf would also commit 80,000 Pakistani troops to operations in Pakistan's Federally Administered Tribal Areas (FATA) along the Afghanistan border. Their mission, in 2004 and 2006, was to root out suspected Al-Qaeda and Afghani Taliban hideouts occupied after the fall of Kabul. The United States became more directly involved in 2005, when the CIA launched its first Predator strikes in FATA. It has since been revealed by Wikileaks that the Musharraf regime was complicit. In exchange for such support, some sanctions imposed on Pakistan after its 1998 nuclear tests were lifted, and mostly military aid ran into the billions of dollars, promised in the form of annual payments to the government and monthly payments to the military.

Relations with India, like those with the US, were also overtaken by the 'War on Terror' during Musharraf's tenure. On 13 December 2001, the Indian Parliament was attacked by five militants, and India blamed the attack on the Lashkar-i Taiba and Jaish-i Muhammad, formerly involved in the insurgency in Indian-administered Kashmir. Tensions between the two countries led to the amassing of hundreds of thousands of troops along their shared border and a ban on the two accused groups. The standoff continued in one form or another until 2003. By 2005, a bus link between the Indian and Pakistani-administered portions of Kashmir signaled a retreat from the brink, and both countries cooperated to some degree with the distribution of humanitarian aid following a deadly earthquake that struck the region on 8 October 2005. The earthquake had its epicenter in the Pakistani-administered part of Kashmir, killing tens of thousands and displacing millions. Nevertheless, no progress was made toward normalizing relations.

On the domestic front, Musharraf's policies drew increasing fire from media and judicial activists, as well as civilian political parties. Nevertheless, in April 2002, a referendum conferred 98% majority on Musharraf's bid for another 5-year term as President.

In August, he unilaterally implemented 29 amendments to the constitution to grant himself the power to dissolve Parliament and to remove the Prime Minister. He also gave the military a formal role in governing the country for the first time by setting up a National Security Council that would oversee the performance of Parliament, the Prime Minister, and his or her government. Parliamentary elections were held on 10 October 2002, with the PML (Quaid-i Azam Group), a political faction of the Muslim League supportive of Musharraf, taking the most seats.

Musharraf's tussle with the judiciary centered on his insistence on remaining Army Chief and President. In the election held on 6 October 2007, Musharraf won the most votes. However, the Supreme Court declared no winner could be formally announced until it ruled if the Army Chief had been eligible to stand for election. On 18 October, Bhutto was cheered by about 200,000 of her PPP supporters as she made her way home to Karachi; however, two bombs exploded just feet from her truck, killing some 140 people and wounding more than 400. Bhutto was unhurt, but the bombing undermined a power-sharing deal concluded between herself and Musharraf. On 3 November, Musharraf declared a state of emergency, suspending the constitution, shutting down independent news organizations on the pretext that the country was under threat by Islamic extremists. The Supreme Court was expected to rule within days on the legality of Musharraf's reelection as President. Musharraf then took the further step of arresting lawyers, thousands of whom posed the first organized civil resistance to Musharraf's emergency rule. Indeed, on 3 November, the day emergency rule was declared, Musharraf placed Chief Justice Chaudhry under house arrest, along with most of the other justices of the Supreme Court, who refused to swear a new oath.

By mid-November 2007, Musharraf had arrested some 2,500 opposition politicians, lawyers, and human rights activists. He put Bhutto under house arrest, but released her on 16 November; the same day the Supreme Court, now packed with Musharraf supporters, legitimated his reelection. On 28 November, Musharraf resigned as Army Chief and was sworn in to a second five-year presidential term the next day. Hours after being sworn in, he announced the state of emergency would be lifted on 16 December 2007, leaving barely three weeks of election campaigning before parliamentary elections. The two main opposition parties led by Benazir Bhutto and Sharif (who had also recently returned to Pakistan) said they would participate in the January 2008 poll. But Bhutto was assassinated on 27 December 2007, and public sentiment turned more strongly against Musharraf. When the February 2008 election results were tallied, Musharraf's party had been soundly defeated. A new government was formed by Sharif and Asif Ali Zardari, widower of Benazir Bhutto. Although the two were fighting each other for control of the government, they together called for impeachment proceedings against Musharraf, which they announced on 7 August 2008. Musharraf responded by resigning as President on 18 August. In September 2008, Zardari was elected by legislators as the new President, while Sharif's PML led the opposition.

Musharraf's policies have been broadly consequential for Pakistanis. Military operations in FATA alone led to mass civilian casualties and internal displacement. CIA Predator strikes add to the list of civilian casualties. Armed resistance also pushed the formal creation of Tehrik-i Taliban Pakistan (TTP) in 2007. The related siege of the Red Mosque in Islamabad that same year, contributed to the banned Lashkar-i Taiba, Jaish-i Muhammad and Sipah-i Sahaba Pakistan launching suicide attacks on civilian and military targets in Pakistan that have passed on to the PPP government of President Zardari and Prime Minister Yusuf Raza Gilani.

Although brought to power on a surge of judicial and media activism driven to reinstate Chief Justice Chaudhry, restore judicial autonomy and return the supremacy of Parliament, the Zardari government lost considerable support by resisting the reinstatement of the Chief Justice until March 2009, and waiting to April 2010 to approve a series of constitutional amendments limiting the power of the President. Esteem was also diminished due a stayed course of close Pakistan-US relations, cemented by the Kerry-Lugar Bill (2009) which tripled non-military aid from the United States. The CIA's continuing Predator program is popularly perceived as a violation of Pakistani sovereignty, as is the US Navy Seal operation that killed Osama bin Laden in Abbotabad on 2 May 2011. Military-to-military relations, as well, have soured, most publically since that day to the end of the year. Relations with India, however, took a turn for the worse as early as 26 November 2008, when the brutal Mumbai attack was judged in India to be linked to the already banned Lashkar-i Taiba and the Pakistani Inter-Services Intelligence (ISI). A thaw appears to be in the offing as agreements to increase trade were announced after ministerial level talks in November 2011.

Domestic conditions have also suffered as bombings attributed to a number of militant Islamist groups stoked by the continuation of Musharraf's policies have claimed civilian and military lives at an unprecedented rate. As well, running street battles in Karachi between the militias and hired enforcers of 'secular' parties associated with the government have taken more than 1,500 innocents in 2011 alone. The Asian Legal Resource Center reports that between May 2010 and 2011, more than 120 people were extra-judicially killed by the state, while thousands have been subjected to arbitrary arrest, abduction, torture and disappearance. According to the World Association of Journalists and Newspaper Publishers, Pakistan topped the list for journalists killed in 2010, and was running second only to Iraq in 2011. In total, some 35,000 people are reported to have been killed since 2001, the highest casualty rates occurring since 2007. The monsoon floods of 2010 and 2011 added thousands dead and millions more displaced as of December 2011. In the midst of such turmoil, coupled with endemic corruption and mismanagement, the economy has understandably not fared well; inflation rose, the Pak-Rupee and stock markets plummeted and foreign investments dropped significantly between 2010 and 2011. By December 2011, the government had not announced or implemented any strategies to deal with the surge in violence or to calm growing political unrest rooted in popular dissatisfaction.

13 GOVERNMENT

When Pakistan gained its independence from Britain, under the Indian Independence Act of 1947, it was to be governed by the Government of India Act of 1935 until a Constituent Assembly could write a sovereign constitution. The Constituent Assembly, comprising 69 (later 79) members, also served as the country's legislature and exercised all the powers and functions of the central government.

After nine years of debate, primarily on the role of Islam and the division of powers between East and West 'wings' of the state, the first Constitution of Pakistan was adopted on 29 February 1956, and came into effect on 23 March 1956. This lengthy document declared the state the 'Islamic Republic of Pakistan.' It stipulated a Federal system, dividing powers between the center and provinces, and a unicameral legislature (the 'National Assembly') consisting of 300 members (150 from each 'wing') elected by adult franchise. Following the Parliamentary system, a President, elected by the National Assembly, would serve as head of state, and a Prime Minister, elected by the National Assembly, would act as head of government. An independent judiciary was required, including a Supreme Court empowered to interpret the constitution. Fundamental rights of citizens included the right of free movement, speech and religion. Urdu and Bengali were named as national languages. Specifically Islamic provisions were limited to the principle that no law should be passed that transgresses Koran and Sunnah; the President, as head of state, must be Muslim; and, slavery, prostitution, alcohol and narcotics prohibited.

The Constitution of 1956 was short lived. It was abrogated on 7 October 1958, when President Iskandar Mirza staged a coup d'état, appointing General Ayub Khan Chief Martial Law Administrator. Three weeks later, Ayub Khan assumed the presidency and ruled under martial law until 1962, when a new constitution was issued. The Constitution of 1962 maintained much of the character of its predecessor, including a federal system, unicameral legislature, independent judiciary, the same fundamental rights, parity between East and West 'wings,' provisions for Urdu and Bengali and for the role of Koran and Sunnah. However, it switched to a Presidential system, with the president elected by an Electoral College comprising 80,000 'Basic Democrats' – district level elected officials (40,000 from each 'wing'). The number of provinces was reduced to two: 'East' and 'West Pakistan,' and the state was renamed the 'Republic of Pakistan.'

On 25 March 1969, following President Ayub Khan's resignation, the Constitution of 1962 was abrogated and martial law declared. Between then and 1972, civil war, the Indo-Pak war of 1971 and the secession of East Pakistan to form Bangladesh, fundamentally changed the character of Pakistan. The federation, now comprising only the former West Pakistan, took on its present borders and promulgated a new constitution to reflect its provincial make-up under the government of Zulfikar Ali Bhutto. The Constitution of 1973 remained in effect as of 2011.

According the Constitution of 1973, which came into effect on 14 August 1973, the state was again declared the 'Islamic Republic of Pakistan.' It also returned to a Parliamentary System and did away with the system of Basic Democrats to re-established the provinces. A bicameral legislature was now instituted, adding a Senate providing equal representation for each province (70 members) and seats in the National Assembly based on population (216 members). The President was to be elected by Parliament, and Prime Minister by the National Assembly. Reflecting the provisions for Islam, contrasting with the 1956 constitution, both the President and Prime Minister were required to be Muslim, though male or female candidates were accepted. A 'Muslim' was also defined for the first time and an 'Islamic Council' constituted to align federal and provincial legislation with Koran and Sunnah. Prostitution, gambling, alcohol, and literature deemed obscene were prohibited.

Between August 1973 and December 2011, this constitution was suspended and restored twice. The first suspension came with the military coup d'état under General Zia ul-Haq. Martial law governed from 5 July 1977 to 30 December 1981. The second suspension fell on 15 October 1999, precipitated by General Pervez Musharraf's coup d'état, and was restored on 31 December 2002.

The constitution has also been amended multiple times. Most significantly, under the government of Zulfikar Ali Bhutto, the Second Amendment (1974) declared members of the Ahmadi community non-Muslims. Under the government of Zia ul-Haq, the Eighth Amendment (1985) provided the President discretionary powers to dissolve the National Assembly. Under the government of Pervez Musharraf, the Seventeenth Amendment (2003) validated all measures enacted (including the coup d'état) by the President since 1999. And finally, under the government of Asif Ali Zardari, the Eighteenth Amendment (2010) abrogated the Seventeenth Amendment, curtailed the powers of the President enacted by the Eighth Amendment and raised the number of seats in the National Assembly to 342, including 60 reserved for women and 10 for non-Muslims. The number of Senators stood at 100 as of 2011.

14 POLITICAL PARTIES

Although the military has interrupted party politics in Pakistan on various occasions and for lengthy periods, political parties have weathered bans and restrictions, or collaborated with the military, to play a central role in Pakistan's governance at federal and provincial levels.

The tradition of party politics began in era of British colonial rule, most significantly with the founding of the All-India Muslim League in 1906. This party, under the leadership of Muhammad Ali Jinnah, spearheaded the Pakistan Movement and upon Pakistan's independence in 1947, was renamed the Pakistan Muslim League (PML). Factionalization has since led to the formation of multiple incarnations. Those in play as of 2011 are the Pakistan Muslim League (Functional—PML-F); the Pakistan Muslim League (Nawaz Sharif Group—PML-N); and, the Pakistan Muslim League (Quaid-I Azam Group—PML-Q). In 2010, former President Musharraf also launched the All-Pakistan Muslim League, as a precursor to his return to Pakistan and his intent to run for office in the 2013 elections. All incarnations of the Muslim League have espoused largely right-of-center policies.

Before the emergence of Bangladesh in 1971, the Awami League (Awami Muslim League, from 1949 to 1955), also played a significant role as the prime advocate of East Pakistani interests. Under Mujibur Rehman's leadership, it successfully led the campaign for East Pakistani autonomy and then independence. It has played a leading role in Bangladesh since.

Other parties of significance to have emerged before 1971 include the National Awami Party, founded in 1957, as an umbrella for a variety of leftist groups. It was banned in 1975, under the government of Zulfikar Ali Bhutto. The National Awami Party's rival and prosecutor, the Pakistan People's Party, was founded by Zulfikar Ali Bhutto in 1967. The latter has ideologically ranged from left-of-center to centrist, and has been led by Zulfikar Ali

Bhutto, Nusrat Bhutto, Benazir Bhutto, Asif Ali Zardari and Bilawal Bhutto Zardari.

After 1971, the only national party formed and set to influence Pakistani politics is the Pakistan Tehrik-i Insaf, founded in 1996. However, a number of regional parties had taken shape. Prime among these were: the Jeay Sindh Qaumi Mahaz, founded in 1972 to represent Sindhi interests; the Muhajir/Muttahida Qaumi Movement, formed in 1984 to represent the interests of Urdu-speaking immigrants from India; the Awami National Party, rising in 1986 out of the ashes of the banned National Awami Party to represent Pashtun interests; and, the Baluchistan National Party, founded in 1996, to represent Baluchi interests.

A number of Islamist parties with parliamentary leanings have also played an important part in Pakistani politics. These are primarily represented by the Jamaat-i Islami, founded in 1941; the Jamaat-i Ulama-i Islam, founded in 1945; and, the Jamaat-i Ulama-i Pakistan, founded in 1948.

A total of 13 parties hold seats in Pakistan's Parliament as of December 2011, reflecting the general elections of 2008.

15 LOCAL GOVERNMENT

Since 1971, Pakistan was divided into four provinces, in order of population: Punjab (capital: Lahore), Sindh (capital: Karachi), Khyber-Pukhtunkhwa (formerly NWFP; capital: Peshawar) and Baluchistan (capital: Quetta). The majority of the population in each was bound ethno-linguistically and by Sunni Islam, but each was also home to ethno-linguistic, sectarian and religious minorities. Outside the provinces, but administered by them, were the Federally Administered Tribal Areas (FATA) along the border with Afghanistan and the Federal Capital of Islamabad. As well, Pakistani-administered Kashmir comprised two areas: Gilgit-Baltistan (formerly the Federally Administered Northern Areas [FANA]; capital: Gilgit) and Azad Jammu and Kashmir (capital: Muzaffarabad).

Under the Constitution of 1973, in effect as of 2011, provinces were administered by a Governor appointed by the President and a Chief Minister popularly elected through a Provincial Assembly (with reserved seats for women and non-Muslims). Each province was divided into Divisions, Districts (*zillas*) and Sub-Districts (*tehsils*/*talukas*). Divisions were headed by Commissioners who were senior members of the Pakistan Civil Service (CSP). Districts were headed (depending on local usage) by Deputy Commissioners, District Officers, or Collectors, also members of the CSP, who managed development funds, collect revenues, supervise the police, adjudicate disputes, administer justice, and interfaced with the Sub-Districts' elected councils (since 2001), which had limited taxing authority, but decided priorities for local development programs and trying certain local legal cases. Women were allotted a minimum of 33% seats in these councils; there was no upper limit to the number of women in these councils. Some districts, incorporating large metropolitan areas, were called City Districts. A City District could contain subdivisions called Towns and Union Councils.

The two units of Pakistani-administered Kashmir were differently governed. Azad Jammu and Kashmir (AJK) was linked with Pakistan by the Azad Jammu and Kashmir Council, consisting of 11 members, six from the government of AJK and five from the government of Pakistan. Its Chairman/Chief Executive was the

President of Pakistan. The government of AJK has been headed by its own elected President, Prime Minister and Legislature since 1974.

Until 2009, Gilgit-Balistan was directly administered by the government of Pakistan through a Northern Areas Council. However, the Gilgit-Baltistan Empowerment and Self-Governance Order (2009), represented a major step toward provincial status, by establishing a Presidentially-appointed Governor alongside an elected local government structure mirroring those of constitutional provinces, without constitutionally including the region as a province.

16 JUDICIAL SYSTEM

The judicial system of Pakistan is an amalgam of British colonial and late Islamic jurisprudence and institutions. With the May 2010 passage of the Eighteenth Amendment to constitution, the apex court in the system, the Supreme Court of Pakistan seated in Islamabad, regained a degree of independence deprived by a cycle of abrogations and amendments initiated by successive military regimes since the late 1970s. Rather than being appointed by the President of Pakistan, decades of judicial activism won a Judicial Commission and Parliamentary Committee, comprising Supreme Courts judges (5), the Attorney General, Federal Justice Minister and a member of the Pakistan Bar Council, to appoint the 17 member Supreme Court. An identical process would also deprive the President power to appoint the judges of the provincial (4) and capital (1) High Courts. As the Supreme Court has jurisdiction of the High Courts and the latter over District and Sessions Courts, the provisions of the Eighteenth Amendment translated into an unprecedented degree of independence in Pakistan's judicial history.

While the jurisprudential and structural particulars of the Supreme, High and Lower Courts were inherited from the period of British rule, the Islamic element of this system was primarily represented by the Federal Shariat Court (FSC), established by the Presidential order of General Zia ul-Haq in 1980. This court, comprising eight Muslim judges drawn from the general court system (5) and three from the ranks of clerical jurists (ulama), was decided by a Judicial Commission, the Chief Justice of the FSC and the Chief Justice of the Supreme Court. It was empowered to oversee all legislation and require address from the government when that legislation was judged against Koran and Sunnah. As of 2011, the jurisprudential approach has been largely restricted in practice to the puritanical 19th century CE Deobandi movement of the Hanafi school. A Shariat Appellate Bench of the Supreme Court, comprising three Muslim members of the Supreme Court and two clerical jurists, hears appeals against Federal Shariat Court rulings.

Despite this elaborate system, for many Pakistanis disputes continued to be decided, and punishments decreed, by equally elaborate and far more deeply rooted tribal jirgas and community-based panchayats.

17 ARMED FORCES

The International Institute for Strategic Studies reports that the Pakistan Armed Forces (PAF) totaled 617,000 active members in 2011, making it the 7th largest force in the world. It comprised 550,000 from the army, 22,000 from the navy, and 45,000 members of the air force. There were also 513,000 reservists and 304,000 in paramilitary forces. All 1,451,000 personnel were volunteers, conscription never having been inducted. In 2011, military spending totaled $13.9 billion, or approximately 3% of GDP.

The PAF has played an instrumental role in Pakistani history, fighting three wars with India (1948; 1965; 1971) and playing a major part in Afghan wars from the Soviet invasion in 1979 to the on-going US-led NATO occupation as of 2011. It has further been deployed to quell various domestic insurgencies, as well as in times of natural disasters, and has governed Pakistan under four Martial Law regimes (1958–62; 1969–71; 1978–85; 1999–2002), followed by protracted periods of Chief Marshal Law Administrators serving as President of Pakistan. As of 1998, Pakistan became a declared nuclear-state, never having signed the Nuclear Non-Proliferation Treaty (NPT) to hold an arsenal of between 24 and 48 weapons, officially as a deterrent against conventional disparities with India. The conflict with India has also fostered close ties with the US since the 1950s. The US has been one of Pakistan's major conventional arms suppliers, though China has increasingly compensated for sporadic US restrictions since the 1965 and 1971 Indo-Pak wars. Joint ventures with China and others (e.g., France) have also spawned a large domestic weapons industry, including the development of the JF-17 fighter jet, the al-Khalid tank and the Agosta 90B submarine. Pakistan exported weapons to an estimated 50 countries, revenues reaching into hundreds of millions of dollars by 2006.

As part of the US strategic ambit since the 1950s (CENTO and SEATO), the PAF has also maintained close ties with US allies in the Middle East. Pakistani trainers and personnel have served in Saudi Arabia, Kuwait, the United Arab Emirates, Bahrain and Jordan. Since the Iranian Revolution of 1979, this cooperation grew closer, at the expense of previous relations with Iran. In South Asia, Sri Lanka and Nepal were the largest buyers of Pakistani military equipment. The PAF was also one of the largest participants in UN operations. 10,000 Pakistani personnel were deployed in 2007, serving from Western Sahara to East Timur.

18 INTERNATIONAL COOPERATION

Pakistan became a member of the United Nations on 30 September 1947 and has been a member of several specialized agencies, such as ESCAP, the FAO, UNESCO, UNHCR, the World Bank, ILO, UNIDO, and the WHO. The PAF has also served in various UN peacekeeping operations. Pakistan also belonged to the Asian Development Bank, the Colombo Plan, the Commonwealth of Nations, G-24, G-77, and the WTO. Pakistan entered the US-led Cold War alliances of CENTO and SEATO in the 1955, but withdrew from SEATO in 1972, following the independence of Bangladesh. CENTO members Pakistan, Turkey, and Iran, however, established a tripartite organization of Regional Cooperation for Development (RCD) in 1964, but CENTO and the RCD lapsed with the Iranian Revolution in 1979, leading to bilaterally agreed relations with the US and the ratification of the Turkish-Pakistani Economic Cooperation Organization (ECO) in 1985. That same year, Pakistan and six other South Asian countries, including India and Bangladesh, formed the South Asian Association for Regional Cooperation (SAARC). As a Muslim-majority state, Pakistan was an active member of the Organization of the

Islamic Conference (OIC). The state also held observer status in the Organization of American States (OAS).

In environmental cooperation, Pakistan was part of the South Asia Cooperative Environment Program (SACEP), the Basel Convention, the Convention on Biological Diversity, Ramsar, CITES, the London Convention, the Kyoto Protocol, the Montréal Protocol, MARPOL, and the UN Conventions on the Law of the Sea, Climate Change, and Desertification.

19 ECONOMY

The gross domestic product of Pakistan as of January 1, 2011, was $464.9 billion (GDP-PPP) or $174.9 billion (GDP-CER), with a rate of change, as of the second quarter of 2011, at 2.4% (down from 4.6% in 2010). GDP-PPP per capita income was $2500. This made Pakistan the 27th largest world economy in terms of Purchasing Power Parity (PPP). Breakdown by sector was agriculture: 21.2%; industry: 25.4%; services: 53.4%. As well, according to the State Bank of Pakistan, remittances from citizens living abroad totaled $11.2 billion, accounting for more than 2% of GDP. The labor force was 55.77 million, with 43% in agriculture; 20.3% in industry and 36.6% in services. Unemployment was reported at 15.4% and inflation at 13.9% (up from 7.7% in 2007).

As of 2010, exports totaled $21.46 billion and imports $32.88 billion. Major export partners included the US (15.8%), Afghanistan (8.1%), UAE (7.9%), China (7.3%), UK (4.3%) and Germany (4.2%). Prime exports are agricultural, cotton alone accounting for 60%. Manufactured products include textiles, pharmaceuticals, processed foods and construction materials. Pakistani imports were led by China (17.9%) for manufactured products and oil from the Middle East, including Saudi Arabia (10.7%), the United Arab Emirates (10.6%) and Kuwait (5.5%). External debt was $61.85 billion as of June 2011, and public debt was 50.6% of GDP. Foreign exchange reserves stood at $17.2 billion and a budget deficit of -6.2% of GDP was posted.

Since the liberalization of the economy beginning in the 1980s, foreign investment rose to a high of $484 million in 2001, since when it has declined. According to the State Bank of Pakistan, the downward trend continues into 2011. Investment fell 60.8 percent in the first month of 2011/12 fiscal year (July-June) to $61.9 million, from $157.8 million in July 2010. This severely retarded the development of crucial energy, oil and gas, and mining sectors, which were reported to hold great prospects. The under-performance of the economy was largely accredited to rising debt-servicing burdens since the 1970s, low tax revenues (14.2% of GDP in 2010), high levels of defense spending and US-led sanctions (1990–2001). Endemic corruption was also a major concern, Transparency International ranking Pakistan consistently toward the bottom of their findings in the last three years, resting at 134th out of 176 countries polled in 2011. In the last decade, instability created by the Afghan war and natural disasters such as the 2005 Kashmir earthquake and the 2010–11 monsoon floods further eroded growth potential.

20 INCOME

As of 2011, the World Bank estimated that Pakistan, with 2.51% of the world's population, accounted for 0.67% of the world's GDP. By comparison, the United States, with 4.85% of the world's population, accounted for 22.51% of world GDP. Actual individual consumption in Pakistan was 79.7% of GDP and accounted for 0.84% of world consumption. By comparison, the United States accounted for 25.44% of world individual consumption. The World Bank also estimated that 39.6% of Pakistan's GDP was spent on food and beverages, 12.8% on housing and household furnishings, 6.0% on clothes, 5.8% on health, 4.1% on transportation, 1.5% on communications, 2.1% on recreation, 0.5% on restaurants and hotels, and 3.6% on miscellaneous goods and services and purchases from abroad.

Household consumption as of 2009 totaled $115.9 billion or about $619 per capita, measured in current US dollars rather than PPP. It was estimated that household consumption was growing at an average annual rate of 11.3%. However, disparities in income must be taken into account. Household consumption by percentage share, based on the latest available figures from 2005, reveals that the lowest 10% of the population accounted for 3.9% of consumption, while the highest 10% accounted for 26.5%, in comparison with US rates of lowest 10% consumption at 2% and highest 10% consumption of 30% in 2007. As of 2008, the World Bank reported a poverty rate of 17.2%, down from about 24% in 2006. Nevertheless, the 2010 Human Development Index found 60.3% of Pakistan's population lived on under $2/day, and 22.6% under $1/day, ranking Pakistan at 145 out of 187 states included.

21 LABOR

By the Constitution of 1973 and subsequent legislation, the 2011 Pakistani labor force of 55.77 million was guaranteed numerous safeguards. The prohibition of human trafficking, slavery, child and bonded labor, workdays and weeks capped at international standards, paid leave, benefits and severance, and the right to collective bargaining number among the rights enjoined. Abuses of all these rights, however, were endemic.

For example, in 2002 the US Department of Labor (International Labor Office) estimated that 14.4 percent of children ages 10 to 14 years in Pakistan were working. Most working children (officially under the age of 15 years) were found in agriculture, followed by informal activities in the non-agricultural sector, such as domestic work, street vending, and work in family businesses. More egregiously by international and official Pakistani standards, children were also employed or bonded in several hazardous sectors, including leather tanning, surgical instruments manufacturing, coal mining, deep sea fishing, brick-making, and glass bangle manufacturing, and further exploited by the illicit sex and drug trades. Anywhere from two to 19 million children were thought to work in violation of Pakistani law as of 2011. Pakistan was also a source, transit, and destination country for child trafficking victims, primarily involving Bangladesh, Afghanistan, Iran, Burma, Nepal, and Central Asia.

Beyond government apathy in enforcement, the violation of labor laws was driven by chronic unemployment and underemployment. Structural inadequacies, combined with lack of educational opportunities, have been identified as major contributors to low labor standards. Although there were dozens of active trade unions in Pakistan, periodic government clamp-downs and cooption have limited their activities. In 2010 only 3% of the total workforce was unionized. Low participation contributed to broader violations, including those rooted in a lack of awareness of existing labor rights among the workforce. The answer to such problems for many in Pakistan has been to join ex-patriot labor forces, mostly in the Middle East and Europe, sometimes illegally and often for less than adequate wages. Nevertheless, according to the State Bank of Pakistan in 2011, remittances from citizens living abroad totaled $11.2 billion, accounting for more than 2% of GDP.

22 AGRICULTURE

Agriculture in Pakistan is a gift of the Indus River and the largest contiguous irrigation system in the world. As a sector of the economy in 2011, it accounted for 21.2% of Pakistan's GDP-PPP, only recently overshadowed by industry (25.4%) and services (53.4%). Yet it still employed 43% of the working population. Roughly 34% of the total land was farmed as of 2011, and the country's major crops included cotton, wheat, rice and sugarcane. Cereal production amounted to 38.1 million tons, fruit production 6.3 million tons, and vegetable production 5.3 million tons, making it is a net food exporter. According to the UN Food and Agriculture Organization in 2005, Pakistan was in the top ten producers of 11 staples and fruits world-wide, including cotton (4th), sugarcane (5th) and wheat (9th).

The expansion of price controls since the establishment of the Agricultural Price Commission (1980) and the availability of credit through the Zarai Taraqiati Bank Limited (formerly Agricultural Development Bank of Pakistan [1961]) enhanced development to a peak of 5.7% real growth during the mid-1990s, from when the agricultural sector has slowed. In August 2009, for example, a shortfall in sugar production resulted in a 15% increase in sugar prices and the need for emergency imports of over 175,000 tons. Decreased production may be attributed to weak harvests and on-going regional conflicts. Periodic natural disasters have also added to decreased productivity. With the devastating 2010 monsoon floods between early August to mid-September, at least 570,000 hectares (1,400,000 acres) of cropland were destroyed in Punjab and Sindh, including 3,000 sq km(1,158 sq mi) of cotton, 800 sq km (309 sq mi) of rice and the same amount of sugarcane, 500,000 tons of wheat and 1,000 sq km (386 sq mi) of animal fodder and 500,000 tons of wheat. Official estimates of losses totaled just below $9 billion. Similar losses, particularly in Sindh, were posted for the 2011 floods.

A more persistent problem was the distribution of landholdings. With less than 1% of farms accounting for more than 25% of agricultural land, and one-third of farmers (50% in Sindh) working as tenants, much of the wealth generated was held by an entrenched landed elite. The incidence of bonded labor was also high in this sector. The military government of Ayub Khan decreed in 1959 that the maximum holding for any person should be 200 hectares (500 acres) of irrigated land or 400 hectares (1,000 acres) un-irrigated. Land in excess of these amounts was acquired by the government and paid for in interest-bearing 30-year bonds. However, exceptions such as title transfers failed to undermine large holdings and the political power of the landed elite, limiting land surrendered to approximately 1 million hectares with only 250,000 hectares sold to roughly 50,000 tenants by 1971. In 1972, Zulfikar Ali Bhutto's government reduced the maximum size of holdings by an additional two-thirds, with the government empowered to confiscate without payment all excess land for free redistribution to landless peasants and small tenants. By 1977, according to of-

ficial figures, only 520,000 hectares (1.28 million acres) had been appropriated with less than 285,000 hectares (704,250 acres) redistributed to approximately 71,000 farmers. Although contemporary figures are scant, the maintenance of large holdings and commensurate political power for landed elites continued into 2011. Most controversially, agricultural income tax was the sole prerogative of provincial governments and it was not until the 1990s that legislation was passed to levy a negligible rate. In 2009, only PKR1 billion ($11.5 million) in agricultural tax was collected from all four provinces out of total tax revenue of PKR1.38 trillion ($15.87 billion).

23 ANIMAL HUSBANDRY

Some 30 to 35 million of Pakistan's workforce was engaged in animal husbandry in 2011. The UN Food and Agriculture Organization (FAO) reported that Pakistan dedicated 5 million hectares (12.4 million acres) to permanent pasture or meadow in 2009. During that year, the country tended 295 million chickens and 33 million head of cattle. The production from these animals and other animals amounted to 1.35 million tons of beef and veal, 319 tons of goat, 560,111 tons of poultry, 414,507 tons of eggs, and 27.5 million tons of milk. Pakistan also produced 134,590 tons of cattle hide and 41,540 tons of raw wool. Livestock accounted for 10.8% of GDP.

Livestock played a vital role in the lives of the rural poor. Herds animals have long been built up in times of plenty and sold to supplement income in times of scarcity. Camels, donkeys and bullocks have alos long been used for transport and as draft animals. Dung has also been a vital source of fuel and fertilizer. As such, sheep ranged widely over the grazing lands of middle and northern Pakistan; the bulk of their wool exported. Among local breeds of cattle, the Red Sindhi, the Tharparker, the Sahiwal were renowned for milk, and the Bhagnari and Dhanni for draft purposes. The production of powdered milk, cheese, butter and ice cream was carried out by several large dairy plants. From 1984 to 1990, milk production increased by 41%, and meat production rose 48%. Further increases were recorded in the 2000's, following the oubreak of mad cow disease elsewhere in the world and increased demand on the international market. Poultry production was also prominent as of late, especially through scientific research in breeding, feeding, and disease control. The government, with the aid of the Asian Development Bank, has also broadened extension and artificial breeding services, taken measures to improve slaughterhouses, and introduced high-yield fodder varieties. However, the UN FAO reported that the 2010 monsoon floods resulted in the deaths of millions of livestock animals, poultry being entirely wiped out in certain areas, severely affecting the income of the rural poor and the productivity of the sector. The picture was worsened by the 2011 floods, particularly in Sindh, projecting a significant decrease in this sector's contribution to the economy.

24 FISHING

With a coastline of 814 km (506 mi), and the Indus River and its tributaries, Pakistan is rich in marine and riverine fishery resources that remain to be fully developed. Almost the entire population of the coastal areas of Sindh and Balochistan depends on fisheries for its livelihood. There were 5,920 decked commercial fishing boats in 2008 (approximately constant since 2000). The 2008 capture totaled 451,414 tons according to the UN FAO. Species caught included salmon, mullet, pomfret, mackerel, shrimp, and local varieties. About 10% of the annual catch was exported, amounting to $136.9 million in 2003 and $196 million in 2006. To exploit potential fishery resources, the government has undertaken such projects as construction of a modern harbor for fishing vessels at Karāchi, procurement of diesel-powered vessels, establishment of cold storage and marketing facilities, export of frozen shrimp, and encouragement of cooperative fish-marketing societies. Aquaculture projects have also increased production from around 10–15,000 tons in 2000 to 100,000 tons in 2006 and 2007, yet fisheries in total only contributed 0.3% to overall GDP and less than 1% to national employment in 2011.

25 FORESTRY

According to the UN FAO, 2.2% (1,687,000 hectares) of Pakistan was covered by forest, representing a decline of 42,000 hectares (1.66% per year) from 1990 to 2010, reaching 2.6% from 2005 to 2010. Irrigated plantation forests grew such species as sheesham, mulberry, bakain, and semal, mostly for timber, furniture, and sporting goods production. In 2009, roundwood harvests stood at 2.99 million cu m (105.6 million cu ft), about 500,000 cu m (17.6 million cu ft) of which was produced annually by state forests under the authority of the Pakistan Forest Institute. The value of all forest products, including roundwood, totaled $133 million in 2005. Woodfuel harvests was 31.6 million cu m in 2005, with a total value of $1.38 billion. Pakistan has a 25-year forestry master plan outlining the development of the industry through 2018, but its ineffectiveness is evident in rising rates of deforestation and growing imports for construction timber.

26 MINING

Except for petroleum and natural gas, mineral reserves in Pakistan were meager and of poor quality. Chromite was one of the few valuable minerals available. Production of chromium (by metal content) rose to an estimated 50,000 metric tons in 2009 from an estimated 32,900 metric tons in 2005. Construction materials were a leading industry in the country. In 2003 small quantities were produced of aragonite and marble, barite, bauxite, bentonite, chalk, dolomite, natural emery, feldspar, fire clay, fluorspar, fuller's earth, crude gypsum, kaolin (china clay), limestone and other stone, crude magnesite, nitrogen, ammonia, phosphate rock, natural mineral pigments, rock and marine salt, bajir and common sand, glass sand, caustic soda, soapstone, strontium minerals (celestite), native sulfur, soapstone talc and related materials.

Remote and hazardous locations, regional conflicts and inadequate investments account for the lack of development. The Saindak copper-gold reserves were to be developed through a $350 million Sino-Pak joint venture. The project was leased for 10 year to a Chinese company (Metallurgical Construction Corp), but the lease was due to expire in September 2012. Under the lease agreement, an annual rent of $500,000 plus a 50% share of sales was to be paid to the Pakistani government. Such agreements have been a significant source of tension between provincial and federal governments, as well as between transparency advocates and government in general, explaining delays in operations. For example, the Reqo Diq copper-gold reserves were under contract to be developed by Tethyan Copper, a joint venture of Chile's Antofagasta and Canada's Barrick Gold, but the Baluchistan government blocked the project in 2011, seeking to renegotiate terms. In 2010, Engro Chemical announced intensions to develop Thar coal fields, as well as coal gasification plants, but actual investment remains unspecified.

27 ENERGY AND POWER

The World Bank reported in 2008 that Pakistan produced 91.6 billion kWh of electricity and consumed 72.4 billion kWh, or 387 kWh per capita. The major power producers were WAPDA (Water & Power Development Authority), KESC (Karachi Electric Supply Company), IPPs (Independent Power Producers) and PAEC (Pakistan Atomic Energy Commission). Roughly 65% of generation relied on fossil fuels, 33% on hydropower and 2% nuclear. Wind, solar and other alternative energy sources have not been seriously pursued.

Despite late increases in installed generating capacity, Pakistan faced electricity shortages due to lack of investment in new generators, rapid demand growth, transmission losses due to outdated infrastructure, power theft, $1.38 billion government debt to power producers, and seasonal reductions in the availability of hydropower. Rotating power outages of 6–8 hours daily were common in many areas, urban and rural. In 2010, with shortfalls estimated between 6000 and 7500 MW, the government responded by formulating a Pakistan National Energy Policy. At the end of 2011, promises to pay debt were announced, but the only measures implemented center on cutting consumption by ordering the closure of markets early, cutting air conditioner usage in government offices, and other such policies conceived to reduce consumption by 500 MW. The energy crisis has hampered the economy and led to mass demonstrations and sporadic riots in 2011.

28 INDUSTRY

As of 2011, industry accounted for 25.4% of Pakistan's GDP and employed 20.3% of the labor force. Textile and garment manufacturing accounted for approximately 66% of the total export earnings from manufactured goods. Some long and extra-long staple cotton was imported to meet demand for finer cottons. About 80% of the textile industry was based on cotton, but factories also produced synthetic fabrics, worsted yarn, and jute textiles. Jute textile output amounted to 70,100 tons in 1999/00. The textile industry as a whole employed about 38% of the industrial work force, accounting for 8.5% of GDP, 31% of total investment, and 27% of industrial value-added. In January 2005, the WTO lifted textile-import quotas in Europe and the United States, and Pakistan, having invested $4 billion in the four years up to the lifting of the quotas, was well-placed for growth in the textile industry.

Other important industries included food processing, chemicals manufacture, and the iron and steel industries. Food processing was considered Pakistan's second largest industry, accounting for slightly more than 27% of value-added production. Pakistan Steel, the country's only integrated steel mill, employed about 14,500 workers and has an annual production capacity of 1.1 million tons. The government planned to expand the mill's annual capacity to 3 million tons. Pakistan Steel produced coke, pig iron, billets, hot and cold rolled coils and sheets, and galvanized sheets.

In June 1999, the first tin-plating plant began operation, a joint venture with Japan.

As of 2005, Pakistan had 10 fertilizer plants, four state-owned and six private, with a total annual production capacity of 5.75 million tons. There were 24 cement plants, four state-owned and 20 private, with an annual production capacity of 19.55 million tons. Pakistan's chemical industry produced a number of basic chemicals used in its other industries, including soda ash, caustic soda and sulfuric acid. Industrial output from other major industries also included refined sugar, vegetable ghee, urea, rubber tubes, electric motors, electrical consumer products (light bulbs, air conditioners, fans, refrigerators, freezers, TV sets, radios, and sewing machines), and pharmaceuticals.

Much of Pakistan's industrial output was fostered by government planning and investment during the 1960's and 1970's. For example, large government investments in the 1970's, under the government of Zulfikar Ali Bhutto, established the country's first large-scale ship-building and steel milling operations; the production of chemical fertilizers was also given special government support. A nationalization program also brought most privately-owned basic industrial units under the public sector. The Pakistan Industrial Development Corp., established in the early 1980s with IDA credit, developed industrial estates for small- and medium-scale industries, assisting their occupants in obtaining credit, raw materials, technical and managerial assistance, access to production facilities, as well as marketing support. Despite steady overall industrial growth during the 1980s, the sector remained concentrated in cotton processing, textiles, food processing and petroleum refining.

The public sector continued to dominate in steel, heavy engineering, automobiles, petroleum and defense-related production, but since 1991, successive governments have moved toward privatization, auctioning off majority control in nearly all public sector industrial enterprises, including those manufacturing chemicals, fertilizers, engineering products, petroleum products, cement, automobiles, and other industrial products requiring a high level of capital investment, to private investors. The majority of the 74 production enterprises controlled by eight public holding companies—Pakistan Steel, the State Cement Corporation (PACO), Federal Chemical and Ceramics Corporation (FCCC), State Petroleum Refining and Petrochemical Corporation (PERAC), State Engineering Corporation (SEC), the Pakistan Industrial Development Corporation (PIDC), the state fertilizer corporation, and Pakistan Automobile Corporation, have been privatized, and most of those remaining were scheduled to be sold.

29 SCIENCE AND TECHNOLOGY

As of 2011, 44 of Pakistan's 132 recognized universities specialized in scientific fields including engineering, medical sciences, agricultural sciences and information technologies, while many more offered basic degrees in the sciences. More specialized research was also fostered by the Pakistan Academy of Sciences, established in 1953 by researchers in natural sciences. This was followed by such institutions as the High Tension Laboratories (HTL), the Institute of Theoretical Physics (ITP), the Institute of Nuclear Science and Technology and the Centre for Nuclear Studies. High

technology exports in 2002 totaled $36 million or 1% of Pakistan's manufactured exports.

The government did not become directly involved in research and development until 1972, when Zulfikar Ali Bhutto's government established the Ministry of Science. Under Z.A. Bhutto, the Ministry of Science was particularly focused on the promotion military research and development, including the nuclear bomb, increasing government funding many times. However, the advancement of physics and mathematics, in which Pakistani scientists had begun winning international recognition, had already begun to wane by the time the physicist Dr. Abdus Salam became Pakistan's only Nobel Laureate in 1979.

During the 1980s, under Zia ul-Haq's tenure as President, increased military orientation further eroded pure research. However, the Karāchi Export Processing Zone (EPZ), established in 1980, has attracted foreign capital investment in advanced technologies. By 2011, the EPZ included computer assembly and parts manufacture, television assembly, other electrical and electronic products, and engineering. As well, the Pakistan Atomic Energy Commission (AEC) developed a nuclear plant for electric power generation and research programs. The AEC's three nuclear centers for agricultural research have employed nuclear techniques to improve crop varieties. Six nuclear medical centers provide diagnosis and treatment of patients with radioisotopes produced from Pakistan's own uranium resources. Although it was not until May 1998, that Pakistan conducted nuclear weapons tests, firing five nuclear devises, it is believed that these weapons were developed by 1983.

Research received renewed government attention under the rule of Pervez Musharraf, with the establishment of the Higher Education Commission (HEC). Major research was undertaken by Pakistan's institutes in the field of natural sciences, but the situation soon deteriorated, as evinced by the dissolution of the HEC in 2011. In 2002, research and development expenditures totaled 1.67% of GDP. According to the World Bank, it had fallen to 0.67% of GDP by 2009.

30 DOMESTIC TRADE

According to the Pakistan Ministry of Commerce, domestic commerce, which includes retail and wholesale traders, hotels and restaurants, transport, storage, communications, financial and real estate services, accounted for 50% of the service sector's contribution to GDP in 2006, or approximately 25% of total GDP, while employing 35–40% of the workforce. The government supervised the supply and pricing of essential commodities, including fruits, vegetables, livestock, and dairy products, and had established several cooperative marketing and distribution organizations. Foreign goods were brought in by large importing concerns, centered at Karāchi, and distributed to retailers through many intermediaries. There were several produce exchanges in major cities and towns, and trade organizations were represented by the Federation of Chambers of Commerce and Industry. Growth potential was hampered by regional conflicts, power shortages, transpor-

Principal Trading Partners – Pakistan (2010)

(In millions of US dollars)

Country	Total	Exports	Imports	Balance
World	59,193.0	21,410.0	37,783.0	-16,373.0
China	9,202.0	1,573.0	7,629.0	-6,056.0
United Arab Emirates	6,224.0	1,699.0	4,525.0	-2,826.0
United States	5,479.0	3,389.0	2,090.0	1,299.0
Somalia	4,653.0	83.0	4,570.0	-4,487.0
India	2,760.0	282.0	2,478.0	-2,196.0
Maldives	2,711.0	132.0	2,579.0	-2,447.0
Kuwait	2,450.0	94.0	2,356.0	-2,262.0
Afghanistan	1,876.0	1,724.0	152.0	1,572.0
Germany	1,872.0	899.0	973.0	-74.0
Japan	1,769.0	323.0	1,446.0	-1,123.0

(…) data not available or not significant.

(n.s.) not specified.

SOURCE: *2011 Direction of Trade Statistics Yearbook,* New York: United Nations, 2011.

Balance of Payments – Pakistan (2010)

(In millions of US dollars)

Current Account		-1,490.0
Balance on goods	-11,416.0	
Imports	-32,879.0	
Exports	21,463.0	
Balance on services	-678.0	
Balance on income	-3,178.0	
Current transfers	13,782.0	
Capital Account		132.0
Financial Account		2,580.0
Direct investment abroad	-46.0	
Direct investment in Pakistan	2,016.0	
Portfolio investment assets	6.0	
Portfolio investment liabilities	-114.0	
Financial derivatives	…	
Other investment assets	-295.0	
Other investment liabilities	1,013.0	
Net Errors and Omissions		-528.0
Reserves and Related Items		-694.0

(…) data not available or not significant.

SOURCE: *Balance of Payment Statistics Yearbook 2011,* Washington, DC: International Monetary Fund, 2011.

tation shortfalls, lack of government investments, oversight and corruption.

31 FOREIGN TRADE

As of 2010, Pakistan's exports totaled $21.46 billion and imports $32.88 billion. Major export partners included the United States (15.8%), Afghanistan (8.1%), UAE (7.9%), China (7.3%), UK (4.3%) and Germany (4.2%). Prime exports were agricultural, cotton alone accounting for 60%. Manufactured products included textiles, pharmaceuticals, processed foods and construction materials. Pakistani imports were led by China (17.9%) for manufactured products and oil from the Middle East, including Saudi Arabia (10.7%), the United Arab Emirates (10.6%) and Kuwait (5.5%). Pakistan's Ministry of Commerce estimated that up to $1.5 billion of unregistered trade occured annually, mostly from smuggled imports. Pakistan has suffered a weak trade position since the early 1970s, as the cost of oil imports have risen while prices for the country's main exports have declined and the rupee has been consistently devalued on the international market.

32 BALANCE OF PAYMENTS

In 2010, Pakistan's exports totaled $21.46 billion and imports $32.88 billion, amounting to a foreign trade deficit of approximately $12 billion, or 2.5% of GDP-PPP. External debt was $61.85 billion as of June 2011, and public debt was 50.6% of GDP. Foreign exchange reserves stood at $17.2 billion. The current account balance was $-1.585 billion.

Pakistan's deficit financing has been chronic since the 1970s. The cost of oil/petroleum product imports, as well as machinery, were primarily responsible for the imbalance. By the mid-1990's, imports were growing at an annual rate of 16%, relative to export growth of 6%. The rupee was devalued by 11% during 1995 and 1996 to encourage exports. Nevertheless, foreign reserves fell to around $800 million by mid-1997. By 2000, foreign debt equaled 100% of GDP. Subsequent growth of exports and remittances from Pakistanis working abroad (mostly in the Middle East) helped Pakistan to keep the payments deficit in check, although fluctuating commodity prices and regional conflicts continued

to leave Pakistan in a vulnerable position. During the 1991 Gulf War, for example, nearly 80,000 Pakistanis in Kuwait and Iraq lost their jobs, and only about 25% of these jobs had been regained by 1993, resulting in remittances as low as $1.4 billion in 1997/98 and $1 billion from 1999 to 2001, after having peaked at near $3 billion in 1982/83. In 2011, the State Bank of Pakistan reported a record $11.2 billion in remittances, contributing to the government declining the last tranche of an IMF loan signed in 2008. Nevertheless, a World Bank loan of $5.5 billion was still needed to offset slowed development largely due damage sustained during the devastating 2010 and 2011 monsoon floods.

33 BANKING AND SECURITIES

The central banking institution was the State Bank of Pakistan (SBP), established in 1948. The government held 51% of the bank's paid-up capital; 49% was held by corporations, societies, and individuals. The State Bank had exclusive responsibility for the issuance of currency; it was the financial agent of the central and provincial governments, and was responsible for the flotation and management of the public debt. The discount rate as of December 2010 was 0.07%.

The nation's largest commercial banks were nationalized by the government of Zulfikar Ali Bhutto in 1974. In 1981, in accordance with the Islamic condemnation of usury, virtually all banks opened special accounts for depositors who preferred, in lieu of interest, to share in the profits or losses from investments made with their money. In 1985, all savings accounts stopped yielding interest and converted to sharing in profit and loss. So-called Islamic banking has continued to win shares in the commercial banking sector into 2011. Pakistan instituted banking reforms in 1991, as part of its economic liberalization under the government of Nawaz Sharif. The Muslim Commercial Bank and the Allied Bank of Pakistan Ltd. reverted to private ownership shortly thereafter. In 1991, banking licenses were granted to private commercial banks that wanted to establish foreign bank branches in the country. Privatization measures continued as of 2011. The commercial banks' prime lending rate as of December 2010 was 13.462%.

Consumer banking in Pakistan was largely undeveloped; commercial banks lend predominantly to corporations. The rate of non-performing loans in 2011 was approximately 15%. Major weaknesses persisted and, as Moody's Investors Service in a Banking System Outlook published in December 2011 suggested, the negative outlook reflected two key factors: a weak operating environment; and high exposure to the Pakistani government's weak fiscal position. Further risks included an escalation of ongoing political instability and growing deterioration in investor confidence. Partly ameliorating these negatives were low-cost deposit-funding profiles, which supported overall liquidity and solid earnings-generating capacity.

There were stock exchanges at Lahore, Karāchi, and Islāmābād, with Karāchi accounting for a major share of the business. In 2009, there were 654 companies listed on the Karachi Stock Exchange (KSE), down from a peak of 782 in 1996. Market capitalization has fluctuated since the 1990s, standing at $12.2 billion in 1994, dropping to $4.9 billion in 2001, but rising to approximately $35 billion by mid-2011.

³⁴INSURANCE

Pakistan's life insurance sector, nationalized in 1972, operated under the aegis of the State Life Insurance Corp. and Postal Life Insurance until 1992, when the government opened it to private sector participation. Foreign companies were no longer barred from the life insurance business, but they were restricted to minority ownership. Private companies functioned in nonlife insurance areas, but the government insurance business was controlled by the National Insurance Corp. Political instability since the 1990s, together with the widespread poverty of households, constrained investment and the development of insurance. One of the state's first steps was to standardize and reduce premium rates and to encourage coverage among a wider segment of the population. In 2003, the value of all direct insurance premiums written totaled $434 million, of which nonlife premiums accounted for $269 million. In 2002 Pakistan's top nonlife insurer was Adamjee, which had gross domestic written nonlife premiums of $75.4 million, while the country's leading life insurer was State Life, which had gross written life insurance premiums of $140.4 million. The monsoon floods of 2010 and 2011 severely tested the sector as life and nonlife claims rose. Consequently, the government began striving to encourage the development of crop insurance and micro-insurance.

³⁵PUBLIC FINANCE

In 2010 the budget of Pakistan included $25.33 billion in public revenue and $36.24 billion in public expenditures. The budget deficit amounted to 6.3% of GDP. Public debt was 49.9% of GDP, with $56.13 billion of the debt held by foreign entities. From 2004 to 2011, government outlays by function generally remained constant as follows: general public services (including debt servicing), 66.5%; defense, 19.9%; public order and safety, 1.7%; economic affairs, 8.5%; housing and community amenities, 0.3%; health, 0.8%;

Public Finance – Pakistan (2011)

(In billions of rupees, budgetary central figures)

Revenue and Grants	**2,510.68**	**100.0%**
Tax revenue	1,778.72	70.8%
Social contributions	...	...
Grants	99.69	4.0%
Other revenue	632.28	25.2%
Expenditures	**3,312.91**	**100.0%**
General public services	2,582.94	78.0%
Defense	442.17	13.3%
Public order and safety	53.16	1.6%
Economic affairs	143.34	4.3%
Environmental protection	0.45	<0.1%
Housing and community amenities	6.63	0.2%
Health	21.52	0.6%
Recreational, culture, and religion	4.79	0.1%
Education	55.61	1.7%
Social protection	2.31	0.1%

(…) data not available or not significant.

SOURCE: *Government Finance Statistics Yearbook 2010*, Washington, DC: International Monetary Fund, 2010.

recreation, culture, and religion, 0.3%; education, 1.9%; and social protection, 0.2%.

Pakistan's fiscal year extends from 1 July to 30 June. The federal government frames two separate budgets: revenue (current account) and capital. Deficits have appeared since 1971/72, a combined result of the loss of revenues from East Pakistan, stepped-up defense expenditures, lax spending controls, and a low and inelastic tax base. Tax revenues have not kept pace with expenditure growth due to widespread evasion, corruption among tax officials, overreliance on foreign trade taxes, and a tax exemption for agricultural income, which comprises 24% of GDP. To increase tax revenues, largely under the direction of the IMF and World Bank, successive governements have sought to raise revenues by expanding the tax base beyond the 1% of Pakistanis who then paid income tax. Other proposals included a reduction in government payrolls, improved tax administration, and an end to the tax exemption for agricultural income. That public debt has continued to rise while tax revenue earned in 2010 amounted to no more than 14.2% of GDP, attests to the minimal effect of government policies over the decades.

³⁶TAXATION

As of 2011, Pakistan's tax revenues were dependent on a variety of levies. From 2007, Pakistan effectively had one corporate tax rates: a 35% rate for public companies; a 35% rate for private companies; and a 35% rate for banking companies. There was also a 0.5% tax on turnover. Generally, capital gains for companies and individuals were taxed as part of income. Capital gains resulting from assets held 12 months or less were taxed at the full corporate rate. Gains resulting from the sale of assets held longer than 12 months were taxed only at 75% of the total capital gains amount. Dividends were subject to a withholding tax of 5% (for those paid to public firms or insurance companies); 7.5% (dividends paid by power companies, certain privatized power projects, and by those firms solely engaged in mining operations, except petroleum); and 10% (for all other dividends). Generally, interest income was subject to a 30% tax rate, while royalties and technical services fees were each subject to a 15% rate. A sales tax of 15% is levied on the value of goods. However, there were exemptions for certain items and for certain classes of people. Exports were zero-rated. Established proportions of the various taxes levied by the federal government were distributed to the provincial governments. In addition, the provinces collected, for their exclusive use, taxes on land revenue, immovable property, vehicles, professions and services, and mineral rights, as well as excise taxes. Municipalities and other local governments may also levy taxes.

Taxation has been a vexed issue for successive governments. The federal government has an officially progressive income tax regime, rising from 5% in the lowest category to 35% in the highest, with a net wealth tax of up to 2.5%. Reflecting the elite commercial and landowning background of most government legislators, however, the federal government did not levy income tax on agricultural income and only about 1% of the population paid income tax. Thus, in 2010, total tax revenues collected only amounted to 14.2% of GDP.

37 CUSTOMS AND DUTIES

Pakistan's customs tariffs brought in the largest single share of national revenue. Most dutiable items were subject to ad valorem duties that range from 0–30%. There was, in many cases, a 15% sales tax on imported goods (food, raw materials, and capital goods are exempt from this tax). Alcohol was levied at a rate up to 65%, but could be as high as 225%. However, maximum rates averaged at around 35%. Tariffs were also levied on major items of export, but these rates were subject to change as measures were taken to encourage or discourage the export of raw materials. Exports of certain foods, used copper and brass utensils, and some hides and skins were banned.

38 FOREIGN INVESTMENT

Foreign direct investment (FDI) in Pakistan was a net inflow of $2.39 billion according to World Bank figures published in 2009. FDI represented 1.47% of GDP. According to the State Bank of Pakistan, however, a downward trend had set in by 2011, investment falling 60.8 percent in the first month of 2011/12 fiscal year (July-June) to $61.9 million, from $157.8 million in July 2010.

Foreign aid and investment have played a critical role in Pakistan's economic development since the first years of independence. Since 1954, the government has tried to attract foreign investment to maintain economic development, provide specialized technical knowledge, and bring in much-needed foreign exchange. Incentives for private investment included guarantees for the repatriation of capital invested in approved industries, facilities for remittance of profits, and guarantees for equitable compensation in the event of nationalization of an industry. In addition, special tax concessions available to certain local industries were also available to foreign investors. Since the late 1980s, a series of regulatory reforms related to exchange controls, repatriation of profits, credit for foreign-owned firms, issuing of equity shares, foreign currency accounts, and transactions on the stock exchange have significantly reduced the restrictions on general foreign investor activity in the wider Pakistani economy.

Due largely to endemic corruption and political instability, the record of foreign direct investment in Pakistan has been a rollercoaster. In 1995/96, FDI stood at $1.1 billion, then dropped to $548 million in 1996/97 in response to a foreign-exchange crisis. Investors were also deterred by Pakistan's listing as the second-most-corrupt nation in the world, after Nigeria, that year. In the tension leading up to the nuclear bomb tests in May 1998, FDI fell to $432.7 million in 1998/99, and then decreased further after the military coup in 1999, to $420 million, in 1999/00. In 2000/01, FDI fell to an annual rate of less than $275 million. After the 11 September 2001 terrorist attacks on the United States, however, the overall investment climate in terms of security was worsened by Pakistan's role in the US-led war on terrorism, though US aid increased.

In 2004/05, total FDI inflows amounted to $1.524 billion, with the UAE investing $367.5 million in the country, the United States $326 million, and the United Kingdom $181.5 million. From July to November 2005, Saudi Arabia invested $265.6 million in Pakistan, the United States $170.8 million, the United Kingdom $56.2 million, while the UAE's FDI total was in the negative figures, at -$31.5 million. Such shifts in investment were due in part to foreign countries' reactions to Pakistan's privatization efforts: certain Gulf states, flush with capital, have placed bids on Pakistani contracts only to pull out. This happened in the case of the Pakistan Telecommunications Co. Ltd. (PTCL). In June 2005, the UAE's company Etisalat (Emirates Telecommunications) offered the highest bid of $2.6 billion to acquire 26% shares and management control of PTCL. This bid price offered by Etisalat was 100% higher than market price and reserve price fixed by the government. The second-highest bidder was China Mobile of China, offering a bid of $1.4 billion, followed by Sing Tel of Singapore, with a bid of $1.17 billion for 26% shares. In October 2005, the PTCL privatization transaction failed to materialize when Etisalat failed to make payment of the balance bid amount by the agreed-upon timeline. This was the second major privatization deal that had failed within a year: earlier in 2005, Kanooz-al-Watan of Saudi Arabia, the highest bidder of Karāchi Electric Supply Corp. (KESC), backed out of its offer. However, in January 2006, Etisalat and the Pakistani government came to an agreement over payments for PTCL, so the deal went through.

39 ECONOMIC DEVELOPMENT

After the founding of the state in 1947, the government's economic policy concentrated attention on developing an economic infrastructure, achieving self-sufficiency in food, and developing export industries. Under the government of Zulkifar Ali Bhutto, a major new land reform program introduced in March 1972 had resulted by March 1975 in the confiscation (for eventual redistribution) of 45.3% of all privately cultivated farmland. By November 1973, the government had nationalized industries in 10 major categories of production. In a third major step, most of the commercial banks were nationalized on 1 January 1974, resulting in control of more than 90% of all banking business by the State Bank and the five newly created units.

By the late 1970s, however, Pakistan's martial law government under General Zia ul-Haq, claiming the nationalization program had stifled production and discouraged private investment, moved to restore private sector confidence by fostering economic stability and by redressing the balance-of-payments deficit, which was causing large overseas debt obligations. A new five-year plan (1978–83), Pakistan's fifth, reserved 48% of industrial investment for the private sector and set goals for an annual economic growth rate of 7.2%, a 4.2% rise in per capita income, and increases of 6% in agricultural output and 10% in industrial production. The plan was allocated a budget of $21 billion, of which 25% was to come from external sources. Indications were that the agricultural sector would meet its target, but that rising oil costs and the burden of providing for the Afghan refugees had impeded progress in other sectors. A sixth five-year plan (1983–88) envisioned further investments in water and power development, deregulation to increase private sector activity, and a new emphasis on provision of social services and infrastructural improvements for rural areas.

By the late 1980s, a number of structural factors resulted in increasingly critical fiscal and balance of payment deficits. With less than 30% of the budget devoted to infrastructural development and other needs in health and education, the prognosis for long-term social and economic development remained poor. In response, a medium-term structural reform program was developed under the government of Benazir Bhutto for implementation in 1989–91. Aimed at correcting fiscal and external imbalances, the program targeted a reform of the tax collection system, tighter government spending controls and monetary management, the privatization of state-owned industrial enterprises, banks and utilities, the phasing out of state monopolies in the transportation, insurance, telecommunications and energy sectors, and liberalization of investment and foreign exchange regulations. Implementation of the ambitious program proceeded under the government of Nawaz Sharif who assumed the prime minister's office in 1991. Results were somewhat uneven, with little effective improvements scored in the country's tax system or its fiscal and balance of payments deficits. With the rapid change of government in 1993 and again in 1996 and 1999, ongoing political tensions dampened private investment, but officials assured that structural reform and privatization would continue.

Fiscal indecision and post-nuclear test economic sanctions dried up foreign investments while budget and trade deficits soared by 1999. New economic aid from the United States was halted in 1990, under the terms of a Congressional amendment requiring certification of Pakistan's status as a nuclear weapons-free country. These sanctions were alleviated in 1996 by the Brown Amendment, but the nuclear tests of 1998 caused further economic sanctions that were only partially lifted by 2000. The United States lifted some sanctions, clearing the way for the IMF to negotiate a bailout package of $1.5 billion with Pakistan. Key demands included cuts in government budget deficits, further privatization, and improved tax collections. After suspension of payments under a previous arrangement, Pakistan entered into a 10-month stand-by arrangement as a prerequisite to rescheduling. Since the 11 September 2001 terrorist attacks on the United States, however, Pakistan has received substantial international financial resources and concessions have been mobilized in exchange for the government's support of the US-led war in Afghanistan. Its chief recipient, the martial law government of General Musharraf, therefore, entered into a three-year program under the Poverty Reduction and Growth Facility (PRGF) in preparation for a sec-

ond rescheduling of debt by Paris Club members, in this case for more than $12 billion.

Since 2008, when the government of Asif Ali Zardari assumed office, the economic and institutional reforms initiated by the military government have continued, but slowed. The government announced the privatization program would follow an accelerated course, as would the expansion of exports, and the maintenance of inflows of remittances through official channels. Inflation, however, remained a significant threat to the economy, rising from 6.7% in 2007 to 13.9% in 2010, and the devastating monsoon floods of 2010 and 2011 further retarded development and forced a new World Bank loan of $5.5 billion in 2011.

40 SOCIAL DEVELOPMENT

Pakistan's social development is primarily represented by a social security plan that covered employees of firms with 10 or more workers. Family and self-employed labor was excluded, and there were separate systems for the armed forces, police, and other public employees. Social security coverage included old age, disability, and survivor benefits, as well as sickness and maternity payments, workers' compensation, and unemployment benefits. This program was funded by contributions from employers and employees and subsidies from the government. The Worker's Compensation Act was supplemented by a Social Insurance Law and provided disability and worker's injury benefits to workers earning RS. 3,000 or less a month. The labor code required employers with more than 20 employees to pay a severance gratuity in the amount of 30 days wages for each year of employment. As well, an Islamization program to promote social welfare in accordance with Islamic precepts was introduced in 1977 under martial law. Islamic welfare taxes, the zakat and ushr, were levied to redistribute wealth. The ushr tax on landowners took effect in 1983.

Despite legislated provisions for social security and welfare, most segments of Pakistani society faced grave insecurities as of 2011. First and foremost, as less than 4% of annual federal budgets since the 1980s have been allocated to housing, community amenities, health, recreation, culture, religion, education and social protection, it is clear that the state has not allocated significant funds to support social development. With discriminatory legislation and customs also in place, while pro-development legislation is inadequately enforced, various segments of society are vulnerable to abuse. Sectarian and religious minorities are both culturally and institutionally discriminated against, best evinced by blasphemy laws (introduced in the early 1980s) widely reported to be employed for less than religious reasons. Women, like religious minorities, are protected by some laws and customs, while prosecuted by others. Here, the range of abuses extends from sexual harassment to honor killings. Lack of access to education leaves most women unaware of their legal rights. Child labor is also prevalent, affecting millions of children. And finally, bonded labor, particularly in rural areas, is widely recorded. Human rights violations, including arbitrary arrest, prolongs detention. Torture, having long been present, has grown particularly acute since the beginning of Pakistan's participation in the US-led 'War on Terror.'

41 HEALTH

Life expectancy in Pakistan was 67 years in 2011. The fertility rate was estimated between 3.17 and 3.9 children born per woman, while the infant mortality rate was between 63 and 71 per 1,000 live births. In 2008 the maternal mortality rate, according to the World Bank, was 260 per 100,000 births. Major causes of infant mortality were immunizable diseases, diarrhea, malnutrition, and poor environmental sanitation. The leading causes of death more generally were diarrhea, pneumonia, tuberculosis, cardiovascular diseases and cancer.

Health facilities in Pakistan were inadequate in 2011, mainly due to a lack of resources and a high population growth rate. In 2011, total expenditure on healthcare was 2.6% of GDP, amounting to $23 per person. As expenditure throughout the last decade has been no better (2.2% of GDP in 2007), there were only 8 physicians, 6 nurses and midwives, and 6 hospital beds per 10,000 inhabitants. There were no more than 5 dentists per 100,000 inhabitants. It was estimated that 88% of the population had access to safe drinking water, but only 61% had adequate sanitation. Approximately 36% of children under five years old were considered malnourished. The goiter rate remained high in school aged children. Around 90% of children up to one year of age were immunized against tuberculosis; 72% against diphtheria, pertussis, and tetanus; 74% against polio; and 78% against measles. Leprosy remains a major concern, however. The incidence of tuberculosis was 181 per 100,000 people in 2007, and the prevalence of HIV/AIDS was estimated to be about 0.1% in 2009. In 2011, the UN noted concern over the rising number of polio cases within the country. In the first seven months of 2011, there were 63 reported cases, up from 36 cases reported during the first seven months of 2010. A polio vaccination campaign targeting 16.5 million children in high-risk district of the country was set for 19–21 September 2011.

42 HOUSING

Rapid rates of urbanization, coupled with a rising population, began creating pressures on housing in urban areas by the late-1960's. The Ministry of Housing and Works (and the Pakistan Housing Authority since 1987) and various city-level development authorities, have been charged with addressing the shortfall, but 25% of the people in large cities were estimated to live in *katchi abadis* (shantytowns) in 2011. Initiatives have included the granting of proprietary rights to shantytown dwellers, as well as the extention of amenities (water, sewerage, electricity, etc.) into these communities. Authorities have launched various schemes for low-cost housing, such as the one revived in 2011 by the Capital Development Authority's to constuct housing untis for low-rank government employees and low-income families in Islamabad. Housing authorities have also worked closely with the private sector to provide affordable housing. Apart from issuing contracts, the Karachi Development Authority, for example, has provided discounted lands to private development firms.

As the high incidence of shantytowns suggests, the results have less than required. By 1998, there were 19,211,738 housing units nationwide with an average of 6.8 occupants per unit. About 54.97% of all units had two to four rooms; 38.11% had one room. About 81% of all dwellings were owner occupied. The most common building materials for residential dwellings were baked bricks, blocks or stones for walls (58% of all units) and wood or bamboo for the roofs (57%). Only 32% of all housing units were linked to piped drinking water. Only 32.7% of all housing units

had a separate kitchen and 33.29% had a separate bathroom. Shortfalls have been attributed to widespread corruption in contracts and allocations, substandard building and the eventual turn of the legitimate private construction industry from low-income housing schemes as in the 1960s and 1970s, to highend construction for the growing middle and upper classes since the 1990s.

43 EDUCATION

The education system in Pakistan, overseen by the Ministry of Education and the provincial governments, includes primary, middle, high and intermediate schools, leading to secondary degrees, and universities and colleges providing undergraduate and graduate degrees. All education is in Urdu and English. Since 1972, the government has aimed at providing free and universal education through the 10th year of formal schooling for both boys and girls. However, public expenditure on education hovered about 2.5% of GDP from 1972 to 2011.

As of 2011, there were 132 recognised universities, 44 of which specialized in scientific fields including engineering, medical sciences, agricultural sciences and information technologies. Arts and sciences colleges were affiliated with the universities of the Punjab (at Lahore, established 1882), Sind (at Hyderābād, 1947; at Karāchi, 1951), Peshāwar (1950), Baluchistan (1970), and Multan (1975). An agricultural university was established in 1961 at Lyallpur (now Faisalābād). There were also an estimated 40,000 madrasas (seminaries), largely beyond government regulation, whose curriculum ranged from reading and Koranic recitation in the smaller to law and theology in the larger.

In 2009 the World Bank estimated that 66% of age-eligible children in Pakistan were enrolled in primary school. Secondary enrollment for age-eligible children stood at 33%. Tertiary enrollment was estimated at 6%. Of those enrolled in tertiary education, there were 100 male students for every 85 female students. In 2000, of those enrolled in secondary education, there were 100 male:67 female, at the middle level, 100:68, and at the primary level, 100:74. These ratios represented at significant decrease in gender disparity since 1990.

Literacy rates stood at 49.9% in 2011. However, literacy rates are subject to great regional and urban-rural variations. For example, in 2007, Islamabad had a literacy rate of 87%, while nearby Sialkot was 59%. In 2009, Punjab's literacy rate was 59%, while Baluchistan's was 45%. Higher literacy rates are also recorded among young adults as opposed to seniors.

44 LIBRARIES AND MUSEUMS

The National Library of Pakistan in Islāmābād, established in 1993, holds 130,000 volumes, including 555 manuscripts dating to the early Islamic period. The largest university library in Pakistan is that of the Punjab University at Lahore, with a collection of about 398,000 volumes, including some 20,000 manuscripts. Sizable collections are also found at the University of Karāchi (105,000 volumes) and the University of Sindh (244,000 volumes). Other important libraries are the Punjab Public Library in Lahore (259,000 volumes), the Liaquat Memorial Library (147,000 volumes), the Central Secretariat Library (110,000 volumes), and the National Archives (35,000 volumes), all in Karāchi. The International Islamic University in Islāmābād holds 100,000 volumes. There are about 300 public libraries in the country, but only about 30 libraries had a collection of 10,000 or more volumes.

The National Museum of Pakistan was inaugurated in 1950, adding to the seven museums inherited from the colonial era. Since then, the number of museums had risen to 27 (1 in Baluchistan, 4 in Khyber Pukhtunkhwa, 14 in Punjab and 8 in Sindh) by 2011. The National Museum of Pakistan (Karāchi) contains material spanning the long history of the region, from the ancient Indus Valley culture to the renowned Mughal period. The Peshāwar Museum features a splendid collection of Buddhist sculpture of the Gandhara style. The Lahore Museum has an outstanding collection of Greco-Buddhist sculpture, in addition to works from other periods. The 5,000 year-old ruins at Mohenjodaro, the 2,000 year-old ruins at Taxila and the 1,000-year old ruins of Bhanbore are three of the pre-Islamic sites with museums showcasing local finds. Fine forts, mosques, shrines, gardens and mausoleums of the Islamic centuries are scattered throughout the country, major sites also hosting museums.

45 MEDIA

Pakistan's media, including print, radio, television and telecommunications system, witnessed dramatic development from the 1990s. In 2009, the CIA reported that there were 4.1 million telephone landlines in Pakistan. This represented only marginal growth and rural areas have difficulty in accessing main line phone service. However, the number of mobile cellular phone service subscribers had risen sharply, and fiber-optic systems were under construction or expanding. Some 103 million mobile cellular phones were in use and subscriptions averaged 61 per 100 people. Domestic service was provided through a mix of microwave radio relay, satellite, cellular, and coaxial and fiber-optic cable systems. International service was provided by satellite ground stations, international gateway exchanges, and microwave radio relay systems.

Government-run Pakistan-TV broadcasts at least 10 hours a day through 28 transmitters. Through Azad Kashmir Radio and the Pakistan Broadcasting Corporation, the government operates 18 shortwave radio stations. Karāchi is the broadcasting center, and there are important transmitters at Hyderābād, Quetta, Lahore, Rāwalpindi, Peshāwar, Multan, Bahawalpur, and Islāmābād. There are 31 AM and 68 FM radio stations and 20 television stations in use, 5 of which are state run. About 26.7 of every 1,000 people are cable subscribers. In 2010, the country had 330,466 Internet hosts. In 2009, there were some 20.4 million Internet users in Pakistan, or about 12 per 100 citizens.

Daily newspapers—most of them with very small circulations—are published in Urdu, English, and a few other languages. English-language newspapers are read by less than 1% of the population but are very influential, especially *Dawn* (2002 estimated circulation, 80,000), published in Karāchi, and *Pakistan Times* (50,000), published in Lahore and Rāwalpindi. Leading Urdu-language dailies (with approximately 2,000 circulations)are *Jang* (750,000) and *Hurriyet* (600,000), both in Karāchi, and *Jang Lahore* (1,200,000) and *Nawa-e-Waqt* (560,000), in Lahore.

While freedom of the press has always been provided for constitutionally, censorship was imposed on the press by martial law governments. Between 1979 and 1982, for example, local censors reviewed items prior to publication, and some books and periodicals were confiscated. Even after the lifting of censorship, the government continued to influence press coverage by controlling the availability of newsprint, which must be imported, and the placement of government advertising, which is a source of newspapers' revenue. Media was most thoroughly freed from direct censorship and regulation by the government of General Musharraf, leading to a burgeoning of satellite TV channels and radio stations. However, constitutional prohibition on offending Islam and the Army remained in effect and attempts to curtail press freedom continued to occur. According to the World Association of Journalists and Newspaper Publishers, Pakistan topped the list for journalists killed in 2010, and was running second only to Iraq in 2011.

46 ORGANIZATIONS

Numerous civic or non-governmental organizations are active in Pakistan, some dating back to the colonial era. Most major cities contain chambers of commerce and there are numerous employers' associations, such as the All-Pakistan Textile Mills Association, the Pakistan Carpet Manufacturers' and Exporters' Association, and the Pakistan Shipowners' Association. There are also professional associations representing a variety of fields, including lawyers, doctors, journalists and academics. Those specifically involved in the promotion of national culture included the Pakistan Historical Society, the Scientific and Cultural Society of Pakistan, and the Research Society of Pakistan. Religious communities are also represented by a host of flourishing organizations. National youth organizations included a number of student unions, the Pakistan Boy Scouts Association, and the YMCA/YWCA. There are also a number of sports associations for all ages. National women's organizations include the All Pakistan Women's Association, the Pakistan Association for Women's Studies, the Pakistan Federation of University Women and the Women's Resource Center. International organizations with national chapters include Amnesty International, Caritas, Habitat for Humanity, the Society of St. Vincent de Paul, and the Red Crescent Society.

47 TOURISM, TRAVEL, AND RECREATION

Despite a broad range of topographies and climates, a rich array of historical treasures—including five sites on the UNESCO World Heritage List—and a vibrant array of regional cultures, tourism remains a sector awaiting development. Pakistan's political instability, involvement in regional conflicts and lack of intrastructure mostly account for low levels of inbound travel and occupancy rates of 51% for the 61,757 available hotel beds. The *Tourism Factbook*, published by the UN World Tourism Organization, reported 855,000 incoming tourists in 2009, who spent a total of $903 million. Of those incoming tourists, there were 379,000 from Europe, 178,000 from South Asia, and 162,000 from the Americas.

Most visitors to Pakistan are required to have a visa and a valid passport. Tourists planning to stay more than 30 days are required to register with the government. Road permits are available for land crossings into India at Wagah (between Lahore and Amritsar in India). There are no health restrictions on visitors entering Pakistan except in regard to cholera and yellow fever immunizations for those who have been in infected areas. Their estimated daily cost to visit Islamabad, the capital, is $110. The cost of visiting other cities averages $217.

Violence issuing from involvement in the Afghan War since 2001, as well as such natural calamites as the October 2005 earthquake, have dipped an already underdeveloped sector into severe crisis. By 2009, tour operators had begun focusing on domestic tourism to survive, while the government issued its third master plan since 1974 to promote international and domestic tourism, blaming low appeal on erroneous perceptions of Pakistan as much as security concerns.

⁴⁸FAMOUS PERSONS

A number of Pakistanis have received wide recognition in a variety of fields, besides achieving iconic status in Pakistani culture.

From the political classes, Muhammad Ali Jinnah (1876–1948), known as Quaid-i Azam (Great Leader), is acknowledged for his leading role in the Pakistan Movement that created the state. The poet-philosopher Muhammad Iqbal (1873–1938)is seen as the spiritual father of the state, having proposed its creation as part of his approach to Islamic modernism. Both their tombs are sites of state functions. Fatima Jinnah (1893–1967) plays the role of Madr-i Millat (Mother of the Nation), for her role in mobilizing women for the Pakistan Movement. She was also the first woman in the world to win the popular vote in a Presidential election (1965), only to be denied power by the constitutional aborations of military rule. Zulfikar Ali Bhutto (1928–79) and his daughter, Benazir Bhutto (1953–2007), have since added their names to the list of civilian leaders held in esteem. Benazir Bhutto was the first woman to head the government of a Muslim state (1988–91; 1993–96).

Among the intelligentsia, Maulana Maududi (1903–79), founder of the Jamaat-i Islami, has been widely influential in the global Islamist movement. Largely participatory in electoral politics, his puritanical approach to Islam and the structure of his party has formed the model for parties across the Muslim world. By way of contrast, Fazlur Rahman Malik (1919–88), briefly head of the Pakistan Central Institute of Islamic Research, made his mark in Islamic modernist thought and was an honored professor at McGill University, UCLA and the University of Chicago. In the sciences, Dr. Abdus Salam (1926–96) remains most celebrated as Pakistan's only Nobel Laureate.

The arts have been graced by such recognizable poets and novelists as Iqbal, Faiz Ahmad Faiz (1911–84), Hasan Manto (1912–55), Zulfikar Ghose (b. 1935), Bapsi Sidwa (b. 1938), and Mohsin Hamid (b. 1971). In the fine arts, Abd al-Rahman Chughtai (1899–1975) remains iconic for his modernism, followed by the likes of Sadequain (1930–87), Ismail Gulgee (1926–2007), and Jamil Naqsh (b. 1938), who pushed into cubism and surrealism, while redefining Islamic calligraphy. The world of ghazals, qaw-walis and naats have been defined by the likes of Nusrat Fateh Ali Khan (1948–97), Abida Parveen (b. 1954), the Sabri Brothers, Noor Jehan (1926–2000), Muhammad Rafi (1924–80), and Farida Khanum (b. 1935). In the realm of popular music, meanwhile, such singers as Nazia (1965–2000) are noteworthy for introducing disco rhythms, while bands like Junoon began fusing rock and tablas with a Sufi mystic's lilt.

Pakistani culture also has its sports heroes. Most issue from the game of international cricket, dating back to Hanif Muhammad (b. 1934), who held the record for most runs scored in a Test inning (499) for decades, and forward to the masters of swing bowling, Wasim Akram (b. 1966) and Waqar Yunus (b. 1971). However, the captain who led Pakistan to raise the World Cup in 1992, Imran Khan (b. 1952), is perhaps held in highest regard. From beyond the world of cricket, as well, squash players such as the Jehangir Khan (b. 1963) and Jansher Khan (b. 1969), who dominated the international game for decades, as well as members of the World Cup and Olympic gold winning field hockey teams, win honorable mention.

⁴⁹DEPENDENCIES

Pakistan has no territories or colonies.

⁵⁰BIBLIOGRAPHY

Burki, Shahid Javed. *Historical Dictionary of Pakistan*. 3rd ed. Metuchen, NJ: Scarecrow Press, 2008.

Khan, Adeel. *Politics of Identity: Ethnic Nationalism and the State in Pakistan*. Thousand Oaks, CA: Sage, 2005.

Kukreja, Veena and M.P. Singh, eds. *Pakistan: Democracy, Development, and Security Issues*. Thousand Oaks, CA: Sage, 2005.

Lyon, Peter. *Conflict between India and Pakistan: An Encyclopedia*. Santa Barbara, CA: ABC-CLIO, 2008.

Malik, Iftikhar H. *Culture and Customs of Pakistan*. Westport, CT: Greenwood Press, 2006.

Mitra, Subrata K., ed.. *A Political and Economic Dictionary of South Asia*. Philadelphia: Routledge/Taylor and Francis, 2006.

Pakistan Investment and Business Guide: Strategic and Practical Information. Washington, DC: International Business Publications USA, 2012.

Saliba, Therese, Carolyn Allen, and Judith A. Howard, eds. *Gender, Politics, and Islam*. Chicago: University of Chicago Press, 2002.

Stern, Robert W. *Democracy and Dictatorship in South Asia: Dominant Classes and Political Outcomes in India, Pakistan, and Bangladesh*. Westport, CT: Praeger, 2001.

PALAU

Republic of Palau
Belau

CAPITAL: Melekeok, Babelthuap

FLAG: The flag, adopted 1 January 1981, is light blue, with a yellow disc set slightly off center toward the hoist.

ANTHEM: Belau Rekid, (Our Palau).

MONETARY UNIT: The US dollar is the official medium of exchange.

WEIGHTS AND MEASURES: Imperial units are used.

HOLIDAYS: New Year's Day, 1 January; Youth Day, 15 March; Senior Citizens Day, 5 May; Constitution Day, 9 July; Labor Day, 1st Monday in September; United Nations Day, 24 October; Thanksgiving Day, 4th Thursday in November; Christmas, 25 December.

TIME: 8 p.m. = noon GMT.

¹LOCATION, SIZE, AND EXTENT

Palau (also known as Belau) is located in the western extremities of the Pacific Ocean. It consists of the Palau group of islands, in the western Caroline Islands, and four remote islands to the sw. Palau is isolated from larger land masses, with Papua New Guinea/Irian Jaya (Indonesia) 660 km (410 mi) to the S, the Philippines 885 km (550 mi) to the W, and Japan 3,042 km (1,890 mi) to the N. Yap Island in the Federated States of Micronesia lies 579 km (360 mi) to the NE. The country consists of more than 200 islands, with a total land area of 458 sq km (177 sq mi). Babelthuap (also known as Babeldaob) is the largest island, with an area of 397 sq km (153.2 sq mi); Koror Island has an area of 18 sq km (7.1 sq mi). The islands of Peleliu and Angaur are about 50 km (30 mi) S of Koror. Sonsorol and Hatohobei, the two smallest island states, lie 560–640 km (350–400 mi) SW of Koror. Kayangel is a coral atoll 45 km (28 mi) N of Babelthuap.

²TOPOGRAPHY

The islands include four types of topographical formation: volcanic, high limestone, low platform, and coral atoll. The Palau barrier reef encircles the Palau group, except Angaur Island and the Kayangel atoll. The reef encloses a lagoon (1,267 sq km/489 sq mi) on the western side, containing a large number of small elevated limestone islets known as the Rock Islands. Babelthuap and Koror, with peak elevations of 217 m (713 ft) and 628 m (2,061 ft), respectively, contain elevated limestone and volcanic formations. Arakabesan, Malakal, and several small northern islands are volcanic formations. Peleliu and Angaur are low-platform reef islands.

³CLIMATE

Located near the equator, Palau's climate is maritime tropical, characterized by little seasonal and diurnal variation. The annual

mean temperature is 28°C (82°F) in the coolest months. There is high precipitation throughout the year and a relatively high humidity of 82%. Heavy rainfall occurs from May to November. The short torrential nature of the rainfall produces up to 380 cm (150 in) of precipitation annually. Typhoons and tropical storms occur from June through November.

⁴FLORA AND FAUNA

The World Resources Institute estimates that Palau is home to 8 species of mammals, 112 species of birds, 21 species of reptiles, and 1 species of amphibian. Plant life, abundant throughout most of the islands, includes mangrove swamps, savanna land, and rain forest in upland areas. Food crops, such as taros, cassavas, sweet potatoes, coconuts, bananas, papayas, and citrus fruits, are mostly wild. Marine life is also abundant, with more than 1,500 species of tropical fish and 700 species of coral and anemones in the lagoons and reefs. Fauna includes the sea turtle, which is consumed as a delicacy, and the dugong, or sea cow, a marine mammal that is close to extinction.

⁵ENVIRONMENT

While much of Palau's fragile natural environment remains free of environmental degradation, there are several areas of concern, including illegal fishing with the use of dynamite, inadequate facilities for disposal of solid waste in Koror, and extensive sand and coral dredging in the Palau lagoon.

Like the other Pacific island nations, a major environmental problem is global warming and the related rising of sea level. Water coverage of low-lying areas is a threat to coastal vegetation, agriculture, and the purity of the nation's water supply. Palau also has a problem with inadequate water supply and limited agricultural areas to support the size of the population. The nation is also vulnerable to earthquakes, volcanic activity, and tropical storms. Sewage treatment is a problem, along with the handling of toxic waste from fertilizers and biocides. The UN reported in 2008 that carbon dioxide emissions in Palau totaled 213 kilotons.

In 2010 top officials from Palau and thirteen other developing Pacific Island nations and dependencies met to discuss the progress made in addressing some of the issues unique to these low-lying, developing island states, including climate change, sea-level rise, natural disasters, remoteness from major markets, and poverty. One key objective of the meeting was to address the progress each nation had made in adopting the 2005 Mauritius Strategy, the only global blueprint that exists to combat the development challenges of small-island developing states.

According to a 2011 report issued by the International Union for Conservation of Nature and Natural Resources (IUCN), threatened species included 4 mammals, 4 birds, 2 reptiles, 14 fish, 5 mollusks, and 4 plants. Threatened species included the hawksbill turtle, tiger sharks, grey dolphins, coconut crabs, and green turtles. The Palau flying fox has become extinct.

6 POPULATION

The US Central Intelligence Agency (CIA) estimates the population of Palau in 2011 to be approximately 20,956, which placed it at number 193 in population among the 196 nations of the world. In 2011, approximately 6.5% of the population was over 65 years of age, with another 21.5% under 15 years of age. The median age in Palau was 32.6 years. There were 1.13 males for every female in the country. The population's annual rate of change was 0.363%. The projected population for the year 2025 was 20,000. Population density in Palau was calculated at 46 people per sq km (119 people per sq mi).

The UN estimated that 83% of the population lived in urban areas in 2010, and that urban populations had an annual rate of change of 1.4%. The largest urban area is the city of Koror, on the island of the same name, at approximately 14,000 in 2004.

7 MIGRATION

According to the CIA in 2011, Palau's net migration rate amounted to 0.76 migrants per 1,000 citizens. The total number of emigrants living abroad was 8,000. Persons not Palau-born account for about 30% of the total population. Most were born in the Philippines, China, and Bangladesh; there were also significant numbers from the Federated States of Micronesia, the United States, and Japan. Most were workers; in 2010 there were 6,000 foreign workers in the country. The vast majority of these foreigners were located in Koror.

8 ETHNIC GROUPS

Palauans are a composite of Polynesian, Malayan, and Melanesian races. At the 2000 census, Palauans accounted for about 69.9% of the total population. The largest non-Palauan ethnic groups included Filipinos (15.3%), Chinese (4.9%), other Asians (2.4%), Carolinians (1.4%), other Micronesians (1.1%), and people of European descent (1.9%).

9 LANGUAGES

English is the official language in all of Palau's 16 states; however, it is only spoken by about 9.4% of the population. Palauan, a Malayo-Polynesian language related to Indonesian, is the most commonly spoken language, used by 64.7% of the population. Palauan is used, in addition to English, as an official language in 13 states. Sonsorolese is official in the state of Sonsoral; Anguar and Japanese in the state of Anguar; and Tobi in the state of Tobi. About 13.5% of the population speak Filipino. 5.7% speak Chinese, 1.5% speak Carolinian, 1.5% Japanese, and 2.3% other Asian languages.

10 RELIGIONS

Most Palauans are Christians. The Roman Catholic Church holds the largest number of members at about 65% of the population. Other significant denominations include the Evangelical Church, the Seventh-Day Adventists, The Church of Jesus Christ of Latter-Day Saints, and Jehovah's Witnesses. Modekngei, which is indigenous to Palau and combines both pagan and Christian beliefs and customs, is practiced by about 1,800 people. There are a small number of Bangladeshi Muslims. Several foreign missionaries are active in the country. Freedom of religion is guaranteed by the constitution. Religious groups are expected to register as non-profit organizations through the Office of the Attorney General. There is no state religion. By application, the government does offer some financial support to religious schools of any religion. Christmas is observed as a national holiday.

11 TRANSPORTATION

Though Palau's total road network was not published in 2011, the nation's roads at last estimate totaled 61 km (37.9 mi), of which 36 km (22 mi) were paved. Asphalt roads are found only in Koror, Airai, and Melekeok. A two-lane concrete bridge, constructed in 1976, links Koror with Airai. The Koror state government provides a public bus service. Palau's deepwater harbor at Malakal in Koror offers international port facilities. Heavy reliance is placed on small private watercraft throughout the country.

As of 2010 there were three airports, one of which had a paved runway. The international airport is located in Airai, 10 km (6 mi) from Koror. Three airlines provide international service: Air Micronesia/Continental, Air Nauru, and South Pacific Island Airways. There are three domestic airlines: Palau Paradise Air, Aero Belau, and Freedom Air.

Commercial port facilities are available at the Malakal Commercial Port, which receives merchant vessels, fishing fleets, and international cruise lines.

12 HISTORY

As part of the Carolinian archipelago, the islands were sighted by European navigators as early as the 16th century. In 1686, the Spanish explorer Francisco Lezcano named Yap Island (now in the Federated States of Micronesia) "La Carolina" after King Charles II of Spain. The name was later generalized to include all the islands. Spanish sovereignty was established in 1885. In 1899, after Spain's defeat in the Spanish-American War of 1898, Palau, with the rest of the Carolines, was sold to Germany. At the outbreak of World War I in 1914, the islands were taken by the Japanese. As a member of the League of Nations, Japan was given a mandate over Palau in 1920, and Koror was developed as an administrative center of Japanese possessions in the north Pacific.

In 1947, following occupation by US forces in World War II, Palau became part of the UN Trust Territory of the Pacific Islands, which was administered by the United States. After the adoption of a constitution in 1980, Palau became a self-governing republic in 1981. Beginning in 1982, the republic was involved in negotiating a Compact of Free Association (CPFA) with the United States. Negotiations stalled because the United States wanted to use the islands as a military site, while Palau's 1980 constitution prohibited any placement of nuclear weapons.

On 1 October 1994 Palau became an independent nation in free association with the United States; under the 1994 CPFA, the United States took on responsibility for Palau's defense for a period of 50 years. In addition, CPFA funds were allocated to finance the building of roads and infrastructure on Babelthuap in order to attract people and economic activity. A comprehensive review of the compact was completed in September 2010, resulting in the renewal of several federal programs for a 15-year period.

In October 2006, the official seat of government was moved from the Koror state on Koror Island to Melekeok state on Babelthuap. Johnson Toribiong took the office of president in 2009.

13 GOVERNMENT

The government comprises three branches: the executive, the legislative, and the judicial. The executive branch is headed by the president, who is elected by popular vote for not more than two terms of four years each. The president is assisted by a cabinet of ministers, one of whom is the vice president. The president and vice president run on the same ticket. Presidential elections take place on the same schedule as the presidential elections in the United States. A council of chiefs, based on Palau's clan system, advises the president on traditional and customary matters.

The legislative branch, known as the Olbiil Era Kelulau, or National Congress, is a bicameral form of legislature comprised of a senate and a house of delegates, with 13 senators and 16 delegates. The senators, elected for four-year terms, are apportioned throughout Palau on the basis of population and traditional regional political groupings. The delegates are elected from each of the 16 states and have the same four-year term as the senators.

14 POLITICAL PARTIES

No political parties exist in Palau. All legislators and presidential candidates run as independents. In June 1985, President Haruo Remeliik was assassinated; Vice President Alfonso Oiterang served as acting president until August 1985, when he was defeated in an election by Lazarus E. Salii. President Salii committed suicide in August 1988. Vice President Tommy E. Remengesau, Sr. stepped in as acting president until Ngiratkel Etpison was elected in 1988. In November 1992 Kuniwo Nakamura was elected as president with Remengesau as vice president. Both Nakamura and Remengesau were reelected in 1996. In the 2000 general elections, Remengesau was elected president, and Sandra Pierantozzi became Palau's first woman vice president. In November 2004, Remengesau was reelected, taking 64% of the popular vote, while Camsek Chin took 70% of the votes to become vice president. In the November 2008 elections, Johnson Toribiong won the presidential race with 51% of the vote. The post of vice president was won by Kerai Mariur.

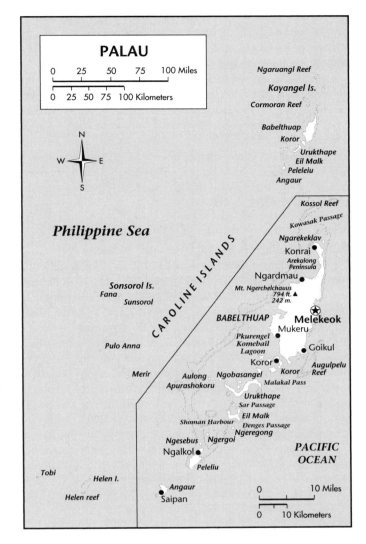

LOCATION: 131° to 135° E; 3° to 8° N.

15 LOCAL GOVERNMENT

Each of Palau's 16 states has a government headed by a governor, who is popularly elected, in most cases, for a four-year term. The members of the state legislatures are popularly elected for a four-year term, although in a few states, the term of office is limited to two years. The states are empowered to make their own laws, which must not be in conflict with the national constitution or any existing laws.

16 JUDICIAL SYSTEM

The Supreme Court is the highest court in the land and consists of trial and appellate divisions. Other courts include the Court of Common Pleas and the Land Court. Court appointments are for life. While the constitution provides for the development of separate National Court (just below the Supreme Court), this court was inactive as of 2011.

In October 1990, US Interior Secretary Manuel Lujan issued an order granting the Interior Department in Washington the power to veto laws and reverse decisions by Palau's courts. This reassertion of legal authority by the United States was partially in response to the decade of unsuccessful negotiations concerning a plan for eventual self-government.

The constitution provides for an independent judiciary and the government respects this provision in practice. Palau has an independent prosecutor and an independent public defender system.

17ARMED FORCES

The United States is responsible for defense. Palau has no armed forces and does not have US armed forces within its borders except for a small contingent of US Navy Seabees who undertake civil action projects.

18INTERNATIONAL COOPERATION

Palau became a member of the United Nations (UN) on 15 December 1994; it participates in ESCAP, the World Bank, the FAO, ICAO, IMF, IFC, UNCTAD, UNESCO, and WHO. Palau is also a member of the ACP Group, the Asian Development Bank, G-77, the Pacific Island Forum, and the Alliance of Small Island States (AOSIS). The country is part of the Organization for the Prohibition of Chemical Weapons. Under the Compact of Free Association, the United States is responsible for the island nation's defense. In environmental cooperation, Palau is part of the Convention on Biological Diversity, the Kyoto Protocol, the Montréal Protocol, and the UN Conventions on the Law of the Sea, Climate Change and Desertification. In 2003, Palau became a member of SOPAC, the South Pacific Applied Geoscience Commission, a group which has among its aims the sustainable development of mineral and other nonliving resources, and the reduction of poverty for the people of the Pacific.

19ECONOMY

Palau is one of the wealthier Pacific Island nations, with a per capita gross domestic product (GDP) of $8,941 in 2011. The GDP rate of change was -2.1%. Inflation stood at 2.7%, and unemployment was reported at 4.2%.

Tourism is the most important industry, though construction has been growing in importance as well as the nation has embarked on several major infrastructure projects. The service sector employs more than half the workforce and accounts for more than 80% of GDP. Subsistence agriculture and fishing employ 20% of the labor force, with primary crops including coconuts, taro, and bananas. Tuna fishing is a small source of revenue, but the industry is in decline because catches have decreased. Most fishing revenue is generated through license fees.

The economy is still highly dependent on foreign aid. Palau has been a party to a Compact of Free Association with the United States since 1 October 1994, with some amendments to the agreement made in 2010. With the amendments, Palau accepted a financial package of $250 million to be paid out through 2025. In return, the government of Palau is expected to institute a number of economic and financial reforms that will lead to greater self-sufficiency.

20INCOME

The CIA estimated that in 2008 the GDP of Palau was $164 million. The CIA defines GDP as the value of all final goods and services produced within a nation in a given year and computed on the basis of purchasing power parity (PPP) rather than value as measured on the basis of the rate of the exchange based on current dollars. The per capita GDP was estimated at $8,941 in 2011. The annual growth rate of GDP was -2.1%. The average inflation rate in 2005 was 2.7%. It was estimated that agriculture accounted for 6.2% of GDP, industry 12%, and services 81.8%.

21LABOR

As of 2005, Palau had a total labor force of 9,777 people. As of 2011, more than half of the workforce was employed in the service sector, while an estimated 20% were employed in agricultural, primarily subsistence. Though employers are encouraged to hire residents, in 2010 there were 6,000 foreign workers in the country, about 60% of whom were from the Philippines. About 30% of the workforce is employed by the government. Unemployment has been estimated at about 4.2%.

There are no specific provisions granting the right to strike or organize unions, but the issue has never come up. There were no organized trade unions, presumably due in part to the fact that most local businesses are smaller, family-owned and operated establishments that tend to hire friends and extended family members.

There is no minimum age for resident employment, but children do not typically work, except to help out in small-scale family enterprises such as fishing or agriculture. Education is compulsory until age 14, and this is enforced by the government. The minimum age for foreign workers is 21 years.

As of 2011, the minimum wage was established at a rate of $2.50 per hour for resident workers. The minimum wage does not apply to foreign workers, who often receive housing and food in addition to wages. There are no legally proscribed work hours, but many businesses are closed on Saturday or Sunday.

22AGRICULTURE

Out of 46,000 hectares (113,668 acres) of land in Palau, 1,000 hectares (2,471 acres) are arable. Roughly 11% of the total land is farmed. Most households outside Koror are fully or partially engaged in subsistence agriculture, with taro, cassava, and sweet potatoes as primary crops. Commercial produce is marketed mainly in Koror, consisting mostly of copra and coconut oil, vegetables, and a wide variety of tropical fruits.

23ANIMAL HUSBANDRY

The UN Food and Agriculture Organization (FAO) reported that Palau dedicated 2,000 hectares (4,942 acres) to permanent pasture or meadow in 2009. Livestock is limited to pigs, chickens, ducks, cattle, and goats. Pigs and chickens are raised by most households. Several small commercial egg-producing operations supply eggs to the Koror market. The Livestock Branch of the Division of Agriculture maintains breeding herds of pigs, cattle, and goats.

24 FISHING

Palau's marine resources are rich and diverse. Subsistence fishing within the reef is a major activity and dominates market production. Seasonal trochus harvesting for shell button manufacture is an important source of income for most fishermen. Other marine resources include pearls, shrimp, ornamental fish, seaweed (agar agar), and mollusks. Palau is also known for having some of the best diving, snorkeling, and sport fishing areas in the world. In 2008, the annual capture totaled 1,007 tons according to the UN FAO.

As of 2010, the government began considering new legislation that would promote the domestic tuna industry by limiting the number of foreign fishing agreements. Big eye and yellow fin tuna are fairly common in the waters around Palau, and are especially valuable to the Japanese sushi market. However, domestic income from the tuna industry has been reported as less than $1 million annually. Some officials believe that the imposition of higher fish import taxes and higher access fees for foreign companies in local waters will provide a much needed boost for the economy; but many would like to see an increase in the number of Palauan fishermen participating in the industry instead.

Also in 2010, the First Presidential Summit of the Parties of the Nauru Agreement (PNA) was held in Koror. The PNA was established in 1982 and is comprised of the nations of Palau, Micronesia, Marshall Islands, Tuvalu, Kiribati, Papua New Guinea, Nauru, and the Solomon Islands. The purpose of the group is to work together for the conservation and management of tuna resources within their exclusive economic zones (EEZ). At the March 2010 meeting, called the Tuna Summit, members adopted the Koror Declaration, which aims to initiate management practices that will enhance commercial and economic opportunities for member states and work toward the conservation and restoration of migratory stocks. The waters of the PNA nations account for nearly 60% of all tuna catches in the western and central Pacific Ocean and 25% of the global tuna catches that supply canneries and processing facilities around the world.

25 FORESTRY

Approximately 87% of Palau is covered by forest. Forestry resources consist of coastal mangrove, coconut and pandanus palms, and rain forest species in upland areas. Palau is heavily dependent on imported forestry products, including furniture and lumber for house construction. The government's forestry station at Nekken on Babelthuap Island, of which more than half of the 1,257 hectares (3,105 acres) consists of natural forest, provides primarily mahogany seedlings to farmers. Palau imported $1.1 million in forest products during 2004.

26 MINING

Crystalline calcite from glistening limestone caves was first quarried as many as 1,500–2,000 years ago. The doughnut-shaped finished carved products would be transported by canoe some 400 km (250 mi) to Yap (now part of the Federated States of Micronesia), and used as currency.

The Koror state government engages in some commercial production of dredged sand and coral from the Palau lagoon. Other states are also involved in coral dredging.

27 ENERGY AND POWER

The economy is almost totally dependent on imported petroleum for energy. Electricity is supplied from the Malakal power plant, located in the state of Koror, with an installed capacity of approximately 8,000 kW. There are state-owned power plants with capacities ranging from 30 kW to 120 kW in Peleliu, Angur, Ngiwal, Ngeremlengui, Airai, Ngaraard, and Ngerchelong. Total electricity consumption in 2006 was reported by the government at more than 114.2 million kWh.

28 INDUSTRY

Manufacturing plays a limited role in the economy. Production of handicrafts and garments is primarily targeted at local and tourist markets. Copra is processed as an export product. Construction has become a growth industry, accounting for about 15% of the GDP in 2010. The Ngardmau Free Trade Zone was established in 2001 in an effort to promote investment in light manufacturing (including computer hardware and electronic components) and financial and trade related services.

29 SCIENCE AND TECHNOLOGY

The World Bank reported in 2009 that there were no patent applications in science and technology in Palau. Palau's Micronesian Mariculture Demonstration Center, established in 1973, promotes the cultivation of commercially valuable and ecologically threatened marine species. The center attracts visiting marine scientists. Its giant clam hatchery was the first and remains the largest of its kind. The Palau International Coral Research Center, managed jointly by the United States and Japan, conducts research in coral reef and marine diversity.

30 DOMESTIC TRADE

Domestic trade is primarily centered in Koror, with a large number of retail and wholesale establishments handling imported goods. There are several retail establishments targeting tourists in this area. Many retail establishments are small, family owned and operated businesses.

31 FOREIGN TRADE

The nation relies heavily on imported goods. Primary imports include food, beverages, and tobacco; manufactured goods, machinery and transportation equipment; and mineral fuel and lubricants; along with many other consumer goods. The country's low volume and limited range of exports include shellfish, tuna, copra, and garments.

Major import partners in 2009 were the United States, Guam, Japan, Singapore, Taiwan, and Korea. Its major export partners were the United States, Japan; and Taiwan.

^{32}BALANCE OF PAYMENTS

With a strong reliance on imported goods, Palau's economy sustains a large trade deficit. According to a government report, Palau imported about $115.2 million worth of goods and services (FOB) in 2005/06, while exporting $13.5 million worth of goods and services, resulting in a deficit of $101.7 million.

^{33}BANKING AND SECURITIES

As of 2008, there were 12 commercial banks and 11 non-bank financial institutions, including some small credit unions. At least three of the commercial bank branches were affiliated with US companies. The National Development Bank of Palau was established in 1982.

^{34}INSURANCE

There are several local and international insurance firms with offices in the country. Social security and pension fund contributions are made by the government on behalf of its employees.

^{35}PUBLIC FINANCE

In 2008 the budget of Palau included $114.8 million in public revenue and $99.5 million in public expenditures. The budget surplus amounted to 9.3% of GDP. Tax revenues only cover a minor portion of the national budget. The government relies somewhat heavily on financial assistance from the United States, Japan, and China.

^{36}TAXATION

There is an annual graduated income tax of 6% on the first $8,000 of wages and salaries and 12% on any amount over $8,000. There is no corporate tax and no taxes are imposed on income for business owners. There are, however, some special fees imposed employers who hire foreign workers, including a fee of $500 per year for each foreign worker employed.

^{37}CUSTOMS AND DUTIES

There are no import duties on raw materials if they are processed for sale outside Palau. Import taxes of varying amounts are imposed on other products, with most products levied at 3%.

^{38}FOREIGN INVESTMENT

Foreign direct investment (FDI) in Palau was unreported according to World Bank figures published in 2009. However, FDI was estimated at $18.7 million in 2004. The government encourages investments in tourism and, to a lesser extent, in light manufacturing and agricultural development.

There is a Foreign Investment Board for processing applications from foreign investors; the Division of International Trade of the Bureau of Foreign Affairs is responsible for establishing contacts with foreign companies to promote Palau's trade interests. Foreign investors must commit to an investment of more than $500,000 or undertake a project in which at least 20% of those employed are Palauan.

^{39}ECONOMIC DEVELOPMENT

Palau has been a party to a Compact of Free Association with the United States since 1 October 1994. The compact provided Palau with $700 million in US aid for 15 years in return for furnishing military facilities. When that assistance ended at the end of 2009, the governments of Palau and the United States began a review of the compact to consider options for further aid. An agreement was finally approved in September 2010, as Palau accepted a financial package of $250 million to be paid out through 2025. This includes $21 million in subsidies for the US Postal Service operations in the country. The government also receives development assistance from the Asian Development Bank (ADB), as well as other countries.

Assistance from the United States and the ADB comes with an expectation that the nation is actively working toward developing greater levels of self-sufficiency. Toward that end, the government has published a National Master Development Plan that sets forth goals and strategies for both short-term and long-term progress toward economic stability. Key growth sectors include tourism, agriculture and fisheries, and light manufacturing. The government also expects to continue work on infrastructure development and improvement.

^{40}SOCIAL DEVELOPMENT

A system of old age, disability, and survivor's pensions was first introduced in 1967. This program covers all gainfully employed persons, and provides old age pensions after the age of 60. It is financed by 6% of employee earnings, matched by an equal contribution from employers. There is voluntary coverage for some self-employed persons. The government contributes only as an employer.

In the traditional social structure, rank and inheritance are matrilineal. Women are accorded considerable respect within the clan system. However, weakening extended family ties and the rise of drug and alcohol abuse are leading to an increase in domestic violence and abuse of women. In urban areas, women face minimal gender based discrimination in employment. The government adequately funds education and medical care for children.

Foreigners residing in Palau are barred from owning land or obtaining citizenship. Some foreigners complain of discrimination in access to housing, education, and employment. Human rights are well respected in Palau, and nongovernmental organizations operate without government interference.

^{41}HEALTH

Hospital services are provided by the MacDonald Memorial Hospital in Koror. As of 2008, there were an additional four primary care super-dispensaries and four community-based dispensaries on outlying islands. There were also at least three private primary care clinics, with two in Koror and on free clinic in Airai operated by the US Navy.

In 2011, there were an estimated 13 physicians, 59 nurses and midwives, and 50 hospital beds per 10,000 inhabitants. Healthcare expenditure totaled 16.6% of GDP, amounting to $981 per person.

The total fertility rate in 2011 was 1.73 children per woman. In 2011 life expectancy averaged an estimated 71.78 years and the infant mortality rate was 12.43 deaths per 1,000 births. A 100% immunization rate for children under one was achieved for diphtheria, hepatitis B, measles, tetanus, pertussis, and polio.

Obesity is becoming a major concern for the nation, which was ranked as having the seventh highest obesity rate in the world by the World Health Organization in 2010. At that time, it was estimated that 18.5% of the nation's schoolchildren were obese, with another 15% considered to be at risk. In response, the Ministry of Health teamed up with the Ministry of Education to design and implement a new Healthy Lifestyle curriculum that will focus on healthy eating habits and the need for exercise. The government expects to receive additional funding and expert assistance from Israel for programs that address obesity in both children and adults. Diabetes, hypertension, and cardiovascular diseases are also emerging problems.

A national health insurance scheme is under development as part of the 2008 National Healthcare Coverage and Savings Act.

42 HOUSING

According to a 2005 survey (the latest data available from the government) there were 5,355 housing units within the nation, of which 60% were located in Koror. The average household consisted of 3.86 persons. About 57% of all units were owner occupied, while 31% were renter-occupied and 12% were vacant. Most house walls are constructed from metal sheets, wood, or concrete blocks, and roofs are of corrugated material. About 80% of all houses have water and electricity. About 48% of the occupied units were connected to the public sewer system. The majority of homeowners finance their house construction under the traditional *ocheraol* system, whereby clan members contribute to construction costs.

43 EDUCATION

Elementary education is free and compulsory for all Palauan children ages 6–14. In 2009 the World Bank estimated that 96% of age-eligible children in Palau were enrolled in primary school.

The number of students has declined each year since 2004, due to a decrease in the number of children born in the country. The student-to-teacher ratio for primary school was at about 11:1 in 2007; the ratio for secondary school was about 10:1. In 2005, private schools accounted for about 19.1% of primary school enrollment and 27.1% of secondary enrollment.

In 2009, there were 22 public and 2 private elementary schools in Palau. There was one public high school (Palau High School) and five private high schools the same year. Postsecondary education is provided by the College of Micronesia's Micronesian Occupational College (MOC) in Koror and the Palau Community College. In 2006, Palau Community College had about 54 teachers; student enrollment for the fall 2006 was 683. As of 2005, an estimated 70% of the adult population had completed one or more years of post secondary education. The adult literacy rate has been estimated at about 92%.

As of 2003, public expenditure on education was estimated at 11.1% of GDP, or 20% of total government expenditures.

44 LIBRARIES AND MUSEUMS

The Palau Community College Library is the largest in the country, with a collection of about 26,000 items. The PCC library also serves as a depository library for the Secretariat of the Pacific Community, the United Nations, and the World Health Organization. There is a small public library in Koror, with a collection comprising about 17,000 books. The Palau Congressional Library, established in 1981, has about 5,000 volumes and offers reading rooms open to the public.

The Belau National Museum, established in 1973, is also located in Koror as is the Etpison Museum; both museums contain collections on art and history. The Palau International Coral Reef Center on Koror houses an aquarium, a nursery of giant clams, a crocodile farm, an old Japanese shrine, WWII relics and monuments, and a traditional Bai meeting house.

45 MEDIA

The Palau National Communications Corp., established in 1982, provides domestic and international telephone connections, radio broadcasting, telex and telegram communications, and navigational and weather services. In 2009, there were 7,100 main phone lines and 13,200 cellular phones in use, or 64 mobile phone subscriptions for every 100 people.

A radio station in Koror broadcasts to listeners in the outer islands. As of 2011, there was 1 FM radio station, 4 AM radio stations, and 1 shortwave radio station. There are no local television stations, but cable television service is available. As of 1997, there were 478 radios and 85 television sets in use per 1,000 population. In 2010, there were three Internet hosts in the nation. In 2011, Internet users numbered 27 per 100 citizens. Most Internet access is made through public places, such as schools and Internet cafes.

There are no daily papers. Tia Belau and Palau Horizon are English-language weeklies, and Roureur Belau is a Palauan language weekly. The constitution provides for free speech and a free press, and the government respects these rights in practice.

46 ORGANIZATIONS

The clan system forms the basic unit of social organization. Youth, women's, and community development organizations provide economic self-help, community involvement and leadership training, skills training, and sports and recreation. There are also a few sports associations affiliated with international organizations. The Pacific Endowment for Art Culture and Environment supports the arts and the preservation of native culture. The Lion's Club has programs in the country. There is a national chapter of the Red Cross Society.

47 TOURISM, TRAVEL, AND RECREATION

Palau's scenic areas include the Rock Islands, a large number of small, mushroom-shaped islands that are unique in the region, and the Floating Garden Islands. The marine environment is rich in live coral formations and tropical fish, making the country a prime destination for snorkeling and scuba diving. Many tourists visit the World War II battlefields, war memorials, and shrines.

In 2005, the US television show "Survivor: Palau" was aired on CBS. The US Department of State found this heightened the level international awareness of the small nation. A new luxury hotel affiliated with Japan Airlines opened on Palau that same year.

Tourism is the nation's primary industry. As a result of the 2008–09 global financial crisis, there was a significant decline in the number of tourists to Palau. In March 2009, the number of tourist arrivals declined by 11% in comparison to figures from 2008; in April 2009, the number declined by nearly 20%. In 2010, there were an estimated 85,593 visitors, of which about 34% were from Japan. The government hopes to attract more foreign investment in the tourist industry in years to come. One development idea for the industry is to create a casino gambling sector.

In 2011 estimated daily cost to visit Melekeok, the capital, was $255.

⁴⁸FAMOUS PERSONS

Haruo Remeliik (1933–85) was the first president of Palau, serving from 1981 until his assassination in 1985. Tommy Remengesau (b. 1956) was elected president in 2000 and reelected in 2004.

⁴⁹DEPENDENCIES

Palau has no territories or colonies.

⁵⁰BIBLIOGRAPHY

Gillespie, Rosemary G., and David A. Clague, eds. *Encyclopedia of Islands.* Berkeley: University of California Press, 2009.

Kirch, Patrick Vinton, and Jean-Louis Rallu. *The Growth and Collapse of Pacific Island Societies.* Honolulu: University of Hawaii Press, 2007.

Leibo, Steven A. *East and Southeast Asia, 2005.* 38th ed. Harpers Ferry, WV: Stryker-Post Publications, 2005.

Leibowitz, Arnold H. *Embattled Island: Palau's Struggle for Independence.* Westport, CT: Praeger, 1996.

May, Stephen J. *Michener's South Pacific.* Gainesville: University of Florida Press, 2011.

Sloan, Bill. *Brotherhood of Heroes: The Marines at Peleliu, 1944: The Bloodiest Battle of the Pacific War.* New York: Simon and Schuster, 2005.

Wright, Derrick. *To the Far Side of Hell: The Battle for Peleliu, 1944.* Tuscaloosa: University of Alabama Press, 2005.

PALESTINIAN TERRITORIES

CAPITAL: The headquarters of the Palestinian National Authority (PNA) is located in Ramallah, while the headquarters of Hamas's government is in Gaza City. Both the PNA and Hamas seek Jerusalem as the capital of a future Palestinian state.

FLAG: The national flag is a tricolor of black, white, and green horizontal stripes with a red triangle at the hoist.

ANTHEM: The official anthem of the PNA is *Fida'i* (*My Redemption*). A popular, unofficial national anthem is *Mawtini* (*My Homeland*).

MONETARY UNIT: The major monetary unit in Palestine is the Israeli Shekel. The Jordanian Dinar, Egyptian Pound (Gaza), Euro and US Dollar are also often used.

WEIGHTS AND MEASURES: The metric system is used the West Bank, Gaza and East Jerusalem.

HOLIDAYS: New Year's Day; the Prophet Muhammad's birthday; Land Day, 20 March; Labor Day, 1 May; the Prophet's ascension; Eid al-Fitr (end of Ramadan); Independence Day, 15 November; Eid al-Adha; the Islamic New Year; and Christmas Day, 25 December. Other Muslim and Christian holidays are observed as well.

TIME: 2 p.m.= noon GMT.

¹LOCATION, SIZE, AND EXTENT

Historically, Palestine included all the territories of present-day Israel, the West Bank, East Jerusalem, and the Gaza Strip. The geographical area constituting Jordan was often considered part of Palestine as well. The PNA seeks a state in the West Bank, East Jerusalem, and the Gaza Strip (references to Palestine below refer to these territories, except when describing the history of Palestine prior to 1948).

Slightly smaller than the US state of Delaware, the West Bank spans 5,860 sq km (2,263 sq mi) and shares an expansive border with Israel to the W, S, and N, and Jordan to the E.

The Gaza Strip is located between Israel and Egypt, on the eastern edge of the Mediterranean Sea. The area totals 578 sq km (223 sq mi). The Mediterranean coastline stretches for about 40 km (25 mi).

²TOPOGRAPHY

The terrain ranges from flat to rolling. In the West Bank, altitudes vary considerably throughout the region. The Dead Sea rests below sea level, at -408 m (-1,339 ft). The highest peak, Tall Asur, stands 1,022 m (3,353 ft) above sea level.

Dune-like desert plains dot the landscape of Gaza, which is sometimes referred to as the Gaza Strip, because of its long, narrow shape. The highest point, Abu 'Awday (Joz Abu 'Auda) reaches 105 m (346 ft).

³CLIMATE

The climate of Palestine is temperate, with warm to hot summers and cool to mild winters.

⁴FLORA AND FAUNA

The West Bank is home to a number of plants including *Oronis natrix* and *Poa bulbosa*. Other plants such as *Bullota undulate* and *Hordeum bulbosum* can be found on the Eastern slopes of the West Bank. In the semi-coastal region of the West Bank, shrubs such as *Thymus capitata* are prevalent. Along the Gaza Strip's seashores, plants such as *Artemisia monosperma* and *Retama raetam* are present. In Palestine, there are more than 500 species of birds, including the blue-cheeked bee-eater, greater flamingo, and the great grey shrike. Mammals include Palestinian mountain gazelles, Arabian wolves, the Gaza house mouse, and Persian honey badgers.

⁵ENVIRONMENT

A number of environmental concerns have impacted the Palestinian ecosystem such as desertification and the adequacy of the freshwater supply. In the West Bank, the Palestinian water supply is polluted by wastewater emanating from Israeli settlements. Israeli settlers have been responsible for uprooting olive trees and farms. In the Gaza Strip, the environment is plagued by soil degradation, inadequate water resources, and desertification.

⁶POPULATION

The total population of Palestinians living in the West Bank (including East Jerusalem) and the Gaza Strip was approximately 4.02 million in 2007 with a 3.2% growth rate. These areas are also inhabited by roughly 470,000 Israeli settlers.

[7] MIGRATION

During the period 2005–2009, 7,000 Palestinians emigrated to a number of destinations, including Jordan, the United States and Arab Gulf countries. Some left to pursue educational opportunities, while others wanted to attain better living conditions. During the same period, however, between 5,000 and 6,000 Palestinians returned to the West Bank and Gaza Strip. Little internal migration takes place, mostly within Palestinian governorates.

[8] ETHNIC GROUPS

Most of the population (excluding Israeli Jewish settlers) is Arab. There are also small communities of Armenians, Circassians, and Kurds.

[9] LANGUAGES

The dominant language is Arabic. Hebrew and English are also understood by many Palestinians.

[10] RELIGIONS

Islam (Sunni sect) is the dominant religion in the West Bank and Gaza Strip. Some 97% of the Palestinian population is Muslim, while 3% is Christian.

[11] TRANSPORTATION

Roads covered close to 113 sq km (44 sq mi) of land in Palestine according to a 2007 study. These roads include main roads, district roads, bypass roads and local/access roads. There were 78,609 registered vehicles in the country in 2008. Private cars, buses, taxis, bicycles, mopeds, motorcycles, tractors and trailers are used by Palestinians.

Israel's separation barrier, designed to protect the Jewish state from terrorist attacks, hinders Palestinian mobility, cuts into Palestinian land, and increases transportation costs.

The Yasser Arafat International Airport in Rafah on the Gaza Strip was bombed by the Israeli air force in 2001 and was still closed as of January 2012.

[12] HISTORY

Palestine was initially inhabited by the Canaanites between c. 3000 and 1500 BC. The term Palestine was used by the 5th-century-BC Greek scholar Herodotus to refer to the geographical region defined today as Israel, the West Bank and Gaza Strip. The term was derived from the Philistines, a Greek people who established themselves on the region's coastal area during the Iron Age (1175 BC). A number of alternative names were also used to describe this region, including the terms Israel and Southern Syria. The land was home to many peoples throughout the ages, such as the Canaanites, Greeks, Jews, Romans, Arabs, Persians, European Crusaders, and many others. For most of its modern history, Palestine was inhabited by a majority of Arab Muslims, an Arab Christian minority (both ancestors of modern-day Palestinians) and a Jewish minority. The area was governed as part of the province of Syria by the Ottoman Empire. The Ottomans ruled Palestine from 1516 until the end of World War I (1918).

Beginning in 1882, Jewish communities began to migrate to Palestine in substantial numbers. Jewish thinkers also wrote about the need for a Jewish national home and Jewish self-determination.

Theodor Herzl's *The Jewish State* was a particularly influential text, published in 1896, a time when the Jewish population in Palestine accounted for no more than 5% of the population.

The World Zionist Congress was formed in 1897 and was followed by the establishment of the Jewish National Fund in 1901. During World War I, the British government promised Jewish leaders that it would seek the creation of a Jewish national home in Palestine, a promise made in the Balfour Declaration of 1917. According to the Arabs, the Balfour Declaration and British plans with the French for a post-war Middle East contradicted promises made to their side in the Husayn-McMahon correspondence of 1916. The Arabs perceived the correspondence to have promised the creation of an independent, unified Arab Kingdom that included Palestine as part of its territories, after the War. Britain subsequently prevailed over the Ottoman armies in Palestine, occupying the region in 1918. British and French plans were set in motion, and a system of colonial mandatory control was established during this time. The British Mandate for Palestine was established by the League of Nations in 1922.

The British pursued a policy that sparked opposition from both Arabs and Jews. The former aimed to restrict Jewish immigration into their homeland, while the latter wanted to increase the migration of their kin to allow for the creation of a new state. In 1936–39 an Arab revolt took place that was eventually suppressed by Britain. Arab-Jewish tensions simmered in the 1940s, leading to a United Nations (UN) recommendation to partition Palestine into an Arab and a Jewish state. Jewish leaders agreed to the recommendation, while the Arabs refused because the partition resolution carved up an area in which they still constituted the clear majority.

The Arabs of Palestine, aided by brethren across the frontiers, at once rose up in arms to thwart partition. The Jews of Palestine accepted the plan; on 14 May 1948, the last day of the mandate, they proclaimed the formation of the State of Israel. The next day, the Arab League states—Egypt, Iraq, Jordan, Lebanon, Saudi Arabia, and Syria—launched a concerted armed attack. There followed a mass flight of hundreds of thousands of Palestinian Arabs abroad, partly at the urging of foreign Arab leaders and partly owing to actions of Israeli forces. Following the war, the West Bank was annexed to Jordan and the Gaza Strip was administered by Egypt. Arab-Israeli relations did not improve in the 1950s and 1960s. In 1964, the Palestinian Liberation Organization (PLO) was formed, and in 1965 the Palestinian resistance movement Fatah, led by Yasser Arafat, commenced raids against Israel.

In 1967, under the pan-Arab leadership of Gamal Abdel Nasser, Egypt expelled UN peacekeepers from Gaza and the Sinai Peninsula and mobilized its troops along Israel's border. Israel responded by launching a preemptive strike on Egypt and a war ensued between Israel and several Arab states (Egypt, Syria and Jordan). Israel again captured Arab territory, including the West Bank, East Jerusalem, the Gaza Strip and the Golan Heights. More Palestinians became refugees as a consequence of the 1967 War. UN Resolution 242 called for Israel to withdraw from "territories occupied in the recent conflict." Israel returned the Sinai lands captured in the 1967 war to Egypt in the 1979 Camp David Accords and the Israel-Egypt Peace Treaty of 1980, but continued to occupy the West Bank.

In 1969, Arafat was elected Chairman of the PLO. Palestinian political groups that did not adhere to the authority of Arab states, such as Fatah and the Popular Front for the Liberation of Palestine, were becoming more popular during this period. They espoused a leftist, secular, nationalist ideology and advocated armed struggle based on a guerilla model as a means to liberate Palestine. Palestinian fighters came to be known as the *fidayyin* (redeemers) and symbolized the Palestinian struggle. Eventually, many of these groups based themselves in Jordan and challenged the authority of the Jordanian state, leading to the Black September civil conflict between Jordan and the Palestinians in 1970–1971. By 1971 the Palestinian groups were expelled to Lebanon, where they were later embroiled in the Lebanese Civil War (1975–91).

During the 1970s and 1980s, Palestinian political groups were responsible for a number of terror attacks against Israeli civilians, including the Munich massacre of Israeli athletes during the Olympic Games of 1972. For its part, Israel pursued a violent occupation in the West Bank and Gaza Strip and a settlement program that violated international law. In 1982, Israel invaded Lebanon, where it defeated the PLO. Tensions mounted between Palestinians living in Gaza and the West Bank and Israel in the 1980s, leading to the First Intifada of 1987, a popular revolt against Israeli forces. The Intifada accelerated peace efforts such as the Madrid Peace Process, which culminated in the 13 September 1993 signing of a Declaration of Principles by Israel and the PLO. The document established a framework for transferring authority over Gaza and the West Bank from Israel to Palestinian control. Over the next years, more documents were signed: on 4 May 1994 Israel and the PLO signed the Gaza-Jericho Agreement, and on 29 August 1994 both parties signed the Agreement on Preparatory Transfer of Powers and Responsibilities. The process was neither smooth nor simple. Peace talks broke down in 2000, and the Second Intifada erupted later that year.

Both Israelis and Palestinians have been responsible for the killing of civilians since the late 1980s. Palestinian suicide bombings and rocket attacks, carried out mostly by Islamist groups Hamas and Islamic Jihad, killed many Israeli civilians. Israeli Defense Forces' (IDF) incursions into Palestinian areas and air attacks also led to numerous Palestinian civilian deaths.

On 15 August 2005, Israel began disengaging from Gaza, withdrawing the IDF from the Strip and dismantling 17 Jewish settlements. With the help of many Western governments and institutions, Gaza's economy experienced a marked improvement following Israeli disengagement.

In the January 2006 elections, Hamas took a majority of seats in the Palestinian Legislative Council elections. Hamas's message of violent resistance against Israel had won considerable support. Internal struggles within the Palestinian leadership divided Hamas and Fatah. With Hamas blacklisted internationally for refusing to renounce violence and recognize the state of Israel, critical international aid was withheld from the PNA. Facing this grave situation, moderate Fatah leader and president of the PNA, Mahmoud Abbas, tried to negotiate with Hamas to establish an internationally and politically acceptable unity platform. Unable to reach an agreement with Hamas, violence erupted between Hamas and Fatah, and the unity government was dissolved. In 2007 Hamas staged a coup-like takeover in Gaza, leaving the

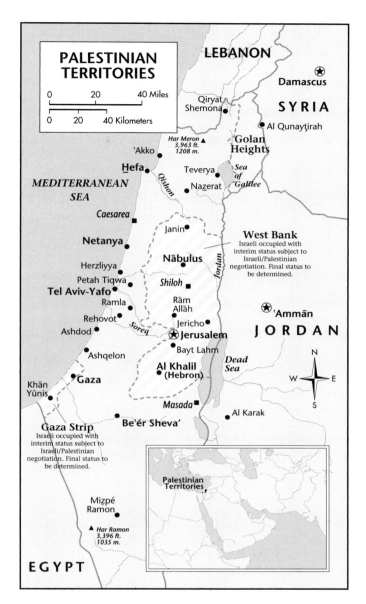

LOCATION: 31°35′ to 31°13′ N; 34°13′ to 34°33′ E (Gaza); 32°29′ to 31°21′ N; 35° to 35°32′ E (West Bank). BOUNDARY LENGTHS: In Gaza, Egypt, 11 kilometers (7 miles); Israel, 51 kilometers (32 miles); Mediterranean coastline, 40 kilometers (25 miles); In the West Bank, Israel, 307 kilometers (191 miles), Jordan, 97 kilometers (60 miles).

Palestinian leadership essentially divided—Fatah in the West Bank, Hamas in Gaza.

In 2009 a major conflict erupted between Israel and Hamas in Gaza, leading to further civilian casualties. By the end of 2011, Israel and the Palestinians had not made significant additional progress toward a final peace agreement.

¹³GOVERNMENT

According to the 1994 Oslo Accords signed between the PLO and Israel—and subsequent agreements and talks—the PNA was formed to serve as an interim body responsible for administering the West Bank and Gaza Strip, pending a final status peace agreement.

The PNA is governed by an elected president, an appointed prime minister and an elected legislature known as the Palestinian Legislative Council (PLC).

The PLO represents Palestinian refugees and members of the Palestinian diaspora as well as the Palestinians in the West Bank, Gaza and East Jerusalem in negotiations with Israel. As of 2011, Israel and the PLO have failed to arrive at a final status agreement. The PLO has been able to gain widespread international recognition for the State of Palestine. Israel, the United States, and a number of European countries have not recognized Palestine as an independent state.

14 POLITICAL PARTIES

A wide range of parties participated in Palestinian political life during the 20th and into the 21st century. These included Fatah, a secular, nationalist party formed in 1965; Hamas, an Islamist political party founded in 1988 during the First Intifada; the leftist Popular Front for the Liberation of Palestine (PFLP) established in 1967; the communist group, the Palestinian People's Party, formed in 1982; the Democratic Front for the Liberation of Palestine, a Marxist-Leninist organization, established in 1969; the Palestinian Islamic Jihad founded in the 1970s; and the Palestinian National Initiative (al-Mubadara), established in 2002 by independent figures in the Palestinian community.

The first PNA president was PLO Chairman Yasser Arafat, who came to office in 1994 and was then elected in 1996. He remained president until his death in November 2004. After a brief period during which PLC speaker Rawhi Fattuh served as Acting President of the PNA, Fatah and PLO chief and former PNA prime minister Mahmoud Abbas became president. Abbas was elected in January 2005 for a four-year term, winning 62% of the vote. Despite the expiration of his term in 2009, Abbas continued as president throughout 2009–2011.

The office of PNA prime minister was created in 2003 to oversee the Palestinian cabinet. Abbas was the first person vested with this position (March 2003–October 2003) and was succeeded by Ahmad Qurei (October 2003–February 2006, with a brief interruption in December 2005).

After Hamas's successful electoral campaign in the PLC elections of January 2006, Hamas leader Ismail Haniyeh became PNA prime minister in March 2006. Abbas replaced Haniyeh with independent economist Salam Fayyad in June 2007. Fayyad was reappointed in 2009.

Hamas did not recognize Fayyad and, since 2007, has been the *de facto* governing authority in the Gaza Strip. Hamas recognizes its own leader, Haniyeh, as PNA prime minister and has its own cabinet.

While Hamas has exercised authority in the Gaza Strip, the PNA under Abbas and Fayyad has retained security and civil authority in the Oslo-defined Area A of the West Bank and civil authority in Area B of the West Bank. Security authority for Area B and complete authority for Area C has been retained by Israel.

15 LOCAL GOVERNMENT

Government at the local level is administered by governorates, municipal and village councils, and refugee camps. As of 2008, there were 11 governorates in the West Bank (Bethlehem, Hebron, Jenin, Tubas, Tulkarem, Qalqilya, Salfit, Nablus, Ramallah and al-Bireh, Jerusalem, Jericho) and 5 in the Gaza Strip (Jabalya, Gaza City, Deir al-Balah, Khan Younis and Rafah).

16 JUDICIAL SYSTEM

The Palestinian judicial system draws on Ottoman, British Mandate, Jordanian and Egyptian legal codes and Israeli military decrees. A Palestinian Basic Law was ratified in 2002 and outlines public laws and freedoms, the nature and powers of the legislative, executive and judicial authorities, and the laws governing the police, security forces and law enforcement, local administration, general finance and other matters of state, society and government. The Palestinian court system includes a Supreme Court, appeals courts, first instance courts, and magistrate courts.

17 ARMED FORCES

PNA security forces have limited their activities to the West Bank and have not been present in the Gaza Strip since June 2007 when Hamas seized power. Since that time, security functions in Gaza have been managed by Hamas.

18 INTERNATIONAL COOPERATION

The PNA receives support from the European Union and the United States as well as from Arab states.

19 ECONOMY

The GDP was estimated at $11.95 billion in 2008.

Gaza's economy is restricted by limited land, high population density, and external controls imposed by Israel for security reasons. Compared to the West Bank, Gaza is the smaller of the two areas under the PNA. An economic downturn followed the Second Intifada of September 2000, when Israel closed access to the territory ostensibly because of security concerns. When Israel withdrew from the Gaza Strip in September 2005, prospects for economic growth appeared to improve. However, Israeli-imposed lack of access to the territory persisted. The 2007 rise to power by Hamas led to further private sector layoffs and shortages of most goods. Economically crippling sanctions imposed by Israel on Gaza continued through 2011, allowing only the most basic goods to flow into the territory.

The West Bank's economy also underwent some decline since the Second Intifada. Israel enforced a series of closures and access restrictions that crippled the West Bank's economy. Israeli security measures drove businesses to close in the territory. Economic life-support for the West Bank (and Gaza) came by way of international aid, which in 2004 totaled nearly $1.15 billion.

When Hamas was elected to run the Palestinian Legislative Council (2006–07), however, the West Bank's economy suffered even further, as almost all international aid was withheld. The PNA was then forced to cut all social services and withhold the salaries of PNA employees. The situation improved under PNA Prime Minister Salam Fayyad.

20 INCOME

The GDP per capita for the West Bank (excluding East Jerusalem) and Gaza Strip was estimated at $1,261 in 2007. The poverty rate was estimated at 19% for the West Bank and 51.8% for the Gaza Strip.

21 LABOR

The Palestinian unemployment rate was 25.8% as of 2008 (16.3% in the West Bank and 45.5% in the Gaza Strip). 61.3% of those employed worked in the private sector, while 22.7% were in the public sector. About 10.8% of the labor force worked in Israel and in settlements. The two most active areas of employment were service branches and commercial enterprises.

22 AGRICULTURE

The total cultivated area in Palestine accounted for 1,834 sq km (708 sq mi). In the central highlands region stretching from Jenin in the north to Hebron in the south, olives, grapes, vegetables, cereals, and grain legumes are cultivated. The agricultural sector accounted for 25% of Palestinian exports, including fruits, olives and olive oil, vegetables, and flowers.

23 ANIMAL HUSBANDRY

On the eastern slopes of the West Bank, shepherds and farmers graze sheep and goats. Beef and dairy cattle are the only commercial livestock raised in Palestine.

24 FISHING

As of 2005, there were nearly 3,000 Palestinian fishermen using over 700 fishing boats. They caught 1,818 tons of fish.

25 FORESTRY

The Palestinian ecosystem contained 232 sq km (90 sq mi) of forested areas. These areas provide fruits, honey, dyes, and timber that are important components to Palestinian industry and to the Palestinian economy. They also allow for the retention of water and biological diversity in the area.

26 MINING

Mining and quarrying accounted for 0.5% of Palestinian GDP in 2008. Quarrying takes place in Bethlehem, Nablus, Hebron, and other locations.

27 ENERGY AND POWER

Gaza imported 120,000 kWh of electricity from the Israel Electric Company in 2009. The West Bank produced 400 million kWh of electricity and imported 3.2 billion kWh, mostly from Israel. The Jerusalem District Electricity Company provided electric power to Palestinians in East Jerusalem.

28 INDUSTRY

Palestinian industrial production mostly occurs in the private sector and includes manufacturing, construction, pharmaceuticals, and textile production. Employment in industrial ventures has declined, especially in Gaza, where thousands of industrial businesses went under in the 2000s. An estimated 98% of Gaza's industries had collapsed by 2008.

29 SCIENCE AND TECHNOLOGY

A number of Palestinian universities publish scientific journals. Al-Najah University's *Journal of Research* (Natural Sciences) was established in 1988. The *Journal of the Islamic University of Gaza* has published a series on natural studies and engineering since 1993. Other universities also promote and publish research and teaching in science and technology. The Palestine Academy for Science and Technology (PALAST), an independent organization located in East Jerusalem with branches in Ramallah and Gaza, was established in 1997. PALAST is considered the primary organization dedicated to science and technology in the Palestinian territories.

30 DOMESTIC TRADE

Palestinian domestic trade is encumbered by Israeli restrictions on Palestinian mobility.

31 FOREIGN TRADE

Palestinian trade with Israel constituted 90% of overall Palestinian trade as of 2008. Palestinian exports included food, live animals, and manufactured goods. Palestinian imports come in the form of investment goods and raw materials. Palestinian foreign trade is hindered by Israeli restrictions and by the difficult political circumstances in the region. Still, Palestine exports to countries in the Arab world, non-Arab Asian countries, North America, and the EU.

32 BALANCE OF PAYMENTS

According to the Palestine Monetary Authority and the Palestinian Central Bureau of Statistics, the Palestinian balance of payments for the third quarter of 2011 showed a deficit of $291.6 million in the current account.

33 BANKING AND SECURITIES

Some 21 banks operate in Palestine, with a total of 140 branches. Prominent banks include the Bank of Palestine, a Palestinian bank that has 25 branches, and the Arab Bank, an international bank that has 22 branches. In 1995 the Palestine Exchange (PEX) was set up. Trading commenced on the al-Quds Index in 1997. The PEX is now a public shareholding company regulated by the Palestinian Capital Market Authority. On 30 November 2011, the PEX listed 46 companies possessing a total market capitalization of $2.7 billion.

34 INSURANCE

Health insurance was available to 65.8% of the West Bank population and to 93.8% of Gazans in 2004. Sources of health insurance included the Palestinian government and security forces, the UN Relief and Works Agency for Palestine Refugees (UNRWA), social security, and private insurance.

35 PUBLIC FINANCE

The PNA's revenues are drawn from tax collection, foreign grants from international organizations, grants from other countries, property income, sales of goods and services, and fines and

Public Finance – Palestine (2009)

(In millions of U.S. dollars, budgetary central government figures)

Revenue and Grants	**3,094.3**	**100.0%**
Tax revenue	1,491.4	48.2%
Social contributions	...	...
Grants	1,416.5	45.8%
Other revenue	186.4	6.0%
Expenditures	**3,060.3**	**100.0%**
General public services	582.1	19.0%
Defense	...	...
Public order and safety	835.1	27.3%
Economic affairs	73.9	2.4%
Environmental protection	2.7	0.1%
Housing and community amenities	87.7	2.9%
Health	342.3	11.2%
Recreational, culture, and religion	95.6	3.1%
Education	492.5	16.1%
Social protection	548.7	17.9%

(...) data not available or not significant.

SOURCE: *Government Finance Statistics Yearbook 2010*, Washington, DC: International Monetary Fund, 2010.

penalties. Tax collection and foreign grants are the largest sources of revenue for the PNA.

36 TAXATION

The PNA was sanctioned to administer taxation in the Palestinian territories according to the Gaza-Jericho Accord of May 1994 and the subsequent Early Empowerment Agreement of August 1994. Some taxes are administered by Israel and then distributed to the PNA. Israel has sometimes withheld taxes owed to the PNA. In January 2012 Fayyad announced an increase in taxes to meet budget deficits. Income tax rates for high earners doubled from 15% to 30% under the new plan, among other changes.

37 CUSTOMS AND DUTIES

The Palestinian tariff structure is based on the Israeli model with limited variations. The PNA levies the Israeli VAT rate of 17% and adjusts it by a 2% increase or decrease for certain goods. Tariffs and VAT taxes on imports are collected by Israel and dispensed to the PNA.

38 FOREIGN INVESTMENT

At the end of 2009, the total stocks of foreign investments in Palestine were estimated at $1.586 billion. This figure includes foreign direct investment, portfolio investments, stocks of Palestinian deposits abroad, trade credits, and loans given to non-residents.

39 ECONOMIC DEVELOPMENT

The PNA has exerted significant efforts to identify potential avenues for economic development. It has compiled a comprehensive development program entitled the Palestinian Reform and Development Plan (PRDP). One of the national goals articulated in the plan is the provision of economic security in the Palestinian territories and a rise in private sector employment.

40 SOCIAL DEVELOPMENT

Palestinian women have achieved a high level of enrollment in secondary schools and universities. An estimated 54% of university students in Palestine were women in 2007. Nonetheless, women's labor force participation has been 15.2% of the formal labor force.

41 HEALTH

Health expenditure constituted 13% of the GDP of Palestine as of 2007. In 2005 Palestine contained a total of 619 primary health care centers and 78 hospitals; the latter administered by the Ministry of Health, nongovernmental organizations, UNRWA, and private boards. Infant mortality rates were 24 per 1,000 live births, while maternal mortality for women between the ages of 15–49 was 12.7 out of 100,000 live births. The separation barrier erected by the Israeli government in the West Bank has obstructed access to medical care and the transport of medical personnel to work locations. In the Gaza Strip, similar problems have occurred as a result of the closure of border crossings between the Strip and Egypt.

42 HOUSING

Palestinian rights to housing have been compromised by the Israeli-Palestinian conflict. IDF demolitions of homes and building units, the Israeli government's erection of the separation barrier, and the expropriation of Palestinian land have considerably impacted the ability of many Palestinians to maintain or find adequate shelter. Housing projections undertaken in 2011 highlighted the need to provide more Palestinian housing, as housing units were forecasted to increase by 63% from 2007 numbers. The Palestinian Housing Council, based in Jerusalem, is one of the organizations attempting to find solutions for the Palestinian housing crisis.

43 EDUCATION

During 2005–2009, 94% of Palestinians in the West Bank and Gaza Strip were literate. The primary school net enrollment ratio for the same period stood at 75%. Secondary school net enrollment ratios were also high, recorded at 85% for males and 90% for females.

As of 2010–2011, there were a total of 2,652 primary and secondary schools in Palestine. The majority of these schools catered to a single-sex student body, although as many as 787 were coeducational. Some 1,573 schools were public, while 344 were registered as private schools. The rest were supervised by UNRWA.

A number of vocational schools respectively specialized in industrial, agricultural, commercial, hotel, and religious training were established over the years in the West Bank and Gaza Strip.

In 2005–2006, the two territories contained 13 colleges, 19 community colleges, and 11 universities. Birzeit University and al-Quds University are among the most famous.

44 LIBRARIES AND MUSEUMS

As of 2009 there were 12 museums in the West Bank, attended by nearly 9,000 visitors. These museums included the Bethlehem Folklore Museum and the al-Bad Museum for Olive Oil

Production. The Gaza Museum of Archaeology (al-Mathaf) is located in the Gaza Strip.

In addition to university libraries, Palestine has a number of private and public libraries.

45 MEDIA

Several private Palestinian daily newspapers are in circulation including *al-Quds* and *al-Ayyam*. The PNA's daily newspaper is called *al-Hayat al-Jadida*, while the daily *Filastin* is affiliated with Hamas. The PNA and Hamas each have their own satellite TV, terrestrial TV and radio station outlets. The PNA outlets are run by the Palestinian Broadcasting Corporation (PBC), while Hamas outlets are distributed by the al-Aqsa Media Network. There are several major news agencies including the official Palestine News Agency, known as Wafa, the Ma'an News Agency, and the Palestine News Network.

46 ORGANIZATIONS

There are numerous Palestinian non-governmental organizations based in the West Bank and Gaza Strip. These include the al-Badil Resource Center for Palestinian Residency and Refugee Rights, the Democracy and Workers' Rights Center, al-Haq and al-Mawrid Teacher Development Center.

47 TOURISM, TRAVEL, AND RECREATION

In the first half of 2008, 213,317 tourists visited Palestine. These visitors included Palestinians living abroad, Europeans, Israelis, Canadians, US citizens, Arabs of various nationalities, and other nationalities. There were 82 hotels according to the Palestine Central Bureau of Statistics. Attractions in the area include the Church of the Nativity in Bethlehem, the Tomb of the Patriarchs in Hebron, the Old City in Jerusalem, and the modern cities of Ramallah and Nablus.

48 FAMOUS PERSONS

Yasser Arafat (1929–2004) was the founder of Fatah and the Chairman of the PLO (1969–2004). Mahmoud Abbas (b. 1935) is the President of the PNA and Chairman of the PLO. Economist Salam Fayyad (b. 1952) is the internationally-recognized prime minister of the PNA. Ismail Haniyeh (b. 1963) is the prime minister in charge of the Gaza Strip and a Hamas leader.

During the last 50 years, several internationally prominent literary figures and scholars have hailed from Palestine. These included the famed literary and cultural critic and Columbia University Professor, Edward Said (1935–2003), the poets Mahmoud Darwish (1941–2008) and Ibrahim Touqan (1905–1941), and the novelist Ghassan Kanafani (1936–1972).

49 DEPENDENCIES

There are no dependencies.

50 BIBLIOGRAPHY

Baracskay, Daniel. *The Palestine Liberation Organization: Terrorism and Prospects for Peace in the Holy Land.* Santa Barbara, CA: Praeger, 2011.

Mitchell, Thomas G. *Native vs. Settler: Ethnic Conflict in Israel/Palestine, Northern Ireland, and South Africa.* Westport, CT: Greenwood Press, 2000.

Palestine Investment and Business Guide. Washington, DC: International Business Publications USA, 2009.

Smith, Charles D. *Palestine and the Arab-Israeli Conflict: A History with Documents.* New York: Bedford/St. Martin's, 2006.

PAPUA NEW GUINEA

Independent State of Papua New Guinea

CAPITAL: Port Moresby

FLAG: The flag is a rectangle, divided diagonally. The upper segment is scarlet with a yellow bird of paradise; the lower segment is black with five white stars representing the Southern Cross.

ANTHEM: *O, Arise All You Sons.*

MONETARY UNIT: The kina (PGK) of 100 toea is linked with the Australian dollar. There are coins of 5, 10, 20, and 50 toea and 1 kina, and notes of 2, 5, 10, 20, 50, and 100 kina. PGK1=US$0.4493 (or US$1=PGK2.1813) as of 2011.

WEIGHTS AND MEASURES: The metric system is the legal standard.

HOLIDAYS: New Year's Day, 1 January; Queen's Birthday, 1st Monday in June; Remembrance Day, 23 July; National Day of Repentance, 26 August; Independence Day, 16 September; Christmas, 25 December; Boxing Day, 26 December. Movable religious holidays include Good Friday and Easter Monday.

TIME: 10 p.m. = noon GMT.

¹LOCATION, SIZE, AND EXTENT

Situated to the north of Australia, Papua New Guinea has a total land area of 462,840 sq km (178,704 sq mi), including the large islands of New Britain, New Ireland, and Bougainville and hundreds of smaller islands. Comparatively, the area occupied by Papua New Guinea is slightly larger than the state of California. The country extends 2,082 km (1,294 mi) NNE–SSW and 1,156 km (718 mi) ESE–WNW. Mainland Papua New Guinea shares the island of New Guinea, the second-largest island in the world, with Indonesia. To the N is the Federated States of Micronesia; to the E, the Solomon Islands; to the W, Indonesia; and about 160 km (100 mi) to the S, Australia. Papua New Guinea has a total boundary length of 5,972 km (3,711 mi), of which 5,152 km (3,201 mi) is coastline.

Papa New Guinea's capital city, Port Moresby, is located on the country's southern coast.

²TOPOGRAPHY

Papua New Guinea is situated between the stable continental mass of Australia and the deep ocean basin of the Pacific. The largest section is the eastern half of the island of New Guinea. This region is dominated by a massive central cordillera, or system of mountain ranges, extending from the Indonesian half of New Guinea to East Cape in Papua New Guinea at the termination of the Owen Stanley Range, which includes the nation's highest peak, Mt. Wilhelm (4,509 m/14,793 ft).

A second mountain chain fringes the north coast and runs parallel to the central cordillera. In the lowlands there are many swamps and floodplains. Important rivers are the Sepik, flowing about 1,130 km (700 mi) to the north coast and the Fly, which is navigable for 800 km (500 mi) in the southwest. The Bougainville-New Ireland area comprises the Bougainville and Buka islands, the Gazelle Peninsula of New Britain, New Ireland, New Hanover, the St. Matthias group, and the Admiralty Islands. The smaller islands of Papua New Guinea are also areas of extreme topographical contrast and generally feature mountain ranges rising directly from the sea or from narrow coastal plains.

Papua New Guinea contains the most active volcanoes in the southwest Pacific region, with a total of 80 volcanoes. 14 are active, with eruptions in the last 150 years; 22 are dormant; and the remainder are extinct. An eruption in September 1994 of two volcanoes caused the destruction of half of the town of Rabaul on New Britain Island. The Manam volcano erupted on 20 May 2002, sending an ash plume as high as 9 km. On 11 July 2002 the Langila volcano on New Britain erupted.

Papua New Guinea experiences frequent earthquakes, some of them of high-magnitude. On 16 November 2000 the New Ireland region experienced a quake that hit 8.0 on the Richter scale. It was recorded as the largest earthquake of the year worldwide, but fatalities were limited to two people. On 11 March 2003 a 6.8 magnitude earthquake hit the same region, and on 9 September 2005 a 7.7 magnitude quake occurred; both quakes caused some damage but no reported deaths.

Two quakes of magnitude 6.2 and 5.1 hit the New Ireland region on 25 July 2011; a week later, on 31 July 2011, a 6.8 magnitude quake struck off the northern coast of Papua New Guinea. No injuries were reported for the three July 2011 quakes.

³CLIMATE

The climate of Papua New Guinea is chiefly influenced by altitude and monsoons. The northwest or wet monsoon prevails from December to March and the southeast or dry trade winds from May to October. Annual rainfall varies widely with the monsoon pattern, ranging from as little as 127 cm (50 in) at Port Moresby to an average of 584 cm (230 in) in the western river basin. Most of the lowland and island areas have daily mean temperatures of about 27°C (81°F), while in the highlands temperatures may fall to 4°C (39°F) at night and rise to 32°C (90°F) in the daytime. Relative humidity is uniformly high in the lowlands at about 80% and averages between 65% and 80% in the highlands.

⁴FLORA AND FAUNA

Boasting an estimated 11,544 plant species, the flora of Papua New Guinea is rich and varied, with habitats ranging from tidal swamps at sea level to alpine conditions. In low-lying coastal areas, various species of mangroves form the main vegetation, together with casuarina, sago, and palm. Most of the country is covered by tropical and savanna rain forest, in which valuable trees such as kwila and cedar are found. Orchids, lilies, ferns, and creepers abound in the rain forests. There are large stands of pine at elevations of 910–1,220 m (3,000–4,000 ft). At the highest altitudes, mosses, lichens, and other alpine flora prevail.

Papua New Guinea provides a home for an estimated 720 types of birds, and is the major center for a number of bird families, particularly the bird of paradise, bower bird, cassowary, kingfisher, and parrot. Many of its 260 mammal species are nocturnal; rodent and marsupial orders predominate. Butterflies of Papua New Guinea are world famous for their size and vivid coloring. In addition, the World Resources Institute estimates that there are 338 reptile species and 253 amphibian species in Papua New Guinea. (Calculations in this section reflect the total number of distinct species residing in the country, not the number of endemic species.)

⁵ENVIRONMENT

Papua New Guinea's environmental concerns include pollution, global warming, and the loss of the nation's forests. Coastal waters are polluted with sewage and residue from oil spills. Another significant source of pollution is open-pit mining. The country's cities have produced an average of 0.1 million tons of solid waste per year. Global warming and the resulting rise in sea level are threats to Papua New Guinea's coastal vegetation and water supply. The UN reported in 2008 that carbon dioxide emissions in Papua New Guinea totaled 3,364 kilotons.

In 2010 top officials from Papua New Guinea and 13 other developing Pacific island nations and dependencies met in Vanuatu to discuss the progress made in addressing some of the issues unique to these low-lying, developing island states. These include climate change, sea-level rise, natural disasters, remoteness from major markets, and poverty. Another key objective of the meeting was to address the progress each nation had made in adopting the 2005 Mauritius Strategy, the only global blueprint that exists to help deal with the development challenges of small-island developing states.

The Department of Physical Planning and Environment is responsible for integrating environmental planning and conserving natural resources. According to a 2011 report issued by the International Union for Conservation of Nature and Natural Resources (IUCN), threatened species in Papua New Guinea included 39 mammals, 37 birds, 11 reptiles, 11 amphibians, 42 fish, 2 mollusks, 169 other invertebrates, and 143 plants. Threatened species in Papua New Guinea also included four species of turtle (green sea, hawksbill, olive ridley, and leatherback) and Queen Alexandra's birdwing butterfly.

The World Resources Institute reported that Papua New Guinea had designated 3.62 million hectares (8.95 million acres) of land for protection as of 2006. Water resources totaled 801 cu km (192.2 cu mi) while water usage was 0.1 cu km (0.024 cu mi) per year. Domestic water usage accounted for 56% of total usage, industrial for 43%, and agricultural for 1%. Per capita water usage totaled 17 cu m (600 cu ft) per year.

⁶POPULATION

The US Central Intelligence Agency (CIA) estimated the population of Papua New Guinea in 2011 to be approximately 6,187,591, which placed it at number 106 in population among the 196 nations of the world. In 2011 approximately 3.6% of the population was over 65 years of age, with another 36.4% under 15 years of age. The median age in Papua New Guinea was 21.8 years. There were 1.06 males for every female in the country. The population's annual rate of change was 1.985%. The projected population for the year 2025 was 9,100,000. Population density in Papua New Guinea was calculated at 13 people per sq km (34 people per sq mi).

The UN estimated that 13% of the population lived in urban areas, and that urban populations had an annual rate of change of 2.9%. The largest urban area was Port Moresby, with a population of 314,000.

⁷MIGRATION

Estimates of Papua New Guinea's net migration rate, carried out by the CIA in 2011, amounted to zero, meaning that the numbers of emigrants and immigrants were roughly equal. The total number of emigrants living abroad was 61,200, and the total number of immigrants living in Papua New Guinea was 24,500. Papua New Guinea also accepted 10,177 refugees. In the 1980s many came as refugees from Indonesian New Guinea. In earlier years, emigration of non-indigenous residents may have been influenced by constitutional provisions that restricted eligibility for naturalization to those with eight years' residency, but limited their tax and business rights to the same status as those of aliens.

In November 2010 the governments of the Autonomous Region of Bougainville (ARB) and Papua New Guinea finalized planned to relocate residents from the low-lying atolls of the ARB to the Bougainville mainland. The relocation was necessary because atolls, including Cartaret, Tasman, and Fead Island, were losing ground to rising sea levels which caused flooding and destroyed gardens and wells. These climate-change driven relocations are expected to continue through 2023, with about 40 families moving each year. A large section of land from the constituencies of Peit and Halia was designated as the new homeland for the displaced population, which will be allowed to maintain some level of governmental autonomy in its new location.

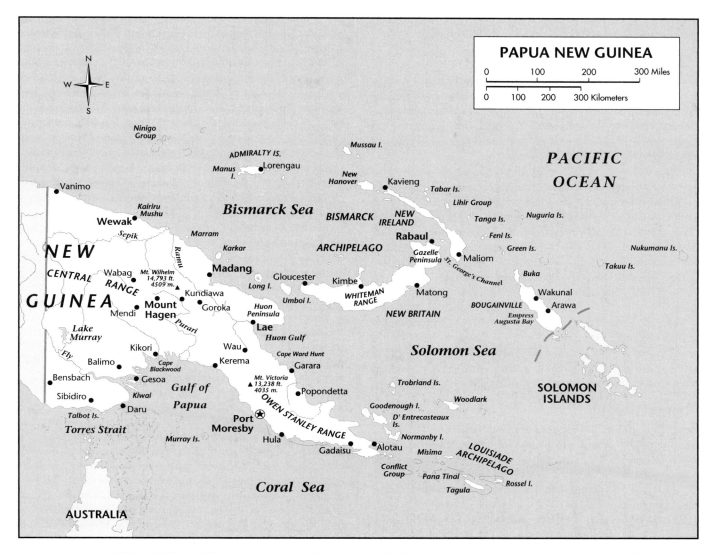

LOCATION: 140°51' to 160°E; 0° to 12° S. BOUNDARY LENGTHS: Total coastline, 5,152 kilometers (3,202 miles); Indonesia, 820 kilometers (509 miles).
TERRITORIAL SEA LIMIT: 12 miles.

8 ETHNIC GROUPS

Papua New Guinea has more than 1,000 different ethnic groups. Papua New Guineans vary considerably in ethnic origins, physical appearance, and spoken languages. The indigenous people are Melanesians. They are usually classified by language group, with Papuans representing the descendants of the original Australoid migration and Austronesian speakers descended from later migrants. The former are generally found in the highlands and the latter in coastal areas and on the islands other than New Guinea. Other groups with significant populations include Negritos, Micronesians, and Polynesians.

9 LANGUAGES

Papua New Guinea has three official languages: English, which is only spoken by 1–2% of the population; Tok Pisin, a Melanesian lingua franca with roots primarily in English and German; and Hiri Motu, a lingua franca of Papuan derivation, spoken by 1–2% of the population. Tok Pisin, which is sometimes referred to as

Pidgin, is the most widely understood. In all, there are about 860 indigenous languages, most of them spoken by a few hundred to a few thousand people.

10 RELIGIONS

Indigenous religions, varying widely in ritual and belief, remain important in tribal societies in Papua New Guinea, with about one-third of the population practicing some form of traditional belief either exclusively or, more commonly, in conjunction with another faith. However, most of the population (96.6%) is nominally Christian. About 27% are Roman Catholics; 19.5% are Evangelical Lutherans; another 11.5% are members of the United Church; and 10% are Seventh-Day Adventists. The Evangelical Alliance accounts for 5.2% of the population, followed by Anglicans at 3.2%, Baptists at 2.5%, and members of the Salvation Army at 0.2%. Another set of Protestant groups, including The Church of Jesus Christ of Latter-Day Saints (Mormons) and Jehovah's Witnesses, make up about 8.9% of the population. Other Protestant sects account for 8.6% of the population. The Baha'i and Muslim communities each account for less than 1% of the population.

11 TRANSPORTATION

Transportation is a major problem in Papua New Guinea because of the difficult terrain. Large population centers are linked chiefly by air and sea, although road construction has increased to supplement these expensive means of transport. The CIA reports that Papua New Guinea has a total of 9,349 km (5,809 mi) of roads, of which 3,000 km (1,864 mi) are paved.

Papua New Guinea has approximately 11,000 km (6,835 mi) of navigable waterways. The government operates a fleet of coastal work boats, none more than nine m (30 ft) long. The principal harbors are Madang, Port Moresby, and Lae. There are international shipping services by refrigerated container ships and other cargo vessels. There is also some passenger service to Australia, Southeast Asia, Pacific island countries, the US west coast, and Europe. The main shipping lines are government owned. In 2008 the merchant fleet was comprised of 21 ships of 1,000 GRT or more.

There were 562 airports, which transported 847,353 passengers in 2009 according to the World Bank. Only 21 of the airports had paved runways. There were also two heliports. Papua New Guinea's national air carrier, Air Niugini, established in 1973, has undertaken most of the services previously provided by Australian lines.

12 HISTORY

Papua New Guinea appears to have been settled by 14,000 BC, with migrations first of hunters and later of agriculturists probably coming from the Asian mainland by way of Indonesia. Early communities had little contact with each other because of rough terrain and so maintained their autonomy, as well as their distinct languages and customs.

New Guinea was first sighted by Spanish and Portuguese sailors in the early 16th century and was known prophetically as Isla del Oro (Island of Gold). The western part of the island was claimed by Spain in 1545 and named New Guinea because the people there resembled those living on the West African coast. ("Papua" is a Malay word for the typically frizzled quality of Melanesian hair.) Traders began to appear in the islands in the 1850s and, at about that same time, the Germans sought coconut oil available in northern New Guinea. The Dutch and the British had earlier agreed on a division of their interests in the island and, starting in 1828, the Dutch began to colonize the western portion.

Although the British flag was hoisted on various parts of eastern New Guinea, the British government did not ratify annexation. Some Australian colonists were eager to see New Guinea become a British possession for trade, labor, gold mining, and missionary reasons. However, it was not until 1884, after an unsuccessful Australian annexation attempt and under fear of German ambitions in the area, that Britain established a protectorate over the southern coast of New Guinea and the adjacent islands. The Germans followed by laying claim to three different parts of northern New Guinea. British and German spheres of influence were delineated by the Anglo-German Agreement of 1885. Germany took control of the northeastern portion of the island, as

well as New Britain, New Ireland, and Bougainville, while Britain took possession of the southern portion and the adjacent islands.

British New Guinea passed to Australian control in 1902 and was renamed the Territory of Papua in 1906. German New Guinea remained intact until the outbreak of war in 1914, when Australian forces seized it. Although the territories retained their separate identities and status, they were administered jointly by Australia from headquarters at Port Moresby. In 1921 the former German New Guinea was placed under a League of Nations mandate administered by Australia. Papua New Guinea was contested territory during World War II. Rabaul was captured by Japanese forces in 1942 and became one of their largest bases in the region. Fighting between Japanese and Allied forces continued through the end of the war in 1945.

In 1947 the former German New Guinea became the Trust Territory of New Guinea, still administered by Australia but now subject to the surveillance of the United Nations (UN) Trusteeship Council. The Trust Territory of New Guinea and the Territory of Papua were merged into the Territory of Papua and New Guinea in 1949. A Legislative Council, established in 1953, was replaced by the House of Assembly in 1964. Eight years later, the territory was renamed Papua New Guinea, and on 1 December 1973, it was granted self-government. Separatist movements in Papua in 1973 and secessionist activities on the island of Bougainville in 1975 flared briefly and then subsided, though debates over citizenship and land-reform provisions were vigorous until the passage of a constitution in 1975. Papua New Guinea achieved complete independence on 16 September 1975, with Michael Somare as prime minister of a coalition government.

Somare was voted out of office in 1980 but reelected in 1982; subsequently, he put through a constitutional change giving the central government increased authority over the provincial governments. In November 1985 Somare was again voted out of office on a no confidence motion and replaced by his previous deputy, Paias Wingti. Elections in mid-1987 returned Wingti to office at the head of a shaky five-party coalition, but his government was defeated in a no confidence vote in July 1988, and a coalition government led by Rabbie Namaliu replaced the People's Democratic Movement (PDM) government.

A secessionist crisis on Bougainville dominated domestic politics during 1990–91. The Bougainville Revolutionary Army (BRA) declared the island of Bougainville to be independent from Papua New Guinea in May 1990, and in response government forces landed on the north of Bougainville in April 1991. Paias Wingti, the leader of the PDM, was reelected prime minister in July 1992 as the leader of a new coalition government with the support of the People's Progress Party and the League for National Advancement. During 1993 the government continued to extend its control over Bougainville, partly because of popular revulsion against human rights violations by members of the BRA. In September 1994 rebel troops withdrew to the surrounding hills of the Bougainville copper mine allowing government forces to reclaim it. In 1995 the prime minister halted cease-fire talks.

Julius Chan was elected prime minister on 30 August 1994, but stepped aside pending a judicial inquiry into his hiring a group of mercenaries to put down the rebellion in Bougainville. In 1997 reformist premier Bill Skate, governor of Port Moresby, was elected by members of the People New Guinea Party's (PNGP) 109-seat parliament, defeating Michael Somare. Skate represented Julius Chan who lost his seat in the elections but who supported Skate's selection as premier.

A resolution to the Bougainville problem remained elusive until April 1998, when a government truce with the rebels resulted in a permanent cease-fire agreement, and the reconstruction of war-torn Bougainville commenced. Up to 20,000 people had been killed during nine years of conflict. In 1999 the rebel leaders and the PNGP government signed an agreement known as the Matakana and Okataina Understanding which established an agreement to continue discussions about the island's political future. In August 2001 the Bougainville Peace Agreement was signed, which provided for an autonomous Bougainville government and secured a plan of disarmament. A referendum on independence would be conducted in 10–15 years' time.

In July 1999 Bill Skate resigned as prime minister as allegations regarding the misappropriation of development funds arose. On 14 July 1999 the National Assembly chose Sir Mekere Morauta as prime minister in a 99–5 vote. Morauta sought to restore damaged relations with the People's Republic of China, which had been angered by the Skate government's decision to accept normal relations with Taiwan in return for economic assistance. The Morauta government engaged in a privatization program and successfully negotiated with the International Monetary Fund (IMF) and World Bank for an aid package in 2000. On 14 March 2001 hundreds of soldiers led a mutiny against Morauta's government in protest of a proposed defense force restructuring plan. They seized an armory and only relinquished their weapons a week later when Morauta promised a full amnesty for the soldiers involved in the revolt and a withdrawal of the controversial military restructuring plan.

Former Prime Minister Michael Somare became prime minister once again on 5 August 2002 when his National Alliance Party (NA) won the parliamentary elections in June that year. The elections were marked by violence and widespread irregularities, including vote-rigging. Somare was elected unopposed by a vote of 88–0, with members from Morauta's PDM and a section of the Papua and Niugini Party (PANGU) abstaining. Somare immediately set out to halt Morauta's privatization program, stating that the government would need more time to assess state assets. Somare headed a coalition of 13 parties and 20 independent members of parliament. He named a 28-member cabinet, including 19 new members of parliament.

In 2003 the PNG government formally began planning to set up an autonomous government in Bougainville, with a multinational team in place to monitor the effort. In December 2004 the cabinet gave formal approval to a draft constitution granting the province of Bougainville free elections and an autonomous government. The cabinet also requested for the UN Security Council to keep its mission in place in Bougainville for 6–12 months to oversee elections. In May 2005 elections took place with 293 candidates competing for 40 assembly seats. One month later, Bougainville elected Joseph Kabui president. Kabui named a caretaker cabinet comprising 10 members, with 8 of the ministries going to members of the ruling Bougainville People's Congress Party.

Following the deadly tsunamis of December 2004, in 2005 the Japanese Meteorological Agency began providing Papua New Guinea and five other western Pacific nations with alerts of any tsunamis following earthquakes of 6.5 or greater on the Richter scale.

Australia deployed a number of police officers to help fight rampant crime in Papua New Guinea in August 2004. In December 2004 an Australian study found that Papua New Guinea was headed for social and economic collapse. However, in May 2005, Australia withdrew its police officers after the PNGP Supreme Court ruled that their deployment was unconstitutional. In May 2007 parliament passed a law to allow casinos and online gambling, in hopes of improving the economy.

In March 2010 Papua New Guinea and fellow members of the Parties of the Nauru Agreement (PNA) met for their First Presidential Summit. The PNA was established in 1982 and is comprised of the nations of Palau, Micronesia, Marshall Islands, Tuvalu, Kiribati, Papua New Guinea, Nauru, and Solomon Islands. The purpose of the group is to work together for the conservation and management of tuna resources within their exclusive economic zones (EEZ). At the March meeting, which has been called the Tuna Summit, members adopted the Koror Declaration which aimed, among other things, to establish cooperative management practices that would enhance commercial and economic opportunities for member countries and to work toward the conservation and restoration of migratory tuna stocks. The waters of the PNA nations account for nearly 60% of all tuna catches in the western and central Pacific Ocean and 25% of the global tuna catches that supply canneries and processing facilities around the world.

A surge in piracy off the coast of New Ireland province has become a major concern for national and local officials. In October 2010 the police force of the province noted that there had been a substantial increase in piracy within the preceding months, with crimes ranging from hijacking small boats from coastal villages to armed attacks against boats further out at sea. Police noted that travel by sea had become quite dangerous, but claimed that the lack of effective resources has limited their ability to handle the newest wave of pirates, who are equipped with high-tech devices such as GPS devices, mobile phones, computers, high-powered guns, and high-speed boats. The provincial police commander estimated that at least 15 incidents of piracy were occurring each week. Incidents of crime on land have also increased within the province.

The national government underwent a chaotic political struggle in 2011. Prime Minister Somare was in ill-health and spent several months receiving treatment in Singapore. In June, his family announced his retirement, and in August 2011 a new government was sworn in, with the election in parliament of Peter O'Neill as prime minister. However, in September Somare declared that his family's announcement had been made without his knowledge while he was in intensive care, was invalid, and that he was still prime minister. O'Neill insisted this was not the case. Over the next several months the crisis escalated, with the rivals forming separate cabinets, and appointing their own police commissioners to command police forces loyal to their sides. On December 12, the Supreme Court declared that O'Neill's election had been invalid and that Somare was still prime minister; parliament responded by once again electing O'Neill prime minister. A week later the governor general, who had voiced support for Somare, declared that he had acted in error and that O'Neill was the rightful prime minister because he had the support of parliament. The heads of the public service, military, and police were reported to have recognized the O'Neill government as well. Therefore, in early 2012 O'Neill's government had effective control, but Somare continued to press his claim in the courts.

13 GOVERNMENT

Papua New Guinea is an independent, parliamentary democracy in the Commonwealth of Nations, with a governor-general representing the British crown.

Under the 1975 constitution, legislative power is vested in the National Parliament (formerly the house of assembly) of 109 members, including 20 representing provincial electorates and 89 from open electorates, serving a term of up to five years. Suffrage is universal and voting compulsory for adults at age 18. The government is formed by the party or coalition of parties that has a majority in the national parliament, and executive power is undertaken by the national executive council, selected from the government parties and chaired by the prime minister.

The government has constitutional authority over the defense force, the Royal Papua New Guinea Constabulary, and intelligence organizations.

14 POLITICAL PARTIES

Political parties in Papua New Guinea lack ideological conviction and rely almost exclusively on patronage politics, personalism, and regional bases. Generally, party allegiances have been fluid, with regional and tribal politics impacting greatly on political events. More than 40 parties registered to participate in the June 2002 elections. In those elections, Michael Somare's NA took 19 seats and formed a 13-party coalition. Former Prime Minister Mekere Morauta's PDM took 13 seats. Other parties winning seats included the United Resources Party (URP), the People's Progressive Party (PPP), the PANGU, the People's Action Party (PAP), and the People's Labor Party (PLP). Somare was chosen as prime minister.

In the June 2007 elections, the NA won 27 seats in parliament, followed by the PNGP with 8, the PAP with 6, the URP with 6, the PANGU with 5, and the PDM with 5. 19 seats were won by independent candidates. The remaining 33 seats were filled by members from 15 other parties. Somare retained his post as prime minister, but after a prolonged period of illness, he was replaced by Peter O'Neill in a controversial 2 August 2011 election in parliament.

15 LOCAL GOVERNMENT

Papua New Guinea is divided into 18 provinces, one autonomous region (Bougainville), and one district (the National Capital District). Each province, region, and district has its own government, headed by a premier. In addition, there are more than 160 locally elected government councils. The local government system went through a process of reform in 1995, when the then 19 provincial governments were replaced by regional authorities.

Bougainville presently exercises significant autonomy in its administrative affairs.

16 JUDICIAL SYSTEM

The legal system is based on English common law. The Supreme Court is the nation's highest judicial authority and final court of appeal. Other courts are the national court; district courts, which deal with summary and non-indictable offenses; and local courts, established to deal with minor offenses, including matters regulated by local customs.

The Papua New Guinea government has undertaken a process of legal reform, under which village courts have been established to conserve and reactivate traditional legal methods. Special tribunals deal with land titles and with cases involving minors. An ombudsman commission has been established to investigate and refer cases involving abuse of official authority to the public prosecutor.

The constitution declares the judiciary independent of executive, political, or military authority. It also provides a number of procedural due process protections including the right to legal counsel for criminal defendants. The chief justice of the Supreme Court is appointed by the governor-general upon nomination by the national executive council in consultation with the minister for justice. The Judicial and Legal Services Commission appoint other judges.

17 ARMED FORCES

The International Institute for Strategic Studies (IISS) reported that armed forces in Papua New Guinea totaled 3,100 members in 2011. The force was comprised of 2,500 members in the army, 200 in the air force, and 400 in the maritime-based component. Armed forces represented 0.1% of the labor force in Papua New Guinea. Defense spending totaled $210 million and accounted for 1.4% of Gross Domestic Product (GDP).

Australia provides a 38-member training unit.

18 INTERNATIONAL COOPERATION

Papua New Guinea became a member of the UN on 10 October 1975 and participates in ESCAP and several UN non-regional specialized agencies, such as the UN Food and Agricultural Organization (FAO), the World Bank, ILO, UNESCO, UNIDO, and the World Health Organization (WHO). It also belongs to the World Trade Organization (WTO), the ASEAN Regional Forum, APEC, the Colombo Plan, the ACP Group, the Asian Development Bank, the Alliance of Small Island States (AOSIS), the Commonwealth of Nations, G-77, the Pacific Island Forum, the South Pacific Commission, and the South Pacific Regional Trade and Economic Cooperation Agreement (Sparteca). The country is part of the Nonaligned Movement.

In environmental cooperation, Papua New Guinea is part of the South Pacific Regional Environmental Program, the Antarctic Treaty, the Basel Convention, the Convention on Biological Diversity, the Ramsar Convention, CITES, the London Convention, International Tropical Timber Agreements, the Kyoto Protocol, the Montréal Protocol, MARPOL, the Nuclear Test Ban Treaty, and the UN Conventions on the Law of the Sea, Climate Change, and Desertification. Papua New Guinea is a member of the PNA, which was established in 1982 among the nations of Palau, Micronesia, Marshall Islands, Tuvalu, Kiribati, Solomon Islands, and Nauru. The purpose of the group is to work together for the conservation and management of tuna resources within their EEZ.

19ECONOMY

Papua New Guinea is rich in natural resources, but has had trouble exploiting these resources for its own economic growth, with issues ranging from dealing with the physical problems of the rough terrain to regaining investor confidence and restoring integrity to state institutions.

Economic activity is concentrated in two sectors: agriculture and mining. More than 85% of the population is involved in subsistence farming, producing livestock, fruit, and vegetables for local consumption. Agricultural products for export include copra, palm oil, coffee, cocoa, and tea. Rubber production has declined, and in the mid-1980s coffee crops were threatened by the spread of coffee rust fungus through Western Highlands Province. Again in the late-1990s the coffee crop suffered due to drought.

Mining of gold, copper, and oil make up approximately two-thirds of the nation's export income. The Bougainville copper mine had been a chief foreign exchange earner since the early 1970s, but it was closed in 1989. New mines located at Ok Tedi in the Star Mountains, on Misima Island, and at Porgera have replaced it as sources of mineral revenues. Papua New Guinea also has rich oil and natural gas resources in its Southern Highlands Province. In 2004 Papua New Guinea's first oil refinery began operation. In addition, a new liquefied natural gas production facility being constructed through a group led by a major US oil dealer was anticipated to begin processing in 2014 and expected to double the nation's GDP and potentially triple its export revenues. Forestry and fishing hold increasing importance.

The GDP rate of change in Papua New Guinea, as of 2010, was 7%. Inflation stood at 6.8%, and unemployment was reported at 1.8%.

Papua New Guinea has experienced a number of economic and political issues and is now working on regaining investor confidence, restoring integrity to state institutions, promoting economic efficiency by privatizing moribund state institutions, and balancing relations with Australia. The Somare government brought stability to the national budget. However, Australia, the country's former colonial ruler, supplied more than $300 million to Papua New Guinea for the 2007/2008 fiscal year, amounting to almost 20% of the national budget. In August 2010 the government signed two agreements with the World Bank for a total of $40 million in concessional financing earmarked for the improvement of rural communities. The money funded the Productive Partnership in Agriculture Project (PPAP) and the Rural Communications Project (RCP), both of which provided much needed support for improvements in agriculture and telecommunications. The PPAP assists coffee and cocoa farmers by teaching them improved farming practices, facilitating relationships between small farmers and agribusiness, and providing improved infrastructure for access to markets. In April 2011 the $46.3 million PPAP launched in Goroka, benefiting up to 30,000 farmers. The PPAP also launched in two other locations, Kokopo

and Buka. The RCP will provide access to telecommunications for 420,000 rural people in the Chimbu and East Sepik provinces and facilitate public internet access in about 60 districts.

20INCOME

The CIA estimated that in 2010 the GDP of Papua New Guinea was $14.95 billion. The CIA defines GDP as the value of all final goods and services produced within a nation in a given year and computed on the basis of purchasing power parity (PPP), rather than value as measured on the basis of the rate of the exchange based on current dollars. The per capita GDP was estimated at $2,500. The annual growth rate of GDP was 7%. The average inflation rate was 6.8%. It was estimated that agriculture accounted for 31.9% of GDP, industry 35.5%, and services 32.6%.

According to the World Bank, remittances from citizens living abroad totaled $12 million, or about $2 per capita, and accounted for approximately 0.1% of GDP.

The World Bank reports that in 2009, household consumption in Papua New Guinea totaled $5.6 billion or about $909 per capita, measured in current US dollars rather than PPP.

It was estimated that in 2002 about 37% of the population subsisted on an income below the poverty line established by Papua New Guinea's government.

21LABOR

As of 2010 Papua New Guinea had a total labor force of 3.809 million people. Within that labor force, CIA estimates in 2005 noted that 85% were employed in agriculture.

Legislation covers working conditions and wages and provides for collective bargaining. There are some 50 trade unions in Papua New Guinea; the Papua New Guinea Trade Union Congress is the main union federation. Unions have the right to organize and bargain collectively, but the government may cancel wage agreements if they are deemed to be against "public policy." The right to strike is protected, and it is prohibited to discriminate against union activity. However, there have been some reports of retaliation against union members. Approximately half of the nation's wage earners are union members.

The minimum working age is 18, although children may be employed in family-related work as young as 11. Few children work in any capacity outside of subsistence farming. The minimum weekly wage in January 2010 was PGK2.29 ($1.08) per hour. New entrants into the work force age 16–21 are paid a reduced minimum wage equal to 75% of the adult wage. The law provides for minimum occupational health and safety standards; however, due to a shortage of inspectors, workplaces are not inspected regularly but only at the request of a union or worker.

22AGRICULTURE

Agriculture in Papua New Guinea is divided into a large subsistence sector and a smaller monetary sector for export. In 2009 agriculture contributed about 31.9% to GDP. About 85% of the population engages in subsistence agriculture, growing such crops as yams, taro, and other staple vegetables. Cash crops are increasing in rural areas, stimulated by government-financed developmental programs. Production by small farmers of coffee, copra, cocoa, tea, rubber, and oil palm is important for export, although production on plantations, which are usually foreign-owned, is also significant. Such plantations are gradually being sold back to nationals. Papua New Guinea grows very little rice, the staple food for many of its inhabitants. A single Australian company imports over 150,000 tons per year to satisfy demand.

Roughly 3% of the total land is currently farmed, and the country's major crops include coffee, cocoa, copra, palm kernels, tea, sugar, rubber, sweet potatoes, fruit, vegetables, and vanilla. Cereal production amounted to 15,731 tons, fruit production 2.3 million tons, and vegetable production 495,810 tons.

23 ANIMAL HUSBANDRY

The FAO reported that Papua New Guinea dedicated 190,000 hectares (469,500 acres) to permanent pasture or meadow in 2009. During that year, the country tended 4 million chickens, 94,000 head of cattle, and 1.8 million pigs. Papua New Guinea also produced 535 tons of cattle hide.

Livestock in 2005 included an estimated 7,500 sheep. Cattle production is encouraged, with the aim of achieving self-sufficiency in meat supplies. Local poultry and beef production is almost sufficient to meet domestic demand. Beef imports are subject to quota controls. The farming of crocodiles, whose hides are exported, has also been expanded. Total crocodile production in 2003 was 27,000 tons.

24 FISHING

In many coastal parts of Papua New Guinea, fishing is of great economic importance. In 2008 the nation had 15 decked commercial fishing boats, with an annual capture that totaled 223,631 tons, according to the FAO. The export value of seafood totaled $112.9 million. The government is involved in the development of fishing through supply of freezers, transport, and research facilities.

Although the government has faced some challenges in establishing trust with foreign investors, at least three major overseas investment groups have made plans to develop tuna processing facilities within the nation. As of June 2010 Majestic Seafood—a joint venture of Frabelle Fishing Corp of the Philippines, Century Canning Corp. (Philippines), and Thai Union Manufacturing Co. (Thailand)—had already begun construction on a new tuna canning facility in Malahang, Lae. With an initial investment of about $30 million, the cannery is expected to create 6,000 new jobs and produce about 350 metric tons of tuna per day. The Papua New Guinea National Fisheries Authority had also approved a second tuna processing plant in Malahang that will be built and operated by Zho Shan Zheyeng Deep Sea Fishing (ZZDF) of China. Trans Pacific Journey Fishing (Philippines) is hoping to receive approval for the development of an offshore processing plant.

25 FORESTRY

Approximately 63% of Papua New Guinea is covered by forest. Exploitable forests account for roughly 40% of the total land area and include a great variety of hardwood and softwood species. The FAO estimated the 2009 roundwood production at 3.04 million cu m (107.4 million cu ft). The value of all forest products, including roundwood, totaled $165.5 million. Plywood, hardwoods, and logs are regularly exported to Japan, New Zealand, Australia, and Europe.

People in Papua New Guinea rely heavily on firewood in their cooking and celebrations. A 2011 report cited that 96% of rural dwellers and nearly all highlanders use wood for fuel. But firewood is becoming expensive and collecting is problematic. In 2011 scientists were working on a new agricultural model called short rotation coppicing that would make wood more of an agricultural crop, suitable for smallholders.

26 MINING

The mining of gold, silver, and copper are leading industries in Papua New Guinea. As of 2009, there were between 25 and 30 recognized base and precious metal operations active for exploration, target outline, reserve development, or production. The country also produces cement, common clays, sand and gravel, stone, natural gas, natural gas liquids, and crude petroleum.

Gold output in 2009 was estimated at 63,600 kg, down from 67,463 kg in 2008. In 1888 gold was discovered on Misima Island, marking the start of mining on Papua New Guinea. Prior to World War II, gold mining contributed 75% of export earnings. This proportion declined greatly in subsequent years, reaching 44% in 2009. Reserves on Lihir Island have been estimated to contain 895 tons of recoverable gold, and deposits at Porgera, near Ok Tedi in the Star Mountains, were considered to hold another 470 tons.

Copper output (metal content) in 2009 was estimated at 166,700 metric tons. All copper came from the Ok Tedi mine, near the Indonesian border. In 1971-72, the Bougainville copper mine, one of the richest in the world, began to export copper ores and concentrates, which totaled 220,000 tons in 1988 and accounted for 44% of all exports in the years the mine operated. The mine closed in 1989 because of civil unrest caused by BRA militants. Nine years of civil unrest were temporarily halted by a cease-fire in 1997.

Mineral exploration is being expanded. Bauxite is known to exist on Manus Island, in the Admiralty Islands, and on New Ireland Island. Additionally, lead, manganese, molybdenum, zinc, limestone, and phosphate guano and rock deposits are present. Major deposits of chromite, cobalt, and nickel are believed to be recoverable at a site on the Ramu River, northeast of Ok Tedi. Mineral resources in Papua New Guinea are difficult and expensive to mine, and exploration and mining are hampered by rugged terrain, the nation's poor road infrastructure, and the high cost of developing infrastructure. Ethnic strife has become commonplace and has had a negative impact on mining exploration and investment. Land disputes have become common as well, because land is communally held and there is no real system of land registration. Exploration permits are issued for an initial two-year period; leases may be granted for up to 20 years.

27 ENERGY AND POWER

The World Bank reported in 2008 that Papua New Guinea produced 2.97 billion kWh of electricity. Oil production totaled 30,356 barrels of oil a day.

ExxonMobil has begun work on a liquefied natural gas plant and pipeline project centered at Port Moresby. The project was tentatively scheduled for completion in 2014; however, construction has been halted from time to time as a result of protests from local landowners who object to the presence of the foreign oil company. The project could result in governmental revenues of $30 billion

Principal Trading Partners – Papua New Guinea (2010)

(In millions of US dollars)

Country	Total	Exports	Imports	Balance
World	14,450.5	9,885.4	4,565.1	5,320.3
Australia	4,658.3	2,778.4	1,879.9	898.5
Japan	1,200.7	906.0	294.7	611.3
China	1,062.1	709.5	352.7	356.8
Singapore	627.4	40.5	586.9	-546.4
Malaysia	340.6	119.4	221.2	-101.8
United States	283.7	92.0	191.7	-99.7
Germany	280.8	255.3	25.5	229.7
Philippines	277.3	266.3	11.0	255.4
South Korea	265.7	182.9	82.9	100.0
Thailand	194.2	53.7	140.5	-86.8

(…) data not available or not significant.

(n.s.) not specified.

SOURCE: *2011 Direction of Trade Statistics Yearbook,* New York: United Nations, 2011.

over 30 years, but some analysts fear that the government, which already struggles with political corruption, is not prepared to responsibly handle such an infusion of wealth. If political corruption continues, and the government refuses to adequately address the issues and concerns of local landowners, the new wealth could lead to greater political and social upheaval. If the government does not develop new spending plans to responsibly manage new revenues, poverty could persist for a majority of citizens.

28 INDUSTRY

The industrial sector, constrained by the small domestic market and the population's low purchasing power, is largely undeveloped. Industries are concentrated in industrial metals, timber processing, machinery, food, drinks, and tobacco. Industrial production, including construction and the provision of utilities (electricity and water) has grown steadily, increasing at a rate of at least 5% per year for the period 2007–2010.

The relative importance of manufacturing has declined as the result of growth in the construction sector, including projects such as the building of new schools, infrastructure for the Papua New Guinea Liquefied Natural Gas (LNG) production plant, and installation of a 14.8 km security fence at the Port Moresby airport. Handicraft and cottage industries have expanded. A government-sponsored program assists Papua New Guineans in setting up businesses and purchases equity in existing firms. It has also encouraged small-scale import-substitution operations.

In 2010 industry accounted for 35.5% of the GDP, followed by services with 32.6%, and agriculture with 32.6%. However, 85% of the 3.4 million labor force continues to be engaged in subsistence agriculture.

29 SCIENCE AND TECHNOLOGY

The Papua New Guinea Scientific Society, founded in 1949 at Boroko, promotes the sciences, exchanges scientific information, preserves scientific collections, and establishes museums. The University of Papua New Guinea, founded in 1965 at Waigani, and the Papua New Guinea University of Technology, founded in 1965 at Lae, provide scientific and technical training. The

Lowlands Agricultural Experiment Station, founded in 1928, is in Kerevat. The Papua New Guinea Institute of Medical Research was founded in 1968.

According to the World Bank, there was one patent application in science and technology in 2009.

30 DOMESTIC TRADE

Trade in rural areas is mostly informal and cash is used in transactions. The local market, particularly in fruit and vegetables, is an important feature of economic and social life. Domestic trade in urban centers is primarily through modern supermarket chains and independent stores. The companies sponsoring supermarkets tend to be in both the importing and wholesale businesses and take responsibility for distribution of goods to outlying villages, which are generally somewhat isolated. Domestic trade is hampered by street gangs that terrorize local and foreign residents and merchants. There are a few Australian-based franchises within the country.

Most stores are open weekdays from 8 a.m. to 5 p.m. and until noon on Saturdays. Banks are open from 9 a.m. to 3 p.m. Monday–Thursday and from 9 a.m. to 4 p.m. on Fridays. Other businesses operate from 8 a.m. to 4:30 p.m. weekdays. Most businesses and government offices are not open on the weekends.

31 FOREIGN TRADE

Papua New Guinea imported $3.529 billion worth of goods and services in 2010, while exporting $5.746 billion worth of goods and services. Major import partners in 2009 were Australia, 41.9%; China, 14.8%; Singapore, 9.3%; the United States, 6.2%; and Japan, 4.5% . Its major export partners were Australia, 29.4%; Japan, 7.9%; and China, 4.1%.

Papua New Guinea imports consumer goods, machinery, transportation equipment, and food and beverages. It exports, among other items, crude petroleum, copper ore, coffee, palm oil, and rough wood.

32 BALANCE OF PAYMENTS

In 2010 Papua New Guinea had a foreign trade deficit of $223 million. Exports of goods and services totaled $5.746 billion in 2010, while imports grew to $3.529 billion. Foreign exchange reserves (including gold) increased to $3.092 billion in 2010.

Papua New Guinea relies heavily on imported goods and services, both for consumption and as inputs for its exports. The country registered deficits on current accounts during the early 1980s, after recording annual surpluses in the late 1970s. In the late 1980s mine closings, civil unrest, and sustained deterioration in prices for the country's principal agricultural exports severely tested the economy and led to a program of structural adjustment supported by the World Bank and IMF. When the economy rebounded in the early 1990s, however, the government lost interest in the reforms and instituted expansionist fiscal policies that led to a decline in international reserves. To restore foreign exchange levels, the government devalued the currency in 1994. When that failed to solve the problem, the government let the kina float, resulting in a depreciation of about 28% by 1996. In 1995 Papua New Guinea reached an agreement with the World Bank and IMF on a series of economic reforms. The subsequent receipt of approximately $200 million in loans in August 1995 substantially

Balance of Payments – Papua New Guinea (2010)

(In millions of US dollars)

Current Account		**-913.6**
Balance on goods		2,215.8
Imports	-3,528.9	
Exports	5,744.7	
Balance on services		-2,446.3
Balance on income		-592.4
Current transfers		-90.6
Capital Account		**37.2**
Financial Account		**1,037.3**
Direct investment abroad		-0.2
Direct investment in Papua New Guinea		28.9
Portfolio investment assets		-104.4
Portfolio investment liabilities		...
Financial derivatives		-7.5
Other investment assets		1,182.0
Other investment liabilities		-61.6
Net Errors and Omissions		**-75.9**
Reserves and Related Items		**-85.0**

(…) data not available or not significant.

SOURCE: *Balance of Payment Statistics Yearbook 2011*, Washington, DC: International Monetary Fund, 2011.

bolstered foreign reserves. Another agreement with the IMF in 2000 brought in an additional $115 million in loans to the country.

The PNG LNG project was expected to have major economic impact on Papua New Guinea once the project went into full operation, which was to take place in 2015. Over the length of the project, annual value added was expected to be approximately PGK2.0 billion, representing a 20–25% increase in GDP per year. During the construction phase the large amount of imports were expected to result in large deficits in the balance of payments; however, once production began it was expected that the resulting exports would move the balance of payments into surplus.

33 BANKING AND SECURITIES

The Bank of Papua New Guinea, the country's central bank, was established in 1973. The currency, the kina, was first issued in April 1975 and is backed by a standby arrangement with Australia. The value of the kina was tied to the Australian dollar until 1994, since then the currency has traded as a floating currency.

The Papua New Guinea Banking Corp. was set up in 1973 to take over the savings and trading business of the former Australian government-owned bank operating in Papua New Guinea. It competes with seven other private commercial banks, three of which are subsidiaries of Australian banks. The IMF reported that in 2009 currency and demand deposits-an aggregate commonly known as M1-were equal to $5.555 billion. In that same year, M2—an aggregate equal to M1 plus savings deposits, small time deposits, and money market mutual funds—was $10 billion.

In 2010 the money market rate, the interest rate at which financial institutions lend to one another in the short term, was 10.45%. The discount rate, the interest rate at which the central bank lends to financial institutions in the short term, was 14%. At the end of 2010 the nation's reserve of gold bullion was 0.06 million ounces. This amount has remained unchanged since 1997.

The Port Moresby Stock Exchange, Ltd. (POMSoX) is Papua New Guinea's only stock exchange. Trading began in June 1999. The POMSoX is closely aligned with, and follows, the procedures of the Australian stock exchange. Share transactions are exempt from capital gains tax, the Goods and Service Tax (GST), and stamp duty. In November 2011 five companies were listed on the POMSoX.

34 INSURANCE

The Papua New Guinea Insurance Commission is responsible for introducing legislation governing the insurance industry. Life insurance is regulated by the Life Insurance Act of 2000, revised in 2002. In 2008 five companies were licensed to offer life insurance. Several companies offer other non-life insurance. In 2010 an Australian firm advised the insurance commission regarding new contract legislation aimed at providing foreign investors an attractive stable market in which to invest.

35 PUBLIC FINANCE

In 2010 the budget of Papua New Guinea included $2.917 billion in public revenue and $2.765 billion in public expenditures. The budget surplus amounted to 0.7% of GDP. Public debt was 27.8% of GDP, with $1.604 billion of the debt held by foreign entities.

Papua New Guinea receives most of its bilateral aid from Australia, which donates about $200 million a year in assistance. Foreign budgetary support was phased out in 2000; aid is now concentrated on project development. Other major sources of aid include Japan, the European Union (EU), China, Taiwan, the UN, the Asian Development Bank, the IMF, and the World Bank.

The 2010 budget showed the following outlays by function: general government affairs (including law and public order, and defense), 17.4%; community and social affairs (including education and health), 16.5%; economic affairs (including agriculture, land administration, transport, and communication), 3.9%; multifunctional expenditures (including general transfers to provincial and local governments), 20.3%; and public debt charges, 41.9%.

36 TAXATION

In 2009 company incomes were taxed at a rate of 30–48%. Additional profits tax was calculated on the net profits of mining and petroleum companies at a rate of 30–50%. In addition, progressive tax rates were applied to individuals' wages and salaries, with taxes automatically withheld from paychecks. Tax rates ranged from 22–42%. Land and property taxes, estate and death taxes, gift taxes, stamp taxes, excise taxes, and sales taxes were also imposed.

37 CUSTOMS AND DUTIES

Papua New Guinea acceded to the WTO in 1996 and has liberalized its trade to conform to WTO standards, removing all nontariff barriers to trade including quotas, bans, and license requirements. The government put a value-added tax (VAT) into effect in 1998 with the intent of reducing all non-protective tariffs to zero, using the VAT. In 2009 the rate was 10%. There are import duty rates of 5%, 8%, and 11%. The protective tariff is 40% and there are higher rates applied to luxury items such as tobacco and liquor.

³⁸FOREIGN INVESTMENT

Foreign direct investment (FDI) in Papua New Guinea was a net inflow of $423.2 million according to World Bank figures published in 2009. FDI represented 5.36% of GDP. The bulk of foreign investment is in the mining and petroleum sector. Statistics on foreign equity holdings for 2007 show that Australia was the largest investor with over half of all foreign equity investment in Papua New Guinea, followed by China, the United Kingdom, the Bahamas, Malaysia, Singapore, and Japan.

The Investment Promotion Authority (IPA), established in 1992, facilitates and certifies foreign investment. All foreign businesses must apply for a formal Investment Promotion Authority Certificate, which is processed by the Companies Office of Papua New Guinea, a division of the IPA. A number of free trade zones were in development in 2009.

Foreign investment in Papua New Guinea took on an air of international intrigue when it was revealed that in early 1997 Prime Minister Julius Chan had entered into a $46 million contract with Sandline Incorporated, a mercenary military organization, to retake Bougainville Island, in particular the copper mining complex there that had been occupied by separatists since 1989. Money behind the contract was traced to the British-Australia mining company, RTZ-CRA. The army prevented the use of the mercenaries. Chan lost his parliamentary seat in the 1997 elections, and a peace agreement was signed with the BRA in 1998.

³⁹ECONOMIC DEVELOPMENT

The fundamental purposes of Papua New Guinea's economic strategy have been distilled into the nation's eight aims: a rapid increase in the proportion of the economy under the control of Papua New Guineans; a more equal distribution of economic benefits; decentralization of economic activity; an emphasis on small-scale artisan, service, and business activity; a more self-reliant economy; an increasing capacity for meeting government spending from locally raised revenue; a rapid increase in the equal and active participation of women in the economy; and governmental control and involvement in those sectors where control is necessary to achieve the desired kind of development.

In March 2000 Papua New Guinea's economic reform efforts came under the supervision of an IMF Structural Adjustment Program (SAP) financed by a stand-by credit line of $120 million that ran from 29 March 2000 to 29 September 2001. The IMF was critical of policies through which the government had intervened heavily in the economy—through tax incentives, licensing and approval requirements, trade restrictions, tariffs and price controls—to create an economy dominated by a few privately-owned, highly protected, noncompetitive, import substitution enterprises. The SAP called for privatization of the few state owned enterprises, liberalization of trade and investment, reduction in public service employment, and the decontrol of prices.

Papua New Guinea experienced economic recovery in 2007 and 2008, with growth of 6.5% and 6.6%, respectively. The nation has the advantage of being rich in natural resources. It has excellent horticultural growth conditions supporting a variety of crops. There is great potential for future development in the tourism sector. Challenges to be overcome include crime and corruption that make it unattractive to foreign investors, low economic output, and great economic disparities among the population and between regions.

Reliance on mineral resources leaves the nation vulnerable to the issue of what happens when resources are exhausted. The Papua New Guinea Sustainable Development Program, Ltd. was created with the objective of supporting sustainable development, especially in the Western Province, home of the Ok Tedi gold mine, which will end production around 2013.

⁴⁰SOCIAL DEVELOPMENT

A mandatory occupational retirement system covers persons employed by firms with 20 or more workers, providing old age, disability, and survivor benefits. The system is financed by 5% contribution of earnings from employees and 7% of payroll from employers. Retirement is set at age 55, or at any age with 12 years of contributions. Benefits are provided as a lump sum and include total contributions plus interest. Workers' compensation is provided by employers through direct provision of benefits or insurance premiums. Medical services, where available, are provided free or at a nominal cost. Rural communities traditionally assume communal obligations to those in need.

The constitution and other laws provide extensive rights for women, however traditional patterns of discrimination still prevail. Women are considered second-class citizens. A 2009 report indicated that two-thirds of all women experienced domestic violence. Village courts tend to enforce these patterns, and intertribal warfare often involves attacks on women. In some cases women are reported to have been killed on accusation of sorcery. Polygamy is common, and the tradition of paying a bride-price persists. Violence against women is widespread and few victims press charges. Much of the violence is committed by women against another of their husband's wives. The government does not adequately fund programs to protect the rights and welfare of children.

The spread of HIV/AIDS may be one factor in another growing problem, baby selling. In 2010 the Papua New Guinea Family Sexual Violence Action Committee, a family welfare agency, warned the government that baby selling seemed to be on the rise. Though no official statistics could be cited, the group claims to have heard of an increase in the practice from various sources. According to the group, in most cases women are selling infants born as a result of rape or incest, since the mothers do not want to keep them and other families are reluctant to adopt such children. Children who are orphaned when their parents die from HIV/AIDS are also considered to be at risk for abduction and sale, since relatives may have few resources to care for the children and rural orphanages are considered good targets for child traffickers. Some government officials claim that the practice is most prevalent among the poor, who do not have enough resources to keep a child, or by young unmarried women who sell their infants to escape condemnation by their community. A spokesperson for the Family Sexual Violence Action Committee rejected these latter views, stating that there is a growing acceptance of unwed mothers and that the relatives and families of these women are usually willing to support the children in question, if they have the resources. She argued that there are simply not enough services available to help women make well-informed decisions on keeping their children and few credible agencies to care for children who could be put up for adoption, rather than sold.

41 HEALTH

According to the CIA, life expectancy in Papua New Guinea was 61 years in 2011. Total healthcare spending was 3.2% of GDP, amounting to $37 per person. There were five nurses and midwives and one physician per 10,000 inhabitants. The fertility rate was 3.46 in 2009, while the infant mortality rate was 43.29 per 1,000 live births. In 2008 the maternal mortality rate, according to the World Bank, was 250 per 100,000 births. It was estimated that 58% of children were vaccinated against measles.

The CIA calculated HIV/AIDS prevalence in Papua New Guinea to be about 0.9% in 2009. There were about 3,200 new cases in 2009, some 3,100 were children. The government has been actively working on projects to prevent, diagnose, and treat the disease. The number of testing service clinics in the nation rose from 17 in 2005 to 174 in 2009 and access to treatment has improved. The government pledged to continue in its efforts, with particular focus on reaching those who are in the highest risk groups.

In 2009 a cholera outbreak in Morobe province of western Papua New Guinea affected over 800 people, resulting in the deaths of at least 40. The outbreak represented the first reported instance of the disease in the country and caused concern for many domestic and international health observers, who feared that the country's health system might be strained under a prolonged outbreak. Cholera is an intestinal disease that usually spreads through contaminated food and water. Treatable if addressed early, the severe dehydration caused by the disease can be fatal without medical help.

42 HOUSING

Traditional housing in rural areas appears to be adequate, but in urban areas there are acute shortages due to population migration. In most urban areas, there are squatter settlements with households accommodating a far greater number of people (as many as 15–20) than the normal 5.8 people per household found in rural areas. In 2007 it was estimated that an additional 500,000 housing units were needed in the nation's urban areas. As of 2007 about 85% of the population lived in rural areas.

43 EDUCATION

The present government aims at upgrading and improving the educational system as well as the quality. Children attend state-run community schools for primary education and provincial and national high schools for secondary education. Primary school covers nine years of schooling, including one year of preschool and grades 1-8. The provincial secondary schools cover a two-year program, which may be followed by a two-year national high school program. Students may choose to enter a two-year technical school for their secondary education. In addition to the national government system, there is an international school system that ends at high school. Fees are considerably higher than the government run schools, and the curriculum is based on the British system. There are also privately run preschools and primary schools. The academic year runs from February to November.

In 2002 about 59% of age-eligible children were enrolled in some type of preschool program. Primary school enrollment in 2005 was estimated at about 75% of age-eligible students, while secondary school enrollment was about 26% of age-eligible students. It is estimated that about 55% of all students complete their primary education. The student-to-teacher ratio for primary school was at about 35:1 in 2005; the ratio for secondary school was about 23:1.

The University of Papua New Guinea in Port Moresby offers degrees in law, science, medicine, and arts. The University of Technology in Lae offers degrees in technical subjects such as engineering, business, architecture, and forestry. The Pacific Adventist College, a privately run university outside Port Moresby, offers courses in education, business, accounting, secretarial studies, and theology. In 1999 (the latest year for which data was available), about 2% of the tertiary age population were enrolled in some type of higher education program. The adult literacy rate for 2004 was estimated at about 57.3%, with 63.4% for men and 50.9% for women.

In the 2010 budget allocated 4.7% to education.

44 LIBRARIES AND MUSEUMS

The largest libraries are at the University of Papua New Guinea (440,000 volumes) and at the Papua New Guinea University of Technology (130,000 volumes). Local libraries are well established in urban centers. The National Library Service in Boroko has 85,000 volumes. The Papua New Guinea Institute of Public Administration in Boroko holds 90,000 volumes.

The Papua New Guinea National Museum and Art Gallery in Boroko has a good collection of art and general ethnography. The museum is implementing the National Cultural Property Act to protect the country's cultural heritage and to further establish appropriate museums. In 1981 the country opened the Madang Museum, Culture and Tourism Center in Yomba. The J. K. MacCarthy Museum, an ethnological collection, is located in Goroka.

45 MEDIA

In 2009 the CIA reported that there were approximately 60,000 telephone landlines and 900,000 mobile cellular phones in use in Papua New Guinea. There were 8 FM radio stations, 19 AM radio stations, and 28 shortwave radio stations. A coastal radio service provides communications between land-based stations and ships at sea. Internet users numbered 2 per 100 citizens.

In 2009 the government-owned National Broadcasting Commission was operating three radio networks with multiple repeaters and approximately 20 provincial stations. NBC broadcasts in English, Pidgin, Hiri Motu, and a dozen other vernaculars. EMTV, owned by a private Fijian company, was the only television broadcaster in 2004. There are also two independent local cable companies. The privately owned NAU-FM radio network is based in Port Moresby. In addition, there are several commercial radio stations and several community stations.

Prominent newspapers in 2010, with circulation numbers listed parenthetically, included the National (20,000) and the Papua New Guinea Post-Courier (26,262). Other local news sheets are published, many in Pidgin. Niugini Nius, also in Boroko, is published Tuesday–Friday (circulation 31,000) and also has a weekend edition (16,000). The constitution provides for free speech and free media, and the government is said to generally respect these rights in practice.

⁴⁶ORGANIZATIONS

The Papua New Guinea Chamber of Commerce and Industry is located in Port Moresby. There are some organizations dedicated to the promotion of specific industries, such as the Papua New Guinea Tourism Promotion Authority and the Papua New Guinea Chamber of Mines and Petroleum.

National youth organizations include the Papua New Guinea National Union of Students, Young Men's Christian Association/ Young Women's Christian Association (YMCA/YWCA), and the Scout Association of Papua New Guinea. There are several sports associations organizing amateur competitions for pastimes such as cricket, track and field, baseball, lawn tennis, tae kwon do, and squash. Women's organizations include the East Sepik Women and Children's Health Project and the Simbu Women's Resource Center. There are national chapters of the Red Cross Society and Caritas.

⁴⁷TOURISM, TRAVEL, AND RECREATION

The *Tourism Factbook*, published by the UN World Tourism Organization, reported 114,000 incoming tourists to Papua New Guinea in 2008, who spent a total of $3.8 million. Of those incoming tourists, there were 94,000 from East Asia and the Pacific. The estimated daily cost to visit Port Moresby, the capital, was $550. The cost of visiting other cities averaged $353.

The Tourism Promotion Authority of Papua New Guinea works with the government to actively promote tourism as a priority for economic development. There are large-scale resorts and basic lodges to accommodate all travelers. Ecotourism is the main attraction, since there is an abundance of vibrant flora and fauna in the rain forest and national parks. Water sports, golf, tennis, and rock climbing are popular pastimes. Tourists must have a

valid passport, round-trip ticket, proof of sufficient funds, and an entry permit. A 60 day visa may be issued upon arrival to visitors from Australia, Cyprus, Japan, Portugal, Austria, Denmark, Netherlands, Switzerland, Belgium, France, Norway, Sweden, Canada, Germany, New Zealand, the United States, and the United Kingdom.

⁴⁸FAMOUS PERSONS

The best known Papua New Guineans are Michael Thomas Somare (b. 1936), chief minister during colonial rule and the nation's first prime minister; Sir Albert Maori Kiki (b. 1931–d. 1993), author of *Kiki: Ten Thousand Years in a Lifetime*; and Vincent Eri (b. 1936–d. 1993), author of *The Crocodile*.

⁴⁹DEPENDENCIES

Papua New Guinea has no territories or colonies.

⁵⁰BIBLIOGRAPHY

Leibo, Steven A. *East and Southeast Asia, 2011*. Harpers Ferry, WV: Stryker-Post Publications, 2011.

Lilley, Ian, ed. *Archaeology of Oceania: Australia and the Pacific Islands*. Malden, MA: Blackwell, 2006.

Mead, Margaret. *Growing Up in New Guinea*. Middlesex: Penguin, 1973 (orig. 1930).

Papua New Guinea Investment and Business Guide: Strategic and Practical Information. Washington, DC: International Business Publications USA, 2012.

Turner, Ann. *Historical Dictionary of Papua New Guinea*. 2nd ed. Lanham, MD: Scarecrow, 2001.

Waiko, John. *A Short History of Papua New Guinea*. 2nd ed. New York: Oxford University Press, 2007.

PHILIPPINES

Republic of the Philippines
Republika ng Pilipinas

CAPITAL: Manila

FLAG: The national flag consists of a white equilateral triangle at the hoist, with a blue stripe extending from its upper side and a red stripe extending from its lower side. Inside each angle of the triangle is a yellow five-pointed star, and in its center is a yellow sun with eight rays.

ANTHEM: *Bayang Magiliw (Nation Beloved).*

MONETARY UNIT: The peso (PHP) is divided into 100 centavos. There are coins of 1, 5, 10, and 25 centavos and 1, 5, and 10 pesos, and notes of 5, 10, 20, 50, 100, 200, 500, and 1000 pesos. The 5 and 10 peso notes have been replaced by coins, but are still in circulation. PHP1 = US$0.0231 (or US$1 = PHP43.51) as of 2011.

WEIGHTS AND MEASURES: The metric system is the legal standard, but some local measures also are used.

HOLIDAYS: New Year's Day, 1 January; Freedom Day, 25 February; Labor Day, 1 May; Independence Day (from Spain), 12 June; Heroes' Day, 29 August; Jose Rizal's Birthday, 20 June; All Saints' Day, 1 November; Eid al-Adha, 7 November; Bonifacio Day, 30 November; Christmas, 25 December; Rizal Day, 30 December; Last Day of the Year, 31 December. Movable religious holidays include Holy Thursday and Good Friday.

TIME: 8 p.m. = noon GMT.

¹LOCATION, SIZE, AND EXTENT

The Republic of the Philippines consists of an archipelago of 7,107 islands situated SE of mainland Asia and separated from it by the South China Sea. The total land area is approximately 300,000 sq km (115,831 sq mi), 67% of which is contained within the two largest islands: Luzon, 108,171 sq km (41,765 sq mi) and Mindanao, 99,078 sq km (38,254 sq mi).

Other large islands include Samar, Negros, Palawan, Panay, Mindoro, Leyte, Cebu, Bohol, and Masbate. Comparatively, the area occupied by the Philippines is slightly larger than the state of Arizona. The Philippines' length is 1,851 km (1,150 mi) SSE-NNW, and its width is 1,062 km (660 mi) ENE-WSW.

The Philippines is separated from Taiwan on the N by the Bashi Channel (forming part of the Luzon Strait) and from Sabah, Malaysia (northern Borneo), on the SW by the Balabac Strait (off Palawan) and the Sibutu Passage (off the Sulu Archipelago). Bordering seas include the Philippine Sea and the Pacific Ocean on the E, the Celebes Sea on the S, the Sulu Sea on the SW, and the South China Sea on the W. The Philippines has a total coastline of 36,289 km (22,549 mi).

The Philippines claims a portion of the Spratly Islands, in the South China Sea, as do China, Malaysia, Taiwan, and Vietnam. An undisclosed number of Philippine military troops were stationed on Pagasa and other Spratly islands in 2011. The Philippines also has a claim on Sabah, dating back to 1670.

The Philippines' capital city, Manila, is located on the island of Luzon.

²TOPOGRAPHY

The topography is extremely varied, with volcanic mountain masses forming the cores of most of the larger islands. The range culminates in Mt. Pulog (elevation 2,928 m/9,606 ft) in northern Luzon and in Mt. Apo, the highest point in the Philippines (elevation 2,954 m/9,692 ft), in Mindanao. A number of volcanoes are active, and the islands have been subject to destructive earthquakes. On 16 July 1990, a 7.7 magnitude earthquake occurred on Luzon causing the death of 1,621 people; it was recorded as the strongest earthquake that year worldwide. A 6.5 magnitude earthquake occurred in Samar on 18 November 2003, causing structural damage to buildings and roads, but few injuries. Another 6.5 magnitude tremor occurred in Mindoro on 8 October 2004. Negros Island was struck by a 6.2 magnitude earthquake on 11 July 2011. Eight quakes struck the Moro Gulf off Mindanao in one 24 hour period, on 24 July 2010.

Of the Philippines' 37 volcanoes, 18 are described as active. People living near the Mayan volcano were evacuated from their homes in December 2009 when a major eruption seemed imminent; while the volcano oozed and produced much steam and lava, the expected major eruption did not occur and the people returned to their homes. In February 2011, Mt. Bulusan erupted, sending ash and steam as high as 2 kilometers.

Lowlands are generally narrow coastal strips except for larger plains in Luzon (Cagayan Valley and Central Plains), Mindanao (Cotabato and Davao-Agusan valleys), and others in Negros and Panay. Rivers are short and generally seasonal in flow. Important ones are the Cagayan, Agno, Abra, Bicol, and Pampanga in Luzon and the Cotabato and Agusan in Mindanao. Flooding is a frequent hazard. The shores of many of the islands are embayed (Manila

Bay is one of the finest harbors in East Asia); however, several islands lack adequate harbors and require offshore lightering for sea transport. The only two inland water bodies of significant size are Laguna de Bay in Luzon and Lake Sultan Alonto in Mindanao.

³CLIMATE

The Philippine Islands, in general, have a maritime tropical climate and, except in the higher mountains, temperatures remain warm, the annual average ranging from about 23° to 32°C (73 to 90°F) throughout the archipelago. Daily average temperatures in Manila range from a minimum of 21°C (70°F) to a maximum of 30°C (86°F) in January and from 24°C (75°F) to 33°C (91°F) in June. Annual normal relative humidity averages 80%. Rainfall and seasonality differ markedly throughout the islands, owing to varying exposures to the two major wind belts, northeast trades or monsoon (winter) and southwest monsoon (summer). Generally, the east coasts receive heavy winter rainfall and the west coasts heavy summer rainfall. Intermediate and southern locales receive lesser amounts more equally distributed. The average annual rainfall in the Philippines ranges from 96 to 406 cm (38 to 160 in).

In October 2010, typhoon Megi destroyed several homes and cut power to many areas of the country. At least 26 people died as a result of the typhoon and 200,000 people were left homeless. The department of agriculture reported that at least 10% of the rice crop in the Cagayan valley (the second-largest agricultural production area in the country) was damaged. In January 2011, after weeks of monsoon rain following the typhoon, at least 40 were reported dead, with more missing. Over one million people were affected by the typhoon and its aftermath, many of them left homeless.

⁴FLORA AND FAUNA

The World Resources Institute estimates that there are 8,931 plant species in the Philippines. The Philippines has close botanical connections to Indonesia and mainland Southeast Asia. Forests are typically tropical, with the dominant family, Dipterocarpaceae, representing 75% of the stands. The forest also has vines, epiphytes, and climbers. Open grasslands, ranging up to 2.4 m (8 ft) in height, occupy one-fourth of the land area; they are man-made, the aftermath of the slash-and-burn agricultural system, and most contain tropical savanna grasses that are nonnutritious and difficult to eradicate. The diverse flora includes 1,000 kinds of ferns and 800 species of orchids.

The Philippines is home to 222 mammal species, the most common of which include the wild hog, deer, wild carabao, monkey, civet cat, and various rodents. There are 590 bird species; some of the more numerous are the megapodes (turkey-like wildfowl), button quail, jungle fowl, peacock pheasant, dove, pigeon, parrot, and hornbill. The Philippines is home to 274 reptile and 110 amphibian species. Crocodiles, pythons, and several varieties of cobra are prominent among the reptilian life.

⁵ENVIRONMENT

Many of the environmental challenges facing the Philippines are man-made. Uncontrolled deforestation in watershed areas, with consequent soil erosion and silting of dams and rivers, constitutes a major environmental problem, as do the rising levels of air and water pollution in Manila and other urban areas. The NPCC

has established standards limiting automobile emissions but has lagged in regulating industrial air and water pollution. The UN reported in 2008 that carbon dioxide emissions in the Philippines totaled 70,858 kilotons.

Pollution has also damaged the coastal mangrove swamps, which serve as important fish breeding grounds, and provide shelter to hundreds of fish, crustacean, and invertebrate species. Between the 1920s and 1990s, the Philippines lost 70% of its mangrove area. Starting in the late 1980s, conservation groups planted 44,000 hectares of land across the archipelago with millions of mangrove seedlings; however, they did this without a good understanding of the plant's biological needs, so that many of the plantings failed.

A 2009 study showed that the Philippines had lost of third of its forest cover between 1990 and 2005, and that this loss continues at 2% per year, but that the rate was slowing. The loss of forests is attributed to multiple causes, including logging, conversion of forest to farmland, spread of human settlement, natural disasters, and forest fires. Deforestation has lead to erosion and loss of groundwater, and has posed a threat to wildlife.

Primary responsibility for environmental protection rests with the National Pollution Control Commission (NPCC), under whose jurisdiction the National Environmental Protection Council (NEPC) serves to develop national environmental policies and the Environmental Center of the Philippines implements such policies at the regional and local levels. The World Resources Institute reports that the Philippines had designated 3 million hectares (7.41 million acres) of land for protection as of 2006. Water resources totaled 479 cu km (114.9 cu mi) while water usage was 28.52 cu km (6.84 cu mi) per year. Domestic water usage accounted for 17% of total usage, industrial for 9%, and agricultural for 74%. Per capita water usage totaled 343 cu m (12,113 cu ft) per year.

The coral reefs of the Philippines are among the most endangered in the world, with only 5% described as in excellent condition in 2007. They are threatened by pollution and by destructive fishing techniques that include dynamiting and the use of cyanide. In June 2009, an extension of land was officially added to the Tubbataha Reef Marine Park, which has been a UNESCO World Heritage site since 1993. The 32,000-hectare park is a nesting site for birds and marine turtles and home to a wide variety of marine species. The nation has four additional UNESCO World Heritage sites

The nation is also vulnerable to typhoons, earthquakes, floods, and volcanic activity. At the end of September 2009, typhoon Ketsana swept westward across the main northern island of Luzon. High winds, heavy rainfall, and flooding resulted in at least 240 deaths. The government declared a state of calamity and sent out a plea for immediate international aid. One week later, typhoon Parma swept across the northern Philippines, killing at least 200 people in floods and landslides. Numerous roads and bridges were submerged under water and mud, making rescue and aid operations more difficult. Over 500,000 people were displaced as a result of Ketsana and Parma.

In April 2011, a volcano in the capital city of Manila showed potential activity after 21 earthquakes were recorded at its location in a 24-hour period. The earthquakes were seen as an indication that magma was moving towards the center of Taal Volcano's surface.

Evidence of potential eruption was seen in January of the same year when an unusually high level of toxic gas was recorded near the volcano and there was an intensified steaming of the main crater lake. The volcano last erupted in 1977.

A study completed by the Asian Development Bank (ADB) in 2009 projected a general sea level rise of up to 70 cm (28 in) within 100 years. According to models and projections used in the study, a sea level rise of about 30 cm (12 in) before 2045 could cause flooding of about 5,000 acres of coastal land in the Philippines, affecting about 500,000 people.

According to a 2011 report issued by the International Union for Conservation of Nature and Natural Resources (IUCN), threatened species included 38 types of mammals, 74 species of birds, 38 types of reptiles, 48 species of amphibians, 71 species of fish, 3 types of mollusks, 210 species of other invertebrates, and 223 species of plants. Threatened species in the Philippines included the monkey-eating eagle, Philippine tarsier, tamarau, four species of turtle (green sea, hawksbill, olive ridley, and leatherback), Philippines crocodile, sinarapan, and two species of butterfly. The Cebu warty pig, Panay flying fox, and Chapman's fruit bat have become extinct.

6 POPULATION

The US Central Intelligence Agency (CIA) estimated the population of the Philippines in 2011 to be approximately 101,833,938, which placed it at number 12 in population among the 196 nations of the world. In 2011, approximately 4.3% of the population was over 65 years of age, with another 34.6% under 15 years of age. The median age in the Philippines was 22.9 years. There were 1.00 males for every female in the country. The population's annual rate of change was 1.903%. The projected population for the year 2025 was 117,600,000. Population density in the Philippines was calculated at 339 people per sq km (882 people per sq mi).

The UN estimated that 49% of the population lived in urban areas, and that urban populations had an annual rate of change of 2.3%. The largest urban areas, along with their respective populations, included Manila, 11.4 million; Davao, 1.5 million; Cebu City, 845,000; and Zamboanga, 827,000.

7 MIGRATION

Estimates of Philippines's net migration rate, carried out by the CIA in 2011, amounted to -1.29 migrants per 1,000 citizens. The Philippine government in 2009 listed 8.58 million as the total number of emigrants living abroad, with 4.06 of those permanent emigrants. The ten top destinations were the US, Saudi Arabia, Canada, UAE, Australia, Malaysia, Japan, the UK, Hong Kong, and Singapore. The total number of immigrants living in Philippines was 435,400. The rapid growth of the Philippine population has led to considerable internal migration. On Luzon, frontier-like settlements have pushed into the more remote areas. The Mindoro and Palawan islands also have attracted numerous settlers, and hundreds of thousands of land-hungry Filipinos have relocated to less densely populated Mindanao. There also has been a massive movement to metropolitan Manila, especially from central Luzon. Emigration abroad is substantial.

In the years following the 1975 fall of Saigon, 2,500 Vietnamese refugees fled to the Philippines. Many stayed in a refugee camp on the island of Palawan. The last of these refugees left in 2008, go-

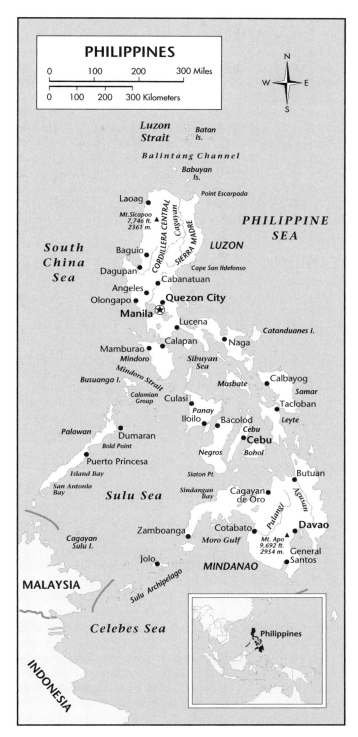

LOCATION: 4°23′ to 21°25′N; 116° to 127°E. TERRITORIAL SEA LIMIT: 12 miles.

ing to Canada as part of a program called Freedom at Last. Distinctions between Indochinese and other nationalities have been dropped, and all are now referred to as urban refugees. Many refugees became legal exiles while studying in the Philippines following political or military upheavals in their homelands; a majority has since married Filipino nationals. The number of migrants in 2000 was 160,000.

8 ETHNIC GROUPS

Filipinos of Malay (Malayan and Indonesian) stock constitute about 95.5% of the total population. They are divided into nine main ethnic groups: the Tagalog, Ilocanos, Pampanguenos, Pangasinans, and Bicolanos, all concentrated in Luzon; the Cebuanos, Boholanos, and Ilongos of the Visayas; and the Waray of the Visayas, Leyte, and Samar. The largest single group is the Tagalog, accounting for about 28.1% of the total population. The Cebuano is the next largest group, representing about 13.1% of the population. They are followed by the Ilocana at 9%, the Bisaya/Binisaya at 7.6%, the Hiligaynon Ilonggo at 7.5%, the Bikol at 6%, and the Waray at 3.4%. Numerous smaller ethnic groups inhabit the interior of the islands, including the Igorot of Luzon and the Bukidnon, Manobo, and Tiruray of Mindanao. There are small groups of Chinese and Muslims.

9 LANGUAGES

There are two official languages: Filipino (based on Tagalog), the national language adopted in 1946 and understood by a majority of Filipinos; and English, which is also widely spoken and understood. Spanish, introduced in the 16th century and an official language until 1973, is now spoken by only a small minority of the population. More than 80 indigenous languages and dialects (basically of Malay-Indonesian origin) are spoken. Besides Tagalog, which is spoken around Manila, the principal dialects include Cebuano (spoken in the Visayas), Ilocano (spoken in northern Luzon), and Panay-Hiligaynon. The teaching of Filipino is mandatory in public and private primary schools, and its use is encouraged by the government.

10 RELIGIONS

Most of the population (between 80% and 85%) belongs to the Roman Catholic Church. Other Christian churches represent about 8% of the population and include such denominations as Seventh-Day Adventist, United Methodist, the Episcopal Church in the Philippines, United Church of Christ, Assemblies of God, the Church of Jesus Christ of Latter-Day Saints, and Philippine Baptist (associated with Southern Baptist). In addition, there are three churches established by Filipino religious leaders, the Independent Church of the Philippines, also called Aglipayan; the Iglesia ni Cristo (Church of Christ); and the Ang Dating Daan (an offshoot of the Church of Christ). Muslims represent between 5% and 9% of the population and are commonly called Moros by non-Muslims. They are concentrated in Mindanao and the Sulus. Most Muslims are Sunni. The term Balik Islam refers to those Filipinos who converted from Christianity to Islam while living and working overseas, and who retained their Muslim practice on returning to the Philippines. Buddhists make up less than 1% of the population. There are also small communities of Hindus and Jews. It is believed that a majority of the indigenous population includes elements of native religions within their practice of other faiths. Freedom of religion and the separation of church and state are guaranteed by the constitution.

The National Commission on Muslim Filipinos (NCMF) was established in 2010 as a cabinet-level commission dedicated to the promotion and protection of rights for Muslim Filipinos. Through the Bureau of Pilgrimage and Endowment, the commission provides assistance for those Muslims participating in the Hajj. The NCMF replaced the Office of Muslim Affairs, which was established in the 1980s. Interfaith cooperation and dialogue is encouraged by the National Ecumenical Consultative Committee.

Certain Christian and Muslim holidays are recognized as national holidays. These include Maundy Thursday, Good Friday, Easter, All Saints' Day, Christmas Day, Eid al-Fitr, and Eid al-Adha.

11 TRANSPORTATION

The CIA reports that the Philippines has a total of 213,151 km (132,446 mi) of roads, of which 54,481 km (33,853 mi) are paved. Luzon contains about one-half of the total road system, and the Visayas about one-third.

In 2010, the Philippine railroad system consisted of 995 km (618 mi) of railroad track on Luzon and Panay. However, the system only plays a minor role in transportation. Waterways were limited to vessels with a draft of less than 1.5 m (4.5 ft).

Water transportation is of paramount importance for inter-island and intra-island transportation. A small offshore fleet registered under the Philippine flag is engaged in international commerce, but most ocean freight is carried to and from the Philippines by ships of foreign registry. There are 25 major ports. Manila is the busiest Philippine port in international shipping, followed by Cebu and Iloilo. Other ports and harbors include Batangas, Cagayan de Oro, Davao, Guimaras Island, Iligan, Jolo, Legaspi, Masao, Puerto Princesa, San Fernando, Subic Bay, and Zamboanga. The Philippines has approximately 3,219 km (2,000 mi) of navigable waterways.

There are 254 airports, which transported 10.48 million passengers in 2009 according to the World Bank. Aquino International Airport, formerly Manila International Airport, is the principal international air terminal. Five other airports serve international flights as well. Philippine Air Lines (PAL), the national airline, provides domestic and international flights. Under the Aquino government there were plans to sell PAL stock to the private sector.

12 HISTORY

Evidence of human habitation dates back some 250,000 years. In more recent times, experts believe that the Negritos, who crossed then existing land bridges from Borneo and Sumatra some 30,000 years ago, settled the Philippine Islands. Successive waves of Malays, who arrived from the south, at first by land and later on boats called barangays—a name also applied to their communities—came to outnumber the Negritos. By the 14th century, Arab traders made contact with the southern islands and introduced Islam to the local populace. Commercial and political ties also linked various enclaves in the archipelago with Indonesia, Southeast Asia, India, China, and Japan. Ferdinand Magellan, a Portuguese-born navigator sailing for Spain, made the European discovery of the Philippines on 15 March 1521 and landed on Cebu on 7 April, claiming the islands for Spain, but the Filipino chieftain Lapulapu killed Magellan in battle. The Spanish later named the islands in honor of King Philip II, and an invasion under Miguel Lopez de Legaspi began in 1565. The almost complete conversion of the natives to Christianity facilitated the Spanish conquest; by 1571, it was concluded, except for the Moro lands (Moro is the Spanish word for Moor). The Spanish gave this name to Muslim Filipinos, mostly inhabitants of southern and eastern Mindanao, the Sulu Archipelago, and Palawan. The Spanish administered the Philippines, as a province of New Spain, from Mexico. Trade became a monopoly of the Spanish government; galleons shipped Oriental goods to Manila, from there to Acapulco in Mexico, and from there to the mother country.

Although Spain governed the islands until the end of the 19th century, its rule was constantly threatened by the Portuguese, the Dutch, the English (who captured Manila in 1762, occupying it for the next two years), the Chinese, and the Filipinos themselves. After the 1820s, which brought the successful revolts of the Spanish colonies in the Americas, Filipinos openly agitated against the government trade monopoly, the exactions of the clergy, and the imposition of forced labor. This agitation brought a relaxation of government controls: the colonial government opened ports to world shipping, and the production of such typical Philippine exports as sugar, coconuts, and hemp began. Filipino aspirations for independence, suppressed by conservative Spanish rule, climaxed in the unsuccessful rebellion of 1896–98. Jose Rizal, the most revered Filipino patriot, was executed, but Gen. Emilio Aguinaldo and his forces continued the war. During the Spanish-American War (1898), Aguinaldo declared independence from Spain on 12 June. When the war ended, the United States acquired the Philippines from Spain for $20,000,000. US rule replaced that of the Spanish, but Philippine nationalists continued to fight for independence. In 1899, Gen. Aguinaldo became president of the revolutionary First Philippine Republic and continued guerrilla resistance in the mountains of northern Luzon until his capture in 1901, when he swore allegiance to the United States. Over the long term, the effect of US administration was to make the Philippines an appendage of the US economy, as a supplier of raw materials to and a buyer of finished goods from the American mainland. Politically, US governance of the Philippines was a divisive issue among Americans, and the degree of US control varied with the party in power and the US perception of its own security and economic interests in the Pacific. In the face of continued nationalist agitation for independence, the US Congress passed a series of bills that ensured a degree of Philippine autonomy. The Tydings-McDuffie Independence Law of 1934 instituted commonwealth government and further stipulated complete independence in 1944. In 1935, under a new constitution, Manuel Luis Quezon y Molina became the first elected president of the Commonwealth of the Philippines.

On 8 December 1941, Japan invaded the Philippines, which then became the focal point of the most bitter and decisive battles fought in the Pacific during World War II. By May 1942, the Japanese had achieved full possession of the islands. US forces, led by Gen. Douglas MacArthur, recaptured the Philippines in early 1945, following the Battle of Leyte Gulf, the largest naval engagement in history. In September 1945, Japan surrendered. On 4 July 1946, Manuel A. Roxas y Acuna became the first president of the new Republic of the Philippines. Both casualties and war damage wreaked on the Philippines were extensive, and rehabilitation was the major problem of the new state. Communist guerrillas, called Hukbalahaps, threatened the republic. Land reforms and military action by Ramon Magsaysay, the minister of national defense, countered the Huks revolutionary demands. Magsaysay was

elected to the presidency in 1953 but died in an airplane crash in 1957. Carlos P. Garcia succeeded Magsaysay and then won election to the office in 1958. Diosdado Macapagal became president in November 1961. He was succeeded by Ferdinand Edralin Marcos following the 1965 elections. Marcos was reelected in 1969 with a record majority of 62%. The Marcos government brutally suppressed the renewed Hukbalahap insurgency, but armed opposition by Muslim elements organized as the Moro National Liberation Front (MNLF), the Maoist-oriented New People's Army (NPA), and by other groups gathered force in the early 1970s.

Unable under the 1935 constitution to run for a third term in 1973, President Marcos, on 23 September 1972, placed the entire country under martial law, charging that the nation was threatened by a "full-scale armed insurrection and rebellion." Marcos arrested many of his more vehement political opponents, some of whom remained in detention for several years. In January 1973, the Marcos administration introduced a new constitution, but many of its provisions remained in abeyance until 17 January 1981, when Marcos finally lifted martial law. During the intervening period, Marcos consolidated his control of the government through purges of opponents, promotion of favorites, and delegation of leadership of several key programs-including the governorship of metropolitan Manila and the Ministry of Human Settlements-to his wife, Imelda Romualdez Marcos. Although Marcos made headway against the southern guerrillas, his human-rights abuses cost him the support of the powerful Roman Catholic Church, led by Jaime Cardinal Sin. Elections were held in April 1978 for an interim National Assembly to serve as the legislature until 1984, but local elections held in 1980 were widely boycotted. Pope John Paul II came to Manila in February 1981, and even though martial law was no longer in effect, he protested the violation of basic human rights. In June 1981, Marcos won reelection for a new six-year term as president under an amended constitution preserving most of the powers he had exercised under martial rule. New threats to the stability of the regime came in 1983 with the rising foreign debt, a stagnant economy, and the public uproar over the assassination on 21 August of Benigno S. Aquino, Jr. Aquino, a longtime critic of Marcos, was shot at the Manila airport as he returned from self-exile to lead the opposition in the 1984 legislative elections. The gunman was immediately killed, and 26 others suspected of conspiracy in the assassination were acquitted in December 1985 for lack of evidence. Public sympathy gave opposition parties 59 out of 183 elective seats in 1984.

In 1985, political pressures forced Marcos to call for an election in February 1986 in view of a widespread loss of confidence in the government. The Commission on Elections and the National Assembly, controlled by his own political party, proclaimed Marcos the winner. His opponent, Maria Corazon Cojuangco Aquino, the widow of Benigno S. Aquino, claimed victory, however, and charged the ruling party with massive election fraud. The National Movement for Free Elections, the United States, and other international observers supported Aquino's charge. Accordingly, other countries withheld recognition of Marcos. On 21 February 1986, a military revolt grew into a popular rebellion, urged on by Jaime Cardinal Sin. US president Ronald Reagan gave Marcos an offer of asylum, which Reagan guaranteed only if Marcos left the Philippines without resistance. Marcos went into exile in Hawaii.

After Marcos

On 25 February 1986, Corazon Aquino assumed the presidency. Her government restored civil liberties, released political prisoners, and offered the NPA a six-month cease-fire, with negotiations on grievances, in exchange for giving up violence. Because Aquino came to power through the forced departure of an officially proclaimed president, the legality of her regime was suspect. Consequently, she operated under a transitional "freedom constitution" until 11 February 1987, when the electorate ratified a new constitution. On 11 May 1987, the first free elections in nearly two decades were held under the new constitution. More than 83% of eligible voters cast their ballots, 84 candidates ran for the 24 senate seats, and 1,899 candidates ran for the 200 house seats. There were 63 election-related killings. Old-line political families still controlled the system, as 169 House members out of the 200 elected either belonged to or were related to these families.

On 20 December 1987 one of the worst disasters in maritime history occurred when an overcrowded passenger ship collided with an oil tanker off Mindoro Island and at least 1,500 people perished. This delayed local elections until 18 January 1988. Nationwide 150,000 candidates ran for 16,000 positions as governor, vice governor, provincial board member, mayor, vice mayor, and town council member. In 1988 election-related violence killed more than 100 people. Members of the pro-government parties, a faction of the PDP-Laban and Lakas ng Bansa, formed a new organization, Laban ng Demokratikong Pilipino (LDP) in June 1988. In March 1989 the thrice-postponed election for barangay officials was held, electing some 42,000 barangay captains. In August 1989 President Aquino signed a law giving limited autonomy to provinces where most Philippine Muslims lived: Mindanao, Palawan, Sulu, and Tawi-Tawi islands.

There were five coup attempts between the time Aquino took office and the end of 1987. This continuing succession of coup plots culminated in a large, bloody, well-financed attempt in December 1989. Led by Colonel Gregorio Honasan (who participated in the 1987 coup attempt, and was a close associate of Senator Juan Ponce Enrile) and involving more than 3,000 troops that targeted several bases; US air support helped to quell this attempt. The Senate granted Aquino emergency powers for six months. President Aquino's administration lost international credibility with the appeal for US military support to quell the coup attempt. The authorities made arrests, but the Supreme Court ruled that Senator Juan Ponce Enrile could not be charged with murder, nullifying a criminal case against him. He was charged in a lower court with rebellion. In September 1990, 16 military members were convicted of the assassination of Senator Benigno Aquino in 1983 and sentenced to life in prison.

Former president Ferdinand Marcos had appealed to Aquino to allow him to attend the funeral of his mother, as he had appealed several times to visit his mother while she was ill; Aquino denied each request. The Philippine government had traced at least $5 billion in deposits to Swiss bank accounts made by Marcos. Marcos attempted to negotiate his return to the Philippines, promising his support for Aquino and the return of $5 billion to the Philippines. Aquino also rejected his wife Imelda's plea for her husband's return. The Philippine government filed an antigraft civil suit for $22.6 billion against Marcos in 1987. Marcos and his wife, Imelda, were indicted in the United States, charged with the illegal transfer

of $100 million in October 1988. On 28 September 1989 former President Ferdinand Marcos died in Honolulu. Aquino refused to allow his burial in the Philippines.

Under pressure from Communist rebels Aquino removed the US military bases from the Philippines in 1989. Three US servicemen were murdered outside Clark Air Force Base and the Communists took responsibility for the murders. A Communist guerrilla who admitted participating in the 21 April 1989 assassination of US Army Colonel James Row was arrested. In September 1989 US vice president Dan Quayle met with Aquino to discuss the renewal of the lease on US military bases. Prior to his arrival two American civilians working on the bases were killed; the government attributed these deaths to Communist guerrillas. The Communists continued to threaten US servicemen and local politicians. Anti-American demonstrations at Clark Air Base and in Manila led to clashes with the police and to injuries. The Communists continued their threats and two more US servicemen were killed near the Clark Air Base. In June of 1990 the Peace Corps removed 261 volunteers from the Philippines after Communist threats against them. In September 1990 Aquino said it was time to consider an "orderly withdrawal" of US forces from the Philippines.

Within a year the Philippines was pummeled with three major natural disasters. In July 1990 an earthquake measuring 7.7 on the Richter scale struck. The epicenter was 89 km (55 mi) north of Manila and more than 1,600 people were killed. A super-typhoon devastated the central Visayas in November 1990. An even more destructive natural disaster occurred on 12 June 1991 when Mount Pinatubo in Zambales province, a volcano dormant for more than 500 years, violently erupted, causing the abandonment of Clark Air Base in Angeles City; 20,000 US military, their dependents, and civilian employees evacuated to the United States from Clark and the Subic Bay Naval Station.

The Philippine-American Cooperation Talks (PACT) reached agreement on military base and nonbase issues, but the Philippine Senate refused to ratify the proposed treaty. On 6 January 1992 the Philippines government served notice of the termination of the US stay at Subic Naval Base in Zambales. After almost a century of US military presence, on 30 September 1992 the United States handed over Subic Naval Base to the Philippines. The Philippine government turned it into a free port, headed until 1998 by Dick Gordon.

Amnesty International (AI), the human rights organization, published a report in 1992 that was critical of the Aquino administration's assent to human rights violations perpetrated by the military; AI alleged that 550 extra judicial killings occurred during 1988–91. The military refuted the AI report citing its oversight of rebel activities.

In March 1991 President Aquino stated that Imelda Marcos could return to the Philippines, but that she faced charges that her husband stole $10 billion during his 20 years as president. Mrs. Marcos returned in November, after five years in Hawaii, to face civil and criminal charges, including tax fraud. In January 1992 Imelda Marcos announced that she would run for election in 1992; in the same month she was arrested, and then released, for failing to post bail on charges that she unlawfully maintained accounts in Switzerland. In September 1993 the government permitted the embalmed body of Ferdinand Marcos to return to the

Philippines for burial near his home in northern Luzon. On 24 September 1993 Imelda Marcos was found guilty of participating in a deal that was "disadvantageous to the government" under the Anti-Graft and Corruption Practices Act. She faced a maximum prison sentence of 24 years, but she remained free on bail while her appeal was considered.

In national and local elections held 11 May 1992, Fidel V. Ramos and Joseph E. Estrada were elected president and vice president, respectively. On 30 June 1992 Fidel Ramos succeeded Corazon Aquino as president of the Philippines with a plurality of 23.6%. Nearly 85% of eligible voters turned out to elect 17,205 officials at national, regional, and local levels. The election was relatively peaceful with only 52 election-related deaths reported. Rules required voters to write the names of the candidate they wanted for office. This, combined with the number of candidates, meant it was several weeks before the votes were completely tallied. Ramos, a Methodist and the Philippine's first non-Catholic president, considered the country's population growth rate as an obstacle to development. A rally of 300,000 Catholics led by Cardinal Sin took place in Manila in 1993 to protest the Ramos administration's birth control policies and the public health promotion of prophylactics to limit the spread of AIDS.

Domestic insurgency by the Muslim population continued throughout the 1980s. By the 1990s, however, internal divisions among the Muslims, reduced external support, military pressure, and government accommodations, including the creation of the Autonomous Region in Muslim Mindanao in 1990, had greatly reduced the threat. In January 1994 the government signed a ceasefire agreement with the Moro National Liberation Front, ending 20 years of guerrilla war. Splinter groups among the Muslim population continue, however, to cause difficulties for both the MNLF and the government.

The last remaining communist insurgency in Asia was reduced temporarily by the Ramos government's peaceful signal, the 1992 Anti-Subversion Law, and the 1993 split in the ranks of the NPA that created a lull until issues related to the weakened leadership were resolved. The NPA returned to violent opposition sporadically throughout the 1990s, especially by the Revolutionary Proletarian Army, an offshoot of the NPA. The NPA significantly increased its use of children as armed combatants and noncombatants during this same time.

In January 1994 the congress passed a law restoring the death penalty for 13 crimes including treason, murder, kidnapping and corruption. Police reform was a particular goal of the legislation. This legislation was partly in response to a series of abductions of wealthy ethnic Chinese Filipinos abducted for ransom, in which the Philippine National Police were found to be involved.

China, Vietnam, Taiwan, the Philippines, Malaysia, and Brunei all lay claim to all, or a portion, of the Spratly Islands in the South China Sea. These conflicting claims are a source of tension between the Philippines and the People's Republic of China. In 1989 Chinese and Philippine warships exchanged gunfire in the vicinity of the Spratly Islands. The incident was resolved by diplomatic means. In 1994 China protested an oil exploration permit granted to Vaalco Energy of the United States, and to Alcorn Petroleum and Minerals, its Philippine subsidiary. The Philippine response was to refer to a principle of "common exploration" and development of the Spratlys. China had employed this same principle

when the Philippines had protested China's granting the United States permission to explore in the Spratlys in 1993. In June 1994 a 5-day conference on East Timor held in Manila ended with an agreement to establish a coalition for East Timor in the Philippines and proposed a peace plan based on the gradual withdrawal of Indonesian troops.

But turmoil in the Spratlys did not end. In 1995 China briefly occupied Mischief Reef in a part of the islands claimed by the Philippines. In spring of 1997, Chinese warships were seen near Philippine-occupied islands in the chain. The two countries have also traded occupation of Scarborough Shoal, heightening tensions and prompting Manila to seek renewed American military presence. In May 1999 the Philippine Senate ratified a new Visiting Forces Agreement with the United States, despite claims by opponents that the VFA would give the US military the opportunity to bring nuclear weapons, without declaration, into the Philippines, violating the Philippine constitution.

The issue of Filipino women forced to work abroad, long a controversy in the country's large impoverished class, came to a head in 1995. In March, Filipina domestic worker Flor Contemplacion was executed in Singapore for the murder of a maid and a child. Outraged Filipinos claimed the girl was framed; they filled the streets of Manila in protest. The crisis, the product of unemployment and underemployment forcing families to export their children to low-wage overseas jobs, culminated in Ramos's sacking of two cabinet ministers.

Muslim rebels in Mindanao continued their insurgencies against the government, raiding the trading town of Ipil in April 1996. The terrorists killed 57 people and burned the town's business district. The rebels also took part in the resurgence of kidnappings and bank robberies in Manila and Mindanao. More than 100 kidnappings were reported in 1996, many in which police officers were also suspected. A peace agreement between the Philippine government and the MNLF was signed on 2 September 1996, ending the 24-year-old war in Mindanao. The agreement was signed by the government chief negotiator Manuel Yan, Nur Misuari, Indonesian Foreign Minister Ali Alatas, and Secretary General Hamid Algabid of the Organization of Islamic Conference (OIC). Later, Misuari ran for and won the governorship of the Autonomous Region for Muslim Mindanao (ARM) in the 9 September 1996 elections.

The Philippine economy suffered a harsh blow in 1995 when a typhoon ravaged the rice harvest, trebling the destruction of the rice acreage lost to the Mount Pinatubo eruption. But the economy rebounded in late 1995 and through 1996, buoyed by the government's massive infrastructure improvements and plans to develop former US military bases Subic Bay and Clark Air Force Base as tourist attractions and economic zones.

President Ramos introduced the Philippines 2000 movement, which was both a strategy and a movement; he called it the Filipino people's vision of development by the year 2000. As envisioned, the Philippines by the year 2000 would have a decent minimum of food, clothing, shelter, and dignity. The major goal of Philippines 2000 was to make the Philippines the next investment, trade, and tourism center in Asia and the Pacific. The Ramos administration achieved several of its economic goals but few of the social changes envisioned.

On 30 June 1998 the newly elected President, Joseph Ejercito Estrada, took office. The new Vice President was Gloria Macapagal-Arroyo. In November 2000, impeachment proceedings began against Estrada on allegations of corruption, betrayal of the public trust, and violation of the constitution. Estrada stepped down as president on 20 January 2001 after months of protests, and Arroyo was sworn in as president. Estrada in April 2001 was charged with taking more than $80 million from state funds while in office; he was arrested and placed in custody. Arroyo faced a sluggish economy upon coming into office; the economy was still recovering from the 1997–98 Asian financial crisis. She initiated privatization and deregulation policies, especially in agriculture and the power-generating industry. On 30 December 2002, Arroyo declared she would not seek a second term in the 16 May 2004 presidential elections, so that she could focus on her economic reform agenda, restore peace and order, reduce corruption, and "heal political rifts." Despite this promise, she did participate in the 2004 presidential elections.

The separatist conflict on Mindanao had claimed more than 140,000 lives in three decades as of 2005. In March 2001, the 12,500-member Moro Islamic Liberation Front declared a cease-fire and declared it was ready to hold talks with the government. However, on 11 February 2003, more than 2,000 government soldiers advanced toward an MILF base near Pikit, attempting to disband a group of kidnappers known as the "Pentagon gang," which is on the list of US terrorist organizations. Approximately 135 MILF fighters were killed in three days of fighting. In January 2002, nearly 700 US troops, including 160 Special Forces soldiers, were sent to Mindanao to assess the military situation, provide military advice, and train the 7,000 Philippine soldiers pursuing the guerrillas of the Abu Sayyaf group operating in the southern islands of Basilan and Jolo. The Philippine constitution forbids foreign troops fighting on its territory. A cease-fire between the government and the MILF that was agreed to in 2003 was broken in January 2005 with heavy fighting between government troops and MILF rebels. However, that April, a breakthrough on the contentious issue of ancestral land was achieved at peace talks in Malaysia between the government and the MILF.

Following the 11 September 2001 terrorist attacks on the United States, the United States urged countries around the world to increase their antiterrorist measures. Southeast Asia was a primary focus of attention. In May 2002, the 10 members of ASEAN pledged to form a united antiterror front and to set up a strong regional security framework. The steps include introducing national laws to govern the arrest, investigation, prosecution, and extradition of suspects. They also agreed to exchange intelligence information and to establish joint training programs such as bomb detection and airport security.

The militant Islamic group Abu Sayyaf ("Bearer of the Sword") is one of several guerrilla organizations involved in a resurgence of violence in the Philippines after 2000. It split off from the Moro National Liberation Front (MNLF) in 1991 to pursue a more fundamentalist course against the government. Actions taken since the early 1990s include bombings, assassinations, and kidnappings of priests and businessmen. One of its goals is an independent Islamic state in Mindanao, but its activities have been linked to international terrorism as well, including ties to the al-Qaeda network, according to the US government. Financial links have been found between Abu Sayyaf, Jemaah Islamiyah, and al-Qaeda. It continued to launch sporadic attacks against government and civilian targets through 2011.

The 2004 presidential elections were extremely close, but Arroyo was able to retain the presidency with 40% of the vote, defeating Fernando Poe Jr. who netted 37%. However, the Philippines continued to be plagued by accusations of corruption in the government, business arena, and security forces. President Arroyo was credited with increasing economic growth—4.3% in 2002 to 4.7% in 2003 and to about 6% in 2004—but there were substantial criticisms levied against her government. Intense poverty remained a central problem in the Philippines, as did counterinsurgency groups like the MNLF, Abu Sayyaf, Jemaah Islamiyah, and the communist New People's Army. Despite Arroyo's efforts, trafficking of women and children still remained a prominent issue.

From July-September 2005, Arroyo was pressured to resign over allegations of election fraud in the 2004 election. In September she survived an impeachment attempt. In February 2006, Arroyo declared a weeklong state of emergency after the army declared it had foiled a plan to overthrow her government. In August 2006, Arroyo survived another attempt to impeach her over allegations of corruption, human rights abuses, and election fraud. Arroyo left office at the end of her term in 2010 and was prevented from leaving the country by government officials, who suspected her of corruption, although Arroyo claimed that her international travel was necessary for medical treatment. She was later arrested on corruption charges and appeared in court in early 2012, where she pleaded not guilty.

In November-December 2005, scores of people were killed during clashes between government troops and Abu Sayyaf rebels on the southern island of Jolo. In January 2007, tests confirmed that a body found in a remote area was that of Abu Sayyaf leader Khaddafy Janjalani, who the army had claimed killing in 2006. In April 2007, the military ramped up its offensive against Abu Sayyaf, after the group beheaded seven Christian hostages on Jolo.

In November 2009, a group of about thirty politicians, reporters, and civilian supporters were abducted by armed men as they travelled to the election office in Manguindanao to file papers for the nomination of Ismael Mangudadatu, who planned to run for governor of the province in the May 2010 elections. A few days after the abduction, twenty-one members of the group, including thirteen women and eight men, were found dead. While Mangudadatu had not been part of the group, his wife and two sisters were among the dead. Andal Ampatuan, Jr., son of the governor of Maguindanao and a candidate in the next election, was charged with twenty-five counts of murder, but he denied any involvement in the massacre.

The 10 May 2010 presidential election pitted former president Joseph Estrada against opposition senator Benigno "Noynoy" Aquino. At the time of the elections, the Philippine presidency was suffering from extensive allegations of graft and corruption, and both candidates attempted to distance themselves from the outgoing president, Gloria Arroyo. Aquino actively campaigned on an anti-corruption platform, juxtaposing his reputation for honesty with Arroyo's corruption scandal, and pledging, once in office, to have her investigated for graft. Analysts said that Aquino's other policies, such as his plan to deal with the Muslim insurgency in the south and to revive the underperforming Philippine economy, were more ambiguous. In the final election results, Aquino, of the Liberal Party, took the presidency by a landslide, capturing 15 million votes. Estrada, of the Force of the Philippine Masses, received 9.3 million votes.

13 GOVERNMENT

Under the constitution of 11 February 1987 the Philippines is a democratic republican state. Executive power is vested in a president elected by popular vote for a six-year term, with no eligibility for reelection. The president is assisted by a vice president, elected for a six-year term, with eligibility for one immediate reelection, and a cabinet, which can include the vice president. Legislative power rests with a bicameral legislature. Congress consists of a senate, with 24 members elected for six-year terms (limited to two consecutive terms). Senators are chosen at large. Senators must be native-born Filipinos and at least 35 years old. A house of representatives is elected from single-member districts for three-year terms (limited to three consecutive terms). Districts are reapportioned within three years of each census. In 2004, 212 members were elected. Up to 52 more may be appointed by the president from "party lists" and "sectoral lists," but the constitution prohibits the house of representatives from having more than 250 members. Representatives must be native-born Filipinos and at least 25 years of age.

The 1987 constitution also allows for autonomous regions in the Muslim areas of Mindanao and the Cordillera region of Luzon where many aboriginal tribes are found.

14 POLITICAL PARTIES

The first Philippine political party, established in 1900, was the Federal Party, which advocated peace and eventual statehood. Later, the Nationalist Party (NP) and the Democratic Party were established. They did not produce an actual two-party system, since the Nationalists retained exclusive control and the Democrats functioned as a "loyal opposition." However, following Japanese occupation and the granting of independence, an effective two-party system developed between the Liberal Party (LP) and the NP. The Progressive Party, formed in 1957 by adherents of Ramon Magsaysay, polled more than one million votes in the presidential election of 1958.

In the elections of November 1965, Senator Ferdinand Marcos, the NP candidate, received 55% of the vote. In the 1969 election, he was elected to an unprecedented second term. All political activity was banned in 1972, following the imposition of martial law, and did not resume until a few months before the April 1978 elections for an interim National Assembly. The Marcos government's New Society Movement (Kilusan Bagong Lipunan—KBL) won that election and the 1980 and 1982 balloting for local officials, amid charges of electoral fraud and attempts by opposition groups to boycott the voting.

The principal opposition party was the People's Power Movement-Fight (Lakas Ng Bayan—Laban), led by Benigno S. Aquino, Jr., until his assassination in 1983. This party joined with 11 other opposition parties in 1982 to form a coalition known as the United Nationalist Democratic Organization (UNIDO). Following Aquino's murder, some 50 opposition groups, including the members of the UNIDO coalition, agreed to coordinate their anti-Marcos efforts. This coalition of opposition parties enabled Corazon

Aquino to campaign against Marcos in 1986. In September 1986 the revolutionary left formed a legal political party to contest congressional elections. The Partido ng Bayan (Party of the Nation) allied with other left-leaning groups in an Alliance for New Politics. This unsuccessful attempt for electoral representation resulted in a return to guerrilla warfare on the part of the Communists.

After assuming the presidency, Aquino formally organized the People's Power Movement (Lakas Ng Bayan), the successor to her late husband's party. In the congressional elections of May 1987, Aquino's popularity gave her party a sweep in the polls, making it the major party in the country. Marcos's KBL was reduced to a minor party. Some of its members formed their own splinter groups, such as the Grand Alliance for Democracy (GAD), a coalition of parties seeking distance from Marcos. Others revived the LP and the NP, seeking renewed leadership. The left-wing People's Party (Partido Ng Bayan), which supports the political objectives of the NPA, was a minor party in the elections.

In May 1989 Juan Ponce Enrile reestablished the Nacionalista Party. A new opposition party, the Filipino Party (Partido Pilipino), organized in 1991 as a vehicle for Aquino's estranged cousin Eduardo "Danding" Cojuangco's presidential campaign. He ran third in the election, taking 18.1% of the vote, behind Miriam Defensor Santiago with 19.8% of the vote. On 30 June 1992 Fidel Ramos succeeded Corazon Aquino as president of the Philippines with a plurality of 23.6%. In September 1992 Ramos signed the Anti-Subversion Law signaling a peaceful resolution to more than 20 years of Communist insurgency, with the repeal of the anti-subversion legislation in place since 1957. On 26 August 1994 Ramos announced a new political coalition that would produce the most powerful political group in the Philippines. Ramos' Lakas-National Union of Christian Democrats (Lakas/NUCD) teamed with the Democratic Filipino Struggle (Laban ng Demokratikong Pilipino, Laban). Following the 1995 elections, the LDP controlled the Senate with 14 of the 24 members. The elections in 1998 changed the political landscape once more. In the Senate the newly created Laban Ng Masang Pilipino, led by presidential candidate, Joseph Estrada, captured 12 seats to the Lakas 5, PRP 2, LP 1, independents 3. The LAMP party also dominated the House of Representatives with 135 seats to the Lakas 37, LP 13, Aksyon Demokratiko 1, and 35 independents.

The elections in 2004 again changed the political landscape dramatically. The Senate became a majority Lakas with 7 seats, LP with 3 seats, KNP (coalition) with 3 seats, independents with 4 seats, others with 6 seats (there were 23 rather than 24 sitting senators because one senator was elected vice president). Fourteen senators were pro-government, 9 were in opposition. Lakas also were a majority in the House of Representatives with 93 seats, NPC with 53, LP with 34, LDP with 11, and others with 20.

Legislative and local elections were held on 14 May 2007. The number of seats in the House of Representatives following the election were as follows: Lakas, 70 seats; the Kabalikat ng Malayang Pilipino coalition, 47 seats; the NPC, 26 seats; the Liberals 16; the Nacionalistas 6; other parties won four or fewer seats. The opposition held a majority in the Senate

Liberal Party Senator Benigno Aquino won the 2010 presidential election.

Political parties and their leaders in 2011 included: Laban Ng Demokratikong Pilipino (Struggle of Filipino Democrats— LDP),

Lakas, Liberal Party (LP), Nacionalista Party, National People's Coalition (NPC), PDP-Laban, and the People's Reform Party (PRP).

15 LOCAL GOVERNMENT

Under the constitutions of 1935, 1973, and 1987, the country has been divided into provinces, municipalities, and chartered cities, each enjoying a certain degree of local autonomy. Each of the 73 provinces and subprovinces elects a governor, a vice-governor, and two provincial board members for terms of six years. There are 61 chartered cities headed by a mayor and a vice-mayor. Chartered cities stand on their own, are not part of a province, do not elect provincial officials, and are not subject to provincial taxation, but have the power to levy their own taxes. Municipalities, of which each province is composed, are public corporations governed by municipal law. There are approximately 1,500 municipalities, and within each municipality are communities (*barangays*), each with a citizens' assembly. There are about 42,000 *barangays*.

The 1987 constitution provides for special forms of government in the autonomous regions created in the Cordilleras in Luzon and the Muslim areas of Mindanao. Any region can become autonomous by a referendum. The Local Government Code of 1991 provided for a more responsive and accountable local-government structure. Local governments are to be given more powers, authority, responsibilities and resources through a system of decentralization.

16 JUDICIAL SYSTEM

Under the 1973 constitution, the Supreme Court, composed of a chief justice and 14 associate justices, was the highest judicial body of the state, with supervisory authority over the lower courts. The entire court system was revamped in 1981, with the creation of new regional courts of trials and of appeals. Justices at all levels were appointed by the president. Delays in criminal cases were common, and detention periods in national security cases were long. Security cases arising during the period of martial law (1972–81) were tried in military courts. The 1987 constitution restored the system to what it had been in 1973. Despite the reinstitution of many procedural safeguards and guarantees, the slow pace of justice continues to be a major problem.

The constitution calls for an independent judiciary and defendants in criminal cases are afforded the right to counsel. The legal system is based on both civil and common law, and is especially influenced by Spanish and Anglo-American laws. The Philippines accepts the compulsory jurisdiction of the International Court of Justice.

The national court system consists of four levels: local and regional trial courts; a national Court of Appeals divided into 17 divisions; the 15-member Supreme Court; and an informal local system for arbitrating or mediating certain disputes outside the formal court system. There is no jury system. Defendants enjoy a presumption of innocence and have the right to confront witnesses, to present evidence and to appeal. A Shari'ah (Islamic law) court system, with jurisdiction over domestic and contractual relations among Muslim citizens, operates in some Mindanao provinces. Supreme Court justices may hold office, on good behavior, until the age of 70.

The government allows free press although several journalists have been killed in revenge for reporting on crimes committed by local authorities. Issues affecting women, such as rape, domestic violence, and sexual discrimination, continue to be problematic although banned by law. Drug trafficking, forced labor and child prostitution continue to be problems for the law enforcement community.

17 ARMED FORCES

The International Institute for Strategic Studies reports that armed forces in the Philippines totaled 125,000 members in 2011. The force is comprised of 86,000 from the army, 24,000 from the navy, and 15,000 members of the air force. Armed forces represent 0.4% of the labor force in the Philippines. Defense spending totaled $3.2 billion and accounted for 0.9% of gross domestic product (GDP).

The Philippines has participated in a number of UN peacekeeping missions, in 2001 sending 600 peacekeeping troops to East Timor, and in 2009 sending 336 to Syria's Golan Heights.

18 INTERNATIONAL COOPERATION

The Philippines is a charter member of the United Nations, having joined on 24 October 1945, and belongs to ESCAP and several non-regional specialized agencies, such as the FAO, ILO, UNESCO, UNHCR, UNIDO, the World Bank, IAEA, and the WHO. The Philippines is a member of ASEAN and led in the formation of the Asian Development Bank, which opened its headquarters in Manila in 1966. The nation is also a member of APEC, the Colombo Plan, G-24, G-77, and the WTO. It has observer status in the OAS.

The Philippines is part of the Nonaligned Movement. The government has offered support to UN missions and operations in Kosovo (est. 1999), Liberia (est. 2003), East Timor (est. 2002), and Burundi (est. 2004), among others. In environmental cooperation, the Philippines is part of the Basel Convention, the Convention on Biological Diversity, Ramsar, CITES, the London Convention, International Tropical Timber Agreements, the Kyoto Protocol, the Montréal Protocol, MARPOL, the Nuclear Test Ban Treaty, and the UN Conventions on the Law of the Sea, Climate Change and Desertification.

19 ECONOMY

The Philippine economy has been based primarily on the agricultural production of crops for subsistence and export. Efforts to transform it to a more diversified growth economy, led by manufactured exports commanding more favorable terms of trade, have been repeatedly hindered by natural disasters and external economic shocks. In 1990–91 the islands suffered the triple blow of earthquake, super-typhoon, and volcanic eruption. In succession, there were the even more devastating typhoon of 1995, the Asian financial crisis of 1997, and the global economic slowdown of 2001. The breakdown of the GDP has remained roughly the same, with (in 2010), 12.3% of the GDP attributable to agriculture, 32.6% to industry, and 55.1% to services. In that same year, 33% of the labor force was engaged in agriculture, compared with 15% in industry and 52% in services.

The fastest growing segment of the economy in 2011 was the business process outsourcing (BPO) industry. The Philippines' BPO industry accounts for 15% of the worldwide market, and generated more than $6 billion in 2008 and $7.2 billion in 2009.. This industry has remained strong where others have slowed in response to global financial difficulties. An estimated 525,000 Filipinos were employed in BPO at the end of 2010.

The manufacturing sector consists largely of the processing and assembly of food, beverages, tobacco, pharmaceuticals, textiles, clothing, and other diverse products. Heavier industries include the production of cement, glass, fertilizers, fabricated metal parts, and machinery. Newer industries involve the production of semiconductors and other consumer electronic components and the building of automobiles. This newer technology takes place largely in special economic zones. In general, the industrial segment of the Philippine economy is located in urban areas far from the rural economy.

The economy is marked by many disparities—in ownership of assets, in income, in levels of technology in production, and in the geographic concentration of economic activity. Those living in poverty were estimated at 32.9% of the nation's population in 2006, but figures varied widely among provinces and municipalities. The NCR, the richest region of the country, had an incidence rate of poverty among families in 2006 of only 7.1%, compared to the municipality of Carara, which at 45.5% had the highest rate. In 2006, the top 1% of the country's families earned the equivalent of what the bottom 30% combined earned.

Widespread unemployment and underemployment plague the labor market. In 2010, the unemployment rate was 7.3% and the underemployment rate was 19.1%. High rates of labor migration abroad provide some relief and accounts for a substantial portion of the country's foreign exchange earnings.

The Philippines has great potential as a tourist destination. The tourism industry has at times been hobbled by natural disasters, high fuel costs, and political difficulties, particularly with the emergence of the Abu Sayyaf (Bearers of the Sword) Islamic fundamentalist group. The industry took a downturn following the 11 September 2011 terrorist attacks in the United States, but showed signs of recovery in 2004. By 2011, an estimated 3 million visitors per year were traveling to the Philippines.

The GDP rate of change in Philippines, as of 2010, was 7.3%. Inflation stood at 3.8%. Remittances are a recognizable part of the economy and contributed to the growth in 2011.

20 INCOME

The CIA estimated that in 2010 the GDP of the Philippines was $351.4 billion. The CIA defines GDP as the value of all final goods and services produced within a nation in a given year and computed on the basis of purchasing power parity (PPP) rather than value as measured on the basis of the rate of the exchange based on current dollars. The per capita GDP was estimated at $3,500. The annual growth rate of GDP was 7.3%. The average inflation rate was 3.8%. It was estimated that agriculture accounted for 12.3% of GDP, industry 32.6%, and services 55.1%.

According to the World Bank, remittances from citizens living abroad totaled approximately $21.3 billion or about $209 per capita and accounted for approximately 6% of GDP.

The World Bank reports that in 2010, household consumption in the Philippines totaled $142.8 billion or about $1,400 per capita, measured in current US dollars rather than PPP. Household consumption includes expenditures of individuals, households, and nongovernmental organizations on goods and services, excluding the purchases of dwellings. It was estimated that household consumption was growing at an average annual rate of 4.1%.

In 2010, the World Bank estimated that the Philippines, with 1.39% of the world's population, accounted for 0.473% of the world's GDP. By comparison, the United States, with 4.85% of the world's population, accounted for 22.51% of world GDP.

As of 2011, the most recent study by the World Bank reported that actual individual consumption in the Philippines was 72.8% of GDP and accounted for 0.50% of world consumption. By comparison, the United States accounted for 25.44% of world individual consumption. The World Bank also estimated that 33.4% of the Philippines's GDP was spent on food and beverages, 11.6% on housing and household furnishings, 1.6% on clothes, 2.5% on health, 4.0% on transportation, 2.9% on communications, 0.8% on recreation, 2.3% on restaurants and hotels, and 7.3% on miscellaneous goods and services and purchases from abroad.

It was estimated that in 2006 about 32.9% of the population subsisted on an income below the poverty line established by the Philippines's government.

21 LABOR

As of 2010, the Philippines had a total labor force of 38.9 million people. Within that labor force, CIA estimates in 2010 noted that 33% were employed in agriculture, 15% in industry, and 52% in the service sector.

In May 1974, the government passed a new labor code that restructured the trade union movement on a one-industry, one-union basis. In 2008, there were 17,305 unions, but only 1,456 had collective bargaining agreements, with only 227,000 workers represented by these agreements. In addition, there were 15,758 worker associations, 129 of which had collective negotiation agreements on record. These agreements covered 29,000 workers. While Philippine regulations allow unions, only one in ten unions can represent the workers, and less than 1% of the labor force is represented by those unions. The trade unions are small; industrial unions have been united in the Philippines Trade Union Congress, and agricultural workers in the Federation of Free Farmers. Strikes are prohibited in such essential services as transportation, communications, and health care. While the right to strike and bargain are recognized by law, numerous instances of intimidation of union officials have been reported. During 2006, 33 union leaders, organizers, and sympathizers were killed, in most cases shot by masked gunmen on motorcycles.

In 2011, the legal daily minimum wage for non-agricultural workers ranged from P216 ($5.00) in the provinces to P426 ($9.85) in the capital area. For agricultural workers, daily minimum wages ranged from P195 to P389 ($4.50 to $9.00). Perhaps as many as one-fifth of businesses in the Philippines do not pay the minimum wage. The minimum working age is 15, although children even younger may work under the supervision of a parent or guardian. In practice, many children work in the informal economy, although serious efforts are being made by the government to reduce the number of children who are working.

22 AGRICULTURE

Roughly 40% of the total land of the Philippines is farmed, with three-fourths of the cultivated area devoted to subsistence crops and one-fourth to commercial crops, mainly for export. The country's major crops include sugarcane, coconuts, rice, corn, bananas, cassavas, pineapples, and mangoes. Cereal production in 2009 amounted to 23.3 million tons, fruit production 16 million tons, and vegetable production 5.7 million tons. Farms tend to be small, and many areas are double-cropped. Soils are generally fertile, but 30% of the agricultural land is suffering from erosion.

Roughly half the cultivated land is devoted to the two principal subsistence crops, palay (unhusked rice) and corn. Long-term production of palay has increased, mainly through the use of high-yielding hybrid seeds under a government development program begun in 1973. The Philippines attained self-sufficiency in rice in 1974 and became a net exporter of rice for the first time in 1977. A similar development plan was aimed at raising yields of corn, which is the chief food crop in areas unsuitable for rice-growing and is increasingly important as feed for use in the developing livestock and poultry industries. The Philippines has been self-sufficient in corn for human consumption since the late 1970s, but since production of animal feed lags behind the demand, imports are still necessary.

Commercial agriculture, dominated by large plantations, centers on coconuts and copra, sugarcane, tobacco, bananas, and pineapples. Coconut products are the most important export crop. While coconut farms account for nearly 30% of all farmland in the Philippines, coconuts have the lowest farm value per hectare of all crops grown in the nation. The government spent $5.2 million replacing old trees in 2011, but this only covered 10% of the over-age trees. Copra production, in 2011 was 2.57 million tons, while coconut oil production was 1.5 billion tons. Sugarcane production was down in 2010, 1.9 million metric tons, compared to the previous two years' milled harvests of 26.8 and 21.6 million metric tons. The decrease was blamed on reduced fertilizer use, reduced amount of land devoted to sugarcane, and the hot, dry conditions of the El Nino weather pattern. Pineapple production was estimated to be 1,709,000 tons in 2010.

In 1973, the Marcos government began a land-reform program that intended to transfer landownership to about half of the country's 900,000 tenant farmers. Thirteen years after its inception, 75% of the intended beneficiaries had not become landowners, and over one-half of the area—about 600,000 hectares (1,482,600 acres)— had not been distributed. The Aquino administration proposed a program in two stages: the first, covering 1.5 million hectares (3.7 million acres) in 1987–89, involved previously undistributed land and other land held by the state; the second, covering 3.9 million hectares (9.6 million acres) in 1990–92, involved land cultivating sugar, coconuts, and fruits. A more detailed 1990–95 plan sought to increase productivity of small farms, maintain self-sufficiency in rice and corn production, and increase the agricultural sector's role in the trade balance.

In August 2009, the European Union (EU) allocated over $9.2 million (€6.4 million) in grant funds to benefit small farmers in the Philippines. As part of the EU Food Facility program, funds were used to support projects in crop diversification and collective farming, with the aim of improving the efficiency of small farms and boosting local production. In association with the UN World Food Program, additional projects provided food in exchange for work on irrigation and flood prevention projects. All of these projects were designed to address the challenge of food security in the nation and boost the local economy.

23 ANIMAL HUSBANDRY

Animal husbandry has never been important in the Philippines because meat consumption is very low. The carabao, or water buffalo, is the principal draft animal, particularly in the rice paddies; hogs are the chief meat animals (except in Muslim sections). The Philippines is self-sufficient in pork and poultry, but imports of beef and dairy products are still necessary. In 2005 there were 6.5 million goats and 3.2 million buffaloes. The livestock and poultry sectors each contribute about 13% to the total value of agricultural production. In 2004, exports of livestock, meat, and skins were valued at nearly $7.6 million.

The UN Food and Agriculture Organization (FAO) reported that the Philippines dedicated 1.5 million hectares (3.71 million acres) to permanent pasture or meadow in 2009. During that year, the country tended 158.4 million chickens, 2.6 million head of cattle, and 13.6 million pigs. The production from these animals amounted to 350,679 tons of beef and veal, 1.67 million tons of pork, 732,793 tons of poultry, 500,926 tons of eggs, and 1.58 million tons of milk. The Philippines also produced 16,160 tons of cattle hide.

24 FISHING

Fish are the primary source of protein in the Filipino diet. Some 2,000 species abound in Philippine waters. Despite more than a doubling in output since the 1960s, the fishing industry remains relatively undeveloped, and large quantities of fish are imported. The Bureau of Fisheries and Aquatic Resources (BFAR) cites the continued environmental degradation of Philippine waters as a major constraint on fish production.

Six species are most important, according to BFAR, because each has yielded 100,000 tons per year or more since the mid-1980s. These species are: sardines, roundscad, frigate tuna, anchovies, milkfish, and tilapia. Indian mackerel, skipjack and yellowfin tuna, sea bass, red snapper, mullet, kawakawa, squid, and prawn are also plentiful. Principal commercial fishing grounds are off Palawan, north of Panay and Negros, and to the south and west of Mindanao. Subsistence fishing is conducted throughout the archipelago. Fish ponds, chiefly for cultivation of bangos or milkfish, are principally in the swampy coastal areas of western Panay and around Manila Bay. Pearl shells (including cultured pearls), sponges, sea cucumbers (trepang), shark fins, and sea turtles are exported.

The Philippines had 1,485 decked commercial fishing boats in 2008. The annual capture totaled 2.56 million tons according to the UN FAO. The export value of seafood totaled $347.8 million.

25 FORESTRY

Forests are an important economic resource in the Philippines. Approximately 26% of the Philippines is covered by forest. Major commercial forest reserves are located in Mindanao, Luzon, Samar, Negros, and Palawan. Deforestation has been recognized as a serious problem for the nation. Applications to operate new sawmills were suspended in 2003, when it was determined that most sawmills had been utilizing illegally acquired logs. A series of devastating typhoons and the ensuing mudslides in central Luzon in December 2004 revealed the seriousness of both legal and illegal deforestation, prompting the government to review existing forestry laws. The House of Representatives passed an act in 2009 establishing a self-sustaining program to provide incentives for planting trees on public or private lands. In May 2011 it was reported that the University of the Philippines at Los Banos was using cloning to produce the trees needed for a six year reforestation program that will plant 1.5 billion trees on 1.5 million hectares of public lands. The trees to be planted are all indigenous species.

The UN FAO estimated the 2009 roundwood production at 3.8 million cu m (134.1 million cu ft). The value of all forest products, including roundwood, totaled $194.7 million. In the early 1980s, the Philippines was a significant exporter of tropical hardwood logs and lumber, but production fell by over 50% over the decade, leaving the country a net importer of tropical hardwood logs by 1990.

Among other forest products are bamboo, rattan, resins, tannin, and firewood.

26MINING

The mining and quarrying sector contributed about 2% to the to the country's 2010 GDP. Production for much of the last quarter of the 20th century was slowed by political instability, declining foreign investment, low international prices, high operation and production costs, labor problems, an inadequate mining law, and natural disasters such as earthquakes, volcanic eruptions, landslides, tsunamis, typhoons, floods, and drought. Similar problems hampered mining in the first decade of the 21st century. Nevertheless, the Philippines ranked second in the Asia-Pacific region, after Indonesia, in terms of mineral prospectivity and resources. The Philippines reportedly had the world's largest source of refractory chromite, from Masinloc, and substantial resources of copper, gold, nickel, and silver. The production of chemicals and petroleum refining were leading industries in 2011.

Copper output was estimated at 21,235 metric tons (metal content) in 2008. Mined gold output was estimated at 37,047 kg in 2009, with mined nickel output estimated at 27,000 metric tons in 2009. The Philippines also produced sizable quantities of metallurgic chromite. Chromite ore production totaled an estimated 15,268 metric tons (gross weight) in 2008. In addition, 33.81 metric tons of silver were produced for export in 2009. The industrial mineral sector was dominated by the production of limestone, marble, and sand and gravel. In 2009, the Philippines also produced bentonite, hydraulic cement, clays (including red and white), feldspar, lime, perlite, phosphate rock, pyrite and pyrrhotite (including cuprous), marine salt, silica sand, stone (including dolomite, volcanic cinder, tuff, quartz), and sulfur. Approximately 2 metric tons per year of guano phosphate were produced in 2009.

Exploitation of the Philippines' mineral resources was stimulated by the Mining Act of 1995, which was designed to promote the mining industry to the international community and to provide incentives to ensure efficiency and economic viability for mining endeavors. The law also aimed to help the domestic mining industry regain its competitiveness by allowing companies (contractors) to obtain an exploration permit for a specific area for up to four years. For a viable deposit, the code provided four production agreements—production sharing, co-production, joint venture, or financial/technical assistance—with a duration of up to 50

years. A serious accident in 1996 involving spilled mine tailings from a copper mine on Marinduque led the government to freeze almost all applications for exploration licenses by foreign companies for one year; however, in 2004 the Supreme Court upheld the Mining Act, regenerating international interest in the Philippines' mining potential.

The mining industry employed 400,000 people—300,000 of them engaged in small-scale mining and panning activities, chiefly in artisanal gold workings.

27ENERGY AND POWER

The World Bank reported in 2008 that the Philippines produced 60.8 billion kWh of electricity and consumed 53.1 billion kWh, or 522 kWh per capita. Roughly 57% of energy came from fossil fuels, while 25% came from alternative fuels. Per capita oil consumption was 455 kg. Oil production totaled 32,945 barrels of oil a day.

The Philippines has modest reserves of oil, but more robust reserves of natural gas that could make the country a significant producer. The country is also one of the world's largest producers of geothermal power. Large hydroelectric plants have been installed on the Agno and Angat rivers on Luzon and at María Cristina Falls on the Agusan River in Mindanao.

28INDUSTRY

Exports of electronics first surpassed food products and textiles in value in the late 1990s, as the government sought to shift from an economy based on agricultural produce and sweatshop factory output to one anchored by the assembly of computer chips and other electronic goods. Over 50 chip assemblers and computer components makers have invested in Philippine operations. Technology companies with major investments in the Philippines include Intel, Philips, Acer, Toshiba, Hitachi, Fujitsu, Cypress Semiconductor, and Amkor Technology.

Antilock braking systems used in Mercedes-Benz, Volvo, and BMW automobiles are made in Philippine factories, as are Honda motorcycles and several American and Japanese car brands. In 2011 China's Chery Automobile announced it would be setting up a plant within the next five years to provide cars for the ASEAN market.

In 2010, consumer goods, such as food, beverages, apparel, shoes, and tobacco, accounted for 57% of industrial output. Intermediate goods including petroleum products, coal, and chemicals, accounted for 25%, while capital goods, such as electronics, semiconductors, iron, and steel, accounted for 18%. The industrial production growth rate in 2010 was 12.1%.

Historically, manufacturing production has been geographically concentrated in the Metro Manila area and the adjoining regions of Southern Tagalog and Central Luzon. With the progress in electrification, this geographic concentration has decreased. Most industrial output is concentrated in a relatively few large firms. Although small and medium-sized businesses account for about 80% of manufacturing employment, they account for only about 25% of the value-added in manufacturing. In 2010, industry accounted for 32.6% of GDP.

A major natural gas discovery in the Malampaya field was a promising development, formally inaugurated in 2001 with the completion of a 312 mile (504 km) sub-sea pipeline and the con-

Principal Trading Partners – Philippines (2010)

(In millions of US dollars)

Country	Total	Exports	Imports	Balance
World	109,661.0	51,432.0	58,229.0	-6,797.0
Japan	14,574.0	7,827.0	6,747.0	1,080.0
United States	13,433.0	7,568.0	5,865.0	1,703.0
Singapore	12,515.0	7,331.0	5,184.0	2,147.0
China	10,311.0	5,702.0	4,609.0	1,093.0
South Korea	6,056.0	2,228.0	3,828.0	-1,600.0
Hong Kong	5,802.0	4,334.0	1,468.0	2,866.0
Thailand	5,650.0	1,784.0	3,866.0	-2,082.0
Taiwan	5,429.0	1,752.0	3,677.0	-1,925.0
Malaysia	3,834.0	1,396.0	2,438.0	-1,042.0
Germany	3,769.0	2,657.0	1,112.0	1,545.0

(…) data not available or not significant.

(n.s.) not specified.

SOURCE: *2011 Direction of Trade Statistics Yearbook,* New York: United Nations, 2011.

version of three power plants in Batangas to natural gas usage. In the Philippine Energy Plan 2000–2009 (PEP) the government envisioned domestic energy production increasing to over 50% self-sufficiency from about 42% self-sufficiency in 2001. Oil production has not been promising: in 2001 only 2.3% of the oil consumed was produced in the Philippines. The Malampaya Deepwater Gas-to-Power Project has shifted the government focus to an emphasis on the development of natural gas resources.

29 SCIENCE AND TECHNOLOGY

As of 2009, according to the World Bank, patent applications in science and technology totaled 216 in the Philippines. Leadership in formulating and implementing national science policy is exercised by the Department of Science and Technology. Special training in science is offered by the Philippine Science High School, whose graduates are eligible for further training through the department's scholarship program. The International Rice Research Institute in Los Banos, founded by the Rockefeller and Ford foundations and US AID in 1960, conducts training programs in the cultivation, fertilization, and irrigation of hybrid rice seeds. The Southeast Asian Regional Center for Graduate Study and Research in Agriculture maintains genotype and information banks for agricultural research.

The Philippine Nuclear Research Institute, founded in 1958, is located in Quezon City. In 2011 its projects included crop improvement through mutation breeding and sterile insect techniques for pest control. In 2011, the Philippines had 71 universities and colleges offering courses on basic and applied sciences. In 2009, high-tech exports were valued at $26.875 billion and accounted for 66.9% of manufactured exports.

30 DOMESTIC TRADE

The archipelagic structure of Philippine marketing requires the establishment of regional centers and adds considerably to distribution costs, foreign domination of much of marketing, direct government participation, and the proliferation of small firms. About 90% of all imported goods come through the Port of Manila. Makati City is the business center of the country and hosts a number of distribution centers, trading firms, commercial banks, and high-end retail establishments. Cebu City is the trading center of the south.

Small stores typify retail trade. Manila has major shopping centers and malls. Generally, sales are for cash or on open account. Retailing is conducted on a high markup, low-turnover basis. A law provides for price-tagging on retail items. Direct marketing, particularly of foreign name-brand products, has gained in popularity. English is the general language of commercial correspondence. Most advertising is local; the chief media are newspapers, radio, television, posters, billboards, and sound trucks.

Franchising is one of the fastest growing business sectors in the Philippine economy. Population growth, increasing economic activity, and consumer preferences have all fueled expansion in this sector. US-based franchise operations dominate, with a 70% share. In 2011, there were more than 13,000 franchisers with 125,000 franchisees operating in the Philippines, up from only 50 franchisers in the early 1990s. Franchise sales totaled $9.45 billion in 2010, up from $1.875 billion in 2001. The output from franchises accounted for 30% of the nation's total output; this percentage was expected to continue to increase in coming years, adding jobs. In 2010, the industry generated more than one million jobs. The fastest growing sub-sectors are in services and food.

Electronic commerce (e-commerce) in the Philippines is increasing, with business-to-consumer (B2C) websites experiencing rapid growth in such areas as banking and financial services, travel, shopping, movie reservations, and bill payment. In 2009, an estimated 29.7% of the general population used the internet, accessing it through personal computers at home, in schools and corporate offices, and in Internet cafes.

Shops are usually open from 10 a.m. to 8 p.m., Monday through Saturday, but these hours can vary. Most department stores and supermarkets are open on Sunday. Banking hours are weekdays from 9 a.m. to 3 p.m. Office hours, and hours for the Philippine government are generally from 8 a.m. to 5 p.m. Monday through Friday, with a one-hour lunch break from 12 to 1 p.m. Some offices are open from 8 a.m. to 12 p.m. on Saturday. Staggered hours, with up to three shifts, are common in the metropolitan Manila area.

31 FOREIGN TRADE

The Philippines' traditional exports were primary commodities and raw materials. However, by 2000, machinery and transport equipment made up the majority of exports. In 2004, the major exports were: electronic products (67.3% of all exports); semiconductors (47.1%); garments (5.5%); coconut oil (1.5%); and petroleum products (1%). Primary imports were: capital goods (38.1% of all imports); semi-processed raw materials (34%); parts for the manufacture of electronic equipment (15.4%); mineral fuels (11.7%); and chemicals (7.9%). By 2010, with the loss of related quotas, apparel exports had dropped below those of coconut oil.

The Philippines imported $59.9 billion worth of goods and services in 2008, while exporting $50.72 billion worth of goods and services. Major import partners in 2009 were Japan, 12.6%; the United States, 12%; China, 8.9%; Singapore, 8.6%; South Korea, 6.9%; Thailand, 5.7%; and Indonesia, 4.2% . Its major export partners were the United States, 17.7%; Japan, 16.3%; Netherlands,

9.5%; Hong Kong, 8.4%; China, 7.6%; Singapore, 6.7%; Germany, 6.6%; and South Korea, 4.7%.

In January 2010 a new free trade area was established between China and the six founding members of the Association of South East Asian Nations (ASEAN), including the Philippines. A major point of the free trade agreement was the elimination of tariffs on nearly 90% of imported goods. The free trade area agreement was expected to allow for a major increase in exports and export earnings among the ASEAN countries. In terms of population, this is the largest free trade area in the world.

In another expected boost for trade, the ASEAN Trade in Goods Agreement (ATIGA), approved in 2009, entered into force on 17 May 2010. The ATIGA represents the next step in realizing the free flow of goods within the region by simplifying the processes and procedures necessary to create a single market and production base—known as the ASEAN Economic Community (AEC)—by 2015. Major points of ATIGA include tariff liberalization, a simplification of the rules of origin, and implementation of such rules. The comprehensive agreement also demands greater transparency in regional trade liberalization, aiding the work of businesses and investors. As a member of ASEAN, the government of the Philippines is expected to approve any domestic legislation necessary to be within full compliance of the agreement within 90 days. The ATIGA supersedes the Common Effective Preferential Tariff Scheme (CEPT) adopted in 1992.

32 BALANCE OF PAYMENTS

In 2010, the Philippines had a foreign trade deficit of $7.3 billion, amounting to 3.9% of GDP. The Central Bank expected a balance of payments surplus of $6–8 billion in 2011, down from 2010's record surplus of $14.4 billion. Foreign investments were up in the first quarter of 2011, more than double for the same period the previous year. These figures reflect the IMF's analysis in 2010 which indicated that the Philippine economy had recovered from the slowdown it had weathered in relation to the global financial crisis. Investor confidence was good in response to a variety of factors, including the smooth transition in July 2010 to a new administration, low inflation, and a surplus in the balance of payments. The IMF predicted growth to average 7% in 2010 and 5% in 2011. In November 2010 Standard and Poor's upgraded its listing of the Philippines long-term foreign currency debt to BB in recognition of the Philippines' stronger financial position.

The economic outlook for the Philippines had not always been so optimistic. Political instability and global economic developments have from time to time taken their toll. The Aquino assassination in August 1983 had immediate economic consequences for the Marcos government, as did the broader Third World Debt Crisis. Hundreds of millions of dollars in private capital fled the Philippines, leaving the country with insufficient foreign exchange reserves to meet its payments obligations. The government turned to the IMF and its creditor banks for assistance in rescheduling the nation's foreign debt. An austerity program was set up during 1984–85. In December 1986, under IMF guidance, the Aquino government launched a privatization program with the establishment of the Assets Privatization Trust (APT). Monopolies established under the Marcos administration in coconuts, sugar, meat, grains, and fertilizer were dismantled and a ban on copra exports was lifted. All export taxes were abolished and the government allowed free access to lower-cost or higher-quality imports as a means of improving the cost-competitiveness of domestic producers.

Many difficulties remained, however. The prices of commodity exports, such as sugar, copper, and coconut products, were still weak, while demand for nontraditional manufactured products, such as clothing and electronic components, failed to rise. The structural reforms produced an initial recovery between 1986 and 1989, but this was arrested by the series of natural disasters in 1990–91. In 1986, Aquino had also embarked on a Comprehensive Agrarian Reform Programme, but its goals remain unfulfilled. Merchandise exports, in double digits through most of the 1990s, slowed to a single-digit growth pace in 2000, reflecting fewer export receipts from electronics and telecommunications parts and equipment. This decline was attributed by the electronics industry to weaker prices for maturing products and technologies, and to the decline in electronic industry investments from the 1994–97 boom years.

In the 1990s, the government concluded three additional financial arrangements with the IMF—a stand-by agreement signed 20 February 1991 for about $240 million; an arrangement under the Extended Fund Facility (EFF) signed 24 June 1994 for about $554 million, and a stand-by agreement signed 1 April 1998 for about $715 million. The country also had five debt reschedulings in the period 1984 to 1991 with the Paris Club—for official debt owed to aid donor countries—on which some payments were still owed in 2011.

33 BANKING AND SECURITIES

The government-owned Bangko Sentral ng Pilipinas replaced the Central Bank of the Philippines in 1993. It acts as the government's fiscal agent and administers the monetary and banking system. Some 38 commercial and universal banks, of which many are foreign-majority-owned, operate in the Philippines. Other variet-

Balance of Payments – Philippines (2010)

(In millions of US dollars)

Current Account		**8,924.0**
Balance on goods		-10,966.0
Imports	-61,714.0	
Exports	50,748.0	
Balance on services		2,939.0
Balance on income		347.0
Current transfers		16,604.0
Capital Account		**98.0**
Financial Account		**9,530.0**
Direct investment abroad		-487.0
Direct investment in Philippines		1,713.0
Portfolio investment assets		-3,460.0
Portfolio investment liabilities		9,845.0
Financial derivatives		-191.0
Other investment assets		-2,979.0
Other investment liabilities		5,089.0
Net Errors and Omissions		**-1,959.0**
Reserves and Related Items		**-16,593.0**

(…) data not available or not significant.

SOURCE: *Balance of Payment Statistics Yearbook 2011,* Washington, DC: International Monetary Fund, 2011.

Public Finance – Philippines (2009)

(In billions of pesos, budgetary central government figures)

Revenue and Grants	**1,123.13**	**100.0%**
Tax revenue	981.63	87.4%
Social contributions	...	...
Grants	0.19	<0.1%
Other revenue	141.31	12.6%
Expenditures	**1,425.34**	**100.0%**
General public services	626.32	43.9%
Defense	64.99	4.6%
Public order and safety	84.58	5.9%
Economic affairs	267.3	18.8%
Environmental protection	15.12	1.1%
Housing and community amenities	5.77	0.4%
Health	38.44	2.7%
Recreational, culture, and religion	10.95	0.8%
Education	221.64	15.5%
Social protection	90.21	6.3%

(...) data not available or not significant.

SOURCE: *Government Finance Statistics Yearbook 2010*, Washington, DC: International Monetary Fund, 2010.

ies of banking institutions exist, including thrift banks, rural and cooperative banks, private development banks, savings banks, and investment houses, and two specialized government banks. Rural banks in every province offer microfinance services. The government operates about 1,145 postal savings banks and the Development Bank of the Philippines, the Land Bank of the Philippines, and the Philippine Amanah Bank (for Mindanao). There are also 13 offshore banking units in the country, and 26 foreign bank representative offices. The CIA reported in 2010 that the stock of narrow/broad money was $97.35 billion.

Based on total assets, the five largest banks in the Philippines in 2009 were Banco de Oro, Metrobank, Bank of the Philippine Islands, Landbank of the Philippines, and Development Bank of the Philippines. Those five banks represented nearly half of the total bank assets for 2009 of $143.22 billion.

In 2010, the money market rate, the interest rate at which financial institutions lend to one another in the short term, was 7.673%. The discount rate, the interest rate at which the central bank lends to financial institutions in the short term, was 3.8%. At the end of 2009, the nation's gold bullion deposits totaled 5.295 million fine troy ounces.

The Philippine stock exchange is self-governing, although the Philippine Securities and Exchange Commission (SEC), established in 1936, has supervisory power over registrants. As of November 2011, 245 companies were listed. In 2010, the PSE had a market capitalization of $202.3 billion. At the beginning of December 2011, the PSE Composite Index (PSEI) was up 6.8% from the previous year, to 4290.2. The PSEI is a capitalization-weighted index composed of 30 stocks representing services, industry, properties, mining and oil, finance, and holding firm sectors of the economy.

34INSURANCE

The Government Service Insurance System (GIS), a government organization set up in 1936, provides life, permanent disability, ac-

cident, old age pension, burial insurance and salary and real estate loan benefits. Compulsory third-party motor liability insurance went into effect on 1 January 1976. In addition, workers' compensation and personal accident insurance for workers abroad are compulsory. The Insurance Commission of the Department of Finance oversees the insurance industry.

Life and nonlife insurance companies provide coverage against theft, fire, marine loss, accident, embezzlement, third-party liability, and other risks. In 2010, a total of $2.72 billion in direct insurance premiums were written, of which life insurance premiums accounted for $1.62 billion. In 2010, Malayan Insurance was the Philippines' top nonlife insurer, with gross written nonlife premiums of $134.21 million. In 2010, the leading life insurer was Philam Life and General, with gross written life insurance premiums of $257.87 million.

35PUBLIC FINANCE

In 2010 the budget of Philippines included $26.84 billion in public revenue and $33.82 billion in public expenditures. The budget deficit amounted to 3.7% of GDP. Public debt was 56.5% of GDP, with $63.75 billion of the debt held by foreign entities.

The principal sources of revenue are income taxes, taxes on sales and business operations, and excise duties. Infrastructural improvements, defense expenditures, and debt service continue to lead among the categories of outlays. The Philippines was not affected as severely by the Asian financial crisis of 1998 as many of its overseas neighbors, as a result of over $7 billion in remittances annually by workers overseas.

Late in November 2011 the government presented its proposed $41.61 billion budget for 2012, representing 16.5% of GDP. It passed with a 10.4% increase and was expected to be ratified by mid-December. Roughly one third of this budget was for automatic appropriations, such as debt servicing and internal revenue allotment. Allocated outlays by function included the following: social services, 28.8%; education, 11.9%; defense, 5.4%; agriculture, 2.7%; interior and local government (DILG), 5%; public works and highways (DPWH), 6.3%.

36TAXATION

The individual income tax consists of taxes on compensation income (from employment), business income, and passive income (interests, dividends, royalties, and prizes). As of 2010, personal income was taxed on a progressive scale with a top rate of 32%.

In 2010, the business income tax rate was 30%. For resident foreign corporations, after-tax profits remitted abroad to the head office are subject to a 15% tax. Corporations registered with the Philippine Economic Zone Authority (PEZA), the Board of Investment (BOI), the Bases Conversion Development Authority, or operating in independent special economic zones (ecozones), are eligible for special tax and customs incentives, exemptions and reductions designed to attract foreign, new, necessary and/or export-oriented foreign investment. The capital gains tax is 6% on real property; 5% on gains of PHP100,000 or less from the sale of stock not listed on the stock exchange, and 10% on gains over PHP100,000. Dividends are not subject to taxation if paid from one domestic corporation to another domestic corporation, or to resident foreign corporations. However, dividends paid to non-resident companies are generally subject to a 32% withholding tax, which can be reduced to 15%, under certain circumstances. Some cities, such as Manila, levy their own wholesale and retail sales taxes.

Taxes on transactions include a value-added tax (VAT) of 12% as of 2010. For smaller businesses not registered with the VAT a percentage sales tax of 3% on quarterly sales is applied. Higher rates for activities involving issues of public morality: cockpits are taxed 18%, cabarets, 18% and jai-alai and racetracks, 30%.

Excise taxes are imposed on selected commodities such as alcoholic beverages, tobacco products, jewelry, and petroleum products. In addition, the government levies a variety of other taxes, including mining and petroleum taxes, residence taxes, a head tax on immigrants above a certain age and staying beyond a certain period, document stamp taxes, donor (gift) taxes, estate taxes, and capital gains taxes. A document stamp tax is charged on stock certificates, proofs of indebtedness, proofs of ownership, etc.

³⁷CUSTOMS AND DUTIES

The Philippines, under its commitments to ASEAN, has reduced or eliminated tariffs on manufactured goods on the AFTA Common Preferential Tariff (CEPT) Inclusion List. The Philippines, as a member of the Asia Pacific Economic Cooperation (APEC) forum, is also committed to the establishment of free trade in the region and is expected to eliminate intra-regional barriers by 2020. There is also a value-added tax (VAT) of 12% on almost all imports and excise taxes are levied on alcohol and tobacco products, automobiles, and other luxury items.

³⁸FOREIGN INVESTMENT

In the first five months of 2011 foreign investment in the Philippines was up 189% over same period the previous year, with the Netherlands posting $171.75 million, and the United States and Japan posting investments of $164.60 million and $148.90 million respectively. This contrasts with an earlier report warning that tax policies favoring local businesses over foreign companies was discouraging foreign investment. Foreign direct investment (FDI) in the Philippines was a net inflow of $1.95 billion according to World Bank figures published in 2009. FDI represented 1.21% of GDP.

While investments have traditionally been concentrated in manufactures for exports, utilities, mining, petroleum refining, and export-oriented agriculture, there is accelerating interest in labor-intensive textiles, footwear, electronics, and other nontraditional export industries. Call center operation and business process outsourcing (BPO) are a growing source of foreign investment. The Philippine government has put BPO at the top of its priority plan.

The government has historically restricted foreign investment in favor of developing local businesses and corporations. The Omnibus Investments Code of 1987 generally limited foreign equity ownership to 40%, but allowed 100% foreign ownership in a "pioneer" priority industry identified in the annual Investment Priorities Plan (IPP). Special encouragement was given to pioneer manufacturing endeavors, export-oriented and labor-intensive industries, projects outside metropolitan Manila, and to joint ventures with a minimum of 60% Filipino capitalization.

The Foreign Investment Act of 1991 (FIA) further liberalized the investment climate of the Philippines by permitting 100% foreign ownership, without prior BOI approval, of companies engaged in any activity not included in the foreign investment negative list (FINL). The FINL is comprised of three categories where foreign investment is totally or partially restricted by the constitution or by specific laws. Restriction on setting up export processing zones has also been considerably relaxed. The development of special economic zones began with the transformation of the former US military bases into enterprise zones, the Subic Bay Freeport Zone (SBFZ) and the Clark Special Economic Zone (CSEZ) according to the Bases Conversion Act of 1992.

The Export Development Act of 1994 signaled the government's conversion from an import substitution model of industrial development to an export-led growth model, more in line with the neighboring economies of the so-called Asian Tiger nations. The banking and insurance sectors were also significantly liberalized by legislation in 1994. Under a 1994 law, each bank was allowed to open up to six new branches, plus up to 10 new foreign full-service banks could be licensed with up to six branches each. Insurance was opened to 100% foreign ownership but such that the higher the percent foreign ownership, the higher minimum capital requirements. Rural banking, however, continues to remain closed to foreign investment. In 1995, the Special Economic Zone Act established the framework for the collection of four government-managed ecozones and over 40 private ecozones, all with liberalized incentives to attract foreign investment. In 2000 the Estrada administration opened the retail trade and grain milling businesses to foreign investment.

In 2001, Arroyo, a trained economist, launched a high profile campaign to attract foreign investment. Former president Fidel Ramos and four other senior government officials were appointed as envoys to promote trade and investment. Against strong nationalist opposition, her administration passed the Electric Power Industry Reform Act that required the National Power Corporation (NPC) to privatize at least 70% of its generating assets by 2004. NPCs transmission assets were fully privatized and opened up to the maximum 40% foreign ownership allowed for public utilities.

There remain, however, major restrictions on foreign investments in the Philippines, not the least of which is the complexity and detail of the investment regime. Under the FIA, the government is obliged to promulgate a Foreign Investment Negative List (FINL) consisting of a List A of foreign ownership limited by the constitution and specific laws, and a List B of foreign ownership limited for reasons of security, defense, risk to health and morals and protection of small- and medium-scale enterprises. In 2010 president Arroyo issued the Eighth FINL. On List A, by its terms, no foreign equity was to be allowed in the mass media except recording, nor in any of the licensed professions including law, medicine, accounting, engineering, environmental planning, interior design, teaching, and architecture. Small scale retail and mining, private security, utilization of marine resources, the operation of cockpits, and the manufacture of fireworks, are off-limits to foreigners, as are, on another level, the manufacture and stockpiling of nuclear, biological, chemical and radiological weapons. Only a maximum of 20% ownership is allowed a private radio communications network; only up to 25% in employee recruitment industries, public works construction projects (though with important exceptions for infrastructure/development projects, and those built with foreign aid); only up to 30% in ad agencies; only up to

40% in natural resource extraction projects (though the president can authorize up to 100%), ownership of private lands, ownership of condominiums, educational institutions, public utilities, commercial deep sea fishing, government procurement contracts, adjustment companies, and rice and corn processing (with at least 60% divestment to Filipino citizens required after 30 years of operation); and only up to 60% in financial and investment houses. On the B list for 2010, foreign ownership was restricted to 40% in manufacture of firearms, ammunition, explosives, military ordnance, dangerous drugs, saunas, steam baths, massage parlors, all forms of gambling, local businesses not engaged in exporting with paid-in capital of less than $200,000 and local businesses that involved advanced technology or employed at least 50 persons with paid-in capital of less than $100,000.

The Philippine government, despite its attempts to attract more foreign investment, has failed to invest in the infrastructure—roads, communications, healthcare, and education—that is crucial to foreign and domestic investors. The government has been unable to address issues of congestion and pollution in Manila.

39 ECONOMIC DEVELOPMENT

Beginning in 1972, the main tenets of the Marcos government's economic policies included substantial development of infrastructure, particularly through the use of labor-intensive rather than capital-intensive (i.e., mechanized) methods, and a shift in export emphasis from raw materials to finished and semi-finished commodities. The policies of the Aquino administration stressed labor-intensive, small and medium-scale agricultural projects and extensive land reform. Long-range planning has followed a series of economic plans, most of them covering five-year periods. The development program for 1967–70 was aimed at increasing the growth rate of per capita income, increasing national income, and reducing unemployment. The government invested $3.5 billion in integrating the traditional and modern sectors of the economy. Marcos's first long-range plan following the 1972 declaration of martial law was a four-year (1974–77) infrastructure development program calling for 35% to be expended on transportation, 33% on energy and power, 20% on water resources, 10% on education, health, and welfare, and 2% on telecommunications. A 1974–78 plan, announced in late 1975, envisioned energy as the major focus of the new plan, with 34% of expenditures, followed by transportation, 30%; water resources, 23%; social programs, 7%; and other sectors, 6%. The goals of the 1978–82 plan included an 8% annual growth in GNP, rural development, tax incentives for export-oriented industries, continued self-sufficiency in grain crops despite rapid population growth, and accelerated development of highways, irrigation, and other infrastructure. The 1983–87 plan called for an annual expansion of 6.2% in GNP, improvement of the rural economy and living standards, and amelioration of hunger.

Under the Aquino administration the goals of the 1987–92 plan were self-sufficiency in food production, decentralization of power and decision making, job creation, and rural development. Economic performance for real growth fell far short of plan targets by 25% or more. Structural changes to provide a better investment climate were made. The Foreign Investment Act of 1991 liberalized the environment for foreign investment. An executive order issued in July 1991 reduced the number of tariff levels over

five years and reduced the maximum duty rate from 50% to 30%. Quantitative restrictions were removed from all but a few products. The foreign exchange market was fully deregulated in 1992.

A new six-year medium-term development plan for 1993–98 stressed people empowerment and international competitiveness within the framework of sustainable development. To do this, the government planned to disperse industries to regions outside the metropolitan Manila area. The plan also called for technological upgrading of production sectors, poverty alleviation, and human/social development. The Medium-Term Philippine Development Plan (MTPDP) for 1999 through 2004 focused on rural development, especially on the modernization of the agricultural sector. The MTPDP targeted agricultural growth from 2.6% to 3.4% during the plan's time-frame, as well as growth in the industrial and service sectors. The Philippines finished three years of IMF supervision in March 1998, only to be hit by the Asian financial crisis. Financial assistance continued in 1998 and 1999 through the Asian Development Bank, World Bank, and Japan's Overseas Economic Cooperation Development Fund.

By 2006, the primary economic policy challenge confronting the government was to bring the public finances back into balance, allowing increased expenditure on areas such as infrastructure, education, and healthcare. The fiscal deficit had increased due to poor tax administration, and public debt ballooned to 77.4% of GDP in 2005. Interest payments accounted for a third of all public spending. Nevertheless, the stock market in mid-2005 was at a five-year peak, and the peso at its highest against the dollar since mid-2003. Applications for investment incentives more than doubled in 2004 and were also high in 2005.

In the mid-2000s, the economies of Southeast Asia revolved around trade. In 2004, the region experienced a 6.3% GDP growth rate, largely due to a double-digit increase in exports. However, growth in the domestic economy was still believed necessary to insulate the Philippines from fluctuations in the world market. The only country where exports did not make a significant contribution to growth by 2005 was the Philippines, where almost all growth was attributable to domestic demand. Instead of being a mark of strength, however, this was a mark of economic weakness.

GDP growth slowed to 38% in 2008, and fell further to 1.1% in 2009, but rebounded to 7.3% year on year during 2010. The rebound was attributed to election-related spending and the peaceful transition to a new government, among other factors. Overseas remittances increased by 8.2% in 2010, to $18.7 billion. Overall the GDP has grown during the first decade of the 21st century, but not enough to alleviate poverty.

In 2010, business process outsourcing was the fastest growing segment of the Philippine economy, generating more than $6 billion in 2008, $7.2 billion in 2009, and $9 billion in 2010. Merchandise exports grew by nearly 35% in 2010, with electronics revenue especially high. The national government debt decreased significantly from its peak in 2004, when debt was equal to 78% of GDP, amounting in 2010 to 58% of GDP.

Due to the billions of dollars of remittances that Filipinos working overseas send to their families back home, consumer spending in the Philippines is robust. However, the economy does not grow fast enough to provide jobs for all Filipinos, driving many to seek work overseas.

⁴⁰SOCIAL DEVELOPMENT

The Government Service Insurance System covers employees up to age 60, including domestic workers and the self-employed. Membership for employers is compulsory. Benefits include compensation for confinement due to injury or illness, pensions for temporary incapacity, indemnities to families in case of death, old age pensions, and benefits to widows and orphans. Charges to cover the system are paid jointly by employers and employees and according to 29 wage classes. The government funds any deficit. A medical care plan for employees provides hospital, surgical, medicinal, and medical-expense benefits to members and their dependents, as well as paid maternity leave. Retirement is at age 60 for most workers; a social security system exists.

A handful of women enjoy high prestige and visibility, but most women occupy traditional social roles and occupations. Unemployment rates are higher for women, and women continue to earn less than men. Sexual harassment in the workplace is widespread, and goes largely unreported because women are afraid of losing their jobs. Spousal abuse and violence remain serious concerns. The absence of divorce laws and lack of economic opportunity keep women in destructive relationships. The government has enacted various measures to safeguard the rights of children. Child prostitution, while illegal, is widespread and has contributed to the growing sex-tourism industry. Some human rights violations remain, including arbitrary arrest and detention, torture, and disappearances.

⁴¹HEALTH

According to the CIA, life expectancy in the Philippines was 72 years in 2011. The country spent 3.7% of its GDP on healthcare, amounting to $67 per person. There were 12 physicians, 60 nurses and midwives, and 5 hospital beds per 10,000 inhabitants. The fertility rate was 3.0, while the infant mortality rate was 19 per 1,000 live births. In 2008 the maternal mortality rate, according to the World Bank, was 94 per 100,000 births. It was estimated that 88% of children were vaccinated against measles. The CIA calculated HIV/AIDS prevalence in the Philippines to be about less than 0.1% in 2009.

Malnutrition remained a health problem despite government assistance in the form of Nutripaks (consisting of indigenous foods such as mung beans and powdered shrimp) that were made available for infants, children, and pregnant women. Protein malnutrition, anemia, and vitamin A and iodine deficiencies were commonly found in children. The goiter rate was high. Heart disease was a prevalent cause of death in the Philippines.

During the 1980s, a nationwide primary health care program was implemented. As a result, community involvement in health services increased, the prevalence of communicable diseases decreased, and the nutritional state of the population improved. Obesity and hypertension were more common in the cities.

⁴²HOUSING

At the 2000 census, there were 14,891,127 housing units in the Philippines with an average household size of 5 members. Most housing units are single-family detached homes. About 71% of all housing was owner occupied. In 2008, 93% of the urban population had access to an improved water source, compared to 87% of the rural population. 80% of the urban population and 69% of the rural population had access to improved sanitation facilities.

Tens of thousands of barrios are scattered throughout the Philippines, each consisting of a double row of small wood or nipa cottages strung out along a single road. Each cottage is generally built on stilts and has a thatched roof, veranda, and small yard. In the towns and cities, a variety of building materials, including nipa, wood, concrete, brick, and bamboo, are used.

Public spending on housing in the Philippines is very low, averaging less than 0.1% of GDP. Over the years, various government programs have addressed the issue of inadequate housing. The Housing and Urban Development Coordinating Council (HUDCC) was created in 1986, replacing the scandal-ridden Bagong Lipunon Improvement of Sites and Services (BLISS) program from the Marcos years. HUDCC is the highest housing policy making body and serves to coordinate the National Shelter Program (NSP). The NSP regulates housing production and financing, but has been unable to keep up with demand; in 2011, the Philippines had a housing shortage of at least one million units. The shortage was anticipated to get worse, due to increasing poverty and migration to urban areas. Many factors have worked to keep the NSP from meeting its goals: the high cost of resettlement, the unwillingness of local government units to accept low income migrants, difficulty in identifying beneficiaries, and government red tape.

Two pieces of legislation—the Urban Development and Housing Act, passed in 1992, and the Comprehensive Shelter Finance Act, passed in 1994—have not yet provided the quantity of housing needed for the nation's poor.

⁴³EDUCATION

Education is free for primary school and compulsory for six years and is coeducational. English is the main medium of instruction, although Filipino or the local vernacular is used for instruction in the lower primary grades. Primary school lasts for four years, followed by two years of intermediate school. Students may then move on to four years of secondary school. The academic year runs from June to March. Overall, the CIA estimates that the Philippines has a literacy rate of 92.6%. Public expenditure on education represented 2.8% of GDP in 2008.

In 2008 the World Bank estimated that 92% of age-eligible children in the Philippines were enrolled in primary school. Secondary enrollment for age-eligible children stood at 61%. The overall student-to-teacher ratio for primary and secondary schools was 50 to one, with the teacher shortage due in part to poor pay for teachers. It is estimated that about 97% of all students complete their primary education. In 2005, private schools accounted for about 7.6% of primary school enrollment and 19.9% of secondary enrollment. Tertiary enrollment was estimated at 29%. Of those enrolled in tertiary education, there were 100 male students for every 124 female students.

The University of the Philippines, in Quezon City, with branches in major islands, is the leading institution of higher learning. In addition, there are some 50 other universities, including the University of Santo Tomás, founded in 1611 and run by the Dominican friars.

44 LIBRARIES AND MUSEUMS

The National Library in Manila has an estimated 1.2 million volumes. The Filipiniana and Asia Division contains over 100,000 Filipiniana books. Large libraries are in the universities, notably the University of the Philippines (948,000 volumes), the University of Santo Tomás (822,000), the University of the East (177,900), and the University of San Carlos. The International Rice Research Institute in Manila holds 160,000 volumes. There are over 940 public libraries across the country; about 580 are city or municipal libraries.

The National Museum in Manila collects and exhibits materials and conducts research in anthropology, ethnography, archaeology, botany, geology, history, and maps. The University of Santo Tomás Museum contains an art gallery and archaeology and anthropology collections. Three relatively new museums in Manila exhibit primarily art: the Lopez Memorial Museum (1960) exhibits Filipino painters; the Metropolitan Museum (1976) exhibits a variety of art forms; and the Philippines Presidential Museum (1986) exhibits fine and decorative arts. The Ateneo Art Museum in Quezon City features post-World War II Philippine paintings, and there is a Mabini Shrine in Tonauan, featuring relics of Apolinaria Mabina, a leader of Philippine independence.

45 MEDIA

The quality of domestic and inter-island communications in the Philippines is generally adequate, while international service, by way of radiotelephone and submarine cable, is rated as good. Domestic service is dominated by cellular communications. In 2009, the CIA reported that there were some 6.8 million telephone land lines, as well as 81 cellular phones per 100 people.

In 2011, there were 381 FM radio stations, 628 AM radio stations, 4 shortwave radio stations and more than 300 television stations. Radio and television are operated by both government agencies and private concerns.

In 2010, the country had 394,990 Internet hosts, with approximately 7 internet users per 100 citizens. Prominent newspapers in 2010, with circulation numbers listed parenthetically, included *People Tonight* (500,000), *People's Bagong Taliba* (508,000), and *Abante* (350,000), as well as 21 other major newspapers.

The censorship of the press, radio, and television of the Marcos years was revoked under the Aquino administration, however, there are still reports of threats, assaults, and killings of journalists who report on illegal activities such as gambling, logging, prostitution, and the drug trade among powerful individuals or groups, especially outside Manila.

46 ORGANIZATIONS

The Philippine Chamber of Commerce and Industry has branches in metropolitan Manila and other important cities, and there are associations of producers and industrial firms in many areas. The Trade Union Congress of the Philippines, based in Quezon City, represents over 1.4 million people. There are many associations of persons active in such fields as agriculture, architecture, art, biology, chemistry, economics, library service, literature, engineering, medicine, nutrition, veterinary service, and the press. The multinational ASEAN Confederation of Employers is located in Makati City, with that office coordinated in part by the Employers' Confederation of the Philippines.

The Philippine Academy is the oldest and best-known scholarly organization. The National Research Council of the Philippines promotes research and education in physical and social sciences and the humanities. A number of professional associations also promote public research and education in specific fields, particularly those involved in medical research and healthcare, such as the Philippine Medical Association, the Philippine National AIDS Council, and the Philippine Diabetes Association.

National youth organizations include the National Youth Parliament, League of Filipino Students, National Indigenous Youth, Junior Chamber, National Union of Students of the Philippines, Student Christian Federation of the Philippines, Young Christian Workers of The Philippines, Boy Scouts of the Philippines, and YMCA/YWCA. Sports associations are popular throughout the country. The International Bowling Federation is based in Pasig City.

There are several national organizations focusing on women's rights, including the Philippine Association of University Women and the National Commission on the Role of Filipino Women. Kiwanis and Lion's Clubs have programs in the country. The Asian Volunteers' Network for Human Rights in the Philippines is based in Quezon City. International organizations with national chapters include CARE Philippines, Defense for Children International, UNICEF, Habitat for Humanity, Amnesty International, and the Red Cross.

47 TOURISM, TRAVEL, AND RECREATION

The increase in tourism that followed the ouster of Ferdinand Marcos was dampened by the national disasters of the early 1990s. The tourism industry has since rebounded. Manila remains the chief tourist attraction. Other points of interest are the 2,000-year-old rice terraces north of Baguio; Vigan, the old Spanish capital; Cebu, the oldest city; numerous beaches and mountain wilderness areas; and homes formerly owned by the Marcoses. Basketball is the national sport, followed in popularity by baseball and football (soccer). Jai-alai is popular in Manila and Cebu. Cockfighting is legal and often televised. Each tourist must have a valid passport and an onward/return ticket; no visa is required for stays of up to 21 days.

The *Tourism Factbook*, published by the UN World Tourism Organization, reported 3.02 million incoming tourists to the Philippines in 2009, who spent a total of $2.84 billion. Of those incoming tourists, 1.6 million were from East Asia and the Pacific. There were 43,204 hotel beds available in the Philippines, with an occupancy rate of 65%. The estimated daily cost to visit Manila, the capital, was $237. The cost of visiting other cities averaged $188.

48 FAMOUS PERSONS

Filipinos have made their most important marks in the political arena. Foremost are José Rizal (1861–96), a distinguished novelist, poet, physician, linguist, statesman, and national hero; Andrés Bonifacio (1863–97), the leader of the secret Katipunan movement against Spain; and Emilio Aguinaldo y Famy (1869–1964), the commander of the revolutionary forces and president of the revolutionary First Philippine Republic (1899). Notable Filipinos of the 20th century include Manuel Luis Quezon y Molina

(1878–1944), the first Commonwealth president; Ramón Magsaysay (1907–57), a distinguished leader in the struggle with the Hukbalahaps; and Carlos Peña Rómulo (1899–1985), a Pulitzer Prize-winning author and diplomat and the president of the fourth UN General Assembly. Ferdinand Edralin Marcos (1917–89), who won distinction as a guerrilla fighter during the Japanese occupation, was the dominant political figure in the Philippines from his first election to the presidency in November 1965 to his ouster in February 1986. His wife, Imelda Romualdez Marcos (b. 1929), emerged as a powerful force within her husband's government during the 1970s. Leading critics of the Marcos government during the late 1970s and early 1980s were Benigno S. Aquino, Jr. (1933–83) and Jaime Sin (1928–2005), who became the archbishop of Manila in 1974 and a cardinal in 1976. Maria Corazon Cojuangco Aquino (1933–2009), the widow of Benigno, opposed Marcos for the presidency in February 1986 and took office when he went into exile in the same month. Fidel Valdez Ramos (b. 1928) succeeded Corazon Aquino and governed from 1992 until 1998, when he was succeeded by Joseph Estrada (b. 1937). Estrada led the country from 1998–2001.

Lorenzo Ruiz (fl. 17th century) was canonized, along with 15 companion martyrs, as the first Filipino saint. Fernando M. Guerrero (1873–1929) was the greatest Philippine poet in Spanish. Two painters of note were Juan Luna y Novicio (1857–99) and Félix Resurrección Hidalgo y Padilla (1853–1913). Contemporary writers who have won recognition include Claro M. Recto (1890–1960), José García Villa (1914–97), and Carlos Bulosan (1914–56). José A. Estella (1870–1945) is the best-known Filipino composer. Filipino prizefighters have included two world champions, Pancho Villa (Francisco Guilledo, 1901–25) and Ceferino García (1910–81).

⁴⁹DEPENDENCIES

The Philippines has no territories or colonies.

⁵⁰BIBLIOGRAPHY

Altbach, Philip G., and Toru Umakoshi, eds. *Asian Universities: Historical Perspectives and Contemporary Challenges*. Baltimore, Md.: Johns Hopkins University Press, 2004.

Goldoftas, Barbara. *Green Tiger: The Costs of Economic Decline in the Philippines*. New York: Oxford University Press, 2005.

Guillermo, Artemio R. and May Kyi Win. *Historical Dictionary of the Philippines*. Lanham, MD: Scarecrow, 2005.

Leibo, Steven A. *East and Southeast Asia, 2011*. Harpers Ferry, WV: Stryker-Post Publications, 2011.

Nadeau, Kathleen M. *The History of the Philippines*. Westport, CT: Greenwood Press, 2008.

Philippines Investment and Business Guide: Strategic and Practical Information. Washington, DC: International Business Publications USA, 2012.

Rodell, Paul A. *Culture and Customs of the Philippines*. Westport, CT: Greenwood Press, 2002.

Smith, Paul J., ed. *Terrorism and Violence in Southeast Asia: Transnational Challenges to States and Regional Stability*. Armonk, NY: M.E. Sharpe, 2005.

QATAR

State of Qatar

Dawlat Qatar

CAPITAL: Doha (Ad-Dawhah)

FLAG: Maroon with white serrated border at the hoist.

ANTHEM: *Al-Salam Al Amiri (The Peace for the Anthem).*

MONETARY UNIT: The Qatar riyal (QAR) of 100 dirhams was introduced on 13 May 1973. There are coins of 1, 5, 10, 25, and 50 dirhams, and notes of 1, 5, 10, 50, 100, and 500 riyals. QAR1 = US$0.27473 (or US$1 = QAR3.64) as of 2011.

WEIGHTS AND MEASURES: The metric system is the legal standard, although some British measures are still in use.

HOLIDAYS: Independence Day, 3 September; National Day, 18 December. Muslim religious holidays include Eid al-Fitr, Eid al-Adha, and Milad an-Nabi.

TIME: 3 p.m. = noon GMT.

1 LOCATION, SIZE, AND EXTENT

Comprising an area of 11,586 sq km (44730 sq mi), the State of Qatar consists of a peninsula projecting northward into the Persian Gulf, extending about 160 km (100 mi) N–S. The width of the peninsula ranges between 55 km (34 mi) and 90 km (55 mi) E–W. Comparatively, the area occupied by Qatar is slightly smaller than the state of Connecticut. It is bordered by Saudi Arabia and has a total boundary length of 623 km (387 mi), of which 563 km (350 mi) is coastline. Qatar also includes a number of islands, of which the most important is Halul.

Qatar's capital city, Doha, is located on the Persian Gulf coast.

2 TOPOGRAPHY

The terrain is generally flat and rocky, with some hills and sand dunes in the northern and western parts of the country. About 56 km (35 mi) long, the Dukhan anticline rises from the west coast as a chain of hills of up to 100 m (325 ft) in height. Some low cliffs mark the northern end of the east coast. The presence of extensive salt flats at the base of the peninsula supports the theory that Qatar was once an island. Rainwater draining basins in north and central Qatar offer fertile ground for agriculture.

3 CLIMATE

Qatar's summer, from May to October, is extremely hot. Mean temperatures in June are 42°C (108°F), dropping to 15°C (59°F) in winter. The winter is general mild and pleasant from October through May. Humidity is high along the coast. Rainfall is minimal.

4 FLORA AND FAUNA

Vegetation is generally sparse and typical of Persian Gulf desert regions. The World Resources Institute estimated that Qatar has 355 plant species, 8 species of mammals, 151 species of birds, and 11 species of reptiles. The national animal, the oryx, is widely seen, thanks to the help of three wildlife reserves where the once endangered oryx has been bred in captivity and gradually reintroduced to the wild. The gazelle, also once nearly extinct in Qatar, was reintroduced in captivity, and its numbers were reported to exceed 3,500 in 2009. Jerboas (desert rats) and an occasional fox are found. Birds include the flamingo, cormorant, osprey, kestrel, plover, lark, and other migrants. Reptiles include monitors, other lizards, and land snakes. Life in the seas around Qatar is considerable and varied, including prawn, king mackerel, shark, grouper, and swordfish.

5 ENVIRONMENT

Environmental protection responsibility is vested in the Supreme Council for the Environment and National Sanctuaries. The council protects endangered habitat, monitors environmental and wildlife protection policies, and works toward developing sustainable practices. Conservation of oil supplies, preservation of natural wildlife, and efforts to protect marine and air resources from an ongoing problem of desertification were among the council's top priorities in 2011.

Air, water, and land pollution are significant environmental issues in Qatar. Pollution from the oil industry poses a threat to the nation's water. Water resources totaled 0.1 cu km (0.024 cu mi) while water usage was 0.29 cu km (0.07 cu mi) per year. Domestic water usage accounted for 24% of total usage, industrial for 4%, and agricultural for 72%. Per capita water usage totaled 358 cu m

(12,643 cu ft) per year. The United Nations (UN) reported in 2008 that carbon dioxide emissions in Qatar totaled 63,003 kilotons.

The World Resources Institute reported had Qatar had designated 100 hectares (247 acres) of land for protection as of 2006. According to a 2011 report by Earth's Endangered Creatures, there were 68 endangered species in Qatar, including numerous fish and marine creatures, three mammals, and five birds. Endangered animals included the black-tailed godwit, Indo-Pacific humpbacked dolphin, and the saker falcon. Recognition of Qatar's environmental issues has prompted the country to designate 26 February as National Environment Day.

6 POPULATION

The World Bank estimated the population of Qatar in 2011 to be approximately 1,758,793, although roughly three-quarters were foreign workers. In 2011 approximately 1.5% of the population was over 65 years of age, with another 21.8% under 15 years of age. The median age in Qatar was 32.9 years for males and 25.5 years for females. There were 1.99 males for every female in the country. The population's annual rate of change was 0.81%. The projected population for 2025 was 2,100,000. Population density in Qatar was calculated in 2010 at 130 people per sq km (337 people per sq mi).

The UN estimated that 96% of the population lived in urban areas in 2010, and that urban populations had an annual rate of change of 1.6%. The largest urban area was Doha, with a population of 427,000.

7 MIGRATION

Estimates of Qatar's net migration rate, carried out by the CIA in 2011, amounted to -4.94 migrants per 1,000 citizens. The total number of emigrants living abroad was 9,900. The US State Department reported in 2011 that foreign workers made up 85% of Qatar's population and 90% of its work force. Most foreign workers were from South Asia, Southeast Asia, Egypt, the Palestinian territories, Jordan, Lebanon, Syria, Yemen, and Iran. About 8,000 US citizens were estimated to be living in Qatar in 2011, and the total number of immigrants living in Qatar was 1.31 million.

8 ETHNIC GROUPS

The US State Department estimated about 40% of Qatar's population to be Arabs in 2011. Indians made up 20% of the population, Nepalis 13%, Filipinos 10%, Pakistanis 7%, Sri Lankans 5%; and other ethnic backgrounds made up 5%.

9 LANGUAGES

Arabic is the official language, but English was widely spoken, and Farsi is used by smaller groups in Doha.

10 RELIGIONS

Islam, the official religion of Qatar, is practiced by nearly all native Qataris. Most Muslims followed the Sunni tradition in 2011, though some identified with the Shi'a tradition. The constitution and laws provide for freedom of workship and public assembly within limits. Followers are required to follow Qatar laws based on Islamic jurisprudence and rules about how to dress and behave in public. These laws also prohibit proselytizing by non-Muslims, and require religious groups to register with the government for

legal recognition. Catholic, Anglican, Greek Orthodox, Coptic, and Indian Christian churches have been recognized by the government. According to the US State Department, Hindus and Buddhists also have been able to worship in private locations without governmental or societal harassment.

The Ministry of Islamic Affairs oversees the building of mosques, clerical matters, and Islamic education. Additionally, the emir finances travel to Mecca for the Hajj pilgrimage for those who cannot afford the expense.

11 TRANSPORTATION

The CIA reports that Qatar had 7,790 km (4,840 mi) of roads. The country's six airports transported 10.21 million passengers in 2009, according to the World Bank. Qatar has overland truck routes from Europe through Saudi Arabia via the Trans-Arabia Highway and road links with the United Arab Emirates and Oman. Doha International Airport is served by 20 international airlines. Qatar maintains modern deepwater ports at Doha, Umm Sa'id, and Ra's Laffan. A private company, Mowasalat, began bus service in 2005.

Groundbreaking began in 2010 on the world's longest marine causeway. The 40-kilometer (24.85-mile) causeway, known as the Friendship Bridge, will connect the east coast of Bahrain with the west coast of Qatar and will feature passenger and freight rail lines, as well as a marine highway. Analysts estimate the cost of the project to fall between $3 billion and $4 billion, a significant sum shared equally by the governments of Qatar and Bahrain. Project officials expect the project to be completed by 2015.

12 HISTORY

Archaeological evidence shows that human habitation existed in Qatar for many centuries prior to the modern age; however, little is known of Qatar's history until the 18th century. The Al Thani family, forebears of the present rulers, arrived in Qatar then from what is now Saudi Arabia. During the same century, the Al Khalifah family, who currently rule Bahrain, arrived from Kuwait.

In 1868 Great Britain intervened on behalf of the Qatari nobles and negotiated the Perpetual Maritime Truce, signed by Muhammad bin Thani, an accord that terminated the Bahraini claim to Qatar in exchange for a tribute payment. In 1872, however, Qatar fell under Ottoman occupation, and Jasim bin Muhammad bin Thani became Turkish deputy governor of Qatar. Turkish dominion prevailed until the outbreak of World War I (1914–18),and the subsequent withdrawal of the Turks from the Arabian Peninsula. Qatar thereupon established its independence, and in 1916 Sheikh 'Abdallah bin Jasim Al Thani signed a treaty with the United Kingdom granting British protection in exchange for a central role for the United Kingdom in Qatar's foreign affairs. A 1934 treaty further strengthened this relationship. A year later the Qatar Petroleum Company, a consortium of Anglo-Dutch, French, and US interests, received a 75-year oil concession, and discovered oil at Dukhan on the country's west side in 1940. Full-scale exploitation of these resources began in 1949.

Oil revenues brought wealth, social progress, and a wave of new migrants into Qatar. The British announced in 1968 that it would end its treaty relationships with the Gulf sheikdoms. At this point, Qatar attempted to form a union of Arab emirates with eight other states under British protection. The effort failed, however, and Qatar declared independence as a separate entity on 3 September 1971. The United Kingdom, United States, and most nations in the Arab world immediately recognized Qatar's sovereignty, and the country joined the UN and the Arab League soon after independence. The United States opened an embassy in Qatar in March 1973, and the first US ambassador in residence arrived the following year. Qatar also was a founding member of the Gulf Cooperation Council in 1981, and an early member of the Organization of Oil Exporting Countries (OPEC). It established diplomatic relations with China and the Union of Soviet Socialist Republics (USSR) in 1988. Qatar generally has maintained good relations with its Arab neighbors.

Oil production and revenue continued to grow, helping Qatar move from being one of the world's poorest countries to one of its richest. Qatar also completed a natural gas development project in 1991, known as Phase I of the North Field project, at a cost of $1.5 billion. North Field was one of the largest natural gas production fields in the world in 2011 and was shared by Qatar and Iran. The development project allowed Qatar to begin exporting liquefied natural gas to Japan in 1996. The nation has since entered into export agreements with the United Arab Emirates, Spain, Turkey, Italy, the United States, France, South Korea, India, China, Taiwan, and Great Britain. Despite this growth, falling oil prices and production quotas led to a downturn in Qatar's economy in the mid-1990s. The country recovered from the recession, however, and continued to show strong growth in the 21st century and into the second decade.

The Al Thani family maintained its rule of Qatar through independence and continued to rule the country through 2011. Heir apparent Sheikh Khalifa bin Hamad assumed power in February 1972, deposing his cousin, Emir Ahmad, from the throne. Emir Khalifa continued to rule until 27 June 1995 when his son Sheikh Hamad bin Khalifa, who had been ruling as deputy emir, deposed him in a bloodless coup. An unsuccessful counter-coup occurred in 1996. The father and son, however, reconciled shortly after. Emir Hamad announced an intention to move Qatar toward a more democratic regime soon after assuming power. Qatari citizens approved a constitution via a referendum vote in April 2003, and the constitution took effect in June 2005. The constitution guarantees the hereditary rule of the Al Thani family but also allows for municipal and parliamentary elections. Municipal elections first took place in 1999, and the fourth round occurred in 2011. Parliamentary elections were scheduled for 2012. Sheik Hamad bin Jassem al Thani, who is the son of Emir Hamad, held the position of prime minister in 2011, but by mutual approval his younger brother, Sheik Hamad bin Tamim, had been designated as successor to emir.

13 GOVERNMENT

Qatar is a monarchy ruled by an emir. The hereditary ruling family, Al Thani, has held power since Qatar's independence from Britain in 1971 and has received no significant challenge to its rule. The constitution formalizes this rule, but it also establishes an elected legislature. The US State Department described governance in Qatar as influenced by a tradition of consultation and a willingness on the part of the emir to rule by consensus. The emir cannot violate Islamic law, and generally has considered the views of leading Qatari families and religious leaders in making

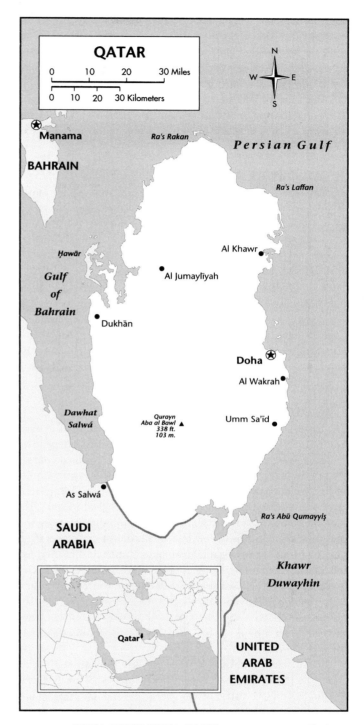

LOCATION: 26°23′ to 24°31′N; 50°43′ to 51°41′ E. BOUNDARY LENGTHS: Persian Gulf coastline, 563 kilometers (350 miles); United Arab Emirates, 45 kilometers (28 miles); Saudi Arabia, 60 kilometers (38 miles).
TERRITORIAL SEA LIMIT: 3 miles.

decisions. Citizens can appeal grievances directly to the emir, and both men and women vote for representatives to the municipal council.

A Basic Law established in 1970 on the eve of Qatar's independence included a bill of rights and provided for a nine-member executive council of ministers (cabinet) and a 30-member legislative advisory council, with members serving three-year terms. The council of ministers, appointed by the emir and led by a prime minister (the head of government), formulates public policy and directs the ministries. The ruling Al Thani family continues to hold a majority of cabinet positions and most of the key posts.

Qataris ratified a new constitution on 29 April 2003, which took effect on 9 June 2005. This constitution provides for a 45-member advisory council, or Majlis al-Shura, of which 30 members are to be elected by the public.

14 POLITICAL PARTIES

No organized political parties or serious opposition movements have formed in Qatar. The first legislative elections for the 45-member Majlis al-Shura (established by the 2003 constitution) were scheduled for 2013.

15 LOCAL GOVERNMENT

Qatar is divided into seven municipalities (*baladiyat*; singular, *baladiyah*): Ad Dawhah, Al Khawr wa adh Dhakhira, Al Wakrah, Ar Rayyan, Ash Shamal, Az Za'yain, and Umm Salal. Municipal councils have been established in Doha, Khor, Ash-Shamal, and several other towns. The councils manage their own planning and development programs, but they remain directly accountable to the Ministry of Municipal Affairs.

16 JUDICIAL SYSTEM

The legal system is based on the Shari'ah (Islamic law). The Basic Law of 1970, however, provided for the creation of an independent judiciary, including a court of appeal, a higher criminal court, a lower criminal court, the civil court, and the labor court. Courts of first instance, appeal, and cassation, as well as an administrative court and constitutional court were established in 2007. The Shari'ah court has jurisdiction in family and criminal cases and may also assume jurisdiction in commercial or civil cases if requested by a Muslim litigant. Muslims and non-Muslims may ask the Shari'ah courts to assume jurisdiction in family, commercial, and civil cases. The losing party in all types of courts may submit his or her case to an appeals court. Under the new judiciary law issued in 2003, the two court systems, civil and Islamic law, were merged under a higher court, the court of cassation, established for appeals.

The judiciary is attached to three different ministries. The civil courts are subordinate to the Justice Ministry. Shari'ah courts fall under the Ministry of Endowments and Islamic Affairs. Prosecutors fall under the Ministry of the Interior.

17 ARMED FORCES

The International Institute for Strategic Studies reported that armed forces in Qatar totaled 11,800 members in 2011. The force is comprised of 8,500 from the army, 1,800 from the navy, and 1,500 members of the air force. Qatar also maintained a public security force of about 8,000 that included a coast guard, national firefighting force, air wing, marine police, and internal security force.

Armed forces represented 1.2% of the labor force in Qatar. Defense spending totaled $15.1 billion and accounted for 10% of gross domestic product (GDP).

Qatar also has established defense pacts with the United States, the United Kingdom, and France. Its forces have participated in collective defense efforts of the Gulf Cooperation Council and supported US military operations during the Persian Gulf War (1990–91) and the Iraq War beginning in 2003. Qatar also took part in military action against the Qadhafi regime in Libya during 2011, including air strikes and the deployment of ground forces to support the rebels who eventually toppled Qadhafi.

18 INTERNATIONAL COOPERATION

Qatar joined the UN on 21 September 1971, and its UN ambassador, Nassir Abdulaziz al-Nasser, was elected in July 2011 as president of the General Assembly for a one-year term. Qatar has been part of the UN Security Council, Human Rights Council, Commission on Sustainable Development and Economic and Social Council. UN Secretary-General Ban Ki-moon told media that the 2011 selection of al-Nasser as General Assembly president signified Qatar's increasingly important presence on the international scene.

Qatar also has participated in ESCWA and several nonregional specialized agencies, such as the FAO, IAEA, the World Bank, ILO, UNESCO, UNIDO, and the WHO. Qatar is a member of the WTO, the Arab Bank for Economic Development in Africa, the Arab Fund for Economic and Social Development, the Arab League, the Organization of the Islamic Conference (OIC), OPEC, OAPEC, G-77, and the GCC. The country has observer status in the OAS. Qatar is part of the Nonaligned Movement.

In environmental cooperation, Qatar is part of the Basel Convention, the Convention on Biological Diversity, CITES, the Kyoto Protocol, the Montréal Protocol, and the UN Conventions on the Law of the Sea, Climate Change, and Desertification.

19 ECONOMY

Historically, the Qatari peninsula was an undeveloped, impoverished area, with a scant living provided by the traditional occupations of pearl diving, fishing, and nomadic herding. In 1940 a major oil discovery was made at Dukhan and, in the ensuing decades, oil has been the dominant factor in the Qatari economy. Oil revenues have provided Qataris with the highest per-capita income, and in 2010 Qatar had the world's highest growth rate, according to the CIA. Although the country's economic policy aims to develop more of Qatar's natural gas reserves and to encourage investment in non-energy sectors, oil and gas accounted for more than 50% of Qatar's GDP, 85% of its export earnings, and 70% of its government revenues in 2011.

Other economic activities remain limited. Agriculture has received considerable attention in recent years, but most food is still imported. The state encourages free enterprise, provided it does not conflict with the public interest. Real property, however, may be acquired only by Qatari nationals.

Qatar's per capita GDP stood at $179,000 in 2010, the highest in the world. In a year when many countries suffered from large contractions in their economies, Qatar's grew at a rate faster than any other nation in the world. Despite the impact of the 2008–09 global financial crisis, Qatari authorities protected local banks with direct investments. The GDP rate of change in Qatar as of 2011 was 16.3%. Inflation stood at -2.4%, and unemployment was reported at 0.5%.

20 INCOME

The CIA estimated that in 2010 the GDP of Qatar was $150.6 billion. The CIA defines GDP as the value of all final goods and services produced within a nation in a given year and computed on the basis of purchasing power parity (PPP) rather than value as measured on the basis of the rate of the exchange based on current dollars. The per capita GDP was estimated at $179,000. The annual growth rate of GDP was 16.3%. The average inflation rate was -2.4%. It was estimated that agriculture accounted for 0.1% of GDP, industry 69.8%, and services 30.1%.

The World Bank reports that in 2009 household consumption in Qatar totaled $20.5 billion or about $24,213 per capita, measured in current US dollars rather than PPP.

As of 2011 the most recent study by the World Bank reported that actual individual consumption in Qatar was 21.9% of GDP and accounted for 0.03% of world consumption. By comparison, the United States accounted for 25.44% of world individual consumption.

21 LABOR

As of 2010, Qatar had a total labor force of 1.242 million people. Unemployment was estimated at 0.5%, one of the lowest rates in the world.

The law allows for only one official trade union for private sector employees, the General Union for the Workers of Qatar. Enterprises with more than 100 citizen workers are permitted to form other organizations or workers committees that are granted the right of collective bargaining, but there are strict government rules involving the bargaining process. While workers do have a right to strike, there are several restrictions that make most strikes illegal. Noncitizens and government sector employees are not permitted to join the union.

The minimum age for employment is 16, with parental consent. There is no minimum wage. As of 2010 the median wage of noncitizen workers was not considered enough to provide a decent standard of living for a worker with a family. The law establishes a workweek of up to 48 hours, but most government offices follow a 36-hour workweek. Overtime pay is required for employees during the Islamic holy month of Ramadan.

22 AGRICULTURE

Roughly 6% of the total land is farmed, and the country's major crops include fruits, vegetables, poultry, beef, fish, and dairy products. Rice is also grown for the domestic market. Cereal production in 2009 amounted to 9,948 tons, fruit production 23,152 tons, and vegetable production 49,013 tons. According to government estimates, Qatar imported about 90% of its food.

Agriculture is constrained by a lack of adequate fertile soil, rainfall, and underground water sources; the aquifers that supply the crops are expected to soon run dry. Treated wastewater has been used for irrigation.

23 ANIMAL HUSBANDRY

The UN Food and Agriculture Organization (FAO) reported that Qatar dedicated 50,000 hectares (123,553 acres) to permanent pasture or meadow in 2009. During that year, the country tended 4.7 million chickens and 7,500 head of cattle. Qatar also had 148,000 sheep, 140,000 goats, 34,000 camels, and 4,900 horses. Meat production in 2009 included about 9,400 tons of lamb and mutton, 5,431 tons of chicken, 2,100 tons of goat, and 342 tons of cattle. Qatar also produced 51 tons of cattle hide.

According to government estimates, less than 4% of cattle, 7% of sheep, 8% of poultry, and 6% of dairy products consumed by Qataris came from domestic sources. The government has initiated several programs to increase food security in Qatar.

24 FISHING

Climate change has threatened fish stocks in the Gulf, and the government's National Food Security program has been monitoring fish stocks and the impacts of climate change. The government has planned to establish fishing regimes and to establish or expand fish farming in Ras Matbakh and other parts of the country.

In 2008 the annual capture totaled 17,688 tons according to the UN FAO. The government estimated fish self-sufficiency at 96% and annual per capita consumption at 12kg (26.4 lbs).

25 FORESTRY

There are no forests in Qatar. Imports of forestry products totaled about 42,000 tons in 2010.

26 MINING

Much of Qatar's economy is based on the production of natural gas, petrochemicals, crude oil, and refined petroleum products. Among other exploitable minerals, production in 2009 included limestone, estimated at 1.1 million metric tons; hydraulic cement, estimated at 4.1 million metric tons; nitrogen (ammonia), 2.04 metric tons; and nitrogen (urea), estimated at 1.38 million metric tons. The country also produced clay, gypsum, sand, and gravel.

27 ENERGY AND POWER

The CIA reported in 2009 that Qatar produced 19.18 billion kWh of electricity and consumed 18.79 billion kWh. All energy came from fossil fuels.

Qatar has large reserves of oil and the world's third-largest natural gas reserves, trailing only Russia and Iran. Nearly all of Qatar's natural gas reserves are in the North Dome Field, considered to be the largest natural gas field (unassociated with oil) in the world. It is also emerging as a major exporter of liquefied natural gas (LNG), and is a member of the Organization of Petroleum Exporting Countries (OPEC). Qatar's largest-producing oil field is the onshore Dukhan field on the western coast of the peninsula. Offshore production accounts for about 40% of the total, mainly from three of Qatar's six offshore fields about 50 miles from the coast.

Oil consumption totaled 166,000 barrels a day in 2010. Oil production totaled 1.437 million barrels a day. Most of the oil produced was exported, mainly to Japan and other Asian countries. In 2011 proved oil reserves were estimated at 25.3 billion barrels.

Natural gas consumption in 2010 was estimated at 21.89 billion cubic meters while production was estimated at 116.7 billion cubic meters. Proved reserves of natural gas were estimated at 25.37 trillion cubic meters in 2011.

28 INDUSTRY

The discovery and exploitation of oil in the 1940s established the initial structure of Qatar's industrial base. Oil continued to account for the bulk of the country's GDP in 2011, but the government's Ministry of Business and Trade has been making a strong effort to diversify its industry. The ministry encouraged foreign investment in a variety of industrial projects including liquefied natural gas, infrastructure, and educational facilities. There were three primary industrial centers in 2011: Mesaieed, an industrial city and oil exporting port; Ras Laffan, a center for LNG exports; and Dukhan, an area administered by the state-run Qatar Petroleum for oil.

The main offices of most of Qatar's industrial companies are housed in Mesaieed Industrial City. These companies include Qatar Petroleum, Qatar Fertilizer Company, Qatar Steel, Qatar Petrochemical Company, Qatar Vinyl Company, Qatar Chemicals Company, and Qatar Aluminum.

Industrial production grew 27.1% in 2010, according to the CIA. Key industries included liquefied natural gas; crude oil production and refining; commercial ship repair; and production of ammonia, fertilizers, petrochemicals, steel reinforcing bars, and cement.

Major construction projects in Qatar included the Doha New Port, scheduled for completion in 2014; a comprehensive rail project that consisted of the Doha Metro Network and new passenger and cargo train service; the Bahrain-Qatar Friendship Bridge; a planned city being built at al Khor by the Barwa Group at a cost of $35 billion; and an Entertainment City consisting of hotels, theme parks, theatres, housing, and a snow dome.

29 SCIENCE AND TECHNOLOGY

The World Bank reported in 2009 that there were no patent applications in science and technology in Qatar. The Office of Academic Research oversees scientific, engineering, and technology research projects underway at Qatar University. Projects underway in 2011 included: work on designing new cooling drums for the manufacture of ready-mix concrete; development of an assistive computerized system to facilitate learning for children with special needs; the development of voice recognition computer software in Arabic; and continued work on a project to develop a family of biodegradable polymers to treat cancer.

30 DOMESTIC TRADE

Qatar's relatively affluent society has led to the development of many retail establishments, including fast food and casual dining franchises, fitness centers, car rental agencies, computer learning centers, clothing shops, real estate brokerages, and language learning centers. The government requires that foreign investors form a relationship with a commercial agent of Qatari nationality and that franchises of international businesses have a Qatari sponsor. Private supermarkets accounted for about 60% of grocery sales in Qatar, and consumer cooperatives accounted for 80% of the rest of such sales.

Principal Trading Partners – Qatar (2010)

(In millions of US dollars)

Country	Total	Exports	Imports	Balance
World	83,500.0	61,500.0	22,000.0	39,500.0
Japan	20,978.0	19,723.0	1,255.0	18,468.0
South Korea	11,352.0	10,832.0	520.0	10,312.0
India	5,880.0	5,468.0	412.0	5,056.0
Singapore	5,222.0	4,998.0	224.0	4,774.0
United Kingdom	4,104.0	2,742.0	1,362.0	1,380.0
United States	3,923.0	443.0	3,480.0	-3,037.0
China	3,169.0	2,223.0	946.0	1,277.0
Italy	3,080.0	1,877.0	1,203.0	674.0
Thailand	2,227.0	1,934.0	293.0	1,641.0
Germany	2,163.0	130.0	2,033.0	-1,903.0

(…) data not available or not significant.

(n.s.) not specified.

SOURCE: *2011 Direction of Trade Statistics Yearbook*, New York: United Nations, 2011.

Normal business hours are from 8 a.m. to 12 noon and from 4 p.m. to 8 p.m., Sunday through Thursday. Government offices are open from 7 a.m. to 2 p.m., Sunday through Thursday. Banks are open from 8 a.m. to 12:30 p.m. Private-sector business hours are usually 8 a.m. to 12:30 p.m. and 4 p.m. to 7:30 p.m., Saturday through Thursday. Most businesses are closed on Friday.

31 FOREIGN TRADE

Qatar imported $20.94 billion worth of goods and services in 2010, while exporting $72.04 billion worth of goods and services. Major import partners in 2010 were the United States, 15.5%; Germany, 9%; the United Arab Emirates, 7.3%; South Korea, 6.5%; the United Kingdom, 6.1%; Japan, 5.6%; Saudi Arabia, 5.4%; Italy, 5.3%; France, 4.5%; and China, 4.2%. Major export partners were Japan, 30.3%; South Korea, 13.1%; India, 8%; Singapore, 7.7%; and the United Kingdom, 4.2%.

Qatar's most important commodity exports were liquefied natural gas, petroleum products, fertilizers, and steel. Its imports included machinery and transport equipment, food, and chemicals.

32 BALANCE OF PAYMENTS

The CIA reported that Qatar had a current account balance of $15.04 billion in 2010, compared with $5.672 billion in 2009. Exports totaled $72.04 billion in 2010 and $48.31 billion in 2009, while imports totaled $20.94 billion in 2010 and $22.45 billion in 2009. The country's external debt in 2010 totaled $75.13 billion. Economy Watch predicted that Qatar's current account balance would reach $42.21 billion by 2015.

33 BANKING AND SECURITIES

In 2010 there were 18 banks were operating in Qatar, 11 of which were Qatari institutions, and 7 of which were foreign branch banks. Three of Qatar's national banks operated as Islamic institutions while the remaining were commercial banks.

The CIA reported Qatar's stock of narrow money (the amount of total currency in circulation) at $15.98 billion in 2010. Total assets held in Qatar banks totaled $65.95 billion. Publicly traded

Public Finance – Qatar (2009)		
(In millions of riyals, budgetary central government figures)		
Revenue and Grants	**169,078**	**100.0%**
Tax revenue	70,928	41.9%
Social contributions	...	...
Grants	...	...
Other revenue	98,150	58.1%
Expenditures	**114,575**	**100.0%**
General public services	35,127	30.7%
Defense	7,092	6.2%
Public order and safety	6,204	5.4%
Economic affairs	28,173	24.6%
Environmental protection	468	0.4%
Housing and community amenities	2,327	2.0%
Health	6,813	5.9%
Recreational, culture, and religion	13,348	11.7%
Education	14,255	12.4%
Social protection	739	0.6%

(…) data not available or not significant.

SOURCE: *Government Finance Statistics Yearbook 2010,* Washington, DC: International Monetary Fund, 2010.

stock shares totaled $123.6 billion, and domestic credit extended by banks to both the public and private sector was $89.61 billion. The Doha Securities Market was reorganized in 2009 as the Qatar Exchange, which serves as the primary stock market for Qatar. According to a 2010 annual report issued by the Qatar Central Bank, gold holdings totaled $566 million.

On 30 May 2010 Qatar's central bank announced that it would issue its first-ever local currency bond in an effort to diversify its funding away from the US dollar. The move would also give central bankers greater tools to soak up excesses in liquidity, officials said, which develop when there are "hot money inflows" (i.e., high gas prices). Qatar's central bank stated that it would sell $1.1 billion worth of riyal-denominated conventional and Islamic bonds to its banks.

34 INSURANCE

In 2011 there were nine insurance companies represented in Qatar, four of which were foreign owned. The Qatar National Insurance Company has the largest market share and manages the government's insurance business.

35 PUBLIC FINANCE

In 2010 the budget of Qatar included $44.62 billion in public revenue and $29.69 billion in public expenditures. The budget surplus amounted to 12.1% of GDP. Public debt was 10.3% of GDP, with $75.13 billion of the debt held by foreign entities.

Revenues from oil and gas constituted about 70% of total government income in 2011. From 1986 to 1990 the government ran a deficit due to the drop in oil revenues from falling prices. These deficits resulted in the procrastination of payments by the government, which created a financial difficulty for many private companies. To address this problem the government took measures to boost the oil industry, which achieved positive results by the late 1990s.

36 TAXATION

Qatar has cut its corporate income tax rate to 10% in 2010, ending a practice of levying between 5% and 35% on foreign companies. Qatari companies do not pay any tax. The only other commercial tax as of 2011 was a trade license renewal tax, assessed annually at QAR100 ($27). There was no personal income tax.

37 CUSTOMS AND DUTIES

Customs duties included 5% on most processed foods and 100% on cigarettes and other tobacco products in 2010, according to the US State Department. No import duties are levied for live animals, fresh fruits and vegetables, seafood, grains, flours, tea, sugar, spices, and seeds for plantings. Qatar banned imports of U.S. beef from 2005 through mid-2008, and continued in 2011 to prohibit the importation of pork products for cultural reasons.

Qatar is a member of the World Trade Organization and the Gulf Cooperation Council (GCC), through which it signed a free trade agreement that provides duty-free access to goods from GCC member nations.

38 FOREIGN INVESTMENT

The CIA reported foreign direct investment in Qatar to be $26.38 billion as of 31 December 2010, compared with $20.71 billion a year earlier.

The government limits foreign ownership of local companies to 49% to encourage majority-Qatari ownership in national firms. This restriction does not include investments in agricultural, industry, health care, education, tourism, natural resource development, technical and information consultancy, distribution services, and cultural, sports, and entertainment areas. Investments must be approved by the government. Generally, Qatar has prohibited foreign investment in commercial agencies and real estate, although it has allowed foreigners to own real estate in select areas such as the West Bay Lagoon, Al-Khor district, and Pearl of the Gulf Development.

The US State Department reported in 2010 that Qatar had attracted an estimated $100 billion in investment in its energy sector during the preceding decade, with as much as $70 billion of that amount coming from the United States. In addition, it was expected that Qatar would spend up to $100 billion on infrastructure projects in preparation for hosting the 2022 FIFA World Cup.

39 ECONOMIC DEVELOPMENT

Qatar's economic development policy, as outlined in its National Vision 2030 statement, continues to seek a more diversified industrial and commercial base so as to reduce its dependence on oil. The government called in 2011 for responsible exploitation of its existing oil and natural gas reserves. The government also sought to encourage small-scale agricultural development, fishing, and light industrial enterprises.

Qatar has planned for the construction of several new petrochemical plants in its industrial Mesaieed region through joint ventures between its state-owned Qatar Petroleum company and US, European, and Japanese firms. US companies also have supplied equipment to the country's oil and gas industry.

While Qatar has encouraged foreign investment, it has also pursued a "Qatarization" program that aims to move Qatari nationals into leadership positions. Foreign-educated Qataris have begun to return home to assume positions previously held by expatriates.

The government has described its diversification efforts as being focused on technical and information industries, knowledge-based services, education, and a strong infrastructure. The government has encouraged the development of a world-class educational system and has encouraged foreign universities to establish branch campuses in its Education City complex. As of 2011 Cornell University had established a degree-granting branch medical school campus in Doha, and Texas A&M, Carnegie Mellon University, the Virginia Commonwealth University School of Design, Georgetown School of Foreign Service, and Northwestern University had opened branch campuses in the Education City complex.

40 SOCIAL DEVELOPMENT

Many of those residing in Qatar are foreigners who do not hold citizenship rights. Although women hold the right to vote and to run for public office, Shari'ah law has influenced Qatar rules and often has restricted the activities of Qatari women. However, women have been held high public office positions in such roles as heading the Qatar Foundation, General Authority for Museums, and Qatar University. Women also have served on the Supreme Council for Family Affairs, the Central Municipal Council, and as judges in the courts of first instance.

No laws exist regarding domestic violence. The Qatari Foundation reported that 109 cases of domestic abuse were brought to its attention in 2010. Foreign embassies also have reported cases of rape and abuse of domestic workers. A 2007 study by Qatar University reported 2,778 females claiming to have been victims of physical abuse. In response, the Supreme Council for Family Affairs established a shelter in 2007 to accommodate abused women. The shelter also offers women financial assistance, legal aid, and counseling.

Some foreigners have been sentenced to flogging in accordance with Islamic law for smoking or drinking in public, practices that go against Islamic custom.

41 HEALTH

According to the CIA, life expectancy in Qatar was 76 years in 2011. The country spent 2.5% of its GDP on healthcare. There were 28 physicians, 74 nurses and midwives, and 14 hospital beds per 10,000 inhabitants. The fertility rate was 2.43 children per woman, while the infant mortality rate was 12 deaths per 1,000 live births. In 2008 the maternal mortality rate, according to the World Bank, was 8 deaths per 100,000 births. It was estimated that 99% of children were vaccinated against measles. The CIA has calculated the HIV/AIDS prevalence rate in Qatar to be less than 0.1% in 2009.

42 HOUSING

Qatar's Department of Housing oversees housing policies for the government. The department has initiatives aimed at different family sizes and income levels, and has a goal of ensuring that every family has suitable housing. An ambitious development known as The Pearl–Qatar was underway in 2011. This called for the construction of 18,000 luxury housing units on a man-made island along the country's eastern shore. The project allowed international investors a freehold title ownership, and the first residents

began to occupy the area in 2009. When complete, the Pearl will include beachfront villas, town homes, luxury apartments, penthouses, five-star hotels, marinas, and upscale restaurants and retail establishments.

43 EDUCATION

Education is compulsory and free for all residents 6–16 years of age. All children receive free books, meals, transportation, clothing, and boarding facilities if required. Primary school covers six years of study. This is followed by three years of general preparatory school or religious preparatory school; the latter is only available for boys. Secondary school programs cover a three-year course of studies. Girls are permitted to attend general academic studies at the secondary level, but only boys are given the option of attending religious, commercial, or technical secondary schools.

In 2009 the World Bank estimated that 93% of age-eligible children in Qatar were enrolled in primary school. Secondary enrollment for age-eligible children stood at 77%. Tertiary enrollment was estimated at 10%. Of those enrolled in tertiary education, there were 100 male students for every 605 female students. Overall, the CIA estimated that Qatar had a literacy rate of 89%.

The leading higher education institution is the University of Qatar, founded at Doha in 1973. In addition to faculties of education, science, humanities, social sciences, Islamic studies, and engineering, the university offers a Language Teaching Institute (founded in 1972) and a Regional Training Center, established in 1979 with UN Development Program technical assistance. Scholarships for higher education abroad are given to all who qualify.

Public expenditures on education were estimated at 3.3% of GDP in 2005.

44 LIBRARIES AND MUSEUMS

The Qatar National Library, founded in 1962, is one of the oldest national libraries in the Persian Gulf region. It was the main library in Qatar in 2011, although plans were underway to build a new library adjacent to the government's National Council for Culture, Arts, and Heritage at a cost of $120 million. Qatar University also maintains a library.

Museums in Qatar included the Qatar National Museum, Maritime Museum, Weaponry Museum, al-Khor Museum, al-Zubarah Fort Museum, and the Doha Fort Museum.

45 MEDIA

Qatar serves as the base for al-Jazeera, a highly influential pan-Arab and international news television network. The Qatari government owns the media outlet, which began broadcasting in 2006. Although al-Jazeera is highly praised for its coverage of Middle Eastern affairs, its editors avoid any direct criticism of the Al Thani family. Although Qatar eased its censorship rules in the mid-1990s, authorities have continued to filter political criticism, material deemed offensive to Islam, and pornographic content.

In addition to al-Jazeera, there are three state-run media organizations—Qatar TV, Qatar Broadcasting Service (a radio service), and the English-language Qatar News Service. The country also has six newspapers, three of which are English-language presses, six FM radio stations, five AM radio stations, and one shortwave radio station. *The Economist* reported that Qatar had nearly 564,000 Internet users by March 2011.

Qatar enjoys excellent international telecommunications service based on a mix of troposcatter radio, submarine cable, microwave radio relay, and satellite ground station communications. In 2009 there were 285,300 main phone lines and 2.4 million mobile cellular phones in use.

46 ORGANIZATIONS

The Qatar Chamber of Commerce was founded in Doha in 1963. Numerous social service organizations also exist in the country, including Qatar Charity Foundation, Qatar Center for Voluntary Activities, Qatar Red Crescent, and Shafallah Center Qatar. The quasi-governmental Qatar Foundation also serves as an umbrella for many cultural and social organizations including The Heritage Library, Qatar Philharmonic Orchestra, Qatar Music Academy, and the Al Shaqab equestrian center.

47 TOURISM, TRAVEL, AND RECREATION

The *Tourism Factbook*, published by the UN World Tourism Organization, reported 1.66 million incoming tourists to Qatar who spent a total of $874 million in 2009. Of those incoming tourists, there were 628,000 from the Middle East and 329,000 from elsewhere. There were 11,308 hotel beds available in Qatar, which had an occupancy rate of 50%. The estimated daily cost to visit Doha, the capital, was $341.

The Qatar Tourism Authority has been developing a plan to make the country a destination for business travelers. The plan includes an investment of $17 billion over five years in hotel and conference center developments, beginning in 2011. The Doha Exhibitions Center hosted 25 gatherings in 2009, and two new facilities were set to open by the end of 2012. Doha also has a Museum of Islamic Art and other museums, mosques, and historic sites. Other sites of interest to tourists are Sealine Beach Resort, Palm Tree Island, and Entertainment City (the Kingdom of Aladdin). Qatar hosted the Asian Nations Cup in 2011 and was awarded the privilege of hosting the FIFA International World Cup in 2022.

48 FAMOUS PERSONS

Sheikh Khalifa bin Hamad Al Thani (b. 1932) was emir of Qatar from 1972 to 1995. The heir apparent Sheikh Hamad bin Khalifa Al Thani (b. 1948) became emir in June 1995 following a bloodless coup that ousted his father. Sheikh Tamim bin Hamad Al Thani was designated heir apparent in 2003.

49 DEPENDENCIES

The State of Qatar has no territories or colonies.

50 BIBLIOGRAPHY

Chaddock, David. *Qatar: The Business Travellers' Handbook.* Northampton, Mass.: Interlink Books, 2003.

Held, Colbert C. *Middle East Patterns: Places, Peoples, and Politics.* 4th ed. Boulder, Colo.: Westview Press, 2006.

Hourani, Albert Habib. *A History of the Arab Peoples.* Cambridge, Mass.: Belknap Press of Harvard University Press, 2002.

Miles, Hugh. *Al-Jazeera: The Inside Story of the Arab News Channel That Is Challenging the West.* New York: Grove Press, 2005.

Qatar Investment and Business Guide: Strategic and Practical Information. Washington, DC: International Business Publications USA, 2012.

Qatar: Live, Work, Explore. Brentford, Eng.: Portfolio, 2011.

Seddon, David (ed.). *A Political and Economic Dictionary of the Middle East.* Philadelphia: Routledge/Taylor and Francis, 2004.

Tétreault, Mary Ann, Gwenn Okruhlik, et al. *Political Change in the Arab Gulf States.* Boulder, CO: Lynne Rienner Publishers, 2011.

SAMOA

Independent State of Samoa
Malo Sa'oloto Tuto'atasi o Samoa i Sisifo

CAPITAL: Apia

FLAG: The upper-left quarter of the flag is blue and bears five white, five-rayed stars representing the Southern Cross; the remainder of the flag is red.

ANTHEM: *O le Fu'a o le Sa'olotoga o Samoa (The Banner of Freedom)*.

MONETARY UNIT: The Samoan tala (WST) is a paper currency of 100 sene. There are coins of 1, 2, 5, 10, 20, and 50 sene and 1 tala, and notes of 2, 5, 10, 20, and 100 talas. WST1 = US$0.438500 (or US$1 = WST2.80) as of 2011.

WEIGHTS AND MEASURES: The metric system is in official use, but British weights and measures are still used in some areas.

HOLIDAYS: New Year's, 1–2 January; Independence Holidays (first three workdays of June); Anzac Day, 25 April; Christmas Day, 25 December; Boxing Day, 26 December. Movable religious holidays are Good Friday, Easter Monday, and Whitmonday.

TIME: 2 a.m. = noon GMT.

¹LOCATION, SIZE, AND EXTENT

Samoa consists of the islands of Savai'i and Upolu and several smaller islands, of which only Manono and Apolima are inhabited. The country, situated almost centrally both in the Pacific Ocean and among the South Sea islands, has a total land area of 2,944 sq km (1,137 sq mi), extending 150 km (93 mi) ESE–WNW and 39 km (24 mi) NNE–SSW. Savai'i and Upolu, separated by the Apolima Strait at a distance of nearly 18 km (11 mi), have a combined coastline of 403 km (250 mi). Comparatively, the area occupied by Samoa is slightly smaller than the state of Rhode Island.

For more than 100 years, world maps have placed Samoa on the east side of the International Date Line, as the nation aligned its clocks and calendar to coincide with same-day business hours in Europe and the United States. However, this has placed the nation's clocks more than 20 hours behind those of Australia and New Zealand, now Samoa's largest trading partners, making it more challenging to conduct business with those countries, since Friday in Samoa is Saturday in New Zealand and Monday in Australia is Sunday in Samoa. In order to align itself more closely with these major partners, the government decided to jump one day ahead by realigning itself to the west of the International Date Line. The government contacted the cartographers of Collins Bartholomew in April 2011 to begin the process of marking the change on the 2012 editions of world time zone maps. On 29 December 2011 Samoa's clocks were reset from 21 hours behind those of Sydney, Australia, to 3 hours ahead, meaning that Samoa effectively skipped 30 December and went directly to 31 December.

²TOPOGRAPHY

Located on the Pacific tectonic plate near the boundary of the Australian Plate, the country lies within the "Ring of Fire," a seismically active band surrounding the Pacific Ocean. The islands are, therefore, volcanic in origin, with coral reefs surrounding most of them. Rugged volcanic ranges rise on both islands. Volcanoes on Savai'i include Mauga Afi and Mauga Silisili, the latter of which is the highest point in Samoa, with an elevation of 1,857 m (6,094 ft). Mauga Fito is the highest point on Upolu, with an elevation of 1,116 m (3,660 ft). There are numerous swift-flowing, seasonal rivers on both islands.

Apolima is a volcanic crater whose wall is pierced by a passage that connects its harbor with the sea. Manono, about 70 m (230 ft) high, consists chiefly of coral sand. These two islands lie within the Apolima Strait. There are also a number of underwater volcanoes in the region.

Its location on the Ring of Fire makes the nation vulnerable to earthquakes and related events. On 29 September 2009, a deadly tsunami swept over Samoa, causing the death of at least 135 people and leaving more than 150 injured. The tsunami was triggered by an 8.3-magnitude earthquake in the South Pacific, striking about 190 kilometers (120 miles) to the south of Apia at a depth of about 33 kilometers (20 miles). There were three additional aftershocks, each measuring a magnitude of at least 5.6. The disaster struck too quickly for evacuations to take place and officials reported that some residents ignored warning sirens, believing they were false alarms. Villages along the west coast of Samoa were leveled and numerous homes and buildings inland were destroyed or severely damaged.

³CLIMATE

The climate is tropical, but because of the oceanic surroundings, temperature ranges are not considerable. The hottest month is December, and the coldest is July; the mean daily temperature is about 27°C (81°F). The year is divided into a dry season (May to

October) and a wet season (November to April). Rainfall averages 287 cm (113 in) annually, and the average yearly relative humidity is 83%. Although the islands lie outside the normal track of hurricanes, severe storms occurred in 1889, 1966, and 1968. Trade winds from the southeast are fairly constant throughout the dry season.

4 FLORA AND FAUNA

The World Resources Institute estimates that Samoa is home to 6 species of mammals, 49 species of birds, and 19 species of reptiles. These figures reflect the total number of distinct species residing in the country, not the number of endemic species. Lush vegetation covers much of the land. Along the coast there are mangrove forests, pandani, Barringtonia, hibiscus, and strand vegetation, commonly found throughout the Pacific. The adjacent lowland forest, which originally stretched inland over the lower slopes of the mountains, has been cut down extensively on Upolu and in more limited areas on Savai'i. Inland and at higher elevations, the rain forests contain trees and lianas of many genera and species. The higher elevations of Savai'i contain moss forests and mountain scrub.

Of the bird species, about 16 are seabirds, and many visit Samoa only during the breeding season. Land birds include small doves, parrots, pigeons, and wild ducks. The most interesting bird, scientifically, is the tooth-billed pigeon (Didunculus strigirostris Peale), which some ornithologists regard as the connecting link between bird life of the present and the tooth-billed birds of zoological antiquity.

The only indigenous mammals in Samoa are the rat (Mus exulans Peale) and the flying fox (Pteropus samoensis Peale). Several species of birds and mammals, chiefly domesticated, have been introduced by the Samoans and Europeans. Two species of snakes, several different lizards, and the gecko are found. Insect life includes many species of moths, beetles, spiders, and ants. The mosquito (Stegomyia pseudoscutellaris) is a carrier of human filaria.

5 ENVIRONMENT

Samoa's environmental problems include soil erosion, damage to the nation's forests, and the need for protection of its wildlife. The lack of adequate sewage disposal facilities, as well as siltation and industrial by-products, threaten the nation's marine habitats. Samoa's water supply is too small to support its current population. The United Nations (UN) reported in 2008 that carbon dioxide emissions in Samoa totaled 161 kilotons.

In February 2010, top officials from Samoa and thirteen other developing Pacific island nations and dependencies met in Vanuatu to discuss the progress made in addressing some of the issues unique to these low-lying, developing island states. These include climate change, sea-level rise, natural disasters, remoteness from major markets, and poverty. Another key objective of the meeting was to address the progress each nation had made in adopting the 2005 Mauritius Strategy, the only global blueprint that exists to combat the development challenges of small-island developing states.

The World Resources Institute reported that Samoa had designated 5,700 hectares (14,085 acres) of land for protection as of 2006. Lake Lanoto'o (Goldfish Lake), located on Upolu, is a Ramsar wetland site. The deep lake fills a volcanic crater with pea-green-colored water; wild goldfish inhabit its shorelines. According to a 2011 report issued by the International Union for Conservation of Nature and Natural Resources (IUCN), threatened species include 2 types of mammals, 6 species of birds, 3 types of reptiles, 12 species of fish, one type of mollusk, and two species of plants. Threatened species include the humpbacked whale, albacore tuna, hawksbill turtle, Samoan moorhen, and Samoan flying fox.

6 POPULATION

The US Central Intelligence Agency (CIA) estimated the population of Samoa in 2011 to be approximately 193,161, which placed it at number 176 in population among the 196 nations of the world. In 2011, approximately 5.2% of the population was over 65 years of age, with another 35.4% under 15 years of age. The median age in Samoa was 22.1 years. There were 1.05 males for every female in the country. The population's annual rate of change was 0.6%. The projected population for the year 2025 was 190,000. Population density in Samoa was calculated at 63 people per sq km (163 people per sq mi).

The UN estimated that 20% of the population lived in urban areas, and that urban populations had no change during the previous year. The largest urban area was Apia, with a population of 36,000.

7 MIGRATION

Under German colonial rule, many Chinese laborers were imported to work on plantations. More recently, there has generally been a net annual loss of population through migration. Emigration occurs mainly through students going to New Zealand to continue their education and Samoans seeking work there. In addition, several thousand Samoans live in American Samoa and other parts of the United States.

The CIA estimated Samoa's net migration rate at -11.16 migrants per 1,000 citizens in 2011. The total number of emigrants living abroad was about 150,000, and the total number of immigrants living in Samoa was 9,000.

8 ETHNIC GROUPS

Samoans compose about 92.6% of the total population. The Samoans are the second-largest branch of the Polynesians, a people occupying the scattered islands of the Pacific from Hawaii to New Zealand and from eastern Fiji to Easter Island. Most of the remaining Samoans are of mixed Samoan and European or Asian descent. Euronesians (persons of European and Polynesian descent) make up 7% of the total, and Europeans constitute 0.4%. For many years, all inhabitants of Samoa were accorded a domestic status as Samoan or European. Residents are now officially classed as either citizens or foreigners. Among Samoan citizens, however, the distinction between persons of Samoan or European status is still recognized. Most Samoans live in foreshore villages, while non-Samoans predominate in Apia and its environs.

9 LANGUAGES

Samoan is the universal language, but both Samoan and English are official. Some Chinese is also spoken. Most of the part-Samoans and many others speak English, and it is taught in the schools.

10 RELIGIONS

Over 99% of Samoans profess some form of Christianity, and religious observance is strong among all groups. The Congregational Christian Church of Western Samoa, a successor to the London Missionary Society, is self-supporting and the largest religious body in the country, representing about 33.6% of the population. The Roman Catholic (19.4%) and Methodist churches (14.3%) also have large followings. The Church of Jesus Christ of Latter-Day Saints (Mormons, 13.2%), Assemblies of God (6.9%), and Seventh-Day Adventists (3.5%) have grown in recent years. Other Christian groups include Jehovah's Witnesses, the Congregational Church of Jesus, Nazarenes, nondenominational Protestants, Baptists, the Worship Center, Peace Chapel, Samoa Evangelism, Elim Church, and Anglicans. The country is home to one of seven Baha'i Houses of Worship in the world. There are small numbers of Muslims, Jews, Buddhists, and Hindus. The constitution provides for religious freedom but describes the state as "based on Christian principles and Samoan customs." Religious groups do not have to register with the government. Good Friday, Easter Monday, White Monday (Children's Day), and Christmas are observed as national holidays.

11 TRANSPORTATION

Most roads are on the northern coast of Upolu. Buses and taxis provide public transportation. According to a 2001 report from the CIA (representing the latest figures available as of 2011), there are about 2,337 km (1,452 mi) of roads, of which 332 km (206 mi) are paved.

Diesel-powered launches carry passengers and freight around the islands, and small motor vessels maintain service between Apia and Pago Pago in American Samoa. Fortnightly cargo and passenger connections are maintained with New Zealand, and scheduled transpacific services connect Samoa with Australian, Japanese, United Kingdom, and North American ports. Apia is the principal commercial port. Three other deepwater ports are located at Mulifaunua, Salelologa, and Asau. As of 2010, there were two vessels of 1,000 GRT or more in the merchant fleet.

As of 2010, there were four airports, one of which had a paved runway. Faleolo Airport, 35 km (22 mi) west of Apia, is the principal air terminal. Polynesian Airlines provides daily air connections with Pago Pago and regularly scheduled flights to other Pacific destinations; through Pago Pago there are connecting flights to New Zealand, Australia, and the United States. Air Samoa and Samoa Aviation provide internal air service between Upolu and Savai'i, and Hawaiian Airlines provides direct service between Honolulu and Faleolo and commuter service between Faleolo and Pago Pago.

12 HISTORY

Archaeological evidence on Upolu indicates that Samoa was colonized by maritime traders of the Lapita culture at least as early as the 1st millennium BC. From the mid-13th century AD, genealogies, important titles, traditions, and legends give considerable information on the main political events. The first Europeans to sight the islands were the Dutch explorer Jacob Roggeveen in 1722 and the French navigator Louis de Bougainville in 1768. But the world knew little about Samoa until after the arrival of the

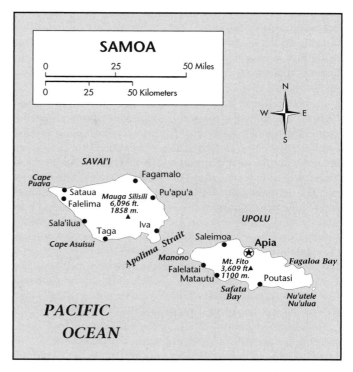

LOCATION: 13° to 15°S; 171° to 173° W. BOUNDARY LENGTHS: Savai'i 188 kilometers (117 miles); Upolu coastline, 183 kilometers (114 miles). TERRITORIAL SEA LIMIT: 12 miles.

missionary John Williams in 1830 and the establishment of the London Missionary Society.

Williams' arrival coincided with the victory of one group of chiefs over another, ending a series of violent internecine wars. Runaway sailors and other Europeans had already settled among the Samoans and assisted the chiefs in their campaigns. Whalers also visited the islands, and from time to time the warships of the great powers visited Apia to oversee the activities of whaling crews and settlers. Naval officers and missionaries began to consult with the dominant group of chiefs as if it represented a national government and treated its leader as a king. In time, semiofficial representatives of Great Britain and the United States were stationed in Apia. Between 1847 and 1861, the United States appointed a commercial agent, and Britain and the city of Hamburg appointed consuls.

Factional rivalries took a new turn as British, US, and German consular agents, aided sometimes by their countries' warships, aligned themselves with various paramount chiefs. Intrigues among the chiefs and jealousies among the representatives of the great powers culminated in civil war in 1889. In the Berlin Treaty, which followed, Britain, the United States, and Germany set up a neutral and independent government under King Malietoa Laupepea, and their consuls were authorized to constitute Apia as a separate municipality. The death of King Malietoa in 1898 led to a dispute over succession, and the three powers intervened once again. In 1899, they abolished the kingship, and in 1900, they signed a series of conventions that divided the Samoan islands into American and German protectorates. The German protectorate, encompassing the western portion of the islands, is what would eventually become independent Samoa. The German administration continued to experience difficulties, leading to the exile of several Samoan leaders and the suspension of others from office. With the outbreak of World War I in 1914, New Zealand military forces occupied Samoa, and from 1919 to 1946, New Zealand administered the islands as a mandate of the League of Nations.

In 1946, a trusteeship agreement was approved by the UN General Assembly, and New Zealand formally committed itself to promoting the development of Samoa toward ultimate self-government. The passage of the Samoa Amendment Act of 1947 and a series of further amendments governed Samoa's subsequent evolution toward independence. An executive council was reconstituted in 1957, and the New Zealand high commissioner withdrew from the Legislative Assembly, which thenceforth was presided over by an elected speaker. In 1959, an executive cabinet was introduced, and in 1960, the constitution of the Independent State of Samoa was adopted. This was followed by a plebiscite under UN supervision in 1961, in which an overwhelming majority of voters approved the adoption of the constitution and supported independence. On 1 January 1962, Samoa became an independent nation under the name of Western Samoa.

During the 1970s and 1980s, Western Samoa suffered from a worsening economy and growing political and social unrest. In July 1997, following an affirmative vote by the legislative assembly, the country officially changed its name from Western Samoa to the Independent State of Samoa, or simply Samoa.

In the early 2000s, Samoa again faced economic concerns, primarily as a result of declining fish catches. A much greater blow to the economy came in the form of natural disaster. On 29 September 2009, a deadly tsunami swept over the island nation, causing the death of at least 77 people and leaving over 150 injured. The tsunami was triggered by an 8.3-magnitude earthquake in the South Pacific, striking about 190 km (120 mi) to the south of Apia at a depth of about 33 km (20 mi). There were an additional three aftershocks, each of at least 5.6 magnitude. The disaster struck too quickly for evacuations to take place and officials reported that some residents ignored warning sirens, believing it was a false alarm. A full recovery from the tsunami was expected to take several years.

While the nation's economic growth and stability was linked to those of the United States and Europe for many years, the nation's largest trading partners have since become Australia and New Zealand. In an effort to promote even stronger economic connections with these two nations, the government decided to realign itself with them by changing time zones. For more than 100 years, Samoa was positioned on the east side of the International Date Line, with clocks and calendars aligned to coincide with same-day business hours in Europe and the United States, but one day behind Australia and New Zealand. In April 2011 the government decided to align itself to the west of the dateline instead. The change took place on 29 December 2011, when clocks were reset from 21 hours behind those of Sydney, Australia, to 3 hours ahead. This meant that 30 December was skipped, and Samoa went directly to 31 December.

13 GOVERNMENT

Executive power is vested in the chief of state. Malietoa Tanumafili II, the first official chief of state, was granted lifetime tenure and

served at his post until his death in 2007. According to the constitution of 1962, all successors are to be elected for a term of five years by the Fono, or legislative assembly. There are no term limits. The powers and functions of the head of state are far-reaching. All legislation must have his assent before it becomes law. He also has power to grant pardons and reprieves and to suspend or commute any sentence by any court. Executive authority is administered by a cabinet consisting of a prime minister, who is the head of government, and 12 other ministers appointed by the chief of state upon the advice of the prime minister. The head of state and the cabinet members make up the executive council. The constitution also calls for a Council of Deputies consisting of one to three members appointed to serve in place of the chief of state if necessary. These deputies are pulled from some of the most senior traditional chiefs.

The prime minister is appointed by the chief of state after legislative elections, with the approval of the newly seated legislative assembly. The leader of the majority party in the Fono is usually chosen for this post.

The 49-member Fono consists of 47 matai—traditional chiefs or heads of families—who are elected by Samoan voters from traditional village-based electoral districts. As of 2011, there were more than 30,000 matai registered with the government, though only about 16,000 were resident in the country. Approximately 8% of the matai are women. The two remaining seats are reserved for citizens of non-Samoan origin who qualify for registration on the individual voters' roll and are elected by non-Samoans. Universal suffrage was established in 1990, with the voting age at 21 years and over.

14 POLITICAL PARTIES

Technically, candidates for public office campaign as individuals, since all candidates for the Fono must be among the registered matai (traditional chiefs or heads of families); however, political parties have become increasingly important in representing various issues and policies. The Human Rights Protection Party (HRPP) was founded in 1979 as an opposition party to the government of Prime Minister Tupuola Efi. Tupuola's followers, although not yet formally organized at the time, had constituted the ruling party; Tupuola later became the head of the Christian Democratic Party (CDP). In 1988, the CDP merged with the Samoa National Party to form the Samoan National Development Party (SNDP). There are occasional disputes within the Samoan legislature that have led to the creation or reorganization of political parties. The TSP and the People's Party, for instance, were formed in 2008 as a result of opposition to new "road code" legislation that changed the driving side of the road from the right to the left beginning on 7 September 2009. Other parties include the Samoa Christian Party (TCP), the Samoa Democratic United Party (SDUP), and the Samoa Progressive Political Party (SPPP).

The HRPP first took control of the government in 1982 remained the dominant party through the March 2011 elections, winning 36 of the 49 seats in parliament. The TSP won the remaining 13. About 90% of all registered voters participated in the election. Tuila'epa Lupesoliai Sailele Malielegaoi, who was first chosen as prime minister in 1998, was unopposed to retain his post, making him the longest serving premier in the nation's history.

Tupua Tamasese Meaoli and Malietoa Tanumafili II served as joint heads of state beginning in 1962. When the former died on 5 April 1963, the latter became the sole head of state and retained that post until his death in 2007. Former prime minister Tupuola Efi (1976–82), now of the Samoa National Development Party, was unanimously elected to serve as head of state in his place.

15 LOCAL GOVERNMENT

With the exception of the Apia area, local government is carried out by the village fono, or council of matai and orators, and where and when necessary, through meetings of matai and orators of a district. The main administrative link between the central government and the outside districts is provided by part-time officials in each village who act as government agents in such matters as the registration of vital statistics; local inspectors represent the various government departments. For administrative purposes, the nation is divided into 11 districts.

16 JUDICIAL SYSTEM

Court procedure is patterned after practices in British courts; however, Samoan custom is taken into consideration in certain cases. English is the official language of the court, but Samoan is also used. The Supreme Court has full civil and criminal jurisdiction over the administration of justice in Samoa. It is under the jurisdiction of a chief judge and an unspecified number of additional justices who are appointed by the head of state, acting on the advice of the prime minister. The Court of Appeal consists of three judges, who may be judges of the Supreme Court or other persons with appropriate qualifications, including judges from overseas.

Magistrates' courts or district courts are subordinate courts with varying degrees of authority. The highest, presided over by the senior magistrate, may hear criminal cases involving imprisonment of up to three years or cases involving only fines. The Land and Titles Court has jurisdiction in disputes over Samoan land and succession to Samoan titles. Samoan assessors and associate judges possessing a good knowledge of Samoan custom must be present at all sittings of the court. Lawyers are not permitted to appear in the Land and Titles Court; each party appoints its own leader, usually a chief or an orator. Court decisions are based largely on Samoan custom.

Some civil and criminal matters are handled by village fonos (traditional courts), which apply a considerably different procedure than that used in the official Western-style courts. The Village Fono Law of 1990 affords legal status to the decision of the village fono and allows the appeal of fono decisions to the Land and Titles Court and to the Supreme Court. In July 2000, the Supreme Court ruled that the Village Fono Law could not be used to infringe upon villagers' freedom of religion, speech, assembly, or association.

17 ARMED FORCES

Samoa has no armed forces and relies on its police force for internal security. The government foresees no military development because of financial considerations and the absence of threats from abroad. There are informal defense ties with New Zealand under the terms of the 1962 Treaty of Friendship. There is a small Samoa Police Force.

18 INTERNATIONAL COOPERATION

Samoa became a member of the United Nations (UN) on 15 December 1976; it belongs to ESCAP and several nonregional specialized agencies, such as the FAO, the World Bank, UNCTAD, UNESCO, and WHO.

The nation also participates in the ACP Group, the Asian Development Bank, the Commonwealth of Nations, G-77, the South Pacific Commission, the South Pacific Regional Trade and Economic Cooperation Agreement (Sparteca), the Alliance of Small Island States (AOSIS), and the Pacific Island Forum. Samoa has observer status in the World Trade Organization.

An Inter-Samoa Consultative Committee, made up of representatives from Samoa and American Samoa, holds meetings alternately in both countries to discuss matters of mutual interest. By treaty, New Zealand is the exclusive representative of Samoa in the conduct of its foreign affairs outside the Pacific region. In environmental cooperation, Samoa is part of the Convention on Biological Diversity, the Kyoto Protocol, the Montréal Protocol, MARPOL, the Nuclear Test Ban Treaty, and the UN Conventions on the Law of the Sea, Wetlands of International Importance, Climate Change, and Desertification.

19 ECONOMY

The gross domestic product (GDP) rate of change in Samoa for 2010 was 0%. Inflation stood at 1% that year. The economy is based largely on tourism, which has grown considerably in terms of revenues and number of visitors since the 1990s. The effects of the global financial crisis of 2008–09 and the devastating tsunami of 2009 and resulted in a temporary decline in the industry, and a negative economic growth rate for both years. But the sector rebounded in 2010 and was expected to continue on in an upward trend. As of 2011, the service sector (including financial services) accounted for about 75% of the GDP. The industrial section has shown some signs of growth in the 2000s, primarily in construction and light manufacturing. Agricultural accounts for a small portion of the GDP. In 2010, remittances from citizens working abroad accounted for nearly 24% of GDP.

20 INCOME

The CIA estimated that in 2010 the GDP of Samoa was $1.055 billion. The CIA defines GDP as the value of all final goods and services produced within a nation in a given year and computed on the basis of purchasing power parity (PPP) rather than value as measured on the basis of the rate of the exchange based on current dollars. The per capita GDP was estimated at $5,500. The GDP was constant, neither shrinking nor growing. The average inflation rate was 1%. In 2011, it was estimated that agriculture accounted for 3.6% of GDP, industry 13.1%, and services 75.3%.

In 2010 remittances from citizens living abroad totaled $128.2 million.

21 LABOR

As of 2010, Samoa had a formal labor force of 25,000 people. Into 2011, only 18% of the total population were formal wage or salary earners. Others are employed in a variety of subsistence level activities. More than 50% of the formal workforce are employed in services. Less than 6% are employed in industry and 2% are employed in agriculture. Over the years, thousands of skilled and semiskilled Samoans have left the islands, drawn away mainly by better economic opportunities in New Zealand, Australia, and the United States.

Although small, a trade union movement has been established. Public employees are represented by the Public Service Association. As of 2010, approximately 20% of the workforce was unionized.

Labor is generally restricted to a 40-hour week or 8 hours per day. As of 2010, the hourly minimum wage for the public sector was $1.14, while the minimum wage for the private sector was set at $0.86 per hour. These wages do not provide a decent standard of living for a family, with the result that many wage workers also continue in subsistence agriculture or fishing activities. Samoan labor law provides for rudimentary safety and health standards, but these standards are not always effectively enforced. Children under the age of 15 may only be employed in safe and light work, but the law does not apply to service rendered to family members, such as work on family farms, or to the matai, who sometimes require children to work on village farms. Moreover, increasing numbers of children work as street vendors in Apia. To minimize the use of child labor as street vendors, the government enacted a new law in 2009 that prohibits any child under age 14 from working in light or heavy industry activity during school hours. Labor laws prohibit women from working during the hours of midnight and 6 a.m.

22 AGRICULTURE

Out of 283,000 hectares (699,308 acres) of land in Samoa, 25,000 hectares (61,776 acres) are arable. The commercial agriculture sector is relatively small, accounting for about 3.6% of GDP in 2011. Coconut products, including coconut oil, coconut cream, and copra cake, are the primary agricultural exports. Exports of cocoa have fallen in recent years, thereby discouraging production. Since 1991, no production over 1,000 tons has been reported. Banana exports fluctuate greatly from year to year. In 2009, fruit production amounted to 50,544 tons and vegetable production to 1,224 tons.

Most Samoans grow food crops for home consumption and cash crops for export. Village agriculture, in which the family is the productive unit, involves the largest areas of land, occupies the preponderance of the labor force, and produces the major portion of food and cash crops. Coconut products, cocoa, taro, and bananas are produced for export, and bananas, taro, and taamu are grown for local sale. Village plantings are invariably mixed, containing some or all of the following crops: coconuts, cocoa, bananas, taro, taamu, breadfruit, sugarcane, yams, manioc, and various fruits. Plantation agriculture has been controlled mainly by nonindigenous residents.

23 ANIMAL HUSBANDRY

The UN Food and Agriculture Organization (FAO) reported that Samoa dedicated 3,000 hectares (7,413 acres) to permanent pasture or meadow in 2009. During that year, the country tended 620,000 chickens, 30,000 head of cattle, and 202,000 pigs. The production from these animals amounted to 1,989 tons of beef and veal, 4,003 tons of pork, 6,253 tons of poultry, 614 tons of eggs,

and 3,625 tons of milk. Samoa also produced 210 tons of cattle hide.

Pigs and cattle form the bulk of the livestock. Pigs are common in the villages. A small number of cattle are kept for milk; the remainder are raised for beef. Nearly one-half of the cattle population is owned by Western Samoa Trust Estate Corporation (WSTEC), the most progressive cattle breeder. Other livestock in 2005 included an estimated 7,000 donkeys and 1,800 horses.

24 FISHING

The government has sought to expand the fishing industry, but most fishing is still conducted along the reefs and coasts; deep-sea fishing, save for bonito and shark, is not developed. The local fish catch steadily fell from 4,020 tons in 1982 to 565 tons in 1991; by 2003, the catch rebounded to 10,267 tons, with tuna comprising about 40%. In 2008, the annual capture totaled 3,800 tons according to the UN FAO.

25 FORESTRY

Approximately 60% of Samoa is covered by forest. The UN FAO estimated the 2009 roundwood production at 5,700 cu m (201,294 cu ft). The value of all forest products, including roundwood, totaled $86,000.

Reforestation projects are concentrated on Savai'i, which accounts for 80% of the nation's forest area. A large-scale timber-milling enterprise, established on Savai'i in 1970, began to produce kiln-dried sawn timber and veneer sheets for export. The most common timber available in Samoa is tava, which is used for flooring and furniture. Timber imports were estimated at $6 million in 2009.

26 MINING

No minerals of commercial value were known to exist in Samoa.

27 ENERGY AND POWER

Samoa formerly depended heavily on imported energy, but hydroelectric power, first available in 1985, has greatly increased its generating capacity. The World Bank reported in 2008 that Samoa produced 106 million kWh of electricity. In 2007, consumption of electricity totaled 101.4 million kWh. Total installed capacity in 2002 was 0.029 million kW.

Samoa has no reserves of oil, natural gas, or coal, nor any refining capacity. All fossil fuel needs were met by imports of refined petroleum products. In 2009, oil consumption averaged 1,000 barrels per day. In 2007, oil imports were estimated at 1,105 barrels per day. Gasoline and distillates made up the majority of those imports.

28 INDUSTRY

The government has encouraged growth in this industry, primarily through the development of light manufacturing. Manufactured products include beer, cigarettes, soap, paint, soft drinks, fruit juices, processed foods, and timber products. A coconut oil mill, an additional coconut cream factory, a veneer mill, and a meat cannery began operations in the 1980s.

Principal Trading Partners – Samoa (2010)

(In millions of US dollars)

Country	Total	Exports	Imports	Balance
World	291.5	13.5	278.0	-264.5
New Zealand	103.2	2.0	101.3	-99.3
China	77.1	0.0	77.1	-77.0
Fiji	76.6	1.2	75.3	-74.1
Australia	70.1	41.0	29.1	11.9
American Samoa	62.9	61.8	1.2	60.6
Singapore	60.5	0.4	60.1	-59.8
Japan	35.2	0.3	34.9	-34.7
United States	24.7	3.6	21.1	-17.6
Taiwan	12.7	6.2	6.6	-0.4
Indonesia	10.4	0.2	10.2	-10.0

(…) data not available or not significant.

(n.s.) not specified.

SOURCE: *2011 Direction of Trade Statistics Yearbook,* New York: United Nations, 2011.

Balance of Payments – Samoa (2010)

(In millions of US dollars)

Current Account		**-57.9**
Balance on goods	-244.5	
Imports	-280.0	
Exports	35.5	
Balance on services	71.6	
Balance on income	-17.6	
Current transfers	132.6	
Capital Account		**82.4**
Financial Account		**11.8**
Direct investment abroad	…	
Direct investment in Samoa	0.7	
Portfolio investment assets	-1.7	
Portfolio investment liabilities	…	
Financial derivatives	…	
Other investment assets	-36.0	
Other investment liabilities	48.8	
Net Errors and Omissions		**-12.0**
Reserves and Related Items		**-24.3**

(…) data not available or not significant.

SOURCE: *Balance of Payment Statistics Yearbook 2011,* Washington, DC: International Monetary Fund, 2011.

In 1991, the Japanese Yazaki Samsa Co. began manufacturing automotive seat belts and electrical wiring systems for Toyota vehicles. This plant was the largest manufacturer in the country in 2008, employing more than 2,000 people. However, due to the global financial crisis of 2008–09 and a devastating 2011 earthquake in Japan, about 50% of these workers had been laid off by 2011. It was unclear whether or not the company would reinvest in the short-term. As of 2011, industry accounted for about 13.1% of GDP.

29 SCIENCE AND TECHNOLOGY

The World Bank reported in 2009 that there were no patent applications in science and technology in Samoa. New Zealand provides extensive scientific and technical aid to Samoa. Other donors include Japan, the Federal Republic of Germany (FRG), Australia, the United States, the United Kingdom, and the United Nations Development Program (UNDP). United Nations Educational, Scientific and Cultural Organization (UNESCO) has an integrated field office in Apia to promote science in the Pacific States. The National University of Samoa, founded in 1988 at Apia, has a faculty of science. The University of the South Pacific, founded in 1977 at Apia, has a school of agriculture.

30 DOMESTIC TRADE

Apia is the primary center of commercial life. Many firms act as agents for shipping and airlines and for overseas commercial organizations generally. Outside Apia, trading stations, linked with the capital by launch and road transport, collect produce and distribute consumer goods. Several major firms operate about 200 stations in the outer districts and secure a large share of the total commercial business. There are also a number of smaller firms and independent traders. In Apia, various firms and small shops sell imported commodities and domestic products.

Open markets sponsoring local produce vendors are a common food retailing situation for a nation where most of the population is employed in some level of agriculture. The largest such market is Meketi Fou in Apia. Shops are generally open from 9 a.m. to 5 p.m. Monday through Friday and 8 a.m. to 12:30 p.m. on Saturdays.

31 FOREIGN TRADE

The fact that Samoa has a limited number of exports—principally agricultural and timber—renders its economy extremely vulnerable to weather conditions and market fluctuations. Imports consist chiefly of machinery and equipment, industrial supplies, fuel, and food. The principal exports include fish, coconut oil and cream, copra, taro, garments, and beer.

Major import partners in 2009 were New Zealand, 24.2%; Fiji, 17.4%; Singapore, 12.6%; China, 12%; Australia, 9.9%; and the United States, 6%. Its major export partners were American Samoa, 40.8%; Australia, 24.5%; China, 5.8%; and the United States, 4%.

32 BALANCE OF PAYMENTS

In the early 1970s, Samoa's heavy trade deficits were largely offset by tourism revenues, remittances from Samoans working abroad, and long-term investment capital. By the early 1980s, however, rising import costs and declining export earnings led to a critical balance-of-payments situation. By 1992, the external account deficit (excluding grants) had increased to about 28% of GDP. Samoa's external debt stood at $192 million in 1999. Samoa imported $324 million worth of goods and services in 2008, while exporting $131 million worth of goods and services, resulting in a trade deficit of $193 million.

33 BANKING AND SECURITIES

Legislation in 1974 set up the Monetary Board to act as the central bank. The activities of the Monetary Board were taken over in May 1984 by the new Central Bank of Samoa. An Australian bank, ANZ, acquired the government's 25% stake in the Bank of Western Samoa (BWS), becoming its outright owner of what is now known as ANZ Samoa. The government has sold its Post Office Savings Bank (POSB) to a consortium of local businesses. The bank, to be renamed the National Bank of Samoa, was the country's first locally owned commercial bank. The other banks are Pacific Commercial Bank (owned by Westpac, the Bank of Hawaii, and local shareholders) and the Development Bank of Western Samoa.

Parliament passed legislation in early 1988 to allow banks to set up offshore banking centers. More the 1,000 companies have registered in Apia under the new tax haven legislation, contributing substantially to the national budget. In 1998, the International Finance Center opened within the Central Bank of Samoa in 1998 and has since become a leading offshore center in the South Pacific. The Samoa International Finance Authority was established in 2005 to monitor and supervise the international finance services provide within the nation's banking system and to promote the International Finance Center.

³⁴INSURANCE

There is a private life insurance company in Apia, National Pacific Insurance Ltd., managed by the National Insurance Co. of New Zealand. Other insurance companies within the nation include Apia Insurance Company, Pacific Insurance Underwriters, Progressive Insurance, and Talofa Insurance.

³⁵PUBLIC FINANCE

Samoa's financial year ends on 31 December. Government budgets commonly show deficits.

According to the CIA, in 2010 the budget of Samoa included $201.2 million in public revenue and $281.7 million in public expenditure. The budget deficit amounted to 14.5% of GDP. In total $235.5 million of the debt was held by foreign entities in 2009. In 2010 remittances from citizens living abroad totaled about $128.2 million and accounted for approximately 24% of GDP. The nation also continued to rely on development assistance from other countries.

For the 2010/11 fiscal year, the national budget allocated about $10 million for the tourist sector, with about 70% provided for marketing. More than $2.5 million was designated for tourist marketing efforts in Australia.

³⁶TAXATION

Individuals and companies are liable for the payment of income tax. The basic nonresident company tax rate is 27% on taxable income derived from the Samoa source. The resident company tax rate is 27% on its global taxable income. Personal income tax rates range from 10% to 27%. There are also gift, inheritance, and stamp taxes. A 15% value added goods and service tax is applied to on all goods and services, except for imported goods and some goods that are liable to excise duties.

³⁷CUSTOMS AND DUTIES

Customs duties are levied on all imports except those specifically exempted. Basic foodstuffs are generally exempt or at a very low rate. Though some rates are as high as 60%, the most common rate is 35%. Preferential rates for imports from Commonwealth countries were abolished in 1975.

³⁸FOREIGN INVESTMENT

Foreign direct investment (FDI) in Samoa was a net inflow of $3.03 million according to World Bank figures published in 2009. FDI represented 0.61% of GDP.

The government actively promotes the establishment of industries financed by overseas companies. Areas open for new development include tourism, business and financial services, food and beverage manufacturing, and agriculture and fisheries.

³⁹ECONOMIC DEVELOPMENT

Despite the temporary setbacks presented by the global financial crisis of 2008–09 and the 2009 tsunami, the economy appears to have a great deal of growth potential, and the government is eager to work toward greater levels of economic sustainability. The *Strategy for the Development of Samoa 2008–2012* sets three priority areas for ensuring sustainable economic and social progress. These include improved economic policies, particularly those that inspire sustained macroeconomic stability and private sector growth; improved social policies that promote better health and education, along with improved economic stability at the village level; and improvements in public sector management and environmental sustainability.

⁴⁰SOCIAL DEVELOPMENT

A social security system was established in 1972 under the Samoan National Provident Fund. It provides for employee retirement pensions, disability benefits, and death benefits. Employees contribute 5% of their earnings, and this amount is matched by their employers. Retirement is allowed at age 55. Workers' compensation is funded by employers and is compulsory. This program covers reasonable medical expenses and is paid for entirely by employer contributions.

Though the constitution provides for equal rights and prohibits abuse against women, domestic abuse is common and considered culturally acceptable, except in the most extreme cases. Police are rarely notified and domestic issues are usually resolved within the village structure. Punishment for abuse was generally made by the village fono only if the abuse was considered extreme (leaving physical marks). The government sponsors literacy programs to assist in integrating women into the economic mainstream. While the law and local traditions prohibit severe child abuse, there appeared to be an increase in the number of reported child abuse cases in 2010. These cases were aggressively prosecuted by the government.

Universal suffrage was enacted in 1990. Human rights are generally well respected in Samoa.

⁴¹HEALTH

The Department of Health oversees health care on the islands. The country spent about 5.9% of its GDP on healthcare, amounting to $205 per person. District nurses are stationed at strategic points throughout the islands. Child health clinics, particularly clinics for young children and infants, are a regular feature of their work.

As of 2011, there were about 3 physicians, 9 nurses and midwives, and 10 hospital beds per 10,000 inhabitants. It was estimated that 49% of children were vaccinated against measles. A mobile dental clinic operates in the villages, while all schools in Apia are visited at regular intervals by a team of dental practitioners.

Diabetic retinopathy is common in Polynesian Samoans. The increase in diabetes has been linked to the Westernization of the Samoan diet. According to the CIA, life expectancy was estimated at 72.4 years of 2011. During that same year, the infant mortality rate was an estimated 22.74 per 1,000 births. The total fertility rate in 2011 was estimated at 3.22 children born per woman. Tuberculosis and AIDS were present but not considered major problems. The incidence of tuberculosis was 28 per 100,000 people in 2007. In 2006, injuries and accidents were a leading cause of death. That year, the teenage fertility rate was high, at 28.6 births per 1,000 girls.

42 HOUSING

Most Samoans live in villages in traditional Samoan houses called *fales*. A fale is usually round or oval, with pebble floors and a thatch roof. It has no walls, being supported on the sides by posts. Coconut-leaf blinds can be lowered to exclude wind and rain. In areas more affected by contact with Europeans, the fale may have a concrete floor, corrugated iron roof, and latticework walls. Another fused Samoan-European type, much used by chiefs and pastors, is an oblong concrete house with some walls, often with separate rooms in each corner; like the fale it is open at the sides. Fales are grouped around an open area in the center of the village and have separate cookhouses behind them.

More modern housing has been constructed since about the 1990s, primarily through international assistance. Solid wall structures with concrete foundations and iron roofs have been built to withstand the natural elements of harsh wind, rain, and cyclones. However, low-income families are not able to purchase or build such structures without assistance. The Housing Corporation of Samoa was established by the Housing Corporation Act of 1989 to offer loans and assistance for prospective homeowners.

At the 2006 census, there were 46,048 buildings serving 23,813 households. (Larger households may occupy more than one fale). About 84% of these buildings were occupied at the time of the census. About 6.7% were noted as guesthouses.

On 29 September 2009, a deadly tsunami was triggered by an 8.3-magnitude earthquake in the South Pacific, striking about 190 km (120 mi) to the south of Apia at a depth of about 33 km (20 mi). There were an additional three aftershocks, each of at least 5.6 magnitude. The disaster struck too quickly for evacuations to take place and officials reported that some residents ignored warning sirens, believing it was a false alarm. Villages along the west coast were leveled and numerous homes and buildings inland were destroyed or severely damaged. Though several countries and international relief organizations offered immediate aid, by May 2010, several families in the affected areas remained without adequate permanent shelter. That month, an inspection of shelters conducted by a team of researchers from the University of Auckland in New Zealand revealed that, while many islanders have rebuilt their homes and communities on higher ground, most new buildings are not sufficiently storm-proof to withstand future cyclones,

tsunamis, or earthquakes. In many cases, residents were given materials to build their own homes, but most communities lack the human resources of trained carpenters or other construction engineers to build more than the most basic shelters. The research team also noted the lack of coordinated efforts to distribute construction materials and relief supplies once they arrive. Some areas still lacked an adequate supply of clean drinking water.

43 EDUCATION

Samoa launched its first free education program in January 2010. The program, which supports free and compulsory education for students of ages 5–14, is expected to cost the nation about $2 million per year. For the first three years of the program, the governments of Australia and New Zealand pledged to cover the total cost of program under the Samoa School Fee Grant Scheme. This free education covers both government and church sponsored schools and will include special needs classes as well. While the program marks a major step for the nation's people, some have criticized the move as not enough, claiming that the lack of free secondary education (covering grades 9–13) puts the future of the nation's skilled trade workforce at great risk. Also, as of 2010, some families were still required to pay administrative fees, which are imposed by individual school boards.

Formal education is provided by the Department of Education and five religious missions. Government and mission schools have a uniform syllabus and common examinations. The government school system is more comprehensive, with almost all teachers holding Samoan teachers' certificates. Village schools provide four years of primary schooling. District schools draw the brighter pupils from village schools and educate them through the upper primary level. In the Apia area, urban schools provide a lower-through upper-primary curriculum. A major educational goal has been to make Samoans bilingual, with English as their second tongue. In some senior classes of the primary schools, all instruction is in English.

The government maintains secondary schools, in which the medium of instruction is English. Samoa College is patterned after a New Zealand secondary school; each year, 100 pupils from government and mission schools are selected for admission by competitive examination. Vaipouli High School, in Savai'i, provides a general secondary curriculum.

Avele College, in Apia, offers training in modern agricultural methods. In addition, the University of the South Pacific School of Agriculture maintains a campus at Alafua, on the outskirts of Apia. Other institutes of higher learning include the Oceania Medical University and the National University of Samoa. The medium of instruction in mission secondary schools is English, with curriculum and textbooks similar to those used in New Zealand.

In 2002, about 49% of age-eligible children were enrolled in some type of preschool program. In 2009 the World Bank estimated that 90% of age-eligible children in Samoa were enrolled in primary school. Overall, the CIA estimated that Samoa had a literacy rate of 99%. It is estimated that nearly all students complete their primary education. The student-to-teacher ratio for primary school was at about 25:1 in 2005; the ratio for secondary school was about 21:1. In 2005, private schools accounted for about 17% of primary school enrollment and 32.2% of secondary enrollment.

Samoa was one of the founders of the regional University of the South Pacific. The National University, which was established in 1984, was upgraded and provided with a new campus in 1997. Other tertiary institutions include the College of Tropical Agriculture and a Trades Training College. In 2001, it was estimated that about 7% of the tertiary-age population was enrolled in tertiary education programs.

Public expenditure on education represented 5.7% of GDP in 2009. The commitment to education was reflected in the 2010/11 fiscal year national budget, as the government has increased its investment in education by 25% more than the previous year, allocating $85.2 million. About $3 million of this total is earmarked for the ongoing tsunami recovery program in the education sector. More than $47.3 million was provided for daily operations of the Ministry of Education, Sports, and Culture.

44 LIBRARIES AND MUSEUMS

The Nelson Memorial Public Library in Apia has 90,000 volumes. The library of the University of the South Pacific has around 22,000 volumes, and the Legislative Assembly has a library with 6,000 volumes. A bookmobile service operates on Upolu and Savai'i. A number of primary and secondary schools have their own libraries. The Library Association of Samoa was established in 1988. The National Museum and Culture Center in Apia, established in 1984, includes a local museum, library, and theater and offers crafts workshops. Vailima is home to the Robert Louis Stevenson Museum, featuring the author's house and estate.

45 MEDIA

Internal and overseas wireless telegraph services are available. According to the CIA, in 2009, there were 31,900 main phone lines and 151,000 mobile cell phones in use, with about 84 mobile phone subscription per 100 people.

The government-controlled Samoan Broadcasting Service, in Apia, transmits radio programs on two stations in Samoan and English and provides direct broadcasts from the Fono. In 2009, there were 2 FM radio stations and 5 AM radio stations. In 2004, there was a satellite cable system available in parts of Apia. One of the two television stations was owned by the government. In 2006, about 89.1% of all households had a radio and 61.9% had a television set. In 2010, the country had about 17,044 Internet hosts. In 2009 Internet users numbered 5 per 100 citizens.

There are several bilingual weeklies, including *Le Samoa* and *Savali*, published in Samoan and English. There are two dailies, the *Samoan Times* and *Samoa Observer*. *Talamua Magazine* is published monthly in Samoan and English. The constitution provides for free speech and a free press, and the government is said to respect these provisions in practice.

46 ORGANIZATIONS

The Samoa Chamber of Commerce and Industry is based in Apia. Youth clubs include the Boy's Brigade Samoa, University of South Pacific Student Association, and YMCA/YWCA. There are several sports associations representing such pastimes as squash, weightlifting, badminton, tae kwon do, and sailing. Many of these are affiliated with the national Olympic Committee and other international organizations. Volunteer service organizations, such as the Lions Clubs International and the Calliope Lodge of Freemasons, are present. Women's organizations include Soroptimist International of Samoa, Mothers' Club, Federation of Women's Committees, and the South-East Asia and Pan-Pacific Women's Association. Mapusaga O Aiga Samoa is a national organization promoting public awareness of issues concerning child abuse and domestic violence. The Samoa Family Health Association serves as an advocate for greater access to improved health care. There are national chapters of the Red Cross Society and Habitat for Humanity.

47 TOURISM, TRAVEL, AND RECREATION

The *Tourism Factbook*, published by the UN World Tourism Organization, reported 129,000 incoming tourists to Samoa in 2009, spending an estimated total of $116.2 million. Of those incoming tourists, there were 113,000 from East Asia and the Pacific. There were 2,525 hotel beds available in Samoa. The estimated daily cost to visit Apia was $266.

Until 1965, official policy in Samoa was opposed to tourism, but during 1966–67, there was a complete reversal of policy. The government hired international tourism consultants to advise it on long-term means of developing a tourism industry. Samoa joined the Pacific Area Travel Association, extended tax holidays and import-duty concessions to hotel builders, and appropriated money for the building of new hotels. Tourism has since become a major industry.

The major tourist attractions are the beaches and traditional villages. In Apia is Vailima, the residence of the head of state and once the home of Robert Louis Stevenson; Stevenson's grave is nearby. Pastimes include swimming, waterskiing, and fishing. Football (soccer), cricket, and rugby are popular local sports.

Travelers to Samoa must have a passport valid for at least six months, as well as an onward/return ticket. Visitors do not require a visa or entry permit for stays of up to 60 days.

48 FAMOUS PERSONS

The Scottish author Robert Louis Stevenson (1850–94) lived principally on Upolu from 1889 until his death. Samoans famous since independence include Malietoa Tanumafili II (1913–2007), who was named head of state in 1962, and Fiame Faumuina Mataafa (1921–75), who served as prime minister from 1962 to 1970 and again from 1973 until his death. Tupuola Taisi Efi (b. 1938) was prime minister from 1976 to 1982; he was elected as head of state in 2007. Tofilau Eti (b. American Samoa, 1924–99) was prime minister from December 1982 to December 1985, when he resigned and was succeeded by Va'ai Kolone, the founder of the Human Rights Protection Party (1911–2001). Sailele Malielegaoi Tuila'epa (b. 1945) has served as prime minister since 1998, most recently reelected in 2011.

49 DEPENDENCIES

Samoa has no territories or colonies.

50 BIBLIOGRAPHY

Craig, Robert D. *Historical Dictionary of Polynesia.* Lanham, MD: Scarecrow, 2002.

Gillespie, Rosemary G., and David A. Clague, eds. *Encyclopedia of Islands*. Berkeley: University of California Press, 2009.

Kirch, Patrick Vinton, and Jean-Louis Rallu. *The Growth and Collapse of Pacific Island Societies*. Honolulu: University of Hawaii Press, 2007.

Leibo, Steven A. *East and Southeast Asia, 2005*. 38th ed. Harpers Ferry, WV: Stryker-Post Publications, 2005.

Lockwood, Victoria S., ed. *Globalization and Culture Change in the Pacific Islands*. Upper Saddle River, NJ: Pearson/Prentice Hall, 2004.

Mead, Margaret. *Coming of Age in Samoa*. London: Penguin, 1961 (orig. 1928).

Samoa and Tonga. Oakland, CA: Lonely Planet, 2009.

SAUDI ARABIA

Kingdom of Saudi Arabia

Al-Mamlakah al-ʿArabiyah as-Saʿudiyah

CAPITAL: Riyadh (Ar-Riyad)

FLAG: The national flag bears in white on a green field the inscription, in Arabic, "There is no god but Allah, and Mohammad is the messenger of Allah." There is a long white sword beneath the inscription; the sword handle is toward the fly.

ANTHEM: *Aash Al-Malik (Long Live Our Beloved King).*

MONETARY UNIT: The Saudi riyal (SAR) is divided into 20 qursh (piasters), in turn divided into 5 halalah. There are coins of 1, 5, 10, 25, 50, and 100 halalah and notes of 1, 5, 10, 50, 100, and 500 riyals. SAR1 = US$0.26667 (or US$1 = SAR3.75) as of 2010.

WEIGHTS AND MEASURES: The metric system has been officially adopted.

HOLIDAYS: Muslim religious holidays include 1st of Muharram (Muslim New Year), Eid al-Fitr, and Eid al-Adha.

TIME: 3 p.m. = noon GMT.

¹LOCATION, SIZE, AND EXTENT

Saudi Arabia constitutes about four-fifths of the Arabian Peninsula in Southwest Asia. Although Saudi Arabia is known to be the third-largest country in Asia, after China and India, its precise area is difficult to specify because several of its borders are incompletely demarcated. Saudi Arabia has an area of 1,960,582 sq km (756,985 sq mi); it extends 2,295 km (1,426 mi) ESE–WNW and 1,423 km (884 mi) NNE–SSW. Comparatively, the area occupied by Saudi Arabia is slightly less than one-fourth the size of the United States. Saudi Arabia is bounded on the N by Jordan and Iraq; on the NE by Kuwait; on the E by the Persian Gulf, Qatar, and the United Arab Emirates (UAE); on the SE by Oman; on the S and SE by Yemen; and on the W by the Red Sea and the Gulf of Aqaba, with a total estimated land boundary length of 4,431 km (2,753 mi) and a coastline of 2,640 km (1,640 mi).

The Farasān Islands, belonging to Saudi Arabia, include about 120 islands in the Red Sea, the largest of which is Farasān al Kabir, with an area of about 395 sq km (152 sq mi).

An agreement was reached in 1965 whereby the neutral zone separating Saudi Arabia from Kuwait was divided administratively between the two countries; however, Kuwait and Saudi Arabia continue to debate the maritime boundary with Iran. A dispute between Saudi Arabia and the newly formed UAE over control of the Buraymi oasis was settled in 1974, when they reached an accord fixing their common border; however, the details of this treaty had not been made public.

Saudi Arabia's capital city, Riyadh, is located in the east-central part of the country.

²TOPOGRAPHY

A narrow plain, the Tihamat ash-Sham, parallels the Red Sea coast, as do, farther north, the Hijaz Mountains (with elevations of 910–2,740 m/3,000–9,000 ft), which rise sharply from the sea. The highest mountains (more than 2,740 m/9,000 ft) are in ʿAsir in the south. ʿAsir is a region extending about 370 km (230 mi) along the Red Sea and perhaps 290–320 km (180–200 mi) inland. East of the Hijaz, the slope is more gentle, and the mountains give way to the central uplands (Najd), a large plateau ranging in elevation from about 1,520 m (5,000 ft) in the west to about 610 m (2,000 ft) in the east. The Dahna, a desert with an average width of 56 km (35 mi) and an average altitude of 460 m (1,500 ft), separates Najd from the low plateau (Hasa) to the east (average width, 160 km/100 mi; average altitude, 240 m/800 ft). This, in turn, gives way to the low-lying Gulf region.

At least one-third of the total area is sandy desert. The largest of the deserts is the famed Ar-Rub' al-Khali in the south, with an area of roughly 647,500 sq km (250,000 sq mi). An-Nafud, its northern counterpart, has an area of about 57,000 sq km (22,000 sq mi). There are no lakes, and except for artesian wells in the eastern oases, there is no perennially flowing water.

³CLIMATE

The climate is generally very dry and very hot; dust storms and sandstorms are frequent. Day and night temperatures vary greatly. From May to September, the hottest period, daytime temperatures reach 54°c (129°f) in the interior and are among the highest recorded anywhere in the world. Temperatures are slightly lower along the coasts, but humidity reaches 90%, especially in the east, which is noted for heavy fogs. From October through April, the climate is more moderate, with evening temperatures between 16°

and 21°c (61° and 70°f). Average annual rainfall is 9 cm (3.5 in), with most rain falling from November to May. Between 25 and 50 cm (10 and 20 in) of rain falls in the mountainous 'Asir area, where there is a summer monsoon. In late spring and early summer, a strong northwesterly wind known as the shamal produces sometimes severe sand and dust storms.

⁴FLORA AND FAUNA

The World Resources Institute estimates that there are 2,028 plant species in Saudi Arabia. In addition, Saudi Arabia is home to 94 mammal, 433 bird, 103 reptile, and 6 amphibian species. The calculation reflects the total number of distinct species residing in the country, not the number of endemic species.

Vegetation is sparse, owing to aridity and soil salinity. The date palm, mangrove, tamarisk, and acacia are prevalent. Wild mammals include the oryx, jerboa, fox, lynx, wildcat, monkey, panther, and jackal. The favorite game bird is the bustard. The camel and Arab stallion are renowned, as is the white donkey of Al-Ahsa. Fish abound in the coastal waters and insects, scorpions, lizards, and snakes are numerous. Some beaches of the Farasãn Islands are nesting grounds for turtles. An annual gathering of harid parrotfish takes place on these islands, and the waters surrounding them are home to several types of dolphins, whales, and dugong (an aquatic mammal related to the manatee).

⁵ENVIRONMENT

The Saudi government has traditionally not given priority to environmental protection, but in recent years it has become concerned about the continuing encroachment of sand dunes on agricultural land, the preservation and development of water resources, and pollution and sanitation problems. Legislation enacted in May 1978 forbade the felling of trees and regulated the protection of forestland. The World Resources Institute reported that Saudi Arabia had designated 81.83 million hectares (202.2 million acres) of land for protection as of 2006.

Saudi Arabia's natural environment was threatened by the Persian Gulf War. The dumping of up to six million barrels of oil in the surrounding waters and the destruction of Kuwait's oil wells by fire polluted the nation's air and water. It has been estimated that the nation's water supply may be exhausted by 2025. Water resources totaled 2.4 cu km (0.576 cu mi) while water usage was 17.32 cu km (4.16 cu mi) per year. Domestic water usage accounted for 10% of total usage, industrial for 1%, and agricultural for 89%. Per capita water usage totaled 705 cu m (24,897 cu ft) per year. Saudi Arabia produces an average of 12 million tons of municipal solid waste per year. The UN reported in 2008 that carbon dioxide emissions in Saudi Arabia totaled 402,120 kilotons.

The Meteorological and Environmental Protection Administration and the National Commission for Wildlife Conservation and Development promote and develop environmental projects. In the late 1970s, the 'Asir Kingdom Park, in the southwest, was created to preserve the landforms, flora, and fauna of the 'Asir region, which forms part of the Great Rift Valley. Drakensberg Park became a UNESCO World Heritage Site in 2000.

According to a 2011 report issued by the International Union for Conservation of Nature and Natural Resources (IUCN), threatened species included 9 types of mammals, 15 species of birds, 2 types of reptiles, 23 species of fish, 53 species of invertebrates, and

3 species of plants. Threatened species in Saudi Arabia include the Asiatic cheetah (possibly extinct), South Arabian leopard, northern bald ibis, and two species of turtle (green sea and hawksbill). The Arabian gazelle, Queen of Sheba's gazelle, Saudi gazelle, and the Syrian wild ass have become extinct.

⁶POPULATION

The US Central Intelligence Agency (CIA) estimated the population of Saudi Arabia in 2011 to be approximately 26,131,703, which placed it at number 46 in population among the 196 nations of the world. In 2011, approximately 3% of the population was more than 65 years of age, with another 29.4% less than 15 years of age. The median age in Saudi Arabia was 25.3 years. There were 1.17 males for every female in the country. The population's annual rate of change was 1.536%. The projected population for the year 2025 was estimated at 35,700,000. Population density in Saudi Arabia was calculated at 13 people per sq km (34 per sq mi).

The UN estimated that 82% of the population lived in urban areas, and that urban populations had an annual rate of change of 2.2%. The largest urban areas, along with their respective populations, included Riyadh, 4.7 million; Jeddah, 3.2 million; Mecca, 1.5 million; Medina, 1.1 million; and Ad Dammam, 902,000.

⁷MIGRATION

Estimates of Saudi Arabia's net migration rate, carried out by the CIA in 2011, amounted to -0.64 migrants per 1,000 citizens. The total number of emigrants living abroad was 178,700, and the total number of immigrants living in Saudi Arabia was about 6 million. Saudi Arabia also accepted 240,015 refugees from Palestinian Territories. Emigration is limited. Immigration of professionals, technicians, and others from the surrounding Arab states and growing numbers from outside the region have been spurred by the development of the oil industry and by the lack of adequately trained and educated Saudi personnel.

In the early 1990s, there were significant numbers of expatriate workers from the United States, European countries, Turkey, Jordan, Syria, Kuwait, Yemen, the Republic of Korea (ROK), Pakistan, India, Sri Lanka, and the Philippines. In 1990, when Iraq invaded Kuwait, Saudi Arabia reacted by expelling workers from Jordan, Yemen, and Palestine, for their countries' support of Iraq.

⁸ETHNIC GROUPS

At least 90% of Saudis have a common Arabian ancestry, making the population fairly homogeneous in ethnicity, religion, and language. Divisions are based mainly on tribal affiliation or descent; the primary distinction is between groups with a tradition of being sedentary agriculturalists or traders, and the Bedouins, who have a tradition of nomadic pastoralism. The two groups traditionally have been antagonistic. There has been some loosening of tribal ties, however, caused by rapid economic development. Afro-Asians account for the remaining 10% of the population. Admixtures of Turks, Iranians, Indonesians, Pakistanis, Indians, various African groups, and other non-Arab Muslim peoples appear in the Hijaz, mostly descendants of pilgrims to Mecca. The foreign population stands at an estimated 6.5 million, including Bangladeshis, Pakistanis, Indians, Filipinos, Egyptians, Palestinians, Lebanese, Sri Lankans, Indonesians, Eritreans, and Americans.

9 LANGUAGES

Arabic, the native language of the indigenous population, is a Semitic language related to Hebrew and Aramaic. Local variations in pronunciation do not prevent oral communication between people from opposite sections of the Arabian Peninsula. The language is written in a cursive script from right to left. The 28 letters of the alphabet have initial, medial, and terminal forms; short vowels are seldom indicated. Most businesspeople and merchants in oil-producing areas and commercial centers understand English. Government correspondence must be written in Arabic.

10 RELIGIONS

Islam is the state religion and all citizens must be Muslims. Between 85% and 90% of the people of Saudi Arabia are Sunni Muslims who adhere to the practices of the Hanbali school of jurisprudence, a fundamentalist Muslim reform movement first preached by the 18th-century religious leader Muhammad bin 'Abd al-Wahhab. Other Sunnis adhere to the Hanafi, Maliki, and Shafii schools of jurisprudence. Most other Saudis are Shi'a Muslims, most of whom are Twelvers, the term for those who follow Muhammad ibn Hasan as the twelfth imam. There are also Shi'a Seveners, who follow the seventh imam, Ismail ibn Jafar. Other Islam groups include Ashraf, Nakhawala, and Zaydis. The holy city of Mecca is the center of Islam and the site of the sacred Ka'bah sanctuary, toward which all Muslims face at prayer. A pilgrimage to Mecca is one of the five basic obligations of Islam and is incumbent upon every Muslim who is physically and financially able to perform it. There are several thousand foreign Christian employees—Arab, North American, and European. There are also small communities of Jews, Hindus, and Buddhists. The government claims that the Holy Koran and Shari'ah (Islamic law) are the country's constitution. Shari'ah is the basis of the judicial system. As such, the government strictly controls all religious activities. The public worship of non-Muslim faiths is prohibited. While non-Muslim foreigners are theoretically permitted to worship privately, the guidelines that distinguish between public and private worship are ambiguous, leading to severe restrictions on non-Muslim worship. Proselytizing of non-Muslim religions is illegal and conversion of Muslims to other faiths is a capital offense. Eid al-Fitr and Eid al-Adha are observed as national holidays.

11 TRANSPORTATION

The CIA reported that Saudi Arabia had a total of 221,372 km (137,554 mi) of roads as of 2006, of which 47,529 km (29,533 mi) are paved. Railroads extend for 1,378 km (634 mi). There are 217 airports, which transported 17.51 million passengers in 2009 according to the World Bank.

Once the camel was the chief means of transportation in Saudi Arabia, but enormous strides have been made since the early 1970s. Modern roads link Jeddah, Mecca, Medina, Aṭ Ṭā'if, and Riyadh. A new highway connects Saudi Arabia with Jordan, and a causeway completed in 1986 offers a direct connection with Bahrain. Most within-country freight is hauled by truck. The Saudi Government Railroad, which operates between Ad Dammām and Riyadh over a length of 575 km (357 mi), was built by the Arabian American Oil Co. (ARAMCO) during the 1950s.

The government-owned Saudi Arabian Airlines (Saudia) operates regular domestic and foreign flights to major cities. Because of the large distances that separate the main cities, air travel is preferred within the kingdom.

Jeddah, on the Red Sea, is the chief port of entry for Muslim pilgrims going to Mecca. Saudi Arabia has the largest seaport network in the Near East, with 21 ports and nearly 200 piers. Ports include Ad Dammām, Yanbu' al-Bahr, Jizan, Duba, Jeddah, Jizan, Rabigh, Ra's al Khafji, Mishab, Ras Tanura, Madinat Yanbu' al Sinaiyah, and Jubail (Al-Jubayl). In 2010, there were 74 ships of 1,000 gross registered tons or more in the merchant fleet. The traditional dhow is still used for coastal trade.

12 HISTORY

For several thousand years, Arabia has been inhabited by nomadic Semitic tribes. Towns were established at various oases and along caravan routes. During the 7th century ad, followers of Muhammad expanded beyond the Mecca-Medina region and within a century had conquered most of the Mediterranean region between Persia in the east and Spain in the west. Although Arabs were dominant in many parts of the Muslim world and there was a great medieval flowering of Arab civilization, the peninsula itself (except for the holy cities of Mecca and Medina) declined in importance and remained virtually isolated for almost a thousand years. Throughout this period, Arabia was barely more than a province of successive Islamic caliphates that established their capitals in Damascus, Baghdād, Cairo, and Constantinople (now Istanbul).

The foundations of the Kingdom of Saudi Arabia were laid in the 18th century by the fusion of the military power of the Sa'ud family and Wahhabism, an Islamic puritan doctrine preached by Muhammad bin 'Abd al-Wahhab. Muhammad ibn-Sa'ud (r. 1744–65) and his son, 'Abd al-'Aziz (r. 1765–1803), gave the religious reformer refuge at Ad-Dar'iyah, in central Arabia, and together they embarked on a program of religious reform and territorial expansion. By 1801, Najd and Al-Ahsa were occupied. 'Abd al-'Aziz's son and successor, Sa'ud (r. 1803–14), brought the Hijaz under Saudi control and took the holy city of Mecca. The Ottoman Turks called on their governor of Egypt, Muhammad 'Ali, to put down the Saudis. A long struggle (1811–18) finally resulted in Saudi defeat. During that time, Sa'ud died, and his son, 'Abdallah (r. 1814–18), was captured and beheaded.

When international conditions forced Muhammad 'Ali to withdraw his occupation forces in 1840, the Saudis embarked upon a policy of reconquest. Under Faisal (Faysal, r. 1843–67), Wahhabi control was reasserted over Najd, Al-Ahsa, and Oman, with Riyadh as the new capital. (Hijaz remained under the control of the sharifs of Mecca until 1925.) After Faisal's death, conflict between his sons led to a decline in the family's fortunes. Taking advantage of these quarrels, the Ibn-Rashids, a former Saudi vassal family, gained control of Najd and conquered Riyadh. The Saudi family fled to Kuwait in 1891.

In January 1902, 'Abd al-'Aziz, a grandson of Faisal, who was to gain fame under the name Ibn-Sa'ud, succeeded in driving the Ibn-Rashid garrison out of Riyadh. At a decisive battle in 1906, the Rashidi power was broken. In 1913, the Saudis again brought

Al-Ahsa under their control, and in December 1915, Ibn-Sa'ud signed a treaty with the British that placed Saudi foreign relations under British control in return for a sizable subsidy.

Warfare broke out again in Arabia in 1919, when Hussein ibn-'Ali (Husayn ibn-'Ali), the sharif of Mecca, who had become an independent king, attacked the Saudis. Hussein was defeated, and Ibn-Sa'ud annexed 'Asir. In 1921, he finally rid Arabia of the Rashids, and by 1923, he had consolidated his kingdom by occupying the districts west and north of Ha'il. Hussein of Mecca provoked another conflict with Ibn-Sa'ud in March 1924 by proclaiming himself caliph. War broke out, and the Saudis captured Aṭ Ṭa'if, Mecca, and Medina (December 1925). 'Ali ibn-Hussein ('Ali ibn-Husayn), who had replaced his father as king of Hijaz, then abdicated, and in November 1925, Ibn-Sa'ud entered Jeddah. This increase in Ibn-Sa'ud's territory was acknowledged by the British in a treaty of 20 May 1927 that annulled the 1915 agreement and recognized his independence. On 22 September 1932, the various parts of the realm were amalgamated into the Kingdom of Saudi Arabia, with much the same boundaries that exist today.

With the discovery of oil in the 1930s, the history of Saudi Arabia was irrevocably altered. Reserves have proved vast—about one-fourth of the world's total—and production, begun in earnest after World War II, has provided a huge income, much of it expended on infrastructure and social services. Saudi Arabia's petroleum-derived wealth has considerably enhanced the country's influence in world economic and political forums. Following the 1967 Arab-Israeli War, the Saudi government undertook a vast aid program in support of Egypt, Syria, and Jordan. Saudi Arabia joined the 1973 Arab boycott against the United States and the Netherlands and, as a key member of Organization of the Petroleum Exporting Countries (OPEC), lent its support to the huge rise in oil prices during the 1970s. This move had stunning consequences for the world economy and also caused a dramatic upsurge in Saudi Arabia's wealth and power. Since the 1980s, the government has regulated its petroleum production to stabilize the international oil market and has used its influence as the most powerful moderate member of OPEC to restrain the more radical members.

Political life in Saudi Arabia remained basically stable in the last third of the 20th century, despite several abrupt changes of leadership. In November 1964, Crown Prince Faisal (Faysal ibn 'Abd al-'Aziz as-Sa'ud), a son of Ibn-Sa'ud, became king and prime minister following the forced abdication of his brother, King Sa'ud. His first act as prime minister was to announce a sweeping reorganization of the government, and his major social reform was the abolition of slavery. In March 1975, King Faisal was assassinated by a nephew in an apparently isolated act of revenge. Faisal was succeeded by Crown Prince Khaled (Khalid ibn-'Abd al-'Aziz as-Sa'ud), who embarked on an expanded development program. King Khaled died of a heart attack in June 1982, and his half-brother, Crown Prince Fahd ibn-'Abd al-'Aziz as-Sa'ud, ascended the throne. King Fahd encouraged continuing modernization while seeking to preserve the nation's social stability and Islamic heritage. King Fahd, who had been frail since suffering a debilitating stroke in 1995, died at the age of 82 on 1 August 2005. He had delegated the daily affairs of state to Crown Prince Abdullah bin Abd al-Aziz al Sa'ud, his half-brother, since his stroke. Upon Fahd's death, Abdullah became king.

As the custodian of the holy Muslim shrines at Mecca and Medina, the monarchy has been deeply embarrassed by several incidents: the seizure of the Grand Mosque in Mecca by about 500 Islamic militants in 1979, which led to the deaths of more than 160; a riot by Iranian pilgrims during the 1987 pilgrimage, which cost 400 lives; and the suffocation of more than 1,400 pilgrims in a tunnel at the Grand Mosque in 1990. Misfortune continued in 1994, when a stampede in Mecca killed 270 pilgrims rushing toward a cavern for a symbolic stoning ritual, and in 1997, when as many as 300 pilgrims were killed in a fire at a campsite outside the holy city. In 2004, a stampede during the Hajj pilgrimage left 251 dead. In 2006, 363 Hajj pilgrims were crushed in a crowd during a stone-throwing ritual in Mecca.

When Iraq invaded Kuwait in 1990, Saudi Arabia, fearing Iraqi aggression, radically altered its traditional policy to permit the stationing of foreign troops on its soil. (The government was criticized by senior Saudi religious scholars for taking this step.) Riyadh made substantial contributions of arms, oil, and funds to the allied victory. It also expelled workers from Jordan, Yemen, and members of the Palestine Liberation Organization (PLO) for giving support to Iraq in the period after the invasion. Saudi Arabia's wealth and selective generosity has given it great political influence throughout the world and especially in the Middle East. It suspended aid to Egypt after that country's peace talks with Israel at Camp David, Maryland, but renewed relations in 1987. It secretly made substantial funds available to US president Ronald Reagan's administration for combating Marxist regimes in Central America. The kingdom played a key role in creating the Gulf Cooperation Council (GCC) and in working for an end to the civil strife in Lebanon. It actively supported Iraq during the war with Iran and tried, in vain, to prevent the conflict with Kuwait.

Saudi Arabia and the United States consult closely on political, economic, commercial, and security matters. The United States, with the United Kingdom, is a major supplier of arms and offers training and other support to the kingdom's defenses. These supports grew more visible following the Gulf War and continued Iraqi intransigence in the face of increased US and international pressure to disarm. The increased US military presence in Saudi Arabia in 1993–94 caused considerable irritation among conservative elements of Saudi society, who felt that the US military presence was blasphemous to Islam. In 1995, seven people, including five Americans, were killed in a terrorist attack on a Saudi National Guard Training Center in Riyadh. In June 1996, a car bomb detonated in front of a housing complex for US military personnel, killing 19 US servicemen, causing considerable uproar in the United States, and leading military planners to relocate US military bases to remote desert areas.

By the end of the 1990s, the Islamist backlash that followed Saudi-US cooperation in the Gulf War had been contained through the (mostly) temporary detention of hundreds of Islamic radicals and the long-term detention of their most prominent leaders. At the turn of the 21st century, much of the Saudis' attention was focused on unaccustomed economic pressures resulting from a 40% drop in oil prices in 1998. With almost half its GDP coming from oil, the country's budget deficit had soared as export revenues plummeted. Crown Prince Abdullah was instrumental in pushing through the production cutbacks agreed to by the OPEC countries in March 1999.

LOCATION: 16°23′ to 32°14′N; 34°30′ to 56°22′ W. BOUNDARY LENGTHS: Jordan, 728 kilometers (455 miles); Iraq, 814 kilometers (505 miles); Kuwait, 222 kilometers (138 miles); Persian Gulf coastline, 751 kilometers (468 miles); Qatar, 60 kilometers (37 miles); UAE, 457 kilometers (285 miles); Oman, 676 kilometers (420 miles); Yemen 1,458 kilometers (906 miles); Red Sea coastline, 1,889 kilometers (1,170 miles). TERRITORIAL SEA LIMIT: 12 miles.

At a summit held in Beirut in March 2002, the Arab League accepted a Saudi proposal for peace between Israel and the Palestinians, put forward by Crown Prince Abdullah. Known as the "Beirut Declaration," the plan offered Israel normalized relations with the Arab states and a guarantee of peace and security in exchange for a full Israeli withdrawal from the territories occupied by Israel after the 1967 Arab-Israeli War, a "just solution to the Palestinian refugee problem," and Israeli recognition of a Palestinian state

with its capital at East Jerusalem. The proposal was introduced against the backdrop of an escalation in violence in Israel and the occupied territories in spring 2002. In April, Crown Prince Abdullah met with US president George W. Bush, and presented him with an eight-point list of proposed agreements for immediate peace in the Middle East. After the peace plan was put forward, however, the violence in Israel and the West Bank and Gaza increased. Nevertheless, at a summit in Riyadh in March 2007, the

Arab League resurrected Abdullah's peace plan; Israel, however, said it would not agree to the clause in the plan regarding the right of return for Palestinian refugees.

Because 15 of the 19 hijackers involved in the 11 September 2001 terrorist attacks on the United States were Saudis, in addition to al-Qaeda leader Osama bin Laden, the US placed pressure on Saudi Arabia to undertake counterterrorism measures. In the run-up to the 2003 Iraq War, Saudi Arabia debated what degree of support it would offer the US in the event of a war with Iraq. On 26 February 2003, Saudi Arabia stated that it would allow the use of the Prince Sultan Air Base, where most of the 5,000 US troops based in the kingdom were located, only for the enforcement of a "no-fly" zone over southern Iraq. It stated that it would not agree to allow US troops and planes based in the country to undertake a war with Iraq. The war began on 19 March 2003. In April, the US announced it would pull nearly all of its military forces out of Saudi Arabia. Both countries stressed that they would remain allies.

Saudi Arabia's stability began to be seriously rocked in the early 2000s, with a series of suicide bombings and terrorist attacks aimed at Western and local targets. During April 2004, four police officers and a security officer were killed in attacks near Riyadh, and a car bomb at a security forces' headquarters left four dead and 148 wounded. A group linked to the terrorist organization al-Qaeda claimed responsibility for the act. Al-Qaeda has long demanded that the Saudi regime sever its ties to the West and to America in particular. It also holds that the Saudi regime is corrupt.

While the Saudi regime was being destabilized by terrorist attacks, calls for political reform caused concern among the rulers and pointed to a need to respond to such demands for change. In September 2003, 300 intellectuals, both men and women, signed a petition calling for far-reaching political reforms. In October, the police broke up an unprecedented rally for political reform in the center of Riyadh; more than 270 people were arrested. In November 2003, King Fahd granted wider powers to the Majlis al Shura (Consultative Council), enabling it to propose legislation without his permission. From February to April 2005, the first-ever nationwide municipal elections were held, although women were not permitted to take part in the vote.

After King Fahd's death in 2005, the royal family took measures to formalize the royal succession, in October 2006, in an attempt to prevent infighting among the next generation of princes. In October 2007, the royal family issued a decree ordering an overhaul of the judicial system.

In May 2009, the Council of Ministers announced that local council elections scheduled for later that year would be postponed for another two years. In the official statement, the Saudi government claimed that the delay was necessary in order to allow time to initiate reforms that would grant more power to the councils and expand the electoral process. When the local councils were formed in 2005, voters chose half of the representatives, while the other half were appointed. Some political activists claimed that the delay was simply a sign of the ruling family's reluctance to share power.

After the death of the Crown Prince Sultan on 5 November 2011, King Abdullah appointed Prince Naif bin Abdul Aziz as Crown Prince. By appointing Prince Salman as the new Minister of Defense, King Abdullah also placed Salman in the lead position

to become Crown Prince when Naif becomes king. If the king dies before Crown Prince Naif, who is 11 years younger, Naif would be appointed king.

In March 2011, following the beginning of several revolutionary uprisings in North Africa, the government of Saudi Arabia issued a ban against all citizen protests and marches, stating that such demonstrations were contrary to Islamic Shari'ah law and the values of Saudi Arabian society. Earlier in the year, there had been a series of small protests among the Shi'a minority in the eastern province. In an effort to further discourage the eruption of anti-government protests among the people, the king announced a $37 billion package of new benefits for citizens, which included a 15% pay increase for state employees and new funding for housing, social security, and education abroad. Because of this benefits package, it is estimated that about $130 billion was added to spending projections over the next five years. The total number of public-sector jobs was increased. In addition, King Abdullah pledged large numbers of new housing units. Under the banner of the Gulf Cooperation Council (GCC), Saudi troops marched into Bahrain to quell demonstrations in 2011. The Saudi government promised Bahrain $10 billion through the GCC over the next decade and made large financial commitments to both Oman and Jordan, Saudi allies, to provide support against mass protests.

13 GOVERNMENT

Saudi Arabia is a religiously based monarchy in which the sovereign's dominant powers are regulated according to Muslim law (Shari'ah), tribal law, and custom.

There is no written constitution; laws must be compatible with Islamic law. In a decree of March 1992, the king was granted exclusive power to name the crown prince his successor. The Council of Ministers, first set up in 1953, is appointed by the king to advise on policy, originate legislation, and supervise the growing bureaucracy. The post of prime minister is reserved for the king and the crown prince is appointed first deputy prime minister. Most other important posts in the cabinet are reserved for members of the royal family.

In 1992, King Fahd announced the creation of the Majlis al Shura, or Consultative Council, an advisory body that would provide a forum for public debate. The king appointed 60 male citizens not belonging to the royal family to four-year terms on this body, which held its first meeting on 29 December 1992. In 1997, King Fahd increased the size of the Majlis to 90 members. In 2001, membership was increased to 120. In 2003, King Fahd expanded the powers of the Majlis al Shura. In 2005, nationwide municipal elections were held, although women did not participate. King Fahd died in 2005, and his half-brother Crown Prince Abdullah became king.

In 2006, King Abdallah announced the formation of the Allegiance Commission, which would select a king and crown prince upon the death or incapacitation of either. Only direct male descendants of Abdul Aziz, the kingdoms' founder, are eligible to become crown prince or king.

14 POLITICAL PARTIES

Although there are no political parties in Saudi Arabia, various groups do function as blocs, contending for influence. Important among these groups are the conservative *'ulama* (religious scholars) and members of the royal family. Other alliances—among merchants, businessmen, professionals, and leading families—are concerned with economic matters. There is also a small but growing middle class that seems to want greater political participation and a less restrictive social environment. Each group brings its weight to bear on the policy-making bodies of the government and the king, whose leadership is upheld so long as he adheres to Islamic law, tradition, and the collective decisions of the 'ulama. In opposition to the royal family are small, strictly outlawed groups of prodemocracy activists and extremist Islamists. The latter have engaged in terrorist attacks, principally against signs of Western influence. Identified groups connected with Islamists include the Committee for the Defense of Legitimate Rights, the Reform Movement, and the Islamic Awakening.

15 LOCAL GOVERNMENT

The kingdom is divided into 13 provinces, each headed by a crown-appointed governor, often a prince, other member of the royal family, or a member from an allied family. The provinces are subdivided into 118 governorates. Tribal and village leaders (sheikhs) report directly to provincial governors, giving the central government some control over outlying regions. Provincial governors, in turn, report to the minister of the interior. Each sheikh traditionally rules in consultation with a council. A large segment of the population remains tribally organized: tribes, headed by paramount sheikhs, are divided into subtribes, headed by local sheikhs. Decisions are made by tribal sheikhs, emirs, or other chiefs and their councils (*majlis*).

16 JUDICIAL SYSTEM

The king acts as the highest court of appeal and has the power of pardon; access to the king and the right to petition him are well-established traditions. The judiciary consists of lower courts that handle misdemeanors and minor civil cases; high courts of Islamic law (Shari'ah); and courts of appeal. Islamic law of the Hanbali school prevails in Saudi Arabia, but justice is also based on tribal and customary law. Capital and corporal punishment are permitted; the Supreme Court reviews all sentences of execution, cutting, or stoning. A separate military justice system exercises jurisdiction over uniformed personnel and civilian government authorities.

There is no written constitution. In 2007 the Supreme Court was created as the highest court of authority to replace the Supreme Judicial Council. Before 2007, the Justice Ministry was responsible for appointment and promotion of judges. The 2007 law transferred the power to appoint and promote judges, as well as to establish and abolish courts, to the Supreme Court. Although independence of the judiciary is guaranteed by law, courts are subject to the influence of royal family members. At the provincial level, governors also reportedly exercise influence over local judges.

Shari'ah summary courts have jurisdiction over common criminal cases and civil suits regarding marriage, divorce, child custody, and inheritance. While summary courts try cases involving small penalties, more serious crimes go to the Shari'ah courts of common pleas. Appeals from both courts are heard by the appeals courts in Mecca and Riyadh. There is also a Court of Cassation, as well as administrative tribunals that deal with proceedings involving claims against the government and enforcement of foreign judgments.

The military tribunals have jurisdiction over military personnel and civil servants charged with violation of military regulations.

17 ARMED FORCES

The International Institute for Strategic Studies reports that armed forces in Saudi Arabia totaled 233,500 members in 2011. The force is comprised of 75,000 from the army, 13,500 from the navy, 20,000 from the air force, 16,000 from air defense, 9,000 from an industrial security force, and 100,000 members of a national guard. Armed forces represent 2.9% of the labor force in Saudi Arabia. Defense spending totaled $62.2 billion and accounted for 10% of GDP.

18 INTERNATIONAL COOPERATION

Saudi Arabia is a charter member of the UN, having joined on 24 October 1945, and participates in ESCWA and several nonregional specialized agencies, such as the FAO, UNESCO, UNIDO, UNCTAD, the ILO, the World Bank, the IAEA, and the WHO. It is a founding member of the Arab League, OPEC, and OAPEC. Saudi Arabia is also a member of the Arab Bank for Economic Development in Africa, the Arab Fund for Economic and Social Development, the African Development Bank, G-77, the Organization of the Islamic Conference (OIC), and the GCC. The nation has observer status with the OAS and the WTO.

Saudi Arabia has played a key role in promoting Israeli-Palestinian peace negotiations. Although supporting the Palestinian cause and the Arab League's boycott of Israel, the Saudi government in 1981 proposed that the Arab nations show willingness to extend diplomatic recognition to Israel in return for its withdrawal from lands occupied in the 1967 war (including the West Bank and East Jerusalem). Saudi Arabia supported international efforts against Iraq in the 1990–91 Gulf War and the 2003 Operation Iraqi Freedom. In February 2005, the Saudi government sponsored the first-ever Counterterrorism International Conference in Riyadh. Saudi Arabia is part of the Nonaligned Movement.

Saudi Arabia announced support for the establishment of a unified, independent, and sovereign Iraq, and in 2008 Foreign Minister Prince Saud al-Faisal reiterated Saudi Arabia's intention to open a diplomatic mission in Baghdad and appoint an ambassador. The kingdom is a charter member of the International Compact with Iraq and participates in the Expanded Iraq Neighbors process.

In environmental cooperation, Saudi Arabia is part of the Basel Convention, the Convention on Biological Diversity, CITES, the Convention on Migratory Species, the Kyoto Protocol, Stockholm Convention on Persistent Organic Pollutants, the Vienna Convention and its Montréal Protocol, and the UN Conventions on the Law of the Sea, Climate Change, and Desertification.

19 ECONOMY

The GDP rate of change in Saudi Arabia, as of 2010, was 3.7%. Inflation stood at 5.7%, and unemployment was reported at 10.8%. The economy is heavily dependent on oil production, which provides approximately 40% of GDP, 90% of export value, and 75% of government revenues. The country has the largest reserves of petroleum in the world, 25% of the proven total, with its northern neighbor, Iraq, holding second place and two other Arab neighbors, the United Arab Emirates and Kuwait, third and fourth.

Rapidly increasing oil income after the first oil shock, 1973–74, led by the Organization of Petroleum Exporting Countries (OPEC) group, was used to increase disposable income, defense expenditures, and economic development. OPEC was able to enforce a quadrupling of oil prices (from $2.50 per barrel to $10 per barrel) largely because of King Faisal's agreement to deploy the oil weapon in conjunction with the Yom Kippur War. Per capita income in current dollars peaked at $15,700 in 1980 after the second oil shock, in 1978–79, in conjunction with the Iranian Islamic revolution, sent oil prices to all-time highs, peaking at a little more than $40 per barrel in September 1980 at the start of the Iran-Iraq War. From there, population growth, a decreasing OPEC share of world oil production, oil conservation efforts among consumers, and limited success in diversifying the economy combined to reduce per capita income by 2004. The contribution of the oil sector (crude oil and refined products) to overall GDP, nevertheless, has substantially decreased, from 70% in 1980 to a 45% in 2006, and to an estimated 40% in 2010.

The government has always made economic diversification a top priority, seeking to develop industries using petroleum, such as petrochemicals, as well as to finance industrialization. In the capital-intensive oil industry, the Saudis have relied heavily on foreign workers. The kingdom's intolerance of democratic processes, labor unions, women's participation in the workplace, and foreign influences are impediments to development. The government encourages growth in agriculture as a means of reducing Saudi Arabia's reliance on food imports, but dramatic reductions in farm subsidies have resulted in a continuing decline in agricultural output.

20 INCOME

The CIA estimated that in 2010 the GDP of Saudi Arabia was $622 billion. The CIA defines GDP as the value of all final goods and services produced within a nation in a given year and computed on the basis of purchasing power parity (PPP) rather than value as measured on the basis of the rate of the exchange based on current dollars. The per capita GDP was estimated at $24,200. The annual growth rate of GDP was 3.7%. The average inflation rate was 5.4%. It was estimated that agriculture accounted for 2.6% of GDP, industry 61.8%, and services 35.6%.

According to the World Bank, remittances from citizens living abroad totaled $236.5 million.

As of 2011 the most recent study by the World Bank reported that actual individual consumption in Saudi Arabia was 36.8% of GDP and accounted for 0.43% of world consumption. By comparison, the United States accounted for 25.44% of world individual consumption. The World Bank also estimated that 6.6% of Saudi Arabia's GDP was spent on food and beverages, 8.3% on housing and household furnishings, 2.3% on clothes, 3.2% on health, 3.4% on transportation, 0.8% on communications, 1.2% on recreation, 1.4% on restaurants and hotels, and 2.7% on miscellaneous goods and services and purchases from abroad.

21 LABOR

As of 2010, Saudi Arabia had a total labor force of 7.337 million people. Within that labor force, CIA estimates in 2005 noted that 6.7% were employed in agriculture, 21.4% in industry, and 71.9% in the service sector.

Approximately 80% of the Saudi labor force were foreigners, working mostly in the oil and construction sector. By 2010, unemployment was estimated at 10.8% (this data is only for males). Employment rates for women are not tallied by the government.

Labor unions are illegal and collective bargaining is forbidden as well. Workers have few protections against employers. This is especially true of foreign workers, who are often forced to work long hours and beyond the terms specified by their contracts. Foreign workers have little redress against Saudi employers, since the labor system usually sides with the latter and employers can delay cases until the workers have to return home. Saudi employers routinely prevent workers from obtaining exit visas. The government allowed the formation of labor committees, which are permitted to make recommendations to employers. In 2005, labor laws were put into place, but domestic workers were excluded. The Majlis al-Shura, a consultative assembly with a role in the legislative process, passed a law covering domestic workers, which is now with the King and the Council of Ministers for review.

By royal decree, an eight-hour day and 48-hour week are standard. It is reported that domestic workers labor up to 20 hours a day, seven days a week. Labor outdoors is prohibited when the temperature exceeds 50°c (122°f). Foreign workers report that these regulations are seldom enforced. With the consent of parents, children may work as young as 13, and children rarely work in Saudi Arabia outside of family businesses. There is no minimum wage. The minimum age for employment is 14. Saudi Arabia did not conform to the International Labor Organization's (ILO) convention safeguarding workers' rights. A 2004 decree addressed non-Saudi workers' rights, and the Ministry of Labor began taking employers to the Board of Grievances. Some of the penalties include banning employers from recruiting foreign and/or domestic workers for a minimum of five years.

22 AGRICULTURE

The country's major crops include wheat, barley, tomatoes, melons, dates, and citrus. Cereal production in 2009 amounted to 1.4 million tons, fruit production 1.8 million tons, and vegetable production 2.4 million tons. Small owner-operated farms characterize Saudi Arabia's land-tenure system. About 96% of the farm area is owned, and only 4% rented. Less than 3% of the agricultural holdings are of eight hectares (20 acres) or more, and 45% are 0.4 hectare (1 acre) or less in size. Although Saudi Arabia has more than 18 million date palms and provides more than 13% of the world's supply of dates, the growing of dates has declined in favor of wheat, barley, sorghum, tomatoes, onions, grapes, watermelon, and a variety of other fruits and vegetables. Nevertheless, dates remain the only major staple food crop with production sufficient to meet local demand.

Aquifers supply 80% of agriculture's water requirements but are not renewable. Agricultural irrigation accounts for 88% of total water needs, with wheat production alone using about one-third of the country's annual water supply.

23 ANIMAL HUSBANDRY

The UN Food and Agriculture Organization (FAO) reported that Saudi Arabia dedicated 170 million hectares (420.1 million acres) to permanent pasture or meadow in 2009. During that year, the country tended 146 million chickens and 421,000 head of cattle. The production from these animals amounted to 149,754 tons of beef and veal and 2.4 million tons of milk. Saudi Arabia also produced 3,180 tons of cattle hide and 12,160 tons of raw wool.

As imports of animal foodstuffs have increased and as greater varieties of agricultural products have been produced locally, camels have declined steadily in importance as a source of food. Arabia has long been famed for its horses, but the importance of the Arabian horse as an export item is now virtually nil. Donkeys and mules are still valued as pack animals, and the white donkeys of Al-Ahsa are well known. Sheep are found in all parts of Saudi Arabia where pasturage is available; they are raised for milk, as well as for meat and wool. Goats are kept for milk; their hair is used in rugs and tents, and the skins serve as water bags. Because sheep production in Saudi Arabia increased, import of sheep decreased significantly to 1,452,930 sheep in 2008.

The consumption of chicken meat in the Kingdom ranks among the highest in the world and is still slowly increasing. Poultry meat is the main meat consumed on a weight basis. Saudi Arabia is self-sufficient in milk production. There is no hog raising, and importation of pork products is banned, as it is contrary to Islamic law.

24 FISHING

Saudi Arabia had 170 decked commercial fishing boats in 2008. The annual capture totaled 68,000 tons according to the UN FAO. Fishing provides employment and self-sufficiency to some communities on both Saudi coasts, although cash earnings are negligible. With rare exceptions, traditional fishing techniques are used. One of the few growth areas in this sector has been the export of Gulf shrimp.

25 FORESTRY

Approximately 0.5% of Saudi Arabia is covered by forest. The value of all forest products, including roundwood, totaled $59.5 million. The only forest growth is found in the mountainous area that extends from southern Hijaz to 'Asir, accounting for no more than 0.6% of the total area. The principal varieties—acacia, date, juniper, wild olive, sidr, tamarind, and tamarisk—are generally not useful for timber, but some wood from date palms is used for construction.

26 MINING

Oil continues to dominate Saudi Arabia's mining sector. The country supplied 12.4% of the world's crude oil output in 2009. Petroleum and petroleum products accounted for 90% of the country's export earnings in 2008 and 70% of government revenues. Crude oil and natural gas accounted for 61% of GDP; other minerals contributed 0.4% of GDP. Saudi Arabia has nevertheless diversified by expanding its gold production, as well as production of cement, fertilizer, petrochemicals, and steel. Cement production and fertilizer manufacturing were also among the country's leading industries.

Production of ore concentrate and bullion (metal content) in 2009 included copper, 2,000 metric tons; gold, 5,500 kg, and silver, 9,500 kg (estimated). In 2009 the country also produced lead, zinc, barite, basalt clays phosphatic fertilizer, granite, crude gypsum, lime, limestone marble, nitrogen, nitrogenous fertilizers, pozzo-

lan, salt, sand and gravel, silica sand, scoria, and sulfur. Mining operations continue at the ancient gold and silver underground mine Mahd adh-Dhahab (literally, "cradle of gold"), which is located southeast of Medina and probably dates from the time of King Solomon (10th century BC). Other gold producers are the open-pit silver and gold Amar Mine, southwest of Riyadh, which began operations in 2000, and the Sukhaybirat surface mine, northwest of Riyadh.

Feasibility studies at the Balghah Mine estimated resources to be 40 million tons at a grade of 1 grams per ton of gold. The remote Zabirah bauxite deposit has minable resources of 102 million tons. About 3,000 showings for at least 50 metallic and nonmetallic minerals have been located. Substantial national reserves of gold, iron ore, silver, copper, zinc, lead, pyrites, phosphate, magnesite, barite, marble, and gypsum have been suspected. An intensive search was under way by Saudi and foreign companies.

All minerals, including petroleum and natural gas, are owned by the government. A modern mining code encourages foreign participation, although majority holdings by national interests have increasingly been stressed. The Foreign Investment Act of 2000 gave international investors the same rights and privileges as Saudi investors. The government was also considering a revised mineral policy to attract additional investment in the mining sector. In 2000, the government established the Supreme Council for Petroleum and Mineral Affairs. The state-owned Saudi Arabian Mining Co. (Ma'aden) was created in 1997 and participated actively in and promoted mineral exploration and mining activities throughout the kingdom. Several metal and industrial mineral mining projects were expected to come onstream by 2020.

27 ENERGY AND POWER

The World Bank reported in 2008 that Saudi Arabia produced 204.2 billion kWh of electricity and consumed 186.7 billion kWh, or 7,146 kWh per capita. All energy came from fossil fuels. Per capita oil consumption was 6,514 kg. Oil production totaled 8.9 million barrels of oil a day. Saudi Arabia has one-fourth of the world's proven oil reserves and some of the lowest oil production costs. For the foreseeable future, Saudi Arabia will likely remain the largest net exporter of oil in the world. It is also a member of the Organization of Petroleum Exporting Countries (OPEC).

In 2011 Saudi Arabia had proven oil reserves estimated at 263 billion barrels, which includes 2.5 billion barrels, or half of the oil reserves in the Saudi-Kuwaiti divided, or neutral, zone. About two-thirds of the country's reserves are graded as "light" or "extra light," with the remainder in the "medium" or "heavy" grades. Saudi Arabia has around 100 major oil and gas fields and more than 1,500 wells. However, more than 50% of the country's oil reserves are in only eight fields. This includes the Ghawar and the Safaniya fields. The former has estimated reserves of 70 billion barrels and is the world's largest oil field, while the latter is the world's largest offshore oil field, with reserves estimated at 35 billion barrels. As a member of OPEC, Saudi Arabia is subject to OPEC's production quotas. Saudi Arabia has seven domestic oil refineries with a refining capacity of 2.1 million barrels a day.

In addition to its vast oil reserves, Saudi Arabia also has proven natural gas reserves estimated at 275 trillion cu ft (including the neutral zone), which places the country fourth in the world behind Russia, Iran, and Qatar, respectively. About 60% of the coun-

Principal Trading Partners – Saudi Arabia (2010)

(In millions of US dollars)

Country	Total	Exports	Imports	Balance
World	348,224.0	251,147.0	97,077.0	154,070.0
United States	42,434.0	29,684.0	12,750.0	16,934.0
China	40,280.0	28,875.0	11,405.0	17,470.0
Japan	39,747.0	32,618.0	7,129.0	25,489.0
South Korea	29,394.0	24,382.0	5,012.0	19,370.0
India	23,188.0	18,235.0	4,953.0	13,282.0
Taiwan	11,883.0	10,781.0	1,102.0	9,679.0
Singapore	11,114.0	10,219.0	895.0	9,324.0
France	9,258.0	3,016.0	6,242.0	-3,226.0
Germany	7,847.0	532.0	7,315.0	-6,783.0
Italy	7,558.0	3,884.0	3,674.0	210.0

(…) data not available or not significant.

(n.s.) not specified.

SOURCE: *2011 Direction of Trade Statistics Yearbook,* New York: United Nations, 2011.

try's natural gas reserves are associated or produced along with oil, and come from the Ghawar, Safaniya, and Zuluf fields. One-third of the country's natural gas reserves are in the Ghawar field alone. Natural gas production was estimated at 2.7 trillion cu ft in 2007, while 13 to 14 percent of total production was lost to venting, flaring, reinjection and natural processes.

Two major pipelines operated actively in Saudi Arabia: the five million barrel per day Petroline, used to transport crude oil to refineries in western Saudi Arabia and to the Red Sea for export, and the 290,000 barrel per day Abqaiq-Yanbu pipeline, which carries natural gas liquids to petrochemical plants in Yanbu. The IPSA pipeline had been closed indefinitely since Iraq invaded Kuwait in 1990.

Saudi Arabia has limited waterpower resources, and oil-powered diesel engines generate most of its electric power. Solar energy is becoming increasingly important as an alternative to diesel power, particularly for use in the desalination of seawater.

28 INDUSTRY

Although the Saudi economy has been virtually synonymous with crude oil, the country is attempting to diversify its manufacturing. Industrial products include cement, steel, glass, metal manufactures, automotive parts, and building materials, along with petroleum refinery products and petrochemicals (primarily methanol, ethylene, and polypropylene).

Industries producing consumer goods for the local market rely for the most part on imported raw materials. The most notable growth has occurred in food processing, such as meat-packing plants, flour mills, ice cream, yogurt, other dairy processing plants, and vegetable canneries. Other companies produce canvas cloth, surgical supplies, paper products, plastic pipes, electric appliances, paints, detergents, and pharmaceuticals.

29 SCIENCE AND TECHNOLOGY

Patent applications in science and technology as of 2007, according to the World Bank, totaled 128 in Saudi Arabia. Public financing of science was 0.05% of GDP. The government encourages importation of high technology, especially in the oil industry, but its own commitment to national technological development has

been limited. The Industrial Studies and Development Center is located in Riyadh, and the King Fahad University of Petroleum and Minerals, founded in 1963, is in Dhahran. Other institutions offering courses in basic and applied sciences include King Abdulaziz University, founded in 1967 at Jeddah; King Faisal University, founded in 1975 at Dammam and Al-Hassa; King Sa'ud University, founded in 1957 at Riyadh; and Yanbu Industrial College, founded in 1989 at Yanbu al-Sinaiyeh. In 1987–97, science and engineering students accounted for 17% of college and university enrollments. The King Abdul Aziz City for Science and Technology was founded in 1977 at Riyadh to formulate national policy for science and technology development and to draw up strategy and plans for its implementation.

30 DOMESTIC TRADE

Jeddah and Riyadh are the commercial and business centers of the country. Most major cities host large, modern supermarkets and specialty retail stores offering wide varieties of goods and services. Franchising has become popular with a wide range of goods and service-based establishments. Barter is the traditional means by which nomads and farmers obtain each other's products, and weekly markets are held in villages and small towns. However, the economy is being progressively monetized and is now completely so in the towns and cities. Newspapers, magazines, and billboards are the principal means of advertising.

Normal business hours vary in different provinces but are usually from 8 a.m. to 12 noon and from 3 to 6 p.m., Saturday through Wednesday. During the month of Ramadan, the workday is limited to six hours. Banks are generally open from 8 a.m. to 12 noon, Saturday through Wednesday. Government offices and private businesses are closed Thursdays and Fridays. Markets and shops are open until 9 p.m. Most businesses, including stores and restaurants, take breaks at the designated Muslim prayer times, which occur five times throughout the day. These breaks generally last about a half hour each.

31 FOREIGN TRADE

Saudi Arabia imported $88.35 billion worth of goods and services in 2010, while exporting $237.9 billion worth of goods and services. Major import partners in 2010 were the United States, 12.4%; China, 11.1%; Germany, 7.1%; Japan, 6.9%; UK, 4.9%; France, 6.1%; India, 4.7%; South Korea, 4.6%; and Italy, 4%. Its major export partners were Japan, 14.3%; China, 13.1%; the United States, 13%; South Korea, 8.8%; India, 8.3%; and Singapore, 4.5%.

Saudi Arabia's commodity exports are dominated by mineral fuels. Crude petroleum (79% of total exports, 16.3% of world crude petroleum exports) and refined petroleum products (12% and 7.1%, respectively) are the largest exports. Other exports include polymers (1.2%) and industrial alcohols (1.4%, accounting for 8.1% of the world's industrial alcohol exports).

32 BALANCE OF PAYMENTS

In 2010 Saudi Arabia had a foreign trade surplus of $41 billion. Foreign worker remittances, approximately $27 billion in 2010, continued to drain the current account. There are roughly six to seven million foreign workers and their families living in the

Balance of Payments – Saudi Arabia (2010)

(In millions of US dollars)

Current Account		**66,751.0**
Balance on goods		153,717.0
Imports	-97,432.0	
Exports	251,149.0	
Balance on services		-66,089.0
Balance on income		170,044.0
Current transfers		-27,921.0
Capital Account		...
Financial Account		**-7,176.0**
Direct investment abroad		-3,907.0
Direct investment in Sa'udi Arabia		21,560.0
Portfolio investment assets		-18,939.0
Portfolio investment liabilities		1,503.0
Financial derivatives		...
Other investment assets		-6,523.0
Other investment liabilities		-870.0
Net Errors and Omissions		**-24,320.0**
Reserves and Related Items		**-35,255.0**

(…) data not available or not significant.

SOURCE: *Balance of Payment Statistics Yearbook 2011,* Washington, DC: International Monetary Fund, 2011.

country, and the remittances cause the currency to be subject to a mild devaluating pressure.

In 2000, the current account recorded a $14.3 billion surplus, which declined (in line with oil revenue) to $9.4 billion in 2001, despite a significant fall in service debits. Higher oil prices and output in 2002 and 2003 saw the current account surplus widen again, to $11.9 billion and $28 billion, respectively. This surplus increased $51.5 billion in 2004. Due to increased oil prices, surplus in 2008 reached a record $137 billion. In 2009, Saudi Arabia experienced a deficit for the first time in seven years of $17 billion, and in 2010 it reverted back to a surplus of $28.9 billion.

33 BANKING AND SECURITIES

Until the mid-20th century, Saudi Arabia had no formal money and banking system. To the degree that money was used, Saudis primarily used coins having a metallic content equal to their value (full-bodied coins) for storing value and limited exchange transactions in urban areas. For centuries, foreign coins had served the local inhabitants' monetary needs. Development of banking was inhibited by the Koranic injunction against interest. A few banking functions existed, such as money changers (largely for pilgrims visiting Mecca), who had informal connections with international currency markets. A foreign bank was established in Jeddah in 1926, but its importance was minor.

Foreign and domestic banks were formed as oil revenues began to increase. Their business consisted mostly of making short-term loans to finance imports, commercial trading, and businesses catering to pilgrims. Although lending at interest is prohibited by Islamic law, banking has flourished in Saudi Arabia as a conduit for the investment of oil money. The Saudi Arabian Monetary Agency (SAMA) was established by royal decree in 1952 to maintain the internal and external value of currency. The agency issues notes and coins with 100% cover in gold and convertible foreign exchange and regulates all banks and exchange dealers.

In 2011, there were 12 commercial banking houses, the largest of which was the National Commercial Bank. The major foreign partners include Citibank, Arab Bank Ltd., Banque Indosuez, HSBC Holdings, and ABN Amro.

In 2009, currency and demand deposits—an aggregate commonly known as M1—were equal to $139,082.1 billion. In that same year, M2—an aggregate equal to M1 plus savings deposits, small time deposits, and money market mutual funds—was $225,316 billion. At the end of 2010, the nation's gold bullion deposits totaled 332.9 tons.

SAMA runs a stock exchange in Saudi Arabia, created in 1990 as an over-the-counter market in which the commercial banks buy and sell shares by means of an electronic trading system. Although this system has facilitated easy access to transactions, the market remains relatively illiquid because of the small numbers of issuers and the narrow investor base. The market is closed to direct foreign investment, but foreigners can buy and trade shares of Saudi companies within a closed-end fund listed in the United Kingdom.

34 INSURANCE

The National Company for Cooperative Insurance was founded by royal decree in 1985 and is owned by three government agencies. Premiums cover oil facilities, major projects, and marine, aviation, motor, medical, and fire liabilities. In 2003, the government enacted the Control Law for Co-Operative Insurance Companies, requiring all insurance companies in Saudi Arabia to be locally incorporated joint-stock companies and to operate on a cooperative or mutual basis. In 2006, cooperative health insurance became mandatory, and employers were required to pay insurance coverage of foreign workers and their dependents.

35 PUBLIC FINANCE

Public expenditures typically have acted as the vanguard for economic growth and development since the early 1970s. After completing the infrastructure in the 1970s and early 1980s, the emphasis of development expenditures moved to education and training to encourage private enterprise. By 1987, 70% of non-oil GDP was coming from the private sector. Deficits have been common since 1983, as oil revenues have declined. Oil revenues typically account for nearly 75% of government revenues. Deep budget cuts over the past years; higher charges on energy, electricity, water, telephone, worker and visa fees; and reduced subsidies on fuels, utilities, and airline fares have combined to reduce the deficit. To finance the deficit, the government borrows from domestic financial markets. However, Saudi government finances are not transparent; a perennial uncertainty is the difference between the revenues received by the national oil company, Aramco, and what is turned over to the Ministry of Finance to fund government expenses. The difference goes to Aramco's operating expenses and numerous off-budget expenditures. Observers believe that one major use of the off-budget money has been to pay down arrears on contracts.

The US Central Intelligence Agency (CIA) estimated that in 2010 Saudi Arabia's central government took in revenues of approximately $197.3 billion and had expenditures of $167.1 billion. Public debt in 2010 amounted to 16.6% of GDP. Total external debt was $80.95 billion.

³⁶TAXATION

As of 2009, the corporate tax rate in Saudi Arabia for companies in the natural gas sector is 30%, with an 85% rate applied to businesses in the oil sector. Other companies are taxed at a flat rate of 20%. Generally, capital gains are treated as ordinary income and taxed the corporate rate of 20%. However, there is no capital gains tax if the shares sold by non-Saudi shareholders are traded on the Saudi stock exchange and were acquired after 30 July 2004. Gains derived from the sale of property, other than those assets used in business activity, are also exempt. Dividends and interest are subject to a 5% withholding tax. Royalties are subject to a 15% withholding rate. Foreigners who are self-employed professionals or general partners in Saudi partnerships are subject to these taxes.

Saudi Arabia has a flat 20% individual income tax rate on income that is domestically sourced. This income tax only applies to foreign citizens. Citizens of Saudi Arabia and other Gulf Cooperation Council (GCC) members pay a religious tax called the Zakat, an Islamic tax derived from the Shari'ah, which is applied directly to equity, less fixed assets, at a rate of 2.5%. The income of members of the royal family is tax exempt. There is no value-added tax (VAT) or sales tax.

³⁷CUSTOMS AND DUTIES

Saudi Arabia has increasingly used the tariff to protect local industries. The general tariff rate is 5%; new Saudi industries are protected by a 20% tariff rate. Importation of liquor, firearms, ammunition, narcotics, and certain other items is strictly forbidden, as are all imports from Israel and South Africa. No import taxes are levied beyond import tariffs.

³⁸FOREIGN INVESTMENT

Foreign direct investment (FDI) in Saudi Arabia was a net inflow of $21.6 billion according to World Bank figures published in 2010. FDI represented 1% of GDP.

A small group of upper-class Saudis have traditionally held substantial investments overseas. These Saudis hold large demand deposits in US and Western European banks and considerable investments in commercial ventures, especially real estate, in Egypt and other Middle Eastern countries. Since the early 1970s, the Saudi government has vastly increased its overseas investments in the United States, Western Europe, and Japan.

The Saudi government generally encourages foreign direct investment, especially in the case of joint ventures with Saudi partners. The foreign capital investment code specifies that foreign investments (1) must be a "development project," (2) must generate technology transfer, and (3) must have a minimum of 25% Saudi-owned equity in the project. However, in 1999, the government began revising its laws on foreign investment in an effort to attract more overseas capital and to lure back the large private Saudi capital that is invested abroad. Principal foreign investors include the United States, Japan, the United Kingdom, Switzerland, France, and Germany.

In 2000, the government approved a new Foreign Direct Investment (FDI) Law, which allows 100% foreign ownership of investments, and established the General Investment Authority (SAGIA) to provide information and assistance for foreign investors. By the first quarter of 2005, SAGIA showed a dramatic increase in the number of licenses issued to international and domestic projects involving ventures valued at $6.4 billion. That was an 800% increase over the same period in 2004. Saudi Arabia considers privatization to be a pathway to increased foreign investment.

There are different tax systems for Saudis and non-Saudis. Non-Saudi businesses are subject to a corporation tax of up to a maximum of 20% (with the exception of profits in the hydrocarbons sector, which are taxed on a sliding scale between 30% and 85%). Joint ventures between Saudis and non-Saudis are liable to tax on the non-Saudi portion of the profits.

³⁹ECONOMIC DEVELOPMENT

Saudi Arabia's first two development plans (1971–75 and 1976–80) stressed improvement of the country's economic infrastructure by expanding the highway system, port capacity, electric power output, water supply, and irrigated land. The third plan (1981–85), continuing the Saudi program of modernization without Westernization, aimed at diversifying and expanding the productive economic sectors of industry, mining, and agriculture. The government's long-term goal was to reduce the nation's dependence on oil exports and foreign labor. Expenditures for the 1981–85 plan were initially estimated (at current prices) at $235.8 billion, compared with $140 billion for the 1975–80 plan. At the end of the third development plan, most of the infrastructure had been put in place. The fourth development plan (1985–90) emphasized consolidation of the gains of the previous 15 years and rational planning of economic activity. From the plan's emphasis on cost reduction and improvement of economic performance, it was clear that it had been drawn up under the assumption that the days of huge surpluses in the oil sector were over. Planned expenditures for the fourth plan were reduced several times.

The fifth plan (1990–95) followed the goals of the fourth plan closely. Stressing economic diversification, this plan supported industry, agriculture, finance, and business services. An important goal of the sixth plan (1995–2000) was to reduce water consumption by 2% annually over the plan's period. The seventh development plan (2000–05) was geared toward offering foreign investors opportunities to tap into sectors of the economy that had recently undergone privatization: health care, electrical power generation, and water desalination. In addition to privatization, the seventh development plan focused on diversification of national revenue resources, expansion of the production base, and the creation of more jobs for Saudis. During the five-year period, the government planned to create 817,000 new jobs for Saudi citizens (non-Saudi residents held 488,600 of those jobs at the time). The service sector was projected to realize the greatest increase in jobs. Funds were also devoted to the health care industry, including the construction of hospitals and medical colleges (some exclusively for women), and to education.

The eighth plan (2005–2010) also focused on economic diversification, as well as education and inclusion of women in society. The plan called for creating new universities and colleges with technical specializations. The ninth plan (2010–2014) aimed to eliminate poverty and increase development in infrastructure, medical services, education, and housing. The plan focuses on increasing GDP by 15% and calls for government investment in human resource development to lower Saudi unemployment from 9.6% to 5.5%.

40 SOCIAL DEVELOPMENT

Social insurance provides health care, disability, death, old-age pension, and survivor benefits for workers and the self-employed, with some exclusions. There is a special system in place for government workers. Retirement is allowed at age 60. This system is funded by 9% payroll deductions from workers, 9% payroll contributions from employers, and some government funds. Firms with 10 or more workers are required to provide 100% of wages for a month of sick leave and 75% of wages for two additional months.

The customs and regulations governing the behavior of women are strict even by the standards of the Islamic world. Despite the shortage of Saudi labor, the government is unsympathetic to the participation of women in the workplace: only 5% of the labor force is female. Extreme modesty of dress is required. Women wear the abaya, a long black garment, and they must also cover their face and hair. Women are not permitted to drive motor vehicles. Women must enter public buses through a rear door and sit in a segregated area. Women may not travel without a male member of the family. By law, women can only enter a hospital for treatment with the consent of a male relative. Domestic abuse is prevalent.

The government does not recognize international standards on human rights. Rights of privacy, freedom of speech, the press, assembly, association, religion, and movement are strictly curtailed. Security forces commit human rights abuses with the acquiescence of the government, even though they are nominally illegal. Corporal punishment, including amputation of limbs, beheading, and stoning, are used. Executions are carried out for crimes including alcohol trafficking, armed robbery, adultery, and the practice of witchcraft. Most of those executed were foreigners.

41 HEALTH

According to the CIA, life expectancy in Saudi Arabia was 74 years in 2011. The country spent 3.6% of its GDP on healthcare, amounting to $714 per person. There were 9 physicians, 21 nurses and midwives, and 22 hospital beds per 10,000 inhabitants. The fertility rate was 3.0, while the infant mortality rate was 18 per 1,000 live births. In 2008 the maternal mortality rate, according to the World Bank, was 24 per 100,000 births. It was estimated that 98% of children were vaccinated against measles. HIV/AIDS prevalence in Saudi Arabia was about 0.01% in 2001 (most recent available statistics as of February 2012).

Targets for improving health care included improving immunization coverage and achieving better regional coverage. The public health care system was supplemented by a small but generally excellent private health sector.

Despite recent advances, Saudi Arabia still suffered from severe health problems. A major cause of disease is malnutrition, leading to widespread scurvy, rickets, night blindness, and anemia, as well as low resistance to tuberculosis. Dysentery attacked all ages and classes and trachoma was common. A government campaign was successful in eradicating malaria. Typhoid was endemic, but acquired immunity prevented serious outbreaks of this disease.

42 HOUSING

In 2007, there were about 4.3 million occupied households in the country. About 44.5% of all occupied housing is owner occupied. Around 44.4% live in rented units, while 11.1% of households are employer-provided housing units. The continuing influx of rural people to towns and cities, coupled with the rise in levels of expectation among the urban population, has created a serious housing problem; improvement in urban housing is one of Saudi Arabia's foremost economic needs. Some 506,800 dwelling units were built in the period 1974–85: 389,000 by the private sector, with the help of the Real Estate Development Fund, and 117,800 by the Deputy Ministry of Housing and other government agencies. In the oil districts, Aramco, through loans and other assistance, has encouraged construction of private homes and has built accommodations for its unmarried Saudi staff members. The Real Estate Development Fund, established in 1975, continues to provide interest-free loans for home construction to individuals as well as private companies.

43 EDUCATION

In 2009 the World Bank estimated that 86% of age-eligible children in Saudi Arabia were enrolled in primary school. Secondary enrollment for age-eligible children stood at 72%. Tertiary enrollment was estimated at 33%. Of those enrolled in tertiary education, there were 100 male students for every 125 female students. The World Bank also estimated that Saudi Arabia had a literacy rate of 78.8%. Public expenditure on education represented 5.6% of GDP.

Until the mid-1950s, Saudi Arabia's educational system was primarily oriented toward religious schooling that stressed knowledge of the Koran and Hadith (sayings of Muhammad and his companions). Except for basic arithmetic, reading, and writing, secular subjects were not taught in the schools. There was a highly developed oral culture, however. Nearly all of the students were boys; education of girls was virtually nonexistent and took place in the home, if at all. The first school for girls was built in 1964, and now girls' schools exist around the country. Schools continue to be segregated by gender. The General Presidency for Girls' Education administers girls' schools and colleges.

Education is free at all levels, including college and postgraduate study. Elementary school covers six years of study. This is followed by three years of basic intermediate school. Students may then choose to attend either a three-year general secondary school or a three-year technical school (junior college) that offers vocational, commercial, and agricultural studies. The academic year runs from October to July.

Higher education is offered in at least 11 universities and 83 colleges. The principal universities are King Sa'ud University (formerly Riyadh University), founded in 1957, and King Abd al-'Aziz University of Jeddah, founded in 1967. In 2009, it was estimated that about 33% of the tertiary-age population was enrolled in tertiary education programs.

44 LIBRARIES AND MUSEUMS

The King Fahd National Library, founded in Riyadh in 1968, has 462,000 volumes. The largest library system is that of King Sa'ud University established in 1957, with 14 branches and a collection of more than 1.8 million volumes; the library at King 'Abd al-'Aziz University has 560,000 volumes. The library of the University of Petroleum and Minerals in Dhahran, with almost 335,000 volumes, is the nation's largest specialized collection. The largest public library, at Riyadh, contains 275,000 volumes.

There are 10,150 documented monuments and about a dozen museums in Saudi Arabia. The National Museum, originally opened at Riyadh in 1978, focuses on archaeology and ethnography. Major renovations were completed in 1999. Many of the other historic and cultural sites are religious in nature and the high figures for attendance reflect the huge numbers of Muslim pilgrims who visit the kingdom each year. Riyadh is also home to a local museum, an archaeological museum at King Sa'ud University, and a geological museum.

⁴⁵MEDIA

In 2009 the CIA reported that there were 4.2 million telephone landlines in Saudi Arabia. In addition to landlines, mobile phone subscriptions averaged more than one per person (177 per 100). There were 43 FM radio stations, 31 AM radio stations, and 2 shortwave radio stations. Internet users numbered 39 per 100 citizens. Prominent newspapers in 2010, with circulation numbers listed parenthetically, included *Saudi Gazette* (676,000), *Asharq Alawsat* (224,992), and *Ar-Riyadh* (150,000), as well as 8 other major newspapers.

Saudi Arabia has a modern, well-developed telecommunications system. Domestic service is provided by a mix of fiber-optic cable, microwave radio relay, and coaxial cable systems. International service is provided by a system of coaxial and submarine cables, satellite ground stations, and microwave radio relay stations.

The Broadcasting Service of the Kingdom of Saudi Arabia (BSKSA) is owned and operated by the state, sponsoring four television networks. Private broadcasters are not allowed in the country. However, there are millions of satellite dishes in the country receiving foreign broadcasts. The Ministry of Culture and Information oversees radio and television broadcasts, with the right to censor any references to religions other than Islam, politics, sex, alcohol, and pigs or pork.

All Internet servers are monitored by the government. In 2009, a group of Saudi investors started NaqaTube, a "religiously safe," Arabic language alternative to YouTube. The site allows users to surf through prescreened online videos that avoided material deemed racy or impure. Site administrators remove content that is critical of the Saudi government, the royal family, and Islamic scholars.

The government is said to severely limit freedom of speech and the press, punishing any criticism of Islam, the ruling family, or the government with detention and arrest.

⁴⁶ORGANIZATIONS

Saudi social tradition, which emphasizes the exclusiveness of family, clan, and tribe, generally militates against the formation of other social organizations. The absence of political and economic organizations is also a result of the prevalence of tradition. However, there are chambers of commerce in Ad Dammām, Jeddah, Mecca,

Medina, and Riyadh. The umbrella organization of the Council of Saudi Chambers of Commerce and Industry is in Riyadh.

There are several professional associations, particularly in medical and health care fields. Many of these, such as the Saudi Pediatric Association, promote public education and research while also serving as a professional networking organization. The King Faisal Center for Research and Islamic Studies serves as a multinational cultural and educational organization.

National youth organizations include the Saudi Arabian Assembly of Muslim Youth and the Saudi Arabian Boy Scouts Association. The World Assembly of Muslim Youth, based in Riyadh, offers a variety of camping, recreational, and educational programs for youth. There are a number of national and multinational sports associations based in the country, representing such pastimes as cricket, tennis, tae kwon do, and horse racing. Several sports associations are affiliated with the national Olympic Committee.

The Muslim World League works for the welfare of women and children. The Red Crescent Society and UNICEF are active.

⁴⁷TOURISM, TRAVEL, AND RECREATION

The *Tourism Factbook*, published by the UN World Tourism Organization, reported 13.3 million incoming tourists to Saudi Arabia in 2009; they spent a total of $6.69 billion. Of those incoming tourists, there were 8.7 million from the Middle East. There were 570,714 hotel beds available in Saudi Arabia, which had an occupancy rate of 50%. The estimated daily cost to visit Riyadh, the capital, was $397. The cost of visiting other cities averaged $386.

Saudi Arabia was once one of the hardest places in the world to visit due to heavy restrictions on tourism. In 2000, the government opened up the country and added tourist visas; the Tourism Higher Authority was also created to expand the tourism facilities. Every year, however, there is a great influx of pilgrims to Mecca and Medina. In 2010, 2.8 million pilgrims traveled to Mecca.

All visitors, including pilgrims, are required to have a passport valid for at least six months and an onward/return ticket. Visitors in transit or from a Gulf Cooperation Council country are not required to have a visa. Women must have proof of accommodations for their stay, and if they arrive alone, their sponsor or husband must pick them up at the airport. Female visitors are also not allowed to drive cars. Pilgrims who travel to Mecca are required to have the meningococcal vaccine. Precautions against typhoid, malaria, hepatitis, and meningitis are recommended for all who travel to Saudi Arabia.

Traditional sports include hunting with salukis, falconry, and horse and camel racing. Modern sports facilities include the King Fahd International Stadium, complete with Olympic-standard running tracks and football (soccer) fields.

⁴⁸FAMOUS PERSONS

Although Saudi Arabia has a relatively short history as a nation-state, it is heir to an Islamic civilization that developed from the teachings of Muhammad (570–632), born of the tribe of Quraysh in Mecca. The branch of Islam that claims most contemporary Saudis is that preached by Muhammad bin 'Abd al-Wahhab (1703?–91), a fundamentalist reformer.

The Saudi who has gained greatest renown outside the modern kingdom of Saudi Arabia is 'Abd al-'Aziz ibn 'Abd ar-Rahman al-

Faysal as-Sa'ud, better known as Ibn-Sa'ud (1880–1953), the father of his country. Forced into exile with his family at a young age, he reconquered his patrimony and left behind him the state of Saudi Arabia.

In 1964, Faisal (Faysal ibn-'Abd al-'Aziz as-Sa'ud, 1906–75) was proclaimed king. In his role as prime minister, Faisal instituted many economic and social reforms, including the abolition of slavery. Upon his assassination in March 1975, he was succeeded as king and prime minister by Khaled (Khalid ibn-'Abd al-'Aziz, 1913–82). Together with Crown Prince Fahd ibn-'Abd al-'Aziz (1923–2005), King Khaled broadened the country's development policies.

After Khaled's death, Fahd became king; he pursued the same cautious program of modernization as his two predecessors. Abdullah bin Abdulaziz al-Saud (b. 1924), Fahd's half-brother and de facto ruler of the country since Fahd became incapacitated from a stroke in 1995, became king upon Fahd's death in 2005. Ahmad Zaki Yamani (b. 1930), a former minister of petroleum and mineral resources, gained an international reputation as a spokesman for the oil-exporting countries.

⁴⁹ DEPENDENCIES

Saudi Arabia has no territories or colonies.

⁵⁰ BIBLIOGRAPHY

Bradley, John R. *Saudi Arabia Exposed: Inside a Kingdom in Crisis.* New York: Palgrave Macmillan, 2005.

Champion, Daryl. *The Paradoxical Kingdom: Saudi Arabia and the Momentum of Reform.* New York: Columbia University Press, 2003.

Cordesman, Anthony H. *Saudi Arabia: National Security in a Troubled Region.* Santa Barbara, CA: Praeger Security International, 2009.

Holden, David, and Richard Johns. *The House of Saud.* New York: Holt, Rinehart and Winston, 1981.

Hourani, Albert Habib. *A History of the Arab Peoples.* Cambridge, MA: Belknap Press of Harvard University Press, 2002.

Long, David E. *The Kingdom of Saudi Arabia.* 2nd ed. Gainesville: University Press of Florida, 2010.

The Middle East. Washington, DC: CQ Press, 2005.

Peterson, J. E. *Historical Dictionary of Saudi Arabia.* Lanham, MD: Scarecrow Press, 2003.

Saudi Arabia Investment and Business Guide: Strategic and Practical Information. Washington, DC: International Business Publications USA, 2012.

Seddon, David, ed. *A Political and Economic Dictionary of the Middle East.* Philadelphia: Routledge/Taylor and Francis, 2004.

Vasil'ev, Aleksei M. *The History of Saudi Arabia.* New York : New York University Press, 2000.

Zuhur, Sherifa. *Saudi Arabia.* Santa Barbara, CA: ABC-CLIO, 2011.Harrison, Martin..

SINGAPORE

Republic of Singapore

CAPITAL: Singapore

FLAG: The flag consists of a red stripe at the top and a white stripe on the bottom. On the red stripe, at the hoist, are a white crescent opening to the fly and five white stars.

ANTHEM: *Majulah Singapore (Onward Singapore).*

MONETARY UNIT: The Singapore dollar (SGD) of 100 cents is a freely convertible currency. There are coins of 1, 5, 10, 20, and 50 cents and 1 dollar and notes of 2, 5, 10, 50, 100, 500, 1,000, and 10,000 dollars. SGD1 = US$0.7642 (or US$1 = SGD$1.3085) as of 2011.

WEIGHTS AND MEASURES: The metric system is the norm, but some local measures are used.

HOLIDAYS: Major Christian, Buddhist, Hindu, and Muslim holidays are celebrated, some of which fall on annually variable dates because of the calendars used. The public holidays include New Year's Day, 1 January; Chinese New Year; Good Friday; Vesak Day (Buddhist festival); Labor Day, 1 May; Hari Raya Puasa (Muslim festival); National Day, 9 August; Hari Raya Haji (Malay Muslim festival); Dewali; Christmas, 25 December.

TIME: 8 p.m. = noon GMT.

1 LOCATION, SIZE, AND EXTENT

The Republic of Singapore, the second smallest country in Asia, consists of Singapore Island and several smaller adjacent islets. Situated in the Indian Ocean off the southern tip of the Malay Peninsula, Singapore had an area of 712 sq km (275 sq mi), including land reclamation, as of 2011. Comparatively, the area occupied by Singapore is about four times the size of Washington, DC. Singapore Island extends 41.8 km (26 mi) ENE–WSW and 22.5 km (14 mi) SSE–NNW and has a coastline of 193 km (120 mi), including about 84 km (52 mi) along the water channel between the island and the Malay Peninsula, dimensions which have been expanded through land reclamation in the 21st century.

Singapore is connected to the nearby western portion of Malaysia by a causeway, 1,056 m (3,465 ft) in length, across the Johore Strait. Singapore's position at the eastern end of the Strait of Malacca, which separates western Malaysia and the Indonesian island of Sumatra, has given it economic and strategic importance out of proportion to its small size. Singapore is a city state. Parliament House and government offices are located on Singapore Island's southern coast.

2 TOPOGRAPHY

Singapore Island is mostly low-lying, undulating country with a small group of hills at the center. The highest point of the island is Bukit Timah (166 m/545 ft). There are sections of rainforest in the center and some remaining natural wetlands along the northwest coast. The island's rivers have been converted into canals and reservoirs. Singapore's harbor is wide, deep, and well protected.

3 CLIMATE

The climate is tropical, with heavy rainfall and high humidity. The range of temperature is slight; the average annual maximum is 31°C (88°F), and the average minimum 24°C (75°F). The annual rainfall of 237 cm (93 in) is distributed fairly evenly throughout the year, ranging from 39 cm (15 in) in December to 28 cm (11 in) in May. There is rain about one out of every two days.

4 FLORA AND FAUNA

The World Resources Institute estimates that there are 2,282 plant species in Singapore. In addition, Singapore is home to 73 mammal, 400 bird, 106 reptile, and 11 amphibian species. The calculation reflects the total number of distinct species residing in the country, not the number of endemic species.

The dense tropical forest that originally covered Singapore Island is mostly cleared. The greatest concentration of plant life can be found in the rainforest ecosystem Bukit Timah Nature Reserve, at the center of the island. As of 2010, Singapore had about 7 sq km (2.7 sq mi) of mangroves, mostly in the northwest of the island, particularly at Sungei Buloh Wetland Reserve. Threatened species of seagrass are found in the remaining shoreline meadows.

5 ENVIRONMENT

The World Resources Institute reported that Singapore had designated 2,900 hectares (7,166 acres) of land for protection as of 2006. According to a 2011 report issued by the International Union for Conservation of Nature and Natural Resources (IUCN), threatened species included 11 types of mammals, 15 species of birds, 5 types of reptiles, 25 species of fish, 162 species of invertebrate, and 57 species of plants. Threatened species in Singapore include knobby sea stars and mangrove horseshoe crabs; coastal horseshoe crabs are considered endangered.

The government promotes a "Clean and Green" motto and identity for Singapore, with recycling strongly encouraged and heavy penalties for littering. Green Port and Green Shipping plans were announced in 2011. Environmental responsibility for Singapore is vested in the Ministry of the Environment and Water Resources. Regulations limiting the lead content of gasoline were imposed in 1981, and emissions standards for motor vehicles were tightened in 1986, but air pollution from vehicles continues to be a problem. The United Nations reported in 2008 that carbon dioxide emissions in Singapore totaled 54,147 kilotons. The government was promoting "Low Carbon Singapore" goals through efficient use of electricity, providing incentives for solar power firms, and encouraging bicycle transportation, as of 2011. As a low elevation island nation, Singapore was vulnerable to rising sea levels from global warming, and the government considered building protective sea walls. Singapore imported sand for landfill and construction cement, and was accused of damaging coastal ecosystems in Cambodia and other Southeast Asian countries by sand-dredging.

Water resources total 0.6 cu km (0.144 cu mi) while water usage is 0.19 cu km (0.046 cu mi) per year. Domestic water usage accounts for 45% of total usage, industrial for 51%, and agricultural for 4%. Per capita water usage totals 44 cu m (1,554 cu ft) per year. Pollution from the nation's petroleum and petrochemical industry has been a significant problem. Wastewater is treated and recycled to conserve water supplies, and sewers have been built to keep canals filled only with rainwater. As of 2011, Singapore was implementing a project to turn its artificial canals and drainage systems back into natural streams.

6 POPULATION

The US Central Intelligence Agency (CIA) estimated the population of Singapore in 2011 to be approximately 4,740,737, which placed it at number 117 in population among the 196 nations of the world. In 2011, approximately 9.2% of the population was over 65 years of age, with another 13.8% under 15 years of age. The median age in Singapore was 40.1 years. There were 0.95 males for every female in the country. The population's annual rate of change was 0.817%, one of the world's lowest rates, and government programs tried to promote marriage and childbearing. The projected population for the year 2025 was 5,700,000. Population density in Singapore was calculated at 6,802 people per sq km (17,617 people per sq mi).

7 MIGRATION

Singapore had only a few Malay fishermen as inhabitants at the time of its founding as a British trading post in 1819. It was subsequently and quite rapidly populated by immigrant peoples, primarily Chinese, but also Malays (from Sumatra as well as adjacent Malaya), and Indians (who took advantage of common British governance to migrate to Singapore in search of better employment). In 1965, following separation from Malaysia, Singapore's newly independent government introduced measures to restrict the flow of Malaysians entering the country in search of work. These immigrants, who averaged 10,000 a year up to 1964, had to establish residence for several years to qualify for citizenship. In addition, all non-citizens were required to apply for a work permit or employment pass.

Estimates of Singapore's net migration rate, according to the CIA in 2011, amounted to 4.63 migrants per 1,000 citizens. The total number of emigrants living abroad was 297,200, and the total number of immigrants living in Singapore was 1.97 million. Migrant workers came to Singapore mainly from Indonesia, the Phil-

ippines, China, Sri Lanka, India, Bangladesh, Myanmar, and other Asian countries, and mostly worked in construction, manufacturing, and services. As of 2011, Singapore employed over 200,000 foreign domestic workers, who had no guaranteed days off and were vulnerable to abuse.

8 ETHNIC GROUPS

According to the 2010 census, the people of Singapore are predominantly of Chinese origin, with the ethnic Chinese accounting for about 74.1% of the population. About 13.4% are Malays and 9.2% are Indians (also including Pakistanis, Bangladeshis, and Sri Lankans). People of mixed European-Asian ethnicity accounted for 3.3% of the population.

9 LANGUAGES

There are four official languages in Singapore: Chinese (Mandarin dialect), Malay, English, and Tamil. The government encourages learning Mandarin instead of other Chinese dialects. In 1987, under a government mandate, English was made the primary language of the school system. Learning a second language is emphasized in the schools, and most Singaporeans are bilingual. English is the principal medium of government and is widely used in commerce; it was spoken as a first language by about 32% of the population, as of the 2010 census. A local slang dialect of English, known as "Singlish" has become popular. As of 2010, Mandarin was the most widely spoken first language, spoken as a first language by about 48% of the population, while 19% speak other Chinese dialects, including Hokkien and Teochew. Malay was the first language for 13% of Singaporeans.

10 RELIGIONS

The ethnic Chinese adhere in varying degrees to Buddhism, Taoism, Confucianism, and Christianity, as well as traditional ancestor worship. Malays and people with origins in Pakistan and Bangladesh are almost exclusively Muslim. The Indian population is split, with about 55% practicing Hinduism, 25% Islam, and 12% Christianity. There are also small Sikh, Jewish, Zoroastrian, and Jain communities. There is complete separation of state and religion in Singapore and freedom of religion is constitutionally guaranteed. However, all religious groups must be registered under the Societies Act, and the government has maintained a ban on the registration of Jehovah's Witnesses and the Unification Church. The government has a semiofficial relationship with the Islamic Religious Council. Observed national holidays include Hari Raya Haji and Hari Raya Puasa (Islamic); Good Friday and Christmas (Christian); Dewali (Hindu); and Vesak Day (Buddhist).

11 TRANSPORTATION

Singapore's important regional role has been as a transportation link between East and West, and between the mainland and island portions of Southeast Asia. As long ago as 1822—only three years after the establishment of a British colonial presence on the island—1,575 ships called at the new port of Singapore from nearby islands, Europe, India, and China. With a natural deepwater harbor that is open year-round, and anchorage facilities that can accommodate supertankers, Singapore is one of the three busiest container ports in the world. Ships of over 600 shipping lines, flying the flags of nearly all the maritime nations, regularly call at

Singapore. The merchant marine fleet totaled 1,422 as of 2010, according to the CIA. International piracy has disturbed shipping in the Malacca Straits and Singapore Straits, with violence including the murder of crew members, in the early 21st century.

The CIA reported that Singapore has a total of 3,356 km (2,085 mi) of roads, all of which are paved, as of 2011. There are 150 vehicles per 1,000 people in the country. Singapore's sole rail facility is a 38.6-km (24-mi) section of the Malayan Railways, which links Singapore to Kuala Lumpur. There is also an 83-km (52-mi) mass rapid transit system with 89 stations.

Commercial air service was inaugurated in Singapore in 1930. The principal airport is Changi International, with flights to over 60 countries. Singapore also has Seletar Airport (mainly charter flights), and six military air facilities. There were 18.43 million air passengers in 2009 according to the World Bank. Singapore's national carrier is Singapore Airlines, with subsidiaries including SilkAir. Singapore's low cost carriers include Tiger Airways, and Jetstar Asia.

¹²HISTORY

Some historians believe that a town was founded on the Singapore Island as early as the 7th century, while other sources claim that "Singapura" (Lion City) was first established by an Indian prince in 1299. During the 13th and 14th centuries, a trading center existed until it was devastated by a Javanese attack in 1377. Singapore was virtually uninhabited when Sir Stamford Raffles, in 1819, established a trading station of the British East India Company on the island. In 1824, the island was ceded outright to the company by the Sultan of Johore, the Malay state at the extreme southern end of the peninsula. In 1826, it was incorporated with Malacca (Melaka, Malaysia) and Penang (Pinang, Malaysia) to form the Straits Settlements, a British Crown colony until World War II. The trading center grew into the city of Singapore and attracted large numbers of Chinese, many of whom became merchants. With its excellent harbor, Singapore also became a flourishing commercial center and the leading seaport of Southeast Asia, handling the vast export trade in tin and rubber from British-ruled Malaya. In 1938, the British completed construction of a large naval base on the island, which the Japanese captured in February 1942 during World War II, following a land-based attack from the Malay Peninsula to the north.

Recaptured by the United Kingdom in 1945, Singapore was detached from the Straits Settlements to become a separate Crown colony in 1946. Under a new constitution, on 3 June 1959, Singapore became a self-governing state, and on 16 September 1963, it joined the new Federation of Malaysia (formed by bringing together the previously independent Malaya and Singapore and the formerly British-ruled northern Borneo territories of Sarawak and Sabah). However, Singapore, with its predominantly urban Chinese population and highly commercial economy, began to find itself at odds with the Malay-dominated central government of Malaysia. On 9 August 1965, Singapore separated from Malaysia to become wholly independent as the Republic of Singapore. Lee Kuan Yew, a major figure in the move toward independence, served as the country's prime minister from 1959 until 1990. Singapore, Indonesia, Malaysia, the Philippines, and Thailand formed the Association of South-East Asian Nations (ASEAN) in 1967.

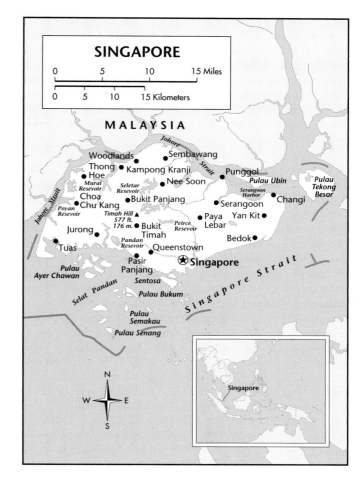

LOCATION: 1°9′ to 1°29′N; 103°38′ to 104°6′ E. TERRITORIAL SEA LIMIT: 3 miles.

Lee Kuan Yew's People's Action Party (PAP), founded in 1954, has been the dominant political party, winning every general election since 1959. The PAP's popular support rested on law-and-order policies buttressed by economic growth and improved standards of living; it did not tolerate expressions of dissent and discouraged the growth of any opposition. Although the PAP regularly carried 60–75% of the popular vote, it repeatedly managed to capture virtually all seats in the National Assembly. In 1987 the government detained 22 people under the Internal Security Act (ISA) for alleged involvement in a "Marxist conspiracy." Dissident Chia Thye Poh remained in custody without charges until 1990.

On 28 November 1990, Lee Kuan Yew, prime minister of Singapore for over 31 years, transferred power to Goh Chok Tong, the former first deputy prime minister. Lee remained in the cabinet as senior minister to the prime minister's office and retained the position of secretary-general of the PAP. Singapore's first direct presidential elections were held on 28 August 1993, with Ong Teng Cheong becoming the first elected president.

An incident that garnered worldwide attention was the Singapore government's October 1993 arrest of nine foreign youths charged with vandalism, including Michael Fay, an 18-year-old American student. Fay confessed and his sentence included being flogged with a rattan cane. President Bill Clinton urged Singapore to reconsider the caning, but the sentence was carried out. In response to international criticism, Singaporean leaders claimed that "Asian values" eschewed the precedence of individual liberty over social stability and that such values promoted an increasingly wealthy, clean, and hospitable city-state devoid of social pathologies that plagued both the West and other large Asian cities. In 1994, Singapore made international news when the government sued the *International Herald Tribune* for libel over an editorial the paper published suggesting that Prime Minister Goh was simply a figurehead, and that ultimate power rested with former prime minister Lee.

Parliamentary elections were held in 1997 and the PAP retained its vast majority-opposition parties won only 2 of 83 seats. One seat, won by Tang Liang Hong, remained vacant in 1997 as Tang fled the country fearing government persecution—including lawsuits, freezing of bank accounts, and restrictions on travel—which began in earnest after his election. On 28 April 2001, an unprecedented antigovernment rally was held, the first legally sanctioned demonstration outside of an election campaign. Over 2,000 people gathered in support of opposition leader J. B. Jeyaretnam, who faced bankruptcy and thus expulsion from parliament. Jeyaretnam owed hundreds of thousands of dollars in defamation lawsuits brought by senior government officials and their supporters.

In December 2001, Singapore arrested 15 individuals believed to be part of a terrorist cell with links to Osama bin Laden's al-Qaeda network. Two suspects were released, but the others belonged to Jemaah Islamiya (JI), an Islamic organization with cells in Singapore, Malaysia, and Indonesia. The cell's plot was reportedly to destroy key buildings in Singapore, including the American Embassy. In August 2002, Singapore arrested 21 terrorist suspects who had allegedly carried out reconnaissance of potential terrorist attack targets in Singapore, including Changi Airport. They were purportedly members of Jemaah Islamiyah. The group's leader, Mas Selamat bin Kastari, escaped from jail in Singapore in February 2009, and was eventually caught in Malaysia in March 2009.

On 12 August 2004, Lee Hsien Loong took office as prime minister of Singapore, while Goh Chok Tong became senior minister and Lee Kuan Yew filled the newly created post of minister mentor, overseeing the cabinet. Singapore's President S.R. Nathan was sworn in for his second term of office on 1 September 2005, without running for reelection, because Singapore's Presidential Election Committee had ruled that he was the only candidate fit for the presidency. When parliamentary elections were held in May 2011, PAP won its usual majority with 81 of the 87 seats, but its share of the popular vote was just 60%, after a coordinated effort by opposition parties. In August 2011, in the first direct election for president in 18 years, PAP's Tony Tan won by a narrow margin. Discontent with inflation and the large presence of foreign workers had eroded Singaporean confidence in the long-ruling PAP, and the opposition was increasingly able to use alternative media, such as social networking, to organize support.

13 GOVERNMENT

The constitution of the Republic of Singapore, as amended in 1965, provides for a unicameral parliamentary form of government, with a president who, prior to 1991, served as head of state. Voting has been compulsory for all citizens over 21 since 1959, despite some calls to lower the age to 18. The maximum term for parliamentary sessions is five years, although elections may be called at any time within that period. A general election is held within three months of dissolution. The number of parliamentary seats has increased with each general election since the seating of Singapore's first parliament, to 87 seats as of 2011. There are up to nine appointed non-constituency members (NCMP). Since 1990 there have also been up to 9 nominated members (NMPs) appointed by the president, who serve two-and-a-half year terms.

Until the 1988 election, all constituencies were single-member constituencies. In 1988, 60 of the original 81 constituencies (out of the increased number for 1988, i.e., from 79 in 1984 to 81 in 1988) were reorganized into 13 group representation constituencies (GRCs). In each GRC teams of three candidates must be fielded, one of who must be of an ethnic minority group, such as Malay, Indian, or an "Other", in an effort to ensure that parties are multi-racial rather than purely Chinese.

The prime minister, who commands the confidence of a majority of parliament, acts as effective head of government. The prime minister appoints a cabinet that as of 2011 had 14 members, including two deputy prime ministers.

Since 1991, under an amendment to the constitution passed by parliament, the president is no longer elected by parliament but by the electorate, and has custodial powers over the country's reserves, as well as a major role in deciding key appointments to the judiciary, civil service, and statutory boards. The president is elected for a term of six years. The first direct presidential elections were held on 28 August 1993, electing Ong Teng Cheong. Several constitutional reforms were enacted in 1996 and 1997. In 1996, parliament enacted governmental reforms limiting the power of the president and curtailing his veto power—which had been granted in 1991.

14 POLITICAL PARTIES

Since independence, Singapore has been governed by a single party, the ruling People's Action Party (PAP) of former prime minister Lee Kuan Yew. The PAP won all parliamentary seats in the general elections from 1968 to 1980. The Workers' Party (WP) won its first parliamentary seat in a 1981 by-election; under its leader, J. B. Jeyaretnam, the WP has been critical of undemocratic practices within the PAP government. In the 1984 general elections, the PAP won 77 of the 79 seats, even though it captured only 62.9% of the popular vote, compared with 75.5% in 1980.

J. B. Jeyaretnam, secretary-general of the Workers' Party, maintained his seat in 1984, and Chiam See Tong, leader of the Singapore Democratic Party (SDP), won another seat for the opposition in the same election. The two main opposition parties, WP and SDP, were subjected to almost continual harassment by the government. In 1984, Jeyaretnam was accused of making false statements involving irregularities in the collection of the WP's funds; he was acquitted of two of three charges and fined. In 1986, the government appealed the case and the higher court set aside the initial judgment; Jeyaretnam was again fined and jailed for one month, enough to disqualify him from parliament and ban him from contesting elections for five years. On the basis of his criminal convictions he was disbarred and denied a pardon. On appeal to the Privy Council against the decision to disbar him, he was vindicated and allowed to practice law again. In 1991, Jeyaretnam avoided bankruptcy by paying legal costs in a defamation suit he lost, filed by Lee Kuan Yew over remarks made by Jeyaretnam in a 1988 election rally. In November 1991, the ban on Jeyaretnam standing for election expired.

In the 1988, and 1991 general elections, opposition parties gained small ground, and the PAP continued to garner a declining percentage of the total votes. In the 1991 elections, Chiam See Tong was again the winner for the SDP, along with Ling How Doong and Cheo Chai Chen. The Workers' Party MP was Low Thai Khiang. Smaller minority parties included the United People's Front, which is also critical of antidemocratic aspects of the government rule and pro-Malaysian; the Singapore Malays' National Organization; and the Singapore Solidarity Party, formed in 1986 by three former leaders of the SDP.

In 1997, parliamentary elections were held and again the PAP maintained its virtual monopoly of seats. Of 83 seats up for election, the long-ruling party captured 81, with 47 unopposed. The opposition leaders, Jeyaretnam and Tang Liang Hong, both with the WP, won seats. After the election, leaders of the PAP, including Prime Minister Goh and Senior Minister (and longtime leader) Lee, sued Tang for defamation. Tang promptly fled the country, saying he feared for his safety as the government froze his assets and imposed travel restrictions on his family. Jeyaretnam continued to face bankruptcy and the loss of his parliamentary seat as well, from a defamation payment awarded against him. In the 1997 elections, the SDP lost all three seats it had won in the 1991 round. In 1998, the government banned all political parties from producing videos and appearing on television to discuss politics. The government moved to tighten control over the political process in 1999 with the PAP filing a petition to close the Workers' Party for failure to pay damages and costs associated with a defamation case.

In parliamentary elections held in 2001, the PAP won 82 of 84 seats with 75.3% of the vote. Opposition candidates contested only 29 of the seats. The WP took one seat, as did the Singapore Democratic Alliance (SDA), which included the Singapore People's Party (SPP), Singapore Democratic Party (SDP), National Solidarity Party, Singapore Justice Party, and Singapore Malay National Organization. The opposition parties complained that constituency changes and a range of regulations imposed by the PAP made it more difficult for them to win votes. The Parliamentary Elections Act was amended, restricting the use of the Internet for political campaigning and banning the publication of opinion polls during elections.

On 12 August 2004, Lee Hsien Loong, the son of Lee Kuan Yew, took office as prime minister of Singapore, while Goh Chok Tong became senior minister and Lee Kuan Yew filled the newly created post of minister mentor, overseeing the cabinet. The 2005 presidential election was cancelled after the Elections Committee disqualified three new presidential candidates. As the only remaining candidate, S. R. Nathan was appointed to another term. Parliamentary elections were held on 6 May 2006. The PAP, under prime minister Lee Hsien Loong, won 66.6% of the vote and 82 seats. The WP won 16.34% of the vote and 1 seat. The SDA won 12.99% of the vote and 1 seat. The SDP ran apart from the SDA, and won 4% of the vote, but no seats in parliament. The leader of the SDP, Chee Soon Juan, became known for challenging Singapore's restrictions on public assembly and free speech.

In the 7 May 2011 legislative elections, considered a show of strengthening opposition, the PAP won 60% of the vote (81 seats), followed by the WP with 12.8% (6 seats). The NSP won 12% of the vote, but no seats in parliament. Lee Hsien Loong of the PAP retained his post as prime minister (which he had held since 2004). Tony Tan of the PAP narrowly won the August 2011 presidential election with 35% of the vote, in a four-way race which included another PAP candidate.

15 LOCAL GOVERNMENT

When the People's Action Party (PAP) came to power in 1959, Singapore's postcolonial city council and rural board were integrated into departments of the central government. The Town Councils Act, enacted in June 1988, reintroduced a limited local organizational structure. Town councils were formed to take over the management and maintenance of the common properties of housing estates. As of 2011, there were 15 town councils. Community Development Councils (CDCs) were set up after the 1997 general election as social parallels to the town councils, to improve community bonding and to manage a spectrum of social services, from child care centers to public welfare assistance. As of 2011, there were five CDCs: South West, North West, Central Singapore, South East, and North East. Each is managed by an appointed council including a mayor (often a member of parliament) and 12 to 80 council members.

16 JUDICIAL SYSTEM

Singapore's legal system is based on British common law. The judiciary includes the Supreme Court as well as subordinate courts. The subordinate courts include the magistrates' courts; the district courts; the juvenile courts, for offenders below the age of 16; the coroners' courts; and the small claims courts. The Supreme Court is headed by a chief justice and is divided into the High Court and the Court of Appeal. The High Court has unlimited original jurisdiction in both criminal and civil cases but ordinarily chooses to exercise such jurisdictional authority only in major cases. In its appellate jurisdiction, the High Court hears criminal and civil appeals from the magistrates' and district courts. Appeals to the Privy Council in London were eliminated in 1994. The president appoints judges of the Supreme Court on the recommendation of the prime minister, after consultation with the chief justice. A Legal Service Commission supervises and assigns the placement of the subordinate court judges and magistrates who have the status of civil servants; however, the president appoints subordinate courts judges on the recommendation of the chief justice.

Defendants have the right to be present at trials, to have an attorney, and to confront witnesses against them. While the constitution provides for an independent judiciary and the judicial system provides a fair and efficient judicial process, the Internal Security Act allows the government to conduct searches without warrants, and detain without charges for unlimited periods, suspects who are deemed to threaten national security. Laws aimed at fighting narcotics, organized crime, and "undesirable publications" also allow detention without trial and warrantless searches. Civil lawsuits have often been directed by the dominant PAP against opposition parties and their leaders. Singapore's executions of foreign nationals for narcotics possession have been highly controversial, and the country has often been criticized and ridiculed internationally for punishments such as the imposition of high fines for littering, spitting, or public smoking. Caning is a common form of punishment for many different offenses. Cases of police abuse are generally investigated by the government and reported in the media.

[17] ARMED FORCES

The International Institute for Strategic Studies reported that armed forces in Singapore totaled 72,500 members in 2011. The force was comprised of 50,000 from the army, 9,000 from the navy, and 13,500 from the air force. Armed forces represent 5.5% of the labor force in Singapore. Service is compulsory for men over age 18. Defense spending totaled US$14.3 billion and accounted for 4.9% of gross domestic product (GDP). Singapore's military has participated in UN peacekeeping and humanitarian missions, and was a member of the US-led military coalition in Iraq from 2003 to 2008.

[18] INTERNATIONAL COOPERATION

Having joined the UN on 21 September 1965, Singapore participates in ESCAP and several non-regional specialized agencies such as the IAEA, the World Bank, ILO, UNCTAD, and the WHO. Singapore served on the UN Security Council in 2001–02. It is a participant in APEC, the Asian Development Bank, the Colombo Plan, the WTO, the Commonwealth of Nations, the Alliance of Small Island States (AOSIS), and G77. Singapore has played a leading part in ASEAN, the Association of South-East Asian Nations. Singapore is part of the Nonaligned Movement.

In environmental cooperation, Singapore is part of the Basel Convention, the Convention on Biological Diversity, the RAMSAR Convention on Wetlands, CITES, the Montréal Protocol, the Kyoto Protocol, MARPOL, the Nuclear Test Ban Treaty, and the UN Conventions on the Law of the Sea, Climate Change, and Desertification.

Indonesia and Singapore pledged in 2005 to finalize their 1973 maritime boundary agreement by defining unresolved areas north of Batam Island. Singapore has sometimes had tense relations with neighboring Malaysia, particularly regarding disagreements about possible plans to replace the causeway between the two nations with a tunnel or bridges. The Five Power Defense Arrangements is an ongoing defense pact between Singapore, Malaysia, Australia, New Zealand, and the United Kingdom, first signed in 1971. Singapore has long been an ally of the United States, actively supporting US anti-terrorism policies and participating in the US-led Iraq war coalition. The US military uses air force and naval port facilities in Singapore.

[19] ECONOMY

The 2008–09 global economic crisis had a significant impact on Singapore; the economy contracted by 12.7% in the first quarter of 2009. A decline in productivity for the manufacturing sector, which accounted for about 25% of the economy, was the primary cause for the recession. The second quarter, however, showed an unexpected expansion at an annualized rate of 20.4%. This increase was the result of a jump in pharmaceutical production and sales attributed to the demand for H1N1 influenza vaccines and an increase in sales of electronics attributed to inventory restocking. The economic contrast between the fourth quarter 2009 and the first quarter 2010 was even more pronounced. In that short period, Singapore's economy grew 7.2%, or what amounted to 32.1%

at an annualized rate. This caused Singapore's monetary authority to allow a modest 1.2% revaluation in the Singapore dollar. The monetary authority also indicated that it would allow the currency to float more naturally in the future. Singapore's monetary authority uses a "managed float" system to control the value of the Singapore dollar. A managed float functions as a middle ground between a pure fixed exchange rate system (as in China and Hong Kong in 2009 and 2010), and a full float system (as in Japan during that period).

In 2010 the Canada-based Fraser Institute ranked Singapore as the second most economically free nation in the world (after Hong Kong) in their Economic Freedom of the World report. The Economic Freedom reports compare five aspects of an economy, including the size of government (expenditures, taxes, and enterprises), legal structure and security of property rights, access to sound money, freedom to trade internationally, and regulation of credit, labor, and business. Singapore received an overall score of 8.7 out of 10 in the analysis. The GDP rate of change in Singapore, in of 2010, was 14.5%, the world's second highest rate. Inflation stood at 2.8%, and unemployment was reported at 2.2%.

In 2011 Singapore's outward-looking economy was driven by manufacturing (including high tech electronics and biomedical products), information technology, financial services, petroleum refining, and tourism. As a difficult global economy weakened demand for products like computer chips in 2011, and crises in Europe challenged the financial services sector, Singapore's economic growth slowed considerably. As of October 2011, the government was projecting a rate of 5% for the year.

[20] INCOME

The CIA reported that in 2010 the GDP of Singapore was an estimated US$291.9 billion. The CIA defines GDP as the value of all final goods and services produced within a nation in a given year and computed on the basis of purchasing power parity (PPP) rather than value as measured on the basis of the rate of the exchange based on current dollars. The per capita GDP was estimated at US$62,100. The annual growth rate of GDP was 14.5%. It was estimated that industry accounted for 27.2% of GDP and services for 72.8%.

The World Bank estimated that Singapore, with 0.07% of the world's population, accounted for 0.33% of the world's GDP. By comparison, the United States, with 4.85% of the world's population, accounted for 22.51% of world GDP. As of 2011, the most recent study by the World Bank reported that actual individual consumption in Singapore was 44.9% of GDP and accounted for 0.18% of world consumption. By comparison, the United States accounted for 25.44% of world individual consumption. The World Bank also estimated that 4.7% of Singapore's GDP was spent on food and beverages, 9.1% on housing and household furnishings, 1.6% on clothes, 3.8% on health, 7.4% on transportation, 1.1% on communications, 5.5% on recreation, 3.4% on restaurants and hotels, and 4.8% on miscellaneous goods and services and purchases from abroad.

[21] LABOR

As of 2010, Singapore had a total labor force of 3.156 million people. Within that labor force, CIA estimates in 2010 noted that 30.2% were employed in industry, and 69.7% in the service sector, with only 0.1% employed in agriculture. Trade unions are allowed in Singapore, and most unions are part of the PAP-associated National Trade Union Congress. Workers have the right to strike but rarely do so; collective bargaining is utilized. Labor by children under 13 is prohibited, and labor by children 13 to 16 is highly restricted. Singapore did not have a minimum wage, as of 2011, although the National Wages Council produces wage guidelines each year. The government has set minimum workplace health and safety regulations. However, foreign migrant workers have been exposed to unsafe, unpaid, or abusive working conditions, particularly in construction and domestic service. As of 2011, the standard legal workweek was 44 hours, with one day off each week, although domestic servants had no mandatory time off.

22 AGRICULTURE

Urbanization and industrialization took land away from agricultural activity in Singapore. Apartment blocks and factories stand where rubber and coconut trees used to grow. Roughly 1% of the total land is farmed, according to the FAO as of 2009, and the country's few crops include orchids for export, and vegetables for local consumption. Fruit production amounted to 12 tons in 2009 and vegetable production to 19,420 tons. Only about 7% of vegetables consumed in Singapore were locally grown, as of 2009. Several vegetable farms, including organic operations, are located in the Kranji Countryside area in the north of the Singapore island. Some Singaporeans grow their own fruits and vegetables in housing estate community gardens, which have been encouraged since 2005 as part of the nation's efforts to reduce the carbon footprint.

23 ANIMAL HUSBANDRY

In 2009 the country tended 3.2 million chickens, according to the FAO. Singapore's needs for meat and dairy products have been met by imports from Indonesia, Malaysia, China, and elsewhere in the 21st century. Singapore's last pig farms were phased out, and a high-intensity pig farming operation was planned for Sarawak, Malaysia, in order to supply pork demand in Singapore. A massive pig-raising operation was also part of the planned Jilin-Singapore Agriculture and Food Zone, a production area in China dedicated to supplying Singapore. A few poultry farms produced eggs for the local market, and there were very limited cattle and goat dairies as of 2011.

24 FISHING

Singapore had 90 decked commercial fishing boats in 2008. The annual capture totaled 1,623 tons according to the UN FAO. The export value of seafood totaled US$402.1 million. Fresh fish are auctioned at the Jurong Fisher Port, which provides modern shore-support assistance and processing plants; in 2010 the Jurong Fishery Port handled over 60,000 tons of fish. The Senoko Port is for local fishing vessels and handled over 9,000 tons of fish in 2010. According to the Singapore government, there were over 100 seafood processing operations as of 2010. Aquaculture concentrates on the breeding of grouper, sea bass, mussels, and prawns. A marine fish-farming scheme to encourage aquaculture in designated coastal waters was implemented in 1981; as of 2010, 112 marine fish farms were in operation. There are also compa-

nies on Singapore island which breed and raise aquarium fish for export.

25 FORESTRY

As of 2011, approximately 3% of Singapore was covered by forest, which was entirely public protected land. Singaporean companies have set up factories in other Asian countries, including China, Indonesia, and Malaysia, to process timber into products such as flooring and furniture, for the Singapore market and for international markets.

26 MINING

There is no mining in Singapore. However, although the city-state has limited natural resources, it is one of the most important shipping centers in the world. Singapore has the world's third-largest oil-refining center, behind Houston, Texas, and Rotterdam, Netherlands, and the major oil and metal futures trading market in Asia. The production of chemicals accounted for 12% of exports in 2009, and manufactured ferrous, nonferrous, and nonmetallic products accounted for 3% of exports that year. Chemicals, mineral fuels, and petroleum products ranked among the top five export commodities. Singapore has no integrated cement plant and local operations ground imported clinker to produce cement.

27 ENERGY AND POWER

The World Bank reported in 2008 that Singapore produced 41.7 billion kWh of electricity and consumed 39.6 billion kWh, or 8,355 kWh per capita. All energy came from fossil fuels. Per capita oil consumption was 3,828 kg. According to the government's Energy Market Authority, in 2010, 79% of electricity was produced from natural gas, and 15% from oil. The government was promoting a goal of "Low Carbon Singapore" through energy conservation measures and technological innovation, as of 2011. Singapore Energy Week, a conference for petroleum industry executives and other experts, is an annual event that started in 2008. A Clean Energy Expo was held in Singapore in 2011, to promote alternative sources such as wind, geothermal, and solar power. Singapore's Solar Energy Research Institute was developing photovoltaic technology, and the government had prioritized smart grid electricity use technology, as of 2011.

28 INDUSTRY

Singapore's major industries were once rubber milling and tin smelting. The modern industrialization of Singapore began in 1961 with the creation of the Economic Development Board to formulate and implement an ambitious manufacturing scheme. Large-scale foreign manufacturing operations in Singapore commenced in 1967 with the establishment of plants by several major multinational electronics corporations. Industry's share of GDP rose from 12% in 1960 to 29% in 1981. Such dramatic achievements were in large measure made possible by the most developed economic infrastructure in Southeast Asia, as well as by the government efforts to provide a skilled workforce.

As of 2010, according to the CIA, industry accounted for 28.3% of GDP and employed about 30% of the labor force. Labor-intensive operations have been encouraged to move offshore by the government, while service and high-technology industries are encouraged. Major industries include electronics manufacture,

Principal Trading Partners – Singapore (2010)

(In millions of US dollars)

Country	Total	Exports	Imports	Balance
World	662,658.0	351,867.0	310,791.0	41,076.0
Malaysia	78,271.0	41,913.0	36,358.0	5,555.0
China	70,162.0	36,496.0	33,666.0	2,830.0
United States	58,638.0	23,005.0	35,633.0	-12,628.0
Hong Kong	44,265.0	41,326.0	2,939.0	38,387.0
Japan	40,866.0	16,412.0	24,454.0	-8,042.0
South Korea	32,428.0	14,398.0	18,030.0	-3,632.0
Taiwan	31,338.0	12,820.0	18,518.0	-5,698.0
Thailand	22,941.0	12,702.0	10,239.0	2,463.0
India	22,574.0	13,341.0	9,233.0	4,108.0
Philippines	16,386.0	7,174.0	9,212.0	-2,038.0

(…) data not available or not significant.

(n.s.) not specified.

SOURCE: 2011 Direction of Trade Statistics Yearbook, New York: United Nations, 2011.

financial services, petroleum-related operations (including refining and equipment), rubber processing, processed food, pharmaceuticals, and biotechnology. The most important manufacturing sector is electronics. During the 1990s, Singapore was the world's leading producer of computer disk drives, and there has been significant investment in computer chip fabrication plants. However, this dependence upon electronics can have negative consequences as well as positive ones: when world demand for electronics, particularly computer chips, declines, as it did in 2011, Singapore can be hard hit.

Petroleum refining is a well-established industry in Singapore. After Rotterdam and Houston, Singapore is the world's third-largest refining center. Production capacity from its three main refineries (capable of processing 40 different types of crude oil) was 1.3 million barrels per day in 2009. Singapore Petroleum Company was taken over by PetroChina, mainland China's state-owned petroleum multinational, in 2009. The petrochemical industry was a direct result of Singapore's refinery capacity. The Petrochemical Corporation of Singapore is a government-linked company (GLC). GLCs are majority government owned but operate commercially, unlike traditional parastatals. Industrial GLCs include Singapore Technologies Engineering (aerospace and electronics manufacturer); Keppel Corporation (oil drilling and related equipment manufacturer); and Sembcorp Industries Corporation (construction and engineering).

29 SCIENCE AND TECHNOLOGY

Patent applications in science and technology as of 2009 totaled 750 in Singapore, according to the World Bank. Public financing of science was 2.56% of GDP. Expenditures for research and development in 2010 totaled 2.2% of GDP (short of the government's stated target of 3%). The Agency for Science, Technology and Research (known as A*STAR) is the government's R&D funding and oversight body. The National Research Foundation was founded in 2006 to implement R&D strategy.

The Singapore National Academy of Sciences, established in 1967, promotes science and technology, and its member organization, the Singapore Association for the Advancement of Science, founded in 1976, disseminates science and technology for the general public, especially young people. Other major scientific and technical learned societies and research facilities include an academy of medicine, an institute of physics, an institute of technical education, botanical gardens, a mathematical society, and a medical association. The Singapore Science Park, located near the National University of Singapore, was developed in 1987. In 1993, the National Computer Board announced an effort towards an "intelligent island" through information infrastructure linking all of Singapore. The Institute of Systems Science researches information technology, and the Institute of Molecular and Cell Biology is a center for biotech research. Biopolis and Fusionopolis are linked research laboratories. An Agri-Bio Park has facilities for companies in research and development on subjects including plant and animal diseases, and pest resistance. In 2010, a Clean Tech Park was established as a "living laboratory" for environmental innovation.

Scientific education is stressed at the university level and supported by training programs for students in the nation's technical and vocational institutes. Courses in engineering, medicine, and other basic and applied sciences are offered at Nanyang Technical University (founded in 1981), the National University of Singapore (founded in 1980 by merger), Singapore Institute of Technology (2009), Ngee Ann Polytechnic (1963), Singapore Polytechnic (1954), Temasek Polytechnic (1990), and Republic Polytechnic (2002). Singapore University of Technology and Design was scheduled to open in April 2012, in partnership with Massachusetts Institute of Technology (MIT).

30 DOMESTIC TRADE

Marketing and transshipment of goods have always been important activities in Singapore. Warehousing, packaging, freight forwarding, and related services are of a high standard. Advertising is done by radio and television, outdoor display, print media, internet, and mobile phones. There are many local agencies as well as branches of international companies in advertising and market research.

A wide range of consumer goods, such as luxury, electronic, handicraft, and food items, are available in Singapore from international department stores, brand name specialty stores, local department store chains, and neighborhood shops and markets. Prices are fixed in most larger retail establishments, however, bargaining is still common in smaller shops. Credit cards are widely accepted. Singapore has been well positioned to take advantage of the growth offered by e-commerce. It was one of the first countries in the world to enact legislation that addressed issues arising from electronic contacts and digital signatures. Selling counterfeit goods and pirated media are illegal in Singapore, and the laws were strictly enforced as of 2011.

Usual business hours are 9 a.m. to 5 p.m., with many businesses closed from 1 p.m. to 2 p.m. Most major enterprises and foreign firms operate Monday through Friday and are open a half day on Saturday. Retail stores are open from 10 a.m. to 9 p.m., Monday through Saturday, with most shops also open for at least part of the day on Sunday.

31 FOREIGN TRADE

Since World War II, Singapore has changed from merely a center for the incoming and outgoing traffic of its neighbors in Southeast

Asia, to an exporting power in its own right, with a variety of capital-intensive manufactures. Except for an occasional slowdown, annual levels of trade regularly record double-digit expansion. During the late 1990s, expansion in the high-end manufacturing and services sectors began replacing capital-intensive production. Re-export trade has remained important due to Singapore's favorable location in the Strait of Malacca and its excellent port facilities.

Singapore imported US$310.4 billion worth of goods and services in 2010, while exporting US$358.4 billion worth of goods and services, according to the CIA. According to the CIA, Singapore's major export partners in 2010 were: Malaysia, 11.9%; Hong Kong, 11.7%; China, 10.4%; Indonesia, 9.4%; the United States, 6.5%; Japan, 4.7%; and South Korea, 4.1%. Major exports included electronics and other machinery, consumer goods, pharmaceuticals, fuel, and chemicals. Major import partners in 2010 were Malaysia, 11.7%; United States, 11.5%; ; China, 10.8%; Japan, 7.9%; Indonesia, 5.8%; South Korea, 5.8% and Indonesia, 5.4%. Imports included machinery, equipment, fuel, chemicals, and food.

In 2003 Prime Minister Goh Chok Tong signed a free trade agreement with the United States. Depicted as the "gold standard" for free trade agreements, it helped Singapore fix its position as a leading financial and trading nation in the region, especially after the Asian financial crisis of 1997–1998 and the effect of Severe Acute Respiratory Syndrome (SARS) in the region.

The ASEAN Trade in Goods Agreement (ATIGA), approved in 2009, entered into force on 17 May 2010. ATIGA represented the next step in realizing the free flow of goods within the region by simplifying the processes and procedures necessary to create a single market and production base—known as the ASEAN Economic Community (AEC)—by 2015. Major points of ATIGA include tariff liberalization, a simplification of the rules of origin, and implementation of such rules. The comprehensive agreement also demands greater transparency in regional trade liberalization, aiding the work of businesses and investors. On 1 January 2010, a new free trade area was established between China and the six founding members of the Association of South East Asian Nations (ASEAN), including Singapore. A major point of the free trade agreement is the elimination of tariffs on nearly 90% of imported goods. The free trade area agreement was expected to allow for a major increase in exports and export earnings among the ASEAN countries.

³²BALANCE OF PAYMENTS

In 2010 Singapore had a foreign trade surplus of US$39 billion, amounting to 1.7% of GDP. Total official reserves were estimated to be equal to about 9 months of imports, as of 2010. Despite having to import virtually all food and fuel for its population, along with raw materials and components for its manufacturing industries, Singapore has had strong surplus figures in the early 21st century, as a high tech value-added exporter with an emphasis on innovation. The current account surplus has often been driven by demand for electronics products such as computer chips, for export to the United States, Japan, and regional countries with elec-

Balance of Payments – Singapore (2010)

(In millions of US dollars)

Current Account		**49,558.0**
Balance on goods	46,758.0	
Imports	-311,727.0	
Exports	358,485.0	
Balance on services	15,845.0	
Balance on income	-8,230.0	
Current transfers	-4,815.0	
Capital Account		**-333.0**
Financial Account		**-6,603.0**
Direct investment abroad	-19,740.0	
Direct investment in Singapore	38,638.0	
Portfolio investment assets	-25,132.0	
Portfolio investment liabilities	3,265.0	
Financial derivatives	...	
Other investment assets	-37,339.0	
Other investment liabilities	33,704.0	
Net Errors and Omissions		**-325.0**
Reserves and Related Items		**-42,297.0**

(…) data not available or not significant.

SOURCE: *Balance of Payment Statistics Yearbook 2011,* Washington, DC: International Monetary Fund, 2011.

tronics production facilities. The account also benefits from high net investment income receipts.

³³BANKING AND SECURITIES

Singapore's development was closely linked to efficient financial management. Conservative fiscal and monetary policies generated high savings, which, along with high levels of foreign investment, allowed growth without the accumulation of external debt. The banking system was opened to foreign banks in the late 1960s. In 1988, Singapore had foreign reserves worth about US$533 billion, which, per capita, put it ahead of Switzerland, Saudi Arabia, and Taiwan. Many sources of finance are available to organizations doing business in Singapore. The Monetary Authority of Singapore (MAS) performs the functions of a central bank, except for the issuing of currency. The Board of Commissioners of Currency deals with currency issues. The MAS seeks to strike a balance between supervision on the one hand, and development of the financial markets on the other.

Singapore has not encouraged the freewheeling financial services culture of Hong Kong, nor has it resorted to a strongly controlled approach, as in South Korea or Taiwan. Banks in Singapore operate under strong secrecy laws, similar to the Swiss banking system. This has led to international criticism of Singapore's banking sector for providing a safe haven for the hidden wealth of criminals or corrupt officials from countries like Myanmar. Two sovereign wealth funds, Government of Singapore Investment Corporations and Temasek Holdings, were Singapore's state investment companies as of 2011. After sustaining losses from international investments in 2011, both were criticized for lack of transparency by Singapore's opposition politicians.

Singapore's citizens have long had high savings rates of over 25%, including mandatory contributions to the Central Provident Fund. The CIA reported that in December 2010, currency and

Public Finance – Singapore (2009)

(In millions of Singapore dollars, central government figures)

Revenue and Grants	48,161	100.0%
Tax revenue	36,584	76.0%
Social contributions	...	...
Grants	...	...
Other revenue	11,577	24.0%
Expenditures	47,774	100.0%
General public services	3,601	7.5%
Defense	11,379	23.8%
Public order and safety	2,366	5.0%
Economic affairs	7,792	16.3%
Environmental protection	...	...
Housing and community amenities	3,228	6.8%
Health	3,687	7.7%
Recreational, culture, and religion	995	2.1%
Education	8,758	18.3%
Social protection	5,968	12.5%

(...) data not available or not significant.

SOURCE: *Government Finance Statistics Yearbook 2010*, Washington, DC: International Monetary Fund, 2010.

demand deposits—an aggregate commonly known as M1—were equal to US$87.35 billion. In that same year, M2—an aggregate equal to M1 plus savings deposits, small time deposits, and money market mutual funds—was US$313.1 billion. In December 2010, the commercial bank prime lending rate was 5.38%.

As of 2011 Singapore had over 100 commercial banks and nearly 50 merchant banks. There were more than 100 branches representing overseas banks, several of which were characterized as Qualifying Full Banks, eligible to provide services at multiple locations. Singapore had wholesale and offshore banks concentrating on foreign exchange transaction as well. Singapore's locally incorporated banks included, as of 2011, Bank of Singapore, Overseas Chinese Banking (OCBC), United Overseas Bank, and DBS Bank (with a subsidiary Islamic Bank of Asia). The Post Office Savings Bank (POSBank) was the national savings bank (est. 1877); it merged with DBS Bank in 1998. Singapore's banks offer internet and mobile phone banking, credit cards, and ATMs. Bank hours are 9:30 a.m. to 3 p.m., Monday through Friday, and Saturday from 9:30 a.m. to 1 p.m.

The Stock Exchange of Malaysia and Singapore was founded in 1964 as the Stock Exchange of Malaysia. In 1973, all of the Singapore stocks moved to the Stock Exchange of Singapore (SES), and the Malaysian companies moved to the Kuala Lumpur Stock Exchange. The Singapore International Monetary Exchange (SIMEX) opened in 1984, to trade in futures contracts; it merged with the SES, forming the Singapore Exchange (SGX) in 1999. SGX offers trading in securities and derivatives. As of August 2011, a total of 775 companies were listed on the Singapore Stock Exchange, which had a market capitalization of US$635 billion. In 1995 Nick Leeson, a Singapore-based investment banker, singlehandedly destroyed the UK's Barings Bank with falsified currency trading leading to enormous failed investments; he was imprisoned in Singapore until 1999.

34 INSURANCE

The regulatory authority is the insurance commissioner of the Monetary Authority of Singapore. As of 2010, there were 158 insurance companies and 63 insurance brokers in Singapore, according to government statistics. Many insurance firms are branches or agencies of UK (or other Commonwealth), European, and US companies, although local participation in insurance, particularly business insurance, has increased. Marine and warehouse insurance constitutes most of the business insurance, but almost all types of commercial insurance are available. Workers' compensation, third-party automobile liability, and professional liability are all compulsory insurance in Singapore, and must be placed with local companies.

As of the second quarter of 2011, the value of all direct insurance premiums written, including offshore risks, was estimated at SGD28.769 billion, of which SGD20.125 billion was accounted for by life insurance premiums. In the second quarter of 2011, the top nonlife insurers were Chartis/American Home, NTUC Income, and AXA Singapore; the nation's leading life insurers were AIA, Great Eastern Life, and NTUC Income. Great Eastern Life, which operates in Singapore and Malaysia, was founded in 1908, and is a subsidiary of OCBC Bank. NTUC Income is a cooperative insurance society formed in Singapore in 1970.

35 PUBLIC FINANCE

In 2010 the budget of Singapore included US$32.7 billion in public revenue and US$32.31 billion in public expenditures, according to the CIA. The budget surplus amounted to .2% of GDP. Public debt was 105.8% of GDP, primarily Singapore Government Securities, issued for the Central Provident Fund (public pensions). Singapore had US$21.82 billion in external debt as of 2010, according to the CIA.

In Singapore's budget for fiscal year 2010 showed that 23% of operating revenue came from corporate income tax, 17% from goods and services tax, and 14% from personal income tax. Government outlays by function for fiscal year 2010 were as follows: social development, 43.6% (of which education accounted for 10.1%); security and external relations, 32.5%; economic development, 20.7%; and government administration, 3.2%. The budget emphasized education and housing infrastructure, with an increase in defense operational costs, and included a "Grow and Share" package of tax rebates and other special transfers.

36 TAXATION

Individual and commercial incomes are taxed, whether derived in Singapore or from outside sources. Types of direct taxation include income, property, and payroll taxes; the Inland Revenue Authority of Singapore is responsible for the assessment and collection of all such levies. As of 2011, Singapore's corporate income tax ranged from 8.5% to 17%, and dividends were not taxed. Industrial establishments, companies, and various other businesses are eligible to deduct varying and usually generous depreciation allowances from their gross profits for building, plants, and machinery. There were tax exemptions for newly incorporated Singapore companies, and a number of tax incentive packages were available for foreign companies starting investments in Singapore, including the Pioneer Incentive for new industries (a full tax holiday of up to 15 years.)

As of 2011, personal income tax rates ranged from 0% (first SGD20,000) to 20% (above SGD320,000).Other taxes, as of 2011, included a goods and services tax (GST) at a rate of 7%, a stamp tax, motor vehicle taxes, betting taxes, and a property tax based on expected rental income. As of 2011, Singapore had no capital gains tax and no estate tax.

37 CUSTOMS AND DUTIES

During 2011, Singapore, considered a free port, charged excise duties only on imports in four categories of goods: alcohol, tobacco, motor vehicles, and petroleum products (gasoline). Vehicles with four or more wheels were generally dutiable at 20%, while motorcycles were dutiable at 12%. As of 2011, there were controls on imports of several types of goods, including weapons, pharmaceuticals, and media (film and print). Prohibited items included narcotics, chewing gum, firecrackers, pirated media, "seditious and treasonable materials", and "obscene" items.

Singapore has seven free trade zones (FTZs), where no import duties are charged. Five FTZs are for seaborne cargo: Brani Terminal, Keppel Distripark, Pasir Panjang Terminal, Sembawang Wharves, Jurong Port, and Tanjong Pagar Terminal; and one FTZ is for air cargo, at Changi Airport. The GST (goods and service tax) of 7%, which is levied on all imports, is not levied on goods stored in the free trade zones.

38 FOREIGN INVESTMENT

Singapore's attractions for foreign investment include Singapore's development as a total international business center, an international air-sea cargo center, a location for the regional operational headquarters of multinational corporations, and a major exporter of services. Political stability, clear policies, low taxes, perceived lack of corruption, and availability of skilled labor have been factors attracting investment in the industrial and service sectors. Foreign investment in manufacturing is encouraged in areas of high technology, particularly scientific innovation, and the design and production of value-added "clean industry" products. Singapore does not require that foreign investors take on private-sector or government joint-venture partners.

Foreign direct investment (FDI) in Singapore was a net inflow of US$18.898 billion in 2010, according to the IMF. FDI represented 17.35% of GDP. According to Singapore government statistics, 21.8% of FDI for 2009 was in manufacturing (pharmaceuticals, 31%; electronics, 28.5%; petroleum products, 16.4%; chemicals, 6.5%; machinery and equipment, 4.8%.) Another 41.8% of FDI was in financial and insurance services. Leading FDI countries, as of 2009, included the United States, the Netherlands, Japan, United Kingdom, and British Virgin Islands. According to the US State Department, as of 2010, Singapore had investments from over 7,000 multinational corporations from the US, Europe and Japan, and an estimated 1,500 each from China and India.

Singapore's foreign direct investment net outflows for 2010 amounted to 8.86% of GDP, according to the IMF. As of the end of 2009, the leading recipients of DIA from Singapore were China, United Kingdom, British Virgin Islands, and Malaysia, according to Singapore government statistics.

39 ECONOMIC DEVELOPMENT

Historically, Singapore's economy was based primarily on its role as a transshipment port for neighboring countries due to its strategic geographic location at the entrance to the Strait of Malacca. It did not have minerals or other primary products of its own to export. Its most significant natural resource is a deep water harbor. As a result of these circumstances, Singapore became highly active in shipbuilding and repair, tin smelting, and rubber and copra milling.

After independence, it was obvious that prospects for economic growth would be severely limited if Singapore remained bound by its old economic role, completely dependent on facilitating trade. The decision to industrialize—and to do so rapidly—was deliberate policy. The initial emphasis in the government's economic development program was on employment. By the end of the 1960s, Singapore boasted one of the lowest unemployment rates in Asia. Emphasis in the mid-1970s was on labor skills and technology, especially for such modern industries as machine tools, petrochemicals, electronics, and other precision work. A high level of participation by private foreign capital provided an important cornerstone to this development.

By the early 1980s, Singapore had built a much stronger and diversified economy, which gave it an economic importance in Southeast Asia out of proportion to its small size. Government plans during the first half of the 1980s called for realigning industrial activities from traditional labor-intensive, low-wage activities to capital-intensive, high-wage and high-technology activities, notably the electronic industries (especially computers), and oil refining. In 1985, however, Singapore's economy declined for the first time in 20 years. One of the reasons for the decline was high wages, which made Singaporean products less competitive on the world market. Other reasons for the economic downturn included a slumping demand for oil and electronic products and the economic woes of Malaysia, Indonesia, and other important trading partners. Following the recession of 1985–86, the government concentrated on developing new markets and on turning Singapore into a manufacturing, financial, and communications center for multinational corporations. One of the fastest-growing sectors of Singapore's economy was international banking and finance, accounting for some 25% of GDP in the late 1980s.

In the 1990s, emphasis was placed on promoting investment in manufacturing. The Strategic Economic Plan (SEP), announced in 1991, focused on education and human resources to enhance export competitiveness. Development of the service sector was supported and enhanced by the Operational Headquarters (OHQ) program, encouraging companies to use Singapore as their regional headquarters or as a central distribution center. Singapore's globalization strategy has hinged on making a transformation from a production-driven economy to an innovation-driven one. Singapore initiated the formation of a growth triangle, linking Johor, Malaysia; Singapore; and Indonesia's Riau Province. Singapore benefited by tapping into a supply of low-wage workers and offshore land to sustain its more labor-intensive industries. Export growth in high-technology manufactured goods signaled Singapore's success in shifting to higher value-added production. The electronics industry accounted for the largest share of value-added in manufacturing. Manufacturing was dominated by the production of computer peripherals and oil processing. In the five years

1993 to 1997, GDP growth averaged 8.84%. Due to the 1997–98 Asian financial crisis, Singapore's GDP growth dropped to 1.5% in 1998. Nevertheless, Singapore weathered the crisis without a contraction, and in 1999, growth recovered to 5.4%.

Driven by the worldwide boom in information technology demand, and robust recoveries in domestic consumption and investment, GDP growth soared to 9.9% in 2000. However, the dot com crisis in 2001 led to the economy's first yearly contraction since 1985. Recovery began in the second quarter of 2002, and though weak because of continued low export demand, growth was positive for the year. GDP growth in 2003 was a sluggish. This was somewhat due to a slowdown in the technology sector as well as the outbreak of Severe Acute Respiratory Syndrome (SARS) in 2003. But, in 2004 growth soared, thanks to the recovery of the tourism sector, double-digit retail sales gains, rising investment rates, increased manufacturing production, and the construction industry's recovery from a two-year slump, among other factors. Bilateral free-trade agreements, including one with the United States, which came into force in 2004, were negotiated in order to improve market access and encourage foreign investment inflows. By the end of 2005, the Singapore economy was growing at a healthy clip of around 5%. At that point, Singapore's central bank (the Monetary Authority of Singapore) stated that its policy of allowing the Singapore dollar to strengthen against a basket of currencies would be maintained. This effective monetary tightening reflected continued confidence in the health of the local economy. Protected sectors, such as financial services, were liberalized in 2006, in an effort to increase overall efficiency. Real GDP growth averaged 7% between 2004 and 2007.

The global financial crisis in 2008–2009 decreased demands for Singapore's exports, plunging GDP growth rates down to 1.5% in 2008 and -0.8% in 2009, but the economy rebounded enormously in 2010, with a 14.5% GDP growth rate, the second highest in the world. In 2011, with export demand still weak and financial services affected by Europe's difficulties, the government projected a more modest, though still healthy, growth rate of 5%. In the 2010s, Singapore's government is seeking to encourage innovation, and to diversify the economy toward new services and consumer industries. Singapore wants to foster the development of a knowledge-based economy, with new campus-type facilities integrating academic and corporate research and development. The financial sector continued to attract foreign investment and environmentally friendly industries were increasingly promoted. Gambling and medical tourism were expected to further boost the services sector. Challenges for future growth included an aging workforce and reliance on foreign migrant labor, the need to import food and fuel, and dependence on volatile export markets for manufactured goods.

40 SOCIAL DEVELOPMENT

The Central Provident Fund (CPF) was established in 1955 as a social security plan. Covering most employed persons and the self-employed, it provides benefits for a wide range of social services, including retirement, housing, education, disability, death, sickness, and maternity. Mandatory employee contributions are based on income; employers pay 16% of monthly earnings. Retirement benefits under the plan can begin as early as age 55, as long as minimum contributions to the account have been made;

age 62 is the age when monthly payments from CPF accounts usually start. Employers also fund workers' compensation benefits for job-related injuries. In addition, employers are required to provide 14 days of paid sick leave per year, and twelve weeks of paid maternity leave.

Women's legal rights are equal to those of men in most areas, including employment, business, property, and education. Women are approximately 55% of the labor force, but are under-represented in politics. Despite the legal principle of equal pay for equal work, women tend to earn less than men. In 2004, the constitution was amended to remove the inequality that a female citizen could not automatically convey citizenship to her children. Rape, spousal abuse and domestic violence were covered by laws, and there were voluntary organizations providing shelters and other services for abused women. Domestic servants, usually foreign migrants, were particularly vulnerable to abuse.

With a birth rate below replacement levels, Singapore's government set up financial incentives for marriage and childbearing, particularly for citizens with higher education levels. Women who have children at a young age are given tax rebates. As of 2011, these measures were unsuccessful at boosting marriage and birth rates. Despite the overall high standard of living, Singaporeans often experienced stress from a completely urban existence, with long work hours, high prices, and the competitive business and education climates.

Under a 2009 law, all outdoor events require permits, making it very difficult for Singaporeans to assemble freely in public for protests or any other reason. Permits are also needed for indoor events with race or religion as topics. An area of Hong Lim Park called Speaker's Corner is less restricted, although registration is still required for events or speeches there. Since 2009, gay rights activists have held annual gatherings at Speaker's Corner. In October 2007, Singapore's parliament rejected a bill to decriminalize sex between men, upholding the rarely enforced official ban on homosexual sex.

41 HEALTH

According to the CIA, life expectancy in Singapore was 81 years in 2011. The country spent 3.3% of its GDP on healthcare, amounting to US$1,501 per person. There were 18 physicians, 59 nurses and midwives, and 31 hospital beds per 10,000 inhabitants. The fertility rate was 1.2, while the infant mortality rate was 2 per 1,000 live births. In 2008 the maternal mortality rate, according to the World Bank, was 9 per 100,000 births. It was estimated that 95% of children were vaccinated against measles.

Singapore has state healthcare funds including Medisave accounts, Medishield catastrophic insurance coverage, and Medifund for low income citizens. Singapore's advanced hospitals and medical specialists attract medical tourism; over 610,000 foreign patients and their relatives arrived for medical procedures in 2008.

In 2003, Singapore was shaken medically and financially by Severe Acute Respiratory Syndrome (SARS). As the disease was identified, Singapore took stringent precautions by closing markets, screening air passengers with thermal imaging, and establishing quarantines. About 33 people in Singapore died from SARS. A sharp economic contraction occurred as tourists stayed away and local people stayed home. In 2005, a Campaign Against Dengue was launched in Singapore, with town councils playing a major oversight role. In 2011, according to the Ministry of Health, there were over 4,500 dengue fever cases, and 17 cases of hemorrhagic dengue fever. Singapore's x-Dengue project offered alerts about clusters of dengue fever outbreaks, through a smartphone app, social media, and email. The CIA calculated HIV/AIDS prevalence in Singapore to be about 0.1% in 2009.

42 HOUSING

Sustained rapid population growth in the years preceding and following World War II caused an acute housing shortage in Singapore. In 1947, a housing committee determined that 250,000 persons required immediate housing, while another 250,000 people would need new housing by the late 1950s. In 1960, the Housing and Development Board (HDB) was established by the new PAP government. During its first five-year building program (1960–65), it built 53,000 apartment units for more than 250,000 people. It was during this period that Queens Town, Singapore's first satellite community, was developed. By the mid-1970s, Queens Town had a total of 27,000 living units in seven neighborhood complexes, housing upwards of 150,000 people. By 1985, as a result of government-sponsored efforts, 2,148,720 persons (84% of the total population of Singapore) lived in 551,767 apartments under the management of the HDB. Some 397,180 units were sold to the public.

As of 2010, according to Singapore government statistics, the average household size was 3.5 persons. The home ownership rate was 87.2%, with 74.4% of householders living in HDB four room or larger flats, or in houses. According to the CIA, 100% of people in Singapore had access to improved water sources and improved sanitation as of 2008. Nearly all housing stock consisted of concrete high-rise apartment buildings, with very few of Singapore's traditional shop-houses or private dwellings remaining. Only 5.1% of Singapore residents lived in landed property. Foreign migrant workers were often housed in substandard, crowded conditions, including construction sites and converted shipping containers.

43 EDUCATION

As of 2010, according to Singapore government statistics, the literacy rate was 95.9% among residents 15 years old and over. Public expenditure on education represented 3.2% of GDP in 2009, according to the World Bank. According to Singapore government statistics, as of 2010 there were 698,544 students in 173 primary schools, and 263,906 students in 155 secondary schools. The student-to-teacher ratio was 19 to 1 for primary school, and 16 to 1 for secondary school, as of 2008, according to the World Bank.

All children are entitled to free education for ten years. Bilingual education—English plus a "mother tongue"—is emphasized in primary schools. There is a national curriculum, with an examination after completion of primary school to help determine placement in different types of secondary education. Specialized independent secondary schools are geared toward students with particular talents in sports, mathematics and science, or the arts.

Students eligible to consider university studies enter a three-year preparatory program to complete their secondary education. The National University of Singapore (founded in 1980 by merger of the University of Singapore and Nanyang University) offered nine degree courses as of 2010, including graduate schools of law,

medicine, public policy, and engineering, and has created specialized science research facilities. Nanyang Technological University was derived from Nanyang University in 1981. Singapore Management University (2000) offers graduate and undergraduate degrees in business and related subjects. Singapore Institute of Technology (2009) provides higher education for polytechnic graduates. Singapore University of Technology and Design is scheduled to begin its programs in Apirl 2012, offering undergraduate degrees in architecture, engineering, and information systems, in collaboration with the Massachusetts Institute of Technology (MIT). Singapore also has five polytechnics, and other vocational schools, including arts colleges, as well as an Institute of Technical Education. Singapore offers extensive adult education and skills training courses. As of 2010, according to Singapore government statistics, enrollment in Singapore's institutions of higher learning was close to equal for male and female students.

44 LIBRARIES AND MUSEUMS

The National Library Board oversees the National Library, and Public Libraries Singapore (PLS), as well as an international library consulting company called Cybrarian Ventures. The free PLS system included 24 libraries as of 2011, and offered extensive online resources. The National Library of Singapore (founded in 1844 and known, until 1960, as Raffles National Library) contains over 9 million items; it includes the Lee Kong Chian Reference Library, with a collection of about 530,000 items and many electronic resources. The National Library moved into a new building in 2005, which also houses the Central public library as well as performance space. Singapore has several major academic libraries, including the National University of Singapore Library system, with 1,495,000 items as of 2010; Singapore Polytechnic Library with over 200,000 volumes, in addition to periodicals and electronic resources; and the Institute of Southeast Asian Studies, a research center with over 500,000 items.

The National Museum (formerly Raffles Museum), established in 1849, has collections of natural history, ethnology, and archaeology. Since 1965, it has also specialized in the art, culture, and way of life of Singapore's ethnic communities. The National University of Singapore (NUS) has the NUS Center for the Arts, which includes the Lee Kong Chian Art Museum (Chinese art) as well as South and Southeast Asian collections. The Singapore Art Museum opened in 1996 and focuses on modern and contemporary works by Asian artists. The Asian Civilizations Museum opened in 1997. Science Center Singapore has a popular museum geared toward young people. The lotus-shaped ArtScience Museum opened in 2011, hosting international traveling exhibitions in the Marina Bay Sands resort and casino complex.

45 MEDIA

Singapore has a long and ongoing pattern of interference with press freedom. Magazines, films, plays, websites, computer games, and other media are censored for sexual content, political views, and presentation of sensitive ethnic or religious topics. In addition to official censorship of local and foreign media, libel litigation and the government's access to electronic surveillance technology have led to a climate of self-censorship in Singapore's local media.

Bloggers and social media users who comment on controversial subjects usually do so anonymously.

Singapore Press Holdings and MediaCorp, two corporations linked to the ruling PAP, were owners of most of the print and broadcast media, as of 2011. There are English, Chinese, Malay, and Tamil daily newspapers. Prominent newspapers in 2010, with circulation numbers listed parenthetically, included the *Straits Times* (founded in 1845, 392,611), the *Sunday Times* (387,000), and *Lianhe Zaobao* (205,158), as well as 6 other major newspapers.

Virtually all broadcasting services are operated by the government-linked MediaCorp, with 8 broadcast television channels and 14 radio stations (3 on shortwave) as of 2011. Satellite dishes for television reception were banned, as of 2011, but cable television with foreign channels was available, although sometimes censored. Radio and television broadcasts are available in Mandarin, Malay, Tamil, and English.

According to Singapore government statistics, as of October 2011, there were 2.0 million landline subscriptions in Singapore, and 7.7 million mobile telephone subscriptions. Mobile phone subscriptions averaged 150 per 100 people, as of 2011, according to Singapore government statistics. Singapore has excellent domestic and international telecommunication services and facilities. In February of 2005, the country initiated third-generation (3G) wireless phone service; as of mid- 2011, nearly 70% of mobile subscriptions were for 3G. 4G wireless availability was planned for 2012. Mobile phones are used for text messaging, internet access, and e-commerce.

In 2010 the country had 992,786 Internet hosts, according to the CIA. As of October 2011, according to Singapore government statistics, there were more than 8.8 million broadband Internet subscriptions. E-commerce, blogs, and social networking were extremely popular, with leading sites including Facebook (an estimated 2.4 million users as of mid-2011) YouTube, and Twitter. Social media was increasingly used by the political opposition, particularly during the 2011 election.

46 ORGANIZATIONS

Organizations of ten or more members were required to register with the government, as of 2011, and were subject to government approval. Groups which had not registered as political parties or organizations were not allowed to participate in political activities.

Maruah works for human rights in Singapore and internationally, and TWC2 (Transient Workers Count Too) is an advocacy group for migrant labor. Women's organizations include the Association of Women for Action and Research (AWARE), and Singapore Council of Women's Organizations. Groups supporting the Lesbian, Gay, Bisexual, and Transgender communities include Pink Dot Singapore, founded in 2008, and Sisters in Solidarity, founded in 2009.

The Singapore Chamber of Commerce is the nation's oldest business organization. There are also chambers of commerce for the Chinese, Indian, and Malay communities, and for expatriate business people. The National Trades Union Congress is the dominant labor group. The Consumers' Association of Singapore was founded in 1971. There are professional associations covering a variety of fields. Organizations including the Academy of Medicine, the Singapore National Academy of Sciences, and the Institute of Physics promote public interest and education in various

branches of science. There are several other associations dedicated to research and education for specific fields of medicine, and particular diseases and conditions.

The government's National Council of Social Service assists in coordinating volunteer services through member service organizations, professional associations, retirement homes, and children's homes. There are service clubs belonging to international associations, such as national chapters of Lions Clubs, Kiwanis International, the Red Cross, and Habitat for Humanity. Singapore International Foundation is a volunteer group that works in developing countries.

In 1960, the government established the People's Association to organize and promote community participation in social, cultural, educational, and recreational activities. National youth organizations include the Singapore Scout Association, Singapore Girl Guides, YMCA/YWCA, Junior Chamber, and Outward Bound. Singapore has many clubs and associations for sports, as well as clubs for hobbyists and games enthusiasts. The government's National Arts Council promotes arts education and organizes events including the Singapore Writers' Festival, and Singapore Arts Festival. Culture and arts organizations include the Indian Fine Arts Society and the Singapore Art Society.

47 TOURISM, TRAVEL, AND RECREATION

The *Tourism Factbook*, published by the UN World Tourism Organization, reported 9.68 million incoming tourists to Singapore in 2009 who spent a total of US$9.2 billion. Of those incoming tourists, 6.8 million were from East Asia and the Pacific. The estimated daily cost to visit Singapore was US$490.

Shopping in Singapore has long been a major draw for tourists from all over the world. Singapore is known for its extraordinary food culture, with outdoor food hawkers' centers featuring a huge variety of Chinese, Indian, and Southeast Asian cuisines. Places of interest for visitors include the Singapore Zoo and Night Safari, Jurong Bird Park, the Botanic Gardens, the Haw Par Villa folk art statue park, and the tallest Ferris wheel in the world-the Singapore Flyer. Although Singapore has been relentlessly modernized, pockets of the old architecture have been preserved or reconstructed, including colonial government buildings now serving as museums, the Raffles Hotel, the Alkaff Mansion, and parts of Chinatown, Arab Street, and Little India. Ways to reach the island of Sentosa include boardwalk and cable car; beach resorts and the Underwater World aquarium are located there. As part of the government's continuing effort to promote tourism, two casinos opened in 2010, at Sentosa Island and Marina Bay Sands. They quickly became profitable and contributed to Singapore's high GNP growth rates in 2010 and 2011.

All visitors to Singapore must carry a passport valid for at least six months upon entry. Proof of sufficient funds and an onward/return ticket are also necessary and checked by the Immigration and Checkpoints Authority (ICA). Nationals of most countries did not need a visa for a visit of up to 90 days, as of 2011, but visas were required for nationals of 34 countries, including China, India, Myanmar, Bangladesh, Russia, Egypt, and Iraq.

48 FAMOUS PERSONS

Singapore's dominant contemporary figure is Lee Kuan Yew (b. 1923), prime minister of the Republic of Singapore from 1965 to

1990. His son, Lee Hsien Loong (b. 1952), became the nation's third prime minister in 2004. Goh Chok Tong (b. 1941) was the nation's second prime minister. Singapore's marginalized elected opposition has been exemplified by J. B. Jeyaretnam (1926–2008) and Chee Soon Juan (b. 1962). Dissident Chia Thye Poh (b. 1941) endured decades under arrest.

In the arts, Ng Eng Teng (1934–2001) was known for his large scale ceramic sculptures; Arthur Yap (1943–2006) was a notable poet and painter; Catherine Lim (b. 1942) is a short story writer and novelist; and Kumarason Chinnadurai, known as Kumar (b. 1968) is a popular cross-dressing comedian. Sim Wong Hoo (b. 1955) is a high tech inventor and entrepreneur.

⁴⁹DEPENDENCIES

Singapore has no territories or colonies.

⁵⁰BIBLIOGRAPHY

Altbach, Philip G. and Toru Umakoshi, eds. *Asian Universities: Historical Perspectives and Contemporary Challenges*. Baltimore, MD: Johns Hopkins University Press, 2004.

Aspalter, Christian. *Conservative Welfare State Systems in East Asia*. Westport, CT: Praeger, 2001.

Barr, Michael D. *Lee Kuan Yew, the Beliefs Behind the Man*. Washington, DC: Georgetown University Press, 2000.

Corfield, Justin J, and K Mulliner. *Historical Dictionary of Singapore*. Lanham, MD: Scarecrow Press, 2011.

Koh, Jaime, and Lee-Ling Ho. *Culture and Customs of Singapore and Malaysia*. Santa Barbara, CA: Greenwood Press, 2009.

Leibo, Steven A. *East and Southeast Asia, 2011*. Lanham, MD: Stryker-Post Publications, 2011.

Singapore Investment and Business Guide: Strategic and Practical Information. Washington, DC: International Business Publications USA, 2012.

Managing Political Change in Singapore: The Elected Presidency. Edited by Kevin Tan and Peng Er Lam. London: Routledge, 1997.

Mulliner, K. *Historical Dictionary of Singapore*. Metuchen, N.J.: Scarecrow Press, 1991.

Murray, Geoffrey. *Singapore: The Global City-State*. Kent, U.K.: China Library, 1996.

Peebles, Gavin. *The Singapore Economy*. Cheltenham, U.K.: Edward Elgar, 1996.

Rahim, Lily Z. *The Singapore Dilemma: The Political and Educational Marginality of the Malay Community*. New York: Oxford University Press, 1998.

SOLOMON ISLANDS

CAPITAL: Honiara

FLAG: The flag consists of two triangles, the upper one blue, the lower one green, separated by a diagonal gold stripe; on the blue triangle are five white, five-pointed stars.

ANTHEM: *God Save Our Solomon Islands.*

MONETARY UNIT: The Solomon Islands dollar (SBD), a paper currency of 100 cents, was introduced in 1977, replacing the Australian dollar, and became the sole legal tender in 1978. There are coins of 1, 2, 5, 10, 20, and 50 cents and 1 dollar, and notes of 2, 5, 10, 20, and 50 dollars. SBD1 = US$0.13 (or US$1 = SBD7.47) as of 2011.

WEIGHTS AND MEASURES: The metric system is in force.

HOLIDAYS: New Year's Day, 1 January; Queen's Birthday, 10 June; Independence Day, 7 July; Christmas, 25 December; Thanksgiving Day, 26 December. Movable religious holidays include Good Friday, Easter Monday, and Whitmonday.

TIME: 11 p.m. = noon GMT.

¹LOCATION, SIZE, AND EXTENT

The Solomon Islands consist of a chain of six large and numerous small islands situated in the South Pacific, some 1,900 km (1,200 mi) NE of Australia and about 485 km (300 mi) E of Papua New Guinea. Extending 1,688 km (1,049 mi) ESE–WNW and 468 km (291 mi) NNE–SSW, the Solomon Islands have an area of 28,450 sq km (10,985 sq mi). Comparatively, the Solomon Islands are slightly smaller than the state of Maryland. The largest island is Guadalcanal, covering 5,302 sq km (2,047 sq mi); other major islands are Malaita, Makira (formerly San Cristobal), Vella Lavella, Choiseul, Rennell, New Georgia, and the Santa Cruz group. The total coastline of the Solomon Islands is 5,313 km (3,301 mi).

The capital city of the Solomon Islands, Honiara, is located on the island of Guadalcanal.

²TOPOGRAPHY

The topography varies from the volcanic peaks of Guadalcanal to low-lying coral atolls. Densely forested mountain ranges are intersected by precipitous, narrow valleys. The highest peak is Mt. Makarakomburu, at 2,447 m (8,127 ft), on Guadalcanal, an island that also contains the country's most extensive alluvial grass plains. Rivers are narrow and impassable except by canoe. Extensive coral reefs and lagoons surround the island coasts. The nation is located within a seismically active area known as the Pacific "Ring of Fire." Two earthquakes (at magnitudes of 7.2 and 6.5) and a resulting tsunami hit near the Western Province of Gizo in the first few days of January 2010, leaving nearly 1,000 people homeless from home collapse, flooding, and landslides. Two earthquakes of similar magnitude (7.1 and 6.9) occurred in April 2011 but did not cause major damage or trigger a tsunami.

³CLIMATE

The climate is tropical. From December to March, northwest equatorial winds bring hot weather and heavy rainfall; from April to November, the islands are cooled by drier southeast trade winds. Damaging cyclones occasionally strike during the rainy season. The annual mean temperature is 27°C (81°F); annual rainfall averages 305 cm (120 in), and humidity is about 80%.

⁴FLORA AND FAUNA

Dense rain forest covers about 89% of the islands, with extensive mangrove swamps and coconut palms along the coasts. Other tree species include teak, African and Honduras mahogany balsa, and Queensland maple. There are over 230 varieties of orchids and other tropical flowers and 3,172 total plant species.

The World Resources Institute estimates that animal species include 72 mammals, 248 birds, 70 reptiles, and 12 amphibians. The calculation reflects the total number of distinct species residing in the country, not the number of endemic species.

⁵ENVIRONMENT

Many of the environmental challenges faced by the Solomon Islands result from its status as a low-lying island state. As such, it is impacted critically by sea-level rise and climate change. Other environmental issues facing the country include destruction of coral reefs, deforestation, soil erosion, and water pollution. Most of the coral reefs surrounding the islands are dead or dying. Deforestation is significant, and the related problem of soil erosion threatens the country's agricultural productivity. Sources of water pollution include sewage, pesticides, and mining byproducts.

In 2010 top officials from the Solomon Islands and 13 other developing Pacific island nations and dependencies met in Vanuatu to discuss the progress made in addressing some of the issues unique to these low-lying, developing island states. These include climate change, sea-level rise, natural disasters, remoteness from major markets, and poverty. Another key objective of the meeting was to address the progress each nation had made in adopting the 2005 Mauritius Strategy, the only global blueprint to combat the development challenges of small-island developing states.

The World Resources Institute reported that the Solomon Islands had designated 20,900 hectares (51,645 acres) of land for protection as of 2006. Water resources totaled 44.7 cu km (10.72 cu mi). The United Nations (UN) reported in 2008 that carbon dioxide emissions in the Solomon Islands totaled 198 kilotons.

According to a 2011 report issued by the International Union for Conservation of Nature and Natural Resources (IUCN), threatened species included 20 mammals, 20 birds, 6 reptiles, 2 amphibians, 16 fish, 2 mollusks, 139 other invertebrates, and 16 plants. Specific species included the gizo white-eye and the hawksbill, green sea, and leatherback turtles. The Solomon Islands' crowned pigeon, the emperor rat, and the Nendo tube-nosed fruit bat have become extinct.

6 POPULATION

The US Central Intelligence Agency (CIA) estimates the population of the Solomon Islands in 2011 to be approximately 571,890, which placed it at number 169 in population among the 196 nations of the world. In 2011 approximately 3.9% of the population was over 65 years of age, with another 37.8% under 15 years of age. The median age in Solomon Islands was 20.9 years. There were 1.02 males for every female in the country. The population's annual rate of change was 2.22%. Population density in the Solomon Islands in 2010 was calculated at 19 people per sq km (49 people per sq mi). In 2011 the US Census Bureau projected the 2025 population of the Solomon Islands to be 747,000.

The UN estimated that 19% of the population lived in urban areas, and that urban populations had an annual rate of change of 4.2%. The largest urban area was Honiara, with a population of 72,000.

7 MIGRATION

Estimates of the Solomon Islands' net migration rate, carried out by the CIA in 2011, amounted to -1.9 migrants per 1,000 citizens. The total number of emigrants living abroad was 5,400, and the total number of immigrants living in the Solomon Islands was 7,000. Since 1955, immigrants from the Gilbert Islands (now Kiribati) have settled in underpopulated areas. Movements from the countryside to Honiara and northern Guadalcanal have created problems of overcrowding. The resentment engendered by those who moved from the heavily populated island of Malaita to Guadalcanal resulted in violence in 1999.

8 ETHNIC GROUPS

Melanesians account for about 94.5% of the total population. Polynesians make up about 3% and Micronesians account for about 1.2%. Europeans and Chinese each account for less than 1% of the population. Melanesians live mainly on the larger islands; Polynesians tend to inhabit the smaller islands and atolls.

9 LANGUAGES

English is the official language but is spoken by only 1–2% of the population. Melanesian pidgin is the lingua franca. Some 120 indigenous languages and dialects are spoken, each within a restricted geographic area.

10 RELIGIONS

Christianity, introduced by missionaries in the 19th and early 20th centuries, is the principal organized religion. The primary groups are the Anglican Church of Melanesia (32.8% of the population), Roman Catholics (19%), South Seas Evangelicals (17%), United Church Methodists (10.3%), and Seventh-Day Adventists (11.2%). These groups are all part of the Solomon Islands Christian Association, which plays an important role in society. Indigenous churches that are offshoots of other established Christian churches are attended by about 5% of the population. Other groups represented are Jehovah's Witnesses, the Church of Jesus Christ of Latter-Day Saints (Mormons), and the Unification Church. The Muslim community is estimated at 350 people. The constitution provides for freedom of religion. The Department of Home and Cultural Affairs has a policy-making role in religious affairs; however, this regulation is meant only as a precaution for maintaining public order, and there have been no reports of major restrictions on religious groups. Christianity is taught in public schools, but the course is not required. Easter and Christmas are observed as national holidays.

11 TRANSPORTATION

The CIA reports that the Solomon Islands have a total of 1,360 km (845 mi) of roads, of which 33 km (20.5 mi) are paved. There are 36 airports, which transported 94,027 passengers in 2009 according to the World Bank. There were only two airports with paved runways in 2010. There were also three heliports. Honiara International Airport (formerly known as Henderson's Field), on the northern coast of Guadalcanal, is the site of Honiara's civil airport. Solomon Airlines provides regular flights between islands and to nearby Papua New Guinea, Fiji, Australia, and Vanuatu.

About 800 km (497 mi) of the country's roads belong to private plantations. Shipping services link the Solomons with other Pacific islands, Australia, Japan, and Europe. Honiara is the principal port, followed by Ringi Cove. A fleet of government vessels provides interisland connections and handles about one-third of total tonnage carried.

12 HISTORY

The islands now known as the Solomon Islands are thought to have been inhabited originally by Melanesians, whose language has affinities with Malay but whose precise origin has not been determined. The first European contact with the Solomons, in 1567, was the sighting of Santa Isabel Island by the Spanish explorer Alvaro de Mendaña; the following year, Mendaña and another Spaniard, Pedro de Queirós, explored the islands. Mendaña named the islands Islas de Salomon, thinking that the gold source for King Solomon's riches was located there.

European contact with the Solomons was cut off for nearly two centuries until they were visited by the English navigator Philip Carteret in 1767. Following Carteret's visit, the British navy began to make periodic calls at the islands. During the period 1845–93, the Solomons were visited frequently by missionaries and traders. Indigenous peoples were also subjected to exploitation by "black-birders," who impressed their captives into forced labor, often on colonial sugar plantations in Fiji, Hawaii, Tahiti, or Queensland. The brutality of the kidnappers provoked reprisals by the islanders, resulting in mass slayings of both Europeans and local peoples.

In 1893 the British government established a protectorate over certain islands in the southern Solomons, including Guadalcanal, Malaita (now Makira), San Cristobal, and the New Georgia group. The remainder of the Solomons had fallen under German dominion; some of these, including Choiseul and Santa Isabel, were transferred by treaty to the United Kingdom in 1900. The British Solomon Islands Protectorate, as the entire group came to be known, was initially under the jurisdiction of the Office of the British High Commissioner for the Western Pacific.

During World War II, the Solomons provided the theater for some of the bitterest fighting of the Pacific war after Japanese troops invaded and occupied Guadalcanal in 1942. A Japanese airfield on the island's northern coast—later known as Henderson's Field—was captured by US Marines on 7 August 1942, the opening foray in the Battle of Guadalcanal, which cost the lives of about 1,500 US and 20,000 Japanese soldiers. Guadalcanal was evacuated by Japan in February 1943, although Japanese forces remained elsewhere in the Solomons until 1945. Widespread destruction and loss of life were visited on the local peoples during the war, and the legacy of social dislocation gave impetus to the development of a pro-independence nationalist movement in Malaita known as the Marching Rule.

In 1953 local advisory councils were set up in Malaita, eventually spreading to other islands of the protectorate. In 1960 the territorial government appointed executive and legislative councils, which were granted their first elected minority in 1964. A new constitution promulgated in April 1970 replaced the two councils with a unitary Governing Council, the majority of whose members were to be elected. During May and June, the Solomon Islands' first general election was held, with voters selecting 17 of the council's 26 members. On 21 August 1974, a new constitution introduced a ministerial system of government headed by a Council of Ministers. A Legislative Assembly subsequently chose Solomon Mamaloni as the Solomons' first chief minister. In May 1975 a delegation from the Solomon Islands, led by Mamaloni, met with UK officials in London and set up a timetable for internal self-government and full independence. On 22 June 1975, the territory's name was officially changed from the British Solomon Islands Protectorate to the Solomon Islands.

The islands achieved internal self-government in 1976 and became an independent member of the Commonwealth of Nations on 7 July 1978. Peter Kenilorea was prime minister until his coalition government collapsed in August 1981, after which Mamaloni returned to power. In October 1984 Sir Peter Kenilorea (as he had become) was reelected prime minister, but he resigned in November 1986, following allegations of mismanagement of funds; Ezekiel Alebua, deputy prime minister, succeeded him. In the general elections of February 1989, the People's Alliance Party (PAP), led by Solomon Mamaloni, defeated the Alebua government. Mamaloni became the new prime minister in March 1989. Mamaloni resigned as PAP leader in October 1990 and formed

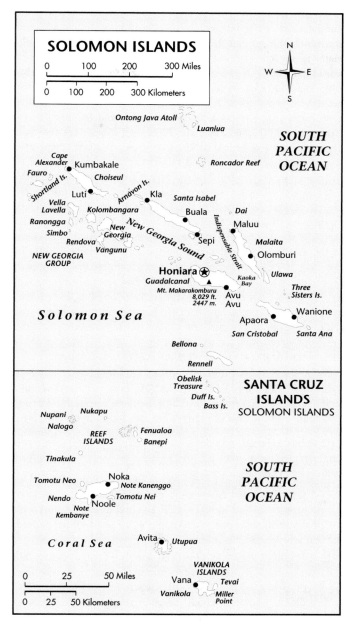

LOCATION: 5° to 12°30′ S; 155° to 170°E. TERRITORIAL SEA LIMIT: 12 miles.

a coalition government with several members of the opposition. Francis Billy Hilly, an independent supported by members of the National Coalition Partners (a loose six-party coalition), became the Solomon Islands' new prime minister in June 1993. Hilly worked with the Melanesian Spearhead Conference to ease tensions between the Solomon Islands and Papua New Guinea. In 1994 parliament voted to replace Hilly with Mamaloni, now leader of the Group for National Unity and Reconciliation (GNUR), the largest political party in parliament.

In the 1997 national parliamentary elections, the GNUR retained its majority, and Bartholomew Ulufa'alu was elected prime minister. He pledged to resolve the Solomons' financial crisis by improving revenue collections and downsizing government ministries. He also grappled with the problem of finding a resolution to the ethnic conflict in Guadalcanal, which had dominated all other domestic political issues since late 1998. Disputed were issues of land ownership, access to education, employment, and economic development between the people of Guadalcanal and Malaitan settlers on the island. That year, the Isatubu Freedom Movement (IFM), representing Guadalcanal's native people, forcibly began to evict Malaitans, who responded by forming the Malaita Eagle Force (MEF). In May 2000, the MEF took Ulufa'alu hostage, staging a coup. Ulufa'alu resigned, and in June he was replaced by Manasseh Sogavare. Fighting between the two factions left over 100 people dead and more than 20,000 displaced. A peace agreement was signed in October 2000, but it failed to end the violence. Unarmed peacekeepers from Australia and New Zealand were sent to supervise disarmament and demilitarization. In September 2001 IFM rebel leader Selwyn Sake was killed, threatening the peace agreement. In November the MEF reported that 90% of its weapons had been surrendered. Allan Kemakeza of the PAP was elected prime minister in December 2001. In February 2003 a member of the country's National Peace Council, Sir Frederick Soaki, was assassinated. He had worked with the UN to demobilize former militants still employed by the government as police officers on Malaita. In 2003 Kemakeza's government was criticized for failing to curb the actions of militia members, three of whom were convicted in 2005 of the April 2003 murder of six Melanesian brothers on the Weathercoast of Guadalcanal.

An Australian-led intervention force, the Regional Assistance Mission to Solomon Islands (RAMSI), came to the Solomon Islands in July 2003 to assist ending the lawlessness and corruption following the years of unrest. In July 2004 the first anniversary of RAMSI's partnership with the people of the Solomon Islands was celebrated with festivities in Honiara; however, not all were happy with the governmental welcome afforded to RAMSI.

In May 2005 a group of 66 rebel militants, calling themselves the Malaita Separatist Movement, demanded the resignation of Prime Minister Allan Kemakeza. They cited dissatisfaction with his pro-Australian views and accused RAMSI of ethnic hatred, particularly against Malaitans.

In July 2005 the cabinet approved voting reforms to eliminate the election fraud caused by voters selling their unmarked ballots. Under the proposed plan, each voter was to have a finger marked with indelible ink, after which the voter would go into a private voting booth to mark the ballot, and then cast the marked ballot into a central ballot box, in view of the election officials.

Fierce rioting occurred soon after the April 2006 general election and the election of Snyder Rini as prime minister. Most of the violence was directed against businesses owned by ethnic Chinese in Honiara, with the almost complete destruction of the Chinatown commercial district. Mr. Rini resigned shortly after the riots, and a parliamentary vote elected Manasseh Sogavare as the new prime minister in May 2006.

Relations between RAMSI and the Sogavare government were increasingly strained after the controversial July 2007 appointment of Julian Moti—wanted by Australia on child sex-offense charges—as attorney general. On 13 December Sogavare's coalition government lost a parliamentary vote of no confidence, and on 20 December, parliament elected Derek Sikua as prime minister. The Sikua government dismissed Moti and deported him to Australia.

Australian Prime Minister Kevin Rudd's visit to the Solomon Islands in March 2008 began a new era of bilateral relations; however as 2011 drew to a close, relations again were threatened when the *Solomon Star* revealed documents alleging an Australian political agenda in the handling of the 2006 riots. It was alleged that Australian appointees in the Solomon Islands were advised not to dispatch riot squads during the riots, in order to drive the Chinese out of Honiara and thus weaken China's position in the Solomon Islands.

13GOVERNMENT

Under the independence constitution of 1978, the Solomon Islands are a parliamentary democracy with a ministerial system and a unicameral national parliament consisting of 50 members elected to four-year terms. Suffrage is universal for citizens over the age of 21. The prime minister, who must command a parliamentary majority, selects the 20-member cabinet. The head of state is the British monarch, represented by the governor-general. A constitutionally provided ombudsman provides protection against improper administrative treatment.

14POLITICAL PARTIES

Members of the first parliament formed after independence in 1978 had no party affiliations. However, political parties emerged shortly before the elections of August 1980, in which the Solomon Islands United Party, headed by Peter Kenilorea, won 14 seats; the PAP, led by Solomon Mamaloni, received 8 seats; the National Democratic Party (NDP), 2 seats; and independents, 14 seats.

In the December 2001 elections, the dominant parties were the PAP, led by Kemakeza, which won 16 seats; the Alliance for Change Coalition, led by Ulufa'alu, which took 13 seats; the People's Progressive Party, led by Sogavare, which took 2 seats; and the Labor Party, led by Joses Tuhanuku, which won 1 seat. Independents held 18 seats.

In the April 2006 elections, the National Party and the Solomon Islands Party for Rural Advancement each took four seats in parliament. The Democratic Party and the PAP each won three seats while the Liberal Party, the Social Credit Party, and the LAFARI Party each had two seats. Thirty seats were won by independents.

On 15 June 2009, retired judge Frank Ofagioro Kabui was elected governor-general designate, replacing incumbent Sir Nathaniel Waena. Kabui was chairman of the Law Reform Commission.

The first women's political party was launched on 30 May 2010. The Twelve Pillars to Peace and Prosperity Party (TP4) was founded through the efforts of political activist Delma Nori and a number of like-minded women, with the hope of providing a forum for a gender friendly democratic process. At the official launch, Nori, the interim president of the group, highlighted the major concerns of the party, which included the absence of women in the national parliament and national policies, thus denying women the opportunity to participate fully in the political process. The 12 pillars represent issues related to a strong economy, fair education, state security, healthy living, environment and a secure infrastructure, strong finance policies, good governance, lands, business and foreign investors, work and employment, family, and religion. Membership is not restricted to women but is open to anyone who identifies with the twelve pillars of the group's charter.

In the August 2010 legislative elections, the Democratic Party gained the most party-affiliated seats with 12 out of 50; however, with 28 independents, no single party gained enough votes to secure control of the government. Political analysts initially feared that the haggling and bribery associated with the formation of a coalition would lead to protests and a lack of confidence in an already unstable political climate. But after three weeks of negotiations, Danny Philip of the Reform Democratic Party was selected prime minister with 26 votes. His rival, Steve Abana, received 23 votes. The announcement of Philip's election did not cause any protests in the capital. However, a few days later, a newly elected member of parliament who supported Philip, Steve Laore, passed away, leaving a temporarily vacant seat and changing the balance of power to 25 for Philip and 23 in opposition. Shortly after that, one member of Philip's camp joined the opposition, bringing the official government coalition down to 24. There were rumors that the opposition was planning for a vote of no confidence at the first seating of parliament, but these rumors were dismissed shortly after Abana was elected as the head of the Solomon Islands Opposition. Abana declared that reports of a no-confidence vote were fabricated and that there were no plans to unseat Philip. Sir Allan Kemakeza, a former prime minister, was elected as speaker of parliament.

15 LOCAL GOVERNMENT

The islands are divided into ten administrative districts, of which nine are provinces, each with an elected assembly and a premier; the other is the town of Honiara, governed by an elected council. In outlying areas, village headmen exercise administrative responsibilities.

16 JUDICIAL SYSTEM

The judicial system is based on a blend of British and traditional systems and consists of the High Court, magistrate's courts, and local courts. Appeals from magistrate's courts go to the High Court; customary land appeals courts hear appeals from the local courts.

Defendants in criminal cases are entitled to counsel and the writ of habeas corpus. Violations of civil liberties are punishable by fines and jail sentences. An ombudsman with the power of subpoena can investigate complaints of violations of civil liberties. Traditional culture, in addition to legal provisions, provides strong protection against arbitrary interference with privacy, home, family, and correspondence.

17 ARMED FORCES

The Solomon Islands have no military forces. There is a 500-member police force that also engages in border protection. Maritime surveillance is provided by this police force, which is headed by a commissioner. In 2010 defense spending totaled US$48.8 million and accounted for 3% of gross domestic product (GDP).

18 INTERNATIONAL COOPERATION

The Solomon Islands joined the UN on 19 September 1978 and belong to ESCAP and several nonregional specialized agencies, such as the FAO, the World Bank, ILO, UNCTAD, UNESCO, and WHO. The Solomon Islands participate in the Asian Development Bank, the ACP Group, the Commonwealth of Nations, WTO, G-77, the South Pacific Regional Trade and Economic Cooperation Agreement (Sparteca), the Alliance of Small Island States (AOSIS), and the Pacific Island Forum. In environmental cooperation, the Solomon Islands are part of the Convention on Biological Diversity, the London Convention, the Montréal Protocol, and the UN Conventions on the Law of the Sea, Climate Change, and Desertification.

19 ECONOMY

The GDP rate of change in the Solomon Islands, as of 2010, was 5.6%. Inflation stood at 6.3%, and unemployment was described as high.

At least 75% of the population is tied to subsistence agriculture. The capital sector is dependent on the production of copra, timber, and fish for export, but outputs of other cash commodities—particularly cocoa, spices, and palm oil—have grown in recent years. The development of large-scale lumbering operations has increased timber production considerably, and concern about the preservation of forest resources led to a government restriction on log exports in 1993.

In the late 1990s the economic downturn in Asia led to the collapse of the export market for logs, which were exported primarily to Japan and South Korea. In 1997 the government devalued the currency to encourage the development of other export products and discourage the growth of imports.

The economy declined by 10% in 1998, and the government initiated cutbacks in its agencies. The GDP growth rate was -15% over the 2001–03 period. The islands are rich in mostly undeveloped mineral resources such as lead, zinc, nickel, and gold. In 1998, however, Ross Mining of Australia began producing gold at Gold Ridge on Guadalcanal. In the wake of ethnic violence in 2000, exports of palm oil and gold ceased, and exports of timber fell.

In 2003 RAMSI helped to rescue the country from economic collapse by restoring law and order. Negotiations were underway in 2005 to reopen the Gold Ridge Mine and the major palm oil plantation, but each could take years to reopen.

In July 2011 the Finance Minister of the Solomon Islands announced that there would be a 5% appreciation applied to the Solomon Islands dollar. Increasing the dollar's value was an effort to cope with rising inflation.

20 INCOME

The CIA estimated that in 2010 the GDP of Solomon Islands was US$1.627 billion. The CIA defines GDP as the value of all final goods and services produced within a nation in a given year and computed on the basis of purchasing power parity (PPP) rather than value as measured on the basis of the rate of the exchange based on current dollars. The per capita GDP was estimated at US$2,900. The annual growth rate of GDP was 5.6%. The average inflation rate was 6.3%. In 2010 the CIA estimated that agriculture accounted for 31.7% of GDP, industry 6.7%, and services 61.6%.

According to the World Bank, remittances from citizens living abroad totaled US$2.4 million or about US$4 per capita and accounted for approximately 0.1% of GDP.

21 LABOR

As of 2009 the Solomon Islands had a total labor force of 202,500 people. Within that labor force, CIA estimates noted that 75% were employed in agriculture, 5% in industry, and 20% in the service sector.

The country suffers from an acute shortage of skilled workers, and an estimated 80% of professional and technical employees are recruited from overseas.

Most employed persons have a standard workday of between five and six hours, six days a week, with overtime bringing the average workweek to 45 hours. The minimum working age is 12 (15 for work in factories or on ships). In practice, given low wages and high unemployment, there is little reason to hire children. The minimum wage was US$0.53 per hour in 2010. The Solomon Islands' largest trade union is the Solomon Islands National Union of Workers. Unions are free to organize and strike, although unions seldom strike. About 55% of public employees were unionized as of 2010, compared to 25% of those in the private sector. Government regulations require employers to provide housing for workers whose jobs do not permit them to travel to and from home each day. Unions regularly engage in collective bargaining.

With unemployment at about 24% in 2009, the government reached out to the international community for much-needed assistance. In May 2010 the International Monetary Fund (IMF) approved a grant of US$3.2 million for the Solomon Islands Rapid Employment Project, which was designed to provide short-term employment for residents in and around the capital city of Honiara. The first stage of the project was to create about 500,000 days of work over a five-year period (2010–2015). The jobs offered primarily involved labor on public works projects, such as construction, road repair, and trash collection. A second phase included the launch of a new Life Skills Development program to offer training opportunities for participating workers. The estimated total cost of the program was US$7.2 million. Funding came from the World Bank, AusAid (Australia), and the government of New Zealand.

22 AGRICULTURE

Roughly 3% of the total land was farmed, and the country's major crops included cocoa beans, coconuts, palm kernels, rice, potatoes, vegetables, and fruit. In 2009 cereal production amounted to 4,434 tons, fruit production 30,566 tons, and vegetable production 8,214 tons.

Copra (coconut meat) is typically the dominant export and the economic lifeline of the Solomons; world copra prices strongly affect the economy. About 75% of copra is produced by small holders, principally on Guadalcanal, Choiseul, the Russell Islands, Makira, Santa Isabel, and Vella Lavella. Development plans called for crop diversification and the construction of a copra mill on the islands. The overseas marketing of copra is a monopoly of the government's Solomon Islands Copra Board. Exports of palm, copra, and cocoa typically account for more than 20% of total exports.

Over 75% of the population depends on subsistence farming and fishing for their livelihood. Small family farms have suffered from changes in weather patterns, and severe storms and floods that have begun to occur more frequently. The major food crops are coconuts, breadfruit, yams, taro, sweet potatoes, cassava, and green vegetables. The government has encouraged the cultivation of rice, rotated with soybeans, in the Guadalcanal plains.

23 ANIMAL HUSBANDRY

The UN Food and Agriculture Organization (FAO) reported that the Solomon Islands dedicated 8,000 hectares (19,768 acres) to permanent pasture or meadow in 2009. During that year, the country tended 235,000 chickens, 14,500 head of cattle, and 54,000 pigs. The production from these animals amounted to 2,030 tons of beef and veal, 2,445 tons of pork, 766 tons of poultry, 558 tons of eggs, and 3,575 tons of milk. The Solomon Islands also produced 100 tons of cattle hide.

Cattle traditionally have been kept on coconut plantations as a means of controlling the growth of grass; many large copra plantations raise cattle for slaughter. Over 40% of the cattle are raised by small holders. The government's Livestock Development Authority (LDA) maintains about 3,200 head in Guadalcanal and Western Province. The LDA is mostly a producer of trader pigs and poultry, raising 25,000 chicks and 120 piglets per month for sale. Production of pork has doubled since the early 1980s yet has failed to keep up with domestic demand.

24 FISHING

Fish are an essential part of the local diet, and fishing an important source of revenue for the Solomon Islands, both as an export item, and also in the licensing of domestic and foreign fishing fleets. In 2008 the Solomon Islands had 130 decked commercial fishing boats. The annual capture totaled 26,235 tons, with a seafood export value totaling US$26.57 million, according to the UN FAO.

In 2010 Prime Minister Sikua met with fellow members of Parties of the Nauru Agreement (PNA) for their First Presidential Summit. The PNA was established in 1982 and is comprised of the nations of Palau, Micronesia, the Marshall Islands, Tuvalu, Kiribati, Papua New Guinea, Nauru, and the Solomon Islands. The purpose of the group is to work together for the conservation and management of tuna resources within their exclusive economic zones (EEZ). At the meeting, which has been called the Tuna Summit, members adopted the Koror Declaration, which aimed, among other things, to establish cooperative management practices to enhance commercial and economic opportunities for member states and to work toward the conservation and restoration of migratory tuna stocks. The waters of PNA nations account for nearly 60% of all tuna catches in the western and central Pacific Ocean and 25% of the global tuna catch, supplying canneries and processing facilities around the world.

25 FORESTRY

Approximately 79% of the Solomon Islands are covered by forest. Important forest timbers are kuari, balsa, teak, Honduras and African mahoganies, Queensland maple, silky oak, and black bean. The UN FAO estimated 2009 roundwood production at 1.23 million cu m (43.5 million cu ft). The value of all forest products, including roundwood, totaled US$114.8 million.

Several hundred chainsaw operators and about 40 portable sawmills produce over one-fifth of all sawn timber. Logging at current rates (15,000–16,000 hectares/37,000–39,000 acres per year) exceeds the estimated sustainable level by a factor of three. A report published by Oxfam in 2008 estimated that if logging continued at the present legally licensed rate, all accessible forest would be depleted by 2015. Forest preservation and management legislation has been proposed, but there is no long-term viable silvicultural plan in place.

26 MINING

Although the archipelago was named in the 16th century for the fabled gold mines of King Solomon and had long-term mining potential, there have been insufficient high-quality mineral deposits to justify extensive mining investment. Mining was nevertheless the second-leading industry in 2002. Mineral production is limited to small quantities of common clays, crushed stone, and sand and gravel, and no gold or silver mining was reported (a minor amount of gold, and possibly associated silver, was obtained from primitive panning and sluicing by individuals). In 2000 production of gold was 338 kg, with silver output estimated at 200 kg. There was no recorded gold or silver output since 2001. The Gold Ridge Mine, at Mavu, which closed in mid-2000, had undertaken a study to upgrade production from 3,100 kg per year to 4,500–4,700 kg per year, which could increase the mining sector's contribution to GDP from 1 to 15%. The country's main industrial prospects focused on undeveloped mineral resources of gold-silver, lead-zinc, nickel, and phosphate. Deposits of bauxite, copper, chromite, and manganese ores also have been found.

27 ENERGY AND POWER

The World Bank reported in 2008 that the Solomon Islands produced 78 million kWh of electricity, and electricity consumption was estimated at 72.54 million kWh. The Solomon Islands, with no proven reserves of oil, natural gas, or coal, rely entirely upon imports to meet all petroleum, natural gas, and coal needs. In 2009 oil imports were estimated at 1,485 barrels per day. In 2010 oil consumption was estimated at 2,000 barrels per day. Most electric power is supplied by the government-controlled Solomon Islands Electricity Authority, although some private undertakings produce their own electricity.

28 INDUSTRY

Industrial activity in the Solomon Islands is rudimentary, lacking in both the capital and skilled labor necessary for significant development. The leading industries are fish processing and timber milling; soaps are made from palm oil and coconut oil. Small firms produce a limited array of goods for the local market: biscuits, tobacco products, rattan furniture, baskets and mats, concrete blocks, boats, and fiberglass products. Tuna is processed at Noro's Soltai Cannery, which has suffered limited closures due to unresolved issues regarding shares in the company and labor grievances. The Solomon Islands sought investors in 2009 for a cannery in Malaita, but that development was derailed by concerns that the tuna could not be judged dolphin-safe due to mass dolphin killings in the area. Products from the cannery would therefore not be marketable in Europe, New Zealand, Australia, or the United States.

29 SCIENCE AND TECHNOLOGY

The Solomon Islands College of Higher Education is comprised of seven schools: the School of Industrial Development; the School of Humanities, Science, and Media; the School of Nursing and

Principal Trading Partners – Solomon Islands (2010)

(In millions of US dollars)

Country	Total	Exports	Imports	Balance
World	808.6	438.5	370.1	68.4
China	289.4	260.9	28.4	232.5
Australia	109.8	5.0	104.8	-99.9
Singapore	80.8	2.5	78.3	-75.8
South Korea	36.3	14.3	22.0	-7.7
Malaysia	26.1	6.0	20.1	-14.0
New Zealand	24.2	2.2	22.0	-19.7
Thailand	21.8	14.8	7.0	7.8
Japan	20.5	8.5	12.0	-3.5
Papua New Guinea	20.3	5.2	15.1	-9.9
Fiji	16.0	0.5	15.6	-15.1

(…) data not available or not significant.

(n.s.) not specified.

SOURCE: *2011 Direction of Trade Statistics Yearbook*, New York: United Nations, 2011.

Health Studies; the School of Natural Resources; the School of Finance and Administration; the School of Marine and Fisheries Studies; and the School of Education. The World Bank reported in 2009 that there were no patent applications in science and technology in the Solomon Islands.

30 DOMESTIC TRADE

Honiara is the commercial center, with a highly developed port and a wide variety of services to support trade and tourism. However, growth in both domestic trade and tourism has been hindered by inadequate infrastructure and security concerns. Most commercial enterprises have been controlled by the Chinese or Europeans. A large segment of the population still rely on bartering. Normal banking hours are 8:30 a.m. to 3 p.m., Monday through Friday, with some banks also open from 9 a.m. to noon on Saturday. Normal business hours are 8 a.m. to 4:30 p.m., Monday through Friday, and 9 a.m. to noon on Saturday.

31 FOREIGN TRADE

The distribution of the Solomon Islands' trade continues to be limited by the huge distances to potential export markets. The Solomon Islands' major exports are copra, timber, fish, palm oil, and cocoa.

The Solomon Islands imported US$256 million worth of goods and services in 2008, while exporting US$237 million worth of goods and services. Major import partners in 2009 were Singapore, 24.5%; Australia, 22.9%; China, 6.1%; New Zealand, 5.2%; Fiji, 4.4%; Papua New Guinea, 4.3%; and Malaysia, 4.3%. Major export partners were China, 57.1%; Spain, 5.1%; and South Korea, 4.1%.

32 BALANCE OF PAYMENTS

Although the Solomon Islands' economy suffered in 2009 as a result of the 2008–09 global financial crisis, it recovered in 2010, growing an estimated 4%, due in large part to high prices and increased demand for logs. Prices for other cash crops rose as well.

The country receives approximately US$28 million annually in economic aid, primarily from Australia. Other important aid donors include New Zealand, the European Union, Japan, and Taiwan. Most manufactured goods and petroleum products must be imported. In 2009 the Solomon Islands had a foreign trade deficit of US$75.8 million.

33 BANKING AND SECURITIES

The Central Bank of the Solomon Islands (CBSI) was established in January 1983 to perform various official functions, including advising the government on banking issues, promoting monetary stability, and regulating the issuance and supply of money. Three commercial banks also operate on the islands: The Australia and New Zealand Banking Group, Westpac, and the National Bank of Solomon Islands (NBSI)—which has operated since April 2007 as a subsidiary of the Bank of the South Pacific Ltd (BSP). Only the NBSI has branches outside the capital. Most villages rely on credit unions. The National Provident Fund, which owned 51% of NBSI, purchased equivalent BSP shares.

The government participates in private investment projects through a holding company, the Investment Corporation of the Solomon Islands (ICSI), the successor to the Government Shareholding Agency. It holds the government's equity in other financial institutions, notably the Development Bank of the Solomon Islands (DBSI), as well as in many other companies, some of which are foreign controlled. The government, via the ICSI, uses locally borrowed funds and foreign aid to assist industry. The government also guarantees commercial bank loans to companies in which the ICSI has an equity holding.

The IMF reported in 2009 that currency and demand deposits (an aggregate commonly known as M1) were equal to US$73.2 million. In that same year, M2 (an aggregate equal to M1 plus savings deposits, small-time deposits, and money market mutual funds) was US$227 million.

34 INSURANCE

Insurance is sold through representatives of foreign firms. In 2011 GRE Insurance, Tower Insurance Limited, QBE Insurance, and Zürich Australian Insurance were operating in the Solomon Islands.

35 PUBLIC FINANCE

In 2010 the CIA reported that the budget of Solomon Islands included US$186 million in public revenue and US$173.6 million in public expenditures. The budget surplus amounted to 1.7% of GDP. The total external debt was US$166 million.

36 TAXATION

In 2006 individual incomes were taxed on a graduated scale ranging from 11% on the first SBD15,100 of taxable income to 42% on taxable income exceeding SBD60,000. Companies incorporated in the Solomon Islands were taxed at a fixed rate of 30%; a rate of 35% applied to those incorporated elsewhere. A value-added tax (10%, with some exceptions) was charged on various goods and services, including telephone services, restaurant food, and overseas travel tickets. Employers contributed 7.5% of employee wages for social security; employees contributed a minimum of 5%. A resident withholding tax was levied for royalties, fishing operations, sales of copra and cocoa, and certain other sources of income.

Balance of Payments – Solomon Islands (2010)

(In millions of US dollars)

Current Account		-372.6
Balance on goods	-133.8	
Imports	-360.3	
Exports	226.5	
Balance on services	-81.0	
Balance on income	-121.1	
Current transfers	-36.6	
Capital Account		49.8
Financial Account		270.1
Direct investment abroad	-2.3	
Direct investment in Solomon Islands	237.9	
Portfolio investment assets	-2.7	
Portfolio investment liabilities	...	
Financial derivatives	...	
Other investment assets	-7.2	
Other investment liabilities	44.3	
Net Errors and Omissions		-12.4
Reserves and Related Items		74.6

(…) data not available or not significant.

SOURCE: *Balance of Payment Statistics Yearbook 2011,* Washington, DC: International Monetary Fund, 2011.

A goods tax was levied on the sale value of items manufactured in the Solomon Islands as well as those imported for home consumption. Some goods were declared exempt from the goods tax. The non-taxed items included medical supplies, coffins, and works of art. In 2006 the goods tax varied from 5% for rice to 15% for imported goods.

37 CUSTOMS AND DUTIES

All products imported into the Solomon Islands are subject to customs duties. In 2006 an ad valorem duty ranging from 5% to 20% was levied against most imported goods. In addition, export duties applied to the export of various goods, including minerals, copra, and crocodile skin.

Specific duties apply to alcoholic beverages, tobacco, rice, and sugar. Concessionary rates have been granted to imports of industrial machinery and equipment, raw materials, chemicals, and building materials. Licenses are required for the importation of firearms, ammunition, animals, seeds, soil, and plant material.

38 FOREIGN INVESTMENT

The government encourages foreign direct investment (FDI) through tax concessions, remission of customs duties, and other forms of assistance. Foreigners may repatriate profits (after taxes) and, under most conditions, capital investments. A primary role in the development of resources is reserved for the government. According to World Bank figures published in 2009, net inflows of FDI amounted to US$117.6 million, representing 17.91% of GDP.

39 ECONOMIC DEVELOPMENT

The government has attempted to diversify agricultural production in order to make the economy less vulnerable to world price fluctuations of such key cash crops as copra. In 2011 the Secretariat of the Pacific Community provided support to the

Solomon Islands' Maraghoto Holdings in reviving the ngali nut industry with the goal of exporting the product in 2012.

In 2009 Australia and the Solomon Islands signed a bilateral development plan called the Partnership for Development. This plan involved road improvement, educational funding, and other quality of life improvements. Foreign assistance has played an essential role in the nation's development strategy. As of the mid-2000s, the country was receiving approximately US$28 million annually in economic aid, primarily from Australia. Other important aid donors include New Zealand, the European Union, Japan, and Taiwan. Aid is also received from the IBRD and ADB. Net inflows of official development assistance were US$306.74 million in 2006.

40 SOCIAL DEVELOPMENT

A National Provident Fund covering certain categories of wage workers age 14 and older provides old-age, disability, and survivor benefits in lump-sum payments. This program is financed from worker and employer contributions. Employers cover the cost of workers' compensation. The Employment Act mandates that employers pay dismissal indemnity of two weeks' wages for each year of employment. The bulk of organized welfare services are provided by church missions. In small villages and outlying areas, assistance traditionally is provided through the extended family.

Although women are accorded equal rights by law, their role is limited by customary family roles in most Solomon Islands societies. Due to cultural barriers, a majority of women are illiterate, which contributes to a general shortage of employment opportunities for women. Domestic abuse and violence are common.

The government generally respects the human rights of its citizens. However, armed conflict between rival militias has resulted in the deterioration of human rights.

41 HEALTH

According to the CIA, life expectancy at birth was 74 years in 2011. The fertility rate was 3.59, while the infant mortality rate was 17.82 per 1,000 live births. In 2008 the maternal mortality rate, according to the World Bank, was 100 per 100,000 births. The country spent 5.3% of its GDP on healthcare, amounting to US$72 per person. There were 2 physicians and 15 nurses and midwives per 10,000 inhabitants. It was estimated that 60% of children were vaccinated against measles. Poor standards of general hygiene and inadequate sanitation continue to make malaria and tuberculosis endemic. The incidence of tuberculosis was 59 per 100,000 people in 2007.

A food shortage occurred in mid-2009 that was particularly severe in the eastern province of Temotu along the Reef Islands. An unusually low harvest of breadfruit, a staple crop, was the primary cause. The rising cost of food imports has placed a greater burden on the food security of the nation and has led to unhealthy eating habits. Coconuts are a primary crop for the islands and the diet of most Solomon Islanders is rich in coconut cream, which is added to a wide variety of local dishes, including fish, rice, cassava, bananas, and cabbage. Coconut cream is also very high in saturated fat. Many foods are fried in palm oil, another major agricultural product. Some officials have begun a campaign to convince more islanders to grow their own vegetable gardens as a means of saving money and switching to a healthier diet.

42 HOUSING

The government has built low-cost housing projects in Honiara to help ease congestion. Outside Honiara, housing is primitive, with overcrowding a problem even in smaller villages. The majority of the population lives in villages of less than 300 people. According to a 2009 census, there were 91,251 households, 98% of which were single-family households. The average household had 5.5 members.

CIA estimates from 2000 show that access to modern sanitation and piped water vary greatly between urban and rural locations. While 94% of urban dwellers reported having access to an improved water source, only 65% of rural dwellers did, for a combined figure of 70%. Similarly, 98% of urban dwellers had access to modern sanitary facilities, but only 18% of rural dwellers did, for a combined figure of 31%.

Since 1998, the Ministry of Lands and Housing has focused on programs for improved housing and utilities for all.

43 EDUCATION

Education is not compulsory in the Solomon Islands. In 2007 the World Bank estimated that 81% of age-eligible children were enrolled in primary school. Secondary enrollment for age-eligible children stood at 30%. Overall, the US State Department estimated that the Solomon Islands had a literacy rate of 77% as of 2010.

While many schools traditionally have charged fees, in 2011 Australia provided financial support for a Solomon Islands government initiative to remove school fees, making education available to more of the population. New Zealand has also been active in supporting education in the Solomon Islands and has stressed the need to educate all the nation's children, regardless of gender.

Primary school lasts for six years. This is followed by three years of lower-secondary schooling, which is offered through provincial and community schools. An additional two years of upper-secondary education is offered through a national secondary school. Students planning to enter university studies take a final year (sixth form). The academic year runs from February to November.

Higher education is provided by the Solomon Islands Teachers College (Honiara), the Honiara Technical Institute, and the University of the South Pacific Solomon Islands Center, also in Honiara. As of 2003 public expenditures on education were estimated at 3.2% of GDP, or 15.4% of total government expenditures. A great deal of foreign aid has been provided for educational programs, with investments in career training, computer technology, and scholarships for higher education offered through such countries as Japan and Papua New Guinea. In 2009 Papua New Guinea awarded the government of the Solomon Islands a grant of US$1.5 million to assist students from the islands who wished to study at PNG colleges.

44 LIBRARIES AND MUSEUMS

The National Library (founded in 1974) in Honiara has two branches and a collection of over 100,000 volumes. It is responsible for school and public library services. The library at the Solomon Islands Center of the University of the South Pacific holds 9,000 volumes. The Solomon Islands National Museum and Cultural Center began collecting in the 1950s and opened a permanent site in 1969. The center promotes and provides research into all aspects of Solomon Islander culture.

45 MEDIA

In 2009 the CIA reported that there were 8,200 telephone landlines in the Solomon Islands. In addition to landlines, mobile phone subscriptions averaged 6 per 100 people. There was one FM radio station, one AM radio station, and one shortwave radio station. Internet users numbered 2 per 100 citizens. The nation's prominent newspaper in 2010 was the *Solomon Star,* with a circulation of 5,000. An online newspaper, the *Solomon Times Online,* was launched in April 2007.

The main post office is in Honiara. In 2009 there were 30,000 mobile cellular phones in use nationwide. Two television channels were sponsored by Australia's Asia-Pacific Service and British Broadcasting Corporation International.

In 2009 parliament passed a telecommunications bill that ended the monopoly of Our Telekom, opening the market to competition for Internet services and mobile communications. The passage of the bill was hailed as a step forward in the development of telecommunications, the establishment of more competitive markets, and, perhaps, the attraction of foreign investment.

The government is said to generally respect constitutional provisions for freedom of speech and the press.

46 ORGANIZATIONS

Cooperative societies are important in rural areas for the distribution of locally produced goods. Honiara has a chamber of commerce. YMCA and YWCA chapters are active. There are active sports associations in the country, including those representing such pastimes as tae kwon do, tennis, yachting, and weightlifting; most sports groups are affiliated with the national Olympic committee. The Solomon Island Graduate Women's Association helps support the advancement of women in business and education. There are also chapters of Habitat for Humanity and the Red Cross.

47 TOURISM, TRAVEL, AND RECREATION

Tourism, although encouraged by the government's Tourist Authority, is not seen as a major growth area due to lack of investment. Visitors are drawn to the ecotourism resorts of the Marovo Lagoon. Fishing and diving are the main attractions. Popular pastimes include rugby, football (soccer), basketball, and water sports. All visitors are required to carry a passport and an onward/return ticket.

The *Tourism Factbook,* published by the UN World Tourism Organization, reported 18,300 incoming tourists to Solomon Islands in 2009, who spent a total of US$52.4 million. Of those incoming tourists, there were 15,900 from East Asia and the Pacific. There were 2,544 hotel beds available in the Solomon Islands. The estimated daily cost to visit Honiara, the capital, was US$306.

48 FAMOUS PERSONS

Sir Peter Kenilorea (b. 1943), Solomon Mamaloni (1943–2000), Ezekiel Alebua (b. 1947), and Sir Allan Kemakeza (b. 1951) were among the country's political and government leaders from independence into the mid-2000s.

49 DEPENDENCIES

The Solomon Islands have no territories or colonies.

50 BIBLIOGRAPHY

Dutson, Guy C. L., et al. *Birds of Melanesia: The Bismarcks, Solomons, Vanuatu, and New Caledonia.* London, Eng.: Christopher Helm, 2011.

Leibo, Steven A. *East and Southeast Asia 2011.* Lanham, MD: Stryker-Post Publications, 2011.

Lilley, Ian (ed.). *Archaeology of Oceania: Australia and the Pacific Islands.* Malden, Mass.: Blackwell, 2006.

Solomon Islands Investment and Business Guide: Strategic and Practical Information. Washington, DC: International Business Publications USA, 2012.

SRI LANKA

Democratic Socialist Republic of Sri Lanka
Sri Lanka Prajathanthrika Samajavadi Janarajaya

CAPITAL: Colombo is the capital, while the seat of Parliament is Sri Jayewardenepura Kotte.

FLAG: The national flag contains, at the hoist, vertical stripes of green and saffron (orange-yellow) and, to the right, a maroon rectangle with yellow bo leaves in the corners and a yellow lion symbol in the center. The entire flag is bordered in yellow, and a narrow yellow vertical area separates the saffron stripe from the dark maroon rectangle. The lion is meant to represent Sinhalese ethnicity, national strength, and bravery. The sword represents national sovereignty. The bo leaves symbolize Buddhism and its four virtues of kindness, friendliness, happiness, and equanimity. The color represent various ethnic minorities within Sri Lanka: orange represents Tamils; green represents Moors; maroon represents both the European Burghers as well as the colonial heritage of the country; and yellow represents other ethnic groups.

ANTHEM: *Sri Lanka Matha (Mother Sri Lanka).*

MONETARY UNIT: The Sri Lanka rupee (LKR) of 100 cents is a paper currency with one official rate. There are coins of 1, 2, 5, 10, 25, and 50 cents and 1 and 2 rupees, and notes of 10, 20, 50, 100, 500, and 1,000 rupees. LKR1 = US$0.00879 (or US$1 = LKR113.69) as of January 2012.

WEIGHTS AND MEASURES: The metric system is the national standard, but British weights and measures and some local units also are used.

HOLIDAYS: New Year's Day, 1 January; National Day, 4 February; May Day, 1 May; and Christmas , 25 December. Movable holidays include Duruthu Full Moon Poya Day; Tamil Thai Pongal Day; Navam Full Moon Poya Day; Nikini Full Moon Poya Day; Milad an-Nabi (Birth of the Prophet); Medin Full Moon Poya Day; Bak Full Moon Poya Day; Good Friday; Vesak (Buddha Day); Poson Full Moon Poya Day; Escala Full Moon Poya Day; Eid al-Fitr (End of Ramadan); Binara Full Moon Poya Day; Vap Full Moon Poya Day; Eid al-Adha (Hadji Festival Day); Il Full Moon Poya Day; Deepavali; and Unduvap Full Moon Poya Day. The Poya days commemorate the rise of the full moon in every month of the Buddhist calendar.

TIME: 5:30 p.m. = noon GMT.

¹LOCATION, SIZE, AND EXTENT

Sri Lanka is an island in the Indian Ocean situated S and slightly E of the southernmost point of India, separated from that country by the 23 km- (14 mi-) wide Palk Strait. Including 870 sq km (336 sq mi) of inland water, Sri Lanka has a total area of 65,610 sq km (25,332 sq mi), extending 435 km (270 mi) N–S and 225 km (140 mi) E–W. Sri Lanka's total coastline is 1,340 km (833 mi). Comparatively, the area occupied by Sri Lanka is slightly larger than the state of West Virginia. Sri Lanka's capital city, Colombo, is located on the southwest coast.

²TOPOGRAPHY

Sri Lanka, one of the world's most scenic places, is comprised primarily by three geographic zones: the Central Highlands, plains and coastal belt.

The Central Highlands lie in south-central Sri Lanka. The area includes a high plateau that runs north-south for 65 km (40 mi), and some of the country's highest mountains including Pidurutalagala at 2,524 m (8281 ft). Two lower plateaus flank the high central ridges: to the west is Hatton Plateau and to the east is the Uya Basin. The steep escarpments, gorges and peaks of the Knuckles Massif lie to the north. The land from the Central Highlands de-

scends through a series of escarpments and ledges before beginning to slope toward the coastal plains.

The plains lie between 30 m (98 ft) and 200 m (656 ft) above sea level. In the southwest, ridges and valleys rise, and gradually merge with the Central Highlands. Extensive erosion has left rich soil deposits for agriculture downstream. The southeast is characterized by red soil, and flat grounds studded with monolithic hills. In the east and north, the plains are flat and are dissected by long, narrow ridges of granite.

The coastal belt at 30 m (98 ft) above sea level surrounds the island. It consists of sandy beaches indented by lagoons. Limestone beds form low-lying cliffs in the Jaffna Peninsula. In the northeast and southwest, the coast cuts across rocks, cliffs, and bays. Offshore islands are located in this area.

Sixteen major rivers longer than 100 km (62 mi) start in the Central Highlands and flow in a radial pattern toward the ocean. There also are several shorter rivers. In the north, east, and southeast, the rivers feed several artificial lakes or reservoirs. Large-scale dam projects in the 1970s and 1980s helped create these lakes. In addition, canals built by the Dutch in the 18th century connect inland waterways in southwestern Sri Lanka.

Both the eastern and western coasts of Sri Lanka were hit by the catastrophic Indian Ocean Tsunami on 26 December 2004. Stemming from an underwater earthquake 324 km (180 mi) south of Indonesia's Sumatra island, waves reaching 12 m (40 ft) rolled onto the coasts, killing almost 40,000 residents and tourists. More than 1.5 million were left without homes.

³CLIMATE

Sri Lanka is located just north of the equator between 5° and 10° north latitude. As a result, the climate is warm, wet, and moderated by ocean winds. Mean temperatures range from 15.8°C (60.4°F) in Nuwara Eliya in the Central Highlands to 29°C (84°F) in Trincomalee on the northeast coast. The average yearly temperature is between 26°C (78°F) and 28°C (82°F). The coolest month is January and the hottest month is May.

The monsoon winds of the Indian Ocean and Bay of Bengal influence rainfall and have formed four seasons. From mid-May to October, southwest winds bring moisture from the Indian Ocean, producing heavy rains on the mountain slopes and southwest of the island. Some windward slopes receive up to 250 cm (98.4 in) of rain per month while the leeward slopes in the east and northeast receive very little rain. Squalls and occasional tropical cyclones occur in October and November in the southwest, northeast, and east. Monsoon winds from the northeast bring moisture from the Bay of Bengal between December and March. March through mid-March is characterized by light, variable winds and evenings thundershowers.

⁴FLORA AND FAUNA

The World Resources Institute estimates that there are 3,314 plant species in Sri Lanka. In addition, Sri Lanka is home to 123 species of mammals, 381 bird species, 181 reptile species, and 66 amphibian species. The calculation reflects the total number of distinct species residing in the country, not the number of endemic species.

Most plants and animals are those common to southern India, but there are additional varieties. The plant life ranges from that of the equatorial rain forest to that of the dry zone and the more temperate climate of the highlands. Tree ferns, bamboo, palm, satinwood, ebony, and jak trees abound. The wide range of mammals, birds, and reptiles once found in Sri Lanka has been reduced by the conversion of forests into rice fields, but water buffalo, deer, bear, elephants, monkeys, and leopards are among the larger animals still present. The Ceylon elk (*sambhur*) and the polonga snake are unique to Sri Lanka. Many varieties of birds from colder countries winter on the island. Sri Lanka has well-organized game and bird sanctuaries. Insects abound and numerous fish are found in the shallow offshore waters.

Threatened wildlife in Sri Lanka included the sloth bear and some leopard species.

Sri Lanka has established several protected areas and national parks to provide safe habitat for its plants and wildlife. The Sinharaja Forest hosts hundreds of indigenous plants, birds, mammals, and reptiles. Leopards inhabit the Yala National Park. Elephants, tigers, deer, sambur, wild boar, pythons, cobras, and vipers have found a safe haven in the Randenigala forest cover.

⁵ENVIRONMENT

The World Resources Institute reported that Sri Lanka had designated 1.13 million hectares (2.8 million acres) of land for pro-

tection as of 2006. Water resources totaled 50 cu km (12 cu mi) while water usage was 12.61 cu km (3.03 cu mi) per year. Domestic water usage accounted for 2% of total usage, industrial for 3%, and agricultural for 95%. Per capita water usage totaled 608 cu m (21,471 cu ft) per year.

The UN reported in 2008 that carbon dioxide emissions in Sri Lanka totaled 12,304 kilotons.

Sri Lanka's principal environmental problem has been rapid deforestation, leading to soil erosion, destruction of wildlife habitats, and reduction of water flow. The government began a reforestation program in 1970, and since 1977, it has banned the export of timber and the felling of forests at elevations over 1,500 m (5,000 ft). Nevertheless, between 1981 and 1985, some 58,000 hectares (143,000 acres) of forestland were lost each year. From 1990–2000, the annual rate of deforestation was 1.6%.

The nation's water has been polluted by industrial, agricultural, and mining by-products along with untreated sewage. Air pollution from industry and transportation vehicles is another significant environmental concern. The main environmental agency is the Central Environmental Authority within the Ministry of Industry and Scientific Affairs.

Although legislation to protect flora and fauna and to conserve forests has been enacted, there has been inadequate enforcement of the laws, and the nation's wildlife population has been reduced by poaching. According to a 2011 report issued by the International Union for Conservation of Nature and Natural Resources (IUCN), the number of threatened species includes 29 types of mammals, 15 species of birds, 11 types of reptiles, 55 species of amphibians, 44 species of fish, 120 species of invertebrates, and 285 species of plants. Threatened species include the Asian elephant, green labeo, spotted loach, and four species of turtle (green sea, hawksbill, olive ridley, and leatherback). Over a dozen species of amphibians have become extinct.

Sri Lanka in 2011 was party to international environmental agreements on biodiversity, climate change, desertification, endangered species, environmental modification, hazardous wastes, law of the sea, ozone layer protection, ship pollution, wetlands, and marine life conservation.

⁶POPULATION

The US Central Intelligence Agency (CIA) estimates the population of Sri Lanka in 2011 to be approximately 21,283,913, which placed it at number 57 in population among the 196 nations of the world. In 2011, approximately 7.9% of the population was over 65 years of age, with another 24.9% under 15 years of age. The median age in Sri Lanka was 30.8 years. There were 0.97 males for every female in the country. The population's annual rate of change was 0.934%. The projected population for the year 2025 is 23,200,000. Population density in Sri Lanka was calculated at 324 people per sq km (839 people per sq mi).

The UN estimates that 14% of the population lives in urban areas, and that urban populations have an annual rate of change of 1.1%. The largest urban area is Colombo, with a population of 681,000 in 2009.

⁷MIGRATION

Estimates of Sri Lanka's net migration rate, carried out by the CIA in 2011, amounted to -2.16 migrants per 1,000 citizens. The total number of emigrants living abroad was 1.85 million, and the total number of immigrants living in Sri Lanka was 339,900.

Military activities in 1995 and 1996 internally displaced an estimated 650,000 people. The civil war continued through the first decade of the 21st century, ending with the Sinhalese-dominant government's defeat of the Libertation Tigers of Tamil Eelam (also known as Tamil Tigers or LTTE) in May 2009. Although the government had resettled 75% of people displaced in the fighting by December 2011, the CIA reported that 460,000 individuals were still internally displaced. The International Organization for Migration reported that most of those displaced were in the northern and eastern parts of the country. The internal displacement resulted in a pressing need for emergency shelters, water, sanitation facilities, and health care.

The US State Department reported in its 2010 Human Rights Report on Sri Lanka that nearly all of the internally displaced persons were ethnic Tamils, include 80,000 Tamil-speaking Muslims whom the LTTE had displaced from their stronghold in Jaffna in 1990. Displaced individuals were residing in government-run camps, host communities, or with relatives or friends.

The after-effects of the civil war have resulted in an estimated increase in out-migration, though figures were unavailable in 2011. A 2008 report by the University of California at Davis based Migration News found that Sri Lanka had sent more than 200,000 workers abroad in 2007, about 55% of which were women. Many of these women went to the Middle East to serve as domestic labor. 460,000 Sri Lankans were estimated to be in Saudi Arabia; 212,000 in Kuwait; and 130,000 in Qatar.

Historically, India pledged in 1964 to repatriate 525,000 of the 975,000 persons of Indian origin (Tamils) then on the island, while Sri Lankan (then known as Ceylon) agreed to absorb 300,000 and grant them Ceylonese citizenship. Of the remaining 150,000, 75,000 were repatriated by a separate agreement concluded in 1974, and an equal number became citizens of Sri Lanka. Repatriation activities ceased with the outbreak of civil war.

8 ETHNIC GROUPS

Provisional data from 2002 showed that Sri Lanka's population was 74% Sinhalese, 12% Sri Lankan Tamil, 5% Indian Tamil, 7% Muslim, and 2% others.

The other groups included the Dutch-descended Burghers; Malays of Arab extraction; and the aboriginal Veddas.

Most of the Sinhalese population reside in the southwest. Tamils comprise two groups. Sri Lankan Tamils, whose genealogies in Sri Lanka go back centuries, live all over the island but are dominant in the Northern Province. Indian Tamils, who also are known as Estate Tamils, first arrived in Sri Lanka in the 19th century as tea and rubber plantation workers for British colonialists and reside mostly in the south-central part of the country.

The US State Department's 2010 Human Rights Report on Sri Lanka indicated that ethnic Tamils of Sri Lankan as well as Indian origin continued to suffer harassment and systematic discrimination in university education, government employment, and housing.

The US State Department also reported in 2010 that fewer than 1,000 Kaffari or Kaffirs resided in the Negombo, Trincomalee, and Batticaloa coastal areas. This group, thought to be descendents of African slaves who had been brought to the country by the Por-

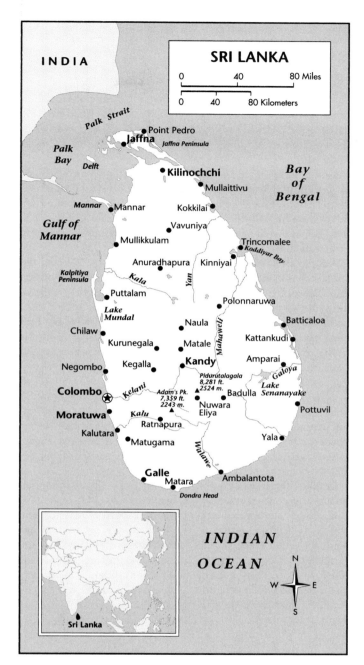

LOCATION: 5°55′ to 9°50′N; 79°42′ to 81°53′ E. TERRITORIAL SEA LIMIT: 12 miles.

tuguese in the 16th century, were struggling to maintain a distinct cultural identity as intermarriage and deaths caused their numbers to dwindle. The aboriginal Veddas also were estimated at fewer than 1,000. Many members of this community felt that the creation of protected forest areas had deprived them of their traditional livelihoods.

9 LANGUAGES

Both Sinhala (spoken by an estimated 74% of the population) and Tamil (spoken by 18%) are national languages, although Sinhala also was the official language of the government. English is also used in governmental and business affairs and is spoken by about 10% of the population.

10 RELIGIONS

The US State Department estimated in its 2010 Religious Freedom report on Sri Lanka that 70% of the population was Buddhist; 15% Hindu; 8% Christian; and 7% Muslim. Christians tend to reside in the western part of the country, Muslims in the east, and Hindus in the north.

Most Buddhists are Sinhalese and follow the Theravada Buddhist tradition. Most of the Hindus are Tamil. Muslims are primarily Sunni, though small numbers in the Bohra community follow the Shi'a tradition. Of the Christians, 80% are Roman Catholic. The remainder follow a range of Anglican and mainstream Protestant faiths.

Although the 1983–2009 civil war between the LTTE and the Sinhala-dominant government was not fought on grounds of religious difference, the US State Department reported that religious hostilities erupted during the fighting. After the war ended, some outbreaks of religious tension were reported in 2009–10, but religious hostility is not a major issue in Sri Lanka.

The government has designated a variety of Buddhist, Hindu, Muslim, and Christian holy days as public holidays.

11 TRANSPORTATION

The CIA reported that Sri Lanka has a total of 91,907 km (57,108 mi) of roads. There are 61 vehicles per 1,000 people in the country. There are 18 airports, which transported 2.42 million passengers in 2009 according to the World Bank. Sri Lanka has approximately 160 km (99.4 mi) of navigable waterways.

In 2007, there was 1,449 km (901 mi) of railroad tracks, all broad gauge, owned and operated by the state.

Colombo, one of the great commercial seaports of Asia, formerly was an open roadstead, but the construction of breakwaters has made it one of the world's greatest artificial harbors. In 2010, the merchant fleet consisted of 22 ships of 1,000 gross registered tons (GRT) or more. Ports of the open roadstead type are Trincomalee, Galle, Batticaloa, Kankesanturai, Kayts, and Jaffna. A car ferry service links Mannar Island with the Indian mainland. In May 2011, ferry services running from Sri Lanka to India resumed after a 30-year delay of operation. The delay was said to be a result of technical difficulties, though some sources cited terrorist activity in Sri Lanka as the main cause. The re-opening of the ferry service, which runs between Tuticorin, India, and Colombo, Sri Lanka, is expected to boost tourism.

Sri Lanka had 14 airports with paved runways in 2010. The principal international airport is Katunayaka, 39 km (24 mi) north of Colombo. Air Lanka (formerly Air Ceylon), the national airline company, serves international routes only. Upali Travels, a private carrier, provides domestic service.

12 HISTORY

The Sinhalese, early Indo-European-speaking settlers, arrived in what is present-day Sri Lanka, in the 6th century BC, probably from northern India. Later arrivals from India brought Buddhism beginning about 240 BC. The practice of Buddhism set Sri Lanka apart from southern India, where Hinduism was the major reli-

gion. The presence of Tamil Dravidian speakers is noted in many ancient texts from the region, and for much of the first millennium AD, the Sri Lankan peninsula was controlled by Tamil Dravidians, whose primary religion was Hinduism. However, following a series of civil wars between the Sinhalese and Tamils, Vijayabahu reestablished the Sinhalese dynasty in the 11th century. In the 12th century, the Sinhalese king Parakrma Bahu I united the entire island.

The Portuguese East India Company brought the first European rulers in the early 16th century, and in time, the Portuguese conquered the entire island, with the exception of the Sinhalese kingdom in Kandy in the central plateau. By the middle of the 17th century, the Portuguese had been driven out of Sri Lanka (and southern India) by the Dutch East India Company, which governed for more than 100 years, introduced plantation agriculture, developed trade, and left a legacy that includes Roman-Dutch law and a group of people of Dutch-Sinhalese ancestry known as Burghers. But they, too, found themselves displaced.

Having won their struggle with France for mastery in India (and in North America), the British laid claim to Sri Lanka, which they called Ceylon, at the end of the 18th century after the Netherlands fell under French control. After a brief period as part of the British East India Company's Indian domain, Ceylon was designated a Crown colony in 1802, and by 1815, the entire island was united under British rule. The British introduced coffee, tea, coconut, and rubber plantations, and their own form of administration.

With the development of a nationalist movement across the Palk Strait in India in the 20th century, nationalists in Ceylon also pressured for greater self-rule, leading to further democratic political reforms in constitutions enacted in 1910, 1920, 1924, 1931, and 1947; included in the 1931 enactment was limited self-rule under universal suffrage. In 1948, with little actual struggle, and a year after Indian independence, Ceylon became a self-governing dominion within the British Commonwealth.

The period from 1948 through 1970 saw the evolution of Ceylon's multiparty parliamentary system, in which orderly and constitutional elections and changes of government took place. Beginning in 1970, executive power began to be highly centralized under Prime Minister Sirimavo Bandaranaike, who from 1971 to 1977 ruled with the use of unpopular emergency powers in support of her socialist, pro-Sinhalese policies. She introduced a new constitution in 1972, converting the dominion of Ceylon to the republic of Sri Lanka, reaffirming a parliamentary system under a weak, ceremonial presidency, and making the protection of Buddhism a constitutional principle.

The defeat of the Sri Lanka Freedom Party (SLFP) in the July 1977 elections brought Junius Richard Jayewardene of the more moderate United National Party (UNP) to power. He became Sri Lanka's first elected executive president in February 1978, under a constitutional amendment of fall 1977 establishing a presidential form of government. Seven months later, a new, more liberal constitution came into effect. As his prime minister, Jayewardene chose Ranadive Premadasa, a long-time follower with lower-caste support. In October 1982, Jayewardene was popularly elected to a new six-year term, and two months later, in a successful effort to avoid general elections, the life of the sitting parliament was extended through July 1989 by means of a constitutional amendment endorsed by popular referendum.

Since 1978, rising tensions and violence between the majority (mostly Buddhist) Sinhalese and minority (mostly Hindu) Sri Lankan Tamil communities that have long shared the island have dominated political life. The tensions began with independence when the Tamil minority feared that the Sinhalese majority would abuse Tamil rights. The fears gained currency in 1956 when S.W.R.D. Bandaranaike used appeals to Sinhalese nationalism to win the presidential election. He declared Sinhala as the official language, instituted an educational policy that replaced English with separate language tracks in education for Sinhala and Tamil speakers, and established agricultural programs that encouraged Sinhalese farmers to move to newly irrigated lands in the east. Outbreaks of communal violence began occurring and continued through the 1970s and 1980s, causing Tamil groups to grow more radical. By the mid-1970s Tamil politicians began demanding a separate Tamil state – known as Tamil Eelam – in the north and east parts of the country, where they had traditionally settled.

The Tamil United Liberation Front won all seats in Tamil areas in 1977 elections through campaigns that rallied for separatism. In the meantime, other groups, including the Liberation Tigers of Tamil Eelam (LTTE or Tamil Tigers), began using force to agitate for a separate state.

In 1983, the LTTE murdered 13 Sinhalese soldiers, and the country erupted into communal violence. Hundreds of Tamils were killed, tens of thousands left homes, and more than 100,000 Tamils fled to south India. The Sri Lankan government accused India of supporting the Tamil fighters, and established an economic blockade to prevent food and other supplies from reaching the Jaffna Peninsula where the Tamil insurgency was based. India began air-dropping supplies to the peninsula in mid-1987.

A 29 July 1987 accord between Indian Prime Minister Rajiv Gandhi and President Jayewardene led to a series of concessions. The Sri Lankan government agreed to a devolution of power away from the capital and toward the provinces, a merger of the northern and eastern Tamil dominant provinces, and to grant the Tamil language official status. India agreed to establish an Indian Peace-Keeping Force, and militant groups surrendered their arms to the Indian troops. In the fall of 1987, LTTE attacks resumed, killing about 300 people. The LTTE refused the Indian Peace-Keeping Force's protection, causing the Indian troops to launch an offensive on Jaffna. Fighting between the Indian Peace-Keeping Force and the LTTE continued for 18 months. The Sri Lankan government engaged in talks with the LTTE leaderships from April 1989 through June 1990, and India withdrew its forces in early 1990. During this time, a militant Sinhalese nationalist party known as Janatha Vimukhti Peramuna sought to overthrow the government for allowing Indian troops to enter Sri Lanka. President Premadasa, who had replaced Jayewardene in 1988, brutally quelled the rebellion. After Indian troops left in 1990, fighting between the LTTE and government resumed and continued through 2001 with sporadic efforts to negotiate peace settlements.

The Union National Party won elections in 2001, and its government and the LTTE declared a unilateral cease-fire in December 2001. A ceasefire agreement was signed in February 2002, and peace talks began in Norway in December 2002. The LTTE, however, dropped out of the talks in February 2003, and a suicide bomb was detonated in Colombo in July 2004. Eastern Tiger commander Karuna broke with the LTTE in March 2004, went underground with supporters, and registered as a political party in March 2006. This move resulted in low-level attacks between the LTTE and Karuna faction. In the meantime, more than 30,000 Sri Lankans died in the 26 December 2004 Indian Ocean tsunami, and while an agreement to share $3 billion in international aid was brokered, it was not implemented. The LTTE assassinated Foreign Minister Lakshman Kadirgamar, an ethnic Tamil, in August 2005 and enforced a voting boycott in November 2005 in areas under its control. A pro-LTTE Tamil National Alliance Member of Parliament was assassinated in December 2005.

The government and the LTTE engaged in talks in Geneva in early 2006, and renewed their commitment to the ceasefire agreement signed in 2002 in February 2006. However, violence erupted again in April 2006, and an LTTE suicide bomber killed the Army's third-in-command general in June 2006.

The government took control of the LTTE's eastern stronghold of Vakari in January 2007, and began moving into LTTE territory, reclaiming the former eastern province in July 2007, killing the LTTE's number two leader in November 2007, and reclaiming all of the northern province by May 2009. The government declared victory on 19 May 2009 after the capture of the last LTTE-held territory and the death of LTTE leader Velupillai Prabhakaran.

In June 2009, Tamil leader Selvarasa Pathmanathan announced the formation of a new provisional transnational government to continue the political struggle for self-rule. By November 2009, opposition groups were openly critical of President Mahinda Rajapaksa for what was perceived as a failure to return the nation to normalcy after the war. The ruling administration was accused of repressing the freedom of the media and of stalling in efforts to resettle refugees from the war. In late November the electoral office announced that new presidential elections would take place on 27 January 2010, two years ahead of schedule.

Former military general Sarath Fonseka, who was credited for the LTTE defeat, was the primary opposition candidate, running on a platform that focused on social justice, media freedom, and the strengthening of democracy. However, Rajapaksa was reelected in January 2010, dissolved the parliament on 9 February 2010, and, in accordance with Sri Lankan law, scheduled new elections for April 2010. Rajapaksa's ruling coalition triumphed in the elections. In the meantime, Fonseka was arrested in February 2010 for allegedly breaking military rules by holding talks with politicians during his term on the national security council. He was found guilty in a military court in August 2010 and sentenced to a dishonorable discharge. The Parliament approved a constitutional amendment in September 2010 that would allow the president to seek an unlimited number of terms.

A UN report in April 2011 found that both the government and LTTE committed atrocities against civilians in the long-running civil war, and called for an international investigation into possible war crimes. The report stated that tens of thousands of civilians were killed in the final phases of war, mostly as a result of government shelling, and that the army deliberately targeted hospitals, UN centers, and ships belonging to the Red Cross. It also contended that the LTTE used civilians as human shields and shot those who tried to escape. The government denounced the report as biased, and in July 2011 the Tamil National Alliance won two-thirds of the local council seats in the north and east. President

Rajapaksa announced in August 2011 that state emergency laws would be allowed to expire.

The Lessons Learnt and Reconciliation Commission, which had been formed to internally investigate the civil war delivered a report containing its findings to the government in November 2011, and Defense Secretary Gotabhaya Rajapaksa, the president's brother, announced that the government would prepare a census of those who died or went missing during the war.

13 GOVERNMENT

The constitution of September 1978 established the Democratic Socialist Republic of Sri Lanka as a free, sovereign, independent state based on universal suffrage at 18 years of age.

The president is directly elected for a six-year term and serves as head of state and as executive head of government. The president appoints and heads a cabinet of ministers, members of which also become members of parliament. The president also has the power to summon, suspend or end a legislative session and dissolve the parliament.

The prime minister serves as the president's deputy and leads the ruling party in Parliament. A parliamentary no-confidence vote requires that the cabinet be dissolved and a new one be appointed by the president.

The parliament is a unicameral body consisting of 225 members who are directly elected to six-year terms through a system of proportional representation. The parliament makes laws, and can remove the president from office by a two-thirds vote with concurrence of the Supreme Court.

Legislation approved by parliament cannot be vetoed by the president. The constitution can be amended by a two-thirds majority vote in the parliament, subject to ratification (for certain provisions) by popular referendum. The constitution provides that popular referenda also may be held on issues of national importance, but the normal business of legislation is in the hands of a unicameral parliament.

As of 2011, the 225-member parliament included 10 female representatives, 28 Tamil representatives, and 17 Muslim representatives.

A two-term limit on the presidency was abolished in August 2010 after President Rajapaksa's cabinet submitted a proposal to parliament. Additions to the proposed amendment also included measures to give the president sole power in appointing top judges and high commissioners for human rights, elections, and other matters. The amendment was approved by parliament on 8 September 2010 by a vote of 161 to 17. The opposition United National Party boycotted the election and accused the government of bribing and threatening members of parliament to secure their votes. Many officials who opposed the amendment believe the president is leading the country further into a dictatorship.

Elections for both the president and parliament are scheduled for 2016.

14 POLITICAL PARTIES

Sri Lanka's two major political parties are the United National Party and the Sri Lanka Freedom Party. Numerous other parties participate in the country's political life including the Janatha Vimukthi Peramuna, National Freedom Front, Jathika Hela Urumaya, Tamil National Alliance, Tamileela Makkal Viduthalai Pulikal, Sri Lankan Muslim Congress, National Unity Alliance, Ceylon Workers' Congress, and the Up-Country People's Front, among others.

The major parties historically have embraced democratic values and international non-alignment. They also have been Sinhala dominant. However, in 2010, a coalition government led by the Sri Lanka Freedom Party consolidated political power in the executive, limited media freedom, and stifled the role of civil society.

The United National Party (UNP) was the main party of the independence movement, and its widely respected leader, D. S. Senanayake, as head of a coalition of which the UNP was the chief unit, became Ceylon's first prime minister after independence. He remained in power until he died in 1956. Solomon Bandaranaike left the UNP to form the Sri Lanka Freedom Party (SLFP).

Shortly before the 1956 elections, Bandaranaike formed the People's United Front (Mahajana Eksath Peramuna—MEP), composed of his own SLFP, the Trotskyite Lanka Sama Samaja (LSSP), and a group of independents. The MEP called for the extension of state control, termination of British base rights, nationalization of tea and rubber plantations, and a foreign policy of strict non-alignment. In the elections, the MEP won 51 seats, and Bandaranaike became prime minister, holding power until September 1959 when he was assassinated by a Buddhist monk.

In the elections of March 1960, the UNP won 50 of the 151 seats at stake; the SLFP, 46 seats; and other parties, the remaining 55. UNP leader Dudley Senanayake failed to muster a majority, and new elections were called for July. In this second round of polling, the UNP won a majority of the popular vote but only 30 seats. The SLFP, led by its slain leader's widow, Sirimavo Bandaranaike, won 75, and with her supporters on the left, she was able to form a government, becoming the first woman in the world to hold office as prime minister. She committed her government to pursuing continuation of her husband's agenda, including nationalization of enterprises.

The UNP and SLFP alternated in power from 1960–77. The SLFP's Sirimavo Bandaranaike was returned to power in the 1970 elections and in response to an insurrection fomented in 1971 by the Janatha Vimukhti Peramuna (JVP), a militant Sinhalese party in the south, imposed a state of emergency on the island that lasted for six years. She pushed through a new constitution in 1972.

In 1977, J. R. Jayewardene's UNP was returned to power with 51% of the popular vote and 142 of 168 seats in parliament. The moderate Tamil United Liberation Front (TULF), which had swept Tamil areas of the north and east, became the major opposition party in parliament with 16 seats, and the SLFP representation in the house fell to a bare eight seats.

Jayewardene's sweeping victory enabled him to fulfill the UNP's campaign pledge to introduce a French-style presidential system of government. Forsaking the now-eclipsed office of prime minister, he set out as president to use his new powers to open the economy and to make a new effort to reconcile with the increasingly disaffected Tamil minority. In the local elections and parliamentary by-elections of May 1983, the UNP strengthened its commanding position by gaining control of a majority of municipal and urban councils and winning 14 of 18 parliamentary seats contested.

Several leftist parties were banned in 1983 on charges of playing a role in the ethnic riots that swept the island in July and leaders of the Communist Party were subsequently arrested. Parliamentary elections in February 1989 saw the emergence of several small Tamil parties with reputed ties to the LTTE-led rebellion.

In December 1988, Prime Minister Premadasa beat the SLFP's Sirimavo Bandaranaike in a close race marred by ethnic violence. He was sworn in as Jayewardene's successor on 2 January 1989. In February, he led the UNP to a strong victory in parliamentary polling, capturing 125 of the 225 seats under a new proportional voting system. In a rising tide of violence and assassinations of governmental officials across the island, President Premadasa himself became a victim of a Tamil bomber on 1 May 1993. The Parliament unanimously elected Prime Minister Wijetunga as his successor on 7 May 1993.

Chandrika Bandaranaike Kumaratunga, the daughter of Sirimavo Bandaranaike, became prime minister in 1994, and won election on the promise of ending the civil war. In November 1994, presidential elections were held. UNP leader Gamini Dissanayake fell victim to the island's endemic violence and his widow Srima Dissanayake was appointed to run against Kumaratunga. While the latter's political party won only a slim plurality and had to govern by coalition, in the presidential race she won a commanding majority (63–36%) and, upon becoming president, appointed her mother prime minister. Despite criticisms over the handling of Sri Lanka's tsunami relief efforts, the SLFP retained its leadership on 17 November 2005 when Mahinda Rajapakse won a slim majority.

In the April 2010 parliamentary elections, President Rajapaksa's United People's Freedom Alliance (UPFA) gained 144 of the 225 seats in parliament, followed by the United National Party with 60 seats. Although the UPFA's strong performance in the elections gives it considerable power in the parliament, the alliance falls short of the coveted supermajority position (150 seats) that would allow it to press through constitutional changes. D. M. Jayaratne, a former teacher, was sworn in as prime minister on 21 April 2010.

15 LOCAL GOVERNMENT

The 13th amendment to the Sri Lankan constitution established in 1987 three levels of government in Sri Lanka: national, provincial, and local.

The provincial level included nine provincial councils. The nine provinces were created on the basis of Sri Lanka's traditional geographic divisions and included as of 2012 the following provinces: Eastern, Northern, Central, Southern, Western, North Western, North Central, Uva, and Sabaragamuwa. Provincial councils were responsible for the enforcement of internal law and order, the establishment of provincial economic plans, education, housing, and agriculture. Within the provinces were a total of 25 districts and 335 secretariats, which were roughly co-terminous with the municipal, urban, and rural councils of the local tier.

The provinces gained significant authority under the Indo-Sri Lankan Accord of 1987. Citizens in each province elect council members to five-year terms, and the leader of the council majority serves as the province's chief minister. In addition, the president appoints a provincial governor. Much of the council powers are shared with the central government or subjected to central governmental oversight. According to the US State Department, the provincial councils generally have not functioned effectively. With the end of the civil war, governmental officials began considering ways to strengthen the councils further.

The local level includes 330 local authorities: 18 municipal councils, 42 urban councils, and 270 rural pradeshiya sabhas. Local governments operate with the support of grants from the provinces and central government, and are responsible for collecting taxes and user fees, setting property tax rates, rents, and grants. Local authorities are also responsibility for roads, and health and utility services. The rural pradeshiya sabhas also hold some developmental responsibilities.

The municipal councils serve larger cities and are headed by a mayor who is nominated by the ruling party to fill a four-year term. The urban councils serve smaller cities and are led by a chairperson nominated by the ruling party to a four-year term. The rural pradeshiya sabhas also are led by a chairperson nominated by the ruling party to a four-year term.

16 JUDICIAL SYSTEM

The judiciary as of 2011 consists of a Supreme Court, Court of Appeal, High Court, and several lower-level courts. The legal system reflects the country's history of foreign influence. While criminal law is based on the British tradition, civil law follows the Roman-Dutch code introduced during the period of Dutch rule. Laws pertaining to marriage, divorce, and inheritance are communal.

Lower level courts include district courts, magistrates' courts, courts of request (restricted to civil cases), and rural courts.

17 ARMED FORCES

The International Institute for Strategic Studies reports that armed forces in Sri Lanka totaled 160,900 members in 2011. The force is comprised of 117,900 from the army, 15,000 from the navy, and 28,000 members of the air force. Armed forces represent 2.7% of the labor force in Sri Lanka. Defense spending totaled $2.8 billion and accounted for 2.6% of GDP.

Sri Lankan forces are deployed in four countries as UN peacekeepers.

18 INTERNATIONAL COOPERATION

Sri Lanka joined the UN under the name Ceylon on 14 December 1955. It was a founding member of the Non-Aligned Movement, and participates in multilateral diplomacy at the UN, particularly in promoting sovereignty, independence, and development of poorer nations. As of 2010, Sri Lanka is a member of the Commonwealth, the South Asian Association for Regional Cooperation, the World Bank, International Monetary Fund, Asian Development Bank, and the Colombo Plan.

Foreign assistance to Sri Lanka totaled nearly $1 billion in 2009. Major lenders were China, Japan, Iran, Indian, and the United States. US aid totaled more than $2 billion from 1948 to 2010, and included economic development and housing projects, relief following the 2004 tsunami, and humanitarian assistance in the aftermath of the civil war.

19 ECONOMY

The GDP rate of change in Sri Lanka, as of 2010, was 9.1%. Inflation stood at 5.6%, and unemployment was reported at 5.4%. According to 2010 CIA estimates, agriculture accounted for 12.8% of GDP and employed 32.7% of Sri Lanka's 8,074,000 workers. Industry accounted for 29.4% of GDP and employed 26.3% of the labor force. Services accounted for 57.8% of GDP and employed 41% of the labor force.

About 23% of the population was estimated to be living below the poverty line in 2008. The CIA reported that Sri Lanka was working to combine private investment and state policies to encourage economic growth in poorer areas, develop small and medium businesses, and encourage agricultural development, which had served as the country's traditional mainstay and was devastated during the civil war. According to the US State Department, income inequality in Sri Lanka was severe, though poverty had begun to decrease after 2009 with the cessation of civil war.

Sri Lanka had followed a socialist orientation from independence through the mid-1970s. In 1978, it shifted toward a more market-oriented approach. The government lifted most price controls, shifted government spending into capital investment, liberalized foreign exchange and import restrictions, and eliminated some government monopolies to permit more business competition. GDP growth surged to 6% from 1978–81 but began to fall in the 1980s with the onset of inflation and outbreak of violence between the government and LTTE. By 1989, GDP growth had fallen to 2%, while annual export growth fell to 5% and the official unemployment rate reached 18%. These indicators prompted the government to try and stabilize the economy through structural adjustment programs that emphasized tighter monetary and fiscal policies and privatization.

Average economic growth rebounded in the 1990s to above 5%, led by expansions in manufactures and services. Strong growth in 2000 foundered in 2001 due to the global economic slowdown; an attack on Colombo's international airport by the Liberation Tigers of Tamil Eelam (LTTE), which harmed the tourism industry; a severe drought; and the 11 September 2001 terrorist attacks on the United States, which sharply reduced foreign direct investment and resulted in reductions in travel and spending. A moderate recovery occurred in 2002,

The December 2004 Indian Ocean tsunami caused an estimated $1 billion in damage to the country. Overall, however, the impact was less severe than expected, with the economy growing by 6% in 2005 and 7.7% in 2006. Such growth was attributed to the boost of construction and related industries as the nation rebuilt. The global financial crisis of 2008–09 caused the economy to falter somewhat, with notable declines in exports and remittances. In 2009, the GDP grew by 3.5%. In the summer of 2009, The International Monetary Fund (IMF) approved a $2.6 billion loan to Sri Lanka to keep the economy strong during the crisis. The money was also meant to help the nation continue its post-war reconstruction programs. The IMF loan was contingent on the nation's promise to initiate significant tax reforms and the development of private sector investment. In June 2010, Sri Lanka unveiled a new budget aimed at cutting the deficit by 8% of GDP by year-end; the deficit stood at 9.9% of GDP at the end of 2009. To achieve this goal, the government announced it would implement a more business friendly, simplified tax system that would include lower rates for income and company taxes. The CIA reported that the end of the civil war and the IMF loan had restored investor confidence in Sri Lanka. GDP grew 8% in 2010.

The US State Department described Sri Lanka in 2010 as a lower-middle income developing nation. The service sector, which is the largest component of the country's GDP, grew 8% in 2010 compared with 3% in 2009. The main contributors to this growth were tourism, shipping, aviation, telecommunications, trading, and finance services. In addition, information technology training and software development were growth areas. As of 2011, the country's main economic focus was to re-build after 26 years of civil war. Projects included rebuilding the road and rail network and expanding access to electricity. These rebuilding efforts also have fueled economic growth.

²⁰INCOME

The CIA estimated that in 2010 the GDP of Sri Lanka was $106.5 billion. The CIA defines GDP as the value of all final goods and services produced within a nation in a given year and computed on the basis of purchasing power parity (PPP) rather than value as measured on the basis of the rate of the exchange based on current dollars. The per capita GDP was estimated at $5,000. The annual growth rate of GDP was 9.1%. The average inflation rate was 5.6%.

According to the World Bank, remittances from citizens living abroad totaled $3.4 billion or about $158 per capita and accounted for approximately 3.2% of GDP. The US State Department reported that foreign remittances increased to $4.1 billion in 2010. Income from remittances had surpassed earnings from apparel exports by 2010 and accounted for Sri Lanka's most important source of foreign exchange.

The World Bank reports that in 2009, household consumption in Sri Lanka totaled $27 billion or about $1,269 per capita, measured in current US dollars rather than PPP.

The World Bank estimates that Sri Lanka, with 0.32% of the world's population, accounted for 0.12% of the world's GDP. By comparison, the United States, with 4.85% of the world's population, accounted for 22.51% of world GDP.

As of 2011 the most recent study by the World Bank reported that actual individual consumption in Sri Lanka was 76.3% of GDP and accounted for 0.14% of world consumption. By comparison, the United States accounted for 25.44% of world individual consumption. The World Bank also estimated that 30.9% of Sri Lanka's GDP was spent on food and beverages, 10.5% on housing and household furnishings, 7.0% on clothes, 2.6% on health, 12.8% on transportation, 0.7% on communications, 2.8% on recreation, 1.3% on restaurants and hotels, and 5.5% on miscellaneous goods and services and purchases from abroad.

²¹LABOR

As of 2010, Sri Lanka had a total labor force of 8.074 million people. Within that labor force, CIA estimates in 2008 noted that 32.7% were employed in agriculture, 26.3% in industry, and 41% in the service sector.

The unemployment rate was 4.5% in the fourth quarter of 2010 compared with 5.7% in the fourth quarter of 2009. According to the US State Department, unemployment was highest among the 20–29 year old age group, particularly for women and high school and college graduates.

Although Sri Lanka has a strong trade union tradition, union membership was declining in the first decade of the 21st century. As of 2010, approximately 20% of the work force was unionized. The country had more than 1,900 registered trade unions in 2010. The Ceylon Workers Congress and the Lanka Jathika Estate Workers Unions are the two largest unions and represent plantation workers. Other strong unions are the Ceylon Mercantile Union, Sri Lanka Nidhahas Sevaka Sangamaya, Jathika Sevaka Sangayama, the Celong Federation of Trade Unions, Ceylon Bank Employees Union, the Union of Post and Telecommunication Officers, the Conference of Public Sector Independent Trade Unions, and the Inter-Company Trade Union.

About 31% of the labor force included self-employed workers. The US State Department estimated that 61% of the employed in 2010 were in the informal sector.

The US State Department reported that 1.7 million Sri Lankan citizens were working abroad as of 2010, a majority of which were women employed as housemaids.

The minimum age for employment in Sri Lanka is 14. Although employment laws prohibit the hiring of persons under age 18 in businesses where work conditions are considered dangerous, the US State Department's 2010 Human Rights Report for Sri Lanka found that children are working under hazardous conditions as street and mobile vendors and as domestic helpers. Children alsoworki in agriculture, mining, construction, manufacturing, transport services, tile factories, and fishing. Much of this situation resulted from the displacement of children by the civil war. The government outlined a plan in 2010 to eliminate the worst forms of child labor by 2016 with assistance from workers representatives, the International Labor Organization, and UN Children's Fund. The government in December 2010 defined 51 occupations as hazardous and prohibited for children.

Forty-three wage boards established by the Ministry of Labor Relations and Manpower are tasked with setting minimum wages and working conditions by sector in consultation with unions and employers. The minimum monthly wage in the private sectors covered by these boards is $71. The minimum monthly wage in the public sector is $105. The maximum workweek is 45 hours.

The US State Department reported that 122,000 people were employed in Sri Lanka's export processing zones, where minimum wages and working conditions were set by the Board of Investment. In response to complaints about working conditions, the Labor Ministry established mediation centers in three of the export processing zones, and in 2010 began conducting inspections at plants based in the zones.

22 AGRICULTURE

Roughly 29% of the total land is farmed, and the country's major crops includ rice, sugarcane, grains, pulses, oilseed, spices, vegetables, fruit, tea, rubber, and coconuts. Cereal production in 2009 amounted to 3.8 million tons, fruit production 710,207 tons, and vegetable production 731,228 tons.

Agriculture once dominated the Sri Lankan economy. Its importance to GDP has diminished since 1977 as the country's industrial and services sectors have grown. From 1988 to 2000, agriculture's share of GDP declined from 26.3% to 21%, although employing still about 35% of the labor force.

Agricultural production fell during the 1983–2009 civil war as ongoing hostilities between the government and LTTE led to the internal displacement of tens of thousands of people from the northern and eastern provinces where much of Sri Lanka's agricultural production was based. Since the war ended, the domestic cultivation of rice and other food crops increased in 2010–11, although floods in early 2011 damaged a large area of agricultural land.

Rice is cultivated extensively as a staple crop, with major growing districts in the Northwestern, Eastern, North Central provinces and the Mahaweli area.

Tea, rubber, and coconuts are cultivated on plantations.

Under the Land Reform Law of 1972, all property holdings exceeding 20 hectares (50 acres), except for property controlled by publicly owned companies, are vested in the Land Reform Commission for redistribution; a total of 226,373 hectares (559,377 acres) were redistributed, including one-fifth of the land under tea. Under the Land Reform Amendment Bill of 11 October 1975, all publicly owned estates (including the major British-owned tea and rubber plantations) were nationalized.

The government established a Small Holder Plantations Entrepreneurship Development Program in 2007 that allowed for 134,000 small crop farmers to take up rubber cultivation.

In November 2010, an anti-wheat campaign led by the National Freedom Front (NFF) resulted in a ban on wheat products from various public institutions, such as schools and hospitals. Government subsidies toward wheat prices were also slashed. NFF officials claimed that wheat was a costly and unhealthy foreign import and stated that the promotion of wheat in a country where rice is the staple crop is part of a multinational "conspiracy" to undermine the food security of Sri Lanka. The party called on bakers to substitute rice flour for wheat flour in their products, which many claimed is difficult to do. With government imposed price increases and cuts in subsidies, the cost of wheat rose so high that nearly 2,000 bakers across the country were forced to close their businesses in 2010.

23 ANIMAL HUSBANDRY

The UN Food and Agriculture Organization (FAO) reported that Sri Lanka dedicated 440,000 hectares (1.09 million acres) to permanent pasture or meadow in 2009. During that year, the country tended 13.6 million chickens, 1.1 million head of cattle, and 81,311 pigs. The production from these animals amounted to 27,584 tons of beef and veal, 2,277 tons of pork, 103,745 tons of poultry, 43,090 tons of eggs, and 716,966 tons of milk. Sri Lanka also produced 3,360 tons of cattle hide.

24 FISHING

Sri Lanka had 2,877 decked commercial fishing boats in 2008. The annual capture totaled 327,575 tons according to the UN FAO. The export value of seafood totaled $106.7 million.

Although Sri Lanka has large fresh and brackish water resources, aquaculture is not traditionally practiced. Fisheries have been identified in the early 21st century as a potential area of economic development. The US Agency for International Development formed a partnership with a Sri Lankan company in the first decade of the 21st century to establish an aquaculture supply chain of seafood products. The partnership increased farm-based income for more than 1,300 families.

The US State Department identified sea bass and shellfish as areas with sustainable growth potential in its 2011 guide to Doing Business in Sri Lanka.

25 FORESTRY

Approximately 30% of Sri Lanka is covered by forest. The UN FAO estimated the 2009 roundwood production at 611,000 cu m (21.6 million cu ft). The value of all forest products, including roundwood, totaled $31.4 million.

26 MINING

Sri Lanka's major mineral commodities are graphite and colored gemstones. However, 18 years of civil war, prolonged drought, high oil prices, and an electricity crisis have crippled its economy. In 2009, the country's gross domestic product (GDP) grew by 3.5%. Mining and quarrying accounted for 1.5% of GDP in 2009. Graphite production (all grades) totaled 7,000 metric tons in 2009, up from 3,000 metric tons in 2005. The island's gem industry is world famous. In the Ratnapura district, there are considerable deposits of sapphire, star sapphire, ruby, star ruby, cats eye, chrysoberyl, beryl, topaz, spinel, garnet, zircon, tourmaline, quartz, and moonstone. A lapidary industry was established for the international marketing of cut and polished precious and semiprecious gemstones. Although output of star rubies and star sapphires were not available for 2009, production of cat's-eye totaled 51,000 carats, while production of rubies came to 50,000 carats; sapphires to 600,000 carats; and all other gemstones (other than diamonds, precious and semiprecious), came to 2,400,000 carats in 2009.

Large quantities of kaolin and apatite have been found, and there are large surface deposits of quartz sand, with kaolin and quartz sand mined. Limestone dating from the Miocene era is quarried from the Jaffna peninsula and used in the manufacture of cement. In the dry-zone coastal areas, salt is manufactured by solar evaporation of seawater. In addition, Sri Lanka produces clays (brick, tile, and for cement production), feldspar, and phosphate rock, and presumably produces varieties of stone and sand and gravel. Cement production and petroleum refining were among the Sri Lanka's leading industries in 2003, with diamonds and petroleum products import exports. The beach sands contain large quantities of ilmenite, rutile, monazite, and zircon, although none were produced from 2000 through 2003. There are plans to revive mineral sands operations, including of garnet sands discovered along the southern coastline. The cerium, yttrium, zirconium, niobium, tantalum, thorium, and uranium groups have been found, and thorianite appears to be widely distributed.

27 ENERGY AND POWER

The World Bank reported in 2008 that Sri Lanka produced 9.24 billion kWh of electricity and consumed 8.23 billion kWh, or 387 kWh per capita. Roughly 43% of energy came from fossil fuels, while 4% came from alternative fuels. Per capita oil consumption was 443 kg.

As of 2010, Sri Lanka had the capacity to generate 2,619 MW of electricity, 52% from hydroelectricity, 47% from oil, and about 1% from wind power and biomass. Total power generation grew by 8% in the first half of 2010, with substantial increases in hydropower generation.

The government is working to reduce the country's dependence on oil.

28 INDUSTRY

The CIA estimated the industrial production rate of change at 8.4% for 2010. Key industries are the processing of rubber, tea, coconuts, tobacco, and other agricultural commodities; telecommunications; apparel and textile production; cement making; petroleum refining; information technology services; and construction.

Industry was Sri Lanka's second-largest component of GDP, accounting for nearly 30%. Manufacturing, the largest industrial subsector, accounted for 17% of GDP. Construction accounted for 7% of GDP; mining and quarrying 2%; and electricity, gas, and water 2%.

The second largest subsector is textiles, apparel, and leather. The apparel industry accounted for 33% of manufacturing employment in 2010, and apparel exports formed a major component of Sri Lanka's exports. The US State Department described the industry as world class in its 2011 guide to Doing Business in Sri Lanka, and noted that most of the larger factories are locally owned enterprises that work with international partners.

The third largest sector is the production of chemical, petroleum, rubber, and plastic products.

The US State Department identified two strong areas of growth in the industrial sector: oil exploration and drilling, and software production. Seismic surveys conducted by an Australian subsidiary of Norway's TGS-NOPEC in 2003 and 2005 indicated that Sri Lanka probably has offshore oil reserves in an area known as the Cauvery basin in the Palk Straits that separate the country from India off the northern coast and in the Mannar basin along its western coast. The Ministry of Petroleum and Petroleum Resources Developed identified eight exploratory blocks in the Mannar Basin and issued an exploration license to Cairn India in July 2008. The company was to drill three wells from 2011–14, and planned to invest more than $100 million in the effort. The government planned to open new blocks for exploration in the second decade of the 21st century.

Production of software and information technology enabled services were expected to grow by 26% in 2011, and Sri Lanka had set a target of $1 billion revenue and employment of 100,000 by 2015.

Since 1977, industrial growth has been aided by market-oriented policies that encouraged private ownership of small and medium sized enterprises. The government continued in early 2012 to hold ownership in most of its larger industries, particularly oil refining and electricity generation. The government's industrial policy has encouraged investment in industries in which it believed Sri Lanka held a comparative advantage.

29 SCIENCE AND TECHNOLOGY

Patent applications in science and technology as of 2009, according to the World Bank, totaled 201 in Sri Lanka. Public financing of science was 0.17% of GDP. With the launch in 1978 of a free-trade zone north of Colombo, Sri Lanka was able to establish such high-technology enterprises as the manufacture of integrated circuits and control and relay panels. In 1982, two US electronics manufacturers contracted to build semiconductor assembly plants in the zone.

The National Science Foundation was established in 1998 under the Ministry of Technology & Research. On 30 June 2011, it released its first national strategy for Science, Technology & Innovation, 2011–15. The document called for an increase in high-tech exports from 1.5% of GDP in 2010 to 10% by 2015, and estimated per capita investments in research & development in 2010 at $2,041. The strategy also highlighted challenges that Sri Lanka faced in reversing a "brain drain" of technical talent. As of 2010, there were about 75 software development companies in the country. The country had 4,600 researchers in research-related positions at 31 state research institutes, 16 universities and a few private sector industries. There also were 1,160 PhD-holding researchers in the country. Fewer than 300 were supervising doctoral research projects, which meant that about 20 to 50 doctoral degrees were being produced annually by the country's 16 universities.

30 DOMESTIC TRADE

Much of Sri Lanka's economic production has been oriented toward producing goods for export. The domestic market is relatively small and undeveloped. The domestic market was also still recovering at the end of 2011 from the 26 December 2004 tsunami, which affected fishing, hotel and restaurant, banking, small industry, and domestic trade particularly hard.

Most retail stores are small and the government retains control over distribution and pricing of food products through 2011. Business hours generally are 8:30 a.m. to 5 p.m. Monday through Friday. In addition, banks, government offices and private companies generally close for the numerous holidays celebrated in Sri Lanka.

Major commercial centers are Colombo, Kandy, Galle, Negombo, and Jaffna.

31 FOREIGN TRADE

Sri Lanka imported $11.6 billion worth of goods and services in 2008, while exporting $7.908 billion worth of goods and services. Imports were estimated to increase to $12.16 billion in 2010 and exports to $8.307 billion.

Major import partners in 2009 were India, 17.5%; China, 15.9%; Singapore, 7.7%; and Iran, 7.1%. Major import commodities were oil, raw materials for the textile industry, machinery and transportation equipment, building materials, mineral products, and foods.

Sri Lanka's major export partners in 2009 were the United States, 20.5%; UK, 12.8%; Italy, 5.5%; Germany, 5.3%; Belgium, 4.4%; and India, 4%. Major export commodities were textiles and apparel, tea, spices, rubber products, precious stones, coconuts, and fish.

The US State Department estimated machinery and mechanical imports at $1.1 billion in 2010, and reported that such imports were likely to continue to increase through the second decade of the 21st century as Sri Lanka expanded its tourism sector, rehabilitated infrastructure and industries affected by the 2004 tsunami, and continued post-civil war reconstruction. Key suppliers of these items were India, Taiwan, Japan, and the European Union. Some of these imports also serviced Sri Lanka's software and information technology enabled services sector, a fast-growing export area. Export earnings in the software and IT-services sector were about $390 million in 2010.

Principal Trading Partners – Sri Lanka (2010)				
(In millions of US dollars)				
Country	**Total**	**Exports**	**Imports**	**Balance**
World	21,818.7	8,307.0	13,511.7	-5,204.7
India	4,084.9	437.2	3,647.7	-3,210.4
China	2,287.6	93.1	2,194.5	-2,101.4
United States	1,860.5	1,664.7	195.8	1,468.9
Singapore	1,398.2	79.2	1,319.0	-1,239.8
United Kingdom	1,082.1	884.4	197.7	686.7
Iran	1,057.2	44.8	1,012.4	-967.6
Japan	904.7	200.2	704.5	-504.3
Belgium	687.4	349.0	338.4	10.6
United Arab Emirates	684.4	284.8	399.6	-114.9
Italy	668.5	436.8	231.7	205.2

(…) data not available or not significant.

(n.s.) not specified.

SOURCE: *2011 Direction of Trade Statistics Yearbook,* New York: United Nations, 2011.

Apparel manufacturers imported nearly 90% of the fabric used in the garment industry. Fabric imports—particularly woven and knitted items—were about $1.2 billion annually as of 2010. The primary importers of fabric were China, South Korea, Taiwan, India, Italy, and France. In addition, Sri Lanka imported approximately $500 million annually of raw cotton, yarn and other cotton materials, primarily from Hong Kong, India, Indonesia, and South Korea. These materials serviced Sri Lanka's largest export item. The apparel sector in 2010 accounted for 40% of total exports and about 33% of Sri Lanka's manufacturing employment. Apparel exports totaled $3.3 billion in 2010, a 4% increase from 2009. The largest market for apparel exports was the US. The US State Department reported in its 2011 guide to Doing Business in Sri Lanka that the apparel industry had maintained its international competitiveness through a commitment to make high quality, eco-friendly, and ethically manufactured products. Exports comprised four basic categories: active/sportswear, casual wear, children's wear, and intimate wear. The industry was expected to increase its exports to $5 billion annually by 2015.

While domestically cultivated rice is a staple crop, Sri Lanka also imported about 1 million tons of wheat in 2010, mostly from Canada. Prima Ceylon Ltd., a Singaporean concern, is the largest producer of wheat flour. A second mill owned by a United Arab Emirates company was commissioned in August 2008. Sri Lanka also was a strong importer of lentils, with annual imports valued at more than $40 million. The main supplier was India.

The growth of Sri Lanka's apparel and software industries has lessened the significance of traditional export items such as tea, natural rubber, spices, and coconut products. Reliance on these commodities in the past had made the nation's economy more vulnerable to adverse weather conditions and global economic conditions.

As of 2011 there were 12 export processing zones in Sri Lanka, with nearly 200 foreign export processing companies in operation. There also were two industrial parks, and a privately-owned apparel company opened Sri Lanka's first privately run fabric park in 2007.

Balance of Payments – Sri Lanka (2010)

(In millions of US dollars)

Current Account		**-1,471.0**
Balance on goods	-3,853.0	
Imports	-12,161.0	
Exports	8,307.0	
Balance on services	-653.0	
Balance on income	-573.0	
Current transfers	3,608.0	
Capital Account		**164.0**
Financial Account		**-952.0**
Direct investment abroad	-43.0	
Direct investment in Sri Lanka	478.0	
Portfolio investment assets	172.0	
Portfolio investment liabilities	-1,049.0	
Financial derivatives	...	
Other investment assets	249.0	
Other investment liabilities	-760.0	
Net Errors and Omissions		**-523.0**
Reserves and Related Items		**2,782.0**

(…) data not available or not significant.

SOURCE: *Balance of Payment Statistics Yearbook 2011*, Washington, DC: International Monetary Fund, 2011.

³²BALANCE OF PAYMENTS

In 2010 Sri Lanka had a foreign trade deficit of $2.7 billion, amounting to 6.6% of GDP.

Sri Lanka's balance-of-payments position is highly sensitive to price changes in the world market because it has traditionally depended in large part on a few export crops to pay for its imports. From 1983–2010, sharply rising defense expenditures, a decline in tourism caused by continuing civil violence, and slumping world tea and coconut prices have combined to exert pressure on the balance of payments. The deficit has been partially offset by substantial foreign exchange earnings from tourism, apparel export revenue, and remittances by Sri Lankans working abroad. Sri Lanka saw a rebound in tourism in 2010–11 with the end of the civil war.

The current account deficit, which was $860 million in 1994, had declined to $291 million by 2009. However, it climbed sharply to $1.691 billion in 2010, according to CIA estimates. The International Monetary Fund attributed the jump to an increase in imports, in response to domestic demand. In November 2011, the government unveiled its 2012 budget and announced a 3% devaluation of the Sri Lanka rupee against the US dollar. The Economic Intelligence Unit suggested that while this move would support exporters, it also would lead to an increase in inflation.

As of 31 December 2010, Sri Lanka's reserves of foreign exchange and goal were estimated at $7.197 billion compared with $5.358 at the end of 2009.

³³BANKING AND SECURITIES

The Central Bank of Sri Lanka, established in 1949, administers and regulates the country's monetary and banking systems. As of 2010, there were two state-owned commercial banks, nine private domestic commercial banks, 11 foreign banks, a national savings bank, six regional development banks, two long-term lending in-

stitutions, two housing banks, two private savings banks, and 12 merchant banks operating in Sri Lanka.

All commercial banks have foreign currency banking units, and carry out off-shore business and finance projects that have been approved by the Board of Investment.

Total assets of the commercials were $22 billion as of 31 December 2009. The two state-owned commercial banks – Bank of Ceylon and People's Bank – had assets of $4.8 billion and $4.4 billion respectively. Although regarded as inefficient, these two banks accounted for more than 40% of all assets.

The Colombo Stock Exchange was established by the Association of Stockbrokers in 1987. As of 31 December 2010, there were 241 companies listed on the stock exchange. The top ten market capitalization positions were held by conglomerates, telecommunications companies, banks, and food and beverage companies. The exchange ended 2010 as the world's second best performing stock market for the second year in a row. It gained 96% in 2010 and 125% in 2009.

There were nine new companies listed on the Colombo Stock Exchange in 2010, and the US State Department reported in its 2011 guide to Doing Business in Sri Lanka that an additional 75 companies were expected to list on the exchange in 2011.

Foreign stockbrokers are allowed to hold up to 100% equity in stock brokerage firms at the exchange.

³⁴INSURANCE

There were 19 insurance companies registered with Sri Lanka's National Insurance Board at the end of 2011. Twelve companies were composite insurers who offered both life and general insurance; five offered general insurance only; and two offered life insurance only. There were 42 insurance brokerage companies at the end of 2010.

Gross written premiums totaled $601.34 million in 2010, compared with $502.65 million in 2009.

Sri Lanka nationalized its insurance sector in 1962, and established the Sri Lanka Insurance Corporation Ltd. as a monopoly company. The government established the National Insurance Board in 1980, and liberalized the insurance market in 1988 by permitting private companies to register with the board. The Sri Lanka Insurance Corporation was reorganized in 1993 as a government-owned limited liability company and sold to a private consortium in 2003. The Parliament found irregularities in the privatization procedure in 2006, and on 4 June 2009, the Supreme Court ordered the consortium to return its stake to the government. The company was re-nationalized in 2009 and was the largest insurer as of January 2012.

³⁵PUBLIC FINANCE

In 2010 the budget of Sri Lanka included $7.415 billion in public revenue and $11.18 billion in public expenditures. The budget deficit amounted to 7.9% of GDP. Public debt was 86.7% of GDP, with $17.81 billion of the debt held by foreign entities.

The US State Department reported that the government forecast a deficit of 6.8% in its 2011 budget. The budget aimed to simplify the tax structure, reduce a number of taxes, and clarify investment incentives.

High military expenditures, losses by nationalized corporate entities, welfare and pension expenditures, and spiraling debt

Public Finance – Sri Lanka (2008)

(In millions of rupees, budgetary central government figures)

Revenue and Grants	**686.5**	**100.0%**
Tax revenue	585.6	85.3%
Social contributions	6.8	1.0%
Grants	31.2	4.5%
Other revenue	62.8	9.1%
Expenditures	**1,007.5**	**100.0%**
General public services	281.1	27.9%
Defense	134.7	13.4%
Public order and safety	41.2	4.1%
Economic affairs	249.2	24.7%
Environmental protection	...	...
Housing and community amenities	31.6	3.1%
Health	74.5	7.4%
Recreational, culture, and religion	...	...
Education	100.1	9.9%
Social protection	95.1	9.4%

(…) data not available or not significant.

SOURCE: *Government Finance Statistics Yearbook 2010*, Washington, DC: International Monetary Fund, 2010.

service costs caused Sri Lanka's public debt to grow to unsustainable levels, according to an International Monetary Fund report in 2011. In September 2002, the government enacted a Welfare Benefit Law aimed at clarifying welfare eligibility and establishing penalties to reduce politicization and mistargeting. In January 2003, the government passed the Fiscal Management Responsibility Act (FMRA), setting medium-term deficit targets and passed a new Board of Investment (BOI) law eliminating the BOI's power to grant extralegal incentives. These measures helped secure International Monetary Fund (IMF) approval in 2003 for a three-year program under the combined Poverty Reduction and Growth Facility and Extended Fund Facility (PRGF and EFF). The PRGF-EFF program was in direct support of the government's program for 2003–06 aimed at poverty reduction through private-sector growth. Sri Lanka received an additional $2.6 billion loan from the IMF in 2009. Sri Lanka's public debt-to-GDP ratio was one of the highest among the world's developing countries in 2011, but the IMF reported that the ratio was expected to fall as the country's economy rebounds.

36 TAXATION

Sri Lanka completed a major overhaul of its tax structure in 2011. The government announced in the 2011 budget the elimination of several taxes including a social responsibility levy, a debits tax, a levy on cellular mobile telephone subscribers, an environmental conservation levy, and a regional infrastructure development levy. The budget also reduced the personal income tax rate from 5% to 35% to 4% to 24%.

Other reforms introduced in the 2011 budget included reducing the value added tax from 15% to 10%; cutting income tax rate for export companies from 15% to 12%; reducing taxes on financial services from 20% to 12%; reducing profit taxes of banking and financial institutions from 35% to 28%; reducing taxes on tourism earnings from 15% to 12%; and instituting a $20 per bed

tax on five-star hotels that charged a room rate of less than $125 per night.

37 CUSTOMS AND DUTIES

Changes to Sri Lanka's tax structure introduced in 2011 led to increases in tax rates on several imported items. According to the US State Department's 2011 guide to Doing Business in Sri Lanka importers were required to pay a customs-import tariff, an export development board levy, a port and airport tax, a nation building tax, port handling charges, and agent commissions. Importers also were charged a value added tax, which was one of Sri Lanka's most important sources of taxation revenue.

Excise fees also were added to some products included aerated water, liquor, beer, motor vehicles, cigarettes, and some household electronics.

The customs import tariffs were based on a harmonized system of classification and included, as of 2010, tariff bands of 0%, 5%, 15% and 30%. Basic raw materials, textiles, pharmaceuticals, medical equipment, telecommunications equipment, software machinery and some consumer electronics had no tariff. Semi-processing raw materials were subjected to the 5% tariff; intermediate products were at the 15% tariff; and most agricultural and food products, consumer goods, and finished products were at the 30% rate.

Imported items used to prepare commodities for export were not subject to import duties. These items included fabrics, yarns, and other materials used by apparel manufacturers.

Sri Lanka has free trade agreements with India and Pakistan. A South Asia Free Trade Area was established on 1 January 2006 for the nations belonging to the South Asian Association for Regional Cooperation.

38 FOREIGN INVESTMENT

FDI represented 0.96% of GDP, according to 2009 World Bank figures.

Sri Lanka's agricultural enterprises, insurance companies, and banks were developed originally by foreign capital. In 1959, foreigners owned almost 36% of the country's rubber acreage and 6% of the tea plantations; 80% of the insurance business was written by foreign companies, and the banking business was largely a monopoly of British and Indian firms. After 1961, when nationalization became widespread, private investors were reluctant to place new funds in Sri Lanka. Consequently, during the 1960s, the country had to depend almost entirely on loans and short-term credits. During the 1970–77 period, foreign companies, principally Japanese, were more willing to collaborate with public-sector enterprises.

With the change of direction in the government's economic policy since 1977, foreign investment began to flow more freely into the private sector.

FDI flows to Sri Lanka were modest from 1998–2001, averaging about $150 million a year. In late 2002, the government relaxed its investment rules, allowing 100% foreign equity in a number of services—banking, finance, insurance, stock brokerage, construction of residential buildings and roads, supply of mass transportation, telecommunications, production and distribution of energy and professional services.

Foreign direct investment increased to $600 million in 2007 and to $750 million in 2008. World Bank figures published in 2009 put FDI at $404 million, and the US State Department estimated FDI at $450 million in 2010. The US State Department's 2011 guide to Doing Business in Sri Lanka reported that Sri Lanka expected FDI to increase to $1.5 billion in 2011 with investments in hotel construction and other tourism related activities.

The top sources of FDI were Malaysia, the UK, the US, Singapore, India, China, the United Arab Emirates, and South Korea. Major investors were Unilever, Nestle, British American Tobacco Company, Mitsui, Pacific Dunlop/Ansell, Prima, FDK, Telecom Malaysia Bhd, SP Tao, HSBC, and the Indian Oil Corporation.

US investment in Sri Lanka included a range of companies such as Energizer Battery, Mast Industries, Chevron, Citibank, Coca-Cola, and SmartShirts. IBM, Lanier, NCR, GTE, Motorola, Proctor & Gamble, Liz Claiborne, Tommy Hilfiger, JC Penney, Sun Microsystems, Microsoft, Bates Strategic Alliance, McCann-Erickson, Ernst and Young, and KMPG also have branches, affiliated offices or local distributorships. There are also Kentucky Fried Chicken, Pizza Hut, Federal Express, UPS, and McDonald's franchises in the country.

The main law governing foreign investment is Law No. 4 of 1978, amended in 1980, 1983, and 1992, after which it has been generally known as the BOI Act. Under the BOI Act, foreign companies are separated into two categories: Those that fall under Section 16 are subject to the "normal" laws, and those falling under Section 17 qualify for special BOI-specified incentives. In general, incentives are targeted at investments that are export oriented, infuse substantial capital into the economy, and/or transfer advanced technology.

³⁹ECONOMIC DEVELOPMENT

Since independence, successive governments have attempted ambitious economic development programs with mixed results. The nationalization in 1962 of three Western oil companies and in 1975 of large rubber and tea plantations was intended to end the nation's economic dependence and neocolonialism, and to create an egalitarian socialist society.

The United National Party (UNP) government, elected in 1977, chose as the centerpiece of its development strategy the Mahaweli hydroelectric irrigation resettlement program, the largest development project ever undertaken in Sri Lanka. The project involved diverting the Mahaweli Ganga in order to irrigate 364,000 hectares (900,000 acres) and generate 2,037 million kWh of hydroelectricity annually from an installed capacity of 507 Mw. Launched in 1978, construction was largely completed by 1987, at a cost of about $2 billion. Even as the UNP government launched this massive capital program, it sought to encourage private investors, limit the scope of government monopolies, and reduce subsidies on consumer products.

While government development policies resulted in moderate growth during the late 1970s and early 1980s, the outbreak of civil war in 1983 led to a rapid rise in defense spending (from 1% of GDP in 1980 to over 4% in 1996), exacerbating structural weaknesses in the Sri Lankan economy. By 1989, rapidly declining economic growth and worsening fiscal and balance-of-payment problems reached crisis proportions, prompting renewed stabilization and adjustment efforts. These measures resulted in greatly improved economic performance in the early 1990s, despite unfavorable weather and the ongoing insurgency.

In 1996, as the market showed signs of weakening, the government reaffirmed its free-market policies. From 1997 to 2001, however, the economy was whipsawed between a series of exogenous shocks and political pressures to maintain welfare expenditures. In 1998, the insecurity arising from the Tamil Tiger separatist campaign was aggravated by nuclear tests in Pakistan and India, and the aftermath of the Asian financial crisis. Recovery in 1999 and 2000 was cut short in 2001 by the global economic slowdown, the LTTE terrorist attack on the country's international airport in July, the 11 September terrorist attacks on the United States, and the onset of severe drought, all of which combined to produce Sri Lanka's first year of economic contraction on record.

Laws encompassing welfare reform, tax reform, and investment deregulation were passed in 2002, and, in January 2003, the Financial Responsibility Act (FRA) was adopted, setting a course to bringing the budget deficit down to below 5% of GDP by 2006, and limiting government borrowing to less than 10% total revenue. In all, 36 new laws were introduced by the government to buttress the economy's financial stability and the government's economic program. The program was pursued in conjunction with a three-year arrangement with the IMF under its Poverty Reduction and Growth Facility and Extended Fund Facility (PRGF/EFF) with a credit line of $567 million approved in April 2003. The focus was on restoring raising revenues by 2.5% of GDP; implementing deregulation and privatization measures; creating opportunities for the poor to share more fully in the benefits of economic growth through improvements in infrastructure and education; and garnering resources for reconstruction, including though donor assistance and government investments. By 2006, Sri Lanka had made impressive progress on privatization and reform of the tax, tariff, and foreign investment regimes.

The end of civil war in May 2009 opened a new era of economic opportunity. The government has set ambitious goals for economic development in the second decade of the 21st century. President Rajapaksa outlined his country's economic strategy in 2005 and 2010 election manifestos known as Mahinda Chintana (Mahinda's Thoughts). These manifestos called in 2010 for a doubling of Sri Lanka's per capita income to $4,000 by 2016; development of small and medium enterprises; and development of Sri Lanka as a regional hub for air and sea transportation, trading, energy, and knowledge based services. A 10-year development framework encourages a series of large infrastructure projects. Generally, the plan maintains state ownership of its bank, airports, and electrical utilities but calls for management of these enterprises that enables them to become profitable.

Expansion of the Port of Colombo was identified as a major infrastructure project. As of 2010, 23 major shipping lines serviced the port, and it had an annual cargo handling capacity of 4 million 20-foot terminal equivalent units (TEUs). The government planned to increase capacity to 10 million TEUs by 2023 through the addition of three terminals. It had received a loan of $300 million from the Asian Development Bank to expand the port's southern breakwater. A Chinese company was awarded a contract to construct the first terminal, and the second and third terminals were expected to be completed in 2016 and 2023. The government also planned to develop an additional breakwater and container terminal in 2028.

The government also had initiated a series of infrastructure projects aimed at economic development of its southern province. In the area surrounding the rural town of Hambantota, projects in 2010 included the development of a deep water port, an adjacent industrial area, and an international airport.

As of 2010, Sri Lanka was providing electricity to 86% of the country, and the government set a goal of 100% by 2012. A 900 MW coal power plant and a 150 MW hydropower plant were being built in 2011. The government was negotiating with the government of India to develop an additional 500 MW coal power plant, and had hoped to encourage private-sector investment in wind, small hydropower, biomass, and other renewable energy resources. A $120 million loan from the Asian Development Bank was funding the construction of transmission lines, the strengthening of distribution systems, and rural electrification projects.

Much of the infrastructure development was being financed with assistance from the World Bank and Asian Development Bank, as well as loans from China, Iran, and Japan. The US Agency for International Development, which had provided more than $2 billion to Sri Lanka from 1948–2010, is also investing in the country's economic development. Foreign grants totaled $230 million in 2009, and loans were just under $1 billion.

40 SOCIAL DEVELOPMENT

Historically, Sri Lanka, though low on per capita income, has been relatively high on other social welfare indicators such as adult literacy (90%), school enrollment, infant mortality, and life expectancy (72 years). The country faces a significant challenge to find ways to maintain welfare and educational standards while bringing the budget deficit under control.

Through a provident fund system, the government pays monthly allotments to the aged, sick, and disabled, to destitute widows, and to wives of imprisoned or disabled men. The program is financed by 8% employee contributions and 12% employer contributions. Old-age benefits are paid as a lump-sum grant equal to total contributions plus interest. Medical care is available free of charge in government hospitals and clinics. The law provides for a system of family allowances for families earning less than 1,000 rupees per month.

Some human rights observers have worried that the government, while based on a strong tradition of multi-party pluralism, was growing increasingly statist after 2005. President Mahinda Rajapaksa was elected in 2005; under his leadership, a constitutional limit of two six-year terms for the presidency was eliminated. The government as of 2010 was dominated by Rajapaksa's family: his brothers held positions of defense secretary, minister of economic development, and speaker of parliament.

Sri Lanka's human rights record continued to be weak in early 2012, although the government had taken steps to address institutional discriminatory practices against ethnic Tamils and other non-ethnic Sinhalese individuals after the country's long-running civil war ended 2009. A Lessons Learned and Reconciliation Commission was established to gather evidence of wartime atrocities and to attempt to heal hatred. At the same time, independent investigations found serious human rights abuses were committed by military forces in the final years of the 1983–2009 civil war. The government continued to search for and detain persons suspected of being affiliated with the Liberation Tigers of Tamil Eelam (LTTE), even after the war ended. Journalists are harassed for being critical of the government.

Although citizens are allowed to travel throughout the country, police and military checkpoints that had been established during the civil war were still common in 2010. Tamils are also harassed at military checkpoints, and ae required to carry national identification cards printed in Sinhala as well as Tamil.

The US State Department's 2010 Human Rights Report on Sri Lanka cited reports that torture is used in prisons and detention centers. In the Tamil dominant northern and eastern provinces, military intelligence often work with armed paramilitaries to detain individuals with suspected LTTE connections. These arrests often were followed by interrogations including torture. Human rights groups estimated 2,400 LTTE suspects were in regular detention centers, with an additional 1,200 being held in police stations, army or paramilitary camps, and other information detention facilities.

In an effort to reduce violence against Tamils, the government hired 500 Tamil police officers to work in the northern and eastern provinces. At the start of 2010, approximately 11,700 former LTTE fighters were being held in detention centers. About 5,000 were released in 2010, while about 1,400 were transferred to other prisons and charged with crimes related to LTTE activity.

Laws against rape and domestic violence ae not effectively enforced, and sexual assault, rape, and spousal abuse are pervasive. The Bureau for the Protection of Children and Women within the Sri Lankan police force received 714 complaints of violent crimes and 2,391 minor crimes against women in 2009.

41 HEALTH

According to the CIA, life expectancy in Sri Lanka was 74 years in 2011. The country spent 4.1% of its GDP on healthcare, amounting to $84 per person. There were 5 physicians, 19 nurses and midwives, and 31 hospital beds per 10,000 inhabitants. The fertility rate was 2.3, while the infant mortality rate was 13 per 1,000 live births. In 2008 the maternal mortality rate, according to the World Bank, was 39 per 100,000 births. It was estimated that 96% of children were vaccinated against measles.

The CIA calculated HIV/AIDS prevalence in Sri Lanka to be about less than 0.1% in 2009. The CIA cited a high degree of risk for bacterial diarrhea, hepatitis A, dengue fever, chikungunya, leptospirosis, and rabies.

Government policy allows for free health care at public hospitals, and government expenditures on the health care sector totaled $530 million in 2010. Easing some of the cost of this policy has been a growth in private sector investments in health care since 2009. As of 2010, there were 619 government hospitals, nearly 200 private hospitals and nursing homes, 5,000 private pharmacies, and 1,000 laboratories.

US companies exported medical equipment worth $2 million and pharmaceuticals worth $6 million in 2010.

⁴²HOUSING

Housing statistics on Sri Lanka had not been updated since a partial census was conducted in 2001. A nationwide census was carried out in 2011.

The 2001 census found 3,969,211 occupied housing units, a 59.4% increase from a previous census taken in 1981. The average household had 4.5 members. About 64% of all households were nuclear families. About 96% of urban dwellings and 73% of rural dwellings had access to safe drinking waters. Only 73% of all households had access to safe sanitation systems.

About 88,544 housing units were completely destroyed or severely damaged during the 26 December 2004 tsunami. In addition, Sri Lanka in 2011 had an internally displaced population of 460,000 individuals as a result of the long-running civil war. Many of those displaced were in the northern and eastern provinces, and were residing in government-run camps, host communities, or with relatives and friends.

As of 2010, the population was largely rural, with only 14% of the people residing in urban areas. A Sri Lankan newspaper article published in 2010 cited a 2006 government survey that had found 54% of the housing in Colombo was huts and slums. Many of those homes were built from plaited palm leaves, old planks, and corrugated iron. The survey also found that 43,462 families in the capital city lacked access to clean drinking water.

The government's National Housing Development Authority cited a few home-building projects, including a plan to construct 150,000 housing units for estate workers living in rooms built in the early 20th century, a Nagamu Purawara program to upgrade housing in rural settlements, and a program to build 10,210 housing units in rural areas with participation of Buddhist temples.

Tamils experience discrimination in housing, and landlords are required to register Tamil tenants as well as report their presence to the police.

⁴³EDUCATION

In 2009 the World Bank estimated that 95% of age-eligible children in Sri Lanka were enrolled in primary school.

A report by the US-Sri Lanka Fulbright Commission put the literacy rate at 97%. The report stated that there were 10,390 government schools as of 2007. Education is state funded and offered free of charge at all levels, including the university level. Instruction is offered in Sinhala, Tamil, or English, and English is widely taught as a second language. Children ages 5–13 are required to attend school and receive free textbooks from the government.

Students take a general certificate of education exam at the end of the 11th year of schooling, and an advanced level exam at the end of their 13th years. There are 15 national universities and seven post-graduate institutes in the country. Undergraduate admission is based on the examination results and are extremely competitive. Only 6% of the students who take the exams are admitted to Sri Lankan universities, prompting an increasing number of students to consider study opportunities outside the country.

⁴⁴LIBRARIES AND MUSEUMS

The National Library and Documentation Services Board oversees management of the country's libraries. There are approximately 1,135 public libraries in Sri Lanka.

The National Library of Sri Lanka serves as the national repository library, with 206,300 volumes. There are also seven science and technology libraries and 15 college and university libraries.

Sri Lanka's long-running civil war has had an effect on libraries. The Jaffna Public Library, once one of the largest in Asia with more than 97,000 books and manuscripts, was burned in 1981 following clashes between Tamil separatists and ethnic Sinhala police. News reports indicated that an organized mob of ethnic Sinhalese individuals were responsible for the destruction. The library was rebuilt and reopened in 2007.

The Colombo National Museum was established on 1 January 1877, and is one of four national museums as of 2012. The others are in Galle, Kandy, and Ratnapura. Other museums include the National Museum of Natural History, the Dutch Museum, Maritime Museum, Anuradhapura Folk Museum, and Independence Memorial Museum.

⁴⁵MEDIA

In 2009 the CIA reported that there were 3.5 million telephone landlines in Sri Lanka. In addition to landlines, mobile phone subscriptions averaged 69 per 100 people. There are 15 FM radio stations, 52 AM radio stations, and 4 shortwave radio stations.

Major English-language newspapers in Sri Lanka include *Daily News, Daily Mirror, Sunday Observer, The Island, Sunday Times, The Sunday Leader,* and *Daily FT.*

Sinhala newspapers are *Dinamina. Silumina, Divavina,* and *Lankadeepa.* Tamil newspapers are *Thinkaran* and *Virakesan.*

The central government owns and operates all telephone, telegraph, cable, and radio facilities, except in a few rural districts, which are served by private exchanges. Domestic telephone service is reportedly inadequate, while international service is good. In 2009, there were 15.8 million mobile cell phones in use.

The government operates both commercial and noncommercial radio broadcasting services in Sinhala, Tamil, and English and began television service in 1982. The state-owned Sri Lanka Broadcasting Corporation airs broadcasts on AM, FM, and shortwave. There are several privately owned broadcasting stations.

In 2010 the country had 8,865 Internet hosts. In 2009, there were some 1.7 million Internet users in Sri Lanka.

The constitution provides for free speech and a free press and these rights are generally respected by the government. However, in the past the government has imposed restrictions on the media on the grounds of national security. In 2002, several criminal defamation laws were eliminated.

⁴⁶ORGANIZATIONS

A large number of non-governmental, political, professional, student, religious, and community organizations were present in Sri Lanka as of 2011. The Radio Society of Sri Lanka hosted monthly gatherings for amateur radio enthusiasts and the Model Railroad Club brought together railway enthusiasts. There also was a Lion's

Club, Surangany Voluntary Services, and a number of community groups operating in diaspora.

Chambers of commerce included the National Chamber of Commerce of Sri Lanka, the Ceylon Chamber of Commerce, the Indian Chamber of Commerce, and the Moor Chamber of Commerce. There are numerous trade and industrial organizations. Social action organizations include the Center for Society and Religion and the Civil Rights Movement of Sri Lanka. There is a national chapter of the Red Cross Society.

47 TOURISM, TRAVEL, AND RECREATION

The US State Department reported in its 2011 guide to Doing Business in Sri Lanka that tourist arrivals rose 46% in 2010 to 654,000. Of those incoming tourists, there were 199,000 from Europe and 127,000 from South Asia. The *Tourism Factbook*, published by the UN World Tourism Organization, reported that tourists to Sri Lanka in 2009 spent a total of $754 million. There were 39,998 hotel beds available in Sri Lanka, which had an occupancy rate of 48%. The estimated daily cost to visit Colombo, the capital, was $320. The cost of visiting other cities averaged $119.

The tourism industry took a big hit when the 2004 tsunami severely damaged hotels and facilities, causing many resorts to close. Damage occurred mainly in the eastern and southern areas of Sri Lanka.

The government has identified tourism as a growth industry for the second decade of the 21st century, and hoped to increase tourist arrivals to 2.5 million in 2016. The US State Department stated that an additional 36,000 hotel rooms would be needed to meet that target. Hilton was the only international hotelier in Sri Lanka as of 2010, but the government was reaching out to international and regional hotel chains such as Shangri-La, Six Senses, and Movenpick Hotels.

The *New York Times* identified Sri Lanka as one of the world's top 31 places to go in 2010. The newspaper described Nilaveli Beach in the formerly war-ravaged northern province and the seaside village of Galle and Unawatuna beach in the south as prime areas to visit. Nilaveli was off-limits for nearly three decades during the civil war, and the southern areas were ravaged by the 2004 tsunami, but recovery efforts have helped rebuild the areas.

Besides beaches, there are wildlife parks, rain forests, tea plantations, ruins, and a variety of Buddhist cultural sites.

Visitors must have a valid passport. All foreign nationals are required to carry a visa, except those of the South Asian Association for Regional Cooperation (SAARC).

48 FAMOUS PERSONS

One of the great rulers of the Anuradhapura period was Dutugemunu (fl. 100 BC), who is famous for having saved Ceylon and its religion from conquest by Indian invaders. Mahasen, a king in the 3rd century AD, built many fine dagobas and other monuments that delight and amaze visiting art lovers. The classical period of Ceylonese art flourished under Kassapa, a king of the 5th century. The great figure of the Polonnaruwa period was Parakramabahu I (the Great, r. 1153–86), who unified the government of Ceylon, built many magnificent structures, and organized the economy. The most famous political figure in modern Ceylon was Don Stephen Senanayake (1884–1952), leader of the independence movement and first prime minister of independent Ceylon. Solomon West Ridgway Dias Bandaranaike (1899–1959), prime minister from 1956 to 1959, is regarded as the founder of Ceylon as a socialist state. His widow, Sirimavo Bandaranaike (1916–2000), was prime minister during 1960–65, 1970–77, and 1994–2000. She was the world's first female prime minister. Her daughter, Chandrika Bandaranaike Kumaratunga (b. 1945) was president from 1994 to 2005. Junius Richard Jayewardene (1906–96), who helped usher in economic reforms and a free enterprise system, became Sri Lanka's first president in 1978 and served until 1982. Science fiction writer Sir Arthur C. Clarke (b. England, 1917–2008) is one of Sri Lanka's most famous expatriate residents. Born in Sri Lanka, Canadian author and poet Michael Ondaatje (b. 1943) received the 1992 Booker McConnell Prize for his novel *The English Patient*.

49 DEPENDENCIES

Sri Lanka has no territories or colonies.

50 BIBLIOGRAPHY

Dos, Santos A. N. *Military Intervention and Secession in South Asia: The Cases of Bangladesh, Sri Lanka, Kashmir, and Punjab.* Westport, CT: Praeger Security International, 2007.

Hasbullah S. H. and Barrie M. Morrison, eds. *Sri Lankan Society in an Era of Globalization: Struggling to Create a New Social Order.* Thousand Oaks, CA: Sage, 2004.

Orizio, Riccardo. *Lost White Tribes: The End of Privilege and the Last Colonials in Sri Lanka, Jamaica, Brazil, Haiti, Namibia, and Guadeloupe.* New York: Free Press, 2001.

Peebles, Patrick. *The History of Sri Lanka.* Westport, CT: Greenwood Press, 2006.

Sri Lanka Investment and Business Guide: Strategic and Practical Information. Washington, DC: International Business Publications USA, 2012.

Wood, Alan Thomas. *Asian Democracy in World History.* New York: Routledge, 2004..

SYRIA

Syrian Arab Republic

Al-Jumhuriyah al-'Arabiyah as-Suriyah

CAPITAL: Damascus (Dimashq)

FLAG: The national flag is a horizontal tricolor of red, white, and black stripes; in the white center stripe are two green five-pointed stars.

ANTHEM: *Humat ad-Diyar (Guardians of the Homeland).*

MONETARY UNIT: The Syrian pound (SYP) is a paper currency of 100 piasters. There are coins of 25 and 50 piasters and 1 Syrian pound and notes of 1, 5, 10, 25, 50, 100, and 500 Syrian pounds. SYP1 = US$0.02015 (US$1 = SYP49.628) as of November 2011.

WEIGHTS AND MEASURES: The metric system is the legal standard, but local units are widely used.

HOLIDAYS: New Year's Day, 1 January; Revolution Day, 8 March; Egypt's Revolution Day, 23 July; Union of Arab Republics Day, 1 September; National Day, 16 November. Muslim religious holidays include Eid al-Fitr, Eid al-Adha, Milad an-Nabi, and Laylat al-Miraj. Christian religious holidays include Easter (Catholic); Easter (Orthodox); and Christmas, 25 December.

TIME: 2 p.m. = noon GMT.

¹LOCATION, SIZE, AND EXTENT

Situated in southwest Asia at the eastern end of the Mediterranean Sea, Syria has an area of 185,180 sq km (71,498 sq mi). Comparatively, the area occupied by Syria is slightly larger than the state of North Dakota. Included in this total is the Golan Heights region (1,176 sq km/454 sq mi), which Israel captured in 1967 and annexed on 14 December 1981; the annexation was denounced by Syria and unanimously condemned by the United Nations (UN) Security Council. Syria extends 793 km (493 mi) ENE–WSW and 431 km (268 mi) SSE–NNW. It is bounded on the N by Turkey, on the E and SE by Iraq, on the S by Jordan, on the SW by Israel, and on the W by Lebanon and the Mediterranean Sea, with a land boundary length of 2,253 km (1,400 mi) and a coastline of 193 km (120 mi).

²TOPOGRAPHY

There are five main geographic zones: (1) the narrow coastal plain along the Mediterranean shore; (2) the hill and mountain regions, including the Ansariyah (Alawite) Mountains in the northwest paralleling the coast, the eastern slopes of the Anti-Lebanon Mountains, and the Jabal Ad-Duruz in the southeast; (3) the cultivated area east of the Ansariyah and Anti-Lebanon ranges, which is widest in the north, discontinuous between Homs and Damascus; (4) the steppe and desert region, traversed by the Euphrates (Al-Furat) River; and (5) the Jazirah in the northeast, steppe country with low rolling hills.

The Anti-Lebanon Mountains, extending southward along the Lebanese border, serve as a catchment for the rainfall of central Syria. To the north of this range, the Ansariyah Mountains, which reach heights of over 1,500 m (5,000 ft), slope westward to the Mediterranean. The Orontes (Asi) River irrigates areas on the eastern side of the Ansariyah Mountains.

³CLIMATE

The climate varies from the Mediterranean type in the west to extremely arid desert conditions in the east. The coastal regions have hot summers and mild winters; in the mountains, summer heat is moderated according to elevation, and the winters are much more severe.

The steppe and desert areas have extremely hot, arid summers and greatly varying winter temperatures ranging from 21°C (70°F) to below freezing. Average temperatures for Damascus range from about 21 to 43°C (70 to 109°F) in August and from about -4 to 16°C (25 to 61°F) in January. Rainfall averages about 75 cm (30 in) on the coast, around 125 cm (50 in) in some mountain areas, and less than 25 cm (10 in) in the eastern three-fifths of the country. In dry years, rainfall may be reduced by half.

⁴FLORA AND FAUNA

The World Resources Institute estimates that there are 3,000 plant species in Syria. In addition, Syria is home to 82 species of mammals, 350 species of birds, 82 species of reptiles, and 5 species of amphibians. This calculation reflects the total number of distinct species residing in the country, not the number of endemic species.

The coastal plain is highly cultivated, and the little wild growth found is mainly of the brushwood type, such as tamarisk. On the northern slopes of the Ansariyah range are remnants of pine forests, while oak and scrub oak grow in the less well-watered central portion. Terebinth is indigenous to the low-hill country of the steppes, and wormwood grows on the plains. Some sections of the Jabal Ad-Duruz are covered with a dense maquis.

The wildlife of Syria includes types common to the eastern Mediterranean region, together with typical desert species. There are a diminishing number of bears in the mountains. Antelope are found wherever grazing is available and human competition not too severe. There are also deer in some sections. Smaller animals include squirrel, wildcat, otter, and hare. In the desert, the viper, lizard, and chameleon are found in relatively large numbers. Native birds include flamingo and pelican, as well as various ducks, snipe, and other game birds.

5 ENVIRONMENT

Water resources totaled 46.1 cu km (11.06 cu mi) while water usage was 19.95 cu km (4.79 cu mi) per year. Domestic water usage accounted for 3% of total usage, industrial for 2%, and agricultural for 95%. Per capita water usage totaled 1,048 cu m (37,010 cu ft) per year.

The UN reported in 2008 that carbon dioxide emissions in Syria totaled 69,836 kilotons.

Much of Syria's natural vegetation has been depleted by farming, livestock grazing, and cutting of trees for firewood and construction. The thick forests that once covered western Syria have been drastically reduced; as a result, soil erosion and desertification are extensive. The salinity of the soil is also a problem, causing a loss of more than $300 million worth of agricultural products per year. Other environmental problems include drought, pollution of coastal waters from oil spills and human waste, and contamination of inland waterways by industrial waste and sewage.

Environmental awareness has been a growing concern in the Arab world. The UN and Middle Eastern environmental organizations have sponsored Arab Environment Day to focus the nation's attention on environmental problems. The quantity of native wildlife had been so seriously depleted that in 1979 the government banned hunting for five years.

According to a 2011 report issued by the International Union for Conservation of Nature and Natural Resources (IUCN), threatened species includes 16 mammals, 14 birds, 6 reptiles, 34 fish, and 7 invertebrates. The Mediterranean monk seal, bald ibis, and African softshell turtle are endangered. The Anatolian leopard, cheetah, Syrian wild ass, Israel painted frog, and Persian fallow deer are extinct.

6 POPULATION

The US Central Intelligence Agency (CIA) estimated the population of Syria in 2011 to be approximately 22,517,750, which placed it at number 52 in population among the 196 nations of the world. In 2011 approximately 3.8% of the population was over 65 years of age, with another 35.2% under 15 years of age. The median age in Syria was 21.9 years. There were 1.03 males for every female in the country. The population's annual rate of change was 0.913%. The projected population for the year 2025 was 28,600,000. Population density in Syria was calculated at 122 people per sq km (316 people per sq mi).

The UN estimated that 56% of the population lived in urban areas, and that urban populations had an annual rate of change of 2.5%. The largest urban areas, along with their respective populations, included Aleppo, 3 million; Damascus, 2.5 million; Homs, 1.3 million; and Hama, 854,000.

7 MIGRATION

Estimates of Syria's net migration rate, carried out by the CIA in 2011, amounted to -11.18 migrants per 1,000 citizens. The total number of emigrants living abroad was 944,600, and the total number of immigrants living in Syria was 2.21 million. Syria was home to an estimated 1.2 million refugees in 2011, a large number of whom have come from Iraq since 2003. Since World War I, there has been substantial internal migration from the coastal mountains to the central plains and, in general, from rural areas to the towns. There is considerable migration across the borders with Lebanon and Jordan. As of January 2011 there were approximately 500,000 Palestinian refugees in Syria according to the UN. In 1997 the Syrian government accepted the protection mandate of the UN High Commissioner for Refugees (UNHCR) for all recognized refugees in the country.

8 ETHNIC GROUPS

Ethnic Syrians are primarily of a Semitic stock; however, racial types have generally become intermixed. It is estimated that Arabs make up about 90.3% of the population. Other ethnic groups make up the remaining 9.7%, including Kurds, Armenians, and others. The Kurdish minority faces widespread social and governmental discrimination.

9 LANGUAGES

The official language and the language of the majority is Arabic, but dialect variations are distinct from region to region and even from town to town. The written language, classical Arabic, based on the Koran, is the basis of the standard spoken form. Kurdish and Armenian are the principal minority languages. Aramaic, the language of Jesus, and Circassian are also widely understood. French and English are somewhat understood.

10 RELIGIONS

Islam is the religion of the vast majority. About 74% of the population are Sunni Muslims. Alawite, Druze, Ismailis, Shi'a, and Yazidis account for another 13% of the population. The Alawite constitute an important minority in Syria and hold a disproportionate share of political power; although they consider themselves Muslims, they combine their avowed creed with Christian rituals and esoteric cults. Also important are the Druze (most of whom live in the Jabal Ad-Duruz), whose religion is an offshoot of Shi'a Islam. The Druze account for about 3% of the population. There are about 100,000 Yazidis. About 10% of the population are Christian, with Greek Orthodox the largest denomination. Other Christian churches include Armenian Catholic, Greek Catholic, Armenian Orthodox (Gregorian), Syrian Catholic, Maronite, Baptist, Mennonite, Anglican, Baptist, Church of Jesus Christ of Latter-Day Saints, and Nestorian (Chaldean). The small Jewish population of about 100 is urban, living primarily in Damascus, Al Qamishli, and Aleppo.

Under the 1973 constitution, Islam is no longer the religion of the state, but the president of Syria still must be a Muslim, and Islamic law (Shari'ah) is a major source of legislation. Freedom of worship is guaranteed by the constitution, but there are a number of restrictions on religious practice. Public proselytizing is strongly discouraged by the government, as is the conversion of Muslims to other faiths. All religious groups must register with the government. The government retains the right to monitor all fundraising efforts by religious groups, and all groups must receive government permission for any meetings other than worship services. Religious affiliation is included on legal documents, and everyone is required to identify themselves as Christian, Jewish, or Muslim. The Birth of the Prophet Muhammad, Orthodox and Western Easter, Eid al-Fitr, Eid al-Adha, the Islamic New Year, and Western Christmas are observed as national holidays.

11 TRANSPORTATION

The CIA reports that Syria has a total of 97,401 km (60,522 mi) of roads, of which 19,490 km (12,111 mi) are paved. There are 62 vehicles per 1,000 people in the country. Railroads extend for 1,801 km (1,119 mi). There are 104 airports, which transported 1.34 million passengers in 2009 according to the World Bank. Syria has approximately 900 km (559 mi) of navigable waterways.

Three sections of Syrian railway are the old Baghdād Railway; the main line from Damascus to Aleppo, with connections to Tartus, points in Lebanon, and the phosphate mines; and the railway linking Al Lādhiqiyah, Halab, and Al-Qamishli, built with Soviet help and completed in 1981. There are also 251 km (156 mi) of narrow-gauge line, part of which is the pre-World War I Hejaz Railway, linking Damascus to Jordan and Lebanon. Syria is also connected by rail with Turkey (thus with Europe) and Iraq.

The road system, though growing, remains inadequate in view of the demands imposed by increased economic activity. There are road connections between the major towns and with Iraq, Jordan, Lebanon, and Turkey.

Tartus and Al Lādhiqiyah are the main ports. Jablah and Baniyas are minor ports. In 2010 the merchant fleet comprised 41 vessels of 1,000 gross registered tons or more. Syria's navigable inland waterways have had little economic impact. In 2010 Syria had 29 airports with paved runways. There were also seven heliports. Damascus is a connecting point for a number of major airlines; the main passenger terminal of its international airport was completed in 1982. Another principal airport is Aleppo International at Aleppo (Halab). Syrian Arab Airlines provides service to Halab, Al-Qamishli, Al Lādhiqiyah, and other airports; it also flies to other Arab countries and to Europe and Africa.

12 HISTORY

Archaeological excavations at Ebla, in northern Syria, have revealed that Syria was the center of a great Semitic empire extending from the Red Sea north to Turkey and east to Mesopotamia around 2500 BC. At that time, Damascus, traditionally the world's oldest continuously occupied city and certainly one of the world's oldest cities, was settled. Later, an advanced civilization was developed along the Syrian and Lebanese coastlands under the Phoenicians (c. 1600–c. 800 BC), among whom trade, industry, and seafaring flourished. The wealth of the land attracted many conquerors, and Syria was invaded successively by the Hittites, Egyptians, Assyrians, Persians, and others. In the 4th century BC Syria fell to Alexander the Great, first in a long line of European conquerors. After the breakup of his empire, dominion over Syria was disputed by the Seleucid and Ptolemaic successor states, and Persians invaded when the opportunity arose; eventually the Seleucids gained control. In the 1st century BC, all of Syria, Lebanon, Palestine, and Transjordan was conquered by the Romans and organized as the province of Syria; these areas are termed "geographic" Syria. Christianity, particularly after its

official recognition in the early 4th century AD by Constantine the Great, spread throughout the region.

In 637 Damascus fell to the Arabs. Most Syrians were converted to Islam, and Arabic gradually became the language of the area. Under the Umayyad caliphs, Damascus became the capital of the Islamic world and a base for Arab conquests. Under the 'Abbasids, the caliphate was centered at Baghdād, and Syria was reduced to provincial status. Thereafter, geographic Syria fell prey to a succession of invaders, including Byzantines and Crusaders from Western Europe. Some parts of Syria came under the sway of Seljuks and Ayyubids, a Kurdish dynasty. The latter was most prominent under its leader Saladin (Salah ad-Din). During the 13th century Mongols frequently invaded Syria, and for 200 years parts of Syria were controlled by the Mamluks, who ruled it from Egypt through local governors. In 1516 the Ottoman forces of Sultan Selim I defeated the Mamluks, and for the next four centuries, Syria was a province of the Ottoman Empire.

During World War I Sharif Hussein (Husayn Ibn-'Ali) of Mecca threw in his lot with the Allies and revolted against Ottoman rule. After the war, with British forces in control, the formal entry of Allied troops into Damascus was made by Arab forces under Faisal (Faysal), Hussein's son, on 30 October 1918. Faisal and the Arab nationalists, whose number had been growing since 1912, opposed French aspirations to Syria and claimed independence under the terms of agreements between the British government and Hussein. In March 1920 Faisal was proclaimed king by a congress representing Syria, Lebanon, and Palestine. However, geographic Syria was divided into British and French mandates. In June the French, who had been allotted a mandate for Syria and Lebanon by the Agreement of San Remo (April 1920), ejected Faisal and installed local administrations of their own choosing. Arab nationalists resented French rule; there was a major revolt from 1925 to 1927, and unrest persisted until the outbreak of World War II. In 1941 Free French and British forces wrested control of Syria from Vichy France. Two years later, under pressure from the United Kingdom and the United States, the French permitted elections and the formation of a nationalist government. The United Kingdom and the United States recognized Syria's independence in 1944, and the last French troops departed on 17 April 1946.

Two parties that had led the struggle for independence, the Nationalist Party and the People's Party, dominated Syrian political life in the immediate postwar period. However, the Palestine War of 1948–49, which resulted in the defeat of the Arab armies and the establishment of Israeli statehood, discredited the Syrian leadership. In December 1948 riots against the government were put down by the army, and several army factions struggled for more than a year to gain control of the Syrian state. Col. Adib Shishakli ruled Syria for most of the period from December 1949 to March 1954, when he was ousted by another army coup.

The years from 1954 to 1958 were marked by the growth of pan-Arab and left-of-center political forces at the expense of the traditional merchant landowner class, which dominated the Nationalist and People's parties. Foremost among these forces was the Arab Socialist Ba'ath Party, which saw in Gamal Abdel Nasser (Nasir), the president of Egypt, a kindred pan-Arabist. Military officers remained active in political affairs but were split into competing factions. Some elements of the Nationalist and People's parties sought to counter the left by seeking help from Iraq and other countries. In late 1957 influential military officers decided to seek unity with Egypt as a means of suppressing factionalism. Enthusiastically supported by the Ba'ath and other pan-Arabists, they appealed to Cairo. Nasser agreed, and on 1 February 1958, Egypt and Syria proclaimed the union of Syria and Egypt as the United Arab Republic.

A monolithic single-party structure replaced the lively Syrian political tradition; decisions were made in Cairo; land reforms were introduced. Syrians chafed under Egyptian rule, and in September 1961, after a military coup, Syria seceded from the United Arab Republic. A period of political instability followed until, on 8 March 1963, power was seized by a group of leftist army officers calling themselves the National Council of the Revolutionary Command, and a radical socialist government dominated by the Ba'ath Party was formed.

The period that followed was marked by internal struggles between the founders of the Ba'ath Party and a younger generation of party militants, many in the military. That generation came to power in 1966 but split in succeeding years. In the June 1967 war between Israel on one side, and Syria, Egypt, and Jordan on the other, Israel gained control of the Golan Heights. Gen. Hafez al-Assad (Hafiz al-Asad), a former chief of the Air Force and defense minister, became chief of state on 16 November 1970; he assumed the presidency, a reinstituted office, for the first of four seven-year terms beginning in March 1971, and a permanent constitution was ratified by popular referendum on 12 March 1973. Assad would rule Syria until his death in 2000.

On 6 October 1973 of that year, Syrian troops launched a full-scale attack against Israeli forces in the Golan Heights, as the Egyptians attacked in the Suez Canal area. After the UN ceasefire of 24 October, Israel remained in control of the Golan Heights, and Syria boycotted peace negotiations in Geneva. However, on 31 May 1974, Syria signed a US-mediated disengagement accord with Israel, restoring part of the Golan Heights to Syria and creating a buffer zone, manned by a UN peacekeeping force. The occupied sector of the Golan Heights was annexed by Israel in 1981; outside powers criticized and did not recognize the annexation.

In recent years Syria has intervened militarily in neighboring Arab states to secure political ends. In September 1970 Syrian armored forces crossed the border into Jordan to support the Palestinians during the Jordanian civil war, but the Syrians were driven back by troops loyal to Jordan's King Hussein (Husayn) and by the threat of Israeli intervention. In 1976 Syrian troops entered Lebanon, nominally to enforce a ceasefire between Christian and Muslim forces but actually to help the Christian forces prevent a victory by leftist Muslims and Palestinians. Syria strongly opposed the Egyptian-Israeli peace treaty of 1979 and was one of the few Arab states to support Iran in its war against Iraq, with which Syria had hoped to merge. Another merger plan, this one with Libya, was announced in September 1980, but the effort was stillborn. In October of that year, Syria signed a 20-year friendship treaty with the Soviet Union; subsequently, Syria received large quantities of Soviet arms, including antiaircraft missiles, which it deployed in the Bekaa (Biqa') Valley in Lebanon. After Israel invaded southern Lebanon in June 1982, the Israelis knocked out the missile batteries, crippled Syria's Soviet-equipped air force, and trapped Syrian as well as Palestinian fighters in Beirut before

allowing their evacuation. Having reequipped its army with Soviet weapons, Syria maintained 25,000–35,000 troops in Lebanon until 2005. In the Lebanese civil war, Syria supported the Druze and Muslim militias against the Maronite Lebanese Forces.

Syria made repeated attempts to establish a ceasefire among Lebanon's factions. In 1989 it endorsed the Taif Accord for ending the conflict and, later, when Christian militia general Michel Aoun declared himself president of Lebanon and sought to expel the Syrian forces, assaulted his enclave with artillery and drove him out of the country. In 1991 Syria backed moves to disarm and disband the militias and signed a treaty with Beirut to put relations on a stable and peaceful basis. Under the Taif Accord, Syria was to have withdrawn its forces from Beirut and coastal areas by September 1992. Syria's withdrawal from Beirut took place in June 2001.

The authoritarian Assad regime was condemned by outsiders for assisting terrorist and drug smuggling groups. Both charges were played down after Syria joined the coalition of forces against Iraq in 1990 and agreed to participate in direct peace talks with Israel in 1991. The collapse of the Soviet Union removed Syria's most important source of external support, nullifying Assad's proclaimed strategy of refusing to negotiate with Israel until Syria gained military parity.

Internally, the regime was resented for its denial of democracy and the concentration of power with members of the Assad family's minority religious sect, the Alawites. A serious internal threat came from Islamic militants in the late 1970s and early 1980s. In 1982 Assad sent the army against their stronghold in Hama, devastating a section of the city and causing tens of thousands of casualties. The force of the response deterred further threats to the regime and the Ba'ath Party continued to control the country. In the 1990s Assad took steps to liberalize economic controls and to permit some political freedoms. About 300 political prisoners were released in 1992, and Syrian Jews were again allowed to travel. Still, the country remained on the US State Department's list of countries that support terrorism, and US trade was severely restricted. In 1994 Syrian officials met with representatives of Israel's Yitzhak Rabin-led government on the return of the Golan Heights—something Assad had wanted for decades. After Rabin's assassination, however, the talks were discontinued, and the stalemate between Syria and Israel continued. In 1997 US Secretary of State Madeleine Albright announced that she would visit Syria in an effort to get the stalled peace process back on track. Syria was officially guarded about the prospects for success, as it remained deeply suspicious of Israel's right-wing government led by Benjamin Netanyahu. In the same year, the Assad regime entered into negotiations with Iraq to open up its ports to the latter. Syria broke off diplomatic relations with Iraq after backing Iran in the 1980–88 war.

With the election of Labor leader Ehud Barak as prime minister of Israel in May 1999, new hope arose for improved relations with Israel, and a new round of peace talks between Syria and Israel was held in the United States, near Washington, DC, in January 2000. In May 2000 Israel withdrew from southern Lebanon. By the late 1990s serious concerns had been raised about the health and mental status of Syria's president, who was reportedly having "mental lapses" and suspected to be suffering from some form of dementia, as well as other infirmities. Nevertheless, Assad was elected to

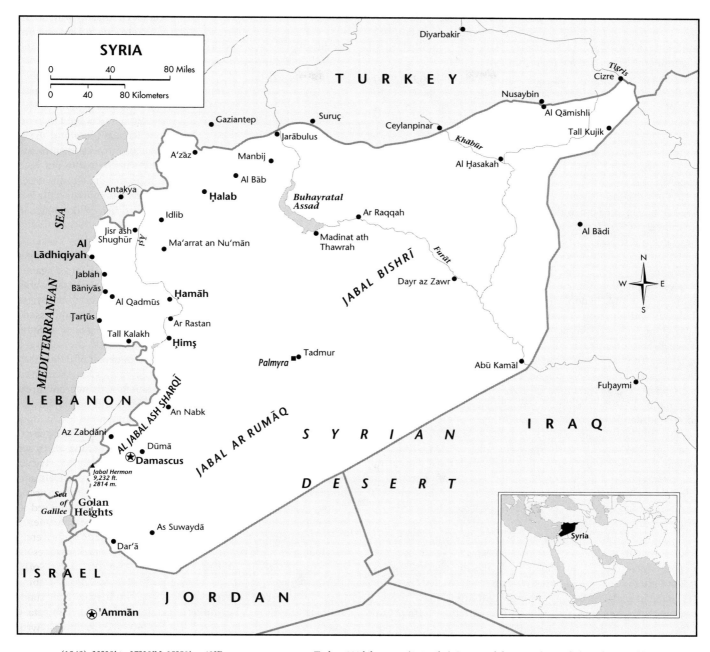

LOCATION: (1949): 32°30′ to 37°30′N; 35°50′ to 42°E. BOUNDARY LENGTHS: Turkey, 822 kilometers (510 miles); Iraq, 605 kilometers (378 miles); Jordan, 375 kilometers (234 miles); Israel, 76 kilometers (47 miles); Lebanon, 375 kilometers (234 miles); Mediterranean coastline, 193 kilometers (117 miles). TERRITORIAL SEA LIMIT: 35 miles.

a fifth seven-year term in 1999 in a nearly unanimous vote. After the 1994 death in an automobile accident of Basel, the son whom the Syrian leader had been grooming to succeed him, another of Assad's sons, Bashar, was given increased responsibilities. Assad died on 10 June 2000 of a heart attack; 34-year-old Bashar Assad was unanimously elected secretary-general by the Ba'ath Party one week later. Parliament amended the constitution to lower the minimum age for a president from 40 to 34. In a July referendum, Bashar won overwhelming support to succeed his father, and he officially began a seven-year term as president on 17 July 2000.

In November 2000 President Assad ordered the release of more than 600 political prisoners. However, in September 2001, members of parliament and pro-reform activists were detained,

which dulled hopes that Bashar would usher in a new climate of reform in the aftermath of his father's death. Although more than 100 dissidents were released from prison in November, human rights organizations maintained that hundreds of political prisoners remained in jail in Syria. In April 2001 the outlawed Muslim Brotherhood, whose members were targeted during the 1982 Hama massacre, announced its intention to resume political activity.

Following the terrorist attacks on the United States on 11 September 2001, Bashar Assad publicly emphasized Syria's stance against terrorism, although it did not support the US-led war on terrorism, stating military action was not the appropriate response to terrorism. The United States continued to list Syria as a state sponsor of terrorism and in 2004 imposed economic sanctions on Syria over what it called its support for terrorists, including the militant anti-Israeli groups Hamas and Hezbollah, and failure to stop militants from entering Iraq from Syria.

Syrian troops withdrew from Beirut in June 2001 to redeploy in other parts of Lebanon, in response to greater Lebanese criticism of Syria's presence there. In April 2005, as a result of massive Lebanese street protests following the 14 February 2005 assassination of former Lebanese Prime Minister Rafik al-Hariri, Syria withdrew all of its military forces from Lebanon. By October 2005 an investigation into Hariri's death implicated senior Syrian officials.

One of the main reasons Israel has not pulled out of the Golan Heights has to do with water. The Golan Heights provides approximately 30% of Israel's water needs. The Dan, the Banyas, and the Hatzbani, tributaries of the upper Jordan River, originate in the Golan Heights. Israel's water needs are also tied to Lebanon. Lebanon has begun to divert 50 million cu m (1.77 billion cu ft) a year from the Wazzani and Hatzbani Rivers to supply villages in southern Lebanon with water. The Wazzani feeds into the Hatzbani, which in turn flows into the Jordan River watershed and Lake Kinneret (Lake Tiberias or the Sea of Galilee), a major source of Israel's water supply. In 2002 Sharon identified measures to divert water from Israel as a cause for war. In 1964 Syria tried to dam the waters that fed Lake Kinneret, but Israel destroyed the dams as one of the events leading to the 1967 Six-Day War. Since then, Syria has built 23 dams on the Yarmouk River, a tributary flowing into the Jordan River south of Lake Kinneret, affecting the water supplies of Israel and Jordan.

In July 2006 the extremist group Hezbollah seized two Israeli soldiers on Israel's northern border. Israel responded with a full air, water, and land assault on Hezbollah's bases of operation in Lebanon. Ss a result of the fighting in Lebanon, thousands of Lebanese temporarily fled to Syria to escape Israel's bombardment of their country.

By 2006–07 the international community increasingly sought to involve Syria in dealing with the Iraq debacle. In November 2006 Iraq and Syria restored diplomatic relations after nearly 25 years. In December of that year, humanitarian agencies stated they were struggling to deal with the large number of Iraqis fleeing into Syria to escape the violence in Iraq. That same month the US Iraq Study Group recommended Iraq's neighboring states form a support group to reinforce security and national reconciliation in Iraq. Syria agreed to participate. In March 2007 the European Union (EU) reopened dialogue with Syria. In April 2007 the Speaker of the US House of Representatives, Nancy Pelosi, traveled to Syria to meet with Assad. She was the highest-level US politician to visit Syria in several years. The Bush administration condemned the visit, saying it sent the wrong signal to Syria.

In the wake of anti-government protests that swept through North Africa in early 2011, a series of protests began in the southern city of Daraa and in the capital, Damascus, in March 2011. Protests started in several other cities throughout the country as the weeks progressed, with many breaking into violence between protesters and local security forces as demonstrators called for the ouster of Assad. The government asserted that violence was caused by armed foreign fighters. In an effort to appease the crowds, Assad promised a series of government reforms, but the

rallies continued. On 29 March the cabinet of Assad resigned in a symbolic gesture addressing the public protests, prompting the president to form a new cabinet with the hopes of calming the masses. International journalists were banned from the country as of 25 April 2011.

Anti-government demonstrations and reports of government attacks on protestors continued, and by November the unrest had not ended. On 2 November the Syrian government agreed to an Arab League-brokered peace plan, but ten days later the Arab League voted to suspend Syria's membership in the organization in response to new violence in the country. In December the Arab League secured Syrian approval to allow observers from the organization to supervise a military withdrawal from Syrian cities. The UN estimated that at least 4,000 people had been killed in Syria between March and December 2011; the Syrian government disputed the figure.

13 GOVERNMENT

After independence, Syria made several attempts at establishing a constitution. The constitution of 1950 was revived in amended form in 1962 and then abrogated. A provisional constitution adopted in April 1964 was suspended in 1966 and replaced to some extent by a series of edicts. The fundamental law that emerged considered Syria a socialist republic forming part of the Arab homeland, required that the head of state be a Muslim, recognized Islamic law as a main source of legislation, ordained collective ownership of the means of production, but permitted some private ownership.

The constitution of 12 March 1973, embodying these principles and ratified by popular referendum, vests strong executive power in the president, who is nominated by the Ba'ath Party and elected by popular vote to a seven-year term. The president appoints the cabinet (headed by a prime minister) and also serves as commander-in-chief of the armed forces and as secretary-general of the Ba'ath Party. There can be multiple vice presidents at one time; three vice presidents were named in March 1984, including President Assad's younger brother Rifaat, who was dismissed from his post in 1998. In 2011 there were two sitting vice presidents. The unicameral People's Assembly (Majlis al-shaab) has 250 members who are elected every four years, but who have no real power. Suffrage is universal, beginning at age 18. Syria had been under a state of emergency since 1963 (except for 1973–74), which gave the Assad regime broad powers to stifle dissent. Although Bashar Assad announced in January 2001 that the emergency law was "frozen" and "not applied," the state of emergency still remained in force. In April 2011, in response to uprisings in the country, Assad announced that the state of emergency was being lifted, but this was largely a symbolic gesture and the regime continued to use force to suppress dissent.

14 POLITICAL PARTIES

The Arab Socialist Ba'ath Party is Syria's dominant political institution. It has a countrywide organization and controls mass organizations for youth, students, women, and the like. Only the Ba'ath may carry on political activity in the armed forces. It is far larger and more influential than the combined strength of its five partners in the National Progressive Front (NPF). This official political alignment, formed by President Hafez Assad in 1972, groups the Communist Party of Syria (SCP) and small leftist parties—the Syrian Arab Socialist Union (ASU), the Socialist Unionist Movement (ASUM), the Democratic Socialist Union Party (DSUP), and the Arab Socialist Party (ASP)—with the Ba'ath. The Ba'ath Party was founded in 1947 with the goals of Arab liberation, Arab unity, and socialism. Ba'athists attained control of the government in 1963, but the party became divided into two factions, a wing of doctrinaire socialists and a more pragmatic wing. Assad, then minister of defense and a strong nationalist, seized power in a bloodless coup in November 1970 and purged the doctrinaire Ba'athists from the government. The Ba'athists have relied on the minority Alawite sect, of which Assad was a member, and on the rural sector of the population generally. During his years as president, Assad appointed Ba'athist Alawites to influential positions in the government and in the military and security services. When Assad died on 10 June 2000, the Ba'ath Party held a party congress—its first since 1985—and elected Bashar Assad secretary-general.

While Syria conducts regular elections, in practice the Ba'ath Party and (in recent decades) the Assad family are guaranteed victory through their control of the political process. Hafez Assad, the sole presidential candidate for over 20 years, won national plebiscites by 99% majorities on 12 March 1971, 8 February 1978, 13 March 1985, 2 December 1991, and 10 February 1999. His son, Bashar, won in July 2000 by a vote of 8.6 million to 22,000. At the end of his first presidential term, a referendum was held on 27 May 2007 to confirm Assad as president. It was officially reported that he won over 97% of the vote.

In elections on 1 December 1998, the Ba'ath Party won 135 seats; the ASU, 8; SCP, 8; ASUM, 7; ASP, 5; DSUP, 4; and independents, 83. In the March 2003 elections, the NPF won 167 seats (with the Ba'ath winning 135 seats once again), and independents held 83 seats. The next parliamentary elections were held on 22 April 2007. The NPF won 169 seats, while independents won the other 81 seats. Ba'athists took 134 seats. The next elections were scheduled for 2014.

15 LOCAL GOVERNMENT

Syria is divided into 14 provinces (*muhafazat*); every province has a governor (*muhafiz*) and council. Each province is in turn divided into districts (*mantiqat*), each headed by a *qaimmaqam*. Each district is further subdivided into subdistricts, each in the charge of a *mudir*. Governors are appointed by and are directly responsible to the authorities in Damascus.

16 JUDICIAL SYSTEM

The Syrian legal system is based partly on French law and partly on Syrian statutes. Investigating magistrates determine whether a case should be sent to trial. Minor infringements are handled by peace courts, and more serious cases go to courts of first instance. There are civil and criminal appeals courts, the highest being the court of cassation. Separate state security courts have jurisdiction over activities affecting the security of the government. In addition, Shari'ah courts apply Islamic law in cases involving personal status. The Druze and non-Muslim communities have their own religious courts.

A Supreme Constitutional Court investigates and rules on petitions submitted by the president or one-fourth of the members of the People's Assembly challenging the constitutionality of laws or legislative decrees. This court has no jurisdiction to hear appeals for cases from the civil or criminal courts.

The constitution provides for an independent judiciary. The regular court system is independent; however, the state security courts are not completely independent from the executive.

There are no jury trials. The regular courts respect constitutional provisions safeguarding due process. The supreme state security court tries political and national security cases. The economic security court tries cases involving financial crimes. Both courts operate under the state-of-emergency rules overriding constitutional defendants' rights.

17 ARMED FORCES

The International Institute for Strategic Studies reports that armed forces in Syria totaled 295,000 members in 2011. The force was comprised of 220,000 from the army, 5,000 from the navy, 30,000 from the air force, and 40,000 members of an air defense force. Armed forces represented 5.8% of the labor force in Syria. Defense spending totaled $6.3 billion and accounted for 5.9% of gross domestic product (GDP).

In 2005 Syria removed its 18,000 troops from Lebanon.

18 INTERNATIONAL COOPERATION

Syria is a founding member of the UN, having joined on 24 October 1945, and belongs to ESCWA and several nonregional specialized agencies, such as the FAO, the World Bank, UNESCO, UNIDO, the ILO, and the WHO. Syria served on the UN Security Council from 2002 to 2003. It is a charter member of the Arab League, set up in 1945 to foster cooperation in foreign and domestic affairs. Syria also belongs to the Arab Bank for Economic Development in Africa, the Arab Fund for Economic and Social Development, the Council of Arab Economic Unity, G-24, G-77, the Islamic Development Bank, the Organization of the Islamic Conference (OIC), and OAPEC.

Syria is a member of the Nonaligned Movement. Despite a long history of tense relations, Syria established full diplomatic relations with Egypt in 1989. Lebanon and Syria signed a treaty of brotherhood, cooperation, and coordination in 1991. Syria is officially in a state of war with Israel. Syria cooperated with the US-led multinational coalition of forces in the Gulf War (1990–91) and has offered limited cooperation in the war on terrorism.

In environmental cooperation, Syria is part of the Basel Convention, the Convention on Biological Diversity, Ramsar, the Montréal Protocol, MARPOL, the Nuclear Test Ban Treaty, and the UN Conventions on Climate Change and Desertification.

19 ECONOMY

The GDP rate of change in Syria, as of 2010, was 3.2%. Inflation stood at 5.9%, and unemployment was reported at 8.3%.

Statistics on the Syrian economy are subject to government manipulation and revision, and may be inaccurate and inconsistent. Traditionally, Syria has been an agricultural economy, although the sector has been declining in part because of climatic conditions, including drought. In 2001 agriculture accounted for 40% of the labor force and 27% of GDP; 10 years later those numbers had declined to 17% each.

Development of the state-owned oil industry and exploitation of other mineral resources, notably phosphates, have helped to diversify Syrian industry, which was formerly concentrated in light manufacturing and textiles. Although Syria's oil production is small by Middle Eastern standards, in 2001 oil accounted for 70% of Syria's exports and 20% of its GDP. Syria became an oil exporter in 1987, but at present levels of proven reserves, it will eventually become a net importer.

Economic growth in Syria has depended on oil prices, foreign aid, and good weather. Low oil prices and drought dampened growth in the late 1980s, but in the first half of the 1990s, due to increased oil production, recovery from drought and nearly $5 billion in foreign aid as a "reward" for its participation in the Gulf War combined to help the economy register average annual growth rates of 5.3% in the late 1990s. Oil production peaked in 1996, after which it declined due to technical problems and depletion. Modest growth was restored in 2000 and 2001 with the increase in oil prices.

On 14 July 1998 Iraq and Syria signed a memorandum of understanding to reopen the Iraqi Petroleum Co. (IPC) pipeline built in 1934 connecting the Kirkuk oil fields with the Syrian port of Banias on the Mediterranean. Syria had closed the pipeline in 1982 when it broke off diplomatic relations with Iraq and shifted to Iran as an oil supplier. The IPC pipeline had been severely damaged during the Gulf War, and it was not until March 2000 that it was reported serviceable. In mid-November 2000, numerous press reports began circulating claiming that the IPC pipeline was being used to ship Iraqi oil to Syrian refineries on favorable terms, allowing Iraq to obtain oil revenues above the limits set by the UN Oil-for-Food program. Iraq and Syria denied the allegations, but according to the US Department of Energy, independent analysts determined that Syria's export levels of crude oil in 2001 could not have been attained without importing from Iraq in the range of 150,000 and 200,000 barrels per day. In November 2001 Iraq and Syria reportedly signed an agreement on building a new $200 million pipeline to replace the aging IPC line. In April 2003, as part of the invasion of Iraq, American troops shut down the IPC pipeline. The cost to Syria of the shutdown was estimated at $500 million to $1 billion a year.

The GDP growth rate decreased in the mid 2000s. The inflation rate has been fairly stable; it did not pose any major problems to the economy. The unemployment rate has been fairly stable. The government has implemented modest economic reforms, but most of the economy continues to be under its control. Declining oil production and population growth pressure on water supplies are long-term problems not yet resolved.

Historically, Syria has failed to participate effectively in the world economy. It resigned from the GATT because of Israel in 1951 and is not a member of the WTO. Syria did become part of the Greater Arab Free Trade Agreement in 2005, in which all duties were eliminated between members. In 2007 Syria signed a free-trade agreement with Turkey. In May 2010 US President Barack Obama renewed sanctions on Syria.

20INCOME

The CIA estimated that in 2010 the GDP of Syria was $107.4 billion. The CIA defines GDP as the value of all final goods and services produced within a nation in a given year and computed on the basis of purchasing power parity (PPP) rather than value as measured on the basis of the rate of the exchange based on current dollars. The per capita GDP was estimated at $4,800. The annual growth rate of GDP was 3.2%. The average inflation rate was 5.9%. It was estimated that agriculture accounted for 17.6% of GDP, industry 26.8%, and services 55.6%.

According to the World Bank, remittances from citizens living abroad totaled $1.3 billion or about $59 per capita and accounted for approximately 1.2% of GDP.

The World Bank reported that in 2009 household consumption in Syria totaled $35.1 billion or about $1,561 per capita, measured in current US dollars rather than PPP. Household consumption includes expenditures of individuals, households, and nongovernmental organizations on goods and services, excluding the purchases of dwellings. It was estimated that household consumption was growing at an average annual rate of 4.8%.

As of 2011 the most recent study by the World Bank reported that actual individual consumption in Syria was 74.2% of GDP and accounted for 0.15% of world consumption. By comparison, the United States accounted for 25.44% of world individual consumption. The World Bank also estimated that 31.2% of Syria's GDP was spent on food and beverages, 20.1% on housing and household furnishings, 6.5% on clothes, 6.1% on health, 2.4% on transportation, 0.2% on communications, 1.0% on recreation, 1.4% on restaurants and hotels, and .4% on miscellaneous goods and services and purchases from abroad.

It was estimated that in 2006—the most recent year for which figures were available—about 11.9% of the population subsisted on an income below the poverty line established by Syria's government.

21LABOR

As of 2010 Syria had a total labor force of 5.527 million people. Within that labor force, CIA estimates in 2008 noted that 17% were employed in agriculture, 16% in industry, and 67% in the service sector.

The Syrian labor force is well educated and well trained in comparison to other Arab countries, but its size is small because about half the population is under 15 years of age and because many skilled workers are employed abroad in Organization of the Petroleum Exporting Countries (OPEC) member nations. There is a high level of underemployment. Many unskilled persons in agriculture and industry work only seasonally. The government is attempting to meet the demand for trained workers by establishing vocational schools.

The public sector workweek is 35 hours, and the private sector workweek 48 hours. In 2010 there were four levels of minimum wage, depending on education and job type; these ranged from $132 per month to $218 per month. The law mandates one day of rest per week. These regulations are enforced through the ministry of labor and social affairs. The legal minimum age for employment is between 15 and 17 years depending on the type of employment. The Labor Law of 1959 established the right of workers to form unions and empowered the government to regulate hours of work, vacations, sick leave, health and safety measures, and workers' compensation. However, unions must belong to the government's bureaucratic labor confederation. The confederation acts merely as a conduit to transfer directives from government decision makers to unions and workers. Thus, there is no meaningful right to strike or bargain collectively. The government also is authorized to arbitrate labor disputes.

22 AGRICULTURE

Roughly 29% of the total land is farmed, and the country's major crops include wheat, barley, cotton, lentils, chickpeas, olives, and sugar beets. In 2009 cereal production amounted to 4.7 million tons, fruit production 2.3 million tons, and vegetable production 3.1 million tons.

Because only 25% of cultivated land is irrigated, agriculture depends on rainfall, which is uncertain, and in lean years Syria becomes a net importer of wheat and barley; this strains the whole economy and hampers development. The government has two approaches to this problem: to increase the use of fertilizers in low rainfall areas and to add substantially to irrigated cultivation. The irrigated area was expected to double through the Euphrates Dam project, which was completed in 1978. Lake Assad, formed by the dam, was planned to provide irrigation for some 640,000 hectares (1,581,000 acres). Costs of land reclamation, technical difficulties due to gypsum in the soil, and low water, in part caused by Turkish damming upstream, have slowed progress.

Beginning in 2006 the country experienced four years of successive drought, which the UN estimated affected more than one million people and destroyed the livelihoods of some 800,000. The northeast region of the country was most affected. The drought forced thousands to migrate from rural areas. The drought severely impacted the country's wheat crop and forced Syria to become a net importer of wheat.

Traditionally, much of Syria's agricultural land was held by landowners in tracts of more than 100 hectares (250 acres); sharecropping was customary. This picture was greatly altered by the government's agrarian reform program, begun in 1958. The law, as modified in 1963, fixed the maximum holding of irrigated land at 15–50 hectares (37–124 acres) per person and nonirrigated land at 80 hectares (198 acres) per person. All expropriated land available for cultivation has been allotted to farmers.

The principal cash crop is cotton, but cotton's share of total export value declined from 33% in 1974 to 2.3% by 2004. Other cash crops are cereals, vegetables, fruit, and tobacco. Since the government suspended convertibility of the Syrian pound, grain and other agricultural products have been smuggled to Lebanon in exchange for goods not available through the state importing agencies.

23 ANIMAL HUSBANDRY

The UN Food and Agriculture Organization (FAO) reported that Syria dedicated 8.2 million hectares (20.3 million acres) to permanent pasture or meadow in 2009. During that year, the country tended 24.5 million chickens and 1.1 million head of cattle. The production from these animals amounted to 66,243 tons of beef and veal, 180,233 tons of poultry, 139,785 tons of eggs, and 2.28 million tons of milk. Syria also produced 7,140 tons of cattle hide and 53,001 tons of raw wool.

Stock raising contributes significantly to the Syrian economy. Since 1975 the number of model farms, veterinary units, and livestock artificial insemination centers has increased considerably.

Sheep are the most important livestock animals in Syria, grazing on poorly developed wheat and barley fields and on the remains of crops such as wheat and corn.

24 FISHING

Syria had 16 decked commercial fishing boats in 2008. The annual capture totaled 6,996 tons according to the UN FAO. There is some fishing off the Mediterranean coast and from rivers and fish farms. Common carp and tilapia from inland waters account for about 40% of the catch.

25 FORESTRY

Approximately 3% of Syria is covered by forest. The UN FAO estimated the 2009 roundwood production at 39,800 cu m (1.41 million cu ft). The value of all forest products, including roundwood, totaled $8.48 million. Syria is almost entirely denuded of native forests. Approximately 4,910 sq km (1,896 sq mi) were forested in 2010. Most of the designated forestland consists either of wholly barren land or of rangeland with arboreous shrubs. The substantial forests are mainly on the northern slopes of the Ansariyah range, on the windward side of the Anti-Lebanon Mountains, and in the Al Lādhiqiyah region.

26 MINING

Syria's mineral resources are not extensive, but deposits of iron, petroleum, and phosphate have been exploited. Syria is a leading exporter of phosphate rock, while petroleum has become a leading source of foreign currency earnings. In 2009 the production of phosphate rock (gross weight) totaled 2,466,000 tons, down from 3,221,000 million tons in 2008. Syria's phosphate production that year was ninth in the world and accounted for 1.9% of global production. Other mineral deposits include asphalt, salt, chromite, and marble. Marble and salt were mined in commercial quantities. In 2009 an estimated 202 metric tons of marble blocks were quarried, with salt output in that same year at 78,263 metric tons. Syria also produces hydraulic cement, refractory-grade dolomite, natural gas, natural gas liquids, gravel and crushed rock, gypsum, nitrogen, phosphatic fertilizers, phosphoric acid, construction and industrial sand, steel, dimension stone, sulfur, and volcanic tuff. No metal was mined in 2009. Deposits of silica sand in al-Qaristyn had resources of 150 million tons. The mineral industry is owned and controlled by the government. In 2001 the government began opening the mineral industry to local and foreign private investors. Several private local and international investors are involved in building new cement and steel production plants. The rapid expansion of the construction sector in the near future was expected to increase Syria's demand for cement, gypsum, limestone, gravel, sand, and steel.

27 ENERGY AND POWER

The World Bank reported in 2008 that Syria produced 41 billion kWh of electricity and consumed 31.3 billion kWh, or 1,390 kWh per capita. Roughly 99% of energy came from fossil fuels, while 1% came from alternative fuels.

Syria's proven reserves of oil have made it the largest oil producer in the eastern Mediterranean region (includes Israel, Jordan and Lebanon). It also has reserves of natural gas, but no known reserves of coal.

As of 1 January 2011 Syria had proven oil reserves estimated at 2.5 billion barrels. In 1996 Syria's oil output peaked at 590,000 barrels per day, and has generally been declining as reserves have become depleted, and as older fields reach maturity.

Syria has two refineries, one at Homs, and the other at Banias. Oil production totaled 367,128 barrels a day in 2008, and increased to just over 400,000 barrels a day in 2010. Oil consumption was estimated at 292,000 barrels a day. Oil exports were 263,000 barrels a day in 2009, making Syria the 46th largest exporter of oil in the world that year.

As of 1 January 2011 Syria's proven reserves of natural gas were estimated at 8.5 trillion cu ft. In 2010 natural gas production was estimated at 316 billion cu ft. Natural gas consumption was 340 billion cu ft, and natural gas imports were 24 billion cu ft.

28 INDUSTRY

Syria has been renowned since ancient times for such handicrafts as Damascus brocade and Syrian soap. Some of these traditions endured even after 1933, when the first mechanized plant for spinning and weaving was set up in Aleppo. In 1965 the textile industry was nationalized and reorganized into 13 large state corporations. A series of nationalization measures after 1963 resulted in public control of most industry, but efforts have been made to stimulate the expansion of the private sector, as state-owned industries suffer from low productivity. In the 1970s government policy began emphasizing domestic industrial production (coupled with high tariffs on imported consumer goods) of iron and steel, fertilizers, chemicals, and household appliances. In 1995 manufacturing and mining accounted for 14% of GDP. In 2002 the government announced that priority would be shifted from efforts to privatize the state-owned enterprises (SOEs) to continued efforts to increase their efficiency. By 2010 industry accounted for 27% of GDP.

Important industries include the chemical and engineering industries, the food industry, and oil refining. The largest component of the General Establishment of Chemical Industries (GECI) is the cement industry, which is considered strategic and wholly state owned. Syria's fertilizer industry rests on its ample deposits of natural gas and phosphates, and produces ammonia, urea, and nitrogenous fertilizers. Syria also has an iron-rolling mill at Homs and factories producing furniture, refrigerators, paper, glass and plastic products, and television sets. In 2010, out of a labor force of 5.5 million people, 16% were engaged in industrial activities.

29 SCIENCE AND TECHNOLOGY

Patent applications in science and technology as of 2009, according to the World Bank, totaled 124 in Syria. Courses in basic and applied science are offered at Al-Ba'ath University (founded in 1979 at Homs), the University of Aleppo (Halab) (founded in 1960), the University of Damascus (founded in 1903), and Tishreen University (founded in 1971 at Lattakia). Major scientific research institutions in Syria include the International Center for Agricultural Research in the Dry Areas (ICARDA), founded in 1977 at Aleppo and the Arab Center for the Study of Arid Zones and Dry Lands (ACSAD), founded in 1971 at Damascus. The country's advanced petrochemical technologies have been installed by foreign oil companies. In 2008 high technology exports were valued at slightly more than $83 million, or 2% of the country's manufactured exports.

30 DOMESTIC TRADE

Damascus and Aleppo are the principal commercial centers. Virtually all importers, exporters, and wholesalers have offices in one or both cities. The chief retail centers have general and specialized stores as well as large bazaars. Smaller bazaars and open markets are found in many Syrian towns and villages. Advertising agencies use newspapers, magazines, moving picture theaters, signs on buses, and other media.

The Syrian government cracked down on smuggling in the early 1990s. Most of the previously smuggled commodities can now be imported through official channels. Commodity smuggling from Lebanon, however, is still present and provides an "unofficial market" for imported products at the free-market exchange rate reflective of world price levels.

Usual business hours are from 9 a.m. to 1 p.m. and from 3:30 p.m. to 7 p.m. Friday is the weekly day of rest. Banking hours are Saturday–Thursday, 8 a.m. to 2 p.m.

The Damascus International Fair and the Syrian Industrial Marketing Fair are annual events.

31 FOREIGN TRADE

Syria imported $13.57 billion worth of goods and services in 2008, while exporting $12.84 billion worth of goods and services. Major import partners in 2009 were China, 10.8%; Saudi Arabia, 10.1%; Turkey, 7%; United Arab Emirates, 5%; Italy, 4.9%; South Korea, 4.7%; Germany, 4.5%; Russia, 4.2%; Lebanon, 4.1%; and Egypt, 4.1%. Its major export partners were Iraq, 31.4%; Lebanon, 12.7%; Germany, 9.2%; Saudi Arabia, 5.2%; and Italy, 4.7%.

Major imports in 2010 were machinery and transport equipment, electric power machinery, food and livestock, metals, and chemicals. Major exports were crude oil, minerals, petroleum products, fruits and vegetables, wheat, and textiles.

During the 1980s, Syria focused on increasing its trade with socialist nations. However, when the Soviet Union broke apart in 1991, Syria increased trade with European nations.

Principal Trading Partners – Syria (2010)

(In millions of US dollars)

Country	Total	Exports	Imports	Balance
World	30,950.0	14,000.0	16,950.0	-2,950.0
Iraq	5,546.0	4,662.0	884.0	3,778.0
Sa'udi Arabia	3,752.0	777.0	2,975.0	-2,198.0
Lebanon	3,001.0	1,826.0	1,175.0	651.0
Italy	2,827.0	1,364.0	1,463.0	-99.0
China	2,725.0	37.0	2,688.0	-2,651.0
Turkey	2,631.0	602.0	2,029.0	-1,427.0
Germany	2,184.0	1,373.0	811.0	562.0
United Arab Emirates	1,901.0	439.0	1,462.0	-1,023.0
South Korea	1,520.0	138.0	1,382.0	-1,244.0
Russia	1,249.0	39.0	1,210.0	-1,171.0

(…) data not available or not significant.

(n.s.) not specified.

SOURCE: 2011 Direction of Trade Statistics Yearbook, New York: United Nations, 2011.

Balance of Payments – Syria (2010)

(In millions of US dollars)

Current Account		-367.0
Balance on goods		-3,663.0
Imports	-15,936.0	
Exports	12,273.0	
Balance on services		3,860.0
Balance on income		-1,514.0
Current transfers		950.0
Capital Account		287.0
Financial Account		1,252.0
Direct investment abroad		...
Direct investment in Syria		1,469.0
Portfolio investment assets		-193.0
Portfolio investment liabilities		...
Financial derivatives		...
Other investment assets		61.0
Other investment liabilities		-85.0
Net Errors and Omissions		905.0
Reserves and Related Items		-2,076.0

(…) data not available or not significant.

SOURCE: *Balance of Payment Statistics Yearbook 2011*, Washington, DC: International Monetary Fund, 2011.

32 BALANCE OF PAYMENTS

Syria has had serious deficits in its trade balance since 1976, but import restrictions, foreign aid (especially from other Arab governments), and the drawdown of foreign exchange holdings enabled the government to cover the losses. Since the late 1980s, the government has been encouraging private-sector trade. Private-sector exports consequently skyrocketed from $79 million in 1987 to $517 million in 1990, thus reducing the trade deficit. An upturn in world oil prices at the end of the 1990s and into the early 2000s—and an improvement in the country's agricultural exports—greatly improved the balance of payments situation.

In 2010 the country had a current account balance of $-1.379 billion. In order to reduce its debt burden, Syria made bilateral repayment deals with a number of key European creditors. In 2008 Russia forgave nearly three-quarters of Syria's $14.5 billion debt.

33 BANKING AND SECURITIES

Syria's financial services sector is underdeveloped, although Assad's government has undertaken reform efforts. The Central Bank, founded in 1956, is the bank of issue for currency, the financial agent of the government, and the cashier for the treasury. The Agricultural Bank makes loans to farmers at low interest; the Industrial Bank (nationalized in 1961), the People's Credit Bank and the Real Estate Bank (both founded in 1966), and the Commercial Bank of Syria (formed in 1967 by a merger of five nationalized commercial banks) make loans in their defined sectors. In 2003 the government revoked the law that had previously criminalized the private exchange of foreign currencies and Syrian pounds.

Privatization of banks, which had been prohibited for 30 years, arrived in 2001 with new banking reform laws. In March of that year President Assad issued Law 28, authorizing the establishment of private and joint-venture banks, with foreigners permitted up to 49% ownership. As of 2010, 13 private banks had opened in the country. In March 2009 Syria opened its first stock exchange.

In 2010 the discount rate—the interest rate at which the central bank lends to financial institutions in the short term—was 0.75%. At the end of 2010, the nation's gold reserves were valued at $20.57 billion, ranking it 58th in the world in terms of gold reserves.

34 INSURANCE

All insurance in Syria was nationalized in 1963; thereafter, insurance was controlled solely by a government-owned company. In 2005 reforms were passed, permitting the establishment of private insurance companies. Motor vehicle insurance is compulsory.

35 PUBLIC FINANCE

In 2010 the budget of Syria included $12.53 billion in public revenue and $15.3 billion in public expenditure. The budget deficit amounted to 4.5% of GDP. Public debt was 29.8% of GDP, with $7.572 billion of the debt held by foreign entities.

Although Syria was able to balance its budget in 1992, large military expenditures and continued subsidization of basic commodities and social services have produced deficits in subsequent years. State intervention in business and price controls put a damper on growth.

36 TAXATION

Relatively low salaries have kept the tax base narrow, and price controls have restricted the taxable profits from industry. Earners of less than SYP6,000 per year are exempt from income taxes. There are taxes on individual income at progressive rates of 5–22%.

Business profits are taxed at progressive rates from 10 to 28%. Joint stock companies are taxed at 22%; private banks are taxed at 25%. Capital gains are included in taxable income and are taxed at the applicable corporate rate. However, capital gains resulting from the sale of shares by the shareholder are not taxed. Dividends distributed by Syrian companies are not subject to a withholding tax if paid out of profits that have already been taxed. For Syrian and non-Syrian companies and individuals, income from movable capital (interest, royalties, and foreign sources of dividends) is taxed at a flat rate of 7.5%. There is no general sales tax, but consumption taxes are assessed on specific items such as petrol, rice and sugar. Other taxes include excise taxes, property taxes, stamp duties, and social security contributions.

37 CUSTOMS AND DUTIES

Goods imported into Syria are subject to a customs duty and "unified" tax. Rates are progressive and depend on the government's view of the necessity for the product. Food and industrial raw materials carry low rates while luxury goods, such as automobiles, have rates of 150–200%. The unified tax is a surcharge on all imported goods and ranges from 6 to 35%. The tax helps to support the military, schools, and municipalities.

Syria has free-trade agreements with Bahrain, Kuwait, Iraq, Jordan, Lebanon, Qatar, Sudan, Saudi Arabia, and the United Arab Emirates. Trade agreements with Libya, Morocco, Oman, and Tunisia are in negotiations. There is a single-column tariff modified by trade and transit agreements with other Arab League states, under which member countries are granted preferential

Public Finance – Syria (2008)

(In millions of pounds, central government figures)

Revenue and Grants	**490,904**	**100.0%**
Tax revenue	348,848	71.1%
Social contributions	...	...
Grants	...	...
Other revenue	142,056	28.9%
Expenditures	**548,394**	**100.0%**
General public services	...	...
Defense	130,591	23.8%
Public order and safety	109,851	20.0%
Economic affairs	204,499	37.3%
Environmental protection	...	...
Housing and community amenities	...	...
Health	...	...
Recreational, culture, and religion	1,787	0.3%
Education	64,627	11.8%
Social protection	8,136	1.5%

(...) data not available or not significant.

SOURCE: *Government Finance Statistics Yearbook 2010*, Washington, DC: International Monetary Fund, 2010.

duties on some products and duty-free entry for others. Syria accepts the Arab League boycott of Israel.

38 FOREIGN INVESTMENT

Foreign direct investment (FDI) in Syria was a net inflow of $1.43 billion according to World Bank figures published in 2009. FDI represented 2.75% of GDP. Although a government decree prohibits confiscation of foreign investments, there are no safeguards against nationalization of property. In principle, the judicial system upholds the obligations of contracts, but in practice decisions are subject to outside pressures. In addition, poor infrastructure, power outages, an inadequate banking sector, and lack of transparency have all contributed to Syria's failure to attract significant amounts of foreign investment.

Beginning in 1984, a number of pieces of legislation have been passed to encourage foreign investment. Decision 186, issued in 1985, aimed at encouraging investment in tourism. Decree 10 in 1986 was designed to encourage joint-venture agricultural companies. In June 1991, in the wake of the Gulf War, the government issued Investment Law 10, aimed at promoting investment in all sectors of the economy by providing the same incentives to local and foreign investors. Qualifying investors were granted tax holidays and duty-free privileges for the import of capital goods. The law succeeded in attracting investments particularly in textiles, pharmaceuticals, food processing, and other light industries. The primary investors have been from Gulf states. In 1999 it was estimated that nearly 1,500 projects valued at $6.5 billion had been approved since the reforms of 1991. In May 2000 Decree 7 amended Law 10 of 1991 to make investment more attractive by extending tax holiday periods, increasing hard currency flexibility, reducing income taxes on shareholding companies, and offering sector and regional incentives. A tax holiday of five years was extended to seven years for enterprises that export over 51% of their output.

Additional decrees since 2007—including allowing foreigners to own or lease land for business purposes and the free repatriation of profits once tax liabilities have been met—have been intended to further encourage foreign investment. Despite these reforms, overall progress with regard to foreign investment has been slow. With the exception of cotton ginning, water bottling, and cigarette production, all sectors are open to foreign investment.

In 2011 the World Bank ranked Syria 134th out of 183 economies in its global "Doing Business" report. That was a slight improvement over Syria's ranking of 138th in 2009.

US investment in Syria has been hampered by US sanctions in place since 1979; these included restrictions on supplying Syria with "dual use" items such as computers and oil exploration equipment, and, since 2004, a ban on the export of almost all US products. Other US-imposed restrictions having to do with taxes and the transfer of money have caused a number of US companies—namely in the oil and gas sector—to pull out of Syria since 2006.

39 ECONOMIC DEVELOPMENT

The transformation of Syria's economy began with the Agrarian Reform Law in 1958, which called for the expropriation of large tracts of land. During the union with Egypt, laws were passed for the nationalization of banks, insurance companies, and large industrial firms. After the Ba'ath Party came to power in 1963, the socialist trend reasserted itself with greater force. A series of laws created a new banking system and instituted public ownership of all large industries. By the early 1970s, however, the government had relaxed many restrictions on trade, foreign investment, and private-sector activity in an effort to attract private and foreign, especially Arab, contributions to Syria's economic growth.

Since 1961 a series of five-year plans has concentrated on developing the nation's infrastructure and increasing agricultural and industrial production. Investments reached 60% of the target under the first plan (1961–65); the second plan (1966–70) aimed to expand real GDP by 7.2% annually but achieved a yearly growth rate of only 4.7%. The third plan (1971–75) was disrupted by the 1973 Arab-Israeli War, but thanks to aid from other Arab states and large oil price increases, Syria experienced an economic boom with a high annual growth rate of 13%. The fourth plan (1976–80) was hampered by the high cost of Syria's military intervention in Lebanon and a cutoff of aid from Gulf states; economic growth varied widely, from 2.8% in 1977 to 9.2% in 1980.

Under the fifth plan (1981–85), development projects begun during the previous plan were to be continued or completed. Total investment was estimated at £101 billion, of which 23% was to be provided by the private sector. Real GDP was to grow by 7.7% annually; actual growth rates ranged from 10.2% in 1981 to 3.6% in 1984, averaging 2.3% for the period.

Syria's sixth development plan (1986–90) emphasized increased productivity rather than new projects, with special emphasis on agriculture and agro-industries. Actual investment in agriculture accounted for 18.7% of total spending. The share of the industry and energy sector was at 19.7%, far below the planned 30.9%. Services received the highest share, with 53% of the total.

The seventh five-year plan (1991–95) proposed total investments of SYP259 billion, more than double the amount spent under the previous plan. It aimed at spending 81.7% of the total on the public sector and 18.3% on the mixed-sector/private-sector cooperatives. Officials at the Supreme Planning Commission stated that agriculture and irrigation would continue to receive top priority, with self-sufficiency in cereal production a policy objective. Output in agriculture and manufacturing was planned to expand by 5.6% per annum.

During 1949–86, multilateral assistance to Syria totaled $822.7 million, of which 77% came through the IBRD. US loans and grants during the same period amounted to $581.9 million. Financial aid to Syria from Arab oil-producing states has not been made public. Because Syria was in arrears on payments to the World Bank, disbursements were halted in 1988 and projects canceled. Syria has been in violation of the Brooke Amendment since 1985. The improvement in Syria's external payment position in 1989 as well as the resumption of aid flows to Syria in 1990 due to its participation in the coalition against Iraq helped to restore its ability to repay its debt.

In March 2009 Syria took steps to address and liberalize its ailing economy, opening the Damascus Securities Exchange, the country's first stock exchange. Although the exchange began modestly—with just six companies trading two days a week—the move was enthusiastically welcomed by Syrians who have long hungered for market reform.

In 2011 the Syrian economy was facing a number of long-term challenges, including declining oil production, variable climatic conditions, population growth, and high unemployment.

40 SOCIAL DEVELOPMENT

A system of social insurance provides old-age pensions and disability and death benefits. The pension system is funded by 14% contributions from employers and 7% from employees. Retirement is set at age 60 for men and age 55 for women with at least 15 years of contributions, or age 55 for men and age 50 for women with 20 years of contributions. Survivors' pensions are paid to widows only; widowers are covered only if disabled. Employers also contribute 3% of payroll to fund workers' compensation providing temporary and permanent disability benefits, as well as medical and survivor benefits. Funeral grants amount to one month's earnings.

Although the government supports equal pay for equal work and encourages education for women, Islamic precepts govern many areas of women's lives, including marriage, divorce, child custody, and inheritance. Some secular laws also discriminate against women. Victims of domestic violence do not seek redress due to social stigma, and there are no reliable statistics regarding abuse and rape. Children's rights are generally protected.

The human rights situation is poor, and fundamental rights are denied. Arbitrary arrest and incommunicado detention are common. Detainees' relatives are also arrested to force confessions. Torture is common. Public criticism of the Ba'ath Party or of government officials is not permitted. Local human rights organizations are banned, although one international organization was allowed to conduct a limited fact-finding mission.

41 HEALTH

According to the CIA, life expectancy in Syria was 74 years in 2011. The country spent 3.1% of its GDP on healthcare, amounting to $72 per person. There were 15 physicians, 19 nurses and midwives, and 15 hospital beds per 10,000 inhabitants. The fertility rate was 3.1, while the infant mortality rate was 14 per 1,000 live births. In 2008 the maternal mortality rate, according to the World Bank, was 46 per 100,000 births. It was estimated that 81% of children were vaccinated against measles. The CIA calculated HIV/AIDS prevalence in Syria to be about less than 0.1% in 2001. The HIV/AIDS adult prevalence rate was less than 1% in 2007. The incidence of tuberculosis was 41 per 100,000 people in 2007. About 45% of women used contraception in 2007.

In 1947 Syria had only 37 hospitals, with a total of 1,834 beds, but by 1985, the number of hospitals had increased to 195, with 11,891 beds. The government also maintains mobile hospital units, modern laboratories, x-ray centers, sanatoriums, and dispensaries.

Since World War II, malaria has been virtually eliminated with the aid of the WHO, but intestinal and respiratory diseases associated with poor living conditions are still common, particularly in rural areas. Cases of malaria, tuberculosis and leprosy persist. Approximately 80% of the population had access to safe drinking water and 90% had adequate sanitation.

In April 2010 Syria became the first Arab nation to implement a ban on smoking in public places, including businesses, restaurants, schools, theaters, sports arenas, and on public transportation. The law was approved by President Assad, who is a medical doctor, in November 2009. It has raised a great deal of controversy nationwide because smoking is a favorite pastime of many Syrians, particularly through the use of the traditional nargile, or hubble-bubble pipe. Many business owners feared that the ban would lead to a significant loss of business. Violators of the ban were subject to penalties of between $11 and $2,000.

42 HOUSING

A development plan from 1981–85 allocated SYP2.6 billion to construction projects, including housing. Migration from the rural areas to the cities has at times led to a housing shortage. Affordable housing in the major cities remains a challenge; housing units are very expensive in relation to average salaries. Consequently home ownership remains out of reach for many low and middle-income citizens.

In December 2010 the government passed legislation that makes it easier for foreigners to buy property.

43 EDUCATION

In 2009 the World Bank estimated that 95% of age-eligible children in Syria were enrolled in primary school. Secondary enrollment for age-eligible children stood at 69%. Overall, the CIA estimated that Syria had a literacy rate of 79.6%. Public expenditure on education represented 4.9% of GDP.

Elementary schooling is free and compulsory for nine years, which are covered in two stages (five years plus four years) of basic school. Secondary schools offer three-year programs in general (scientific or literary), technical, and vocational studies. The academic year runs from September to June.

In 2009 about 9% of age-eligible children were enrolled in some type of preschool program. It is estimated that nearly all students complete their primary education. The student-to-teacher ratio for primary school was at about 18:1 in 2008; the ratio for secondary school was about 15:1.

There are some two dozen public and private universities in Syria. They include the University of Damascus (founded in 1923); the University of Aleppo (Halab, 1960); Tishrin University (Al Lādhiqiyah, 1971); and Al-Ba'ath University (Homs, 1979).

44 LIBRARIES AND MUSEUMS

The Assad National Library, founded in 1984 in Damascus and an adjunct of the Arab Academy, has 262,000 volumes and is well known for rare books and manuscripts. The library of the University of Damascus has 169,000 volumes. The Al Zahiriah public library in Damascus has 100,000 volumes. There are also public libraries in Halab, Damascus, Homs, and Al Lādhiqiyah.

The most important museum is the National Museum in Damascus, founded in 1919. It contains ancient Oriental, Greek, Roman, Byzantine, and Islamic collections and houses the Directorate-General of Antiquities, established in 1947, which supervises excavations and conserves antiquities under the Antiquities Law. Also in Damascus, there is the Museum of Art and Popular Traditions and the Museum of Arabic Medicine and Science. There are small museums in Halab, Hama, Homs, Palmyra, Tartos, and other cities.

45 MEDIA

In 2009 the CIA reported that there were 3.9 million telephone landlines in Syria. In addition to landlines, mobile phone subscriptions averaged 46 per 100 people. There were 14 FM radio stations, 2 AM radio stations, and 1 shortwave radio station. Internet users numbered 19 per 100 citizens. In 2010 the country had 8,114 Internet hosts. Prominent newspapers in 2010, with circulation numbers listed parenthetically, included *Al Baath* (40,000), *Ath Thawra* (40,000), *Syria Times* (3,000), and *Tishrin* (50,000). Most Syrian newspapers are published by government ministries and popular organizations. In 2000, the government authorized publication of the first private paper since 1963.

Nearly all communications facilities are owned and operated by the government, including the postal service, telegraph, telephone, radio, and television.

The government-controlled Syrian Broadcasting Service transmits on medium wave and shortwave, and broadcasts in Arabic and 10 foreign languages. Syrian television has two stations. While there are a few private radio stations, they are not permitted to transmit any news or political information.

Though the constitution provides for free expression of opinion in speech and writing, in practice the government is reported to restrict these rights significantly. Written criticism of the president, the president's family, the Ba'ath Party, the military, and the regime are not permitted.

46 ORGANIZATIONS

Syria has chambers of commerce, industry, and agriculture, most of which are members of the Federation of Syrian Chambers of Commerce. The International Center for Agricultural Research in the Dry Areas is based in Aleppo. Other multination groups based in Syria include the Arab Institute for Occupational Health and Safety and the Arab Inter-Parliamentary Union. The cooperative movement is well developed. There are some professional associations.

The most prominent cultural and educational organizations are the Arab Academy and the Arab Club for Information (Arabcin), both in Damascus. There are a number of sports associations promoting amateur competition for athletes of all ages in a variety of pastimes.

The General Women's Federation was established in 1967 as one of several organizations through which the Ba'ath Party has tried to mobilize popular energies and consolidate its control. Analogous groups include the General Union of Peasants, the General Federation of Trade Unions, the General Union of Students, and the Revolutionary Youth Organization.

There is a national chapter of the Red Crescent Society.

47 TOURISM, TRAVEL, AND RECREATION

The *Tourism Factbook*, published by the UN World Tourism Organization, reported 7.72 million incoming tourists to Syria in 2009, who spent a total of $3.78 billion. Of those incoming tourists, there were 4.7 million from the Middle East. There were 50,903 hotel beds available in Syria. The estimated daily cost to visit Damascus, the capital, was $344.

Syria has many famous tourist attractions, such as the Krak des Chevaliers, a Crusaders' castle; Ra's Shamrah, site of the ancient city of Ugarit; Ar-Rusafah, with its early Christian monuments and Muslim palace; and the ancient town of Dura Europus (now As-Salihiyah). Palmyra, the capital of Queen Zenobia, is a fairly well-preserved ruin of an Arabo-Hellenic city. The Umayyad Mosque, which incorporates parts of the Byzantine Cathedral of St. John the Baptist, in Damascus, is popular. Damascus' old city is a UNESCO World Heritage Site. Syria's mountains and Mediterranean beaches also attract visitors.

A vaccination for meningitis is required for pilgrims traveling to Mecca for the annual Hajj. All travelers are strongly recommended to take precautions against malaria, typhoid, and meningitis.

48 FAMOUS PERSONS

Among the famous Syrians of earlier periods are Queen Zenobia of Palmyra (3rd century AD), who led a series of military campaigns against the Romans in order to reopen trade routes; the philosopher Al-Farabi (Muhammad bin Muhammad bin Tarkhan abu Nasr al-Farabi, 872–950), considered by the Arab world as second only to Aristotle; the poet Al-Mutanabbi (Abu at-Tayyib Ahmad bin al-Husayn al-Mutanabbi, 915–65); the mystic philosopher Shihab ad-Din as-Suhrawardi (d. 1191); and the theologian philosopher Taqi ad-Din Ahmad bin Taymiyah (1263–1328).

Of the Umayyad caliphs, Umar bin 'Abd-al-'Aziz (r. 717–720) is still revered as a restorer of true Islam. In a later era, Nureddin

(Nur ad-Din, 1118–74), ruler of Aleppo, annexed Damascus and brought Egypt under his control. By unifying Muslim forces against the Crusaders, he made possible the victories of the renowned Saladin (Salah ad-Din, 1138–93), sultan of both Syria and Egypt, whose tomb is in Damascus. Hafez al-Assad (Hafiz al-Asad, 1928–2000) ruled Syria from 1970–2000.

⁴⁹ DEPENDENCIES

Syria has no territories or colonies.

⁵⁰ BIBLIOGRAPHY

Ball, Warwick. *Syria: A Historical and Architectural Guide.* Northampton, MA: Interlink Books, 2010.

Commins, David. *Historical Dictionary of Syria.* 2nd ed. Lanham, MD: Scarecrow, 2004.

Hourani, Albert Habib. *A History of the Arab Peoples.* Cambridge, MA: Belknap Press of Harvard University Press, 2002.

The Middle East. Washington, D.C.: CQ Press, 2005.

Rabil, Robert G. *Syria, the United States, and the War on Terror in the Middle East.* Westport, CT: Praeger Security International, 2006.

Seddon, David, ed. *A Political and Economic Dictionary of the Middle East.* Philadelphia: Routledge/Taylor and Francis, 2004.

Shoup, John A. *Culture and Customs of Syria.* Westport, CT: Greenwood Press, 2008.

Syria Investment and Business Guide: Strategic and Practical Information. Washington, DC: International Business Publications USA, 2012.

Tauber, Eliezer. *The Formation of Modern Syria and Iraq.* London: Routledge, 2007.

TAIWAN

CAPITAL: T'aipei

FLAG: The flag is red with a 12-pointed white sun on the blue upper left quadrant. The 12 points of the sun represent the 12 two-hour periods of the day in Chinese tradition, and symbolize progress. The colors red, white, and blue represent the Three Principles of the people (San Min Chu I) of Sun Yat-sen, father of the Republic of China, and symbolize the spirit of liberty, fraternity, and equality.

ANTHEM: *Zhonghua Minguo guoge* (*National Anthem of the Republic of China*).

MONETARY UNIT: The new Taiwan dollar (TWD) is a paper currency of 100 cents. There are coins of 50 cents and 1, 5, and 10 dollars, and notes of 50, 100, 500, and 1,000 new Taiwan dollars. TWD1 = US$0.033 (or US$1 = TWD30.303) as of 2011.

WEIGHTS AND MEASURES: The metric system is employed in government and industrial statistics. Commonly used standards of weights and measures are the catty (1.1 lbs or 0.4989 kg), the li (0.5 km or 0.31 mi), the ch'ih (0.33 m or 1.09 ft), and the chia (0.97 hectare or 2.39 acres).

HOLIDAYS: New Year's Day and the Founding of the Republic of China (1912), 1 January; Chinese New Year's Eve, the last day of the 12th lunar month; Spring Festival (Chinese New Year), from the 1st to the 3rd day of the first lunar month; Farmer's Day and the Beginning of Spring, 3 February, 4 February or 5 February; Children's Day 4 April; Tomb-Sweeping Day, 4 or 5 April; May Day, 1 May; Dragon Boat Festival, the 5th day of the 5th lunar month; Armed Forces Day, 3 September; Birthday of Confucius and Teachers' Day, 28 September; Mid-Autumn Festival (Moon Festival), the 15th day of the 8th lunar month; National Day (Double Tenth Day), 10 October; Taiwan Retrocession Day, 25 October; Sun Yat-Sen's Birthday, 12 November; Constitution Day, 25 December.

TIME: 8 p.m. = noon GMT.

¹LOCATION, SIZE, AND EXTENT

Taiwan lies in the western Pacific Ocean astride the Tropic of Cancer, less than 161 km (100 mi) from the southeast coast of mainland China, from which it is separated by the Taiwan (Formosa) Strait. To the NE, less than 129 km (80 mi) away, is the W end of the Japanese Ryukyu Islands; to the E is the Pacific Ocean; the Philippine island of Luzon lies 370 km (230 mi) to the S.

Besides the island proper, Taiwan comprises 21 small islands in the Taiwan group and 64 islands in the Penghu (Pescadores) group; the total area is 35,980 sq km (13,892 sq mi). Comparatively, the area occupied by Taiwan is slightly larger than the states of Maryland and Delaware combined. Leaf-shaped Taiwan island extends 394 km (245 mi) NNE–SSW and 144 km (89 mi) ESE–WNW; it has a coastline of 1,566 km (973 mi). The Penghu group, lying 40 km (25 mi) west of Taiwan island, has a total area of 127 sq km (49 sq mi).

Also under the control of the Taiwan government are Quemoy (Chinmen) and Matsu, two island groups located strategically close to the mainland Chinese province of Fujian (Fukien). Quemoy is the biggest of a group of six islands, two of which are occupied by the People's Republic of China; it is situated in Xiamen (Amoy) Bay at 118°23 E and 24°27 N and has a total area of 176 sq km (68 sq mi). The Matsu group, consisting of Nankan (the largest), Peikan, Tungyin, and about 10 small islets, is located at 119°56 E and 26°9 N, 30.6 km (19 mi) off the mainland port city of Fuzhou; it has a total area of 28.8 sq km (11.1 sq mi).

The capital city of T'aipei is located on northern Taiwan.

²TOPOGRAPHY

Taiwan perches on the margin of the continental shelf. Along the west coast, the sea is rather shallow, averaging 90 m (300 ft) and not exceeding 210 m (690 ft) at the deepest point; however, it deepens abruptly along the east coast, dropping to a depth of 4,000 m (13,000 ft) only 50 km (31 mi) offshore. The terrain is precipitous on the east coast, with practically no natural harbor except Suao Bay in the north. The west coast is marked by wide tidal flats. Kaohsiung, the southern port, is situated in a long lagoon called Haochiung Bay. The north coast, with its many inlets, provides Taiwan with its best harbor, Chilung (Keelung).

The eastern two-thirds of the island are composed of rugged foothill ranges and massive mountain chains. A low, flat coastal plain, extending from north to south, occupies the western third. Yü Shan, with an elevation of 3,997 m (13,113 ft), is the highest peak on the island.

Located on the Eurasian tectonic plate near the border of the Philippine plate, Taiwan is part of the Ring of Fire, a seismically active band surrounding the Pacific Ocean. Mild to moderate earthquake tremors are common, with over 200 minor shocks recorded each year.

All the rivers originate in the mountains in the central part of the island. They have short courses and rapid streams. The longest river, Choshui, draining westward, is only 190 km (118 mi) long. Only the Tanshui, which flows past T'aipei in the north, is navigable.

3 CLIMATE

Taiwan enjoys an oceanic, subtropical monsoon climate. The warm and humid summer lasts from May until September, the mild winter from December until February. The average lowland temperature in January is 16°C (61°F) in the north and 20°C (68°F) in the south; the average July temperature is 28°C (82°F) in both the north and south. The growing season lasts throughout the year, except at elevations above 1,200 m (4,000 ft), where frost and snow occasionally occur.

The average rainfall is 257 cm (101 in), ranging from 127 cm (50 in) at the middle of the western coast to 635 cm (250 in) or more on exposed mountain slopes. Southwest monsoon winds blow from May through September and northeast monsoon winds from October to March. Only the extreme southwest has a distinct dry season. As a result of the tropical cyclonic storms that sweep out of the western Pacific, typhoons occur between June and October. In September 2010, typhoon Fanapi hit Taiwan, bringing high winds, flooding, and as much as 44 inches of rain to southern regions. The storm left about 100 people injured.

4 FLORA AND FAUNA

The flora is closely related to that of southern China and the Philippines. Taiwan has almost 190 plant families, about 1,180 genera, and more than 3,800 species, of which indigenous members constitute about one-third of the total flora. Mangrove forest is found in tidal flats and coastal bays. From sea level to a height of 2,000 m (6,600 ft) is the zone of broad-leaved evergreen tropical and subtropical forest, where ficua, pandanus, palms, teak, bamboos, and camphors are commonly found. The mixed forest of broad-leaved deciduous trees and conifers occupies the next zone, extending from a height of 2,000 m to 3,000 m (6,600 ft to 9,800 ft). Pines, cypresses, firs, and rhododendrons are grown in this region. Above this level is the zone of coniferous forests, composed mainly of firs, spruce, juniper, and hemlock.

The mammals so far discovered number more than 60 species, 45 of which appear to be indigenous to the island. The largest beast of prey is the Formosan black bear. Foxes, flying fox bats, deer, wild boar, bats, squirrels, macaques, and pangolins are some of the mammals seen on the island. There are more than 330 species and subspecies of birds, of which 33 are common to the island, China, and the Philippines, and about 87 are peculiar forms. More than 65 species of reptiles and amphibians inhabit the island. There is an abundance of snakes, of which 13 species are poisonous. The insect life is rich and varied.

5 ENVIRONMENT

The Environmental Protection Administration (EPA) has the main responsibility for environmental policy. Water pollution from raw sewage and industrial effluents is a significant problem in Taiwan. Outside the larger hotels and urban centers, the water is likely to be impure and health problems such as hepatitis result from waterborne contaminants. Water quality is regulated under the provisions of the Drinking Water Management Act of 1972 and the 1974 Water Pollution Control Act. According to statistics collected in 2000, the renewable water resources in Taiwan totaled 67 cu km (16.07 cu mi).

Air pollution is another significant problem, complicated by a high pollen count. Solid waste disposal regulations and air quality standards were adopted in 1975. All factories are required to comply with established standards, with the cost of installing antipollution devices being written off as a depreciable item over two years. In 1978, Taiwan adopted the safety procedures for nuclear facilities issued by the International Atomic Energy Agency (IAEA). In the mid-1980s the government began tightening emission standards for automobiles and ordered many factories and power plants to install filters and dust collectors. The EPA announced plans in 1987 to install an island-wide pollution-monitoring system. The UN reported in 2008 that carbon dioxide emissions in Taiwan totaled 270,000 kilotons.

Typhoons and tropical storms that cause severe damage to the environment are frequent in the season from July through September. During an average year, a total of 26–27 tropical systems develop. On 9 and 10 August 2009, the nation was hit first by Tropical Storm Etau and then by Typhoon Morakot. The storms, along with the resulting floods (the worst in 50 years) and mudslides, took the lives of at least 62 people. A massive landslide near the southern mountain village of Hsiaolin trapped over 700 people, leaving an unknown death toll. Numerous homes and businesses were destroyed. The amount of damage to agricultural land was initially estimated at US$152 million.

Wildlife management is the responsibility of the National Wildlife Protection Association of the Republic of China. The nation's marine life is threatened by the use of driftnets. According to a 2011 report issued by the International Union for Conservation of Nature and Natural Resources (IUCN), threatened species included 11 types of mammals, 23 species of birds, 7 types of reptiles, 10 species of amphibians, 59 species of fish, and 78 species of plants. Threatened species include the Formosan sika, hawksbill turtle, Oriental white stork, and Lan Yü scops owl. Trade in endangered species has been reported.

6 POPULATION

The population of Taiwan in 2011 was estimated by the US Central Intelligence Agency (CIA) at approximately 23,071,779, which placed it at number 50 in population among the 196 nations of the world. In 2011 approximately 10.9% of the population was over 65 years of age, with another 15.6% under 15 years of age. There were 1.084 males for every female in the country. The population's annual rate of change was 0.193%. Population density in Taiwan was calculated at 641 people per sq km (1,661 people per sq mi).

The largest urban areas, along with their respective populations, included Taipei, 2.6 million; Kaohsiung, 1.5 million; and Taichung, 1.1 million.

7 MIGRATION

Estimates of Taiwan's net migration rate, carried out by the CIA in 2011, amounted to 0.03 migrants per 1,000 citizens. In 1963 the Nationalist government stated that since the completion of the Communist conquest of the mainland in 1949–50 a total of

146,772 Chinese refugees had come to Taiwan for resettlement. The number of refugees has varied from year to year.

In 2006, the Overseas Compatriot Affairs Commission, ROC (Republic of China) reported that there were 39,379,784 overseas Chinese (30,976,784 in Asia, 5,920,000 in the Americas, 1,700,000 in Europe, 1,000,000 in Oceania, and 103,000 in Africa), including those with dual nationality.

There may be as many as 100,000 illegal immigrants. Taiwan is pressured by the Chinese perception that Taiwan is a "land of fortune." In 2003, the Taiwanese government cracked down on illegal Chinese immigrants, especially the smuggling of Chinese women, which had increased tenfold from 1999. As reported in the *Asia Times Online*, the phenomenon of "foreign brides" is another unique aspect of Taiwanese immigration. In 2003 about 25% of marriages involved Taiwanese men marrying foreign women. The Ministry of the Interior noted that there were about 280,000 foreign women in Taiwan married to Taiwanese nationals. More than half of these women were from China and the remainder from Southeast Asian countries, predominantly Vietnam and Indonesia. Illegal immigration of Chinese to Taiwan continued to be a concern in 2011.

8 ETHNIC GROUPS

The term "Taiwanese" is often used when referring to those Chinese who are natives of the island as distinct from the two million "mainlanders" who migrated from China after the end of World War II (1939–45). Most of the more than 20 million inhabitants of Taiwan are descendants of earlier immigrants from Fujian and Guangdong (Kwangtung) provinces in South China. They form several distinct groups. The Hakka are descendants of refugees and exiles from Guangdong who came to Taiwan before the 19th century; they are farmers and woodsmen who occupy the frontiers of settlement. The more numerous Fujians are descendants of peasants from Fujian who migrated to Taiwan in the 18th and 19th centuries; they form the bulk of the agricultural population. The aboriginal population is primarily of Indonesian origin. They live mainly in central and eastern Taiwan. They are mainly divided into nine major tribes, with the Ami, Atayal, Paiwan, and Bunun accounting for about 88%; the balance is mainly distributed among the Puyuma, Rukai, Saisiyat, Tsou, and Yami. The language and customs of the aborigines suggest a close resemblance to the Malays. About 84% of the total population is Taiwanese and 14% are mainland Chinese. About 2% of the total population is aborigine.

9 LANGUAGES

Most people on Taiwan now speak Mandarin Chinese (Peking dialect). It is the official language and is used in administration, jurisprudence, education, and, to a large extent, in commerce; it has come into increasingly common use since the 1990s. The Wade-Giles system of Romanization, which has been replaced on the mainland by the Pinyin system, is still used in Taiwan. Native Taiwanese speak a variety of southern Chinese dialects, but mainly Southern Fukienese. This is the native tongue of about 70% of the population. It has also influenced the vocabulary of Mandarin spoken on Taiwan. There is also a sizable population of Hakka speakers. This dialect is mainly spoken in Kwantung Province on the mainland. As a result of 50 years of Japanese rule, most

LOCATION: 21°45′25″ to 25°56′39″ N; 119°18′3″ to 124°34′30″ E.
TERRITORIAL SEA LIMIT: 12 miles.

Taiwanese and aborigines over the age of 60 speak or understand Japanese. Tribal peoples speak dialects of the Malay-Polynesian family, which have no written script.

10 RELIGIONS

The Chinese are traditionally eclectic in their religious beliefs. The Taiwanese folk religion is a fluid mixture of shamanism, ancestor worship, magic, ghosts and spirits, and aspects of animism. These commonly overlap with an individual's belief in Buddhism, Confucianism, Taoism, or other traditional Chinese religions. Natural phenomena have been deified, and ancestors, sages, virtuous women, and historical personalities have been given the status of gods. Some traditional religions include I Kuan Tao, Tien Ti Chiao (Heaven Emperor Religion), Tien Te Chiao (Heaven Virtue Religion), Li-ism, Hsuan Yuan Chiao (Yellow Emperor Religion), Tian Li Chiao (Tenrikyo), Universe Maitreya Emperor Religion, Hai Tze Tao, Zhonghua Sheng Chiao (Chinese Holy Religion), Da Yi Chiao (Great Changes Religion), Pre-cosmic Salvationism, and Huang Chung Chiao (Yellow Middle Religion). The CIA reported that as of 2011 Buddhists and Taoists constituted 93% of the population, Christians accounted for 4.5%, and other religions made up the remaining 2.5%.

11 TRANSPORTATION

As of 2011, Taiwan had 1,580 km (982 mi) of railroad track. The main trunk line, now electrified, links the main cities of the populous west coast between Chilung and Kaohsiung. A second trunk line, the North Link between T'aipei and Hualien on the east coast, was completed in 1979. It connects with an eastern line between Hualien and T'aitung, which was modernized in the early 1980s. Construction of the 98 km (61 mi) South Link (between T'aitung and P'ingtung) has been completed. Forming the last link in the round-the-island rail system, the South Link opened on six December 1991; it took over 11 years and US$770 million to complete.

In 2011 the CIA reported that Taiwan had a total of 41,475 km (25,771 mi) of roads, of which 41,033 km (25,497 mi) are paved. As reported by the Directorate General of Budget, Accounting and Statistics of the executive yuan of ROC, the number of registered motor vehicles in Taiwan as of the end of 2010 had reached 21,720,000.

Taiwan has five international seaports, all of them extensively modernized in the 1970s. Kaohsiung in the southwest is by far the largest, handling about two-thirds of all imports and exports. Other major ports are Chilung, on the north coast; Hualien and Suao, both on the east coast; and T'aichung, on the west coast. As of 2008 Taiwan's merchant marine consisted of 102 vessels of 1,000 GRT or more.

In 2010 there were 41 airports, of which 38 had paved runways. There were also four heliports. There are two international airports. The main one, opened in 1979, is Chiang Kai-shek International Airport, at T'aoyüan, southwest of T'aipei; the other serves Kaohsiung. T'aipei Airport handles only domestic flights. Regular domestic flights also reach Hualien, T'aitung, Chiai, T'ainan, and several other cities. Principal air service is provided by China Air Lines, Taiwan's international airline, and other international carriers, and by Taiwan's leading domestic airline, Far Eastern Air Transport.

12 HISTORY

Although Taiwan can be seen on a clear day from mainland China, ancient Chinese accounts contain few references to the island. The earliest inhabitants were Malayo-Polynesian aborigines. Historians have surmised from the brief information available in the early dynastic histories that Chinese emigration to Taiwan began as early as the T'ang dynasty (618–907). During the reign of Kublai Khan (1263–94), the first civil administration was established in the neighboring Pescadores. Taiwan itself, however, remained outside the jurisdiction of the Mongol Empire. During the Ming dynasty (1368–1644), Japanese pirates and Chinese outlaws and

refugees wrested the coastal areas from the native aborigines. The Chinese settled in the southwest region, while the Japanese occupied the northern tip of the island. Significant Chinese settlement, by immigrants from Fujian and Guangdong, began in the 17th century.

In 1517 the Portuguese sighted the island and named it Ilha Formosa (Beautiful Island). The Dutch, who were disputing the monopoly of Far Eastern trade held by the Portuguese, captured the Pescadores in 1622 and used them as a base for harassing commerce between China, Japan, and the Philippines. Two years later, the Chinese offered the Dutch a treaty that gave them certain commercial privileges if they withdrew from the Pescadores and occupied instead a trading post on Taiwan. The Dutch complied by building Fort Zeelandia and Fort Providentia in the southwestern part of the island. The Spaniards, wishing to compete, seized the northern part of Chilung in 1626 and later extended their domain to nearby Tanshui. The Japanese, constrained by the policy of national seclusion adopted by the Tokugawa Shogunate, withdrew voluntarily in 1628. The Dutch captured the Spanish settlement in 1642 and, after putting down a Chinese uprising in 1656 with the aid of the aborigines, gained complete control of the island.

While the Dutch were consolidating their hold on Taiwan, the Ming dynasty on the China mainland was overthrown by the Manchus, who established the Qing (Ch'ing) dynasty (1644–1912). Remnants of the Ming forces, led by Zheng Chenggong (Cheng Ch'eng-kung Koxinga, 1624–62), son of a Chinese pirate and a Japanese mother, decided to establish an overseas base in Taiwan. They landed on the island in 1661 and ousted the Dutch in the following year. It was not until 1683 that the Manchus succeeded in wresting Taiwan from Zheng Chenggong's successors.

From 1683 to 1885 Taiwan was administered as a part of Fujian Province. During this period, Chinese colonization proceeded steadily, as the aborigines were either assimilated into the Chinese population or pushed back into the mountains. The imperial government, however, paid scant attention to the island administration. As a result, official corruption and inefficiency often provoked armed rebellions. In the latter part of the 19th century, the strategic importance of Taiwan for the defense of the South China coast was recognized by the authorities, particularly after the French bombardment and blockade of the island in 1884 during the Sino-French War over Annam. The local administration was reorganized, and the island was made into a separate province in 1885.

Upon the conclusion of the First Sino-Japanese War in 1895, Taiwan was ceded to Japan. Refusing to submit to Japanese rule, the islanders declared their independence and established a republic, although organized resistance against the Japanese lasted only a few months. Ineffective armed resistance, chiefly by aborigines, continued. Under the Japanese, the island's agricultural resources were developed rapidly to supply the needs of the home islands and the transportation infrastructure experienced modernization. A policy of Japanization of the Taiwan population was adopted and, by 1944, 71% of children attended primary school. During World War II (1939–45), Japanese administrators began to orchestrate the island's industrialization in support of Japanese expansionism in south Asia.

In accordance with the Cairo Declaration of 1943 and the Potsdam Proclamation of 1945, Taiwan was restored to China in September 1945. The carpetbagging malpractices of the mainland Chinese officials, however, aroused the resentment of the local population. In February 1947 a police incident touched off a popular revolt, which was suppressed with bloodshed. In May more troops were brought from the mainland and the Taiwanese leadership was systematically killed. Estimates of the dead ranged from 5,000 to 50,000. On 8 December 1949, as the Chinese Communists were sweeping the Nationalist armies off the mainland, the government of the Republic of China (ROC), led by General Chiang Kai-shek (Jiang Jieshi), was officially transferred to Taiwan.

The Republic of China

With the removal of the ROC government to Taiwan, two million mainland Chinese came to the island, where they instituted an authoritarian rule under martial law. Initially Chiang Kai-shek remained myopically focused on retaking the mainland, but as the stalemate continued, the government gradually shifted its attention to industrializing Taiwan. Strong government policies contributed to steady economic progress, first in agriculture and then in industry. In the 1950s, with US aid and advice, the ROC undertook a successful program of land redistribution. Japan built an infrastructure; the Nationalists brought skills and capital; and the United States poured in excess of US$2 billion in aid by 1968. Furthermore, Japanese investment and procurement boom during the Vietnam War in the 1960s further stimulated economic growth.

In 1951 Japan signed the San Francisco Peace Treaty, thereby formally renouncing its claim to the island of Taiwan. In 1954 the ROC and the United States concluded a mutual defense treaty, and the United States and Western nations supported Taiwan possession of a UN Security Council seat, while the Eastern Bloc nations supported the People's Republic of China (PRC). Support for Taiwan's representation gradually eroded over the years, and on 25 November 1971 the General Assembly voted 75–36 (with 17 abstentions) to remove recognition from the ROC and recognize the PRC. In a significant policy reversal, the United States voted with the majority to seat the mainland government. Although maintaining full diplomatic ties with Taiwan, the United States took the occasion of President Nixon's visit to China to acknowledge, in what became known as the Shanghai Communiqué of February 1972, that "all Chinese on either side of the Taiwan Strait maintain there is but one China and that Taiwan is part of China. The United States government does not challenge that position."

By 1975 most nations shifted recognition from the ROC to the PRC. On 1 January 1979 the United States formally recognized the PRC as the sole legal government of China and severed diplomatic ties with Taiwan. It also announced the unilateral termination of the 1954 US-ROC Mutual Defense Treaty, effective 1 January 1980, and withdrew its remaining military personnel. Nonetheless, the United States continued to sell arms to Taiwan, and commercial and cultural contacts were unofficially maintained through the American Institute in Taiwan and the Coordination Council for North American Affairs. Taiwan successfully warded off worldwide political and economic isolation by maintaining a host of similar contacts with other countries.

When President Chiang Kai-shek died at age 87 on 5 April 1975, he was succeeded in office by former vice president Yen Chia-kan (Yan Jiagan). Leadership of the Nationalist Party (Kuomintang,

Guomindang—KMT) and, hence, of the government, passed to Chiang's elder son, Chiang Ching-kuo (Jiang Jingguo). The younger Chiang was elected to a six-year term as president in March 1978 and reelected in 1984. While control of the central government had remained in the hands of mainlanders in the first decades of KMT rule on Taiwan, Taiwanese Chinese increasingly won elections at local levels, and Chiang Ching-kuo instituted a policy of bringing more Taiwanese into the KMT. By the 1980s economic development had produced a new middle class, and the passage of time, together with intermarriage between mainlanders and Taiwanese, had brought a new generation for which the distinction between mainlander and Taiwanese held diminished importance. These factors contributed to popular pressure for a more democratic government. In November 1986 between 5,000 and 10,000 people demonstrated in support of an exiled dissident, Hsu Hsin-liang (Xu Xinliang), when he was not allowed to return to Taiwan. Thousands protested the 38th anniversary of martial law in May 1987. In March 1990 more than 10,000 demonstrators demanded greater democracy and direct presidential elections. This was followed in the same month by a demonstration involving some 6,000 students.

In 1987 martial law was revoked, and with that press restrictions were eased, citizens were allowed to visit relatives on the mainland, and opposition political parties formed. Then in January 1988 Chiang Ching-kuo died, and was succeeded as president by the vice president, Lee Teng-hui (Li Denghui, b. 1923). Lee, a protégé of Chiang Ching-kuo, was a native Taiwanese. In March 1990 the national assembly reelected Lee as president for a six-year term. In July he was also named Chairman of the Nationalist Party by the party congress.

In the early 1990s, as Taiwan increasingly opened its political system to greater democracy, the KMT's corrupt practices were revealed. However, after the 1992 legislative elections, the KMT emerged victorious, as it still controlled most national media and opposition parties failed to mobilize voters. Vote-buying and other forms of fraud were also widespread. By the 1995 elections, however, the political environment changed because the KMT lost control of the media. Furthermore, the control yuan, the branch of government responsible for oversight, began to assert its independence by investigating KMT corruption. In local elections of 1994, for instance, state prosecutors convicted more than one-third of 858 city and county representatives for vote-buying. Just prior to the 1995 national elections, it was revealed that the Minister of Justice had evidence of another extensive ring of vote buying. The KMT took 54% of the vote (83 seats), its lowest majority ever and its major rival, the Democratic People's Party (DPP) obtained 54 seats and the Chinese New Party (CNP) captured 21 with 6 going to various independents. The constitution was rewritten in 1995, calling for direct election of the president with the first election slated to be held in 1996.

Amid these democratic reforms, Taiwan faced a major international crisis in 1995 when President Lee was given a US visa to visit Cornell University, his alma mater. China objected vociferously and threatened military action against Taiwan. In a show of support for Taiwan and in opposition to PR China's launching of missiles into Taiwan's territorial waters, the United States dispatched a naval force to the region, which further irritated PR China.

Prior to the presidential elections of March 1996, the formerly united KMT began to splinter. Dissidents within the party and those who had previously left the KMT announced their intentions to run against Lee, who had been chosen by a party plenum in August 1995 as the official KMT candidate. Primary among these were Lin Yang-gang, a former judicial yuan president and current vice-chairman of the KMT, and Chien Li-an, president of the control yuan and former Minister of National Defense. Campaigning was intense, with scandals being revealed on all sides, but Lee received a resounding 54% compared to 21% for his nearest competitor.

President Lee was criticized by political opponents in 1997 as an increased wave of crime swept the island. In May 1997 more than 50,000 protestors gathered in the capital protesting the government's lack of action on issues of crime. Multiple members of the executive yuan resigned and Lee reshuffled his cabinet. However, late in 1997 the KMT suffered severe losses in local and magistrate elections. The main opposition, the DPP, won 12 of the 23 constituency positions contested and led to the reorganization of the KMT following the resignation of the party's secretary general. In 1998 the KMT recovered in the next set of elections, only to suffer a setback in summer elections that year. As the economy weakened from the Asian financial crisis, the government sought to deregulate the economy and decrease taxes. Relations with PR China again worsened as Taiwan prepared for presidential elections in 2000. On 18 March 2000 Chen Shui-bian, the DPP candidate and a former dissident leader imprisoned for his opposition to the KMT, was elected president in a hotly contested race. He obtained 39.3% of the vote and Lien Chan (KMT) captured 23.1%, while ex-KMT businessman James Soong ran as an independent and garnered 36.8%. Leading up to and following the election, the PRC warned the Taiwanese that the election of a pro-independence DPP candidate would lead to possible military action. In his inaugural address in May, Chen stated that he would not declare independence as long as China did not attack the island. He said he would not call for a referendum on independence, nor abolish Taiwan's plan for an eventual reunion with the PRC. China responded by saying that Chen had evaded the question as to whether he considered Taiwan to be part of China.

In April 2001 the Dalai Lama met with President Chen during a visit which drew strong opposition from China. That month, the United States announced it would sell submarines, warships, and antisubmarine aircraft to Taiwan, but not the Aegis naval combat radar system, as Taiwan had requested. China protested the sale, and US president George W. Bush pledged to come to Taiwan's aid in the event of a Chinese invasion. That November, Taiwan lifted a 50-year ban on direct trade and investment with China.

In August 2002, President Chen referred to Taiwan and China as two countries, and stated he supported legislation for a referendum to be held on independence, contrasting with his inaugural pledge not to hold a referendum.

President Chen was able to reduce the amount of corruption, bribery, and organized crime that pervaded Taiwanese politics prior to the end of his first term. However, allegations of vote buying and electoral inconsistencies remained. The 2004 presidential elections resulted in a surprising electoral result with Chen emerging victorious over the opposition by 0.2%. Hours before the vote, Chen and his vice president, Annette Lu, were shot, although not fatally. The opposition blamed the loss of the presidential election on sympathy votes gained by the shooting and claimed the shooting was staged. A commission was set up in late 2004 to investigate the shooting. Starting in May 2006 President Chen and his family were accused of a series of scandals involving bribery, embezzlement, and insider trading. Chen's approval ratings dropped down to 5.8% in the same month. In November 2006 the Taiwan High Court filed charges of embezzlement and forgery of documents against Chen's wife, Wu Shu-chen. The prosecutors claimed to have enough evidence to charge President Chen with corruption as well, but the sitting president was protected by presidential immunity. On 11 September 2009, nearly four months after Chen stepped down as the president of Taiwan, he was sentenced to life in prison for corruption, fraud, and money laundering. On 11 June 2010 the High Court reduced Chen's life sentence to 20 years. Chen was the first president to receive a prison sentence in the history of ROC. His defenders claimed that Chen's charges were politically motivated.

In February 2006 Taiwan abolished its National Unification Council, a body that was established in 1990 to bring about reunification with the mainland. Although the council had not met under President Chen's administration since 2000, and was a relatively toothless body, China reacted harshly. China's Taiwan Affairs department stated: "The escalated secessionist push of Chen Shui-bian will certainly trigger a serious crisis across the Taiwan Straits and destroy peace and stability in the Asia Pacific region." In August 2007 the government applied for membership in the United Nations under the name Taiwan for the first time, instead of as the official Republic of China. The application was refused.

In 2005 a constitutional amendment was passed that decreased the legislative yuan to about half, from 225 to 113 seats. In the January 2008 elections, the first to be held under this new structure, the Nationalist Party won an absolute majority of 81 seats to the Democratic Progressive Party's 27 seats, with the remaining five seats going to independent and small party candidates.

Ma Ying-jeou won the March 2008 presidential election by a substantial majority and took office on May 20, 2008. In 2009 he was reelected as chairman of the KMT. In his inaugural speech, Ma announced his cross-strait policy to be "no reunification, no independence, no use of force," which is to retain the status quo across the strait. Despite his claim that he would not discuss unification with PRC during his presidential term, Ma was criticized by his political opponents for steering Taiwan toward an "eventual unification." On 5 December 2008 Taiwan and mainland China resumed direct shipping, air, and postal links after a six decade ban. Also during Ma's presidency, Taiwan was opened to tourists, students, and stock investors from mainland China for the first time. Ma was reelected in January 2012.

13GOVERNMENT

The government of the Republic of China in T'aipei claims to be the central government of all of China. Its constitution was drafted by a constitutional convention at Nanjing (Nanking) on 15 November 1946; the constitution was adopted on 25 December 1946 and promulgated by the national government on 1 January 1947. All governmental powers originally emanated from a national assembly; however, the powers of the assembly have been curtailed. The first assembly, which was elected in November 1947, had

2,961 delegates, selected on the basis of regional and occupational representation. The original delegates held their seats "indefinitely," until control of the mainland could be reestablished. Since 1969, the number of seats gradually increased with the addition of new seats for Taiwan. In April 1990, President Lee Teng-hui revoked the emergency decree of 1948 which had allowed the 1,947 deputies to remain in office and the "indefinite" deputies had to retire by December 1991. With the promulgation of constitutional amendments on 25 April 2000, the assembly's functions are limited to amending the constitution and altering the national territory after a public announcement by the legislative yuan. In addition, the assembly may impeach the president or vice president within three months of a petition initiated by the legislative yuan. The assembly's 300 delegates are selected by proportional representation of the political parties in the legislative yuan.

The president is the head of state and of the executive yuan, which functions as a cabinet. Previously, the assembly chose the president. After amendments to the constitution in 1992, however, citizens now elect the president by direct popular vote. The president may serve a maximum of two consecutive four-year terms. Under the president, there are five government branches known as yuans (councils or departments): legislative, executive, control, examination, and judicial. The legislative yuan, elected by popular vote, is the highest lawmaking body. As in the assembly, many members of the 1948 legislative yuan held their seats until 1991.

The executive yuan, comparable to the cabinet in other countries, is the highest administrative organ in the government. There are eight ministries, two commissions, and a number of subordinate organs under the executive yuan. The premier-the president of the executive yuan-is appointed by the president of the republic, with the consent of the legislative yuan. The president is empowered to compel the premier to resign by refusing to sign decrees or orders presented by the latter for promulgation.

The legislative yuan is the highest legislative organ of the state. It has a binding vote of no confidence which would lead to the dissolution of the executive yuan. Of its 225 members, 168 are chosen by universal suffrage and the remaining members are appointed through a system of proportional representation; members serve three-year terms. The number of seats in the legislature was reduced from 225 to 113 beginning with the election in 2008.

The control yuan, the highest supervisory organ, exercises censorial and audit powers over the government and may impeach officials. It also supervises the execution of the government budget. It has 29 members, all of whom serve six-year terms and are appointed by the president with the consent of the legislative yuan.

The examination yuan is the equivalent of a civil service commission. It consists of two ministries. The Ministry of Examination appoints government personnel through competitive examination. The Ministry of Civil Service registers, classifies, promotes, transfers, retires, and pensions civil servants. Its president, vice president, and 19 commissioners are appointed by the president of the republic with the consent of the control yuan.

14 POLITICAL PARTIES

The Chinese Nationalist Party, better known as the Kuomintang–KMT, was, until 2000, the dominant political party in Taiwan. The teachings of Sun Yat-sen (Sun Zhongshan), which stress nationalism, democracy, and people's livelihood, form the ideology of the party. After the fall of the mainland to the Communists in 1949, a reform committee was organized to chart a new program for the party.

The KMT's organization is similar to that of the Chinese Communist Party. The basic unit is the cell, which represents neighborhoods. The next levels include the district, county, and provincial congresses and committees. The highest levels include the national congress and the central committee. The congress delegates serve four-year terms and are charged with the tasks of amending the party charter, determining the party platform and other important policies. It also elects the party chairman and the central committee members, and approves candidates nominated by the chairman to serve as vice chairmen and members of the central advisory council. When the congress is in recess, the supreme party organ is the central committee, which holds a plenary session every year.

The central standing committee, which represents the central committee when that body is not in session, is the most influential organ in the KMT. The day-to-day affairs of the party are managed by the secretariat. All organizations within the KMT are funded by profits from party-owned and operated business enterprises, ranging from newspapers and TV stations to electrical appliance companies and computer firms.

At the party's 14th congress, held in August 1993, significant changes to the conduct of party affairs were made. It decided that the party chairman was to be elected by the congress through secret ballot. President Lee Teng-hui won 83% of the votes cast and was reelected chairman of the party. In addition, four vice-chairmen were added to the central committee after being nominated by the chairman and approved by the Congress. It also decided that the chairman would appoint only 10 to 15 of the 31 members of the standing committee, with the remaining members elected by the central committee. Finally, it decided to hold the congress every two years instead of four years.

Under martial law, from 1949 through 1986, the formation of new political parties was illegal, although there were two nominal, previously formed parties. Non-KMT candidates ran as independents or "nonpartisans," with increasing success by the end of the 1970s. In September 1986 a group of nonpartisans formed a new opposition party, the Democratic Progressive Party (DPP), which had an orientation toward the Taiwanese population and advocated self-determination. Although technically illegal, the DPP's candidates took 22% of the vote in the December 1986 elections, winning 12 out of 73 contested seats in the legislative yuan; the KMT won 59. The lifting of martial law in 1987 made the formation of new parties legal, although a new security law continued to restrict political activity. In the first fully competitive, democratic national elections, in December 1992 the KMT won 53% and the DPP 31% of the votes for the legislative yuan. Before the 1995 legislative elections, the KMT began to splinter and in 1994 the Chinese New Party (CNP) was formed by KMT defectors who favored strengthened ties with the mainland. In the 1995 balloting, however, the KMT was able to maintain its majority, winning 83 of the 164 seats in the legislative yuan. The DPP took 54, the CNP took 21 and six seats were won by independents. In the national assembly (334 seats) the KMT took 183, the DPP 99, the CNP 46, and six were won by others.

The DPP's organizational structure closely resembles that of the KMT. The DPP's national congress elects members to the central executive committee and to the central advisory committee. The executive committee in turn elects the members of the central standing committee. Its leader is President Chen Shui-bian. At the party's sixth congress, held in April and May of 1994, a two-tier primary system was initiated under which ordinary members of the DPP voted for candidates in one primary election and party cadres vote in a second primary. The results of the two would then be combined, with equal weight given to both. At the second plenary meeting of the sixth congress held in March 1995, the nomination process for the presidential and gubernatorial candidates was modified to add open primaries for DPP members and nonmembers. It was further decided at the meeting that the party chairman would be elected directly by all members of the party starting in 1998. What most distinguishes the DPP from the two other major parties is its support of Taiwan independence, or the permanent political separation of Taiwan from the Chinese mainland. Although the DPP has incorporated Taiwan independence into its official platform, the urgency accorded to its realization is a source of factional contention within the party.

The Chinese New Party (NP) was formed in August 1993, shortly before the KMT's 14th congress, by a group of KMT reformers who broke away from the party in protest of the undemocratic practices of the KMT. The NP adopted an anticorruption platform and championed social justice. The goal of the NP was to attract voters who were dissatisfied with the performance of the ruling KMT and opposed to the DPP's advocacy of Taiwan independence.

In 2005 a constitutional amendment was passed that decreased the seats in the legislative yuan to about half, from 225 to 113 seats. In the 12 January 2008 elections, the first to be held under this new structure, the KMT won an absolute majority of 81 seats with 53.5% of the vote. The DPP took 38.2% of the vote for 27 seats. The Non-Partisan Solidarity Union, established in 2004, won 2.4% of the vote and three seats. The People's First Party gained one seat with less than 1% of the vote. In 2011, a total of 175 political parties had registered with the Ministry of the Interior.

Ma won the March 2008 presidential election by a substantial majority and took office on May 20, 2008. He was reelected in January 2012.

15 LOCAL GOVERNMENT

The Taiwan provincial government holds jurisdiction over the main island of Taiwan, 21 smaller islands in adjacent waters, and the 64 islands of the Penghu (Pescadores) group. The provincial capital is located at Zhongxin New Village, Nantou County. The province is divided into 12 county administrative areas (*hsien*) and three municipalities under the direct jurisdiction of the provincial government. In addition, T'aipei (since 1967), Kaohsiung (since 1979), New Taipei (since 2010), Taichung (since 2010), and Tainan (since 2010) are self-governing special municipalities under the direct jurisdiction of the executive yuan. Subdivisions of the county are the township (*chen*), the rural district or group of villages (*hsiang*), and the precinct. Quemoy and Matsu are administered by the military. At the local level and under the Taiwan provincial government, there are three cities—Chilung, Hsinchu,

and Chiayi —and 12 counties, and under each county there are county municipalities.

The province is headed by a governor who is nominated by the president of the executive yuan and appointed by the president of the republic. Department heads and members of the provincial council are recommended by the governor for appointment by the executive yuan. The governor is the ex officio chairman of the appointed provincial council, the policy making body, and holds veto power over its resolutions. The provincial government can issue ordinances and regulations for the administration of the province as long as they do not conflict with laws of the central government. The head of a municipality is a mayor, who is directly elected for a term of four years.

The provincial assembly, an elected body, meets for two yearly sessions of two months each. Nominally it possesses broad legislative powers; however, its prerogatives are circumscribed by a provision in its organic law that in the event of a disagreement between the provincial executive and the assembly, the former may request reconsideration. Should the assembly uphold its original resolution, the provincial executive may submit the dispute to the executive yuan for final judgment. The executive yuan may dissolve the provincial assembly and order a new election if it holds that the assembly is acting contrary to national policy.

At the end of 1996 a national development conference was convened to streamline local government operations. The county government is headed by an elected magistrate (*hsien-chang*) and the municipal government by a mayor (*shih-chang*). Each county or municipality has a representative body called the *hsien*, or municipal assembly. Further down are the councils and assemblies of townships and rural districts, each headed by a chief officer. All of these officials are elected by universal suffrage of citizens over age 20.

On 25 December 2010 Taipei County (renamed New Taipei City), Taichung City (encompassing Taichung City and Taichung County), and Tainan City (encompassing Tainan City and Tainan County) were upgraded as special municipalities; meanwhile, Kaohsiung County was merged with Kaohsiung City, which was already a special municipality.

16 JUDICIAL SYSTEM

The judicial yuan is Taiwan's highest judicial organ. It interprets the constitution and other laws and decrees, adjudicates administrative suits, and disciplines public functionaries. The president and vice president of the judicial yuan are nominated and appointed by the president of the republic, with the consent of the legislative yuan. They, together with 15 grand justices, form the Council of Grand Justices, which is charged with the power and responsibility of interpreting the constitution, laws, and ordinances. The judicial system is based on the principle of three trials in three grades of courts: district court, high court, and the Supreme Court of the ROC. The supreme court, the highest tribunal of the land, consists of a number of civil and criminal divisions, each of which is formed by a presiding judge and four associate judges. The judges are appointed for life.

In 1993 a separate constitutional court was established. Staffed by the then-16 grand justices of the judicial yuan, but with the judicial yuan excluded from the court, the new court was charged with resolving constitutional disputes, regulating the activities of political parties and accelerating the democratization process.

There is no right to trial by jury, but the right to a fair public trial is protected by law and respected in practice. Defendants are afforded a right to counsel and to a right to appeal to the high court and the supreme court in cases in which the sentence exceeds three years. Those sentenced to three years or less may appeal only to the high court. The supreme court automatically reviews all sentences to life imprisonment or death. There is also an administrative court.

In late 2004 the legislative yuan approved constitutional changes, effective 2008, which included halving the number of seats in the legislative yuan and extending all legislators' terms from three to four years. Taiwan employs a quota system which allows for minorities and aboriginal persons to gain access into government positions. Although banned by law, minorities and aboriginal persons claim to face discrimination in the socio-economic realm.

The judicial system is based on civil law and Taiwan accepts compulsory jurisdiction of the International Court of Justice. Military service is mandatory for Taiwanese males.

Taiwanese citizens are able to organize, protest and gain access to any type of material without fear of reprisal. Trade unions are independent and collective bargaining is legal. The law does restrict the right to strike by ordering mediation sessions and banning work stoppages while mediation is in progress.

17 ARMED FORCES

Two years' military service is compulsory for all male citizens from 19 to 35 years of age. The International Institute for Strategic Studies reports that armed forces in Taiwan totaled 290,000 members in 2011. The force is comprised of 200,000 from the army, 45,000 from the navy, and 45,000 members of the air force. Defense spending totaled US$12.3 billion and accounted for 3.1% of gross domestic product (GDP).

18 INTERNATIONAL COOPERATION

The ROC, a charter member of the UN, became the first government to lose its recognition from that body following a General Assembly vote on 25 November 1971 to recognize the PRC as the sole legitimate representative of China. The ROC subsequently lost its membership in most UN bodies, as well as in several other international organizations-usually with its place taken by the PRC. Taiwan is a member of APEC, the Asian Development Bank, the International Chamber of Commerce, the International Confederation of Free Trade Unions, the World Confederation of Labor, and the World Trade Organization.

As of 2011 Taiwan had formal diplomatic ties with only 23 countries. The government claims to have substantive trade relations with more than 140 countries and territories, however. In November 2001 Taiwan lifted a 50-year ban on direct trade and investment with China. On 5 December 2008 Taiwan and mainland China resumed direct shipping, air, and postal links after a six decade ban.

In March 2009 the Chinese government offered to begin peace talks with Taiwan. The Taiwanese government has agreed to a number of economic deals, but officials were not ready to commit to a promise of political reunification based on the "one China" principle favored by the mainland.

In the wake of the H1N1 (Swine Flu) pandemic scare in April 2009, the Chinese agreed to allow the Taiwanese government to participate as an observer at the World Health Assembly of the World Health Organization (WHO), a body of the United Nations. During the 2003 SARS outbreak, mainland authorities had refused to allow WHO to provide direct assistance to Taiwan, a move that further strained relationships between mainland authorities and Taiwanese independence advocates. The Taiwanese government agreed to attend the 2009 WHO assembly using the name Chinese Taipei instead of its legal name of the Republic of China or Taiwan.

Taiwan is involved in several land disputes, most notably a complex dispute with China, Malaysia, Philippines, Vietnam, and possibly Brunei over the Spratly Islands. The Paracel Islands are occupied by China, but claimed by Taiwan and Vietnam. In 2003 China and Taiwan became more vocal in rejecting both of Japan's claims to the uninhabited islands of the Senkaku-shoto (Diaoyu Tai). Taiwan also disputes Japan's unilaterally declared claim to the exclusive economic zone in the East China Sea.

19 ECONOMY

Under the Japanese, the island was developed as a major source of foodstuffs for Japan. Production of rice and sugar increased rapidly, but little effort was directed toward industrialization until after 1937. Immediately after World War II, a number of factors—including repatriation of Japanese technicians, dismantling of industrial plants, and lack of fertilizer for agriculture—caused a rapid deterioration of the economy, which was aggravated by the influx of refugees from the mainland. The situation improved after 1949 with the removal of the ROC government to Taiwan. The arrival of technical and experienced personnel and capital equipment from the mainland facilitated the island's economic rehabilitation. Currency and tax reforms stabilized the monetary situation. The supply of fertilizer from the United States and a land reform program aided the revival of agricultural production.

Energetic government measures in the form of successive four-year plans, at first supplemented by US aid, resulted in substantial economic progress. In the first decade (1951–60) the stress was on agricultural development and the establishment of textile and other labor-intensive industries. From 1961 to 1970 the promotion of industrial products for export was emphasized. In 1963 Taiwan registered its first favorable trade balance. By 1965 the economy appeared stable enough to warrant the cessation of US economic aid programs. Medium and light industry led the expansion, with striking gains registered in electronics, household goods, and chemicals. The decade 1971–80 saw the development of such capital-intensive industries as steel, machinery, machine tools, and motor vehicle assembly. Such industries, based on imports of raw materials, were encouraged through massive government support for major infrastructural improvements in roads, railroads, ports, and electricity. During the 1980s emphasis was placed on the development of high-technology industries. As a result, between 1981 and 1991 the share of high-technology industries in total manufactures increased from 20% to 29%, making Taiwan the seventh-largest producer of computer hardware on the global market. The 1990s brought an influx of capital-rich investment, especially after 1996 when the first democratic elections were held. High-technology industries accounted for over 73% of total manufacturing and 67% of exports in 1999. Growth accelerated in the late 1990s, measuring 4.6% in 1998, 5.4% in 1999 and 6% in 2000, spurred by the boom in the PC and IT industries. Exports played an increasing role, accounting for 47.8% of GDP in 1998, 48.3% in 1999 and 54% in 2000. Growth in high-tech exports peaked at 54% in the third quarter of 2000.

Taiwan's GNP advanced at an average annual rate of 9% in real terms between 1952 and 1980. In contrast to Taiwan's industry-led economic growth of previous decades, since the late 1980s the country has undergone a shift towards a services-dominated economy.

Though still expanding in absolute terms, industry's share of the GDP declined from 52% in 1986 to 31.1% in 2010. Agriculture has continued to claim only a small share of the economy, making up 1.4% of the GDP in 2010. A lack of domestic resources hampers the development of agriculture and primary industries. An earthquake in September of 1999 caused major damages to Taiwanese lives and property, but reconstruction was complete by 2000. What affected the economy more was the burst of the dot.com bubble beginning in late 2000, and the global slowdown in 2001, aggravated by the aftermath of the 11 September 2001 terrorist attacks on the United States. Taiwan experienced its first recorded decline in real GDP, -2.2%. Recovery began in the last quarter of 2001, and in 2002 real growth of 3.2% was recorded; by 2007 GDP annual growth had reached a healthy 5.7%. Inflation generally fell in the late 1990s, from 3.1% in 1996 to 0% in 2001, and was reported at 1.8% in 2007. Unemployment, by contrast, increased steadily, from 2.6% in 1996 to 5.2% in 2002, but stood at 3.9% in 2007.

The global recession of 2008–09 had a significant effect on the economy as world demand for export products dropped. Damage caused by Typhoon Morakot added to the economic crisis. In August 2009 the unemployment rate had risen to 6%. In November 2009 after posting 14 consecutive months of contraction in global demand for its exports, analysts forecast a surge in Taiwanese exports for the month. Strong Chinese demand for high-tech electronics contributed to the rosy forecast, as did the slow rate at which export demand fell in October 2009, the slowest in more than one year. Government reports released in February 2010, however, showed a strong rebound in Taiwan's economy. Despite contracting 1.9% by year-end 2009, Taiwan's economy grew at a better-than-expected 9.2% in the final quarter of 2009. Those numbers were believed to be fed by stimulus-inspired demand from mainland China, where consumers indulged in the high-tech gadgetry that remains Taiwan's specialty. Also, the closer cross-strait economic relationship that Taiwan had developed with mainland China since President Ma Ying-jeou took office in 2008 opened the island to greater opportunities. As of 2011 the GDP rate of change in Taiwan was 10.8%. Inflation stood at 1%, and unemployment was reported at 5.2%.

20INCOME

The CIA estimated that in 2010 the GDP of Taiwan was US$821.8 billion. The per capita GDP was estimated at US$35,700. The annual growth rate of GDP was 10.8%. The average inflation rate was 1%. It was estimated that agriculture accounted for 1.4% of GDP, industry 31.1%, and services 67.5%. The World Bank estimated that Taiwan, with 0.37% of the world's population, accounted for 1.07% of the world's GDP. By comparison, the United States, with

4.85% of the world's population, accounted for 22.51% of world GDP.

As of 2011 the most recent study by the World Bank reported that actual individual consumption in Taiwan was 66.1% of GDP and accounted for 1.02% of world consumption. By comparison, the United States accounted for 25.44% of world individual consumption. The World Bank estimated that 11.3% of Taiwan's individual consumption was spent on food and beverages, 13.7% on housing and household furnishings, 2.4% on clothes, 5.5% on health, 6.7% on transportation, 2.1% on communications, 5.5% on recreation, 5.0% on restaurants and hotels, and 6.7% on miscellaneous goods and services and purchases from abroad.

It was estimated that in 2010 about 1.16% of the population subsisted on an income below the poverty line established by Taiwan's government.

21LABOR

The civilian labor force in Taiwan was last estimated at 11.07 million in 2010. The share of persons employed in farming, forestry, and fishing has been declining steadily, while the share of the workforce employed in mining, manufacturing, construction, and utilities has increased. As of 2010 only 5.2% of the labor force was employed in agriculture; 35.9% was employed in industry, and 58.8% in the service sector. Unemployment was reported at 5.2%

The law provides for an 8-hour day (which may be extended to 11 hours for men and 10 for women) and a 5-day workweek; overtime is paid at 40–100% above the regular wage. Most large firms give allowances for transportation, meals, housing, and other benefits, which can increase base pay by 60–80%. A minimum of one week's vacation is provided after a year's employment, and there are 14 or 15 other paid holidays. As of October 2011 the monthly minimum wage was US$619. This amount provides a decent standard of living in rural areas but is not sufficient for urban life.

Trade unions are weak and cannot be called unions in the real sense of the term, for the law does not provide for effective collective bargaining and also prohibits strikes, shutdowns, and walkouts in vital industries. The trade unions, organized under government supervision, tend to be used for carrying out government policies, but they carry on a considerable amount of welfare work. At of the end of 2007 there were 4,574 registered unions in Taiwan with over three million members. The minimum age for employment is 15. Current occupational health and safety regulations provide only minimal protection and have a mixed record of enforcement.

22AGRICULTURE

About 24% of the land is under cultivation. Although still important as both an export earner and a domestic food source, agriculture has fallen far from the preeminent position it long held in the Taiwan economy. High production costs and low return have driven much of the agricultural work force away to industry. Part-time farming households have accounted for over 80% of all farming households since 1980.

Rice, the principal food crop, is grown along the western plain and in the south. There were 255,415 hectares of rice fields in Taiwan as of 2009, when more than 1.58 million tons of rice were produced for a production value of US$1 billion. Taiwan's annual rice production exceeds demand; the island's per capita rice consumption has declined by over 50% since the mid-1970s due to changing diet preferences. Other food crops include sweet potatoes, bananas, peanuts, soybeans, and wheat. Sugar, pineapples, citrus fruits, crude tea, and asparagus are plantation-grown and are the principal cash and export crops. Small amounts of Taiwan's world-famous oolong tea, cotton, tobacco, jute, and sisal are also produced. A fast-rising industry, mushroom canning, led to the development of mushroom cultivation, a specialty crop well suited to Taiwan since it is labor-intensive and requires little space and small investment. Betel nuts have become Taiwan's second most valuable cash crop after rice. In 2008 betel nut production totaled 144,195 tons.

Generally, Taiwanese agriculture is characterized by high yields, irrigation, terracing, multiple cropping, intertillage, and extensive use of fertilizers. Farms are small, averaging 1.1 hectares (2.7 acres) of cultivable land per farm family. Mechanization, once confined largely to sugarcane and rice production, is increasing rapidly as a result of government subsidies and other incentives. Since there is an oversupply of rice, the government has encouraged farmers to grow soybeans, wheat, and corn, which are more profitable. The growing scarcity of land on Taiwan is causing serious disagreements over land resources between agricultural, industrial, and housing interests.

23 ANIMAL HUSBANDRY

Pastures in Taiwan occupy only 0.1% of the total land area. Hog production is Taiwan's most valuable farm product. In 2009 Taiwan's pork production was valued at TWD65.9 billion (US$2.1 billion). In 1997 a major outbreak of hoof and mouth disease affected 6,147 hog farms. As a result, one-third of the hog population had to be destroyed. The government helped compensate pig farmers with US$1.1 billion in low interest loans. Livestock production declined by 13% from 1996 to 2001, and fell another 3.9% from 2001 to 2004. After 2007 livestock production began to regain its status. In 2009 the livestock sector production reached TWD142 billion (US$4.7 billion). Chickens and ducks are raised by most households.

24 FISHING

Production of fish products totaled 1.1million tons in 2009, valued at TWD85.9 billion (US$2.8 billion). Exports of seafood products were US$2 billion, accounting for 37% of Taiwan's total agricultural export. Squid, skipjack and yellowfin tuna, chub mackerel, shark, and milkfish are the main species of the marine catch. Deep-sea fishing, which was practically wiped out by World War II (1939–45), has shown strong gains following heavy investments in vessels and harbors. Milkfish, tilapias, clams, oysters, and eels are the main species farmed. While marine culture output remained relatively stable, inland fisheries production continued to grow. In 2009 the inland aquacultural area covered 41,013 hectares (101,344 acres), with production of 286,300 tons, valued at TWD28.3 billion (US$933 million).

25 FORESTRY

Native stands of cypress, fir, camphor, and oak were cut to help fund Japan's development when Taiwan was under Japanese imperial rule (1895–1945). Logging provided hard currency exports for the Nationalist Chinese regime after its retreat from mainland China to the island in 1949. Nearly 60% of Taiwan is covered with forests, with the total forest area estimated at 2.1 million hectares (5.2 million acres) in 2009. The geographical distribution was highly unbalanced. While 93% of the mountain areas in central Taiwan are covered by forest, only one-third of flat land is forested.

The roundwood harvest was estimated at 27,891 cu m (0.98 million cu ft) in 2009 (90% softwood, valued at TWD416.2 million/US$13.7 million). Forestry production declined by 20.6% between 2004 and 2009; domestic timber production only meets 1% of total demand. Taiwan's timber production has declined since the 1980s due to local labor shortages, intensifying environmental concerns, and logging restrictions. In 1992, Taiwan banned all logging from nonplantation forests. Principal timbers are oak, cedar, and hemlock. Taiwan is a major furniture exporter that relies heavily on imported wood products to support the industry.

26 MINING

Mining accounts for only 0.1% by value of Taiwan's total industrial output. Iron and steel lead the metal production sector on the island. In 2009 Taiwan ranked 12th in the world and 5th in Asia in crude steel production. Value-added products made from aluminum and copper are dependent upon scrap or imported metals. Dolomite, limestone, and marble are the most important nonfuel mineral commodities. The western third of the island has adequate amounts of sand, gravel, and limestone for building purposes, although there has been a recent slowdown in the construction sector. The demand for mineral products has increased over the years, while local supplies have dwindled. Mineral production in 2009 included (in metric tons): dolomite, 70,000, down from 104,000 in 2008; limestone, 232,000, up from 227,000 in 2008; marble, 22,186, down from 25,811 in 2008; and serpentine, 242,000, down from 264,000 in 2008. Taiwan also produces hydraulic cement, fire clay, feldspar, precipitated gypsum, lime, mica, marine salt, caustic soda, soda ash, sulfur, and talc.

27 ENERGY AND POWER

The island's total installed power capacity reached 40,823 MW as of July 2010. Natural gas-fueled generators accounted for 37% of the total capacity, coal-fired stations 29%, and nuclear reactors 13%. Taiwan imports 99% of its energy. The CIA reported in 2009 that Taiwan produced 229.1 billion kWh of electricity (ranked 18th in the world) and consumed 220.8 billion kWh. Nuclear power has taken an increasingly significant role in the electricity supply. In 2011 Taiwan had six nuclear reactors operating at three plants with a combined installed capacity of 5,307 MW, with two advanced reactors under construction.

Power is controlled by the Taiwan Power Co. (Taipower), a government-owned corporation, but some enterprises generate power for their own consumption. The principal sources for consumption in 2009 were oil (52.13%), coal (30.66%) and nuclear energy (8.44%). In 2010 Taiwan consumed 1.001 million barrels of oil per day, ranking 21st in the world. Oil is imported from the Middle East, Indonesia, Brunei, and Venezuela. River basin development is being vigorously pushed for irrigation, flood control, and power generation. In addition, experiments during the late 1970s and 1980s concentrated on developing Taiwan's geothermal potential.

Taiwan has very limited coal resources, and domestic coal production stopped in 2000 due to government policies designed to close unsafe coal mines, high production costs, and reduced domestic reserves. Taiwan meets all of its current coal consumption with imports, primarily from Indonesia, Australia and PR China. Natural gas production amounted to 310 million cu m in 2009, while crude oil production was an estimated 26,680 barrels per day in 2010. As of 1 Jan 2010 proven natural gas reserves amounted to 6.229 billion cu m.

28 INDUSTRY

Under the Japanese, about 90% of the industrial enterprises were owned by the government or by Japanese corporations with government assistance. After the restoration of Taiwan to China in 1945, the ROC government took over these enterprises. Some were sold to private owners, and the rest were grouped under the management of 18 public corporations, operated either by the national government or by the provincial government, or by both. Added to the confiscated enemy properties were public enterprises evacuated from the mainland. As a result, government-operated enterprises came to dominate Taiwanese industry. Since 1992 Taiwan authorities made efforts to reduce the size of the public sector. These efforts gained momentum after democratization in 1996. By 2002 the government had sold equity shares and reduced public ownership to below 50% in 23 state-owned enterprises (SOEs), mostly banks and insurance companies, but including a steel mill and one fertilizer company. In 1998 and 1999 privatization announcements included the Chinese Petroleum Corp., Chunghwa Telecom Corp., and Taiwan Power Corp. Plans for privatization have been announced for SOEs involved in power, oil, tobacco, wine, railway transport, mining and telecommunications. Since 1998 a number of construction projects—the north–south high speed railway, the mass rapid transit (MRT) systems in Kaohsiung (KMRT) and the bridge between T'aipei and the CKS Airport—were given to private firms, including many foreign companies, on a build-operate-transfer (BOT) basis.

The average annual growth rate in manufacturing was 13% during 1953–62, 20% during 1963–72, 9.6% during 1973–85 and 5.9% for 1986–92. The private sector outpaced the public sector during each of these periods. The number of workers in manufacturing rose from 362,000 in 1952 to 736,000 in 1967 and to almost 2.8 million in 1987. By 1992, however, this number declined to about 2.6 million as the rapidly expanding service sector absorbed more of the workforce. Manufacturing for export has been encouraged by the establishment of free trade export processing zones (EPZs) in the Kaohsiung harbor area, at Nantze (near Kaohsiung), and at T'aichung. Since the late 1980s rising production costs and a 40% appreciation of the New Taiwan dollar have prompted many export-oriented companies to relocate their manufacturing plants to mainland China and Southeast Asia. In particular; labor-intensive industries, such as toys, footwear, umbrellas, and garments, have relocated. In 1986 industrial production accounted for nearly half of GDP. By 1997 this figure had dropped to about 35% and in 2000, it was an estimated 31.9%, including manufacturing at 26.4% of GDP; construction at 3.4% and electricity, gas and water at 2.1% of GDP. In 2009 industrial production accounted for 28.8% of GDP, with manufacturing accounting for 24.8%. The industrial production growth rate in 2010 was estimated to be 26.4%.

Production rose spectacularly after the end of World War II (1939–45), especially between 1952 and the early 1980s. Slower economic growth since the mid-1980s, and greater investment emphasis on heavy and high-technology industries as well as services, has resulted in declining production figures for traditional manufactures such as cotton yarn and fertilizer. Labor intensive industries have gradually been replaced by capital and technology intensive industries. In 2009 electronics and information technology (IT) products accounted for 34.2% of industrial output. The two largest made-to-order computer chip manufacturers are Taiwan Semiconductor Manufacturing Company (TSMC), Taiwan's second-largest company, and United Microelectronics Company (UMC). In 2009 Taiwan's global share in motherboards was 92.4%; notebook computers, 95.3%; Mask ROM, 94%; cable modems, 88.3%, and portable navigation devices, 65.9%. As of 2011 Taiwan was the world's second-largest IT hardware manufacturer. Taiwan has become the world's leading supplier of computer peripherals, including motherboards, monitors, mice, interfaces, network cards, and graphic cards; and holds the largest market share of notebook computers and semiconductors. The structure of Taiwan's IT industry is a pyramid, with a handful of large companies that make the major investments in research and development, and over 1000 small and medium-sized operations that account for about 85%s of the output. The sector employs about 130,000.

Taiwan's petrochemical industry consists mainly of 45 upper- and middle-stream manufacturers, many concentrated in the Kaohsiung special chemical zone. In 1999 Taiwan's petrochemical production capacity was only 51% of domestic demand. As of 2000 this was raised to 79% with the completion of a naphtha cracking plant in the Mailiao industrial zone. The Mailiao zone also includes its newest oil refinery, a 450,000 barrels per day facility built by Formosa Petrochemical Company (FPC), which, with Taiwan's three other refineries--a 270,00 barrels-per-day refinery at Kaohsiung, a 270,000 barrels-per-day refinery at Ta-Lin, and a 200,000 barrels-per-day refinery at Taoyuan--establishes refinery capacity in excess of domestic demand.

In heavy industry, Taiwan has 10 manufacturing companies, most of them contractual joint ventures with Japan. In 2010 Taiwan's automobile production totaled 251,490, ranking 27th in the world. Taiwan's small size and the availability of efficient public transportation limit the demand for automobiles.

Textiles were the leading export until the 1980s, when labor costs, land prices and environmental protection concerns led to a relocation of much of the industry to Southeast Asia and China. The domestic industry is based on man-made fibers. In 2010 Taiwan was third in the world in the production of man-made fibers, and second in the production of polyester, which constitutes 80% of its output.

Overall industrial production fell 2.6% in 1998, from an increase of 7.4% in 1997, due largely to the effects of the Asian financial crisis. Industrial production recovered quickly to growth rates of 7.5% and 7.4% in 1999 and 2000, but then slid 10.4% in 2001 in the wake of the dot.com bust. In 2002 the economy recovered, registering a 3.3% growth rate. In 2003 and 2004 industrial production regained rapid growth rates at 8.4% and 12.2%, respectively. The years of 2005, 2006, and 2007 continued to witness a healthy growth of 6.6% per year, until the 2008–09 global financial crisis brought Taiwan's industrial production down to 1.2% and 2% in 2008 and 2009, respectively. In 2010 Taiwan's industrial production rocketed to an annual growth rate of 26.4%, the highest growth its kind in 40 years, due to the booming outputs of high-tech and electronic industries, according to the Ministry of Economic Affairs.

In 2010, Industry made up 31.1% of the economy, and employed 35.9% of the working population.

29 SCIENCE AND TECHNOLOGY

In the 1970s Taiwan instituted its Science and Technology Development Program. Coordinated by the National Science Council, the program seeks to encourage the development of "knowledge-intensive" industries through grants for the training of scientific personnel, subsidies for recruitment of distinguished scientists from abroad, and grants to universities to promote scientific research. Specific goals of the program are to integrate and promote research in geothermal energy, battery-powered vehicles, electronics, cancer treatment, pharmaceuticals, nuclear safety, and the development of high-precision instrumentation and computers.

The Industrial Technology Research Institute is charged with the transfer of pertinent technologies developed to manufacturing and other industries. College students are encouraged to build careers in engineering and science. In 1979 the Hsinchu Science and Industrial Park was established near the National Tsinghua University, with the objective of encouraging computer manufacturing and other high-technology industries by offering loans, tax incentives, and low-cost housing and factory buildings. By 1990 over 60 companies had established research and development (R&D) and joint production facilities there. These include computer, semiconductor, precision electronics and instrumentation, telecommunications, and biotechnology firms.

The highest institution for scientific research on Taiwan is the Academia Sinica (Chinese Academy of Sciences), founded in 1928 and now located in T'aipei. Its 18 associated institutes carry on research in mathematics, statistics, history and philology, economics, modern history, physics, botany, zoology, ethnology, chemistry, molecular biology, biological chemistry, biomedical sciences, atomic and molecular sciences, earth sciences, information science, nuclear energy, social sciences and philosophy, and American culture. An Atomic Energy Council, founded in 1955, promotes atomic research.

In T'aipei, the National Taiwan Science Education Center has a planetarium and various exhibits; the Taiwan Museum has exhibits on natural history, geology, and ethnography, and a spectroscopic dating laboratory for fossils. Taiwan has 23 universities and colleges that offer courses in basic and applied sciences.

30 DOMESTIC TRADE

Before 2000 Taiwan's marketing system was partly free and partly controlled. Salt, tobacco, alcoholic beverages, and certain commodities were produced and distributed by the government. Prices of basic living commodities were controlled. Retail sales in cities were handled by small department stores, specialty shops, general stores, convenience stores, roadside stands, and peddlers. Since roadside stands and peddlers had little overhead and were satisfied with a small profit, their prices were generally lower than those of the large stores and shops, if the customer bargained. However, the entry of modern retail stores, shopping malls, department stores, hypermarkets, supermarkets and convenience

stores since the beginning of the 21st century has widely replaced Taiwan's old retail landscape, which was characterized by "mom-and-pop" stores and traditional open markets. The nation's first shopping malls opened in 1999 and 2001. As of 2010 department stores, shopping malls and shopping centers shared more than one-quarter of domestic sales, amounting to US$6 billion; convenient stores shared another quarter, and hypermarkets nearly one-fifth.

Chilung and T'aipei are the distribution centers for the northern end of the island, while Kaohsiung and T'ainan are the principal distribution centers for the southern area. Most registered import and export trading firms are located in T'aipei. Accounts are usually settled during festival periods, according to Chinese custom.

Direct marketing techniques such as mail order, television and home shopping, and Internet marketing are expanding rapidly in Taiwan. In 2005 there were about 720 companies registered as multi-level sales or direct marketing enterprises. Of that total, there were 415 major direct marketing firms, specializing mainly in such things as health care products, cosmetics, skin care, and household cleaning items. As of 2010 Taiwan has become one of the world's most densely populated direct sales markets. Asian New Zealand Foundation reported that over four million Taiwanese are involved in direct sales, generating around US$1.64 billion a year.

Electronic commerce (e-commerce) is still evolving in Taiwan, even though the country's Internet infrastructure is highly developed and completely able to support the development of e-commerce. More than 90% of the country's businesses have internal networks and the supporting infrastructure. In addition, the country as of June 2010 had 16.1 million (70.1% of the population) Internet users.

Taiwan imposes a 5% value-added tax on most goods and services.

Local markets open about 7 a.m. and close at 6 p.m. or later. Business firms and stores are usually open from 9 a.m. to 5:30 p.m., and in the morning on Saturdays, and some stores close as late as 10 p.m. Most stores are open seven days a week. Banks are open six days a week: Monday-Friday, 9 a.m. to 3:30 p.m., and Saturday, 9 a.m. to noon.

31 FOREIGN TRADE

Foreign trade is of ultimate importance to the island economy. To fulfill both production and consumer needs, Taiwan must import large quantities of energy, industrial raw materials, food, and manufactured goods. With rising consumer wealth within Taiwan as well as tariff reductions and other liberalization measures by the government, imports have risen rapidly from US$24 billion in 1986 to an estimated US$251.4 billion in 2010.

The export pattern has changed significantly since the end of World War II. In 1952 industrial products represented only 10% of Taiwan's total exports and agricultural exports made up the rest; but by 1992, industrial exports (excluding processed agricultural products) had jumped to an overwhelming 95.7% share of the total. Exports increased from US$8.2 billion in 1976 to an estimated US$274.4 billion in 2010. Most of Taiwan's export commodities are electronic equipment and other small manufactured goods.

In June 2010, in a sign of growing Chinese influence across Asia, Taiwan signed a historic bilateral trade agreement with China that would eliminate tariffs on more than 800 goods traded between the countries—267 that China exports to Taiwan and 539 that Taiwan exports to China. The agreement, known as the Economic Co-operation Framework Agreement (ECFA), was signed in the southwestern Chinese city of Chongqing. In addition to reflecting growing economic ties between the countries, the agreement also represented shifting geopolitical realities in Asia, where China's rising power enabled it to increasingly hammer out a geopolitical landscape that conformed to its desires. The favorable trading terms granted to Taiwan in the deal, analysts said, reflected China's underlying motivation behind the agreement-to woo Taiwan to accept the mainland's primacy and control.

As of 2010 the major export partners of Taiwan were China, 28.1%; Hong Kong, 13.8%; the United States, 11.5%; Japan, 6.6%; and Singapore, 4.4%.

32 BALANCE OF PAYMENTS

There was a consistent trade surplus after the mid-1970s, which exceeded US$10 billion after the mid-1980s through the mid-1990s. The account surplus in 2009 was US$42.9 billion, up from US$27 billion in 2008. Taiwan's total foreign exchange reserves are the world's fourth-largest after China, Japan, and Russia; they stood at a record US$392.6 billion in March 2011. Total foreign debt was only US$75.3 billion in 2010.

The CIA reported that in 2010 the purchasing power parity of Taiwan's exports was US$274.4 billion, while imports totaled US$251.4 billion resulting in a trade surplus of US$23 billion.

33 BANKING AND SECURITIES

Many banking institutions are either owned or controlled by the government. There were 11 public banks in 1998, with total assets of US$261 billion. The Bank of Taiwan (with 75 branches) used to issue currency notes, handle foreign exchange, act as the government's bank, and perform central banking functions in addition to its commercial banking activities, before reactivating the Central Bank of China (CBC) in T'aipei in 1961. The functions of the central bank include regulation of the money market, management of foreign exchange, issuance of currency, and service as fiscal agent for the government. The Bank of China is a foreign exchange bank with branch offices in major world capitals. The Bank of Communications is an industrial bank specializing in industrial, mining, and transportation financing. The Export-Import Bank of China, inaugurated 1 February 1979, assists in the financing of Taiwan's export trade. The Central Trust of China acts as a government trading agency and handles most of the procurements of government organizations. The Postal Savings System accepts savings deposits and makes domestic transfers at post offices.

The government holds majority status in several of the most important banks, including the Bank of Taiwan, the Cooperative Bank of Taiwan, and the First Commercial Bank. The two largest private banks are the International Commercial Bank of China and the Overseas Chinese Commercial Banking Corp.

In 1990 the government announced the goal of establishing the island as a regional financial center. On 18 February 1997 the finance ministry set up a 37-member financial reform task force, headed by the finance minister. This group spent 10 months de-

vising proposals in the following four areas: improving the overall efficiency of the banking system; development of capital and derivatives markets, and relaxation of the rules governing the kinds of business banks may conduct; improving market-regulating procedures such as credit evaluation systems, asset management, investor insurance, and insider trading rules; and strengthening banks' internal financial controls. By 1998 three large government-owned provincial banks were privatized, and others were set to follow. At the end of 2009 there were 37 domestic commercial banks with 3,155 branches, only 1 medium business bank, and 32 local branches of foreign banks. There were also 26 credit cooperatives, 275 farmers' credit unions, and 25 fishermen's credit unions.

Taiwan's first private corporate bond issue was floated in 1958. The first stock exchange in Taiwan opened on 4 February 1962. Volume was low until liberalization measures opened the market to foreigners, and the Taiwan stock market surged in the early months of 1997, with the index smashing through the 8,000-point barrier for the first time since 5 March 1990. This milestone immediately prompted rumblings from the CBC that the market was overheated. Yet, by May 1997 the market was flirting with the next resistance level, at 8,500 points. Authorities raised the limits to foreign ownership in companies listed on the TAIEX from 30% to 50% in 1999. Most limits on foreign ownership were ended in 2000, and the index was up by the 10,000 mark in that year. However, it has since dropped off considerably, especially in the wake of the Asian financial crisis of 1998. The TAIEX was at 5,551.2 at the end of 2001, and trading value, at US$545 billion, was only slightly more than half of the previous year's level. As of 2010 the TAIEX stood at 8,972.50, up 1% from the previous year. Trading value that year totaled US$751.5 billion. As of 31 December 2010 a total of 758 companies were listed on the Taiwan Stock Exchange, which had a market capitalization of US$787.977 billion.

34 INSURANCE

Insurance in Taiwan is supervised by the Ministry of Finance and may be written only by a limited liability company or a cooperative association. Aside from group insurance operated by the government, life and annuity insurance are comparatively undeveloped in Taiwan. The Chinese tradition that the family should take care of its members in sickness and old age lowered demand in the past, but social change and rapid economic growth have modified this situation, especially in industrial areas. In 1986 the Taiwanese government agreed to allow US companies to compete equally for insurance business. In 1999 nine foreign nonlife insurers were authorized to run full branches in Taiwan. Foreign insurers must receive approval from the government, however, and secure a business license. According to statistics released by the Taiwan Insurance Institute at the end of 2010, there were 54 insurance companies in Taiwan, of which 31 were life insurance companies and 23 were non-life insurance companies. In Taiwan, third-party automobile liability, health insurance, pension, unemployment insurance, and workers' compensation are all compulsory. In 2010 the value of all direct insurance premiums written totaled

US$32.402 billion, of which life insurance premiums accounted for US$79.8 billion.

35 PUBLIC FINANCE

Central government revenues come mostly from taxation, customs and duties, and income from government monopolies on tobacco and wines; other revenues are derived from profits realized by government enterprises. Government accounts showed surpluses through the early 1980s. Public authorities anticipated a growing fiscal deficit throughout the 1990s as Taiwan's six-year development plan required over US$300 billion of investment in public infrastructural construction projects and in upgrading industries. In 1996 the government's deficit was equal to 4% of GDP. Growing demands for social welfare spending and increased defense spending (up 20% in 1996/97, the largest rise in over a decade) continued to put pressure on the budget. Outstanding debt reached 16% of GDP in 1998, up from 6% in 1991, and debt service payments consumed 15% of the central budget in 1999. The government was committed to balancing the budget by 2001. Austerity measures included controlling public sector consumption expenditures, limiting expansion of government expenditures, freezing government employment, limiting public employee pay raises, and encouraging private participation in major public projects. The government was also committed to reducing the public sector's role in the economy. National defense expenditures as a portion of the central budget dropped from over 40% in 1960 to 20% in 1999, and were set to fall to 2.2% in 2009. In the same year, President Ma Ying-jeou pledged to maintain Taiwan's defense expenditure at 3% of GDP or higher. The 2011 defense spending was estimated at 2.73%.

The CIA estimated that in 2010 Taiwan's central government took in revenues of approximately US$73.54 billion and had expenditures of US$81.72 billion. Revenues minus expenditures totaled -US$8.18 billion. The budget deficit amounted to 1.9% of GDP. In total US$92.07 billion of the debt was held by foreign entities. In 2010 public debt amounted to 33.3% of GDP.

36 TAXATION

All taxes are collected by the local government and transferred to the relevant provincial or central government agency. The CIA estimated that Taiwan's tax revenues in 2010 equaled 17.1% of GDP. Tax revenues reserved for the central government include the income tax, estate (inheritance) tax, gift taxes (4–50%); customs duty, stamp tax, commodity tax, securities transaction tax, and mine tax.

As of 2011 individual income taxes were progressive, with a top rate of 40%. Dividends paid to resident individuals are not subject to a withholding tax. Nonresident individuals were subject to a 18% withholding rate on wages and salaries, 20% on commissions, bank interest, royalties, fees for professional practices, rental income, and prizes exceeding TWD2,000 (US$66). Beginning in 2010 a 15% withholding tax is levied on interest on short-term bills, securitized certificates, corporate bonds, government bonds, or financial debentures, as well as interest derived from repurchase transactions with the aforementioned bonds or certificates. The rate is 20% in all other cases.

Taiwan's corporate income tax rate was lowered from 20% to 17% in 2010. Capital gains are subject to the same corporate tax rates, although gains incurred by a nonresident company are taxed at a flat rate of 20%. In 2010 a 20% withholding tax was levied on dividends paid to a nonresident firm, unless otherwise reduced under a tax treaty. Banking, insurance and investment services are subject to a 2% turnover tax. Higher rates apply to entertainment.

Taiwan also has a value-added tax (VAT) of 5% on sales and services. Items zero-rated from the VAT include international transport, exports, services performed in Taiwan but for use abroad, and services performed overseas. Basic foodstuffs, land, water, certain agricultural inputs, some financial and insurance products, and education and health are exempt from the VAT. However, certain businesses not subject to the VAT pay a tax on their gross business receipts that ranges from 0.1%-25%. Sales taxes are 1% for reinsurance activities, 5% for bank activities, insurance and brokerage services; and 15–25% for bars and restaurants. There is a 60% ad valorem merchandise tax on petrol. Other taxes include building, commodity, deed, estate, gift and land value taxes. There are no social security or local income taxes in Taiwan.

37 CUSTOMS AND DUTIES

Customs duties are important revenue earners and consist principally of import duties and tonnage dues. The former are levied on dutiable commodities, the latter on ships that call at Taiwan ports. Duties range from 2 to 60% and are assessed on seven commodity categories that include rubber tires, cement, beverages, oil and gas, electrical appliances, flat glass, and automobiles. Articles imported for military use, for relief, or for educational or research purposes are exempted from import duty. Duties on imported raw materials for business can be rebated. Some agricultural products are prohibited from importation, such as rice, sugar, chicken, some pork cuts, peanuts, and certain dairy products. Imports from Japan and mainland China are restricted due to balance of payments problems. There is also a 5% VAT that is applied to the CIF (cost, insurance, freight) value, plus the duty and a 0.3% harbor construction fee that is not applied to items arriving by parcel post or air freight duty.

38 FOREIGN INVESTMENT

From 1952 to 2010 cumulative foreign direct investment (FDI) approvals came to approximately US$81 billion, of which more than one-quarter was in the electronics and electrical industries. Other industries attracting relatively heavy foreign investment include banking and insurance services, chemicals, trade and basic metals. The rate of foreign investment has been rapidly accelerating as Taiwan, in preparation for its accession to the World Trade Organization (WTO), has liberalized its economy and improved its investment environment. Foreign firms are generally accorded national treatment and trade-related capital flows are unrestricted. In January 2001 the 50% foreign ownership limit was lifted, with exceptions in a few designated industries. Most limits on the amount of portfolio investment in companies listed on the Taiwan Stock Exchange (TWSE) were also lifted. About 1% of manufacturing industries and 5% of services industries continue to have limits on foreign ownership. Investment incentives are offered for investments in emerging or strategic industries, pollution control systems, production automation, and energy conservation. Since the goal was first announced in 1995, increasing effort has been put into making Taiwan an Asia-Pacific Regional Operations

Center (APROC). In 2010 Taiwan's foreign direct investments declined 20.6% from 2009 due to a weaker momentum from Europe and the United States. However, the approved investment cases expanded at a rate of 19.4% in the same year.

Taiwan outward investment has been such that by 2000 over 50% of Taiwan manufacturing was being conducted outside of the country, and by 2001, 53% was being out-sourced. The top five sectors for outward investment were banking and finance, services, electronics and electrical appliances, marketing, and transportation. In 1992 investment in mainland China was legalized and, despite a fall off due to tensions in 1996, by 2001 Taiwan had become China's fourth-largest source of foreign investment. In 2002 the government changed its official investment stance towards China from "patience over haste" to "active opening and effective management."

Taiwan uses the cheap labor force from the mainland to assemble and process domestically produced high tech goods, and then exports them to the developed markets (like the United States, Japan, and Europe). Taiwan's direct investments in China grew from US$1.3 billion in 1999 to US$5.4 billion in the first 10 months of 2004. China (including Hong Kong) has thus become Taiwan's largest export market. Capital inflows have also been high, with FDI levels amounting to 20.8% of the GDP in 2003. Investors complain, however, that the business environment is not as streamlined and transparent as it could be.

³⁹ECONOMIC DEVELOPMENT

Since 1950 the government has adopted a series of economic plans to help guide and promote economic growth and industrialization. The first four-year economic development plan (1953–56) emphasized reconstruction and increased production of rice, fertilizers, and hydroelectric power; it resulted in an increase of 37% in GNP and 17% in income per capita. In the second four-year plan (1957–60), import substitution industries were encouraged. Industry and agriculture both registered significant gains; GNP increased by 31%, and national income per capita by 13%. The third four-year plan (1961–64) emphasized labor-intensive export industries, basic services, energy development, industries contributing to agricultural growth, and exploration and development of the island's limited natural resources. The results were a 42% increase in GNP and a 31% increase in per capita income. US loans and grants, totaling US$2.2 billion, and foreign (mostly overseas Chinese) investment financed these early stages of development.

Following the curtailment of assistance in 1965, the fourth four-year plan (1965–68) was introduced, followed by the fifth four-year plan (1969–72); increases in GNP for these periods were 46% and 55%, respectively. By 1971 exports of manufactured goods had registered spectacular increases, and Taiwan's foreign trade pattern changed from one of chronic deficit to consistent trade surpluses. At this point, the government began to redirect its priorities from labor-intensive industries to the development of such capital-intensive sectors as shipbuilding, chemicals, and petrochemicals. The sixth four-year plan (1973–76), adversely affected by the worldwide recession, was terminated in 1975 after producing only a 19% increase in GNP. It was replaced by a six-year plan (1976–81) that focused on expansion of basic industries and completion of 10 major infrastructural projects, including rail electrification, construction of the North Link railroad, development of

nuclear energy, and construction of the steel mill at Kaohsiung and of the new port of T'aichung.

In 1978 the six-year plan was revised, and 12 new infrastructural projects were added, including completion of the round-the-island railroad, construction of three cross-island highways, expansion of T'aichung Port's harbor, and expansion of steel and nuclear energy facilities. A subsequent four-year plan (1986–89), designed to supplement a longer-range 10-year plan (1980–89), had as a target average annual GNP increase of 6.5%. Among its goals were price stability, annual growth of 7.5% in the service sector, trade liberalization, encouragement of balanced regional development, and redirection of new industrial growth into such high-technology industries as computers, robotics, and bioengineering. In response to flagging export growth and a slowdown in private investment following a stock market collapse in 1990, the government devised a six-year plan for 1991–97 aimed at economic revitalization. This plan targeted investment mainly in transportation, telecommunications, power generation, and pollution control. A "Statute for Upgrading Industries" enacted in early 1991 continued the government's efforts to provide incentives for private investment in research and development and high-technology sectors of the economy. Economic development in the late 1990s focused on a continuing privatization of government enterprises, the opening of the Taiwan market to foreigners, and high investment in the technological sector.

Taiwan's six-year national development plan for 2002–08 was titled *Challenge 2008*. It had seven specified goals: 1) expanding the number of products and technologies that meet the world's highest standards; 2) doubling the number of foreign visitors; 3) increasing expenditures on research and development to 3% GDP; 4) reducing unemployment to less than 4%; 5) increasing the average growth rate to over 5%; 6) increasing the number of broadband internet users to over six million; and 7) creating about 700,000 jobs. There were 10 major areas of emphasis, including cultivating talent for the E-generation (with a special emphasis on mastering English); developing the cultural arts industry; developing a digital Taiwan, using information technologies to make government more efficient and industries more competitive; developing Taiwan as a regional headquarters for multinational corporations; and constructing culturally rich hometown communities as a means of retaining talent, in addition to more standard goals of increasing value-added industrial production, improving the transportation infrastructure, conserving water resources and doubling the number of tourists.

The global recession of 2008–09 had a significant effect on the economy as world demand for export products dropped. However, strong Chinese demand for high-tech electronics helped the nation rebound. Also, the closer cross-strait economic relationship that Taiwan developed with mainland China since President Ma Ying-jeou took office in 2008 opened the island to greater opportunities. The 2009–12 development plan aims to increase competitive advantage through innovation, upgrading of industrial infrastructure, and lessening of income inequality.

⁴⁰SOCIAL DEVELOPMENT

A social insurance system provides medical, disability, old age, survivor, and other benefits, with employers paying 3.85% of payroll and workers contributing 1.1% of earnings. Benefits are paid in lump sums depending on years of contribution. The retirement age is set at age 60 for men and 55 for women. The National Health Insurance Bureau provides medical care for all workers and dependents. Firms with five or more employers are required to fund a workers' compensation program. Unemployment benefits are funded by employers, employees, and the government.

All enterprises and labor organizations must also furnish welfare funds for workers and "welfare units," such as cafeterias, nurseries, clinics, and low-rent housing. Fishermen, farmers, and salt workers have their own welfare funds. Government programs include relief for mainland refugees, calamity-relief assistance, and direct assistance to children in needy families.

The law provides equal rights to women, and protects against sex discrimination. Sections of the legal code that discriminated against women have been eliminated. Now the law permits married women to retain their maiden names, gives them an equal voice in child custody disputes, and clarifies their property rights. In the workplace, women tend to receive lower salaries and less frequent promotion, and are often denied federally mandated maternity leave. Violence against women, especially domestic abuse, is extremely widespread. Child abuse is also a serious problem. The Child Welfare Act mandates that any citizen aware of child abuse or neglect must report it to the authorities. As of 2010 Taiwan remained a significant transit point for trafficked persons.

Human rights are generally well respected, but some cases of corruption, violence, discrimination against women and children, the trafficking in persons, and abuses of foreign workers continue to be reported.

41 HEALTH

As a result of improved living conditions and mass vaccinations, significant progress has been made in controlling malaria, tuberculosis, venereal disease, leprosy, trachoma, typhoid, diphtheria, and encephalitis. According to the CIA, life expectancy in Taiwan was 78 years in 2011. The fertility rate was 1.2 children per woman, while the infant mortality rate was 5 deaths per 1,000 live births. It was estimated that 93% of children were vaccinated against measles. The CIA calculated the HIV/AIDS prevalence rate in Taiwan to be about less than 0.1% in 2011.

42 HOUSING

The evacuation of more than two million persons from the mainland to an already densely populated island in 1949 made the provision of low-cost housing an early priority. By 1979 more than 150,000 units of public housing had been built. Since the 1970s government housing programs have focused on the cities, with slum clearance and the construction of high-rise apartment dwellings for low-income groups the major priorities. Two new towns were constructed in the early 1980s. The government set a target of 600,000 new housing units for the 1979–89 decade, but only 236,106 units were completed as of 1986. In 2000 the total housing stock was at about 6,977,770 units with about 3.4 people per dwelling. Some 29% of all housing was built in the period 1971–

80; about 32% was built in the period 1991–2000. About 83% of all dwellings were owner occupied.

43 EDUCATION

All children receive nine years of free and compulsory education provided at government expense, including six years in public primary school and three years in junior high. After completing nine years of compulsory schooling, approximately 90% of students continue their studies at a senior high (general studies) or vocational school. Agriculture, engineering, commerce, maritime navigation, home economics, and nursing are some of the skills taught in vocational schools, which offer three-year programs. In order to attend high school, students must pass an examination after junior high. Salaries of the teaching staff are paid by local governments.

As of 2009 there were 1.59 million students enrolled in primary schools and 1.7 million enrolled in secondary schools. The same year there were 99,164 primary school teachers and 104,035 secondary school teachers. The student-teacher ratio was 16.07 in primary schools and 16.4 in secondary schools.

As of 2009 Taiwan had over 150 institutions of higher education. More than 100,000 students take the joint college entrance exam each year. Approximately 60% of candidates are admitted to a college or university. In 2009–10, there were 49,191 teachers in Taiwanese universities. The government relaxed many restrictions that prevented students from studying abroad in the 1980s. Although Taiwan has a highly developed college curriculum, many students do travel abroad to study. Taiwanese college and graduate students are particularly interested in engineering, computer science, natural science, and business management. The number of foreign students studying in Taiwan also has grown from around 7,500 in 1999–2000 to 19,376 in 2009–10. In 2011 Taiwan opened doors to students from mainland China for the first time. About 2,000 Chinese students enrolled in full degree programs in Taiwan in 2011. Overall, the CIA estimated that Taiwan had a literacy rate of 96.1% in 2011.

44 LIBRARIES AND MUSEUMS

The National Central Library in T'aipei holds more than 1,615,000 items, including a collection of rare Chinese books (180,000 volumes). The National Taiwan University in T'aipei has more than 1,500,000 volumes in collected holdings. The T'aipei Public Library of Taiwan consists of a main library, 30 branch libraries, and 12 neighborhood reading rooms within the metropolitan area with a combined collection of about 4,386,601 volumes, plus periodicals and multimedia materials.

The major museums, all in T'aipei, are the National Palace Museum, National Museum of History, and the Taiwan Museum. The National Palace Museum houses one of the world's largest collections of Chinese art-the collection consists primarily of treasures brought from the mainland. The T'aipei Contemporary Arts Museum was completely renovated in 2001. The National Museum of History, founded in 1955, has more than 30,000 items in its collections of oracle bones and ritual vessels of the Shang and Chou dynasties, earthenware of the Sui and T'ang dynasties, stone engravings of the Han dynasty, and jade articles of the Chou dynasty. The Taiwan Museum has the most complete collection of natural history specimens in the country. The National Taiwan Science

Education Center in T'aipei houses a planetarium and scientific exhibits.

45 MEDIA

Taiwan's telecommunications system is capable of meeting every private and business need. Domestic service is fully digital and modern. International service is provided by submarine cable and satellite ground stations. In 2009 the CIA reported that there were 14.6 million main phone lines and 26.9 million mobile cellular phones in use. Mobile phone subscriptions averaged 117 per 100 people.

Radio broadcasting stations in Taiwan are under the supervision of the Ministry of Communications. The largest network is the Broadcasting Corp. of China, which operates three systems: an overseas service, known as the Voice of Free China; the mainland service, known as the Central Broadcasting Station, aimed at the Chinese mainland; and the domestic service. These stations broadcast in 14 languages and dialects. Television was introduced in 1962. In 2010 the country had about 6.3 million Internet hosts. In 2009 there were some 16.1 million Internet users in Taiwan, or about 70 per 100 citizens.

The leading newspapers are *United Daily News*, *China Times*, *Central Daily News*, *Min Sheng Daily*, *Liberty Times*, *Taiwan Hsin Sheng Pao*, *China Times Express*, and *China Daily News*. The Central News Agency was established on the mainland by the KMT in 1924.

Though authorities generally respect constitutionally provided rights to free speech and free press, these rights are formally circumscribed by a law excluding the advocacy of communism or division of national territory. Controls over radio and television are said to be under a process of liberalization and privatization.

46 ORGANIZATIONS

The most influential private organizations are the occupational or trade associations. These include associations of farmers, fishermen, trade unions, business leaders, and professional persons. Organizations devoted to social welfare and relief work are sponsored by the government, by religious groups, and by civic clubs. The Taiwan Federation of Chambers of Commerce has branches in all the principal cities.

Cooperatives are an important adjunct to economic life, especially in the urban centers. In rural areas, agricultural cooperatives help farmers transport and market special farm products such as fruits, tea, citronella oil, and handicrafts. Cooperative farms, organized with the help of the government, operate either on a community basis, with the products distributed among the members, or on an individual basis, with the cooperative functioning as a purchasing, processing, and marketing agency.

Agricultural services and 4-H clubs in various parts of Taiwan provide training and social activities for boys and girls. Both the YMCA and YWCA are active in Taiwan, as is Little League baseball. There is an active Junior Chamber in Taiwan and there are several other sports associations based in T'aipei.

Cultural and educational organizations include the Historical Research Commission of Taiwan, the National Science Council, Academia Sinica, and Modern Fine Arts Association of Southern Taiwan. The Taiwan Medical Association is one of many professional organizations that promote research and education in medical and scientific fields.

Social action groups include the Taiwan Grassroots Women Worker's Center and the Taiwan Association of Human Rights. Volunteer service organizations, such as the Lions Clubs and Kiwanis International, are also present. There are national chapters of Amnesty International and the Society of St. Vincent de Paul.

47 TOURISM, TRAVEL, AND RECREATION

T'aipei is the chief tourist attraction, with such popular sites as the seat of government in Presidential Square, Lungshan Temple, and the nearby National Palace Museum and famous Yangmingshan National Park. Attractions outside the capital include the Shihmen Dam recreation area, Lake Tzuhu, and the mausoleum of Chiang Kai-shek. The many temples and Dutch relics of T'ainan, Taiwan's oldest city, and Sun Moon Lake, near T'aichung, also attract numerous visitors. The national sports are baseball, football (soccer), and basketball.

In 2010 tourist arrivals totaled 5.57 million, up 27% from the 4.4 million during the previous year. Some 58.1% were foreign visitors and 41.9% overseas Chinese. All visitors need a valid passport and visa.

48 FAMOUS PERSONS

Among the many Chinese scholars who have lived in Taiwan since 1949 are Hu Shih (1891–1962), philosopher and president of the Academia Sinica; Chiang Monlin (1886–1964), educator and chairman of the Joint Commission on Rural Reconstruction; Li Chi (1896–1979) and Tung Tso-pin (1895–1963), archaeologists, whose discoveries at the Anyang site laid the foundation for modern Chinese archaeology; and Tsiang Ting-fu (Ting-fu Fuller Tsiang, 1895–1965), historian and long-time delegate to the UN. Chang Ta-chien (1899–1983) is known for his painting of landscapes and figures and his copies of the famous Buddhist mural paintings of Tunhwang caves in Gansu Province. Lin Yutang (1895–1976), poet, philosopher, lexicographer, and historian, was one of China's foremost interpreters for Western cultures.

The outstanding political and military figure of Nationalist China and postwar Taiwan was Chiang Kai-shek (Chiang Chungcheng, 1887–1975), who was responsible for sustaining the spirit of anticommunism in Taiwan. His son, Chiang Ching-kuo (1910–88), assumed leadership of the Taiwan government from Chiang Kai-shek's death to his own. Chen Shui-bian (b. 1950) became president in 2000; his controversial views regarding Taiwanese independence have caused consternation with mainland China. In 2008 Ma Ying-jeou (b. 1950) became the 12th term president of Taiwan. Since he took office as president, Ma has pursued warmer relations with mainland China.

49 DEPENDENCIES

Taiwan has no territories or colonies.

50 BIBLIOGRAPHY

Aspalter, Christian. *Conservative Welfare State Systems in East Asia*. Westport, CT: Praeger, 2001.

Chang, Sung-sheng. *Literary Culture in Taiwan: Martial Law to Market Law*. New York: Columbia University Press, 2004.

Clark, Cal, and Alexander C. Tan. *Taiwan's Political Economy: Meeting Challenges, Pursuing Progress.* Boulder, CO: Lynne Rienner Publishers, 2012.

Copper, John F. *The A to Z of Taiwan (Republic of China).* Lanham, MD: Scarecrow Press, 2010.

Copper, John F. *Historical Dictionary of Taiwan (Republic of China).* Lanham, MD: Scarecrow Press, 2007.

Hoare, Jim and Susan Pares. *A Political and Economic Dictionary of East Asia.* Philadelphia: Routledge/Taylor and Francis, 2005.

Manthorpe, Jonathan. *Forbidden Nation: A History of Taiwan.* New York: Palgrave Macmillan, 2005.

Taiwan Investment and Business Guide: Strategic and Practical Information. Washington, DC: International Business Publications USA, 2012.

Wei, C. S. George. *China-Taiwan Relations in a Global Context: Taiwan's Foreign Policy and Relations.* New York: Routledge, 2012.

TAJIKISTAN

Republic of Tajikistan

Jumhurii Tojikistan

CAPITAL: Dushanbe

FLAG: The national flag contains three horizontal stripes: red at the top, a wider stripe of white in the middle, and green at the bottom. A gold crown and seven gold stars is in the center of the white stripe. The red represents sun, victory, and national unity. The white represents purity, cotton, and mountain snows. The green represents Islam and the bounty of nature. The crown represents the Tajik peoples and the stars signify the magic number of seven, which symbolizes perfection and happiness.

ANTHEM: *Surudi Milli (National Anthem).*

MONETARY UNIT: The Tajikistani Somoni (TJS) replaced the Tajik ruble as the primary currency in 2000. TJS1 = US$0.210128 (or US$1 = TJS4.75900) as of 2011.

WEIGHTS AND MEASURES: The metric system is used.

HOLIDAYS: New Year's Day (1 January), International Women's Day (8 March) Navrus (Persian New Year), International Labour Day (1 May), Victory Day (9 May), National Unity Day (27 June), Eid-i-Ramazon (End of Ramadan), Independence Day (9 September), Eid-i-Kurbon (Feast of the Sacrifice, and Constitution Day (6 November). Dates vary for religious holidays.

TIME: 6 p.m. = noon GMT.

¹LOCATION, SIZE, AND EXTENT

Tajikistan is located in central Asia, between Kyrgyzstan and Uzbekistan to the north and west, China to the east, and Afghanistan to the south. Comparatively, it is slightly smaller than the state of Wisconsin with a total area of 143,100 sq km (55,251 sq mi). Tajikistan's boundary length totals 3,651 km (2,269 mi).

Its capital city, Dushanbe, is located in the western part of the country.

²TOPOGRAPHY

The Pamir and Alay mountains dominate Tajikistan's landscape. The western Ferghana Valley lies in the north, and the Kofarnihon and Vakhsh Valleys are in the southwest. The Pamir and Alay mountains ranges have some of the world's highest mountains. Ninety-three percent of Tajikistan is mountainous with altitudes ranging from 984 feet to 24,589 feet. Nearly 50% of the country is above 10,000 feet.

Hundreds of canyons and gorges cut through the mountains. Most of the country's people live and work in large river valleys formed by streams running through the canyons and gorges. Both the Amu Darya and Syr Darya flow through Tajikistan and are fed by melting snow and glaciers.

³CLIMATE

The climate ranges from semiarid to polar. In the semiarid regions, extreme temperatures have reached 48°C (118°F) in the summer. In the eastern Pamirs, winter temperatures have dropped as low as -60°C (-76°F). The national mean temperature in July is 30°C (86°F). The mean temperature in January is 0°C (32°F). Rainfall in most of the country averages 70 to 160 cm (28 to 63 in).

Earthquakes of varying degrees are frequent. Flooding and landslides sometimes occur during the annual spring thaw.

⁴FLORA AND FAUNA

The World Resources Institute estimates that there are 5,000 plant species in Tajikistan. In addition, Tajikistan is home to 76 species of mammals, 351 bird species, 51 reptile species, and 7 amphibian species. The calculation reflects the total number of distinct species residing in the country, not the number of endemic species.

The international non-governmental conservation organization Flora & Fauna International described Tajikistan in 2011 as having a biological richness equivalent to Kazakhstan. However, habitat fragmentation, soil erosion, and overuse of natural resources have threatened its flora and fauna. Snow leopard, wolves, Marco Polo sheep, and the bar-headed goose are among the animals inhabiting Zorkul Lake in the Pamir Mountains. The Siberian ibex can also be found in the mountains, and its forests include wild fruit and nut trees. The Childukhtaron Forest contains walnut, apple, cherry, mulberry, and juniper trees.

⁵ENVIRONMENT

The World Resources Institute reported that Tajikistan had designated 1.96 million hectares (4.84 million acres) of land for protection as of 2006. Water resources totaled 99.7 cu km (23.92 cu mi) while water usage was 11.96 cu km (2.87 cu mi) per year. Domestic water usage accounted for 4% of total usage, industrial for 5%, and agricultural for 91%. Per capita water usage totaled 1,837 cu m (64,873 cu ft) per year.

Protected areas include five Ramsar wetland sites. According to a 2011 report issued by the International Union for Conservation of Nature and Natural Resources (IUCN), threatened species included 8 mammal species, 12 bird species, 2 species of reptiles, 5 fish species, 2 invertebrate species, and 13 plant species. Threatened species include the argali, Aral salmon, Tadjik markhor, tiger, and snow leopard.

Inadequate sanitation facilities, increasing soil salinity, industrial pollution, and excessive pesticide use are some of the major environmental issues confronting Tajikistan. The country is party to international environmental agreements on biodiversity, climate change, desertification, environmental modification, ozone layer protection, and wetlands. Tajikistan has been identified as a biodiversity hotspot within the Central Asian mountain areas. Flora & Fauna International noted that the mix of fruit and nut trees in Tajikistan's forests are vital to the population's survival and is working with the Forestry Department, local communities, and national non-governmental organizations to improve forestry management.

The United Nations (UN) reported in 2008 that carbon dioxide emissions in Tajikistan totaled 7,222 kilotons.

6 POPULATION

The US Central Intelligence Agency (CIA) estimated the population of Tajikistan in 2011 to be 7,627,200, which placed it at number 96 in population among the 196 nations of the world. In 2011, approximately 3.4% of the population was over 65 years of age, with another 33.9% under 15 years of age. The median age in Uzbekistan was 22.6 years. There were 1.05 males for every female in the country. The population's annual rate of change was 1.846%. The life expectancy for males in 2011 was about 63 years for males and 69 years for females. About 26% of the population lived in urban areas. The largest city is Dushanbe with a population in 2009 of 704,000.

7 MIGRATION

Estimates of Tajikistan's net migration rate, carried out by the CIA in 2011, amounted to -1.24 migrants per 1,000 citizens. The total number of emigrants living abroad was 791,100, and the total number of immigrants living in Tajikistan was 284,300.

As a result of the civil war that began in 1992, more than 600,000 people were internally displaced, and 60,000 were forced into Northern Afghanistan by January 1993. Also, between 1991–95, 300,000 Russians, 30,000 Ukrainians, and 10,000 Belarusians all left Tajikistan. By April 1997, virtually all of the internally displaced people had returned to their homes. When the peace agreement was reached in June 1997, the UN High Commissioner for Refugees (UNHCR) completed the repatriation of Tajik refugees from northern Afghanistan to Tajikistan. In 1998 the UNHCR started the voluntary repatriation of Tajik refugees from other countries. By 1999, some 20,000 refugees had returned to their places of origin.

Refugees from Afghanistan and former Soviet republics bordering Tajikistan entered the country in increasing numbers in the latter half of the 2000–09 decade. As of December 2010, the government reported that Tajikistan had 2,538 registered refugees in the country and 1,676 asylum seekers trying to gain refugee status. The UN High Commission on Refugees, which maintains an observer status in the Refugee Status Determination Commission, has stated that the government might have underestimated these figures. Refugees and asylum seekers included Afghans, Iranians, and Kyrgyz, with about 98% of the total being Afghan.

A 2000 law has prohibited refugees and asylum seekers from living in urban areas, and refugees are often subject to police raids.

8 ETHNIC GROUPS

Using data from a 2000 census, the CIA reported in 2011 that 80% of the population was Tajik, 15% was Uzbek, and that Russians and others accounted for the remaining 5%. Russian and Kyrgyz peoples each comprised about 1.1% of the total population.

9 LANGUAGES

Tajik, a derivative language of Persian, was named the official state language in 1994, and reaffirmed as such in 2009. Russian is widely used in governmental and business settings, but Tajik is the main language spoken in the rural areas where 74% of the population reside.

Tajik has no genders or cases, and its vocabulary is borrowed from Arabic, Uzbeki, and Russian. Since the 1940s, the Tajik alphabet has been a modified version of the Russian Cyrillic alphabet. Since the adoption of Tajik as the national language, instruction of the Arabic-based Persian alphabet in schools has been encouraged, with teaching materials provided by Iran.

10 RELIGIONS

About 97% of the population in 2011 was Muslim, and the US State Department reported that active observance of Islam was increasing, especially among youth. Most Muslims follow the Hanafi school of Sunni Islam. About 4% of the Muslims were Ismaili Shi'a, and resided in the eastern Gorno-Badakhshan Autonomous Region as well as in some parts of Khatlon Region.

There were 74 registered non-Muslim religious organizations as of 2011. The US State Department estimated that approximately 150,000 Christians, most of whom are ethnic Russians or other immigrants from the Soviet era, live in Tajikistan. There are also some Baha'is and Jews. The largest Christian group is Russian Orthodox.

The government forbade Muslim women from attending mosques through a 2004 Council of Ulemo fatwa (religious ruling), and placed restrictions on the wearing of the hijab (traditional head scarf). In addition, a 2009 Law on Religion required all registered religious organizations to re-register with the government by 1 January 2010. That procedure resulted in the temporary closure of at least 28 mosques.

11 TRANSPORTATION

The CIA reported that Tajikistan has a total of 27,767 km (17,254 mi) of roads. Railroads extend for 616 km (383 mi). There are 26 airports, which transported 764,505 passengers in 2009 according to the World Bank. Eighteen of those airports have paved runways. Tajikistan has approximately 200 km (124 mi) of navigable waterways.

The US government funded a $36 million bridge project over the Pyanzh River connecting Sher Khan, Afghanistan with Nizhniy Pyanzh, Tajikistan. The bridge opened for commercial traffic in October 2007 and about 200 trucks crossed daily as of 2011.

As of 2008 all of Tajikistan's railroads were broad gauge. A 258-km (160-mi) line connects Dushanbe with Termez, Uzbekistan,

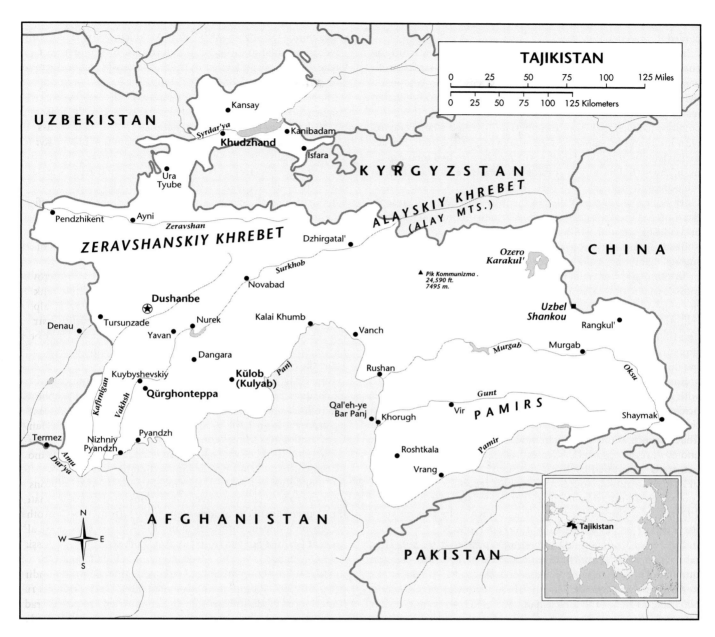

LOCATION: 15°0′ N; 39°0′ E. BOUNDARY LENGTHS: Afghanistan, 1,206 kilometers (749.4 miles); China, 414 kilometers (257.3 miles); Kyrgyzstan, 870 kilometers (541 miles); Uzbekistan, 1,161 kilometers (721.4 miles).

and ultimately with the other rail systems of the former Soviet Union.

The major roads connect Khudzhand in the north to Kulyab in the south via Dushanbe. Only one main road services the eastern Gorno-Badakhshanskaya region, meandering from Khrough to Kyrgyzstan.

12 HISTORY

The roots of present-day Tajikistan can be traced back to the Persian based Samanid Empire (AD 875–999), although the area has been continuously inhabited and ruled by a variety of groups since the early Stone Age. Parts of present-day Tajikistan lay in the states of Sogdia and Bactria in the first millennium BC; the terri-

tory was Persian-controlled from the 6th century BC until it was conquered by Alexander the Great in 329 BC. Much of Tajikistan was included in the Greco-Bactrian kingdom in 3rd century BC, but displaced by the Tochari tribes who invaded Sogdia a century later. The Kushana kingdom was established in the first centuries of the Christian era, when a number of cities were established and agriculture and commerce grew. In the 5th and 6th centuries, parts of Tajikistan were conquered by nomadic tribes, the Chionites, and, later, the Ephthalites. At the end of the 6th century the large Ephthalite empire was displaced by the Eastern Turkic Kaganate. Arabs conquered the area in the 8th century and introduced Islam. The area came under the Samanid Empire in AD 875. The Samanids, who were the last Persians to rule in Central Asia, encouraged the revival of written Persian as well as the development of trade and material culture.

Tajikistan fell under rule of a number of kingdoms from the 10th to 13th centuries, including the Ghaznavids, Karakhanids, Ghorids, Karakitai, and Khwarzmites. Genghiz Khan conquered the area in 1291–21, and Tajikistan became part of lands given to his son, Chagatai.

In the 14th century Timur (Tamerlane) created a large empire, with its capital in Samarqand (Samarkand). In the 16th century Tajikistan was conquered by the Sheibanids, who had their capital in Bukhoro (Bukhara). Portions of territory were included later in the Ashtarkhanid state and then in the Kokand Khanate, which emerged in the Fergana Valley in the mid-18th century. Present-day Tajikistan was split between the Khanates of Bukhoro (Bukhara) and Kokand in the 18th and 19th centuries.

In 1863, Russia asserted a right to exercise dominance in Central Asia, and began the military conquest of the khanates. Bukhoro (Bukhara) and Samarqand (Samarkand) were incorporated into Russia in 1868. Kokand was eliminated in 1876, and the border with Afghanistan was set by accord with England in 1895. At that point, part of Tajikistan was in the Emirate of Bukhara, and part of it was in Turkestan. When the Tsar's draft call-up of 1916 was announced, rebellions broke out all over Central Asia, including in Tajikistan. These were suppressed, at great loss of life.

Russian rule collapsed after the Russian Revolution of 1917 when the Bolsheviks consolidated their power and were embroiled in a civil war in other regions of the former Russian Empire. An indigenous Central Asian movement in the Ferghana Valley known as the "Basmachi movement" challenged Bolshevik efforts to regain control of Central Asia in the 1920s. The movement was suppressed by 1925. The Soviet Union established Tajikistan as an autonomous Soviet socialist republic within Uzbekistan in 1924 and as an independent Soviet socialist republic in 1929. In 1929, the northern Sughd region, which had been part of the Uzbek republic, was added to the Tajik republic.

The Soviet Union's establishment of separate Uzbek and Tajik republics was an administrative decision that led to the creation of two separate nationalities based on language: Uzbeks spoke Turkic and Tajiks spoke Persian. These identities were unnatural because Persian and Turkic had been used interchangeably for centuries. The Soviet boundaries also put two major Tajik cities—Bukhara and Samark—into Uzbekistan. This decision left Tajikistan with smaller cities and little arable land. Despite widespread resistance, the Soviet Union completed a collectivization of agriculture in Tajikistan, and by the 1960s the republic was the third largest cotton-producing republic in the Soviet Union. Aluminum production also was introduced. Despite these changes, Tajikistan was the poorest and least developed republic by the 1980s.

In the late Soviet period Tajikistan comprised four separate areas, and elites from each of these areas competed for power. Traditionally, power was held by people from Khojent, which is geographically and culturally closest to Uzbekistan's Fergana valley. They were contested by families and clans from Kulyab, south of Dushanbe. Poorest were people from the Gorno Badakhshan Autonomous Province, most of which is in the Pamir Mountains. The final area was Kurgan-Tyube, in the extreme south, where the influence of Islam was strong; public calls for establishing an Islamic state were heard there as early as 1976.

In 1985 Mikhail Gorbachev replaced longtime republic leader Rakhmon Nabiyev with Kakhar Makhkamov, whose control never penetrated to the most local levels. At the same time, Gorbachev's glasnost policy led to the formation of political groups and an interest in reviving Tajik culture. The Tajik Supreme Soviet declared Tajik (a derivation of Persian) to be the republic's official language in 1989, a decision that was formalized with Tajikistan's establishment as an independent nation.

The years leading up to Tajikistan's declaration of independence and first decade as a sovereign nation were marked by internal rife, massive displacements of people, and bloodshed. A state of emergency was declared in 1990 and the Soviet Union deployed 5,000 troops to the capitol city Dushanbe following pro-democracy protests. Makhkamamov supported the August 1991 Soviet coup attempt, and after the coup failed, he was forced to resign. Nabiyev returned to power, and after Tajikistan declared independence on 9 September 1991, prevailed in presidential elections on 27 October 1991. However, he was forced to resign at gunpoint, and was replaced in November 1992 by Emomali Rahmonov, who ruled Tajikistan in an authoritarian style through 2011. Meanwhile, factions that were disenfranchised from the traditional ruling elites organized into a loose coalition known as the United Tajik Opposition (UTO). They began to challenge the elites and by 1992, the country had fallen into civil war.

The UTO included representatives from disenfranchised regions, democratic reformists, and Islamists. In addition, numerous militias and other armed groups launched challenges to the government from 1992–97. The result, according to the US State Department, was a breakdown in central authority.

By 1997, the civil war had resulted in 20,000 deaths, the displacement of 600,000 people, and economic devastation. After Rahmonov gained control, the government banned opposition political parties and took over the nation's media. It also gained the consent to place peacekeeping forces from the Commonwealth of Independent States along the Afghan-Tajik border to prevent Islamist fighters from entering Tajikistan.

In December 1996, the government and United Tajik Opposition agreed to set up a National Reconciliation Commission. On June 27, 1997, Rahmonov and United Tajik Opposition (UTO) leader Seyed Abdullo Nuri signed a comprehensive peace agreement, under which Rakhmanov remained president but 30% of ministerial posts were allocated to the opposition and Nuri headed the NRC. The power-sharing agreement took effect on 26 March 2000, and the NRC was disbanded. Legislative elections took place, the UN Security Council withdrew UN observers, and the benchmarks of the peace process were largely met. These benchmarks included a return of refugees, demilitarization of rebel forces, the legalization of opposition parties, and the holding of presidential elections. Stability in Tajikistan remained fragile, however, and as of 2011, Rahmono had consolidated power and removed most oppositionists from the government.

New Islamist militant activity, along with the US war on terror, confronted Tajikistan through the first decade of the 21st century. The Islamic Movement of Uzbekistan, which seeks to establish an Islamic state in Central Asia, and the Hizb-ut-Tahrir (Freedom Party) both operated in the country. Tajikistan offered the use of its airports to the US for its campaign in Afghanistan following the 11 September 2001 terrorist attacks on the US. Russia also established a 3,000-person tactical air base and increased its border troops along the Tajik-Afghan border in 2001. Russia withdrew the border guard in June 2005, but US and French troops continued to be stationed in the country.

The Economist Intelligence Unit reported that regional Islamist groups have been building their presence and ability to stage attacks in Tajikistan, and predicted further instability for the country in 2012–13.

13 GOVERNMENT

The Soviet Socialist Republic of Tajikistan was renamed the Republic of Tajikistan on 31 August 1991, and declared independence from the Soviet Union on 9 September 1991. A constitutional amendment passed through a 26 September 1999 referendum increased the president's term of office from five to seven years.

The legislative branch consists of a bicameral parliament with a 63-seat lower house known as the Council of Representatives and a 33-seat upper house known as the National Council.

Elections for the presidency last took place in 2006, and were set for 2013. Elections for parliament last took place in 2010 and were set for 2015. President Rahmonov first took control of the government in April 1992, and was re-elected in 1999 and 2006 in elections that international observers have described as neither free nor fair. Rahmonov has retained extensive power, and has kept elite supporters from the Kulyab region dominant in the government. A June 2003 constitutional amendment approved by a reported 93% of voters allowed for the president to serve two additional seven-year terms beyond the 2006 election, allowing Rahmonov to remain in office theoretically until 2020.

According to the Rahmonov-designed constitution, the Oliy Majlis (legislature) enacts laws, interprets the constitution, determines basic directions of domestic and foreign policy, sets dates for referenda and elections, and approves key ministerial and other appointments. The legislature also approves the state budget, determines tax policy, ratifies treaties, and approves a state of war or emergency as decreed by the president. The constitution also calls for creation of a presidium to "organize work," to be elected by the legislators and to be headed by the speaker. Laws are required to be passed by a two-thirds majority of the total number of deputies, and a presidential veto may be overridden by the same margin. The prime minister is appointed by the president.

The ruling party won an overwhelming victory in parliamentary elections held in February 2005 and again in 2010. Foreign observers declared in both cases that these elections did not meet international standards.

From 2004–06, the government arrested opposition party leaders, often on allegations of involvement with terrorism. Opposition Democratic Party leader Mahmadruzi Iskandarov was sentenced in October 2005 to 23 years in prison on terrorism and corruption charges, and Gaffor Mirzoyev, a former military commander, was sentenced in August 2006 to life imprisonment after being convicted on charges of terrorism and plotting to overthrow the government.

The US State Department noted in 2011 that corruption was pervasive in the Tajikistan government, and that power has not been equally shared.

14 POLITICAL PARTIES

Political parties active in Tajikistan as of December 2011 included the People's Democratic Party of Tajikistan (PDPT), which was headed by President Rahmonov; the Islamic Revival Party (IRPT), headed by Muhiddin Kabiri; the Tajik Communist Party (CPT), headed by Shodi Shabdolov; the Democratic Party (DPT), a government-recognized faction which was headed by Masud Sobirov while the chair of the original party, Mahmadruzi Iskandarov was serving a 23-year prison term; the Social Democratic Party (SDPT), headed by Rahmatullo Zoyirov; the Socialist Party of Tajikistan (SPT), a government-recognized faction which was headed by Abdukhalim Gafforov while the original party which was not recognized by the government was headed by Murhuseyn Narziev; the Agrarian Party (APT), headed by Amir Birievich; and the Party of Economic Reform (PERT), headed by Olimjon Boboyev.

In the February 2010 elections, the president's political party, the People's Democratic Party, captured 71% of the vote and 55 seats in the assembly. The main opposition party, the Islamic Revival Party, won 8.2% of the vote and two seats in the assembly. The Tajik Communist Party, the Agrarian Party, and the Party of Economic reform each gained two seats.

15 LOCAL GOVERNMENT

The local governance structure of Tajikistan since independence has consisted of two provinces (viloyat); one autonomous province (viloyati mukhtor); and 52 districts that are ruled directly from the capitol city of Dushanbe. The provinces are Khation and Sughd, and the autonomous province is Gorno Badakhshon. The viloyat Khation includes the Qurghonteppa and Kulyab regions, which were separate oblasts under Soviet rule.

16 JUDICIAL SYSTEM

The judicial system consists of a Supreme Court, with judges appointed by the president. Civil cases are heard in general civil courts, economic courts, and military courts. According to the US State Department, there were no known cases of individuals filing civil cases for alleged human rights violations.

The president appoints judges and the procurator general to five-year terms with confirmation by the legislature, and the president has the power to dismiss them. The court system suffers from a lack of trained judges and lawyers and from pressures applied by local political factions and the central government.

17 ARMED FORCES

The International Institute for Strategic Studies reports that armed forces in Tajikistan totaled 8,800 members in 2011. The force is comprised of 7,300 from the army and 1,500 members of the air force and air defense. Armed forces represent 0.6% of the labor force in Tajikistan. Defense spending totaled $222.6 million and accounted for 1.5% of gross domestic product (GDP).

Russian troops patrolled the Tajik-Afghan border before withdrawing in 2005, replacing the border troops with Tajikistan soldiers.

[18]INTERNATIONAL COOPERATION

Tajikistan became a member of the UN on 2 March 1992; it is part of ESCAP, and several nonregional specialized agencies, such as the FAO, ILO, UNESCO, UNIDO, the IAEA, the World Bank, and the WHO. Tajikistan is also a member of the Asian Development Bank, the Commonwealth of Independent States (CIS), the Euro-Atlantic Partnership Council, the European Bank for Reconstruction and Development, OSCE, and the Organization of the Islamic Conference (OIC). It has observer status at the WTO.

Afghanistan was a primary security concern through 2011, although the ousting of the Taliban government helped make relationships friendlier between Tajikistan and Afghanistan. Relationships with Uzbekistan also have been tense, especially over Tajikistan's plans to develop hydropower. Tensions also have flared up periodically between Tajikistan and Kyrgyzstan.

US-Tajik relationships have deepened with Tajikistan's support to the United States following the 11 September 2001 terrorist attacks on the United States.

[19]ECONOMY

The GDP rate of change in Tajikistan, as of 2010, was 6.5%. Inflation stood at 5.8%, and unemployment was reported at 2.2%.

According to the US State Department, Tajikistan in 2011 was the poorest of the former Soviet republics and one of the poorest countries in the world. Its foreign revenue was dependent on exports of cotton and aluminum as well as remittances from overseas Tajik workers living primarily in Russia.

The 1992–97 civil war damaged an already weak economy. Through strict fiscal and monetary policies, the country experienced a period of steady growth beginning in the late 1990s, but it was not enough to stabilize the economy. The US State Department notes that despite the strict fiscal and monetary policies, government interference and massive corruption have stifled economic growth and private investment. After the National Bank of Tajikistan admitted in December 2007 to improper lending practices, the International Monetary Fund canceled its program. The IMF support was later restated.

The CIA estimated that 49.8% of Tajikistan's work force was in agriculture in 2009. Drug trafficking along the Afghan border was on the rise in 2011, and has impacted Tajikistan's economy.

The CIA assessed Tajikistan's economy in 2011 as fragile due to a lack of economic reform, corruption, weak governances, seasonal power shortages, and external debt.

In the midst of the global economic crisis that began in 2008, an estimated 500,000 Tajiks (primarily men) left to find jobs in Russia and Kazakhstan. Because those nations went into recession, however, many Tajik migrants soon became unemployed, with some returning home. As foreign recessions translated into a drop in remittances, thousands of families found themselves in greater depths of poverty. Women and children have been most drastically affected, especially as many men choose to stay abroad with at least the hope of employment, rather than return home, knowing that no jobs are available. An estimated 53% of the population lived below the poverty line in 2009.

[20]INCOME

The CIA estimated that in 2010 the GDP of Tajikistan was $14.74 billion. The CIA defines GDP as the value of all final goods and services produced within a nation in a given year and computed on the basis of purchasing power parity (PPP) rather than value as measured on the basis of the rate of the exchange based on current dollars. The per capita GDP was estimated at $2,000. The annual growth rate of GDP was 6.5%. The average inflation rate was 5.8%. It was estimated that agriculture accounted for 19.2% of GDP, industry 22.6%, and services 58.1%.

According to the World Bank, remittances from citizens living abroad totaled $1.7 billion or about $229 per capita and accounted for approximately 11.9% of GDP.

The World Bank reported that in 2009, household consumption in Tajikistan totaled $3.9 billion or about $512 per capita, measured in current US dollars rather than PPP. Household consumption includes expenditures of individuals, households, and nongovernmental organizations on goods and services, excluding the purchases of dwellings. It was estimated that household consumption was growing at an average annual rate of 4.9%.

The World Bank estimates that Tajikistan, with 0.11% of the world's population, accounted for 0.02% of the world's GDP. By comparison, the United States, with 4.85% of the world's population, accounted for 22.51% of world GDP.

As of 2011 the most recent study by the World Bank reported that actual individual consumption in Tajikistan was 89.3% of GDP and accounted for 0.03% of world consumption. By comparison, the United States accounted for 25.44% of world individual consumption. The World Bank also estimated that 46.4% of Tajikistan's GDP was spent on food and beverages, 11% on housing and household furnishings, 4.3% on clothes, 3.1% on health, 7.3% on transportation, 1.7% on communications, 1.7% on recreation, 0.2% on restaurants and hotels, and 8% on miscellaneous goods and services and purchases from abroad.

[21]LABOR

As of 2009, Tajikistan had a total labor force of 2.1 million people. Within that labor force, CIA estimates in 2009 noted that 49.8% were employed in agriculture, 12.8% in industry, and 37.4% in the service sector.

Tajikistan laws allow workers to form and join unions, and according to the government, approximately 1.3 million people or about 63% of the labor force belonged to unions as of 2010. However, the government often tried to influence union leadership and activities, and an umbrella organization known as the Federation of Trade Unions was not found to represent worker interests. Citizens often were reluctant to strike because they feared government retaliation.

Average monthly wages were $73 in 2010; in many sectors, however, the average wage was considerably lower. Agricultural workers earned an average of $24.50 a month. To offset the low wages, the government provided subsidies for workers and families who earned a minimum wage of $17 a month, and some employers included food commodities or products produced by their enterprises in the employee compensation. Employers often sold or bartered these goods in local markets.

The standard workweek is 40 hours for adults over 18. The minimum age for children to work is 16, although 15 year olds are allowed to work with permission from local trade unions. The maximum workweek for children under 18 is 36 hours. Children are allowed to participate in household labor and agricultural work starting at age seven, and many children work during cotton harvests, in bazaars, or selling goods on the street.

22 AGRICULTURE

Roughly 7% of the total land is currently farmed, and the country's major crops include cotton, grain, fruits, grapes, and vegetables. Cereal production amounted to 1.2 million tons, fruit production 350,000 tons, and vegetable production 1.5 million tons.

Agriculture employed 49.8% of the labor force in 2009, and accounted for 19% of GDP.

Food production declined dramatically following independence and the 1992–97 civil war. According to the World Bank, Tajikistan could not afford to import enough food to feed its people and only averted food shortages through the acceptance of foreign aid. Because of the country's mountainous terrain, Tajik agriculture relies extensively on irrigation. A network of canals expands agriculture into semidesert areas. Cotton is the major commercial crop; three irrigated valleys (Vakhsh, Kofarnihon, and Zeravshan) are the sites of most production.

Wheat is the staple grain and is grown mainly in the northern and southern plains. About one-third of the wheat crop is irrigated.

Horticulture has been important since antiquity. Most orchards and vineyards are located in the northern valleys, where apricots, pears, plums, apples, cherries, pomegranates, figs, and nuts are grown.

Foreign aid has provided small farmers with agricultural equipment, and the government has distributed seedlings to farmers and gardeners through a 2010–14 State Programme for the Development of Horticulture.

23 ANIMAL HUSBANDRY

The UN Food and Agriculture Organization (FAO) reported that Tajikistan dedicated 3.9 million hectares (9.53 million acres) to permanent pasture or meadow in 2009. During that year, the country tended 3.7 million chickens and 1.8 million head of cattle. The production from these animals amounted to 35,617 tons of beef and veal, 5,675 tons of poultry, 9,000 tons of eggs, and 387,388 tons of milk. Tajikistan also produced 3,290 tons of cattle hide and 5,447 tons of raw wool.

Livestock herding has formed a major part of Tajikistan's economy. A 2011–16 project to develop livestock and pasture was being support by the International Fund for Agricultural Development. The agreement would provide $14.5 million from the fund to the Ministry of Agriculture.

24 FISHING

In 2008, the annual capture totaled 146 tons according to the UN FAO.

The Ministry of Agriculture has supported the establishment of trout-breeding fisheries in the Gomo Badakhshan Autonomous Region, where clean lakes are present. About 70 fish farms were operating there and in the Khatlon region as of 2011, and the government was supporting a fish farming program through 2015 to meet domestic demand for fish. The UN Agricultural Organization provided $27,000 to establish a water analysis laboratory, and planned to help increase the variety of fish farmed.

25 FORESTRY

Approximately 3% of Tajikistan is covered by forest. The UN FAO estimated the 2009 roundwood production at zero. The value of all forest products, including roundwood, totaled $80,000.

Ninety percent of Tajikistan's forests disappeared through the 20th and early 21st century.

26 MINING

Although Tajikistan is an important gold producer, the possessor of the largest deposits of antimony in the former Soviet Union, and had more than 400 explored mineral deposits, containing 70 types of minerals, it is primary aluminum that is the country's most important mineral-based product. In 2009, Tajikistan Aluminum Co. aluminum smelter was the country's only large-scale production enterprise in the minerals sector.

In 2009 gold production was estimated at 1,361 kg. Silver production in 2009 totaled 4,500 kg, down from an estimated 5,000 kg in 2008. In 2009, Tajikistan also produced antimony, lead, and mercury. Gypsum production in 2009 totaled 8,500 metric tons, unchanged since 2005. Tajikistan also produces cement, and fluorspar. No copper, molybdenum, tungsten, or zinc has been produced in recent years. Gold is mined southeast of Gharm, in the Pamir Mountains, in the Yakhsu Valley, in Chkalovsk, and in the Jilau, Taror, and Aprelevka deposits; mercury is mined at the Dzhizhikrutskoye deposit, north of Dushanbe; antimony, at Isfara and Dzhizhikrutskoye; arsenic, cadmium, tungsten, and lead-zinc, in the Yuzhno-Yangikanskiy deposit, north of the Zeravshan River; and uranium and graphite, northeast of Khudzhand. Uranium mining was conducted during 1945–1992 in Chkalovsk; interest in exploration and processing has resumed.

Other metal and industrial resources includ alunite, bauxite, iron, manganese, nepheline syenite, nickel, rare metals, selenium, strontium, tin, barite, boron, construction materials, dolomite, phosphates, precious and semiprecious stones, and salt.

27 ENERGY AND POWER

The World Bank reported in 2008 that Tajikistan produced 16.2 billion kWh of electricity and consumed 14.2 billion kWh, or 1,857 kWh per capita. Roughly 42% of energy came from fossil fuels, while 55% came from alternative fuels. Per capita oil consumption was 365 kg. Oil production totaled 215 barrels of oil a day.

Tajikistan has experienced severe electricity shortages with most of its residents receiving little or no electricity for weeks at a time during the winter months. Despite these shortages, its potential for hydroelectrical power development is considered strong. The country expanded its output of electricity with the completion of the Sangtuda I hydropower dam in 2009, a project that was supported with Russian investment. A smaller dam, Sangtuda 2, was being built with Iranian support and was scheduled to be completed in 2012. The Roghun dam would be the tallest dam in the world, if completed. The World Bank has agreed to finance feasibility studies for the dam, but the project has generated fric-

Principal Trading Partners – Tajikistan (2010)

(In millions of US dollars)

Country	Total	Exports	Imports	Balance
World	3,850.2	1,194.7	2,655.5	-1,460.8
Russia	958.3	101.8	856.5	-754.7
China	685.1	447.0	238.2	208.8
Turkey	437.0	377.0	60.0	317.0
Kazakhstan	312.6	19.9	292.7	-272.8
Iran	201.3	59.6	141.6	-82.0
Ukraine	200.1	11.3	188.7	-177.4
United States	95.1	0.1	95.0	-94.8
Afghanistan	92.1	52.3	39.9	12.4
Turkmenistan	84.8	1.2	83.5	-82.3
Uzbekistan	80.4	8.6	71.8	-63.1

(…) data not available or not significant.

(n.s.) not specified.

SOURCE: *2011 Direction of Trade Statistics Yearbook,* New York: United Nations, 2011.

tion with neighboring Uzbekistan. The government sold shares in the Roghun project beginning in January 2010. It raised more than $180 million, but numerous reports indicated that Tajik residents and businesses were forced to buy shares.

28 INDUSTRY

Industry accounted for 22.9% of Tajikistan's GDP in 2010 and employed 12.9% of its work force, according to CIA estimates. The industrial production growth rate was estimated at 7.5% and major industrial items produced were aluminum, lead, zinc, cement, fertilizers, vegetable oil, textiles, metal-cutting machine tools, and refrigerators and freezers. Factories are small and obsolete. Despite these obstacles, Tajikistan possesses silver, gold, uranium, and tungsten mineral resources.

The 1992–97 civil war damaged much of the country's industrial infrastructure, and rebuilding has been slow.

As of 2011, only a few large industrial enterprises accounted for the bulk of Tajikistan's industrial activities. Although the government has made a privatization and development of industry a goal, ongoing corruption has hindered industrial growth.

29 SCIENCE AND TECHNOLOGY

Patent applications in science and technology as of 2009, according to the World Bank, totaled 11 in Tajikistan. Public financing of science was 0.06% of GDP.

Tajikistan in 1992 became part of a newly-established International Science and Technology Center, a consortium dedicated to engaging weapons scientists, technicians, and engineers from the Commonwealth of Independent States in research and development projects aimed at peaceful civilian activities. Prior to the formation of this consortium, the former Soviet Union had exploited much of Tajikistan's mineral resources for the development of nuclear weaponry.

The Tajik Academy of Sciences, founded in 1951 at Dushanbe, has departments of physical-mathematical, chemical, and technical sciences; earth sciences; biological and medical sciences; and 10 associated research institutes. Tajik State University has faculties of mechanics and mathematics, physics, chemistry, geolo-

gy, and biology. Tajik Abu-Ali Ibn-Cina (Avicenna) State Medical Institute was founded in 1939. Tajik Agricultural Institute was founded in 1951. Tajik Technical University was founded in 1956. All four educational institutions are in Dushanbe.

30 DOMESTIC TRADE

Although trade is still dominated by the state sector, the government has been working on programs to transfer of much of the retail and wholesale trade sector into private ownership. Most small enterprises are in private hands. Privatization of medium and large-sized businesses, land reform, and banking reforms are still in the works. Price liberalization lifted controls on most consumer and wholesale trade, although subsidies and lowered ceilings have been applied to staple goods like flour, sugar, oil, bread, meat, and children's footwear. Most large towns have large marketplaces, or bazaars, where individual merchants sell a variety of consumer goods, many of which are imported. Trade on the black market has expanded significantly with the growing economic disarray since independence.

31 FOREIGN TRADE

Tajikistan imported $3.301 billion worth of goods and services in 2008, while exporting $1.318 billion worth of goods and services. Major import partners in 2009 were Russia, 31.7%; Kazakhstan, 11.1%; China, 10.6%; Uzbekistan, 5%; and Ukraine, 4.6%. Its major export partners were China, 40.2%; Turkey, 15.1%; Russia, 10.2%; Uzbekistan, 7.1%; and Iran, 4.8%.

Key exports in 2009 included aluminum, electricity, cotton, gold, fruits, vegetable oil, and textiles. Key imports were electricity, petroleum products, aluminum oxide, machinery and equipment, and foodstuffs.

32 BALANCE OF PAYMENTS

In 2010 Tajikistan had a foreign trade deficit of $1.8 billion.

The CIA estimated that Tajikistan had a negative current account balance of $381.1 million in 2010 compared with a negative current account balance of $179.9 million in 2009. Foreign exchange reserves (including gold) were estimated at $506 million as of 31 December 2010 compared with $469.1 million on 31 December 2009.

Foreign income earnings depend on cotton and aluminum exports, and remittances from Tajik workers living abroad. The World Bank estimated that there were more than 1.5 million Tajik workers in Russia and Kazakhstan, and that migrant remittance inflows in 2010 were equivalent to 42% of GDP.

33 BANKING AND SECURITIES

The National Bank of Tajikistan was formally established in 1991 as the country's central bank. As of 2008, there were 10 banks in the country, along with one branch of a foreign bank, seven credit societies, and one non-banking financial institution. There also were eight micro-credit deposit organizations, 24 micro-lending organizations, and 38 micro-lending funds.

The CIA estimated Tajikistan's stock of narrow money (the amount of total currency in circulation) at $882.4 million in 2010 compared with an estimate of $675.1 million in 2009. The stock of broad money (which includes the total currency along with banking and credit union deposits, money market funds, short-term

Balance of Payments – Tajikistan (2010)

(In millions of US dollars)

Current Account		**-382.8**
Balance on goods		-1,633.7
Imports	-2,936.4	
Exports	1,302.7	
Balance on services		-183.4
Balance on income		-78.7
Current transfers		1,513.1
Capital Account		**68.5**
Financial Account		**382.4**
Direct investment abroad		...
Direct investment in Tajikistan		15.8
Portfolio investment assets		...
Portfolio investment liabilities		6.5
Financial derivatives		...
Other investment assets		22.4
Other investment liabilities		337.7
Net Errors and Omissions		**31.0**
Reserves and Related Items		**-99.1**

(…) data not available or not significant.

SOURCE: *Balance of Payment Statistics Yearbook 2011,* Washington, DC: International Monetary Fund, 2011.

repurchase agreements, and other large liquid assets) was estimated at $1.2 billion for 2010 and $924.7 million for 2009. The stock of domestic credit was estimated at $931.2 million in 2010, compared with $709.2 million in 2009.

There is no securities exchange.

34 INSURANCE

The World Bank reported that there were 14 insurance companies in Tajikistan as of June 2007. The organization found that the sector was growing in a largely unregulated environment. Gross premiums totaled $20 million in 2006, and many insurance firms were undercapitalized. Two state-owned firms held a monopoly on mandatory insurances and government business.

35 PUBLIC FINANCE

In 2010 the budget of Tajikistan included $1.482 billion in public revenue and $1.538 billion in public expenditures. The budget surplus amounted to .4% of GDP. In total $1.988 billion of the debt held by foreign entities.

Taxes and other revenues accounted for 26.5% of GDP, according to 2010 estimates.

36 TAXATION

Business taxes in Tajikistan included a social tax of 25% on gross salaries, a 1% minimum income tax, a sales tax of 3%, a value-added tax of 18%, and a corporate income tax of 15%. There also were land, vehicle, road, and interest income taxes. The maximum personal tax was 40%, and employees also were required to contribute 1% of their income to a social security fund. A new tax code was being developed in 2011.

37 CUSTOMS AND DUTIES

The government maintains a list of commodities and services subject to import licensing and quotas. Generally, imports are free

of restrictions, including tariffs and quotas, with the exception of narcotics and firearms, which are forbidden. Goods traded within the former Soviet Union are mostly free from import duties. There is a 28% VAT and excise taxes are levied on some products.

Four special economic zones—Khujand, Panj, Ishkoshim, and Dangara—have been granted special trade privileges and exceptions from taxation.

38 FOREIGN INVESTMENT

Foreign direct investment (FDI) in Tajikistan was a net inflow of $15.8 million according to World Bank figures published in 2009. FDI represented 0.32% of GDP.

After independence, Tajikistan's government emphasized the promotion of foreign investment particularly to develop labor-intensive manufacturing industries. With civil unrest, however, few investments flowed into the country.

From 1997–2004 Tajikistan attracted $224 million in FDI. President Rakhmanov made numerous statements calling for increased foreign investment in the early- and mid-2000s, particularly in the hydropower sector, but his administration as of 2011 had yet to fully implement key reforms and regulations to create an attractive business climate.

Tajikistan's foreign direct investment grew substantially between 2005 and 2008, and totaled about $1.1 billion, from $54 million in 2005 to $376 million in 2008. Top investors were the U.K., Korea, the Russian Federation, Cyprus, Italy, the US and Canada.

The government announced in December 2011 that it hoped to attract $15 billion in foreign direct investment by 2015.

39 ECONOMIC DEVELOPMENT

Tajikistan, the poorest of the former Soviet Republics, endured much economic hardship during its first two decades as an independent nation.

Soviet development policies for the Tajik Republic prioritized agricultural and natural resources development. After Tajikistan became independent in 1991, the government's initial economic development plans were to develop hydroelectric power production, and the silk, fertilizer, coal, metal and marble industries, and to expand fruit and vegetable processing. The government also introduced price liberalization, privatization measures, and fiscal reforms. The outbreak of civil war in 1992, however, brought economic development to a standstill.

After the civil war ended, the government initiated proposals in 1996–97 to convert state-owned enterprises to joint stock companies. In addition, legislation was passed to create a securities market. The government also initiated plans to turn land over to private farmers and to privatize the cotton industry. The private sector accounted for less than 30% of GDP in 1997. Tajikistan's government also entered a three-year arrangement with the International Monetary Fund's Poverty Reducion and Growth Facility in 1998, which was only partially completed due to a lack of transparency and lack of independence of the Tajik Central Bank. A new structural reform program was begun in 2002, and the Tajikistan parliament adopted a three-year National Poverty Reduction Strategy that was aimed at increasing real income and improving the living standards of the country's poorest peoples.

Although Tajikistan's economic growth resumed after the civil war ended in 1997, and accelerated after 2002, its macroeconomic picture has remained fragile and vulnerable to fluctuations in the world prices of aluminum and cotton. Tajikistan's economic growth has also been increasingly tied to the economy of Russia, where many Tajik laborers reside because remittances from these workers have formed an important source of revenue.

The International Monetary Fund reported that real GDP growth was 6.5% in 2010 compared with 3.9% in 2009. Since 2005, gains in hydroelectricity production have boosted industrial activity. The external current account balance had an average 5% deficit from 2005–09 but shifted to a surplus of 2.2% in 2010.

Foreign aid from Russia, Uzbekistan, and international lending organizations support Tajikistan's basic needs, and aid officials have described the country's infrastructure and health and education systems as fragile. Illegal drug trafficking along the Afghanistan border have also imperiled country's security situation.

Although Tajikistan has maintained strict fiscal and monetary controls on its economy, poverty, unemployment and underemployment continued to be major problems as of 2011. The country has also faced problems with electrical supply and clean water access. One prospect that aid officials have cited has been the ongoing construction of hydropower facilities, which would allow Tajikistan to export electricity for profit.

40 SOCIAL DEVELOPMENT

The government's social security systems have been threatened by war and economic turmoil. Refugees returning from Afghanistan after the war suffered from malnutrition and had high mortality rates in resettlement camps.

The human rights situation in Tajikistan continued to be weak through 2011. According to the US State Department, political participation of citizens was severely restricted; torture and abuse of prison detainees was widespread; government corruption hindered democratic and social reforms; and restrictions on the freedom of speech, press, association, and religion were widely imposed.

During a period of violence in the country's Rasht Valley from September to December 2010, the government blocked five Web sites, and refused to allow three newspapers to be published. Journalists who covered the violence were charged with supporting terrorism. In addition, villagers who protested the imposition of new toll stations on the road between Dushanbe and Khujand in April 2010 were threatened with imprisonment.

Government officials also extorted money from citizens and businesses in 2010 by ordering teachers, doctors, government employees, students, and villagers to buy shares toward the purchase of the Roghun hydroelectric dam. The demands often were in excess of people's salaries. Students also were forced to pay bribes to enter universities or to earn good grades on exams.

Violence against women has also continued to be widespread, with one-third to one-half of Tajik women experiencing some form of domestic violence. Female suicide and female susceptibility to the HIV virus are also prevalent.

41 HEALTH

According to the CIA, life expectancy in Tajikistan was 67 years in 2011. The country spent 5.0% of its GDP on healthcare, amounting to $38 per person. There were 20 physicians, 50 nurses and midwives, and 61 hospital beds per 10,000 inhabitants. The fertil-

ity rate was 3.4, while the infant mortality rate was 52 per 1,000 live births. In 2008 the maternal mortality rate, according to the World Bank, was 64 per 100,000 births. It was estimated that 89% of children were vaccinated against measles. The CIA calculated HIV/AIDS prevalence in Tajikistan to be about 0.2% in 2009.

42 HOUSING

A 2009 report by Habitat for Humanity highlighted Tajikistan's housing conditions. The report noted that the economic collapse that accompanied the 1992–97 civil war had left thousands without acceptable housing, and that little effort had been put toward improving the situation.

As of 2009 homes were often overcrowded, had leaking roofs, and inadequate heating systems. Access to improved water systems also was weak. The CIA reported that nearly 39% of families residing in rural areas in 2008 lacked access to clean drinking water.

The most common building materials for new homes are prefabricated ferro-cement slabs. In rural areas, traditional materials of paksha, brick, mortar, and stone are used.

43 EDUCATION

In 2008 the World Bank estimated that 97% of age–eligible children in Tajikistan were enrolled in primary school. Secondary enrollment for age–eligible children stood at 83%. Tertiary enrollment was estimated at 20%. Of those enrolled in tertiary education, there were 100 male students for every 40 female students. Overall, the CIA estimated that Tajikistan had a literacy rate of 99.5%. Public expenditure on education represented 3.5% of GDP, compared with approximately 8% in 2005.

Before the country came under Soviet control in 1920, there were no state-supported schools, only Islamic ones. Since then, many schools have been built. Education is free and compulsory between the ages of 7 and 17. Primary school covers four years of study, followed by eight years of secondary school. Vocational and technical programs are offered at the secondary level. Since 1989, there has been an increased emphasize on Tajik language, literature, and culture.

A 2009 report by the EurasiaNet news service described Tajikistan's educational system as deteriorating. A lack of teachers due to low salaries had produced understaffing in schools as well as a large number of unqualified instructors. The situation was considered so bad that parents were likely to have received a better primary and secondary education than their children.

There were 28 higher educational institutes as of 2011. The main universities are Tajik State National University, the Academy of Science, and Khujand Polytechnic Institute. Many regional colleges and universities also exist.

44 LIBRARIES AND MUSEUMS

The Tajikistan National Library serves as the country's main depository. Museums include the Museum of National Antiquities, a center for Tajik and Russian scholars; the Tajik State Regional Museum; the Gurminj Museum of Musical Instruments; the Ziyadullo Shahidi Museum of Musical Culture, located in the former home of Tajik composer Ziyadullo Shahidi; and museums honoring two Tajik poets Tursunzoda and Sadridden Aini. The

Fortress of Hissar outside Dushanbe also contains indoor and outdoor museums.

⁴⁵MEDIA

In 2009 the CIA reported that there were 290,000 telephone landlines in Tajikistan. In addition to landlines, mobile phone subscriptions averaged 70 per 100 people, with 4.9 million cell phones in use. There were 8 FM radio stations, 10 AM radio stations, and 2 shortwave radio stations. Internet users numbered 10 per 100 citizens.

Tajik Radio broadcasts in Russian, Tajik, Persian, and Uzbek; Tajik Television, with four channels, broadcasts in Tajik, Russian, and Uzbek. Repeater television stations relay programs from Russia, Iran, and Turkey. Satellite earth stations receive Orbita and INTELSAT broadcasts. There are only a few private radio stations and no private television stations. In 2010, the country had 1,504 Internet hosts. As of 2009, there were some 700,000 Internet users.

Despite a 1991 law protecting already constitutionally provided free speech and press, the government has continued to restrict these freedoms severely. Editors and journalists practice careful self-censorship, and supplies of newsprint, broadcasting facilities, and operating monies are controlled by the authorities.

⁴⁶ORGANIZATIONS

The Association of Microfinance Organizations and the Tajikistan Chamber of Commerce and Industry are key economic organizations. In addition, there were nearly 3,000 civil society organizations operating in Tajikistan as of 2006. These organizations include women's groups, arts and crafts organizations, educational entities, and organizations pressing for political and economic reforms.

Many international organizations have chapters in Tajikistan including the Red Crescent Society, UNICEF, and Habitat for Humanity.

⁴⁷TOURISM, TRAVEL, AND RECREATION

The *Tourism Factbook*, published by the UN World Tourism Organization, reported 325,000 incoming tourists to Tajikistan in 2008, who spent a total of $19.5 million. Of those incoming tourists, there were 310,000 from Europe. The estimated daily cost to visit Dushanbe, the capital, was $325. The cost of visiting other cities averaged $155.

Visitors to Tajikistan can partake in trekking, mountaineering, horse or camel riding, rock climbing and other sports. Many remnants of the area's ancient Zoroastrian, Hindu, Buddhist, and Christian civilizations remain as well as examples of Islamic architecture and Central Asian art. A statue of Bolshevik leader Vladimir Lenin that was believed to be the largest in Central Asia was removed from the central square in Khujand in 2011, and was to be replaced with a statue of Ismoili Somoni, founder of Tajik statehood.

⁴⁸FAMOUS PERSONS

Outstanding representatives of culture and literature in Tajikistan are the Tadzhik poet Rudaki (d. 941) and the scientist and poet Avicenna (Hussayn ibn 'Abd' Addallah ibn Sine, 980?–1037), born near Bukhoro (Bukhara). Avicenna wrote an encyclopedia of science. Pre-Soviet Tajik cultural figures include the author Abdalrauf Fitrat, who wrote *Last Judgement,* and Sadridalin Aymi, author of the novels *Slaves* and *Dokhunala.*

⁴⁹DEPENDENCIES

Tajikistan has no territories or colonies.

⁵⁰BIBLIOGRAPHY

Abazov, Rafis. *Tajikistan.* New York: Marshall Cavendish Benchmark, 2006.

Abdullaev, Kamoludin, and Shahram Akbarzadeh. *Historical Dictionary of Tajikistan.* 2nd ed. Lanham, MD: Scarecrow Press, 2010.

Dannreuther, Roland. *European Union Foreign and Security Policy: Towards a Neighbourhood Strategy.* New York: Routledge, 2004.

Kort, Michael. *Central Asian Republics.* New York: Facts On File, 2004.

Roi, Yaacov. *Democracy and Pluralism in Muslim Eurasia.* New York: Frank Cass, 2004.

Tajikistan Investment and Business Guide: Strategic and Practical Information. Washington, DC: International Business Publications USA, 2012.

THAILAND

Kingdom of Thailand
Prates Thai

CAPITAL: Bangkok (Krung Thep)

FLAG: The national flag, adopted in 1917, consists of five horizontal stripes. The outermost are red (symbolizing the Thai people); those adjacent are white (symbolizing Buddhism); the blue center stripe (representing the monarchy) is twice as thick as each of the other four.

ANTHEM: There are three national anthems: *Pleng Sansen Phra Barami (Anthem Eulogizing His Majesty)*; *Pleng Chard Thai (Thai National Anthem)*; and *Pleng Maha Chati (Anthem of Great Victory)*, an instrumental composition.

MONETARY UNIT: The baht is divided into 100 satang. There are coins of 1, 5, 10, 25, and 50 satang and 1, 5, and 10 baht, and notes of 50 satang and 1, 5, 10, 20, 50, 60, 100, and 500 baht. BAHT1 = US$0.0321 (or US$1 = BAHT31.20) as of 2011.

WEIGHTS AND MEASURES: The metric system is the legal standard, but some traditional units also are used.

HOLIDAYS: New Year's Day, 1 January; Chakkri Day, 6 April; Songkran, several days mid-April; Coronation Day, 5 May; Queen's Birthday, 12 August; Chulalongkorn Day, 23 October; King's Birthday, 5 December; Constitution Day, 10 December. Movable holidays include Makabuja Day, Plowing Festival, and Visakabuja Day.

TIME: 7 p.m. = noon GMT.

¹LOCATION, SIZE, AND EXTENT

Comprising an area of 514,000 sq km (198,456 sq mi) in Southeast Asia, Thailand (formerly known as Siam) extends almost two-thirds down the Malay Peninsula, with a length of 1,648 km (1,024 mi) N–S and a width of 780 km (485 mi) E–W. Comparatively, Thailand is slightly more than twice the size of Wyoming. It is bordered on the NE and E by Laos, on the SE by Cambodia and the Gulf of Thailand (formerly the Gulf of Siam), on the S by Malaysia, on the SW by the Andaman Sea, and on the W and NW by Myanmar (Burma), with a total boundary length of 8,082 km (5,022 mi), of which 3,219 km (2000 mi) is coastline.

Thailand's capital city, Bangkok, is located on the Chao Phraya River, north of the Gulf of Thailand.

²TOPOGRAPHY

Thailand can be thought of as five major physical regions: the central valley, the continental highlands of the north and northwest, the northeast, the southeast coast, and the peninsula. The heartland of the nation is the central valley, fronting the Gulf of Thailand and enclosed on three sides by hills and mountains. This valley, the alluvial plain of the Chao Phraya River and of its many tributaries and distributaries, is 365 km (227 mi) from north to south and has an average width of 160–240 km (100–150 mi). On this plain, and especially on its flat delta land bordering the Gulf, are found Thailand's main agricultural wealth and population centers.

The continental highlands lie north and west of the central valley. They include North Thailand, surrounded on three sides by Myanmar and Laos, which is a region of roughly parallel mountain ranges between which the Nan, Yom, Wang, Ping, and other rivers flow southward to join and create the Chao Phraya in the central valley. In the northernmost tip, drainage is northward to the Mekong River; on the western side, drainage runs westward to the Salween in Myanmar. Most of the people of North Thailand live in small intermontane plains and basins. Doi Inthanon (2,576 m/8,451 ft) is the highest point in Thailand. Along the Myanmar border from North Thailand to the peninsula is a sparsely inhabited strip of rugged mountains, deep canyons, and restricted valleys. One of the few natural gaps through this wild mountain country is Three Pagodas Pass along the Thailand-Myanmar boundary, used by the Japanese during World War II for their "death railway" (now dismantled) between Thailand and Myanmar.

The northeast, much of it often called the Khorat, is a low, undulating platform roughly 120 to 210 m (400–700 ft) above sea level in the north and west, gradually declining to about 60 m (200 ft) in the southeast. Hill and mountain ranges and scarps separate the northeast from the central valley on the west and from Cambodia on the south, while its northern and much of its eastern boundaries are marked by the Mekong River. Most of the northeast is drained by the Mun River and its major tributary, the Chi, which flow eastward into the Mekong. The northeast, in the rain shadow of the Indochina Cordillera, suffers from shortage of water and from generally thin and poor soils.

The small southeast coast region faces the Gulf of Thailand and is separated from the central valley and Cambodia by hills and mountains that rise in places to over 1,500 m (5,000 ft). The area is well-watered, and the vegetation is, for the most part, lush and tropical. Most of the people live along the narrow coastal plain and the restricted river valleys that drain southward to the Gulf.

Peninsular Thailand extends almost 960 km (600 mi) from the central valley in the north to the boundary of Malaysia in the south and is anywhere from 16 to 217 km (10–135 mi) wide between the Gulf of Thailand on the east and the Andaman Sea (Indian Ocean) and Myanmar on the west. At the Isthmus of Kra, the peninsula itself is only 24 km (15 mi) wide. A series of north-south ridges, roughly parallel, divide the peninsula into distinct west and east coast sections. The west coastal plain is narrow—nonexistent in many places—and the coast itself is quite indented and often very swampy. The east coastal plain is much wider, up to 32 km (20 mi) in sections, and the coast is smooth, with long beach stretches and few bays. Well-watered (especially the west coast), hot, and densely forested, the peninsula, unlike most of Thailand, lies within the humid tropical forest zone.

A disastrous tsunami struck southern Thailand and other countries along the Indian Ocean on 26 December 2004. Stemming from an underwater earthquake about 324 km (180 mi) south of Sumatra, the tsunami caused more than 5,400 deaths in Thailand. Many of the beaches were severely damaged, as well as the island of Phi Phi Lei, which was almost completely leveled.

3 CLIMATE

Thailand has a tropical climate. For much of the country, there are three distinct seasons: the hot season, from March through May; the rainy or wet monsoon, June to October; and the cool season, November through February. While continental Thailand receives most of its precipitation from June through October, rain occurs at all seasons in peninsular Thailand, the largest amount along the west coast from May to October and along the east coast from October to January.

For most of Thailand, the temperature rarely falls below 13°C (55°F) or rises above 35°C (95°F) with most places averaging between 24°C and 30°C (75°F and 86°F). The annual rainfall ranges from 102 cm (40 in) in the northeast to over 380 cm (150 in) in the peninsula. Bangkok has an average annual temperature of 28°C (82°F); monthly mean temperatures range from a low of around 25°C (77°F) in December to a high of around 30°C (86°F) in May, and annual rainfall is about 150 cm (59 in).

Heavy rainstorms and flooding are among the natural disasters that affect Thailand. In October–November 2010, a series of heavy rains and flash floods left more than 200 people dead and millions affected by damage to homes and farms. In late March 2011, two weeks of heavy rains caused flooding in ten southern provinces, damaging buildings and roads and leading to the deaths of at least 53 people. Catastrophic flooding occurred again in August–November 2011, causing over 350 deaths and leaving over 100,000 homeless, as flood waters inundated rural areas and towns, then swept into parts of Bangkok.

4 FLORA AND FAUNA

The World Resources Institute estimates that there are 11,625 plant species in Thailand. The remaining forests include hardwood species (notably teak), pine, bamboos, and betel and coconut palms;

in the coastal lowlands, mangroves and rattan are found. Forests produce orchids and wild fruits, such as rambutan.

Thailand is home to 300 mammal species, 971 bird species, 341 reptile species, and 103 amphibian species. The calculation reflects the total number of distinct species residing in the country, not the number of endemic species. Small populations of wild elephants, tigers, rhinoceroses, wild cattle, bears, and tapirs still survive, mainly in designated wildlife sanctuaries. Primates include gibbons and several species of monkey. Crocodiles, lizards, snakes, and turtles are numerous. A variety of fish and crustacean species live in the rivers and coastal waters.

5 ENVIRONMENT

The Promotion and Enhancement of Environmental Quality Act of 1975 charges the National Environment Board with coordination of environmental protection programs in Thailand. The nation's water supply is at risk due to contamination by industry, farming activity, sewage, and salt water, especially in the Bangkok area. Watershed regions have been deforested by increased cultivation of upland areas. Parts of Bangkok have been reported as sinking at a rate of 10 cm (4 in) a year because of depletion of the water table. Water resources totaled 409.9 cu km (98.34 cu mi), while water usage was 82.75 cu km (19.85 cu mi) per year. Domestic water usage accounted for 2% of total usage, industrial for 3%, and agricultural for 95%. Per capita water usage totaled 1,288 cu m (45,485 cu ft) per year.

Land use in urban areas is regulated by the City Planning Act of 1975, the Control of Construction of Buildings Act of 1936, and the 1960 Act for Cleanliness and Orderliness of the Country. Thailand's cities produce an average of 2.5 million tons of solid waste per year. Urban air and noise pollution is severe, largely as a result of increasingly congested motor vehicle traffic. In 1992, Thailand was among 50 nations with the world's highest levels of industrial carbon dioxide emissions. The UN reported in 2008 that carbon dioxide emissions in Thailand totaled 277,284 kilotons.

The World Resources Institute reported that Thailand had designated 10.17 million hectares (25.12 million acres) of land for protection as of 2006. Wildlife is partially protected under the Wild Animals Preservation and Protection Act of 1960, but species have been depleted through habit loss and degradation as well as illegal hunting and trapping. According to a 2011 report issued by the International Union for Conservation of Nature and Natural Resources (IUCN), threatened species included 57 types of mammals, 46 species of birds, 23 types of reptiles, 4 species of amphibians, 97 species of fish, 9 types of mollusks, and 96 species of plants. Threatened/endangered species in Thailand include the pileated gibbon, tiger, Asian elephant, Malayan tapir, Fea's muntjac, Thailand brow-antlered deer, kouprey, green turtle, hawksbill turtle, olive ridley turtle, leatherback turtle, river terrapin, estuarine crocodile, Siamese crocodile, and the false gavial. By the 1980s, Thailand had lost about 25% of its original mangrove forest area. Overexploitation and pollution of freshwater and marine fisheries have yet to be remedied.

6 POPULATION

The US Central Intelligence Agency (CIA) estimates the population of Thailand in 2011 to be approximately 66,720,153, which placed it at number 20 in population among the 196 nations of the world. In 2011, approximately 9.2% of the population was over 65 years of age, with another 19.9% under 15 years of age. The median age in Thailand was 34.2 years. There were 0.98 males for every female in the country. The population's annual rate of change was 0.566%. The projected population for the year 2025 is 72,600,000. Population density in Thailand was calculated at 130 people per sq km (337 people per sq mi). The UN estimated that 34% of the population lived in urban areas and that urban populations had an annual rate of change of 1.8%. The largest urban area was Bangkok with a population of 6.9 million.

7 MIGRATION

Thailand's estimated net migration rate, according to the CIA in 2011, amounted to zero. The total number of emigrants living abroad was 810,800, and the total number of immigrants living in Thailand was 1.16 million. Immigration to Thailand, except for by the Chinese, had historically been comparatively small. The decade of the 1920s was a period of large-scale Chinese immigration of 70,000 to 140,000 a year. Strict immigration regulations introduced in the 1940s all but stopped the legal flow of Chinese into the country.

As of December 1992, the United Nations (UN) estimated that 63,600 refugees were living in Thailand; these represented part of the over four million refugees who had left Cambodia, Laos, and Vietnam since the 1970s. Some 370,000 Cambodians on the Thai-Cambodian border were repatriated during 1992–93. The 36,000 Cambodian refugees who fled their country after the political and military events of 1997 were repatriated by 1999, and three border camps were subsequently closed. In 1986, the Thai government began forcibly repatriating many refugees from Laos. The last refugee camp for Vietnamese was closed in February 1997.

In June 1998, the Thai government formally requested increased assistance from the UN High Commissioner for Refugees (UN-HCR) for some 100,000 Karen and Karenni refugees from Myanmar, who were living in 11 camps in Thailand along the Myanmar border. A comprehensive registration of the border population was completed through the joint efforts of the Thai government and UNHCR in 1999.

In 2003, immigration authorities arrested 280,937 illegal foreigners, including 189,486 unauthorized workers; the workers were from Myanmar, Cambodia, and Laos. In 2004, some 1.3 million foreigners, from Cambodia, Laos, and Myanmar, registered as migrant workers in Thailand under a government effort to better regulate their presence. They were further required to re-register in 2005, but to do so they needed a Thai employer. Over 132,000 refugees and migrant workers from Myanmar live in Thailand, although their legal status is precarious. Third countries, particularly the United States, have increasingly accepted Myanmar refugees, particularly of the Karen ethnic group, from Thailand's border camps.

8 ETHNIC GROUPS

Thailand contains more than 30 ethnic groups varying in history, language, religion, and culture. The ethnic Thai, related to the Lao of Laos (the Shan of Myanmar, or Burma), and the Tai of southern China comprise about 75% of the total population of Thailand. The Thai may be divided into four major groups and three minor groups. Major groups are the Central Thai (Siamese) of

LOCATION: 97° to 106°E; 6° to 21°N. BOUNDARY LENGTHS: Cambodia, 803 kilometers (499 miles); Laos, 1,754 kilometers (1,090 miles); Malaysia, 506 kilometers (316 miles); Myanmar, 1,799 kilometers (1,118 miles).

the Central Valley; the Eastern Thai (Lao) of the Northeast (Khorat); the Northern Thai (Lao) of North Thailand; and the Southern Thai (Chao Pak Thai) of peninsular Thailand. Minor groups are the Phuthai of northeastern Khorat, the Shan (Tai Yai) of the far northwestern corner of northern Thailand, and the Lue in the northeastern section of northern Thailand. The several branches of Thai are united by a common language family.

A major ethnic minority are the Chinese, who account for about 14% of the total population. They are largely assimilated into the majority Thai culture, and most have Thai names. Other varied ethnic groups account for the remaining 11% of the population. Malays (3–4%) live in the southern peninsula near the border and, to a lesser extent, along the southeast coast; Khmers (1%) are settled all along the Cambodian border from the Mekong to the Gulf of Thailand, and Vietnamese or Annamese are found in the southern Khorat and on the southeast coast. Mons live mainly on the peninsula along the Burmese border. Small numbers of residents from India, Europe, and the United States live mainly in urban areas.

Principal tribal groups, mainly hill peoples, include the Kui and Kaleung in the northeast and the Karens along the northern Burmese border. There are, in addition, some 20 other minority groups, including the Akha, Lahu, Meo (H'mong), Lisu and Lawa; most of these peoples traditionally live by shifting cultivation in rugged, isolated mountain terrain. Many of the "hill tribe" people have faced government restrictions due to lack of legal documentation of nationality and citizenship, as well as discrimination. Citizenship is not granted automatically to children born of undocumented parents.

9 LANGUAGES

The Thai language, with central (Bangkok or official Thai), northern, eastern and southern dialects, all distantly related to Chinese, prevails throughout the country. Spoken Thai is considered part of the Sino-Tibetan language family, although links to Indian languages are also evident. Thai is written with a Khmer-related, southern-Indian-derived alphabet with marks denoting tones. Although the ethnic minorities generally speak their own languages, Thai is widely understood. The Chinese population is largely bilingual. All official documents are in the central Thai language, although English, taught in many secondary schools and colleges, is also used in official and commercial circles.

10 RELIGIONS

According to government statistics, Theravada Buddhism is the religion of about 94% of the population. However, other nongovernmental agencies and religious groups estimate that the number of Buddhists is only about 85–90%. The religious life of Thailand also includes animist elements and Brahman beliefs from Hinduism. While the government estimates that 5% of the population is Muslim, non-governmental agencies place the number at about 10% of the population, including the Malay ethnic minority. Among the other ethnic minorities, the Chinese practice a traditional mixture of Mahayana Buddhism, Taoism, Confucianism, and ancestor worship. Most Vietnamese are Mahayana Buddhists, and most Indians (0.1% of the population) are Hindus. Christians have been active in Thailand since the 17th century and account for an estimated 1% of the population. Christian churches are pri-

marily Protestant, belonging to one of four umbrella organizations in the country—the Church of Christ in Thailand (Protestant), the Evangelical Fellowship of Thailand (Protestant), Saha Christchak (Baptist), and the Seventh Day Adventist Church of Thailand. The Catholic Mission of Bangkok (Roman Catholic) claims 335,100 members. There are small Baha'i, Sikh, and Jewish communities.

Though the constitution does not designate a state religion, Theravada Buddhism is granted significant preference by the government. The constitution stipulates that the monarch must be a Buddhist and allows the government to take measures to protect Buddhism as a traditional faith while promoting religious harmony among faiths. Religious groups must register under the Religious Affairs Department. To be approved for registration, each group must be aligned with one of the five officially recognized religions—Buddhism, Islam, Brahmin Hinduism, Sikhism, and Christianity. The Buddhist holy days—Maka Bucha Day (the full moon of the third lunar month), Visakha Bucha Day (the full moon day of the sixth lunar month), Asalaha Bucha Day (the full moon day of the eighth lunar month), and Khao Phan Sa Day—are observed as national holidays.

11 TRANSPORTATION

The CIA reports that Thailand has a total of 180,053 km (111,880 mi) of roads. The highway system, significantly expanded during the 1960s and 1970s, serves many areas inaccessible by railway. Modern two-lane highways connect Bangkok with the rest of the country

Owned and operated by the government, railways extend for 4,429 km (2,752 mi). Rail lines radiate from Bangkok to Malaysia in the south, to the Cambodian border in the east, to Ubon Ratchathani and Nong Khai in the northeast, and to Chiang Mai in the north.

Thailand has approximately 4,000 km (2,485 mi) of navigable waterways. Waterways, both river and canal, carry much of the nation's bulk freight. The Chao Phraya River, with its tributaries, is the main traffic artery, and Bangkok is its focal point. The modern port of Bangkok at Klong Toey is the chief port for international shipping. Lying some 40 km (25 mi) inland from the sea, its harbor is navigable for vessels up to 10,000 tons, but constant dredging of the Chao Phraya is necessary. To relieve the congestion at Klong Toey, the modern Juksamet Port was developed at Sattahip, a former US naval base, and new seaports at Laem Chabang and Hap Ta Phut. Phuket Harbor in southern Thailand was improved to accommodate 15,000-ton cargo ships. An extensive shipping service also exists along the Gulf of Thailand, and a Thai merchant fleet plies between local and neighboring ports. In 2008, there were 398 oceangoing vessels of more than 1,000 gross registered tons, 56 of which were foreign-owned or registered in foreign countries.

After the end of World War II, Bangkok became an important center of international aviation. Suvarnabhumi International Airport opened in 2006 to replace the old Don Muang International Airport. In 2009, Thailand had 105 airports, which transported 19.62 million passengers, according to the World Bank. Principal airports include Chiang Mai, Hat Yai, and Phuket. The government-owned Thai Airways International and Thai Airways Co. handle international and domestic air traffic, respectively. A number of privately owned Thai budget airlines, such as Nok Air, Happy Air, and Sunny Airways appeared in the 2000s, competing on local and regional routes.

12 HISTORY

Archaeological excavations in the 1970s in Ban Chiang, northeastern Thailand, yielded traces of a Bronze Age people dating as far back as 3600 BC, predating Bronze cultures in China and the Middle East. The technical achievements of the Ban Chiang society, as surmised from archaeological evidence, indicate the existence of a settled agrarian people with advanced knowledge of bronze and iron metallurgy. Moreover, the skills demonstrated in their pottery, housing, and printing of silk textiles reflect at least 2,000 years of prior development, a finding that challenged previous concepts of incipient civilization and technology and Southeast Asia's role in it.

The Thai descended from the ancient Pamir plateau peoples. The Pamir, who are racially related to the Chinese, migrated from southern China to mainland Southeast Asia. While in southern China, the Thai created the powerful Nan-Chao kingdom, but continued pressure from Chinese and Tibetans and the final destruction by Kublai Khan in 1253 forced the Thai southward across the mountain passes into Southeast Asia. After entering the valley of the Chao Phraya River, they defeated and dispersed the Khmer settlers, ancestors of the Cambodians, and established the Kingdom of Thailand.

By the mid-14th century, the Thai expanded and centralized their kingdom at the expense of the Lao, Burmese, and Cambodians. While Thailand, then known as Siam, developed trading contacts with the Dutch and Portuguese and with the French and British in the 16th and 17th centuries, respectively, it remained a feudal state with a powerful court of nobles. Diplomacy and trade enabled the Thai kingdom to evade the Western colonization that was taking over all the neighboring countries. During the reigns of Mongkut (1851–68) and his son Chulalongkorn (1868–1910), however, Thailand emerged from feudalism and entered the modern world. A cabinet of foreign advisers was formed; commercial treaties of friendship were signed with the British (1855) and with the United States and France (1856); the power of nobles was curtailed, slavery abolished, and many court practices, such as prostration in the royal presence, were ended.

The Thai government continued as an absolute monarchy despite the progressive policies of Mongkut and Chulalongkorn. In 1932, however, a bloodless revolution of intellectuals led to a constitutional monarchy. Since then, Thailand has experienced multiple constitutions, changes of government, and military coups. With the government in a state of flux, political parties tended to cluster around strong personalities rather than political ideologies. At the start of World War II, Thailand, after annexing Burmese and Malayan territories, signed an alliance with Japan and declared war on the United States and the United Kingdom. From 1932 through the 1940s, political life in Thailand centered around Pridi Banomyong and Marshal Phibul Songgram and thereafter around Marshal Sarit Thanarat, until his death in 1963. Sarit's handpicked heir, Marshal Thanom Kittikachorn, subsequently emerged as the country's political leader.

After World War II, Thailand became an ally of the United States through their common membership in the Southeast Asia Treaty Organization (SEATO) and various other bilateral treaties and agreements. As a SEATO member, Thailand took a direct role in the Vietnam War and supplied a small number of troops in support of the Republic of Vietnam (RVN). Furthermore, it granted US forces the use of air bases in Thailand for massive bombing sorties against the Democratic Republic of Vietnam and the Vietcong. US forces stationed in Thailand increased to as many as 25,000 by the end of 1972. With the termination of the direct US combat role in Vietnam in early 1973, the United States began a gradual withdrawal of military personnel from Thailand. In March 1976, the Thai government ordered the United States to close its remaining military installations in the country.

Internally, Thailand weathered a series of political upheavals in the 1970s. In November 1971, Marshal Thanom, who had been reconfirmed as prime minister in the 1969 general elections, led a bloodless military coup that abrogated the constitution and imposed a state of martial law. In December 1972, an interim constitution that preserved military rule caused student and labor groups to agitate for greater representation in Thai politics. By early October 1973, demonstrations erupted into riots, and on 14 October, Marshal Thanom resigned and quit the country. King Bhumibol Adulyadej stepped into the vacuum and named a national legislative assembly to draft a new constitution. On 7 October 1974, the new constitution—the tenth such document to be promulgated in Thailand since 1932—went into effect. On 26 January 1975, Thailand held its first truly open parliamentary elections since 1957. Some 42 parties competed in the balloting, which produced a coalition government under Seni Pramoj. In March 1975, Seni's government resigned following a no-confidence vote, and a right-wing coalition government led by Kukrit Pramoj (Seni's brother) subsequently assumed control, but it, too, resigned in January 1976. Elections held in April restored Seni Pramoj to power as head of a four-party coalition, but when civil disorder again erupted among students in Bangkok, he was overthrown by the military. The military-led government declared martial law, banned strikes and political parties, and enacted yet another constitution. Promulgation of a subsequent constitution in December 1978 paved the way for elections in 1979, 1983, and 1986. General Prem Tinsulanonda was appointed for a third term as prime minister following the 1986 elections.

Communist insurgents based in Laos and Cambodia contributed to the nation's political instability in the 1970s by launching guerrilla attacks on the country, and an upsurge in the number of refugees from Laos and Cambodia contributed to a humanitarian crisis. In 1979, the government estimated the number of insurgents at 10,000. Following the Vietnamese victory in Cambodia in January 1979, thousands of insurgents took advantage of a government offer of amnesty and surrendered to Thai security forces, while others were apprehended subsequently.

During 1985 and 1986, the Progress Party gained power when cabinet ministers were replaced. A parliamentary defeat over proposed vehicle tax legislation resulted in the dissolution of the House of Representatives. In July 1986, a general election for an enlarged House took place. General Prem formed a coalition government and served as prime minister, but opposition parties accused his government of corruption and mismanagement. In 1988, General Prem dissolved summarily the House of Representatives and announced a general election. In the July 1988 election, the Chart Thai gained the largest number of seats. Although its leader, General Chatichai Choonhavan, declared his unsuitability for prime minister, he was appointed to the position. General Chatichai took an active role in foreign affairs and made bold initiatives to improve relations with Laos, Vietnam, and Cambodia. His support declined because his preoccupation with foreign affairs was considered a detriment to his handling of domestic issues, especially regarding government response in the aftermath of a devastating typhoon in November 1989. In December 1990, General Chatichai resigned as prime minister only to be reappointed the next day, enabling him to form a new coalition government. On 23 February 1991, a bloodless military coup led by the National Peace Keeping Council (NPKC) ousted Chatichai's government, alleging massive and systemic corruption. The NPKC declared martial law, abrogated the constitution, and dissolved the cabinet. An interim constitution approved by the King was published in March 1991. A former diplomat and business executive, Anand Panyarachun was appointed prime minister. Despite public protest, a draft constitution presented in November was approved on 7 December 1991.

In March 1992, General Suchinda became prime minister amid continued unrest. Two months later, Major General Chamlong called for the resignation of Suchinda and an amendment to the constitution at a rally attended by 100,000 demonstrators. On 17 May 1992, about 150,000 demonstrators met in central Bangkok, and the protests turned violent. Government forces arrested Chamlong and killed over 100 demonstrators and detained several thousand. Four days of violence ended with intervention by the King, and, on 24 May, Suchinda resigned. A general election followed on 13 September 1992, and Chuan Leekpai, leader of the winning Democratic Party, became prime minister. Beginning in 1993 and continuing into 1994, Chuan's government faced two "no confidence" motions in parliament, but the government emerged stronger. In 1994, Chamlong and Palang Dharma became more assertive in demands for constitutional reform, decentralization of state power, and progress in solving Bangkok's traffic problems. Ultimately, corruption charges brought Chuan's governing coalition down. In late 1994, the New Aspirations Party (NAP), led by Chavalit Yongchaiyadh, left the ruling coalition over a planned electoral reform. In May 1995, prior to a vote of no confidence, Chuan dissolved parliament and called for new elections.

During the campaigning leading to the July 1995 elections, politicians spent 17 billion baht buying votes, a seemingly intractable problem. The balloting was won by the Chart Thai party, which took 92 (of 391) seats. Former Prime Minister Chuan's Democrats secured 86; the NAP took 57; and Palang Dharma lost heavily, going from 47 to 23 seats. Chart Thai selected as its prime minister Banharn Silpa-archa. In appointing his cabinet, however, Banharn was immediately perceived as favoring the old, corrupt elite. Banharn's government collapsed before the end of 1996, and elections took place on 17 November 1996. Chart Thai went from 92 seats to 39, as the NAP, led by coalition parties and Minister of Defense Chavalit Yongchaiyudh, emerged victorious. They swept into power, going from 57 seats to 125. 1997 was a disastrous year for the Thai economy. In mid-May, the stock market collapsed, and speculative currency trading hammered the baht. The government intervened, but conditions deteriorated so badly that, by July, the government decided to float the baht, which had been pegged to the US dollar, causing a precipitous drop. In one day,

the currency fell more than 17% against the dollar. The floating of the baht caused international headlines as neighboring Asian countries frantically scrambled to protect their own currencies. By September 1997, the crisis had spread to Singapore, the Philippines, Malaysia, and Indonesia. Prime Minister Chavalit resigned on November 6. In November, Chuan Leepkai formed a coalition government that included his Democratic Party, Chart Thai, the SAP, Ekkaparb, the Seirtham Party, Palang Dharma, the Thai Party, and a majority of the Prachakorn Thai Party.

By May 1998, the Thai economy stabilized and began to recover slowly despite the swirling of allegations of corruption that led to the resignation of two ministers. The government accepted a significant International Monetary Fund bailout package and promised to deregulate the economy and adopt transparency. In March 1999, a major privatization bill that allowed government enterprises to become corporate entities without legislative action passed the National Assembly. On 5 October 1998, Chuan reorganized the government and invited Chart Pattana into the government, extending the coalition's majority in the House of Representatives to 257.

In March 2000, the first ever Senate elections took place in accord with the 1997 constitution. The nonpartisan elections fielded 1,521 candidates who, by law, refrained from campaigning. In January 2001 general elections marked by voting irregularities, media tycoon Thaksin Shinawatra's Thai Rak Thai (Thais Love Thais) Party won a major victory, making him prime minister. The new party took 248 of 500 seats in the House of Representatives, and Thaksin formed a coalition government with the Chart Thai (Thai Nation) Party and New Aspiration Party. Thaksin promised to help small businessmen and farmers in Thailand, pledging to postpone farmers' debts for three years and allocate credit of approximately $23,000 each to more than 70,000 villages.

During 2001 and 2002, relations between Myanmar's military government and Thailand improved. The two countries held talks in June 2001, attempting to ameliorate disagreements over the drug trade and border tensions. Thailand benefited from resources such as petroleum, minerals, and timber extracted from Myanmar, and the two governments regarded themselves as good neighbors. However, in May 2002, Myanmar closed its border with Thailand after the Thai army fired shells into Myanmar's territory during a battle between Myanmar's army and ethnic Shan rebels. The border was reopened in October.

On 29 January 2003, riots broke out in the Cambodian capital of Phnom Penh over comments attributed to a Thai actress that Cambodia's Angkor Wat temple complex was stolen from Thailand. Thailand initially suspended all economic cooperation and business dealings with Cambodia, and closed the border. Cambodian Prime Minister Hun Sen promised to pay $46.7 million in compensation for the damage done to Thai businesses.

Thailand became a focal point for unrest in January 2004, when a militant movement revived an insurgency in the predominantly Muslim southern part of the country. In an effort to contain the violence, the Thai government imposed emergency powers on the region. This action did little to quell the insurgency, and, as of March 2012, violence related to Islamic insurgent activity had claimed more than 5,000 lives. Although the insurgency did not appear to be drawing support from international Islamic terrorist organizations, fears that such groups would enter the conflict persisted. Both sides were accused of human rights violations, as the insurgents targeted civilians, such as teachers and Buddhist monks, and the government forces used heavy-handed detention and interrogation tactics. The Thaksin government was also criticized for extrajudicial executions in its national campaign against suspected narcotics dealers.

On 26 December 2004, catastrophic tsunami waves triggered by a massive undersea earthquake off the Indonesian coast swept Thailand's southwestern region, causing devastation at many of its beach resorts. More than 5,400 people were killed in Thailand, and Thai officials reported in June 2005 estimated losses to the tourism industry as high as $1.2 billion.

In March 2005, Thaksin Shinawatra began a second term as prime minister after his Thai Rak Thai party won general elections held in February by a landslide. However, by April and May 2006, a snap election, called by Thaksin amid mass protests against him, was boycotted by the opposition and subsequently annulled, leaving a political vacuum. On 19 September 2006, Thai military leaders staged a bloodless coup while Thaksin was attending the UN General Assembly in New York City. Retired General Surayud Chulanont was appointed interim prime minister in October. The international community condemned the coup, but the King endorsed the new leadership. It was Thailand's first coup in 15 years but its 18th since it became a constitutional monarchy in 1932. The coup leaders, called the Council for National Security, said they seized power to unite the nation after months of political turmoil. The Council promised to return the country to civilian rule. The Council introduced an interim constitution, giving the coup leaders the power to form and dismiss the government as well as the acting parliament. The interim constitution also allowed the Council to select the people who would draw up a new constitution and to vet the draft before it was subjected to a referendum. Surayud Chulanont was appointed interim governor.

In a national referendum on 19 August 2007, a majority of Thai voters approved a new constitution drafted by the appointed assembly. Under this new constitution, the national assembly was defined with two chambers—the Senate and the House of Representatives. The Senate is a non-partisan body with 150 members, 76 of whom are directly elected (one per province). The remaining 74 are appointed by a panel comprised of judges and senior independent officials from a list of candidates compiled by the Election Commission. The House was given 480 members, 400 of whom are directly elected from constituent districts and the remainder drawn proportionally from party lists.

The interim government held multi-party elections under provisions of the new constitution on 23 December 2007, which resulted in the People's Power Party (PPP) winning a plurality of 233 of the 480 seats in the lower house of Parliament. PPP leader Samak Sundaravej formed a coalition government and formally took office as prime minister on 6 February 2008. Urban royalist demonstrators, the People's Alliance for Democracy, known as the Yellow Shirts, called for the government to step down. The Yellow Shirts caused widespread civil unrest in 2008, taking over Government House, blockading the Parliament building, and occupying Bangkok's international airport

A new wave of protests took place in August 2009, as some 30,000 rural-based Thaksin supporters, the United Front for Democracy Against Dictatorship, also known as Red Shirts, gathered

in Bangkok to submit a petition requesting the royal pardon of Thaksin. The twice-elected premier had fled the country in 2008 after being sentenced to two years in prison for corruption. Beloved by large numbers of Thailand's poor but despised by the military elite and members of the Thai monarchy, Thaksin has remained a controversial and defiant figure.

More antigovernment protests rocked Thailand from March through May 2010, as the Red Shirts called for the dissolution of parliament and new elections, claiming that the existing government was created through parliamentary deals rather than a legitimate vote of the people. By May, the protesters had occupied sections of Bangkok, leading the government to call in the military to maintain the peace. The protests resulted in more than 80 deaths, at least 1,800 injuries, and the declaration of a state of emergency. Prime Minister Abhisit Vejjajiva came under fire for his decision to involve the military, with opposition leaders claiming the move was an excessive show of force. Nonetheless, Abhisit survived a legislative vote of no confidence in June 2010 with a vote of 246 to 186.

General elections were held in July 2011. With Thaksin still unable to return to Thailand without being arrested, his sister Yingluck Shinawatra, a 44-year-old businesswoman with no prior political or government experience, ran in his place, opposing Abhisit as the Pheu Thai candidate. Her party won a landslide victory, winning 265 of the parliamentary seats. She became Thailand's first female prime minister in August 2011, pledging policies of reconciliation. An early challenge for her administration was the catastrophic flooding that swept through Thailand in the second half of 2011, killing hundreds and inundating rice fields, towns and cities.

13 GOVERNMENT

Thailand has been a constitutional monarchy since 1932. The present king, Bhumibol Adulyadej, ascended to the monarchy in 1946 and became King Rama IX on 5 May 1950. Until 1958, Thailand was governed under a constitution originally promulgated in December 1932. In October 1958, however, the constitution was suspended, and, three months later, the King proclaimed an interim basic law providing for a constituent assembly to draft a new constitution. Nine years in the making, a new constitution was promulgated in June 1968, and the first elections under it were held in 1969. In November 1971, Marshal Thanom Kittikachorn overturned the document despite being chosen by its rules.

A period of martial law under a national executive council ensued, with the military continuing in power through an interim constitution. A new constitution, promulgated in 1974, was suspended and replaced by martial law in 1976 when civil disorder ensued. The 1976 constitution was abrogated after an October 1977 coup, and, under an interim constitution, the king empowered a legislative assembly to draft a new governing document. This constitution, approved by the legislature on 18 December 1978, lifted the ban on political parties and eased some of the martial law provisions imposed in 1976.

On 23 February 1991, the National Peacekeeping Council (NPKC), led by the supreme commander of the Royal Thai Armed Forces, General Sundhara Kongsompong, took over the administration of the country. On 9 December 1991, the NPKC promulgated a new constitution, which provided for a cabinet headed by an appointed prime minister and a national assembly comprised of elected representatives and an appointed senate. This charter was sympathetic to the needs of the military and gave the junta power over the senate. Protests that resulted in the deaths of pro-democracy demonstrators between 17–20 May 1992 quickly led to a constitutional amendment to provide for an elected prime minister and to curb some of the appointed senate's power. This constitutional amendment was approved by the national assembly on 10 June 1992 and required the prime minister to be a member of the house of representatives. The senate was also barred from initiating, or taking part in, no-confidence motions. The first elections under these reforms were held on 13 September 1992.

Efforts to amend the constitution again came before parliament in April 1994, and seven government-sponsored amendments were defeated. Those amendments sought to reform Thailand's political structure by institutionalizing political parties and increasing the role of the legislature. Prolonged debate and political indecision prevented the passage of these amendments until 27 September 1997, when the new constitution passed with the King's endorsement. According to this constitution, the house of representatives would consist of 500 members, with 400 selected by respective constituencies and 100 seats allocated by proportional representation of all parties exceeding the 5% threshold of popular votes. In an attempt to stabilize the political situation and institutionalize parties, the new constitution required representatives to resign their seats if they renounced or switched their party memberships.

As of the result of the military coup of September 2006, the constitution was suspended and an interim constitution established. In a national referendum on 19 August 2007, a majority of Thai voters approved a new constitution drafted by the appointed assembly. Under this new constitution, the national assembly was defined with two chambers—the Senate and the House of Representatives. The Senate is a non-partisan body with 150 members, 76 of whom are directly elected (one per province). The remaining 74 are appointed by a panel comprised of judges and senior independent officials from a list of candidates compiled by the Election Commission. The House was given 500 members, 375 of whom are directly elected from constituent districts and the remainder drawn proportionally from party lists.

14 POLITICAL PARTIES

In the 20th century, political parties were mostly formed by military personalities rather than around political issues, ideology, or programs. Military leader Phibul Songgram, who became prime minister in 1938, did not favor political parties. Phibul's immediate postwar successor, the pro-Japanese Pridi Banomyong, encouraged the growth of parties, but these were generally ineffective, primarily because of Thai inexperience with such institutions.

Upon Phibul and other military leaders' return to power in 1947, parties were banned. In a move designed to undercut a growing threat from other soldiers, Phibul reinstated political parties in 1955 in preparation of the elections for 1957. A new coup, led by Marshal Sarit Thanarat, deposed Phibul in 1957 and again banned political parties. Following the promulgation of a new constitution in June 1968, parties were again legalized and hotly contested the 1969 parliamentary elections. Prime Minister Thanom Kittikachorn's United Thai People's Party won a plurality (76)

of the 219 seats in the House of Representatives, giving it a majority in partnership with 72 "independents" supported by Deputy Premier (and army chief) Praphas Charusathien. The Democrat Party, led by civilian politician Seni Pramoj, won 56 seats, becoming the chief opposition party. Following Marshal Thanom's 1971 coup, political activity again subsided in favor of the military. The collapse of military rule in October 1973 led to a resurgence of civilian political groups. In the parliamentary elections of 26 January 1975, 2,193 candidates from 42 political parties contested 269 seats in the House of Representatives. Voter apathy remained a problem, however, as only 47% of the electorate (33% in Bangkok) took part. The conservative Bangkok-based Democrat Party emerged with a meager plurality of 72 seats, failing to secure a majority coalition. On 13 March, Kukrit Pramoj, leader of the Social Action Party (SAP), which held 18 seats, was elected prime minister in a controversial vote; he formed a ruling right-wing coalition with the Social Justice Party (45 seats), the Chart Thai (28 seats), and four smaller groups. The coalition collapsed in January 1975, and, in new elections held on 4 April, Seni Pramoj gained the premiership.

In the wake of the 1976 coup, massive arrests were made of liberal and leftist political elements, political parties were banned, and martial law was instituted. Political activity was restored and martial rule partially relaxed under the 1978 constitution. Subsequent elections, held on 22 April 1979, gave no party a clear majority. The SAP won a plurality of 82 seats, and the Thai Nation Party finished second with 38. Gen. Prem Tinsulanonda, who became prime minister in March 1980, formed a new coalition government after the April 1983 elections in which the SAP emerged with a plurality of 92 seats. Several days after the elections, the Thai Nation Party, which had won 73 seats, subsumed the Siam Democratic Party, which controlled 18. In subsequent elections on 27 July 1986, the Bangkok-based Democrat Party improved its position greatly, winning 100 seats. The Thai Nation Party won 63 and the SAP, 51. These three parties, along with the small Rassadorn—or People's—Party, which won 18 seats, formed a new coalition, again with Gen. Prem as prime minister.

In the bloodless military coup of 23 February 1991 by the National Peacekeeping Council (NPKC), General Chatichai's government was turned out. The NPKC promulgated a provisional constitution and, after a brief period, paved the way for a civilian interim government headed by Anand Panyarachun. A general election was held 22 March 1992. Persistent vote buying marred the election in which 59.2% of the electorate voted. A coalition government controlling 195 seats in the House of Representatives was comprised of Samakkhi Tham, Chart Thai, Pratchakorn Thai, the SAP, and Rassadorn parties. In April 1992, General Suchinda was named prime minister. His appointment as an unelected prime minister met with immediate protest. Agreement was reached to amend the constitution to prevent an unelected prime minister, but an apparent change of mind by the government resulted in violent rioting. Suchinda resigned, and constitutional amendments were approved by parliament on 10 June. The National Democratic Front, four parties that had opposed the military government—the DP, the New Aspiration Party, Palang Dharma, and Ekkaparb—formed an alliance to contest the elections called for in September 1992.

In the 13 September 1992 general election, 12 parties contested 360 seats in the House of Representatives. Voter turnout was 62.1%. Election results were the DP (79), Chart Thai (77), Chart Pattana (60), New Aspiration Party (51), and SAP (22). The DP formed a coalition party with Palang Dharma (47 seats) and Ekkaparb (Solidarity) for control of 185 of the 360 seats. The SAP was invited to join the coalition. The leader of the DP, Chuan Leekpai, was named prime minister. Chuan served for two years—then the longest continuous civilian rule in modern times—before scandal brought his government down in May 1995. Elections were held in July 1995, which were won by Chart Thai, taking 92 of the expanded body's 391 seats. Chuan's Democratic Party was next with 86 seats; the NAP took 57; and Phalang Dharma slipped from 47 to 23 seats. Banharn Silpa-archa was appointed prime minister and was almost immediately assailed by the press—and even the King—for assembling a government of largely discredited cronies.

Banharn's coalition lasted barely 14 months, and new elections were held in November 1996, the results of which were as follows: NAP, 125 seats; Democratic Party, 123; Chart Pattana, 52; Chart Thai, 39; SAP, 20; Prachakorn Thai Party, 18; Solidarity Party, 8; Seritham Party, 4; Muan Chan Party, 2; Phalang Dharma, 1; Thai Party, 1. Chavalit Yongchaiyudh became prime minister in January 1997. He resigned in November, and Chuan Leekpai once again formed a coalition government including his Democratic Party, Chart Thai, the SAP, Ekkaparb, the Sirtham Party, Palang Dharma, the Thai Party, and a majority of the Prachakorn Thai Party. Constitutional changes, promulgated on 11 October 1997, increased party discipline and loyalty by requiring representatives to resign their seats if they switched or renounced their party affiliations.

General elections were held on 6 January 2001, which were won by the new Thai Rak Thai ("Thais Love Thais") Party, led by Thaksin Shinawatra, who became prime minister. Thaksin, a billionaire telecommunications tycoon, took almost twice as many seats as his rivals but fell short of an outright majority. Thai Rak Thai took 248 of 500 seats in the House of Representatives, and the Democratic Party of outgoing Prime Minister Chuan Leekpai won 128 seats. Thaksin's coalition included the New Aspiration Party and the Chart Thai Party. The elections were marred by allegations of fraud and vote-buying. The results of 62 constituencies were thrown out because of voting irregularities, with more than half of the disqualifications earned by candidates from Thai Rak Thai. Those constituencies held reelections on 29 January.

Thaksin retained a secure grip on power and was reappointed prime minister on 11 March 2005 following the Thai Rak Thai's victory in the lower House of Representatives on 6 February 2005. Thai Rak Thai's showing in the elections was unusual; it marked only the second time in Thailand's 73 years of democratic elections that a single party controlled the country. The election outcome also made Thaksin the first prime minister in Thailand's history to have completed a full four-year term. The Thai Rak Thai leadership was supported by the Machachon Party, with the Democrat and Chart Thai parties comprising the main opposition.

In elections held for the House of Representatives on 2 April 2006, the Thai Rak Thai party won in a landslide, taking 460 of 500 seats (61.1% of the vote, or 15,866,031 votes). Approximately 37.9% of the eligible electorate cast no vote (9,842,197 voters), and opposition parties boycotted the election. The Supreme Court in-

validated the results of the House of Representatives election. The Senate elections were also held on 2 April 2006; the Senate's 200 seats were held by nonpartisans.

On 19 September 2006, Thai military leaders staged a bloodless coup while Thaksin was attending the UN General Assembly in New York City. Retired General Surayud Chulanont was appointed interim prime minister in October. Coup leaders drafted a new constitution that was accepted in a national referendum on 19 August 2007. Under this new constitution, the bicameral Rathasapha was defined as a 150-member nonpartisan Senate (76 members elected by popular vote representing 76 provinces, 74 appointed by judges and independent government bodies) and a 480-member House of Representatives (400 members elected from multi-seat constituencies and 80 elected on a proportional party-list basis).

The interim government held multi-party elections under provisions of the new constitution on 23 December 2007, which resulted in the People's Power Party (PPP) winning a plurality of 233 of the 480 seats in the House of Representatives. The Democratic Party (DP) took 164 seats, followed by the Thai National Party (TNP) with 34 seats, the Motherland party with 24 seats, the Middle Way Party with 11, the Thai Unity Party with 9, and the Royalist People's Party with 5. PPP leader Samak Sundaravej formed a coalition government and formally took office as prime minister on 6 February 2008. On 19 February 2008, 74 senators were appointed by a seven-member committee headed by the chief of the Constitutional Court; 76 senators were elected on 2 March 2008. Elections to the Senate are non-partisan; registered political party members are disqualified from being senators.

Following several years of civil unrest in opposition to Thaksin and in support of him, general elections were held on 3 July 2011. With Thaksin living in Dubai under threat of imprisonment in Thailand on a corruption charge, his sister Yingluck Shinawatra ran in his place with the opposition Pheu Thai party against Prime Minister Abhisit Vejjajiva's Democratic Party. In a landslide upset, Pheu Thai won 265 seats to the Democratic Party's 160, enabling Yingluck to become the first female prime minister of Thailand in August 2011. The election had over 65% participation.

15 LOCAL GOVERNMENT

Thailand is divided into 76 administrative provinces (*changwats*), each under the control of an appointed governor responsible to the Ministry of the Interior. Bangkok is sub-divided into 50 districts or *khets*. As of 2010, outside of Bangkok, there were 878 districts, 7,255 subdistricts, or *tambon,* and over 70,800 villages. Numerous changes went into effect with the promulgation of the constitution of 1997 and were maintained by the constitution of 2007. Local administrators are now elected directly by popular suffrage or by the approval of a local assembly. Furthermore, local government officials are prohibited from holding permanent national positions or receiving additional compensation from government-related positions. Governors of provinces are still appointed rather than elected, which has spurred popular calls for decentralization reforms.

16 JUDICIAL SYSTEM

The 1997 and 2007 constitutions provided for an independent judiciary and the guarantee of basic civil liberties. The 2007 constitution gave the judiciary a more political role, with the power to appoint senators and dissolve political parties.

Courts of the first instance, juvenile courts, and magistrates' courts exist in Bangkok and in each of the provincial capitals. There are nine regional courts of appeal, and a Court of Appeal, sitting in Bangkok, which hears cases for the entire kingdom. The Supreme Court, also in Bangkok, consists of at least three judges and decides only on points of law. Judges in Thailand are appointed (and removed) by the King. All appointments are subject to initial approval by a judicial commission.

Military courts deal primarily with military justice, but have broader jurisdiction when martial law is in force. There is no appeal of decisions by military courts. Defendants in ordinary criminal courts are afforded a wide range of procedural due process protections. Although there is no right to counsel during the investigative phase of cases, detainees are afforded access to counsel during trial. There is no trial by jury in Thailand.

[17]ARMED FORCES

The International Institute for Strategic Studies reports that armed forces in Thailand totaled 305,860 members in 2011. The force is comprised of 190,000 from the army, 69,860 from the navy, and 46,000 members of the air force. Armed forces represent 1.1% of the labor force in Thailand. Defense spending totaled $10.6 billion and accounted for 1.8% of gross domestic product (GDP).

[18]INTERNATIONAL COOPERATION

Thailand, a member of the UN since 16 December 1946, is the headquarters for ESCAP and belongs to several non-regional specialized agencies, such as UNSECO, UNHCR, the FAO, the World Bank, ILO, IAEA, and the WHO. The country is a member of the Asian Development Bank, ASEAN, the Colombo Plan, G-77, and the WTO. Thailand has observer status in the OAS and the Organization of the Islamic Conference (OIC) and is a partner in the OSCE.

Thailand has long had a close alliance with the United States, which includes military cooperation with annual joint training exercises, but Thailand also has significant diplomatic and economic ties to China. In 1995, Thailand, Cambodia, Laos, and Vietnam established the Mekong River Commission (MRC) to coordinate development in the region. Thailand is a signatory of the Basel Convention, Ramsar, CITES, International Tropical Timber Agreements, the Kyoto Protocol, the Montréal Protocol, the Nuclear Test Ban Treaty, and the UN Conventions on Climate Change and Desertification.

Thailand's relations with neighbors have sometimes been strained over resource extraction and other issues. In 1987–88, a territorial dispute with Laos caused hundreds of casualties. Dozens of Thai border guards and civilians have been killed by Myanmar military incursions and shelling since 1988, which has led to sporadic temporary border trade shutdowns. Cambodia and Thailand have clashed for many years over an ownership dispute involving the 11th-century Hindu temple Preah Vihear. Officially declared as Cambodian territory in 1962, the temple has caused controversy between Cambodia and Thailand, which also claims it as its own. The site was listed as a UNESCO World Heritage Site in 2008. In that year, the International Court of Justice ruled that the temple belonged to Cambodia. The ruling was based on a French colonial map that Cambodia and Thailand have been in dispute over for years. Military clashes occurred in the region in February and April 2011, despite attempts to enforce a ceasefire. After becoming prime minister, Yingluck worked on forging a rapprochement between the two countries through "football diplomacy" with a friendly soccer match.

[19]ECONOMY

Thailand's "Asian Tiger" economy more than tripled in the decade after 1986, achieving approximately 9% real growth annually from 1989 to 1996 before it became an epicenter of the Asian financial crisis of 1997, a regional crisis of investor confidence. Thailand's real GDP declined 1.4% in 1997 and then plunged 10.5% in 1998. In early 1997, the Bank of Thailand spent about $30 billion in foreign exchange reserves trying to defend the baht's value in terms of a basket of currencies speculating against it and then, on 2 July 1997, abandoned the peg and allowed the currency to float. The subsequent rapid fall in the baht's value—from 25 baht to 1 US dollar down to a low of about 53 baht to 1 US dollar by January 1998—was the proximate cause of the financial crisis that left most business in Thailand technically bankrupt. A $17.2 billion international bailout package was quickly arranged through the IMF, which seeded the loans with a standby line of credit running from 20 August 1997 to 19 June 2000 of about $2 billion, subject to a program of economic reform conditionals. Moderate growth returned in 1999 and 2000, but then dropped to an anemic 1.8% in 2001 in the face of a global economic slowdown and the halving of foreign direct investment worldwide following the 11 September 2001 terrorist attacks on the United States.

By 2002, the economy had recovered to its pre-crisis level with a 5.41% GDP growth rate. From 2002 to 2006, the growth rate averaged 5.6% per year. There was a drop from 2004 to 2005 due to high oil prices, a drought, the 2004 Indian Ocean tsunami, unrest in the Muslim south of the country, and a downturn in the global electronics industry. Subsequent growth was driven by higher investment demand as Thaksin's government embarked on an ambitious infrastructure development program, including electricity generation, transportation, housing, irrigation, health, and education. High amounts of exports also account for much of economic growth in Thailand, the GDP of which is over two-thirds dependent on exports of goods and services.

The coup in 2006 led to weaker private investment and investment demand in Thailand. The political uncertainty slowed the economy somewhat. By 2007, the tourism industry had almost fully recovered from the 2004 tsunami. While Thailand had in the past welcomed foreign investment, amendments to the Foreign Business Act in 2007 applied greater restrictions to non-Thais controlling business in the Thai service sector.

Reliance on exports led to recession in Thailand during the global financial crisis in 2008–09. In May 2009, exports took a record drop of 26.6% due to the global decrease in demand for exports including textiles, footwear, computer hardware, and electronics. Then, in 2010, exports rebounded, driving economic recovery to an industrial production growth rate of 14.4%. The Thai manufacturing sector also produces jewelry, automobiles, furniture, and wood products for domestic use and export. In export markets Thailand faces strong competition from the cheaper labor industries of China, Indonesia, Vietnam, Pakistan, and Bangladesh.

In 2008, according to the CIA, nearly 43% of the population was employed in agriculture. Rice is the country's most important cash crop, and Thailand is the largest rice exporter in the world market. Thailand has developed a mobile labor market in which many workers migrate between agricultural jobs in the country and self-employment and/or light industry jobs in the cities and industrialized zones. The unemployment rate in the nation was estimated at 1.1% in 2010. Official figures do not adequately reflect the seasonal unemployment of about two million agricultural workers during one third of the year. Overall, the shift of workers out of agriculture continues, particularly in the northeast, where agriculture is less productive, providing to Bangkok and other industrialized areas a steady inflow of workers who contribute to Thailand's expanding and diversified manufacturing and construction sectors.

The average inflation rate from 2000 to 2010 was 2.51% with a high in 2008 of 9.20%. As of mid-2011, Thailand's inflation rate was 4.3%. The gross domestic product (GDP) rate of change in Thailand, as of 2010, was 7.8%. Unemployment was reported at 1.2%.

²⁰INCOME

The CIA estimated that, in 2010, the GDP of Thailand was $586.9 billion. The CIA defines GDP as the value of all final goods and services produced within a nation in a given year and computed on the basis of purchasing power parity (PPP) rather than value as measured on the basis of the rate of the exchange based on current dollars. The per capita GDP was estimated at $8,700. It was estimated that agriculture accounted for 10.4% of GDP, industry 45.6%, and services 44%. According to the World Bank, remittances from citizens living abroad totaled $1.6 billion or about $25 per capita and accounted for approximately .3% of GDP.

According to the CIA, it was estimated that in 2006 about 9.6% of the population subsisted on an income below the poverty line established by Thailand's government.

The World Bank reported that in 2009, household consumption in Thailand totaled $145 billion or about $2,173 per capita, measured in current US dollars rather than PPP. Household consumption includes expenditures of individuals, households, and nongovernmental organizations on goods and services, excluding the purchases of dwellings. It was estimated that household consumption was growing at an average annual rate of 1.1%.

As of 2011, the most recent study by the World Bank reported that actual individual consumption in Thailand was 63.1% of GDP and accounted for 0.78% of world consumption. By comparison, the United States accounted for 25.44% of world individual consumption. The World Bank also estimated that 12.8% of Thailand's GDP was spent on food and beverages, 8.3% on housing and household furnishings, 4.4% on clothes, 5.3% on health, 9.2% on transportation, 0.8% on communications, 3.7% on recreation, 9.4% on restaurants and hotels, and 3.5% on miscellaneous goods and services and purchases from abroad.

²¹LABOR

As of 2010, Thailand had a total labor force of 38.64 million people. Within that labor force, CIA estimates in 2008 noted that 42.4% were employed in agriculture, 19.7% in industry, and 37.9% in the service sector.

Because of persisting government opposition to unions, organized labor was not a major factor in Thai life prior to the 1970s. Labor legislation in 1969 delineated certain basic workers' rights, and unions were granted greater freedom to organize under the Labor Relations Act of 1975. Under 2% of all workers were trade union members (10% in industrial occupations and 59% in the public sector) in 2010. The Thai Trade Union Congress is the largest labor federation. Minimum daily wage rates varied depending on the cost of living in different provinces. The minimum wage was raised significantly in 2010, to 215 baht per day in and around Bangkok and from 151 to 205 baht in other provinces. Legislation regulating hours and conditions of labor, workers' compensation, and welfare also exists, but these laws are weakly enforced.

The minimum working age was raised to 15 in 1998, but this law has not traditionally been effectively enforced, particularly in the case of migrant workers. As of 2002, it was estimated that there were one million children working on family farms. Another 240,000 to 410,000 children were working in urban areas. In 2009, the US Department of Labor reported continued use of child labor in Thailand's shrimp, sugarcane, and garment industries.

While forced labor is prohibited by the Thai constitution, there are reports that workers are physically prevented from leaving some manufacturing sweatshops, especially ones that employ illegal immigrants from Laos, Cambodia, and Burma. These same sweatshops have also been accused of using physical coercion to meet production goals. There have also been credible reports of forced labor on fishing boats (usually workers from Myanmar) and of forced prostitution or sex slavery, including the use of trafficked children.

²²AGRICULTURE

Roughly 39% of the total land is farmed, according to the World Bank (2008), and the country's major crops include rice, cassava (tapioca), rubber, corn, sugarcane, coconuts, and soybeans. According to the UN FAO, in 2009, cereal production amounted to 36.3 million tons, fruit production 8.6 million tons, and vegetable production 3.5 million tons.

Thailand continues to rely heavily on agriculture, although the country has suffered from declining export prices in recent years. Rice is the major crop, and Thailand is the world's biggest rice exporter. The government has embarked on large-scale irrigation projects and introduced higher-yielding varieties of rice in an effort to increase production.

Rubber, also a major export, is grown on the peninsula and, to a lesser extent, on the southeast coast. Total production in 2004 was the highest in the world and accounted for 31% of all production that year. Thailand provides about 95% of the world's cassava exports. Much of the harvest is processed into chips and pellets and exported to the EU for fodder. Higher EU tariffs, however, have caused the Thai government to promote dairy, fruit, and cashew farming as well. Corn production has increased significantly in recent decades. One third of annual corn production is consumed annually as fodder, with the remainder exported to Europe and Japan. Kenaf, tobacco, cotton, and kapok are cultivated mainly for domestic use, but quantities of jute, cocoa, peanuts, soybeans, and medical plants are exported. Canned pineapple and fresh flowers, especially orchids, are important exports. The Thai government's official policy of encouraging mountain villagers to grow coffee, apples, strawberries, beans, and other temperate crops instead of opium poppies and marijuana has been successful.

In the mid-1970s, farmers began to organize to express their discontent over the disparity between farm and non-farm incomes. To improve farm conditions, the government legitimized squatters' rights to nearly 500,000 hectares (1,236,000 acres) of land classified as forest reserve and established credit and crop insurance programs for farmers. The Marketing Organization for Farmers, founded in 1975 by the Thai government, allows farmers to buy fertilizers, machinery, and equipment at the lowest possible prices and assists in crop marketing. It is also government policy to channel revenues from agricultural export taxes to a welfare fund called the Farmers Assistance Fund. Thaksin's debt moratorium for farmers and subsidized small agriculture loans earned him loyal support in many rural areas.

23 ANIMAL HUSBANDRY

The UN Food and Agriculture Organization (FAO) reported that Thailand dedicated 800,000 hectares (1.98 million acres) to permanent pasture or meadow in 2009. During that year, the country tended 228.2 million chickens, 6.7 million head of cattle, and 7.5 million pigs. The production from these animals amounted to 293,797 tons of beef and veal, 868,565 tons of pork, 732,212 tons of poultry, 644,438 tons of eggs, and 1.51 million tons of milk. Thailand also produced 45,000 tons of cattle hide.

Cattle and water buffalo are still used for plowing and harrowing for rice farming, and most rural households own cattle as well as hogs, chickens, and ducks. In 2005, Thailand had 1.8 million head of buffalo and 50,000 sheep. Other livestock included 17 million ducks. Crocodiles, raised for their skins, are a specialty livestock product. About 1,600 tons of silk were produced in 2005. Elephants are employed in the tourism sector.

24 FISHING

Fish is a major protein element in the Thai diet. Thailand had 18,439 decked commercial fishing boats in 2008. The annual capture totaled 2.46 million tons in 2008, according to the UN FAO. The export value of seafood totaled $4.47 billion. Leading marine species include sardines, anchovies, mackerels, and breams. Thailand exports cured fish to neighboring countries and frozen shrimp and prawns. Giant tiger prawn, tilapia, hybrid catfish, and green mussels accounted for most of the farmed fish and shellfish. Thailand's shrimp-farming industry reportedly damages mangrove ecosystems.

25 FORESTRY

Thailand's forested area declined from 53% of the nation's land area in 1961 to only 28% by 2000, due to agriculture and logging. Of Thailand's 17.01 million hectares (42.03 million acres) of forest in 2004, over 50% was in the north, where teak and pine predominated. Teak, once a major export, declined in importance, largely because of government restrictions on cutting and past depletion of the forests through excessive harvesting and inadequate replanting. The remainder consists of yang (keruing) plantations and rosewood, other species used as fuel, and smaller mangrove forests and conifers.

Thailand imposed a ban on logging government-owned timber in 1989. Conservation efforts and reforestation have improved the level of forest cover in the 21st century. Approximately 37% of Thailand is covered by forest, reported the UN FAO as of 2010. Thailand is now a negligible exporter of tropical logs and lumber. However, Thailand exports value-added wood products (mostly furniture). Exports of wood products in 2004 totaled $870.9 million. Imports of logs, timber, and wood products in 2004 were valued at $1,033 million. Hardwood logs are imported, often illegally, from neighboring Myanmar and Laos.

Rubber trees, planted mostly in the south of Thailand, make up 10% of the forest area. Rubber wood, considered a sustainable timber, is used in furniture and handicrafts. Other important forestry products include bamboo, rattan, charcoal, gums and resins, and kapok fiber and seed. The UN FAO estimated the 2009 roundwood production at 8.7 million cu m (307.2 million cu ft). The value of all forest products, including roundwood, totaled $1.78 billion.

26 MINING

In 2009 Thailand was one of the world's leading producers of feldspar and gypsum and was a leading exporter of each, as well as of cement. In addition to feldspar and gypsum, tin metal, tantalum powder and zinc metal are leading export minerals for Thailand. The country also has considerable resources of diatomite, dolomite, limestone, potash, rock salt, and a wide variety of other industrial minerals. Other important minerals are barite, natural gas, gemstones, lead, crude petroleum, and silica. Except for gypsum, and tin and its by-products (ilmenite, monazite, struverite, tantalum, and zircon), most mineral production is for domestic consumption. Thailand is a net importer of minerals, mainly because of its large import bills for coal, crude petroleum, iron and steel, primary aluminum, refined copper, gold, refined lead, and silver. Thailand's resources of most metallic minerals and fuel minerals are small.

Tin concentrate production (gross weight) in 2009 totaled 210 metric tons, up from 235 metric tons in 2008. Tin was mined mainly on the southern peninsula, of which 52% was produced from offshore dredging. Tin production has been declining steadily in the face of falling world prices and output curbs. Tungsten concentrate output (gross weight) in 2009 was 950 metric tons. Other metal minerals exploited on a small scale included antimony, cadmium, iron ore, lead, manganese, tantalum, zinc, and zirconium. Iron ore production (gross weight) which totaled 50 metric tons in 2001, grew to 570,110 metric tons in 2002, fell to 9,675 metric tons in 2003, shot upward again in 2004 to 135,580 metric tons, and then to 1,400,800 metric tons in 2009. Gold and silver output in 2009 totaled 5,400 kg and 15,300 kg, respectively. There has been no production of monazite rare earths since the 1990s.

Among industrial minerals produced in 2009 were the following: feldspar output was 600,000 metric tons, up from 670,618 metric tons in 2009; gypsum production was 8.5 million metric tons; hydraulic cement production was 31,181,000 metric tons. The Somboon potash deposit was estimated to contain more than 300 million tons of sylvinite ore, with prospects for a two million ton per year potash mine, and the Udon deposit was estimated to contain more resources than the Somboon deposit. One copper deposit, at the Puthep project, near Loei, had ore reserves of 42 million tons of heap-leachable ore at a grade of 0.52% copper.

The government's underlying policy has been to conserve the country's mineral resources and to shift the emphasis to exploration, development, and exploitation of minerals consumed domestically, such as ball clay, feldspar, gypsum, kaolin, silica sand, limestone, lignite, phosphate, potash, rock salt, and zinc, and away from minerals that were predominantly exported, such as antimony, barite, fluorite, tantalum-columbium, tin, and tungsten. Thailand's mining industry consisted of a small mining and mineral-processing sector for ferrous and nonferrous metals, and a large mining and mineral-processing sector for industrial minerals. All mining and mineral-processing businesses except coal, natural gas, and crude petroleum were owned and operated by private companies.

²⁷ENERGY AND POWER

The World Bank reported in 2008 that Thailand produced 147.4 billion kWh of electricity and consumed 140.1 billion kWh, or 2,099 kWh per capita. Roughly 81% of energy came from fossil fuels, while 1% came from alternative fuels. Per capita oil consumption was 1,591 kg. Oil production totaled 241,801 barrels of oil a day. Thailand produces natural gas from offshore deposits in the Gulf of Thailand and imports natural gas from Myanmar. Plans to obtain electricity for Thailand by building hydropower dams in Myanmar and Laos have been opposed by environmentalists. Thailand's own massive Nam Choen dam project was cancelled due to environmental concerns in 1988. Use of renewable energy sources such as biomass, solar and wind power is increasing, with a government plan for 20% of Thailand's energy needs to be met by renewables by 2022.

By 2005, Thailand had four oil refineries. The largest refineries are run by Shell Company of Thailand Ltd. at Rayong, Thai Oil Company Ltd. at Sriracha, and Esso Standard Thailand Ltd. at Sriracha. Distillate fuel oil, gasoline, residual fuel oil, jet fuel, and liquefied natural gas are produced in Thailand.

²⁸INDUSTRY

Seven government agencies supervise the Thai industrial sector: the Ministries of Finance, Commerce, and Industry, the Board of Investment, the Industrial Finance Corporation, the Bank of Thailand, and the National Economic and Social Development Board (NESDB), are in charge of formulating five-year development plans. In 1982, an eighth agency, the Industrial Restructuring Committee, was created to coordinate the other seven and to formulate policy proposals in line with economic development plans.

Manufacturing grew at an average rate of 12% annually in the 1960s and 10% in the 1970s. However, in the wake of the second oil shock in 1978–79, rising interest rates reduced global demand, and falling commodity prices adversely affected manufacturing growth. From 1971 to 1985, Thailand continued to import most of its manufactured goods, although there was impressive growth in some sectors. The production of food products nearly tripled, textiles grew by over 500%, and transportation equipment showed even greater growth. With the collapse of oil prices in 1986, Thailand was propelled into a decade-long boom led by its industri-

al sector in which the economy more than tripled, which ended when the baht collapsed in early July 1997.

Annual growth for automobile production averaged 42.6% from 1986 to 1990, and, after a 7% decline in the global recession of 1991, 15% from 1992 to 1996. It was the world's fastest-expanding automotive industry, and Thailand also became the world's second-largest producer of motorcycles and pickup trucks. With the onset of the Asian financial crisis in 1997, automobile production fell 35.6%. Recovery began in 1999, with a 106.9% increase. By 2004, Thailand had dubbed itself the "Detroit of Asia," and set a production target of one million automobiles for that year. Thailand's automobile sector consists of 17 companies, the four largest being Auto Alliance Thailand, Toyota Motor Thailand, MMC Sittiphol, and Isuzu Motor Thailand, which together account for over 70% of production capacity. In 2010, more foreign companies, including Ford, were basing major production facilities in Thailand. Despite global economic woes and domestic political instability, Thailand's industrial sector grew by 14% in 2010, according to the government.

By contrast, the cement industry, dependent more on the recovery of domestic demand, has not achieved pre-crisis production levels. Construction, one of the three leading growth sectors in the boom (with manufacturing and financial services), was the most severely affected by the financial crisis. While the overall economy decreased 1.4% in 1997 and 10.5% in 1998, construction fell about 25% in 1997 and then over 38% in 1999, as landscapes that had been dominated by construction cranes were transformed into ones dominated by "For Sale" signs and unfinished buildings. Growth did not return to construction until 2002. Annual cement production, which grew from 18,834,000 metric tons in 1990 to a peak of 36,943,000 metric tons in 1997, was at 28,611,000 metric tons in 2002. Thailand produced 35,626,000 metric tons of cement in 2004. In 2010, there was some growth in the construction sector, driven mainly by public building and infrastructure projects.

Textiles and garments remain Thailand's largest industry. About two-thirds of the output are ready-to-wear garments destined for markets in the United States and Western Europe. In 2005, there were an estimated 4,500 textile firms employing more than one million workers. In 2004, Thailand produced 845,820 metric tons of spun textile products and 893,859 metric tons of synthetic fiber products. The global downturn for exports affected the Thai garment industry in 2008–10 with hopes for a rebound in 2011 driven by local fashion designers' styles and branding.

Since 1985, electronics has been Thailand's leading manufacturing export sector, employing about 300,000 workers. Annual growth in electronics production averaged over 20% over the 1990s, with about 80% of the output exported. In 2000, electronics constituted one third of all exports. Unlike most other manufacturing sectors, electronics production continued to grow during the financial crisis; the devaluation of the baht only made Thai electronic exports more competitive. Leading products include fully assembled computers, computer accessories, and integrated circuits in addition to a wide range of consumer electronics products. In 2004, Thailand produced 9.8 billion integrated circuits. In 2010, Thailand was the world's leading hard disc drive producer and continued to increase production of integrated circuits and semiconductors.

29SCIENCE AND TECHNOLOGY

Research and development (R and D) expenditures in 2006 were 0.25% of GDP, according to the World Bank. High technology exports in 2008 accounted for 25.39% of the country's manufactured exports, and, according to the World Bank, patent applications in science and technology as of 2009 totaled 802.

Scientific organizations include the Medical Association of Thailand (founded in 1921), the Thailand Institute of Scientific and Technological Research (1963), and the Science Society of Thailand (1948), all headquartered in Bangkok. National science policy is the responsibility of the Ministry of Science, Technology, and Energy.

Many students seek technical training in other countries, while some receive postgraduate education in specialized technical subjects at the Asian Institute of Technology in Bangkok (founded in 1959), which offers advanced degrees in agricultural engineering, human settlements, and computer applications. The institute also operates receiving equipment for LANDSAT transmissions that provide Southeast Asian countries with aerial surveys for agricultural development, forest inventories, and city planning. In addition to the Asian Institute of Technology, 15 other universities offer courses in basic and applied sciences.

30DOMESTIC TRADE

Bangkok, the distribution point for the whole country, is the commercial center of Thailand; most foreign firms have their main offices there. Other commercially important cities include Chiangmai (tourism, rice, and textiles), Ubon Ratchathani (rice, jute, and leather), Phuket (tourism and tin), and Songkhla (rubber).

Many essential commodities are grown and consumed by the producer or distributed at the local level. Production for the domestic market has continued to increase, led by high-growth industries such as construction materials, foods and beverages, and electronic appliances. In the greater Bangkok metropolitan area, almost every kind of retail outlet is represented, including specialty shops and over 100 department stores. Indoor shopping malls are popular in urban areas. Department stores, discount stores, hypermarkets, and convenience stores are all available. Outdoor day and night markets for food and other goods remain attractive to locals as well as to tourists. Trade fairs take place year-round, in Bangkok and other cities, and as promotions for provincial specialties. Franchising for convenience stores and restaurants has grown rapidly in Thailand. With Thai cuisine internationally known, individually owned restaurants, bars and food carts continue to be ubiquitous in cities, towns, and villages.

Direct marketing and Internet and television shopping have all become popular, corresponding with a greater use of credit cards for consumer purchases. Newspaper, radio, television, Internet, and cinema advertising are available. Usual business office hours are from 8:00 a.m. to 5 p.m., Monday through Friday. Shops are open from 9 or 10 a.m. to 8 or 9 p.m., and banks from 8:30 a.m. to 3:30 p.m.

31FOREIGN TRADE

Thailand imported $156.9 billion worth of goods and services in 2008 while exporting $191.3 billion worth of goods and services. Major import partners in 2009 were Japan, 18.7%; China, 12.7%;

Principal Trading Partners – Thailand (2010)

(In millions of US dollars)

Country	Total	Exports	Imports	Balance
World	379,965.0	195,375.0	184,590.0	10,785.0
Japan	58,740.0	20,420.0	38,320.0	-17,900.0
China	46,005.0	21,479.0	24,526.0	-3,047.0
United States	31,128.0	20,243.0	10,885.0	9,358.0
Malaysia	21,406.0	10,569.0	10,837.0	-268.0
Singapore	15,387.0	9,019.0	6,368.0	2,651.0
Australia	15,345.0	9,372.0	5,973.0	3,399.0
China, P.R.: Hong Kong	14,976.0	13,136.0	1,840.0	11,296.0
Indonesia	13,094.0	7,350.0	5,744.0	1,606.0
South Korea	11,775.0	3,608.0	8,167.0	-4,559.0
United Arab Emirates	11,599.0	2,844.0	8,755.0	-5,911.0

(…) data not available or not significant.

(n.s.) not specified.

SOURCE: *2011 Direction of Trade Statistics Yearbook,* New York: United Nations, 2011.

and Malaysia, 6.4%. Its major export partners were the United States, 10.9%; China, 10.6%; and Japan, 10.3%. Thailand supplies the world with a large proportion of its natural rubber, rice, and seafood. Thailand is an exporter of automobiles and auto parts, electronic goods, and textiles and apparel. In 2004, the major exports in percentage terms were machinery and mechanical appliances (13.5% of all exports); electrical apparatuses for circuits (13.2%); computers and parts (9.4%); and electrical appliances (8.8%). The major imports were electrical machinery (14% of all imports); fuel and lubricants (10.8%); non-electronic machinery (10.2%); and base metals (9.8%).

As of 1 January 2010, a new free trade area has been established among China and the six founding members of the Association of South East Asian Nations (ASEAN), including Thailand. A major point of the free trade agreement was the elimination of tariffs on nearly 90% of imported goods. The free trade area agreement was expected to allow for a major increase in exports and export earnings among the ASEAN countries. In terms of population, this is the largest free trade area in the world. Cambodia, Laos, Vietnam, and Myanmar, the newer members of ASEAN, are expected to gradually become full members of the free trade area by 2015.

In another boost to trade, the ASEAN Trade in Goods Agreement (ATIGA), approved in 2009, entered into force on 17 May 2010. ATIGA represented the next step in realizing the free flow of goods within the region by simplifying the processes and procedures necessary to create a single market and production base—known as the ASEAN Economic Community (AEC)—by 2015. Major points of ATIGA included tariff liberalization, a simplification of the rules of origin, and implementation of such rules. The comprehensive agreement also demands greater transparency in regional trade liberalization, aiding the work of businesses and investors. The ATIGA supersedes the Common Effective Preferential Tariff Scheme (CEPT) adopted in 1992.

32BALANCE OF PAYMENTS

In 1996, a weakening economy and a decline in export growth created a current account deficit that amounted to 8% of GDP. Simultaneously, high interest rates and a currency tied to the dollar

Balance of Payments – Thailand (2010)

(In millions of US dollars)

Current Account		**14,754.0**
Balance on goods	32,340.0	
Imports	-161,270.0	
Exports	193,610.0	
Balance on services	-11,809.0	
Balance on income	-10,581.0	
Current transfers	4,803.0	
Capital Account		...
Financial Account		**17,211.0**
Direct investment abroad	-5,287.0	
Direct investment in Thailand	6,306.0	
Portfolio investment assets	1,171.0	
Portfolio investment liabilities	9,005.0	
Financial derivatives	-268.0	
Other investment assets	-6,315.0	
Other investment liabilities	12,599.0	
Net Errors and Omissions		**-719.0**
Reserves and Related Items		**-31,246.0**

(…) data not available or not significant.

SOURCE: *Balance of Payment Statistics Yearbook 2011,* Washington, DC: International Monetary Fund, 2011.

attracted money to an economy without sufficient productive assets to support the inflow. The government was forced to pursue a high interest-rate policy to protect the currency. When the cost of doing so got too high, the government let the currency float against the dollar, which resulted in a 20% devaluation. By mid-1997, Thailand's short-term debt obligations had reached $23.4 billion, consuming three-quarters of its foreign reserve holdings. In August of 1997, Thailand agreed to an economic restructuring package with the IMF that included $10–20 billion in standby credits. The economy since the 1997–98 crisis subsequently rebounded, and strong export performance drove economic growth in 1999–2000. Growth declined in 2001, due in part to the global economic downturn, a downturn in export demand, a slow pace of corporate debt restructuring, and a struggling financial sector. Severe Acute Respiratory Syndrome (SARS) negatively impacted trade and travel in 2003. The global economic crisis and Thailand's political turmoil had dampening but not permanent effects on exports and tourism from 2008 to 2010. In 2010, as Thailand recovered, there was a foreign trade surplus of $25 billion, amounting to 3% of GDP.

33 BANKING AND SECURITIES

The central bank is the Bank of Thailand, established in 1942. It operates as an independent body under government supervision; its entire capital is owned by the government. The Bank issues notes, a function previously handled by the Ministry of Finance.

The financial sector is broad and diverse. In 2007, there were 30 commercial banks operating in Thailand, 15 domestic and 15 foreign-owned. The top three Thai banks are Krung Thai Bank, Bangkok Bank, and Thai Farmers Bank. Shareholdings in even the largest banks, led by Bangkok Bank and the Thai Farmers Bank, are structured to ensure private family control. US banks with full branches in Thailand include Citibank, JP Morgan Chase, and Bank of America.

The 1990s baht currency crisis dealt a severe blow to the banking industry and prompted a major restructuring of the banking industry. By mid-2000, non-performing loans accounted for about one-third of total lending, down from a peak of almost 48% in mid-1999. Thai banks were forced to accept big write-offs by selling nonperforming loans for as little as 30% of the loan's face value. In addition, Thailand's domestic banking system has been criticized for failing to mobilize adequate domestic savings and for not offering adequate incentives to savers. The International Monetary Fund reported that, in 2001, currency and demand deposits—an aggregate commonly known as M1—were equal to $14.4 billion. In that same year, M2—an aggregate equal to M1 plus savings deposits, small-time deposits, and money-market mutual funds—was $119.3 billion. In 2005, the money market rate, the rate at which financial institutions lend to one another in the short term, was 2.62%. The discount rate, the interest rate at which the central bank lends to financial institutions in the short term, was 5.5%. As of mid-2011 the nation's gold bullion deposits totaled 4.10 million fine troy ounces, according to the IMF.

Thailand's first public stock exchange was opened in Bangkok on 30 April 1975 (the Securities Exchange of Thailand). All of its 30 members were Thai-owned securities firms. The Ministry of Finance encourages companies to go public by reducing income tax for listed companies and also by according favorable tax treatment of dividends. It was not until the late 1980s that the market was taken seriously by the international and domestic financial communities. In 1991, the name was changed to Stock Exchange of Thailand (SET). According to the World Federation of Exchanges, the SET as of June 2011 listed 544 companies with a combined market capitalization of $279 billion and a share turnover value of 15.9.

34 INSURANCE

There are a wide variety of insurance companies doing business in Thailand, including the American International Assurance Co., Asia Insurance Thailand, Assets Insurance Co., Bangkok Insurance, Indara Insurance Public Co., Navakij Insurance Public Co., Paiboon Insurance Co., Phatra Insurance Co., Safety Insurance Co., and the Viriyah Insurance Co. In Thailand, both workers' compensation and third-party automobile liability are compulsory. The government's Workmen's Compensation Fund, under the Social Security department, holds a monopoly on workers' compensation insurance. As of 2003, foreign investors were only allowed to own 25% of a Thai insurance company, but, in 2008, the law was amended to allow foreign ownership of up to 49%. According to Business Monitor International, in 2009, Thailand's top non-life insurer was Viriyah, with a 15% market share, while the country's leading life insurer was AIA with a 33% market share. In 2011's first quarter, the Office of Insurance Commission reported growth of over 13% with the value of all direct insurance premiums written totaling $3.7 billion.

35 PUBLIC FINANCE

Only a few utilities in power generation, transportation, and communications are owned by the government. Following the Asian financial crisis of 1998, the Royal Government of Thailand took strong macroeconomic steps to stimulate the economy. By 2005, it appeared the country was among the few in the region that had

Public Finance – Thailand (2009)

(In billions of baht, central government figures)

Revenue and Grants	**1,686.7**	**100.0%**
Tax revenue	1,371	81.3%
Social contributions	82.8	4.9%
Grants	2.2	0.1%
Other revenue	230.7	13.7%
Expenditures	**1,962.5**	**100.0%**
General public services	274.5	14.0%
Defense	150	7.6%
Public order and safety	118.4	6.0%
Economic affairs	400.8	20.4%
Environmental protection	4.1	0.2%
Housing and community amenities	50	2.5%
Health	281.5	14.3%
Recreational, culture, and religion	20.4	1.0%
Education	397.8	20.3%
Social protection	265	13.5%

(…) data not available or not significant.

SOURCE: *Government Finance Statistics Yearbook 2010,* Washington, DC: International Monetary Fund, 2010.

recovered. Government outlays by function were as follows: general public services, 13.5%; defense, 7.3%; public order and safety, 6.0%; economic affairs, 23.3%; environmental protection, 0.1%; housing and community amenities, 3.8%; health, 10.7%; recreation, culture, and religion, 0.8%; education, 22.8%; and social protection, 11.6%.

In 2010, the budget of Thailand included $56.33 billion in public revenue and $56.87 billion in public expenditures. The budget deficit amounted to 1.3% of GDP. Public debt was 42.3% of GDP, with $81.82 billion of the debt held by foreign entities.

³⁶TAXATION

Thailand, as of 2011, had a progressive personal income tax structure with a top rate of 37% applied to a person's total income, including dividends from stock and capital gains. Business and individual citizens are also subject to indirect taxes, including customs duties, sales tax, and excise taxes. Corporate income taxes on net profits are levied at a flat rate of 30%. However, small and medium companies and those firms newly listed on the national stock exchange can opt for lower rates. Companies involved in certain types of projects can also qualify for various reliefs and exemptions. Capital gains are treated as ordinary business income and are subject to the corporate rate. Dividends are subject to a 10% withholding tax. Generally, interest income and royalty income are subject to withholding taxes of 15%.

As of October 2011, Thailand had a value-added tax (VAT) rate of 7% on goods, services, and imports. However, exports and international transport are zero-rated. Domestic transport, rents from immovable property, and educational and health services are exempt. In addition, a municipal tax is levied on certain businesses. There are excise taxes on tobacco, petroleum products, alcoholic beverages, soft drinks, and other products. Automobiles are subject to a special tax based on engine size.

Thailand has double taxation treaties with 33 countries, including the United States, Canada, Australia, Belgium, Denmark, Fin-

land, France, and Germany. The US treaty has been in force since January 1998.

³⁷CUSTOMS AND DUTIES

Tariffs, low in the 1960s, were increased in the 1970s, some to above 90%, and price controls were pervasive. As part of the fifth economic development plan, 1982–86, the government began to lower tariffs and relax price controls. In the economic boom of the early 1990s, trade liberation was continued, particularly as the protection of industries became less important for Thailand's industrial growth than reducing the cost of imported capital goods and spare parts for rapidly expanding sectors like the automotive industry and electronics. The Thai government began to reduce tariffs in 1994, although progress was impeded in 1997 due to a shortfall in government revenue.

Thailand's customs tariff is primarily for revenue, although in a limited fashion it protects local industry. No preferential treatment is afforded any country, and all goods are subject to the general rate. Only a few goods require import licenses, including some foods, materials, and industrial products. Products banned from import include aerosol mixtures of vinyl chloride monomers (for health reasons) and products constituting trademark infringement.

³⁸FOREIGN INVESTMENT

Growth of the Thai economy has been directly related to the flow of investments from abroad. In order to stimulate such investment, the government passed the Industrial Promotion Act (1962), which established the Board of Investment for Industry, renamed the Board of Investment (BOI) in 1972. National Executive Council Announcement Number 218, otherwise known as the Alien Business Law of 1972, restricted the participation of non-Thai nationals in certain types of business activities. The BOI, the powers and responsibilities of which were broadened in 1977, granted the following benefits to promoted industries: guarantees against nationalization and competition from government industries; exemption from import duties and business tax on plant, machinery, spare parts, and raw materials; exemption from duty on exports; exemption from tax on corporate income for a specified period; and repatriation of capital and remittance of profits abroad. In the wake of the Asian financial crisis, the Thai government embarked on an IMF-supervised program designed to make the economy more open and transparent for foreign investment. The 1972 Alien Business Law was replaced by the Alien Business Act of 1999, which opened additional business sectors to foreign investors and raised the maximum ownership in some cases to above the old 49% limit. Limits on foreign ownership are most prominent in the financial sector, although now up to 100% ownership is permitted in Thai financial institutions for up to 10 years. A number of restrictions affect portfolio investments so that Thai authorities can track foreign investment.

In 2001 in the wake of the 11 September 2001 terrorist attacks on the United States, there was a world-wide contraction in foreign direct investment (FDI), and the government instituted a number of incentives to compete for scarcer investment funds, including tax incentives for firms to locate their regional headquarters in Thailand and several new government-backed investment funds to attract foreign money. To support its industrial exports,

Thailand has an extensive network of export processing zones located within industrial estates to which businesses may import raw materials and export finished products duty-free. Also, factories may apply to establish bonded warehouses on their premises to which raw materials used exclusively to produce exports may be imported duty-free.

Foreign Direct Investment (FDI), including inflows from the banking sector, totaled $610 million in 2004 (January to October), compared with $1.4 billion in 2003 (January to October). Major FDI recipients included metal and nonmetallic processing, petroleum products, and service sectors. Japan was the largest source of FDI in 2004, followed by Germany and the United States. FDI in Thailand was a net inflow of $4.98 billion according to World Bank figures published in 2009. FDI represented 1.89% of GDP. Japan, the EU, and China were the top FDI sources in 2009.

³⁹ECONOMIC DEVELOPMENT

The Thai government, historically vulnerable in its financial dependence on a few primary commodities (rice, rubber, tin, and teak), has pursued a policy of economic diversification through industrial development and increased agricultural production. With the beginning of the first development plan in 1961, the government committed itself to the primacy of private enterprise and to a policy of fostering and assisting it. Thailand has also followed a policy of foreign trade and exchange liberalization. Foreign exchange control is nominal.

Thailand's first five-year plan, covering the period 1961–66, aimed to raise the standard of living by means of greater agricultural, industrial, and power production. In the second development plan (1967–71), emphasis was placed on agricultural development, highways, irrigation, education, and industrial development in the private sector. The third development plan (1972–76) placed special emphasis on improvements in the rural infrastructure, growth in the financial and commercial sectors, and further assistance to crop diversification and to import-substitution industries. The government also committed itself to a reduction in the role of state-owned enterprises. The first three plans did much to increase the standard of living and to bring new roads, irrigation schemes, and land reform to the prosperous Bangkok region, but these changes also increased the income gap between rural and urban Thailand and drew increasing numbers of migrants to the city in search of work. Accordingly, the fourth economic plan, covering the years 1977–81, emphasized decentralization of industry and economic growth from the capital region to the provinces. It also ended the policy of encouraging import-substitution industries and began the promotion of export-oriented industries able to benefit from the nation's relatively low wage rates. Industrial estates were established.

The fifth development plan, covering the years 1982–86, stressed reduction of rural poverty and social tensions and expansion of employment opportunities in the poorer regions. To this end, four investment promotion zones were established. After completion in 1981 of the natural gas pipeline from the Gulf of Thailand, investment priority was reassigned to the Eastern Seaboard Development Program. This ambitious program called for the creation of a new urban-industrial complex in the Rayong-Sattahip region that was expected to draw industries from the congested Bangkok area. Heavy industries were to be emphasized, with early construction of a natural gas separator and plants for the manufacture of soda ash, fertilizers, and petrochemicals. The sixth national economic and social development plan (1986–91) stressed continuing export promotion, streamlining of the public sector, and strict monetary and fiscal policies with growth targeted at only about 5% yearly. Emphasis was placed on the less-capital-intensive industries, and more emphasis was given to improved utilization of resources. The plan targeted private sector investment and initiatives. Privatization of state enterprises would proceed in clear-cut phases, and enterprises were required to seek their own revenue. Agricultural production was forecast to grow at 2.9% per year. The development of small-scale industry, particularly in rural areas, was emphasized. In 1993, the Eastern Seaboard Development Plan southeast of Bangkok—begun 10 years before as a $4 billion investment—demonstrated results with the new port Laem Chabang.

The sixth national development plan coincided with the early part of Thailand's ten-year boom, and most of its economic targets were more than met. The actual average annual rate of real GDP growth—10.5%—was more than twice the targeted 5%. In the seventh development plan, 1992 to 1997, coinciding with the second half of the decade of boom, targets had shifted to a stronger emphasis on balanced, sustained development and less on growth per se. The three official emphases were 1) sustained, moderate growth (though with the target set at a rather heady 8.2% annual real growth rate); 2) redistribution of income and decentralization of planning to achieve reductions in the percent in poverty and in the widening gap between rich and poor; and 3) human resource development. The real GDP growth target was met, though with concern that this was through a combination of an explosive industrial sector growing at an above-target average annual rate of 11.4% and a moribund agricultural sector, growing at a below-target annual rate of 1.5%. Inflation averaged only 4.13% a year, better than the 5.6% targeted, but goals to eliminate Thailand's large balance of trade and current account deficits were not met. Poverty reduction, however, was substantial, with the percent of the population living in poverty falling from 32.6% in 1988 to 11.4% in 1996. Themes for each region guided development. In the north, light and clean industries were encouraged, such as clothing, high-value electronics, and agro-industry. In the south, transport links and natural gas networks developed between the Andaman Sea and the Gulf of Thailand would attract heavy industry such as petrochemicals, and cross-border development with Malaysia would link with Penang's industrial sector. Development plans for the impoverished northeast included linking with Laos, Cambodia, and Vietnam to process raw materials from those countries and to provide services involved with investment and manufacturing in those countries.

Thailand's eighth national development and social development plan, emphasizing again the concern with qualitative as well as quantitative growth, coincided with the onset of the Asian financial crisis and Thailand's struggle back to pre-crisis levels of economic activity, 1997 to 2001. The plan, assuming a continuation of economic growth, put priority on two long-range economic development goals: human development and the replacement of top-down administration with bottom-up processes. Virtually none of the goals of the plan were met as the economy was plunged into recession and high inflation with the collapse of the baht in July 1997. Whereas about a million people a year had been lifted out of poverty during the decade of boom, from 1997 to 1999 about a million and a half a year were plunged back into poverty, as the estimated number in poverty rose from 6.8 million to 9.8 million (16% of the population). In August 1997 the eighth economic plan was essentially superceded by the IMF-guided international bailout program that involved a three-year, $17.2 billion support package conditioned on a program of economic reforms. The IMF program did provide from the outset for "the protection of vital health and education expenditures in the central government budget," and, in fact, health expenditures rose by 8% during 1997–98 even as revenues fell. The government adhered sufficiently close to the reform program to bring down inflation and replenish foreign reserves. Thailand began repaying the IMF in November 2000 and repaying other lenders in 2001. Net capital flows were negative throughout the five-year planning period but by 2001 had improved to a -$4.9 billion balance from -$12.6 billion in 1998.

The introduction of the ninth national development and social development plan, to run 2001 to 2006, took a philosophical turn as the government presented it as embodying the King's concept of "sufficiency economy" as its guiding principle bestowed on the people as a means of helping his subjects overcome the economic crisis. "Sufficiency economy" was explained as based on adherence to the middle path, and involving moderation not just as a guide for economic policies but as a way of life. Balanced development was to be achieved through a combination of patience, perseverance, diligence, wisdom, and prudence. The four pillars of the holistic approach of the ninth plan were social protection, competitiveness, governance, and environmental protection. The more specific elements of the Thaksin government's economic policy strategy in 2001 included the following seven elements: 1) farm debt restructuring, including a three-year suspension of some debts owed by poor farmers to state banks; 2) village funds financed by grants of one million baht (about $24,000) to each of the country's roughly 70,000 villages to provide locally administered micro-loans; 3) the transfer of nonperforming loans (NPLs) to the newly established Thai Asset Management Corporation (TAMC), required of state-owned operations and voluntary for private ones, to promote more efficient debt restructuring; 4) special attention to small- and medium-sized enterprises (SMEs) by state-owned lending agencies; 5) promotion of product specialization by village groups, a scheme inspired by a similar Japanese program; 6) the establishment of the People's Bank, administered through the Government Savings Bank (GSB), allowing GBS account-holders to apply for small loans (up to about 30,000 baht or $370) mainly for small retailing or commercial ventures; and 7) a restructuring of the economy away from heavy dependence on imports and towards more reliance on local resources, especially agricultural.

By 2006, the Thaksin government was using expansionary fiscal policy to enhance economic growth. In its first term, the focus was on boosting rural incomes and development, but infrastructure development was the priority for Thaksin's second term. From 2006–09, the government planned to invest $41 billion, or 26% of GDP, in infrastructure, spanning electricity generation, transportation, housing, irrigation, health, and education. Thailand was in need of new investment in 2006; transportation costs weighed heavily upon business, and the telecommunications network was outdated. The government wanted to turn Thailand into a center for regional trade and business. Thailand, by 2006, had expanded into a few specialist markets with higher, more defensible profits, such as medical tourism (affordable but high-quality heart bypasses, cancer care, and cosmetic surgery are a few of the services offered to foreigners), long-stay tourism, and a beginning fashion industry.

Other economic policy objectives include the restoration of a solvent banking sector and poverty reduction. In 2005, Thaksin declared that Southeast Asia must not look solely to exports to resuscitate its economic fortunes but should try to revive domestic consumption, which would help insulate the region from the vagaries of the world economy. His policies (suspending farmers' debts, instituting inexpensive universal health care, and the granting of loans to villagers, small businesses, and homebuyers) were undertaken to this end, as well as creating a rural power base for his party. The government also subsidized a variety of goods, from computers to cows, to increase Thais' spending power. Nevertheless, exports have remained the chief engine of Thailand's growth, including automobiles, integrated circuits, and rice.

Corruption, with losses estimated at over $3 billion a year, has remained a severe problem, and Thaksin was found guilty on corruption charges in 2008. Hoping for a strong recovery from the global financial crisis, the administration of Prime Minister Vejjajiva produced a Capital Market Development plan in 2009. Exports again led the rebound, with international trading processes increasingly streamlined, and incentives were introduced to attract more foreign investment.

40 SOCIAL DEVELOPMENT

A 1990 law established a social security system, which began paying disability and death benefits in 1991. Old age benefits (pensions) were introduced in 1998. The pension system is funded by employers, employees, and the government. Old age pensions begin at age 55, and employment must cease at that time. There is a provision for deferred pensions. The social security law also provides for sickness and maternity benefits, which are provided to employees of firms with 10 or more workers. Employers are required to provide workers' compensation coverage, including temporary and permanent disability benefits, and medical and survivor benefits. Maternity benefits are available for two childbirths only. While prime minister, Thaksin instituted government subsidized health coverage programs that resulted in 96% of the population having access to low-cost or no-cost medical care.

Women have equal legal rights in most areas, but inequities remain in domestic areas, including divorce and child support. Women constitute more than half of university graduates. Discrimination in hiring persists, and there is a gender gap in wages. Domestic abuse and violence remain a huge problem. Many women, often trafficked from neighboring countries, are trapped into prostitution through a system of debt bondage. Brothels provide a loan to parents of young women, and these women are required to work as prostitutes to pay off the loan. In many cases, this is done without the consent of the woman involved. As of 2011, prostitution thrived, and sex tourism continued. Human trafficking is prevalent for cheap labor in agriculture, construction, and fishing boats, as well as the sex trade.

Many Thai minorities lack any type of documentation. As noncitizens, they do not have full access to education and health care. They lack titles to their land and may not vote in elections. Human rights are generally well-respected, but some abuses occur. During the Thaksin administration, hundreds of suspected narcotics dealers were extrajudicially executed. Government forces involved in suppression of the Muslim insurgents in the south and control of protesters in Bangkok were accused of excessive, often lethal use of force. Coerced confessions and the torture of suspects are occasionally reported. Overcrowding in prisons has resulted in poor conditions. Credible reports emerged of refugees and migrants from Myanmar being abused in detention and of "boat people" from Myanmar being pushed back out to sea by local Thai authorities. Refugees and migrants remained particularly vulnerable to exploitation and even enslavement in prostitution, fishing, construction, agriculture, and manufacturing.

41 HEALTH

According to the CIA, life expectancy in Thailand was 69 years in 2011. The country spent 4.1% of its GDP on healthcare, amounting to $168 per person. There were 3 physicians, 15 nurses and midwives, and 22 hospital beds per 10,000 inhabitants. The fertility rate was 1.8, while the infant mortality rate was 12 per 1,000 live births. In 2008, the maternal mortality rate, according to the World Bank, was 48 per 100,000 births. It was estimated that 98% of children were vaccinated against measles.

The CIA calculated HIV/AIDS prevalence in Thailand to be about 1.3% in 2009. Thailand has been a regional leader in prevention of HIV/AIDS, and medications for HIV/AIDS are subsidized by the government. Other infectious diseases include drug-resistant malaria, dengue fever, and H5N1 avian flu.

42 HOUSING

In 1973, to house Bangkok residents who had been living in makeshift shelters, the government formed the National Housing Authority (NHA), which undertook overall responsibility for coordination of public and private housing programs. By 1979, the NHA had completed 54,780 housing units, and, from 1979 to 1984, a total of 1,442,250 housing units were built in Thailand. Although urban slums persist, most Thai citizens live in dwellings that compare favorably to living facilities elsewhere in Southeast Asia. The Thai government has stimulated housing and community development by means of a housing plan that provides government mortgages for building, renovation, or purchase of government land and houses. Under a self-help settlement scheme, the government sets up whole new communities, surveys sites, constructs roads and irrigation systems, and provides public utilities and medical care.

According to the results of the 2000 census, there were about 15,349,500 dwelling units serving 15,662,300 households nationwide. The average household had 3.9 people. About 81% of all dwellings were owner-occupied. Nearly 80% of all households lived in detached houses. About 67% of all households lived in non-municipal areas. Cement, brick, and wood were the main construction material for about 47.9% of all dwelling units; another 44.7% were made of a mixture of permanent and nonpermanent materials. According to the CIA, as of 2008, 99% of the population has access to improved drinking water sources, and 95% had improved sanitation facilities.

43 EDUCATION

In 2009, the World Bank estimated that 90% of age-eligible children in Thailand were enrolled in primary school. Secondary enrollment for age-eligible children stood at 71%. Tertiary enrollment was estimated at 45%. Of those enrolled in tertiary education, there were 100 male students for every 122 female students. Public expenditure on education represented 4.1% of GDP. The CIA estimated that Thailand had an adult literacy rate of 92.6%.

Schooling is compulsory for nine years, including six years of primary school and three years of lower secondary school. Three-year upper secondary schools offer general or vocational studies. Both teacher training and technical and vocational training (especially in agriculture) have been stressed in Thailand's development plans. The academic year runs from June to March.

In Bangkok, Chulalongkorn University (founded 1917) is Thailand's most eminent university. Also in Bangkok are Thammasart Univeristy (founded 1933), specializing in social and political sciences, and Kasetsart University (founded 1943) specializing in agriculture. Newer universities established in provincial areas include Chiang Mai University (founded in 1964), Khon Kaen University (founded in the northeast in 1966), and Prince of Songkhla University (founded in 1968). King Mongkut's Institute of Technology was formed in 1971 through the amalgamation of three institutes, and eight colleges of education were combined into Sri Nakharinwirot University in Bangkok in 1974. A distance learning institution, Ramkhamhaeng University, opened in 1974 and Sukhothai Thammathirat Open University began operations in 1978. There are 16 public universities in addition to numerous regional and private universities, colleges, institutes, and teacher training colleges.

44 LIBRARIES AND MUSEUMS

The National Library (founded in 1905) contains over 2.4 million books and over 300,000 manuscripts; the National Library maintains a main library site and eight other sites in Bangkok as well as 17 provincial branch locations. Other important libraries in Bangkok include the Asian Institute of Technology (over 200,000 volumes), Chulalongkorn University (264,700), the University of Thammasat (231,000), Kasetsart University (313,000), and Sri Nakharinwirot University (299,500). The Library of the Department of Science Services maintains a special collection of 450,000 volumes. Outside Bangkok, sizable collections are maintained at the University of Chiang Mai (655,000) and Khon Kaen University (340,000). The Economic and Social Commission for Asia and the Pacific holds 150,000 volumes. The public library system includes over 70 Chalermrajgumaree Public Libraries. There are over 70 additional provincial public libraries and over 650 small district libraries.

The National Museum in Bangkok (founded in 1926) has an extensive collection of Thai artifacts, including sculptures, textiles, ceramics, jewels, coins, weapons, and masks. Many of Bangkok's temples and palaces contain excellent examples of Thai frescoes and sculptures. The Temple of the Emerald Buddha has a famous mural of the Ramayana, the Sanskrit epic, and the Marble Temple contains a fine collection of bronze and stone Buddhas. Bangkok also houses the Bhirasi Institute of Modern Art, the Science Museum, Jim Thompson's House, and the Sood Sanquichien Prehistoric Museum and Laboratory. The Hall of Opium Museum and the Hill Tribes Museum are near Chiang Rai in the north. There are dozens of other provincial, palace, private and specialized museums throughout the country.

45 MEDIA

Domestic telecommunications services are provided by government-owned and private fixed-line systems and an extensive wireless system. International service is provided by submarine cable and satellite ground stations. In 2009, there were some 7 million main phone lines and 83 million mobile telephones in use, averaging 123 per 100 people. Thailand is a member of INTELSAT and maintains trans-Pacific and Indian Ocean satellite communications stations..

The first daily newspaper, the *Siam Daily Advertiser,* appeared in 1868. Dozens of daily newspapers are now published in Bangkok, including several in Chinese and two in English; there are also numerous provincial newspapers. Thailand also has a variety of weekly and monthly periodicals, most appearing in Thai. Prominent newspapers in 2010, with circulation numbers listed parenthetically, included *Thai Rath* (10,000,000), *Naew Na* (200,000), *Matichon Daily Newspaper* (180,000), as well as 11 other major newspapers.

Ownership of broadcasting is both public and private. There are about six government and military radio networks. The first mainland Asian television station was established in Bangkok in 1955. There were 238 FM radio stations, 351 AM radio stations, and 6 shortwave radio stations as of 2010. Thailand has 6 terrestrial television channels and over 100 cable and satellite television stations.

In 2010, the country had 1.3 million Internet hosts. Internet users numbered 26 per 100 citizens, with broadband catching up to dial-up. Social networking and online shopping sites have rapidly grown in popularity in Thailand and are accessed by mobile telephone or computer. Numerous Thai bloggers cover culture, politics, and other issues. The Thai government blocks Internet sites for reasons including pornography, political issues, and perceived insults to the monarchy.

Citizens enjoy constitutionally provided freedom of speech and a free press. However, the law prohibits criticism of the royal family, threats to national security, and insults to Buddhism. Prohibitions of criticism or insults directed at the monarchy have resulted in the banning of a foreign-published biography of the King, high-profile arrests—including of foreign writers—and the blocking of YouTube. Libel laws have caused some media sources to practice self-censorship.

46 ORGANIZATIONS

Thailand has an extensive cooperative movement. Credit societies are the dominant type of cooperative; consumer cooperatives are the next-largest, followed by agricultural marketing and processing cooperatives. Trade organizations under the Ministry of Economic Affairs include the Thai Chamber of Commerce, the Board of Trade, and several foreign trade associations. There are many organizations that promote the interests of workers, such as the Thai Trade Union Congress and for promoting particular industries, such as the Thai Silk Association and the Thai Tapioca

Trade Association. Professional associations promoting research and development include the Agricultural Science Society of Thailand, the Medical Association of Thailand, and the Science Society of Thailand. Environmental groups include the Thailand Environmental Institute and Wildlife Friends of Thailand.

Cultural organizations include the Royal Institute (founded 1933); the Thai-Bhara Cultural Lodge (founded 1940), which sponsors studies in the fields of linguistics, philosophy, and religion; and the Siam Society (founded 1904), which issues studies on Thai art, literature, and science. The National Culture Commission was established in 1979. The multinational organization of the World Fellowship of Buddhists is based in Bangkok. Thailand has a number of gay, lesbian, and transgender organizations, with annual Pride parades in several cities.

National youth organizations include the Student Federation of Thailand, Junior Chamber of Thailand, Girl Guides, the National Scout Organization of Thailand, and YMCA/YWCA. There are many sports associations promoting competition for amateur athletes of all ages in variety of pastimes, such as squash, golf, Thai boxing, and football (soccer).

There are a number of ASEAN organizations based in Thailand, including the ASEAN Institute for Health Development, ASEAN Institute for Physics, and the ASEAN Solar Energy Network. Social action groups include the Asian Coalition for Housing Rights, Asian Forum for Human Rights and Development, and the National Council of Women of Thailand. There is also the Center for the Protection of Children's Rights Foundation and the multinational Committee for Asian Women. There are national chapters of the Red Cross, UNICEF, Habitat for Humanity, and Amnesty International. Many Myanmar exile organizations and media outlets are based in Thailand.

47 TOURISM, TRAVEL, AND RECREATION

Tourism has become a vital industry in Thailand, offering a range of attractions from outdoor activities to museums and cultural events. The Thai tourist industry has proved resilient, recovering from the 2004 tsunami, SARS and H1N1 flu epidemics, economic crises, and political turmoil, which included the 2008 Yellow Shirt protest occupation of the main international airport. According to the Tourism Authority of Thailand, the average stay of foreign tourists in Thailand in 2007 was 9 days. The *Tourism Factbook*, published by the UN World Tourism Organization, reported 14.2 million incoming tourists to Thailand in 2009, who spent a total of $19.4 billion. Of those incoming tourists, there were 8 million from East Asia and the Pacific and 4 million from Europe. The estimated daily cost to visit Bangkok, the capital, was $218. The cost of visiting other cities averaged $106.

Most tourists visit Bangkok and Chiangmai, with their Buddhist temples (wats) and markets. Beach resorts and northern hill resorts draw many visitors as well. Thai cuisine and performing arts are important tourist attractions. Sports include football (soccer), Thai boxing, golf, badminton, and kite fighting. Medical tourism is promoted, with some hospitals resembling resort hotels. Sex tourism remains a problem, with arrests of foreigners involved in child prostitution.

Visitors from 48 countries, including the US, EU countries, and some ASEAN countries, can stay for up to 30 days without a visa, if arriving by air, or 15 days if arriving by land. Sixty-day tourist visas are available in advance from Thailand's embassies.

⁴⁸FAMOUS PERSONS

Many ancient Thai kings enjoy legendary reputations. Rama Khamheng (the Great), a 13th-century monarch, is traditionally regarded as the inventor of the Thai alphabet; Rama Tibodi I in the 14th century promulgated the first-known Thai laws; Trailok instituted lasting governmental reforms in the 15th century; and Phya Tak in the 18th century rebuilt a war-defeated Thailand. Two great monarchs, Mongkut (r. 1851–68) and his son Chulalongkorn (r. 1868–1910), became famous for introducing Thailand to the modern world. Further modernization was accomplished in by three premiers: Phibul Songgram (1897–1964), Pridi Banomyong (1900–83), and Sarit Thanarat (1900–63). Prince Wan Waithayakon (1891–1976), foreign minister and Thailand's representative to the UN, played a major role in diplomacy following World War II. Marshal Thanom Kittikachorn (1911–2004) was leader of Thailand from 1963 until October 1973, when political protests compelled his resignation as prime minister. King Bhumibol Adulyadej (b. 1927) ascended the throne in 1946 and is Thailand's longest-reigning monarch, with a particular interest in rural health and development. Sulak Sivaraksa (b. 1933) is a Buddhist social justice and environmental activist. Meechai Viravaidya (b. 1941) is a social activist who has had major impacts on Thailand's population policies and HIV/AIDS awareness education.

Prince Akat Damkoeng (1905–32) was the author in 1930 of the first modern novel written in Thailand, *Yellow Skin or White Skin.* Modern styles in painting and sculpture are reflected in the work of Chitr Buabusaya and Paitun Muangsomboon (b. 1922), and the traditional manner in the art of Apai Saratani and Vichitr Chaosanket. Notables in Thai film include avant-garde director Apichatpong Weerasethakul (b. 1970), martial arts star Tony Jaa (b. 1976), and action movie director Prachya Pinkaew (b. 1962). Thakoon Panichgul (b. 1974) is an internationally known Thai fashion designer, based in the US.

⁴⁹DEPENDENCIES

Thailand has no territories or colonies.

⁵⁰BIBLIOGRAPHY

Altbach, Philip G. and Toru Umakoshi, eds. *Asian Universities: Historical Perspectives and Contemporary Challenges.* Baltimore, MD: Johns Hopkins University Press, 2004.

Kislenko, Arne. *Culture and Customs of Thailand.* Westport, CT: Greenwood Press, 2004.

Leibo, Steven A. *East and Southeast Asia, 2011.* Lanham, MD: Stryker-Post Publications, 2011.

Mishra, Patit P. *The History of Thailand.* Santa Barbara, CA: Greenwood, 2010.

Smith, Harold E., Gayla S. Nieminen, and May Kyi Win. *Historical Dictionary of Thailand.* Lanham, MD: Scarecrow, 2005.

Summers, Randal W., and Allan M. Hoffman, eds. *Domestic Violence: A Global View.* Westport, CT: Greenwood Press, 2002.

Thailand Investment and Business Guide: Strategic and Practical Information. Washington, DC: International Business Publications USA, 2012.

TONGA

Kingdom of Tonga
Pule'anga Tonga

CAPITAL: Nuku'alofa, Tongatapu

FLAG: The flag, adopted in 1862, is crimson with a cross of the same color mounted in a white square in the upper left corner.

ANTHEM: *Ko e fasi 'o e tu'i 'o e 'Otu Tonga (Song of the King of the Tonga Islands).*

MONETARY UNIT: The Tongan pa'anga (TOP) is comprised of 100 seniti. There are coins of 1, 2, 5, 10, 20, and 50 seniti, and 1 and 2 Tongan pa'angas, and notes of 1, 2, 5, 10, 20, and 50 pa'angas. TOP1 = US$0.57460 (or US$1 = TOP1.74058) as of 2011.

WEIGHTS AND MEASURES: The metric system is the legal standard, but some imperial and local weights and measures also are employed.

HOLIDAYS: New Year's Day, 1 January; ANZAC Day, 25 April; Crown Prince's Birthday, 4 May; Independence Day, 4 June; King's Birthday, 4 July; Constitution Day, 4 November; Tupou I Day, 4 December; Christmas, 25–26 December. Movable religious holidays include Good Friday and Easter Monday.

TIME: 1 a.m. (the following day) = noon GMT.

¹LOCATION, SIZE, AND EXTENT

The Tonga archipelago, also known as the Friendly Islands, lies scattered east of Fiji in the South Pacific Ocean. Nuku'alofa, the capital, is about 690 km (430 mi) from Suva, Fiji, and about 1,770 km (1,100 mi) from Auckland, New Zealand. Consisting of 171 islands of various sizes, only 45 of which are inhabited, Tonga has a total area of 747 sq km (288 sq mi), including inland waters and Teleki Tokelau and Teleki Tonga (formerly the Minerva Reefs). Comparatively, the area occupied by Tonga is slightly more than four times the size of Washington, DC. It extends 631 km (392 mi) NNE–SSW and 209 km (130 mi) ESE–WNW. The major islands are Tongatapu and 'Eua, Ha'apai, Vava'u, Niuatoputapu and Tafahi, and Niuafo'ou. Tonga's total coastline is about 419 km (260 mi). The capital city of Nuku'alofa is located on Tongatapu.

²TOPOGRAPHY

The islands run roughly N–S in two parallel chains; the western islands are volcanic, and the eastern are coralline encircled by reefs. At 10,800 m (35,400 ft) deep, the Tonga Trench is one of the lowest parts of the ocean floor. The soil on the low-lying coral islands is porous, being a shallow layer of red volcanic ash, devoid of quartz, but containing broken-down limestone particles.

The volcanic islands range in height to a maximum of 1,033 m (3,389 ft) on Kao. Fonuafo'ou (formerly Falcon Island), about 65 km (40 mi) northwest of Nuku'alofa, is famous for its periodic submergences and reappearances, as a result of earthquakes and volcanic action. There are few lakes or streams. Tofua, Vava'u, Nomuka, and Niuafo'ou each have a lake, and there are creeks on 'Eua and one stream on Niuatoputapu. Other islands rely on wells and the storage of rainwater to maintain a water supply.

³CLIMATE

The climate of Tonga is basically subtropical. Because the islands are in the southeast trade wind area, the climate is cooler from May to December, when the temperature seldom rises above 27°C (81°F). The mean annual temperature is 23°C (73°F), ranging from an average daily minimum of 10°C (50°F) in winter to an average maximum of 32°C (90°F) in summer. Average annual rainfall, most of which occurs from December to March during the hot season, is 160 cm (63 in) on Tongatapu, 257 cm (101 in) on Niuatoputapu, and 221 cm (87 in) on Vava'u. The mean relative humidity is 80%.

On 30–31 December 2001, Cyclone Waka tore through the northern islands of Niuafo'ou and Vava'u destroying an estimated 90% of the crops and causing severe damage to hundreds of homes and buildings. Total damages were estimated at $50 million. On 29 September 2009, a deadly tsunami swept through the region, causing the death of at least 10 people on the island of Niuatoputatu. The tsunami was triggered by an 8.3-magnitude earthquake in the South Pacific, striking about 190 km (120 mi) south of neighboring Samoa. There were an additional three aftershocks, each of at least 5.6 magnitude. The coastal region experienced significant flooding from the waves.

⁴FLORA AND FAUNA

The World Resources Institute estimates that there are about 463 plant species in Tonga. In addition, Tonga is home to 5 species of mammals, 46 species of birds, and 18 species of reptiles. These figures reflect the total number of distinct species residing in the country, not the number of endemic species.

Some original forest growth can be found on islands in the Vava'u and Ha'apai groups. Tree species include coconut palms and paper mulberry. Tropical bushes and flowers are abundant, including hibiscus and datura. A wide variety of fish are found in the coastal waters. Tonga is famous for its flying foxes (which are actually a type of fruit bat).

5 ENVIRONMENT

Agricultural activities in Tonga have exhausted the fertility of the soil. The forest area is declining because of land clearing, and attempts at reforestation have had limited success. Water pollution is also a significant problem due to salinization, sewage, and toxic chemicals from farming activities. The impurity of the water supply contributes to the spread of disease. The nation is also vulnerable to cyclones, flooding, earthquakes, and drought.

In 2010 top officials from Tonga and thirteen other developing Pacific island nations and dependencies met in Vanuatu to discuss the progress made in addressing some of the issues unique to these low-lying, developing island states. These include climate change, sea-level rise, natural disasters, remoteness from major markets, and poverty. Another key objective of the meeting was to address the progress each nation had made in adopting the 2005 Mauritius Strategy, the only global blueprint that exists to combat the development challenges of small-island developing states. The United Nations (UN) reported in 2008 that carbon dioxide emissions in Tonga totaled 176 kilotons.

The World Resources Institute reported that Tonga had designated 6,200 hectares (15,321 acres) of land for protection as of 2006. According to a 2011 report issued by the International Union for Conservation of Nature and Natural Resources (IUCN), threatened species included 2 species of mammals, 4 species of birds, 3 species of reptiles, 11 species of fish, 2 species of mollusks, and 4 species of plants. The Fiji banded iguana, and the loggerhead, green sea, and hawksbill turtles are endangered. The Tonga ground skink has become extinct. There has been some damage to the nation's coral reefs from starfish and from coral and shell collectors. Overhunting threatens the native sea turtle populations.

Fiji and Tonga have an unresolved border dispute over the Minerva Reef. Both countries claim the reef, which provides important boating and mineral exploration.

6 POPULATION

In 2012, the US Central Intelligence Agency (CIA) estimated the population of Tonga be approximately 106,146, which placed it at number 181 in population among the 196 nations of the world. In 2011 approximately 6.1% of the population was over 65 years of age, with another 37.2% under 15 years of age. The median age in Tonga was 21.4 years. There were 0.99 males for every female in the country. The population's annual rate of change in 2012 was 0.192%. The projected population for the year 2025 was 110,000. Population density in Tonga was calculated at 142 people per sq km (368 people per sq mi).

The UN estimated that 23% of the population lived in urban areas, and that urban populations had an annual rate of change of 0.8%. The largest urban area was Nuku'alofa, with a population of 34,000.

7 MIGRATION

CIA estimates of Tonga's net migration rate in 2011 amounted to -17.94 migrants per 1,000 citizens. The total number of emigrants living abroad was 47,400, and the total number of immigrants living in Tonga was 800. There is considerable movement toward the larger towns as population pressure on agricultural land increases. Some ethnic non-Tongans born on the islands migrate mainly to Fiji and New Zealand. Emigration by Tongan workers, both skilled and unskilled, has long been of concern to the government. Many Tongans live in the United States, Australia, and New Zealand, with expatriate Tongan communities in Brisbane and Sydney (Australia), Auckland (New Zealand), San Francisco (United States), and on Hawaii. Persons wishing to reside in Tonga must obtain a government permit; permission is granted only to those taking up approved employment. Immigrant settlement is not encouraged because of the land shortage.

8 ETHNIC GROUPS

The Tongans are a racially homogeneous Polynesian people. Less than 2% of the population is of European, part-European, Chinese, or non-Tongan Pacific island origin.

9 LANGUAGES

Tongan, a Polynesian language not written down until the 19th century, is the language of the kingdom, but government publications are issued in both Tongan and English, and English is taught as a second language in the schools.

10 RELIGIONS

According to the 2006 census, 37.3% of the population were members of the Free Wesleyan Church of Tonga (Methodist), 16.8% were members of the Church of Jesus Christ of Latter-Day Saints, 15.6% were of the Free Church of Tonga, and 11.3% were Roman Catholics. Other Christian groups include Seventh-Day Adventists, the Assembly of God, the Tokaikolo Church (a local offshoot of the Methodist Church), and Anglicans. There are also groups of Baha'is, Muslims, Buddhists, and Hindus. Though freedom of religion is provided for in the constitution and there is no state religion, the constitution stipulates that Sunday is the official Sabbath day. As such, the government restricts the operation of a large number of businesses on Sunday. The Tongan Broadcasting Commission also maintains a policy that restricts broadcasts of any religious tenets not within the mainstream Christian tradition. Good Friday, Easter Monday, and Christmas Day are observed as national holidays.

11 TRANSPORTATION

The CIA reports that Tonga has a total of about 680 km (423 mi) of roads, of which 184 km (114 mi) are paved. There are no bridges in Tonga, but three islands in the Vava'u group are connected by two causeways. Tonga has no railways.

Nuku'alofa and Neiafu are the ports of entry for overseas vessels. An additional port is located at Pangal. In 2010 the merchant fleet consisted of 10 ships of 1,000 GRT or more, some of them foreign owned and registered as a flag of convenience. Shipping lines offering regular international routes include the Pacific Forum Line, the Pacific Direct Line, and the South Pacific Inter Line, among others. Internal sea connections are maintained by the government-owned Shipping Corp. of Polynesia and private sector operators.

In 2010 there were six airports. The two major airports are Fua'amotu International at Tongatapu and Lupepau'u International Airport (also known as Vava'u International). Air Pacific, Air New Zealand, and Pacific Blue operate scheduled international flights from Fua'amotu.

12 HISTORY

Since the Tongan language was not written down until the 19th century, the early history of Tonga (which means "south") is based on oral tradition. Hereditary, absolutist kings (Tu'i Tonga) date back to Ahoeitu in the 10th century. Around the 14th century, the twenty-third king, Kau'ulufonua, while retaining his sacred powers, divested himself of most executive authority, transferring it to his brother Ma'ungamotu'a, whom he thereafter called the Tu'i Ha'atakalaua. In the middle of the 17th century, the seventh temporal king, Fotofili, transferred the executive power to his brother Ngala, called the Tu'i Kanokupolu, and thereafter the powers gradually passed into the hands of the latter and his descendants. According to tradition, in the mid-19th century, upon the death of the then Tu'i Tonga, those powers were conferred upon the 19th Tu'i Kanokupolu, Taufa'ahu Tupou, founder of the present dynasty.

European chronicles disclose that the island of Niuatoputapu was discovered by the Dutch navigators Jan Schouten and Jacob le Maire in 1616. In 1643 Abel Tasman discovered Tongatapu, and from then until 1767, when Samuel Wallis anchored at Niuatoputapu, there was no contact with the outside world. Capt. James Cook visited the Tongatapu and Ha'apai groups in 1773 and again in 1777, and called Lifuka in the Ha'apai group the "friendly island" because of the gentle nature of its people—hence the archipelago received its nickname, the Friendly Islands. It was in the waters of the Ha'apai group that the famous mutiny on the British ship *Bounty* occurred in 1789. The first Wesleyan missionaries landed in Tonga in 1826.

The first half of the 19th century was a period of civil conflict in Tonga, as three lines of kings all sought dominance. They were finally checked during the reign of Taufa'ahu Tupou, who in 1831 took the name George. By conquest, George Tupou I (r.1845–93) gathered all power in his own hands and united the islands; he abolished the feudal system of land tenure and became a constitutional monarch in 1875. Meanwhile, by the middle of the century, most Tongans had become Christians, the great majority being Wesleyans, and the king himself was strongly influenced by the missionaries.

In the latter part of the century, there were religious and civil conflicts between the Wesleyan Mission Church and the newly established Free Wesleyan Church of Tonga. After the dismissal of Prime Minister Rev. Shirley Waldemar Baker in 1890, the new government allowed full freedom of worship. Ten years later, during the reign (1893–1918) of George II, a treaty of friendship was concluded between the United Kingdom and Tonga, and a protectorate was proclaimed. During World War II (1939–45), Tongan soldiers under Allied command fought the Japanese in the Solomon Islands, and New Zealand and US forces were stationed on Tongatapu, which served as an important shipping point.

Two more treaties of friendship between the United Kingdom and Tonga were signed in 1958 and 1968, according to which Tonga remained under British protection, but with full freedom in

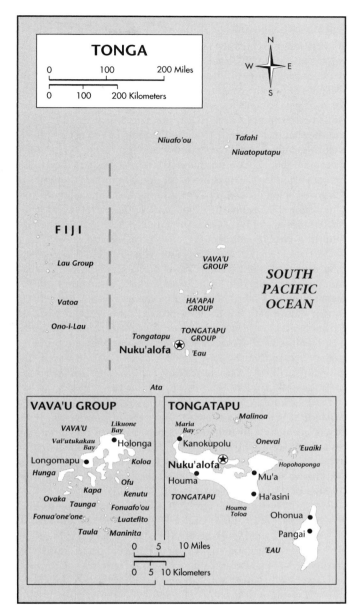

LOCATION: 15° to 23°30′S; 173° to 177°W. TERRITORIAL SEA LIMIT: 12 miles.

internal affairs. On 4 June 1970, Tonga ceased being a British protectorate and became an independent member of the Commonwealth of Nations, with King Taufa'ahau Tupou IV—who had succeeded to the throne upon the death of his mother, Queen Salote Tupou (r.1918–65)—as head of state. The new status brought few immediate changes, though it added Tongan control of foreign affairs to self-rule in domestic matters.

Many of the government's strongest critics gained seats in the 1987 legislative elections; the unprecedented turnover was thought to reflect changing attitudes toward traditional authority. However, the hereditary nobility continued to be in charge of the government. The island's dissident pro-democracy movement, led by Akilisi Pohive, won the February 1990 general election but remained a minority within the legislature. Pro-democracy sentiments continued to grow and spread throughout the 1990s and into the 2000s.

In 2005, public workers declared Tonga's first national strike. The 47-day strike ended when the chairman of the Public Servants Association presented the king with a petition calling him to dismiss Prime Minister Prince 'Ulukalala Lavaka Ata and all 14 cabinet ministers. The petition also demanded a commission be established to review the constitution and called for a more democratic form of government, as well as the return of royal family-controlled government assets. As a result, parliament voted to establish the National Committee of the Kingdom of Tonga for Political Reforms, with the goal of examining and improving Tonga's form of government. Committee members were to be drawn from the executive and legislative (both noble and commoner) branches of the government, as well as from the nongovernmental population. One major step occurred in 2006, when Feleti Sevele became the first commoner to be elected prime minister. He gained the post following the resignation of Prince 'Ulukalala Lavaka Ata.

On 10 September 2006, King Taufa'ahau Tupou IV died after a long illness. His eldest son, Crown Prince Tupouto'a, succeeded him (taking on the title King Siaosi Tupou V, also known as King George Tupou V), but his official coronation was delayed as the former king's death inspired new protests for political reforms. In November 2006, rioting erupted in Nuku'alofa, in protest at the lack of substantial democratic reforms. Eight people were killed in the riots, and much of the business district was destroyed. The government declared a state of emergency that remained in effect until February 2011.

The new king expressed a willingness to consider reforms that would lead to a more democratic government. Shortly before his official coronation in 2008, King George Tupou V ceded much of his role in day-to-day affairs to the prime minister. The king also approved a plan to restructure the legislature, which had been dominated by members of the royal family, to include a greater number of elected representatives.

For the 2010 legislative elections, there were 17 people's representative seats to be filled. Twelve seats were won by the Friendly Islands Democratic Party, but this was not enough to secure a majority. In the end the independent candidates among the commoners sided with the members of the nobility to elect Lord Siale'ataonga Tu'ivakano as the new prime minister. The choice was still significant, however, since this was the first time that a prime minister was elected by his peers, rather than appointed by the monarch.

On 18 March 2012, King George Tupou V died. His brother, Crown Prince Tupouto'a Lavaka, succeeded him and took the throne name Tupou VI.

13 GOVERNMENT

Tonga is a constitutional monarchy. The executive branch includes the hereditary monarch, the prime minister, and the cabinet, who together form the Privy Council. The prime minister is elected by and from the members of the parliament and appointed by the monarch. The cabinet members are nominated by the prime minister from among the members of parliament and appointed by the monarch. The Privy Council proposes ordinances that may become law when approved by the legislature. The unicameral legislative assembly, Fale Alea, consists of 26 seats. Seventeen members are elected as people's representatives, one from each electoral constituency, by popular vote to serve four-year terms. All

citizens 21 years of age or older are eligible to vote. Nine seats are reserved for members of the nobility, who are elected by and from the nobility. As of 2011 there were 33 peers with titles inherited through their estates. There were also eight life peers who had been granted titles by the crown.

14 POLITICAL PARTIES

The People's Democratic Party was formed in 2005, having been established from the roots of the still active Tonga Human Rights and Democracy Movement that was formalized in the 1990s. The Sustainable Nation-Building Party was established in 2007, followed by the Democratic Party of the Friendly Islands and the Tonga Democratic Labor Party, both established in 2010.

In the 25 November 2010 parliamentary elections, the Democratic Party of the Friendly Islands led by Akalisi Pohiva won 12 of the 17 seats for elected representatives in the new parliament. Five of the seats went to independent candidates. The remaining nine seats were filled by hereditary nobles selected by and from their own council. Falling short of a majority, the party needed to form a coalition government with the independents in order to decide on who would become prime minister. For their part, the nobles agreed to allow a commoner to take the seat of prime minister; however, a few days after the election, it was reported that the nobles were pursuing an alliance with the independents in order to control the government. That proved to be true, as the nobles secured the support of all of the independents and elected the former education minister Lord Tu'ivakano as prime minister in a vote of 14 to 12 against Akalisi Pohiva.

15 LOCAL GOVERNMENT

The islands are divided administratively into three districts: Vava'u in the north, Ha'apai in the center, and Tongatapu in the south. Ha'apai, Vava'u, and the outlying islands are administered by governors who are responsible to the prime minister. Town and district officials have been popularly elected since 1965. The town officials represent the central government in the villages; the district official has authority only over a set group of villages.

16 JUDICIAL SYSTEM

The Supreme Court exercises jurisdiction in major civil and criminal cases. Other cases, heard in the magistrate's courts or the land court, may be appealed to the Supreme Court and then to the court of appeal, the appellate court of last resort. The Privy Council has jurisdiction over cases on appeal from the Land Court dealing with titles of nobility and estate boundaries. In 2010 the king dissolved the Judicial Services Commission, which once had oversight of the court system, and created instead the Office of Lord Chancellor. The lord chancellor is appointed by the monarch and has the authority to appoint judges and to oversee complaints against judges. Criminal defendants are afforded the right to counsel, and the right to a fair public trial is protected by law and honored in practice.

17 ARMED FORCES

The Tonga Defense Force was first organized during World War II. It consists of a Royal Guard (a light infantry land force company) and a Maritime Force (sometimes referred to as the Royal Marines, including a small coastal naval unit and an air wing. The primary mission of the force is to maintain public order and patrol coastal waters. However, the force has become active in some multinational operations. In 2004–08, the force deployed four contingents of soldiers to Iraq. In 2010, 55 soldiers were sent to Afghanistan in support of the British Armed Forces wing of the International Security Assistance Force.

The International Institute for Strategic Studies reports that armed forces in Tonga totaled more than 500 members in 2011. Armed forces represent about 1.2% of the labor force in Tonga. Defense spending totaled $6.8 million and accounted for 0.9% of GDP in 2006.

18 INTERNATIONAL COOPERATION

Tonga was admitted to the UN on 14 September 1999. It participates in ESCAP and several nonregional specialized agencies, such as the FAO, UNCTAD, UNESCO, the World Bank, and WHO. Tonga is also a member of the Asian Development Bank, the Commonwealth of Nations, the ACP Group, G-77, the South Pacific Regional Trade and Economic Cooperation Agreement (Sparteca), the Alliance of Small Island States (AOSIS), and Pacific Island Forum (formally called the South Pacific Forum). It became the 150th member of the World Trade Organization in 2005.

In environmental cooperation, Tonga is part of the Convention on Biological Diversity, the London Convention, the Montréal Protocol, MARPOL, the Nuclear Test Ban Treaty, and the UN Conventions on the Law of the Sea, Climate Change, and Desertification.

19 ECONOMY

The economy still contains a substantial nonmonetary sector, with most citizens involved in agriculture, including both plantation and subsistence farming. Most of the monetary sector is dominated by the nobility and members of the royal family. With a strong reliance on imports and very few exports, the government generally sustains high trade deficits, which are offset by external aid and remittances from expatriate Tongans. Although the tourism industry is underdeveloped, the country recognizes its potential.

The nation suffered several economic setbacks in the early 2000s. Cyclone Waka, which tore through the northern islands of Niuafo'ou and Vava'u on 30–31 December 2001, destroyed an estimated 90% of the crops and hundreds of homes and buildings, with total damage estimated at $50 million. Donor countries—principally New Zealand, Australia, French Polynesia, and the United States—responded with food aid and emergency assistance, as did several missions and charities. Another economic shock, in 2002, was the discovery of the loss of most assets (about $26.5 million) from the Tonga Trust Fund (TTF) through failed investments and, perhaps, simple fraud by its American managers.

Tonga's dependence on remittances caused economic turmoil during the 2008–09 global recession. Remittance-based income fell consistently during the downturn, and Tongans were forced to cut back on retail purchases. Demand for imported goods in particular, which are subject to government tax, fell precipitously. As a result, government income dropped, straining social services. Sensing Tonga's vulnerability, the Asian Development Bank (ASN) issued Tonga a $10 million grant in 2009 to help the government continue basic social services as it weathered the weak-

ened economy. The gross domestic product (GDP) rate of change in Tonga, as of 2011, was 1.4%. Inflation stood at 8.4%.

20 INCOME

The CIA estimates that in 2011 the GDP of Tonga was $816 million. The CIA defines GDP as the value of all final goods and services produced within a nation in a given year and computed on the basis of purchasing power parity (PPP) rather than value as measured on the basis of the rate of the exchange based on current dollars. The per capita GDP was estimated at $7,500. The annual growth rate of GDP was 1.4%. The average inflation rate was 8.4%. It was estimated that agriculture accounted for 20.8% of GDP, industry 18.1%, and services 61.1%. In 2004 remittances from Tongans living and working abroad amounted to about 42.5% of the GDP. The World Bank reports that in 2009, household consumption in Tonga totaled $310 million or about $2,924 per capita, measured in current US dollars rather than PPP. It was estimated that in 2004 about 24% of the population subsisted on an income below the poverty line established by Tonga's government.

21 LABOR

According to the CIA, Tonga had a total resident labor force of 36,960 people. About 65% of the official workforce is involved in some type of paid employment, while the remainder is involved in subsistence work. About one-third are employed in agriculture or fishing (primarily men) and another third in some type of craft manufacturing or related trade (primarily women). A relatively large number of Tongans live and work abroad.

Workers have the right to form unions under the 1964 Trade Union Act, but as of 2010, none had been formed. The Friendly Islands Teachers Association and the Tonga Nurses Association have formed under the Incorporated Societies Act, but these do not have the formal bargaining rights afforded to unions. The Public Servants Association represents government employees.

There are no specific child labor laws, but child labor is not a problem in the wage sector. Some children work on family farms. The workweek is limited to 40 hours. There is no set minimum wage. According to a 2005 survey of communities conducted by the Asian Development Bank, about 23% of workers earned less than $16 per week, which was not a sufficient wage to provide a decent standard of living for a family.

22 AGRICULTURE

Out of 72,000 hectares (177,916 acres) of land in Tonga, 16,000 hectares (39,536 acres) are arable. According to the constitution of 1875, all the land in the kingdom belongs to the crown and cannot be alienated. Much of it, however, consists of hereditary estates bestowed upon various chiefs, who lease the lands to farmers at a nominal annual rent. As of 2009 an estimated 35% of the total land was farmed.

With increasing population pressure on the land, more land is being cultivated, and less is available for fallow. The use of fertilizers, high-protein strains of corn, and similar methods to improve the efficiency of land use has become increasingly necessary.

Principal subsistence crops are yams, taro, sweet potatoes, and manioc. The principal cash crops are squash (particularly pumpkins), fish, copra and coconut products, vanilla bean extract, and bananas. Agriculture accounts for about 20.8% of the GDP. In

2009 fruit production amounted to an estimated 11,199 tons and vegetable production to 28,076 tons.

23 ANIMAL HUSBANDRY

The UN Food and Agriculture Organization (FAO) reported that Tonga dedicated 4,000 hectares (9,884 acres) to permanent pasture or meadow in 2009. Beef cattle often graze in coconut plantations to lessen undergrowth and provide additional income. Every householder has several hogs, which generally are not sold but used for feasts. Sheep were brought into Tonga in 1954 but did not thrive, and in 1956 the entire flock was slaughtered. In 2009 livestock totals included 330,000 chickens, 11,300 head of cattle, and 81,200 pigs. Tonga also produced 53 tons of cattle hide. Other livestock (in 2005) included 12,500 goats and 11,400 horses.

24 FISHING

Fish are abundant in the coastal waters, but the fishing industry is relatively undeveloped, and the supply of fish is insufficient to meet local demand; thus, canned fish has been imported in recent years. Nearly one-third of all households participate in some type of fishing activities, either for personal consumption or to sell locally. Principal commercial species include tuna and marlin. Tonga had 41 commercial fishing boats in 2008. The annual capture totaled 2,141 tons according to the UN FAO. The export value of seafood totaled $2.02 million.

25 FORESTRY

Estimates on Tonga's forest resources vary, with the average amount of forestland falling between 5% and 13% of total land area in 2009. Forest resources are diminishing fairly quickly, and much wood for construction must be imported. There is a government sawmill on 'Eua. Charcoal is manufactured from logs and coconut shells. The FAO estimated the 2009 roundwood production at 2,000 cu m (70,629 cu ft). The value of all forest products, including roundwood, totaled $25,000.

26 MINING

Tonga had few known mineral resources. A limited amount of crushed stone is produced at local quarries.

27 ENERGY AND POWER

Tonga has no proven reserves of oil, natural gas, or coal, making the nation dependent upon imports to meet its hydrocarbon needs. Tonga's primary energy source is electricity, all of it powered by fossil fuels. The World Bank reported in 2008 that Tonga produced 40 million kWh of electricity. For 2007 the CIA estimated electricity consumption at 39.99 million kWh. In 2009 oil consumption was estimated at 1,000 barrels per day.

28 INDUSTRY

Encouragement of new manufacturing ventures has been a part of Tonga's development plans since 1966. The primary manufacturing activities include metal fabrication (with imported materials), furniture making, food and beverage processing (including soft drinks, beer, and bakeries), small boat building, and the manufacturing of paint and construction materials. At the government-backed Small Industry Center in Nuku'alofa, more ad-

vanced products are made, including refrigerators, jewelry, bicycles, toys, furniture, wheelbarrows, and mini-excavators; other consumer goods are assembled for use locally and in neighboring countries. A small but growing construction sector has developed as well. Long-established industries include coconut processing, sawmilling, and local handicrafts. Industry accounted for about 18.1% of GDP in 2011.

29 SCIENCE AND TECHNOLOGY

The World Bank reported in 2009 that there were no patent applications in science and technology from Tonga. There are no major institutions participating in research activities. Some government ministries support research projects related to their particular field of interest, such as the Ministry of Agriculture, Food, Forestry, and Fisheries. The Ministry of the Tonga Science Network is a website created by a team from the University of Canterbury in New Zealand to share scientific information related to Tonga with local schools and communities and fellow scientists. The project was approved by the Tongan Ministry of Education.

30 DOMESTIC TRADE

Nuku'alofa is the primary commercial and urban center, offering a wide range of retail outlets for imported goods. Many of these establishments have been rebuilt following the anti-government riots of 2006, which led to the destruction of a large number of businesses owned and operated by immigrants and members of the nobility. Village stores typically carry a stock of flour, sugar, canned meats, textiles, hardware, soap, kerosene, tobacco, and matches. Many retail establishments on Tongatapu are owned by Chinese immigrants. Private business hours are typically 8 a.m. to 1 p.m. and 2 p.m. to 5 p.m., Monday through Friday and 8 a.m. to noon on Saturdays. All shops are usually closed on Sunday.

31 FOREIGN TRADE

With a heavy reliance on imported goods, Tonga suffers from chronic trade deficits. Agricultural products, including squash, root crops, vanilla, and copra, are the primary export products, along with fish. Food and beverage, mineral fuels, machinery and

Principal Trading Partners – Tonga (2010)

(In millions of US dollars)

Country	Total	Exports	Imports	Balance
World	167.1	8.3	158.8	-150.5
Fiji	67.6	1.4	66.2	-64.9
New Zealand	47.8	1.0	46.8	-45.8
United States	24.9	2.3	22.7	-20.4
Japan	23.8	0.8	23.0	-22.2
Australia	12.1	0.5	11.7	-11.2
China	10.7	0.0	10.7	-10.7
South Africa	6.7	...	6.7	-6.7
Canada	5.0	0.0	4.9	-4.9
Samoa	4.8	1.1	3.7	-2.5
China, P.R.: Hong Kong	3.7	3.4	0.3	3.1

(…) data not available or not significant.

(n.s.) not specified.

SOURCE: *2011 Direction of Trade Statistics Yearbook,* New York: United Nations, 2011.

Balance of Payments – Tonga (2009)

(In thousands of US dollars)

Current Account		**-54,216.0**
Balance on goods		-131,205.0
Imports	-139,640.0	
Exports	8,435.0	
Balance on services		-13,460.0
Balance on income		3,847.0
Current transfers		86,603.0
Capital Account		**54,867.0**
Financial Account		**17,650.0**
Direct investment abroad		...
Direct investment in Tonga		-36.0
Portfolio investment assets		...
Portfolio investment liabilities		...
Financial derivatives		1,657.0
Other investment assets		10,381.0
Other investment liabilities		5,648.0
Net Errors and Omissions		**-37,266.0**
Reserves and Related Items		**18,965.0**

(…) data not available or not significant.

SOURCE: *Balance of Payment Statistics Yearbook 2011*, Washington, DC: International Monetary Fund, 2011.

transport equipment, and manufactured goods are major imports. Tonga imported $139 million worth of goods and services in 2008, while exporting $22 million worth of goods and services. Major import partners in 2010 were Fiji, 31.6%; New Zealand, 22.3%; Japan, 11%; the United States, 10.8%; Australia, 5.6%; and China, 5.1%. Major export partners were Hong Kong, 26.8%; the United States, 17.9%; Fiji, 10.7%; Samoa, 9%; New Zealand, 7.9%; Japan, 6.1%; and American Samoa, 5.7%.

³²BALANCE OF PAYMENTS

Since 1960 Tonga has had a growing trade deficit, offset by funds from the United Kingdom, New Zealand, Australia, and the Asian Development Bank (ADB). Tonga had a 2008 trade deficit of $117 million.

³³BANKING AND SECURITIES

The nation's first commercial bank, the Bank of Tonga, was opened in 1974, with the government holding 40% of shares, and the Bank of Hawaii, the Bank of New Zealand, and the Bank of New South Wales each holding 20% of the remaining shares. The Tongan Development Bank (TDB) was founded in 1977 and offers both commercial banking and business advisory services. A locally incorporated commercial bank, MBF Bank, opened in 1993. ANZ Tonga was also established on the islands in 1993.

Tonga's fiscal policy has traditionally been cautious, with taxation and expenditure measures balancing in the recurrent budget and the development budget being financed mainly through grants and soft loans. Legislation to set up a central bank was passed in late 1988, and the National Reserve Bank came into existence the following year. The Ministry of Finance, the Board of Currency Commissioners, the Board of Coinage Commissioners, and the island's only commercial bank, the Bank of Tonga, had until then jointly performed central bank functions.

Tonga has no stock issues or securities trading.

³⁴INSURANCE

ANZ Tonga offers home and vehicle insurance, and Dominion Insurance Tonga provides a range of home, business, motor vehicle, health, and life insurance products.

³⁵PUBLIC FINANCE

In 2010 the budget of Tonga included $80.4 million in public revenue and $109.8 million in public expenditures, resulting in a deficit of $29.4 million. Total external debt as of 2009 was $104.5 million. About half of all public revenues accrued from customs duties on imported goods; the remainder came mainly from export duties, port fees, income taxes, and stamp revenues. Principal items of expenditure were public health, medical services, education, and agriculture.

³⁶TAXATION

As part of the government's revenue reform program, a series of new tax laws were passed in 2007. These included the Customs Act 2007, Income Tax Act 2007, Customs and Excise Repeal Act 2007, Customs and Excise Management Act 2007, Excise Tax Act 2007, and Revenue Service Administration Amendment Act 2007.

Under the new income tax regulations, the personal income tax is levied at a rate of 10% for income between TOP7,401 and TOP30,000. Higher incomes are taxed at a rate of TOP2,260 plus 20% of each TOP over TOP30,000. The standard business tax is levied at 25% on chargeable income. There is also a 5% sales tax.

³⁷CUSTOMS AND DUTIES

Customs duties on imports (when applicable) are levied at rates of 15% or 20% of the transaction value of the goods (the price actually paid for them) plus the cost of transporting the goods to Tonga. A consumption tax of 15% is then calculated on the duty-inclusive value plus international freight and/or insurance charges. Excise taxes are imposed on a number of items, including tobacco and alcoholic beverages.

³⁸FOREIGN INVESTMENT

In an effort to encourage foreign investment, the government initiated a new Foreign Investment Act for Tonga in 2007, with regulations drawn from the Foreign Investment Act 2002 and Foreign Investment Regulations 2006. Under the act, there are 13 business activities reserved for Tongans, such as taxi services, retailing activities, and the production of certain agricultural crops. Investment opportunities are encouraged in agribusiness, fisheries, import substitution and export industries, information technology and telecommunication services, and tourism. Foreign direct investment (FDI) in Tonga was a net inflow of $14.6 million according to World Bank figures published in 2009. FDI represented 4.71% of GDP.

There are no free trade zones in Tonga, but in 1980 the government established the Small Business Center near Nuku'alofa, which serves as an improved industrial park for small enterprises.

³⁹ECONOMIC DEVELOPMENT

Tonga's first seven development plans (1966–2006) emphasized development of the islands' economic infrastructure, with particular attention toward increasing agricultural production by revitalizing the copra and banana industries, improvements in telecommunications and transport, and expansion of tourism, industry, and exports. While there was some growth in these sectors, a number of economic and political setbacks hindered efforts toward greater economic development. On the economic side, these included damages caused by Cyclone Waka in 2001 and the scandal involving the mismanagement of the Tonga Trust Fund, which was discovered in 2002. The eruption of pro-democracy demonstrations in 2006 interrupted development plans as the government answered to call for political reforms.

The eighth development plan (2006–08) reflected the need for political change by emphasizing good governance as the key to economic growth. The ninth development plan (2009–13) maintains much of the same goals and strategies of the eighth, presenting a vision for a higher standard of living for all Tongans through good governance, private sector growth, improved health and education standards, and cultural development. To this end, the government planned to continue on a program of constitutional and regulatory reforms with an eye toward community development and greater support for economic growth in the public sector. Strategies under the ninth plan are also designed to continue work toward developing and maintaining infrastructure, improving the health and education systems, and ensuring environmental protection and sustainability. Financial and technical support for the implementation of the ninth development plan was secured from the Secretariat of the Pacific Community, as outlined in the *Joint Country Strategy 2009–2013*.

40 SOCIAL DEVELOPMENT

The law supports a social structure in which members of the royal family and the hereditary nobility enjoy special status and significant advantages over commoners. For example, the nobility are the primary landowners and control most of the monetary sector of the economy. An original constitutional mandate granting a plot of land to every male at age 16 has been disregarded as the population has become too large to provide the necessary land. In addition, the dictates of traditional culture, particularly in defining family roles, began to change as the population became more aware of Western influences through expanded educational opportunities, foreign media, and reports from Tongans living abroad. These influences likely contributed to a rise in pro-democracy sentiments, which has led the government to initiate a number of political reforms.

Polynesian cultural traditions have kept most women in somewhat subservient roles, and few have risen to positions of leadership. The first woman was elected to the legislative assembly in 2005. As of 2012, there was still only one woman serving in the legislative assembly. Inheritance laws discriminate against women, and women may not own land. However, there have been no reports of discrimination against women in access to education. There have been no major reports of discrimination against women in terms of generally employment, though more men than women are employed in paid work. Domestic violence has been an issue, but there are no laws specifically relating to domestic abuse or spousal rape. Some incidents have been prosecuted under the law of physical assault. The Center for Women and Children focuses on improving the economic and social conditions for women. Child abuse is rare.

There is no social welfare department. Care for the elderly, disabled, widows, and orphans is offered through extended family. While this traditional standard is still prevalent, shifting cultural views and migration of some family members from rural to urban areas have posed some challenges. The medical and education departments and religious missions provide what welfare services are available. The only pension scheme is for civil servants.

Human rights are generally respected in Tonga.

41 HEALTH

Tongans receive free medical and dental treatments through the public healthcare system. There was a government medical department hospital in Tongatapu, Vava'u, Ha'apai, and Eau Island, with several dispensaries. As of 2008 there were 4 hospitals and 14 healthcare centers in the country. In 2011 there were an estimated 3 physicians, 29 nurses and midwives, and 24 hospital beds per 10,000 inhabitants.

Life expectancy as of 2012 was estimated at 75.38 years. Infant mortality was an estimated 13.21 deaths per 1,000 live births, and the fertility rate was 3.55. It was estimated that 99% of children were vaccinated against measles. The incidence of tuberculosis was 28 per 100,000 people in 2007. In 2009 it was estimated that the country spent 5.0% of its GDP on healthcare each year.

42 HOUSING

Village houses usually have reed sides and a sloping roof thatched with sugarcane or coconut leaves; the posts are of ironwood, and braided cord takes the place of nails. More modern houses, especially in the towns, are built of wood, with roofs of corrugated iron. Unlike the village houses, they often contain more than one room and have verandas. At the 2006 census, there were 17,462 private households reported with an average household size of 5.8 people.

43 EDUCATION

Primary education is free and compulsory for six years. General secondary school lasts for five years, but students pay tuition at the public secondary school. Private mission schools are available for all ages with varying fees. Students may choose to continue with one or two more years of upper secondary education. Selected Tongan students prepare for the New Zealand school certificate examination.

In 2005 about 23% of age-eligible children were enrolled in some type of preschool program. Primary school enrollment that year was estimated at about 95.4% of age-eligible students, while secondary school enrollment was about 67.7% of age-eligible students. It is estimated that nearly all students complete their primary education. The student-to-teacher ratio for primary school was at 20:1 in 2005; the ratio for secondary school was about 14:1. In 2005 private schools accounted for 8.8% of primary school enrollment.

The University of the South Pacific operates an extension center in Tonga. A teacher-training college, established in 1944, provides a two-year course. The Tonga Institute of Science and Technology in Nuku'alofa offers two-year programs in selected trades. A government scholarship program provides the opportunity for Tongan students to pursue higher education abroad. Overall, the CIA estimated that Tonga had a literacy rate of 98.9% in 2011. As of 2004 public expenditure on education was 4.8% of GDP.

⁴⁴LIBRARIES AND MUSEUMS

Since 1971, the Ministry of Education has operated a joint library service with the University of the South Pacific. Its library in Nuku'alofa has 9,000 volumes covering agriculture, small business management, adult education, and an important collection of Pacificana. The Ministry of Education library has 12,500 volumes. Most of the secondary and high schools have libraries. The Tonga College Museum's collection includes artifacts from Tongan history. Notable monuments include the great trilithon known as the Ha'amanga and some 45 *langis*, great rectangular platforms of recessed tiers of coral limestone blocks erected as tombs for medieval kings.

⁴⁵MEDIA

In 2010 the CIA reported that there were 31,000 telephone landlines in Tonga, with an additional 54,300 mobile cell phones in use nationwide. Mobile phone subscriptions averaged 51 per 100 people; land and mobile phone density combined was 70 per 100 people.

The government's radiotelegraph station at Nuku'alofa has substations at Neiafu (Vava'u), Pangai, Ha'afeva and Nomuka (in the Ha'apai group), 'Eua, and Niuatoputapu. There is also a direct overseas telegraph service linking Nuku'alofa with Wellington, Suva, Apia, and Pago Pago. An internal radiotelephone service connects Nuku'alofa, 'Eua, Nomuka, Ha'afeva, and Vava'u, and a direct overseas radiotelephone service links Nuku'alofa to other Pacific island capitals.

The Tonga Broadcasting Commission's Radio Tonga was established in 1961. It broadcasts about 75 hours a week in Tongan, English, Fijian, and Samoan; commercial advertising is accepted. In 2009 there was one FM radio station, four AM radio stations, and one shortwave radio station. The government owned one of the three television stations operating in 2004. In 1997 Tonga had 600 radios and 18 television sets in use per 1,000 inhabitants. In 2011 the country had 20,766 Internet hosts. As of 2009 there were some 8,400 Internet users in Tonga, with internet subscriptions at about eight per 100 citizens.

The government publishes a weekly newspaper, *Tonga Chronicle*, which had an average circulation (in 2002) of 7,000 copies in Tongan and English. *Matangi Tonga* is a privately owned monthly magazine that also publishes online. There are church newspapers issued by missions and a few private publications printed at regular intervals.

In 2010 two women launched a new full-color, bilingual newspaper targeted primarily for women in rural areas. The biweekly publication *Faite* features articles in English and Tongan on issues of concern for women.

The constitution provides for free speech and a free press, although occasional infringements of press freedoms do occur. In nongovernmental publications, opposition opinion appears regularly, usually without interference, but journalists were targeted for prosecution in civil lawsuits by the minister of police.

⁴⁶ORGANIZATIONS

Extension of consumer cooperatives has been actively encouraged by the government. The Tonga Chamber of Commerce and Industry is in Nuku'alofa.

National youth organizations are typically affiliated with religious or educational institutions, including the Catholic Youth Association, Free Church of Tonga Youth Association, Free Wesleyan Church Youth Association, Tonga Ex-Commonwealth Youth Programme Diplomats Association, and Tupou Farmers. Scouting and YMCA/YWCA programs are also available. Meetings of Christian Endeavor societies and Bible classes are well attended by all ages. There are sports associations promoting amateur competitions for athletes of all ages in a variety of pastimes.

Every Tongan village has a community house. The Civil Society Forum of Tonga formed in 2001 to promote community development and issues of equality and social justice. The Tongan Women's Progressive Association, formed in 1956, conducts programs for the betterment of village conditions and holds classes in a variety of subjects. The National Center for Women and Children and the Women and Children Crisis Center provide some health and support services for women, particularly those who are victims of domestic violence. The Tonga National Women's Congress promotes equal rights for women. There is a national chapter of the Red Cross Society.

⁴⁷TOURISM, TRAVEL, AND RECREATION

The tourist industry is a small but growing source of foreign exchange revenues. In 2004 there were 41,208 tourist arrivals, with 57% of travelers coming from Australia and New Zealand. Popular tourist sites are the royal palace and terraced tombs in Nuku'alofa. Most visitors enjoy a traditional evening feast of suckling pig, crayfish, chicken, and assorted accompaniments. Fishing, swimming, and sailing are popular. Rugby is a favorite spectator sport.

Tourists must have a valid passport as well as an onward/return ticket. Visitor's visas are required for nationals of many countries; they are provided upon arrival and valid for one month. Estimates from the 2011 *Tourism Factbook*, published by the UN World Tourism Organization, indicated that the daily cost to visit Nuku'alofa, the capital, was $271.

⁴⁸FAMOUS PERSONS

King George Tupou I (Taufa'ahu Tupou, 1797–1893) ruled for 48 years; during his reign, Tonga became a Christian nation, abolished serfdom, and acquired a constitution. His prime minister, Shirley Waldemar Baker (1831–1903), was a Wesleyan clergyman who, after being deposed in 1890, became an Episcopal minister and then returned to Tonga. The most famous Tongan of this century was Queen Salote Tupou (1900–65), whose rule began in 1918. Her dynasty, the Tupou, is the third branch of the royal family and traces its descent back to Ahoeitu, the first Tu'i Tonga of whom there is record. Queen Salote's son, King Taufa'ahau Tupou IV (1918–2006), succeeded to the throne in 1965 and was formally crowned in 1967. His son Siaosi Tupou V (1948–2012), also known as King George Tupou V, succeeded to the throne in his place and was formally crowned in 2008. After King George Tupou's death on 18 March 2012, his brother, Crown Prince Tupouto'a

Lavaka (b. 1959), succeeded to the throne with the crown name King Tupou VI.

49 DEPENDENCIES

Tonga has no territories or colonies.

50 BIBLIOGRAPHY

Besnier, Niko. *On the Edge of the Global: Modern Anxieties in a Pacific Island Nation.* Stanford, CA: Stanford University Press, 2011.

Cook, James. *The Explorations of Captain James Cook in the Pacific, as Told by Selections of His Own Journals, 1768–1779.* New York: Heritage, 1958.

Craig, Robert D. *Historical Dictionary of Polynesia. 3rd ed.* Lanham, MD: Scarecrow, 2010.

Ellem, Elizabeth W. *Queen Salote of Tonga: The Story of an Era 1900–1965.* Auckland, NZ: Auckland University Press, 1999.

Gillespie, Rosemary G., and David A. Clague, eds. *Encyclopedia of Islands.* Berkeley: University of California Press, 2009.

Kirch, Patrick Vinton, and Jean-Louis Rallu. *The Growth and Collapse of Pacific Island Societies.* Honolulu: University of Hawaii Press, 2007.

Leibo, Steven A. *East and Southeast Asia 2011.* Lanham, MD: Stryker-Post Publications, 2011.

Samoa and Tonga. Oakland, CA: Lonely Planet, 2009.

Tonga Investment and Business Guide: Strategic and Practical Information. Washington, DC: International Business Publications USA, 2012.

TURKEY

Republic of Turkey
Türkiye Cumhuriyeti

CAPITAL: Ankara

FLAG: The national flag consists of a white crescent (open toward the fly) and a white star on a red field.

ANTHEM: *Istiklâl Marşi (March of Independence).*

MONETARY UNIT: As of 1 January 2009 the official monetary unit became the Turkish lira (TRY), replacing the Turkish new lira (YTL). The YTL existed from 1 January 2005 to 31 December 2009 to facilitate the re-valuing of the lira following decades of gradual depreciation. There are coins of 1, 5, 10, 25 and 50 kuruş, and 1 lira. TRY1 = US$0.54 (or US$1 = TRY1.85) as of October 2011.

WEIGHTS AND MEASURES: The metric system is the legal standard for all units of measurement. Some regions of Turkey have retained the weight unit oka, which equals 1.28 kg (2.82 lbs).

HOLIDAYS: New Year's Day (Yılbaşı, 1 January); National Sovereignty and Children's Day (Ulusal Egemenlik ve Çocuk Bayramı, 23 April); May Day (Emek ve Dayanışma Günü, 1 May; officially legal again as of 1 May 2010); Atatürk Day/Youth and Sports Day (Anma Gençlik ve Spor Bayramı, 19 May); Victory Day (Zafer Bayramı, 30 August); and Independence Day (Anniversary of the Republic, Cumhuriyet Bayramı, 29 October). Movable religious holidays include Eid al-Fitr (Şeker Bayrami, lasting three days); and Eid al-Adha (Kurban Bayrami, lasting four days) 70 days after Ramadan.

TIME: 3 p.m. = noon GMT.

¹LOCATION, SIZE, AND EXTENT

The Republic of Turkey has a total area of 783,562 sq km (301,384 sq mi), and is slightly larger than the state of Texas. It encompasses the entire Black Sea straits system—the Dardanelles, the Sea of Marmara, and the Bosporus—and controls it through international law. Turkey is bordered on the N by the Black Sea, on the NE by Georgia and Armenia, on the E by Iran, on the SE by Iraq, on the S by Syria and the Mediterranean Sea, on the W by the Aegean Sea, and on the NW by Greece and Bulgaria, with a total land boundary of 2,648 km (1,645 mi) and a coastline of 7,200 km (4,474 mi). Turkey's capital city, Ankara, is located in the northwest central part of the country.

The peninsula-like region has had several names over time, but the most commonly known designations are Asia Minor and Anatolia. It is often considered the border region between Asia and Europe. Modern Turkey is geographically divided into seven regions: the Aegean, the Black Sea, Central Anatolia, East Anatolia, Southeast Anatolia, Marmara (including Thrace), and the Mediterranean.

²TOPOGRAPHY

Other than the low, rolling hills of Turkish Thrace, the fertile river valleys that open to the Aegean Sea, the warm plains of Antalya and Adana on the Mediterranean, and the narrow littoral along the Black Sea, the country is wrinkled by rugged mountain ranges that surround and intersect the high, semiarid Anatolian plateau. Average elevations range from 600 m (2,000 ft) above sea level in the west to over 1,800 m (6,000 ft) amid the wild eastern highlands. The highest point is Mount Ararat (Büyük Agri Dagi, 5,166 m/16,949 ft), which rises just within Turkey at the intersection of the Turkish, Armenian, and Iranian frontiers. There are over 100 peaks with elevations of 3,000 m (10,000 ft) or more.

Turkey has a small network of rivers, the most prominent being the Tigris and Euphrates, which originate in eastern Anatolia. Because the watersheds of most streams are semibarren slopes, the seasonal variations in flow are great. The largest lake is Lake Van (3,675 sq km/1,419 sq mi), which lies near the Iranian border. The other major lake is Lake Tuz (1665 km2/643 sq mi), near the center of the country, which has a salinity level so high that it serves as a commercial source of salt. Turkey's 7,200 km (5,474 mi) of coastline and beaches, including the Turkish Riviera, are a prominent tourist destination.

Most of Turkey lies within an earthquake zone, and recurrent tremors are recorded. On 28 March 1970 a 6.9-magnitude earthquake hit the Gediz region of western Turkey, killing 1,086 persons and destroying 33 towns. The most destructive earthquake in the country was that of 29 December 1939–near Erzincan, at a magnitude of 7.8—which killed 30,000 persons. On 17 August 1999 a 7.6 magnitude quake near Izmit was followed two days later by two aftershocks of about 4.8 and 5.0 in magnitude. At least 17,118 people died in the quake and nearly 50,000 injured were injured. A 6.1 magnitude earthquake on 1 May 2003 in eastern Turkey left 150 people dead and over 1,000 injured. A 7.2 magnitude earthquake in October 2011 destroyed nearly 1,000 buildings and killed several hundred people.

³CLIMATE

Turkey's southern coast enjoys a Mediterranean climate, and the Aegean coastal climate as far north as İzmir is much the same. The mean temperature range in these regions is 17–20°C (63–68°F), and the annual rainfall ranges from 58 to 130 cm (23 to 51 in). The Black Sea coast is relatively mild (14–16°C/57–60°F) and very moist, with 71–249 cm (28–87 in) of rainfall. The central Anatolian plateau is noted for its hot, dry summers and cold winters: the average annual temperature is 8–12°C (46–54°F), and annual precipitation is 30–75 cm (12–30 in). With the exception of some warmer pockets in the valleys, the eastern third of Turkey is colder (4–9°C /39–48°F), and rainfall averages 41–51 cm (16–20 in). The little precipitation there is on the central plateau tends to be concentrated during the late fall and winter months.

⁴FLORA AND FAUNA

A moderate degree of biodiversity can be found within Turkey's borders, from semitropical to temperate, and desert to alpine regions. The World Resource Institute estimates that there are 8,650 plant species in Turkey. In addition, Turkey is home to about 145 species of mammals, 436 species of birds, 133 species of reptiles, 23 species of amphibians, and 184 species of fish (this calculation reflects the total number of distinct species residing in the country, not the number of endemic species). In the mountains of southern, southwestern, and northern Turkey, there are extensive coniferous stands of commercial importance and some deciduous forest. Licorice, valonia oaks, and wild olive trees grow in the southwest. Principal varieties of wild animals are the fallow deer, red deer, roe deer, eastern mouflon, wild boar, hare, Turkish leopard, brown bear, red fox, gazelle, beech marten, pine marten, wildcat, lynx, otter, and badger. There is a large variety of birds, including the snow partridge, quail, great bustard, little bustard, widgeon, woodcock, snipe, and a variety of geese, ducks, pigeons, and rails. About 30 species of snakes are indigenous. Bees and silkworms are grown commercially.

According to a 2007 report issued by the International Union for Conservation of Nature and Natural Resources (IUCN), threatened species included 18 types of mammals, 15 species of birds, 13 types of reptiles, 9 types of amphibians, 54 species of fish, 12 species of invertebrates, and 3 species of plants. Threatened species include the Anatolian leopard, Mediterranean monk seal, bald ibis, slender-billed curlew, Atlantic sturgeon, and hawksbill and green sea turtles. Wild goats are among the vulnerable species.

⁵ENVIRONMENT

The Turkish government has been steadily increasing its efforts at environmental conservation, integrating many of its agricultural and forestry policies with those of the European Union. The World Resource Institute reported that Turkey had designated 1.27 million hectares (3.14 million acres) of land for protection as of 2006. Water resources totaled 234 cu km (56.14 cu mi) while water usage was 39.78 cu km (9.54 cu mi) per year. Domestic water usage accounted for 15% of total usage, industrial for 11%, and agricultural for 74%. As of 2010 the European Commission for Agricultural and Rural development noted that 55% of Turkey's ecosystem was designated for agricultural use, 13% as forestland, and 33% as arid shrub or grassland. Per capita water usage totaled 544 cu m (19,211 cu ft) per year.

Environmental responsibilities are vested in the Under Secretariat for Environment and in the Ministry of Energy and Natural Resources. Among Turkey's principal environmental problems is air pollution in Ankara and other cities. The smog in Ankara grew worse after 1979, when the government banned oil heating systems in new buildings in order to reduce costly oil imports. As a result, the increased burning of Turkish lignite, which is high in sulfur content, greatly increased the levels of sulfur dioxide and dust in the air. In 1983 the government reversed itself and banned the conversion of heating systems to coal. At the same time, it introduced an antipollution program designed to reduce air pollution levels by more than 50% within a year. In addition to heating restrictions, the plan called for strict traffic controls, the closing of the worst industrial polluters, a prohibition on the import of high-sulfur fuel oil, special emergency hospital wards for smog victims, and the building of green areas and parks in and around cities. In 1992 Turkey had the world's highest level of industrial carbon dioxide emission, which totaled 145.5 million metric tons, a per capita level of 2.49 metric tons. Emissions increased to 178.3 million metric tons in 1996 and to 221.6 million metric tons in 2000. The United Nations (UN) reported in 2008 that carbon dioxide emissions in Turkey totaled 288 million metric tons.

A $220-million project to clean up the polluted water in the Golden Horn, an inlet of the Bosporus forming a harbor in Istanbul, was implemented in the 1980s. The World Bank World Development Institute stated in 2003 that the most prominent source of freshwater pollution, at 44% of total pollution, comes from food industry waste. Chemicals constitute 8%, with the remaining spread among various manufacturing and development industries. As of 2002 the UN Environmental Program's Water Quality Monitoring System calculated Turkey's freshwater pollution level at 1.1 tons per cubic km, 31st in the world. Soil erosion affects both coastal and internal areas; the combination of water and wind eliminates about 500 metric tons of soil each year.

⁶POPULATION

The US Central Intelligence Agency (CIA) estimated the population of Turkey in July 2011 to be approximately 78,785,548, which placed it at number 17 in population among the 196 nations of the world. In 2011 approximately 6.3% of the population was over 65 years of age, with another 26.6% under 15 years of age. The median age in Turkey was 28.5 years. There were 1.02 males for every female in the country. The population's annual rate of change was 1.235%. The projected population for the year 2025 was 85,000,000. Population density in Turkey was calculated at 101 people per sq km (262 people per sq mi). A 2010 report by the same agency stated that 70% of the population lived in urban areas, and that urban populations had an annual rate of change of 1.7%. The largest urban areas, along with their respective populations, included Istanbul, 10.4 million; Ankara, 3.8 million; Izmir, 2.7 million; Bursa, 1.6 million; and Adana, 1.3 million.

⁷MIGRATION

Estimates of Turkey's net migration rate, carried out by the CIA in 2011, amounted to 0.51 migrants per 1,000 citizens. The total number of emigrants living abroad was 4.26 million, and the total number of immigrants living in Turkey was 1.41 million. Much Turkish emigration has consisted of workers under contract for employment in European Community countries. In the 1960s several European countries (including Russia) signed bilateral treaties with Turkey permitting immigrant guest workers. In most cases, the de facto arrangement became permanent; however, the

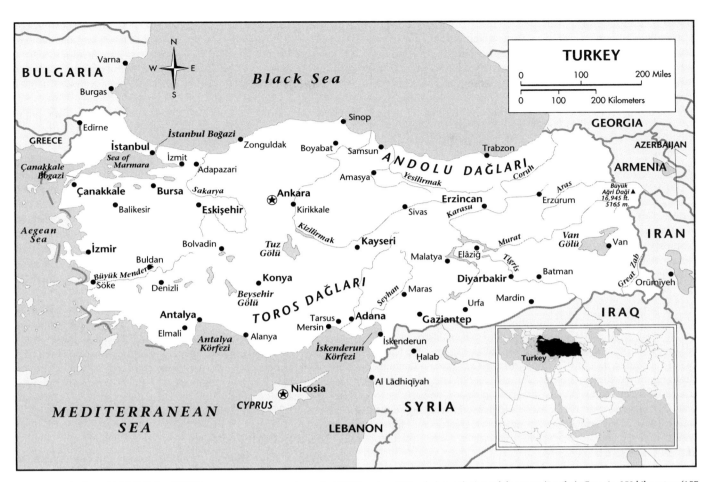

LOCATION: 25°40′ to 44°48′E; 35°51′ to 42°6′ N. BOUNDARY LENGTHS: Armenia, 268 kilometers (167 miles); Azerbaijan, 9 kilometers (5 miles); Georgia, 252 kilometers (157 miles); Iran, 499 kilometers (311 miles); Iraq, 331 kilometers (206 miles); Syria, 822 kilometers (500 miles); Greece, 206 kilometers (128 miles); Bulgaria, 240 kilometers (150 miles); total coastline, 7,200 kilometers (4,482 miles). TERRITORIAL SEA LIMIT: 6 miles, Aegean Sea; 12 miles, Mediterranean and Black Seas.

de jure status of the Turkish workers became unclear. While the European Union has a workers' treaty with Turkey as well, the rules between this treaty and those of individual countries are not consistent. Between 2004 and 2006 the Council of Europe conducted a survey of the situations of Turkish workers and their remittances across Europe, as well as an analysis of laws and regulations. They then submitted a proposal to update and integrate these laws in order to clarify the position of migrant Turks in Europe. As of 2004, there were an estimated 3.03 million Turkish migrants living in Europe, with 1.06 million employed and 241,988 actively seeking employment. The vast majority of the total, 1.9 million, were in Germany.

The Council of Europe also conducted surveys outside of Europe and estimated that there were 19,800 Turkish migrants living in the republics of Central Asia, 108,070 in the Middle East, and 363,789 elsewhere in the world. Low numbers in Central Asia reflect high unemployment in most Central Asian republics, and, because a Turkic language is the primary language in Central Asian countries, many unemployed are themselves drawn to Turkey for work.

The Kurdish situation is another point of controversy regarding migrants in Turkey. After the 1990–91 Gulf War, 500,000 Iraqi Kurds fled to Turkey. While most of these refugees have since re-patriated or resettled in third countries, the lack of documentation of Kurdish refugees makes the data difficult to determine. Further, in 1992 about 20,000 Bosnians came to Turkey, and in 1999 nearly 18,000 Kosovar refugees sought asylum, including 8,000 people evacuated from Macedonia. Nearly all were voluntarily repatriated, as non-European refugees are granted only temporary protection in Turkey.

8 ETHNIC GROUPS

The constitution provides a single designation of nationality for all Turks; however, ethnic identification among the citizens themselves is strong. Between 70% and 75% of the population is Turkish. The major ethnic minority (by mother tongue), the Kurds, is estimated at 18%. Arabs, Turkmen, Circassians, Greeks, and others do account for a small percentage of the population. The number of Roma within the country may be significant; however, many are unwilling to disclose their ethnic identity since discrimination against Roma has been common.

Hundreds of thousands of Armenians were either killed or forced to flee by the Ottoman Turks during 1915–16. The Armenians regard the killings as genocide, a view that is formally held by several other countries. Turkey denies the allegations of genocide, insisting that the killings were simply a result of the widespread fighting of World War I (1914–18). Armenians mark the death toll at about 1.5 million; Turkey claims that only about 300,000 died. Bitterness between Armenians and Turks continues over this situation to this day. In March 2012 US senators introduced legislation to recognize the mass killings as genocide. The administration of US president Barack Obama opposed the measure. As of March 2012, 19 nations had recognized the Armenian Genocide.

The Greek component in Turkey was reduced as a result of the 1919–22 hostilities with Greece, the 1923 Treaty of Lausanne (which provided for an exchange of population with Greece), and the post-World War II Cyprus controversy.

The Arabs live in the south along the Syrian and Iraqi frontiers, and the Greeks, Armenians, and Jews live primarily in Istanbul. In 1984 the Kurdistan Workers' Party (PKK), now known as the People's Congress of Kurdistan or Kongra-Gel (KGK), began a separatist insurgency, towards which the government took considerable action. The Turkish Kurds, who heavily populate eleven provinces in the southeast portion of Turkey, have been fighting to establish an independent Kurdish state for decades. In the call for national unity, the Turkish government does not recognize separate minority groups. The government has been criticized by some international organizations for discrimination against the Kurds, including a government ban on the use of the Kurdish language. The militant Kurdish faction of Kongra-Gel has been designated as a terrorist group by Turkey, the United States, and the European Union. However, many Turkish Kurds are working within the structure of the legal system to guarantee greater civil rights.

9 LANGUAGES

Turkish, which belongs to the Ural-Altaic group, is the official language. Modern Turkish uses the Roman alphabet, with the inclusion of transliterated letters ç, ş, ğ, ö, ı, and ü. With only minor exceptions, words are spelled phonetically. The language is agglutinative and phonetic, with minimal use of diphthongs or dropped letters. A 1928 language reform substituted the Roman alphabet for the Arabic script, which had been used by the Turks since their conversion to Islam. During the 1930s there was a state-sponsored effort to rid the language of Arabic and Persian words and grammatical constructions, though many Persian and Arabic expressions persist. Traditionally, there was a great difference between vernacular Turkish and written Ottoman Turkish, the latter being heavily influenced by Arabic and Persian and almost unintelligible to the mass of Turks. This difference has been almost obliterated, though some regional differences in dialect, particularly in the villages, still make effective communication difficult. Kurdish and Arabic are also spoken. Kurmanci Kurdish, the branch of Kurdish primarily spoken in Turkey, is a language of the Iranian group; it has traditionally been written in Arabic script; however, in the 21st century, a standardized Latin transliteration has developed. Armenian and Greek are also spoken in Turkey.

10 RELIGIONS

About 99% of the population is officially Muslim; however, the number of practicing Muslims may be much lower. The vast majority of Turkish Muslims are Sunni, but there is a substantial Shi'a minority. About 15–20 million Muslims are believed to be Alevis, incorporating traditions of Sunni and Shi'a practices as well as other indigenous beliefs of Anatolia. A small number of people in western Anatolia practice a blend of Islam and shamanism. The Alevis and Tahtacilar are regarded as non-Muslim sects by the government.

The only religious minorities officially recognized by the government are Greek Orthodox Christians, Armenian Orthodox Christians, and Jews. The Greek Orthodox patriarch at Istanbul is considered first among equals of the seven patriarchs in the Eastern Orthodox churches. The Greek Orthodox Church has about 2,500 members. The Armenian Orthodox church has about 60,000 members. Turkey was a haven for Jewish refugees from Spain and Portugal in the late 15th and 16th centuries, and Jews have lived there in relative peace until recent years. There are about 23,000 Jews in the country. Other unofficial religious groups include about 10,000 Baha'is, 20,000 Syrian Orthodox Christians, 5,000 Yezidi, 3,600 Jehovah's Witnesses, 3,500 Protestants, and smaller numbers of Chaldean and Nestorian Christians, Syrian Orthodox, Syriac Catholics, Bulgarian Orthodox, Roman Catholics, and Maronite Christians.

There is no official state religion, and the constitution establishes the nation as a secular state. While the freedom of religion is guaranteed, some practices are restricted. Proselytizing by non-Muslims is generally discouraged. Laws against the use of religion for political purposes are rigorously enforced. Religious groups are not required by law to register with the government, but have no legal standing unless they do. Eid al-Fitr and Eid al-Adha are observed as national holidays.

11 TRANSPORTATION

Turkey's difficult terrain and its limited economic resources have proved obstacles to the construction of transportation facilities. When the republic was founded in 1923 there were about 4,000 km (2,500 mi) of railway track and 7,400 km (4,600 mi) of motor roads in Anatolia and Thrace, all in disrepair. In October 1973 the Bosporus Bridge in Istanbul was opened, facilitating the crossing of the strait of Bosporus by motorists. This six-lane steel suspension bridge has a main span of 1,074 m (3,524 ft). As of 2008, the CIA reported that Turkey had a total of 352,046 km (218,751 mi) of roads, of which 313,151 km (194,583 mi) are paved. World Bank statistics indicated that in 2008 there were 138 vehicles per 1,000 people in the country.

Railways connect most of the important points in the country with Ankara, Istanbul, and the Black Sea and Mediterranean ports. According to the State Ministry for Infrastructure and Investment (ISPAT), Turkey has 8,690 km (5,400 mi) of railways, operated by the General Directorate of Turkish State Railways (TCDD). Since most of the railways have been long in service, a budget of $23.5 billion has been allocated to railway development through 2023. A long-closed rail link between Mosul, Iraq, and Gazientep, Turkey, reopened 16 February 2010, indicating renewed economic partnerships between the two countries.

Turkey has approximately 1,200 km (746 mi) of navigable inland waterways, and 8,333 km (5,157 mi) of coastal borders; approximately 55% of all commercial trade is conducted via maritime transport, with a domestic fleet of 1,631 vessels. Marine transport is primarily conducted through the Istanbul-Izmit, Izmir, Adana-Mersin and Samsun ports; however, there are dozens of smaller ports throughout the Mediterranean and the Aegean.

There are 45 airports (16 serving international flights) that transported 85.2 million passengers in 2009. The major international airports are Atatürk in Istanbul, Esenboğa in Ankara, Adnan Menderes in Izmir, Antalya, and Dalaman. With minor exceptions, domestic air transportation is the monopoly of the semipublic Turkish Airways Corp. (Türk Hava Yollari), which connects most major centers within the country on a regular schedule and operates some international flights. The new Sabiha Gokcen International Airport on Istanbul's Asian side can handle 3.5 million passengers, with a potential capacity for 10 million passengers.

12 HISTORY

In ancient times Turkey was known as Asia Minor or Anatolia. Among the many inhabitants were the Hittites (c. 1800–1200 BC), the first people to use iron; the Greeks, who according to legend destroyed Troy (or Ilium) about 1200 BC and who colonized the Aegean coast from about 1000 BC on; the Phrygians (c. 1200–600 BC); the Lydians (c. 700–546 BC), the first people to mint coins; the Persians (546–333 BC); and the Romans, beginning in the 2nd century BC. Roman Emperor Constantine I (the Great) changed the name of the city of Byzantium to Constantinople (now Istanbul) and made it his capital in AD 330. A division between the Western and Eastern Roman Empires, with their respective capitals at Rome and Constantinople, became official in 395. Constantinople, seat of the Byzantine Empire, became the center of Eastern Orthodox Christianity, which officially separated from Roman Catholicism in 1054.

The Turks are an Altaic people whose origins are not thoroughly understood. They seem to have emerged from the plains between the Ural Mountains in Europe and the Altay Mountains in Asia around the 7th or 8th century AD. The forerunners of present-day Turkey, known as the Seljuk Turks (named after the Turkish conqueror Seljuk of the 10th century), defeated the Byzantines in the battle of Malazgirt (1071) and established themselves in Anatolia. They attained a highly developed Muslim culture in their great capital at Konya in central Turkey. The Turkish conquest of Syria, including Palestine, led to the Crusades (1096–1270), a series of intermittent and inconclusive wars. Various Latin (Roman Catholic) and Greek (Eastern Orthodox) states were formed in parts of the Turkish Empire, but none lasted. The sacking of the Christian city of Constantinople by Crusaders in 1204, followed by the establishment of the Latin Empire there (1204–61), shocked Europe and tended to discredit the Crusading movement.

Seljuk power was shattered when the Mongols, another Altaic people, swept across Asia Minor in 1243. As the Mongols withdrew, Turkish power revived and expanded under the Ottoman Turks, a group of frontier warriors whose first chief was Osman I (called Ottoman in the West, r. 1300?–26). In 1453, the Ottomans under Mehmet II (the Conqueror) occupied Constantinople and made it their capital. In 1516, they conquered Syria and in 1517, Egypt. In 1529 they were at the gates of Vienna, at which point the European expansion of Turkish power was stopped. The Turkish fleet was decisively defeated in a battle near Lepanto (now Navpaktos) in Greece in 1571. At its peak, generally identified with the reign of Sultan Süleyman I (the Magnificent, r. 1520–66), the Ottoman Empire encompassed an estimated 28 million inhabitants of Asia Minor, much of the Arabian Peninsula, North Africa

as far west as modern Algeria, the islands of the eastern Mediterranean, the Balkans, the Caucasus, and the Crimea. During the 17th, 18th, and 19th centuries, as a result of the rise of nationalism and encroachment by the European powers, the Ottoman Empire gradually shrank in size, the independence of the remainder being maintained only by shrewd balance-of-power diplomacy.

The process of modernization began with the Imperial Rescript of 1839, promulgated by Sultan Abdul Mejid (r. 1839–61), and by a body of reforms known as the Tanzimat, which to some extent curbed the absolute powers of the sultan-caliph. (The Turkish sultans had added the title "caliph" following the conquest of Egypt in 1517.) The Illustrious Rescript of 1856 was largely dictated by Britain, France, and Austria as part of the negotiations leading to the settlement of the Crimean War (1853–56), which was a clash between the Russian and Ottoman Empires. The Illustrious Rescript of 1856 ensured equal rights for non-Muslims, provided for prison reform and the codification of Turkish law, and opened Turkey to European skills and capital. A constitution was introduced in 1876 by Sultan Abdul Hamid II (r. 1876–1909), but was suspended in the following year. Thereafter, an absolute monarchy prevailed until the Young Turk revolution of 1908, at which time the constitution of 1876 was reinstated. In 1913, leaders of the Committee for Union and Progress (the organizational vehicle of the Young Turks) took effective control of the government under Sultan Mehmet V (r. 1909–18). The principal leaders were Talat and Enver Pasha, who, at the outbreak of World War I (1914–18) , threw what little remained of Ottoman strength behind the Central Powers, which had sided with Turkey in its fruitless attempt to retain its last major European possessions in the Balkan Wars of 1912–13. Although the Turks were unable to make any headway against British forces defending the Suez Canal, they did offer a heroic defense at Gallipoli (the Gelibolu Peninsula) and the Dardanelles, in a prolonged battle between Turkish and British-French forces that lasted from February 1915 to January 1916 and took the lives of about 100,000 soldiers on each side. In 1917, however, Turkish resistance collapsed, and the British pushed Turkey out of Syria, Palestine, Iraq, and Arabia. An armistice was concluded on 30 October 1918, and Enver Pasha and his colleagues fled the country. Before and during the war, Armenians sought to establish their independence and were brutally repressed by the Turks. Over a million people are said to have died being driven from their homes; many survived in exile.

On the basis of a series of earlier Allied agreements, the Ottoman Empire was to be stripped of all non-Turkish areas, and much of what remained-Asia Minor-was to be divided among the United Kingdom, France, Greece, and Italy. A substantial portion was actually occupied. In 1919, with Allied assistance, the Greeks invaded Anatolia through İzmir, but a Turkish nationalist resistance movement under the leadership of Mustafa Kemal (later called Atatürk), who had commanded a division at Gallipoli, finally defeated them in 1922. The sultan, being virtually captive in Istanbul, was disgraced in Turkish eyes by his identification with Allied policy. After much maneuvering, a rival nationalist government under Mustafa Kemal was established in Ankara and gained national and international recognition. On 1 November 1922, the sultanate was abolished by Mustafa Kemal's provisional government. The following year, the Ankara government negotiated the Treaty of Lausanne with the Allies, which recognized Turkish sovereignty over Asia Minor and a small area in Thrace. There was a massive exchange of Greek and Turkish populations. On 29 October 1923 a republic was proclaimed, with Ankara as its capital, and on 3 March 1924 the caliphate was abolished and all members of the dynasty banished.

During the next few years of the republic, a series of social, legal, and political reforms, collectively known as the Atatürk Reforms, were implemented. They included the substitution of secular law for religious law, the writing of a republican constitution based on popular sovereignty, suppression of religious education in Turkish schools, introduction of a Roman alphabet to replace the Arabic script, and the legal upgrading of the position of women. With minor exceptions, political power resided in a single party, the Republican People's Party, and, to a substantial extent, in Mustafa Kemal personally until his death in 1938. His chief of staff, Ismet Inönü (Pasha), became president and established a two-party system of government with the formation of the opposition Democrat Party (DP) in 1946.

Turkey remained neutral during most of World War II (1939–45), however, on 23 February 1945 it declared war on the Axis. Following the war, Turkey became a charter member of the UN. In 1947 the Truman Doctrine pledged US support to Turkey in the face of mounting Soviet pressure, and in 1951 the joint US-Turkish Air Force Base Incirlik was constructed outside the city of Adana, near the Syrian border.

The DP came to power in 1950. Under Prime Minister Adnan Menderes the government stressed rapid industrialization and economic expansion at the cost of individual liberties. Restrictive press laws were passed in 1954 and 1956, and by 1960 the Menderes government had curtailed judicial independence, university autonomy, and the rights of opposition parties. On 27 May 1960, after student demonstrations (joined by War College cadets and some army officers) were harshly suppressed, Prime Minister Menderes, President Celâl Bayar, and other government leaders were arrested by a newly formed Committee of National Unity. Gen. Cemal Gürsel became acting president and prime minister. Menderes was found guilty of violating the constitution and was hanged in 1961. A new constitution was popularly ratified in 1961, and elections were held in October. Gen. Gürsel was elected president by the New Grand National Assembly, and Inönü became prime minister of a coalition government.

The opposition Justice Party (JP) won 52.3% of the vote in the 1965 elections and formed a new government under Süleyman Demirel. Four years later, the JP was returned to power, and Prime Minister Demirel began a new four-year term. But Turkey's four top military commanders forced the resignation of Demirel's government in 1971 and called for a "strong and credible government" that would restore economic and political stability and suppress student disorders, which had steadily grown more frequent and more violent since 1968. Martial law had been imposed from June to September 1970, and a new "above party" government under Nihat Erim reimposed martial law in 11 provinces (including Ankara and Istanbul) from 1971 to 1973.

Political stability proved no easier to achieve. A succession of weak coalition governments, headed alternately by Demirel and Republican leader Bülent Ecevit, held office between 1973 and 1980. Ecevit's government was in power during the Greco-Turkish war on Cyprus in July–August 1974. Relations with Greece,

strained by a dispute over mineral rights on the Aegean continental shelf, reached the breaking point on 15 July, when Cypriot President Makarios was overthrown in a Greek-led military coup. Fearing the island would be united with Greece, Turkish forces invaded on 20 July. A UN cease-fire came into effect two days later, but after peace talks at Geneva broke down, Turkish troops consolidated their hold over the northern third of the island by 16 August. As the result of this action, the United States embargoed shipments of arms to Turkey until 1978.

During the late 1970s escalating acts of violence by political groups of the extreme left and right, coupled with economic decline, threatened the stability of Turkey's fragile democracy. By April 1980, 47,000 people had been arrested, and martial law had spread to 20 of Turkey's 67 provinces. At midyear more than 5,000 persons had been killed (including former prime minister Nihat Erim), and the factional strife was claiming an average of 20 victims each day. With the legislature deadlocked, the military intervened in the political process for the third time in 20 years. A five-man military National Security Council (NSC), headed by Gen. Kenan Evren, took power in a bloodless coup on 12 September 1980. The NSC suspended the 1961 constitution, banned all political parties and activities, and arrested thousands of suspected terrorists. With the entire country under martial law, factional violence was drastically reduced. By April 1982, about 40,000 alleged political extremists had been arrested and 23,000 had been tried and convicted in martial law courts, some 6,000 of them for "ideological offenses." Under an NSC edict forbidding Turkey's former political leaders from speaking out on political matters, former prime minister Ecevit was twice arrested and imprisoned during 1981–82. In protest against the treatment of Ecevit, the EEC froze payment of $650 million in loans and grants previously pledged to Turkey.

In a national referendum on 7 November 1982, Turkish voters overwhelmingly approved a new constitution (prepared by a constituent assembly chosen by the NSC), under which Gen. Evren became president of the republic for a seven-year term. Campaigning against ratification had been illegal under martial law. Legislative elections were held in November 1983, although martial law remained in effect. Following the elections, Turgut Özal, leader of the victorious Motherland Party, was installed as prime minister. Martial law was lifted in most provinces over the next two years, but emergency rule remained in effect; legislation was passed to broaden police powers, freedom of expression remained limited, and trials of alleged extremists continued. Human-rights groups complained of torture, suspicious deaths, overcrowding, and substandard conditions in Turkish jails; the government denied any improprieties. Özal's Motherland Party retained its legislative majority in November 1987 elections, and he was reelected for a second five-year term. In 1989 Özal was elected president. His Motherland Party continued in power but with declining popularity as shown in 1989 municipal elections. Özal's ambition was to tie Turkey closely to Europe but, despite improvements in Turkey's human rights record, its application for full membership in the European Union was deferred indefinitely. Özal also sought to give Turkey a leading role with the Turkic republics of former Soviet Central Asia. He continued Turkey's long-standing policy of quiet contacts with Israel while seeking better ties with the Arab states. During the Gulf War, he joined the embargo against Iraq, closed Iraq's oil pipelines, provided facilities for allied air raids and later supported protective measures for Iraqi Kurds. In compensation, Turkey received increased aid worth $300 million.

In October 1991 elections the Motherland Party lost its legislative majority to the True Path and Social Democratic Party in coalition. True Path leader Demirel was named prime minister. He succeeded to the presidency in May 1993 following the death of Özal. Tansu Ciller, True Path chairperson, became Turkey's first female prime minister in July. In 1994 Ciller faced three major tasks: dealing with the problems of high inflation (about 70%) and unemployment as she continued Özal's free market policies of export-led growth (7–8%), reducing government regulations and privatization; pacifying the rebellious Kurdish areas of eastern Turkey where large numbers of troops have been tied down; and responding to the rising challenge to Turkey's secular nationalism from politically militant Islamic groups. These problems continued, and in some cases escalated, and the Ciller government also faced scandals and a weakened resolve due to its fragile coalition majority. Corruption allegations ultimately led to a parliamentary investigation and the collapse of Ciller's ruling coalition, which allowed Necmettin Erbakan to become modern Turkey's first conservative Islamic prime minister in June 1996. The instability, as well as Erbakan's anti-West, antisecular slogans, caused Turkey's economy to lapse and slowed foreign investment significantly.

The "Kurdish Question" has been an issue in Turkey since the Lausanne Treaty was signed by the new post-Ottoman government in 1923. In the initial Serve treaty that was drafted in 1920, ending World War I, Kurdish concentrations were to receive either autonomy or independence; however, this was excluded in the final version. Turkish history up to the 1960s consisted of attempts to merge the Kurdish populations into Turkish society. These efforts were unsuccessful, and it is a source of severe contention whether the methods used were constructive or repressive.

The 1960s saw renewed efforts toward greater autonomy and independence by members of the Kurdish communities, and on 27 November 1978 Kurdistan Workers' Party (*Partiya Karkerên Kurdistan*, or PKK) was officially established by Abdullah Öcalan. The general violence that began shortly after World War II and continued throughout the 20th century regarding the Kurdish Question was the prime reasoning behind the Turkish government's consideration of the PKK as a terrorist organization. In fighting since 1984, more than 37,000 people have died. Given that Kurdish populations existed outside of Turkey—into Iraq, Iran, and Syria—this conflict did not remain within its borders,. On 20 March 1995, 35,000 troops backed by tanks and jets pursued rebels into northern Iraq. In the biggest military operation in the history of the Turkish republic, the troops hunted for suspected PKK bases. The PKK maintained the area was home only to Iraqi Kurds, not the PKK. Turkey said it was targeting 2,400 guerrillas who had been mounting cross-border raids and that it would not pull out until a buffer zone or other plan was set up to keep the PKK from moving back into the area. Western leaders condemned the incursion, and the eventual Turkish pullout was seen as a reaction to that negative pressure. Meanwhile, Turkey promised reforms to improve the lives of the 11 million Kurds living there. It said it would lift restrictions on broadcasts in Kurdish and allow Kurds to establish their own schools after the PKK was crushed.

The Kurdish question took a new turn by 1990, after Turgut Özal rose in political power. His tenure was marked by new attempts at loosening laws against Kurdish language and culture. Nevertheless, the issue was never settled, and advocates on both sides continue to project strong opinions on how to resolve the conflict.

Beginning in early 1997 Turkey's military leaders began to speak openly of their displeasure with the Islamist turn the country had taken under Erbakan's government-even intimating that if the government did not return to secular policies instituted by Ataturk nearly a century earlier, then it would overthrow the government militarily. Erbakan had angered the military, which considers itself the defenders of the country's secularism, by proposing mandatory Islamic education and by making political overtures to Libya and Iran. Pressure from the military increased in late spring and early summer 1997, and Turkey's neighbors in Europe and allies in the United States also expressed concern over the direction the NATO member was taking. The crisis was resolved in July 1997, when the Welfare Party's coalition fell apart, and its leader, Erbakan, resigned his post. After the resignation, Mesut Yilmaz, leader of the Motherland Party, was asked by President Demirel to form a government. Erbakan, upon resigning, said he did so with the full intention of returning to office one day.

By November 1998 Yilmaz's government fell victim to another corruption scandal and Ecevit returned as interim prime minister. Within two months of returning to power, Ecevit scored a major victory for his government through the capture of Kurdish terrorist leader Abdulah Ocalan in Nairobi, Kenya. Ocalan had taken refuge in the Greek embassy in Nairobi and was apprehended while on the way to the airport. Ocalan's capture brought relations with Greece to a new low as Ecevit accused Greece of being a state sponsor of terrorism.

In the wake of the terrorist leader's arrest, Ecevit called for early elections to be held in April 1999. The balloting resulted in a plurality for Ecevit's DSP (Democratic Left Party) which captured 136 out of 550 seats (22.3% of the vote) in the assembly. The MHP came second with 129 (18.1%), the Virtue Party (successor to the outlawed Welfare Party) dropped to 111 seats (15.5%), while the Motherland Party received 86 seats (13.3%). Ecevit formed a coalition with MHP and Motherland thus strengthening his position with the secularist military and isolating the Islamists.

Ecevit continued to make progress in foreign affairs throughout 1999 and into 2000. Relations in Greece saw marked improvement following a major earthquake that killed 20,000 Turkish citizens in August 1999. Greece was among the first nations to send aid-an act of humanitarian assistance warmly received by the Turkish government and public. When Greece suffered a smaller earthquake the following month, Turkey returned the favor. A dialogue on cooperation between the two countries in areas of mutual interest subsequently resulted in accords in the areas of trade and the fight against terrorism. Many international observers placed emphasis on the warm personal relationship between Turkish foreign minister Ismail Cem and his Greek counterpart George Papandreou. Finally, at the December 2000 EU summit in Helsinki, the EU member states placed Turkey's name on the list of candidates for entry. Although most observers ruled out Turkish membership for at least 10–15 years, the decision was a symbolic victory for Turkey, as it recognized the efforts of most Turks to identify with the West.

In October 2001 the Turkish assembly voted for 34 changes to the constitution, as a way of improving Turkey's chances of joining the European Union. Among the reforms were the abolition of the death penalty, except in times of war and for acts of terrorism, ending torture in prisons, and allowing for the use of the Kurdish language in broadcasting and education. However, in May 2002, the assembly approved a law increasing government control over the media, including the Internet. At an EU summit held in Copenhagen in December 2002, Turkey was not listed among 10 countries to be included in an expanded European Union. Then US president George W. Bush had pressed for early accession talks on Turkey, but EU members stated the country needed more time to demonstrate progress on improving human rights, the economy, and on reducing the influence of the military on Turkish politics. Talks on Turkey's application were deferred until December 2004.

The situation on EU enlargement was made more difficult for Turkey as Cyprus was included in the group of 15 prospective new members. The European Union accepted the Greek Cypriot government as a member in 2004, even though reunification was not achieved. The EU has stated that Turkey will have to formally recognize Cyprus in order to join the organization.

Ahmet Necdet Sezer was elected president on 5 May 2000. He was the first president in modern Turkish history to be neither an active politician nor a military commander. He is seen as a secularist. Early legislative elections were held on 3 November 2002, after eight ministers, including foreign minister Ismail Cem, resigned in July, protesting Prime Minister Ecevit's refusal to leave office despite a dire economic and political climate. Ecevit's health was poor, Turkey was in its most severe recession since World War II, the domestic political situation was volatile, and a US-led war with Iraq was looming, one that would depend upon Turkish cooperation. In the November elections, the newly formed Islamist-based Justice and Development Party (Adalet ve Kalkinma Partisi or AKP) won a landslide victory, allowing it to rule without a coalition and amend the constitution by taking 363 of 550 seats in the assembly. The AKP pledged to adhere to the secular principles of the constitution. Abdullah Gül was named prime minister, largely because the party's leader, Recep Tayyip Erdogan, was barred from the assembly due to a 1998 criminal conviction for inciting religious hatred, after he recited a religious poem deemed to be seditious. In February 2003 the assembly amended the constitution, allowing Erdogan to be eligible as a candidate in parliamentary by-elections in March, which paved the way for him to become prime minister. He became prime minister on 14 March 2003.

During 2002 and into 2003 the international community placed pressure on Iraq to rid itself of weapons of mass destruction (WMD). Erdogan supported a military strike against Iraq. He stated that Turkey was concerned that the territorial integrity of Iraq be preserved after a war—that the economic effects of such a conflict should be taken into consideration—but that weapons of mass destruction in Iraq could not be tolerated. Turkey was also concerned about the possible effects of war on its Kurdish population: if the 3.5 million Kurds in northern Iraq organized following a defeat of Iraqi President Saddam Hussein's forces, Turkey feared they might want to form an independent Kurdish state, and to potentially unite with the 12 million Kurds in southeastern Turkey.

In February 2003, the United States negotiated a deal with Turkey for the use of its military bases in the event of an attack on Iraq. The United States also agreed to allow Turkish troops to cross into Iraq to observe the disarmament of Kurds once fighting had stopped. The Turkish assembly voted to allow as many as 62,000 US troops and 320 military aircraft to use Turkish bases in the event of war, in exchange for $26 billion in aid. At the time, 95% of the Turkish population was against a war with Iraq. Just prior to the launching of the Iraq War on 19 March 2003, the assembly decided not to allow US troops to cross Turkish territory in order to set up a northern front in Iraq. However, Turkey did allow the United States to use its airspace in the war with Iraq. On 17 October 2007, Turkey's assembly authorized sending troops into northern Iraq against Kurdish rebels there. The 507–19 vote was the result of months of frustration in Turkey with the United States, which had criticized Kurdish rebels who attack Turkey from Iraq, but failed to persuade its Kurdish allies in Iraq to act against them.

Turkey was the site of several terrorist attacks from various sources in the early 2000s. In November 2003, 25 people were killed and more than 200 injured when two car bombs exploded near Istanbul's main synagogue. Just days later, two coordinated suicide bombings at the British consulate and a British bank in Istanbul killed 28 people. In March 2004, at least two people were killed in a suspected suicide attack on a building housing a Masonic lodge in Istanbul. In July 2004, three people died in a car bomb attack in the southeastern town of Van. Authorities accused the PKK of involvement, which the group denied. In July 2005, six people were killed in a bomb attack on a passenger train in the eastern part of the country. Again the authorities blamed the PKK for the act. That month, in the resort town of Kusadasi, an explosion on a minibus killed four people. Violence continued to wrack Turkey in 2006. In March 2006, security forces killed 14 suspected Kurdish rebels. In April 2006, in clashes between Kurdish protesters and security forces in the southeast, at least 12 people were killed. In addition, several people were killed in related unrest in Istanbul. In May 2006, an Islamist gunman opened fire in the Constitutional Court, Turkey's highest, killing a prominent judge. In August and September 2006, certain Turkish resorts and Istanbul were bombed. The separatist group Kurdistan Freedom Falcons (TAC) claimed responsibility for some of the attacks.

The issue of separation of church and state is another strong debate in Turkish politics. In 2007, Turkey's status as a secular state since Ataturk's time was called into question by the election of an Islamist president. In April 2007, tens of thousands of supporters of secularism protested in Ankara, with the intent of pressuring Erdogan not to run for president due to his Islamist background. The AKP party put forward Foreign Minister Abdullah Gül as its candidate after Erdogan decided not to stand. In May 2007, the assembly moved up national elections to 22 July to try to end the standoff between secularists and Islamists over the choice of the next president. In the 22 July elections the AKP won the most seats, 341 of 550, or over 46% of the vote. After the elections, the newly composed Grand National Assembly restarted the election for president. In August 2007, Abdullah Gül was elected president.

13 GOVERNMENT

The 1961 constitution vested legislative power in the Grand National Assembly, consisting of a house of representatives, with a membership of 450 elected for four-year terms, and a senate of 165 members, of whom 150 were elected and 15 appointed by the president. The president of the republic—the head of state—was elected for a single seven-year term by a joint session of the assembly. The president was empowered to designate the prime minister from among the assembly members; the prime minister in turn chose other cabinet ministers, who were responsible for general government policy.

The constitution ratified in November 1982, which replaced the 1961 document, declared Turkey to be a democratic and secular republic that respects the human rights of its citizens and remains loyal to the nationalistic principles of Atatürk. It vested executive powers in the president of the republic and the council of ministers. The president was elected by the assembly for a seven-year term. Legislative functions were delegated to a unicameral Grand National Assembly of Turkey, consisting of 400 members elected for five-year terms. Under the constitution's "temporary articles," the five-person National Security Council (NSC) remained in power until the new assembly convened, at which time the NSC became a presidential council, to function for a period of six years before dissolving. These "temporary" provisions expressly forbade all former leaders of either the Justice or the Republican People's Party from participating in politics for 10 years. All former members of the previous assembly were forbidden from founding political parties or holding public office for five years. A referendum in September 1987 approved a proposal to lift the 10-year ban on political participation by leaders of the Justice and Republican People's Parties and numerous other politicians. Proposals to change the voting age from 21 to 20 years and expand the assembly from 400 to 450 members were approved in May 1987. Following further constitutional amendments in 1995, 2001, 2007 and 2010, the assembly has grown to 550 seats, and the voting age has been lowered to 18. Assembly members are directly elected to serve four-year terms. A 2007 amendment also provides for direct public election of the president, who may serve a total of two five-year terms.

Although the constitution guarantees individual freedoms, exceptions may be made in order to protect the republic and the public interest, or in times of war or other national emergency. The provision holding that an arrested person cannot be held for more than 48 hours without a court order may likewise be suspended in the case of martial law, war, or other emergency.

14 POLITICAL PARTIES

The first significant nationwide party, the Republican People's Party (Cumhuriyet Halk Partisi or CHP), was organized by Mustafa Kemal in 1923. Strong, centralized authority and state economic planning marked its 27 years of power (1923–50). It deemphasized everything religious to the point of subordinating religious activity and organization to state control.

Not until 1946 did a second popular party, the Democrat Party (Demokratik Parti or DP), come into being. Initially formed by a small group of dissident CHP members of parliament, the DP demanded greater political and economic liberalism, specifi-

cally a relaxation of central controls. When they came to power in 1950, the Democrats put into effect their policies of economic expansion through rapid mechanization and free enterprise. They also emphasized rural development through liberal credit terms to farmers. These policies, aimed at broadening the base of the economy, helped to return the Democrats to power three times in succession. After 1954, however, the Democrat regime reinstituted many of the former controls and instituted others, notably over the press. The CHP condemned these moves and the lack of economic planning and inadequate fiscal and commercial controls. Both the Democrats and the CHP supported a firmly pro-Western, anti-Communist foreign policy.

In the first elections of the Second Republic (October 1961), none of the four competing parties won a controlling majority in either chamber, and a coalition government was formed for the first time in 1962. The coalition, however, was short-lived, for the newly formed Justice Party (Adalet Partisi or AP) withdrew from the governing group of parties and became the chief political opposition. The AP, which became the main political force in the country after the 1965 elections, favored private enterprise (in this respect it can be considered the successor of the DP, which was banned in 1960). Organized originally by local Democrat leaders, the AP came to reflect the views of modernization-minded professionals as well as workers and villagers. In the 1965 elections, the AP won 53.8% of the seats in the house of representatives and 61% of the senate seats. The elections of October 1969 confirmed its legislative predominance.

In December 1970, dissident members of the AP created the Democratic Party. Another new organization, the Republican Reliance Party (Cumhuriyetçi Güven Partisi or CGP), formed by dissident members of the CHP, put up its first candidates in the 1969 elections. The National Salvation Party (Milli Selâmet Partisi or MSP) was created in March 1973 for the purpose of preserving Islamic traditions and bringing about economic and social reforms. In the general elections of 14 October 1973, the CHP replaced the AP as the most popular party in Turkey, although it did not achieve a legislative majority, and the CHP and MSP formed a coalition government under Bülent Ecevit. After the Ecevit government fell in September 1974, more than six months passed before a new permanent government was formed by Süleyman Demirel. His minority government of the Nationalist Front, which included representatives of the AP, CGP, MSP, and National Action Party (Milliyetçi Hareket Partisi), commanded 214 out of 450 assembly seats. After the CHP won 213 assembly seats in the 1977 elections, Ecevit, having formed a minority cabinet, lost a legislative vote of confidence and had to resign. But his rival, Demirel, fared little better as prime minister, and his coalition government soon dissolved. Each served another brief stint as head of government prior to the 1980 military coup.

The new military government banned all political parties and, under the 1982 constitution, forbade the leaders of the AP and CHP from active participation in politics for 10 years. After the new constitution was approved, however, the government allowed the formation of new political groups. The first new party, the Nationalist Democracy Party, was formed in May 1983 by certain retired military officers, former government officials, and business leaders. It received support from the military but fared poorly in local and national elections and was disbanded three years later.

Another new group, the rightist Great Turkey Party, was abolished by the government soon after its founding because of alleged close resemblances to the banned AP. The True Path Party (Dogru Yol Partisi or DYP) was established in its place but was not allowed to participate in the elections to the assembly on 6 November 1983. Also barred were the newly formed Welfare Party and the Social Democratic Party, and Demirel and other politicians were temporarily placed under military detention. The Populist Party, which the military was said to regard as a loyal opposition, and the Motherland Party (Anatavan Partisi or ANAP), formed by conservative business leaders and technocrats, won approval to run. In the balloting, the ANAP won a majority in the assembly, with 212 out of 400 seats, and its leader, Turgut Özal, became prime minister on 13 December 1983.

Subsequently, all parties were allowed to participate in local elections. In 1985 the Populist Party merged with the Social Democratic Party to form the Social Democratic Populist Party (Sosyal Demokrasi Halkçi Partisi or SDHP). The Free Democrat Party was formed in 1986 as a successor to the Nationalist Democracy Party. In September 1987, the 10-year ban on political participation by over 200 leaders of the AP and CHP was lifted after a referendum indicated approval by a bare majority of just over 50%. At the same time, Özal announced elections in November of that year and had a law passed requiring nomination of candidates by party leaders rather than by popular choice. After challenges from opposition groups, the Constitutional Court declared the new procedure illegal. In the November 1987 elections, Özal was reelected as prime minister with 36.3% of the vote; the ANAP won 292 of the 450 seats in the assembly (although polling only 36% of the vote), the SDHP won 99 seats, and the DYP took 59 seats. A coalition of True Path and Social Democrats defeated the Motherland Party in 1991. Outside the established political system are the Kurdistan Workers Party (PKK) and other smaller separatist parties which have been banned.

In 1993, Motherland Party leader Turgut Özal died while serving as president. He was succeeded by True Path leader Suleyman Demirel. In July of that year, Tansu Ciller, chairperson of True Path, became prime minister (Turkey's first female prime minister). Ciller headed a shaky coalition and, in a budgetary debate in September 1995, her government collapsed. She lost a vote of confidence in October and new elections were held in December. The elections were won by the Welfare Party, which took 158 of 550 seats. Although hardly a majority, this was 23 more seats than Ciller's True Path. Fearing an Islamic government, secularists scrambled to form a majority but failed, and in 1996 President Demirel invited Welfare Party leader Necmettin Erbakan to form a government.

The Erbakan government lasted only until mid-1997. While popular in rural areas, it faced strong opposition from the business elite—which tends to be pro-Western—and the military. Beginning in 1997, the military let it be known that if Erbakan did not uphold Turkey's secular traditions, it would overthrow the government and return it to secular parties. In July 1997, Erbakan resigned and Motherland Party leader Mesut Yilmaz was asked to form a government. Following allegations of corruption, the Yilmaz government fell in November 1998 and was replaced by an interim minority government headed by Ecevit pending early elections.

Ecevit returned to head a minority government pending early elections in 1999. On 18 April 1999 Turkish voters gave Ecevit's DSP a plurality with 136 seats (22.3% of the vote). Ecevit went on to form a coalition government with the MHP and Motherland. In May 2000, President Demirel's long political career came to an end with the election of Ahmet Necdet Sezer as his successor.

Political pressure brought to bear on the Ecevit government in mid-2002 led to the resignation of eight of his cabinet ministers and a call for early legislative elections. The elections were won by the Islamic-based Justice and Development Party (Adalet ve Kalkinma Partisi, or AKP), in a landslide victory. The AKP took 363 of 550 seats in the assembly with 34.3% of the vote; the CHP took 178 seats with 19.4% of the vote; and independents took 9 seats, as other parties participating in the elections did not meet the 10% threshold for obtaining seats. Abdullah Gül became prime minister, but the AKP leader, Recep Tayyip Erdogan, retained power in the party, and later became prime minister. The rise of the AKP is one demonstration of the popularity of Islamic parties in Turkey, although the country is officially attempting to align itself with the West. The Islamic Welfare Party, which had appeal among the middle class, was banned and closed in 1998, and Erbakan was banned from participating in politics for five years. The Welfare Party's successor, the Virtue Party (Fazilet Partisi), was the main opposition party in 2001 when it was banned that June by the constitutional court for posing a threat to the state. A new party, the Felicity or Happiness Party (Saadet Partisi) was established by banned members of the Virtue Party. The AKP also had its roots in the Virtue Party.

The next legislative elections were held on 22 July 2007. The AKP won 341 of 550 seats, or more than 46% of the vote. The CHP won 112 seats, followed by the Nationalist Movement Party with 71 seats. Independent candidates won 26 seats. The new assembly elected Abdullah Gül of the AKP as president in 2007. He has the distinction of being the first head of state from an Islamist background since the republic was established. Recep Tayyip Erdogan of AKP retained his post as prime minister (which he has held since 2003).

In the 2011 assembly elections the AKP won 326 seats (with 49.8% of the vote), followed by the CHP with 135 seats (25.9%) and the MHP with 53 seats (13%). Thirty-six seats were won by independent candidates.

[15]LOCAL GOVERNMENT

The chief administrative official in each of Turkey's 81 provinces (*vilayets* or *iller*) is the provincial governor (*vali*), an appointee of the central government who is responsible to the Ministry of Internal Affairs. During the military takeover in the 1980s, governors were made responsible to the military authorities, and provincial assemblies were suspended. In 11 mainly Kurdish southeastern provinces, a regional governor exercised authority under a state of emergency declared in 1987. The state of emergency was lifted in November 2002. For administrative purposes, provinces are subdivided into districts (*kazas* or *ilces*), which in turn are divided into communes (*nahiyes* or *bucaks*), comprising kasabas and villages. In municipalities and villages, locally elected mayors and councils perform government functions. Both levels of government have specified sources of income and prepare budgets for the allocation of such income, which are then subject to approval by the central government. Most public revenue, however, is collected by the Ministry of Finance in Ankara.

16 JUDICIAL SYSTEM

The judicial system was left substantially intact by the 1982 constitution, except for the addition of special state security courts to handle cases involving terrorism and state security. There are four branches of courts: general law courts, military courts, state security courts, and a constitutional court.

The general law courts include civil, administrative, criminal, and military courts. The high court system includes a constitutional court responsible for judicial review of legislation, a court of cassation (or supreme court of appeals), a council of state serving as the high administrative and appeals court, a court of accounts, and the military court of appeals. The High Council of Judges and Prosecutors, appointed by the president, supervises the judiciary. The state security courts are composed of five-member panels. They are found in eight cities and try cases dealing with terrorism, gang-related crimes, drug smuggling, membership in illegal organizations, and sedition.

The constitutional court reviews the constitutionality of legislation at the time of passage when requested by the required percentage of members of parliament and in the context of review of constitutional issues which emerge during litigation. The constitution guarantees the independence of the judiciary from the executive and provides for life tenure for judges. It also explicitly prohibits state authorities from issuing orders or recommendations concerning the exercise of judicial power. A high council of judges and prosecutors selects judges and prosecutors for the higher courts and oversees those in lower courts. In practice the courts act independently of the executive. The constitution guarantees defendants the right to a public trial. The bar association is responsible for providing free counsel to indigent defendants. There is no jury system. All cases are decided by a judge or a panel of judges. The European Court of Human Rights is the final arbiter in cases concerning human rights.

In May 2010 the Turkish assembly approved a bill to amend the constitution in order to allow for an overhaul in the judiciary. The measures were widely supported by the ruling Justice and Development Party (AKP), but opposed by the opposition Republican People's Party (CHP) and members of the military, all of whom claim the amendment would give the AKP too much power over the judiciary. The divisiveness of the bill prevented it from achieving the two-thirds assembly majority necessary for immediate adoption. Instead, the measures were added into a larger package of proposed constitutional reforms that went to a national referendum in September 2010. The reform package included a total of 26 amendments, including measures to protect the rights of children and women, the implementation of privacy laws for personal data, and the right for civil servants to form unions. The referendum passed by a vote of about 58%. Although the reforms were hailed by international observers as a step toward greater democracy, opposition leaders still believed that the government retained too much control over the judiciary and lamented the fact that amendments relating to the court system could not be separated from the package of reforms.

17 ARMED FORCES

The Turkish Armed Forces consists of the Land Forces Command (Turk Kara Kuvvetleri, TKK), Naval Forces Command (Turk Deniz Kuvvetleri, TDK) and Air Forces Command (Turk Hava Kuvvetleri, THK), which are subordinate to Turkish General Staff. The Gendarmerie General Command and the Coast Guard Command are subordinate to the Ministry of Internal Affairs in peacetime and to the Land Forces and the Naval Forces Commands in wartime. The International Institute for Strategic Studies reports that armed forces in Turkey totaled 510,600 members in 2011. The force is comprised of 402,000 from the army, 48,600 from the navy, and 60,000 members of the air force. Armed forces represent 2.4% of the labor force in Turkey. In 2009 the World Bank listed Turkey's military expenditures at 2.8% of gross domestic product (GDP). Civil and internal defense expenditures increased this number to 5.1%.

An estimated 36,000 Turkish soldiers were stationed on Cyprus. Turkey is a member of NATO and currently contributes 800 soldiers to the International Security Assistance Force in Afghanistan. It also contributes representative forces to several other international conflict zones through participation in the OSCE, UN Peacekeeping Missions, and NATO. The United States maintains a joint air base near Incirlik, as well as support facilities at Izmir and Ankara.

18 INTERNATIONAL COOPERATION

Turkey is a charter member of the UN, having joined on 24 October 1945, and belongs to ECE and several non-regional specialized agencies, such as the IAEA, the World Bank, UNHCR, UNESCO, UNCTAD, ILO, and the WHO. Turkey is also a member of the WTO, the Asian Development Bank, the Black Sea Economic Cooperation Zone, the Euro-Atlantic Partnership Council, the Islamic Development Bank, the Council of Europe, the OSCE, the Organization of the Islamic Conference (OIC), NATO, and the OECD. As of 2005, Turkey was a candidate for membership to the European Union. The nation holds observer status in the OAS and is an associate member of the Western European Union. Examples of numerous additional international agreements and coalitions include the Australia Group, the Zangger Committee, the Nuclear Suppliers Group (London Group), the Nuclear Energy Agency, and the Organization for the Prohibition of Chemical Weapons. It holds observer status in the European Organization for Nuclear Research (CERN).

Relations with the United States, Turkey's principal aid benefactor, were strained during the 1970s over the Cyprus issue. After the Turkish military forces, using US-supplied equipment, had occupied the northern third of the island, the US Congress in 1975 embargoed military shipments to Turkey in accordance with US law. In response Turkey abrogated its 1969 defense cooperation agreement with the United States and declared that it would take over US military installations in Turkey (except the NATO base at Adana). The US government then relaxed the arms embargo and finally ended it in 1978, after which Turkey lifted its ban on US military activities. Relations between the two countries improved markedly thereafter, and a new defense and economic cooperation agreement between Turkey and the United States was signed in 1980. In 1986, the 1980 agreement was renewed, allowing the United States to use some 15 Turkish military bases in exchange for continuing military and economic subsidies. Relations between Greece and Turkey remain strained over the issue of Cyprus.

Tension between Turkey and neighboring Armenia stems from the highly charged issue of the mass killings of Armenians by Ottoman Turks during 1915–16. The Armenians regard the killings as genocide, a view that is formally held by several other countries. Turkey denies the allegations of genocide, insisting that the killings were simply a result of the widespread fighting of World War I. The two countries have had no diplomatic ties since 1991. Tension between the governments also exists over the Nagorno-Karabakh conflict, involving Azerbaijan and Armenia, in which Turkey has allied with Azerbaijan. As a result, Turkey closed its border to Armenia in 1993. In April 2009, officials from Turkey and Armenia met and announced an agreement on a process to normalize relations between their two countries.

In environmental cooperation, Turkey is part of the Antarctic Treaty, the Basel Convention, Conventions on Biological Diversity and Air Pollution, Ramsar, CITES, the Montréal Protocol, MARPOL, the Nuclear Test Ban Treaty, and the UN Conventions on Climate Change and Desertification.

¹⁹ECONOMY

According to the CIA, the GDP rate of change in Turkey was 8.2% in 2010—a dramatic change from -4.7% in 2009 and 0.7% in 2008. Inflation in 2010 stood at 8.6% (compared to 6.3% in 2009), and unemployment was 12% (14.1% in 2009).

The economy in Turkey is in transition, as the services sector has been consistently increasing. With the hope of joining the European Union (EU), the government has begun planning and, to some extent, implementing a number of economic reforms that would lead to increased modernization of the economy and open the door for increased foreign investment. Despite strong economic gains from 2000 to 2010, the country still suffers from outstanding debt with the International Monetary Fund (IMF). Primary trading partners are Russia, Germany, the United Kingdom, and China.

During the late 1960s and early 1970s, Turkey enjoyed a high economic growth rate, averaging about 7% annually. This growth was financed largely by foreign borrowing, increased exports, and remittances from Turkish workers in Western Europe. As a result of the large increases in oil import costs during 1973–74, however, Turkey's economic growth declined in real terms during 1974–80, and the country suffered a severe financial crisis. Stabilization programs implemented in 1978 and 1979 under a standby agreement with the IMF proved inadequate, but in January 1980, as a condition of further IMF aid, Turkey imposed a more stringent economic reform program, involving currency devaluation, labor productivity improvements, and restructuring of the nation's inefficient state enterprises.

In response to the reforms, the GDP grew on average by 4.8% from 1980 to 1994, the highest rate of any OECD economy. In 1994, structural problems, including inflation rates between 60–90% and budget deficits between 6–12%, eventually took their toll, plunging the economy into its worst recession since World War II. Real GDP declined by 6% and the inflation rate exceeded 130%. The underlying strength of the economy, together with a govern-

ment austerity program designed to rein in spending, led to a turnaround in 1996, and in 1997 GDP grew by 8%. In 1998 real GDP growth slowed and then turned negative as the economy was affected by the Russian financial crisis and domestic political turmoil. Conditions worsened in 1999 when on 17 August 1999 Turkey was hit by the Kocaeli earthquake (between Bursa and Izmik), the worst ever to hit the country. The earthquake caused 15,000 deaths, 28,000 serious injuries, 500,000 homeless and an estimated $5 billion worth of damages. In 1999, nominal GDP growth was 46.3%, but inflation, as measured by the consumer price index (CPI), was 68.8%, and real GDP declined 6.1%.

At the end of 1999, Turkey entered into a three-year stand-by arrangement with the IMF, with a stringent set of conditions designed to bring Turkey's chronic inflation under control. The World Bank followed in 2000 with a Country Assistance Strategy (CAS) that provided external program lending, technical assistance, analytical and policy advice. In 1999 the government took over 10 insolvent private banks and then began criminal investigations into their operations. Several arrests were made of key bankers, including the nephew of a former president, accused of siphoning off funds in various ways. During 2000, real GDP grew at 6.3% and CPI inflation decreased to 39%. However, in late November 2000, the economy was suddenly beset with a banking crisis as foreign investors, apparently more concerned about what further investigations might reveal than convinced that banking was being cleansed, began to rapidly sell their Turkish assets and cut lending. An estimated $6 billion left Turkey in 10 days, $2.5 billion on 22 November 2000 alone. Overnight interbank interest rates climbed to an annualized 1700%, at one point reaching 1950%. Domestic interest rates rose to 60%, almost double the pre-crisis level.

By early 2001, Turkey's stock market had lost nearly half of its value. A break in the precipitous divestment was achieved when the IMF announced an agreement to supply an additional $7.5 billion credit in a one-year program under its Supplemental Reserve Facility (SRF) to run from 21 December 2000 to 20 December 2001. The reversal of the outflow proved only temporary, however. By late February 2001 the economy was plunged into a full-blown financial crisis, precipitated by the president's criticism of the prime minister's handling of the banking investigations during a meeting on 19 February 2001. The interbank overnight rate reached an annualized 7500% and the stock market lost nearly 18% of its value within a day. The central bank reportedly sold $5 billion of its $28 billion of reserves trying to defend the lira's exchange rate, but on 22 February 2001 it announced its decision to allow the lira to float. Its value dropped 36% in two days, as the exchange rate for the lira moved to 1,223,140 per US dollar. For the year, real GDP fell 9.4% and inflation, measured by 12-month end-of-period CPI, increased nearly 30% to 68.5%. Net public debt rose to 93.4% of GDP, up from 57.7% the year before. Net external debt doubled as a percent of GDP from 18.5% to 37.1%. In July 2001 the World Bank revised its 2000 CAS program to include an additional $1.2 billion on Special Structural Adjustment Loan (SSAL) terms, for a total possible lending of $6.2 billion in the period 2001 to 2003. On 4 February 2001, the day Turkey's three-year stand-by arrangement with the IMF expired, the government entered into a new two-year stand-by arrangement with an $11.3 billion line of credit.

Turkey has a long-held objective of becoming a member of the European Union, and EU accession negotiations were opened in October 2005, as if to cement confidence in Turkey's economic recovery. Exports did well in 2005—even those to Iraq—and the war in Iraq did not deter tourists from visiting Turkey.

The banking system was restructured with a large injection of public funds. On 1 January 2005 Turkey introduced a new lira, eliminating six zeros from the old one. The current-account deficit was estimated at 8% of GDP in 2006. The government's large debt was reduced to 45% of GDP by the end of 2006. However, debt remains a vulnerability to the country. Strong economic gains from 2002–07 were largely due to renewed investor interest in emerging markets, IMF backing, and tighter fiscal policy.

20 INCOME

The CIA estimated that in 2010 the GDP of Turkey was $960.5 billion. The CIA defines GDP as the value of all final goods and services produced within a nation in a given year and computed on the basis of purchasing power parity (PPP) rather than value as measured on the basis of the rate of the exchange based on current dollars. The per capita GDP was estimated at $12,300. The annual growth rate of GDP was 8.2%. The average inflation rate was 8.6%. It was estimated that agriculture accounted for 9.6% of GDP, industry 16.7%, and services 63.8%.

According to the World Bank, 18.1% of the population is estimated to be living at or below the national poverty line; in urban areas the rate was 8.9%, while in rural areas it was 38.7%. The GINI index rate, or distribution of wealth, in 2008 was approximately 40, in comparison to 45 in the United States (the range measures 0–100, with 0 rated as completely equal distribution of wealth among individuals). In 2010 approximately $874 million in remittances were transferred from citizens living abroad.

In 2010 GNI per capita, based on purchasing power parity, was $15,180. The World Bank reported that in 2005 actual individual consumption in Turkey was 73.7% of GDP and accounted for 1.1% of world consumption. By comparison, the United States accounted for 25.44% of world individual consumption. It was also estimated at that time that 19.8% of Turkey's GDP was spent on food and beverages, 22.3% on housing and household furnishings, 4.2% on clothes, 2.8% on health, 8.6% on transportation, 3% on communications, 1.7% on recreation, 3% on restaurants and hotels, and 3.9% on miscellaneous goods and services and purchases from abroad.

21 LABOR

Turkey had a total labor force of 24.67 million people in 2010. Within that labor force, it was estimated that 22.9% were employed in agriculture, 25.9% in industry, and 47.3% in the service sector. Unemployment was estimated at 12%.

A 1946 law authorized the formation of labor unions and enabled them to engage in collective bargaining, and the right to strike was legally permitted in 1963, although general, solidarity, and wildcat strikes are explicitly prohibited. Employers' unions also exist, but members of one kind of union are prohibited from joining the other. As of 2005 about 25% of the country's wage and salaried workforce were unionized. Union membership was largest in the textile industry, tobacco manufacturing, public utilities, transport and communications, and coal mining. After the 1960 overthrow of the Menderes government, trade unions pressed the government to act upon their demands for the right to strike, for collective labor contracts, and for various social benefits, which were provided for in law but had not been fully implemented. However, the right to strike and the right to bargain collectively remained restricted as of 2005.

A detailed labor code administered by the Ministry of Labor controls many aspects of labor-management relations. As of 2010 Turkey had a basic 45-hour workweek with a weekly day of rest, although flexibility is given for Muslims to leave work on Fridays to attend prayer. This often translates into one paid day off per week. Overtime was technically limited, although this factor was considered negotiable and in higher, white-collar jobs was codified in an employment contract. The minimum wage as of July 2011, adjusted to the purchasing power standard, was $574 per month. Minimum wage rates are set semiannually by Turkey's minimum wage commission. The minimum working age is 15, and in urban areas child labor is minimal (although growing in the services sector). In rural areas, child labor continues to be widespread, particularly in agriculture. The UN Statistics Division reported in 2009 that 469,404 of the total children between the ages of 12 and 14 were working, with 374,426 engaged in agriculture, hunting, forestry, and fishing.

22 AGRICULTURE

Roughly 33% of the total land is used for agriculture. The average holding is not more than 4 or 5 hectares (10–12 acres). Large farms are concentrated mainly in the Konya, Adana, and İzmir regions. Agricultural methods are mechanically on par with most of the developed world; for every 100 sq km (38.6 sq mi) of arable land there were estimated to be 489 tractors (in comparison to 265 in the United States). Research indicates, however, that the technology is not as advanced.

The country's major crops include tobacco, cotton, grain, olives, sugar beets, hazelnuts, pulse, and citrus. Cereal production in 2009 amounted to 33.6 million tons, fruit production 14.2 million tons, and vegetable production 26.7 million tons. Turkish tobacco is world famous for its lightness and mildness. Most of the crop is grown in the Aegean region, but the finest tobacco is grown around Samsun, on the Black Sea coast. Most of the cotton crop is grown around Adana and İzmir. Turkey usually leads the world in the production and export of hazelnuts and also is a leading producer of pistachio nuts.

The government stimulates production through crop subsidies, low taxation, price supports, easy farm credit, research and education programs, and the establishment of model farms. The government also controls the conditions under which farm products can move into world markets. For some products, such as grain, the government is the sole exporter. Turkey began exporting vegetables and fruits abroad, which affected domestic market prices. Cotton and tobacco production levels are increasing as demands by the textile and cigarette industries have risen.

Turkey is one of seven countries authorized under the 1961 UN Convention on Narcotic Drugs to grow opium poppies for legitimate pharmaceutical purposes. In June 1971, after persistent US complaints that up to 80% of all opiates smuggled into the United States were derived from Turkish poppies, the Turkish government banned poppy growing. After efforts to find substitute crops failed, however, the government decided to rescind the ban on 1 July 1974. Areas authorized for poppy cultivation were estimated at 37,500 hectares (92,700 acres) in 1983; 5,000 hectares (12,350 acres) of opium capsule were sown in 1985. Government steps to curtail illegal cultivation, refining, and export of opiates were reportedly successful. In 2010 the DEA reported findings that illegal poppy export from Turkey was minimal, particularly in comparison to Central Asia; however, illegal export of hashish had grown exponentially.

23 ANIMAL HUSBANDRY

The UN Food and Agriculture Organization (FAO) reported that Turkey dedicated 14.6 million hectares (36.1 million acres) to permanent pasture or meadow in 2009. During that year, the country tended 244.3 million chickens, 10.9 million head of cattle, 6.3 million goats, 25.5 million sheep, and 1,717 pigs. The production from these animals amounted to 430,135 tons of beef and veal, 157 tons of pork, 1.03 million tons of poultry, 663,091 tons of eggs, and 10.1 million tons of milk. Turkey also produced 25,535 tons of cattle hide and 40,270 tons of raw wool.

Many animals are used for transport and draft purposes, as well as to supply meat and dairy products. The principal animals of non-consumption commercial importance are mohair goats and sheep. The sheep wool is used mainly for blankets and carpets, and Turkey is a leading producer of mohair. According to a 2006 presentation by the Agriculture and Rural Development of the European Union, Turkey is second in the world in their number of bee colonies (4.1 million), and eighth in honey production (16 kg per hive). They also export wax, pollen, and propolis.

24 FISHING

According to the FAO, fisheries represent about 0.3% of Turkey's GDP and 2.7% of the country's total agricultural production. In 2009 all fishing production totaled approximately 623 thousand tons; 25% of this came from aquacultural farming (157 thousand tons), although this equated to 53% by value ($670 million of $1,260 million). Turkey had 1,106 decked commercial fishing boats in 2008. The export value of seafood totaled $243.3 million.

Aquaculture is one of the fastest growing industries in Turkey having grown in volume by over 20% for the past ten years. During the 1990s production from three major species—rainbow trout, seabass and seabream—increased rapidly until 2000, and then declined during the following two years, due to a national economic crisis. The years 2005–08 saw growth in the fishing industry, however 2009–10 showed a renewed decline. Aquaculture is dominated by finfish production. Shellfish culture is represented by just 89 tons per year of mussel culture. Trout farms are widely spread across the country in freshwater and marine environments, while most seabream and seabass farms are located on the southern Aegean coast, which provides optimum ecological conditions for marine aquaculture. The Black Sea region also makes an important contribution, with around 24% of the total production. Less important areas include the Marmara Sea, the Mediterranean, and the Central Anatolian regions. Rainbow trout is the main species cultured in the Central Anatolian region and is farmed in both land-based raceways and sea cages, followed by seabass and common carp. The Black Sea also provides a good ecological supply for trout culture in marine environment thanks to low salinity.

25 FORESTRY

Approximately 15% of Turkey is covered by forest. Forestry is regulated by the Ministry of Environment and Forestry (Çevre ve Orman Bakanlığı), which states that primary forested woods consist of oak, red pine, larch, beech, and scotch pine. A Global Forest Resources assessment was conducted by the FAO in 2010, noting that viable forestland was occupied 11.3 million hectares (27.9 million acres). State forests include almost all the forestland—roughly 10.7 million hectares (26.4 million acres)—while community or municipal forests and private forests are of insignificant size. The FAO estimated the 2009 roundwood production at 14.4 million cu m (507.9 million cu ft). The value of all forest products, including roundwood, totaled $519.4 million. In 2010 an estimated 7.9 million hectares were considered by the FAO, based on Ministry regulations, to be reserved for production purposes; the remaining were considered protected.

26 MINING

Turkey has a 9,000-year history of metal mining. Although Turkey has a wide variety of minerals, its resources are only partially developed. Turkey is a leading producer of boron, and is known for such industrial minerals as barite, celestite (strontium), clays, emery, feldspar, limestone, magnesite, marble, perlite, pumice, and trona (soda ash). Other minerals actively exploited and marketed are copper, chromite, iron ore, sulfur, pyrite, manganese, mercury, lead, zinc, and meerschaum. Mineral products exported in 2009 included: iron and steel, $7.6 billion; jewelry and precious or semiprecious stones, $5.9 billion; alumina and aluminum articles, $1.4 billion; building stone, $1.2 billion; chromium ore, $287 million; copper ore, $263 million; and boron ore, $105 million.

In 2009 preliminary production included copper (metal content) at 105,000 metric tons, up from 100,000 metric tons in 2008; dolomite at 11,152,094 metric tons; limestone (other than for cement) at 7 million metric tons; marble at 2,715,601 cu m, compared to 2,262,537 in 2008; quartzite at 1.943,877 metric tons; boron concentrates at 1.8 million metric tons, down from 2.1 million metric tons in 2008; feldspar at 4,215,547 metric tons; iron ore (metal content), 4.17 million metric tons, down from 4.7 million metric tons in 2008; and meerschaum and attapulgite at 3,448 kg. Eskisehir, in northwestern Anatolia, is the world center of meerschaum (sepiolite). Turkey is famous for its meerschaum pipes. Also produced in 2009 were alumina, antimony, gold, lead, manganese, silver, alumina sulfate (alunite), barite, hydraulic cement, clays (including bentonite and kaolin), emery, fluorspar, crude glass, graphite, gypsum, lime, magnesite, nitrogen, perlite, pumice, cupreous pyrite, sand and gravel, silica sand, sodium compounds (salt, soda ash [trona], and sodium sulfate), stone (basalt, diabase, granite, onyx, sandstone, serpentine, slate, and travertine), sulfur, talc, and zeolite. No mercury, molybdenum, nickel, or celestite were produced in 2009.

Despite the divestment of a large portion of the state-owned minerals sector holdings, to domestic and foreign investors the government remains a significant factor in most sectors of the minerals industry, through shareholdings in a number of private companies and various state-owned industrial corporations. In the 2000s, the government has been encouraging mineral exports as well as domestic and foreign private mining investment. Ongoing privatization costs are expected to result in layoffs and the closure of inefficient operations. Most of the nation's 3,000 mines are small. Resources of metallic commodities minable by large-scale methods are known for bauxite, chromite, copper and copper-zinc, gold, iron, and silver.

27 ENERGY AND POWER

Turkey sits as a hub of energy transit between oil and gas fields around the Caspian Sea and Europe and the Middle East. Functioning hydrocarbon pipelines, as of 2010, include the BTC oil pipeline (Caspian to Europe), Turkey-Greece Interconnector (TGI), Kirkuk-Ceyhan (Middle East), Blue Stream (from Russia), and Samsun-Ceyhan (Kazakhstan to the Bosporus). Nabucco (Central Asia to Europe) is scheduled to open in 2015.

Turkey has only modest reserves of oil and natural gas, while its coal reserves are generally of indifferent quality and highly polluting. According to the International Energy Agency, as of 2011 approximately 70% of Turkey's domestic oil and gas are imported, primarily from Russia and Iran.

The World Bank reported in 2008 that Turkey produced 198.4 billion kWh of electricity and consumed 170.6 billion kWh, or 2,165 kWh per capita. Roughly 91% of energy came from fossil fuels, while 5% came from alternative fuels. Per capita oil consumption was 1,333 kg. Oil production totaled 48,337 barrels of oil a day.

28 INDUSTRY

Overall industrial production, which had increased by annual rates of close to or over 10% from 1973 to 1977, fell sharply because of Turkey's financial crisis in 1978–79, and actually declined by 5% in 1979 and 1980. After the government's economic reform program slowed inflation and stabilized the lira, industrial production improved. Production rose 28% during 1985–87. State enterprises were restructured to reduce their government subsidies and to make them more productive and competitive with private firms. However, industry has continued to suffer from structural weaknesses, and in many firms production facilities are obsolete. Production rose by an annual average of almost 5% from 1980 to 1993 but fell more than 6% in the recession of 1994 as the chronic double-digit inflation rose to triple digits (128%).

As of 2010 industry accounted for about 26.7% of GDP and 24.7% of employment. Construction contributes about 4–5% of GDP. The industrial production growth rate in 2010 was 13.1%.

The textile industry, Turkey's largest manufacturing sector (accounting for one-third of industrial employment), is centered in İzmir, Istanbul, Adana, and Kayseri. The removal of EU quotas on imports of textiles and apparel when Turkey joined in a customs union with the European Union in 1996 has improved growth prospects, but the removal of global quotas in 2005 caused Turkey to face stiff competition on international markets for its textiles and clothing. Nevertheless, export value in the textile sector grew from $1.1 million in 1990 to $5.4 billion in 2009. According to the WTO, in 2008 Turkey was seventh in the world in textile exports with 3.8% of the market, and that same year Eurostat ranked it second in the EU market at 17.5%.

Mining, steelmaking, petroleum, and construction have grown into leading industries in Turkey. Secondary mineral commodities, including refined petroleum products, steel, cement, glass, and certain chemicals account for over two-thirds of manufacturing output. Turkey's largest industry is petroleum refining, due to its strategic location as a hydrocarbon transit hub. Turkey has six oil refineries, four operated by the state. The four state refineries—at Izmit, at Aliaga, at Kirikkale, and at Batman—were built by the National Oil and Gas Company of Turkey (TPAO—Turkiye Petrolleri A.O.). The major private refinery in Turkey is Anadolu Tasfiyehanesi A.S. (ATAS). A small refinery in the southeast was bought in 1997 by Aladdin Middle East Ltd., a US-based company concerned mainly with oil exploration and development in this Kurdish-dominated region. Total refinery production suffered in the Russian financial crisis of 1998 and the Izmit earthquake of 1999, which damaged the Izmit Refinery in Kocaeli Province, the epicenter of the earthquake.

Major industrial complexes include the government-owned iron and steel mill at Karabuk and the Eregli iron and steel works. Other important Turkish enterprises are brick and tile, glass, leather, chemicals and pharmaceuticals, metalworking, cordage, flour milling, vegetable-oil extraction, fats and oils, paper products, printing and publishing, plastic products, and rubber processing. The sugar-beet industry ranks first among food-processing industries and produces more than domestic consumption requires. The automobile industry expanded rapidly in the 1970s and continued to be a growth sector in the mid-2000s. Tofas, a joint venture between Fiat and Koc Holding A.S., Turkey's biggest industrial conglomerate, is the leading automotive producer.

29 SCIENCE AND TECHNOLOGY

The government body that coordinates scientific research is the Scientific and Technical Research Council of Turkey, founded in 1963 in Ankara. The Mavmara Scientific and Industrial Research Institute (1972), in Istanbul, conducts research on basic and applied sciences and industrial research. The Ankara Nuclear Research and Training Center (1967), attached to the Turkish Atomic Energy Authority, studies health physics, nuclear electronics, and plasma physics. The General Directorate of Mineral Research and Exploration (1935), also in Ankara, conducts the Geological Survey of Turkey and evaluates mineral resources. The Turkish Natural History Museum was founded in 1968 at Ankara. Turkey has 29 universities that offer courses in basic and applied sciences. In 2008, of all bachelor's degrees awarded, 57.1% were for the sciences (natural, mathematics and computers, engineering). Patent applications in science and technology as of 2009 totaled 2,555 in Turkey, according to the World Bank. Public financing of science was 0.72% of GDP.

In 2008 total expenditures on research and development (R&D) amounted to $5.22 billion, or 0.71% of GDP. Of that amount, the government accounted for 50.6%, followed by the business sector at 41.3%. Private nonprofit organizations and foreign sources accounted for 6.9% and 1.3%, respectively. In that same year, there were 680 researchers and technicians engaged in research and development per million people. High technology exports in 2008 totaled $1.81 billion, or 1.7% of the country's manufactured exports.

Principal Trading Partners – Turkey (2010)

(In millions of US dollars)

Country	Total	Exports	Imports	Balance
World	299,427.0	113,883.0	185,544.0	-71,661.0
Germany	29,028.0	11,479.0	17,549.0	-6,070.0
Russia	26,229.0	4,628.0	21,601.0	-16,973.0
China	19,450.0	2,269.0	17,181.0	-14,912.0
Italy	16,711.0	6,507.0	10,204.0	-3,697.0
United States	16,164.0	3,841.0	12,323.0	-8,482.0
France	14,235.0	6,057.0	8,178.0	-2,121.0
United Kingdom	11,917.0	7,236.0	4,681.0	2,555.0
Iran	10,689.0	3,044.0	7,645.0	-4,601.0
Spain	8,376.0	3,536.0	4,840.0	-1,304.0
Iraq	7,391.0	6,036.0	1,355.0	4,681.0

(…) data not available or not significant.

(n.s.) not specified.

SOURCE: *2011 Direction of Trade Statistics Yearbook,* New York: United Nations, 2011.

30 DOMESTIC TRADE

Individual firms tend to be small and specialized. There is virtually no commercial activity in villages; the villager comes into the market town to buy and sell. Government-operated exchanges for cereals are located in municipalities. If the price of grain in the free market falls below the supermarket price, the government-operated exchanges purchase the grain and market it. In this manner, the government controls the price range of cereals. Franchising has grown in the past few years, primarily in foreign fast-food and apparel firms. Value-added taxes (VAT) apply to most goods and services with different rates for different products. In most cases an 18% VAT is levied. However, reduced rates of 1% and 8% are imposed on certain goods and services as defined by law.

Electronic commerce (e-commerce) transactions in Turkey are mostly in the area of Internet banking. Specifically, online banking and financial services account for almost 70% of all e-commerce transactions. The remaining volume of e-commerce transactions involves food delivery, books, CDs, entertainment, clothing, and other consumer products.

Because of the scarcity of some commodities, the government controls the distribution of various essential goods, notably cement, coal, lignite, and steel. Under a 1954 law, municipal authorities enforce specified profit margins on designated commodities. These margins are established at four levels: importer or manufacturer, distributor, wholesaler, and retailer. Customarily, a Turkish wholesaler supplies credit to retailers who, in turn, often extend credit beyond their own means to consumers. Wholesalers' margins tend to be small because of low overhead and keen competition. Due to Turkey's high inflation rate, wholesalers usually try to maintain minimal stocks to reduce carrying costs.

Most commercial firms belong to chambers of commerce, which exist in all cities. Chambers of industry are increasingly important in larger manufacturing centers. The government sponsors an international trade fair every year at İzmir. Shops are normally open from 9 a.m. to 5 p.m., Monday through Friday; some establishments tend to stay open later in the evenings, some shops often have Sunday hours, and some close Friday nights for Muslim religious observances. Banking hours are from 9 a.m. to 5 p.m., Monday through Friday. Business office hours are from 9 a.m. to 5 p.m., Monday through Friday, with an hour for lunch.

31 FOREIGN TRADE

Turkey's trade balance has long been negative, but the deficit reached crisis proportions in 1974–75 and again in 1980–81, when import value was nearly double that of exports, and the annual trade deficit approached $5 billion. In 1985 the government mandated the creation of four free trade and export processing zones aimed at expansion and diversification of exports. By 1990 the deficit had risen to over $9 billion and the ratio of exports to imports fell to 58%, compared to 81% in 1988. The gap narrowed slightly in 1991 and 1992, but widened in 1993. Exports increased from $18.1 billion in 1994 to $21.6 billion in 1995 and to $24.5 billion in 1996. Total imports in 1994 amounted to $23.3 billion, and rose to $35.7 billion in 1995 and to $45 billion in 1996.

After 1994, strong domestic demand caused imports to surge, along with the reduction of import duties that accompanied the introduction of a customs union with the European Union in 1996. By 2000, exports equaled only slightly more than half of imports (50.8%), bringing back memories of trade balances of the 1970s and 1980s. The share of exports of goods and services in GDP surged to over 30% in the 2001 recession year, in which domestic demand contracted sharply, but exports rose sharply, particularly due to the devaluation of the lira. That was the first time exports accounted for more than 25% of GDP. In 2002, the share of exports was 28.8%, and imports of goods and services amounted to about 30% of GDP. The foreign trade gap continued to widen in 2005, driven in part by high international oil prices. Turkey imported $166.3 billion worth of goods and services in 2008, while exporting $117.4 billion worth of goods and services. Major import partners in 2009 were Russia, 13.8%; Germany, 10%; China, 9%; the United States, 6.1%; Italy, 5.4%; and France, 5%. Its major export partners were Germany, 9.6%; France, 6.1%; the United Kingdom, 5.8%; Italy, 5.8%; and Iraq, 5%.

32 BALANCE OF PAYMENTS

In 2000 and 2001 a trade deficit and a weak banking sector forced Turkey to float the lira, which caused the country to fall into recession. The economy improved in 2002, however, due in part to support from the IMF and tighter fiscal policies. The share of exports of goods and services in GDP rose to 31.5% in 2001, the first time it surpassed 25%. That year imports of goods and services amounted to 29.2% of GDP. Total external debt by September 2001 stood at $118.3 billion. In 2004 exports amounted to $67 billion, while imports were $90.9 billion, leaving a trade deficit of $23.9 billion, compared with $14 billion in 2003. The foreign trade gap continued to widen in 2005, due in large measure to high international oil prices. In 2010 Turkey had a foreign trade deficit of $8.6 billion, amounting to 5.5% of GDP.

33 BANKING AND SECURITIES

The Central Bank of the Republic of Turkey was founded in 1930 as a privileged joint-stock company. It possesses the sole right of note issue and has the obligation of providing for the monetary requirements of the state agricultural and commercial enterprises by discounting the treasury-guaranteed bonds they issue. All foreign exchange transfers are handled exclusively by the central

Balance of Payments – Turkey (2010)

(In millions of US dollars)

Current Account		**-47,739.0**
Balance on goods		-56,445.0
Imports	-177,347.0	
Exports	120,902.0	
Balance on services		14,699.0
Balance on income		-7,322.0
Current transfers		1,329.0
Capital Account		**-56.0**
Financial Account		**58,063.0**
Direct investment abroad		-1,464.0
Direct investment in Turkey		9,278.0
Portfolio investment assets		-3,491.0
Portfolio investment liabilities		19,617.0
Financial derivatives		...
Other investment assets		7,049.0
Other investment liabilities		27,074.0
Net Errors and Omissions		**4,703.0**
Reserves and Related Items		**-14,971.0**

(…) data not available or not significant.

SOURCE: *Balance of Payment Statistics Yearbook 2011*, Washington, DC: International Monetary Fund, 2011.

bank, which operates the clearing accounts under separate agreements with foreign countries. The bank has 25 domestic branches, plus a banknote printing plant and foreign branch offices in New York, London, Frankfurt, and Zürich.

As of 2011, the Banks Association of Turkey had 44 registered banks, 3 of which were state-owned and 20 of which were foreign owned. Banks supervised by the central bank play a declining role in the banking system; 49% of total bank assets are still concentrated in three state-owned banks. The major private banks are linked mostly to industrial conglomerates, such as the Cukurova Group, which owns the Construction and Credit Bank (Yapi ve Kredi Bankasi), Pamukbank, Interbank, and the Sabanci Group, which owns Akbank. Several Western commercial banks are also active, as are some Middle Eastern trading banks. There are also a few specially designated finance houses, which have adopted Islamic banking practices. Many observers predict large-scale bank consolidation as Turkey continues liberalizing its economy.

Two of Turkey's most important banks, the Sümerbank and Etibank, are also state investment-holding companies. Another important state financial institution is the agricultural bank, which supplies credit to the farm population. The largest private commercial bank is the business bank. Another private bank, the Industrial Development Bank of Turkey, stimulates the growth of private industrial development and channels the flow of long-term debt capital into the private industrial sector for both short- and long-range development programs.

In 2010, the World Bank calculated Turkey's total reserves at $86 billion. The money market rate, the rate at which financial institutions lend to one another in the short term, was recorded in 2008 at 17.72%. While this was higher than the 2008 average rate in the European Union, since 1990 Turkey has suffered severe fluctuations in this figure. The discount rate, the interest rate at which the central bank lends to financial institutions in the short term, was 15% in December 2009, compared to 25% in Decem-

ber 2008. At the end of 2009, the nation's gold bullion deposits totaled 3.73 million fine troy ounces, or 116 tons. This figure had not changed since 2001.

The Istanbul Stock Exchange was established on 26 December 1985. Because of the shortage of foreign exchange, with few exceptions, trading is in government bonds and virtually all securities issued by private enterprises are sold privately through personal arrangements between buyers and sellers. International Bonds Market started its operations within the ISE Foreign Securities Market on 16 April 2007. As of 2008 approximately 320 companies were listed, total market capitalization was $98.3 billion, and trading value that year came to $147.4 billion, with a turnover ratio of 182.3%. In August 2009 the Istanbul Stock Exchange Emerging Companies Market Regulation was published in order to increase market organization and transparency.

34 INSURANCE

Government regulations, effective 1929 and subsequently amended, require all insurance companies to reinsure 30% of each policy with the National Reinsurance Corp., a state organization. In 1954 life policies were exempted from this requirement. It is possible to secure insurance policies for flood damage, third-party liability, earthquake, commercial shipments, theft, fire, accident, and life. Varied social security schemes are administered directly by the state. Third-party automobile liability, workers' compensation, and employers' liability have all been consistently compulsory. Workers' compensation has been covered solely by the government as a part of the Social Security scheme. The insurance market is officially regulated through the Ministry of Commerce. According to the Association of Insurance and Reinsurance Companies of Turkey, in August 2011 the value of all direct insurance premiums written totaled $8.95 billion, of which life premiums were statistically insignificant ($115,000).

35 PUBLIC FINANCE

Beginning in 1983, the fiscal year was shifted to the calendar year, starting on 1 January. (It had formerly begun on 1 March.) The consolidated budget includes the general budget of the government (by ministry) and a number of annexed budgets, which pertain to semiautonomous state activities, such as universities. Additionally, each section is divided into operating and investment expenditures. The budget is invariably in deficit. In 1994, when budget deficits led to an economic crisis with inflation peaking at 150%, the government launched an austerity program that reduced inflation but sent the economy into recession. When conditions improved, the government's commitment to austerity measures waned, and expenditures again exceeded revenues. In 1999 the government initiated structural reforms under ongoing programs of standby agreements with the IMF. However, in 2000-01, banking crises, political disputes, and a rapidly growing current account deficit set the economy into a deep downturn that forced the government to adopt a floating exchange rate regime, an ambitious reform program, a tight fiscal policy, additional structural reforms, and unparalleled levels of IMF lending. By 2005 the economy was on stronger footing, with continued support from the IMF.

In 2010 the budget of Turkey included $159.4 billion in public revenue and $189.6 billion in public expenditures. The budget

Public Finance – Turkey (2009)

(In trillions of liras, central government figures)

Revenue and Grants	**303,610**	**100.0%**
Tax revenue	180,146	59.3%
Social contributions	68,623	22.6%
Grants	519	0.2%
Other revenue	54,322	17.9%
Expenditures	**28,702**	**100.0%**
General public services	...	...
Defense	...	...
Public order and safety	...	...
Economic affairs	...	...
Environmental protection	...	...
Housing and community amenities	...	...
Health	...	...
Recreational, culture, and religion	...	...
Education	...	...
Social protection	...	...

(...) data not available or not significant.

SOURCE: *Government Finance Statistics Yearbook 2010*, Washington, DC: International Monetary Fund, 2010.

deficit amounted to 3.6% of GDP. Public debt was 48.1% of GDP, with $290.7 billion of the debt held by foreign entities.

36 TAXATION

All persons domiciled in Turkey, whether of Turkish citizenship or otherwise, are subject to taxation on income. Certain categories of foreigners are taxed only on income earned in Turkey, specifically, foreign business representatives, consultants, scientists, government officials, press correspondents, and others who do not intend to become permanent residents regardless of length of stay. As of 2011 the progressive personal income tax rates ranged from 15% to 35%. Dividends paid to resident individuals were taxed at only 50% of the distribution. In addition, the withholding tax paid on that portion can be taken as a credit against the taxable dividend income. Tax rates for gifts were between 10% and 30%, and inheritance tax, paid over 3 years, was between 1% and 10%.

As of 1 January 2011 the basic corporate tax rate was 20%. Capital gains, as of that date, were also taxed at 20% and were included in ordinary income. Dividends paid by resident corporations to other resident companies are not subject to a withholding tax. However, a 10% withholding rate may apply to those dividends if: the recipients are residents not subject to or exempt from income or corporate taxes; are nonresident corporations without a permanent representative or office in Turkey; and if the nonresident recipients are exempt from Turkish corporate and income taxes. Interest income from Turkish government treasury bills and bonds, and on loans made by foreign financial institutions, are not subject to a withholding tax. Interest income derived from other sources is subject to varying withholding tax rates. Royalties paid to nonresident companies or under licenses of rights are subject to a 22% withholding rate. A higher 25% rate applies payments on the sales of rights.

A value-added tax (VAT) with a standard rate of 18% applies to most transactions. However, an 8% rate is applied to basic foodstuffs, medical services, private education, books, and some en-

tertainment services. An even lower rate of 1% is applied to some immovable property, agricultural products, newspapers, and used cars. In December 2001 two higher rates of 26% and 40% applied to luxury goods were abolished. Exemptions to the VAT include transactions subject to Turkey's insurance and banking transactions tax, the pipeline transport of petroleum and crude oil, and the leasing of immovable property. Exports, international transport services provided abroad, and the supply of aircraft and ships are zero-rated.

Other taxes include excise taxes, stamp taxes, sales taxes, and consumption and property taxes. Business establishments are subject to an old-age insurance tax and an illness and disability tax, shared by employers and employees.

37 CUSTOMS AND DUTIES

Most imports are subject to the 18% VAT (with a ceiling of 26%) which is applied on the CIF (cost, insurance, freight) plus duty value. Turkey is a member of the World Trade Organization (WTO) and aligns its customs policies with WTO regulations. Turkish customs duties are assessed on an ad valorem basis only. Present customs classification conforms to standardized international nomenclature. Duty-free entry is provided for many types of imports, such as some raw materials, imports by government agencies, and capital goods. In 1996 Turkey aligned its tariffs with the EU's common external tariff system. Importers no longer need an import license and import authorization from a bank. A government monopoly, TEKEL, controls alcohol and cigarette imports. Narcotics and weapons are strictly prohibited.

38 FOREIGN INVESTMENT

Although Turkey has been the recipient of considerable foreign aid, its leaders have also recognized the need for private foreign investment. By 1970 foreign capital could operate in any field of economic activity open to Turkish private capital, and there was no limit on the percentage of foreign participation in equity capital. However, direct capital investment by foreign companies from 1960 to 1979 averaged no more than $20 million annually, which was very low by OECD standards. This changed dramatically in 1980 with new foreign investment policies that cut red tape to gain more rapid approval for investment applications; inflows of private capital increased to $97 million in 1980, $337 million in 1981, and $913 million in 1992. Foreign direct investment (FDI) in Turkey was a net inflow of $8.4 billion according to World Bank figures published in 2009. FDI represented 1.37% of GDP. The primary sources of investment are Germany and the United Kingdom, followed by Russia.

39 ECONOMIC DEVELOPMENT

Economic policy is formulated by the State Planning Organization. In June 1961 an integrated 15-year plan was announced, consisting of three five-year plans designed to achieve a 7% yearly increase in national income. In March 1963 the first five-year plan was inaugurated. The 1963–68 program fell short of its goals to some extent, but its average annual increase of 6.7% in GNP was still impressive. Two objectives of the second five-year plan (1968–72) were economic viability and social justice. The role of the public sector under this program was twofold: creation and expansion of the economic and social infrastructure, and development of modern manufacturing industries. Economic policy, however, still sought the largest possible active role for private enterprise in the development of industries, and the government sought with limited success to encourage private activity through fiscal concessions, financial assistance, and state participation in mixed enterprises. The third five-year plan was inaugurated in 1973 with the objective of helping Turkey prepare for its future membership in the EC. The long-term goals were to increase the per capita GNP from $400 in 1972 to $1,500 by 1995, to reduce agriculture's share of the GDP to 12%, and to increase industry's share to 37%. One of the main aims of the third five-year plan, still largely unmet, was to increase the efficiency of the tax-collection service. In agriculture the objectives were to increase food supplies for export and to feed a growing population through improved irrigation, technical advice to farmers, and the establishment of more cooperative farms.

All these efforts required large new investments and massive foreign loans which, coupled with the huge increases in the cost of oil imports after 1973, led to the financial crisis of 1977–78. Since 1980 Turkey has deliberately pursued a deflationary policy, allowing the international exchange rate of the lira to fluctuate on a daily basis from 1 May 1981. The government also delayed several ambitious development proposals, mainly because new foreign credits were not available. However, a number of smaller projects financed by the IBRD went forward. Meanwhile, the fourth (1979–83) and fifth (1985–90) five-year plans continued to stress industrial development, deflationary monetary policy, and export promotion. The creation of free trade zones in the mid-1980s was a major step in line with these policies.

Long-term economic programs adopted in 1991 and 1994 planned to reform social security and subsidy programs, implement tax reforms and improve tax administration, and restructure state enterprises, transferring certain inefficient ones to the private sector. By 1996 these plans had reduced the government's role in the economy, but huge budget deficits continued to plague the economy and further reforms are needed if Turkey is to solve its economic problems.

Turkey's geostrategic significance received a big boost in 1999 when its leaders, along with those of Azerbaijan and Georgia, agreed to the construction of an oil pipeline from the Caspian Sea port of Baku to the Turkish Mediterranean port of Ceyhan. The first section of the 1,100-mile pipeline opened in May 2005. The $3.2 billion pipeline has a capacity of one million barrels of oil per day.

At the December 1999 EU summit in Helsinki, Turkey formally became a candidate for accession in the next round of EU enlargement. Turkey's economic problems, along with reservations about human rights have, put a brake on early Turkish entry to the European Union. Nevertheless, Turkey's status as a candidate member provides clear goals for Turkish development, and accession negotiations were opened in October 2005. These goals include addressing the high government debt, inflation, unemployment, and income inequality. National debt has dropped consistently since 2001, from 91% of GDP, to 64% in 2005 and 46.3% in 2009. Turkey is working to become more globally competitive, and government policies have shifted toward liberalization. However, efforts to reduce the role of the state have been hindered by special-interest groups and political instability. On the World Bank's scale for ease of doing business in the country, 1 being easiest and 181 being hardest, Turkey was given a 65 in 2010.

40 SOCIAL DEVELOPMENT

The social insurance system provides old age, disability, and death pensions for employees in industry, commerce, and the service sector. Special systems cover other workers. The benefits are funded by payroll taxes and employee contributions. Sickness and maternity benefits are also covered. Employers contribute additional funds to cover worker's injury insurance. Unemployment benefits are available for most workers and are available after 600 days of contributions in the three years before loss of work. The Social Insurance Institution provides medical services in its own hospitals and other facilities.

The civil code explicitly bans sex-based privileges yet proclaims the male as the legal head of the household. This grants the male the right to choose the place of residence, and most assets are held in the name of the husband. Women in urban areas are increasingly working outside the home. Women generally receive equal pay for equal work in their professions but are underrepresented in managerial positions. Spousal abuse and violence are widespread. In 2004 a study showed that over 31% of women were beaten by their husbands, and 39% of women believed that men were justified in beating their wives in certain situations. Authorities hesitate to intervene in domestic matters, and violence against women goes largely unreported. Honor killings continue in some rural areas, and forced marriages are common. Reports of child abuse have increased in recent years. Kurds are the largest ethnic minority and suffer discrimination, especially in less-industrialized areas.

41 HEALTH

According to the CIA, life expectancy in Turkey was 72 years in 2011. The country spent 6.1% of its GDP on healthcare, amounting to $571 per person. There were 15 physicians, 19 nurses and midwives, and 24 hospital beds per 10,000 inhabitants. In 2008, the World Bank calculated the maternal mortality rate at 23 deaths per 100,000 births, and the infant mortality rate at 19 deaths per 1,000 live births. It was estimated that 97% of children were vaccinated against measles. The CIA calculated the HIV/AIDS prevalence rate in Turkey to be about less than 0.1% in 2009.

Free medical treatment, given at state hospitals or health centers, is provided by the state to any Turkish citizen who obtains a certificate of financial need from a local administrator.

42 HOUSING

In 1999, major earthquakes in August and November left about 800,000 people homeless. The disasters brought to light the issues of substandard housing and illegal construction permits. The Turkish Chamber of Commerce estimated that about 65% of all buildings were built with illegal permits or below regulations, producing structures that are in no way suited to withstand the earthquakes to which Turkey is prone. International assistance has helped to rebuild and repair a number of homes. In 2000 there were about 16.2 million dwelling units nationwide. The average household had 4.5 members, and in 2006 the home ownership rate was 70%, with 77.8% of properties having 3–4 rooms. The Collective Housing Administration Directorate, founded in 1984, provides credit for residential construction projects. Government regulation in housing and mortgaging, however, has been almost non-existent. As in most of the developed world, housing prices dropped significantly in 2008 but, in 2010 and 2011, prices recovered to almost the same numbers as before the crash.

43 EDUCATION

Primary, secondary, and some higher education are free. Education is compulsory for children ages 6–14 or until graduation from primary school (grade five). Since 1997 the regular school system has consisted of eight years of basic school and three years of secondary school. Technical, trade, and commercial schools are available at the secondary level. Some Anatolian high schools offer courses in English, French, or German in the first year and use those languages in instruction for the following years. There are also Anatolian fine arts high schools. Among private schools in operation are a number of foreign schools and those maintained by ethnic or religious minorities. The academic year runs from October to June.

As of 2008 public expenditure on education was estimated at 4.1% of GDP. According to the UN Children's Fund (UNICEF), in 2008 about 12% of age-eligible children were enrolled in some type of preschool program. Primary school enrollment that year was estimated at about 96% of age-eligible students, while secondary school enrollment was about 74% of age-eligible students. It is estimated that about 95% of all students complete their primary education.

Among Turkey's 97 universities are the universities of Istanbul (founded 1453) and Ankara (founded 1946), the Technical University of Istanbul (founded 1773), and the Middle East Technical University at Ankara (founded 1957). Thirty of Turkey's higher education institutions are private and five are military. In 2007 it was estimated that about 34% of the tertiary age population was enrolled in a higher education program—substantially lower than the average in most European countries (45%–55%). Of those enrolled in tertiary education, there were 100 male students for every 78 female students. The adult literacy rate for 2008 was estimated at about 87.7%, with 95.4% for men and 81.3% for women.

44 LIBRARIES AND MUSEUMS

The National Library in Ankara has over 960,000 volumes. There are also two provincial branches of the library system: the Beyazit State Library in Istanbul with 500,000 volumes and the National Library of İzmir with 350,000 volumes. Major university collections include the Istanbul University and Documentation Center with 1.5 million volumes and one of the Middle East's finest rare book collections; the Middle East Technical University with 145,000 volumes, and the University of Ankara with 750,000 volumes.

The most famous museums and ancient buildings are located in Istanbul. The old seraglio, now Tip-top Museum, is perhaps the most famous; it houses a large collection of paintings, manuscripts, and historically important items. Nearby is the Ayasofya (Saint Sophia), the world-renowned Byzantine church that draws thousands of tourists to Istanbul. Next to it is the Blue Mosque, famous for the beauty of its interior and the grace of its dome. Also in Istanbul are the museums of archaeology and of the ancient Orient, housing one of the world's finest collections of Greek

art, including the sarcophagus of Alexander the Great. Additionally, the city is home to the Museum of Turkish Written Art, the Istanbul Museum of Painting and Sculpture, and the Museum of Revolution.

The Museum of Archaeology in Ankara contains the world's outstanding collection of Hittite works. Also in Ankara are Ataturk's Mausoleum and Museum, the Museum of Anatolian Civilizations, and the Museum of the Turkish Independence War and Turkish Republic. In Konya there are museums of Islamic art, one of which is housed in the mausoleum of Mevlana. Newer facilities include the decorative arts museums at the Beyler beyi and Dolmahbace palaces (both opened in Istanbul in 1984) and the Fire Brigade Museum in Fatib (1992). Along Turkey's Aegean coast are the ruins of Ephesus, Pergamum, Troy (Ilium), Halicarnassus, and other famous ancient cities. A zoological garden is located in Ankara.

45 MEDIA

Turkey's telecommunications system is undergoing rapid modernization and growth, particularly in cellular telephone usage. Fiber-optic cable and digital microwave radio relay systems are being installed to create advanced intercity trunk lines to facilitate inter-city communications. Remote areas are reached by a domestic, satellite-based communications system. Meanwhile, the number of subscribers to mobile cellular telephone service is growing rapidly. International service is provided by submarine, fiber-optic cables in the Black and Mediterranean Seas and permanent and mobile satellite ground stations. Land telephone usage as of 2009 stood at 23 out of 100 people, while mobile subscriptions numbered 87 out of 100.

The government owns and operates the Turkish Radio and Television Corporation (TRT). According to the Ministry of the Directorate General of Press and Information of Turkey (DGPI), in 2009 there were 226 local, 15 regional, and 16 national officially registered television stations, and 959 local, 104 regional, and 36 national radio stations. Foreign broadcasts are available via satellite. All broadcasts are monitored by the government through The High Board of Radio and Television. In 2003 there were an estimated 470 radios and 423 television sets for every 1,000 people. About 14.8 of every 1,000 people were cable subscribers. Based on 2009 World Bank data, 37 out of every 100 people had regular internet access.

Statistics from the DGPI for 2009 showed 5,665 circulating periodicals (including daily and weekly newspapers and journals), many of which had small local circulations. The independent leftist *Cumhuriyet* (circulation 59,251) has been closed and reopened a number of times. Other leading dailies in 2009 were *Zaman* (753,250); *Posta* (541,629); *Hurriyet* (474,417); and *Sabah* (371,147). Although the constitution guarantees freedom of expression, it also authorizes newspaper confiscations and closures in the cases of crimes against the unity, security, or republican principles of the state.

46 ORGANIZATIONS

Professional organizations, charitable associations, student organizations, and athletic clubs are active in the major cities. Chambers of commerce and chambers of industry are semiofficial agencies for the control of import license and foreign exchange allocations. The Union of Chamber of Commerce, Industry, and

Maritime Commerce and Commodity Exchanges of Turkey, established in 1952, is based in Ankara.

There are several Masonic lodges and branches of the Rotary and Lions clubs. Women are active in a number of their own charitable organizations. National women's rights and development organizations include the Federation of Women's Associations, the Turkish Cypriot Association of University Women, Women for Women's Human Rights/New Ways, and the Association of Women's Rights Protection. National youth organizations include the International Islamic Federation of Student Organizations, Youth for Habitat, the Youth Services Center, Junior Chamber, the Scouting and Guiding Federation of Turkey, and YMCA/YWCA. There are active sports associations promoting amateur competitions in a variety of pastimes; many such clubs are affiliated with international organizations as well as with the national Olympic Committee.

Since World War II, international cultural associations have appeared, chief among them being Turkish-American, Turkish-French, Turkish-German, and Turkish-English. The Research Center for Islamic History, Art and Culture, based in Istanbul, is a multinational subsidiary organization of the Organization of the Islamic Conference (OIC). The Scientific and Technical Research Council of Turkey and the Turkish Academy of Sciences promote public interest, education, and research in a broad range of scientific fields. The Medical Association of Turkey also promotes public health and advanced research in fields of medicine.

There are national chapters of the Red Crescent Society, UNICEF, UNESCO, Habitat for Humanity, and Amnesty International.

47 TOURISM, TRAVEL, AND RECREATION

The World Tourism Organization of the UN shows a steady increase in tourism since data publication began in 1995. For 2009, it reported 25.5 million inbound tourists, spending approximately $24.6 billion. The majority of tourists from a single country in 2009 came from Germany, with 4.4 million; however, approximately 21.4 million originated in Europe, which includes the Russian Federation. According to Turkey's National Tourism Industry Report, accommodation bed capacity (including hotels, villas, and other rentals) in 2008 was 567,470, primarily along the Aegean and Mediterranean, with an average occupancy rate of 49%. In 2008 the estimated daily cost to visit Ankara, the capital, was $229. The cost of visiting other cities averaged $202; costs were substantially less outside of larger cities.

Istanbul was designated by the European Union as a "European Capital of Culture" for 2010, along with Essen in Germany and Peç in Hungary. In addition to the museums and monuments of Istanbul, places of interest include the Aegean ports of İzmir and Bodrum; the ancient cities of Troy (Ilium), Ephesus, Tarsus, Konya, Samsun, Erzurum, and Trabzon; Mt. Ararat, traditionally considered the landing place of Noah's Ark, the remains of which some expeditions have tried to find; the ski resort of Uludag, 36 km (22 mi) south of Bursa; and the sea resort of Antalya, on the Mediterranean coast. Water sports, mountaineering, and football (soccer) are popular forms of recreation, as are such traditional Turkish sports as camel fighting (*deve güreşi*) and a horseback javelin competition (*cirit oyunu*) played mainly in eastern Turkey.

In November 2010 the Kirkpinar oil wrestling festival of Edirne, Turkey, was officially inscribed on the UNESCO Representative List of the Intangible Heritage of Humanity, an offshoot of the World Heritage program. The festival was deemed a living tradition by UNESCO, meaning that it is still passed from generation to generation and continues to create a sense of identity and community for those who participate. Such traditions have been approved by UNESCO for special consideration since 2001. A special program is designed to protect and promote the practice and understanding of the tradition. The annual oil wrestling is attended by thousands of spectators from across the country who come to watch this championship bout of the *pehlivan* (wrestlers). The pehlivan are comprised of men from all regions, representing many religions and languages. They are trained in the sport through a master-apprentice tradition, which includes training in social attributes of generosity, honesty, respectfulness, and adherence to traditions and customs. The *semah*, a religious ritual involving rhythmic movements accompanied by music performed on traditional instruments, was also inscribed. Semahs are performed by men and women who are adherents of Alevi-Bektasi, a belief system based on adoration of Ali, the fourth caliph after the prophet Muhammad.

All visitors need a valid passport and a visa. Entering the country from Iraq is problematic for visitors of any nationality. There are no immunizations required, although precautions are recommended for typhoid, malaria, and hepatitis, as well as standard routine vaccinations.

48 FAMOUS PERSONS

The most famous rulers before the coming of the Turks were Croesus (r. 560–546 BC), a king of Lydia noted for his wealth and for the loss of his kingdom to the Persians; Constantine I (the Great; Flavius Valerius Aurelius Constantinus, b. Moesia, AD 280?–337), the first Roman emperor to accept Christianity and to use Constantinople as a capital; and Justinian I (the Great; Flavius Petrus Sabbatius Justinianus, b. Illyricum, 483–565), a Byzantine emperor whose collection of laws and legal principles has been the model for European law down to modern times. Outstanding political figures since the arrival of the Turks include Sultan Mehmet II (1429–1481), conqueror of Constantinople in 1453; Sultan Süleyman I (the Magnificent, 1495–1566); the Barbarossa brothers, Aruj (1473?–1518) and Hayreddin Paşa (Khayr ad-Din, 1466?–1546), naval commanders, born in Mytilene, who established Turkish supremacy in the Mediterranean; Mehmet Köprülü Paşa (1583–1661), Mehmet IV's grand vizier and founder of a family line of outstanding grand viziers; Sultan Abdul Hamid II (1842–1918), a despotic ruler whose tyranny led to the formation of the Young Turk movement; Enver Paşa (1881–1922), Young Turk leader who was the ruler of Turkey during World War I; Mustafa Kemal Atatürk (1881–1938), World War I military commander, nationalist leader, and first president of the republic; Ismet Inönü (Paşa, 1884–1973), Atatürk's chief of staff and prime minister, who succeeded him as president (1938–50) and was the first prime minister of the Second Republic (1961–65); Celâl Bayar (1883–1986), who helped found the Democrat Party and was president (1950–60) until ousted by the military; and Adnan Menderes (1899–1961), prime minister (1950–60) until he was forced to resign and then executed. Outstanding religious figures include Haci Bektaş Veli (1242–1337), founder of the Bektashi dervishes, and Mevlana

(Celâleddin-i Rumi or Jalal al-Din Rumi, 1207–73), author of the epic *Mesnevi* (or *Mathnavi*) and founder of the Mevlevi dervishes.

Revered literary figures include the mystical poets Yunus Emre (1238?–1320?) and Süleyman Çelebi (d. 1422), author of *Mevlidi Sherif (Birth Song of the Prophet)*. Other significant poets of the imperial epoch are Ahmedi (1334–1413), Şeyhi (d.1429?); Fuzulî (1494–1555), renowned for his lyrical verses about platonic love; Ali Şir Nevâî (1441–1501); Nef'î (1582?–1636); Nabî (1642?–1712); Ahmet Nedim (1681–1730), perhaps Ottoman Turkey's greatest love poet; and Şeyh Galib (1757–98), the last great poet of the mystical and classical tradition. Renowned for his geographical and historical writings is Kâtip Çelebi (known in Europe as Haji Khalifa, 1609–57); the great traveler Evliya Çelebi (1611–82) is noted for his books on travel and history. The greatest folk poet was the 17th-century minstrel Karacaoglan.

Sinasi (1826–71), a dramatist, journalist, and essayist, was the first Turkish writer in the Western tradition. Other significant playwrights are Musaipzade Celal (1870–1959), Haldun Taner (1916–86), and Necati Cumali (1921–2001). The poet Ziya Paşa (1825–80) was the outstanding literary figure of the reform period. Namik Kemal (Ahmed Kemal, 1840–88) and Mehmet Emin Yurdakul (1869–1944) dedicated their poetry to the achievement of political ideals. Four widely read novelists are Huseyin Rahmi Gurpinar (1864–1944), Ahmet Rasim (1864–1932), Halit Ziya Usakligil (1865–1945), and Mehmet Rauf (1871–1931). Omer Seyfettin (1884–1920) was a major short-story writer. Ziya Gökalp (1875–1924) was a noted poet and sociologist. Significant contemporary novelists include Halide Edib Adivar (1884–1966), Yakup Kadri Karaosmanoglu (1888–1974), Refik Halit Karay (1888–1974), Reşat Nuri Güntekin (1892–1957), Kemal Tahir Demir (1910–74), Orhan Kemal (1914–70), and Yasar Kemal Gokceli (b. 1922). Two fine modern poets were Yahya Kemal Beyatli (1884–1958) and Nazim Hikmet Ran (1901–60). Two prominent journalists and political writers were Hüseyin Çahit Yalçin (1875–1957) and Ahmet Emin Yalman (1889–1973). Outstanding historians were Naima (1752–1815), Mehmet Fuat Köprülü (1890–1966), and Ahmet Zekî Velidî Togan (1890–1970).

Other famous Turks include the architect Sinan (1490–1588), the miniaturist Abducelil Celebi Levni (d. 1732), and the modern painter Bedri Rahmi Eyuboglu (1913–75). Famous contemporary composers include Ulvi Cemal Erkin (1906–72) and Ahmet Adnan Saygun (1907–93). The operatic soprano Suna Korad (1935–2003) and bass-baritone Ayhan Baran (b. 1929) have won renown in European musical circles.

49 DEPENDENCIES

Turkey has no territories or colonies, excepting minor islands in the Aegean and the disputed territory in Cyprus.

50 BIBLIOGRAPHY

Alexander, Yonah (ed.). *Combating Terrorism: Strategies of Ten Countries*. Ann Arbor, Mich.: University of Michigan Press, 2002.

Altinay, Ayse Gul. *The Myth of the Military Nation: Militarism, Gender, and Education in Turkey*. New York: Palgrave Macmillan, 2004.

Heper, Metin and Bilge Criss. *Historical Dictionary of Turkey*. 2nd ed. Lanham, MD: Scarecrow, 2009.

Kuru, Ahmet T., and Alfred C. Stepan. *Democracy, Islam, and Secularism in Turkey*. New York: Columbia University Press, 2012.

Musil, Pelin Ayan. *Authoritarian Party Structures and Democratic Political Setting in Turkey*. New York: Palgrave Macmillan, 2012.

Park, Bill. *Modern Turkey: People, State and Foreign Policy in a Globalized World*. New York: Routledge, 2012.

Seddon, David (ed.). *A Political and Economic Dictionary of the Middle East*. Philadelphia: Routledge/Taylor and Francis, 2004.

Somel, Selcuk Aksin. *Historical Dictionary of the Ottoman Empire*. Lanham, MD: Scarecrow Press, 2012.

Swan, Suzanne. *DK Eyewitness Turkey*. London, Eng.: DK Publishing, 2012.

TURKMENISTAN

CAPITAL: Ashgabat (Ashkhabad)

FLAG: The flag of Turkmenistan reflects the country's long tradition of carpet-making and is highly intricate. It consists of a green field with a vertical stripe near the hoist side. The stripe contains five tribal guls, which are designs used in carpet making, placed over two cross olive branches. In addition, five white stars and a white crescent moon appears in the upper corner of the green field. The green color and crescent moon represent Islam. The stars symbolize the regions of Turkmenistan, and the guls represent the country's national identity.

ANTHEM: *Garassyz, Bitarap Turkmenistanyn (Independent, Neutral, Turkmenistan State Anthem).*

MONETARY UNIT: The Turkmenistani Manat (TMT), introduced in 1993, is the primary currency. TMT1 = US$0.350877 (or US$1 = TMT2.85) as of 2011.

WEIGHTS AND MEASURES: The metric system is used.

HOLIDAYS: New Year's Day (1 January), Remembrance Day (12 January), National Flag Day (19 February), International Women's Day (8 March), Novruz Bairam—Turkmen New Year (20 March), Heroes Day (8 May), Victory Day (9 May), Constitution Day or Day of Revival, Unity and Poetry of Magtymguly Pyragy (18 May), Remembrance Day observing the anniversary of the 1948 Earthquake (6 October), Independence Day (27 October), and Neutrality Day (12 December). Other holidays are Kurban Bairam and Oraza Bairam, which mark the end of Ramadan. Kurban Bairam is celebrated 70 days after Oraza Bairam.

TIME: 4 p.m. = noon GMT.

¹LOCATION, SIZE, AND EXTENT

Turkmenistan is located in central Asia, bordering the Caspian Sea, between Iran and Uzbekistan. Comparatively, Turkmenistan is slightly larger than the state of California, with a total area of 488,100 sq km (188,456 sq mi). Turkmenistan shares boundaries with Kazakhstan and Uzbekistan on the N, Afghanistan on the SE, Iran on the SW, and the Caspian Sea on the W. Turkmenistan's boundary length totals 5,504 km (3,420 mi), of which 1,768 km (1,099 mi) is shoreline along the Caspian Sea. Turkmenistan's capital city, Ashgabat meaning "city of love"), is located in the southwestern part of the country near its border with Iran.

²TOPOGRAPHY

The topography features flat to rolling sandy desert with dunes to the Caspian Sea, which lies in the west. The Kara Kum desert (also spelled Garagum) occupies over 80% of Turkmenistan's total area. The desert is bounded by oases in the north that are watered by the Amu Darya, and by the Murgab, Tejen, and Atrek rivers in the south. About 4% of Turkmenistan's land is arable with approximately 2.5% under irrigation.

The highest point in Turkmenistan is the Gora Ayribaba (3,139 m/10,299 ft), located along the eastern border near Uzbekistan. The lowest point in the country is Vpadina Akchanaya (Akdzhakaya Depression) at 81 m (266 ft) below sea level in the north central region of the country. The Sarygamysh Koli lake in the northern part of the country has a water level that fluctuates significantly. It can rise higher than Vpadina Akchanaya, but has also has dropped to 110 m (361 ft) below sea level.

The Kopet-Dag Mountains of the southern border are part of a seismically active region that has experienced devastating earthquakes. One of the most destructive earthquakes in history occurred near Ashgabat on 6 October 1948 when a 7.3 magnitude quake resulted in the death of 110,000 people.

³CLIMATE

The climate is arid continental. In July the mean temperature is 28°C (82°F). The mean temperature in January is -4°C (25°F). It can become very hot in the Kara Kum desert, with daytime temperatures of 50°C (122°F) not unusual. It does not rain much in Turkmenistan. The annual precipitation varies from 80 mm (3.15 in) in the northwest to 300 mm (11.8 in) in the Kopet-Dag Range near the Iranian border.

⁴FLORA AND FAUNA

Turkmenistan is home to 103 mammal species, 318 bird species, 97 reptile species, and 7 amphibian species. The calculation reflects the total number of distinct species residing in the country, not the number of endemic species.

The Kara Kum (Black Sea) desert that covers most of the country has limited plant and animal life. Herders raise goats, camels, and sheep in the desert.

In the southwest part of the country, the Kopet-Dag Mountains are rich with such plants as the Turkmen mandragora, Komarov's atropa, almonds, Blinov cherries, pomegranates, figs, and persimmon. Other wild fruits, berries, herbs, spices, and honey-bearing plants are used for consumption, food processing, and medicinal purposes.

The delta of the Amu Darya River contains a liquorice that is used in tobacco, liqueurs, cordials, beers, drinks, and sweets.

5 ENVIRONMENT

The World Resources Institute reported that Turkmenistan had designated 1.26 million hectares (3.13 million acres) of land for protection as of 2006. Water resources totaled 60.9 cu km (14.61 cu mi) while water usage was 24.65 cu km (5.91 cu mi) per year. Domestic water usage accounted for 2% of total usage, industrial for 1%, and agricultural for 97%. Per capita water usage totaled 5,104 cu m (180,246 cu ft) per year.

The United Nations (UN) reported in 2008 that carbon dioxide emissions in Turkmenistan totaled 45,771 kilotons.

The most significant environmental problems in Turkmenistan include salinization of the soil and water pollution. The nation's water supply is threatened by chemical contaminants from farming activity. The problem is complicated by a lack of adequate sewage treatment facilities. A large share of the Amu Darya River's flow is diverted for irrigation, decreasing its contribution to the water supply of the rapidly shrinking Aral Sea. Water cycles have also affected the Garabogazol Aylagy, a lagoon-like appendage in the northwest that adjoins the Caspian Sea. It became fully enclosed because of a drop in the volume of the Caspian Sea, but is starting to rise again as the sea returns to previous levels.

According to a 2011 report issued by the International Union for Conservation of Nature and Natural Resources (IUCN), threatened species included 9 types of mammals, 16 species of birds, 2 types of reptiles, 11 species of fish, and 5 species of invertebrates. Threatened species include the cheetah, tiger, Aral salmon, slender-billed curlew, and white-headed duck.

The National Institute of Deserts, Flora and Fauna within the Ministry of Nature Protection has sponsored research into the biology, ecology, and human environment of Turkmenistan. The country is party to international environmental agreements on biodiversity, climate change, desertification, hazardous wastes, and ozone layer protection.

6 POPULATION

The US Central Intelligence Agency (CIA) estimates the population of Turkmenistan in 2012 to be approximately 5,054,828, which placed it at number 118 in population among the 196 nations of the world. In 2011, approximately 4.1% of the population was over 65 years of age, with another 27.4% under 15 years of age. The median age in Turkmenistan was 25.3 years. In 2012, there were 1.05 males for every female in the country. The population's annual rate of change was 1.143% . The life expectancy for males in 2012 was about 66 years for males and 72 years for females. About 50% of the population lived in urban areas in 2010. The largest city is Ashgabat, which had a population in 2009 of 637,000.

7 MIGRATION

Estimates of Turkmenistan's net migration rate, carried out by the CIA in 2012, amounted to -1.9 migrants per 1,000 citizens. The to-tal number of emigrants living abroad was 261,000, and the total number of immigrants living in Turkmenistan was 207,700.

Turkmenistan severely restricts cross-border movement. According to a January 2011 report by the UN High Commission on Refugees, human rights groups had found that the government had barred between 12,000 and 17,000 citizens from going abroad. Many of these individuals were journalists, civil activists, dissidents, relatives of political prisoners, and émigrés. Prior to 2006, the country required transit passengers and people with relatives residing in border areas to secure entry permits . This requirement was relaxed following the death of President Saparmurat Niyazov in late 2006. Other human rights reports indicated that a presidential decree issued on 16 August 2010 prohibited 37,057 individuals from leaving the country. In addition, it would not allow 8,000 others as well as international human rights organizations to enter the country.

Emigration to other Union of Soviet Socialist Republics (USSR) countries exceeded immigration by 20,600 during 1979–90. More than 40,000 people fled from Tajikistan to Turkmenistan in 1992 to escape civil war. Repatriation of the Tajik refugees started in early 1998. There were also some 13,000 Tajik refugees, mostly ethnic Turkmen, who expressed the desire to remain in Turkmenistan. Between 1993 and 1995, 100,000 Russians left Turkmenistan.

Turkmenistan established the State Service for the Registration of Foreign Citizens in 2003 to monitor foreign visitors, whose activities are strictly regulated. In that same year, Niyazov ordered the forced relocation of ethnic Uzbeks living along the Turkmen border with Uzbekistan on the ground that "unworthy people" should be replaced with ethnic Turkmen.

Turkmenistan has not issued reports on asylum seekers since 2005. However, the US State Department reported in its 2010 Human Rights Report on Turkmenistan that the State Migration Service had registered 12,000 individuals who had difficulty determining their nationality. Most of these individuals were former Soviet Union passport holders who had not selected a new national affiliation when their passports expired in 1999. The report indicated that some of these residents may have received residency permits, but Turkmen citizenship has not been granted to any individual since 2005.

8 ETHNIC GROUPS

According to unofficial estimates in 2003, about 85% of the population consisted of ethnic Turkmen. Uzbeks accounted for 5% of the population, and Russians for about 4%. The remaining 6% of the population included about 100 distinct ethnic groups. The Turkmen generally divide themselves into five main tribes: the Teke, Yomut, Ersary, Yasyr, and Goklen. Smaller groups of people included Kazakhs, Ukrainians, Armenians, Azeris, Tatars, Beluji, Belarusians, Germans, Jews, Georgians, Moldovans, Uighurs, and Koreans.

Non-ethnic Turkmen have faced discrimination in employment and educational activities. The US State Department reported in its 2010 Human Rights Report on Turkmenistan that applicants for government jobs were required to provide information about ethnicity going back three generations. In addition, non-Turkmen often were targeted first for dismissal when layoffs occurred.

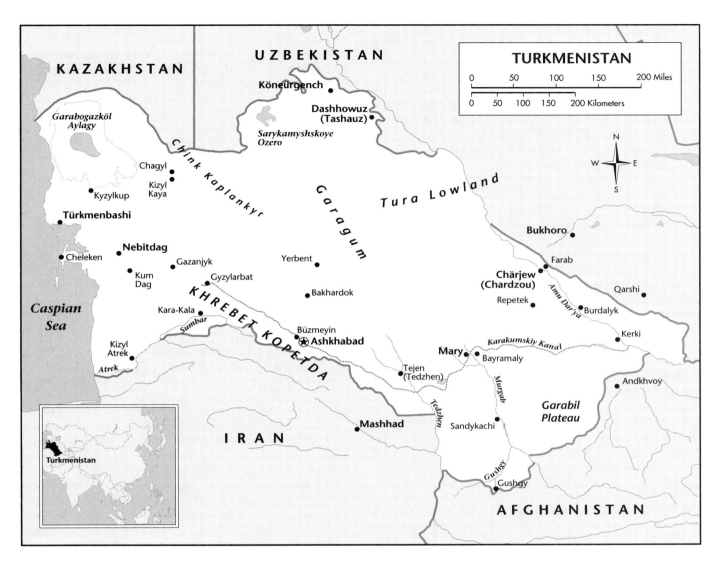

LOCATION: 40°0′ N; 60°0′ E. BOUNDARY LENGTHS: Afghanistan, 744 kilometers (462.3 miles); Iran, 992 kilometers (616.4 miles); Kazakhstan, 379 kilometers (236 miles); Uzbekistan, 1,621 kilometers (1007.3 miles).

⁹LANGUAGES

Turkmen, the official language of Turkmenistan, is spoken by 72% of the population. Russian is spoken by about 12% of the people and Uzbek by 9%. A variety of other languages are spoken by about 7% of the population.

Russian was used widely in commerce, but the government has been trying to impose Turkmen as the sole language used in government and business. Ministry employees were required to take tests demonstrating their knowledge of Turkmen, and resources to learn Turkmen were only offered to children in primary and secondary schools. The government has mandated since 2007 that English be taught, but few citizens understand English.

¹⁰RELIGIONS

The US State Department reported that official statistics on religious affiliation were not known as of 2010. The majority religion was Sunni Islam, and Russian Orthodox Christians constituted the largest religious minority. There also were believed to be small numbers of practicing Catholics, Lutherans, and Jews.

The traditional Islamic culture of Turkmenistan prior to its 19th-century occupation by Russia was not mosque-based. Since independence in 1991, mosque-based Islam has seen a resurgence. There were three mosques in Turkmenistan in 1991, and 398 at the end of 2010. There also were 13 Russian Orthodox churches. The government formally registered the Catholic Church in 2010, 13 years after the organization submitted its application.

The government has incorporated some aspects of Islam into the country's cultural activities in an effort since independence to create a national identity. It has financed the construction of mosques and organized events around traditional Turkmen shrines. In 2010, the government did not support travel to Mecca for the Hajj but instead organized an 18-day internal pilgrimage that allowed a group of believers to visit 38 Turkmen shrines.

11 TRANSPORTATION

The CIA reports that Turkmenistan had a total of 58,592 km (36,407 mi) of roads, of which 47,577 km (29,563 mi) were paved, in 2002. There were 106 vehicles per 1,000 people in the country. Railroads extended for 3,095 km (1,923 mi) according to the World Bank. There were 27 airports, which transported 1.71 million passengers in 2009 according to the World Bank. Twenty-two of those airports had paved runways; five did not. There was also one heliport in 2010. Turkmenistan has approximately 1,300 km (808 mi) of navigable waterways in 2008.

Nebitdag, Ashgabat, Mary, and Chärjew (Chardzhou) are connected by railroad to the nation's main port of Turkmenbashi on the Caspian Sea. Other lines include a railroad from Mary along the Murgab and Kushka rivers to Afghanistan and a line from Chärjew (Chardzhou) along the Amu Darya, which nearly parallels Uzbekistan's border. Smaller rail spurs are located at Dashhowuz (Tashauz) and Kerki. Turkmenistan's navigable inland waterways include the Amu Darya River and the Kara Kum canal. In 2008, the country's merchant marine consisted of seven ships of 1,000 GRT or more.

Despite the large number of rail links between Turkmenistan and Uzbekistan in the north and northeast, rail and road crossings at Turkmenabat were more widely used. Trucks entering from Uzbekistan cross the Amu Darya River by pontoon bridge. A road linking Turkmenistan to Kazakhstan via Bekdash was in poor shape as of 2011, but plans were underway to rebuild it.

A new international railway Uzen-Gyzylgaya-Bereket-Etrek-Gorgan was under construction during 2011. This railway was expected to transport 6 million tons of goods annual, and would link the Kazakh and Iranian railway systems through Turkmenistan.

12 HISTORY

The territory of present-day Turkmenistan has been inhabited since the Stone Age, with evidence of agricultural communities as early as 6000 BC and of planned irrigation works from 3500 BC. The first states were Margiana and Parthia, from about 1000 BC. In the 7th–6th centuries BC, Margiana was part of Bactria, while Parthia was part of the Median state.

Horse-breeding tribal Turkmen were believed to have entered the area from the Altay Mountains and to have established grazing areas along the outskirts of the Kara Kum desert and extending into Persia, Syria, and Anatolia.

In the 6th–4th centuries BC, the region was ruled by the Achaemenids, who were conquered by Alexander the Great at the end of the 4th century. In Alexander's wake there emerged a Parthian Empire which lasted until AD 224, when Persians of the Sassanid dynasty seized the territory. In the 5th century, much of Turkmenistan was conquered by Ephthalites, who in turn were conquered in the 6th century by the Tiu-chue nomads of Turkic origin. The Arab caliphate conquered Turkmenistan in 716 and began to introduce Islam. In the 10th century, part of Turkmenistan was under Samanid control.

Oghuz Turks began to migrate into Turkmenistan in the 9th century. In 1040 the Seljuk clan took control of the territory and held sway until the 13th century, when Turkmenistan was part of the Khwarazm-Shah state. The entire region was conquered by Mongols in 1219–21, and Turkmenistan was split between the Golden Horde and the Chagatai Khanate, as well as the Hulaguid Khanate of Persia.

In the 1380s, Turkmenistan became part of the empire of Timur (Tamerlane). By the 16th century, part of the territory was ruled by the Khiva Khanate, part by Bukhara, and part by Persia. The course of the Amu Darya River changed, and the Kara Kum desert claimed a great deal of once arable land.

Beginning in the 16th century, Turkmen raiders on horseback would prey on caravans passing through the area to take prisoners for the slave trade. Russia began to make commercial contacts with the Turkmens as early as the 16th century; by the 18th century almost all trade between Europe and Central Asia passed through Turkmenistan. Local tribes were used diplomatically by the Persians, Russians, and British as part of the Great Game of the 18th and 19th centuries.

Russia sent troops into Turkmenistan in 1865 in an effort to consolidate the Tsarist Empire in Central Asia, using the claim that they were freeing Russian citizens from slavery as justification. In 1881, fighting between the Russian troops and Turkmen climaxed with a massacre of 7,000 Turkmen at the desert fortress of Gokdepe. An additional 8,000 Turkmen were killed while trying to flee across the desert. The area came under Russian control by 1885, and in 1894 the tsarist regime incorporated Turkmenistan into the Russian Empire, calling it the Transcaspian District.

Turkmen joined the uprising of 1916 when the tsar attempted to draft Central Asians into work battalions. It remained in general rebellion throughout the period of the revolution and civil war. Muslim and nationalist opposition, whom the Russians called basmachi, resisted the Bolsheviks until 1924, when the area was made part of the Trans-Caspian Republic. In 1925, the present-day territory became a Soviet Socialist Republic.

Throughout the Soviet period, Turkmenistan was the poorest and least assimilated of the republics. In 1985, longtime Communist Party boss M. Gapurov was fired by then-General Secretary of the Communist Party of the Soviet Union Mikhail Gorbachev, who picked Sapamurat Niyazov as new republic head. On 27 October 1990, Niyazov received 98.3% of the popular vote in an uncontested election to the new post of president of Turkmenistan. Turkmenistan declared independence on 27 October 1991. After independence, Niyazov won another uncontested presidential election in June 1992 with 99.95% of the vote. In a referendum in January 1994, he received the support of 99.99% of the vote for extending his term until 2002. An elaborate cult of personality grew up around Niyazov, who came to prefer the title "Turkmenbashi," or "chief of all Turkmen." Niyazov was president, supreme commander of the armed forces, first secretary of the Democratic Party of Turkmenistan, head of the quasi-legislative Khalk Maslakhaty (People's Council), and chairman of the Cabinet of Ministers and the National Security Council. Changes to the constitution were introduced in late December 1999 during a joint meeting of the Mejlis (legislature), the Khalk Maslakhaty, and Niyazov's National Revival Movement, to include naming Niyazov president for life. Niyazov remained in power from then until his death in December 2006.

Following the 11 September 2001 terrorist attacks on the United States, Turkmenistan offered to aid the US-coalition in its military and humanitarian campaign in Afghanistan. On 25 November 2002, an assassination attempt was made on Niyazov. Following the attack on president's motorcade, the Niyazov government began a wide investigation and 61 people were arrested in connection with the assassination plot. Turkmenistan's National Assembly granted powers to the Supreme Court to administer "special punishment" to people found guilty of involvement in the plot. The resolution permits the Supreme Court to hand out life sentences to those convicted, with no possibility of amnesty, pardon, early release, or change of prison. Former foreign minister Boris Shikhmuradov was sentenced to life in prison for his involvement. By 2003, more than 30 people had been given lengthy sentences by Turkmen courts, including at least three life sentences amid reports of torture and coerced confessions. The US State Department expressed concern with Turkmenistan's conduct in the investigations into the assassination plot, stating that while the United States recognized the government's right to apprehend those involved, the US government could not condone actions that violated international practice. The United States claimed the Turkmen government conducted summary trials of alleged suspects without due process of law, and cited credible reports of torture and abuse of suspects.

In January 2003, the Turkmen government announced parliamentary elections would be held on 6 April, nearly two years ahead of schedule (elections had been scheduled for December 2004) for the unicameral People's Council or Halk Maslahaty. There was no election campaign. The state media did not provide information about the candidates, all of whom were nominated by the presidential administration. All candidates at the elections of April 2003 belonged to Niyazov's party, or the Democratic Party of Turkmenistan (DPT). The 2004 elections for the unicameral Parliament or Mejlis, which consists of 50 seats, were also all won by the DPT.

In May 2005, Deputy Prime Minister Elly Kurbanmuradov was fired. He had been a senior official in charge of the energy sector. He was sentenced to 25 years in prison on corruption and other charges. That July, Rejep Saparov was fired as head of the presidential administration. He was sentenced to 20 years in prison for corruption. In September 2006, Radio Liberty journalist and human rights activist Ogulsapar Muradova died in prison. Government authorities declared her death was from natural causes, but her family suspected foul play.

Niyazov died of heart failure at the age of 66 on 21 December 2006. Under the constitution, the chairman of the People's Council should have been named president. However, the chairman Ovezgeldy Atayev became the subject of a criminal investigation shortly after Niyazov's death, and Deputy Prime Minister Gurbanguly Berdymukhammedov was named interim leader. Many international observers likened the succession to a coup. On 11 February 2007, presidential elections were held. Six candidates were allowed to run for office. Berdymukhammedov was declared the victor.

Berdymukhammedov once served as Niyazov's personal dentist. He became Turkmenistan's health minister in 1997 and was elevated to the position of deputy prime minister in 2001. Since 2007, Berdymukhammedov has continued to rule in the authoritarian style of his predecessor, but has introduced some reforms. In April 2008 Berdymukhammedov abolished the calendar set in place by his predecessor, Niyazov, and officially instituted the return to the Gregorian calendar used most widely throughout the world. Niyazov had renamed months and days of the calendar after himself and his family members. Berdymukhammedov also eased restrictions on Internet access and restored pensions to more than 100,000 elderly citizens that had been cut by Niyazov. In 2011, he ended the practice of using a spiritual guide Niyazov had composed called the *Ruhnama* in school graduation exams, replacing it with courses on computer science. At the same time, Berdymukhammedov has replaced some of the personality cult of his successor with his own. A new mosque was named after him in 2009, and he has placed his own writings in Turkmenistan bookshops.

At the end of 2011, the government continued to hold control over all media, by monitoring news services, dictating editorial policies, and operating all printing presses. The political system remained authoritarian. Although President Berdymukhammedov had shown some willingness to undertake minor reforms, little was expected to change.

13 GOVERNMENT

Turkmenistan's constitution, enacted in May 1992, declares the country to be a secular democracy and presidential republic. In reality, Turkmenistan operated as an authoritarian state, at the start of 2012. The president served as both chief of state and the head of the government. The president appointed a prime minister and cabinet. The economy was centrally planned, and presidential edicts had the force of law. All judges and local officials also were appointed by the president.

Turkmenistan was ruled by Saparmurat Niyazov in its final years as a Soviet republic from 1985–91. Niyazov was designated President for Life in 1999 and continued to rule the country until his death on 21 December 2006. The People's Council (Halk Maslahaty) decided 10 days after the death that his successor would be chosen in a public election 11 February 2007. Former Deputy Prime Minister Gurbanguly Berdymukhammedov emerged as the winner of a six-person race. International observers deemed the election as flawed.

A new constitution was adopted on 28 September 2008, which called for elections for the president to be held every five years, with elections scheduled to take place in February 2012. The new constitution eliminated the 2,507-member People's Council (Halk Maslahaty) that had held mixed executive and legislative powers. It was replaced with a stronger and bigger Meijlis (parliament) . The new Meijlis consisted of 125 members who were elected by popular vote to five-year terms. Elections took place on 26 September 2008 and were scheduled for December 2013. All candidates were required to have presidential approval to run for office.

The Meijlis under Niyazov's rule routinely supported presidential decrees and had little legislative initiative.

14 POLITICAL PARTIES

There was no legal political opposition in Turkmenistan as of December 2011. The only legally registered party was the Democratic Party of Turkmenistan, which had been the Communist Party until September 1991. A 2007 paper by the Strategic Studies Institute reported that Niyazov's policies had effectively destroyed civil society in Turkmenistan and suppressed opposition through imprisonment or exile.

All of the candidates who ran in the 2007 presidential election were from the Democratic Party of Turkmenistan. Gurbanguly Berdymukhammedov won with 89.23% of the vote. Five other candidates contested the election; each of them won less than 4% of the vote. Electoral officials in Turkmenistan reported that 95% of voters cast ballots in the election. Western observers described the vote as fundamentally flawed.

All elected members of the Meijlis must belong to either the Democratic Party of Turkmenistan or the National Revival Movement, a political bloc that Niyazov created in 1994 to unite cultural, religious, and public groups. Candidates also must be preapproved by the president.

A few small opposition movements were in existence abroad, including the National Democratic Movement of Turkmenistan, the Republican Party of Turkmenistan, and the Watan (Fatherland) Party.

In February 2010, Berdymukhammedov announced that new political parties might be welcome in the country, but later said such a development was unlikely to occur soon.

15 LOCAL GOVERNMENT

There are five large regional subdivisions, called velayets. Beneath these are shekhers, then etraps, then ovs. Velayets, shekhers, and etraps have executives called vekils who are appointed and dismissed by the president. In addition, each administrative subunit has an elected assembly called a gengeshchi, the chairman of which is an archyn.

The clan system is still said to be very strong in Turkmenistan, and the velayets reflect distribution of the five major clans, whose totems are represented in the state flag.

16 JUDICIAL SYSTEM

The judicial system follows a Supreme Court model. All judges are appointed by the president and can be dismissed at the president's will.

Authorities often deny due process to defendants, provide no jury trials, and refuse to allow defendants or their attorneys to view government evidence.

There are 61 district and city courts and six provincial courts (including one for the capital city of Ashgabat) in addition to the Supreme Court. A supreme economic court hears cases involving disputes between business enterprises and ministries. Military courts were abolished in 1997 and cases involving the armed forces are now tried in civilian courts. Decisions of lower courts are appealable to higher courts.

The constitution declares the establishment of an independent judiciary. In practice, the president's role in selecting and dismissing judges compromises judicial independence. The president appoints all judges for a term of five years, without legislative review, except for the chairman of the Supreme Court.

17 ARMED FORCES

The International Institute for Strategic Studies reports that armed forces in Turkmenistan totaled 22,000 members in 2011. The force is comprised of 18,500 from the army, 500 from the navy, and 3,000 members of the air force. Armed forces represent 0.9% of the labor force in Turkmenistan. Defense spending totaled $1.3 billion and accounted for 3.4% of gross domestic product (GDP).

18 INTERNATIONAL COOPERATION

Turkmenistan joined the UN on 2 March 1992, and its declaration of "permanent neutrality" was formally recognized by the UN in 1995. The government has forged commercial relations with the United States, Turkey, Russia, Iran, and China. Turkmenistan also had established cross-border trade relationships with Afghanistan, which ended on 11 September 2001 following the terrorist attacks on the United States.

Turkmenistan, as of 2010, was a member of the Organization for Security and Cooperation in Europe, the International Monetary Fund, Organization of the Islamic Conference, and the European Bank for Reconstruction and Development. It held associate membership status in the Commonwealth of Independent States, and it initiated a Partnership and Cooperation Agreement with the EU in May 1998, which was not in force as of 2011.

Turkmenistan's relationships with its neighboring countries have been tense, and disputes over water supplies, environmental issues, drug trafficking, organized crime, and cross-border migration occurred sporadically in the country's first two decades of independence. President Berdymukhammedov has worked to improve regional relations since becoming president in 2007, both through the hosting of regional leaders and through travels to their respective countries.

Turkmenistan resolved a boundary dispute with Kazakhstan in 2001. In 2004, it settled a boundary dispute with Uzbekistan, signed an agreement on water resources for cotton production, and established a declaration of friendship between the two countries' presidents.

An ongoing dispute over the allocation of seawaters and seabed in the Caspian Sea remained stalled at the end of 2011 between Turkmenistan, Kazakhstan, Iran, and Azerbaijan. According to the CIA, the lack of resolution lay in Turkmenistan's indecision over how to allocate the resources. In addition, a dispute over how to divide the seabed and oilfields in the Caspian Sea with Azerbaijan remained unresolved. Turkmenistan had announced in July 2009 that it would take the dispute to international arbitration, which Azerbaijan did not agree to. The dispute with Azerbaijan dates back to October 2001 when Azerbaijan announced the planned trans-Caspian gas pipeline would not be realized. It had discovered its own huge gas reserves in Shahdeniz, and subsequently demanded a share of the exports to the amount of half of the trans-Caspian pipeline's capacity. Turkmenistan regarded such demands as contrary to its interests. In July 2002, an Azerbaijani tanker exploded in the Turkmen port of Turkmenbashi, killing six Azeri sailors. Some blamed the Turkmen government for the incident.

Turkmenistan was part of the US Caspian Basin Energy Initiative in the 1990s, which involved the building of a pipeline under the Caspian Sea to export Turkmen gas to Turkey. The initiative aimed to facilitate negotiations between businesses and the governments of Turkmenistan, Georgia, Azerbaijan, and Turkey. Turkmenistan removed itself from the talks in 2000 by demanding billion-dollar "pre-financing" of the project. Berdymukhammedov, however, rekindled the possibility of building the pipeline in the future during a May 2007 summit with the presidents of Russia and Kazakhstan.

In August 2009, Turkmenistan announced plans to increase its natural gas export to Iran to 14 billion cubic meters (bcm) per year, up from its current export of 8 bcm. The plan came at a time when a new Turkmenistan-Iran natural gas pipeline neared completion. In addition to growing trade ties with Iran, Turkmenistan is also interested in cultural ties with the approximately one million Turkmen residing in Iran. Russian military and border troops assisted Turkmenistan until it built up its own forces, and Russia's presence has been used to counter Uzbek policies in the region. In 1993, Russia and Turkmenistan agreed that Russian border guards would work with Turkmen border guards under Turkmen command at borders with Iran and Afghanistan. In 1999, Turkmenistan canceled this agreement, and the last of Russia's 1,000 border troops in Turkmenistan left in late 1999.

In February 2011, officials from the European Union (EU) visited Turkmenistan, where they met with Berdymukhammedov to discuss the country's relations with the EU. The European Parliament gave the go-ahead to form closer relations with Turkmenistan. The EU has been criticized for supporting a repressive regime in Turkmenistan, but the country's gas reserves have caused the EU to step up plans to address concerns about human rights. A spokesperson from the EU told reporters that Turkmenistan must honor human rights and pro-democracy clauses of the agreement with the EU.

¹⁹ ECONOMY

The GDP rate of change in Turkmenistan, as of 2010, was 9.2%. Inflation stood at 12%, and unemployment was reported at 6%. Agriculture constituted 8.3% of GDP, based on 2010 estimates, while industry accounted for 21.8% and services 69.9%.

Although agriculture made up a relatively small share of GDP, it employed nearly half of the work force.

Turkmenistan's greatest potential for economic growth lay in its large oil and natural gas reserves, as well as its rich deposits of potassium, sulfur, and salts. However, the country has had difficulty developing these industries because of its slow move away from the command economy practices that dominated the Soviet system of government. A lack of strong export routes and a dispute between nations bordering the Caspian Sea over the legal status of offshore oil also have hindered development. At the end of 2011, Turkmenistan remained one of the poorest and least developed countries that was once part of the Soviet Union.

Turkmenistan's transition from a command economy to a free market economy was initially cushioned by its relatively low level of development, as well as by the central government's plans for a gradual reform over a 10-year period with the state continuing to play strong directive and protective roles in the economy. Even in the first decade of the 21st century, the government continued to rely upon cotton and gas exports to sustain its economy. However, mismanagement and poor irrigation methods through the first decade of the 21st century had led to a substantial decline in cotton production as of 2011.

Government-owned enterprises dominated the economy in 2011 and controlled industrial production in hydrocarbons, transportation, refining, electricity generation and distribution, chemicals, rail and air transport, and construction. In addition, the government owned and tightly controlled the country's educational, health care, and media enterprises. The government also was heavily involved in agriculture, food processing, textiles, communications, trade, and services. Although President Berdymukhammedov promised to open up the economy and encourage privatization following his election in 2007, little progress had been made as of 2011. The private sector's share of the economy was less than 25% and concentrated in retail trade. Private ownership of land was prohibited as well. The slow pace of privatization has meant that much of the economy has not been exposed to market disciplines, and it remained subject to the inefficiencies and distortions inherent in central controls. Although evidence suggests that living standards remain low and that structural development has been impeded, assessment is difficult because the government has treated economic statistics like state secrets.

Like most of the former Soviet republics, Turkmenistan's economy was devastated by the break-up of the former socialist state. Independence in 1991 came with a 90% increase in retail prices in 1991 and an 800% increase in 1992. Industrial output fell while government investments in agriculture and transportation spurred growth in those sectors. The government also offered large subsidies, wages, and family allowances, and it reinstated price controls to ease the impact of rising prices. It also introduced its own currency in November 1993. In the same month, Russia, on whose Gazprom pipelines Turkmenistan relied to take its natural gas to market, cut Turkmenistan's access to the hard currency markets of Western Europe, diverting its competitor's gas instead to the cash-strapped markets of Ukraine and the former Soviet republics of the Transcaucasus. The result was one of the worst bouts of hyperinflation experienced by one of the newly independent states. The manat, introduced at two to a dollar, was at 125 to the dollar before the end of 1994; unofficial rates were often three times as high. In November 1995, with inflation at over 1000% for the year and the Turkmeni government threatening to cut off gas to its late paying customers, an agreement was reached with Russia for the creation of a joint stock company TurkmanRosGaz (TRAO)-51% Turkmen, 44% Gazprom, and 5% Itera International Energy Corp. (US)-whereby Gazprom would purchase and transport all the gas that Turkmenistan could sell to Ukraine and the Transcaucasus countries. A poor cotton harvest in 1996 and substantial gas debts from Azerbaijan, Kazakhstan, and Ukraine kept inflation at 992% and resulted in GDP declines. By 1997, the government faced an external debt of $1.77 billion.

Although not officially under an IMF program, the government chose to follow IMF recommendations about controlling credit expansion, reducing budget deficits, and liberalizing foreign exchange. These changes helped bring inflation down from 1997 to 2001.

From 1998 to 2005, Turkmenistan suffered from a lack of adequate export routes for its natural gas and from its external debt burden. Nevertheless, due to high international oil and natural gas prices over the 2003 to 2005 period, Turkmenistan registered a 20–30% rise in exports per year. In 2005, the IMF estimated Turkmenistan's GDP growth rate at 7%. The CIA estimated the unemployment rate in 2004 to be 60% and the percentage of people living below the poverty line to be 30% in 2004.

Turkmenistan's main natural gas export pipeline initially ran through Russia, which closely controlled the volume, price, and destination. The government began to seek alternatives in the mid-1990s. Turkmenistan in December 1997 opened a 200-km (125-mi) gas pipeline to connect with the Iranian pipeline system. On 18 November 1999, Turkmenistan, Azerbaijan, Georgia, and Turkey signed a declaration on a trans-Caspian and trans-Caucasus gas pipeline territory that would deliver Turkmen gas to Turkey. In 2001 agreement was reached on a route whereby Turkmenistan gas could be delivered to Armenia. On 14 May 2001 Turkmenistan and Ukraine reached an agreement for the supply of natural gas between 2002 and 2006 in exchange for 60% payment in cash and the rest in participation in 20 construction and industrial projects in Turkmenistan worth $412 million. In May 2002, Turkmenistan led the reopening of discussions on the Trans-Afghan pipeline, and in December 2002, Turkmenistan, Afghanistan, and Pakistan signed an agreement to build a 1,500-km (932-mi) pipeline to carry gas from Turkmenistan's Dauletabad-Donmez field through Afghanistan to Pakistan. In 2002, a $190 million, 39-km (24-mi) Korpedzhe Kurt-Kui pipeline connecting Turkmenistan to the Iranian gas pipeline system also was completed.

By an agreement reached with Russia in 1998, Turkmenistan was supposed to export 20 billion cu m (706 billion cu ft) of natural gas to Russia by 2000 and increase this figure by 10 billion cu m (353 billion cu ft) per year until a level of 50–60 billion cu m (1,765–2,118 billion cu ft) was reached in 2004 or 2005.

Russia signed a 25-year contract in 2003 and China signed a 30-year contract in 2006 for natural gas sales from Turkmenistan. In 2010, Turkmenistan was the 44th largest producer of oil and 24th largest producer of natural gas in the world. The Economist Intelligence Unit forecast in December 2011 that real GDP would grow 6% in 2012 and 7% in 2013 with increases in natural gas exports.

20 INCOME

The CIA estimated that in 2011 the GDP of Turkmenistan was $41.5 billion. The CIA defines GDP as the value of all final goods and services produced within a nation in a given year and computed on the basis of purchasing power parity (PPP) rather than value as measured on the basis of the rate of the exchange based on current dollars. The per capita GDP was estimated at $7,500. The annual growth rate of GDP was 9.9%. The average inflation rate was 15%. It was estimated that agriculture accounted for 7.8% of GDP, industry 24.1%, and services 68.1%.

The World Bank reports that in 2009, household consumption in Turkmenistan totaled $9.8 billion or about $1,952 per capita, measured in current US dollars rather than PPP.

The CIA estimated that in 2004 about 30% of the population subsisted on an income below the poverty line established by Turkmenistan's government.

21 LABOR

In 2008, Turkmenistan had a total labor force of 2.3 million people. The division of labor, according to CIA estimates in 2004 was: 48.2% were employed in agriculture, 14% in industry, and 37.8% in the service sector.

The CIA reported in 2011 that the unemployment rate in Turkmenistan was 60%, based on a 2004 estimate. The US State Department reported in its 2011 guide to Doing Business in Turkmenistan that the government did not acknowledge rises in unemployment and put the rate at about 50%.

The only union allowed to exist was the Center for Professional Union, an umbrella organization that was led by a presidential appointee. The organization included professional unions in medicine, construction, banking, accounting, economics, entrepreneurship, and lease holding. None of these organizations had an independent voice.

Rights to bargain collectively were not protected by law.

The minimum monthly wage for public sector employment was $116. The US State Department's 2010 Human Rights Report on Turkmenistan noted that this amount was not sufficient to provide for basic needs of workers and their families.

The standard workweek was 40 hours with weekends off, but many employees were required to work 10-hour days or to add a sixth day without compensation. Laws prohibiting children from working in cotton production were generally enforced.

22 AGRICULTURE

Roughly 5% of the total land is farmed, and the country's major crops include cotton and grain. Cereal production in 2009 amounted to 3.2 million tons, fruit production 390,000 tons, and vegetable production 936,500 tons.

Almost 80% of the sown agricultural land is under irrigation. Yields are relatively low because of poor water usage, desalinity, inefficient irrigation, and overdevelopment of cotton cultivation.

Cotton is the main crop, with production on the Mary and Tejen oases and along the Amu Darya. The US State Department estimated the 2009 harvest of cotton at 823,000 tons, which made Turkmenistan the second-largest cotton producer in the former Soviet Union after Uzbekistan. Much of the cotton produced is exported. The crop yield has declined steadily since 1991 because of poor irrigation and management practices.

Wheat also is cultivated, primarily for domestic consumption. Citrus fruit, dates, figs, grapes, pomegranates, olives, and sugarcane are grown in irrigated groves and fields in the southwest. Sesame, pistachios, and oilseeds are other important export crops.

Agriculture accounted for 7.8% of GDP based on 2011 estimates, and 48.2% of the labor force according to 2004 estimates.

23 ANIMAL HUSBANDRY

The UN Food and Agriculture Organization (FAO) reported that Turkmenistan dedicated 30.7 million hectares (75.9 million acres) to permanent pasture or meadow in 2009. During that year, the country tended 14.6 million chickens, 2.2 million head of cattle, and 29,800 pigs. The production from these animals amounted to 97,558 tons of beef and veal, 293 tons of pork, 12,537 tons of poultry, 31,471 tons of eggs, and 698,428 tons of milk. Turkmenistan also produced 14,778 tons of cattle hide and 37,500 tons of raw wool.

An inability to raise sufficient fodder has impeded livestock development in the past. However, the US State Department reported in its 2011 guide to Doing Business in Turkmenistan that meat and dairy production has increased. Mutton, lamb, beef, pork, and poultry were raised in the country, and the government offered loans and tax benefits to poultry producers. Despite these increases, the country relies on imports from Ukraine, Belarus, Kazakhstan, Iran, Turkey, Azerbaijan, India, and Pakistan.

Akhaltekin horses, raised at the Akhaltekin oasis, are a breed that dates to the 3rd century. Bucephalus, the favorite horse of Alexander the Great, was Akhaltekin. In 1986, an Akhaltekin horse, Dancing Brave, was sold for $50 million. Akhaltekins have a large share of the racehorse breeding market worldwide, and they are depicted on Turkmenistan's national emblem.

24 FISHING

In 2008 the annual capture totaled 15,000 tons according to the UN Food and Agriculture Organization.

The fisheries sector was relatively small in Turkmenistan but has been regarded by the government as a potential source of future food and export value. Efforts were being made in 2011 to preserve the sturgeon population in the Caspian Sea, and a Fishing Industry of Turkmenistan International Exhibition took place in 2008 in Ashgabat.

25 FORESTRY

Approximately 9% of Turkmenistan is covered by forest. The value of all forest products, including roundwood, totaled $501,000. Arid conditions and the expansive Kara Kum desert inhibit the development of commercial forestry. Forestry imports amounted to $3.88 million in 2010.

26 MINING

Turkmenistan had the world's third-largest reserves of sulfur in 2009, and was a leading producer of natural gas. Its top industries in 2009 were the production of natural gas, oil, and petroleum products.

In 2009 estimated outputs included: sulfur (mined at the Gaurdak complex, in the Gora deposit), 9,000 metric tons; gypsum, 100,000 metric tons; sodium sulfate (from an extensive mirabilite site in the Gararbogazköl), 60,000 metric tons; iodine, 270,000 metric tons; and nitrogen (content of ammonia), 270,000 metric tons. Turkmenistan also produced bentonite, bentonite powder, bischofite, cement, and a majority of the former Soviet Union's supply of epsomite, ferrous bromide, lime, and salt (north of Nebitdag).

Ozocerite, iodine, and bromine were found on the Cheleken Peninsula and in Vyshka, Stantsiya. The Garabogaz Aylagy lagoon, off the Caspian Sea, was one of the world's largest sources of raw materials for the chemical industry. Commercial interest in the salts of the region began at the end of the 19th century, and it supplied all of the FSU's supply of medicinal Glauber's salt. Other mineral deposits included potassium and polymetallic ores.

27 ENERGY AND POWER

The World Bank reported in 2008 that Turkmenistan produced 15 billion kWh of electricity and consumed 11.5 billion kWh, or 2,294 kWh per capita.

Turkmenistan in 2010 had nine gas-fired power stations and one hydroelectric station. Its total existing generation capacity was estimated at 4,100 megawatts. While much of the electricity produced was used domestically, approximately 1.6 billion kWh were exported to Afghanistan, Iran, and Turkey in 2010.

Per capita oil consumption was 3,730 kg. Oil production totaled 178,188 barrels of oil a day in 2008. The CIA estimated oil production in 2010 to be 202,400 barrels per day. As of 1 January 2011, Turkmenistan was estimated to have 600 million bbl in proven reserves.

Natural gas production was estimated at 38.1 billion cu m in 2009. As of 1 January 2011, Turkmenistan's proven natural gas reserves were estimated at 7.504 trillion cu m.

28 INDUSTRY

The CIA estimated Turkmenistan's industrial production growth rate at 7.3% in 2010. The major industries were natural gas, oil, petroleum products, textiles, and food processing.

The hydrocarbons sector made up the country's largest industry in 2010, and the government was making substantial investments in petroleum refining and processing facilities. There were two oil refineries in the country: one in Turkmenbashy had a refining capacity of 6 million tons a year and plans were underway to increase the capacity to 9 million tons. The other refinery was at Seydi . Through the refineries, Turkmenistan produces unleaded gasoline, petroleum coke, laundry detergents, and hydro-treated diesel and lubrication oils. It also was producing 83,000 tons of propane and polypropylene annually in 2010 and 412,000 tons of LPG a year. Turkmenistan's largest natural gas fields were at Yoloten, Osman, and Yashlar.

The US State Department reported in its 2011 guide to Doing Business in Turkmenistan that the country had nine chemical plants producing 700,000 tons annually of nitrogen and phosphorous fertilizers. Sulfuric and nitric acids, iodine, bromine, and mineral salts also were being made. In 2011, construction was underway on a new urea plant with a capacity of 640,000 tons per year and an ammonia plant with a production capacity of 400,000 tons a year.

Textile production began to develop in the early 1990s through joint ventures with Turkish companies. In 2011, there were more than 20 textile companies operating in Turkmenistan, and total investment exceeded $1 billion, with 20% direct investment from Turkish partners. About 90% of the textile products were exported. Turkmen carpets are known worldwide for their quality and are a source of national pride: ornaments of Turkmen carpets are components of the national flag and the national emblem of Turkmenistan. They are sometimes erroneously identified in Western markets by the label "Bukhara," which is actually the Uzbekistan city where the carpets are sold. Turkmen carpets feature deep red wool, with stylized geometric patterns.

The State Food Industry Association controlled 125 food processing plants that produced cotton seed oil, meat and dairy products, and wine. Fruits, vegetables, and grains also were processed.

After growing at an average rate of 2.3% during the 1980s, the industrial sector declined after the breakup of the Soviet Union. Industrial output declined by 15% in 1992, and fell 25% in 1994 when it became clear that Turkmenistan's gas exports were going to be diverted from hard currency markets, and therefore from external sources of capital finance. After a further decline of 7% in 1995, gross industrial output reportedly surged ahead 17.9% in 1996, despite a 7.7% decline in the wider economy, as agreements were reached for gas supplies to Ukraine and the Trans-Caucasus. However, in 1997 deepening financial problems stemming from Russia's cutoff of Turkmenistan's access to its Gazprom lines over a price dispute, arrears in payments from its ex-Soviet customers, and declines in cotton processing helped to produce a fall in industrial production of 29.3%. From this low point, however, industrial output expanded consistently through 2011.

Principal Trading Partners – Turkmenistan (2010)				
(In millions of US dollars)				
Country	Total	Exports	Imports	Balance
World	8,961.4	3,366.6	5,594.8	-2,228.2
Turkey	1,605.0	351.2	1,253.8	-902.6
China	1,523.8	949.6	574.3	375.3
Russia	925.6	134.6	791.1	-656.5
United Arab Emirates	719.5	239.6	479.9	-240.4
Germany	439.4	82.4	357.0	-274.6
Iran	394.1	159.5	234.7	-75.2
Italy	281.1	177.9	103.2	74.7
Ukraine	258.4	28.6	229.8	-201.3
Azerbaijan	233.4	12.7	220.8	-208.1
Afghanistan	215.3	215.3	…	215.3

(…) data not available or not significant.

(n.s.) not specified.

SOURCE: *2011 Direction of Trade Statistics Yearbook*, New York: United Nations, 2011.

29 SCIENCE AND TECHNOLOGY

The World Bank reported in 2009 that there were no patent applications in science and technology in Turkmenistan. Research was being carried out at the Turkmensuvylymtaslama Institute, the Institute of Chemistry, the Research Institute of the Grain Cultures, the State Institute of Cultural Heritage, the National Institute of Deserts, Flora and Fauna, the Strategic Planning and Economic Development Institute, and the Turkmenistan Scientific-Clinical Center of Oncology.

30 DOMESTIC TRADE

Like the rest of the Turkmenistan economy, much of the country's retail and wholesale sector remain under the control of the central government. However, informal markets also operate in the country, at which a wide variety of consumer goods, including food, clothing and household wares, may be purchased. In 1994, the government established the State Commodity and Raw Materials Exchange as a means to regulate all trade and to restrict foreign competitors from controlling the market during the economic transition to a free market economy.

In 2011, Coca-Cola was the only franchise in Turkmenistan.

The government required food items to be labeled in Turkmen and/or Russia. However, labeling in Turkish, Persian, and Arabic also was common. Most home appliances and electronics were labeled in English.

The workweek is from 9 a.m. to 6 p.m., Monday to Saturday.

31 FOREIGN TRADE

Turkmenistan imported $4.888 billion worth of goods and services in 2008, while exporting $9.672 billion worth of goods and services. Major import partners in 2009 were Turkey, 16.1%; Russia, 15.9%; China, 15.6%; Germany, 6.1%; the United Arab Emirates, 5.7%; Ukraine, 5.5%; the United States, 5.3%; and France, 4.2%. Major imported items were machinery and equipment, chemicals, and food stuffs.

Its major export partners were Ukraine, 22.2%; Turkey, 10.1%; Hungary, 6.7%; the United Arab Emirates, 6.2%; Poland, 6.1%; Af-

ghanistan, 5.8%; and Iran, 5.2%. Major export items were natural gas, crude oil, petroleum products, textiles, and cotton fiber.

Turkmenistan is heavily dependent on imports for industrial equipment, industrial raw materials, and a number of basic food items such as grain, milk and dairy products, potatoes, and sugar. The country also has invested in its civil aviation through numerous aircraft purchases from the US-based Boeing Co. in 2009–11.

The US State Department's 2011 guide to Doing Business in Turkmenistan noted that slow, bureaucratic customs procedures have inhibited trade, as have visa regime and taxation policies. A 1 June 2004 Trade and Investment Framework Agreement between Turkmenistan, the US, Kazakhstan, Tajikistan, Kyrgyzstan, and Uzbekistan has sought to create a regional forum for improving the investment climate and trade relationships within Central Asia.

Turkmenistan also has established 10 free economic zones under a 1993 law that forbids nationalization of businesses operating in the zones and discrimination against foreign investors. However, the government has continued to interfere in the business decisions of those enterprises, which has stifled foreign participation.

32 BALANCE OF PAYMENTS

The value of Turkmenistan's exports was estimated at $10.55 billion in 2010 compared with $8.946 billion in 2009, and imports were estimated at $8.277 billion in 2010 compared with $8.071 billion in 2009. The current account balance was estimated at -$1.105 billion in 2010 compared to -$2.808 billion in 2009.

Reserves of foreign exchange and gold were estimated at $17.6 billion as of 31 December 2010 compared with $17.06 billion as of 31 December 2009.

33 BANKING AND SECURITIES

The State Central Bank of Turkmenistan (SCBT) is charged with issuing currency and executing a monetary policy, and it represents the top tier of a two-tiered banking system. Commercial banks are responsible for collection, settlement, and handling of assets for clients and other banks. The State Bank for Foreign Economic Activities has been established to provide hard currency credits for foreign economic activities.

Money laundering became a growing problem in the first decade of the 2000s. In 2010, Turkmenistan formed a Financial Intelligence Unit under the Ministry of Finance to deter money laundering and to fight the financing of terrorism. It also joined the Eurasian Group and Financial Action Task Force as part of an effort to improve its compliance with international standards. The president of Turkmenistan signed a decree in July 2010 that ordered all Turkmen banks to adhere to International Finance Reporting Standards by 1 January 2011.

The financial system in Turkmenistan remained underdeveloped as of 2012. The largest state banks were State Bank for Foreign Economic Relations (Vnesheconombank), Dayhanbank, Turkmenbashy Bank, Turkmenistan Bank, Haik Bank, and President Bank. Two smaller state banks—Senagat and Garagum—provided general banking services. Five foreign commercial banks were in operation: a joint Turkmen-Turkish bank, a National Bank of Pakistan branch, the German Deutsche and Commerz banks, and a Saderat Bank of Iran branch.

Turkmenistan has no securities exchange, although a 1993 law on securities and stock exchanges outlines a procedure for issuing, selling, and circulating securities.

34INSURANCE

The State Insurance Organization of Turkmenistan offered a wide range of insurances. As of 2011, there was no private insurance market in the country.

35PUBLIC FINANCE

In 2010 the budget of Turkmenistan included $1.97 billion in public revenue and $1.878 billion in public expenditures. The budget surplus amounted to 3% of GDP. In total $511.3 million of the debt was held by foreign entities.

Although still a centrally planned economy, Turkmenistan has slowly begun to decrease the size of the public sector's influence. Among the steps it has taken are a drive toward a unified market-based exchange rate, the allocation of government credits by auction, and stricter limits on budget deficits.

36TAXATION

A new tax code was adopted in 2005, and subsequently amended in 2006, 2007, and 2008. The code as of 2011 set the value added tax rate at 15% and charged an income tax of 8% on joint ventures as well as a 20% income tax to wholly owned foreign companies and state-owned enterprises. Foreign investors and their subcontractors also pay a social welfare tax that amounts to 20% of the local staff payroll. The government also taxes dividends at 15% and has set a personal income tax rate of 10%.

Domestic private companies are exempt from paying the value added tax and property taxes, and they are charged an income tax of 2%. Excise taxes were raised in August 2006 on imported beer (50%) and wine (100%), while taxes on domestically produced beer and hard liquor have remained at 10% for beer and 15% to 40% for hard liquor.

A 2008 Petroleum Production Sharing Agreement subjected companies working in the oil and gas sector to a 20% income tax and royalties of 1% to 15% depending on the level of production. Employees and subcontractors to the companies who are part of this agreement pay a personal income tax of 10%.

Turkish textile factories that used Turkmenistani materials and labor have enjoyed tax breaks.

37CUSTOMS AND DUTIES

Turkmenistan's value added tax was 15% in 2011. Although the country does not apply tariffs on imported goods, it does levy customs duties and higher excise taxes on items that pose significant barriers to trade. In 2011, there was a customs duty on 49 types of imported merchandise, with the rates ranging from 5% to 100%. Importers also were charged administrative fees to the Customs Service. These fees included a 0.2% customs fee payment and a charge of $1.76 for every hour spent by a customs official inspecting imported goods.

Excise taxes were applied to imported beer, wine, spirits, tobacco products, jewelry, and automobiles.

Twenty export items also were subject to customs duties, as of 2011. State-owned enterprises often were exempted from paying these duties.

Turkmenistan established the Awaza Tourist Zone to promote tourism development along the Caspian Sea coast in May 2007. Legislation passed in October 2007 exempted hotel and recreational facilities construction within the zone from the value added tax, as well as catering, accommodation, and other services. It also waived income taxes on those providing accommodation and catering services for the first 15 years.

38FOREIGN INVESTMENT

Foreign direct investment (FDI) in Turkmenistan was a net inflow of $1.36 billion according to World Bank figures published in 2009. FDI represented 6.79% of GDP.

The government of Turkmenistan announced its desire regularly through the independent nation's first 20 years of existence to attract foreign investment. However, tight governmental controls over the economy, a slow pace of reform, and visa restrictions have deterred investors. Nevertheless, the country's political stability and rich natural resources have been seen as attractive incentives. Since independence, Turkmenistan has established bilateral trade agreements with Turkey, China, France, Malaysia, Pakistan, Romania, Slovakia, the UK, Ireland, Egypt, India, Uzbekistan, Iran, Armendia, Georgia, Germany, the Ukraine, and the United Arab Emirates. Negotiations to establish bilateral trade with the US began in 1991 but were suspended in 1994. The EU ministers established a trade agreement with Turkmenistan in July 2009 on the grounds that economic engagement with the country might stimulate political reforms.

Foreign investors have looked primarily to the oil and gas, agricultural, and construction sectors.

Most foreign investment in Turkmenistan in the first two decades of its existence as an independent state was in the oil and gas sector. There are three Production Sharing Agreements for on shore operations: Nebitdag Contractual Territory with Burren Energy UK/ENI; Khazar which is operated jointly between the Turkmennebit state oil concern and Mitro International of Austria; and Bagtyarlyk Contractual Territory operated by the Chinese National Petroleum Corporation. There also are six Production Sharing Agreements for offshore operations that involve Petronas of Malaysia, Dragon Oil of the United Arab Emirates, Buried Hill of Canada, Maersk Oil of Denmark, Wintershall and RWE of Germany, and Itera of Russia.

Turkish and French companies have proposed several billion dollars in construction projects to the Turkmenistan government, and contracts of more than $500 million were signed with contractors from the two nations in late 2009.

According to the US State Department, Turkmenistan received a loan of reportedly $4 billion from the Chinese Development Bank in 2009 as well as a $1 billion loan from the Islamic Development Bank for road and infrastructure projects. It also received smaller loans from the Chinese Export-Import Bank for transportation and communications projects.

A Law on Foreign Investment, which was passed in 1991 and amended in 2008, defines a foreign investor as an entity that owns at least 20% of a company's assets. Despite the protections that the law purports to provide, overseas companies who have invested in Turkmenistan have experienced difficulties. According to the US State Department, litigation between a Western oil and gas company and the government-owned Turkmennebit oil company that began in 1996 was still continuing in 2010. The Western company was awarded $495 million in damages to be paid by the Turkmenistan government. As of 2010, the award had not been paid. In addition, a US telecommunications company has been trying to collect payment from the Ministry of Turkmenistan since 2006 on an outstanding debt.

39 ECONOMIC DEVELOPMENT

Saparmurat Niyazov, the first president of Turkmenistan, envisioned his country as having a high standard of living, a comprehensive welfare program, and industrial development from the invested proceeds of natural gas, oil, and cotton operations – all of which would be state-owned. As of 2011, that vision had not yet been realized. Turkmenistan in 2011 was economically poor, politically isolated, and geographically distant from much of the rest of the world. Nevertheless, some steps were being taken to realize that vision.

The government adopted a National Program for Socio-Economic Development 2011–30 in May 2010. The program called for diversification of the economy, increased market competition, and economic and institutional reforms. It also included a plan to step up privatization of small and medium sized businesses.

According to the US State Department's 2011 guide to Doing Business in Turkmenistan, key economic development priorities were to create natural gas refining facilities to produce polyethylene, polyvinyl chloride, methanol, formaldehyde, amino-formaldehyde resin, synthetic rubber, and paint materials; to increase its power generation capacities to 26 billion kWh by 2020 and 35 billion kWh by 2030; and to increase fertilization production to 5 million tons a year and iodine production to 1,515 tons a year by 2030.

The government economic development program emphasized a need also to attract foreign investment. Turkmenistan hoped to seek joint ventures to make chemicals based on local raw materials and to produce more consumer products.

After becoming president in 2007, Gurbanguly Berdymukhammedov announced a policy of providing "Internet access to every home, school, and kindergarten." In 2007–08, the government began introducing educational software into university and secondary school classrooms while expanding Internet access across the country. As of 2010, there were only 18 public Internet centers in the country. Although the number of subscribers reportedly increased from 5,000 to 75,000, general receptiveness to information technology has been low due to a lack of technical training.

Turkmenistan's relatively well-educated population and natural resources provide a promising foundation for the national economy to prosper. However, the pace at which economic growth and a rise in living standards would occur was seen in 2011 as dependent upon the willingness of the post-Niyazov regime to open the economy, privatize businesses, and enact political reforms.

40 SOCIAL DEVELOPMENT

Turkmenistan's human rights record has been extremely poor since independence through 2011. The US State Department wrote in its 2010 Human Rights Report on Turkmenistan that ar-

bitrary arrests, denials of due process and fair trials, media censorship, and restrictions on travel outside the country were rampant.

A February 2010 survey by the Turkmenistan Independent Lawyers Association and Turkmen Initiative for Human Rights that was cited by the State Department report found that nearly half of all suspects arrested and placed in temporary holding facilities were subjected to abusive treatment and torture. In addition, military hazing was widespread and was believed to have contributed to a sharp increase in military suicides. Prisons were unsanitary, overcrowded, and unsafe, with guards and other inmates engaging in widespread violence.

The government was found to routinely destroy residential units without providing inhabitants with replacement facilities or compensation in favor of urban renewal projects. Physical surveillance, wire-tapping, and electronic eavesdropping were used by security officials, and personal mail was often was intercepted and opened. Although Internet access has expanded, the government monitored e-mail accounts in an effort to identify political dissidents. Travel restrictions were imposed on journalists, and many representatives of the media practiced self-censorship for personal safety.

Academic degrees received abroad were not accepted unless they were obtained through educational programs that the government approved in advance. Foreign grant recipients also were harassed. The government also continued to refuse to register domestic human rights organizations and to deny entry to international human rights representatives.

Women are entitled to equal rights with men under the law, however due to societal constraints the woman's role is primarily that of homemaker and mother. Opportunities for education and careers outside the home were limited. Laws against rape, domestic violence, and marital rape were weak and often not enforced. The US State Department also noted that honor killings were common.

Turkmenistan's social security system has traditionally provided old age, disability, and survivor pensions to employed persons. Social pensions for those not eligible for employment-related pensions, old age benefits, unemployment benefits, workers compensation, and sickness and maternity benefits also were traditionally provided. However, the deteriorating state of Turkmenistan's economy put some of those benefits in limbo in the first decade of the early 21st century. The International Crisis Group stated in a 2007 briefing following the death of President Niyazov that "Niyazov left a country on the verge of a grave humanitarian and socio-economic crisis."

41 HEALTH

According to the CIA, life expectancy in Turkmenistan was 68.8 years in 2012. The country spent 1.9% of its GDP on healthcare, amounting to $77 per person. There were 24 physicians, 45 nurses and midwives, and 41 hospital beds per 10,000 inhabitants. The fertility rate was 2.14, while the infant mortality rate was 41 per 1,000 live births. In 2008 the maternal mortality rate, according to the World Bank, was 77 per 100,000 births. It was estimated that 99% of children were vaccinated against measles. The CIA calculated HIV/AIDS prevalence in Turkmenistan to be less than 0.1% in 2007.

Access to health care grew increasingly limited in the first decade of the 21st century, according to the International Crisis Group. The human rights organization as well as other observers attributed governmental cuts to a decline in revenue that resulted from money from oil and gas exports being placed in off-budget and offshore accounts controlled by the former president Niyazov.

42 HOUSING

Turkmenistan as of 2011 lacked a private commercial real estate industry. The government would finance the construction of new apartments and sell the units to the public. Housing loans were made available at low rates (1–1.5%). All land was owned by the state.

Citizens lacked residence rights, which made them vulnerable to eviction. The government frequently evicted residents of properties slated for demolition in the name of urban renewal. In June 2011, about 50 residents staged a rare protest in Ashgabat to protest the demolition of their homes. Police broke up the protest, and the government claimed that the units had been illegally constructed. Much of the demolition activity was being done to build 12–14 story Western style apartment buildings, hotels, shopping centers, theaters, fountains, and parks.

The Turkmenistan Meijlis began reviewing legislation in 2011 that would privatize housing.

The CIA reported that 83% of the population had access to improved drinking water (2000) and 98% to improved sanitation facilities (2008).

43 EDUCATION

President Gurbanguly Berdymukhammedov announced in 2007 ambitious plans to upgrade Turkmenistan's educational system. According to a 2010 report by the European Training Foundation, the educational system was inherited from the Soviet era. The first president, Sapamurat Niyazov, established a State Program for Implementation of a New Education Policy in 1993 that focused primary and secondary education on the learning of national history and values. A key text in this learning was Niyazov's *Ruhnama* spiritual guide.

Education was compulsory for nine years in the Niyazov era, and students were eligible to pursue higher education after gaining at least two years of work experience. College enrollments were estimated at 2.6% of the population in 2002, according to the report.

UNICEF estimated that Turkmenistan had an adult literacy rate of 100% between 2005 and 2010. UNICEF reported that in 2003–08 primary school attendance was 99% and secondary school attendance 84%.

The European Training Foundation cited poor infrastructure, a lack of teaching and learning materials, and a lack of teaching training opportunities as areas of concern.

Shortly after assuming office in 2007, President Berdymukhammedov raised the compulsory education requirement to 10 years, abolished the 2-year compulsory work rule, and expanded higher education from 3 years to 5 years. He also sought to introduce information technology into classrooms, and replaced the *Ruhnama* with his own authored text as a primary teaching guide.

According to a government website, there were 10 institutions of higher learning in 2011.

44 LIBRARIES AND MUSEUMS

The National Library of Turkmenistan in Ashgabat holds 5.5 million volumes and is the largest in the country. The Republican Scientific and Technical Library of Turkmenistan holds 900,000 volumes and the Turkmen Academy of Sciences, in the capital, holds 2.1 million volumes. Turkmen University has the nation's largest academic library, holding 542,000 volumes.

In early 2005, President Saparmurat Niyazov closed nearly all of the nation's public libraries, with the exception of the National Library and some libraries associated with educational institutions. The president called for these closings claiming that most of the citizens don't read books or visit libraries. About 140 libraries across the country were affected. The libraries reopened on 1 April 2010 following a decree from President Berdymukhammedov.

Museums in Turkmenistan include the National Museum of History and the Carpet Museum, which celebrates the centuries-old craft of carpet weaving.

45 MEDIA

In 2010 the CIA reported that there were 520,000 telephone landlines in Turkmenistan. In addition to landlines, mobile phone subscriptions were 3.2 million. There were 16 FM radio stations, 8 AM radio stations, and 2 shortwave radio stations. Internet users numbered 80,400 citizens in 2009.

Telephone links to other former Soviet republics and Iran are provided by land link or microwave and to other countries through Moscow.

Journalists face severe restrictions on what they can report. Even mild criticism of the president is forbidden. Subscription to foreign magazines or other media is also forbidden. Freedom of assembly is also restricted; there is only one union, the Colleagues Union, and it is government-controlled.

All media is government-controlled. President Berdymukhammedov indicated in July 2010 that some private newspapers might be permitted in the future.

The state-run Turkmentelecom controlled Internet access, and foreign-based opposition websites were blocked as well as YouTube and the blog platform LiveJournal.

Newspapers as of 2011 included the Russian-language *Neytralnyy Turkmenistan*, and five Turkmen-language publications: *Watan, Galkynys, Turkmen Dunyasi, Adalat*, and *Edebiyat we Sungat*. The state-owned Turkmen TV carried the Altyn Asyr channel, and the state-owned Turkmen radio operated four networks. The official news agency was Turkmen State News Service.

46 ORGANIZATIONS

The economic affairs and other concerns of workers are handled by the Chamber of Commerce and Industry and the Federation of Trade Unions of Turkmenistan, respectively. The ruling political party—the Democratic Party of Turkmenistan (formerly the Communist Party)—controls all aspects of Turkmenistan's politics, society and culture. Its organizations of control are the Committee on National Security, Ministry of Internal Affairs, and various trade unions. The trade unions, all controlled by the state, serve to promote government production plans and policies.

The government registered the Society of Guitarists in December 2010. It was the first nongovernmental association to be registered since 2008.

⁴⁷TOURISM, TRAVEL, AND RECREATION

The *Tourism Factbook*, published by the UN World Tourism Organization, reported 8,200 incoming tourists to Turkmenistan in 2007. Of those incoming tourists, there were 4,300 from Europe. There were 1,675 hotel beds available in Turkmenistan, which had an occupancy rate of 19%. The estimated daily cost to visit Ashgabat (Ashkhabad), the capital, was $258. The cost of visiting other cities averaged $165.

The government made tourism a priority after President Niyazov's death. In July 2007, a National Tourist Zone was established in Ayaza along the Caspian Coast with a goal of attracting $4 billion in foreign investment to build hotels, recreational facilities, and entertainment sites. Contracts worth more than $500 million were signed between 2007–10 to improve the infrastructure in Turkenbashy City, which is where the zone is located. These projects included expansions to the airport to support international flights, renovations to water and sewage networks, building a water desalination plant, and constructing an artificial navigable river. Eight foreign companies had announced intentions as of December 2007 to invest nearly $200 million in resort hotels, villas, office buildings, shopping malls, and tennis complexes.

All hotels in Turkmenistan were state-owned, and as of 2011, there were only about 20 hotels in the country. However, the government has given management rights over the country's largest hotel, Oguzkent, to Sofitel, a French company. It also has allowed an Italian company to take management rights over two other hotels.

The State Migration Services controls the movement of foreigners. It requires visitors to register upon entry. Travel to border areas required a special permit.

Turkish Airlines and Lufthansa Airlines offered flights to Ashgabat. Turkmenistan Airlines offered flights to Abu Dhabi, United Arab Emirates; Almaty, Kazakhstan; Amritsar, India; Bangkok; Beijing; Birmingham, England; London; Frankfurt; Istanbul; Minsk, Belarus; Moscow; and New Delhi. There also were some flights by other airlines between Moscow and Ashgabat. From Ashgabat, travelers can fly to Balkanabt, Dashoguz, Mary, Turkenabat, and Turkmenbashy.

⁴⁸FAMOUS PERSONS

Saparmurat A. Niyazov (1940–2006) was the first president of Turkmenistan. His successor was Gurbanguly Berdymukhammedov (b. 1957), who became president in 2007. Representatives of culture and literature of Turkmenistan include Abdulhekin Qulmukam Medoghli, a writer, researcher and political activist who was killed in 1937 during one of Russian leader Joseph Stalin's purges, and the poet and thinker, Maktum Kuli, who first envisioned an independent Turkmenistan.

⁴⁹DEPENDENCIES

Turkmenistan has no territories or colonies.

⁵⁰BIBLIOGRAPHY

Abazov, Rafis. *Historical Dictionary of Turkmenistan.* Lanham, MD: Scarecrow, 2005.

Bramwell, Martyn. *Northern and Western Asia.* Minneapolis: Lerner Publications Company, 2000.

Hiro, Dilip. *Inside Central Asia: A Political and Cultural History of Uzbekistan, Turkmenistan, Kazakhstan, Kyrgyzstan, Tajikistan, Turkey, and Iran.* New York: Overlook Press, 2011.

Kort, Michael. *Central Asian Republics.* New York: Facts on File, 2004.

Seddon, David, ed. *A Political and Economic Dictionary of the Middle East.* Philadelphia: Routledge/Taylor and Francis, 2004.

Turkmenistan Investment and Business Guide: Strategic and Practical Information. Washington, DC: International Business Publications USA, 2012.

TUVALU

CAPITAL: Funafuti

FLAG: The national flag has the Union Jack in the upper quarter nearest the hoist; nine yellow stars on a light blue field are arranged in the same pattern as Tuvalu's nine islands.

ANTHEM: *Tuvalu mo te Atua (Tuvalu for the Almighty)*.

MONETARY UNIT: Both the Australian dollar (AUD) and the Tuvaluan dollar (TVD) of 100 cents are legal tender. There are coins of 1, 2, 5, 10, 20, and 50 Tuvaluan cents; 1 and 5 TVD; and notes of 5, 10, 20, 50, and 100 AUD. TVD1 = US$0.977915 (or US$1 = TVD1.02) as of 2011.

WEIGHTS AND MEASURES: The metric system is in official use.

HOLIDAYS: New Year's Day, 1 January; National Children's Day, first Monday in August; Tuvalu Day, 1 October; Christmas Day, 25 December; Boxing Day, 26 December. Movable holidays include Commonwealth Day (March), Queen's Official Birthday (June), and Prince of Wales's Birthday (November); movable religious holidays include Good Friday and Easter Monday.

TIME: Midnight = noon GMT.

¹LOCATION, SIZE, AND EXTENT

Tuvalu (formerly the Ellice Islands) comprises a cluster of nine islands, plus islets, located in the southwestern Pacific Ocean just south of the Equator. These remote atolls are situated about 1,050 km (650 mi) N of Suva, Fiji, and 4,000 km (2,500 mi) NE of Sydney, Australia. They lie in a 595-km-long (370-mi) chain extending over some 1,300,000 sq km (500,000 sq mi) of ocean and have a total land area of 26 sq km (10 sq mi).

Comparatively, the area occupied by Tuvalu is about 0.1 times the size of Washington, D.C. Tuvalu has a coastline of 24 km (15 mi). Tuvalu's capital city, Funafuti, is located on the island of Funafuti.

²TOPOGRAPHY

Tuvalu consists entirely of low-lying coral atolls, none of which is more than 5 m (16 ft) above sea level; few of the atolls are more than 0.8 km (0.5 mi) wide. The islands are coral reefs on the outer arc of ridges formed by pressure from the Central Pacific against the ancient Australian landmass.

On five islands, the reefs enclose sizable lagoons; the others are mere pinnacles rising abruptly from the ocean floor. Only two of the islands, Funafuti and Nukufetau, have natural harbors for oceangoing ships. There are no rivers on the islands.

³CLIMATE

Tuvalu has a tropical climate with little seasonal variation. The annual mean temperature of 30ºC (86ºF) is moderated by trade winds from the east. Rainfall averages over 355 cm (140 in), with most rain falling between November and February. Although the

islands lie north of the main cyclone belt, Funafuti was devastated in 1894, 1972, and 1990.

⁴FLORA AND FAUNA

The surrounding sea is rich in flora and fauna, but land vegetation is limited to coconut palm, pandanus, and imported fruit trees. Pigs, fowl, and dogs, all of which were imported in the 19th century, flourish on the islands. The only indigenous mammal is the Polynesian rat. Birds include reef herons, terns, and noddies. There are 22 known species of butterfly and moth.

⁵ENVIRONMENT

Environmental dangers include uncontrolled spread of the crown of thorns starfish, which flourishes in deepened channels and is destructive to coral reefs; erosion of beachheads from the use of sand for building materials; and excessive clearance of forest undergrowth for firewood. About 40% of Funafuti island is uninhabitable because the United Kingdom authorized the United States to dig an airstrip out of the coral bed during World War II (1939-45). Global warming/climate change and the related rise of sea level are also a significant environmental concern for Tuvalu's residents. The encroachment of seawater also poses a threat of contamination to the nation's limited water supply, whose purity is already at risk due to untreated sewage and the by-products of the mining industry and farming. Natural hazards include earthquakes, cyclones, and volcanic activity.

In the late 1990s, Tuvalu, Nauru, and Kiribati aligned with the Cook Islands and Niue to put pressure on Australia to reduce its production of greenhouse gases. These low-lying island nations are particularly vulnerable to global warming. Already flooding in stormy weather, they pressed for a worldwide cut of 20% of 1990 emission levels by 2005. Australia rejected the proposal, cit-

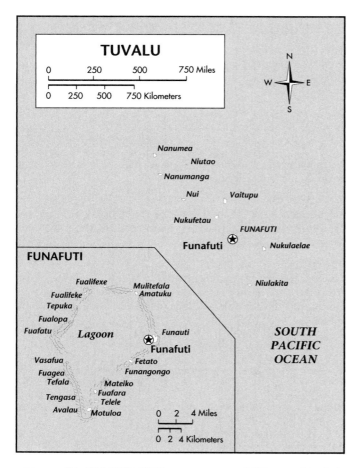

LOCATION: 5° to 11° S; 176° to 180°E. TOTAL COASTLINE: 24 kilometers (15 miles).
TERRITORIAL SEA LIMIT: 12 miles.

ing 90,000 jobs would be lost if Australia was forced to reduce emissions. None of Tuvalu's islands rise more than 16 feet (5 m) above sea level, and their future existence may be imperiled. There is concern that many Tuvalu residents will become climate-change refugees.

Tuvalu's ambitious climate proposal at the 2009 United Nations climate conference in Copenhagen, Denmark, was rebuffed on the third day of talks. Tuvalu proposed a deal that would require the world's nations to limit the rise in global temperatures to no more than 1.5°C (2.7°F) above preindustrial levels. However, oil producing and more developed nations deemed such measures unrealistic, underscoring the challenge of building consensus on an issue that required the participation of the world. The UN reported in 2008 that carbon dioxide emissions in Tuvalu totaled 5 kilotons.

In 2010 top officials from Tuvalu and 13 other developing Pacific island nations and dependencies met in Vanuatu to discuss the progress made in addressing some of the issues unique to these low-lying, developing island states, including climate change, natural disasters, remoteness from major markets, and poverty. Another key objective of the meeting was to address the progress each nation had made in adopting the 2005 Mauritius Strategy, the only global blueprint that exists to combat the development challenges of small-island developing states.

According to a 2011 report issued by the International Union for Conservation of Nature and Natural Resources (IUCN),

threatened species included 1 species of bird, 2 types of reptiles, 10 species of fish, and 1 type of mollusk. Current fishing methods threaten Tuvalu's marine life. The green sea turtle, hawksbill turtle, bay shark, and the leatherback turtle are endangered.

6 POPULATION

The US Central Intelligence Agency (CIA) estimates the population of Tuvalu in 2012 to be approximately 10,619, which placed it at number 194 in population among the 196 nations of the world. In 2011, approximately 5.4% of the population was over 65 years of age, with another 30.6% under 15 years of age. The median age in Tuvalu was 24.1 years. There were 0.97 males for every female in the country. The population's annual rate of change was 0.725% in 2012. The projected population for the year 2025 was 10,000. Population density in Tuvalu was calculated at 406 people per sq km (157 people per sq mi).

The CIA estimated that 50% of the population lived in urban areas, and that urban populations had an annual rate of change of 1.4%. The largest urban area was Funafuti.

7 MIGRATION

In 2012, the CIA estimated Tuvalu's net migration rate at -6.97 migrants per 1,000 citizens. During the 19th century, recruitment of Tuvaluans to work on plantations in other Pacific islands, Australia, and South America reduced the resident population from about 20,000 to 3,000. Migrants account for about 3% of the total population. A steady rate of emigration has resulted in little population growth between 2000 and 2010.

8 ETHNIC GROUPS

Apart from a few Europeans, the islanders are almost entirely Polynesian (96%) and have strong ties with the Samoans and Tokelauans. Language and tradition indicate that the Tuvaluans were part of a Samoan-Tongan migration from the 14th through the 17th century. Micronesians account for most of the remaining population.

9 LANGUAGES

English and Tuvaluan, a Polynesian tongue related closely to Samoan, are the principal languages. A Gilbertese dialect (Kiribati) is spoken on Nui. Samoan is also spoken.

10 RELIGIONS

In 1865, a member of the London Missionary Society reached Tuvalu from Samoa and Samoan pastors were sent to the islands. Tuvaluans rapidly embraced the Christian faith. According to a 2010 report, about 91% of Tuvaluans are members of the Church of Tuvalu, a Congregationalist group. Seventh-Day Adventists account for 3% of the population, Baha'is for 3%, Jehovah's Witnesses for 2%, and Catholics for 1%. There are also small numbers of Muslims, Baptists, Mormons (The Church of Jesus Christ of Latter-Day Saints), and Tuvalu Brethren (charismatic). The constitution provides for freedom of religion and the separation of church and state; however, the government seems to favor Christian practices, even by opening sessions of parliament with Christian prayer. Traditional chiefs from all of the nine island groups are members of the Church of Tuvalu. Religious groups are required to register with the government and may be prosecuted for failure to do so.

Good Friday, Easter Monday, Gospel Day, and Christmas are observed as national holidays.

11 TRANSPORTATION

Transportation is inadequate. Most roads are little more than tracks, although Funafuti has about 19.5 km (12.1 mi) of coral-impacted roads for use by the island's few cars and trucks. The CIA reports that the nation had about 8 km (5 mi) paved roads in 2002. Funafuti and Nukufetau are the only seaports, used chiefly by freighters in the copra trade. Ships drawing up to 9 m (30 ft) can dock in Funafuti harbor at a deepwater wharf completed in 1980. In 2010, Tuvalu had a merchant fleet of 66 ships of 1,000 GRT or more, many of which were foreign-owned. All the islands are served by Tuvalu's one interisland ferry. Funafuti International Airport was the only airstrip providing international services in 2011.

12 HISTORY

The islands were probably settled between the 14th and 17th centuries by Polynesians drifting west with prevailing winds from Samoa and other large islands. The first European to discover Tuvalu is thought to have been the Spanish navigator Alvaro de Menda-a de Neyra, who sighted Nui in 1568 and Niulakita in 1595. Further European contact was not made until the end of the 18th century. Between 1850 and 1875, the islands were raided by ships forcibly recruiting plantation workers for South America, Fiji, Hawaii, Tahiti, and Queensland. To help suppress such abuses, the Office of British High Commissioner for the Western Pacific was created in 1877.

In 1892, after ascertaining the inhabitants' wishes, the United Kingdom proclaimed the Ellice Islands (as Tuvalu was then known), together with the Gilberts, as a British protectorate. After further consultation, the protectorate became the Gilbert and Ellice Islands Colony in 1916. After the Japanese occupied the Gilberts in 1942 during World War II, US forces occupied the Ellice group in 1943 and drove the Japanese out of the Gilberts. After the war, the ethnic differences between the Micronesians of the Gilberts and the Polynesians of the Ellice Islands led the Ellice Islanders to demand separation. In 1973, a British commissioner appointed to examine the situation recommended administrative separation of the two island groups. The British government agreed, provided that the Ellice Islanders declared their wishes by referendum. The vote, held during August-September 1974 with UN observers in attendance, produced an overwhelming majority of 3,799–293 for separation. Accordingly, on 1 October 1975, the Ellice Islands were established as the separate British colony of Tuvalu, and a ministerial system was instituted. Pursuant to a constitutional conference held in London in February 1978, Tuvalu became an independent member of the Commonwealth of Nations on 1 October 1979. In 2000, Tuvalu was admitted to the United Nations.

13 GOVERNMENT

Tuvalu is a parliamentary democracy within the Commonwealth of Nations. The head of state is the British monarch, whose representative on the islands is the governor-general, who is appointed by the monarch on the advice of the prime minister. There is a unicameral legislature, or Fale I Fono, also referred to as the House of Assembly, with 15 members elected to four-year terms by universal adult suffrage. Seven islands elect two members each and one island elects one member. The prime minister and deputy prime minister are elected by and from the members of parliament. The cabinet is headed by the prime minister and has up to five ministers (all assembly members). Suffrage is 18 years of age and over.

14 POLITICAL PARTIES

There are no political parties, and political life and elections are dominated by personalities. Most members of parliament maintain a strong interest for their home island. In the 16 September 2010 parliamentary elections, .10 of the 15 incumbent members were reelected. Matia Toafo was elected as prime minister with nine out of 15 votes from parliament. Toafo was ousted in December 2010 following a vote of no confidence. Willie Telavi was elected as prime minister in his place. Taeia Italeli was appointed as governor general in May 2010.

15 LOCAL GOVERNMENT

Local governments were established on the eight inhabited islands by a 1965 ordinance that provided the framework for a policy aimed at financing local services at the island level. Funafuti's town council and the other seven island councils each consist of six elected members, including a president. Under the Falekapule Act of 1997, increasing power devolved from the central government to the island councils.

16 JUDICIAL SYSTEM

The judicial system consists of a High Court of Justice, a court of appeals, district magistrates, island courts, and land courts. The eight island courts (with limited jurisdiction) were constituted in 1965 to deal with land disputes, among other local matters. The High Court of Justice was set up in 1975 to hear appeals from district courts. Appeals from the High Court may go to the Court of Appeals in Fiji. In the High Court a chief justice visits twice a year to preside over its sessions.

The right to a fair public trial is respected in practice. Services of the public defender are available to all Tuvaluans free of charge. Defendants have the right to confront witnesses, present evidence, and to appeal. The judiciary is independent and free of governmental interference.

17 ARMED FORCES

Tuvalu has no armed forces except for the local police, which includes a maritime surveillance unit. For defense the islands rely on Australian-trained volunteers from Fiji and Papua New Guinea.

18 INTERNATIONAL COOPERATION

Tuvalu became a member of the Commonwealth of Nations on 1 September 2000, and the 189th member of the United Nations on 5 September 2000. Tuvalu serves on the FAO, IMO, ITU, UNCTAD, UNESCO, UPU, and the WHO. The country is also part of the Asian Development Bank, the ACP Group, the South Pacific Regional Trade and Economic Cooperation Agreement (Sparteca), the Alliance of Small Island States (AOSIS), and the Pacific Island Forum. In 1979, Tuvalu signed a treaty of friendship with the United States, which in 1983 formally dropped its prior claim to four of the nine islands. Tuvalu opposes French nuclear testing in the South Pacific and signed the 1985 Rarotonga Agreement declaring the region a nuclear-weapons-free zone. In environmental cooperation, Tuvalu is part of the Kyoto Protocol, the Montréal Protocol, MARPOL, and the UN Conventions on the Law of the Sea, Climate Change, and Desertification. Tuvalu became a member of the International Monetary Fund in June 2010.

19 ECONOMY

With limited natural resources, government jobs and government enterprises, including the sale of stamps, coins, and ".tv" internet domains, are the dominant forces in the national economy. In 1990, the government leased the right to the suffix .tv to Idealab, a California company, for AUD90 million over 12 years, retaining a 20% share in the .tv Corporation. Some of the funds generated were put in other investments and some were used for infrastructure projects like airport development, electrification, and the construction of roads, office buildings and hospitals. In January 2002, .tv Corp. became a wholly owned subsidiary of VeriSign Corp., which bought it for US$45 million in an agreement by which Tuvalu maintains control of the management of its domain name. While still considered an important source of government income, royalties from .tv Corp. have been highly variable.

The stabilizing factor of the economy has been the Tuvalu Trust Fund (TTF), set up in 1987 with AUD27 million derived from contributions from Tuvalu, Australia, New Zealand, the United Kingdom, Japan, and South Korea. Helped by occasional lump sum contributions from Australia, and modest withdrawals by Tuvalu, the TTF had grown to an estimated AUD100 million by 2008. From 1990 through 2011, the TTF contributed about 11% per year to the annual government budget.

Remittances from those living and working abroad and from Tuvaluan seafarers working on foreign vessels account for a fairly significant source of revenues as well. Most citizens are employed in subsistence agriculture or fishing. The islands are too small and too remote for development of a tourist industry. The gross domestic product (GDP) rate of change in Tuvalu, as of 2010, was 0.2%. Inflation stood at 3.8%

20 INCOME

The CIA estimated that in 2010 the GDP of Tuvalu was $36 million. The CIA defines GDP as the value of all final goods and services produced within a nation in a given year and computed on the basis of purchasing power parity (PPP) rather than value as measured on the basis of the rate of the exchange based on current dollars. The per capita GDP was estimated at $3,400. The annual growth rate of GDP was 0.2%. The average inflation rate was 3.8%. As of 2002 (the latest figures available in 2011), it was estimated that agriculture accounted for 16.6% of GDP, industry 27.2%, and services 56.2%. From 1990 through 2011, about 11% of government revenues came from the Tuvalu Trust Fund. Remittances continue an estimated AUD4 million in revenues each year.

21 LABOR

The estimated workforce numbered 3,615 in 2004. Only about 25% of the workforce is involved in the formal wage economy. The government is the primary employer, providing jobs to about 69% of the formal workforce in 2011. These included direct government jobs (39%) and employment in public or semipublic corporations (30%). In Funafuti, the government-controlled philately bureau is the largest single employer, with a staff of several dozen workers. In the informal workforce (comprising 75% of the population), more than 50% of workers are employed in subsistence ventures including agriculture, fishing, and handicrafts. It has been estimated that about 15% of the total adult male population are seafarers working on foreign vessels. Remittances from these and other laborers working abroad are an important source of income for families and the government.

In 2010, the nation's only registered trade union was the Tuvalu Seamen's Union, which had about 1,350 members who work abroad on foreign merchant vessels. Many public sector employees, such as teachers and nurses, belong to professional associations that are not registered as unions. The law protects the right to strike, but no strike has ever occurred.

The minimum working age is 14 (15 for industrial employment). The minimum age for shipboard employment is 18, primarily due to a law stipulating that children under this age are not permitted to enter into formal contracts of any kind. An exception to this law allows children to enter into apprenticeships of up to five years beginning at age 15. Generally children do not work outside of the traditional economy. As of 2010, the biweekly minimum wage for the public sector was AUD130 (about US$130). There was no minimum wage for the private sector. According to a 2008 business report, the average minimum wage for unskilled casual labor was about AUD2.25. The law sets the workday at eight hours. Basic health and safety standards, such as clean drinking water, are mandated by law but irregularly enforced.

22 AGRICULTURE

While more than 50% of the population practices subsistent farming, agricultural production is limited because of poor soil quality (sand and rock fragments), uncertain rains, and primitive catchment. Coconuts form the basis of both subsistence and cash cropping. Other food crops are pulaka (taro), pandanus fruit, bananas, and papayas. Fruit production amounted to 789 tons and vegetable production to 543 tons in 2009.

23 ANIMAL HUSBANDRY

Some families raise pigs and chickens for personal consumption or to provide a small income in local trade.

24 FISHING

Sea fishing, especially for tuna and turtle, is excellent. Although fishing is mainly a subsistence occupation, fish is sold in the capital, and bêche-de-mer is exported. The Republic of Korea and Taiwan are both licensed to fish within the territorial waters of Tuvalu. In October 1986, Tuvalu, along with several other Pacific island nations, signed an agreement with the United States giving US tuna boats the right to fish its offshore waters. The sale of fishing licenses annually contributes about AUD80,000 to the government's revenues. In 2008, the annual capture totaled 2,200 tons according to the UN FAO.

Tuvalu is one of the Parties of the Nauru Agreement (PNA), which held its first presidential summit in 2010. The PNA was established in 1982 and is comprised of the nations of Palau, Micronesia, Marshall Islands, Tuvalu, Kiribati, Papua New Guinea, Nauru, and the Solomon Islands. The purpose of the group is to work together for the conservation and management of tuna resources within their exclusive economic zones (EEZ). At the March 2010 meeting, which has been called the Tuna Summit, members adopted the Koror Declaration, which aims, among other things, to establish cooperative management practices that will enhance commercial and economic opportunities for member states and to work toward the conservation and restoration of migratory tuna stocks. The waters of the PNA nations account for nearly 60% of all tuna catches in the western and central Pacific Ocean and 25% of the global tuna catches that supply canneries and processing facilities around the world.

25 FORESTRY

Approximately 33% of Tuvalu is covered by forest. There is little useful timber on the islands.

26 MINING

There is no commercial mining.

27 ENERGY AND POWER

With no fossil fuel reserves, the islands are highly dependent on imported fuels to provide for their energy needs. Most electricity is generated from petroleum-fed generators. Funafuti has a limited amount of electricity to operate its meteorological and broadcasting stations and for use by its hospital and hotel; very few private households have electrical service. Both production and consumption of electricity amounted to 3,000,000 kWh, or 330 kWh per capita, in 1995. The Tuvalu Solar Electric Cooperative Society, formed in 1984, provides a limited supply of photovoltaic electricity.

In an effort to lead by example, Tuvalu has initiated a plan to eliminate the use of generator fuels on the nine inhabited islands by 2020. With assistance from a non-profit consortium of electric companies from the G8 nations, known as e8, a large solar energy system has already been built in Funafuti that supplies about 5% of the electricity needed in that city. Solar and wind projects are in the works for the entire nation.

28 INDUSTRY

There is no industry apart from handicrafts, baking, and small-scale construction; the islands lack the population, capital, and resources to make commercial enterprises cost effective. In 1995, the latest year for which data was available, manufacturing accounted for 3% of GDP and construction about 14%.

29 SCIENCE AND TECHNOLOGY

The World Bank reported in 2009 that there were no patent applications in science and technology in Tuvalu. There is no advanced science and technology except for that imported under foreign aid programs.

30 DOMESTIC TRADE

The local economy is based primarily on agriculture, which employs a majority of the resident population. Most residents of smaller villages and islands can grow or create their own necessary goods. Barter remains an important part of this subsistence economy. In larger communities, cooperative societies dominate commercial life, controlling many retail outlets (relying heavily on imported goods), the marketing of local handicrafts, and the supply of fish to the capital.

31 FOREIGN TRADE

Copra, the main cash crop, is affected by fluctuating market prices (although there is a subsidy to producers). Other exports include handicrafts and postage stamps. Most food, fuel, and manufactured goods are imported. Tuvalu imported $12.91 million worth of goods and services in 2008, while exporting $1 million worth of goods and services. Major import partners in 2009 were Australia, Fiji, Singapore, and New Zealand. Its major export partners were Fiji, Australia, and New Zealand.

Tuvalu is party to the Pacific Island Countries Trade Agreement (PICTA) that took effect in 2002. This agreement represents a commitment to reduce and eliminate tariffs among the 14 members of the Pacific Island Forum.

32 BALANCE OF PAYMENTS

Tuvalu imported US$12.91 million worth of goods and services in 2008, while exporting $1 million worth of goods and services, resulting in a trade deficit of US$11.91 million. Such recurring trade deficits are offset by the Tuvalu Trust Fund and additional economic aid from international donors. Tuvalu's main economic aid donors are Australia, Japan, and the United States. Official development assistance (ODA) net inflows amounted to US$8 million in 2004.

33 BANKING AND SECURITIES

The government-owned National Bank of Tuvalu was founded in Funafuti in 1980 and has commercial branches on all the islands. The Development Bank of Tuvalu, also government owned, began operations in 1993 to provide financing for a variety of business ventures.

34 INSURANCE

Insurance plays a minimal role in Tuvaluan life.

35 PUBLIC FINANCE

In 2006 the budget of Tuvalu included US$21.54 million in public revenue and US$23.05 million in public expenditures, resulting in a deficit of US$1.51 million. The budget deficit amounted to 4.7% of GDP. Revenue is obtained principally by means of indirect taxation through stamp sales, the copra export tax, fishing licenses, telephone line leasing, earnings from the Tuvalu Trust Fund, and profits from .tv Corporation.

36 TAXATION

Under the Income Tax Act of 1992, the personal income tax rate is set at 30% of taxable income. The company income tax rate on chargeable income is also 30%, down from 40%. The income of both nonresidents and foreign resident companies is taxed at a flat rate of 40%. There are a variety of sales taxes applied to a variety of goods and services. Island councils also levy a head tax and a land tax based on territorial extent and soil fertility.

³⁷CUSTOMS AND DUTIES

Since a single-line tariff was implemented on 1 January 1975, trade preferences are no longer granted to imports from Commonwealth countries. Tariffs, applying mostly to private imports, are levied as a source of revenue. Most duties are ad valorem, with specific duties on alcoholic beverages, tobacco, certain chemicals, petroleum, cinematographic film, and some other goods.

³⁸FOREIGN INVESTMENT

The cash economy is not sufficiently developed to attract substantial foreign investment. In 1981, the government established the Business Development Advisory Board to promote local and foreign investment in the Tuvalu economy; in 1993, the board became the Development Bank of Tuvalu, the country's only commercial bank.

The Foreign Investment Facilitation Board has been established within the Ministry of Tourism, Trade, and Commerce to facilitate and oversee all foreign investment activities.

UNCTAD reported that the annual flow of foreign direct investment (FDI) to Tuvalu for 1997 and 1998 was no more than US$100,000, zero for 1999, US$100,000 in 2000, and zero again in 2001. In 2004, net FDI inflow amounted to US$8.5 million. Foreign direct investment (FDI) in Tuvalu was unreported according to World Bank figures published in 2009.

³⁹ECONOMIC DEVELOPMENT

The government relies heavily on international assistance for development projects. Much of the financial assistance comes in the form of contributions to the Tuvalu Trust Fund, provided by Australia, New Zealand, the United Kingdom, Japan, Korea, and Tuvalu itself. The net income from the fund is paid to the Tuvalu government annually. In 2008, the fund amounted to an estimated AUD100 million.

In 2002, the government announced the Island Development Program (IDP) designed to reduce the disparity between household income on the main island, Funafuti, and the outer islands, and thereby slow the migration to the capital city. The program centers around the creation of a trust fund, the Falekanpule Trust Fund (FTF), modeled on the successful TFF. The FTF was capitalized at US$8.2 million, contributed by the government and donor countries (principally New Zealand and Australia). Four types of policies are to be followed to achieve IDP goals: 1) decentralization of administration; 2) improvement of public service delivery; 3) promotion of small business development, and 4) a sustained augmentation of money available for the IDP through the prudent management of the FTF. In the first distribution of earnings from the FTF, the island councils were each given US$318,000 for development projects, and US$104,000 was allocated to a buffer account.

The Asian Development bank and AusAID have each provided technical assistance in designing comprehensive development plans for the nation. Under the *Australia Partnership for Development with Tuvalu*, the nation has received support for improving public financial management and increasing access to health and educational services for residents. Tuvalu's own *National Strategy for Sustainable Development 2005–2015 (Te Kakeega II)* outlines government objectives in eight key strategic areas: good governance; macroeconomic growth and stability; social development (health, welfare, youth, gender, housing, and poverty alleviation); outer island development; employment and private sector development; human resource development; natural resources (agriculture, fisheries, tourism, and environmental management); and infrastructure and support services.

All development efforts in Tuvalu are overshadowed by the real possibility that an increase in global warming that ends up raising normal sea level could mean the disappearance altogether of the nine low-lying coral islands that constitute the country. The government has consequently pushed hard on two fronts: urging industrialized countries to ratify and adhere to the Kyoto Protocol on limiting greenhouse gasses, and, in other countries, particularly, Australia, to have a plan for accepting displaced Tuvaluans.

⁴⁰SOCIAL DEVELOPMENT

Villages are organized on a communal rather than a clan basis and have a customary system of social welfare. There is no constitutional protection against sex discrimination. Women generally play a subordinate role within the family and society at large. Working women are primarily concentrated in the clerical, retail, education, and health sectors. Violence against women and domestic abuse are not widespread problems. Children's welfare is protected, and free medical care is provided until 18 years of age. The law does not prohibit discrimination against those who are physically or mentally challenged; however, there have not been any significant reports of such discrimination. Human rights are generally well respected in Tuvalu. Serious crime is virtually nonexistent, and most prisoners are held for one night for offenses such as public drunkenness.

⁴¹HEALTH

In 2009, there were an estimated 6 physicians, 58 nurses and midwives, and 56 hospital beds per 10,000 inhabitants. Approximately 85% of the population had access to sanitation, and the entire population had access to safe water. The infant mortality rate was estimated at 33.55 deaths per 1,000 live births in 2012. In the same year, the fertility rate was an estimated 3.08 children born per woman. In 2007, immunization rates for a child under one were as follows: diphtheria, pertussis, and tetanus, 93%, and polio, 92%. About 49% of children under one had been immunized for hepatitis B. In 2011, child immunizations for measles were estimated at 90%. The average life expectancy in 2012 was estimated at 65.11 years. The incidence of tuberculosis was 28 per 100,000 people in 2007. In 2009, it was estimated that the country spent 8.0% of its GDP on healthcare, amounting to $290 per person.

⁴²HOUSING

Most islanders live in small villages and provide their own housing from local materials. Government-built housing is largely limited to that provided for civil servants. At the 2002 census (the most recent as of 2011), the housing stock stood at about 1,568 houses. About 640 houses, or 40% of the housing stock, are on Funafuti. Niulakita only reported eight houses at the time of the census. About 74% of all houses are single-family permanent structures. These are made of wood or concrete or both. A little over

17% of all homes are of traditional construction, primarily with thatch and mud walls and thatched or iron-sheeted roofs. About 22% of the housing stock was between 21 and 50 years old. Another 26% was between 11 and 20 years old. Only about 30% of all houses had an indoor flush toilet. About 89% of all households had kerosene stoves for cooking. Only 40 households had microwave ovens.

43 EDUCATION

All children receive free primary education from the age of seven. Education is compulsory for 10 years. The Tuvaluan school system has seven years of primary and six years of secondary education. Secondary education is provided at Motufoua, a former church school on Vaitupu now jointly administered by the government. In 2004, there were 2,010 students enrolled in primary schools with a student-teacher ratio of about 19:1. The same year, there were about 446 students enrolled in secondary schools with a student-teacher ratio of 11:1. Overall, the CIA estimated that Tuvalu had a literacy rate of 95%.

Tuvalu Marine School was opened in 1979 with Australian aid. In the same year, the University of the South Pacific (Fiji) established an extension center in Funafuti. The Tuvalu Technical Education Center offers technical and vocational training for adults. The Tuvalu Business Center provides specialized training courses that support local businesses.

44 LIBRARIES AND MUSEUMS

The first book published in Tuvalu was the Bible, in 1977. The National Library and Archives of Tuvalu is located on Funafuti; documents from parliamentary proceedings are collected there. The Ministry of Finance and Economic Planning maintains a small depository library for the Asian Development Bank.

45 MEDIA

In 2009, there were 1,700 main phone lines and 2,000 mobile cellular phones in use nationwide, with mobile phone subscriptions averaging 19 per 100 people. The government-owned Tuvalu Broadcasting Service, on Funafuti, transmits daily in Tuvaluan and also broadcasts news in English. In 2009, there was 1 FM radio station and 1 AM radio station. There is no national television station, but some islanders own satellite dishes to receive foreign broadcasts. Internet access is available through the management of the Office of the Prime Minster and the Department of Telecommunications. In 2010, there were 109,478 Internet hosts in the nation. As of 2008, there were about 4,200 Internet users nationwide. In 2009, Internet subscriptions stood at 40 per 100 citizens.

There is no commercial press, but *Tuvalu Echoes* (2010 circulation, 250) is published biweekly by the government. Other local publications are produced by the churches or the government. The government is reported to respect freedom of speech and of the press.

46 ORGANIZATIONS

Young men's clubs and women's committees are standard features of social life, concerning themselves with sailing, fishing, crafts, and child welfare. Organized youth groups include the Boy's Brigade, the Tuvalu Youth Fellowship and Pathfinder, and Girl Guide and Boy Scout troops. The Tuvalu Amateur Sports Association and the Pacific Red Cross are also notable. The Tuvalu Association of Nongovernmental Organizations is an umbrella group that provides a network for several religious organizations and some political and human rights advocacy groups. The National Council of Women of Tuvalu serves as an umbrella organization for women's cooperatives. The Fusi Alofa Association provides some services for the disabled.

47 TOURISM, TRAVEL, AND RECREATION

Tuvalu's remoteness has discouraged tourism; the few visitors are on commercial or official business. The many atolls, flora and fauna, and the World War II remains are the primary attractions of the islands. In 2007, about 1,130 tourists visited Tuvalu; half of the visitors were there on business. A valid passport, onward/return ticket, and proof of sufficient funds are required to enter Tuvalu. Visitor permits are issued upon arrival and are valid for up to three months. The *Tourism Factbook*, published by the UN World Tourism Organization in 2011, indicated that the estimated daily cost to visit Funafuti, the capital, was $194.

48 FAMOUS PERSONS

Tuvalu's first prime minister was Toaripi Lauti (b. Papua New Guinea, 1928). He later became governor-general of Tuvalu. Sir Tomasi Puapua (b. 1938) was prime minister from 1981–89, and the governor-general from 1998–2003. Faimalaga Luka (1940–2005) was governor-general (2003–05) and prime minister of Tuvalu (2001).

49 DEPENDENCIES

Tuvalu has no territories or colonies.

50 BIBLIOGRAPHY

Craig, Robert D. *Historical Dictionary of Polynesia*. Lanham, MD: Scarecrow, 2002.

Gillespie, Rosemary G., and David A. Clague, eds. *Encyclopedia of Islands*. Berkeley: University of California Press, 2009.

Kirch, Patrick Vinton, and Jean-Louis Rallu. *The Growth and Collapse of Pacific Island Societies*. Honolulu: University of Hawaii Press, 2007.

Leibo, Steven A. *East and Southeast Asia*. Harpers Ferry, WV: Stryker-Post Publications, 2005.

Lockwood, Victoria S., ed. *Globalization and Culture Change in the Pacific Islands*. Upper Saddle River, NJ: Pearson and Prentice Hall, 2004.

UNITED ARAB EMIRATES

United Arab Emirates

Al-Imarat al-'Arabiyah al-Muttahidah

CAPITAL: Abu Dhabi (Abu Zaby)

FLAG: The national flag contains three horizontal bands of green, white, and black that are equal in size, and one vertical band of red on the hoist side. The colors represent the pan-Arab colors of fertility (green), neutrality (white), petroleum resources (black), and unity (red).

ANTHEM: *Nashid al-Watani al-Imarati (National Anthem of the United Arab Emirates).*

MONETARY UNIT: The Arab Emirati Dirham (AED) is the primary currency. AED1 = US$0.2723 (or US$1 = AED3.6724).

WEIGHTS AND MEASURES: The metric system and imperial and local measures are used.

HOLIDAYS: New Year's Day (1 January), Milad an-Nabi (Birth of the Prophet), Leilat al-Meiraj (Ascension of the Prophet), Eid al-Fitr, Eid al-Adha, al-Hijra (Islamic New Year), and National Day (2 December). Dates vary for Muslim holidays.

TIME: 4 p.m. = noon GMT.

¹LOCATION, SIZE, AND EXTENT

Comprising a total area of approximately 82,880 sq km (32,000 sq mi), including some 6,000 sq km (2,300 sq mi) of islands, the United Arab Emirates (UAE), located in the eastern Arabian Peninsula, consists of seven states: Abu Dhabi (Abu Zaby), Dubai (Dubayy), Sharjah, Ra's al-Khaimah (Ra's al-Khaymah), Fujairah (Al-Fujayrah), Umm al-Qaiwain (Umm al-Qaywayn), and 'Ajman. Comparatively, the area occupied by United Arab Emirates is slightly smaller than the state of Maine. Extending 544 km (338 mi) NE–SW and 361 km (224 mi) SE–NW, the United Arab Emirates is bordered on the N by the Persian (or Arabian) Gulf, on the E by Oman, on the S and W by Saudi Arabia, and on the NW by Qatar, with a total boundary length of 2,185 km (1,358 mi), including a coastline of 1,318 km (819 mi).

In the late 1970s, Saudi Arabia and Qatar reached a boundary agreement according to which a narrow corridor of land was ceded by Abu Dhabi, thus allowing Saudi Arabia access to the Persian Gulf near the Khawr Duwayhin and eradicating the former Qatar-UAE frontier. However, the agreement had not been ratified by the United Arab Emirates as of 2011. A 1999 border treaty with Oman also remained unratified as of 2011.

The United Arab Emirates's capital city, Abu Dhabi, is located on the Persian Gulf.

²TOPOGRAPHY

The United Arab Emirates consists mainly of sandy desert. It is bounded on the west by an immense *sebkha*, or salt flat, extending southward for nearly 112 km (70 mi). The eastern boundary runs northward over gravel plains and high dunes until it almost reaches the Hajar Mountains in the Ra's Musandam near Al 'Ayn. The flat coastal strip that makes up most of the United Arab Emirates has an extensive area of sebkha subject to flooding. Some sand spits and mud flats tend to enlarge, and others enclose lagoons. A sandy desert with limestone outcroppings lies behind the coastal plain in a triangle between the gravel plain and the mountains of the east and the sands of Saudi Arabia to the south. Far to the south, the oases of Al-Liwa' are aligned in an arc along the edge of dunes, which rise above 90 m (300 ft).

The main gravel plain extends inland and southward from the coast of Ra's al-Khaimah to Al 'Ayn and beyond. Behind Ra's al-Khaimah and separating Fujairah from the Persian Gulf is an area of mountains that rise over 900 m (3,000 ft) in height, with isolated cultivation. Finally, alluvial flats on the Gulf of Oman fill the bays between rocky spurs. South of Khor Fakkan (Sharjah), a continuous, well-watered fertile littoral strip known as the Batinah Coast runs between the mountains and the sea and continues into Oman. In addition, there are many islands, most of which are owned by Abu Dhabi including Das, the site of oil operations, and Abu Musa, exploited for oil and red oxide.

³CLIMATE

The United Arab Emirates experiences a subtropical, dry, hot desert climate. Annual rainfall is low. The months between May and October are extremely hot, with shade temperatures of between 38–49°C (100–120°F) and high humidity near the coast. Winter temperatures can fall as low as 2°C (36°F) but average between 17–20°C (63–68°F). Normal annual rainfall is from 5–10 cm (2–4 in), with considerably more in the mountains; most rainfall occurs between November and February.

The *shamal*, a hot dust-laden wind, blows through the United Arab Emirates from March through August, and often can cause sandstorms.

⁴FLORA AND FAUNA

There are an estimated 678 terrestrial plant species in the United Arab Emirates. In addition, the United Arab Emirates is home to 30 species of mammals, 268 species of birds, 39 species of reptiles, and 2 species of amphibians. The calculation reflects the total number of distinct species residing in the country, not the number of endemic species.

Plant species included a number of flowering plants, ferns, bryophytes and mosses. In the coastal areas, various seaweeds, sea grasses and microalgae could be found. Many species have adapted themselves to the desert climate.

Apart from cultivated plants, there are two categories of plant life in the United Arab Emirates: the restricted salt-loving vegetation of the marshes and swamps, including the dwarf mangrove, and the desert plant community, which includes a wide range of flora that is most abundant after the fall of rain.

Animal and reptile life is similar to that of Bahrain, with the addition of the fox, wolf, jackal, wildcat, and lynx. Hedgehogs have been seen. Many of the larger birds, including kites, buzzards, eagles, falcons, owls, and harriers, have been seen in the United Arab Emirates. However, the number of breeding species in the country may be much less than 100. Sea birds include a variety of gulls, terns, ospreys, waders, and flamingos. Popular game birds include the houbara (ruffed bustard), as well as species of ducks and geese.

⁵ENVIRONMENT

The World Resources Institute reported that the United Arab Emirates had designated 18,800 hectares (46,456 acres) of land for protection as of 2006. Water resources totaled 0.2 cu km (0.048 cu mi) while water usage was 2.3 cu km (0.552 cu mi) per year. Domestic water usage accounted for 23% of total usage, industrial for 9%, and agricultural for 68%. Per capita water usage totaled 511 cu m (18,046 cu ft) per year.

The United Nations (UN) reported in 2008 that carbon dioxide emissions in the United Arab Emirates totaled 135,429 kilotons.

In 2011 there were 86 endangered species found in United Arab Emirates. This figure included 45 species of corals; 17 species of fish; 16 species of birds, including the Egyptian vulture and Eurasian peregrine falcon; and 6 species of mammals, including the Arabian gazelle, duqong, sand cat, and goitered gazelle.

Key environmental issues in the United Arab Emirates are a lack of natural freshwater sources, desertification, and beach pollution from oil spills.

⁶POPULATION

The US Central Intelligence Agency (CIA) estimated the population of United Arab Emirates in 2011 to be approximately 5,148,664, which placed it at number 115 in population among the 196 nations of the world. In 2011 approximately 0.9% of the population was over 65 years of age, with another 20.4% under 15 years of age. The median age in United Arab Emirates was 30.2 years. There were 2.2 males for every female in the country. The population's annual rate of change was 3.28%.

About 84% of the population lived in urban areas in 2010, and about 74% of the individuals between ages 16 and 64 were non-

nationals. The largest city was Abu Dhabi with a population in 2009 of 660,000.

⁷MIGRATION

Estimates of the UAE's net migration rate, carried out by the CIA in 2011, amounted to 19.00 migrants per 1,000 citizens. The total number of emigrants living abroad was 55,900, and the total number of immigrants living in the United Arab Emirates was 3.29 million.

More than 80% of UAE residents were foreigners in 2010, and about 85% of the total workforce was comprised of non-UAE nationals. The US State Department reported that about 98% of private sector workers were non-UAE nationals. The government established the UAE Emiratization Council in May 2009 to formulate policies and standards to promote Emiratization of the workforce.

⁸ETHNIC GROUPS

The US State Department estimated that native Emirati made up only 890,000 of the country's 5.14 million residents in 2011. The rest of the population consisted of 1.75 million Indians, 1.25 million Pakistanis, 500,000 Bangladeshis, 1 million other Asians, and 500,000 Europeans and Africans. The population traditionally has included other Arabs, Iranians, Jordanians, Palestinians, Egyptians, Iraqis, and Bahrainis in its Asian and African totals.

⁹LANGUAGES

Arabic is the official and universal language. English, Hindi, Urdu, and Bengali also are widely spoken.

¹⁰RELIGIONS

Islam is the official religion in all seven emirates. However, because about 85% of UAE residents are non-citizens, much religious diversity exists.

Approximately 96% of the citizen population are Muslims, with about 85% Sunni and the remainder Shi'a. Christians, Hindus, Buddhists. Parsis, Baha'is, Sikhs, and Jews also reside in the United Arab Emirates.

The constitution guarantees freedom of religious worship, but prohibits Muslims from changing religions. It also allows for Muslims to proselytize people of other faiths, but restricts others from proselytizing Muslims. Both Muslims and non-Muslims are prohibited from eating in public during the Ramadan fast.

The US State Department reported 35 Christian churches in the United Arab Emirates, a Sikh temple, and two Hindu temples, one of which shared space with a second Sikh temple. Jews observed holidays in their homes, and the Sri Lankan embassy held a monthly Buddhist service.

¹¹TRANSPORTATION

The CIA reports that the United Arab Emirates has a total of 4,080 km (2,535 mi) of roads, all of which are paved. There were 41 airports, which transported 31.76 million passengers in 2009 according to the World Bank. Two of the world's fasting growing airlines–Emirates and Etihad–are based in the United Arab Emirates.

The government was continuing to expand its transportation infrastructure in 2011, and has been working to develop aviation policies that will promote Dubai as an international hub for trade and passenger flights. A "cargo village" at Dubai Airport has the ability to transfer cargo received at the port into air containers ready for airlift in three hours. Nearly all international airlines are permitted to land in Dubai and the fees imposed are very low. Projects to expand the international airport at Abu Dhabi also were underway in 2011, and the United Arab Emirates also had international airports in Sharjah and Ra's al-Khaimah.

With most of the population concentrated in coastal towns and the Al 'Ayn oasis, road links between these centers have been given priority. There is now a paved coastal road linking Abu Dhabi, Dubai, Sharjah, 'Ajman, Umm al-Qaiwain, and Ra's al-Khaimah. Roads linking the interior to the main towns have been constructed; of particular importance is the transpeninsular road from Fujairah through the Hajar Mountains. A six-lane, 209-km (130-mi) highway has been built between Abu Dhabi and Al- 'Ayn, and two bridges connect Abu Dhabi island with the mainland. Another highway links the UAE coastal network with the Trans-Arabian Highway at As-Silah on the Qatar border.

There are no railways or waterways in the United Arab Emirates. However, a $7 billion Union Rail project is underway to create an intermodal rail system throughout the country.

The United Arab Emirates is well provided with port facilities, with eight ports operational throughout the country in 2011. Dubai's Port Rashid, with its deepwater berths and warehouses, is one of the largest artificial harbors in the Middle East. Other ports are the Jabal 'Ali complex, also in Dubai; Abu Dhabi's Port Zayid; Sharjah's Port Khalid; and the deepwater port at Ra's al-Khaimah. Sharjah constructed a port at Khor Fakkan in the early 1980s; the Fujairah port became fully operational in 1983. Port Khalifa, a greenfield offshore port, became operational in 2010.

Jabal 'Ali in Dubai is the largest man-made port in the world. In 2008 the merchant fleet consisted of 58 ships of 1,000 gross register tonnage (GRT) or more.

12 HISTORY

The Trucial Coast for centuries was situated on one of the main trade routes between Asia and Europe. The United Arab Emirates itself was formed from a group of tribally organized sheikhdoms along the southern coast of the Persian Gulf and northwest coast of the Gulf of Oman. The sheikhdoms historically were embroiled in dynastic disputes, and through the 17th to 19th centuries foreign shippers endured a great deal of harassment from raiders. During this time period, the area came to be known as the Pirate Coast.

Abu Dhabi island was settled by its present ruling family, Al-Nuhayyan, toward the end of the 18th century, and Dubai was founded by an offshoot of the same family in 1833. The late 18th and 19th centuries brought the division of the area between the Nuhayyan and the Qawasim, who ruled Ra's al-Khaimah and neighboring territories.

British efforts to protect its India trade at Ra's al-Khaimah led to additional British naval expeditions in 1819. A general peace treaty signed in 1820 established a formal relationship between the sheikhdoms of the southern Gulf and Britain, and an 1835 treaty ended the intermittent raids when the sheikhs agreed to a maritime truce that would be enforced by the British Navy. The bond between the British and the sheikhdoms was further strengthened in 1892 when Britain promised to protect the Trucial Coast and

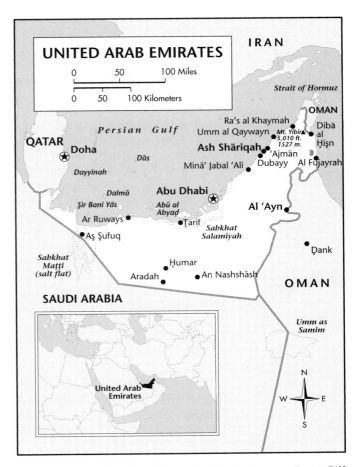

LOCATION: 51°3' to 56°23'E; 22°30' to 26°17' N. BOUNDARY LENGTHS: Persian Gulf coastline, 1,318 kilometers (817 miles); Oman, 410 kilometers (256 miles); Saudi Arabia, 457 kilometers (285 miles). TERRITORIAL SEA LIMIT: 3 miles, except Ash Shariqah (12 miles).

to assist the sheikhs in a possible land attack in exchange for the sheikhs agreeing not to form foreign relationships without consent from the United Kingdom.

The rulers of the seven sheikhdoms comprising the Trucial Sheikhdoms formed the Trucial Council in 1952 with a goal of developed common administrative policies and creating a future federation of the states.

Offshore petroleum was discovered beneath the coastal waters of Abu Dhabi in 1958, and onshore in 1960. Commercial drilling began in 1962. Oil in the 1960s replaced the pearling industry that had been the mainstay of the area as the top revenue generator.

The British announced in 1968 that it would end the treaty relationships it had held with the seven Trucial Sheikhdoms (Abu Dhabi, Dubai, Sharjah, Umm al-Qaiwain, Ajman, Fujairah, and Ra's al-Khaimah) along with Bahrain and Qatar. After the nine entities attempted to form a union of emirates, Bahrain and Qatar established themselves as independent nations in 1971. The seven Trucial Sheikhdoms also became independent when their treaty with the British expired on 1 December 1971. Six of the sheikhdoms formed the United Arab Emirates on 2 December 1971, and the seventh, Ra's al-Khaimah, joined the union in early 1972. Sheikh Zayid bin Sultan Al-Nuhayyan of Abu Dhabi was elected president, and Sheikh Rashid bin Said al Maktum of Dubai became prime minister.

The advent of independence led Saudi Arabia and Iran to assert territorial claims on some of the oases and islands within the emirates. Disputes over these claims persisted through 2011. Although the United Arab Emirates and Saudi Arabia signed a border agreement on the Liwa' oases in 1974, neither nation had fully recognized the terms of the agreement.

The United Arab Emirates provided aid to Iraq during the Iran-Iraq war of the 1970s, though it maintained diplomatic relations with Iran. In 1981, the United Arab Emirates became a founding member of the Gulf Cooperation Council (GCC), with a goal of curbing Iran. The dispute with Iran over the Abu Musa and Tumb Islands became tense when Iranian forces unilaterally asserted control over the UAE section of Abu Musa in 1992. In 1996 Iran rejected a proposal by the GCC to put the dispute over the islands to the International Court of Justice (ICJ) for arbitration. Iran has refused to accede to these calls and, as of 2011, continued to occupy some islands.

UAE forces sided with the US campaign to liberate Kuwait during the 1990–91 Gulf War, and have participated in peacekeeping missions in Lebanon, Somalia, Bosnia, Albania, Kosovo, and Afghanistan.

In 2004 Sheikh Zayid bin Sultan Al-Nuhayyan died. His son, Khalifa bin Zayid Al-Nuhayyan succeeded him as ruler of Abu Dhabi, and in accordance with the UAE constitution was elected UAE president by the country's Supreme Council of Rulers. In December 2005 Sheikh Khalifa announced plans for the United Arab Emirates's first national elections. Half of the members of the consultative federal national council (Majlis al-Ittihad al-Watani) were to be elected by a limited number of citizens. The elections were held on 16 December 2006. A small number of hand-picked voters chose half of the members of the council.

Oil and global finance have driven the UAE economy through the late 20th and early 21st centuries. The confluence of falling oil prices, collapsing real estate values, and an international banking crisis in 2008–09 hit the nation especially hard, and resulted in calls for political reforms. In March 2011 about 100 Emirati activists and intellectuals petitioned the government to establish a parliament with full legislative powers and to expand the nation's electorate. The government, attempting to quell unrest, announced a multiyear, $1.6 billion infrastructure investment plan for poorer emirates in the north, and expanded voting in the September 2011 federal national council elections to about 12% of the Emirate population, from 6,600 in 2006.

13 GOVERNMENT

There is a unicameral national council (Majlis al-Ittihad al-Watani) of 20 appointed and 20 elected, with members from each of the emirates. The council holds only a consultative role. The seven emirs, who represent each of the emirates, form the Supreme Council of Rulers. This council was charged in the 2 December 1971 constitution (which was formally ratified in 1996) with the task of electing the president from among its rulers.

The Supreme Council of Rulers formulates UAE policies, ratifies federal laws, and monitors the national budget. This council also appoints a council of ministers, or cabinet, led by the prime minister. Each emirate is represented by at least one minister, and senior posts are allocated to the larger emirates. The council of

ministers was reshuffled in February 2008; its members initiate legislation for ratification by the supreme council.

Pressure to establish a fully elected national parliament mounted in 2011, prompting the supreme council to expand the number of eligible voters.

14 POLITICAL PARTIES

No political parties existed in the United Arab Emirates as of 2011.

15 LOCAL GOVERNMENT

The United Arab Emirates is a federation of seven emirates: Abu Dhabi, Dubai, Sharjah, 'Ajman, Ra's al-Khaimah, Umm al-Qaiwain, and Fujairah. Each emirate has a separate ruler who oversees the local government. Most of the emirates are governed in accordance with tribal traditions. There are a handful of traditional councils known as *majalis* and *amiri diwans*, through which citizens may speak directly to rulers in open meetings.

16 JUDICIAL SYSTEM

The United Arab Emirates maintains a dual court system. Shari'ah courts handle criminal and family law matters based on the individual emirates' interpretation of Islamic law. Civil courts handle civil law matters and are accountable to the Federal Supreme Court, which holds the power of judicial review. The larger Dubai, Abu Dhabi, and Ra's al-Khaimah emirates are not subject to Federal Supreme Court review, though they hold the power to refer individual cases to the court.

Cases involving military personnel are heard by military tribunals, but the Federal Supreme Court hears national security cases.

Local rulers' offices, known as *diwans*, review several cases, which often results in delays in decision making and lengthier prison terms.

Although the 1971 constitution provided for an independent judiciary, the US State Department reported in 2011 that the federal intelligence service and directorate of state security routinely intervened in judicial matters and that operation of the judiciary suffered from nepotism.

17 ARMED FORCES

The International Institute for Strategic Studies reported that armed forces in the United Arab Emirates totaled 51,000 members in 2011. The force is comprised of 44,000 from the army, 2,500 from the navy, and 4,500 members of the air force. Armed forces represent 1.8% of the labor force in the United Arab Emirates. Defense spending totaled $7.7 billion and accounted for 3.1% of gross domestic product (GDP).

The armed forces of the United Arab Emirates were placed under a unified command in 1976, and the forces of Abu Dhabi, Dubai, Ra's al-Khaimah, and Sharjah were merged.

Many military personnel are expatriates from Oman, Jordan, and other countries. The US maintained a military presence of approximately 140 troops in the United Arab Emirates, as of 2010.

18 INTERNATIONAL COOPERATION

The United Arab Emirates became a member of the UN on 9 December 1971, shortly after becoming independent. In 2011, the United Arab Emirates was a member of the Arab League, Organization of the Islamic Conference, the Gulf Cooperation Council,

Organization of Petroleum Exporting Countries, and the Organization of Arab Petroleum Exporting Countries. It had established diplomatic relations with more than 60 countries including the United States, Japan, Russia, China, and most western European countries.

According to the US State Department, the United Arab Emirates also has provided more than $15 billion in development assistance to Arab and Muslim countries. It pledged $300 million to Lebanon in 2007, and had fulfilled the pledge by 2010. It also has pledged $215 million in economic and reconstruction assistance to Iraq, and provided aid to Afghanistan, Pakistan, and the Palestinian Authority.

The International Renewable Energy Agency is headquartered in Abu Dhabi.

19 ECONOMY

The GDP rate of change in the United Arab Emirates, as of 2010, was 3.2%. Inflation stood at 2.2%, and unemployment was reported at 2.4%.

Before the discovery of oil in 1962, pearl production, fishing, agriculture, and herding dominated the UAE economy. Petroleum has been the dominant activity since 1973, and crude oil accounted for 45% of UAE exports in 2010. The US State Department estimated the country's proven oil reserves at 97.8 billion barrels in 2011 and placed its natural gas reserves at 214.2 trillion cubic feet. Oil production was estimated at 2.813 billion barrels a day in 2010, and the United Arab Emirates was the world's fourth largest exporter of oil. Its reserves were expected to last more than 150 years.

The Economist Intelligence Unit predicted that the United Arab Emirates would enjoy annual average growth of 4.6% a year from 2011–20. Although GDP growth would remain dependent on oil production, the Economist Intelligence Unit also noted that a huge accumulation of overseas investments (estimated at $600 billion) and ongoing diversification of the economic base would start to have more of an effect on overall GDP. Dubai was one of the two largest shareholders of the London Stock Exchange, the world's third largest stock exchange, in September 2007. The CIA noted that economic diversification efforts had helped reduce the portion of GDP based on oil and gas output to 25% as of 2011. The United Arab Emirates has increased its imports of manufactured goods, machinery, and transportation equipment.

The United Arab Emirates also has earned export income from re-exports, primarily through its Jabal 'Ali deepwater port and free trade zone in Dubai. More than 6,000 companies representing about 120 countries operate at the complex. All goods for re-export or transshipment are 100% duty free.

Tourism and construction have been major growth areas, despite contractions in investment due to the 2008–09 global financial crisis. Although the government tried to ease the crisis through increased spending and liquidity boosts to the banking sector, depressed real estate prices hit Dubai especially hard. The emirate was unable to meet its debt obligations, which prompted global fears of its solvency. The UAE Central Bank and Abu Dhabi banks bought some shares, the emirate of Abu Dhabi provided Dubai with a $10 billion loan in December 2009. Into 2010, the economy recovered fairly well, with growth of real GDP estimated at 2.5% for year-end.

Much of the tourism and construction growth has been centered in Dubai, the world's fastest-growing city. Dubai was the Middle East's prime destination for luxury tourism and shopping as of 2011. It has become known worldwide for its conferences, trade exhibitions, and festivals. It is also a hub for international air travel. As of 2011 there were about $100 billion worth of projects either underway or planned for the near future.

Although 'Ajman has a small shipbuilding and ship repair yard and a cement company, and Umm al-Qaiwain has a fish hatchery, a cement plant, and some small handicraft operations, these poorer emirates depend on federal aid, which is tantamount to revenue sharing by Abu Dhabi and Dubai.

20 INCOME

The CIA estimated that in 2010 the GDP of the United Arab Emirates was $246.8 billion. The CIA defines GDP as the value of all final goods and services produced within a nation in a given year and computed on the basis of purchasing power parity (PPP) rather than value as measured on the basis of the rate of the exchange based on current dollars. The per capita GDP was estimated at $49,600. The annual growth rate of GDP was 3.2%. The average inflation rate was 2.2%. It was estimated that agriculture accounted for 0.9% of GDP, industry 51.5%, and services 47.6%. Despite having one of the highest per capita incomes in the region, some 19.5% of the population is living under the poverty line.

21 LABOR

As of 2010, the United Arab Emirates had a total labor force of 3.908 million people. Within that labor force, CIA estimates in 2000 noted that 7% were employed in agriculture, 15% in industry, and 78% in the service sector. Unemployment was reported at 2.4% in 2010.

The government has made Emiratization of the workforce a national goal. However, as of 2010, it had limited mandatory hiring of nations to a few sectors including banking with a 4% quota, insurance with a 5% quota, and trade with a 2% quota for companies employing more than 50 people.

The workforce included a large number of both skilled and unskilled foreign nationals in 2010. The unskilled laborers included 268,000 domestic servants who were primarily women from South and East Asia as well as unskilled male workers from South Asia. Many workers in the unskilled ranks were subject to poor working conditions and were dependent on employee sponsorships.

A labor law, proposed in 2007 but not ratified as of 2011, did not allow for labor unions or collective bargaining. However, it did call upon businesses to streamline and improve foreign worker contracts, make timely salary payments, and provide adequate housing for employees. The Ministry of Labor also introduced an electronic wage protection system in 2009 to fight non-payment of wages.

There was no minimum wage in the United Arab Emirates as of 2010, and the US State Department reported that the standard work week of eight hours per day, six days a week, was not effectively enforced. Wages were not adequate to provide a decent standard of living. Foreign unskilled laborers, particularly female domestic workers, were especially vulnerable to abuse.

22 AGRICULTURE

Roughly 7% of the total land is farmed, and the country's major crops included dates, vegetables, and pumpkins, squashes, and gourds. Cereal production in 2009 amounted to 45 tons, fruit production 790,493 tons, and vegetable production 448,915 tons.

About 230,000 UAE residents were estimated to be working in agriculture in 2010, compared with 160,000 in 2005. Although the agricultural labor force grew, it was declining as a percentage of the overall labor by about 4.32% annually between 2005 and 2010.

According to the government, many farms fell into decline in the first decade of the 21st century because farm owners did not live near their lands. In an effort to reverse that decline, the United Arab Emirates established the Abu Dhabi Farmers' Service Center in 2009. The government hoped to use the Center to make the agricultural sector more sustainable and to raise the share of locally grown produce from 15% in 2011 to 40% by 2016.

The most productive region was Ra's al-Khaimah, which receives underground water supplies from the nearby mountains of Oman and which enjoys the most plentiful rainfall. Government initiatives have promoted greenhouse gardening, experimental farms for local Bedouins, and irrigation and hydroponic practices.

23 ANIMAL HUSBANDRY

The UN Food and Agriculture Organization (FAO) reported that the United Arab Emirates dedicated 305,000 hectares (753,671 acres) to permanent pasture or meadow in 2009. During that year, the country tended 15.5 million chickens and 62,000 head of cattle. The production from these animals amounted to 37,868 tons of beef and veal and 480,262 tons of milk. The United Arab Emirates also produced 440 tons of cattle hide.

Livestock production was increasing in the United Arab Emirates in the first decade of the 21st century, and chicken and meat production grew by 2.6% between 2008 and 2009 while egg production grew 4.6%, according to government reports.

The government was investing in agricultural, livestock, and fisheries production through 2011 in an effort to attain food security for the emirates.

24 FISHING

In 2008, the annual capture totaled 74,075 tons according to the UN FAO, and was estimated to be 78,000 tons for 2009.

Fishing was an important source of domestic food and fodder through 2011. UAE coastal waters abound in fish and shellfish, and the country borders two high-potential fishing regions, the Persian Gulf and the Gulf of Oman. Demand for fish products in the United Arab Emirates has led to the development of new fisheries and investment in fishing activities. The government stated that production of fish, mollusks, and crustaceans increased 2.8% between 2008 and 2009. Many varieties of fish were caught, including rock cod, tuna, mackerel, sardines, anchovies, jack, marlin, red mullet, bream, and snapper.

25 FORESTRY

Approximately 4% of the United Arab Emirates is covered by forest. The value of all forest products, including roundwood, totaled $124 million in 2009.

Natural woodland is scarce, apart from palm groves along the northern and eastern coasts. The government in the early 21st century invested in the planting of native trees and shrubs in an effort to stop desertification and to minimize the effects of sandstorms.

26 MINING

Apart from oil and natural gas, the minerals sector includes fertilizer production and production of construction materials, marble, and stone quarried from the Hajar Mountains. Copper and chromium have been found in Fujairah and Ra's al-Khaimah. In 2009 mineral production included 24 metric tons of chromium, 150,000 metric tons of crushed stone, 380,000 metric tons of ammonia (nitrogen content); and 284,000 metric tons of urea (nitrogen content). Lime, gypsum, hydraulic cement, common clays, diabase, gravel, limestone, marble sand, and shale were also produced.

27 ENERGY AND POWER

The World Bank reported in 2008 that the United Arab Emirates produced 81.1 billion kWh of electricity and consumed 75.8 billion kWh, or 14,714 kWh per capita. All energy came from fossil fuels. Per capita oil consumption was 13,030 kg. Oil production totaled 2.41 million barrels of oil a day.

The United Arab Emirates contains almost 8% of the world's proven oil reserves and is ranked fifth in the world by the size of its natural gas reserves. The United Arab Emirates is also a significant exporter of liquefied natural gas (LNG) and a member of the Organization of Petroleum Exporting Countries (OPEC). Proven petroleum reserves totaled 97.8 billion barrels in 2011. Natural gas reserves were estimated at 227.9 trillion cu ft.

The Abu Dhabi National Company, comprised of 14 operating companies, was expanding oil output in 2010 from 2.7 million barrels per day to 3.5 million barrels per day, and was working to manufacture more petrochemical and plastics products. In addition, Abu Dhabi was investing in the building of a series of nuclear power plants to meet growing energy needs of Abu Dhabi and the northern emirates. The first plant, being built by a consortium of Korean firms, was to be operational in 2017.

28 INDUSTRY

The CIA estimated the industrial production growth rate at 3.2% in 2010. Primary industries were petroleum and petrochemicals, fishing, aluminum, cement, fertilizers, commercial ship repair, construction materials, boat building, handicrafts, and textiles.

The process of industrialization gathered momentum after the formation of the federation in 1971. By 2010, industry accounted for 51.5% of the United Arab Emirates's total GDP, with about 15% of its labor force employed in the sector. The US State Department anticipated that growth in aircraft and parts, security and safety equipment, information technology, medical equipment, architecture, construction, engineering, environmental and pollution control equipment, and water and power programs would occur in the second decade of the 21st century. As of 2010 the UAE government was investing heavily in infrastructure projects that included road improvements, power generation and distribution systems, desalination plants, sewage systems, public housing, recreational facilities, hospitals, schools, sports facilities, refineries, airports, and government buildings.

In the private sector, hotel and luxury resort development dominated construction projects, particularly in Dubai. Although the global financial crisis of 2008–09 caused real estate prices in Dubai to fall by about 40%, construction continued to grow in the emirate. Among the construction projects were the Burj Khalifa skyscraper which was the tallest human-made structure ever built, and the artificial palm-shaped Palm Islands that were developed as part of a futuristic land reclamation project.

²⁹ SCIENCE AND TECHNOLOGY

The World Bank reported in 2009 that there were no patent applications in science and technology in the United Arab Emirates. A report prepared for UNESCO on research and development activity in the United Arab Emirates concluded that such activities were relatively weak in the emirates in comparison with other developed countries. However, the United Arab Emirates has been investing in research and development through its colleges and universities. The Masdar Institute of Science and Technology was established in 1999 to promote education and innovation in advanced energy and sustainability. As of 2011, 170 graduate students had enrolled at the institution from 32 nations. About 43% of the student body included Emirati nationals. More than 30 research projects were underway. Research also was being conducted at the United Arab Emirates's 12 higher technology colleges.

³⁰ DOMESTIC TRADE

Dubai is the most important center of trade and commerce, both for the nation and the region. US fast-food outlets, casual dining, and organic foods are gaining popularity, and several large malls cater to the Emirati middle class. Although much of the distribution of retail goods is handled through middle men, franchising has become popular in a variety of retail sectors including restaurants, clothing, hardware supplies, beauty products, health care products, toys, and sporting goods.

Government offices generally are open from 7:30 a.m. to 2 p.m. Sunday through Thursday, and local business hours often would close between 1–4:30 p.m. Most companies were closed Friday and Saturday.

³¹ FOREIGN TRADE

The United Arab Emirates imported $159 billion worth of goods and services in 2008, while exporting $195.8 billion worth of goods and services. Export receipts in 2010 rose by 10.7% to $212.3 billion over the previous year, and import spending by 7.8% to $161.4 billion. The Economist Intelligence Unit estimated that the merchandise trade surplus increased to $50.8 billion in 2010, and that the current account surplus was $11.2 billion, or 3.8% of GDP.

Crude oil made up 28.3% of the total exports, natural gas accounted for 5.5%, and re-exports for 40.6% Major export partners were Japan, 17.5%; India, 11.9%; South Korea, 7.2%; Iran, 6.9%; and Thailand, 5.2%.

Machinery and electrical equipment made up 14% of the total imports, precious stones and metals, 20.7%, and vehicles and oth-

Principal Trading Partners – United Arab Emirates (2010)

(In millions of US dollars)

Country	Total	Exports	Imports	Balance
World	405,000.0	235,000.0	170,000.0	65,000.0
India	55,975.0	23,575.0	32,400.0	-8,825.0
Japan	34,678.0	26,615.0	8,063.0	18,552.0
China	27,329.0	3,967.0	23,362.0	-19,395.0
Iran	21,364.0	20,406.0	958.0	19,448.0
South Korea	17,100.0	11,064.0	6,036.0	5,028.0
United States	13,889.0	1,087.0	12,802.0	-11,715.0
Thailand	11,087.0	7,959.0	3,128.0	4,831.0
Singapore	9,981.0	5,792.0	4,189.0	1,603.0
Germany	9,804.0	439.0	9,365.0	-8,926.0
Oman	9,084.0	5,055.0	4,029.0	1,026.0

(…) data not available or not significant.

(n.s.) not specified.

SOURCE: *2011 Direction of Trade Statistics Yearbook,* New York: United Nations, 2011.

er transport equipment, 9%. Major import partners in 2009 were India, 15%; China, 13.5%; the United States, 8.8%; Germany, 6.1%; and Japan, 4.7%.

³² BALANCE OF PAYMENTS

The CIA estimated United Arab Emirates to have a current account balance of $6.053 billion in 2010 compared with $7.826 billion in 2009. The current account balance shrank in these two years over surpluses that reached $12.7 billion in 2004.

Oil and natural gas exports have allowed the United Arab Emirates to sustain a trade surplus for many years, but changes in oil prices have caused the surplus to fluctuate widely from year to year. For 2010, exports were estimated at $212.3 billion compared with $191.8 billion in 2009, while imports were estimated at $161.4 billion for 2010 and $149.7 billion for 2009.

³³ BANKING AND SECURITIES

The CIA estimated the United Arab Emirates's stock of narrow money (the amount of total currency in circulation) at $63.43 billion in 2010 compared with an estimated $60.84 billion in 2009. The stock of broad money (which includes the total currency along with banking and credit union deposits, money market funds, short-term repurchase agreements, and other large liquid assets) were estimated at $214.1 billion for 2010 and $201.6 billion for 2009. The country's reserves of foreign exchange and gold were estimated at $42.79 billion for 2010, an increase from $36.1 billion in 2009. The stock of domestic credit was estimated at $274.7 billion in 2010, compared with $263.6 billion in 2009. The market value of publicly traded shares was estimated at $104.7 billion in 2010. This figure declined from an estimated $109.6 billion in 2009 due to the global financial crisis, but was up slightly from $97.85 billion in 2008.

The UAE Central Bank regulates the banking system. With the 1980s oil boom, commercial banks proliferated in the emirates, making it one of the most over-banked countries in the world. By 1987 strains were beginning to show and two banks collapsed. Bad loans were prevalent and some borrowers used the Islamic prohibition on *riba* (interest) as an excuse not to repay debts. UAE banks were hit hard again by the invasion of Kuwait in 1990, when partial withdrawals amounted to an estimated $1.9 billion, or 7% of total deposits.

These crises had made the UAE Central Bank hesitant to issue licenses to new foreign banks in the 1990s, but the restrictions eased toward the end of the first decade of the early 21st century. The US State Department reported that as of 2010 the United Arab Emirates had 24 locally incorporated banks with 745 branches, 28 foreign banks with 82 branches, 1 restricted license bank, 3 investment banks, and 80 representative offices. While a number of US financial institutions have established a presence in the Dubai International Financial Center's financial free zone, Citibank was the only US bank that offered full banking services as of 2010. The largest banks in the United Arab Emirates that year were Emirates NBD, the National Bank of Abu Dhabi, Mashreq Bank, and Abu Dhabi Commercial Bank. The UAE Ministry of Finance announced a merger of two Sharia real estate finance providers—Amlak Finance PJSC and Tamwell—under the UAE Real Estate Bank in 2008.

The Economist Intelligence Unit reported that deposits in the United Arab Emirates for the first nine months of 2011 grew by 5.3% year on year. Lending continued to be sluggish, growing at 3.5% for the year on year time period. Lending was expected to increase in 2012.

The Dubai Financial Market and the Abu Dhabi Securities Market both opened in 2000. Total capitalization of the 134 companies listed on the two exchanged was more than $104 billion as of January 2010. In addition, the United Arab Emirates has a free finance zone in Dubai known as the Dubai International Financial Center. The Dubai Financial Market announced plans in December 2009 to acquire the NASDAQ Dubai Stock Exchange for $121 million.

34 INSURANCE

About half of the insurance companies operating in the United Arab Emirates were foreign-owned as of 2010, despite a law requiring that 75% of such companies must be owned by a UAE national or corporation.

The Emirates Insurance Authority regulates the sector, and reported 60 companies operating in the United Arab Emirates as of November 2011. Gross premiums written growth was 3% in the first six months of 2011, and the sector was forecast to grow at a compound annual growth rate of 19% to $18.3 billion by 2015.

35 PUBLIC FINANCE

In 2010 the budget of the United Arab Emirates included $65.02 billion in public revenue and $60.02 billion in public expenditures. The budget surplus amounted to 0.7% of GDP. Public debt was 44.6% of GDP, with $152.3 billion of the debt held by foreign entities.

A federal budget is prepared according to the United Arab Emirates's development policy, while each emirate is responsible for municipal budgets and local projects. Abu Dhabi's oil income accounts for the bulk of federal revenues; under the constitution, each emirate contributes 50% of its net oil income to the federal budget.

36 TAXATION

The United Arab Emirates had no personal income tax in 2011, and levied corporate taxes only on foreign banks and energy companies. Each emirate sets its own corporate tax rate. The Economist Intelligence Unit reported in 2011 that Dubai was generating an increasing amount of revenue by extending fees and charges for services. Islamic banks and financial institutions also were levied a *zakat*, or Islamic tax, of 2.5% of their net operating capital.

37 CUSTOMS AND DUTIES

The United Arab Emirates continued to maintain a liberal trading policy through the first decade of the 21st century. Imports into the emirates for the purpose of re-export were exempt from customs duty, although a deposit or bank guaranteed to the local customs authority was required. Duties for all but some restricted items were calculated at a rate of 5%. Liquor imports were subject to a 70% customs duty, and tobacco products 100%. The United Arab Emirates prohibited imports of irradiated food products and required a health and Halal slaughter certificate on all imported meats.

Dubai, the major area for foreign trade, is a free trade zone and free port with no restrictions on imports or exports. The individual emirate governments exert no control over imports, except for licensing.

38 FOREIGN INVESTMENT

Foreign direct investment (FDI) in the United Arab Emirates was unreported according to World Bank figures published in 2009. The Economist Intelligence Unit estimated foreign direct investment flows at 3.7% of GDP from 2006–10.

The CIA estimated the stock of FDI in the United Arab Emirates at $74.13 billion in 2010, compared with $70.18 billion in 2009. These figures represent investments made by foreigners, other than purchases of stock shares. The stock of FDI made by UAE residents in other countries was estimated at $53.43 billion in 2010 compared with $51.41 billion in 2009.

The US State Department, citing figures from the UN Conferences on Trade and Development, reported that inward FDI flow rose to $13.7 billion in 2008, and that the United Arab Emirates was ranked 34th in the 196 nations of the world in terms of attracting foreign investment. Leading FDI sectors were oil and gas field machinery and services, power and water, computers and peripherals, medical equipment and supplies, airport development, telecommunications, and franchising.

The government requires that investments be of a joint venture nature, with the local partner owning at least 51% of the venture. Full foreign ownership is allowed, however, in the free trade zones.

39 ECONOMIC DEVELOPMENT

The discovery of oil in 1962 rapidly shifted the UAE economy from one based on pearl fishing, herding, and agriculture to a more industrialized nation. As the federation of emirates formally organized into a sovereign nation, government policy focused on using the vast oil wealth to build and expand roads, ports, airports, communications facilities, electric power plants, and water desalination facilities, as well as to construct huge oil-processing complexes. With the completion of major infrastructural projects by the early 1980s, the focus of development shifted to diversifying the economy by establishing capital-intensive industries based on oil and gas resources.

The 2008–09 global financial crisis shifted economic policy toward protecting the banking and real estate sectors, particularly in Dubai.

Diversification of the economy remained a priority for the United Arab Emirates in 2011, although the nation's rich oil and gas reserves were expected to last at least 150 years. The reliance on oil has made the country vulnerable to global shifts in oil commodity prices.

Much of the country's labor force continued to be comprised of non-nationals in 2011, and Emiratization of the work force was a key policy aim for the government. The strategic plan outlined goals to increase employment of nationals in the private sector and to improve the educational system. The government also announced in 2011 a plan to consider requiring non-nationals to contribute to a national pension system for the first time. The change would replace a system in which expatriates were paid a lump sum upon their departure from the country. Both employers and employees would contribute to the pension scheme.

40 SOCIAL DEVELOPMENT

The United Arab Emirates in 2011 was generally more liberal in its social practices than other Arab nations. Although women continued to suffer discrimination, employment and educational opportunities were growing for women in government, education, and health areas. Women in the larger, more cosmopolitan emirates of Abu Dhabi and Dubai often wore western attire and appeared in public in the company of men.

Despite the modernization of the UAE economy, many social problems persist. Citizens do not have a right to change their government, and the dispensation of law and order often is subject to the leadership of each individual emirate. The US State Department in 2010 reported instances of flogging as a judicially sanctioned punishment, arbitrary arrests, restrictions on civil liberties, domestic abuse, and human trafficking.

There is no social security law in the United Arab Emirates, but many welfare benefits are available to citizens, among them free hospital treatment and medical care, and subsidies for education. Relief for any domestic catastrophe is provided from a disaster fund. If the father of a family is unable to work because of illness, disability, or old age, he receives help under the National Assistance Law; should he die or divorce his wife, the woman's future is secured. UAE nationals receive many government services, including health care, water, and electricity, free of charge.

41 HEALTH

According to the CIA, life expectancy in the United Arab Emirates was 78 years in 2011. The country spent 2.5% of its GDP on healthcare, amounting to $1,520 per person. There were 19 physicians, 41 nurses and midwives, and 19 hospital beds per 10,000 inhabitants. The fertility rate was 1.9 children born per woman, while the infant mortality rate was 7 deaths per 1,000 live births. In 2008 the maternal mortality rate, according to the World Bank,

was 10 deaths per 100,000 births. It was estimated that 92% of children were vaccinated against measles.

Health facilities have expanded rapidly since independence. Modern hospitals have been built in Abu Dhabi, Dubai, and other cities and towns.

42 HOUSING

About 84% of the total population lived in urban areas as of 2010, and the rate of change of urbanization was 2.3% annually. The federal government has initiated several plans to make modern low-cost homes available to poorer families, supplying them with amenities such as piped water, sewerage systems, and electricity. As of 2010 the entire UAE population had access to clean water and virtually all (97%) had access to improved sanitation facilities.

Among the initiatives underway in 2011 were home safety programs initiated by the Dubai Police, and affordable lending and housing development programs initiated by the national government and the rulers of Dubai.

43 EDUCATION

In 2009 the World Bank estimated that 90% of age-eligible children in the United Arab Emirates were enrolled in primary school. Secondary enrollment for age-eligible children stood at 83%. Tertiary enrollment was estimated at 30%. Overall, the CIA estimated that the United Arab Emirates had a literacy rate of 77.9%. Public expenditure on education represented 1.2% of GDP.

Since its formation as a sovereign nation, the United Arab Emirates has established a strong higher educational system. Emirati nationals can attend governmental institutions free of charge. According to the UNESCO study, 95% of women and 80% of men who complete the final year of secondary school continue to pursue education in the United Arab Emirates or abroad. Numerous colleges and universities were present in the United Arab Emirates in 2011. Some of the larger institutions included Zayed University for women, with campuses in Abu Dhabi and Dubai; American Universities of Sharjah; United Arab Emirates University; Abu Dhabi University; and Al Hosn University.

Despite the expansion of the educational system, government restrictions on academic freedom persist. Students in secondary schools are prohibited from reading texts featuring sexuality or showing illustrations of the human body. Conferences that discuss political issues require government permission. Islamic studies continue to be mandatory in public schools as well as private schools serving Muslim children. Any schools that are found to be teaching subjects offensive to Islam face penalties. Arabic is a required subject, and sex segregation of classrooms is required.

44 LIBRARIES AND MUSEUMS

The UAE Public Library in Dubai houses a 1 million volume national library, auditorium, and exhibit center. Dubai Public Libraries, the oldest system in the emirates, has eight branches in Dubai. Other major libraries include the National Library in Dubai, the Juma Al-Majid Heritage and Cultural Centre, the Higher Colleges of Technology Library and the United Arab Emirates University Library.

Most of the emirates have museums of historic and cultural value. Among the major museums are the Dubai National Museum, housed in the Al Fahidi Fort, the Al ʿAyn Museum, the Sharjah

Archeology Museum, Sharjah Heritage Museum, Sharjah Natural History Museum, Sharjah Science Museum, and a children's museum called the Discovery Center.

⁴⁵MEDIA

The telecommunications system of the United Arab Emirates is marked by modern, fiber-optic integrated services, digital networks, and a growing mobile cellular telephone sector. Domestic services are provided by a mix of coaxial and fiber-optic cable systems, and microwave radio relay stations. International service is provided by submarine cable, microwave radio relay stations, and satellite ground stations. In 2009 the CIA reported that there were 1.6 million telephone landlines in the United Arab Emirates. In addition to landlines, mobile phone subscriptions averaged 232 per 100 people.

Nearly all of the television and radio broadcasting stations are owned and operated by the government through Abu Dhabi Radio and TV or Emirates TV. There is a Media Free Zone in Dubai where private stations are located, including those broadcasting in English and Arabic. In 2009 there were 13 FM radio stations, 8 AM radio stations, and 2 shortwave radio stations. In 2010, the country had 379,309 Internet hosts. Internet users numbered 82 per 100 citizens.

Prominent newspapers in 2010, with circulation numbers listed parenthetically, included *Khaleej Times* (100,000), *Gulf News* (91,534), and *Al Khaleej* (85,000), as well as nine other major newspapers.

The provisional constitution provides for free expression; however, the government restricts expression in practice. All published materials must be licensed by the Ministry of Education, which governs content and allowable subjects. The media practice self-censorship on the subjects of government policy, the ruling families, national security, religion, and international relations.

⁴⁶ORGANIZATIONS

Numerous philanthropic organizations were based in the United Arab Emirates as of 2011, and each emirate had its own chamber of commerce. Several associations represent foreign businesses, and professional and sporting organizations thrive. The Federation of United Arab Emirates Chambers of Commerce and Industry is located in Abu Dhabi.

⁴⁷TOURISM, TRAVEL, AND RECREATION

Tourists visiting the United Arab Emirates spent a total of $7.16 billion in 2009. The estimated daily cost to visit Abu Dhabi, the capital, was $526. The cost of visiting other cities averaged $413.

The UN World Tourism Institute reported 7.43 million tourist visits to the United Arab Emirates in 2009.

Aggressive marketing increased tourism in Dubai substantially in 2011. Figures from the emirate's Department of Tourism and Marketing estimated that 6.64 million guests stayed in Dubai hotels in the first nine months of 2011, an 11% increase from the same period in 2010.

Except for Gulf nationals and citizens of the United Kingdom, most visitors must secure a visa in advance. Tourism is encouraged by all the emirates, whose varied scenery includes mountains, beaches, deserts, and oases. Activities include visits to Bedouin markets, museums, zoos, and aquariums. Many large world-class hotels have opened in recent years. In January 2010 Dubai celebrated the opening of the world's largest tower, the Burj Khalifa. The tower itself soars 828 m (2,717) ft in the air. The Burj has the world's first Armani hotel, the world's highest swimming pool, the highest mosque, and the highest observation deck.

⁴⁸FAMOUS PERSONS

Sheikh Zayid bin Sultan Al-Nuhayyan (1918–2004) was ruler of Abu Dhabi after 1966 and president of the United Arab Emirates from 1971 until his death in 2004. His son, Sheikh Khalifa bin Zayid Al-Nuhayyan (b. 1948) became president of the United Arab Emirates upon his father's death. Other famous Emiratis included H.E. Sheikha Lubna Khalid Sultan al Qasimi (b. 1962), of Sharjah, the first female to hold a ministerial post; artist Abdul Qader al-Rais (b. 1951); and singer Hussain al-Jasmi (b. 1979).

⁴⁹DEPENDENCIES

The United Arab Emirates has no territories or colonies.

⁵⁰BIBLIOGRAPHY

Elsheshtawy, Yasser. *Dubai: Behind an Urban Spectacle*. New York: Routledge, 2010.

Etheredge, Laura. *Persian Gulf States: Kuwait, Qatar, Bahrain, Oman, and the United Arab Emirates*. New York: Britannica Educational Publications, 2011.

McCoy, Lisa. *United Arab Emirates*. Philadelphia: Mason Crest Publishers, 2004.

Oman and the United Arab Emirates. London: Lonely Planet, 2009.

Seddon, David, ed. *A Political and Economic Dictionary of the Middle East*. Philadelphia: Routledge/Taylor and Francis, 2004.

Stannard, Dorothy, ed. *Oman and the United Arab Emirates*. Singapore: APA Publications, 2007.

United Arab Emirates Investment and Business Guide: Strategic and Practical Information. Washington, DC: International Business Publications USA, 2012.

UNITED STATES PACIFIC DEPENDENCIES

AMERICAN SAMOA

American Samoa is a US territory that lies in the South Pacific Ocean. It is made up of seven small islands in the Samoan archipelago (chain of islands). American Samoa lies between 14° and 15° S and 168° and 171° W). The islands of American Samoa lie east of longitude 171° W. (The rest of the Samoan islands comprise the independent state of Western Samoa.) American Samoa has a total area (land and water) of 197 sq km (76 sq mi). Five of the islands are volcanic, with rugged peaks rising sharply, and two are coral atolls.

The climate is hot and rainy; normal temperatures range from 24°C (75°F) in August to 32°C (90°F) during December–February; mean annual rainfall is 330 cm (130 in). The rainy season lasts from December through March. Hurricanes are common. Native plants include tree ferns, coconut, hardwoods, and rubber trees. There are few wild animals.

As of mid-2012, the estimated population was 68,061, an increase over the 1986 population of 37,500. The inhabitants, who are concentrated on the island of Tutuila, are almost entirely Polynesian. Most people are bilingual: English and Samoan are the official languages. Most Samoans are Christians, belonging to the Congregationalist denomination.

The capital of the territory, Pago Pago, lies on Tutuila. Pago Pago has one of the finest natural harbors in the South Pacific and is a duty-free port. Passenger cruise ships stop there on South Pacific tours. Passenger and cargo ships arrive regularly from Japan, New Zealand, Australia, and the US west coast.

There are regular air and sea services between American Samoa and Western Samoa, and scheduled flights between Pago Pago and Honolulu.

American Samoa was settled by Melanesian migrants in the first millennium BC. The Samoan islands were visited in 1768 by the French explorer Louis-Antoine de Bougainville. He named them the Îles des Navigateurs (Islands of the Navigators) as a tribute to the skill of their native boatmen.

In 1889, the United States, the United Kingdom, and Germany agreed to share control of the islands. The United Kingdom later withdrew its claim. Under the 1899 Treaty of Berlin, the United States was acknowledged internationally as having rights over all the islands of the Samoan group lying east of 171° W. Germany was acknowledged to have similar rights to the islands west of that meridian.

The islands of American Samoa were officially ceded to the United States by the various ruling chiefs in 1900 and 1904. On 20 February 1929 the US Congress formally accepted sovereignty over the entire group. From 1900 to 1951, the territory was administered by the US Department of the Navy, and thereafter by the Department of the Interior. The basic law is the constitution of 1966.

In June 2010, officials in American Samoa publicly raised the issue of a referendum for full autonomy for the territory, arguing that full autonomy is the only way to protect the region's local laws and culture from the effects of a political process intended for the mainland United States. Popular support for the idea remained uncertain.

The executive branch of the government is headed by a governor who, along with the lieutenant governor, is elected by popular vote. Before 1977, the governor and lieutenant governor were appointed by the US government. Village, county, and district councils have full authority to regulate local affairs. The legislature (Fono) is composed of the House of Representatives and the Senate. The 15 counties elect 18 *matais* (chiefs) to four-year terms in the senate, while the 21 house members are elected for two-year terms by popular vote within the counties. (There is one appointed member from Swains Island.)

The judiciary, an independent branch of the government, functions through the high court and five district courts. Those born in Samoa are nationals of the United States. The territory sends one delegate to the US House of Representatives.

Small plantations occupy about one-third of the land area; 90% of the land is communally owned. The principal crops are bananas, coconuts, breadfruit, taro, papayas, pineapples, sweet potatoes, tapioca, coffee, cocoa, and yams. Hogs and poultry are the principal livestock raised; dairy cattle are few. The principal cash crop is copra. A third of the total labor force is employed by the federal and territorial government. The largest employers in the private sector, accounting for 80% of employment, are two modern tuna canneries supplied with fish caught by Japanese, US, and Taiwanese fishing fleets. Canned tuna is the primary export. Most foreign trade is conducted with the United States. The GDP was $575.3 million in 2007, or $8,000 per capita.

The 2008–09 global financial crisis had a significant effect on the personal income of many workers. To alleviate some of the strain, the US Treasury Department issued an economic stimulus package of $20.4 million, to be distributed by the American Samoa government in the form of tax rebates for qualifying workers and their families. The rebates were issued throughout 2010 and 2011, based on returns filed for the 2009 and 2010 tax years.

Samoans are entitled to free medical treatment, including hospital care. Besides district dispensaries, the government maintains a central hospital, a tuberculosis unit, and a leprosarium. US-trained staff physicians work with Samoan medical practitioners and nurses. The LBJ Tropical Medical Center opened in 1986. Obesity is a major problem, with a prevalence rate of 74.6% as of 2007—the highest of any territory in the world. The infant mortality rate was 9.42 deaths per 1,000 live births in 2012; the fertility rate was 3.1 children born per woman. Life expectancy was 74.44 years as of 2012.

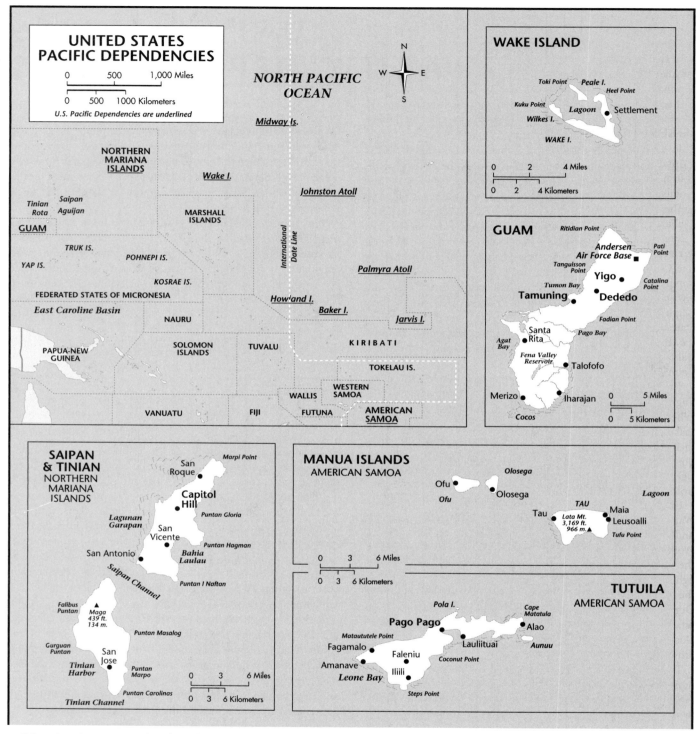

Education is a joint undertaking between the territorial government and the villages. School attendance is compulsory for all children from ages 6 through 18. In 2010 more than $30 million was granted to American Samoa under the American Recovery and Reinvestment Act. The funds were to be used primarily for the improvement of the education system. About 97% of the population is literate.

There were 10,400 telephone landlines in 2010 and 2,200 mobile cellular telephones (2004). Three television stations broadcast lo-cally, and additional pay-per-view services are available. Internet hosts numbered 2,368 in 2011.

GUAM

Guam is the largest and most populous of the Mariana Islands in the Western Pacific. Guam (13° 28′ N and 144° 44′ E) has an area, including land and water, of 540 sq km (208 sq mi) and is about 48 km (30 mi) long and 6–12 km (4–7 mi) wide.

The island is of volcanic origin; in the south, the terrain is mountainous, while the northern part is a plateau with shallow fertile soil. The central part of the island (where the capital, Agana, is located) is hilly.

Guam lies in the typhoon belt of the Western Pacific and is occasionally subject to widespread storm damage. In May 1976, a typhoon with winds of 306 km/hour (190 mi/hour) struck Guam, causing an estimated $300 million in damage and leaving 80% of the island's buildings in ruins. Guam has a tropical climate with little seasonal variation. Average temperature is 26°C (79°F). Rainfall is substantial, reaching an annual average of more than 200 cm (80 in). Endangered species include the giant Micronesian kingfisher and Marianas crow.

The mid-2012 population, excluding transient US military and civilian personnel and their families, was estimated at 185,674, an increase over the 1986 population of 117,500. The increase was attributed largely to the higher birthrate and low mortality rate. The Chamorro comprise about 37% of the permanent resident population. The Chamorro descend from the intermingling of the few surviving original Chamorro (Pacific Islander) with Spanish, Filipino, and Mexican settlers, and later arrivals from the United States, United Kingdom, Korea, China, and Japan. Filipinos (26%) are the largest ethnic minority. English and Chamorro are official languages. The predominant religion is Roman Catholicism, claimed by 85% of the population.

The earliest known settlers on Guam were the Chamorro, who migrated from the Malay Peninsula to the Pacific around 1500 BC. When Ferdinand Magellan landed on Guam in 1521, it is believed that as many as 100,000 Chamorro lived on the island; by 1741, their numbers had been reduced to 5,000—most of the population either had fled the island or been killed through disease or war with the Spanish. A Spanish fort was established in 1565, and from 1696 until 1898, Guam was under Spanish rule.

Under the Treaty of Paris that ended the Spanish-American War in 1898, the island was ceded to the United States and placed under the jurisdiction of the Department of the Navy. During World War II (1939–45), Guam was occupied by Japanese forces; the United States recaptured the island in 1944 after 54 days of fighting. In 1950, the island's administration was transferred from the Navy to the US Department of the Interior. Under the 1950 Organic Act of Guam passed by the US Congress, the island was established as an unincorporated territory of the United States. Guamanians were granted US citizenship, and internal self-government was introduced.

The governor and lieutenant governor have been elected directly since 1970. A 15-member unicameral legislature elected for two years by adult suffrage is empowered to legislate on all local matters, including taxation and appropriations. The US Congress reserves the right to annul any law passed by the Guam legislature, but must do so within a year of the date it receives the text of any such law.

Judicial authority is vested in the district court of Guam. Appeals may be taken to the regular US courts of appeal and ultimately to the US Supreme Court. An island superior court and other specialized courts have jurisdiction over certain cases arising under the laws of Guam. The judge of the district court is appointed by the US president; the judges of the other courts are appointed by the governor. Guam's laws were codified in 1953.

Guam is one of the most important US military bases in the Pacific. The island's economy has been profoundly affected by the large sums of money spent by the US defense establishment. During the late 1960s and early 1970s, when the United States took the role of a major combatant in the Vietnam conflict, Guam served as a base for long-range US bombers.

Prior to World War II, agriculture and animal husbandry were the primary activities. By 1947, most adults were wage earners employed by the US armed forces, although many continued to cultivate small plots to supplement their earnings. A considerable amount of arable land is taken up by military installations. Fruits and vegetables are grown, and pigs and poultry are raised for local consumption, but most food is imported. About 26% of the labor force is employed in agriculture, while 10% are employed in industry, and 64% in services. Tourism became a major industry and sparked a boom in the construction industry in the mid-1980s. As of 2011, tourism was second only to US defense spending in economic importance. In fiscal year 2010, the combined dollar value of civilian and military construction projects on Guam was $649.2 million. This represented an increase of 47% from the previous year, primarily through military build-up in the region. The projects resulted in the creation of 6,500 new jobs on Guam. Construction projects expanded during fiscal year 2011 as well. Officials expected that 38,000 new jobs would be created by 2014.

Guam's foreign trade usually shows large deficits. Exports were $45 million in 2004, while imports were $701 million. The bulk of Guam's trade is with the United States, Japan, Singapore, and South Korea. Primary imports are petroleum and petroleum products, food, and manufactured goods; main exports are refined petroleum products, construction materials, fish, food, and beverage products.

US income tax laws are applicable in Guam; all internal revenue taxes derived by the United States from Guam are paid into the territory's treasury. US customs duties, however, are not levied. Guam is a duty-free port.

Typical tropical diseases are practically unknown today in Guam. The Guam Memorial Hospital has a capacity of 208 beds. Village dispensaries serve both as public health units and first-aid stations. In addition, there are a number of physicians in private practice. Specialists from the US Naval Hospital in Guam, assisting on a part-time basis, have made possible a complete program of curative medicine. The infant mortality rate was 5.72 deaths per 1,000 live births in 2012; the fertility rate was 2.45 children born per woman. Life expectancy was 78.5 years. School attendance is compulsory from the age of 6 through 16. The literacy rate is nearly 100%. As of 2010 there were 65,500 telephone landlines and 98,000 mobile cellular phones (2004). Internet users numbered 90,000 in 2009; Internet hosts totaled 23 in 2011.

HOWLAND, BAKER, AND JARVIS ISLANDS

Howland Island (0° 48′ N and 176° 38′ W), Baker Island (0° 14′ N and 176° 28′ W), and Jarvis Island (0° 23′ S and 160° 1′ W) are three small coral islands. Each measures about 2.6 sq km (1 sq mi) in area. They belong to the Line Islands group of the central Pacific Ocean. All three are administered by the US government as unincorporated territories. Public entry is by special permit and is generally restricted to scientists and educators.

Howland was discovered in 1842 by US sailors. It was claimed by the United States in 1857. It was worked for guano by US and British companies until about 1890. Howland Island was formally proclaimed a US territory in 1935–36.

Baker Island lies 64 km (40 mi) S of Howland. Jarvis Island lies 1,770 km (1,100 mi) E of Howland. Both were claimed by the United States in 1857, and their guano deposits were similarly worked by US and British enterprises. The United Kingdom annexed Jarvis in 1889. In 1935, the United States sent colonists from Hawaii to all three islands, which were placed under the US Department of the Interior in 1936. Baker Island was captured by the Japanese in 1942 and recaptured by the United States in 1944.

The three islands are administered as part of the National Wildlife Refuge system. All lack fresh water and have no permanent inhabitants. They are visited annually by the US Coast Guard. A lighthouse on Howland Island is named in honor of the US aviatrix Amelia Earhart, who vanished en route to the island on a round-the-world flight in 1937.

JOHNSTON ATOLL

Johnston Atoll is located in the North Pacific 1,151 km (715 mi) SW of Honolulu, Hawaii. It consists of two islands—Johnston (16° 44′ N and 169° 31′ W) and Sand (16° 45′ N and 169° 30′ W)—with a total land and water area of about 2.6 sq km (1 sq mi). The islands are enclosed by a semicircular reef. It was discovered by English sailors in 1807 and claimed by the United States in 1858. For many years, it was worked for guano and was a bird reservation. Commissioned as a naval station in 1941, it remains an unincorporated US territory under the control of the US Department of the Air Force. In the 1950s and 1960s, it was used primarily for the testing of nuclear weapons. Until late 2000, it was maintained as a storage and disposal site for chemical weapons. Munitions destruction is now complete, and cleanup and closure of the facility was completed by May 2005.

The population usually stood at 1,100 government personnel and contractors, but decreased significantly after the September 2001 departure of the US Army Chemical Activity Pacific (US-ACAP). All US government personnel had left the island by 2005. The atoll is equipped with an excellent satellite and radio telecommunications system.

MIDWAY

The Midway Islands (28° 12′–17′ N and 177° 19′–26′ W) consist of an atoll and two small islets, Eastern Island (177° 20′ W) and Sand Island (177° 22′–24′ W), 2,100 km (1,300 mi) WNW of Honolulu, Hawaii. Total land and water area is 5 sq km (2 sq mi). As of 2011, about 40 people made up the staff of the US Fish and Wildlife service on the atoll.

Midway Island was discovered and claimed by the United States in 1859 and formally annexed in 1867. It became a submarine cable station early in the 20th century and an airlines station in 1935. Midway became a US naval base in 1941 (during World War II) and was attacked twice by the Japanese, in December 1941 and January 1942. In one of the great battles of World War II, a Japanese naval attack on 3–6 June 1942 was repelled by US warplanes.

Midway is a US unincorporated territory; there is a closed naval station, and the islands are important nesting places for seabirds. In 1993, administrative control of Midway was transferred from the US Department of the Navy to the US Department of the Interior's Fish and Wildlife Service.

NORTHERN MARIANAS

The Northern Marianas, a US commonwealth in the Western Pacific Ocean, is comprised of the Mariana Islands excluding Guam (a separate political entity). Located between 12° and 21° N and 144° and 146° E, it consists of 16 volcanic islands with a total land area of about 475 sq km (184 sq mi). Only six of the islands are inhabited, and most people live on the three largest islands—Rota, 85 sq km (33 sq mi); Saipan, 122 sq km (47 sq mi); and Tinian, 101 sq km (39 sq mi).

The climate is tropical, with relatively little seasonal change; temperatures average 21–29°C (70–85°F). Relative humidity is generally high. Rainfall averages 216 cm (85 in) per year. The southern islands, which include Rota, Saipan, and Tinian, are generally lower in elevation. They are covered with moderately heavy tropical vegetation. The northern islands are more rugged, reaching a high point of 959 m (3,146 ft) on Agrihan. The northern islands are generally barren due to erosion and insufficient rainfall. Pagan and Agrihan have active volcanoes, and typhoons are common from August to November. Insects are numerous and ocean birds and ocean wildlife are abundant. The endemic Marianas mallard is extinct.

The Northern Marianas had an estimated population of 44,582 in mid-2012. Three-fourths of the population is descended from the original Micronesian inhabitants, known as Chamorros. There are also many descendants of migrants from the Caroline Islands and smaller numbers of Filipino and Korean laborers and settlers from the US mainland. English and Chamorro are official languages. However, only 10.8% of the population speaks English in the home. Philippine languages and Chinese are each spoken by about one-quarter of the population. Most people are Roman Catholic.

It is believed that the Marianas were settled by migrants from the Philippines and Indonesia. Excavations on Saipan have yielded evidence of settlement around 1500 BC. The first European to reach the Marianas, in 1521, was Ferdinand Magellan.

The islands were ruled by Spain until the Spanish defeat by the United States in the Spanish-American War (1898). Guam was then ceded to the United States and the rest of the Marianas were sold to Germany. When World War I (1914–18) broke out, Japan took over the Northern Marianas and other German-held islands in the Western Pacific. These islands (the Northern Marianas, Carolines, and Marshalls) were placed under Japanese administration as a League of Nations mandate on 17 December 1920. Upon its withdrawal from the League in 1935, Japan began to fortify the islands. In World War II the islands served as important military bases.

Several of the islands were the scene of heavy fighting during the war. In the battle for control of Saipan in June 1944, some 23,000 Japanese and 3,500 US troops lost their lives in one day's fighting. As each island was occupied by US troops, it became subject to US authority in accordance with international law. The US planes that dropped atomic bombs on Hiroshima and Nagasaki, bringing an end to the war, took off from Tinian.

On 18 July 1947, the Northern Mariana, Caroline, and Marshall islands formally became a United Nations (UN) Trust Territory under US administration. This Trust Territory of the Pacific Islands was administered by the US Department of the Navy until 1 July 1951, when administration was transferred to the Department of the Interior. From 1953 to 1962, the Northern Marianas, with the exception of Rota, were administered by the Department of the Navy.

The people of the Northern Marianas voted to become a US commonwealth by a majority of 78.8% in a plebiscite held on 17 June 1975. A covenant approved by the US Congress in March 1976 provided for the separation of the Northern Marianas from the Caroline and Marshall island groups, and for the Marianas' transition to a commonwealth status similar to that of Puerto Rico.

The islands became internally self-governing in January 1978. On 3 November 1986, US president Ronald Reagan proclaimed the Northern Marianas a self-governing commonwealth; its people became US citizens. The termination of the trusteeship was approved by the UN Trusteeship Council in May 1986 and received the required approval from the UN Security Council. On 3 November 1986, the Constitution of the Commonwealth of the Northern Marianas Islands came into force.

A governor and a lieutenant governor are popularly elected for four-year terms. The legislature consists of 9 senators elected for four-year terms and 20 representatives elected for two-year terms. A district court handles matters involving federal law, and a commonwealth court has jurisdiction over local matters.

The traditional economic activities were subsistence agriculture, livestock raising, and fishing, but much agricultural land was destroyed or damaged during World War II, and agriculture has never resumed its prewar importance. Following the decline of the agricultural sector, garment production and tourism became the mainstays of the economy. However, the garment industry collapsed in the wake of the 2008–09 global financial crisis, as the drastic drop in demand for exports led to the closing of the last garment factory on the islands. This left tourism as the primary industry, at a time when a weak economy meant fewer travelers were venturing to the islands. The US Department of the Interior's Office of Insular Affairs (OIA) committed $1 million in financial aid for economic revitalization in May 2011. These funds were earmarked for use in tourism, labor market training (for US citizens), and renewable energy and agriculture/aquaculture projects. A basic goal was to create jobs that would reduce the territories' dependence on fossil fuels and contribute to the food supply. However, the OIA also recognized healthcare, education, transportation, and communication as sectors of concern. Tourism employs about 50% of the work force and accounts for one-fourth of GDP. Most tourists come from Japan, with annual tourist arrivals often exceeding 500,000. Exports, mainly garments, totaled $98.2 million in 2008, and imports totaled $214 million. Although the Northern Marianas is heavily dependent on funds from the US government—paid to lease property on Saipan, Tinian, and Farallon de Medinilla islands for defense purposes—US funding has declined as the domestic economy has grown.

Healthcare is primarily the responsibility of the commonwealth government and has improved substantially since 1978. There is a hospital on Saipan and health centers on Tinian and Rota. The infant mortality rate was 5.69 deaths per 1,000 live births in 2012; the fertility rate was 2.09 children born per woman. Life expectancy was 77.27 years. By mid-2011, the health system had accumulated a $3 million debt to suppliers, resulting in a scarcity of necessary supplies for diagnoses and treatments. Additionally, many residents had been forced to drop their health insurance coverage and were no longer able to pay for services. In July 2011, the governor declared a state of emergency, which allowed for the transfer of $1.7 million from the Commonwealth Development Authority to the Commonwealth Health Center.

Education is free and compulsory for children between the ages of 8 and 14, and literacy is high, approaching 100%. Northern Marianas College was founded in 1981. There were nine broadcast radio stations and one television station in 2009. Internet hosts numbered 17 in 2011. There were 25,500 telephone landlines in 2010, and 20,500 mobile cellular telephones (2004).

PALMYRA ATOLL

Palmyra, an atoll in the Central Pacific Ocean, contains 50 islets with a total area of some 10 sq km (4 sq mi). Palmyra is situated about 1,600 km (1,000 mi) SSW of Honolulu, Hawaii, at 5° 52′ N and 162° 5′ W.

Palmyra was discovered in 1802 by the USS *Palmyra* and formally annexed by the United States in 1912. It was under the jurisdiction of the city of Honolulu until 1959, when Hawaii became the 50th state of the United States. Palmyra is now the responsibility of the US Fish and Wildlife Service. The atoll is privately owned by the Nature Conservancy.

Kingman Reef, northwest of Palmyra Atoll at 6° 25′ N and 162° 23′ N, was discovered by the United States in 1874, annexed by the United States in 1922, and became a naval reservation in 1934. Now abandoned, it is under the control of the US Department of the Navy. The reef has an elevation of only 1 m (3 ft) and is awash most of the time, making it hazardous for ships.

WAKE ISLAND

Wake Island is actually a coral atoll and three islets (Wake, Peale, and Wilkes). Wake Island is about 8 km (5 mi) long by 3.6 km (2.25 mi) wide. It lies in the North Pacific 3,380 km (2,100 mi) W of Honolulu, Hawaii, at 19° 17′ N and 166° 35′ E. The total land and water area is about 8 sq km (3 sq mi). Discovered by the British in 1796, Wake was long uninhabited.

In 1898, a US expeditionary force en route to Manila, Philippines, landed on the island. The United States formally claimed Wake in 1899. It was made a US naval reservation in 1934, and became a civil aviation station in 1935. Captured by the Japanese during World War II on 23 December 1941, Wake was subsequently the target of several US air raids. It was surrendered by the Japanese in September 1945 and has thereafter remained a US unincorporated territory under the jurisdiction, since 1972, of the Department of the Air Force.

The island is no longer used for missile launches by the US Army's Space and Strategic Defense Command. It is a stopover and fueling station for civilian and military aircraft flying between Honolulu, Guam, and Japan. In August 2006, all military employees and civilian contractors were evacuated from the island because of Typhoon Ioke, a category-five storm. One month later, an assessment team was sent to the island to inspect the damage and determine whether US activity could resume. Soon after, it was determined that military activities could return to Wake Island.

UZBEKISTAN

Republic of Uzbekistan
Uzbekiston Respublikasi

CAPITAL: Tashkent (Toshkent)

FLAG: The flag features three horizontal bands of blue, white, and green, equal in length. Smaller stripes of red separate each of the bands. A white crescent moon and 12 white stars are placed near the hoist. The blue represents the Turkick peoples and sky; the white represents peace and purity; and green represents nature and the color of Islam. The red stripes stand for the vital force of all living things, while the crescent moon represents Islam. The stars represent the months and constellations of the Uzbek calendar.

ANTHEM: *O'zbekiston Respublikasining Davlat Madhiyasi (National Anthem of the Republic of Uzbekistan).*

MONETARY UNIT: The Som (UZS) has been the primary currency since November 1993 when Uzbekistan left the ruble system. UZS1 = US$0.00056038 (or US$1 = UZS1,784) as of 2011.

WEIGHTS AND MEASURES: The metric system is used.

HOLIDAYS: New Year's Day (1 January), the Prophet's Birthday. International Women's Day (8 March), Navruz (Persian New Year), Labour Day (1 May), Day of Memory and Respect (9 May), Hait (End of Ramadan), Independence Day (1 September), Qurban-Hait (Feast of the Sacrifice), and Constitution Day (8 December). Dates vary by year for religious holidays.

TIME: 5 p.m. = noon GMT.

¹LOCATION, SIZE, AND EXTENT

Uzbekistan is located in central Asia bordering the Aral Sea, between Kazakhstan and Turkmenistan. Comparatively, it is slightly larger than the state of California, with a total area of 447,400 sq km (172,742 sq mi). Uzbekistan shares boundaries with Kazakhstan on the N, Kyrgyzstan and Tajikistan on the E, Afghanistan on the S, and Turkmenistan on the SW. Uzbekistan's boundary length totals 6,221 km (3,866 mi). Its capital city, Tashkent, is located in the eastern part of the country.

²TOPOGRAPHY

Nearly 85% of Uzbekistan is desert or semi-desert. The land consists of mostly flat to rolling sandy desert with dunes, although the country also has high mountain ranges, wetlands, and the Aral Sea. The Fergana Valley lies in the east surrounded by the Tian Shan mountains of Tajikistan and Kyrgyzstan. The Alai mountains lie to the extreme southeast. The highest point in the country is Adelunga Toghi, at an elevation of 4,301 meters (14,111 feet). The lowest point is Sariqarnish Kuli, which dips to 12 meters (39 feet) below sea level. The country is located in a seismically active region along the Eurasian Tectonic Plate, resulting in frequent earthquakes.

The Kyzyl Kum desert covers most of the interior of the country. With an area of about 297,850 square kilometers (115,000 square miles), it is the largest desert region in Central Asia and the ninth-largest in the world. In the northwest, the Aral Sea is shared with Kazakhstan. Covering an area of about 64,500 square kilometers (24,900 square miles), it is the largest lake in the country and the fourth-largest lake in the world. The longest river in the country is the Amu Dar'ya, which has a total length of 2,540 kilometers (1,580 miles), only a portion of which runs through Uzbekistan.

³CLIMATE

The climate is mid-latitude climatic desert, with semi-arid grassland toward the east. Temperatures range from 26 to 32°C (79 to 90°F) in the summer, with much higher figures in the desert. Average winter temperatures are between -6 and 2°C (21 to 36°F). Summers are generally long and hot while the winters are relatively mild. There is very little rainfall in the country. The best watered areas only receive about 30 cm (12 in) annually.

⁴FLORA AND FAUNA

The World Resources Institute estimated that there were 4,800 plant species in Uzbekistan. In addition, Uzbekistan was home to 91 mammal species, 343 bird species, 55 reptile species, and 5 amphibian species. The calculation reflects the total number of distinct species residing in the country, not the number of endemic species.

Uzbekistan is an important flyway for migratory bird species traveling between northern Europe and Africa and Asia. However, chronic use of water for irrigation during the Soviet era has threatened much of the country's wildlife.

⁵ENVIRONMENT

The World Resource Institute reported that Uzbekistan had designated 868,900 hectares (2.15 million acres) of land for protection as of 2006. Water resources totaled 72.2 cu km (17.32 cu mi) while water usage was 58.34 cu km (14 cu mi) per year. Domestic water usage accounted for 5% of total usage, industrial for 2%, and agricultural for 93%. Per capita water usage totaled 2,194 cu m (77,480 cu ft) per year.

The United Nations (UN) reported in 2008 that carbon dioxide emissions in Uzbekistan totaled 115,995 kilotons. Fertilizers and pesticides have contaminated water and other parts of the natural environment. These threats have exacerbated an ongoing loss of wildlife habitat. The organization Fauna & Flora International has been developing a landscape scale conservation project on the Ustyurt Plateau between Kazakhstan and Uzbekistan.

The draining and evaporation of the Aral Sea has been considered one of the worst ecological disasters in the world. Irrigation withdrawals from the Amu Darya and Syr Darya rivers have been a major cause of lake shrinkage. This shrinkage is creating a growing concentration of chemical pesticides and natural salts. These substances have been blowing away from an increasingly exposed lake bed and are contributing to desertification. Uzbekistan also faces increasing soil salination, and soil contamination from buried nuclear processing and agricultural chemicals.

Uzbekistan is party to international environmental agreements on biodiversity, climate change, desertification, endangered species, environmental modification, hazardous wastes, ozone layer protection and wetlands.

In 1992 Uzbekistan had the world's 27th highest level of carbon dioxide emissions, which totaled 123.5 million metric tons, a per capita level of 5.75 metric tons. In 2000, the total of carbon dioxide emissions was at 118,600 kilotons.

According to a 2011 report issued by the International Union for Conservation of Nature and Natural Resources (IUCN), threatened species included 10 types of mammals, 15 species of birds, 2 types of reptiles, 7 species of fish, 1 species of invertebrate, and 15 species of plants. Threatened or rare species include the markhor, Central Asia cobra, Aral salmon, slender-billed curlew, and Asiatic wild dog. The Jeseter hladky has become extinct.

6 POPULATION

The US Central Intelligence Agency (CIA) estimates the population of Uzbekistan in 2011 to be 28,128,600, which placed it at number 44 in population among the 196 nations of the world. In 2011, approximately 4.7% of the population was over 65 years of age, with another 26.5% under 15 years of age. The median age in Uzbekistan was 25.2 years. There were 1.06 males for every female in the country. The population's annual rate of change was 0.94%. The life expectancy for males in 2011 was about 69 years for males and 76 years for females. About 36% of the population lived in urban areas. The largest city is Tashkent, with a population in 2009 of 2.201 million.

7 MIGRATION

Estimates of Uzbekistan's net migration rate, carried out by the CIA in 2011, amounted to -2.74 migrants per 1,000 citizens. The total number of emigrants living abroad was 1.96 million, and the total number of immigrants living in Uzbekistan was 1.18 million. Uzbekistan also accepted 39,202 refugees from Tajikistan and 1,060 from Afghanistan.

A 24 September 2010 report by The Institute for War and Peace Reporting stated that Uzbekistan has failed to acknowledge the large number of residents who have left the country to work abroad. Many of these residents enter Russia illegally and work in poorly paid positions at building sites, farms, logging facilities, or in catering and cleaning. The per capita remittance of these migrants was reported to be $1,500 annually. In addition to Russia, migrants also sought work in Kazakhstan, the United Arab Emir-

ates, and South Korea. The government often denied the workers pensions and other benefits, and would not intervene in cases of mistreatment or abuse.

8 ETHNIC GROUPS

The US State Department used 1996 figures to report in 2011 that about 80% of the population was Uzbek. Russians constituted 5.5%, Tajiks made up 5%, Kazakhs accounted for 3%, Karakalpaks for 2.5%, Tatars 1.5%, and others 2.5%. There are small numbers of ethnic Koreans, Meskhetian Turks, Germans, and Greeks.

9 LANGUAGE

Uzbek, the official language, is spoken by 74.3% of the people. About 14.2% of the population speak Russian, about 4.4% Tajik, and various other languages are used by 7.1% of the people. Uzbek is a Turkic language and bears similarities to Tajik. Uzbek is the most widely spoken non-Slavic language in the former USSR.

10 RELIGIONS

According to government reports, about 93% percent of the population was Muslim in 2010. All but 1% of the Muslim population is Sunni, of the Hanafi school, with the remaining 1% being Shi'a and residing primarily in Bukhara and Samarkhand. About 4% of the population was Russian Orthodox, and the remaining 3% was comprised of Roman Catholics, Korean Christians, Baptists, Lutherans, Seventh-day Adventists, Pentecostal Christians, Jehovah's Witnesses, Buddhists, Baha'is and Hare Krishnas. There also were an estimated 10,000 Ashkenazi and Bukharan Jews, primarily in Tashkent, Bukhara, and Samarkhan. Approximately 80,000 Jews emigrated to the United States and Israel between 1990 and 2010.

A 1998 Law on Freedom of Conscience and Religious Organizations prohibits activities including proselytizing and private religious instruction, requires groups to register, and provides strict criteria for their registration. Although the government generally does not interfere with worshippers at sanctioned worship sites, the US State Department found in its Report on Religious Freedom that the government deals harshly with Muslims who discuss religious issues outside of mosques. Children are discouraged from attending mosque or church services, and Muslim girls are rebuked for wearing the traditional hijab.

11 TRANSPORTATION

The CIA reported that Uzbekistan has a total of 86,496 km (53,746 mi) of roads, of which 75,511 km (46,920 mi) are paved. Railroads extend for 4,230 km (2,628 mi). There are 54 airports, which transported 1.85 million passengers in 2009 according to the World Bank. Uzbekistan has approximately 1,100 km (684 mi) of navigable waterways.

Separate rail lines serve eastern and western regions. As a doubly landlocked nation, there is no direct connection to the open sea. The closest route to the sea is to the south through Termiz on the Afghanistan border. Conflict in Afghanistan blocks this route. The Zeravshan River is the largest inland waterway. Uzbekistan has 33 airports with paved runways in 2009.

The Uzbekistan government began pouring money into new road and bridge construction and maintenance in 2009, spending about $180 million on construction and maintenance, and an additional $56 million in equipment. At the center of this develop-

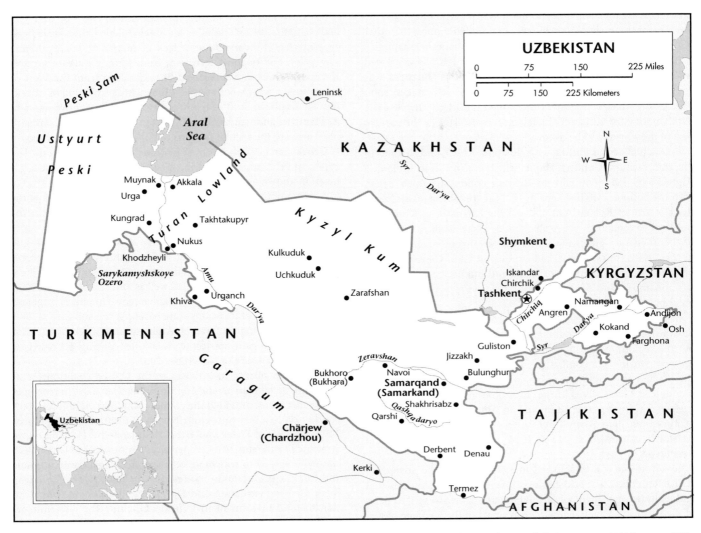

LOCATION: 41°0′ N; 64°0′ E. BOUNDARY LENGTHS: Afghanistan, 137 kilometers (85 miles); Kazakhstan, 2,203 kilometers (1,369 miles); Kyrgyzstan, 1,099 kilometers (683 miles); Tajikistan, 1,161 kilometers (722 miles); Turkmenistan, 1,621 kilometers (1,007 miles).

ment is an International Transport Road that will run through the country, much as the Silk Road once connected Europe with Asia. The project was supported financially by several international development agencies.

¹²HISTORY

Uzbekistan has a long heritage. The leading cities of the Silk Road – Samarkand, Bukhara, and Khiva – are all located in the present-day country, which meant that many conquerors made their way through the land. Some parts of present-day Uzbekistan have been inhabited since the Paleolithic era. The first states in the region were Khwarazm, Bactria, Sogdiana, and the Parthian Empire, in the first millennium BC. The territory was consolidated under the Achaemenids in the 6th century BC, until it was conquered by Alexander the Great, 329–327 BC. Alexander stopped near Samarkand en route to India and married Roxanna, the daughter of a local chieftain.

The Greeks were displaced by the Tochari in the 3rd century BC. From the 1st century BC to the 4th century AD Uzbekistan was part of the Kushana Kingdom. This in turn was replaced by the Ephthalite state.

In the 6th century the area was part of the West Turkic Kaganate, a loose confederation of largely nomadic tribes. By the 8th century the region was conquered by the Arabs, who introduced Islam. The Ummayid dynasty was displaced by the Abbasids in 747–750. In the 9th century the Samanids, an indigenous dynasty, took control of most of Central Asia, including Uzbekistan.

Turkic tribes again began to push into the area from the east in the 10th century, eventually forming the Karakhanid state. A lesser part of that state, Khwarazm, grew more powerful in the 12th century and came to dominate most of Central Asia.

Genghiz Khan's Mongols invaded in 1219, conquering all of Central Asia by 1221. In 1224 Genghiz Khan's son Chagatai was made ruler of this area. As Chingisid influence waned, Timur (Tamerlane, 1336–1405) established an empire in Samarkand. Upon his death it split into Khorasan, ruled by his son Shah Rukh, and Maweranahr, ruled by his grandson, Ulgh Beg. Although Timur is now claimed as the father of the modern Uzbeks, more likely candidates are the Sheibanid, nomadic Uzbeks who fought to take the area in the early 16th century. They settled among the other populations and became farmers, making Bukhara their capital.

In the 16th century Khwarazm, Balkh, and Khiva separated from Bukhara, becoming separate principalities. Bukhara was conquered by Persia in 1740, but sovereignty was retaken soon after by the Mangyt dynasty, which ruled until 1920. In the early 19th century the Kokand Khanate grew powerful in the eastern part of present-day Uzbekistan.

Russia had begun trading with Bukhara, Khiva, and Kokand in the 18th century. Concern about British expansion in India and Afghanistan led eventually to Russian conquest, which began with the conquest of Tashkent in 1865. In 1876, Russia dissolved the Khanate of Kokand but allowed the Khanates of Khiva and Bukhara to remain direct protectorates. Uzbekistan became part of the Turkestan guberniia under this arrangement. By the end of the 19th century, Russia had conquered all of Central Asia. It placed all but the Khanates of Khiva and Bukhara under colonial administration and began promoting cotton growing and settlement by Russian colonists in the area.

In 1916 Tsar Nicholas II issued a call for Central Asian males to be drafted into labor battalions. This sparked resistance throughout the region, including in Uzbekistan, which was violently repressed. During the conflict from 1917–20, Uzbekistan was the site of competing attempts to create governments; the Bolsheviks announced a short-lived Turkestan Autonomous Republic, while a Muslim Congress also attempted an Autonomous Government of Turkestan. Red Army forces intervened savagely, but armed resistance continued as late as 1924, in the so-called Basmachi Rebellion.

Soviet power was established in 1924. In 1925, the Soviet Socialist Republic of Uzbekistan was formed out of territories that had included the Khanates of Bukhara and Khiva as well as parts of the Ferghana Valley that had been a part of the Khanate of Kokand. The Soviet Union exploited Uzbekistan's natural resources and cotton growing potential, using an inefficient irrigation system that had resulted by the early 21st century in shrinking the Aral Sea to less than one-third of its original size.

The borders of Uzbekistan were altered in 1929 when Tajikistan, formerly an administrative sub-unit, was established as a full republic, and again in 1936.

Under the leadership of long-time leader S. Rashidov, Uzbekistan was politically conservative during the 1970s and early 1980s. The republic was targeted for anticorruption purges in the mid-1980s, when considerable fraud in the cotton industry was discovered.

The Soviet Union appointed Islam Karimov, former First Secretary of the Central Committee of the Uzbek Soviet Socialist Republic Communist Party, as leader of the Uzbek republic in 1989. He was elected by the Uzbek Supreme Soviet to a newly created post of president in March 1990, and Uzbekistan declared independence on 1 September 1991 following the disintegration of the Soviet Union. Karimov was elected to a five-year term in a December 1991 election. He was reelected in 1995, 2000, 2002, and 2007 through elections or referendums that the US State Department has deemed unfair. Karimov continued to serve as president as of December 2011.

Karimov has been hostile to democratic reforms, and Uzbekistan's first two decades as an independent nation have been characterized by corruption, a lack of human rights, economic stagnation and ongoing terrorism from Islamic militant groups. Karimov, however, has received little criticism from the West or from Russia, which has supplied him with ample military backing. He has been seen as a buffer against Islamist movements in Afghanistan and neighboring Tajikistan, and Uzbekistan has supplied arms to the secular factions of both countries' civil wars.

Uzbekistan began battling a low-intensity insurgency in the late 1990s. In February 1999, Karimov accused a radical Islamic organization known as the Islamic Movement of Uzbekistan (IMU) of five car bombings in Tashkent. Karimov further claimed that the organization was attempting to assassinate him and destabilize the country. The IMU broadcast a declaration of jihad from a radio station in Iran and demanded that the country's leaders resign. IMU fighters began a series of engagements with government forces, while militants took four Japanese geologists and eight Kyrgyz soldiers hostage in 1999 as well as four US citizens in 2000.

The IMU allied itself with the Taliban government in Afghanistan, where most of its troops were based, in the summer of 2001 and began engaging US forces in Afghanistan. IMU military leader Juma Namangani apparently was killed during a US-led air strike in Afghanistan in November 2001.

Uzbekistan offered its airbases to the US-led coalition for its campaign in Afghanistan beginning in October 2001. In response, the United States provided the country with $60 million for 2002, in addition to a one-time contribution of $100 million. In March 2002, the United States and Uzbekistan signed a Declaration on Strategic Partnership and Cooperation Framework, in which both countries agreed to cooperate on economic, legal, humanitarian, and nuclear proliferation matters. In April 2004, the European Bank for Reconstruction and Development announced its decision to limit investment in Uzbekistan, citing the government's lack of progress on democratic and economic reform benchmarks established one year earlier. Similarly, in July, the United States suspended $18 million of the $55 million originally earmarked for Uzbekistan in 2004. The decision was based on the 2002 Strategic Partnership and Cooperation Framework, which makes US assistance to the Uzbek government conditional on Tashkent's introduction of meaningful political reforms and curbs in human rights abuses. In August 2005, the upper house of parliament voted to evict US forces from the air base at Khanabad used for the campaign in Afghanistan.

Terrorist activity occurred sporadically in Uzbekistan from 1999 through 2011. The US and Israeli embassies in Tashkent were attacked in 2004. In May 2005, a gunman in Andijon attacked a police station, seized weapons and stormed a prison, freeing 4,000 members of a local Islamic organization that the government had accused of extremism. The attackers then gathered in the town's square along with thousands of residents. Shooting erupted between the government's forces and the insurgents. The Uzbek government put the death toll at 187; the US State Department estimated the toll to be as high as 800. In November 2005, the Supreme Court convicted 15 men of having organized the Andijan unrest and sentenced them to 14 to 20 years in prison. In March 2006, Sanjar Umarov, head of the Sunshine Uzbekistan opposition movement, was sentenced to 11 years in prison, later reduced to eight, for economic crimes. The Sunshine group had criticized the Andijan massacre and had called for economic reforms. That month, human rights activist Mukhtabar Tojibayeva, a critic of the Andijan crackdown, was sentenced to eight years in prison for economic crimes. Karimov has refused to allow an independent international investigation into the killings.

In May 2009, a suicide bomber in Andijon and an attack on a border post near Khanabad on the Uzbekistan-Kyrgyzstan border resulted in the Uzbek government temporarily closing its border and putting some parts of the Ferghana Valley under lockdown. As many as 100,000 ethnic Uzbeks fled from Kyrgyzstan to Uzbekistan in June 2010 following ethnic clashes in southern Kyrgyzstan. Uzbekistan worked with international organizations to provide food and shelter to the refugees until they returned to Kyrgyzstan later that month.

Terrorist activity continued in 2011 with a suspected terrorist attack on a railway line linking Uzbekistan to Afghanistan on 16 November. The route reportedly was being used by NATO to transport US troops into Afghanistan after the killing of Osama bin Laden in May 2011 in Pakistan made the transport of troops from that country unsafe.

13 GOVERNMENT

A new constitution adopted on 8 December 1992 declared Uzbekistan a multi-party democracy and presidential republic. The executive branch includes the president and a prime minister and Cabinet of Ministers, both of whom the president appoints.

The legislative branch was initially a unicameral 250-member legislature. This body was replaced with a bicameral parliament known as the Oliy Majlis (Supreme Assembly) in two elections in December 2004 and January 2005. The lower house of the new parliament, known as the Legislative Chamber, was comprised of 135 members chosen by direct election following elections in December 2009. The upper house, the Senate, consisted of 84 senators elected by local governments and 16 senators appointed by the president.

The president is the head of state and has responsibility for the functioning of the other branches of government as well as for making sure the constitution is observed. The president of Uzbekistan has essentially ruled by decree through the country's first two decades of independence. Karimov banned opposition parties in 1992. He also appoints regional governors who report directly to him, and appoints members of the judiciary to five- and 10-year terms.

Elections for both the parliament and president were expected to take place in 2014.

14 POLITICAL PARTIES

No meaningful political opposition existed in Uzbekistan as of December 2011. Five political parties, all of whom support the president, held all of the seats in parliament and independent political parties have been suppressed since the early 1990s.

Active political parties as of 2011 included the Adolat (Justice) Social Democratic Party; the Democratic National Rebirth Party; the People's Democratic Party; the Liberal Democratic Party of Uzbekistan; and the Ecological "Green" Movement. Other political groups in Uzbekistan were the Birlik (Unity) Movement; the Erk (Freedom) Democratic Party, which was banned in December

1992; the party of Agrarians and Entrepreneurs of Uzbekistan; the Ozod Dehkon (Free Farmers) Party; the Human Rights Society of Uzbekistan; and the Independent Human Rights Society of Uzbekistan. Many of these parties formed as mass-based organizations in 1989–90, as Soviet control began to disintegrate.

The Islamic Militant Union and Hizb-ut-Tahrir are radical Islamic organizations that operate in Uzbekistan.

15 LOCAL GOVERNMENT

The local government is divided into 12 provinces known as *viloyat* in the singular and *viloyatlar* in the plural; one autonomous republic, and one city. The viloyatlar include Andijon, Buxuro, Farg'ona, Jizzax, Namangan, Navoiy, Qashqadaryo, Samarkand, Sirdaryo, Surxondaryo, Tashkent (province), and Xorazm. The republic is Karakalpakstan, and the city is Tashkent.

Administration is performed by locally elected councils, overseen by presidential appointees.

The smallest communal units in Uzbekistan are *mahallas*, traditional institutions charged with regulating communal life and carrying out such social functions as community policing, political surveillance, and the distribution of welfare payments. The US State Department reported in 2011 that the government was relying on an estimated 12,000 such units for information about political extremists.

16 JUDICIAL SYSTEM

Uzbekistan law stipulates that the president appoint all judges to renewable five-year terms. The parliament is required to confirm removal of Supreme Court judges.

The Karakalpakstan Supreme Court has jurisdiction over the Karakalpakstan republic, a semiautonomous region, and defendants may appeal decisions of district and provincial courts within 10 days of a ruling. A constitutional court also has been established to review laws, decrees, and other decisions to ensure that they comply with the constitution. Military courts handled civil and criminal matters within the military. The Supreme Court handles selected cases of national significance.

There was no provision for jury trials in Uzbekistan as of 2011. Trials are generally open to the public, and citizens are permitted to file suit in civil courts on cases of alleged human rights violations. According to judicial reforms made in 2008, detainees have the right to request hearings before a judge to determine whether they remain incarcerated or are released.

17 ARMED FORCES

The International Institute for Strategic Studies reports that armed forces in Uzbekistan totaled 67,000 members in 2011. The force is comprised of 50,000 from the army and 17,000 members of the air force. Armed forces represent 0.7% of the labor force in Uzbekistan. Defense spending totaled $3 billion and accounted for 3.5% of gross domestic product (GDP).

The US State Department reported Uzbekistan's military force to be the largest in Central Asia. Although the military structure was inherited from the former Soviet model, the military is restructuring its organization around light and Special Forces. Both equipment and training are inadequate.

Uzbekistan received US Foreign Military Financing (FMF) and International Military Education and Training funds from the late

1990s until 2004. The funding was stopped when it appeared unclear whether the government was meeting human rights and economic reform commitments stipulated under the US-Uzbekistan Strategic Framework Agreement. US President Barack Obama included $100,000 of FMF assistance in his fiscal year 2012 budget request to Congress.

18 INTERNATIONAL COOPERATION

Uzbekistan was admitted to the UN on 2 March 1992. As of 2011, it was a member of the Shanghai Cooperation Organization, the Collective Security Treaty Organization, the Commonwealth of Independent States, the Euro-Atlantic Partnership Council, NATO Partnership for Peace, the Organization for Security and Cooperation in Europe, and the Organization of the Islamic Conference. It has hosted the Shanghai Cooperation Organization's Regional Anti-Terrorist Structure in Tashkent.

Uzbekistan also has been part of the Economic Cooperation Organization with Azerbaijan, Turkey, Iran, Afghanistan, and Pakistan. It joined the GUAM alliance with Georgia, Ukraine, Azerbaijan, and Moldova in 1999 but withdrew in 2005. Uzbekistan also joined the Eurasian Economic Community with Belarus, Kazakhstan, Kyrgyzstan, Russia, and Tajikistan but withdrew in 2008.

The government has accepted arms control obligations of the former Soviet Union, acceded to the Nuclear Non-Proliferation Treaty, and supports US-led efforts to demilitarize and clean former weapons of mass destruction facilities in its western provinces. It has participated in a peacekeeping force in Tajikistan, and has supported anti-terrorist operations in Afghanistan.

19 ECONOMY

The GDP rate of change in Uzbekistan, as of 2010, was 8.5%. Inflation stood at 15%, and unemployment was reported at 1.1%. The CIA estimated that agriculture accounted for 22.3% of Uzbekistan's GDP in 2010, industry for 38.4%, and services 39.3%.

Uzbekistan was subject to intense production of cotton and grains during the Soviet era. The production methods led to an overuse of agricultural chemicals and water resources; as a result, the land is heavily contaminated and many of its rivers and the Aral Sea have been left half dry.

After becoming independent in 1991, the government maintained a Soviet-style command economy and imposed subsidies and controls on production and prices. Most production and employment continued to remain governmentally controlled as of 2011, and efforts to institute market reforms have been slow.

In 2003 the government accepted Article VIII obligations under the International Monetary Fund that provided for full currency convertibility. However, currency controls and a tightening of borders has lessened the effects of this provision and led to shortages. An increase in the inequality of income distribution since independence also has hurt many Uzbeks.

As of 2011, Uzbekistan was trying to decrease its dependence on agriculture while developing its mineral and petroleum resources. The economy is based primarily on agriculture and natural resource extraction. Although the country is a major exporter of cotton, it also exports natural gas, gold, uranium, and strategic minerals.

The US State Department has reported strong economic growth in the past few years, but notes that the wealth remained in the hands of elites. The CIA reported 26% of Uzbeks lived below the poverty line.

20 INCOME

The CIA estimated that in 2010 the GDP of Uzbekistan was $85.85 billion. The CIA defines GDP as the value of all final goods and services produced within a nation in a given year and computed on the basis of purchasing power parity (PPP) rather than value as measured on the basis of the rate of the exchange based on current dollars. The per capita GDP was estimated at $3,100. The annual growth rate of GDP was 8.5%. The average inflation rate was 15%.

The World Bank reports that in 2009, household consumption in Uzbekistan totaled $18 billion or about $641 per capita, measured in current US dollars rather than PPP.

21 LABOR

As of 2010, Uzbekistan had a total labor force of 16 million people. Within that labor force, CIA estimates in 1995 noted that 44% were employed in agriculture, 20% in industry, and 36% in the service sector.

The labor code adopted in 1992 recognizes the right for all workers to voluntarily create and join unions, which may in turn associate with international affiliations. Unions were also granted independence from government administrative and economic bodies (except where provided by law), and were encouraged to develop their own charters, structure, and executive bodies. However, as of 2011, the union structure remained the same as under Soviet rule. There are no independent unions.

The standard workweek is 40 hours, with a required 24-hour rest period. The US State Department noted that while overtime pay exists in theory, it rarely is paid. The minimum of $25 per month from December 2009 to August 2010 of $25 was raised to $28 per month on 1 August 2010.

The constitution prohibits forced or compulsory labor. However, the US State Department found in its 2011 Human Rights Report that school administrators, teachers, and other public sector employers were forced to work in the cotton fields during the harvest period. The use of children to pick cotton also was widespread. During the fall harvest, authorities closed schools and universities and required students to work in the cotton fields. Many university students were threatened in 2009 with expulsion if they did not participate in the harvest.

22 AGRICULTURE

Roughly 11% of the total land is farmed, and the country's major crops include cotton, vegetables, fruits, and grain. Cereal production in 2009 amounted to 7.4 million tons, fruit production 2.4 million tons, and vegetable production 6.8 million tons.

The CIA reported in 2011 that more than 60% of the population lived in densely populated rural communities, and that Uzbekistan had become the world's second largest exporter of cotton and the fifth largest producer. The country had a bumper cotton crop in 2010 amid record high prices.

The US State Department reported that Uzbekistan also produced silk. Because the country's terrain is dry and land-locked, nearly all of its agricultural production has required heavy irrigation. The president signed a decree in 2008 that redistributed the land of small farmers to create larger private farms.

During the Soviet era, cotton was grown on almost half of all sown land. Cotton is grown in the crescent beginning in the Fergana Valley and extending south along the Tien Shan Mountains to Samarqand (Samarkand) and Bukhoro (Bukhara), and then west along the Amu Darya River. All cotton is flood irrigated. Plantings are generally in April, with the harvest coming in late August or early September. Fields are usually planted with alfalfa or corn every four or five years, but many fields are planted without rotation, leading to declining yields.

Rice, wheat, barley, and corn are important grain crops. Rice is produced on 48 specialized state farms, and about 85% of the rice crop comes from the southwestern part of Karakalpakistan and the Khorezm region.

23 ANIMAL HUSBANDRY

The UN Food and Agriculture Organization (FAO) reported that Uzbekistan dedicated 22 million hectares (54.4 million acres) to permanent pasture or meadow in 2009. During that year, the country tended 12.2 million sheep, 29.1 million chickens, and 8 million head of cattle. The production from these animals amounted to 551,361 tons of beef and veal, 27,895 tons of poultry, 111,700 tons of eggs, and 3.86 million tons of milk. Uzbekistan also produced 65,728 tons of cattle hide and 24,980 tons of raw wool.

Sheep are the main livestock product, with Karakyl sheep (noted for their black wool) raised in the Bukhara region. Mulberry trees have been grown for silkworm breeding since the 4th century.

24 FISHING

Uzbekistan had 44 decked commercial fishing boats in 2008. The annual capture totaled 2,800 tons according to the UN FAO. The export value of seafood totaled $337,000.

Fishing occurs mainly in the Fergana Valley. The Aral Sea in the north is too saline to support fishing.

25 FORESTRY

Approximately 8% of Uzbekistan is covered by forest. The UN FAO estimated the 2009 roundwood production at 8,000 cu m (282,517 cu ft). The value of all forest products, including roundwood, totaled $6.27 million.

26 MINING

The mineral sector remains one of the chief contributors to the country's economic development. Along with natural gas and uranium, in which Uzbekistan is a world leader, and crude oil, in which it is self-sufficient, the country is significant to world mineral markets as a gold producer—it has, at times, been a world leader. Gold was the second-leading export commodity in 2008, providing 20% of export earnings. Production of fertilizers is an important part of the domestic chemical industry, as fertilizers are used for the production of cotton.

Uzbekistan produced an estimated 85,000 kg of gold in 2008. Uzbekistan also mines copper (95,000 metric tons in 2008), molybdenum, silver, and tungsten. Copper, molybdenum, and lead-zinc are mined at the Almalyk mining and metallurgical complex, Uzbekistan's major nonferrous-metals-producing enterprise, northeast of Tashkent. No bismuth, cadmium, lead, palladium,

tin, or zinc has been mined since 1997. Control of one of the main lead-mining deposits, Altyn-Topkan, in the Kurama mountain range, was transferred to Tajikistan in 1999. Uzbekistan also produces cement, kaolin clays (an estimated 250,000 metric tons in 2008), feldspar, graphite, iodine, mineral fertilizer, nitrogen, phosphate rock, and sulfur. Fluorspar output totaled 90,000 metric tons in 2008. Uzbekistan also manufactures copper, gold, lead, molybdenum, rhenium, selenium, silver, steel, tellurium, tungsten, and zinc metals.

Uzbekistan's explored resources of gold were 5,300 tons. The main reserves, amounting to 3,200 tons, are in the central Kyzylkum region, containing the Muruntau deposit (2,230 tons), the largest gold deposit in Eurasia and among the largest in the world; Muruntau's milling operation, near Zarafshan, processes more than 22 million tons per year of ore. Uzbekistan has a reported 115,000 metric tons of lithium oxide reserves in the Shavuzsay deposit in Toshkent Viloyatti, with byproduct components of rubidium oxide and cesium oxide. Uzbekistan's rare earth minerals could be of increasing importance as technologies advance to replace use of hydrocarbons as fuel.

27 ENERGY AND POWER

The CIA estimated electricity production in 2009 at 47.42 billion kWh, and consumption of 40.1 billion kWh. Uzbekistan exported 11.52 billion kWh and imported 11.44 billion kWh, according to the CIA's 2009 estimates.

Roughly 98% of energy came from fossil fuels, while 2% came from alternative fuels. Per capita oil consumption was 1,849 kg. Oil production was estimated at 58,660 barrels of oil a day in 2010, and consumption was estimated at 144,000 barrels a day. According to 1 January 2011 estimates, Uzbekistan had proved oil reserves of 594 million barrels.

Natural gas production was estimated at 61.41 billion cu m in 2009, and consumption was estimated at 46.21 billion cu m. Proved reserves were estimated to be 1.841 trillion cu m as of 1 January 2011.

28 INDUSTRY

The US State Department estimated Uzbekistan's industrial production growth rate at 8% in 2010. The major industries were textiles, food processing, machine building, metallurgy, gold, oil and natural gas production, and chemicals.

Manufacturing has gained importance as Uzbekistan has tried to make its economy less reliant on agriculture. Its automotive sector has grown as companies manufacture vehicles for export to Russia. Uzbekistan also was the world's seventh-largest producer of gold in 2010, mining about 80 tons a year. It also has large reserves of copper, lead, zinc, tungsten, and uranium.

During the Soviet era, most industry was based on the processing of local agricultural products. Soft goods (mainly cotton, wool, and silk fiber) and processed foods (including cottonseed oil, meat, dried fruit, wines, and tobacco) accounted for about 39% and 13% of industrial production respectively in 1990 and their manufacture was concentrated in Tashkent and the Fergana Valley. Much of the antiquated food processing and packaging equipment used in those industries has continued to be used, and needs to be updated.

Principal Trading Partners – Uzbekistan (2010)

(In millions of US dollars)

Country	Total	Exports	Imports	Balance
World	14,364.7	5,825.6	8,539.1	-2,713.5
Russia	3,205.8	1,375.9	1,829.9	-454.0
China	2,476.9	1,181.0	1,295.9	-114.9
South Korea	1,602.5	20.0	1,582.5	-1,562.5
Turkey	1,094.0	783.1	310.9	472.1
Kazakhstan	953.2	460.0	493.2	-33.2
Germany	809.6	37.8	771.8	-733.9
Bangladesh	524.7	517.7	7.0	510.7
Kyrgyz Republic	445.4	161.7	283.7	-122.0
Italy	422.3	290.4	131.9	158.4
Japan	242.1	157.1	85.0	72.1

(…) data not available or not significant.

(n.s.) not specified.

SOURCE: *2011 Direction of Trade Statistics Yearbook,* New York: United Nations, 2011.

The US State Department reported 22 new textile projects worth $108 million began operations in 2006, with investment from a Turkish-US company, Korean Kabul Textiles, Spentex of India, and Daewoo International of South Korea. Uzbekistan launched 20 additional new textile companies between 2008 and 2010.

A state-owned joint-stock company known as Uzbekyengilsanoat (Uzbek light industry) has developed a program to improve existing companies and start new ones. These efforts increased yarn production by 45,100 tons, textile production by 2,400 tons, and ready products by 22.85 min pieces between 2008 and 2011. In addition, 8,000 new jobs in the textile sector were created. An additional 17 textile enterprises were slated for modernization between 2009 and 2011.

Other industry in Uzbekistan includes machines and heavy equipment production; aerospace; metal-processing; chemical fertilizer production; oil and natural gas.

29 SCIENCE AND TECHNOLOGY

Patent applications in science and technology as of 2009, according to the World Bank, totaled 238 in Uzbekistan. The Uzbek Academy of Sciences, headquartered in Tashkent, has departments of physical-mathematical sciences; mechanics; control processes; informatics; chemical-technological and earth sciences; and biological sciences.

Uzbekistan became a significant center for scientific research in Central Asia following its independence. As of 2011, nearly 300 scientific institutions existed, and more than 25,000 scientists and researchers were conducting work in the country. Key scientific projects are in micro-electronics, astronomy, biophysics, genetics, and geology. Areas of interest include the use of genetic engineering to produce new kinds of silkworm cocoons; solar thermal system development, and improved irrigation and water conservation technologies.

30 DOMESTIC TRADE

A 2009 report by the International Development Corporation reported that more than 16,000 laws regulating private sector business activities had been adopted between 1991 and 2008. Those laws, high taxes, and heavy permitting and reporting requirements have hurt private sector development.

Since 1992, thousands of small businesses have been privatized or leased to worker collectives, with the most progress in retail trade, consumer services, public catering, and local industry. However, the shift from state control to a free-market economy continues to move at a very slow pace. As of 1 January 2008, there were 436,500 businesses in Uzbekistan, of which 392,000 were small businesses. About 64% of these businesses were in the agricultural sector and about 12% were in trade and catering. There were about 15 small businesses per 1,000 people in 2007.

Business hours are 9 a.m. to 6 p.m., Monday to Friday, and banks are open from 9 a.m. to 4 p.m. Department stores are open from 10 a.m. to 6 p.m., Monday through Saturday.

31 FOREIGN TRADE

Uzbekistan imported $9.44 billion worth of goods and services in 2008, while exporting $13.13 billion worth of goods and services. Major import partners in 2009 were Russia, 22.1%; China, 20.3%; South Korea, 15%; Germany, 6%; Ukraine, 5.3%; and Kazakhstan, 4.6%. Its major export partners were Ukraine, 30.5%; Russia, 15.8%; Turkey, 7.7%; Kazakhstan, 7.4%; Bangladesh, 7%; and China, 6.5%.

Natural gas, oil, and other hydrocarbon exports accounted for about 40% of foreign exchange earnings in 2009. Other export earners were gold and cotton.

Uzbekistan has placed strict controls on foreign trade in an effort to prevent capital outflow. The US State Department stated that the country needs to introduce structural reforms to improve the investment climate for foreign investors and liberalize the agricultural sector. Other factors that have restricted foreign trade have been high customs and duties, long delays in currency conversion, import and export restrictions, and periodic border closings.

A new commercial and military supply route through Uzbekistan opened in March 2009 to ship cargo to US and North Atlantic Treaty Organization (NATO) forces in Afghanistan. The route provided coalition forces with an alternative to the major supply route through Pakistan, which was increasingly threatened by instability.

32 BALANCE OF PAYMENTS

The CIA estimated external debt of $4.221 billion as of 31 December 2010, compared with $4.109 billion a year earlier. The current account balance was estimated at $5.843 billion in 2010 compared with $3.58 billion in 2009.

Foreign exchange reserves (including gold) were estimated at $9.8 billion as of 31 December 2010 compared with $9 billion as of 31 December 2009.

Uzbekistan was extremely reliant on cotton exports as a means of trade throughout its association with the former USSR, but earnings fluctuated widely from year to year depending on the performance of the agricultural sector.

The country lost almost half of its foreign exchange reserves in 1996, after the government imposed strict currency controls. As of the early 2000s, Uzbekistan was able to maintain reserve levels at or close to $1.2 billion, in large measure by restricting imports.

33 BANKING AND SECURITIES

The Central Bank of Uzbekistan has been charged with regulation of the banking sector. However, a series of government laws and decrees put much of the sector's control in the hands of the government. As of 2011, there were 31 banks in Uzbekistan. The banking system is tightly controlled by the state, and most assets are in state-operated banks. The sector includes the government-controlled banks such as the National Bank of Uzbekistan, Uzpromstroybank, Asaka Bank, and Uzjilsberbank; banks with foreign investments such as RBS Bank, NB Uzbekistan A.O., KDB Bank, Uzbekistan-Turkish Bank, and Soderat Bank; and medium and small private banks.

Citizens and private businesses often have difficulty obtaining credit due to a lack of reforms. Only foreign investors with joint venture status are able to obtain credit on the local market. Because branches are not recognized as legal entities, they can not provide services that use the capital of the parent company.

Uzbekistan introduced currency convertibility in October 2003. Although the government committed itself to the provisions of IMF's Article VIII, multiple restrictions have continued to hinder the conversion of currency. Private businesses in 2009 reported currency conversion delays of more than six months, and cash shortages were common.

The Tashkent Stock Exchange was established in 1995, and in 2011 hosted a low volume of equity and secondary market transactions. Accurate financial reports are difficult to obtain, and the State Property Committee generally makes decisions as to who could buy and sell shares and at what prices.

34 INSURANCE

There were 33 insurance companies operating in Uzbekistan in 2011. According to a report from the Central Asia-Caucasus Institute, total insurance premiums were $64.5 million in 2008.

A state insurance company known as Uzgosstrah was restructured in 1997, and in the late 1990s the state began created government-run insurance companies. As of 2011, there were four types of available insurance: property, liability, personal, and mandatory insurance.

35 PUBLIC FINANCE

In 2010 the budget of Uzbekistan included $12.25 billion in public revenue and $12.3 billion in public expenditures. The budget surplus amounted to 0.3% of GDP. Public debt was 9% of GDP, with $3.884 billion of the debt held by foreign entities.

Uzbekistan's spiraling inflation as a member of the ruble zone necessitated the introduction of a transition currency after it left the ruble zone in November 1993. In 1994, the government undertook economic reforms, but privatization efforts have fallen short of expectations. Subsidies for basic consumer goods (except some food staples and energy products) and subsidized credit to industrial enterprises were substantially reduced during 1994 and 1995. The external debt, $1.5 billion at the end of 1994, more than doubled to $3.3 billion by 1997. By 2005, it had exceeded $5 billion. An enterprise profit tax, a value-added tax, and an excise tax on cotton supply the bulk of government revenues.

36 TAXATION

The US State Department's 2010 Country Commercial Guide on Uzbekistan describes the system of taxation as complicated and ambiguous. Business tax deductions for marketing, communications, and training expenses are limited, and corruption is endemic. Tax laws also regarded a company that failed to show a profit for six months as bankrupt.

A new Tax Code took effect on 1 January 2008, but had not significantly changed the tax structure as of 2011. Payroll taxes also are high: employee income taxes, compulsory social security charges, and other payments made up nearly 50% of wages employers paid to employees.

As of November 2010, Uzbekistan taxed personal income at a progressive rate ranging from 11% to 22%. Joint filing of taxes is prohibited. Residents are also levied a stamp tax on general government services, a land tax on private property of approximately 0.5%, and a 4% withholding of gross salary for a social security fund.

Corporate taxes as of November 2010 was 9% and 15% for banks. There also was a value added tax of 20%

37 CUSTOMS AND DUTIES

As of 2010, Uzbekistan imposed custom duties and levies, the value added tax, an excise tax, and a custom clearance fee on imports. Custom duties generally average 30%, and as of 2009, these duties were lifted on imported live animals, milk and cream, wheat, x-ray films, and computer hardware. Duties of 10% to 30% were imposed on clothing, furniture, metals, and food imports; and 50% duties were applied to luxury consumer goods. The customs duty on Imported ice cream products was very high.

Excise taxes were required for such products as cigarettes, vodka, ice cream, fuels, cars, and carpets. These rates varied significantly, ranging from 5% for passenger cars in 2010 to 140% for jewelry.

The value added tax was 20% and the customs clearance fee was 0.2% of the declared customs value.

High tariffs and import duties and the occasional closure of bridges and border checkpoints have allowed the government to restrict imports considerably.

38 FOREIGN INVESTMENT

Foreign direct investment (FDI) in Uzbekistan was a net inflow of $750 million according to World Bank figures published in 2009. FDI represented 2.34% of GDP.

US companies invested approximately $500 million in Uzbekistan from independence through 2011. GM-DAT, a Korean subsidiary of GM, signed a joint venture agreement with UzDaewoo in 2007 to assemble Korean made cars for export and domestic sale. Chevrolets were among the cars being produced and, as of 2011, many lines of cars under the Chevrolet nameplate were being assembled for export to Russia.

In 2010 GM began producing powertrain engines at a plant outside Tashkent. The Boeing Co., Coca Cola, Baker Hughes, Nukem, and Hewlett Packard are among some of the other US corporations operating in Uzbekistan.

Russian and Chinese companies were considering investments in Uzbekistan's gas and oil industry in 2011, and South Korean firms have worked with the country in civil aviation. Uzbekistan President Karimov signed an alliance with Russian President Vladimir Putin in November 2005 that included economic and business cooperation. Uzbekistan took steps to rejoined the Collective Security Treaty Organization and the Eurasian Economic Community in 2006, both of which were dominated by Russia. Uzbekistan subsequently withdrew from the Eurasian Economic Community in 2008.

As of 2011, Uzbekistan was a member of the IMF, World Bank, Asian Development Bank, Islamic Development Bank, and European Bank for Reconstruction and Development. It also had stated an intention to accede to the World Trade Organization.

39 ECONOMIC DEVELOPMENT

Centralized economic planning under the former Soviet Union focused Uzbekistan's economic growth largely on agricultural production. Large stretches of land were brought under irrigation to cultivate cotton. Uzbekistan continued to be a significant producer of cotton through the first decade of the 21st century, but its reliance on agriculture has lessened as its economy has diversified.

Since independence the government has aimed at facilitating a greater market orientation in the economy. Development of oil and natural gas fields, bolstering cotton exports, and sustaining gold exports were initial goals. Uzbekistan relied heavily on foreign aid for its economic development in its early years of independence and continued to do so into the second decade of the 21st century. Uzbekistan has received financial support from the International Monetary Fund, World Bank, European Bank for Reconstruction and Development, and the Asian Development Bank (ADB).

In 2002 the government and the Central Bank embarked on an IMF staff monitored program (SMP) primarily designed to convince the IMF to approve a financial program. The SMP was aimed at accelerating the transition to a market economy and achieving macroeconomic stability. The World Bank developed a three-year Country Assistance Strategy (CAS) to prepare the country and its decision-makers for currency and trade liberalization. Projects supported by the European Bank for Reconstruction and Development have included the rehabilitation of oil refineries and power plants, building of new production facilities, development of gold mines, and assistance to small and medium enterprises (SMEs), and others.

The World Bank and UN Development Program provided additional technical assistance in 2007 in an effort to reform the Central Bank and Ministry of Finance.

The Asian Development Bank's country strategy and program Uzbekistan for 2006–2010 was based on the country's first national medium-term development strategy. That Welfare Improvement Strategy set transformation and diversification of the economy, the adoption of market principles, and broader participation of the private sector as its goals. The Asian Development Bank's program focused on rural development, private sector development, regional transport, customs transit, and human capital development. In 2010–11, the ADB added the following projects: microfinance development, modernization of the Amu Bukhara irrigation system, a clean power development project, and basic education and early childhood development projects.

In 2010 the US government trained more than 1,200 farmers (25% of whom were women) in plant pest and disease identification, agronomic best practices, orchard pruning, thinning, and grafting; cold storage management, drip irrigation, fruit and vegetable drying, and post-harvest practices.

In September 2010, President Islam Karimov pledged in a speech marking the 19th anniversary of Uzbekistan's independence to transform the country into a developed democracy and raise the per capita earnings of its people. Repressive economic policies remain a barrier to growth, but according to a news analysis from the Central Asia Newswire, Karimov began growing more receptive to introduce and extend economic reforms to speed the technological and socioeconomic growth of the country.

40 SOCIAL DEVELOPMENT

Government benefits in Uzbekistan have followed a socialistic model through 2011. The social security system includes old age, disability and survivor's pensions, in addition to sickness, maternity, work injury, and unemployment benefits. Pensions are provided at age 60 for men and age 55 for women. Women are entitled to 126 days of maternity benefits plus three years unpaid maternity leave. Unemployment benefits are funded entirely by employers, with subsidies as needed from the government. All residents have medical benefits.

Despite these benefits, governmental policies often curtail freedoms in other areas. The US State Department's 2011 Human Rights Report on Uzbekistan found that crimes against women such as domestic violence and rape are often not prosecuted, and that trafficking of women and children persists. Local authorities often use children as free or cheap labor during the cotton harvest. In addition, prisons suffer from overcrowding and food and medicine shortages. The US State Department estimated that 5,000 to 6,000 political prisoners are being held in Uzbekistan. The country also restricts foreign travel, and retains control over major media outlets and newspaper printing and distribution sites.

41 HEALTH

According to the CIA, life expectancy in Uzbekistan was 68 years in 2011. The country spent 4.9% of its GDP on healthcare, amounting to $62 per person. There were 26 physicians, 108 nurses and midwives, and 48 hospital beds per 10,000 inhabitants. The fertility rate was 2.7, while the infant mortality rate was 32 per 1,000 live births. In 2008 the maternal mortality rate, according to the World Bank, was 30 per 100,000 births. It was estimated that 95% of children were vaccinated against measles. The CIA calculated HIV/AIDS prevalence in Uzbekistan to be about 0.1% in 2009.

Ninety-nine cases of acute flaccid paralysis were reported in 2010 when Central Asia experienced a large outbreak of polio. Thirty of the 99 cases were confirmed as cases of polio.

The government has subsidized health care, but low wages for doctors and poor funding of the health sector have led to corruption, with informal payments required for services. This system has limited access to health care for the poor. Street children and children of migrant workers often lack access to government health facilities because they do not possess an officially registered address.

42 HOUSING

The CIA reported that 98% of Uzbekistan's urban population and 81% had access to improved drinking water in 2008, and that the entire population had access to improved sanitation facilities. The Asian Development Bank in 2011 introduced a $500 million lending program to help moderate to low income rural families finance home purchases. About 70% of Uzbekistan's poor population resided in rural areas as of 2011. The lending program was being offered in support of a governmental Housing for Integrated Rural Development Investment Program in which $3 billion was being pumped into the construction of 40,000 new homes in rural areas.

43 EDUCATION

In 2009 the World Bank estimated that 87% of age-eligible children in Uzbekistan were enrolled in primary school. Secondary enrollment for age-eligible children stood at 92%. Tertiary enrollment was estimated at 10%. Of those enrolled in tertiary education, there were 100 male students for every 68 female students. Overall, the CIA estimated that Uzbekistan had a literacy rate of 99.3%.

The government has invested heavily in education through the first two decades of independence. At the pre-school level kindergarten complexes have been established for children to take art, music, foreign languages, and computer studies. More than 400 academic lyceums, secondary schools, and colleges also have been formed. These programs encourage children to identify special talents or skills and to master them as they proceed through school. Children receive free and compulsory education for 12 years, though supply shortages often force families to pay expenses. Teachers are poorly paid and sometimes are found to demand payments from students and their parents in exchange for good grades.

The government also has invested in higher education. As of 2011, there were 16 universities and 39 teacher training institutes, medical, technical, economic, agricultural, and other vocational institutes. These universities and institutes enrolled about 300,000 students. The oldest institutions are the National University and the Technical Institute.

For centuries, Uzbekistan was a noted Muslim educational center. Muslim schools in the cities of Bukhoro (Bukhara), Samarqand (Samarkand), Tashkent, and Khiva attract students from other Muslim countries. In 1920, after the Soviet Union took control of the region, schools and mosques were closed down, and a secular state-funded educational system was established. In recent years, there has been an increased emphasis on Uzbek literature, culture, and history.

44 LIBRARIES AND MUSEUMS

There were 30 libraries and library systems listed in Uzbekistan's online Golden Pages directory in December 2011. The National Library of Uzbekistan is the legal deposit and copyright library. Other libraries are the Alisher Navoi State Public Library, the Central State Archive, the Republic Library for Science and Technology, the Foundation Library of the Uzbek Academic of Sciences, and the Pedagogical Institute.

Museums in Uzbekistan includd the State Museum of Applied Art in Tashkent, the Museum of Arts in Tashkent, the Museum of Amir Timur in Tashkent, the Afrosiyob Museum in Samarkand, the History Museum in Samarkan, the Ichan Kala Museum in Khiva, and the Ark Museum in Bukhara.

45 MEDIA

In 2009 the CIA reported that there were 1.9 million telephone landlines in Uzbekistan. In addition to landlines, mobile phone subscriptions averaged 59 per 100 people. There were four FM radio stations, six AM radio stations, and three shortwave radio stations. Internet users numbered 17 per 100 citizens.Prominent newspapers in 2010, with circulation numbers listed parenthetically, included *Khalk Suzi* (52,000) and *Pravda Vostoka* (35,000).

Telephone links to other former Soviet Republics are provided by land link or microwave and to other countries through Moscow.

Radio Tashkent, established in 1947, broadcasts in Uzbek, English, Urdu, Hindi, Farsi, Arabic, and Uighur. There is also a television station in Tashkent, and satellite earth stations receive Orbita and INTELSAT. In 2010 the country had 47,718 Internet hosts. In 2009 there were some 4.6 million Internet users.

Though there are privately-owned newspapers, the government owns the entire publishing house and must grant approval for all publications printed.

46 ORGANIZATIONS

An umbrella organization known as the Fund Forum has established a number of organizations in Uzbekistan. Among these groups are the Children's Creativity Centers Network, the Junior Sport Children's Sports Complex, the Centre for National Arts, and several associations dedicated to promoting Uzbek handicrafts, antiques, arts, and traditional medicines.

The Uzbekistan Chamber of Commerce and Industry promotes the country's exports in world markets. An umbrella organization, the Federation of Trade Unions of Uzbekistan, coordinates the activities of the country's trade unions. Other organizations promote foreign trade.

The Academy of Sciences was established in 1943 to promote public interest in science while encouraging the work of scientific researchers and educators. The Physicians Association of Uzbekistan serves as a professional networking group and promotes research and education on public health issues.

Women's organizations include the governmental Women's Committee, and non-governmental Business Women's Association, 'Olima" Scholarly Women's Association, the 'Perzent' Karakalpak Center of Humand Reproduction and Planning, and the Women's Resource Center.

47 TOURISM, TRAVEL, AND RECREATION

The *Tourism Factbook*, published by the UN World Tourism Organization, reported 1.22 million incoming tourists to Uzbekistan in 2009, who spent a total of $99 million. Of those incoming tourists, there were 649,000 from East Asia and the Pacific and 333,000 from Europe. There were 52,862 hotel beds available in Uzbekistan, which had an occupancy rate of 54%. The estimated daily cost to visit Tashkent , the capital, was $206. The cost of visiting other cities averaged $77.

Hotels are required to register foreign visitors with the government on a daily basis, and foreigners who stay in private homes are mandated to register their location within three days of their arrival.

Uzbekistan tourist attractions include the Islamic cities of Samarqand (Samarkand), Bukhoro (Bukhara), Khiva, and Kokand. Muslims from Pakistan, Iran, and the Middle East have been drawn to these sites with their palaces, mosques, *madrassas* (religious colleges), and pre-Islamic remains.

48 FAMOUS PERSONS

Islam A. Karimov (b. 1938) has been president of Uzbekistan since 1991. A famous 20th century writer is Abdullah Quaisi, who wrote the historical novels *Days Gone By* and the *Scorpion from the Pulpit*, published in the 1920s. Quaisi was killed in the 1930s during Stalin's purges. Ilyas Malayev (1936–2008) was a popular poet and musician.

49 DEPENDENCIES

Uzbekistan has no territories or colonies.

50 BIBLIOGRAPHY

Doi, Mary M. *Gesture, Gender, Nation: Dance and Social Change in Uzbekistan.* Westport, CT: Bergin and Garvey, 2002.

Ferguson, Robert W. *The Devil and the Disappearing Sea: A True Story about the Aral Sea Catastrophe.* Vancouver, BC: Raincoast Books, 2003.

Human Rights and Democratization in Uzbekistan and Turkmenistan. Washington, DC: Commission on Security and Cooperation in Europe, 2000.

Kort, Michael. *Central Asian Republics.* New York: Facts On File, 2004.

Melvin, Neil. *Uzbekistan: Transition to Authoritarianism on the Silk Road.* Amsterdam: Harwood Academic, 2000.

Northrop, Douglas Taylor. *Veiled Empire: Gender and Power in Stalinist Central Asia.* Ithaca: Cornell University Press, 2004.

Seddon, David, ed. *A Political and Economic Dictionary of the Middle East.* Philadelphia: Routledge/Taylor and Francis, 2004.

Uzbekistan Investment and Business Guide: Strategic and Practical Information. Washington, DC: International Business Publications USA, 2012.

VANUATU

Republic of Vanuatu
[French] *République de Vanuatu*
[Bislama] *Ripablik blong Vanuatu*

CAPITAL: Port-Vila

FLAG: Red and green sections are divided horizontally by a gold stripe running within a black border and widening at the hoist into a black triangle on which is a pig's tusk enclosing two crossed yellow mele leaves.

ANTHEM: *Yumi, Yumi, Yumi* (We, We, We).

MONETARY UNIT: As of 1 January 1981, the vatu (VUV) replaced at par value the New Hebridean franc as the national currency. There are coins of 100 vatu and notes of 100, 500, 1,000, and 5,000 vatu. VUV1 = US$0.0111 (or US$1 = VUV90.25) as of 2011.

WEIGHTS AND MEASURES: The metric standard is used.

HOLIDAYS: New Year's Day, 1 January; May Day, 1 May; Independence Day, 30 July; Assumption, 15 August; Constitution Day, 5 October; National Unity Day, 29 November; Christmas Day, 25 December; Family Day, 26 December. Movable religious holidays include Good Friday, Easter Monday, and Ascension.

TIME: 11 p.m. = noon GMT.

¹LOCATION, SIZE, AND EXTENT

Vanuatu, formerly the Anglo-French condominium of the New Hebrides, is an irregular Y-shaped chain of some 80 islands, with a total land area of about 12,200 sq km (4,710 sq mi) and a total coastline of 2,528 km (1,571 mi). Comparatively, the area occupied by Vanuatu is slightly larger than the state of Connecticut. Of the 70 inhabited islands, the largest is Espiritu Santo; the island of Éfaté is the administrative center. The island chain is about 800 km (500 mi) long and lies about 1,000 km (600 mi) W of Fiji and 400 km (250 mi) NE of New Caledonia.

Vanuatu is in dispute with France over the nearby uninhabited islands of Mathew and Hunter, which are claimed by France as part of the territory of New Caledonia. In November 2010 the government of Vanuatu warned France of its intention to file a suit in the International Court of Justice if France did not renounce its claim. The government claimed that the two islands had been geographically a part of Vanuatu since the creation of the world. The dispute continued through 2011.

Vanuatu's capital city, Port-Vila, is located on the island of Éfaté.

²TOPOGRAPHY

The islands are of coral and volcanic origin; there are active volcanoes on several islands, including Ambrym, Lopevi, and Tanna. Most of the islands are forested and mountainous, with narrow coastal strips. The highest peak, Tabwemasana, on Espiritu Santo, rises 1,878 m (6,161 ft) above sea level. The islands are generally well watered. Being formed in a geologically active area, the islands experience occasional earthquakes. Though these are generally minor, a 6.8 magnitude earthquake was recorded at 90 miles (140 km) north of Luganville, Espiritu Santo, on 5 February 2005.

³CLIMATE

The tropical oceanic climate is moderated by southeastern trade winds, which blow between the months of May and October. Winds are variable during the remainder of the year, and cyclones may occur. Average midday temperatures in Port-Vila range from 25°C (77°F) in winter to 29°C (84°F) in summer. Humidity averages about 74%, and rainfall on Éfaté is about 230 cm (90 in) a year.

⁴FLORA AND FAUNA

The World Resource Institute estimates that there are 870 plant species in Vanuatu. In addition, Vanuatu is home to 22 mammal species, 108 species of birds, and 25 reptile species. The calculation reflects the total number of distinct species residing in the country, not the number of endemic species.

There are no indigenous large mammals, poisonous snakes, or spiders. The native reptile species include the flowerpot snake, found only on Éfaté. There are 11 species of bat, three of which are native to Vanuatu. While the small Polynesian rat is thought to be indigenous, the large species arrived with Europeans, as did domesticated hogs, dogs, and cattle. The wild pig and fowl appear to be indigenous.

The region is rich in sea life, with more than 4,000 species of marine mollusks. Coneshell and stonefish carry poison fatal to humans. The giant East African snail arrived only in the 1970s but already has spread from the Port-Vila region to Luganville.

⁵ENVIRONMENT

The World Resource Institute reported that Vanuatu had designated 8,200 hectares (20,263 acres) of land for protection as of 2006. The UN reported in 2008 that carbon dioxide emissions in Vanuatu totaled 103 kilotons.

Vanuatu's population growth has caused concern for the environment in several areas. Water pollution in urban areas is a problem due to inadequate sanitation systems. The nation's logging industry threatens the forests and contributes to the problem of soil erosion. The reefs on Vanuatu's coasts, which are the home of the country's marine life, are threatened by inappropriate fishing methods and siltation.

In 2009 the Gaua volcano (on the island of the same name) began erupting, creating damaging mudflows and thick plumes of ash and volcanic gases that contaminated the air and water of the surrounding area. At least 400 people were immediately evacuated to relocation centers. However, the volcano continued to erupt, at varying degrees, for several months. Also in 2010, the eruption of Mount Yasur on Tanna Island caused large volcanic rocks and plumes of ash to fall on at least ten surrounding villages.

Vanuatu hosted a meeting of top officials from fourteen developing Pacific island nations and dependencies in 2010 to discuss the progress made in addressing some of the issues unique to these low-lying, developing island states. These include climate change, sea-level rise, natural disasters, remoteness from major markets, and poverty. Another key objective of the meeting was to address the progress each nation had made in adopting the 2005 Mauritius Strategy, the only global blueprint that exists to combat the development challenges of small-island developing states.

According to a 2011 report issued by the International Union for Conservation of Nature and Natural Resources (IUCN), threatened species included 8 types of mammals, 8 species of birds, 3 types of reptiles, 15 species of fish, and 10 species of plants. The estuarine crocodile, hawksbill turtle, Fiji banded iguana, and insular flying fox are threatened species.

⁶POPULATION

The US Central Intelligence Agency (CIA) estimates the population of Vanuatu in 2011 to be approximately 224,564, which placed it at number 175 in population among the 196 nations of the world. In 2011 approximately 4.3% of the population were over 65 years of age, with another 29.6% under 15 years of age. The median age in Vanuatu was 24.9 years. There were 1.04 males for every female in the country. The population's annual rate of change was 1.343%. The projected population for the year 2025 is 350,000. Population density in Vanuatu was calculated at 18 people per sq km (7 people per sq mi).

The UN estimated that 26% of the population lived in urban areas, and that urban populations had an annual rate of change of 4.2%. The largest urban areas, along with their respective populations, included Port Vila, 44,040; and Luganville.

⁷MIGRATION

Estimates of Vanuatu's net migration rate, carried out by the CIA in 2011, amounted to zero. The total number of emigrants living abroad was 3,900, and the total number of immigrants living in Vanuatu was 800. Vanuatu's earliest known settlers probably migrated from the northwestern Pacific about 3,000 years ago. They were followed a thousand years later by migrants from the Solomon Islands. Tradition describes a series of subsequent incursions. In the 19th century, thousands of New Hebrides islanders were recruited as indentured laborers for plantation work in Australia, Fiji, New Caledonia, and Samoa. This migration gradually died down after the establishment of the Anglo-French Condominium, although voluntary emigration to New Caledonia continued un-

til independence. Adverse economic conditions have encouraged emigration to Fiji, New Zealand, and the United States.

⁸ETHNIC GROUPS

Approximately 98.5% of the total population are of Melanesian origin. French, Vietnamese, Chinese, and other Pacific Islanders are also found.

⁹LANGUAGES

More than 100 languages and dialects are spoken in Vanuatu. Melanesian, the principal language, is related to Fijian and New Caledonian speech. Pidgin English, known as Bislama or Bichelama, is recognized by the constitution as the lingua franca, although English and French are also official languages. The national anthem is in Bislama, which is also used in parliamentary debate, with the proceedings reported in English and French as well. Children often speak as many as four languages and every aspect of public life—including education, law, and the media—is complicated by language problems.

¹⁰RELIGIONS

A majority of the population is considered to be Christian, though many include indigenous customs with their practice. The Anglican, Presbyterian, and Roman Catholic churches first began missionary work in the New Hebrides during the 19th century. More recently, the Seventh-Day Adventists and other nontraditional Protestant groups have been active in mission work. While most of the mission schools have been handed over to the government, missionaries have continued to make important contributions to education and health. According to the latest estimates, about 31.4% of the population were Presbyterians, 13.1% were Roman Catholics, 13.4% were Anglican, and 10.8% were Seventh-Day Adventists. The Church of Christ, the Apostolic Church, and the Assemblies of God also have active congregations. Jehovah's Witnesses and Mormons (The Church of Jesus Christ of Latter-Day Saints) together account for about 9.6% of the population. Since 1940, the John Frum Movement (political party and indigenous religion based on a rejection of the white Christian's beliefs but not his goods) has flourished, mainly on Tanna and provides a remarkable example of religious development in a situation of cultural challenge and transition. Membership, however, is only about 5% of the population. Muslims are also active within the country.

The constitution allows for religious freedom while making a commitment to traditional values of Christian principles. Some subsidies are offered to Christian churches and the government maintains good relations with the Vanuatu Christian Council through the Ministry of Home Affairs. Religious organizations must register with the government, but this rule is not generally enforced. Father Lini Day (commemorating the former prime minister and Anglican priest), Good Friday, Easter Monday, Ascension, Assumption, and Christmas are observed as national holidays.

¹¹TRANSPORTATION

During World War II, Vanuatu became an important Allied base, and many roads and airstrips were built by the US forces. By 2010, the CIA reported that Vanuatu had a total of 1,070 km (665 mi) of roads, of which 256 km (159 mi) were paved.

Small usable airfields serve the main islands; only three had paved runways in 2009. The chief airports are Bauerfield, on Éfaté, and Pekoa, on Espiritu Santo; both have been upgraded to handle jet aircraft. Air Vanuatu, the national airline operated by Ansett Airlines of Australia, maintains regular service to Australia; an internal airline, Air Melanesiae, links 22 airfields on various islands. Air travel transported 112,169 passengers in 2009 according to the World Bank.

Port-Vila and Luganville are the chief seaports. Small ships provide frequent interisland service. Vanuatu maintains a policy of open registry for merchant ships, allowing foreign shipowners to avoid the higher costs and regulations of registration under their own flags. As of 2008, there were 54 ships of 1,000 gross registered tons or more in the Vanuatuan merchant fleet.

12 HISTORY

Although the Portuguese navigator Pedro Fernandes de Queir established a short-lived settlement on Espiritu Santo in 1606, little more is known about the history of the New Hebrides until French and British explorers arrived in the late 18th century. Captain James Cook discovered, named, and charted most of the southern islands in 1774. The next century brought British and French missionaries, planters, and traders, and for many years the islanders suffered from the depredations of the recruiting ships and from other lawless acts by Europeans in the region.

By the Anglo-French Convention of 1887, a joint naval commission was established, with a resident commissioner to protect the lives and interests of the islanders. In 1906, following a London conference, the Anglo-French Condominium was established, largely to settle land claims and to end difficulties caused by lack of clear local jurisdiction. Indigenous political activity developed after World War II, with increasing native concern over land alienation and European dominance.

In 1975 a representative assembly replaced the nominated advisory council under which the New Hebrides had been governed; 29 assembly members were elected by universal suffrage, nine members represented economic interests, and four members represented the traditional chiefs. In 1977 the National Party (Vanuaaku Pati), which held 21 of 42 assembly seats, demanded independence and staged a boycott of the legislature; in response, at a conference in Paris, self-government was agreed on for 1978, to be followed by a 1980 referendum on independence. After considerable difficulty, a constitutional conference in 1979 finally agreed on an independence constitution. In the November 1979 elections for a newly constituted, fully elective assembly, the National Party, led by Father Walter Lini, obtained 26 of the 39 seats.

In May 1980 however, a dissident francophone group, based on Espiritu Santo, attempted to break away and declared an independent government of Vemarana, under Jimmy Stevens and the Nagriamal Party. Attempts made during June to resolve the differences between the new central government and the rebels failed, and UK and French troops were sent to Luganville on 24 July. No shots were fired, but the soldiers remained until Vanuatu's formal declaration of independence on 30 July 1980. They were then replaced at the new government's request by forces from Papua New

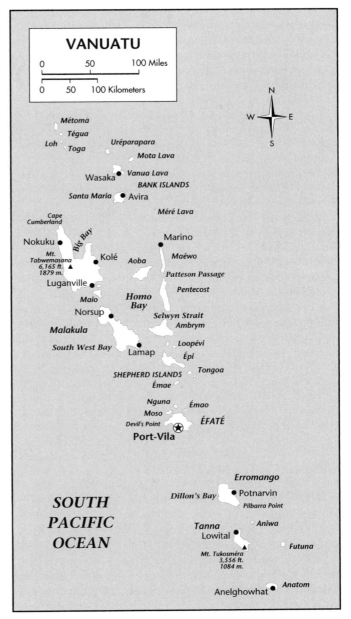

LOCATION: 13° to 21°S; 166° to 171° E. TOTAL COASTLINE: 2,528 kilometers (1,571 miles). TERRITORIAL SEA LIMIT: 12 miles.

Guinea, who were assisted by the local police in putting down the rebellion.

Since independence, Vanuatu (Our Land Forever) has followed a nonaligned foreign policy. It became the first South Pacific nation to join the nonaligned movement, and in January 1987 it signed a controversial fishing agreement with the USSR. In May 1987 Vanuatu announced a ban on all military ships and aircraft in a dispute over a proposed Libyan diplomatic mission. The dispute ended with the expulsion of two Libyan diplomats. Relations with the French government remained strained throughout much of the Lini government's rule, though they improved at the end of 1989 with the signing of the Matignon Accord relating to New Caledonia.

In December 1988 President George Ati Sokomanu attempted to dismiss the Lini government by ordering the dissolution of the country's parliament. Sokomanu appointed Barak Sope as prime minister. Lini refused to surrender office and reconvened parliament. Sope and several supporters were arrested and charged with inciting mutiny. Sope was sentenced to six years' imprisonment.

Fr. Lini lost a parliamentary vote of confidence in September 1991 and he was replaced by Donald Kalpokas. In December 1991 the francophone Union of Moderate Parties (UMP), led by Maxime Carlot Korman, won the largest bloc of seats and formed a coalition government with the National United Party (NUP), led by Lini. Strains between the coalition members led to Lini joining the opposition in August 1993, but Carlot Korman's government survived the defection.

Parliamentary elections were again held in 1995, with the UMP winning slightly more seats than the Vanuatu Party (VP), led by Donald Kalpokas. Rialuth Serge Vohor was prime minister from November 1995 until a no-confidence vote in parliament forced his resignation on 7 February 1996. Maxime Carlot Korman was elected prime minister, forming a coalition, and parliament appointed Kalpokas deputy prime minister. The coalition was considered to be weak, however. On 30 September 1996 Korman was ousted by a no-confidence motion. Vohor was reelected as prime minister. The Vohor government repealed the Ombudsman's Act, but President Jean Marie Leye refused to declare this piece of legislation as law. Leye, in the face of dissent and political crises, took action to dissolve parliament. The ruling coalition refused to step down, questioning the constitutional right of Leye to do this. The Court of Appeal ruled in January 1998 that Leye's actions were legal, thus opening the way for a new general election. In the election held 6 March 1998 the VP of Kalpokas improved its earlier performance, but could not claim a majority. Kalpokas rejoined forces with Fr. Lini and the NUP and coalesced with minority party legislators to gain a clear majority. Kalpokas was elected prime minister. Willie Jimmy was named deputy prime minister on 19 October 1998. Kalpokas resigned to avoid a no-confidence vote in late 1999, and Barak Sope of Melanesian Progressive Party (MPP) became prime minister. In 1999, the government introduced a Comprehensive Reform Program, to combat corruption and abuse of power by government officials. It included a revamping of state administration, an increase in private sector development, a reduction in the public service sector, and the enactment of a leadership code of conduct.

At the South Pacific Forum in June 1999 Vanuatu supported a proposed Pacific Free Trade Area (FTA) that would initially include 14 countries in the region. The South Pacific Forum set up the Pacific Kava Council to work at protecting the regional rights to kava and its uses. The kava plant's reputed relaxation properties had attracted the attention of producers of herbal medicines. The establishment of kava plantations in Central America threatened the Pacific Islands' production. Vanuatu joined with other small island developing states (SIDS) through the United Nations SIDSnet, an Internet project linking over 40 island nations worldwide to address issues like the economic hurdles of isolation and small markets. The United Nations Environment Program (UNEP) issued a report assessing the ecological and population threats faced by SIDS, Vanuatu included. The UN's Intergovernmental Panel on Climate Change announced its predictions on the consequences of global warming. Vanuatu was mentioned as already affected by inundation of low-lying areas and coastal regions by rising oceans.

In April 2001 Barak Sope was ousted as prime minister in a vote of no confidence, and Edward Natapei became prime minister. The new government undertook investigations into Sope's business dealings, and in November, Sope was charged with two counts of forgery. He was sentenced to three years' imprisonment but was subsequently pardoned by President Fr. John Bani. Natapei was reelected prime minister in May 2002, after parliamentary elections held on 30 April, in which his Vanua'aku Party took 15 seats and the Union of Moderate Parties took 14 seats.

Presidential and legislative elections were held in 2004. The controversial prime minister Serge Vohor, who took office in July 2004, was ousted following a no-confidence vote that December; Vohor had attempted to switch Vanuatu's diplomatic recognition of China to Taiwan. Ham Lini became prime minister in December 2004. In April and May 2004, Alfred Masing Nalo was elected president, but was later removed from office after the Supreme Court invalidated the result of the election. Kalkot Matas Kelekele was elected president in August 2004. The 2008 elections reinstated Natapei as prime minister; Natapei was replaced in 2010 by Sato Kilman, who was in office for only a year before a no-confidence vote installed former prime minister Vohor. Vohor's victory was rescinded by the Supreme Court, and he was succeeded by Kilman in June 2011.

13 GOVERNMENT

Under the independence constitution adopted in 1979 and effective in 1980, Vanuatu is an independent republic within the Commonwealth of Nations. The head of state is the president (Iolu Johnson Abbil as of September 2011); the head of government is the prime minister (Sato Kilman as of September 2011). The unicameral legislature consists of 52 members (39 before 1987, and 50 before 1998) elected by universal adult suffrage to four-year terms. The cabinet is responsible to parliament, and the president is chosen by an electoral college for a five-year term. The electoral system includes a degree of proportional representation. A Council of Chiefs chosen by their peers in the chiefs' district councils advises the government on the protection of Vanuatuan languages and culture.

14 POLITICAL PARTIES

In the elections of 2008, the Vanua'aku Pati (VP; Our Land Party) took 11 of the 52 seats in the unicameral parliament. The National United Party (NUP) came in next with eight seats, followed by the Union of Moderate Parties (UMP) with seven seats, the Vanuatu Republic Party (VRP) with another seven seats, the People's Progressive Party (PPP) with four seats, and the Greens Confederation with two seats. The Melanesian Progressive Party (MPP), Nagriamel movement (NAG), Namangi Aute (NA), and People's Action Party (PAP) each gained one seat.

Edward Natapei came into office as prime minister following Vanuatu's September 2008 parliamentary elections, when the VP won 11 of 52 seats in parliament. However, Natapei had a number of conflicts with various members of parliament. In December 2010, he lost a vote of confidence brought against him after a clash with members of parliament to block the military commander Commodore Frank Bainimarama from taking the rotating lead in the regional Melanesian Spearhead Group. Natapei was replaced by the deputy prime minister Sato Kilman on 3 December 2010, following a special parliamentary vote to which the media was denied access. Opposition leaders claimed that by denying media access, the vote represented a circumvention of the democratic process. As a result, nearly two weeks later the group made a motion for a vote of no confidence against Kilman. Kilman boosted support for his coalition government by reshuffling his cabinet to include eight members from the Union of Moderate Parties. With this move, the Kilman coalition secured the support of 34 members of parliament, while the Natapei opposition had only 18.

However, on 24 April 2011, parliament issued a vote of no confidence against Kilman and elected Serge Vohor of the Union of Moderate Parties as the new prime minister by a vote of 26 to 25. Kilman contested the vote, citing a constitutional stipulation that an absolute majority, or at least 27 votes, is necessary, for the vote of no confidence and the selection of a new prime minister. The court of appeals agreed, and Kilman was reinstated as prime minister on 13 May.

The next scheduled legislative elections were set for 2012, and presidential elections were scheduled for 2014.

15 LOCAL GOVERNMENT

Vanuatu is divided into six provinces (Malampa, Penama, Sanma, Shefa, Tafea, and Torba). There are municipal councils in Port-Vila and Luganville, and community councils elsewhere. Espiritu Santo and Tanna have special regional councils.

16 JUDICIAL SYSTEM

Despite the great difficulty in unifying laws based on the very different English and French traditions, Vanuatu has sought to establish a single system based on British criminal procedure and the French penal code. The constitution establishes a Supreme Court, with a chief justice and three other judges, as well as an appeals court. The chief justice is appointed by the president in consultation with the prime minister and opposition leader. The other three judges are appointed by the president based on recommendations from the Judicial Service Commission. Village and island courts have jurisdiction over customary and other matters.

The judiciary is independent of the executive and free from military influence. The constitution guarantees a range of procedural due process protections including the presumption of innocence, fair public trial, habeas corpus, and the prohibition against double jeopardy.

17 ARMED FORCES

Though there were no regular military forces in 2011, the nation maintained close links with Papua New Guinea, where Vanuatuan cadets trained as part of the Vanuatu Mobile Force under the auspices of the Australian Ministry of Defense. Vanuatu also maintained a police force with a maritime wing.

18 INTERNATIONAL COOPERATION

Vanuatu joined the United Nations on 15 September 1981 and participates in ESCAP and several nonregional specialized agencies, such as the FAO, the World Bank, UNESCO, UNIDO, and the WHO. It also belongs to the Asian Development Bank (which opened a regional office in Port-Vila in 1984), the ACP Group,

G-77, the Pacific Island Forum, the South Pacific Regional Trade and Economic Cooperation Agreement (Sparteca), the Alliance of Small Island States (AOSIS), and the Commonwealth of Nations. The country holds observer status in the WTO.

Vanuatu has taken an active role in Pacific affairs, campaigning for a nuclear-free zone and advocating independence for New Caledonia. Vanuatu has established diplomatic relations with a number of OECD countries, as well as China, Cuba, Vietnam, and Libya. The country is part of the Nonaligned Movement.

In environmental cooperation, Vanuatu is part of the Convention on Biological Diversity, CITES, the London Convention, the Kyoto Protocol, the Montréal Protocol, MARPOL, and the UN Conventions on the Law of the Sea, Climate Change, and Desertification.

Vanuatu announced in 2011 that it would join the World Trade Organization (WTO) and the UN Convention Against Corruption (UNCAC).

19 ECONOMY

The gross domestic product (GDP) rate of change in Vanuatu, as of 2010, was 2.2%. Inflation stood at 3.9%, and unemployment was reported at 1.7%. Vanuatu's economy is based largely on small-scale agriculture, which employs some 80% of the population. Copra is the most important cash crop, accounting for about 35% of the nation's exports. Other agricultural products included coconuts, cocoa, coffee, taro, yams, fruits, and vegetables.

Tourism accounts for about 20% of the GDP in 2007. Financial services and the service industry have also become increasingly important in foreign exchange. Beginning in 2002, the country has taken measures to tighten the regulation of its offshore financial center, which is internationally known as a tax haven. The government also earns fees from a "flag of convenience" shipping registry. Unskilled laborers often find work in New Zealand or Australia through what is known as the Recognized Seasonal Employer program. In 2009 Vanuatu traded primarily with regional partners such as Thailand, Japan, and Australia.

GDP grew by less than 3% a year in the 1990s. For the three years 2000 to 2002, GDP growth averaged 3% and inflation averaged 3%. During this period the islands had to deal with the extensive damage from two severe earthquakes, each followed by sizeable tsunamis: in November, 1999 on the northern island of Pentecote, and in January 2002, centered on the capital and surrounding areas. Growth continued during the 2000s, reaching a peak of nearly 6% in 2008 before declining as a result of the global recession. Nonetheless, relatively high commodity prices have sustained growth in the face of the economic downtown.

Major economic development is hindered by the geographic isolation of the country, its vulnerability to natural disasters, and its dependency on relatively few export commodities. Australia and New Zealand are the main sources of tourism and foreign aid.

20 INCOME

The CIA estimated that in 2010 the GDP of Vanuatu was $1.137 billion. The CIA defines GDP as the value of all final goods and services produced within a nation in a given year and computed on the basis of purchasing power parity (PPP) rather than value as measured on the basis of the rate of the exchange based on current dollars. The per capita GDP was estimated at $5,100. The annual growth rate of GDP was 2.2%. The average inflation rate was 3.9%. It was estimated that agriculture accounted for 26% of GDP, industry 12%, and services 62%.

According to the World Bank, remittances from citizens living abroad totaled $6.5 million or about $29 per capita and accounted for approximately 0.6% of GDP.

21 LABOR

As of 2007 Vanuatu had a total labor force of 115,900 people. Within that labor force, CIA estimates in 2000 noted that 65% were employed in agriculture, 5% in industry, and 30% in the service sector; other estimates place agricultural employment as high as 80%.

A seasonal employment program permits unskilled workers from Vanuatu to work in New Zealand as fruit pickers and farm workers. In 2007 alone, the program had a financial inflow worth VUV20 million.

For persons engaged in government enterprises, port work, construction, and certain other jobs, the terms of employment and wages are set by legislation. The nation's first trade unions were formed in 1984. The Vanuatu Council of Trade Unions is the umbrella group for organized labor.

The law prohibits children under 12 from working. Children between 12 and 18 may work under restricted hours and conditions. The Labor Department effectively enforces these laws. In 2002 the minimum wage was $143 per month for all workers; it was raised to $285 per month in 2008. This increase still failed to provide an adequate living, and most families subsidized their income with subsistence farming. The law mandates a 44-hour maximum workweek that included at least one 24-hour rest period. The Employment Act provides health and safety standards but these are not effectively enforced. An amendment to that act, added in 2008, increased maternity leave from half salary to full salary for a period of 12 weeks.

22 AGRICULTURE

Out of 1.2 million hectares (3 million acres) of land in Vanuatu, 20,000 hectares (49,421 acres) are arable. Roughly 15% of the total land is currently farmed, and the country's major crops include copra, coconuts, cocoa, coffee, taro, yams, fruits, and vegetables. Cereal production in 2009 amounted to 846 tons, fruit production 25,642 tons, and vegetable production 11,563 tons.

While most crops are raised for local consumption, cash crops like copra, cocoa, and coffee have been increasingly important. Although sustained high prices for its cash crops have fostered economic growth through 2010, both the agricultural sector and the broader economy were susceptible to fluctuations in commodity prices.

In 1983, Vanuatu's first agricultural census was taken, with British assistance. A land alienation act passed in 1982 limits land ownership to indigenous owners and their descendants, but expatriates can lease land for up to 75 years.

23 ANIMAL HUSBANDRY

The UN Food and Agriculture Organization (FAO) reported that Vanuatu dedicated 42,000 hectares (103,784 acres) to permanent pasture or meadow in 2009. During that year, the country tended 800,000 chickens, 170,000 head of cattle, and 89,000 pigs. The pro-

Principal Trading Partners – Vanuatu (2010)

(In millions of US dollars)

Country	Total	Exports	Imports	Balance
South Korea	591.0	0.8	590.2	-589.4
World	380.0	60.0	320.0	-260.0
Thailand	128.1	121.0	7.1	113.9
Japan	103.9	52.3	51.6	0.7
Australia	74.8	1.0	73.8	-72.8
Singapore	73.2	2.4	70.7	-68.3
New Zealand	36.7	2.2	34.5	-32.4
Fiji	33.0	0.2	32.8	-32.5
China	25.5	0.6	24.9	-24.3
United States	22.3	1.6	20.7	-19.0
New Caledonia	21.9	3.6	18.3	-14.7

(…) data not available or not significant.

(n.s.) not specified.

SOURCE: *2011 Direction of Trade Statistics Yearbook,* New York: United Nations, 2011.

duction from these animals amounted to 2,445 tons of beef and veal, 3,590 tons of pork, 1,442 tons of poultry, 382 tons of eggs, and 6,480 tons of milk. Vanuatu also produced 520 tons of cattle hide.

Vanuatu is ideal for cattle, and large numbers are raised on plantations. The growing meat-packing industry produces frozen, chilled, and tinned bee. The beef industry is centered on the island of Espiritu Santo, where the country's main abattoir is located. Beef is exported primarily to Japan, with a lesser amount going to New Caledonia. By 2011 beef exports trailed only copra exports in agricultural importance.

24 FISHING

Vanuatu had 80 decked commercial fishing boats in 2008. The annual capture totaled 60,881 tons according to the UN FAO. The export value of seafood totaled $83.19 million. Vanuatu lays claim to an exclusive economic zone of 735,893 sq km (284,130 sq mi).

Although the South Pacific Fishing Co., a joint Vanuatuan government and Japanese venture, has facilities at Luganville that freeze and export both tuna and bonito to Japan and the United States, the full fishery potential has not been realized— most fishing ventures are conducted by foreigners.

A 2007 government census reported that 75% of rural households were involved in fishing for domestic consumption. Vanuatu charges a 4% levy on all fish exported by processing plants.

25 FORESTRY

Approximately 36% of Vanuatu is covered by forest. The UN FAO estimated the 2009 roundwood production at 28,000 cu m (988,811 cu ft). The value of all forest products, including roundwood, totaled $951,000.

The government approved the establishment of a large commercial forestry plantation on Espirito Santo in 1987. The quality of timber and the accessibility to it have limited commercial development in subsequent years. A focus on sustainable harvesting has created the opportunity for investment in tree farms and the exploitation of previously underutilized tree species.

Balance of Payments – Vanuatu (2007)

(In millions of US dollars)

Current Account		-53.8
Balance on goods	-142.9	
Imports	-176.5	
Exports	33.6	
Balance on services	110.3	
Balance on income	-24.8	
Current transfers	3.6	
Capital Account		30.0
Financial Account		15.0
Direct investment abroad	0.6	
Direct investment in Vanuatu	34.2	
Portfolio investment assets	1.7	
Portfolio investment liabilities	...	
Financial derivatives	...	
Other investment assets	51.3	
Other investment liabilities	-71.5	
Net Errors and Omissions		-4.3
Reserves and Related Items		13.2

(…) data not available or not significant.

SOURCE: *Balance of Payment Statistics Yearbook 2011*, Washington, DC: International Monetary Fund, 2011.

26 MINING

Vanuatu has few known minerals, although gold deposits have been discovered. A small manganese mine on Éfaté ceased exports in 1980.

27 ENERGY AND POWER

The World Bank reported in 2008 that Vanuatu produced 43 million kWh of electricity while consuming 40 million kWh. Temporary generators established throughout the islands by the United States during World War II (1939–45) have mostly deteriorated.

All hydrocarbon needs were met by imports. In 2010 demand for refined petroleum products averaged 1,000 barrels per day, up from 610 barrels per day in 2002.

In October 2009, Vanuatu received $7 million from the European Investment Bank for the construction of the nation's first wind farm on the island of Éfaté. The wind farm was to be built by Unelco Vanuatu, a company that is part of the International GDF-Suez Energy Group. Officials hoped the project will not only satisfy local energy needs, but also serve as an example of sustainable energy production for other Pacific islands.

28 INDUSTRY

The industrial sector is small, accounting for roughly 10% of GDP in the 1990s and 2000s. The leading industries are fish and food freezing, wood processing, and meat canning. The small manufacturing sector, accounting for is geared to toward domestic consumption. Indigenous crafts include basketry, canoe building, and pottery.

The government has continually sought out new manufacturing investment. The production and refinement of coconut fuel is one notable sector. Others include the production of soft drinks, bread, furniture, and clothing.

29 SCIENCE AND TECHNOLOGY

The World Bank reported in 2009 that there were no patent applications in science and technology in Vanuatu. There is no advanced technology apart from overseas aid programs.

30 DOMESTIC TRADE

In Port-Vila, European businesses dominate commercial life; there are hotels, supermarkets, fashion shops, and patisseries, as well as Australian steak houses and small Chinese restaurants. Some Vanuatuans have entered the cash economy in urban areas. There is a very small light industry section that supplies the local markets. The nation's numerous cooperative societies handle most of the distribution of goods on the islands. A value-added tax applies to most goods and services.

Normal business hours in the capital are 7:30 to 11:30 a.m. and 1:30 to 4:30 p.m., Monday through Friday. Banks in Vanuatu are open on weekdays from 8 to 11:30 a.m. and 1:30 to 3 p.m.

31 FOREIGN TRADE

Vanuatu imported $156 million worth of goods and services in 2008, while exporting $40 million worth of goods and services. Major import partners in 2009 were Japan, 17.5%; Australia, 13.7%; Singapore, 12.2%; China, 11.3%; NZ, 7%; Poland, 6.7%; France, 5.9%; and Fiji, 5.6% . Imports included machinery and transport equipment, food and live animals, basic manufactures, and mineral fuels. Major export partners were Thailand, 57.7%; Japan, 13.3%; and Poland, 12.8%. Exports included copra, beef, cocoa, timber, kava, and coffee. A commodities marketing board exported copra and cocoa until its repeal in 2011.

32 BALANCE OF PAYMENTS

Trade figures from 2008 showed a trade deficit of $116 million. Service receipts have helped offset the traditionally adverse trade balance. Vanuatu has Continuing trade deficits have been offset by aid from the United Kingdom and France, but this assistance is being steadily reduced.

33 BANKING AND SECURITIES

Vanuatu's banking system includes a the Reserve Bank of Vanuatu, the country's central bank established in 1980, as well as local retail banks and departmental development banks that provides loans for agricultural projects, housing, and industrial development.

Vanuatu's financial sector was considered a tax haven for years, and reforms to offshore banking began in 2002. It was removed from the OECD blacklist in 2003. New legal reforms to the sector in 2011 were developed in collaboration with the Asian Development Bank. The financial services sector grew during the 2000s, though a 2008 financial crisis and increasingly stringent regulation diminished profitability.

In 2009 the discount rate, the interest rate at which the central bank lends to financial institutions in the short term, was 6%. The commercial bank prime lending rate, the rate at which banks lend to customers, was 5.5% in 2010. There is no stock exchange.

³⁴INSURANCE

Insurance coverage is available through agents of overseas companies, mainly British and French.

³⁵PUBLIC FINANCE

Budget projections for 2012 anticipated revenues and expenditures at 19% of GDP in order to sustain a balanced budget. The government, which felt it would meet or exceed balanced budget obligations, also projected its debt level to remain below 40% of GDP.

In 2005 the budget of Vanuatu included $78.7 million in public revenue and $72.23 million in public expenditures. The budget surplus amounted to .9% of GDP. All $81.2 million of debt was held by foreign entities.

³⁶TAXATION

Vanuatu has no income, corporation, or sales tax. Government revenues are derived from indirect taxes, which include a 12.5% VAT tax.

³⁷CUSTOMS AND DUTIES

Tariff rates for household goods average 5–15%; however, rates for luxury goods average closer to 50%. Export duties are levied on the country's primary products. Exempt items include items imported for humanitarian relief and other charitable ends. Other goods that serve economic development, such as hotel goods and mining equipment, may also be exempt.

³⁸FOREIGN INVESTMENT

Foreign direct investment (FDI) in Vanuatu was a net inflow of $34.6 million according to World Bank figures published in 2009. FDI represented 5.33% of GDP. The government encourages all forms of foreign investment, especially if there is joint local participation. Duty exemptions are available on application to the Ministry of Finance.

In late 1999 Vanuatu's Department of Trade announced that prior to consideration, all foreign investment proposals must be accompanied by an application fee. This action was taken because of the high number of project proposals approved but not implemented. Application fees varied from VUV15,000 to VUV50,000 based on the investment cost. Foreign direct investment (FDI) in Vanuatu during previous years totaled $30.2 million (1997) and $20.3 million (2001).

³⁹ECONOMIC DEVELOPMENT

The British independence settlement provided grants of £23.4 million to Vanuatu, including £6.4 million in budgetary aid (with additional grants provided annually), £4 million for technical aid, and £13 million for development projects aimed at promoting national economic self-sufficiency. Projects under the five-year development plan for 1982–86 included harbor development, agricultural training, and road improvements. Aid for other infrastructural development is provided by Australia, New Zealand, the UN, and the EU.

Government development projects have emphasized local participation and preservation of Vanuatu's cultural heritage. In 1995, Vanuatu received $45.8 million in aid from international sources.

In 2000, Vanuatu was listed on the OECD's blacklist of tax havens, though reforms prompted its removal in 2003.

Economic growth continued throughout the 2000s, as Vanuatu weathered global economic turmoil in 2008–09 through its valuable agricultural exports. Tourism revenues are similarly important and one of the government's main targets for foreign investment. A balanced budget and low debt burden provided the government with financial flexibility, although natural disasters or a drop in commodity prices remained a potential threat.

⁴⁰SOCIAL DEVELOPMENT

A majority of the people retain a traditional village life. The extended family system ensures that no islanders starve, while church missions and the social development section of the Education Ministry concentrate on rural development and youth activities. The government incorporates family planning into its overall maternal and child health program. A provident fund system provides lump-sum benefits for old age, disability, and death. Workers contributed 4% of earnings and employers contribute 6% of payroll. Pensions are provided at the age of 55.

Although human rights are generally well respected, women are still largely confined to traditional cultural roles, and most marriages include a "bride-price" that encourages men to consider their wives as possessions. Women generally do not own land. Village chiefs usually act to reinforce the subordinate roles of women and are thus viewed as a primary obstacle to female advancement. A disproportionate number of women lost their jobs due to cutbacks in government employment. Violence against women, especially domestic abuse, is common. The 2008 Family Protection Act addressed concerns of violence against women; it was sponsored by the Department of Women's Affairs.

Prison conditions are considered substandard, and the issue reached Vanuatu's Supreme Court in 2007 leading to further investigations through 2009 and at least one court case on behalf of an inmate.

⁴¹HEALTH

According to the CIA, life expectancy in Vanuatu was 71 years in 2011. The country spent 3.9% of its GDP on healthcare, amounting to $106 per person. There was one physician, 17 nurses and midwives, and 17 hospital beds per 10,000 inhabitants. The fertility rate was 3.9, while the infant mortality rate was 14 per 1,000 live births. It was estimated that 52% of children were vaccinated against measles. Malaria is the most serious of the country's diseases, which also include leprosy, tuberculosis, filariasis, and venereal diseases.

The Ministry of Health serves the rural population through its six Community Health Services offices. Access to health care remains a primary concern, as some remote populations have to travel by boat or canoe for up to two days to reach an adequate medical facility.

⁴²HOUSING

In urban areas only the emerging middle class can afford government-built housing. Other migrants to the towns buy plots of land and build cheap shacks of corrugated iron and waste materials, principally near Port-Vila and Luganville. The vast majority of villagers still build their own homes from local materials. Most dwellings are traditional Melanesian houses with earth or coral floors, no glass windows, and palm, bamboo, or cane walls and roofing. An estimated 60% of households qualified as substandard in 2006. The rainy season and cyclones are major threats to the population living in substandard housing.

43 EDUCATION

In 2009 the World Bank estimated that 97% of age-eligible children in Vanuatu were enrolled in primary school. Overall, the CIA estimated that Vanuatu had a literacy rate of 74%. Public expenditure on education represented 4.8% of GDP.

Primary education is available for almost all children except in a few remote tribal areas. Education is provided in either English or French. Full secondary education is provided by the Anglophone Malapoa College and the French Lycée at Port-Vila. For postsecondary education, especially medical and technical training, selected students go principally to Fiji, Australia, and New Zealand.

In 2010 the Ministry of Education presented the first local education curriculum to be developed solely by the Vanuatuan government. The previous curriculum was a holdover from the British and French systems in place when the country gained its independence in 1980. Officials believed that a local curriculum, addressing points of local culture and customs, was necessary to ensure a stronger future for the nation. A focus on agriculture, a mainstay of the economy, represented a major shift. Some argued that the previous curriculum trained students to look beyond the borders of their own nation for employment, rather than teach those skills that could be used to strengthen the local economy. The new curriculum is to be presented in both English and French.

44 LIBRARIES AND MUSEUMS

The National Library is housed at the Vanuatu Cultural Centre in Port-Vila, as is the National Museum, and the National Photo, Film, and Sound Archive. The Vanuatu Cultural Centre was established in the 1960s in an effort to codify both history and culture. In particular it sought to record oral histories from the myriad indigenous cultures on the islands.

Secondary schools also have libraries, and there is a small library in the parliament building. Éfaté has a small museum displaying South Pacific artifacts and current works of art. There is a private fine arts museum located in Port-Vila.

45 MEDIA

In 2009 the CIA reported that there were 7,200 telephone landlines in Vanuatu. In addition to landlines, mobile phone subscriptions averaged 53 per 100 people. There were 2 FM radio stations, 4 AM radio stations, and 1 shortwave radio station. Internet subscriptions stood at 7 per 100 citizens.

The government owns one television station and two radio stations. Multi-channel cable subscriptions are available. *The Vanuatu Independent*, published weekly, and the *Vanuatu Daily Post* are major newspapers. The *Vanuatu Weekly* is published by the government. The constitution provides for free speech and a free press; however, in practice these provisions are not always honored, threatening opposition groups and media representatives with revocations of licenses and permits.

46 ORGANIZATIONS

There are a great number of European organizations, but the cooperative movement has had the greatest local impact. Cooperative units have organized a training center in Port-Vila for such skills as accounting, management, law, and marketing. Cooperatives receive British aid and government support but remain firmly independent. There is an active Vanuatu Credit Union League offering educational opportunities as well as financial services to members.

National youth organizations include the Vanuatu National Youth Council and the Vanuatu National Union of Students. There are several active sports associations promoting amateur competition for all ages in a variety of pastimes, including cricket, tennis, tae kwon do, and track and field. Many sports clubs are affiliated with the national Olympic Committee. The Vanuatu Association of Women Graduates promotes higher education opportunities for women. There are national chapters of the Red Cross Society, and UNICEF, and Habitat for Humanity.

47 TOURISM, TRAVEL, AND RECREATION

The *Tourism Factbook*, published by the UN World Tourism Organization in 2011, reported 101,000 incoming tourists to Vanuatu who spent a total of $142 million. Of those incoming tourists, there were 91,000 from East Asia and the Pacific. There were 2,450 hotel beds available in Vanuatu. The estimated daily cost to visit Port-Vila (on Éfaté), the capital, was $364. The cost of visiting other cities averaged $33.

The most popular recreations in Vanuatu include marine sightseeing, deep-sea fishing, sailing, and beachcombing for shells. Citizens from most nations do not require visas. However, a valid passport and onward/return ticket are necessary.

48 FAMOUS PERSONS

Father Walter Hayde Lini (1943–99), ordained as an Anglican priest in 1970, served as prime minister in Vanuatu from 1980 to 1991.

49 DEPENDENCIES

Vanuatu has no territories or colonies.

50 BIBLIOGRAPHY

Bennett, Michelle. *Vanuatu.* 4th ed. London, Eng.: Lonely Planet, 2003.

Bolton, Lissant. *Unfolding the Moon: Enacting Women's Kastom in Vanuatu.* Honolulu: University of Hawaii Press, 2003.

Craig, Robert D. *Historical Dictionary of Polynesia.* Lanham, MD: Scarecrow Press, 2002.

Eriksen, Annelin. *Gender, Christianity and Change in Vanuatu.* Burlington, VT: Ashgate, 2007.

Gillespie, Rosemary G., and David A. Clague, eds. *Encyclopedia of Islands.* Berkeley: University of California Press, 2009.

Kirch, Patrick Vinton, and Jean-Louis Rallu. *The Growth and Collapse of Pacific Island Societies.* Honolulu: University of Hawaii Press, 2007.

Leibo, Steven A. *East and Southeast Asia, 2005.* 38th ed. Harpers Ferry, WV: Stryker-Post Publications, 2005.

VIETNAM

Socialist Republic of Vietnam
Cong Hoa Chu Nghia Viet Nam

CAPITAL: Hanoi

FLAG: The flag is red with a five-pointed gold star in the center.

ANTHEM: *Tien Quan Ça (Forward, Soldiers!).*

MONETARY UNIT: The dong (VND) is a plastic polymer currency with banknotes of 10,000, 20,000, 50,000, 100,000, 200,000 and 500,000 dong. Older paper notes in smaller denominations still circulate and there are coins in 200, 500, 1,000, 2,000 and 5,000 dong. VND1 = US$0.00004792 (or US$1 = VND20,864) as of October 2010.

WEIGHTS AND MEASURES: The metric system is the legal standard, but some traditional measures are still used.

HOLIDAYS: Liberation of Saigon, 30 April; May Day, 1 May; Independence Day, 2 September. Movable holidays include the Vietnamese New Year (Tet).

TIME: 7 p.m. = noon GMT.

1 LOCATION, SIZE, AND EXTENT

Situated on the eastern coast of mainland Southeast Asia, the Socialist Republic of Vietnam (SRV) has an area of 329,560 sq km (127,244 sq mi), extending 1,650 km (1,025 mi) N–S and 600 km (373 mi) E–W. Comparatively, Vietnam is slightly larger than New Mexico. At its narrowest, Vietnam is only 50 km (31 mi) across. The nation is bordered on the N by China, on the E by the Gulf of Tonkin, on the E and S by the South China Sea, on the SW by the Gulf of Thailand, and on the W by Cambodia and Laos, with a total land boundary of 4,639 km (2,883 mi) and a coastline of 3,444 km (2,140 mi). Before unification, which was proclaimed on 3 July 1976, Vietnam was divided in two by the 17th parallel. To the S was the Republic of Vietnam (RVN), also known as South Vietnam; to the N, the Democratic Republic of Vietnam (DRV), also known as North Vietnam.

Vietnam, China, the Philippines, Brunei, Taiwan, and Malaysia claim all or part of the Spratly Islands and Paracel Islands, located in the South China Sea roughly 600 km (350 mi) east of Ho Chi Minh City and 400 km (250 mi) east of Da Nang, respectively. The Paracel Islands are known in Vietnamese as the Hoang Sa archipelago, and the Spratlys as the Truong Sa. Both archipelagoes are reportedly surrounded by rich undersea oil reserves, and are productive fishing grounds. China has occupied the Paracel Islands since 1974, when Chinese troops drove a South Vietnamese garrison from the western islands. Vietnam occupies six of the Spratlys and has unsuccessfully engaged in negotiations with Malaysia and the Philippines over the remainder. Periodic clashes between Chinese and Vietnamese naval forces have taken place in the vicinity of both island groups.

Vietnam's capital city, Hanoi, is located in the northern part of the country.

2 TOPOGRAPHY

Vietnam has been described as a carrying pole with a rice basket hanging from each end. The description is a fitting one, for a single mountain chain, the Annam Cordillera (in Vietnamese, Truong Son), extends along Vietnam's western border from north to south, connecting two "rice baskets," which are formed by the densely populated Red River Delta of the Tonkin region in the north and the rich Mekong River Delta in the south. Over two-thirds of the entire population of the country lives in the two low-lying delta regions, both of which are composed of rich alluvial soils brought down from the mountainous regions of southern China and mainland Southeast Asia. The remainder of the population lives along the narrow central coast, in the hilly regions of the Central Highlands north of Ho Chi Minh City (formerly Saigon), or in the mountains north and west of the Red River Delta. The highest mountain peak is Fan Si Pan (3,143 m/10,312 ft), near the northern border.

3 CLIMATE

Vietnam is entirely located in the tropical belt lying between the equator and the Tropic of Cancer. While there are slight variations in temperature, depending on the season and the altitude, the primary seasonal changes are marked by variations in rainfall.

In the north, the rainy season extends from mid-April to mid-October; the city of Hanoi has a mean annual rainfall of 172 cm (68 in), and, in the mountains, annual rainfall sometimes exceeds 406 cm (160 in). Daily temperatures fluctuate considerably in the Red River Delta region, particularly in the dry season, when the thermometer may drop as low as 5°C (41°F) in the region of Hanoi. During the rainy season, the average temperature in Hanoi is about 30°C (86°F).

The south is more tropical; temperatures in Ho Chi Minh City vary only from 18–33°c (64–91°f) throughout the year. Temperatures in the Central Highlands are somewhat cooler, ranging from a mean of about 17°C (63°F) in winter to 20°C (68°F) in summer. The rainy season extends from early May to November, with annual rainfall averaging about 200 cm (79 in) in lowland regions. The typhoon season lasts from July through November, with the most severe storms occurring along the central coast. Typhoons in this region frequently lead to serious crop damage and loss of life. In late September 2009, high winds, heavy rains, flooding, and mudslides left at least 37 people dead as typhoon Ketsana swept into central Vietnam.

⁴FLORA AND FAUNA

The World Resources Institute estimates that there are 10,500 plant species in Vietnam. In addition, Vietnam is home to 279 mammal, 837 bird, 286 reptile, and 132 amphibian species. The calculation reflects the total number of distinct species residing in the country, not the number of endemic species.

The mountainous regions of Tonkin and the Annam Cordillera are characterized by tropical rainforest broken by large areas of monsoon forest. In the higher altitudes, of the far northwest there are pine forests. Shifting cultivation has resulted in many sections of secondary forest. Tropical grasses are widespread, and there are mangrove forests fringing parts of the Red River Delta and in the Ca Mau peninsula, which juts into the Gulf of Thailand. Tropical evergreen forests predominate in the south, with extensive savanna in the southwest.

Deer and wild oxen are found in the more mountainous areas. Two of the seven new species of mammals identified worldwide in the 20th century were found in a nature reserve in the northwest corner of Vietnam: the giant muntjac (a barking deer) and the Vu Quang ox.

⁵ENVIRONMENT

During the Vietnam War, massive bombing raids and defoliation campaigns caused severe destruction of natural foliage, especially in the Central Highlands in the south. In addition, dioxin, a toxic residue of the herbicide known as Agent Orange, leached into water supplies. Over 50% of the nation's forests have been eliminated. However, reforestation projects have begun in some areas of the country.

According to a 2011 report issued by the International Union for Conservation of Nature and Natural Resources (IUCN), threatened species included 54 types of mammals, 43 species of birds, 30 types of reptiles, 16 species of amphibians, 68 species of fish, and 147 species of plants. Endangered species include the tiger (fewer than 200), elephant (fewer than 100 in the wild), Javan rhinoceros (probably ten or fewer survive), Thailand brow-antlered deer, kouprey, river terrapin, Siamese crocodile (probably extinct), estuarine crocodile, and the pileated, crowned, and caped gibbons. Poaching for the wildlife trade is a danger to many of those species.

Water resources total 891.2 cu km (213.8 cu mi), while water usage is 71.39 cu km (17.13 cu mi) per year, according to the US Central Intelligence Agency (CIA). Domestic water usage accounted for 8% of total usage, industrial for 24%, and agricultural for 68%. Per capita water usage totals 847 cu m (29,912 cu ft) per year. Large-scale mining projects have been opposed by environmentalists and indigenous peoples in the mining regions. A

Chinese bauxite mine in the Central Highlands has been the subject of particular controversy, with opponents imprisoned by the government.

Salinization and alkalinization are a threat to the quality of the soil, as are excessive use of pesticides and fertilizers. Environmental damage, including deforestation and soil erosion, has also been caused by agriculture, particularly commercial plantations. The United Nations (UN) reported in 2008 that carbon dioxide emissions in Vietnam totaled 111,287 kilotons.

⁶POPULATION

The CIA estimates the population of Vietnam in 2011 to be approximately 90,549,390, which placed it at number 14 in population among the 196 nations of the world. In 2011, approximately 5.5% of the population was over 65 years of age, with another 25.2% under 15 years of age. The median age in Vietnam was 27.8 years. There were 0.99 males for every female in the country. The population's annual rate of change was 1.077%. The projected population for the year 2025 was 103,200,000. Population density in Vietnam was calculated at 273 people per sq km (707 people per sq mi).

The UN estimated that 30% of the population lived in urban areas and that urban populations had an annual rate of change of 3.0%. The largest urban areas, along with their respective populations, included Ho Chi Minh City, 6 million; Hanoi, 2.7 million; Haiphong, 1.9 million; and Da Nang, 807,000.

A 2010 report from the UN Population Fund showed an increasingly imbalanced sex ratio for Vietnam, with birth rates indicating that 110.6 males are born for every 100 females. According to UN reports, the increase in the number of boys was most dramatically noted from 2005 through 2010. In 2005, the sex ratio stood at 105 males for every 100 females. The increase is attributed to a cultural preference for sons. Although sex selection practices have been officially banned since 2003, couples who decide to have a male child may turn to selective abortion as a means to ensure the desired outcome, particularly if the couple feels socially or economically pressured to keep their family small. Officials from the Vietnam General Office for Population and Family Planning hope to implement programs to raise awareness of the issue and promote greater acceptance of gender equality, dispelling the traditions that favor men over women.

⁷MIGRATION

Estimates of Vietnam's net migration rate, carried out by the CIA in 2011, amounted to -0.35 migrants per 1,000 citizens. The total number of emigrants living abroad was 2.23 million, and the total number of immigrants living in Vietnam was 69,300. The 1954 partition of Vietnam resulted in the exodus of over 820,000 refugees, the majority of them Catholics, from the northern part of the country. Most eventually settled with government assistance in the Central Highlands or on the outskirts of the capital city of Saigon (now Ho Chi Minh City). During the same period, about 80,000 Viet-Minh troops and their dependents moved from the south to the north.

The Vietnam War caused severe disruption of living patterns in both the north and the south. In the north, intensive US bombing of major industrial cities led to a dispersal of the population from urban areas, while a government-sponsored program resulted in the resettlement of nearly one million Vietnamese from crowded areas in the Delta to less-densely populated regions in upland areas of the country. In the south, migration was primarily from the countryside to the cities, as millions of peasants fled their villages to escape the effects of the war or to seek employment in the affluent cities of Saigon and Da Nang. At the end of the war in 1975, nearly one half of the population lived in urban areas, many in refugee camps on the edges of the major cities.

After seizing control of the south in 1975, the Hanoi government announced a new program that called for the resettlement of over 10 million Vietnamese into less-crowded areas of the country by the end of the century. Many were to be moved from refugee camps in the south to new economic zones established in the Central Highlands or along the Cambodian border. Although the zones were unpopular because of poor living conditions, nearly 1.5 million Vietnamese were resettled into new areas between the end of the war and 1981. The overall aim was to disperse the entire population into several hundred "agro-industrial districts" that would provide the basis for development of an advanced Socialist economy. Since 1981, another 2.1 million have been resettled.

In addition to this migration within the country, since the war, there has been a substantial outflow of Vietnamese to other countries. About 150,000 were evacuated from the south in the final weeks of the war, many of them eventually settling in the United States. There were 593,213 people of Vietnamese ancestry in the United States in 1990. In 1978, a new exodus began after the government nationalized all private trade and manufacturing in the country. During 1978–87, an estimated one million Vietnamese fled by sea to other countries in Southeast Asia or by land to China. Many later resettled in Australia, France, the United States, and other countries. From 1979–84, 59,730 people emigrated legally through the US Orderly Departure Program; this program was suspended by the Vietnamese government in 1986 but later resumed, with 57,000 immigrating to the United States in 1993 alone. In 1984, the United States started a program that offered asylum to Vietnamese political prisoners and all Asian-American children. This program was restarted in September 1987. Between 1975 and 1984, about 554,000 people, known as the "boat people," emigrated illegally. In 1992, Vietnam signed agreements with the United Kingdom providing for the forcible repatriation of almost all the 55,700 "boat people" remaining in Hong Kong. The major refugee community was in China, which harbored 285,500 Vietnamese of Chinese ancestry at the end of 1992.

⁸ETHNIC GROUPS

About 85.7% of the population is composed of ethnic Vietnamese. The origins of the Vietnamese are obscure, although many scholars believe they represent a mixture of Australoid peoples who lived in mainland Southeast Asia during the Stone Age with peoples who migrated into the area from southern China. In addition to the ethnic Vietnamese, there are 53 other ethnic groups. Many, like the Tay, the Thai, the Nung, the Rhadé, and the Jarai, are tribal peoples living in the mountainous areas of the Central Highlands and along the Sino-Vietnamese border. The overseas Chinese (Hoa) are descendants of peoples who migrated into the area in recent centuries. The Cham and the Khmer are remnants of past civilizations that controlled the southern parts of the country. The largest ethnic minority in the country is the ethnic Chi-

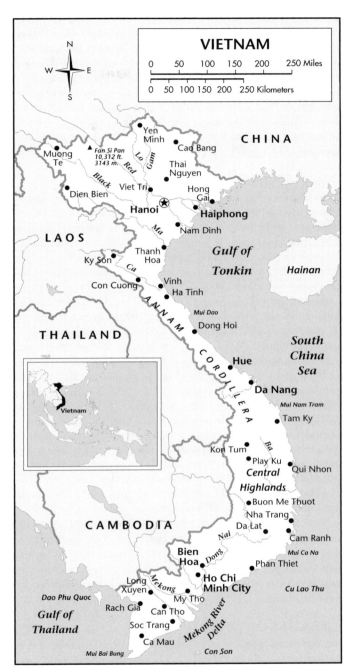

LOCATION: 102°10′ to 109°30′E; 8°30′ to 23°22′ N. BOUNDARY LENGTHS: China, 1,281 kilometers (796 miles); Cambodia, 982 kilometers (610 miles); Laos, 1,555 kilometers (966 miles). COASTLINE: 3,444 kilometers (2,140 miles).
TERRITORIAL SEA LIMIT: 12 miles.

nese, numbering more than two million. The next largest minority group is the Montagnards (mountain people) of the central highlands. The Khmer Krom (Cambodians) number about 600,000, primarily living along the Cambodian border and at the mouth of the Mekong River. Other sizable minority groups are the Muong, the Tay, Meo, Man, and Cham.

⁹LANGUAGES

The official language of the SRV is Vietnamese (*Quoc ngu*). A tonal language, it has elements of Khmer, Thai, and Chinese, and at least one-third of the vocabulary is derived from Chinese. Formerly, Vietnamese was written in Chinese characters, but under French rule a Romanized alphabet, originally developed by Roman Catholic missionaries in the 17th century, was adopted as the standard written form of the language. Most of the minority groups have their own spoken languages, and some have their own writing systems, but all children in the SRV receive instruction in the national language. Other languages include Chinese, English, French, Khmer, and the tribal languages, which are of the Mon-Khmer, Sino-Tai and Malayo-Polynesian language families.

10 RELIGIONS

The dominant religious belief is Buddhism; however, many believers practice a mixture of Mahayana Buddhism, Taoism, and Confucianism, sometimes called Vietnam's "Triple Religion." Though 50% of the population is nominally Buddhist, the government's Office of Religious Affairs estimates that only 11% of the population actively practices Buddhism. Like many other Asian peoples, the Vietnamese also practice spirit worship.

Christianity was first brought to Vietnam in the 17th century by Roman Catholic missionaries sponsored by the French, the Spanish, the Portuguese, or the papacy. Eventually, however, propagation of the Christian faith was forbidden by the imperial court, and Catholicism could only be practiced in secret. French priests were especially active in provoking the French decision to conquer Vietnam in the 19th century. Under French rule, Christianity prospered, and when Vietnam restored its independence in 1954, there were more than two million Catholics in the country, a population that increased to between six and seven million in 1998. Estimates for 2010 indicate that 7% of the population is Roman Catholic and between 1% and 2% is Protestant. The largest Protestant churches are the Southern Evangelical Church of Vietnam and the Evangelical Church of Vietnam North. According to the US State Department, Protestant house churches, particularly in highland ethnic minority areas, have been subject to violent harassment by government authorities. There have also been arrests of Catholic and Buddhist activists. Muslims account for less than 1% of the population, with Bani Islam, a practice unique to the ethnic Cham, being the most prevalent practice, following by Sunni Islam.

11 TRANSPORTATION

The war wreaked massive damage on Vietnam's transportation network, especially its railways, roads, and bridges. Despite Vietnam's economic growth, transport infrastructure remains under developed.

Domestic goods are often transported by small barges or sampans. Vietnam has approximately 17,702 km (11,000 mi) of navigable waterways. About 29% of waterways are navigable year-round by vessels with less than a 1.8 m draft. The major export/import seaports are Haiphong in the north, Da Nang in the center, and a recently developed complex of four container ports in the south. In 2008, Vietnam had a merchant fleet of 387 ships of 1,000 GRT or more.

The CIA reports that Vietnam has a total of 171,392 km (106,498 mi) of roads, of which 125,789 km (78,162 mi) are paved. Railroads extend for 2,347 km (1,458 mi). There is a rail link to China, but not to Cambodia or Laos.

There are 44 airports, which transported 11.07 million passengers in 2009, according to the World Bank. The international airpots are Noi Bai (Hanoi), Tan Son Nhat (Ho Chi Minh City) and Da Nang. There are direct flights from Southeast and East Asia, Europe and Australia. Vietnam Airlines is the national airline, with international flights. Other airlines operating within Vietnam include Jetstar Pacific and Air Mekong.

12 HISTORY

During the first millennium BC, the Lac peoples, the ancestors of the modern-day Vietnamese, formed a Bronze Age civilization in the vicinity of the Red River Delta in northern Vietnam. The Lac were primarily rice farmers. In the 3rd century BC, the Vietnamese kingdom of Van Lang was conquered by a Chinese military adventurer who incorporated the Red River Delta area into his own kingdom in southern China. A century later, Vietnam was integrated into the expanding Chinese empire. During 1,000 years of Chinese rule, Vietnamese society changed significantly as it was introduced to Chinese political and social institutions, Chinese architecture, art, and literature, and the Chinese written language. In AD 939, during a period of anarchy in China, Vietnamese rebels restored national independence.

During the next several hundred years, the Vietnamese Empire, then known as Dai Viet (Great Viet), gradually developed its own institutions and expanded steadily to the south. Under two great dynasties, the Ly (1009–1225) and the Tran (1225–1400), the Vietnamese fended off periodic attempts by China to re-subjugate Vietnam while gradually expanding southward at the expense of their southern neighbor, Champa. In the early 15th century, Chinese rule was briefly restored, but a national uprising led by Le Loi led to the expulsion of the Chinese and the formation of an independent Le Dynasty (1428–1788). Under the Le, expansion to the south continued, and the entire Mekong River Delta came under Vietnamese rule during the 17th century. But expansion brought problems, as a weakened Le court slipped into civil war between two princely families, the Trinh in the north and the Nguyen in the south.

The division of Vietnam into two separate political entities came at a time when Europeans were beginning to expand their commercial and missionary activities into East and Southeast Asia. In 1771, a major peasant revolt led by the Tay Son brothers destroyed the Nguyen and the Trinh and briefly united the entire country under Emperor Nguyen Hue, ablest of the Tay Son. But a prince of the defeated Nguyen house enlisted the aid of a French Roman Catholic bishop and raised a military force that conquered the Tay Son and reunited the country under a new Nguyen Dynasty (1802–1945). When the founding emperor, Gia Long, died in 1820, his son Minh Mang refused to continue the commercial and missionary privileges granted by his predecessor to the French. In 1858, French forces attacked near Saigon and forced the defeated Vietnamese Empire to cede territory in the area to the French, which became the colony of Cochin China. In 1884, France completed its conquest of the country, establishing a protectorate over central and northern Vietnam (now renamed Annam and Tonkin). In 1895, the three sections of Vietnam were included with the protectorates of Laos and Cambodia into a French-ruled Indochinese Union.

The first Vietnamese attempts to resist French rule were ineffectual. Western-style nationalist movements began to form after World War I, and an Indochinese Communist Party, under the leadership of the veteran revolutionary Ho Chi Minh, was formed in 1930. After the collapse of France in World War II, Japan forced the French administration to accept a Japanese military occupation of Indochina. During the joint French-Japanese rule, Communist forces under the umbrella of the Viet-Minh Front began to organize for a national uprising at the end of the war. In March 1945, the Japanese, nearing defeat, disarmed the French and seized full administrative control over French Indochina. At the same time, Japan set up a puppet government, with Bao Dai, the figurehead emperor of Vietnam, as nominal ruler. Shortly after Japan surrendered to Allied forces in August 1945, Viet-Minh forces, led by the Indochinese Communist Party, launched the nationwide August Revolution to restore Vietnamese independence. On 2 September, President Ho Chi Minh declared the formation of an independent Democratic Republic of Vietnam (DRV) in Hanoi. Under the Potsdam agreements, Nationalist Chinese troops occupied all of Indochina north of the 16th parallel, while British troops occupied the remainder of the old Indochinese Union. Chinese commanders permitted the Viet-Minh to remain in political control of the north, but the British assisted the French to restore their authority in the south.

In March 1946, France and the DRV signed a preliminary agreement (the Ho-Sainteny Agreement) recognizing Vietnam as a "free state" in the new French Union. The agreement also called for a plebiscite in Cochin China to permit the local population in that colony to determine their own future. During the summer of 1946, French and Vietnamese negotiators attempted without success to complete an agreement on the future of Vietnam. Clashes between Vietnamese and French troops in the DRV led to the outbreak of war in December 1946. The Franco-Viet-Minh war lasted nearly eight years, ending in July 1954 after a successful siege of the French garrison at Dien Bien Phu by Viet-Minh forces.

According to the Geneva agreement signed on 21 July 1954, Vietnam was temporarily partitioned along the 17th parallel, pending general elections to bring about national reunification. North of the parallel, the DRV began to build a Socialist society, while in the south, an anti-Communist government under the Roman Catholic politician Ngo Dinh Diem attempted with US aid to build a viable and independent state. In the summer of 1955, Prime Minister Diem refused to hold consultations with the DRV on elections called for by the Geneva accords. On 26 October, Diem proclaimed the Republic of Vietnam (RVN), with its capital at Saigon. In a referendum held three days earlier, Diem had defeated ex-Emperor Bao Dai, and in 1956, Diem became president of the RVN under a new constitution written with US support. With the Geneva accords thus abrogated, Vietnamese guerrillas, supported by the DRV, initiated low-level political and military activities to destabilize the Saigon regime. Their efforts were assisted by Diem's own shortcomings, as he brutally suppressed all political opposition and failed to take effective measures to bring to an end the unequal division of landholding in South Vietnam.

In December 1960, revolutionary forces in the south formed a National Liberation Front (NLF) to coordinate political activities against the Diem regime. Guerrilla activities by the People's Liberation Armed Forces (known as the Viet Cong) were stepped up, and Hanoi began to infiltrate trained cadres from the north to provide leadership to the revolutionary movement. Despite increasing economic and military assistance from the United States, the Diem regime continued to decline, and in November 1963, Diem was overthrown by a military coup waged with the complicity of US president John F. Kennedy's administration, which had watched in dismay as Diem had alienated Buddhist elements by his open favoritism toward Roman Catholics. A Military Revolutionary Council, led by the popular southern general Duong Van (Big) Minh, was formed in Saigon. General Minh promised to continue efforts to defeat the insurgency movement in the south but was unable to reverse the growing political crisis in Saigon. Early in 1964, he was replaced by another military junta. During the next 15 months, a number of governments succeeded each other, while the influence of the NLF, assisted by growing numbers of regular troops that were infiltrating from the north, steadily increased in the countryside. By early 1965, US intelligence was warning that without US intervention, South Vietnam could collapse within six months.

Beginning in February 1965, US president Lyndon Johnson took two major steps to reverse the situation in South Vietnam. American combat troops were introduced in growing numbers into the south, while a campaign of heavy bombing raids was launched on military and industrial targets in the north. In Saigon, the political situation stabilized with the seizure of power by a group of army officers led by Nguyen Van Thieu and Nguyen Cao Ky. Encouraged by the United States, the new military regime drafted a constitution, and in elections held in September 1967, Gen. Thieu was elected president of the country. By 1967, US troop strength in South Vietnam had reached over 500,000, while US air strikes over DRV territory were averaging about 100 sorties a day. The Hanoi regime attempted to match the US escalation by increasing infiltration of North Vietnamese military units into the south, but under the sheer weight of US firepower, the revolution began to lose momentum, and morale was ebbing.

On 30 January 1968, in an effort to reverse the military decline on the battlefield and encourage the growing popular discontent with the war in the United States, Hanoi launched the Tet Offensive, a massive effort to seize towns and villages throughout the south. The attempt to seize Saigon or force the collapse of the Saigon regime failed to achieve its objective, but the secondary aim of undermining support for the war in the United States succeeded. President Johnson canceled plans to increase the US military commitment and agreed to pursue a political settlement. To bring about negotiations with Hanoi, a complete bombing halt was ordered on 1 November, just before the US presidential election that brought Richard M. Nixon to office as the new Republican president. President Nixon announced a policy of "Vietnamization," according to which US forces would be gradually withdrawn and the bulk of the fighting in the south would be taken over by RVN forces. On 30 April 1970, in order to destroy enemy sanctuaries beyond the South Vietnamese border, US and South Vietnamese forces invaded neutral Cambodia. The invasion backfired, however, stimulating the rise of revolutionary activities by the Hanoi-supported Cambodian Communist movement and arousing protests in the United States that the war was being expanded. The withdrawal of US military forces continued, and, in March 1972, the DRV attempted to test the capability of the South Vietnamese forces by launching a direct offensive across the 17th parallel. The "Easter Offensive" succeeded in capturing the provincial capital of Quang Tri, but further gains were prevented by the resumption of US bombing raids.

By this time, both sides were willing to compromise to bring the war to an end; on 26 October 1972, the DRV announced that secret talks between US secretary of state Henry Kissinger and its representative, Le Duc Tho, had produced a tentative agreement. Hanoi agreed to recognize the political authority of President Nguyen Van Thieu in Saigon, while the United States agreed to complete the withdrawal of US forces without demanding the removal of existing North Vietnamese troops in the south. The Paris Agreement was formally signed on 27 January 1973.

The Paris Agreement and the withdrawal of US forces by no means signaled the end of the conflict. Clashes between revolutionary forces and South Vietnamese units continued in the south, while provisions for a political settlement quickly collapsed. In January 1975, North Vietnamese forces in the south launched a major military offensive in the Central Highlands. President Thieu resigned on 21 April, but his successor, General Duong Van Minh, was unable to achieve a negotiated settlement. The capital of the RVN, Saigon, was occupied by North Vietnamese troops on 30 April. Thus ended a war in which some 2,000,000 Vietnamese and more than 56,000 Americans were killed. In the DRV, US bombing was estimated to have destroyed 70% of the industrial plant; in the RVN, more than four million were homeless. During the 1950–74 period, total US economic and military aid to Vietnam was $23.9 billion (including $16.1 billion in direct military aid). Chinese aid to the DRV (according to intelligence estimates) probably averaged over $200 million a year. No complete figures are available on the extent of Soviet assistance to the DRV, but some scholars estimate it at about $1 billion annually.

During the next 15 months, the DRV moved to complete national reunification of north and south. Nationwide elections for a new National Assembly were held on 25 April 1976. The first Assembly of the unified country proclaimed the establishment on 2 July of the Socialist Republic of Vietnam (SRV), with its capital remaining at Hanoi. In December, the Communist Party, known as the Vietnamese Workers' Party since 1951, was renamed the Vietnamese Communist Party. The NLF was dissolved into a nationwide Fatherland Front for the entire country. The nation's Communist leadership, with Le Duan the general secretary of the Communist Party and Pham Van Dong the prime minister, remained unchanged, while loyal members of the revolutionary movement in the south were given positions of prominence at the national level. Ton Duc Thang, figurehead president of the DRV after the death of Ho Chi Minh in 1969, remained in that position until his death in 1980.

Economic reconstruction and the building of a fully Socialist society proved more difficult than reunification. Nationalization of industry and collectivization of agriculture had been achieved in the north in the late 1950s, but the south proved more resistant to official efforts to end private enterprise after 1975. When the regime attempted to destroy the remnants of capitalism and private farming in the south in 1978, thousands fled, and the economy entered a period of severe crisis. Its problems were magnified by the outbreak of war with China. In December 1978, Vietnamese forces had invaded neighboring Kampuchea (Cambodia) to over-

throw the anti-Vietnamese government of Pol Pot. A pro-Vietnamese government was installed in early January 1979. China, which had been supporting Pol Pot to retain its own influence in Southeast Asia, mounted a punitive invasion of North Vietnam in February 1979. After a short but bitter battle that caused severe casualties on both sides, the Chinese forces withdrew across the border.

During the 1980s, the SRV attempted to recover from its economic crisis. Party leaders worked out a compromise permitting the survival of a small private sector while maintaining a program of gradual Socialist transformation. With the death of Le Duan in June 1986, a new leadership emerged under General Secretary Nguyen Van Linh at the Sixth National Party Congress. This leadership promised a new "openness" in political affairs and a policy of economic renovation (*doi moi*) to improve the livelihood of the population. A strong conservative coalition of party leaders seriously reduced Linh's effectiveness as they stressed the dangers of political liberalization and slowed the pace of economic reform. In March 1988, Prime Minister Pham Hung died, and Linh's choice of a conservative replacement, Do Muoi, was a clear concession to these groups.

Economic recovery continued to be difficult due to a serious lack of investment capital, resources, and technical skills. The SRV's internal problems were compounded by the continuing dispute with China. To protect itself from Chinese intimidation, Hanoi had formed a military alliance with the USSR and was deeply dependent upon Soviet economic assistance. The continuing civil war in Cambodia also represented a steady drain on the SRV's slender resources and prevented foreign economic assistance, particularly from the United States. In December 1988, the constitution was amended to remove derogatory references to the United States, China, France, and Japan, as an attempt to improve international relations. In August 1991, Do Muoi resigned as prime minister. His successor, Vo Van Kiet, favored free-market reforms. A new constitution was adopted by the National Assembly in April 1992. A general election took place in July 1992, and, for the first time, independent candidates were allowed to present themselves, but neither of the two deemed qualified were elected. On 23 September 1992, the National Assembly elected Lu Duc Anh as president and reelected Vo Van Kiet as prime minister.

In January 1989, the first direct talks between Vietnam and China since 1979 resulted in Vietnam's agreement to withdraw its troops from Cambodia by the end of September 1989 and China's agreement to end aid to the Khmer Rouge guerrillas once the Vietnamese withdrawal was achieved. Later, Vietnam insisted that the withdrawal was contingent on the end of all foreign military aid to factions opposing Cambodian Prime Minister Hun Sen. Hanoi hoped to use the September 1989 withdrawal of its troops from Cambodia as leverage for improved relations with the Association of Southeast Asian Nations (ASEAN), Japan, and the West. On 23 October 1991, a Cambodian peace agreement was signed, paving the way for Vietnam's eventual entry into ASEAN, which occurred in 1995.

The Soviet economic assistance on which Vietnam had depended withered away with the collapse of the USSR, and Vietnam's relations with the West began to warm considerably. In June 1992, Vietnam announced that all South Vietnamese officials had been released from reeducation camps, a US-mandated prerequisite for lifting its embargo against Vietnam. As a result, on 3 February 1994, President Bill Clinton lifted the US trade embargo against Vietnam. At the time Clinton lifted the embargo, there were still 2,238 US servicemen listed as missing. Vietnam agreed to cooperate with their recovery to the "fullest possible extent." Vietnam and the United States established full diplomatic relations in 1995.

During the 1990s, Vietnam stepped up its efforts to attract foreign capital from the West and regularize relations with the world financial system. After joining ASEAN in 1995, Vietnam began reframing its trade laws and instituting legal reforms aimed at codifying its sometimes-capricious statutory system. During 1995, a significant year in Vietnam's opening up to the world, the Communist Party held two meetings to discuss the establishment of a law-based civil society to replace the decades-old system of rule by fiat. In this spirit, the National Assembly passed a series of laws aligning the country with international standards on copyright protection—needed for World Trade Organization (WTO) membership—and other areas. An extensive document, called the Civil Code, was passed containing 834 articles ostensibly granting the Vietnamese people greater civil liberties. Other measures were decidedly investor-unfriendly, such as Prime Minister Kiet's decree that no more land would be turned over from rice production to industrial use. Subsequently, Vietnam's foreign investment rate slid from a peak of $8.6 billion in 1996 to just $1.4 billion in 1999.

In June 1996, the Communist Party held its eighth congress, its first full congress since 1991. Much was expected from the congress in light of the country's ambiguous and, at times, conflicting moves toward openness and reform over the 12 years of *doi moi*. The congress returned to power the aging leadership, granting additional five-year terms to General Secretary Do Muoi, President Le Duc Anh, and Prime Minister Vo Van Kiet. The Party issued decrees in favor of continued economic reform and international investment.

Severe, violent unrest in the countryside during 1997 led to increased awareness of agricultural concerns and punishment of rural officials for corruption. As aftereffects of the 1997 Asian economic crisis stunted the growth of Vietnam's economy, the country remained poor at the beginning of the 21st century. In spite of strides in rice production, literacy, and education, unemployment outpaced economic growth. Rural infrastructure languished, and the urban gap between a rich elite and struggling masses was enormous. Socialist rhetoric and retrenchment failed to heal the divide, which also existed between North and South. The reformists within the Party were never completely marginalized, only outmaneuvered by the old-time Marxists. Retired General Tran Do's open criticism of corruption and other failures of the system resulted in his expulsion from the Party in January 1999. General Tran Do endured other forms of harassment, but it was not as severe as that meted out to other dissidents, due to his revered war veteran, communist-faithful status. He died on 9 August 2002.

At the ninth Party congress held in April 2001, reform-minded National Assembly chairman Nong Duc Manh was chosen as General Secretary to replace the unpopular Le Kha Phieu, who was increasingly seen as an obstacle to Vietnam's modernization. In 2002, the Party revised its rules to allow members to engage in private business. At the meeting of the National Assembly in July 2002, Prime Minister Phan Van Khai and General Secretary Nong Duc Manh, among others, identified corruption as one of the government's main challenges. By September, more than 100 government officials had been arrested, more than 50 police officers had been suspended from duty, and two members of the Central Committee were expelled from the Party for dealings with Nam Cam, a crime figure involved in drug, prostitution, and protection rackets.

In National Assembly elections held on 19 May 2002, approximately 700 candidates, including some independents, competed for 498 seats. However, a government body, the Fatherland Front, was responsible for screening candidates. No opposition parties contested the vote. In July 2002, President Tran Duc Luong was reappointed for a second term by the National Assembly, which also reappointed Prime Minister Phan Van Khai for a second five-year term.

Stronger trade ties helped Vietnam's economy grow considerably. The World Bank, for instance, had rated 58% of Vietnam's population as poor in 1993; by 2002, that figure stood at 29%. Through the mid-1990s into the early 21st century, the country's economy grew at an annual 7.4% rate with a 6.8% rate in 2010, according to the CIA.

In June 2006, as part of an anticipated political shake-up, the prime minister and president were replaced by younger leaders: Nguyen Tan Dung (prime minister) and Nguyen Minh Triet (president.) In October 2007, the voting members of the UN General Assembly held elections for the ten two-year rotating seats on the UN Security Council. Vietnam received 183 votes and was elected to one of the rotating seats. National assembly elections were held on 20 May 2007 and 22 May 2011 with minimal non-Communist Party participation. Truong Tan San became president on 25 July 2011.

The US government (particularly members of Congress) has remained critical of Vietnam's human rights policies, including arbitrary arrest and detention of citizens. In contradiction to assertions of commitment to the cause of human rights, authorities continued to severely limit freedom of speech, press, religion, assembly and association, workers' rights, and rights of citizens to change their government.

In November 2003, the first US warship to visit the country since the end of the Vietnam War arrived in port near Ho Chi Minh City; in December 2004, the first US commercial flight since the end of the war arrived at Ho Chi Minh City. In another first, in June 2005, Prime Minister Phan Van Khai made the first visit to the US by a Vietnamese leader since the war ended in 1975. Also representing a greater openness to the West, in January 2007, after 12 years of negotiations, Vietnam became the 150th member of the World Trade Organization (WTO).

An ongoing controversy between the People's Republic of China and Vietnam over the control of the Spratly and Paracel archipelagoes in the South China Sea dates to the early part of the 20th century. After the Vietnam War, when oil supplies became an issue, the dispute intensified, leading to numerous armed clashes between China and Vietnam. Vietnam, China, the Philippines, Brunei, Taiwan, and Malaysia claim all or part of the Spratly and Paracel archipelagoes. These competing claims have broad geopolitical implications regarding oil reserves, fishing rights, rights of passage for ships, prevention of nuclear dumping, and security in the region. In 1995, China occupied Mischief Reef on an island in the area claimed by the Philippines, and later that year China signed an agreement with a US oil exploration firm to drill for oil in waters claimed by Vietnam. As a member of ASEAN, Vietnam took its complaint to that body. In March 1997, a meeting of the ASEAN ambassadors was convened in Hanoi, and the regional bloc emerged united in opposition to China's move against what they officially recognized as Vietnam's legal territory, marking the first time the ASEAN nations stood up in defiance of Beijing. Vietnam staked its own claim to the islands when it fired on a Philippines jet in 2002. In June-July 2011, unusual street demonstrations took place in Vietnam's cities to protest China's naval presence around the Spratly and Paracel islands, following confrontations between Vietnamese and Chinese ships.

13 GOVERNMENT

The Communist Party-controlled government of Vietnam has ruled under four state constitutions. The first was promulgated in 1946, the second in 1960, the third in 1980, and the fourth in 1992.

The 1946 constitution of the Democratic Republic of Vietnam (DRV), adopted shortly before the war with the French, was never fully implemented because of wartime conditions. On 1 January 1960, a new constitution was promulgated, instituting a largely presidential system to capitalize on Ho Chi Minh's considerable prestige. In the Republic of Vietnam (RVN), formerly South Vietnam, two constitutions were promulgated. The first, by the regime of Ngo Dinh Diem was introduced in 1956. The second was put forth when Nguyen Van Thieu was elected president in 1967. Like the DRV constitution, it created a modified presidential system with a cabinet responsible to the legislative branch. Following the fall of the RVN in 1975, the north moved quickly toward national reunification. A nationwide National Assembly was elected in April 1976, and the Socialist Republic of Vietnam was proclaimed in early July. In December 1980, the SRV adopted a new constitution for the entire country. The new charter, more doctrinaire than its predecessors, described Vietnam as a "proletarian dictatorship" led by the Communist Party, and called for an early transition to full Socialist ownership. The highest state authority was the National Assembly. Members were elected for five-year terms by universal adult suffrage at age 18. The Assembly appointed the Council of Ministers (a cabinet of 33 ministers), the chairman of which ranked as premier. The Council of State (12 members in 1987) served as the collective presidency of Vietnam, elected by the National Assembly from among its own members and accountable to them.

In 1992, a new constitution was adopted by the National Assembly. Like the 1980 constitution, it affirmed the central role of the Communist Party, stipulating that the party must be subject to the law. In support of a free-market economy, constitutional protection of foreign investment was guaranteed. However, land remained the property of the state, with individuals or enterprises entitled to the right to long-term leases that can be inherited or sold. The newly created position of president replaced the Council of State; the president has the right to appoint a prime minister subject to the approval of the National Assembly. The National Assembly, with a maximum of 400 members, retained legislative power. Members are elected to five-year terms by universal adult suffrage. As of 2011, there were 500 members of the National Assembly, with the next election to be held in 2016.

14 POLITICAL PARTIES

The government of the SRV is a de facto one-party state ruled by the Vietnamese Communist Party (VCP). The Vietnamese Communist Party is the political successor to the Indochinese Communist Party, created in 1930 and formally dissolved in 1945. From 1945 until 1951, the party operated in secret until it emerged once more as the Vietnamese Workers' Party at the Second National Congress in 1951. The party assumed its current name in 1976, shortly after the unification of the country into the Socialist Republic of Vietnam.

The Communist Party is administered through an assembly of national delegates. National party conventions elect a Central Committee to guide party affairs between sessions of the national convention. The Central Committee, in turn, elects the Politburo, the highest policy-making body, and a secretariat to direct day-to-day party operations.

The Fatherland Front is the linear successor of the Viet-Minh Front, formed in 1941 to provide the Communist Party with a broad organization to unify all elements in Vietnam against the French colonial regime. The Fatherland Front was formed in North Vietnam in 1955 as a device to mobilize the population to support the regime's goals. A similar organization, the National Liberation Front (NLF), was established in South Vietnam in 1960 by Nguyen Huu Tho to provide a political force in favor of national reunification. After the fall of the RVN in 1975, the NLF was merged into the Fatherland Front.

Under the RVN government, development of a political party system in the Western sense never passed the rudimentary stage. President Thieu, who headed the People's Alliance for Social Revolution, tried to consolidate anti-Communist political organizations in the RVN through a multiparty National Social Democratic Front, but formal political organizations were weak and plagued with religious and regional sectarianism. Wartime conditions and the lack of a national tradition of political pluralism were additional factors preventing the rise of a multiparty system. All such parties were abolished after the fall of Saigon in 1975.

In the SRV, elections for national and local office are controlled by the Communist Party and the state. In the July 1992 general elections, 601 candidates contested 395 National Assembly seats. For the first time independent candidates—not Communist Party members or endorsed by organizations affiliated with the Party— were permitted to contest seats, although they did require Party approval in order to present themselves. Two candidates qualified, but neither was elected. In 1996, the Communist Party held its eighth congress, at which it was widely expected a new generation of leaders would be inaugurated; however, again the aging hard-line leaders were given another five-year term in office as the country struggled with the consequences of 12 years of economic reform and increased international openness. In 1998's national elections, the first three "self-nominated" candidates (not proposed by the Party or the Fatherland Front) managed to gain seats in the 450-member National Assembly. At the ninth party congress held in April 2001, National Assembly chairman Nong Duc Manh was chosen as general secretary, which was seen as a step toward reform. In the May 2002 elections for the 498-member National Assembly, some independents competed for seats, although the Fatherland Front was responsible for approving them. No opposition parties contested the vote. The May 2007 elections gave all but one of the 493 seats to the Communist Party. Women had about 25% of National Assembly seats, and Nguyen Thi Kim Ngan was vice chairwoman of the assembly.

In the May 2011 elections, the Communist Party won 458 out of the 500 seats directly. Thirty-eight seats were won by approved non-party candidates, and four seats were won by self-nominated candidates.

15 LOCAL GOVERNMENT

Vietnam is divided into 58 provinces (*tinh*), and five municipalities (*thanh pho*)—Can Tho, Da Nang, Hanoi, Haiphong, and Ho Chi Minh City. All are administered by the national government. Districts, towns, and villages are governed by locally elected people's councils. Council candidates are screened by the party. Council members' responsibilities include upholding the constitution and laws and overseeing local armed forces units. The councils, in turn, elect and oversee executive organs, called people's committees, to provide day-to-day administration. The entire system functions in a unitary fashion, with local governing bodies directly accountable to those at higher levels.

16 JUDICIAL SYSTEM

The judicial system of the SRV parallels that of the former DRV. The highest court in Vietnam is the Supreme People's Court, whose members are appointed for five-year terms by the National Assembly on the recommendation of the president. In addition, there are local people's courts at each administrative level, military courts, and "special courts," established by the National Assembly in certain cases. Law enforcement is handled by the People's Organs of Control; the president, or procurator-general, of this body is appointed by the National Assembly.

The legal system is based on communist legal theory and French civil law. Although the constitution provides for the independence of judges and jurors, there is close control of the entire governmental system by the Vietnamese Communist Party (VCP) and a judicial selection process that favors appointment of jurists supportive of the VCP. Prison sentences are frequently imposed through administrative procedures without the protections of procedural due process or judicial review.

Trials are generally open to the public. Defendants have the right to be present at the trial, to have an attorney, and to cross-examine witnesses. A crackdown beginning in 2009 brought convictions of 22 pro-democracy and human rights activists in short trials with limited defense and observation, according to Amnesty International. Rising crime, including violent robbery and extortion, in the cities, plus endemic corruption and smuggling, provide challenges for under-funded law enforcement agencies and the criminal justice system.

17 ARMED FORCES

The International Institute for Strategic Studies reports that armed forces in Vietnam totaled 482,000 members in 2011. The force is comprised of 412,000 from the army, 40,000 from the navy, and 30,000 members of the air force. Armed forces represent 1.1% of the labor force in Vietnam. Defense spending totaled $6.9 billion and accounted for 2.5% of GDP.

18 INTERNATIONAL COOPERATION

Issues of importance which are relevant to Vietnam's reintegration into the international system include the status of Vietnamese refugees; border and troop withdrawal disputes with Cambodia, Thailand, and the People's Republic of China; the recovery of the remains of US soldiers missing-in-action (MIA); and conflicts over the Spratly and Paracel island groups in the South China Sea. The island disputes remain unresolved as of late 2011.

Vietnam was admitted to the UN on 20 September 1977. The nation belongs to ESCAP and several non-regional specialized agencies, such as the World Bank, IAEA, the FAO, UNESCO, UNIDO, UNCTAD, and the WHO. Vietnam is also a member of the Asian Development Bank, APEC, ASEAN, the Colombo Plan, and G-77. Vietnam joined the WTO on 11 January 2007. Vietnam is part of the Nonaligned Movement.

In environmental cooperation, Vietnam is part of the Basel Convention, the Convention on Biological Diversity, Ramsar, CITES, the Kyoto Protocol, the Montréal Protocol, MARPOL, and the UN Conventions on the Law of the Sea, Climate Change, and Desertification.

19 ECONOMY

Vietnam's economy suffered through the Vietnam War (roughly 1960–75) and did not begin recovering until the 1980s, when it began to take immense steps towards economic liberalization and international integration. The war took its heaviest economic toll on Vietnam's infrastructure, which even in the best of times was far from adequate for the country's agricultural and industrial resources. Further setbacks came in the late 1970s. According to official sources, in 1978, floods destroyed 3 million tons of rice, submerged over 1 million hectares (2.5 million acres) of cultivated land, and killed 20% of all cattle in the affected areas along the central coast. The termination of all Chinese aid in the same year and the Chinese attack on the north in February-March 1979 dealt the economy further blows.

In 1979, faced with serious shortages of food and consumer goods, Vietnamese leaders approved a new program granting incentives for increased productivity and delaying the construction of farm collectives in the southern provinces. During the 1981–85 five-year plan, emphasis was placed on agriculture and the production of consumer goods. Economic performance improved in the early 1980s, with the growth rate estimated at about 10% annually.

On 3 February 1994, US President Clinton lifted the trade embargo against Vietnam that had been in place for 33 years. Reforms helped Vietnam's economy to grow at a rate of 9% per year during most of the 1990s and by almost 10% in 1996. Growth in the industrial sector was especially strong at over 12% annually between 1988 and 1997. The growth rate averaged 6.6% between 1997 and 2004. The pace of growth was 8.5% in 2007, aided by solid growth in industry.

In 2001, the Bilateral Trade Agreement (BTA) between the US and Vietnam was signed. This marked an important "normalization" with US relations and helped to liberalize the economy. In 2007, Vietnam became a formal member for the WTO. This gave Vietnam unconditional normal trade status with the United States, and, because of WTO regulation, Vietnam became more attractive to foreign investment. Vietnam also became a member of the ASEAN Free Trade Area. In July 2010, Vietnam's General Statistics Office released a second-quarter economic report that showed Vietnam's economy continuing its surge forward. From April to June 2010, Vietnam's economy expanded at a robust 6.4%. The statistics office attributed Vietnam's economic acceleration to stronger industrial output, construction, and exports.

In May 2011, inflation reached a 29-month high at 19.8%. Rising prices created pressure on the government to curb inflation through monetary policy reform. The GDP rate of change in Vietnam, as of 2010, was 6.8%. Inflation stood at 11.8%, and unemployment was reported at 2.9%. The growth rate was estimated at 6.8% for 2010, according to the CIA.

Wet-rice agriculture continues to be an important sector of the economy, employing more than half of Vietnam's workforce. While agriculture has continued to grow, transforming Vietnam from a net importer into the second-largest exporter of rice, industry has grown even faster. Foods, garments, shoes, machines, cement, chemical fertilizer, glass, tires, oil, coal, steel, and paper are the main industrial products. Also significant are petroleum reserves and diverse mineral resources.

20 INCOME

The CIA estimated that, in 2010, the GDP of Vietnam was $276.6 billion. The CIA defines GDP as the value of all final goods and services produced within a nation in a given year and computed on the basis of purchasing power parity (PPP) rather than value as measured on the basis of the rate of the exchange based on current dollars. The per capita GDP was estimated at $3,100. The annual growth rate of GDP was 6.8%. The average inflation rate was 11.8%. It was estimated that agriculture accounted for 20.6% of GDP, industry 41.1%, and services 38.3%.

In 2007, the World Bank estimated that Vietnam, with 1.36% of the world's population, accounted for 0.32% of the world's GDP. By comparison, the United States, with 4.85% of the world's population, accounted for 22.51% of world GDP. According to the World Bank, remittances from citizens living abroad totaled $6.6 billion or about $73 per capita and accounted for approximately 2.4% of GDP.

The World Bank reports that, in 2009, household consumption in Vietnam totaled $64.6 billion or about $713 per capita, measured in current US dollars rather than PPP. Household consumption includes expenditures of individuals, households, and non-governmental organizations on goods and services, excluding the purchases of dwellings. It was estimated that household consumption was growing at an average annual rate of 3.7%.

As of 2011, the most recent study by the World Bank reported that actual individual consumption in Vietnam was 62.9% of GDP and accounted for 0.29% of world consumption. By comparison, the United States accounted for 25.44% of world individual consumption. The World Bank also estimated that 21.1% of Vietnam's individual consumption was spent on food and beverages, 12.5% on housing and household furnishings, 2.2% on clothes, 5.1% on health, 6.0% on transportation, 0.5% on communications, 3.0% on recreation, 4.2% on restaurants and hotels, and 2.2% on miscellaneous goods and services and purchases from abroad.

It was estimated that in 2010 about 10.6% of the population subsisted on an income below the poverty line established by Vietnam's government, according to the CIA.

21 LABOR

As of 2010, Vietnam had a total labor force of 47.37 million people. Within that labor force, CIA estimates in 2009 noted that 53.9% were employed in agriculture, 20.3% in industry, and 25.8% in the service sector.

As of 2011, Vietnamese workers were not free to form or join independent unions. The government-controlled Vietnam General Confederation of Labor (VGCL) oversees all unions. Strikes are restricted in scale and are prohibited at enterprises that serve the public or are important to the national economy or defense, and the Prime Minister decides what enterprises conform to that definition. Several prominent labor activists have been harassed and imprisoned by the government since 2006. Illegal strikes took place against foreign-owned companies in 2011, as workers demanded more pay to cope with inflation as high as 19.8% (May 2011).

The minimum age for full-time employment is 18, with special provisions for those between 15 and 18 years of age. However, many children work in violation of this law, especially in the informal economy. The Labor Law requires the government to set a minimum wage, which, as of October 2011, varies regionally, with foreign and domestic companies paying the same. In the major cities, the monthly minimum wage was 2 million dong ($95). Working hours are set by law at eight hours per day with a mandatory 24-hour rest period per week.

22 AGRICULTURE

Vietnam's agriculture has been concentrated in the lowland areas of the Red River Delta in the north and along the central coast. The Mekong Delta, among the great rice-producing regions of the world, is the dominant agricultural region of the south. Excess grain from the area is shipped to the northern parts of the country.

Agriculture in the north reached an advanced stage of collectivization after a land-reform program completed in 1956 distributed 810,000 hectares (2,002,000 acres) to 2,104,000 peasant families. The share of the Socialist sector in agricultural land increased from 1% in 1955 to 95% in 1975. By 1977, the north had 15,200 agricultural cooperatives and 105 state farms.

In the south, rapid collectivization began in 1978, when the government announced a program to place the majority of southern farmers in low-level cooperative organizations by the end of the 1976–80 five-year plan. Popular resistance was extensive, however, and, by 1981, less than 10% of the rural population was enrolled in full-scale collectives, and a roughly equal number was enrolled in low-level, semi-Socialist production solidarity teams and production collectives. In an effort to make collectivization more palatable, the regime announced a "household contract" system, permitting members of cooperatives to lease collective land in return for an agreed proportion of total output. This system apparently encouraged many peasants to join cooperative organizations, and the regime announced in mid-1986 that collectivization at the low level had been "basically completed" in the south, with 86.4% of the rural population enrolled in some form of collective organization.

Roughly 32% of the total land is currently farmed, and the country's major crops include paddy rice, coffee, rubber, cotton, tea, pepper, soybeans, cashews, sugar cane, peanuts, and bananas. According to the UN Food and Agriculture Organization (FAO), in 2009, cereal production amounted to 43.3 million tons, fruit production 6 million tons, and vegetable production 8 million tons.

In 2009, the Vietnamese rice industry—second-largest in the world in terms of exports—proved invaluable to the country's economy, pulling Vietnam away from the grips of recession. Whereas the global economic downturn caused other nations to post dramatic economic contractions, Vietnam boasted a 3.2% GDP growth rate in the first half of 2009, largely due to the resilient rice industry. Rice occupies 94% of arable land. In the north, two and in some cases three crops a year are made possible through an extensive system of irrigation, utilizing upward of 4,000 km (2,500 mi) of dikes. Single-cropping remains the rule in the south, where heavy rains fall for six months of the year with virtually no rain at all during the other six months. The southern region's extensive network of canals is used mainly for transport and drainage, although some irrigational use was attempted under the RVN government. Annual food-grain production averaged 20 million tons in the early 1990s, reaching 39.6 million tons in 2004. As of October 2011, high regional demand for rice exports from Vietnam was outpacing supply, with export of 7.5 million tons passing 2010's record volume of 6.8 million tons. Severe flooding from typhoons damaged the rice harvest in the Mekong delta region in September-October 2011.

Rubber, formerly a major crop and a leading source of foreign exchange, was grown mostly on large plantations organized under the French colonial regime. As a result of the Vietnam War, practically all of the large plantations in the south were shut down, and damage to the trees was severe. In 1975, the SRV announced that rubber workers had resumed the extraction of latex from hundreds of thousands of rubber trees on plantations north and northwest of Ho Chi Minh City, most of which had lain fallow for years. Rubber production was given high priority by the Hanoi regime and increased from 40,000 tons in 1975 to 782,200 tons in 2010. In the 2010–2011 season, 1.12 tons of coffee were produced (second in the world after Brazil). Confiscation of land from indigenous highland peoples for coffee and other export-driven plantation agriculture was reported in the early 21st century.

23 ANIMAL HUSBANDRY

Draft animals for rice farming are important in Vietnam, and poultry (ducks and chickens) are raised throughout the country. During 2004, the appearance of H5N1 avian flu necessitated the mass slaughter of poultry stocks and other birds in Vietnam.

The UN FAO reported that Vietnam dedicated 642,000 hectares (1.59 million acres) to permanent pasture or meadow in 2009. During that year, the country tended 196.1 million chickens, 6.1 million head of cattle, and 27.6 million pigs. The production from these animals amounted to 318,131 tons of beef and veal, 2.55 million tons of pork, 598,974 tons of poultry, 206,325 tons of eggs, and 1.03 million tons of milk. Vietnam also produced 34,800 tons of cattle hide.

24 FISHING

Fresh and dried fish and fish sauce (known as nuoc mam) are major ingredients of the Vietnamese diet, and fishing is an important occupation. Shrimp, lobster, and more than 50 commercial species of fish are found in Vietnamese waters. Fish also abound in Vietnam's rivers and canals.

The fishing industry was severely depleted after the Vietnam War, when many fishing people fled the country. The government has increased marine production into a major export industry. In 2008, the annual capture totaled 2.09 million tons according to the UN FAO. Vietnamese aquaculture produces carp, pangasius, tilapia and prawns. Industrial fish farming in Vietnam has been criticized as an unsustainable industry producing fish in polluted conditions.

25 FORESTRY

Approximately 45% of Vietnam was covered by forest as of 2009. Depletion of forests has been serious, not only through US defoliation campaigns in the south during the war, but also through converting forestland to agriculture. Planted forests are mainly found in the northeast, where they serve as watershed protection and supply materials for the mining and paper industries. In 1998, the government began a reforestation program. Official policy has encouraged the replacement of natural forests with export crops such as cinnamon, aniseed, rubber, coffee, and bamboo. Vietnam has become a world-class producer of wooden furniture. The UN FAO estimated the 2009 roundwood production at 5.85 million cu m (206.6 million cu ft). The value of all forest products, including roundwood, totaled $226 million. Important forestry products include fuel wood, bamboo, and resins.

26 MINING

Vietnam has a wide variety of important mineral resources, but the mining sector is relatively small and undeveloped. The principal reserves, located mainly in the north, are bauxite, carbonate rocks, chrome, clays, anthracite coal, copper, natural gas, gemstones, gold, graphite, iron ore, lead, manganese, mica, nickel, crude petroleum, phosphate rock (apatite), pyrophyllite, rare earths, silica sand, tin, titanium, tungsten, zinc, and zirconium. Coal dominates the mining sector, and, along with carbonate rocks, crude petroleum, and phosphate rocks, is produced in large quantity. Iron reserves are estimated at 520 million tons, and apatite reserves, 1.7 billion tons. Bauxite mines in the Central Highlands Province (Lam Dong) are capable of producing 1.7 million tons per year of ore. Mining and quarrying contributed 4.4% to GDP in 2009. Also among leading industries are the production of cement, chemical fertilizer, oil, coal, and steel; crude oil was its top export commodity. Vietnam's movement toward a free market has resulted in increased international trade.

Estimated production outputs in 2009 included: chromium ore (gross weight), 37,105 metric tons, down from 55,880 metric tons in 2008; ilmenite (gross weight), 686,800 metric tons, down from 672,000 tons in 2008; mined zinc, 45,600 metric tons, unchanged from 2008; mined tin, 5,400 metric tons; gold, 3,000 kg, unchanged from 2008; lime, 1.5 million tons; and silica sand, 200 million tons, unchanged from 2008. Vietnam also produced barite, bauxite, bentonite, hydraulic cement, chromium, kaolin clay, refractory clay, construction aggregates, copper, fluorspar, gemstones, granite, graphite, ilmenite, iron ore, lead, lime, marble, nitrogen, phosphate rock, pyrite, pyrophyllite, rare earths, salt, silica sand, sulfur, building stone, and zirconium. Most chromite, ilmenite, and zirconium, and some granite, kaolin, salt, and silica sand, was exported. Asian Mineral Resources started two diamond drilling programs at nickel deposits. The mining industry comprised state-owned companies, several state-and-foreign mining and mineral-processing company joint ventures, many small-scale local government-owned mining companies, local government-private mining company joint ventures, and local private miners.

27 ENERGY AND POWER

The World Bank reported in 2008 that Vietnam produced 73.1 billion kWh of electricity and consumed 68.9 billion kWh, or 761 kWh per capita. Roughly 54% of energy came from fossil fuels, while 4% came from alternative fuels. Per capita oil consumption was 689 kg. Oil production totaled 318,178 barrels of oil a day. PetroVietnam is the government-owned company that develops petroleum resources; it has joint ventures with multinational partners and also operates overseas.

Control over the Spratly Islands remains a contentious issue between Vietnam, China, Taiwan, the Philippines, Brunei, and Malaysia. The reefs, many of which are partially submerged, lie atop an oil field containing an estimated 1–7 billion barrels of oil.

28 INDUSTRY

Most heavy and medium industry is concentrated in the north, including the state-owned coal, tin, chrome, and other mining enterprises. There are also an engineering works at Hanoi, power stations, and modern tobacco, tea, and canning factories. The industrial sector in the south is characterized by light industry and the consumer goods industry, including pharmaceuticals, textiles, and food processing, although there are some large utilities and cement works. Much of the industrial sector in the north was badly damaged by US bombing raids during the war. In the south, the private sector was permitted to continue in operation after 1975, but all industry and commerce above the family level was nationalized in March 1978. The results were disastrous, and the regime began some privatization in the 1980s with the *doi moi* economic reforms. Industrial production in the 1980s increased at an average annual rate of 9.5%. During the 1990s, industrial production grew by about 12% per year.

The government has continued to own the majority of nonagricultural enterprises. Industry accounted for 41.1% of GDP in 2010, up from 28% in 1985. The industrial production growth rate for 2010 was an estimated 14%, according to the CIA, which lists leading industrial sectors as food processing, garments, shoes, machine building, mining, cement, chemical fertilizers, glass, tires, oil, coal, steel, and paper.

Vietnam exports about $3 billion worth of footwear a year, its third-largest export earner after crude oil and textiles. Garment production and food processing are also significant export earners. In 2004, Vietnam was Asia's third-largest oil producer, with crude oil production averaging 403,300 barrels per day. Construction has been one of the driving forces of the economy, growing at 7% in 2008. Vietnam has a large-scale wood processing industry and in 2008 was the fifth-largest exporter of furniture and other wood products in the world.

29 SCIENCE AND TECHNOLOGY

The World Bank reported in 2009 that there were no patent applications in science and technology in Vietnam. Science and technology have been one of the key weak spots in the Vietnamese economy. Vietnam's learned societies include the Union of Scientific and Technical Associations (founded in 1983) and the General Association of Medicine (founded in 1955), both in Hanoi. The State Commission for Science and Technology supervises research at the universities and institutes attached to the Ministry of Higher Education; the Institute of Science organizes research at other institutions. All research institutes are attached to government ministries. According to Vietnam's Ministry of Science and Technology, as of 2010, Vietnam had 1,500 science institutes with 60,000 researchers employed.

Courses in basic and applied sciences are offered at Cantho University (founded in 1966), Hanoi University of Technology (founded in 1956), University of Hanoi (re-founded 1956), University of Ho Chi Minh City (founded in 1977), Ho Chi Minh City Pedagogical University of Technology (founded in 1962), and various other colleges. Hue College of Sciences—Hue University (founded 1976) conducts research in biotechnology, environmental science, information technology, agriculture, and other fields. There are eight university medical programs in Vietnam.

30 DOMESTIC TRADE

Since 1979, the government has permitted the existence of a private commercial sector. Most private businesses are small shops and restaurants. In 1991, private enterprise and company laws were adopted by the National Assembly. It is estimated that private businesses account for 70% of domestic trade.

Wholesalers in Vietnam consist of state-owned trading companies and private local wholesalers. The retail sector in Vietnam is undergoing rapid transformation, as new sales outlets and merchandising techniques have emerged. In the major urban areas, mini-markets and privately owned convenience stores have opened. Showrooms and service centers for electronics, appliances, and industrial goods offer wholesale and retail sales. In 1996, the Saigon Superbowl opened in Ho Chi Minh City as Vietnam's first entertainment and retail center. Urban areas have numerous indoor shopping malls, department stores, and supermarkets. Ho Chi Minh City has boutiques for foreign luxury brands and specialty stores for electronic goods. Outside of the larger cities, retail outlets consist mostly of family-operated market stalls and small street-front shops. A strong "gray market" of smuggled and counterfeit goods persists. A value-added tax (VAT) applies to most goods and services. Advertising appears in many forms.

Business and government office hours are usually Monday through Friday between 8 a.m. and 5 p.m., with a midday break between noon and 1:00 p.m. Commercial offices are also open on Saturdays from 8 to 11:30 a.m. Banks are open from 8 a.m. until 4 p.m. weekdays and until 11:30 a.m. on Saturdays. Shops and restaurants are open into the evenings and on Sundays.

<table>
<tr><td colspan="5">

Principal Trading Partners – Vietnam (2010)

(In millions of US dollars)
</td></tr>
</table>

Country	Total	Exports	Imports	Balance
World	155,437.0	71,658.0	83,779.0	-12,121.0
China	27,328.0	7,309.0	20,019.0	-12,710.0
United States	18,005.0	14,238.0	3,767.0	10,471.0
Japan	16,744.0	7,728.0	9,016.0	-1,288.0
South Korea	16,744.0	7,728.0	9,016.0	-1,288.0
Taiwan	8,420.0	1,443.0	6,977.0	-5,534.0
Thailand	6,785.0	1,183.0	5,602.0	-4,419.0
Singapore	6,222.0	2,121.0	4,101.0	-1,980.0
Malaysia	5,506.0	2,093.0	3,413.0	-1,320.0
Germany	4,115.0	2,373.0	1,742.0	631.0
Switzerland	3,659.0	2,652.0	1,007.0	1,645.0

(…) data not available or not significant.

(n.s.) not specified.

SOURCE: *2011 Direction of Trade Statistics Yearbook,* New York: United Nations, 2011.

Balance of Payments – Vietnam (2010)

(In millions of US dollars)

Current Account		**-4,287.0**
Balance on goods		-5,147.0
Imports	-77,339.0	
Exports	72,192.0	
Balance on services		-2,461.0
Balance on income		-4,564.0
Current transfers		7,885.0
Capital Account		…
Financial Account		**6,201.0**
Direct investment abroad		-900.0
Direct investment in Vietnam		8,000.0
Portfolio investment assets		-13.0
Portfolio investment liabilities		2,383.0
Financial derivatives		…
Other investment assets		-7,063.0
Other investment liabilities		3,794.0
Net Errors and Omissions		**-3,679.0**
Reserves and Related Items		**1,765.0**

(…) data not available or not significant.

SOURCE: *Balance of Payment Statistics Yearbook 2011,* Washington, DC: International Monetary Fund, 2011.

31 FOREIGN TRADE

Beginning in 1980, emphasis was placed on the development of potential export commodities such as cash crops, marine products, and handicrafts, while imports were severely limited. To promote trade expansion with Japan, Singapore, and Hong Kong, several export-import firms were set up in Ho Chi Minh City under loose official supervision. The results were favorable, but the experiment aroused distrust among communist party leaders, and the freewheeling enterprises were integrated into a single firm strictly supervised by the government.

The economic reforms of the late 1980s, including currency devaluation, adoption of a flexible exchange rate system, and lifting restrictions on foreign trade, contributed to the rapid growth in exports in the early 1990s. The US lifting of economic sanctions in 1994 pushed the volume of foreign trade even further upwards. Investments in Vietnam contributed to the development and expansion of tourism. Vietnam joined the ASEAN Free Trade Area (AFTA) in 1995, committing itself to tariff reductions among member nations.

Since 2001, the government has moved toward economic liberalization and international in order to modernize the economy and produce more competitive, export-driven industries. In 2001, the United States-Vietnam Bilateral Trade Agreement (BTA) was concluded, which, by 2004, had resulted in a fourfold increase in bilateral trade between the two countries. Trade between the two countries totaled $6.4 billion by 2004, compared to $451 million in 1995. By April 2005, around the 30th anniversary of the fall of Saigon, the United States had become Vietnam's largest export market.

In another boost to trade, the ASEAN Trade in Goods Agreement (ATIGA), approved in 2009, entered into effect on 17 May 2010. The ATIGA represented the next step in realizing the free flow of goods within the region by simplifying the processes and procedures necessary to create a single market and production base—known as the ASEAN Economic Community (AEC)—by 2015. Major points of ATIGA include tariff liberalization, a simplification of the rules of origin, and implementation of such rules. The comprehensive agreement also demands greater transparency in regional trade liberalization, aiding the work of businesses and investors. The ATIGA supersedes the Common Effective Preferential Tariff Scheme (CEPT) adopted in 1992. Vietnam was expected to become a full member of the ASEAN-China free trade area by 2015. This new trade agreement went into force 1 January 2010 between the founding members of ASEAN and China. A major point of the free trade agreement is the elimination of tariffs on nearly 90% of imported goods.

Import commodities include petroleum and steel products, motor vehicles and tractors, tires, foodstuffs, raw cotton, sugar, and grain. The most important export commodities for Vietnam are crude petroleum, footwear and apparel, rice, shellfish, and coffee.

Vietnam imported $84.3 billion worth of goods and services in 2008 while exporting $72.03 billion worth of goods and services. Major import partners in 2009 were China, 23.8%; South Korea, 11.6%; Japan, 10.8%; Taiwan, 8.4%; Thailand, 6.7%; and Singapore, 4.9%. Its major export partners were the United States, 20%; Japan, 10.7%; China, 9.8%; and South Korea, 4.3%.

32 BALANCE OF PAYMENTS

Vietnam has received increasing foreign loans, aid, and direct investment, with an estimated $8 billion in international development aid pledged for 2011. Despite huge growth in exports, Vietnam experienced a balance of payments crisis from 2008. In 2010, exports were $72 billion, and imports were $79 billion, and external debt was estimated at $32.81 billion, with an account balance of -$12.22 billion according to the CIA. Foreign exchange and gold reserves were estimated at $13.36 billion in December 2010, down from $16.8 billion in December 2009.

33 BANKING AND SECURITIES

The State Bank of Vietnam, created in 1951, was the central bank of issue for the DRV with numerous branches throughout the territory and an extensive agricultural and industrial loan service; in

1976, it became the central bank of the SRV. All private Vietnamese and foreign banks were closed in 1976.

Since the banking reorganization of July 1988, but particularly since 1992, Vietnam has moved to a diversified system in which state-owned, joint-stock, joint-venture, and foreign banks provide services to a broader customer base. The first foreign-representative bank office arrived in 1989. In 1992, foreign banks were granted permission to open full commercial branches. In addition to state-owned commercial banks, there are numerous joint-stock banks, foreign bank branches, joint-venture banks, and foreign banks with representative offices.

Two banking decrees, issued in October 1990 and governing respectively commercial banks, credit cooperatives and other financial institutions, and the State Bank, aimed to regulate the financial system more strictly. Credit cooperatives had to be licensed by the State Bank rather than by local People's Committees. The first decree also gave the state commercial banks greater autonomy, and permitted them to compete with each other and to seek capital from sources other than the state. The second decree introduced new instruments by which the State Bank could control the banking sector, including open-market operations and varying reserve requirements and discount rates. In October 2011, with Vietnam's economy beset by inflation and trade deficit troubles, the discount rate (the interest rate at which the central bank lends to financial institutions in the short term) was 13%.

The state banks still dominate the system, state enterprises are still the main borrowers, and their lending is still predominantly short-term because of the skewed interest rate structure. The state-owned banks include Joint Stock Commercial Bank for Foreign Trade of Vietnam (Vietcombank), Vietnam Industrial and Commercial Bank (Incombank), the Vietnam Bank for Agriculture and Rural Development (BARD), Vietnam Bank for Social Policies, Vietnam Bank for Investment and Development (BIDV), and Mekong Housing Bank. Vietnam Technological and Commercial Joint Stock Bank (Techcombank) is a leading joint-stock bank. Bank use has grown rapidly, with an estimated 20% of Vietnam's population having a bank account as of 2010. Vietcombank and other banks have ATM networks. Credit cards are accepted in major cities and tourist areas.

In July of 2000, Vietnam's first stock exchange, the Ho Chi Minh City Stock Exchange, opened. The Hanoi Securities Trading Center opened in 2005. As of mid 2011, the two exchanges had a total of 596 listed companies.

34 INSURANCE

Before May 1975, life and property insurance coverage was available in the RVN from three small Vietnamese insurance companies and through local representatives of French, UK, and US insurance firms. By the end of 1975, all private insurance facilities had ceased to operate, and the Vietnam Insurance Co., established in the DRV in 1965, had become the nation's lone insurance firm. In 2002, foreign insurers were allowed to do business in Vietnam.

In 2009, the value of general insurance premiums written totaled $769 million, of which life insurance premiums accounted for $679 million. About 50 companies provide insurance in Vietnam as of 2011, including BaoViet Life, Prudential Vietnam, AIA Vietnam, Manulife Vietnam, and Dai-Ichi Life Vietnam. Types of insurance offered include motor vehicle, personal accident, hull

and cargo, offshore exploration, aviation, and third-party risk. In Vietnam, third-party automobile insurance and employers' liability insurance are compulsory.

35 PUBLIC FINANCE

In 2010 the budget of Vietnam included $27.08 billion in public revenue and $29.65 billion in public expenditures. The budget deficit amounted to 5.5% of GDP. Public debt was 56.7% of GDP, with $32.81 billion of the debt held by foreign entities. Main sources of monetary revenue are income taxes, VAT, the sale of state-owned enterprises, foreign aid, and customs taxes.

36 TAXATION

All taxes are national; there are no provincial or local taxes. Individual income is subject to a progressive tax ranging from 0–35%. The capital gains tax rate is 25%.

The main corporate tax rate is 25%. In addition, companies deriving income from land use rights are subject to a surtax ranging from 10–25%. Gains stemming from the sale of shares in a foreign-invested company are taxed at a 25% rate. There is no tax on dividends, although income from interest and/or royalties are each subject to a 10% withholding rate. A fuel tax ranges from 30% to 50%.

Other taxes include capital transfer taxes, natural resources and environmental protection taxes, technology transfer fees, import and export duties. There are also special consumption taxes applied to tobacco products, spirits, beer, and other items ranging from 15–100%. Vietnam also imposes a VAT with a standard rate of 10%, which covers all goods and services, except for exports.

37 CUSTOMS AND DUTIES

Tariffs are imposed by the National Assembly with the Ministry of Finance. Customs duty is generally charged on imports and exports, with many exemptions and duty reductions available (including imports related to an aid program and goods to be used for security, national defense, scientific and educational training, or research purposes). Tariff rates are divided into three categories according to the import source country's trade relationship with Vietnam: ordinary rates apply to goods imported from countries that have not exchanged normal trade relations (NTR) agreements with Vietnam; preferential rates apply to goods from countries that have exchanged NTRs with Vietnam; and special preferential rates apply to goods from countries that have made special trade arrangements with Vietnam. Ordinary tariff rates are about 50% higher than preferential rates.

38 FOREIGN INVESTMENT

France was the dominant foreign investor in Indochina before World War II. Resident Chinese played a major role in rice milling, retailing, and other activities (and continued to do so in the south through the early 1970s). Following the 1954 partition agreement, the French economic position in the DRV was completely liquidated, and the participation of private foreign investors in the DRV economy was prohibited. In 1977, the SRV issued a new investment code in an effort to attract private foreign capital to help develop the country. However, because of stringent regulations and a climate of government suspicion of private enterprise, the 1977 code attracted little enthusiasm among potential investors. Only the USSR and France made sizable investments, although Japan subsequently laid the foundation for future investment by bank loans. Beginning in 1984, the government began to encourage the formation of joint ventures and announced that preparations were underway for a new foreign investment code.

In 1987, the National Assembly passed a liberalized investment law seeking to improve the overall investment climate and emphasize the development of export industries and services. The code permitted wholly owned foreign enterprises in Vietnam, levied low taxes on profits, allowed full repatriation of profits after taxes, and guaranteed foreign enterprises against government appropriation. The law also encouraged petroleum exploration. The Vietnamese government controls both upstream and downstream oil and gas industries, but since 1998 foreign investment has been permitted. BP entered Vietnam in 1989, discovering important gas fields; in 2010, BP put its Vietnam assets up for sale, with India's Oil and Natural Gas Corporation bidding in partnership with PetroVietnam. In 2001, a consortium that included Conoco, the Korean National Oil Company (KNOC), SK Corporation of South Korea, and Geopetrol of France made a major find of oil in the Cuu Long Basin. In 2002, the Japan Vietnam Petroleum Company (JVPC) made its first sizeable discoveries.

In early 1994, the government announced three proposals intended to improve the investment environment and increase foreign trade: expedited decisions on small investment projects; the elimination of the requirement for import-export licenses for many commodities; and a reduced list of industries that would be off-limits to foreign investors. Foreign investments were allowed in insurance companies and brokerages. Under amendments to the Foreign Investment Law in 1996, more authority over investment licensing was given to local governments.

Vietnam's primary investors in 2008 were, in order: Malaysia, Taiwan, Japan, Singapore, Brunei, Canada, Thailand, and British Virgin Islands. Vietnam's encouragement of foreign investment includes its ability to attract and utilize large amounts of foreign capital, both in the form of foreign direct investment (FDI) and official development assistance (ODA). For the 2001–05 period, the government set targets for FDI at $11 billion in disbursements from existing and newly licensed foreign investments and for approximately $10 to $11 billion in ODA disbursed by foreign donors for a total of $21 to $22 billion from foreign sources. FDI in Vietnam was a net inflow of $7.6 billion according to World Bank figures published in 2009. FDI represented 7.82% of GDP. Factors that have continued to hinder performance of foreign investors are bureaucracy, lack of management expertise, smuggling, intellectual property violations, corruption, inflation, and strikes due to low wages.

According to the government, as of mid 2011 Vietnam had invested in 600 projects worth over $10 billion in other countries including Cambodia, Laos, Myanmar (Burma), Malaysia, Indonesia, Mongolia, Algeria and Iraq. The investments included projects in telecommunications, petroleum exploration and production, real estate, and rubber plantations.

³⁹ECONOMIC DEVELOPMENT

With the defeat of the RVN forces in April 1975, Vietnam faced the task of restoring its infrastructure, devastated by the war, while working toward the goal of a technologically advanced so-

ciety. Long-range planning centered on the second five-year plan (1976–80), which called for major emphasis on heavy industry and rapid agricultural growth. Due to factors including unfavorable weather, decreased foreign aid, and high military expenditures—combined with managerial inefficiency—the plan was a disaster. Industrial production grew by only 0.6% and agriculture by 1.9%. The third five-year plan (1981–85) was more modest in its objectives. Emphasis was placed on agricultural development and the promotion of consumer goods, with industrial development in the background. Growth figures in industry (9.5%) and agriculture (4.9%) improved significantly over the previous five years.

The fourth five-year plan (1986–90) continued the previous plan's emphasis on agricultural growth and expansion of exports and light industry. Efforts to promote Socialist transformation were to continue, but at a gradual pace and "by appropriate forms." Development aid continued to come primarily from the former USSR. This aid and trade waned with the decline of the USSR, with the full cutoff occurring in 1991. The SRV's new economic emphasis, *doi moi* (renovation), was instituted by Nguyen Van Linh following the sixth national party congress (1986). His plan included policy and structural reforms for a market-based economic system: price decontrol (liberalized prices), currency devaluation, private sector expansion through de-collectivization of agriculture (food production), legal recognition of private business, new foreign investment laws, autonomy of state enterprises, devolution of government decision-making in industry to enterprise level, and limiting government participation to macroeconomic issues. Implementation of these policies was achieved with varied success. Inflation policy and agricultural reform resulted in immediate increases in rice production. Vietnam changed from a net importer of rice to the third-largest rice exporter after Thailand and the United States. It became the second-largest world rice exporter in 2005, holding that position into 2011.

A privatization program in the early 1990s met with resistance from conservative politicians, companies, and from foreign investors. Conservatives feared that privatization undermined the economic basis of socialism, and foreign investors were wary of poor investments with meager legal underpinnings, and privatized companies were badly affected by corruption.

US president Bill Clinton's lifting of the 30-year-old trade embargo in 1994 opened the way for American companies to do business in Vietnam. International assistance during the mid 1990s was from the World Bank for education and agricultural reforms, the Japan Overseas Economic Cooperation Fund for infrastructure programs, the United Kingdom for soft loans, technical training and refugee resettlement, and from the Asian Development Bank. A continuation of reforms promoting foreign investment and minimizing the state's role in the economy moved slowly in the late 1990s due to political corruption and inefficiencies.

The Asian financial crisis of the late 1990s negatively affected investor confidence in the region, severely reducing Vietnam's main focus of economic development. Vietnam's increasing integration in regional and international economic organizations, including ASEAN and the WTO made Vietnam more economically attractive to foreign investment and competitive with exports. Vietnam by 2006 had largely overcome the negative effects of the Asian financial crisis, with GDP growth ticking along at 7.4% over the 2001–05 period. The GDP growth rate was estimated at 6.8% for 2010, according to the CIA.

Industry replaced agriculture as the main engine of the economy and, by 2005, accounted for 40.9% of GDP. Agriculture remains important, however, accounting for about 20% of GDP (2010) and about 54% of the labor force (2009). The government has made progress in reducing poverty: as of 1993, the World Bank declared 58% of the population to be poor, and, by 2002, that had fallen to 29%. By 2010, just 10% were under the poverty line, according to the CIA. Poverty remains concentrated in remote, rural districts, especially those populated mainly by ethnic minorities.

Many economic challenges remain, in terms of strengthening the financial sector and the legal framework, reforming state-owned enterprises, controlling inflation, and ending corruption. Small businesses are booming, but Vietnam lacks mid-sized private firms between small family companies and large exporters backed by foreign investors.

40 SOCIAL DEVELOPMENT

A social security plan provides old age, disability and survivorship benefits, as well as worker's injury and some limited medical insurance. All private- and public-sector employees with employment contracts of at least three months are covered. Pensions are funded by 5% of employee wages, 10% of employer payroll, and government contributions; retirement age is low (55 for women and 60 for men), but pensions start at minimum wage level, and only an estimated 22% of senior citizens are in pension-receiving households. Since 2002, the government has instituted a Hunger Eradication and Poverty Reduction program, including a Free Health Card for the Poor, which provides subsidized health insurance, but the free coverage is still not widely available. Maternity benefits are payable at 100% of wages for 4 months, and are also available to women who adopt a newborn baby; there is also paid leave in the case of miscarriage or abortion. Families are legally limited to two children; this is enforced mainly through family planning education campaigns. Workers' compensation is provided according to the level of disability.

Women have full legal rights under the law but are subject to some social discrimination. Few women are found in senior management or high-level government positions, although industry, business, and the public sector employ many women. Women also generally receive lower wages than do their male counterparts. Domestic violence against women is common, and NGOs have set up crisis centers and hotlines to combat the problem.

Vietnam's human rights record is poor, and there are continuing reports of arbitrary detention and the mistreatment of detainees during interrogation, including deaths in custody from beatings by police. Religious activists, pro-democracy lawyers and bloggers, indigenous people in land disputes, and environmental protestors are among those detained or imprisoned since 2008. Human rights organizations are not permitted to operate in Vietnam, and criticism of human rights violations is not tolerated by the government.

41 HEALTH

According to the CIA, life expectancy in Vietnam was 72 years in 2011. The government spent 7.2% of its GDP on healthcare, amounting to $80 per person (2009). There were 12 physicians,

10 nurses and midwives, and 29 hospital beds per 10,000 inhabitants. The fertility rate was 2.0, while the infant mortality rate was 20 per 1,000 live births as of 2011. The maternal mortality rate was 56 per 100,000 births (2008). Government-mandated and -subsidized healthcare coverage only covered about 41% of the population as of 2010.

The CIA calculated HIV/AIDS prevalence in Vietnam to be about 0.4% in 2009. H5N1 avian flu broke out in Southeast Asia in 2003, and Vietnam was one of the first and hardest-hit countries, with 58 fatalities. Other infectious diseases include dengue fever, malaria, hepatitis A, typhoid fever, and diarrhea. An outbreak of hand, foot, and mouth disease killed over a hundred children and caused numerous preschools to close in September 2011.

42 HOUSING

Traditional rural houses have been built of bamboo and wood, with thatched roofs. Brick, stone, and concrete houses have appeared with rising incomes in the countryside. Urban housing shortages have been a serious problem in Vietnam. In cities of the north, war damage caused overcrowding. By 1986, housing had become a critical problem in Hanoi, particularly in the central sections of the city, where per capita living space was reduced to four sq m. (43 sq ft). Subsequent building booms increased housing stock significantly. According to the government's 2009 Population and Housing Census, the average per capita living space was 16.7 sq m, (179.7 sq ft) with a 15.7 sq m (179 sq ft) rural average and 19.2 sq m (206.6) urban average. The larger towns and cities have concrete shop-houses and apartment buildings, including luxury high-rises. Real estate speculation has affected housing prices in the cities.

As of 2005, 81% of all households used electricity, according to the World Bank. About 94% of all households had improved drinking water, and 75% of all households had access to improved sanitation as of 2008, according to the CIA.

43 EDUCATION

In 2009, the World Bank estimated that 94% of age-eligible children in Vietnam were enrolled in primary school. Vietnam had 94% literacy in 2009 (96% for men, 92% for women). Public expenditure on education represented 5.3% of GDP as of 2008, according to the CIA.

After 1975, the educational system in the south was restructured to conform to the Socialist guidelines that had been used in the DRV. The 12-year school cycle was reduced to 10 years, and the more than 20,000 teachers in the south were among those subjected to "reeducation." By 1976, some 1,400 tons of textbooks printed in the DRV had been shipped to the south, and the books used previously under the RVN were destroyed. In addition, more than 1,000 formerly private schools in the south were brought under state control.

Education is free at all levels, and five years of primary education are compulsory. Seven years of secondary school are offered through two cycles of four, then three years. Students progress to the upper level only through completion of an entrance examination. Vocational studies are also offered at the upper-secondary level. The academic year runs from September to June.

In 2005, about 60% of age-eligible children were enrolled in some type of preschool program. Primary school enrollment that year was estimated at about 88% of age-eligible students, while secondary school enrollment was about 69% of age-eligible students. It is estimated that about 94% of all students complete their primary education. The student-to-teacher ratio for primary school was at about 22:1 in 2005; the ratio for secondary school was about 24:1.

Vietnam has numerous public and private universities and colleges, offering courses in sciences, humanities, arts, technology, and medicine. Highly competitive entrance exams are required for university enrollment. Universities include Can Tho, Vietnam National University (in Hanoi and Ho Chi Minh City), University of Technology, Foreign Trade University, and National Economics University. There are also specialized academies and vocational schools.

44 LIBRARIES AND MUSEUMS

The École Française d'Extrême-Orient once maintained an extensive research library in Hanoi, which was transferred intact to the DRV; it is now the National Library, housing about one million volumes, as well as historical archives. Vietnam's public library systems include 64 provincial/municipal libraries, 577 district libraries, and thousands of commune or village libraries. There are also thousands of post office reading rooms. The Ho Chi Minh City General Scientific Library maintains a collection of over 800,000 volumes, and there are numerous other specialized and academic libraries. Vietnam National University at Hanoi Library holds 1.4 million volumes.

Vietnam has five national museums: the Ho Chi Minh Museum (founded in 1977, with a section devoted to the revolution and another to ancient arts), The Museum of the Vietnamese Revolution (memorabilia of Vietnam's struggle for independence), the Viet Nam Fine Arts Museum (1966, exhibits of folk and modern art), the Vietnam National Museum of Nature, and the Museum of the Cultures of Viet Nam's Ethnic Groups. Dozens of other museums are state-owned, and provinces and cities operate many others. Private museums are allowed, as well.

45 MEDIA

Vietnam's postal and telephone services are under the Ministry of Communications (MIC). The country made significant progress in upgrading its telecommunications system in the 1990s. Fiber-optic and microwave transmission systems were extended from the major cities to the provinces. 3G networks are available for smart phones. According to the MIC, as of October 2011, there were 15.5 million telephone landlines and 30 million cell phone users in Vietnam, with 62% of mobile users in rural areas. Mobile phones, usually with prepaid plans, are used for text messaging, business, and entertainment. A telecommunications company owned by Vietnam's military, Viettel, has expanded into overseas markets. Other carriers include Vinaphone and MobiFone. Vinasat-1, Vietnam's first communications satellite, was launched in 2008, with Vinasat-2 planned to launch in 2012.

Even though the constitution provides for freedom of speech and of the press, the government places major restrictions and regulations on all media, with harassment, fines, and even prison time for journalists who produce content objectionable to the MIC and the Communist Party Propaganda and Education Commission. Print and broadcast media remain firmly state-owned.

In January 2002, the Communist Party ordered the seizure and destruction of unauthorized books written by leading dissidents.

Prominent newspapers in 2010, with circulation numbers listed parenthetically, included *Nhan Dan* (200,000), *Sai Gon Giai Phong* (100,000), and *Quan Doi Nhan Dan* (60,000). The English-language *Saigon Times* was established in 1995, and the Vietnam News Agency started its English-language *Viet Nam News* in 1991. There are also newspapers in Chinese and French.

As of 2008, Vietnam had 7 FM radio stations, 65 AM radio stations, and 29 shortwave radio stations. The Voice of Vietnam is the primary international shortwave station and also broadcasts on six domestic channels. Television was introduced into the RVN in 1966. A pilot television station was inaugurated in the DRV in 1971. Many of the major cities have television stations, all under MIC guidance. In 2006, there were six national and 61 provincial television stations. The national news outlet, Vietnam News Agency, offered a news channel, VNEWS in 2010. Satellite dishes are popular and provide access to foreign television.

According to a 2011 report by the MIC, 2.5 million households in Vietnam have personal computers. According to the CIA, there were 120,318 Internet hosts (2010) and 23 million Internet users (2009). The arrival of Internet access in Vietnam has begun to provide a means for free expression, although Internet content is government-monitored, with the Internet service providers state-owned. Regulations require cybercafes to keep records of their customers, but this practice is often ignored. Vietnam has over a million bloggers. Some bloggers have been detained and imprisoned for expressing opinions that the government finds objectionable. Pro-democracy, religious, and environmental websites (such as Bauxite Vietnam) are repeatedly blocked or hacked. Social networking is popular with millions of users in Vietnam, particularly the local Zing Me and the officially blocked Facebook.

46 ORGANIZATIONS

The principal mass organization is the Fatherland Front, which, in January 1977, combined with the National Liberation Front and with the Vietnam Alliance of National, Democratic, and Peace Forces. The Fatherland Front draws up single slates of candidates in all elections and seeks to implement the political, economic, and social policies of the Communist Party. Other organizations that form part of the Fatherland Front are the Vietnam National Farmers Union, with some 14 million members; the Ho Chi Minh Communist Youth Union, with more than 6 million members; and the Vietnamese Women's Union (VMU), with over 13 million members. The VMU is active on issues including domestic violence and human trafficking. Industrial and commercial enterprises are represented by the Chamber of Commerce of the SRV in Hanoi.

There are some professional organizations that promote education and research in specific fields, such as the Chemical Society of Vietnam and the Vietnam Medical Association. There are numerous charitable organizations and sustainable development projects, often in partnership with international organizations, such as the Red Cross and Habitat for Humanity. Cultural organizations include the Viet Nam Writers' Association and many performing arts groups. The government promotes "Villages of Culture" as a way to preserve rural traditions.

47 TOURISM, TRAVEL, AND RECREATION

In 1986 and 1987, the government made plans to expand international and domestic airline service, double hotel capacity in the major cities, simplify complicated visa restrictions, and grant shore leave passes to passengers on cruise ships at Vietnamese ports. As a result of these measures, tourism grew rapidly.

Vietnam possesses a number of historic and scenic areas of interest to tourists. In the north, the beauty of Ha Long Bay, with its countless grottoes and rock formations, is well-known. Hanoi itself, with its historical monuments, lakes and pagodas, and its extensive French colonial architecture, is extremely picturesque. A wide array of accommodations are available, from budget to 5-star luxury. The cuisine of Vietnam, performing arts, and the indigenous cultures of the northern highlands are particular draws for foreign tourists.

The *Tourism Factbook*, published by the UN World Tourism Organization, reported 3.75 million incoming tourists to Vietnam in 2009, who spent a total of $3.05 billion. Of those incoming tourists, there were 2.4 million from East Asia and the Pacific. The estimated daily cost to visit Hanoi was $278. The cost of visiting other cities averaged $207. Hotels had an occupancy rate of 52% in 2011. As of 2007 there 140,000 hotel rooms available in Vietnam. That year, China, South Korea, the US, Japan, Taiwan, Australia, and France had the largest numbers of visitors to Vietnam. Visitors (except for citizens of some Asian and Scandinavian countries) must obtain visas issued by Vietnam's diplomatic missions or consulates in advance.

48 FAMOUS PERSONS

Important figures in Vietnamese history include the sisters Trung Trac and Trung Nhi, national heroines who led a revolt (AD 40–43) against China when that nation was imperial master of Tonkin and North Annam; Ngo Quyen, who regained Vietnamese independence from China in 938; Tran Hung Dao, who defeated the forces of Kublai Khan in 1288; Emperor Le Loi, national hero and brilliant administrator, in whose reign the Vietnamese legal code was promulgated in 1407; Emperor Gia Long (d. 1820), who reunified Vietnam in the early 19th century; and Le Van Duyet (1763–1832), a military leader who helped the emperor to unify the country.

Phan Boi Chau (1875–1940) was Vietnam's first modern nationalist. Ho Chi Minh ("The Enlightener"), born Nguyen That Thanh (1890–1969) was a founding member of the French Communist Party in 1920 and founded the Vietnamese Communist Party in 1930. He was president of the DRV from 1945 until his death. General Vo Nguyen Giap (1912–75), organized the first anti-French guerrilla groups in 1944, led the Viet-Minh in its eight-year struggle against France, and defeated the French at Dien Bien Phu; subsequently, he served as minister of defense, commander-in-chief of the army, and vice-premier of the DRV. Truong Chinh (1906–88), the DRV's foremost Communist thinker, was secretary-general of the Vietnamese Communist Party from 1940 until 1956. Pham Von Dong (1908–2000), a member of the nobility, joined the Vietnamese revolutionary movement at its inception and became premier of the SRV in 1976; he resigned in 1987. Le Duan (1907–86), first secretary of the Communist Party, presided over Vietnam's reunification and the formation of the SRV. Le Duc

Tho (1911–90), a member of the Communist Party Politburo, was the DRV's chief negotiator in talks that led to the 1973 Paris Peace Agreement; for his role, Le shared with US Secretary of State Henry Kissinger the 1973 Nobel Peace Prize.

Prominent political figures in the formation of the RVN included Bao Dai (1913–97), who had served as nominal emperor of Annam under the Japanese and had attempted to form a unified national government after the war, and Ngo Dinh Diem (1901–63), who served as president of the RVN from its founding on 26 October 1955 until his overthrow and death in November 1963. Nguyen Cao Ky (1930–2011), an RVN air force commander, took control of the government in the coup of June 1965. General Nguyen Van Thieu (1923–2001) was elected president of the RVN in the elections of September 1967 (with Ky as his vice presidential running mate), an office he retained until the RVN's defeat in 1975. The new leadership in the south, following the 1975 NLF victory, was headed by Pham Hung (1912–88), chairman of the southern wing of the Communist Party since 1967; Huynh Thanh Phat (1913–89), the PRG premier, who later became a member of the Council of State; and Nguyen Thi Binh (b. 1927), the PRG's foreign affairs minister who had headed the NLF delegation at the Paris talks and who also became a Council of State Member. Nguyen Van Linh (1915–98) became general secretary of the Communist Party in December 1986.

The 13th-century writer Nguyen Si Co is regarded as one of the first truly Vietnamese authors; he is best known for his collection titled *Chieu Quan Cong Ho*. Other leading literary figures are two 15th-century poets, Ho Huyen Qui and Nguyen Binh Khien. Nguyen Du (1765–1820) wrote a famous novel in verse, *Kim Van Kieu*. Hoang Ngoc Phach, who wrote the novel *To Tam*, is credited with the introduction of Western literary styles into Vietnamese literature. Duong Thu Huong (b. 1947) is a contemporary Vietnamese author and political dissident; her first two books were published in Vietnam, but subsequent novels were only published abroad. Xuan Dieu (1916–1985) earned fame for his romantic poetry. His nephew, Cu Huy Ha Vu (b. 1957) is a lawyer who has been imprisoned for his human rights and environmental activism. Thich Nhat Hanh (b. 1926) is a Buddhist monk and world peace activist, based in France, who has published many books of poetry and spiritual instruction.

Tran Anh Hung (b. 1962), a film director based in France, won international acclaim and awards for movies about contemporary Vietnam such as *Cyclo* and *The Scent of Green Papaya*. Vietnam is known for its thriving visual arts scene, from Impressionist-influenced landscape paintings to conceptual works. Pham Luan (b. 1954) paints urban landscapes. Contemporary artist Truong Tan (b. 1963) examines gender issues with his installations and ceramics.

49 DEPENDENCIES

Vietnam has no territories or colonies.

50 BIBLIOGRAPHY

Altbach, Philip G. and Toru Umakoshi (eds.). *Asian Universities: Historical Perspectives and Contemporary Challenges.* Baltimore, MD: Johns Hopkins University Press, 2004.

Ashwill, Mark A. *Vietnam Today: A Guide to a Nation at a Crossroads.* Yarmouth, ME: Intercultural Press, 2005.

Dutton, George Edson, Jayne Susan Werner, et al. *Sources of Vietnamese Tradition.* New York: Columbia University Press, 2012.

Frankum, Ronald Bruce. *Historical Dictionary of the War in Vietnam.* 2nd ed. Lanham, MD: Scarecrow Press, 2011.

Kelley, Michael. *Where We Were in Vietnam: A Comprehensive Guide to the Firebases, Military Installations, and Naval Vessels of the Vietnam War.* Central Point, OR: Hellgate Press, 2002.

Kerkvliet, Benedict J. *The Power of Everyday Politics: How Vietnamese Peasants Transformed National Policy.* Ithaca, NY: Cornell University Press, 2005.

Lockhart, Bruce McFarland and William J. Duiker. *Historical Dictionary of Vietnam.* Lanham, MD: Scarecrow, 2006.

Moise, Edwin e. *The A to Z of the Vietnam War.* Lanham, MD: Scarecrow Press, 2005.

SarDesai, D. R. *Vietnam, Past and Present.* 4th ed. Boulder, CO: Westview Press, 2005.

Vietnam Investment and Business Guide: Strategic and Practical Information. Washington, DC: International Business Publications USA, 2012.

YEMEN

Republic of Yemen
Al-Jumhuriyah al-Yamaniyah

CAPITAL: Şan'ā'

FLAG: The national flag contains three horizontal bands of red, white, and black that are equal in size. The colors are derived from the Arab Liberation flag and represent oppression (black,) victory through struggle (red), and a new future (white).

ANTHEM: *Al-Qumhuriyatu l-Muttahida (United Republic).*

MONETARY UNIT: The Yemeni riyal (YER) is a paper currency of 100 fils. There are coins of 1, 5, 10, 25, and 50 fils and notes of 1, 5, 10, 20, 50, and 100 riyals. YER1 = US$0.00469373 (or US$1 = YER213) as of 2011.

WEIGHTS AND MEASURES: The metric system is being introduced, but local measures remain in common use.

HOLIDAYS: New Year's Day, Milad an-Nabi, Labour Day (1 May), National Unity Day (22 May), Eid al-Fitr, Revolution Day (14 October), National Day (6 November), Eid al-Adha, Muharram (Islamic New York), and Independence Day (30 November).

TIME: 3 p.m. = noon GMT.

¹LOCATION, SIZE, AND EXTENT

Yemen is located in the southern part of the Arabian Peninsula. It is slightly larger than twice the size of the state of Wyoming with a total area of 527,970 sq km (203,850 sq mi). Yemen shares boundaries with Saudi Arabia on the N, Oman on the E, Gulf of Aden on the S, and the Red Sea on the W, and has a total land boundary length of 1,746 km (1,085 mi) plus a coastline of 1,906 km (1,184 mi).

²TOPOGRAPHY

Yemen's coastline is long (450 km/279 mi) and narrow (45 km/27.9 mi). Its general topography is that of semi-desert. Mountains of the southern Arabian Peninsula range run through the country with the highest peak, Hadur Shu'ayb, at 3,760 meters (nearly 12,336 feet). Fertile highland plateaus allow for tropical and temperate zone crops. Wadis—river valleys which go dry in the summer—run through the highlands. Regular rainfall makes the northern region rich and fertile in comparison with the dry southern region. In the northeast, the mountains merge with the Rub al-Khali desert.

³CLIMATE

Yemen's climate is dry and hot. The country experiences low annual rainfall, high temperatures in the summer, and big differences between its maximum and minimum temperatures in the inland areas. Temperatures between June and September can reach 54°C (129°F). The winter months are cooler, and the spring and fall seasons are warm, mostly dry and pleasant. Spring and fall temperatures range between 25°C (77°F) and 35°C (95°F) in the daytime and 15°C (59°F) and 22°C (72°F) at night.

The hot, dusty wind known as the Shamal blows from March through August, and can cause sandstorms. Most rainfall occurs in the winter, generally in sudden, short, heavy cloudbursts.

⁴FLORA AND FAUNA

The World Resources Institute estimates that there are 1,650 plant species in Yemen. In addition, Yemen is home to 74 mammal, 385 bird, 100 reptile, and 7 amphibian species. The calculation reflects the total number of distinct species residing in the country, not the number of endemic species.

Intense cultivation and wildlife hunting have depleted Yemen of its once-rich flora and fauna.

⁵ENVIRONMENT

Data from Earth's Endangered Creatures found 405 endangered species in Yemen in 2010. These figures included 27 species of birds; 158 coral, jellyfish, and sea anemone species; 10 mammal species; and 171 plant species. Endangered species include the northern bald ibis, the South Arabian leopard, slender-billed curlew, and two species of turtle (green sea and hawksbill). Queen of Sheba's gazelle and the Saudi Gazelle have become extinct in the wild.

Major environmental issues were a lack of natural fresh water and potable water, overgrazing, soil erosion, and desertification. Sandstorms and dust storms are common in the summer months, and several volcanoes were historically active. Jebel al-Tair erupted in 2007 after awakening from dormancy.

Yemen was party in 2011 to international agreements on biodiversity, climate change, desertification, endangered species, environmental modification, hazardous wastes, law of the sea, and ozone layer protection.

The CIA reported that Yemen's total renewable water resources were 4.1 cu km (less than 1 cu mi), and that its fresh water withdrawal for domestic, industrial, and agricultural uses was about 6.3 cu km per year. Domestic water usage accounted for 4% of total usage, industrial for 1%, and agricultural for 95%. Per capita water usage totaled 316 cu m (11,159 cu ft) per year.

Natural forests in mountainous areas have been destroyed by agricultural clearing and livestock overgrazing. In response to the nation's environmental needs, the government of Yemen has created laws governing the use of the country's water supply. Law Number 42 (1991) protects water and marine life.

The UN reported in 2008 that carbon dioxide emissions in Yemen totaled 21,958 kilotons.

6 POPULATION

The US Central Intelligence Agency (CIA) estimates the population of Yemen in 2011 to be 24,133,492 million, which placed it at number 49 in population among the 196 nations of the world. In 2011, approximately 2.6% of the population was over 65 years of age, with another 43% under 15 years of age. The median age in Yemen was 18.1 years. There were 1.04 males for every female in the country. The population's annual rate of change was 2.647%. The life expectancy for males in 2011 was about 62 years and for females about 65 years. About 32% of the total population lived in cities in 2010.

7 MIGRATION

Estimates of Yemen's net migration rate, carried out by the CIA in 2011, amounted to zero. The total number of emigrants living abroad was 1.13 million, and the total number of immigrants living in Yemen was 517,900. Yemen also accepted 91,587 refugees from Somalia. Most were working in Saudi Arabia and other Gulf states.

Many people from the Wadi Hadramawt in southern Yemen have worked abroad in East Africa, India, and Indonesia for centuries. Following independence and the establishment of a leftist regime in the PDRY, more than 300,000 people fled to the north, including about 80,000 Yemenis from the Yemen Arab Republic, and virtually all minority groups left the country. Subsequent political upheavals resulted in further emigration.

Large Yemeni communities are present throughout the world, particularly in Persian Gulf countries, Indonesia, India, East Africa, the United Kingdom and the United States. Remittances from residents of these overseas communities have supported Yemen's economy in the past. At least 850,000 Yemenis living in Saudi Arabia and the neighborhood Gulf states returned to the country in 1991 during the outbreak of the 1991 Persian Gulf war.

In early January 2011, several boat accidents near the coast of Yemen resulted in the drowning of over 80 Ethiopian and Somali migrants. The instability in the Horn of Africa caused a 50% increase of refugees fleeing their countries in 2009. Despite hundreds of deaths among refugees fleeing to Yemen, the number of migrants heading towards south Yemen continued to grow in 2011.

8 ETHNIC GROUPS

The population was almost entirely Arab in 2011. However, there were some Afro-Arabs in western coastal locations, South Asians in southern regions, and small European communities in major metropolitan areas. Yemenis are primarily Semitic in origin, though some residents in coastal areas can claim African descent. Most minority groups left the area when the former states of north and south Yemen attained independence.

Many ethnologists contend that the purest "Arab" stock is to be found in Yemen. Classified as Joktanic Semites, the Yemenis claim descent from Himyar, great-grandson of Joktan, who, according to the book of Genesis, was descended from Shem, the son of Noah. Yemenis were prominent in the early armies of Islam and thus helped to Arabize much of the Middle East.

9 LANGUAGES

Arabic is the official language. English also is used in official and business circles.

10 RELIGIONS

Nearly all of Yemen's citizens are Muslim and belong either to the Zaydi order of Shi'a Islam or the Shafa'i order of Sunni Islam. Zaydis were estimated to make up about 45% of the population and Shafa'is 55% in 2008. A few thousand Islmaili Muslims resided in the north, and about 150 Baha'is and 250 Jews lived in the country.

Jews comprised an indigenous non-Muslim minority in Yemen, but the US State Department reported that the government had failed to protect the community and that most Jews had fled. A Saada Governorate community of 60 Jews was living since January 2007 in Şan'ā' under governmental protection after threats for al-Houthi rebels forced them to abandon their homes. Increasing violence against Jews in the Amran Governorate forced the closure of two synagogues in 2008 and 2009.

About 3,000 Christians resided in Yemen, mostly refugees or temporary foreign residents in 2009. There were four churches in Aden. In addition, 40 Hindus lived in Aden, and the community housed one Hindu temple.

Although Yemen's constitution contains protections for freedom of religion, violence against non-Muslims has often hindered the free practice of Judaism and Christianity.

11 TRANSPORTATION

Through the 1950s, Yemen's transportation system consisted of a few primitive mud tracks connecting the larger towns. Major road projects in 1961–69 and in 1999 developed the country's major highways. The CIA reported that Yemen had a total of 71,300 km (44,304 mi) of roads in 2011, of which 6,200 km (3,853 mi) were paved.

There were 55 airports, which transported 1.05 million passengers in 2009 according to the World Bank. In 2011, there were 17 airports with paved runways. The principal airfield, capable of handling modern jet aircraft, was Ar-Rahba International Airport, north of Şan'ā'. There are smaller international airports at Al Hudaydah, Ta'izz, and 'Aden. Yemen Airways (Alyemda), the national airline, offered flights between Şan'ā', Ta'izz, Al Hudaydah, and Al-Bayda as well as flights to Egypt, Ethiopia, Kuwait, Saudi Arabia, and the United Arab Emirates.

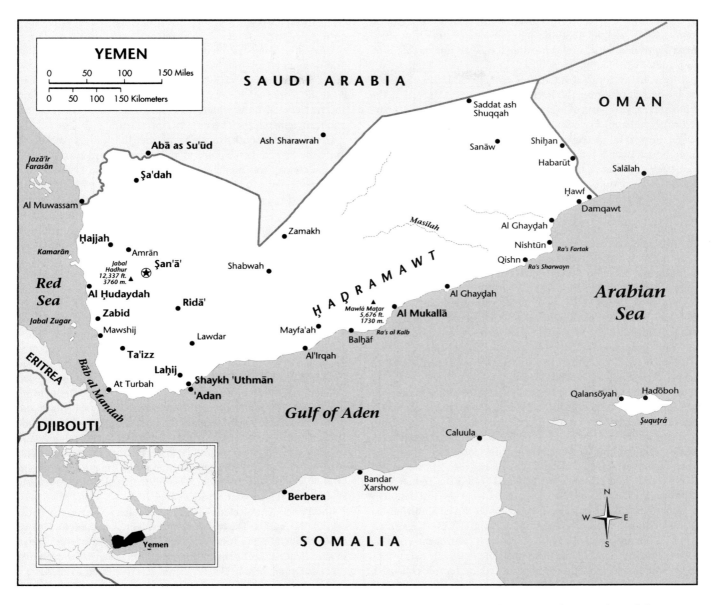

In 2011, Yemen had eight ports. The Port of Aden received 2,183 vessels in 2008 carrying 15.2 million tons of cargo. Its facilities include a container terminal, refineries terminal, and general cargo port. The Port of Hodeidah had 2 container berths, 6 conventional berths, and 2 oil terminals.

Smaller ports included the Ash Shihr Terminal; the ports of Mokha, Mukalia, Nishtun, Saleef, and the Ras Isa Marine Terminal.

In 2008 Yemen had a merchant fleet of four ships of 1,000 gross registered tons or more.

12 HISTORY

Yemen is one of the oldest Near East centers of civilization. Classical geographers divided Arabia into three regions: Arabia Petraea ("rocky"), Arabia Deserta ("deserted"), and Arabia Felix ("fortunate"). The last, the southwestern corner, included the territory now occupied by Yemen. The region was the site of a series of rich kingdoms that dominated world trade, one of which was Sheba. The prosperity of this kingdom (10th to 2nd centuries BC) was based on the spice and incense trade. Competition from new trade routes undermined the kingdom of Sheba's prosperity and caused it to decline. From the 2nd century BC to the 6th century AD, the Himyarite dynasty, of ethnic stock similar to that of the Sabaeans, ruled in Arabia Felix, until the area came under first Christian Ethiopian and then Persian rule.

Islamic caliphs began to vie for parts of Yemen in the 7th century. Imams from various dynasties of the Zaydi sect took control of the former north Yemen and established a theocratic political structure. Through the 11th century Egyptian Sunni caliphs occupied much of north Yemen. The area became part of the Ottoman Empire in the 16th century and again in the 19th century. Imams also exerted control over south Yemen during these centuries. From about 1630 through the 19th century, the Ottomans controlled the coastal area while the Zaydi imams ruled the highlands.

British forces occuped Aden as a coaling station in 1834 and established control over the Port of Aden in 1839, as well as the south and eastern parts of present-day Yemen. Aden became part of British India and remained so until 1937 when the UK converted the port into a crown colony and designated the remaining lands under British influence as east Aden and west Aden protectorates. A series of tribal states continued to exist within the crown colony and protectorates and by 1965 most of these states had joined together as the British-sponsored Federation of South Arabia.

In north Yemen, Ottoman control continued in cities and the Imam's suzerainty over tribal areas was recognized. After Turkish forces withdraw in 1918, Imam Yahya Muhammad Hamid al-din strengthened his control over the north. This part of Yemen became a member of the Arab League in 1945 and the United Nations in 1947. Imam Yahya died during an unsuccessful coup attempt in 1948. His son Ahmad ruled until September 1962. Imam Ahmad's rule was characterized by increased repression, friction between Yemen and the UK over the continuing British presence in the south, and pressures to support the Arab nationalist goals of Egypt's president, Gamal Abdul Nasser.

After Ahmad's death, his son Muhammad assumed power but was soon deposed by revolutionary forces who seized control of Şan'a' and created the Yemen Arab Republic with support from Egypt. Conflict grew as Saudi Arabia and Jordan stepped in to support Muhammad's royalist forces, and continued until 1967 when Egypt withdrew its troops. The opposing leaders reconciled in 1968, and Saudia Arabia formally recognized the Yemen Arab Republic in 1970. Meanwhile, in south Yemen, two rival nationalist groups—the Front for the Liberation of Occupied South Yemen (FLOSY) and the National Liberation Front (NLF)—began carrying out terrorist activities in a struggle to control the country. As the violence mounted to uncontrollable levels, British troops began withdrawing from the region, the federation rule collapsed, and the Marxist-inspired NLF took control. South Arabia declared independence on 30 November 1967, and renamed itself the People's Republic of South Yemen. A radical wing of the NLF gained power in June 1969 and renamed the country on 1 December 1970 the People's Democratic Republic of Yemen (PDRY). The People's Republic established close ties with the former Soviet Union, China, Cuba, and radical Palestinians. Both the former Soviet Union and China provided substantial economic aid during this time.

The People's Democratic Republic of Yemen and the Yemen Arab Republic declared approval for a future union of the two entities in 1972. However, relations between the two governments often were strained, and fighting broke out out in 1979. Even as the heads of state reaffirmed a goal for unity, the People's Democratic Republic of Yemen began sponsoring an anti-Yemen Arab Republic insurgency. The president of the People's Democratic Republic of Yemen, Abdul Fattah Ismail, resigned in April 1980 and went into exile. The former president returned on 13 January 1986 and a violent struggle broke out him and his successor Ali Nasir Muhammad. After a month of fighting, Ismail was killed and Ali Nasir was removed from power. He and about 60,000 of his supporters fled to the Yemen Arab Republic.

Unification talks resumed in May 1988, a draft unity constitution was agreed upon in November 1989, and the Republic of Yemen was declared on 22 May 1990. Ali Abdullah Saleh, who had been the leader of the Yemen Arab Republic, became president and Ali Salim al-Bidh, who had been the People's Democratic Republic of Yemen leader, became vice president.

During a 30-month transition period, the leaders worked to unify the two country's political and economic systems. A presidential council was established, and it appointed a Prime Minister who formed a Cabinet. A 301-seat provisional parliament also was formed and included 159 members from the north, 111 members from the south, and 31 independent members appointed by the council chairman. Citizens ratified a final unity constitution in May 1991. Parliamentary elections took place on 27 April 1993.

Meanwhile, the economy was hard hit by the consequences of Yemen's support for Iraq after the 1990 Kuwait invasion. It is estimated that Saudi Arabia expelled between 800,000 and one million Yemeni workers, thus depriving Yemen of some $3 billion in foreign exchange. In addition, the Saudis and Gulf states ended $2 billion in foreign aid. Unemployment in Yemen reached 30%.

At the same time, cordiality between the unified elements was short-lived. As conflicts within the ruling coalition mounted, Vice President Ali Salim al-Bidh retreated to Aden in a self-imposed exile and civil war broke out in May 1994. Most of the fighting occurred in the south and, with support from neighboring states, the south declared secession and the establishment of the Democratic Republic of Yemen on 21 May 1994. Ali Nasir Muhammad's troops captured Aden on 7 July 1994, causing the resistance to collapse. A general amnesty was announced for everyone except 16 individuals. Most of those who participated in the resistance returned to Yemen after a brief exile.

The Parliament elected Ali Abdullah Saleh to a five-year term on 1 October 1994. The first direct presidential election took place in September 1999. President Saleh won a second five-year term in this election, and constitution amendments in 2000 extended the presdential term by 2 years. Saleh was re-elected in 2006.

The civil war left Yemen in dire economic straits. Inflation in 1995 was 70% to 90%, and the country's deficit constituted 17% of its GDP. The International Monetary Fund and World Bank instituted structural adjustment programs, helping to bring Yemen's inflation rate below 10%. Yemen continued to require international support through the first decade of the 21st century.

Yemen's first two decades as a unified republic were marked by political corruption, economically motivated kidnappings, frequent outbreaks of violence, and economic instability as the kidnappings damaged the country's tourist industry while falling world oil prices reduced the country's export revenue. Anti-US and Islamist terrorist groups believed to have ties to al-Qaeda were responsible for a suicide attack on 12 October 2000 that killed 17 US sailors and wounded 39 others on the *USS Cole*. Clashes between government security forces and Shia rebels in the north between 2004 and 2007 resulted in the deaths of hundreds of people. A separatist movement continued to gain strength in the south, and a group known as al-Qaeda in the Arabia Peninsula established itself along the Saudi Arabian border. The government called a state of emergency in the northern border province of

Saada in August 2009 as the Yemen army engaged in military offensives against rebel camps. These incidents left the unified governnance of Yemen in an extremely precarious state at the end of 2011.

Anti-government protests broke out in the capital city of Şan'ä' in early 2011, demanding that President Ali Abudullah Saleh step down. Violent clashes erupted, exacerbating the country's financial crisis and prompting the government to seek $6 billion in aid from the Gulf Cooperation Council. The violence continued through 2011, with increasing pressure placed on Saleh to resign. Saleh signed a GCC transition plan on 23 November 2011 in which he formally agreed to resign, transferring power to vice president Abd Rabbo Mansour Hadi. Hadi appointed opposition leader Muhammad Basindwa to form a national unity cabinet, and set 21 February 2012 for presidential elections. Observers warned that the transition had a high risk of turning violent.

13 GOVERNMENT

Efforts to reconcile the political systems of the former Yemen Arab Republic and People's Democratic Republic of Yemen have been difficult, and a new government was in the stages of being formed in late 2011.

Following the 1990 unification, leaders set a 30-month transition period during which legislative bodies from the two former republics jointly elected a presidential council. The presidential council appointed a Prime Minister who formed a Cabinet. A provision unified Parliament also included 301 seats: 159 for representatives from the north, 111 for representatives from the south, and 31 seats for independent members appointed by the council chairman.

The leaders agreed upon a unity constitution in May 1990, which was ratified the following year in a popular referendum. The constitution established Yemen's commitment to free elections, a multiparty political system, the right to own private property, equality under the law, and respect for basic human rights.

Parliamentary elections on 27 April 1993 resulted in a legislative body of 143 General People's Congress party representatives, 69 Yemeni Socialist Party members, and 63 members of Islah, a party comprised of tribal and religious groups. Islah's head, Abdullah bin Hussein al-Ahmar, paramount sheikh of the powerful Hashid tribal confederation, was elected speaker of the parliament and filled that role until his death in 2007.

Constitutional amendments eliminated the presidential council in 1994, and on 1 October of that year, the parliament elected President Ali Abdullah Saleh to a five-year term. Multi-party parliamentary elections were held in April 1997, and the first direct presidential elections took place in September 1999. Constitutional amendments in 2000 extended the presidential term to seven years, extended parliamentary terms to six years, and provided that the president would be elected by popular vote from at least two candidates selected by the parliament. A constitutional amendment on 20 February 2001 created a bicameral legislature with an 111-seat Shura Council whose members would be appointed by the president, and a 301-seat House of Representatives whose members would be elected by popular vote. Yemen held its first municipal elections in February 2001.

Parliamentary elections took place in 2003 and had been scheduled for April 2009. These elections were delayed to 2011, and then to 2013. Presidential elections took place in 2006 and were scheduled for 2013. The resignation of President Saleh, however, indicated that a new date for elections might be set in 2012.

14 POLITICAL PARTIES

In 2011, Yemen had 22 legal political parties, five of which had parliamentary representation. The ruling party in 2011 was the General People's Congregation (GPC). Other parties with representation in parliament were the Yemeni Congregation for Reform (also known as Islaah, a religious party with tribal and Islamist factions); the Arab Socialist Baath Party, the Yemeni Socialist Party; and the Nasserist Union Party. These parties formed a coalition known as the Joint Meeting Parties with two opposition groups: the Union of Public Forces and Al-Haq.

Political parties did not exist in North Yemen before unification; tribal allegiances were more important political factors. After unity, the northern leader, General Saleh, formed the GPC, which became the country's largest party. The second-largest bloc in the parliament was held by the Islaah Party (The Yemeni Congregation for Reform). After the 1994 civil war, the GPC and Islaah formed a coalition government to establish civil order.

Tribalism, election boycotts, and favoritism has marred the unified Yemen's political process. In 1997, the Yemeni Socialist Party, representing the defeated south, announced that it would boycott the elections in protest of the GPC's collusion with Islaah. The GPC won a landslide victory and no longer governed in coalition with Islaah. The Yemeni Socialist Party also boycotted presidential elections in 1999. Women's rights activists in 2006 accused the GPC of rigging the elections against women.

As of 2011, the GPC controlled 238 of the 301 seats in parliament while Islah controlled 46 seats.

15 LOCAL GOVERNMENT

Yemen was divided, as of 2011, into 21 governorates (*muhafazat*), each headed by a governor. Local councils in each of the governorates elected governors in 2008; previously those positions had been appointed by the president. However, the opposition parties boycotted the council elections, which allowed the ruling GPC to dominate the local seats.

16 JUDICIAL SYSTEM

Yemen's unified constitution provided for an independent judiciary consisting of separate commercial courts and a Supreme Court in Şan'ä'.

A Supreme Judicial Council administers the judiciary, appointing and promoting judges and reviewing policies regarding the structure and functioning of the judicial system. There are courts of first instance, which hear civil, criminal, commercial, and family matters; decisions can be appealed to courts of appeal. The Supreme Court rules on the constitutionality of laws, hears cases brought against high government officials, and is the last court of appeal for all lower court decisions.

The US State Department reported in a 2011 Human Rights report that the judiciary system was weak and politically corrupt. A Specialized Criminal Court is charged with hearing cases involving defendants regarded as public dangers; the court, however, heard a number of non-security cases in 2011. A press court established in May 2009 to try media and publication cases declared guilty verdicts in nearly all its cases and suspended numerous journalists.

The judiciary, especially at the lower levels, was susceptible to pressure and influence from the executive branch. All laws are codified from Shariah, and there are no jury trials. In addition to regular courts, a system of tribal adjudication exists for some noncriminal issues, although the tribal "judges" often hear criminal cases as well.

17 ARMED FORCES

The International Institute for Strategic Studies reports that armed forces in Yemen totaled 66,700 members in 2011. The force is comprised of 60,000 from the army, 1,700 from the navy, 3,000 from the air force, and 2,000 members of air defense. Armed forces represent 2.2% of the labor force in Yemen. Defense spending totaled $4.2 billion and accounted for 6.6% of GDP.

The country's paramilitary forces totaled 70,000 personnel, which were comprised of 50,000 Ministry of Interior Forces, and tribal levies in excess of 20,000. A coast guard is slowly being established.

18 INTERNATIONAL COOPERATION

Yemen's international relationships underwent numerous shifts through the 20th and early 21st centuries, as the area was reorganized from a series of imam-led kingdoms in the north and British colonial holdings in the south.

Before unification, north Yemen's relationships with British colonial authorities in Aden and south Yemen were tense. The Taif Agreement of 1934 established a framework for commercial and diplomatic relations between the region and Saudi Arabia, and has been reaffirmed periodically. Soviet and Chinese aid missions were begun in 1958 and 1959, and the former ruling imams were heavily dependent on Egypt following the 1962 revolution. Since formation of the Yemen Arab Republic, north Yemen has received substantial support from Saudi Arabia. North Yemen formed the Arab Cooperation Council in February 1989 with Iraq, Jordan, and Egypt, and the new Republic of Yemen was accepted as a member of the council following the 1990 unification. The council has been inactive since the 1991 Persian Gulf War.

In the south, the People's Democratic Republic of Yemen joined the Arab League in 1945, and the United Nations in 1947. Although it had diplomatic relations with many nations, its major ties were to the former USSR and other Marxist countries. Relations with other Arab states were strained. The southern republic clashed with Saudi Arabia in 1969 and 1973, and supported the Dhofar rebellion against the Sultanate of Oman. It also offered support to several international terrorist groups.

Since unification, Yemen has been a member of the UN, Arab League, Organization of the Islamic Conference, and has participated in the nonaligned movement. Yemen was not a member of the Gulf Cooperation Council but was allowed limited participation in some affairs.

Yemen's seeming support for Iraq during 1991 Gulf war resulted in a curtailing of diplomatic contacts and aid programs by Western and Gulf states. At least 850,000 Yemenis returned from Saudi Arabia and other Gulf states during this time.

Yemen was admitted to the United Nations on 30 September 1947; it participates in the ESCWA and several nonregional specialized UN agencies such as the World Bank, the FAO, ILO, UNESCO, UNHCR, UNCTAD, and the WHO. The country is also a member of the Arab Fund for Economic and Social Development, the Arab Monetary Union, the Council of Arab Economic Unity, the Islamic Development Bank, the Arab League, G-77, and the Organization of the Islamic Conference (OIC). Yemen has observer status in the OAS and the WTO.

19 ECONOMY

The gross domestic product (GDP) rate of change in Yemen, as of 2010, was 8%. Inflation stood at 12.2%, and unemployment was reported at 35%.

The CIA described Yemen in 2011 as a low income country that depended on declining oil resources for its revenue. More than one-third of the population lived below the poverty line, and Yemen was among the world's "Heavily Indebted Poor Countries" in 2011. Oil production accounted for 25% of GDP and 70% of government revenue. A structural adjustment program by the International Monetary Fund was initiated in the mid-1990s following the 1994 civil war. However, difficulties in implementing the financial and monetary reforms demanded by the IMF caused the program to lapse. A new IMF program was implemented in August 2010 in which Yemen received an Extended Credit Facility of approximately $370 million over three years. The IMF demanded a series of economic reforms in exchange for the funds. The political instability that erupted in 2011 had put the IMF program on hold. The World Bank also maintained 20 projects in public sector government, water, and education as of 2011.

Historically an agricultural and herding economy, northern Yemen was able to sustain itself until the outbreak of civil war in the 1960s and a prolonged drought in the early 1970s. The economy of southern Yemen developed through foreign assistance, and the southern city of 'Aden has continued to be the economic and commercial center of the country. The Port of 'Aden relied on seaborne transit trade for much of its income until this sector collaborated with Great Britain's withdrawl from 'Aden in 1967. Aid from China and the former USSR as well as remittances from overseas Yemeni workers sustained the economy from the 1950s through early 1990. The economy of southern Yemen collapsed with the break-up of the Soviet Republic in 1991.

Despite government efforts to integrate the two economic systems since the 1990 unification, severe economic shocks, including the return in 1990 of 850,000 Yemenis from the Persian Gulf states, cuts in foreign aid, and the 1994 civil war, hampered economic growth. Oil production, which began in 1982, peaked in 2001.

An economic diversification program was initiated in 2006 to counter the effects of Yemen's declining oil resources. The CIA reported that Yemen exported its first liquefied natural gas as part of this diversification effort in October 2009. The diversification effort was supported by an international Friends of Yemen group that formed in January 2010 as well as the IMF's $370 million reform program that was initiated in August 2010. Although political unrest threatened the diversification effort, the Economist Intelligence Unit reported that record high oil prices in 2011 were able to sustain Yemen through the turmoil. Exports of crude oil were estimated at 207,700 billion barrels a day in 2009, while exports of natural gas were estimated at 420 million cubic meters in that year. Yemen's oil reserves were estimated at 3 billion and its natural gas reserves at 478.5 billion cubic meters in 2011.

20 INCOME

The CIA estimated that in 2010 the GDP of Yemen was $63.4 billion. The CIA defines GDP as the value of all final goods and services produced within a nation in a given year and computed on the basis of purchasing power parity (PPP) rather than value as measured on the basis of the rate of the exchange based on current dollars. The per capita GDP was estimated at $2,700. The annual growth rate of GDP was 8%. The average inflation rate was 12.2%. It was estimated that agriculture accounted for 8.2% of GDP, industry 38.8%, and services 53%.

According to the World Bank, remittances from citizens living abroad totaled $1.2 billion or about $48 per capita and accounted for approximately 1.8% of GDP.

The World Bank estimates that Yemen, with 0.33% of the world's population, accounted for 0.08% of the world's GDP. By comparison, the United States, with 4.85% of the world's population, accounted for 22.51% of world GDP.

As of 2011 the most recent study by the World Bank reported that actual individual consumption in Yemen was 68.9% of GDP and accounted for 0.08% of world consumption. By comparison, the United States accounted for 25.44% of world individual consumption. The World Bank also estimated that 29.7% of Yemen's GDP was spent on food and beverages, 14.2% on housing and household furnishings, 6.0% on clothes, 2.6% on health, 3.6% on transportation, 0.5% on communications, 0.9% on recreation, 1.7% on restaurants and hotels, and 5.4% on miscellaneous goods and services and purchases from abroad.

21 LABOR

All unions in Yemen in 2011 were part of the General Federation of Trade Unions of Yemen. The national umbrella group claimed 42,000 members in 21 unions in 2007. Labor laws allowed unions the right to strike and to bargain collectively on behalf of workers. Laws prohibiting forced labor and child labor generally were not enforced. In 2010, the US State Department reported that approximately 12% of children between ages 6 and 14 worked. Many children worked in subsistence farming in rural areas and in stores and workshops in urban areas. Children also sold goods and begged on streets. Many children worked instead of attending school.

There was no minimum wage as of 2010, and the average daily wage did not provide workers and their families a decent standard of living, according to the US State Department. The minimum civil service wage also did not allow workers to live above the poverty level. The maximum work week of 48 hours in the private sector often was violated without penalty. Government employees generally worked a 35-hour work week, Saturday through Wednesday.

22 AGRICULTURE

Roughly 3% of the total land was arable or under permanent crops, and the country's major crops included grain, fruits, vegetables, pulses, qat, coffee, and cotton. Cereal production in 2009 amounted to 674,488 tons, fruit production 981,431 tons, and vegetable production 820,261 tons.

Yemen, with its wide range of arable climatic zones, has the greatest potential for agricultural development of any nation on the Arabian Peninsula. The northern region is rich and fertile, with regular rainfall. Despite these assets, frequent periods of drought in the late 20th and early 21st centuries have stifled agricultural growth. Declines in water resources also have impeded Yemen's agricultural development. Agriculture accounted for 8% of Yemen's GDP in 2010, and more than 75% of its labor force.

Traditionally, Yemen was famous for its coffee, shipped from the port of Al-Mukha, from which the English word mocha derives. However, production of coffee has declined in favor of the main cash crop, qat. Qat is a mild stimulant chewed by many Yemenis on a daily basis. Qat cultivation in 2011 took up one-third of the country's cropland while cereal cultivation was unable to meet the needs of more than 75% of the population.

23 ANIMAL HUSBANDRY

The UN Food and Agriculture Organization (FAO) reported that Yemen dedicated 22 million hectares (54.4 million acres) to permanent pasture or meadow in 2009. During that year, the country tended 58 million chickens and 1.6 million head of cattle. The production from these animals amounted to 74,757 tons of beef and veal, 366 tons of pork, 212,154 tons of poultry, 42,864 tons of eggs, and 687,329 tons of milk. Yemen also produced 18,071 tons of cattle hide and 7,593 tons of raw wool.

Although Yemen's poultry production grew in the first decade of the 21st century, a September 2011 report from the US Department of Agriculture noted that poultry production was expected to significantly decline as a result of the ongoing hostilities in the country.

24 FISHING

Yemen had 144 decked commercial fishing boats in 2008. The annual capture totaled 127,132 tons according to the UN FAO. The export value of seafood totaled $116.9 million.

Fishermen work along the Arabian Sea, Gulf of Aden, and Red Sea coasts. Principal species of that catch include Indian and Spanish mackerel, cuttlefish, lobster, and scavengers. Fish-processing plants are located at Al-Hudaydah and Al-Mukalla. Pearl and coral diving have been practiced for centuries.

25 FORESTRY

Overgrazing by goats and the systematic cutting of timber for fuel and construction have eliminated most of Yemen's once abundant forest cover. Approximately 1% of Yemen is covered by forest. The value of all forest products, including roundwood, totaled $752,000.

26 MINING

Until the discovery of petroleum, the preeminent segment of the Yemeni economy, the mineral industry, had been limited to the production of cement, dimension stone, gypsum, and salt. In 2009, production of cement amounted to 2,118,000 metric tons. Other mineral commodities produced in 2009 were: marble, 250,000 sq m; gypsum, 100,000 metric tons; and salt, 65,000 metric tons. The government was focusing on creating conditions fa-

Principal Trading Partners – Yemen (2010)

(In millions of US dollars)

Country	Total	Exports	Imports	Balance
World	18,200.0	8,500.0	9,700.0	-1,200.0
China	3,872.3	2,525.9	1,346.4	1,179.4
India	2,567.7	2,025.0	542.7	1,482.3
United Arab Emirates	1,843.0	350.6	1,492.4	-1,141.9
Sa'udi Arabia	915.2	211.4	703.7	-492.3
Thailand	740.2	485.0	255.2	229.8
Japan	720.7	391.7	329.0	62.6
Kuwait	718.7	192.9	525.9	-333.0
United States	627.6	187.0	440.6	-253.6
South Korea	608.2	382.5	225.7	156.7
France	518.6	38.5	480.1	-441.6

(…) data not available or not significant.

(n.s.) not specified.

SOURCE: *2011 Direction of Trade Statistics Yearbook,* New York: United Nations, 2011.

vorable to foreign investment, to develop the nation's mineral resources. The government had exclusive domain over the precious stone and hydrocarbon industries; mining legislation guaranteed the rights of private property for all other commodities. ZincOx Resources, of the United Kingdom, continued evaluating the Al-Jabail zinc deposit, which Anglo American Corp. had explored in the late 1990s.

27 ENERGY AND POWER

The World Bank reported in 2008 that Yemen produced 6.55 billion kWh of electricity and consumed 5.04 billion kWh, or 209 kWh per capita. Roughly 99% of energy came from fossil fuels. Per capita oil consumption was 326 kg. Oil production totaled 258,800 barrels of oil a day in 2010, according to the CIA.

Yemen is a small non-OPEC producer of oil and has the potential to be an exporter of natural gas. Whatever gas is produced results from the oil extraction process and is re-injected. Most of the known reserves are concentrated in the Marib-Jawf fields.

28 INDUSTRY

Industry accounted for 38.5% of GDP in 2010, although less than a quarter of the labor force was employed in that sector. Yemen's oil production was minor in comparison with other Gulf nations, but energy exports generated the majority of the government's revenue.

Oil production peaked in 2001 at 440,000 bbls per day and has since then declined to about 258,800 as of 2010. Oil exports generated approximtely $1 billion in revenues in 1995 and had grown to approximately 5.5 billion by 2010. Although some new oil discoveries have been made in the Jannah and east Shabwah blocks, dwindling resources and a lack of equipment maintenance and new investment in exploration activities have resulted in steady production declines.

US-based Hunt Oil had a 20-year contract to manage Yemen's Block 18 fields. The contract ended in 2005, and disputes over its extension resulted in a lawsuit brought by Hunt against Yemen. The decision was not made public, and while the company con-

tinued to operate in Yemen in 2011, its activities were of a smaller scope.

Oil near Marib has been found to contain associated natural gas. Several projects have been launched to use Yemen's liquefied natural gas to fuel power plants. The Yemen LNG project at the Port of Balhaf became commercially operational in October 2009.

In addition to oil and natural gas production, Yemen also had some small-scale production of cotton textiles and leather goods, food processing, and handicrafts. It also produced cement, maintained a small aluminum products factory, and engaged in commercial ship repair.

29 SCIENCE AND TECHNOLOGY

Patent applications in science and technology as of 2009, according to the World Bank, totaled 11 in Yemen. The University of Aden, founded in 1975 at Al-Mansoora, has faculties of science, arts, and education; agriculture; engineering; and medicine. Șan'ā' University, founded in 1970, has faculties of science, medicine and health sciences, engineering, and agriculture.

30 DOMESTIC TRADE

At the center of most towns is a market place (*sug*), the lanes of which are lined with open-front booths where food, clothing, and implements are displayed and sold. Some goods are bartered. Others are sold for cash, usually after bargaining. The production of *qat*, a mild stimulant which many Yemenis chew, plays an important role in domestic trade.

Businesspeople in Yemen are generally expected to dress formally for meetings and conduct transactions in English. Appointments are often required and visitors are expected to be punctual. Business hours are generally 8 a.m. to 3 p.m. Saturday through Wednesday, and 10 a.m. to 3 p.m. during the holy month of Ramadan.

31 FOREIGN TRADE

Yemen imported $9.2 billion worth of goods and services in 2010, while exporting $7.462 billion worth of goods and services. Major import partners in 2009 were China, 13.4%; UAE, 11.8%; India, 8.5%; Saudi Arabia, 5.6%; the United States, 4.4%; Brazil, 4.3%; Turkey, 4.3%; Kuwait, 4.2%; and France, 4.1% . Its major export partners were China, 23%; India, 21.4%; Thailand, 19.4%; South Africa, 6.8%; Japan, 6.1%; and UAE, 5.5%.

The Yemen Chamber of Commerce reported in 2011 that merchandise imports dropped as much as 80% in the first six months of the year. This drop resulted from a demand by foreign companies for full up-front payments of goods, and put the economy in a precarious position as Yemen relied on imports for up to 90% of its food needs as well as medical supplies.

Oil accounted for 70% of Yemen's exports in 2010, compared with 90% in 2004. Other major exports were liquefied natural gas, refined oil products, seafoods, fruits, vegetables, animal hides, and tobacco products. Key imports were petroleum products, cereals, feed grains, food, machinery, transportation equipment, iron, sugar, and honey

Balance of Payments – Yemen (2009)

(In millions of US dollars)

Current Account		**-2,564.9**
Balance on goods		-2,012.8
Imports	-7,867.8	
Exports	5,855.0	
Balance on services		-895.6
Balance on income		-1,171.3
Current transfers		1,514.9
Capital Account		...
Financial Account		**-317.2**
Direct investment abroad		...
Direct investment in Yemen		129.2
Portfolio investment assets		-13.5
Portfolio investment liabilities		...
Financial derivatives		...
Other investment assets		-574.9
Other investment liabilities		142.1
Net Errors and Omissions		**1,589.6**
Reserves and Related Items		**1,292.4**

(...) data not available or not significant.

SOURCE: *Balance of Payment Statistics Yearbook 2011*, Washington, DC: International Monetary Fund, 2011.

Public Finance – Yemen (2009)

(In millions of rials, general government central government figures)

Revenue and Grants	**1,277**	**100.0%**
Tax revenue	406	31.8%
Social contributions	...	...
Grants	21	1.6%
Other revenue	850	66.6%
Expenditures	**1,773**	**100.0%**
General public services	338	19.1%
Defense	288	16.2%
Public order and safety	129	7.3%
Economic affairs	482	27.2%
Environmental protection	20	1.1%
Housing and community amenities	97	5.5%
Health	62	3.5%
Recreational, culture, and religion	23	1.3%
Education	286	16.1%
Social protection	48	2.7%

(...) data not available or not significant.

SOURCE: *Government Finance Statistics Yearbook 2010*, Washington, DC: International Monetary Fund, 2010.

32 BALANCE OF PAYMENTS

In 2010 Yemen had a foreign trade deficit of $2.9 billion.

The CIA estimated that Yemen had a negative current account balance of $1.944 billion in 2010 compared with a negative balance of $2.565 billion in 2009. Foreign exchange reserves (including gold) were estimated at $5.942 billion in December 2010 compared with $6.993 billion in December 2009.

Yemen's balance of payments was adversely affected in the early 1990s, as other nations sought to economically punish Yemen for its support of Iraq during the Persian Gulf War.

33 BANKING AND SECURITIES

The Central Bank of Yemen, based in Şan'ā', regulates the banking sector and manages foreign exchange transactions. The Yemen Bank for Reconstruction and Development and the National Bank of Yemen are the country's largest commercial banks. Foreign banks in Yemen include Bank Indosuez (France), United Bank (Pakistan), and the Arab Bank (Jordan). The commercial bank prime lending rate was 25% in December 2010 compared with 18% in December 2009.

The CIA estimated Yemen's stock of narrow money (the amount of total currency in circulation) at $3.679 billion in 2010 compared with an estimate of $3.659 billion in 2009. The stock of broad money (which includes the total currency along with banking and credit union deposits, money market funds, short-term repurchase agreements, and other large liquid assets) were estimated at $10.13 billion for 2010 and $9.346 billion for 2009. The stock of domestic credit was estimated at $6.183 billion in 2010. The market value of publicly traded shares was estimated at $4.988 billion. This figured declined from an estimated $109.6 billion in 2009 due to the global financial crisis, but was up slightly from $97.85 billion in 2008.

Yemen's deteriorating economy led to more depositors moving money out of Yemen banks in 2010 and 2011. While the Central Bank was able to prevent depreciation of the Yemeni riyal, political instability and a draining of foreign reserves made devaluation of the currency a risk.

Yemen had no securities exchange in 2011.

34 INSURANCE

There were at least 13 insurance firms in the Yemen in 2010. The largest insurance company, United Insurance, held a 44% share of the market. Some other insurance companies were Mareb, founded in the mid-1970s as Yemen's first insurance company; Watania and Saba.

Yemeni Insurance Union president Ali Mohamed Hashem reported in December 2011 that political turmoil had resulted in a 40% loss in premiums during the year. The breakdown in security had led companies to opt out of insuring goods being transported through Yemen because of kidnapping and robbery risks.

35 PUBLIC FINANCE

In 2010 the budget of Yemen included $7.581 billion in public revenue and $9.345 billion in public expenditures. The budget deficit amounted to 5.1% of GDP. Public debt was 39.1% of GDP, with $6.477 billion of the debt held by foreign entities.

Amid the 2011 economic crisis, the government had begun to minimize expenditures. It reduced outlays on capital projects, and prioritized salaries and basic costs. A diesel subsidy also was reduced in 2011.

Political unrest posed significant threats to Yemen's domestic reserves in late 2011. The Economist Intelligence Unit reported that reserves in the Central Bank were at $4.7 billion and that $300 million was being pumped into the economy every month to support the Yemeni riyal.

³⁶TAXATION

Yemen residents and businesses pay several taxes.

Workers and self-employed individuals paid personal income taxes, while businesses paid taxes on profits, capital gains, dividends, interest earnings, and royalties. Yemen also levied excise duties, road and vehicle taxes, port fees, rental taxes, and telegraph fees. Another tax was the 2.5% Zakat (the religious charity tax) which is state-enforced, but under the republican regime, its estimation has become a voluntary concern of each individual.

Yemen has been working to reform its tax system. In 2011, the Tax Authority prepared a draft anti-tax avoidance law, and a by-law aimed at simplifying and unifying collection procedures. Proposed reforms included amendments to a vehicle tax law and the imposition of a draft consul fees law.

³⁷CUSTOMS AND DUTIES

According to the Muslim Trade Network, import duties in Yemen were generally levied at rates varying from 5% on essential goods to 30% on luxury items. Duties on food products were 15%. The import of pork and pork products, coffee, alcohol, narcotics, fresh fruits and vegetables, weapons and explosives, and rhinoceros horn was prohibited. Imports also were assessed a 1% tax for reconstruction related to earthquakes, and imports for industrial use were subjected to an additional excise tax.

Yemen has also agreed in principal to join the Arab Common Market under an arrangement that would allow a 50% initial cut in duties on imports from other member states. Yemen also has established a cooperation agreement with the European Union.

Yemen maintains a free-trade zone at the Port of Aden.

³⁸FOREIGN INVESTMENT

Foreign direct investment (FDI) in Yemen was a net inflow of $129.2 million according to World Bank figures published in 2009. FDI represented 0.49% of GDP.

Although the Yemeni government has encouraged foreign investment, the country's political turmoil has deterred foreign investment in recent years.

The Yemen General Investment Authority (GIA) was established in 1992, and worked with the World Bank's Foreign Investment Advisory Service, to revise Yemen's Investment Law 22 of 1991 (as amended) to refocus it on promotion rather than regulation of foreign investment. Investment law restructuring was also part of the IMF-World Bank-sponsored economic reform program that began in 1995. The Yemeni Free Trade Zone Public Authority was established in 1991 to develop the 'Aden Free Trade Zone. The port was developed as a joint venture between the Port of Singapore Authority (PSA) and the Bin Mahfouz Group of Saudi Arabia

US investment has mainly been in the oil and gas sector. The Houston-based Yemen Hunt Oil Company has been operating since 1984 but constantly faces security threats. The first shipments of LNG began in 2009.

³⁹ECONOMIC DEVELOPMENT

A September 2011 report by The Economist on Yemen depicted the country's economy as being on the verge of collapse. Famine threatened the interior of the country in late 2011, and attacks on oil pipelines made the transport of food and water excessively expensive and forced the government to import fuel. Factories were closing because of a lack of fuel, and jobs were being cut.

As the poorest of the Arab countries, Yemen has faced particular hardship. Following the unification of north and south Yemen, the new government assumed all debts incurred by former governments. Domestic political strains ultimately culminated in civil strife in 1994. As a result, the economy was further burdened with reconstruction costs. In addition, Yemen's long-standing president Ali Abdullah Saleh did little to encourage economic development through the late 1990s and early years of the 21st century. Yemen's refusal to endorse military action against Iraq in 1990 also led to a loss in overseas remittances as hundreds of thousands of Yemeni migrant workers were forced to leave Saudi Arabia and Kuwait.

While the discovery of oil in the early 1990s helped boost the economy, it made many who had been economically autonomous dependent on the new wealth that flowed into the state. Corruption among governmental and business leaders was rife.

International aid has an ongoing role in the economy's development. A structural adjustment program by the International Monetary Fund was initiated in the mid-1990s following the 1994 civil war. However, difficulties in implementing the financial and monetary reforms demanded by the IMF caused the program to lapse. A new IMF program was implemented in August 2010 in which Yemen received an Extended Credit Facility of approximately $370 million over three years. The IMF demanded a series of economic reforms in exchange for the funds. The political instability that erupted in 2011 had put the IMF program on hold. The World Bank also maintained 20 projects in public sector government, water, and education as of 2011.

An economic diversification program was initiated in 2006 to counter the effects of Yemen's declining oil resources. The diversification effort was supported by an international Friends of Yemen group that formed in January 2010 as well as the IMF's $370 million reform program that was initiated in August 2010. Although political unrest threatened the diversification effort, the Economist Intelligence Unit reported that record high oil prices in 2011 were able to sustain Yemen through the turmoil.

⁴⁰SOCIAL DEVELOPMENT

A social insurance system provides old age, disability, survivor, and workers' compensation benefits. This program covers most employees, including Yemeni nationals working overseas. Workers contribute 6% of their wages, and employers pay 6% of payroll. The government contributes as an employer only. Old age benefits are payable at age 60 with at least 15 years of contributions for men, and age 55 with at least 10 years of contributions for women. A health insurance program exists only for public employees. While the government has expanded its role in providing assistance, traditional means still predominate.

An April 2011 a Human Rights report by the US State Department found that armed conflicts with Houthi rebels in the north, elements of the Southern Mobility Movement in the south, and Al-Qaida terrorist activities in the Arabian Peninsula had severely diminished the security and personal freedoms of Yemeni citizens. According to the report, more than 300,000 people had been internally displaced, and discrimination against women was widespread. Early marriage, child labor, and child trafficking were widely reported, and discrimination on the basis of religion, sect, and ethnicity was common.

Although the constitution provides for equal rights and opportunity for all, women faced considerable official and social discrimination. Polygamy is legal, and the practice of paying large dowries continues to be widespread. Women are required to obtain permission from a male member of the family in order to leave the house, and are rarely allowed to travel unaccompanied. Women have limited access to education. Women were permitted to vote, but social customs discourage most women from becoming politically active.

41 HEALTH

According to the CIA, life expectancy in Yemen was 63 years in 2011. The country spent 4.8% of its GDP on healthcare, amounting to $64 per person. There were 3 physicians, 7 nurses and midwives, and 7 hospital beds per 10,000 inhabitants. The fertility rate was 5.1, while the infant mortality rate was 51 per 1,000 live births. In 2008 the maternal mortality rate, according to the World Bank, was 210 per 100,000 births. It was estimated that 58% of children were vaccinated against measles. The CIA calculated HIV/AIDS prevalence in Yemen to be about 0.1% in 2001.

Malnutrition and the diseases associated with it were major health problems. Malaria, typhus, tuberculosis, dysentery, whooping cough, measles, hepatitis, schistosomiasis, and typhoid fever were widespread, and sewage disposal of the most rudimentary type constituted a general health hazard.

42 HOUSING

Housing in Yemen was generally of poor quality in 2011. Houses in the coastal regions were made primarily of reed, thatch, and mud brick while houses of stone and mud brick were found in the highlands. Access to fresh water, electricity, and hygienic sewage systems was rare, particularly in the rural areas.

The condition of Yemen's early 21st century housing stood in sharp contrast to its centuries-old tradition of using stone and mud to build high impressive structures with stained glass windows, communal gathering areas, and private courtyards at the ground level. Many of the older Yemeni homes have been converted to hotels, particularly in Şan'ä'.

In the first decade of the 21st century, about one-fourth of the urban housing units were huts, tents, or other makeshift structures. Wealthier Yemenis, however, lived in larger houses in which the lower part was built of sandstone, basalt, or granite, while the upper part, which may rise from two to eight stories, would be baked brick with windows.

43 EDUCATION

In 2008 the World Bank estimated that 73% of age-eligible children in Yemen were enrolled in primary school. Tertiary enrollment was estimated at 10%. Public expenditure on education represented 5.2% of GDP.

The CIA reported that the literacy rate among Yemeni adults, age 15 and older was 50.2%, based on 2003 figures. The literacy rate was noticeably higher for adult males (70.5%) than for adult females (30%). Overall, the CIA estimated that Yemen had a literacy rate of 50.2%. Public expenditure on education represented 5.2% of GDP. Males on average completed 11 years of school and females completed seven years.

The literary rate was improving in the first decade of the 21st century among Yemeni children. A September 2010 World Bank news report commented that efforts by the World Bank's International Development Association and partner countries had increased primary education enrollments to 87% in 2008–09 from 68% in 1998–99, and that the enrollment rate for girls had increased to 78% in 2008–09 from 49% in 1998–99.

New classrooms have been built in rural areas with international assistance, and teacher training programs have been initiated. Yemen, however, still faces many challenges. Although the law requires universal, compulstory and tuition-free education for children from the ages of six to 15, compulsory attendance is not enforced and fees for books and school uniforms makes education unaffordable for many. In addition, many girls fail to continue their schooling to the secondary and post-secondary levels.

The Catalogue of World Universities listed 12 colleges and universities in Yemen as of July 2011. The universities included Şan'ä' University (founded in 1970) and University of Aden (founded in 1975). Other institutions were Al Ahgaff University, Al Eman University, Hadhramout University of Science & Technology, Hodeidah University, Ibb University, Queen Arwa University, Saba University, Thamar University, Yemen University of Science & Technology, and Şan'ä' Community College.

Early Yemeni education, with regard to medieval disciplines of law, religion, history and poetry, was sophisticated and, for a country of its type, remarkably widespread. Its people contributed nobly to medieval Islamic civilization. The Al-Azhar University of Cairo was well known for its education during the 10th and 11th centuries and it attracted students from nearby countries such as Ethiopia, Arabia, and Somalia. However, in the 19th and 20th centuries, there was slow progress in the field of education. Prior to the 1962 revolution, no proper educational system was in place. Civil war and internal political upheaval worsened the situation.

44 LIBRARIES AND MUSEUMS

Yemen has many public and private libraries, which are believed collectively to contain 50,000 ancient manuscripts about the country's geography, history, and scholarly communities. Many of these manuscripts had been held since 1929 at the Library of the Great Mosque of Şan'ä'. In an effort to digitize all of the Yemeni manuscripts, the German Foreign Office and Freie Universität Berlin launched The Yemen Manuscript Digitization Project in 2009, along with the Yemen Manuscript Digitization Initiative, which began in 2010, with a mission of preserving the Arabic manuscripts in Yemen's private libraries.

The country's largest public libraries are the Yemen National Library and the Miswal Library, each with a collection of 30,000 volumes, located in 'Aden. In addition, the British Council maintains two libraries: at 'Aden (3,000 volumes) and at Şan'ä' (10,400 volumes).

Şan'ä' has three museums: the National Museum, founded in 1971; the Yemeni Military Museum, and the House of Folklore, founded in 2004.

⁴⁵MEDIA

In 2009 the CIA reported that there were 997,000 telephone land-lines in Yemen. In addition to landlines, mobile phone subscriptions averaged 16 per 100 people. There were six FM radio stations, one AM radio station, and two shortwave radio stations. Internet users numbered 2 per 100 citizens. Yemen had 255 Internet hosts. The government operates or controls all of the broadcast networks through the Ministry of Information and the Public Corporation for Radio and Television.

Since unification, efforts have been underway to upgrade the country's telecommunications infrastructure. Two-way radio links Yemen directly with Cairo and Rome. Telephone and telegraph facilities are available in major cities, and a modern dial telephone system has been installed in Şan'ä', Ta'izz, and Al-Hudaydah.

The most prominent newspapers in 2010 was *Al Jumhuriya* (circulation 100,000).

⁴⁶ORGANIZATIONS

The government has encouraged the formation of cooperatives, but private associations with political overtones are suspect. There are chambers of commerce in the major cities. The Federation of Yemen Chamber of Commerce and Industry is located in Şan'ä'.

There were more than 3,000 charitable organizations in Yemen and more than 200 non-governmental organizations doing human rights work in the country in 2011.

⁴⁷TOURISM, TRAVEL, AND RECREATION

The *Tourism Factbook*, published by the UN World Tourism Organization, reported 434,000 incoming tourists to Yemen in 2009, who spent a total of $496 million. Of those incoming tourists, 290,000 were from the Middle East. There were 52,891 hotel beds available in Yemen. The estimated daily cost to visit Şan'ä', the capital, was $242. The cost of visiting other cities averaged $173.

Terrorism threats through the 2000s and political unrest in 2011 prompted the US State Department to advise Americans against traveling to Yemen. British authorities also advised UK civilians to avoid travel to Yemen.

Tourists can visit historic and religious sites (such as the Ghumdau Palace and the Great Mosque in Şan'ä') and exotic markets, and enjoy scenic areas including the Red Sea coast. Passports and visas are required of foreign visitors. Vaccination against meningitis is required for pilgrims to Mecca. Precautions against meningitis, typhoid, and hepatitis are recommended for all visitors.

⁴⁸FAMOUS PERSONS

Imam Yahya ibn Muhammad Hamid ad-Din (1869–1948) ruled during the period when Yemen established its independence; he was assassinated during an uprising. 'Ali 'Abdullah Saleh (b. 1942) became president of the Yemen Arab Republic in 1978, ending a period of upheaval in which his two immediate predecessors were assassinated. He became united Yemen's first directly-elected president in 1999. Field Marshal 'Abdallah as-Sallal (1920–94) was the first president of the Yemen Arab Republic and held power from 1962 until a coup ousted him in 1967. Other famous Yemenis have been filmmaker Bader Ben Hirsi (b. 1968), the alchemist Abu Musa Jābir ibn Hayyān (c. 721–c. 815), and Sheikh Mohammed bin Awad bin Laden (1908–1967), who was a businessman, investor, and patriarch of the bin Laden family.

⁴⁹DEPENDENCIES

Yemen has no territories or colonies.

⁵⁰BIBLIOGRAPHY

Burrowes, Robert D. *Historical Dictionary of Yemen*. 2nd ed. Lanham, MD: Scarecrow, 2010.

Caton, Steven Charles. *Yemen Chronicle: An Anthropology of War and Mediation*. New York: Hill and Wang, a division of Farrar, Straus and Giroux, 2005.

Jones, Clive. *Britain and the Yemen Civil War, 1962–1965: Ministers, Mercenaries and Mandarins: Foreign Policy and the Limits of Covert Action*. Portland, OR: Sussex Academic Press, 2004.

Mackintosh-Smith, Tim. *Yemen: The Unknown Arabia*. Woodstock, NY: Overlook Press, 2000.

The Middle East. Washington, DC: CQ Press, 2005.

Saliba, Therese, Carolyn Allen, and Judith A. Howard, eds. *Gender, Politics, and Islam*. Chicago: University of Chicago Press, 2002.

Rushby, Kevin. *Eating the Flowers of Paradise: A Journey through the Drug Fields of Ethiopia and Yemen*. New York: St. Martin's Press, 2000.

Seddon, David, ed. *A Political and Economic Dictionary of the Middle East*. Philadelphia: Routledge/Taylor and Francis, 2004.

Yemen Investment and Business Guide: Strategic and Practical Information. Washington, DC: International Business Publications USA, 2012.

Weber, Sandra. *Yemen*. Philadelphia: Chelsea House Publishers, 2003.

INDEX TO COUNTRIES AND TERRITORIES

This alphabetical list includes countries and dependencies (colonies, protectorates, and other territories) described in the encyclopedia. Countries and territories described in their own articles are followed by the continental volume (printed in *italics*) in which each appears. Country articles are arranged alphabetically in each volume. For example, Argentina, which appears in *Americas*, is listed this way: Argentina—*Americas*. Dependencies are listed here with the title of the volume in which they are treated, followed by the name of the article in which they are dealt with. In a few cases, an alternative name for the same place is given in parentheses at the end of the entry. The name of the volume *Asia and Oceania* is abbreviated in this list to *Asia*.

Juan Fernandez Island—*Americas:* Chile

Kampuchea—*Asia:* Cambodia
Kashmir—*Asia:* India; Pakistan
Kazakhstan—*Asia*
Kazan Islands—*Asia:* Japan (Volcano Islands)
Kenya—*Africa*
Khmer Republic—*Asia:* Cambodia
Kiribati—*Asia*
Korea, Democratic People's Republic of (DPRK)—*Asia*
Korea, North—*Asia:* Korea, Democratic People's Republic of
Korea, Republic of (ROK)—*Asia*
Korea, South—*Asia:* Korea, Republic of
Kosovo—*Europe*
Kuwait—*Asia*
Kyrgyzstan—*Asia*

Laccadive, Minicoy, and Amindivi Islands—*Asia:* India: Lakshadweep
Lakshadweep—*Asia:* India
Lao People's Democratic Republic—*Asia*
Laos—*Asia:* Lao People's Democratic Republic
Latvia—*Europe*
Lebanon—*Asia*
Leeward Islands—*Americas:* UK American Dependencies; Antigua and Barbuda; St. Kitts and Nevis
Lesotho—*Africa*
Liberia—*Africa*
Libya—*Africa*
Liechtenstein—*Europe*
Line Islands—*Asia:* Kiribati
Lithuania—*Europe*
Luxembourg—*Europe*

Macau—*Asia:* China
Macedonia, Former Yugoslav Republic of—*Europe*
Macquarie Island—*Asia:* Australia
Madagascar—*Africa*
Madeira—*Europe:* Portugal
Malagasy Republic—*Africa:* Madagascar
Malawi—*Africa*
Malaya—*Asia:* Malaysia
Malaysia—*Asia*
Malden and Starbuck Islands—*Asia:* Kiribati
Maldive Islands—*Asia:* Maldives
Maldives—*Asia*
Mali—*Africa*
Malta—*Europe*
Malvinas—*Americas:* UK American Dependencies (Falkland Islands)
Mariana Islands—*Asia:* US Pacific Dependencies
Marquesas Islands—*Asia:* French Pacific Dependencies: French Polynesia
Marshall Islands—*Asia*
Martinique—*Americas:* French American Dependencies
Matsu Islands—*Asia:* Taiwan
Mauritania—*Africa*

Mauritius—*Africa*
Mayotte—*Africa:* French African Dependencies
Melilla—*Europe:* Spain
Mexico—*Americas*
Micronesia, Federated States of—*Asia:* Federated States of Micronesia
Midway—*Asia:* US Pacific Dependencies
Moldova—*Europe*
Monaco—*Europe*
Mongolia—*Asia*
Montenegro—*Europe*
Montserrat—*Americas:* UK American Dependencies: Leeward Islands
Morocco—*Africa*
Mozambique—*Africa*
Muscat and Oman—*Asia:* Oman
Myanmar—*Asia*

Namibia—*Africa*
Nauru—*Asia*
Navassa—*Americas:* US
Nepal—*Asia*
Netherlands—*Europe*
Netherlands American Dependencies—*Americas*
Netherlands Antilles—*Americas:* Netherlands American Dependencies
Nevis—*Americas:* St. Kitts and Nevis
New Caledonia—*Asia:* French Pacific Dependencies
New Guinea—*Asia:* Papua New Guinea
New Hebrides—*Asia:* Vanuatu
New Zealand—*Asia*
Nicaragua—*Americas*
Nicobar Islands—*Asia:* India
Niger—*Africa*
Nigeria—*Africa*
Niue—*Asia:* New Zealand
Norfolk Island—*Asia:* Australia
North Borneo—*Asia:* Malaysia
Northern Ireland—*Europe:* United Kingdom
Northern Mariana Islands—*Asia:* US Pacific Dependencies
Northern Rhodesia—*Africa:* Zambia
North Korea—*Asia:* Korea, Democratic People's Republic of
North Vietnam—*Asia:* Vietnam
Northwest Territories—*Americas:* Canada
Norway—*Europe*
Nosy Boraha and Nosy Be—*Africa:* Madagascar
Nyasaland—*Africa:* Malawi

Ocean Island—*Asia:* Kiribati (Banaba)
Ogasawara Islands—*Asia:* Japan (Bonin Islands)
Okinawa—*Asia:* Japan
Oman—*Asia*
Outer Mongolia—*Asia:* Mongolia

Pacific Islands, Trust Territory of the—*Asia:* Federated States of Micronesia; Marshall Islands; Palau; US Pacific Dependencies
Pakistan—*Asia*

FOR REFERENCE

Do Not Take From This Room

ISBN-13: 978-1-4144-3394-3
ISBN-10: 1-4144-3394-8

90000

9 781414 433943

FOR REFERENCE

Afghanistan

Australia

Azerbaijan

Bahrain

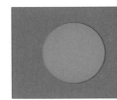
Bangladesh

East Timor

Fiji

India

Indonesia

Iran

Kiribati

Korea, Democratic People's Republic of

Korea, Republic of

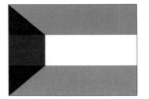
Kuwait

Kyrgyzstan

Micronesia, Federated States of

Mongolia

Myanmar

Nauru

Nepal

Philippines

Qatar

Samoa

Saudi Arabia

Singapore

Thailand

Tonga

Turkey

Turkmenistan

Tuvalu